The Celebrity Black Book

D1608258

Over 40,000 Celebrity Addresses!

Edited by Jordan McAuley

Contact Any Celebrity
www.contactanycelebrity.com

ISBN 0-9707095-3-6

Library of Congress Control Number 2004115012

ATTENTION CORPORATIONS, UNIVERSITIES, COLLEGES AND PROFESSIONAL ORGANIZATIONS: Quantity discounts are available on bulk purchases of this book for educational training purposes, fundraising or gift giving. Special books, booklets or book excerpts can also be created to fit your specific needs. For more information contact Marketing Department, Mega Niche Media, 8721 Santa Monica Boulevard #431, West Hollywood, CA 90069.

Edited by Jordan McAuley
Cover by Matt Burkhalter Design

Register This Book!
(And Get a Free Month of Database Access!)

Register your copy of *The Celebrity Black Book* now and get a free month of access to Contact Any Celebrity, our exclusive online database located at www.contactanycelebrity.com!

Contact Any Celebrity contains the agent, manager, publicist, attorney, business manager and production company of each celebrity as well as their contact address, phone and fax number. You'll also get a free subscription to our online newsletter and access to free reports including *How to Contact Any Celebrity...and Get Great Responses*, *How to Raise Money for Your Nonprofit Organization by Holding a Celebrity Autograph Auction*, *How to Get High-Profile Testimonials for Your Products and Services*, and much more!

Simply mail or fax us the completed form below, and as soon as we process it we'll contact you with your username and password to Contact Any Celebrity. Register now—you don't want to miss out!

....

First Name: _____ Last Name: _____

Company: _____

Address: _____

City: _____ State: _____ Zip: _____

Country: _____

Phone: _____ Fax: _____

Email Address: _____

Signature: _____

I am already a member and my username is _____. Please add an additional free month to my account.

I understand that by submitting the form above, I give Contact Any Celebrity permission to add my email address to their mailing list contact me in the future regarding their products and services. I also understand that I may opt-out of these mailings at any time by sending an email to blackbook@contactanycelebrity.com or by clicking on the opt-out link at the bottom of the message.

Simply mail or fax this completed form to (310) 362-8771 (24 hours) or mail to:

Contact Any Celebrity
8721 Santa Monica Boulevard #431
West Hollywood, CA 90069-4507

....

112 *Music Group*
Da Twelve Music Inc, 3060 Peachtree Rd #1420, Atlanta, GA 30305 USA

12 Stones *Music Group*
Wind-up Records, 72 Madison Ave, New York, NY 10016 USA

2 Live Crew *Music Group*
250 W 57th St #821, New York, NY 10107 USA

3 (Three) Doors Down *Music Group*
In De Goot Entertainment, 119 W 23rd St #609, New York, NY 10011 USA

311 *Music Group*
311 Touring Inc, 946 N Croft Ave, Los Angeles, CA 90069 USA

3LW *Music Group*
1211 S Highland Ave, Los Angeles, CA 90019

3T *Music Group*
23726 Long Valley Rd, Hidden Hills, CA 91302-2508 USA

4th (Fourth) Ward *Music Group*
PO Box 1890, Indian Trail, NC 28079-1890 USA

5th (Fifth) Dimension, The *Music Group*
Paradise Artists, PO Box 1821, Ojai, CA 93024 USA

98 Degrees *Music Group*
40 W 57th St, New York, NY 10019 USA

A

A R S *Actor*
15 Sarangapani Street, T Nagar, Chennai, TN 600 017, INDIA

A*Teens *Music Group*
Evolution Talent Agency LLC, 1776 Broadway Fl 15, New York, NY 10019 USA

A1 *Music Group*
Concorde Intl Artists Ltd, 101 Shepherds Bush Rd, London, W6 7LP, UNITED KINGDOM (UK)

Aadland, Beverly *Actor*
27617 Ennismore Ave, Canyon Country, CA 91351 USA

Aaker, Lee *Actor*
PO Box 8013, Mammoth Lakes, CA 93546-8013 USA

Aames, Willie *Actor*
10209 SE Division St, Portland, OR 97266 USA

Aamni *Actor, Bollywood*
6 Parthasarathi Puram Extension, Chennai, TN 600017, INDIA

Aamodt, Kjetil Andre *Skier*
Holmenkollvn 105, Oslo, 0391, NORWAY

Aaron, Angela *Stylist*
Rex Agency, The, 4446 Ambrose Ave, Los Angeles, CA 90027 USA

Aaron, Caroline *Actor*
Framework Entertainment (LA), 9057 Nemo St #C, W Hollywood, CA 90069 USA

Aaron, Chester *Writer*
PO Box 388, Occidental, CA 95465 USA

Aaron, Hank *Baseball Player*
Milwaukee Braves, 1611 Adams Dr SW, Atlanta, GA 30311-3625 USA

Aaron, Henry J *Economist*
1326 Hemlock St SW, Washington, DC 20012 USA

Aaron, Paul *Director*
1604 Courtney Ave, Los Angeles, CA 90046

Aaron, Tommy *Golfer*
440 E Lake Dr, Gainesville, GA 30504-1740 USA

Aarsleff, Hans *Linguist*
Princeton University, English Dept, Princeton, NJ 08544 USA

Aarthi *Actor, Bollywood*
18 Senthil Andavar Koil Street, Dhanalakshmi Colony Saligramam, Chennai, TN 600079, INDIA

Aas, Roald *Speed Skater*
Enebakkvn 252, Oslo 11, 1187, NORWAY

Aase, Donald W (Don) *Baseball Player*
Boston Red Sox, 5055 Via Ricardo, Yorba Linda, CA 92886-4526 USA

Abad, Andy *Baseball Player*
Oakland A's, 1600 Lance Rd, Jupiter, FL 33469-2924 USA

Abair, Mindy *Musician*
PO Box 931513, Los Angeles, CA 90093 USA

Abakanowicz, Magdalena *Artist*
Ul Bzowa 1, Warsaw, 02-708, POLAND

Abalakin, Victor K *Astronomer*
Main Observatory, Pulkovskoye Shosse 65, Moscow, 117218, RUSSIA

Abalkin, Leonid I *Economist*
Academy of Scienes, Nakhimovsky Prospekt 32, Moscow, 117218, RUSSIA

Abams, John N *General*
Commanding General, US Training/Doctrine Command, Fort Monroe, VA 23651

ABBA *Music Group*
Postbus 3079, Roosendaal, NL-4700 GB, HOLLAND

Abbado, Claudio *Conductor*
Piazzetta Bossi 1, Milan, 20121, ITALY

Abbas *Bollywood, Actor*
C-24 1702 BBA QTRS AUSTIN TOWN, Bangalore, KA, INDIA

Abbatiello, Carmine *Athlete*
176 Stone Hill Rd, Colts Neck, NJ 07722 USA

Abbe, Elfriede M *Artist*
Applewood, Manchester Center, VT 05255

Abbott, Bruce *Actor*
Metropolitan Talent Agency (MTA), 4526 Wilshire Blvd, Los Angeles, CA 90010 USA

Abbott, D Thomas *Business Person*
Salvin Corp, 333 Ludlow St, Stamford, CT 06902 USA

Abbott, Diahnne *Actor*
460 W Ave 46, Los Angeles, CA 90065

Abbott, Glenn *Baseball Player*
Oakland A's, 4413 Dawson Dr, North Little Rock, AR 72116-7037 USA

Abbott, Gregory
Box 68, Bergenfield, NY 07621-0068

Abbott, James A (Jim) *Baseball Player*
California Angels, 3449 Quiet Cove, Corona Del Mar, CA 92625-1637 USA

Abbott, Jeff *Baseball Player*
Chicago White Sox, 6403 Chastain Dr NE, Atlanta, GA 30342-4181 USA

Abbott, Kurt *Baseball Player*
Oakland A's, 613 Howard Creek Ln, Stuart, FL 34994-9114 USA

Abbott, Kyle *Baseball Player*
California Angels, 171 Lockford, Irvine, CA 92602-0952 USA

Abbott, Paul *Baseball Player*
Minnesota Twins, 1945 Dana Pl, Fullerton, CA 92831-1216 USA

Abbott, Preston S *Doctor*
1305 Namassin Rd, Alexandria, VA 22308

Abboud, A Robert *Business Person*
A Robert Abboud Co, 212 Stone Hill Center, Lake Zurich, IL 60047 USA

Abboud, Joseph M *Fashion Designer*
650 5th Ave #2700, New York, NY 10019 USA

Abdnor, James *Politician, Senator*
PO Box 217, Kennebec, SD 57544-0217 USA

Abdrashitov, Vadim Y *Director*
3D Frunzenskaya 8 #211, Moscow, 119270, RUSSIA

Abdul, Paula *Musician*
American Idol, 7800 Beverly Blvd #251, Los Angeles, CA 90036 USA

Abdul-Jabbar, Kareem *Basketball Player*
Kareem Productions, 5458 Wilshire Blvd, Los Angeles, CA 90036

Abdullah II *General, King*
Royal Palace, Amman, JORDAN

Abdulov, Aleksandr G *Actor*
Peschanaya Str 4 #3, Moscow, 125252, RUSSIA

Abdur-Rahim, Shareef *Basketball Player*
Atlanta Hawks, 1 CNN Center #405, Atlanta, GA 30303

Abed, Rodrigo *Actor*
Gabriel Blanco Iglesias (Mexico), Rio Balsas 35-32, Colonia Cuauhtemoc, DF, 06500, Mexico

Abel, Jessica *Artist*
Fantagraphics Books, 7563 Lake City Way, Seattle, WA 98115 USA

Abel, Joy *Bowler*
PO Box 296, Lansing, IL 60438 USA

Abell, Tim *Actor*
Personal Management Company, 425 N Robertson Dr, Los Angeles, CA 90048 USA

Abelson, Alan *Writer*
Barron's Magazine - Editorial Dept, 200 Liberty St, New York, NY 10281

Abelson, John *Biologist*
1097 Blanche St #316, Pasadena, CA 91106 USA

Abelson, Philip *Physicist*
4244 50th St NW, Washington, DC 20016
USA

Abelson, Robert P *Doctor*
1155 Whitney Ave, Hamden, CT 06517

Abercrombie, Ian *Actor*
Cunningham-Escott-Dipene & Associates
Inc (CED-NY), 257 Park Ave S #900, New
York, NY 10010 USA

Abercrombie, John L *Musician*
Joel Chriss, 300 Mercer St #3J, New York,
NY 10003 USA

Abernathie, Bill *Baseball Player*
Cleveland Indians, 35808 Avenue E,
Yucaipe, CA 92399-4935 USA

Abernathy, Brent *Baseball Player*
Tampa Bay Devil Rays, 508 Cascade Cir,
Palm Harbor, FL 34684-3505 USA

Abernathy, Frankie *Reality TV Star*
Bunim/Murray Productions Inc, 6007
Sepulveda Blvd, Van Nuys, CA 91411
USA

Abernathy, Frederick H *Engineer*
43 Islington Rd, Newton, MA 02166 USA

Abernathy, Robert *Commentator*
Public Broadcasting Service (PBS), 1320
Braddock Pl, Alexandria, VA 22314 USA

Abernathy, Tal *Baseball Player*
Philadelphia Athletics, 1621 Fairfield Dr,
Gastonia, NC 28054-5171 USA

Abernathy, Ted *Baseball Player*
Washington Senators, 2211 Armstrong
Park Dr, Gastonia, NC 28054-4833 USA

Abert, Donald B *Publisher*
Milwaukee Journal, 333 W State St,
Milwaukee, WI 53203

Abhishek, Bachchan *Actor, Bollywood*
Prateeksha, 10th Rd Juhu Scheme,
Mumbai, MS 400049, INDIA

Abhishek, V B *Actor*
10 ALS Garden 83 A, Natarajan Salai
Dhanalakshmi Colony, Chennai, TN 600
026, INDIA

Abiodun, Oyewole *Musician*
Agency Group, The (UK), 370 City Rd,
London, EC1V 5QA, UNITED KINGDOM
(UK)

Abizaid, John P *General*
Commander, US Central Command,
MacDill Air Force Base, FL 33621 USA

Able, Forest
507 Candlelight Lane, Louisville, KY
40213

Ablon, Ralph E *Business Person*
Ogden Corp, PO Box 2615, Fairfield, NJ
07004 USA

Abner, Shawn *Baseball Player*
San Diego Padres, 2295 Towne Lake
Parkway Ste 116, Woodstock, GA 30189-
5520 USA

Aboud, John *Writer*
Principato/Young Management, 9665
Wilshire Blvd #500, Beverly Hills, CA
90212 USA

Abourezk, James G *Politician, Senator*
21 Dupont Cir NW #400, Washington,
DC 20036 USA

Abragam, Anatole *Scientist*
33 Rue Croulebarbe, Paris, 75013,
FRANCE

Abraham, F Murray *Actor*
William Morris Agency (WMA-LA), 1
William Morris Pl, Beverly Hills, CA
90212 USA

Abraham, Jay

Abraham, John *Football Player*
New York Jets, 1000 Fulton Avenue,
Hempstead, NY 11550 USA

Abraham, Spencer E *Politician, Senator*
Energy Dept, 1000 Independence Ave
SW, Washington, DC 20585 USA

Abrahamian, Emil *Cartoonist*
147 Woodleaf Dr, Winter Springs, FL
32708 USA

Abrahams, Jim S *Director*
Endeavor Agency LLC (LA), 9601 Wilshire
Blvd Fl 3, Beverly Hills, CA 90210 USA

Abrahams, Jonathan (Jon) *Actor*
3 Arts Entertainment Inc, 9460 Wilshire
Blvd Fl 7, Beverly Hills, CA 90212 USA

Abrahamse, Taylor
Rockyz Kidz, 146 Shuter St, Studio B,
Toronto, ON M5A 1V9, Canada

Abrahamson, James A *Business Person,
General*
3557 Havercamp Rd, Hibbig, MN 55746
USA

Abrahamson, Leslie *Lawyer*
4929 Wilshire Blvd, Los Angeles, CA
90010

Abram, Norm *Entertainer*
This Old House, PO Box 130, Concord,
MA 01742 USA

Abramovitz, Max *Architect*
176 Honey Hollow Rd, Pound Ridge, NY
10576 USA

Abramowicz, Daniel (Danny) *Football
Player*
10018 Evergreen Ct N, Minneapolis, MN
55443 USA

Abrams, Dan *Television Host*
Abrams Report, The, 1 MSNBC Plaza,
Secaucus, NJ 07094 USA

Abrams, Eliot
Dogwood Farm Lane 10607, Great Falls,
VA 22066-2937

Abrams, Elliott *Government Official*
10607 Dogwood Farm Ln, Great Falls, VA
22066 USA

Abrams, Jeffrey *Writer, Producer, Actor*
William Morris Agency (WMA-LA), 1
William Morris Pl, Beverly Hills, CA
90212 USA

Abramson, Leslie *Actor*
4929 Wilshire Blvd, Los Angeles, CA
90010 USA

Abramson, Neil *Director, Writer*
United Talent Agency (UTA), 9560
Wilshire Blvd, Beverly Hills, CA 90212
USA

Abrego, Johnny *Baseball Player*
Chicago Cubs, 6222 Flint Rock Dr, San
Antonio, TX 78238-3907 USA

Abreu, Aldo *Musician*
Concert Artists Guild, 850 7th Ave #1205,
New York, NY 10019 USA

Abreu, Bobby *Baseball Player*
Houston Astros, 2611 Miami Circle,
Philadelphia, PA 19121 USA

Abreu, Irina *Actor*
Televisa, Blvd Adolfo Lopez Mateos 232,
Colonia San Angel INN, DF, CP 01060,
MEXICO

Abrikosov, Alexei A *Nobel Prize Laureate*
804 Houston St, Lemont, IL 60439 USA

Abril, Victoria *Actor*
IFPM Representation, 11 rue Chanez,
Paris, 75016, FRANCE

Abroms, Edward M *Director*
EMA Enterprises, 1866 Marlowe St,
Thousand Oaks, CA 91360 USA

Abronzino, Umberto *Soccer Player*
1336 Seattle Ave, San Jose, CA 95125
USA

Abrunhosa, Pedro *Musician*
Polygram Records, Worldwide Plaza, 825
8th Ave, New York, NY 10019 USA

Abruzzo, Ray *Actor*
Peter Strain & Associates Inc (LA), 5724 W
3rd St #302, Los Angeles, CA 90036 USA

Abshire, David M *Diplomat*
Strategic/International Studies Center,
1800 K St NW, Washington, DC 20006
USA

Abul-Ragheb, Ali *Prime Minister*
Prime Minister's Office, PO Box 80,
Amman, 35215, JORDAN

AC/DC *Music Group*
Prager & Fenton, 12424 Wilshire Blvd
#1000, Los Angeles, CA 90025 USA

Accardo, Salvatore *Musician*
Columbia Artists Mgmt Inc, 165 W 57th
St, New York, NY 10019 USA

Accola, Paul *Skier*
Bolgenstr 17, Davos Platz, 7270,
SWITZERLAND

Acconci, Vito *Artist*
39 Pearl St, Brooklyn, NY 11201 USA

Ace, Buddy *Musician*
Rodgers Redding, 1048 Tatnall St, Macon,
GA 31201

Ace of Base *Music Group*
Evolution Talent Agency LLC, 1776
Broadway Fl 15, New York, NY 10019
USA

Acevedo, Hernan F *Scientist*
Allegheny-Singer Research Institute, 320 E
North Ave, Pittsburgh, PA 15212

Acevedo, Juan *Baseball Player*
Colorado Rockies, 2801 N Litchfield Rd
Unit 47, Goodyear, AZ 85338-2005 USA

Acevedo, Kirk *Actor*
Paradigm (LA), 10100 Santa Monica Blvd,
Fl 25, Los Angeles, CA 90067 USA

Achebe, Chinua *Writer*
Bard College, Language & Literature Dept,
PO Box 41, Annandale, NY 12504 USA

Achica, George *Football Player*
3165 Lone Bluff Way, San Jose, CA 95111
USA

Acid Test *Music Group*
83 Riverside Dr, New York, NY 10024
USA

Ackeman, Leslie *Actor*
950 2nd St #201, Santa Monica, CA
90403 USA

Acker, Amy *Actor*
Lesher Entertainment Inc, 800 S Robertson
Blvd #8, Los Angeles, CA 90035 USA

Acker, Jim *Baseball Player*
Toronto Blue Jays, PO Box AA, Freer, TX
78357-2027 USA

Acker, Joseph E *Doctor*
1307 Old Weisgarber Rd, Knoxville, TN
37909

Acker, Sharon *Actor*
332 N Palm Dr #401, Beverly Hills, CA
90210 USA

Acker, Tom *Baseball Player*
Cincinnati Reds, 1 Marwood Dr, Palmyra,
VA 22963-2810 USA

Ackeren, Robert V *Director*
Kurfurstendamm 132A, Berlin, 10711,
GERMANY

Ackerman, Andrew (Andy) *Director,
Producer, Editor*
Kaplan-Stahler-Gumer Agency, 8383
Wilshire Blvd #923, Beverly Hills, CA
90211 USA

Ackerman, Bettye *Actor*
100 Sunset Blvd, W Columbia, SC 29169-
7500 USA

Ackerman, F Duane *Business Person*
BellSouth Corp, 1155 Peachtree St NE,
Atlanta, GA 30309 USA

Ackerman, Joshua *Actor*
Burstein Company, The, 15304 Sunset
Blvd #208, Pacific Palisades, CA 90272
USA

Ackerman, Leslie *Actor*
4439 Worster Ave, Studio City, CA 91604
USA

Ackerman, Michael W *General*
Pentagon, HqUSA - Inspector General,
Washington, DC 20310 USA

Ackerman, Roger G *Business Person*
Coming Inc, Houghton Park, Coming, NY
14831 USA

Ackerman, Thomas E *Cinematographer*
1644 San Leandro Ln, Montecito, CA
93108 USA

Ackerman, William *Composer*
Drake Assoc, 177 Woodland Ave,
Westwood, NJ 07675 USA

Ackermann, Rosemarie *Track Athlete*
Str der Jugend 72, Cottbus, 03050,
GERMANY

Ackland, Joss *Actor*
Jonathan Altaras Assoc Ltd, 13 Shorts
Gardens, London, WC2H 9AT, UNITED
KINGDOM (UK)

Ackles, Jensen *Actor*
Anonymous Content, 8522 National Blvd
#101, Culver City, CA 90232 USA

Ackroyd, David *Actor*
273 N Many Lakes Dr, Kalispell, MT
59901 USA

Ackroyd, Peter *Writer*
Anthony Shell Assoc, 43 Doughty St,
London, WC1N 2LF, UNITED KINGDOM
(UK)

Acohido, Byron *Journalist*
Seattle Times Editorial Dept, 1120 John St,
Seattle, WA 98109 USA

Acord, Lance *Cinematographer*
Dattner Disposto and Associates, 10635
Santa Monica Blvd, Suite 165, Los
Angeles, CA 90025 USA

Acosta, Eduardo *Baseball Player*
Pittsburgh Pirates, 22822 Boltana, Mission
Viejo, CA 92691-1717 USA

Acovone, Jay *Actor*
GVA Talent Agency Inc, 9229 Sunset Blvd
#320, Los Angeles, CA 90069 USA

Acquanetta *Actor*
6721 E Cheney Dr, Paradise Valley, AZ
85253 USA

Acres, Mark *Basketball Player*
1001 Marina Dr #906, N Quincy, MA
02171 USA

Acrivos, Andreas *Scientist*
145 W 67th St, New York, NY 10023
USA

Acton, Loren W *Astronaut*
PO Box 1857, Bozeman, MT 59771-1857
USA

Acuff, Amy
1 RCA Dome #140 Box 120, Indianapolis,
IN 46206-0120

Acuþa, Jason "Wee Man" *Actor*
LW 1 Inc, 7257 Beverly Blvd Fl 2, Los
Angeles, CA 90036 USA

Aczel, Janos D *Mathematician*
97 McCarron Crescent, Waterloo ON,
N2L 5M9, CANADA

Adade, Manohar *Bollywood, Actor*
199 Vellala Street, Purasawakkam,
Chennai, TN 600 084, INDIA

Adair, Deborah *Actor*
Cast Images, 2530 J St, Ste 330,
Sacramento, CA 95816 USA

Adair, Paul N (Red) *Misc*
Adair Enterprise, PO Box 747, Bellville,
TX 77418 USA

Adair, Red
Box 747, Bellville, TX 77418

Adam, Robert *Architect*
Winchester Design, 9 Upper High St,
Winchester, Hants, SO23 8UT, UNITED
KINGDOM (UK)

Adam, Theo *Opera Singer*
Schillerstr 14, Dresden, 01326,
GERMANY

Adamek, Donna *Bowler*
Ladies Professional Bowling Tour, 7200
Harrison Ave #7171, Rockford, IL 61112
USA

Adamie, Mike *Football Player,
Sportscaster*
ESPN, 935 Middle St, Bristol, CT 06010
USA

Adamkus, Valdas *Politician, President*
Presidential Office (Lithuania), Gediminas
53, Vilnius, 232026, Lithuania

Adamkus, Valdas *President*
President's Office, Gediminas 53, Vilnius,
232026, LITHUANIA

Adamle, Mike *Football Player*
ABC-TV - Sports Dept, 77 W 66th St, New
York, NY 10023

Adams, Ace *Baseball Player*
New York Giants, PO Box 72046, Albany,
GA 31708-2046 USA

Adams, Alvan *Basketball Player*
5617 N Palo Cristi Rd, Paradise Valley,
AZ 85253

Adams, Amy *Actor*
Firm, The, 9465 Wilshire Blvd, Beverly
Hills, CA 90212 USA

Adams, Bob *Baseball Player*
Detroit Tigers, 31713 157th St E, Llano,
CA 93544-1222 USA

Adams, Brock *Senator, Secretary*
138 Tanners Point Dr, Stevensville, MD
21666 USA

Adams, Brooke *Actor*
248 S Van Ness Ave, Los Angeles, CA
90004

Adams, Bryan *Musician*
SL Feldman & Associates, 1505 W 2nd
Ave #200, Vancouver BC, V6H 3Y,
CANADA

Adams, Charles *Baseball Player*
Chicago Cubs, 6058 Puerto Dr, Rancho
Murieta, CA 95683-9314 USA

Adams, Charles J *Religious Leader*
Progressive National Baptist Convention,
601 50th St NE, Washington, DC 20019

Adams, Dick *Baseball Player*
Philadelphia Athletics, 4650 Dulin Rd Spc
136, Fallbrook, CA 92028-9362 USA

Adams, Don *Actor*
Artist's Agency, The (LA), 1180 S Beverly
Dr #301, Los Angeles, CA 90035 USA

Adams, Doug *Baseball Player*
Chicago White Sox, 1129 Harmony Cir
NE, Janesville, WI 53545-2072 USA

Adams, Edie *Actor*
8040 Ocean Ave, Los Angeles, CA 90046

Adams, Evan *Actor*
Characters Talent Agency, The (Toronto),
150 Carlton St Fl 2, Toronto ON, M5A
2K1, CANADA

Adams, George R *Musician*
Joel Chriss, 300 Mercer St #3J, New York,
NY 10003

Adams, Gerard (Gerry) *Politician*
Sinn Fein/IRA, 51/55 Falls Road, Belfast,
Northern Ireland, BT 12, United Kingdom

Adams, Glenn *Baseball Player*
San Francisco Giants, RR 1, Sedan, NM
88436-9801 USA

Adams, Greg *Hockey Player*
Cowichan Valley Capitals, 2687 James St,
Duncan, BC V9L 2X5, CANADA

Adams, Herb *Baseball Player*
Chicago White Sox, 903 S Williston St,
Wheaton, IL 60187-6635 USA

Adams, Jane *Actor*
13080 Mindanao Way #69, Marino del
Rey, CA 90292

Adams, Joey Lauren *Actor*
Seven Summits Pictures & Management, 8906 West Olympic Blvd, Ground Floor, Beverly Hills, CA 90211 USA

Adams, John C *Musician*
Elektra Records, 75 Rockefeller Plaza, 17th Floor, New York, NY 10019 USA

Adams, John H *Religious Leader*
African Methodist Church, 1134 11th St, Washington, DC 20001

Adams, Jonathan *Actor*
Crouch Assoc, 59 Firth St, London, W1V 5TA, UNITED KINGDOM (UK)

Adams, Julie *Actor*
Sutton Barth Vennari, 145 S Fairfax Ave #310, Los Angeles, CA 90036

Adams, Julius T *Football Player*
2135 Jefferson Davis St, Macon, GA 31206

Adams, Kenneth S (Bud) *Football Player*
Tennessee Titans, Baptist Sports Park, 460 Great Circle Rd, Nashville, TN 37228

Adams, Kim *Actor*
LA Talent, 8335 Sunset Blvd #200, Los Angeles, CA 90069

Adams, Lorraine *Journalist*
Washington Post - Editorial Dept, 1150 15th St, Washington, DC 20071

Adams, Mark *Artist*
3816 22nd St, San Fransisco, CA 94114 USA

Adams, Marla *Actor*
247 S Beverly Dr #102, Beverly Hills, CA 90212 USA

Adams, Mary Kay *Actor*
Roe Enterprises, PO Box 2023, Fairfield, IA 52556 USA

Adams, Mason *Actor*
570 Park Ave #9B, New York, NY 10021 USA

Adams, Maud *Actor*
PO Box 10838, Beverly Hills, CA 90213 USA

Adams, Michael F *Educator*
University of Georgia, President's Office, Athens, GA 30602 USA

Adams, Mike *Baseball Player*
Minnesota Twins, 13205 Jo Ln NE, Albuquerque, NM 87111-7112 USA

Adams, Noah *Commentator*
National Public Radio, 635 Massachusetts Ave NW, Washington, DC 20001 USA

Adams, Oleta *Music Group*
Engine Entertainment, 4840 Peninsula Pointe Dr, Hermitage, TN 37076 USA

Adams, Pat *Artist*
370 Elm St, Bennington, VT 05201 USA

Adams, Patch *Doctor*
6855 Washington Blvd, Arlington, VA 22213 USA

Adams, Ranald T Jr *General*
1002 Emerald Dr, Alexandria, VA 22308 USA

Adams, Richard G *Writer*
Benwell's, 26 Church St, Whitechurch, Hants, RG28 7AR, UNITED KINGDOM (UK)

Adams, Richard N *Doctor, Misc*
P O Box ZZ, Basalt, CO 81621 USA

Adams, Ricky *Baseball Player*
California Angels, 6437 Garnet St, Alta Loma, CA 91701-4009 USA

Adams, Ryan *Songwriter, Music Group*
High Road, 751 Bridgeway #300, Sausalito, CA 94965 USA

Adams, Sam E *Football Player*
12010 Holly Stone Dr, Houston, TX 77070 USA

Adams, Sassoon Beverly *Model*
1923 Selby Ave #203, Los Angeles, CA 90025 USA

Adams, Scott *Cartoonist*
Harper Business Publishers, 10 East 53rd St, New York, NY 10022 USA

Adams, Terry *Music Group*
Skyline Music, P O Box 31, Lancaster, NH 03584 USA

Adams, Terry *Baseball Player*
Chicago Cubs, 866 Homestake Ct, Castle Rock, CO 80108-9081 USA

Adams, Trace *Music Group*
Borman, 1222 16th Ave S #23, Nashville, TN 37212 USA

Adams, Willie *Baseball Player*
Oakland A's, 11903 Kibbee Ave, La Mirada, CA 90638-1518 USA

Adams, Yolanda *Musician, Music Group*
Mahogany Entertainment, P O Box 4367, Upper Marboro, MD 20775 USA

Adams, Yolonda *Musician*
Elektra Records, 75 Rockefeller Plaza, New York, NY 10019

Adams Jr, Robert McCornick *Misc*
PO Box ZZ, Basalt, CO 81621 USA

Adamson, Andrew *Director*
United Talent Agency (UTA), 9560 Wilshire Blvd, Beverly Hills, CA 90212 USA

Adamson, James C *Astronaut*
16459 Frederick Road, Woodbine, MD 21797 USA

Adamson, Joel *Baseball Player*
Florida Marlins, 14832 S 46th Pl, Phoenix, AZ 85044-6872 USA

Adamson, Mike *Baseball Player*
Baltimore Orioles, 17610 Canterbury Dr, Monument, CO 80132-8310 USA

Adamson, Robert E Jr *Admiral*
1801 Patriots Colony Dr, Williamsburg, VA 23188 USA

Aday, Michael (Meat Loaf / Meatloaf) Lee *Musician*
James/Levy/Jacobson Management, 3500 W Olive Ave #1470, Burbank, CA 91505 USA

ADC Band
17397 Santa Barbara, Detroit, MI 48221

Addabbo, Anthony *Actor*
SDB Partners Inc, 1801 Ave of the Stars #902, Los Angeles, CA 90067 USA

Adderly, Herb
PO Box 219, Mantua, NJ 08051-0219

Adderly, Herbert A (Herb) *Football Player*
1058 Tristam Circle, Mantua, NJ 08051 USA

Addiction, Jane's *Musician*
Creative Artists Agency LCC (CAA-LA), 9830 Wilshire Blvd, Beverly Hills, CA 90212 USA

Addis, Bob *Baseball Player*
Boston Braves, 7466 Hollycroft Ln, Mentor, OH 44060-5611 USA

Addis, Don *Cartoonist*
Creators Syndicate, 5777 W Century Blvd #700, Los Angeles, CA 90045 USA

Adduci, Jim *Baseball Player*
St Louis Cardinals, 10429 Lamon Ave, Oak Lawn, IL 60453-4742 USA

Addy, Mark *Actor*
International Creative Mgmt, 8942 Wilshire Blvd #219, Beverly Hills, CA 90211 USA

Ade, King Sunny *Music Group*
Monterey International, 200 W Superior #202, Chicago, IL 60610 USA

Adelman, Kenneth L *Government Official*
Int'l Contemporary Studies Institute, 4018 27th St N, Arlington, VA 22207 USA

Adelman, Rick *Basketball Player, Coach*
1905 Lane Ave NE, Salem, OR 97314 USA

Adelstein, Paul *Actor*
Principal Entertainment (LA), 1964 Westwood Blvd #400, Los Angeles, CA 90025 USA

Adema *Music Group*
William Morris Agency (WMA-LA), 1 William Morris Pl, Beverly Hills, CA 90212 USA

Adey, Christopher
137 Anson Road, Willesden Green, NW2 4AH, UNITED KINGDOM (UK)

Adie, Kate *Journalist*
BBC Television Centre, Incoming Mail, Wood Lane, London, W12 7RJ, UNITED KINGDOM (UK)

Adjani, Isabelle *Actor*
ArtMedia, 20 Ave Rapp, Paris, 75007, FRANCE

Adjodhia, Jules *Prime Minister*
Prime Minister's Office, Kleine Combeweg 1, Paramaribo, SURINAME

Adkins, John
28208 Village 28, Camarillo, CA 93012-7619

Adkins, Jon *Baseball Player*
Chicago White Sox, RR 2 Box 2306, Wayne, WV 25570-8102 USA

Adkins, Seth *Actor*
Paradigm (LA), 10100 Santa Monica Blvd, Fl 25, Los Angeles, CA 90067 USA

Adkins, Steve *Baseball Player*
New York Yankees, 5001 Derry Way, Tampa, FL 33647-1338 USA

Adkins, Trace *Musician, Music Group*
Borman Entertainment, 1222 16th Ave S #23, Nashville, TN 37212 USA

Adkisson, Perry L *Educator, Misc*
9211 Lake Forest Court N, College Station, TX 77845 USA

Adleman, Leonard *Scientist*
University of Southern California, Computer Math Dept, Los Angeles, CA 90089 USA

Adler, Brian *Composer*
Gorfaine/Schwartz, 13245 Riverside Dr #450, Serman Oaks, CA 91423 USA

Adler, Charles *Actor*
Arlene Thomton Assoc, 12001 Ventura Place #20, Studio City, CA 91604 USA

Adler, Jerry *Actor*
Paradigm Agency, 10100 Santa Monica Blvd #2500, Los Angeles, CA 90067 USA

Adler, Lee *Artist*
Lime Kiln Farm, Climax, NY 12042 USA

Adler, Lou *Actor, Producer, Director*
Ode Sounds & Visuals, 3969 Villa Costera, Malibu, CA 90265 USA

Adler, Matt
PO Box 1866, Studio City, CA 90067

Adler, Richard *Composer, Songwriter*
PO Box 1151, Southampton, NY 11969 USA

Adler, Stephen L *Physicist*
Institute for Advanced Study, Einstein Lane, Princeton, NJ 08540 USA

Adler, Steven *Music Group*
Big FD Entertainment, 301 Arizona Ave #200, Santa Monica, CA 90401 USA

Adlesh, Dave *Baseball Player*
Houston Colt 45's, 9770 Avenida Monterey, Cypress, CA 90630-3446 USA

Adni, Daniel *Musician*
64A Menelik Road, London, NW2 3RH, UNITED KINGDOM (UK)

Adoboli, Koffi Eugene *Prime Minister*
Prime Minister's Office, BP 5618, Lome, TOGO

Adoor, Gopalkrishnan *Director*
Darsanam, Trivandrum, Kerala, 695017, INDIA

Adorf, Mario *Actor*
Perlacher Str 28, Grunwald, D-82031, GERMANY

Adoti, Rasaaq *Actor*
Coast to Coast Talent Group, 3350 Barham Blvd, Los Angeles, CA 90068 USA

Adotta, Kip *Actor, Comedian*
PO Box 5734, Santa Rosa, CA 95402 USA

Adria, Ferran *Chef*
El Bulli, En Cala Montjoi Roses, Girona, 17480, SPAIN

Adulyadey, King
BhumibolVilla Chitralada, Bangkok, THAILAND

Adway, Dwayne *Actor*
McKeon-Valeo Management, 9107 Wilshire Blvd #321, Beverly Hills, CA 90210 USA

Adyrkhayeva, Svetlana D *Ballerina*
1 Smolensky Pereulor 9, #74, Moscow, 121099, RUSSIA

Aedo, Daniela *Actor*
Televisa, Blvd Adolfo Lopez Mateos 232, Colonia San Angel INN, DF, CP 01060, MEXICO

Aerle, Taree *Artist, Music Group*
William Morris Agency, 1325 Ave of Americas, New York, NY 10019 USA

Aerosmith *Music Group*
Monterey Peninsula Artists (Monterey), 509 Hartnell St, Monterey, CA 93940 USA

Afanasiyev, Viktor M *Cosmonaut*
Potchta Kosmonavtov, Moskovskoi Oblasti, Syvisdny Goroduk, 141160, RUSSIA

Afenir, Troy *Baseball Player*
Houston Astros, 459 Old Via Rancho Dr, Escondido, CA 92029-7959 USA

Affeldt, Jeremy *Baseball Player*
Kansas City Royals, 969 Crestwood Rd, Englewood, FL 34223-3905 USA

Affleck, Ben *Actor*
LivePlanet, 2644 30th St, Santa Monica, CA 90405 USA

Affleck, Casey *Actor*
United Talent Agency (UTA), 9560 Wilshire Blvd, Beverly Hills, CA 90212 USA

Affleck, James G *Business Person*
American Cyanamid, 5 Giralda Farms, Madison, NJ 07940 USA

AFI *Music Group*
Leave Home Booking, 1216 California St, Huntington Beach, CA 92648 USA

Afinogenov, Maxim *Hockey Player*
Buffalo Sabres, HSBC Arena 1 Seymour St, Buffalo, NY 14210 USA

Afrika, Bambaataa *Artist, Musician*
KLB Productions, 70A Greenwich Ave #441, New York, NY 10011 USA

Afroman *Artist, Music Group*
Crescent Moon, 20 Music Square W, Nashville, TN 37203 USA

Aftermath *Music Group*
Starcrest Entertainment Corp, 4585 N River Rd E, Zanesville, OH 43701-8174 USA

Afwerki, Isaias *President*
State Council, Asmara, ERITREA

Aga Khan IV, Prince Karim *Religious Leader*
Aiglemont, Gouvieux, 60270, FRANCE

Agajanian, Benjamin (Ben) *Football Player*
5251 E Los Altos Plaza, Long Beach, CA 90815 USA

Agam, Yaacov *Artist*
26 Rue Boulard, Paris, 75014, FRANCE

Agarwal, Anu *Actor, Bollywood*
503 Godavari, Khan Pochkhawala Road Worli, Mumbai, MS 400025, INDIA

Agase, Alex
1281 Pine Ridge Circle #C-2, Tarpon Springs, FL 33469-6409

Agase, Alexander G (Alex) *Coach, Football Player, Football Coach*
1281 Pine Ridge Circle E #G1, Tarpon Springs, FL 34688 USA

Agassi, Andre *Tennis Player*
8921 Andre Dr, Las Vegas, NV 89148 USA

Agbayani, Benny *Baseball Player*
New York Mets, 66-948 Kolu Pl, Waialua, HI 96791-9743 USA

Agena, Keiko *Actor*
c/oGilmore Girls, 4000 Warner Blvd, Building 2222, Burbank, CA 91522

Aghayan, Ray *Designer*
431 S Fairfax Ave #3, Los Angeles, CA 90036 USA

Agna, Tom *Actor, Writer, Producer*
Endeavor Agency LLC (LA), 9601 Wilshire Blvd Fl 3, Beverly Hills, CA 90210 USA

Agnelo, Geraldo Majella Cardinal *Religious Leader*
Rue Martin Alfanso de Souza 270, Salvador, BA, 40100-050, BRAZIL

Agnew, Harold M *Physicist*
322 Punta Baja Dr, Solana Beach, CA 92075 USA

Agnew, Valerie *Musician*
Rave Booking, PO Box 310780, Jamaica, NY 11431 USA

Agnihotri, Atul *Actor, Bollywood*
Ashwini, Pali Mala Road Bandra, Mumbai, MS 400050, INDIA

Agnus, Michael *Business Person*
Whitbread PLC, Chiswell St, London, EC1Y 4SD, UNITED KINGDOM (UK)

Agoos, Jeff *Soccer Player*
4628 Buckhorn Ridge, Fairfax, VA 22030 USA

Agostini, Didier *Actor*
Cineart, 36 Rue de Ponthieu, Paris, 75008, FRANCE

Agosto, Juan *Baseball Player*
Chicago White Sox, 3815 65th St E #175, Bradenton, FL 34208-6613 USA

Agranoff, Bernard W *Biologist, Doctor*
1942 Boulder Dr, Ann Arbor, MI 48104 USA

Agre, Bernard Cardinal *Religious Leader*
Archeveche, Ave Jean-Paul II, Abidjan, 01 BP 1287, IVORY COAST

Agre, Peter *Nobel Prize Laureate*
7033 Lenleigh Road, Baltimore, MD 21212 USA

Agt, Andries A M Van *Prime Minister*
Europa House, 9-15 Sambancho Chiyodaku, Tokyo, 102, JAPAN

Aguayo, Luis *Baseball Player*
Philadelphia Phillies, 23 Dorado Bch E, Dorado, PR 00646-2047 USA

Aguilar, Pepe *Music Group*
Agency Group Ltd, 1775 Broadway #430, New York, NY 10019 USA

Aguilera, Christina *Musician, Songwriter*
azoffmusic management, 1100 Glendon Ave #200, Los Angeles, CA 90024 USA

Aguilera, Hellweg Max *Photographer*
144 Magazine St #3, Cambridge, MA 02139 USA

Aguilera, Richard W (Rick) *Baseball Player*
New York Mets, P O Box 174, Roncho Santa Fe, CA 92067-0174 USA

Aguirre, Beatriz *Actor*
Televisa, Blvd Adolfo Lopez Mateos 232, Colonia San Angel INN, DF, CP 01060, MEXICO

Aguirre, Mark *Athlete*
125 S Pennsylvania St, Indianapolis, IN
46204

Aguirre, Mark A *Basketball Player, Misc*
LifeCast.com, Park Central II 12750 Merit
Dr #1020, Dallas, TX 75251 USA

Agustoni, Gilberto Cardinal *Religious Leader*
Piazzi della Citla Leorina 9, Rome, 00193,
ITALY

Agutter, Jenny *Actor*
73930 Shadow Lake Dr, Palm Desert, CA
92260 USA

Ahana *Actor, Bollywood*
26-B-17 Elegant Apts, Hindi Prachara
Sabha Road, Chennai, TN 600017, INDIA

Aheam, Kevin *Hockey Player*
174 Marlborough St, Boston, MA 02116
USA

Ahearne, Pat *Baseball Player*
Detroit Tigers, 246 Milam Ln, Bastrop, TX
78602-3108 USA

Ahern, Bertie *Prime Minister*
Prime Minister's Office, Upper Merrion St,
Dublin, IRELAND

Ahern, Neal *Producer*
William Morris Agency (WMA-LA), 1
William Morris Pl, Beverly Hills, CA
90212 USA

Ahith, Kumar *Actor*
8/10 Norton Apartment, I Floor
Mandavelli, Chennai, TN 600 028, INDIA

Ahmed, Kazi Zafar *Prime Minister*
Jatiya Sangsad, Dhaka, BANGLADESH

Aho, Esko *Prime Minister*
Centre Party, Pursimiehenkatu 15,
Helsinki, 00150, FINLAND

Ahrens, Lynn *Musician*
Willaim Morris Agency, 151 El Camino
Dr, Beverly Hills, CA 90212 USA

Ahrens, Thomas J *Geophysicist*
California Institute of Technology,
Seismology Laboratory, Pasadena, CA
91125 USA

Ahronovitch, Yuri
Stockholm Philharmonic, Hotorget 8,
Stockholm, SWEDEN

Aida, Takefumi *Architect*
1-3-2 Okubo, Shinjukuku, Tokyo, 169,
JAPAN

Aiello, Danny *Actor*
Manhattan Pictures International, 369
Lexington Ave, New York, NY 10017 USA

Aiken, Clay *Musician*
RCA Records, 1540 Broadway #3500,
New York, NY 10036 USA

Aiken, Kimberly
PO Box 119, Atlantic City, NJ 08404

Aiken, Linda H *Social Activist*
2209 Lombard St, Philadelphia, PA 19146
USA

Aikens, Curtis *Chef*
William Morris Agency (WMA-LA), 1
William Morris Pl, Beverly Hills, CA
90212 USA

Aikens, Willie *Baseball Player*
California Angels, PO Box 01732-031 A3-
611, Atlanta, GA 30315 USA

Aikman, Laura Holly *Actor*
551 Green Lanes, Palmers Green, London,
N13 3DR, UNITED KINGDOM (UK)

Aikman, Troy K *Football Player, Athlete*
325 Brock St, Coppell, TX 75019 USA

Ailes, Roger E *Business Person*
218 Truman Dr, Cresskill, NJ 07626 USA

Aimee, Anouk *Actor*
ArtMedia, 20 Ave Rapp, Paris, 75007,
FRANCE

Aimi, Milton *Soccer Player*
5703 W Bellfort St, Houston, TX 77035
USA

Ainge, Daniel R (Danny) *Basketball Player*
Toronto Blue Jays, 140 Wellesly Ave,
Wellesly Hills, MA 02481-7209 USA

Ainsleigh, H Gordon *Track Athlete*
17119 Placer Hills Road, Meadow Vista,
CA 95722 USA

Ainslie, Ben *Yachtsman*
RYA House, Romsey Road, Eastleigh,
Hampshire, S050 9YA, United Kingdom
(UK)

Ainsworth, Kurt *Baseball Player*
San Francisco Giants, 6317 Hope Estate
Dr, Baton Rouge, LA 70820-5098 USA

Air Supply *Music Group*
Agency for the Performing Arts (APA-LA),
9200 Sunset Blvd #900, Los Angeles, CA
90069 USA

Aitay, Victor *Musician*
800 Deerfield Road, #203, Highland Park,
IL 60035 USA

Aitken, John *Artist*
University College, Slade Art School,
London, WC1E 6BT, UNITED KINGDOM
(UK)

Aitmatov, Chingiz T *Writer*
Ulitsa Toklogulstz 98, #9, Bishkek,
720003, Kyrgyzstan

Aizenberg Selove, Fay *Physicist*
118 Cherry Lane, Wynnewood, PA 19096
USA

Ajayrathnam *Actor*
78 Gajapathy Street, Shenoy Nagar,
Chennai, TN 600 030, INDIA

Akayev, Askar *President*
President's Office, Government House,
Bishkek, 720003, KYRGYZSTAN

Akbar, Taufik *Astronaut*
Jalan Simp, Pahlawan III/24, Bandung,
40124, INDONESIA

Akebono *Wrestler*
Azumazeki Stable, 4-6-4 Higashi
Komagala, Ryogoku, Tokyo, JAPAN

Akens, Jewell
5228 Marburn Ave, Los Angeles, CA
90043

Aker, Jack *Baseball Player*
Kansas City A's, 44 Slayback Dr,
Princeton Junction, NJ 08550-1912 USA

Akerfelds, Darrel *Baseball Player*
Oakland A's, 12834 W Rosewood Dr, El
Mirage, AZ 85335-7209 USA

Akerlof, George A *Nobel Prize Laureate*
University of California, Economics Dept,
Evans Hall, Berkeley, CA 94720 USA

Akerlund, Jonas *Director*
International Creative Management
(ICM-LA), 8942 Wilshire Blvd, Beverly
Hills, CA 90211 USA

Akerman, Malin *Actor*
Alan Siegel Entertainment, 345 N Maple
Dr #375, Beverly Hills, CA 90210 USA

Akers, Fred *Football Coach*
Purdue University, Athletic Dept, West
Lafayette, IN 47907 USA

Akers, John F *Business Person*
PO Box 194, Pebble Beach, CA 93953
USA

Akers, Michelle *Soccer Player*
SOI, 2875 S Orange Ave, #500, Orlando,
FL 32806 USA

Akers, Thomas D (Tom) *Astronaut*
11770 Timberline Dr, Rolla, MO 65401
USA

Akerson, Daniel F *Business Person*
Nexiel Communications, 2001 Edmund
Halley Dr, Reston, VA 20191 USA

Akhtar, Javed *Songwriter, Writer*
702 Sagar Samrat Green Field Road, Near
Juhu P O Juhu, Bombay, MS 400 049,
INDIA

Akihito *King*
Imperial Palace, 1-1 Chiyoda, Chiyodaku,
Tokyo, 100, JAPAN

Akihoto, EmperorThe Palace
1-1 ChiyodaChiyoda-Ku, Tokyo, JAPAN

Akil, Salim *Director*
International Creative Management
(ICM-LA), 8942 Wilshire Blvd, Beverly
Hills, CA 90211 USA

Akinnuoye-Agbaje, Adewale *Actor*
Untitled Entertainment (NY), 23 E 22nd St
Fl 3, New York, NY 10010 USA

Akins, Rhett *Musician*
RPM Mgmt, 209 10th Ave S, #229,
Nashville, TN 37203 USA

Akiyama, Kazuyoshi *Conductor*
Columbia Artists Mgmt Inc, 165 W 57th
St, New York, NY 10019 USA

Akiyama, Toyohiro *Astronaut, Journalist*
Tokyo Broadcasting Systems, 3-6-5
Akasaka, Minaloku, Tokyo, 107, JAPAN

Akiyoshi, Toshiko *Composer, Musician*
Berkeley Agency, 2608 9th St, Berkeley,
CA 94710 USA

Akoshino *Royalty*
Imperial Palace, Tokyo, JAPAN

Aksyonov, Vassily P *Writer*
Random House, 1745 Broadway, #B1,
New York, NY 10019 USA

Aksyonov, Vladimir V *Cosmonaut*
Astrakhansky Per 5, Kv 100, Moscow,
129010, RUSSIA

Al Fayed, Mohammed
The Ritz Hotel Place Vendome, Paris,
FRANCE

Al-Assad, Bashar *Politician, President*
Presidential Office (Syria), Muharreem
Abu Rumanch, Al-Rashid Street,
Damascas, Syria

al-Aziz, Abdullah Ibn Abdul *Prince*
Council of Ministers, Murabba, Riyadh,
11121, SAUDI ARABIA

Al-Hoss, Selim *Prime Minister*
Premier's Office, Serail, Place de l'Eloile, Beirut, LEBANON

Al-Yawer, Sheik Ghazi Mashal Ajll *President*
President's Office, Al-Sijound Majalis, Karradat Mariam, Baghdad, IRAQ

al-Zubi, Mahmoud *Prime Minister*
Premier's Office, Damascas, SYRIA

Alabama *Music Group*
William Morris Agency (WMA-TN), 2100 W End Ave #1000, Nashville, TN 37203 USA

Alagna, Roberto *Opera Singer*
Levon Sayan, 2 Rue du Prieure, Nyon, 1260, SWITZERLAND

Alagu, K *Actor*
17 T N H B Staff Quarter Dr Ramaswamy Road, Chennai, TN 600 078, INDIA

Alaia, Azzeddine *Fashion Designer*
18 Rue de la Verrerie, Paris, 75008, FRANCE

Alaigal, Selvakumar *Actor*
9A Pari St, Avvai Nagar Choolaimedu, Chennai, TN 600 094, INDIA

Alan, Buddy *Musician*
600 E Gilbert Dr, Tempe, AZ 85281 USA

Alarcon, Arthur L *Judge*
US Court of Appeals, 312 N Spring St, Los Angeles, CA 90012 USA

Alatorre, Javier *Actor*
TV Azteca, Periferico Sur 4121, Colonia Fuentes del Pedregal, DF, CP 14141, Mexico

Alba, Jessica *Actor*
Endeavor Agency LLC (LA), 9601 Wilshire Blvd Fl 3, Beverly Hills, CA 90210 USA

Albanese, Licia *Opera Singer*
Nathan Hale Dr, Wilson Point, South Norwalk, CT 06854 USA

Albano, Lou *Wrestler*
16 Mechanic St, Carmel, NY 10512 USA

Albarn, Damon *Musician, Songwriter*
CMO Mgmt, Ransomes Dock, 35 Parkgale Road #32, London, SW11 4NP, UNITED KINGDOM (UK)

Albeck, Stan *Basketball Player, Coach*
Toronto Raptors, Air Canada Center, 40 Bay St, Toronto, ON M5J 2NB, CANADA

Albee, Edward
PO Box 697, Montauk, NY 11954

Albee, Edward F *Writer*
14 Harrison St, New York, NY 10013 USA

Alberghetti, Anna Maria *Actor, Musician*
10333 Chrysanthemum Lane, Los Angeles, CA 90077 USA

Albers, Hans *Business Person*
BASF AG, Carl-Bosch-Str 38, Ludwigshafen, 78351, GERMANY

Alberstein, Chara *Musician*
DL Media, PO Box 2728, Bala Cynwyd, PA 19004 USA

Albert, Calvin *Artist*
6525 Brandywine Dr S, Margate, FL 33063 USA

Albert, Eddie *Actor*
719 Amalfi Dr, Pacific Palisades, CA 90272 USA

Albert, Edward *Actor*
Hawks Ranch, 27320 Winding Way, Malibu, CA 90265 USA

Albert, John G *General*
Albert Farms, RR2, Monroe, VA 24574 USA

Albert, Marv *Sportscaster*
TNT-TV, Sports Department, 1050 Techwood Dr, Atlanta, GA 30318 USA

Albert (Prince) *Royalty*
Palais de Monaco, Boite Postale 518, Monacode Cedex, 98015, MONACO

Albert II *King*
Koninklijk Palais, Rue de Brederode, Brussels, 1000, BELGIUM

Alberto, Padre *Actor*
Telemundo, 2470 West 8th Avenue, Hialeah, FL 33010 USA

Alberts, Trev *Football Player*
10430 E Hickory Ridge Dr, Rochelle, IL 61068 USA

Albita *Musician*
Estefan Enterprises, 6205 SW 40th St, Miami, FL 33155 USA

Albom, Mitch *Writer*
Hyperion Books, 114 5th Ava, New York, NY 10011 USA

Albrecht, A Chim *Wrestler*
Physique Promotions, 9668 Moss Glen Ave, Fountain Valley, CA 92708 USA

Albrecht, Gerd
Mariedi Anders Artists, 535 El Camino del Mar, San Francisco, CA 94121 USA

Albright, Gerald *Musician*
Richard Walters, 1800 Argyle Ave, #408, Los Angeles, CA 90028 USA

Albright, Lola *Actor*
213 N Valley St #136, Burbank, CA 91505 USA

Albright, Madeleine K *Politician, Secretary*
1318 34th St NW, Washington, DC 20007 USA

Albright, Malvin Marr (Zsissly) *Artist*
1500 N Lake Shore Dr, Chicago, IL 60610 USA

Albright, Tenley E *Doctor*
186 Windswept Way, Osterville, MA 02655 USA

Albuquerque, Lita *Artist*
305 Boyd St, Los Angeles, CA 90013 USA

Alcaraz, Lalo *Editor, Cartoonist*
PO Box 63052, Los Angeles, CA 90063 USA

Alcock, Charles *Physicist*
Lawrence Livemore Laboratory, 7000 East St, Livemore, CA 94550 USA

Alcott, Amy S *Golfer*
Giaciolli Intersport, 1301 Montana Ave, Santa Monica, CA 90403 USA

Alda, Alan *Actor*
International Creative Management (ICM-LA), 8942 Wilshire Blvd, Beverly Hills, CA 90211 USA

Alda, Rutanya *Actor*
18645 Collins St, #19, Tarzana, CA 91356 USA

Alden, Ginger *Model, Actor, Musician*
Ron Leyser, 25 Rolling Hill Court W, Sag Harbor, NY 11963 USA

Alden, Norman *Actor*
Twentieth Century Artists, 15760 Ventura Blvd, Ste 700, Encino, CA 91436 USA

Alden, Richard *Actor*
Icon Talent Agency, 3800 Barham Blvd #303, Burbank, CA 90068

Alden Robinson, Phil *Director*
Creative Artists Agency, 9830 Wilshire Blvd, Beverly Hills, CA 90212 USA

Alderman, Darrell *Race Car Driver*
D A Construction Co, 8145 Flemingsburg Road, Morehead, KY 40351 USA

Alderman, Grady C *Football Player*
10395 W Colfax Ave, #340, Lakewood, CO 80215 USA

Aldisert, Ruggero J *Judge*
120 Cremona Dr, #0, Goleta, CA 93117 USA

Aldiss, Brian W *Writer*
Hambledon, 39 Saint Andrews Road, Old Headington, Oxford, OX3 9DL, UNITED KINGDOM (UK)

Aldred, Sophie *Actor*
1 Duchess St, #1, London, S1N 3EE, UNITED KINGDOM (UK)

Aldredge, Theoni V *Designer*
425 lalayette St, New York, NY 10003 USA

Aldrich, John H *Politician, Scientist*
Duke University, Political Science Dept, Durham, NC 27708 USA

Aldrich, Lance *Cartoonist*
University Press Syndicate, 4520 Main St, Kansas City, MO 64111 USA

Aldridge, Donald O *General*
1004 incol Road, #168, Bellevue, NE 68005 USA

Aldridge, Edward C (pete) Jr *Government Official*
Aerospace Corp, 2350 E El Segundo Blvd, El Segundo, CA 90245 USA

Aldrin, Buzz *Astronaut*
10380 Wilshire Blvd, Suite 703, Los Angeles, CA 90024-4745 USA

Aldrin, Edwin E (Buzz) Jr *Astronaut*
Shapiro-Lichtman Talent Agency, 8827 Beverly Blvd, Los Angeles, CA 90048 USA

Aleandro, Norma *Actor*
Blanco Encalada 1150, Buenos Aires, 1428, ARGENTINA

Alechinsky, Pierre *Artist*
2 Bis Rue Henri Barbusse, Bougival, 78380, FRANCE

Aleksiy II *Religious Leader*
Moscow Patriarchy, Chisty Per 5, Moscow, 119034, RUSSIA

Aleno, Charles
601 Marion Ct, Deland, FL 32720

Alerlol, George *Nobel Prize Laureate*
University of California, Economics Dept, Berkeley, CA 94720 USA

Alesi, Jean *Race Car Driver*
HWA GmbH, Benzstr 8, Affalterbach, 71563, GERMANY

Aletter, Frank *Actor*
5430 Corbin Ave, Tarzana, CA 91356
USA

Alex *Actor*
2 Rajaji North Street, Pushpa Nagar
Nungambakkam, Chennai, TN 600 034
USA

Alexakis, Art *Musician*
Pinnacle Entertainment, 30 Glenn St,
White Plains, NY 10603 USA

Alexander, A Lamar *Secretary, Educator,
Governor, Senator*
2233 Blue Springs Road, Ashland City, TN
37015 USA

Alexander, Bruce E *Football Player*
508 Englewood Dr, Lufkin, TX 75901 USA

Alexander, Christopher W J *Architect*
2701 Shasta Road, Berkeley, CA 94708
USA

Alexander, Clifford L Jr *Government
Official*
412 A St SE, Washington, DC 20003 USA

Alexander, Corey *Basketball Player*
440 Alpha St, Waynesboro, VA 22980
USA

Alexander, Denise *Actor*
270 N Canon Dr, #1919, Beverly Hills,
CA 90210 USA

Alexander, Derrick S *Football Player*
18508 Monte Vista St, Detroit, MI 48221
USA

Alexander, Doyle
5416 Hunter Park Ct, Arlington, TX 76017

Alexander, Eric *Musician*
Joel Chriss, 300 Mercer St, #3J, New York,
NY 10003 USA

Alexander, Erika *Actor*
Innovative Artists (LA), 1505 Tenth St,
Santa Monica, CA 90401 USA

Alexander, Flex *Actor*
Bragman/Nyman/Cafarelli, 9171 Wilshire
Blvd #300, Beverly Hills, CA 90210 USA

Alexander, Jamie *Game Show Host*
William Morris Agency (WMA-LA), 1
William Morris Pl, Beverly Hills, CA
90212 USA

Alexander, Jane *Actor, Government
Official*
William Morris Agency, 1325 Ave of
Americans, New York, NY 10019 USA

Alexander, Jason *Actor, Producer*
Baker/Winokur/Ryder, 9100 Wilshire Blvd,
#600, Beverly Hills, CA 90212 USA

Alexander, Jules *Musician*
Variety Artists, 1924 Spring St, Paso
Robles, CA 93446 USA

Alexander, Keith *Actor*
Cunningham-Escott-Dipene & Associates
Inc (CED-LA), 10635 Santa Monica Blvd
#130, Los Angeles, CA 90025 USA

Alexander, Khandi *Actor*
Innovative Artists, 1505 10th St, Santa
Monica, CA 90401 USA

Alexander, Lloyd *Writer*
1005 Drexel Hills Blvd, New
Cumberland, PA 17070 USA

Alexander, Monty *Musician*
Bennett Morgan, 1282 RR 376,
Wappingers Falls, NY 12590 USA

Alexander, R Minter *General*
824 Eden Court, Alexandria, VA 22308
USA

Alexander, Robert M *Misc*
14 Moor Park Mount, Leeds, LS6 4BU,
UNITED KINGDOM (UK)

Alexander, Sasha *Actor*
William Morris Agency (WMA-LA), 1
William Morris Pl, Beverly Hills, CA
90212 USA

Alexander, Shana *Journalist*
PO Box 429, Wainscott, NY 11975 USA

Alexander, Shasha *Actor*
Endeavor Talent Agency, 9701 Wilshire
Blvd, #1000, Beverly Hills, CA 90212
USA

Alexander, Shaun *Football Player*
Seattle Seahawks, 11220 NE 53rd St,
Kirkland, WA 98033 USA

Alexander, Susana *Actor*
TV Azteca, Periferico Sur 4121, Colonia
Fuentes del Pedregal, DF, CP 14141,
Mexico

Alexander, Victor *Basketball Player*
8405 Holcomb Bridge Road, Alpharetta,
GA 30022 USA

Alexander, Willie *Musician*
Tournmaline Music Group, 894 Mayville
Road, Bethel, PA 04217 USA

Alexander (Prince Yogoslavia) *Prince*
36 Park Lane, London, W1Y 3LE, UNITED
KINGDOM (UK)

Alexander of Weedon, Robert S *Financier*
National Westminster Bank, 41 Lothbury,
London, EC2P 2BP, UNITED KINGDOM
(UK)

Alexandre, Boniface *President, Judge*
President's Office, Palacio Nacional, Port-
au-Prince, HAITI

Alexandrov, Alexander P *Cosmonaut*
Hovanskaya UI 3, #27, Moscow, 129515,
RUSSIA

Alexie, Sherman *Writer*
PO Box 376, Wellpinit, WA 99040 USA

Alexis, Kim *Model, Actor*
2219 W Olive Ave, PO Box 10038,
Burbank, CA 91506 USA

Alfaro, Victor *Fashion Designer*
130 Barrow St, New York, NY 10014 USA

Alferov, Zhores *Nobel Prize Laureate*
Ioffe Institute, 26 Polytekhnicheskaya, Saint
Petersburg, 194021, RUSSIA

Alfieri, Janet *Cartoonist*
15 Bumpus road, Plymouth, MA 02360
USA

Alfonseca, Antonio *Baseball Player,
Athlete*
Florida Marlins, 2269 Dan Marino Blvd,
Miami, FL 33056 USA

Alfonso, Kristian *Actor*
Metropoliton Talent Agency, 4526
Wilshire Blvd, Los Angeles, CA 90010
USA

Alford, Steve *Basketball Player*
831 Forest Hill Dr, Coralville, IA 90010
USA

Alford, William *Writer*
150 Federal St, #2600, Boston, MA 02110
USA

Alfredsson, Helen *Golfer*
Int'l Mgmt Group, 1 Erieview Plaza, 1360
E 9th St #1300, Cleveland, OH 44114
USA

Algabid, Hamid *President*
National Assembly, Vice President's
Office, Niamey, NIGER

Ali, Laila *Athlete, Boxer*
Trident Media Group LLC, 41 Madison
Ave Fl 33, New York, NY 10010 USA

Ali, May May *Actor*
Wallis Agency, 4444 Riverside Dr #105,
Burbank, CA 91505 USA

Ali, Muhammad *Athlete, Boxer*
Ali Farm, PO Box 187, Berrien Springs, MI
49103 USA

Ali, Somy *Actor, Bollywood*
208 Vindhyachal 22 Mount Mary Road,
Bandra, Bombay, MS 400 050, INDIA

Ali, Tatyana *Actor*
Evolution Talent, 1776 Broadway, #1500,
New York, NY 10019 USA

Ali Khan, Saif *Actor, Bollywood*
Bungalow 5, Belscot Tower, Lokhandwala
Complex Andheri Link Road, Mumbai, MS
400058, INDIA

Alice In Chains *Music Group*
The Plaza, 535 Kings Rd, London, SW10
0SZ, UNITED KINGDOM (UK)

Alicia, Karen *Actor*
Televisa, Blvd Adolfo Lopez Mateos 232,
Colonia San Angel INN, DF, CP 01060,
MEXICO

Alien Ant Farm *Music Group*
Creative Artists Agency LCC (CAA-LA),
9830 Wilshire Blvd, Beverly Hills, CA
90212 USA

Alikhan, Anwar *Actor*
Parkavi Apartments Phase IV No 15-F 18
Mariamman Koil Street, West K K Nagar,
Chennai, TN 600 078, INDIA

Alington, William H *Architect*
60 Homewood Crescent, Wellington,
NEW ZEALAND

Alis, Robert *Cinematographer*
13920 72nd Road, Flushing, NY 11367
USA

Alisha *Musician*
Famous Artists Agency, 250 W 57th St,
New York, NY 10107 USA

Alison, Jane *Writer*
FarrarStraus Giroux, 19 Union Square W,
New York, NY 10003 USA

Alito, Samuel A Jr *Judge*
US Court of Appeals, US Courthouse, 50
Walnut St, Newark, NJ 07102 USA

Aliyev, Ilham *President*
President's Office, Baku, 370066,
AZERBAIJAN

All For One / All-4-One *Music Group*
Performers Of the World/ Management
Interests Associates (POW/MIA), 8901
Melrose Avenue, 2nd Floor, West
Hollywood, CA 90069 USA

All Saints *Music Group*
72 Chancellors Rd, London, W6 9SG,
UNITED KINGDOM (UK)

All-American Rejects, The *Music Group*
PO Box 1413, Stillwater, OK 74076 USA

Allaben, Maureen *Stylist*
6536 Jamestown Pl, Atlanta, GA 30084
USA

Allain, William A *Governor*
970 Momingside St, Jackson, MS 39202
USA

Allais, Emile *Skier*
Imeuble Cassiopee, Cluses, 7430,
FRANCE

Allais, Maurice *Nobel Prize Laureate*
60 Blvd Saint-Michel, Paris, 75006,
FRANCE

Allam, Mark W *Doctor*
Strath Haven, #809, Swathmore, PA
19081 USA

Allan, Gabrielle *Producer*
United Talent Agency (UTA), 9560
Wilshire Blvd, Beverly Hills, CA 90212
USA

Allan, Gary *Musician*
Lytle Management Group, 1101 18th Ave
S, Nashville, TN 37212 USA

Allan, Jed *Actor*
76470 Minaret Way, Palm Desert, CA
92211 USA

Allan, Stephen D (Steve) *Golfer*
gaylord Sports Mgmt, 14646 N Kierland
Blvd, #230, Scottsdale, AZ 85254 USA

Allard, Linda M *Fashion Designer*
Ellen Tracy Corp, 575 Fashion Ave, New
York, NY 10018 USA

Allawi, Iyad *Prime Minister*
Prime Minister's Office, Karradat Mariam,
Baghdad, IRAQ

Allbaugh, Joseph *Government Official*
Federal Emergency Management Agency,
500 C St SW, Washington, DC 20472
USA

Allegre, Claude J *Misc*
Recherce/Technologie Institute, 110 Rue
Grenelle, Paris, 75700, FRANCE

Allem, Fulton P *Golfer*
Professional Golfer's Assc, PO Box
109601, Palm Beach Gardens, FL 33410,
u

Allen, Andrew M *Astronaut*
782 Killamey Court, Memitt Island, FL
32953 USA

Allen, Betty *Opera Singer*
Harlem School of Arts, 645 Saintt
Nicholas Ave, New York, NY 10030 USA

Allen, Bruce *Race Car Driver*
Reger-Morrison Racing Engines, 1120
Enterprise Place, Arlington, TX 76001
USA

Allen, Byron *Comedian*
Schwartzman & Associates PR, 1925
Century Park East, Penthouse 2300, Los
Angeles, CA 90067 USA

Allen, C Keith *Hockey Player*
10000 Highland Ave, Long Beach
Township, NJ 08008 USA

Allen, Chad *Actor*
Creative Management Group, 3815
Hughes Ave Fl 3, Culver City, CA 90232
USA

Allen, Chuck *Athlete*
192 Victoria Loop, Port Townsend, WA
98368-9400 USA

Allen, Clarence R *Misc, Scientist*
1763 Royal Oaks Dr, #F207, Duarte, CA
91010 USA

Allen, Corey *Actor, Director*
8642 Hollywood Blvd, Los Angeles, CA
90069 USA

Allen, Danielle Sherie *Actor*
Privilege Agency, 9229 Sunset Blvd, Los
Angeles, CA 90069 USA

Allen, Debbie *Actor, Choreographer*
607 Marguerita Ave, Santa Monica, CA
90402 USA

Allen, Deborah *Musician*
Morningstar, 595 Hicks Road, #38,
Nashville, TN 37221 USA

Allen, Doug *Artist*
Fantagraphics Books, 7563 Lake City
Way, Seattle, WA 98115 USA

Allen, Duane D *Musician*
88 New Shackle Island Road,
Hendersonville, TN 37075 USA

Allen, Elizabeth Anne *Actor*
Innovative Artists (LA), 1505 Tenth St,
Santa Monica, CA 90401 USA

Allen, Frances E *Scientist*
Finney Farm, Croton on Hudson, NY
10520 USA

Allen, George F *Senator, Governor*
PO Box 17704, Richmond, VA 23226
USA

Allen, Geri *Composer, Musician*
Clayton Ross Productions, 307 Lake St,
San Francisco, CA 94118 USA

Allen, Henry *Critic*
Washington Post, Editorial Dept 1150
15th St NW, Washington, DC 20071 USA

Allen, J Presson *Writer, Producer*
Lewis Allen Productions, 1501 Broadway
#1614, New York, NY 10036 USA

Allen, Joan *Actor*
International Creative Mgmt, 8942
Wilshire Blvd #219, Beverly Hills, CA
90211 USA

Allen, Jonelle *Actor*
Silver Massetti & Szatmary (SMS-LA),
8730 Sunset Blvd #440, Los Angeles, CA
90069 USA

Allen, Joseph P IV *Astronaut*
Veridian, 1200 S Hayes St #1100,
Arlington, VA 22202 USA

Allen, Karen *Actor*
P O Box 237, Monterey, MA 01245 USA

Allen, Kevin *Director*
William Morris Agency, 52/53 Poland
Place, London, W1F 7LX, UNITED
KINGDOM (UK)

Allen, Krista *Actor*
Stone Manners, 6500 Wilshire Blvd #550,
Los Angeles, CA 90048 USA

Allen, Larry C *Football Player*
2001 Piner Road, Santa Rosa, CA 95403
USA

Allen, Leo *Writer*
Principato/Young Management, 9665
Wilshire Blvd #500, Beverly Hills, CA
90212 USA

Allen, Lew Jr *General*
Draper Laboratory, 555 Technology
Square, Cambridge, MA 02139 USA

Allen, Loy Jr *Race Car Driver*
3197 Steamboat Ridge Road, Port Orange,
FL 32128 USA

Allen, Marcus *Business Person*
International Creative Management
(ICM-LA), 8942 Wilshire Blvd, Beverly
Hills, CA 90211 USA

Allen, Marcus L *Sportscaster, Football
Player*
CBS-TV, Sports Dept 51 W 52nd St, New
York, NY 10019 USA

Allen, Marty *Actor, Comedian*
8704 Carlitas Joy Court, Las Vegas, NV
89117 USA

Allen, Maryon P *Senator*
3215 Cliff Road, Birmingham, AL 35205
USA

Allen, Nancy *Actor*
Creative Artists Agency, 9830 Wilshire
Blvd, Beverly Hills, CA 90212 USA

Allen, Nancy *Misc, Music Group,
Musician*
Columbia Artists Mgmt Inc, 165 W 57th
St, New York, NY 10019 USA

Allen, Natalie *Commentator*
Cable News Network, News Dept, 1050
Techwood Dr NW, Atlanta, GA 30318
USA

Allen, Pam *Golfer*
809 Delphinium Dr, Billings, MT 59102
USA

Allen, Paul G *Misc, Scientist*
Vulcan Northwest, 505 5th Ave S #900,
Seattle, WA 98104 USA

Allen, Rae *Actor*
Kyle Fritz Management, 1979 Grace Ave
#5A, Hollywood, CA 90068 USA

Allen, Rax Jr *Music Group*
209 10th Ave #527, Nashville, TN 37203
USA

Allen, Ray *Basketball Player, Actor*
3 Arts Entertainment Inc, 9460 Wilshire
Blvd Fl 7, Beverly Hills, CA 90212 USA

Allen, Richard *Actor*
89 Saltergate, Chesterfield, S40 IUS,
UNITED KINGDOM (UK)

Allen, Richard A (Richie) *Baseball Player*
RR2 Possum Hollow Road, Wampum, PA
16157 USA

Allen, Richard J (Rick) *Music Group*
Q Prime Mgmt, 729 7th Ave #1400, New York, NY 10019 USA

Allen, Richard V *Government Official*
905 16th St NW, Washington, DC 20006 USA

Allen, Robert E *Business Person*
60 Stewart Road, Short Hills, NJ 07078 USA

Allen, Rosalind *Actor*
Agency for Performing Arts, 9200 Sunset Blvd #900, Los Angeles, CA 90048 USA

Allen, Scott *Figure Skater*
40 Brayton St, Englewood, NJ 07631 USA

Allen, Sian Barbara *Actor*
732 S Plymouth Blvd #E, Los Angeles, CA 90005 USA

Allen, Sin Barbara *Actor*
732 South Plymouth Blvd, #E, Los Angeles, CA 90005

Allen, Ted *Television Host*
Queer Eye for the Straight Guy, 119 Braintree St, Boston, MA 02134

Allen, Thomas B *Opera Singer*
I C M Artists, 40 W 57th St, New York, NY 10019 USA

Allen, Tim *Actor, Comedian*
Messina Baker Entertainment, 955 Carillo Dr #100, Los Angeles, CA 90048 USA

Allen, Willard M *Doctor*
211 Key Haighway, Baltimore, MD 21230 USA

Allen, William L *Editor*
National Geographic Magazine, 17th & M NW, Washington, DC 20036 USA

Allen, Woody *Director, Actor, Comedian*
48 E 92nd St, New York, NY 10128 USA

Allen-Moritt, Krista *Actor*
Brillstein-Grey Entertainment, 9150 Wilshire Blvd #350, Beverly Hills, CA 90212 USA

Allenby, Robert *Golfer*
Master's Int'l Hurst Grove, Sanford Lane, Hurts, Berks, RG10 0SQ, UNITED KINGDOM (UK)

Allende, Fernando *Actor*
El Dorado Pictures, 725 Arizona Ave #100, Santa Monica, CA 90401

Allende, Isabel *Writer*
92 Fernwood Dr, San Rafael, CA 94901 USA

Allesandro, Nivola
ICM, 9830 Wilshire Blvd, Beverly Hills, CA 90212

Alley, Alphonse *President*
Carre 181-182, BP 48, Cotonou, BENIN

Alley, Kirstie *Actor, Producer*
True BlueProductions, PO Box 27127, Los Angeles, CA 90027-0127

Alley, Kristie *Actor*
Untitled Entertainment, 8436 W 3rd St #650, Los Angeles, CA 90048 USA

Alley, L Eugene (Gene) *Baseball Player*
10236 Steuben Dr, Glen Allen, VA 23060 USA

Alley Cats
ThePO Box 1031, Montrose, CA 91021-1031

Allfrey, Vincent G *Misc*
24 Winthrop Court, Tenafly, NJ 07670 USA

Allimadi, E Otema *Prime Minister*
PO Box Gulu, Gulu District, UGANDA

Allinson, Michael
112 Knollwood Dr, Larchmont, NY 10538

Allione, Tsultrim *Religious Leader*
Tara Mandala Retreat Center, PO Box 3040, Pagosa Springs, CO 81147 USA

Allison, Dave *Hockey Player, Coach*
P O Box 1416, International Falls, MN 56649 USA

Allison, Donnie *Race Car Driver*
355 Quail Dr, Salisbury, NC 28147 USA

Allison, Glenn *Bowler*
1844 S Haster St #138, Anaheim, CA 92802 USA

Allison, Herbert M *Business Person*
TIAA-CREF, 730 3rd, New York, NY 10017 USA

Allison, Jerry *Songwriter, Musician*
8455 New Bethal Road, Lyles, TN 37098 USA

Allison, John A IV *Financier*
BB&T Corp, 200 W 2nd St, Winston Salem, NC 27101 USA

Allison, John V *War Hero*
2007 Banshore Dr, Niceville, FL 32578 USA

Allison, Mose J Jr *Musician, Composer*
34 Dogwood Dr, Smithtown, NY 11787 USA

Allison, Richard C *Judge*
24 Circle Dr, Manhasset, NY 11030 USA

Allison, Robert J Jr
Anadarko Petroleum Corp, 1201 Lake Robbins Dr, Spring, TX 77380 USA

Allison, Stacy *Mountaineer*
7003 SE Reed College Place, Portland, OR 97202 USA

Allison Jr, Graham T *Educator*
69 Pinhurst Road, Belmont, MA 02478 USA

Alliss, Peter *Sportscaster*
Int'l Mgmt Group, 1 Erieview Plaza, 1360 E 9th St #1300, Cleveland, OH 44114 USA

Allman, Greg *Musician*
Allman Brothers Band Inc, 18 Tamworth Road, Waban, MA 02468 USA

Allnut, Robert *Scientist, Doctor*
5400 Edgemoor Lane, Bethesda, MD 20814 USA

Allouache, Merzak *Director*
Cite des Asphodeles Bt D15, 183 Ben Aknoun, Algiers, ALGERIA

Allport, Chris M *Actor*
1324 Pine St, Santa Monica, CA 90405 USA

Allport, Christopher *Actor*
Pakula/King & Associates, 9229 Sunset Blvd #315, Los Angeles, CA 90069 USA

Allred, Gloria R *Lawyer, Attorney General*
Allred Maroko Goldberg, 6300 Wilshire Blvd #1500, Los Angeles, CA 90048 USA

Allsopp, Kirstie *Actor*
Arlington Enterprises Ltd, 1-3 Charlotte St, London, W1P 1HD, UNITED KINGDOM (UK)

Allsup, Mike *Music Group, Musician*
Mckenzie Accountancy, 5171 Caliente St #134, Las Vegas, NV 89119 USA

Allsup, Tommy *Music Group*
Tophands Talent, P O Box 1547, Arlington, TX 76004 USA

Allyson, June *Actor*
1651 Foothill Rd, Ojai, CA 93023 USA

Almanzar, Carlos *Baseball Player, Athlete*
San Diego Padres, 8880 Rio San Diego Drive #400, San Diego, CA 92108 USA

Almeda, Alex
5067 Woodley Ave, Encino, CA 91436

Almee, Anouk *Actor*
ICM France, 37 Rue de Acacias, Paris, 75017, FRANCE

Almen, Lowell G *Religious Leader*
Evangelical Lutheran Church, 8765 W Higgins Road, Chicago, IL 60631 USA

Almodovar, Pedro *Director*
El Deseo SA, Ruiz Perello 25, Madrid, 28028, SPAIN

Almond, Marc *Music Group*
Take Out Productions, 630 9th Ave #216, New York, NY 10036 USA

Almunia, Amann Joaquin *Government Official*
Piaza de las Cortes #9, 4A Planta, Madrid, 28014, SPAIN

Alois *Prince*
Schloss Vaduz, Vaduz, 9490, LIECHTENSTEIN

Alomar, Roberto *Baseball Player*
3803 54th Dr W #103, Bradenton, FL 34210 USA

Alomar, Roberto V (Robbie) *Baseball Player*
3803 54th Dr W #103, Bradenton, FL 34210 USA

Alomar, Santos C (Sandy) Jr *Baseball Player*
P O Box 367, Salinas, FL 00751 USA

Alonsa, Alicia *Ballerina*
Calzada 510 Entre D & E, El Vedada, Havana, CP 10400, CUBA

Alonso, Alicia *Ballerina*
Calzada 510 Entre D&E, El Vedada, Havana, 10400, CP, CUBA

Alonso, Anabel *Actor*
GRPC SL, Calles Fuencarral 17, Madrid, 28004, SPAIN

Alonso, Daniella *Actor*
Gersh Agency, The (LA), 232 N Canon Dr, Beverly Hills, CA 90210 USA

Alonso, Maria Conchita *Actor, Music Group*
118 Beverly Dr #201, Beverly Hills, CA 90212 USA

Alosio, Ryan *Actor*
Marshak/Zachary Company, The, 8840 Wilshire Blvd Fl 1, Beverly Hills, CA 90211 USA

Alou, Felipe *Baseball Player, Misc*
80119 Heather Cove Dr, Boynton Beach, FL 33467 USA

Alou, Moises *Baseball Player*
13095 NW 13 St, Pembroke Pines, FL 33028 USA

Alpert, Herb *Musician*
31930 Pacific Coast Hwy, Malibu, CA 90265 USA

Alpert, Hollis
Box 142, Shelter Island, NY 11964

Alpert, Joseph S *Doctor*
3440 E Cathedral Rock Circle, Tucson, AZ 85718 USA

Alphand, Luc *Skier*
Chalet Le Balme Chantemarie, Sierra Chavalier, 05330, FRANCE

Alpher, Ralph A *Physicist*
253 Ascot Lane, Schenectady, NY 12309 USA

Alsgaard, Thomas *Skier*
Cathinka Guldbergsveg 16, Holter, 2034, NORWAY

Alsop, Marin *Musician*
International Creative Management (ICM-LA), 8942 Wilshire Blvd, Beverly Hills, CA 90211 USA

Alsop, Will *Architect*
Bishop's Wharf, 39-49 Parkgate Road, London, SW11 4NP, UNITED KINGDOM (UK)

Alston, Alyce Carolyn *Publisher*
Oprah Magazine, 224 W 57th St #900, New York, NY 10019 USA

Alston, Barbara *Music Group*
Superstars Unlimited, P O Box 371371, Las Vegas, NV 89137 USA

Alston, Reeves Shirley *Music Group*
GHR Entertainment, 6014 N Pointe Place, Woodland Hills, CA 91367 USA

Alstott, Mike *Football Player*
7800 9th Ave S, Saint Petersburg, FL 33707 USA

Alt, John M *Football Player*
1 Scotch Pine Road, Saint Paul, MN 55127 USA

Altenberg, Wolfgang *General*
Birkenhof 44, Brenen-Saint-Magnus, 28759, GERMANY

Alter, Hobie *Designer, Misc, Yachtsman*
P O Box 1008, Oceanside, CA 92051 USA

Alther, Lisa *Writer*
1086 Silver St, Hinesburg, VT 05461 USA

Altman, Chelsea *Actor*
Innovative Artists (LA), 1505 Tenth St, Santa Monica, CA 90401 USA

Altman, Jeff *Actor*
Richard De La Font Agency, 4845 S Sheridan Rd, Tulsa, OK 74145 USA

Altman, Robert *Director, Producer*
International Creative Mgmt, 8942 Wilshire Blvd, #219, Beverly Hills, CA 90211 USA

Altman, Scott D *Astronaut*
3011 Harvest Hill Dr, Friendswood, TX 77546 USA

Altman, Sidney *Nobel Prize Laureate*
71 Blake Road, Hamden, CT 06517 USA

Altman, Stuart H *Educator*
11 Bakers Hill Road, Weston, MA 02493 USA

Altmeyer, Jeannine T *Opera Singer*
Im Muhlader, Herrliberg, 8709, SWITZERLAND

Altobelli, Joseph (Joe) *Baseball Player*
10 Stowell Dr, #3, Rochester, NY 14616 USA

Altomar, Tony
44 Norvel Lane, Stamford, CT 06905-1316

Altschul, Serena *Commentator*
MTV, News Dept, 1515 Broadway, New York, NY 10036 USA

Alva, Luigi
via Moscova 46/3, Mailand, ITALY, 20121

Alvarado, Natividad (Naty) *Misc*
Equitable of Lowa, 2700 N Main St, Santa Ana, CA 92705 USA

Alvarez, Barry *Football Coach*
University of Wisconsin, Athletic Dept, Medison, WI 53711 USA

Alvarez, Gabe *Baseball Player*
Detroit Tigers, 4401 La Madera Ave, El Monte, CA 91732-2009 USA

Alvarez, Jose *Baseball Player*
Minnesota Twins, 210 Murphy Ln, Greenville, SC 29607-4934 USA

Alvarez, Mario Roberto *Architect*
Marlo Roberto Alvarez Assoc, Solis 370, Buenos Aires, ARGENTINA

Alvarez, Orlando *Baseball Player*
Los Angeles Dodgers, Cummunidad Dolores 37, Rio Grande, PR 00745 USA

Alvarez, Rogelio *Baseball Player*
Cincinnati Reds, 5010 NW 183rd St, Carol City, FL 33055-2929 USA

Alvarez, Victor *Baseball Player*
Los Angeles Dodgers (LA Dodgers), 1000 Elysian Park Avenue, Los Angeles, CA 90012 USA

Alvarez, Wilson *Baseball Player*
Texas Rangers, 6927 Westchester Cir, Bradenton, FL 34202-2584 USA

Alvarez Martinez, Francisco Cardinal *Religious Leader*
Arco de Palacio 3, Toledo, 45002, SPAIN

Alvarez-Buylla, Arturo *Biologist*
Rockefeller University, Medical Center, 1230 York Ave, New York, NY 10021 USA

Alves, Joe *Director*
4176 Rosario Road, Woodland Hills, CA 91364 USA

Alvin, Dave *Musician, Songwriter*
Mark Pucci, 5000 Oak Bluff Court, Atlanta, GA 30350 USA

Alvina, Anicee *Actor*
41 Rue de l'Echese, Le Visinet, 75008, FRANCE

Alvis, Max *Baseball Player*
Cleveland Indians, 806 Hunterwood Dr, Jasper, TX 75951-2820 USA

Alworth, Lance D *Football Player*
242 22nd St, Del Mar, CA 92014 USA

Alyea, Brant *Baseball Player*
Washington Senators, 119 Lockhardt Rd, Tryon, NC 28782-3900 USA

Ama, Shola *Musician*
12 One Mgmt, Executive Suite, 20 Damien St, London, E1 2HX, UNITED KINGDOM (UK)

Amaker, Tommy *Basketball Player, Coach*
University of Michigan, Athletic Dept, Ann Arbor, MI 48109 USA

Amalfitano, J Joseph (Joe) *Baseball Player*
265 Bowstring Dr, Sedona, AZ 86336 USA

Amalfitano, Joey *Baseball Player*
New York Giants, 265 Bowstring Dr, Sedona, AZ 86336-6523 USA

Amalou, J K *Director*
William Morris Agency, 52/53 Poland Place, London, W1F 7LX, UNITED KINGDOM (UK)

Aman, Zeenat *Actor, Bollywood*
Neelam Apartments 3rd Floor, Mount Mary Road Bandra, Bombay, MS 400 050, INDIA

Amanar, Simona *Gymnast*
Gymnastic Federation, Str Vasile Conta 16, Budapest, 70139, ROMANIA

Amandes, Tom *Actor*
Writers & Artists, 8383 Wilshire Blvd, #550, Beverly Hills, CA 90211 USA

Amanpour, Christiane *Journalist, Correspondent*
Cable News Network, 2 Stephen St, #100, London, W1P 1PL, UNITED KINGDOM (UK)

Amara, Lucine *Opera Singer*
260 W End Ave, #7A, New York, NY 10023 USA

Amaral, Bob
14643 Hamlin, Van Nuys, CA 91406

Amaral, Richard L (Rich) *Baseball Player*
Seattle Mariners, 6525 Silverspur Ln, Huntington Beach, CA 92648-1516 USA

Amarjargal, Rinchinnyamiyn *Prime Minister*
Prime Minister's Office, Ulan Bator, Great Hural, 12, MONGOLIA

Amaro Jr, Ruben *Baseball Player*
California Angels, 1063 Country Hills Rd, Yardley, PA 19067-6024 USA

Amaro Sr, Ruben *Baseball Player*
St Louis Cardinals, 4098 Cinnamon Way, Weston, FL 33331-3810 USA

Amato, Giuliano *Prime Minister*
Carmera dei Deputati, Piazza di Montecitorio, Rome, 00186, ITALY

Amato, Joe *Race Car Driver*
Amato Racing, 44 Tunkhannuck Ave, Exeter, PA 18643 USA

Amaya, Armando *Artist*
Lopex 137, Depto 1, Mexico City, 06070 CP, MEXICO

Amazing Jonathan, The *Actor*
International Creative Management (ICM-LA), 8942 Wilshire Blvd, Beverly Hills, CA 90211 USA

Amazing Rhythm Aces *Music Group*
Fat City Artists, 1906 Chet Atkins Pl #502, Nashville, TN 37212

Ambasz, Emilio *Architect*
8 E 62nd St, New York, NY 10021 USA

Amber *Musician*
Artists & Audience Entertainment, PO Box 35, Pawling, NY 12564 USA

Ambler, Wayne
305 Tournament Rd, Ponte Vedra, FL 32082

Ambro, Thomas L *Judge*
US Court of Appeals, Federal Building, 844 N King St, Wilmington, DE 19801 USA

Ambrose, Ashley A *Football Player*
2877 Major Ridge Trail, Duluth, GA 30097 USA

Ambrose, Lauren *Actor*
United Talent Agency, 9560 Wilshire Blvd, #500, Beverly Hills, CA 90212 USA

Ambroslus, Marsha *Songwriter, Musician*
DreamWorks Records, 9268 W 3rd St, Beverly Hills, CA 90210 USA

Ambrozic, Aloysius Matthew Cardinal
Religious Leader
Archdiocese, 1155 Yonge St, Toronto, ON M4T 1W2, CANADA

Ambuehl, Clindy *Actor*
Paul Kohner, 9300 Wilshire Blvd, #555, Beverly Hills, CA 90212 USA

Amdahl, Gene M *Business Person, Engineer*
4 Hallmark Circle, Menlo park, CA 94025 USA

Amedori, John Patrick *Actor*
Creative Management Group (CMG), 9465 Wilshire Blvd #335, Beverly Hills, CA 90212 USA

Ameling, Elly *Musician, Music Group*
Hubstein Artist Services, 65 W 90th St, #13F, New York, NY 10024 USA

Amelio, Gilbert F *Business Person*
13416 Middle Fork Lane, Los Altos, CA 94022 USA

Amelung, Ed *Baseball Player*
Los Angeles Dodgers, 16681 Cedar Cir, Fountain Valley, CA 92708-2310 USA

Amen, Irving *Artist*
90 SW 12th Terrace, Boca Raton, FL 33486 USA

Amenabar, Alejandro *Director, Writer, Musician*
Maxmedia, 1620 Broadway, Santa Monica, CA 90404 USA

Amend, Bill *Artist, Cartoonist*
Universal Press Syndicate, 4520 Main Street, Kansas City, MO 64111 USA

Amendola, Tony *Actor*
Michael Bloom, 9255 Sunset Blvd, #710, Los Angeles, CA 90069 USA

Ament, Jeff *Musician*
Annie Ohayon Media Relations, 525 Broadway, #600, New York, NY 10012

Amer, Nicolas
14 Great Russell St, London, ENGLAND, WC1B 3NH

America *Musician*
William Morris Agency (WMA-LA), 1 William Morris Pl, Beverly Hills, CA 90212 USA

Ames, Aldrich
PO Box 3000, White Deer, PA 17887

Ames, Bruce N *Misc*
1324 Spruce St, Berkeley, CA 94709 USA

Ames, Denise *Actor*
Studio Talent Group, 1328 12th St, Santa Monica, CA 90401 USA

Ames, Ed *Actor, Musician*
1457 Claridge Dr, Beverly Hills, CA 90210 USA

Ames, Frank Anthony *Musician*
1235 Potamac St NW, Washington, DC 20007 USA

Ames, Rachel *Actor*
Atkins Assoc, 8040 Ventura Canyon Ave, Panorama City, CA 91402 USA

Amick, Madchen *Actor*
Lynch-Frost Productions, PO Box 1723, North Hollywood, CA 91614 USA

Amiez, Sebastien *Skier*
Ave Chasse-Foret, Pralognan, FRANCE

Amigo Vallejo, Carlos Cardinal *Religious Leader*
Archdiocese, Piaza Virgin de los Reyes S/N, Seville, 41004, SPAIN

Amin, Idi
Box 8948, Jidda, SAUDI ARABIA, 21492

Amini *Actor, Bollywood*
6 Parthasarathipuram, T Nagar, Chennai, TN 600017, INDIA

Amis, Martin *Journalist, Writer*
P F D, Drury House, 34-43 Russell St, London, WC2B 5HA, UNITED KINGDOM (UK)

Amis, Suzy *Actor, Model*
International Creative Mgmt, 8942 Wilshire Blvd, #219, Beverly Hills, CA 90211 USA

Amitri, Del *Musician, Songwriter*
Progressive Global Agency, PO Box 50294, Nashville, TN 37205 USA

Amlong, Joe *Athlete*
HC 36 Box 73, Sand Coulee, MT 59472 USA

Amlong, Thomas *Athlete*
166 Four Mile River Road, Old Lyme, CT 06371 USA

Ammaccapane, Danielle *Golfer*
13214 N 13th St, Phoenix, AZ 85022 USA

Ammachi *Religious Leader*
Amrita IInstitutions, Ettimadai, Coimbatore, Tamil Nadu, 641105, INDIA

Ammann, Simon *Speed Skater*
Ski Verband, Worbstr 52, Muri, 3074, SWITZERLAND

Amonte, Tony *Hockey Player*
5245 E Saguaro Place, Paradise Valley, AZ 85253 USA

Amor, Vincente *Baseball Player*
Chicago Cubs, 3905 W 8th Ct, Hialeah, FL 33012-7291 USA

Amorosi, Vanessa *Musician*
Mar Jac Productions, PO Box 51, Caulfield South, VIC, AUSTRALIA

Amos, John *Actor*
Innovative Artists, 1505 10th St, Santa Monica, CA 90401 USA

Amos, Paul S *Business Person*
AFLAC Inc, AFLAC Center, 1932 Wynnton Road, Columbus, GA 31999 USA

Amos, Tori *Musician, Songwriter*
Spivak Entertainment, 11845 W Olympic Blvd, #1125, Los Angeles, CA 90064 USA

Amos, Wally (Famous) *Business Person*
Rosica Mulhern Assoc, 627 Grove St, Ridgewood, NJ 07450 USA

Amoyal, Pierre A W *Musician*
Jacques Thelen, 252 Rue de Faubourg Saint-Honore, Paris, 75008, FRANCE

Amplas, John *Actor*
443 Meridian Dr, Pittsburgh, PA 15228 USA

Amram, David W III *Composer, Musician*
Peekskill Hollow Farm, Peekskill Hollow Road, Putnam Valley, NY 10579 USA

Amrapurkar, Sadashiv *Actor, Bollywood, Comedian*
A/201 Panchdhara Off Yari Road, Versova Andheri, Bombay, MS 400 058, INDIA

Amritraj, Ashok *Actor, Producer, Writer*
Hyde Park Entertainment, 2500 Broadway St, Santa Monica, CA 90404 USA

Amritraj, Vijay *Tennis Player*
First Serve Entertainment, 7277 Havenhurst Ave, Van Nuys, CA 91406 USA

Amsterdam, Anthony G *Attorney General, Educator*
68 Middle Lane Highway, Southampton, NY 11968 USA

Amte, Baba *Religious Leader*
Maharogi Sewa Samiti, Waora Anandwan, Dist Chandrapur, Maharashtra, 442914, INDIA

Amurri, Eva *Actor*
United Talent Agency (UTA), 9560 Wilshire Blvd, Beverly Hills, CA 90212 USA

Ana-Alicia *Actor*
S D B Partners, 1801 Ave of Stars, #902, Los Angeles, CA 90067 USA

Anagarano, Michael *Actor*
Coast to Coast Talent Group, 3350 Barham Blvd, Los Angeles, CA 90068 USA

Anagnostopoulos, Constantine E *Doctor*
213 N Bemiston Ave, Clayton, MO 63105 USA

Anahi *Actor*
Televisa, Blvd Adolfo Lopez Mateos 232, Colonia San Angel INN, DF, CP 01060, MEXICO

Anakin, Douglas *Athlete*
PO Box 27, Windermere, BC V0B 2L, CANADA

Anand, Babu N *Actor*
1 A Officers Defence Colony St, Thomas Mount, Chennai, TN 600 097, INDIA

Anand, Dev *Actor, Bollywood*
2 Iris Park, Juhu, Mumbai, MS 400049, INDIA

Anand, J N *Actor*
No 8 B N Reddy Road, T Nagar, Chennai, TN 600 017, INDIA

Anand, Sabita *Actor, Bollywood*
61 Sivan Koil Ist Cross Street, Kodambakkam, Chennai, TN 600024, INDIA

Anand, Tinnu *Actor, Bollywood, Director, Filmmaker*
101 Lakshadeep Glmohar Cross Road No 4, JVPD Scheme, Bombay, MS 400 049, INDIA

Anand, Tinu *Actor, Bollywood, Director*
101 Lakshyadeep 4th X Road, Juhu Scheme, Mumbai, MS 400049, INDIA

Anand, Vijay *Actor, Director, Filmmaker, Producer, Bollywood*
Ketnav 17 Union Park Pali Hill, Khar, Bombay, MS 400 052, INDIA

Ananiashvill, Nina G *Ballerina*
Bolshoi Theatre, 1 Ploschad Sverdlove, Moscow, 103009, RUSSIA

Anantha, Raaj *Actor*
25 2nd Cross Street, Lake Area, Chennai, TN 600 034, INDIA

Anapau, Kristina *Actor*
Untitled Entertainment (NY), 23 E 22nd St Fl 3, New York, NY 10010 USA

Anastacia *Musician*
Braude Mgmt, PO Box 69978, West Hollywood, CA 90069 USA

Anastasio, Trey *Musician*
Dionysian Productions, 431 Pine St, Burlington, VT 05401 USA

Anaya, Rudolfo *Writer*
5324 Canada Vista NW, Albuquerque, NM 87120 USA

Anaya, Toney *Governor*
711 E May Ave, Las Cruces, NM 88001 USA

Anbusrinivas *Actor*
12 Ramanajum Street, Nungambakkam, Chennai, TN 600 034, INDIA

Ancheta, Bernie *Director, Writer*
Lenhoff & Lenhoff, 830 Palm Ave, West Hollywood, CA 90069

Anchia, Juan-Ruiz *Cinematographer*
Stanford-Beckett-Skouras, 1015 Gayley Ave, Los Angeles, CA 90024 USA

Ancker-Johnson, Betsy *Physicist*
222 Harbour Dr #311, Naples, FL 34103 USA

Anddrson, Rebecca Moesta
PO Box 767, Monument, CO 80132-0767

Andere, Jacqueline *Actor*
Televisa, Blvd Adolfo Lopez Mateos 232, Colonia San Angel INN, DF, CP 01060, MEXICO

Anders, David *Actor*
Liberman/Zerman Management, 252 N Larchmont Blvd #200, Los Angeles, CA 90004 USA

Anders, Edward *Misc*
Hintere Engehaldenstr 12, Beme, 3004, SWITZERLAND

Anders, William A *Astronaut, General*
1 Aeroview Lane, Eastsound, WA 98245 USA

Andersen, Anthony *Actor*
1619 Broadway, #900, New York, NY 10019 USA

Andersen, Barbara *Actor*
PO Box 10118, Santa Fe, NM 87504 USA

Andersen, Elmer L *Governor*
1483 Bussard Court, Arden Hills, MN 55112 USA

Andersen, Eric *Musician, Songwriter*
Drake, 177 Woodland Ave, Westwood, NJ 07675 USA

Andersen, Greta *Swimmer*
19332 Brooktrail Lane, Huntington Beach, CA 92648 USA

Andersen, Hjalmar (Hjallis) *Speed Skater*
Velferden for Handelsflaten, Trondheimsvn 2, Oslo 5, 0560, NORWAY

Andersen, Ladell *Coach*
41 W Cedar Dr, Hermiston, OR 97838 USA

Andersen, Larry *Baseball Player*
Cleveland Indians, 8600 SW Carmel Cir, Wilsonville, OR 97070-9430 USA

Andersen, Lee Pamela *Model, Actor*
5699 Kanan Road, #255, Agoura Hills, CA 91301 USA

Andersen, Linda *Yachtsman*
Aroysund, Torod, 3135, NORWAY

Andersen, Mogens *Football Player*
Strandagervej 28, Hellerup, Copenhagen, 2900, DENMARK

Andersen, Morten *Football Player*
6501 Old Shadburn Ferry Road, Buford, GA 30518 USA

Andersen, Reidar *Skier*
National Ski Hall of Fame, PO Box 191, Ishperning, MI 49849 USA

Andersen, Watts Teresa *Swimmer*
2582 Marsha Way, San Jose, CA 95125 USA

Anderson, Allan *Baseball Player*
Minnesota Twins, 1491 Lancaster Kirkersville Rd NW, Lancaster, OH 43130-8969 USA

Anderson, Anthony *Actor, Producer*
Principato/Young Management, 9665 Wilshire Blvd #500, Beverly Hills, CA 90212 USA

Anderson, Audrey Marie *Actor*
Untitled Entertainment (NY), 23 E 22nd St Fl 3, New York, NY 10010 USA

Anderson, Bill *Musician, Songwriter*
PO Box 6721, San Bernardino, CA 92412 USA

Anderson, Bob *Baseball Player*
Chicago Cubs, 4209 E 104th St, Tulsa, OK 74137-6216 USA

Anderson, Brad *Race Car Driver*
1240 S Cucamonga Ave, Ontario, CA 91761 USA

Anderson, Brad *Director*
422 Santa Monica Court, Escondido, CA 92029 USA

Anderson, Bradley J (Brad) *Cartoonist*
13022 Wood Harbour Dr, Montgomery, TX 77536 USA

Anderson, Brady *Baseball Player*
Baltimore Orioles, 959 Fairview Blvd, Incline Village, NV 89451-8942 USA

Anderson, Brett *Musician*
Lookout! Records, 3264 Adeline St, Berkeley, CA 94703 USA

Anderson, Brett *Musician*
Interceptor Enterprises, 98 White Lion St, London, N1 9PF, UNITED KINGDOM (UK)

Anderson, Brian *Baseball Player*
California Angels, 80 Park Ln, Chagrin Falls, OH 44022-2427 USA

Anderson, Bruford
44 Oswald Close Fetcham, Leatherhead, ENGLAND, KT22 9UG

Anderson, Bud *Baseball Player*
Cleveland Indians, 240 Twin Ln E, Wantagh, NY 11793-1963 USA

Anderson, C Neal *Football Player*
35 Farms, 3351 SE State Road 121, Morriston, FL 32668 USA

Anderson, Camille *Actor*
Jerry Shandrew PR, 1050 South Stanley Avenue, Los Angeles, CA 90019-6634 USA

Anderson, Chantelle *Basketball Player*
Cleveland Rockers, Gund Arena, 1 Center Court, Cleveland, OH 44115 USA

Anderson, Christopher *Writer*
Avon/William Morrow, 1350 Ave of Americas, New York, NY 10019 USA

Anderson, Clayton C *Astronaut*
1909 Summer Reef Dr, League City, TX 77573 USA

Anderson, Craig *Baseball Player*
St Louis Cardinals, 19217 SW 96th Loop, Dunnellon, FL 34432-4201 USA

Anderson, Dan
17440 NW Brugger Rd, Portland, OR 97229

Anderson, Daryl *Actor*
24136 Friar St, Woodland Hills, CA 91367 USA

Anderson, Dave
8 Inness Rd, Tenafly, NJ 07670-2715

Anderson, David *Baseball Player*
Los Angeles Dodgers, 207 Athletic Office Bldg, Memphis, TN 38152-3730 USA

Anderson, David P (Dave) *Writer*
8 Inness Road, Tenafly, NJ 07670 USA

Anderson, Derek *Basketball Player*
Portland Trail Blazers, Rose Garden, 1 Center Court St, Portland, OR 97227 USA

Anderson, Dion *Actor*
S D B Partners, 1801 Ave of Stars, #902, Los Angeles, CA 90067 USA

Anderson, Don (Donny) *Football Player*
4516 Lovers Lane, #133, Dallas, TX 75225 USA

Anderson, Don L *Misc*
669 Alameda St, #E, Altadena, CA 91001 USA

Anderson, Donny *Athlete*
4516 Lovers Lane, #133, Dallas, TX 75225

Anderson, Duwayne M *Scientist*
PO Box 468, Hamilton, WA 98255 USA

Anderson, Dwain *Baseball Player*
Oakland A's, 1807 Fallbrook Dr, Alamo,
CA 94507-2810 USA

Anderson, Edward G (Ed) III *General*
Senior Representative, United Nations
Military Committee, Washington, DC
20318 USA

Anderson, Erich *Actor*
Paradigm Agency, 10100 Santa Monica
Blvd, #2500, Los Angeles, CA 90067 USA

Anderson, Erika *Actor, Model*
Artists Agency, 1180 S Beverly Dr, #301,
Los Angeles, CA 90035 USA

Anderson, Erriestine I *Musician*
Thomas Cassidy, 11761 E Speedway Blvd,
Tucson, AZ 85748 USA

Anderson, Garret J *Baseball Player*
California Angels, 11268 Overlook Point,
Tustin, CA 92782-4314 USA

Anderson, Gary A *Football Player*
5563 Wingwood Court, Minnetonka, MN
55345 USA

Anderson, Gary L *Writer*
National Rifle Assn, 11250 Waples Mill
Road, Fairfax, VA 22030 USA

Anderson, George L (Sparky) *Baseball
Player*
Philadelphia Phillies, PO Box 6415,
Thousands Oaks, CA 91359-6415 USA

Anderson, Gerry *Director, Entertainer*
Gerry Anderson Magazine, 332 Lytham
Road, Blackpool, FY4 1DW, UNITED
KINGDOM (UK)

Anderson, Gillian *Actor*
Creative Artists Agency, 9830 Wilshire
Blvd, Beverly Hills, CA 90212 USA

Anderson, H George *Religious Leader*
Evangelical Lutheran Church, 8765 W
Higgins Road, Chicago, IL 60631 USA

Anderson, Hans Christian *Misc*
Stanford University, Chemistry Dept,
Stanford, CA 94305 USA

Anderson, Harry *Actor*
100 Bourbon St, PO Box 372, New York,
NY 10008 USA

Anderson, Ho Che *Artist*
Fantagraphics Books, 7563 Lake City
Way, Seattle, WA 98115 USA

Anderson, Howard A *Actor*
PO Box 2230, Los Angeles, CA 90028
USA

Anderson, Howard A Jr *Cinematographer*
4943 Sunnyslope Ave, Sherman Oaks, CA
91423 USA

Anderson, Ian *Musician, Songwriter*
43 Brook Green, London, W6 7ER,
UNITED KINGDOM (UK)

Anderson, Jack N *Writer*
PO Box TT, McLean, VA 22101 USA

Anderson, James F *Religious Leader*
12 Surf Ave, Ocean Grove, NJ 07756 USA

Anderson, James G *Misc*
Harvard Unviversity, Eatrh-Planetary
Physics Center, Cambridge, MA 02138
USA

Anderson, James W *Doctor*
University of Kentucky, Medical Center,
Endocrinology Dept, Lexington, KY 40506
USA

Anderson, Janet *Golfer*
Outlings on Links, PO Box 10475,
Phoenix, AZ 85064 USA

Anderson, Jim *Baseball Player*
California Angels, 21301 Bottletree Ln
Unit 1128, Newhall, CA 91321-4451 USA

Anderson, Jo
1505 10th St, Santa Monica, CA 90401

Anderson, John *Songwriter, Musician*
Bobby Roberts, PO Box 1547,
Goodlettsville, TN 37070 USA

Anderson, John B *Misc*
3300 NE 36th St, #1016, Fort Laudedale,
FL 33308 USA

Anderson, John E *Attorney General*
Kindel & Anderson, 555 S Flower St
#2601, Los Angeles, CA 90071 USA

Anderson, John Jr *Governor*
16609 W 133rd St, Olathe, KS 66062
USA

Anderson, Jon *Musician*
Sun Artists, 9 Hillgate St, London, W8
7SP, UNITED KINGDOM (UK)

Anderson, June *Opera Singer*
Herbert Breslin, 119 W 57th St, #1505,
New York, NY 10019 USA

Anderson, Kenneth A (Ken) *Football
Player, Football Coach*
Jacksonville Jaguars, 1 AllTel Stadium
Place, Jacksonville, FL 32202 USA

Anderson, Kenny *Basketball Player*
270 N Canon Dr, #1289, Beverly Hills,
CA 90210 USA

Anderson, Kent *Baseball Player*
California Angels, 925 E Twin Church Rd,
Timmonsville, SC 29161-8528 USA

Anderson, Kevin *Actor*
Writers & Artists, 8383 Wilshire Blvd,
#550, Beverly Hills, CA 90211 USA

Anderson, Kevin C *Actor*
McKeon-Valeo Management, 9107
Wilshire Blvd #321, Beverly Hills, CA
90210 USA

Anderson, Kevin J *Writer*
Trident Media Group LLC, 41 Madison
Ave Fl 33, New York, NY 10010 USA

Anderson, Laurie *Musician*
Maine Road, 195 Chrystie St, #501F, New
York, NY 10002 USA

Anderson, Loni *Actor*
Innovative Artists (LA), 1505 Tenth St,
Santa Monica, CA 90401 USA

Anderson, Loni *Actor*
20652 Lassen, #98, Chatsworth, CA
91311 USA

Anderson, Louie *Actor, Comedian*
109 N Sycamore Ave, Los Angeles, CA
90036 USA

Anderson, Loule *Actor, Comedian*
8033 Sunset Blvd #605, West Hollywood,
CA 90046 USA

Anderson, Lynn *Musician*
Anders Productions, 4925 Tyne Valley
Road, Nashville, TN 37220 USA

Anderson, Marlon *Baseball Player*
Philadelphia Phillies, 2747 Via Capri Unit
1128, Clearwater, FL 33764-5900 USA

Anderson, Mary *Actor*
1127 Norman Place, Los Angeles, CA
90049 USA

Anderson, Matt *Baseball Player*
Detroit Tigers, 14626 Anderson Woods
Trce, Louisville, KY 40245-8428 USA

Anderson, Melissa Sue *Actor*
PO Box 1148, Beverly Hills, CA 90213
USA

Anderson, Melody *Actor*
PO Box 350, New York, NY 10028 USA

Anderson, Michael *Musician, Songwriter*
Brock Assoc, 7106 Moores Ln, #200,
Brentwood, TN 37027 USA

Anderson, Michael H *Physicist*
University of Colorado, Physics Dept,
Boulder, CO 80309 USA

Anderson, Michael J *Director*
Paul Burford, 52 Yorkminster Road, North
York, ON M2P 1M3, CANADA

Anderson, Mike *Baseball Player*
Cincinnati Reds, 140 Clear Springs Rd,
Georgetown, TX 78628-2611 USA

Anderson, Mike *Baseball Player*
Philadelphia Phillies, RR 1, Timmonsville,
SC 29161-9801 USA

Anderson, Mitchell *Actor*
Badgley Connor Talent, 9229 Sunset Blvd,
#311, Los Angeles, CA 90069 USA

Anderson, Nick *Basketball Player*
9163 Port Cypress Dr, Orlando, FL 32836
USA

Anderson, Nick *Editor, Cartoonist*
Courier Journal, Editorial Dept, 525 W
Broadway, Louisville, KY 40202 USA

Anderson, Ottis J (O J) *Football Player*
47 Duffield Dr, South Orange, NJ 07079
USA

Anderson, Pamela *Actor*
Rocket Photographic, 984 Monument
Street, Suite 205, Pacific Palisades, CA
90272 USA

Anderson, Paul Thomas *Director, Writer*
2402 Grand Canal, Venice, CA 90291
USA

Anderson, Paul Thomas *Director*
Endeavor Agency LLC (LA), 9601 Wilshire
Blvd Fl 3, Beverly Hills, CA 90210 USA

Anderson, Paul WS *Director*
United Talent Agency (UTA), 9560
Wilshire Blvd, Beverly Hills, CA 90212
USA

Anderson, Philip W *Nobel Prize Laureate*
Princeton University, Physics Dept,
Princeton, NJ 08544 USA

Anderson, Poul
3 Las Palomas, Orinda, CA 94563

Anderson, R John *Football Player*
14730 Crestwood Court, Elm Grove, WI
53122 USA

Anderson, R Lanier III *Judge*
US Court of Appeals, 56 Forsyth St NW,
Atlanta, GA 30303 USA

Anderson, Randy *Race Car Driver*
Brad Anderson Enterprises, 2356 1st St, La Verne, CA 91750 USA

Anderson, Ray *Musician*
James faith Entertainment, 318 Wynne Lane, Port Jefferson, NY 11777 USA

Anderson, Reid B *Dancer, Director*
Stuttgart Ballet, Ober Schlossgarten 6, Stuttgart, 70173, GERMANY

Anderson, Renee *Actor*
2818 Laurel Canyon Blvd, Los Angeles, CA 90046 USA

Anderson, Richard *Actor*
10120 Cielo Dr, Beverly Hills, CA 90210 USA

Anderson, Richard Dean *Actor*
Gekko Film Corporation, 2500 Broadway St, Santa Monica, CA 90404 USA

Anderson, Richard P (Dick) *Football Player*
4603 Santa Maria St, Coral Gables, FL 33146 USA

Anderson, Rick *Baseball Player*
New York Mets, 8495 Ashford Rd, Saint Paul, MN 55125-8481 USA

Anderson, Robert *Business Person*
Rockwell International, 5836 Corporate Ave, #100, Cypress, CA 90630 USA

Anderson, Robert G W *Misc*
British Museum, Great Russell St, London, WC1B 3DG, UNITED KINGDOM (UK)

Anderson, Robert W *Writer*
14 Sutton Place S, New York, NY 10022 USA

Anderson, Ross *Journalist*
Seattle Times, Editorial Dept, 1120 John St, Seattle, WA 98109 USA

Anderson, Scott *Baseball Player*
Texas Rangers, 13555 Fielding Rd, Lake Oswego, OR 97034-2422 USA

Anderson, Shandon *Basketball Player*
8 Oak Valley Lane, Purchase, NY 10577 USA

Anderson, Shelly *Race Car Driver*
1240 S Cucamonga Ave, Ontario, CA 91761 USA

Anderson, Stephen H *Judge*
US Court of Appeals, Federal Building, 125 S State St, Salt Lake City, UT 84138 USA

Anderson, Sunshine *Musician*
Family Tree, 135 E 57th St, #2600, New York, NY 10022 USA

Anderson, Terence (Terry) *Journalist*
17 Sunlight Hill, Yonkers, NY 10704 USA

Anderson, Terry *Producer*
Pinewood Studios, Iverheath, Iver, Bucks, SL0 0NH, UNITED KINGDOM (UK)

Anderson, Theodore W *Economist, Mathematician*
746 Santa Ynez St, Stanford, CA 94305 USA

Anderson, Tom *Actor*
William Morris Agency, 151 El Camino Dr, Beverly Hills, CA 90212 USA

Anderson, Vickey Ray *Athlete*
1145 SW 132nd St, Oklahoma City, OK 73170-6957

Anderson, W French *Misc*
USC Medical School, 144 E Lake View Terrace, Los Angeles, CA 90039 USA

Anderson, Warren M *Business Person*
270 Park Ave, New York, NY 10017 USA

Anderson, Webster *War Hero*
3044 US Highway 321 N, Winnsboro, SC 29180 USA

Anderson, Wendell R *Governor, Senator*
Larkin & Hoffman, 1700 First Bank Plaza W, Minneapolis, MN 55402 USA

Anderson, Wes *Director, Writer*
United Talent Agency, 9560 Wilshire Blvd, #500, Beverly Hills, CA 90212 USA

Anderson, Wessell *Musician*
Fat City Artists, 1906 Chet Atkins Place, #502, Nashville, TN 37212 USA

Anderson, Weston *Physicist*
Varian Assoc, 611 Hansen Way, Palo Alto, CA 94304 USA

Anderson, Wilford C *War Hero*
3585 Round Barn Blvd, Santa Rosa, CA 95403 USA

Anderson, William R *Misc*
10505 Miller Road, Oakton, VA 22124 USA

Anderson, Willie *Basketball Player*
Toronto Raptors, Air Canada Center, 40 Bay St, Toronto, ON M5J 2N8, CANADA

Anderson III, N Christian *Editor, Publisher*
Gazette Telegraph, 30 S Prospect St, Colorado Springs, CO 80903 USA

Andersson, Benny *Musician, Composer*
Mono Music, Sodra Brobaeken 41-A, Stockholm, 111 49, SWEDEN

Andersson, Bibi *Actor*
Agents Associes Beaume, 201 Faubourg Saint Honore, Paris, 75008, FRANCE

Andersson, Harriet *Actor*
Roslagsgatan 15, Stockholm, SWEDEN, 113 55

Andersson, Henrik *Musician*
MOB Agency, 6404 Wilshire Blvd, #505, Los Angeles, CA 90048 USA

Andersson, Kent-Erik *Hockey Player*
Persiljav 9, Karlstad, 65 351, SWEDEN

Anderszewski, Piotr *Conductor, Musician*
Virgin Classics Records, 90 University Plaza, New York, NY 1000

Anderszewski, Piotr *Musician*
Virgin Classics Records, 90 University Plaza, New York, NY 10003 USA

Andes, Karen *Misc*
G P Putnam's Sons, 375 Hudson St, New York, NY 10014 USA

Ando, Tadao *Architect*
Tadao Ando Architect, 5-23-2 Toyosaki, Kitaku, Osaka, 531, JAPAN

Andov, Stojan *President*
Sobranje, 11 Oktombri Blvd, Skopje, 91000, MACEDONIA

Andrade, Sergio *Musician*
DreamWorks Records, 9268 W 3rd St, Beverly Hills, CA 90210 USA

Andrade, William T (Billy) *Golfer*
4439 E Brookhaven Dr NE, Atlanta, GA 30319 USA

Andre, Carl *Artist*
689 Crown St, Brooklyn, NY 11213 USA

Andre, Maurice *Musician*
Presles-en-Brie, Tournan-en-Brie, 77220, FRANCE

Andre, Peter *Musician*
55 Drury Ln, London, 4217, UNITED KINGDOM (UK)

Andre-Deshays, Claudie *Misc*
Hopital Cochin, Rhumatologie Dept, Paris, 75000, FRANCE

Andreas, Dwayne O *Business Person*
181 Southmoreland Place, Decatur, IL 62521 USA

Andreas, G P Allen *Business Person*
Archer-Daniels-Midland, 4666 Faries Parkway, Decatur, IL 62526 USA

Andreasen, Nancy C *Doctor*
200 Hawkings Dr, Iowa City, IA 52242 USA

Andreason, Larry *Yachtsman*
10874 Kyle St, Los Alamitos, CA 90720 USA

Andreeff, Starr *Actor*
C N A Assoc, 1875 Century Park East, #2250, Los Angeles, CA 90067 USA

Andreessen, Marc *Designer*
Opsware, 599 N Mathilda Ave, Sunnyvale, CA 94085 USA

Andrei, Alessandro *Track Athlete*
Via V Bellini 1, Scandicci, Firenze, 50018, ITALY

Andreone, Leah *Songwriter, Musician*
Metropolitan Entertainment, 363 US Highway 46, #300F, Fairfield, NJ 07004 USA

Andreotti, Giulio
Piazza Montecitorio 13, Rome, ITALY, I-00186

Andres, Ernie *Baseball Player*
Boston Red Sox, 5714 Garden Lakes Dr, Bradenton, FL 34203-7226 USA

Andress, Tuck *Musician*
Windham Hill Records, PO Box 5501, Beverly Hills, CA 90209 USA

Andress, Ursula *Actor*
Via Francesco Siacci 38, Rome, 00186, ITALY

Andretti, John *Race Car Driver*
107 Keats Rd, Mooresville, NC 28117 USA

Andretti, Mario *Race Car Driver*
630 Setvaggio Dr, #340, Nazareth, PA 18109 USA

Andretti, Michael M *Race Car Driver*
3310 Airport Rd, Allentown, PA 18109 USA

Andrew, C Robert (Rob) *Athlete, Misc*
Newcastle RFC, Newcastle-upon-Tyne, NE3 2DT, UNITED KINGDOM (UK)

Andrew, HRH
PrinceSunninghill Park, Windsor, ENGLAND

Andrew, Kim *Baseball Player*
Boston Red Sox, 10052 Densmore Ave, Sepulveda, CA 91343-1454 USA

Andrew, Phillip *Actor*
Career Management Corp, 1850 Sawtelle Blvd #450, Los Angeles, CA 90025

Andrew, Prince *Royalty, Prince*
Buckingham Palace, London, SW1A 1AA, UNITED KINGDOM (UK)

Andrews, Al *Boxer*
1119 River St, Rhinelander, WI 54501 USA

Andrews, Andy *Actor, Comedian*
PO Box 17321, Nashville, TN 37217 USA

Andrews, Anthony *Actor*
13 Manor Place, Oxford, Oxon, UNITED KINGDOM (UK)

Andrews, Donna *Golfer*
Ladies Pro Golf Assn, 100 International Golf Dr, Daytona Beach, FL 32124 USA

Andrews, Fred *Baseball Player*
Philadelphia Phillies, PO Box 178016, Chicago, IL 60617-8016 USA

Andrews, Giuseppe *Actor*
PO Box 24561, Ventura, CA 93002 USA

Andrews, Hub *Baseball Player*
New York Giants, 2305 N 2nd Ave, Dodge City, KS 67801-2534 USA

Andrews, Inez *Musician*
Subrena Artists, 330 W 56th St, #18M, New York, NY 10019 USA

Andrews, James *Doctor*
American Sports Medicine Institute, 1313 13th St S, Birmingham, AL 35205 USA

Andrews, James E *Misc*
Presbyterian Church (USA), 100 Witherspoon St, Louisville, KY 40202 USA

Andrews, Jessica *Musician*
RPM Management LLC, 209 Tenth Ave S #229, Nashville, TN 37203 USA

Andrews, John *Baseball Player*
St Louis Cardinals, 9292 Gordon Ave, La Habra, CA 90631-2452 USA

Andrews, John H *Architect*
John Andrews Int'l, PO Box 7087, McMahon's Point, NSW, 2060, AUSTRALIA

Andrews, Julie (Dame) *Actor, Musician*
PO Box 491668, Los Angeles, CA 90049 USA

Andrews, Lee *Musician*
Mars Talent, 27 L'Ambiance Court, Bardonia, NY 10954 USA

Andrews, Mark *Senator*
3354 165th Ave SE, Mapleton, ND 58059 USA

Andrews, Mike *Baseball Player*
Boston Red Sox, 375 Longwood Ave, Boston, MA 02215-5395 USA

Andrews, Naveen *Actor*
International Creative Mgmt, 76 Oxford St, London, W1N 0AX, UNITED KINGDOM (UK)

Andrews, Patricia (Patt) *Musician*
9823 Aldea Ave, Northridge, CA 91325 USA

Andrews, Patricia (Patti) *Musician*
9823 Aldea Ave, Northridge, CA 91325 USA

Andrews, Patty *Musician*
9823 Aldea Ave, Northridge, CA 91354 USA

Andrews, Rob *Baseball Player*
Houston Astros, 1280 Mountbatten Ct, Concord, CA 94518-3927 USA

Andrews, Robert *Writer*
G P Putnam's Sons, 375 Hudson St, New York, NY 10014 USA

Andrews, Robert F *Misc*
5879 Beulah Land, Lakeland, FL 33810 USA

Andrews, Russell *Actor*
William Morris Agency (WMA-LA), 1 William Morris Pl, Beverly Hills, CA 90212 USA

Andrews, Shane *Baseball Player*
Montreal Expos, 1818 N Guadalupe St, Carlsbad, NM 88220-8813 USA

Andrews, Theresa *Swimmer*
2004 Homewood Rd, Annapolis, MD 21402 USA

Andrews, Tige *Actor*
Dade/Schultz, 6442 Coldwater Canyon Ave, #206, Valley Green, CA 91606 USA

Andrews, Tina *Actor*
William Morris Agency (WMA-LA), 1 William Morris Pl, Beverly Hills, CA 90212 USA

Andrews II, George E *Football Player*
10195 Overhill Dr, Santa Ana, CA 92705 USA

Andreychuck, Dave *Hockey Player*
38 Bishopsgate Ave, Hamilton, ON L8V 3K4, CANADA

Andrianarivo, Tantely *Prime Minister*
Prime Minister's Office, Mahazoarivo, Antananarivo, MADAGASCAR

Andrie, George J *Football Player*
26536 E Zeerip, Drummond Island, MI 49726 USA

Andriessen, Louis *Composer*
Nonesuch Records, 75 Rockefeller Plaza, New York, NY 10019 USA

Androsky, Carol *Actor*
Henderson/Hogan, 8285 W Sunset Blvd, #1, West Hollywood, CA 90046 USA

Andrulis, Greg *Football Coach*
Columbus Crew, 2121 Velman Ave, Columbus, OH 43211 USA

Andrus, Cecil *Senator, Governor*
1280 Candleridge Rd, Boise, ID 83712 USA

Andrus, Lou *Football Player*
739 W 550 S, Orem, UT 84058 USA

Andrusyshyn, Zenon *Football Player*
2823 Lake Saxon Dr, Land O Lakes, FL 34639 USA

Andujar, Joaquin *Baseball Player*
Houston Astros, Ave Lamiama Tio #47, San Pedro de Macoris, Dominican Republic

Ane, Charles T (Charlie) III *Football Player*
749 16th Ave, Honolulu, HI 96816 USA

Anemone
82 rue Bonaparte, Paris, FRANCE, 75006

Angarano, Michael *Actor*
Coast to Coast Talent, 3350 Barham Blvd, Los Angeles, CA 90068 USA

Angel, Ashley Parker *Musician*
Trans Continental Records, 7380 Sand Lake Road, #350, Orlando, FL 32819 USA

Angel, Criss *Entertainer, Magician, Musician*
Angel Productions Inc, PO Box 503, E Meadow, NY 11554-0503 USA

Angel, Heather H *Photographer*
Highways, 6 Vicarage Hill, Farnham, Surrey, GU9 8HJ, UNITED KINGDOM (UK)

Angel, James R P *Astronomer*
University of Arizona, Steward Observatory, Tucson, AZ 85721 USA

Angel, Vanessa *Actor*
Bauer Company, The, 9300 Wilshire Blvd #PH, Beverly Hills, CA 90212 USA

Angelini, Florenzo Cardinal *Religious Leader*
Via Anneo Lucano 47, Rome, 00136, ITALY

Angelini, Norm *Baseball Player*
Kansas City Royals, 15063 E Chenango Pl, Aurora, CO 80015-2136 USA

Angell, Wayne D *Government Official, Financier*
Bear Steams Co, 383 Madison Ave, New York, NY 10017 USA

Angelopoulos, Theodoros (Theo) *Director, Writer, Producer, Actor*
Solmou 18, 106 82, Athens, GREECE

Angelou, Maya *Writer*
3240 Valley Road, #MB-9, Winston-Salem, NC 27106 USA

Angels, Anaheim
Edison Field, 2000 Gene Autry Way, Anaheim, CA 92806 USA

Angelycal Musical *Music Group*
Sony Music Miami, 605 Lincoln Rd, Miami Beach, FL 33138 USA

Angelyne *Actor, Model, Artist*
PO Box 16595, Encino, CA 91416 USA

Angerer, Paul *Composer*
Esteplatz 3/26, Vienna, 1030, AUSTRIA

Angerer, Peter *Athlete*
Wagenau 2, Hammer, 17326, GERMANY

Angle, Kurt *Wrestler*
Hawk & Co, PO Box 97007, Pittsburgh, PA 15229 USA

Angler, Natalie M *Journalist*
New York Times, Editorial Dept, 229 W 43rd St, New York, NY 10036 USA

Anglim, Philip *Actor*
2404 Grand Canal, Venice, CA 90291 USA

Anglin, Jennifer *Actor*
651 N Kilkea Dr, Los Angeles, CA 90048 USA

Anguiano, Raul *Artist*
Anaxagoras 1326, Colonia Narvate, Mexico City, 13 DF, MEXICO

Anhalt, Edward *Actor*
13906 Fiji Way #148, Marina del Rey, CA 90292-6930

Anikulap-Kuti, Femi *Songwriter, Musician*
MCA Records, 70 Universal City Plaza, Universal City, CA 91608 USA

Animals, The *Music Group*
PO Box 1821, Ojai, CA 93024 USA

Anissina, Marina *Figure Skater*
Sports de Glace Federation, 35 Rue Felicien David, Paris, 75016, FRANCE

Aniston, Jennifer *Actor*
Creative Artists Agency LCC (CAA-LA), 9830 Wilshire Blvd, Beverly Hills, CA 90212 USA

Aniston, John *Actor*
3110 Summit Pointe Dr, Topanga, CA 90290 USA

Anjali *Bollywood, Actor*
14 Ganapathi Colony, 1 Street Gopalpuram, Chennai, TN 600006, INDIA

Anjali, Devi *Actor, Bollywood*
6 Bags Road, Raja Annamalai Puram, Chennai, TN 600028, INDIA

Anjard Sr, Ronald P *Business Person*
PO Box 420950, San Diego, CA 92142 USA

Anju *Actor, Bollywood*
37 Nagarathanammal Nagar, Janaki Nagar, Chennai, TN 600017, INDIA

Anka, Paul *Musician, Songwriter, Actor*
12078 Summit Circle, Beverly Hills, CA 90210 USA

Ankiel, Rick *Baseball Player*
St Louis Cardinals, 126 Sandpiper Cir, Jupiter, FL 33477-8433 USA

Anlyan, William G *Doctor*
Duke Medical Center, 100 Seeley Mudd Building #109, Durham, NC 27710 USA

Annakin, Kenneth (Ken) *Director*
Denise Denny, 9233 Swallow Dr, Los Angeles, CA 90069 USA

Annan, Kofi A *Politician, Secretary*
Secretary General's Office, 1 United Nations Plaza, New York, NY 10017 USA

Annan, Kofi A *General*
Secretary-General's Office, 1 United Nations Plz, New York, NY 10017 USA

Annand, Richard Wallace *War Hero*
Springwell House, Whitesmocks, Durham City, DH1 4ZL, UNITED KINGDOM (UK)

Annaud, Jean-Jacques *Director*
Reperage, 16 Rue Saint-Vincent, Paris, 75018, FRANCE

Anne *Royalty*
Gatecombe Park, Gloucestershire, UNITED KINGDOM (UK)

Anne of Bourbon-Palma *Royalty*
Villa Serena, 77 Chemin Louis-Degallier, Versoix-Geneva, 1290, SWITZERLAND

Annenberg, Wallis *Publisher*
10273 Century Woods Dr, Los Angeles, CA 90067 USA

Annett, Chloe *Actor*
Innovative Artists (LA), 1505 Tenth St, Santa Monica, CA 90401 USA

Annis, Francesca *Actor*
International Creative Mgmt, 76 Oxford St, London, W1N 0AX, UNITED KINGDOM (UK)

Annu, Kapoor *Actor, Bollywood*
F-19 Flat No. 504 Green Crest Yamuna Nagar, Opp Parasrampuria Tower Andheri(W), Mumbai, MS 400053, INDIA

Annunziata, Robert *Business Person*
Global Crossing Ltd, Wessex House, 45 Reid St, Hamilton, HM, 12, BERMUDA

Ansa, Tina McElroy *Writer*
William Morris Agency, 151 El Camino Dr, Beverly Hills, CA 90212 USA

Ansara, Edward *Actor*
Jack Scagnetti, 5118 Vineland Ave #102, North Hollywood, CA 91601 USA

Ansara, Michael *Actor*
4624 Park Mirasol, Calabasas, CA 91302 USA

Anschutz, Philip F *Business Person*
Qwest Communications, 700 Qwest Tower, 555 17th St, Denver, CO 80202 USA

Anselmo, Philip *Musician*
Concrete Mgmt, 361 W Broadway, #200, New York, NY 10013 USA

Anspach, Susan *Actor*
PO Box 5605, Santa Monica, CA 90409 USA

Anspaugh, David *Director, Producer*
Creative Artists Agency, 9830 Wilshire Blvd, Beverly Hills, CA 90212 USA

Ant, Adam *Musician*
Peters Fraser & Dunlop (PFD - UK), Drury House, 34-43 Russell St, London, WC2 B5, UNITED KINGDOM (UK)

Ant, Adam *Musician*
Kathleen Denney Co, 18685A Main St, #627, Huntington Beach, CA 92648 USA

Antes, Horst *Artist*
Hohenbergstr 11, Karlsruhe (Wolfartsweier, 76228, GERMANY

Anthony, Barbara Cox *Business Person*
Cox Enterprises, 1400 Lake Hearn Dr NE, Atlanta, GA 30319 USA

Anthony, Carl *Misc*
Harvard University, Kennedy Government School, Cambridge, MA 02138 USA

Anthony, Carmelo *Basketball Player*
Denver Nuggets, Pepsi Center, 1000 Chopper Circle, Denver, CO 80204 USA

Anthony, Eric *Baseball Player*
Houston Astros, 42 Fosters Ct, Sugar Land, TX 77479-5872 USA

Anthony, Greg *Basketball Player*
520 S 4th St, Las Vegas, NV 89101 USA

Anthony, Jason *Model*
Boss Models, 1 Gansevoort St, New York, NY 10014 USA

Anthony, Lysette *Actor*
46 Old Compton St, London, WV 5PB, UNITED KINGDOM (UK)

Anthony, Marc *Musician, Actor, Songwriter*
Marc Anthony Productions, 146 W 57th St #38C, New York, NY 10019 USA

Anthony, Piers
PO Box 2289, Inverness, FL 34451-2289

Anthony, Plers *Writer*
PO Box 2289, Inverness, FL 34451 USA

Anthony, Ray *Musician*
9288 Kinglet Dr, Los Angeles, CA 90069 USA

Anthrax
15 Haldane Crescent Piners Heath, Wakefield, ENGLAND, WF1 4TE

Antin, Steve *Actor, Writer*
International Creative Mgmt, 8942 Wilshire Blvd, #219, Beverly Hills, CA 90211 USA

Antion, Tom

Anton, Alan *Musician*
Macklam Feldman Mgmt, 1505 W 2nd Ave, #200, Vancouver, BC V6H 3Y4, CANADA

Anton, Craig *Actor*
United Talent Agency, 9560 Wilshire Blvd, #500, Beverly Hills, CA 90212 USA

Anton, Susan *Actor, Live Show*
Susan Anton Inc, 16830 Ventura Blvd, Suite 300, Encino, CA 91499-3465 USA

Anton, Susan *Misc*
Institute of Human Origins, 1288 9th St, Berkeley, CA 94710 USA

Antonakakis, Dimitris *Architect*
Atelier 66, Emm Benaki 118, Athens, 114-73, GREECE

Antonakakis, Suzana M *Architect*
Atelier 66, Emm Benaki 118, Athens, 114-73, GREECE

Antonelli, Dominic A *Astronaut*
4106 Oak Blossom Court, Houston, TX 77059 USA

Antonelli, Ennio Cardinal *Religious Leader*
Archdiocese, Piazza S Giovanni 3, Florence, 50129, ITALY

Antonelli, Johnny *Baseball Player*
Boston Braves, 198 Brittany Ln, Pittsford, NY 14534-4311 USA

Antonelli, Laura *Actor*
Pietrovalle, Via B Buozzi 51, Rome, 00197, ITALY

Antonetti, Lorenzo Cardinal *Religious Leader*
Patrimony of the Holy See, Palazzo Apostolico, Vatican City, 00120

Antonio *Dancer*
Caslada 7, Madrid, SPAIN

Antonio, Jim *Actor*
Epstein-Wyckoff, 280 S Beverly Dr #400, Beverly Hills, CA 90212 USA

Antonio, Lou *Actor*
530 S Gaylord Dr, Burbank, CA 91505 USA

Antonio dos Santos R, Eanes *President, General*
Partido Renovador Democratico, Travessa do Falo 9, Lisbon, 1200, Portugal

Antonioni, Michelangelo *Director*
Via Vincenzo Tiberio 18, Rome, 00191, ITALY

Antoun (Khouri), Bishop *Religious Leader*
Antiochian Orthodox Christian Archdiocese, 358 Mountain Rd, Englewood, NJ 07631 USA

Antrobus, Charles *Governor*
Governor General's Office, Kingstown, Saint Vincent & Grenadlines

Antuofermo, Vito *Boxer*
16019 81st St, Howard Beach, NY 11414
USA

Antwine, Houston *Football Player*
28074 Dobbel Ave, Hayward, CA 94542
USA

Anu, Christine *Musician*
Robert Bamham Mgmt, 432 Tyagarah
Road, Myocum, NSW, 2481, AUSTRALIA

Anuja *Actor, Bollywood*
4-B Periyar Street Happee Home Apts,
Gandhi Nagar Saligram, Chennai, TN
600093, INDIA

Anusha *Actor, Bollywood*
Flat Non 202 II Floor, 167 Eldams Road,
Chennai, TN 600018, INDIA

Anuszkiewicz, Richard J *Artist*
76 Chestnut St, Englewood, NJ 07631
USA

Anwar, Gabrielle *Actor*
United Talent Agency, 9560 Wilshire
Blvd, #500, Beverly Hills, CA 90212 USA

Aoki, Chieko N *Business Person*
Westin Hotels Co, Westin Building, 777
Westchester Ave, White Plains, NY 10604
USA

Aoki, Devon *Actor*
International Creative Management
(ICM-LA), 8942 Wilshire Blvd, Beverly
Hills, CA 90211 USA

Aoki, Isao *Golfer*
International Mgmt Group, 1 Eriview
Plaza, 1360 E 9th St #1300, Cleveland,
OH 44114 USA

Aoki, Rocky *Business Person, Athlete*
Benihana of Tokyo, 8685 NW 53rd Terr,
#201, Miami, FL 33166 USA

Aouita, Said *Track Athlete*
Abdejil Bencheikh, 9 Rue Soivissi,
Loubira, Rabat, MOROCCO

Apap, Gilles *Musician*
Columbia Artists Mgmt Inc, 165 W 57th
St, New York, NY 10019 USA

Aparicio, Luis E *Baseball Player*
Chicago White Sox, Calle 67 #26-82,
Maracalbo, VENEZUELA

Apel, Katrin *Athlete*
Suedlung 9, Grafenroda, 99330,
GERMANY

Apodaca, Bob *Baseball Player*
New York Mets, 2999 SW Van Buren Ter,
Port Saint Lucie, FL 34953-4262 USA

Apodaca, Raymond S (Jerry) *Governor*
6223 Utah Ave NW, Washington, DC
20015 USA

Apodaka, Bob
Box 7845, Columbia, SC 29202

Apollonia *Actor, Model*
8271 Melrose Ave, #110, Los Angeles, CA
90046 USA

Aponte Martinez, Luis Cardinal *Misc*
Arzobispado, Apatado S-1967, 201 Calle
San Jorge, Santurce, PR 00912 USA

Appel, Deena *Designer*
Montana Artists Agency, 625 Montana
Ave Fl 2, Santa Monica, CA 90403 USA

Appel, Fiona *Songwriter, Musician*
H K Mgmt, 9200 W Sunset Blvd, #530,
Los Angeles, CA 90069 USA

Appel, Karel C *Artist*
Galerie Statier, 51 Rue de Seine, Paris,
FRANCE

Appice, Carmine *Musician*
Long Distance Entertainment, 568 SE
Woodbright #234, Boynton Beach, FL
33435 USA

Appier, Kevin
Kansas City Royals, 24761 Goldcrest Dr,
Bonita Springs, FL 34134-0945 USA

Apple, Fiona *Musician*
HK Management, 9200 Sunset Blvd #530,
Los Angeles, CA 90069

Apple Jr, Raymond W *Journalist*
New York Times, Editorial Dept, 1627 I St
NW, Washington, DC 20006 USA

Applebaum, Judy

Appleby, Shiri *Actor*
United Talent Agency (UTA), 9560
Wilshire Blvd, Beverly Hills, CA 90212
USA

Appleby, Stuart *Golfer*
Int'l Mgmt Group, 1 Erieview Plaza, 1360
E 9th St #1300, Cleveland, OH 44114
USA

Applegate, Christina *Actor*
20411 Chapter Dr, Woodland Hills, CA
91364 USA

Applegate, Eddie *Actor*
Studio Talent Group, 1328 12th St, Santa
Monica, CA 90401 USA

Applegate, Jodi *Commentator*
NBC-TV, News Dept, 30 Rockefeller
Plaza, New York, NY 10112 USA

Applen, Henry E *Misc*
Plant Guard Workers Union, 25510 Kelly
Road, Roseville, MI 48066 USA

Appleton, James R *Educator*
University of Redlands, President's Office,
Redlands, CA 92373 USA

Appleton, Myra *Editor*
Cosmopolitan Magazine, Editorial Dept,
224 W 57th St, New York, NY 10019
USA

Appleton, Steven R *Business Person*
Micron Technology, PO Box 6, Boise, ID
83707 USA

Appolonia (Kotero) *Actor*
TalentWorks (LA), 3500 W Olive Ave
#1400, Burbank, CA 91505 USA

Aprea, John *Actor*
401 S Detroit, #113, Los Angeles, CA
90036 USA

April, Johnny *Musician*
William Morris Agency, 151 El Camino
Dr, Beverly Hills, CA 90212 USA

April Wine *Music Group*
Mascioli Entertainment Corp, 2202 Curry
Ford Rd #E, Orlando, FL 32806 USA

Apt, Jerome (Jay) *Astronaut*
4 Shadycourt Dr, Pittsburgh, PA 15232
USA

Apted, Michael *Actor*
Creative Artists Agency LCC (CAA-LA),
9830 Wilshire Blvd, Beverly Hills, CA
90212 USA

Apted, Michael D *Director*
360 N Saltair Ave, Los Angeles, CA 90049
USA

Aqua *Music Group*
TG Management Productions &
Publishing, Badehusvej 1, 2 sal tv,
Aalborg, 9000, DENMARK

Aquilino, Thomas J Jr *Judge*
US Court of International Trade, 1 Federal
Plaza, New York, NY 10278 USA

Aquino
AmyPO Box 5617, Beverly Hills, CA
90210

Aquino, Amy *Actor*
9615 Brighton Way, #300, Beverly Hills,
CA 90210 USA

Aquino, Corazon C *President, Nobel Prize
Laureate*
119 de la Rosa Comer, Castro St, Makati
City, Manila, PHILIPPINES

Arafat, Yasser *Politician, President, Nobel
Prize Laureate*
President's Office, PO Box 115, Jericho,
Palestine, ISRAEL

Aragall Garriga, Glacomo *Opera Singer*
Stafford Law Assoc, 6 Barham Close,
Weybridge, Surrey, KT1 9PR, UNITED
KINGDOM (UK)

Aragon, Art *Boxer*
19050 Wells Dr, Tarzana, CA 91356 USA

Aragones, Sergio *Cartoonist*
PO Box 696, Ojai, CA 93024 USA

Araiza, Armando *Actor*
Televisa, Blvd Adolfo Lopez Mateos 232,
Colonia San Angel INN, DF, CP 01060,
MEXICO

Araiza, Francisco *Opera Singer*
Columbia Artists Mgmt Inc, 165 W 57th
St, New York, NY 10019 USA

Arakawa, Toyozo *Artist*
4-101 O-Hatacho, Tokyo, JAPAN

Araki, Greg *Director*
United Talent Agency (UTA), 9560
Wilshire Blvd, Beverly Hills, CA 90212
USA

Arambula, Aracely *Actor*
Televisa, Blvd Adolfo Lopez Mateos 232,
Colonia San Angel INN, DF, CP 01060,
MEXICO

Aramburu, Juan Carlos Cardinal *Religious
Leader*
Arzobispado, Suipacha 1034, Buenos
Aires, 1008, ARGENTINA

Arana, Facundo *Actor*
Telefe - Argentina, Pavon 2444
(C1248AAT), Buenos Aires, ARGENTINA

Arana, Tomas *Actor*
Paradigm Agency, 10100 Santa Monica
Blvd, #2500, Los Angeles, CA 90067 USA

Arango, Juan Carlos *Actor*
Gabriel Blanco Iglesias (Mexico), Rio
Balsas 35-32, Colonia Cuauhtemoc, DF,
06500, Mexico

Ararktsyan, Babken G *Government Official*
National Assembly, Marshal Bagzamyan Prosp 26, Yerevan, 375019, ARMENIA

Arashi, Qadi Abdul Karim al
Constituent People's Assembly, Sana'a, Yemen

Araskog, Rand V *Business Person*
ITT Corp, 1330 Ave of Americas, New York, NY 10019 USA

Arau, Alfonso *Director*
Productions AA, Privada Rafael Oliva 8, Coyoacan, 04120, MEXICO

Arau, Fernando *Actor*
Univision, 314 Main St, Chico, CA 95928 USA

Araujo, Serafim Fernandes de Cardinal *Religious Leader*
Curia Metropolitana, Av Brasil 2079, Belo Horizonte, MG, 30240-002, Brazil

Aravind, Ramesh *Actor, Bollywood*
F1 4th Block, Bajaj Apartments Nandanam Extn, Chennai, TN 600035, INDIA

Araya, Zeudy *Actor*
Carol Levi Co, Via Giuseppe Pisanelli, Rome, 00196, ITALY

Arbaaz, Ali Khan *Actor, Bollywood*
602 Sea King Apts, Band Stand Bandra (W), Mumbai, MS 400050, INDIA

Arbanas, Frederick V (Fred) *Football Player*
3350 SW Hook Road, Lees Summit, MO 64082 USA

Arbeid, Murray *Fashion Designer*
202 Ebury St, London, SW1W 8UN, UNITED KINGDOM (UK)

Arber, Werner *Nobel Prize Laureate*
70 Klingelbergstr, Basel, 4056, SWITZERLAND

Arbour, Louise *Government Official*
UN Human Rights Commision, 1 United Nations Plaza, New York, NY 10017 USA

Arbulu Galliani, Guillermo *Prime Minister*
Prime Minister's Office, Urb Corpac, Calle 1 Oesta S/N, Lima, 27, PERU

Arbus, Alan *Actor*
2208 N Beverly Glen, Los Angeles, CA 90077 USA

Arbus, Loreen
8841 Appian Way, Los Angeles, CA 90046

Arcain, Janeth *Basketball Player*
Houston Comets, 2 Greenway Plaza #400, Houston, TX 77046 USA

Archambault, Lee J *Astronaut*
4318 Sweet Cicely Court, Houston, TX 77059 USA

Archana *Actor, Bollywood*
8 North Cresent Road, T Nagar, Chennai, TN 600017, INDIA

Archer, Annee *Actor*
13201 Old Oak Lane, Los Angeles, CA 90049 USA

Archer, Bernard
Holt Barton, Witham Frairy Somerset, ENGLAND

Archer, Beverly *Actor*
Judy Schoen, 606 N Larchmont Blvd, #309, Los Angeles, CA 90004 USA

Archer, George *Golfer*
774 Mays Blvd, #10-184, Incline Village, NV 89451 USA

Archer, Glenn L Jr *Judge*
US Court of Appeals, 717 Madison Place NW, Washington, DC 20439 USA

Archer, Jeffrey *Actor, Writer*
Curtis Brown Ltd, Hay Market House 28/29, Hay Market Fl 4, London, SW1 Y45, UNITED KINGDOM (UK)

Archer, Jim *Baseball Player*
Kansas City A's, 1414 Oleander Dr, Tarpon Springs, FL 34689-2308 USA

Archer, John *Writer*
10901 176th Circle NE, #3601, Redmond, WA 98052 USA

Archer, Tasmin
20 Manchester Sq, London, ENGLAND, W1M 5AE

Archer of Weston-Super-Mare, Jeffrey H *Government Official, Writer*
93 Albert Embankment, London, SE1 7TY, UNITED KINGDOM (UK)

Archerd, Army *Journalist*
Variety Magazine - Editorial Dept, 5700 Wilshire Blvd, Los Angeles, CA 90036 USA

Archibaid, Nathaniel (Nate) *Basketball Player*
2920 Holland Ave, Bronx, NY 10467 USA

Archibald, Nolan D *Business Person*
Black & Decker Corp, 701 E Joppa Road, Towson, MD 21286 USA

Archipoeski, Ken *Musician*
PO Box 656507, Fresh Meadows, NY 11365 USA

Arcia, Jose *Baseball Player*
Chicago Cubs, 7325 NW 3rd St, Miami, FL 33126-4211 USA

Arcieri, Leila *Actor*
Catch 23 Management, 301 N Canon Dr #207, Beverly Hills, CA 90210 USA

Arcieri, Leila *Actor*
Paradigm (LA), 10100 Santa Monica Blvd, Fl 25, Los Angeles, CA 90067 USA

Arcineiga, Tomas A *Educator*
California State College, President's Office, Bakersfield, CA 9331 USA

Ard, William D (Bill) *Football Player*
41 Vail Lane, Watchung, NJ 07069 USA

Ardalan, Nader *Architect*
KEO International Consultants, PO Box 3679, Safat, 13037, KUWAIT

Ardant, Fanny *Actor*
Artmedia, 20 Ave Rapp, Paris, 75007, FRANCE

Ardell, Donald B *Doctor*
3301 Bayshore Blvd, #802 SW, Tampa, FL 33629 USA

Arden, Jann *Musician, Songwriter*
Macklam Feldman Mgmt, 1505 W 2nd Ave, #200, Vancouver, BC V6H 3Y4, CANADA

Arden, John *Writer*
Cassarotto, 60/66 Wardour St, London, W1V 4ND, UNITED KINGDOM (UK)

Arden, Toni *Musician*
3434 75th St, Jackson Heights, NY 11372 USA

Arditi, Pierre
6-8 rue Lalande, Paris, FRANCE, 75014

Ardito Barletta, Nicolas *President*
PO Box 7737, Panama City, 9, PANAMA

Arditti, Irvine *Musician*
Lattidue Arts, 109 Boul Saint-Joseph Quest, Montreal, PA H2T 2P7, CANADA

Ardolino, Todd *Director*
Creative Artists Agency, 9830 Wilshire Blvd, Beverly Hills, CA 90212 USA

Ardolino, Tom *Musician*
Skyline Music, PO Box 31, Lancaster, NH USA

Aregood, Richards L *Journalist*
Philadelphia Daily News, Editorial Dept, 400 N Broad St, Philadelphia, PA 19130 USA

Arena, Bruce *Soccer Player, Coach*
DC United, 14120 Newbrook Dr, Chantilly, VA 20151 USA

Arena, Tina *Musician*
Magnus Entertainment, 5 Darley St, Neutral Bay, NSW, 2089, AUSTRALIA

Arenas, Joe *Football Player*
12508 E Ventura Dr, Galveston, TX 77554 USA

Arenberg, Lee *Actor*
Gage Group, The (LA), 14724 Ventura Blvd #505, Los Angeles, CA 91403 USA

Arens, Moshe *Government Official*
Ministry of Defence, Rehov Kapian, Hakirya, Tel-Aviv, 67695, ISRAEL

Arent, Eddi
Am Postplatz 5, Titisee-Neustadt, GERMANY, 79822

Aretsky, Ken *Business Person*
21 Club, 21 W 52nd St, New York, NY 10019 USA

Arfons, Arthur E (Art) *Race Car Driver*
PO Box 1409, Saint Charles, MO 63302 USA

Argento, Asia *Actor*
Via Pisanelli 2, Rome, 00196, ITALY

Argento, Dario *Director*
ADC, Via Balemonti 2, Rome, ITALY

Argento, Dominick *Composer*
Universit of Minnesota, Music Dept, Ferguson Hall, Minneapolis, MN 55455 USA

Argerich, Martha *Musician*
Jacques Thelen Agence, 252 Rue Faubourg, Saint Honore, Paris, 75008, FRANCE

Arguello, Alexis
1 Hall of Fame Dr, Canastota, NY 13032

Arian, David *Misc*
International Longshoremen's Union, 1188 Franklin St, San Francisco, CA 94109 USA

Arias, Mariana *Actor*
Telefe - Argentina, Pavon 2444 (C1248AAT), Buenos Aires, ARGENTINA

Arias, Ricardo M *President*
Apdo 4549, Panama City, PANAMA

Arias, Yancey *Actor*
Henze Management, 1925 Century Park E #2320, Los Angeles, CA 90067 USA

Arias-Sanchez, Oscar *Politician, Nobel Prize Laureate, President*
Arias Foundation for Peace, Apdo 8-6410-1000, San Jose, COSTA RICA

Arie, India *Musician, Music Group, Songwriter*
Helter Skelter, Plaza, 535 Kings Road, London, SW10 0S, UNITED KINGDOM (UK)

Arigoni, Dulio *Misc*
Im Glockenacker 42, Zurich, 8053, SWITZERLAND

Arima, Akito *Physicist*
Physical Research Institute, Hirosawa 2-1, Wakoshi, Saltarna, 351-01, JAPAN

Arinze, Francis Cardinal *Religious Leader*
Pontifical Council for Inter-Religious Dialogue, Vatican City, 00120

Aris, Ben
47 West Sq, London, ENGLAND, SE11 4SP

Arison, M Micky *Business Person*
Camivai Corp, 3655 NW 87th Ave, Miami, FL 33178 USA

Aristide, Jean-Bertrand *President*
President's Office, Palace du Gouvernement, Port-Au-Prince, HAITI

Ariyoshi, George R *Governor*
745 Fort St, #500, Honolulu, HI 96813 USA

Arizin, Paul J *Basketball Player*
227 Lewis Road, Springfield, PA 19064 USA

Arjun *Actor*
B3-C Block, 109 G N Chetty Road T Nagar, Chennai, TN 600 017, INDIA

Arkadius *Fashion Designer*
Arkadius, 41 Brondesbury Road, London, England, NW6 6BP, United Kingdom

Arkangel R-15 *Music Group*
Sony Music Miami, 605 Lincoln Rd, Miami Beach, FL 33138 USA

Arkhipova, Irina K *Opera Singer*
Bryusov Per 2/14, #27, Moscow, 103009, RUSSIA

Arkin, Adam *Actor*
2372 Veteran Ave, Los Angeles, CA 90064 USA

Arkin, Alan *Actor*
21 E 40th St, #1705, New York, NY 10016 USA

Arm, Mark *Musician*
Legends of 21st Century, 7 Trinity Row, Florence, MA 01062 USA

Armacost, Michael H *Diplomat*
State Department, 2201 C St NW, Washington, DC 20520 USA

Arman *Artist*
Arman Studios, 430 Washington St, New York, NY 10013 USA

Armani, Giorgio *Fashion Designer*
Via Borgonuovo 21, Milan, 20121, ITALY

Armaou, Lindsay *Musician*
Clintons, 55 Drury Lane, Covent Garden, London, WC2B 5SQ, UNITED KINGDOM (UK)

Armas, Antonio R (Tony) *Baseball Player*
Los Mercedes #37, P Piruto-Edo, Anzoatequi, VENEZUELA

Armas, Chris *Soccer Player*
Chicago Fire, 980 N Michigan Ave, #1998, Chicago, IL 60611 USA

Armatrading, Joan *Musician, Songwriter*
21 Ramilles St, London, W1V 1DF, UNITED KINGDOM (UK)

Armedariz, Pedro Jr *Actor*
Diamond Artists, 215 N Barrington Ave, Los Angeles, CA 90049 USA

Armenante, Jilian *Actor*
Susan Smith, 121A N San Vincente Blvd, Beverly Hills, CA 90211 USA

Armenante, Jillian *Actor*
Metropolitan Talent Agency (MTA), 4526 Wilshire Blvd, Los Angeles, CA 90010 USA

Armitage, Alison *Actor, Model*
Twentieth Century Artists, 15760 Ventura Blvd, Ste 700, Encino, CA 91436 USA

Armitage, Karole *Choreographer, Dancer*
350 W 21st St, New York, NY 10011 USA

Armour, Thomas D (Tommy) III *Golfer*
4211 Saint Andrews Blvd, Irving, TX 75038 USA

Arms, Russell *Actor, Musician*
2918 Davis Way, Palm Springs, CA 92262 USA

Armstead, Jessie *Football Player*
1316 Mill Stream Dr, Dallas, TX 75232 USA

Armstrong, A James *Misc*
Broadway Methodist Church, 1100 W 42nd St, Indianapolis, IN 46208 USA

Armstrong, Alan *Actor*
Markham & Froggatt, Julian House, 4 Windmill St, London, W1P 1HF, UNITED KINGDOM (UK)

Armstrong, Anne
Armstrong Ranch, Armstrong, TX 78338

Armstrong, Anne L *Educator, Diplomat*
Armstrong Ranch, Armstrong, TX 78338 USA

Armstrong, B J *Basketball Player*
1220 Boden Place, Fort Washington, PA 19034 USA

Armstrong, Bess *Actor*
William Morris Agency, 151 El Camino Dr, Beverly Hills, CA 90212 USA

Armstrong, Billie Joe *Musician, Songwriter*
Warner Bros Records, 3300 Warner Blvd, Burbank, CA 91505 USA

Armstrong, Clay M *Scientist*
University of Pennsylvania, Medical School 3400 Spruce, Philadelphia, PA 19104 USA

Armstrong, Curtis *Actor*
3867 Shannon Rd, Los Angeles, CA 90027 USA

Armstrong, Darrell *Basketball Player*
2238 Kettle Dr, Orlando, FL 32835 USA

Armstrong, Debbie
Box 710 Taos Sky Valley, Taos, NM 87525

Armstrong, Deborah (Debbie) *Skier*
P O Box 710, Taos Ski Valley, NM 87252 USA

Armstrong, Garner Ted
Box 2525, Tyler, TX 75710

Armstrong, Gillian *Director*
Harry Linstead, 500 Oxford St, Bondi Junction, NSW, 2022, AUSTRALIA

Armstrong, Kerry *Actor*
Barbara Leane Mgmt, 261 Miller St, North Sydney, NSW, 2060, AUSTRALIA

Armstrong, Lance *Athlete*
Lance Armstrong Foundation, PO Box 161150, Austin, TX 78716-1150 USA

Armstrong, Michael *Director*
114 Doheny Dr, West Hollywood, CA 90048 USA

Armstrong, Murray A *Hockey Player, Coach*
104 Augusta Circle, Saint Augustine, FL 32086 USA

Armstrong, Neil *Astronaut*
CTA Inc, PO Box 436 Rt 123, Lebanon, OH 45036 USA

Armstrong, Neil *Referee*
1169 Sherwood Trail, Sarnia, ON N7V 2H3, CANADA

Armstrong, Otis *Football Player*
7183 S Newport Way, Centennial, CO 80112 USA

Armstrong, RG *Actor*
3856 Reklaw Dr, Studio City, CA 91604 USA

Armstrong, Robb *Cartoonist*
United Feature Syndicate, 200 Madison Ave, New York, NY 10016 USA

Armstrong, Russell P *War Hero*
425 Bench Road, Fallen, NV 89406 USA

Armstrong, Samaire *Actor*
International Creative Management (ICM-LA), 8942 Wilshire Blvd, Beverly Hills, CA 90211 USA

Armstrong, Sheila A *Opera Singer, Musician*
Harvesters Tilford Road, Hindhead, Surrey, GU26 6SQ, UNITED KINGDOM (UK)

Armstrong, Spence M *General*
9714 Bluedale St, Alexandria, VA 22308 USA

Armstrong, Thomas *Race Car Driver*
PacWest Racing Group, 150 Gasoline Alley Road, Indianapolis, IN 46222 USA

Armstrong, Thomas H W *Misc*
1 East St, Olney, Bucks, MK46 4AP, UNITED KINGDOM (UK)

Armstrong, Tom *Cartoonist*
North American Syndicate, 235 E 45th St, New York, NY 10017 USA

Armstrong, Trace *Football Player*
18 Oyster Shaols, Alameda, CA 94502 USA

Armstrong, Valorie *Actor*
Contemporary Artists, 610 Santa Monica Blvd #202, Santa Monica, CA 90401 USA

Armstrong, Vaughn *Actor*
4416 Union Ave, La Canada, CA 91011
USA

Armstrong, William *Writer*
6 Roland St, Newton, MA 02461 USA

Armstrong, William L *Senator*
1900 E Girard Place # 1004, Englewood,
CO 80113 USA

Army of Lovers
78 Stanley Gardens, London, ENGLAND,
W3 7SN

Arnatt, John
3 Warren Cottage Woodland Way, Surrey,
ENGLAND, KT20 6NN

Arnaud, Jean-Loup *Government Official*
55 Rue de Seine, Paris, 75006, FRANCE

Arnault, Bernard *Business Person*
Moet Hennessy Louis Vuitton, 30 Ave
Hoche, Paris, 75008, FRANCE

Arnaz, Lucie *Actor*
Scott Stander & Associates, 13701
Riverside Dr #201, Sherman Oaks, CA
91423 USA

Arnaz, Lusie *Actor*
P O Box 636, Cross River, NY 10518 USA

Arnaz Jr, Desi *Actor*
1361 Ridgecrest, Beverly Hills, CA 90210
USA

Arndt, Denis *Actor*
Artist Group International (NY), 150 East
58th Street, Fl 19, New York, NY 10155
USA

Arneil, Richard A S *Composer*
Benhall Lodge, Benhall, Suffolk, IP17 1DJ,
UNITED KINGDOM (UK)

Arnesen, Lasse
Fagerborggata 34, Oslo, Norway, N-0360

Arnesen, Liv *Skier*
Yourexpidition 119 N 4th St #406,
Minneapolis, MN 55401 USA

Arness, James *Actor*
PO Box 492163, Los Angeles, CA 90049
USA

Arnett, Jon D *Football Player*
P O Box 4077, Palos Verdes Peninsula,
CA 90274 USA

Arnette, Jay *Basketball Player*
2 Hillside Court, Austin, TX 78746 USA

Arnette, Jeanetta *Actor*
466 N Harper Ave, Los Angeles, CA
90048 USA

Arngrim, Alison *Actor*
PO Box 98, Tujunga, CA 91043 USA

Arning, Lisa *Actor*
The Morgan Agency, 7080 Hollywood
Blvd, Ste 1009, Hollywood, CA 90028
USA

Arno, Ed
11220 72nd Dr, Flushing, NY 11375 USA

Arnold, Anna Bing *Philanthropist*
Anna Bing Arnold Foundation, 9700 W
Pico Blvd, Los Angeles, CA 90035 USA

Arnold, Ben *Musician*
Golden Guru, 227 Pine St, Philadelphia,
PA 19106 USA

Arnold, Brian A *General*
Commander Space & Missile Systems
Center, Los Angeles Air Force Base, CA
90245 USA

Arnold, Debbie *Actor*
M Arnold Mgmt, 12 Cambridge Park, Ease
Twickenham, Middx, TW1 2PF, UNITED
KINGDOM (UK)

Arnold, Eddy *Actor*
PO Box 97, Brentwood, TN 37027

Arnold, Edward (Eddy) *Music Group*
P O Box 97 Franklin Road, Brentwood,
TN 37024 USA

Arnold, Eve *Photographer*
Magnum Photographic Agency, 5 Old St,
London, EC1V 9HL, UNITED KINGDOM
(UK)

Arnold, Gary H *Critic*
5133 N 1st St, Arlington, VA 22203 USA

Arnold, Jackson D *Admiral, War Hero*
Los Pinos Box 185, Rancho Santa Fe, CA
92067 USA

Arnold, James R *Misc*
University of California, Chemistry Dept,
Code 0524, La Jolla, CA 92093 USA

Arnold, Kristine *Music Group*
Monty Hitchcock Mgmt, 5101 Overton
Road, Nashville, TN 37220 USA

Arnold, Malcolm H *Composer*
26 Springfields, Attleborough, Norfolk,
NR17 2PA, UNITED KINGDOM (UK)

Arnold, Monica *Musician, Actor*
Handprint Entertainment, 1100 Glendon
Ave #1000, Los Angeles, CA 90024 USA

Arnold, Morris S *Judge*
US Court of Appeals, 600 W Capitol Ave,
Little Rock, AR 72201 USA

Arnold, Murray *Basketball Player, Coach*
Western Kentucky University, Athletic
Dept, Bowling Green, KY 42101 USA

Arnold, Richard S *Judge*
US Court of Appeals, 600 W Capitol Ave,
Little Rock, AR 72201 USA

Arnold, Stuart *Publisher*
Fortune Magazine, Rockefeller Center,
New York, NY 10020 USA

Arnold, Tichina *Actor*
Metropolitan Talent Agency, 4526
Wilshire Blvd, Los Angeles, CA 90010
USA

Arnold, Tom *Actor, Comedian*
Clean Break Productions, 14046 Aubrey
Road, Beverly Hills, CA 90210

Arnold Jr, Harry L *Doctor, Writer*
250 Laurel St #301, San Francisco, CA
94118 USA

Arnoldi, Charles A *Artist*
721 Hampton Dr, Venice, CA 90291 USA

Arnott, Jason *Hockey Player*
Budget Rent-a-Car, 412 Dunlop St W,
Barrie, ON L4N 1C1, CANADA

Arnoul, Francoise *Actor*
53 Rue Censier, Paris, 75005, FRANCE

Arns, Paulo E Cardinal *Religious Leader*
Alvenida Higienopolos 890, CP 6778, Sao
Paulo, SP, 01064, BRAZIL

Arnstein, Rolly *Music Group*
Bad Boy Entertainment, 1540 Broadway
#3000, New York, NY 10036 USA

Arnsten, Stefan
1017 Laurel Way, Beverly Hills, CA
90210

Aronofsky, Darren *Director*
International Creative Mgmt, 8942
Wilshire Blvd #219, Beverly Hills, CA
90211 USA

Arons, Arnold B *Physicist*
10313 Lake Shord Blvd NE, Seattle, WA
98125 USA

Arora, Amrita *Actor, Bollywood*
Amrita Arora Plot No198 Poojakunj Apts,
Sher-e-Punjab Colony Plot No. 195
Andheri (E), Mumbai, MS 400093, INDIA

Arp, Halton C *Astronomer*
Max Pianck Physic/Radiology Institute,
Garching Munich, 84518, GERMANY

Arpel, Adrien *Beauty Pageant Winner*
Adrien Arpel Cosmetics, 400 Hackensack
Ave, Hackensack, NJ 07601 USA

Arpey, Gerard *Business Person*
AMR Corp, 433 Amon Carter Blvd, Forth
Worth, TX 76155 USA

Arpino, Gerald P *Choreographer*
City Center Joffrey Ballet, 70 E Lake St
#1300, Chicago, IL 60601 USA

Arquette, Alexis *Actor*
Innovative Artists, 1505 10th St, Santa
Monica, CA 90401 USA

Arquette, David *Actor*
Baker Winokur Ryder (BWR-LA), 9100
Wilshire Blvd Fl 6, W Tower, Beverly
Hills, CA 90212 USA

Arquette, Patricia *Actor*
United Talent Agency, 9560 Wilshire Blvd
#500, Beverly Hills, CA 90212 USA

Arquette, Rosanna *Actor*
P O Box 69646, Los Angeles, CA 90069
USA

Arrants, Rod *Actor*
1173 Regent St, Alameda, CA 94501 USA

Arras, Maria Celeste *Actor*
Telemundo, 2470 West 8th Avenue,
Hialeah, FL 33010 USA

Arredondo, Rosa *Actor*
TalentWorks (LA), 3500 W Olive Ave
#1400, Burbank, CA 91505 USA

Arrindell, Clement A *Governor*
Lark, Bird Rock, Saint Kitts & Nevis

Arrington, Buddy *Race Car Driver*
2620 Kings Mountain Road, Martinsville,
VA 24112 USA

Arrington, Jill *Sportscaster*
CBS-TV, Sports Dept 51 W 52nd St, New
York, NY 10019 USA

Arrington, LaVar *Football Player*
Washington Redskins, 21300 Redskin Park
Dr, Ashburn, VA 20147 USA

Arriola, Dante *Director*
International Creative Management
(ICM-LA), 8942 Wilshire Blvd, Beverly
Hills, CA 90211 USA

Arriola, Gus
Box 3275, Carmel, CA 93921

Arriota, Gus *Cartoonist*
P O Box 3275, Carmel, CA 93921 USA

Arrow, Kenneth J *Nobel Prize Laureate*
580 Constanzo St, Stanford, CA 94305 USA

Arroyo, Carlos *Basketball Player*
Utah Jazz, Delta Center, 301 West South Temple, Salt Lake City, UT 84101 USA

Arroyo, Jose *Writer*
Kaplan-Stahler-Gumer Agency, 8383 Wilshire Blvd #923, Beverly Hills, CA 90211 USA

Arroyo, Luis E *Baseball Player*
Box 354, Penuelas, PR 00624 USA

Arroyo, Martina *Opera Singer*
Berkshire Corsert Artists, 20 Alfred Dr, Pittsfield, MA 01201 USA

Art of Noise, The *Music Group*
PO Box 199, London, W11 4AN, UNITED KINGDOM (UK)

Arteage, Rosalia *President*
Vice President's Office, Gobiemo Palacio, Garcia Morena, Quito, ECUADOR

Artemas, Cole *Cartoonist*
15 Regency Manor #15-8, Rutland, VT 05701 USA

Artemis, Cole
1050 Colonial Dr, Rutland, VA 05701-9575

Artest, Ron *Basketball Player*
800 S Wells, Chicago, IL 60607 USA

Arteta, Miguel *Director*
William Morris Agency (WMA-LA), 1 William Morris Pl, Beverly Hills, CA 90212 USA

Arthur, Beatrice (Bea) *Actor*
2000 Old Ranch Road, Los Angeles, CA 90049 USA

Arthur, Joseph *Music Group, Songwriter*
Evolution Talent, 1776 Broadway #1500, New York, NY 10019 USA

Arthur, Maureen *Actor*
9171 Wilshire Blvd #530, Beverly Hills, CA 90210 USA

Arthur, Owen *Prime Minister*
Prime Minister's Office, Bay St, Saint Michael, Bridgetown, BARBADOS

Arthur, Perry *Golfer*
7513 Zurich Dr, Plano, TX 75025 USA

Arthur, Rebeca *Actor*
Epstein-Wyckoff, 280 S Beverly St #400, Beverly Hills, CA 90212 USA

Arthurs, Paul (Bonehead) *Musician*
Ignition Mgmt, 54 Linhope St, London, NW1 6HL, UNITED KINGDOM (UK)

Artschwager, Richard E *Artist*
P O Box 12, Hudson, NY 12534 USA

Artsebarsky, Anatoli P *Cosmonaut*
Potchta Kosmonavtov, Moskovskoi Oblasti, Syvisdny Goroduk, 141160, RUSSIA

Artzt, Alice J *Musician*
180 Claremont Ave #31, New York, NY 10027 USA

Artzt, Edwin L *Business Person*
3849 Hedgewood Dr, Lawrenceburg, IN 47025 USA

Arulmani *Actor*
15 Pookara Street, Saidapet, Chennai, TN 600 015, INDIA

Arum, Robert (Bob) *Boxer*
36 Gulf Stream Court, Las Vegas, NV 89113 USA

Arun, Ila *Actor, Bollywood*
401 Paradise Apartments, 7th Road Santacruz East, Bombay, MS 400055, INDIA

Arvesen, Nina *Actor*
412 Culver Blvd #9, Playa del Rey, CA 90293 USA

Arvind, V *Actor*
1 65th Street 12th Avenue, Ashok Nagar, Chennai, TN 600 083, INDIA

Arvindasamy *Actor*
29A Muthiah Street, Cathedral Road, Chennai, TN 600 086, INDIA

Arzu Irigoyen, Alvaro E *President*
President's Office, Palacio Nacional, Guatemala City, GUATAMALA

Asay, Chuck *Cartoonist*
Colorada Springs Gazette, 303 S Prospect St, Colorado Springs, CO 80903 USA

Asbury, Kelly *Actor*
Creative Artists Agency LCC (CAA-LA), 9830 Wilshire Blvd, Beverly Hills, CA 90212 USA

Asbury, Martin *Cartoonist*
Stoneworld, Pitch Green, Princes Risborough, Bucks, HP27 9QG, UNITED KINGDOM (UK)

Ascencio, Nelson *Actor*
Heidi Rotbart Management, 4000 Warner Blvd, Bldg 160 Room 716, Burbank, CA 91522

Aschenbrener, Frank *Football Player*
16372 E Jacklin Dr, Fountain Hills, AZ 85268 USA

Ash, Mary Kay *Business Person*
Mary Kay Ash Charitable Foundation, PO Box 799044, Dallas, TX 75379-9044 USA

Ash, Roy L *Business Person, Government Official*
655 Funchal Road, Los Angeles, CA 90077 USA

Ashanti *Musician*
International Creative Mgmt, 8942 Wilshire Blvd #219, Beverly Hills, CA 90211 USA

Ashbery, John L *Writer*
326 Belmont Ave, Buffalo, NY 14223 USA

Ashbrook, Dana *Actor*
Rigberg Roberts Rugolo, 1180 S Beverly Dr #601, Los Angeles, CA 90035 USA

Ashbrook, Daphne *Actor*
Innovative Atrists, 1505 10th St, Santa Monica, CA 90401 USA

Ashbrook, Stephen *Musician*
Green Room, 2280 NW Thurman St, Portland, OR 97210 USA

Ashby, Alan *Baseball Player*
15826 Roseview Ln, Cypress, TX 77429 USA

Ashby, Alan D *Baseball Player*
15826 Roseview Lane, Cypress, TX 77429 USA

Ashby, Jeffrey S *Astronaut*
NASA, Johnson Space Center 2101 NASA Road, Houston, TX 77058 USA

Ashby, Linden *Actor*
639 N Larchmont Blvd #207, Los Angeles, CA 90004 USA

Ashcroft, John D *Attorney General, Senator, Governor*
Justice Department, 10th St & Constitution Ave NW, Washington, DC 20530 USA

Ashcroft, Richard *Musician, Songwriter*
Little Big Man Booking, 39A Grammercy Park N #1C, New York, NY 10010 USA

Ashdown, J J D (Paddy) *Government Official*
Vane Cottage, Norton Sub Hamdon, Somerset, TA14 6SG, UNITED KINGDOM (UK)

Ashdown, Paddy
House of Commons, London, ENGLAND, SW1A 0AA

Ashe, Danni *Adult Film Star, Business Person*
Video Bliss, 520 Washington Blvd #445, Marina del Rey, CA 90292 USA

Ashenfelter III, Horace *Track Athlete*
100 Hawthome Ave, Glen Ridge, NJ 07028 USA

Asher, Barry *Bowler*
Professional Bowlers Assn, 719 2nd Ave #701, Seattle, WA 98104 USA

Asher, Jane *Actor*
24 Cale St, London, SW3 3QU, UNITED KINGDOM (UK)

Asher, Peter *Musician, Business Person*
Peter Asher Mgmt, 644 N Doheny Dr, Los Angeles, CA 90069 USA

Asher, William *Director, Writer*
54337 Oak Hill Blvd, La Quinta, CA 92253 USA

Asherson, Renee *Actor*
28 Elsworthy Road, London, NW3, UNITED KINGDOM (UK)

Ashford, David
53 Moat Dr Harrow, Middlesex, ENGLAND

Ashford, Evelyn
818 Plantation Lane, Walnut, CA 91789

Ashford, Mandy *Music Group*
Evolution Talent, 1776 Broadway #1500, New York, NY 10019 USA

Ashford, Matthew *Actor*
J Michael Bloom, 9255 Sunset Blvd #710, Los Angeles, CA 90069 USA

Ashford, Michelle *Writer, Producer*
William Morris Agency (WMA-LA), 1 William Morris Pl, Beverly Hills, CA 90212 USA

Ashford, Nicholas (Nick) *Songwriter, Music Group*
Associated Booking Corp, 1995 Broadway #501, New York, NY 10023 USA

Ashford, Roslyn *Music Group*
Thomas Cassidy, 11761 E Speedway Blvd, Tucson, AZ 85748 USA

Ashford, Washington Evelyn *Track Athlete*
38997 Cherry Point Lane, Murrieta, CA 92563 USA

Ashida, Jun *Fashion Designer*
1-3-3 Aobadai, Meguroku, Tokyo, 153, JAPAN

Ashihara, Yoshinobu *Architect*
Ashihara Architects, 31-15 Sakuragaokacho, Shibuyaku, Tokyo, 150, JAPAN

Ashkenasi, Shmuel *Musician*
3800 N Lake Shore Dr, Chicago, IL 60613 USA

Ashkenazy, Vladimir D *Musician*
Savinka, Kappelistr 15, Meggen, 6045, SWITZERLAND

Ashley *Model*
Ford Model Agency, 142 Greene St #400, New York, NY 10012 USA

Ashley, Elizabeth *Actor*
1223 North Ogden Dr, West Hollywood, CA 90046 USA

Ashley, Jennifer *Actor*
129 W Wilson #202, Costa Mesa, CA 92627 USA

Ashley, John *Hockey Player, Referee*
Hockey Hall of Fame, BCE Place, 30 Yonge St, Toronto, ON M5E 1X8, CANADA

Ashley, Laurence *Actor*
Cineart, 36 Rue de Ponthieu, Paris, 75008, FRANCE

Ashley, Leon *Musician*
PO Box 567, Hendersonville, TN 37077 USA

Ashley, Merrill *Ballerina*
New York City Ballet, Lincoln Center Plaza, New York, NY 10023 USA

Ashmore, Edward B *Admiral*
Naval Secretary, Victor Bldg, HM Naval Base, Portsmouth, Hants, UNITED KINGDOM (UK)

Ashmore, Shawn *Actor*
Evolution Entertainment, 901 N Highland Ave, Los Angeles, CA 90038 USA

Ashrawl, Hanan *Politician*
Higher Education Ministry, PO Box 17360, Jerusalem, West Bank, ISRAEL

Ashton, John *Actor*
PO Box 272489, Ft Collins, CO 80527 USA

Ashton, Peter S *Scientist*
233 Herald Road, Carlisle, MA 01741 USA

Ashton, Susan *Music Group*
Bob Doyle Assoc, 1111 17th Ave S, Nashville, TN 37212 USA

Ashton-Griffiths, Roger
16 Chelmsford Rd, London, ENGLAND, E11 1BS

Ashworth, Gerald (Gerry) *Track Athlete*
7 Athena Circle, Andover, MA 01810 USA

Ashworth, Jeanne C *Speed Skater*
Whiteface Highway, Wilmington, NY 12997 USA

Asia
63 Main St, Cold Spring, NY 10516

Askew, Desmond *Actor*
Envision Entertainment, 9255 Sunset Blvd #300, Los Angeles, CA 90069 USA

Askew, Luke *Actor*
Media Artists Group, 6300 Wilshire Blvd #1470, Los Angeles, CA 90048 USA

Askew, Reubin O *Governor*
P O Box 1512, Burnsville, NC 28714 USA

Askin, Leon *Actor*
Hutteldorferstr 349, Vienna, 1140, AUSTRIA

Asleep At The Wheel
PO Box 463, Austin, TX 78767

Asner, Ed *Actor*
Envoy Entertainment, 1640 S Sepulveda Blvd #530, Los Angeles, CA 90025 USA

Asner, Edward *Actor*
3556 Mound View Ave, Studio City, CA 91604 USA

Asner, Jules *Television Host*
E! Entertainment Television (LA), 5750 Wilshire Blvd, Los Angeles, CA 90036 USA

Asomugha, Nnamdi *Football Player*
Oakland Raiders, 1220 Harbor Bay Parkway, Alameda, CA 94502 USA

Aspen, Jennifer *Actor*
B & B Entertainment, 1640 S Sepulveda Blvd #530, Los Angeles, CA 90025 USA

Asplin, Edward W *Business Person*
601 Carlson Parkway #1050, Hopkins, MN 55305 USA

Aspromonte, Kenneth J (Ken) *Baseball Player*
2 Derham Park St, Houston, TX 77024 USA

Asrani *Actor, Bollywood*
B3 Beach House Apartments, Gandhigram Rd Juhu, Mumbai, MS 400049, INDIA

Assante, Armand *Actor*
RR 1 Box 561, Campbell Hall, NY 10916 USA

Assante, Armand *Actor*
Patricola Lust PR, 8383 Wilshire Blvd, Suite 530, Beverly Hills, CA 90211 USA

Assenmacher, Ivan *Doctor*
419 Ave d'Occitanie, Montpellier, 34090, FRANCE

Assuras, Thalia *Television Host*
CBS Weekend Evening News, 524 W 57th St Fl 8, New York, NY 10019 USA

Astin, John *Actor, Director*
3801 Canterbury Road #505, Baltimore, MD 21218 USA

Astin, Mackenzie *Actor*
William Morris Agency (WMA-LA), 1 William Morris Pl, Beverly Hills, CA 90212 USA

Astin, Sean *Actor*
PO Box 57858, Sherman Oaks, CA 91413 USA

Astley, Rick *Musician*
Unit 4 Plato St, 72-74 Saint Dionis Road, London, SW6 4UT, UNITED KINGDOM (UK)

Astley, Thea *Writer*
PO Box 23, Cambewarra, NSW, 2540, AUSTRALIA

Astor, Brooke *Misc*
Vincent Astor Foundations, 405 Park Ave, New York, NY 10022 USA

Astroth, Joe C *Athlete*
151Moyer Rd, Chalfont, PA 18914

Asturaga, Nova *Government Official*
Permanent Mission of Nicaragua, 820 2nd Ave #801, New York, NY 10017 USA

Asuma, Linda *Actor*
Chasin Agency, The, 8899 Beverly Blvd #716, Los Angeles, CA 90048 USA

Aswanikumar, G *Actor*
Plot 780 29th Street, T N H B Korattur, Chennai, TN 600 080, INDIA

Atala, Anthony *Doctor*
Harvard Medical School, 25 Shattuck St, Boston, MA 02115 USA

Atchison, David W *Religious Leader*
Southern Baptist Convention, 5452 Grannywhite Pike, Brentwood, TN 37027 USA

Atchison, Michael *Cartoonist*
Associated Press, 50 Rockefeller Plaza, New York, NY 10020 USA

Atchison, Scott
3112 Olympic Dr, Bakersfield, CA 93308

Aterciopelados *Musician*
BMG, 1540 Broadway, New York, NY 10036 USA

Atherton, William *Actor*
5102 San Feliciano Dr, Woodland Hills, CA 91364 USA

Athfield, Ian C *Architect*
105 Amritser St, Khandallah, Wellington, NEW ZEALAND

Athow, Kirk L *Misc*
2104 Crestview Court, Lafayette, IN 47905 USA

Atilla
2350 Benedict Canyon, Beverly Hills, CA 90210

Atiyeh, Victor *Governor*
Victor Atiyeh Co, 509 SW Park Ave #205, Portland, OR 97205 USA

Atkin, Harvey *Actor*
527 S Curson St, Los Angeles, CA 90036 USA

Atkins, Christopher *Actor*
Michael Mann Talent Mgmt, 617 S Olive St #510, Los Angeles, CA 90014 USA

Atkins, Doug
PO Box 14007, Knoxville, TN 37914

Atkins, Douglas L (Doug) *Football Player*
P O Box 14007, Knoxville, TN 37194 USA

Atkins, Erica *Songwriter, Music Group*
The Firm, 9100 Wilshire Blvd #100W, Beverly Hills, CA 90210 USA

Atkins, Essence *Actor*
Abrams Artists Agency (LA), 9200 Sunset Blvd Fl 11, Los Angeles, CA 90069 USA

Atkins, Sharif *Actor*
Christopher Wright Management, 3340 Barham Blvd, Los Angeles, CA 90068

Atkins, Tina *Songwriter, Music Group*
The Firm, 9100 Wilshire Blvd #100W, Beverly Hills, CA 90210 USA

Atkins, Tom *Actor*
Paradigm Agency, 10100 Santa Monica Blvd #2500, Los Angeles, CA 90067 USA

Atkinson, Jayne *Actor*
Innovative Atrists, 1505 10th St, Santa Monica, CA 90401 USA

Atkinson, Ray N *Business Person*
Guy F Atkinson Co, 1001 Bayhill Dr, San Bruno, CA 94066 USA

Atkinson, Rick *Journalist, Writer*
Kansas City Times, Editorial Dept 1729 Grand Ave, Kansas City, MO 64108 USA

Atkinson, Ron *Soccer Player*
Nottingham Forest, Pavillion Road, Bridgeford, Nottingham, N62 5JF, UNITED KINGDOM (UK)

Atkinson, Rowan *Actor*
PBJ Management, 7 Soho Street, London, W1D 3DQ, United Kingdom

Atkinson, Ted
1735 Log Cabin Rd, Beaverdam, VA 23015

Atkinson, Theodore F (Ted) *Jockey*
1735 Log Cabin Road, Beaverdam, VA 23015 USA

Atkinson Hudson, Dianne *Producer*
Harpo Productions, Harpo Studios, 110 N Carpenter St, Chicago, IL 60607 USA

Atkisson, Sharyl *Commentator*
Cable News Network, News Dept 1051 Techwood Dr NW, Atlanta, GA 30318 USA

Atkov, Oleg Y *Cosmonaut*
Potchta Kosmonavtov, Moskovskoi Oblasti, Syvisdny Goroduk, 141160, RUSSIA

Atler, Vanessa
PO Box 860847, Plano, TX 75086-0847

Atomic Kitten *Music Group*
Concorde Intl Artists Ltd, 101 Shepherds Bush Rd, London, W6 7LP, UNITED KINGDOM (UK)

Atopare, Silas *Governor*
Governor General's Office, Konedobu, Port Moresby, Papua New Guinea

Attack, Massive *Music Group*
Monterey Peninsula Artists (Monterey), 509 Hartnell St, Monterey, CA 93940 USA

Attal, Yvan *Actor, Director*
Artmedia, 20 Ave Rapp, Paris, 75007, FRANCE

Attell, Dave *Comedian*
Gersh Agency, The (NY), 41 Madison Ave Fl 33, New York, NY 10010 USA

Attenborough, David *Actor, Writer*
5 Park Road, Richmond Surrey, ENGLAND, TW10 6NS, United Kingdom

Attenborough, David F *Business Person, Writer*
5 Park Road, Richmond, Surrey, TW10 6NS, UNITED KINGDOM (UK)

Attenborough, Richard S *Actor, Director*
Old Farms, Beaver Lodge, Richmond Green, Surrey, TW9 1NQ, UNITED KINGDOM (UK)

Atterton, Edward *Actor*
PFD, Drury House, 34-43 Russell St, London, WC2B 5HA, UNITED KINGDOM (UK)

Attlee, Frank III *Business Person*
Monsanto Co, 800 N Lindbergh Blvd, Saint Louis, MO 63167 USA

Attles, Al *Basketball Player, Coach*
3555 Lincoln Ave #26, Oakland, CA 94602 USA

Atun, Hakki *Prime Minister*
Gov't Assembly, North Cyprus Republic, Via Mersin 10, Lefkosa, TURKEY

Atwater, H Brewster Jr *Business Person*
IDS Center, 80 S 8th St, Minneapolis, MN 55402 USA

Atwater, Stephen D (Steve) *Football Player*
565 Plandome Road, Manhasset, NY 11030 USA

Atwell, Alfred *Astronaut*
3253 Ennis Court, Las Vegas, NV 89121 USA

Atwood, Casey *Race Car Driver*
Ultra/Evemham Motorsports, 160 Munday Road, Statesville, NC 28677 USA

Atwood, Margaret E *Writer*
McClelland/Stewart, 481 University Ave, #900, Toronto, ON M5G 2E9, CANADA

Atwood, Susie (Sue) *Swimmer*
5624 E 2nd St, Long Beach, CA 90803 USA

Atzmon, Moshe
Marignanostr 12, Basel, 4059, SWITZERLAND

Auber, Brigitte
56 rue Guy-Moquet, Paris, FRANCE, F-75017

Auberjonois, Rene *Actor*
448 S Arden Blvd, Los Angeles, CA 90020 USA

Aubert, KD *Actor*
Endeavor Agency LLC (LA), 9601 Wilshire Blvd Fl 3, Beverly Hills, CA 90210 USA

Auboin, Jean A *Misc*
27 Ave des Baumettes, Nice, 06000, FRANCE

Aubrey, Emlyn *Golfer*
2013 Surrey Lane, Bossier City, LA 71111 USA

Aubrey, James *Actor*
Van Gelder, 18-21 Jermyn St #300, London, SW1Y 6HP, UNITED KINGDOM (UK)

Aubry, Cecile *Actor*
Le Moulin Bleu, 6 Chemin Moulin Bleu, Sant-Cyr-sous-Dourdan, 91410, FRANCE

Aubry, Cristina *Actor*
Carol Levi Co, Via Giuseppe Pisanelli, Rome, 00196, ITALY

Aubry, Eugene E *Architect*
8021 Marina Isles Lane, Holmes Beach, FL 34217 USA

Aubuchon, Chet *Basketball Player*
107 2nd St NW, Ruskin, FL 33507 USA

Aubuchon, Remi *Producer*
International Creative Management (ICM-LA), 8942 Wilshire Blvd, Beverly Hills, CA 90211 USA

Auburn, David *Writer*
97 W Elmwood Ave, Clawson, MI 48017 USA

Auchincloss, Louis S *Writer*
1111 Park Ave #14D, New York, NY 10128 USA

AuCoin, Les *Misc*
Bogle & Gates, 601 13th St NW #370, Washington, DC 20005 USA

Audioslave *Music Group*
Creative Artists Agency LCC (CAA-LA), 9830 Wilshire Blvd, Beverly Hills, CA 90212 USA

Audran, Stephane *Actor*
2F De Marthod, 11 Rue Chanez, 70016E, FRANCE

Auel, Jean M *Writer*
PO Box 8278, Portland, OR 97207 USA

Auer, Barbara *Actor*
Agentur Carola Studlar, Neurieder Str 1C, Planegg, 82152, GERMANY

Auerbach, Arnold J (Red) *Coach, Misc*
780 Boylston St, Boston, MA 02199 USA

Auerbach, Frank *Artist*
Marlborough Fine Art Gallery, 6 Albermarle St, London, W1X 4BY, UNITED KINGDOM (UK)

Auerbach, Stanley I *Misc*
3314 W End Ave #202, Nashville, TN 37203 USA

Auermann, Nadia *Model*
Elite Models, 4 Rue de la Paiz, Paris, 75002, FRANCE

Auermann, Nadja
Via San Vittore 40, Milan, ITALY, I-20123

AufDerMaur, Melissa *Music Group, Musician*
Artist Group International, 9560 Wilshire Blvd #400, Beverly Hills, CA 90212 USA

Auger, Brian *Music Group, Musician*
Earthtone, 8306 Wilshire Blvd #981, Beverly Hills, CA 90211 USA

Auger, Claudine *Actor*
Artmedia, 20 Ave Rapp, Paris, 75007, FRANCE

Auger, Pierre V *Physicist*
12 Rue Emile Faguet, Paris, 75014, FRANCE

Augmon, Stacey *Basketball Player*
4212 Kessler Ridge Dr, Marietta, GA 30062 USA

August, Bille *Director*
2800 Lyngby, DENMARK

August, Don *Baseball Player*
28372 Lorente, Mission Viejo, CA 92692 USA

August, John *Writer, Producer, Director, Musician*
United Talent Agency (UTA), 9560 Wilshire Blvd, Beverly Hills, CA 90212 USA

August, Pernilla *Actor*
Royal Dramatic Theater, Box 5037, Stockholm, 102 41, SWEDEN

Augustain, Ira *Actor*
Diamond Artists, 215 N Barrington Ave, Los Angeles, CA 90049 USA

Augustine, Norman R *Business Person*
24131 Doreen Dr, Gaithersburg, MD 20882 USA

Augustnyiak, Jerry *Music Group, Musician*
Agency for Performing Arts, 9200 Sunset Blvd #900, Los Angeles, CA 90069 USA

Augustus, Sherman *Actor*
Richard Schwartz Management, 2934-1/2 Beverly Glen Cir #107, Los Angeles, CA 90077

Auker, Eldon L *Baseball Player*
15 Sailfish Road, Vero Beach, FL 32960 USA

Aulby, Michael (Mike) *Bowler*
1591 Springmill Ponds Circle, Carmel, IN 46032 USA

Aulby, Mike
1591 Springmill Ponda Circle, Carmel, IN 46032

Aulenti, Gae *Architect*
4 Piazza San Marco, Milan, 20121, ITALY

Ault, Chris *Football Coach*
University of Nevada, Athletic Dept, Reno, NV 89557 USA

Ault, James M *Religious Leader*
1 Amoskegan Dr, Brunswick, ME 04011 USA

Aumont, Michel
8 rue Herold, Paris, FRANCE, 75001

Aurel, Jean
40 rue Lauriston, Paris, FRANCE, F-75116

Auriemma, Geno *Basketball Player, Coach*
University of Connecticut, 2095 Hillside Road, Storrs Mansfield, CT 06269 USA

Aurilla, Richard S (Rich) *Baseball Player*
1164 67th St, Brooklyn, NY 11219 USA

Ausoin, Derek *Baseball Player*
Montreal Expos, 233 W 77th St Apt 5E, New York, NY 10024-6809 USA

Aust, Dennis *Baseball Player*
St Louis Cardinals, 16614 Willow Glen Dr, Odessa, FL 33556-2315 USA

Austen, W Gerald *Doctor*
163 Wellesley St, Weston, MA 02493 USA

Auster, Paul *Director, Writer*
Henry Holt, 115 W 18th St, New York, NY 10011 USA

Austin, A Woody *Golfer*
705 SE Melody Lane #B, Lees Summit, MO 64063 USA

Austin, Alana *Actor*
Roklin Management, 8265 Sunset Blvd #101, Los Angeles, CA 90046 USA

Austin, Charles *Track Athlete*
514 Duncan Dr, San Marcos, TX 78666 USA

Austin, Dallas *Actor*
4523 Wieuca Road NE, Atlanta, GA 30342 USA

Austin, Darlene
PO Box 110332, Nashville, TN 37211

Austin, Debbie *Golfer*
6733 Bittersweet Lane, Orlando, FL 32819 USA

Austin, Denise *Physicist, Misc*
Peter Pan Industries, 88 St Francis St, Newark, NJ 07105 USA

Austin, Jeff *Baseball Player*
Kansas City Royals, 3903 Spruce Bay Dr, Kingwood, TX 77345-2063 USA

Austin, Jim *Baseball Player*
Milwaukee Brewers, 44256 Mossy Brook Sq, Ashburn, VA 20147-3362 USA

Austin, Karen *Actor*
3356 Rowena Ave #3, Los Angeles, CA 90027 USA

Austin, Patti *Music Group*
3 Loudon Dr #8, Fishkill, NY 12524 USA

Austin, Rick *Baseball Player*
Cleveland Indians, 26424 Highway 11 #347, Saint Catharine, MO 64628-8004 USA

Austin, Sherie *Music Group, Musician, Actor*
P O Box 551, Gallatin, TN 37066 USA

Austin, Sherrie *Musician*
William Morris Agency (WMA-TN), 2100 W End Ave #1000, Nashville, TN 37203 USA

Austin, Steve (Stone Cold) *Wrestler*
World Wrestling Entertainment (WWE), 1241 E Main St, Stamford, CT 06905 USA

Austin, Teri *Actor*
4245 Laurel Grove, Studio City, CA 91604 USA

Austin, Tracy *Tennis Player*
1751 Pinnacle Dr #1500, McLean, VA 22102 USA

Austin Jr, M P *Business Person*
BMC Software, 2101 City West Blvd, Houston, TX 77042 USA

Austin-Grow, Vivian
140 Via Lola, Palm Springs, CA 92662

Auston, Jim
PO Box 60896, Nashville, TN 37206

Austregesilo de Athayde, Belarmino M *Journalist*
Rua Cosme Velho 599, Rio de Janeiro RJ, BRAZIL

Austrian, Robert *Physicist*
Univ of Pennsylvania, Med Center 36 Hamilton Circle, Philadelphia, PA 19130 USA

Auteuil, Daniel *Actor*
Artmedia, 20 Ave Rapp, Paris, 75007, FRANCE

Auth, Tony *Editor, Cartoonist*
Philadelphia Inquirer, Editorial Dept 1830 Town Center Dr, Langhome, PA 19047 USA

Autolitano, Astrid *Business Person*
Mattel Inc, 333 Continental Blvd, El Segundo, CA 90245 USA

Autry, Alan *Actor*
David Shapira, 15821 Ventura Blvd #235, Encino, CA 91436 USA

Autry, Albert *Baseball Player*
Atlanta Braves, 1119 Princeton Ave, Modesto, CA 95350-4919 USA

Autry, Darnell *Football Player*
510 E Greenway Dr, Tempe, AZ 85282 USA

Autry, Jim *Golfer, Misc*
Professional Golfer's Assn, P O Box 109601, Palm Beach Gardens, FL 33410 USA

Avalon, Frankie *Actor, Music Group*
4303 Spring Forest Lane, Westlake Village, CA 91362 USA

Avari, Erick *Actor*
Henderson/Hogan, 8285 W Sunset Blvd #1, West Hollywood, CA 90046 USA

Avary, Roger *Director*
Creative Artists Agency LCC (CAA-LA), 9830 Wilshire Blvd, Beverly Hills, CA 90212 USA

Avdelsayed, Gabriel *Religious Leader*
Coptic Orthodox Curch, 427 Westside Ave, Jersey City, NJ 07304 USA

Avdeyev, Sergei V *Cosmonaut*
Potchta Kosmonavtov, Moskovskoi Oblasti, Syvisdny Goroduk, 141160, RUSSIA

Avedon, Doe
4333 Hayvenhurst Ave, Encino, CA 91436

Avedon, Richard (Dick) *Photographer*
407 E 75th St, New York, NY 10021 USA

Avellan, Elizabeth *Producer*
International Creative Management (ICM-LA), 8942 Wilshire Blvd, Beverly Hills, CA 90211 USA

Aven, Bruce *Baseball Player*
Cleveland Indians, 1097 NW 167th Ave, Pembroke Pines, FL 33028-1479 USA

Averell, Tom
PO Box 95, Ingomar, PA 15127-0095

Averill Jr, Earl *Baseball Player*
Cleveland Indians, 1806 19th Dr NE, Auburn, WA 98002-3465 USA

Averre, Berton *Music Group, Musician*
17510 Posetano Road, Pacific Palisades, CA 90272 USA

Avery, James *Actor*
195 S Beverly Dr #400, Beverly Hills, CA 90212 USA

Avery, Margaret *Actor*
Artists Agency, 1180 S Beverly Dr #301, Los Angeles, CA 90035 USA

Avery, Mary Ellen *Doctor, Physicist*
52 Liberty St, Plymouth, MA 02360 USA

Avery, Phyllis *Actor*
609 Sterling Place, South Pasadena, CA 91030 USA

Avery, Steven T (Steve) *Baseball Player*
Atlanta Braves, 22721 Coachlight Circle, Taylor, MI 48180-6381 USA

Avery, Val *Actor*
84 Grove St #19, New York, NY 10014 USA

Avery, William H *Governor*
P O Box 6, Wakefield, KS 67487 USA

Avery, William J *Business Person*
Crown Cork & Seal, 1 Crow Way, Philadelphia, PA 19154 USA

Avi *Writer*
Orchard Books, 95 Madison Ave, New York, NY 10016 USA

Avila, Alejandro *Actor*
Televisa, Blvd Adolfo Lopez Mateos 232, Colonia San Angel INN, DF, CP 01060, MEXICO

Avila, Mariana *Actor*
Televisa, Blvd Adolfo Lopez Mateos 232, Colonia San Angel INN, DF, CP 01060, MEXICO

Avila, Roberto F G (Bobby) *Baseball Player*
Navegantes FR-19, Reforma-Veracruz, MEXICO

Avila, Roberto F G (Bobby, Beto) *Baseball Player, Athlete*
Navegantes FR 19, Reforma, Vera Cruz, MEXICO

Avildsen, John G *Director*
2423 Briarcrest Road, Beverly Hills, CA 90210 USA

Aviles, Ramon *Baseball Player*
Boston Red Sox, 2 Calle E #C19, Manati, PR 00674-4028 USA

Avital, Mili *Actor*
Creative Artists Agency, 9830 Wilshire Blvd, Beverly Hills, CA 90232 USA

Avnet, Jon *Producer, Director*
Brooklyn Films, 3815 Hughes Ave, Culver City, CA 90232-2715

Avnet, Jonathan M (Jon) *Director, Producer*
3815 Hughes Ave, Culver City, CA 90232 USA

Avory, Mike *Musician*
Larry Page, 29 Rushton Mews, London, W11 1RB, UNITED KINGDOM (UK)

Awrey, Donald W (Don) *Hockey Player*
14960 Collier Blvd #1036, Naples, FL 34119 USA

Awsome
10 Bourlit Close, London, ENGLAND, W1T 7PJ

Awtrey, Dennis *Basketball Player*
509 W Granada, Phoenix, AZ 85003 USA

Ax, Emmanuel *Music Group, Musician*
173 Riverside Dr #12G, New York, NY 10024 USA

Axelrod, Jonathan H *Biologist*
Salk Institute, 10100 NTorrey Pines Road, La Jolla, CA 92037 USA

Axelrod, Julius *Nobel Prize Laureate*
10401 Grosvenor Place, Rockville, MD 20852 USA

Axtell, George C *War Hero*
41 High Bluff Dr, Weaverville, NC 28787 USA

Ay-O *Artist*
2-6-38 Matsuyama, Kiyoseshi, Tokyo, JAPAN

Ayala, Alexis *Actor*
Televisa, Blvd Adolfo Lopez Mateos 232, Colonia San Angel INN, DF, CP 01060, MEXICO

Ayala, Fransisco J *Biologist, Misc*
2 Locke Court, Irvine, CA 92612 USA

Ayala, Paul *Boxer*
7524 Creek Meadow Dr, Fort Worth, TX 76123 USA

Ayanna, Charlotte *Actor*
Industry Entertainment, 955 Carillo Dr #300, Los Angeles, CA 90048 USA

Aybar, Manny *Athlete*
401 E Jefferson, Phoenix, AZ 85004

Aybar, Manuel *Baseball Player*
St Louis Cardinals, 3020 SW 189th Ter, Miramar, FL 33029-5861 USA

Ayckbourn, Alan *Writer, Director*
M Ramsay, 14A Goodwins Ct, Saint Martin's Lane, London, WC2N 4LL, UNITED KINGDOM (UK)

Aycock, Alice *Artist*
62 Green St, New York, NY 10012 USA

Aycock, H David *Business Person*
Nucor Corp, 2100 Resford Road, Charlotte, NC 28211 USA

Aycock, Thomas *Golfer*
425 Seco Dr, Portland, TX 78374 USA

Aycox, Nicki *Actor*
Booh Schut Company, 11350 Ventura Blvd #200, Studio City, CA 91604 USA

Ayer, David *Producer, Writer*
William Morris Agency (WMA-LA), 1 William Morris Pl, Beverly Hills, CA 90212 USA

Ayers, Chuck *Cartoonist*
Unversal Press Syndicate, 4520 Main St, Kansas City, MO 64111 USA

Ayers, Dick *Cartoonist*
64 Beach St W, White Plains, NY 10604 USA

Ayers, Randy *Basketball Player, Coach*
Philadelphia 76ers, 1st Union Center 3601 S Broad St, Philadelphia, PA 19148 USA

Ayers, Roy E Jr *Music Group, Musician*
Associated Booking Corp, 1995 Broadway #501, New York, NY 10023 USA

Ayers, Sam *Actor*
Bobby Ball Talent Agency, 4342 Lankershim Blvd, Universal City, CA 91602 USA

Aykroyd, Dan *Actor, Comedian*
Creative Artists Agency, 9830 Wilshire Blvd, Beverly Hills, CA 90212 USA

Aylesworth, Reiko *Actor*
Innovative Artists (LA), 1505 Tenth St, Santa Monica, CA 90401 USA

Aylward, John *Actor*
J Michael Bloom, 9255 Sunset Blvd #710, Los Angeles, CA 90069 USA

Aylwin Azocar, Patricio *President*
Teresa Salas 786, Providencia, Santiago, CHILE

Ayrault, Bob *Baseball Player*
Philadelphia Phillies, 3012 Green Dr, Carson City, NV 89701-3363 USA

Ayrault, Joe *Baseball Player*
Atlanta Braves, 2338 Vintage St, Sarasota, FL 34240-8317 USA

Ayres, Leah
15718 Milbank, Encino, CA 91436

Ayres, Rosalind *Actor*
Lou Coulson Agency, 37 Berwick St Fl 1, London, WIV 3RF, UNITED KINGDOM (UK)

Aytes, Rochelle *Actor*
Kazarian/Spencer & Assoc, 11365 Ventura Blvd #100, Box 7403, Studio City, CA 91604 USA

AZ, Martyo *Reality TV Star*
Creative Artists Agency LCC (CAA-LA), 9830 Wilshire Blvd, Beverly Hills, CA 90212 USA

Azar, Steve *Music Group*
Gold Mountain, 2 Music Circle S #212, Nashville, TN 37203 USA

Azaria, Hank *Actor*
Endeavor Talent Agency, 9701 Wilshire Blvd #1000, Beverly Hills, CA 90212 USA

Azcue, Jose *Baseball Player*
Cincinnati Reds, 7609 W 115th St, Overland Park, KS 66210-2614 USA

Azenberg, Emanuel *Producer*
165 W 46th St, New York, NY 10036 USA

Azimov, Yakhyo *Prime Minister*
Prime Minister's Office, Rudaki Prosp 42, Dushaube, 743051, TAJIKISTAN

Azinger, Paul W *Golfer*
Leader Enterprises, 1101 N Kentucky Ave #100, Winter Park, FL 32789 USA

Aziz, Tariq *Prime Minister*
Prime Minister's Office, Karadat Mariam, Baghdad, IRAQ

Azizi, Anthony *Actor*
Geddes Agency, The, 8430 Santa Monica Blvd #200, Los Angeles, CA 90069

Azlan, Muhibuddin Shah *King*
Sultan's Palace, Istana Bukit Serene, Kuala Lumpur, MALAYSIA

Azmi, Shabana *Actor, Bollywood*
702 Sagar Samrat, Greenfields Juhu, Mumbai, MS 400049, INDIA

Aznar, Jose Maria *Prime Minister*
Prime Minister's Office, Complejo de las Moncloa, Madrid, 28071, SPAIN

Aznavour, Charles *Musician, Actor, Songwriter*
Levon Sayan, 76-78 Ave Champs-Elysees, Paris, 75008, FRANCE

Azria, Max *Fashion Designer*
BCBG/Max Azaria, 2761 Fruitland Ave, Vemon, CA 90058 USA

Azul Azul *Music Group*
Sony Music Miami, 605 Lincoln Rd, Miami Beach, FL 33138 USA

Azuma, Norio *Artist*
276 Riverside Dr, New York, NY 10025 USA

Azuma, Takamitsu *Architect*
Azuma Architects, 3-6-1 Minami-Aoyama, Minatoku, Tokyo, 107, JAPAN

Azumah, Jerry *Football Player*
39 King St, Worcester, MA 01610 USA

Azzara, Candice *Actor*
Meridian Artists, 9229 Sunset Blvd #310, Los Angeles, CA 90069 USA

Azzaro, Chrissy *Fashion Designer*
Perception Public Relations LLC, 13333 Ventura Blvd #203, Sherman Oaks, CA 91423 USA

Azzi, Jennifer *Basketball Player*
San Antonio Silver Stars, 1 SBC Center,
San Antonio, TX 78219 USA

B

B, Jon *Musician, Songwriter*
Devour Mgmt, 6399 Wilshire Blvd, #426,
Los Angeles, CA 90048 USA

B*Witched *Music Group*
Concorde Intl Artists Ltd, 101 Shepherds
Bush Rd, London, W6 7LP, UNITED
KINGDOM (UK)

B-52's, The *Music Group*
Monterey Peninsula Artists (Monterey),
509 Hartnell St, Monterey, CA 93940 USA

B-Real *Artist, Musician*
William Morris Agency, 151 El Camino
Dr, Beverly Hills, CA 90212 USA

B2K *Music Group*
Ultimate Group, The, 848 N La Cienega
Blvd #201, W Hollywood, CA 90069 USA

Baab, Mike *Football Player*
1705 Windlea Circle, Euless, TX 76040
USA

Baba, Enclik Abdul Ghafar Bin *Prime Minister*
Rural Development Ministry, Jalan Raja
Laut, Kuala Lumpur, 50606, MALAYSIA

Babashoff, Jack *Swimmer*
4859 Monroe Ave, San Diego, CA 92115
USA

Babashoff, Shirley *Swimmer*
17254 Santa Clara St, Fountain Valley, CA
92708 USA

Babatunde, Obba *Actor*
Stone Manners, 6500 Wilshire Blvd #550,
Los Angeles, CA 90048 USA

Babb, Charlie *Football Player*
371 Heron Ave, Naples, FL 34108 USA

Babb-Sprague, Kristen *Swimmer*
4677 Pine Valley Dr, Stockton, CA 95219
USA

Babbar, Raj *Actor, Bollywood*
Nepathaya Plot 20, Gulmohar Road JVPD
Scheme, Mumbai, MS 400049, INDIA

Babbidge, Homes D Jr *Educator*
3 Diving St, Stonington, CT 06378 USA

Babbit, Jamie *Director, Writer, Producer*
Innovative Artists (LA), 1505 Tenth St,
Santa Monica, CA 90401 USA

Babbitt, Bruce E *Secretary, Governor*
5169 Watson St NW, Washington, DC
20016 USA

Babbitt, Milton B *Composer*
222 Western Way, Princeton, NJ 08540
USA

Babbitt, Natalie *Writer*
Farrar Strous Giroux, 19 Union Square W,
New York, NY 10003 USA

Babcock, Barbara *Actor*
PO Box 222271, Carmel, CA 93922 USA

Babcock, Bob *Baseball Player*
Texas Rangers, 1192 Johns Ln, New
Castle, PA 16101-6774 USA

Babcock, Mike *Hockey Player, Coach*
Anaheim Mighty Ducks, 2000 E Gene
Autry Way, Anaheim, CA 92806 USA

Babcock, Tim M *Governor*
Ox Bow Ranch, P O Box 877, Helena,
MT 59624 USA

Babcock, Todd *Actor*
Gage Group, The (LA), 14724 Ventura
Blvd #505, Los Angeles, CA 91403 USA

Babenco, Hector E *Director*
International Creative Mgmt, 8942
Wilshire Blvd #219, Beverly Hills, CA
90211 USA

Babich, Bob *Football Player*
4994 Mt Ashmun Dr, San Diego, CA
92111 USA

Babilonia, Tai *Figure Skater*
13889 Valley Vista Blvd, Sherman Oaks,
CA 91423 USA

Babin, Rex *Editor, Cartoonist*
Sacramento Bee, Editorial Dept 21st & Q
Sts, Sacramento, CA 95852 USA

Babitt, Shooty *Baseball Player*
Oakland A's, 4912 Plaza Way, Richmond,
CA 94804-4346 USA

Babu, Ganesh *Actor*
No 1 Janaki Avenue, Abhiramapuram,
Chennai, TN 600 028, INDIA

Baby, Oje *Artist, Music Group*
William Morris Agency, 1325 Ave of
Americas, New York, NY 10019 USA

Baby, Peggy *Actor*
2219 Canyon Brook Lane, Newman, CA
95360 USA

Baby's
1545 Archer Rd, Bronx, NY 10462

Babych, Dave *Hockey Player*
6 Willow Brook Lane, Glastonbury, CT
06033 USA

Baca, John P *War Hero*
PO Box 9203, San Diego, CA 92169 USA

Baca, Susana *Music Group*
Todo Mondo, P O Box 652 Cooper
Station, New York, NY 10276 USA

Bacall, Lauren *Actor*
Dakota Hotel, 1 W 72nd St #43, New
York, NY 10023 USA

Bacall, Michael *Writer*
International Creative Management
(ICM-LA), 8942 Wilshire Blvd, Beverly
Hills, CA 90211 USA

Baccarin, Morena *Actor*
Lee Daniels Entertainment, 625 Broadway
#6M, New York, NY 10012 USA

Bach, Barbara *Actor*
2 Glynde Mews, London, SW3 1SB,
UNITED KINGDOM (UK)

Bach, Catherine *Actor*
C N A Assoc, 1925 Century Park East
#750, Los Angeles, CA 90067 USA

Bach, Emmanuelle *Actor*
Artmedia, 20 Ave Rapp, Paris, 75007,
FRANCE

Bach, Jillian *Actor*
Metropolitan Talent Agency (MTA), 4526
Wilshire Blvd, Los Angeles, CA 90010
USA

Bach, Pamela *Actor*
William Morris Agence, 151 El Camino
Dr, Beverly Hills, CA 90212 USA

Bach, Richard *Writer*
Dell Publishing, 1540 Broadway, New
York, NY 10036 USA

Bach, Sebastian *Actor, Music Group*
Premier Talent, 3 E 54th St #1100, New
York, NY 10022 USA

Bach, Steven K *Producer*
101 Park Ave #4300, New York, NY
10178 USA

Bachan, Abhishek *Bollywood*
Pratiksha, 10th Rd, JVPD Scheme,
Mumbai, 400049, INDIA

Bachan, Jaya *Bollywood, Actor*
Pratiksha 10th Road, JVPD Scheme,
Mumbai, 400049, India

Bachanan, Jaya *Bollywood, Actor*
Pratiksha 10th Road, JVPD Scheme,
Mumbai, 400049, India

Bachans *Actor*
Pratiksha 10th Rd, JVPD Scheme,
Mumbai, 400049, India

Bacharach, Burt *Musician, Composer*
681 Amalfi Dr, Pacific Palisades, CA
90272 USA

Bachardy, Don *Writer*
145 Adelaide Dr, Santa Monica, CA
90402 USA

Bachchan, Amitabh *Actor, Bollywood*
Pratiksha, 10th Road Juhu Scheme,
Mumbai, MS 400049, INDIA

Bachchan, Jaya *Actor, Bollywood*
Pratiksha 10rh Road, JVPD Scheme,
Mumbai, MS 400049, INDIA

Bacher, Avron (Ali) *Cricketer, Misc*
United Cricket Board, PO Box 55009,
Northlands, 2116, SOUTH AFRICA

Bacher, Robert F *Physicist*
1300 Hot Springs Road, Montecito, CA
93108 USA

Bachleda-Curus, Alicja *Actor*
Leverage Management, 1610 Broadway,
Santa Monica, CA 90404 USA

Bachman, Randy *Songwriter, Music Group*
Entertainment Services, 6400 Pleasant
Park Dr, Chanhassen, MN 55317 USA

Bachman, Tal *Songwriter, Music Group, Musician*
Q Prime, 729 7th Ave #1600, New York,
NY 10019 USA

Bachmann, Maria *Music Group, Musician*
Columbia Artists Mgmt Inc, 165 W 57th
St, New York, NY 10019 USA

Bachrach, Howard L *Misc*
355 Dayton Road, Southod, NY 11971
USA

Bachrach, Louis F Jr *Photographer*
Bachrach Inc, 647 Boylston St #2, Boston,
MA 02116 USA

Baciocco, Albert Juozas Cardinal *Admiral*
747 Pitt St, Mount Pleasant, SC 29464
USA

Backe, Brandon *Baseball Player*
Tampa Bay Devil Rays, 2550 Quaker Dr,
Texas City, TX 77590-3740 USA

Backe, John D *Business Person*
Backe Group, 83 General Warren Blvd
#100, Malvem, PA 19355 USA

Backis, Audrys Juozas Cardinal *Religious Leader*
Sventaragio 4, Vilnius, LITHUANIA

Backley, Stephen (Steve) *Track Athlete*
Cambridge Harriers, 56A-60 Glenhurst Ave, Bexley, Kent, DA5 3QN, UNITED KINGDOM (UK)

Backman, Jules *Economist, Writer*
59 Crane Road, Scarsdale, NY 10583 USA

Backman, Walter W (Wally) *Baseball Player*
New York Mets, 421 N Main St, Prineville, OR 97754-1855 USA

Backstreet Boys *Music Group*
Evolution Talent Agency LLC, 1776 Broadway Fl 15, New York, NY 10019 USA

Backus, Billy *Boxer*
308 N Main St, Canastota, NY 13032 USA

Backus, George E *Geophysicist*
9362 La Jolla Farms Road, La Jolla, CA 92037 USA

Backus, Gus *Musician*
Lustig Talent, PO Box 770850, Orlando, FL 32877 USA

Backus, John *Mathematician*
91 Saint Germaine Ave, San Francisco, CA 94114 USA

Backus, Sharon *Coach*
University of California, Athletic Dept, Los Angeles, CA 90024 USA

Bacon, Coy *Football Player*
1017 S 8th St, Ironton, OH 45638 USA

Bacon, Edmund N *Architect*
2117 Locust St, Philadelphia, PA 19103 USA

Bacon, James *Writer*
10982 Topeka Dr, Northridge, CA 91326 USA

Bacon, Kelvin *Actor*
PO Box 668, Sharon, CT 06069 USA

Bacon, Kevin *Actor*
PMK/HBH Public Relations (PMK-LA), 8500 Wilshire Blvd #700, Beverly Hills, CA 90211 USA

Bacon, Michael *Actor*
Circle Talent Associates, 433 N Camden Dr #400, Beverly Hills, CA 90210 USA

Bacon, Nicky D *War Hero*
Medal of Honor Society, 40 Patriots Point Road, Mount Pleasant, SC 29464 USA

Bacon, Roger F *Admiral*
24285 Johnson Road NW, Poulsbo, WA 98370 USA

Bacot, J Carter *Financier*
48 Porter Place, Montclair, NJ 07042 USA

Bacquier, Gabriel *Opera Singer*
141 Rue de Rome, Paris, 75017, FRANCE

Bacs, Ludovic *Composer*
31 D Golescu, Sc III E7 V Ap 87, Bucharest, 1, ROMANIA

Bacsik, Mike *Baseball Player*
Texas Rangers, 4014 Falcon Lake Dr, Arlington, TX 76016-4126 USA

Bacsik, Mike *Baseball Player*
Cleveland Indians, 4014 Falcon Lake Dr, Arlington, TX 76016-4126 USA

Bacuicchi, Antonello *Misc*
Co-Regent's Office, Government Palace, San Marino, 47031, SAN MARINO

Bad Company *Music Group*
Creative Artists Agency LCC (CAA-LA), 9830 Wilshire Blvd, Beverly Hills, CA 90212 USA

Bada, Jeffrey *Misc*
Scripps Institute of Oceanography, Chemistry Dept, La Jolla, CA 92093 USA

Badalamenti, Angelo *Composer*
11 Fidelian Way, Lincoln Park, NJ 07035 USA

Badalucco, Michael *Actor*
Manhattan Beach Studios, 1600 Rosecrans Ave, #1A, Manhattan Beach, CA 90266 USA

Badawi, Abdullah Ahamad *Prime Minister*
Prime Minister's Office, Jalan Dato Onn, Kuala Lumpur, 50502, MALAYSIA

Baddour, Raymond F *Engineer*
6495 SW 122nd St, Miami, FL 33156 USA

Badel, Sarah
4 Ovington Gardens, London, ENGLAND, SW3 1LS

Badelt, Klaus *Musician*
Gorfaine/Schwartz, 13245 Riverside Dr #450, Sherman Oaks, CA 91423 USA

Bader, Diedrich *Actor*
131 N June St, Los Angeles, CA 90004 USA

Badgley, Mark *Fashion Designer*
Badgley Mischka, 525 Fashion Ave, New York, NY 10018 USA

Badham, John M *Director*
Badham Company, 344 Clerendon Road, Beverly Hills, CA 90210 USA

Badham, Mary *Actor*
3344 Clarendon Road, Beverly Hills, CA 90210 USA

Badie, Mina *Actor*
Rigberg-Rugolo Entertainment, 1180 S Beverly Dr #601, Los Angeles, CA 90035 USA

Badu, Erykah *Musician, Songwriter*
Motown Records, 6255 Sunset Blvd, Los Angeles, CA 90028 USA

Badura-Skoda, Paul *Musician, Composer*
Zuckerkandlgass 14, Vienna, 1190, AUSTRIA

Baer, Amy *Business Person*
Columbia Pictures, 10202 W Washington Blvd, Culver City, CA 90232

Baer, Gordy *Bowler*
8577 Tullamore Dr, Tinley Park, IL 60477 USA

Baer, Olaf *Opera Singer*
Olbersdorferstr 7, Dresden, 01324, GERMANY

Baer, Parley
4967 Bilmoor Ave, Tarzana, CA 91356

Baer, Robert J (Jacob) *General*
6213 Militia Court, Fairfax Station, VA 22039 USA

Baer Jr, Max *Actor, Producer, Director*
PO Box 1831, Zephyr Cove, NV 89448 USA

Baerga, Carlos *Baseball Player*
Cleveland Indians, Ciudad Jardin 74 Calle Sauco, Toa Alta, PR 00953 USA

Baerwald, David *Musician*

Baez, Joan *Songwriter, Musician*
Mark Spector C, 44 Post Road W, Westport, CT 06880 USA

Baez, Jose *Baseball Player*
Seattle Mariners, 153 Lexington Ave, Jersey City, NJ 07304-1203 USA

Baez, Kevin *Baseball Player*
New York Mets, 975 S 4th St, Lindenhurst, NY 11757 USA

Baeza, Braulio *Jockey*
650 Huntington Ave, Boston, MA 02115 USA

Baeza, Paloma *Actor*
PFD, Drury House, 34-43 Russell St, London, WC2B 5HA USA

Bafaro, Michael *Director, Writer*
Lenhoff & Lenhoff, 830 Palm Ave, West Hollywood, CA 90069

Bafile, Corrado Cardinal *Religious Leader*
Via P Pancrazio Pfeiffer 10, Rome, 00193, ITALY

Bagabandi, Ntsaagiyn *President*
President's Office, Great Hural, Ulan Bator, MONGOLIA

Bagdasarian Jr, Ross *Actor, Producer*
Bagdasarian Productions, 1192 E Mountain Dr, Montecito, CA 93108

Bagge, Peter *Artist*
Fantagraphics Books, 7563 Lake City Way, Seattle, WA 98115 USA

Baggetta, Vincent *Actor*
3928 Madelia Ave, Sherman Oaks, CA 91403 USA

Baggio, Roberto *Soccer Player*
Bologna FC, Via Casteldebole 10, Bologna, 40132, ITALY

Baggott, Julianna *Writer*
Pocket Books, 1230 Ave of Americas, New York, NY 10020 USA

Bagian, James P *Astronaut*
21537 Holmbury Road, Northville, MI 48167 USA

Bagley, John *Basketball Player*
828 Beechwood Ave, Bridgeport, CT 06605 USA

Bagley, Lorri
PO Box 5617, Beverly Hills, CA 90210

Bagnal, Charles W *General*
Ratchford Assoc, 221 W Springs Road, Columbia, SC 29223 USA

Bagwell, Buff *Wrestler*
213 Morning Mist Way, Woodstock, GA 30189

Bagwell, Jeffrey R (Jeff) *Baseball Player*
Houston Astros, 4 Saddle Creek, Houston, TX 77024-6834 USA

Bahcall, John N *Physicist*
21 Adams Dr, Princeton, NJ 08540 USA

Bahns, Maxine *Actor, Athlete*
Jerry Shandrew PR, 1050 South Stanley Avenue, Los Angeles, CA 90019-6634 USA

Bahnsen, Stanley R (Stan) *Baseball Player*
New York Yankees, 3500 217th Pl SW,
Pompano Beach, FL 33064-2026 USA

Bahouth, Peter *Misc*
Greenpeace, 702 H St NW, Washington,
DC 20001 USA

Bahr, Chris *Football Player*
122 Kaywood Dr, Boalsburg, PA 16827
USA

Bahr, Ed *Baseball Player*
Pittsburgh Pirates, 326 217th Pl SW,
Bothell, WA 98021-8228 USA

Bahr, Egon *Government Official*
Ollenhauerster 1, Bonn, 53113,
GERMANY

Bahr, Matthew D (Matt) *Football Player*
53 Parkridge Lane, Pittsburgh, PA 15228
USA

Bahr, Morton *Misc*
Communications Workers Union, 501 3rd
St NW, Washington, DC 20001 USA

Bahr, Walter *Soccer Player*
250 Elks Road, Boalsburg, PA 16827 USA

Bai, Pandari *Actor, Bollywood*
54 Pillayar Koil Street, Vadapalani,
Chennai, TN 600026, INDIA

Bai, Yang *Actor*
978 Huashan Road, Shanghai, 200050,
CHINA

Bailar, Benjamin F *Government Official,
Educator*
410 Walnut Road, Lake Forest, IL 60045
USA

Bailes, Scott *Baseball Player*
Cleveland Indians, 2415 E Edgewood St,
Springfield, MO 65804-3905 USA

Bailey, Bob *Baseball Player*
Pittsburgh Pirates, 3081 Lido Isle Ct, Las
Vegas, NV 89117-3534 USA

Bailey, Cory *Baseball Player*
Boston Red Sox, 3822 2nd Dr NE,
Bradenton, FL 34208-5074 USA

Bailey, David *Photographer*
Robert Montgomery, 3 Junction Mews,
Sale Place, London, W2, UNITED
KINGDOM (UK)

Bailey, Donovan *Track Athlete*
625 Hales Chapel Rd, Gray, TN 37615
USA

Bailey, Ed *Baseball Player*
Cincinnati Reds, 642 Broome Rd,
Knoxville, TN 37909-2107 USA

Bailey, Eion *Actor*
I/D PR (LA), 8409 Santa Monica Blvd,
West Hollywood, CA 90069 USA

Bailey, F Lee *Attorney General*
Beverly & Freeman, 823 N Olive Ave,
West Palm Beach, FL 33401 USA

Bailey, G W *Actor*
22935 Frisca Dr, Valencia, CA 91354
USA

Bailey, Howard *Baseball Player*
Detroit Tigers, 11674 156th Ave, West
Olive, MI 49460-9388 USA

Bailey, Jim *Actor, Musician*
5909 W Colgate Ave, Los Angeles, CA
90036 USA

Bailey, Jim *Baseball Player*
Cincinnati Reds, PO Box 212, Fairburn,
GA 30213-0212 USA

Bailey, Joel
6550 Murietta, Van Nuys, CA 91401

Bailey, John *Cinematographer*
United Talent Agency, 9560 Wilshire
Blvd, #500, Beverly Hills, CA 90212 USA

Bailey, Johnny L *Football Player*
1282 Kingsbury Road, Abilene, TX 79602
USA

Bailey, Keith E *Business Person*
Williams Companies, 1 One Williams
Center, Tulsa, OK 74172 USA

Bailey, Leonard L *Doctor*
Loma Linda University, Medical School,
Loma Linda, CA 92350 USA

Bailey, Mark *Baseball Player*
Houston Astros, 32703 Waltham Xing,
Fulshear, TX 77441-4203 USA

Bailey, Maxwell C *General*
306 2nd St, Paris, KY 40361 USA

Bailey, Michael *Doctor*
Northwestern University, Psychology
Dept, Evanston, IL 60208 USA

Bailey, Norman S *Opera Singer*
84 Warham Road, South Croydon, Surrey,
CR2 6LB, UNITED KINGDOM (UK)

Bailey, Paul *Writer*
79 Davisville Road, London, W12 9SH,
UNITED KINGDOM (UK)

Bailey, Philip *Musician*
Covenant Agency, 1011 4th St, #315,
Santa Monica, CA 90403 USA

Bailey, Razzy *Songwriter, Musician*
Doc Sedelmeier, PO Box 62, Geneva, NE
68361 USA

Bailey, Robert M *Football Player*
15325 SW 99th Ave, Miami, FL 33157
USA

Bailey, Roger *Baseball Player*
Colorado Rockies, 11045 Puma Run,
Littleton, CO 80124-9420 USA

Bailey, Steve *Baseball Player*
Cleveland Indians, 4600 Queen Anne
Ave, Lorain, OH 44052-5648 USA

Bailey, Steven W *Reality TV Star*
Fox Broadasting Company, PO Box 900,
Beverly Hills, CA 90213

Bailey, T Wayne *Politician, Social Activist*
Stetson University, Political Science Dept,
Stetson, FL 32720 USA

Bailey, Thomas H *Financier*
Janus Capital Corp, 100 Fillmore St,
Denver, CO 80206 USA

Bailey, Thurl *Basketball Player*
6406 S Crestmont Circle, Salt Lake City,
UT 84121 USA

Bailey, William *Artist*
223 E 10th St, New York, NY 10003 USA

Bailey II, Irving W *Business Person*
Providian Corp, 400 W Market St,
Louisville, KY 40202 USA

Bailon, Adrienne *Actor, Musician*
Pyramid Entertainment, 89 5th Ave, #700,
New York, NY 10003 USA

Bailor, Bob *Baseball Player*
Baltimore Orioles, 1950 Swan Ln, Palm
Harbor, FL 34683-6275 USA

Bailyn, Bernard *Historian*
170 Clifton St, Belmont, MA 02478 USA

Bain, Anthony *Actor*
Stein Entertainment Group, 11271 Ventura
Blvd #477, Studio City, CA 91604 USA

Bain, Barbara *Actor*
1501 Skylark Lane, Los Angeles, CA
90069 USA

Bain, Conrad *Actor*
1230 Chickory Lane, Los Angeles, CA
90049 USA

Bain, Michael *Actor*
Stein Entertainment Group, 11271 Ventura
Blvd #477, Studio City, CA 91604 USA

Bain, William E (Bill) *Football Player*
27661 Paseo Barona, San Juan Capo, CA
92675 USA

Bainbridge, Beryl *Actor, Writer*
42 Albert St, London, NW1 7NU,
UNITED KINGDOM (UK)

Bainbridge, Merril *Musician, Songwriter*
001 Productions, PO Box 1760,
Collingswood, VIC, 3068, AUSTRALIA

Baines, Harold D *Baseball Player*
Chicago White Sox, PO Box 335, Saint
Michaels, MD 21663-0335 USA

Baio, Jimmy *Actor*
11662 Duque Dr, Studio City, CA 91604
USA

Baio, Scott *Actor*
4333 Forman Ave, Toluca Lake, CA
91602 USA

Baiocchi, Hugh *Golfer*
Int'l Mgmt Group, 1 Erieview Plaza, 1360
E 9th St #1300, Cleveland, OH 44114
USA

Bair, Doug *Baseball Player*
Pittsburgh Pirates, 560 Ohio Pike,
Cincinnati, OH 45255-3315 USA

Baird, Briny *Golfer*
Pro's Inc, 9 S 12th St, #300, Richmond,
VA 23219 USA

Baird, Butch *Golfer*
PO Box 2633, Carefree, AZ 85377 USA

Baird, James M *Religious Leader*
Presbyterian Church, PO Box 1428,
Decatur, GA 30031 USA

Baird, Stuart *Director*
William Morris Agency, 151 El Camino
Dr, Beverly Hills, CA 90212 USA

Bairstow, Scott H *Actor*
4333 Forman Ave, Toluca Lake, CA
91602 USA

Baiul, Oksana *Figure Skater*
Bob Young, PO Box 988, Niantic, CT
06357 USA

Bajanowsky, Louis J *Architect*
Cambridge Seven Assoc, 1050
Massachusetts Ave, Cambridge, MA
02138 USA

Bajardi, Lane *Television Host*
Bloomberg Television, 499 Park Ave Fl
17, New York, NY 10022 USA

Bajcsy, Ruzena *Engineer*
University of California, Electrical
Engineering Dept, Berkeley, CA 94720
USA

Bajor, Jim *Musician*
34841 Mound Rd #114, Sterling Heights,
MI 48310

Bajpai, Manoj *Actor, Bollywood*
304 Victoria Shastrinagar, Lokhandwala
Complex Andheri(W), Mumbai, MS
4000593, INDIA

Bakalyan, Richard *Actor*
1070 S Bedford St, Los Angeles, CA
90035 USA

Bakatin, Vadim V *Government Official*
Kotelnicheskaya Nab 17, Moscow,
103240, RUSSIA

Bakay, Nick *Actor*
United Talent Agency (UTA), 9560
Wilshire Blvd, Beverly Hills, CA 90212
USA

Bakenhaster, Dave *Baseball Player*
St Louis Cardinals, 3710 Rome Corners
Rd, Galena, OH 43021-9490 USA

Baker, Anita *Musician*
Associated Booking Corp, 1995
Broadway, #501, New York, NY 10023
USA

Baker, Bill *Baseball Player*
Cincinnati Reds, 250 Manor Cir, Myrtle
Beach, SC 29588-7202 USA

Baker, Blanche *Actor*
2501 Palisade Ave #B2, Bronx, NY 10463
USA

Baker, Brenda *Actor*
Agency for Performing Arts, 9200 Sunset
Blvd #900, Los Angeles, CA 90069 USA

Baker, Buddy *Race Car Driver*
4860 Moonlite Bay Dr, Sherrills Ford, NC
28673 USA

Baker, Carroll *Actor*
Abrams Artists, 9200 Sunset Blvd, #1125,
Los Angeles, CA 90069 USA

Baker, Chuck *Baseball Player*
San Diego Padres, 3035 Mescalero Dr,
Lake Havasu City, AZ 86404-9605 USA

Baker, Colin *Actor*
Evans & Reiss, 100 Fawe Park Road,
London, SW15 2EA, UNITED KINGDOM
(UK)

Baker, Dave *Baseball Player*
Toronto Blue Jays, 22234 S23 Hwy,
Lacona, IA 50139-6669 USA

Baker, Diane *Actor*
2733 Outpost Dr, Los Angeles, CA 90068
USA

Baker, Donald K *Cinematographer*
11789 Lakeshore N, Auburn, CA 95602
USA

Baker, Doug *Baseball Player*
Detroit Tigers, 2676 S Mission Rd,
Fallbrook, CA 92028-4536 USA

Baker, Dylan *Actor*
Paradigm Agency, 10100 Santa Monica
Blvd, #2500, Los Angeles, CA 90067 USA

Baker, Earl P Jr *War Hero*
10100 Cypress Cove Dr, Fort Myers, FL
33908 USA

Baker, Ellen Shulman *Astronaut*
2207 Garden Stream Court, Houston, TX
77062 USA

Baker, Floyd *Baseball Player*
St Louis Browns, 3033 Idlewood Ave,
Youngstown, OH 44511-3135 USA

Baker, Frank *Misc, Bowler*
13900 W Burleigh Road, Brookfield, WI
53005 USA

Baker, Frank *Baseball Player*
New York Yankees, 4105 A Pl, Meridian,
MS 39301-1038 USA

Baker, Ginger *Musician*
Twist Mgmt, 4230 Del Rey Ave, #621,
Marina Del Rey, CA 90292 USA

Baker, Graham *Director*
10 Buckingham St, London, WC2,
UNITED KINGDOM (UK)

Baker, Jack *Baseball Player*
Boston Red Sox, 5513 Hunters Hill Rd,
Irondale, AL 35210-3011 USA

Baker, Janet A *Opera Singer, Musician*
Transart Ltd, 8 Bristol Gardens, London,
W9 2JG, UNITED KINGDOM (UK)

Baker, Joe Don *Actor*
23339 Hatteras St, Woodland Hills, CA
91367 USA

Baker, John F Jr *War Hero*
Medal of Honor Society, 40 Patriots Point
Road, Mount Pleasant, SC 29464 USA

Baker, John H Jr *Football Player*
5 Famham Park Dr, Houston, TX 77024
USA

Baker, John R *General*
Vice Commander, Air Mobility Command,
Scott Air Force Base, IL 62225 USA

Baker, Johnnie B (Dusty) *Baseball Player*
Minnesota Twins, 40 Livingston Terrace
Dr, San Bruno, CA 94066-2800 USA

Baker, Kathy *Actor*
1146 N Central Ave #163, Glendale, CA
91202 USA

Baker, Kendall L *Educator*
University of North Dakota, President's
Office, Grand Forks, ND 58202 USA

Baker, Kenny *Actor*
51 Mulgrave Ave, Ashton, Preston,
Lancashire, PR2 1HJ, UNITED KINGDOM
(UK)

Baker, Laurie *Hockey Player*
67 Prairie St, Concord, MA 01742 USA

Baker, Leslie M Jr *Financier*
Wachovia Corp, 301 N Main St, Winston
Salem, NC 27150 USA

Baker, Lewis *Musician*
Joe Terry Mgmt, PO Box 1017,
Turnersville, NJ 08012 USA

Baker, Mark *Bowler*
11751 Steele Dr, Garden Grove, CA
92840 USA

Baker, Michael A (Mike) *Astronaut*
NASA, Johnson Space Center, 2101 NASA
Road, Houston, TX 77058 USA

Baker, Nicholson *Writer*
Melanie Jackson Agency, 256 W 57th St
#1119, New York, NY 10019 USA

Baker, Paul T *Misc*
1000 Escalon Ave, #A3005, Sunnyvale,
CA 94085 USA

Baker, Rae *Actor*
Marmont Management, Langham House,
308 Regent St, London, W1B 3AT,
UNITED KINGDOM (UK)

Baker, Raymond *Actor*
253A 26th St, #312, Santa Monica, CA
90402 USA

Baker, Robby *Musician*
Management Trust, 219 Dufferin St
#309B, Toronto, ON M5K 3J1, CANADA

Baker, Robert *Actor*
Evolution Entertainment, 901 N Highland
Ave, Los Angeles, CA 90038 USA

Baker, Robert *Attorney General*
Baker Silberberg Keener, 2850 Ocean
Park Blvd, Santa Monica, CA 90405 USA

Baker, Roy Ward
125 Gloucester Rd, London, ENGLAND,
SW7 4TE

Baker, Russell W *Writer*
New York Times, Editorial Dept, 229 W
43rd St, New York, NY 10036 USA

Baker, Scott *Baseball Player*
Oakland A's, 508 Red Shale Ct,
Henderson, NV 89052-2886 USA

Baker, Scott Thompson *Actor*
17651 Sidwell, Granada Hills, CA 91344
USA

Baker, Shaun *Actor*
Michael Slessinger & Assoc, 8730 Sunset
Blvd #270, Los Angeles, CA 90069 USA

Baker, Simon *Actor*
Norman House, Cambridge Palace,
Cambridge, CB2 1NS, UNITED
KINGDOM (UK)

Baker, Steve *Baseball Player*
Detroit Tigers, 27527 Easy Acres Dr,
Eugene, OR 97405-9726 USA

Baker, Terry *Football Player*
3208 SW Fairmount Blvd, Portland, OR
97239 USA

Baker, Tom *Actor*
JM Associates, 77 Beak St, London, W1R
3LE, UNITED KINGDOM (UK)

Baker, Tyler Christopher *Actor*
Beddingfield Company, The, 9255 Sunset
Blvd #920, Los Angeles, CA 90069 USA

Baker, Vernon J *War Hero*
650 Vemon Lane, Saint Maries, ID 83861
USA

Baker, Vin *Basketball Player*
PO Box 179, Old Saybrook, CT 06475
USA

Baker, W Thane *Track Athlete*
6704 Saint John Court, Granbury, TX
76049 USA

Baker, William (Bill) *Hockey Player*
6005 Sugarbush Trail, Brainerd, MN
56401 USA

Baker, William O *Misc*
AT&T Bell Lucent Laboratory, 600
Mountain Ave, New Providence, NJ
07974 USA

Baker III, James A *Politician*
Baker & Botts, 1 Shell Plz, 910 Louisiana, Houston, TX 77002 USA

Baker Jr, Howard H *Politician, Senator, Diplomat*
US Embassy, 10-1-1 Akasaka, Minatoku, Tokyo, 1-7, JAPAN

Baker-Finch, Ian *Golfer*
IBF Enterprises, PO Box 176, Sanctuary Grove, QLD, 4212, AUSTRALIA

Bakhtair, Rudi *Commentator*
Cable News Network, News Dept, 1050 Techwood Dr NW, Atlanta, GA 30318 USA

Bakis, Kristen *Writer*
Farrar Straus Giroux, 19 Union Square W, New York, NY 10003 USA

Bakke, Brenda *Actor*
28128 Pacific Coast Highway, #258, Malibu, CA 90265 USA

Bakken, Earl *Inventor, Doctor*
68-1399 Mauna Lani Dr, Kamuela, HI 96743 USA

Bakken, James L (Jim) *Football Player*
230 Glen Hollow Road, Madison, WI 53705 USA

Bakker, James O (Jim) *Religious Leader*
123 E End Road, Branson, MO 65616 USA

Bakker Messner, Tammy Faye *Religious Leader*
1527 Wood Creek Road, Matthews, NC 28105 USA

Bako, Brigitte *Actor*
Kritzer, 12200 W Olympic Blvd, #400, Los Angeles, CA 90064 USA

Bako, Paul *Baseball Player*
Detroit Tigers, 110 Coventry St, Lafayette, LA 70506-6149 USA

Bakshi, Ralph *Animator*
7950 Sunset Blvd, Los Angeles, CA 90046 USA

Bakula, Scott *Actor*
15300 Ventura Blvd, #315, Sherman Oaks, CA 91403 USA

Balaban, Bob *Director, Producer, Writer*
Chicago Films, 250 W 57th St #2217, New York, NY 10107 USA

Balaban, Liane *Actor*
International Creative Management (ICM-LA), 8942 Wilshire Blvd, Beverly Hills, CA 90211 USA

Baladmenti, Angelo *Composer*
4146 Lankershim Blvd, #401, North Hollywood, CA 91602 USA

Balambika *Actor, Bollywood*
3 Indira Gandhi Street, Chennai, TN 600093, INDIA

Balandin, Aleksandr N *Cosmonaut*
Potcha Kosmonavtov, Moskovskoi Oblasti, Syvisdny Goroduk, 141160, RUSSIA

Balaski, Belinda *Actor*
Epstein-Wyckoff, 280 S Beverly Dr, #400, Beverly Hills, CA 90212 USA

Balassa, Sandor *Composer*
18 Sumegvar Str, Budapest, 1118, HUNGARY

Balasubramaniyam, S P *Actor, Musician*
16 Kamdar Nagar, Nungambakkam, Chennai, TN 600 034, INDIA

Balboa, Marcelo *Soccer Player*
13139 Hedda Dr, Cerritos, CA 90703 USA

Baldacci, David *Writer*
Warner Books, 1271 Ave of Americas, New York, NY 10020 USA

Baldavin, Barbara *Actor*
228 17th St, Manhattan Beach, CA 90266 USA

Balderstone, James S *Business Person*
115 Mont Albert Road, Canterbuy, VIC, 3126, AUSTRALIA

Baldeschwieler, John D *Misc*
PO Box 50065, Pasadena, CA 91115 USA

Baldessari, John *Artist*
2001 1/2 Main St, Santa Monica, CA 90405 USA

Balding, Rebecca *Actor*
2001 Winnetka Place, Woodland Hills, CA 91364 USA

Baldinger, Brian *Sportscaster*
Fox-TV, Sports Dept, 205 W 67th St, New York, NY 10021 USA

Baldock, Bobby R *Judge*
US Court of Appeals, PO Box 2388, Roswell, NM 88202 USA

Baldridge, Letitia *Business Person, Writer*
2339 Massachusetts Ave NW, Washington, DC 20008 USA

Baldrige, Leticia *Writer*
Letitia Baldrige Enterprises Inc, 2339 Massachussetts Ave NW, Washington, DC 20008

Baldry, Long John *Musician*
Macklam Feidman Mgmt, 1505 W 2nd Ave #200, Vancouver, BC V6H 3Y4, CANADA

Baldschun, Jack E *Baseball Player*
311 Erie Road, Green Bay, WI 54311 USA

Baldwin, Adam *Actor*
1301 Caryle Ave, Santa Monica, CA 90402 USA

Baldwin, Alec *Actor*
El Dorado Pictures, 725 Arizona Ave, 100, Santa Monica, CA 90401 USA

Baldwin, Burr *Football Player*
2000 Ashe Road, Bakersfield, CA 93309 USA

Baldwin, Daniel *Actor*
William Morris Agency, 151 El Camino Dr, Beverly Hills, CA 90212 USA

Baldwin, Jack *Race Car Driver*
4748 Balmoral Way NE, Marietta, GA 30068 USA

Baldwin, Jack E *Misc*
Oxford University, Dyson Perrins Lab, S Park Rd, Oxford, OX1 3QY, UNITED KINGDOM (UK)

Baldwin, John A (Jack) Jr *Admiral*
1371 Millersville Road, Millersville, MD 21108 USA

Baldwin, John W *Historian*
Johns Hopkins University, History Dept, Baltimore, MD 21218 USA

Baldwin, Judy *Actor*
PO Box 4723, Valley Village, CA 91617 USA

Baldwin, Margaret *Writer*
PO Box 1106, Williams Bay, WI 53191 USA

Baldwin, Robert E *Economist*
125 Nautilus Dr, Madison, WI 53705 USA

Baldwin, Stephen *Actor*
Edmonds Management, 1635 N Cahuenga Blvd Fl 5, Los Angeles, CA 90028 USA

Baldwin, William *Editor*
Forbes Magazine, Editorial Dept, 60 5th Ave, New York, NY 10011 USA

Baldwin, William (Billy) *Actor*
Firm, The, 9465 Wilshire Blvd, Beverly Hills, CA 90212 USA

Bale, Christian *Actor*
Endeavor Agency LLC (LA), 9601 Wilshire Blvd Fl 3, Beverly Hills, CA 90210 USA

Balenda, Carla
15848 Woodvale, Encino, CA 91316

Balfanz, John C *Skier*
7770 E lliff Ave, #G, Denver, CO 80231 USA

Balfour, Eric *Actor*
United Talent Agency, 9560 Wilshire Blvd #500, Beverly Hills, CA 90212 USA

Balgimbayev, Nurlan *Prime Minister*
Dom Pravieelstva, Pl im VI Lenina, Astana, 148008, KAZAKHSTAN

Baliani, Marco *Actor*
Carol Levi Co, Via Giuseppe Pisanelli, Rome, 00196, ITALY

Baliga Bantval, Jayant *Engineer*
2612 Bembridge Dr, Raleigh, NC 27613 USA

Baliles, Gerald L *Governor*
Riverfront Plaza East Tower, 951 E Byrd St, Richmond, VA 23219 USA

Balin, Marty *Musician, Songwriter*
Joe Buchwald, PO Box 170040, San Francisco, CA 94117 USA

Balitran, Celine *Model*
Ford Model Agency, 142 Greene St, #400, New York, NY 10012 USA

Balk, Fairuza *Actor*
Rigberg Roberts Rugolo, 1180 S Beverly Dr, #601, Los Angeles, CA 90035 USA

Balkenende, Jan-Peter *Prime Minister*
Premier's Office, Binnenhof 20, Postbus 20001, EA Hague, NETHERLANDS

Balkenhol, Klaus *Athlete*
Narzissenweg 11A, Hilden, 40723, GERMANY

Ball, Alan *Producer*
United Talent Agency (UTA), 9560 Wilshire Blvd, Beverly Hills, CA 90212 USA

Ball, David *Musician*
Buddy Lee, 38 Music Square E, #300, Nashville, TN 37203 USA

Ball, Edward *Writer*
Farrar Straus Giroux, 19 Union Square W, New York, NY 10003 USA

Ball, Eric C *Football Player*
10614 Margate Terrace, Cincinnati, OH 45241 USA

Ball, Jeff
8311 East Via de Ventura, #1013,
Scottsdale, AZ 85258-6601

Ball, Jerry L *Football Player*
3311 Meadowside Dr, Sugar Land, TX
77478 USA

Ball, Michael A *Musician, Actor*
PO Box 2073, Colchester, Essex, CO4
3WS, UNITED KINGDOM (UK)

Ball, Robert M *Government Official*
1776 Massachusetts Ave NW,
Washington, DC 20036 USA

Ball, Sam *Actor*
Gersh Agency, 232 N Canon Dr, Beverly
Hills, CA 90210 USA

Ball, Taylor *Actor*
William Morris Agency (WMA-LA), 1
William Morris Pl, Beverly Hills, CA
90212 USA

Balladur, Edouard *Prime Minister*
5 Rue Jean Formige, Paris, 75015,
FRANCE

Ballantine, Carl *Actor*
2575 N Beachwood Dr, Los Angeles, CA
90068 USA

Ballantine, Sara *Actor*
Talent Group, 5670 Wilshire Blvd #820,
Los Angeles, CA 90036 USA

Ballantyne *Fashion Designer*
Ballantyne, 4-6 Savile Road, London,
England, W1S 3PD, United Kingdom

Ballard, Carroll *Director*
PO Box 556, Saint Helena, CA 94574
USA

Ballard, Del Jr *Bowler*
Ebonite International, PO Box 746,
Hopkinsville, KY 42241 USA

Ballard, Donald E *War Hero*
PO Box 34593, North Kansas City, MO
64116 USA

Ballard, Glenn *Songwriter*
Sorfaine/Schwartz, 13245 Riverside Dr,
#450, Sherman Oaks, CA 91423 USA

Ballard, Greg *Basketball Player*
4440 Harbor Lane N, Minneapolis, MN
55446 USA

Ballard, James Graham (JG) *Writer*
36 Old Charlton Rd, Shepperton, Middx,
TW17 8AT, UNITED KINGDOM (UK)

Ballard, Kaye *Actor*
PO Box 922, Rancho Mirage, CA 92270
USA

Ballard, Robert D *Oceanographer*
Institute for Exploration, 55 Coogan Blvd,
Mystic, CT 06355 USA

Ballerini, Edoardo *Actor*
Thruline Entertainment, 9250 Wilshire
Blvd, Ground Floor, Beverly Hills, CA
90210 USA

Ballesteros, Roberto *Actor*
Televisa, Blvd Adolfo Lopez Mateos 232,
Colonia San Angel INN, DF, CP 01060,
MEXICO

Ballesteros, Seveiano (Seve) *Golfer*
Fareway SAE, Pasage de Pena 10, Curata
Planta, Santander, 39008, SPAIN

Ballestros, Anderson *Actor*
LatinActors, 920 Leavenworth St #302,
San Francisco, CA 94109

Ballhaus, Florian M *Cinematographer*
115 Berkeley Place, Brooklyn, NY 11217
USA

Ballhaus, Michael *Cinematographer*
11 Elm Place, Rye, NY 10580 USA

Ballmer, Steven A *Business Person*
Microsoft Corp, 1 Microsoft Way,
Redmond, WA 98052 USA

Ballon, Adrienne *Actor*
International Creative Management
(ICM-LA), 8942 Wilshire Blvd, Beverly
Hills, CA 90211 USA

Ballou, Mark *Actor*
145 Ave of the Americas, #200, New
York, NY 10013 USA

Ballou, Tyson *Model*
Ford Model Agency, 142 Greene St, #400,
New York, NY 10012 USA

Balmaseda, Liz *Journalist*
Miami Herald, Editorial Dept, 1 Herald
Plaza, Miami, FL 33132 USA

Balmer, Jean Francois *Actor*
ArtMedia, 20 Ave Rapp, Paris, 75007,
FRANCE

Balmer, Jean-Francois *Actor*
Artmedia, 20 Ave Rapp, Paris, 75007,
FRANCE

Balon, David A (Dave) *Hockey Player*
1246 Gilmor Crescent, Prince Albert, SK
S6V 6A7, CANADA

Balraaj, Anand *Actor, Bollywood*
72/1 AV Villa, Kakori Camp, Aram Nagar,
Seven Bungalows Versova Andheri,
Mumbai, MS 400058, INDIA

Balsam, Talia *Actor*
1 Bank St, #6H, New York, NY 10014
USA

Balser, Glennon *Religious Leader*
Advent Christian Church, 6315 Studley
Road, Mechanicsville, VA 23116 USA

Balsley, Philip E *Musician*
191 Abbington Road, Swoope, VA 24479
USA

Baltes, Jameson *Actor*
Hervey/Grimes, PO Box 64249, Los
Angeles, CA 90064 USA

Baltica, Kremerata *Musician*
International Creative Management
(ICM-LA), 8942 Wilshire Blvd, Beverly
Hills, CA 90211 USA

Baltimore, David *Nobel Prize Laureate,
Educator*
31460 Beach Park Road, Malibu, CA
90265 USA

Baltray, Charies *Astronomer*
Yale University, Astronomy Dept, New
Haven, CT 06520 USA

Baltron, Donna *Actor*
C N A Assoc, 1925 Century Park East,
#750, Los Angeles, CA 90067 USA

Baltsa, Agnes *Opera Singer*
Manuela Kursidem, Wasagasse 12/1/3,
Vienna, 1090, AUSTRIA

Baltz, Lewis *Photographer*
11693 San Vincente Blvd #527, Los
Angeles, CA 90049 USA

Balukas, Jean *Billiards Player*
9818 4th Ave, Brooklyn, NY 11209 USA

Balul, Oksana *Figure Skater*
Bob Young, PO Box 988, Niantic, CT
06357 USA

Balzary, Michael (Flea) *Musician, Actor*
Innovative Artists (LA), 1505 Tenth St,
Santa Monica, CA 90401 USA

Bama, Jim *Artist*
PO Box 148, Wapiti, WY 82450 USA

Bamber, Jamie
Alan Siegel Entertainment, 345 N Maple
Dr #375, Beverly Hills, CA 90210 USA

Bamman, Gerry *Actor*
Writers & Artists, 8383 Wilshire Blvd
#550, Beverly Hills, CA 90211 USA

Ban Breathnach, Sarah *Writer*
Warner Books, 1271 Ave of Americas,
New York, NY 10020 USA

Bana, Eric *Actor, Comedian*
8-12 Sandilands St #2, S Melbourne,
Victoria, 3205, AUSTRALIA

Banach, Edward (Ed) *Wrestler*
2128 Country Club Blvd, Ames, IA 50014
USA

Banach, Louis (Lou) *Wrestler*
3276 E Fairfax Road, Cleveland Heights,
OH 44118 USA

Banachowski, Andy *Volleyball Player,
Coach*
University of California, Athletic Dept, Los
Angeles, CA 90024 USA

Banaszak, John A *Football Player*
420 Robinhood Lane, McMurray, PA
15317 USA

Banaszak, Pete *Football Player*
612 W Surf Spray Lane, Ponte Vedra
Beach, FL 32082 USA

Banaszek, Cas *Football Player*
1018 Cohen Court, Petaluma, CA 94952
USA

Banaszynski, Jacqui *Journalist*
Saint Paul Pioneer Press, Editorial Dept,
345 Cedar St, Saint Paul, MN 55101 USA

Banbury, F H Frith *Director*
18 Park Saint James, Prince Albert Road,
London, NW8 7LE, UNITED KINGDOM
(UK)

Bancroft, Ann *Skier*
Yourexpedition, 119 N 4th St, #406,
Minneapolis, MN 55104 USA

Bancroft, Anne *Actor*
23868 Malibu Road, Malibu, CA 90265
USA

Bancroft, Cameron *Actor*
Gersh Agency, The (LA), 232 N Canon Dr,
Beverly Hills, CA 90210 USA

Band, Richard H *Composer*
24053 Bessemer St, Woodland Hills, CA
91367 USA

Banda El Limon, Arrolladora *Music Group*
Sony Music Miami, 605 Lincoln Rd,
Miami Beach, FL 33138 USA

Banda Pachuco *Music Group*
Sony Music Miami, 605 Lincoln Rd, Miami Beach, FL 33138 USA

Bandar, Prince Sultan-al-saud
601 New Hampshire NW, Washington, DC 20037

Banderas, Antonio *Actor, Producer, Musician, Director*
Creative Artists Agency LCC (CAA-LA), 9830 Wilshire Blvd, Beverly Hills, CA 90212 USA

Bandholz, Antonio *Misc*
Sohnholm 92, Westerholz, 24977, GERMANY

Bando, Salvatore L (Sal) *Baseball Player*
W308N 6225 Shore Acres Road, Hartland, WI 53029 USA

Bandy, Moe *Musician, Songwriter*
Blackwood Mgmt, PO Box 5331, Sevierville, TN 37864

Banes, Lisa *Actor*
Don Buchwald & Associates Inc (LA), 6500 Wilshire Blvd #2200, Los Angeles, CA 90048 USA

Banfield, Ashleigh *Commentator*
NBC-TV, News Dept, 30 Rockfeller Plaza, New York, NY 10112 USA

Bang, Molly *Writer*
43 Drumlin Road, Falmouth, MA 02540 USA

Bangemann, Martin *Government Official*
European Commission, 200 Rue de la Loi, Brussels, 1049, BELGIUM

Bangerter, Norman H *Governor*
603 E South Temple, Salt Lake City, UT 84102 USA

Bangles, The *Music Group*
Creative Artists Agency LCC (CAA-LA), 9830 Wilshire Blvd, Beverly Hills, CA 90212 USA

Bani, John *President*
President's Office, Port Vila, VANUATU

Bank, Frank *Actor*
PO Box 902, North Palm Springs, CA 92258 USA

Banke, Paul *Boxer*
1926 Bobolink Way, Pomona, CA 91767 USA

Banks, Brianna *Adult Film Star*
Atlas Multimedia Inc, 22940 Burbank Blvd, Woodland Hills, CA 91367 USA

Banks, Chip *Football Player*
2600 Peachtree Road NW, #3, Atlanta, GA 30305 USA

Banks, David *Actor*
Shane Collins Assoc, 2-5 Stedham Pl, Bloomsbury, London, WC1A 1BU, ENGLAND

Banks, Dennis *Misc*
General Delivery, Oglala, SD 57764 USA

Banks, Elizabeth *Actor*
Untitled Entertainment (LA), 8436 W 3rd St #650, Los Angeles, CA 90048 USA

Banks, Ernie *Baseball Player*
520 Washington Blvd #284, Marina del Rey, CA 90292-5442 USA

Banks, Gene *Basketball Player*
Bluefield State College, Athletic Dept, 219 Rock St, Bluefield, WV 24701 USA

Banks, Jonathan *Actor*
909 Euclid St, #8, Santa Monica, CA 90403 USA

Banks, Kelcie *Boxer*
3040 E Charleston Blvd, Las Vegas, NV 89104 USA

Banks, Lynne Reid *Writer*
Avon Books, 1350 Ave of Americas, New York, NY 10019 USA

Banks, Morwenna *Actor, Writer*
International Creative Management (ICM-LA), 8942 Wilshire Blvd, Beverly Hills, CA 90211 USA

Banks, Russell *Writer*
Princeton University, English Debt, Princeton, NJ 08544 USA

Banks, Steven *Actor, Comedian*
Gersh Agency, 232 N Canon Dr, Beverly Hills, CA 90210 USA

Banks, Steven Gary *Writer, Producer*
International Creative Management (ICM-LA), 8942 Wilshire Blvd, Beverly Hills, CA 90211 USA

Banks, Ted *Coach*
Riverside Community College, Athletic Dept, Riverside, CA 92506 USA

Banks, Tom *Football Player*
358 Wisteria St, Fairhope, AL 36532 USA

Banks, Tyra *Model, Actor*
Handprint Entertainment, 1100 Glendon Ave #1000, Los Angeles, CA 90024 USA

Banks, William A (Willie) III *Track Athlete*
250 Williams St NW, #6000, Atlanta, GA 30303 USA

Bankston, Warren *Football Player*
4201 Bordeaux Dr, Kenner, LA 70065 USA

Banner, Bob *Producer, Director*
1158 Wellesley Ave #101, Los Angeles, CA 90049 USA

Banner, Penny
6810 Cabot Circle, Charlotte, NC 28226-3928

Bannerman, Isabella *Cartoonist*
41 South Drive, Hastings-on-Hudson, NY 10706 USA

Bannister, Floyd F *Baseball Player*
6701 Caball Dr, Paradise Valley, AZ 85253 USA

Bannister, Reggie *Actor, Musician*
Magic Inc, 4450 California Place, Box 315, Long Beach, CA 90807 USA

Bannister, Roger G *Track Athlete, Scientist*
21 Bardwell Road, Oxford, OX2 6SV, UNITED KINGDOM (UK)

Bannister, Trevor *Actor*
David Daly, 68 Old Brompton Road, London, SW7 3LQ, UNITED KINGDOM (UK)

Bannon, Jack *Actor*
5923 Wilbur Ave, Tarzana, CA 91356 USA

Bannon, Shaun *Musician*
Artist Group International, 9560 Wilshire Blvd #400, Beverly Hills, CA 90212 USA

Bano, Al
I-72020 Cellino San Marco, (Brindise), ITALY

Banois, Vincent J *Football Player*
24256J Tamarack Trail, Southfield, MI 48075 USA

Banowsky, William S *Educator, Business Person*
Gaylord Broadcasting Co, PO Box 25125, Oklahoma City, OK 73125 USA

Bantock, Nick *Writer, Misc*
Chronicle Books, 85 2nd St, San Francisco, CA 94105 USA

Bantom, Michael (Mike) *Basketball Player*
NBA Properties, Olympic Tower, 122 E 55th St, New York, NY 10022 USA

Banuchandar *Actor*
26 B N Reddy Road, Chennai, TN 600 017, INDIA

Bao, Joseph Y *Doctor*
17436 Terry Lyn Lane, Cerritos, CA 90703 USA

Bapitha *Actor, Bollywood*
7 Ayyappan Nagar 2nd Street, Cinmaya Nagar, Chennai, TN 600111, INDIA

Baptista, Juan Alfonso *Actor*
Gabriel Blanco Iglesias (Mexico), Rio Balsas 35-32, Colonia Cuauhtemoc, DF, 06500, Mexico

Baquet, Dean P *Journalist*
New York Times, Editorial Dept, 229 W 43rd St, New York, NY 10036 USA

Bar, Olaf *Opera Singer*
Organisation of Int'l Artistique, 16 Ave FD Roosevelt, Paris, 75008, FRANCE

Bar-Josef, Ofer *Archaeologist*
Harvard University, Archaeology Dept, Cambridge, MA 02138 USA

Barak, Ehud *Prime Minister, General*
Israel Labor Party, 16 Hayarkon St, Tel-Aviv, 63571, ISRAEL

Baran, Paul *Inventor*
Com21 Inc, PO Box 36308, San Jose, CA 95158 USA

Baranova, Anastasia *Actor*
Gersh Agency, The (LA), 232 N Canon Dr, Beverly Hills, CA 90210 USA

Baranski, Christine *Actor*
Creative Artists Agency, 9830 Wilshire Blvd, Beverly Hills, CA 90212 USA

Barany, Istvan *Swimmer*
I Attila Utca 87, Budapest, 01012, HUNGARY

Baratta, Adam *Actor*
9 Yards Entertainment, 8530 Wilshire Blvd Fl 5, Beverly Hills, CA 90211 USA

Barbacid, Mariano *Misc*
CNIO, Melchor Fernandez Almagro 3, Madrid, 28029, SPAIN

Barbara, Kingsolver E *Writer*
PO Box 31870, Tucson, AZ 85751 USA

Barbarin, Phillipe X I Cardinal *Religious Leader*
Archdiocese, 1 Place de Fouriere, Lyon Cedex 05, 69321, FRANCE

Barbaro, Gary W *Football Player*
1000 Giuffrias Ave, Metairie, LA 70001
USA

Barbat, Roxanne *Producer, Director, Writer*
Fantastic Films, 3854 Clayton Ave, Los
Angeles, CA 90027 USA

Barbeau, Adrienne *Actor, Musician*
Shefrin Co, 808 S Ridgeley Dr, Los
Angeles, CA 90036

Barber, Andrea *Actor*
Savage Agency, 6212 Banner Ave, Los
Angeles, CA 90038 USA

Barber, Bill *Hockey Player, Coach*
12 Hunter Dr, Herry Hill, NJ 08003 USA

Barber, Chris *Musician*
Cromwell Mgmt, 45 High St, Huntington,
Cambridgeshire, PE29 3TE, UNITED
KINGDOM (UK)

Barber, Glynis *Actor*
Susan Sharper, Queen's House, 1
Leicester, London, WC2H 7BP, UNITED
KINGDOM (UK)

Barber, Mike *Football Player*
PO Box 2424, DeSoto, TX 75123 USA

Barber, Miller *Golfer*
Myers, PO Box 11807, Marina del Rey,
CA 90295 USA

Barber, Paul *Actor, Writer, Producer*
Paradigm (LA), 10100 Santa Monica Blvd,
Fl 25, Los Angeles, CA 90067 USA

Barber, Stephen D (Steve) *Baseball Player*
1997 Joy View Lane, Henderson, NV
89012 USA

Barber, Stewart C (Stew) *Football Player*
2138 Country Manor Dr, Mount Pleasant,
SC 29466 USA

Barber, Tiki *Football Player*
PO Box 20595, Roanoke, VA 24018 USA

Barber, William *Cinematographer*
2509 White Chapel Place, Thousand
Oaks, CA 91362 USA

Barber of Wentbridge, Anthony P L
Financier, Government Official
House of Lords, Westminster, London,
SW1A 0PW, UNITED KINGDOM (UK)

Barbera, Joseph (Joe) *Animator*
12003 Briarvale Lane, Studio City, CA
91604 USA

Barberie, Jillian *Actor, Television Host*
Modus Entertainment, 110 S Fairfax Ave
#250, Los Angeles, CA 90038 USA

Barberos, Alessandro *Business Person*
Fiat Spa, Corso G Marconi 10/20, Turin,
10125, ITALY

Barbi, Shane *Model*
480 Westlake Blvd, Malibu, CA 90265
USA

Barbi, Sia *Model*
480 Westlake Blvd, Malibu, CA 90265
USA

Barbieri, Gato *Musician*
Central Entertainment Services, 123
Hardvard Ave, Staten Island, NY 10301

Barbieri, Paula *Actor, Model*
PO Box 20483, Panama City, FL 32411
USA

Barbot, Ivan *Lawyer*
4 Rue Marguerite, Paris, 75017, FRANCE

Barbour, Ian *Physicist, Scientist*
Carleton College, Theology Dept,
Northfield, MN 55057 USA

Barbour, John *Comedian, Actor, Writer*
54 Pine Isle Court, Henderson, NV 89074
USA

Barbour, Ross *Musician*
Four Freshmen, PO Box 93534, Las
Vegas, NV 89193 USA

Barbutti, Pete *Musician*
Thomas Cassidy, 11761 E Speedway Blvd,
Tucson, AZ 85748 USA

Barcelona, Custo *Fashion Designer*
Custo Barcelona, 2 Michael Road, 1927
Bldg, North Entrance, London, England,
SW6 2AD, United Kingdom

Barclay, Paris *Actor*
Lovett Mgmt, 918 6th St #5, Santa
Monica, CA 90403 USA

Bard, Allen J *Misc*
6202 Mountainclimb Dr, Austin, TX
78731 USA

Bardem, Javier *Actor*
Jose Marzilli Represente de Actores, Calle
Rafael Calvo 42 5* Dcha, Madrid, 28010,
SPAIN

Bardem, Javier E *Actor*
United Talent Agency, 9560 Wilshire
Blvd, #500, Beverly Hills, CA 90212 USA

Bardis, Panos D *Writer*
University of Toledo, Sociology Dept,
Toledo, OH 43606 USA

Bardot, Brigitte *Actor*
La Madrigue, Saint Tropez, Var, 83990,
FRANCE

Bare, Bobby *Musician*
The Bobby Roberts Company Inc, PO Box
1547, Goodlettsville, TN 37070-1547
USA

Bare, Robert J (Bobby) *Songwriter, Musician*
2401 Music Valley Dr, Nashville, TN
37214 USA

Bareikis, Arija *Actor*
Gersh Agency, The (NY), 41 Madison Ave
Fl 33, New York, NY 10010 USA

Bareikis, Arlia *Actor*
360 W 23rd St, New York, NY 10011
USA

Barenaked Ladies, Barenaked Ladies
Music Group
Nettwerk Management (LA), 8730
Wilshire Blvd #304, Beverly Hills, CA
90211 USA

Barenboim, Daniel *Musician, Conductor*
29 Rue de la Coulouvreeniere, Geneva,
1206, SWITZERLAND

Baretto, Ray *Musician*
Creative Music Consultants, 181 Christle
St #300, New York, NY 10002 USA

Barfield, Jesse L *Baseball Player*
5814 Spanish Moss Court, Spring, TX
77379 USA

Barfod, Hakon *Yachtsman*
Jon Ostensensy 15, Nesbru, 1360,
NORWAY

Barfoot, Van T *War Hero*
Leaning Oaks Farm, 4801 Namozine
Road, Ford, VA 23850 USA

Barierre, Tony *Actor*
Stein Entertainment Group, 11271 Ventura
Blvd #477, Studio City, CA 91604 USA

Barinholtz, Ike *Comedian*
William Morris Agency (WMA-LA), 1
William Morris Pl, Beverly Hills, CA
90212 USA

Barisich, Carl J *Football Player*
PO Box 982091, Park City, UT 84098
USA

Barjatya, Sooraj *Director, Bollywood, Producer*
Bhana 1st Floor, 422 Veer Sawarkar Road
Prabhadevi Dadar, Mumbai, MS 400025,
INDIA

Barkauskas, Antanas S *President*
Akmenu 71, Vilnus, LITHUANIA

Barkely, Douglas (Doug) *Hockey Player, Coach*
523-3131 63 Ave NE, Calgary, AB T3E
6N4, CANADA

Barker, Bob *Game Show Host*
Price Is Right, The, 2700 Colorado Ave Fl
4, Santa Monica, CA 90404 USA

Barker, Clive *Writer, Director*
PO Box 691885, Los Angeles, CA 90069
USA

Barker, Clyde F *Doctor*
3 Coopertown Road, Haverford, PA
19041 USA

Barker, David J P *Biologist*
Manor Farm, East Dean near Salisbury,
Wilts, SP5 1HB, UNITED KINGDOM (UK)

Barker, Jordan *Actor*
Select Artists Ltd (CA-Westside Office),
1138 12th Street, Suite 1, Santa Monica,
CA 90403 USA

Barker, Pat *Writer*
Gillion Aitken, 29 Fernshaw Road,
London, SW10 0TG, UNITED KINGDOM
(UK)

Barker, Richard A *Religious Leader*
Orthodox Presbyterian Church, PO Box P,
Willow Grove, PA 19090 USA

Barker, Robert W (Bob) *Entertainer*
Goodson-Todman Productions, 5757
Wilshire Blvd, #206, Los Angeles, CA
90036 USA

Barker, Tom *Actor*
London Mgmt, 2-4 Noel St, London, W1V
3RB, UNITED KINGDOM (UK)

Barker, Travis *Musician*
Creative Artists Agency, 9830 Wilshire
Blvd, Beverly Hills, CA 90212 USA

Barkin, Ellen *Actor*
Baker/Winokur/Ryder, 9100 Wilshire Blvd,
#600, Beverly Hills, CA 90212 USA

Barkley, Charles W *Basketball Player, Television Host*
7815 E Vaquero Dr, Scottsdale, AZ 85258
USA

Barkley, Dean M *Politician*
2840 Evergreen Lane N, Minneapolis, MN
55441 USA

Barkley, Iran *Boxer*
2645 3rd Ave, Bronx, NY 10451 USA

Barkman, Tyler Jane (Janie) *Swimmer*
Princeton University, Athletic Dept,
Princeton, NJ 08544 USA

Barksdale, James (Jim) *Business Person*
Barksdale Group, 2730 Sand Hill Road,
Menlo Park, CA 94025 USA

Barksdale, LaQuanda *Basketball Player*
San Antonio Silver Stars, 1 SBC Center,
San Antonio, TX 78219 USA

Barksdale, Rhesa H *Judge*
US Court of Appeals, 245 E Capitol St,
Jackson, MS 39201 USA

Barkum, Jerome P *Football Player*
1302 Mills Ave, Gulfport, MS 39501 USA

Barkworth, Peter
47 Flask Walk, London, ENGLAND, NW3
1HH

Barletta, Joseph *Publisher*
TV Guide Magazine, 100 Matsonford
Road, Radnor, PA 19080 USA

Barlow, Gary *Musician, Songwriter*
Int'l Talent Booking, 27A Floral St, #300,
London, WC2E 9DQ, UNITED
KINGDOM (UK)

Barlow, Perry *Cartoonist*
New Yorker Magazine, Editorial Dept, 4
Times Square, New York, NY 10036 USA

Barmes, Bruce *Baseball Player*
Washington Senators, 509 McDonald Ave,
Charlotte, NC 28203-5321 USA

Barnaby, Matthew *Hockey Player*
134 King Anthony Way, Getzville, NY
14068 USA

Barner, Bob *Writer*
1880 Jackson St, San Francisco, CA 94109
USA

Barnes, Benny J *Football Player*
5003 Fleming Ave, Richmond, CA 94804
USA

Barnes, Brian *Baseball Player*
Montreal Expos, 860 River Cove Dr,
Dacula, GA 30019-2090 USA

Barnes, Christopher Daniel *Actor*
3824 Fairway Ave, Studio City, CA 91604
USA

Barnes, Clive A *Critic*
New York Post, 1211 Avenue of
Americas, New York, NY 10036 USA

Barnes, Edward Larrabee *Architect*
975 Memorial Dr, Cambridge, MA 02138
USA

Barnes, Erich *Football Player*
712 Warburton Ave, Yonkers, NY 10701
USA

Barnes, Frank *Baseball Player*
St Louis Cardinals, 1508 Brazil St,
Greenville, MS 38701-2622 USA

Barnes, Frank S *Engineer*
University of Colorado, Engineering Dept,
Boulder, CO 80309 USA

Barnes, Jhane *Fashion Designer*
Jhane Barnes Inc, 575 Fashion Ave, New
York, NY 10018 USA

Barnes, Jim (Bad News) *Basketball Player*
2243 Oakgrove Circle, Valdosta, GA
31602 USA

Barnes, Jimmy *Musician*
Harbour Agency, 135 Forbes St,
Wooloomooloo, NSW, 2011, AUSTRALIA

Barnes, Joanna *Actor*
267 Middle Road, Santa Barbara, CA
93108 USA

Barnes, John *Baseball Player*
Minnesota Twins, 9860 E Lindner Ave,
Mesa, AZ 85212-2569 USA

Barnes, Julian P *Writer*
P F D Drury House, 34-43 Russell St,
London, WC2B 5HA, UNITED KINGDOM
(UK)

Barnes, Lute *Baseball Player*
New York Mets, 292 Juniper Dr, Palm
Springs, CA 92264-6432 USA

Barnes, Norm *Hockey Player*
17 Meadow Crossing, Simsbury, CT
06070 USA

Barnes, Priscilla *Actor*
270 N Canon, #1140, Beverly Hills, CA
90210 USA

Barnes, Rich *Baseball Player*
Chicago White Sox, 2845 Wilderness Rd,
West Palm Beach, FL 33409-2030 USA

Barnes, Rick *Basketball Player*
Texas University, Athletic Dept, Austin,
TX 78713 USA

Barnes, Robert H *Psychic*
Texas Tech University, Medical School,
PO Box 4349, Lubbock, TX 79409 USA

Barnes, Rod *Basketball Player*
Mississippi State University, Athletic Dept,
Mississippi State, MS 39762 USA

Barnes, Roosevelt Jr *Football Player*
922 E Belmont Dr, Fort Wayne, IN 46806
USA

Barnes, Skeeter *Baseball Player*
Cincinnati Reds, 11544 Winding Wood
Dr, Indianapolis, IN 46235-9731 USA

Barnes, Stu *Hockey Player*
5069 Royal Creek Lane, Plano, TX 75093
USA

Barnes, Wallace *Business Person*
Barnes Group, 123 Main St, Bristol, CT
06010 USA

Barnes Jr, Harry G *Diplomat*
Hapenny Road, Peacham, VT 05862 USA

Barnet, Will *Artist, Educator*
National Arts Club, 15 Gramercy Park S,
New York, NY 10003 USA

Barnett, Dick *Basketball Player*
Athletic Role Model Educational Institute,
51 E 42nd St, New York, NY 10017 USA

Barnett, Gary *Football Coach*
Colorado University, Athletic Dept,
Boulder, CO 80309 USA

Barnett, Jim *Basketball Player*
7 Kittiwake Road, Orinda, CA 94563 USA

Barnett, Jonathan *Architect*
4501 Connecticut Ave NW, Washington,
DC 20008 USA

Barnett, Mandy *Musician*
Monterey Peninsula Artists (Nashville),
124 12th Ave S #410, Nashville, TN
37203 USA

Barnett, Sabrina *Model*
Next Model Mgmt, 23 Watts St, New
York, NY 10013 USA

Barnett, Steven (Steve) *Athlete, Misc*
433 Queens Court, Campbell, CA 95008
USA

Barnette, Curtis H *Business Person*
Bethlehem Steel, 1170 8th Ave,
Bethlehem, PA 18016 USA

Barney, Matthew *Artist, Entertainer*
Barbara Gladstone Gallery, 515 W 24th
St, New York, NY 10011

Barney Jr, Lemuel J (Lem) *Football Player*
775 Kentbrook Dr, Commerce Township,
MI 48382 USA

Barnhart, Vic *Baseball Player*
Pittsburgh Pirates, 13102 Unger Rd,
Hagerstown, MD 21742-1428 USA

Barnowski, Ed *Baseball Player*
Baltimore Orioles, 7843 Donegal Cv,
Eden Prairie, MN 55347-1072 USA

Barnwell, Ysaye *Musician*
Sweet Honey Agency, PO Box 600099,
Newtonville, MA 02460 USA

Barocco, Rocco *Fashion Designer*
Via Occhio Marion, Capri/Napoli, 80773,
ITALY

Baron, Blaire *Actor*
Irv Schechter, 9300 Wilshire Blvd #410,
Beverly Hills, CA 90212 USA

Baron, Crespo Enrique *Government
Official*
European Parliament, 97/113 Rue
Velliard, Brussels, 1040, BELGIUM

Baron, Joanne *Actor*

Baron, Lita
1508 La Verne Way, Palm Springs, CA
92262

Baron, Martin D *Editor*
Boston Globe, Editorial Dept, 135 WT
Morrissey Blvd, Dorchester, MA 02125
USA

Barone, Anita *Actor*
1180 S Beverly Dr, #608, Beverly Hills,
CA 90212 USA

Barone, Dick *Baseball Player*
Pittsburgh Pirates, 1220 Heather Glen Cir,
Hollister, CA 95023-5153 USA

Barone, Richard *Musician, Songwriter*
Richard Barone Music, 240 Waverly
Place, New York, NY 10014 USA

Barr, Dave *Athlete*

Barr, Doug *Actor*
PO Box 63, Rutherford, CA 94573 USA

Barr, Jim *Baseball Player*
San Francisco Giants, 6335 Oak Hill Dr,
Granite Bay, CA 95746-8908 USA

Barr, Julia *Actor*
Saint Laurent Assoc, Cherokee Station, PO
Box 20191, New York, NY 10028 USA

Barr, Nevada *Writer*
G P Putnam's Sons, 375 Hudson St, New
York, NY 10014 USA

Barr, Roseanne *Actor, Comedian*
Creative Management Group (CMG),
9465 Wilshire Blvd #335, Beverly Hills,
CA 90212 USA

Barr, Steve *Baseball Player*
Boston Red Sox, 2520 14th St SE, Winter Haven, FL 33884-1908 USA

Barragan, Cuno *Baseball Player*
Chicago Cubs, 1824 Saint Ann Ct, Carmichael, CA 95608-5643 USA

Barranca, German *Baseball Player*
Kansas City Royals, 389 School St, York, PA 17402-9556 USA

Barrasso, Thomas (Tom) *Hockey Player*
40 Alder Lane, North Falmouth, MA 02556 USA

Barratt, Michael R *Astronaut*
2102 Pleasant Palm Circle, League City, TX 77573 USA

Barrault, Marie-Christine *Actor*
Cineart, 36 Rue de Ponthlieu, Paris, 75008, FRANCE

Barraza, Maria *Actor*
TV Caracol, Calle 76 #11 - 35, Piso 10AA, Bogota DC, 26484, COLOMBIA

Barre, Raymond *Prime Minister*
4-6 Ave Emile-Acollas, Paris, 75007, FRANCE

Barreto, Alexandra *Actor*
Michael Slessinger & Assoc, 8730 Sunset Blvd #270, Los Angeles, CA 90069 USA

Barreto, Bruno *Director*
22 W 68th St, New York, NY 10023 USA

Barrett, Alice *Actor*
Alliance Talent, 9171 Wilshire Blvd #441, Beverly Hills, CA 90210 USA

Barrett, Brendan Ryan *Actor*
Stone Manners Talent Agency, 6500 Wilshire Blvd, Ste 550, Los Angeles, CA 90048 USA

Barrett, Brendon Ryan *Actor*
9255 Sunset Bvd, #1010, West Hollywood, CA 90069 USA

Barrett, Colleen *Business Person*
Southwest Airlines, PO Box 36611, 2702 Love Field Dr, Dallas, TX 75235 USA

Barrett, Craig R *Business Person*
Intel Corp, 2200 Mission College Blvd, Santa Clara, CA 95054 USA

Barrett, Jacinda *Actor*
1836 Courtney Terrace, Los Angeles, CA 90046 USA

Barrett, James E *Judge*
US Court of Appeals, 2120 Capitol Ave, Cheyenne, WY 82001 USA

Barrett, Martin G (Marty) *Baseball Player*
Boston Red Sox, 9708 Buckhorn Dr, Las Vegas, NV 89134-7836 USA

Barrett, Michael (Mike) *Basketball Player*
5721 Templegate Dr, Nashville, TN 37221 USA

Barrett, Stanton *Race Car Driver*
Rocking K Ranch, Bishop, CA 93514 USA

Barrett, Stephen *Social Activist, Doctor*
PO Boc 1747, Allentown, PA 18105 USA

Barrett, Thomas J *Admiral*
Vice Commandant US Court Guard, 2100 2nd St SW, Washington, DC 20593 USA

Barrett, Tim *Baseball Player*
Montreal Expos, 5588 Jandel Dr, Aurora, IN 47001-3010 USA

Barrett, Tom *Baseball Player*
Philadelphia Phillies, 5941 W Venus Way, Chandler, AZ 85226-7531 USA

Barrett, Wade *Soccer Player*
San Jose Earthquakes, 3550 Stevens Creek Blvd, #200, San Jose, CA 95117 USA

Barrett, William *Misc*
34 Harwood Ave, Sleepy Hollow, NY 10591 USA

Barrett-Roddenberry, Majel *Actor*
Lincoln Enterprises, PO Box 691370, West Hollywood, CA 19151 USA

Barrett-Roddenberry, Majel *Actor*
Lincoln Enterprises, PO Box 691370, West Hollywood, CA 90069 USA

Barretto, Ray *Musician*
Pan American Music, 6407 Overbrook Ave, Philadelphia, PA 19151 USA

Barrichello, Rubens *Race Car Driver*
Jaguar Racing Ltd, Bradbourne Drive, Tilbrook, Milton Keynes, MK7 8BJ, United Kingdom

Barrie, Barbara *Actor*
Innovative Artists (LA), 1505 Tenth St, Santa Monica, CA 90401 USA

Barrie, Chris *Actor, Comedian*
International Creative Mgmt, 76 Oxford St, London, W1N 0AX, UNITED KINGDOM (UK)

Barrile, Anthony *Actor*
Alliance Talent, 9171 Wilshire Blvd #441, Beverly Hills, CA 90210 USA

Barrileaux, James *Misc*
Dryden Flight Research Center, PO Box 273, Edwards, CA 93523 USA

Barrino, Fantasia *Musician*
American Idol, 7800 Beverly Blvd #251, Los Angeles, CA 90036 USA

Barrios, Jose *Baseball Player*
San Francisco Giants, 6484 SW 25th St, Miami, FL 33155-2958 USA

Barris, Chuck *Television Host*
Hyperion Books, 77 West 66th Street, 11th Floor, New York, NY 10023 USA

Barriw, Barbara *Actor*
15 W 72nd St, #2A, New York, NY 10023 USA

Barron, Alex *Race Car Driver*
Gurney Racing, 2334 S Broadway, Santa Ana, CA 92707 USA

Barron, Dana *Actor*
Coast to Coast Talent Group, 3350 Barham Blvd, Los Angeles, CA 90068 USA

Barron, Kenneth (Kenny) *Musician, Composer*
Joel Chriss, 300 Mercer St, #3J, New York, NY 10003 USA

Barron, Tony *Baseball Player*
Montreal Expos, 12211 135th St E, Puyallup, WA 98374-4674 USA

Barros, Dana *Basketball Player*
17 Clarkwood St, Mattapan, MA 02126 USA

Barrow, Geoff *Musician*
Fruit, Saga Center, 326 Kensal Road, London, W10 5BZ, UNITED KINGDOM (UK)

Barrow, Michael C *Football Player*
204 Lorraine Ave, Monclair, NJ 07043 USA

Barrowman, John *Actor*
Innovative Artists (LA), 1505 Tenth St, Santa Monica, CA 90401 USA

Barrowman, Mike *Swimmer*
706 N Wamer St, Bay City, MI 48706 USA

Barrs, Jay *Athlete*
6395 Senoma Dr, Salt Lake City, UT 84121 USA

Barrueco, Manuel *Musician*
Columbia Artists Mgmt Inc, 165 W 57th St, New York, NY 10019 USA

Barry, A L *Religious Leader*
Lutheran Church Missouri Synod, 1333 S Kirkwood Road, Saint Louis, MO 63122 USA

Barry, Brent *Basketball Player*
2302 4th Ave N, Seattle, WA 98109 USA

Barry, Claudia *Musician*
Talent Consultants Int'l, 1560 Broadway, #1308, New York, NY 10036 USA

Barry, Claudja *Musician*
Talent Consultants International, 1560 Broadway, #1308, New York, NY 10036 USA

Barry, Daniel T (Dan) *Astronaut*
46 Ashton Lane, South Hadley, MA 01075 USA

Barry, Dave *Journalist, Writer*
Miami Herald, Editorial Dept, 1 Herald Plaza, Miami, FL 33132 USA

Barry, Gene *Actor*
12178 Ventura Blvd, #205, Studio City, CA 91604 USA

Barry, Jeff *Composer*
BMI, 8730 Sunset Blvd #300W, Los Angeles, CA 90069 USA

Barry, Jeff *Baseball Player*
New York Mets, 322 N Barneburg Rd, Medford, OR 97504-6683 USA

Barry, John *Composer*
540 Centre Island Rd, Oyster Bay, NY 11771 USA

Barry, John J *Misc*
Int'l Brotherhood of Electrical Workers, 1125 15th St NW, Washington, DC 20005 USA

Barry, Jon *Basketball Player*
Detroit Pistons, Palace, 2 Championship Dr, Auburn Hills, MI 48326 USA

Barry, Len *Musician*
Cape Entertainment, 1161 NW 76th Ave, Plantation, FL 33322 USA

Barry, Lynda *Cartoonist*
PO Box 447, Footville, WI 53537 USA

Barry, Marion S *Politician*
161 Raleigh St SE, Washington, DC 20032 USA

Barry, Marion S Jr *Senator*
161 Raleigh St SE, Washington, DC 20032 USA

Barry, Maryanne Trump *Judge*
US Court of Appeals, US Courthouse, 50 Walnut St, Newark, NJ 07102, u

Barry, Maryanne Trump *Judge*
US Court of Appeals, US Courthouse, 50 Walnut St, Newark, NJ 07102 USA

Barry, Patricia *Actor*
12742 Highwood St, Los Angeles, CA 90049 USA

Barry, Raymond J *Actor*
Metropolitan Talent Agency, 4526 Wilshire Blvd, Los Angeles, CA 90010 USA

Barry, Rich *Baseball Player*
Philadelphia Phillies, 12020 Hoffman St Apt C, Studio City, CA 91604-2075 USA

Barry, Seymour (Sy) *Cartoonist*
34 Saratoga Dr, Jericho, NY 11753 USA

Barry, Thomas (Thom) *Actor*
Don Buchwald & Associates Inc (LA), 6500 Wilshire Blvd #2200, Los Angeles, CA 90048 USA

Barry, Todd *Comedian*
3 Arts Entertainment Inc, 9460 Wilshire Blvd Fl 7, Beverly Hills, CA 90212 USA

Barry III, Richard F D (Rick) *Basketball Player*
5240 Broadmoor Bluffs Dr, Colorado Springs, CO 80906 USA

Barrymore, Drew *Actor, Producer*
Flower Films, 9220 W Sunset Blvd, #309, Los Angeles, CA 90069 USA

Barrymore, John III *Actor*
2825 Forest Hill Blvd, Pacific Grove, CA 93950 USA

Barsh, Gregory S *Doctor*
Stanford University, Medical Center, Pediatrics Dept, Stanford, CA 94305 USA

Barsotti, Charles *Cartoonist*
419 E 55th St, Kansas City, MO 64110 USA

Bart, Peter *Writer*
Trident Media Group LLC, 41 Madison Ave Fl 33, New York, NY 10010 USA

Bartee, Kimera *Baseball Player*
Detroit Tigers, 14300 N 83rd Ave Apt 1025, Peoria, AZ 85381-4625 USA

Bartek, Steve *Musician*
Kraft-Engel Management, 15233 Ventura Blvd #200, Sherman Oaks, CA 91403 USA

Bartel, Jean
229 Bronwood Ave, Los Angeles, CA 90049

Bartels, Wolfgang *Skier*
Womdihof Hintersee, Ransau, 83486, GERMANY

Barth, Robert *Religious Leader*
Churches of Christ in Christian Union, Po Box 30, Circleville, OH 43113 USA

Bartha, Justin *Actor*
International Creative Management (ICM-LA), 8942 Wilshire Blvd, Beverly Hills, CA 90211 USA

Bartholome, Earl *Hockey Player*
6024 W 35th St, Minneapolis, MN 55416 USA

Bartholomew, Dave *Musician*
4732 Odin St, New Orleans, LA 70126 USA

Bartholomew, Reginald *Diplomat*
State Department, 2201 C St NW, Washington, DC 20520 USA

Bartirome, Tony *Baseball Player*
Pittsburgh Pirates, 1104 Palma Sola Blvd, Bradenton, FL 34209-3342 USA

Bartiromo, Maria *Commentator*
CBS-TV, News Dept, 51 W 52nd St, New York, NY 10019 USA

Bartkowski, Steven J (Steve) *Football Player*
10745 Bell Road, Duluth, GA 30097 USA

Bartle, Cheryl *Actor*
8281 Melrose #200, Los Angeles, CA 90046 USA

Bartlett, Bonnie *Actor, Musician*
12805 Hortense St, Studio City, CA 91604 USA

Bartlett, Erinn *Actor*
Untitled Entertainment (LA), 8436 W 3rd St #650, Los Angeles, CA 90048 USA

Bartlett, Jennifer L *Artist*
Paula Cooper Gallery, 534 W 21st St, New York, NY 10011 USA

Bartlett, Jim *Hockey Player*
8718 Chadwick Dr, Tampa, FL 33635 USA

Bartlett, Neil *Misc*
6 Oak Dr, Orinda, CA 94563 USA

Bartlett, Robin *Actor*
Gersh Agency, The (LA), 232 N Canon Dr, Beverly Hills, CA 90210 USA

Bartlett, Thomas A *Educator*
1209 SW 6th St, #904, Portland, OR 97204 USA

Bartletti, Don *Journalist*
Los Angeles Times, Editorial Dept, 202 W 1st St, Los Angeles, CA 90012 USA

Bartley, Boyd *Baseball Player*
Brooklyn Dodgers, 7500 Noreast Dr, Fort Worth, TX 76180-6736 USA

Bartoe, John-David F *Astronaut*
2724 Lighthouse Dr, Houston, TX 77058 USA

Bartoletti, Bruno *Conductor*
Chicago Lyric Opera, 20 N Wacker Dr, Chicago, IL 60606 USA

Bartolo, Sal *Boxer*
422 Border St, East Boston, MA 02128 USA

Bartolomew, Ken *Speed Skater*
4820 Bryant Ave S, Minneapolis, MN 55409 USA

Barton, Austin *Artist*
100 N Lake, Joseph, OR 97846 USA

Barton, Bob *Baseball Player*
San Francisco Giants, 37193 Stardust Way, Murrieta, CA 92563-5076 USA

Barton, Dorie *Actor*
Evolution Entertainment, 901 N Highland Ave, Los Angeles, CA 90038 USA

Barton, Eileen *Musician*
8740 Holloway Dr, Los Angeles, CA 90069 USA

Barton, Glenys *Artist*
Angela Flowers Gallery, 199-205 Richmond Road, London, E8 3NJ, UNITED KINGDOM (UK)

Barton, Gregory (Greg) *Athlete*
6657 58th Ave NE, Seattle, WA 98115 USA

Barton, Harris S *Football Player*
765 Market St, #32 E, San Francisco, CA 94103 USA

Barton, Jacqueline K *Misc*
California Institute of Technology, Chemistry Dept, Pasadena, CA 91125 USA

Barton, Lou Ann *Musician*
2010 Kinney Ave, Austin, TX 78704 USA

Barton, Mischa *Actor*
William Morris Agency (WMA-LA), 1 William Morris Pl, Beverly Hills, CA 90212 USA

Barton, Peter *Actor*
2265 Westwood Blvd, #2619, Los Angeles, CA 90064 USA

Barton, Rachel *Musician*
I C M Artists, 40 W 57th St, New York, NY 10019 USA

Barton, Shawn *Baseball Player*
Seattle Mariners, 1239 Fredrick Blvd, Reading, PA 19605-1184 USA

Bartosch, Dave *Baseball Player*
St Louis Cardinals, 849 Glendale Dr, Clarksville, TN 37043-4823 USA

Bartosik, Alison *Swimmer*
Premier Management Group, 200 Merry Hill Dr, Cary, NC 27511 USA

Bartow, Gene *Coach*
Memphis Grizzlies, 175 Toyota Plaza, #150, Memphis, TN 38103 USA

Bartucelli, Jean-Louis
9 rue Benard, Paris, FRANCE, F-75014

Bartz, Carol A *Business Person*
Autodesk Inc, 111 McInnis Parkway, San Rafael, CA 94903 USA

Bartz, Gary L *Musician, Composer*
Joel Chriss, 300 Mercer St #3J, New York, NY 10003 USA

Baruchel, Jay *Actor*
Glenn Talent Management, 3981 St Laurent #730, Montreal QB, H2W 1Y5, CANADA

Baryshnikov, Mikhail *Actor, Dancer*
Creative Artists Agency, 9830 Wilshire Blvd, Beverly Hills, CA 90212 USA

Barzini, Benedetta *Model*
Donna Karan Co, 361 Newbury St, Boston, MA 02115 USA

Barzun, Jacques M *Educator*
597 5th Ave, New York, NY 10017 USA

Basañez, Sergio *Actor*
TV Azteca, Periferico Sur 4121, Colonia Fuentes del Pedregal, DF, CP 14141, Mexico

Basaraba, Gary *Actor*
Paradigm (LA), 10100 Santa Monica Blvd, Fl 25, Los Angeles, CA 90067 USA

Basch, Harry *Actor*
920 1/2 S Serrano Ave, Los Angeles, CA 90006 USA

Basche, David Alan *Actor*
60 W 84th St, #GDX, New York, NY 10024 USA

Baschnagel, Brian D *Football Player*
1823 Sunset Ridge Road, Glenview, IL
60025 USA

Basco, Dante *Actor*
Don Buchwald, 6500 Wilshire Blvd
#2200, Los Angeles, CA 90048 USA

Basco, Derek *Actor*
GVA Talent Agency Inc, 9229 Sunset Blvd
#320, Los Angeles, CA 90069 USA

Basco, Dion *Actor*
Schiowitz/Clay/Rose, 1680 N Vine St
#1016, Los Angeles, CA 90028 USA

Basgall, Monty *Baseball Player*
Pittsburgh Pirates, 2745 Saint Andrews Dr,
Sierra Vista, AZ 85650-5221 USA

Bashir, Martin *Commentator*
ABC-TV, News Dept, 77 W 66th St, New
York, NY 10023 USA

Bashkirov, Dmitri A *Musician*
25 Martirez Oblatos, Pozuelo, Madrid,
SPAIN

Bashmet, Yuri *Musician*
International Creative Management
(ICM-LA), 8942 Wilshire Blvd, Beverly
Hills, CA 90211 USA

Basia *Music Group*
Creative Artists Agency LCC (CAA-LA),
9830 Wilshire Blvd, Beverly Hills, CA
90212 USA

Basilio, Carmen *Boxer*
67 Boxwood Dr, Rochester, NY 14617
USA

Basinger, Kim *Actor*
11288 Ventura Blvd #414, Studio City, CA
91604 USA

Basinski, Ed *Baseball Player*
Brooklyn Dodgers, 4110 SE Jackson St,
Milwaukie, OR 97222-5936 USA

Bass, Bob *Basketball Player, Coach, Misc*
2266 Deerfield Dr, Fort Mill, SC 29715
USA

Bass, Dick
14001 Bayside Dr, Norwalk, CA 90650

Bass, Fontella *Music Group, Musician*
Cape Entertainment, 1181 NW 76th Ave,
Plantation, FL 33322 USA

Bass, George F *Archaeologist*
1600 Dominik Dr, College Station, TX
77840 USA

Bass, Kevin *Baseball Player*
Houston Astros, 3630 Maranatha Dr,
Sugar Land, TX 77479-9665 USA

Bass, Lance *Musician*
Wright Entertainment, 7680 Universal
Blvd #500, Orlando, FL 32819 USA

Bass, Laura
PO Box 293, Mountainside, NJ 07092

Bass, Randy *Baseball Player*
Minnesota Twins, 2709 SW Coombs Rd,
Lawton, OK 73501-8640 USA

Bass, Richard L (Dick) *Football Player*
14001 Bayside Dr, Norwalk, CA 90650
USA

Bass, Ronald *Writer*
Creative Artists Agency LCC (CAA-LA),
9830 Wilshire Blvd, Beverly Hills, CA
90212 USA

Bass, Ronald (Ron) *Writer*
Creative Artists Agency, 9830 Wilshire
Blvd, Beverly Hills, CA 90212 USA

Bassett, Angela *Actor*
Creative Artists Agency, 9830 Wilshire
Blvd, Beverly Hills, CA 90212 USA

Bassett, Brian *Editor, Cartoonist*
Seattle Times, Editorial Dept 1120 John St,
Seattle, WA 98109 USA

Bassett, Leslie R *Composer*
1618 Harbal Dr, Ann Arbor, MI 48105
USA

Bassey, Dame Shirley
24 Avenue Princess Grace #1200, Monte
Carlo, MONACO

Bassey, Jennifer *Actor*
12 E 86th St #1728, New York, NY 10028
USA

Basslitz, Georg *Artist*
Schloss Demeberg, Holle, 31188,
GERMANY

Bast, William
6691 Whitley Terrace, Los Angeles, CA
90068

Bastedo, Alexandra *Actor*
Charlesworth, 68 Old Brompton Rd #280,
London, SW7 3LQ, UNITED KINGDOM
(UK)

Bastian, Noah *Actor, Musician*
Amsel Eisenstadt & Frazier Inc, 5757
Wilshire Blvd #510, Los Angeles, CA
90036 USA

Batali, Dean *Writer*
Genesis, 8530 Wilshire Blvd, 3rd Floor,
Beverly Hills, CA 90211 USA

Batali, Mario *Television Host, Chef*
Ciao America with Mario Batali, 1180 6th
Ave Fk 12, New York, NY 10036 USA

Batch, Charlie *Football Player*
1844 Willow Oak Dr, Wexford, PA 15090
USA

Batchelor, Amelia
14811 Mulholland Dr, Los Angeles, CA
90024

Batchelor, Rich *Baseball Player*
St Louis Cardinals, 1004 Pineneedle Rd,
Hartsville, SC 29550-8452 USA

Bateman, Jason *Actor*
8828 Wonderland Park Ave, Los Angeles,
CA 90046 USA

Bateman, Justine *Actor*
11288 Ventura Blvd #190, Studio City, CA
91604 USA

Bates, Alfred *Track Athlete*
4506 Mulberry St, Philadelphia, PA 19124
USA

Bates, Bill *Baseball Player*
Milwaukee Brewers, 300 N Vista Dr Apt
1421, Houston, TX 77073-5216 USA

Bates, Charles C *Oceanographer*
136 W La Pintura, Green Valley, AZ
85614 USA

Bates, Del *Baseball Player*
Philadelphia Phillies, 8213 NE 115th
Way, Kirkland, WA 98034-3506 USA

Bates, Dick *Baseball Player*
Seattle Pilots, 5859 W Cielo Grande,
Glendale, AZ 85310-3631 USA

Bates, Jason *Baseball Player*
Colorado Rockies, 9856 W Freiburg Dr
Unit F, Littleton, CO 80127-5949 USA

Bates, Jeff
Hallmark Direction Company, 15 Music
Square West, Nashville, TN 37203 USA

Bates, Kathy *Actor*
PO Box 472, Culver City, CA 90232 USA

Bates, Patrick J *Football Player*
10101 Harvin Dr #298, Houston, TX
77036 USA

Bates, Robert T *Misc*
Railroad Signalman Brotherhood, 601 W
Golf Road, Mount Prospect, IL 60056 USA

Bateson, Mary Catherine *Misc*
10220 Bushman Dr #211, Oakton, VA
22124 USA

Bathe, Bill *Baseball Player*
Oakland A's, 7990 E Snyder Rd Apt
14201, Tucson, AZ 85750-9030 USA

Bathgate, Andy
43 Brentwood Dr, Brampton, CANADA,
ON L6T 1R1

Batinkoff, Randall *Actor*
1330 4th St, Santa Monica, CA 90401
USA

Batista, Tony *Athlete*
333 W Camden St, Baltimore, MD 21201

Batiste, Kevin *Baseball Player*
Toronto Blue Jays, 3624 Avenue M,
Galveston, TX 77550-4145 USA

Batiste, Kim *Baseball Player*
Philadelphia Phillies, 16163 Aikens Rd,
Priarieville, LA 70769-4903 USA

Batiuk, Thomas M (Tom) *Cartoonist*
Universal Press Syndicate, 4520 Main St,
Kansas City, MO 64111 USA

Batra, Pooja *Actor, Bollywood*
403H Gokul Vihar II, Thakur Complex
Kandivli (E), Mumbai, MS 400068, INDIA

Battaglia, Matt *Actor*
Main Title Entertainment, 5225 Wilshire
Blvd #500, Los Angeles, CA 90036 USA

Battaglia, Rik *Actor*
Viale Montegrappa 10, Colle Verde
Guidonia, Rome, 00012, ITALY

Battelle, Ann *Skier*
1355 Walton Creek Road, Steamboat
Springs, CO 80487 USA

Battier, Shane *Basketball Player*
Memphis Grizzlies, 175 Toyota Plaza
#150, Memphis, TN 38103 USA

Battista, Bobbie
1 CNN Center Box 105366, Atlanta, GA
30349-5366

Battle, Allen *Baseball Player*
St Louis Cardinals, 106 Donette Loop,
Daphne, AL 36526-7764 USA

Battle, Hinton *Dancer, Actor*
Abrams Artists, 9200 Sunset Blvd #1125,
Los Angeles, CA 90069 USA

Battle, Howard *Baseball Player*
Toronto Blue Jays, 420 Fayard St, Biloxi,
MS 39530-2070 USA

Battle, Kathleen D *Opera Singer*
Columbia Artists Mgmt Inc, 165 W 57th
St, New York, NY 10019 USA

Battle, Lois *Writer*
Viking Press, 375 Hudson St, New York, NY 10014 USA

Batton, Chris *Baseball Player*
Oakland A's, 42370 Meadowlark Rdg, Murrieta, CA 92562-8915 USA

Batts, Matt *Baseball Player*
Boston Red Sox, 17927 Silver Creek Ct, Baton Rouge, LA 70810-8918 USA

Batts, Warren L *Business Person*
Premark International, 3600 W Lake Ave, Glenview, IL 60025 USA

Bauchau, Patrick *Actor*
DS WebDesign, 107 N Reno Road #184, Newbury Park, CA 91320 USA

Baudry, Patrick
305 Ave Mairie, Eaunas, 31600, FRANCE

Bauer, Belinda *Actor*
2580 Amherst Ave, Los Angeles, CA 90064 USA

Bauer, Chris *Actor*
Framework Entertainment (LA), 9057 Nemo St #C, W Hollywood, CA 90069 USA

Bauer, Erwin A *Photographer*
PO Box 3730, Sequim, WA 98382 USA

Bauer, Henry A (Hank) *Baseball Player*
New York Yankees, 11284 Pflumm Road, Shawnee Mission, KS 66215-4811 USA

Bauer, Jaime Lyn *Actor*
Tyler Kjar, 5116 Lankershim Blvd, North Hollywood, CA 91601

Bauer, Kristin *Actor*
Envision Entertainment, 9255 Sunset Blvd #300, Los Angeles, CA 90069 USA

Bauer, Linda Susan
2476 Glendale Circle, Smyrna, GA 30080

Bauer, Peggy *Photographer*
P O Box 3730, Sequim, WA 98382 USA

Bauer, Peter *Publisher*
People Magazine, Time-Life Building, Rockefeller Center, New York, NY 10020 USA

Bauer, Rick *Baseball Player*
Baltimore Orioles, 13334 W Fernleaf St, Boise, ID 83713-1962 USA

Bauer, Steven *Actor*
Innovative Artists, 1505 10th Ave St, Santa Monica, CA 90401 USA

Bauer, William J *Judge*
US Court of Appeals, 111 N Canal St, Chicago, IL 60606 USA

Baugh, Laura *Golfer*
5225 Timberview Terrace, Orlando, FL 32819 USA

Baugh, Samuel A (Sammy) *Football Player, Coach*
General Delivery, Rotan, TX 79546 USA

Baughan, Maxie C *Football Player, Coach*
3355 Lawndale Road, Reisterstown, MD 21136 USA

Baughman, J Ross *Journalist, Photographer, Misc*
203 S Payne St, Alexandria, VA 22314 USA

Baughman, Justin *Baseball Player*
Anaheim Angels, 4052 NE 21st Ave, Portland, OR 97212-1433 USA

Baum, Herbert M *Business Person*
Quarker State Corp, 700 Milam St, Houston, TX 77002 USA

Bauman, John Bowzer
3168 Oakshire Dr, Los Angeles, CA 90068

Bauman, Jon (Bowzer) *Music Group*
Cape Entertainment, 1161 NW 76th St Ave, Plantation, FL 33322 USA

Baumann, Frank M *Baseball Player*
Boston Red Sox, 7712 Sunray Lane, Saint Louis, MO 63123-1938 USA

Baumann, Herbert K W *Composer*
Franziskaserster 16 #1419, Munich, 81669, GERMANY

Baumgarten, Ross *Baseball Player*
Chicago White Sox, 1020 Bluff Rd, Glencoe, IL 60022-1152 USA

Baumgartner, Bruce *Wrestler*
RR 2, Cambridge Springs, PA 16403 USA

Baumgartner, John *Baseball Player*
Detroit Tigers, 1215 Oxford Ct, Birmingham, AL 35242-4676 USA

Baumgartner, William *Doctor*
Johns Hopkins Hospital, 600 N Wolfe St, Baltimore, MD 21287 USA

Baumhower, Robert G (Bob) *Football Player*
21201 Ayrshire Lane, Fairhope, AL 36532 USA

Baumler, Hans-Jurgen
18 chemin du Casteller, Le Rouret, FRANCE F-, 06650

Bauta, Ed *Baseball Player*
St Louis Cardinals, 4820 Bitterbrush Dr, Boise, ID 83703-3804 USA

Baute, Joseph A *Business Person*
Nashua Corp, 11 Trafalgar Square #200, Nashua, NH 03063 USA

Bavaro, Mark *Football Player*
17 Long Hill, Boxford, MA 01921 USA

Bax, Kylie *Actor, Model*
Men/Women Model Inc, 199 Lafayette St #700, New York, NY 10012 USA

Baxendale, Helen *Actor*
Yakety Yak, 8 Bloomsbury Sq, London, WC1A 2UA, UNITED KINGDOM (UK)

Baxter, James *Animator*
Dream Works SKG, 100 University City Plaza, University City, CA 91608 USA

Baxter, Jeff (Skunk) *Music Group, Musician*
Monterey Peninsula Artists, 509 Hartnell St, Monterey, CA 93940 USA

Baxter, Meredith *Actor*
2049 Century Park E #2500, Los Angeles, CA 90067 USA

Bay, Frances *Actor*
Henderson/Hogan, 8285 W Sunset Blvd #1, West Hollywood, CA 90046 USA

Bay, Howard *Designer*
159 W 53rd St, New York, NY 10019 USA

Bay, Michael *Director, Producer*
Propaganda Films Mgmt, 1741 Ivar Ave, Los Angeles, CA 90028 USA

Bay, Susan *Actor*
801 Stone Canyon Road, Los Angeles, CA 90077 USA

Bay, Willow
1050 Techwood Dr, Atlanta, GA 30318

Bay City Rollers *Music Group*
297-101 Kinderkamack Road, Oradell, NJ 07649

Baye, Nathalie
10 avenue George V, Paris, FRANCE, F-75008

Bayes, G E *Religious Leader*
Free Methodist Church, PO Box 535002, Winona Lake, IN 46590 USA

Bayle, Silvia *Actor*
Telefe - Argentina, Pavon 2444 (C1248AAT), Buenos Aires, ARGENTINA

Bayley, Aaron *Musician*
Pop Idol (Fremantle Media), 2700 Colorado Ave #450, Santa Monica, CA 90404 USA

Bayliss, Rachel
Somerset Park Farm, Congelton Chelshire, ENGLAND

Baylon, Noah *Writer*
International Creative Management (ICM-LA), 8942 Wilshire Blvd, Beverly Hills, CA 90211 USA

Baylor, Don *Baseball Player*
56325 Riviera, La Quinta, CA 92253 USA

Baylor, Elgin *Basketball Player*
2480 Briarcrest Road, Beverly Hills, CA 90210 USA

Bayo, Maria *Opera Singer*
Opera et Concert, Maxifilianstr 22, Munich, 80539, GERMANY

Bayona, Alvaro *Actor*
Gabriel Blanco Iglesias (Mexico), Rio Balsas 35-32, Colonia Cuauhtemoc, DF, 06500, Mexico

Baz, Farouk El- *Geophysicist*
Boston University, Remot Sensing Center, Boston, MA 02215 USA

Bazell, Robert J *Commentator*
NBC-TV News Dept, 4001 Nebraska Ave NW, Washington, DC 20016 USA

Bazer, Fuller W *Scientist*
8600 Creekview Court, College Station, TX 77845 USA

BBMak *Music Group*
Evolution Talent Agency LLC, 1776 Broadway Fl 15, New York, NY 10019 USA

Beach, Adam *Actor*
Paradigm Agency, 10100 Santa Monica Blvd, #2500, Los Angeles, CA 90067 USA

Beach, Bill *Bowler*
435 Koehler Dr, Sharpsville, PA 16150 USA

Beach, Gary *Actor*
62 W 62nd St, #6F, New York, NY 10023 USA

Beach, Michael *Actor*
1823 Virginia Rd, Los Angeles, CA 90019 USA

Beach, Roger C *Business Person*
Unocal Corp, 2141 Rosecrans Ave, El Segundo, CA 90245 USA

Beacham, Stephanie *Actor*
Peters Fraser & Dunlop (PFD - UK), Drury House, 34-43 Russell St, London, WC2 B5, UNITED KINGDOM (UK)

Beachy, Roger N *Scientist*
526 W Polo Dr, Saint Louis, MO 63105 USA

Beadle, Jeremy *Actor*
MPC Entertainment, 7979 Old Georgetown, Bethesda, MD 20814 USA

Beagle, Ronald G (Ron) *Football Player*
3830 San Ysidro Way, Sacramento, CA 95864 USA

Beal, Jack *Artist*
80 Epps Road, Oneonta, NY 13820 USA

Beal, Jeff *Composer*
Gorfaine/Schwartz, 13245 Riverside Dr, #450, Sherman Oaks, CA 91423 USA

Beale, Betty *Writer*
2926 Garfield St NW, Washington, DC 20008 USA

Beals, Jennifer *Actor*
Innovative Artists, 1505 10th St, Santa Monica, CA 90401 USA

Beals, Vaughn L Jr *Business Person*
Harley-Davidson Inc, 3700 W Juneau Ave, Milwaukee, WI 53208 USA

Beam, C Arlen *Judge*
US Court of Appeals, Federal Building, 100 Centennial Mall N, Lincoln, NE 68508 USA

Beaman, Lee Anne *Actor*
Cavaleri Assoc, 178 S Victory Blvd, #205, Burbank, CA 91502 USA

Beamer, Frank *Football Coach*
Virginia Polytechnic Institute, Athletic Dept, Blacksburg, VA 24061 USA

Beamer, Lisa *Writer*
The Todd M Beamer Foundation, PO Box 32, Cranbury, NJ 08512

Beamon, Autry Jr *Football Player*
12200 River Ridge Blvd, Bumsville, MN 55337 USA

Beamon, Robert *Athlete*
Florida Atlantic University, Athletic Dept, Boca Raton, FL 33431

Beamon, Robert (Bob) *Athlete*
Florida Atlantic University, Athletic Dept, Boca Raton, FL 33431 USA

Bean, Alan L *Astronaut*
9173 Briar Forest Dr, Houston, TX 77024-7222 USA

Bean, Andy *Golfer*
2912 Grasslands Dr, Houston, TX 77024 USA

Bean, Andy *Golfer*
2912 Grasslands Dr, Lakeland, FL 33803 USA

Bean, Dawn Pawson *Swimmer*
11902 Red Hill Ave, Santa Ana, CA 92705 USA

Bean, Henry *Director*
William Moris Agency, 151 El Camino Dr, Beverly Hills, CA 90212 USA

Bean, Orson *Actor, Comedian*
444 Carol Canal, Venice, CA 90291 USA

Bean, Sean *Actor*
Creative Artists Agency, 9830 Wilshire Blvd, Beverly Hills, CA 90212 USA

Bean, William Bennett *Doctor*
11 Rowland Court, Iowa City, IA 52246 USA

Bear, Greg
10430 Nate Way, Santee, CA 92071

Bearak, Barry *Journalist*
New York Times, Editorial Dept, 229 W 43rd St, New York, NY 10036 USA

Beard, Alana *Basketball Player*
Washington Mystics, MCI Center, 601 F St NW, Washington, DC 20004 USA

Beard, Alfred (Butch) *Basketball Player, Coach*
3834 Berleigh Hill Court, Burtonsville, MD 20866 USA

Beard, Amanda *Swimmer*
3792 Carmel Ave, Irvine, CA 92606 USA

Beard, Frank *Golfer*
70 Rocio Court, Palm Desert, CA 92260 USA

Beard, Frank *Musician*
Lone Wolf Mgmt, PO Box 163690, Austin, TX 78716 USA

Bearden, Gene
PO Box 176, Helena, AR 72342

Bearse, Amanda *Actor*
Blueprint Management, 5670 Wilshire Blvd #2525, Los Angeles, CA 90036 USA

Beart, Emmanuelle
10 avenue George V, Paris, FRANCE, F-75008

Beart, Guy *Musician, Songwriter*
Editions Temporel, 2 Rue du Marquis de Mores, Garches, 92380, FRANCE

Beasley, Allyce *Actor*
SBV, 145 S Fairfax Ave, #310, Los Angeles, CA 90036 USA

Beasley, Alyce *Actor*
TalentWorks (LA), 3500 W Olive Ave #1400, Burbank, CA 91505 USA

Beasley, Bruce M *Artist*
322 Lewis St, Oakland, CA 94607 USA

Beasley, John *Actor*
Bauman Redanty & Shaul Agency, 5757 Wilshire Blvd #473, Los Angeles, CA 90036 USA

Beasley, Terry P *Football Player*
3248 Highfield Dr, Moody, AL 35004 USA

Beatrix, HM Queen
Kasteel Drakesteijn, Lage Vuursche, HOLLAND, 3744 BA

Beattle, Ann *Writer*
Janklow & Nesbit, 445 Park Ave, #1300, New York, NY 10022 USA

Beattle, Bob *Skier*
210 Aabc, #N, Aspen, CO 81611 USA

Beattle, Bruce *Cartoonist*
Daytona Beach News-Journal, Editorial Dept, 901 6th St, Daytona Beach, FL 32117 USA

Beatty, James T (Jim) *Athlete*
1516 LaRochelle Lane, Charlotte, NC 28226 USA

Beatty, Jim
1516 Larochelle Lane, Charlotte, NC 28226

Beatty, Ned *Actor*
2706 N Beachwood Dr, Los Angeles, CA 90068 USA

Beatty, Warren *Actor, Director, Producer*
13671 Mulholland Dr #700, Beverly Hills, CA 90210 USA

Beaty, Zelmo *Basketball Player*
2808 120th Ave NE, Bellevue, WA 98005 USA

Beau Brummels
PO Box 53664, Indianapolis, IN 46253

Beauford, Carter *Musician*
Red Light Mgmt, 3302 Lobban Place, Charlottesville, VA 22903 USA

Beaufoy, Simon *Writer*
Creative Artists Agency, 9830 Wilshire Blvd, Beverly Hills, CA 90212 USA

Beaumont, Jimmy
2002 Duquesne Ave, McKeesport, PA 15132

Beaumont, Thomas *Actor*
Scott Stander & Associates, 13701 Riverside Dr #201, Sherman Oaks, CA 91423 USA

Beaupre, Don *Hockey Player*
5020 Scriver Road, Edina, MN 55436 USA

Beauvais-Nilon, Garcelle *Actor, Model*
Nina Blanchard, 8826 Burton Way, Beverly Hills, CA 90211 USA

Beaver, Jim *Actor*
Artists Agency, 1180 S Beverly Dr, #301, Los Angeles, CA 90035 USA

Beaver, Joe *Rodeo Rider*
Po Box 1595, Huntsville, TN 77342 USA

Beaver, Terry *Actor*
Paradigm Agency, 10100 Santa Monica Blvd #2500, Los Angeles, CA 90067 USA

Beban, Gary
1334 Edgewood Lane, Northbrook, IL 60062-4716

Beban, Gary J *Football Player*
20 Timber Lane, Northbrook, IL 60062 USA

Bech, Debra *Actor*
A Prairie Home Companion, 45 East 7th Street, St Paul, MN 55101-2274 USA

Becherer, Hans W *Business Person*
Deere Co, 1 John Deere Place, Moline, IL 61265 USA

Bechtel, Riley P *Business Person*
Bechtel Group, 50 beale St, San Francisco, CA 94105 USA

Bechtel, Stephen D Jr *Business Person*
Bechtel Group, 50 beale St, San Francisco, CA 94105 USA

Bechtol, Hubert E (Hub) *Football Player*
7917 taranto Dr, Austin, TX 78729 USA

Beck *Musician*
Creative Artists Agency LCC (CAA-LA), 9830 Wilshire Blvd, Beverly Hills, CA 90212 USA

Beck *Musician, Songwriter*
GAS Entertainment, 8935 Lindblade St, Culver City, CA 90232 USA

Beck, Aaron T *Doctor*
3600 Market St #700, Philadelphia, PA 19104 USA

Beck, Charles H (Chip) *Golfer*
Int'l Mgmt Group, 1 Eriview Plaza, 1360 E 9th St #1300, Cleveland, OH 44114 USA

Beck, Jeff *Musician*
Creative Artists Agency LCC (CAA-LA), 9830 Wilshire Blvd, Beverly Hills, CA 90212 USA

Beck, Maria *Actor*
Lichtman/Salners Company, 12216 Moorpark Street, Studio City, CA 91604 USA

Beck, Marilyn M *Writer*
2152 El Roble Lane, Beverly Hills, CA 90210 USA

Beck, Martin *Actor*
Lichtman/Salners, 12216 Moorpark St, Studio City, CA 91604 USA

Beck, Mat *Cinematographer*
621 Via de la Paz, Pacific Palisades, CA 90272 USA

Beck, Michael *Actor*
Paradigm (LA), 10100 Santa Monica Blvd, Fl 25, Los Angeles, CA 90067 USA

Beck, Ray M *Football Player*
745 N College St, Cedartown, GA 30125 USA

Beck, Robin *Musician*
Cavaricci & White, 156 W 56th St #1803, New York, NY 10019 USA

Beck Hilton, Kimberly *Actor*
Badgley Connor Talent, 9229 Sunset Blvd, #311, Los Angeles, CA 90069 USA

Beckel, Robert D *General*
New Mexico Military Institute, Superintendent's Office, Roswell, NM 88201 USA

Becker, Boris *Tennis Player*
Grafenau, Grafenauweg, Zug, 6300, SWITZERLAND

Becker, Edward R *Judge*
US Court of Appeals, US Couthouse, 601 Market St, Philadelphia, PA 19106 USA

Becker, Gary S *Nobel Prize Laureate*
1308 E 58th St, Chicago, IL 60637 USA

Becker, George *Misc*
United Steelworkers of America, 5 Gateway Center, Pittsburgh, PA 15222 USA

Becker, Gerry *Actor*
Paradigm (LA), 10100 Santa Monica Blvd, Fl 25, Los Angeles, CA 90067 USA

Becker, Gretchen *Actor*
Acme Talent, 4727 Wilshire Blvd, #333, Los Angeles, CA 90010 USA

Becker, Harold *Director*
Creative Artists Agency, 9830 Wilshire Blvd, Beverly Hills, CA 90212 USA

Becker, Isaura *Actor*
Televisa, Blvd Adolfo Lopez Mateos 232, Colonia San Angel INN, DF, CP 01060, MEXICO

Becker, Kuno *Actor*
Arenas Group, The, 8010 Hollywood Blvd, Los Angeles, CA 90046

Becker, Margaret *Musician*
Sparrow Communications, 101 Winners Circle, Brentwood, TN 37027 USA

Becker, Quinn H *Doctor, General*
PO Box 2388, Dillon, CO 80435 USA

Becker, Rob *Comedian, Actor*
William Moris Agency, 151 El Camino Dr, Beverly Hills, CA 90212 USA

Becker, Robert J *Misc*
6 Oakbrook Club Dr #J101, Oak Brook, IL 60523 USA

Becker, Thomas *Athlete*
Hagedomweg 6A, Solingen, 42697, GERMANY

Becket, MacDonald G *Architect*
Becket Group, 2501 Colorado Blvd, Santa Monica, CA 90404 USA

Beckett, Josh *Baseball Player*
Florida Marlins, Pro Player Stadium 2269 Dan Marino Blvd, Miami, FL 33056 USA

Beckett, Wendy (Sister)
BBC-TV, Center Wood Ln, London, ENGLAND, W12 7R3

Beckford, Roxanne *Actor*
9255 Sunset Blvd #401, Los Angeles, CA 90069 USA

Beckford, Tyson *Actor, Model*
Bethann Model Mgmt, 36 N Moore St #36N, New York, NY 10013 USA

Beckham, Brice *Actor*
6561 Espanita St, Long Beach, CA 90815

Beckham, Brice *Actor*
17070 Knollbrook Place, Riverside, CA 92503 USA

Beckham, David *Soccer Player*
Global Talent Group, 119 Mercer Street, 2nd Floor, New York, NY 10012 USA

Beckham, Victoria Adams *Musician*
Lee & Thompson, 15 St Christopher's Pl, London, W1M 5HE, UNITED KINGDOM (UK)

Beckinsale, Kate *Actor*
Creative Artists Agency LCC (CAA-LA), 9830 Wilshire Blvd, Beverly Hills, CA 90212 USA

Beckley, Gerry *Music Group, Musician*
Agency for Performing Arts, 9200 Sunset Blvd #900, Los Angeles, CA 90069 USA

Beckwith, Alan *Actor*
3928 Carpenter Ave, Studio City, CA 91604 USA

Becton, C W *Religious Leader*
United Pentacostal Free Will Baptist Church, 8855 Dunn Rd, Hazelwood, MO 63042 USA

Becton, Julius W Jr *General, Educator*
Prairie View A & M University, President's Office, Prairie View, TX 77446 USA

Bedard, Irene *Actor*
Don Buchwald, 6500 Wilshire Blvd #2200, Los Angeles, CA 90048 USA

Bedard, Myriam *Athlete*
3329 Pinecourt, Neufchatel, QC, G2B 2E4, CANADA

Bedelia, Bonnie *Actor*
International Creative Management (ICM-LA), 8942 Wilshire Blvd, Beverly Hills, CA 90211 USA

BeDell, Chad Ryan
Box 699, Clark, CO 80428

Bedford, Brian *Actor*
Arts Management Group, 1133 Broadway #1025, New York, NY 10010 USA

Bedford, Steuart J R
Harrison/Parrott, 12 Penzance Place, London, W11 4PA, UNITED KINGDOM (UK)

Bedi, Kabir *Actor, Bollywood*
B4 Beach House Apt, Gandhigram Road, Mumbai, MS 400054, INDIA

Bedingfield, Daniel *Musician*
Island Def Jam Music Group, The, 825 Eighth Avenue, New York, NY 10019

Bednarik, Charles P (Chuck) *Football Player*
6379 Winding Road, Coopersburg, PA 18036 USA

Bednarski, John *Hockey Player*
11 2nd St, Scottsville, NY 14546 USA

Bedrosian, Stephen W (Steve) *Baseball Player*
3335 Gordon Road, Senoia, GA 30276 USA

Bedsole, Harold (Hal) *Football Player*
146 Balboa Lane, Tustin, CA 92780 USA

Beebe, Dion *Cinematographer*
International Creative Mgmt, 8942 Wilshire Blvd #219, Beverly Hills, CA 90211 USA

Beeby, Thomas H *Architect*
Hammond Beeby Babka, 440 N Wells St, Chicago, IL 60610 USA

Beem, Rich *Golfer*
Gaylord Sports Mgmt, 14646 N Keirland Blvd #230, Scottsdale, AZ 85254 USA

Beene, Geoffrey *Fashion Designer*
Geoffrey Beene Inc, 1770 W Maine St, Riverhead, NY 11901 USA

Beer, A M *Editor*
Spectator, Editorial Dept, 44 Frid St, Hamilton, ON L8N 3G3, CANADA

Beering, Steven C *Educator*
Purdue University, President's Office, West Lafayette, IN 47907 USA

Beesley, Max *Actor*
Untitled Entertainment (LA), 8436 W 3rd St #650, Los Angeles, CA 90048 USA

Beeson, Jack H *Composer*
18 Seaforth Lane, Lloyd Harbor, NY 11743 USA

Beeson, Paul B *Physicist, Doctor*
7 Riverwoods Dr #F125, Exeter, NH 03833 USA

Beezer, Robert R *Judge*
US Court of Appeals, US Courthouse 1010 5th Ave, Seattle, WA 98104 USA

Bega, Leslie *Actor*
31 1/2 Buccaneer Ave, MDR, CA 90292 USA

Bega, Lou
Postfach 80 01 49, Munich, GERMANY, D-81601

Begala, Paul *Television Host*
Crossfire, 820 First St NE Fl 10, Washington, DC 20002 USA

Begay, Notah *Golfer*
Professional Golfer's Assn, P O Box 109601, Palm Beach Gardens, FL 33410 USA

Begert, William J *General*
Commander Pacific Air Force, Hickam Air Force Base, HI 96853 USA

Begg, Varyl *Admiral*
Copyhold Cottage Chilbotton, Stockbridge, Hants, UNITED KINGDOM (UK)

Beggs, James M *Government Official, Misc*
1177 N Great Southwest Parkway, Grand Prairie, TX 75050 USA

Beghe, Jason *Actor*
7473 Mulholland Dr, Los Angeles, CA 90046 USA

Beghe, Renato *Judge*
US Tax Court, 400 2nt St NW, Washington, DC 20217 USA

Begler, Michael *Producer*
William Morris Agency (WMA-LA), 1 William Morris Pl, Beverly Hills, CA 90212 USA

Begley Jr, Ed *Actor*
Sterling/Winters Company, The, 1900 Ave of the Stars Fl 5, Los Angeles, CA 90067 USA

Behagen, Ron *Basketball Player*
1101 Juniper St NE, #401, Atlanta, GA 30309 USA

Behar, Joy *Actor*
William Morris Agency, 151 El Camino Dr, Beverly Hills, CA 90212 USA

Behe, Michael *Writer, Misc*
Lehigh University, Biochemistry Dept, Bethlehem, PA 18015 USA

Behl, Mohnish *Actor, Bollywood*
Sagar Sangeet 30th Floor, Opp Colaba Post Office, Bombay, MS 400 005, INDIA

Behle, Jochen *Skier*
Sonnenhof 1, Willingen, 34508, GERMANY

Behm, Forrest E *Football Player*
3 Briarcliff Dr, Coming, NY 14830 USA

Behnken, Robert L *Astronaut*
43708 Dejay St, Lancaster, CA 93536 USA

Behr, Aaron *Actor*
Acme Talent & Literary Agency (LA), 4727 Wilshire Blvd #333, Los Angeles, CA 90010 USA

Behr, Dani
195 March Wall #24 Norex, London, ENGLAND, E14 9SG

Behr, Jason *Actor*
Rogers & Cowan, 1888 Century Park E #500, Los Angeles, CA 90067 USA

Behrend, Marc *Hockey Player*
1808 Savannah Way, Waunakee, WI 53597 USA

Behrens, Hildegard *Opera Singer*
Herbert Breslin, 119 W 57th St #1505, New York, NY 10019 USA

Behrens, Sam *Actor*
530 Bryant Drive, Canoga Park, CA 91304 USA

Beilina, Nina *Musician*
400 W 43rd St #7D, New York, NY 10036 USA

Bel Biv Devoe
8942 Wilshire Blvd, Beverly Hills, CA 90211

Belafonte, Harry *Musician, Model*
William Morris Agency, 1325 Ave of Americas, New York, NY 10019 USA

Belafonte, Harry *Musician, Actor*
William Morris Agency, 1325 Ave of Americas, New York, NY 10019 USA

Belaga, Julie *Financier*
Export-Import Bank, 811 Vermont Ave NW, Washington, DC 20571 USA

Belchlavek, Jiri *Conductor*
Czechoslovakia Philharmonic, Alsovo Nabr 12, Prague, 11001, CZECH REPUBLIC

Belen, Ana *Musician, Actor*
Rompeolas Productions, Alabama St #1761 San Gerardo, Rio Piedras, PR 00926 USA

Belew, Adrian *Musician*
Umbrella Artists Mgmt, 2612 Erie Ave, Cincinnati, OH 45208 USA

Belford, Christina *Actor*
10635 Santa Monica Blvd, #130, Los Angeles, CA 90025 USA

Belfour, Edward (Ed) *Hockey Player*
Promo Athlete Inc, 9810 Sarle Road, Freeland, MI 48623 USA

BelGeddes, Barbara *Actor*
PO Box 869, Northeast Harbor, ME 04662 USA

Belichick, Steve *Football Player*
3035 Aberdeen Road, Annapolis, MD 21403 USA

Belichik, William S (Bill) *Football Coach*
New England Patriots, Gillette Stadium RR1, 60 Washington, Foxboro, MA 02035 USA

Belin, Gaspard D *Attorney General*
4 Willard St, Cambridge, MA 02138 USA

Belin, Nat *Cartoonist*
Drawing Board, PO Box 1162, Winston Salem, NC 27102 USA

Belisle, Danny *Hockey Player*
3967 Glen Oaks Manor Dr, Sarasota, FL 34232 USA

Belita
44 Crabtree Lane, London, ENGLAND, SW6 6LW

Beliveau, Jean
155 rue Victoria, Longueuil, CANADA, QC J4H 2J4

Belka, Marek *Prime Minister*
UI Ursad Rady Ministrow, UI Wiejska 4/8, Warsaw, 00-583, POLAND

Belkirch, Gary B *War Hero*
68 South Ave, Hilton, NY 14468 USA

Belknap, Anna *Actor*
Cornerstone Talent Agency, 37 W 20th St #1108, New York, NY 10011 USA

Bell, Anthony D *Football Player*
172 Daisy Court, Hercules, CA 94547 USA

Bell, Archie *Musician*
Speer Entertainment Services, PO Box 49612, Atlanta, GA 30359 USA

Bell, Art *Business Person*
Court TV, 600 Third Ave Fl 2, New York, NY 10016 USA

Bell, Bobby
208 Shagbark, Lee's Summit, MO 63063

Bell, C Gordon *Scientist*
Microsoft Corp, 1 Microsoft Way, Redmond, WA 98052 USA

Bell, Catherine *Actor*
Innovative Artists, 1505 10th St, Santa Monica, CA 90401 USA

Bell, Charles *Business Person*
McDonald's Corp, 1 McDonald's Plaza, 1 Kroc Dr, Oak Brook, IL 60523 USA

Bell, Clyde R (Bob) *Admiral*
1301 Harney St, Omaha, NE 68102 USA

Bell, Coby
Vincent Cirrincione Associates, 8721 Sunset Blvd #205, Los Angeles, CA 90069 USA

Bell, David *Composer*
Gorfaine/Schwartz, 13245 Riverside Dr #450, Sherman Oaks, CA 91423 USA

Bell, David G (Buddy) *Baseball Player*
PO Box 11718, Chandler, AZ 85248 USA

Bell, Derek N *Baseball Player*
PO Box 261286, Tampa, FL 33685 USA

Bell, Drake *Actor*
Osbrink Talent Agency, 4343 Lankershim Blvd #100, Universal City, CA 91602 USA

Bell, Felicia M *Actor*
1365 Riverside Dr, #317, North Hollywood, CA 91607 USA

Bell, Gary *Baseball Player*
American Sports, 1436 N Flores St, San Antonio, TX 78212 USA

Bell, Gregory (Gerg) *Track Athlete*
831 W Miami Ave, Logansport, IN 46947 USA

Bell, Gregory (Greg) *Track Athlete*
831 W Miami Ave, Logansport, IN 46947 USA

Bell, James D *Diplomat*
154 Zinfandel Circle, Scotts Valley, CA 95066 USA

Bell, Jamie *Actor*
PO Box 1116, Belfast, BT2 7AJ, Ireland

Bell, Jay S *Baseball Player*
Cleveland Indians, PO Box 50249, Phoenix, AZ 85076-0249 USA

Bell, Jerry *Baseball Player*
Milwaukee Brewers, 631 Audrey Rd, Mount Juliet, TN 37122-3844 USA

Bell, John *Musician*
Brown Cat Inc, 400 Foundry St, Athens, GA 30601 USA

Bell, John Anthony *Actor, Director*
Bell Shakespeare Co, 88 George St, Level 1, Rocks, NSW, 200, AUSTRALIA

Bell, Jorge A M (George) *Athlete, Baseball Player*
Lamiama #14, Bell 2nd Planto, San Pedro de Macoris, Dominican Republic

Bell, Joshua *Musician*
I M G Artists, 3 Burlington Lane, Chiswick, London, W4 2TH, UNITED KINGDOM (uk)

Bell, Judie
PO Box 121626, Nashville, CA TN 37212

Bell, Kevin *Baseball Player*
Chicago White Sox, 621 Sue St, Little Chute, WI 54140-2424 USA

Bell, Kristen *Actor*
Brookside Artists Management (LA), 450 N Roxbury Dr Fl 4, Beverly Hills, CA 90210 USA

Bell, Lake *Actor*
Burstein Company, The, 15304 Sunset Blvd #208, Pacific Palisades, CA 90272 USA

Bell, Larry S *Artist*
PO Box 4101, Taos, NM 87571 USA

Bell, Lauralee *Actor*
9950 Beverly Grove Dr, Beverly Hills, CA 90210 USA

Bell, Lynette *Swimmer*
149 Henry St, Merwether, NSW 22, Australia

Bell, Madison Smartt *Writer*
Random House, 1745 Broadway, #B1, New York, NY 10019 USA

Bell, Marshall *Actor*
IFA Talent Agency, 8730 Sunset Blvd #490, Los Angeles, CA 90069 USA

Bell, Michael *Actor*
Dade/Schulz, 6442 Coldwater Canyon Ave #206, Valley Green, CA 91606 USA

Bell, Mike *Race Car Driver*
American Motorcycle Assn, 13515, Yarmouth Dr, Pickerington, OH 43147 USA

Bell, Mike *Baseball Player*
Atlanta Braves, 1331 Noah Ave, Spring Hill, FL 34608-5767 USA

Bell, Mike J *Football Player*
7405 Lakewood Circle, Wichita, KS 67205 USA

Bell, Pat

Bell, Rini *Actor*
Main Title Entertainment, 5225 Wilshire Blvd #500, Los Angeles, CA 90036 USA

Bell, Robert *Musician*
J Bird Entertainment Agency, 4905 S Atlantic Ave, Daytona Beach, FL 32127 USA

Bell, Robert L (Bobby) Sr *Football Player*
208 NW Shagbark St, Lees Summit, MO 64064 USA

Bell, Sam *Coach*
2310 E Woodstock Place, Bloomington, IN 47401 USA

Bell, Sean *Actor*
Daniel Sladek Entertainment Corporation, 8306 Wilshire Blvd #510, Beverly Hills, CA 90212 USA

Bell, Terry *Baseball Player*
Kansas City Royals, 8352 Normandy Creek Dr, Dayton, OH 45458-3284 USA

Bell, Tobin *Actor*
Saffron Management, 1701 N Beverly Dr, Beverly Hills, CA 90210 USA

Bell, Tom *Actor*
Shepherd & Ford, 13 Randor Walk, London, SW3 4BP, UNITED KINGDOM (uk)

Bell, Tommy *Astronaut*
205 S Redondo Ave, Manhattan Beach, CA 90266 USA

Bell Biv Devoe
8942 Wilshire Blvd, Beverly Hills, CA 90211

Bell Calloway, Vanessa *Actor*
9 Yards Entertainment, 8530 Wilshire Blvd Fl 5, Beverly Hills, CA 90211 USA

Bell-Lundy, Sandra *Cartoonist*
255 Northwood Dr, Welland, ON L3C 6V1, Canada

Bella, Ivan *Cosmonaut*
Potchta Kosmonavtov, Moskovskoi Oblasti, Syvisdny Goroduk, 141160, RUSSIA

Bella, John *Baseball Player*
New York Yankees, 409 N Cypress Dr Apt 7, Tequesta, FL 33469-2656 USA

Bella, Rachael *Actor*
3 Arts Entertainment Inc, 9460 Wilshire Blvd Fl 7, Beverly Hills, CA 90212 USA

Bella, Rachel *Actor*
3 Arts Entertainment Inc, 9460 Wilshire Blvd Fl 7, Beverly Hills, CA 90212 USA

Bellamy, Bill *Actor, Comedian*
Talent Entertainment Group, 9111 Wilshire Blvd, Beverly Hills, CA 90210 USA

Bellamy, Carol *Misc*
United Nations Children's Fund, 3 United Nations Plaza, New York, NY 10017 USA

Bellamy, David *Songwriter, Musician*
Webster Assoc, 811 18th Ave S, #200, Nashville, TN 37203 USA

Bellamy, David J *Writer*
Mill House Bedbum, Bishop Auckland, County Durham, DL13 3NN, UNITED KINGDOM (UK)

Bellamy, Howard *Songwriter, Musician*
Webster Assoc, 811 18th Ave S, #200, Nashville, TN 37203

Bellamy, Walt
2884 Lakeshore Dr, College Park, GA 30337-4420

Bellamy, Walter J (Walt) *Basketball Player*
2884 Lakeshore Dr, College Park, GA 30337 USA

Bellar, Clara *Actor*
IFA Talent Agency, 8730 Sunset Blvd #490, Los Angeles, CA 90069 USA

Belle, Albert J *Baseball Player*
Cleveland Indians, 9574 E Ann Way, Scottsdale, AZ 85260-5016 USA

Belle, Camilla *Actor*
Creative Artists Agency LCC (CAA-LA), 9830 Wilshire Blvd, Beverly Hills, CA 90212 USA

Belle, Regina *Musician*
Green Light, PO Box 3172, Beverly Hills, CA 90212 USA

Bellecourt, Vernon *Social Activist*
American Indian Vovement, 1209 4th St SE, Minneapolis, MN 55414 USA

Beller, Kathleen *Actor*
PO Box 806, Half Moon Bay, CA 94019 USA

Bellhorn, Mark *Basketball Player*
Oakland A's, 1544 Chipmunk Ln, Oviedo, FL 32765-6666 USA

Belliard, Rafael *Baseball Player*
Pittsburgh Pirates, 10846 King Bay Dr, Boca Raton, FL 33498-4548 USA

Belliard, Ronnie *Baseball Player*
Milwaukee Brewers, 9120 NW Brown Road, Miami, FL 33143 USA

Bellinger, Clay *Baseball Player*
New York Yankees, 1390 E Horseshoe Dr, Chandler, AZ 85249-4761 USA

Bellingham, Norman *Misc*
208 Morgan St NW, Washington, DC 20001 USA

Bellini, Mario *Architect*
Architecture Center, 66 Portland Place, London, W1, UNITED KINGDOM (UK)

Bellino, Joe
45 Hayden Lane, Bedford, MA 01730-1140

Bellino, Joseph M (Joe) *Football Player*
45 Hayden Lane, Bedford, MA 01730 USA

Bellisario, Donald P *Actor, Writer, Producer, Director*
Broder Kurland Webb Uffner, 9242 Beverly Blvd, #200, Beverly Hills, CA 90210 USA

Bellmon, Henry *Governor, Senator*
RR 1, Red Rock, OK 74651 USA

Bello, Maria *Actor*
Creative Artists Agency, 9830 Wilshire Blvd, Beverly Hills, CA 90212 USA

Belloir, Bob *Baseball Player*
Atlanta Braves, 335 Mimosa Dr, Fayetteville, GA 30214-1753 USA

Bellotti, Mike *Football Coach*
University of Oregon, Athletic Dept, Eugen, OR 97403 USA

Bellovin, Steven M *Scientist*
AT & T Research Labs, 180 Park Ave, PO Box 971, Florham Park, NJ 07932 USA

Bellow, Saul C *Nobel Prize Laureate*
Boston University, 745 Commonwealth Ave, Boston, MA 02215 USA

Bellows, Brian *Hockey Player*
9470 Foxford Road, Chanhassen, MN 55317 USA

Bellows, Gil *Actor*
International Creative Mgmt, 8942 Wilshire Blvd, #219, Beverly Hills, CA 90211 USA

Bellson, Louie
901 Winding River Rd, Vero Beach, FL 32963

Bellson, Louis (Louie) *Composer, Musician*
Ted Schmidt Assoc, 901 Winding River Road, Vero Beach, FL 32963 USA

Bellucci, Monica *Actor, Model*
Agence Intertalent, 5 Rue Clement Marot, Paris, 75008, FRANCE

Bellugi, Piero
50027 Strada In Chianti, Florence, ITALY

Bellwood, Pamela *Actor*
1696 San Leandro Ln, Santa Barbara, CA
93108 USA

Belm, Michaela *Model*
Agentur Talents, Ohmstr 5, Munich,
80802, GERMANY

Belmondo, Jean-Paul *Actor*
9 Rue des Saint Peres, Paris, 75007,
FRANCE

Belo, Carlos Filipe Ximenes *Nobel Prize Laureate, Religious Leader*
Catholic Bishop Dili, EAST TIMOR

Belote Hamlin, Melissa *Swimmer*
7311 Exmore St, Springfield, VA 22150
USA

Belousova, Ludmila *Figure Skater*
Chalet Hubel, Grindelwald, 3818,
SWITZERLAND

Belov, Sergei *Basketball Player*
Basket Cassino, Vis Appia Nuova,
Cassino, Rome, ITALY

Beltrami, Marco *Composer*
Air-Edel, 1416 N La Brea Ave, Los
Angeles, CA 90028 USA

Beltran, Carlos *Baseball Player*
Kansas City Royals, I-18 Calle 17, Manati,
PR 00674-5430 USA

Beltran, Rigoberto *Baseball Player*
St Louis Cardinals, 4612 Fairhope Dr, La
Mirada, CA 90638-6120 USA

Beltran, Robert *Actor*
2210 Talmadge St, Los Angeles, CA
90027 USA

Beltre, Adrian *Baseball Player, Athlete*
Los Angeles Dodgers (LA Dodgers), 1000
Elysian Park Avenue, Los Angeles, CA
90012 USA

Belushi, James (Jim) *Actor*
Brillstein-Grey Entertainment, 9150
Wilshire Blvd #350, Beverly Hills, CA
90212 USA

Belzer, Richard *Actor, Comedian*
Wolf Chelsea Pier, 62 W 23rd St & 12th
Ave, New York, NY 10010 USA

Beman, Deane R *Golfer*
255 Deer Haven Dr, Ponte Vedra, FL
32082 USA

Bemhard *Prince*
Soestdijk Palace, Baarn, NETHERLANDS

Bemis, Cliff *Actor*
Halpern & Associates, 12304 Santa
Monica Blvd #104, Los Angeles, CA
90025 USA

Ben Ali, Zine al-Abidine *President, General*
President's Office, Palais Presidentiel,
Tunis, Tunisia

Ben Ali, Zine al-Abidine *President, General*
President's Office, Palais Presidentiel,
Tunis, TUNISIA

Ben-Victor, Paul *Actor*
Leverage Management, 1610 Broadway,
Santa Monica, CA 90404 USA

Benabib, Kim *Writer*
Harper Collins Publishers, 10 E 53rd St,
New York, NY 10022 USA

Benacerraf, Baruj *Nobel Prize Laureate*
111 Perkins St, Boston, MA 02130 USA

Benackova, Gabriela *Opera Singer*
Oper et Concert, Maximilianstr 22,
Munich, 80539, GERMANY

Benade Leo, Edward *General*
417 Pine Ridge Road, #A, Carthage, NC
28327 USA

Benanti, Laura *Actor*
Creative Artists Agency LCC (CAA-LA),
9830 Wilshire Blvd, Beverly Hills, CA
90212 USA

Benard, Marvin *Baseball Player*
San Francisco Giants, 1006 Country Ct,
Richland, WA 99352-9500 USA

Benard, Maurice *Actor*
Stone Manners Talent Agency, 6500
Wilshire Blvd, Ste 550, Los Angeles, CA
90048 USA

Benatar, Pat *Musician, Songwriter*
Sonder, 250 W 57th St, #1830, New York,
NY 10107 USA

Benavides, Fortunato P (Pete) *Judge*
US Court of Appeals, 903 San Jacinto
Blvd, Austin, TX 78701 USA

Benavides, Freddie *Baseball Player*
Cincinnati Reds, 2502 Garfield St, Laredo,
TX 78043-3030 USA

Benavides, Osvaldo *Actor*
Televisa, Blvd Adolfo Lopez Mateos 232,
Colonia San Angel INN, DF, CP 01060,
MEXICO

Benben, Brian *Actor*
Gersh Agency, The (LA), 232 N Canon Dr,
Beverly Hills, CA 90210 USA

Bench, John L (Johnny) *Baseball Player*
Cincinnati Reds, 528 4 Mile Rd,
Cincinnati, OH 45230-5209 USA

Benchley, Peter B *Writer*
35 Boudinot St, Princeton, NJ 08540 USA

Benchoff, Dennis L (Den) *General*
380 Arbor Road, Lancaster, PA 17601
USA

Bender, Candace
PO Box 341489, Los Angeles, CA 90034

Bender, Gary N *Sportscaster*
TNT-TV, Sports Dept, 1050 Techwood Dr
NW, Atlanta, GA 30318 USA

Bender, Thomas *Historian*
54 Washington Mews, New York, NY
10003 USA

Bendix, Simone *Actor*
Joy Jameson, 2/19 Plaza, 535 Kings Road,
London, SW10 0SZ, UNITED KINGDOM
(UK)

Bendlin, Kurt *Track Athlete*
DLV, Asfelder Str 27, Leverkusen, 64289,
GERMANY

Bendre, Sonali *Actor, Bollywood*
A/203 43 Paradise Apts, Swami Samarth
Nagar 1st Cross Lane Andheri(W),
Mumbai, MS 400053, INDIA

Benedek, George B *Physicist*
Massachusetts Institute of Technology,
Physics Dept, Cambridge, MA 02139 USA

Benedek, Joana *Actor*
Televisa, Blvd Adolfo Lopez Mateos 232,
Colonia San Angel INN, DF, CP 01060,
MEXICO

Benedeti, Paulo *Actor*
Kazarian/Spencer & Assoc, 11365 Ventura
Blvd #100, Box 7403, Studio City, CA
91604 USA

Benedict, Bruce *Baseball Player*
Minnesota Twins, 335 Quiet Water Ln,
Atlanta, GA 30350-3724 USA

Benedict, Dirk *Actor, Director, Writer*
PO Box 634, Bigfork, MT 59911-0634
USA

Benedict, Manson *Engineer*
108 Moorings Park Dr, #206, Naples, FL
34105 USA

Benedict, Paul *Actor*
84 Rockland Pl, Newton, MA 02464 USA

Benedicto, Lourdes *Actor*
Paradigm (LA), 10100 Santa Monica Blvd,
Fl 25, Los Angeles, CA 90067 USA

Benes, Alan *Baseball Player*
St Louis Cardinals, 13005 Wheatfield
Farm Rd, Saint Louis, MO 63141-8546
USA

Benes, Andrew C (Andy) *Baseball Player*
San Diego Padres, 1127 Highland Point
Dr, Saint Louis, MO 63131-1420 USA

Benet, Eric *Musician, Songwriter*
Family Tree Entertainment, 135 E 57th St,
#2600, New York, NY 10022 USA

Benetton, Giuliana *Business Person*
Benetton Group SpA, Via Minelli,
Ponzano Treviso, 31050, ITALY

Benetton, Luciano *Business Person*
Benetton Group SpA, Via Minelli,
Ponzano Treviso, 31050, ITALY

Benflis, Ali *Prime Minister*
Prime Minister's Office, Palais du
Gouvernement, Algiers, ALGERIA

Benford, Gregory *Writer*
Created By, 1041 N Formosa Ave,
Formosa Bldg #10, W Hollywood, CA
90046 USA

Benglis, Lynda *Artist*
222 Bowery St, New York, NY 10012
USA

Bengston, Billy Al *Artist*
805 Hampton Dr, Venice, CA 90291 USA

Benhamou, Eric A *Business Person*
ThreeCom Corp, 5400 Bayfront Plaza,
Santa Clara, CA 95054 USA

Benhima, Mohamed *Prime Minister*
Km 5.5, Route des Zaers, Rabat,
MOROCCO

Benigni, Roberto *Actor*
Nancy Seltzer & Associates, 6220 Del
Valle Drive, Los Angeles, CA 90048

Benignl, Roberto *Actor, Director*
Via Traversa 44, Vergaglio, Provinz di
Prato, ITALY

Bening, Annette *Actor*
13671 Mulholland Dr, Beverly Hills, CA
90210 USA

Benioff, David *Writer, Producer*
Management 360, 9111 Wilshire Blvd,
Beverly Hills, CA 90210 USA

Benirschke, Rolf J *Football Player*
4326 Vista de la Tierra, San Diego, CA
92130 USA

Benitez, Armando G *Baseball Player*
Batey El Soco, Ramon Santana,
DOMINICAN REPUBLIC

Benitez, John (Jellybean)
William Morris Agency, 151 El Camino
Dr, Beverly Hills, CA 90212 USA

Benitez, Yamil *Baseball Player*
San Francisco Giants, 13 Calle Rev
Francisco Colon B, Rio Piedres, PR
00925-3009 USA

Benitz, Max *Actor*
Handprint Entertainment, 1100 Glendon
Ave #1000, Los Angeles, CA 90024 USA

Benjamin, Andre (Dre) *Artist*
LaFace/Arista Records, 3423 Piedmont
Road NE, Atlanta, GA 30305 USA

Benjamin, Jill *Actor*
Power Entertainment, 12200 W Olympic
Blvd #499, Los Angeles, CA 90064 USA

Benjamin, Richard *Actor, Director*
Bartels Co, PO Box 57593, Sherman
Oaks, CA 91413 USA

Benjamin, Stan *Baseball Player*
Philadelphia Phillies, 46 Allen St,
Greenfield, MA 01301-2322 USA

Benjamin, Stephen *Yachtsman*
40 Quintard Ave, Norwalk, CT 06854
USA

Benkovic, Stephen J *Misc*
771 Teaberry Lane, State College, PA
16803 USA

Benmosche, Robert H *Business Person*
Metropolitan Life Insurance, 1 Madison
Ave, New York, NY 10010 USA

Benn, Anthony N W (Tony) *Government
Official*
House of Commons, Westminster,
London, SW1A 0AA, UNITED KINGDOM
(UK)

Benn, Nigel *Boxer*
Matchroom Boxing, 10 Western Road,
Romford Essex, RM1 3JT, UNITED
KINGDOM (UK)

Bennack Jr, Frank A *Publisher*
Hearst Corp, 250 W 55th St, New York,
NY 10019 USA

Bennett, A L *Basketball Player*
3446 S Gary Ave, Tulsa, OK 74105 USA

Bennett, Bob *Musician, Songwriter*
Jeff Roberts Assoc, 909 Meadowland
Lane, Goodlettsville, TN 37072 USA

Bennett, Brooke *Swimmer*
2585 Rowe Road, Milford, MI 48380 USA

Bennett, Bruce
2702 Forester Rd, Los Angeles, CA 90064

Bennett, Bruce (Herman Brix) *Track
Athlete, Actor*
2702 Forester Road, Los Angeles, CA
90064 USA

Bennett, Clay *Cartoonist*
Christian Science Monitor, Editorial Dept,
1 Norway St, Boston, MA 02115 USA

Bennett, Darren *Football Player*
PO Box 705, Solano Beach, CA 92075
USA

Bennett, Dave *Baseball Player*
Philadelphia Phillies, 408 N Fairchild St,
Yreka, CA 96097-2219 USA

Bennett, Dennis *Baseball Player*
Philadelphia Phillies, 630 N 5th St,
Klamath Falls, OR 97601-3028 USA

Bennett, Donnell *Football Player*
8055 W Leitner Dr, Coral Springs, FL
33067 USA

Bennett, Erik *Baseball Player*
California Angels, 517 3rd St Apt 884,
Yreka, CA 96097-2437 USA

Bennett, Fleur
25 Whitehall, London, ENGLAND, SW1A
2BS

Bennett, Fran *Actor*
749 N Lafayette Park Place, Los Angeles,
CA 90026 USA

Bennett, Gary *Baseball Player*
Philadelphia Phillies, 39895 N Delany Rd,
Wadsworth, IL 60083-9516 USA

Bennett, Hywel *Actor*
Gavin Barker, 45 S Molton St, London,
W1Y 3RD, UNITED KINGDOM (UK)

Bennett, Jeff *Baseball Player*
Nashville Sounds, 534 Chestnut St,
Nashville, TN 37203

Bennett, Jimmy *Actor*
Untitled Entertainment (LA), 8436 W 3rd
St #650, Los Angeles, CA 90048 USA

Bennett, Joe C *Educator*
4101 Altamont Road, Birmingham, AL
35213 USA

Bennett, Joel *Baseball Player*
Baltimore Orioles, 401 Riley Rd, Windsor,
NY 13865-1043 USA

Bennett, John *Governor*
New Jersy State Senate, 125 W State St,
Trenton, NJ 08608 USA

Bennett, Jonathan *Actor*
Amplitude Entertainment, 8033 Sunset
Blvd #823, Los Angeles, CA 90046

Bennett, Michael *Football Player*
Minnesota Vikings, 9520 Viking Dr, Eden
Prairie, MN 55344 USA

Bennett, Nelson *Skier*
807 S 20th Ave, Yakima, WA 98902 USA

Bennett, Nigel *Actor*
PO Box 14, Rossford, OH 43460 USA

Bennett, Richard Rodney *Composer*
Novello Co, 8-9 Firth St, London, W1V
5TZ, UNITED KINGDOM (UK)

Bennett, Robert (Bob) *Swimmer*
70 Rivo Alto Canal, Long Beach, CA
90803 USA

Bennett, Robert R *Business Person*
Home Shopping Network, 2501 118th
Ave N, Saint Petersburg, FL 33716 USA

Bennett, Robert S *Attorney General*
1840 24th St NW, Washington, DC 20008
USA

Bennett, Tony *Musician*
Tony Bennett Enterprises, 130 W 57th St
#9D, New York, NY 10019-3311 USA

Bennett, Tracie *Actor*
Annette Stone, 9 Newburgh St, London,
W1V 1LA, UNITED KINGDOM (UK)

Bennett, William *Politician, Secretary*
862 Venable Place NW, Washington, DC
20012 USA

Bennett, William J *Secretary*
1701 Pennsylvania Ave NW, #900,
Washington, DC 20006 USA

Bennie, Dan
22121 Cleveland St, Dearborn, MI 48124

Bennington, Chester *Musician*
Warner Bros Records (LA), 3300 Warner
Blvd, Burbank, CA 91510 USA

Bennis, Warren G *Educator, Writer*
University of Southern California,
Management School, Los Angeles, CA
90007 USA

Benny, Joan
1131 Coldwater Canyon, Beverly Hills,
CA 90210

Benoit, Chris *Wrestler*
World Wrestling Entertainment (WWE),
1241 E Main St, Stamford, CT 06905 USA

Benoit, David *Musician*
Fitzgerald-Hartley, 34 N Palm St, #100,
Ventura, CA 93001 USA

Benoit-Samuelson, Joan *Track Athlete*
95 Lower Flying Point Rd, Freeport, ME
04032 USA

Benrubi, Abraham *Actor*
Stone Manners Talent Agency, 6500
Wilshire Blvd, Ste 550, Los Angeles, CA
90048 USA

Benson, Amber *Actor*
United Talent Agency (UTA), 9560
Wilshire Blvd, Beverly Hills, CA 90212
USA

Benson, Andrew A *Misc*
6044 Folsom Dr, La Jolla, CA 92037 USA

Benson, Doug *Comedian*
OmniPop Inc (LA), 10700 Ventura Blvd Fl
2, Studio City, CA 91604 USA

Benson, George *Musician*
374 Poll St, #205, Ventura, CA 93001
USA

Benson, Harry *Photographer*
181 E 73rd St, #18A, New York, NY
10021 USA

Benson, Herbert *Doctor*
Mind/Body Medical Institute, Beth Israel
Hospital, Brookline, MA 02146 USA

Benson, Kent *Basketball Player*
3003 Daniel Court, Bloomington, IN
47401 USA

Benson, Kris *Baseball Player*
Pittsburgh Pirates, 248 Whetherburn Dr,
Wexford, PA 15090-8868 USA

Benson, Renaldo
ICM, 40 W 57th St, New York, NY 10019

Benson, Renaldo (Obie) *Musician*
William Morris Agency, 151 El Camino
Dr, Beverly Hills, CA 90212 USA

Benson, Robby *Actor*
Innovative Artists, 1505 10th St, Santa
Monica, CA 90401 USA

Benson, Stephen R (Steve) *Cartoonist*
Arizona Republic, Editorial Dept, 200 E
Van Buren St, Phoenix, AZ 85004 USA

Benson, Sydney W *Misc*
1110 N Bundy Dr, Los Angeles, CA 90049 USA

Benson, Vern *Baseball Player*
Philadelphia Athletics, PO Box 127, Granite Quarry, NC 28072-0127 USA

Benson Jr, Johnny *Race Car Driver*
PO Box 150619, Grand Rapids, MI 49515 USA

Benson-Landes, Wendy *Actor*
Northern Exposure Talent Management, 1077 Marinaside Cresc #2502, Vancouver BC, V6Z 2Z5, CANADA

Bentley, Eric *Writer*
194 Riverside Dr, New York, NY 10025 USA

Bentley, John *Actor*
Wedgewood House, Peterworth, Sussex, UNITED KINGDOM (UK)

Bentley, Ray *Sportscaster*
Fox-TV, Sports Dept, 205 W 67th St, New York, NY 10021 USA

Bentley, Stacey *Misc*
PO Box 26, Santa Monica, CA 90406 USA

Bentley, Wes *Actor*
151 W 74th St, #600, New York, NY 10023 USA

Benton, Andrew K *Educator*
Pepperdine University, President's Office, Malibu, CA 90263 USA

Benton, Barbi *Actor, Model*
40 N 4th St, Carbondale, CO 81623 USA

Benton, Butch *Baseball Player*
New York Mets, 12314 SE 60th Ave, Belleview, FL 34420-5200 USA

Benton, Fletcher *Artist*
250 Dore St, San Francisco, CA 94103 USA

Benton, Robert *Director*
International Creative Mgmt, 40 W 57th St, #1800, New York, NY 10019 USA

Bentsen Jr, Lloyd M *Senator, Secretary*
Verner Lipfert Bernhard, 901 15th St NW, #700, Washington, DC 20005 USA

Benvenuti, Giovanni (Nino) *Boxer*
FPI Viaie Tiziano 70, Rome, 00196, ITALY

Benvenuti, Nino
Via Giuseppe Ferrari 35, Rome, ITALY, 00127

Benz, Julia *Actor*
Innovative Artists, 1505 10th St, Santa Monica, CA 90401 USA

Benz, Julie *Actor*
William Morris Agency (WMA-LA), 1 William Morris Pl, Beverly Hills, CA 90212 USA

Benz, Sepp *Athlete*
Kiefernweg 37, Zurich, 8057, SWITZERLAND

Benza, AJ *Actor*
5670 Wilshire Blvd, #400W, Los Angeles, CA 90036 USA

Benzali, Daniel *Actor*
Diverse Talent Group, 1875 Century Park E #2250, Los Angeles, CA 90067 USA

Benzer, Seymour *Biologist*
2075 Robin Road, San Marino, CA 91108 USA

Benzi, Roberto
12 Villa Sainte Foy, Neuilly-sur-Seine, 92200, FRANCE

Benzinger, Todd *Baseball Player*
Boston Red Sox, 3502 Behymer Rd, Cincinnati, OH 45245-3104 USA

Beotti, Valentina *Actor*
Carol Levi Co, Via Giuseppe Pisanelli, Rome, 00196, ITALY

Beranek, Josef *Hockey Player*
Pittsburgh Penguins, Melton Arena, 66 Mario Lemieux Place, Pittsburgh, PA 15219 USA

Berberet, Lou *Baseball Player*
New York Yankees, 2500 Keppel Sands Dr, Las Vegas, NV 89134-7586 USA

Berblinger, Jeff *Baseball Player*
St Louis Cardinals, 102 Swanee Dr, Goddard, KS 67052-9420 USA

Bercaw, John E *Misc*
California Institute of Technology, Chemistry Dept, Pasadena, CA 91125 USA

Bercu, Michaeala
Habaal-Shem Tov #10--#93, Herzelia, SRAEL, 46342I

Bercu, Michaela *Model, Actor*
Habaal-Shem Tov #10, Apt 93, Herzelia, 46342, CANADA

Berdahl, Robert M *Educator*
University of California, Chancellor's Office, Berkeley, CA 94720 USA

Bere, Jason *Baseball Player*
Chicago White Sox, 101 Lowell St, Reading, MA 01867-2112 USA

Berenblum, Isaac *Doctor*
Weizmann Institute of Science, Pathology Dept, Rehovot, ISRAEL

Berendzen, Richard E *Educator*
1300 Crystal Dr, Arlington, VA 22202 USA

Berenger, Tom *Actor*
International Creative Management (ICM-LA), 8942 Wilshire Blvd, Beverly Hills, CA 90211 USA

Berenguer, Juan *Baseball Player*
New York Mets, 14347 Raymond Ln, Eden Prairie, MN 55347-4171 USA

Berenson, Ken (Red) *Coach, Hockey Player*
3555 Daleview Dr, Ann Arbor, MI 48105 USA

Berenyi, Bruce *Baseball Player*
Cincinnati Reds, 5630 Pacific Blvd Apt 816, Boca Raton, FL 33433-6712 USA

Beresford, Bruce *Director*
3 Marathon Road, #13 Darling Point, Sydney, NSW, AUSTRALIA

Beresford, Meg *Social Activist*
Wiston Lodge, Wiston, Biggar, ML12 6HT, SCOTLAND

Berezhnaya, Yelena *Figure Skater*
Ice House Skating Rink, 111 Midtown Bridge Approach, Hackensack, NJ 07601 USA

Berezin, Sergei *Hockey Player*
3200 N Military Trail #201, Boca Raton, FL 33431 USA

Berezovsky, Boris V *Musician*
IMG Artists, 3 Burlington Lane, Chiswick, London, W4 2TH, UNITED KINGDOM (UK)

Berezovy, Anatoli N *Cosmonaut*
Potchia Kosmonavtov, Moskovskoi Oblasti, Syvisdny Goroduk, 141160, RUSSIA

Berfield, Justin *Actor*
Reel Talent Management, 980 N Bundy, Los Angeles, CA 90049 USA

Berg, A Scott *Writer*
G P Putnam's Sons, 375 Hudson St, New York, NY 10014 USA

Berg, Aki-Petteri *Hockey Player*
Octagon, 1751 Pinnacle Dr, #1500, McLean, VA 22102 USA

Berg, Dave *Baseball Player*
Florida Marlins, 1917 Stonecastle Dr, Roanoke, TX 76262-4912 USA

Berg, Matraca *Musician*
Joe's Garage, 4405 Belmont Park Terr, Nashville, TN 37215 USA

Berg, Patrica J (Patty) *Golfer*
William Harvey, PO Box 1607, Fort Myers, FL 33902 USA

Berg, Patty
PO Box 1607, Fort Myers, FL 33902-1607

Berg, Paul *Nobel Prize Laureate*
Stanford University, Medical School, Beckman Center, Stanford, CA 94305 USA

Berg, Peter *Actor*
H S I Productions, 3630 Eastham Dr, Culver City, CA 90232 USA

Berg, Yehuda *Religious Leader*
Kabbalah Center International, 1066 S La Cienega Blvd, Los Angeles, CA 90035 USA

Berganza, Teresa *Opera Singer*
La Rossinlana Archanda 5, 28200 San Lorenzo del Escorial, Madrid, SPAIN

Berge, Francine *Actor*
Cineart, 36 Rue de Ponthiew, Paris, 75008, FRANCE

Berge, Ole M *Misc*
Maintenance of Way Brotherhood, 12050 Woodward Ave, Detroit, MI 48203 USA

Berge, Pierre V G *Business Person*
Yves Saint Laurent SA, 5 Ave Marceau, Paris, 75116, FRANCE

Bergen, Candice *Actor*
William Morris Agency (WMA-NY), 1325 Ave of the Americas, New York, NY 10019 USA

Bergen, Candice P *Actor*
222 Central Park South, New York, NY 10019 USA

Bergen, Frances *Actor*
1485 Carla Ridge Dr, Beverly Hills, CA 90210 USA

Bergen, Polly *Actor, Writer, Musician, Producer*
Jan McCormack, 1746 S Britain Rd, Southbury, CT 06488 USA

Berger, Brandon *Baseball Player*
Kansas City Royals, 99 W Orchard Rd, Ft Mitchell, KY 41011-2633 USA

Berger, Gerhard *Race Car Driver*
Berger Motorsport, Postfach 1121, Vaduz, 9490, AUSTRIA

Berger, Helmut *Actor*
Viale Parioli 50, Rome, 00197, ITALY

Berger, John *Writer*
Quincy, Mieussy, Taninges, 74440, FRANCE

Berger, Lee *Actor*
57 Fellows Dr, Brentwood, NH 03833 USA

Berger, Senta *Actor*
Sentana Films, Gebsattelstr 30, Munich, 81541, GERMANY

Berger, Thomas L *Writer*
PO Box 11, Palisades, NY 10964 USA

Bergeron, Michel *Coach*
CHL T630, 25 Rue Bryant, Sherbrooke QC, J1J 3Z5, CANADA

Bergeron, Peter *Baseball Player*
Montreal Expos, 13 Arnold Ln, Greenfield, MA 01301-9743 USA

Bergeron, Tom *Actor, Producer*
International Creative Management (ICM-LA), 8942 Wilshire Blvd, Beverly Hills, CA 90211 USA

Bergevin, Marc *Hockey Player*
409 S Bodin St, Hinsdale, IL 60521 USA

Bergey, John *Inventor*
1807 Mayflower Circle, Lancaster, PA 17603 USA

Bergey, William E (Bill) *Football Player*
2 Hickory Lane, Chadds Ford, PA 19317 USA

Berggren, Jenny *Musician*
Basic Music Mgmt, Norrtullsgatan 51, Stockholm, 113 45, SWEDEN

Berggren, Jonas *Musician*
Basic Music Mgmt, Norrtullsgatan 51, Stockholm, 11345, SWEDEN

Berggren, Malin *Musician*
Basic Music Mgmt, Norrtullsgatan 51, Stockholm, 11345, SWEDEN

Berggren, Thommy *Actor*
Swedish Film Institute, PO Box 27126, Stockholm, 102 52, SWEDEN

Bergi, Emily *Actor*
Innovative Artists, 1505 10th St, Santa Monica, CA 90401 USA

Bergin, Michael *Actor, Model*
300 Park Ave, #200, New York, NY 10010 USA

Bergin, Patrick *Actor*
Hyler Mgmt, 25 Sea Colony Dr, Santa Monica, CA 90405 USA

Bergkamp, Dennis *Soccer Player*
Arsenal FC, Arsenal Stadium, Avenell Road, London, N5 1BU, UNITED KINGDOM (UK)

Bergland, Robert S (Bob) *Secretary*
1104 7th Ave SE, Roseau, MN 56751 USA

Berglind (Icey) *Television Host*
E! Entertainment Television (LA), 5750 Wilshire Blvd, Los Angeles, CA 90036 USA

Berglund, Paavo A E *Conductor*
Munkkiniemenranta 41, Helsinki 33, 00330, FINLAND

Bergman, Alan *Musician*
714 N Maple Dr, Beverly Hills, CA 90210 USA

Bergman, Andrew C *Writer, Director*
555 W 57th St, #1230, New York, NY 10019 USA

Bergman, Arnfinn *Skier*
Nils Collett Vogtsv 58, Oslo 7, 0765, NORWAY

Bergman, Dave *Baseball Player*
New York Yankees, 728 Canterbury Ct, Grosse Pointe Woods, MI 48236-1294 USA

Bergman, Ingmar *Director*
Box 73, Farosund, 62036, SWEDEN

Bergman, Jaime
Writers & Artists Agency, 8383 Wilshire Blvd #550, Beverly Hills, CA 90211

Bergman, Marilyn K *Musician*
714 N Maple Dr, Beverly Hills, CA 90210 USA

Bergman, Martin *Producer*
641 Lexington Ave, New York, NY 10022 USA

Bergman, Peter *Actor*
4799 White Oak Ave, Encino, CA 91316 USA

Bergman, Robert G *Misc*
501 Coventry Road, Kensington, CA 94707 USA

Bergman, Sean *Baseball Player*
Detroit Tigers, 18405 jW Donohue Rd, Wilmington, IL 60481-8235 USA

Bergoglio, Jose Mario Cardinal *Religious Leader*
Arzobispado, Rivadavia 415, Buenos Aires, 1002, ARGENTINA

Bergomi, Giuseppe
via Trento 1, Settala (MI), ITALY, 20090

Bergonzi, Cario *Opera Singer*
I C M Artists, 40 W 57th St, New York, NY 10019 USA

Bergoust, Eric *Skier*
228 W Main, Missoula, MT 59802 USA

Bergquist, Curt *Doctor*
Allergon AB, Valinge 2090, Angelhoim, 262 92, SWEDEN

Bergsten, C Fred *Economist*
4106 Sleepy Hollow Road, Annandale, VA 22003 USA

Bergstrom, K Sune *Nobel Prize Laureate*
Karolinska Institute, Box 270, Stockholm, 17177, SWEDEN

Berio, Luciano
11 Colombaig Radiocobdoli, Siena, ITALY, 53100

Beristain, Gabriel L *Cinematographer*
United Talent Agency, 9560 Wilshire Blvd, #500, Beverly Hills, CA 90212 USA

Berkeley, Elizabeth *Actor, Model*
Handprint Entertainment, 8436 W 3rd St, Los Angeles, CA 90048 USA

Berkeley, Michael F *Composer*
Rogers Coleridge White, 20 Powis Mews, London, W11 1JN, UNITED KINGDOM (UK)

Berkeley, Xander *Actor*
Abrams Artists, 9200 Sunset Blvd #1125, Los Angeles, CA 90069 USA

Berkley, Elizabeth *Actor*
Innovative Artists (LA), 1505 Tenth St, Santa Monica, CA 90401 USA

Berkman, Lance *Baseball Player*
Houston Astros, 285 Bryn Mawr Cir, Houston, TX 77024-6811 USA

Berkoff, David *Swimmer*
Harvard University, Athletic Dept, Cambridge, MA 02138 USA

Berkowitz, Bob *Entertainer*
CNBC-TV, 2200 Fletcher Ave, Fort Lee, NJ 07024 USA

Berkus, Nate *Designer*
Nate Berkus Associates, 311 W Superior #110, Chicago, IL 60610

Berlant, Anthony (Tony) *Artist*
Los Angeles Louver Gallery, 55 N Venice Blvd, Venice, CA 90291 USA

Berlanti, Greg *Producer*
Everwood, 1000 West/2610 South, Salt Lake City, UT 84119 USA

Berlin, Clay *Publisher*
2935 Franciscan Way, Carmel, CA 93923 USA

Berlin, Mike *Bowler*
12 Coventry Lane, Muscatine, IA 52761 USA

Berlin, Steve *Musician*
Gold Mountain, 3575 Cahuenga Blvd W, #450, Los Angeles, CA 90068 USA

Berliner, Alain *Director*
United Talent Agency, 9560 Wilshire Blvd #500, Beverly Hills, CA 90212 USA

Berliner, Jane *Producer, Business Person*
Handprint Entertainment, 1100 Glendon Ave #1000, Los Angeles, CA 90024 USA

Berlinger, Warren *Actor*
10642 Arnel Place, Chatsworth, CA 91311 USA

Berlinsky, Dmitri *Musician*
35 W 64th St #7F, New York, NY 10023 USA

Berlioux, Daniel *Actor*
Cineart, 36 Rue de Ponthieu, Paris, 75008, FRANCE

Berlusconi, Silvio *Prime Minister*
Premier's Office, Palazzo Chigi, Piazza Colonna, Rome, 00187, ITALY

Berman, Andy *Actor*
Gersh Agency, The (LA), 232 N Canon Dr, Beverly Hills, CA 90210 USA

Berman, Boris *Musician*
Columbia Artists Mgmt Inc, 165 W 57th St, New York, NY 10019 USA

Berman, Chris *Sportscaster*
ESPN-TV, Sports Dept ESPN Plaza, 935 Middle St, Bristol, CT 06010 USA

Berman, Jennifer *Doctor*
University of California, Women's Sexual Health Center, Los Angeles, CA 90024 USA

Berman, Josh *Producer*
Jackoway Tyerman Wertheimer Austen Mandelbaum & Morris, 1888 Century Park E Fl 18, Los Angeles, CA 90067 USA

Berman, Laura *Doctor*
University of California, Women's Sexual Health Center, Los Angeles, CA 90024 USA

Berman, Lazar N *Musician*
World Touring Productions, 26 Middlesex Dr, Dix Hills, NY 11746 USA

Berman, Rick *Producer, Writer*
Rick Berman Productions, 5555 Melrose Ave, Cooper Bldg #232, Los Angeles, CA 90038 USA

Berman, Shari Springer *Director*
Creative Artists Agency LCC (CAA-LA), 9830 Wilshire Blvd, Beverly Hills, CA 90212 USA

Berman, Shelley *Actor, Comedian*
268 Bell Canyon Rd, Bell Canyon, CA 91307 USA

Bermudez, Gustavo *Actor*
Telefe - Argentina, Pavon 2444 (C1248AAT), Buenos Aires, ARGENTINA

Bern, Howard A *Biologist*
1010 Shattuck Ave, Berkeley, CA 94707 USA

Bernabei, Ray *Soccer Player*
541 Woodview Dr, Longwood, FL 32779 USA

Bernadotte, Princess Marianne
Villagatan 10, Stockholm, SWEDEN, S-11432

Bernadotte af Wisborg, Count Lennart
Insel Mainau, Konstanz, GERMANY, D-78465

Bernal, Gael Garcia *Actor*
Endeavor Talent Agency, 9701 Wilshire Blvd #1000, Beverly Hills, CA 90212 USA

Bernal, Vic *Baseball Player*
San Diego Padres, 4632 Abner St, Los Angeles, CA 90032-3847 USA

Bernard, Betsy *Business Person*
American Telephone & Telegraph Corp, 32 Ave of Americas, New York, NY 10013 USA

Bernard, Carlos *Actor*
CunninghamEscottDipene, 10635 Santa Monica Blvd #130, Los Angeles, CA 90025 USA

Bernard, Claire M A *Musician*
53 Rue Rabelais, Lyon, 69003, FRANCE

Bernard, Crystal *Actor, Musician, Songwriter*
Creative Artists Agency, 9830 Wilshire Blvd, Beverly Hills, CA 90212 USA

Bernard, Dwight *Baseball Player*
New York Mets, 5120 N Norwich Ln, Belle Rive, IL 62810-2703 USA

Bernard, Ed *Actor*
PO Box 7965, Northridge, CA 91327 USA

Bernard, Henry *Architect*
44 Av D'Ilena, Paris, 75116, FRANCE

Bernard, James
#1 Oakley Gardens Chelsea, London, ENGLAND, SW3 5QH

Bernard, Robyn
3227 Cardiff Ave, Los Angeles, CA 90034

Bernazard, Tony *Baseball Player*
Montreal Expos, Santa Av D-25 Urb Santa Elvira, Caguas, PR 00625 USA

Berner, Robert A *Misc*
15 Hickory Hill Road, North Haven, CT 06473 USA

Bernero, Adam *Baseball Player*
Detroit Tigers, 1231 Sibley Rd, Toledo, OH 43615-4660 USA

Bernero, Edward Allen *Writer*
Endeavor Agency LLC (LA), 9601 Wilshire Blvd Fl 3, Beverly Hills, CA 90210 USA

Berners-Lee, Timothy J *Scientist*
Massachusetts Institute of Technology, Computer Sci Lab, Cambridge, MA 02139 USA

Berney, Bob *President*
Newmarket Films, 597 5th Ave Fl 7, New York, NY 10017 USA

Bernhard, Ruth *Photographer*
2982 Clay St, San Francisco, CA 94115 USA

Bernhard, Sandra *Actor, Comedian, Musician*
9465 Wilshire Blvd, #308, Beverly Hills, CA 90212 USA

Bernhardt, Daniel *Actor*
6500 Wilshire Blvd #2200, Los Angeles, CA 90048

Bernhardt, Glenn R *Cartoonist*
PO Box 3772, Carmel, CA 93921 USA

Bernhardt, Juan *Baseball Player*
New York Yankees, Eduardo Brito 13, San Pedro de Macoris, Dominican Republic

Bernhardt, Kevin *Writer*
Lichter Grossman Nichols Adler & Goodman, 9200 Sunset Blvd #1200, Los Angeles, CA 90069 USA

Bernheim, Emmanuele *Writer*
Viking Press, 375 Hudson St, New York, NY 10014 USA

Bernheimer, Martin *Musician*
17350 Sunset Blvd, #702C, Pacific Palisades, CA 90272 USA

Bernier, Sylvie *Race Car Driver*
Olympic Assn, Cite du Harve, Montreal, QC H3C 3R4, CANADA

Berning, Susie Maxwell *Golfer*
1701 Rock Springs Dr, Las Vegas, NV 89128 USA

Bernsen, Corbin *Actor*
13535 Hatteras St, Van Nuys, CA 91401 USA

Bernstein, Besil *Misc*
90 Farquhar Road, Dulwich, SE19 1LT, UNITED KINGDOM (UK)

Bernstein, Carl *Journalist*
William Moris Agency, 151 El Camino Dr, Beverly Hills, CA 90212 USA

Bernstein, Carlc *Journalist*
2753 Ontario Road NW, Washington, DC 20009

Bernstein, Charles *Composer*
FMA, 6525 Sunset Blvd, #300, Los Angeles, CA 90028 USA

Bernstein, Jay *Producer, Director, Writer*
Jay Bernstein Productions, PO Box 1148, Beverly Hills, CA 90213

Bernstein, Kenny *Race Car Driver*
King Racing, 26231 Dimension Dr, Lake Forest, CA 92630 USA

Berov, Lyuben *Prime Minister*
Rights & Freedom Movement, Tzarigradsko Shosse 47/1, Sofia, 1408, BULGARIA

Berra, Dale *Baseball Player*
Pittsburgh Pirates, 19 Highland Ave, Montclair, NJ 07042-1909 USA

Berra, Lawrence P (Yogi) *Baseball Player*
New York Yankees, 19 Highland Ave, Montclair, NJ 07042-1909 USA

Berres, Ray *Baseball Player*
Brooklyn Dodgers, 111 Hawthorne Dr, Twin Lakes, WI 53181-9564 USA

Berresford, Susan V *Misc*
Ford Foundation, 320 E 43rd St, New York, NY 10017 USA

Berri, Claude *Director, Producer*
Renn Espace d'Art Contemporain, 7 Rue de Lille, Paris, 75007, FRANCE

Berridge, Elizabeth *Actor*
Judy Schoen, 606 N Larchmont Blvd, #309, Los Angeles, CA 90004 USA

Berridge, Michael J *Biologist*
13 Home Close, Histon, Cambridge, CB4 4JL, UNITED KINGDOM (UK)

Berrigan, Daniel *Social Activist*
220 W 98th St, #11L, New York, NY 10025 USA

Berruti, Livio *Social Activist*
Via Avigliana 45, Torino, 10138, ITALY

Berry, Bertice
Inner City Faith, PO Box 721244, San Diego, CA 92172-1244

Berry, Bill *Writer*
839 N Center St, Reno, NV 89501 USA

Berry, Bill *Musician*
REM/Athens Ltd, 170 College Ave, Athens, GA 30601 USA

Berry, Charles E (Chuck) *Musician, Songwriter*
Berry Park, 691 Buckner Rd, Wentzville, MO 63385 USA

Berry, Dave *Actor*
5139 Monticello Avenue, Dallas, TX 75206

Berry, David *Actor*
5903 Winton St, Dallas, TX 75206 USA

Berry, Halle *Actor, Model*
Image Public Relations, 8721 Sunset Blvd #208, Los Angeles, CA 90069 USA

Berry, Jim *Cartoonist*
United Feature Syndicate, 200 Madison Ave, New York, NY 10016 USA

Berry, John *Musician*
Firstars Mgmt, 14724 Ventura Blvd, #PH, Sherman Oaks, CA 91403 USA

Berry, Ken *Actor*
13911 Fenton Ave, Sylmar, CA 91342 USA

Berry, Kevin *Swimmer*
28 George St, Manly, NSW, 2295, AUSTRALIA

Berry, Michael J *Misc*
PO Box 1421, Pebble Beach, CA 93953
USA

Berry, R Stephen *Misc*
5317 S University Ave, Chicago, IL 60615
USA

Berry, Raymond E *Football Player,
Football Coach*
1972 Montane Dr E, Golden, CO 80401
USA

Berry, Robert V (Bob) *Hockey Player,
Coach*
640 3rd St, Hermosa Beach, CA 90254
USA

Berry, Stephen J (Steve) *Journalist*
6527 Ellenview Ave, West Hills, CA
91307 USA

Berry, Vincent *Actor*
Academy Kids Mgmt, 4942 Vineland Ave
#103, North Hollywood, CA 91601 USA

Berry, Wendell E *Writer*
River Road, Port Royal, KY 40058 USA

Berryman, Michael *Actor*
PO Box 1746, Middletown, CA 95461
USA

Bersia, John *Journalist*
Orlando Sentinel, Editorial Dept, 633 N
Orange Ave, Orlando, FL 32801 USA

Bertelmann, Fred
Am Hohenberg 9, Berg/Starnberger -See
Y, GERMAN, D-82335

Berteotti, Missy *Golfer*
3221 Annandale Dr, Preston, PA 15142
USA

Berthold, Helmut *Misc*
Meyerstr 21, Hamburg, 21075,
GERMANY

Bertie, Diego *Musician*
Gabriel Blanco Iglesias (Mexico), Rio
Balsas 35-32, Colonia Cuauhtemoc, DF,
06500, Mexico

Bertil *Prince*
Hert Av Halland, Kungl Slottel,
Stockholm, 1130, SWEDEN

Bertinelli, Valerie *Actor*
1850 Pleasant St, Walla Walla, WA 99362
USA

Bertini, Catherine *Misc*
United Nations, 1 United Nations Plaza,
New York, NY 10017 USA

Bertolucci, Bernardo *Actor*
Via Della Lungara 3, Rome, 00165, ITALY

Berton, Pierre *Historian*
Pierre Berton Enterprises, 21 Sackville St,
Toronto, ON M5A 3E1, CANADA

Bertone, Tarcisco Cardinal *Religious
Leader*
Archdiocese Piazza Matteotti 4, Genoa,
16123, ITALY

Berzon, Marsha S *Judge*
US Court of Appeals, Court Building, 95
7th St, San Francisco, CA 94103 USA

Bess, Daniel *Actor*
Anonymous Content, 8522 National Blvd
#101, Culver City, CA 90232 USA

Bessillieu, Donald A (Don) *Football Player*
4787 Gardiner Dr, Columbus, GA 31907
USA

Bessmertnova, Natalia *Ballerina*
Sretenskii Blvd 6/1, #9, Moscow, 101000,
RUSSIA

Bessmertnykh, Aleksandr *Government
Official*
Yelizarova Str 10, Moscow, 103064,
RUSSIA

Besson, Luc *Director*
CBC, 11 Rue de la Croix Boissee,
Mennecy, 91540, FRANCE

Best, George *Soccer Player, Sportscaster*
British Sky Broadcasting, Grant Way,
Middlesex, TW7 5QD, UNITED
KINGDOM (UK)

Best, James *Actor*
PO Box 621027, Oviedo, FL 32762 USA

Best, John O *Soccer Player*
1065 Lomita Ave, Harbor City, CA 90710
USA

Best, Kevin
PO Box 1164, Hesperia, CA 92345

Best, Pete *Musician*
8 Hymans Green, W Derby, Liverpool,
12, UNITED KINGDOM (UK)

Best, Travis *Basketball Player*
703 Bradley Road, Springfield, MA 01109
USA

Bestar, Maria *Musician*
Sony Music Miami, 605 Lincoln Rd,
Miami Beach, FL 33138 USA

Bestwicke, Martine *Actor*
Goldey Co, 1156 S Carmelia Ave #B, Los
Angeles, CA 90049 USA

Beswicke, Martine *Actor*
Goldey Co, 1156 S Carmelina Ave, #8,
Los Angeles, CA 90049 USA

Betancurt, Natalia *Actor*
TV Caracol, Calle 76 #11 - 35, Piso
10AA, Bogota DC, 26484, COLOMBIA

Bethe, Hans A *Nobel Prize Laureate*
324 Savage Farm Dr, Ithaca, NY 14850
USA

Bethea, Elvin L *Football Player*
16211 Leslie Lane, Missouri City, TX
77489 USA

Bethune, Patricia *Actor*
Impact Artists Group LLC, 10508 La
Maida St, Toluca Woods, CA 91601 USA

Bethune, Zina *Actor*
3096 Lake Hollywood Dr, Los Angeles,
CA 90068 USA

Bettany, Paul *Actor*
Personal Management Company, 425 N
Robertson Dr, Los Angeles, CA 90048
USA

Bettenhausen, Gary *Race Car Driver*
2741 Chesterfield Dr, Bettendori, IA
52722 USA

Betters, Doug L *Football Player*
3352 E Lakeshore Dr, Whitefish, MT
59937 USA

Bettis, Angela *Actor*
1122 S Roxbury Dr, Los Angeles, CA
90035 USA

Bettis, Jerome A *Football Player*
17600 Fairway Dr, Detroit, MI 48221
USA

Bettman, Gary B *Misc*
National Hockey League, 1251 Ave of
Americas, New York, NY 10020 USA

Betts, Austin W *General*
6414 View Point, San Antonio, TX 78229
USA

Betts, Dickey *Musician*
Intrepid Artists, Midtown Plz, 1300 Baxter
St #405, Charlotte, NC 28204 USA

Betts, Dickie *Musician*
FreeFalls, PO Box 604, Chagrin Falls, OH
44022 USA

Betts, Katherine *Editor*
Harper's Bazaar, Editorial Dept, 1770
Broadway, New York, NY 10019 USA

Betz Addie, Pauline *Tennis Player*
18560 SE Wood Haven Lane, #F,
Tequesta, FL 33469 USA

Beuchel, Ted *Musician*
Variety Artists, 1924 Spring St, Paso
Robles, CA 93446 USA

Beueriein, Stephen T (Steve) *Football
Player*
15624 McCullers Court, Chariotte, NC
28277 USA

Beutel, Bill *Commentator*
WABC-TV, News Dept, 7 Lincoln Square,
New York, NY 10023 USA

Beutler, Ernest *Doctor*
2707 Costebelle Dr, La Jolla, CA 92037
USA

Bevan, Timothy H *Financier*
Barclay's Bank, 54 Lombard St, London,
EC3P 3AH, UNITED KINGDOM (UK)

Beverley, Frankie *Musician*
115 Cherokee Rose Lane, Fairburn, GA
30213 USA

Beverley, Nick *Coach, Hockey Player*
Chicago Blackhawks, United Center, 1901
W Madison St, Chicago, IL 60612 USA

Bevill, Lisa *Musician*
Jeff Roberts, 206 Bluebird Dr,
Goodlettsville, TN 37072 USA

Bevington, Terry P *Baseball Player, Misc*
2600 Halle Parkway, Collierville, TN
38017 USA

Bevis, Leslie *Actor*
Epstein-Wyckoff, 280 S Beverly Dr #400,
Beverly Hills, CA 90212 USA

Bewkes, Jeff *Business Person*
Time Warner, 75 Rockefeller Plaza, New
York, NY 10019 USA

Bey, Andy *Musician*
Megaforce Entertainment, PO Box 779,
New Hope, PA 18938 USA

Bey, Richard *Entertainer*
445 Park Ave #1000, New York, NY
10022 USA

Bey, Turhan *Actor*
Paradisgasse Ave 47, Vienna, XIX, 1190,
AUSTRIA

Beyer, Brad *Actor*
William Morris Agency (WMA-NY), 1325
Ave of the Americas, New York, NY
10019 USA

Beyer, Frank M *Composer*
Sohtstra 6, Berlin, 12203, GERMANY

Beyer, Troy *Actor*
Don Buchwald, 6500 Wilshire Blvd, #2200, Los Angeles, CA 90048 USA

Beymer, Richard *Actor*
1818 N Fuller Ave, Los Angeles, CA 90046 USA

Beyonce *Musician*
Columbia Records, 2100 Colorado Ave, Santa Monica, CA 90404 USA

Bezos, Jeff *Business Person*
Amazon.com, PO Box 81226, Seattle, WA 98108 USA

BG *Musician*
JL Entertainment Inc, 18653 Ventura Blvd, #340, Tarzana, CA 91356

Bhagwan *Actor, Bollywood*
25 Lallubhai Mansion Shankarrao Palav Marg, Mumbai, MS 400014, INDIA

Bhagwati, Jagdish N *Economist*
Columbia University, Economics Dept, New York, NY 10027 USA

Bhagyashree *Actor, Bollywood*
96/B Hirak Society, SV Rd Vile Parle, Mumbai, MS 400056, INDIA

Bhan Bhagta Gurung *War Hero*
Victoria Cross Assn, Old Admiralty Building, London, SW1A 2BL, UNITED KINGDOM (UK)

Bhanu, Prakash (Bharathan) *Actor*
12/2 Circular Road United India Colony, Kodambakkam, Chennai, TN 600 024, INDIA

Bhanupriya *Actor, Bollywood*
4 1st Cross Street, Vijayaraghava Road, Chennai, TN 600017, INDIA

Bhatnagar, Deepti *Actor, Bollywood*
42 Ashok Apts, Gandhigram Road Juhu, Mumbai, MS 400049, INDIA

Bhatnagar, Dipti *Actor, Bollywood*
42 Ashoka Apts, Gandhigram Rd Juhu, Mumbai, MS 400049, INDIA

Bhatt, Mahesh *Director, Bollywood, Filmmaker*
205 Silver Beach Apartments, Near Sun-N-Sand Hotel Juhu, Bombay, MS 400049, INDIA

Bhatt, Mukesh *Director, Filmmaker, Producer, Bollywood*
10 Shubh Jeevan Co-op Society, JVPD Scheme, Bombay, MS 400 049, INDIA

Bhattacharya, Basu *Actor, Bollywood, Director*
36 Carter Road Bandra, Mumbai, MS 400050, INDIA

Bhattarai, Krishna Prasad *Prime Minister*
Nepali Congress Central Office, Baneshwar, Kathmandu, NEPAL

Bhave, Ashwini *Actor, Bollywood*
A-9 Green View, Suburban Soc Shiv Shrushti, Mumbai, MS 400024, INDIA

Bhumibol, Adulyadej *King*
Royal Residence, Chirtalad a Villa, Bangkok, THAILAND

Biafra, Jello
PO Box 419092, San Francisco, CA 94141

Biagiotti, Laura *Fashion Designer*
Studio Biagiotti, Via Borgopesco 19, Milan, 20121, ITALY

Biakabutuka, Tshimanga (Tim) *Football Player*
Carolina Panthers, Ericsson Stadium, 800 S Mint St, Charlotte, NC 28202 USA

Bialik, Mayim *Actor*
Coppage Co, 5411 Camelia Ave, North Hollywood, CA 91601 USA

Biancalana, Buddy *Baseball Player*
7901 30th Ave N, St Petersburg, FL 33710 USA

Bianchi, Rosa Maria *Actor*
Televisa, Blvd Adolfo Lopez Mateos 232, Colonia San Angel INN, DF, CP 01060, MEXICO

Bianchl, Alfred (Al) *Basketball Player, Coach*
Miami Heat, American Airlines Arena, 601 Biscayne Blvd, Miami, FL 33132 USA

Biasucci, Dean *Football Player*
3355 Allegheny Court, Westlake Village, CA 91362 USA

Bibb, John *Writer*
Nashville Tennessean, Editorial Dept, 1100 Broadway, Nashville, TN 37203 USA

Bibb, Laslie *Actor*
9615 Brighton Way, #300, Beverly Hills, CA 90210 USA

Bibb, Leslie *Actor*
International Creative Management (ICM-LA), 8942 Wilshire Blvd, Beverly Hills, CA 90211 USA

Bibby, Mike *Basketball Player*
Sacramento Kings, Arco Arena, 1 Sports Parkway, Sacramento, CA 95834 USA

Bichette, A Dante *Baseball Player*
4207 S Atlantic Ave, #2S, New Smyrna, FL 32169 USA

Bickerstaff, Bernard T (Bernie) *Coach*
Charlotte Bobcats, 129 W Trade St, #700, Charlotte, NC 28202 USA

Bidart, Frank *Writer*
Wellesley College, English Dept, 106 Central St, Wellesley, MA 02481 USA

Biddle, Adrian *Cinematographer*
Whitelands, Saint George Hill Weybridge, Surrey, KT13 0LB, UNITED KINGDOM (UK)

Biddle, Martin *Archaeologist*
19 Hamilton Road, Oxford, OX2 7OY, UNITED KINGDOM (UK)

Biddle, Melvin E *War Hero*
918 Essex Dr, Anderson, IN 46013 USA

Bidwell, Charles E *Misc*
5835 S Kimbark Ave, Chicago, IL 60637 USA

Bieber, Owen F *Misc*
United Auto Workers Union, 8000 E Jefferson Ave, Detroit, MI 48214 USA

Biebl-Prelevic, Heidi *Skier*
Haus Olympia, Oberstaufen, 87534, GERMANY

Biederman, Charles J *Artist*
5840 Collischan Road, Red Wing, MN 55066 USA

Biegler, David W *Business Person*
Texas Utilities Co, Energy Plaza, 1601 Bryan St, Dallas, TX 75201 USA

Biehn, Michael *Actor*
11220 Valley Spring Lane, North Hollywood, CA 91602 USA

Bieka, Silverstre Siale *Prime Minister*
Prime Minister's Office, Malabo, EQUATORIAL GUINEA

Biel, Jessica *Actor*
Creative Artists Agency, 9830 Wilshire Blvd., Beverly Hills, CA 90212 USA

Bielecki, J Krzysztof *Prime Minister*
Urzad Rady Ministrow, Al Ujazdowskie 9, Warsaw, 00-918, POLAND

Biellmann, Denise *Figure Skater*
Im Brachli 25, Zurich, 8053, SWITZERLAND

Bien, Fijate *Musician*
William Morris Agency (WMA-LA), 1 William Morris Pl, Beverly Hills, CA 90212 USA

Bienen, Andy *Writer*
United Talent Agency (UTA), 9560 Wilshire Blvd, Beverly Hills, CA 90212 USA

Bieniemy, Eric *Football Player*
325 Westwood Plaza, Los Angeles, CA 90095 USA

Bierko, Craig *Actor, Musician*
Talent Entertainment Group, 9111 Wilshire Blvd, Beverly Hills, CA 90210 USA

Bies, Don *Golfer*
1262 NW Blakely Court, Seattle, WA 98177 USA

Bies Susan, Schmidt *Government Official*
Federal Reserve Board, 20th St & Constitution Ave, Washington, DC 20551 USA

Bieshu, Mariya L *Opera Singer*
24 Pushkin Str, Chisinau, 2012, MOLDOVA

Bietila, Walter *Skier*
General Delivery, Iron Mountain, MI 49801 USA

Biffen, John *Government Official*
Tanat House, Llanyblodwel Oswestry, Shropshire, SY10 8NQ, UNITED KINGDOM (UK)

Biffi, Giacomo Cardinal *Religious Leader*
Archdiocese of Bologna, Via Altabella 6, Bologna, 40126, ITALY

Biffle, Greg *Race Car Driver*
122 Knob Hill Road, Mooresville, NC 28117 USA

Biffle, Jerome *Track Athlete*
3205 Monaco Parkway, Denver, CO 80207 USA

Big, Boi *Musician*
Family Tree Entertainment, 135 E 57th St, #2600, New York, NY 10022 USA

Big Bad Voodoo Daddy
Creative Artists Agency LCC (CAA-LA), 9830 Wilshire Blvd, Beverly Hills, CA 90212 USA

Big Blue, The *Music Group*
Pop Idol (Fremantle Media), 2700 Colorado Ave #450, Santa Monica, CA 90404 USA

Big Dismal *Music Group*
Wind-up Records, 72 Madison Ave, New York, NY 10016 USA

Big Tymers *Music Group*
International Creative Management (ICM-LA), 8942 Wilshire Blvd, Beverly Hills, CA 90211 USA

Bigeleisen, Jacob *Misc*
PO Box 217, Saint James, NY 11780 USA

Bigelow, Kathryn *Director*
Creative Artists Agency, 9830 Wilshire Blvd, Beverly Hills, CA 90212 USA

Bigelow, Tom
RR #1Box 158A, Winchester, IN 47394

Biggerstaff, Sean *Actor*
International Creative Management (ICM-UK), Oxford House, 76 Oxford St, London, W1N OAX, UNITED KINGDOM (UK)

Bigglo, Craig A *Baseball Player*
6520 Belmont St, Houston, TX 77005 USA

Biggs, Jason *Actor*
Innovative Artists, 1505 10th St, Santa Monica, CA 90401 USA

Biggs, John H *Business Person*
240 E 47th St, #47D, New York, NY 10017 USA

Biggs, Peter M
Willows, London Road, Saint Ives, Huntingdon Cam, PE17 4ES, UNITED KINGDOM (UK)

Biggs, Ronald
201 rue Monte Alegre Santa Teresa, Rio de Janeiro, BRAZIL

Biggs-Dawson, Roxann *Actor*
Innovative Artists, 1505 10th St, Santa Monica, CA 90401 USA

Biggs-Dawson, Rozann
Innovative Artists (LA), 1505 Tenth St, Santa Monica, CA 90401 USA

Bigley, Thomas J *Admiral*
1329 Carpers Ferry Way, Vienna, VA 22182 USA

Bignotti, George *Race Car Driver*
9413 Steeplehill Dr, Las Vegas, NV 89117 USA

Bijan *Fashion Designer*
420 N Rodeo Dr, Beverly Hills, CA 90210 USA

Bikel, Theodore *Actor*
94 Honey Hill Rd, Wilton, CT 06897 USA

Bila, Lucie *Actor, Musician*
Theate Ta Fantastika, Karlova UI 8, Prague 1, 110 00, CZECH REPUBLIC

Bilal *Musician*
Creative Artists Agency, 9830 Wilshire Blvd, Beverly Hills, CA 90212 USA

Bilderback, Nicole *Actor*
Lloyd and Kass Entertainment, 10202 W Washington Blvd, Bldg Astaire 2210, Culver City, CA 90232 USA

Bildt, Carl *Prime Minister*
Svenges Riksdag, Stockholm, 10012, SWEDEN

Biletnikoff, Frederick (Fred) *Football Player, Coach*
516 Iris Lane, San Ramon, CA 94583 USA

Bilheimer, Robert S *Religious Leader*
15256 Knightwood Road, Cold Spring, MN 56320 USA

Bill, Tony *Actor, Director, Producer*
Market Street Productions, 73 Market St, Venice, CA 90291 USA

Billick, Brian *Football Player*
Baltimore Ravens, 11001 Owings Mills Blvd, Owings Mills, MD 21117

Billie *Musician*
CIA, Concorde House, 101 Sherpherds Bush Road, London, W6 7LP, UNITED KINGDOM (UK)

Billingham, John E (Jack) *Baseball Player*
8945 Lake Irma Pointe, Orlando, FL 32817 USA

Billings, Earl *Actor*
Artists Group (LA), 10100 Santa Monica Blvd #2490, Los Angeles, CA 90067 USA

Billings, Marland P *Misc*
Westside Road, RFD, North Conway, NH 03860 USA

Billingslea, Beau *Actor*
6025 Sepulveda Blvd, #201, Van Nuys, CA 91411 USA

Billingsley, Barbara *Actor, Model*
Cosden, 129 W Wilson St, #202, Costa Mesa, CA 92627 USA

Billingsley, Hobie *Coach*
746 PePPerridge Dr, Bloomington, IN 47401 USA

Billingsley, John *Actor*
Don Buchwald & Associates Inc (LA), 6500 Wilshire Blvd #2200, Los Angeles, CA 90048 USA

Billingsley, John *Actor*
AKA Talent Agency, 6310 San Vicente Blvd #200, Los Angeles, CA 90048 USA

Billingsley, Peter
9028 Sunset Blvd PH #1, Los Angeles, CA 90069

Billingsley, Ray *Cartoonist*
King Features Syndicate, 888 7th Ave, New York, NY 10106 USA

Billington, David P *Engineer*
45 Hodge Road, Princeton, NJ 08540 USA

Billington, Kevin *Director*
33 Courtnell St, London, W2 5BU, UNITED KINGDOM (UK)

Billups, Chauncey *Basketball Player*
Detroit Pistons, Palace, 2 Championship Dr, Aubum Hills, CA 91604 USA

Billy Vera and the Beaters *Music Group*
Agency for the Performing Arts (APA-LA), 9200 Sunset Blvd #900, Los Angeles, CA 90069 USA

Bilson, Bruce *Director*
Downwind Enterprices, 12505 Sarah St, Studio City, CA 91604 USA

Bilson, Malcolm *Musician*
132 N Sunset Dr, Ithaca, NY 14850 USA

Bilson, Rachel *Actor*
Creative Artists Agency LCC (CAA-LA), 9830 Wilshire Blvd, Beverly Hills, CA 90212 USA

Binchy, Maeve *Writer*
Irish Times, 11-15 D'Olier St, Dublin, 2, Ireland

Binder, John *Religious Leader*
North American Baptist Conference, 1S210 Summit, Oakbrook Terrace, IL 60181 USA

Binder, Mike *Actor, Director, Writer*
Three Arts Entertainment, 9460 Wishire Blvd, #700, Beverly Hills, CA 90212 USA

Binder, Theodor *Physicist*
Taos Canyon, Taos, NM 87571 USA

Bindu *Actor, Bollywood*
C1-2 Eden Hall Opp Lotus Cinema, Worli, Mumbai, MS 400018, INDIA

Bindugosh *Actor, Bollywood*
76A 1st Cross Street, Ventatesa Nagar, Chennai, TN 600093, INDIA

Bing, David (Dave) *Basketball Player*
Bing Manufacturing, 1111 Rosedale Ct, Detroit, MI 48211 USA

Bing, Jonathan
Trident Media Group LLC, 41 Madison Ave Fl 33, New York, NY 10010 USA

Bingham, Barry Jr *Editor, Publisher*
Louisville Courier Journal & Times, 525 W Broadway, Louisville, KY 40202 USA

Bingham, Gregory R (Greg) *Football Player*
3710 W Valley Dr, Missouri City, TX 77459 USA

Bingham, Traci *Actor, Model*
Vincent Cirrincione, 8721 Sunset Blvd, #205, Los Angeles, CA 90069 USA

Binkley, Gregg *Actor*
Artists Group (LA), 10100 Santa Monica Blvd #2490, Los Angeles, CA 90067 USA

Binkley, Leslie J (Les) *Hockey Player*
RR 3, Main Station, Hanover, ON N4N 3B9, CANADA

Binmore, Kenneth G *Economist*
Newsmills, Whitebrooks, Monmouth, Gwent, NP5 4TY, UNITED KINGDOM (UK)

Binnig, Gerd K *Nobel Prize Laureate*
IBM Research Laboratory, Saumerstr 4, Ruschlikon, 8803, SWITZERLAND

Binns, Malcolm *Musician*
233 Court Road, Orpington, Kent, BR6 9BY, UNITED KINGDOM (UK)

Binoche, Juliette *Actor*
United Talent Agency (UTA), 9560 Wilshire Blvd, Beverly Hills, CA 90212 USA

Binoche, Juliette *Actor*
Artmedia, 20 Ave Rapp, Paris, 75007, FRANCE

Bintley, David *Choreographer*
Royal Ballet, Covent Garden, Bow St, London, WC2E 9DD, UNITED KINGDOM (UK)

Biondi, Frank J Jr *Business Person*
Seagram Co, 1430 Peel St, Monstreal, QC, H3A 1S9, CANADA

Biondi, Matthew N (Matt) *Swimmer*
Nicholas A Biondi, 1404 Rimer Dr,
Moraga, CA 94556 USA

Birch, L Charles *Misc*
5A/73 Yarranabbe Road, Darling Point,
NSW, 2027, AUSTRALIA

Birch, Stanley F Jr *Judge*
US Court of Appeals, 56 Forsyth St NW,
Atlanta, GA 30303 USA

Birch, Thora *Actor*
Creative Artists Agency, 9830 Wilshire
Blvd, Beverly Hills, CA 90212 USA

Birchard, Bruce *Religious Leader*
Friends General Conference, 1216 Arch
St, Philadelphia, PA 19107 USA

Birck, Michael J *Business Person*
Tellabs Inc, 1415 W Diehl Road,
Naperville, IL 60563 USA

Bird, Antonia *Director*
International Creative Mgmt, 76 Oxford
St, London, W1N 0AX, UNITED
KINGDOM (UK)

Bird, Brad *Director, Writer*
Creative Artists Agency LCC (CAA-LA),
9830 Wilshire Blvd, Beverly Hills, CA
90212 USA

Bird, Caroline *Writer, Social Activist*
60 Grammercy Park, New York, NY
10010 USA

Bird, Forrest M *Inventor*
212 N Cerritos Dr, Palm Springs, CA
92262 USA

Bird, Larry *Athlete, Basketball Player*
6278 North Federal Hwy, Suite 298, Ft
Lauderdale, FL 33308 USA

Bird, Larry J *Basketball Player, Coach*
Indiana Pacers, Conseco Fieldhouse, 125
S Pennsylvania, Indianapolis, IN 46204
USA

Bird, Lester B *Prime Minister*
Prime Minister's Office, Factory Road,
Saint John's, ANTIGUA

Bird, R Byron *Engineer*
University of Wisconsin, Chemical
Engineering Dept, Madison, WI 53706
USA

Bird, Sue *Basketball Player*
Seatle Storm, Key Arena, 351 Elliot Ave W
#500, Seattle, WA 98119 USA

Bird, Thora *Actor*
Old Loft 21 Leinster Mews, Lancaster
Gate, London, W2, UNITED KINGDOM
(UK)

Bird, Vicki
PO Box 428, Portland, TN 37148-0428

Birdsong, Carl *Football Player*
1807 Clubview Dr, Amarillo, TX 79124
USA

Birdsong, Otis *Basketball Player*
3202 Farrow Ave, Kansas City, KS 66104
USA

Birk, Roger E *Business Person*
Federal National Mortgage Assn, 3900
Wilconsin Ave NW, Washington, DC
20016 USA

Birkavs, Valdis *Prime Minister*
Foreign Affairs Ministry, Brivbas Blvd 36,
Riga, 1395, LATVIA

Birkell, Lauren *Actor*
Evolution Entertainment, 901 N Highland
Ave, Los Angeles, CA 90038 USA

Birkerts, Gunnar *Architect*
Gunnar Birkets Assoc, 28105 Greenfield
Road, Southfield, MI 48076 USA

Birkett, Zoe *Musician*
Pop Idol (Fremantle Media), 2700
Colorado Ave #450, Santa Monica, CA
90404 USA

Birkin, Jane *Actor*
Cineart, 36 Rue de Ponthieu, Paris,
75008, FRANCE

Birkitt, Stephanie
Late Show with David Letterman, 1697
Broadway, 11th Floor, New York, NY
10019 USA

Birman, Len *Actor*
Michael Mann talent, 617 S Olive St,
#311, Los Angeles, CA 90014 USA

Birmingham, Stephen *Writer*
Brandt & Brandt, 1501 Broadway, New
York, NY 10036 USA

Birney, David *Actor*
20 Ocean Park Blvd, #118, Santa Monica,
CA 90405 USA

Birney, Earle *Writer*
1204-130 Carlton St, Toronto, ON M5A
4K3, CANADA

Birney, Frank *Actor*
Bauman Redanty & Shaul Agency, 5757
Wilshire Blvd #473, Los Angeles, CA
90036 USA

Birren, James E *Misc*
University of California, Borun
Gerontology Center, Los Angeles, CA
90024 USA

Birtwistle, Harrison *Composer*
Allied Artists, 42 Montpelier Square,
London, SW7 1JZ, UNITED KINGDOM
(UK)

Bisher, J Furman *Writer*
431 Lester Road, Fayetteville, GA 30215
USA

Bishop, Ed *Actor*
29 Sunbury Court Island, Sunbury-on-
Thames, Middx, TW16 5PP, UNITED
KINGDOM (UK)

Bishop, Elvin *Musician*
DeLeon Artists, 4031 Panama Court,
Piedmont, CA 94611 USA

Bishop, J Michael *Nobel Prize Laureate*
University of California, Hooper
Foundation, San Francisco, CA 94143
USA

Bishop, Joey *Actor, Comedian*
534 Via Lido Nord, Newport Beach, CA
92660 USA

Bishop, Kevin *Actor*
Gavin Barker Assoc, 2D Wimpole St,
London, W1G 0EB, UNITED KINGDOM
(UK)

Bishop, Michael *Football Player*
PO Box 168, 113 Philpot St, Willis, TX
77378 USA

Bishop, Robert R *Business Person*
Silicon Graphics, 1600 Amphitheatre
Parkway, Mountain View, CA 94043 USA

Bishop, Stephen *Musician, Songwriter*
2310 Apollo Dr, Los Angeles, CA 90046
USA

Bisoglio, Val *Actor*
House of Representatives, 400 S Beverly
Dr, #101, Beverly Hills, CA 90212 USA

Bisplinghoff, Raymond L *Engineer*
Tyco Laboratories, 273 Corporate Dr,
#100, Portsmouth, NH 03801 USA

Bissell, Charles O *Editor, Cartoonist*
1006 Tower Place, Nashville, TN 37204
USA

Bissell, Charles P (Phil) *Cartoonist*
Cartoon Corner, 4 Cross Hill Circle,
Forestdale, MA 02644 USA

Bissell, Jean G *Judge*
US Court of Appeals, 717 Madison Place
NW, Washington, DC 20439 USA

Bissell, Mina J *Physicist*
Lawrence Berkeley Laboratory, 1
Cyclotron Road, Berkeley, CA 94720 USA

Bisset, Jacqueline *Actor*
1815 Benedict Canyon Dr, Beverly Hills,
CA 90210 USA

Bissett, Josie *Actor*
8033 Sunset Blvd, #4048, West
Hollywood, CA 90046 USA

Bista, Kirti Nidhi *Prime Minister*
Gyaneshawor, Kathmandu, NEPAL

Bittinger, Ned *Designer*
410 Graham Ave, Santa Fe, NM 87501
USA

Bittle, Ryan *Actor*
Hollander Talent, 3518 Cahuenga Blvd,
#103, Los Angeles, CA 90068 USA

Bittner, Armin *Skier*
Rauchbergstr 30, Izell, 83334, GERMANY

Biya, Paul *President*
Palais Presidentiel, Rue de L'Exploration,
Yaounde, CAMEROON REPUBLIC

Bizkit, Limp *Music Group*
Creative Artists Agency LCC (CAA-LA),
9830 Wilshire Blvd, Beverly Hills, CA
90212 USA

Bizzy, Bone *Artist, Musician*
Creatice Artists Agency, 9830 Wilshire
Blvd, Beverly Hills, CA 90212 USA

Bjarni V, Tryggvason *Astronaut*
Space Agency, 6767 Route de Aeroport,
Saint Hubert, QC, J3Y 8Y9, CANADA

Bjedov-Gabrilo, Djurdjica *Swimmer*
Brace Santini 33, 5800 Split, Serbia &
Montenegro, SERBIA & MONTENEGRO

Bjorge, Jamie
10061 Riverside Dr, Box 113, Toluca
Lake, CA 91602

Bjork *Musician, Songwriter, Actor*
16 Rue des Fosses Saint Jacques, Paris,
75007, FRANCE

Bjork, Anita *Actor*
AB Baggensgatan 9, Stockholm, 111 31,
SWEDEN

Bjorklund, Anders *Doctor*
University of Lund, Neurology Dept,
Lund, SWEDEN

Bjorkman, Jonas *Tennis Player*
Octagon, 1751 Pinnacle Dr, #1500,
McLean, VA 22102 USA

Bjorkman, Olle E *Biologist*
3040 Greer Road, Palo Alto, CA 94303
USA

Bjorlin, Nadia *Actor*
Days of Our Lives, 3000 W Alameda Ave,
Burbank, CA 91523 USA

Blachnik, Gabriele *Fashion Designer*
Blachnik Gabriele KG, Marstallstr 8,
Munich, 80539, GERMANY

Black, Alex *Actor*
Innovative Artists (LA), 1505 Tenth St,
Santa Monica, CA 90401 USA

Black, Barbara A *Attorney General,
Educator*
Columbia University, Law School, 435 W
116th St, New York, NY 10027 USA

Black, Bibi *Musician*
Columbia Artists Mgmt Inc, 165 W 57th
St, New York, NY 10019 USA

Black, Brantley *Actor*
Cinema Talent Agency, 2609 W Wyoming
Ave #A, Burbank, CA 91505

Black, Carole *Business Person*
Lifetime Entertainment, 39 W 49th St,
New York, NY 10112 USA

Black, Cathleen P *Publisher*
Hearst Corp, Magazine Division, 250 W
55th St, New York, NY 10019 USA

Black, Cilla *Actor, Musician*
Bobsons Productions, 10 Abbet Orchard
St, London, SW1P 2JP, UNITED
KINGDOM (UK)

Black, Claudia *Actor*
Farscape, PO Box 20726, New York, NY
10023-1488 USA

Black, Clint *Musician, Songwriter*
Flitzgerald-Hartley, 1908 Wedgewood
Ave, Nashville, TN 37212 USA

Black, Conrad M *Publisher*
1 Canada Square, Canary Wharf, London,
E14 5DT, UNITED KINGDOM (UK)

Black, David *Producer, Writer*
Parseghian/Planco LLC, 23 E 22nd St Fl 3,
New York, NY 10010 USA

Black, Jack *Actor, Musician, Comedian*
United Talent Agency (UTA), 9560
Wilshire Blvd, Beverly Hills, CA 90212
USA

Black, James W *Nobel Prize Laureate*
3 Ferrings, Dulwich, London, SE21 7LU,
UNITED KINGDOM (UK)

Black, Jay *Musician*
Charles Rapp, 1650 Broadway, #1410,
New York, NY 10019 USA

Black, Karen *Actor*
Contemporary Artists, 610 Santa Monica
Blvd, #202, Santa Monica, CA 90401 USA

Black, Larry *Track Athlete*
14401 Pierce St, Miami, FL 33176 USA

Black, Lewis *Comedian, Actor*
Agency for Performing Arts, 9200 Sunset
Blvd, #900, Los Angeles, CA 90069 USA

Black, Lisa Hartman *Actor*
Innovative Artists (LA), 1505 Tenth St,
Santa Monica, CA 90401 USA

Black, Lucas *Actor*
Agency for Performing Arts, 9200 Sunset
Blvd, #900, Los Angeles, CA 90069 USA

Black, Marina *Actor*
Bragman/Nyman/Cafarelli, 9171 Wilshire
Blvd #300, Beverly Hills, CA 90210 USA

Black, Mary *Musician*
International Music Network, 278 S Main
St, #400, Gloucester, MA 01930 USA

Black, Michael Ian *Actor, Architect*
United Talent Agency, 9560 Wilshire
Blvd, #500, Beverly Hills, CA 90212 USA

Black, Robert P *Financier, Government
Official*
10 Dahlgren Road, Richmond, VA 23233
USA

Black, Thought *Musician*
William Morris Agency, 1325 Ave of
Americas, New York, NY 10019 USA

Black, Todd *Producer*
International Creative Management
(ICM-LA), 8942 Wilshire Blvd, Beverly
Hills, CA 90211 USA

Black Eyed Peas *Music Group*
DAS Communications, 83 Riverside Dr,
New York, NY 10024 USA

Black Mambazo, Ladysmith *Musician,
Actor*
William Morris Agency (WMA-LA), 1
William Morris Pl, Beverly Hills, CA
90212 USA

Black Oak Arkansas
6400 Pleasant Park Dr, Chanhassen, MN
55317

Black Sabbath *Music Group*
Creative Artists Agency LCC (CAA-LA),
9830 Wilshire Blvd, Beverly Hills, CA
90212 USA

Blackburn, Elizabeth *Misc*
294 Yerba Buena Ave, San Francisco, CA
94127 USA

Blackburn, Greta *Actor*
Dade/Schultz, 6442 Coldwater Canyon
Ave, #206, Valley Green, CA 91606 USA

Blackiedge, Todd A *Football Player,
Sportscaster*
2711 Glenmont Dr NW, Canton, OH
44708 USA

Blackiston, Caroline *Actor*
Caroline Dawson, 125 Gloucester Road,
London, SW7 4IE, UNITED KINGDOM
(UK)

Blackjack
35 Brentwood, Farmingville, NY 11738

Blackman, Honor *Actor*
Michael Ladkin Mgmt, 1 Duchess St, #1,
London, W1N 3DE, UNITED KINGDOM
(UK)

Blackman, Robert R Jr *General*
Commanding General, III Expeditionary
Force Okinawa, FPO, AP, 96602 USA

Blackman, Rolando *Basketball Player,
Sportscaster*
CBS-TV, Sports Dept, 51 W 52nd St, New
York, NY 10019 USA

Blackmore, Ritchie *Musician*
Performers of the World, 8901 Melrose
Ave, #200, West Hollywood, CA 90069
USA

Blackwell, Harolyn *Opera Singer*
Columbia Artists Mgmt Inc, 165 W 57th
St, New York, NY 10019 USA

Blackwell, Richard *Misc*
531 S Windsor, Los Angeles, CA 90020

Blackwood, Nina *Entertainer*
22968 Victory Blvd, #158, Woodland
Hills, CA 91367 USA

Blackwood, Sarah *Musician*
Primary Talent Int'l, 2-12 Petonville Road,
London, N1 9PL, UNITED KINGDOM
(UK)

Blacque, Taurean *Actor*
5049 Rock Springs Road, Lithonia, GA
30038 USA

Bladd, Stephen Jo *Musician*
Nick Ben-Meir, 652 N Doheny Dr, Los
Angeles, CA 90069 USA

Blade, Brian *Musician*
Ted Kurland, 173 Brighton Ave, Boston,
MA 02134 USA

Blades, Brian K *Football Player*
1900 SW 70th Terrace, Plantation, FL
33317 USA

Blades, H Benedict (Bennie) *Football
Player*
1900 SW 70th Terrace, Plantation, FL
33317 USA

Blades, Ruben *Musician, Songwriter,
Actor*
1187 Coast Village Road, #1, Montecito,
CA 93108 USA

Blaese, R Michael *Doctor*
National Cancer Institute, 9000 Rockville
Pike, Bathesda, MD 20892 USA

Blaese, R Michael *Doctor*
National Cancer Institute, 9000 Rockville
Pike, Bethesda, MD 20892 USA

Blaha, John E *Astronaut*
18219 Indian Row, San Antonio, TX
78259 USA

Blahnik, Manolo *Fashion Designer*
49-51 Old Church St, London, SW3 5BS,
UNITED KINGDOM (UK)

Blahoski, Alana *Hockey Player*
7045 James Ave S, Richfield, MN 55423
USA

Blaine, David *Magician*
Creative Artists Agency LCC (CAA-LA),
9830 Wilshire Blvd, Beverly Hills, CA
90212 USA

Blaine, David *Artist*
Evolution Talent, 1775 Broadway, #1500,
New York, NY 10019 USA

Blaine, Hal *Musician*
SpikeArt, PO Box 11864, Costa Mesa, CA
92627 USA

Blair, A Matthew (Matt) *Football Player*
308 Deton Court, Hoopkins, MN 55343
USA

Blair, Anthony C L (Tony) *Politician,
Prime Minister*
Prime Minister's Office, 10 Downing St,
London, SW1A 2AA USA

Blair, Barry *Cartoonist*
PO Box 612, Murray Hill Station, New
York, NY 10156 USA

Blair, Betsy *Actor*
11 Chalcot Gardens, Englands Lane,
London, NW3 4YB, UNITED KINGDOM
(UK)

Blair, Bonnie *Speed Skater*
1223 Aspen Court, Delafield, WI 53018
USA

Blair, Isla *Actor*
Mayer & Eden, Grafton House, 2/3
Golden House, London, W1R 3AD,
UNITED KINGDOM (UK)

Blair, Janet *Actor*
3661 1/2 Glendon Ave, Los Angeles, CA
90034

Blair, Linda *Actor*
4727 Wilshire Blvd, #333, Los Angeles,
CA 90010 USA

Blair, Lionel *Dancer*
68 Old Brompton Road #200, London,
England, SW7 3LQ, United Kingdom

Blair, Paul L D *Baseball Player*
10829 Sherwood Hill Road, Owings Mills,
MD 21117 USA

Blair, Selma *Actor*
Creative Artists Agency LCC (CAA-LA),
9830 Wilshire Blvd, Beverly Hills, CA
90212 USA

Blair, William *Director*
New Star Entertainment, PO Box 84172,
San Diego, CA 92138 USA

Blair, William Draper Jr *Attorney
General, Diplomat*
2510 Foxhall Road NW, Washington, DC
20007 USA

Blais, Madeleine H *Journalist*
Miami Herald, Editorial Dept, 1 Herald
Plaza, Miami, FL 33132 USA

Blake, Andre *Actor*
Kerin-Goldberg Associates, 155 East 55th
Street, #5D, New York, NY 10022

Blake, Asha *Commentator*
NBC-TV, News Dept, 30 Rockefeller
Plaza, New York, NY 10112 USA

Blake, Bud
PO Box 146, Darariscotta, ME 04543

Blake, Casey *Baseball Player*
Toronto Blue Jays, 208 W Kentucky Ave,
Indianola, IA 50125-1112 USA

Blake, Ed *Baseball Player*
Cincinnati Reds, 208 Willow Creek Ct,
Belleville, IL 62223-4207 USA

Blake, Geoffrey *Writer*
Creative Artists Agency LCC (CAA-LA),
9830 Wilshire Blvd, Beverly Hills, CA
90212 USA

Blake, George R *Editor*
Cincinnati Enquirer, Editorial Dept, 617
Vine St, Cincinnati, OH 45202 USA

Blake, Jeff *Football Player*
Philadelphia Eagles, 1 Novacare Way,
Philadelphia, PA 19145 USA

Blake, John C *Artist*
Oz Voorburgwal 131, Amsterdam, 1012
ER, NETHERLANDS

Blake, Josh *Actor*
Pakula/King & Associates, 9229 Sunset
Blvd #315, Los Angeles, CA 90069 USA

Blake, Julian W (Bud) *Cartoonist*
PO Box 146, Damariscotta, ME 04543
USA

Blake, Marcia *Writer*
Creative Artists Agency LCC (CAA-LA),
9830 Wilshire Blvd, Beverly Hills, CA
90212 USA

Blake, Norman *Musician*
Scott O'Malley Assoc, 433 E Cucharras St,
Colorado Springs, CO 80903 USA

Blake, Peter *Architect*
80 Cedar St, #311, Branford, CT 06405
USA

Blake, Peter T *Artist*
Waddington Galleries, 11 Cork St,
London, W1X 1PD, UNITED KINGDOM
(UK)

Blake, Quentin *Artist, Philanthropist*
The Roald Dahl Foundation, 92 High
Street, Great Missenden,
Buckinghamshire, HP16 0AN, United
Kingdom

Blake, Rob *Hockey Player*
4 Gooseberry Lane, Englewood, CO
80113 USA

Blake, Rockwell *Opera Singer*
1 Onondaga Lane, Plattsburgh, NY 12901
USA

Blake, Stephanie *Actor*
First Artists, 1631 N Bristol St, #820, Santa
Ana, CA 92706 USA

Blake, Susan *Commentator*
News Center 4, 1001 Van Ness Ave, San
Francisco, CA 94109 USA

Blake, Tchad *Musician*
Monterey International, 200 W Superior,
#202, Chicago, IL 60610 USA

Blake, Teresa *Actor*
Stone Manners, 6500 Wilshore Blvd,
#550, Los Angeles, CA 90048 USA

Blakeley, Ronee *Actor, Musician*
8033 Sunset Blvd, #693, West
Hollywood, CA 90046 USA

Blakely, Rachel *Actor*
Melbourne Artists, 21 Cardigan Place,
Albert Park, VIC, 3206, AUSTRALIA

Blakely, Susan *Actor, Model*
Jaffe Co, 9663 Santa Monica Blvd, #214,
Beverly Hills, CA 90210 USA

Blakemore, Colin B *Doctor*
University Laboratory of Physiology, Parks
Road, Oxford, OX1 3PT, UNITED
KINGDOM (UK)

Blakemore, Michael *Actor, Writer,
Director*
18 Upper Park Rd, London, NW3 2UP,
UNITED KINGDOM (UK)

Blaker, Clay *Musician, Songwriter*
Texas Sounds Entertainment, 2317 Pecan,
Dickinson, TX 77539 USA

Blakey, Marion *Government Official*
Federal Aviation Agency, 800
Independence Ave SW, Washington, DC
20591 USA

Blalack, Robert *Cinematographer*
12251 Huston St, North Hollywood, CA
91607 USA

Blalock, Jane *Golfer*
Flagship Wharf, 197 8th St, Charlestown,
MA 02129 USA

Blalock, Jolene *Actor*
Don Buchwald, 6500 Wilshire Blvd,
#2200, Los Angeles, CA 90048 USA

Blanc, Georges *Chef*
Le Mere Blanc, Vonnas, Ain, 01540,
FRANCE

Blanc, Jennifer *Actor*
Writers & Artists, 8383 Wilshire Blvd,
#550, Beverly Hills, CA 90211 USA

Blanc, Raymond R A *Chef*
Le Manoir, Church Road, Great Milton,
Oxford, OX44 7PD, UNITED KINGDOM
(UK)

Blancas, Homero *Golfer*
6826 Queensclub Dr, Houston, TX 77069
USA

Blanchard, Felix A (Doc) *Football Player,
General*
30395 Olympus, Bulverde, TX 78163
USA

Blanchard, Felix Doc
30395 Olympus, Bulverde, TX 78163-
2726

Blanchard, George S *General*
9110 Belvoir Woods Parkway, #126, Fort
Belvoir, VA 22060 USA

Blanchard, James H *Financier*
Synovus Financial Corp, 901 Front Ave,
PO Box 120, Columbus, GA 31902 USA

Blanchard, James J *Governor, Diplomat*
426 4th St NE, Washington, DC 20002
USA

Blanchard, John *Baseball Player*
New York Yankees, 230 Central Ave N
Apt 314, Wayzata, MN 55391-1219 USA

Blanchard, John A *Business Person*
Delux Corp, 3680 Victoria St N,
Shoreview, MN 55126 USA

Blanchard, Kenneth *Business Person,
Writer*
2048 Aldergrove, #B, Escondido, CA
92029 USA

Blanchard, Nina *Misc*
3610 Wrightwood Dr, Studio City, CA
91604 USA

Blanchard, Rachel *Actor*
Creatice Artists Agency, 9830 Wilshire
Blvd, Beverly Hills, CA 90212 USA

Blanchard, Tammy *Actor*
International Creative Mgmt, 8942
Wilshire Blvd, #219, Beverly Hills, CA
90211 USA

Blanchard, Terence *Musician, Composer*
BMI, 8730 Sunset Blvd, #300W, Los
Angeles, CA 90069 USA

Blanchard, Tim *Religious Leader*
Conservative Baptist Assn, 1501 W
Mineral Ave, #B, Littleton, CO 80120
USA

Blanchett, Cate *Actor*
Robyn Gardiner Mgmt, 397 Riley St,
Surrey Hills, NSW, 2010, AUSTRALIA

Blanco, Gil *Baseball Player*
New York Yankees, 18403 N 16th Pl,
Phoenix, AZ 85022-1355 USA

Blanco-Cervantes, Raul *President*
Apdo 918, San Jose, COSTA RICA

Bland, Bobby (Blue) *Musician*
It's Happening Presents, PO Box 8073, Pittsburg, CA 94565 USA

Bland, Bobby Blue
1995 Broadway #501, New York, NY 10023

Bland, Nate *Baseball Player*
Houston Astros, 1342 W Esplanade Ave, Kenner, LA 70065-6237 USA

Blanda, George *Football Player*
18 Forest Gate Circle, Oak Brook, IL 60523 USA

Blandford, Roger D *Astronomer*
California Institute of Technology, Astrophysics Dept, Pasadena, CA 91125 USA

Blandon, Roberto *Actor*
TV Azteca, Periferico Sur 4121, Colonia Fuentes del Pedregal, DF, CP 14141, Mexico

Blaney, Dave *Race Car Driver*
1751 W Lexington Ave, High Point, NC 27262 USA

Blaney, George
31 Mark Circle, Holden, MA 01520

Blank, Matt *Baseball Player*
Montreal Expos, 5226 Overridge Dr, Arlington, TX 76017-1211 USA

Blankenship, Kevin *Baseball Player*
Chicago Cubs, 5014 Regency Dr, Rocklin, CA 95677-4420 USA

Blankenship, Lance *Baseball Player*
Oakland A's, 340 Kimberwicke Ct, Alamo, CA 94507-2703 USA

Blankers-Koen, Fanny *Track Athlete*
Olympic Committe, Surinamestraat 33, La Harve, 2585, NETHERLANDS

Blankfield, Mark 5 *Actor*
Artists Group (LA), 10100 Santa Monica Blvd #2490, Los Angeles, CA 90067 USA

Blanks, Larvell *Baseball Player*
Atlanta Braves, 886 N Cofco Center Ct Unit 1103, Phoenix, AZ 85008-6445 USA

Blarikfield, Mark *Actor*
Artists Group, 10 100 Santa Monica Blvd, #2490, Los Angeles, CA 90067 USA

Blasco, Chuck *Musician*
Media Promotion Enterprises, 423 6th Ave, Hurlington, WV 25701 USA

Blashford-Snell, John N *Misc*
Exploration Society, Motcome, Shaftesbury, Dorset, SP7 9PB, UNITED KINGDOM (UK)

Blasi, Rosa *Actor*
8060 Melrose Ave, Los Angeles, CA 90046 USA

Blasingame, Don *Baseball Player*
St Louis Cardinals, 9040 N Longfeather, Fountain Hills, AZ 85268-6413 USA

Blasingame, Wade *Baseball Player*
Milwaukee Braves, 5207 Riverhill Rd NE, Marietta, GA 30068-4865 USA

Blass, Stephen R (Steve) *Baseball Player*
Pittsburgh Pirates, 1756 Quigg Dr, Pittsburgh, PA 15241-2023 USA

Blasucci, Dick *Producer*
Kaplan-Stahler-Gumer Agency, 8383 Wilshire Blvd #923, Beverly Hills, CA 90211 USA

Blateric, Steve *Baseball Player*
Cincinnati Reds, 2855 S Monaco Pkwy Apt 2-304, Denver, CO 80222-7191 USA

Blatnick, Jeff *Actor*
848 Whitney Drive, Schenectady, NY 12309

Blatnick, Jeffrey C (Jeff) *Wrestler*
848 Whitney Dr, Schenectady, NY 12309 USA

Blatnik, Johnny *Baseball Player*
Philadelphia Phillies, 68615 Chermont Rd, Bridgeport, OH 43912-8757 USA

Blatt, Melanie *Musician*
Concorde Intl Artists Ltd, 101 Shepherds Bush Rd, London, W6 7LP, UNITED KINGDOM (UK)

Blatter, Joseph (Sepp) *Football Executive*
Federation Int'l Football Assn, PO Box 85, Zurich, 8030, SWITZERLAND

Blattner, Bud
576 Highway 44, Lake Ozark, MO 65049

Blattner, Buddy *Baseball Player*
St Louis Cardinals, 576 E Highway 42, Lake Ozark, MO 65049-9761 USA

Blatty, William Peter *Writer*
7018 Longwood Dr, Bethesda, MD 20817 USA

Blau, Daniel *Artist*
Belgradstr 26, Munich, 80796, GERMANY

Blauser, Jeff *Baseball Player*
Atlanta Braves, 3005 Compton Ct, Alpharetta, GA 30022-7127 USA

Blaylock, Bob *Baseball Player*
St Louis Cardinals, RR 2 Box 96, Muldrow, OK 74948-9607 USA

Blaylock, Gary *Baseball Player*
St Louis Cardinals, PO Box 241, Maiden, MO 63863-0241 USA

Blaylock, Mookie *Basketball Player*
Golden State Warriors, 1001 Broadway, Oakland, CA 94607 USA

Blazelowski, Carol A *Basketball Player*
New York Liberty, Madison Square Garden, 2 Penn Plaza, New York, NY 10121 USA

Blazier, Ron *Baseball Player*
Philadelphia Phillies, 610 N 9th St, Bellwood, PA 16617-1524 USA

Bleak, David B *War Hero*
355 Louise Dr, Arco, ID 83213 USA

Bleaney, Brebis *Physicist*
Garford House, Garford Road, Oxford, OX1 3PU, UNITED KINGDOM (UK)

Bledel, Alexis *Actor, Model*
P M K Public Relations, 8500 Wilshire Blvd, #700, Beverly Hills, CA 90211 USA

Bledsoe, Drew *Football Player*
PO Box 786, East Aurora, NY 14052-0786 USA

Bledsoe, Tempestt *Actor*
Artists Group, 10100 Santa Monica Blvd, #2490, Los Angeles, CA 90067 USA

Bleek (Cox), Memphis (Malik) *Musician, Artist*
Green Light Talent Agency, PO Box 3172, Beverly Hills, CA 90212 USA

Bleeth, Yasmine *Actor*
Creatice Artists Agency, 9830 Wilshire Blvd, Beverly Hills, CA 90212 USA

Blegen, Judith *Opera Singer*
91 Central Park West, #1B, New York, NY 10023 USA

Bleier, Robert P (Rocky) *Athlete*
801 Larchmont Rd, Pittsburgh, PA 15243

Bleier, Robert P (Rocky) *Football Player*
801 Larchmont Road, Pittsburgh, PA 15243 USA

Blessed, Brian *Actor*
Associated International Mgmt, 5 Denmark St, London, WC2H 8LP, UNITED KINGDOM (UK)

Blessen, Karen A *Journalist*
Karen Blessen Illustration, 6327 Vickery Blvd, Dallas, TX 75214 USA

Blessitt, Ike *Baseball Player*
Detroit Tigers, 19712 Anglin St, Detroit, MI 48234-1469 USA

Blethen, Frank A *Publisher*
Seattle Times Publisher's Office, 1120 John St, Seattle, WA 98109 USA

Blethyn, Brenda A *Actor*
61-63 Portobello Road, London, W1N OAX, UNITED KINGDOM (UK)

Bleu, Corbin *Actor*
TalentWorks (LA), 3500 W Olive Ave #1400, Burbank, CA 91505 USA

Blevins, Michael *Actor*
13 W 100th St #2C, New York, NY 10025 USA

Bley, Carla B *Composer, Musician*
Watt Works, PO Box 67, Willow, NY 12495 USA

Bley, Paul *Musician, Composer*
Legacy Records, 550 Madison Ave, #1700, New York, NY 10022 USA

Blick, Richard (Dick) *Swimmer*
2505 Tamarack Court, Kingsburg, CA 93631 USA

Blier, Bertrand *Director*
11 Rue Margueritte, Paris, 75017, FRANCE

Blige, Mary J *Musician*
International Creative Mgmt, 40 W 57th St, #1800, New York, NY 10019 USA

Blim, Richard D *Doctor*
304 W 172nd St, Belton, MO 64012 USA

Blinder, Alan S *Government Official, Financier*
Princeton University, Economics Dept, Princeton, NJ 08544 USA

Blink 182 *Music Group*
Creative Artists Agency LCC (CAA-LA), 9830 Wilshire Blvd, Beverly Hills, CA 90212 USA

Bliss, Caroline
34-43 Russell, London, ENGLAND, WC2B 5HA

Blitt, Ricky *Writer*
Leverage Management, 1610 Broadway, Santa Monica, CA 90404 USA

Blitz, Andy *Writer*
3 Arts Entertainment Inc, 9460 Wilshire
Blvd Fl 7, Beverly Hills, CA 90212 USA

Blitzer, Wolf *Television Host,
Commentator*
8929 Holly Leaf Lane, Bathesda, MD
20817 USA

Blobel, Erich *Engineer, Scientist*
National Science Foundation, 1800 C St
NW, Was

Blobel, Gunter K J *Nobel Prize Laureate*
Rockefeller University, Cell Biology Dept,
1230 York Ave, New York, NY 10021
USA

Bloch, Erich *Engineer, Scientist*
National Science Foundation, 1800 C St
NW, Washington, DC 20550 USA

Bloch, Henry W *Business Person*
H & R Block Inc, 4410 Main St, Kansas
City, MO 64111 USA

Bloch, Phillip *Stylist*
Cloutier Agency, 1026 Montana Ave,
Santa Monica, CA 90403 USA

Blochwitz, Hans-Peter *Opera Singer*
Matthew Sprizzo, 477 Durant Ave, Staten
Island, NY 10308 USA

Block, Cy *Baseball Player*
Chicago Cubs, 10 S Middle Neck Rd,
Great Neck, NY 11021-3463 USA

Block, Hunt
Box 462, Green's Farms, CT 06436-0462

Block, John R *Secretary*
National Wholesale Grocers Assn, 201
Park Washington, Falls Church, VA 22046
USA

Block, Lawrence *Writer*
299 W 12th St #12D, New York, NY
10014 USA

Block, Ned J *Misc*
29 Washington Square, New York, NY
10011 USA

Blocker, Dirk *Actor*
5063 La Ramada Dr, Santa Barbara, CA
93111 USA

Blocker, Terry *Baseball Player*
New York Mets, 745 Guide Post Ln, Stone
Mountain, GA 30088-1943 USA

Bloemstedt, Herbert T
Kunstleragentur Raab & Bohm,
Plankengasse 7, Vienna, 1010, AUSTRIA

Blomberg, Ron *Baseball Player*
New York Yankees, 11660 Mountain
Laurel Dr, Roswell, GA 30075-1329 USA

Blombergen, Nicolaas *Nobel Prize
Laureate*
13835 W Langtree Lane, Tucson, AZ
85747 USA

Blomdahl, Ben *Baseball Player*
Detroit Tigers, 5370 Nottingham Rd,
Riverside, CA 92506-1511 USA

Blomgren, Michael *Actor*
Select Artists Ltd (CA-Westside Office),
1138 12th Street, Suite 1, Santa Monica,
CA 90403 USA

Blomquist, Rich *Actor*
Creative Artists Agency LCC (CAA-LA),
9830 Wilshire Blvd, Beverly Hills, CA
90212 USA

Blondie *Musician*
Artist Group International (NY), 150 East
58th Street, Fl 19, New York, NY 10155
USA

Blong, Jenni *Actor*
Susan Smith Company, The, 121 A North
San Vicente Blvd, Beverly Hills, CA 90211
USA

Blood, Edward J *Skier*
2 Beech Hill, Durham, NH 03824 USA

Bloodgood, Moon *Actor*
Paradigm (LA), 10100 Santa Monica Blvd,
Fl 25, Los Angeles, CA 90067 USA

Bloodworth-Thomason, Linda *Producer,
Writer*
Badgely Connor Talent, 9229 Sunset Blvd
#311, Los Angeles, CA 90069 USA

Bloom, Alfred H *Educator*
Swarthmore College, President's Office,
Swarthmore, PA 19081 USA

Bloom, Anne *Actor*
Abrams Artists, 9200 Sunset Blvd #1125,
Los Angeles, CA 90069 USA

Bloom, Brian *Actor*
Agency for the Performing Arts (APA-LA),
9200 Sunset Blvd #900, Los Angeles, CA
90069 USA

Bloom, Claire *Actor*
Conway Van Gelder Robinson, 18-21
Jermyn St, London, SW1Y 6NB, UNITED
KINGDOM (UK)

Bloom, Floyd E *Physicist*
628 Pacific View Dr, San Diego, CA
92109 USA

Bloom, Lindsay *Actor*
PO Box 412, Weldon, CA 93263 USA

Bloom, Luka *Music Group*
Mattie Fox Mgmt, Derryneel Ballinalee,
Longford, IRELAND

Bloom, Orlando *Actor*
International Creative Management
(ICM-LA), 8942 Wilshire Blvd, Beverly
Hills, CA 90211 USA

Bloom, Ursula *Writer*
Newton House Walls Dr Ravenglass,
Cumbria, UNITED KINGDOM (UK)

Bloom, Verna *Actor*
327 E 82nd St, New York, NY 10028 USA

Bloomberg, Michael R *Politician, Misc*
Mayor's Office, Gracie Mansion, New
York, NY 10007 USA

Bloomfield, Clyde *Baseball Player*
St Louis Cardinals, 14250 State Highway
180, Gulf Shores, AL 36542-8222 USA

Bloomfield, Michael J (Mike) *Astronaut*
14302 Autumn Canyon Terrace, Houston,
TX 77062 USA

Bloomfield, Sara *Director, Misc*
Holocaust Memorial Museum, 100
Wallenberg Place SW, Washington, DC
20024 USA

Blosser, Greg *Baseball Player*
Boston Red Sox, 5525 47th Ct E,
Bradenton, FL 34203-5655 USA

Blount, Lisa *Actor*
William Morris Agency (WMA-LA), 1
William Morris Pl, Beverly Hills, CA
90212 USA

Blount, Mel
RD #1Box 91, Claysville, PA 15323

Blount, Melvin C (Mel) *Football
Executive, Football Player*
6 Mel Blount Dr, Claysville, PA 15323
USA

Blount, Winton M III *Business Person*
Blount Inc, 4909 SE Internationl Way,
Portland, OR 97222 USA

Blout, Elkan R *Misc*
1010 Memorial Dr #12A, Cambridge, MA
02138 USA

Blow, Kurtis *Music Group*
Entertainment Artists, 2409 21st Ave
#100, Nashville, TN 37212 USA

Blowers, Mike *Baseball Player*
New York Yankees, 22211 42nd Ave E,
Spanaway, WA 98387-6889 USA

Blu, D K *Musician*
Working Artists Agency, 13525 Ventura
Blvd, Sherman Oaks, CA

Blucas, Marc *Actor*
Endeavor Agency LLC (LA), 9601 Wilshire
Blvd Fl 3, Beverly Hills, CA 90210 USA

Blucker, Sara *Actor*
Stein Entertainment Group, 11271 Ventura
Blvd #477, Studio City, CA 91604 USA

Blue *Musician*
Concorde Intl Artists Ltd, 101 Shepherds
Bush Rd, London, W6 7LP, UNITED
KINGDOM (UK)

Blue, Callum *Actor*
Untitled Entertainment (LA), 8436 W 3rd
St #650, Los Angeles, CA 90048 USA

Blue, Vida *Baseball Player*
Oakland A's, PO Box 1449, Pleasanton,
CA 94566-0349 USA

Blues Traveler *Music Group*
William Morris Agency (WMA-LA), 1
William Morris Pl, Beverly Hills, CA
90212 USA

Bluford Jr, Guion S (Guy) *Astronaut*
PO Box 549, N Olmstead, OH 44070
USA

Bluhm, Kay *Athlete*
Bahnorstr 104, Potsdam, 14480,
GERMANY

Blum, Arlene *Mountaineer*
University of California, Biochemistry
Dept, Berkeley, CA 94720 USA

Blum, Geoff *Baseball Player*
Montreal Expos, 9723 La Jolla Dr Apt C,
Rancho Cucamonga, CA 91701-6115
USA

Blum, H Steven *General*
Chief National Guard Bureau, HqUSA
Pentagon, Washington, DC 20310 USA

Blum, Stephanie *Comedian*
Don Buchwald & Associates Inc (LA),
6500 Wilshire Blvd #2200, Los Angeles,
CA 90048 USA

Bluma, Jaime *Baseball Player*
Kansas City Royals, 15219 Reeds St,
Overland Park, KS 66223-3241 USA

Blumas, Trevor *Actor*
Premier Artists Management Ltd, 1502
Stoneybrook Cresc, London ON, N5X
1C5, CANADA

Blumberg, Baruch S *Nobel Prize Laureate*
324 N Lowrence St, Philadelphia, PA
19106 USA

Blume, Judy *Writer*
Tashmdo, 244 5th Ave #1100, New York,
NY 10001 USA

Blume, Martin *Physicist*
Brookhaven National Laboratory, 2 Center
St, Upton, NY 11973 USA

Blumenthal, W Michael *Secretary,
Financier, Misc*
227 Ridgeview Road, Princeton, NJ 08540
USA

Blundell, Mark *Race Car Driver*
4001 Methanol Lane, Indianpolis, IN
46268 USA

Blundell, Pamela *Fashion Designer*
Copperwheat Blundell, 14 Cheshire St,
London, E2 6EH, UNITED KINGDOM
(UK)

Blunstone, Colin *Music Group*
Barry Collins, 21A Cliftown Southend-on-
Sea, Sussex, SS1 1AB, UNITED
KINGDOM (UK)

Blur *Music Group*
United Talent Agency (UTA), 9560
Wilshire Blvd, Beverly Hills, CA 90212
USA

Blurth, Ray *Bowler*
569 Beauford Dr, Saint Louis, MO 63122
USA

Bly, Dre' *Football Player*
4312 Topsail Landing, Chesapeake, VA
23321 USA

Bly, Robert *Writer, Misc*
1904 Girard Ave S, Minneapolis, MN
55403 USA

Blyleven, Bert *Baseball Player*
Minnesota Twins, 1501 McGregor Reserve
Drive, Fort Myers, FL 33901-9658 USA

Blyth, Ann *Actor, Music Group*
Box 9754, Rancho Santa Fe, CA 92067
USA

Blyth, Chay *Yachtsman, Misc*
Inmans House 12 London Road Sheet
Petersfield, Hamps, GU31 4BE, UNITED
KINGDOM (UK)

Blythe, Jamie *Reality TV Star*
Esterman Events, 220 Park Rd, Riva, MD
21140 USA

Blyzka, Mike *Baseball Player*
St Louis Browns, 2816 E 7th St, Cheyenne,
WY 82001-5612 USA

Boal, Mark *Writer*
Creative Artists Agency LCC (CAA-LA),
9830 Wilshire Blvd, Beverly Hills, CA
90212 USA

Boatman, Michael *Actor*
Sanders/Armstrong Management, 2120
Colorado Blvd #120, Santa Monica, CA
90404 USA

Bob, Tim *Music Group, Musician*
ArtistDirect, 10900 Wilshire Blvd #1400,
Los Angeles, CA 90024 USA

Bobek, Nicole *Figure Skater*
19220 Seaview Road #100, Jupiter, FL
33469 USA

Bobko, Karol J *Astronaut*
14214 Lake Scene Trail, Houston, TX
77059 USA

Bobo, DJ *Music Group*
Postfach, Wauwil, 6242, SWITZERLAND

Boccabella, John *Baseball Player*
Chicago Cubs, 1035 Lea Dr, San Rafael,
CA 9493794903-3747 USA

Bocek, Milt *Baseball Player*
Chicago White Sox, 2342 S 61st Ct,
Cicero, IL 60804-2607 USA

Bocelli, Andrea *Music Group, Musician*
Galleria del Corso 4, Milan, 201122,
ITALY

Bochco, Steven *Producer, Writer*
Steven Bochco Productions, P O Box 900,
Beverly Hills, CA 90213 USA

Bochner, Hart *Actor*
Gersh Agency, 232 N Canon Dr, Beverly
Hills, CA 90210 USA

Bochner, Lloyd *Actor*
42 Halderman Rd, Santa Monica, CA
90402 USA

Bochte, Bruce *Baseball Player*
California Angels, 311 Rydal Ave, Mill
Valley, CA 94941-3441 USA

Bochtler, Doug *Baseball Player*
San Diego Padres, 4277 Forest Ln, Palm
Springs, FL 33406-7501 USA

Bochy, Bruce *Baseball Player*
Houston Astros, 16144 Brittany Park Ln,
Poway, CA 92064-2069 USA

Bock, Charles
PO Box 4197, Incline Village, NV 89450-
4197

Bock, Charles Jr *Misc*
P O Box 4197, Incline Village, NV 89450
USA

Bock, Edward J *Football Player, Business
Person*
2232 Clifton Forge Dr, Saint Louis, MO
63131 USA

Bock, Jerrold L (Jerry) *Composer*
145 Wellington Ave, New Rochelle, NY
10804 USA

Bockman, Eddie *Baseball Player*
New York Yankees, 1400 Millbrae Ave
#2, Millbrae, CA 94030-2831 USA

Bockus, Randy *Baseball Player*
San Francisco Giants, 560 Helena Dr,
Tallmadge, OH 44278-2667 USA

Bocuse, Paul *Business Person, Misc*
40 Rue de la Plage, Collonges-au-Mont
d'Or, 69660, FRANCE

Boddicker, Michael J (Mike) *Basketball
Player*
Baltimore Orioles, 11324 W 121st
Terrace, Overland Park, KS 66213-1978
USA

Bode, John R *War Hero*
1100 Warm Sands Dr SE, Albuquerque,
NM 87123 USA

Bode, Ken *Commentator, Educator*
Northwestern University, Journalism
School, Evanston, IL 60206 USA

Bodemann, Joe
Meinholz 1, Meine, GERMANY, D-38527

Boden, Margaret A *Misc*
Brighton University, Cognitive Science
School, Brighton, BN1 9QH, UNITED
KINGDOM (UK)

Bodett, Tom *Writer, Entertainer*
PO Box 3249, Homer, AK 99603 USA

Bodine, Brett *Race Car Driver*
Brett Bodine Racing, 304 Performance Rd,
Mooresville, NC 28115 USA

Bodine, Geoff
PO Box 1790, Monroe, NC 28111-1790

Bodine, Geoffrey (Geoff) *Race Car Driver*
Brett Bodine Racing, 304 Performance
Road, Moorseville, NC 28115 USA

Bodine, Todd *Race Car Driver*
PO Box 2427, Cornelius, NC 28031 USA

Bodison, Wolfgang *Actor*
J Michael Bloom, 9255 Sunset Blvd #710,
Los Angeles, CA 90069 USA

Bodmer, Walter F *Scientist, Misc*
Oxford University, Hertford College,
Oxford, OX1 3BW, UNITED KINGDOM
(UK)

Boede, Marvin J *Misc*
Plumbing & Pipe Fitting Union, 901
Massachusetts Ave NW, Washington, DC
20001 USA

Boeheim, James A (Jim) Jr *Basketball
Player, Coach*
Syracuse University, Manley Field House,
Syracuse, NY 13244 USA

Boehm, Gottfried K *Architect, Historian*
Sevogelplatz 1, Basel, 4052,
SWITZERLAND

Boehmer, Len *Baseball Player*
Cincinnati Reds, 206 Townview Ct,
Wentzville, MO 63385-2925 USA

Boehne, Edward G *Financier*
Federal Reserve Bank, Independance Mall
100 N 6th St, Philadelphia, PA 19106
USA

Boehringer, Brian *Baseball Player*
New York Yankees, 7 Sunset, Festus, MO
63028-1770 USA

Boen, Earl
PO Box 11086, Beverly Hills, CA 90213-
4586

Boerner, Jacqueline *Speed Skater*
Bemhard-Bastlein-Str 55, Berlin, 10367
USA

Boesch, Rudy *Reality TV Star*
Survivor, 1661 Lincoln Blvd, Ste 200,
Santa Monica, CA 90404

Boeschenstein, William W *Business
Person*
10617 Cardiff Road, Perrysburg, OH
43551 USA

Boesel, Raul *Race Car Driver*
9181 W Bay Harbor Dr #2, Bay Harbor
Island, FL 33154 USA

Boesen, Dannis L *Astronaut*
6613 Sandra Ave NE, Albuquerque, NM
87109 USA

Boever, Joe *Baseball Player*
St Louis Cardinals, 13085 Morris Rd Unit
11112, Alpharetta, GA 30004-4113 USA

Boff, Leonardo G D *Misc*
Pr M Leao 12/204 Alto Vale Encantado, Rio de Janeiro, 20531-350, BRAZIL

Boffill, Angela *Music Group*
1385 York Ave #6B, New York, NY 10021 USA

Bofill, Ricardo *Architect*
Taller de Arguitectura, 14 Ave de la Indurstria, Barcelona, 08960, SPAIN

Bofinger, Heinz *Architect*
Beibricher Allee 49, Wiesbaden, 65187, GERMANY

Bogalusa, Los Angeles
CA, 70429-0958

Bogar, Tim *Baseball Player*
New York Mets, 0N032 Pauley Sq, Geneva, IL 60134-4442 USA

Bogart, Andrea *Actor*
Kazarian/Spencer & Assoc, 11365 Ventura Blvd #100, Box 7403, Studio City, CA 91604 USA

Bogart, Paul *Television Host, Director*
1801 Century Park E #2160, Los Angeles, CA 90067 USA

Bogdanovich, Peter *Director*
468 N Camden Dr #200, Beverly Hills, CA 90210 USA

Bogeberg, J B *Misc*
Bandana Mgmt, 11 Elvaston Place #300, London, SW7 5QC, UNITED KINGDOM (UK)

Bogener, Terry *Baseball Player*
Texas Rangers, 411 E McCabe Ave, Palmyra, MO 63461-2012 USA

Boggs, Haskell *Cinematographer*
3710 Goodland Ave, Studio City, CA 91604 USA

Boggs, Tommy *Baseball Player*
Texas Rangers, 703 Botany Bay Cir, Pflugerville, TX 78660-8007 USA

Boggs, Wade A *Baseball Player*
Boston Red Sox, 6006 Windham Place, Tampa, FL 33647-1149 USA

Bogguss, Suzy *Songwriter, Music Group*
Brokaw Co, 9255 Sunset Blvd #804, Los Angeles, CA 90069 USA

Bogle, John C *Financier*
612 Shipton Lane, Bryn Mawr, PA 19010 USA

Bogle, Warren *Baseball Player*
Oakland A's, 11605 SW 103rd Ave, Miami, FL 33176-4001 USA

Bogner, Willy *Fashion Designer*
Bogner Film GmbH, Saint-Veit-Str 4, Munich, 81673, GERMANY

Bogosian, Eric *Actor, Artist*
Ararat Productions P O Box 24, New York, NY 10013 USA

Bogues, Tyrone (Muggsy) *Athlete*
310 North Kings Drive, Charlotte, NC 28204

Bohan, Justin *Actor*
Don Buchwald & Associates Inc (LA), 6500 Wilshire Blvd #2200, Los Angeles, CA 90048 USA

Bohan, Marc *Fashion Designer*
35 Rue du Bourg a Mont, Chatillon Sur Seine, 21400, FRANCE

Bohanon, Brian *Baseball Player*
Texas Rangers, 243 W Thorn Way, Houston, TX 77015-2069 USA

Bohay, Heidi *Actor*
48 Main St, South Bound Brook, NJ 08880 USA

Bohem, Les *Writer, Producer*
United Talent Agency (UTA), 9560 Wilshire Blvd, Beverly Hills, CA 90212 USA

Bohigas, Guardiola Oriol *Architect*
Calle Calvert 71, Barcelona, 21, SPAIN

Bohlen, Dieter
Carla Fornells Peguera, (Mallorca), SPAIN, 35E-07160

Bohlmann, Ralph A *Religious Leader*
Lutheran Church Missouri Synod, 1333 S Kirkwood Road, Saint Louis, MO 63122 USA

Bohn, Parker III *Bowler*
25 Pitney Lane, Jackson, NJ 08527 USA

Bohnet, John *Baseball Player*
Cleveland Indians, 224 Panorama Dr, Benicia, CA 94510-1523 USA

Bohr, Aage N *Nobel Prize Laureate*
Strangade 34 1-Sal, Copenhagen, 1401, DENMARK

Bohrer, Corinne *Actor*
Abrams-Rubaloff Lawrence, 8075 W 3rd St #303, Los Angeles, CA 90048 USA

Bohrer, Thomas *Athlete*
77 Crest St, Concord, MA 01742 USA

Bohringer, Romaine
5 rue Clement-Marot, Paris, FRANCE, F-75008

Boies, David *Lawyer, Attorney General*
Cravath Swaine Moore, 1 Chase Manhattan Plaza, New York, NY 10005 USA

Boileau, Linda *Editor, Cartoonist*
Frankfort State Journal, Editorial Dept 321 W Main St, Frankfort, KY 40601 USA

Boisson, Christine *Actor*
Artmedia, 21 Ave Rapp, Paris, 75007, FRANCE

Boitano, Brian *Figure Skater*
Brian Boitano Enterprises, 101 First St. #370, Los Altos Hills, CA 94022 USA

Boiteux, Jean *Swimmer*
51 Ave de Merignac, Bordeaux, Cauderan, 33200, FRANCE

Boivin, Leo J *Hockey Player*
PO Box 406, Prescott ON, K0E 1T0, CANADA

Bok, Bart J *Astronomer, Educator*
200 N Sierra Vista Dr, Tucson, AZ 85719 USA

Bok, Chip *Editor, Cartoonist*
709 Castle Blvd, Akron, OH 44313 USA

Bok, Derek C *Educator*
Harvard University, Kennedy Government School, Cambridge, MA 02138 USA

Bok, Sissela *Misc*
75 Cambridge Parkway #610, Cambridge, MA 02142 USA

Bokadia, K C *Director, Producer, Filmmaker, Bollywood*
A12 Neha Apartments Juhu Tara Road, Juhu, Bombay, MS 400 049, INDIA

Bokamper, Kim *Football Player*
301 NW 127th Ave, Plantation, FL 33325 USA

Bolaṇos, Enrique *President*
President's Office, Casa de Gobierno #2398, Managua, Nicaragua

Bolcom, William E *Composer*
3080 Whitmore Lake Road, Ann Arbor, MI 48105 USA

Bolden, Charles F Jr *Astronaut, General*
2952 Holly Hall St, Houston, TX 77054 USA

Boldon, Ato *Track Athlete*
PO Box 3703, Santa Cruz, Trinidad, TRINIDAD & TOBAGO

Boles, John E *Baseball Player, Misc*
7901 Timberlake Dr, West Melbourne, FL 32904 USA

Bolger, James B (Jim) *Prime Minister*
New Zealand Embassy, 37 Observatory Circle NW, Washington, DC 20008 USA

Bolin, Bobby D *Baseball Player*
P O Box 1948, Easley, SC 29641 USA

Bolkiah, Mu'izuddin Waddaulah *Misc*
Istana Darul Hana, Brunei Darussalam

Bolleau, Linda *Editor, Cartoonist*
Frankfort State Journal, Editorial Dept 321 W Main St, Frankfort, KY 40601 USA

Bollen, Roger *Cartoonist*
Tribune Media Services, 435 N Michigan Ave #1500, Chicago, IL 60611 USA

Bolles, Richard N *Writer*
2378 Hagen Oaks Dr, Alamo, CA 94507 USA

Bollettieri, Nick *Tennis Player, Coach*
Nick Bollettieri Tennis Academy, 5500 34th St W, Bradenton, FL 34210 USA

Bolling, Claude *Composer, Music Group*
20 Ave de Lorrainne, Garches, FRANCE

Bolling, Tiffany *Actor*
12483 Braddock Dr, Los Angeles, CA 90066 USA

Bollinger, Lee C *Educator*
Columbia University, President's Office, New York, NY 10027 USA

Bollman, Ryan *Actor*
Lichtman/Salners Company, 12216 Moorpark Street, Studio City, CA 91604 USA

Bologna, Joseph *Actor*
16830 Ventura Blvd #326, Encino, CA 91436 USA

Bolt, John F *War Hero*
705 N Atlantic Ave #303, New Smyrna Beach, FL 32169 USA

Bolt, Mae *Bowler*
1321 Highland Ave, Berwyn, IL 60402 USA

Bolt, Tommy *Golfer*
Cherokee Village Public Golf Course, Cherokee Village, AR 72525 USA

Bolten, Joshua *Government Official*
Office of Management/Budget, Executive Office Building, Washington, DC 20503 USA

Bolten, Michael *Songwriter, Music Group*
130 W 57th St #10B, New York, NY 10019 USA

Bolton, Ruthie *Basketball Player*
Sacramento Monarchs, ARCO Arena, One Sports Parkway, Sacramento, CA 95834 USA

Bolton-Holifield, Ruthie *Basketball Player*
Sacramento Monarchs, Arco Arena 1 Sports Parkway, Sacramento, CA 95834 USA

Bolvin, Leo J *Hockey Player*
P O Box 406, Prescott, ON KOE 1TO, CANADA

Bombassaro, Gerald *Misc*
Tile Marble & Granit Cutters Union, 801 N Pitt St, Alexandria, VA 22314 USA

Bomer, Matthew *Actor*
Carlson Menashe Agency, 159 West 25th Street, Suite 1011, New York, NY 10001

Bon Jovi, Jon *Music Group, Songwriter, Actor*
Bon Jovi Mgmt, 248 W 17th St #501, New York, NY 10011 USA

Bonaduce, Danny *Actor, Music Group*
2651 La Cuesta Dr, Los Angeles, CA 90046 USA

Bonaly, Surya *Figure Skater*
35 Rue Felicien David, Paris, 750l6, FRANCE

Bonamy, James *Musician*
Hallmark Direction, 15 Music Square West, Nashville, TN 37203 USA

Bonanno, Louie
PO Box 583, Laguna Beach, CA 92652-0583

Bonanno, Louis *Actor*
P O Box 583, Laguna Beach, CA 92652 USA

Bond, Alan *Business Person, Yachtsman*
89 Watkins Road, Dalkeith, WA 6069, AUSTRALIA

Bond, Christopher S (Kit) *Governor, Senator*
308 E High St #202, Jefferson City, MO 65101 USA

Bond, Edward *Writer*
Orchard Way, Great Wilbraham, Cambridge, CB1 5KA, UNITED KINGDOM (UK)

Bond, H Julian *Social Activist*
54435 41st Place NW, Washington, DC 20015 USA

Bond, J Max Jr *Architect*
Davis Broder Assoc, 100 E 42nd St, New York, NY 10017 USA

Bond, Larry *Writer*
Trident Media Group LLC, 41 Madison Ave Fl 33, New York, NY 10010 USA

Bond, Samantha *Actor*
Conway Van Gelder Robinson, 18-21 Jermyn St, London, SW1Y 6NB, UNITED KINGDOM (UK)

Bond, Steve *Actor*
14050 Marquesas Way, Marina del Rey, CA 90292 USA

Bond, Tommy (Butch) *Actor*
993 Delaware St, Imperial Beach, CA 91932 USA

Bond, Victoria A *Composer*
Roanoke Symphony, 541 Luck Ave SW #200, Roanoke, VA 24016 USA

Bondar, Roberta L *Astronaut*
Space Agency, P O Box 7014 Station V, Vanier, ON K1L8E2, CANADA

Bondevik, Kjell Magne *Prime Minister*
Statsministerens Kontor, Postboks 8001 Dep, Oslo, 0030, Norway

Bondi, Hermann *Mathematician*
61 Mill Lane, Impington, Cambridgeshire, CB4 4XN, UNITED KINGDOM (UK)

Bonds, Barry *Athlete, Baseball Player*
San Fransisco Giants, Pacific Bell Park 24 Mays Plz, San Fransisco, CA 94103 USA

Bonds, Gary U S *Music Group*
Entity Communications, 875 Ave of Americas #1908, New York, NY 10001 USA

Bone Thugs-N-Harmony *Music Group*
Sony Music Entertainment, 555 Madison Avenue, New York, NY 10022-3211 USA

Boneham, Rupert *Reality TV Star*
Survivor, 1661 Lincoln Blvd, Ste 200, Santa Monica, CA 90404

Bonell, Carlos A *Music Group, Composer*
Upbeat Mgmt, Sutton Business Centre, Wallington, Surrey, SM6 7AH, UNITED KINGDOM (UK)

Bonerz, Peter *Actor, Comedian, Director*
3637 Lowry Road, Los Angeles, CA 90027 USA

Bonet, Lisa *Actor*
5534 Encino Ave #103, Encino, CA 91316 USA

Bonet, Pep *Architect*
C/Pujades 62, Barcelona, 08005, SPAIN

Bongo, Albert-Bernard Omar *President*
President's Office, Blvd de Independence, Libreville, BP 546, GABON

Bonham, Tracy *Songwriter, Music Group*
Artists Management Group, 207 Crabapple Dr, Baytown, TX 77520 USA

Bonham Carter, Helena *Actor*
7 West Heath Ave, London, NW11 7S, UNITED KINGDOM (UK)

Bonifant, J Evan *Actor*
Pacific Artists Management, 1404-510 W Hastings St, Vancouver, BC V6B 1L, CANADA

Bonilla, Hector *Actor*
TV Azteca, Periferico Sur 4121, Colonia Fuentes del Pedregal, DF, CP 14141, Mexico

Bonilla, Roberto M A (Bobby) *Baseball Player*
390 Round Hill Road, Greenwich, CT 06831 USA

Bonin, Gordie *Race Car Driver*
12471 Stanford St, Los Angeles, CA 90066 USA

Bonington, Christian J S *Mountaineer*
Badger Hill Nether Row Hesket Newmarket, Cumbria, UNITED KINGDON (UK)

Bonnaire, Sandrine
36 rue de Ponthieu, Paris, FRANCE, F-75008

Bonner, Elayna
Uliza Tschakalowa 48, Moscow, RUSSIA

Bonner, Frank *Actor*
Stone Manners, 6500 Wilshire Blvd #550, Los Angeles, CA 90048 USA

Bonner, John T *Biologist*
52 Patton Ave #A, Princeton, NJ 08540 USA

Bonness, Rik *Football Player*
1650 Famam St, Omaha, NE 68102 USA

Bonneville, Hugh *Actor*
Paradigm (LA), 10100 Santa Monica Blvd, Fl 25, Los Angeles, CA 90067 USA

Bonney, Barbara *Opera Singer*
Gunnarsbyn, Edane, 671 94, SWEDEN

Bono *Music Group, Songwriter*
Regine Moylett, 145A Ladbroke Grove, London, W10 6HJ, UNITED KINGDOM (UK)

Bono, Chastity *Actor, Music Group*
8968 Vista Grande, West Hollywood, CA 90069 USA

Bono, Mary *Politician*
Mary Bono, 1555 South Palm Canyon Drive, Suite D105, Palm Springs, CA 92264 USA

Bono, Steven C (Steve) *Football Player*
1100 Hamilton Ave, Palo Alto, CA 94301

Bonoff, Karla *Music Group, Songwriter*
2122 E Valley Road, Santa Barbara, CA 93108 USA

Bonsall, Joseph S (Joe) Jr *Music Group*
New Leaf Press, PO Box 726, Green Forest, AR 72638 USA

Bontemps, Ronald (Ron) *Basketball Player*
133 S Illinois Ave, Morton, IL 61550 USA

Bonvicini, Joan *Basketball Player, Coach*
University of Arizona, Atheletic Dept McKale Memorial Center, Tucson, AZ 85721 USA

Bonynge, Richard A
Chale Monet Rte de Sonloup, Les Avants, 1833, SWITZERLAND

Boo, Katherine *Journalist*
Washington Post, Editorial Dept 1150 15th St NW, Washington, DC 20071 USA

Boochever, Robert *Judge*
US Court of Appeals, 125 S Grand Ave, Pasadena, CA 91105 USA

Booker, Chris *Correspondent*
Entertainment Tonight (ET), 5555 Melrose Ave, Mae West Bldg Fl 2, Hollywood, CA 90038 USA

Bookwalter, J R *Director*
P O Box 6573, Akron, OH 44312 USA

Boom, Benn *Actor*
William Morris Agency (WMA-LA), 1 William Morris Pl, Beverly Hills, CA 90212 USA

Boomer, Linwood *Producer, Writer*
Endeavor Agency LLC (LA), 9601 Wilshire
Blvd Fl 3, Beverly Hills, CA 90210 USA

Boon, David C *Cricketer*
Durham Cricket Club, Chester-le-Street,
County Durham, DH3 3QR, UNITED
KINGDON (UK)

Boone, Bret *Baseball Player*
5112 Isleworth Country Club Dr,
Windermere, FL 34786 USA

Boone, Debby *Actor, Musician*
4334 Kester Ave, Sherman Oaks, CA
91403 USA

Boone, Pat *Musician, Actor*
904 N Beverly Dr, Beverly Hills, CA
90210 USA

Boone, Randy *Actor*
4150 Arch St #223, Studio City, CA
91604 USA

Boone, Raymond O (Ray) *Baseball Player*
3728 Paseo Vista Famosa, Rancho Santa
Fe, CA 92091 USA

Boone, Robert R (Bob) *Baseball Player,
Misc*
18571 Villa Dr, Villa Park, CA 92861
USA

Boone, Ron *Basketball Player*
3877 Pheasant Ridge Road, Salt Lake City,
UT 84109 USA

Boone, Steve *Music Group, Musician*
Pipeline Artists Mgmt, 620 16th Ave S,
Hopkins, MN 55343 USA

Boorem, Mika *Actor*
Gilbertson-Kincaid Management, 1330
Fourth St, Santa Monica, CA 90401 USA

Boorman, John *Director*
Merlin Films, 16 Upper Pembroke St,
Dublin 2, IRELAND

Boosler, Elayne *Actor, Comedian*
Gersh Agency, The (LA), 232 N Canon Dr,
Beverly Hills, CA 90210 USA

Booth, Adrian *Actor*
3922 Glenridge Dr, Sherman Oaks, CA
91423 USA

Booth, Connie *Actor*
Kate Feast, Primrose Hill Studios, Fitzroy
Rd, London, NW1 8TR, UNITED
KINGDOM (UK)

Booth, George *Cartoonist*
P O Box 1539, Stony Brook, NY 11790
USA

Booth, James *Actor*
Hillard/Elkins, 8306 Wilshire Blvd #438,
Beverly Hills, CA 90211 USA

Booth, Lindy *Actor*
Characters Talent Agency, The (Toronto),
150 Carlton St Fl 2, Toronto ON, M5A
2K1, CANADA

Boothe, Powers *Actor*
23629 Long Valley Road, Hidden Hills,
CA 91302 USA

Boothroyd, Betty *Government Official*
House of Commons, Westminster,
London, SW1A 0AA, UNITED KINGDOM
(UK)

Boozer, Carlos *Basketball Player*
Cleveland Cavaliers, Gund Arena 1 Center
Court, Cleveland, OH 44115 USA

Boozer, Robert (Bob) *Basketball Player*
100 S 19th St, Omaha, NE 68102 USA

Borboni, Paola
Via degli Artisti 23, Rome, ITALY,
I-000187

Borcherds, Richard E *Mathematician*
University of California, Mathematics
Dept, Berkeley, CA 94720 USA

Bordaberry, Arocena Juan M *President*
Juaquin Suarez 2868, Montevideo,
URUGUAY

Borden, Amanda *Gymnast*
Cincinnati Gymnastics Acadamy, 3536
Woodridge Blvd, Fairfield, OH 45014
USA

Borden, Lynn *Actor*
Associated Artists, 6399 Wilshire Blvd
#211, Los Angeles, CA 90048 USA

Borden, Robert *Producer*
United Talent Agency (UTA), 9560
Wilshire Blvd, Beverly Hills, CA 90212
USA

Borden, Scott *Actor*
Progressive Artists Agency, 400 S Beverly
Dr #216, Beverly Hills, CA 90212

Borden, Steve (Sting) *Wrestler*
World Wrestling Entertainment (WWE),
1241 E Main St, Stamford, CT 06905 USA

Border, Allan R *Cricketer*
Cricket Board, 90 Jolimont St, Jolimont
VIC, 3002, AUSTRATIA

Boreanaz, David *Actor*
Visionary Mgmt, 8265 Sunset Blvd #104,
West Hollywood, CA 90046 USA

Boren, David L *Governor, Senator,
Educator*
705 W Boyd, Norman, OK 73019 USA

Borg, Bjorn R *Tennis Player*
International Management Group, Pier
House Chiswick, London, W4M 3NN,
UNITED KINGDOM (UK)

Borg, Kim *Opera Singer*
Osterbrogade 158, Copenhagen, 2100,
DENMARK

Borges, YamilRaimundtheatre
Wallgasse 18-20, Vienna, AUSTRIA, 1060

Borghi, Frank *Soccer Player*
4123 Poepping St, Saint Louis, MO 63123
USA

Borgman, James A (Jim) *Cartoonist, Editor*
Cincinnati Enquirer, Editorial Dept, 617
Vine St, Cincinnati, OH 45202 USA

Borgnine, Ernest *Actor*
3055 Lake Glen Drive, Beverly Hills, CA
90210 USA

Boris, Angel *Actor*
Acme Talent & Literary Agency (LA), 4727
Wilshire Blvd #333, Los Angeles, CA
90010 USA

Boris, Ruthanna *Ballerina, Choreographer*
Center for Dance, 555 Pierce St #1033,
Albany, CA 94706 USA

Bork, Erik *Writer*
CAA, 9830 Wilshire Blvd, Beverly Hills,
CA 90212

Bork, George *Football Player*
7316 Conventry Dr S, Spring Grove, IL
60081 USA

Bork, Judge Robert
5171 Palisade Lane, Washington, DC
20016

Bork, Robert H *Judge*
6520 Ridge St, McLean, VA 22101 USA

Borkh, Inge *Opera Singer*
Haus Weitblick, Wienacht, 9405,
SWITZERLAND

Borkowski, Bob *Athlete*
1031 Gerhard St, Dayton, OH 45404

Borlaug, Norman E *Nobel Prize Laureate*
P O Box 6-641, Mexico City DF, SP
06600, MEXICO

Borlenghi, Matt *Actor*
Independent Group, The, 8721 W Sunset
Blvd #105, Los Angeles, CA 90069 USA

Borman, Frank *Astronaut, Business Person*
Patlex Corp, PO Box 1139, Fairacres, NM
88033 USA

Borntrager, Mary Christner *Writer*
Herald Press, 616 Walnut Ave, Scottsdale,
PA 15683 USA

Borodina, Olga V *Opera Singer*
Lies Askonas, 6 Henrietta St, London,
WC2E 8LA, UNITED KINGDOM (UK)

Borofsky, Jonathan *Artist*
57 Market St, Venice, CA 90291 USA

Boron, Kathrin *Athlete*
Potsdamer RG, An Der Pirschheide,
Potsdam, 14471, GERMANY

Boros, Guy *Golfer*
2540 SE 8th St, Pompano Beach, FL
33062 USA

Boross, Peter *Prime Minister*
Kossouth Lajos Ter 1-3, Budapest, 1055,
HUNGARY

Borowiak, Tony *Music Group*
MPI Talent, 9255 Sunset Blvd #407, Los
Angeles, CA 90069 USA

Borowy, Henry L (Hank) *Baseball Player*
57 Nina Court, Brick, NJ 08723 USA

Borrego, Jesse *Actor*
PO Box 785, Bellport, NY 11713 USA

Borrero, Alejandra *Actor*
Gabriel Blanco Iglesias (Mexico), Rio
Balsas 35-32, Colonia Cuauhtemoc, DF,
06500, Mexico

Borris, Angel *Actor*
Lara Rosenstock Management, 8371
Blackburn Ave #1, Los Angeles, CA 90048
USA

Borst, Plet *Misc*
Meentweg 87, Bussum, 1406 KE,
NETHERLANDS

Borstein, Alex *Actor*
Mosaic Media Group, 9200 Sunset Blvd Fl
10, Los Angeles, CA 90069 USA

Borten, Per *Prime Minister*
7095 Ler, NORWAY

Borton, Della (D B) *Writer*
Ohio Wesleyan University, Dept of
English, Delaware, OH 43015 USA

Boryla, Vince *Basketball Player, Misc*
5577 S Emporia Circle, Englewood, CO
80111 USA

Borysenko, Joan *Writer, Doctor*
Mind-Body Health Sciences Inc, 393
Dixon Rd, Boulder, CO 80302 USA

Borzov, Valeri F *Track Athlete*
Sport & Youth Ministry, Esplanadna St 42, Kiev 23, 252023, UKRAINE

Boschman, Ed *Religious Leader*
Mennonite Brethren Churches General Conference, P O Box 347, Newton, KS 67114 USA

Bosco, Philip *Actor*
Judy Schoen, 606 N Larchmont Blvd #309, Los Angeles, CA 90004 USA

Bose, Amar G *Inventor*
Bose Corp Mountain, Framington, MA 01701 USA

Bose, Bimal K *Engineer*
215 Ski Mountain Road, Gatlinburg, TN 37738 USA

Bose, Eleanora *Model*
I M G Models, 304 Park Ave S #1200, New York, NY 10010 USA

Bose, Miguel *Actor, Songwriter, Music Group*
RLM Producciones, Puerto Santa Maria 65, Madrid, 28043, SPAIN

BoseIII, Tony *Football Player*
6 Glendenning Lane, Houston, TX 77024 USA

Boskin, Michael J *Government Official*
Stanford University, Hoover Instution, Stanford, CA 94305 USA

Bosley, Tom *Actor*
Burton Moss, 8827 Beverly Blvd #L, Los Angeles, CA 90048 USA

Bossard, Andre *Lawyer, Misc, Judge*
228 Rue de la Convention, Paris, 75015, FRANCE

Bosseler, Don J *Football Player*
7420 SW 133rd St, Miami, FL 33156 USA

Bossidy, Lawrence A (Larry) *Business Person*
Honeywell Inc, Honeywell Plaza, Minneapolis, MN 55408 USA

Bosson, Barbara *Actor*
694 Amalfi Dr, Pacific Palisades, CA 90272 USA

Bossy, Michael (Mike) *Hockey Player*
136 Ducharne St, Rosemere, QC, J7A 4HB, CANADA

Bostelle, Tom *Artist*
Aeolian Palace Gallery, P O Box 8, Pocopson, PA 19366 USA

Bostic, Jeff *Football Player*
10701 Miller Road, Oakton, VA 22124 USA

Boston *Music Group*
Agency for the Performing Arts (APA-LA), 9200 Sunset Blvd #900, Los Angeles, CA 90069 USA

Bostridge, Ian *Musician*
International Creative Management (ICM-LA), 8942 Wilshire Blvd, Beverly Hills, CA 90211 USA

Bostrom, Zachary *Actor*
Kazarian/Spencer, 11365 Ventura Blvd #100, Box 7403, Studio City, CA 91604

Bostwick, Barry *Actor*
Melissa Prophet Management, 1640 S Sepulveda Blvd #218, Los Angeles, CA 90025 USA

Bostwick, Dunbar *Race Car Driver*
1623 Dewey Ave, Pompano Beach, FL 33060 USA

Boswell, David W (Dave) *Baseball Player*
309 Roxbury Court, Joppa, MD 21085 USA

Boswell, Thomas M *Writer*
Washington Post, Sports Dept 1150 15th St NW, Washington, DC 20071 USA

Bosworth, Brian *Actor, Football Player*
Artist's Agency, 1180 S Beverly Dr #301, Los Angeles, CA 90035 USA

Bosworth, Kate *Actor*
United Talent Agency, 9560 Wilshire Blvd #500, Beverly Hills, CA 90212 USA

Boteach, Rabbi Shmuley *Writer, Social Activist*
Trident Media Group LLC, 41 Madison Ave Fl 33, New York, NY 10010 USA

Botehho, Joao *Director*
Assicuacai de Realizadores, Rua de Palmeira 7 R/C, Lisbon, 1200, PORTUGAL

Botero, Fernando *Artist*
Nohra Haime Gallery, 41 E 57th St #600, New York, NY 10022 USA

Botha, Francois (Frans) *Boxer*
White Buffalo, P O Box 3982, Clearwater, FL 33767 USA

Botha, Pieter W *President*
Die Anker, Wildemess, 6560, SOUTH AFRICA

Botha, Roelof F *Government Official*
P O Box 16176, Pretoria North, 0116, SOUTH AFRICA

Botham, Ian T *Cricketer*
Ludorum Mgmt, 33 Tooley St, London, SE1 2QF, UNITED KINGDOM (UK)

Botsford, Beth *Swimmer*
405 Ivy Church Road, Timonium, MD 21093 USA

Botsford, Sara *Actor*
Kordek Agency, 8490 W Sunset Blvd #403, West Hollywood, CA 90069 USA

Bott, Raoul *Mathematician*
1 Richdale Ave #9, Cambridge, MA 02140 USA

Botta, Mario *Architect*
Via Ciani 16, Lugano, 6904, SWITZERLAND

Bottcher, Martin
Via Longhena 3, Lugano, SWITZERLAND, CH-6900

Bottom, Joe *Swimmer*
PO Box 3840, Chico, CA 95927 USA

Bottomley, Virginia *Government Official*
House of Commons, Westminster, London, SW1A 0AA, UNITED KINGDOM (UK)

Bottoms, Joseph *Actor*
Stanford-Gross, 6715 Hollywood Blvd #238, Los Angeles, CA 90028 USA

Bottoms, Sam *Actor*
4719 Willowcrest Ave, North Hollywood, CA 91602' USA

Bottoms, Timothy *Actor*
532 Hot Springs Road, Santa Barbara, CA 93108 USA

Botts, Mike
6269 Mulholland Hwy, Los Angeles, CA 90068

Boublil, Alain A *Songwriter*
Cameron Mackintosh Ltd, 1 Bedford Square, London, WCIB 3RA, UNITED KINGDOM (UK)

Boucha, Henry *Hockey Player*
314 Minnesota St, Warroad, MN 56763 USA

Bouchard, Emile
213 Marie Victoria, Vercheres, CANADA, PQ J0L 2T0

Bouchard, Emile J (Butch) *Hockey Player*
CSAS, P O Box 60036 RPO Glen Abbey, Oakville, ON L6M 3H2, CANADA

Boucher, Gaetan *Speed Skater*
Center Sportif, 3850 Edger, Saint Hubert, QC, J4T 368, CANADA

Boucher, Pierre *Photographer*
L'Ermitage 7th Ave Massoul Faremountiers, Coulomiers, 77120, FRANCE

Boucher, Savannah *Actor*
H W A Talent, 3500 W Olive Ave #1400, Burbank, CA 91505 USA

Bouchez, Elodie *Actor*
Untitled Entertainment (LA), 8436 W 3rd St #650, Los Angeles, CA 90048 USA

Bouck, Brittany Page *Actor*
Penner PR, 8225 Santa Monica Blvd, West Hollywood, CA 90046

Bouck, Jonathan
PO Box 1398, Burbank, CA 91507

Boudart, Michel *Engineer, Misc*
512 Gerona Road, Stanford, CA 94305 USA

Boudin, Michael *Judge*
US Appeals Court, McCormack Federal Building, Boston, MA 02109 USA

Boudreau, Lou
415 Cedar Lane, Frankfort, IL 60423-1003

Bouillon, Jean-Christophe
Wildbacher 9, Hinwil, SWITZERLAND, CH 8340

Boujenah, Michael
35 rue de Rivoli, Paris, FRANCE, 75004

Boulez, Pierre *Composer, Conductor*
IRCAM, 1 Place Igor Stravinsky, Paris, 75004, FRANCE

Boulos, Frenchy *Soccer Player*
20 Elvin St, Staten Island, NY 10314 USA

Boulud, David *Chef*
Daniel Restaurant, 60 E 65th St, New York, NY 10021 USA

Boulware, Peter *Football Player*
305 Leaning Tree Road, Columbia, SC 29223 USA

Bouquet, Carole *Actor, Model*
Agents Associes Beaume, 201 Faubourg Saint Honore, Paris, 75008, FRANCE

Bourdeaux, Brandy *Actor*
Coralie Jr Theatrical Agency, 4789 Vineland Ave #100, N Hollywood, CA 91602 USA

Bourdeaux, Michael *Religious Leader*
Keston College, Heathfield Road Keston, Kent, BR2 6BA, UNITED KINGDOM (UK)

Bourdian, Anthony *Chef*
Food Network, 1180 Ave of Americas
#1200, New York, NY 10036 USA

Bourgeois, Louise *Misc*
347 W 20th St, New York, NY 10011
USA

Bourgignon, Serge *Director*
18 Rue de General-Malterre, Paris, 75016,
FRANCE

Bourjaily, Vance *Writer*
Redbird Farm RR 3, Iowa City, IA 52240
USA

Bourne, Judith
707 Crestmoore Pl, Venice, CA 90291

Bourne, Shae-Lynn *Figure Skater*
Connecticut Skating Center, 300 Alumni
Road, Newington, CT 06111 USA

Bournissen, Chantal *Skier*
1983 Evolene, SWITZERLAND

Bourque, Pierre *Misc*
Hotel de Ville, 275 Rue Notre Dame Est,
Montreal, QC, H2Y 1C6, CANADA

Bourque, Raymond J (Ray) *Hockey Player*
78 Coppermine Road, Topsfield, MA
01983 USA

Bourret, Caprice *Actor*
Richard Schwartz Management, 2934-1/2
Beverly Glen Cir #107, Los Angeles, CA
90077

Boushka, Richard (Dick) *Basketball Player*
7676 E Polo Dr #38, Wichita, KS 67206
USA

Bouteflika, Abdul Aziz *President*
President's Office, Al-Mouradia, Algiers,
Algeria

Bouton, James A (Jim) *Baseball Player,
Writer*
P O Box 188, North Edgemont, MA
01252 USA

Bouton, Jim
PO Box 188, North Edremont, MA 01252-
0188

Boutros-Ghali, Boutros *Secretary*
Inter'l Francophonie Org, 28 Rue de
Bourgogne, Paris, 75007, FRANCE

Bouvet, Didier *Skier*
Bouvet-Sports, Abondance, 74360,
FRANCE

Bouvia, Gloria *Bowler*
658 NE 23rd Place, Gresham, OR 97030
USA

Bova, Raoul *Actor*
Alan Siegel Entertainment, 345 N Maple
Dr #375, Beverly Hills, CA 90210 USA

Bow, Chuck *Race Car Driver*
National Assn of Stock Car Racing, 1801
Speedway Blvd, Daytona Beach, FL
32114 USA

Bow, Wow *Actor, Music Group*
Primier Talent, 1790 Broadway, New
York, NY 10019 USA

Bowa, Lawrence R (Larry) *Baseball
Player, Misc*
129 Upper Gulph Road, Radnor, PA
19087 USA

Bowab, John
2598 Green Valley, Los Angeles, CA
90046

Bowden, Robert (Bobby) *Football Coach*
Florida State University, Athletic Dept,
Tallahassee, FL 32306 USA

Bowden, Terry *Football Coach,
Sportscaster*
ABC-TV, Sports Dept 77 W 66th St, New
York, NY 10023 USA

Bowden, Tommy *Football Coach*
Clemson University, Athletic Dept,
Clemson, SC 29364 USA

Bowdler, William G *Diplomat*
State Department, 2201 C St NW,
Washington, DC 20520 USA

Bowe, David *Actor*
Karg/Weissenbach, 329 N Wetherly Dr
#101, Beverly Hills, CA 90211 USA

Bowe, Riddick L *Boxer*
714 Ahmer Dr, Fort Washington, MD
20744 USA

Bowe, Rosemarie *Actor*
321 St Pierre Rd, Los Angeles, CA 90077
USA

Bowen, Michael *Actor*
Diverse Talent Agency, 1875 Century Park
East #2250, Los Angeles, CA 90067 USA

Bowen, Otis R *Secretary*
P O Box 348, Bremen, IN 46506 USA

Bowen, Pamela
1140 Avenue of the Americas #500, New
York, NY 10036-5803

Bowen, William G *Educator, Misc*
Andrew Mellon Foundation, 140 E 62nd
St, New York, NY 10021 USA

Bower, Antoinette *Actor*
1529 N Beverly Glen Blvd, Los Angeles,
CA 90077 USA

Bower, John W (Johny) *Hockey Player*
3937 Parkgate Dr, Mississauga, ON L5N
7B4, CANADA

Bower, Robert W *Inventor*
University of California, Microelectronics
Dept, Davis, CA 95616 USA

Bowers, John *Misc*
International Longshoremen's Assn, 17
Battery Place, New York, NY 10004 USA

Bowers, John W *Religious Leader*
Foursquare Gospel Int'l Church, 1100
Glendale Blvd, Los Angeles, CA 90026
USA

Bowersox, Kenneth D *Astronaut*
16907 Soaring Forest Dr, Houston, TX
77059 USA

Bowie, David *Actor, Music Group*
Outside, 180-182 Thttenham Court Road,
London, W1P 9LE, UNITED KINGDOM
(UK)

Bowie, Sam *Basketball Player*
901 Curtilage, Lexington, KY 40502 USA

Bowker, Albert H *Educator*
1523 New Hampshire Ave NW,
Washington, DC 20036 USA

Bowker, Judi *Actor*
66 Berkeley House 5 Hay Hill, London,
W1X 7LH, UNITED KINGDOM (UK)

Bowles, Crandall C *Business Person*
Springs Industries, 205 N White St, Fort
Mill, SC 29715 USA

Bowles, Erskine B *Government Official*
6725 Old Providence Road, Charlotte, NC
28226 USA

Bowles, Lauren *Actor*
Endeavor Agency LLC (LA), 9601 Wilshire
Blvd Fl 3, Beverly Hills, CA 90210 USA

Bowles, Peter
125 Gloucester Rd, London, ENGLAND,
SW7

Bowlin, Michael R *Business Person*
Atlantic Richfield Co, 333 S Hope St, Los
Angeles, CA 90071 USA

Bowman, Christopher *Figure Skater*
5653 Kester Ave, Van Nuys, CA 91411
USA

Bowman, Harry W *Business Person*
Outboard Marine, P O Box 410,
Waukegan, IL 60079 USA

Bowman, Pasco M II *Judge*
US Court of Appeals, US Courthouse 811
Grand Ave, Kansas City, MO 64106 USA

Bowman, W Scott (Scotty) *Hockey
Player, Coach, Misc*
56 Halsten Parkway, East Amherst, NY
14051 USA

Bowyer, William *Artist*
12 Cleveland Ave Chiswick, London, W4
1SN, UNITED KINGDOM (UK)

Boxberger, Loa *Bowler*
P O Box 708, Russell, KS 67665 USA

Boxleitner, Bruce *Actor*
23679 Calabasas Road #181, Calabasas,
CA 91302 USA

Boy Hits Car *Music Group*
Wind-up Records, 72 Madison Ave, New
York, NY 10016 USA

Boyar, Lombardo *Actor*
Greene & Associates, 526 North
Larchmont Blvd, #201, Los Angeles, CA
90004

Boyce, Kim *Music Group*
200 Nathan Dr, Hollister, MO 65672 USA

Boycott, Geoffrey *Cricketer*
Cricket Club, Headingley Cricket Ground
Leeds, Yorks, LS6 3BY, UNITED
KINGDOM (UK)

Boyd, Alan S *Secretary, Misc*
2922 Larranaga Dr, Lady Lake, FL 32162
USA

Boyd, Billy *Actor*
Seven Summits Pictures & Management,
8906 West Olympic Blvd, Ground Floor,
Beverly Hills, CA 90211 USA

Boyd, Bob *Athlete*
2811 N Vassar St, Wichita, KS 67220

Boyd, Brandon *Musician*
Creative Artists Agency LCC (CAA-LA),
9830 Wilshire Blvd, Beverly Hills, CA
90212 USA

Boyd, Brent *Writer*

Boyd, Cayden *Actor*
James/Levy/Jacobson Management, 3500
W Olive Ave #1470, Burbank, CA 91505
USA

Boyd, Cletis L (Clete) *Baseball Player*
2034 20th Avenue Parkway, Indian Rocks
Beach, FL 33785 USA

Boyd, Davis (Oil Can) *Baseball Player*
1611 20th St, Meridian, MS 39301 USA

Boyd, Herbert W *Misc, Inventor*
P O Box 7318, Rancho Santa Fe, CA 92067 USA

Boyd, Jenna *Actor*
James/Levy/Jacobson Management, 3500 W Olive Ave #1470, Burbank, CA 91505 USA

Boyd, Malcolm *Writer, Religious Leader*
Saint Augustine-by-Sea Episcpal Church, 1227 4th St, Santa Monica, CA 90401 USA

Boyd, Paul D *Nobel Prize Laureate*
1033 Somera Road, Los Angeles, CA 90077 USA

Boyd, Richard A *Misc*
Fraternal Order of Police, 2100 Gardiner Lane, Louisville, KY 40205 USA

Boyd, Tanya *Actor*
Amsel Eisenstadt Frazier, 5757 Wilshire Blvd #510, Los Angeles, CA 90036 USA

Boyer, Jacqueline
162 rue Perronet, Neuilly s/s, FRANCE, 92200

Boyet, William
PO Box 1805, Studio City, CA 91614

Boykin, William G *General*
DepUndersecretary Intelligence, Defense Dept Pentagon, Washington, DC 20301 USA

Boylan, Jeanne
William Morris Agency (WMA-LA), 1 William Morris Pl, Beverly Hills, CA 90212 USA

Boyle, Clune Charlotte *Swimmer*
50 Brown's Grove Box 31, Scottsville, NY 14546 USA

Boyle, Danny *Director*
International Creative Management, 76 Oxford St, London, W1N 0AX, UNITED KINGDOM (UK)

Boyle, Lara Flynn *Actor*
International Creative Management (ICM-LA), 8942 Wilshire Blvd, Beverly Hills, CA 90211 USA

Boyle, Lisa *Actor, Model*
7336 Santa Monica Blvd #776, W Hollywood, CA 90046 USA

Boyle, Peter *Actor*
130 E End Ave, New York, NY 10028 USA

Boyle, T Coraghessan *Writer*
University of Southern California, English Dept, Los Angeles, CA 90089 USA

Boynton, Robert M *Doctor, Misc*
376 Bellaire St, Del Mar, CA 92014 USA

Boynton, Sandra *Artist, Misc*
Recycled Paper Products, 3636 N Broadway, Chicago, IL 60613 USA

Boys, Beach, The *Musician*
International Creative Management (ICM-NY), 40 W 57th St, New York, NY 10019 USA

Boys, Pet Shop *Music Group*
Creative Artists Agency LCC (CAA-LA), 9830 Wilshire Blvd, Beverly Hills, CA 90212 USA

Boysen, Sarah *Misc*
Ohio State University, Psychology Dept, Columbus, OH 43210, u

Boysen, Sarah *Misc*
Ohio State University, Psychology Dept, Columbus, OH 43210 USA

boysetsfire *Music Group*
Wind-up Records, 72 Madison Ave, New York, NY 10016 USA

Boyz II Men *Music Group*
Wright Entertainment Group (WEG), 7680 Universal Blvd #500, Orlando, FL 32819 USA

Bozilovic, Ivana *Actor*
Exposure (Xposure) Public Relations, 9171 Wilshire Blvd #300, Beverly Hills, CA 90210 USA

Boznic, Josip Cardinal *Religious Leader*
Zagreb Archdiocese, Kaptol 31 PP 553, Zagreb Hrvatska, 10001, CROATIA

Bozo, Laura *Actor*
Telemundo, 2470 West 8th Avenue, Hialeah, FL 33010 USA

BR5-49
9830 Wilshire Blvd, Beverly Hills, CA 90212

Braase, Ordeil *Football Player*
15549 W Clear Canyon Dr, Surprise, AZ 85374 USA

Brabham, John A (Jack) *Race Car Driver*
5 Ruxley Lane Ewell, Surrey, KT19 0JB, UNITED KINGDOM (UK)

Brabham, Sir Jack
Box 654, Miranda, AUSTRALIA, NSW 2228

Bracco, Lorraine *Actor*
Innovative Artists, 1505 10th St, Santa Monica, CA 90401 USA

Brace, William F *Geophysicist, Misc*
49 Liberty St, Concord, MA 01742 USA

Bracewell, Ronald N *Engineer*
836 Santa Fe Ave, Stanford, CA 94305 USA

Bracher, Karl D *Politician, Historian, Misc*
Unversitat Bonn, Stationsweg 17, Bonn, 53127, GERMANY

Brack, Kenny *Race Car Driver*
Team Rahal, 4601 Lyman Dr, Hillard, OH 43026 USA

Brack, Reginald K Jr *Publisher*
12 Huntzinger Dr, Greenwich, CT 06831 USA

Brackett, Griffin *Model*
860 NE 73rd St, Miami, FL 33138-5228

Bradbury, Janette Lane *Actor*
10817 King St, Toluca Lake, CA 91602 USA

Bradbury, Ray D *Writer*
10265 Cheviot Dr, Los Angeles, CA 90064 USA

Brademas, John *Educator*
New York University, Presindent's Emeritus Office, New York, NY 10012 USA

Braden, Vic *Tennis Player, Coach*
22000 Trabuco Canyon Road, Trabuco Canyon, CA 92678 USA

Bradford, Barbara Taylor *Writer*
Bradford Enterprises, 450 Park Ave, New York, NY 10022 USA

Bradford, Jesse *Actor*
William Morris Agency (WMA-LA), 1 William Morris Pl, Beverly Hills, CA 90212 USA

Bradford, Richard *Actor*
2511 Canyon Dr, Los Angeles, CA 90068 USA

Bradford, William *Business Person*
Halliburton Co, Lincoln Plaza 500 N Akard St, Dallas, TX 75201 USA

Bradlee, Benjamin C *Editor*
3014 N St NW, Washington, DC 20007 USA

Bradley, Bob *Soccer Player, Coach*
Chicago Fire, 980 N Michigan Ave #1998, Chicago, IL 60611 USA

Bradley, Brian *Hockey Player*
6417 MacLaurin Dr, Tampa, FL 33647 USA

Bradley, Bruce *Athlete, Misc*
262 Saint Joseph Ave, Long Beach, CA 90803 USA

Bradley, Dick *Cartoonist, Misc*
10176 Corporate Square Dr #200, Saint Louis, MO 63132 USA

Bradley, Edward R (Ed) *Commentator*
285 Central Park West, New York, NY 10024 USA

Bradley, Gordon *Soccer Player, Coach*
14300 Bakerwood Place, Haymarket, VA 20169 USA

Bradley, James *Actor*
1565 Riverside Dr #4, Glendale, CA 91201 USA

Bradley, Kathleen *Actor*
Kazarian/Spencer, 11365 Ventura Blvd #100, Studio City, CA 91604 USA

Bradley, Marion Zimmer *Writer*
Scovil-Chichak-Galen Literary Agency, 381 Park Ave S #1020, New York, NY 10016 USA

Bradley, Michael *Basketball Player*
6150 Blackjack Court N, Punta Gorda, FL 33982 USA

Bradley, Michael (Mike) *Golfer*
5203 Sand Trap Place, Valrico, FL 33594 USA

Bradley, Pat
PO Box 488, Camp Hill, PA 17001-0488

Bradley, Patricia E (Pat) *Golfer*
Opus, P O Box 116, Cheboygan, MI 49721 USA

Bradley, Rebecca *Golfer*
14443 W Lee Shore Dr, Willis, TX 77318 USA

Bradley, Robert A *Physicist*
2465 S Downing St, Denver, CO 80210 USA

Bradley, Shawn *Basketball Player*
P O Box 744 Highway 10, Castle Dale, UT 84513 USA

Bradley, William W (Bill) *Senator, Basketball Player*
Legal Center, 395 Pleasant Valley Way, West Orange, NJ 07052 USA

Bradley-Boyd, Grace
23872 Marmaro Bay, Monarch Beach, CA 92629

Bradshaw *Wrestler*
139 Denny Ln, Athens, TX 75751

Bradshaw, John E *Writer, Actor, Director*
Becsey/Wisdom/Kalajian, 9200 Sunset Blvd #820, Los Angeles, CA 90069 USA

Bradshaw, Terry *Football Player, Sportscaster*
8911 Shady Lane Dr, Shreveport, LA 71118 USA

Brady, Beau *Actor*
Darren Gray Management, 2 Marston Lane, Portsmouth, Hampshire, PO3 5T, England

Brady, Charles E *Astronaut*
287 Ben Ure Island, Oak Harbor, WA 98277 USA

Brady, James S (Jim) *Government Official, Journalist*
Handgun Control, 1225th St NW #1100, Washington, DC 20005 USA

Brady, Kyle *Football Player*
2221 Alicia Lane, Atlantic Beach, FL 32233 USA

Brady, Nicholas F *Secretary, Senator, Misc*
Darby Overseas Investments, 1133 Connecticut Ave NW, Washington, DC 20036 USA

Brady, Pat *Cartoonist*
United Feature Syndicate, 200 Madison Ave, New York, NY 10016 USA

Brady, Patrick H *War Hero*
2809 179th Ave E, Sumner, WA 98390 USA

Brady, Ray *Commentator*
CBS-TV, News Dept 524 W 57th St, New York, NY 10019 USA

Brady, Roscoe O *Misc*
6026 Valerian Lane, Rockville, MD 20852 USA

Brady, Sarah *Social Activist*
Handgun Control, 1225 I St NW #1100, Washington, DC 20005 USA

Brady, Tom *Actor*
Endeavor Agency LLC (LA), 9601 Wilshire Blvd Fl 3, Beverly Hills, CA 90210 USA

Brady, Tom *Football Player*
New England Patriots, Gillette Stadium - RR 1, 60 Washington, Foxboro, MA 02035 USA

Brady, Wayne *Actor, Comedian*
Wayne Brady Show, The, 7800 Beverly Blvd E #214, Los Angeles, CA 90036 USA

Braeden, Eric *Actor*
13723 Romany Dr, Pacific Palisades, CA 90272 USA

Braff, Zach *Actor*
P M K Public Relations, 8500 Wilshire Blvd, #700, Beverly Hills, CA 90211 USA

Braga, Brannon *Writer*
Endeavor Agency LLC (LA), 9601 Wilshire Blvd Fl 3, Beverly Hills, CA 90210 USA

Braga, Sonia *Actor*
41 River Terrace, #1403, New York, NY 10282 USA

Bragan, Robert R (Bobby) *Baseball Player*
7201 W Vickery Blvd, Benbrook, TX 76116 USA

Bragg, Billy *Musician*
Sincere Mgmt, 6 Bravington Road, #6, London, W9 3AH, UNITED KINGDOM (UK)

Bragg, Darrell B *Misc*
University of British Columbia, Vancouver, BC V6T 2AZ, CANADA

Bragg, Don
PO Box 171, New Gretna, NJ 08224

Bragg, Donald G (Don) *Track Athlete*
90 State St, Penns Grove, NJ 08069 USA

Bragg, Melvyn *Writer*
12 Hampstead Hill Gardens, London, NW3 2PL, UNITED KINGDOM (UK)

Bragin, Rob *Writer*
William Morris Agency (WMA-LA), 1 William Morris Pl, Beverly Hills, CA 90212 USA

Brahaney, Thomas F (Tom) *Football Player*
17 Winchester Court, Midland, TX 79705 USA

Brainin, Nobert *Musician*
19 Prowse Ave, Busbey Heath, Herts, WD2 1JS, UNITED KINGDOM (UK)

Brainville, Ives
34 Cours de Vincennes, Paris, FRANCE, 75012

Bramall of Busfield, Edwin N W *Misc*
House of Lords, Westminster, London, SW1A 0PW, UNITED KINGDOM (UK)

Bramlett, Delaney *Musician*
PO Box 177, Sunland, CA 91041 USA

Branagh, Kenneth *Actor, Director*
Marmont Mgmt, Langham House, 320/8 Regent St, London, W1R 5AL, UNITED KINGDOM (UK)

Branca, John G *Attorney General*
Ziffren Brittenham Branca, 1801 Century Park West, Los Angeles, CA 90067 USA

Branca, Ralph
Westchester Country Club, Rye, NY 10580

Branca, Ralph T J *Baseball Player*
National Pension, 1025 Westchester, White Plains, NY 10604 USA

Brancato, John D (JD) *Writer, Producer*
Broder Webb Chervin Silbermann Agency, The (BWCS), 9242 Beverly Blvd #200, Beverly Hills, CA 90210 USA

Brancato Jr, Lillo *Actor*
Innovative Artists (LA), 1505 Tenth St, Santa Monica, CA 90401 USA

Branch, Clifford (Cliff) *Football Player, Football Coach*
2071 Stonefield Lane, Santa Rosa, CA 95403 USA

Branch, Michelle *Musician, Songwriter*
PO Box 20425, Sedona, AZ 86341 USA

Branch, Vanessa *Actor*
Jerry Shandrew PR, 1050 South Stanley Avenue, Los Angeles, CA 90019-6634 USA

Branch, William B *Writer*
53 Cortlandt Ave, New Rochelle, NY 10801 USA

Brand, Colette *Skier*
Rigistr 24, Baar, 6340, SWITZERLAND

Brand, Daniel (Dan) *Wrestler*
4321 Bridgeview Dr, Oakland, CA 94602 USA

Brand, Elton *Basketball Player*
Los Angeles Clippers, Staples Center, 1111 S Figueroa St, Los Angeles, CA 90015 USA

Brand, Glen *Wrestler*
PO Box 6069, Omaha, NE 68106 USA

Brand, Jolene
8321 Beverly Blvd, Los Angeles, CA 90048

Brand, Joshua *Producer*
William Morris Agency (WMA-LA), 1 William Morris Pl, Beverly Hills, CA 90212 USA

Brand, Myles *Educator*
Indiana University, President's Office, Bloomington, IN 47405 USA

Brand, Neville *Actor*
International Creative Management (ICM-LA), 8942 Wilshire Blvd, Beverly Hills, CA 90211 USA

Brand, Oscar *Songwriter, Musician*
Gypsy Hill Music, 141 Baker Hill Road, Great Neck, NY 11023 USA

Brand, Robert *Designer*
508 W End Ave, New York, NY 10024 USA

Brand, Steven *Actor*
Bauer Company, The, 9300 Wilshire Blvd #PH, Beverly Hills, CA 90212 USA

Brand, Vance D *Astronaut*
NASA Dryden Flight Center, PO Box 273, Edwards, CA 93523 USA

Brandauer, Klaus Maria *Actor*
Novapool Gmbh, Paul Lincke Ufer 42-43, Berlin, 10999, GERMANY

Brandenstein, Daniel C *Astronaut*
12802 Tri-City Beach Road, Baytown, TX 77520 USA

Brandi *Model*
Next Model Mgmt, 23 Watts St, New York, NY 10013 USA

Brando, Marion *Actor*
Brown Craft Co, 11940 San Vicente Blvd, Los Angeles, CA 90049 USA

Brando, Marlon
Special Artists Agency, 345 North Maple Drive, #302, Beverly Hills, CA 90210 USA

Brandon, Barbara *Cartoonist*
Universal Press Syndicate, 4520 Main St, Kansas City, MO 64111 USA

Brandon, Clark *Actor*
Jennings Assoc, 28035 Dorothy Dr, #210A, Agoura, CA 91301 USA

Brandon, Jeb *Actor*
Endeavor Agency LLC (LA), 9601 Wilshire Blvd Fl 3, Beverly Hills, CA 90210 USA

Brandon, John *Actor*
Coast to Coast Talent, 3350 Barham Blvd, Los Angeles, CA 90068 USA

Brandon, Michael *Actor*
Epstein-Wyckoff, 280 S Beverly Dr, #400, Beverly Hills, CA 90212 USA

Brands, Tom *Wrestler*
4494 Taft Ave SE, Iowa City, IA 52240 USA

Brands, X *Actor*
17171 Roscoe Blvd, #104, Northridge, CA 91325 USA

Brandt, Hank *Actor*
Contemporary Artists, 610 Santa Monica Blvd, #202, Santa Monica, CA 90401 USA

Brandt, Jon *Musician*
Monterey Peninsula Artists, 509 Hartnell St, Monterey, CA 93940 USA

Brandt, Paul *Musician*
Creative Trust, 2105 Elliston Place, Nashville, TN 37203 USA

Brandt, Victor *Actor*
H David Moss, 733 Seward St, #PH, Los Angeles, CA 90038 USA

Branduardi, Angelo
Viale di Trastevere 1-108, Rome, ITALY, I-00153

Brandy, J C *Actor*
Henderson/Hogan, 8285 W Sunset Blvd, #1, West Hollywood, CA 90046 USA

Brandywine, Marcia *Commentator*
743 Huntley Dr, Los Angeles, CA 90069 USA

Brannan, Charles F *Secretary*
3131 E Alameda Ave, Denver, CO 80209 USA

Brannon, Ronald *Religious Leader*
Wesleyan Church, PO Box 50434, Indianapolis, IN 46250 USA

Branson, Richard *Business Person*
Virgin Group, 120 Campden Hill Rd, London, W8 7AR, UNITED KINGDOM (UK)

Branson, Sir, Richard *Business Person*
Manor Royal, Crasley, West Sussex, England, RH10 2ND

Brant, Tim *Sportscaster*
ABC-TV, Sports Dept, 77 W 66th St, New York, NY 10023 USA

Braschler Family PO Box 1408, Branson MO, 65615

Brashear, Carl *Misc*
804 Tenure Lane, Virginia Beach, VA 23462 USA

Brasi, Tino Via Ferraioli
Isola Farnesi, Rome, ITALY, I-00123

Braslow, Paul *Artist*
82 Neds Way, Bel Tiburon, CA 94920 USA

Brassette, Amy *Actor*
Marv Dauer Management, 11661 San Vicente Blvd #104, Los Angeles, CA 90049 USA

Brasseur, Claude *Actor*
Artmedia, 20 Ave Rapp, Paris, 75007, FRANCE

Brathwaite, Nicholas *Prime Minister*
House of Representatives, Saint George's, GRENADA

Bratkowski, Edmund R (Zeke) *Football Player, Coach*
224 Anchors Lake Dr N, Santa Rosa Beach, FL 32459 USA

Bratt, Benjamin *Actor*
11777 San Vicente Blvd, #700, Los Angeles, CA 90049 USA

Bratton, Creed *Musician*
Thomas Cassidy, 11761 E Speedway Blvd, Tucson, AZ 85748 USA

Bratton, Joseph K *General*
1465 Goldrush Ave, Melbourne, FL 32940 USA

Bratton, William J *Lawyer*
Los Angeles Police Dept, 150 S Los Angeles St, Los Angeles, CA 90012 USA

Bratz, Mike *Basketball Player*
7503 Tillman Hill Road, Colleyville, TX 76034 USA

Brauer, Arik *Artist*
Academy of Fine Arts, Schillerplatz 3, Vienna, 1010, AUSTRIA

Braugher, Andre *Actor*
361 Charlton Ave, South Orange, NJ 07079 USA

Brauman, John *Misc*
849 Tolman Dr, Palo Alto, CA 94305 USA

Braun, Allen *Scientist*
National Institute on Deafness, 9000 Rockville Pike, Bethesda, MD 20892 USA

Braun, Carl *Basketball Player, Coach*
5603 SE Foxcross Place, Stuart, FL 34997 USA

Braun, Lillian Jackson *Writer*
Blanche Gregory Inc, 2 Tudor Place, New York, NY 10017 USA

Braun, Pinkas *Actor, Director*
Unterdorf, 8261, Hemishofen/SH, SWITZERLAND

Braun, Richard L *War Hero*
1912 Whittle Wood Road, Williamsburg, VA 23185 USA

Braun, Steve *Actor*
Evolution Entertainment, 901 N Highland Ave, Los Angeles, CA 90038 USA

Braun, Tamara *Actor*
General Hospital, 4151 Prospect Ave, Los Angeles, CA 90027 USA

Braun, Wendy *Actor*
House of Representatives, 400 S Beverly Dr #101, Beverly Hills, CA 90212 USA

Braun, Zev *Producer*
Zev Braun Pictures, 1438 N Gower St, #26, Los Angeles, CA 90028 USA

Braunduardi, Angelo
Viale Travestere, Rome, ITALY, 1-10800153

Braunwald, Eugene *Physicist*
Partners Healthcare, 800 Boylston St, Boston, MA 02199 USA

Braver, Rita *Commentator*
CBS-TV, News Dept, 2020 M St NW, Washington, DC 20036 USA

Braverman, Bart *Actor*
House of Representatives, 400 S Beverly Dr, #101, Beverly Hills, CA 90212 USA

Bravo, Tony *Actor*
Televisa, Blvd Adolfo Lopez Mateos 232, Colonia San Angel INN, DF, CP 01060, MEXICO

Braxton, Anthony *Composer*
Berkeley Agency, 2608 9th St, Berkeley, CA 94710 USA

Braxton, Toni *Musician, Songwriter*
Blackground, 10345 W Olympic Blvd, Los Angeles, CA 90064 USA

Braxton, Tyrone S *Football Player*
455 Keamey St, Denver, CO 80220 USA

Bray, Deanne *Actor*
Craig Management, 125 South Sycamore Avenue, Los Angeles, CA 90036 USA

Brayton, Tyler *Football Player*
Oakland Raiders, 1220 Harbor Bay Parkway, Alameda, CA 94502 USA

Brazadskas, Algirdas *President*
Tumiskiu 30, Vilnius, 2016, LITHUANIA

Brazelton, T Berry *Doctor*
23 Hawthorn St, Cambridge, MA 02138 USA

Brazen, Randi
3205 Evergreen Point Rd, Media, WA 98039

Brazil, Jeff *Journalist*
Orlando Sentinel, Editorial Dept, 633 N Orange Ave, Orlando, FL 32801 USA

Brazil, John R *Educator*
Bradley University, President's Office, Peoria, IL 61625 USA

Brazile, Robert L Jr *Football Player*
263 Woodland Ave, Satsuma, AL 35672 USA

Brazile, Trevor *Rodeo Rider*
4609 US Highway, 277 S, Anson, TX 79501 USA

Bready, Richard L *Business Person*
166 President Ave, Providence, RI 02906 USA

Breaking Point *Music Group*
Wind-up Records, 72 Madison Ave, New York, NY 10016 USA

Bream, Julian *Musician*
Hazard Chase, Richmond House, 16-20 Regent St, Cambridge, CB2 1DB, UNITED KINGDOM (UK)

Breathed, Berkeley *Cartoonist*
Washington Post Writers Group, 1150 15th St NW, Washington, DC 20071 USA

Breathwaite, Edward *Writer*
University of West Indies, History Dept, Mona, Kingston, 7, JAMAICA

Breck, Jonathan *Actor*
Chasin Agency, The, 8899 Beverly Blvd #716, Los Angeles, CA 90048 USA

Breck, Peter *Actor*
Artists Group, 10100 Santa Monica Blvd, #2490, Los Angeles, CA 90067 USA

Breckenridge, Alex *Actor*
Kohner Agency, The, 9300 Wilshire Blvd #555, Beverly Hills, CA 90212 USA

Brecker, Michael *Musician*
International Music Network, 278 S Main St, #400, Gloucester, MA 01930 USA

Brecker, Randy *Musician*
Tropix International, 163 3rd Ave, #206,
New York, NY 10003 USA

Breder, Charles M *Misc*
6275 Manasola Key Road, Englewood, FL
34223 USA

Bredsen, Espen *Skier*
Hellerud Gardsvei 18, Oslo, 0671,
NORWAY

Breeden, Richard C *Government Official*
Coopers & Lybrand, 1800 M St NW,
Washington, DC 20036 USA

Breedlove, N Craig *Race Car Driver*
200 N Front St, Rio Vista, CA 94571-1420
USA

Breen, Bobby *Actor*
10550 NW 71st Pl, Tamarac, FL 33321
USA

Breen, Edward D *Business Person*
Tyco International, 273 Corporate Dr,
#100, Portsmouth, NH 03801 USA

Breen, George *Swimmer*
425 Pepper Mill Court, Sewell, NJ 08080
USA

Breen, John G *Business Person*
18800 N Park Blvd, Shaker Heights, OH
44122 USA

Breen, Monica *Writer*
Endeavor Agency LLC (LA), 9601 Wilshire
Blvd Fl 3, Beverly Hills, CA 90210 USA

Breen, Patrick *Actor*
Gersh Agency, 232 N Canon Dr, Beverly
Hills, CA 90210 USA

Breen, Shelley *Musician*
TBA Artists Mgmt, 300 10th Ave S,
Nashville, TN 37203 USA

Breen, Stephen (Steve) *Cartoonist*
San Diego Union-Telegram, PO Box
120191, San Diego, CA 92112 USA

Brees, Drew *Football Player*
San Diego Chargers, 4020 Murphy
Canyon Road, San Diego, CA 92123 USA

Bregman, Buddy *Actor*
11288 Ventura Blvd #700, Studio City, CA
91604 USA

Bregman, Martin *Producer*
Bregman/Baer Productions, 641 Lexington
Ave, New York, NY 10022 USA

Bregman Recht, Tracey *Actor*
Bell-Phillip Productions, 7800 Beverly
Blvd, #3371, Los Angeles, CA 90036 USA

Breidenbach, Warren *Doctor*
Jewish Hospital, Surgery Dept, 217 E
Chestnut, Louisville, KY 40202 USA

Breiman, Valerie *Director*
Industry Entertainment, 955 S Carrillo Dr
#300, Los Angeles, CA 90048 USA

Breitner, Paul
Kuckucksweg 4, Brunnthal, GERMANY,
D-85649

Breitschwerdt, Werner *Business Person*
Daimler-Benz AG, Mercedesstr 136,
Stuttgart, 70322, GERMANY

Breland, Mark *Boxer*
5355 Carolina Highway, Denmark, SC
29042 USA

Bremmer, Rory
BBC Artist Mail, PO Box 1116, Belfast,
BT2 7AJ, United Kingdom

Bremner, Ewen *Actor*
International Creative Mgmt, 76 Oxford
St, London, W1N 0AX, UNITED
KINGDOM (UK)

Brenan, Gerald *Writer*
Alhaurin El Grande, Malaga, SPAIN

Brendel, Alfred *Musician*
Vanguard/Omega Classics, 27 W 72nd St,
New York, NY 10023 USA

Brendel, Wolfgang *Opera Singer*
Manuela Kursiden, Wasagasse 12/1/3,
Vienna, 1090, AUSTRIA

Brenden, Hallgeir *Skier*
2417 Torberget, NORWAY

Brendon, Nicholas *Actor*
Platform, 2666 N Beachwood Dr, Los
Angeles, CA 90068 USA

Breneman, Curtis E *Misc*
38 Cartyle Ave, Troy, NY 12180 USA

Brenly, Robert E (Bob) *Basketball Player*
9726 E Laurel Lane, Scottsdale, AZ 85260
USA

Brennaman, Marty *Sportscaster*
Cincinnati Reds, Cinergy Field, 100
Riverfront Stadium, Cincinnati, OH 45202
USA

Brennaman, Thom *Sportscaster*
Fox-TV, Sports Dept, PO Box 900, Beverly
Hills, CA 90213 USA

Brennan, Amy *Actor*
Creative Artists Agency, 9830 Wilshire
Blvd, Beverly Hills, CA 90212 USA

Brennan, Bernard F *Business Person*
Montgomery Ward, PO Box 5238, Elgin,
IL 60121 USA

Brennan, Christine *Writer*
Washington Post, Sports Dept, 1150 15th
Ave NW, Washington, DC 20071 USA

Brennan, Edward A *Business Person*
AMR Corp, 433 Amon Carter Blvd, Fort
Worth, TX 76155 USA

Brennan, Eileen *Actor*
4380 Troost Ave, Studio City, CA 91604
USA

Brennan, Joseph E *Governor*
104 Frances St, Portland, ME 04102 USA

Brennan, Kevin *Actor, Comedian*
United Talent Agency, 9560 Wilshire
Blvd, #500, Beverly Hills, CA 90212 USA

Brennan, Maire *Musician, Songwriter*
Soho Agency, 55 Fulham High St,
London, SW6 3JJ, UNITED KINGDOM
(UK)

Brennan, Melissa *Actor*
6520 Platt Ave, #634, W Hills, CA 91307
USA

Brennan, Terrance P (Terry) *Football
Player, Coach*
1731 Wildberry Dr, #C, Glenview, IL
60025 USA

Brenneman, Amy *Producer, Writer, Actor*
Tavel Entertainment, 9171 Wilshire Blvd
#406, Beverly Hills, CA 90210 USA

Brenner, David *Actor, Comedian*
3749 Amber Lantern Cir, Las Vegas, NV
89147 USA

Brenner, Dori *Actor*
210 W 101st St #15C, New York, NY
10025 USA

Brenner, Lisa *Actor*
7729 Sunset Blvd, Los Angeles, CA 90046
USA

Brenner, Sydney *Nobel Prize Laureate*
Salk Institute, 10100 N Torrey Pines Road,
La Jolla, CA 92037 USA

Brenner, Teddy *Boxer*
24 W 55th St, #9C, New York, NY 10019
USA

Brent, Eve *Actor*
Craig Mgmt, 125 S Sycamore Ave, Los
Angeles, CA 90036 USA

Bresee, Bobbie *Actor*
PO Box 1222, Hollywood, CA 90078
USA

Breslawsky, Marc C *Business Person*
Pitney Bowes Inc, 1 Elmcroft Road,
Stamford, CT 06926 USA

Breslin, Abigail *Actor*
Envision Entertainment, 9255 Sunset Blvd
#300, Los Angeles, CA 90069 USA

Breslin, Jimmy *Journalist*
Newsday, Editorial Dept, 235 Pinelawn
Road, Melville, NY 11747 USA

Breslin, Spencer *Actor*
Cunningham/EscottDipene, 10635 Santa
Monica Blvd, #130, Los Angeles, CA
90025

Breslow, Lester *Physicist*
10926 Verano Road, Los Angeles, CA
90077 USA

Breslow, Ronald C *Misc*
295 Three Mile Harbor Road, East
Hampton, NY 11937 USA

Brest, Martin *Director, Producer*
831 Paseo Miramar, Pacific Palisades, CA
90272 USA

Brett, George
PO Box 419969, Kansas City, MO 64141

Brett, George H *Baseball Player*
2360 Guilford Lane, Mission Hills, KS
66208 USA

Brett, Jonathan *Actor*
Agency for Performing Arts, 9200 Sunset
Blvd, #900, Los Angeles, CA 90069 USA

Breuer, Grit *Track Athlete*
Konrad-Adenauer-Str 16, Garbsen, 30823,
GERMANY

Breuer, Jim *Comedian*
Brillstein-Grey Entertainment, 9150
Wilshire Blvd #350, Beverly Hills, CA
90212 USA

Breunig, Robert P (Bob) *Football Player*
9215 Westview Circle, Dallas, TX 75231
USA

Brewer, Albert P *Governor*
2520 Ashford Place, Birmingham, AL
35243 USA

Brewer, Derek Stanley *Educator*
Emmanuel College, English Dept,
Cambridge, CB2 3AP, UNITED
KINGDOM (UK)

Brewer, Donald *Musician*
Lustig Talent, PO Box 770850, Orlando, FL 32877 USA

Brewer, Gay
7736 Glen Devon Lane, Del Ray Beach, FL 33446

Brewer, Gay Jr *Golfer*
7736 Glendevon Lane, Delray Beach, FL 33446 USA

Brewer, Jim T *Basketball Player, Coach*
29710 Whitley Collins Dr, Rancho Palos Verdes, CA 90275 USA

Brewer, Leo *Misc*
5739 SW Downs View Court, Portland, OR 97221 USA

Brewer, Richard G *Physicist*
730 De Soto Dr, Palo Alto, CA 94303 USA

Brewer, Teresa *Musician*
384 Pinebrook Blvd, New Rochelle, NY 10804 USA

Brewster, Jordana *Actor*
Creative Artists Agency LCC (CAA-LA), 9830 Wilshire Blvd, Beverly Hills, CA 90212 USA

Brewster, Paget *Actor*
Burstein Company, The, 15304 Sunset Blvd #208, Pacific Palisades, CA 90272 USA

Brewton, Maia *Actor*
PB Management, 6523 West Sixth Street, Los Angeles, CA 90048 USA

Brey, Mike *Coach*
Notre Dame University, Athletic Dept, Notre Dame, IN 46556 USA

Breyer, Stephen G *Judge*
US Supreme Court, 1 1st St NE, Washington, DC 20543 USA

Breytenbach, Breyten *Writer*
Harcourt Brace, 525 B St, San Diego, CA 92101 USA

Breziner, Salome
PO Box 5617, Beverly Hills, CA 90210

Brezis, Haim *Mathematician*
18 Rue de la Glaciere, Paris Cedex 13, 75640, FRANCE

Brezner, Larry *Producer*
MBST Entertainment, 345 N Maple D #200, Suite 200, Beverly Hills, CA 90210 USA

Brialy, Jean-Claude *Actor*
25 Quai Bourbon, 75004, Paris, 75004, FRANCE

Brian, Earl W *Publisher*
United Press International, 1400 I St NW, Washington, DC 20005 USA

Brice, William J *Artist*
427 Beloit St, Los Angeles, CA 90049 USA

Bricekel, James R *General*
4798 Hanging Moss Lane, Sarasota, FL 34238 USA

Bricekell, Beth *Director*
PO Box 119, Paron, AR 72122 USA

Bricekell, Edie *Musician, Songwriter*
88 Central Park West, New York, NY 10023 USA

Brickell, Beth
PO Box 26, Paron, AR 72122-0026

Brickell, Edie *Musician*
88 Central Park W, New York, NY 10023 USA

Bricker, Neal S *Physicist*
4240 Piedmont Mesa Road, Claremont, CA 91711 USA

Brickhouse, Smith N *Religious Leader*
Church of Christ, PO Box 472, Independence, MO 64051 USA

Bricklin, Daniel S *Designer*
Trellix Corp, 300 Bahr Ave, Concord, MA 01742 USA

Brickman, Jim *Actor*
Brickman Music, 11288 Ventura Blvd, #606, Studio City, CA 91604 USA

Brickman, Paul *Director*
4116 Holly Knoll Dr, Los Angeles, CA 90027 USA

Bricusse, Lesile *Musician, Composer*
8730 Sunset Blvd, #300W, Los Angeles, CA 90069 USA

Bridgers, Sean *Actor*
Daris Hatch Management, 9538 Brighton Way #308, Beverly Hills, CA 90210 USA

Bridges, Alan J S *Director*
28 High St, Shepperton, Middx, TW7 9AW, UNITED KINGDOM (UK)

Bridges, Alicia
1560 Broadway #1308, New York, NY 10036

Bridges, Allcia *Songwriter, Musician*
Talent Consultants International, 1560 Broadway, #1308, New York, NY 10036 USA

Bridges, Angelica *Actor, Model*
Marv Dauer Management, 11661 San Vicente Blvd #104, Los Angeles, CA 90049 USA

Bridges, Beau *Actor*
United Talent Agency, 9560 Wilshire Blvd, #500, Beverly Hills, CA 90212 USA

Bridges, Bill *Basketball Player*
145 Bay St, #19, Santa Monica, CA 90405 USA

Bridges, Chris (Ludacris) *Musician, Actor, Producer*
William Morris Agency (WMA-LA), 1 William Morris Pl, Beverly Hills, CA 90212 USA

Bridges, Jeff *Actor, Producer*
988 Hot Springs Road, Montecito, CA 91308 USA

Bridges, Todd A *Actor*
2621 Oakwood Ave, Venice, CA 90291 USA

Bridges Jr, Roy D *Astronaut, General*
750 N Atlantic Ave, #405, Cocoa Beach, FL 32931 USA

Bridgewater, Dee Dee *Musician*
B H Hopper Mgmt, Elvirastr 25, Munich, 80636, GERMANY

Bridwell, Norman *Writer*
PO Box 869, Edgartown, MA 02539 USA

Brierley, Ronald A *Business Person*
Guinness Peat Group, 21-26 Garlick Hill, London, EC4 2AU, UNITED KINGDOM (UK)

Briers, Richard *Actor, Comedian*
Hamilton Hodell Ltd, 24 Hanway St Fl 24, London, W1T 1UH, UNITED KINGDOM (UK)

Brigati, Eddie *Musician, Songwriter*
Dassinger Creative, 32 Ardsley Road, #201, Montclair, NJ 07042 USA

Briggs, Edward S *Admiral*
3648 Lago Sereno, Esxondido, CA 92029 USA

Briggs, Raymond R *Cartoonist, Writer*
Weston, Underhill Lane, Westmeston near Hassocks, Sussex, UNITED KINGDOM (UK)

Briggs, Robert W *Biologist*
480 Rale St, Palo Alto, CA 94301 USA

Briggs of Lewes, Asa *Historian*
Caprons Keere St, Lewes, Sussex, UNITED KINGDOM (UK)

Bright, Kevin S *Director, Producer, Writer*
Bright Kauffman Crane Productions, 4000 Warner Blvd, Bldg 160 #750, Burbank, CA 91522

Bright, Myron H *Judge*
655 1st Ave N, #340, Fargo, ND 58102 USA

Brightman, Sarah *Musician*
Feinstein Mgmt, 420 Lexington Ave, #2150, New York, NY 10170 USA

Briles, Nelson K *Baseball Player*
78 Lakewood Road, Greensburg, PA 15601 USA

Brill, Charlie *Actor*
3635 Wrightwood Dr, Studio City, CA 91604 USA

Brill, Francesca *Actor*
Kate Feast Primrose Hill Studios, Fitzroy Road, London, NW1 8TR, UNITED KINGDOM (UK)

Brill, Steven *Editor, Publisher*
American Lawyer Magazine, 600 3rd Ave, New York, NY 10016 USA

Brill, Steven *Director, Writer*
International Creative Mgmt, 8942 Wilshire Blvd, #219, Beverly Hills, CA 90211 USA

Brill, Winston J *Misc*
12529 237th Way NE, Redmond, WA 98053 USA

Brillstein, Bernie *Producer*
Brillstein-Grey Entertainment, 9150 Wilshire Blvd #350, Beverly Hills, CA 90212 USA

Brimley, Wilford *Actor*
B7 Ranch, 10000 North, Lehi, UT 84043 USA

Brimmer, Andrew F *Economist, Government Official*
Brimmer Co, 4400 MacArthur Blvd NW, Washington, DC 20007 USA

Brin, Sergey *Business Person, Engineer*
Google Inc, 2400 Bayshore Parkway, Mountain View, CA 94043 USA

Brinegar, Claude S *Secretary, Business Person*
Po Box 4346, Stanford, CA 94309 USA

Bring, Murray H *Business Person*
Altria Group, 120 Park Ave, New York, NY 10017 USA

Brink, Andre P *Writer*
University of Cape Town, English Dept, Rondebosch, 7700, SOUTH AFRICA

Brink, Frank Jr *Physicist*
Pine Run, #E1 Ferry & Iron Roads, Doylestown, PA 18901 USA

Brink, K Robert *Publisher*
Town & Country Megazine, 1700 Broadway, New York, NY 10012 USA

Brink, R Alexander *Misc*
8301 Old Sauk Road, #326, Middleton, WI 53562 USA

Brinker, Bob *Business Person, Radio Personality*
AdPad Inc, 5226 E Wagoner Rd, Scottsdale, AZ 85254-7636

Brinker, Nancy *Business Person*
The Susan G. Komen Breast Cancer Foundation, Inc, 5005 LBJ Freeway, Suite 250, Dallas, TX 75244

Brinkley, Christie *Model*
Ford Model Agency, 142 Greene St, #400, New York, NY 10012 USA

Brinkman, John A *Historian*
1321 56th St, #4, Chicago, IL 60637 USA

Brinkman, William F *Physicist*
20 Constitution Hill W, Princeton, NJ 08540 USA

Brinkmann, Robert S *Cinematographer*
Spyros Skouras, 631 Wilshire Blvd, #2C, Santa Monica, CA 90401 USA

Brinster, Ralph L *Biologist*
University of Pennsylvania, Veterinary Medicine School, Philadelphia, PA 19104 USA

Brion, Francoise
11 rue de Seine, Paris, FRANCE, 75006

Brion, John *Composer*
Gortaine/Schwartz, 13245 Riverside Dr, #450, Sherman Oaks, CA 91423 USA

Brisco, Jack *Wrestler*
19018 Blake Road, Odessa, FL 33556 USA

Brisco, Marlin *Football Player*
379 Newport Ave, #107, Long Beach, CA 90814 USA

Brisco, Valerie *Track Athlete*
USA Track & Field, 4341 Starlight Dr, Indianapolis, IN 46239 USA

Briscoe, Brent *Actor*
United Talent Agency (UTA), 9560 Wilshire Blvd, Beverly Hills, CA 90212 USA

Briscoe, Dolph Jr *Governor*
338 Pecan St, Uvalde, TX 78801 USA

Briscoe, Mary Beck *Judge*
US Appeals Court, 4839 W 15th St, Lawrence, KS 66049 USA

Brisebois, Danielle *Actor, Musician*
Haber Corp, 16830 Ventura Blvd, #501, Encino, CA 91436 USA

Brissie, Leland V (Lou) *Baseball Player*
1908 White Pine Dr, North Augusta, SC 29841 USA

Brisson, Lance
4570 Noeline Way, Encino, CA 91436

Brister, Walter A (Bubby) III *Football Player*
139 Fontainbleau Dr, Mandeville, LA 70471 USA

Bristow, Allan M *Coach, Basketball Player*
PO Box 635, Gloucester Point, VA 23062 USA

Britain, Radie *Composer*
PO Box 17, Smithville, IN 47458 USA

Britt, Chris *Cartoonist*
State Journal-Register, Editorial Dept, 1 Copley Plaza, Springfield, IL 62701 USA

Britt, Michael *Musician*
Borman Entertainment, 1222 16th Ave S, #23, Nashville, TN 37212 USA

Brittany, Morgan *Actor, Model*
3434 Cornell Road, Agoura Hills, CA 91301 USA

Britten, Roy J *Misc*
Kerckhoff Marine Laboratory, 101 Dahlia Ave Ave, Corona del Mar, CA 92625 USA

Brittenham, Harry *Attorney General*
Ziffren Brittenham Branca, 1801 Century Park West, Los Angeles, CA 90067 USA

Britton, Benjamin *Inventor*
University of Cincinnati, Fine Arts Dept, Cincinnati, OH 45221 USA

Britton, Connie *Actor*
Handprint Entertainment, 1100 Glendon Ave #1000, Los Angeles, CA 90024 USA

Britton, Tony *Actor*
International Creative Mgmt, 76 Oxford St, London, W1N 0AX, UNITED KINGDOM (UK)

Britz, Jerilyn *Golfer*
415 E Lincoln St, #7, Luverne, MN 56156 USA

Brizan, George *Prime Minister*
Prime Minister's Office, Botanical Gardens, Saint George's, GRENADA

Broadbent, Jim *Actor*
International Creative Mgmt, 76 Oxford St, London, ENGLAND, W1N 0AX, UNITED KINGDOM (UK)

Broadbent, John Edward *Government Official*
1386 Nicola, #30, Vancouver, BC V6G 2G2, CANADA

Broaddus, J Alfred Jr *Financier*
Federal Reserve Bank, PO Box 27622, Richmond, VA 23261 USA

Broadhead, James L *Business Person*
FPL Group, 700 Universe Blvd, Juno Beach, FL 33408 USA

Brobeck, John R *Physicist*
224 Vassar Ave, Swarthmore, PA 19081 USA

Broberg, Gus *Basketball Player*
208 El Pueblo Way, Palm Beach, FL 33480 USA

Broccoli, Barbara *Producer*
Creative Artists Agency LCC (CAA-LA), 9830 Wilshire Blvd, Beverly Hills, CA 90212 USA

Broches, Aron *Attorney General*
44 Pond St, Wakefield, RI 02879 USA

Brochtrup, William (Bill) *Actor*
S D B Partners, 1801 Ave of Stars, #902, Los Angeles, CA 90067 USA

Brock, Lou
61 Berkley Pl, Saint Charles, MO 63301-4569

Brock, Louis C (Lou) *Baseball Player*
61 Barkley Place, Saint Charles, MO 63301 USA

Brock, Stanley J (Stan) *Football Player*
2555 SW 81st Ave, Portland, OR 97225 USA

Brock, Stevie *Actor*
Official International Fan Club, PO Box 5308, Bellingham, WA 98227 USA

Brock III, William E (Bill) *Secretary, Senator*
16 Revell St, Annapolis, MD 21401 USA

Brockert, Richard C *Misc*
United Telegraph Workers, 701 E Gude Dr, Rockville, MD 20850 USA

Brockington, John *Football Player*
Equitable Insurance, 701 B St, #1500, San Deigo, CA 92101 USA

Brockovich, Erin *Writer*
5707 Corsa Ave, Westlake Village, CA 91362 USA

Brodbin, Kevin *Writer*
Creative Artists Agency, 9830 Wilshire Blvd, Beverly Hills, CA 90212 USA

Broder, David S *Writer*
4024 27th St N, Arlington, VA 22207 USA

Broder, Samuel *Misc*
IVAX Corp, 4400 Biscayne Blvd, Miami, FL 33137 USA

Broderick, Beth *Actor*
Innovative Artists, 1505 10th St, Santa Monica, CA 90401 USA

Broderick, Matthew *Actor*
3 Arts Entertainment Inc, 9460 Wilshire Blvd Fl 7, Beverly Hills, CA 90212 USA

Brodeur, Martin *Hockey Player*
New Jersey Devils, Continental Arena, 50 Rt 120 N, E Rutherford, NJ 07073 USA

Brodeur, Martin (Marty) *Hockey Player*
40 Fox Run, North Caldwell, NJ 07006 USA

Brodie, H Keith H *Misc*
63 Beverly Dr, Durham, NC 27707 USA

Brodie, John R *Football Player, Sportscaster, Golfer*
49350 Avenida Fernando, La Quinta, CA 92253 USA

Brodie, Kevin *Actor*
20023 Lull St, Winnetka, CA 91306 USA

Brodsky, Julian A *Business Person*
Comcast Corp, 1500 Market St, Philadelphia, PA 19102 USA

Brody, Adam *Actor*
Endeavor Agency LLC (LA), 9601 Wilshire Blvd Fl 3, Beverly Hills, CA 90210 USA

Brody, Adrien *Actor*
Creative Artists Agency LCC (CAA-LA), 9830 Wilshire Blvd, Beverly Hills, CA 90212 USA

Brody, Jane E *Journalist*
New York Times, Editorial Dept 229 W 43rd St, New York, NY 10036 USA

Brody, Kenneth D *Financier*
Export-Import Bank, 811 Vermont Ave NW, Washington, DC 20571 USA

Brody, Lane *Music Group*
Black Stallion Country Productions, PO Box 368, Tujunga, CA 91043 USA

Broecker, Wallace S *Geophysicist, Misc*
Lamont-Doherty Earth Observatory, P O Box 1000, Palisades, NY 10964 USA

Broeg, Robert W (Bob) *Writer*
60 Frontenac Estates Dr, Saint Louis, MO 63131 USA

Broelsch, Christopher E *Doctor, Misc*
University of Chicago, Medical Center Surgery Dept Box 259, Chicago, IL 60690 USA

Brogdon, Cindy *Basketball Player*
4932 Shawdowwood Parkway SE, Atlanta, GA 30339 USA

Broglio, Ernest G (Ernie) *Baseball Player*
2838 Via Carmen, San Jose, CA 95124 USA

Broglio, Ernie
2838 Via Carmen, San Jose, CA 95124 USA

Brokaw, Gary *Basketball Player, Coach, Misc*
1477 Langham Terrace, Lake Mary, FL 32746 USA

Brokaw, Tom *Journalist, Television Host*
NBC Nightly News, 30 Rockefeller Plaza, Room 300S, New York, NY 10112

Broken Lizard *Comedian*
United Talent Agency (UTA), 9560 Wilshire Blvd, Beverly Hills, CA 90212 USA

Brolin, James *Actor*
Metropolitan Talent Agency, 4526 Wilshire Blvd, Los Angeles, CA 90010 USA

Brolin, Josh *Actor*
8200 Dover Canyon Road, Paso Robles, CA 93446 USA

Brolly, Shane *Actor*
Marsh Entertainment, 12444 Ventura Blvd #203, Studio City, CA 91604 USA

Bromberg, David *Musician*
Agency Group, The (LA), 8490 Sunset Blvd #403, W Hollywood, CA 90069 USA

Bromfield, John *Actor*
Box 2655, Lake Havasu City, AZ 86405 USA

Bromley, D Allan *Government Official, Physicist*
35 Tokeneke Dr, North Haven, CT 06473 USA

Bron, Eleanor *Actor*
Rebecca Blond, 69A King's Road, London, SW3 4WX, UNITED KINGDOM (UK)

Bronars, Edward J *General*
3354 Rose Lane, Falls Church, VA 22042 USA

Bronfman, Charles R *Baseball Player, Business Person, Misc*
501 N Lake Way, Palm Beach, FL 33480 USA

Bronfman, Yefin *Musician*
I C M Artists, 40 W 57th St, New York, NY 10019 USA

Bronfman Jr, Edgar M *Business Person, Philanthropist*
Seagram Company, 1430 Peel Street, Montreal, Quebec, H3A 1S9, Canada

Bronfman Sr, Edgar M *Business Person, Philanthropist*
Seagram Company, 1430 Peel Street, Montreal, Quebec, H3A 1S9, Canada

Bronfman Sr, Edgar M *Business Person*
31122 Broad Beach Road, Malibu, CA 90265 USA

Bronleewe, Matt *Musician*
Flood Burnstead McCready McCarthy, 1700 Hayes St, #304, Nashville, TN 37203 USA

Bronson, Oswald P Sr *Educator*
Bethune-Cookman College, President's Office, Daytona Beach, FL 32114 USA

Bronson, Po *Writer*
Random House, 1745 Broadway, #B1, New York, NY 10019 USA

Bronstein, Elizabeth *Producer*
Creative Artists Agency LCC (CAA-LA), 9830 Wilshire Blvd, Beverly Hills, CA 90212 USA

Brook, Jayne *Actor*
Brillstein-Grey Entertainment, 9150 Wilshire Blvd #350, Beverly Hills, CA 90212 USA

Brook, Kelly *Actor*
Hyler Management, 20 Ocean Park Blvd #25, Santa Monica, CA 90405 USA

Brook, Peter S P *Director*
CICT, 13 Blvd de Rochechouart, Paris, 75009, FRANCE

Brooke, Allison *Music Group, Songwriter*
2-K/EMI Records, 6920 Sunset Blvd, Los Angeles, CA 90028 USA

Brooke, Edward W III *Senator*
O'Connor & Hannan, 1919 Pennsylvania Ave NW, #800, Washington, DC 20006 USA

Brooke, Jonatha *Songwriter, Musician*
Patrick Rains Assoc, 220 W 93rd St, #7B, New York, NY 10025 USA

Brooke, Paul
19 Sydney Mews, London, ENGLAND, SW3 6HL

Brooke-Taylor, Tim *Actor, Comedian*
Jill Foster Ltd, 3 Lonsdale Road, London, SW13 9ED, UNITED KINGDOM (UK)

Brookens, Tom *Baseball Player*
488 Black Gap Rd, Fayetteville, PA 17222 USA

Brooker, Gary *Songwriter, Musician*
5 Cranley Gardens, London, SW7, UNITED KINGDOM (UK)

Brookes, Harvey *Physicist*
Harvard University, Aiken Computation Laboratory, Cambridge, MA 02138 USA

Brookes, Jacqueline *Actor*
William Morris Agency, 151 El Camino Dr, Beverly Hills, CA 90212 USA

Brookes, Peter *Cartoonist*
London Times, Editorial Dept, 1 Pennington St, London, E98 1S5, UNITED KINGDOM (UK)

Brookfield, Price *Basketball Player*
90 Fox Run Road, #HC57, Pinehurst, NC 28374 USA

Brookhart, Maurice S *Misc*
University of North Carolina, Chemistry Dept, Chapel Hill, NC 27514 USA

Brookins, Gary *Cartoonist*
Richmond Newspapers, Editorial Dept, PO Box 85333, Richmond, VA 23293 USA

Brooklyn Bridge
PO Box 309M, Bayshore, NY 11706

Brookner, Anita *Writer*
68 Elm Park Gardens, #6, London, SW10 9PB, UNITED KINGDOM (UK)

Brooks, Aaron *Football Player*
LPS, PO Box 6282, Newport News, VA 23606 USA

Brooks, Albert *Actor, Director, Writer*
William Morris Agency (WMA-LA), 1 William Morris Pl, Beverly Hills, CA 90212 USA

Brooks, Angelle *Actor*
Pakula/King & Associates, 9229 Sunset Blvd #315, Los Angeles, CA 90069 USA

Brooks, Avery *Actor*
Lynn Coles Productions, PO Box 4082, Oakland, CA 94614 USA

Brooks, Conrad *Actor*
PO Box 1192, Falling Waters, WV 25419 USA

Brooks, Danny *Musician*
American Promotions, 2011 Ferry Ave, #U19, Camden, NJ 08104 USA

Brooks, David Allen (David A) *Actor*
Orange Grove Group Inc, 12178 Ventura Blvd #205, Studio City, CA 91604 USA

Brooks, Derrick *Football Player*
1713 Cedrus Lane, Pensacola, FL 32514 USA

Brooks, Donald M *Fashion Designer*
Costume Guild, 13949 Ventura, #309, Sherman Oaks, CA 91423 USA

Brooks, Donnie *Musician*
Al Lampkin Entertainment, 1817 W Verdugo Ave, Burbank, CA 91506 USA

Brooks, E R *Business Person*
Central & South West Corp, 1616 Woodall Rogers Freeway, Dallas, TX 75202 USA

Brooks, Frederick P Jr *Mathematician, Scientist*
413 Granville Road, Chapel Hill, NC 27514 USA

Brooks, Garth *Musician, Songwriter*
GB Management, 1111 17th Ave S, Nashville, TN 37212 USA

Brooks, Geraldine *Writer*
Viking Press, 375 Hudson St, New York, NY 10014 USA

Brooks, Golden *Actor*
Abrams Artists Agency (LA), 9200 Sunset Blvd Fl 11, Los Angeles, CA 90069 USA

Brooks, Herb *Athlete*
180 Birchwood Ave, St Paul, MN 55110-1612

Brooks, Hubert (Hubie) *Baseball Player*
15001 Olive St, Hesperia, CA 92345 USA

Brooks, James *Football Player*
Baltimore Ravens, Ravens Stadium, 11001 Russell St, Baltimore, MD 21230 USA

Brooks, James L *Actor*
International Creative Management (ICM-LA), 8942 Wilshire Blvd, Beverly Hills, CA 90211 USA

Brooks, Jason *Actor*
289 S Robertson Blvd, #424, Beverly Hills, CA 90211 USA

Brooks, Joel *Actor*
Gage Group, The (LA), 14724 Ventura Blvd #505, Los Angeles, CA 91403 USA

Brooks, John E *Educator*
College of Holy Cross, President's Office, Worcester, MA 01610 USA

Brooks, Karen *Musician*
5408 Clear View Lane, Waterford, WI 53185 USA

Brooks, Kimberly A *Actor*
Coast to Coast Talent Group, 3350 Barham Blvd, Los Angeles, CA 90068 USA

Brooks, Kix *Musician, Songwriter*
TBA Mgmt, 300 10th Ave S, Nashville, TN 37203 USA

Brooks, Lala *Misc*
Superstars Unlimited, PO Box 371371, Las Vegas, NV 89137 USA

Brooks, Larry L Sr *Football Player, Coach*
12721 NE 192nd Place, Kirkland, WA 98033 USA

Brooks, Mark *Golfer*
6417 Forest Highlands Dr, Fort Worth, TX 76132 USA

Brooks, Mel *Director, Actor*
23868 Malibu Colony Road, Malibu, CA 90265 USA

Brooks, Meredith *Musician*
Capitol Records, 1750 N Vine St, Los Angeles, CA 90028 USA

Brooks, Michael *Basketball Player*
495 Bethany St, San Diego, CA 92114 USA

Brooks, Michael *Football Player*
604 Spring Leaf Court, Greensboro, NC 27455 USA

Brooks, Nathan *Boxer*
3139 Albion Road, Cleveland, OH 44120 USA

Brooks, Randi *Actor, Model*
3205 Evergreen Point Road, Medina, WA 98039 USA

Brooks, Rich *Football Coach*
University of Kentucky, Athletic Dept, Lexington, KY 40506 USA

Brooks, Richard *Actor*
333 Washington Blvd, #102, Marina del Rey, CA 90292 USA

Brooks, William (Bud) *Football Player*
302 Doubtoon Circle, Hot Springs, AR 71913 USA

Brooks & Dunn *Music Group*
William Morris Agency (WMA-TN), 2100 W End Ave #1000, Nashville, TN 37203 USA

Brookshier, Thomas (Tom) *Football Player, Sportscaster*
1130 Riverview Lane, Conshohouken, PA 19428 USA

Brophy, Kevin *Actor*
15010 Hamlin St, Van Nuys, CA 91411 USA

Brophy, Theodore F *Business Person*
60 Arch St, Greenwich, CT 06830 USA

Brorby, Wade *Judge*
US Court of Appeals, 2120 Capitol Ave, Cheyenne, WY 82001 USA

Broshears, Robert *Artist*
Robert Broshears Studio, 8020 NW Holly Road, Bremerton, WA 98312 USA

Brosius, Scott D *Baseball Player*
3207 NW Westside Road, McMinnville, OR 97128 USA

Broski, David C *Educator*
University of Illinois, President's Office, Chicago, IL 60607 USA

Brosky, Albert (Al) *Football Player*
2031 Yellow Dalsy Court, Naperville, IL 60563 USA

Brosnan, Pierce *Actor, Producer*
24955 Pacific Coast Highway, #C-205, Malibu, CA 90265 USA

Brostek, Bern *Football Player*
Saint Louis Rarns, 901 N Broadway, Saint Louis, MO 63101 USA

Broten, Neal *Hockey Player*
N8216 690th St, Eagan, MN 55123 USA

Broth, Ed
Trident Media Group LLC, 41 Madison Ave Fl 33, New York, NY 10010 USA

Brotherhood of Man, Rochdale
PO Box 106, ENGLAND, 0L16 4HW

Brothers, Bellamy, The *Musician*
Agency for the Performing Arts (APA-LA), 9200 Sunset Blvd #900, Los Angeles, CA 90069 USA

Brothers, Dr Joyce *Doctor, Actor*
William Morris Agency (WMA-NY), 1325 Ave of the Americas, New York, NY 10019 USA

Brothers, Joyce D *Physicist*
NBC Westwood One Radio Network, 524 W 57th St, New York, NY 10019 USA

Brotman, Jeffrey *Business Person*
Costco Wholesale Corp, 999 Lake Dr, Issaquah, WA 98027 USA

Brough, Randi *Actor*
11684 Ventura Blvd, #476, Studio City, CA 91604 USA

Brough Clapp, A Louise *Tennis Player*
1808 Voluntary Rd, Vista, CA 92083 USA

Broughton, Bruce *Composer*
Air-Edel, 1416 N La Brea Ave, Los Angeles, CA 90028 USA

Broussard, Rebecca *Actor*
9911 W Pico Blvd, #PH A, Los Angeles, CA 90035 USA

Broussard, Steve *Football Player*
2028 Englewood Dr, Biloxi, MS 39532 USA

Brouwenstyn, Gerada
Bachplein 3, Amsterdam, NETHERLANDS, NL-1077 GH

Brouwenstyn, Gerarda *Opera Singer*
3 Bachpiein, Armsterdam, NETHERLANDS

Browder, Ben *Actor*
PO Box 5617, Beverly Hills, CA 90210

Browder, Felix E *Mathematician*
37 Quince Place, North Brunswick, NJ 08902 USA

Brower, Jordan
9100 Wilshire Blvd #503E, Beverly Hills, CA 90212

Brown, Aaron *Commentator*
Cable News Network, News Dept, 1050 Techwood Dr NW, Atlanta, GA 30318 USA

Brown, Alison *Songwriter, Musician*
SRO Artists, 6629 University Ave, #206, Middleton, WI 53562 USA

Brown, Alton *Chef*
Food Network, 1180 Ave of Americas, #1200, New York, NY 10036 USA

Brown, Amanda *Writer*
EP Dutton, 375 Hudson St, New York, NY 10014 USA

Brown, Arthur E Jr *General*
35 Fairway Winds Place, Hilton Head Island, SC 29928 USA

Brown, Ashley Nicole *Actor*
Hervey/Grimes, PO Box 64249, Los Angeles, CA 90064 USA

Brown, Bailey *Judge*
US Court of Appeals, Federal Building, 167 N Main St, Memphis, TN 38103 USA

Brown, Billy Aaron *Actor*
Stone Manners Talent Agency, 6500 Wilshire Blvd, Ste 550, Los Angeles, CA 90048 USA

Brown, Blair *Actor*
18 E 53rd St, #140, New York, NY 10022 USA

Brown, Bo *Cartoonist*
3500 West Chester Pike, #A210, Newtown Square, PA 19073 USA

Brown, Bobby *Musician, Songwriter, Dancer*
1324 Thomas Place, Fort Worth, TX 76107 USA

Brown, Bruce *Photographer*
15550 Calle Real, Gaviota, CA 93117 USA

Brown, Bryan *Actor*
June Cann Mgmt, 110 Queen St, Woollahra, NSW, 2025, AUSTRALIA

Brown, Buck *Cartoonist*
PO Box 122, Park Forest, IL 60466 USA

Brown, C Edward (Eddie) *Football Player*
3465 Commodore Point, Knoxville, TN 37922 USA

Brown, Campbell *Commentator*
NBC-TV, News Dept, 30 Rockefeller Plaza, New York, NY 10112 USA

Brown, Chad *Actor*
Sterling/Winters Company, The, 1900 Ave of the Stars Fl 5, Los Angeles, CA 90067 USA

Brown, Chadwick (Chad) *Football Player*
2827 Holliston Ave, Altadena, CA 91001 USA

Brown, Charlie *Football Player*
3017 Valley Brook Place, Decatur, GA 30033 USA

Brown, Chucky *Basketball Player*
102 Balsamwood Court, Cary, NC 27513 USA

Brown, Cindy *Basketball Player*
Detroit Shock, Palace, 2 Championship Dr, Auburn Hills, MI 48326 USA

Brown, Clancy *Actor*
3141 Oakdell Lane, Studio City, CA 91604 USA

Brown, Clarence
PO Box 958

Brown, Clarence (Gatemouth) *Musician*
Po Box 958, Bogalusa, LA 70429 USA

Brown, Courtney *Football Player*
Cleveland Browns, 76 Lou Groza Blvd, Berea, OH 44017 USA

Brown, Curtis L Jr *Astronaut*
204 Starrwood, Hudson, WI 54016 USA

Brown, Dale *Writer*
Trident Media Group LLC, 41 Madison Ave Fl 33, New York, NY 10010 USA

Brown, Dale D *Coach, Sportscaster*
ESPN-TV, Sports Dept ESPN Plaza, 935 Middle St, Bristol, CT 06010 USA

Brown, Dan *Writer*
Doubleday Press, 1540 Broadway, New York, NY 10036 USA

Brown, Daniel G *General*
Deputy CinC, US Transportation Command, Scott Air Force Base, IL 62225 USA

Brown, Dave M *Football Player*
18451 NE 155th Place, Woodinville, WA 98072 USA

Brown, David *Producer*
Zanuck/Brown Co, 200 W 57th St, New York, NY 10019 USA

Brown, David P *Athlete*
155 Valley View Road, Talent, OR 97540 USA

Brown, Dee *Basketball Player*
5103 Isleworth Country Club Dr, Windermere, FL 34786 USA

Brown, Denise
PO Box 3777, Monarch Bay, CA 92629

Brown, Derek V *Football Player*
1410 Eleanore Dr, Tallahassee, FL 32301 USA

Brown, Donald David *Biologist*
5721 Oakshire Road, Baltimore, MD 21209 USA

Brown, Dwier *Actor*
Michael Slessinger & Assoc, 8730 Sunset Blvd #270, Los Angeles, CA 90069 USA

Brown, Edmund G (Jerry) Jr *Governor*
Mayor's Office, City Hall, Frank Ogawa Plaza, Oakland, CA 94612 USA

Brown, Edward (Ed) *Football Player*
3395 S Higuera St, SPC 61, San Luis Obispo, CA 93401 USA

Brown, Edward R *Cinematographer*
10607 Angelo Tenero Ave, Las Vegas, NV 89135 USA

Brown, Errol
PO Box 106, Rochdale, ENGLAND, OL16 4HW

Brown, Faith *Actor*
Million Dollar Music Co, 12 Praed Mews, London, W2 1QY, UNITED KINGDOM (UK)

Brown, Foxy *Musician*
William Morris Agency (WMA-LA), 1 William Morris Pl, Beverly Hills, CA 90212 USA

Brown, Fred *Coach, Basketball Player*
3696 72nd Place SE, Mercer Island, WA 98040 USA

Brown, G Hanks (Hank) *Senator*
Daniels Fund, 55 Madison St, #255, Denver, CO 80206 USA

Brown, Georg Stanford *Actor*
2565 Greenvalley Road, Los Angeles, CA 90046 USA

Brown, George C Jr *Football Player*
12817 Lakeshore Dr, Lakeside, CA 92040 USA

Brown, Gordie *Comedian*
William Morris Agency (WMA-LA), 1 William Morris Pl, Beverly Hills, CA 90212 USA

Brown, Harold *Secretary*
Strategic/International Studies Center, 1800 K St NW, #1800, Washington, DC 20006 USA

Brown, Helen Gurley *Writer, Editor*
1 W 81st St, #22D, New York, NY 10024 USA

Brown, Henry *Actor*
1101 E Pike St, #300, Seattle, WA 98122 USA

Brown, Henry W *War Hero*
2389 Mount Vernon Dr, Sumter, SC 29154 USA

Brown, Herbert C *Nobel Prize Laureate*
1014 Lincoln Trail, West Lafayette, IN 47906 USA

Brown, Heritage Doris *Track Athlete*
Seattle Pacific College, Athletic Dept, Seattle, WA 98119 USA

Brown, Himan *Director*
285 Central Park W, New York, NY 10024 USA

Brown, Hubie *Coach*
120 Foxridge Road NW, Atlanta, GA 30327 USA

Brown, Hyman *Engineer*
Colorado State University, Civil Engineering Dept, Fort Collins, CO 80523 USA

Brown, J Cristopher (Cris) *Baseball Player*
5015 Brighton Ave, Los Angeles, CA 90062 USA

Brown, J Gordon *Government Official*
House of Commons, Westminister, London, SW1A 0AA, UNITED KINGDOM (UK)

Brown, James *Musician*
James Brown Enterprises, PO Box 1051, Augusta, GA 30903 USA

Brown, James *Sportscaster*
Fox-TV, Sports Dept, 205 W 67th St, New York, NY 10021 USA

Brown, James (Jim) *Actor*
20543 Tiara St, Woodland Hills, CA 91367 USA

Brown, James N (Jim) *Actor, Football Player*
11176 Huston St, #201, North Hollywood, CA 91601 USA

Brown, James R *General*
1591 Stowe Road, Reston, VA 20194 USA

Brown, Jay W Jr *Financier*
MBIA Inc, 113 King St, Armonk, NY 10504 USA

Brown, Jim *Actor*
1851 Sunset Plaza Drive, Los Angeles, CA 90069 USA

Brown, Jim Ed *Musician*
Billy Deaton Talent, 5811 Still Hollow Road, Nashville, TN 37215 USA

Brown, Joe *Boxer*
1615 N Broad St, New Orleans, LA 70119 USA

Brown, John *Basketball Player*
1329 N Florissant Road, Saint Louis, MO 63135 USA

Brown, John Y Jr *Governor*
2601 Old Cave Hill Lane, Lexington, KY 40513 USA

Brown, Judge Joe *Judge*
Judge Joe Brown, 1438 N Gower St #62, Los Angeles, CA 90028

Brown, Julie *Actor, Comedian*
11288 Ventura Blvd #728, Studio City, CA 91604 USA

Brown, Julie (Downtown) *Entertainer*
Michael Slessinger & Assoc, 8730 Sunset Blvd #270, Los Angeles, CA 90069 USA

Brown, Junior *Musician*
Force Inc, 1505 16th Ave S, Nashville, TN 37212 USA

Brown, Kale *Actor*
Gage Group, The (LA), 14724 Ventura Blvd #505, Los Angeles, CA 91403 USA

Brown, Katie *Designer, Television Host*
Style Network, 5750 Wilshire Blvd, Los Angeles, CA 90036 USA

Brown, Kedrick *Basketball Player*
Boston Celtics, 151 Merrimac St, #1, Boston, MA 02114 USA

Brown, Kenneth J *Misc*
Graphic Communications Int'l Union, 1900 L St NW, Washington, DC 20036 USA

Brown, Kevin D *Basketball Player*
New York Yankees, Yankee Stadium, 161st St & River Ave, Bronx, NY 10451 USA

Brown, Kimberlin Ann *Actor*
Pakula/King & Associates, 9229 Sunset
Blvd #315, Los Angeles, CA 90069 USA

Brown, Kimberly J *Actor*
2069 Troon Dr, Henderson, NV 89074
USA

Brown, Koffee *Musician*
Red Entertainment Group, 481 Eight Ave,
#1750, New York, NY 10001

Brown, Kwarne *Basketball Player*
Washington Wizards MCI Centre, 601 F St
NW, Washington, DC 20004 USA

Brown, Larry *Hockey Player*
5781 Eucalyptus Dr, Garden Valley, CA
95633 USA

Brown, Lawrence (Larry) Jr *Football
Player*
4390 Parliament Place, #A, Lanham, MD
20706 USA

Brown, Lawrence H (Larry) *Coach,
Basketball Player*
Detroit Pistons, Palace, 2 Championship
Dr, Aubum Hills, MI 48326 USA

Brown, Lee P *Government Official*
Mayor's Office, City Hall, 901 Bagby St
#300, Houston, TX 77002 USA

Brown, Lester R *Misc*
Worldwatch Institute, 1776 Massachusetts
Ave NW, Washington, DC 20036 USA

Brown, Mack *Coach*
University of Texas, Athletic Dept, Austin,
TX 78712 USA

Brown, Mark N *Astronaut*
80 Earlsgate Road, Dayton, OH 45440
USA

Brown, Marty *Musician*
Mitchell Fox Mgmt, 212 3rd Ave N,
Nashville, TN 37201 USA

Brown, Matt *Director*
William Morris Agency (WMA-NY), 1325
Ave of the Americas, New York, NY
10019 USA

Brown, Melanie *Musician*
Spice Girls Ltd, 66-68 Bell St, London,
NW1 6SP, UNITED KINGDOM (UK)

Brown, Michael S *Nobel Prize Laureate*
5719 Redwood Lane, Dallas, TX 75209
USA

Brown, Mike *Misc*
Cincinnati Bengals, 1 Paul Brown
Stadium, Cincinnati, OH 45202 USA

Brown, Mike *Astronomer*
California Institute of Technology,
Astronomy Dept, Pasadena, CA 91125
USA

Brown, Napoleon (Nappy) *Musician*
1023 Moretz Ave, Charlotte, NC 28206
USA

Brown, Norman W *Business Person*
Foote Cone Belding, 101 E Erie St,
Chicago, IL 60611 USA

Brown, Olivia *Actor*
David Shapira, 15821 Ventura Blvd,
#235, Encino, CA 91436 USA

Brown, Orlando *Actor*
Abrams Artists Agency (LA), 9200 Sunset
Blvd Fl 11, Los Angeles, CA 90069 USA

Brown, Owsley II *Business Person*
Brown-Forman Corp, 850 Dixie Highway,
Louisville, KY 40210 USA

Brown, P J *Basketball Player*
903 Beverly Dr, Carthage, TX 75633 USA

Brown, Patrick *Misc*
Stanford University, Medical School,
Biochemistry Dept, Stanford, CA 94305
USA

Brown, Peter *Actor*
5328 Alhama Dr, Woodland Hills, CA
91364 USA

Brown, Philip *Actor*
8721 Sunset Blvd, #200, Los Angeles, CA
90069 USA

Brown, Phill *Actor*
28388 Mulholland Dr, #305, Woodland
Hills, CA 91364 USA

Brown, R Hanbury *Astronomer*
White Cottage, Penton Mewsey, Andover
Hants, SP11 0RQ, UNITED KINGDOM
(UK)

Brown, Ray *Football Player*
Detroit Lions, 222 Republic Dr, Allen
Park, MI 48101 USA

Brown, Reb *Actor*
5454 Virgenes Rd, Calabasas, CA 91302
USA

Brown, Reggie *Football Player*
2242 NW 93rd Terrace, Miami, FL 33147
USA

Brown, Richard E (Tex) III *General*
Deputy CofS for Personnel, HqUSAF
Pentagon, Washington, DC 20330 USA

Brown, Robert (Bobby) *Baseball Player*
4100 Clark Ave, Fort Worth, TX 76107
USA

Brown, Robert D *Business Person*
Milacron Inc, 2090 Florence Ave,
Cincinnati, OH 45206 USA

Brown, Robert S (Bob) *Football Player*
1200 Lakeshore Ave, Oakland, CA 94606
USA

Brown, Roger L *Football Player*
9 N Point Dr, Portsmouth, VA 23703 USA

Brown, Ron J *Track Athlete, Football
Player*
3363 Milbury Ave, Baldwin Park, CA
91706 USA

Brown, Ruben *Football Player*
170 Fox Meadow Lane, Orchard Park, NY
USA

Brown, Ruth *Musician*
Rosebud Agency, PO Box 170429, San
Francisco, CA 94117 USA

Brown, Samantha *Actor*
Carlson Menashe Agency, 159 West 25th
Street, Suite 1011, New York, NY 10001

Brown, Sandra *Writer*
1306 W Abram St, Arlington, TX 76013
USA

Brown, Sara *Actor*
Media Artists Group, 6300 Wilshire Blvd,
#1470, Los Angeles, CA 90048 USA

Brown, Shay
499 Erin Dr, Knoxville, TN 37919

Brown, Susan *Actor*
11931 Addison St, N Hollywood, CA
91607 USA

Brown, Sylvia *Psychic*
PO Box 5100, Carlsbad, CA 92018

Brown, T Graham *Musician*
Bobby Roberts, 909 Meadowlark Lane,
Goodlettsville, TN 37072 USA

Brown, Theotis J *Football Player*
9604 W 121st Terrace, Overland Park, KS
66213 USA

Brown, Thomas Wilson
3033 Vista Crest, Los Angeles, CA 90068

Brown, Timothy D (Tim) *Football Player*
505 S Farrell Dr, #E28, Palm Springs, CA
92264 USA

Brown, Tom *Football Player*
679 Aldfrod Ave, Delta, BC V3M 5P5,
CANADA

Brown, Tracy *Ballerina*
Royal Ballet, Convent Garden, Bow St,
London, WC2E 9DD, UNITED KINGDOM
(UK)

Brown, Trisha *Dancer, Choreographer*
Trisha Brown Dance Co, 211 W 61st St,
New York, NY 10023 USA

Brown, Vincent B *Football Player*
1615 Thoreau Dr, Suwanee, GA 30024
USA

Brown, W Earl *Actor*
Artists Group (LA), 10100 Santa Monica
Blvd #2490, Los Angeles, CA 90067 USA

Brown, William D (Bill) *Football Player,
Coach*
Bromley Printing, 514 Northdale Blvd,
Minneapolis, MN 55448 USA

Brown, William F (Willie) *Coach, Football
Player*
27138 Lillegard Ct, Tracy, CA 95304 USA

Brown, Woody
6548 Colbath Ave, Van Nuys, CA 91401-
1503

Browne, Chris *Cartoonist*
King Features Syndicate, 888 7th Ave,
New York, NY 10106 USA

Browne, E John P *Business Person*
BP Exploration Co, 1 Finsbury Circus,
London, EC2M 7BA, UNITED KINGDOM
(UK)

Browne, Gerald *Writer*
Warner Books, 1271 6th Ave, New York,
NY 10020 USA

Browne, Jackson *Musician, Songwriter*
Donald Miller Management, 12746 Kling
St, Studio City, CA 91604

Browne, Kale *Actor*
Gage Group, The (LA), 14724 Ventura
Blvd #505, Los Angeles, CA 91403 USA

Browne, Kathy
PO Box 2939, Beverly Hills, CA 90213

Browne, Leslie *Actor, Ballerina*
2025 Broadway, #6F, New York, NY
10023 USA

Browne, Olin *Golfer*
Larry Hayes, 1051 Runnymede Road,
Dayton, OH 45419 USA

Browne, Roscoe Lee *Actor*
465 W 57th St, #1A, New York, NY
10019 USA

Browne, Secor D *Engineer, Government Official*
2101 L St NW, #207, Washington, DC
20037 USA

Browne, Victor *Actor*
Lara Rosenstock Management, 8371
Blackburn Ave #1, Los Angeles, CA 90048
USA

Browne, Zachary *Actor*
Iris Burton Agency, 8916 Ashcroft Ave,
Los Angeles, CA 90048

Browner, Joey *Football Player*
P O Box 571, Pierz, MN 56364 USA

Browner, Keith *Football Player*
10200 Gandy Blvd N #620, Saint
Petersburg, FL 33702 USA

Browner, Ross *Football Player*
Ross Browner Enterprises, 1135 Flamingo
Dr SW, Atlanta, GA 30311 USA

Browning, Dominique *Editor*
Mirabella Magazine, Editorial Dept 200
Madison Ave, New York, NY 10016 USA

Browning, Edmond L *Religious Leader*
5164 Imai Road, Hood River, OR 97031
USA

Browning, James R *Judge*
US Court of Appeals, Court Building 95
7th St, San Fransisco, CA 94103 USA

Browning, Kurt *Figure Skater*
Int'l Management Group, 175 Bloor St E
#400, Toronto, ON M4W 3R8, CANADA

Browning, Ricou *Actor*
5221 SW 196th Lane, Southwest Ranches,
FL 33332 USA

Browning, Ryan *Actor*
United Talent Agency, 9560 Wilshire Blvd
#500, Beverly Hills, CA 90212 USA

Browning, Thomas L (Tom) *Baseball Player*
3094 Friars St, Edgewood, KY 41017 USA

Brownlow, Kevin *Producer*
Photoplay Productions, 21 Princess Road,
London, NW1, UNITED KINGDOM (UK)

Brownmiller, Susan *Social Activist*
61 Jane St, New York, NY 10014 USA

Brownstein, Carrie *Music Group, Musician*
Legends of 21st Century, 7 Trinity Row,
Florence, MA 01062 USA

Brownstein, Michael L *Publisher*
Ladies Home Journal, 125 Park Ave, New
York, NY 10017 USA

Browny, Jann *Musician*
Tracy Gershon Mgmt, PO Box 158400,
Nashville, TN 37215 USA

Broyles, Frank F *Football Player, Coach, Sportscaster*
University of Arkansas, Broyles Athletic
Complex, Fayetteville, AR 72701 USA

Brubeck, Dave *Musician*
221 Millstone Rd, Wilton, CT 06897

Brubeck, David W (Dave) *Music Group, Musician*
221 Millstone Road, Wilton, CT 06897
USA

Brubeck, William H *Government Official*
7 Linden St, Cambridge, MA 02138 USA

Bruce, Aundray *Football Player*
1730 Wentworth Dr, Montgomery, AL
36106 USA

Bruce, Bruce *Comedian*
Agency for the Performing Arts (APA-LA),
9200 Sunset Blvd #900, Los Angeles, CA
90069 USA

Bruce, Carol *Actor, Musician*
1055 N Kingsley Dr #AD-405, Los
Angeles, CA 90029 USA

Bruce, Christopher *Choreographer*
Rambert Dance Co, 94 Chiswick High
Road, London, W4 1SH, UNITED
KINGDOM (UK)

Bruce, Ed
1022 16th Ave S, Nashville, TN 37212
USA

Bruce, George
3 rue de Plaisance, Paris, FRANCE,
F-75014

Bruce, Isaac I *Football Player*
373 NW 29th Avenue, Fort Lauderdale, FL
33311 USA

Bruce, Jack *Songwriter, Music Group*
International Creative Mgmt, 40 W 57th St
#1800, New York, NY 10019 USA

Bruce, Robert V *Historian*
3923 Westpark Court NW, Olympia, WA
98502 USA

Bruce, Thomas (Tom) *Swimmer*
122 Seaterrace Way, Aptos, CA 95003
USA

Bruce, Tom
122 Sea Terrace Way, Aptos, CA 95003

Brucie, Cousin
PO Box 50, New York, NY 10101

Bruckheimer, Jerry *Director, Producer*
Jerry Bruckheimer Films, 1631 10th St,
Santa Monica, CA 90404 USA

Bruckner, Agnes *Actor*
Curtis Talent Management, 9607 Arby Dr,
Beverly Hills, CA 90210 USA

Brudzinkski, Robert L (Bob) *Athlete*
1057 Lido Court, Weston, FL 33326

Brudzinski, Robert L (Bob) *Football Player*
5466 W Sample Road, Margate, FL 33073
USA

Bruel, Patrick *Music Group*
Artmedia, 20 Ave Rapp, Paris, 75007,
FRANCE

Brueland, Lowell K *Misc*
118 Fairview Circle, Brewton, AL 36426
USA

Bruen, John D *General, Business Person*
6104 Greenlawn Court, Springfield, VA
22152 USA

Bruestle, Martin *Director*

Bruggink, Eric G *Judge*
US Claims Court, 717 Madison Place NW,
Washington, DC 20439 USA

Bruguera, Sergi *Tennis Player*
C'Escipion 42, Barcelona, 08023, SPAIN

Brumback, Charles T *Publisher*
1500 N Lake Shore Dr, Chicago, IL 60610
USA

Brumbly, Charlie *Actor*
DDO Artist Agency, 8322 Beverly Blvd
#301, Los Angeles, CA 90048 USA

Brumel, Valeryi
Louknetzkaya Nab 8, Moscow, RUSSIA

Brumfield, Jacob D *Baseball Player*
43275 Tillman Dr, Hammond, LA 70403
USA

Brumm, Donald D (Don) *Football Player*
511 County Road 442, New Franklin, MO
65274 USA

Brummer, Renate *Astronaut*
NOAA/FSL, 325 Broadway, Boulder, CO
80305 USA

Brunansky, Thomas A (Tom) *Baseball Player*
13411 Summit Circle, Poway, CA 92064
USA

Brundage, Howard D *Publisher*
RR 2 Box 332-47, Old Lyme, CT 06371
USA

Brundige, Bill *Football Player*
RR 2, Moneta, VA 24121 USA

Brunell, Mark *Football Player*
911 Ponte Vedra Blvd, Ponte Vedra, FL
32082 USA

Bruner, Jerome S *Misc*
200 Mercer St, New York, NY 10012 USA

Bruner, Michael L (Mike) *Swimmer*
1518 Hillview Dr, Los Altos, CA 94024
USA

Brunet, Andree Joly *Figure Skater*
2805 Boyne City Road, Boyne City, MI
49712 USA

Brunetti, Melvin T *Judge*
US Court of Appeals, 40 W Liberty St,
Reno, NV 89501 USA

Brunetti, Wayne H *Business Person*
New Century Energies, 1225 17th St,
Denver, CO 80202 USA

Brungardt, Kurt
Trident Media Group LLC, 41 Madison
Ave Fl 33, New York, NY 10010 USA

Bruni, Carla *Model, Songwriter, Music Group*
Marilyn Gauthier Agency, 4 Rue de la
Paix, Paris, 75002, FRANCE

Brunner, J Terrance *Misc*
Better Government Assn, 230 N Michigan
Ave, Chicago, IL 60601 USA

Bruno, Chris *Actor*
Stone Manners, 6500 Wilshire Blvd #550,
Los Angeles, CA 90048 USA

Bruno, Corbucci
Via dei Colli della Farnesina 144, Rome,
ITALY, I-00194

Bruno, Dylan *Actor*
Gersh Agency, 223 N Canon Dr, Beverly
Hills, CA 90210 USA

Bruno, Frank
Box 2266, Brentwood Essex, ENGLAND,
CM1S 0AQ

Bruno, Franklin R (Frank) *Boxer*
P O Box 2266 Brentwood, Essex, CM15
0AQ, UNITED KINGDOM (UK)

Bruns, Breck *Actor*
Stein Entertainment Group, 11271 Ventura
Blvd #477, Studio City, CA 91604 USA

Bruschi, Tedy *Football Player*
21 Red Oak Road, North Attleboro, MA 02760 USA

Bruskin, Grisha *Artist*
236 W 26th St #705, New York, NY 10001 USA

Bruson, Renato *Opera Singer*
Columbia Artists Mgmt Inc, 165 W 57th St, New York, NY 10019 USA

Brusteln, Robert S *Educator, Producer, Critic*
Harvard University, Loeb Drama Center 64 Brattle St, Cambridge, MA 02138 USA

Bruton, John G *Prime Minister*
Qomelstown, Dunboyne, County Meath, IRELAND

Bry, Ellen *Actor*
Media Artists Group, 6300 Wilshire Blvd #1470, Los Angeles, CA 90048 USA

Bryan, Alan *Archaeologist*
University of Alberta, Archaeology Dept, Edmonton, AB T6G 2J8, CANADA

Bryan, David *Misc*
Bon Jovi Mgmt, 248 W 17th St #501, New York, NY 10011 USA

Bryan, Donald S *Misc*
702 Melba St, Adel, GA 31620 USA

Bryan, Dora *Actor*
11 Marine Parade Brighton, Sussex, UNITED KINGDOM (UK)

Bryan, Mark *Music Group, Musician*
FishCo Mgmt, P O Box 5656, Columbia, SC 29250 USA

Bryan, Rick D *Football Player*
804 E South St, Coweta, OK 74429 USA

Bryan, Sabrina *Actor*
Abrams Artists Agency (LA), 9200 Sunset Blvd Fl 11, Los Angeles, CA 90069 USA

Bryan, Wright *Journalist*
3747 Peachtree Road #516, Atlanta, GA 30319 USA

Bryan, Zachary Ty *Actor*
Evolution Entertainment, 901 N Highland Ave, Los Angeles, CA 90038 USA

Bryant, Anita *Social Activist, Music Group*
Blackwood Mgmt, P O Box 5331, Sevierville, TN 37864 USA

Bryant, Brad *Golfer*
2622 Northampton Ave, Orlando, FL 32828 USA

Bryant, Clark Rosalyn *Track Athlete*
3901 Somerset Dr, Los Angeles, CA 90008 USA

Bryant, Gray *Editor*
34 Horatio St, New York, NY 10014 USA

Bryant, Gyude *President*
President's Office, Executive Mansion Capitol Hill, Monrovia, LIBERIA

Bryant, Joshua *Actor*
216 Paseo Del Pueblo Norte #M, Taos, NM 87571 USA

Bryant, Joy *Actor*
Creative Artists Agency LCC (CAA-LA), 9830 Wilshire Blvd, Beverly Hills, CA 90212 USA

Bryant, Kelvin *Football Player*
1803 Chiles Higgins Court, Greensboro, NC 27406 USA

Bryant, Kobe *Basketball Player*
P O Box 491787, Los Angeles, CA 90049 USA

Bryant, Mark *Basketball Player*
107 Kirkwood Court, Suger Land, TX 77478 USA

Bryant, Ray *Music Group, Musician*
Maxine Harvard Unlimited, 7942 W Bell Road, Glendale, AZ 85308 USA

Bryant, Todd *Actor*
9150 Wilshire Blvd #175, Beverly Hills, CA 90212 USA

Bryant, W Cullen *Football Player*
6495 Timber Bluff Point, Colorado Springs, CO 80918 USA

Bryant, Waymond *Football Player*
2440 Covington Dr, Flower Mound, TX 75028 USA

Bryant, Wendell *Football Player*
Arizona Cardinals, P O Box 888, Phoenix, AZ 85001 USA

Bryars, R Gavin *Composer*
Bolton-Quinn Ltd, 8 Pottery Lane, London, W11 4LZ, UNITED KINGDOM (UK)

Bryniarski, Andrew *Actor*
Flutie Entertainment, 270 Lafayette St, #1400, New York, NY 10012 USA

Bryson, John E *Business Person*
Edison International, 2244 Walnut Grove Ave, Rosemead, CA 91770 USA

Bryson, Peabo *Musician, Songwriter, Music Group*
Agency for the Performing Arts, 9200 Sunset Blvd #900, Los Angeles, CA 90069 USA

Bryson, William C *Judge*
US Appeals Court, 717 Madison Place NW, Washington, DC 20439 USA

Brzeska, Magdalena *Gymnast*
Vitesse Karcher GmbH, Porschestr 6, Fellbach, 70736, GERMANY

Brzezinski, Zbigniew *Government Official, Educator*
Strategic/International Studies Center, 1800 K NW, Washington, DC 20006 USA

Brzezinski, Zbignlew *Government Official, Educator*
Strategic/International Studies Center, 1800 K NW, Washington, DC 10006 USA

Buatta, Mario *Designer*
120 E 80th St, New York, NY 10021 USA

Bubas, Vic *Basketball Player, Coach*
133 Robert E Lane, Bluffton, SC 29909 USA

Bubka, Sergie N *Track Athlete*
Andresi Kulikowski, Vasavagen 13, Solna, 171 39, SWEDEN

Bubka, Surgei N *Track Athlete*
Andresi Kulikowski, Vasavagen 13, Solna, 171 39, SWEDEN

Bubna, P F *Religious Leader*
Christian & Missionary Alliance, P O Box 3500, Colorado Springs, CO 80935 USA

Bucatinsky, Dan *Writer, Producer, Actor*
Endeavor Agency LLC (LA), 9601 Wilshire Blvd Fl 3, Beverly Hills, CA 90210 USA

Buccellati, Giorgio *Misc*
University of California, Near Eastern Languages Dept, Los Angeles, CA 90024 USA

Buccellato, Benedetta *Actor*
Carlo Levi Co, Via Giuseppe Pisanelli, Rome, 00196, ITALY

Bucha, Paul W *War Hero*
601 Salem Road, Ridgefield, CT 06877 USA

Buchanan, Edna *Journalist*
P O Box 403556, Miami Beach, FL 33140 USA

Buchanan, Ian *Actor, Model*
Gold Marshak Liedtke, 3500 W Olive Ave #1400, Burbank, CA 91505 USA

Buchanan, Isobel *Opera Singer*
Marks Mgmt, 14 New Burlington St, London, W1X 1FF, UNITED KINGDOM (UK)

Buchanan, James M *Nobel Prize Laureate*
George Mason University, Study of Public Choice Center, Fairfax, VA 22030 USA

Buchanan, Jensen *Actor*
Paradigm Agency, 10100 Santa Monica Blvd #2500, Los Angeles, CA 90067 USA

Buchanan, John M *Misc*
56 Meriam St, Lexington, MA 02420 USA

Buchanan, John M *Religious Leader*
Presbyterian Church USA, 100 Witherspoon St, Louisville, KY 40202 USA

Buchanan, Ken *Boxer*
45 Marmion Road Greenfaulds, Cumbemaul, G67 4AN, SCOTLAND

Buchanan, Larry *Director*
4154 Via Andorra #B, Santa Barbara, CA 93110 USA

Buchanan, Patrick J (Pat) *Government Official, Commentator*
8233 Old Courthouse Road #200, Vienna, VA 22182 USA

Buchanan, Raymond L (Ray) *Football Player*
1010 Ridgewood Dr, Bolingbrook, IL 60440 USA

Buchanan, Robert S *Astronaut*
3 Lariat Lane, Rolling Hills, CA 90274 USA

Buchanan, Tom *Reality TV Star*
3130 Valley Rd, Saltville, VA 24370

Buchanan, Willie J *Football Player*
227 Cottingham Court, Oceanside, CA 92054 USA

Buchanon, Willie J *Football Player*
227 Cottingham Ct, Oceanside, CA 92054 USA

Buchbinder, Rudolf *Music Group, Musician*
Columbia Artists Mgmt Inc, 165 W 57th St, New York, NY 10019 USA

Buchel, Lloyd M *Misc*
16296 Rostrata Hill, Poway, CA 92064 USA

Buchel, Marco *Skier*
Ramschwagweg 55, Balzers, 9496, SWITZERLAND

Bucher, Lloyd M *Captain*
16296 Rostrata Hill, Poway, CA 92064 USA

Buchheim, Lothar-Gunther *Writer*
Johann-Biersack-Str 23, Feldafing, 82340, GERMANY

Buchholz, Christopher
17 rue Pierre Lescot, Paris, FRANCE, F-75001

Buchli, James F (Jim) *Astronaut*
1602 Fairoaks St, Seabrook, TX 77586 USA

Buchmann, Ralner *Race Car Driver, Misc*
Project Indy, 43

Buchmann, Ralner *Race Car Driver, Misc*
Project Indy, 434 E Main St, Brownsburg, IN 46112 USA

Buchwald, Art *Writer, Misc*
4327 Hawthorne St NW #W, Washington, DC 20016 USA

Buck, Craig *Volleyball Player*
P O Box 603, Goleta, CA 93116 USA

Buck, Detlev *Director*
Agentur Sigrid Narjes, Goethestr 17, Munich, 80336, GERMANY

Buck, Joe *Sportscaster*
Fox-TV, Sports Dept P O Box 900, Beverly Hills, CA 90213 USA

Buck, John E *Artist*
11229 Cottonwood Road, Bozeman, MT 59718 USA

Buck, Mike E *Football Player*
321 Fox Den Court, Destin, FL 32541 USA

Buck, Peter *Musician, Music Group*
Rem/Athens Ltd, 170 College Ave, Athens, GA 30601 USA

Buck, Robert T Jr *Director, Misc*
Brooklyn Museum, 200 Eastern Parkway, Brooklyn, NY 11238 USA

Buck, Scott *Producer*
William Morris Agency (WMA-LA), 1 William Morris Pl, Beverly Hills, CA 90212 USA

Buckbee, Ed *Scientist, Misc*
47 Revere Way, Huntsville, AL 35801 USA

Buckey, Jay C Jr *Astronaut*
14 Valley Road, Hanover, NH 03755 USA

Buckingham, Gregory (Greg) *Swimmer*
338 Ridge Road, San Carlos, NH 94070 USA

Buckingham, Lindsay
900 Airole Way, Los Angeles, CA 90077

Buckingham, Lindsey *Music Group, Musician*
East End Mgmt, 8209 Melrose Ave #200, Los Angeles, CA 90046 USA

Buckingham, Marcus *Writer*
Simon & Schuster/Pocket/Summit, 1230 Ave of Americas, New York, NY 10020 USA

Buckinghams, The *Music Group*
Paradise Artists, PO Box 1821, Ojai, CA 93024-1821 USA

Buckland, Jonny *Music Group, Musician*
Nettwerk Mgmt, 1650 W 2nd Ave, Vancouver, BC V6J 4R3, CANADA

Buckles, Bradley *Government Official, Misc*
Alcohol Tobacco Firearms Agency, 650 Massachusetts NW, Washington, DC 20001 USA

Bucklew, Neil S *Educator*
West Virginia University, President's Office, Morgantown, WV 26506 USA

Buckley, A J *Actor*
Innovative Artists, 1505 10th St, Santa Monica, CA 90401 USA

Buckley, Betty *Actor, Musician, Director*
Park Ave Talent, 404 Park Ave S #1000, New York, NY 10016 USA

Buckley, Carol *Misc*
Elephant Sanctuary, P O Box 393, Hohenwald, TN 38462 USA

Buckley, D Terrell *Football Player*
4215 Palmetto Trail, Weston, FL 33331 USA

Buckley, James L *Senator, Judge*
4952 Sentinel Dr #302, Bathesda, MD 20816 USA

Buckley, Marcus W *Football Player*
7100 Monterey Dr, Forth Worth, TX 76112 USA

Buckley, Richard E *Conductor*
310 W 55th St #1K, New York, NY 10019 USA

Buckley, William F Jr *Commentator, Editor*
215 Lexington Ave, New York, NY 10016 USA

Buckman, James E *Business Person*
Cendant Corp, 9 W 57th St, New York, NY 10019 USA

Buckner, Betty
10643 Riverside Dr, Toluca Lake, CA 91602

Buckner, Pam *Bowler*
645 Utah St, Reno, NV 89506 USA

Buckner, Shelley *Actor*
Cunningham-Escott-Dipene & Associates Inc (CED-LA), 10635 Santa Monica Blvd #130, Los Angeles, CA 90025 USA

Buckner, William (Quinn) *Basketball Player, Coach*
1608 Dowling Dr, Irving, TX 75038 USA

Buckson, David P *Governor*
110 N Main St, Camden Wyoming, DE 19934 USA

Bucyk, John P (Chief) *Hockey Player*
17 Boren Lane, Boxford, MA 01921 USA

Buczkowski, Bob *Football Player*
1205 Bowling Green Dr, Monroeville, PA 15146 USA

Budarin, Nikolai M *Cosmonaut*
Potchta Kosmonavtov, Moskovskoi Oblasti, Syvisdny Goroduk, 141160, RUSSIA

Budd, Frank *Athlete, Track Athlete, Football Player*
138 Dorchester Road, Mount Laurel, NJ 08054 USA

Budd, Harold *Composer, Misc*
Opal/Warner Bros Records, 6834 Camrose Dr, Los Angeles, CA 90068 USA

Budd, Julie *Actor, Music Group*
Julie Budd Productions, 163 Amsterdam Ave #224, New York, NY 10023 USA

Budd, Pieterse Zola *Track Athlete*
General Delivery, Bloemfontein, SOUTH AFRICA

Budd, Zola
1 Church Row Wandsworth Plain, London, ENGLAND, SW18

Budde, Brad E *Football Player*
34316 Via Fortuna, Capistrano Beach, CA 92624 USA

Budde, Ed *Football Player*
5121 W 159th Terrace, Stilwell, KS 66085 USA

Budden, Joe *Actor*
International Creative Management (ICM-NY), 40 W 57th St, New York, NY 10019 USA

Budig, Eugene A (Gene) *Baseball Player, Educator, Misc*
Baseball Commissioner's Office, 350 Park Ave, New York, NY 10022 USA

Budig, Rebecca
13576 Cheltenham Dr, Sherman Oaks, CA 91423

Budko, Walter *Basketball Player, Coach*
2525 Pot Spring Road #703, Lutherville Timon, MD 21093 USA

Budney, Albert J Jr *Business Person*
Niagara Mohawk Holdings, 300 Erie Blvd W, Syracuse, NY 13202 USA

Budnick, Neil G *Financier*
MBIA Inc, 113 King's St, Armonk, NY 10504 USA

Bueche, Wendell F *Business Person*
IMC Global, 2100 Sanders Road, Northbrook, IL 60062 USA

Buechler, John Carl *Director*
12031 Vose St #19-21, North Hollywod, CA 91605 USA

Buechler, Jud *Basketball Player*
1515 West Lane, Del Mar, CA 92014 USA

Buechrle, James *Baseball Player*
Chicago White Sox, Comiskey Park 333 W 35th St, Chicago, IL 60616 USA

Bueno, Maria *Tennis Player*
Rua Consolagao 3414 #10 Edificio Agustus, Sao Paulo, 1001, BRAZIL

Buerge, Aaron *Reality TV Star*
Maximum Talent, 1660 South Albion Street, Suite 1004, Denver, CO 80222 USA

Buerger, Martin J *Misc*
Weston Road, Lincoln, MA 01773 USA

Buffa, Dudley W *Writer*
Henry Holt, 115 W 18th St, New York, NY 10011 USA

Buffenbarger, R Thomas *Misc*
International Machinists Assn, 9000 Machinists Place, Upper Marlboro, MD 20772 USA

Buffett, Jimmy *Music Group, Songwriter*
Margaritaville, 424 Flemming St #A, Key West, FL 33040 USA

Buffett, Warren E *Business Person*
Berkshire Hathaway, 1440 Kiewit Plz, Omaha, NE 68131 USA

Buffkins, Archie Lee *Misc*
Kennedy Center, Executive Suite,
Washington, DC 20566 USA

Buffone, Douglas J (Doug) *Football Player*
WSCR-Radio, Sports Dept 4949 W
Belmont, Chicago, IL 60641 USA

Bufi, Ylli *Prime Minister*
Privatization Ministry, Keshilli i
Ministrave, Tirana, Albania

Bufi, Ylli *Prime Minister*
Privatization Ministry, Keshilli i
Ministrave, Tirana, ALBANIA

Bufman, Zev *Producer*
520 Brickett Key Dr #612, Miami, FL
33131 USA

Buford, Damon J *Baseball Player*
15412 Valley Vista Blvd, Sherman Oaks,
CA 91403 USA

Bugliosi, Vincent T *Writer*
3699 Wilshire Blvd #850, Los Angeles,
CA 90010 USA

Bugner, Joe *Boxer*
22 Buckingham St, Surrey Hills, NSW,
2010, AUSTRALIA

Buhari, Muhammadu *President, General*
GRA, Daura, Katsina State, NIGERIA

Buhner, Jay C *Baseball Player*
1420 NW Gilman Blvd #2666, Issaquah,
WA 98027 USA

Buhrmaster, Robert C *Business Person*
Jostens Inc, 5501 Norman Center Dr,
Minneapolis, MN 55437 USA

Bujold, Genevieve *Actor*
Blake Agency, 1327 Ocean Parkway #J,
Santa Monica, CA 90401 USA

Buktenica, Raymond *Actor*
Special Artists Agency, 345 N Maple Dr
#302, Beverly Hills, CA 90210 USA

Bulaich, Norman B (Norm) *Football Player*
421 Linndale Court, Hurst, TX 76054 USA

Bulatovic, Momir *President*
Vlada Savezne Republike, Lenina 2,
Belgrade, 11070, SERBIA &
MONTENEGRO

Bulifant, Joyce *Actor*
James/Levy/Jacobson, 3500 W Olive Ave
#1470, Burbank, CA 91505 USA

Bull, John S *Astronaut*
P O Box 1106, South Lake Tahoe, CA
96156 USA

Bull, Richard *Actor*
200 E Delaware Pl #20F, Chicago, IL
60611 USA

Bull, Ronald D (Ronnie) *Football Player*
15 Redspire Court, Bolingbrook, IL 60490
USA

Bullard, Louis E *Football Player*
3129 Friars Bridge Pass, Franklin, TN
37064 USA

Bullen, Voy M *Religious Leader*
Church of God, 1207 Willow Brook,
Huntsville, AL 35802 USA

Bullins, Ed *Writer*
425 Lafayette St, New York, NY 10003
USA

Bullitt, John C *Attorney General, Government Official*
Shearman Sterling, 53 Wall St, New York,
NY 10005 USA

Bullmann, Maik *Wrestler*
AC Bavaria Goldbach, Postfach 1112,
Goldbach, 63769, GERMANY

Bulloch, Jeremy *Actor*
Fett Photos, 10 Birchwood Rd, London,
SW17 9BQ, UNITED KINGDOM (UK)

Bullock, Dona *Actor*
Writers & Artists, 8383 Wilshire Blvd
#550, Beverly Hills, CA 90211 USA

Bullock, Donna
10000 Santa Monica Blvd. #305, Los
Angeles, CA 90067

Bullock, J R *Business Person*
Laidlaw Inc, 3221 N Service Road,
Burlington, ON L7R 3Y8, CANADA

Bullock, Jim J *Actor*
612 Lighthouse Ave #200, Pacific Grove,
CA 93950 USA

Bullock, Keith *Football Player*
641 Old Hickory Blvd #301, Bentwood,
TN 37027 USA

Bullock, Sandra *Actor, Producer*
Fortis Films, 8581 Santa Monica Blvd #1,
West Hollywood, CA 90069 USA

Bullock, Theodore H *Biologist*
University of California, Neurosciences
Dept, La Jolla, CA 92093 USA

Bullock, Vicki *Basketball Player*
Charlotte Sting, 100 Hive Dr, Charlotte,
NC 28217 USA

Bulriss, Mark P *Business Person*
Great Lakes Chemical, 9025 River Road
#400, Indianapolis, IN 46240 USA

Bumbeck, David *Artist*
Drew Lane RD 3, Middleburry, VT 05753
USA

Bumbry, Alonzo B (Al) *Baseball Player*
28 Tremblant Court, Lutherville, MO
21093 USA

Bumbry, Grace *Opera Singer*
Opera et Concert, Maximilianstr 22,
Munich, 80539, GERMANY

Bumgarner, Wayne
PO Box 208, Clairmont, NC 28610

Bumiller, William
9255 Sunset Blvd. #515, Los Angeles, CA
90069

Bumpers, Dale *Senator, Governor*
7613 Honesty Way, Bethesda, MD 20817
USA

Bunch, Jimmy Castor *Musician*
Universal Attractions, 145 W 57th St,
New York, NY 10019-2220 USA

Bund, Karlheinz *Business Person*
Huyssenallee 82-84, Essen Ruhr, 45128,
GERMANY

Bundchen, Gisele *Model*
IMG Models, 304 Park Ave S Fl 12, New
York, NY 10010 USA

Bundy, Brooke *Actor*
833 N Martel Ave, Los Angeles, CA
90046 USA

Bunim, Mary-Ellis *Producer*
Bunim/Murray Productions Inc, 6007
Sepulveda Blvd, Van Nuys, CA 91411
USA

Bunker, Edward *Writer*
Saint Martins Press, 175 5th Ave, New
York, NY 10010 USA

Bunker, Wallace E (Wally) *Baseball Player*
6149 Muskingum River Road, Lowell, OH
45744 USA

Bunker, Wally
502 1st St., Langley, WA 98260

Bunkowsky-Scherbak, Barb *Golfer*
Ladies Pro Golf Assn, 100 International
Golf Dr, Daytona Beach, FL 32124 USA

Bunnell, Dewey *Music Group, Musician*
Agency for Performing Arts, 9200 Sunset
Blvd #900, Los Angeles, CA 10069 USA

Bunnett, Joseph F *Misc*
608 Arroyo Seca, Santa Cruz, CA 95060
USA

Bunnetta, Bill *Bowler*
1176 E San Bruno Ave, Fresno, CA 93710
USA

Bunning, James P D (Jim) *Senator, Baseball Player*
4 Fairway Dr, Southgate, KY 41071 USA

Bunning, Jim *Politician, Senator*
United States Senate (Hart Office), 316
Hart Senate Office Building, Washington,
DC 20510 USA

Bunt, Dick
11 Irving Pl., Greenlawn, NY 11740

Bunting, Eve *Writer*
Harper Collins Publishers, 10 E 53rd St,
New York, NY 10022 USA

Bunting, John *Football Player*
202 Oak Park Dr, Chapell Hill, NC 27517
USA

Bunton, Emma *Musician, Music Group*
Lee & Thompson, Green Garden House
15 22nd St, London, WC1M 5HE,
UNITED KINGDOM (UK)

Buoniconti, Nicholas A (Nick) *Football Player, Business Person*
445 Grand Bay Dr #803, Key Biscayne, FL
33149 USA

Buono, Cara *Actor*
8675 W Washington Blvd #203, Culver
City, CA 90232 USA

Buono, Carla
25 Sea Colony Dr, Santa Monica, CA
90405-5321

Buraas, Hans-Peter *Skier*
Norges Skiforbund, Postboks 3853,
Ulleval Hageby, Oslo, 0805, NORWAY

Burba, Edwin H Jr *General*
256 Montrose Dr, McDonough, GA
30253 USA

Burbank, Daniel C (Dan) *Astronaut*
3210 Water Elm Way, Houston, TX 77059
USA

Burbidge, E Margaret P *Astronomer*
University of California, Astrophysics
Center 9500 Gilman, La Jolla, CA 92093
USA

Burbules, Peter G *General*
6321 Pasadena Point Blvd S, Gulfport, FL 33707 USA

Burch, Elliot *Race Car Driver, Misc*
402 Corey Lane, Middletown, RI 02842 USA

Burchfiel, Burrell C *Geophysicist, Misc*
9 Robinson Park, Winchester, MA 01890 USA

Burchuladze, Paata *Opera Singer*
Raab & Bohm, Piankengasse 7, Vienna, 1010, AUSTRIA

Burckhalter, Joseph H *Inventor*
705 Valley Brook Road, Wilmington, NC 28412 USA

Burd, Steven A *Business Person*
Safeway Inc, 5918 Stoneridge Mall Road, Pleasanton, CA 94588 USA

Burden, Ross *Chef*
Roseman Organisation, The, 51 Queen Anne St, London, W1G 9HS, UNITED KINGDOM (UK)

Burden, William A M *Diplomat, Financier*
820 5th Ave, New York, NY 10021 USA

Burdette, Lou
2019 Beveva Rd., Sarasota, FL 34232

Burdette, S Lewis (Lew) *Baseball Player*
17709 Deer Isle Cirlce, Winter Garden, FL 34787 USA

Burditt, Joyce *Writer*
Knopf, 201 E 50th St, New York, NY 10022 USA

Burdon, Eric *Songwriter, Music Group*
Lustig Talent, PO Box 770850, Orlando, FL 32877 USA

Bure, Paval
V100 N. Renfrew St., Vancouver, BC V5K 3N7, CANADA

Bure, Pavel *Hockey Player*
12335 NW 10th Dr #5, Coral Springs, FL 33071 USA

Bure, Valeri *Hockey Player*
10371 Golden Eagle Court, Plantation, FL 33324 USA

Burford, Christopher W (Chris) *Football Player*
1215 Broken Feather Court, Reno, NV 89511 USA

Burge, Gregg
420 Madison Ave. #1400, New York, NY 10017

Burgee, John H *Architect*
Perelanda Farm Skunks Misery Road, Millerton, NY 12546 USA

Burger, Neil *Director*
Endeavor Agency LLC (LA), 9601 Wilshire Blvd Fl 3, Beverly Hills, CA 90210 USA

Burgere, Andre
67 quai d'Orsay, Paris, F-75007, FRANCE

Burgess, Adrian *Mountaineer*
109 North St, Anderson, SC 29621 USA

Burgess, Annie *Athlete*
601 F Street NW, Washington, DC 20004

Burgess, Bobby
11684 Ventura Blvd. #691, Studio City, CA 91604

Burgess, Christian
33 Gastein Rd, London, W6 8LT, ENGLAND

Burgess, Don *Cinematographer*
Gersh Agency, 232 N Canon Dr, Beverly Hills, CA 90210 USA

Burgess, Greg
1144 Holly Oaks Cove, Jacksonville, FL 32259

Burgess, Mitchell *Writer*
Broder Webb Chervin Silbermann Agency, The (BWCS), 9242 Beverly Blvd #200, Beverly Hills, CA 90210 USA

Burgess, Neil *Engineer*
201 E 5th St #2200, Cincinnati, OH 45202 USA

Burgess, Robert K *Business Person*
Pulte Corp, 33 Bloomfield Hills Parkway, Bloomfield Hills, MI 48304 USA

Burgess, Tony *Misc*
US Geological Survey, 119 National Center, Reston, VA 22092 USA

Burgess, Warren D *Religious Leader*
Reformed Church in America, 475 Riverside Dr, New York, NY 10115 USA

Burgett, Gordon

Burghardt, Raymond F *Diplomat*
US Embassy, 7 Lang Ha St, Ba Dinh, Hanoi, VIETNAM

Burghardt, Walter J *Misc*
19 I St NW, Washington, DC 20001 USA

Burghoff, Gary *Actor*
Scott Stander, 13701 Riverside Dr, #201, Sherman Oaks, CA 91423 USA

Burgi, Richard *Actor*
124 Sunset Terrace, Laguna Beach, CA 92651 USA

Burgin, C David *Editor*
Oakland Tribune, Editorial Dept, 409 13th St, Oakland, CA 94612 USA

Burgon, Geoffrey *Composer*
Chester Music, 8-9 Firth St, London, W1V 5TZ, UNITED KINGDOM (UK)

Burham, Daniel *Business Person*
Raytheon Co, 141 Spring St, Lexington, MA 02421 USA

Burham, James B *Financier*
Mellon Bank, 1 Mellon Bank Center, #0400, Pittsburgh, PA 15258 USA

Burhoe, Ralph Wendell *Misc*
Montgornery Place, 5550 S South Shore Dr #715, Chicago, IL 60637 USA

Burke, Alfred *Actor*
Jameson, 219 The Plaza, 535 Kings St, London, SW10 0SZ USA

Burke, Bernard F *Physicist*
10 Bloomfield St, Lexington, MA 02421 USA

Burke, Billy *Actor*
Writers & Artists, 8383 Wilshire Blvd, #550, Beverly Hills, CA 90211 USA

Burke, Brooke *Actor, Model*
BLB Inc, 1880 Century Park E #1600, Los Angeles, CA 90067 USA

Burke, Chris *Actor*
426 S Orange Grove Ave, Los Angeles, CA 90036 USA

Burke, Clement (Clem) *Musician*
Shore Fire Media, 32 Court St, #1600, Brooklyn, NY 11201 USA

Burke, David *Actor*
Writers & Artists, 8383 Wilshire Blvd, #550, Beverly Hills, CA 90211 USA

Burke, Delta *Actor*
4270 Farmdale Ave, Studio City, CA 91604 USA

Burke, Ed
285 E. Main St., Los Gatos, CA 95030

Burke, Hederman Lynn *Swimmer*
26 White Oak Tree Road, Syosset, NY 11791 USA

Burke, Jack
13722 Champion's Dr., Houston, TX 77079

Burke, Jack Sr *Golfer*
Champions Golf Club, 13722 Champions Dr, Houston, TX 77069 USA

Burke, James *Commentator*
Henley House, Terrace Bames, London, SW13 0NP, UNITED KINGDOM (UK)

Burke, James D *Director*
Saint Louis Art Museum, Forest Park, Saint Louis, MO 63110 USA

Burke, James E *Business Person*
Johnson & Johnson, 317 George St, #200, New Brunswick, NJ 08901 USA

Burke, James Lee
114 Fifth Ave., New York, NY 10011

Burke, James Lee *Writer*
Boubleday Press, 1540 Broadway, New York, NY 10036 USA

Burke, John F *Educator, Doctor*
984 Memorial Dr, #503, Cambridge, MA 02138 USA

Burke, Joseph C *Educator*
Rockefeller Institute, 411 State St, Albany, NY 12203 USA

Burke, Kathy *Actor*
Stephen Halton Mgmt, 83 Shepperton Road, London, N1 3DF, UNITED KINGDOM (UK)

Burke, Kelly H *General*
Stafford Burke Hecker, 1006 Cameron St, Alexandria, VA 22314 USA

Burke, Michael Reilly
10100 Santa Monica Blvd. #2500, Los Angeles, CA 90067

Burke, Patrick *Golfer*
24 Saint Georges Court, Coto de Caza, CA 92679 USA

Burke, Paul
2217 Avenida Caballeros, Palm Springs, CA 92262

Burke, Paul Timothy *Actor*
2217 Avenida Caballeros, Palm Springs, CA 92262 USA

Burke, Robert John *Actor*
Gersh Agency, 232 N Canon Dr, Beverly Hills, CA 90210 USA

Burke, Soloman
1048 Tatnall St., Macon, GA 31201

Burke, Solomon *Musician*
Rodgers Redding, 1048 Tatnall St, Macon, GA 31201 USA

Burket, Harriet *Editor*
700 John Ringling Blvd, Sarasota, FL 34236 USA

Burkett, John D *Baseball Player*
104 Craydon Circle, Beaver, PA 15009 USA

Burkhalter, Edward A Jr *Admiral*
4128 Fort Washington Place, Alexandria, VA 22304 USA

Burkhardt, Francois *Architect*
3 Rue de Venise, Paris, 75004, FRANCE

Burkhardt, Lisa *Sportscaster*
Madison Square Garden Network, 4 Pennsylvania Plaza, New York, NY 10001 USA

Burkholder, JoAnn *Physicist*
North Carolina State University, Botany Dept, Raleigh, NC 27695 USA

Burkholder, Owen E *Religious Leader*
421 S 2nd St, #600, Elkhart, IN 46516 USA

Burkl, Fred A *Misc*
United Retail Workers Union, 9865 W Roosevelt Road, Westchester, IL 60154 USA

Burkley, Dennis *Actor*
5145 Costello Ave, Sherman Oaks, CA 91423 USA

Burks, Arthur W *Mathematician*
3445 Vintage Valley Road, Ann Arbor, MI 48105 USA

Burks, Ellis R *Baseball Player*
1427 Fitzroy St, Westlake, OH 44145 USA

Burleson, Richard P (Rick) *Baseball Player*
241 E Country Hills Dr, La Habra, CA 90631 USA

Burleson, Tom *Basketball Player*
PO Box 861, Newland, NC 28657 USA

Burlinson, Tom *Actor*
June Cann Mgmt, 110 Queen St, Woollahra, NSW, 2025, AUSTRALIA

Burn, Scott *Writer*
Creative Artists Agency LCC (CAA-LA), 9830 Wilshire Blvd, Beverly Hills, CA 90212 USA

Burnell, Jocelyn Bell *Astronomer*
Bell Open University, Physics Dept, Milton Keynes, MK7 6AA, UNITED KINGDOM (UK)

Burner, David L *Business Person*
B F Goodrich Co, 3 Coliseum Centre, 2550 W Tyvola Road, Charlotte, NC 28205 USA

Burnes, Karen *Commentator*
CBS-TV, News Dept, 51 W 52nd St, New York, NY 10019 USA

Burnett, Carol *Comedian, Actor*
Kalola Productions, 270 N Canon Dr, #1186, Beverly Hills, CA 90210 USA

Burnett, Howard J *Educator*
Washington & Jefferson College, President's Office, Washington, PA 15301 USA

Burnett, James E *Government Official*
Transportations Safety Board, 800 Independence Ave SW, Washington, DC 20594 USA

Burnett, Mark *Producer*
Mark Burnett Productions, 1661 Lincoln Blvd #200, Santa Monica, CA 90404 USA

Burnett, Nancy
7800 Beverly Blvd. #3305, Los Angeles, CA 90036

Burnett, T-Bone *Musician, Songwriter, Producer*
Immortal Ent Group, 1650 21st St, Santa Monica, CA 90404 USA

Burnette, Olivia
121 N. San Vicente Blvd, Beverly Hills, CA 90211

Burnette, Rocky *Musician*
1900 Ave of Stars, #2530, Los Angeles, CA 90067 USA

Burnette, Thomas N Jr *General*
Deputy Cinc, US Joint Forces Command, Norfolk, VA 23551 USA

Burnin' Daylight
PO Box 150245, Nashville, TN 37215

Burning, Spear *Musician*
13034 231st St, Springfield Gardens, NY 11413 USA

Burnley, James H IV *Secretary*
Shaw Pittman Potts Trowbridge, 2300 N St NW, Washington, DC 20037 USA

Burns, Annie *Musician, Songwriter*
Drake Assoc, 177 Woodland Ave, Westwood, NJ 07675 USA

Burns, Bob *Musician*
Vector Mgmt, 1607 17th Ave S, Nashville, TN 37212 USA

Burns, Brooke *Model, Actor*
Paradigm (LA), 10100 Santa Monica Blvd, Fl 25, Los Angeles, CA 90067 USA

Burns, Charles *Artist*
Fantagraphics Books, 7563 Lake City Way, Seattle, WA 98115 USA

Burns, Christian *Musician*
Day Time, Crown House, 225 Kensington High St, London, W8 8SA, UNITED KINGDOM (UK)

Burns, Edward *Actor, Director*
Firm, The, 9465 Wilshire Blvd, Beverly Hills, CA 90212 USA

Burns, Eileen
4000 W. 43rd St., New York, NY 10036

Burns, Eric *Entertainer*
Fox News Watch, 1211 Ave of the Americas, New York, NY 10036-8701 USA

Burns, Heather *Actor*
Endeavor Talent Agency, 9701 Wilshire Blvd, #1000, Beverly Hills, CA 90212 USA

Burns, James MacGregor *Historian, Scientist*
High Mowing, Bee Hill Road, Williamstown, MA 01267 USA

Burns, Jeannie *Musician, Songwriter*
Drake Assoc, 177 Woodland Ave, Westwood, NJ 07675 USA

Burns, Jere
1465 Lindacrest Dr., Beverly Hills, CA 90210

Burns, Jere II *Actor*
Binder, 1465 Lindacrest Dr, Beverly Hills, CA 90210 USA

Burns, Jerry
9520 Viking Dr., Eden Prairie, MN 55344

Burns, Jim
2706 Lincoln Ave., Evanston, IL 60201

Burns, John F *Journalist*
New York Times, Editorial Dept, 229 W 43rd St, New York, NY 10036 USA

Burns, Ken *Director, Producer*
Florentine Films, 59 Maple Grove Rd, PO Box 613, Walpole, NH 03608

Burns, Kenneth L (Ken) *Director*
Florentine Films, Maple Grove Road, Walpole, NH 03608 USA

Burns, M Anthony *Business Person*
Ryder System Inc, 3600 NW 82nd Ave, Miami, FL 33166 USA

Burns, Marie *Songwriter, Musician*
Drake Assoc, 177 Woodland Ave, Westwood, NJ 07675 USA

Burns, Megan *Actor*
Peters Fraser & Dunlop (PFD - UK), Drury House, 34-43 Russell St, London, WC2 B5, UNITED KINGDOM (UK)

Burns, Pat *Coach*
New Jersey Devils, Continental Arena, 50 RR 120 N, East Rutherford, NJ 07073 USA

Burns, Regan *Actor*
OmniPop Inc (LA), 10700 Ventura Blvd Fl 2, Studio City, CA 91604 USA

Burns, Robert H *Misc*
1015 University Bay Dr, Madison, WI 53705 USA

Burns, Steven *Actor*
Davis Spylios Management, 244 West 54th Street #707, New York, NY 10019

Burnside, R L *Musician*
Billions Corp, 833 W Chicago Ave, #101, Chicago, IL 60622 USA

Burr, Bill *Comedian*
William Morris Agency (WMA-LA), 1 William Morris Pl, Beverly Hills, CA 90212 USA

Burrell, Garland L Jr *Judge*
US District Court, 5011 St, Sacramento, CA 95814 USA

Burrell, Kenneth E (Kenny) *Composer, Musician*
Tropix International, 163 3rd Ave, #143, New York, NY 10003 USA

Burrell, Kenny
163 Third Ave. #206, New York, NY 10003

Burrell, Leroy *Track Athlete*
University of Houston, Athletic Dept, Houston, TX 77023 USA

Burrell, Scott *Basketball Player*
331 Evergreen Ave, Hamden, CT 06518 USA

Burress, Plaxico *Football Player*
Pittsburgh Steelers, 3400 S Water St, Pittsburgh, PA 15203 USA

Burris, Jeffrey L (Jeff) *Football Player*
PO Box 5.35, Zionsville, IN 46077 USA

Burris, Kurt (Buddy) *Football Player*
2617 Fairfield Dr, Norman, OK 73072 USA

Burris, Robert H *Misc*
6225 Mineral Point Road, #96, Madison, WI 53705 USA

Burrough, Kenneth O (Ken) *Football Player*
206 Sweetgum Dr, Haughton, LA 71037 USA

Burroughs, Jeffrey A (Jeff) *Baseball Player*
6155 Laguna Court, Long Beach, CA 90803 USA

Burroughs, William S *Musician*
PO Box 147, Lawrence, KS 66044 USA

Burrow, Bob
520 Crocus, Radcliff, KY 41060

Burrowes, Norma E *Opera Singer*
56 Rochester Road, London, NW1 9JG, UNITED KINGDOM (UK)

Burrows, Darren E *Actor*
Writers & Artists, 8383 Wilshire Blvd, #550, Beverly Hills, CA 90211 USA

Burrows, Edwin G *Writer*
Oxford University Press, 198 Madison Ave, New York, NY 10016 USA

Burrows, Eva *Religious Leader*
102 Domain Park, 193 Domain Road, South Yarra, VIC, 3141, AUSTRALIA

Burrows, J Stuart *Opera Singer*
Nirvana, 35 Saint Fagans Dr Saint Fagans, Cardiff, Wales, CF5 6EF, UNITED KINGDOM (UK)

Burrows, James *Director*
Broder Webb Chervin Silbermann Agency, The (BWCS), 9242 Beverly Blvd #200, Beverly Hills, CA 90210 USA

Burrows, Saffron *Actor*
Jonathan Altaras, 13 Shorts Gardens, London, WC2H 9AT, UNITED KINGDOM (UK)

Burrows, Stephen *Fashion Designer*
10 W 57th St, New York, NY 10019 USA

Burrus, William *Misc*
American Postal Workers Union, 1300 L St NW, Washington, DC 20005 USA

Bursch, Daniel W *Astronaut*
1119 Montecito Ave, Pacific Grove, CA 93950 USA

Burshnick, Anthony J *General*
7715 Carrleigh Parkway, Springfield, VA 22152 USA

Burstyn, Ellen *Actor*
Matrix Movies, PO Box 217, Washington Springs Road, Palisades, NY 10964 USA

Burt, Adam *Hockey Player*
1508 Weiskopf Loop, Round Rock, TX 78664 USA

Burt, James M *War Hero*
1621 Sherwood Road, Colony Park, Wyomissing, PA 19610 USA

Burt, Robert N *Business Person*
FMC Corp, 200 E Randolph Dr, Chicago, IL 60601 USA

Burtnett, Wellington *Hockey Player*
1703 Poullot Place, Wilmington, MA 01887 USA

Burton, Amanda *Actor*
International Creative Mgmt, 8942 Wilshire Blvd, #219, Beverly Hills, CA 90211 USA

Burton, Brandie *Golfer*
Int'l Mgmt Group, 1 Erieview Plaza, 1360 E 9th St #1300, Cleveland, OH 44114 USA

Burton, Ed
660 West Hile Rd., North Shores, MI 49441

Burton, Gary *Musician*
Berklee College of Music, 1140 Boylston St, Boston, MA 02215 USA

Burton, Glenn W *Misc*
421 10th St W, Tifton, GA 31794 USA

Burton, Hilarie *Actor*
Endeavor NY, 23 Watts St Fl 6, New York, NY 10013 USA

Burton, Jake *Skier*
Burton Snowboards, 80 Industrial Parkway, Burlington, VT 05401 USA

Burton, Jeff *Race Car Driver*
15555 Huntersville Concord Road, Huntersville, NC 28078 USA

Burton, Kate *Actor, Musician*
Gersh Agency, 232 N Canon Dr, Beverly Hills, CA 90210 USA

Burton, Lance *Misc*
Monte Carlo Hotel, 3770 S Las Vegas Blvd, Las Vegas, NV 89109 USA

Burton, LeVar *Actor*
The Marion Rosenberg Office, PO Box 69826, Los Angeles, CA 90069-0826

Burton, Nelson Jr *Bowler*
9359 SW Eagles Landing, Stuart, FL 34997 USA

Burton, Norman *Actor*
3641 Meadville Dr, Sherman Oaks, CA 91403 USA

Burton, Robert G *Publisher*
World Color Press, 101 Park Ave, New York, NY 10178 USA

Burton, Steve *Actor*
4814 Lemore Ave, Sherman Oaks, CA 91403 USA

Burton, Tim *Director*
William Morris Agency (WMA-LA), 1 William Morris Pl, Beverly Hills, CA 90212 USA

Burton, Timothy W (Tim) *Director*
1041 N Formosa Ave, #10, West Hollywood, CA 90046 USA

Burton, Tony
3500 W. Olive Ave. #1400, Burbank, CA 91505

Burton, Warren
280 S. Beverly Dr. #400, Beverly Hills, CA 90212

Burton, Willie *Basketball Player*
18900 Fleming St, Detroit, MI 48234 USA

Burum, Stephen H *Cinematographer*
Mirisch Agency, 1801 Century Park E, #1801, Los Angeles, CA 90067 USA

Burwell, Barbara
1100 Millstone Rd., Wayzata, MN 55391

Burwell, Carter *Composer*
Creative Artists Agency, 9830 Wilshire Blvd, Beverly Hills, CA 90212 USA

Bury, Pol *Artist*
12 Vallee da la Taupe-Perdreauville, Mantes-La-Jolie, 78200, FRANCE

Busby, Wayne
287 S. Tampa Ave., Orlando, FL 32805

Buscemi, Steve *Actor, Director*
Endeavor Agency LLC (LA), 9601 Wilshire Blvd Fl 3, Beverly Hills, CA 90210 USA

Busch, August A III *Business Person*
Anheuser-Busch Cos, 1 Busch Place, Saint Louis, MO 63118 USA

Busch, Charles *Actor, Writer*
Eighth Square Entertainment, 606 N Larchmont #307, Los Angeles, CA 90004 USA

Busch, Frederick M *Writer*
RR 1 Box 31A, New Turnpike Road, Sherburne, NY 13460 USA

Buse, Don *Basketball Player*
7300 W State Road 64, Huntingburg, IN 47542 USA

Busemann, Frank *Track Athlete*
Borkumstr 13A, Recklinghausen, 45665, GERMANY

Buser, Martin *Race Car Driver*
PO Box 520997, Big Lake, AK 99652 USA

Busey, Gary *Actor*
Vicki M Roberts, PO Box 642326, Los Angeles, CA 90064

Busey, Jake *Actor*
International Creative Mgmt, 8942 Wilshire Blvd, #219, Beverly Hills, CA 90211 USA

Busfield, Timothy *Actor*
2416 G St, #D, Sacramento, CA 95816 USA

Bush
William Morris Agency (WMA-LA), 1 William Morris Pl, Beverly Hills, CA 90212 USA

Bush, Barbara P *First Lady*
9 W Oak Dr, Houston, TX 77056 USA

Bush, Billy *Correspondent*
Access Hollywood, 3000 W Alameda Ave, Trailer E, Burbank, CA 91523 USA

Bush, Dave *Musician*
CMO Mgmt, Ransomes Dock, 35-37 Parkgate Road, London, SW11 4NP, UNITED KINGDOM (UK)

Bush, Dick
8 Grande Parade #16 Plymouth, Devon, PL1 3DF, ENGLAND

Bush, Jeb (Governor)
36 Pine St., Orlando, FL 32801

Bush, Jim *Coach*
5106 Bounty Lane, Culver City, CA 90230 USA

Bush, Kate *Musician, Songwriter*
PO Box 120 Welling, Kent, DA16 3DS, UNITED KINGDOM (UK)

Bush, Laura *Politician, First Lady*
White House, The, 1600 Pennsylvania Ave NW, Washington, DC 20500 USA

Bush, Lesley L *Misc*
65 Birch Ave, Princeton, NJ 08542 USA

Bush, Robert E *Misc*
3148 Madrona Beach Road NW,
Olympia, WA 98502 USA

Bush, Sophia *Actor*
Joan Green Management, 1836 Courtney
Terr, Los Angeles, CA 90046 USA

Bush, Walter L *Misc*
5200 Malibu Dr, Minneapolis, MN 55436
USA

Bush, William Green *Actor*
Gold Marshak Liedtke, 3500 W Olive
Ave, #1400, Burbank, CA 91505 USA

Bush Jr, George H *Politician, President*
White House, 1600 Pennsylvania Ave
NW, Washington, DC 20500 USA

Bushinsky, Joseph M (Jay) *Commentator*
Rehov Hatsafon 5, Savyon, 56540, ISRAEL

Bushkin, Joe
435 E. 52nd St., New York, NY 10022

Bushland, Raymond C *Misc*
200 Concord Plaza Dr, San Antonio, TX
78216 USA

Bushnell, Bill *Director*
2751 Pelham Place, Los Angeles, CA
90068 USA

Bushnell, Candace *Writer*
Greater Talent Network, 437 5th Ave,
New York, NY 10016 USA

Bushy, Ronald (Ron) *Musician*
Entertainment Services Int'l, 6400 Pleasant
Park Dr, Chanhassen, MN 55317 USA

Busino, Orlando *Cartoonist*
12 Shadblow Hill Road, Ridgefield, CT
06877 USA

Buss, Jerry H *Business Person*
Los Angeles Lakers, Staples Center, 1111 S
Figueroa St, Los Angeles, CA 90015 USA

Bussard, Robert W *Physicist*
9705 Carroll Centre Road, #103, San
Diego, CA 92126 USA

Bussell, Darcey A *Ballerina*
155 New King's Road, London, SW6 4SJ,
UNITED KINGDOM (UK)

Bussey, Dexter M *Football Player*
2565 Bloomfield Crossing, Bloomfield
Hills, MI 48304 USA

Bustamante, Carlos *Scientist*
University of California, Howard Hughes
Medical Institute, Berkeley, CA 94720
USA

Busted *Music Group*
Helter Skelter (UK), The Plaza, 535 Kings
Rd, London, N13 5H, UNITED
KINGDOM (UK)

Buster, Dolly
Am Schornacker 66, Wesel, GERMANY,
D-46485

Buster, John E *Misc*
Harbor-UCLA Medical Center, PO Box
2910, Torrance, CA 90509 USA

Butala, Tony *Musician*
PO Box 151, McKees Rocks, PA 15136
USA

Butcher, Clyde *Photographer*
52388 Tamiami Trail E, Chokoloskee, FL
34138 USA

Butcher, Donnie
1745 Burns Rd., Milford, MI 48381

Butcher, Susan H *Dog Sled Racer*
Trail Breaker Kennel, 1 Eureka, Manley,
AK 99756 USA

Butcher, Willard C *Financier*
101 Park Ave, New York, NY 10178 USA

Butera, Sam
L PO Box 43295, as Vegas, NV 89116

Buthelezi, Chief Mangosuthu G *Politician*
Home Affairs Ministry, Private Bag x741,
Pretoria, 0001, SOUTH AFRICA

Buthelezi, Minister Mangosuthu
Union Bldg, Pretoria, SOUTH AFRICA,
0001

Butkus, Richard J (Dick) *Football Player,
Actor*
21647 Rambla Vista, Malibu, CA 90265
USA

Butler, Bernard *Musician*
Interceptor Enterprises, 98 White Lion St,
London, N1 9PF, UNITED KINGDOM
(UK)

Butler, Bill C *Cinematographer*
1097 Aviation Blvd, Hermosa Beach, CA
90254 USA

Butler, Brett *Actor, Comedian*
William Morris Agency, 151 El Camino
Dr, Beverly Hills, CA 90212 USA

Butler, Brett (baseball player)
315 Longvue Ct., Duluth, GA 30155-1837

Butler, Brett M *Baseball Player*
2286 Flowering Crab Dr E, Lafayette, IN
47905 USA

Butler, Caron *Basketball Player*
Miami Heat, American Airlines Arena,
601 Biscayne Blvd, Miami, FL 33132 USA

Butler, Conrad *Actor*
Paradigm Agency, 10100 Santa Monica
Blvd, #2500, Los Angeles, CA 90067 USA

Butler, Dan
8730 Sunset Blvd. #480, Los Angeles, CA
90069

Butler, David
10 Highgate West Hill, London,
ENGLAND, NW 6JR

Butler, Dean *Actor*
1310 Westholme Ave, Los Angeles, CA
90024 USA

Butler, Gary C *Business Person*
Automatic Data Processing, 1 ADP Blvd,
Roseland, NJ 07068 USA

Butler, George L *General*
Peter Kiewit & Sons, 11122 William
Plaza, Omaha, NE 68144 USA

Butler, Gerard *Actor*
Paradigm Agency, 10100 Santa Monica
Blvd, #2500, Los Angeles, CA 90067 USA

Butler, Jerry *Doctor*
164 Woodstone, Buffalo Grove, IL 60089
USA

Butler, Jerry (Iceman) *Musician,
Songwriter*
Jerry Butler Productions, 164 Woodstone
Dr, Buffalo Grove, IL 60089 USA

Butler, Jerry O *Football Player*
2820 W Park Blvd, Shaker Heights, OH
44120 USA

Butler, Joe *Musician*
Pipeline Artists Mgmt, 620 16th Ave S,
Hopkins, MN 55343 USA

Butler, Kevin G *Football Player*
262 Hawthorn Village Common, Vernon
Hills, IL 60061 USA

Butler, LeRoy *Football Player*
4119 Westloop Lane, Jacksonville, FL
32277 USA

Butler, Martin *Composer*
Princeton University, Music Dept,
Princeton, NJ 08544 USA

Butler, Paul *Astronomer*
University of California, Astronomy Dept,
Berkeley, CA 94720 USA

Butler, Robert *Director*
650 Club View Dr, Los Angeles, CA
90024 USA

Butler, Robert N *Misc*
Mount Sinai Medical Center, Geriatrics
Dept, 1 Levy Plaza, New York, NY 10029
USA

Butler, Robert Olen *Writer*
1009 Concord Road, #230, Tallahassee,
FL 32308 USA

Butler, Samuel C *Attorney General*
Cravath Swain Moore, 825 8th Ave, New
York, NY 10019 USA

Butler, William E *Business Person*
Eaton Corp, Eaton Center, 1111 Superior
Ave, Cleveland, OH 44114 USA

Butler, Yancy *Actor*
Writers & Artists, 8383 Wilshire Blvd,
#550, Beverly Hills, CA 90211 USA

Butor, Michael *Writer*
A L'Ecart, Lucinges, Bonne, 74380,
FRANCE

Butsavage, Bernard *Misc*
Molders & Allied Workers Union, 1225 E
McMillan St, Cincinnati, OH 45206 USA

Butt, Yondani
Gurtman & Murtha, 450 Fashion Ave,
#603, New York, NY 10123 USA

Buttafuoco, Joey *Actor*
Ruth Webb Enterprises, 10580 Des
Moines Ave, Northridge, CA 91326 USA

Butterfield, Alexander P *Government
Official*
3410 Brookwood Dr, Fairfax, VA 22030
USA

Butterfield, Deborah K *Artist*
11229 Cottonwood Road, Bozeman, MT
59718 USA

Butterfield, Jack *Misc*
55 Pineridge Drive, Westfield, MA 08085
USA

Butthole Surfers
315 S. Coast Hwy. #100, Encinitas, CA
92024

Buttle, Gregory E (Greg) *Football Player*
5 Hollacher Dr, Northport, NY 11768
USA

Button, Richard T (Dick) *Producer, Figure
Skater*
Candio Productions, 765 Park Ave, #6B,
New York, NY 10021 USA

Buttons, Red *Actor*
2142 Century Park Lane, #210, Los Angeles, CA 90067 USA

Butts, Earl
2741 N. Salisbury St. #2116, W. Lafayette, IN 47906-1499

Butts, James *Track Athlete*
16950 Belforest Dr, Carson, CA 90746 USA

Butz, David E (Dave) *Football Player*
65 Oak Grove Dr, Belleville, IL 62221 USA

Butz, Earl *Secretary*
2741 N Salisbury St, West Lafayette, IN 62221 USA

Butzer, Hans E *Architect*
University of Oklahoma, Architecture Division, Gould Hall, Norman, OK 73019 USA

Butzner, John D Jr *Judge*
US Court of Appeals, PO Box 2188, Richmond, VA 23218 USA

Buxbaum, Richard M *Attorney General, Educator*
University of California, Boalt Hall, Berkeley, CA 94720 USA

Buxton, Sarah *Actor*
Jerry Shandrew PR, 1050 South Stanley Avenue, Los Angeles, CA 90019-6634 USA

Buzek, Jerzy *Prime Minister*
Kancelaria Prezesa Ministrow, Al Ujazdowskie, 1/3, Warsaw, 00-583, POLAND

Buzzi, Ruth *Actor, Comedian*
Entertainment Alliance, PO Box 5734, Santa Rosa, CA 95402 USA

Byars, Betsy C *Writer*
401 Rudder Ridge, Seneca, SC 29678 USA

Byatt, Antonia Susan (A S) *Writer*
37 Rusholme Road, London, SW15 3LF, UNITED KINGDOM (UK)

Bychkov, Semyon
Buffalo Symphony Orchestra, 71 Symphony Circle, Buffalo, NY 14201 USA

Bye, Karyn *Hockey Player*
335 Soo Line Road, Hudson, WI 54016 USA

Bye, Kermit E *Judge*
US Court of Appeals, 657 2nd Ave N, Fargo, ND 58102 USA

Byers, Nina *Physicist*
University of California, Physics Dept, Los Angeles, CA 90024 USA

Byers, Steve *Actor*
Evolution Entertainment, 901 N Highland Ave, Los Angeles, CA 90038 USA

Byers, Walter *Misc*
PO Box 96, Saint Marys, KS 66536 USA

Bykovsky, Valeri F *Cosmonaut*
Potchta Kosmonavtov, Moskovskoi Oblasti, Syvisdny Goroduk, 141160, RUSSIA

Byner, Earnest A *Football Player*
850 Stembridge Road SE, Milledgeville, GA 31061 USA

Byner, John *Actor*
American Mgmt, 19948 Mayall St, Chatsworth, CA 91311 USA

Bynes, Amanda *Actor, Comedian*
Tollin/Roberts, 10960 Ventura Blvd, Studio City, CA 91604 USA

Bynoe, Peter C B *Misc*
Denver Nuggets, Pepsi Center, 1000 Chopper Circle, Denver, CO 80204 USA

Byrd, Benjamin F Jr *Doctor*
4220 Hardling Pike, #380, Nashville, TN 37205 USA

Byrd, Dennis
PO Box 90, Owasso, OK, 74056

Byrd, Donald *Musician*
DL Media, PO Box 2728, Bala Cynwyd, PA 19004 USA

Byrd, Eugene *Actor*
Creative Management Group (CMG), 9465 Wilshire Blvd #335, Beverly Hills, CA 90212 USA

Byrd, Gill A *Football Player*
510 E Glenbrook Dr, Pulaski, WI 54162 USA

Byrd, Harry F Jr *Senator*
Rockingham Publishing Co, 2 N kent St, Winchester, VA 22601 USA

Byrd, Robin
Box 305 Lenox Hill Sta., New York, NY 10021

Byrd, Tom *Actor*
United Talent Agency, 14011 Ventura Blvd, #213, Sherman Oaks, CA 91423 USA

Byrd, Tracy *Musician*
Carter & Co, 1114 17th Ave S, #103, Nashville, TN 37212 USA

Byrds, The
PO Box 1333, Manomet, MA 02345

Byrne, Brendan T *Governor*
6 Becker Farm Road, Roseland, NJ 07068 USA

Byrne, Chris *Actor*
Central Artists, 269 West Alameda Avenue, A, Burbank, CA 91502

Byrne, David *Musician, Songwriter*
Maine Road, 48 Laight St, New York, NY 10013 USA

Byrne, Gabriel *Actor*
Industry Entertainment, 955 Carillo Dr, #300, Los Angeles, CA 90048 USA

Byrne, Garry *Publisher*
Variety Inc, 5700 Wilshire Blvd, Los Angeles, CA 90036 USA

Byrne, John *Cartoonist*
DC Cornics, 1700 Broadway, #700, New York, NY 10019 USA

Byrne, Josh *Actor*
Hervey/Grimes, PO Box 64249, Los Angeles, CA 90064 USA

Byrne, Martha
40 W. 57th St., New York, NY 10019

Byrne, Michael *Actor*
Conway Van Gelder Robinson, 18-21 Jermyn St, London, SW1Y 6NB, UNITED KINGDOM (UK)

Byrne, Rose *Actor*
RGM Associates (Australia), PO Box 128, Surry Hills NSW, 2010, AUSTRALIA

Byrne, Thomas J (Tommy) *Baseball Player*
1104 Chilmark Ave, Wake Forest, NC 27587 USA

Byrnes, Edd *Actor*
PO Box 1623, Beverly Hills, CA 90213 USA

Byrnes, Jim *Actor*
Characters Talent Agency, The (Toronto), 150 Carlton St Fl 2, Toronto ON, M5A 2K1, CANADA

Byrnes, Kevin P *General*
Assistant Vice Chief of Staff, HqUSA, Pentagon, Washington, DC 20310 USA

Byron, Jeffrey *Actor*
8827 Beverly Blvd, Los Angeles, CA 90048 USA

Byron, Jeffrey *Actor*
Shapiro-Lichtman, 8827 Beverly Blvd, Los Angeles, CA 90048 USA

Byrorn, Don *Musician*
Hans Wendl Productions, 2220 California St, Berkeley, CA 94703 USA

Byrorn, Monty *Musician, Songwriter*
Gurley Co, 1204B Cedar Lane, Nashville, TN 37212 USA

Byrum, John W *Director*
7435 Woodrow Wilson Dr, Los Angeles, CA 90046 USA

Bywater, William H *Misc*
International Electronic Workers, 1126 16th St NW, Washington, DC 20036 USA

Bzdelik, Jeff *Coach*
Denver Nuggets, Pepsi Center, 1000 Chopper Circle, Denver, CO 80204 USA

C

Caan, James *Actor*
PO Box 6646, Denver, CO 80206 USA

Caan, Scott *Actor*
United Talent Agency, 6560 Wilshire Blvd #500, Beverly Hills, CA 90212 USA

Caballe, Monserrat
Avenida Madronos 27, Madrid, SPAIN, 28043

Caballe, Montserrat *Opera Singer*
Opera Carlos Caballe, Via Augusta 59, Barcelona, 08006, SPAIN

Cabana, Robert D *Astronaut*
18315 Cape Bahamas Lane, Houston, TX 77058 USA

Cabas *Musician*
Creative Artists Agency LCC (CAA-LA), 9830 Wilshire Blvd, Beverly Hills, CA 90212 USA

Cabell, Enos M *Baseball Player*
4103 Frost Court, Missouri City, TX 77549 USA

Cabibbo, Nicola *Physicist*
ENEA, Viale Regina Margherita 125, Rome, 00198, ITALY

Cable Guy, The, Larry *Comedian*
Parallel Entertainment, 8380 Melrose Ave #310, Los Angeles, CA 90069 USA

Cabot, Louis W *Business Person*
Brookings Institution, 1775 Massachusetts Ave NW, Washington, DC 20036 USA

Cabral, Sam A *Misc*
Police Associations International Union, 1421 Prince St, Alexandria, VA 22314 USA

Cabranes, Jose A *Judge*
US District Court, 141 Church St, New Haven, CT 06510 USA

Cabrera, Jolbert *Baseball Player*
Los Angeles Dodgers (LA Dodgers), 1000 Elysian Park Avenue, Los Angeles, CA 90012 USA

Caccialanza, Lorenzo *Actor*
Ambrosio/Mortimer, P O Box 16758, Beverly Hills, CA 90209 USA

Cacciavillan, Agnostino Cardinal *Religious Leader*
Patrimony of Holy See, Palazzo Apostolico, Vatican City, 00120, VATICAN CITY

Caceres, Kurt *Actor*
Pakula/King & Associates, 9229 Sunset Blvd #315, Los Angeles, CA 90069 USA

Cackowski, Liz *Actor, Comedian*
Creative Artists Agency LCC (CAA-LA), 9830 Wilshire Blvd, Beverly Hills, CA 90212 USA

Cacoyannis, Michael *Director*
15 Mouson St, Athens, 117-41, GREECE

Cadall, Ava
8484 Wilshire Blvd. #745, Beverly Hills, CA 90211

Cadbury, Adrian *Business Person*
Bank of England, Threadneedle St, London, EC2R 8AH, UNITED KINGDOM (UK)

Caddell, Patrick H *Mathematician, Misc*
Cambridge Research Inc, 1625 I St NW, Washington, DC 10006 USA

Cade, J Robert *Inventor, Misc*
University of Florida, Medical School Physiology Dept, Gainesville, FL 32610 USA

Cade, Mossy *Football Player*
6112 N 67th Ave, #127, Glendale, AZ 85301 USA

Cadell, Ava *Actor, Model*
Levin, 8484 Wilshire Blvd #745, Beverly Hills, CA 90211 USA

Cadillacs, The
PO Box 8406, Santa Cruz, CA 95061

Cadogan, William J *Business Person*
ADC Communications, PO Box 1101, Minneapolis, MN 55440 USA

Cadorette, Mary *Actor*
8831 Sunset Blvd, #304, Los Angeles, CA 90069 USA

Cady, Sherry *Scientist*
Portland State University, Geology Dept, Portland, OR 97207 USA

Caesar, Shirley *Music Group*
Shirley Caesar Outreach Ministries, 3310 Croasdaile Dr #902, Durham, NC 27705 USA

Caesar, Sid *Actor, Comedian*
1910 Loma Vista Dr, Beverly Hills, CA 90210 USA

Cafego, George
10121 El Pinar, Knoxville, TN 37922

Cafferata, Hector A Jr *War Hero*
1807 Plum Lane, Venice, FL 34293 USA

Caffery, Stephen
8271 Melrose Ave. #208, Los Angeles, CA 90046

Caffey, Charlotte *Music Group, Musician*
4800 Bryn Mawr Rd, Los Angeles, CA 90027 USA

Caffey, Jason *Basketball Player*
6701 Cedarwood Court, Mobile, AL 36695 USA

Caffrey, Stephen *Actor*
Peter Strain, 5724 W 3rd St, #302, Los Angeles, CA 90036 USA

Cafu *Soccer Player*
AS Roma, Via di Trigoria Km 3.600, Rome, 00128, ITALY

Cagatay, Mustafa *Prime Minister*
60 Cumhuriyet Caddesi, Kyrenia, Cyprus

Cage, Michael *Basketball Player*
New Jersey Nets, 390 Murray Hills Parkway, East Rutherford, NJ 07073 USA

Cage, Nicolas *Actor*
Creative Artists Agency, 9830 Wilshire Blvd, Beverly Hills, CA 90212 USA

Cagle, Chris *Musician*
Mark Hybner Entertainment, 50 Music Square W, #503, Nashville, TN 37203 USA

Cagle, J Douglas *Business Person*
Cagle's Inc, 2000 Hills Ave NW, Atlanta, GA 30318 USA

Cagle, Jim *Football Player*
745 Sharpshooters Ridge NW, Marietta, GA 30064 USA

Cagle, Yvonne D *Astronaut*
10190 N Foothill Blvd #F15, Cupertino, CA 65014 USA

Caglini, Umperto
via Don Crocetti #3, Fabriano (Ancona), ITALY, 60044

Cahill, James *Actor*
31 Chambers St #311, New York, NY 10007 USA

Cahill, John C *Business Person*
Trans World Airlines, City Center 515 N 6th St, Saint Louis, MO 63101 USA

Cahill, Laura *Writer*
Broder Webb Chervin Silbermann Agency, The (BWCS), 9242 Beverly Blvd #200, Beverly Hills, CA 90210 USA

Cahill, Teresa M *Opera Singer*
65 Leyland Road, London, SE12 8DW, UNITED KINGDOM (UK)

Cahill, Thomas *Writer*
Doubleday Press, 1540 Broadway, New York, NY 10036 USA

Cahn, John W *Misc*
6610 Pyle Road, Bathesda, MD 20817 USA

Cahouet, Frank V *Financier*
Mellon Bank Corp, 1 Mellon Bank Center 500 Grant St, Pittsburgh, PA 15219 USA

Caifanes *Music Group*
BMG, 1540 Broadway, New York, NY 10036 USA

Cain, Carl *Basketball Player*
3045 Sun Valley Dr, Pickerington, OH 43147 USA

Cain, Dean *Actor*
Paradigm (LA), 10100 Santa Monica Blvd, Fl 25, Los Angeles, CA 90067 USA

Cain, John Paul *Golfer*
8002 Woodway Dr, Houston, TX 77063 USA

Cain, Jonathan *Musician*
Hemming Morse, 160 Spear St, #1900, San Francisco, CA 94105 USA

Cain, Mick
7800 Beverly Blvd. #3371, Los Angeles, CA 90036

Caine, Michael *Actor*
International Creative Management, 76 Oxford St, London, W1N 0AX, UNITED KINGDOM (UK)

Caio, Francesco *Business Person*
Ing C Olivetti Co, Via G Jervos 77, Ivrea/Truin, 10015 USA

Cairns, Hugh J F *Biologist*
Holly Grove House, Wilcote, Shipping Norton, Oxon, OX7 3EA, UNITED KINGDOM (UK)

Calabresi, Guido *Judge*
US Appeals Court, 157 Church St, New Haven, CT 06510 USA

Calabro, Thomas *Actor*
12400 Ventura Blvd #369, Studio City, CA 91604 USA

Calatrava, Santiago *Architect, Engineer*
Santiago Calatrava SA, Hoschgasse 5, Zurich, 8008, SWITZERLAND

Calcevecchi, Mark *Golfer*
2785 Hawthome Lane, West Palm Beach, FL 33409 USA

Caldeiro, Fernando (Frank) *Astronaut*
2211 Summer Reef Dr, League City, TX 77573 USA

Calder, David
1 Winterwell Rd., London, ENGLAND, SW2 5TB

Calder, Nigel
8 The Chase Furnace Green, Crawley W. Sussex, ENGLAND, RH10 6HW

Caldera, Rodriguez Rafael *President*
Ave Urdaneta 33-2 Apdo 2060, Caracas, 1010, VENEZUELA

Calderon, Leticia *Actor*
Televisa, Blvd Adolfo Lopez Mateos 232, Colonia San Angel INN, DF, CP 01060, MEXICO

Calderon, Sila Maria *Governor*
Governer's Office, La Fortaleza P O Box 9020082, San Juan, PR 00902 USA

Calderon Fournier, Rafael A *President*
Partido Unidad Social Cristiana, San Jose, COSTA RICA

Caldicott, Helen *Social Activist, Doctor, Misc*
Physicians for Responsibility, 639 Massachusetts Ave, Cambridge, MA 02139 USA

Caldwell, Bobby *Musician, Songwriter*
Public Relations Partners, 12702 Landale St, Studio City, CA 91604 USA

Caldwell, Gail *Journalist*
Boston Globe, Editorial Dept 135 W T Morrissey Blvd, Dorchester, MA 02139 USA

Caldwell, John *Cartoonist*
King Features Syndicate, 888 7th Ave, New York, NY 10106 USA

Caldwell, Joseph (Joe) *Basketball Player*
1750 Boulder St, Colorado Springs, CO 80890 USA

Caldwell, Kimberly *Musician, Reality TV Star*
FremantleMedia North America (LA), 2700 Colorado Ave #450, Santa Monica, CA 90404 USA

Caldwell, Philip *Business Person*
Smith Barney Shearson, 200 Vesey St, New York, NY 10285 USA

Caldwell, Sarah *Producer*
Boston Opera Co, P O Box 50, Newton, MA 02456 USA

Caldwell, William A *Editor*
Vineyard Gazette, Editorial Dept S Summer St, Edgartown, MA 02539 USA

Caldwell, Zoe *Actor*
Whitehead-Stevens, 1501 Broadway, New York, NY 10036 USA

Cale, J J *Music Group, Musician*
Rosebud Agency, P O Box 170429, San Fransisco, CA 94117 USA

Cale, John *Music Group, Musician*
Firebrand Mgmt, 12 Rickett St, West Brompton, London, SW6 1RU, UNITED KINGDOM (UK)

Cale, Paula
345 N. Maple Dr. #200, Beverly Hills, CA 90210

Cale, Puala *Actor*
Gersh Agency, 232 N Canon Dr, Beverly Hills, CA 90210 USA

Calegari, Maria *Ballerina*
New York City Ballet, Lincoln Center Plaza, New York, NY 10023 USA

Calfa, Don *Actor*
Richard Sundel, 1910 Holmby Ave, #1, Los Angeles, CA 90025 USA

Calfa, Marian *Prime Minister*
Calfa Pravni Kancelar Premyslovska 28, Prague 3, 130 00 USA

Calhoon, Jesse M *Misc*
Marine Engineers Union, 17 Battery Place, New York, NY 10004 USA

Calhoun, Corky *Yachtsman, Misc*
Surfer Magazine, P O Box 1028, Dana Point, CA 92629 USA

Calhoun, Donald C (Don) *Football Player*
1308 N Crestway St, Wichita, KS 67208 USA

Calhoun, Jim *Basketball Player, Coach*
Connecticut University, 2111 Hillside Road, Storrs Mansfield, CT 06269 USA

Calhoun, Monica *Actor*
Innovative Artists, 1505 10th St, Santa Monica, CA 90401 USA

Cali, Joseph *Actor*
25630 Edenwild Road, Monte Nido, CA 91302 USA

Caliendo, Frank *Actor*
Creative Artists Agency LCC (CAA-LA), 9830 Wilshire Blvd, Beverly Hills, CA 90212 USA

Califano, Joseph
3551 Springfield Lane, Washington, DC 20008

Califano, Joseph A Jr *Secretary*
Casa at Columbia, 633 3rd Ave #1900, New York, NY 10017 USA

Caligiuri, Paul *Soccer Player*
P O Box 4444, Blue Jay, CA 92317 USA

Calipari, John *Basketball Player, Coach*
University of Memphis, Athletic Dept, Memphis, TN 38152 USA

Calisher, Hortense *Writer*
Marion Boyars, 365 5th Ave #5406, New York, NY 10016 USA

Calkins, Buzz *Race Car Driver*
2261 Blake St #6A, Denver, CO 80205 USA

Call, Anthony *Actor*
Michael Thomas Agency, 134 E 10th St, New York, NY 10021 USA

Call, Brandon *Actor*
5918 Van Nuys Blvd, Van Nuys, CA 91401 USA

Callaghan of Cardiff, L James *Prime Minister*
House of Lords, Vestminster, London, SW1A 0PW, UNITED KINGDOM (UK)

Callahan, Bill *Football Coach*
University of Nebraska, Athletic Dept, Lincoln, NE 68588 USA

Callahan, James *Actor*
1159 Via Estrellada, Fallbrook, CA 92028 USA

Callahan, John *Actor*
Levin Representatives, 2402 4th St #6, Santa Monica, CA 90405 USA

Callahan, John *Cartoonist*
Viking Press, 375 Hudson St, New York, NY 10014 USA

Callan, Cecile *Actor*
SMZ, 8730 Sunset Blvd #480, Los Angeles, CA 90069 USA

Callan, K *Actor*
4957 Matilija Ave, Sherman Oaks, CA 91423 USA

Callan, Michael *Actor*
1651 Camden Ave #3, Los Angeles, CA 90025 USA

Callas, Charlie *Actor, Comedian*
2180 Center Ave, Fort Lee, NJ 07024 USA

Callaway, Howard H (Bo) *Government Official*
Callaway Gardens, Pine Mountain, GA 31822 USA

Callaway, Mark (The Undertaker) *Wrestler*
World Wrestling Entertainment (WWE), 1241 E Main St, Stamford, CT 06905 USA

Callaway, Paul Smith *Music Group, Musician*
Washington Cathedral, Mount Saint Alban, Washington, DC 20016 USA

Callaway, Thomas *Actor*
House of Representatives, 400 S Beverly Dr #101, Beverly Hills, CA 90212 USA

Callen, Bryan *Actor*

Callen, Bryan *Actor*
Innovative Artists (LA), 1505 Tenth St, Santa Monica, CA 90401 USA

Callen, Jones Gloria *Swimmer*
1508 Chafton Road, Charleston, WV 25314 USA

Callery, Sean *Composer*
Gorfaine/Schwartz, 13245 Riverside Dr #450, Sherman Oaks, CA 91423 USA

Callies, Sarah Wayne *Actor*
William Morris Agency (WMA-LA), 1 William Morris Pl, Beverly Hills, CA 90212 USA

Calling, The *Music Group*
William Morris Agency (WMA-LA), 1 William Morris Pl, Beverly Hills, CA 90212 USA

Callis, James *Actor, Director*
Alan Siegel Entertainment, 345 N Maple Dr #375, Beverly Hills, CA 90210 USA

Callow, Simon *Actor*
Marina Martin, 12/13 Poland St, London, WlV 3DE, UNITED KINGDOM (UK)

Callum, Keith Rene
525 Seymour St. #500, Vancouver, CANADA, BC V6B 3H7

Calne, Roy Y *Doctor*
Addenbrooke's Hospital, Hills Road, Cambridge, CB2 2QQ, UNITED KINGDOM (UK)

Caltabiano, Tom *Comedian*
United Talent Agency (UTA), 9560 Wilshire Blvd, Beverly Hills, CA 90212 USA

Calvaer, Andre J *Engineer*
Blvd Louis Mettewie 270, Molenbeek-Saint-Jean, 1080, BELGIUM

Calvert, James F *Admiral, Writer*
P O Box 479, Saint Michaels, MD 21663 USA

Calvet, Jacques *Financier*
31 Ave Victor Hugo, Paris, 75116, FRANCE

Calvin, John *Actor*
2503 Ware Road, Austin, TX 78741 USA

Calvin, William H *Biologist*
University of Washington, Neurobiology Dept, Seattle, WA 98195 USA

Calvo, Paul M *Governor*
Governor's Office, Capitol Building, Agana, GU, 96910 USA

Calvo-Sotelo, Bustelo Leopoldo *Prime Minister*
Buho 1 Somosaguas, Madrid, SPAIN

Cam'ron *Musician*
Famous Artists Agency, 250 W 57th St, New York, NY 10107 USA

Camacho, Andy
4545 Encino Ave., Encino, CA 91316

Camacho, Hector (Macho) *Boxer*
8034 Solitaire Court, Orlando, FL 32836
USA

Camacho, Hector Macho
4751 Yardarm Lane, Boynton Beach, FL
33436-1983

Camarata, Toodie *Musician, Conductor*
12141 Iradell St, Studio City, CA 91604
USA

Camarda, Charles J *Astronaut*
2386 Sabal Park Lane, League City, TX
77573 USA

Camastra, Danielle *Actor*
David Shapira & Associates, 15821
Ventura Blvd #235, Encino, CA 91436
USA

Cambor, Kathleen *Writer*
Farrar Straus Giroux, 19 Union Square W,
New York, NY 10003 USA

Cambre, Ronald C *Business Person*
Newmont Mining, 9903 W Laurel Place,
Littleton, CO 80127 USA

Cambria, John *Cinematographer*
6910 Mayall St, North Hills, CA 91343
USA

Camby, Marcus *Basketball Player*
5 Woods End, Rye, NY 10580 USA

Camden, John *Business Person*
RMC Group, Coldgarbour Lane, Thorpe,
Egham, Surrey, TW20 8TD, UNITED
KINGDOM (UK)

Camdessus, Michel J *Financier*
International Monetary Fund, 700 19th St
NW, Washington, DC 20431 USA

Cameletti, Rob
643 N. La Cienega Blvd., Los Angeles, CA
90048

Camelia-Romer, Susanne *Prime Minister,
Misc*
Primier's Office, Fort Amsterdam 17,
Willemstad, NETHERLANDS ANTILLES

Cameron, Ann *Writer*
Foster Books/Farrar Straus Giroux, 19
Union Square W, New York, NY 10003
USA

Cameron, Candance *Actor*
Barbara Camaron Assoc, 8369 Sausalito
Ave #A, Canoga Park, CA 91304 USA

Cameron, David *Fashion Designer*
Schauspielschule Krauss, Weihburggasse
19, Vienna, 1010, AUSTRIA

Cameron, Dean *Actor*
Landmark Artists Mgmt, 4116 W Magnolia
Ave, Burbank, CA 91505 USA

Cameron, Don R *Educator, Misc*
National Education Association, 1201
16th St NW, Washington, DC 20036 USA

Cameron, Duncan *Music Group,
Musician*
Sawyer Brown Inc, 5200 Old Harding
Road, Franklin, TN 37064 USA

Cameron, Glenn S *Football Player*
250 S Australian Ave, West Palm Beach,
FL 33401 USA

Cameron, James *Producer, Director*
LightStorm Entertainment, 919 Santa
Monica Blvd, Santa Monica, CA 90401
USA

Cameron, Joanna *Actor*
Cameron Productions, PO Box 1011,
Pebble Beach, CA 93953 USA

Cameron, John
. 35 Ragged Hall Lane, St. Albans Herts,
ENGLAND, AL2 3LB

Cameron, Kenneth D *Astronaut*
Austvagen 13, Vastra Frotunda, 42676,
SWEDEN

Cameron, Kirk *Actor*
William Morris Agency (WMA-LA), 1
William Morris Pl, Beverly Hills, CA
90212 USA

Cameron, Laura *Actor*
8383 Wilshire Blvd, #954, Beverly Hills,
CA 90211 USA

Cameron, Mat *Music Group, Musician*
Susan Silver Mgmt, 6523 California Ave
SW #348, Seattle, WA 98136 USA

Cameron, Mechelle *Swimmer*
Box 2 Site 1SS3, Calgary, AL T3C 3N9,
CANADA

Cameron, Paul *Football Player*
3503 Terra Linda Lane, Fallbrook, CA
92028 USA

Cameron, Rhona *Actor*
Jeremy Hicks Associates, 11-12 Tottenham
News, London, W1T 4AG, UNITED
KINGDOM (UK)

Cameron-Bure, Candace *Actor*
Osbrink Talent Agency, 4343 Lankershim
Blvd #100, Universal City, CA 91602 USA

Camilleri, Andrea *Writer*
Viking Press, 375 Hudson St, New York,
NY 10014 USA

Camilleri, Louis C *Business Person*
Altria Group, 120 Park Ave, New York,
NY 10017 USA

Camilo, Michael *Musician*
Joel Chriss, 300 Mercer St, #3J, New York,
NY 10003 USA

Camilo, Michel *Music Group, Musician*
Redondo Music, 590 W End Ave #6, New
York, NY 10024 USA

Caminiti, Kenneth G (Ken) *Baseball
Player*
2210 Quarter Path, Richmond, TX 77469
USA

Caminito, Jerry *Race Car Driver*
Blue Thunder Racing, P O Box 1486,
Jackson, NJ 08527 USA

Cammermeyer, Margarethe
4632 S. Tompkins Rd., Langley, WA
98260-9695

Cammuso, Frank *Cartoonist*
1725 James St, #1, Syracuse, NY 13206
USA

Camoy, Martin *Economist*
Stanford University, Economic Studies
Center, Stanford, CA 94305 USA

Camp, Colleen *Actor*
473 N Tigertail Rd, Los Angeles, CA
90049 USA

Camp, Greg *Musician*
Creative Artists Agency, 9830 Wilshire
Blvd, Beverly Hills, CA 90212 USA

Camp, John *Journalist*
Saint Paul Pioneer Press, Editorial Dept
345 Cedar St, Saint Paul, MN 55101 USA

Camp, Shawn
PO Box 121972, Nashville, TN 37212

Camp, Steve *Music Group*
Third Coast Artists, 2021 21st Ave S #220,
Nashville, TN 37212 USA

Campanella, Joseph *Actor*
4647 Arcola Ave, Toluca Lake, CA 91602
USA

Campaneris, B Dagoberto (Bert) *Baseball
Player*
9797 N 105th Place, Scottsdale, AZ
85258 USA

Campaneris, Bert
PO Box 5096, Scottsdale, AZ 85261

Campau, Thomas E *Cinematographer*
2000 S Hammond Lake Dr, West
Bloomfield, MI 90212 USA

Campbell, A Kim *Prime Minister*
Harvard University, Kennedy School of
Government, Cambridge, MA 02138 USA

Campbell, Alan *Actor*
Gersh Agency, 41 Madison Ave #3300,
New York, NY 10010 USA

Campbell, Allan McCulloch *Biologist*
947 Mears Court, Stanford, CA 94305
USA

Campbell, Bebe Moore *Writer*
Creative Artists Agency LCC (CAA-LA),
9830 Wilshire Blvd, Beverly Hills, CA
90212 USA

Campbell, Ben Nighthorse
456 New Jersey Ave SE, Washington, DC
20003 USA

Campbell, Billy *Actor*
International Creative Mgmt, 8942
Wilshire Blvd #219, Beverly Hills, CA
90211 USA

Campbell, Bruce *Actor*
Agency for the Performing Arts (APA-LA),
9200 Sunset Blvd #900, Los Angeles, CA
90069 USA

Campbell, Carol
Agt. Uschi Drews Droysenstr. 2, Berlin,
GERMANY, D-10629

Campbell, Carroll A Jr *Governor*
101 Constitution Ave #708, Washington,
DC 20001 USA

Campbell, Cheryl *Actor*
Michael Whitehall, 125 Gloucester Road,
London, SW7 4TE, UNITED KINGDOM
(UK)

Campbell, Christian *Actor*
12533 Woodgreen, Los Angeles, CA
90066 USA

Campbell, Colin (Soupy) *Hockey Player,
Coach*
New York Rangers, Madison Square
Garden, 2 Penn Plaza, New York, NY
10121 USA

Campbell, Darian
1 Wandsworth Plain, London, ENGLAND,
SW17 1EH

Campbell, Earl C *Football Player*
2937 Thousand Oaks Dr, Austin, TX
78746 USA

Campbell, Elden *Basketball Player*
17252 Hawthome Blvd #493, Torrance,
CA 90504 USA

Campbell, Garry *Writer, Producer*
Creative Artists Agency LCC (CAA-LA),
9830 Wilshire Blvd, Beverly Hills, CA
90212 USA

Campbell, Gene *Hockey Player*
1554 Wilshire Dr NE, Rochester, MN
55906 USA

Campbell, Glen *Music Group*
28 Biltmore Est, Phoenix, AZ 85016 USA

Campbell, Isobel *Music Group, Musician*
Legends of 21st Century, 7 Trinity Row,
Florence, MA 01062 USA

Campbell, Jennifer
9200 Sunset Blvd. #1130, Los Angeles,
CA 90069

Campbell, Jessica *Actor*
Somers Teitelbaum David, 8840 Wilshire
Blvd, #200, Beverly Hills, CA 90211 USA

Campbell, John *Race Car Driver*
John D Campbell Stable, 823 Allison Dr,
River Vale, NJ 07675 USA

Campbell, Joshua *Actor*
Select Artists Ltd (CA-Westside Office),
1138 12th Street, Suite 1, Santa Monica,
CA 90403 USA

Campbell, Julia *Actor*
Innovative Artists, 1505 10th St, Santa
Monica, CA 90401 USA

Campbell, Keith H S *Biologist, Misc*
Roslin Institute, Roslin Bio Centre,
Midlothlan, EH25 9PS, SCOTLAND

Campbell, Ken *Actor*
Marathon Entertainment, 8060 Melrose
#400, Los Angeles, CA 90046

Campbell, Kim *Prime Minister*
Canadian Consulate, 550 S Hope St, Los
Angeles, CA 90071

Campbell, L Arthur *Misc, Scientist*
Rockefeller University, Medical center,
1230 York Ave, New York, NY 10021
USA

Campbell, Larry Joe *Actor*
Brillstein-Grey Entertainment, 9150
Wilshire Blvd #350, Beverly Hills, CA
90212 USA

Campbell, Lewis B *Business Person*
Textron Inc, 40 Westminster St,
Providence, RI 02903 USA

Campbell, Luther
8400 NE 2nd Ave., Miami, FL 33138

Campbell, Luther (Skywalker) *Music
Group*
Famous Artists Agency, 250 W 57th St,
New York, NY 10107 USA

Campbell, Martin *Director*
International Creative Mgmt, 8942
Wilshire Blvd #219, Beverly Hills, CA
90211 USA

Campbell, Milton (Milt) *Track Athlete,
Football Player*
1132 Saint Marks Place, Planifield, NJ
07062 USA

Campbell, Naomi *Actor, Model, Music
Group*
Men/Women Model Inc, 199 Lafayette St
#700, New York, NY 10012 USA

Campbell, Nell *Actor*
246 W 14th St, New York, NY 10011
USA

Campbell, Neve *Actor*
12533 Woodgreen St, Los Angeles, CA
90066 USA

Campbell, Nicholas *Actor*
1206 N Orange Grove, West Hollywood,
CA 90046 USA

Campbell, Patrick J *Misc*
Carpenter & Joiners Union, 101
Constitution Ave NW, Washington, DC
20001 USA

Campbell, Robert *Architect, Critic, Misc*
54 Antrim St, Cambridge, MA 02139 USA

Campbell, Robert H *Business Person*
Sunoco Inc, 10 Penn Center 1801 Market
St, Philadelphia, PA 19103 USA

Campbell, Scott Michael *Actor*
Allman/Rea Management, 141 Barrington
#E, Los Angeles, CA 90049 USA

Campbell, Stacy Dean
1105-C 16th Ave. So, Nashville, TN
37212

Campbell, Tevin *Music Group*
Pyramind Entertainment, 89 5th Ave
#700, New York, NY 10003 USA

Campbell, Tisha *Actor*
Management 360, 9111 Wilshire Blvd,
Beverly Hills, CA 90210 USA

Campbell, Vivian *Music Group, Musician*
Int'l Talent Booking, 27A Floral St #300,
London, WC2E 9DQ, UNITED
KINGDOM (UK)

Campbell, William *Actor*
21502 Velicata St, Woodland Hills, CA
91364 USA

Campbell, William J *General*
3267 Alex Findlay Place, Sarasota, FL
34240 USA

Campbell-Martin, Tisha *Actor*
Writers & Artists, 8383 Wilshire Blvd
#550, Beverly Hills, CA 90211 USA

Campese, David I *Athlete, Misc*
D C Management Group, 870 Pacific
Highway #4, Gordon, NSW, 2072,
AUSTRALIA

Campion, Jane *Director*
Hilary Linstead, 500 Oxford St, Bondi
Junction, NSW, 2022, AUSTRALIA

Campo, Dave *Football Coach*
Celveland Browns, 76 Lou Groza Blvd,
Berea, OH 44017 USA

Campos, Arsenio *Actor*
Televisa, Blvd Adolfo Lopez Mateos 232,
Colonia San Angel INN, DF, CP 01060,
MEXICO

Campos, Bruno *Actor*
SDB Partners, 1801 Ave of Stars, #902,
Los Angeles, CA 90067 USA

Campos, Francisco *Baseball Player,
Athlete*
Milwaukee Brewers, County Stadium, PO
Box 3099, Milwaukee, WI 53201 USA

Campos, Jorge *Soccer Player*
Federacion de Futbol Assn, Col Juarez,
Mexico City 6, DF, CP 06600, MEXICO

Canada, Ron *Actor*
Christopher Wright Management, 3340
Barham Blvd, Los Angeles, CA 90068

Canadas, Esther *Model, Actor*
Wilhelmina Models, 300 Park Ave S
#200, New York, NY 10010 USA

Canadec, Tony
1746 Carriage Ct., Green Bay, WI 54304-
2812

Canadian Brass
450 7th Ave. #603, New York, NY 10123-
0101

Canady, James (Jim) *Football Player*
303 Sunset Dr, Burnet, TX 78611 USA

Canale, Gianna Maria
8 via A. Richelmy, Rome, ITALY, I-00165

Canals, Maria *Actor*
Agency for the Performing Arts (APA-LA),
9200 Sunset Blvd #900, Los Angeles, CA
90069 USA

Canary, David *Actor*
900 S Mansfield Ave, Los Angeles, CA
90036 USA

Candelaria, John R *Baseball Player*
606 Wingspread, Peachtree City, GA
30269 USA

Candeloro, Philippe *Figure Skater*
Federation des Sports de Glace, 35 Rue
Felicien David, Paris, 75016, FRANCE

Candills, Georges *Architect*
17 Rue Campagne-Premiere, Paris, 75014,
FRANCE

Candiotti, Thomas C (Tom) *Baseball
Player*
1775 Sharon Dr, Concord, CA 94519 USA

Candlebox *Music Group*
Maverick Recording Co (LA), 9348 Civic
Center Dr, Beverly Hills, CA 90210

Cane, Mark A *Oceanographer, Misc*
Lamont Doherty Earth Observatory, Route
9W, Palisades, NY 10964 USA

Canella, Guldo *Architect*
Via Revere 7, Milan, 20123, ITALY

Canerday, Natalie *Actor*
Bauman Redanty & Shaul Agency, 5757
Wilshire Blvd #473, Los Angeles, CA
90036 USA

Canfield, Jack *Writer*
PO Box 30880, Santa Barbara, CA 93130
USA

Canfield, Mary Grace *Actor*
Shelly & Pierce, 13775A Mono Way,
#220, Sonora, CA 95370 USA

Canfield, Paul *Physicist*
Iowa State University, Physics Dept,
Arnes, IA 50011 USA

Canfield, William L (Bill) *Editor,
Cartoonist*
Star Ledger, Editorial Dept ! Star Ledger
Plaza, Newark, NJ 07102 USA

Cangemi, Joseph P *Misc*
1409 Mount Ayr Circle, Bowling Green,
KY 42103 USA

Canibus *Musician*
Famous Artists Agency, 555 Eighth Ave #1803, New York, NY 10018 USA

Canizales, Gaby *Boxer*
2205 Saint Maria Ave, Laredo, TX 78040 USA

Cannatella, Trishelle *Reality TV Star*
Bunim/Murray Productions Inc, 6007 Sepulveda Blvd, Van Nuys, CA 91411 USA

Cannavale, Bobby *Actor*
251 W 95th St #65, New York, NY 10025 USA

Canned Heat
PO Box 3773, San Rafael, CA 94912

Cannell, Stephen J *Writer, Producer*
1220 Hillcrest, Pasadena, CA 91106 USA

Cannon, Ace *Musician*
American Mgmt, 19948 Mayall St, Chatsworth, CA 91311 USA

Cannon, Billy *Athlete*
1640 Sherwood Forest Blvd, Baton Rouge, LA 70815

Cannon, Danny *Producer*
International Creative Management (ICM-LA), 8942 Wilshire Blvd, Beverly Hills, CA 90211 USA

Cannon, Dyan *Actor*
1100 Alta Loma Rd #808, West Hollywood, CA 90069 USA

Cannon, Freddy
18641 Cassandra St., Tarzana, CA 91356

Cannon, Freddy (Boom Boom)
Songwriter, Music Group
Rick Levy Mgmt, 4250 A1A S #D11, Saint Augustine, FL 32080 USA

Cannon, Glenn
1717 Mott Smith Dr., Honolulu, HI 96822

Cannon, Harold *Actor*
Select Artists Ltd (CA-Valley Office), PO Box 4359, Burbank, CA 91503 USA

Cannon, J D *Actor*
RR 2, Hudson, NY 12534 USA

Cannon, Joe *Soccer Player*
Colorado Rapids, 555 17th St #3350, Denver, CO 80202 USA

Cannon, Katherine *Actor*
1310 Westholme Ave, Los Angeles, CA 90024 USA

Cannon, Nick *Actor, Producer*
Tollin/Robbins Management, 10960 Ventura Blvd Fl 2, Studio City, CA 91604 USA

Cannon, William A (Billy) *Football Player*
176 Shirley Circle, Monterey, LA 71354 USA

Cano, Roberto *Actor*
TV Caracol, Calle 76 #11 - 35, Piso 10AA, Bogota DC, 26484, COLOMBIA

Canova, Diana *Actor*
Agency for Performing Arts, 9200 Sunset Blvd #900, Los Angeles, CA 90069 USA

Canseco, Jose *Baseball Player, Athlete*
5601 Collins Avenue, #CU-1, Miami Beach, FL 33140 USA

Canseco, Jose Jr *Baseball Player*
5601 Collins Ave #CU1, Miami Beach, FL 33140 USA

Cantaline, Anita *Bowler*
31455 Pinto Dr, Warren, MI 48093 USA

Cantey, Charisie *Sportscaster*
ABC-TV, Sports Dept 77 W 66th St, New York, NY 10023 USA

Canton, Alan *Writer*

Canton, Joanna *Actor*
Liberman/Zerman Management, 252 N Larchmont Blvd #200, Los Angeles, CA 90004 USA

Cantona, Eric *Soccer Player*
French Federation de Football, 60 Bis Ave D'Ilena, Paris, 75783, France

Cantone, Vic *Editor, Cartoonist*
238 Blackpool Court, Ridge, NY 11961 USA

Cantoni, Giulio L *Biologist, Misc*
6938 Blaisdell Road, Bathesda, MD 20817 USA

Cantor, Charles R *Biologist*
11 Bay Street Road, Boston, MA 02116 USA

Cantoral, Itati *Actor*
Gabriel Blanco Iglesias (Mexico), Rio Balsas 35-32, Colonia Cuauhtemoc, DF, 06500, Mexico

Cantrell, Blu *Music Group*
Arista Records, 8750 Wilshire Blvd, #300, Beverly Hills, CA 90211 USA

Cantrell, Jerry *Actor*
William Morris Agency (WMA-LA), 1 William Morris Pl, Beverly Hills, CA 90212 USA

Cantrell, Lana *Music Group*
300 E 71st St, New York, NY 10021 USA

Cantrell, Wayne
18265 Wakecrest, Malibu, CA 90265

Canup, Robin *Astronomer*

Canup, Robin *Astronomer*
Southwest Reasearch Institute, 1050 Walnut St #400, Boulder, CO 80302 USA

Canyon, Christy
13601 Ventura Blvd. #218, Sherman Oaks, CA 91423

Capa, Cornell *Photographer*
275 5th Ave, New York, NY 10016 USA

Capalbo, Carmen C *Producer, Director*
500 2nd Ave, New York, NY 10016 USA

Caparulo, John *Comedian*
Brillstein-Grey Entertainment, 9150 Wilshire Blvd #350, Beverly Hills, CA 90212 USA

Capasso, Federico *Physicist*
Lucent Technologies, Bell Labs 600 Mountain Ave, New Providence, NJ 07974 USA

Capecchi, Mario R *Biologist*
2529 E 1300 S, Salt Lake City, UT 84108 USA

Capek, Frantisek *Athlete*
Michelangelova 4, Prague 10, 100 00 USA

Capel, Jon
PO Box 120, Indianapolis, IN 46206-0120

Capellas, Michael *Business Person*
MCI, 500 Clinton Center Dr, Clinton, MS 39056 USA

Capellino, Ally *Fashion Designer*
N1R Metropolitan Wharf, Wapping Wall, London, E1 9SS, UNITED KINGDOM (UK)

Capers, Dom *Football Coach*
Houston Texans, 4400 Post Oak Parkway #1400, Houston, TX 77027 USA

Caperton, W Gaston III *Governor, Misc*
College Board, Presiden's Office 45 Columbus Ave, New York, NY 10023 USA

Capilla, Perez Joaquin *Misc*
Torres de Mixcoac, Lomas de Platerce, Mexico City 19, DF, MEXICO

Caplan, Arthur L *Biologist, Misc*
University of Pennsylvania, Biomedical Ethics Center, Philadelphia, PA 19104 USA

Caplan, Lizzy *Actor*
Imparato Fay Management, 1122 S Roxbury Dr, Los Angeles, CA 90035 USA

Capleton *Musician*
Agency Group Ltd, 1775 Broadway, #430, New York, NY 10019 USA

Caplin, Mortimer M *Government Official*
5610 Wisconsin Ave NW, #18E, Bethesda, MD 20815 USA

Capoblanco, Tito *Opera Singer, Director*
Pittsburgh Opera Co, 711 Penn Ave #800, Pittsburgh, PA 15222 USA

Capodice, John *Actor*
Sharp/Karrys, 117 N Orlando Ave, Los Angeles, CA 90048 USA

Capon, Edwin G *Religious Leader*
Swedenborgian Church, 11 Highland Ave, Newtonville, MA 02460 USA

Caponera, John *Actor, Comedian*
Messina Baker Entertainment, 955 Carillo Dr, #100, Los Angeles, CA 90048 USA

Caponi, Donna *Golfer*
Ladies Pro Golf Association (LPGA), 100 International Golf Drive, Daytona Beach, FL 32124 USA

Caponi, Donna M *Golfer*
11 Bedfort St, Burlington, MA 01803 USA

Cappelletti, Gino R M *Football Player*
19 Louis Dr, Wellesley, MA 02481 USA

Cappelletti, John *Football Player*
28791 Brant Lane, Laguna Niguel, CA 92677 USA

Capps, Steve *Designer, Misc*
Microsoft Corp, 1 Microsoft Way, Redmond, WA 98052 USA

Capps, Thomas E *Business Person*
Dominion Resources, 120 Tredegar St, Richmond, VA 23219 USA

Cappuccilli, Piero *Opera Singer*
S A Gorlinsky, 3 Dover St, London, W1X 4NJ, UNITED KINGDOM (UK)

Capra, Francis *Actor*
Melissa Prophet Management, 1640 S Sepulveda Blvd #218, Los Angeles, CA 90025 USA

Capra, Frank Jr *Producer*
602 S Hudson, Los Angeles, CA 90005 USA

Capra, Lee W (Buzz) *Baseball Player*
3249 Lightning Court, New Lenox, IL
60451 USA

Capri, Ahna
8227 Fountain Ave. #2, Los Angeles, CA
90046

Capri, Sophia
5124 Mayfield Rd., Lyndhurst, OH 44124-
2506

Caprice *Model, Music Group, Songwriter*
Mission Control, Business Center Lower
Road, London, SE16 2XB, UNITED
KINGDOM (UK)

Caprio, Giuseppe Cardinal *Religious
Leader*
Palazza del S Uffizio 1, Rome, 00193,
ITALY

Capshaw, Jessica *Actor*
Endeavor Talent Agency, 9701 Wilshire
Blvd #1000, Beverly Hills, CA 90212 USA

Capshaw, Kate *Actor*
PO Box 869, Pacific Palisades, CA 90272
USA

Captain, Raj *Actor*
951 Munuswamy Salai, K K Nagar,
Chennai, TN 600 078, INDIA

Capucill, Terese *Dancer*
Martha Graham dance Center, 440
Lafayette St, New York, NY 10003 USA

Cara, Irene *Actor, Music Group*
110 W 26th St #300, New York, NY
10001 USA

Carafotes, Paul *Actor*
8033 Sunset Blvd #3554, West
Hollywood, CA 90046 USA

Caramanlis, Costas *Prime Minister*
Premier's Office, 17 Stissichoros St, King
George V Ave, Athens, GREECE

Carasco, Joe (King) *Music Group*
Texas Sounds, 2317 Pecan, Dickinson, TX
77539 USA

Caray, Skip *Sportscaster*
Turner Broadcasting System, 1050
Techwood Dr NW, Atlanta, GA 30318
USA

Carazo, Odio Rodrigo *President, Educator*
University for Peace, Apdo 199, San Jose,
COSTA RICA

Carbajal, Michael *Boxer*
914 E Fillmore St, Phoenix, AZ 85006
USA

Carberry, Deirdre *Ballerina*
American Ballet Theater, 890 Broadway,
New York, NY 10003 USA

Carbonara, David *Composer*
Gorfaine/Schwartz, 13245 Riverside Dr,
#450, Sherman Oaks, CA 91423 USA

Carbonell, Nestor *Actor*
Rigberg Roberts Rugolo, 1180 S Beverly
Dr #601, Los Angeles, CA 90035 USA

Carbonneau, Guy *Hockey Player, Misc*
Dallas Stars, StarCenter 211 Cowboys
Parkway, Irving, TX 75063 USA

Carcaterra, Lorenzo *Writer*
William Morris Agency, 151 El Camino
Dr, Beverly Hills, CA 90212 USA

Card, Andrew H Jr *Secretary, Misc*
White House, 1600 Pennsylvania Ave
NW, Washington, DC USA

Card, Michael *Music Group, Musician*
1143 Dora Whitley Road, Franklin, TN
37064 USA

Cardamone, Richard J *Judge*
US Court of Appeals, 10 Broad St, Utica,
NY 13501 USA

Cardellini, Linda *Actor*
Gersh Agency, 232 N Canon Dr, Beverly
Hills, CA 90210 USA

Carden, Joan M *Opera Singer*
Jennifer Eddy, 596 Saint Kilda Road #11,
Melbourne, VIC, 3004, AUSTRALIA

Cardenal, Jose D *Baseball Player*
12 Country Club Dr #UC, Prospect
Heights, IL 60070 USA

Cardenas, Elsa
Altamirano 126, Mexico DF, MEXICO

Cardich, Augusto *Archaeologist*
University of La Plata, Archaeology Dept,
La Plata, ARGENTINA

Cardiff, Jack *Cinematographer*
32 Woodland Rise, London, N10,
UNITED KINGDOM (UK)

Cardigans, The *Music Group*
International Talent Booking (ITB - UK),
27A Floral Street, Third Floor, Covent
Garden, London, WC2E 9, United
Kingdom

Cardin, Pierre *Fashion Designer*
59 Rue du Foubourg-St-Honore, Paris,
75008, FRANCE

Cardinahl, Jessika
Vogelbeerenweg 4, Hamburg, GERMANY,
D-22299

Cardinal, Douglas J *Architect*
7011A Manchester Blvd #315, Alexandria,
VA 22310 USA

Cardinale, Claudia *Actor*
Via Flaminia Km 77, Prima Porta, Rome,
00188, ITALY

Cardona, Manolo *Actor*
TV Caracol, Calle 76 #11 - 35, Piso
10AA, Bogota DC, 26484, COLOMBIA

Cardone, Vivien *Actor*
Everwood, 1000 West/2610 South, Salt
Lake City, UT 84119 USA

Cardos, John Bud
PO Box 7430, Burbank, CCA, 91505

Cardosa, Patricia *Director*
International Creative Management
(ICM-LA), 8942 Wilshire Blvd, Beverly
Hills, CA 90211 USA

Cardoso, Fernando
Palacio do Planalto, Brasilia DF, BRAZIL,
70150-900

Cardoso, Patricia *Director*
Industry Entertainment, 955 S Carrillo Dr
#300, Los Angeles, CA 90048 USA

Cardwell, Donald E (Don) *Baseball Player*
P O Box 454, Clemmons, NC 27012 USA

Care, Peter *Director*
Creative Artists Agency LCC (CAA-LA),
9830 Wilshire Blvd, Beverly Hills, CA
90212 USA

Carell, Steve *Actor*
Media Four, 8840 Wilshire Blvd Fl 2,
Beverly Hills, CA 90211 USA

Carelli, Rick *Race Car Driver*
15764 W 63rd Ave, Golden, CO 80403
USA

Caretto-Brown, Patty *Swimmer*
16079 Mesquite Circle, Santa Ana, CA
92708 USA

Carew, Drew *Actor, Comedian*
Messina Baker Entertainment, 955 Carillo
Dr #100, Los Angeles, CA 90048 USA

Carey, Andrew A (Andy) *Baseball Player*
PO Box 8708, Dept 434, Newport Beach,
CA 92658 USA

Carey, Clare
9255 Sunset Blvd. #620, Los Angeles, CA
90069

Carey, Drew *Comedian, Actor*
Messina Baker/Entertainment, 955 Carrillo
Dr #100, Los Angeles, CA 90048 USA

Carey, Duane G *Astronaut*
15706 Falmouth Dr, Houston, TX 77059
USA

Carey, Ezekiel *Music Group*
509 E Ridge Crest Blvd #A, Ridge Crest,
CA 93555 USA

Carey, Hugh L *Governor*
WR Grace Co, 1114 Ave of Americas,
New York, NY 10036 USA

Carey, Jim (Hockey) *Hockey Player*
4848 Hanging Moss Lane, Sarasota, FL
34238 USA

Carey, Mariah *Musician, Songwriter,
Music Group*
Talent Entertainment Group, 9111
Wilshire Blvd, Beverly Hills, CA 90210
USA

Carey, Mary *Adult Film Star*
Mary Carey Inc, 4850 Vineland Ave #274,
N Hollywood, CA 91601 USA

Carey, Matthew Thomas *Actor*
Evolution Entertainment, 901 N Highland
Ave, Los Angeles, CA 90038 USA

Carey, Michelle *Actor*
H David Moss, 733 Seward St, #PH, Los
Angeles, CA 90038 USA

Carey, Peter *Writer*
International Creative Mgmt, 40 W 57th St
#1800, New York, NY 10019 USA

Carey, Philip
56 W. 66th St., New York, NY 10023

Carey, Rick
119 Rockland Ave., Larchmont, NY
10538

Carey, Ron
NW 25 Louisiana Ave., Washington, DC
20001

Carey, Ron *Actor*
419 N Larchmont Ave, Los Angeles, CA
90004 USA

Carey, Ron (actor)
419 N. Larchmont Blvd, Los Angeles, CA
90004

Carey, Tony
BMG Postfach 800149, Munich,
GERMANY, D-81601

Carey Jr, Harry *Actor*
P O Box 1388, Goleta, CA 93116 USA

Cargo, David F *Governor*
6422 Concordia Road NE, Albuquerque, NM 87111 USA

Carides, Gia *Actor*
Robyn Gardiner Mgmt, 397 Riley St, Surrey Hills, NSW, 2010, AUSTRALIA

Caridis, Miltiades
Himmelhofgasse 10, Vienna, 1130, AUSTRIA

Carille, Lori
1065 Lyndhurst Dr, Pittsburgh, PA 16206

Carillo, Mary *Sportscaster*
822 Boylston St #203, Chestnut Hill, PA 02467 USA

Cariou, Len *Actor*
Paradigm Agency, 10100 Santa Monica Blvd #2500, Los Angeles, CA 90067 USA

Carithers, William Jr *Physicist*
Fermi Net Acceleration Lab, D-Zero Collaboration, PO Box 500, Batavia, IL 60510 USA

Carl, Jann *Television Host*
Entertainment Tonight (ET), 5555 Melrose Ave, Mae West Bldg Fl 2, Hollywood, CA 90038 USA

Carl XVI, Gustaf *King*
Kungliga Slottet, Slottsbacken, Stockholm, 111 30, SWEDEN

Carle, Eric *Artist*
PO Box 485, Northampton, MA 01060 USA

Carlei, Carlo *Director*
Creative Artists Agency, 9830 Wilshire Blvd, Beverly Hills, CA 90212 USA

Carles Gordo, Ricardo M Cardinal *Religious Leader*
Carrer del Bisbe 5, Barcelona, 08002, SPAIN

Carlesimo, Pete J (P J) *Basketball Player, Coach, Sportscaster*
San Antonio Spurs, Alamodome 1 SBC Center, San Antonio, TX 78219 USA

Carlestrom, John E *Astronomer*
University of Chicago, Astronomy Dept 5640 S Ellis Ave, Chicago, IL 60637 USA

Carlile, Forbes *Swimmer, Coach*
16 Cross St, Ryde, NSW, 2112, AUSTRALIA

Carlin, George *Comedian, Actor*
Carlin Productions, 11911 San Vicente Blvd #348, Los Angeles, CA 90049 USA

Carlin, John W *Governor*
18201 Allwood Terrace, Olney, MD 20832 USA

Carlin, Thomas R *Publisher*
Saint Paul Pioneer Press, Publisher's Office, 345 Cdear, Saint Paul, MN 55101 USA

Carling, William D C *Sportscaster, Misc, Athlete*
Insights Ltd, 22 Suffolk St, London, SW1Y 4HG, UNITED KINGDOM (UK)

Carlino, Lewis John *Director, Writer*
991 Oakmont Dr, Los Angeles, CA 90049 USA

Carlisle, Belinda *Model, Songwriter, Music Group*
Firstars Management, 14724 Ventura Blvd #PH, Sherman Oaks, CA 91403 USA

Carlisle, Bob *Songwriter, Music Group*
Ray Ware Artist Mgmt, 251 2nd Ave #5, Franklin, TN 37064 USA

Carlisle, James B *General, Governor*
Governer General's Office, Government House, Saint John's, ANTIGUA

Carlisle, Jodi *Actor, Comedian*
International Creative Management (ICM-LA), 8942 Wilshire Blvd, Beverly Hills, CA 90211 USA

Carlisle, Mary *Actor*
517 N Rodeo Dr, Beverly Hills, CA 90210 USA

Carlisle, Rick *Basketball Player, Coach*
RR 4, Ogdensburg, NY 13669 USA

Carlisle Hart, Kitty *Actor, Music Group*
32 E 64th St, New York, NY 10021 USA

Carlos, John *Track Athlete*
68640 Tortuga Rd, Cathedral City, CA 92234 USA

Carlos I, Juan *King*
Palacio de la Zarzuela, Madrid, 28671, SPAIN

Carlos Moco, Marcolino Jose *Prime Minister*
Movimento Popular de Libertacao de Angola, Luanda, ANGOLA

Carlot, Maxime *Prime Minister*
P O Box 698, Port Vila, VANUATU

Carlson, Arne H *Governor*
22005 Iden Ave N, Forest Lake, MN 55025 USA

Carlson, Dudley L *Admiral*
Navy League, 2300 Wilson Blvd, Arlington, VA 22201 USA

Carlson, Gretchen *Television Host*
CBS Saturday Early Show, 524 W 57th St Fl 6, New York, NY 10019-2902 USA

Carlson, Jack W *Misc*
American Assn of Retired Persons, 1901 K St NW, Washington, DC 20006 USA

Carlson, John A *Business Person*
Cray Research, 655 Lone Oak Dr #A, Eagan, MN 55121 USA

Carlson, K C *Cartoonist*
DC Comics, 1700 Broadway, New York, NY 10019 USA

Carlson, Karen *Actor*
3700 Ventura Canyon Ave, Sherman Oaks, CA 91423 USA

Carlson, Katrina *Actor*
Sara Bennett Agency, 1062 S Alfred St, Los Angeles, CA 90035 USA

Carlson, Kelly *Actor*
Cunningham-Escott-Dipene & Associates Inc (CED-LA), 10635 Santa Monica Blvd #130, Los Angeles, CA 90025 USA

Carlson, Lane *Model*
WARNING Models, 9440 Santa Monica Blvd #400, Beverly Hills, CA 90210 USA

Carlson, Paulette *Music Group*
Mark Sonder Music, Fisk Building 250 W 57th St #1830, New York, NY 10107 USA

Carlson, Richard *Writer*
Pennsylvania State Univ, 613 Mmore Bldg, University Park, PA 16802

Carlson, Richard *Writer*
Pennsylvania State Univ, 613 Moore Bldg, University Park, PA 16802

Carlson, Shane *Model*
WARNING Models, 9440 Santa Monica Blvd #400, Beverly Hills, CA 90210 USA

Carlson, Stuart *Cartoonist*
Universal Press Syndicate, 4520 Main St, Kansas City, MO 64111 USA

Carlson, Tucker *Commentator*
P O Box 1005366, Atlanta, GA 30348 USA

Carlson, Veronica *Actor*
7844 Kavanagh Court, Sarasota, FL 34240 USA

Carlsson, Arvid *Nobel Prize Laureate*
Gotheburg University, P O Box 100, Gotheburg, 405 30, SWEDEN

Carlsson, Ingvar G *Prime Minister*
Riksdagen, Stockholm, 100 12, SWEDEN

Carlton, Carl *Music Group*
Randolph Enterprises, Oakland, Inkster, MI 48141 USA

Carlton, Larry *Musician*
Monterey Peninsula Artists (Monterey), 509 Hartnell St, Monterey, CA 93940 USA

Carlton, Paul K *General*
1716 Briescrest Dr # 702, Bryan, TX 77802 USA

Carlton, Steve
555 S. Camino Del Rio #B2, Durango, CO 81301-6852

Carlton, Steven N (Steve) *Baseball Player*
GW Sports, 555 Camino Del Rio #B2, Durango, CO 81301 USA

Carlton, Vanessa *Musician*
Peter Malkin Management, 410 Park Ave #420, New York, NY 10022 USA

Carlton, Venessa *Music Group*
Peter Malkin Mgmt, 410 Park Ave #420, New York, NY 10022 USA

Carlton-Luff, Rebekah
9300 Wilshire Blvd. #410, Beverly Hills, CA 90212

Carlucci, Dave *Music Group*
Joe Terry Mgmt, P O Box 1017, Tumersville, NJ 08012 USA

Carlucci, Frank C
1001 Pennsylvania Ave NW, Washington, DC 20004-2506 USA

Carlucci, Frank C III *Secretary, Business Person*
Carlyle Group, 1001 Pennsylvania Ave NW, Washington, DC 20004 USA

Carlyle, Joan H *Opera Singer*
Laundry Cottage Hammer, North Wales, SY13 4QX, UNITED KINGDOM (UK)

Carlyle, Randy *Hockey Player, Coach*
Washington Capitals, MCI Center 601 F St NW, Washington, DC 20004 USA

Carlyle, Robert *Actor*
International Creative Management, 76 Oxford St, London, W1N 0AX, UNITED KINGDOM (UK)

Carmack, Chris *Actor*
Jerry Shandrew PR, 1050 South Stanley Avenue, Los Angeles, CA 90019-6634 USA

Carman *Music Group*
Carman Ministries, PO Box 5093, Brentwood, TN 37024 USA

Carman, Gregory W *Judge*
US Court of International Trade, 1 Federal Plaza, New York, NY 10278 USA

Carmen, Eric *Songwriter, Music Group*
David Spero Mgmt, 1679 Belvoir Blvd, South Euclid, OH 44121 USA

Carmen, Jean
PO Box 3367, Laguna Hills, CA 92653

Carmen, Jeanne *Actor, Model*
Brandon James, P O Box 11812, Newport Beach, CA 92658 USA

Carmen, Julie *Actor*
Metropolitan Talent Agency, 4526 Wilshire Blvd, Los Angeles, CA 90010 USA

Carmichael, Greg *Musician*
Monterey International, 200 W Superior #202, Chicago, IL 60610 USA

Carmichael, Ian *Actor*
London Mgmt, 2-4 Noel St, London, W1V 3RB, UNITED KINGDOM (UK)

Carmichael, L Harold *Football Player*
38 Birch Lane, Glassboro, NJ 08028 USA

Carmine, Michael *Cinematographer*
3615 West Dr, Douglaston, NY 11363 USA

Carmona, Richard H *Government Official, Physicist, Misc*
Surgeon General's Office, 200 Independence Ave SW, Washington, DC 20201 USA

Carn, Jean
PO Box 27641, Philadelphia, PA 19150

Carnahan, Joe *Director*
Endeavor Agency LLC (LA), 9601 Wilshire Blvd Fl 3, Beverly Hills, CA 90210 USA

Carne, Jean *Music Group*
Walt Reeder Productions, P O Box 27641, Philadelphia, PA 19118 USA

Carne, Judy *Actor, Comedian*
2 Horatio St #10N, New York, NY 10014 USA

Carner, JoAnne *Golfer*
7641 Mackenzie Court #314, Lake Worth, FL 33467 USA

Carner, Randall
11043 Kling St., No. Hollywood, CA 91602

Carnes, Kim *Songwriter, Music Group*
1829 Tyne Blvd, Nashville, TN 37215 USA

Carnesale, Albert *Educator*
University of California, Chancellor's Office, Los Angeles, CA 90024 USA

Carnevale, Bernard L (Ben) *Basketball Player, Coach*
5109 Dorset Mews, Williamsburg, VA 23188 USA

Carney, Art *Actor*
143 Kingfisher Lane, Westbrook, CT 06498 USA

Carney, John M *Football Player*
2950 Wishbone Way, Encinitas, CA 92024 USA

Carney, Thomas P *General*
9806 Kirktree Court, Fairfax, VA 22032 USA

Carns, Michael P C (Mike) *General*
966 Coral Dr, Pebble Beach, CA 93953 USA

Caro, Anthony A *Artist, Misc*
111 Frognal Hampstead, London, NW3, UNITED KINGDOM (UK)

Caro, Niki *Director, Writer*
Broder Webb Chervin Silbermann Agency, The (BWCS), 9242 Beverly Blvd #200, Beverly Hills, CA 90210 USA

Caro, Robert A *Writer*
Robert A Caro Assoc, 250 W 57th St, New York, NY 10107 USA

Caroline *Misc, Prince*
Villa Le Clos Saint Pierre, Ave San-Martin, Monte Carlo, MONACO

Caroline, James C (J C) *Football Player*
2501 Stanford Dr, Champaign, IL 61820 USA

Caroline, Princess
Villa Le Clos St. Pierre ave. Saint Martin, Monte Carlo, MONACO

Carolla, Adam *Talk Show Host*
Lapides Entertainment, 345 N Maple Dr, Beverly Hills, CA 90210

Caron, Leslie *Actor, Dancer*
6 Rue De Bellechalsse, Paris, 75007, FRANCE

Carothers, A J
2110 The Terrace, Los Angeles, CA 90049 USA

Carothers, Robert L *Educator*
University of Rhode Island, President's Office, Kingston, RI 02881 USA

Carothers, Veronica *Actor*
535 N Heatherstone Dr, Orange, CA 92869 USA

Carp, Daniel A (Dan) *Business Person*
Eastman Kodak Co, 343 State St, Rochester, NY 14650 USA

Carpendale, Howard
200 Admiral's Cove Blvd., Jupiter, FL 33477

Carpenter, Bob *Hockey Player*
PO Box 451, Alton Bay, NH 03810 USA

Carpenter, Carleton *Actor*
RR 2 Chardavoyne Road, Warwick, NY 10990 USA

Carpenter, Charisma *Actor, Model*
Gersh Agency, The (LA), 232 N Canon Dr, Beverly Hills, CA 90210 USA

Carpenter, Dave *Editor, Cartoonist*
PO Box 520, Emmetsburg, IA 50536 USA

Carpenter, George *War Hero*
320 Walnut St, Paris, TN 38242 USA

Carpenter, John *Director*
William Morris Agency (WMA-LA), 1 William Morris Pl, Beverly Hills, CA 90212 USA

Carpenter, John M *Opera Singer*
Maurel Enterprises, 225 W 34th St #1012, New York, NY 10122 USA

Carpenter, Ken *Football Player*
PO Box 172, Seaside, OR 97138 USA

Carpenter, Kip *Speed Skater*
425 N Park Blvd, Brookfield, WI 53005 USA

Carpenter, Liz *Social Activist*
116 Skyline Dr, Austin, TX 78746 USA

Carpenter, M Scott *Astronaut*
PO Box 3161, Vail, CO 81658 USA

Carpenter, Marj C *Religious Leader*
Presbyterian Church USA, 100 Witherspoon St, Louisville, KY 40202 USA

Carpenter, Mary-Chapin *Musician, Songwriter*
AGF Entertainment, 30 W 21st St, #700, New York, NY 10010 USA

Carpenter, Patrick *Race Car Driver*
Team Players, 2015 Peel, #500, Montreal, PQ H3A 1T8, CANADA

Carpenter, Richard *Songwriter, Musician*
960 Country Valley Road, Westlake Village, CA 91362 USA

Carpenter, Russell P *Cinematographer*
Gersh Agency, 232 N Canon Dr, Beverly Hills, CA 90210 USA

Carpenter, Teresa *Journalist*
Village Voice, Editorial Dept, 36 Cooper Square, New York, NY 10003 USA

Carpenter, W M *Business Person*
Bausch & Lomb, 1 Bausch & Lomb Place, Rochester, NY 14604 USA

Carpenter, William S (Bill) Jr *Football Player*
PO Box 4067, Whitefish, MT 59937 USA

Carr, Austin *Basketball Player*
32659 Allenbury Dr, Solon, OH 44139 USA

Carr, Caleb *Writer*
Don Buchwald, 6500 Wilshire Blvd, #2200, Los Angeles, CA 90048 USA

Carr, Catherine (Cathy) *Swimmer*
409 10th St, Davis, CA 95616 USA

Carr, Charmain
4150 Hayvenhurst Dr., Encino, CA 91316

Carr, Charmian *Actor, Musician*
Arete Publishing Co, PO Box 127, Claremont, CA 91711 USA

Carr, Darleen *Actor*
Abrams Artists, 9200 Sunset Blvd #1125, Los Angeles, CA 90069 USA

Carr, David *Football Player*
Houston Texans, 4400 Post Oak Parkway, #1400, Houston, TX 77027 USA

Carr, Gerald F
PO Box 919, Huntsville, AR 72740-0919 USA

Carr, Gerald P (Jerry) *Astronaut*
CAMUS Inc, PO Box 919, Huntsville, AR 72740 USA

Carr, Henry *Track Athlete, Football Player*
11642 Beaverland St, Detroit, MI 48239 USA

Carr, Jane *Actor*
6200 Mount Angelus Dr, Los Angeles, CA 90042 USA

Carr, Jimmy *Actor*
William Morris Agency (WMA-LA), 1 William Morris Pl, Beverly Hills, CA 90212 USA

Carr, Kenneth M *Admiral*
2322 Fort Scott Dr, Arlington, VA 22202 USA

Carr, Kenny *Baseball Player*
24421 SW Valley View Dr, West Linn, OR 97068 USA

Carr, Lloyd *Coach*
University of Michigan, Athletic Dept, Ann Arbor, MI 48109 USA

Carr, Michael L (M L) *Basketball Player, Coach*
Boston Celtics, 151 Merrimac St, #1, Boston, MA 02114 USA

Carr, Paul *Actor*
H David Moss, 733 Seward St, #1, Boston, MA 02114 USA

Carr, Roger D *Football Player*
107 Lake Lane, West Monroe, LA 71291 USA

Carr, Steve *Musician*
Creative Artists Agency LCC (CAA-LA), 9830 Wilshire Blvd, Beverly Hills, CA 90212 USA

Carr, Vikki *Musician*
3102 Iron Stone Lane, San Antonio, TX 78230 USA

Carr of Hadley, L Robert *Government Official*
14 North Court, Great Peter St, London, SW1 3LL, UNITED KINGDOM (UK)

Carra, Raffella
Via Nemea 21, Rome, ITALY, I-00194

Carrabba, Chris *Musician*
Hard 8 Management, 2118 Wilshire Blvd #361, Santa Monica, CA 90403 USA

Carrack, Paul *Musician, Songwriter*
Firstars Mgmt, 14724 Ventura Blvd, #PH, Sherman Oaks, CA 91403 USA

Carradine, David *Actor*
628 S San Fernando Blvd, #C, Burbank, CA 91502 USA

Carradine, Ever *Actor*
Gersh Agency, The (LA), 232 N Canon Dr, Beverly Hills, CA 90210 USA

Carradine, Keith *Actor, Songwriter, Musician*
PO Box 460, Placeville, CO 81430 USA

Carradine, Robert *Actor*
355 So. Grand Ave, #4150, Los Angeles, CA 90071 USA

Carraher, Harlen
2832 Abenel St. #1, Los Angeles, CA 90039

Carrasquel, Alfonso C (Chico) *Baseball Player*
4625 Wisconsin Ave, Berwyn, IL 60402 USA

Carre, Isabelle
8 rue de Duras, Paris, FRANCE, F-75008

Carreno, J Manuel *Ballerina*
Royal Ballet, Covent Garden, Bow St, London, WC2E 9DD USA

Carrera, Asia *Adult Film Star*
Atlas Multimedia Inc, 22940 Burbank Blvd, Woodland Hills, CA 91367 USA

Carrera, Barbara *Actor, Model*
Chasin Agency, 8899 Beverly Blvd, #716, Los Angeles, CA 90048 USA

Carrera, Carlos *Director*
Creative Artists Agency LCC (CAA-LA), 9830 Wilshire Blvd, Beverly Hills, CA 90212 USA

Carreras, Jose *Opera Singer*
Foundacion Jose Carreras, Calle Muntaner 283, Barcelona, 08021, SPAIN

Carrere, Tia *Actor, Model*
836 N La Cienega Blvd, #204, West Hollywood, CA 90069 USA

Carretto, Joseph A Jr *Astronaut*
4534 E 85th St, Tulsa, OK 74137 USA

Carrey, Jim *Actor, Comedian*
Marleah Leslie Assoc, 8370 Wilshire Blvd #210, Beverly Hills, CA 90211 USA

Carrier, George F *Mathematician*
7 Rice Spring Lane, Wayland, MA 01778 USA

Carrier, J Mark *Football Player*
4115 Highland Park Circle, Lutz, FL 33558 USA

Carrier, Mark A *Football Player*
7626 E Cholla Dr, Scottsdale, AZ 85260 USA

Carriere, Jean P J *Writer*
Les Broussanes Domessargues, Ledignan, 30350, FRANCE

Carriere, Mathieu *Actor*
Agentur Schafer, Friesenstr 53, Cologne, 50670, GERMANY

Carril, Pete *Coach*
Sacramento Kings, Arco Arena, 1 Sports Parkway, Sacramento, CA 95834 USA

Carrillo, Elpidia *Actor*
Bresler Kelly Assoc, 11500 W Olympic Blvd, #510, Los Angeles, CA 90064 USA

Carrillo, Erick *Actor*
Three Moons Entertainment Inc, 5441 E Beverly Blvd #G, Los Angeles, CA 90022

Carrillo, Yadhira *Actor*
Televisa, Blvd Adolfo Lopez Mateos 232, Colonia San Angel INN, DF, CP 01060, MEXICO

Carrington, Alan *Misc*
46 Lakewood Road, Chandler's Ford, Hants, SO53 1EX, UNITED KINGDOM (UK)

Carrington, Chuck *Actor*
Catch 23 Management, 301 N Canon Dr #207, Beverly Hills, CA 90210 USA

Carrington, Debbie Lee *Actor*
Jonis, 8147 Tunney Ave, Reseda, CA 91335 USA

Carrington, Lord
Bledlow Aylesbury, Bucks, ENGLAND, HP17 9PE

Carrington, Peter A R *Government Official*
Manor House, Bledlow near Aylesbury, Bucks, HP17 9PE, UNITED KINGDOM (UK)

Carroll, Bruce *Musician, Songwriter*
William Morris Agency, 2100 W End Ave #1000, Nashville, TN 37203 USA

Carroll, Clay P *Baseball Player*
3040 Leisure Place, Sarasota, FL 34234 USA

Carroll, Diahann *Actor, Musician*
William Morris Agency, 1325 Ave of Americas, New York, NY 10019 USA

Carroll, Earl (Speedo) *Musician*
PS #87, 180 W 78th St, New York, NY 10019 USA

Carroll, Earl W *Misc*
United Garment Workers of America, PO Box 239, Hermitage, TN 37076 USA

Carroll, Georgia
504 E. Franklin St., Chapel Hill, NC 27514

Carroll, Joe Barry *Basketball Player*
Denver Nuggets, Pepsi Center, 1000 Chopper Circle, Denver, CO 80204 USA

Carroll, John B *Misc*
2158 Penrose Lane, Fairbanks, AK 99709 USA

Carroll, John S *Editor*
Los Angeles Times, Editorial Dept, 202 W 1st St, Los Angeles, CA 90012 USA

Carroll, Julian M *Governor*
Carroll Assoc, 25 Fountain Place, Frankfort, KY 40601 USA

Carroll, Kent J *Admiral*
Country Club of North Carolina, 1600 Morganton Road, #30X, Pinehurst, NC 28374 USA

Carroll, Lester (Les) *Cartoonist*
1715 Ivyhill Loop N, Columbus, OH 43229 USA

Carroll, Mickey
7225 St. Charles Rock Rd., St. Louis, MO 63113

Carroll, Pat *Actor*
14 Old Tavern Lane, Harwich Port, MA 02646 USA

Carroll, Pete *Football Coach*
University of Southern California, Heritage Hall, Los Angeles, CA 90089 USA

Carroll, Phillip *Business Person*
Fluor Corp, 3353 Michelson Dr, Irvine, CA 92612 USA

Carroll, Rocky
100 Universal City Plaza #507-3D, Universal City, CA 91608-1002

Carroll, Tom
1601 N. Genesee Ave., Los Angeles, CA 90046

Carroll, Willard *Writer, Producer, Director*
Hyperion Pictures, 111 N Maryland Ave #300, Glendale, CA 91206 USA

Carruthers, Garrey E *Governor*
5258 Redman Road, Las Cruces, NM 88011 USA

Carruthers, James H (Red) *Skier*
8 Malone Ave, Garnerville, NY 10923 USA

Carruthers, Kitty *Figure Skater*
22 E 71st St, New York, NY 10021 USA

Carruthers, Peter *Figure Skater*
22 E 71st St, New York, NY 10021 USA

Carry, Jerry
PO Box 919, Huntsville, AR 72740

Carry, Julius
4091 Farmdale Ave., Studio City, CA 91604

Carry, Julius J III *Actor*
4091 Farmdale Ave, Studio City, CA 91604 USA

Carsey, Marcia L P *Producer*
Carsey-Warner Productions, 4024 Radford Ave, Building 3, Studio City, CA 91604 USA

Carsey, Marcy
4024 Radford Ave. #3, Studio City, CA 91604

Carson, Benjamin S *Doctor*
Johns Hopkins University, Medical Center, Baltimore, MD 21218 USA

Carson, Bud *Football Player*
Saint Louis Rams, 901 N Broadway, Saint Louis, MO 63101 USA

Carson, Carlos A *Football Player*
2621 SW Wintercreek Dr, Lees Summit, MO 64081 USA

Carson, David *Director*
10474 Santa Monica Blvd, Los Angeles, CA 90025 USA

Carson, Harold D (Harry) *Football Player*
732 Barrister Court, Franklin Lakes, NJ 07417 USA

Carson, Hunter
8730 Sunset Blvd. #490, Los Angeles, CA 90069

Carson, James (Jimmy) *Hockey Player*
1154 Ridgeway Dr, Rochester, MI 48307 USA

Carson, Jean
190 Sahara Lane, Palm Springs, CA 92264

Carson, Jeff *Musician*
Shipley Biddy Entertainment, 1400 South St, Nashville, TN 37212 USA

Carson, Joanna
400 St. Cloud Rd., Los Angeles, CA 90024

Carson, Joanne
11001 Sunset Blvd., Los Angeles, CA 90049

Carson, Johnny *Entertainer*
6962 Wildlife Road, Malibu, CA 90265 USA

Carson, Lisa Nicole *Actor*
Pinnacle PR, 8265 Sunset Blvd #201, Los Angeles, CA 90046 USA

Carson, T C
1505 10th St, Santa Monica, CA 90401 USA

Carson, William H (Willie) *Jockey*
Minster House, Bamsley, Cirencester, Glos, UNITED KINGDOM (UK)

Carsten, Peter
Via Garibaldi 11, SVN-Piran, Istrien, SLOVAKIA

Carstens, Christiane
Kielortallee 65, Hamburg, GERMANY, D-20144

Cartan, Henri P *Mathematician*
95 Blvd, Jourdan, Paris, 75014, FRANCE

Carter, Aaron *Musician, Actor*
Evolution Talent Agency LLC, 1776 Broadway Fl 15, New York, NY 10019 USA

Carter, Alex *Actor*
Gilbertson-Kincaid Management, 1330 Fourth St, Santa Monica, CA 90401 USA

Carter, Amy
1 Woodland Dr., Plains, GA 31780

Carter, Anthony *Football Player*
4314 Danielson Dr, Lake Worth, FL 33467 USA

Carter, Betsy *Musician*
7561 Brush Lake Road, North Lewisburg, OH 43060

Carter, Carlene *Songwriter, Musician*
Warner Bros Records, 3300 Warner Blvd, Burbank, CA 91505 USA

Carter, Cheryl *Actor*
CunninghamEscottDipene, 10635 Santa Monica Blvd, #130, Los Angeles, CA 90025 USA

Carter, Chris *Producer*
Broder Kurland Webb Uffner, 9242 Beverly Blvd, #200, Beverly Hills, CA 90210 USA

Carter, Clarence *Musician*
Rodgers Redding, 1048 Tatnall St, Macon, GA 31201 USA

Carter, Cris *Football Player*
1500 Mill Creek Dr, Desoto, TX 75115 USA

Carter, Darren *Comedian*
William Morris Agency (WMA-LA), 1 William Morris Pl, Beverly Hills, CA 90212 USA

Carter, Deana *Musician, Songwriter*
PO Box 7877, Fredericksbrg, VA 22404 USA

Carter, Dexter A *Football Player*
13715 Richmond Park Dr N #1205, Jacksonville, FL 32224 USA

Carter, Dixie *Actor*
9100 Hazen Dr, Beverly Hills, CA 90210 USA

Carter, Donald J (Don) *Bowler*
9895 SW 96th St, Miami, FL 33176 USA

Carter, Elliott C Jr *Composer*
31 W 12th St, New York, NY 10011 USA

Carter, Frank *Misc*
Glass Molders Pottery Plastics Union, 608 E Baltimore Pike, Media, PA 19063 USA

Carter, Frederick J (Fred) *Baseball Player, Coach*
5070 Parkside Ave, #3500, Philadelphia, PA 19131 USA

Carter, Gary E *Baseball Player*
Gary Carter Foundation, 560 Village Blvd, #260, West Palm Beach, FL 33409 USA

Carter, Gaylord
555 E. Ocean Blvd. #810, Long Beach, CA 90802-5055

Carter, Herbert E *Educator, Biologist*
2401 Cerrada de Promesa, Tucson, AZ 85718 USA

Carter, Hodding III
211 S. St. Asaph, Alexandria, VA 22314

Carter, Jack *Actor, Comedian*
1023 Chevy Chase Dr, Beverly Hills, CA 90210 USA

Carter, Jay *Musician*
Brothers Mgmt, 141 Dunbar Ave, Fords, NJ 08863 USA

Carter, Jim *Golfer*
12611 E Cortez Dr, Scottsdale, AZ 85259 USA

Carter, Joe *Baseball Player*
300 Bremner Blvd #3200, Toronto ON, MV5 38, CANADA

Carter, John *Musician*
Resort Attractions, 2375 E Tropicana Ave, #304, Las Vegas, NV 89119 USA

Carter, John Mack *Editor*
Good Housekeeping Magazine, Editorial Dept, 959 8th Ave, New York, NY 10019 USA

Carter, Ki-Jana *Athlete*
592 Westbury Woods Ct, Westerville, OH 43081 USA

Carter, Laverne *Bowler*
4750 Madrigal Way, Las Vegas, NV 89122 USA

Carter, Lynda *Actor*
Melissa Prophet Management, 1640 S Sepulveda Blvd #218, Los Angeles, CA 90025 USA

Carter, Marshall N *Financier*
State Street Corp, 225 Franklin St, Boston, MA 02110 USA

Carter, Mel *Musician*
Cape Entertainment, 1161 NW 76th Ave, Plantation, FL 33322 USA

Carter, Michael *Actor*
London Mgmt, 2-4 Noel St, London, W1V 3RB, UNITED KINGDOM (UK)

Carter, Michael D *Football Player, Track Athlete*
901 Red Oak Creek Dr, Ovilla, TX 75154 USA

Carter, Nick *Musician, Songwriter*
Wright-Crear Management, 3815 Hughes Ave, Culver City, CA 90232 USA

Carter, Paula *Bowler*
9895 SW 96th St, Miami, FL 33176 USA

Carter, Powell F Jr *Admiral*
699 Fillmore St, Harpers Ferry, WV 25425 USA

Carter, Rachel
PO Box 1663, Julian, CA 92036

Carter, Ralph
21 St. James Pl., Brooklyn, NY 11205

Carter, Ronald L (Ron) *Composer, Musician*
Bridge Agency, 35 Clark St, #A5, Brooklyn, NY 11201 USA

Carter, Rosalynn *First Lady*
Carter Center, 451 Freedom Parkway NE, Atlanta, GA 30307 USA

Carter, Rosana *Opera Singer*
Angel Records, 150 5th Ave, New York, NY 10011 USA

Carter, Roy
Box 204, Goodlettsville, TN 37072

Carter, Rubin (Hurricane) *Boxer*
Assoc in Defense of the Wrongly
Convicted, 85 King St E #318, Toronto,
ON M5C 1G3, CANADA

Carter, Rublin *Football Player*
3018 Marsh Crossing Dr, Laurel, MD
20724 USA

Carter, Sarah *Actor*
Sanders/Armstrong Management, 2120
Colorado Blvd #120, Santa Monica, CA
90404 USA

Carter, Stephen L *Writer, Attorney General*
Yale University, Law School, New Haven,
CT 06520 USA

Carter, Terry *Actor*
244 Madison Ave, #332, New York, NY
10016 USA

Carter, Thomas *Director*
140 N. Tigertail Raod, Los Angeles, CA
90049 USA

Carter, Vince *Basketball Player*
Toronto Raptors, 20 Bay Street, #1702,
Toronto, Ontario, M5J 2N8, Canada

Carter III, W Hodding *Government Official*
214 N Columbus, Alexandria, VA 22314
USA

Carter Jr, James E (Jimmy) *Politician, Ex-President, Nobel Prize Laureate*
Carter Center, 453 Freedom Pkwy NE,
Atlanta, GA 30307 USA

Carteris, Gabrielle *Actor*
International Creative Mgmt, 8942
Wilshire Blvd, #219, Beverly Hills, CA
90211 USA

Carthy, Eliza *Songwriter, Musician*
Agency Group Ltd, 1775 Broadway, #430,
New York, NY 10019 USA

Cartier, Bresson Henri *Photographer*
Magnum Photos, 5 Passage Piver, Paris,
75011, FRANCE

Cartwright, Angela *Actor*
Rubber Boots, 11333 Moorpark St, #433,
Toluca Lake, CA 91602 USA

Cartwright, Bill *Coach, Basketball Player*
2222 Francisco Dr, #510, El Dorado Hills,
CA 95762 USA

Cartwright, James F *General*
Director Structure Resources Assessment,
HqUSMC Navy Station, Washington, DC
20380 USA

Cartwright, Lionel *Songwriter, Musician*
Long Run Music, 21 Music Square E,
Nashville, TN 37203 USA

Cartwright, Nancy *Actor*
Innovative Artists (LA), 1505 Tenth St,
Santa Monica, CA 90401 USA

Cartwright, Veronica *Actor*
12754 Sarah St, Studio City, CA 91604
USA

Carty, Ricardo A J (Rico) *Baseball Player*
5 Ens Enriquillo, San Pedro de Macoris,
DOMINICAN REPUBLIC

Caruana, Patrick P (Sat) *General*
1922 Havemeyer Lane, Redondo Beach,
CA 90278 USA

Caruana, Peter R *Politician*
Chief Minister's Office, 10/3 Irish Town,
GIBRALTAR

Caruso, David *Actor*
United Talent Agency, 9560 Wilshire
Blvd, #500, Beverly Hills, CA 90212 USA

Carvel, Elbert N *Governor*
107 Carvel Ave, Laurel, DE 19956 USA

Carver, Brent *Actor, Musician*
Live Entertainment, 1500 Broadway,
#902, New York, NY 10036 USA

Carver, Dana *Actor, Comedian*
775 E Blithedale Ave SE, #501, Mill
Valley, CA 94941 USA

Carver, Johnny *Musician*
House of Talent, 9 Lucy Lane, Sherwood,
AR 72120 USA

Carver, Randall *Actor*
Tyler Kjar, 5144 Vineland Ave, North
Hollywood, CA 91601 USA

Carvey, Dana *Actor*
Baker Winokur Ryder (BWR-LA), 9100
Wilshire Blvd Fl 6, W Tower, Beverly
Hills, CA 90212 USA

Carvilie, C James Jr *Politician*
209 Pennsylvania Ave SE, #800,
Washington, DC 20003 USA

Carville, James *Television Host*
Crossfire, 820 First St NE Fl 10,
Washington, DC 20002 USA

Cary, W Sterling *Religious Leader*
206 Lemoyne Parkway, Oak Park, IL
60302 USA

Cary-Hiroyuki, Tagawa *Actor*
Jerry Shandrew, 1050 S Stanley Ave, Los
Angeles, CA 90019 USA

Casablancas, John *Model*
Elite Model Mgmt, 111 E 22nd St, #200,
New York, NY 10001 USA

Casablancas, Julian *Songwriter, Musician*
MVO Ltd, 370 7th Ave, #807, New York,
NY 10001 USA

Casadesus, Jean-Claude *Conductor*
23 Blvd de la Liberte, Lille, 59800,
FRANCE

Casados, Rene *Actor*
Televisa, Blvd Adolfo Lopez Mateos 232,
Colonia San Angel INN, DF, CP 01060,
MEXICO

Casady, Jack *Musician*
Ron Rainey Mgmt, 315 S Beverly Dr,
#407, Beverly Hills, CA 90212 USA

Casali, Kim *Cartoonist*
Times-Mirror Syndicate, Times-Mirror
Square, Los Angeles, CA 90053 USA

Casals, Rosemary (Rosie) *Tennis Player*
Sportswoman Inc, PO Box 537, Sausalito,
CA 94966 USA

Casals, Rosie
PO Box 537, Sausalito, CA 94966

Casanova, Thomas H (Tommy) *Football Player*
141 Gardenia Lane, Crowley, LA 70526
USA

Casares, Adolfo Bioy
Posadas 1650-5, (1112) Buenos Aires,
ARGENTINA

Casares, Ricardo (Rick) *Football Player*
4107 Starfish Lane, Tampa, FL 33615 USA

Casares, Rick *Football Player*
4107 Starfish Ln, Tampa, FL 33615 USA

Casbarian, John *Architect*
Taft Architects, 2370 Rice Blvd, #112,
Houston, TX 77005 USA

Case, Harold
34 Cunningham Park Harrow, Middlesex,
ENGLAND, HA1 4AL

Case, John *Writer*
Random House, 1745 Broadway, #B1,
New York, NY 10019 USA

Case, Peter
976 S. Carmelina Ave., Los Angeles, CA
90049

Case, Scott *Football Player*
4930 Price Dr, Suwanee, GA 30024

Case, Sharon *Actor*
Jerry Shandrew PR, 1050 South Stanley
Avenue, Los Angeles, CA 90019-6634
USA

Case, Stephen M (Steve) *Business Person*
8619 Westwood Center Dr, Vienna, VA
22182 USA

Case, Walter Jr *Race Car Driver*
60 Edgecomb Road, Lisbon Falls, ME
04252 USA

Casel, Nitanju Bolade *Musician*
Sweet Honey Agency, PO Box 600099,
Newtonville, MA 02460 USA

Casella, Max
1505 10th St, Santa Monica, CA 90401

Casely-Hayford, Joe *Fashion Designer*
Joe Casely-Hayford, 128 Shoreditch High
Street, London, England, E1 6JE, United
Kingdom

Casey, Bernie
6145 Flight Ave., Los Angeles, XA, 90056

Casey, Harry W *Musician*
7530 Loch Ness Dr, Miami Lakes, FL
33014 USA

Casey, John D *Writer*
University of Virginia, English Dept,
Charlottesville, VA 22903 USA

Casey, Jon *Hockey Player*
Saint Louis Blues, Sawis Center, 1401
Clark Ave, Saint Louis, MO 63103 USA

Casey, Lawrence
4139 Vanette Pl., No. Hollywood, XA,
91604

Casey, Lee
Paul Kohner Agency Inc, 9300 Wilshire
Blvd #555, Beverly Hills, CA 90212

Casey, Maurice F *General*
7017 Union Mill Road, Clinton, VA
20124 USA

Casey, Peter *Director*
Jim Preminger Agency, 450 N Roxbury
Dr, #1050, Beverly Hills, CA 90210 USA

Cash, Gerald C *Governor*
4 Bristol St, PO Box N476, Nassau,
BAHAMAS

Cash, Keith L *Football Player*
9839 Heritage Farm Road, San Antonio,
TX 78245 USA

Cash, Pat *Tennis Player*
281 Clarence St, Sydney, NSW 2000, AUSTRALIA

Cash, Rosanne *Songwriter, Musician*
Danny Kahn, 45 W 11th St, #7B, New York, NY 10011 USA

Cash, Swin *Basketball Player*
Detroit Shock, Palace, 2 Championship Dr, Auburn Hills, MI 48326 USA

Cash, Tommy *Songwriter, Musician*
PO Box 1230, Hendersonville, TN 37077 USA

Cashman, John Jr *Misc*
PO Box 11889, Lexington, KY 40578 USA

Cashman, Terry *Musician*
15 Engle St, Englewood, NJ 07631 USA

Cashman, Wayne J *Hockey Player*
PO Box 280, Lowell, FL 32663 USA

Casiavska, Vera *Gymnast*
SVS Sparta Prague, Korunovacni 29, Prague 7, CZECH REPUBLIC

Casida, John E *Misc*
1570 La Vereda Road, Berleley, CA 94708 USA

Casiraghi, Pierlulgi *Soccer Player*
Lazio Rorna, Via Novaro 32, Rome, 00197, ITALY

Caskey, C Thomas *Biologist, Scientist*
Baylor College of Medicine, Molecular Genetics Dept, Houston, TX 77030 USA

Casnoff, Philip *Actor*
Daris Hatch Management, 9538 Brighton Way #308, Beverly Hills, CA 90210 USA

Casnoff, Phillip *Actor*
216 S Plymouth Blvd, Los Angeles, CA 90004 USA

Caso, Mark
1252 S. Ogden Dr. #8, Los Angeles, CA 90019

Caspar, Donald L D *Physicist*
911 Gardenia Dr, Tallahassee, FL 32312 USA

Casper, Billy
PO Box 210010, Chula Vista, CA 91921

Casper, David J (Dave) *Football Player*
1525 Alamo Way, Alamo, CA 94507 USA

Casper, John H *Astronaut*
4414 Village Corner Dr, Houston, TX 77059 USA

Casper, Robert *Actor*
CunninghamEscottDipene, 10635 Santa Monica Blvd #130, Los Angeles, CA 90025 USA

Casper, William E (Billy) *Golfer*
PO Box 210010, Chula Vista, CA 91921 USA

Caspersson, Tobjorn O *Doctor*
Emanuel Birkes Vag 2, Ronninge, 14400, SWEDEN

Cass, Christopher *Actor*
Halpern Assoc, PO Box 5597, Santa Monica, CA 90409 USA

Cassady, Howard (Hopalong) *Football Player*
539 Severn Ave, Tampa, FL 33606 USA

Cassady, Howard Hopalong
539 Severn Ave, Tampa, FL 33602

Cassar, Jon *Producer*
Roklin Management, 8265 Sunset Blvd #101, Los Angeles, CA 90046 USA

Cassaveters, Nick *Actor, Director*
22223 Buena Ventura St, Woodland Hills, CA 91364 USA

Cassavetes, Nick *Actor*
William Morris Agency (WMA-LA), 1 William Morris Pl, Beverly Hills, CA 90212 USA

Cassel, Jean-Pierre *Actor*
Agentur Riese-Burghardt, Berliner Allee 32, Dusseldorf 1, 4000, GERMANY

Cassel, Seymour *Actor*
Innovative Artists, 1505 10th St, Santa Monica, CA 90401 USA

Cassel, Vincent *Actor*
United Talent Agency, 9560 Wilshire Blvd, #500, Beverly Hills, CA 90212 USA

Cassell, Sam *Basketball Player*
6000 Reirns Road, #3402, Houston, TX 77036 USA

Cassels, A James H *Misc*
Hamble End Higham Road, Barrow Bury Saint Edmunds, Suffolk, UNITED KINGDOM (UK)

Casserino, Lt Col Frank J
6150 Wilson Rd, Colorado Springs, CO 80919-3501 USA

Casseus, Gabriel *Actor*
Metropolitan Talent Agency, 4526 Wilshire Blvd, Los Angeles, CA 90010 USA

Cassidy, Bruce *Hockey Player, Coach*
1810 Winella Dr SE, Grand Rapids, MI 49506 USA

Cassidy, David *Actor, Musician*
JAG Entertainment, 4265 Hazeltine Ave, Sherman Oaks, CA 91423

Cassidy, Ed
PO Box 1508, Arroyo Grande, CA 93421

Cassidy, Edward I Cardinal *Religious Leader*
Council for Christian Unity, Piazza del S Uffizio 11, Rome, 00193, ITALY

Cassidy, Elaine *Actor*
International Creative Management (ICM-LA), 8942 Wilshire Blvd, Beverly Hills, CA 90211 USA

Cassidy, Joanna *Actor*
PO Box 74123, Los Angeles, CA 90004 USA

Cassidy, Michael *Actor*
Vic Ramos Management, 49 W 9th St #5B, New York, NY 10011 USA

Cassidy, Patrick *Actor*
Innovative Artists, 1505 10th St, Santa Monica, CA 90401 USA

Cassidy, Ryan
4949 Strohm Ave., No. Hollywood, CA 91601

Cassidy, Shaun *Actor, Musician*
19425 Shirley Court, Tarzana, CA 91356 USA

Cassini, Oleg L *Fashion Designer*
15 E 53rd St, New York, NY 10022 USA

Casson, Mel *Cartoonist*
King Features Syndicate, 888 7th Ave, New York, NY 10106 USA

Cast, Edward
4 Bankside Dr Thames Ditton, Surrey, ENGLAND, KT7 0AQ, ENGLAND

Cast, Tricia *Actor*
20 Georgette Road, Rolling Hills Estates, CA 90274 USA

Casta, Laetitia *Actor*
ArtMedia, 20 Ave Rapp, Paris, 75007, FRANCE

Castaneda, Jorge A *Government Official*
Anillo Periferico Sur 3180, #1120, Jardines del Pedregal, 01900, Mexico

Castaneda, Jorge A *Government Official*
Anillo Periferico Sur 3180, #1120, Jardines del Pedregal, 01900, MEXICO

Castel, Nico *Opera Singer*
RPA Mgmt, 4 Adelaide Lane, Washingtonville, NY 10992 USA

Castellaneta, Dan *Actor, Musician, Writer*
Forster Entertainment, 12533 Woodgreen St, Los Angeles, CA 90066 USA

Castellini, Clateo *Business Person*
Becton Dickinson Co, 1 Becton Dr, Franklin Lakes, NJ 07417 USA

Castelluccio, Frederico *Actor*
Nicole Nassar PR, 521 Spoleto Dr, Pacific Palisades, CA 90272 USA

Casteres, Rick
4107 Starfish Lane, Tampa, FL 33615

Castilla, Vinny *Baseball Player, Athlete*
Atlanta Braves, Turner Field, PO Box 4064, Atlanta, GA 30302 USA

Castille, Jeremiah *Football Player*
210 Lorna Square, #160, Birmingham, AL 35216 USA

Castillo, Luis *Baseball Player, Athlete*
Florida Marlins, 2269 Dan Marino Blvd, Miami, FL 33056 USA

Castillo, Patricio *Actor*
Televisa, Blvd Adolfo Lopez Mateos 232, Colonia San Angel INN, DF, CP 01060, MEXICO

Castillo, Vinicio *Baseball Player, Athlete*
Atlanta Braves, Turner Field, PO Box 4064, Atlanta, GA 30302 USA

Castillo Lara, Rosalio Jose Cardinal *Religious Leader*
Palazzo del Governatorato, 00120, VATICAN CITY

Castle, Jo Ann *Musician*
Welk Resort Center, 1984 State Hwy 165, Branson, MO 65616 USA

Castle, John *Actor*
Larry Dalzell, 91 Regent St, London, W1R 7TB, UNITED KINGDOM (UK)

Castle, Michael N *Governor*
300 S New St, Dover, DE 19904 USA

Castle, Nick *Director*
Creative Artists Agency, 9830 Wilshire Blvd, Beverly Hills, CA 90212 USA

Castle of Blackbum, Barbara A *Government Official*
House of Lords, Westminster, London, SW1A 0PW, UNITED KINGDOM (UK)

Castle-Hughes, Keisha *Actor*
Auckland Actors, PO Box 56460, Dominion Road, Auckland, 1030, NEW ZEALAND

Castleman, Albert W Jr *Misc*
425 Hillcrest Ave, State College, PA 16803 USA

Castleman, E Riva *Misc*
Museum of Modern Art, 11 W 53rd St, New York, NY 10019 USA

Castrillon Hoyos, Dario Cardinal *Religious Leader*
Arzobispado, Calle 33 N 21-18, Bucaramanga, Santander, COLOMBIA

Castro, Cristian *Musician*
BMG, 1540 Broadway, New York, NY 10036 USA

Castro, Daniela *Actor*
Televisa, Blvd Adolfo Lopez Mateos 232, Colonia San Angel INN, DF, CP 01060, MEXICO

Castro, Emilio *Religious Leader*
World Council of Churches, 475 Riverside Dr, New York, NY 10115 USA

Castro, Raquel *Actor*
Endeavor Agency LLC (LA), 9601 Wilshire Blvd Fl 3, Beverly Hills, CA 90210 USA

Castro, Raul H *Governor, Diplomat*
429 W Crawford St, Nogales, AZ 85621 USA

Castro Ruz, Fidel *President*
Palacio del Gobierno, Plaza de Revolucion, Havana, CUBA

Castro Ruz, Raul *Prime Minister*
First Vice President's Office, Plaza de la Revolucion, Havana, CUBA

Castroneves, Helio *Race Car Driver*
3138 Commodore Plaza, #307, Miami, FL 33133 USA

Catalano, Eduardo F *Architect*
44 Grozier Road, Cambridge, MA 02138 USA

Catalino, Ken *Editor, Cartoonist*
Creators Syndicate, 5777 W Century Blvd #700, Los Angeles, CA 90045 USA

Catalona, William J *Misc*
Washington University, Medical School, Urology Division, Saint Louis, MO 63110 USA

Catanzaro, Tony *Dancer*
3496 NW 7th St, Miami, FL 33125 USA

Catchings, Tamika *Athlete*
125 S Pennsylvania St, Indianapolis, IN 46024

Catchings, Tamika *Basketball Player*
Indiana Fever, Conseco Fieldhouse, 125 S Pennsylvania, Indianapolis, IN 46204 USA

Cateris, Gabrielle
12953 Greenleaf St., Studio City, CA 49160

Cates, Dariene *Actor*
13340 FM 740, Forney, TX 75126 USA

Cates, Darlene
PO Box 39, Forney, TX 75126

Cates, Gilbert *Director, Producer*
Gilbert Cates Productions, 10920 Wilshire Blvd, #600, Los Angeles, CA 90024 USA

Cates, Phoebe *Actor*
1636 3rd Avenue, #309, New York, NY 10128 USA

Cathcard, Patti *Musician*
Windham Hill Records, PO Box 5501, Beverly Hills, CA 90209 USA

Catlett, Mary Jo *Actor*
4375 Farmdale Ave, Studio City, CA 91604 USA

Catlin, Thomas (Tom) *Football Player, Coach*
22621 NE 25th Way, Redmond, WA 98074 USA

Cato, Robert Milton *Prime Minister*
PO Box 138, Ratho Mill, SAINT VINCENT & GRENADINES

Caton, Jack Joseph *General*
17230 Citronia St, Northridge, CA 91325 USA

Caton Jones, Michael *Director*
William Moris Agency, 52/53 Poland Place, London, W1F 7LX, UNITED KINGDOM (UK)

Catrow, David *Editor, Cartoonist*
Springfield News-Sun, Editorial Dept, 202 N Limestone St, Springfield, OH 45503 USA

Cattaneo, Peter *Director*
International Creative Mgmt, 76 Oxford St, London, W1N OAX, UNITED KINGDOM (UK)

Cattell, Christine *Actor*
Epstein-Wyckoff, 280 S Beverly Dr, #400, Beverly Hills, CA 90212 USA

Catto, Henry E Jr *Diplomat*
110 E Crockett St, San Antonio, TX 78205 USA

Cattrail, Kim *Actor*
Propaganda Films Mgmt, 1741 Ivar Ave, Los Angeles, CA 90028 USA

Cattrall, Kim *Actor*
International Creative Management (ICM-LA), 8942 Wilshire Blvd, Beverly Hills, CA 90211 USA

Caubere, Philippe
10 passage du Charolais, Paris, FRANCE, F-75012

Cauduro, Eugenia *Actor*
Televisa, Blvd Adolfo Lopez Mateos 232, Colonia San Angel INN, DF, CP 01060, MEXICO

Cauffiel, Jessica *Actor*
Koopman Management, 851 Oreo Pl, Pacific Palisades, CA 90272 USA

Caulfield, Emma *Actor*
Metropolitan Talent Agency, 4526 Wilshire Blvd, Los Angeles, CA 90028 USA

Caulfield, Lore *Fashion Designer*
2228 Cotner Ave, Los Angeles, CA 90064 USA

Caulfield, Maxwell *Actor*
5252 Lennox Ave, Sherman Oaks, CA 91401 USA

Caulkins, Tracy
511 Oman St., Nashville, TN 37203

Cause in Effect
4707 N. Maiden, Chicago, IL 60640

Cauterize *Music Group*
Wind-up Records, 72 Madison Ave, New York, NY 10016 USA

Cauthen, Stephen M (Steve) *Misc*
Cauthen Ranch, RFD Boone County, 167 S Main St, Walton, KY 41094 USA

Cauthen, Steve
167 S. Main St., Walton, KY 41094-1139

Cava, Cassandra
911 N. Kings Rd. #301, Los Angeles, CA 90069

Cavadini, Catherine (Cathy) *Actor*
International Creative Management (ICM-LA), 8942 Wilshire Blvd, Beverly Hills, CA 90211 USA

Cavaiani, Jon R *War Hero*
10956 Green St, #230, Columbia, CA 95310 USA

Cavalera, Max *Musician*
Variety Artists, 1924 Spring St, Paso Robles, CA 93446 USA

Cavalier, Carrie
3200 Wyoming Ave., Burbank, CA 91505

Cavaliere, Felix *Musician, Composer*
Primo Productions, PO Box 253, Audubon, NJ 08106 USA

Cavalli, Constanza *Actor*
Gabriel Blanco Iglesias (Mexico), Rio Balsas 35-32, Colonia Cuauhtemoc, DF, 06500, Mexico

Cavalli, Roberto *Fashion Designer*
Via del Cantone 29, Osmannoro Sesto Florentino, Firenze, 50019, ITALY

Cavanagh, Megan *Actor*
Firm, The, 9465 Wilshire Blvd, Beverly Hills, CA 90212 USA

Cavanagh, Tom *Actor*
Endeavor Agency LLC (LA), 9601 Wilshire Blvd Fl 3, Beverly Hills, CA 90210 USA

Cavanaugh, Christine *Actor*
Allman, 342 S Cochran Ave, #30, Los Angeles, CA 90036 USA

Cavanaugh, Joe *Hockey Player*
25 Nathaniel Greene Dr, East Greenwich, RI 02818 USA

Cavanaugh, Matthew A (Matt) *Football Player*
6422 Cloister Gate Dr, Baltimore, MD 21212 USA

Cavanaugh, Michael *Actor*
Ambrosio/Mortimer, 165 W 46th St, New York, NY 10036 USA

Cavanaugh, Page *Musician*
5442 Woodman Ave, Sherman Oaks, CA 914101 USA

Cavaretta, Philip J (Phil) *Baseball Player*
2200 Country Walk, Snellville, GA 30039 USA

Cavazos, Lauro F *Secretary*
173 Annursnac Hill Road, Concord, MA 01742 USA

Cavazos, Lumi *Actor*
Visionary Entertainment, 8265 W Sunset Blvd, #203, West Hollywood, CA 90046 USA

Cave, Nick *Songwriter, Musician*
Billions Corp, 833 W Chicago Ave, #101, Chicago, IL 60622 USA

Caven, Ingrid
91 rue Faubourg St. Honore, Paris,
FRANCE, F-75008

Cavett, Dick *Actor, Writer*
William Morris Agency (WMA-LA), 1
William Morris Pl, Beverly Hills, CA
90212 USA

Caviezel, James (Jim) *Actor*
Beverlee Dean Management, 8924 Clifton
Way #103, Beverly Hills, CA 90211 USA

Cavill, Henry *Actor*
Peters Fraser & Dunlop (PFD - UK), Drury
House, 34-43 Russell St, London, WC2
B5, UNITED KINGDOM (UK)

Cavuto, Neil *Television Host*
Your World with Neil Cavuto, 1211 Ave
of the Americas Fl 2, New York, NY
10036 USA

Cawley, Tucker *Actor*
Creative Artists Agency LCC (CAA-LA),
9830 Wilshire Blvd, Beverly Hills, CA
90212 USA

Cawley, Warren (Rex) *Track Athlete*
1655 San Rafael Dr, Corona, CA 92882
USA

Cawley, Yvonne Goolagong
1360 E. 9th St. #100, Cleveland, OH
44114

Cazenove, Christopher *Actor*
32 Bolingbroke Grove, London, SW11,
UNITED KINGDOM (UK)

Ce Marco, Cardinal *Religious Leader*
S Marco 318, Venice, 30124, ITALY

Ceberano, Kate *Musician*
Richard East Productions, Kildean Lane,
Winchelsea, VIC, 3241, AUSTRALIA

Ceccato, Aldo *Conductor*
Chaunt da Crusch, Zuoz, 7524,
SWITZERLAND

Cech, Thomas R *Nobel Prize Laureate*
PO Box 215, Boulder, CO 80309 USA

Cechmanek, Roman *Hockey Player*
Los Angeles Kings, Staples Center, 1111 S
Figueroa St, Los Angeles, CA 90015 USA

Cecil, Chuck
4636 E. Monte Way, Phoenix, AZ 85004

Cedeno, Cesar E *Baseball Player*
2112 Marisol Loop, Kissimmee, FL 34743
USA

Cedeno, Matt
11365 Ventura Blvd. #100 Box 7403,
Studio City, CA 91604

Cedras, Raoul *General*
Continental Riande Hotel, Panama City,
PANAMA

Cedric the Entertainer *Actor, Comedian*
Creative Artists Agency, 9830 Wilshire
Blvd, Beverly Hills, CA 90212 USA

Cee-Lo *Artist, Musician*
William Morris Agency, 1325 Ave of
Americas, New York, NY 10019 USA

Ceglarski, Leonard (Len) *Hockey Player,
Coach*
61 Lantern Lane, Duxbury, MA 02332
USA

Celant, Gerwano *Misc*
Solomon Guggenheim Museum, 1971 5th
Ave, New York, NY 10128 USA

Cellucci, A Paul *Governor, Diplomat*
State Department, 2201 C St NW,
Washington, DC 20520 USA

Celmins, Vija *Artist*
49 Crosby St, New York, NY 10012 USA

Cena, John *Wrestler*
World Wrestling Entertainment (WWE),
1241 E Main St, Stamford, CT 06905 USA

Cenac, Winston Francis *Prime Minister*
7 High St, Box 629, Castries, Saint Lucia

Cenac, Winston Francis *Prime Minister*
7 High St, Box 629, Castries, SAINT
LUCIA

Cenker, Robert J *Astronaut*
GORCA Inc, 155 Hickory Corner Road,
East Windsor, NJ 08520 USA

Cennamo, Ralph *Misc*
Leather Plastics & Novelty Workers
Union, 265 W 14th St, New York, NY
10011 USA

Centers, Larry *Football Player*
6408 Tempest Circle, Plano, TX 75024
USA

Cepeda, Angie *Actor*
Kuranda Management, 8626 Skyline, Los
Angeles, CA 90046 USA

Cepeda, Oriando M *Baseball Player*
2305 Palmer Court, Fairfield, CA 94534
USA

Cepeda, Orlando M *Baseball Player*
2305 Palmer Ct, Fairfield, CA 94534

Cera, Michael
9 Sultan St. #200, Toronto, CANADA,
Ont. M5S 1

Cerami, Anthony *Misc*
Ram Island Dr, Shelter Island, NY 11964
USA

Cerbone, Jason *Actor*
Tavel Entertainment, 9171 Wilshire Blvd
#406, Beverly Hills, CA 90210 USA

Cerezo, Arevalo M Vincio *President*
Partido Democracia Cristiana, Avda Elena
20-66, Guatemala City, GUATEMALA

Cerf, Vinton G *Scientist*
3614 Camelot Dr, Annandale, VA 22003
USA

Cerha, Friedrich *Composer, Conductor*
Doblinger Music, Dorotheergasse 10, PO
Box 882, Vienna, 1011, AUSTRIA

Cerlan, Paul G *General*
3524 Old Course Lane, Valrico, FL 33594
USA

Cernadas, Segundo *Actor*
Telefe - Argentina, Pavon 2444
(C1248AAT), Buenos Aires, ARGENTINA

Cerny, Jobe *Voice Over Artist*
259 Hazel Ave, Highland Park, IL 60035-
3359

Cerone, Richard (Rick) *Baseball Player*
2 Sandburg Court, Teaneck, NJ 07666
USA

Cerrone, Rick *Athlete*
2 Sandburg Ct, Teaneck, NJ 07666

Cerruda, Ron *Golfer*
7 Fox Briar Court, Hilton Head Island, SC
29926 USA

Cerruti, Nino *Fashion Designer*
3 Place de la Madeleine, Paris, 75008,
FRANCE

Cerv, Robert H (Bob) *Baseball Player*
3130 Williamsburg Dr, Lincoln, NE 68516
USA

Cervantes, Gary *Actor*
2240 Mardel Ave, Whittier, CA 90601
USA

Cervenka, Exene *Musician*
Performers of the World, 8901 Melrose
Ave, #200, West Hollywood, CA 90069
USA

Cerveris, Michael
465 S. Detroit #403, Los Angeles, CA
90036

Cervl, Alfred N (Al) *Basketball Player*
177 Dunrovin Lane, Rochester, NY 14618
USA

Cervl, Valentina *Actor*
Artmedia, 20 Ave Rapp, Paris, 75007,
FRANCE

Cesaire, Aime Ferdinand *Writer*
La Mairie, Fort-de-France, Martinique,
97200, WEST INDIES

Cesarani, Sai *Fashion Designer*
SJC Concepts, 40 E 80th St, New York,
NY 10021 USA

Cetara, Pete
8900 Wilshire Blvd. #300, Beverly Hills,
CA 90211

Cetera, Peter *Musician, Songwriter*
1880 Century Park East, #900, Los
Angeles, CA 90067 USA

Cetlinski, Matthew (Matt) *Swimmer*
13121 SE 93rd Terrace Road,
Summerfield, FL 34491 USA

Cey, Ron
22714 Creole Rd., Woodland Hills, CA
91364

Cey, Ronald C (Ron) *Baseball Player*
22714 Creole Road, Woodland Hills, CA
91364 USA

Chabat, Alain *Actor*
Endeavor Agency LLC (LA), 9601 Wilshire
Blvd Fl 3, Beverly Hills, CA 90210 USA

Chaber, Madelyn J *Attorney General*
101 California St, San Francisco, CA
94111 USA

Chabert, Lacey *Actor*
9 Yards Entertainment, 8530 Wilshire Blvd
Fl 5, Beverly Hills, CA 90211 USA

Chabon, Michael *Writer*
Random House, 1745 Broadway, #B1,
New York, NY 10019 USA

Chabot, Herbert L *Judge*
US Tax Court, 400 2nd St NW,
Washington, DC 20217 USA

Chabraja, Nicholas D *Business Person*
General Dynamics, 3190 Fairview Park
Dr, Falls Church, VA 22042 USA

Chabria, Renee *Director*
Management 360, 9111 Wilshire Blvd,
Beverly Hills, CA 90210 USA

Chabrol, Claude *Director, Producer*
VMA, 40 Rue Francois 1er, Paris, 75008,
FRANCE

Chace, William E *Educator*
Emory University, Prisident's Office, Atlanta, GA 30322 USA

Chacon, Alex Pineda *Soccer Player*
Los Angeles Galaxy, 1010 Rose Bowl Dr, Pasadena, CA 91103 USA

Chacon, Bobby *Boxer*
Main Street III Gym, Huntington Hotel, 752 S Main St, Los Angeles, CA 90014 USA

Chacurian, Chico *Soccer Player*
96 Stratford Road, Stratford, CT 06615 USA

Chad & Jake
PO Box 1160, Whitney, TX 76692-1160

Chadha, Gurinder *Director*
International Creative Management (ICM-LA), 8942 Wilshire Blvd, Beverly Hills, CA 90211 USA

Chadirji, Rifat Kamil *Architect*
28 Troy Court, Kensington High St, London, W8, UNITED KINGDOM (UK)

Chadli, Bendjedid *President*
Palace Emir Abedelkader, Algiers, ALGERIA

Chadwick, Ed *Hockey Player*
998 Daytona Dr, Fort Erie, ON L2A 4Z8, CANADA

Chadwick, J Leslie (Les) *Musician*
Barry Collins, 21A Cliftown Road, Southend-on-Sea, Essex, SS1 1AB, UNITED KINGDOM (UK)

Chadwick, June *Actor*
Contemporary Artists, 610 Santa Monica Blvd, #202, Santa Monica, CA 90401 USA

Chadwick, William L (Bill) *Misc*
PO Box 501, Country Club Dr, Cutchogue, NY 11935 USA

Chafetz, Sidney *Artist*
Ohio State University, Art Dept, Columbus, OH 43210 USA

Chaffee, Don *Director*
7020 La Presa Dr, Los Angeles, CA 90068 USA

Chaffee, Susan (Suzy) *Skier*
5106 Woodwind Lane, Anaheim, CA 92807 USA

Chafin, Brian
4107 Medical Parkway #210, Austin, TX 78756

Chaiken, Ilene *Writer, Producer*
William Morris Agency (WMA-LA), 1 William Morris Pl, Beverly Hills, CA 90212 USA

Chailly, Riccardo *Conductor*
Royal Concertgebrew, Jacob Obrechtstraat 51, Armsterdam, 1071 KJ, 41, HOLLAND

Chairmen of the Board
11320 Pine Valley Club Dr., Charlotte, NC 28277

Chakiris, George *Actor, Musician, Dancer*
7266 Clinton St, Los Angeles, CA 90036 USA

Chakraborty, Pramod *Director, Filmmaker, Producer, Bollywood*
Natraj Studios 194 M V Road, Andheri (E), Bombay, MS 400 069, INDIA

Chakravarthi, Vinu *Actor, Bollywood*
63 Apusali Street, Chennai, TN 600093, INDIA

Chakravarthy, Dheephan *Actor*
Auroammaa 5/17 Royal Villa 4th Main Road Extn, Kottur Gardens, Chennai, TN 600 085, INDIA

Chalayan, Hussein *Fashion Designer*
71 Endell Road, London, WC2 9AJ, UNITED KINGDOM (UK)

Chalfont, A G (Arthur) *Government Official*
House of Lords, Westminster, London, SW1A 0PW, UNITED KINGDOM (UK)

Chalke, Sarah *Actor*
Salt Spring, 8391 Beverly Blvd, #372, Los Angeles, CA 90048 USA

Challis, Christopher
18 Middle Roy, London, ENGLAND, W10 5AT

Chalmers, Judith
23 Eyot Gardens, London, ENGLAND, W10 5AT

Chaloner, William G *Misc*
20 Parke Road, London, SW13 9NG, UNITED KINGDOM (UK)

Chamberlain, Jimmy *Musician*
Creative Artists Agency, 9830 Wilshire Blvd, Beverly Hills, CA 90212 USA

Chamberlain, John A *Artist*
Ten Coconut Inc, 1315 10th St, Sarasota, FL 34236 USA

Chamberlain, Joseph W *Astronomer*
Rice University, Space Physics & Astronomy Dept, Houston, TX 77001 USA

Chamberlain, Owen *Nobel Prize Laureate*
882 Santa Barbara Road, Berkeley, CA 94707 USA

Chamberlain, Richard *Actor*
TalentWorks (LA), 3500 W Olive Ave #1400, Burbank, CA 91505 USA

Chambers, Anne Cox *Business Person, Diplomat*
Cox Enterprises, 1440 Lake Hearn Dr NE, Atlanta, GA 30319 USA

Chambers, Christina *Actor*
Roklin Management, 8265 Sunset Blvd #101, Los Angeles, CA 90046 USA

Chambers, Emma *Actor*
Conway Van Gelder Ltd, 18-21 Jermyn St Fl 3, London, SW1Y 6HP, UNITED KINGDOM (UK)

Chambers, Faune *Actor*
Roklin Management, 8265 Sunset Blvd #101, Los Angeles, CA 90046 USA

Chambers, Faune *Actor*
Kazarian/Spencer & Assoc, 11365 Ventura Blvd #100, Box 7403, Studio City, CA 91604 USA

Chambers, Jerry *Basketball Player*
3443 6th Ave, Los Angeles, CA 90018 USA

Chambers, John
433 S. Fairview St., Burbank, CA 91505

Chambers, Justin *Actor*
Industry Entertainment, 955 S Carrillo Dr #300, Los Angeles, CA 90048 USA

Chambers, Lester *Musician*
Lustig Talent, PO Box 770850, Orlando, FL 32877 USA

Chambers, Rebecca *Actor*
Writers & Artists, 8383 Wilshire Blvd, #550, Beverly Hills, CA 90211 USA

Chambers, Tom *Basketball Player*
153 E 2550 N, Ogden, UT 84414 USA

Chambers, Wallace (Wally) *Football Player*
95 Meadle St, Mount Clemens, MI 48043 USA

Chambers, Willie *Musician*
Noga Mgmt, PO Box 1428, Studio City, CA 91614 USA

Chambers Brothers, The
1601 S Rainbow Blvd #210, Las Vegas, NV 89102, US

Chambliss, C Christopher (Chris) *Baseball Player*
PO Box 440, Briarcliff Manor, NY 10510 USA

Chambon, Pierre H *Misc*
Institute Genetique Moleculaire/Cellulaire, BP 163, Illkirch, 67404, FRANCE

Champion, Marge *Dancer, Actor*
484 W 43rd St, New York, NY 10036 USA

Champion, Will *Musician*
Nettwerk Mgmt, 1650 W 2nd Ave, Vancouver, BC V6J 4R3, CANADA

Champlin, Charles *Critic*
2169 Linda Flora Dr, Los Angeles, CA 90077 USA

Chan, Ernie *Cartoonist*
4131 Vale Ave, Oakland, CA 94619 USA

Chan, Jackie *Actor*
Golden Harvest Studios, 145 Waterloo Road, Kowloon, Hong Kong, CHINA

Chan, Jullus *Prime Minister*
PO Box 6030, Boroto, PAPUA NEW GUINEA

Chan, Sy *Misc*
Premier's Office, Phnorn-Penh, PEOPLE'S REPUBLIC OF KAMPUCHEA

Chana, Ameet *Actor*
EastEnders, BBC Elstree Centre, Clarendon Road, Borehamwood, Herts, UNITED KINGDOM

Chance, Britton *Misc, Yachtsman*
4014 Pine St, Philadelphia, PA 19104 USA

Chance, Dean *Baseball Player*
9505 W Smithville Western Road, Wooster, OH 44691 USA

Chance, Jeff
PO Box 2977, Hendersonville, TN 37077

Chance, Larry *Musician*
Brothers Mgmt, 141 Dunbar Ave, Fords, NJ 08863 USA

Chancellor, Van *Coach*
Houston Cornets, 2 Greenway Plaza, #400, Houston, TX 77046 USA

Chandler, Christopher M (Chris) *Football Player*
2529 12th Ave W, Seattle, WA 98119 USA

Chandler, Colby H *Business Person*
Ford Motor Co, American Road, Dearborn, MI 48121 USA

Chandler, Donald G (Don) *Football Player*
3248 E 93rd St, Tulsa, OK 74137 USA

Chandler, Gene *Musician*
Entertainment Consultants, 164 Woodstone Dr, Buffalo Grove, IL 60089 USA

Chandler, Jeff *Boxer*
6242 Horner St, Philadelphia, PA 19144 USA

Chandler, Kyle *Actor*
Brillstein/Grey, 9150 Wilshire Blvd, #350, Beverly Hills, CA 90212 USA

Chandler, Otis
1421 Emerson, Oxnard, CA 93033

Chandler, Tyson *Basketball Player*
18903 Chickory Dr, Riverside, CA 92504 USA

Chandler, Wesley S (Wes) *Football Player*
525 Island Bay Dr, Coppell, TX 75019 USA

Chandnois, Lynn *Football Player*
2048 Walden Court, Flint, MI 48532 USA

Chandola, Walter *Photographer*
50 Spring Hill Road, Annandale, NJ 08801 USA

Chandra, Asha *Actor, Bollywood*
C6/6 Sangeeta Apartments, Juhu Santacruz, Mumbai, MS 400049, INDIA

Chandran, S S *Actor*
34A Asumpon Muthuramalingum Street, Rajaji Colony, Chennai, TN 600 092, INDIA

Chandran, Sudha *Actor, Bollywood*
4, Mahant Road Extension 6141250, Vile Parkel (E), Mumbai, MS 400057, INDIA

Chandran, T K S *Actor*
D25 Amutham Colony, South Boag Road, Chennai, TN 600 017, INDIA

Chandrasekar *Actor*
34 Senthil Nagar Main Road Chinna Porur, Near Valasaravakkam, Chennai, TN 600 116, INDIA

Chandrasekhar, Bhagwat S *Cricketer*
571 31st Cross, 4th Block Jayanagar, Bangalore, 56011, INDIA

Chandrasekhar, Jay *Comedian*
United Talent Agency (UTA), 9560 Wilshire Blvd, Beverly Hills, CA 90212 USA

Chanel, Patrice
12001 Ventura Blvd. #331, Studio City, CA 91604

Chanel, Tally *Actor, Model*
Don Gerler, 3349 Cahuenga Blvd W, #1, Los Angeles, CA 90068 USA

Chaney, John *Coach*
Temple University, Athletic Dept, Philadelphia, PA 19122 USA

Chang, Christina *Actor*
TalentWorks (LA), 3500 W Olive Ave #1400, Burbank, CA 91505 USA

Chang, Chun-hsiung *Prime Minister*
Premier's Office, 1 Chunghsiao East Road, Section 1, Taipei, TAIWAN

Chang, Jeannette *Publisher*
Harper's Bazaar Magazine, 1700 Broadway, New York, NY 10019 USA

Chang, Michael *Tennis Player*
PO Box 6080, Mission Viejo, CA 92690 USA

Chang, Sarah *Musician*
I C M Artists, 40 W 57th St, New York, NY 10019 USA

Chang-Diaz, Franklin R *Astronaut*
NASA, Johnson Space Center, 2101 NASA Road, Houston, TX 77058 USA

Changeux, Jean-Pierre G *Biologist*
47 Rue du Four, Paris, 75006, FRANCE

Channing, Carol *Actor, Musician*
William Morris Agency (WMA-LA), 1 William Morris Pl, Beverly Hills, CA 90212 USA

Channing, Stockard *Actor*
B & B Entertainment, 1640 S Sepulveda Blvd, #530, Los Angeles, CA 90025 USA

Chantels, The *Music Group*
Creative Entertainment Associates Inc, 2201 S 21st St, Floor 1, Philadelphia, PA 19145

Chanticleer *Musician*
International Creative Management (ICM-LA), 8942 Wilshire Blvd, Beverly Hills, CA 90211 USA

Chantres, Carlos *Baseball Player*
67 Amherst St, Nashua, NH 03064-2561

Chao, Elaine L *Secretary*
Labor Department, 200 Constitution Ave NW, Washington, DC 21210 USA

Chao, Rosalind *Actor*
Don Buchwald, 6500 Wilshire Blvd, #2200, Los Angeles, CA 90048 USA

Chapelle, Dave *Actor*
United Talent Agency (UTA), 9560 Wilshire Blvd, Beverly Hills, CA 90212 USA

Chapin, Doug
9911 W. Pico Blvd, PH I, Los Angeles, 90035-2718

Chapin, Dwight L *Publisher, Government Official*
San Francisco Examiner, 110 5th St, San Francisco, CA 94103 USA

Chapin, Lauren *Actor*
11940 Reedy Creek Dr, #207, Orlando, FL 32836 USA

Chapin, Miles
9200 Sunset Blvd. #1130, Los Angeles, CA 90069

Chapin, Schuyler G *Misc*
650 Park Ave, New York, NY 10021 USA

Chapin, Tom *Musician, Songwriter*
57 Piermont Place, Piermont, NY 10968 USA

Chaplin, Alexander *Actor*
Personal Management Company, 425 N Robertson Dr, Los Angeles, CA 90048 USA

Chaplin, Ben *Actor*
London Mgmt, 2-4 Noel St, London, W1V 3RB, UNITED KINGDOM

Chaplin, Brit
345 N. Maple Dr. #300, Beverly Hills, CA 90210

Chaplin, Geraldine *Actor, Writer*
Manoir de Bau, Vevey, SWITZERLAND

Chaplin, Josephine
10 av. George V., Paris, FRANCE, F-75008

Chaplin, Kiera *Actor, Producer*
Limelight Films Inc, 8913 1/2 Sunset Blvd, W Hollywood, CA 90069 USA

Chapman, Alvah H Jr *Publisher*
Grove Harbour, 1690 S Bayshore Lane, #10A, Miami, FL 33133 USA

Chapman, Ben
300 Wai Nai Way #1612, Honolulu, HI 96815-3994

Chapman, Beth Nielsen *Musician, Songwriter*
Sussman Assoc, 1222 16th Ave S, #300, Nashville, TN 37212 USA

Chapman, Bruce K *Government Official*
Discovery Institute, 1201 3rd Ave #4000, Seattle, WA 98101 USA

Chapman, Dr Philip K *Astronaut*
416 Ives Terrace, Sunnyvale, CA 94087 USA

Chapman, Gary *Entertainer*
PO Box 25330, Nashville, TN 37202 USA

Chapman, Judith *Actor*
11670 SUnset Blvd, #312, Los Angeles, CA 90049 USA

Chapman, Kevin *Actor*
Ellen Meyer Entertainment, 8899 Beverly Blvd #616, Los Angeles, CA 90048 USA

Chapman, Lanei *Actor*
Susan Smith, 121A N San Vicente Blvd, Beverly Hills, CA 90211 USA

Chapman, Lonny *Actor*
3973 Goodland Ave, Studio City, CA 91604 USA

Chapman, Mark David
#81 A 3860 Box 149, Attica Corr. Facility, Attica, NY 14011

Chapman, Marshall *Musician*
1906 South St, #704, Nashville, TN 37212 USA

Chapman, Max C Jr *Financier*
Normura Securities, 2 World Financial Center, 200 Liberty St, New York, NY 10281 USA

Chapman, Michael J *Director, Cinematographer*
501 S Beverly Dr, #300, Beverly Hills, CA 90212 USA

Chapman, Nicki *Actor*
Pop Idol (Fremantle Media), 2700 Colorado Ave #450, Santa Monica, CA 90404 USA

Chapman, Paul
63 Oakwood Rd., London, ENGLAND, NW11 6RJ

Chapman, Rex *Basketball Player*
2248 Terrace Woods Park, Lexington, KY 40513 USA

Chapman, Robert F *Judge*
PO Box 253, Linville, NC 28646 USA

Chapman, Samuel B (Sam) *Football Player, Baseball Player*
11 Andrew Dr, #39, Tiburon, CA 94920 USA

Chapman, Steven Curtis *Musician, Songwriter*
Creative Trust, 2105 Elliston Place, Nashville, TN 37203 USA

Chapman, Thomas F *Business Person*
Equifax Inc, 1550 Peachtree St NE, Atlanta, GA 30309 USA

Chapman, Tracy *Musician, Songwriter*
Gold Mountain, 3575 Cahuenga Blvd, #450, Los Angeles, CA 90068 USA

Chapman, Wes *Ballerina*
American Ballet Theater, 890 Broadway, New York, NY 10003 USA

Chapot, Frank *Horse Racer*
1 Ople Road, Neshanic Station, NJ 08853 USA

Chapoy, Pati *Actor*
TV Azteca, Periferico Sur 4121, Colonia Fuentes del Pedregal, DF, CP 14141, Mexico

Chappell, Crystal *Actor*
35 Chestnut Hill Place, Glen Ridge, NJ 07028 USA

Chappell, Fred D *Writer*
305 Kensington Road, Greensboro, NC 27403 USA

Chappell, Gregory S (Greg) *Cricketer*
S A Cricket Assn, Andelaide Oval, North Adelaide, SA, 5006, AUSTRALIA

Chappell, Len *Basketball Player*
7624 Chestnut Lane, Waterford, WI 53185 USA

Chappelle, Dave *Actor*
Baker Winokur Ryder (BWR-LA), 9100 Wilshire Blvd Fl 6, W Tower, Beverly Hills, CA 90212 USA

Chappelle, David *Actor, Comedian*
Creative Artists Agency, 9830 Wilshire Blvd, Beverly Hills, CA 90212 USA

Chappuis, Bob *Football Player*
3115 Covington Lake Dr, Fort Wayne, IN 46804 USA

Chapuisat, Stephane *Soccer Player*
Borussia Dortmund Soccer Club, Strobeialle, Dortmund, 44139, GERMANY

Charan, Raaj N *Actor*
Shri Renuka Mandir 154, Vasudevan Nagar Jaffarkhanpet, Chennai, TN 600 095, INDIA

Charbonneau, Patricia *Actor*
749 1/2 N Lafayette Park Place, Los Angeles, CA 90026 USA

Charette, William R (Doc) *War Hero*
5237 Limberlost Dr, Lake Wales, FL 33898 USA

Charisse, Cyd *Actor, Dancer*
PO Box 1029, Frazier Park, CA 93225 USA

Charlap, Bill *Musician*
Abby Hoffer, 223 1/2 E 48th St, New York, NY 10017 USA

Charles, Bob *Golfer*
Int'l Mgmt Group, 1 Erieview Plaza, 1360 E 9th St #1300, Cleveland, OH 44114 USA

Charles, Caroline *Fashion Designer*
56/57 Beauchamp Place, London, SW3, UNITED KINGDOM (UK)

Charles, Craig *Actor*
PFD, Drury House, 34-43 Russell St, London, WC2B 5HA, UNITED KINGDOM (UK)

Charles, Daedra *Basketball Player*
Los Angeles Sparks, Staples Center, 111 S Figueroa St, Los Angeles, CA 90015 USA

Charles, Josh *Actor*
International Creative Mgmt, 8942 Wilshire Blvd, #219, Beverly Hills, CA 90211 USA

Charles, Ken *Basketball Player*
621 Putnam Ava, Brooklyn, NY 11221 USA

Charles, Nick *Sportscaster*
Cable News Network, News Dept, 1050 Techwood Dr NW, Atlanta, GA 30318 USA

Charles, Prince *Royalty, Prince*
Clarence House, Stable Tard Gate, London, SW1, UNITED KINGDOM (UK)

Charles, Suzette
2705 Cricket Hollow Ct, Hendersonville, NV 89014-1924 USA

Charleson, Leslie *Actor*
4851 Cromwell Ave, Los Angeles, CA 90027 USA

Charlesworth, James H *Misc*
Princeton Theological Seminary, Theology Dept, Princeton, NJ 08540 USA

Charlton, Janet
7560 Hollywood Blvd. #310, Los Angeles, CA 90046

Charlton, Robert (Bobby) *Soccer Player*
Garthollerton, Cleford Road, Ollerton near Knutsford, Cheshire, UNITED KINGDOM (UK)

Charmila *Actor, Bollywood*
27/1 Habibullah Road, T Nagar, Chennai, TN 600017, INDIA

Charmoli, Tony *Choreographer, Director*
1271 Sunset Plaza Dr, Los Angeles, CA 90069 USA

Charney, Jordan *Actor*
Epstein-Wyckoff, 280 S Beverly Dr #400, Beverly Hills, CA 90212 USA

Charnin, Martin *Producer, Director, Songwriter*
Richard Ticktin, 1345 Ave of Americas, New York, NY 10105 USA

Charo *Musician*
William Morris Agency, 151 El Camino Dr, Beverly Hills, CA 90212 USA

Charpak, Georges *Nobel Prize Laureate*
2 Rue de Poissy, Paris, 75005, FRANCE

Charren, Peggy *Social Activist*
Action for Children's Television, PO Box 383090, Cambridge, MA 02238 USA

Charron, Paul R *Business Person*
Liz Claiborne Inc, 1441 Broadway, New York, NY 10018 USA

Chartoff, Melanie *Actor*
Artists Agency, 1180 S Beverly Dr, #301, Los Angeles, CA 90035 USA

Chartoff, Robert *Producer*
PO Box 3628, Granada Hills, CA 91394 USA

Charuhasan *Actor*
37 Maharani Chinnamani Road, Chennai, TN 600 018, INDIA

Charvet, David *Actor*
510 18th Ave, Honolulu, HI 96816 USA

Charyk, Joseph V *Business Person*
790 Andrews Ave, #A302, Delray Beach, FL 33483 USA

Chase, Alison *Director*
Pilolobus Dance Theater, PO Box 388, Washington Depot, CT 06794 USA

Chase, Alston *Writer*
Bohrman Agency, The, 8899 Beverly Blvd #811, Los Angeles, CA 90048 USA

Chase, Bailey *Actor*
Don Buchwald & Associates Inc (LA), 6500 Wilshire Blvd #2200, Los Angeles, CA 90048 USA

Chase, Barrie *Actor, Dancer*
446 Carrol Canal, Venice, CA 90291 USA

Chase, Chevy *Actor, Comedian*
PO Box 257, Bedford, NY 10506 USA

Chase, Daveigh *Actor*
Curtis Talent Management, 9607 Arby Dr, Beverly Hills, CA 90210 USA

Chase, David *Producer*
United Talent Agency (UTA), 9560 Wilshire Blvd, Beverly Hills, CA 90212 USA

Chase, John *Hockey Player*
170 Broadway, #609, New York, NY 10038 USA

Chase, Lorraine
68 Old Brompton Rd., London, ENGLAND, SW7

Chase, Sylvia B *Commentator*
ABC-TV, News Dept, 77 W 66th St, New York, NJ 10023 USA

Chasez, Joshua Scott (JC) *Musician*
Wright Entertainment, 7680 Universal Blvd, #500, Orlando, FL 32819 USA

Chass, Murray *Writer*
New York Times, Editorial Dept, 229 W 43rd St, New York, NY 10036 USA

Chast, Roz *Comedian*
New Yorker Magazine, Editorial Dept, 4 Times Square, New York, NY 10036 USA

Chastain, Brandi *Soccer Player, Model*
1661 University Way, San Jose, CA 95126 USA

Chastel, Andre *Writer*
30 Rue de Lubeck, Paris, 75116, FRANCE

Chatham, Russell *Artist*
General Delivery, Deep Creek, Livingston, MT 59047 USA

Chatterjee, Moushumi *Actor, Bollywood*
Nibbana annexe 1st Floor, Pali Hill Bandra, Bombay, MS 400 050, INDIA

Chatterji, Basu *Actor, Bollywood, Director, Filmmaker*
Violete Villa 1st Floor West Avenue, Santacruz, Mumbai, MS 400054, INDIA

Chaudhari, Mahima *Actor*
D5 4th Floor Silver View, Versova
Andheri, Bombay, MS 400 061, INDIA

Chaudhary, Mahima *Actor, Bollywood*
D/5 4th Floor Silver View Versova,
Andheri, Mumbai, MS 400061, INDIA

Chauvire, Yvette *Ballerina*
21 Place du Commerce, Paris, 75015,
FRANCE

Chaves, Richard J *Actor*
Sharp/Karrys, 117 N Orlando Ave, Los
Angeles, CA 90048 USA

Chavez, Frias Hugo R *President*
Palacio de Miraflores, Avenida Urdaneta,
Caracas, 1010, VENEZUELA

Chavez, Julio Cesar
1 Hall of Fame Dr., Canastota, NY 13032

Chavez, Marga *Actor*
Select Artists Ltd (CA-Valley Office), PO
Box 4359, Burbank, CA 91503 USA

Chavis, Benjamin
PO Box 1661, Ellicott City, MD 21041

Chavous, Barney L *Football Player,
Football Coach, Coach*
601 Chavous Road, Aiken, SC 29803 USA

Chawla, Juhi *Actor, Bollywood*
153 Oxford Tower Yamuna Nagar,
Oshiwara Complex Andheri (W), Mumbai,
MS 400058, INDIA

Chayanne *Musician, Actor*
Chaf Enterprises, 1717 North Bayshore Dr,
#2146, Miami, FL 33132 USA

Chaykin, Maury *Actor*
Writers & Artists, 8383 Wilshire Blvd,
#550, Beverly Hills, CA 90211 USA

Chazov, Yevgeny I *Doctor*
Cardiology Research Center,
Cherepkovskaya UI 15-A, Moscow,
121552, RUSSIA

Cheadle, Don *Actor*
2454 Glyndon Ave, Venice, CA 90291
USA

Cheaney, Calbert N *Basketball Player*
Golden State Warriors, 1001 Broadway,
Oakland, CA 94607 USA

Cheatham, Maree *Actor*
Yvette Schumer, 8787 Shoreham Dr, West
Hollywood, CA 90069 USA

Chechi, Yuri
Viale Tiziano 70, Rome, ITALY, 00196

Checker, Chubby *Musician, Songwriter*
Twisted Ent, 320 Fayette St, #200,
Conshohocken, PA 19428 USA

Cheek, James E *Educator*
1201 S Benbow Road, Greensboro, NC
27406 USA

Cheek, John *Opera Singer*
ICM Artists, 40 W 57th St, New York, NY
10019 USA

Cheek, Molly *Actor*
Kazarian/Spencer, 11365 Ventura Blvd,
#100, Studio City, CA 91604 USA

Cheeks, Danyel
8033 Sunset Blvd. #851, Los Angeles, CA
90046

Cheeks, Judy
49-50 New Bond St., London, ENGLAND,
W1

Cheeks, Maurica E (Mo) *Basketball Player,
Coach*
7325 SW Childs Road, Portland, OR
97224 USA

Cheena, Manager *Actor*
No 8 Vivekanandapuram Ist Street, West
Mambalam, Chennai, TN 600 033, INDIA

Cheetwood, Derk *Actor*
Bohemia Entertainment Group, 8170
Beverly Blvd #102, Los Angeles, CA
90048 USA

Cheever, Eddie *Race Car Driver*
Team Cheever, 8435 Georgetown Road,
#600, Indianapolis, IN 46268 USA

Cheevers, Gary
905 Lewis Ogray Dr, Saugus, MA 01906-
4406

Chekamauskas, Vitautas *Architect*
State Arts Academy, Maironio 6, Vilnius,
2600, LITHUANIA

Chelberg, Robert D *General*
Cubic Applications, Patch Community,
Unit 30400 Box R65, APO, AE, 09128
USA

Cheli, Giovanni Cardinal *Religious Leader*
Pastoral Care of Migrants Council, Piazza
Calisto 16, Rome, 00153, ITALY

Cheli, Maurizio *Astronaut*
38 Via Ciro Santagata, Modena, ITALY

Cheli-Merchez, Marianne *Astronaut*
132 Rue Van Aliard, Bruxelles, 1180,
BELGIUM

Chelios, Christos K (Chris) *Hockey Player*
790 Falmouth Dr, Bloomfield Hills, MI
48304 USA

Chellgren, Paul W *Business Person*
Ashland Inc, PO Box 391, Covington, KY
41015 USA

Chelsom, Peter *Actor*
International Creative Management
(ICM-LA), 8942 Wilshire Blvd, Beverly
Hills, CA 90211 USA

Chemiakin, Mihail
Rt. 9H Box 0079, Claverack, NY 12513

Chen, Bruce *Baseball Player, Athlete*
Cincinnati Reds, Cinergy Field, 100
Cinergy Field, Cincinnati, OH 45202 USA

Chen, Da *Writer*
Writers and Artists Group Intl (NY), 19 W
44th St #1000, New York, NY 10036 USA

Chen, Edith *Musician*
Columbia Artists Mgmt Inc, 165 W 57th
St, New York, NY 10019 USA

Chen, Irvin S Y *Scientist*
University of California, Med Center,
Hematology Dept, Los Angeles, CA 90024
USA

Chen, Joan *Actor, Director*
2601 Filbert St, San Francisco, CA 94123
USA

Chen, Joie *Commentator*
Cable News Network, News Dept, 1050
Techwood Dr NW, Atlanta, GA 30318
USA

Chen, Julie *Reality TV Star*
CBS-TV, News Dept, 51 W 52nd St, New
York, NY 10019 USA

Chen, Kaige *Director*
International Creative Mgmt, 8942
Wilshire Blvd, #219, Beverly Hills, CA
90211 USA

Chen, Lincoln C *Doctor*
302 Dean Road, Brookline, MA USA

Chen, Lu *Figure Skater*
Skating Assn, 54 Baishiqiao Road, Haidian
District, Beijing, 10044, CHINA

Chen, Lynn *Actor*
International Creative Management
(ICM-LA), 8942 Wilshire Blvd, Beverly
Hills, CA 90211 USA

Chen, Robert *Musician*
Columbia Artists Mgmt Inc, 165 W 57th
St, New York, NY 10019 USA

Chen, Shui-bian *President*
President's Office, Chieshshou Hall,
Chung-King Road, Taipei, 100, TAIWAN

Chen, Steve S *Engineer*
Chen Systems Corp, 1414 W Hamilton
Ave, Eau Claire, WI 54701 USA

Chen, Xieyang
Shanghai Symphony Orchestra, 105
Hunan Road, Shanghai, 200031, CHINA

Chen, Yi *Composer*
University of Missouri, Music Dept,
Kansas City, MO 64110 USA

Chen, Zuohuang *Conductor*
Wichita Symphony Orchestra, Concert
Hall, 225 W Douglas St, Wichita, KS
67202 USA

Chenery, Penny *Misc*
20 Roberts Lane, Saratoga Springs, NY
12866 USA

Cheney, Lynne V *Government Official*
American Enterprise Institute, 1150 17th
St NW, Washington, DC 20036 USA

Cheney, Richad B (Dick) *Politician, Vice
President*
White House, The, 1600 Pennsylvania
Ave NW, Washington, DC 20500 USA

Cheney, Richard B *Vice President,
Secretary*
6613 Madison Dr, McLean, VA 22101
USA

Chenier, Phil *Basketball Player*
12121 Blue Flag Way, Columbia, MD
21044 USA

Chennault, Anna *Business Person*
TAC International, Chennault Building,
1049 30th St NW, Washington, DC 20007
USA

Chenoweth, Kristin *Actor, Musician*
Handprint Entertainment, 1100 Glendon
Ave #1000, Los Angeles, CA 90024 USA

Cher *Musician, Actor*
Lindsay Scott Management, 8899 Beverly
Blvd #600, Los Angeles, CA 90048 USA

Cher *Actor, Musician*
Goldman Grant Tani, 9100 Wilshire Blvd,
#1000W, Beverly Hills, CA 90212 USA

Chereau, Patrice *Director*
Nanterre-Amandiers, 7 Ave Pablo Picasso,
Nanterre, 9200, FRANCE

Cherestal, Jean-Marie *Prime Minister*
Prime Minister's Office, Palais Ministeres,
Port-au-Prince, HAITI

Chermayeff, Peter *Architect*
15 E 26th St, New York, NY 10010 USA

Chernobrovkina, Tatyana A *Ballerina*
Moscow Musical Theater, B Dimitrovka
Str 17, Moscow, 103009, RUSSIA

Chernov, Vladimir K *Opera Singer*
Columbia Artists Mgmt Inc, 165 W 57th
St, New York, NY 10019 USA

Chernow, Ron *Writer*
63 Joralemon St, Brooklyn, NY 11201
USA

Cherrelle *Musician*
Associated Booking Corp, 1995
Broadway, #501, New York, NY 10023
USA

Cherri, Agustina *Actor*
Telefe - Argentina, Pavon 2444
(C1248AAT), Buenos Aires, ARGENTINA

Cherry, Deron *Football Player*
4320 NE Courtney Dr, Lees Summit, MO
64064 USA

Cherry, Don S *Hockey Player, Coach*
Cherry's Grapevine, 1233 Queensway,
Etobicoke, ON M8Z 1S1, CANADA

Cherry, Eagle Eye *Musician*
39A Gramercy Parkway #1C, New York,
NY 10010

Cherry, Fred V *War Hero*
720 Dale Dr, Silver Springs, MD 20910
USA

Cherry, Jonathan *Actor*
ROAR LLC, 2400 Broadway #350, Santa
Monica, CA 90404 USA

Cherry, Neneh *Musician*
PO Box 1622, London, NW10 5TF,
UNITED KINGDOM (UK)

Cherry Poppin' Daddies
83 Riverside Dr., New York, NY 10024

Chertoff, Michael *Attorney General,
Government Official*
Justice Department, 10th St & Constitution
Ave NW, Washington, DC 20530 USA

Chertok, Jack *Producer*
515 Ocean Ave, #305, Santa Monica, CA
90402 USA

Chesney, Kenny *Musician*
PO Box 128558, Nashville, TN 37212
USA

Chesnutt, Mark
1106 16th Ave. So., Nashville, TN 37212

Chester, Colby *Actor*
Talent Group, 5670 Wilshire Blvd #820,
Los Angeles, CA 90036 USA

Chester, Raymond T *Football Player*
4722 Grass Valley Road, Oakland, CA
94605 USA

Chestnut, Cyrus *Musician*
Avenue Management Group, 250 W 57th
St #407, New York, NY 10019 USA

Chestnut, Mary Boykin *Educator*
Sweet Briar College, President's Office,
Sweet Briar, VA 24595 USA

Chestnut, Morris *Actor*
Creative Artists Agency LCC (CAA-LA),
9830 Wilshire Blvd, Beverly Hills, CA
90212 USA

Chestnutt, Mark *Musician, Songwriter*
Ladd Mgmt, 1106 16th Ave S, Nashville,
TN 37212 USA

Chevalier, Tracy *Writer*
EP Dutton, 375 Hudson St, New York, NY
10014 USA

Chevelle *Music Group*
Creative Artists Agency LCC (CAA-LA),
9830 Wilshire Blvd, Beverly Hills, CA
90212 USA

Chew, Geoffrey F *Physicist*
10 Maybeck Twin Dr, Berkeley, CA
94708 USA

Chew Jr, Sam
8075 W 3rd St #303, Los Angeles, CA
90048 USA

Cheyne, Hank
12304 Santa Monica Blvd. #104, Los
Angeles, CA 90025

Chi, Haotian *General*
National Defense Ministry, Jingshanqiq
Jie, Beijing, CHINA

Chi-Lites, The *Music Group*
Universal Attractions, 225 West 57th
Street, 5th Floor, New York, NY 10019

Chia, Sandro *Artist*
Castello Romitorio, Montalcino, Siena,
ITALY

Chiadel, Dana *Athlete*
5302 Flanders Ave, Kensington, MD
20895 USA

Chianese, Dominic *Actor*
RK Talent Management Group, 235 Park
Avenue South, 10th Floor, New York, NY
10003 USA

Chiao, Dr Leroy *Astronaut*
2108 Butler Dr, Friendswood, TX 77546
USA

Chiara, Maria *Opera Singer*
Columbia Artists Mgmt Inc, 165 W 57th
St, New York, NY 10019 USA

Chicago *Music Group*
Howard Rose Agency, The, 9460 Wilshire
Blvd, Suite 310, Beverly Hills, CA 90212

Chicago, Judy *Artist*
ACA Contemporary, 41 E 57th St, New
York, NY 10022 USA

Chiechi, Carolyn P *Judge*
US Tax Court, 400 2nd St NW,
Washington, DC 20217 USA

Chieftans, The *Musician*

Chieftans, The *Music Group*
International Creative Management
(ICM-LA), 8942 Wilshire Blvd, Beverly
Hills, CA 90211 USA

Chiffons, The
PO Box 770850, Orlando, FL 32877

Chihara, Charles S *Misc*
567 Cragmont Ave, Berkeley, CA 94708
USA

Chihara, Paul *Composer*
3815 W Olive Ave, #202, Burbank, CA
91505 USA

Chihuly, Dale P *Artist*
Chihuly Inc, 1111 NW 50th St, Seattle,
WA 98107 USA

Chiklis, Michael *Actor*
4310 Sutton Place, Sherman Oaks, CA
91403 USA

Child, Jane *Musician*
7095 Hollywood Blvd #747, Los Angeles,
CA 90028 USA

Childers, Ernest *War Hero*
13681 S 308th East Ave, Coweta, OK
74429 USA

Childress, Kallie Flynn *Actor*
Stein Entertainment Group, 11271 Ventura
Blvd #477, Studio City, CA 91604 USA

Childress, Raymond C (Ray) Jr *Football
Player*
639 Shady Hill St, Houston, TX 77056
USA

Childress, Richard (R C) *Misc*
Childress Racing, PO Box 1189, Industrial
Dr, Welcome, NC 27374 USA

Childs, Barton *Physicist*
1019 Winding Way, Baltimore, MD
21210 USA

Childs, Billy *Musician*
Integrity Talent, PO Box 961, Burlington,
MA 01803 USA

Childs, Brevard S *Misc*
508 Amity Road, Bethany, CT 06524 USA

Childs, David M *Architect*
Skidmore Owings Merrill, 14 Wall St,
New York, NY 10005 USA

Childs, Toni *Musician, Songwriter*
Geffen Records, 10900 Wilshire Blvd,
#1000, Los Angeles, CA 90024 USA

Chiles, Henry G (Hank) Jr *Admiral*
6436 Pima St, Alexandra, VA 22312 USA

Chiles, Linden *Actor*
2521 Skyline Dr, Topanga, CA 90290
USA

Chiles, Lois *Actor, Model*
Ambrosio/Mortimer, 165 W 46th St, New
York, NY 10036 USA

Chilstrom, Ken *Misc*
20 Selby Lane, Palm Beach Gardens, FL
33418 USA

Chilton, Alex *Musician*
Rick Levy Mgmt, 4250 A1AS, #D11, Saint
Augustine, FL 32080 USA

Chilton, Kevin P *Astronaut*
71 Westover Ave SW, Bolling Air Force
Base, DC 20336 USA

Chin, Tsai *Actor*
Writers & Artists, 8383 Wilshire Blvd,
#550, Beverly Hills, CA 90211 USA

Chinaglia, Giorgio *Soccer Player*
3-9-1 Via Quartara, Genoa, 16148, ITALY

Chinese, Dominic
9150 Wilshire Blvd #350, Beverly Hills,
CA 90212

Chingy *Musician*
Esterman Events, 220 Park Rd, Riva, MD
21140 USA

Chinlund, Nick *Actor*
Writers & Artists, 8383 Wilshire Blvd,
#550, Beverly Hills, CA 90211 USA

Chinny, Jayanth *Actor*
67 1st Main Road, R A Puram, Chennai,
TN 600 028, INDIA

Chirac, Jacques R *President*
Patals de L'Elysee, 55-57 Faubourg Saint
Honore, Paris, 75008, FRANCE

Chiranjeevi *Actor, Bollywood*
No. 4 Porur Somasundaram Street T
Nagar, Chennai, TN 600017, INDIA

Chishholm-Carrillo, Linda *Volleyball
Player*
17213 Vose St, Van Nuys, CA 91406 USA

Chisholm, Melanie *Musician*
Solo Agency Ltd (UK), 55 Fulham High St,
London, SW6 3JJ, United Kingdom

Chisholm, Shirley A S *Politician*
3344 Newbliss Circle, Ormond Beach, FL
32174 USA

Chissano, Joaquim A *President*
President's Office, Avda Julius Nyerere
2000, Maputo, MOZAMBIQUE

Chitalada, Sot *Boxer*
Home Express Co, 242/19 Moo 10,
Sukhumvit Road, Cholburi, 20210,
THAILAND

Chittister, Joan D *Misc*
Saint Scholastica Priory, 335 E 9th St, Erie,
PA 16503 USA

Chitty, Sir Thomas
Bow Cottage W. Hoathly, Sussex,
ENGLAND, RH19 4QF

Chitwood, Joey
4410 W. Alva St., Tampa, FL 33614

Chitwood, Joey Jr *Race Car Driver*
863 Seddon Cove Way, Tampa, FL 33602
USA

Chivers, Warren *Skier*
Vermont Academy, Saxtons River, WI
05154 USA

Chlumsky, Anna *Actor*
David S Lee, 641 W. Lake St, #402,
Chicago, IL 60661 USA

Chmura, Mark W *Football Player*
1901 E Juniper Way, Hartland, WI 53029
USA

Cho *Actor*
26-A Raja Annamataipuram, 2nd Main
Road, Chennai, TN 600 028, INDIA

Cho, Alfred Y *Engineer*
AT & T Bell Lucent Laboratory, 600
Mountain Ave, New Providence, NJ
07974 USA

Cho, Catherine *Musician*
Columbia Artists Mgmt Inc, 165 W 57th
St, New York, NY 10019 USA

Cho, Frank *Cartoonist*
Creators Syndicate, 5777 W Century Blvd
#700, Los Angeles, CA 90045 USA

Cho, Fujio *Business Person*
Toyota Motor Corp, 1 Toyotacho, Toyota
City, Aicji Prefecture, 471, JAPAN

Cho, John *Actor*
William Morris Agency (WMA-LA), 1
William Morris Pl, Beverly Hills, CA
90212 USA

Cho, Margaret *Comedian, Actor*
Cho Taussig Productions, PO Box
252097, Los Angeles, CA 90025 USA

Cho, Paul *Misc*
Full Gospel Central Church, Yoida Plaza,
Seoul, SOUTH KOREA

Choate, Jerry D *Business Person*
Allstate Insurance, Allstate Plaza, 2775
Sanders Road, Northbrook, IL 60062 USA

Choate, Tim
10100 Santa Monica Blvd. #2490, Los
Angeles, CA 90067

Chocolate Milk, PO Box 82
Great Neck, NY CA 11021

Chodorow, Marvin *Physicist, Engineer*
81 Pearce Mitchell Place, Stanford, CA
94305 USA

Choi, Yun *Actor*
Select Artists Ltd (CA-Westside Office),
1138 12th Street, Suite 1, Santa Monica,
CA 90403 USA

Chojnowska-Liskiewicz, Krystyna
Yachtsman
Ul Norblina 29 m 50, Gdansk, Oliwa, 80
304, POLAND

Chokachi, David *Actor*
11693 San Vincente Blvd, #216, Los
Angeles, CA 90049 USA

Chokkalinga, Bhavadhar *Actor*
10 Thiruvalluvar Street, M G R Nagar,
Chennai, TN 600 078, INDIA

Cholodenko, Lisa *Director, Writer,
Producer, Editor*
International Creative Management
(ICM-NY), 40 W 57th St, New York, NY
10019 USA

Chomet, Sylvain *Director, Writer*
International Creative Management
(ICM-LA), 8942 Wilshire Blvd, Beverly
Hills, CA 90211 USA

Chomsky, A Noam *Linguist*
99 Gull haven Lane, Wellfleet, MA 02667
USA

Chomsky, Marvin J *Director*
4707 Ocean Front Walk, Marina del Rey,
CA 90292 USA

Chones, James (Jim) *Basketball Player*
735 Beacon Hill Dr, Chagrin Falls, OH
44022 USA

Chong, Rae Dawn *Actor*
PO Box 691600, Los Angeles, CA 90069
USA

Chong, Thomas
1625 Casale Rd., Pacific Palisades, CA
90272

Chong, Thomas (Tommy) *Comedian,
Actor*
1625 Casale Road, Pacific Palisades, CA
90272 USA

Chopra, B R *Director, Bollywood*
B R House Juhu Tara Road, Santacruz,
Mumbai, MS 400049, INDIA

Chopra, Deepak *Writer, Doctor*
Trident Media Group LLC, 41 Madison
Ave Fl 33, New York, NY 10010 USA

Chopra, Prem *Actor, Bollywood*
144A Nibbana Pali Hill, Bandra, Bombay,
MS 400 050, INDIA

Chopra, Ravi *Director, Filmmaker,
Producer, Bollywood*
B R House, Juhu Tara Road Santacruz,
Bombay, MS 400 049, INDIA

Chopra, Uday *Actor*
Yash Raj Films Private Ltd (India), 17 Vkas
Park, Jalpankhi Society, Juhu, Mumbai,
400 049, India

Chopra, Vidhu Vinod *Director,
Bollywood, Producer, Filmmaker*
B-30 Kalpana Apartments, Sheley Ranjan
Road Bandra, Mumbai, MS 400050,
INDIA

Chopra, Yash *Director, Bollywood,
Producer, Filmmaker*
Yashraj Films, Bungalow No. 17,
Jalpankhi Soc Vikas Park Juhu Tara Road,
Mumbai, MS 400049, INDIA

Chorvat, Scarlett *Actor*
Innovative Artists, 1505 10th St, Santa
Monica, CA 90401 USA

Chorzempa, Daniel W *Misc*
Kunstleragentur Raab & Bohm,
Plankengasse 7, Vienna, 1010, AUSTRIA

Choudhury, Sarita *Actor*
William Morris Agency, 151 El Camino
Dr, Beverly Hills, CA 90212 USA

Chouinard, Marie *Dancer, Choreographer*
Compagnie Chouinard, 3981 Boul Saint-
Laurent, Montreal, PQ H2W 1Y5,
CANADA

Choureau, Etchika
9 rue du Docteur Blanche, Paris, FRANCE,
F-75016

Chow, Amy *Gymnast*
West Valley Gymnastics School, 1190
Dell Ave, #1, Campbell, CA 95008 USA

Chow, China *Actor*
Darren Goldberg Management, 5225
Wilshire Blvd #419, Los Angeles, CA
90036

Chow, Gregory C *Economist*
30 Hardy Dr, Princeton, NJ 08540 USA

Chow, Raymond
23 Barker Rd. Craigside Mansion #5B,
HONG KONG

Chretien, J J Jean *Prime Minister*
Prime Minister's Office, 24 Sussex Dr,
Ottawa, ON K1M 0MS, CANADA

Chretien, Jean-Loup *Astronaut, General*
Astronautes Direction, 2 Place Maurice
Quentin, Paris, 75029, FRANCE

Chrique, Emanuelle *Actor*
Endeavor Agency LLC (LA), 9601 Wilshire
Blvd Fl 3, Beverly Hills, CA 90210 USA

Chriqui, Emmanuelle *Actor*
Endeavor Agency LLC (LA), 9601 Wilshire
Blvd Fl 3, Beverly Hills, CA 90210 USA

Christ, Chad
9200 Sunset Blvd. #900, Los Angeles, CA
90069

Christensen, Erika *Actor*
James/Levy/Jacobson Management, 3500
W Olive Ave #1470, Burbank, CA 91505
USA

Christensen, Hayden *Actor*
PO Box 2459, San Rafael, CA 94912 USA

Christensen, Helena *Model*
Select Model Mgmt, 43 King St, London,
WC2, UNITED KINGDOM (UK)

Christensen, Kai *Architect*
100 Vester Voldgade, Copenhagen V, 1552, DENMARK

Christensen, Todd
991 Sunburst Lane, Alpine, UT 84004-1203

Christensen, Todd J *Football Player, Sportscaster*
991 Sunburst Lane, Alpine, UT 84004 USA

Christian, Christina *Musician*
Fox Television Studios, 10201 W Pico Blvd, Bldg 41, Los Angeles, CA 90035

Christian, Claudia *Actor*
Zard Productions, 8491 Sunset Blvd, #140, West Hollywood, CA 90069 USA

Christian, David W (Dave) *Hockey Player*
3501 Rivershore Dr, Moorhead, MN 56560 USA

Christian, Gordon *Hockey Player*
604 Lake St NW, Warroad, MN 56763 USA

Christian, Richard *Actor*
Select Artists Ltd (CA-Westside Office), 1138 12th Street, Suite 1, Santa Monica, CA 90403 USA

Christian, Roger *Hockey Player*
508 Carrol St NW, Warroad, MN 56763 USA

Christian, Shawn *Actor*
Burstein Company, The, 15304 Sunset Blvd #208, Pacific Palisades, CA 90272 USA

Christian, William (Bill) *Hockey Player*
502 Carrol St NW, Warroad, MN 56763 USA

Christian-Jacque *Director, Writer*
42 Bis Rue de paris, Boulogne, Billancourt, 92100, FRANCE

Christians, F Wilhelm *Financier*
Kobigsallee 51, Dusseldorf, GERMANY

Christians, The
370 City Rd., London, ENGLAND, EC1V 2QA

Christiansen, Helena *Actor*
62 Blvd Sebastopol, Paris, 75003, FRANCE

Christianson, Bob *Musician*
Working Artists Agency, 13525 Ventura Blvd, Sherman Oaks, CA

Christie, Doug *Basketball Player*
851 S Cloverdale Ave, Los Angeles, CA 90036 USA

Christie, Julianna
252 No. Larchmont Blvd. #200, Los Angeles, CA 90004

Christie, Julianne *Actor*
252 N Larchmont Blvd, #200, Los Angeles, CA 90004 USA

Christie, Julie *Actor, Model*
23 Linden Gardens, London, W2 4HD, UNITED KINGDOM (UK)

Christie, Karen
PO Box 111011, Nashville, TN 37211-1101

Christie, Linford *Track Athlete*
Nuff Respect, 107 Sherland Road, Twickenham, Middx, TW9 4HB, UNITED KINGDOM (UK)

Christie, Lou *Musician*
Lightning Strikes Music, PO Box 2172, New Hyde Park, NY 11040 USA

Christie, Tony
C.P. 162 Les Barzette, Montana-Vermala, SWITZERLAND, CH-3962

Christie, William *Musician*
Les Arts Florissants, 2 Rue de Saint-Petersbourg, Paris, 75008, FRANCE

Christine, Andrew (Andy) *Cartoonist*
King Features Syndicate, 888 7th Ave, New York, NY 10106 USA

Christlieb, Peter (Pete) *Musician*
Thomas Cassidy, 11761 E Speedway Blvd, Tucson, AZ 85748 USA

Christo
48 Howard St., New York, NY 10013

Christo (Javacheff) *Artist*
48 Howard St, New York, NY 10013 USA

Christoff, Steven (Steve) *Hockey Player*
542 Fairview Ave S, Saint Paul, MN 55116 USA

Christon, Shameka *Basketball Player*
New York Liberty, Madison Square Garden, 2 Penn Plaza, New York, NY 10121 USA

Christopher, Dennis *Actor*
BR&S, 5757 Wilshire Blvd, #473, Los Angeles, CA 90036 USA

Christopher, Gerald *Actor*
11900 Goshen Ave, #203, Los Angeles, CA 90049 USA

Christopher, Gerard
11900 Goshen Ave. #203, Los Angeles, CA 90049-6380

Christopher, Gretchen *Musician*
509 E Ridgecrest Blvd, #1A, Ridgecrest, CA 93555 USA

Christopher, Thom *Actor*
Ambrosio/Mortimer, PO Box 16758, Beverly Hills, CA 90209 USA

Christopher, Tyler
10100 Santa Monica Blvd. #2500, Los Angeles, CA 90067

Christopher, Warren
1701 Coldwater Canyon, Beverly Hills, CA 90210

Christopher, Warren M *Secretary*
1701 Coldwater Canyon Road, Beverly Hills, CA 90210 USA

Christopher, William *Actor*
Artists Group, 10100 Santa Monica Blvd, #2490, Los Angeles, CA 90067 USA

Christy, George
170 N. Carmelina Ave., Los Angeles, CA 90049

Christy, James W *Astronomer*
Hollinghead, 7285 Golden Eagle Dr, Flagstaff, AZ 86004 USA

Christy, Robert F *Physicist*
1230 Arden Road, Pasadena, CA 91106 USA

Chrysostom, Bishop *Religious Leader*
Serbian Orthodox Church, St Sava Monastery, PO Box 519, Libertville, IL 60048 USA

Chryssa *Artist*
565 Broadway, Soho, New York, NY 10012 USA

Chu, Paul C W *Physicist*
University of Houston, Center for Superconductivity, Houston, TX 77204 USA

Chu, Steven *Nobel Prize Laureate*
636 Alvarado Row, Stanford, CA 94305 USA

Chubais, Anatoly B *Government Official*
United Power Grids, Kitaigorodsky Proyezd 7, Moscow, 103074, RUSSIA

Chuck, D *Musician*
Richard Walters, 1800 Argyle Ave, #408, Los Angeles, CA 90028 USA

Chuck, Wendy *Designer*
Innovative Artists (LA), 1505 Tenth St, Santa Monica, CA 90401 USA

Chuck Wagon Gang
4408 Buffalo Ln, Joshua, TX 76058

Chulack, Christopher *Producer, Director, Writer*
Creative Artists Agency LCC (CAA-LA), 9830 Wilshire Blvd, Beverly Hills, CA 90212 USA

Chung, Connie *Journalist*
Creative Artists Agency LCC (CAA-LA), 9830 Wilshire Blvd, Beverly Hills, CA 90212 USA

Chung, Constance Y (Connie) *Commentator*
Cable News Network, News Dept, 820 1st St NE, Washington, DC 20002 USA

Chung, Mark *Soccer Player*
Columbus Crew, 2121 Velman Ave, Columbus, OH 43211 USA

Chung, Myung-Whun *Musician*
Hans Ulrich Schmid, Postfach 1617, Hanover, 30016, GERMANY

Chupack, Cindy
Trident Media Group LLC, 41 Madison Ave Fl 33, New York, NY 10010 USA

Church, Charlotte *Musician*
7 Dials Cambridge Bridge, Covent Garden, London, WC2H 9HU, UNITED KINGDOM (UK)

Church, Sam *Misc*
United Mine Workers of America, 8315 Lee Highway, #500, Fairfax, VA 22031 USA

Church, Thomas Haden *Actor*
Creative Artists Agency, 9830 Wilshire Blvd, Beverly Hills, CA 90212 USA

Church Lane, North Stoke Wallingford
ENGLAND, 0X10 6BQ

Churches, Brady J *Business Person*
Consolidated Stores, 1105 N Market St, Wilmington, DE 19801 USA

Churchill, Caryl *Writer*
Cassarotto, 60/66 Wardour St, London, W1V 4ND, UNITED KINGDOM (UK)

Chute, Robert M *Biologist, Songwriter*
85 Echo Cove Lane, Poland Spring, ME
04274 USA

Chvatal, Cynthia *Producer*
United Talent Agency (UTA), 9560
Wilshire Blvd, Beverly Hills, CA 90212
USA

Chwast, Seymour *Artist*
Push Pin Group, 18 E 16th St, #1700,
New York, NY 10003 USA

Ciaffa, Chris
627 N. Las Palmas Ave., Los Angeles, CA
90004

Cialini, Julie *Model, Artist*
PO Box 55536, Valencia, CA 91385 USA

Ciampi, Carlo A *Prime Minister*
President's Office, Palazzo del Quirinale,
Rome, 00187, ITALY

Ciampi, Joe *Coach*
Auburn University, Athletic Dept, Auburn,
AL 36831 USA

Ciampl, Joe *Coach*
Aubuin University, Athletic Dept, Auburn,
AL 36831 USA

Cibrian, Eddie *Actor*
Media Four, 8840 Wilshire Blvd Fl 2,
Beverly Hills, CA 90211 USA

Ciccarelli, Dino *Hockey Player*
1872 Clarence St, Sarnia, ON N7X 1C7
USA

Cicciolina, Via Cassia 1818
Rome, ITALY, I-00123

Ciccippio, Joseph
2107 3rd St., Norristown, PA 19401

Ciccolella, Jude *Actor*
McKeon-Valeo Management, 9107
Wilshire Blvd #321, Beverly Hills, CA
90210 USA

Ciccone, Christopher *Designer*
Bernhardt Design/Pacific Design Center,
8687 Melrose Ave, Space B230, West
Hollywood, CA 90069

Cicerone, Aldo *Musician*
Gerhild Baron Mgmt, Dombacher Str 41/
III/3, Vienna, 1170, AUSTRIA

Cicerone, Ralph J *Scientist*
University of Califomia, Earth Science
Dept, Rowland Hall, Irvine, CA 92717
USA

Cichy, Joe J *Football Player*
9806 Island Road, Bismarck, ND 58503
USA

Cid, Celeste *Actor*
Telefe - Argentina, Pavon 2444
(C1248AAT), Buenos Aires, ARGENTINA

Cienfuegos, Mauricio *Soccer Player*
Los Angeles Galaxy, 1010 Rose Bowl Dr,
Pasadena, CA 91103 USA

Cigliuti, Natalia *Actor*
Jerry Shandrew PR, 1050 South Stanley
Avenue, Los Angeles, CA 90019-6634
USA

Cilento, Diane *Actor*
Box 600, Spring Hill, Queensland, 4004,
AUSTRALIA

Cilla
5 Moorland Ave. Sale, Cheshire,
ENGLAND, M33 3FL

Ciller, Tansu *Prime Minister*
True Path Party, Selanik Cod 40, Kizilay,
Ankara, TURKEY

Cimarro, Mario *Actor*
Televisa, Blvd Adolfo Lopez Mateos 232,
Colonia San Angel INN, DF, CP 01060,
MEXICO

Cimino, Leonardo *Actor*
Michael Hartig Agency, 156 5th Ave,
#820, New York, NY 10010 USA

Cimino, Michael *Director*
9015 Alto Cedro, Beverly Hills, CA 90210
USA

Cimmo, Leonardo *Actor*
Michael Hartig Agency, 156 5th Ave
#820, New York, NY 10010 USA

Cincotti, Peter *Musician*
Vector Mgmt, 113 E 55th St, New York,
NY 10022 USA

Cinderella
9200 Sunset Blvd. #900, Los Angeles, CA
90069

Cink, Stewart *Golfer*
2747 NE 10th St, #705, Ocala, FL 34470
USA

Cioffi, Charles *Actor*
Paradigm Agency, 10100 Santa Monica
Blvd, #2500, Los Angeles, CA 90067 USA

Ciokey, Janna *Actor*
J Michael Bloom, 9255 Sunset Blvd, #710,
Los Angeles, CA 90069 USA

Cipriani Thorne, Juan Luis Cardinal
Religious Leader
Arzobispado, Plaza de Armas S/N,
Apartado 1512, Lima, 100, PERU

Circi, Cristian *Architect*
Cirici Arquitecte, Carrer de Pujades 63
2-N, Barcelona, 08005, SPAIN

Ciriani, Henri *Architect*
61 Rue Pascal, Paris, 75013, FRANCE

Cirillo, Jeffrey H (Jeff) *Baseball Player*
8305 213th Dr NE, Redmond, WA 98053
USA

Cirrincione, Vincent
151 El Camino Dr., Beverly Hills, CA
90212

Cisneros, Evelyn *Ballerina*
San Francisco Ballet, 455 Franklin St, San
Francisco, CA 94102 USA

Cisneros, Evelyo *Ballerina*
San Francisco Ballet, 455 Franklin St, San
Francisco, CA 94102 USA

Cisneros, Henry G– *Secretary*
2002 W Houslon St, San Antonio, TX
78207 USA

Citro, Ralph *Boxer*
32 N Black Horse Pike, Blackwood, NJ
08012 USA

Citron, Martin *Biologist*
Amgen Co, 152A 226 Amgen Center,
Thousand Oaks, CA 91320 USA

Citron, Ralph *Boxer*
32 N Black Horse Pike, Blackwood, NJ
08012 USA

Citterio, Antonio *Architect*
Antonio Citterio Partners, Via Cerva 4,
Milan, 20122, ITALY

Citti, Christine *Actor*
Artmedia, 20 Ave Rapp, Paris, 75007,
FRANCE

City High *Music Group*
William Morris Agency (WMA-LA), 1
William Morris Pl, Beverly Hills, CA
90212 USA

Civiletti, Benjamin R *Attorney General*
14 Meadow Road, Baltimore, MD 21212
USA

Cizik, Robert *Business Person*
8839 Hamess Creek Lane, Houston, TX
77024 USA

CK, Louis *Actor, Comedian*
United Talent Agency (UTA), 9560
Wilshire Blvd, Beverly Hills, CA 90212
USA

Clabo, Neal *Football Player*
1100 Beaverton Road, Knoxville, TN
37919 USA

Clack, James T (Jim) *Football Player*
3631 Cherry Hill Dr, Greensboro, NC
27410 USA

Claes, Willy *Government Official*
Berkenlaan 23, Hasselt, 3500, BELGIUM

Claiborne, Chris *Football Player*
5440 Wessex Court, #210, Dearborn, NI,
48126 USA

Claiborne, Craig
30 Park Place, E. Hampton, NY 11937-
2407

Claiborne, Liz
650 Fifth Ave, New York, NY 10019

Claiborne Ortenberg, Elisabeth (Liz)
Fashion Designer
Liz Claiborne Inc, 1441 Broadway, New
York, NY 10018 USA

Clampett, Bobby *Golfer*
PO Box 5849, Cary, NC 27512 USA

Clampi, Cario A *President, Prime Minister*
President's Office, Palazzo del Quirinale,
Rome, 00187, ITALY

Clampi, Joe *Coach*
Auburn University, Athletic Dept, Aubum,
AL 36831 USA

Clancy, Edward B Cardinal *Religious
Leader*
Sydney Archdiocese, Polding House 276
Pitt St, Sydney, NSW, 2000, AUSTRALIA

Clancy, Gil– *Boxer*
47 Morris Ave W, Malveme, NY 11565
USA

Clancy, Thomas J (Tom) *Writer*
1638 Lee Dr, Edgewater, MD 21037 USA

Clancy, Tom
1638 Lee Dr, Edgewater, MD 20137

Clancy Brothers
177 Woodland Ave, Westwood, NJ
07675, US

Clannad
Beverly Hills, CA 90212

Clanton, Jimmy– *Musician*
4425 Kingwood Dr, Kingwood, TX 77339
USA

Clapp, Gordon *Actor*
Paul Kohner, 9300 Wilshire Blvd, #555,
Beverly Hills, CA 90212 USA

Clapp, Nicholas R *Producer*
1551 S Robertson Blvd, Los Angeles, CA
90035 USA

Clapton, Eric *Musician*
46 Kensington Court, London, WE8 5DT,
UNITED KINGDOM (UK)

Clardy, Jon C *Misc*
Cornell University, Chemistry Dept,
Ithaca, NY 14853 USA

Clarin, Hans Joachim
Zellerhornstr. 75, Aschau, GERMANY,
D-83229

Clark, Alan *Musician*
Damage Mgmt, 16 Lambton Place,
London, W11 2SH, UNITED KINGDOM
(UK)

Clark, Anthiony *Actor*
Pinnacle PR, 8265 Sunset Blvd #201, Los
Angeles, CA 90046 USA

Clark, Anthony *Actor, Comedian*
4933 W Craig R3 #268, Las Vegas, NV
89130 USA

Clark, Archie *Basketball Player*
Wayne County Building, 600 Randolph St
#323, Detroit, MI 48226 USA

Clark, Blake
18735 Hillsboro Rd., Northridge, CA
91326

Clark, Bob *Commentator*
ABC-TV, News Dept, 5010 Creston St,
Hyattsville, MD 20781 USA

Clark, Bryan *Actor*
Epstein-Wyckoff, 280 S Beverly Dr, #400,
Beverly Hills, CA 90212 USA

Clark, C Joseph (Joe) *Prime Minister*
707 7th Ave SW, #1300, Calgary, AB T2P
3H6, CANADA

Clark, Candy *Actor*
13935 Hatteras St, Van Nuys, CA 91401
USA

Clark, Carol Higgins *Writer*
300 E 56th St, New York, NY 10022 USA

Clark, Carol Hiqgins *Writer*
300 E 56th St, New York, NY 10022 USA

Clark, Dallas *Football Player*
Indianapolis Colts, 7001 W 56th St,
Indianapolis, IN 46254 USA

Clark, Dick *Producer*
Dick Clark Productions, 3003 W Olive
Ave, Burbank, CA 91505

Clark, Doran
6399 Wilshire Blvd. #414, Los Angeles,
XA, 90048

Clark, Dwight E *Football Player*
98 Inglewood Lane, Atherton, CA 94027
USA

Clark, Earl *Swimmer*
1145 NE 126th St, #4, North Miami, FL
33161 USA

Clark, Eugenie *Biologist*
1255 N Gulfstream Ave, #503, Sarasota,
FL 34236 USA

Clark, Gene *Musician*
Artists Inlernational Mgmt, 9850
Sandaltoot Road, #458, Boca Raton, FL
33428 USA

Clark, George W *Physicist*
Massachusetts Institute of Technology,
Physics Dept, Cambridge, MA 02139 USA

Clark, Guy *Songwriter, Musician*
Keith Case Assoc, 1025 17th Ave S, #200,
Nashville, TN 37212 USA

Clark, Helen *Prime Minister*
Prime Minister's Office, Parliament
Buildings, Wellington, NEW ZELAND

Clark, Jack A *Basketball Player*
10800 E Cactus Road, #14, Scottsdale, AZ
85259 USA

Clark, James (Jim) *Business Person*
Neoteris, 940 Stewart Dr, Sunnyvale, CA
94085 USA

Clark, Joe *Prime Minister*
707 7th Ave SW #1300, Calgary Alb,
CANADA, T2P 3H6, CANADA

Clark, Joe
PO Box 96848, Washington, DC 20090-
6848

Clark, Joe *Educator*
Essex County Detention Center, 208 Essex
Ave, Newark, NJ 07103 USA

Clark, Kelly *Skier*
178 Route 100 PO Box 721, West Dover,
VT 05356 USA

Clark, Kenneth B *Psychic*
17 Pinecrest Dr, Hastings-on-Hudson, NY
10706 USA

Clark, Keon *Basketball Player*
Utah Jazz Delta Center, 301 W South
Temple, Salt Lake Clty, VT 84101 USA

Clark, Kevin Alexander *Actor*
Geddes Agency, The, 8430 Santa Monica
Blvd #200, Los Angeles, CA 90069

Clark, L Hill *Business Person*
Crane Co, 100 Stamford Place, Stamford,
CT 06902 USA

Clark, Larry *Filmmaker*
International Creative Management
(ICM-LA), 8942 Wilshire Blvd, Beverly
Hills, CA 90211 USA

Clark, Laurel B *Doctor*
2006 Town Hill Dr, Houston, TX 77062
USA

Clark, Marcia *Lawyer*
William Morris Agency (WMA-LA), 1
William Morris Pl, Beverly Hills, CA
90212 USA

Clark, Marsha(actress)
335 N. Maple Dr. #360, Beverly Hills,
XA, 90210

Clark, Mary Ellen *Swimmer*
213 Lauderdale Trail, Fort Lauderdale, FL
33312 USA

Clark, Mary Higgins *Writer*
Werimus Brook Road, Saddle River, NJ
07458 USA

Clark, Matt *Actor*
1199 Park Ave, #15D, New York, NY
10128 USA

Clark, Mel *Athlete*
PO Box 97, West Columbia, WV 25287

Clark, Monte D *Football Player*
1482 Lochridge Road, Bloomfield
Township, MI 48302 USA

Clark, Mystro *Actor, Comedian*
International Creative Management
(ICM-LA), 8942 Wilshire Blvd, Beverly
Hills, CA 90211 USA

Clark, Oliver *Actor*
House of Representatives, 400 S Beverly
Dr, #101, Beverly Hills, CA 90212 USA

Clark, Perry *Coach*
Miami University, Athletic Dept, Coral
Gables, FL 33124 USA

Clark, Peter B *Publisher*
7675 La Jolla Blvd, #203, La Jolla, CA
92037 USA

Clark, Petula *Musician*

Clark, Ramsey
36 E. 12th St., New York, NY 10003

Clark, Richard A (Dick) *Entertainer,
Producer*
Dick Clark Enterprise, 3003 W Olive Ave,
Burbank, CA 91505 USA

Clark, Richard C (Dick) *Senator*
4424 Edmunds St NW, #1070,
Washington, DC 20007 USA

Clark, Robert C *Artist*
34 Monterey Court, Manhattan Beach, CA
90266 USA

Clark, Roy *Musician*
Roy Clark Productions, 3225 S Norwood
Ave, Tulsa, OK 74135 USA

Clark, Spencer Treat *Actor*
Don Buchwald & Associates Inc (LA),
6500 Wilshire Blvd #2200, Los Angeles,
CA 90048 USA

Clark, Stephen E (Steve) *Swimmer*
29 Martling Road, San Anselmo, CA
94960 USA

Clark, Susan *Actor*
13400 Riverside Dr, #308, Sherman Oaks,
CA 91423 USA

Clark, Terri *Musician*
William Morris Agency (WMA-TN), 2100
W End Ave #1000, Nashville, TN 37203
USA

Clark, Vernon E *Admiral*
Chief of Naval Operations, HqUSN
Pentagon, Washington, DC 20350 USA

Clark, W G *Architect*
Clark & Menefee Architects, 4048 E Main
St, Charlottesville, VA 22902 USA

Clark, W Ramsey *General*
37 W 12th St, New York, NY 10011 USA

Clark, Wendel *Hockey Player*
Toronto Maple Leafs, 40 Bay St, Toronto,
ON M5J 2K2, CANADA

Clark, Wesley K (Wes) *General*
Stephens Group, 111 Center St, Little
Rock, AR 72201 USA

Clark, William N (Will) Jr *Baseball Player*
55 Tokalon Place, Metairie, LA 70001
USA

Clark, William P *Secretary*
4424 Edmunds St NW #1070,
Washington, DC 20007 USA

Clarke, Allan *Music Group, Musician*
Hill Farm Hackleton, Northantshire, NN7
2DH, UNITED KINGDOM (UK)

Clarke, Angela *Actor*
7557 Mulholland Dr, Los Angeles, CA 90046 USA

Clarke, Bob *Cartoonist*
7480 Rivershore Dr, Seaford, DE 19973 USA

Clarke, Brian Patrick *Actor*
333-D Kenwood, Burbank, CA 91505 USA

Clarke, Elis E I *President*
16 Frederick St, Port of Spain, TRINADAD & TOBAGO

Clarke, Gilby *Music Group, Musician*
Sammy Boyd Entertainment, 212 Allen Ave, Allenhurst, NJ 07711 USA

Clarke, Gilmore D *Architect*
480 Park Ave, New York, NY 10022 USA

Clarke, John *Actor*
Days of Our Lives Show, KNBC-TV 3000W Alameda Ave, Burbank, CA 91523 USA

Clarke, Kenneth H *Government Official*
House of Commons, Westminster, London, SW1A 0AA, UNITED KINGDOM (UK)

Clarke, Lenny *Actor*
8383 Wilshire Blvd #550, Beverly Hills, CA 90211 USA

Clarke, Leon
20078 Vernita Dr., Redding, CA 96003

Clarke, Martha *Dancer, Choreographer*
Sheldon Soffer Mgmt, 130 W 56th St, New York, NY 10019 USA

Clarke, Melinda *Actor*
10600 Holman Ave #1, Los Angeles, CA 90024 USA

Clarke, Michael *Music Group, Musician*
Artists International Mgmt, 9850 Sandalfoot Blvd #458, Boca Raton, FL 33428 USA

Clarke, Richard *Lawyer, Misc*
National Security Council, 1600 Pennsylvania Ave NW, Washington, DC 20500 USA

Clarke, Robert *Actor*
4509 Laurel Canyon Blvd #128, Valley Village, CA 91607 USA

Clarke, Robert E (Bobby) *Hockey Player, Misc*
1930 Glenwood Dr, Ocean City, NJ 08226 USA

Clarke, Robert L *Government Official*
Bracewell & Patterson, 711 Louisiana St #2900, Houston, TX 77002 USA

Clarke, Ronald (Ron) *Track Athlete*
1 Bay St, Brighton, VIC, 3186 USA

Clarke, Sarah *Actor*
William Morris Agency, 151 El Camino Dr, Beverly Hills, CA 90212 USA

Clarke, Sir Arthur C *Writer, Misc*
Leslie's House 25 Barnes Place, Colombo 07, SRI LANKA

Clarke, Stanley *Musician*
Agency Group, The (NY), 1775 Broadway #430, New York, NY 10019 USA

Clarke, Stanley M *Music Group, Musician, Composer*
Agency for Performing Arts, 9200 Sunset Blvd #900, Los Angeles, CA 90069 USA

Clarke, Thomas E *Business Person*
Nice Inc, 1 Bowerman Dr, Beaverton, OR 97005 USA

Clarkson, Adrienne *General, Governor*
Governer General's Office, 1 Sussex Dr, Ottawa, ON K1A 0A2, CANADA

Clarkson, Jeremy *Television Host*
XS Promotions, 57 Fonthill Rd, Aberdeen, AB11 6UQ, UNITED KINGDOM (UK)

Clarkson, Kelly *Musician, Music Group*
RCA Records, 8750 Wilshire Blvd, Beverly Hills, CA 90211 USA

Clarkson, Patricia *Actor*
Gersh Agency, 232 N Canon Dr, Beverly Hills, CA 90210 USA

Clary, Robert *Actor*
10001 Sun Dial Lane, Beverly Hills, CA 90210 USA

Clash, Kevin *Voice Over Artist*
Muppets, The, PO Box 20726, New York, NY 10023-1488 USA

Clash, The
268 Camden Rd., London, ENGLAND, NW1

Clatterbuck, Tamara *Actor*
House of Representatives, 400 S Beverly Dr #101, Beverly Hills, CA 90212 USA

Clatworthy, Robert *Artist, Misc*
Moelfre Cynghordy, Landovery Dyfed, Wales, SA20 0UW, UNITED KINGDOM (UK)

Clatyon, Barry *Voice Over Artist*
Talking Heads, 88-90 Crawford St, London, W1H 2BS, UNITED KINGDOM (UK)

Claudel, Aurelie *Model*
IMG Models, 304 Park Ave S Fl 12, New York, NY 10010 USA

Clausen, Raymond M (Mike) Jr *War Hero*
P O Box 991, Ponchatoula, LA 70454 USA

Clauser, Francis H *Educator, Engineer*
4072 Chevy Chase, Flintridge, CA 91011 USA

Clavel, Bernard *Writer*
Albin Michel 22 Rue Huyghens, Paris, 75014, FRANCE

Clavier, Christian *Actor*
Agents Associes Beaume, 201 Faubourg Saint Honore, Paris, 75008, FRANCE

Clawhammer
Box 1519, Nijnegen, NETHERLANDS, 6501 BM

Clawson, John *Basketball Player*
20 Velasco Court, Danville, CA 94526 USA

Claxton, Craig (Speedy) *Basketball Player*
Golden State Warriors, 1001 Broadway, Oakland, CA 94607 USA

Clay, Andrew *Actor, Comedian*
Artist Group International, 9560 Wilshire Blvd #400, Beverly Hills, CA 90212 USA

Clay, Andrew Dice
836 N. La Cienega Blvd. #202, Los Angeles, CA 90069-4708

Clay, Nicholas
15 Golden Sq. #315, London, ENGLAND, W1R 3AG

Clayborn, Raymond D (Ray) *Football Player*
20610 Aspen Canyon Dr, Katy, TX 77450 USA

Clayburgh, Jill *Actor*
P O Box 432, Lakeville, CT 06039 USA

Clayderman, Richard *Musician*
Denis Vaughan Management, P O Box 28286, London, N21 3WT, UNITED KINGDOM (UK)

Clayman, Ralph V *Doctor, Misc*
Bames Hospital, Surgery Dept, 416 S Kingshighway Blvd, Saint Louis, MO 63110 USA

Claypool, Lee *Music Group, Musician*
Figurehead Mgmt, 3470 19th St, San Fransisco, CA 94110 USA

Claypool, Les *Musician*
Primus/Interscope Records, 2220 Colorado Ave, Santa Monica, CA 90404

Clayson, Jane *Commentator*
CBS-TV, News Dept 51 W 52nd St, New York, NY 10019 USA

Clayton, Adam *Music Group, Musician*
Principle Mgmt, 30-32 Sir John Rogersons Quay, Dublin @, IRELAND

Clayton, Donald D *Misc*
Clemson University, Physic/Astrophysics Dept, Clemson, SC 29634 USA

Clayton, Robert N *Geophysicist, Misc*
5201 S Comell Ave, Chicago, IL 60615 USA

Clayton, Royce S *Baseball Player*
6064 E Jenan Dr, Scottsdale, AZ 85254 USA

Clayton, Thomas David *Music Group, Musician*
Music Avenue Inc, 43 Washington St, Groveland, MA 01834 USA

Cleamons, Jim *Basketball Player, Coach*
1601 1 St, Manhattan Beach, CA 90266 USA

Clearwater, Keith *Golfer*
1077 E Bretonwoods Lane, Orem, UT 84097 USA

Cleary, Beverly A *Writer*
Avon/William Morrow, 1350 Ave of Americas, New York, NY 10019 USA

Cleary, Jon Stephen *Writer*
HarperCollins, 23 Ryde Road, Pymble, NSW, 2073, AUSTRALIA

Cleary, Robert (Bob) *Hockey Player*
18 Juniper Road, Weston, MA 02493 USA

Cleary, William J (Bill) Jr *Hockey Player, Coach*
27 Kingwood Road, Auburndale, MA 02466 USA

Cleave, Mary L *Astronaut*
NASA, Earth Science Office, Code AS Room 7R86, Washington, DC 20546 USA

Cleaver, Alan *Fashion Designer*
Via Vallone 11, Monte Conero, Sirolo, ITALY

Cleaver, Vera *Writer*
5119 N 13th St, Tampa, FL 33603 USA

Cledwyn of Penrhos *Government Official*
Penmorfa Trearddur, Holyhead Gwynedd, Wales, UNITED KINGDOM (UK)

Cleese, John *Actor, Comedian, Writer*
David Wifkinson, 22 Cassius Road, St Margaret's, Middx, TW1 1RU, UNITED KINGDOM (UK)

Cleese, John Otto *Actor*
Creative Artists Agency LCC (CAA-LA), 9830 Wilshire Blvd, Beverly Hills, CA 90212 USA

Clef *Music Group, Musician*
DAS Communications, 83 Riverside Dr, New York, NY 10024 USA

Clegg, Johnny *Musician, Music Group*
Monterey International, 200 W Superior #202, Chicago, IL 60610 USA

Cleghorn, Ellen
9200 Sunset Blvd. #900, Los Angeles, CA 90069

Cleghorne, Ellen *Actor, Comedian*
Brillstein/Grey, 9150 Wilshire Blvd #350, Beverly Hills, CA 90212 USA

Cleland, J Maxwell (Max) *Senator*
340 Mockingbird Lane SE, Smyma, GA 30082 USA

Clemens, Clarence
Vineberg Communications, PO Box 205, Westhampton, NY 11977

Clemens, Donella *Religious Leader*
Monnonite Church, 722 N Main St, Newton, KS 67114 USA

Clemens, Roger *Baseball Player*
11535 Quail Hollow Lane, Houston, TX 77024 USA

Clement, Aurore *Actor*
Artmedia, 20 Ave Rapp, Paris, 75007, FRANCE

Clement F, Haynsworth Jr *Judge*
111 Boxwood Lane, Greenville, SC 29601 USA

Clemente, Carmine D *Physicist, Misc*
11737 Bellagio Road, Los Angeles, CA 90049 USA

Clemente, Fransesco *Artist*
684 Broadway, New York, NY 10012 USA

Clements, John A *Physicist, Misc*
University of California, Cardiovascular Institute, San Fransisco, CA 94143 USA

Clements, Kim *Writer*
Creative Artists Agency LCC (CAA-LA), 9830 Wilshire Blvd, Beverly Hills, CA 90212 USA

Clements, Lennie *Golfer*
1714 Monterey Ave, Coronado, CA 92118 USA

Clements, Nate *Football Player*
Buffalo Bills, 1 Bills Dr, Orchard Park, NY 14127 USA

Clements, Ronald (Ron) *Director, Producer, Writer*
Ziffren Brittenham Branca Fischer Gilbert-Lurie & Stiffman LLP, 1801 Century Park W, Los Angeles, CA 90067 USA

Clements, Ronalds F *Animator, Director*
Disney Animation, P O Box 10200, Burbank, CA 91521 USA

Clements, Suzanne *Fashion Designer*
Clements Ribeiro Ltd, 48 S Molton St, London, W1X 1HE, UNITED KINGDOM (UK)

Clements, William P Jr *Governor*
1901 N Adard St, Dallas, TX 75201 USA

Clemons, Clarence *Music Group, Musician*
Long Distance Enter, 568 E Woodbright Road #234, Boynton Beach, FL 33435 USA

Clemons, Duane *Football Player*
10510 France Ave S #203, Bloomington, MN 55431 USA

Clendenin, Bob *Actor*
Origin Talent, 3393 Barham Blvd, Los Angeles, CA 90068 USA

Clendenon, Donn A *Baseball Player*
2709 S Sandstone Circle, Sloux Falls, SD 57103 USA

Clennon, David *Actor*
2309 27th St, Santa Monica, CA 90405 USA

Cleopatra
WEA/Warner Bros Records, 330 Warner Blvd, Burbank, CA 91505

Clerico, Christian *Business Person, Misc*
Lido-Normandie 116 Bis Ave des Champs Elyees, Paris, 75008, FRANCE

Clervoy, Jean-Francois *Misc*
NASA, Johnson Space Flight Center, 2101 NASA Road 1, Houston, TX 77058 USA

Cleveland, Ashley *Music Group, Songwriter*
Street Level Artists, 106 N Buffalo St #200, Warsaw, IN 46580 USA

Cleveland, J Harlan *Diplomat, Educator*
46891 Grissom St, Sterling, VA 20165 USA

Cleveland, Patience *Actor*
21321 Providencia St, Woodland Hills, CA 91364 USA

Cleveland, Paul M *Diplomat*
989 Saigon Road, McLean, VA 22102 USA

Clevenger, Raymond C III *Judge*
US Court of Appeals, 717 Madison Place NW, Washington, DC 20439 USA

Clexton, Edward W Jr *Admiral*
1000 Bobolink Dr, Virginia Beach, VA 23451 USA

Cliburn, Van *Musician*
PO Box 470219, Fort Worth, TX 76147 USA

Cliche, Karen *Actor*

Click, Cash Money *Music Group*
JL Entertainment Inc, 18653 Ventura Blvd, #340, Tarzana, CA 91356

Cliff, Jimmy *Songwriter, Music Group*
51 Lady Musgrave Rd, Kingston, JAMAICA

Clifford, Linda *Music Group*
T-Best Talent Agency, 508 Honey Lake Court, Danville, CA 94506 USA

Clifford, M Richard (Rich) *Astronaut*
3700 Bay Area Blvd, Houston, TX 77058 USA

Clift, Eleanor
1750 Pennsylvania Ave NW #1220, Washington, DC 20006

Clift, William B III *Photographer*
P O Box 6035, Santa Fe, NM 87502 USA

Cline, Martin J *Educator, Misc*
University of California, Med Center Hematology Dept, Los Angeles, CA 90024 USA

Cline, Richard *Cartoonist*
New Yorker Magazine, Editorial Dept, 4 Times Square, New York, NY 10036 USA

Clinger, Debra *Actor*
1206 Chickasaw Dr, Brentwood, TN 37027 USA

Clinkscale, F Dextor *Football Player*
206 Machaux Dr, Greenville, SC 29605 USA

Clinton, Chelsea
15 Old House Ln, Chappaqua, NY 10514 USA

Clinton, George *Musician, Songwriter, Music Group*
Available Mgmt, 6683 Sunset Blve, Los Angeles, CA 90028 USA

Clinton, Hillary Rodham *Politician, Ex-First Lady*
15 Old House Lane, Chappaqua, NY 10514 USA

Clinton, William J (Bill) *Politician, Ex-President*
55 W 125th St, New York, NY 10027 USA

Clinton-Davis of Hackney, Stanley C *Government Official*
House of Lords, Westminster, London, SW1A 0PW, UNITED KINGDOM (UK)

Clisters, Kim *Tennis Player*
Assn of Tennis Professionals, 200 Tournament Road, Ponte Vedra Beach, FL 32082 USA

Clive, John
4 Court Lodge Chelsea, London, ENGLAND, SW3 AJA

Cloepfil, Brad *Architect*
Allied Works Architecture, 910 NW Hoyt St #200, Portland, OR 97209 USA

Clohessy, Robert *Actor*
Don Buchwald, 6500 Wilshire Blvd #2200, Los Angeles, CA 90048 USA

Cloke, Kristen *Actor*
1450 S Robertson Blvd, Los Angeles, CA 90035 USA

Clokey, Art *Cartoonist*
359 Los Osos Valley Road, Los Osos, CA 93402 USA

Cloninger, Tony L *Baseball Player*
P O Box 1500, Denver, NC 18037 USA

Clooney, George *Actor, Producer*
Creative Artists Agency, 9830 Wilshire Blvd, Beverly Hills, CA 90212 USA

Clooney, Nick
50 Crossways Park W, Woodbury, NY 11797 USA

Close, Bill *Basketball Player*
555 Byron St #409, Palo Alto, CA 94301 USA

Close, Charles T (Chuck) *Artist*
271 Central Park West, New York, NY 10024 USA

Close, Eric *Actor*
Robert Goodman Management, 9647 1/2 Olympic Blvd, Beverly Hills, CA 90212 USA

Close, Glenn *Actor*
Creative Artists Agency LCC (CAA-LA), 9830 Wilshire Blvd, Beverly Hills, CA 90212 USA

Clotet, Lluis *Architect*
Studio PER, Caspe 151, Barcelona, 08013, SPAIN

Clotworthy, Robert *Actor*
4317 Monroe Ave, Woodland Hills, CA 91364 USA

Clotworthy, Robert L (Bob) *Coach, Swimmer, Misc*
HC 74 Box 22313, El Prado, NM 87529 USA

Cloud, Jack M *Football Player*
805 Janice Dr, Annapolis, MD 21403 USA

Clough, Gerald W *Educator*
Georgia Institute of Techonlogy, President's Office, Atlanta, GA 30332 USA

Clough, Ray W Jr *Engineer*
P O Box 4625, Sunriver, OR 97707 USA

Clovers, The
Rt. 1 Box 56, Belvidere, NC 27CA919

Clowes, Dan *Artist*
Fantagraphics Books, 7563 Lake City Way, Seattle, WA 98115 USA

Club, Culture *Musician*
William Morris Agency (WMA-LA), 1 William Morris Pl, Beverly Hills, CA 90212 USA

Clyne, Patricia *Fashion Designer*
353 W 39th St, New York, NY 10018 USA

Coachman, Davis Alice *Track Athlete*
811 Gibson St, Tuskegee, AL 36083 USA

Coase, Ronald H *Nobel Prize Laureate*
University of Chicago, Law School 1111 E 60th St, Chicago, IL 60637 USA

Coasters, The
2756 N. Green Valley Parkway #449, Las Vegas, NV 89014-2100

Coates, Ben *Football Player*
5940 Londonberry Court, Concord, NC 28027 USA

Coates, Kim *Actor*
Paradigm Agency, 10100 Santa Monica Blvd #2500, Los Angeles, CA 90067 USA

Coates, Phyllis *Actor*
PO Box 1969, Boyes Hot Springs, CA 95416 USA

Coats, Dan *Senator*
1300 S Harrison St #3158, Ft. Wayne, IN 46802 USA

Coats, Michael L *Astronaut*
9128 E Star Hill Trail, Lone Tree, CO 81024 USA

Cobb, Geraldyn M (Jerrie) *Astronaut*
1008 Beach Blvd, Sun City Center, FL 33573 USA

Cobb, Henry N *Architect*
Pei Cobb Freed Partners, 88 Pine St, New York, NY 10005 USA

Cobb, Julie *Actor*
S D B Partners, 1801 Ave of the Stars #902, Los Angeles, CA 90067 USA

Cobb, Keith Hamilton *Actor*
Agency for the Performing Arts (APA-LA), 9200 Sunset Blvd #900, Los Angeles, CA 90069 USA

Cobb, Terrie
PO Box 5508, Sun City, FL 33571-5508

Cobbs, Bill *Actor*
TalentWorks (LA), 3500 W Olive Ave #1400, Burbank, CA 91505 USA

Cobert, Bob *Composer*
B M I, 8730 Sunset Blvd #300, Los Angeles, CA 90069 USA

Cobham, William C (Billy) *Music Group, Musician*
Joel Chriss, 300 Mercer St #3J, New York, NY 10003 USA

Coblenz, Walter *Director, Producer*
4310 Cahuenga Blvd #401, Toluca Lake, CA 91602 USA

Cobos, Jesus Lopez *Conductor*
Cincinnati Symphony, 1241 Elm St, Cincinnat, OH 45202 USA

Cobum, Cindy C *Bowler*
Ladies Professional Bowling Tour, 7200 Harrison Ave #7171, Rockford, IL 61112 USA

Cobum, Doris *Bowler*
130 Dalton Dr, Buffalo, NY 14223 USA

Coburn, John G *General*
Commanding General Army Material Command, Alexandra, VA 22333 USA

Cocanower, James S (Jaime) *Baseball Player*
3620 Grisham Dr, Conway, AR 72034 USA

Coccioletti, Philip *Actor*
Fifi Oscard Agency, 110 W 40th St #1601, New York, NY 10018 USA

Cochereau, Pierre *Music Group, Musician*
15 Bis des Ursins, Paris, 75004, u

Cochereau, Pierre *Music Group, Musician*
15 Bis des Ursins, Paris, 75004, FRANCE

Cochran, Anita L *Astronomer*
University of Texas, Astronomy Dept, Austin, TX 78712 USA

Cochran, Barbara Ann *Skier*
213 Brown Hill W, El Prado, NM 87529 USA

Cochran, Hank *Songwriter, Music Group*
RR 2 Box 438 Hunter's Lake, Hendersonville, TN 37075 USA

Cochran, John *Commentator*
ABC-TV, News Dept 5010 Creston St, Hyattsville, MD 20781 USA

Cochran, John *Football Player*
1249 Driftwood Dr, De Pere, WI 54115 USA

Cochran, Leslie H *Educator*
Youngstown State University, President's Office, Youngstown, OH 44555 USA

Cochran, Robert *Writer, Producer*
Agency for the Performing Arts (APA-LA), 9200 Sunset Blvd #900, Los Angeles, CA 90069 USA

Cochran, Shannon *Actor*
Stubbs, 1450 S Robertson Blvd, Los Angeles, CA 90035 USA

Cochran, Tammy *Songwriter, Music Group*
TBA Artists Mgmt, 300 10th Ave S, Nashville, TN 37203 USA

Cochran Jr, Johnnie L *Lawyer, Attorney General*
4929 Wilshire Blvd #1010, Los Angeles, CA 90010 USA

Cochrane, Rory *Actor*
Untitled Entertainment (LA), 8436 W 3rd St #650, Los Angeles, CA 90048 USA

Cockburn, Bruce *Songwriter, Music Group, Musician*
Agency Group Ltd, 1775 Broadway #430, New York, NY 10019 USA

Cocker, Jarvis *Musician, Songwriter, Music Group*
Rough Trade Mgmt, 66 Golborne Road, London, W10 5PS, UNITED KINGDOM (UK)

Cocker, Joe *Music Group*
Mag Dog Ranch, 4345 F Road, Crawford, CO 81415 USA

Cockerill, Franklin *Biologist, Misc*
Mayo Clinic, Microbiology Dept 200 1st St SW, Rochester, MN 55905 USA

Cockey, Tim *Writer*
Hyperion Books, 114 5th Ave, New York, NY 10011 USA

Cockrell, Kenneth D *Astronaut*
2030 Hillside Oak Lane, Houston, TX 77062 USA

Cockroft, Donald L (Don) *Football Player*
2377 Thomhill Dr, Colorado Springs, CO 80920 USA

Code, Arthur D *Astronomer*
University of Wisconsin, WUPPE Project Astronomy Dept, Madison, WI 53706 USA

Codey, Lawrence R *Business Person*
Public Service Enterprise, 80 Park Plaza PO Box 1171, Newark, NJ 07101 USA

Codrescu, Andrei *Writer*
Louisiana State University, English Dept, Baton Rauga, LA 70803 USA

Coduri, Camille *Actor*
International Creative Mgmt, 76 Oxford St, London, W1N 0AX, UNITED KINGDOM (UK)

Cody, Commander *Musician*
Skyline Music, Old Cherry Mountain Road, Jefferson, NH 03583 USA

Coe, Barry
PO Box 100, Sun Valley, ID 83353-0100

Coe, David Allan *Musician, Songwriter, Music Group*
783 Rippling Creek, Nixa, MO 65714 USA

Coe, George *Actor*
Bauman Assoc, 5750 Wilshire Blvd #473, Los Angeles, CA 90036 USA

Coe, Sabastian N *Track Athlete*
Starswood High Barn Road, Effingham, Surrey, KT24 5PW, UNITED KINGDOM (UK)

Coe, Sebastian
Stars Wood High Barn Rd., Effingham Leatherhead, ENGLAND, KT24 5PW

Coe, Sue *Artist*
Galerie Saint Etienne, 24 W 57th St, New York, NY 10019 USA

Coe-Jones, Dawn *Golfer*
Landmark Sports, 277 Richmond St W, Toronto, ON M5V 1X1, CANADA

Coelho, Susie *Actor*
1347 Rossomyne Ave, Glendale, CA 91207 USA

Coen, Ethan *Director, Writer*
United Talent Agency, 9560 Wilshire Blvd #500, Beverly Hills, CA 90212 USA

Coen, Joel *Director, Writer*
United Talent Agency, 9560 Wilshire Blvd #500, Beverly Hills, CA 90212 USA

Coetzee, Gerrie *Boxer*
22 Sydney Road, Ravenswood, Boksburg, 1460, SOUTH AFRICA

Coetzee, John M *Nobel Prize Laureate*
P O Box 92, Rondebosch, Cape Province, 7700, SOUTH AFRICA

Coetzer, Amanda *Tennis Player*
Octagon, 1751 Pinnacle Dr #1500, Mclean, VA 22102 USA

Cofer, J Michael (Mike) *Football Player*
4138 Brighton Lane, Southport, NC 28461 USA

Coffey, John L *Judge*
US Court Appeals, US Courthouse 517 E Wisconsin Ave, Milwaukee, WI 53202 USA

Coffey, Junior L *Football Player*
17228 32nd Ave S, Seatac, WA 98188 USA

Coffey, Kellie *Musician*
William Morris Agency (WMA-TN), 2100 W End Ave #1000, Nashville, TN 37203 USA

Coffey, Paul
633 Hawthorne St., Birmingham, MI 48009-1650

Coffey, Paul D *Hockey Player*
Phoenix Coyotes, Alltel Ice Den, 9375 E Bell Road, Phoenix, AZ 85260 USA

Coffey, Scott
143 Wadsworth Ave, Santa Monica, CA 90405

Coffin, Edmund (Tad) *Horse Racer*
General Delivery, Strafford, VT 05072 USA

Coffin, Fredrick *Actor*
Susan Smith, 121 A N San Vicente Blvd, Beverly Hills, CA 90211 USA

Coffin, William Sloane Jr *Social Activist, Religious Leader*
SANE/Freeze, 55 Van Dyke Ave, Hartford, CT 06106 USA

Coffman, Vance D *Business Person*
Lockheed Martin Corp, 6801 Rockledge Dr, Bethesda, MD 20817 USA

Cogan, Kevin *Race Car Driver*
205 Rocky Point Road, Palos Verdes Estates, CA 90274 USA

Cogdill, Gail *Football Player*
2013 SE Talton Ave, Vancouver, WA 98683 USA

Coghlan, Eamon *Track Athlete*
Int'l Mgmt Group, 1 Erieview Plaza, 1360 E 9th St #1300, Cleveland, OH 44114 USA

Coghlan, Frank (Junior) Jr *Actor*
28506 Ray Court, Saugus, CA 91350 USA

Coghlan, Frank Junior
12522 Argyle Ave, Los Alamitos, CA 90720

Coghlin, Eamonn
4 Fairway Ave., Rye, NY 10580

Cohan, Chris *Basketball Player, Misc*
Goldan State Warriors, 1001 Broadway, Oakland, CA 94607 USA

Cohan, Robert P *Choreographer*
The Place 17 Dukes Road, London, WC1H 9AB, UNITED KINGDOM (UK)

Coheleach, Guy J *Artist*
Pandion Art, PO Box 96, Bernardsville, NJ 07924 USA

Cohen, Aaron *Astronaut, Misc*
1310 Essex Green, College Station, TX 77845 USA

Cohen, Avishai *Music Group, Musician*
Ron Moss Mgmt, 2635 Griffith Park Blvd, Los Angeles, CA 90039 USA

Cohen, Larry *Director*
2111 Coldwater Canyon, Beverly Hills, CA 90210 USA

Cohen, Leonard N *Writer, Music Group, Songwriter*
121 Leslie St, North York, ON M3C 2J9, CANADA

Cohen, Marshall H *Astronomer*
California Institute of Technology, Astronomy Dept, Pasadena, CA 91125 USA

Cohen, Marvin L *Physicist*
10 Forest Lane, Berkeley, CA 94708 USA

Cohen, Mary Ann *Judge*
US Tax Court, 400 2nd St NW, Washington, DC 20217 USA

Cohen, Morris *Engineer*
491 Puritan Road, Swampscott, MA 01907 USA

Cohen, Paul J *Mathematician*
755 Santa Ynez St, Stanford, CA 94305 USA

Cohen, Rob *Director*
United Talent Agency, 9560 Wilshire Blvd #500, Berverly Hills, CA 90212 USA

Cohen, Robert *Music Group, Musician*
Intermusica Artists, 16 Duncan Terrace, London, N1 8BZ, UNITED KINGDOM (UK)

Cohen, Sacha Baron (Ali G) *Actor*
Endeavor Agency LLC (LA), 9601 Wilshire Blvd Fl 3, Beverly Hills, CA 90210 USA

Cohen, Sarah *Journalist*
Washington Post, Editorial Dept 1150 15th St NW, Washington, DC 20071 USA

Cohen, Sasha *Figure Skater*
Ice Palace, 13211 Brooks Dr #A, Baldwin Park, CA 91706 USA

Cohen, Scott *Actor*
Shelley Jefrey Assoc, 12400 Ventura Blvd, Studio City, CA 91604 USA

Cohen, Seymour S *Biologist, Misc*
10 Carrot Hill Road, Woods Hole, MA 02543 USA

Cohen, Sheldon S *Government Official*
5518 Trent St, Chevy Chase, MD 20815 USA

Cohen, Stanley *Nobel Prize Laureate*
Vanderbilt University, Medical Center 1161 21st Ave, Nashville, TN 37232 USA

Cohen, Stanley N *Biologist, Misc*
Stanford University, Medical Center Genetics Dept, Stanford, CA 94305 USA

Cohen, Steve *Actor*
William Morris Agency, 151 El Camino Dr, Beverly Hills, CA 90212 USA

Cohen, William S *Secretary, Senator*
202 Harlow St #204, Bangor, ME 04401 USA

Cohen-Tannoudji, Claude K *Nobel Prize Laureate*
38 Rue des Cordelieres, Paris, 75013, FRANCE

Cohn, Alfred (Al) *Bowler*
13918 S Clark St, Riverdale, IL 60827 USA

Cohn, Ethan *Actor*
Darren Goldberg Management, 5225 Wilshire Blvd #419, Los Angeles, CA 90036

Cohn, Gary *Journalist*
Balitmore Sun, Editorial Dept 501 N Calvert St, Baltimore, MD 21202 USA

Cohn, Marc *Songwriter, Music Group*
Creative Artists Agency, 9830 Wilshire Blvd, Beverly Hills, CA 90212 USA

Cohn, Mildred *Biologist, Physicist, Misc*
226 W Rittenhouse Square, Philadelphia, PA 19103 USA

Cohn, Mindy *Actor*
Osbrink Talent Agency, 4343 Lankershim Blvd #100, Universal City, CA 91602 USA

Cohner, Danny *Musician*
Nine Inch Nails, 63 Main St, Cold Spring, NY 10516

Coia, Arthur A *Misc*
Laborers' International Uinon, 905 16th St NW, Washington, DC 20006 USA

Coifman, Ronald R *Scientist*
11 Hickory Road, North Haven, CT 06473 USA

Cojocaru, Steven *Correspondent*
Entertainment Tonight (ET), 5555 Melrose Ave, Mae West Bldg Fl 2, Hollywood, CA 90038 USA

Coker, Larry *Football Coach*
Miami University, Athletic Dept, Coral Gables, FL 33124 USA

Cokes, Curtis *Boxer*
618 Calcutta Dr, Dallas, TX 75241 USA

Colalillo, Mike *War Hero*
3677 Riley Road, Duluth, MN 55803 USA

Colalucci, Gianluigi *Artist, Misc*
Office of Restoration, Vatican City, 00120, VATICAN CITY

Colander-Richardson, LaTasha *Track Athlete*
26 E Myrtle Dr, Angier, NC 27501 USA

Colangelo, Jerry J *Basketball Player, Misc*
Phoenix Suns, 201 E Jefferson St, Phoenix, AZ 85004 USA

Colantoni, Enrico *Actor*
11931 Hesby St, Valley Village, CA 91607 USA

Colasuonno, Louis C *Editor*
New York Daily News, Editorial Dept 220 E 42nd St, New York, NY 10017 USA

Colbert, Jim *Golfer*
222 S Rainbow Blvd #218, Las Vegas, NV 89145 USA

Colborn, James W (Jim) *Baseball Player*
2932 Solimar Beach Dr, Ventura, CA 93001 USA

Colborn, Richard *Musician*
Legends of 21st Century, 7 Trinity Row, Florence, MA 01062 USA

Cold *Music Group*
Creative Artists Agency LCC (CAA-LA), 9830 Wilshire Blvd, Beverly Hills, CA 90212 USA

Coldplay *Music Group*
Little Big Man Booking, Little Big Man Bldg, 155 6th Avenue, 6th Floor, New York, NY 10013 USA

Cole, Anne *Fashion Designer*
Cole of California, 6040 Bandini Blvd, Los Angeles, CA 90040 USA

Cole, Ashley *Soccer Player*
Arsenal London, Avenell Road Highbury, London, N5 1BU, UNITED KINGDOM (UK)

Cole, Bob *Sportscaster*
Molstar Communications, 250 Bloor St E #805, Toronto, ON M4W 1E6, CANADA

Cole, Bradley *Actor*
Peters Fraser & Dunlop (PFD - UK), Drury House, 34-43 Russell St, London, WC2 B5, UNITED KINGDOM (UK)

Cole, Dennis *Actor*
Scott Stander, 13701 Riverside Dr #201, Sherman Oaks, CA 91423 USA

Cole, Emerson *Football Player*
2142 Riverdale Square W, Columbus, OH 43232 USA

Cole, Eunice *Misc*
American Nurses Assn, 2420 Pershing Road, Kansas City, MO 64108 USA

Cole, Freddy *Music Group*
Producers Inc, 11806 N 56th St, Tampa, FL 33617 USA

Cole, Gary *Actor*
3855 Berry Dr, Studio City, CA 91604 USA

Cole, George *Actor*
Joy Jameson Ltd, 2-19 The Plaza, 535 Kings Road, London, SW10 0SZ, UNITED KINGDOM (UK)

Cole, Holly *Musician*
Alert Music, 41 Britain St, #305, Toronto, ON M5A 1R7, CANADA

Cole, John *Cartoonist*
Durham Herald-Sun, 2828 Pickett Road, Durham, NC 27705 USA

Cole, Julie Dawn *Actor*
Barry Burnett, 31 Coventry St, London, W1V 8AS, UNITED KINGDOM (UK)

Cole, Kenneth *Designer*
Kenneth Cole Productions Inc, 603 West 50th St, New York, NY 10019-9998 USA

Cole, Kimberly Lynn *Actor*
36 Longview Court, Montgomery, AL 36108 USA

Cole, Kyla *Adult Film Star*
J Stephen Hicks Photo, 13323 Washington Blvd #101, Los Angeles, CA 90066 USA

Cole, Larry R *Football Player*
953 Harwood Terrace, Bedford, TX 76021 USA

Cole, Lloyd *Musician, Songwriter*
Agency Group Ltd, 1775 Broadway, #430, New York, NY 10019 USA

Cole, Lloyd *Musician*
Supervision Mgmt, 109B Regents Park Road, London, NW1 8UR, UNITED KINGDOM (UK)

Cole, Michael *Actor*
5121 Varna Ave, Sherman Oaks, CA 91423 USA

Cole, Natalie *Musician, Actor*
Dan Cleary, 1801 Ave of the Stars #1105, Los Angeles, CA 90067 USA

Cole, Nigel *Director, Writer*
Industry Entertainment, 955 S Carrillo Dr #300, Los Angeles, CA 90048 USA

Cole, Olivia *Actor*
Century Artists, PO Box 59747, Santa Barbara, CA 93150 USA

Cole, P K
32522 Bowman Knoll, Westlake Village, CA 91362 USA

Cole, Paula *Musician*
Monterey Peninsula Artists, 509 Hartnell St, Monterey, CA 93940 USA

Cole, Robin *Football Player*
9 Brook Lane, Eighty Four, PA 15330 USA

Cole, Terry *Football Player*
743 Sanders St, Indianapolis, IN 46203 USA

Cole, Tina *Actor*
1540 Castec Dr, Sacramento, CA 95864 USA

Colella, Richard (Rick) *Swimmer*
217 19th Place, Kirkland, WA 98033 USA

Coleman, Catherine G (Cady) *Astronaut*
13619 Willow Heights Court, Houston, TX 77059 USA

Coleman, Cosey *Football Player*
11901 Northumberland Dr, Tampa, FL 33626 USA

Coleman, Cy *Composer*
447 E 57th St, New York, NY 10022 USA

Coleman, Dabney *Actor*
360 N Kenter Ave, Los Angeles, CA 90049 USA

Coleman, Daniel J *Publisher*
Popular Mechanics Magazine, 224 W 57th St, New York, NY 10019 USA

Coleman, Derrick D *Basketball Player*
Philadelphia 76ers, 1st Union Center, 3601 S Broad St, Philadelphia, PA 19148 USA

Coleman, Don E *Football Player*
424 McPherson Ave, Lansing, MI 48915 USA

Coleman, Durell
800 S. Robertson Blvd. #5, Los Angeles, CA 90035

Coleman, Gary *Actor*
4710 Don Miguel Dr, Los Angeles, CA 90008 USA

Coleman, George E *Musician*
63 E 9th St, New York, NY 10003 USA

Coleman, Holly
3579 E. Foothill Blvd. #520, Pasadena, CA 91107

Coleman, Jack *Actor*
11333 Moorpark St, #156, Studio City, CA 91602 USA

Coleman, Jospeh H (Joe) *Baseball Player*
17851 Eagle View Lane, Cape Coral, FL 33909 USA

Coleman, Lisa
3575 Cahuenga Blvd. #450, Los Angeles, CA 90068

Coleman, Marco D *Football Player*
215 Straton Trace SW, Atlanta, GA 30331 USA

Coleman, Mary Sue *Educator*
University of Michigan, President's Office, Ann Arbor, MI 48109 USA

Coleman, Ornette *Composer, Musician*
Monterey International, 200 W Superior, #202, Chicago, IL 60610 USA

Coleman, Sidney R *Physicist*
1 Richdale Ave, #12, Cambridge, MA 02140 USA

Coleman, Signy *Actor*
9200 Sunset Blvd, #625, Los Angeles, CA 90069 USA

Coleman, Vincent M (Vince) *Baseball Player*
1703 Flamm Road, Imperial, MO 63052 USA

Coleman, William T Jr *Secretary*
O'Melveny & Myers, 555 13th St NW, #500, Washington, DC 20004 USA

Coles, Kim *Actor, Comedian*
9000 Cynthia St, #403, West Hollywood, CA 90069 USA

Coles, Robert M *Psychic*
Harvard University, Health Services, 75 Mount Auburn St, Cambridge, MA 02138 USA

Colescott, Warrington W *Artist*
RR1, Hollandale, WI 53544 USA

Coley, Daryl *Musician*
Daryl Coley Ministries, 417 E Regent St, Inglewood, CA 90301 USA

Coley, John Ford *Musician, Songwriter*
Earthtone, 8306 Wilshire Blvd, #981,
Beverly Hills, CA 90211 USA

Colgate, Stirling A *Physicist*
422 Estante Way, Los Alamos, NM 87544
USA

Colgrass, Michael C *Composer*
583 Palmerston Ave, Toronto, ON M6G
2P6, CANADA

Colin, Charlie *Musician*
Jon Landau, 80 Main St, Greenwich, CT
06830 USA

Colin, Margaret *Actor*
41 Bradford Ave, Montclair, NJ 07043
USA

Coll, Stephen W *Journalist*
Washington Post, Editorial Dept, 1150
15th St NW, Washington, DC 20071 USA

Colladay, Martin G *General*
409 Dowding Court, Bellevue, NE 68005
USA

Collard, Jean-Philippe *Musician*
Boite Postal 210, Paris Cedex 09, 75426
USA

Collective Soul *Music Group*
Creative Artists Agency LCC (CAA-LA),
9830 Wilshire Blvd, Beverly Hills, CA
90212 USA

Collen, Phil *Musician*
Q Prime Mgmt, 729 7th Ave, #1400, New
York, NY 10019 USA

Collet, Christopher
8730 Sunset Blvd. #480, Los Angeles, CA
90069

Collett, Elmer *Football Player*
10 Avenida Farralone, PO Box 522,
Stinson Beach, CA 94970 USA

Collette, Buddy *Musician*
5532 S Corning Ave, Los Angeles, CA
90056 USA

Collette, Toni *Actor*
Shanahan Mgmt, PO Box 1509,
Darlinghurst, NSW, 1300, AUSTRALIA

Colley, Dana *Musician*
Creative Performance Group, 48 Laight St,
New York, NY 10013 USA

Colley, Ed *Cartoonist*
404 Holmes St, Hanson, MA 02341 USA

Colley, Kenneth *Actor*
Kenneth McReddie, 91 Regent St, London,
W1R 7TB, UNITED KINGDOM (UK)

Colley, Michael C *Admiral*
444 Magnolia Dr, Gulf Shores, AL 36542
USA

Collie, Mark *Musician, Actor, Songwriter*
Dreamcatcher Artist Mgmt, 2908 Poston
Ave, Nashville, TN 37203 USA

Collier, Don
PO Box 1269, Benson, AZ 85602

Collier, Jason *Basketball Player*
19318 Kristen Pine Dr, Humble, TX
77346 USA

Collier, Lesley F *Ballerina*
Royal Ballet, Convent Garden, Bow St,
London, WC2E 9DD, UNITED KINGDOM
(UK)

Collier, Timothy (Tim) *Football Player*
3116 50th St, Dallas, TX 75216 USA

Collingwood, Chris *Songwriter, Musician*
MOB Agency, 6404 Wilshire Blvd, #505,
Los Angeles, CA 90048 USA

Collins, Arthur D Jr *Business Person*
Medtronic Inc, 7000 Central Ave NE,
Minneapolis, MN 55432 USA

Collins, Bill *Hockey Player*
5000 Town Center, #505, Southfield, MI
48075 USA

Collins, Billy *Writer*
City College of New York, English Dept,
New York, NY 10031 USA

Collins, Blake Jeremy
4942 Vineland Ave. #200, No.
Hollywood, CA 91601

Collins, Bootsy *Musician*
Performers of the World, 8901 Melrose
Ave, #200, West Hollywood, CA 90069
USA

Collins, Brett W *Football Player*
21275 NW Rock Creek Road, Portland,
OR 97229 USA

Collins, Bud *Sportscaster*
822 Boylston St, #203, Chestnut Hill, MA
02467 USA

Collins, Clifton *Actor*
1850 Sawtelle Blvd, #450, Los Angeles,
CA 90025 USA

Collins, David S (Dave) *Baseball Player*
3000 Beal Road, Franklin, OH 45005
USA

Collins, Donald E (Don) *Baseball Player*
127 Deerwood Trail, Sharpsburg, GA
30277 USA

Collins, Douglas (Doug) *Basketball Player,
Coach, Sportscaster*
10040 E Happy Valley Road, #617,
Scottsdale, AZ 85255 USA

Collins, Duane E *Business Person*
Parker Hannifin Corp, 6035 Parkland
Blvd, Cleveland, OH 44124 USA

Collins, Eileen M *Astronaut*
2024 Pebble Beach Dr, League City, TX
77573 USA

Collins, Francis S *Misc*
National Human Genome Research
Institute, 31 Center St, Bethesda, MD
20892 USA

Collins, Gary *Actor*
William Morris Agency, 151 El Camino
Dr, Beverly Hills, CA 90212 USA

Collins, Gary J *Football Player*
221 Lamp Post Lane, Hershey, PA 17033
USA

Collins, Glen L *Football Player*
17 Autumn Park, Jackson, MS 39206 USA

Collins, Jack *Actor*
Contemporary Artists, 610 Santa Monica
Blvd, #202, Santa Monica, CA 90401 USA

Collins, Jackie *Writer*
PO Box 3717, Redondo Beach, CA 90277
USA

Collins, Jason *Basketball Player*
13120 Constable Ave, Granada Hills, CA
91344 USA

Collins, Jessica
723 Westmount Dr. #206, W. Hollywood,
CA 90069-5167

Collins, Joan *Actor*
16 Bulbecks Walk, S Woodham Ferrers,
Chelmsford Essex, CM3 5ZN, UNITED
KINGDOM (UK)

Collins, Joely *Actor*
TalentWorks (LA), 3500 W Olive Ave
#1400, Burbank, CA 91505 USA

Collins, John G *Financier*
Summit Bancorp, Carnegie Center, PO
Box 2066, Princeton, NJ 08543 USA

Collins, John W *Business Person*
Clorox Co, 1221 Broadway, Oakland, CA
94612 USA

Collins, Judy *Musician, Songwriter*
Stan Scottland Entertainment, 157 E 57th
St, #188, New York, NY 10022 USA

Collins, Kate *Actor*
1410 York Ave, #4D, New York, NY
10021 USA

Collins, Kerry *Football Player*
11403 Olde Saint Andrews Court,
Charlotte, NC 28277 USA

Collins, Larry *Writer*
La Biche Niche, Ramatuelle, 83350,
FRANCE

Collins, Lauren *Actor*
Talent Vision, 30 Glen Cameron Rd #100,
Thornhill ON, L3T 1N7, CANADA

Collins, Lewis
22 Westbere Rd, London, ENGLAND,
NW2 3SR

Collins, Martha Layne *Governor, Educator*
Saint Catheine College, President's Office,
Saint Catherine, KY 40061 USA

Collins, Marva *Educator*
Westside Preparatory School, 8035 S
Honore St, Chicago, IL 60620 USA

Collins, Misha *Actor*
S M S Talent, 8730 Sunset Blvd, #440, Los
Angeles, CA 90069 USA

Collins, Mo *Comedian*
Principato/Young Management, 9665
Wilshire Blvd #500, Beverly Hills, CA
90212 USA

Collins, Patrick *Actor*
9200 Sunset Blvd, #702, Los Angeles, CA
90069 USA

Collins, Pauline *Actor*
Michael Whitehall, 125 Gloucester Road,
London, SW7 4TE, UNITED KINGDOM
(UK)

Collins, Phil *Musician, Songwriter*
Soundtrack Music Assoc, 15760 Ventura
Blvd #2021, Encino, CA 91436 USA

Collins, Roosevelt *Football Player*
3600 Holly St, Dension, TX 75020 USA

Collins, Samuel C *Engineer*
12322 Riverview Road, Fort Washington,
MD 20744 USA

Collins, Shawn *Football Player*
2744 Preece St, San Diego, CA 92111
USA

Collins, Stephen *Actor*
12960 Brentwood Terrace, Los Angeles,
CA 90049 USA

Collins, Terry L *Misc*
PO Box 508, Okemos, MI 48805 USA

Collins, Thomas H *Admiral*
Commandant US Coast Guard, 2100 2nd St SW, Washington, DC 20593 USA

Collins, Todd F *Football Player*
1279 Collins Road, New Market, TN 37820 USA

Collinsworth, Cris *Football Player, Sportscaster*
Fox-TV, Sports Dept, 205 W 67th St, New York, NY 10021 USA

Collison, Nick *Basketball Player*
Seattle SuperSonics, 351 Elliott Ave W, #500, Seattle, WA 98119 USA

Collman, James P *Misc*
794 Tolman Dr, Stanford, CA 94305 USA

Colman, Booth *Actor*
2160 Century Park E, #603, Los Angeles, CA 90067 USA

Colmenares, Grecia *Actor*
Telefe - Argentina, Pavon 2444 (C1248AAT), Buenos Aires, ARGENTINA

Colmes, Alan *Commentator*
Conversation Co, 697 Middle Neck Road, Great Neck, NY 11023 USA

Colombini, Aldo
PO Box 7117, Thousand Oaks, CA 91359

Colombo, Emilio *Prime Minister*
Via Aurelia, Rome, 239, ITALY

Colomby, Bobby
1423 Holmby Ave., Los Angeles, CA 90024

Colomby, Scott *Actor*
Borinstein Oreck Bogart, 3172 Dona Susana Dr, Studio City, CA 91604 USA

Colon, Bartolo *Baseball Player, Athlete*
Chicago White Sox, Comiskey Park, 333 West 35th Street, Chicago, IL 60616 USA

Colon, Miriam *Actor*
51 W 52nd St, New York, NY 10019 USA

Colone, Joe *Basketball Player*
534 Carter Ave, Woodbury, NJ 08096 USA

Color Me Badd
PO Box 552113, Carol City, FL 33055-0113

Colosi, Nicholas (Nick) *Misc*
6817 54th Ave, Maspeth, NY 11378 USA

Colquitt, Jimmy *Football Player*
11722 Hardin Valley Road, Knoxville, TN 37932 USA

Colson, Charles W *Religious Leader*
Prison Fellowship, PO Box 1550, Merrifield, VA 22116 USA

Colson, Elizabeth F *Misc*
University of California, Anthropology Dept, Berkeley, CA 94720 USA

Colson, Lloyd A *Baseball Player*
PO Box 128, Hollis, OK 73550 USA

Colson, William (Bill) *Editor*
Sports Illustrated, Editorial Dept, Time-Life Building, New York, NY 10020 USA

Colt, Marshall *Actor*
333 Elm St, Denver, CO 80220 USA

Colter, Jessie *Musician*
1117 17th Ave S, Nashville, TN 37212 USA

Colton, Frank B *Inventor*
6402 N 27th St, Phoenix, AZ 85016 USA

Colton, Graham *Musician*
More Music Group, 3300 Building #305, 397 Little Neck Rd, Virginia Beach, VA 23452 USA

Colton, Lawrence R (Larry) *Baseball Player*
3027 NE 68th Ave, Portland, OR 97213 USA

Colton, Michael *Writer*
Principato/Young Management, 9665 Wilshire Blvd #500, Beverly Hills, CA 90212 USA

Coltraine, Robbie *Actor*
19 Sydney Mews, London, SW3 6HL, United Kingdom

Coltrane, Chi
5955 Tuxedo Terrace, Los Angeles, CA 90068

Coltrane, Robbie *Actor*
Inspirational Artists, PO Box 1AS, London, W1A 1AS, UNITED KINGDOM (UK)

Columbu, Franco *Misc*
2265 Westwood Blvd, #A, Los Angeles, CA 90064 USA

Columbus, Chris *Director, Producer*
1492 Pictures, 4000 Warner Blvd, Producers Bldg 3 #18, Burbank, CA 91522

Columbus, Christopher J (Chris) *Director, Writer*
Leavesden Studios, PO Box 3000, Leavesden, WD2 7LT, UNITED KINGDOM (UK)

Colunga, Fernando *Actor*
Televisa, Blvd Adolfo Lopez Mateos 232, Colonia San Angel INN, DF, CP 01060, MEXICO

Colussy, Dan A *Business Person*
20 Saint Thomas Dr, West Palm Beach, FL 33418 USA

Colville, Alex *Artist*
408 Main St, Wolfville, NS B0P 1XP, CANADA

Colvin, Jack L *Actor*
5828 Colfax Ave, #6, North Hollywood, CA 91601 USA

Colvin, Jim *Football Player*
1310 Rancho Vista Dr, McKinney, TX 75070 USA

Colvin, John O *Judge*
US Tax Court, 400 2nd St NW, Washington, DC 20217 USA

Colvin, Les *Hockey Player*
62 Foxhunt Trail, Courtice, ON L1E 2E4 USA

Colvin, Shawn *Musician, Songwriter*
AGF Entertainment, 30 W 21 St, #700, New York, NY 10010 USA

Colwell, John A *Physicist*
American Diabetes Assn, 1701 N Beauregard St, Alexandria, VA 22311 USA

Colwell, Rita R *Misc, Biologist*
5110 River Hill Road, Bethesda, MD 20816 USA

Comaneci, Nadia *Gymnast*
4421 Hidden Hill Road, Norman, OK 73072 USA

Combes, Willard W *Cartoonist*
1266 Oakridge Dr, Cleveland, OH 44121 USA

Combs, Edwin *Basketball Player*
4103 Shadybrook Dr, Midwest City, OK 73110 USA

Combs, Glenn *Basketball Player*
3627 Dogwood Lane SW, Roanoke, VA 24015 USA

Combs, Holly Marie *Actor*
Gersh Agency, 232 N Canon Dr, Beverly Hills, CA 90210 USA

Combs, Jeffrey *Actor*
1875 Century Park E, #2250, Los Angeles, CA 90067 USA

Combs, Patrick D (Pat) *Baseball Player*
2219 Spanish Forest Lane, Richmond, TX 77469 USA

Combs (P Diddy - Puff Daddy), Sean John *Musician, Producer*
Bad Boy Worldwide Entertainment, 1540 Broadway Fl 30, New York, NY 10036 USA

Comeau, Andy *Actor*
Creative Artists Agency, 9830 Wilshire Blvd, Beverly Hills, CA 90212 USA

Comegys, Dallas *Basketball Player*
73 Water St, Park Forest, IL 60466 USA

Comer, Anjanette *Actor*
Dade/Schultz, 6442 Coldwater Canyon Ave, #206, Valley Green, CA 91606 USA

Comer, James P *Psychic*
Yale University, Child Study Center, 230 S Frontage Road, New Haven, CT 06519 USA

Comess, Aaron *Musician*
DAS Communications, 83 Riverside Dr, New York, NY 10024 USA

Comfort, Brad
PO Box 715, Mercer Island, WA 98040

Comi, Paul *Actor*
2395 Ridgeway Road, San Marino, CA 91108 USA

Comissiona, Sergiu *Conductor*
Helsinki Philharmonic, Karamzininkatu 4, Helsinki, 00100, FINLAND

Commodores, The
1920 Benson Ave., St. Paul, MN 55116

Common *Music Group, Artist*
Artistic Control Management Inc, 685 Lambert Dr NE, Atlanta, GA 30324 USA

Commoner, Barry *Misc*
Queens College, Biology of Natural Systems Center, Flushing, NY 11367 USA

Compagnonl, Deborah *Skier*
Via Frodonfo 3, Santa Catarina Valfurna, 2303, ITALY

Compaore, Blaise *President*
President's Office, Boile Postale 7031, Ouagadougou, BURKINA FASO

Compte, Maurice *Actor*
PMK/HBH Public Relations (PMK-LA), 8500 Wilshire Blvd #700, Beverly Hills, CA 90211 USA

Compton, Ann Woodruff *Commentator*
ABC-TV, News Dept, 5010 Creston St, Hyattsville, MD 20781 USA

Compton, Denis C S *Cricketer*
Sunday Express, 245 Blackfriars Road, London, SE1 9UX, UNITED KINGDOM (UK)

Compton, Forrest *Actor*
CunninghamEscottDipene, 257 Park Ave S, #900, New York, NY 10010 USA

Compton, John G M *Prime Minister*
PO Box 149, Castries, SAINT LUCIA

Compton, Richard *Actor*
Agency for Performing Arts, 9200 Sunset Blvd, #900, Los Angeles, CA 90069 USA

Conacher, Brian *Hockey Player*
120-10 Walder Ave, Toronto, ON M4V 1G2, CANADA

Conant, Kenneth J *Archaeologist*
3 Carlton Village, #T105, Bedford, MA 01730 USA

Conant, Sean *Actor*
Rising Picture, PO Box 2, North Hampton, NH 03862 USA

Conaway, Christi
334 Huntley, Los Angeles, CA 90048-1919

Conaway, Cristi *Actor*
423 Westbourne Dr, West Hollywood, CA 90048 USA

Conaway, Jeff *Actor*
Sharp/Karrys, 117 N Orlando Ave, Los Angeles, CA 90048 USA

Concannon Jr, John J (Jack) *Football Player*
11 Berlin St, Wollaston, MA 02170 USA

Concepcion, David I (Davey) *Baseball Player, Athlete*
Urbanizacion Los Caobos Botalon 5D, 5 Piso, Maracay, Venezuela

Concepion, David I (Davey) *Baseball Player*
Urb Los Caobos Botalon 5D, 5-Piso-Maracay, VENEZUELA

Conde, Ninel *Actor*
Gabriel Blanco Iglesias (Mexico), Rio Balsas 35-32, Colonia Cuauhtemoc, DF, 06500, Mexico

Condit, Philip M *Business Person*
Boeing Co, PO Box 3707, Seattle, WA 98124 USA

Condon, Bill *Director, Writer*
Agency for Performing Arts, 9200 Sunset Blvd, #900, Los Angeles, CA 90069 USA

Condon, Jill *Producer, Writer*
United Talent Agency (UTA), 9560 Wilshire Blvd, Beverly Hills, CA 90212 USA

Condon, Paul *Lawyer*
Metropolitan Police, New Scottland Yard Broadway, London, SW1H 0BG, UNITED KINGDOM (UK)

Condron, Christopher M *Financier*
Melton Financial Corp, Mellon Bank Center, 500 Grant St, Pittsburgh, PA 15258 USA

Cone, David
303 E. 83rd St. #6A, New York, NY 10028

Cone, David B *Baseball Player*
16 Hurlingham Dr, Greenwich, CT 06813 USA

Cone Vanderbush, Carin *Swimmer*
116 Washington Road, #B, West Point, NY 10996 USA

Confederate Railroad
ll8 16th Ave. So. #201, Nashville, TN 37203-3104

Confessional, Dashboard *Musician*
Ellis Industries Inc., 234 Shoreward Dr., Great Neck, NY 11021

Conforti, Gino *Actor*
Orange Gove Group, 12178 Ventura Blvd, #205, Studio City, CA 91604 USA

Conger, Harry M *Business Person*
Homestake Mining Co, 650 California St, San Francisco, CA 94108 USA

Conkey, Margaret *Archaeologist*
University of California, Archaeological Research Facility, Berkeley, CA 94720 USA

Conlan, Shane P *Football Player*
428 Oliver Road, Sewickley, PA 15143 USA

Conlee, John *Musician*
John Conlee Enterprises, 38 Music Square East, #117, Nashville, TN 37203 USA

Conley, Clare D *Editor*
Hemlock Farms, Hawley, PA 18428 USA

Conley, D Eugene (Gene) *Baseball Player, Basketball Player*
2105 Grafton Ave, Clermont, FL 34711 USA

Conley, Darlene *Actor*
1840 S Beverly Glen Blvd, #501, Los Angeles, CA 90025 USA

Conley, Earl Thomas *Songwriter, Musician*
657 Baker Road, Smyrna, TN 37167 USA

Conley, Gene
1 Farrington St., Foxboro, MA 02035

Conley, Jill
10332 Christine Pl, Chatsworth, CA 91311

Conley, Joe *Actor*
PO Box 6487, Thousand Oaks, CA 91359 USA

Conley, Michael (Mike) *Track Athlete*
University of Arkansas, Athletic Dept, Fayetteville, AR 72701 USA

Conlin, Michaela *Actor*
Evolution Entertainment, 901 N Highland Ave, Los Angeles, CA 90038 USA

Conlon, James J
Shuman Assoc, 120 W 58th St, #8D, New York, NY 10019 USA

Conn, Didi *Actor, Musician*
1901 Ave of the Stars, #1450, Los Angeles, CA 90067 USA

Conn, Terri *Actor*
1268 E 14th St, Brooklyn, NY 11230 USA

Conneff, Kevin *Musician*
Macklam Feldman Mgmt, 1505 W 2nd Ave, #200, Vancouver, BC V6H 3Y4, CANADA

Connell, Desmond Cardinal *Religious Leader*
Archbishop's House, Drumcondra, Dublin, 9, IRELAND

Connell, Elizabeth *Opera Singer*
I M G Artists, 3 Burlingtone Lane, Chiswick, London, W4 2TH, UNITED KINGDOM (UK)

Connell, Evan S Jr *Writer*
Fort Macy 13, 320 Artist Road, Santa Fe, NM 87501 USA

Connell, Jane
905 West End Ave., New York, NY 10025

Connell, Thurman C *Financier*
Federal Home Loan Bank, 907 Walnut St, Des Moines, IA 50309 USA

Connelly, Jennifer *Actor*
International Creative Management (ICM-LA), 8942 Wilshire Blvd, Beverly Hills, CA 90211 USA

Connelly, Michael *Writer*
Little Brown, 3 Center Plaza, Boston, MA 02108 USA

Conner, Bart *Gymnast*
4421 Hidden Hill Road, Norman, OK 73072 USA

Conner, Bruce *Artist*
45 Sussex St, San Francisco, CA 94131 USA

Conner, Chris *Actor*
9 Yards Entertainment, 8530 Wilshire Blvd Fl 5, Beverly Hills, CA 90211 USA

Conner, Dennis
1011 Anchorage Lane, San Diego, CA 92106

Conner, Lester *Basketball Player*
45 Kings Way, #8, Waltham, MA 02451 USA

Connery, Jason *Actor*
David Shapira, 15821 Ventura Blvd, #235, Encino, CA 91436 USA

Connery, Sean *Actor*
Nancy Seltzer, 6220 Del Valle Dr, Los Angeles, CA 90048 USA

Connery, Vincent L *Misc*
National Treasury Employees Union, 1730 K St NW, Washington, DC 20006 USA

Connes, Alain *Mathematician*
Leon Motchane I'HES, 35 Route Chartres, Bures-sur-Yvette, 91440, FRANCE

Connick Jr, Harry *Musician, Actor*
Wilkins Mgmt, 323 Broadway, Cambridge, MA 02139 USA

Conniff, Cal *Skier*
157 Pleasantview Ave, Longrneadow, MA 01106 USA

Connolly, Billy *Actor*
Tickety-Boo Ltd, Boathouse, Crabtree Lane, London, SW6 6LU, UNITED KINGDOM (UK)

Connolly, Kevin *Actor*
Ramaker Management, 400 North Gardner Street, Los Angeles, CA 90036 USA

Connolly, Olga Fikotova *Track Athlete*
4561 Montair Ave, #D10, Long Beach, CA 90808 USA

Connor, Chris *Musician*
Maxine Harvard Unlimited, 7942 W Bell Road, #C5, Glendale, AZ 85308 USA

Connor, Christopher M *Business Person*
Sherwin-Williams Co, 101 W Prospect Ave, Clveland, OH 44115 USA

Connor, Joseph E *Business Person, Government Official*
Under-Secretary General's Office, United Nations, UN Plaza, New York, NY 10021 USA

Connor, Kenneth *Actor*
Peter Rogers Productions, Pinewood Films, Iver Heath, SLO 0NH, UNITED KINGDOM (UK)

Connor, Patrick
3 Spring Bank, New Mills nr. Stockport, ENGLAND, SK12 4AS

Connor, Ralph *Misc*
9866 Highwood Court, Sun City, AZ 85373 USA

Connor, Richard L *Publisher*
Fort Worth Star-Telegram, 400 W 7th St, Fort Worth, TX 76102 USA

Connor, Shannon *Model*
4 Rockage Rd, Warren, NJ 07059

Connors, Carol *Songwriter*
1709 Ferrari Dr, Beverly Hills, CA 90210 USA

Connors, James S (Jimmy) *Tennis Player*
1962 E Valley Rd, Santa Barbara, CA 93108 USA

Connors, Mike *Actor*
4810 Louise Ave, Encino, CA 91316 USA

Connway, Craig *Business Person*
PeopleSoft Inc, 4460 Hacienda Dr, Pleasanton, CA 94588 USA

Conombo, Joseph I *Prime Minister*
2003 Ave de la Liberte, BP 613, Dadoya, Ouagadougou, BURKINA FASO

Conover, Lloyd H *Inventor*
27 Old Barry Road, Quaker Hill, CT 06375 USA

Conoway, Christi
PO Box 46515, Los Angeles, CA 90046

Conrad, Barnaby
3530 Pine Valley Dr., Sarasota, FL 34239

Conrad, David *Actor*
Industry Entertainment, 955 Carillo Dr, #300, Los Angeles, CA 90048 USA

Conrad, Eve Burch
23388 Mulholland Dr., Woodland Hills, CA 91364

Conrad, Fred *Photographer*
New York Times, Editorial Dept, 229 W 43rd St, New York, NY 10036 USA

Conrad, James A *Financier*
Source One Mortgage, 27555 Famington Road, Famington Hills, MI 48334 USA

Conrad, Kimberly
10236 Charing Cross Rd, Los Angeles, CA 90077

Conrad, Paul
28649 Crestridge Rd, Palos Verdes, CA 90274

Conrad, Paul F *Cartoonist*
28649 Crestridge Road, Palos Verdes Estates, CA 90275 USA

Conrad, Robert *Actor*
PO Box 5237, Bear Valley, CA 95223 USA

Conrad, Shane
9255 Sunset Blvd. #620, Los Angeles, CA 90069

Conradt, Jody *Coach*
9614 Leaning Rock Circle, Austin, TX 78730 USA

Conran, Jasper A T *Fashion Designer*
Jasper Conran Ltd, 2 Munden St, London, W14 0RH, UNITED KINGDOM (UK)

Conran, Philip J *War Hero*
4706 Calle Reina, Santa Barbara, CA 93110 USA

Conran, Terence O *Designer*
22 SHad Thames, London, SE1 2YU, UNITED KINGDOM (UK)

Conroy, D Patrick (Pat) *Writer*
Houghton Mifftin, 222 Berkeley St, #700, Boston, MA 02116 USA

Conroy, Frances *Actor*
International Creative Mgmt, 8942 Wilshire Blvd, #219, Beverly Hills, CA 90211 USA

Conroy, Kevin
9301 Wilshire Blvd. #312, Beverly Hills, CA 90210-5410

Conroy, Pat *Writer*
5053 Ocean Blvd, #134, Sarasota, FL 34242 USA

Conroy, Patricia
PO Box 1770, Hendersonville, TN 37077

Consagra, Pietro *Artist*
Via Cassia, Rome, 1162, ITALY

Conseco, Jose
5601 Collins Ave #CU1, Miami Beach, FL 33140-2415

Considine, John *Actor*
16 1/2 Red Coal Lane, Greenwich, CT 06830 USA

Considine, Tim *Actor*
3708 Mountain View Ave, Los Angeles, CA 90066 USA

Constable, George *Editor*
Time-Life Books, Editorial Dept, Rockefekker Center, New York, NY 10020 USA

Constantin, Michel
17 blvd. Bartole Beauvallon, St. Maxime, FRANCE, 83120

Constantine, ex-King
4 Linnell Dr.Hampstead Way, London, ENGLAND, NW11

Constantine, Kevin
5928 Jenny Lind Ct., San Jose, CA 95120

Constantine, Michael *Actor*
1604 Bern St, Reading, PA 19604 USA

Constantine II *King*
4 Linnell Dr, Hampstead Way, London, NW11, UNITED KINGDOM (UK)

Consuegra, Sandalio S C (Sandy) *Baseball Player*
3255 W Flagler St, #14, Miami, FL 33135 USA

Consuelos, Mark *Actor*
646 Juniper Place, Franklin Lakes, NJ 07417 USA

Conte, Dino
2325 Fox Hills Dr, Los Angeles, CA 49006 USA

Conte, John *Actor*
75600 Beryl Dr, Indian Wells, CA 92210 USA

Conte, Lansana *President*
President's Office, Conakry, GUINEA

Conte, Lou *Choreographer*
Hubbard Street Dance Co, 1147 W Jackson Blvd, Chicago, IL 60607 USA

Conti, Al
Box 701, Portsmouth, RI 02871

Conti, Bill *Composer*
117 Fremont Place W, Los Angeles, CA 90005 USA

Conti, Tom *Actor*
Chatto & Linnit, Prince of Wales Coventry St, London, W1V 7FE, UNITED KINGDOM(UK)

Contino, Dick *Musician, Music Group*
3355 Nahatan Way, Las Vegas, NV 89109 USA

Contner, James A *Cinematographer*
4146 Ventura Canyon Ave, Sherman Oaks, CA 91423 USA

Contours, The
1161 NW 76th Ave., Ft. Lauderdale, FL 33322

Contreras, Jose *Baseball Player, Athlete*
New York Yankees, Yankee Stadium, 161st Street & River Avenue, Bronx, NY 10451 USA

Converse, Frank *Actor*
Artists Group, 10100 Santa Monica Blvd #2490, Los Angeles, CA 90067 USA

Converse-Roberts, William *Actor*
Innovative Artists, 1505 10th St, Santa Monica, CA 90401 USA

Conway, Billy *Music Group, Musician*
Creative Performance Group, 48 Laight St, New York, NY 10013 USA

Conway, Curtis
27110 Pacific Heights Dr., San Juan Capistrano, CA 92692-5035

Conway, Curtis L *Football Player*
250 Washington Road, Lake Forest, IL 60045 USA

Conway, Gary *Actor*
11240 Chimney Rock Rd, Paso Robles, CA 93446 USA

Conway, James *General*
Commanding General I Marine Expeditionary Force, Camp Pendleton, CA 92055 USA

Conway, James L *Director*
Creative Artists Agency, 9830 Wilshire Blvd, Beverly Hills, CA 90212 USA

Conway, Jill K *Historian*
65 Commonwealth Ave #8B, Boston, MA 02116 USA

Conway, John Horton *Mathematician, Writer*
Princeton Univesity, Mathematics Dept Fine Hall, Princeton, NJ 08544 USA

Conway, John W *Business Person*
Crown Cork & Seal, 1 Crown Way, Philadelphia, PA 19154 USA

Conway, Kevin *Actor*
25 CenturyPark W, New York, NY 10023
USA

Conway, Rob *Wrestler*
World Wrestling Entertainment (WWE),
1241 E Main St, Stamford, CT 06905 USA

Conway, Tim *Actor, Comedian*
Tim Conway Enterprises, P O Box 17047,
Ensino, CA 91416 USA

Conwell, Easther M *Physicist*
800 Philips Road, Webster, NY 14580
USA

Conwell, Tommy *Music Group, Musician*
Brothers Mgmt, 141 Dunbar Ave, Fords,
NJ 08863 USA

Coobar, Abdulmegid *Prime Minister*
Asadu El-Furat St 29, Garden City, Tripoli,
LIBYA

Cooder, Ry *Musician, Music Group,
Composer*
326 Entrada Dr, Santa Monica, CA 90402
USA

Coody, Charles *Golfer*
Int'l Mgmt Group, 1 Erieview Plaza, 1360
E 9th St #1300, Cleveland, OH 44114
USA

Coogan, Dodie
PO Box 413, Palm Springs, CA 92263

Coogan, Keith *Actor*
1640 S Sepulveda Blvd #218, Los
Angeles, CA 90025 USA

Coogan, Richard
5805 Whitsett Ave. #103, No. Hollywood,
CA 91607

Cook, A J *Actor*
United Talent Agency (UTA), 9560
Wilshire Blvd, Beverly Hills, CA 90212
USA

Cook, Ann T
5412 Riverhills Dr, Temple Terrace, FL
33617 USA

Cook, Barbara *Actor, Music Group*
Abby Hoffer, 223 1/2 E 48th St, New
York, NY 10017 USA

Cook, Beryl *Artist*
Coach House 1A Camp Road Clifton,
Bristol, BS8 3LW, UNITED
KINGDOM(UK)

Cook, Brian *Basketball Player*
Los Angeles Lakers, Staples Center 1111 S
Figueroa St, Los Angeles, CA 90015 USA

Cook, Carole *Actor, Comedian*
8829 Ashcroft Ave, West Hollywood, CA
90048 USA

Cook, Dane *Actor*
New Wave Entertainment (LA), 2660 W
Olive Blvd, Burbank, CA 91505 USA

Cook, Donald G *General*
Commander Air Education/Training
Command, Randolph Air Force Base, t

Cook, Donald G *General*
Commander Air Education/Training
Command, Randolph Air Force Base, TX
78155 USA

Cook, Emily *Writer*
Lloyd and Kass Entertainment, 10202 W
Washington Blvd, Bldg Astaire 2210,
Culver City, CA 90232 USA

Cook, Fielder
180 Central Park So, New York, NY
10019

Cook, Jason *Actor*
Coast to Coast Talent Group, 3350
Barham Blvd, Los Angeles, CA 90068
USA

Cook, Jeffrey A (Jeff) *Music Group,
Musician*
P O Box 35967, Fort Payne, AL 35967
USA

Cook, John *Golfer*
1111 Tahquitz E #203, Palm Springs, CA
92262 USA

Cook, Judy *Bowler*
Ladies Professional Bowling Tour, 7200
Harrison Ave #7171, Rockford, IL 61112
USA

Cook, Leigh
9560 Wilshire Blvd. #516, Beverly Hills,
CA 90212

Cook, Paul *Music Group, Musician*
Solo Agency, 55 Fulham High St, London,
SW6 3JJ, UNITED KINGDOM(UK)

Cook, Paul M *Business Person*
SRI International, 333 Ravenswood Ave,
Mento Park, CA 94025 USA

Cook, Peter F C *Architect*
54 Compayne Gardens, London, NW6
3RY, UNITED KINGDOM(UK)

Cook, Rachael Leigh (Lee) *Actor*
Anonymous Content, 8522 National Blvd
#101, Culver City, CA 90232 USA

Cook, Rachel Leigh *Actor*
Moongate Mgmt, 4570 Van Nuys Blvd
#171, Sherman Oaks, CA 91403 USA

Cook, Richard *Scientist*
Jet Propulsion Laboratory, 4800 Oak
Grove Dr, Pasadena, CA 91109 USA

Cook, Robert *Opera Singer*
Quavers 53 Friars Ave, Fiem Barnet,
London, N2O OXG, UNITED
KINGDOM(UK)

Cook, Robert F (Robin) *Government
Official*
House of Commons, Westminster,
London, SW1A 0AA, UNITED
KINGDOM(UK)

Cook, Robin *Writer*
4601 Gulf Shore Blvd #P4, Naples, FL
33940 USA

Cook, Stanton R *Publisher*
224 Raleigh Road, Kenitworth, IL 60043
USA

Cook, Steve *Bowler*
1209 Devonshire Court, Roseville, CA
95661 USA

Cook, Thomas A *Writer*
Bantam Books, 1540 Broadway, New
York, NY 10036 USA

Cooke, Howard F H *General, Governor*
King's House Hope Road, Kingston, 10,
JAMAICA

Cooke, Janis *Journalist*
Washington Post, 1150 15th St NW,
Washington, DC 20017 USA

Cooke, John P *Misc*
290 Branchville Road, Ridgefield, CT
06877 USA

Cooksey, Danny
9300 Wilshire Blvd. #410, Beverly Hills,
CA 90212

Cooksey, Dave *Religious Leader*
Brethren Church, 524 College Ave,
Ashland, OH 44805 USA

Cooksey, Patty *Athlete*
c/oChurchill Downs, Race Office, 700
Central Avenue, Lousiville, KY 40208

Cookson, Peter
30 Norfolk Rd., Southfield, MA 01259

Cool Breeze
PO Box 470642, San Francisco, CA
94147-0642

Cooley, Denton *Doctor, Misc*
3014 Del Monte Dr, Houston, TX 77019
USA

Cooley, Ryan *Actor*
Noble Caplan Agency, 1260 Yonge St Fl
2, Toronto ON, M4T 1W6, CANADA

Coolidge, Charles H *War Hero*
1054 Balmoral Dr, Signal Mountain, TN
37377 USA

Coolidge, Charles H Jr *General*
Vice CinC Air Force Material Command,
Wright-Patterson Air Force Base, OH
45433 USA

Coolidge, Harold J *Misc*
38 Standley St, Beverly, MA 01915 USA

Coolidge, Jennifer *Actor*
Gersh Agency, The (LA), 232 N Canon Dr,
Beverly Hills, CA 90210 USA

Coolidge, Martha *Director*
760 N La Cienega Blvd, Los Angeles, CA
90069 USA

Coolidge, Rita *Music Group*
PO Box 571, Gwynedd Valley, PA 19437
USA

Coolio *Musician, Actor*
William Morris Agency (WMA-LA), 1
William Morris Pl, Beverly Hills, CA
90212 USA

Coombe, George W *Attorney General*
Graham & James, 1Maritime Plaza, San
Fransisco, CA 94111 USA

Coombs, Pat
5 Wendela Ct Harrow-On-The-Hill,
Middlesex, ENGLAND, ENGLAND

Coombs, Philip H *Economist*
617 W Main St, Chester, CT 06412 USA

Coombs-Mueller, Carol
772 Tyrol Ct., Crestline, CA 92325

Coonce, Ricky *Music Group, Musician*
Thomas Cassidy, 11761 E Speedway Blvd,
Tucson, AZ 85748 USA

Cooney, Gerry *Boxer*
22501 Linden Blvd, Cambria Heights, NY
11411 USA

Cooney, Joan Ganz *Educator, Television
Host, Misc*
Children's TV Workshop, 1 Lincoln Plaza,
New York, NY 10023 USA

Coonts, Stephen *Writer*
8200 Crow Valley Lane, Las Vegas, NV
89113 USA

Cooper, Alexander *Architect*
Cooper Robertson & Partners, 311 W 43rd St, New York, NY 10036 USA

Cooper, Alice *Music Group, Songwriter*
4135 E Kelm St, Paradise Valley, AZ 85253 USA

Cooper, Amy Levin *Editor*
60 Sutton Place S #16C, New York, NY 10022 USA

Cooper, Anderson *Commentator*
Cable News Network, News Dept 1050 Techwood Dr NW, Atlanta, GA 30318 USA

Cooper, Ashley
194 Bellevue Ave., Newport, RI 02840-3515

Cooper, Bill *Football Player*
16056 Greenwood Road, Monte Sereno, CA 95030 USA

Cooper, Bradley *Actor*
Brillstein-Grey Entertainment, 9150 Wilshire Blvd #350, Beverly Hills, CA 90212 USA

Cooper, Camille *Basketball Player*
New York Liberty, Madison Square Garden, 2 Penn Plaza, New York, NY 10121 USA

Cooper, Cecil C *Baseball Player*
1431 Misty Bend Dr, Katy, TX 77494 USA

Cooper, Charles *Actor*
Baier/Kleinman International, 3575 Cahuenga Blvd West, Suite 500, Los Angeles, CA 90068 USA

Cooper, Charles G *General*
3410 Barger Dr, Falls Church, VA 22044 USA

Cooper, Chris *Actor*
P M K Public Relations, 8500 Wilshire Blvd #700, Beverly Hills, CA 90211 USA

Cooper, Christian
General Delivery, Sun Valley, ID 83353

Cooper, Christin *Skier*
1001 E Hyman Ave, Aspen, CO 81611 USA

Cooper, Cortz *Religious Leader*
Presbyterian Church in America, 1852 Century Plaza, Atlanta, GA 30345 USA

Cooper, Cynthia *Basketball Player, Coach*
3910 Chatfield Court, Sugar Land, TX 77479 USA

Cooper, Daniel L *Admiral*
121 Leisure Court, Wyomissing, PA 19610 USA

Cooper, Dave *Artist*
Fantagraphics Books, 7563 Lake City Way, Seattle, WA 98115 USA

Cooper, Hal *Director*
2651 Hutton Dr, Beverly Hills, CA 90210 USA

Cooper, Henry *Boxer*
16 Barley House Hildonbroom Farm, Ridings Lane, Kent, TN11 9JN, UNITED KINGDOM(UK)

Cooper, Imogen *Music Group, Musician*
Van Walsum Mgmt, 4 Addison Bridge Place, London, W14 8XP, UNITED KINGDOM(UK)

Cooper, Jackie *Actor, Director*
10430 Wilshire Blvd #1603, Los Angeles, CA 90024 USA

Cooper, Jeanne *Actor*
8401 Edwin Dr, Los Angeles, CA 90046 USA

Cooper, Jilly *Writer*
Desmond Elliott, 38 Bury St, London, SW1Y 6AU, UNITED KINGDOM(UK)

Cooper, Joel D *Doctor*
Washington University, Medical School Surgery Dept, Saint Louis, MO 63110 USA

Cooper, John M *Misc*
182 Western Way, Princeton, NJ 08540 USA

Cooper, Justin *Actor*
Cunningham-Escott-Dipene & Associates Inc (CED-LA), 10635 Santa Monica Blvd #130, Los Angeles, CA 90025 USA

Cooper, L Gordon *Astronaut*
16303 Waterman Dr #B, Van Nuys, CA 91406 USA

Cooper, Lattie F *Educator*
Arizona State University, President's Office, Tempe, AZ 85287 USA

Cooper, Leon N *Nobel Prize Laureate*
49 Intervale Road, Providence, RI 02906 USA

Cooper, Lester I *Producer*
45 Morningside Dr S, Westport, CT 06880 USA

Cooper, Marilyn *Actor*
Gage Group, 315 W 57th St, #4H, New York, NY 10019 USA

Cooper, Matthew T *General*
9326 Fairfax St, Alexandria, VA 22309 USA

Cooper, Minor J *Biologist*
1901 Austin Ave, Ann Arbor, MI 48104 USA

Cooper, Namrata *Actor*
Amsel Eisenstadt & Frazier Inc, 5757 Wilshire Blvd #510, Los Angeles, CA 90036 USA

Cooper, Paula *Misc*
Paula Cooper Gallery, 534 W 21st St, New York, NY 10011 USA

Cooper, Ray *Producer*
@Radical.Media (NY), 435 Hudson St, New York, NY 10014

Cooper, Roxanne *Musician*
Pop Idol (Fremantle Media), 2700 Colorado Ave #450, Santa Monica, CA 90404 USA

Cooper, Scott *Actor*
Diverse Talent Group, 1875 Century Park E #2250, Los Angeles, CA 90067 USA

Cooper, Scott *Baseball Player*
Boston Red Sox, 24 Edgeworth Ave, Maryland Heights, MO 63043-2616 USA

Cooper, Stephen *Business Person*
Enron Corp, 1400 Smith St, Houston, TX 77002 USA

Cooper, Susan Rogers *Writer*
PO Box 92082, Austin, TX 78709-2082

Cooper, Wayne *Artist*
126 W 1025 S, Kouts, IN 46347 USA

Cooper, Wilma Lee *Musician*
Charles Rapp Enterprises, 1650 Broadway, #1410, New York, NY 10019 USA

Cooper, Wima Lee *Musician*
Charles Rapp Enterprises Inc, 1650 Broadway #1410, New York, NY 10019 USA

Cooper Jr, L Gordon *Astronaut*
1338 Nathan Lane, Ventura, CA 93001 USA

Cooperfield, David *Misc*
2000 West Loop S, #1300, Houston, TX 77027 USA

Cooperwheat, Lee *Fashion Designer*
Cooperwheat Blundell, 14 Cheshire St, London, E2 6EH, UNITED KINGDOM (UK)

Coors, William K *Business Person*
Adolph Coors Co, 1221 Ford St, Golden, CO 80401 USA

Coover, Robert *Writer*
Brown University, Linden Press, 49 George St, Providence, RI 02912 USA

Cope, Derrike *Race Car Driver*
CLR Racing, 106 C Motorsports Road, Mooresville, NC 28115 USA

Cope, Jonathan *Dancer*
Royal Ballet, Covent Garden, Bow St, London, WC2E 9DD, UNITED KINGDOM (UK)

Cope, Julian *Musician, Songwriter*
International Talent Group, 729 7th Ave, #1600, New York, NY 10019 USA

Cope, Kenneth
61-63 Kent House 87 Regent St., London, ENGLAND, W1R 7HF

Copeland, Adam (Edge) *Wrestler*
World Wrestling Entertainment (WWE), 1241 E Main St, Stamford, CT 06905 USA

Copeland, Al *Race Car Driver, Business Person*
5001 Folse Dr, Metairie, LA 70006 USA

Copeland, Cyrus
Trident Media Group LLC, 41 Madison Ave Fl 33, New York, NY 10010 USA

Copeland, Joan *Actor*
88 Central Park West, New York, NY 10023 USA

Copeland, Kenneth *Misc*
Kenneth Copeland Ministries, PO Box 2908, Fort Worth, TX 76113 USA

Copeland, Stewart *Composer*
181 N Saltair Ave, Los Angeles, CA 90049 USA

Copley, Helen K *Publisher*
Copley Press, 7776 Ivanhoe Ave, La Jolla, CA 92037 USA

Copley, Jeff E
687 State Hwy 194, Kimper, KY 41539 USA

Copley, Teri *Actor, Model*
13351 Riverside Dr, #D513, Sherman Oaks, CA 91423 USA

Copon, Michael *Actor*
Kazarian/Spencer & Assoc, 11365 Ventura Blvd #100, Box 7403, Studio City, CA 91604 USA

Copp, D Harold *Misc*
4755 Belmont Ave, Vancouver, BC V6T 1A8, CANADA

Coppens, Yves *Misc*
4 Rue du Pont-aux-Choux, Paris, 75003, FRANCE

Copperfield, David *Entertainer*
2000 W Loop S #1300, Houston, TX 77027 USA

Copping, Allen A *Educator*
Louisiana State University System, President's Office, Baton Rouge, LA 70808 USA

Coppinger, Rocky *Baseball Player*
Baltimore Orioles, 7208 Alto Rey Ave, El Paso, TX 79912-2100 USA

Coppola, Alicia *Actor*
William Morris Agency, 151 El Camino Dr, Beverly Hills, CA 90212 USA

Coppola, Chris *Actor*
Independent Management Group (IMG), 717 N Alta Vista Blvd, Los Angeles, CA 90046 USA

Coppola, Francis Ford *Director*
Zoetrope Studios, 916 Kearny St, San Francisco, CA 94133 USA

Coppola, Sofia *Director, Actor, Writer*
Niebaum-Coppola Estate, PO Box 208, Rutherford, CA 94573 USA

Coppolla, Alicia *Actor*
Agency for the Performing Arts (APA-LA), 9200 Sunset Blvd #900, Los Angeles, CA 90069 USA

Coquillette, Trace *Baseball Player*
Montreal Expos, 5200 Mississippi Bar Dr, Orangevale, CA 95662-5717 USA

Cora, Alex *Baseball Player*
Los Angeles Dodgers, F12 Calle 14, Caguas, PR 00727-6935 USA

Cora, Jose M (Joey) *Baseball Player*
San Diego Padres, Calle 17, F12 Villa Nueva, Caguas, PR 00725-5433 USA

Corabi, John *Musician*
Union Entertainment Group, 31225 La Baya Dr, #213, Westlake Village, CA 91362 USA

Coraci, Frank
9701 Wilshire Blvd. #1000, Beverly Hills, CA 90212

Corbet, Brady *Actor*
Bette Smith Management, 499 N Canon Dr, Beverly Hills, CA 90210 USA

Corbett, Doug *Baseball Player*
Minnesota Twins, 861214 N Hampton Club Way, Fernandina Beach, FL 32034-8700 USA

Corbett, Gene *Baseball Player*
Philadelphia Phillies, 1000 Beaglin Park Dr Apt 104, Salisbury, MD 21804-3086 USA

Corbett, Gretchen *Actor*
S D B Partners, 1801 Ave of Stars, #902, Los Angeles, CA 90067 USA

Corbett, John *Actor*
Lovett Management, 1327 Brinkley Ave, Los Angeles, CA 90049 USA

Corbett, Luke R *Business Person*
Kerr-McGee Corp, Kerr-McGee Center, Oklahoma City, OK 73125 USA

Corbett, Michael *Actor*
2665 Chart Place, Los Angeles, CA 90046 USA

Corbett, Mike *Athlete*
PO Box 917, Yosernite National Park, CA 95389 USA

Corbett, Ronnie *Actor, Comedian*
International Artistes, 235 Regent St, London, W1R 8AX, UNITED KINGDOM (UK)

Corbett, Sherman *Baseball Player*
California Angels, 7031 Washita Way, San Antonio, TX 78256-2310 USA

Corbin, Archie *Baseball Player*
Kansas City Royals, 7525 Tram Rd, Beaumont, TX 77713-8723 USA

Corbin, Barry *Actor*
2113 Greta Lane, Fort Worth, TX 76120 USA

Corbin, Ray *Baseball Player*
Minnesota Twins, 922 Liberty St SW, Live Oak, FL 32064-3619 USA

Corbin, Tyrone *Basketball Player*
New York Knicks, Madison Square Garden, 2 Penn Plaza, New York, NY 10121 USA

Corbo, Vincent J *Business Person*
Hercules Inc, Hercules Plaza, 1313 N Market St, Wilmington, DE 19894 USA

Corbucci, Bruno
via dei Colli della Farnesia 144, Rome, ITALY

Corbus, William *Football Player*
1100 Union St, #1100, San Francisco, CA 94109 USA

Corcoran, Kevin *Actor*
8617 Balcom Ave, Northridge, CA 91325 USA

Corcoran, Roy *Baseball Player*
Montreal Expos, 3305 E Main St, Slaughter, LA 70777-3222 USA

Corcoran, Tim *Baseball Player*
Detroit Tigers, 4349 Friar Cir, La Verne, CA 91750-2718 USA

Cord, Alex *Actor*
335 N Maple Dr, #361, Beverly Hills, CA 90210 USA

Cordalis, Costa
Rippoldsauer Str. 32, Freudenstadt, GERMANY, D-72250

Corday, Barbara *Business Person*
2011 Cummings Dr, Los Angeles, CA 90027 USA

Corday, Mara
PO Box 800393, Valencia, CA 91355

Corder, Roger *Inventor*
Queen Mary Medical School, Turner St, London, E1 2AD, UNITED KINGDOM (UK)

Cordero, Angel T Jr *Jockey*
New York Racing Assn, PO Box 170090, Ozone Park, NY 11417 USA

Cordero, Angelo
PO Box 90, Jamaica, NY 11411

Cordero, Chad *Baseball Player*
Montreal Expos, 13305 Noble Pl, Chino, CA 91710-4742 USA

Cordero, Joaquin *Actor*
Televisa, Blvd Adolfo Lopez Mateos 232, Colonia San Angel INN, DF, CP 01060, MEXICO

Cordero, Wilfredo N (Wil) *Baseball Player*
Montreal Expos, 25844 Kensington Dr, Westlake, OH 44145-1472 USA

Cordova, Francisco *Baseball Player, Athlete*
San Diego Padres, 8880 Rio San Diego Drive #400, San Diego, CA 92108 USA

Cordova, Marty *Baseball Player*
Montreal Expos, 9133 Eagle Ridge Dr, Las Vegas, NV 89134-6310 USA

Cordovez, Zegers Diego *Government Official, Educator*
Foreign Affairs Ministry, Avda 10 Agosta y Carrion, Quito, ECUADOR

Corduner, Allan *Actor*
Innovative Artists (LA), 1505 Tenth St, Santa Monica, CA 90401 USA

Corea, Armando (Chick) *Composer, Musician*
Chick Corea Productions, 10400 Samoa Ave, Tujunga, CA 91042 USA

Corella, Angel
890 Broadway, New York, NY 10003-1218

Corey, Bryan *Baseball Player*
Arizona Diamondbacks, 2905 N Rowen Cir, Mesa, AZ 85207-0916 USA

Corey, Elias J *Nobel Prize Laureate*
20 Avon Hill St, Cambridge, MA 02140 USA

Corey, Irwin (Professor) *Actor, Comedian*
Lustig Talent, PO Box 770850, Orlando, FL 32877 USA

Corey, Jill *Musician*
64 Division Ave, Lavittown, NY 11756 USA

Corey, Mark *Baseball Player*
Baltimore Orioles, 9321 Cornell Cir, Highland Ranch, CO 80130-4143 USA

Corey, Mark *Baseball Player*
New York Mets, 6811 Sterrettania Rd, Fairview, PA 16415-2918 USA

Corgan, Billy *Musician, Songwriter*
Creative Artists Agency LCC (CAA-LA), 9830 Wilshire Blvd, Beverly Hills, CA 90212 USA

Cori, Carl T *Business Person*
Sigma-Aldrich Corp, 3050 Spruce St, Saint Louis, MO 63103 USA

Corigliano, John P *Composer*
365 W End Ave, New York, NY 10024 USA

Corkins, Mike *Baseball Player*
San Diego Padres, 3760 Chemehuevi Blvd, Lake Havasu City, AZ 86406-6449 USA

Corley, Al *Actor*
3323 Corinth Ave, Los Angeles, CA 90066 USA

Corley, Annie *Actor*
Bauman Redanty & Shaul Agency, 5757 Wilshire Blvd #473, Los Angeles, CA 90036 USA

Corley, Pat *Actor*
1327 Ocean Ave, #J, Santa Monica, CA 90401 USA

Corley, W Gene *Engineer*
Construction Tech Labs, 5420 Old Orchard Road, Skokie, IL 60077 USA

Corman, Avery *Writer*
International Creative Mgmt, 40 W 57th St, #1800, New York, NY 10019 USA

Corman, Roger
2501 La Mesa Dr, Santa Monica, CA 90402

Corman, Roger W *Director, Producer*
11600 San Vincente Blvd, Los Angeles, CA 90049 USA

Cormier, Rheal *Baseball Player*
St Louis Cardinals, 15711 Cedar Grove Ln, Wellington, FL 33414-6312 USA

Corn, Alfred *Writer*
350 W 14th St, #6A, New York, NY 10014 USA

Corneille *Artist*
Society of Independent Artists, Cours la Reine, Paris, 75008, FRANCE

Corneisen, Rufus *Religious Leader*
415 S Chester Road, Swarthmore, PA 19081 USA

Cornejo, Mardie *Baseball Player*
New York Mets, 321 E 3rd St, Wellington, KS 67152-2706 USA

Cornejo, Nate *Baseball Player*
Detroit Tigers, 1600 N B St, Wellington, KS 67152-4405 USA

Cornelius, Don *Producer*
12685 Mulholland Dr, Beverly Hills, CA 90210 USA

Cornelius, Helen *Musician, Songwriter*
PO Box 121089, Nashville, TN 37212 USA

Cornelius, James *Business Person*
Guidant Corp, 111 Monument Circle, Indianapolis, IN 46204 USA

Cornelius, Reid *Baseball Player*
Montreal Expos, 10117 Hunt Club Ln, West Palm Beach, FL 33418-4568 USA

Cornell, Chris *Musician*
Rebel Waltz, 3165 2nd Ave, Laguna Beach, CA 92651 USA

Cornell, Eric A *Nobel Prize Laureate*
University of Colorado, PO Box 440, Boulder, CO 80309 USA

Cornell, Harry M Jr *Business Person*
leggett & Platt Inc, 1 Leggett Road, Carthage, MO 64836 USA

Cornell, Jeff *Baseball Player*
San Francisco Giants, 1644 SW Jeffrey Cir, Lees Summit, MO 64081-4115 USA

Cornell, Lydia *Actor*
8075 W 3rd St, #303, Los Angeles, CA 90048 USA

Cornett, Brad *Baseball Player*
Toronto Blue Jays, 1301 E VFW Ln, Odessa, TX 79762-3000 USA

Cornett, Leanza *Actor*
Endeavor Agency LLC (LA), 9601 Wilshire Blvd Fl 3, Beverly Hills, CA 90210 USA

Cornforth, John W *Nobel Prize Laureate*
Saxon Down, Cuilfail Lewes, East Sussex, BN7 2BE, UNITED KINGDOM (UK)

Cornish, Frank E *Football Player*
305 Sheffield Dr, Southlake, TX 76092 USA

Cornish, Nick *Actor*
James Levy Jacobson Mgmt, 3500 W Olive Ave, #900, Burbank, CA 91505 USA

Cornog, Robert A *Business Person*
Snap-On Corp, 10801 Corporate Dr, Pleasant Prairle, WI 53158 USA

Cornthwaite, Robert *Actor*
23388 Mulholland Dr, #12, Woodland Hills, CA 91364 USA

Cornutt, Terry *Baseball Player*
San Francisco Giants, 179 W Hazel St, Roseburg, OR 97470-2211 USA

Cornwell, Johnny *Musician*
Overland Productions, 156 W 56th St, #500, New York, NY 10019 USA

Cornwell, Patricia *Writer*
P O Box 5235, Greenwich, CT 06831 USA

Corone, Antoni *Actor*
Miller & Company Management, 427 North Canon Drive, #215, Beverly Hills, CA 90210 USA

Corr, Andrea *Musician*
Paradigm (LA), 10100 Santa Monica Blvd, Fl 25, Los Angeles, CA 90067 USA

Corr, Edwin G *Diplomat*
1617 Jenkins Ave, Norman, OK 73072 USA

Corrado, Fred *Business Person*
Great A & P Tea Co, 2 Paragon Dr, Montvale, NJ 07645 USA

Corrado, Gabriel *Actor*
Telefe - Argentina, Pavon 2444 (C1248AAT), Buenos Aires, ARGENTINA

Corral, Frank *Football Player*
Municipal Building, Graffiti Control 3900 Main St, Riverside, CA 92522 USA

Corrales, Pat *Baseball Player*
Philadelphia Phillies, 571 Big Canoe, Big Canoe, GA 30143-5128 USA

Correa, Charles M *Architect*
Sonmarg Napean Sea Road, Bombay, 40006, INDIA

Correa, Edwin *Baseball Player*
Chicago White Sox, A2 Calle Milagros Cabezas, Carolina, PR 00987-7101 USA

Correia, Kevin *Baseball Player*
San Francisco Giants, 5844 Riley St Apt 1, San Diego, CA 92110-1705 USA

Correia, Rod *Baseball Player*
California Angels, 23 Winter St, Rehboth, MA 02769-1733 USA

Correll, Alston D (Pete) *Business Person*
Georgia-Pacific Corp, 133 Peachtree St NE, Atlanta, GA 30303 USA

Correll, Vic *Baseball Player*
Boston Red Sox, 119 Kentucky Downs, Perry, GA 31069-8508 USA

Correnti, John D *Business Person*
Nucor Corp, 2100 Rexford Road, Charlotte, NC 28211 USA

Corretja, Alex *Tennis Player*
Assn of Tennis Professionals, 200 Tournament Road, Ponte Vedra Beach, FL 32082 USA

Corri, Adrienne
2-4 Noel St., London, ENGLAND, W1V 3RB

Corri, Andrienne *Actor*
London Mgmt, 2-4 Noel St, London, W1V 3RB, UNITED KINGDOM(UK)

Corridon-Mortell, Marie *Swimmer*
13 Heritage Village #A, Southbury, CT 06488 USA

Corrie, Emily *Actor*
Peters Fraser & Dunlop (PFD - UK), Drury House, 34-43 Russell St, London, WC2 B5, UNITED KINGDOM (UK)

Corrigan, E Gerald *Government Official, Financier*
Goldman Sanchs Co, 85 Broad St, New York, NY 10004 USA

Corrigan, Kevin *Actor*
Innovative Artists, 1505 10th St, Santa Monica, CA 90401 USA

Corrigan, Patrick *Editor, Cartoonist*
Toronto Star, Editorial Dept 1 Yonge St, Toronto, ON M5E 1E5, CANADA

Corrigan, Robert A *Educator*
San Fransisco State University, President's Office, San Fransisco, CA 94123 USA

Corrigan, Wilfred J *Business Person*
LSI Logic, 1621 Barber Lane, Milpitas, CA 95035 USA

Corrigan-Maguire, Mairead *Nobel Prize Laureate*
Peace People, 224 Lisbum Road, Belfast, BT9 6GB, NORTHERN IRELAND

Corripio Ahumada, Ernesto Cardinal *Religious Leader*
Apotinar Nieto 40 Col Tetlameyer, Mexico City, 04730, MEXICO

Corroface, Georges
1 rue Guenegaud, Paris, FRANCE, F-75006

Corrs, Andrea *Music Group*
John Hughes, 6 Martello Terr Sandycove, Dunlaoughaire, Dublin, IRELAND

Corrs, Caroline *Music Group*
John Hughes, 6 Martello Terr Sandycove, Dunlaoughaire, Dublin, IRELAND

Corrs, Jim *Music Group*
John Hughes, 6 Martello Terr Sandycove, Dunlaoughaire, Dublin, IRELAND

Corrs, Sharon *Music Group*
John Hughes, 6 Martello Terr Sandycove, Dunlaoughaire, Dublin, IRELAND

Corrs, The *Music Group*
Monterey Peninsula Artists (Monterey), 509 Hartnell St, Monterey, CA 93940 USA

Corsaro, Frank A *Director*
33 Riverside Dr, New York, NY 10023 USA

Corsi, Jim *Baseball Player*
Oakland A's, 9 Queen Anne Rd, Hopkinton, MA 01748-2160 USA

Corso, John A *Cinematographer*
241 W 13th St #21, New York, NY 10011
USA

Corson, Dale R *Physicist, Educator*
401 Savage Farm Dr, Ithaca, NY 14850
USA

Corson, Keith D *Business Person*
Coachmen Industries, P O Box 3300,
Elkhart, IN 46515 USA

Corson, Shayne *Hockey Player*
Richard Curran, 411 Timber Lane, Devon,
PA 19333 USA

Cort, Barry *Baseball Player*
Milwaukee Brewers, 13106 N Florida Ave
#116, Tampa, FL 33612-3420 USA

Cort, Bud *Actor*
2149 Lyric Ave, Los Angeles, CA 90027
USA

Cortazar, Esteban *Fashion Designer*
Esteban Cortazar Inc, 2320 NE 2nd Ave,
Miami, FL 33137

Cortes, Joaquin *Dancer, Choreographer*
William Morris Agency, 151 El Camino
Dr, Beverly Hills, CA 90212 USA

Cortes, Ron *Journalist*
Philadelphia Inquirer, Editorial Dept 400
N Broad St, Philadelphia, PA 19130 USA

Cortese, Dan *Actor*
28873 Via Venezia, Malibu, CA 90265
USA

Cortese, Joe *Actor*
2065 Coldwater Canyon Dr, Beverly Hills,
CA 90210 USA

Cortese, Valentina *Actor*
Pretta S Erasmo 6, Milan, 20121, ITALY

Cortez, Alfonso *Actor*
CunninghamEscottDipene, 10635 Santa
Monica Blvd #130, Los Angeles, CA
90025 USA

Cortright, Edgar M Jr *Astronaut, Engineer,
Misc*
9701 Calvin St, Northbridge, CA 91324
USA

Corvo *Musician*
Sony Music Miami, 605 Lincoln Rd,
Miami Beach, FL 33138 USA

Corwin, Jeff *Actor*
Jeff Corwin Experience, P O Box 2904,
Toluca Lake, CA 91610 USA

Corwin, Lola *Reality TV Star*
Osbrink Talent Agency, 4343 Lankershim
Blvd #100, Universal City, CA 91602 USA

Corwin, Norman *Writer*
USC, 3551 Ironsdale Parkway, Los
Angeles, CA 90089 USA

Coryatt, Quentin J *Football Player*
611 Cannon Lane, Sugar Land, TX 77479
USA

Coryell, Donald D (Don) *Football Coach*
P O Box 1576, Friday Harbor, WA 98250
USA

Coryell, Larry *Music Group, Musician*
Tedd Kurland, 173 Brighton Ave, Boston,
MA 02134 USA

Corzine, Dave *Basketball Player*
2311 N Cahmplain St, Arlington Heights,
IL 60004 USA

Cosbie, Douglas D (Doug) *Football Player*
2838 Royston Place, Beverly Hills, CA
90210 USA

Cosby, Bill *Actor, Comedian*
P O Box 808 Bardwell Ferry Rd,
Greenfield, MA 01302 USA

Coscarelli, Don *Writer, Director, Producer*
Starway International, 12021 Wilshire
Blvd #661, Los Angeles, CA 90025 USA

Cose, Ellis *Social Activist, Misc*
Harper Collins Publisher, 10 E 53rd St,
New York, NY 10022 USA

Cosey, Ray *Baseball Player*
Oakland A's, 139 Byxbee St, San
Francisco, CA 94132-2602 USA

Cosgrave, Liam *Prime Minister*
Beachperk Templeogue County, Dublin,
IRELAND

Cosgrove, Daniel *Actor*
James/Levy/Jacobson Management, 3500
W Olive Ave #1470, Burbank, CA 91505
USA

Cosgrove, Mike *Baseball Player*
Houston Astros, 8813 W Corrine Dr,
Peoria, AZ 85381-8166 USA

Cosgrove, Miranda *Actor*
Cunningham-Escott-Dipene & Associates
Inc (CED-LA), 10635 Santa Monica Blvd
#130, Los Angeles, CA 90025 USA

Cosic, Dobrica *President*
Sciences/Arts Academy, Knez Mikallove
35, Belgrade, SERBIA-MONTENEGRO

Cosiga, Fransesco *President*
Palazzo Giustiniani, Via Della Dogana
Vecchia 29, Rome, 00186 USA

Cosiga, Fransesco *President*
Palazzo Giustiniani, Via Della Dogana
Vecchia 29, Rome, 00186, ITALY

Coslet, Bruce N *Football Coach*
1084 Hickory Ridge Lane, Loveland, OH
45140 USA

Cosman, Jim *Baseball Player*
St Louis Cardinals, 3676 Oakley Ave,
Memphis, TN 38111-6166 USA

Cosmatos, George P *Director*
International Creative Mgmt, 8942
Wilshire Blvd #219, Beverly Hills, CA
90211 USA

Cosmovici, Cristiano B *Astronaut*
Istituto Fisica Spazio Interplanetario, CP
27, Frascati, 00044, ITALY

Cosper, Kina *Music Group*
Green Light Talent Agency, P O Box
3172, Beverly Hills, CA 90212 USA

Cosso, Pierre
13 rue Madeleine Michelis, Neuilly,
FRANCE, 92200

Cossotto, Fiorenza *Opera Singer*
IUMA, Via E Filiberto 125, Rome, 00185,
ITALY

Costa, Dave
102 Compton Circle #B, San Ramon, CA
94583

Costa, David J (Dave) *Football Player*
102 Compton Circle #B, San Ramon, CA
94583 USA

Costa, Don
7920 Sunset Blvd. #300, Los Angeles, CA
90069

Costa, Gal *Music Group*
Bridge Agency, 35 Clark St #A5, Brooklyn
Heights, NY 11201 USA

Costa, Mary *Opera Singer*
3340 Kingston Pike #1, Knoxville, TN
37919 USA

Costa-Gavras, Constantin
244 rue Saint-Jacques, Paris, FRANCE,
75005

Costa-Gavras, Konstaninos *Director*
Artmedia, 20 Ave Rapp, Paris, 75007, u

Costa-Gavras, Konstaninos *Director*
Artmedia, 20 Ave Rapp, Paris, 75007,
FRANCE

Costanza, Margaret (Midge) *Government
Official*
4518 Agnes Ave, Studio City, CA 91607
USA

Costanza, Midge
11811 W. Olympic Blvd, Los Angeles, CA
90064

Costanzo, Paul
UTA, 9560 Wilshire Blvd #500, Beverly
Hills, CA 90212

Costanzo, Paulo *Actor*
United Talent Agency, 9560 Wilshire Blvd
#500, Beverly Hills, CA 90212 USA

Costanzo, Robert *Actor*
Gold Marshak Liedtke, 3500 W Olive Ave
#1400, Burbank, CA 91505 USA

Costas, Carlos
Entenze 332-334 Atico 2a, Barcelona,
SPAIN, E-08029

Costas, Robert Q (Bob) *Sportscaster*
12813 Flushing Meadows Dr, Saint Louis,
MO 63131 USA

Costello, Billy *Boxer*
17 2nd Ave, Kingston, NY 12401 USA

Costello, Elvis *Songwriter, Musician,
Music Group*
125 Parkway, London, NW1 1PS,
UNITED KINGDOM(UK)

Costello, John *Baseball Player*
St Louis Cardinals, 68 Royal Oak Ct Apt
206, Vero Beach, FL 32962-3755 USA

Costello, Mariclare *Actor*
Borinstein Oreck Bogart, 3172 Dona
Susana Dr, Studio City, CA 91604 USA

Costello, Mark *Writer*
Fordham Univesity, Law School, New
York, NY 10458 USA

Costello, Murray *Hockey Player*
105 Kenilworth St, Ottawa, ON K1Y 3Y8
USA

Costello, Patty *Bowler*
2405 Pittston Ave, Scranton, PA 18505
USA

Costello, Sue *Actor*
United Talent Agency, 9560 Wilshire Blvd
#500, Beverly Hills, CA 90212 USA

Costelloe, Paul *Fashion Designer*
Moygashel Mills, Dungannon, BT71 7PB,
NORTHERN IRELAND

Coster, Nicolas *Actor*
1624 N Vista St, Los Angeles, CA 90046
USA

Coster, Ritchie *Actor*
Duva-Flack Associates, 200 West 57th
Street, Suite 1008, New York, NY 10019

Costle, Douglas M *Government Official,
Educator*
Harvard University, Public Health School,
Cambridge, MA 02138 USA

Costner, Kevin *Actor, Director*
PO Box 2759, Toluca Lake, CA 91610
USA

Costo, Tim *Baseball Player*
Cincinnati Reds, 3107 Pintail Ln, Signal
Mountain, TN 37377-1439 USA

Cota, Humberto *Baseball Player*
Cleveland Indians, Jacobs Field, 2401
Ontario Street, Cleveland, OH 44115 USA

Cotchett, Joseph W *Attorney General*
840 Malcolm Road, Burlingame, CA
94010 USA

Cote, David *Business Person*
TRW Inc, 1900 Richmond Road,
Cleveland, OH 44124 USA

Cothran, Sherry *Music Group*
Turner Management Group, 374 Poli St
#205, Ventura, CA 93001 USA

Cotler, Kami
PO Box 124, Schuyler, VA 22969

Cotlow, Lewis N *Misc*
132 Lakeshore Dr, North Palm Beach, FL
33408 USA

Cotrubas, Ileana *Opera Singer*
Royal Opera House, Convent Garden
Bow St, London, WC2, UNITED
KINGDOM(UK)

Cottee, Kay *Yachtsman*
Showcase Productions, 113 Willoughby
Road, Crows Nest, NSW, 2065,
AUSTRALIA

Cottet, Mia *Actor*
Metropolitan Talent Agency, 4526
Wilshire Blvd, Los Angeles, CA 90010
USA

Cotti, Flavio *President*
Christian Democratic Party, Klaraweg 6,
Bem, 3001, SWITZERLAND

Cottier, Chuck *Baseball Player*
Milwaukee Braves, 7129 Lake Ballinger
Way, Edmonds, WA 98026-8545 USA

Cottier, George Cardinal *Religious Leader*
Convento Santa Sabina, Piazza Pierro
d'Illiria, Rome, 00193, ITALY

Cottingham, Robert *Artist*
P O Box 604 Blackman Road, Newtown,
CT 06470 USA

Cotto, Delilah *Actor*
Arenas Entertainment, 100 N Crescent Dr,
Garden Level, Beverly Hills, CA 90210
USA

Cotto, Henry *Baseball Player*
Chicago Cubs, 1141 W Thomas Rd,
Phoenix, AZ 85013-4206 USA

Cotton, Blaine *Actor*
Jack Scagnetti Talent, 5118 Vineland Ave
#102, North Hollywood, CA 91601 USA

Cotton, Francis E (Fran) *Athlete, Misc*
Beechwood Hulme Hall Road, Stockport,
Cheshire, SK8 6JZ, UNITED
KINGDOM(UK)

Cotton, Frank A *Misc*
Twaycliffe Ranch RR 2 Box 230, Bryan,
TX 77808 USA

Cotton, James *Music Group, Musician*
James Cotton Mgmt, 235 W Eugene St #G
10, Chicago, IL 60614 USA

Cotton, Joseph F *Misc*
20 Linda Vista Ave, Atherton, CA 94027
USA

Cotton, Josie *Music Group*
2794 Hume Road, Malibu, CA 90265
USA

Cotton, Robin *Doctor*
20271 Goldenrod Lane #120,
Germantown, MD 20876-4964 USA

Cottrell, Ralph *Religious Leader*
Baptist Missionary Assn, P O Box 1203,
Van, TX 75790 USA

Cotts, Neal *Baseball Player*
Chicago White Sox, 1 McKendree Park
Rd, Lebanon, IL 62254-1266 USA

Couch, John N *Biologist, Misc*
1109 Carol Woods, Chapel Hill, NC
27514 USA

Couch, Tim *Football Player*
3083 Waterfall Way, Westlake, OH
44145 USA

Couchee, Mike *Baseball Player*
San Diego Padres, 3060 N Ridgecrest Unit
155, Mesa, AZ 85207-1080 USA

Couffer, Jack *Cinematographer*
Daniel Ostroff, 9200 W Sunset Blvd #402,
Los Angeles, CA 90069 USA

Coughlan, Marisa *Actor*
International Creative Management, 8942
Wilshire Blvd #219, Beverly Hills, CA
90211 USA

Coughlin, Bernard J *Educator*
Gonzaga University, Chancellor's Office,
Spokane, WA 99258 USA

Coughlin, Kevin
1090 N. Euclid Ave., Sarasota, FL 34237

Coughlin, Tom *Football Coach*
New York Giants, Giants Stadium, East
Rutherford, NJ 07073 USA

Coughtry, Marian *Baseball Player*
Boston Red Sox, 6801 NE 62nd Ct,
Vancouver, WA 98661-1501 USA

Coulier, Dave
9150 Wilshire Blvd. #350, Beverly Hills,
CA 90212-3427

Coulier, David *Actor*
International Creative Mgmt, 8942
Wilshire Blvd #219, Beverly Hills, CA
90211 USA

Coulson, Catherine E *Actor*
1115 Terra Ave, Ashland, OR 97520 USA

Coulson, Christian *Actor*
Artists Rights Group (ARG London), 4
Great Portland St, London, W1W 8PA,
UNITED KINGDOM (UK)

Coulter, Art
500 Spanish Fort Blvd. #203, Spanish Fort,
AL 36527-5998

Coulter, Brian *Music Group, Musician*
Ashley Talent, 2002 Hogback Road #20,
Ann Arbor, MI 48105 USA

Coulter, Catherine *Writer*
PO Box 17, Mill Valley, CA 94942 USA

Coulter, DeWitt E (Tex) *Football Player*
5001 Convict Hill Road #503, Austin, TX
78749 USA

Coulter, Michael *Cinematographer*
35 Carlton Mansions Randolph Ave,
London, W9 1NP, UNITED
KINGDOM(UK)

Coulter, Phil *Music Group*
87th Street Ltd, 24 Upper Mount St,
Dublin, IRELAND

Coulter, Tom *Baseball Player*
St Louis Cardinals, 718 Trenton St,
Toronto, OH 43964-1269 USA

Coulthard, David *Race Car Driver*
Martin Brundle, Kings Lynn, Tottenhill,
Norfolk, PE32 0PX, UNITED KINGDOM
(UK)

Counsell, Craig *Baseball Player*
Colorado Rockies, 1511 1/2 NE 6th Ct,
Fort Lauderdale, FL 33304-2969 USA

Counting Crows *Music Group*
Creative Artists Agency LCC (CAA-LA),
9830 Wilshire Blvd, Beverly Hills, CA
90212 USA

Counts, Mel *Basketball Player*
1581 Matheny Road, Gervais, OR 97026
USA

Couples, Fred
112 TPC Blvd., Ponte Vedra Beach, FL
32082

Couples, Fredrederick S (Fred) *Golfer*
1851 Alexander Bell Dr #410, Reston, VA
20191 USA

Courant, Ernest D *Physicist*
40 W 72nd St #4I, New York, NY 10023
USA

Couric, Katie *Television Host, Journalist*
Dateline NBC, 30 Rockefeller Plz, New
York, NY 10112 USA

Courier, James S (Jim) Jr *Tennis Player*
9533 Blandford Road, Orlando, FL 32827
USA

Courier, Jim
1 Erieview Plaza #1300, Cleveland, OH
44114

Courreges, Andre *Fashion Designer*
27 Rue Delabordere, Neuilly-Sur-Seine,
92, FRANCE

Courtenay, Tom *Actor*
Jonathan Altaras, 13 Shorts Gardens,
London, WC2H 9AT, UNITED
KINGDOM(UK)

Courtland, Jerome
1837 Westleigh Dr., Glenview, IL 60025-
7611

Courtney, Thomas W (Tom) *Track Athlete*
833 Wyndemere Way, Naples, FL 34105
USA

Courtright, John *Baseball Player*
Cincinnati Reds, 316 S Roosevelt Ave,
Columbus, OH 43209-1829 USA

Cousin, Philip R *Religious Leader*
Episcopal Church, District Headquarters, P O Box 2970, Jacksonville, FL 32203 USA

Cousineau, Tom *Football Player*
910 Eaton Ave, Akron, OH 44303 USA

Cousins, Christopher *Actor*
Deborah Miller & Company Management, 427 N Canon Dr #215, Beverly Hills, CA 90210

Cousins, Ralph W *Admiral*
Leconfield House Curzon St, London, W1Y 8JR, UNITED KINGDOM(UK)

Cousins, Robin *Figure Skater*
Billy Marsh, 174-8 N Gower St, London, NW1 2NB, UNITED KINGDOM(UK)

Cousteau, Jean-Michel *Oceanographer*
Ocean Futures Society, 325 Chapala St, Santa Barbara, CA 93101 USA

Cousy, Bob
459 Salisbury St, Worcester, MA 01609

Cousy, Robert J (Bob) *Basketball Player*
427 Salisbury St, Worcester, MA 01609 USA

Coutteure, Ronny
28 rue Basfroi, Paris, FRANCE, 75011

Covay, Don *Songwriter, Music Group*
Rawstock, P O Box 110002, Cambria Heights, NY 11411 USA

Cover, Franklin *Actor*
Sunset Lanai, 1422 N Sweetzer #402, Los Angeles, CA 90069 USA

Cover Girls
141 Dunbar Ave., Fords, NJ 08863

Coverdale, David *Musician, Music Group*
Agency for Performing Arts, 9200 Sunset Blvd #900, Los Angeles, CA 90069 USA

Coverly, Dave *Editor, Cartoonist*
Bloomington Herald-Times, Editorial Dept 1900 Walnut, Bloomington, IN 47401 USA

Covert, Allen *Actor*
Endeavor Agency LLC (LA), 9601 Wilshire Blvd Fl 3, Beverly Hills, CA 90210 USA

Covert, James (Jimbo) *Football Player*
450 Hunter Lane, Lake Forest, IL 60045 USA

Covey, Richard O *Astronaut*
1155 High Lake View, Colorado Springs, CO 80906 USA

Covey, Stephen R *Writer*
3507 N University Ave #100, Provo, Utah, 84604 USA

Covic, Nebojsa *Prime Minister*
Prime Minister's Office, Nemanjina 11, Belgrade, 11000, SERBIA

Coville, Bruce
PO Box 6110, Syracuse, NY 13217

Covington, Warren *Music Group*
1627 Open Field Loop, Brandon, FL 33510 USA

Covington, Wes *Baseball Player*
Milwaukee Braves, 905-10145 119 St NW, Edmonton, AB T5K 1Z2, CANADA

Cowan, Billy *Baseball Player*
Chicago Cubs, 1539 Via Coronel, Palos Verdes Estates, CA 90274-1941 USA

Cowan, Elliot *Actor*
Hofflund/Polone, 9465 Wilshire Blvd #820, Beverly Hills, CA 90212 USA

Cowan, George A *Misc*
Santa Fe Institute, 1399 Hyde Park Road, Santa Fe, NM 87501 USA

Cowan, Ralph Wolfe *Artist*
243 29th St, West Palm Beach, FL 33407 USA

Cowart, Sam *Football Player*
P O Box 12431, Jacksonville, FL 32219 USA

Cowell, Simon *Actor, Producer, Writer*
American Idol, 7800 Beverly Blvd #251, Los Angeles, CA 90036 USA

Cowen, Robert E *Judge*
US Court of Appeals, Judicial Complex, 402 E State St, Trenton, NJ 08608 USA

Cowen, Scott *Educator*
Tulane University, President's Office, New Orleans, LA 70118 USA

Cowen, Wilson *Judge*
US Court of Appeals, 717 Madison Place NW, Washington, DC 20439 USA

Cowen, Zelman *Attorney General, Educator*
4 Treasury Place, East Melbourne, VIC, 3002, AUSTRALIA

Cowens, David W (Dave) *Basketball Player, Coach*
746 Stonehill Run, Cincinnati, OH 45245 USA

Cowher, Bill *Coach*
100 Art Rooney Ave, Pittsburgh, PA 15212-5721 USA

Cowher, William L (Bill) *Football Player, Football Coach, Coach*
313 Olde Chapel Trail, Pittsburgh, PA 15238 USA

Cowhill, William J *Admiral*
1336 Elsinore Ave, McLean, VA 22102 USA

Cowie, Lennox L *Astronomer*
University of Hawaii, Astronomy Dept, 2600 Campus Road, Honolulu, HI 96822 USA

Cowley, Joe *Baseball Player*
Atlanta Braves, 102 Summertree Dr, Nicholasville, KY 40356-9185 USA

Cowper, Nicola *Actor*
Brunskill Mgmt, 169 Queens Gate #A8, London, SW7 5EH, UNITED KINGDOM(UK)

Cowper, Stephen C (Steve) *Governor*
P O Box A, Juneau, AK 99811 USA

Cox, Alex *Actor, Director*
United Talent Agency, 9560 Wilshire Blvd #500, Beverly Hills, CA 90212 USA

Cox, Bobby *Baseball Player*
New York Yankees, 1572 Reids Ferry Way, Marietta, GA 30062-2061 USA

Cox, Brian *Actor*
Conway Van Gelder Robinson, 18-21 Jermyn St, London, SW1Y 6NB, UNITED KINGDOM (UK)

Cox, Bryan K *Football Player*
4484 4 Winds Lane, Northbrook, IL 60062 USA

Cox, Casey *Baseball Player, Athlete*
2840 La Concha Drive, Clearwater, FL 33762-2203 USA

Cox, Charles C *Government Official*
Lexecon Inc, 332 S Michigan Ave, Chicago, IL 60604 USA

Cox, Christina *Actor*
Rysher Entertainment, 3400 Riverside Dr #600, Burbank, CA 91505 USA

Cox, Danny B *Baseball Player, Misc*
306 Feagin Mill Road, Warner Robins, GA 31088 USA

Cox, David R *Doctor, Misc*
Stanford University, Human Genome Center, Stanford, CA 94305 USA

Cox, Deborah *Musician, Songwriter, Music Group*
Evolution Talent, 1776 Braodway #1500, New York, NY 10019 USA

Cox, Emmett R *Judge*
US Court of Appeals, 113 St Joseph St, Mobile, AL 36602 USA

Cox, Frederick W (Fred) *Football Player*
401 E River St, Monticello, MN 55362 USA

Cox, G David *Religious Leader*
Church of God, P O Box 2420, Anderson, IN 46018 USA

Cox, Harvey G Jr *Educator, Misc*
Harvard University, Divinity School, Cambridge, MA 02140 USA

Cox, Jennifer Elise *Actor*
Metropolitan Talent Agency, 4526 Wilshire Blvd, Los Angeles, CA 90010 USA

Cox, Jim

Cox, Johnny *Basketball Player, Coach*
849 N Main St, Hazard, KY 41701 USA

Cox, Lynne *Swimmer*
Advanced Sport Research, 4141 Ball Road #142, Cypress, CA 90630 USA

Cox, Mark *Tennis Player*
Oaks Astead Woods, Astead, Surrey, KT21 2ER, UNITED KINGDOM(UK)

Cox, Nikki *Actor*
United Talent Agency, 9560 Wilshire Blvd, #500, Beverly Hills, CA 90212 USA

Cox, Paul *Director*
Illumination Films, 1 Victoria Ave, Albert Park, VIC, 3208, AUSTRALIA

Cox, Philip S *Architect*
Cox Richardson Architects, 469 Kent St, Sydney, NSW, 2000, AUSTRALIA

Cox, Ralph *Hockey Player*
Massport, 1 Harborside Dr, #200S, East Boston, MA 02128 USA

Cox, Richard
9200 Sunset Blvd. #900, Los Angeles, CA 90069

Cox, Richard Ian
8730 Sunset Blvd. #480, Los Angeles, CA 90069

Cox, Robert G *Financier*
Summit Bancorp, PO Box 2066, Princeton, NJ 08543 USA

Cox, Robert J (Bobby) *Misc*
1572 Reids Ferry Way, Marletta, GA 30062 USA

Cox, Ronny *Actor*
13948 Magnolia Blvd, Sherman Oaks, CA 91423 USA

Cox, Stephen J *Artist*
154 Barnsbury Road, Islington, London, N1 0ER, UNITED KINGDOM (UK)

Cox, Vera
345 N. Maple Dr. #397, Beverly Hills, CA 90210

Cox, Warren J *Architect*
Hartman Cox Architects, 1025 Thomas Jefferson St NW, Washington, DC 20007 USA

Cox Arquette, Courteney *Actor*
Brillstein-Grey Entertainment, 9150 Wilshire Blvd #350, Beverly Hills, CA 90212 USA

Coyne, Colleen *Hockey Player*
267 Lakeshore Dr N, East Falmouth, MA 02536 USA

Coyote, Peter *Actor*
774 Marin Dr, Mill Valley, CA 94941 USA

Cozler, Jimmy *Musician, Songwriter*
J Racords, 745 5th Ave, #600, New York, NY 10151 USA

Cozzarelli, Nicholas R *Biologist*
University of California, Biology Dept, Berkeley, CA 94720 USA

Crabbe, Cuffy
11216 N. 74th St., Scottsdale, AZ 85260

Crable, Bob *Football Player*
564 Miami Trace, Loveland, OH 45140 USA

Craddock, Bantz *General*
Commander, US Southern Command Miami, APO, AA, 34001 USA

Craddock, Billy (Crash) *Musician, Songwriter*
3007 Old Martinsville Road, Greensboro, NC 27455 USA

Craddock, Billy Crash
PO Box 428, Portland, TN 37148-0428

Craft, Chris
14919 Village Elm St., Houston, TX 77062

Craft, Christine *Commentator*
KRBK-TV, News Dept, 500 Media Place, Sacramento, CA 95815 USA

Crafts, Hannah *Writer*
Creative Artists Agency LCC (CAA-LA), 9830 Wilshire Blvd, Beverly Hills, CA 90212 USA

Cragg, Anthony D (Tony) *Artist*
Adolt-Vorwerk-Str 24, Wuppertal, 42287, GERMANY

Craggs, George *Soccer Player*
6223 6th Ave NW, Seattle, WA 98107 USA

Craig, Daniel *Actor*
International Creative Mgmt, 76 Oxford St, London, W1N 0AX, UNITED KINGDOM (UK)

Craig, Elijah *Actor*
Agency for Performing Arts, 9200 Sunset Blvd, #900, Los Angeles, CA 90069 USA

Craig, James D (Jim) *Hockey Player*
15 Jyra Ln, N Easton, MA 02356 USA

Craig, Jenny *Misc, Doctor*
5770 Fleet St, Carlsbad, CA 92008 USA

Craig, Michael *Actor*
Chatto & Linnit, Prince of Wales, Coventry St, London, W1V 7FE, UNITED KINGDOM (UK)

Craig, Richard *Inventor*
Pacific Northwest National Laboratory, 902 Battelle Blvd, Richland, WA 99352 USA

Craig, Roger *Baseball Player*
PO Box 2174, Borrego Spings, CA 92004 USA

Craig, Roger T *Football Player*
271 Vista Verde Way, Portola Valley, CA 94028 USA

Craig, Wendy
29 Roehampton Gate, London, ENGLAND, SW15 5JR

Craig, William *Government Official*
23 Annadale Ave, Belfast, BT7 3JJ, NORTHERN IRELAND

Craig, William (Bill) *Swimmer*
PO Box 629, Newport Beach, CA 92661 USA

Craig, Yvonne *Actor*
YC/MC Ltd, PO Box 827, Pacifc Palisades, CA 90272 USA

Craig of Radley, David B *Misc*
House of Lords, Westminster, London, SW1A 0PW, UNITED KINGDOM (UK)

Craighead, John J *Misc*
5125 Orchard Ave, Missoula, MT 59803 USA

Crain, Keith E *Publisher*
Crain Communications, 1400 Woodbridge Ave, Detroit, MI 48207 USA

Crain, Rance *Publisher*
Crain Communications, 360 N Michigan Ave, Chicago, IL 60601 USA

Crain, William *Director*
Contemporary Artists, 610 Santa Monica Blvd, #202, Santa Monica, CA 90401 USA

Crais, Robert *Writer*
12829 Landale St, Studio City, CA 91604 USA

Cram, Stephen (Steve) *Track Athlete*
General Delivery, Jarrow, UNITED KINGDOM (UK)

Cramer, Douglas
738 Sarbonne Rd., Los Angeles, CA 90077

Cramer, Grant *Actor*
Richard Sindell, 1910 Holmby Ave, #1, Los Angeles, CA 90025 USA

Cramer, James *Television Host*
Kudlow & Cramer, 900 Sylvan Ave, Englewood Cliffs, NJ 07632 USA

Cramer, Richard Ben *Journalist, Writer*
Philadelphia Inquirer, Editorial Dept, 400 N Broad St, Philadelphia, PA 19130 USA

Cramps, The
1775 Broadway #433, New York, NY 10019

Crampton, Barbara *Actor*
Stone Manners, 6500 Wilshire Blvd, #550, Los Angeles, CA 90048 USA

Crampton, Bruce *Golfer*
2404 A J Eagle Blvd, Annapolis, MD 21401 USA

Cramsey, Denise *Producer*
Trading Spaces, The Learning Channel, 7700 Wisconsin Ave, Bethesda, MD 20814 USA

Cramton, Roger C *Attorney General*
49 Highgate Circle, Ithaca, NY 14850 USA

Cranberries, The *Music Group*
Creative Artists Agency LCC (CAA-LA), 9830 Wilshire Blvd, Beverly Hills, CA 90212 USA

Crandall, Delmar W (Del) *Baseball Player*
1355 Clear Lake Place, Brea, CA 92821 USA

Crane, Brian
PO Box 4812, Sparks, NV 89432-4812

Crane, David *Director, Writer, Producer*
Bright Kauffman Crane Productions, 4000 Warner Blvd, Bldg 160 #750, Burbank, CA 91522

Crane, Fred
643 Greenwood St, Barnesville, GA 30204

Crane, Horace R *Physicist*
66 Cavanaugh Lake Road, Chelsea, MI 48118 USA

Crane, John *Writer*
Agency for the Performing Arts (APA-LA), 9200 Sunset Blvd #900, Los Angeles, CA 90069 USA

Crane, Kenneth G *Director*
6627 Linderhurst Ave, Los Angeles, CA 90048 USA

Crane, Tony *Actor*
Abrams Artists, 9200 Sunset Blvd, #1125, Los Angeles, CA 90069 USA

Cranshaw, Patrick *Actor*
Jeff Ross Management, 14560 Benefit Street, Suite 206, Sherman Oaks, CA 91403 USA

Cranston, Bryan *Actor*
United Talent Agency (UTA), 9560 Wilshire Blvd, Beverly Hills, CA 90212 USA

Cranston, Toller *Figure Skater*
Int'l Management Grp, 1st Clair Ave E, #700, Toronto, ON M4T 2V7, CANADA

Cranz, Christl *Skier*
Steibis 61, Oberstaufen, 87534, GERMANY

Crash Test Dummies
1505 W. 2nd St. #200, Vancouver, CANADA, BC V6H 3Y4

Craven, Gemma
42 Hazelbury Rd., London, ENGLAND, SW6 2ND

Craven, Matt *Actor*
11445 Tongareva St, Malibu, CA 90265 USA

Craven, Ricky *Race Car Driver*
5918 Moray Court, Concord, NC 28027 USA

Craven, Wes *Director*
2419 Solar Dr, Los Angeles, CA 90046 USA

Crawford, Bennie (Hank) Jr *Composer, Musician*
Maxine Harvard, PM Box 51, #C5 7942 Bell Road, Glendale, AZ 85308 USA

Crawford, Brad *Football Player*
RR2, Winamac, IL 46996 USA

Crawford, Bryce L Jr *Misc*
3220 Lake Johanna Blvd, #58, Saint Paul, MN 55112 USA

Crawford, Cheyne *Actor*
Joan Green Management, 1836 Courtney Terr, Los Angeles, CA 90046 USA

Crawford, Christina *Writer*
7 Springs Farm Sanders Road, Tensed, ID 83870 USA

Crawford, Cindy *Model, Actor*
Wolf/Kasteller, 335 N Maple Dr, #351, Beverly Hills, CA 90210 USA

Crawford, Clayne *Actor*
Joan Green Management, 1836 Courtney Terr, Los Angeles, CA 90046 USA

Crawford, Henry C (Shag) *Misc*
1530 Virginia Ave, Havetown, PA 19083 USA

Crawford, Jamal *Basketball Player*
Chicago Bulls United Center, 1901 W Madison St, Chicago, IL 60612 USA

Crawford, Joan *Basketball Player*
4728 S Harvard Ave, #9, Tulsa, OK 74135 USA

Crawford, Johnny *Actor, Musician*
Johnny Crawford Entertainment, PO Box 1851, Los Angeles, CA 90078 USA

Crawford, Kirsty *Musician*
Pop Idol (Fremantle Media), 2700 Colorado Ave #450, Santa Monica, CA 90404 USA

Crawford, Michael *Musician, Actor*
Night Ayrton, 10 Argyll St, London, W1V 1AB, UNITED KINGDOM (UK)

Crawford, Rachael *Actor*
Coast to Coast Talent Group, 3350 Barham Blvd, Los Angeles, CA 90068 USA

Crawford, Randy *Musician*
911 Park St SW, Grand Rapids, MI 49504 USA

Crawford, William J *War Hero*
28520 Country Road 14, Rocky Ford, CO 81067 USA

Cray, Robert *Musician*
Rosebud Agency, PO Box 170429, San Francisco, CA 94117 USA

Crazy Mohan *Actor*
5 Chokkalingam Street, Mandavelli, Chennai, TN 600 028, INDIA

Creamer, Roger W *Writer*
44 Fulling Ave, Tuckahoe, NY 10707 USA

Creamer, Timothy J *Astronaut*
5103 Carefree Dr, League City, TX 77573 USA

Crear, Mark *Track Athlete*
Octagon, 1751 Pinnacle Dr, #1500, Mclean, VA 22102 USA

Creber, William
140 Hollister Ave. #3, Santa Monica, CA 90405

Creech, Sharon *Writer*
Harper Collins Publishers, 10 E 53rd St, New York

Creech, Sharon *Writer*
Harper Collins Publishers, 10 E 53rd St, New York, NY 10022 USA

Creech, Wilbur L *General*
20 Quail Run Road, Henderson, NV 89014 USA

Creed *Music Group*
Wind-up Records, 72 Madison Ave, New York, NY 10016 USA

Creedence Clearwater Revisited
40 W. 57th St., New York, NY 10019

Creeggan, Jim *Musician*
Nettwerk Mgmt, 8730 Wilshire Blvd, #304, Beverly Hills, CA 90211 USA

Creek, Luther *Actor*
International Creative Management (ICM-LA), 8942 Wilshire Blvd, Beverly Hills, CA 90211 USA

Creekmur, Louis (Lou) *Football Player*
7521 SW 1st St, Plantation, FL 33317 USA

Creel, Monica
4526 Wilshire Blvd., Los Angeles, CA 90010

Creeley, Robert W *Writer*
PO Box 384, Waldoboro, ME 04572 USA

Creighton, Joanne V *Educator*
Mount Holyoke College, President's Office, South Hadley, MA 01075 USA

Creighton, John D *Publisher*
Toronto Sun, 333 King St E, Toronto, ON M5A 3X5, CANADA

Creighton, John O *Astronaut*
2111 SW 174th St, Burien, WA 98166 USA

Creighton Sr, David T *Coach, Hockey Player*
16113 E Course Dr, Tampa, FL 33624 USA

Creme, Lol *Musician*
Heronden Hall, Tenferden, Kent, UNITED KINGDOM (UK)

Cremins, Bobby *Coach*
150 Bobby John Road, Atlanta, GA 30332 USA

Crenkovski, Branko *Prime Minister*
Prime Minister's Office, Dame Grueva 6, Skopje, 9100, MACEDONIA

Crenshaw, Ben
1800 Nueces St., Austin, TX 78701

Crenshaw, Ben D *Golfer*
1600 Nueces St, Austin, TX 78701 USA

Crenshaw, Marshall *Musician, Songwriter*
Rascoff/Zysblat, 110 W 57th St, #300, New York, NY 10019 USA

Creole, Kid *Musician*
Ron Rainey Mgmt, 315 S Beverly Dr, #407, Beverly Hills, CA 90212 USA

Creskoff, Rebecca *Actor*
Innovative Artists (LA), 1505 Tenth St, Santa Monica, CA 90401 USA

Crespin, Regine *Opera Singer*
Musicaglotz, 3 Ave Frochet, Paris, 75009, FRANCE

Crespo, Elvis *Musician*
Sony Music Miami, 605 Lincoln Rd, Miami Beach, FL 33138 USA

Cresson, Edith *Prime Minister*
Mairie, Chatellerault Cedex, 86018, FRANCE

Cretler, Jean-Luc *Skier*
153 Ave du Marechal Lereic, BP 20, Bourq Saint Maurice, 73700, FRANCE

Creutz, Edward C *Physicist*
PO Box 2757, Rancho Santa, CA 92067 USA

Crevalle, Laura
PO Box 557, Old Orchard Beach, ME 04064

Crew-Cuts, The
29 Cedar St, Creskill, NJ 07626

Crewdson, John M *Journalist*
Chicago Tribune, Editorial Dept, 435 N Michigan Ave, Chicago, IL 60611 USA

Crewe, Albert V *Physicist*
8 Summit Dr, Chesterton, IN 46304 USA

Crews, David P *Biologist*
University of Texas, Zoology Dept, Austin, TX 78712 USA

Crews, Harry E *Writer*
University of Florida, English Dept, Gainesville, FL 32611 USA

Crews, Philip *Misc*
University of California, Chemistry Dept, Santa Cruz, CA 99504 USA

Crews, Terry *Actor*
William Morris Agency (WMA-LA), 1 William Morris Pl, Beverly Hills, CA 90212 USA

Crewson, Wendy *Actor*
438 Queen St E, Toronto, ON M5A 1T4, CANADA

Crialese, Emanuele *Director*
Endeavor Agency LLC (LA), 9601 Wilshire Blvd Fl 3, Beverly Hills, CA 90210 USA

Cribbins, Barnard *Actor*
Hamm Court, Weybridge, Surrey, UNITED KINGDOM (UK)

Cribbs, Joe S *Football Player*
6131 Eagle Point Circle, Birmingham, AL 35242 USA

Crichton, Dr Michael *Writer*
Janklow & Nesbit, 445 Park Ave, New York, NY 10022 USA

Crick, Francis H C *Nobel Prize Laureate*
1792 Colgate Circle, La Jolla, CA 92037 USA

Cricketts, The
3322 West End Ave. #520, Nashville, TN 37203

Crickhowell of Pont Esgob, Nicholas E *Politician*
4 Henning St, London, SW11 3DR, UNITED KINGDOM (UK)

Crider, Melissa *Actor*
Evolution Entertainment, 901 N Highland Ave, Los Angeles, CA 90038 USA

Crider, Melissa *Actor*
Paradigm Agency, 10100 Santa Monica Blvd, #2500, Los Angeles, CA 90067 USA

Crier, Catherine *Television Host, Commentator*
Cable News Network, News Dept, 1050 Technood Dr NW, Atlanta, GA 30318 USA

Crile, Susan *Artist*
168 W 86th St, New York, NY 10024 USA

Crilley, Mark *Writer*
Delacorte Press, 1540 Broadway, New York, NY 10036 USA

Crippen, Robert
691 E. 3550 N., Ogden, UT 84414-7537

Crippen, Robert L *Astronaut*
691 E 3550 N, Ogden, UT 84414 USA

Criqui, Don *Sportscaster*
CBS-TV, Sports Dept, 51 W 52nd St, New York, NY 10019 USA

Crisostomo, Manny *Photographer, Journalist*
Pacific Daily News, PO Box DN, Hagatna, GU, 96932 USA

Crisp, Terry A *Hockey Player, Coach*
805 Cherry Laurel Court, Nashville, TN 37215 USA

Crispin, Anne C *Writer*
PO Box 522, Bryantown, MD 20617 USA

Criss, Peter *Musician*
McGhee Entertainment, 8730 Sunset Blvd, #195, West Hollywood, CA 90069 USA

Crist, George B *General*
CBS-TV, News Dept, 51 W 52nd St, New York, NY 10019 USA

Crist, Judith *Journalist*
180 Riverside Dr, New York, NY 10024 USA

Cristal, Linda *Actor*
9129 Hazen Drive, Beverly Hills, CA 90210 USA

Cristofer, Michael *Writer, Director*
Media Talent Group, 9200 Sunset Blvd #810, W Hollywood, CA 90069 USA

Cristol, Stanley J *Misc*
2918 3rd St, Boulder, CO 80304 USA

Critchfield, Charles L *Physicist*
PO Box 993, Los Alamos, NM 87544 USA

Critelli, Michael *Business Person*
Pitney Bowes Inc, 1 Elmcroft Road, Stamford, CT 06926 USA

Croce, A J
1027 Meade Ave, San Diego, CA 92116 USA

Crockett, Billy *Musician, Songwriter*
Street Level Artists Agency, 106 N Buffalo St, #200, Warsaw, IN 46580 USA

Crockett, Gibson *Cartoonist*
4713 Great Oak Road, Rockville, MD 20853 USA

Crockett, Ray *Television Host*
Best Damned Sports Show Period, The, 10201 W Pico Blvd, Trailer 103, Los Angeles, CA 90035 USA

Croel, Mike *Football Player*
837 Traction Ave, Los Angeles, CA 90013 USA

Croft, Dwayne *Opera Singer*
Columbia Artists Mgmt Inc, 165 W 57th St, New York, NY 10019 USA

Crofts, Dash *Musician, Songwriter*
Nationwide Entertainment, 2756 N Green Valley Parkway, Henderson, NV 89014 USA

Croghan, Emma-Kate *Director*
Hilary Linstead, 500 Oxford St, Bondi Junction, NSW, 2022, AUSTRALIA

Croker, Stephen B (Steve) *General*
2 Byford Court, Chestertown, MD 21620 USA

Croll, Jimmy *Misc*
Thoroughbred Racing Assn, 420 Fair Hill Dr, #1, Elkton, MD 21921 USA

Crombie, Jonathan *Actor*
Sullivan Entertainment, 111 Davenport Road, Toronto, ON M5R 3R3, CANADA

Cromwell, James *Actor*
S D B Partners, 1801 Ave of Stars, #902, Los Angeles, CA 90067 USA

Cromwell, Nolan *Football Player, Football Coach*
2624 140th Ave NE, Bellevue, WA 98005 USA

Cronbach, Lee J *Educator*
2614 Oregon St, Union City, CA 94587 USA

Cronenberg, David *Actor*
David Cronenberg Productions, 217 Avenue Road, Toronto, ON M5R 2J3, CANADA

Cronenweth, Regina
5410 Wilshire Blvd. #227, Los Angeles, CA 90036

Cronin, James W *Nobel Prize Laureate*
5825 S Dorchester St, Chicago, IL 60637 USA

Cronin, Kevin *Musician*
Shapiro Co, 9229 Sunset Blvd, #607, Los Angeles, CA 90069 USA

Cronin, Mark *Producer*
Mindless Entertainment, 1053 Meadowbrook Avenue, Los Angeles, CA 90019 USA

Cronin, Rachel *Actor*
King Talent, 303-228 E 4th Ave, Vancouver BC, V5T 1G5, CANADA

Cronin, Rich *Musician*
Evolution Talent, 1776 Broadway, #1500, New York, NY 10019 USA

Cronkite, Walter
51 W. 52nd St. #1934, New York, NY 10019

Cronkite, Walter L Jr *Commentator*
CBS-TV, News Dept, 51 W 52nd St, New York, NY 10019 USA

Cronnenberg, David *Director*
Toronto Antenna, 244 DuPont St #200, Toronto, ON M5R 1V7, CANADA

Crook, Edward Jr *Boxer*
4512 Moline Ave, Columbus, GA 31907 USA

Crook & Chase
3201 Dickerson Pike, Nashville, TN 37207-2905

Crooke, Edward A *Business Person*
Constellation Energy Group, 39 W Lexington St, Baltimore, MD 21201 USA

Croom, Sylvester *Football Player, Coach*
Mississippi State University, Athletic Dept, Mississippi State, MS 39762 USA

Crosbie, Annette
68 St. James's St., London, ENGLAND, SW1A 1PH

Crosbie, John C *Politician*
235 Water St, Saint John's NF, A1C 5L3, CANADA

Crosby, Alfred W *Historian*
2506 Bowman Ave, Austin, TX 78703 USA

Crosby, Cathy Lee *Actor*
Epstein Wyckoff Corsa Ross & Assoc (LA), 280 S Beverly Dr #400, Beverly Hills, CA 90212 USA

Crosby, David *Musician*
17525 Ventura Blvd, #210, Encino, CA 91316 USA

Crosby, Denise *Actor, Model*
8242 Blackburn Ave, Los Angeles, CA 90048 USA

Crosby, Elaine *Golfer*
3462 Lone Pine Road, West Bloomfield, MI 48323 USA

Crosby, Kathryn
Box 85, Genda, NV 89411

Crosby, Kathryn Grant *Actor*
PO Box 85, Genoa, NV 89411 USA

Crosby, Lucinda *Actor*
4942 Vineland Ave, #200, North Hollywood, CA 91601 USA

Crosby, Mark
3500 W. Olive Ave. #1400, Burbank, CA 91505

Crosby, Mary
3500 W. Olive Ave. #1400, Burbank, CA 91505

Crosby, Norm *Comedian, Actor*
1400 Londonderry Place, Los Angeles, CA 90069 USA

Crosby, Paul *Musician*
Helter Skelter, Plaza, 535 Kings Road, London, SW10 0S, UNITED KINGDOM (UK)

Crosby, Phil *Actor*
21801 Providencia St, Woodland Hills, CA 91364 USA

Crosby, Rob
PO Box 121551, Nashville, TN 37212

Crosby, Robbin
8250 Grandview Dr., Los Angeles, CA 90046

Crosby Stills Nash & Young *Music Group*
William Morris Agency (WMA-LA), 1 William Morris Pl, Beverly Hills, CA 90212 USA

Crosetti, Frankie
65 W. Monterey Ave., Stockton, CA 92504

Croshere, Austin *Basketball Player*
Indiana Pacers, Conseco Fieldhouse, 125 S Pennsylvania, Indianapolis, IN 46204 USA

Cross, Ben *Actor*
Shepherd & Ford, 13 Radnor Walk, London, SW3 4BP, UNITED KINGDOM (UK)

Cross, Christopher *Musician, Songwriter*
1109 Monument St, Pacific Palisades, CA 90272 USA

Cross, David *Actor*
United Talent Agency, 9560 Wilshire Blvd, #500, Beverly Hills, CA 90212 USA

Cross, Irv *Football Player, Sportscaster*
2196 Marison Road, Roseville, MN 55113 USA

Cross, Joseph *Actor*
Innovative Artists, 1505 10th St, Santa Monica, CA 90401 USA

Cross, Marcia *Actor*
Kleinman Agency, 10340 Santa Monica Blvd, Los Angeles, CA 90025 USA

Cross, Randall L (Randy) *Football Player, Sportscaster*
155 Travertine Trail, Alpharetta, GA 30022 USA

Cross, Roger R *Actor*
Lone Star Entertainment, 147 N Poinsettia Pl, Los Angeles, CA 90036 USA

Cross, Russell *Basketball Player*
Elmhurst College, Athletic Dept, 190 S Prospect Ave, Elmhurst, IL 60126 USA

Cross, Terry M *Admiral*
Commander US Coast Guard Pacific, Coast Guard Island, Alameda, CA 94501 USA

Crosse, Liris *Model, Actor*
Wilhelmina Creative Mgmt, 300 Park Ave S, #200, New York, NY 10010 USA

Crossfield, Scott *Misc*
12100 Thoroughbred Road, Herndon, VA 20171 USA

Crotty, John *Basketball Player*
120 Brighton Ave, Spring Lake, NJ 07762 USA

Crouch, Andrae *Musician, Songwriter*
Hervey Co, 300 Park Ave S, #300, New York, NY 10010 USA

Crouch, Eric *Football Player*
ABC-TV, Sports Dept, 3240 S 10th St, Lincoln, NE 68502 USA

Crouch, Lindsay *Actor*
15115 1/2 Sunset Blvd, #A, Pacific Palisades, CA 90272 USA

Crouch, Paul *Misc*
Trinity Broadcasting Network, PO Box A, Santa Ana, CA 92711 USA

Crouch, Roger K *Astronaut*
Carriage Hill Dr, Laurel, MD 20707 USA

Crouch, Sandra *Musician, Songwriter*
Sparrow Communications Group, 101 Winners Circle, Brentwood, TN 37027 USA

Crouch, Stanley *Writer*
Georges Borchardt Agency, 136 E 57th St, New York, NY 10022 USA

Crouch, William T (Bill) *Journalist, Photographer*
5660 Valley Oaks Court, Placerville, CA 95667 USA

Croucher, Juan
45 Cayuse Lane, Rancho Palos Verdes, CA 90274

Crouse, Lindsay
15115 1/2 Sunset Blvd. #A, Pacific Palisades, CA 90272

Crow, F Trammell *Business Person*
Trammell Crow Co, Trammell Crow Center, 2001 Ross Ave, Dallas, TX 75201 USA

Crow, Harian R *Business Person*
Trammell Crow Co, Trammell Crow Center, 2001 Ross Ave, Dallas, TX 75201 USA

Crow, James F *Misc*
24 Glenway St, Madison, WI 53705 USA

Crow, John David *Football Player, Football Coach*
5004 Augusta Circle, College Station, TX 77845 USA

Crow, Lindon *Football Player*
6800 S Strand Ave, #481, Yuma, AZ 85364 USA

Crow, Martin D *Cricketer*
PO Box 109302, New Market, Auckland, NEW ZEALAND

Crow, Sheryl *Musician, Songwriter, Actor*
Kathryn Schenker, 1776 Broadway #1200, New York, NY 10019 USA

Crowded House, 3 Mitchell Rd
Rose Bay, Sydney, AUSTRALIA, NSW 2929, AUSTRALIA

Crowe, Cameron *Director, Writer*
Creative Artists Agency, 9830 Wilshire Blvd, Beverly Hills, CA 90212 USA

Crowe, George D *Baseball Player, Basketball Player*
1554 Silas Tompkins Road, Long Eddy, NY 12760 USA

Crowe, Phil *Hockey Player*
PO Box 115, Willow Grove, PA 19090 USA

Crowe, Russell *Actor*
Bedford/Pearce Mgmt, PO Box 271, Cammeray, NSW, 2062, AUSTRALIA

Crowe, Sara
13 Shorts Garden, London, ENGLAND, WC2H 9AT

Crowe, Tonya *Actor*
13030 Mindanao Way, #4, Marina del Rey, CA 90292 USA

Crowe, William J Jr *Admiral, Diplomat*
Global Options, 1615 L St NW, #300, Washington, DC 20036 USA

Crowell, Craven H Jr *Government Official*
Tennessee Valley Authority, 400 W Summit Hill Dr, Knoxville, TN 37902 USA

Crowell, John C *Misc*
300 Hot Springs Road, Montecito, CA 93108 USA

Crowell, Rodney
2 Music Circle S. #212, Nashville, TN 37203

Crowell, Rodney J *Musician, Songwriter*
Joe's Garage, 4405 Belmont Park Terrace, Nashville, TN 37215 USA

Crowley, Joseph N *Educator*
University of Nevada, President's Office, Reno, NV 89557 USA

Crowley, Mart *Writer*
8955 Beverly Blvd, West Hollywood, CA 90048 USA

Crowley, Patricia *Actor*
TMCE, 270 N Canon Dr, #1064, Beverly Hills, CA 90210 USA

Crown, David A *Misc*
3344 Twin Lakes Lane, Sanibel, FL 33957 USA

Crown, Lester *Business Person*
Henry Crown & Co, 222 N. LaSalle St, Chicago, IL 60601 USA

Crowson, Richard *Cartoonist, Editor*
Wichita Eagle-Beacon, Editorial Dept, 825 E Douglas Ave, Wichita, KS 67202 USA

Crowton, Gary *Football Coach*
Brigham Young University, Athletic Dept, Provo, UT 84602 USA

Crozier, Joseph R (Joe) *Hockey Player, Coach*
Boston Bruins, 1 Fleet Center, Boston, MA 02114 USA

Crudup, Billy *Actor*
Creative Artists Agency, 9830 Wilshire Blvd, Beverly Hills, CA 90212 USA

Cruikshank, Thomas H *Business Person*
5949 Sherry Lane, #1035, Dallas, TX 75225 USA

Cruise, Tom *Actor*
Cruise/Wagner Productions (C/W), 5555 Melrose Ave, Bldg 200, Los Angeles, CA 90038 USA

Crum, E Denzel (Denny) *Coach*
12038 Hunting Crest Dr, Prospect, KY 40059 USA

Crumb, George H *Composer*
240 Kirk Lane, Media, PA 19063 USA

Crumb, Robert *Artist, Cartoonist*
Fantagraphics Books, 7563 Lake City Way, Seattle, WA 98115 USA

Crumb, Robert (R) *Cartoonist*
20 Rue du Pont Vieux, Sauve, 30610, FRANCE

Crumley, James R Jr *Religious Leader*
362 Little Creek Dr, Leesville, SC 29070 USA

Crumm, Denny
12038 Hunting Crest Rd., Prospect, KY 40059-8405

Crutcher, Chris
3405 E. Marion Ct., Spokane, WA 99223-7215

Crutcher, Lawrence M *Publisher*
Book-of-the-Month Club, Rockefeller Center, New York, NY 10020 USA

Crutchfield, Edward E *Financier*
First Union Corp, 1 First union Center, Charlotte, NC 28288 USA

Crutzen, Paul J *Nobel Prize Laureate*
Max Planck Chemistry Institute, J J Becher-Weg 27, Mainz, 55128, GERMANY

Cruyff, Johan *Soccer Player, Coach*
Koninklike Nederk Voetbalbod, Postbus 515, Zeist, AM, 3700, NETHERLANDS

Cruz, Alexis *Actor*
Abrams Artists, 9200 Sunset Blvd, #1125, Los Angeles, CA 90069 USA

Cruz, Deivi *Baseball Player*
Detroit Tigers, 611 Woodward Ave,
Detroit, MI 48226-3408 USA

Cruz, Henry *Baseball Player*
Los Angeles Dodgers, 16 Calle Un W,
Fajardo, PR 00738-4706 USA

Cruz, Jacob *Baseball Player*
San Francisco Giants, 1582 W Commerce
Ave, Gilbert, AZ 85233-4103 USA

Cruz, Jose D *Baseball Player*
St Louis Cardinals, 10718 Braes Forest Dr,
Houston, TX 77071-1502 USA

Cruz, Juan *Baseball Player, Athlete*
Chicago Cubs, Wrigley Field, 1060 West
Addison Street, Chicago, IL 60613 USA

Cruz, Julio *Baseball Player*
Seattle Mariners, 6599 170th Pl SE,
Bellevue, WA 98006-6012 USA

Cruz, Penelope *Actor, Model*
Kuranda Movies SL, Calle Segre 14,
Madrid, 28002, SPAIN

Cruz, Raymond
8383 Wilshire Blvd. #954, Beverly Hills,
CA 90211

Cruz, Smith Martin *Writer*
Random House, 1745 Broadway, #B1,
New York, NY 10019 USA

Cruz, Todd *Baseball Player*
Philadelphia Phillies, 15655 Reed Dr,
Fontana, CA 92336-8710 USA

Cruz, Valerie *Actor*
Innovative Artists (LA), 1505 Tenth St,
Santa Monica, CA 90401 USA

Cruz, Wilson
8383 Wilshire Blvd. #550, Beverly Hills,
CA 90211

Cruz Jr, Jose *Baseball Player*
Seattle Mariners, 10718 Braes Forest Dr,
Houston, TX 77071-1502 USA

Cruz-Romo, Gilda *Opera Singer*
1315 Lockhill-Selma Road, San Antonio,
TX 78213 USA

Crvenkovski, Branko *President*
President's Office, Skopje, MACEDONIA

Cryer, Gretchen *Writer, Songwriter, Actor*
885 W End Ave, New York, NY 10025
USA

Cryer, Jon *Actor*
Media Artists Group, 6300 Wilshire Blvd,
#1470, Los Angeles, CA 90048 USA

Cryer, Suzanne *Actor*
Paradigm (LA), 10100 Santa Monica Blvd,
Fl 25, Los Angeles, CA 90067 USA

Cryner, Bobbie *Musician*
Lonesome Mgmt, 1313 16th Ave S,
Nashville, TN 37212 USA

Cryner, Bobby
PO Box 2147, Hendersonville, TN

Crystal, Billy *Actor, Comedian*
Face Productions/Jennilind Productions,
335 N Maple Dr #175, Beverly Hills, CA
90210

Crystals *Music Group*
27-L Ambiance Ct, Bardonia, NY 10954-
1421

Crystat, Ronald G *Biologist*
435 E 70th St, #34B, New York, NY
10021 USA

Csikszentmihalyi, Mihaly *Misc*
5848 S University Ave, Chicago, IL 60637
USA

Csokas, Marton *Actor*
Creative Artists Agency LCC (CAA-LA),
9830 Wilshire Blvd, Beverly Hills, CA
90212 USA

Csonka, Lawrence R (Larry) *Football
Player*
37256 Hunter Camp Road, Lisbon, OH
44432 USA

Cua, Rick *Musician*
Greg Menza, PO Box 1736, Columbia,
TN 38402 USA

Cuaron, Alfonso *Director*
Endeavor Talent Agency, 9701 Wilshire
Blvd, #1000, Beverly Hills, CA 90212
USA

Cuban, Mark *Business Person*
Dallas Mavericks, 2909 Taylor St, Dallas,
TX 75226 USA

Cubbage, Mike *Baseball Player*
Texas Rangers, 3349 Carroll Creek Rd,
Keswick, VA 22947-9156 USA

Cubitt, David *Actor*
91 Barber Greene Road, Don Mills, ON
M3C 2A2, CANADA

Cuccinello, Al *Baseball Player*
New York Giants, 106 Legion Pl,
Malverne, NY 11565-1324 USA

Cuccurullo, Waren *Musician*
DD Productions, 93A Westbourne Park
Villas, London, W2 5ED, UNITED
KINGDOM (UK)

Cucinotta, Maria Grazia *Actor*
Cucchini Mgmt, Lundolevere del Melini
10, Rome, 00192, ITALY

Cuckney, John G *Financier*
1 Comhill, London, EC3V 3QR, UNITED
KINGDOM (UK)

Cudahy, Richard D *Judge*
US Court of Appeals, 219 S Dearborn St,
Chicago, IL 60604 USA

Cuddy, Jim *Musician*
Agency Group Ltd, 1775 Broadway, #430,
New York, NY 10019 USA

Cuddyer, Michael *Baseball Player*
Minnesota Twins, 10240 Washingtonia
Palm Way, Fort Myers, FL 33912-6915
USA

Cudlitz, Michael *Actor*
Metropolitan Talent Agency (MTA), 4526
Wilshire Blvd, Los Angeles, CA 90010
USA

Cudmore, Daniel *Actor*
Characters Talent Agency, The (Toronto),
150 Carlton St Fl 2, Toronto ON, M5A
2K1, CANADA

Cueliar, Miguel S (Mike) *Baseball Player*
1002 Chesterfield Circle, Winter Springs,
FL 32708 USA

Cuellar, Bobby *Baseball Player*
Texas Rangers, 705 E 6th St, Alice, TX
78332-4651 USA

Cueva, Beto *Musician*
United Talent Agency (UTA), 9560
Wilshire Blvd, Beverly Hills, CA 90212
USA

Cuevas, Alberto *Writer*
Creative Artists Agency LCC (CAA-LA),
9830 Wilshire Blvd, Beverly Hills, CA
90212 USA

Cuevas, Jose Luis
Galeana 109, Col. San Angel Inn (01000)
Mexico DF, MEXICO

Cuevas, Jose Luis *Artist*
Galeana 109, San Angel Inn, Mexico City,
20 DF, MEXICO

Culbertson, Frank L Jr *Astronaut*
15723 Sylvan Lake Dr, Houston, TX
77062 USA

Culbreath, Joshua (Josh) *Track Athlete*
Central State University, Athletic Dept,
Wilberforce, OH 45384 USA

Culkin, Kieran *Actor*
Creative Artists Agency, 9830 Wilshire
Blvd, Beverly Hills, CA 90212 USA

Culkin, Macaulay *Actor*
Endeavor Agency LLC (LA), 9601 Wilshire
Blvd Fl 3, Beverly Hills, CA 90210 USA

Culkin, Rory *Actor*
Endeavor Talent Agency, 9701 Wilshire
Blvd, #1000, Beverly HIlls, CA 90212
USA

Cullen, Brett *Actor*
Gersh Agency, 232 N Canon Dr, Beverly
HIlls, CA 90210 USA

Cullen, Jack *Baseball Player*
New York Yankees, 164 Alexander Ave,
Nutley, NJ 07110-1002 USA

Cullen, Kimberly *Actor*
8916 Ashcroft Ave, West Hollywood, CA
90048 USA

Cullen, Sean M
10100 Santa Monica Blvd #2500, Los
Angeles, CA 90067 USA

Cullen, Tim *Baseball Player*
Washington Senators, 159 W G St,
Benicia, CA 94510-3114 USA

Cullens, E Van *Business Person*
Harris Corp, 1025 W NASA Blvd,
Melbourne, FL 32919 USA

Culler, Glen *Scientist*
Culler Scientific Systems Corp, 100 Burns
Place, Goleta, CA 93117 USA

Culligan, Joe *Writer*
Research Investigative Services, 650 NE
126th St, North Miami, FL 33161 USA

Cullinan, Edward H *Architect*
Wharf, 1 Baldwin Terrace, London, N1
7RU, UNITED KINGDOM (UK)

Cullum, John *Musician, Actor*
Writers & Artists, 19 W 44th St, #1000,
New York, NY 10036 USA

Cullum, Kaitlin *Actor*
Innovative Artists (LA), 1505 Tenth St,
Santa Monica, CA 90401 USA

Cullum, Kimberly
8916 Ashcroft Ave., Los Angeles, CA
90046

Cullum, Leo *Cartoonist*
2900 Valmere Dr, Malibu, CA 90265 USA

Cullum, Mark E *Cartoonist, Editor*
5401 Forest Acres Dr, Nashville, TN
37220 USA

Culp, Curley *Football Player*
12405 Alameda Trace Circle, #1213,
Austin, TX 78727 USA

Culp, Ray *Baseball Player*
Philadelphia Phillies, 7400 Waterline Rd,
Austin, TX 78731-2055 USA

Culp, Robert *Actor*
1324 N Spaulding Ave, Los Angeles, CA
90046 USA

Culp, Steven *Actor*
1680 Las Lunas St, Pasadena, CA 91106
USA

Cult, The
Immortal Entertainment, 12200 Olympic
Blvd, Suite 400, Los Angeles, CA 90064
USA

Cult Jam
PO Box 284, Brooklyn, NY 11203

Culture Beat
Schleiermacher Str. 2, Darmstadt,
GERMANY, D-64283

Culver, Curt S *Financier*
MGIC Investment Corp, 250 E Killbourn
Ave, Milwaukee, WI 53202 USA

Culver, George *Baseball Player*
Cleveland Indians, 5409 Rustic Canyon St,
Bakersfield, CA 93306-7315 USA

Culver, John C *Senator*
5409 Spangler Ave, Bethesda, MD 20816
USA

Culver, Michael
77 Beak St., London, ENGLAND, W1F
9ST

Culver, Molly *Actor*
2658 Griffith Park Blvd, #284, Los
Angeles, CA 90039 USA

Cumberland, John *Baseball Player*
New York Yankees, PO Box 451, Odessa,
FL 33556-0451 USA

Cumberland Gap
159 Madison Ave. #2G, New York, NY
10016

Cumby, George E *Football Player*
22715 Leedstown Lane, Katy, TX 77449
USA

Cumming, Alan *Actor, Musician*
222 W 14th St #2F, New York, NY 10011
USA

Cummings, Burton *Musician, Songwriter*
Lustig Talent, PO Box 770850, Orlando,
FL 32877 USA

Cummings, Constance *Actor*
68 Old Church St, London, SW3 6EP,
UNITED KINGDOM (UK)

Cummings, Dave
4130 La Village Dr. #107, La Jolla, CA
92037

Cummings, Jim *Actor*
Visionary Entertainment, 8265 Sunset Blvd
#104, Los Angeles, CA 90046 USA

Cummings, John *Baseball Player*
Seattle Mariners, 21 Park Paseo, Laguna
Beach, CA 92677-5317 USA

Cummings, Midre *Baseball Player*
Pittsburgh Pirates, 408 Denise St, Tarpon
Springs, FL 34689-1967 USA

Cummings, Quinn *Actor*
Pietragalio Agency, 398 Collins Dr,
Pittsburgh, PA 15235 USA

Cummings, Ralph W *Misc*
PO Box 1266, Clarksville, VA 23927 USA

Cummings, Steve *Baseball Player*
Toronto Blue Jays, 11010 Sagecrest Ln,
Houston, TX 77089-3904 USA

Cummins, Gregory Scott *Actor*
Schiowitz/Clay/Rose, 1680 N Vine St,
#1016, Los Angeles, CA 90028 USA

Cummins, Peggy *Actor*
17 Brockley Road, Bexhill-on-Sea, Sussex,
TN39 4TT, UNITED KINGDOM (UK)

Cumpsty, Michael *Actor*
Innovative Artists (LA), 1505 Tenth St,
Santa Monica, CA 90401 USA

Cundey, Dean R *Cinematographer*
344 Georgian Road, La Canada, CA
91011 USA

Cundieff, Rusty *Actor*
Writers and Artists Group Intl (LA), 8383
Wilshire Blvd #550, Beverly Hills, CA
90211 USA

Cunnane, Will *Baseball Player*
San Diego Padres, 21837 N Scott Ct,
Maricopa, AZ 85239-1681 USA

Cunniff, Jill *Musician*
Metropolitan Entertainment, 2 Penn Plaza,
#2600, New York, NY 10121 USA

Cunningham, Bennie L *Football Player*
PO Box 1147, Clemson, SC 29633 USA

Cunningham, Bill *Musician*
Horizon Mgmt, PO Box 8770, Endwell,
NY 13762 USA

Cunningham, Gunther *Football Player,
Football Coach*
Tennessee Titan, 460 Great Circle Road,
Nashville, TN 37228 USA

Cunningham, Jeffrey M *Publisher*
Forbes Magazine, 60 5th Ave, New York,
NY 10011 USA

Cunningham, Joe *Baseball Player*
St Louis Cardinals, RR 1 Box 80A,
Koshkonong, MO 65692-9526 USA

Cunningham, Liam *Actor*
Marina Martin, 12/13 Poland St, London,
W1V 3DE, UNITED KINGDOM (UK)

Cunningham, Merce *Dancer,
Choreographer*
Cunningham Dance Foundation, 55
Bethune St, New York, NY 10014 USA

Cunningham, Michael *Writer*
Farrar Straus Giroux, 19 Union Square W,
New York, NY 10003 USA

Cunningham, Randall *Football Player*
2035 Helm Dr, Las Vegas, NV 89119
USA

Cunningham, Ray *Baseball Player*
St Louis Cardinals, 3646 Wingtail Way,
Pearland, TX 77584-5024 USA

Cunningham, Samuel L (Sam) Jr *Football
Player*
5595 E 7th St, #238, Long Beach, CA
90804 USA

Cunningham, Sean *Director, Producer*
4420 Hayvenhurst Ave, Encino, CA 91436
USA

Cunningham, Walter *Astronaut*
AVD, PO Box 604, Glenn Dale, MD
20769 USA

Cunningham, William J (Billy) *Basketball
Player, Coach*
Court Restaurant, 31 Front St, #33,
Conshohocken, PA 19428 USA

Cuoco, Kaley *Actor*
SDB Partners Inc, 1801 Ave of the Stars
#902, Los Angeles, CA 90067 USA

Cuomo, Andrew *Politician, Secretary*
Keppler Assoc, 4350 N Fairfax Dr #700,
Arlington, VA 22203 USA

Cuomo, Christopher *Commentator*
ABC News, 147 Columbus Ave, New
York, NY 10023 USA

Cuomo, Jerome J *Inventor*
IBM T J Watson Research Center, PO Box
218, Yorktown Heights, NY 10598 USA

Cuomo, Mario *Governor*
50 Sutton Place S, #11G, New York, NY
10022 USA

Cuomo, Rivers *Musician, Songwriter*
Atlas/Third World Entertainment, 9168
Sunset Blvd, Los Angeles, CA 90069 USA

Cuomo, Secy
Andrew 4571 7th St SW, Washington, DC
20024 USA

Cuozzo, Gary S *Football Player*
4 Swimming River Road, Lincroft, NJ
07738 USA

Cupp, James N *War Hero*
7506 Todd Place, Manassas, VA 20109
USA

Cura, Jose *Opera Singer*
Columbia Artists Mgmt Inc, 165 W 57th
St, New York, NY 10019 USA

Curatola, Vincent *Actor*
Stone Manners Talent Agency, 6500
Wilshire Blvd, Ste 550, Los Angeles, CA
90048 USA

Curb, Michael (Mike) *Composer, Business
Person*
3907 W Alameda Ave, #2, Burbank, CA
91505 USA

Curb, Mike
3907 W. Alameda Ave, Burbank, CA
91505

Curbeam, Robert L Jr *Astronaut*
15806 Virginia Fern Way, Houston, TX
77059 USA

Cure, Armand *Basketball Player, Football
Player*
6136 E Huntdale St, Long Beach, CA
90808 USA

Cure, The *Music Group*
Creative Artists Agency LCC (CAA-LA),
9830 Wilshire Blvd, Beverly Hills, CA
90212 USA

Cureton, Thomas K *Misc*
501 E Washington, Urbana, IL 61801 USA

Curfman, Shannon *Musician*
Monterey International, 200 W Superior,
#202, Chicago, IL 60610 USA

Curie-Good, Louise
1317 Delresto Dr., Beverly Hills, CA 90210

Curl, Carolyn *Skier*
Robert U Curt, 405 N Westridge Dr, Idaho Falls, ID 83402 USA

Curl, Robert F Jr *Nobel Prize Laureate*
1824 Bolsover St, Houston, TX 77005 USA

Curlander, Paul J *Business Person*
Lexmark International, 740 W New Circle Road, Lexington, KY 40550 USA

Curler, James *Business Person*
Bernis Co, 222 S 9th St, Minneapolis, MN 55402 USA

Curley, Edwin M *Misc*
2645 Pin Oak Dr, Ann Arbor, MI 48103 USA

Curley, John J *Publisher*
Gannett Co, 1100 Wilson Blvd, Arlington, VA 22209 USA

Curley, Thomas (Tom) *Publisher*
Associated Press, 50 Rockefeller Plaza, New York, NY 10020 USA

Curley, Walter J P Jr *Diplomat, Financier*
885 3rd Ave, #1200, New York, NY 10022 USA

Curnin, Thomas F *Attorney General*
Cahill Gordon Reindel, 80 Pine St, New York, NY 10005 USA

Curran, Charles E *Misc*
Southern Methodist University, Dallas Hall, Dallas, TX 75275 USA

Curran, Kevin *Tennis Player*
5808 Back Court, Austin, TX 78731 USA

Curran, Mike *Hockey Player*
7615 Lanewood Lane N, Maple Grove, MN 55311 USA

Curran, Tony *Actor*
Personal Management Company, 425 N Robertson Dr, Los Angeles, CA 90048 USA

Currence, Lafayette *Baseball Player*
Milwaukee Brewers, 1238 Stanley Dr, Rock Hill, SC 29730-5068 USA

Currey, Francis S *War Hero*
106 Catfish Landing Circle, Bonneau, SC 29431 USA

Currie, Bill *Baseball Player*
Washington Senators, 125 Lakeside Dr SW, Arlington, GA 39813-2344 USA

Currie, Cherie *Musician, Actor*
Times Productions, 520 Washington Blvd, #199, Marina del Rey, CA 90292 USA

Currie, Daniel (Dan) *Football Player*
2801 Wynadotte St, #15, Las Vegas, NV 89102 USA

Currie, Gordon *Actor*
Characters Talent Agency, The (Toronto), 150 Carlton St Fl 2, Toronto ON, M5A 2K1, CANADA

Currie, Louise *Actor*
1317 Delresto Dr, Beverly Hills, CA 90210 USA

Currie, Malcolm R *Business Person*
Hughes Aircraft Co, PO Box 956, El Segundo, CA 90245 USA

Currie, Nancy J *Astronaut*
2390 Indigo Harbour Lane, League City, TX 77573 USA

Currie, Sondra *Actor*
3951 Longridge Ave, Sherman Oaks, CA 91423 USA

Currin, Perry *Baseball Player*
St Louis Browns, 818 Amberstone Dr, San Antonio, TX 78258-2345 USA

Currington, Billy *Musician*
Universal Music Group (TN), 60 Music Sq E, Nashville, TN 37203 USA

Curris, Constantine W *Educator*
Clemson University, President's Office, Sikes Hall, Clemson, SC 29634 USA

Curry, Alana *Actor*
Epstein Wyckoff Corsa Ross & Assoc (LA), 280 S Beverly Dr #400, Beverly Hills, CA 90212 USA

Curry, Ann *Commentator*
NBC-TV, News Dept, 30 Rockefeller Plaza, New York, NY 10112 USA

Curry, Bill *Football Player, Football Coach*
2730 Bowman Mill Road, Lexington, KY 40513 USA

Curry, Dell *Basketball Player*
8381 Providence Road, Charlotte, NC 28277 USA

Curry, Denise *Basketball Player, Coach*
San Jose Lasers, 230 California St, #510, San Francisco, CA 94111 USA

Curry, Don "DC" *Actor*
Gersh Agency, The (LA), 232 N Canon Dr, Beverly Hills, CA 90210 USA

Curry, Donald *Boxer*
6814 S Hulen St, #135, Fort Worth, TX 76133 USA

Curry, Eddy *Basketball Player*
Chicago Bulls, United Center, 1901 W Madison St, Chicago, IL 60612 USA

Curry, Eric F *Football Player*
1050 E Piedmont Road, #E119, Marietta, GA 30062 USA

Curry, Mark *Actor*
Power Entertainment, 12200 W Olympic Blvd #499, Los Angeles, CA 90064 USA

Curry, Steve *Baseball Player*
Boston Red Sox, 10725 Obee Rd, Whitehouse, OH 43571-9250 USA

Curry, Tim *Actor*
Innovative Artists (LA), 1505 Tenth St, Santa Monica, CA 90401 USA

Curry, Tony *Baseball Player*
Philadelphia Phillies, PO Box 7054, Nassau, BAHAMAS

Curtin, David S *Journalist*
Colorado Springs Gazette Telegraph, 30 S Prospect, Colorado Springs, CO 80903 USA

Curtin, David Y *Misc*
2903 Rutherford Dr, Urbana, IL 61802 USA

Curtin, Jane T *Actor*
International Creative Mgmt, 8942 Wilshire Blvd, #219, Beverly Hills, CA 90211 USA

Curtin, John J Jr *Attorney General*
Bingham Dana Gould, 150 Federal St, #3500, Boston, MA 02110 USA

Curtin, Valeria *Actor*
Writers & Artists, 8383 Wilshire Blvd, #550, Beverly Hills, CA 90211 USA

Curtin, Valerie
15622 Meadowgate Rd., Encino, CA 91316

Curtis, Chad *Baseball Player*
California Angels, 1221 Old Oak Hill Dr, Ada, MI 49301-9416 USA

Curtis, Cliff *Actor*
R Bruce Ugly Agency, 218 Richmond Rd, Grey Lynn, Auckland, 2, NEW ZEALAND

Curtis, Cuneo Ann E *Swimmer*
35 Golden Hinde Blvd, San Rafael, CA 94903 USA

Curtis, Daniel M (Dan) *Director*
143 S Rockingham Ave, Los Angeles, CA 90049 USA

Curtis, Isaac F *Football Player*
711 Clinton Springs Ave, Cincinnati, OH 45229 USA

Curtis, J Michael (Mike) *Football Player*
7917 Rivers Fall Dr, Potomac, MD 20854 USA

Curtis, Jack *Baseball Player*
Chicago Cubs, 4949 Ike Starnes Rd, Granite Falls, NC 28630-8631 USA

Curtis, Jamie Lee *Actor*
Creative Artists Agency LCC (CAA-LA), 9830 Wilshire Blvd, Beverly Hills, CA 90212 USA

Curtis, John *Baseball Player*
Boston Red Sox, 850 E Ocean Blvd Unit 513, Long Beach, CA 90802-5450 USA

Curtis, Kelly *Actor*
651 N. Kilkea Dr, Los Angeles, CA 90048 USA

Curtis, Kenneth M *Governor, Diplomat*
Curtis Thaxter, 1 Canal Plaza, Portland, ME 04112 USA

Curtis, King *Baseball Player*
St Louis Cardinals, 2538 Beechwood Dr, Vineland, NJ 08361-2932 USA

Curtis, Richard *Writer*
PFD, Drury House, 34-43 Russell St, London, ENGLAND, WC2B 5HA

Curtis, Robert *Actor*
Bauman Redanty & Shaul Agency, 5757 Wilshire Blvd #473, Los Angeles, CA 90036 USA

Curtis, Robin *Actor*
1147 Beverly Hill Dr, Cincinnati, OH 45208 USA

Curtis, Todd *Actor*
2046 14th St, #10, Santa Monica, CA 90405 USA

Curtis, Tony *Actor*
William Morris Agency (WMA-LA), 1 William Morris Pl, Beverly Hills, CA 90212 USA

Curtis-Hall, Vondie *Actor*
The Firm, 9100 Wilshire Blvd, #100W, Beverly Hills, CA 90210 USA

Curtola, Bobby *Musician*
ESP Productions, 720 Spadina Ave, #PH2, Toronto, ON M5S 2T9, CANADA

Cusack, Ann *Actor*
Innovative Artists, 1505 10th St, Santa Monica, CA 90401 USA

Cusack, Joan *Actor, Comedian*
Wolf/Kasteller, 335 N Maple Dr #351, Beverly Hills, CA 90210 USA

Cusack, John *Actor*
Barnes Morris Klein Young, 1424 2nd St, #3, Santa Monica, CA 90401 USA

Cusack, Sinead *Actor*
Markham & Froggatt Julian House, 4 Windmill St., London, W1P 1HF, UNITED KINGDOM (UK)

Cushman, David W *Misc*
20 Lake Shore Dr, Princeton Junction, NJ 08550 USA

Cushman, Karen *Writer*
Clarion Books, 215 Park Ave S, New York, NY 10003 USA

Cussler, Clive *Writer*
13764 W 61st Circle, Arvada, CO 80004 USA

Cust, Jack *Baseball Player*
Arizona Diamondbacks, 145 Route 31 N, Pennington, NJ 08534-3615 USA

Custom *Musician*
ArtistDirect, 10900 Wilshire Blvd, #1400, Los Angeles, CA 90024 USA

Cutcliffe, David *Football Coach*
University of Mississippi, Athletic Dept, University, MS 38677 USA

Cuthbert, Elisha *Actor*
Rozon/Mercer Management, 345 N Maple Dr #376, Beverly Hills, CA 90210-5945 USA

Cuthbeth, Elizabeth (Betty) *Track Athlete*
4/7 Karara Close, Halls Head, Mandurah, WA 6210, AUSTRALIA

Cutler, Alexander M *Business Person*
Eaton Corp, Eaton Center, 1111 Superior Ave, Cleveland, OH 44114 USA

Cutler, Bruce *Attorney General*
41 Madison Ave, New York, NY 10010 USA

Cutler, Lloyd N *Government Official*
3115 O St NW, Washington, DC 20007 USA

Cutler, Walter L *Diplomat*
Meridian International Center, 1630 Crescent Place NW, Washington, DC 20009 USA

Cutliffe, Molly *Actor*
Herney/Grimes, PO Box 64249, Los Angeles, CA 90064 USA

Cutrufello, Mary *Musician, Songwriter*
Joe's Garage, 4405 Belmont Park Terrace, Nashville, TN 37215 USA

Cutter, Kiki *Skier*
PO Box 1317, Carbondale, CO 81623 USA

Cutter, Lise *Actor*
PO Box 2665, Sag Harbor, NY 11963 USA

Cutter, Slade D *Football Player*
6102 RIver Crescent Dr, Annapolis, MD 21401 USA

Cuviello, Peter M *General*
Director, Defence Information Systems Agency, Alington, VA 22204 USA

Cuyler, Milt *Baseball Player*
Detroit Tigers, 962 Lamar Rd, Macon, GA 31210-7109 USA

Cwiklinski, Stanley *Athlete*
68 Chowning Dr, Hampton, VA 23664 USA

Cypher, John
9229 Sunset Blvd. #315, Los Angeles, CA 90069

Cypher, Jon *Actor*
498 Manzanita Ave, Ventura, CA 93001 USA

Cyphers, Charles
324 E. 1st St. #300, Los Angeles, CA 90012

Cypress Hill *Music Group*
William Morris Agency (WMA-LA), 1 William Morris Pl, Beverly Hills, CA 90212 USA

Cyr, Conrad K *Judge*
US Courts of Appeals, PO Box 635, Bangor, ME 04402 USA

Cyrus, Billy Ray *Musician, Songwriter*
As Is Mgmt, 704 18th Ave S, Nashville, TN 37203 USA

Czajkowski, Jim *Baseball Player*
Colorado Rockies, 1648 Rivergate Dr, Sevlerville, TN 37862-9321 USA

Czapsky, Stefan *Cinematographer*
RR 3 Box 278, Unadilla, NY 13849 USA

Czemy, Henry *Actor*
438 Queen St E, Toronto, ON M5A 1T4, CANADA

Czerny, Henry *Actor*
Oscars Abrams Zimel & Associates, 438 Queen St E, Toronto ON, M5A 1T4, CANADA

Czrongursky, Jan *Prime Minister*
Prime Minister's Office, Nam Slobody 1, Bratislava, 81370, SLOVAKIA

Czyz, Bobby *Boxer*
110 Pennsylvania Ave, Flemington, NJ 08822 USA

D

D, Deezer *Actor*
Acme Talent & Literary Agency (LA), 4727 Wilshire Blvd #333, Los Angeles, CA 90010 USA

D'Abaldo, Chris *Musician*
Helter Skelter Plaza, 535 Kings Road, London, SW10 0S, UNITED KINGDOM (UK)

D'Abo, Maryam *Actor*
Artist Independent, 32 Tavistock St, London, WC2E 7PB, UNITED KINGDOM (UK)

D'Abo, Olivia *Actor*
International Creative Management (ICM-LA), 8942 Wilshire Blvd, Beverly Hills, CA 90211 USA

D'Acquisto, John F *Baseball Player*
3440 Fir St, San Diego, CA 92104 USA

D'Agosto, Nicholas *Actor*

D'Alema, Massima *Prime Minister*
Prime Minister's Office, Piazza Colomma 370, Rome, 00187, ITALY

D'Aleo, Angelo *Musician*
Paramount Entertainment, PO Box 12, Far Hills, NJ 07931 USA

D'Amboise, Jacques *Dancer, Choreographer*
National Dance Institute, 594 Broadway, #805, New York, NY 10012 USA

D'Ambrosio, Dominick *Misc*
Allied Industrial Workers Union, 3520 W Oklahoma Ave, Milwaukee, WI 53215 USA

D'Amico, Jeff *Baseball Player*
6903 Cedar Ridge Dr, Pinellas Park, FL 33781 USA

D'Amico, John *Referee*
1900 Owlsnest Lane, Mississauga, ON L4W 2J2, CANADA

D'Amico, William D *Athlete*
30 Greenwood St, Lake Placid, NY 12946 USA

D'Angelo *Musician, Songwriter*
Cheeba Mgmt, 304 Park Ave S, New York, NY 10010 USA

D'Angelo, Beverly *Actor*
Chal Productions, 301 W 57th St, #16C, New York, NY 10019 USA

D'Angio, Giulio J *Misc*
Children's Hospital, 34th & Civic Center Blvd, Philadelphia, PA 19104 USA

D'Antoni, Mike *Basketball Player, Coach*
Phoenix Suns, 201 E Jefferson St, Phoenix, AZ 85004 USA

D'Arbanville, Patti *Actor*
Abrams Artists Agency (LA), 9200 Sunset Blvd Fl 11, Los Angeles, CA 90069 USA

D'Arby, Terence Trent *Musician*
Boulevard Mgmt, 21650 Oxnard St, #1925, Woodland Hills, CA 91367 USA

D'Arby, Terence Trent (Sananda Maitreya) *Musician*
Sananda Records, Sempione 38, Milan, 20154, Italy

D'Arcangelo, Ildebrando *Opera Singer*
Lies Askonas, 6 Henrietta St, London, WC2E 8LA, UNITED KINGDOM (UK)

D'Arcy *Musician*
Cohen Brothers Mgmt, 500 Molino St, #104, Los Angeles, CA 90013 USA

D'Arcy, James *Actor*
Markham and Froggatt Agency, 4 Windmill St, London, W1T 2H, England

D'Arcy, Margaretta *Writer*
Cassarotto, 60/66 Wardour St, London, W1V 4ND, UNITED KINGDOM (UK)

D'Ascoli, Bernard *Musician*
Clarion/Seven Muses, 47 Whitehall Park, London, N19 3TW, UNITED KINGDOM (UK)

D'Eath, Tom *Misc*
2011 74th St NW, Bradenton, FL 34209 USA

D'Elia, Chris *Actor, Writer*
3 Arts Entertainment Inc, 9460 Wilshire
Blvd Fl 7, Beverly Hills, CA 90212 USA

D'Elia, Federico *Actor*
Telefe - Argentina, Pavon 2444
(C1248AAT), Buenos Aires, ARGENTINA

D'Errico, Donna *Actor, Model*
Michael Slessinger & Assoc, 8730 Sunset
Blvd #270, Los Angeles, CA 90069 USA

D'Harnoncourt, Anne *Director*
Philadelphia Museum of Art, 25th &
Franklin Parkway, Philadelphia, PA 19101
USA

D'Lyn, Shae *Actor*
James/Levy/Jacobson Management, 3500
W Olive Ave #1470, Burbank, CA 91505
USA

D'Onofrio, Vincent *Actor, Producer*
Ken Christmas Group, The, 1635 N
Cahuenga Blvd Fl 4, Los Angeles, CA
90028 USA

D'Orsay, Brooke *Actor*
MBST Entertainment, 345 N Maple D
#200, Suite 200, Beverly Hills, CA 90210
USA

D'Rivera, Paquito
Charismic Productions, 2704 Mozart
Place NW, Washington, DC 20009 USA

D'Souza, Lawrence *Director, Filmmaker,
Producer, Bollywood*
302B Red Rose New Link Road, Versova
Andheri, Bombay, MS 400 058, INDIA

D-12 *Musician*
Evolution Talent Agency LLC, 1776
Broadway Fl 15, New York, NY 10019
USA

D12 *Music Group*
William Morris Agency (WMA-NY), 1325
Ave of the Americas, New York, NY
10019 USA

Da Band *Music Group*
Bad Boy Worldwide Entertainment, 1540
Broadway Fl 30, New York, NY 10036
USA

Da Brat *Musician*
Artistic Control, 1385 Spring St NW,
#700, Atlanta, GA 30309 USA

Daal, Omar *Baseball Player*
Los Angeles Dodgers, 2940 Paddock Rd,
Weston, FL 33331-3604 USA

Daberko, David A *Financier*
National City Corp, National City Center,
1900 E 9th St, Cleveland, OH 44114 USA

Dacascos, Mark *Actor*
PMK/HBH Public Relations (PMK-LA),
8500 Wilshire Blvd #700, Beverly Hills,
CA 90211 USA

Dacquisto, John *Baseball Player*
San Francisco Giants, 3440 Fir St, San
Diego, CA 92104-5706 USA

Dacruz Policarpo, Jose Cardinal *Religious
Leader*
Curia Patriarcal, Camo dos Martires da
Patria 45, Lisbon, 1150, PORTUGAL

Dacus, Don *Actor*
8455 Fountain Ave, #512, Los Angeles,
CA 90069 USA

Daddario, Alex *Actor*
Jerry Shandrew PR, 1050 South Stanley
Avenue, Los Angeles, CA 90019-6634
USA

Dade, Paul *Baseball Player*
California Angels, 5212 66th Street Ct W,
University Place, WA 98467-3337 USA

Daehlie, Bjorn *Skier*
Cathinka Guldbergs Veg 64, Holler, 2034,
NORWAY

Dafoe, Willem *Actor*
Artists Independent Network (NY), 270 La
Fayette St #402, New York, NY 10012
USA

Daft, Douglas *Business Person*
Coca Cola Co, 1 Coca Cola Plaza, 310
North Ave NW, Atlanta, GA 30313 USA

Daggett, Timothy (Tim) *Gymnast*
134 Country Club Dr, East Longmeadow,
MA 01028 USA

Dagres, Angie *Baseball Player*
Baltimore Orioles, PO Box 27, Rowley,
MA 01969-0027 USA

Dagworthy Prew, Wendy A *Fashion
Designer*
18 Melrose Terrace, London, W6,
UNITED KINGDOM (UK)

Dahl, Ariene *Actor*
Dahlmark Productions, PO Box 116,
Sparkill, NY 10976 USA

Dahl, Arlene
PO Box 116, Sparkill, NY 10976

Dahl, Christopher *Educator*
State University of New York College,
President's Office, Genesco, NY 14454
USA

Dahl, John *Director, Writer*
Creative Artists Agency, 9830 Wilshire
Blvd, Beverly Hills, CA 90212 USA

Dahl, Lawrence F *Misc*
4817 Woodburn Dr, Madison, WI 53711
USA

Dahl, Roald *Writer*
Casarotto Ramsay & Associates td,
National House, 60-66 Wardour Street,
London, W1V 4ND, United Kingdom

Dahl, Sophie *Actor, Model*
Storm Model Mgmt, 5 Jubilee Place,
London, SW3, UNITED KINGDOM (UK)

Dahlbeck, Eva
Box 27126, Stockholm, SWEDEN, 102 52

Dahlberg, A William *Business Person*
Southern Co, 270 Peachtree St NW,
Atlanta, GA 30303 USA

Dahlberg, Kenneth H (Ken) *War Hero*
19360 Walden Trail, Wayzala, MN 55391
USA

Dahlgren, Edward C *War Hero*
PO Box 26, Mars Hill, ME 04758 USA

Dahlke, Jerry *Baseball Player*
Chicago White Sox, 201 S Pine Lake Dr,
Batesville, MS 38606-6468 USA

Dahm, Werner K *Misc*
7605 Martha Dr SE, Huntsville, AL 35802
USA

Dahrendorf, Ralf Gustav
Postfach 5560, Konstanz, GERMANY,
D-78434

Dai, Ailian *Dancer, Choreographer*
Hua Qiao Gong Yu #2-16, Hua Yuan
Cun, Hai Dian, Beijing, 100044, CHINA

Daiches, David *Writer*
22 Belgrave Crescent, Edinburgh, EH4
3AL, SCOTLAND

Daigle, Alexander *Hockey Player*
3510 Rue Bordeaux, Trois-Rivieres-Quest,
QC, G8Y 3P7, CANADA

Daigneault, J J *Hockey Player*
Minnesota Wild, Xcel Energy Arena, 175
Kellogg Blvd W, Saint Paul, MN 55102
USA

Dailey, Bill *Baseball Player*
Cleveland Indians, 5019 Meadow Way,
Dublin, VA 24084-5721 USA

Dailey, Janet *Writer*
HC 4, Box 2197, Branson, MO 65616
USA

Dailey, Peter H *Diplomat*
State Department, 2201 C St NW,
Washington, DC 20520 USA

Dailey, Quintin *Basketball Player*
22808 Hilton Head Dr, #28, Diamond
Bar, CA 91765 USA

Daily, Bill *Actor*
1331 Park Ave SW, #802, Albuquerque,
NM 87102 USA

Daily, E G *Songwriter, Actor, Musician*
T-Best Talent Agency, 508 Honey Lake
Court, Danville, CA 94506 USA

Daily, Gretchen *Misc*
Stanford University, Ecology Dept,
Stanford, CA 94305 USA

Daily, Parker *Religious Leader*
Baptist Bible Fellowship International, PO
Box 191, Springfield, MO 65801 USA

Dainton, Frederick S *Misc*
Fieldside, Water Eaton Lane, Kidlington,
Oxford, OX5 2PR, UNITED KINGDOM
(UK)

Daio, Norberto J D C A *Prime Minister*
Prime Minister's Office, CP 38, Sao Tome,
SAO TOME & PRINCIPE

Dajani, Nadia *Actor*
Innovative Artists, 1505 10th St, Santa
Monica, CA 90401 USA

Dal Canton, Bruce *Baseball Player*
Pittsburgh Pirates, 624 Ray Dr, Carnegie,
PA 15106-1808 USA

Daland, Peter *Coach*
PO Box 2443, Aquebogue, NY 11931
USA

Dalbavie, Andre *Composer*
Van Walsum Mgmt, 4 Addison Bridge
Place, London, W14 8XP, UNITED
KINGDOM (UK)

Dalberto, Michel *Musician*
13 Blvd Henri Plumof, Vevey, 1800,
SWITZERLAND

Daldry, Stephen *Director*
Royal Court Theater, Sloane Square,
London, SW1, UNITED KINGDOM (UK)

Dale, Alan *Actor*
Himber Entertainment Inc, 211 S Beverly
Dr #208, Beverly Hills, CA 90212 USA

Dale, Bruce *Photographer*
National Geographic Magazine, 1145
17th St NW, Washington, DC 20036 USA
Dale, Carroll W *Football Player*
Clinch Valley College, Athletic
Department, 1 College Ave, Wise, VA
24293 USA
Dale, Dick
PO Box 1713, Twentyninepalms, CA
92277 USA
Dale, James Badge *Actor*
Writers and Artists Group Intl (LA), 8383
Wilshire Blvd #550, Beverly Hills, CA
90211 USA
Dale, Jim *Actor*
Mark Sendroff, 230 W 56th St, #63B, New
York, NY 10019 USA
Dale, William B *Economist, Government
Official*
6008 Landon Lane, Bathesda, MD 20817
USA
Dalembert, Samuel *Basketball Player*
Philadelphia 76ers, 1st Union Center,
3601 S Broad St, Philadelphia, PA 19148
USA
Dalena, Pete *Baseball Player*
Cleveland Indians, 4951 N Thorne Ave,
Fresno, CA 93704-2935 USA
Dales-Schuman, Stacey *Basketball Player*
Washington Mystics, MCI Center, 601 F St
NW, Washington, DC 20004 USA
Dalesandro, Mark *Baseball Player*
California Angels, 1908 Arbor Fields Dr,
Plainfield, IL 60544-5729 USA
Daley, Bud *Baseball Player*
Cleveland Indians, 309 Elk Dr, Riverton,
WY 82501-2527 USA
Daley, Pete *Baseball Player*
Boston Red Sox, 4019 Calle Mira Monte,
Newbury Park, CA 91320-1932 USA
Daley, Richard M *Politician*
Mayor's Office, City Hall, 121 N LaSalle
St, Chicago, IL 60602 USA
Daley, Rosle *Chef, Writer*
Harpo Productions, 110 N Carpenter St,
Chicago, IL 60607 USA
Daley, William N (Bill) *Secretary*
SBC Communications, 175 E Houston,
San Antonio, TX 78205 USA
Dalgarno, Alexander *Astronomer*
27 Robinson St, Cambridge, MA 02138
USA
Dalgilsh, Kenneth M (Kenny) *Soccer
Player*
FC Newcastle United, Saint James Park,
Newcastle-on-Tyne, NE1 4ST, UNITED
KINGDOM (UK)
Dalheimer, Patrick *Musician*
Freedman & Smith, 350 W End Ave, #1,
New York, NY 10024 USA
Dalhousie, Simon R *Government Official*
Brechin Castle, Brechin, DD9 6SH,
SCOTLAND
Dali, Bobby *Musician*
H K Mgmt, 9200 W Sunset Blvd, #530,
Los Angeles, CA 90069 USA

Dali, Tracy *Actor, Model*
PO Box 69541, Los Angeles, CA 90069
USA
Dalian, Susan *Actor*
GVA Talent Agency Inc, 9229 Sunset Blvd
#320, Los Angeles, CA 90069 USA
Dalie, Beatrice *Actor*
Artmedia, 20 Ave Rapp, Paris, 75007,
FRANCE
Dalis, Irene *Opera Singer*
1731 Cherry Grove Dr, San Jose, CA
95125 USA
Dallas Cowboys Cheerleaders
1 Cowboys Parkway, Irving, TX 75063-
4727
Dallenbach, Wally *Misc*
5315 Slowe Lane, Harrisburg, NC 89134
USA
Dallesandro, Joe *Actor*
521 W Briar Place, #505, Chicago, IL
60657 USA
Dalm, Jan
DALM, Dv de Merwedestraat, HI
Ambacht, GB, 3341, Netherlands
Dalmacci, Ricardo *Actor*
Gabriel Blanco Iglesias (Mexico), Rio
Balsas 35-32, Colonia Cuauhtemoc, DF,
06500, Mexico
Dalrymple, Clay *Baseball Player*
Philadelphia Phillies, 28248 Mateer Rd,
Gold Beach, OR 97444-9618 USA
Dalrymple, Gary B *Misc*
1847 NW Hillcrest Dr, Corvallis, OR
97330 USA
Dalton, Abby *Actor*
Kathleen Kinmont, 11365 Ventura Blvd
#100, Studio City, CA 91604 USA
Dalton, Audrey *Actor*
2241 Labrusca, Mission Viejo, CA 92692
USA
Dalton, James E *General*
61 Misty Acres Road, Rolling Hills Estate,
CA 90274 USA
Dalton, John H *Government Official*
3710 University Ave NW, Washington,
DC 20016 USA
Dalton, Lacy J *Musician*
820 Cartwright Road, Reno, NV 89521
USA
Dalton, Mike *Baseball Player*
Detroit Tigers, 354 Flynn Ave, Mountain
View, CA 94043-3923 USA
Dalton, Nic *Musician*
Agency Group Ltd, 1775 Broadway, #430,
New York, NY 10019 USA
Dalton, Timothy *Actor*
James Sharkey, 21 Golden Square,
London, W1R 3PA, UNITED KINGDOM
(UK)
Daltrey, Roger *Actor*
TalentWorks (LA), 3500 W Olive Ave
#1400, Burbank, CA 91505 USA
Daltry, Roger *Musician, Actor*
Conway Van Gelder Robinson, 18-21
Jermyn St, London, SW1Y 6NB, UNITED
KINGDOM (UK)

Daly, Cahal Brendan Cardinal *Religious
Leader*
Ard Mhacha, 23 Rosetta Ave, Belfast, BT7
3HG, NORTHERN IRELAND
Daly, Carson *Entertainer*
William Morris Agency, 1325 Ave of
Americas, New York, NY 10019 USA
Daly, Charles J (Chuck) *Coach*
18586 SE Village Circle, Tequesta, FL
33469 USA
Daly, John *Golfer*
Cambridge Sports Int'l, 5335 Wisconsin
Ave NW, #850, Washington, DC 20015
USA
Daly, John *Producer*
Hemdale, 7960 Beverly Blvd, Los
Angeles, CA 90048 USA
Daly, Michael J *War Hero*
155 Redding Road, Fairfield, CT 06824
USA
Daly, Tess *Television Host*
John Noel Management, 10A Belmont St,
Floor 2, London, NW1 8HH, UNITED
KINGDOM (UK)
Daly, Tim *Actor, Producer*
Red House Entertainment, 22287
Mulholland Hwy #129, Calabasas, CA
91302 USA
Daly, Timothy *Actor*
Industry Entertainment, 955 Carillo Dr,
#300, Los Angeles, CA 90048 USA
Daly, Tyne *Actor*
272 S Lasky Dr, #402, Beverly Hills, CA
90212 USA
Dam, Kenneth W *Government Official,
Attorney General*
University of Chicago, Law School, 1111
E 60st St, Chicago, IL 60637 USA
Damadian, Raymond V *Inventor*
FONAR Corp, 110 Marcus Dr, Melville,
NY 11747 USA
Damanchiah, Godfrey *Comedian, Actor*
William Morris Agency (WMA-NY), 1325
Ave of the Americas, New York, NY
10019 USA
Damas, Bertila *Actor*
PO Box 17193, Beverly Hills, CA 90209
USA
Damasio, Antonio R *Doctor*
University of Iowa Hospital, Neurology
Dept, Iowa City, IA 52242 USA
Damaska, Jack *Baseball Player*
St Louis Cardinals, 252 Blackhawk Rd,
Beaver Falls, PA 15010-1404 USA
DaMatta, Cristiano *Race Car Driver*
Newman-Haas Racing, 50 Tower
Parkway, Lincolnshire, IL 60069 USA
Dameshek, David *Actor, Writer*
Creative Artists Agency LCC (CAA-LA),
9830 Wilshire Blvd, Beverly Hills, CA
90212 USA
Damian, Alexa *Actor*
Televisa, Blvd Adolfo Lopez Mateos 232,
Colonia San Angel INN, DF, CP 01060,
MEXICO
Damian, Michael *Actor, Musician*
Gold Marshak Liedtke, 3500 W Olive
Ave, #1400, Burbank, CA 91505 USA

Damiani, Damiano *Director*
Via Delle Terme Deciane 2, Rome, 00153, ITALY

Damico, Jeff *Baseball Player*
Milwaukee Brewers, 6903 Cedar Ridge Dr, Pinellas Park, FL 33781-4904 USA

Dammerman, Dennis D *Business Person*
General Electric Co, 3135 Easton Tumpike, Fairfield, CT 06828 USA

Damon, Johnny D *Baseball Player*
Kansas City Royals, 904 Main St, Windermere, FL 34786-8727 USA

Damon, Mark *Actor*
2781 Benedict Canyon Dr, Beverly Hills, CA 90210 USA

Damon, Matt *Actor*
LivePlanet, 2644 30th St, Santa Monica, CA 90405 USA

Damon, Stuart *Actor*
387 N Van Ness Ave, Los Angeles, CA 90004 USA

Damon, Una *Actor*
Writer's & Artists, 8383 Wilshire Blvd, #550, Beverly Hills, CA 90211 USA

Damone, Vic *Actor, Musician*
International Ventures, 25864 Tournament Road, Suite L, Valencia, CA 91355 USA

Damphousse, Vincent *Hockey Player*
16780 Loma St, Los Gatos, CA 95032 USA

Dampler, Erick *Basketball Player*
2635 Sea View Parkway, Alameda, CA 94502 USA

Dampler, Louie *Basketball Player*
Dampler Ditributing, 2808 New Moody Lane, La Grange, KY 40031 USA

Damus, Mike *Actor*
United Talent Agency (UTA), 9560 Wilshire Blvd, Beverly Hills, CA 90212 USA

Dan-Jumbo, Andrew *Reality TV Star*
The Learning Channel (TLC), 7700 Wisconsin Avenue, Bethesda, MD 20814 USA

Dana, Bill *Actor, Comedian*
5965 Peacock Ridge, #563, Rancho Palos Verdes, CA 90275 USA

Dana, Justin *Actor*
13111 Ventura Blvd, #102, Studio City, CA 91604 USA

Dana, William (Bill) *Misc*
21400 Grand Oaks Ave, Tehachapi, CA 93561 USA

Danby, Gordon T *Inventor*
126 Sound Road, Wading River, NY 11792 USA

Dance, Bill *Fisherman*
Bill Dance's Fishing, PO Box 198, Brownsville, TN 38012 USA

Dance, Charies *Actor*
7812 Forsythe St, Sunland, CA 91040 USA

Dance, Charles *Actor*
International Creative Management (ICM-LA), 8942 Wilshire Blvd, Beverly Hills, CA 90211 USA

Dancer, Stanley F *Race Car Driver*
1624 E Atlantic Blvd, Pompano Beach, FL 33060 USA

Dancy, Hugh *Actor*
Untitled Entertainment (NY), 23 E 22nd St Fl 3, New York, NY 10010 USA

Dancy, John *Commentator*
Harvard University, Kennedy Government School, Cambridge, MA 02138 USA

Dando, Evan *Musician*
Agency Group Ltd, 1775 Broadway, #430, New York, NY 10019 USA

Dandridge, Bob *Basketball Player*
1708 Saint Denis Ave, Norfolk, VA 23509 USA

Dandridge, Ray
PO Box 61139, Palm Bay, FL 32906

Dandy Warholds, The *Music Group*
Tsunami Entertainment, 2525 Hyperion Ave, Los Angeles, CA 90027 USA

Dane, Alexandra *Actor*
Rolf Kruger Mgmt, 205 Chudliegh Road, London, SE4 1EG, UNITED KINGDOM (UK)

Dane, Paul *Misc*
12105 Ambassador Dr, #515, Colarado Springs, CO 80921 USA

Daneker, Pat *Baseball Player*
Chicago White Sox, 1419 Ritchey St, Williamsport, PA 17701-2640 USA

Danelli, Dino *Musician*
Rascals Cassidy, 11761 Speedway Blvd, Tucson, AZ 85748 USA

Danes, Claire *Actor*
Industry Entertainment, 955 Carillo Dr, #300, Los Angeles, CA 90048 USA

Danesh, Darius *Musician*
Pop Idol (Fremantle Media), 2700 Colorado Ave #450, Santa Monica, CA 90404 USA

Danforth, Fred *Artist*
PO Box 828, Middlebury, VT 05753 USA

Danforth, Douglas D *Business Person, Baseball Player*
8720 Bay Colony Dr, #701, Naples, FL 34108 USA

Danforth, John C (Jack) *Senator*
US Permanent Mission, United Nations, 799 UN Plaza, New York, NY 10017 USA

Dangerfield, Rodney *Comedian, Actor*
TalentWorks (LA), 3500 W Olive Ave #1400, Burbank, CA 91505 USA

Daniel, Beth *Golfer*
Ladies Pro Golf Association (LPGA), 100 International Golf Drive, Daytona Beach, FL 32124 USA

Daniel, Brittany *Actor*
Handprint Entertainment, 1100 Glendon Ave, #1000, Los Angeles, CA 90024 USA

Daniel, Elizabeth A (Beth) *Golfer*
1350 Echo Dr, Jupiter, FL 33458 USA

Daniel, Jeffrey *Musician*
Green Light Talent Agency, PO Box 3172, Beverly Hills, CA 90212 USA

Daniel, Margaret Truman *Writer*
Scott Meredith Literary Agency, 1675 Broadway, New York, NY 10019 USA

Daniel, Tony *Cartoonist*
International Creative Mgmt, 8942 Wilshire Blvd, #219, Beverly Hills, CA 90211 USA

Danielpour, Richard *Composer*
Sony Classics Records, 2100 Colorado Ave, Santa Monica, CA 90404 USA

Daniels, Anthony *Actor*
Fifi Oscard Agency, 110 W 40th St #1601, New York, NY 10018 USA

Daniels, Antonio *Basketball Player*
Seattle SuperSonics, 351 Elliot Ave W, #500, Seattle, WA 98119 USA

Daniels, Charlie *Musician, Songwriter*
CDB Mgmt, 14410 Central Pike, Mount Joliet, TN 37122 USA

Daniels, Cheryl *Bowler*
6574 Crest Top Dr, West Bloomfield, MI 48322 USA

Daniels, Clemon (Bo) *Football Player*
1466 High St, Oakland, CA 94601 USA

Daniels, Erin *Actor*
Essential Entertainment Management, 6121 Santa Monica Blvd #201, Hollywood, CA 90038 USA

Daniels, Greg *Actor*
Endeavor Agency LLC (LA), 9601 Wilshire Blvd Fl 3, Beverly Hills, CA 90210 USA

Daniels, Jeff *Actor*
701 Glazier Road, Chelsea, MI 48118 USA

Daniels, Kevin *Actor*
Lesher Entertainment Inc, 800 S Robertson Blvd #8, Los Angeles, CA 90035 USA

Daniels, Melvin (Mel) *Basketball Player*
19789 Centennial Road, Sheridan, IN 46069 USA

Daniels, William *Actor*
12805 Hortense St, Studio City, CA 91604 USA

Daniels, William B *Physicist*
283 Dallam Road, Newark, DE 19711 USA

Danielsen, Egil *Track Athlete*
Roreks Gate 9, Hamar, 2300, NORWAY

Danielson, Gary D *Football Player*
1686 Edinborough Dr, Rochester Hills, MI 48306 USA

Danielsson, Bengt F *Misc*
Box 558, Papette, TAHITI

Daniloff, Nicholas *Journalist*
PO Box 892, Chester, VT 05143 USA

Danko, William D *Writer*
Pocket Books, 1230 Ave of Americas, New York, NY 10020 USA

Dankworth, John
The Old Rectory Wavendon, Milton Keynes, ENGLAND, MK17 8LT

Dankworth, John P W *Musician, Composer*
Old Rectory, Wavendon, Milton Kenyes, MK17 8LT, UNITED KINGDOM (UK)

Danneels, Godfried Cardinal *Religious Leader*
Aartsbisdom, Wollemarkt 15, Mechelen, 2800, BELGIUM

Danner, Blythe *Actor*
304 21st St, Santa Monica, CA 90402
USA

Danner, Christian *Misc*
JAS Engineering, Viale Europa, 72 Strada
Bn 1, Cusago, 20090, ITALY

Danning, Harry *Baseball Player*
212 Fox Chapel Court, Valparaiso, IN
46385 USA

Danning, Sybil *Actor, Model*
Adventures Production, 1438 North
Gower St, Bldg 35, Los Angeles, CA
90028 USA

Danny & The Juniors
PO Box 1017, Turnersville, NJ 08012

Dano, Linda *Actor*
VSMP, 1010 Nautilus Ln, Marnaroneck,
NY 10543 USA

Dano, Paul Franklin *Actor*
Industry Entertainment, 955 S Carrillo Dr
#300, Los Angeles, CA 90048 USA

Danson, Ted *Actor*
Industry Entertainment, 955 Carillo Dr,
#300, Los Angeles, CA 90048 USA

Dante, Joe *Director*
2321 Holly Dr, Los Angeles, CA 90068
USA

Dante, Michael *Actor*
3349 Cahuenga Blvd W, #1, Los Angeles,
CA 90068 USA

Dantine, Nikki *Actor*
707 North Palm Dr, Beverly Hills, CA
90210 USA

Dantley, Adrian D *Basketball Player,
Coach*
1232 Via del Sol, San Dimas, CA 91773
USA

Danto, Arthur C *Misc*
Columbia University, Philosophy Dept,
New York, NY 10024 USA

Dantzig, George B *Scientist*
821 Tolman Dr, Stanford, CA 94305 USA

Dantzig, Rudi Van *Choreographer*
Emma-Straat 27, Amsterdam,
NETHERLANDS

Danza, Tony *Actor*
25000 Malibu Road, Malibu, CA 90265
USA

Danzig
PO Box 884563, San Francisco, CA
94188

Danzig, Frederick P *Editor*
Advertising Age, Editorial Dept, 220 E
42nd St, New York, NY 10017 USA

Danziger, Jeff *Editor, Cartoonist*
RFD, Plainfield, VT 05667 USA

Daoud, Ignace Moussa I Cardinal
Religious Leader
Palazzo del Bramante, Via della
Conciliazione 34, Rome, 00193, ITALY

Daphnis, Nassos *Artist*
362 W Broadway, New York, NY 10013
USA

Dara, Olu *Actor*
Monterey Peninsula Artists (Chicago), 200
West Superior #202, Chicago, IL 60610
USA

Darabont, Frank *Director, Writer*
William Morris Agency, 151 El Camino
Dr, Beverly Hills, CA 90212 USA

Darboven, Hanne *Artist*
Am Burgberg 26, Hamburg, 21079,
GERMANY

Darby, Kim *Actor*
Michael Slessinger, 8730 Sunset Blvd,
#220W, Los Angeles, CA 90069 USA

Darc, Mireille *Actor*
Agents Associes Beaume, 201 Faubourg
Saint Honore, Paris, 75008, FRANCE

Darcum, Max *Skier*
PO Box 189, Dillon, CO 80435 USA

Darcy, Dame *Artist*
Fantagraphics Books, 7563 Lake City
Way, Seattle, WA 98115 USA

Darden, Christopher
William Morris Agency (WMA-LA), 1
William Morris Pl, Beverly Hills, CA
90212 USA

Daredevil *Music Group*
Wind-up Records, 72 Madison Ave, New
York, NY 10016 USA

Darehshori, Nader F *Publisher*
Houghton Mifflin Co, 222 Berkeley St,
Boston, MA 02116 USA

Dark, Alvin *Baseball Player*
103 Cranberry Way, Easley, SC 29642
USA

Darling, Charles (Chuck) *Basketball
Player*
8066 S Kramerie Way, Centennial, CO
80112 USA

Darling, Jennifer *Actor*
13351 Riverside Dr, #427, Sherman Oaks,
CA 91423 USA

Darling, Joan *Actor*
PO Box 6700, Tesuque, NM 87574 USA

Darling, Ronald M (Ron) *Baseball Player*
19 Woodland Street, Milbury, MA 01527
USA

Darmaatmadja, Julius Riyadi Cardinal
Religious Leader
Keuskupan Agung, Jl Katedral 7, Jakarta,
10710, INDONESIA

Darman, Richard G *Government Official*
1137 Crest Lane, McLean, VA 22101 USA

Darnell, James E Jr *Biologist*
Rockefeller University, Medical Center,
1230 York Ave, New York, NY 10021
USA

Darnton, John *Journalist, Writer*
New York Times, Editorial Dept, 229 W
43rd St, New York, NY 10036 USA

Darnton, Robert C *Historian*
6 McCosh Circle, Princeton, NJ 08540
USA

Darren, James *Musician, Actor*
PO Box 1088, Beverly Hills, CA 90213
USA

Darrian, Raquel *Adult Film Star*
49 Eaton Ct, Manhasset, NY 11030

Darrieux, Danielle *Actor*
Nicole Cann, 1 Rue Alfred de Vigny,
Paris, 75008, FRANCE

Darrow, Henry *Actor*
980 Alta Vista Dr, Altadena, CA 91001
USA

Darwin, Danny *Baseball Player*
1300 N Saint James Cir, Pilot Point, TX
76258 USA

Das, Alisha *Actor*
19583 Bowers Dr, Topanga, CA 90290
USA

Dascascos, Marc *Actor*
PO Box 1549, Studio City, CA 91614 USA

Dash, Damon *Actor, Producer, Director,
Writer*
Dash Films, 825 8th Ave Fl 29, New York,
NY 10019-7472 USA

Dash, Leon O Jr *Journalist*
Washington Post, Editorial Dept, 1150
15th Ave NW, Washington, DC 20071
USA

Dash, Sam
110 Newlands, Chevy Chase, MD 20015

Dash, Sarah *Musician*
Talent Consultants International, 1560
Broadway, #1308, New York, NY 10036
USA

Dash, Stacey *Actor*
Michael Slessinger & Assoc, 8730 Sunset
Blvd #270, Los Angeles, CA 90069 USA

Dassier, Uwe *Swimmer*
Stolze-Schrey-Str 6, Wilday, 15745,
GREECE

Dassin, Jules *Director*
8 Melina Mercouri St, Athens, 11521,
GREECE

Dater, Judy L *Photographer*
2430 5th St, #J, Berkeley, CA 94710 USA

Daubechies, Ingrid C *Mathematician*
Princeton University, Mathematics Dept,
Princeton, NJ 08544 USA

Dauben, William G *Misc*
20 Eagle Hill, Kensington, CA 94707 USA

Daugherty, Bradley L (Brad) *Basketball
Player*
1239 Cane Creek Road, Fletcher, NC
28732 USA

Daugherty, Martha Craig *Judge*
US Court of Appeals, 701 Broadway,
Nashville, TN 37203 USA

Daugherty, Michael *Composer*
Argo London Records, 810 7th Ave, New
York, NY 10019, us

Daugherty, Michael *Composer*
Argo London Records, 810 7th Ave, New
York, NY 10019 USA

Dauline, Marie *Musician*
Todo Mundo, PO Box 652, Cooper
Station, New York, NY 10276 USA

Daulton, Darren A *Baseball Player*
5 Meadow, Lane Arkansas City, KS 67005
USA

Dauplaise, Norman *Jockey*
29 W 36th St, #1000, New York, NY
10018 USA

Daurey, Dana *Actor*
S M S Talent, 8730 Sunset Blvd, #440, Los
Angeles, CA 90069 USA

Dausset, Jean B G *Nobel Prize Laureate*
9 Rue de Villersexel, Paris, 75007, FRANCE

Davalos, Elyssa
2934 1/2 Beverly Glen Circle #53, Los Angeles, CA 90077

Davalos, Richard *Actor*
2311 Vista Gordo Dr, Los Angeles, CA 90026 USA

Davenport, A Nigel *Actor*
5 Ann's Close, Kinnerton Street, London, SW1, UNITED KINGDOM (UK)

Davenport, Jack *Actor*
International Creative Management (ICM-LA), 8942 Wilshire Blvd, Beverly Hills, CA 90211 USA

Davenport, Lindsay
Box 10179, Newport Beach, CA 92658

Davenport, Lindsey *Tennis Player*
PO Box 10179, Newport Beach, CA 92658 USA

Davenport, Nigel *Actor*
Green & Underwood, 2 Conduit St, London, W1R9TG, UNITED KINGDOM (UK)

Davenport Jr, Guy M *Writer*
621 Sayre Ave, Lexington, KY 40508 USA

Davenport Jr, Wilbur B *Engineer*
1120 Skyline Dr, Medford, OR 97504 USA

Davi, Robert *Actor*
10044 Calvin Ave, Northridge, CA 91324 USA

Daviau, Allen *Cinematographer*
2249 Bronson Hill Dr, Los Angeles, CA 90068 USA

Davich, Jacob *Actor*
Paradigm (LA), 10100 Santa Monica Blvd, Fl 25, Los Angeles, CA 90067 USA

Davich, Marty *Composer*
530 S Greenwood Lane, Pasadena, CA 91107 USA

David, Craig *Musician*
Wildstar Atlantic Records, 1290 Ave of Americas, New York, NY 10104 USA

David, George A L *Business Person*
United Technologies Corp, United Technologies Building, Hartford, CT 06101 USA

David, Hal *Musician*
10430 Wilshire Blvd, Los Angeles, CA 90024 USA

David, John R *Misc*
Harvard Public Health School, 665 Huntington Ave, Boston, MA 02115 USA

David, Keith *Actor*
Writers & Artists, 8383 Wilshire Blvd, #550, Beverly Hills, CA 90211 USA

David, Larry *Actor, Writer*
Endeavor Talent Agency, 9701 Wilshire Blvd, #1000, Beverly Hills, CA 90212 USA

David, Mack
1575 Toledo Circle, Palm Springs, CA 92262

David, Mohato *Prince*
Royal Palace, PO Box 524, Maseru, LESOTHO

David, Peter *Actor*
PO Box 239, Bayport, NY 11705 USA

David Jr, Edward E *Engineer*
EED Inc, PO Box 435, Bedminster, NJ 07921 USA

Davidovich, Bella *Musician*
Columbia Artists Mgmt Inc, 165 W 57th St, New York, NY 10019 USA

Davidovich, Lolita *Actor*
15200 Friends St, Pacific Pelisades, CA 90272 USA

Davidovsky, Mario *Composer*
Harvard University, Music Dept, Cambridge, MA 02138 USA

Davids, Hollace *Producer*
Universal Studios, 100 Universal City Plz, Bldg 1320 Fl 3 West, Universal City, CA 91608

Davidson, Amy *Actor*
Paradigm (LA), 10100 Santa Monica Blvd, Fl 25, Los Angeles, CA 90067 USA

Davidson, Ben E *Football Player*
4737 Angels Point, La Mesa, CA 91941 USA

Davidson, Bruce O *Misc*
RR 842, Unionville, PA 19375 USA

Davidson, Cotton *Football Player*
435 Old Osage Road, Gatesville, TX 76528 USA

Davidson, Doug
PO Box 5608, Santa Barbara, CA 93150-5608

Davidson, Eileen *Actor*
11300 West Olympic Blvd, #610, Los Angeles, CA 90064 USA

Davidson, Ernest R *Misc*
550 Elm Way, #213, Edmonds, WA 98020 USA

Davidson, George A Jr *Business Person*
Consolidated Natural Gas, 625 Liberty Ave, Pittsburgh, PA 15222 USA

Davidson, Gordon *Producer, Director*
Center Theatre Group, Mark Taper Forum, 135 N Grand Ave, Los Angeles, CA 90012 USA

Davidson, Jeff *Motivational Speaker*
Breathing Space Institute, 2417 Honeysuckle Road, Chapel Hill, NC 27514 USA

Davidson, Jim *Actor*
William Morris Agency, 151 El Camino Dr, Beverly Hills, CA 90212 USA

Davidson, John *Musician, Actor*
16551 Kettler Lane, Huntington Beach, CA 92647 USA

Davidson, John *Hockey Player*
12 Carey Dr, Bedford, NY 10506 USA

Davidson, Owen *Tennis Player*
32 Whisper Lane, Spring, TX 77380 USA

Davidson, Ralph P *Publisher*
494 Harbor Road, Southport, CT 06890 USA

Davidson, Richard K *Business Person*
Union Pacific Corp, 1717 Main St, Dallas, TX 75201 USA

Davidson, Ronald C *Physicist*
Princeton University, Plasma Physics Laboratory, Princeton, NJ 08544 USA

Davidson, Tommy *Actor, Comedian*
Tencer & Associates PR, 9777 Wilshire Blvd, #504, Beverly Hills, CA 90212 USA

Davidtz, Embeth *Actor*
311 N Venice Blvd, #C, Venice, CA 90291 USA

Davie, Alan *Artist*
Gamels Studio, Rush Green, Hertford, SG13 7SB, UNITED KINGDOM (UK)

Davie, Donald A *Writer*
4 High St, Silverton, Exeter, EX5 4JB, UNITED KINGDOM (UK)

Davies, Colin Rex
7A Fitzroy Park, London, ENGLAND, N6 6HS

Davies, Dave *Musician*
Larry Page, 29 Ruston Mews, London, W11 1RB, UNITED KINGDOM (UK)

Davies, Dennis Russell
Am Wichelshof 24, Bonn, 53111, GERMANY

Davies, Gail *Musician*
246 Cherokee Road, Nashville, TN 37205 USA

Davies, Geralnt Wyn *Actor*
Oscars Abrams Zimel, 438 Queen St W, Toronto, ON M5A 1T4, CANADA

Davies, Jeremy *Actor*
United Talent Agency, 9560 Wilshire Blvd, #500, Beverly Hills, CA 90212 USA

Davies, John G *Judge, Swimmer*
520 Madeline Dr, Pasadena, CA 91105 USA

Davies, Lane *Actor*
PO Box 20531, Thousand Oaks, CA 91358 USA

Davies, Laura *Golfer*
Tytherington Club, Tytherington Macclesfield, SK10 2JP, UNITED KINGDOM (UK)

Davies, Linda *Writer*
Calle Once 286, La Molona, Lima, PERU

Davies, Matt *Editor, Cartoonist*
Journal News, Editorial Dept, 1 Gannett Dr, White Plains, NY 10604 USA

Davies, Mike *Architect*
Rogers Partnership, Thames Wharf, Rainville Road, London, N6 94A, UNITED KINGDOM (UK)

Davies, Paul C W *Mathematician, Physicist*
PO Box 389, Burnside, SA, 5066, AUSTRALIA

Davies, Peter *Misc*
Albert Einstein Medical College, Biochemistry Dept, Bronx, NY 10461 USA

Davies, Peter Maxwell *Composer*
Judy Arnold, 50 Hogarth Road, London, SW5 OPU, UNITED KINGDOM (UK)

Davies, Raymond D (Ray) *Musician, Songwriter*
Larry Page, 29 Ruston Mews, London, W11 1RB, UNITED KINGDOM (UK)

Davies, Raymond Douglas (Ray) *Musician, Actor, Director, Writer*
Trident Media Group LLC, 41 Madison Ave Fl 33, New York, NY 10010 USA

Davies, Ryland *Opera Singer*
71 Fairmile Lane, Cobham, Surrey, KT11 2DG, UNITED KINGDOM (UK)

Davies, Tamara *Actor*
Bauman Redanty & Shaul Agency, 5757 Wilshire Blvd #473, Los Angeles, CA 90036 USA

Davies, Terence *Director*
Nigel Britton Mgmt, 11-15 Betterton St, London, WC2H 9BP, UNITED KINGDOM (UK)

Davies, Warrick *Actor*
International Creative Mgmt, 76 Oxford St, London, W1N 0AX, UNITED KINGDOM (UK)

Davies, Wyn *Actor*
Screen Actors Guild (SAG-LA), 5757 Wilshire Blvd, Los Angeles, CA 90036 USA

Davis, A Dano *Business Person*
Winn-Dixie Stores, 5050 Edgewood Court, Jacksonville, FL 32254 USA

Davis, Al
1220 Harbor Bay Parkway, Alameda, CA 94502

Davis, Allen (Al) *Misc*
Oakland Raiders, 1220 Harbor Bay Parkway, Alameda, CA 94502 USA

Davis, Andrew *Director*
The Agency, 1800 Ave of Stars, #400, Los Angeles, CA 90067 USA

Davis, Andrew F
Askonas Holt, 27 Chancerty Lane, London, WC2A 1PF, UNITED KINGDOM (UK)

Davis, Angela Y *Educator, Politician, Social Activist*
Speakout, PO Box 99096, Emeryville, CA 94662 USA

Davis, Ann B *Actor*
23315 Eagle Gap Rd, San Antonio, TX 78255 USA

Davis, Anne B *Actor*
Cassell-Levy Inc, 843 N Sycamore Ave, Los Angeles, CA 90038 USA

Davis, Anthony *Football Player*
9851 Oakwood Crest, Villa Park, CA 92861 USA

Davis, Anthony *Composer, Musician*
Andriolo Communications, 115 E 9th St, New York, NY 10003 USA

Davis, Antone *Football Player*
9034 Village Green Blvd, Clermont, FL 34711 USA

Davis, Antonio *Basketball Player*
625 Willow Glen Dr, El Paso, TX 79922 USA

Davis, Aree *Actor*
Myrna Lieberman Management, 3001 Hollyridge Drive, Hollywood, CA 90068 USA

Davis, Baron *Basketball Player*
New Orleans Hornets, New Orleans Arena, 1501 Girod St, New Orleans, LA 70113 USA

Davis, Bennie L *General*
101 Golden Road, Georgetown, TX 78628 USA

Davis, Beryl
1870 Caminito Del Cielo, Glendal, CA 91208

Davis, Billy Jr *Musician*
Sterling/Winters, 10877 Wilshire Blvd, #15, Los Angeles, CA 90024 USA

Davis, Carl *Composer*
99 Church Road, Barnes, London, SW13 9HL, UNITED KINGDOM (UK)

Davis, Charles T (Chili) *Baseball Player*
620 Juana Ave, San Leandro, CA 94577 USA

Davis, Chip *Musician*
Brokaw Company, The, 9255 Sunset Blvd #804, Los Angeles, CA 90069 USA

Davis, Clifton *Actor*
9200 Sunset Blvd, #900, Los Angeles, CA 90069 USA

Davis, Clive J *Business Person*
RCA Records (LA), 8750 Wilshire Blvd Fl 2, Beverly Hills, CA 90211 USA

Davis, Colin R
Alison Glaster, 39 Huntingdon St, London, N1 1BP, UNITED KINGDOM (UK)

Davis, Dale *Basketball Player*
7945 Beaumont, Indianapolis, IN 46250 USA

Davis, Dana *Actor*
Marshak/Zachary Company, The, 8840 Wilshire Blvd Fl 1, Beverly Hills, CA 90211 USA

Davis, Daniel *Actor*
Innovative Artists (NY), 235 Park Ave S Fl 7, New York, NY 10003 USA

Davis, Danny *Musician*
Danny Davis Productions, PO Box 210317, Nashville, TN 37221 USA

Davis, David (Dave) *Bowler*
DeStasio, 710 Shore Road, Spring Lake Heights, NJ 07762 USA

Davis, David Brion *Writer, Historian*
783 Lambert Road, Orange, CT 06477 USA

Davis, Don *Golfer*
15910 FM 529, #219, Houston, TX 77095 USA

Davis, Don H Jr *Business Person*
Rockwell International, 777 E Wisconsin Ave, #1400, Milwaukee, WI 53202 USA

Davis, Don S *Actor*
Gold Marshak Liedtke, 3500 W Olive Ave, #1400, Burbank, CA 91505 USA

Davis, Elizabeth *Musician*
Rave Booking, PO Box 310780, Jamaica, NY 11431 USA

Davis, Elliot M *Cinematographer*
1328 Arch St, Berkeley, CA 94708 USA

Davis, Emanuel *Basketball Player*
Atlanta Hawks, 190 Marietta St SW, Atlanta, GA 30303 USA

Davis, Eric K *Baseball Player*
5616 Farmland Ave, Woodland Hills, CA 91367 USA

Davis, Eric W *Football Player*
4501 Old Course Dr, Charlotte, NC 28277 USA

Davis, Eugene *Actor*
Artist's Agency, The (LA), 1180 S Beverly Dr #301, Los Angeles, CA 90035 USA

Davis, Geena *Actor*
Susan Geller, 1301 Belfast Dr, Los Angeles, CA 90069 USA

Davis, Glenn
47-650 Eisenhower Dr, La Quinta, CA 92253

Davis, Glenn E *Baseball Player*
45 Cascade Road, Columbus, GA 31904 USA

Davis, Glenn H *Track Athlete*
801 Robinson Ave, Barberton, OH 44203 USA

Davis, Glenn W *Football Player*
6014 Varna Ave, Van Nuys, CA 91401 USA

Davis, H Thomas (Tommy) *Baseball Player*
Los Angeles Dodgers, 9767 Whirlaway St, Alta Loma, CA 91737-1643 USA

Davis, Hope *Actor*
United Talent Agency, 9560 Wilshire Blvd, #500, Beverly Hills, CA 90212 USA

Davis, Hubert *Basketball Player*
7951 Glade Hill Court, Dallas, TX 75218 USA

Davis, James *Football Player*
5701 S Saint Andrews Place, Los Angeles, CA 90062 USA

Davis, James B *General*
3600 Wimber Blvd, Palm Harbor, FL 34685 USA

Davis, James O *Doctor*
612 Maplewood Dr, Columbia, MO 65203 USA

Davis, James R (Jim) *Cartoonist*
5440 E Country Rd 450 N, Albany, IN 47320 USA

Davis, Jason *Baseball Player*
Cleveland Indians, 345 Carriage Ln NE, Cleveland, TN 37312-6708 USA

Davis, Jay *Golfer*
Kevin Richardson, 1551 Forum Place, #300CF, West Palm Beach, FL 33401 USA

Davis, Jeff *Actor*
United Talent Agency (UTA), 9560 Wilshire Blvd, Beverly Hills, CA 90212 USA

Davis, Jerry *Baseball Player*
San Diego Padres, 72 Theresa St, Trenton, NJ 08618-1531 USA

Davis, Jesse *Musician*
Concord Records, 100 N Crescent Dr, #275, Beverly Hills, CA 90210 USA

Davis, Jill A *Writer*
Random House, 1745 Broadway, #B1, New York, NY 10019 USA

Davis, Jody *Baseball Player*
Chicago Cubs, 4445 Shirley Rd, Gainesville, GA 30506-5104 USA

Davis, Joel *Baseball Player*
Chicago White Sox, 609 Matterhorn Rd, Jacksonville, KY 40165-6352 USA

Davis, John *Baseball Player*
Kansas City Royals, 343 Mill Run, Shepherdsville, KY 40165-6352 USA

Davis, Johnny *Basketball Player, Coach*
2200 Alaqua Dr, Longwood, FL 32779
USA

Davis, Jonathan *Musician*
The Firm, 9100 Wilshire Blvd, #100W,
Beverly Hills, CA 90210 USA

Davis, Jonathan Houseman *Musician*
William Morris Agency (WMA-LA), 1
William Morris Pl, Beverly Hills, CA
90212 USA

Davis, Josie *Actor*
CunninghamEscottDipene, 10635 Santa
Monica Blvd, #130, Los Angeles, CA
90025 USA

Davis, Judy *Actor*
Shanahan Mgmt, PO Box 1509,
Darlinghurst, NSW, 1300, AUSTRALIA

Davis, Kane *Baseball Player*
Cleveland Indians, 4794 Ripley Rd,
Reedy, WV 25270-9504 USA

Davis, Kristin *Actor*
Endeavor Talent Agency, 9701 Wilshire
Blvd, #1000, Beverly Hills, CA 90212
USA

Davis, L Edward *Religious Leader*
Evangelical Presbyterian Church, 26049
Five Mile Road, Detroit, MI 48239 USA

Davis, Lee *Director*
Gersh Agency, 232 N Canon Dr, Beverly
Hills, CA 90210 USA

Davis, Leonard *Football Player*
Arizona Cardinals, PO Box 888, Phoenix,
AZ 85001 USA

Davis, Linda *Musician*
5548 Shady Trail, Old Hickory, TN 37138
USA

Davis, Mac *Musician, Actor, Songwriter*
Grant & Tani, 9100 Wilshire Blvd,
#1000-W, Beverly Hills, CA 90212 USA

Davis, Mark *Baseball Player*
California Angels, 1672 E Mountain St,
Pasadena, CA 91104-3935 USA

Davis, Mark *Baseball Player*
Philadelphia Phillies, 9290 E Thompson
Peak Pkwy Unit 474, Scottsdale, AZ
85255-4519 USA

Davis, Mark M *Misc, Biologist*
Stanford University, Medical Center,
Microbiology Dept, Stanford, CA 94305
USA

Davis, Mark W *Baseball Player*
9290 E Thompson Peak Parkway, #474,
Scottsdale, AZ 85255 USA

Davis, Martha *Musician*
Paradise Artists, 108 E Matilija St, Ojai,
CA 93023 USA

Davis, Marvin *Business Person*
Davis Co, Fox Plaza, 2121 Ave of Stars,
Los Angeles, CA 90067 USA

Davis, Matt *Actor*
McKeon-Valeo Management, 9107
Wilshire Blvd #321, Beverly Hills, CA
90210 USA

Davis, Matthew *Actor*
Lynda Goodfriend, 338 S Beachwood,
Burbank, CA 91506 USA

Davis, Mike *Baseball Player*
Oakland A's, 2491 San Ramon Valley
Blvd, #1407, San Ramon, CA 94583-1677
USA

Davis, Musiello
Janette200 Windemere Way, Naples, FL
33999-8125

Davis, N Jan *Astronaut*
2804 Barcody Circle, Huntsville, AL
35801 USA

Davis, Nathaniel *Diplomat*
1783 Longwood Ave, Claremont, CA
91711 USA

Davis, Odie *Baseball Player*
Texas Rangers, 1014 Montana St, San
Antonio, TX 78203-1117 USA

Davis, Ossie *Actor*
44 Cortland Avenue, New Rochelle, NY
10801 USA

Davis, Ossie *Actor*
44 Cortland Ave, New Rochelle, NY
10801 USA

Davis, Otis *Baseball Player*
Brooklyn Dodgers, 1115 Royal Troon Ct,
Tarpon Springs, FL 34688-6327 USA

Davis, Paige *Television Host*
Trading Spaces, The Learning Channel,
7700 Wisconsin Ave, Bethesda, MD
20814 USA

Davis, Paul H (Butch) *Coach*
Clveland Browns, 76 Lou Groza Blvd,
Berea, OH 44017 USA

Davis, Phyllis *Actor*
29330 SE Hillyard Drive, #D14, Boring,
OR 97009 USA

Davis, Rennie *Politician*
Birth of a New Nation, 905 S Gilpin St,
Denver, CO 80209 USA

Davis, Richard *Musician*
SRO Artists, 6629 University Ave, #206,
Middleton, WI 53562 USA

Davis, Robert T (Bobby) Jr *Football Player*
3721 Eaglebrook Dr, Gastonia, NC 28056
USA

Davis, Ron *Baseball Player*
New York Yankees, 11748 N 90th Pl,
Scottsdale, AZ 85260-6841 USA

Davis, Ronald (Ron) *Artist*
PO Box 293, Arroyo Hondo, NM 87513
USA

Davis, Russ *Baseball Player*
New York Yankees, 3351 Crescent Dr,
Hueytown, AL 35023-2919 USA

Davis, Russell C *General*
Chief National Guard Bureau, HqUSAF,
Pentagon, Washington, DC 20310 USA

Davis, Russell S (Russ) *Baseball Player*
3351 Crescent Dr, Hueytown, AL 35023
USA

Davis, Sammy *Football Player*
San Diego Chargers, 4020 Murphy
Canyon Road, San Deigo, CA 92123 USA

Davis, Sammy L *War Hero*
3376 N 100th St, Flat Rock, IL 62427
USA

Davis, Scott *Figure Skater*
1805 Beech Dr, Great Falls, MT 59404
USA

Davis, Spencer
PO Box 1821, Ojai, CA 93024

Davis, Stephen H *Mathematician,
Engineer*
2735 Simpson St, Evanston, IL 60201 USA

Davis, Steve *Misc*
Matchroom Snooker Ltd, 10 Western
Road, Romford, Essex, RM1 3JT, UNITED
KINGDOM (UK)

Davis, Steve *Baseball Player*
Chicago Cubs, 6717 Westbury Ct,
Benbrook, TX 76132-2700 USA

Davis, Storm *Baseball Player*
Baltimore Orioles, 8469 Mizner Cir E,
Jacksonville, FL 32217-4326 USA

Davis, Terrell *Athlete*
Denver Broncos, 13655 East Broncos
Parkway, Englewood, CO 80112

Davis, Tim *Baseball Player*
Seattle Mariners, 19867 NW County Road
67, Bristol, FL 32321-3713 USA

Davis, Todd *Actor*
245 S Keystone St, Burbank, CA 91506
USA

Davis, Tommy *Baseball Player*
Baltimore Orioles, 4685 Cavalier Dr,
Semmes, AL 36575-4467 USA

Davis, Trench *Baseball Player*
Pittsburgh Pirates, 306 40th Street Cir W,
Palmetto, FL 34221-9516 USA

Davis, Truman A *Misc*
Congress of Industrial Unions, 303 Ridge
St, Alton, IL 62002 USA

Davis, Tyrone *Musician*
Associated Booking Corp, 1995
Broadway, #501, New York, NY 10023
USA

Davis, Vicki *Actor*
Handprint Entertainment, 1100 Glendon
Ave #1000, Los Angeles, CA 90024 USA

Davis, Viola *Actor*
Agency for Performing Arts, 9200 Sunset
Blvd, #900, Los Angeles, CA 90069 USA

Davis, W Eugene *Judge*
US Court of Appeals, 556 Jefferson St,
Lafayette, LA 70501 USA

Davis, Warwick
Willow Personal Mgmt, 63 St Martins
Road, Walmer, CT14 9NY, UNITED
KINGDOM (UK)

Davis, William *Actor*
100 W Pender, Floor 7, Vancouver BC,
CANADA, V6B 1RH

Davis, William D (Willie) *Football Player*
7352 Vista Del Mar, Playa del Ray, CA
90293 USA

Davis, William E *Business Person*
Niagara Mohawk Holdings, 300 Erie Blvd
W, Syracuse, NY 13202 USA

Davis, William G *Government Official*
Tory Tory DesLauries, Aetna Tower,
#3000, Toronto, ON M5K 1N2, CANADA

Davis, William H (Willie) *Baseball Player*
1916 W Victory Blvd, #6, Burbank, CA
91506 USA

Davis, William L *Business Person*
R R Donnelley & Sons, 77 W Wacker Dr,
Chicago, IL 60601 USA

Davis, Willie *Baseball Player*
Los Angeles Dodgers, 1916 W Victory Blvd, Burbank, CA 91506-1150 USA

Davis, Woody *Baseball Player*
Detroit Tigers, PO Box 97, Odum, GA 31555-0097 USA

Davis Jr, Raymond *Nobel Prize Laureate*
28 Bergen Lane, Blue Point, NY 11715 USA

Davis-Wrightsil, Clarissa *Basketball Player*
Phoenix Mercury, American West Arena, 201 E Jefferson St, Phoenix, AZ 85004 USA

Davison, Beverly C *Religious Leader*
American Baptist Churches, PO Box 851, Valley Forge, PA 19482 USA

Davison, Bruce *Actor*
Gersh Agency, 232 N Canon Dr, Beverly Hills, CA 90210 USA

Davison, Fred C *Educator*
National Science Foundation, PO Box 15577, Augusta, GA 30919 USA

Davison, Michelle
1830 Grace Ave. #7, Los Angeles, CA 90028

Davison, Mike *Baseball Player*
San Francisco Giants, 578 Prospect St NE, Hutchinson, MN 55350-1715 USA

Davison, Peter *Actor*
18-21 Jermyn St, #300, London, SW1Y 6NB, UNITED KINGDOM (UK)

Davison, Sam *Religious Leader*
International Baptist Bible Fellowship, 720 E Kearnet St, Springfield, MO 65803 USA

Davoli, Andrew *Actor*
Mosaic Media Group, 9200 Sunset Blvd Fl 10, Los Angeles, CA 90069 USA

Dawber, Pam *Actor*
Wings Inc, 2236 Encinitas Blvd, #A, Encinitas, CA 92024 USA

Dawes, Dominique *Gymnast*
129 Ritchie Ave., Silver Spring, MD 20910

Dawes, Dominque *Gymnast*
129 Ritchie Ave, Silver Springs, MD 20910 USA

Dawes, Joseph *Cartoonist*
20 Church Court, Closter, NJ 07624 USA

Dawkins, Brian *Football Player*
Philadelphia Eagles, 1 Novacare Way, Philadelphia, PA 19145 USA

Dawkins, C Richard *Biologist*
Oxford University, Museum Parks Road, Oxford, OX1 3PW, UNITED KINGDOM (UK)

Dawkins, Johnny *Basketball Player*
Duke University, Cameron Indoor Stadium, Athletic Dept, Durham, NC 27708 USA

Dawkins, Peter M (Pete) *Football Player, Business Person*
80 W River Road, Rumson, NJ 07760 USA

Dawkins, Travis (Gookie) *Baseball Player*
Cincinnati Reds, 7113 Biltmore Way, Lithonia, GA 30058-2963 USA

Dawley, Bill *Baseball Player*
Houston Astros, RR 2, Jewett City, CT 06351-9802 USA

Dawley, Joey *Baseball Player*
Atlanta Braves, 12240 Indian St, Moreno Valley, CA 92557-7216 USA

Dawley, Joseph W (Joe) *Artist*
13 Wholly St, Cranford, NJ 07016 USA

Dawsey, Lawrence *Football Player*
13704 Sun Court, Tampa, FL 33624 USA

Dawson, Andre *Baseball Player*
Montreal Expos, 6770 SW 101st St, Miami, FL 33156-3242 USA

Dawson, Anthony
Via Riccione 6 Fregene, Fiumicino RM, ITALY, 00050

Dawson, Ashley Taylor *Actor*
Blackburn Sachs Associates, 88-90 Crawford St, London, W1H 2BS, UNITED KINGDOM (UK)

Dawson, Buck *Swimmer*
Swimming Hall of Fame, 1 Hall of Fame Dr, Fort Lauderdale, FL 33316 USA

Dawson, Douglas A (Doug) *Football Player*
Dawson Financial Services, 1175 Adkins Road, Houston, TX 77055 USA

Dawson, eonard R (Lenny/Len) *Football Player, Commentator, Athlete*
5800 Ward Parkway, Kansas City, MO 64113 USA

Dawson, J Cutler Jr *Admiral*
Commander, Striking Fleet Atlantic/2nd Fleet, FPO, AE, 08506 USA

Dawson, Leonard R (Lenny) *Football Player, Sportscaster*
5800 Ward Parkway, Kansas City, MO 64113 USA

Dawson, Richard *Actor*
1117 Angelo Dr, Beverly Hills, CA 90210 USA

Dawson, Rosario *Actor*
1635 N Cahuenga Blvd, #500, Los Angeles, CA 90028 USA

Dawson, Roxann *Actor*
Innovative Artists, 1505 10th St, Santa Monica, CA 90401 USA

Day, Bill *Cartoonist*
Memphis Commercial-Appeal, Editorial Dept, 495 Union Ave, Memphis, TN 38103 USA

Day, Boots *Baseball Player*
St Louis Cardinals, 283 Greenyard Dr Apt A, Ballwin, MO 63011-5019 USA

Day, Charlie *Actor*
Endeavor NY, 23 Watts St Fl 6, New York, NY 10013 USA

Day, Chon *Cartoonist*
127 Main St, Ashaway, RI 02804 USA

Day, Doris *Actor*
PO Box 223163, Carmel, CA 93922 USA

Day, EJay *Musician*
Fox Television Studios, 10201 W Pico Blvd, Bldg 41, Los Angeles, CA 90035

Day, Felicia *Actor*
Lighthouse Entertainment, 409 North Camden Drive #202, Beverly Hills, CA 90210 USA

Day, Gail *Publisher*
Plaboy Magazine, 680 N Lake Shore Dr, Chicago, IL 60611 USA

Day, Green *Music Group*
Creative Artists Agency LCC (CAA-LA), 9830 Wilshire Blvd, Beverly Hills, CA 90212 USA

Day, Jennifer
PO Box 120479, Nashville, TN 37212

Day, Julian *Business Person*
Kmart, 3100 W Big Beaver Road, Troy, MI 48084 USA

Day, Laraine
10313 Lauriston Ave, Los Angeles, CA 90025-6010

Day, Larraine *Actor*
10323 Lauriston Ave, Los Angeles, CA 90025 USA

Day, Laura *Writer*
Harper Collins Publishers, 10 E 53rd St, New York, NY 10022 USA

Day, Mary *Misc*
Washington Ballet, 3515 Wisconsin Ave NW, Washington, DC 20016 USA

Day, Matt *Actor*
Robyn Gardiner Mgmt, 397 Riley St, Surrey Hills, NSW, 2010, AUSTRALIA

Day, Peter R *Scientist*
394 Franklin Road, New Brunswick, NJ 08902 USA

Day, Robert *Director*
Creative Artists Agency, 9830 Wilshire Blvd, Beverly Hills, CA 90212 USA

Day, Thomas B *Educator*
San Diego State University, President's Office, San Diego, CA 92182 USA

Day, Zach *Baseball Player*
Montreal Expos, 7133 Glenellyn Dr, Cincinnati, OH 45236-3709 USA

Day-George, Lynda *Actor*
10310 Riverside Dr, #104, Toluca Lake, CA 91602 USA

Day-Lewis, Daniel *Actor*
Alastair Reid, 65 Connaught St, London, W2, UNITED KINGDOM (UK)

Dayan, Isaac *Actor*
TV Caracol, Calle 76 #11 - 35, Piso 10AA, Bogota DC, 26484, COLOMBIA

Dayett, Brian *Baseball Player*
New York Yankees, 10 Hemlock Terrace Ext, Deep River, CT 06417-1606 USA

Dayley, Ken *Baseball Player*
Atlanta Braves, 2115 E 12th St, The Dalles, OR 97058-3913 USA

Dayne, Ron *Football Player*
New York Giants, Giants Stadium, East Rutherford, NJ 07073 USA

Dayne, Taylor *Musician, Songwriter, Actor*
7933 Willow Glen Road, Los Angeles, CA 90046 USA

Days, Drews S III *Educator, Government Official*
Yale University, Law School, New Haven, CT 06520 USA

Dayton, June *Actor*
Abrams Artists, 9200 Sunset Blvd, #1125, Los Angeles, CA 90069 USA

dc Talk *Musician*
Creative Artists Agency LCC (CAA-LA),
9830 Wilshire Blvd, Beverly Hills, CA
90212 USA

De Angelis, Rosemary
817 West End Ave., New York, NY 10025

de Aragow, Maria
1159 Tenth Ave., San Diego, CA 92101

De Bankole, Isaach *Actor*
Margrit Polak Management, 1411 Carroll
Ave, Los Angeles, CA 90026 USA

De Bello, James *Actor, Musician*
Innovative Artists (LA), 1505 Tenth St,
Santa Monica, CA 90401 USA

De Benning, Burr *Actor*
4235 Kingfisher Road, Calabasas, CA
91302 USA

De Blanc, Jefferson J *Misc*
321 Saint Martin Street, Saint Martinville,
LA 70582 USA

De Bont, Jan *Producer, Director*
Blue Tulip Productions, 1708 Berkeley St,
Santa Monica, CA 90404

de Cordova, Fred
1875 Carla Ridge, Beverly Hills, CA
90210

de Dios, Sandra *Actor*

de Dios, Silvia *Actor*
TV Caracol, Calle 76 #11 - 35, Piso
10AA, Bogota DC, 26484, COLOMBIA

De Eugenia, Coco *Actor*
Powerhouse Talent, PO Box 1748, Studio
City, CA 91614-0748 USA

de Gruiin, Inge
PO Box 302, Arnhem, NETHERLANDS,
6800 AH

De Heer, Rolf *Director, Producer, Writer*
Vertigo Productions Pty Ltd, 3 Butler Dr,
Hendon SA, 5014, AUSTRALIA

De Jesus, Wanda *Actor*
Abrams Artists Agency (LA), 9200 Sunset
Blvd Fl 11, Los Angeles, CA 90069 USA

de la Fuente, Marian *Actor*
Telemundo, 2470 West 8th Avenue,
Hialeah, FL 33010 USA

De La Garza, Alana *Actor*
SDB Partners Inc, 1801 Ave of the Stars
#902, Los Angeles, CA 90067 USA

De La Hoya, Oscar *Boxer*
633 W 5th St #6700, Los Angeles, CA
90071 USA

de la Reguera, Ana *Actor*
TV Azteca, Periferico Sur 4121, Colonia
Fuentes del Pedregal, DF, CP 14141,
Mexico

de la Rocha, Zach *Musician*
Creative Artists Agency LCC (CAA-LA),
9830 Wilshire Blvd, Beverly Hills, CA
90212 USA

De La Rocha, Zack *Musician*
Creative Artists Agency LCC (CAA-LA),
9830 Wilshire Blvd, Beverly Hills, CA
90212 USA

De La Soul *Music Group*
2697 Heath Avenue, Bronx, NY 10463
USA

De La Tour, Frances *Actor*
Kate Feast, Primrose Hill Studios, Fitzroy
Road, London, England, NW18TR, United
Kingdom

De Laurentis, Dino *Producer*
Dino De Laurentis Company, 100
Universal City Plz, Bungalow 5195,
Universal City, CA 91608

de Leon, Miguel *Actor*
Televisa, Blvd Adolfo Lopez Mateos 232,
Colonia San Angel INN, DF, CP 01060,
MEXICO

de Lint, Derek
Features Creative Management,
Entrepotdok 76-A, Amsterdam, AD,
Netherlands

De Longis, Anthony
PO Box 323, Burbank, CA 91503-0323

De Los Angeles, Victoria *Opera Singer*
Avenida de Pedralbes 57, Barcelona,
08034, Spain

De Matteo, Drea *Actor*
PMK/HBH Public Relations (PMK-LA),
8500 Wilshire Blvd #700, Beverly Hills,
CA 90211 USA

de Mol, John *Producer*
William Morris Agency (WMA-LA), 1
William Morris Pl, Beverly Hills, CA
90212 USA

de Molina, Raul *Actor*
Univision, 314 Main St, Chico, CA 95928
USA

De Munn, Jeffrey (Jeff) *Actor*
Gersh Agency, The (LA), 232 N Canon Dr,
Beverly Hills, CA 90210 USA

De Paul, Lynsey
21A Clifftown Rd, Southend-on-Sea Essex,
ENGLAND, SSl 1AB

de Ravin, Emilie *Actor*
Darren Goldberg Management, 5225
Wilshire Blvd #419, Los Angeles, CA
90036

De Rossi, Portia *Actor*
PMK/HBH Public Relations (PMK-NY),
650 Fifth Ave Fl 33, New York, NY 10019
USA

de Silva, Jorge *Actor*
Televisa, Blvd Adolfo Lopez Mateos 232,
Colonia San Angel INN, DF, CP 01060,
MEXICO

de Vasconcelos, Tasha *Actor*
International Creative Management
(ICM-UK), Oxford House, 76 Oxford St,
London, W1N OAX, UNITED KINGDOM
(UK)

De Vries, Peter
170 Cross Highway, Westport, CT 06880

Deacon, Brian
85 Gladstone Rd., London, ENGLAND,
SW19

Deacon, John *Musician*
The Mill Mill Lane, 367 Windsor
Highway, New Windsor, NY 12553 USA

Deacon, Richard *Artist*
Lisson Gallery, 67 Lisson St, London,
NW1 5DA, UNITED KINGDOM (UK)

Deacon, Terrence *Misc*
Harvard University, Neuroanatomy Dept,
Cambridge, MA 02138 USA

Deadmarsh, Adam *Hockey Player*
PO Box 262, Metaline Falls, WA 99153
USA

Deadsy *Music Group*
Creative Artists Agency LCC (CAA-LA),
9830 Wilshire Blvd, Beverly Hills, CA
90212 USA

DeAgostini, Doris *Skier*
6780 Airolo, SWITZERLAND

Deakin, Paul *Musician*
AristoMedia, 1620 16th Ave S, Nashville,
TN 37212 USA

Deakins, Roger *Cinematographer*
International Creative Mgmt, 8942
Wilshire Blvd, #219, Beverly Hills, CA
90212 USA

Deal, Ellis *Baseball Player*
Boston Red Sox, 9505 Silver Lake Dr,
Oklahoma City, OK 73162-7547 USA

Deal, Kim *Musician*
William Morris Agency, 151 El Camino
Dr, Beverly Hills, CA 90212 USA

Deal, Lance *Track Athlete*
911 Elkay, Eugene, OR 97404 USA

DeAlmeida, Joaquin
2372 Veteran Ave. #102, Los Angeles, CA
90064

Dean, Billy *Musician*
PO Box 870689, Stone Mountain, GA
30087 USA

Dean, Christopher *Dancer*
124 Ladies Mile Road, Brighton, East
Sussex, BN1 8TE, UNITED KINGDOM
(UK)

Dean, Eddie *Actor, Musician*
32161 Sailview Lane, Westlake Village,
CA 91361 USA

Dean, Hazel
7 Kentish Town Rd., London, ENGLAND,
NW1 8N4

Dean, Ira *Musician*
Creative Artists Agency, 9830 Wilshire
Blvd, Beverly Hills, CA 90212 USA

Dean, Jimmy *Musician*
10151 Carver Road, Cincinnati, OH
45242 USA

Dean, John G *Diplomat*
29 Blvd Jules Sandeau, Paris, 75116,
FRANCE

Dean, Kiley *Musician*
Interscope Records (LA) - Main, 2220
Colorado Ave, Santa Monica, CA 90404
USA

Dean, Laura *Choreographer, Composer*
Dean Dance & Music Foundation, 552
Broadway, #400, New York, NY 10012
USA

Dean, Letitia *Actor*
EastEnders, BBC Elstree Centre, Clarendon
Road, Borehamwood, Herts, UNITED
KINGDOM

Dean, Loren *Actor*
Thruline Entertainment, 9250 Wilshire
Blvd, Ground Floor, Beverly Hills, CA
90210 USA

Dean, Mark E *Inventor*
5901 Standing Rock Dr, Austin, TX 78730
USA

Dean, Paula *Chef, Television Host*
The Lady and Son's Restaurant, 311 W
Congress St, Savannah, GA 31401 USA

Dean, Stafford R *Opera Singer*
I C M Artists, 40 W 57th St, New York,
NY 10019 USA

Dean, Tommy *Baseball Player*
Los Angeles Dodgers, PO Box 1014, Iuka,
MS 38852-6014 USA

Dean III, John W *Misc*
9496 Rembert Lane, Beverly Hills, CA
90210 USA

Deane, William Patrick *General*
Government House, Canberra, ACT,
26000, AUSTRALIA

DeAngelis, Beverly *Psychic*
505 S Beverly Dr #1017, Beverly Hills,
CA 90212 USA

Deardan, Robin *Actor*
Commercial Talent, 9255 Sunset Blvd,
Suite 505, West Hollywood, CA 90069
USA

Dearden, James *Director*
International Creative Mgmt, 8942
Wilshire Blvd, #219, Beverly Hills, CA
90211 USA

Deardorff, Jeff *Baseball Player*
Milwaukee Brewers, 2251 Hill Dr,
Clermont, FL 34711-3652 USA

Deardurff-Schmidt, Deena *Swimmer*
742 Murray Dr, El Cajon, CA 92020 USA

Dearie, Blossom *Musician, Songwriter*
F Sharp Productions, PO Box 2040, New
York, NY 10101 USA

DeArmond, Frank *Astronaut*
3086 Ravencrest Circle, Prescott, AZ
86303 USA

Deas, Justin *Actor*
Paradigm Agency, 10100 Santa Monica
Blvd, #2500, Los Angeles, CA 90067 USA

Deavenport, Earnest Jr *Business Person*
Eastman Chemical Co, 100 N Eastman
Road, Kingsport, TN 37660 USA

Deaver, Jeffrey *Writer*
Pocket Star Books, 1230 Ave of Americas,
New York, NY 10020 USA

Deaver, Michael K *Government Official*
Deaver Assoc, 1025 Thomas Jefferson St
NW, Washington, DC 20007 USA

DeBakey, Michael E *Doctor*
Baylor Medical Center, 1200 Moursand
Avenue, Houston, TX 77030 USA

DeBarge, Chico *Musician, Songwriter*
International Creative Mgmt, 8942
Wilshire Blvd, #219, Beverly Hills, CA
90211 USA

Debarr, Denny *Baseball Player*
Toronto Blue Jays, 33843 Juliet Cir,
Fremont, CA 94555-3452 USA

Debela, Kingsford *Governor, General*
PO Box 113, Port Moresby, PAPURA
NEW GULNEA

DeBellevue, Charles B *War Hero*
916 Huntsman Road, Edmond, OK 73003
USA

DeBello, James *Actor*
Innovative Artists (LA), 1505 Tenth St,
Santa Monica, CA 90401 USA

DeBenning, Burr *Actor*
4235 Kingfisher Road, Colabasas, CA
91302 USA

DeBerg, Steve *Coach, Football Player*
17920 Simms Road, Odessa, FL 33556
USA

DeBlanc, Jefferson J *War Hero*
321 Saint Martin St, Saint Martinville, LA
70582 USA

DeBlasis, Celeste *Writer*
9 Kemper Campbell Ranch St, Victorville,
CA 92392 USA

Debney, John *Composer*
Kraft-Benjamin-Engel, 15233 Ventura
Blvd, #200, Sherman Oaks, CA 91403
USA

DeBoer, Harm E *Business Person*
Russell Corp, 755 Lee St, Alexander City,
AL 35010 USA

DeBoer, Nicole *Actor*
3401 Lawrence Ave E, #577,
Scarborough, ON M1H1B2, CANADA

DeBoer, Rick *Actor*
Pacific Artists, 510 W Hastings St, #1404,
Vancouver, BC V6B 1L8, CANADA

DeBold, Adolfo J *Physicist, Doctor*
Ottawa Civic Hospital, 1053 Carling Ave,
Ottawa, ON K1Y 4E9, CANADA

DeBorba, Dorothy *Actor*
PO Box 2723, Livermore, CA 94551 USA

DeBorchgrave, Arnaud *Editor*
2141 Wyoming Ave NW, Washington,
DC 20008 USA

DeBorda, Dorothy *Actor*
PO Box 2723, Livermore, CA 94551 USA

DeBranges, Louis *Mathematician*
Purdue University, Mathematics Dept,
West Lafayette, IN 47907 USA

Debre, Michael *Prime Minister*
20 Rue Jacob, Paris, 75006, FRANCE

Debreu, Gerard *Nobel Prize Laureate*
University of California, Evans Hall,
Economics Dept, Berkeley, CA 94720
USA

DeBrunhoff, Laurent *Writer*
Mary Ryan Gallery, 24 W 57th St, New
York, NY 10019 USA

DeBurgh, Chris *Musician, Songwriter*
Kenny Thomson Mgmt, 754 Fulham Road,
London, SW6 5SW, UNITED KINGDOM
(UK)

Deby, Idriss *President, General*
President's Office, N'Djamena, CHAS

DeCamilli, Pietro V *Biologist*
Yale University, Medical School, Cell
Biology Dept, New Haven, CT 06512
USA

DeCarava, Roy *Photographer*
81 Halsey St, Brooklyn, NY 11216 USA

DeCario, Yvonne *Actor*
1483 Golf Course Lane, Nipomo, CA
93444 USA

DeCarl, Nancy
4615 Winnetka, Woodland Hills, CA
91364

DeCarlo, Yvonne *Actor*
1483 Golf Course Lane, Nipomo, CA
93444 USA

DeCasabianca, Carnille *Actor*
Artmedia, 20 Ave Rapp, Paris, 75007,
FRANCE

DeCastelia, F Robert *Track Athlete*
Australian Institute of Sport, PO Box 176,
Belconnen, ACT, 2616, AUSTRALIA

DeCinces, Douglas V (Doug) *Baseball
Player*
Baltimore Orioles, 124 Riviera Way,
Laguna Beach, CA 92651-1012 USA

Decker, Franz-Paul *Conductor*
Herbert Barrett, 266 W 37th St, #2000,
New York, NY 10018 USA

Decker, Marty *Baseball Player*
San Diego Padres, 1630 Youngs Ln, Yuba
City, CA 95991-1925 USA

Decker, Scott *Business Person*
HEALTHvision, 6330 Commerce Drive,
Suite 100, Irving, TX 75063 USA

Decker, Steve *Baseball Player*
San Francisco Giants, 1024 Laurelridge St
NE, Keizer, OR 97303-7208 USA

Deckers, Daphne *Actor*
Nagtzaan, Hoge Naardenweg 44,
Hilversum, AG, 1217, NETHERLANDS

DeConcini, Dennis *Senator*
6014 Chesterbrook Road, McLean, VA
22101 USA

DeCosta, Sara *Hockey Player*
200 Cowesett Green Dr, Warwick, RI
02886 USA

DeCoster, Roger *Race Car Driver*
MC Sports, 1919 Torrance Blvd, Torrance,
CA 90501 USA

Decter, Midge *Writer*
120 East 81st St, New York, NY 10028
USA

Dedeaux, Raoul M (Rod) *Coach, Baseball
Player*
Brooklyn Dodgers, 1430 S Eastman Ave,
Los Angeles, CA 90023-4006 USA

Dedini, Eldon L *Cartoonist*
PO Box 1630, Monterey, CA 93942 USA

Dedkov, Anatoli I *Cosmonaut*
Potchta Kosmonavtov, Moskovskoi
Oblasti, Syvisdny, Goroduk, 141160,
RUSSIA

Dedler, Karin
Hohenegg 21, Dietmannsried, GERMANY,
D-87463

Dedmon, Jeff *Baseball Player*
Atlanta Braves, 21102 Broadwell Ave,
Torrance, CA 90502-1636 USA

Dedrick, Jim *Baseball Player*
Baltimore Orioles, 8267 SW Pointer Way
Apt A, Portland, OR 97225-6387 USA

DeDuve, Christian R *Nobel Prize Laureate*
80 Central Park West, New York, NY
10023 USA

Dee, Donald (Don) *Basketball Player*
7924 N Pennsylvania Ave, Kansas City,
MO 64118 USA

Dee, Joey *Musician*
Horizon Mgmt, PO Box 8770, Endwell,
NY 13762 USA

Dee, Ruby *Actor*
44 Cortland Avenue, New Rochelle, NY
10801 USA

Dee, Ruby *Actor*
44 Cortland Ave, New Rochelle, NY
10801 USA

Dee, Sandra *Actor, Model*
18915 Nordhoff St, #5, Northridge, CA
91324 USA

Dee-Lite *Musician*
428 Cedar Street NW, Washington, DC
20012 USA

Deeb, Gary *Critic*
Chicago Sun-Times, Editorial Dept, 401 N
Wabash Ave, Chicago, IL 60611 USA

Deedes of Aldington, William F
Government Official
New Hayters, Aldington, Kent, TN25 7DT,
UNITED KINGDOM (UK)

Deedle, Nelson
PO Box 5358, Scottsdale, AZ 85261

Deeley, Cat *Actor*
Sue Terry Voices, 18 Broadwick St Fl 5,
London, W1F 8HS, UNITED KINGDOM
(UK)

Deep Purple
Box 254, Sheffield, ENGLAND, S6 IDF

Deependra Bir, Bikaram Shah Dev *Prince*
Narayanhiti Royal Palace, Durbeg Marg,
Kathmandu, NEPAL

Deer, Ada E *Government Official*
2537 Mutchler Road, Fitchburg, WI
53711 USA

Deer, Rob *Baseball Player*
San Francisco Giants, 21842 N 40th Pl,
Phoenix, AZ 85050-7225 USA

Deering, John *Cartoonist*
6701 Westover Dr, Little Rock, AR 72207
USA

Dees, Archie *Basketball Player*
4405 N Hillview Dr, Bloomington, IN
47408 USA

Dees, Bowen C *Scientist*
29059 Meadow Glen Way W, Escondido,
CA 92026 USA

Dees, Charlie *Baseball Player*
Los Angeles Angels, 1064 Allison Woods
Ct, Lawrenceville, GA 30043-5383 USA

Dees, Morris *Lawyer, Civil Rights Activist*
Southern Poverty Law Center, PO Box
548, Montgomery, AL 36101 USA

Dees, Morris S Jr *Social Activist*
Southern Poverty Law Center, PO Box
548, Montgomery, AL 36101 USA

Dees, Rick *Entertainer, Musician*
KIIS-Radio, 3400 W Riverside Dr, #800,
Burbank, CA 91505 USA

Def Leppard
72 Chancellor's Rd, London, ENGLAND,
W6 9QB

DeFanti, Tom *Inventor*
University of Illinois, Electronic
Visualization Labe, Chicago, IL 60607
USA

Default *Music Group*
Agency Group, The (NY), 1775 Broadway
#430, New York, NY 10019 USA

DeFerran, Gil *Race Car Driver*
524 Royal Plaza Dr, Fort Lauderdale, FL
33301 USA

DeFigueiredo, Rul J P *Engineer*
University of California, Intelligent
Sensors/Systems Lab, Irvine, CA 92717
USA

DeFleur, Lois B *Educator*
State University of New York, President's
Office, Binghamton, NY 13902 USA

Deford, Frank *Writer*
PO Box 1109, Greens Farms, CT 06838
USA

DeForest, Roy *Artist*
PO Box 47, Port Costa, CA 94569 USA

DeForrest, Jeff *Sportscaster*
5211 NE 14th Terrace, Fort Lauderdale, FL
33334 USA

DeFrancisco, Joseph E (Joe) *General*
7754 Chars Lane, Springfield, VA 22153
USA

DeFranco, Buddy *Musician*
22525 Coral Avenue, Panama City, FL
32413 USA

DeFrank, Joe *Race Car Driver*
29 Crescent Hollow Court, Ramsey, NJ
07446 USA

DeFrantz, Anita *Misc*
US Olympic Committee, 1 Olympia
Plaza, Colorado Springs, CO 80909 USA

DeFreitas, Eric *Bowler*
175 W 12th St, New York, NY 10011
USA

Deftones, The *Music Group*
Creative Artists Agency LCC (CAA-LA),
9830 Wilshire Blvd, Beverly Hills, CA
90212 USA

Deganhardt, Johannes J Cardinal
Religious Leader
Erzbischofliches Generalvikariat,
Domplatz 3, Paderborn, 33098,
GERMANY

DeGarmo, Diana *Musician*
American Idol, 7800 Beverly Blvd #251,
Los Angeles, CA 90036 USA

DeGaspa, Philippe *Publisher*
Canadian Living Magazine, 50 Holly St,
Toronto, ON M4S 3B3, CANADA

Degeneres, Ellen *Actor, Comedian*
Ellen DeGeneres Show, The, 3000 W
Alameda Ave, Burbank, CA 91523 USA

DeGennes, Pierre-Gilles *Nobel Prize
Laureate*
11 Place Marcelin-Berthelot, Paris, 75005,
FRANCE

Degerick, Mike *Baseball Player*
Chicago White Sox, 2702 Lake Osborne
Dr, Lake Worth, FL 33461-5665 USA

DeGioia, John *Educator*
Georgetown University, President's Office,
Washington, DC 20057 USA

DeGiorgi, Salvatore Cardinal *Religious
Leader*
Curia Archivescovile, Corso Vittorio
Emanuele 461, Palermo, 90134, ITALY

DeGivenchy, Hubert *Fashion Designer*
3 Avenue George V, Paris, 75008, France

Degler, Carl N *Historian, Writer*
907 Mears Court, Stanford, CA 94305
USA

DeGlvenchy, Hubert T *Fashion Designer*
3 Ave George V, Paris, 75008, FRANCE

Degnan, John J *Business Person*
Chubb Corp, 15 Mountain View Road,
Warren, NJ 07059 USA

DeGrate, Tony *Football Player*
13007 Heinerman Dr, #901, Austin, TX
78727 USA

Dehaan, Kory *Baseball Player*
San Diego Padres, 216 E 12th St, Pella, IA
50219-2218 USA

DeHaan, Richard W *Religious Leader*
3000 Kraft Ave SE, Grand Rapids, MI
49512 USA

Dehaene, Jean-Luc *Prime Minister*
Berkendallaan 52, Vilvoorde, 1800,
BELGIUM

Dehart, Rick *Baseball Player*
Montreal Expos, 1116 NE Chester Ave,
Topeka, KS 66616-1359 USA

DeHaven, Gloria *Actor*
420 N Palm Dr, Beverly Hills, CA 90210
USA

DeHaven, Penny
Box 83, Brentwood, TN 37027

DeHavilland, Olivia *Actor*
Douglas Gorman Rothacker & Wilhelm
Inc, 1501 Broadway #703, New York, NY
10036 USA

Dehmelt, Hans G *Nobel Prize Laureate*
1600 43rd Ave E, Seattle, WA 98112 USA

Deighton, Len
10 Iron Bridge House Bridge Approach,
London, ENGLAND, NW1 8BD

Deighton, Leonard C (Len) *Writer*
Fairymount Blackrock, Dundalk, County
Louth, IRELAND

Deisenhofer, Johann *Nobel Prize Laureate*
3860 Echo Brook lane, Dallas, TX 75229
USA

Deitch, Donna *Director*
International Creative Mgmt, 8942
Wilshire Blvd, #219, Beverly Hills, CA
90211 USA

Deja, Andreas *Animator*
Disney Animation, PO Box 10200, Lake
Buena Vista, FL 32830 USA

Deja Vu
1 Touchstone Lane Chard, Somerset,
ENGLAND, TA20 1RF

DeJager, Cornelis *Astronomer*
Zonnenburg 1, Utrecht, NL, 352,
NETHERLANDS

Dejdel, Jim *Baseball Player*
New York Yankees, 14312 Wright Way,
Broomfield, CO 80020-4045 USA

Dejean, Mike *Baseball Player*
Colorado Rockies, 3188 Glade Gulch Cir,
Castle Rock, CO 80104-7727 USA

Dejesus, Ivan *Baseball Player*
Los Angeles Dodgers, 14608 Velleux Dr,
Orlando, FL 32837-5467 USA

Dejesus, Jose *Baseball Player*
Kansas City Royals, 7E6 Villa Del Carmen,
Cidra, PR 00639 USA

Dejohn, Mark *Baseball Player*
Detroit Tigers, 21 Bunker Hill Rd, New
Britain, CT 06053 2206 USA

DeJohnette, Jack *Composer*
Silver Hollow Road, Willow, NY 11201
USA

DeJong, Pierre *Misc*
Laerence Livermore Laboratory, 7000 East
St, Livermore, CA 94550 USA

DeJordy, Denis E *Hockey Player*
472 Cherrin Des-Patriotes, Saint Charles,
QC, J0L 2G0, CANADA

DeKierk, Albert *Composer*
Crayenesterlaan, Haarlem, 22,
NETHERLANDS

DeKierk, Frederik W *Nobel Prize Laureate*
7 Eaton Square, London, SW1, UNITED
KINGDOM (UK)

DeKieweit, Cornelis W *Historian*
22 Berkeley St, Rochester, NY 14607 USA

Dekker, Desmond *Musician*
Free World Music, 230 12th St, #117,
Miami Beach, FL 33139 USA

DeKlerk, Frederik W *Nobel Prize Laureate*
7 Eaton Square, London, SW1, UNITED
KINGDOM (UK)

Del Arco, Jonathan *Actor*
Kyle Fritz Management, 1979 Grace Ave
#5A, Hollywood, CA 90068 USA

del Boca, Andrea *Actor*
Telefe - Argentina, Pavon 2444
(C1248AAT), Buenos Aires, ARGENTINA

del Castillo, Eric *Actor*
Televisa, Blvd Adolfo Lopez Mateos 232,
Colonia San Angel INN, DF, CP 01060,
MEXICO

Del Greco, Bobby *Baseball Player*
Pittsburgh Pirates, 625 Southview Dr,
Pittsburgh, PA 15226 2540 USA

Del Negro, Vinny (Vincent) *Athlete*
36 Hickory Hill, West Springfield, MA
01089

Del Regil, Estrellita
PO Box 2004, Beverly Hills, CA 90213

del Rincon, Fernando *Actor*
Univision, 314 Main St, Chico, CA 95928
USA

Del Rubio, Millie
PO Box 6923, San Pedro, CA 90734-6923

Del Savio, Garton *Baseball Player*
Philadelphia Phillies, 608 Western Hwy,
Blauvelt, NY 10913 1317 USA

del Solar, Fernando *Actor*
TV Azteca, Periferico Sur 4121, Colonia
Fuentes del Pedregal, DF, CP 14141,
Mexico

Del Toro, Benicio *Actor*
Firm, The, 9465 Wilshire Blvd, Beverly
Hills, CA 90212 USA

Del Toro, Guillermo *Director, Writer*
Exile Entertainment, 732 El Medio Ave,
Pacific Palisades, CA 90272 USA

Del-Vikings, The *Music Group*
PO Box 770850, Orlando, FL 32877 USA

DeLaBilliere, Peter *General*
Robert Fleming Holdings, 25 Copthall
Ave, London, EC2R 7DR, UNITED
KINGDOM (UK)

Delacote, Jacques
Dr Hilbert Maximilianstr 22, Munich,
80539, GERMANY

DeLaCruz, Rosie *Model*
Willhelmina Models, 300 Park Ave S,
#200, New York, NY 10010 USA

DeLaFuente, Cristian *Actor*
Stubbs Agency, 1450 S Robertson Blvd,
Los Angeles, CA 90035 USA

DeLaFuente, Joel *Actor*
LMRK, 130 W 42nd St, #1906, New York,
NY 10036 USA

Delahoussaye, Eddie
Box 250, Lexington, KY 40588-0250

Delahoussaye, Ryan *Musician*
Ashley Talent, 2002 Hogback Road, #20,
Ann Arbor, MI 48105 USA

DeLaHoya, Oscar *Boxer*
633 W 5th St, #6700, Los Angeles, CA
90071 USA

Delahoz, Mike *Baseball Player*
Cleveland Indians, 1367 SW 14th St,
Miami, FL 33145 1645 USA

Delaire, Suzy
46 rue de Varenne, Paris, FRANCE, 75007

Delamaza, Roland *Baseball Player*
Kansas City Royals, 28533 Silverking Trl,
Santa Clarita, CA 91390 5248 USA

DeLamielleure, Joseph M (Joe) *Football
Player*
7818 Ridgeloch Place, Charlotte, NC
28226 USA

DeLancie, John *Actor*
1313 Brunswick Ave, South Pasadena, CA
91030 USA

Delaney, F James (Jim) *Track Athlete*
PO Box 362, Sun Valley, ID 83353 USA

Delaney, Kim *Actor, Model*
Gersh Agency, The (LA), 232 N Canon Dr,
Beverly Hills, CA 90210 USA

Delaney, Pat
PO Box 273, Tamworth, NH 03886

Delaney, Shelagh *Writer*
Tess Sayle, 11 Jubilee Place, London, SW3
3TE, UNITED KINGDOM (UK)

Delano, Diane *Actor*
Gold Marshak Liedtke, 3500 W Olive
Ave, #1400, Burbank, CA 91505 USA

Delano, Robert B *Misc*
American Farm Bureau Federation, 225 W
Tuuhy Ave, Park Ridge, IL 60068 USA

Delany, Dana *Actor*
Brillstein/Grey, 9150 Wilshire Blvd, #350,
Beverly Hills, CA 90212 USA

Delany, Samuel R *Writer*
Vintage Press, 1111 Rancho Conejo Blvd,
Newbury Park, CA 91320 USA

DeLap, Tony *Artist*
225 Jasmine St, Corona del Mar, CA
92625 USA

DeLaPuente, Raygada Oscar *Prime
Minister*
Prime Minister's Office, Urb Corpac, Calle
1 Oeste, Lima, S/N, PERU

DelArco, Jonathan *Actor*
Michael Slessinger, 8730 Sunset Blvd,
#220W, Los Angeles, CA 90069 USA

DeLaRocha, Zack *Musician*
GAS Entertainment, 8935 Lindblade St,
Culver City, CA 90232 USA

DeLaRosa, Evelyn *Opera Singer*
Dorothy Cone Artists, 150 W 55th St,
New York, NY 10019 USA

DeLaRosa, Yvonne *Actor*
Heidi Rotbart Management, 4000 Warner
Blvd, Bldg 160 Room 716, Burbank, CA
91522

DeLarrocha, Alicia *Musician*
Farmaceutic Carbonell, 46-48 Atic,
Barcelona, 34, SPAIN

Delasin, Dorothy *Golfer*
20 Longview Dr, Daly City, CA 94015
USA

DeLatour, David *Actor*
Writers and Artists Group Intl (LA), 8383
Wilshire Blvd #550, Beverly Hills, CA
90211 USA

DeLatour, Frances *Actor*
Kate Feast, Primrose Hill Studios, Fitzroy
Road, London, NW1 8TR, UNITED
KINGDOM (UK)

DeLaurentiis, Dino *Producer*
Via Poutina Ku, Rome, 23270, ITALY

DeLeeuw, Ton *Composer*
Costerusiaan 4, Hilversum,
NETHERLANDS

Delehanty, Hugh *Editor*
AARP Publications, Editorial Dept, 601 E
St NW, Washington, DC 20049 USA

DeLeo, Dean *Musician*
Q Prime, 729 7th Ave, #1600, New York,
NY 10019 USA

DeLeo, Robert *Composer*
Q Prime, 729 7th Ave, #1600, New York,
NY 10019 USA

Deleon, Jose *Baseball Player*
Pittsburgh Pirates, 7021 NW 70th St,
Parkland, FL 33067 1486 USA

Delfino, Carlos Francisco *Basketball
Player*
Detroit Pistons, Palace, 2 Championship
Dr, Auburn Hills, MI 48326 USA

Delfino, Majandra *Actor*
Bragman/Nyman/Cafarelli, 9171 Wilshire
Blvd #300, Beverly Hills, CA 90210 USA

Delfino, Marieh *Actor*
Bragman/Nyman/Cafarelli, 9171 Wilshire
Blvd #300, Beverly Hills, CA 90210 USA

Delfs, Andreas *Conductor*
Saint Paul Chamber Orchestra, 408 Saint
Peter St, Saint Paul, MN 55102 USA

Delgado, Carlos J *Baseball Player*
Toronto Blue Jays, 9 Repto Ramos
Borinquen Plz, Aguadilla, PR 00603 5944
USA

Delgado, Chiquinquira *Actor*
Gabriel Blanco Iglesias (Mexico), Rio
Balsas 35-32, Colonia Cuauhtemoc, DF,
06500, Mexico

Delgado, Issac *Musician*
Ralph Mercado Mgmt, 568 Broadway,
#806, New York, NY 10012 USA

Delhaven, Robert M *War Hero*
3716 Terrace View Dr, Encino, CA 91436
USA

Delhi, Ganesh *Actor*
No12 62nd Street, Ashok Nagar, Chennai, TN 600 083, INDIA

Delhomme, Jake *Football Player*
Carolina Panthers, Ericsson Stadium, 800 S Mint St, Charlotte, NC 28202 USA

Delhoyo, George *Actor*
TalentWorks (LA), 3500 W Olive Ave #1400, Burbank, CA 91505 USA

Deligne, Pierre R *Mathematician*
Institute for Advanced Study, Math School, Einstein Dr, Princeton, NJ 08540 USA

DeLillo, Don *Writer*
57 Rossmore Ave, Bronxville, NY 10708 USA

DeLint, Derek *Actor*
Features Creative Mgmt, Entrepotdok 76A, Amsterdam, AD, 101, NETHERLANDS

DeLislt, Paul *Musician*
Creative Artists Agency, 9830 Wilshire Blvd, Beverly Hills, CA 90212 USA

Delizia, Cara *Actor*
Abrams Artists Agency (LA), 9200 Sunset Blvd Fl 11, Los Angeles, CA 90069 USA

Delk, Joan *Golfer*
830 Forest Path Lane, Alpharetta, GA 30022 USA

Delk, Tony *Basketball Player*
5129 E Desert Jewel Dr, Paradise Valley, AZ 85253 USA

Dell, Michael S *Business Person*
Dell Inc, 1 Dell Way, Round Rock, TX 78682 USA

DellaCasa-Debeljevic, Lisa *Opera Singer*
Schloss Gottlieben, Thurgau, SWITZERLAND

Dellaero, Jason *Baseball Player*
Chicago White Sox, 3313 SE 10th Ave, Cape Coral, FL 33904 4714 USA

DellaMalva, Joseph *Actor*
William Morris Agency, 151 El Camino Dr, Beverly Hills, CA 90212 USA

Dellanos, Myrka *Actor*
Univision, 314 Main St, Chico, CA 95928 USA

Delli Colli, Tomino
Via Pietro Micheli 78, Rome, ITALY, I-00197

Dellinger, Walter *Educator*
Duke University, Law School, Durham, NC 27706 USA

DelloJolo, Norman *Composer*
PO Box 154, East Hampton, NY 11937 USA

Dellucci, Dave *Baseball Player*
Baltimore Orioles, 18489 Lake Tulip Ave, Baton Rouge, LA 70817 9502 USA

DelNegro, Vinny *Basketball Player*
7320 N 71st St, Paradise Valley, AZ 85253 USA

Delo, Ken *Actor*
161 Avondale Drive, #93-8, Branson, MO 65616 USA

Deloach, Nikki *Musician*
Evolution Talent, 1776 Broadway, #1500, New York, NY 10019 USA

Delock, Ivan M (Ike) *Baseball Player*
Boston Red Sox, 433 Cypress Way E, Naples, FL 34110 1107 USA

Delon, Alain *Actor*
Alain Delon Diffusion, 12 Rue Saint-Victor, Geneva, 1206, SWITZERLAND

Delon, Anthony *Actor*
Intertalent, 5 Rue Clement-Marot, Paris, 75008, FRANCE

Delon, Nathalie
3 Quai Malaquais, Paris, FRANCE, 75006

DeLong, Keith A *Football Player*
915 Fairway Oaks Lane, Knoxville, TN 37922 USA

DeLong, Michael P *General*
Deputy Commander, US Central Command, MacDill Air Force Base, FL 33621 USA

DeLong, Steve C *Football Player*
4103 Dyanax St, Chesapeake, VA 23324 USA

DeLonge, Tom *Musician*
750 W Bluff Dr, Encinitas, CA 92024 USA

DeLongis, Anthony *Actor*
PO Box 2445, Canyon Country, CA 91386 USA

Delora, Jennifer *Actor*
Gilla Roos, 9744 Wilshire Blvd, #203, Beverly Hills, CA 90212 USA

DeLorean, John
567 Lamington Rd, Bedminster, NJ 07921-2781

DeLorean, John Z *Business Person*
PO Box 1092, Bedminster, NJ 07921 USA

DeLorenzo, Michael *Actor*
Abrams Artists Agency (LA), 9200 Sunset Blvd Fl 11, Los Angeles, CA 90069 USA

Deloria, Victor (Vine) Jr *Social Activist*
University of Colorado, History Dept, PO Box 234, Boulder, CO 80309 USA

Delorme, Daniele
16 rue de Marignan, Paris, FRANCE, 75008

Delors, Jacques L J *Government Official*
19 Blvd de Bercy, Paris, 75012, FRANCE

DeLosAngeles, Victoria *Opera Singer*
Avenida de Pedralbes 57, Barcelona, 08034, SPAIN

Delp, Brad *Musician*
Agency for Performing Arts, 9200 Sunset Blvd, #900, Los Angeles, CA 90069 USA

DelPiero, Alessandro *Soccer Player*
Juventus FC, Piazza Crimea 7, Turin, 10131, ITALY

Delpino, Robert L *Football Player*
23276 Daisy Dr, Corona, CA 92883 USA

Delpy, Julie *Actor*
Endeavor Talent Agency, 9701 Wilshire Blvd, #1000, Beverly Hills, CA 90212 USA

DelRio, Jack *Football Player, Coach*
177 Archimeds Court, Baltimore, MD 21208 USA

Delsing, Jim *Baseball Player*
Chicago White Sox, 14316 Conway Meadow Ct E Apt 105, Chesterfield, MO 63017 9607 USA

Delson, Brad *Musician*
Artist Group International, 9560 Wilshire Blvd, #400, Beverly Hills, CA 90212 USA

DelToro, Benicio *Actor*
I F A Talent Agency, 8730 Sunset Blvd, #490, Los Angeles, CA 90069 USA

DelTredici, David *Composer*
463 West St, #G121, New York, NY 10014 USA

DeLuca, Mike *Producer*
New Line Cinema, 716 N Robertson Blvd, Los Angeles, CA 90048 USA

DeLucas, Lawrence J *Astronaut*
909 19th St S, Birmingham, AL 35205 USA

DeLucchi, Michele *Architect*
Via Cenisio 40, Milan, 20154, ITALY

DeLucia, Paco *Musician*
International Music Network, 278 S Main St, #400, Gloucester, MA 01930 USA

Delucia, Rich *Baseball Player*
Seattle Mariners, 3 Muirfield Dr, Reading, PA 19607 3348 USA

Delugg, Milton *Musician*
2740 Claray Drive, Los Angeles, CA 90024 USA

DeLuise, David *Actor*
Schachter Entertainment, 1157 S Beverly Dr Fl 3, Los Angeles, CA 90035 USA

Deluise, Dom *Actor, Comedian*
1186 Corsica Drive, Pacific Palisades, CA 90272 USA

Deluise, Michael *Actor*
1186 Corsica Dr, Pacific Palisades, CA 90272 USA

Deluise, Peter *Actor*
Premiere Artists Agency, 1875 Century Park E, #2250, Los Angeles, CA 90067 USA

Delvecchio, Alexander P (Alex) *Hockey Player*
1135 Maryland Blvd, Birmingham, MI 48009 USA

Demaestri, Joe *Baseball Player*
Chicago White Sox, 50 Fairway Dr, Novato, CA 94949 5904 USA

DeMaiziere, Lothar *Prime Minister*
Am Kupfergraben 6/6A, Berlin, 10117, GERMANY

Demarchelier, Patrick *Photographer*
162 W 21st St, New York, NY 10011 USA

DeMarco, Guido *President*
President's Office, Palace, Valletta, MALTA

DeMarco, Jean *Artist*
Cervaro, Prov-Frosinore, 03044, ITALY

DeMarco, Tony *Boxer*
PO Box 53664, Indianapolis, IN 46253 USA

DeMarcus, Jay *Musician*
LGB Media, 1228 Pineview Lane, Nashville, TN 37211 USA

Demarest, Arthur A *Archaeologist*
Vanderbilt University, Anthropology Dept, Nashville, TN 37235 USA

Demars, Billy *Baseball Player*
Philadelphia Athletics, 770 Island Way Apt 305, Clearwater, FL 33767 1824 USA

Demars, Bruce *Admiral*
41 Manters Point Road, Plymouth, MA 02360 USA

DeMatteo, Drea *Actor*
Filthmart, 531 E 13th St, New York, NY 10009 USA

DeMatteo, Drea *Actor*
Writers & Artists, 8383 Wilshire Blvd, #550, Beverly Hills, CA 90211 USA

DeMedeiros, Maria *Actor*
William Morris Agency, 151 El Camino Dr, Beverly Hills, CA 90212 USA

DeMenezes, Fradique *President*
President's Office

DeMenezes, Fradique *President*
President's Office, Pargo do Povo, Sao Tome, SAO TOME & PRINCIPE

DeMent, Iris *Songwriter*
PO Box 28856, Gladstone, MO 64117 USA

DeMent, Jack *Misc*
Oregon Health Care Center, 11325 NE Weidler St, #44, Portland, OR 97220 USA

Dement, Kenneth *Football Player*
316 S Kingshighway St, Sikeston, MO 63801 USA

Dementieva, Elena *Tennis Player*
Octagon, 1751 Pinnacle Dr, #1500, McLean, VA 22102 USA

DeMerchant, Paul *Religious Leader*
Missionary Church, PO Box 9127, Fort Wayne, IN 46899 USA

Demerit, John *Baseball Player*
Milwaukee Braves, 550 W Walters St, Port Washington, WI 53074 1430 USA

Demery, Larry *Baseball Player*
Pittsburgh Pirates, 10715 Petalo Dr, Bakersfield, CA 93311 2289 USA

Demeter, Don *Baseball Player*
Brooklyn Dodgera, 6240 S Country Club Dr, Oklahoma City, OK 73159 1844 USA

Demeter, Steve *Baseball Player*
Detroit Tigers, 6032 Ravine Blvd, Cleveland, OH 44134 3047 USA

Demetral, Chris *Actor*
William Morris Agency, 151 El Camino Dr, Beverly Hills, CA 90212 USA

Demetriadis, Phoklon *Cartoonist*
3rd September St 174, Athens, GREECE

Demetrios *Religious Leader*
Greek Orthodox Church, 89 E 79th St, #19, New York, NY 10021 USA

Demeulemeester, Ann *Fashion Designer*
Ann Demeulemeester, 6 Rue Milne Edwards, Paris, 75017, France

DeMille, Nelson *Writer*
61 Hilton Ave, #23, Garden City, NY 11530 USA

Demin, Lev S *Cosmonaut*
Potchta Kosmonavtov, Moskovskol Oblasti, Syvisdny Goroduk, 141160, RUSSIA

Deming, Peter *Cinematographer*
Sandra Marsh Mgmt, 9150 Wilshire Blvd, #220, Beverly Hills, CA 90212 USA

DeMita, L Ciriaco *Prime Minister*
Partito Democrazia Cristiana, Piazza de Gesu 46, Rome, 00186, ITALY

Demme, Jonathan *Director*
Creative Artists Agency, 9830 Wilshire Blvd, Beverly Hills, CA 90212 USA

Demola, Don *Baseball Player*
Montreal Expos, 352 Village Dr, Hauppauge, NY 11788 3225 USA

DeMont, Rick *Swimmer*
84-596 Upena St, Waianae, HI 96792 USA

DeMontebello, Philippe L *Misc*
Metropolitan Museum of Art, 82nd St & 5th Ave, New York, NY 10028 USA

DeMornay, Rebecca *Actor*
J/P/M, 760 N La Cienega Blvd #200, Los Angeles, CA 90069 USA

DeMott, William (Bill, Hugh Morris, Crash the Terminator) *Wrestler*
World Wrestling Entertainment (WWE), 1241 E Main St, Stamford, CT 06905 USA

Dempsey, Cedric *Misc*
National Collegiate Athletic Assn, 70 W Washington St, Indianapolis, IN 46204 USA

Dempsey, Con *Baseball Player*
Montreal Expos, 1530 Cordilleras Rd, Redwood City, CA 94062 3208 USA

Dempsey, J Rikard (Rick) *Baseball Player*
Los Angeles Dodgers, Stadium, 1000 Elysian Park Ave, Los Angeles, CA 90012 USA

Dempsey, Mark *Baseball Player*
San Francisco Giants, 673 W Martindale Rd, Union, OH 45322 3043 USA

Dempsey, Patrick *Actor*
15260 Ventura Blvd, #2100, Sherman Oaks, CA 91403 USA

Dempsey, Rick *Baseball Player*
Minnesota Twins, 1673 Crown Ridge Ct, Westlake Village, CA 91362 4731 USA

Dempsey, Thomas (Tom) *Athlete, Football Player*
4922 York St, Metairie, LA 70001 USA

Dempster, Ryan *Baseball Player*
Florida Marlins, 21050 NE 38th Ave Apt 2606, Miami, FL 33180 4082 USA

Demsetz, Harold *Economist*
University of California, Economics Dept, Los Angeles, CA 90024 USA

DeMunn, Jeffrey *Actor*
Gersh Agency, 232 N Canon Dr, Beverly Hills, CA 90210 USA

DeMuron, Pierre *Architect*
Herzog & De Meuron Architekten, Rheinschanze 6, Basel, 4056, SWITZERLAND

Demus, Jorg *Musician*
LYRA, Doblinger Hauptstr 77-A/10, Vienna, 1190, AUSTRIA

Demuth, Richard H *Attorney General, Financier*
5404 Bradley Blvd, Bethesda, MD 20814 USA

Den, Tagayasu *Choreographer*
Ondekoza, Koda Performing Arts Co, Sado Island, JAPAN

Denard, Michael *Dancer*
Paris Opera Ballet, Place de l'Opera, Paris, 75009, FRANCE

Dench, Judi *Actor*
Julian Belfarge, 46 Albermarle St, London, W1X 4PP, UNITED KINGDOM (UK)

Denehy, Bill *Baseball Player*
New York Mets, 5096 Eastwinds Dr, Orlando, FL 32819 3517 USA

Denes, Agnes C *Artist*
595 Broadway, New York, NY 10012 USA

Deneuve, Catherine *Actor*
76 Rue Bonaparte, Paris, 75016, FRANCE

Deng, Luol *Basketball Player*
Phoenix Suns, 201 E Jefferson St, Phoenix, AZ 85004 USA

Denhardt, David T *Biologist*
Rutgers University, Nelson Biological Laboratories, Piscataway, NJ 08855 USA

DenHerder, Vern W *Football Player*
1277 S Main Ave, Sioux Center, IA 51250 USA

Denicourt, Marianne *Actor*
Artmedia, 20 Ave Rapp, Paris, 75007, FRANCE

DeNiro, Robert *Actor*
TriBeCa Productions, TriBeCa Film Center, 375 Greenwich St, New York, NY 10013 USA

Denis, Marc *Hockey Player*
1227 Retreat Lane, Gahanna, OH 43230 USA

Denisof, Alexis *Actor*
Evolution Entertainment, 901 N Highland Ave, Los Angeles, CA 90038 USA

Denison, Anthony *Actor*
10100 Santa Monica Blvd, #1060, Los Angeles, CA 90067 USA

Denisov, Edison V *Composer*
Studentcheskaia 44/28, #35, Moscow, 121165, RUSSIA

Denisse, Francois-Jean *Astronomer*
48 Rue Monsieur Le Prince, Paris, 75006, FRANCE

Denisyuk, Yuri N *Engineer*
Vavilov Optical Institute, 12 Burzhevaya, Saint Petersburg, 199034, RUSSIA

Denker, Henry *Writer*
241 Central Park West, New York, NY 10024 USA

Denman, Brian *Baseball Player*
Boston Red Sox, 16 Cindy Dr, Buffalo, NY 14221 3002 USA

Denman, David *Actor*
Hofflund/Polone, 9465 Wilshire Blvd #820, Beverly Hills, CA 90212 USA

Dennard, Preston *Football Player*
4545 Green Ave NW, Albuquerque, NM 87114 USA

Dennard, Robert H *Inventor*
2054 Quaker Ridge Road, Croton on Hudson, NY 10520 USA

Dennehy, Brian *Actor*
Susan Smith, 121A N San Vicente Blvd, Beverly Hills, CA 90211 USA

Dennehy, Kathleen *Actor*
Susan Nathe, 8281 Melrose Ave, #200, Los Angeles, CA 90046 USA

Denneriein, Barbara *Musician*
Tsingtauer Str 66, Munich, 81827, GERMANY

Dennett, Daniel C *Misc*
20 Ironwood Road, North Andover, MA 01845 USA

Denning, Hazel M *Writer*
Llewellyn Worldwide, PO Box 64383, St Paul, MN 55164-0383

Dennings, Kat *Actor*
Creative Management Group, 3815 Hughes Ave Fl 3, Culver City, CA 90232 USA

Dennis, Cathy *Musician*
19 Music, Ransomes Gate #32, 35-37 Parkgate, London, SW11 4NP, UNITED KINGDOM (UK)

Dennis, Don *Baseball Player*
St Louis Cardinals, RR 2, Uniontown, KS 68779 USA

Dennis, Donna F *Artist*
131 Duane St, New York, NY 10013 USA

Dennis, Jim *Race Car Driver*
1810 Little Masters Corner Road, Harrington, DE 19952 USA

Dennis, Mike *Musician*
American Promotions, 2011 Ferry Ave, #U19, Camden, NJ 08104 USA

Dennis, Pamela *Fashion Designer*
Jerry Shandrew PR, 1050 South Stanley Avenue, Los Angeles, CA 90019-6634 USA

Dennison, Rachel *Actor*
Raymond Katz, 345 N Maple Dr, #205, Beverly Hills, CA 90210 USA

Denny, Dorothy
PO Box 1566, Apple Valley, CA 92307

Denny, Floyd W Jr *Misc*
1 Carolina Meadows, #308, Chapel Hill, NC 27517 USA

Denny, John *Baseball Player*
St Louis Cardinals, 13430 E Camino La Cebadilla, Tucson, AZ 85749 8611 USA

Denny, Martin *Composer, Musician*
6770 Hawaii Kai Drive, #402, Honolulu, HI 96825 USA

Denny, Robyn *Artist*
20/30 Wilds Rents, #4B, London, SE14QG, UNITED KINGDOM (UK)

DenOuden, Wilerninintie (Willy) *Swimmer*
Goudsewagenstraat 23B, Rotterdam, HOLLAND

Densham, Pen *Director*
International Creative Mgmt, 8942 Wilshire Blvd, #219, Beverly Hills, CA 90211 USA

Densmore, Elizabeth *Actor*
Lane Management Group, 13331 Moorpark St, #118, Sherman Oaks, CA 91423 USA

Densmore, John *Musician*
49 Halderman Road, Santa Monica, CA 90402 USA

Denson, Drew *Baseball Player*
Atlanta Braves, 1718 Avonlea Ave, Cincinnati, OH 45237 6110 USA

Dent, Frederick B *Secretary*
221 Montgornery St, Spartanburg, SC 29302 USA

Dent, Jim *Golfer*
PO Box 290656, Tampa, FL 33687 USA

Dent, Richard L *Football Coach, Football Player*
4453 RFD, Long Grove, IL 60047 USA

Dent, Russell E "Bucky" *Athlete*
8895 Indian River Run, Boynton Beach, FL 33437

Denton, Derek A *Physicist*
816 Irring Road, Toorak, VIC, 3142, AUSTRALIA

Denton, Sandi (Pepa) *Musician*
Famous Artists Agency, 250 W 57th St, New York, NY 10107 USA

Denton Jr, Jeremiah A *Senator*
11404 Queens Way, #B, Theodore, AL 36582 USA

Denver, Bob *Actor*
GFC, PO Box 269, Princeton, WV 24740 USA

Denzongapa, Danny *Actor, Bollywood*
Dzongrilla 11th Road, Juhu, Mumbai, MS INDIA

Denzongpa, Danny *Actor, Bollywood*
29 D'Zongrilla, 11th Road, JVPD Scheme, Juhu, Bombay, 400049, India

Denzongpa, Danny *Actor, Bollywood*
29 D'Zongrilla, 11th Road, JVPD Scheme, Juhu, Bombay, 400049, India

Deol, Bobby *Actor, Bollywood*
Plot No 22, 11th Road, JVPD Scheme Juhu, Mumbai, MS 400049, INDIA

Deol, Dharmendra *Actor, Bollywood*
Plot No 22 11th Rd, Juhu, Mumbai, MS 400049, INDIA

Deol, Sunny *Actor, Bollywood*
Plot No 22, 11th Road JVPD Scheme, Mumbai, MS 400026, INDIA

DeOre, Bill *Cartoonist*
Dallas News, Editorial Dept, Communications Center, Dallas, TX 75265 USA

DePalma, Brian R *Director*
International Creative Management (ICM-LA), 8942 Wilshire Blvd, Beverly Hills, CA 90211 USA

DePalva, James *Actor*
PO Box 11152, Greenwich, CT 06831 USA

Depardieu, Gerard *Actor*
Creative Artists Agency LCC (CAA-LA), 9830 Wilshire Blvd, Beverly Hills, CA 90212 USA

Depardon, Raymond *Photographer*
18 Bis Rue Henri Barbusse, Paris, 75005, FRANCE

Depastino, Joe *Baseball Player*
New York Mets, 4142 Center Pointe Cir Apt 62A, Sarasota, FL 34233 1681 USA

Depaula, Sean *Baseball Player*
Cleveland Indians, 2 Thomas St, Derry, NH 03038 2988 USA

DePavia, James
PO Box 11152, Greenwich, CT 06831

DePeyer, Gervase
Porto Vecchio 109, 1250 S Washington St, Alexandria, VA 22314 USA

DePortzamparc, Christian *Architect*
Architecte DPLG, 1 Rue de L'Aude, Paris, 75014, FRANCE

DePoyster, Jerry D *Football Player*
11111 Sceptre Ridge Terrace, Germantown, MD 20876 USA

Depp, Johnny *Actor, Director*
United Talent Agency (UTA), 9560 Wilshire Blvd, Beverly Hills, CA 90212 USA

DePree, Hopwood *Actor*
ROAR LLC, 2400 Broadway #350, Santa Monica, CA 90404 USA

DePreist, James A *Conductor*
Konsert AB, Kungsgatan 32, Stockholm, 11135, SWEDEN

DePrume, Cathryn *Actor*
Flick East West Talents Inc, 9057 Nemo Street, Suite A, West Hollywood, CA 90069 USA

Dequenne, Emilie *Actor*
Cineart, 36 Rue de Ponthieu, Paris, 75008, FRANCE

Dequenne, Emilie *Cartoonist*
Houston Post, Editorial Dept, 4888 Loop Cantral Dr #390, Houston, TX 77081 USA

Derbez, Silvia *Actor*
Televisa, Blvd Adolfo Lopez Mateos 232, Colonia San Angel INN, DF, CP 01060, MEXICO

Derbyshire, Andrew G *Architect*
4 Sunnyfield, Hatfield, Herts, AL9 5DX, UNITED KINGDOM (UK)

Derek, Bo *Actor, Model*
PO Box 1940, Santa Ynez, CA 93460 USA

Deriso, Walter M Jr *Financier*
Synovus Financial Corp, 901 Front Ave, PO Box 120, Columbus, GA 31902 USA

Dern, Bruce *Actor*
PO Box 1581, Santa Monica, CA 90406 USA

Dern, Laura *Actor*
Wolf/Kasteler PR, 335 N Maple Dr #351, Beverly Hills, CA 90210 USA

Dernesch, Helga *Opera Singer*
Neutorgasse 2/22, Vienna, 1013

Dernesch, Helga *Opera Singer*
Neutorgasse 2/22, Vienna, 1013, AUSTRIA

Dernier, Bob *Baseball Player*
Cleveland Indians, 13153 Carter St, Overland Park, KS 66213 4655 USA

DeRosa, Mark *Baseball Player, Athlete*
Atlanta Braves, 626 8th St, Carlstadt, NJ 07072-1702 USA

DeRosa, William *Misc*
Columbia Artists Mgmt Inc, 165 W 57th St, New York, NY 10019 USA

DeRosier, David *Physicist*
27 Chesterfield Road, Newton, MA 02465 USA

Derosier, Michael *Musician*
Borman Entertainment, 1250 6th St, #401, Santa Monica, CA 90401 USA

DeRossi, Portia *Actor*
International Creative Management (ICM-LA), 8942 Wilshire Blvd, Beverly Hills, CA 90211 USA

Derow, Peter A *Publisher*
PO Box 534, Bedford, NY 10506 USA

Derr, Kenneth T *Business Person*
Chevron Corp, 6001 Bollinger Canyon Road, San Ramon, CA 94583 USA

Derrick, Jim *Baseball Player*
Boston Red Sox, 107 Oliver St, West Columbia, SC 29169 7627 USA

Derricks, Cleavant *Actor*
480 Burano Court, Agoura Hills, CA 91377 USA

Derrida, Jacques *Misc*
Ecole des Hautes Eludes, 54 Blvd Raspail, Paris, 75006, FRANCE

Derringer, Rick *Musician*
Brothers Management, 141 Dunbar Ave, Fords, NJ 08863 USA

Derrington, Jim *Baseball Player*
Chicago White Sox, 711 Sandlewood Ave, La Habra, CA 90631 7248 USA

Derry, Kathy *Physicist*
PO Box 1656, Laguna Beach, CA 92652 USA

Derry, Russ *Baseball Player*
New York Yankees, 8619 N Myrtle Ave, Kansas City, MO 64156 1298 USA

Dersch, Hans *Swimmer*
7217 E 55th Place, Tulsa, OK 74145 USA

Dershowitz, Alan M *Lawyer, Educator*
1563 Massachusetts Ave, Cambridge, MA 02138 USA

Dervan, Peter B *Misc*
California Institute of Technology, Chemistry Dept, Pasadena, CA 91125 USA

Derwin, Mark *Actor*
Stone Manners, 6500 Wilshire Blvd, #550, Los Angeles, CA 90048 USA

Derwinski, Edward J *Secretary*
Derwinski Assoc, 1800 Diagonal Road, #600, Alexandria, VA 22314 USA

Des Barres, Michael *Actor*
Ellis Talent Group, 4705 Laurel Canyon Blvd, Suite 300, Valley Village, CA 91607 USA

Des'ree *Musician*
Solo Agency, 55 Fulham High St, London, SW6 3JJ, UNITED KINGDOM (UK)

Desai, Anita *Writer*
Deborah Rogers Ltd, 20 Powis Mews, London, W11 1JN, UNITED KINGDOM (UK)

Desai, Ketan *Director, Bollywood, Producer*
3C Swapnalok Jagmohandas Marg, Bombay, MS 400 026, INDIA

Desailly, Jean *Actor*
Babette Pouget, 9 Square Villaret de Joyeuse, Paris, 75017, FRANCE

Desailly, Marcel *Soccer Player*
FC Chelsea Stamford Bridge, Fulham Road, London, SW6 1HS, UNITED KINGDOM (UK)

deSando, Anthony
PO Box 5617, Beverly Hills, CA 90210

deSantis, Guiseppe
Fiano Romano Via del Commercio 1, Rome, ITALY, I-00154

deSantis, Luigi
Via della Villa di Lucina 72, Rome, ITALY, I-00145

Desanto, Tom *Producer*
William Morris Agency (WMA-LA), 1 William Morris Pl, Beverly Hills, CA 90212 USA

Descendants, The
4230 Del Rey Avenue #621, Marina del Rey, CA 90292 USA

Deschanel, Caleb *Cinematographer*
Dark Light Pictures, 812 N Highland Ave, Los Angeles, CA 90038 USA

Deschanel, Emily *Actor*
Anonymous Content, 8522 National Blvd #101, Culver City, CA 90232 USA

Deschanel, Mary Jo *Actor*
844 Chautaugua Blvd, Pacific Palisades, CA 90272 USA

Deschanel, Zooey *Actor*
844 Chautaugua Blvd, Pacific Palisades, CA 90272 USA

Desert, Alex *Actor*
Pakula/King & Associates, 9229 Sunset Blvd #315, Los Angeles, CA 90069 USA

Desfor, Max *Journalist*
15115 Interlachen Dr, #1018, Silver Spring, MD 20906 USA

Deshales, Jim *Baseball Player*
New York Yankees, 151 N Taylor Point Dr, Spring, TX 77382 1240 USA

DeShields, Delino L *Baseball Player*
100 Shady Brook Walk, Fairburn, GA 30213 3466 USA

Desiderio, Robert *Actor*
1475 Sierra Vista Dr, Aspen, CO 81611 USA

Desilva, John *Baseball Player*
Montreal Expos, 32750 Airport Rd, Fort Bragg, CA 95437 9514 USA

DeSimone, Livio D (Desi) *Business Person*
Minnesota Mining & Manufacturing, 3M Center, Saint Paul, MN 55144 USA

DeSimone, Paul *Actor*

Desjardins, Eric *Hockey Player*
4 Danforth Dr, Voorhees, NJ 08043 USA

Deskur, Andrzej Maria Cardinal *Religious Leader*
Palazzo S Carlo, 00120, VATICAN CITY

Deslongchamps, Pierre *Misc*
1884 Rue des Orioles, Laval, QC, H7L 5T8, CANADA

Desmormeaux, Kent *Jockey*
Desmormeaux Racing Stable, 385 W Huntington Dr, Arcadia, CA 91007 USA

Desny, Ivan *Actor*
Casa al Sole, Ascona-Collina, 6612, SWITZERLAND

Despadovich, Nada
6500 Wilshire Blvd #2200, Los Angeles, CA 90048

Despotopoulos, Johannes (Jan) *Architect*
Anapiron Polemou 7, Athens, 11521, GREECE

Dessay, Natalie *Opera Singer*
Herbert Breslin, 119 W 57th St, #1505, New York, NY 10019 USA

Dessens, Elmer *Baseball Player*
Pittsburgh Pirates, PO Box 312, Leipsic, OH 45856 0312 USA

Destiny's Child *Music Group*
Creative Artists Agency LCC (CAA-LA), 9830 Wilshire Blvd, Beverly Hills, CA 90212 USA

Destrade, Orestes *Baseball Player*
New York Yankees, PO Box 20852, Tampa, FL 33622 0852 USA

Destri, Jimmy *Misc*
Shore Fire Media, 32 Court St, #1600, Brooklyn, NY 11201 USA

Desurvive, Emmanuel *Engineer*
Alcatel Submarine Networks, Villarceaux Centre, Nozay, 91625, FRANCE

DeTar, Dean E *War Hero*
7785 Portwood Road, Azle, TZ, 76020 USA

DeThe, Guy Blaudin *Biologist*
14 Rue Le Regrattier, Paris, 75004, FRANCE

Detherage, Bob *Baseball Player*
Kansas City Royals, 322 Turf Ln, Carl Junction, MO 64834 9575 USA

Detmer, Amanda *Actor*
Foundation Management, 100 N Crescent Dr #300, Beverly Hills, CA 90212 USA

Detmer, Tv H *Football Player*
PO Box 942, Jourdanton, TX 78026 USA

Detmers, Maruschka *Actor*
Myriam Bru, 80 Avenue Charles de Gaulle, Neuilly Sur Seine, 92200, FRANCE

Detorie, Rick *Cartoonist*
Creators Syndicate, 5777 W Century Blvd, #700, Los Angeles, CA 90045 USA

Detroit, Marcella *Musician, Songwriter*
MCM Mgmt, 40 Langham St, #300, London, W1N 5RG, UNITED KINGDOM (UK)

Dettmer, John *Baseball Player*
Texas Rangers, 549 Hickory View Ln, Ballwin, MO 63011 1500 USA

Dettore, Tom *Baseball Player*
Pittsburgh Pirates, 1120 McEwen Ave, Canonsburgh, PA 15317 1928 USA

Detweiler, David K *Physicist*
Waverty Heights, 1400 Waverty Road #A212, Gladwyne, PA 19035 USA

Detweiler, Ducky *Baseball Player*
Boston Braves, 312 Holt St, Federalsburg, MD 21632 1403 USA

Detweiler, Robert C *Educator*
1450 Ellis Ave, Cambria, CA 93428 USA

Deukmejian, C George *Ex-Governor*
Sidley & Austin, 555 West 5th Street, Los Angeles, CA 90013 USA

Deukmejian, C George *Governor*
Sidley & Austin, 555 W 5th St, Los Angeles, CA 90013 USA

Deutch, Howard *Director*
International Creative Mgmt, 8942 Wilshire Blvd, #219, Beverly Hills, CA 90211 USA

Deutch, John M *Government Official*
51 Clifton St, Belmont, MA 02478 USA

Deutekom, Cristina *Opera Singer*
Lancasterdreet 41, Dronten, TG, 8251, HOLLAND

Deutsch, Patti *Actor*
Yvette Bikoff, 1040 1st Ave, #1126, New York, NY 10022 USA

Dev, Mukul *Actor, Bollywood*
Karan Apts 5th Floor, Yari Road Versova, Mumbai, MS 40061, INDIA

Deva, Prabhu *Actor, Musician, Dancer, Choreographer, Comedian*
68 T T K Road, Alwarpet, Chennai, TN 600 018, INDIA

DeValeria, Dennis *Writer*
213 Hillendale Road, Pittsburgh, PA 15237 USA

Devan Nair, Chengara Veetil *President*
Istana, Orchard Road, Singapore, 0922, SINGAPORE

Devane, William *Actor*
Innovative Artists, 1505 10th St, Santa Monica, CA 90401 USA

DeVarona, Donna *Swimmer, Sportscaster*
TWI, 420 W 45th Street, #500, New York, NY 10036 USA

Devault, Calvin *Actor*
Amset Eisenstadt Frazier, 5757 Wilshire Blvd, #510, Los Angeles, CA 90036 USA

Devayani *Actor, Bollywood*
51 Indira Gandhi Street, Saligramam, Chennai, TN 600093, INDIA

Dever, Barbara *Opera Singer*
Wolf Artists Mgmt, 788 Columbus Ave, #15A, New York, NY 10025 USA

Deveraux, Jude *Writer*
Pocket Books, 1230 Ave of Americas, New York, NY 10020 USA

Devereaux, Mike *Baseball Player*
Los Angeles Dodgers, 2236 Doublegrove St, West Covina, CA 91790 5607 USA

Devers, Gail *Track Athlete*
Kersee, 8519 Paul Jones Dr, Jacksonville, FL 32208 USA

Devgan, Ajay *Actor, Bollywood*
5/6 Sheetal Apt, Opp. Chandan Cinema Juhu, Mumbai, MS 400049, INDIA

DeVicenzo, Roberto *Golfer*
Nonl Lann, 5025 Veloz Ave, Tarzana, CA 91356 USA

Devicq, Paula *Actor, Model*
William Morris Agency, 151 El Camino Dr, Beverly Hills, CA 90212 USA

Deville, CC *Musician*
H K Mgmt, 9200 W Sunset Blvd, #530, Los Angeles, CA 90069 USA

Deville, Michael *Director*
36 Rue Reinhardt, Boulogne, 92100, FRANCE

Devine, Adrian *Baseball Player*
Atlanta Braves, 271 Timber Laurel Ln, Lawrenceville, GA 30043 USA

Devine, Harold *Boxer*
595 Wyckoff Ave, Wyckoff, NJ 07481 USA

Devine, Loretta *Actor*
3829 Crestway Place, Los Angeles, CA 90043 USA

DeVink, Lodewijk J R *Business Person*
Warner-Lambert Co, 201 Tabor Road, Morris Plains, NJ 07950 USA

Devisree *Actor, Bollywood*
1 Bharathi Apts, Bharathi Nagar 3rd Street T Nagar, Chennai, TN 600017, INDIA

DeVita, Vincent T Jr *Misc*
Yale Comprehensive Cancer Center, 333 Cedar St, New Haven, CT 06510 USA

DeVito, Danny *Actor, Comedian, Director*
PO Box 491246, Los Angeles, CA 90049 USA

Devitt, John *Swimmer*
46 Beacon Ave, Beacon Hill, NSW, 2100, AUSTRALIA

Devlin, Bruce *Golfer*
11429 E Mark Lane, Scottsdale, AZ 85262 USA

Devlin, Dean *Director, Actor, Producer*
Creative Artists Agency, 9830 Wilshire Blvd, Beverly Hills, CA 90212 USA

Devlin, Jim *Baseball Player*
Cleveland Indians, 130 Worman St, Bloomsburg, PA 17815 3193 USA

Devlin, Robert M *Business Person*
American General Corp, 2929 Allen Parkway, Houston, TX 77019 USA

Devo
PO Box 6868, Burbank, CA 91510

Devon *Adult Film Star*
Atlas Entertainment, 6100 Wilshire Blvd #1170, Los Angeles, CA 90048 USA

Devon, Dayna *Television Host*
Extra (LA), 1840 Victory Blvd, Glendale, CA 91201 USA

DeVries, William C *Doctor*
DeVries Associates, 7 Snowmound Court, Rockville, MD 20850 USA

deVry, William J *Actor*
House of Representatives, 400 S Beverly Dr #101, Beverly Hills, CA 90212 USA

DeWaart, Edo *Conductor*
Essenlaan 68, Rotterdam, 3016, NETHERLANDS

Dewar, Jane E *Editor*
Legion Magazine, 359 Kent St, #504, Ottawa, ON K2P 0R6, CANADA

Dewar, Susan *Cartoonist*
Universal Press Syndicate, 4520 Main St, Kensas City, MO 64111 USA

Dewey, Duane E *War Hero*
RR 1 Box 494, Irons, MI 49644 USA

Dewey, Mark *Baseball Player*
San Francisco Giants, PO Box 14, New Era, MI 49446 0014 USA

DeWilde, Edy *Director*
Stedelijk Museum, Amsterdam, NETHERLANDS

Dewillis, Jeff *Baseball Player*
Toronto Blue Jays, 8918 Wind Side Dr, Houston, TX 77040 3460 USA

DeWinne, Frank *Cosmonaut*
349 Squadron, Vilegbaiss, Kleine Brogel, Peer, 10W TAC, 3990, BELGIUM

DeWitt, Bryce S *Physicist*
University of Texas, Physics Dept, Austin, TX 78712 USA

DeWitt, Darrin *Actor*
Edmonds Management, 1635 N Cahuenga Blvd Fl 5, Los Angeles, CA 90028 USA

DeWitt, Doug *Boxer*
2035 Central Ave, Yonkers, NY 10710 USA

DeWitt, Joyce *Actor*
JG Business Management Inc, 1250 6th Street, Santa Monica, CA 90401 USA

Dewitt, Matt *Baseball Player*
Toronto Blue Jays, 7177 Sixshooter Dr, Las Vegas, NV 89119 4517 USA

DeWitt, Willie *Boxer*
605 N Water St, Bumet, TX 78611 USA

DeWitt-Morette, Cecile *Physicist*
2411 Vista Lane, Austin, TX 78703 USA

Dews, Peter B *Psychic*
181 Upland Road, Newtonville, MA 02460 USA

Dexter, Mary *Director*
Hank Tani, 14542 Delaware Dr, Moorpark, CA 93021 USA

Dexter, Peter W *Writer*
Sacramento Bee, Editorial Dept, 21st & Q Sts, Sacramento, CA 95852 USA

Dey, Susan *Actor*
1640 S Sepulveda Blvd, #530, Los Angeles, CA 90025 USA

DeYoung, Cliff *Actor*
481 Savona Way, Oak Park, CA 91377 USA

Dezhurov, Vladimir N *Cosmonaut*
Potchta Kosmonavtov, Moskovskoi Obtasti, Syvisdny Goroduk, 141160, RUSSIA

DeZonie, Hank *Basketball Player*
700 Lenox Ave, New York, NY 10039 USA

Dhabhara, Firdaus S *Scientist*
Rockefeller University, Neurology Dept, 1230 York Ave, New York, NY 10021 USA

Dhamu *Actor*
84 Pycrofts Road 36 ADK Mansion, Triplicane, Chennai, TN 600 005, INDIA

Dhanapal *Actor*
8 A G Block, Pallaku Maa Nagar Luz, Chennai, TN 600 004, INDIA

Dhanoa, Guddu *Actor*
8A My Little Home, 10th Road JVPD Scheme, Bombay, MS 400 049, INDIA

Dharmasakti, Sanya *Prime Minister*
15 Saukhumvit Road, Soi 41, Bangkok, THAILAND

Dhawan, David *Director, Filmmaker*
A-15 Sagar Darshan, Carter Road Khar, Mumbai, MS 400052, INDIA

Di Maggio, Dominic P (Dom) *Baseball Player, Athlete*
6110 North Ocean Blvd #24, Ocean Ridge, FL 33435 USA

Di Meola, Al *Musician*
Entourage Talent, 133 West 25th Street, 5th Floor, New York, NY 10001

Di Montezemolo, Luca *Race Car Driver, Business Person*
Jaguar Racing Ltd, Bradbourne Drive, Tilbrook, Milton Keynes, MK7 8BJ, United Kingdom

Dial, Leroy (Buddy) *Football Player*
115 Anna St, Tomball, TX 77375 USA

Diallo, Mmadou *Soccer Player*
New England Revolution, CMGI Field, 1 Patriot Place, Foxboro, MA 02035 USA

Diamandis, Peter G *Publisher*
Diamandis Communications, 1515 Broadway, New York, NY 10036 USA

Diamandopoulos, Peter *Educator*
530 E 76th St, #32G, New York, NY 10021 USA

Diamini, Barnabas S *Prime Minister*
Prime Minister's Office, PO Box 395, Mbabane, SWAZILAND

Diamond, Abel J *Architect*
Diamond Schmitz Co, 2 Berkeley St, #600, Toronto, ON M5A 2W3, CANADA

Diamond, Bobby
5309 Comercio Way, Woodland Hills, CA 91364

Diamond, David L *Composer*
249 Edgerton St, Rochester, NY 14607 USA

Diamond, Diane *Television Host*
Court TV, 600 Third Ave Fl 2, New York, NY 10016 USA

Diamond, Dustin *Actor*
Jack Koshick Presents, 1626 North Prospect Avenue, Suite 1801, Milwaukee WI, 53202 USA

Diamond, Jared M *Biologist*
University of California, Med School, Physiology Dept, Los Angeles, CA 90024 USA

Diamond, Marian C *Misc*
2583 Virginia St, Berkeley, CA 94709 USA

Diamond, Michael (Mike D) *Musician*
GAS Entertainment, 8935 Lindblade St, Culver City, CA 90232 USA

Diamond, Neil *Musician*
10345 W Olympic Blvd #200, Los Angeles, CA 90064 USA

Diamond, Nell L *Musician, Songwriter*
10345 W Olympic Blvd, #200, Los Angeles, CA 90064 USA

Diamond, Reed *Actor*
William Morris Agency, 151 El Camino Dr, Beverly Hills, CA 90212 USA

Diamond, Seymour *Doctor*
Diamond Headache Clinic, 467 W Deming Place, #500, Chicago, IL 60614 USA

Diamond Rio *Musician*
William Morris Agency (WMA-LA), 1 William Morris Pl, Beverly Hills, CA 90212 USA

Diamonds, The *Music Group*
561 Keystone Avenue #224, Reno, NV 89503 USA

Diamont, Anita *Writer*
Charles Scribner's Sons, 866 3rd Ave, New York, NY 10022 USA

Diamont, Don *Actor*
Craig Mgmt, 125 S Sycamore Ave, Los Angeles, CA 90036 USA

Dias, Ivan Cardinal *Religious Leader*
Archbishop's House, 21 Nathalal Parekh Marg, Mumbai, MS 400001, INDIA

Dias Dos Santos, Fernando da Piedade *Prime Minister*
Prime Minister's Office, Council of Ministers, Luanda, ANGOLA

Diaw, Boris *Basketball Player*
Atlanta Hawks, 190 Marietta St SW, Atlanta, GA 30303 USA

Diaz, Alex *Journalist*
Associated Press, 50 Rockefeller Plaza, New York, NY 10020 USA

Diaz, Arnold *Correspondent*
20/20, 147 Columbus Ave, New York, NY 10023, US

Diaz, Cameron *Actor*
Creative Artists Agency LCC (CAA-LA), 9830 Wilshire Blvd, Beverly Hills, CA 90212 USA

Diaz, Carlos *Baseball Player*
Atlanta Braves, 47-709 Waiohia St, Kaneohe, HI 96744-4938 USA

Diaz, Carlos *Baseball Player*
Toronto Blue Jays, 3037 Homestead Oaks Dr, Clearwater, FL 33759-1626 USA

Diaz, Einar *Baseball Player*
Cleveland Indians, 9518 Old Hyde Park Pl, Bradenton, FL 34202-4089 USA

Diaz, Guillermo *Actor*
Abrams Artists Agency (LA), 9200 Sunset Blvd Fl 11, Los Angeles, CA 90069 USA

Diaz, Helga *Actor*
Gabriel Blanco Iglesias (Mexico), Rio Balsas 35-32, Colonia Cuauhtemoc, DF, 06500, Mexico

Diaz, Laura *Golfer*
Ladies Pro Golf Association (LPGA), 100 International Golf Drive, Daytona Beach, FL 32124 USA

Diaz, Manny *Politician*
Mayor's Office, 3500 Pan American Dr, Miami, FL 33133 USA

Diaz, Matt *Baseball Player*
Tampa Bay Devil Rays, 1124 Afton St, Lakeland, FL 33803-3202 USA

Diaz, Mike *Baseball Player*
Chicago Cubs, 730 N Ithica St, Gilbert, AZ 85233-4002 USA

Diaz, Norberto *Actor*
Telefe - Argentina, Pavon 2444 (C1248AAT), Buenos Aires, ARGENTINA

Diaz, Robison *Actor*
TV Caracol, Calle 76 #11 - 35, Piso 10AA, Bogota DC, 26484, COLOMBIA

Diaz Balart, Jose *Actor*
Telemundo, 2470 West 8th Avenue, Hialeah, FL 33010 USA

Diaz-Balart, Jose *Commentator*
CBS-TV, News Dept, 51 W 52nd St, New York, NY 10013 USA

Diaz-Rahi, Yamila *Model*
Next Model Mgmt, 23 Watts St, New York, NY 10013 USA

Dibble, Dorne *Athlete, Football Player*
18601 Jamestown Circle, Northville, MI 48167 USA

Dibble, Rob *Baseball Player*
Cincinnati Reds, 250 Dino Rd, Bristol, CT 06010-7889 USA

Dibel, John C *Business Person*
Meade Instruments Corp, 6001 Oak Canyon, Irvine, CA 92618 USA

DiBeliglojoso, Lodovico B *Architect*
Studio Architetti BBPR, 2 Via Dei Chiostri, Milan, 20121, ITALY

DiBiaggio, John A *Educator*
Tufts University, President's Office, Medford, MA 02155 USA

DiBlasio, Raul *Musician*
Esterfan Enterprises, 420 Jefferson Ave, Miami Beach, FL 33139 USA

Diblassio, Raul *Musician*
BMG, 1540 Broadway, New York, NY 10036 USA

DiBona, Craig *Cinematographer*
333 E 66th St, #7O, New York, NY 10021 USA

Dibra, Bash
Trident Media Group LLC, 41 Madison Ave Fl 33, New York, NY 10010 USA

Dicamillo, Gary T *Business Person*
1001 Saint Georges Road, Baltimore, MD 21210 USA

DiCaprio, Leonardo *Actor*
Appian Way, 9255 Sunset Blvd #615, West Hollywood, CA 90069

DiCenzo, George *Actor*
Michael Hartig Agency, 156 5th Ave, #820, New York, NY 10010 USA

Dichter, Misha *Musician*
Columbia Artists Mgmt Inc, 165 W 57th St, New York, NY 10019 USA

Dicillo, Tom *Director*
William Morris Agency, 151 El Camino Dr, Beverly Hills, CA 90212 USA

Dick, Andy *Actor, Comedian*
Management 360, 9111 Wilshire Blvd, Beverly Hills, CA 90210 USA

Dick, Douglas *Actor*
604 S Gretna Green Way, Los Angeles, CA 90049 USA

Dickau, Dan *Basketball Player*
Atlanta Hawks, 190 Marietta St SW, Atlanta, GA 30303 USA

Dicken, Paul *Baseball Player*
Cleveland Indians, 1901 NW 28th Ave, Ocala, FL 34475-4709 USA

Dickens, Jimmy *Musician*
5010 W Concord Road, Brentwood, TN 37027 USA

Dickens, Kim *Artist*
Gersh Agency, The (LA), 232 N Canon Dr, Beverly Hills, CA 90210 USA

Dickenson, Gary *Bowler*
501 Wade Martin Dr, Edmond, Ok, 73034 USA

Dickerson, Eric *Football Player, Sportscaster*
26500 W Agoura Road #654, Calabasas, CA 91302 USA

Dickerson, Ernest R *Director*
Gersh Agency, The (LA), 232 N Canon Dr, Beverly Hills, CA 90210 USA

Dickerson, Sandra *Actor*
Howes & Prior, Berkeley House, Hay Hill, London, W1X 7LH, UNITED KINGDOM (UK)

Dickey, Boh A *Business Person*
SAFECO Corp, SAFECO Plaza, Seattle, WA 98185 USA

Dickey, C Lynn *Football Player*
6102 Mission Road, Fairway, KS 66205 USA

Dickey, Eric Jerome *Writer*
Dutton, 375 Hudson St, New York, NY 10014

Dickey, R A *Baseball Player*
Texas Rangers, 206 Paddock Ln, Nashville, TN 37205-3337 USA

Dickinson, Angie *Actor*
1715 Carla Ridge, Beverly Hills, CA 90210 USA

Dickinson, Bruce *Musician*
Sanctuary Music Mgmt, 82 Bishops Bridge Road, London, W2 6BB, UNITED KINGDOM (UK)

Dickinson, David *Actor*
Bargain Hunt, PO Box 229, Bristol, BS99 7JN, ENGLAND

Dickinson, Gary *Bowler*
501 Wade Martin Road, Edmond, OK 73034 USA

Dickinson, Janice *Actor, Model*
Creative Management Group, 3815 Hughes Ave Fl 3, Culver City, CA 90232 USA

Dickinson, Peter *Writer*
Mysterious Press, Warner Books, 1271 Ave of Americas, New York, NY 10020 USA

Dickinson, Steve *Cartoonist*
King Features Syndicate, 888 7th Ave, New York, NY 10106 USA

Dickman, James B *Journalist*
1471 Peach Creek Dr, Splendora, TX 77372 USA

Dickson, Chris *Yachtsman*
Int'l Mgmt Group, 1 Erieview Plaza, 1360 E 9th St #1300, Cleveland, OH 44114 USA

Dickson, Clarence *Lawyer*
Police Department, Metro Justice, 1351 NW 12th St, Miami, FL 33125 USA

Dickson, Jason *Baseball Player*
California Angels, 9022 E Helm Dr, Scottsdale, AZ 85260-2704 USA

Dickson, Jennifer *Artist, Photographer*
20 Osborne St, Ottawa, ON K1S 4Z9, CANADA

Dickson, Jim *Baseball Player*
Houston Colt.45's, 90580 Sunset Lake Rd #1, Warrenton, OR 97146-7236 USA

Dickson, Lance *Baseball Player*
Chicago Cubs, 5501 N Paseo Pescado, Tucson, AZ 85718-5127 USA

Dickson, Neil *Actor*
International Creative Mgmt, 76 Oxford St, London, W1N 0AX, UNITED KINGDOM (UK)

Dickson, Ngila *Designer*
Sandra Marsh Management, 9150 Wilshire Blvd #220, Beverly Hills, CA 90212 USA

Dicus, Charles (Chuck) *Football Player*
1500 E Clark St, Fayetteville, AR 72701 USA

Diddley, Bo *Musician*
PO Box 410, Archer, FL 32618 USA

Diddy, P *Artist*
Wright Entertainment Group, 7680 Universal Blvd, #500, Orlando, FL 32819 USA

Didier, Bob *Baseball Player*
Atlanta Braves, 544 SW 335th St, Federal Way, WA 98023-6189 USA

Didion, Joan *Writer*
Janklow & Nesbit, 445 Park Ave, #1300, New York, NY 10022 USA

Dido *Musician, Songwriter*
Nettwerk Mgmt, 1650 W 2nd Ave, Vancouver, BC V6J $R3, CANADA

Diebold, John *Business Person*
Diebold Group, PO Box 515, Bedford Hills, NY 10507 USA

Diehl, Digby *Journalist*
788 South Lake Avenue, Pasadena, CA 91106 USA

Diehl, Digby R *Journalist*
788 S Lake Ave, Pasadena, CA 91106 USA

Diehl, John *Actor*
Paradigm (LA), 10100 Santa Monica Blvd, Fl 25, Los Angeles, CA 90067 USA

Diehl, William *Writer*
William Morris Agency, 151 El Camino Dr, Beverly Hills, CA 90212 USA

Dieken, Doug H *Football Player*
209 Prospect Ave, Streator, IL 61364 USA

Diemecke, Enrique Arturo *Conductor*
Herbert Barrett, 266 W 37th St, #2000, New York, NY 10018 USA

Diener, Theodor O *Misc*
PO Box 272, 11711 Battersea Dr, Beltsville, MD 20705 USA

Dierassi, Carl *Inventor*
2325 Bear Gulch Road, Redwood City, CA 94062 USA

Dierassi, Issac *Doctor*
2034 Delancey Place, Philadelphia, PA 19103 USA

Dierdof, Daniel L (Dan) *Football Player, Sportscaster*
13302 Buckland Hall Road, Saint Louis, MO 63131 USA

Diering, Chuck *Baseball Player*
St Louis Cardinals, 1 Nob Hill Dr, Saint Louis, MO 63138-1400 USA

Dierker, Lawrence E (Larry) *Baseball Player*
Houston Colt.45's, 8318 N Tahoe Dr, Houston, TX 77040-1258 USA

Dierker, Robert R *General*
Deputy Commander Pacific Fleet, Camp H M Smith, Honolulu, HI 96861 USA

Dierking, Connie *Basketball Player*
5665 Kugler Mill Road, Cincinnati, OH 45236 USA

Diesel
26 Stokescroft #100, Bristol, ENGLAND, BS1 3QD

Diesel, Vin *Actor, Producer, Director, Writer*
One Race Productions, 3800 Barham Blvd #502, Los Angeles, CA 90068 USA

Dietrich, Dena *Actor*
Peter Strain, 5724 West 3rd Street, #302, Los Angeles, CA 90036 USA

Dietrich, William A (Bill) *Journalist*
Seattle Times, Editorial Dept, 1120 John St, Seattle, WA 98109 USA

Dietz, Dick *Baseball Player*
San Francisco Giants, PO Box 753, Snow Hill, NC 28580-0753 USA

Dietzel, Roy *Baseball Player*
Washington Senators, 8421 Coulwood Oak Ln, Charlotte, NC 28214-1165 USA

Difani, Jay *Baseball Player*
Washington Senators, 1186 Weaver Rd, Festus, MO 63028-4242 USA

Difelice, Mike *Baseball Player*
St Louis Cardinals, 9409 Trails End Rd, Knoxville, TN 37931-4218 USA

Diffie, Joe *Musician, Songwriter*
50 Music Square W, #300, Nashville, TN 37203 USA

Diffie, Whitfield *Inventor*
Sun Microsystems, 901 San Antonia Road, MS UMTV29-116, Palo Alto, CA 94303 USA

Diffrient, Niels *Designer*
General Delivery, Ridgefield, CT 06877 USA

DiFranco, Ani *Musician, Songwriter*
Fleming/Tamulevich, 733 N Main St, #735, Ann Arbor, MI 48104 USA

DiGenova, Joseph E *Lawyer*
DiGenova & Toensing, 901 15th St NW, #430, Washington, DC 20005 USA

Diggins, Ben *Baseball Player*
Milwaukee Brewers, PO Box 2887, Vero Beach, FL 32961-2887 USA

Diggs, Taye *Actor*
584 Broadway, #1009, New York, NY 10012 USA

Digible Planets *Music Group*
345 North Maple Drive #123, Beverly Hills, CA 90210 USA

DiGirolamo, Vincent A *Financier*
National City Corp, National City Center, 1900 E 9th St, Cleveland, OH 44114 USA

DiGregorio, Ernie *Basketball Player*
60 Chestnut Ave, Narragansett, RI 02882 USA

Dilauro, Jack *Baseball Player*
New York Mets, 168 E Mohawk Dr,
Malvern, OH 44644-9539 USA

Dilba *Musician*
United Stage Production, PO Box 11029,
Stockholm, 10061, SWEDEN

Dilfer, Trent F *Football Player*
200 Saint Paul St, #2400, Baltimore, MD
21202 USA

Dilip *Actor*
74 Baskara Colony, Virugambakkam,
Chennai, TN 600 092, INDIA

Dill, Laddie John *Artist*
1625 Electric Ave, Venice, CA 90291 USA

Dillahunt, Garret *Actor*
Allman/Rea Management, 141 Barrington
#E, Los Angeles, CA 90049 USA

Dillam, Bradford *Actor*
770 Hot Springs Road, Santa Barbara, CA
93108 USA

Dillane, Stephen *Actor*
Michelle Braidman, 10/11 Lower John St,
#300, London, W1R 3PE, UNITED
KINGDOM (UK)

Dillard, Alex *Business Person*
Dillard's Inc, 1600 Cantrell Road, Little
Rock, AR 72201 USA

Dillard, Annie *Writer*
Russell Volkering, 50 W 29th St, New
York, NY 10001 USA

Dillard, Don *Baseball Player*
Cleveland Indians, 45 Bream Ln,
Waterioo, SC 29384-4868 USA

Dillard, Gordon *Baseball Player*
Baltimore Orioles, 1290 Rider Ave,
Salinas, CA 93905-1259 USA

Dillard, Harrison
3449 Glencairn Rd, Cleveland, OH
44122-4801

Dillard, Steve *Baseball Player*
Boston Red Sox, 133 County Road 1742,
Saltillo, MS 38866-7206 USA

Dillard, W Harrison *Track Athlete*
3449 Glencairn Road, Shaker Heights,
OH 44122 USA

Dillard, William T Jr *Business Person*
Dillard's Inc, 1600 Cantrell Road, Little
Rock, AR 72201 USA

Dillehay, Thomas (Tom) *Misc*
University of Kentucky, Anthropology
Dept, Lexington, KY 40506 USA

Dilleita, Dilleita Mohamed *Prime Minister*
Prime Minister's Office, PO Box 2086,
Djibouti, DJIBOUTI

Diller, Barry
1940 Coldwater Canyon, Beverly Hills,
CA 90210

Diller, Phyllis *Actor, Comedian*
163 S Rockingham Ave, Los Angeles, CA
90049 USA

Dillinger, Bob *Baseball Player*
St Louis Browns, 15380 Rhododendron
Dr, Canyon Country, CA 91387-1851
USA

Dillinger, Darlene
3104-A Highland Ave, Manhattan Beach,
CA 90266

Dillion, Steve *Baseball Player*
New York Mets, 110 Hyatt Ave, Yonkers,
NY 10704-4315 USA

Dillman, Bill *Baseball Player*
Baltimore Orioles, PO Box 5167, Winter
Park, FL 32793-5167 USA

Dillman, Bradford *Actor*
770 Hot Springs Road, Santa Barbara, CA
93103 USA

Dillman, Brooke *Actor*
Sweet Mud Group, 648 Broadway #1002,
New York, NY 10012 USA

Dillon, Corey *Football Player*
9517 E Kemper Road, Loveland, OH
45140 USA

Dillon, David B *Business Person*
Kroger Co, 1014 Vince St, Cincinnati, OH
45202 USA

Dillon, Denny *Actor, Comedian*
International Creative Mgmt, 8942
Wilshire Blvd, #219, Beverly Hills, CA
90211 USA

Dillon, John T *Business Person*
International Paper Co, 2 Manhattanville
Road, Purchase, NY 10577 USA

Dillon, Kevin *Actor*
49 West 9th Street, #5B, New York, NY
10011 USA

Dillon, Marc *Musician*
Pop Idol (Fremantle Media), 2700
Colorado Ave #450, Santa Monica, CA
90404 USA

Dillon, Matt *Actor, Director*
9465 Wilshire Blvd, #419, Beverly Hills,
CA 90212 USA

Dillon, Melinda *Actor*
4065 Michael Ave, Los Angeles, CA
90066 USA

Dilone, Miguel *Baseball Player*
Pittsburgh Pirates, Calle El Sol #190,
Santiago, DOMINICAN REPUBLIC

DiMaggio, Dominic P (Dom) *Baseball
Player*
Boston Red Sox, 6110 N Ocean Blvd,
#24, Boynton Beach, FL 33435-5241 USA

DiMaggio, John *Actor*
Gersh Agency, The (LA), 232 N Canon Dr,
Beverly Hills, CA 90210 USA

DiMarco, Chris *Golfer*
1408 Langham Terrace, Lake Mary, FL
32746 USA

Dimas, Trent *Gymnast*
Gold Cup Gymnastics School, 6009
Carmel Ave NE, Albuquerque, NM 87113
USA

Dimbleby, David *Journalist, Commentator*
14 King St, Richmond, Surrey, TW9 1NF,
UNITED KINGDOM (UK)

Dimebag, Darrell *Musician*
Concrete Mgmt, 361 W Broadway, #200,
New York, NY 10013 USA

DiMeola, Al *Musician*
Don't Worry, 111 W 57th St, #1120, New
York, NY 10019 USA

Dimichele, Frank *Baseball Player*
California Angels, 812 Tasker St,
Philadelphia, PA 19148-1240 USA

Dimitriades, Alex *Actor*
Shanahan Management, PO Box 1509,
Darlinghurst, 1300, AUSTRALIA

Dimitrova, Ghena *Opera Singer*
I C M Artists, 40 W 57th St, New York,
NY 10019 USA

Dimmel, Mike *Baseball Player*
Baltimore Orioles, 526 Country Ln,
Coppell, TX 75019-5129 USA

Dimon, James (Jamie) *Business Person*
J P Morgan Chase, 270 Park Ave, New
York, NY 10017 USA

Dimple *Actor, Bollywood*
The Gallop Broad Acres Stud Farm, Avan
Hali Estate, Bangalore, KA, INDIA

DiMucci, Dion
1650 Broadway #503, New York, NY
10019

diNapoli, Marc
8 rue de Georges-de-Porto-Riche, Paris,
FRANCE, F-75014

DiNardo, Gerry *Football Coach*
Indiana University, Athletic Dept,
Bloomington, IN 47405 USA

Dindal, Mark *Director*
Lichter Grossman Nichols Adler &
Goodman, 9200 Sunset Blvd #1200, Los
Angeles, CA 90069 USA

Dine, James *Artist*
Pace Gallery, 32 E 57th St, New York, NY
10022 USA

Dineen, Gary *Hockey Player*
177 Sawmill Road, West Springfield, MA
01089 USA

Dineen, Kerry *Baseball Player*
New York Yankees, 2155 Arrowhead Dr,
Santa Maria, CA 93455-5762 USA

Dineen, Kevin *Hockey Player*
30 Rivermead, Avon, CT 06001 USA

Dineen, William P (Bill) *Coach*
Saint Louis Blues, Sawis Center, 1401
Clark Ave, Saint Louis, MO 63103 USA

Dinerstein, James *Artist*
Salander-O'Reilly Gallery, 20 E 79th St,
New York, NY 10021 USA

Dingman, Craig *Baseball Player*
New York Yankees, 3573 Del Sienno St,
Wichita, KS 67203-4349 USA

Dini, Paul *Actor, Producer, Writer*
United Talent Agency (UTA), 9560
Wilshire Blvd, Beverly Hills, CA 90212
USA

Dinkeloo, John *Architect*
Roche & Dinkeloo, 20 Davis St, Hamden,
CT 06517 USA

Dinklage, Peter *Actor*
Silver Massetti & Szatmary (SMS-LA),
8730 Sunset Blvd #440, Los Angeles, CA
90069 USA

Dinner, Michael *Director*
Creative Artists Agency LCC (CAA-LA),
9830 Wilshire Blvd, Beverly Hills, CA
90212 USA

Dinnigan, Collette *Fashion Designer*
22-24 Hutchinson St, Surry Hills, Sydney,
NSW, 2010, AUSTRALIA

Dion *Musician*
Fox Entertainment, 1650 Broadway, #503, New York, NY 10019 USA

Dion, Celine *Musician*
Feeling Productions Inc, 2540 Daniel Johnson #755, Laval QB, H7T 2S3, CANADA

Dion, Colleen *Actor*
Abrams Artists, 9200 Sunset Blvd, #1125, Los Angeles, CA 90069 USA

Dionisi, Stefano *Actor*
Carol Levi Co, Via Giuseppe Pisanelli, Rome, 00196, ITALY

Dionne, Joseph L *Business Person, Publisher*
McGraw-Hill Inc, 1221 Ave of Americas, New York, NY 10020 USA

Dionne, Marcel E *Hockey Player*
Dionne Enterprises, 9930 Keller Road, Clarence Center, NY 14032 USA

Diop, DeSagana *Basketball Player*
Cleveland Cavaliers, Gund Arena, 1 Center Court, Cleveland, OH 44115 USA

Diop, Majhemout *President*
210 HCM Guediawaye, Dakar, SENEGAL

Dior, Christian *Designer, Fashion Designer*
St-Anna-Platz 2, Munich, 80538, Germany

Diorio, Nick *Soccer Player*
273 Clark St, Lemoyne, PA 17043 USA

Diorio, Ron *Baseball Player*
Philadelphia Phillies, 2 White Oak Ln, Waterbury, CT 06705-1835 USA

DiPasquale, James *Composer*
Gorfaine/Schwartz, 13245 Riverside Dr, #450, Sherman Oaks, CA 91423 USA

Dipietro, Bob *Baseball Player*
Boston Red Sox, 909 Carriage Hill Dr, Yakima, WA 98908-2414 USA

DiPietro, Rick *Hockey Player*
63 Loring Road, Winthrop, MA 02152 USA

Dipino, Frank *Baseball Player*
Milwaukee Brewers, 5238 E Foxhill Ln, Camillus, NY 13031-9746 USA

Dipoto, Jerry *Baseball Player*
6009 W 142nd Street, Overland Park, KS 66223-2963 USA

DiPreta, Tony *Cartoonist*
North American Syndicate, 235 E 45th St, New York, NY 10017 USA

DiPrete, Edward D *Governor*
555 Wilbur Ave, Cranston, RI 02921 USA

Dirda, Michael *Journalist*
Washington Post, Editorial Dept, 1150 15th St NW, Washington, DC 20071 USA

Dirie, Waris *Model, Social Activist*
London Mgmt, 2-4 Noel Street, London, W1V 3RB, UNITED KINGDOM (UK)

Dirt Band, The
PO Box 1915, Aspen, CO 81611

Disarcina, Gary *Baseball Player*
California Angels, 6 Patrick Ave, Billerica, MA 01821-5503 USA

Disch, Thomas M *Writer*
Karpfinger Agency, 357 West 20th St, New York, NY 10011 USA

Dischinger, Terry *Basketball Player*
1259 Lake Garden Court, Lake Oswego, OR 97034 USA

Disco, Shanthi *Actor, Bollywood*
19 Habibullah Road, T Nagar, Chennai, TN 600017, INDIA

Disel, Vin *Director, Actor*
The Firm, 9100 Wilshire Blvd, #100W, Beverly Hills, CA 90210 USA

Dishman, Cris E *Football Player*
5453 W Venus Way, Chandler, AZ 85226 USA

Dishman, Glenn *Baseball Player*
San Diego Padres, 5400 Fairway Dr, San Jose, CA 95127-1609 USA

Dishy, Bob *Actor*
20 E 9th St, New York, NY 10003 USA

Disi, Ursula *Skier*
Krumme Gasse 10A, Ruhpolding, 83324, GERMANY

Disi, Uschi *Misc*
Unterer Plattenberg 6, Flossenberg, 92696, GERMANY

Disney, Anthea *Editor*
News America Publishing Group, 211 Ave of Americas, New York, NY 10036 USA

Disney, Roy *Business Person*
Walt Disney Company, 500 S Buena Vista St, Burbank, CA 91521 USA

Disney, William *Speed Skater*
1610 Kirk Dr, Lake Havasu City, AZ 86404 USA

DiSpirito, Rocco *Actor, Reality TV Star*
William Morris Agency (WMA-NY), 1325 Ave of the Americas, New York, NY 10019 USA

Distaso, Alec *Baseball Player*
Chicago Cubs, PO Box 78, Colchester, IL 62326-0078 USA

Distefano, Benny *Baseball Player*
Pittsburgh Pirates, 9911 Murray Lndg, Missouri City, TX 77459-6417 USA

Distel, Sascha
20 rue de Fosses-Saint-Jacques, Paris, F-75005, FRANCE

Disturbed *Music Group*
Agency Group, The (NY), 1775 Broadway #430, New York, NY 10019 USA

DiSuvero, Mark *Artist*
PO Box 2218, Astoria, NY 11102 USA

Ditmar, Arthur J (Art) *Baseball Player*
Philadelphia Athletics, 6687 Wisteria Dr, Myrtle Beach, SC 29588-6481 USA

Dittmer, Andreas *Athlete*
Fischerbank 5, Neubrandenburg, 17033, GERMANY

Dittmer, Edward C *Scientist*
702 Old Mescalero Road, Tularosa, NM 88352 USA

Dittmer, Jack *Baseball Player*
Boston Braves, 200 N Main Street, Elkader, IA 52043 USA

Dityatin, Aleksandr N *Gymnast*
Nevski Prosp 18, #25, Saint Petersburg, RUSSIA

Ditz, Nancy *Track Athlete*
524 Moore Road, Woodside, CA 94062 USA

Diulio, Albert J *Educator*
Marquette University, President's Office, Milwaukee, WI 53233 USA

Divac, Viade *Basketball Player*
17535 Camino de Yatasto, Pacific Palisades, CA 90272 USA

Divine, Gary W *Misc*
National Federation of Federal Employees, 1016 16th St, Washington, DC 20038 USA

Diwakar, R R *Writer*
Sri Arvind Krupa, 233 Sadashiv Nagar, Bangalore, Karnataka, 560006, INDIA

Dix, Drew D *War Hero*
1829 S Pueblo Blvd, Pueblo, CO 81005 USA

Dixie Chicks, The *Music Group*
Firm, The, 9465 Wilshire Blvd, Beverly Hills, CA 90212 USA

Dixie Cups, The *Music Group*
2535 Noble Street, North Las Vegas, NV 89030 USA

Dixieland Rhythm Kings, The
PO Box 12403, Atlanta, GA 30355

Dixit, Madhuri *Actor, Bollywood*
Vijaydeep 3rd Floor Iris Park, Juhu, Mumbai, MS 400049, INDIA

Dixon, Alan J *Senator*
7606 Foley Dr, Belleville, IL 62223 USA

Dixon, Becky *Sportscaster*
ABC-TV, Sports Dept, 77 W 66th St, New York, NY 10023 USA

Dixon, Craig *Track Athlete*
10630 Wellworth Ave, Los Angeles, CA 90024 USA

Dixon, D Jeremy *Architect*
41 Shelton St, London, WC2H 9HJ, UNITED KINGDOM (UK)

Dixon, Donna *Actor*
Edrick/Rich Mgmt, 8955 Norma Place, Los Angeles, CA 90069 USA

Dixon, Floyd *Musician*
Folklore Prod, 1671 Appian Way, Santa Monica, CA 90401 USA

Dixon, Frank J *Misc*
2355 Avenida de la Playa, La Jolla, CA 92037 USA

Dixon, Hanford *Football Player*
30166 Lake Road, Bay Village, OH 44140 USA

Dixon, Ivan *Actor, Director*
27350 Barkes Way, Tehachapi, CA 93561 USA

Dixon, Juan *Basketball Player*
Washington Wizards, MCI Centre, 601 F St NW, Washington, DC 20004 USA

Dixon, Ken *Baseball Player*
Baltimore Orioles, 40 Clinton Hill Ct, Catonsville, MD 21228-3678 USA

Dixon, Randolph C (Randy) *Football Player*
9910 Summerlakes Dr, Carmel, IN 46032 USA

Dixon, Robert J *General*
29342 Ridgeview Terrace, Boerne, TX 78015 USA

Dixon, Rodney (Rod) *Track Athlete*
22 Entrican Ave, Remuera, Auckland, 5,
NEW ZEALAND

Dixon, Sonny *Baseball Player*
Washington Senators, 2912 Iron Gate Ln,
Charlotte, NC 28212-3646 USA

Dixon, Steve *Baseball Player*
St Louis Cardinals, 6510 Hollow Tree Rd,
Louisville, KY 40228-1336 USA

Dixon, Tamecka *Basketball Player*
Los Angeles Sparks, Staples Center, 1111
S Figueroa St, Los Angeles, CA 90015
USA

Dixon, Thomas F *Engineer*
1761 Cuba Island Lane, Hayes, VA 23072
USA

Dixon, Tom *Baseball Player*
Houston Astros, 2945 Delaney St,
Orlando, FL 32806-6256 USA

Dizon, Jesse
PO Box 8933, Universal City, CA 91608

DJ, Premier *Artist*
William Morris Agency, 151 El Camino
Dr, Beverly Hills, CA 90212 USA

Djodjov Pejoski, Marjan *Fashion Designer*
Marjan Djodjov Pejoski, 75 Garden Flat,
Warwick Avenue, London, England, W1Y
1DH, United Kingdom

Djoussouf, Abbass *Prime Minister*
Prime Minister's Office, Moroni, BP, 421,
COMOROS

Djukanovic, Milo *President*
Executive Council, Bul Lenjina 2, Novi
Belgrad, 11075, SERBIA &
MONTENEGRO

Dmitriev, Artur *Figure Skater*
Russian Skating Federation, Luchneksaia
Nab 8, Moscow, 119871, RUSSIA

DMX *Actor, Musician*
William Morris Agency (WMA-LA), 1
William Morris Pl, Beverly Hills, CA
90212 USA

Do Amaral, Diogo F *Government Official*
Ave Fontes Perelra de Melo 35, #13A,
Lisbon, 1050, PORTUGAL

Do Muoi *Politician*
Chairman's Office, Council of Ministers,
Hanoi, VIETNAM

Do Nascimento, Alexandre Cardinal
Religious Leader
Arcebispado, CP 87, Luanda, 1230 C,
ANGOLA

Doan, Charles A *Doctor*
4935 Oletangy Blvd, Columbus, OH
43214 USA

Doar, John *Lawyer*
9 E 63rd St, New York, NY 10021 USA

Dobbek, Dan *Baseball Player*
Washington Senators, 4042 SE Yamhill St,
Portland, OR 97214-4445 USA

Dobbin, Edmund J *Educator*
Villanova University, President's Office,
Villanova, PA 19085 USA

Dobbins, Herb *Football Player*
10 Keating Point, Saint Albert, AB T6N
5N8, CANADA

Dobbs, Lou *Commentator*
Cable News Network, News Dept, 820 1st
St NE, Washington, DC 20002 USA

Dobbs, Mattiwilda *Opera Singer*
1101 S Arlington Ridge Road, Arlington,
VA 22202 USA

Dobek, Michelle *Golfer*
292 Chicopee St, Chicopee, MA 01013
USA

Dobelie, William *Inventor*
Dobelle Institute, 1 Lincoln Place, New
York, NY 10023 USA

Dobie, Alan
Pontus Molash, Kent, CT4 8HW,
ENGLAND

Dobkin, David *Director*
H S I Productions, 3630 Eastham Dr,
Culver City, CA 90232 USA

Dobkin, Lawrence
1787 Old Ranch Rd, Los Angeles, CA
90049

Dobkins, Carl Jr *Musician*
7640 Cheviot Road, #212, Cincinnati, OH
45247 USA

Dobler, Conrad F *Football Player*
12600 Fairway Road, Shawnee Mission,
KS 66209 USA

Dobler, David *Religious Leader*
Presbyterian Church USA, 100
Witherspoon St, Louisville, KY 40202 USA

Dobo, Kata *Actor*
Ramaker Management, 400 North
Gardner Street, Los Angeles, CA 90036
USA

Dobslow, Bill *Musician*
945 Handlebar Road, Mishawaka, IN
46544 USA

Dobson, Chuck *Baseball Player*
Kansas City A's, 4208 Locust St, Kansas
City, MO 64110-1017 USA

Dobson, James C *Religious Leader*
Focus on the Family, 8605 Explorer Dr,
Colorado Springs, CO 80920 USA

Dobson, Kevin *Actor*
Side Action, 685 Miramonte Dr, Santa
Barbara, CA 93109 USA

Dobson, Pat *Baseball Player*
Detroit Tigers, 5033 Rolling Hills Pl, El
Cajon, CA 92020-8255 USA

Dobson, Peter *Actor*
1351 N Crescent Heights Blvd, #318,
West Hollywood, CA 90046 USA

Doby, Larry
45 Nishuane, Montclair, NJ 07042-2461

Dockson, Robert R *Financier*
1301 Collingwood Place, Los Angeles, CA
90069 USA

Dockstader, Frederick J *Misc*
165 W 66th St, New York, NY 10022
USA

Doctorow, E L *Writer*
International Creative Management
(ICM-LA), 8942 Wilshire Blvd, Beverly
Hills, CA 90211 USA

Doctorow, Edgar Lawrence (E L) *Writer*
333 E 57th St, #11B, New York, NY
10022 USA

Doda, Carol *Dancer, Actor*
PO Box 387, Fremont, CA 94537 USA

Dodd, Deryl *Songwriter, Musician*
823 Mgmt, PO Box 186, Waring, TX
78074 USA

Dodd, Jamie *Actor*
Nikki Bond Management, Aspect Court,
47 Park Square East, Leeds, LS1 2NL,
United Kingdom

Dodd, Maurice *Cartoonist*
Daily Mirror, Editorial Dept, 1 Canada
Square, London, E14 5AP, UNITED
KINGDOM (UK)

Dodd, Michael T (Mike) *Volleyball Player*
1017 Manhattan Ave, Manhattan Beach,
CA 90266 USA

Dodd, Patty D *Volleyball Player*
1017 Manhattan Ave, Manhattan Beach,
CA 90266 USA

Dodd, Robert *Baseball Player*
Philadelphia Phillies, 500 New York Ave
Apt 12, Dunedin, FL 34698-7858 USA

Dodd, Tom *Baseball Player*
Baltimore Orioles, 3735 NE Shaver St,
Portland, OR 97212 1817 USA

Dodge, Brooks *Skier*
PO Box C, Jackson, NH 03846 USA

Dodge, GeaHrey *Publisher*
Money Magazine, Time-Life Building,
New York, NY 10020 USA

Dodge, Geoffrey *Publisher*
Money Magazine, Time-Life Building,
New York, NY 10020 USA

Dodson, Pat *Baseball Player*
Boston Red Sox, 4104 Holly Hill Rd,
Mebane, NC 27302 8232 USA

Doenges, Bessie R *Writer*
Russell & Volkening, 50 W 29th St, New
York, NY 10001 USA

Doerr, Robert P (Bobby) *Baseball Player*
33705 Illamo-Agness Road, Agness, OR
97406 USA

Doerre-Heinig, Katrin *Track Athlete*
Westring 53, Erbach, 6471, GERMANY

Dog Star *Music Group*
1900 Avenue of the Stars #1040, Los
Angeles, CA 90067 USA

Dogg, Nate *Musician*
Elektra Records, 75 Rockefeller Plaza,
New York, NY 10019 USA

Doherty, Dennis (Denny) *Musician*
1262 Contour Dr, Mississauga, ON L5H
1B2, CANADA

Doherty, John *Baseball Player*
California Angels, 109 Wakefield St,
Reading, MA 01867 1854 USA

Doherty, John *Baseball Player*
Detroit Tigers, 202 Alpine Pl, Tuckahoe,
NY 10107 3086 USA

Doherty, Laura *Musician*
Pop Idol (Fremantle Media), 2700
Colorado Ave #450, Santa Monica, CA
90404 USA

Doherty, Peter C *Nobel Prize Laureate*
172 Kimbrough Place, #506, Memphis,
TN 38104 USA

Doherty, Shannen *Actor*
United Talent Agency, 9560 Wilshire Blvd, #500, Beverly Hills, CA 90212 USA

Dohery, Peter C *Nobel Prize Laureate*
172 Kimbrough Place #506, Memphis, TN 38104 USA

Dohm, Gaby *Actor*
Omnis Agentur, Wiedenmayerstr 11, Munich, 80538, GERMANY

Dohring, Jason *Actor*
Innovative Artists (LA), 1505 Tenth St, Santa Monica, CA 90401 USA

Dohrmann, Angela *Actor*
Innovative Artists, 1505 10th St, Santa Monica, CA 90401 USA

Dohrmann, George *Journalist*
Saint Paul Pioneer Press, Editorial Dept, 345 Cedar St, Saint Paul, MN 55101 USA

Doi, Takako *Government Official*
Daini Giinkaikan, 2-1-2 Nagatacho, Chiyodaku, Tokyo, JAPAN

Doi, Takao *Astronaut*
NASDA, Tsukuba Space Ctr, 2-1-2 Sengern, Tukubashi, Ibaraki, JAPAN

Doig, Ivan *Writer*
Charles Scribner's Sons, 866 3rd Ave, New York, NY 10022 USA

Doig, Lex *Actor*
Andromeda Productions, 8651 Eastlake Drive, Vancouver, BC V5A 4T7

Dokes, Michael *Boxer*
5151 Collins Ave, #522, Miami Beach, FL 33140 USA

Dokken, Don *Musician*
Agency for Performing Arts, 9200 Sunset Blvd, #900, Los Angeles, CA 90069 USA

Doktor, Martin *Athlete*
Canoe Prosport Sezemice, Slinecni 627, Sezemice, 533 04, CZECH REPUBLIC

Dolan, Don *Actor*
14228 Emelita St, Van Nuys, CA 91401 USA

Dolan, Ellen *Actor*
Don Buchwald, 10 E 44th St, New York, NY 10017 USA

Dolan, Louise A *Physicist*
University of North Carolina, Physics Dept, Chapel Hill, NC 27599 USA

Dolan, Michael P *Government Official*
Internal Revenue Service, 1111 Constitution Ave NW, Washington, DC 20224 USA

Dolan, Tom
One Olympic Plaza, Colorado Springs, CO 80909-5770

Dolby, David C *War Hero*
PO Box 218, Pekiomen Ave, Oaks, PA 19456 USA

Dolby, Raymond M (Ray) *Inventor, Engineer*
Dolby Laboratories, 100 Potrero Ave, San Francisco, CA 94103 USA

Dolby, Thomas *Songwriter, Musician*
Inteinational Talent Group, 729 7th Ave, #1600, New York, NY 10019 USA

Dolce, Domenico *Fashion Designer*
Dolce & Gabbana, Via Santa Cecilia 7, Milan, 20122, ITALY

Dolci, Danilo *Writer, Social Activist*
Centro Iniziative Studl, Largo Scalia 5, Partinico/Palermo, Sicily, ITALY

Dold, R Bruce *Journalist*
501 N Park Road, #HSE, La Grange Park, IL 60526 USA

Dole, Elizabeth H *Politician, Secretary*
601 Pennsylvania Ave NW, Floor 10, Washington, DC 20004-3606 USA

Dole, Robert J (Bob) *Senator*
601 Pennsylvania Ave NW, Floor 10, Washington, DC 20004-3606 USA

Dole, Vincent P *Scientist, Misc*
Rockefeller University, 1230 York Ave, New York, NY 10021 USA

Doleac, Michael *Basketball Player*
7372 Comslock Circle, Salt Lake City, UT 84121 USA

Doleman, Christopher J (Chris) *Football Player*
1025 Leadenhall St, Alpharetta, GA 30022 USA

Doleman, ChristopherJ *Football Player*
1025 Leadenhall St, Alphaetta, GA 30022 USA

Dolenz, Ami *Actor*
1860 Bel Air Road, Los Angeles, CA 90077 USA

Dolenz, Micky *Actor, Musician*
22 Baymare Road, Bell Canyon, CA 91307 USA

Doll, W Richard S *Biologist*
12 Rawlinson Road, Oxford, OX2 6UE, UNITED KINGDOM (UK)

Dollar, Linda *Coach*
Southwest Missouri State University, Athletic Dept, Springfield, MO 65804 USA

Dollard, Christopher Edward *Actor*
Gold Marshak Liedtke, 3500 W Olive Ave, #1400, Burbank, CA 91505 USA

Dollens, Ronald *Business Person*
Guidant Corp, 111 Monument Circle, Indianapolis, IN 46204 USA

Dollfus, Audouin *Astronomer, Physicist*
77 Rue Albert Perdreaux, 92370, Chaville, 92370, FRANCE

Dolls, Goo Goo *Musician*
William Morris Agency (WMA-LA), 1 William Morris Pl, Beverly Hills, CA 90212 USA

Dolmayan, John *Musician*
Velvet Hammer, 9911 W pico Blvd, #350, Los Angeles, CA 90035 USA

Dologuele, Anicet Georges *Prime Minister*
Prime Minister's Office, Bangui, CENTRAL AFRICAN REPUBLIC

Dolphin Barn, Dublin 8
IRELAND

Doman, John *Actor*
Peter Strain & Associates Inc (NY), 1501 Broadway, New York, NY 10036

Domar, Evsey D *Economist*
264 Heath's Bridge Road, Concord, MA 01742 USA

Dombasle, Arielle *Actor*
Agence Intertalent, 5 Rue Clemet Marot, Paris, 75008, FRANCE

Dombrowski, James M (Jim) *Football Player*
220 Evangeline Dr, Mandeville, LA 70471 USA

Domi, Tim *Hockey Player*
46 Florence St, Ottawa, ON K2P 0W7, CANADA

Dominczyk, Dagmara *Actor*
Gersh Agency, The (NY), 41 Madison Ave Fl 33, New York, NY 10010 USA

Domingo, Placido *Opera Singer*
Zaungergasse 1-3, Tur 16, Vienna, 1030, AUSTRIA

Dominguez, Fernandez Adolfo *Fashion Designer*
Polingono Industrial Calle 4, San Ciprian de Vinas, Ourense, 32901, SPAIN

Dominis, John *Photographer*
16 Jackson St, East Hampton, NY 11937 USA

Domino, Antoine (Fats) *Musician*
5515 Marais Street, New Orleans, LA 70117 USA

Dominy, Charles E (Chuck) *General*
300 Fox Mill Road, Oakton, VA 22124 USA

Domnanovich, Joseph (Joe)– *Football Player*
3101 Loma Road, #1112, Birmingham, AL 35216 USA

Domres, Martin F (Marty) *Football Player*
24 Mansel Dr, Reistertown, MD 21136 USA

Donahue, Aichie G *War Hero*
2402 Lary Lake Dr, Harlingen, TX 78550 USA

Donahue, Archie G *War Hero*
2402 Lazy Lake Dr, Harlingen, TX 78550 USA

Donahue, Deacon *Baseball Player*
Philadelphia Phillies, 812 Salem Ln, Carpentersville, IL 60110 1520 USA

Donahue, Elinor *Actor*
78533 Sunrise Mountain View, Palm Desert, CA 92211 USA

Donahue, Heather *Actor*
Rigberg Roberts Rugolo, 118D S Bevedy Dr, #601, Los Aneles, CA 90035 USA

Donahue, Kenneth *Misc*
245 S Westgate Ave, Los Angeles, CA 90049 USA

Donahue, Phil *Entertainer*
244 Madison Ave, #707, New York, NY 10016 USA

Donahue, Terry *Football Coach, Sportscaster*
9130 Woolley St, Temple City, CA 91780 USA

Donahue, Thomas M *Scientist*
1781 Arlington Blvd, Ann Arbor, MI 48104 USA

Donahue, Thomas R *Misc*
American Federation of Labor, 815 l6th St NW, Washington, DC 20006 USA

Donald, David Herbert *Writer*
41 Lincoln Road, PO Box l58, Lincoln, MA 01773 USA

Donald, Kirkland H *Admiral*
Commander Submarine Command
Atlantic, 7958 Blandy Road, Norfolk, VA
23511 USA

Donaldson, Colby *Actor, Reality TV Star*
William Morris Agency (WMA-LA), 1
William Morris Pl, Beverly Hills, CA
90212 USA

Donaldson, James *Basketball Player*
2843 34th Ave W, Seattle, WA 98199
USA

Donaldson, John *Baseball Player*
Kansas City A's, 3913 Yates Ct, Charlotte,
NC 28215 3955 USA

Donaldson, Raymond C (Ray) *Football
Player*
3520 W 86th St, Indianapolis, IN 46268
USA

Donaldson, Roger *Director*
Creative Artists Agency, 9830 Wilshire
Blvd, Beverly Hills, CA 90212 USA

Donaldson, Sam *Journalist*
Sam Donaldson Show, The (ABC News),
1717 DeSales St NW, Washington, DC
20036 USA

Donaldson, Samuel A (Sam) *Commentator*
1125 Crest Lane, McLean, VA 22101 USA

Donaldson, Simon K *Mathematician*
Bristol University, Mathematics Dept,
Bristol, BS8 1TH, UNITED KINGDOM
(UK)

Donaldson, William H *Financier,
Government Official*
Securities & Exchange Commision, 450
5th St NW, Washington, DC 20549 USA

Donan, Holland R *Football Player*
5918 Almaden Dr, Naples, FL 34119 USA

Donat, Peter *Actor*
P O Box 441, Wolfville, NS B0P 1X0,
CANADA

Donath, Helen *Opera Singer*
Bergstr 5, Wedemark, 30900, GERMANY

Done, Kenneth S (Ken) *Artist, Misc*
28 Hopetoun Ave, Mosman, NSW, 2088,
AUSTRALIA

Donegan, Dan *Music Group, Musician*
Mitch Schneider Organization, 14724
Ventura Blvd #410, Sherman Oaks, CA
91403 USA

Donelly, Tanya *Music Group, Songwriter*
Helter Skelter, Plaza 535 Kings Road,
London, SW10 0S, UNITED KINGDOM
(UK)

Donen, Stanley *Director*
30 West 63rd Street #25, New York, NY
10023 USA

Dong Ghua, Li
rue des O'Euches 10, Moutier 1, CP 359
274, SWITZERLAND

Doniger, Wendy *Historian, Misc*
1319 E 55th St, Chicago, IL 60615 USA

Donlan, Yolande *Actor*
11 Mellina Place, London, NW8, UNITED
KINGDOM (UK)

Donleavy, James Patrick (J P) *Writer*
Levington Park Mullingar, County
Westmeath, IRELAND

Donlon, Roger H C *War Hero*
2101 Wilson Ave, Leavenworth, KS 66048
USA

Donnan, Jim *Football Coach*
University of Georgia, Athletic Dept,
Athens, GA 30602 USA

Donnas, The *Music Group*
Lookout! Records, 3264 Adeline St,
Berkeley, CA 94703 USA

Donnellan, Declan *Director*
Cheek by Jowl Theatre Co, Aveline St,
London, SW11 5DQ, UNITED KINGDOM
(UK)

Donnelley, James R *Business Person*
R R Donnelley & Sons, 77 W Wacker Dr,
Chicago, IL 60601 USA

Donnelly, Brendan *Baseball Player*
Anaheim Angels, PO Box 66599,
Albuquerque, NM 87193 6599 USA

Donnelly, Declan *Actor, Television Host*
Rabbit Vocal Management, 18 Broad
Wick St Fl 2, London, W1F 8HS, UNITED
KINGDOM (UK)

Donnelly, Russell J *Physicist*
2175 Olive St, Eugene, OR 97405 USA

Donnels, Chris *Baseball Player*
New York Mets, 35 Sunningdale, Coto de
Caza, CA 92679 5103 USA

Donner, Clive *Director*
20 Thames Reach, 80 Rainville Road,
London, W6 9HS, UNITED KINGDOM
(UK)

Donner, Jom J *Director*
Pohjoisranta 12, Helsinki 17, 00170,
FINLAND

Donner, Jorn
Pohjoisranta 12, Helsinki, SF-00170,
FINLAND

Donner, Richard *Director*
1444 Forest Knoll, Los Angeles, CA 90069
USA

Donner, Robert *Actor*
3828 Glenridge Dr, Sherman Oaks, CA
91423 USA

Donnovan, Elisa *Actor*
SMS Talent, 8730 Sunset Blvd #440, Los
Angeles, CA 90069 USA

Donohoe, Amanda *Actor*
Markham & Froggatt, Julian House, 4
Windmill Street, London, W1P 1HF,
UNITED KINGDOM (UK)

Donohoe, Peter *Music Group, Musician*
82 Hampton Lane Solihull, West
Midlands, B91 2RS, UNITED KINGDOM
(UK)

Donohue, Jim *Baseball Player*
Detroit Tigers, 16 Huntleigh Downs, Saint
Louis, MO 63131 3416 USA

Donohue, Terry
11918 Laurelwood, Studio City, CA
91604

Donohue, Timothy *Business Person*
Nextel Communications, 2001 Edmund
Halley Dr, Reston, VA 20191 USA

Donohue, Tom *Baseball Player*
California Angels, 29 Rugby Rd,
Westbury, NY 11590 1224 USA

Donoso, Jose *Writer*
Calceite, Province of Teruel, SPAIN

Donovan *Music Group, Songwriter*
P O Box 1119, London, SW9 9JW,
UNITED KINGDOM (UK)

Donovan, Alan B *Educator*
State University of New York College,
President's Office, Oneonta, NY 13820
USA

Donovan, Anne *Basketball Player, Coach*
3638 Cordwood Lane, Indianapolis, IN
46214 USA

Donovan, Arthur J (Art) Jr *Football
Player, Athlete*
Valley Country Club, 1512 Jeffers Road,
Baltimore, MD 21204 USA

Donovan, Brian *Journalist*
Newsday, Editorial Dept 235 Pinelawn
Road, Melville, NY 11747 USA

Donovan, Elisa *Actor*
Talent Group, 6300 Wilshire Blvd #2100,
Los Angeles, CA 90048 USA

Donovan, Francis R (Frank) *Admiral*
9216 Dellwood Dr, Vienna, VA 22180
USA

Donovan, Jason S *Actor, Music Group*
Richard East Productions, PO Box 342,
South Yarra, VIC, 3141, AUSTRALIA

Donovan, Jeffrey *Actor*
Principal Entertainment (LA), 1964
Westwood Blvd #400, Los Angeles, CA
90025 USA

Donovan, Landon *Soccer Player*
San Jose Earthquakes, 3550 Stevens Creek
Blvd #200, San Jose, CA 95117 USA

Donovan, Martin *Actor*
Paradigm Agency, 10100 Santa Monica
Blvd #2500, Los Angeles, CA 90067 USA

Donovan, Raymond J *Secretary, Misc*
1600 Paterson Park Road, Secaucusm, NJ
07094 USA

Donovan, Tate *Actor*
Gersh Agency, The (LA), 232 N Canon Dr,
Beverly Hills, CA 90210 USA

Donovan (Leich)
PO Box 106, Rochdale, OL16 4HW,
ENGLAND

Doobie Brothers *Music Group*
15140 Sonoma Hwy, Glen Ellen, CA
95442-9614 USA

Doody, Alison *Actor*
Julian Belfarge, 46 Albermarle St, London,
W1X 4PP, UNITED KINGDOM (UK)

Doohan, James *Actor*
DoFame, PO Box 2800, Redmond, WA
98073 USA

Dooley, Paul *Actor*
Innovative Artists, 1505 10th St, Santa
Monica, CA 90401 USA

Dooley, Thomas *Soccer Player*
28391 Daroca, Mission Viejo, CA 92692
USA

Dooley, Vince
PO Box 1472, Athens, GA 30603

Dooley, Vincent J (Vince) *Football Player,
Football Coach, Coach, Misc*
University of Georgia, Athletic Dept P O
Box 1472, Athens, GA 30603 USA

Dooling, Keyon *Basketball Player*
Los Angeles Clippers, Staples Center 1111 S Figueroa St, Los Angeles, CA 90015 USA

Dopazo, Cecilia *Actor*
Telefe - Argentina, Pavon 2444 (C1248AAT), Buenos Aires, ARGENTINA

Dopson, John *Baseball Player*
Montreal Expos, 3337 Old Gamber Rd, Finksburg, MD 21048 2223 USA

Doran, Bill *Baseball Player*
Houston Astros, 11320 Grandstone Ln, Cincinnati, OH 47249 3416 USA

Doran, Walter F *Admiral*
Chairman Joint Chiefs of Staff Pentagon, Washington, DC 20318 USA

Dore, Andre *Hockey Player*
73 Betsys Lane, Kingston, ON K7M 7B6, CANADA

Dore, Jimmy *Comedian*
OmniPop Inc (LA), 10700 Ventura Blvd Fl 2, Studio City, CA 91604 USA

Dore, Patricia *Actor*
Cineart, 36 Rue de Ponthieu, Paris, 75008, FRANCE

Dore, Ronald Philip *Educator*
157 Surrenden Road Brighton, East Sussex, BN1 6ZA, UNITED KINGDOM (UK)

Dorensky, Sergey L *Music Group, Musician*
Bryusov Per 8/10 #75, Moscow, 103009, RUSSIA

Dorff, Stephen *Actor*
International Creative Management (ICM-LA), 8942 Wilshire Blvd, Beverly Hills, CA 90211 USA

Dorfman, Ariel *Writer*
Duke University, International Studies Center, 2122 Campus Dr, Durham, NC 27706 USA

Dorfman, Dan *Commentator, Misc*
CBS-TV, News Dept 51 W 52nd St, New York, NY 10019 USA

Dorfman, David *Actor*
Abrams Artists Agency (LA), 9200 Sunset Blvd Fl 11, Los Angeles, CA 90069 USA

Dorfmeister, Michaela *Skier*
Quellensteig, Neusiedl, 2763, AUSTRIA

Dorin, Francoise *Writer, Actor*
Artmedia, 20 Ave Rapp, Paris, 75007, FRANCE

Dorio, Gabriella *Track Athlete*
Federation of Light Athletics, Viale Tialano 70, Rome, 00196, ITALY

Dority, Douglas R *Misc*
United Food & Commercial Workers Union, 1775 K St NW, Washington, DC 20006 USA

Dorman, David *Business Person*
American Telephone & Telegraph Corp, 32 Ave of Americas, New York, NY 10013 USA

Dorman, Gerald D *Physicist*
2365 Village Lane, Orient, NY 11957 USA

Dorman, Lee *Music Group, Musician*
Entertainment Services Int'l, 6400 Pleasant Park Dr, Chanhassen, MN 55317 USA

Dorn, Dolores (Dody) *Editor*
The Skouras Agency, 631 Wilshire Blvd, 2nd Floor Suite C, Santa Monica, CA 90401 USA

Dorn, Michael *Actor*
115 N Orange Dr, Los Angeles, CA 90036 USA

Dorney, Keith R *Football Player*
2450 Blucher Valley Road, Sebastopol, CA 95472 USA

Doro & Warlock
Postfach 87 21, Dusseldorf, D-40086, GERMANY

Doronina, Tatyana *Actor*
Gorky Arts Theater, 22 Tverskoi Blvd, Moscow, 119146, RUSSIA

Dorough, Howie *Music Group*
Mitch Schneider Organization, 14724 Ventura Blvd #410, Sherman Oaks, CA 91403 USA

Dorow, Al *Athlete*
4933 Loma Loop, Sierra Vista, AZ 85635

Dorrell, Karl *Football Coach*
University of California, Athletic Dept, Los Angeles, CA 90024 USA

Dorroh, Jefferson D *War Hero*
24603 12th Ave S, Des Moines, WA 98198 USA

Dorsen, Norman *Attorney General*
New York University, Law School 40 Washington Square S, New York, NY 10012 USA

Dorsett, Anthony D (Tony) *Football Player, Athlete*
D A Chemical, 2415 Midway Road #105, Carrollton, TX 75006 USA

Dorsett, Brian *Baseball Player*
Cleveland Indians, 700 S Dobbs Glen St, Terre Haute, IN 47803 2480 USA

Dorsey, Jim *Baseball Player*
California Angels, 335 Elm St, Seekonk, MA 02771 1724 USA

Dorsey, Ken *Football Player*
San Francisco 49ers, 4949 Centennial Blvd, Santa Clara, CA 95054 USA

Dorsey Brothers Orchestra *Music Group*
901 Winding River Rd, Vero Beach, FL 32963, US

Dortort, David *Producer*
133 Udine Way, Los Angeles, CA 90024

Dos Santos, Alexandre J M Cardinal *Religious Leader*
Paco Arquiepiscopal, Avenida Eduardo Mondlane, CP Maputo, 1448, MOZAMBIQUE

Doshi, Balkrishna V *Architect*
Sangath Thaltej Road, Ahmedbad, GJ, 380 054, INDIA

Doss, Desmond T *War Hero*
4600 Highway 157 Lookout Mountain, Rising Fawn, GA 30738 USA

Doss, Murphy *Actor*
52 Hospital Road, Saidapet, Chennai, TN 600 015, INDIA

Doster, David *Baseball Player*
Philadelphia Phillies, 9320 Old Grist Mill Pl, Fort Wayne, IN 46835 9301 USA

Dotrice, Roy *Actor*
Lord, 6 Meadow Lane Leasingham, Sleaford, Linconshire, NG34 8LL, UNITED KINGDOM (UK)

Dotson, Richard E (Rich) *Baseball Player*
Chicago White Sox, 7 Colonel Watson Dr, New Richmond, OH 45157 9002 USA

Dotson, Santana *Football Player*
11002 Greenbay St, Houston, TX 77024 USA

Dotter, Bobby *Race Car Driver*
MPH Racing, 118 Stutt Road, Mooresville, NC 28117 USA

Dotter, Gary *Baseball Player*
Minnesota Twins, 17 Edgemere Dr, Roanoke, TX 76262 9736 USA

Doty, Paul M *Biologist, Misc*
4 Kirland Place, Cambridge, MA 02138 USA

Douaihy, Saliba *Artist*
Vining Road, Windham, NY 12496 USA

Doucet, Michael *Music Group, Musician*
Rosebud Agency, P O Box 170429, San Fransisco, CA 94117 USA

Doucett, Linda *Actor, Model*
Michael Slessinger, 8730 Sunset Blvd #220W, Los Angeles, CA 90069 USA

Doug, Doug E *Musician*
4024 Radford Avenue #3, Studio City, CA 91604 USA

Dougan, Angel Serafin Seriche *Prime Minister*
Prime Minister's Office, Malabo, EQUATORIAL GUINEA

Doughboys *Musician*
Box 5559 Station B, Montreal, QC, PQ H3P 4P1, Canada

Dougherty, Dennis A *Misc*
1817 Bushnell Ave, South Pasadena, CA 91030 USA

Dougherty, Ed *Golfer*
448 SW Fairway Vista, Port Saint Lucie, FL 34986 USA

Dougherty, James J *Misc*
Plasters & Cement Masons' Int'l, 14405 Laurel Place, Laurel, MD 20707 USA

Dougherty, Jim *Baseball Player*
Houston Astros, PO Box 1737, Kitty Hawk, NC 27949 1737 USA

Dougherty, Joe *Producer*
William Morris Agency (WMA-LA), 1 William Morris Pl, Beverly Hills, CA 90212 USA

Dougherty, William A Jr *Admiral*
1505 Colonial Court, Arlington, VA 22209 USA

Doughty, Kenny *Actor*
International Creative Management (ICM-LA), 8942 Wilshire Blvd, Beverly Hills, CA 90211 USA

Douglas, Anslem *Entertainer, Composer*
JW Records, 2833 Church Ave, Brooklyn, NY 11226 USA

Douglas, Barry *Music Group, Musician*
I C M Artists, 40 W 57th St, New York,
NY 10019 USA

Douglas, Bobby *Wrestler, Coach*
Iowa State University, Athletic Dept,
Ames, IA 50011 USA

Douglas, Cameron *Actor*
Creative Management Group (CMG),
9465 Wilshire Blvd #335, Beverly Hills,
CA 90212 USA

Douglas, Carl
4132 Don Ibarra, Los Angeles, CA 90008

Douglas, Carol *Music Group*
Famous Artists Agency, 250 W 57th St,
New York, NY 10107 USA

Douglas, Cathleen *Lawyer, Misc*
815 Connecticut Ave NW, Washington,
DC 20006 USA

Douglas, Charles *Baseball Player*
Pittsburgh Pirates, PO Box 231, Hubert,
NC 28539 0231 USA

Douglas, Denzil L *Prime Minister*
Premier's Office, Government Building,
Basseterre, SAINT KITTS & NEVIS

Douglas, Diana *Actor*
Bauman Redanty & Shaul Agency, 5757
Wilshire Blvd #473, Los Angeles, CA
90036 USA

Douglas, Hugh *Football Player*
Jacksonville Jaguars, 1 AllTel Stadium
Place, Jacksonville, FL 32202 USA

Douglas, Ileana *Actor*
Baumgarten Merims Entertainment, 1640
South Sepulveda, Suite 218, Los Angeles,
CA 90025 USA

Douglas, Illeana *Actor*
Baumgarten Agency, 1041 N Formosa
Ave #200, West Hollywood, CA 90046
USA

Douglas, James (Buster) *Boxer, Athlete*
PO Box 342, Johnstown, OH 43031 USA

Douglas, Jerry *Actor*
17336 Rancho Street, Encino, CA 91316
USA

Douglas, Katie *Basketball Player*
Connecticut Sun, Mohegan Sun Arena,
Uncasville, CT 06382 USA

Douglas, Kirk *Actor*
805 N Rexford Dr, Beverly Hills, CA
90210 USA

Douglas, Kyan *Television Host*
Queer Eye for the Straight Guy, 119
Braintree St, Boston, MA 02134

Douglas, Leon *Basketball Player*
P O Box 58, Leighton, AL 35646 USA

Douglas, Michael *Actor*
Further Films, 100 Universal City Plz, Bldg
1320-4G, Universal City, CA 91608

Douglas, Michael K *Actor, Director,
Producer*
William Morris Agency, 151 El Camino
Dr, Beverly Hills, CA 90212 USA

Douglas, Santiago *Actor*
A Management, 9107 Wilshire Blvd #650,
Beverly Hills, CA 90210 USA

Douglas, Sarah *Actor*
Craig Mgmt, 125 S Sycamore Ave, Los
Angeles, CA 90036 USA

Douglas, Sherman *Basketball Player*
New Jarsey Nets, 390 Murray Hill
Parkway, East Rutherford, NJ 07073 USA

Douglass, Dale *Golfer*
100 Coulter Place, Castle Rock, CO
80108 USA

Douglass, Michael R (Mike) *Football
Player*
1725 Porterfield Place, El Cajon, CA
92019 USA

Douglass, Robyn *Actor*
1301 S Federal St, Chicago, IL 60605 USA

Douglass, Sean *Baseball Player*
Baltimore Orioles, 44437 Benald St,
Lancaster, CA 93535 3440 USA

Dourda, Abu Zaid Umar *Prime Minister*
Prime Minister's Office, Bab el Aziziya
Barracks, Tripoli, LIBYA

Dourdan, Gary *Actor*
Original Film, 2045 S Barrington Ave, Los
Angeles, CA 90025 USA

Dourif, Brad *Actor*
Innovative Artists, 1505 10th St, Santa
Monica, CA 90401 USA

Dove, Rita F *Writer*
1757 Lambs Road, Charlottesville, VA
22901 USA

Dove, Robert (Bob) *Football Player*
6 Neff Dr, Canfield, OH 44406 USA

Dove, Ronnie *Music Group*
Ken Keene Artists, P O Box 1875, Gretna,
LA 70054 USA

Dow, Ellen Albertini *Actor*
GVA Talent Agency Inc, 9229 Sunset Blvd
#320, Los Angeles, CA 90069 USA

Dow, Peggy *Actor*
2121 South Yorkstown Ave, Tulsa, OK
74114 USA

Dow, Tony *Actor*
Diamond Artists, 215 N Barrington Ave,
Los Angeles, CA 90049 USA

Dowd, Maureen *Editor, Misc*
New York Times, Editorial Dept 229 W
43rd St, New York, NY 10036 USA

Dowdle, Walter R *Biologist, Misc*
1708 Mason Mill Road, Atlanta, GA
30329 USA

Dowdy, Steven *Scientist, Misc*
Howard Hughes Medical Institute,
Washington Univesity, Saint Louis, MO
63110 USA

Dowell, Anthony J *Ballerina*
Royal Ballet, Convent Garden Bow St,
London, WC2E 9DD, UNITED KINGDOM
(UK)

Dowell, Ken *Baseball Player*
Philadelphia Phillies, 5640 33rd Ave,
Sacramento, CA 95824 1704 USA

Dower, John W *Writer*
Massachusetts Institute of Technology,
History Dept, Cambridge, MA 02139 USA

Dowle, David *Music Group, Musician*
Int'l Talent Booking, 27A Floral St #300,
London, WC2E 9DQ, UNITED
KINGDOM (UK)

Dowler, Boyd H *Football Player*
Carr Assoc, 2303 S Lila Lane, Tampa, FL
33629 USA

Dowling, Dave *Baseball Player*
St Louis Cardinals, 6131 W Rose Garden
Ln, Glendale, AZ 85308 6270 USA

Dowling, John E *Biologist, Misc*
135 Charles St, Boston, MA 02114 USA

Dowling, Robert J *Publisher, Editor*
Hollywood Reporter, 5055 Wilshire Blvd,
Los Angeles, CA 90036 USA

Dowling, Timothy *Actor*
Endeavor Agency LLC (LA), 9601 Wilshire
Blvd Fl 3, Beverly Hills, CA 90210 USA

Dowling, Vincent *Director, Writer*
322 East River Road, Huntington, MA
01050 USA

Down, Lesley-Anne *Actor*
All-Media Public Relations, 5664
Cahuenga Blvd #231, North Hollywood,
CA 90601 USA

Down, Sarah *Cartoonist*
Playboy Magazine, Reader Services 680 N
Lake Shore Dr, Chicago, IL 60611 USA

Down, System of a *Music Group*
Creative Artists Agency LCC (CAA-LA),
9830 Wilshire Blvd, Beverly Hills, CA
90212 USA

Downes, Edward
Royal Opera House, Covent Garden,
London, WC2E 9DD, UNITED KINGDOM
(UK)

Downey, Jim *Writer*
3 Arts Entertainment Inc, 9460 Wilshire
Blvd Fl 7, Beverly Hills, CA 90212 USA

Downey, Robert J *Director*
55 W 900 S, Salt Lake City, UT 84101
USA

Downey, Roma *Actor*
55 W 900 S, Salt Lake City, UT 84101
USA

Downey Jr, Robert *Actor*
International Creative Management
(ICM-LA), 8942 Wilshire Blvd, Beverly
Hills, CA 90211 USA

Downie, Gordon *Music Group*
Management Trust, 219 Dufferin St
#309B, Toronto, ON M5K 3J1, CANADA

Downie, Leonard Jr *Editor*
Washington Post, Editorial Dept 1150
15th St NW, Washington, DC 20071 USA

Downing, Alphonso E (Al) *Baseball Player*
New York Yankees, 752 Edgewood Ave,
Trenton, NJ 08618 5404 USA

Downing, Big Al *Music Group, Musician*
Tessier-Marsh Talent, 2825 Blue Book Dr,
Nashville, TN 37214 USA

Downing, Brian J *Baseball Player*
8095 County Road 135, Celina, TX 75009
USA

Downing, George *Yachtsman, Misc*
Get Wet!, 3021 Waialae Ave, Honolulu,
HI 96816 USA

Downing, Kathryn *Publisher*
Mypotential.com, 2821 Main St, Santa
Monica, CA 90405 USA

Downing, Walt *Football Player, Athlete*
1141 Durham Circle NW, Celina, TX
44646 USA

Downing, Wayne A *General*
11200 N Pawnee Road, Peoria, IL 61615
USA

Downs, Dave *Baseball Player*
Philadelphia Phillies, 925 E 1050 N,
Bountiful, UT 84010 2620 USA

Downs, Hugh H *Commentator*
Arizona State University, Human
Communications Department, Tempe, AZ
85287 USA

Downs, Kelly *Baseball Player*
San Francisco Giants, 244 W 1750 N,
Centerville, UT 84014 3136 USA

Downs, Scott *Baseball Player*
Chicago Cubs, 6814 Barbrook Rd,
Louisville, KY 40258 2668 USA

Dowson, Philip M *Architect*
Royal Academy of the Arts, Piccadilly,
London, W1V 0DS, UNITED KINGDOM
(UK)

Doyle, Brian *Baseball Player*
New York Yankees, PO Box 9156, Winter
Haven, FL 33883 9156 USA

Doyle, Chris *Cinematographer*
10866 Wilshire Blvd #1000, Los Angeles,
CA 90024 USA

Doyle, Danny *Baseball Player*
Boston Red Sox, 322 S Payne St,
Stillwater, OK 74074 3952 USA

Doyle, Denny *Baseball Player*
Philadelphia Phillies, PO Box 9156,
Winter Haven, FL 33883 9156 USA

Doyle, James H Jr *Admiral*
5121 Baltan Road, Bathesda, MD 208 16
USA

Doyle, Jeff *Baseball Player*
Philadelphia Phillies, 5940 SW Banyon
Cir, Corvallis, OR 97333 3960 USA

Doyle, Patrick *Composer*
Air-Edel, 18 Rodmarton St, London, W1H
3FW, UNITED KINGDOM (UK)

Doyle, Paul *Baseball Player*
Atlanta Braves, 5832 Woodboro Dr,
Huntington Beach, CA 92649 4963 USA

Doyle, Roddy *Writer*
Secker & Warburg, 38A West Road
Bromsgrove, Worc, B60 2NQ, UNITED
KINGDOM (UK)

Dozier, Buzz *Baseball Player*
Washington Senators, 2909 Braemar St,
Waco, TX 76710 2122 USA

Dozier, D J *Baseball Player*
New York Mets, 5821 N Cherokee
Cluster, Virginia Beach, VA 23462 3214
USA

Dozier, James L *General*
2150 Channel Way, North Fort Myers, FL
33917 USA

Dozier, Lamont *Music Group, Songwriter*
McMullen Co, 433 N Camden Dr #400,
Beverly Hills, CA 90210 USA

Dozier, Tom *Baseball Player*
Oakland A's, 1231 Willow Ave Apt D7,
Hercules, CA 94547 1200 USA

Dr Demento *Entertainer*
6102 Pimenta Ave, Lakewood, CA 90712
USA

Dr Dre *Musician, Actor*
Interscope Records (LA) - Main, 2220
Colorado Ave, Santa Monica, CA 90404
USA

Dr Dre *Artist*
Richard Walters, 1800 Argyle Ave #408,
Los Angeles, CA 90028 USA

Dr John *Music Group, Musician,
Songwriter*
Impact Artists, 121 W 27th St #1001, New
York, NY 10001 USA

Drabble, Margaret *Writer*
P F D, Drury House 34-43 Russell St,
London, WC2B 5HA, UNITED KINGDOM
(UK)

Drabek, Douglas D (Doug) *Baseball
Player*
New York Yankees, 15 Ivy Pond Pl, The
Woodlands, TX 77381 6326 USA

Drabinsky, Garth H *Producer*
Livent Inc, 165 Avenue Road #600,
Toronto, ON M5R 3S4, CANADA

Drabowsky, Myron W (Moe) *Baseball
Player*
Chicago Cubs, 4741 Oak Run Dr,
Sarasota, FL 34243 4537 USA

Draffen, Willis *Music Group*
16103 Vista Del Mar Dr, Houston, TX
77083 USA

Draglia, Stacy *Track Athlete*
1112 E Monte Cristo Ave, Phoenix, AZ
85022 USA

Drago, Billy *Actor*
3800 Burham Blvd #303, Los Angeles, CA
90068 USA

Drago, Richard A (Dick) *Baseball Player*
Kansas City Royals, 12626 Castle Hill Dr,
Tampa, FL 33624 4141 USA

Dragon
122 McEvoy Street, Alexandria, NSW,
2015, AUSTRALIA

Dragon, Daryl *Musician*
7123 Franktown Road, Carson City, NV
89704 USA

Dragoti, Stan *Director*
1800 Avenue of the Stars #430, Los
Angeles, CA 90067 USA

Dragpejvic, Srdjan *Director, Writer*
William Morris Agency, 151 El Camino
Dr, Beverly Hills, CA 90212 USA

Drahman, Brian *Baseball Player*
Chicago White Sox, 4050 NE 15th Ave,
Oakland Park, FL 33334 4643 USA

Drai, Victor *Producer*
10527 Bellagio Road, Beverly Hills, CA
90210 USA

Draiman, Dave *Music Group*
Mitch Schneider Organization, 14724
Ventura Blvd #410, Sherman Oaks, CA
91403 USA

Drake, Bebe *Actor*
Baron Entertainment, 5757 Wilshire Blvd
#659, Los Angeles, CA 90036

Drake, Betsy *Actor*
10850 Wilshire Blvd #575, Los Angeles,
CA 90024 USA

Drake, Dallas *Hockey Player*
11472 E Cedar Bay Trail, Traverse City,
MI 49684 USA

Drake, Frank D *Astronomer*
University of California, Lick Observatory,
Santa Cruz, CA 9064 USA

Drake, Jeremy *Astronomer*
Harvard-Smithsonian Center for
Astrophysics, Cambridge, MA 02138 USA

Drake, Judith *Actor*
20th Century Artists, 4605 Lankershim
Blvd #305, North Hollywood, CA 91602
USA

Drake, Juel D *Misc*
Iron Workers Union, 1750 New York Ave
NW, Washington, DC 20006 USA

Drake, Larry *Actor*
15260 Ventura Blvd #2100, Sherman
Oaks, CA 91403 USA

Drake, Sammy *Baseball Player*
Chicago Cubs, 4415 Springdale Dr, Los
Angeles, CA 90043 2107 USA

Drake, Solly *Baseball Player*
Chicago Cubs, 1732 S Corning St, Los
Angeles, CA 90035 4302 USA

Drane, Ashley *Actor*
Axiom Management, 10701 Wilshire Blvd
#1202, Los Angeles, CA 90024

Dransfeldt, Kelly *Baseball Player*
Texas Rangers, 1810 Jana Ln, Morris, IL
60450 1162 USA

Draper, E Lynn Jr *Business Person*
American Electric Power, 1 Riverside
Plaza, Columbus, OH 43215 USA

Draper, Mike *Baseball Player*
New York Mets, 18317 Manor Church Rd,
Boonsboro, MD 21713 2502 USA

Draper, Polly *Actor*
1324 N Orange Grove, West Hollywood,
CA 90046 USA

Draper, William H III *Financier*
91 Tallwood Court, Atherton, CA 94027
USA

Drasner, Fred *Publisher*
New York Daily News, 220 E 42nd St,
New York, NY 10017 USA

Dratch, Rachel *Actor, Comedian*
Michael Mann Talent, 617 S Olive St
#311, Los Angeles, CA 90014 USA

Dravecky, David F (Dave) *Baseball Player*
Outreach of Hope, 13840 Gleneagle Dr,
Colorado Springs, CO 80921 USA

Draven, Jamie *Actor*
International Creative Management
(ICM-UK), Oxford House, 76 Oxford St,
London, W1N OAX, UNITED KINGDOM
(UK)

Draves, Victoria (Vickie) *Swimmer, Misc*
23842 Shady Tree Circle, Laguna Niguel,
CA 92677 USA

Drayton, Charlie *Music Group, Musician*
Direct Mangement Group, 947 N La
Cienega Blvd #2, Los Angeles, CA 90069
USA

Dre *Music Group, Musician*
Family Tree Entertainment, 135 E 57th St
#2600, New York, NY 10022 USA

Dream *Music Group*
Evolution Talent Agency LLC, 1776
Broadway Fl 15, New York, NY 10019
USA

Dream So Real
PO Box 8061, Athens, GA 30603

Dream Street *Music Group*
Evolution Talent Agency LLC, 1776
Broadway Fl 15, New York, NY 10019
USA

Dream Warriors
1505 W 2nd Ave #200, Vancouver, BC
V6H 3Y4, Canada

Drechsler, Heike *Track Athlete*
LAC Chemnitz, Reichenhainer Str 154,
Chmnitz, 09135, GERMANY

Drees, Tom *Baseball Player*
Chicago White Sox, 14723 Boulder Pointe
Rd, Eden Prairie, MN 44347 2438 USA

Dreesen, Tom *Comedian, Actor*
14538 Benefit Street #301, Sherman Oaks,
CA 91403 USA

Dreifort, Darren *Baseball Player*
Los Angeles Dodgers, 710 Pinehurst Dr,
Pasadena, CA 91106 4512 USA

Dreifuss, Ruth *President*
Federal Chancellery, Bundeshaus-W,
Bundesgasse, Beme, 3033,
SWITZERLAND

Drell, Persis *Physicist*
Stanford University, Linear Accelerator
Center, Stanford, CA 94305 USA

Drell, Sidney D *Physicist*
570 Alvarado Row, Stanford, CA 94305
USA

Drescher, Fran *Actor*
International Creative Management
(ICM-LA), 8942 Wilshire Blvd, Beverly
Hills, CA 90211 USA

Dreschler, David *Football Player*
1135 Arablan Farms Road, Clover, SC
29710 USA

Drese, Ryan *Baseball Player*
Cleveland Indians, 1030 Sunnyhills Rd,
Oakland, CA 94610 2417 USA

Dresselhaus, Mildred S *Physicist, Engineer*
Energy Department, 1000 Independence
Ave SW, Washington, DC 20585 USA

Dressendorfer, Kirk *Baseball Player*
Oakland A's, 1004 Oaklands Dr, Round
Rock, TX 78681 4033 USA

Dressler, Rob *Baseball Player*
San Francisco Giants, 2037 17th Ave,
Forest Grove, OR 97116 2709 USA

Drew, B Alvin *Astronaut*
2814 Lighthouse Dr, Houston, TX 77058
USA

Drew, Cameron *Baseball Player*
Houston Astros, 31 Highbridge Rd,
Yardville, NJ 08620-9632 USA

Drew, David Jonathan (J D) *Baseball
Player*
Saint Louis Cardinals, Busch Stadium 250
Stadium Plaza, Saint Louis, MO 63102
USA

Drew, Dennis *Music Group, Musician*
Agency for Performing Arts, 9200 Sunset
Blvd #900, Los Angeles, CA 90069 USA

Drew, Elizabeth H *Publisher*
Avon/William Morrow, 1350 Ave of
Americas, New York, NY 10019 USA

Drew, Griffin *Actor, Model*
PO Box 16753, Beverly Hills, CA 90209
USA

Drew, J D *Baseball Player*
St Louis Cardinals, 16649 Equestrian Ln,
Chesterfield, MO 63005-4881 USA

Drew, Larry *Basketball Player*
4942 Densmore Ave, Encino, CA 91436
USA

Drew, Tim *Baseball Player*
Cleveland Indians, 5006 Old Us 41 N,
Hahira, GA 31632-4405 USA

Drew, Urban *War Hero*
451 Neptune Ave, Encinitas, CA 92024
USA

Drexler, Clyde *Basketball Player, Coach*
Dade/Schultz, 6442 Coldwater Canyon
Ave #206, North Hollywood, CA 91606
USA

Dreyer, Steve *Baseball Player*
Texas Rangers, 3005 Elm St, West Des
Moines, IA 50265-6222 USA

Dreyfus, George *Composer*
3 Grace St, Camberwell, VIC, 3124,
AUSTRALIA

Dreyfus, Lee S *Governor*
3159 Madison St, Waukesha, WI 53188
USA

Dreyfuss, Richard S *Actor, Producer*
P O Box 10459, Burbank, CA 91510 USA

Drickamer, Harry G *Engineer*
304 E Pennsylvania Ave, Urbana, IL
61801 USA

Driedger, Florence G *Social Activist, Misc*
3833 Montaigne St, Regina, SK S4S 3J6,
CANADA

Driessen, Dan *Baseball Player*
Cincinnati Reds, 97 William Hilton Pkwy,
Hilton Head Island, SC 29926-1205 USA

Driest, Burkhard
Alter Militarring 8, Koln, 50933,
GERMANY

Drinan, Robert F *Educator, Misc*
Georgetown University, 1507 Isherwood
St NE #1, Washington, DC 20002 USA

Drinfeld, Vladimir *Mathematician*
Steklov Mathematics Institute, 42
Vavilova, ESP-1 Moscow, 117966,
RUSSIA

Driscoll, Jim *Baseball Player*
Oakland A's, 4135 N 81st St, Scottsdale,
AZ 85251-2670 USA

Driskill, Travis *Baseball Player*
Baltimore Orioles, 510 Brookstone Ct,
Round Rock, TX 78681-4081 USA

Driver, Bruce *Hockey Player*
21A Crest Terrace, Montville, NJ 07045
USA

Driver, Minnie *Actor*
Two Drivers Productions, 8899 Beverly
Blvd #800, Los Angeles, CA 90048 USA

Driver, William J *Government Official*
215 W Columbia St, Falls Church, VA
22046 USA

Drnovsek, Janez *Prime Minister*
Prime Minister's Office, Gregorcicova St
20, Ljubljana, 61000, SLOVENIA

Drobny, Jaroslav *Actor*
23 Kenilworth Court, Lower Richmond
Road, London, SW15 1EW, United
Kingdom

Droge, Pete *Music Group, Songwriter*
1423 34th Ave, Seattle, WA 98122 USA

Dropo, Walter (Walt) *Baseball Player*
Boston Red Sox, 104 Brooksby Village Dr
Unit 104, Peabody, MA 01960-1470 USA

Drosdick, John G *Business Person*
Sunoco Inc, 10 Penn Center 1801 Market
St, Philadelphia, PA 19103 USA

Drowning Pool *Music Group*
Wind-up Records, 72 Madison Ave, New
York, NY 10016 USA

Drozdova, Margarita S *Ballerina*
Stanislavsky Musical Theater,
Pushkinskaya Str 17, Moscow, RUSSIA

Dru Hill *Music Group*
Endeavor Agency LLC (LA), 9601 Wilshire
Blvd Fl 3, Beverly Hills, CA 90210 USA

Druck, Mirchea *Prime Minister*
Str 31 August 123 #7, Kishinev, 277012,
MOLDOVA

Drucker, Eugene *Music Group, Musician*
I M G Artists, 3 Burlington Lane,
Chiswick, London, W4 2TH, UNITED
KINGDOM (UK)

Drucker, Mort *Cartoonist*
Famous Artists Agency, 250 W 57th St,
New York, NY 10107 USA

Drucker, Peter F *Educator, Writer, Misc*
636 Wellesley Drive, Claremont, CA
91711 USA

Druker, Brian J *Misc*
Oregon Health Science University, Cancer
Research Center, Portland, OR 97201
USA

Drummond, Alice *Actor*
351 E 50th St, New York, NY 10003 USA

Drummond, Jonathan (Jon) *Track Athlete*
113 Cascade Lake St, Las Vegas, NV
89148 USA

Drummond, Roscoe *Writer, Misc*
6637 MacLean Dr Olde Dominion
Square, McLean, VA 22101 USA

Drummond, Ryan *Actor*
Bobby Ball Talent Agency, 4342
Lankershim Blvd, Universal City, CA
91602 USA

Drummond, Tim *Baseball Player*
Pittsburgh Pirates, 102 Haldane Ct, La
Plata, MD 20646-4308 USA

Drumright, Keith *Baseball Player*
Houston Astros, 1333 W Lindberg St,
Springfield, MO 65807-2385 USA

Drury, Chris *Hockey Player*
57 W Oak Hills Dr, Castle Rock, CO
80108 USA

Drury, James *Actor*
12126 Osage Park Dr, Houston, TX 77065
USA

Drury, Ted *Hockey Player*
64 Glenwood Ave, Point Lookout, NY
11569 USA

Drut, Guy J *Track Athlete*
Maine, Coulommiers, 77120, FRANCE

Dryburgh, Stuart *Cinematographer*
Sandra Marsh Mgmt, 9150 Wilshire Blvd
#220, Beverly Hills, CA 90212 USA

Dryden, Ken *Hockey Player, Athlete*
58 Poplar Plains Road, Toronto, ON M5J
2M8, Canada

Dryden, Kenneth W (Ken) *Hockey Player*
58 Poplar Plains Road, Toronto, ON M4V
2M8, CANADA

Dryer, Fred *Actor, Producer*
Fred Dryer Productions, 1700 W Burbank
Blvd #101, Burbank, CA 91506

Dryer, J Frederick (Fred) *Football Player, Actor*
4117 Radford Ave, Studio City, CA 91604
USA

Dryke, Matthew (Matt) *Misc*
4702 Davis Ave S #2B102, Renton, WA
98055 USA

Drynan, Jeanie *Actor*
Essential Talent Management, 6399
Wilshire Blvd #400, Los Angeles, CA
90048 USA

Drysdale, Cliff *Tennis Player, Sportscaster*
Landfall, 1801 Eastwood Road #F,
Wilmington, NC 28403 USA

du Tertre, Celine *Actor*
Cunningham-Escott-Dipene & Associates
Inc (CED-LA), 10635 Santa Monica Blvd
#130, Los Angeles, CA 90025 USA

Duany, Andres *Architect*
Duany & Plater-Zaberk Architects, 1023
SW 25th Ave, Miami, FL 33135 USA

DuArt, Louise *Religious Leader, Television Host*
Living the Life, 977 Centerville Tpke,
Virginia Beach, VA 23463 USA

Dubbels, Britta *Model*
Ford Model Agency, 142 Greene St #400,
New York, NY 10012 USA

Dubble, Curtis *Religious Leader*
Church of Brethren, 1451 Dundee Ave,
Elgin, IL 60120 USA

Dube, Joseph (Joe) *Wrestler, Misc*
8821 Eaton Ave, Jacksonville, FL 32211
USA

Dube, Lucky *Musician*
Fast Lane Int'l, 4856 Haygood Road,
#200, Virginia Beach, VA 23455 USA

Dubia, John A *General*
1154 N Pitt St, Alexandria, VA 22314
USA

Dubinbaum, Gail *Opera Singer*
Metropolitan Opera Assn, Lincoln Center
Plaza, New York, NY 10023 USA

Dubinin, Yuri V *Government Official*
Gazprom RAO Nametkina Str 16,
Moscow, 117884 USA

Dubinin, Yuri V *Government Official*
Gazprom RAO Nametkina Str 16,
Moscow, 117884, RUSSIA

Dubois, Brian *Baseball Player*
Detroit Tigers, 359 E Ridge St, Braidwood,
IL 60408-2095 USA

DuBois, Marta *Actor*
Three Moons Entertainment, 5441 East
Beverly Blvd #G, Los Angeles, CA 90022
USA

Dubose, Eric *Baseball Player*
Baltimore Orioles, 11814 Lone Hickory
Ct, Houston, TX 77059-5522 USA

DuBose, G Thomas *Misc*
United Transportation Union, 14600
Detroit Ave, Cleveland, OH 44107 USA

Dubus, Andre III *Writer*
Penguin Group, 375 Hudson St, New
York, NY 10014 USA

Dubzinski, Walt *Football Player*
158 Lovewell St, Gardner, MA 01440
USA

Ducasse, Alain *Chef*
Louis XV Restaurant, Hotel de Paris,
Monte Carlo, MONACO

Ducey, Rob *Baseball Player*
Toronto Blue Jays, 699 Richmond Close,
Tarpon Springs, FL 34688-8423 USA

Duchesnay, Isamelle *Dancer*
Im Steinach 30, Oberstdorf, 87561,
GERMANY

Duchesnay, Paul *Figure Skater*
Bundesleistungszentrum, Rossbichstr 2-6,
Oberstdorf, 87561, GERMANY

Duchin, Peter *Musician, Music Group*
Peter Duchin Orchestra, 60 E 42nd
Street#1625, New York, NY 10165 USA

Duchovny, David *Actor*
Creative Artists Agency, 9830 Wilshire
Blvd, Beverly Hills, CA 90212 USA

Duchscherer, Justin *Baseball Player*
Texas Rangers, 4700 Green Oaks Dr,
Colleyville, TX 76034-4765 USA

DuCille, Michel *Photographer, Journalist*
9571 Pine Meadow Lane, Burke, VA
22015 USA

Ducksworth, Sheila *Producer*
Creative Artists Agency LCC (CAA-LA),
9830 Wilshire Blvd, Beverly Hills, CA
90212 USA

Duckworth, Brandon *Baseball Player*
Philadelphia Phillies, 4460 W 6095 S,
Kearns, UT 84118-5289 USA

Duckworth, Jim *Baseball Player*
Washington Senators, 2245 Tradition
Way, Redding, CA 96001-6308 USA

Ducsmal, Agnieszka
Polish Radio Orchestra, Al
Marchinkowskiego 3, Pozna, 61-745,
POLAND

Dudek, Anne *Actor*
Industry Entertainment, 955 S Carrillo Dr
#300, Los Angeles, CA 90048 USA

Dudek, Joseph A (Joe) *Football Player*
17 Adams Dr, Hudson, NH 03051 USA

Duden, H Richard (Dick) Jr *Football Player*
900 Bestgate Road, Annapolis, MD 21401
USA

Duderstadt, James J *Government Official, Educator*
National Science Foundation, 1800 G St
NW, Washington, DC 20006 USA

Dudikoff, Michael *Actor*
Craig Management, 125 South Sycamore
Avenue, Los Angeles, CA 90036 USA

Dudley, Chris *Basketball Player, Athlete*
1150 Fairway Road, Lake Oswego, OR
97034 USA

Dudley, D-Von *Wrestler*
World Wrestling Entertainment (WWE),
1241 E Main St, Stamford, CT 06905 USA

Dudley, Debra
Box 40, Bonnieville, KY 42713

Dudley, Jaquelin *Biologist, Misc*
University of Texas, Microbiology Dept,
Austin, TX 78712 USA

Dudley, Rick *Hockey Player, Coach, Misc*
921 NW 118th Lane, Coral Springs, FL
33071 USA

Dudley, Rickey *Football Player*
23968 Cottage Trail, Olmsted Falls, OH
44138 USA

Dudley, William M (Bill) *Football Player*
303 Barkley Court, Lynchburg, VA 24503
USA

Duenkel Fuldner, Virginia *Swimmer*
2132 NE 17th Terrace #500, Wilton
Manors, FL 33305 USA

Duerson, David R (Dave) *Football Player*
2605 Kelly Lane, Highland Park, IL 60035
USA

Dues, Hal *Baseball Player*
Montreal Expos, PO Box R, Dickinson, TX
77539-2018 USA

Dueto Voces del Rancho *Musician*
Sony Music Miami, 605 Lincoln Rd,
Miami Beach, FL 33138 USA

Dufay, Rick *Music Group, Musician*
H K Mgmt, 9200 W Sunset Blvd #530,
Los Angeles, CA 90069 USA

Duff, Hilary *Actor, Model, Musician*
Walt Disney Rocords, 3800 W Alameda
St, Burbank, CA 91505 USA

Duff, John B *Educator*
Columbia College, President's Office,
Chicago, IL 60605 USA

Duff, John E *Artist, Misc*
7 Doyers St, New York, NY 10013 USA

Duff, Matt *Baseball Player*
St Louis Cardinals, 1701 27th St E,
Bradenton, FL 34208-7831 USA

Duff, T Richard (Dick) *Hockey Player*
4-7 Elmwood Ave S, Mississauga, ON
L5G 3J6, CANADA

Duffalo, Jim *Baseball Player*
San Francisco Giants, PO Box 1082, Du
Bois, PA 15801-1082 USA

Duffell, Peter
29 Roehampton Gate, London,
ENGLAND, SW15 5JR

Duffie, John *Baseball Player*
Los Angeles Dodgers, PO Box 956363,
Duluth, GA 30095-9507 USA

Duffield, David *Business Person*
PeopleSoft Inc, 4460 Hacienda Dr,
Pleasonton, CA 94588 USA

Duffner, Mark *Football Coach*
University of Maryland, Athletic Dept,
College Park, MD 20740 USA

Duffy, Brian *Astronaut*
2260 Marsh Harbor Ave, Merritt Island, FL 32952 USA

Duffy, Brian *Editor, Cartoonist*
Des Moines Regester, Editorial Dept P O Box 957, Des Moines, IA 50304 USA

Duffy, Dorothy *Actor*
PFD, Drury House, 34-43 Russell St, London, WC2B 5HA, UNITED KINGDOM (UK)

Duffy, Frank *Baseball Player*
Cincinnati Reds, 1740 E Silver St, Tucson, AZ 85719-3152 USA

Duffy, J C *Cartoonist*
Universal Press Syndicate, 4520 Main St, Kansas City, MO 64111 USA

Duffy, James *Business Person*
Saint Paul Companies, 385 Washington St, Saint Paul, MN 55102 USA

Duffy, John *Composer*
Meet the Composer, 2112 Broadway, New York, NY 10023 USA

Duffy, Julia *Actor*
Lacey, 5699 Kanan Road #285, Agoura, CA 91301 USA

Duffy, Karen *Actor, Model*
Ford Model Agency, 142 Greene St #400, New York, NY 10012 USA

Duffy, Keith *Music Group*
Carol Assoc-War Mgmt, Bushy Park Road 57 Meadowgate, Dublin, IRELAND

Duffy, Patrick *Actor*
William Morris Agency (WMA-LA), 1 William Morris Pl, Beverly Hills, CA 90212 USA

Duffy, Troy *Actor, Director, Writer*
William Morris Agency (WMA-LA), 1 William Morris Pl, Beverly Hills, CA 90212 USA

Dufresne, John *Writer*
W W Norton, 500 5th Ave, New York, NY 10110 USA

Dugan, Dennis *Actor, Director*
15611 Royal Oak Road, Encino, CA 91436 USA

Dugan, Michael J *General, Misc*
National Multiple Sclerosis Society, 733 3rd Ave, New York, NY 10017 USA

Duggan, Jim *Wrestler*
3941 Wateroak Way, Titusville, FL 32780 USA

Dugger, John S *Artist*
3392 Adeline St, Berkeley, CA 94703 USA

Duguary, Ron *Actor, Hockey Player*
982 Porte Vedra Blvd, Porta Vedra Beach, FL 32082 USA

Duhamel, Josh *Actor*
Gersh Agency, The (NY), 41 Madison Ave Fl 33, New York, NY 10010 USA

Duhe, Adam J (A J) Jr *Football Player*
379 Coconut Circle, Weston, FL 33326 USA

Duhe, John M Jr *Judge*
US Court of Appeals, 556 Jefferson St, Lafayette, LA 70501 USA

Dukakis, Kitty
85 Perry St, Brookline, MA 02146

Dukakis, Michael *Governor*
85 Perry St, Brookline, MA 02446 USA

Dukakis, Olympia *Actor*
684 Broadway #6E, New York, NY 10012 USA

Duke, Bill *Director*
Duke Media, 7510 Sunset Blvd #523, Los Angeles, CA 90046 USA

Duke, Charles
PO Box 310345, New Braunfels, TX 78130

Duke, Charles M Jr *Astronaut, General*
280 Lakeview Blvd, New Braunfels, TX 78130 USA

Duke, George *Songwriter, Music Group*
Associated Booking Corp, 1995 Broadway #501, New York, NY 10023 USA

Duke, Norm *Bowler*
10836 Country Road 561A, Clermont, FL 34711 USA

Duke, Patty *Actor*
Cunningham-Escott-Dipene & Associates Inc (CED-LA), 10635 Santa Monica Blvd #130, Los Angeles, CA 90025 USA

Duke, Patty D *Volleyball Player*
1017 Manhattan Ave, Manhaltan Beach, CA 90266 USA

Dukes, Jan *Baseball Player*
Washington Senators, 959 Helena Dr, Sunnyvale, CA 94087-4126 USA

Dukes, The *Music Group*
11 Chartfield Square, London, England, SW15, United Kingdom

Dukes, Tom *Baseball Player*
Houston Astros, 325 Monte Vista Rd, Arcadia, CA 91007-6147 USA

Dukes of Dixieland, The
PO Box 56757, New Orleans, Los Angeles, 70156-6757

Dulany, Caitlin *Actor*
Gersh Agency, 232 N Canon Dr, Beverly Hills, CA 90210 USA

Dulbecco, Renato *Nobel Prize Laureate*
7525 Hillside Dr, La Jolla, CA 92037 USA

Dulgan, John *Director*
54A Tite St, London, SW3 4JA, UNITED KINGDOM (UK)

Dulhalde, Eduardo *President*
Casa de Gobiemo, Balcarce 50, Buenos Aires, 1064, ARGENTINA

Duliba, Bob *Baseball Player*
St Louis Cardinals, 327 Philadelphia Ave, West Pittston, PA 18643-2146 USA

Dullea, Keir *Actor*
310 West 72nd Street #9B, New York, NY 10023 USA

Dulles, Avery R Cardinal *Misc*
Fordham University, Jesuit Community, Bronx, NY 10458 USA

Dulli, Greg *Music Group*
Real Time, 48 Laight St, New York, NY 10013 USA

Dumars, Joe III *Basketball Player*
3499 Franklin Road, Bloomfield Hills, MI 48302 USA

Dumart, Woodrow W C (Woody) *Hockey Player*
36 Old Farm Road, Needham, MA 02492 USA

Dumas, Amy (Lita) *Wrestler*
World Wrestling Entertainment (WWE), 1241 E Main St, Stamford, CT 06905 USA

Dummar, Melvin
Dummar's Restaurant, Gabbs, NV 89409

Dummett, Michael A E *Misc*
54 Park Town, Oxford, OX2 6SJ, UNITED KINGDOM (UK)

Dumont, J P *Hockey Player*
Buffalo Sabres, HSBC Arena 1 Seymour St, Buffalo, NY 14210 USA

Dumont, Sky *Actor*
ZBF Agentur, Leopoldstr 19, Munich, 80802, GERMANY

Dumont, Tom *Music Group, Musician*
Rebel Waltz Inc, 31652 2nd Ave, Laguna Beach, CA 92651 USA

Dumoulin, Dan *Baseball Player*
Cincinnati Reds, 202 Nancy Dr, Kokomo, IN 46901-5907 USA

Dunagin, Ralph *Cartoonist*
North American Syndicate, 235 E 45th St, New York, NY 10017 USA

Dunaway, Faye *Actor*
901 N Spaulding Ave, West Hollywood, CA 90046 USA

Dunaway, James E *Football Player*
169 Mount Carmel Church Road, Sandy Hook, MS 39478 USA

Dunbar, Bonnie J *Astronaut*
2200 Todville Road, Seabrook, TX 77586 USA

Dunbar, Huey *Musician*
Sony Music Miami, 605 Lincoln Rd, Miami Beach, FL 33138 USA

Dunbar, Matt *Baseball Player*
Florida Marlins, 2325 Winthorp Ridge Rd, Charlotte, NC 28270-2288 USA

Dunbar, Rockmond *Actor*
Writers and Artists Group Intl (LA), 8383 Wilshire Blvd #550, Beverly Hills, CA 90211 USA

Dunbar, Tommy *Baseball Player*
Texas Rangers, 558 Palm Dr S, Aiken, SC 29803-5450 USA

Duncan, Angus *Actor*
Thomas Jennings, 28035 Dorothy Dr #210A, Agoura, CA 90301 USA

Duncan, Charles K *Admiral*
813 1st St, Coronado, CA 92118 USA

Duncan, Charles W Jr *Secretary*
9 Briarwood Court, Houston, TX 77019 USA

Duncan, Cleveland (Cleve) *Music Group*
David Harris Enterprises, 24210 E Fork Road #9, Azusa, CA 91702 USA

Duncan, Courtney *Baseball Player*
Chicago Cubs, 121 Adalene Ln, Madison, AL 35757-8423 USA

Duncan, Dave *Baseball Player*
Kansas City A's, 10166 N Valle Del Oro Dr, Tucson, AZ 85737-7620 USA

Duncan, David Douglas *Photographer, Journalist*
Castellaras Mouans-Sartoux, 06370, FRANCE

Duncan, H Randolph (Randy) *Football Player*
907 Ashworth Road #106, West Des Moines, IA 50265 USA

Duncan, Jeff *Baseball Player*
New York Mets, 825 Lincoln Ln, Frankfort, IL 60423-1087 USA

Duncan, Lindsay *Actor*
Ken McReddie, 91 Regent St, London, W1R 7TB, UNITED KINGDOM (UK)

Duncan, Mariano *Baseball Player*
Los Angeles Dodgers, Ingenio Angelina #137, San Pedro de Macoris, DOMINICAN REPUBLIC

Duncan, Michael Clarke *Actor*
Dolores Robinson, 9250 Wilshire Blvd #220, Beverly Hills, CA 90212 USA

Duncan, Robert *Misc, Astronomer, Physicist*
University of Texas, Astronomy Dept, Austin, TX 78712 USA

Duncan, Sandy *Actor*
Litke/Gale Madden, 1640 S Sepulveda Blvd #530, Los Angeles, CA 90025 USA

Duncan, Taylor *Baseball Player*
St Louis Cardinals, 83 Hampton St, Asheville, NC 28803-1641 USA

Duncan, Tim *Basketball Player*
San Antonio Spurs, Alamodome 1 SBC Center, San Antonio, TX 78219 USA

Dundee, Angelo *Boxer*
1487 Camellia Circle, Weston, FL 33326 USA

Dunderstadt, James *Educator*
University of Michigan, President's Office, Ann Arbor, MI 48109 USA

Dunegan, Jim *Baseball Player*
Chicago Cubs, 1405 S 12th St, Burlington, IA 52601-3701 USA

Dungey, Merrin *Actor*
Evolution Entertainment, 901 N Highland Ave, Los Angeles, CA 90038 USA

Dungy, Tony *Football Coach*
16604 Villalenda de Avila, Tampa, FL 33613 USA

Dunham, Archie W *Business Person*
ConocoPhilips Inc, 600 N Dairy Ashford, Houston, TX 77079 USA

Dunham, Chip *Cartoonist*
Universal Press Syndicate, 4520 Main St, Kansas City, MO 64111 USA

Dunham, Duane R *Business Person*
Bethlehem Steel Corp, 1170 8th Ave, Bethlehem, PA 18016 USA

Dunham, John L *Business Person*
May Department Stores, 611 Olive St, Saint Louis, MO 63101 USA

Dunham, Katherine *Dancer, Choreographer*
Children's Workshop, 532 N 10th St, East Saint Louis, IL 62201 USA

Dunham, Michael (Mike) *Hockey Player*
277 Gloucester, Matawan, NJ 07747 USA

Dunham, Russell E *War Hero*
31405 Sunderland Road, Jerseyville, IL 62052 USA

Dunham, Stephen *Actor*
Tavel Entertainment, 9171 Wilshire Blvd #406, Beverly Hills, CA 90210 USA

Dunitz, Jack D *Misc*
Obere Heslibachstr 77, Kusnacht, 8700, SWITZERLAND

Dunkie, Nancy *Basketball Player*
University of California, Campus Police, Berkeley, CA 94720 USA

Dunlap, Alexander W *Astronaut*
721 Parkside Dr, Woodstock, GA 31088 USA

Dunlap, Carla *Gymnast, Misc*
Diamond, 732 Irvington Ave, Maplewood, NJ 07040 USA

Dunlap, Grant *Baseball Player*
St Louis Cardinals, 1431 Alga Ct, Vista, CA 92081-5016 USA

Dunlap, Robert H *War Hero*
P O Box 584, Monmouth, IL 61462 USA

Dunleavy, Mary *Opera Singer*
Columbia Artists Mgmt, 165 W 57th St, New York, NY 10019 USA

Dunleavy, Michael J (Mike) *Basketball Player, Coach*
555 S Barington Ave, Los Angeles, CA 90049 USA

Dunleavy, Mike *Basketball Player*
Golden State Warriors, 1001 Broadway, Oakland, CA 94607 USA

Dunlop, Andy *Music Group, Musician*
Wildlife Entertainment, 21 Heathmans Road, London, SW6 4TJ, UNITED KINGDOM (UK)

Dunn, Adam *Baseball Player*
Cincinnati Reds, PO Box 105, Porter, TX 77365-0105 USA

Dunn, Andrew W *Cinematographer*
525 Broadway #250, Santa Monica, CA 90401 USA

Dunn, Gregory *Publisher*
Redbook Magazine, 224 W 57th St, New York, NY 10019 USA

Dunn, Halbert L *Mathematician*
3637 Edelmar Terrace, Silver Spring, MD 20906 USA

Dunn, Holly *Songwriter, Music Group*
P O Box 1258, Gallatin, TN 37066 USA

Dunn, Kevin *Actor*
321 E Grandview Ave, Sierra Madre, CA 91024 USA

Dunn, Martin *Editor*
New York Daily News, Editorial Dept 220 E 42nd St, New York, NY 10017 USA

Dunn, Mignon *Opera Singer*
Warden Assoc, 5626 Deer Run Road, Doylestown, PA 18901 USA

Dunn, Mike *Race Car Driver*
Circle A Racing, RR 24 Box 537A Keeney Lane, York, PA 17406 USA

Dunn, Nora *Actor, Comedian*
Innovative Artists, 1505 10th St, Santa Monica, CA 90401 USA

Dunn, Patricia (Tricia) *Hockey Player*
5 Twinbrook Dr, Derry, NH 03038 USA

Dunn, Ron *Baseball Player*
Chicago Cubs, 1161 Husted Ave, San Jose, CA 95125-3633 USA

Dunn, Ronnie *Music Group, Songwriter*
TBA Mgmt, 300 10th Ave S, Nashville, TN 37203 USA

Dunn, Stephen *Writer*
Stockton State College, Humanities/Fine Arts Arts Dept, Pomona, NJ 08240 USA

Dunn, Stephen L *Religious Leader*
Churches of God General Conference, 7176 Glenmeadow Dr, Frederick, MD 21703 USA

Dunn, Steve *Baseball Player*
Minnesota Twins, 3405 Ardennes Dr, Maryville, TN 37801-9591 USA

Dunn, Susan *Opera Singer*
1212 Lancaster, Champaign, IL 61821 USA

Dunn, T R *Basketball Player*
1014 19th St SW, Birmingham, AL 35211 USA

Dunn, Todd *Baseball Player*
Milwaukee Brewers, 5326 Camelot Forest Dr, Jacksonville, FL 32258-2517 USA

Dunn, Warrick *Football Player*
9823 Bay Island Dr, Tampa, FL 33615 USA

Dunne, Dominick *Writer*
155 East 49th St, New York, NY 10017 USA

Dunne, Griffin *Actor, Director*
445 Park Ave #701, New York, NY 10022 USA

Dunne, Mike *Baseball Player*
Pittsburgh Pirates, 5115 W Ancient Oak Dr, Peoria, IL 61615-2247 USA

Dunne, Robin *Actor*
United Talent Agency, 9560 Wilshire Blvd #500, Beverly Hills, CA 90212 USA

Dunne, Roisin *Music Group, Musician*
Rave Booking, P O Box 310780, Jamaica, NY 11431 USA

Dunnigan, Frank J *Publisher*
1500 Palisade Ave, Fort Lee, NJ 07024 USA

Dunnigan, T Kevin *Business Person*
Thomas & Betts Corp, 8155 Thomas & Betts Blvd, Memphis, TN 38125 USA

Dunning, Debbe *Actor, Model*
PO Box 2748, Toluca Lake, CA 91610 USA

Dunning, John *Writer*
Pocket Books, 1230 Ave of Americas, New York, NY 10020 USA

Dunning, Steve *Baseball Player*
Cleveland Indians, 609 Thackeray Ln, Fox River Grove, IL 60021-1839 USA

Dunphy, Marv *Volleyball Player, Coach*
33370 Decker School Road, Malibu, CA 90265 USA

Dunphy, T J Dermot *Business Person*
Sealed Air Corp, Park 80 Plaza E, Saddle Park, NJ 07663 USA

Dunsmore, Barrie *Commentator*
ABC-TV, News Dept, 5010 Creston St, Hyattsville, MD 20781 USA

Dunst, Kirsten *Actor*
Industry Entertainment, 955 S Carrillo Dr
#300, Los Angeles, CA 90048 USA

Dunst, Kristen *Actor*
8916 Ashcroft Ave, West Hollywood, CA
90048 USA

Dunston, Shawon D *Baseball Player*
Chicago Cubs, 957 Corte Del Sol,
Fremont, CA 94539-4925 USA

Dunton, Gary C *Financier*
MBIA Inc, 113 King St, Armonk, NY
10504 USA

Dunwoody, Richard *Race Car Driver,
Jockey*
14 Saint Maur Road Fulham, London,
SW6 4DP, UNITED KINGDOM (UK)

Dunwoody, Todd *Baseball Player*
Florida Marlins, 4167 Farmstead Ln, West
Lafayette, IN 47906-5100 USA

Dunye, Cheryl *Actor, Director, Producer,
Writer*
Broder Webb Chervin Silbermann Agency,
The (BWCS), 9242 Beverly Blvd #200,
Beverly Hills, CA 90210 USA

DuPlessis, Christian *Opera Singer*
Performing Arts, 1 Hinde St, London,
W1M 5RH, UNITED KINGDOM (UK)

Dupont, Jacques *Politician, Misc*
Minister of State's Office, Boite Postale
522, Monaco-Cedex, 98015, MONACO

DuPont, Margaret Osborne *Tennis Player*
415 Camino Real, El Paso, TX 79922 USA

DuPont, Pierre *Ex-Governor*
Richards Layton Finger, 1 Rodney Square,
PO Box 551, Wilmington, DE 19899 USA

DuPont, Pierre S IV *Governor*
Richards Layton Finger, 1 Rodney Square,
P O Box 551, Wilmington, DE 19899
USA

DuPree, Billy Joe *Football Player*
P O Box 720330, Dallas, TX 75372 USA

Dupree, Donald (Don) *Athlete*
3 Center St, Saranac Lake, NY 12983 USA

Dupree, Marcus *Football Player*
Bossier City Battle Wings, 2000 Century
Tel Dr, Bossier City, LA 71112 USA

Dupree, Mike *Baseball Player*
San Diego Padres, 2358 E Richmond Ave,
Fresno, CA 93720-0438 USA

DuPrez, John *Composer*
Air-Edel, 1416 N La Brea Ave, Los
Angeles, CA 90028 USA

Dupri, Jermaine *Musician*
Creative Artists Agency LCC (CAA-LA),
9830 Wilshire Blvd, Beverly Hills, CA
90212 USA

Dupuis, Roy *Actor*
Agence Premier Role Inc, 3451 Hotel de
Ville, Montreal, Quebec, Canada, H2X
3B5

Duque, Bernardo *Musician*
Gabriel Blanco Iglesias (Mexico), Rio
Balsas 35-32, Colonia Cuauhtemoc, DF,
06500, Mexico

Duque, Pedro *Astronaut*
1103 Virginia St, South Houston, TX
77587 USA

Durack, David T *Physicist*
1700 Woodstock Road, Durham, NC
27705 USA

Duran, Dan *Baseball Player*
Texas Rangers, 104 Brisbane Ter,
Sunnyvale, CA 94086-5064 USA

Duran, Micki *Actor*
DDO Artist Agency, 8322 Beverly Blvd
#301, Los Angeles, CA 90048 USA

Duran, Roberto *Boxer*
Nuevo Reperto El Carmen, PANAMA

Duran Duran *Music Group*
DD Productions, 93A Westbourne Park
Villas, London, W2 5ED, UNITED
KINGDOM (UK)

Durand, Kevin *Actor*
Stubbs Agency, 1450 S Robertson Blvd,
Los Angeles, CA 90035 USA

Durang, Christopher *Writer*
Helen Merrill Agency, 337 W 22nd St,
New York, NY 10011 USA

Durant, Graham J *Inventor*
Cambridge NeuroScience, 333 Boston
Providence Tumpike, Norwood, MA
02062 USA

Durant, Mike *Baseball Player*
Minnesota Twins, 7520 Marston Ln,
Dublin, OH 43016-7029 USA

Durante, Viviana P *Ballerina*
20 Bristol Gardens Little Venice, London,
W9, UNITED KINGDOM (UK)

Durao Barroso, Jose Manuel *Prime
Minister*
Prime Minister's Office, Rua du Imprensa
a Estrela 8, Lisbon, 1300, PORTUGAL

Durazo, Erubiel *Baseball Player, Athlete*
Oakland Athletics, 7000 Coliseum Way,
Oakland, CA 94621 USA

Durbin, Chad *Baseball Player*
Kansas City Royals, 15705 Malvem Hill
Ave, Baton Rouge, LA 70817-3120 USA

Durbin, Deanna *Actor, Music Group*
BP 3315, Paris Cedex 03, 75123, FRANCE

Durbin, Mike *Bowler*
Professional Bowlers Assn, 719 2nd Ave
#701, Seattle, WA 98104 USA

Durcal, Rocio *Musician*
BMG, 1540 Broadway, New York, NY
10036 USA

Duren, Rinold G (Ryne) *Baseball Player*
Baltimore Orioles, 5629 Struthers Ct,
Winter Haven, FL 33884-2620 USA

Durham, Don *Baseball Player*
St Louis Cardinals, 2627 Pennington Bend
Rd, Nashville, TN 37214-1107 USA

Durham, Hugh *Basketball Player, Coach*
Jacksonville University, Athletic Dept,
Jacksonville, FL 32211 USA

Durham, Joe *Baseball Player*
Baltimore Orioles, 9715 Mendoza Rd,
Randallstown, MD 21133-2530 USA

Durham, Leon *Baseball Player*
St Louis Cardinals, 1553 Williamson Dr,
Cincinnati, OH 45240-1549 USA

Durham, Ray (Sugar Ray) *Baseball Player*
Chicago White Sox, 3839 Mountain Cove
Dr, Charlotte, NC 28216 7780 USA

Duritz, Adam *Music Group, Songwriter,
Misc*
Direct Mgmt, 947 N La Cienega Blvd
#400, Los Angeles, CA 90069 USA

Durkin, Clare *Model*
Ford Model Agency, 142 Greene St #400,
New York, NY 10012 USA

Durkin, John A *Senator*
60 Lenz St, Manchester, NH 03102 USA

Durnbaugh, Bobby *Baseball Player*
Cincinnati Reds, 1638 N Central Dr,
Dayton, OH 45432 2118 USA

Durning, Charles *Actor*
10590 Wilshire Blvd #506, Los Angeles,
CA 90024 USA

Durocher, Jayson *Baseball Player*
Milwaukee Brewers, 34042 N 43rd St,
Cave Creek, AZ 85331 4016 USA

Durr, Francoise
195 rue de Lourmel, Paris, FRANCE,
F-75015

Durr, Jason *Actor*
Ken McReddie Ltd, Paurelle House, 91
Regent St, London, W1R7TB, UNITED
KINGDOM (UK)

Durr Browning, Francoise *Tennis Player*
195 Rue de Lourmel, Paris, 75015,
FRANCE

Durrance, Samuel T *Astronaut,
Astronomer*
770 Kerry Downs Circle, Melbourne, FL
32940 USA

Durrant, Devin *Basketball Player*
1716 W 1825 N, Provo, UT 84604 USA

Durringer, Annemarie
Hawelgasse 17, Vienna, AUSTRIA, 1180

Durrington, Trent *Baseball Player*
Anaheim Angels, 499 N Canon Dr Apt
400, Beverly Hills, CA 90210 4842 USA

Durslag, Melvin
PO Box 559, Salisbury, NC 28144

Durst, Fred *Musician*
Firm, The, 9465 Wilshire Blvd, Beverly
Hills, CA 90212 USA

Durst, Will *Actor, Comedian*
Entertainment Alliance, P O Box 5734,
Santa Rosa, CA 95402 USA

Dusay, Debra *Actor*
Susan Nathe, 8281 Melrose Ave #200, Los
Angeles, CA 90046 USA

Dusay, Mari *Actor*
320 W 66th St, New York, NY 10023
USA

Dusay, Marj *Actor*
Susan Nathe, 8281 Melrose Ave #200, Los
Angeles, CA 90046 USA

Dusenberry, Ann *Actor*
1615 San Leandro Lane, Montecito, CA
93108 USA

Duser, Carl *Baseball Player*
Kansas City A's, 3021 Cornwall Rd,
Bethlehem, PA 18017 3313 USA

Dushku, Eliza *Actor*
Creative Artists Agency LCC (CAA-LA),
9830 Wilshire Blvd, Beverly Hills, CA
90212 USA

Dussault, Jean H *Misc*
Laval Medical Center, 2705 Blvd Laurier, Sainte Foy, PQ G1V 4G2, CANADA

Dussault, Nancy *Actor, Music Group*
12211 Iredell St, North Hollywood, CA 91604 USA

Dust, Angel *Music Group*
Digger International, Penthouse 1402, 100 East Chicago Street, Elgin, IL 60120

Dutch, Deborah *Actor*
850 N Kings Road #100, West Hollywood, CA 90069 USA

Dutilleux, Henri *Composer*
12 Rue Saint Louis-en-I'sle, Paris, 75004, FRANCE

Dutoit, Charles E
Montreal Symphony, 85 Sainte Catherine St W, Montreal, QC, H2X 3P4, CANADA

Dutt, Hank *Music Group, Musician*
Kronos Quartet, 1235 9th Ave, San Fransisco, CA 94122 USA

Dutt, Sanjay *Actor, Bollywood*
58 Smt Nargis Dutt Road, Pali Hill Bandra(W), Mumbai, MS 400050, INDIA

Dutt, Sunil *Actor, Director, Filmmaker, Producer, Bollywood*
58 Smt Nargis Dutt Road Pali Hill, Bandra, Bombay, MS 400 050, INDIA

Dutta, Divya *Bollywood, Actor*
C-17 Nehru Nagar, Kishore Kumar Gangulay Marg Juhu Tara Road, Mumbai, MS 400049, INDIA

Dutta, Lara *Beauty Pageant Winner*
Miss Universe Organization, The, 1370 Ave of the Americas Fl 16, New York, NY 10019 USA

Dutton, Charles S *Actor*
10061 Riverside Dr #821, Toluca Lake, CA 91602 USA

Dutton, John O *Football Player*
5706 Moss Creek Trail, Dallas, TX 75252 USA

Dutton, Lawrence *Music Group, Musician*
I M G Artists, 3 Burlington Lane Chiswick, London, W4 2TH, UNITED KINGDOM (UK)

Dutton, Simon *Actor*
Marmont Management, Langham House 302/8 Regent St, London, W1R 5AL, UNITED KINGDOM (UK)

Duva, Lou *Boxer, Misc*
Main Events, 811 Totowa Road #100, Totowa, NJ 07512 USA

Duval, David *Golfer*
135 Professional Dr #4, Ponte Vedra, FL 32082 USA

Duval, Helen *Bowler*
1624 Posen Ave, Berkeley, CA 94707 USA

Duval, James (Jimmy) *Actor*
Writers and Artists Group Intl (LA), 8383 Wilshire Blvd #550, Beverly Hills, CA 90211 USA

Duval, Juliette *Actor*
Cineart, 36 Rue de Ponthieu, Paris, 75008, FRANCE

Duval, Mike *Baseball Player*
Tampa Bay Devil Rays, 5246 Cedarbend Dr Apt 3, Fort Myers, FL 33919 7578 USA

Duvall, Carol *Television Host*
HGTV/Home & Garden Television, 9721 Sherrill Blvd, Knoxville, TN 37932 USA

DuVall, Clea *Actor*
Innovative Artists, 1505 10th St, Santa Monica, CA 90401 USA

Duvall, Jed *Commentator*
ABC-TV, News Dept 5010 Creston St, Hyattsville, MD 20781 USA

Duvall, Robert *Actor*
Butchers Run Films, 1041 N Formosa Ave, Santa Monica Bldg E #200, W Hollywood, CA 90046 USA

Duvall, Sammy *Skier*
P O Box 871, Windermere, FL 34786 USA

Duvall, Shelley *Actor*
Gersh Agency, The (LA), 232 N Canon Dr, Beverly Hills, CA 90210 USA

Duvall-Hero, Camille *Skier*
P O Box 871, Windermere, FL 34786 USA

Duvignaud, Jean *Writer*
28 Rue Saint-Leonard, La Rochelle, 1700, FRANCE

Duvillard, Henri *Skier*
Le Monte d'Arbois, Megere, 74120, FRANCE

Duwelius, Rick *Volleyball Player*
345 W Juniper St #5, San Diego, CA 92101 USA

Duwez, Pol E *Physicist*
1535 Oakdale St, Pasadena, CA 91106 USA

Dvorovenko, Irina *Ballerina*
Amirican Ballet Theatre, 890 Broadway, New York, NY 10003 USA

Dvorsky, Peter *Opera Singer*
Bradianska Ulica 11, Bratislave, SK-811 08, SLOVAKIA

Dwight, Edward Jr *Astronaut*
4022 Montview Blvd, Denver, CO 80207 USA

Dwork, Melvin *Designer*
Melvin Dwork Inc, 196 Ave of Americas, New York, NY 10013 USA

Dworkin, Andrea *Writer*
Elaine Markson, 44 Greenwich Ave, New York, NY 10011 USA

Dworkin, Martin *Biologist, Misc*
2123 Hoyt Ave W, Saint Paul, MN 55108 USA

Dworkins, Lenny (Len) *Cartoonist*
2906 Wilmette Ave, Wilmette, IL 60091 USA

Dworsky, Daniel L (Dan) *Football Player, Architect*
9225 Nightingale Dr, Los Angeles, CA 90069 USA

Dwyer, Bil *Game Show Host*
OmniPop Inc (LA), 10700 Ventura Blvd Fl 2, Studio City, CA 91604 USA

Dwyer, Jim *Baseball Player*
St Louis Cardinals, 7607 159th Pl, Tinley Park, IL 60477 1314 USA

Dwyer, Karyn *Actor*
Oscars Abrams Zimel, 438 Queen St E, Toronto, ON M5A 1T4, CANADA

Dybzinski, Jerry *Baseball Player*
Cleveland Indians, 1626 Haywood Pl, Fort Collins, CO 80526 2289 USA

Dychtwald, Ken *Doctor, Misc*
Age Wave Inc, 1900 Powell St, Emeryville, CA 94608 USA

Dydek, Malforzata (Margo) *Basketball Player*
San Antonio Silver Stars, 1 SBC Center, San Antonio, TX 78219 USA

Dye, Cameron *Actor*
13035 Woodbridge St, Studio City, CA 91604 USA

Dye, Ian *Composer*
Gorfaine/Schwartz, 13245 Riverside Dr #450, Sherman Oaks, CA 91423 USA

Dye, Jermaine *Baseball Player*
Atlanta Braves, 6855 N 66th Pl, Paradise Valley, AZ 85253 4340 USA

Dye, John *Actor*
William Morris Agency, 151 El Camino Dr, Beverly Hills, CA 90212 USA

Dye, Lee *Architect, Golfer, Misc*
Dye Designs, 5500 E Yale Ave, Denver, CO 80222 USA

Dye, Melissa Dori *Musician*
Dye Productions, PO Box 111, Bishop, TX 78343 USA

Dye, Nancy Schrom *Educator*
Oberlin College, President's Office, Oberlin, OH 44074 USA

Dyer, Danny *Actor*
International Creative Management (ICM-LA), 8942 Wilshire Blvd, Beverly Hills, CA 90211 USA

Dyer, David W *Judge*
US Court of Appeals, 300 NE 1st Ave, Miami, FL 33132 USA

Dyer, Duffy *Baseball Player*
New York Mets, 742 W Las Palmaritas Dr, Phoenix, AZ 85021 5545 USA

Dyer, Hector *Track Athlete*
1620 E Chapman #214, Fullerton, CA 92831 USA

Dyer, Joseph W Jr *Admiral*
Commander Naval Air Systems Command, Patuxent River, MD 20670 USA

Dyer, Mike *Baseball Player*
Minnesota Twins, 22392 Manacor, Mission Viejo, CA 92692 1188 USA

Dyer, Wayne W *Writer*
Shore Club, Tower House C, 1905 N Atlantic Blvd, Fort Lauderdale, FL 33305 USA

Dyk, Timothy B *Judge*
US Court of Appeals, 717 Madison Place NW, Washington, DC 20439 USA

Dyke, Charles W *General, Misc*
International Technical/Trade Assoc, 1330 Connecticut NW, Washington, DC 20036 USA

Dykes Bower, John *Music Group, Musician*
4Z Artillery Mansions Westminster, London, SW1, UNITED KINGDOM (UK)

Dykhoff, Radhames *Baseball Player*
Baltimore Orioles, 105 Angelfish Ln, Jupiter, FL 33477 7227 USA

Dykinga, Jack *Photographer, Journalist*
2865 N Tomas Road, Tucson, AZ 85745 USA

Dykstra, John *Artist, Animator, Cinematographer*
15060 Encanto Drive, Sherman Oaks, CA 91403 USA

Dykstra, Leonard K (Lenny) *Baseball Player*
New York Mets, 2672 Ladbrook Way, Thousand Oaks, CA 91361 5073 USA

Dylan, Bob *Music Group, Songwriter*
Creative Artists Agency LCC (CAA-LA), 9830 Wilshire Blvd, Beverly Hills, CA 90212 USA

Dylan, Jakob *Music Group*
H K Mgmt, 9200 W Sunset Blvd #530, Los Angeles, CA 90069 USA

Dymally, Mervyn M *Misc*
Dymally International Group, 9111 S La Cienega Blvd, Compton, CA 90220 USA

Dysart, Richard *Actor*
654 Copeland Court, Santa Monica, CA 90405 USA

Dyson, Esther *Business Person, Writer*
Edventure Holdings, 104 5th Ave #2000, New York, NY 10011 USA

Dyson, Freeman J *Physicist, Writer*
105 Battle Road Circle, Princeton, NJ 08540 USA

Dyson, Michael Eric *Writer*
DePaul University, English Dept, Chicago, IL 60604 USA

Dystel, Oscar *Publisher*
Springs Purchase Hills Dr, Purchase, NY 10577 USA

Dzau, Victor *Scientist, Misc*
Stanford University Hospital, Cardiovascular Medicine Div, Stanford, CA 94305 USA

Dzeliwe *Misc*
Royal Palace, Mbabane, SWAZILAND

Dzhanibekov, Vladimir A *Astronaut, General, Misc*
Potchta Kosmonavtov, Moskovskoi Oblasti, Syvisdny Goroduk, 141160, RUSSIA

Dzhanibelkov, Vladimir
Potchka Kosmon 141 160 Svyosdny Gorodok, Moscow, RUSSIA

Dzundza, George *Actor*
PO Box 573250, Tarzana, CA 91357 USA

Dzurlnda, Mikulas *Prime Minister*
Prime Minister's Office, Nam Slobody 1, Bratislava 1, 81370, SLOVAKIA

E

E-Type *Music Group*
Agency Group, The (Denmark), Slotsgade 2 Fl 2, Copenhagen, 2200, DENMARK

Eaddy, Don *Baseball Player*
Chicago Cubs, 5394 Effingham Dr SE, Grand Rapids, MI 49508 6308 USA

Eade, George J *General*
1131 Sunnyside Dr, Healdsburg, CA 95448 USA

Eads, George *Actor*
William Morris Agency (WMA-LA), 1 William Morris Pl, Beverly Hills, CA 90212 USA

Eads, Ora W *Religious Leader*
Christian Congregation, 804 W, Hemlock St, La Follette, TN 37766 USA

Eagan, James *Writer*
International Creative Management (ICM-LA), 8942 Wilshire Blvd, Beverly Hills, CA 90211 USA

Eagle, Ian *Sportscaster*
CBS-TV, Sports Dept, 51 W 52nd St, New York, NY 10019 USA

Eagleburger, Lawrence S *Secretary*
1450 Osensville Rd, Charlottesville, VA 22901 USA

Eaglen, Jane *Opera Singer*
Columbia Artists Mgmt Inc, 165 W 57th St, New York, NY 10019 USA

Eagles, The *Musician*
William Morris Agency (WMA-LA), 1 William Morris Pl, Beverly Hills, CA 90212 USA

Eagleson, Alan *Hockey Player*
37 Maltland St, Toronto, ON M4Y 1C8, CANADA

Eagleton, Thomas *Ex-Senator*
1 Mercantile Center, St. Louis, MO 63101

Eagleton, Thomas F *Senator*
1 Firstar Center, Saint Louis, MO 63101 USA

Eagling, Wayne J *Dancer, Choreographer*
Postbus 16486, 1001 RN, Amsterdam, Netherlands

Eakes, Bobbie *Actor*
William Morris Agency (WMA-LA), 1 William Morris Pl, Beverly Hills, CA 90212 USA

Eakin, Richard R *Educator*
East Carolina University, Chancellor's Office, Greenville, NC 27858 USA

Eakin, Thomas C *Business Person*
2729 Shelley Road, Shaker Heights, OH 44122 USA

Eakins, Dallas *Hockey Player*
751 New Romaine, Peterborough, ON K9L 2G4, CANADA

Eakins, James(Jim) *Basketball Player*
2575 E 9600th St S, Sandy, UT 84092 USA

Ealy, Michael *Actor*
Vic Ramos Management, 49 W 9th St #5B, New York, NY 10011 USA

Earl, Anthony S *Governor*
2810 Arbor Dr, #B, Madison, WI 53711 USA

Earl, Robin D *Football Player*
9 Middlebury Lane, Lincolnshire, IL 60069 USA

Earl, Roger *Musician*
Lustig Talent, PO Box 770850, Orlando, FL 32877 USA

Earl, Scott *Baseball Player*
Detroit Tigers, PO Box 63, North Vernon, IN 47265 0063 USA

Earle, Ed *Basketball Player*
1940 Burton Lane, Park Ridge, IL 60069 USA

Earle, Stacey *Musician*
Grassroots Media, 800 18th Ave S, #B, Nashville, TN 37212 USA

Earle, Steve *Songwriter*
Dan Gillis Mgmt, 1223 17th Ave S, Nashville, TN 37212 USA

Earle, Sylvia Alice *Oceanographer*
12812 Skyline Blvd, Oakland, CA 94619 USA

Earley, Anthony F Jr *Business Person*
Detroit Edison, 2000 2nd Ave, Detroit, MI 48226 USA

Earley, Bill *Baseball Player*
St Louis Cardinals, 783 Sundance Dr, Cincinnati, OH 45233 1454 USA

Earley, Michael M *Business Person*
Triton Group, 550 W C St, San Diego, CA 92101 USA

Early, Gerald L *Writer*
Washington University, English Dept, Saint Louis, MO 63130 USA

Earnhardt, Kerry *Race Car Driver*
FitzBradshaw Racing, 129 Bevan Dr, Mooresville, NC 28115 USA

Earnhardt, R Dale Jr *Race Car Driver*
1675 Coddle Creek Hwy, Mooresville, NC 28115 USA

Earth Wind & Fire *Music Group*
Creative Artists Agency LCC (CAA-LA), 9830 Wilshire Blvd, Beverly Hills, CA 90212 USA

Easler, Mike *Baseball Player*
Houston Astros, 8428 Dutch Hill Ct, Las Vegas, NV 89128 7623 USA

Easley, Bill *Musician*
Hot Jazz Mgmt, 328 W 43rd St, #4FW, New York, NY 10036 USA

Easley, Damlon *Baseball Player*
California Angels, 14125 N 65th Ave, Glendale, AZ 85306 3757 USA

Easley, Logan *Baseball Player*
Pittsburgh Pirates, 748 Washington St N Apt 1, Twin Falls, ID 83301 3887 USA

Easmon, Ricky *Football Player*
6605 n Riviera Manor St, #A4, Tampa, FL 33604 USA

Eason, Eric *Actor*
Creative Artists Agency LCC (CAA-LA), 9830 Wilshire Blvd, Beverly Hills, CA 90212 USA

Eason, Tony *Football Player*
851 Cocos Dr, San Marcos, CA 92078 USA

East, Jeff *Actor*
Vaughn Hart & Associates, 8899 Beverly Blvd, Los Angeles, CA 90048 USA

East 17
Box 153 Stanmore, Middlesex, ENGLAND, HA7 2HF

Easterbrook, Frank *Judge*
US Court of Appeals, 111 N Canal St, Building 6, Chicago, IL 60606 USA

Easterbrook, Leslie *Actor*
5218 bellingham Ave, Valley Village, CA 91607 USA

Easterbrrok, Frank H *Judge*
US Court of Appeals, 111 N Canal St, Building 6, Chicago, IL 60606 USA

Easterling, Ray *Football Player*
2533 Pocoshock Blvd, Richmond, VA 23235 USA

Easterly, David E *Business Person*
Cox Enterprises, 1400 Lake Heam Dr NE, Atlanta, GA 30319 USA

Easterly, Jamie *Baseball Player*
Atlanta Braves, 1306 Plantation Dr, Crockett, TX 75835 2314 USA

Eastham, Dean E *Physicist*
281 Bloomingbank Road, Riverside, IL 60456 USA

Eastham, Richard *Actor*
211 S Spalding Dr, Beverty Hills, CA 90212 USA

Eastin, Steve *Actor*
Agency for the Performing Arts (APA-LA), 9200 Sunset Blvd #900, Los Angeles, CA 90069 USA

Eastman, John *Attorney General*
Eastman & Eastman, 39 W 54th St, New York, NY 10019 USA

Eastman, Kevin *Cartoonist*
Teenage Mutant ninja Turtles, PO Box 417, Haydenville, MA 01039 USA

Eastman, Madeline *Musician*
Prince/SF Productions, 1450 Southgate Ave, #206, Daly City, CA 94015 USA

Eastman, Marilyn *Actor*
Hardman-Eastman Studios, 138 Hawthome St, Pittsburgh, PA 15218 USA

Eastman, Rodney *Actor*
Leslie Allan-Rice Management, 7524 Mulholland Dr, Los Angeles, CA 90046

Easton, Michael *Actor*
2810 Baseline Trail, Los Angeles, CA 90068 USA

Easton, Millard E (Bill) *Coach*
1704 NW Weatherstone Dr, Blue Springs, MO 64051 USA

Easton, Robert
Paul Kohner, 9300 Wilshire Blvd, #555, Beverly Hills, CA 90212 USA

Easton, Sheena *Musician*
Emmis Mgmt, 18136 Califa St, Tarzana, CA 91356 USA

Eastwick, Rawly *Baseball Player*
Cincinnati Reds, 10 River Meadow Dr, West Newbury, MA 01985 1400 USA

Eastwick-Field, Elizabeth *Architect*
Low Farm Low Road, Denham Eye, Suffolk, IP21 5ET, UNITED KINGDOM

Eastwood, Alison *Actor, Model*
McGowan Management, 8733 W Sunset Blvd #103, W Hollywood, CA 90069 USA

Eastwood, Bob *Golfer*
3826 falmouth Court, Stockton, CA 95219 USA

Eastwood, Clint *Actor, Producer*
Hogs Breath Inn, Carlos St PO Box 4366, Carmel, CA 93921 USA

Eastwood, Kyle
2049 Century Park E. #3500, Los Angeles, CA 90067-3127

Easum, Donald B *Diplomat*
801 W End Ave, #3A, New York, NY 10025 USA

Eaton, Adam *Baseball Player*
4322 113th Ave SE, Snohomish, WA 98290 5576 USA

Eaton, Andrew *Producer*
Revolution Films, 10 Little Turnstile, London, WC1V 70X, UNITED KINGDOM (UK)

Eaton, Brando *Actor*
Art Work Entertainment, 260 South Beverly Dr #205, Beverly Hills, CA 90210 USA

Eaton, Craig *Baseball Player*
3307 Baltusrol Ln, Lake Worth, FL 33467 1301 USA

Eaton, Dan L *Doctor*
Genentech Inc, 460 Point San Bruno Blvd, South San Francisco, CA 94080 USA

Eaton, Don (Babtunde) *Musician, Composer*
Agency Group Ltd, 370 City Road, London, EC1V 2QA, UNITED KINGDOM

Eaton, John C *Composer*
4585 N Hartstrait Road, Bloomington, IN 47404 USA

Eaton, Mark E *Basketball Player*
PO Box 982108, Park City, UT 84098 USA

Eaton, Meredith *Actor*
Susan Smith, 121A N San Vicente Blvd, Beverly Hills, CA 90211 USA

Eaton, Shirley *Actor*
Guild House, Upper Saint Martin's Lane, London, WC2H PEG, UNITED KINGDOM

Eave, Gary *Baseball Player*
Atlanta Braves, 1601 King Ave, Bastrop, LA 71220 4957 USA

Ebadi, Shirin *Nobel Prize Laureate*
University of Tehran, Enghelab Ave & 16 Azar St, Tehran, IRAN

Ebashi, Setsuro *Physicist*
17-503 Nahaizumi Myodaiji, Okazaki, 444, JAPAN

Ebel, David M *Judge*
US Court of Appeals, US Courthouse, 1929 Stout St, Denver, CO 80294 USA

Eben, Petr *Composer*
Hamsikova 19, Prague, 150 00 Prague 5, CZECH REPUBLIC

Ebensteiner, June
20100 Wells Dr., Woodland Hills, CA 91364

Eber, Lorenz *Inventor*
2 Byron Close, Laguna Niguel, CA 92677 USA

Eberhart, Ralph E (Ed) *General*
Commander, US Northen Command, Peterson Air Force Base, CO 80914 USA

Eberhart, Richard
80 Lyme Rd. #32, Kendal-At-Hanover, NH 03755-1226

Eberhart, Richard G *Writer*
80 Lyme Road, #32, Hanvover, NH 03755 USA

Eberharter, Stefan *Skier*
Dorfstr 21, 6272 Stumm, AUSTRIA

Eberle, Markus *Skier*
Unterwestweg 27, Rieztem, 87567, GERMANY

Eberle, William D *Business Person*
13 Garland Road, Concord, MO 01742 USA

Ebershoff, David *Writer*
Viking Press, 375 Hudson St, New York, NY 10014 USA

Ebersole, Christine *Actor*
Agency for Performing Arts, 9200 Sunset Blvd, #900, Los Angeles, CA 90069 USA

Ebersole, Dick *Business Person*
174 West St, #54, Litchfield, CT 06759 USA

Ebersole, Drew *Actor*
House of Representatives, 400 S Beverly Dr #101, Beverly Hills, CA 90212 USA

Ebert, Derrin *Baseball Player*
Atlanta Braves, 7932 Newhall Ave, Hesperia, CA 92345 7032 USA

Ebert, Peter *Musician*
Col di Mura, 06010 Lippiano, ITALY

Ebert, Robert D *Physicist*
16 Brewster Road, Wayland, MA 01778 USA

Ebertharter, Stefan *Skier*
Dorfstr 21, 6272 Stumm, Austria

Eberts, Jake *Producer*
National Geographic Feature Films, 9100 Wilshire Blvd #401E, Beverly Hills, CA 90212-3420 USA

Ebi, Ndudi *Basketball Player*
Minnesota Timberwolves, Target Center, 600 1st Ave N, Minneapolis, MN 55403 USA

Ebsen, Bonnie *Actor*
PO Box 356, Agoura, CA 91376 USA

Eccleston, Christopher *Actor*
Hamilton Asper Mgmt, 24 Hanway St, London, England, W1T 1UH, UNITED KINGDOM

Ecclestone, Bernie *Race Car Driver*
Formula One Ltd, 6 Prince's Gate, London, England, SW7 1QJ, UNITED KINGDOM

Ecclestone, Christopher *Actor*
Hamilton Hodell Ltd, 24 Hanway St Fl 24, London, W1T 1UH, UNITED KINGDOM (UK)

Ecclestone, Timothy J (Tim) *Hockey Player*
10095 Fairway Village Dr, Roswell, GA 30076 USA

Ecevit, Bulent *Prime Minister*
Or-An Sehri 69/5, Ankara, TURKEY

Echevarria, Angel *Baseball Player*
Colorado Rockies, 2127 192nd Ave SE, Sammamish, WA 98075 9648 USA

Echeverria Alvarez, Luis *President*
Magnolia 131, San Jeronimo Lidice, Magdalena Contreras, CP, 10200, MEXICO

Echikunwoke, Megalyn *Actor*
Bresler Kelly & Associates, 11500 W Olympic Blvd #352, Los Angeles, CA 90064 USA

Eckenstahler, Eric *Baseball Player*
Detroit Tigers, 305 S Prospect Rd Apt 2, Bloomington, IL 61704 4553 USA

Eckersley, Dennis *Baseball Player*
Cleveland Indians, 2 Gina Dr, Hopkinton, MA 01748 2018 USA

Eckert, Aaron *Actor*
Creative Artists Agency, 9830 Wilshire Blvd, Beverly Hills, CA 90212 USA

Eckert, Robert *Business Person*
Mattel Inc, 333 Continental Ave, El Segundo, CA 90245 USA

Eckert, Shari *Actor*
PO Box 5761, Sherman Oaks, CA 91413 USA

Eckhart, Aaron *Actor*
Creative Artists Agency, 9830 Wilshire Blvd, Beverly Hills, CA 90212 USA

Eckholdt, Steven *Actor*
137 N Larchmont Blvd, #138, Los Angeles, CA 90004 USA

Eckhouse, James
4222 Murietta Ave., Sherman Oaks, CA 91423

Eckstein, David *Baseball Player*
Anaheim Angels, 103 Aldean Dr, Sanford, FL 32771 3612 USA

Eco, Umberto *Tennis Player*
Piazza Castello 13, Milan, ITALY, 20121, ITALY

Econoline Crush
1505 N. 2nd Ave. #200, Vancouver, CANADA, BC V6H 3Y4

Edberg, Stefan *Tennis Player*
ProServe, 1101 Woodrow Wilson Blvd, #1800, Arlington, VA 22209 USA

Eddy, Chris *Baseball Player*
Oakland A's, 47 Winterbury Cir, Wilmington, DE 19808 1429 USA

Eddy, Don *Baseball Player*
Chicago White Sox, PO Box 537, Rockwell, IA 50469 0537 USA

Eddy, Duane *Songwriter*
Orsbom Co, 2700 Neilson Way, Santa Monica, CA 90405 USA

Eddy, Nicholas M (nick) *Football Player*
2225 London Circle, Modesto, CA 95356 USA

Eddy, Steve *Baseball Player*
California Angels, 700 N Dobson Rd Unit 38, Chandler, AZ 85224 6940 USA

Edelen, Joe *Baseball Player*
St Louis Cardinals, PO Box 38, Washington, OK 73093 0038 USA

Edell, Marc Z *Attorney General*
Budd Larner Gross, 150 John F Kennedy Parkway, #1000, Short Hills, NJ 07078 USA

Edelman, Brad M *Football Player*
4041 Williams Blvd, #A9316, Kenner, LA 70065 USA

Edelman, Gerald M *Nobel Prize Laureate*
Scripps Research Institute, Neurobiology Dept, La Jolla, CA 92037 USA

Edelman, Isidore S *Biologist*
464 Riverside Dr, New York, NY 10027 USA

Edelman, Marian Wright *Business Person*
Children's Defense Fund, 25 E St NW, Washington, DC 20001 USA

Edelman, Pawel *Cinematographer*
International Creative Management (ICM-LA), 8942 Wilshire Blvd, Beverly Hills, CA 90211 USA

Edelman, Randy *Composer*
Gorfaine/Schwartz, 13245 Riverside Dr, #450, Sherman Oaks, CA 91423 USA

Edelstein, Jean *Artist*
48 Brooks Ave, Venice, CA 90291 USA

Edelstein, Lisa *Actor*
I F A Talent Agency, 8730 Sunset Blvd, #490, Los Angeles, CA 90069 USA

Edelstein, Michael *Producer*
Industry Entertainment, 955 S Carrillo Dr #300, Los Angeles, CA 90048 USA

Edelstein, Victor *Fashion Designer*
3 Stanhope Mews West, London, SW7 5RB, UNITED KINGDOM (UK)

Eden, Barbara *Actor*
9816 Denbigh Dr, Beverly Hills, CA 90210 USA

Eden, Mike *Baseball Player*
Atlanta Braves, 11531 Forest Hills Dr, Tampa, FL 33612 5121 USA

Eden, Richard *Actor*
The Agency, 1800 Ave of the Stars, #400, Los Angeles, CA 90067 USA

Edenfield, Ken *Baseball Player*
California Angels, 4407 Barbara Dr, Knoxville, TN 37918 4403 USA

Edens, Tom *Baseball Player*
New York Mets, 2033 Quallridge Ct, Clarkston, WA 99403 1787 USA

Eder, Elfriede
Rain 12, Leogang, AUSTRIA, 5771

Eder, Linda *Actor*
Randy Nolan Artists, 115 S 3rd St, #2C, Geneva, IL 60134 USA

Eder, Richard G *Journalist*
Los Angeles Times, Editorial Dept, 202 W 1st ST, Los Angeles, CA 90012 USA

Edgar, David
917 NE 16th Ave. #13, Ft. Lauderdale, FL 33304

Edgar, David (Dave) *Swimmer*
2633 Middle River Dr, #3, Fort Lauderdale, FL 33306 USA

Edgar, Jim *Governor*
State House 207 E Capitol Ave, Springfield, IL 62706

Edgar, Robert W *Religious Leader*
National Council of Churches, 475 Riverside Dr #1880, New York, NY 10115 USA

Edge *Musician*
Regine Moylet, 145A Ladbroke Grove, London, W10 6HJ, UNITED KINGDOM (UK)

Edge, Butch *Baseball Player*
Toronto Blue Jays, 2491 Michelle Dr, Sacramento, CA 95821 2342 USA

Edge, Graeme *Musician*
Insight Mgmt, 1222 16th Ave S, #300, Nashville, TN 37212 USA

Edgerton, Bill *Baseball Player*
Kansas City A's, 1725 E Jefferson Blvd, Mishawaka, IN 46545 7233 USA

Edlen, Bengt *Physicist*
University of Lund, Physics Dept, Lund, SWEDEN

Edler, Dave *Baseball Player*
Seattle Mariners, 1504 S 34th Ave, Yakima, WA 98902 4808 USA

Edler, Inge G *Doctor*
University Hospital, Cadiology Dept, Lund, SWEDEN

Edler, Lee
1725 K St. NW #1202, Washington, DC 20006

Edlund, David J *Inventor*
Northwest Power Systems, PO Box 5339, Bend, OR 97708 USA

Edlund, Richard P *Cinematographer*
2710 Wilshire Blvd, Santa Monica, CA 90403 USA

Edmiston, Mark M *Publisher*
Jordan Edmiston Group, 885 3rd Ave, New York, NY 10022 USA

Edmonds, James P (Jim) *Baseball Player*
California Angels, 114 Hunters Grove Dr, Saint Louis, MO 63141 7669 USA

Edmonds, Kenneth (Babyface) *Musician, Producer*
10231 Charing Cross Road, Los Angeles, CA 90024 USA

Edmonds, Louis
250 W. 57th St. #2317, New York, NY 10107

Edmonds, Tracey E *Producer*
Edmonds Entertainment, 1635 N Cahuenga Blvd Fl 5, Los Angles, CA 90028 USA

Edmondson, Brian *Baseball Player*
Atlanta Braves, 304 Ridgeview Trce, Canton, GA 30114 7000 USA

Edmondson, James L *Judge*
US Court of Appeals, 56 Forsyth St NW, Atlanta, GA 30303 USA

Edmund-Davies, Herbert E *Judge*
5 Gray's Inn Square, London, WC1R 5EU, UNITED KINGDOM (UK)

Edmunds, Dave *Songwriter, Musician*
Entertainment Services, Main Street Plaza 1000, #303, Voorhees, NJ 08043 USA

Edna, Dame *Actor, Comedian*
PBJ Mgmt, 5 Soho Square, London, W1V 5DE, UNITED KINGDOM (UK)

Edner, Ashley *Actor*
Cunningham-Escott-Dipene & Associates Inc (CED-LA), 10635 Santa Monica Blvd #130, Los Angeles, CA 90025 USA

Edner, Bobby *Actor*
Cunningham-Escott-Dipene & Associates Inc (CED-LA), 10635 Santa Monica Blvd #130, Los Angeles, CA 90025 USA

Edney, Leon A (Bud) *Admiral*
1037 Encino Row, Coronado, CA 92118 USA

Edney, Tyus *Basketball Player*
1800 S Floyd Court, La Habra, CA 90631 USA

Edson, Hilary *Actor*
400 S Beverly Road, #216, Beverly Hills, CA 90212 USA

Eduardo dos Santos, Jose *President*
President's Office, Palacio do Povo, Luanda, ANGOLA

Edward *Prince*
Bagshot, Bagshot Park, Surrey, ENGLAND, GU19 5PN, UNITED KINGDOM

Edward, John *Psychic*
Berkley Publishing Group, 375 Hudson St, New York, NY 10014 USA

Edward (Eddie), Adams *Journalist*
Eddie Adams Inc, 538 E 11th St, New York, NY 10009

Edwards, Anthony *Actor, Producer*
Lovett Management, 1327 Brinkley Ave, Los Angeles, CA 90049 USA

Edwards, Antonio *Football Player*
716 2nd St NW, Moultrie, GA 31768 USA

Edwards, Barbara *Actor, Model*
Hansen, 7767 Hollywood Blvd, #202, Los Angeles, CA 90046 USA

Edwards, Bill
17 Bishop's Rd., Tewin Wood Herts., ENGLAND

Edwards, Blue *Basketball Player*
Miami Heat, American Airlines Arena, 601 Biscayne Blvd, Miami, FL 33132 USA

Edwards, Carl *Race Car Driver*
Roush Racing, 122 Knob Hill Road, Mooresville, NC 28117 USA

Edwards, Charles C *Physicist*
Keeney Park, 10666 N Torrey Pines Road, La Jolla, CA 92037 USA

Edwards, Dave *Baseball Player*
Minnesota Twins, 5059 Quail Run Rd Apt 75, Riverside, CA 92507 6485 USA

Edwards, Dennis *Musician, Opera Singer, Songwriter*
Green Light Talent Agency, PO Box 3172, Beverly Hills, CA 90212 USA

Edwards, Don *Hockey Player*
435 Meredith Anne Court, #102, Raleigh, NC 27606 USA

Edwards, Don *Musician, Songwriter, Music Group*
Scott O'Malley Assoc, 433 S Cuchamas St, Colorado Springs, CO 80903 USA

Edwards, Earl *Football Player*
1534 W Saint Thomas Dr, Gilbert, AZ 85233 USA

Edwards, Eric *Cinematographer*
3404 SW Water Ave, Portland, OR 97239 USA

Edwards, Gail
651 N. Kilkea Dr., Los Angeles, CA 90048-2213

Edwards, Gareth *Soccer Player*
211 West Rd, Nottage, Porthcawl, Mid-Clamorgan, CF363RT, WALES

Edwards, Geoff
249 Main, Ilderton, CANADA, Ont. N0M 2

Edwards, Harry *Educator, Social Activist*
University of California, Sociology Dept, Berkeley, CA 94720 USA

Edwards, Harry T *Judge*
US Court of Appeals, 333 Constitution Ave NW, Washington, DC 20001 USA

Edwards, Herman L *Football Coach, Football Player*
1627 Highland St, Seaside, CA 93955 USA

Edwards, Howard *Baseball Player*
Cleveland Indians, 2106 79th Ct, Vero Beach, FL 32966 1365 USA

Edwards, James *Basketball Player*
3890 Lakeland Lane, Bloomfield Township, MI 48302 USA

Edwards, James B *Secretary, Governor*
100 Venning St, Mount Pleasant, SC 29464 USA

Edwards, Jay *Basketball Player*
121 N Washington St #506, Marion, IN 46952 USA

Edwards, Jennifer *Actor*
4123 Saint Clair, Studio City, CA 91604 USA

Edwards, Jesse E *Doctor*
1565 Edgcumbe Road, Saint Paul, MN 55116 USA

Edwards, Joe F Jr *Astronaut*
Enron Broadband Services, P O Box 1188, Houston, TX 77251

Edwards, Joe F Jr *Astronaut*
Enron Broadband Services, P O Box 1188, Houston, TX 77251 USA

Edwards, Joel *Golfer*
280 Benson Lane, Copell, TX 75019 USA

Edwards, John *Psychic*
Get Psych'd Inc, PO Box 383, Huntington, NY 11743 USA

Edwards, John *Musician*
Buddy Allen Mgmt, 3750 Hudson Manor Terr #3AE, Bronx, NY 10463 USA

Edwards, Jonathan *Track Athlete*
MTC, 10 Kendall Place, London, England, W1H3AH, United Kingdom

Edwards, Jonathan *Songwriter, Music Group*
Northern Lights, 437 Live Oak Loop NE, Albuquerque, NM 87122 USA

Edwards, Kalimba *Athlete*
Detroit Lions, 222 Republic Dr, Allen Park, MI 48101 USA

Edwards, Lena F *Physicist*
821 Woodland Dr, Lakewood, NJ 08701 USA

Edwards, Luke *Actor*
Ensemble Entertainment, 10474 Santa Monica Blvd #380, Los Angeles, CA 90025 USA

Edwards, Mario *Football Player*
Dallas Cowboys, One Cowboys Pkwy, Irving, TX 75063-4727

Edwards, Marshall *Baseball Player*
Milwaukee Brewers, 8948 La Cintura Ct, San Diego, CA 92129 3316 USA

Edwards, Mike *Baseball Player*
Pittsburgh Pirates, 11370 Moreno Beach Dr, Moreno Valley, CA 92555 5240 USA

Edwards, Mike *Baseball Player*
Oakland A's, 502 Sharon Ave, Mechanicsburg, PA 17055 6630 USA

Edwards, Paddi
1800 Avenue of the Stars #400, Los Angeles, CA 90067

Edwards, Paul

Edwards, R Lavell *Football Coach, Football Player*
Brighan Young University, Athletic Dept, Provo, UT 84602 USA

Edwards, Ralph *Entertainer*
6922 Hollywood Blvd #415, Los Angeles, CA 90028 USA

Edwards, Robert *Football Player*
931 Knight Road, Tinnille, GA 31089 USA

Edwards, Robert A (Bob) *Commentator*
National Public Radio, News Dept, 635 Massachusetts NW, Washington, DC 20001 USA

Edwards, Robert G *Physicist*
Duck End Farm, Dry Drayton, Cambridge, England, CB38DB, United Kingdom

Edwards, Robert J *Editor*
Williamscot House, near Banbury, England, Oxon OX17 1AE, UNITED KINGDOM

Edwards, Ronnie Claire *Actor*
Artists Group (LA), 10100 Santa Monica Blvd #2490, Los Angeles, CA 90067 USA

Edwards, Sarah

Edwards, Sian *Conductor*
70 Twisden Road, London, England, NW5 1DN, UNITED KINGDOM

Edwards, Stacy *Actor*
Paradigm Agency, 10 100 Santa Monica Blvd, #2500, Los Angeles, CA 90067 USA

Edwards, Stephanie *Actor*
8075 W 3rd St, #303, Los Angeles, CA 90048 USA

Edwards, Steve *Composer*
3980 Royal Oak Place, Encino, CA 91436 USA

Edwards, Teresa *Basketball Player*
291 Union Grove Church Road SE, Calhoun, GA 30701 USA

Edwards, Tommy Lee *Cartoonist*
DC Comics, 1700 Broadway, New York, NY 10019 USA

Edwards, Tonya *Basketball Player*
Phoenix Mercury, American West Arena, 201 E Jefferson St, Phoenix, AZ 85004 USA

Edwards, W Blake *Writer, Director, Actor, Producer*
Pitt Group, The, 9465 Wilshire Blvd #480, Beverly Hills, CA 90212 USA

Edwards, Wayne *Baseball Player*
Chicago White Sox, 9738 Aqueduct Ave, Sepulveda, CA 91343 2035 USA

Edwards Jr, Charles C *Publisher*
Des Moines Register & Tribune, 715
Locust St, Des Moines, IA 50309 USA

Eenhoorn, Robert *Baseball Player*
New York Yankees, Zermilieplaats 15
3068J, Rotterdam, NETHERLANDS

Egan, Dick *Baseball Player*
Cincinnati Reds, 1611 W Thurderhill Dr,
Phoenix, AZ 85045 1802 USA

Egan, Edward M Cardinal *Religious
Leader*
Archdiocese of New York, 1011 1st St,
New York, NY 10022 USA

Egan, Jennifer *Writer*
Doubleday Press, 1540 Broadway, New
York, NY 10036 USA

Egan, John (Johnny) *Basketball Player*
2124 Nantucket Dr, #B, Houston, TX
77057 USA

Egan, John L *Business Person*
130 Wilton Road, London, England,
SW1V 1LQ, UNITED KINGDOM

Egan, Peter *Actor*
James Sharkey, 21 Golden Square,
London, England, W1R 3PA, UNITED
KINGDOM

Egan, Richard J *Business Person*
ECM Corp, 35 Parkwood Dr, Hopkinton,
MA 01748 USA

Egan, Susan *Actor*
Himber Entertainment, 211 S Beverly Dr,
#208, Beverly Hills, CA 90212 USA

Egan, Tom *Baseball Player*
California Angels, 184 E Myrna Ln,
Tempe, AZ 85284 3118 USA

Egdahl, Richard H *Doctor*
333 Commonwealth Ave, #23, Boston,
MA 02115 USA

Ege, Julie *Actor*
Guild House, Upper Saint Martins,
London, England, WC2H 9EG, UNITED
KINGDOM

Egerszegi, Kristina
Feszti A. u 4, Budapest, HUNGARY, 1032

Egerszegi, Krisztina *Swimmer*
Budapest Spartacus, Koer Utca 1/A, 1103
Budapest, HUNGARY

Eggar, Samantha *Actor*
15430 Mulholland Dr, Los Angeles, CA
90077 USA

Eggby, David *Cinematographer*
4324 Promenade Way, #109, Marina del
Ray, CA 90292 USA

Eggers, Dave *Writer*
Simon & Schuster 1230 Ave of Americas,
New York, NY 10020 USA

Eggert, Nicole *Actor*
11360 Brill Dr, Studio City, CA 91604
USA

Eggert, Robert J *Economist*
Eggert Economics Enterprises, PO Box
4313, Sedona, AZ 86340 USA

Eggerth, Marta
Park Dr. No., Rye, NY 10580

Eggleston, William *Photographer*
Robert Miller Gallery, 526 W 26th St,
#10A, New York, NY 10001 USA

Eggleton, Arthur C *Government Official*
National Defence Ministry, 101 Colonel
By Dr, Ottawa, ON K1A OK2, CANADA

Egielski, Richard
525 B St. #1900, San Diego, CA 92101

Egloff, Bruce *Baseball Player*
Cleveland Indians, 3136 S Emporia Ct,
Denver, CO 80231 4739 USA

Egoyan, Atom *Actor*
Ego Film Artiosts, 80 Niagara St, Toronto,
ON M5V 1C5, CANADA

Ehle, Jennifer *Actor*
134 W 70th St, #4, New York, NY 10023
USA

Ehlers, Beth *Actor*
Stone Manners Talent Agency, 6500
Wilshire Blvd, Ste 550, Los Angeles, CA
90048 USA

Ehlers, Walter D *War Hero*
8382 Valley View, Buena Park, CA 90620
USA

Ehrbar, Nicole *Stylist*
Cartier (LA), 370 N Rodeo Dr, Beverly
Hills, CA 90210 USA

Ehrenreich, Barbara *Writer*
Farrar Straus Giroux, 19 Union Square W,
New York, NY 10003 USA

Ehrlich, Paul R *Biologist*
Stanford University, Biological Sciences
Dept, Stanford, CA 94305 USA

Ehrlich, S Paul Jr *Physicist*
1132 Seaspray Ave, Delray Beach, FL
33483 USA

Eiber, Janet
9300 Wilshire Blvd. #410, Beverly Hills,
CA 90212

Eichelberger, Charles B *General*
California Microwave, 124 Sweetwater
Oaks, Peachtree City, GA 30269 USA

Eichelberger, Dave
112 TPC Blvd., Ponte Vedra, FL 33082-
3046

Eichelberger, Juan *Baseball Player*
San Diego Padres, 14674 Silverset St,
Poway, CA 92064 6408 USA

Eichhorn, Lisa *Actor*
1919 W 44th St, #1000, New York, NY
10036 USA

Eichhorn, Mark *Baseball Player*
Toronto Blue Jays, 147 Norma Ct, Aptos,
CA 95003 9789 USA

Eichorn, Lisa
1501 Broadway #2600, New York, NY
10036

Eighth Wonder
50 Lisson St Unit 1B, London, ENGLAND,
NW1 5DF

Eigsti, Roger H *Business Person*
SAFECO Corp, SAFECO Plaza, Seattle,
WA 98185 USA

Eikenberry, Jill *Actor*
197 Oakdale Ave, Mill Valley, CA 94941
USA

Eikenes, Adele *Opera Singer*
Van Walsum Mgmt, 4 Addison Bridge
Place, London, England, W14 8XP,
UNITED KINGDOM

Eiland, Dave *Baseball Player*
New York Yankees, 5923 War Admiral
Dr, Zephyhills, FL 33544 5542 USA

Eilbacher, Cynthia
PO Box 8920, Universal City, CA 91608

Eilbacher, Lisa *Actor*
4600 Petit Ave, Encino, CA 91436 USA

Eilber, Janet *Actor*
Irv Schechter, 9300 Wilshire Blvd #410,
Beverly Hills, CA 90212 USA

Eilers, Dave *Baseball Player*
602 Perkins Ln, Brenham, TX 77833 4394
USA

Eilts, Hermann F *Diplomat*
67 Cleveland Road, Wellesley, MA 02481
USA

Einertson, Darrell *Baseball Player*
New York Yankees, 427 NW Skyline Dr,
Ankeny, IA 50021 8701 USA

Einstein, Bob (Super Dave Osbourne)
Actor
9842 Cardigan Place, Beverly Hills, CA
90210 USA

Einziger, Mike *Music Group*
Artist Direct, 10900 Wilshire Blvd #1400,
Los Angeles, CA 90024 USA

Eischen, Joey *Baseball Player*
Montreal Expos, 1428 E Herring Ave,
West Covina, CA 91791 3111 USA

Eisen, Herman N *Doctor*
9 Homestead St, Waban, MA 02468 USA

Eisen, Tripp *Music Group*
Andy Gould Mgmt, 9100 Wilshire Blvd
#400W, Beverly Hills, CA 90212 USA

Eisenberg, Hallie Kate *Actor*
Endeavor Agency LLC (LA), 9601 Wilshire
Blvd Fl 3, Beverly Hills, CA 90210 USA

Eisenberg, Jesse *Actor*
William Morris Agency (WMA-LA), 1
William Morris Pl, Beverly Hills, CA
90212 USA

Eisenberg, Lee B *Editor*
Edison Project, 3286 N Park Blvd, Alcoa,
TN 37701 USA

Eisenberg, Leon *Doctor*
9 Clement Circle, Cambridge, MA 02138
USA

Eisenberg, Melvin A *Attorney General,
Educator*
1197 Keeler Ave, Berkeley, CA 94708
USA

Eisenberg, Warren *Business Person*
Bed Bath & Beyond, 650 Liberty Ave,
Union, NJ 07083 USA

Eisenhauer, Peggy *Special Effects Designer*
International Creative Mgmt, 40 W 57th St
#1800, New York, NY 10019 USA

Eisenhauer, Stephen S (Steve) *Football
Player*
105 Abbey Road, Winchester, VA 22602
USA

Eisenhower, David
Foxall Lane, Berwyn, PA 19312

Eisenhower, John
27318 Morris Rd., Trappe, MD 21673-
1915

Eisenhower, Julie Nixon
Foxall Lane, Berwyn, PA 19312

Eisenhower, Susan
1050 17th St. NW #600, Washington, DC 20030

Eisenman, Peter D *Architect*
Eisenman Architects, 40 W 25th St, New York, NY 10010 USA

Eisenmann, Ike
6556 Blucher Ave., Van Nuys, CA 91406

Eisenmann, Ike *Actor*
6556 Blucher Ave, Van Nuys, CA 91406 USA

Eisenreich, James M (Jim) *Baseball Player*
Minnesota Twins, 21300 E 34th St S, Independence, MO 64057 3410 USA

Eisenstein, Michael *Music Group*
Little Big Man, 155 Ave of Americas #700, New York, NY 10013 USA

Eisler, Barry *Writer*
Penguin Group, 375 Hudson St, New York, NY 10014 USA

Eisler, Lloyd
211-800 Montarville, Boucherville, CANADA, PQ JYB 125

Eisley, Howard *Basketball Player, Athlete*
20250 Rodeo Court, Southfield, MI 48075 USA

Eisman, Hy *Cartoonist*
99 Boulevard, Glen Rock, NJ 07452 USA

Eisner, Michael *Business Person*
Walt Disney Company, The, 500 S Buena Vista St, Burbank, CA 91521 USA

Eisner, Thomas *Biologist*
Comell University, Biological Department Mudd Hall, Ithaca, NY 14853 USA

Eisner, Will *Cartoonist*
Poorhouse Press, 8333 W McNab Road #131, Tamarac, FL 33321 USA

Eitan, Raphael *Admiral, General*
Tsomet Party, Knesset, Tel-Aviv, ISRAEL

Eitzel, Mark *Songwriter, Music Group*
Legends of 21st Century, 7 Trinity Row, Florence, MA 01062 USA

Eizenstat, Stuart E *Diplomat, Government Official*
9107 Briety Road, Chevy Chase, MD 20815 USA

Ejiofor, Chiwetel *Actor*
International Creative Management (ICM-LA), 8942 Wilshire Blvd, Beverly Hills, CA 90211 USA

Ejogo, Carmen *Actor*
P F D, Drug House, 34-43 Russell St, London, WC2B, UNITED KINGDOM (UK)

Ekberg, Ulf *Musician*
Basic Music Mgmt, Norrtullsgatan 52, Stockholm, 113 45, SWEDEN

Ekberg Anita
Via Aspro N(2 Genzano Di, Roma, ITALY, 00045

Ekland, Britt *Actor*
1888 N Crescent Heights Blvd, Los Angeles, CA 90069 USA

Eklund, A Sigvard *Physicist*
Krapfenwaldgasse 48, Vienna, 1190, AUSTRIA

Eklund, Greg *Music Group*
Pinnacle Entertainment, 30 Glenn St, White Plains, NY 10603 USA

Ektaa *Actor, Bollywood*
Sagar Sangeet, Opp. Colaba Post Office, Mumbai, MS 400005, INDIA

El DeBarge *Musician, Music Group*
Pyramid Entertainment, 89 5th Ave #700, New York, NY 10003 USA

El Fadil, Siddig *Actor*
Paramount, 5555 Melose Ave, Los Angeles, CA 90038 USA

El Sitio (Moris y Santiago) *Musician*
Gabriel Blanco Iglesias (Mexico), Rio Balsas 35-32, Colonia Cuauhtemoc, DF, 06500, Mexico

Elam, Jason *Football Player*
1445 Jay Court, Snellville, GA 30078 USA

Elam, Merrill *Architect*
Scogin Elam Bray, 1819 Peachtree Road NE #700, Atlanta, GA 30309 USA

Elarton, Scott *Baseball Player*
Houston Astros, 7762 E Archer Pl, Denver, CO 80230 6723 USA

Elavarasan *Actor*
7 Mahalinga Road, Chennai, TN 600 034, INDIA

Elbaradel, Mohamed *Government Official*
International Atomic Energy Agency, Wagramserstr, Vienna, 1400, AUSTRIA

Elcar, Dana *Actor*
Artists Group, 10100 Santa Monica Blvd #2490, Los Angeles, CA 90067 USA

Eldard, Ron *Actor*
Talent Entertainment Group, 9111 Wilshire Blvd, Beverly Hills, CA 90210 USA

Elder, Dave *Baseball Player*
2642 High St SW, Conyers, GA 30094 6843 USA

Elder, George *Baseball Player*
St Louis Browns, 5246 Riviera Ave, Banning, CA 92220 5215 USA

Elder, Lee E *Golfer*
Elder Group, 4737 N Ocean Dr #220, Lauderdale by the Sea, FL 33308 USA

Elder, Mark P
Natinal Opera, London Coliseum, London, WC2N 4ES, UNITED KINGDOM (UK)

Elder, Will *Cartoonist*
311 Jutland Dr #A, Monroe Township, NJ 08831 USA

Elders, M Jocelyn *Government Official, Doctor*
University of Arkansas Medical School, Pediatrics Dept, Little Rock, AR 72205 USA

Eldred, Cal *Baseball Player*
Milwaukee Brewers, 170 Abbotsford Rd, Cedar Rapids, IA 52403 7041 USA

Eldredge, Allison *Music Group*
C M Artists, 40 W 25th St, New York, NY 10019 USA

Eldredge, Todd *Figure Skater*
888 Denison Court, Bloomfield Hills, MI 48302, USA3

Eldredge, Todd *Figure Skater*
888 Denison Court, Bloomfield Hills, MI 48302 USA

Electra, Carmen *Actor, Model, Music Group*
United Talent Agency (UTA), 9560 Wilshire Blvd, Beverly Hills, CA 90212 USA

Elegant, Robert S *Writer*
Manor House, Middle Green near Langley, Bucks, SL3 6BS, UNITED KINGDOM (UK)

Eleniak, Erika *Actor, Model*
Deloitte/Touche, 2029 Century Park E #1300, Los Angeles, CA 90067 USA

Elfman, Bodhi *Actor*
Stone Manners Talent Agency, 6500 Wilshire Blvd, Ste 550, Los Angeles, CA 90048 USA

Elfman, Danny *Composer, Music Group, Musician, Musical Director*
3236 Primera Ave, Los Angeles, CA 90068 USA

Elfman, Jenna *Actor, Model*
Talent Entertainment Group, 9111 Wilshire Blvd, Beverly Hills, CA 90210 USA

Elfont, Harry *Director, Writer*
Benderspink, 6735 Yucca St, Hollywood, CA 90028

Elgart, Larry
2065 Gulf of Mexico Dr., Longboat Key, FL 34228

Elgart, Larry J *Music Group*
2065 Gulf of Mexico Dr, Longboat Key, FL 34228 USA

Elgen, Manfred *Nobel Prize Laureate*
Georg-Dehio-Weg 4, 37075 Gottingen, Germany

Elia, Lee *Baseball Player*
Chicago White Sox, 11613 Innfields Dr, Odessa, FL 33556 5407 USA

Elias, Eliane *Composer, Music Group, Musical Director, Musician*
Bennett Morgan, 1282 RR 376, Wappingers Falls, NY 12590 USA

Elias, Hector *Actor*
28 N Mansfield Ave, Los Angeles, CA 90038 USA

Elias, Jonathan *Composer*
Gorfaine/Schwartz, 13245 Riverside Dr #450, Sherman Oaks, CA 91423 USA

Elias, Patrick *Composer*
1005 Smith Manor Blvd #98, West Orange, NJ 07052 USA

Elias, Rosalind *Opera Singer*
Rober Lombardo, Harkness Plaza 61 W 62nd St #6F, New York, NY 10023 USA

Eliason, Donald *Basketball Player, Football Player*
5690 Fisher St, Saint Paul, MN 55110 USA

Eliel, Ernest L *Misc*
345 Carolina Meadows Villa, Chapell Hill, NC 27517 USA

Eliff, Tom *Religious Leader*
Southern Baptist Convention, 901 Commerce St #750, Nashville, TN 37203 USA

Elinson, Jack *Scientist*
1181 E Laurelton Parkway, Teeneck, NJ 07666 USA

Eliot, Alison
2 Ironsides #18, Marina del Rey, CA 90292

Eliot, Jan *Cartoonist*
P O Box 50032, Eugene, OR 97405 USA

Elise, Christine *Actor*
ROAR LLC, 2400 Broadway #350, Santa Monica, CA 90404 USA

Elise, Kimberly *Actor*
Writers & Artists, 8383 Wilshire Blvd #550, Beverly Hills, CA 90211 USA

Elisha, Walter Y *Business Person*
Springs Industries, 205 N White St, Fort Mill, SC 29715 USA

Elizabeth, Princess
1526 N. Beverly Dr., Beverly Hills, CA 90210

Elizabeth, Shannon *Actor*
International Creative Mgmt, 8942 Wilshire Blvd #219, Beverly Hills, CA 90211 USA

Elizondo, Hector *Actor*
5040 Noble Ave, Sherman Oaks, CA 91403 USA

Elk, Jim *Actor*
Dade/Schultz, 6442 Coldwater Canyon Ave #206, Valley Green, CA 91606 USA

Elkes, Joel *Psychic, Doctor*
University of Louisville, Psychiatry/ Behavioral Sci Dept, Louisville, KY 40292 USA

Elkind, Mortimer M *Physicist*
16925 Hierba Dr, San Diego, CA 92128 USA

Elkington, Steve *Golfer*
7010 Kelsey Rae Court, Houston, TX 77069 USA

Elkins, Hillard *Producer*
1335 N Dohney Dr, Los Angeles, CA 90069 USA

Elkins, Larry
111 S. St. Joseph St., South Bend, IN 46601-1901

Elkins, Lawrence C (Larry) *Football Player*
Saline Water Corp, PO Box 60889, Al Riyadh, 11555, SAUDI ARABIA

Ellard, Henry A *Football Player*
161 W Portland Ave, Fresno, CA 93711 USA

Ellena, Jack *Football Player*
Mountain Meadow Ranch, P O Box 610, Susanville, CA 96130 USA

Ellenstein, Robert *Actor*
5212 Sepulveda Blvd #23F, Culver City, CA 90230 USA

Ellenthal, Ira *Publisher*
New York Daily News, 220 E 42nd St, New York, NY 10017 USA

Eller, Carl *Football Player, Misc*
1035 Washburn Ave N, Minneapolis, MN 55411 USA

Ellerbee, Linda *Commentator*
Lucky Duck Productions, 96 Morton St #600, New York, NY 10014 USA

Elliman, Donald M Jr *Publisher*
Sports Illustrated Magazine, Rockefeller Center, New York, NY 10020 USA

Elliman, Yvonne *Music Group*
Talent Consultants International, 1560 Broadway #1308, New York, NY 10036 USA

Ellin, Doug *Director*
Creative Artists Agency, 9830 Wilshire Blvd, Beverly Hills, CA 90212 USA

Elling, Kurt *Music Group*
Open Door Mgmt, 15327 Sunset Blvd #365, Pacific Palisades, CA 90272 USA

Ellingsen, Bruce *Baseball Player*
Cleveland Indians, 5873 Daneland St, Lakewood, CA 90713 1830 USA

Elliot, Larry *Baseball Player*
Pittsburgh Pirates, 13010 Caminito Bracho, San Diego, CA 92128 1808 USA

Elliot, Ross
5702 Graves Ave., Encino, CA 91316

Elliot, Stephan
Box 452, Paddington, AUSTRALIA, NSW 2021

Elliott, Alecia *Actor, Music Group*
PO Box 3075, Muscle Shoals, AL 35662 USA

Elliott, Alison *Actor*
2 Ironsides #18, Marina del Rey, CA 90292 USA

Elliott, Allison
1505 10th St., Santa Monica, CA 90401

Elliott, Bill
3323 Dillard Rd., Blairsvllle, GA 30512

Elliott, Brennan *Actor*
Sanders/Armstrong Management, 2120 Colorado Blvd #120, Santa Monica, CA 90404 USA

Elliott, Chalmers (Bump) *Football Coach, Football Player*
University of Iowa, Athletic Dept, Iowa City, IA 52242 USA

Elliott, Chris *Actor, Comedian*
Hofflund/Polone, 9465 Wilshire Blvd #820, Beverly Hills, CA 90212 USA

Elliott, David James *Actor*
United Talent Agency, 9560 Wilshire Blvd #500, Beverly Hills, CA 90212 USA

Elliott, Dennis *Music Group*
Hard to Handle Mgmt, 16501 Ventura Blvd #602, Encino, CA 91436 USA

Elliott, Donnie *Baseball Player*
San Diego Padres, 1206 Bayou Vista Dr, Deer Park, TX 77536 6902 USA

Elliott, Gordon *Chef*
Food Network, 1180 Ave of Americas #1200, New York, NY 10036 USA

Elliott, Harry *Baseball Player*
St Louis Cardinals, 1154 Random Rd, El Cajon, CA 92020 7743 USA

Elliott, Herbert (Herb) *Track Athlete*
Athletics Australia, 431 St Kilda Rd, #22, Melbourne, VIC, 3004, AUSTRALIA

Elliott, Jack *Songwriter, Music Group*
Day, 300 W 55th St, New York, NY 10019 USA

Elliott, Joe *Music Group*
Q Prime Inc, 729 7th Ave #1400, New York, NY 10019 USA

Elliott, John *Football Player*
P O Box 340, Warren, TX 77664 USA

Elliott, John (Jumbo) *Football Player*
New York Jets, 1000 Fulton Ave, Hempstead, NY 11550 USA

Elliott, Michael *Misc*
45 Larkfield, Ewhurst Cranleigh, Surrey, GU6 7QU, UNITED KINGDOM (UK)

Elliott, Missy *Musician*
Violator Music & Management, 36 West 25th Street, New York, NY 10010 USA

Elliott, Missy Misdemeanor *Songwriter, Music Group*
Violator Mgmt, 205 Lexington Ave #500, New York, NY 10016 USA

Elliott, Osborn *Journalist*
31 E 72nd St #6B, New York, NY 10021 USA

Elliott, Paul H *Cinematographer*
Sandra Marsh Mgmt, 9150 Wilshire Blvd #220, Beverly Hills, CA 90212 USA

Elliott, Peggy Gordon *Educator*
929 Harvey Dunn St, Brookings, SD 57006 USA

Elliott, Pete3
003 Dunbarton Ave. NW, Canton, OH 44708-1818

Elliott, Peter R (Pete) *Football Coach, Football Player*
3003 Dunbarton Ave NW, Canton, OH 44708 USA

Elliott, R Keith *Business Person*
Hercules Inc, Hercules Plaza 1313 N Market St, Wilmington, DE 19894 USA

Elliott, Ralph E *War Hero*
5150 Damascus Road S, Jacksonville, FL 32207 USA

Elliott, Randy *Baseball Player*
San Diego Padres, PO Box 834, Somis, CA 93066 0834 USA

Elliott, Sam *Actor*
33050 Pacific Coast Highway, Malibu, CA 90265 USA

Elliott, Sean
PO Box 530, San Antonio, TX 78292

Elliott, Sean M *Basketball Player*
San Antonio Spurs, Alamodome 1 SBC Center, San Antonio, TX 78219 USA

Elliott, Stephen
3948 Woodfield Dr., Sherman Oaks, CA 91403

Elliott, Stephen *Director*
PO Box 452, Paddington, NSW, 2021, UNITED KINGDOM (UK)

Elliott, Ted *Writer*
Creative Artists Agency LCC (CAA-LA), 9830 Wilshire Blvd, Beverly Hills, CA 90212 USA

Elliott, William C (Wild Bill) *Race Car Driver*
P O Box 665, Dawsonville, GA 30534 USA

Ellis, Albert *Doctor*
Institute of Rational-Emotional Therapy, 45 E 65th St, New York, NY 10021 USA

Ellis, Alton *Musician*
27 McConnell House, Deeley Road, London, SW8, UNITED KINGDOM (UK)

Ellis, Anita
130 East End Ave., New York, NY 10021

Ellis, Aunjanue *Actor*
Creative Artists Agency, 9830 Wilshire Blvd, Beverly Hills, CA 90212 USA

Ellis, Bret Easton *Writer*
International Creative Mgmt, 40 W 57th St #1800, New York, NY 10019 USA

Ellis, Caroline *Actor*
8060 Saint Clair Ave, North Hollywood, CA 91605 USA

Ellis, Chris
Bauman Redanty & Shaul Agency, 5757 Wilshire Blvd #473, Los Angeles, CA 90036 USA

Ellis, Clarence J Jr *Football Player*
3140 Robinwood Trail, Decatur, GA 30034 USA

Ellis, Cliff *Coach, Basketball Player*
Auburn University, Athletic Dept, Auburn, AL 36831 USA

Ellis, Dale *Basketball Player*
18110 SE 41st Place, Bellevue, WA 98008 USA

Ellis, Dock P *Baseball Player*
Pittsburgh Pirates, 13274 Desert Vista Dr, Victorville, CA 92392 6801 USA

Ellis, Don *Bowler*
34 Crestwood Circle, Suger Land, TX 77478 USA

Ellis, Elmer *Historian*
3300 New Haven Ave #223, Columbia, MO 65201 USA

Ellis, James R *General*
4213 Swann Ave, Tampa, FL 33609 USA

Ellis, Janet *Actor*
Arlington Entertainments, 1/3 Charlotte St, London, W1P 1HD, UNITED KINGDOM (UK)

Ellis, Jim *Baseball Player*
Chicago Cubs, 13608 Avenue 224, Tulare, CA 93274 9304 USA

Ellis, Jimmy *Boxer*
5218 St Gabriel Lane, Louisville, KY 40291 USA

Ellis, Joseph J *Writer*
Mount Holyoke College, History Dept, South Hadley, MA 01075 USA

Ellis, Kathleen (Kathy) *Swimmer*
3024 Woodshor Court, Carmel, IN 46033 USA

Ellis, LaPhonso *Basketball Player*
7041 Old Cutler Road, Coral Gables, FL 33143 USA

Ellis, Larry R *General*
Deputy Chief of Staff Operations/Plans HqUSA Pentagon, Washington, DC 20310 USA

Ellis, Leroy *Basketball Player, Coach*
4633 Marine Ave #239, Lawndale, CA 90260 USA

Ellis, Luther *Football Player*
527 Riverside Ave, Mancos, CO 81328 USA

Ellis, M Herbert (Herb) *Music Group*
Producers Inc, 11806 N 56th St, Tampa, FL 33617 USA

Ellis, Mark *Baseball Player*
Oakland A's, 318 Kinney Ave, Rapid City, SD 57702 2332 USA

Ellis, Mary
54 Eaton Square, London, ENGLAND, SW1 W9BE

Ellis, Maurice (Bo) *Basketball Player*
516 N 14th St

Ellis, Maurice (Bo) *Basketball Player*
516 N 14th St, Milwaukee, WI 53233 USA

Ellis, Osian G *Misc*
90 Chandos Ave, London, N20 9DZ, UNITED KINGDOM (UK)

Ellis, Patrick (H J) *Educator*
Catholic University, President's Office, Washington, DC 20064 USA

Ellis, Rob *Baseball Player*
Milwaukee Brewers, 2020 Krislin Dr NE, Grand Rapids, MI 49505 7160 USA

Ellis, Robert *Baseball Player*
California Angels, 2066 75th Ave, Baton Rouge, LA 70807 5836 USA

Ellis, Romallis *Boxer*
2062 San Marco Dr, Ellenwood, GA 30294 USA

Ellis, Ronald J E (Ron) *Hockey Player*
B C E Place, 30 Yonge St, Toronto, ON M5E 1X8, CANADA

Ellis, Sammy *Baseball Player*
Cincinnati Reds, 12511 Forest Highlands Dr, Dade City, FL 33525 8273 USA

Ellis, Samuel J (Sam) *Baseball Player*
12511 Forest Highlands Dr, Dade City, FL 33525 USA

Ellis, Scott *Director*
420 Central Park West #5B, New York, NY 10025 USA

Ellis, Shuan *Football Player*
New York Jets, 1000 Fulton Ave, Hempstead, NY 11550 USA

Ellis, Terry *Music Group*
East West Records, 75 Rockefeller Plaza #1200, New York, NY 10019 USA

Ellis Brothers, PO Box 50221
Nashville, TN CA 37203

Ellison, Harlan
PO Box 55548, Sherman Oaks, CA 91423-0548

Ellison, Harlan J *Writer*
Kilimajaro Group, P O Box 55548, Sherman Oaks, CA 91413 USA

Ellison, Jennifer *Actor*
Brookside, Noumber 10 Brookside Close, Manor Park, Liverpool, England

Ellison, Lawrence J *Business Person*
Oracle Systems, 500 Oracle Parkway, Redwood City, CA 94065 USA

Ellison, Pervis *Basketball Player*
36 Bishop Terrace, Waltham, m

Ellison, Pervis *Basketball Player*
36 Bishop Terrace, Waltham, MA 02452 USA

Ellison, William H (Willie) *Football Player*
3503 Mosley Court, Houston, TX 77004 USA

Elliss, Luther *Football Player*
2521 Plum Creek Court, Oakland, MI 48363 USA

Ellroy, James *Writer*
Sobel Weber Assoc, 146 E 19th St, New York, NY 10003 USA

Ellsberg, Daniel *Politician*
90 Norwood Ave, Kensington, CA 94707 USA

Ellsworth, Frank L *Educator*
254 La Mirada Road, Pasadena, CA 91105 USA

Ellsworth, Richard C (Dick) *Baseball Player*
Chicago Cubs, 1099 W Morris Ave, Fresno, CA 93711 2432 USA

Ellsworth, Steve *Baseball Player*
Boston Red Sox, 546 W Enterprise Ave, Clovis, CA 93611 8356 USA

Ellwood, Paul M Jr *Physicist*
Jackson Hole Group, P O Box 270, Bondurant, WY 82922 USA

Elman, Jamie *Actor*
Kohner Agency, The, 9300 Wilshire Blvd #555, Beverly Hills, CA 90212 USA

Elmes, Fredrick *Cinematographer*
Mirisch Agency, 1801 Century Park E #1801, Los Angeles, CA 90067 USA

Elmore, Len *Basketball Player*
7118 Deer Valley Road, Highland, MD 20777 USA

Elrod, Jack *Cartoonist*
7240 Hunter's Branch Dr NE, Atlanta, GA 30328 USA

Els, Ernie *Golfer*
46 Chapman Rd, Klippoortjie, 1401, SOUTH AFRICA

Elsna, Hebe *Writer*
Curtis Brown, 162/168 Regent St, London, W1R 5TB, UNITED KINGDOM (UK)

Elsner, Hannelore
ZBF Leopoldstr. 19, Munich, GERMANY, D-80802

Elson, Andrea
9255 Sunset Blvd. #515, Los Angeles, CA 90069

Elson, Karen *Model*
Ford Models Agence, 9 Rue Scribe, Paris, 75009, FRANCE

Elster, Kevin D *Baseball Player*
New York Mets, 2076 Jupiter Hills Ln, Henderson, NV 89012 3283 USA

Elsworth, Michael *Actor*
Sharon Power, PO Box 1243, Wellington, NEW ZEALAND

Elswrit, Richard (Rik) *Music Group*
Artists Int'l Mgmt, 9850 Sandalwood Blvd #458, Boca Raton, FL 33428 USA

Elton, Ben *Actor, Comedian*
Phil McIntyre Mgmt, 35 Soho Square, London, W1V 5DG, UNITED KINGDOM (UK)

Elvin, Violetta *Ballerina*
Marina di Equa, 80066 Seiano, Bay of Naples, ITALY

Elvira (Cassandra Peterson) *Actor*
Queen B Productions, P O Box 38246,
Los Angeles, CA 90038 USA

Elway, John A *Football Player*
10531 E Arapahoe Road, Centennial, CO
80112 USA

Elwes, Cary *Actor*
Evolution Entertainment, 901 N Highland
Ave, Los Angeles, CA 90038 USA

Ely, Alexandre *Soccer Player*
5526 N 2nd St, Philadelphia, PA 19120
USA

Ely, Jack *Music Group*
Jeff Hubbard Productions, P O Box 53664,
Indianapolis, IN 46253 USA

Ely, Joe *Songwriter, Music Group*
Fitzgerald-Hartley, 34 N Palm St #100,
Ventura, CA 93001 USA

Ely, Melvin *Basketball Player*
Los Angeles Clippers, Staples Center 1111
S Figueroa St, Los Angeles, CA 90015
USA

Eman, J H A (Henny) *Prime Minister*
Prime Minister's Office, Oranjestad,
ARUBA

Emanuel, Alphonsia *Actor*
Marina Martin, 12/13 Poland St, London,
W1V 2DE, UNITED KINGDOM (UK)

Emanuel, Elizabeth F *Fashion Designer*
42A Warrington Crescent, Maida Vale,
London, W9 1EP, UNITED KINGDOM
(UK)

Emanuel, Frank *Football Player*
16614 E Course Dr, Tampa, FL 33624
USA

Emanuel, Rahm *Journalist, Government
Official*
Whit House, 1600 Pennsylvania Ave NW,
Washington, DC 20500 USA

Embach, Carsten *Athlete*
BSR Rennsteig e V, Grafenrodaer Str 2,
Oberhof, 98559, GERMANY

Emberg, Kelly *Actor, Model*
2835 McConnell Dr, Los Angeles, CA
90064 USA

Embery, Joan
. San Diego Zoo, Park Blvd, San Diego,
92104

Embree, Alan *Baseball Player*
Cleveland Indians, 15203 SE Northshore
Dr, Vancouver, WA 98683 5315 USA

Embry, Ethan *Actor*
William Morris Agency (WMA-LA), 1
William Morris Pl, Beverly Hills, CA
90212 USA

Embry, Wayne *Basketball Player, Misc*
130 W Juniper Lane, Moreland Hills, OH
44022 USA

Emburey, John E *Cricketer*
Northantshire Cricket Club, Wantage
Road, Northampton, NN1 4TJ, UNITED
KINGDOM (UK)

Emerson, Alice F *Educator*
Andrew Mellon Fondation, 140 E 62nd St,
New York, NY 10021 USA

Emerson, David F *Admiral*
1777 Chelwood Circle, Charleston, SC
29407 USA

Emerson, Douglas *Actor*
1450 Belfast Dr, Los Angeles, CA 90069
USA

Emerson, George H *Educator*
Utah State University, President's Office,
Logan, UT 84322 USA

Emerson, J Martin *Misc*
American Federation of Musicians, 1501
Broadway, New York, NY 10036 USA

Emerson, Keith *Musician*
Columbia Artists Mgmt Inc, 165 W 57th
St, New York, NY 10019 USA

Emerson, Roy
2221 Alta Vista Dr., Newport Beach, CA
92660-4l28

Emerson, Roy *Tennis Player*
Private Bag 6060, Richmond South, VIC,
3121, AUSTRALIA

Emerson Drive *Music Group*
Creative Artists Agency (CAA-Nashville),
3310 West End Ave Fl 5, Nashville, TN
37203 USA

Emery, Cal *Baseball Player*
Philadelphia Phillies, 1623 E Omaha St
Apt A6, Broken Arrow, OK 74012 0332
USA

Emery, John *Athlete*
2001 Union St, San Fransisco, CA 94123
USA

Emery, Julie Ann *Actor*
Principal Entertainment (LA), 1964
Westwood Blvd #400, Los Angeles, CA
90025 USA

Emery, Kenneth O *Oceanographer*
35 Horseshoe Lane, North Falmouth, MA
02556 USA

Emery, Lin *Artist, Misc*
7820 Dominican St, New Orleans, LA
70118 USA

Emery, Oren D *Religious Leader*
Wesleyan International, 6060 Castelway
West Dr, Indianapolis, IN 46250 USA

Emery, Ralph *Entertainer*
P O Box 23470, Nashville, TN 37202
USA

Emery, Victor *Athlete*
61 Walton St, London, SW 3J, UNITED
KINGDOM (UK)

Emick, Jarrod *Actor*
Gersh Agency, 232 N Canon Dr, Beverly
Hills, CA 90210 USA

Emilio *Music Group*
Refugee Mgmt, 209 10th Ave S #347
Cummins Station, Nashville, TN 37203
USA

Eminem *Musician*
United Talent Agency (UTA), 9560
Wilshire Blvd, Beverly Hills, CA 90212
USA

Emir of Bahrain
721 Fifth Ave.60th Flr., New York, NY
10022

Emir of Kuwait
Banyan Palace, Kuwait City, KUWAIT

Emmanuel *Musician*
Sendyk Leonard, 532 Colorado Ave, Santa
Monica, CA 90401 USA

Emme *Model*
Ford Model Agency, 142 Greene St #400,
New York, NY 10012 USA

Emmerich, Noah *Actor*
William Morris Agency, 151 El Camino
Dr, Beverly Hills, CA 90212 USA

Emmerich, Roland *Director, Producer*
Centropolis Entertainment, 1445 N Stanley
Fl 3, Los Angeles, CA 90046 USA

Emmerson, Roy
Private Bag 6060, Richmond South,
AUSTRALIA, Vic. 3121

Emmert, Mark *Educator*
Louisiana State University, President's
Office, Baton Rouge, LA 70803 USA

Emmerton, Bill *Track Athlete*
615 Ocean Ave, Santa Monica, CA 90402
USA

Emmett, John C *Inventor*
Oak House Hatfield Broad Oak, Bishop's
Stortford, Herts, CM22 7HG, UNITED
KINGDOM (UK)

Emmons, Howard W *Engineer*
1010 Waltham St #443B, Lexington, MA
02421 USA

Emmott, Bill *Editor*
Economist Magazine, 25 Saint James's St,
London, SW1A 1HG, UNITED KINGDOM
(UK)

Emory, Sonny *Music Group, Misc*
Great Scott Productions, 137 N Wetherly
Dr #403, Los Angeles, CA 90048 USA

Emtman, Steven C (Steve) *Football Player*
19601 S Cheney Spangle Road, Cheney,
WA 99004 USA

En Blanco Y Negro *Music Group*
Sony Music Miami, 605 Lincoln Rd,
Miami Beach, FL 33138 USA

En Vogue *Music Group*
International Creative Management
(ICM-LA), 8942 Wilshire Blvd, Beverly
Hills, CA 90211 USA

Enberg, Alexander *Actor*
TalentWorks (LA), 3500 W Olive Ave
#1400, Burbank, CA 91505 USA

Enberg, Dick *Sportscaster*
1275 Virginia Way, La Jolla, CA 92037
USA

Enbom, John *Writer*
Creative Artists Agency LCC (CAA-LA),
9830 Wilshire Blvd, Beverly Hills, CA
90212 USA

Endelman, Stephen *Composer*
Gorfaine/Schwartz, 13245 Riverside Dr
#450, Sherman Oaks, CA 91423 USA

Ender, Grummt Kornelia *Swimmer*
DSV, Postfach 420140, Kassel, 34070,
GERMANY

Enders, Trevor *Baseball Player*
Tampa Bay Devil Rays, 930 1/2 32nd Ave
N, Saint Petersburg, FL 33704 2047 USA

Endicott, Bill *Baseball Player*
St Louis Cardinals, 14219 Oak Knoll Rd,
Sonora, CA 95370 8822 USA

Enevoldsen, Einar *Astronaut, Misc*
9651 Lewis Ave, California City, CA
93505 USA

Engel, Albert E *Geophysicist*
University of California, Scripps Institute
Geology Dept, La Jolla, CA 92093 USA

Engel, Albert J *Judge*
US Court of Appeals, 110 Michigan Ave
NW, Grand Rapids, MI 94503 USA

Engel, Georgia *Actor*
10820 Camanlio St #3, Nort Hollywood,
CA 91602 USA

Engel, Steve *Baseball Player*
Chicago Cubs, 317 Walnut St, Cincinnati,
OH 45215 3152 USA

Engel, Susan
43A Princess Rd. Regents Park, London,
ENGLAND, NW1 8JS

Engelbart, Douglas C *Scientist*
89 Catalpa Dr, Menlo Park, CA 94027
USA

Engelberger, Joseph F *Engineer*
Transition Research Corp, 15 Durant Ave,
Bethel, CT 06801 USA

Engelbrecht, Constanze
17 pass. du Montenegro, Paris, FRANCE,
F-75019

Engelhard, David H *Religious Leader*
Cristian Reformed Church, 2850
Kalamazoo Ave SE, Grand Rapids, MI
49560 USA

Engelhardt, Thomas A (Tom) *Editor,
Cartoonist*
Saint Louis Post-Dispatch, Editorial Dept
900 N Tucker, Saint Louis, MO 63101
USA

Engen, Corey *Skier*
506 N 40, Lindon, UT 84042 USA

Engen, D Travis *Business Person*
ITT Industries, 4 W Red Oak Lane, White
Plains, NY 10604 USA

Engerman, Stanley L *Economist, Historian*
181 Warrington Dr, Rochestor, NY 14618
USA

Engholm, Bjorn *Government Official*
Jurgen-Wallenwever-Str 9, Lubeck,
GERMANY

Engibous, Thomas J *Business Person*
Texas Instruments, 8505 Forest Lane P O
Box 660199, Dallas, TX 75266 USA

England, Anthony *Astronaut, Geophysicist*
7949 Ridgeway Court, Dexter, MI, 48130
USA

England, Audie
6100 Wilshire Blvd. #1170, Los Angeles,
CA 90048

England, Dan
PO Box 82, Great Neck, NY 10021

England, Gordon R *Secretary*
Homeland Security Department,
Washington, DC 20528 USA

England, Richard *Architect*
26/1 Merchants St, Valletta, MALTA

England, Ty
3322 West End Ave. #520, Nashville, TN
37213

England, Tyler *Music Group*
Buddy Lee, 38 Music Square E #300,
Nashville, TN 37203 USA

Englander, Herold R *Doctor, Scientist*
11502 Wisper Bluff St, San Antonio, TX
78230 USA

Engle, Dave *Baseball Player*
Minnesota Twins, 5343 Castle Hills Dr,
San Diego, CA 92109 1926 USA

Engle, Doug *Baseball Player*
Montreal Expos, 17282 Helser Rd, Berlin
Center, OH 44401 9784 USA

Engle, Joe *Astronaut, General*
3280 Cedar Heights Dr, Colorado Springs,
CO 80904 USA

Engle, Robert F *Nobel Prize Laureate*
New York University, Stem Business
School, New York, NY 10012 USA

Englehart, Robert W (Bob) Jr *Editor,
Cartoonist*
Hartford Courant, Editorial Dept 280
Broad St, Hartford, CT 06105 USA

Engler, John M *Governor*
PO Box 30013, Lansing, MI 48909-0013
USA

English, Alexander (Alex) *Basketball
Player*
596 Rimer Pond Road, Blythewood, SC
29016 USA

English, Diane *Writer*
Shukovsky-English Ent, 4024 Radford Ave,
Studio City, CA 91604 USA

English, Edmond J *Business Person*
TJX Companies, 770 Cochituate Road,
Framingham, MA 01701 USA

English, Floyd L *Business Person*
Andrew Corp, 10500 W 153rd St, Orland
Park, IL 60462 USA

English, James F Jr *Educator*
31 Potter St, Groton, CT 06340 USA

English, Joseph T *Doctor*
Saint Vincent's Hospital, 203

English, Joseph T *Doctor*
Saint Vincent's Hospital, 203 W 12th St,
New York, NY 10011 USA

English, L Douglas (Doug) *Football Player*
4306 Benedict Lane, Austin, TX 78746
USA

English, Michael *Music Group*
Trifecta Entertainment, 209 10th Ave S
#302, Nashville, TN 37203 USA

English, Paul *Actor*
Wurzel Talent Mgmt, 19528 Ventura Blvd
#501, Tarzana, CA 91356 USA

English, Ralna
PO Box 14522, Scottsdale, AZ 86267-
4522

Engluand, Robert *Actor*
1616 Santa Cruz St, Laguna Beach, CA
92651 USA

Englund, Robert
1278 Glenneyre PMB 73, Laguna Beach,
CA 92651

Engstrom, Ted W *Misc*
World Vision, 919 W Huntington Dr,
Arcadia, CA 91007 USA

Engvall, Bill *Actor, Comedian*
Four Points Entertainment, 8380 Melrose
Ave, #310, Los Angeles, CA 90069 USA

Enis, Curtis *Football Player*
305 SE Deerfield Road, Union City, OH
45390 USA

Enke, Werner
Moltkestr. 6, Munich, GERMANY,
D-80803

Enke-Kania, Karin *Skier*
Tolstoistr 3, Dresden, 01326, GERMANY

Enkhbayar, Nambaryn *Prime Minister*
Prime Minister's Office, Great Hural, Ulan
Bator, 12, MONGOLIA

Enn, Hans *Skier*
Hinterglemm 400, Saalbach, 5754,
AUSTRIA

Ennis, Ralph *Musician*
2 Kirklake Bank, Formby, Liverpool, L37
2Y5, UNITED KINGDOM (UK)

Ennis, Ray *Musician*
2 Kirklake Bank, Formby, Liverpool, L37
2Y5, UNITED KINGDOM (UK)

Ennis Sisters, The *Musician*
Herschel Freeman Agency, 7684 Apahon
Lane, Germantown, TN 38138

Eno, Brian *Actor*
Creative Artists Agency LCC (CAA-LA),
9830 Wilshire Blvd, Beverly Hills, CA
90212 USA

Eno, Brian *Composer, Musician*
Opal Music, 3 Pembridge Mews, London,
W11 3Eq, UNITED KINGDOM (UK)

Enoch, Russell
43A Princess Rd. Regents Park, London,
ENGLAND, NW1 8JS

Enos, John *Actor*
Lara Rosenstock Management, 8371
Blackburn Ave #1, Los Angeles, CA 90048
USA

Enrico, Roger A *Business Person*
Pepsi Co Inc, 700 Anderson Hill Road,
Purchase, NY 10577 USA

Enright, George *Baseball Player*
Montreal Expos, 3075 Strawflower Way,
Lake Worth, FL 33467 1465 USA

Enrique, Luis
1350 Avenue of the Americas, New York,
NY 10019

Enriquez, Jocelyn
1135 Francisco St. #7, San Francisco, CA
94109

Enriquez, Joy *Musician*
William Morris Agency (WMA-LA), 1
William Morris Pl, Beverly Hills, CA
90212 USA

Ensberg, Morgan *Baseball Player*
Houston Astros, 1132 3rd St, Hermosa
Beach, CA 90254 4901 USA

Ensher, Jason R *Physicist*
University of Colorado, Physics Dept,
Boulder, CO 80309 USA

Ensign, Michael *Actor*
Abrams Artists, 9200 Sunset Blvd, #1125,
Los Angeles, CA 90069 USA

Ensler, Eve *Actor*
Creative Artists Agency LCC (CAA-LA),
9830 Wilshire Blvd, Beverly Hills, CA
90212 USA

Entner, Warren *Music Group*
Thomas Cassidy, 11761 E Speedway Blvd,
Tucson, AZ 85748 USA

Entremont, Philippe
Schwarzenbergplatz 10/7, Vienna,
AUSTRIA, A-1040

Entremont, Philippe *Musician*
10 Rue de Castuglione, Paris, 75001,
FRANCE

Entwhistle, John
PO Box 241, Lake Peekskill, NY 10537

Enya *Musician, Composer*
Ayesha Castle, County Dublin, IRELAND

Enyart, Terry *Baseball Player*
Montreal Expos, 3444 Foxwood Blvd,
Zephyhills, FL 33543 5155 USA

Enzensberger, Hans M *Writer*
Lindenstr 29, Frankfurt am Maim, 60325,
GERMANY

Eotvos, Peter *Composer*
Naardeweg 56, Blaircum, 1261 BV,
NETHERLANDS

Ephriam, Mablean *Judge*
Endeavor Agency LLC (LA), 9601 Wilshire
Blvd Fl 3, Beverly Hills, CA 90210 USA

Ephron, Nora *Writer, Producer, Director*
390 W End Ave, New York, NY 10024
USA

Epic *Artist, Musician*
Wyze Mgmt, 34 Maple St, London, W1
5GD, UNITED KINGDOM (UK)

Eppard, Jim *Baseball Player*
California Angels, 23115 153rd Ave,
Rapid City, SD 57703 9041 USA

Epperson-Doumani, Brenda *Actor*
kazarian/Spencer, 11365 Ventura Blvd,
#100, Studio City, CA 91604 USA

Eppinger, Dale L *War Hero*
101 Windy Hollow St, Victoria, TX 77904
USA

Epple, Maria *Skier*
Gunzesried 3, Blaicach, 87544,
GERMANY

Epple-Beck, Irene *Skier*
Autmberg 235, Seeg, 87637, GERMANY

Eppler, Dieter
Franziskaweg 17, Stuttgart, GERMANY,
D-70599

Epps, Hal *Baseball Player*
St Louis Cardinals, 4500 Cypresswood Dr
Apt 406, Spring, TX 77379 8359 USA

Epps, Mike *Actor*
MBST Entertainment, 345 N Maple D
#200, Suite 200, Beverly Hills, CA 90210
USA

Epps, Omar *Actor*
Endeavor Talent Agency, 9701 Wilshire
Blvd, #1000, Beverly Hills, CA 90212
USA

Epstein, Daniel M *Writer*
843 W University Parkway, Baltimore,
MD 21210 USA

Epstein, David *Conductor*
Thea Dispeker Artists, 59 E 54th St, New
York, NY 10022 USA

Epstein, Gabriel *Architect*
3 Rue Mazet, Paris, 75006, FRANCE

Epstein, Jason *Editor*
Random House, 1745 Broadway, #B1,
New York, NY 10019 USA

Epstein, Joseph *Writer, Educator*
522 Church St, #6B, Evanston, IL 60201
USA

Epstein, Mike *Baseball Player*
Baltimore Orioles, 5335 S Valentia Way
Apt 457, Greenwood Village, CO 80111
3129 USA

Erardi, Greg *Baseball Player*
Seattle Mariners, 42 Westgate Rd,
Massapequa Park, NY 11762 1953 USA

Erautt, Eddie *Baseball Player*
Cincinnati Reds, 7252 Walte Dr, La Mesa,
CA 91941 7631 USA

Erb, Donald J *Composer*
2073 Bluestone Road, Cleveland, OH
44121 USA

Erb, Fred *Songwriter*
International Creative Mgmt, 8942
Wilshire Blvd #219, Beverly Hills, CA
90211 USA

Erb, Richard D *Government Official*
International Monetary Fund, 700 19th St
NW, Washington, DC 20431 USA

Erbakan, Necmettin *Prime Minister*
National Salvation Party, Balgat, Ankara,
TURKEY

Erbe, Kathryn *Actor*
LMR, 1964 Westwood Blvd, #400, Los
Angeles, CA 90025 USA

Erburu, Robert F *Business Person,*
Publisher
1518 Blue Jay Way, Los Angeles, CA
90069 USA

Erdman, Dennis *Actor, Director, Producer*
International Creative Management
(ICM-LA), 8942 Wilshire Blvd, Beverly
Hills, CA 90211 USA

Erdman, Paul E *Writer*
1817 Lytton Springs Road, Healdsburg,
CA 95448 USA

Erdman, Richard *Actor*
5655 Greenbush Ave, Van Nuys, CA
91401 USA

Erdmann, Susi-Lisa *Athlete*
Karwendelstr 8A, Munich, 81369,
GERMANY

Erdo, Peter Cardinal *Religious Leader*
Mindszenty Hercegprimas Ter 2,
Esztergom Magyarirszay, 2501,
HUNGARY

Erdogan, Recep Tayyip *Prime Minister*
Premier's Office, Eski Basbakanlik,
Bakanliklar, Ankara, TURKEY

Erdos, Todd *Baseball Player*
San Diego Padres, 118 Windsor Ct,
Cranberry Twp, PA 16066 3216 USA

Erdrich, K Louise *Writer*
Rambar & Curtis, 19 W 44th St, New
York, NY 10036 USA

Ergen, Charles W *Business Person*
EchoStar Communications Corp, 5701 S
Santa Fe Dr, Littleton, CO 80120 USA

Erhardt, Warren R *Publisher*
455 Wakefield Dr, Metuchen, NJ 08840
USA

Erhuero, Oris *Actor*
Midwest Talent Management Inc, 4821
Lankershim Blvd #F, PMB 149, N
Hollywood, CA 91601

Eric, B *Music Group, Musician*
Rush Artists, 1600 Varick St, New York,
NY 10013 USA

Eric B *Artist, Musician*
Richard Walters, 1800 Argyle Ave #408,
Los Angeles, CA 90028 USA

Eric Kaplan, Bruce *Producer*
William Morris Agency (WMA-LA), 1
William Morris Pl, Beverly Hills, CA
90212 USA

Ericks, John *Baseball Player*
Philadelphia Phillies, 17000 Oketo Ave,
Tinley Park, IL 60477 2630 USA

Erickson, Arthur C *Architect*
Arthur Erickson Architects, 1672 W 1st
Ave, Vancouver, BC V6J 1G1, CANADA

Erickson, Craig *Football Player*
420 N Country Club Dr, Lake Worth, FL
33462 USA

Erickson, Dennis *Football Coach*
San Francisco 49ers, 4949 Centennial
Blvd, Santa Clara, CA 95054 USA

Erickson, Don *Baseball Player*
Philadelphia Phillies, 1929 Montana Dr,
Springfield, IL 62704 4150, USA|

Erickson, Don *Baseball Player*
Philadelphia Phillies, 1929 Montana Dr,
Springfield, IL 62704 4150 USA

Erickson, Ethan *Actor*
Diverse Talent Group, 1875 Century Park
E #2250, Los Angeles, CA 90067 USA

Erickson, Hal *Baseball Player*
Detroit Tigers, 4000 Brinker Ave Apt 10,
Ogden, UT 84403 2452 USA

Erickson, keith *Basketball Player,*
Volleyball Player
333 23rd St, Santa Monica, CA 90402
USA

Erickson, Robert *Composer*
University of California, Music Dept, La
Jolla, Ca, 92093 USA

Erickson, Roger *Baseball Player*
Minnesota Twins, 2647 Delaware Dr,
Springfield, IL 62702 1213 USA

Erickson, Scott *Actor*
501 Chicago Avenue South, Minneapolis,
MN 55415 USA

Erickson, Scott G *Baseball Player*
Minnesota Twins, PO Box 2790, Stateline,
NV 89449 2790 USA

Erickson, Steve *Writer*
Poseidon Press, 1230 Ave of Americas,
New York, NY 10020 USA

Ericson, John *Actor*
7 Avenida Vista Grande, #310, Santa Fe,
NM 87508 USA

Eriksen, Stein *Skier*
7700 Stein Way, Park City, UT 84060
USA

Erikson, Duke *Misc*
Borman Entertainment, 1250 6th St, #401,
Santa Monica, CA 90401 USA

Erikson, Raymond L *Doctor*
Harvard University, Medical School, 25
Shattuck St, Boston, MA 02115 USA

Erixon, Jan *Hockey Player*
PO Box 90111, Arlington, TX 76004 USA

Erlandson, Eric *Songwriter*
Artist Group International, 9560 Wilshire
Blvd, #400, Beverly Hills, CA 90212 USA

Erman, John *Director*
Creative Artists Agency, 9830 Wilshire
Blvd, #400, Beverly Hills, CA 90212 USA

Ermer, Cal *Baseball Player*
Washington Senators, 1009 Panorama Dr,
Chattanooga, TN 37421 4028 USA

Ermey, R Lee *Actor*
4348 W Ave N3, Palmdale, CA 93551
USA

Ermy, R Lee
4348 W Avenue N3, Palmdale, CA 9355l
USA

Ernaga, Frank *Baseball Player*
Chicago Cubs, 50 N Roop St, Susanville,
CA 96130 3926 USA

Erni, Hans *Artist*
6045 Meggen, Lucerne, SWITZERLAND

Ernst, Bret *Actor, Comedian*
Joan Green Management, 1836 Courtney
Terr, Los Angeles, CA 90046 USA

Ernst, Mark A *Business Person*
H & R Block Inc, 4400 Main St, Kansas
City, MO 64111 USA

Ernst, Richard R *Nobel Prize Laureate*
Kurlistr 24, Winterthur, SWITZERLAND

Eroy, Iran *Actor*
Televisa, Blvd Adolfo Lopez Mateos 232,
Colonia San Angel INN, DF, CP 01060,
MEXICO

Errazuriz Ossa, Francisco J Cardinal
Religious Leader
Casilla 30D, Erasmo Escala 1894,
Santiago, CHILE

Errico, Melissa *Actor*

Erskine, Carl D *Baseball Player*
Brooklyn Dodgera, 4031 Fallbrook Ln,
Anderson, IN 46011 1609 USA

Erskine, Peter *Musician*
1727 Hill St, Santa Monica, CA 90405
USA

Erskine, Ralph *Architect*
Box 156, Gustav III's Vag, Drottningholm,
170 11, SWEDEN

Erstad, Darin C *Baseball Player*
California Angels, 3224 35 1/2 Court Ave
SW, Fargo, ND 58104 8879 USA

Ertl, Martina *Skier*
Erthofe 17, Lenggries, 83661, GERMANY

Eruzione, Michael (Mike) *Hockey Player*
274 Bowdoin St, Winthrop, MA 02152
USA

Erving, Julius
PO Box 914100, Longwood, FL 32791

Erving, Jullus W (Dr J) *Basketball Player*
400 E Colonial Dr, #1607, Orlando, FL
32803 USA

Ervolino, Frank *Politician*
Laundry & Dry Cleaning Union, 107
Delaware Ave, Buffalo, NY 14202 USA

Erwin, Bill *Actor*
12324 Moorpark St, Studio City, CA
91604 USA

Erwin, Hank
4213rd St. NE, Leeds, AL 35094

Erwin, Mike *Actor*
Leverage Management, 1610 Broadway,
Santa Monica, CA 90404 USA

Erwitt, Elliott R *Photographer*
88 Central Park West, New York, NY
10023 USA

Erxleban, Russell A *Football Player*
144 World of Tennis Square, Lakeway, TX
78738 USA

Esaki, Leo *Nobel Prize Laureate*
2484 Uenomuro, Tsukuba Ibaraki, 305,
JAPAN

Esasky, Nick *Baseball Player*
Cincinnati Reds, 1779 Starlight Dr,
Marietta, GA 30062 1942 USA

Escalante, Jaime A *Educator*
Hiram Johnson High School, 6879 14th
Ave, Sacramento, CA 95820 USA

Eschbach, Jesse E *Judge*
US Court of Appeals, US Courthouse, 701
Clematis St, West Palm Beach, FL 33401
USA

Eschelman, Vaughn *Baseball Player*
Boston Red Sox, 30106 Falher Dr, Spring,
TX 77386 1683 USA

Eschen, Larry *Baseball Player*
Philadelphia Athletics, 3649 Garden Blvd,
Gainesville, GA 30506 1552 USA

Eschenbach, Christoph
2 Ave. d'Alena, Paris, FRANCE, 75016

Eschenbach, Christoph *Musician*
Maspalomas, Monte Leon 760625, Gran
Canaria, SPAIN

Eschenmoser, Albert J *Misc*
Bergstra 9, Kusnacht, ZH, 8700,
SWITZERLAND

Eschert, Jurgen *Athlete*
Tornowstr 8, Potsdam, 1447, GERMANY

Esiason, Norman J (Boomer) *Athlete,
Football Player*
25 Heights Road, Plandome, NY 11030
USA

Eskell, Diana
41 Bushgrove Stanmore, Middlesex,
ENGLAND, HA7 2DY

Esler-Smith, Frank *Misc*
Agency for Peroforming Arts, 9200 Sunset
Blvd, #900, Los Angeles, CA 90069 USA

Esmond, Carl *Actor*
576 N Tigertail Road, Los Angeles, CA
90049 USA

Esparza, Moctesuma *Producer*
International Creative Management
(ICM-LA), 8942 Wilshire Blvd, Beverly
Hills, CA 90211 USA

Esperian, Kallen R *Musician*
514 Lindseywood Cove, Memphis, TN
38117 USA

Esperon, Natalia *Actor*
Televisa, Blvd Adolfo Lopez Mateos 232,
Colonia San Angel INN, DF, CP 01060,
MEXICO

Espino, Gaby *Actor*
Gabriel Blanco Iglesias (Mexico), Rio
Balsas 35-32, Colonia Cuauhtemoc, DF,
06500, Mexico

Espinoza, Alvaro *Baseball Player*
Minnesota Twins, 707 SW Lake Charles
Cir, Port Saint Lucie, FL 34986 3447 USA

Espinoza, Mark *Actor*
Howard Entertainment, 10850 Wilshire
Blvd, Suite 1260, Los Angeles, CA 90024
USA

Esposito, Anthony J (Tony) *Hockey Player*
418 55th Ave, Saint Petersburg Beach, FL
33706 USA

Esposito, Frank *Bowler*
200 N State Route 17, Paramus, NJ 07652
USA

Esposito, Giancarlo *Actor*
Untitled Entertainment (LA), 8436 W 3rd
St #650, Los Angeles, CA 90048 USA

Esposito, Jennifer *Actor*
648 Broadway, #912, New York, NY
10012 USA

Esposito, Laura *Actor*
Gersh Agency, 232 N Canon Dr, Beverly
Hills, CA 90210 USA

Esposito, Phil *Hockey Player*
4807 Tea Rose Ct, Lutz, FL 33558

Esposito, Philip A (Phil) *Hockey Player*
4807 Tea Rose Court, Lutz, FL 33558 USA

Esposito, Sammy *Baseball Player*
Chicago White Sox, 7730 Astoria Pl,
Raleigh, NC 27612 7390 USA

Esposito, Tony
418 55th Ave., St. Petersburg, FL 33706-
2311

Espy, A Michael (Mike) *Secretary*
154 Deertrail Lane, Madison, MS 39110
USA

Espy, Cecil *Baseball Player*
Los Angeles Dodgers, 5480 Encino Dr,
San Diego, CA 92114 6307 USA

Esquivel, Laura *Writer*
Creative Artists Agency, 9830 Wilshire
Blvd, Beverly Hills, CA 90212 USA

Esquivel, Manuel *Prime Minister*
United Democratic Party, 19 King St, PO
Box 1143, Belize City, BELIZE

Essany, Michael *Talk Show Host*
E! Entertainment Television (NY), 1300
Broadway, New York, NY 10036 USA

Essegian, Chuck *Baseball Player*
Philadelphia Phillies, 15639 Bronco Dr,
Canyon Country, CA 91387 4717 USA

Essensa, Bob *Hockey Player*
Boston Bruins, 1 Fleet Center, Boston, MA
02114 USA

Esser, Mark *Baseball Player*
Chicago White Sox, 14 Briarwood Dr,
Poughkeepsie, NY 12601 5529 USA

Essex, David
5 Stratford Saye 20-22 Wellington,
Bournemouth Dorset, ENGLAND, BG8
8JN

Essex, Myron E *Biologist*
Harvard School of Public Health, 665
Huntington Ave, Boston, MA 02115 USA

Essian, James (Jim) *Baseball Player*
Philadelphia Phillies, 134 Eckford Dr, Troy, MI 48085 4745 USA

Esslinger, Hartmut *Designer*
FrogDesign, 1327 Chesapeake Terrace, Sunnyvale, CA 94089 USA

Essman, Susie *Comedian*
William Morris Agency (WMA-LA), 1 William Morris Pl, Beverly Hills, CA 90212 USA

Esswood, Paul L V *Opera Singer*
Jasmine Cottage, 42 Ferring Lane, West Sussex, BN12 6QT, UNITED KINGDOM (UK)

Estalelia, Bobby *Baseball Player*
Philadelphia Phillies, 1850 NW 139th Ave, Pembroke Pines, FL 33028 2839 USA

Estefan, Emilio *Musician*
Estefan Enterprises, 420 Jefferson Ave, Miami Beach, FL 33139 USA

Estefan, Gloria *Musician*
Estefan Enterprises, 420 Jefferson Ave, Miami Beach, FL 33139 USA

Estefan, Lili *Actor*
Univision, 314 Main St, Chico, CA 95928 USA

Estefan, Manuel A *Educator*
California State University, President's Office, Chico, CA 95929 USA

Estelle, Dick *Baseball Player*
San Francisco Giants, 2221 Taylor St, Point Pleasant Boro, NJ 08742 3839 USA

Esten, Charles *Actor*
Stone Manners Talent Agency, 6500 Wilshire Blvd, Ste 550, Los Angeles, CA 90048 USA

Estern, Neil *Misc*
82 Remsen St, Brooklyn, NY 89460 USA

Estes, A Shawn *Baseball Player*
San Francisco Giants, 218 Union St Apt 7, San Francisco, CA 94133 3523 USA

Estes, Billy Sol
1004 S. College, Brady, TX 76825

Estes, Bob *Golfer*
4408 Long Champ Dr, #21, Austin, TX 78746 USA

Estes, Clarissa Pinkola *Writer*
Knopf Publishers, 201 E 50th St, New York, NY 10022 USA

Estes, Ellen *Misc*
Stanford University, Athletic Dept, Stanford, CA 94305 USA

Estes, Howell M Jr *General, Business Person*
7603 Shadywood Road, Bethesda, MD 20817 USA

Estes, James *Cartoonist*
1103 Callahan St, Amarillo, TX 79106 USA

Estes, Rob *Actor*
Much and House Public Relations, 8075 West Third Street, Suite 500, Los Angeles, CA 90048

Estes, Robert *Actor*
910 Idaho Ave, Santa Monica, CA 90403 USA

Estes, Simon L *Opera Singer*
Hochstr 43, Feldmeilen, 8706, SWITZERLAND

Estes, Will *Actor*
Kelman & Arletta, 7813 Sunset Blvd, Los Angeles, CA 90046 USA

Estes, William K *Physicist*
2714 E Pine Lane, Bloomington, IN 47401 USA

Esteve-Coll, Elizabeth *Misc*
27 Ursulu St, London, SW11 3DW, UNITED KINGDOM (UK)

Estevez, Emilio *Actor, Director*
PO Box 6448, Malibu, CA 90264 USA

Estevez, Luis *Fashion Designer*
122 E 7th St, Los Angeles, CA 90014 USA

Estevez, Ramon *Actor*
837 Ocean Ave, #101, Santa Monica, CA 90402 USA

Estevez, Renee *Actor*
Michael Mann Talent, 617 S Olive St, #311, Los Angeles, CA 90014 USA

Esthero *Musician*
ArtistDirect, 10900 Wilshire Blvd #1400, Los Angeles, CA 90024 USA

Estleman, Loren Daniel *Writer*
5552 Walsh Road, Whitmore Lake, MI 48189 USA

Estock, George *Baseball Player*
595 Ray St, Sebastian, FL 32958 4245 USA

Estrada, Charle L (Chuck) *Baseball Player*
Baltimore Orioles, 1289 Manzanita Way, San Luis Obispo, CA 93401 7838 USA

Estrada, Erik *Actor*
3768 Eureka Dr, North Hollywood, CA 91604 USA

Estrada, Erik-Michael *Musician*
Trans Continental Records, 7380 Sand Lake Road, #350, Orlando, FL 32819 USA

Estrella, Alberto *Actor*
Televisa, Blvd Adolfo Lopez Mateos 232, Colonia San Angel INN, DF, CP 01060, MEXICO

Estrella, Leo *Baseball Player*
Toronto Blue Jays, 5462 NW Boydga Ave, Port St Lucie, FL 34986 4038 USA

Estrich, Susan *Attorney General*
9255 Doheny Road, #802, West Hollywood, CA 90069 USA

Estrin, Zack *Writer*
Endeavor Agency LLC (LA), 9601 Wilshire Blvd Fl 3, Beverly Hills, CA 90210 USA

Eszterhas, Joe
8942 Wilshire Blvd., Beverly Hills, CA 90211

Eszterhas, Joseph A *Writer*
Rogers & Cowan, 6340 Breckenridge Run, Rex, GA 30273 USA

Etaix, Pierre *Director, Actor*
Cirque Fratellini, 2 Rue de la Cloture, Paris, FRANCE, 75019

Etchebarren, Andy *Baseball Player*
Baltimore Orioles, 1488 Vermeer Dr, Nokomis, FL 34275 4470 USA

Etchegaray, Roger Cardinal *Religious Leader*
Piazza San Calisto, Vatican City, 00120

Etcheverry, Marco *Soccer Player*
DC United, 14120 Newbrook Dr, Chantilly, VA 20151 USA

Etcheverry, Michel *Actor*
47 Rue du Borrego, Paris, 75020, FRANCE

Etebari, Eric *Actor*
Crystal Sky/Artists Only Management, 1901 Ave of the Stars #605, Los Angeles, CA 90067 USA

Etharton, Seth *Baseball Player*
Anaheim Angels, 16 Saint John, Dana Point, CA 92629 4127 USA

Etheridge, Bobby *Baseball Player*
San Francisco Giants, 118 Portland Rd, Eudora, AR 71640 2174 USA

Etheridge, Melissa *Musician, Songwriter*
W F Leopold Mgmt, 4425 Riverside Dr, #102, Burbank, CA 91505 USA

Ethridge, Mark F III *Editor*
5516 Gorham Dr, Charlotte, NC 28226 USA

Etienne-Martin *Artist*
7 Rue du Pot de Fer, Paris, 75005, FRANCE

Etrog, Sorel *Artist*
PO Box 67034, 23 Yonge St, Toronto, ON M4P 1E0, CANADA

Etsel, Edward (Ed) *Misc*
University of Virginia, Athletic Dept, Charlottesville, VA 22906 USA

Etsou-Nzabi-Bamungwabi, Frederic *Religious Leader*
Archdiocese of Kinshasa, BP 8431, Kinshasa 1, CONGO DEMOCRATIC REPUBLIC

Ettinger, Cynthia *Actor*
Thruline Entertainment, 9250 Wilshire Blvd, Ground Floor, Beverly Hills, CA 90210 USA

Ettles, Mark *Baseball Player*
San Diego Padres, 3-10 Rose Avenue, South Perth, 6151, AUSTRALIA

Etzel, Gregory A M *War Hero*
7822 Wonder St, Citrus Heights, CA 95610 USA

Etzioni, Amitai W *Social Activist*
7110 Arran Place, Bethesda, MD 20817 USA

Etzwiler, Donnell D *Doctor*
7611 Bush Lake Dr, Minneapolis, MN 55438 USA

Eubank, Chris *Boxer*
9 Upper Dr, Hove, East Sussex, BN3 6GR, UNITED KINGDOM (UK)

Eubanks, Bob *Television Host*
3617 Roblar Ave, Santa Ynez, CA 93460 USA

Eubanks, Kevin *Musician*
Ted Kurland, 173 Brighton Ave, Boston, MA 02134 USA

Eufernia, Frank *Baseball Player*
Minnesota Twins, 10 Mariners Rd, Seaside Heights, NJ 08751 1335 USA

Eure, Wesley *Actor*
Irv Schechter, 9300 Wilshire Blvd, #410, Beverly Hills, CA 90212 USA

Europe
Box 22036, Stockholm, SWEDEN, S-10422

Eurythmics *Music Group*
William Morris Agency (WMA-LA), 1 William Morris Pl, Beverly Hills, CA 90212 USA

Eusebio, Tony *Baseball Player*
Houston Astros, 2078 Shannon Lakes Blvd, Kissimmee, FL 34743 3648 USA

Evan & Jaron
2100 Colorado Ave, Santa Monica, CA 90404

Evanescence *Music Group*
Dennis Rider Management, 927 Hilldale Avenue, West Hollywood, CA 90069 USA

Evangelista, Daniella *Actor*
Current Entertainment, 1411 Fifth St #405, Santa Monica, CA 90401 USA

Evangelista, Linda *Model*
655 Madison Ave #2300, New York, NY 10021 USA

Evanovich, Janet *Writer*
PO Box 5487, Hanover, NH 03755 USA

Evans, Alice *Actor*
Bauer Company, The, 9300 Wilshire Blvd #PH, Beverly Hills, CA 90212 USA

Evans, Andrea *Actor*
ARL, 8075 W 3rd St, #303, Los Angeles, CA 90048 USA

Evans, Anthony H *Educator*
California State University, President's Office, San Bermardino, CA 92407 USA

Evans, Barry *Baseball Player*
San Diego Padres, 8303 Seven Oaks Dr, Jonesboro, GA 30236 4025 USA

Evans, Bart *Baseball Player*
Kansas City Royals, 332 S Woodstock Avenue, Springfield, MO 65809 USA

Evans, Bill *Misc*
Dept of Field Mgmt, 1501 Broadway, #1304, New York, NY 10036 USA

Evans, Bob O *Engineer*
170 Robin Road, Hillsborough, CA 94010 USA

Evans, Chris *Actor*
Opus Entertainment, 5225 Wilshire Blvd #905, Los Angeles, CA 90036 USA

Evans, Daniel J *Governor, Senator, Educator*
Daniel J Evans Assoc, 1111 3rd Ave, #3400, Seattle, WA 98101 USA

Evans, Darrell W *Baseball Player*
Atlanta Braves, 13262 Mission Tierra Way, Grenada Hills, CA 91344 USA

Evans, David Mickey *Director*
Schachter Entertainment, 1157 S Beverly Dr Fl 3, Los Angeles, CA 90035 USA

Evans, Dick *Writer*
121 Morning Dove Court, Daytona Beach, FL 32119 USA

Evans, Donald L *Secretary*
Commerce Department, 14th St & Constitution Ave NW, Washington, DC 20230 USA

Evans, Dwayne *Athlete*
PO Box 91219, Phoenix, AZ 85066 USA

Evans, Dwight *Baseball Player*
Atlanta Braves, 3 Jordan Rd, Lynnfield, MA 01940 1220 USA

Evans, Edward P *Publisher*
712 5th Ave, #4900, New York, NY 10019 USA

Evans, Evans *Actor*
3114 Abington Dr, Beverly Hills, CA 90210 USA

Evans, Faith *Musician*
J L entertainment, 18653 Ventura Blvd, #340, Tarzana, CA 91356 USA

Evans, George *Cartoonist*
King Features Syndicate, 888 7th Ave, New York, NY 10106 USA

Evans, Glen *Biologist*
Salk Institute, 10100 N Torrey Pines Road, La Jolla, CA 92037 USA

Evans, Greg *Cartoonist*
216 Country Garden Lane, San Marcos, CA 92069 USA

Evans, Harold J *Physicist*
17320 Holy Names Dr, #C105, Lake Oswego, OR 97034 USA

Evans, Harold M *Editor*
Random House, 1745 Broadway, #B1, New York, NY 10019 USA

Evans, J Handel *Educator*
San Jose State University, President's Office, San Jose, CA 95192 USA

Evans, J Thomas *Wrestler*
607 S Fir Court, Broken Arrow, OK 74012 USA

Evans, James B (Jim) *Baseball Player*
1801 Rogge Lane, Austin, TX 78723 USA

Evans, Janet *Swimmer*
8 Barneburg, Dove Canyon, CA 92679 USA

Evans, John *Business Person*
Alcan Aluminium, 1188 Sherbrooke St W, Montreal, PC, H3A 3G2, CANADA

Evans, John E *Business Person*
Allied Group, 701 5th Ave, Des Moines, IA 50391 USA

Evans, John R *Misc*
Rocketfeller Foundation, 113 Ave of Americas, New York, NY 10036 USA

Evans, John V *Governor*
D L Evans Bank, 397 N Overland, Burfey, ID 83318 USA

Evans, Josh
1032 N. Beverly Dr., Beverly Hills, CA 90210

Evans, Karin
Laubenheimer Str. l, Berlin, GERMANY, D-14197

Evans, Lee *Actor*
GAT Productions, 17 Brickwood Road, Croydon, Surrey, CR0 6UL, UNITED KINGDOM (UK)

Evans, Lee E *Actor, Athlete, Track Athlete*
2650 College Place, Fullerton, CA 92831 USA

Evans, Linda *Actor*
TalentWorks (LA), 3500 W Olive Ave #1400, Burbank, CA 91505 USA

Evans, Lynn *Musician*
Richard Paul Assoc, 16207 Mott, Macomb Township, MI 48044 USA

Evans, Marc *Director*
Tessa Sayle Agency, 11 Jubilee Pl, London, SW3 3TE, UNITED KINGDOM (UK)

Evans, Marsha Johnson *Admiral*
American Red Cross, 431 18th St NW, Washington, DC 20006 USA

Evans, Martin J *Scientist, Misc*
Castle Rise 41, Rumney, Cardiff, CF3 9BB, WALES

Evans, Mary Beth
PO Box 50105, Pasadena, CA 91115-0105

Evans, Michael (Mike) *Actor*
12530 Collins St, North Hollywood, CA 91607 USA

Evans, Mike
12530 Collins St., No. Hollywood, CA 91605

Evans, Nicholas (Nick) *Writer*
Delacorte Press, 1540 Broadway, New York, NY 10036 USA

Evans, Norm E *Football Player*
4143 Via Marina, Marina Del Rey, CA 90292 USA

Evans, Raymond R (Ray) *Football Player, Basketball Player*
8449 Somerset Dr, Prairie Village, KS 66207 USA

Evans, Richard *Sportscaster, Misc*
Madison Square Garden, 4 Pennsylvania Plaza, New York, NY 10001 USA

Evans, Richard Paul *Writer*
Simon & Schuster, 1230 Ave of Americans, New York, NY 10020 USA

Evans, Rob *Coach*
Arizona State University, Athletic Dept, Tempe, AZ 85287 USA

Evans, Robert (Bob/ Bobby) *Producer, Actor, Writer*
Robert Evans Company, The, 5555 Melrose Ave, Lubitsch Bldg 117, Los Angeles, CA 90038 USA

Evans, Robert C *Mountaineer*
Ardincaple, Capel Curig, Betws-y-Coed, Northern Wales, WALES

Evans, Robert J (Bob) *Producer*
Robert Evans Productions, Paramount Pictures, 5555 Melrose, Los Angeles, CA 90038 USA

Evans, Robert S *Business Person*
Crane Co, 100 Stamford Plaza, Stamford, CT 06902 USA

Evans, Ronald E
6134 E Mescal, Scottsdale, AZ 85254 USA

Evans, Ronald M *Doctor*
Salk Institute, 10100 N Torrey Pines Road, La Jolla, CA 92037 USA

Evans, Sara *Musician*
William Morris Agency, 2100 W End Ave, #1000, Nashville, TN 37203 USA

Evans, Thomas *Business Person*
Collins & Aikman Corporation, PO Box 7054, Troy, MI 48007-7054

Evans, Troy *Actor*
PO Box 834, Lakeside, MT 59922 USA

Evans, Walker *Race Car Driver*
Walker Evans Racing, PO Box 2469, Riverside, CA 92516 USA

Evashevski, Forest *Football Coach*
5820 Clubhouse Dr, Vero Beach, FL 32967 USA

Evdokimova, Eva *Ballerina*
Gregori Productions, PO Box 1586, New York, NY 10150 USA

Eve *Musician, Actor*
Eve, 1438 N Gower, Bldg 62 Rm 115, Hollywood, CA 90028 USA

Eve *Artist*
Creative Artists Agency, 9830 Wilshire Blvd, Beverly Hills, CA 90212 USA

Eve, Trevor
76 Oxford St., London, ENGLAND, W1N 0AX

Eve, Trevor J *Actor*
International creative Mgmt, 76 Oxford St, London, W1N 0AX, UNITED KINGDOM (UK)

Everclear *Music Group*
Pinnacle Entertainment, 30 Glenn St, White Plains, NY 10603 USA

Everest, Frank K (Pete) Jr *General*
12440 E Barbary Coast Road, Tucson, AZ 85749 USA

Everett, Adam *Baseball Player*
Boston Red Sox, 70 Colonial Way, Dallas, GA 30157 1084 USA

Everett, Carl E *Baseball Player*
Florida Marlins, 19108 Harborbridge Ln, Lutz, FL 33558 9717 USA

Everett, Chad *Actor*
5472 Island Forest Place, Westlake Village, CA 91362 USA

Everett, Danny *Athlete*
Santa Monica Track Club, 1801 Ocean Park Ave, #112, Santa Monica, CA 90405 USA

Everett, James S (Jim) *Football Player*
31741 Contijo Way, Coto de Caza, CA 92679 USA

Everett, Rupert *Actor*
Wolf/Kasteler PR, 335 N Maple Dr #351, Beverly Hills, CA 90210 USA

Everett, Rupert *Actor*
International Creative Mgmt, 76 Oxford St, London, W1N 0AX, UNITED KINGDOM (UK)

Everett, Thomas G *Football Player*
5639 Bent Creek Trail, Dallas, TX 75252 USA

Everhard, Nancy *Actor*
Kazarian /Spencer, 11365 Ventura Blvd, #100, Studio City, CA 91604 USA

Everhart, Angie *Actor*
3751 Muirfield Dr, Uniontown, OH 44685

Everhart, Arigie *Actor, Model*
Karin, 524 Broadway, #404, New York, NY 10012 USA

Everitt, Leon *Baseball Player*
San Diego Padres, 367 Henry Everitt Rd, Marshall, TX 75672 3919 USA

Everlast *Musician, Actor*
Immortal Entertainment, 12200 Olympic Blvd, Suite 400, Los Angeles, CA 90064 USA

Everly, Donald (Don) *Musician*
10414 Camarillo St, Toluca Lake, CA 91602 USA

Everly, Phil *Musician*
10414 Camarillo St, Toluca Lake, CA 91602 USA

Everly Brothers *Music Group*
PO Box 56 Dunmore, KY CA 42339-0056, US

Evers, Bill *Athlete*
PO Box 507, Durham, NC 27702

Evers, Charles *Civil Rights Activist*
1018 Pecan Park Dr, Jackson, MS 39209 USA

Evers, Jackson *Actor*
232 N Crescent Dr, #101, Beverly Hills, CA 90210 USA

Evers, Jason
232 N. Crescent Dr. #101, Beverly Hills, CA 90210

Evers, John *Comedian*
PO Box 169, Mount Airy, NC 27030 USA

Evers-Williams, Myrlie *Misc*
15 SW Colorado Ave, #310, Bend, OR 97702 USA

Eversgerd, Bryan *Baseball Player*
St Louis Cardinals, 634 Quali Run, O Fallon, IL 62269 3142 USA

Eversley, Frederick J *Artist*
1110 W Albert Kinney Blvd, Venice, CA 90219 USA

Everson, Corinna (Cory) *Misc*
23705 Van Owen St, West Hills, CA 91307 USA

Everson, Cory *Athlete*
23705 Vanowen St #209, West Hills, CA 91307

Everson, Mark *Government Official*
Internal Revenue Service, 111 Constitution Ave NW, Washington, DC 20224 USA

Evert, Chris *Athlete*
701 NE 12th Ave, Ft Lauderdale, FL 33304

Evert, Christine M (Chris) *Tennis Player*
6181 Hollow Lane, Delray Beach, FL 33484 USA

Evert, Ray F *Biologist*
810 Woodward Dr, Madison, WI 53704 USA

Evetts, Hayley *Musician*
Pop Idol (Fremantle Media), 2700 Colorado Ave #450, Santa Monica, CA 90404 USA

Evigan, Greg *Actor*
Evolution Entertainment, 901 N Highland Ave, Los Angeles, CA 90038 USA

Evora, Cesar *Actor*
Televisa, Blvd Adolfo Lopez Mateos 232, Colonia San Angel INN, DF, CP 01060, MEXICO

Evora, Cesaria *Musician*
Monterey International, 200 W Superior, #202, Chicago, IL 60610 USA

Evren, Kenan *President, General*
Beyaz Ev Sokak 21, Armutalan, Marmaris, TURKEY

Evron, Ephraim *Government Official*
Ministry of Foreign Affairs, Tel-Aviv, ISRAEL

Ewald, Elwyn *Religious Leader*
Free Lutheran Congregations, 12015 Manchester Road, Saint Louis, MO 63131 USA

Ewald, Reinhold *Cosmonaut*
DLR Astronauterburo WT/AN, Linder Hohe, Cologne, 51140, GERMANY

Ewing, Barbara *Actor*
Scott Marshall, 44 Perryn Road, London, W3 7NA, UNITED KINGDOM (UK)

Ewing, Maria L *Opera Singer*
33 Bramerton St, London, SW3, UNITED KINGDOM (UK)

Ewing, Patrick *Basketball Player*
37 Summit St, Englewood Cliffs, NJ 07632 USA

Ewing, Sam *Baseball Player*
Chicago White Sox, 1048 Cedarview Ln, Franklin, TN 37067 4068 USA

Exile
PO Box 1547, Goodlettsville, TN 37070-1547

Expose *Music Group*
Richard Walters Entertainment, Inc, 1800 Argyle Avenue, Suite 408, Los Angeles, CA 90028 USA

Extreme
189 Carlton St., Toronto, CANADA, Ont. M5A 2

Eyadema, E Gnassingbe *President*
President's Office, Palais Presidentiel, Ave de la Marina, Lome, TOGO

Eyer, Richard
2739 Underwood Lane, Bishop, CA 93514

Eyes, Raymond *Publisher*
McCall's Magazine, 375 Lexington Ave, New York, NY 10017 USA

Eyharts, Leopold
49 Rue Desnouttes, Paris, 75015, FRANCE

Eyler, John *Business Person*
Toys 'R' Us Inc, 461 From Road, Paramus, NJ 07652 USA

Eyre, Richard *Director*
Judy Daish, 2 Saint Charles Place, London, W10 6EG, UNITED KINGDOM (UK)

Eyre, Scott *Baseball Player*
Chicago White Sox, 7010 190th St E, Bradenton, FL 34211 7242 USA

Eyrich, George *Baseball Player*
Chicago White Sox, 565 S 15th St, Reading, PA 19602 2111 USA

Eysenck, Hans J *Misc*
10 Dorchester Dr, London, SE24, UNITED KINGDOM (UK)

Eyskens, Mark *Government Official*
Graaf de Grunnelaan, Heverlee, 3001, BELGIUM

Eytchison, Ronald M *Admiral*
11 Prentice Lane, Signal Mountain, TN 37377 USA

Ezra, Derek *Government Official*
2 Salisbury Road, Wimbledon, London, SW19 4EZ, UNITED KINGDOM (UK)

F

Fabares, Shelley *Actor*
PO Box 6010-909, Sherman Oaks, CA 91413 USA

Fabbricini, Tiziana *Opera Singer*
Gianni Testa, Via Wrenteggio 31/6, Milan, 20146, ITALY

Faber, Sandra M *Astronomer*
16321 Ridgecrest Ave, Monte Sereno, CA 95030 USA

Fabi, Ted
9350 Castlegate Dr., Indianapolis, IN 46256

Fabian *Musician*
All Gold, 2228 Whitefield Road, Springfield, IL 62704 USA

Fabian, Ava *Actor, Model*
Shelly & Pierce, 13445A Mono Way #220, Sonora, CA 95370 USA

Fabian, John M *Astronaut*
100 Shine Rd, Port Ludlow, WA 98365 USA

Fabian, Lara
BP 37, Boussu-1, BELGIUM, 7301

Fabian, Lara *Actor*
Creative Artists Agency LCC (CAA-LA), 9830 Wilshire Blvd, Beverly Hills, CA 90212 USA

Fabian, Lara *Musician, Songwriter*
Alian Productions, 1 Place du Commerce, Nun's Island, PQ H3E 1A2, CANADA

Fabian, Patrick *Actor*
Writers & Artists, 8383 Wilshire Blvd, #550, Beverly Hills, CA 90211 USA

Fabiani, Joe *Reality TV Star*
NBC Television (LA), 3000 W Alameda Ave #5366, Burbank, CA 91523

Fabio *Actor, Model*
Thor Four LLC, 6464 Sunset Blvd, Suite 830, Hollywood, CA 90028 USA

Fabiola Moray Aragon, Dona *Royalty*
Royal Palace of Laeken, Laeken-Brussels, BELGIUM

Fabius, Laurent *Misc*
Mairie, Le Grand-Quevilly, 76120, FRANCE

Fabolous *Musician*
American Talent Agency, 173 Main St, Ossining, NY 10562 USA

Fabray, Nanette *Actor, Musician*
Webb, 13834 Magnolia Blvd, Sherman Oaks, CA 91423 USA

Fabregas, Jorge *Baseball Player*
California Angels, 9504 SW 125th Ter, Miami, FL 33176 5050 USA

Fabulous, Moolah *Wrestler*
101 Moolah Dr, Columbia, SC 29223 USA

Face, Elroy L (Roy) *Baseball Player*
608 Della Dr, #5F, North Versailles, PA 15137 USA

Facinelli, Peter *Actor*
PO Box 1994, Studio City, CA 91614 USA

Faddeyev, Ludwig D *Mathematician, Physicist*
Streklov Math Institute, Nab Fontanki 27, Saint Petersburg, D11, RUSSIA

Faddis, Jonathan (Jon) *Misc*
Carolyn McClair, PO Box 55, Radio Station, New York, NY 10101 USA

Fadeyechev, Aleksei *Dancer*
Bolshoi Theater, Teatralnaya Pl 1, Moscow, 103009, RUSSIA

Fadeyechev, Nicolai B *Dancer*
Bolshoi Theater, Teatralnaya Pl 1, Moscow, 103009, RUSSIA

Fadul, Francisco Jose *Prime Minister*
Prime Minister's Office, Bissau, GUINEA-BISSAU

Faedo, Len *Baseball Player*
Minnesota Twins, 2920 W Collins St, Tampa, FL 33607 6702 USA

Fagan, Garth *Choreographer*
Garth Fagan Dance, 50 Chestnut Plaza, Rochester, NY 14604 USA

Fagan, John J *Misc*
International teamsters Brotherhood, 25 Louisiana NW, Washington, DC 20001 USA

Fagan, kevin *Cartoonist*
26771 Ashford, Mission Viejo, CA 92692 USA

Fagen, Clifford B *Basketball Player*
1021 Royal Saint George Dr, Naperville, IL 60563 USA

Fagen, Donald *Songwriter, Musician*
Howard Rose, 9460 Wilshire Blvd, #310, Beverly Hills, CA 90212 USA

Fagerbakke, Bill *Actor*
1500 Will Geer Rd, Topanga, CA 90290 USA

Faget, Maxime *Scientist*
11822 Orchard Mountain Dr, Houston, TX 77059 USA

Fagg, George G *Judge*
US Court of Appeals, US Courthouse, East 1st & Walnut, Des Moines, IA 50309 USA

Faggin, Federico *Inventor*
Synaptics Inc, 2381 Bering Dr, San Jose, CA 95131 USA

Faggs, Starr H Mae *Track Athlete*
10152 Shady Lane, Cincinnati, OH 45215 USA

Fahd, King *Royalty*
Royal Palace, Riyadh, Saudi Arabia

Fahd bin Ibn, Abdul al-Aziz al Saud *King*
Royal Palace, Royal Court, Riyadh, SAUDI ARABIA

Fahey, Bill *Baseball Player*
Washington Senators, 5740 Mona Ln, Dallas, TX 75236 1722 USA

Fahey, Jeff *Actor*
Elkins Entertainment, 8306 Wilshire Blvd, Beverly Hills, CA 90211 USA

Fahr, Alicia *Actor*
Televisa, Blvd Adolfo Lopez Mateos 232, Colonia San Angel INN, DF, CP 01060, MEXICO

Fahr, Red *Baseball Player*
Cleveland Indians, 7749 Highway 49 N, Marmaduke, AR 72443 9336 USA

Faia, Renee *Actor*
Abrams Artists Agency (LA), 9200 Sunset Blvd Fl 11, Los Angeles, CA 90069 USA

Fain, Farris
PO Box 1357, Georgetown, CA 95634

Faine, Jeff *Football Player*
Cleveland Browns, 76 Lou Groza Blvd, Berea, OH 44017 USA

Fainsilber, Adrien *Architect*
7 Rue Salvador Allende, Nanterre, 92000, FRANCE

Fairbairn, Bruce *Actor*
Century Artists, PO Box 59747, Santa Barbara, CA 93150 USA

Fairbank, Richard W *Financier*
Capital One Financial, 2980 Fairview Park Dr, Falls Church, VA 22042 USA

Fairchild, Barbara *Musician, Songwriter*
Blackwood Mgmt, PO Box 5331, Sevierville, TN 37864 USA

Fairchild, John B *Publisher*
CHalet Bianchina, Talstr GR, Klosters, 7250, SWITZERLAND

Fairchild, Morgan *Actor*
Bartels Co, PO Box 57593, Sherman Oaks, CA 91413 USA

Fairchild, Thomas E *Judge*
US Court of Appeals, 111 N Cancal St, Building 6, Chicago, IL 60606 USA

Faircloth, D McLauchlin (Lauch) *Senator*
813 Beamon St, Clinton, NC 28328 USA

Faircloth, Michael *Fashion Designer*
Lilly Dodson, 33 Highland Park Village, Dallas, TX 75205 USA

Fairey, Jim *Baseball Player*
Los Angeles Dodgers, 218 Strawberry Ln, Clemson, SC 29631 1363 USA

Fairly, Ronald R (Ron) *Baseball Player*
Los Angeles Dodgers, 75369 Spyglass Dr, Indian Wells, CA 92210 7650 USA

Fairstein, Linda *Writer, Attorney General*
Charles Scribner's Sons, 866 3rd Ave, New York, NY 10022 USA

Faison, Donald Aedeosun *Actor*
PMK/HBH Public Relations (PMK-LA), 8500 Wilshire Blvd #700, Beverly Hills, CA 90211 USA

Faison, Matthew *Actor*
13701 E Kagel Canyon Road, Sylmar, CA 91342 USA

Faison, William E (Earl) *Football Player*
7886 Mission Vista Dr, San Diego, CA 92120 USA

Faith No More
5550 Wilshire Blvd. #202, Los Angeles, CA 90036

Faithfull, Marianne *Actor, Songwriter, Music Group*
Susan Dewsap, 235 Gootscray Rd, New Eltham, London, SE9 2EL, UNITED KINGDOM (UK)

Fajardo, Sharif *Basketball Player*
Cleveland Cavaliers, Gund Arena, 1 Center Court, Cleveland, OH 44115 USA

Fakir, Abdul (Duke) *Music Group*
William Morris Agency, 151 El Camino Dr, Beverly Hills, CA 90212 USA

Falana, Lola *Dancer, Music Group*
Capital Entertainment, 217 Seaton Place
NE, Washington, DC 20002 USA

Falcam, Leo A *President*
President's Office, Palikjr, Kolonia,
Pohnpei, FM, 96941, MICRONESIA

Falcao, Jose Freire Cardinal *Religious
Leader*
QL 12-CJ12, Lote 1, Lago Sul, Brasilia DF,
71630-325, BRAZIL

Falcao, Jose Friere Cardinal *Religious
Leader*
QL 12-CJ 12 Lote 1 Lago Sul, Brasilia DF,
71630-325, BRAZIL

Falco, Edie *Actor*
733 3rd Ave #1900, New York, NY 10017
USA

Faldo, Nicholas A (Nick) *Golfer*
IMG, Pier House Strand on Green
Chiswick, London, W4 3NN, UNITED
KINGDOM (UK)

Falik, Yuri *Composer, Conductor*
Fihlyandsky Prospekt 1 #54, Saint
Petersburg, 194044, RUSSIA

Falk, David *Lawyer*
Falk Assoc, 5335 Wiconsin Ave NW
#850, Washington, DC 20015 USA

Falk, David B *Attorney General, Misc*
Falk Assoc, 5335 Wisconsin Ave NW
#850, Washington, DC 20015 USA

Falk, Lisanne
9255 Sunset Blvd. #515, Los Angeles, CA
90069

Falk, Paul *Figure Skater*
Sybelstr 21, Dusseldorf, 40239,
GERMANY

Falk, Peter *Actor*
1004 N Roxbury Dr, Beverly Hills, CA
90210 USA

Falk, Quentin
Old Barn Cottage Little Marlow, Bucks.,
ENGLAND

Falk, Randall M *Religious Leader*
Temple, 5015 Harding Road, Nashville,
TN 37205 USA

Falkenburg, Bob
259 St. Pierre Rd, Los Angeles, CA 90077

Falkenstein, Claire *Artist*
719 Ocean Front Walk, Venice, CA
90291 USA

Falkner, Keith *Musician*
Low Cottages Ilketshall Saint Margaraet,
Bungay, Suffolk, UNITED KINGDOM (UK)

Fall, Jim *Actor*
United Talent Agency (UTA), 9560
Wilshire Blvd, Beverly Hills, CA 90212
USA

Fall, Timothy *Actor*
Gersh Agency, 232 N Canon Dr, Beverly
Hills, CA 90210 USA

Fallaci, Oriana *Journalist*
Rizzoli, 31 W 57th St #300, New York,
NY 10019 USA

Falldin, N O Thorbjom *Prime Minister*
As, Ramvik, 870 16, SWEDEN

Falldin, N O Thorbjorn *Prime Minister*
As, 16 Ramvik, 870, SWEDEN

Fallon, Jimmy *Actor, Comedian*
Creative Artists Agency, 9830 Wilshire
Blvd, Beverly Hills, CA 90212 USA

Falloon, Pat *Hockey Player*
Pittsburgh Penguins, Mellon Arena, 66
Mario Lemieux Place, Pittsburgh, PA
15219 USA

Faloona, Christopher *Cinematographer*
138 Via La Soledad, Redondo Beach, CA
90277 USA

Faloona, Christopher J *Cinematographer*
138 Via La Soledad, Redondo Beach, CA
90277 USA

Falossi, David *Artist*
Adrienne Editions, 377 Geary St, San
Francisco, CA 94102 USA

Faltermayer, Harold *Composer*
Creative Artists Agency, 9830 Wilshire
Blvd, Beverly Hills, CA 90212 USA

Faltings, Gerd *Mathematician*
Princeton University, Mathematics Dept,
Princeton, NJ 08544 USA

Faludi, Susan C *Journalist*
1032 Irving St #204, San Francisco, CA
94122 USA

Falwell, Jerry L *Religious Leader*
3765 Candlers Mountain Road,
Lynchburg, VA 24502 USA

Fambrough, Charles *Musician*
Zane Mgmt, Bellvue, Broad & Walnut Sts,
Philadelphia, PA 19102 USA

Fambrough, Henry *Music Group*
Buddy Allen Management, 3750 Hudson
Manor Terrace #3AG, Bronx, NY 10463
USA

Famiglietti, Mark *Actor*
Robert Stein Management, 345 N Maple
Dr #317, Beverly Hills, CA 90210 USA

Fancher, Hampton *Director*
262 Old Topanga Cnyon, Topanga, CA
90290 USA

Fanchetti, Peter
151 El Camino Dr., Beverly Hills, CA
90212

Fang, Lizhi *Physicist, Social Activist,
Politician, Misc*
University of Arizona, Physics Dept,
Tucson, AZ 85721 USA

Fangio, Juan Manuel II *Race Car Driver*
All-American Racers, 2334 S Broadway,
Santa Ana, CA 92707 USA

Fankhauser, Merrell *Musician, Composer*
PO Box 1504, Arroyo Grande, CA 93421
USA

Fann, Al *Actor*
6051 Hollywood Blvd #207, Hollywood,
CA 90028 USA

Fanning, Dakota *Actor*
Booh Schut Company, 11350 Ventura
Blvd #200, Studio City, CA 91604 USA

Fanning, Elle *Actor*
Booh Schut Company, 11350 Ventura
Blvd #200, Studio City, CA 91604 USA

Fanning, Michael L (Mike) *Football Player*
28808 S 4190 Road, Inola, OK 74036
USA

Fanning, Shawn *Business Person*
Roxio Inc, 455 El Camino Real, Santa
Clara, CA 95050 USA

Fannypack *Music Group*
Famous Celebrity Sound, 29 John St, Suite
230, New York, NY 10038 USA

Fano, Robert M *Scientist, Engineer*
51 Woodland Way, North Chatham, MA
02650 USA

Fantoni, Sergio
Via del Cappellari 35, Rome, ITALY,
00186

Faracy, Stephanie *Actor*
8765 Lookout Mountain Road, Los
Angeles, CA 90046 USA

Farar, Hassan Abshir *Prime Minister*
Prime Minister's Office, People's Palace,
Mogadishy, SOMALIA

Farber, Barry
2211 Broadway #3A, New York, NY
10024

Farber, Stacey *Actor*
Newton-Landry Management, 19 Isabella
Street, Toronto ON, M4Y 1M7, Canada

Faregalli, Lindy *Bowler*
113 N 5th Ave, Manville, NJ 08835 USA

Farenthold, Frances T *Educator, Social
Activist*
2929 Buffalo Speedway #18B, Houston,
TX 77098 USA

Farentino, Debrah
1505 10th St., Santa Monica, CA 90401

Farentino, James *Actor*
1340 Londonderry Place, Los Angeles, CA
90069 USA

Fares, Muhammad Ahmed Al *Cosmonaut*
PO Box 1272, Aleppo, SYRIA

Fargas, Antonio *Actor*
H David Moss, 733 Seward St #PH, Los
Angeles, CA 90038 USA

Fargis, Joe *Horse Racer*
P O Box 2168, Middlebury, CA 20118
USA

Fargo, Donna *Music Group*
P O Box 210877, Nashville, TN 37221
USA

Fargo, Thomas B *Admiral*
Commander Pacific Fleet, Camp H M
Smith, Honolulu, HI 96861 USA

Farha *Actor, Bollywood*
308 Dara Villa A B Nair Road, Juhu,
Mumbai, MS 400049, INDIA

Farina, Battista (Pinin) *Designer*
Pinitarina SpA, Via Lesna 78, Turin,
Grugliasco, 10095, ITALY

Farina, David *Religious Leader*
Chrishtian Church of North America, 41
Sherbrooke Road, Trenton, NJ 08638 USA

Farina, Dennis *Actor*
217 Edgewood Ave, Clearwater, FL 33755
USA

Farina, Johnny *Music Group*
Bellrose Music, 308 E 6th St #13, New
York, NY 10003 USA

Faris, Anna *Actor*
Row Talent, 9615 Brighton Way #300,
Beverly Hills, CA 90210 USA

Faris, Sean *Actor*
Dino May Management, 2401 W Olive Ave #290, Burbank, CA 91506 USA

Farish, William S *Diplomat*
US Embassy, Grosvenor Square 55 Upper Brook St, London, W1A 2LQ, UNITED KINGDOM (UK)

Farkas, Bertalan *Astronaut, Misc*
A Magyar Koztarsasag Kutato Urhajosa, Pf 25, Budapest, 1885, HUNGARY

Farkas, Ferenc *Composer*
Nagyatai Utca 12, Budapest, 1026, HUNGARY

Farley, Carole *Opera Singer, Music Group*
270 Riverside Dr, New York, NY 10025 USA

Farley, David *Writer*
MBST Entertainment, 345 N Maple D #200, Suite 200, Beverly Hills, CA 90210 USA

Farley, Lillian
84 Kenneth Ave., Huntington, NY 11743

Farmer, Art
49 E. 96th St., New York, NY 10128

Farmer, Ed *Athlete*
333 West 35th St, Chicago, IL 60616

Farmer, Evan *Actor, Television Host*
Abrams Artists Agency (LA), 9200 Sunset Blvd Fl 11, Los Angeles, CA 90069 USA

Farmer, John Jr *Governor*
Attorney General's Office, Hughes Justice Complex, Trenton, NJ 08625 USA

Farmer, Mike *Basketball Player, Coach*
308 W McDonald Ave, Richmond, CA 94801 USA

Farmer, Mimsy *Actor*
Cineart, 36 Rue de Ponthieu, Paris, 75008, FRANCE

Farmer, Phillip W *Business Person*
Harris Corp, 1025 W NASA Blvd, Melbourne, FL 32919 USA

Farmer, Richard G *Doctor*
9126 Town Gate Lane, Bethesda, MD 20817 USA

Farmiga, Vera *Actor*
Innovative Artists, 1505 10th Street, Santa Monica, CA 90401 USA

Farner, Donald S *Biologist, Physicist*
University of Washington, Zoology Dept, Seattle, WA 98195 USA

Farner, Mark *Music Group, Musician*
Bobby Roberts, P O Box 1547, Goodlettsville, TN 37070 USA

Farnham, John
Box 6500 St. Kilda Rd., Central Melbourne, AUSTRALIA, 3004

Farnham, John P *Music Group*
TalentWorks, 663 Victoria St, Abbottsford, VIC, 3067, AUSTRALIA

Farnon, Shannon
12743 Milbank St., Studio City, CA 91604

Farquhar, John W *Doctor*
Stanford University, Med School, Disease Prevention Center, Stanford, CA 94305 USA

Farquhar, Marilyn G *Biologist, Misc*
12894 Via Latina, Del Mar, 92014 USA

Farquhar, Robert W *Scientist*
Johns Hopkins University, Applied Physics Laboratory, Laurel, MD 20723 USA

Farr, Bruce *Architect*
Bruce Farr Assoc, 613 3rd St, Annapolis, MD 21403 USA

Farr, Diane *Actor*
Career Management Corp, 1850 Sawtelle Blvd #450, Los Angeles, CA 90025

Farr, Felicia *Actor*
1143 Tower Road, Beverly Hills, CA 90210 USA

Farr, Jaime *Actor*
51 Ranchero Road, Bell Canyon, CA 91307 USA

Farr, Jamie
53 Ranchero, Bell Canyon, CA 91307

Farr, Kimberly *Actor*
Tisherman Agency, 6767 Forest Lawn Dr #101, Los Angeles, CA 90068 USA

Farr, Melvin (Mel) Sr *Football Player*
4525 Lakeview Court, Bloomfield Hills, MI 48301 USA

Farrakhan, Louis *Religious Leader*
Nation of Islam, 734 W 79th St, Chicago, IL 60620 USA

Farrar, Frank L *Governor*
203 9th Ave, Britton, SD 57430 USA

Farrel, Franklin *Hockey Player*
89 Notch Hill Road #223, North Branford, CT 06471 USA

Farreley, Alexander *Governor*
Governor's Office, Government Offices, Charlotte Amalie, VI 00801 USA

Farrell, Christopher *Musician*
Working Artists Agency, 13525 Ventura Blvd, Sherman Oaks, CA

Farrell, Colin *Actor*
10 Herbert Lane, Dublin 2, IRELAND

Farrell, Mike *Actor*
14011 Ventura Blvd, Sherman Oaks, CA 91423 USA

Farrell, Perry *Music Group*
H K Mgmt, 9200 W Sunset Blvd #530, Los Angeles, CA 90069 USA

Farrell, Sean *Football Player*
7 Legends Circle, Melville, NY 11747 USA

Farrell, Sharon *Actor*
360 S Doheny Dr, Beverly Hills, CA 90211 USA

Farrell, Shea *Actor*
Artists Agency, 1180 S Beverly Dr #301, Los Angeles, CA 90035 USA

Farrell, Suzanne *Ballerina*
Kennedy Center for Performing Arts, Education Dept, Washington, DC 20566 USA

Farrell, Terence (Terry) *Architect*
17 Hatton St, London, NW8 8PL, UNITED KINGDOM (UK)

Farrell, Terry *Actor*
Don Buchwald, 6500 Wilshire Blvd #2200, Los Angeles, CA 90048 USA

Farrelly, Bobby *Director*
Creative Artists Agency, 9830 Wilshire Blvd, Beverly Hills, CA 90212 USA

Farrelly, Peter *Director*
9830 Wilshire Blvd, Beverly Hills, CA 90212 USA

Farrimond, Richard A *Astronaut*
Metra Marconi Center, Gunnels Wood Rd Stevenage, Herts, SG1 2AS USA

Farrimond, Richard A *Astronaut*
Metra Marconi Center, Gunnels Wood Rd Stevenage, Herts, SG1 2AS, UNITED KINGDOM (UK)

Farrington, Amy
1450 S. Robertson Blvd., Los Angeles, CA 90035

Farrington, Robert G (Bob) *Race Car Driver*
201 Lake Hinsdale Dr #211, Willowbrook, IL 60527 USA

Farris, Dionne *Music Group*
Creative Artists Agency, 9830 Wilshire Blvd, Beverly Hills, CA 90212 USA

Farris, Jerome
US Court of Appeals, US Courthouse 1010 5th Ave, Seattle, WA 98104 USA

Farris, Joseph *Cartoonist*
68 Sunburst Circle, Fairport, NY 14450 USA

Farris, Rachel *Musician*
Logic House Media, 3013 Brightwood Avenue, Nashville, TN 37212 USA

Farriss, Andrew *Music Group*
8 Hayes St #1, Neutral Bay, NSW, 20891, AUSTRALIA

Farriss, Jon *Music Group, Musician*
8 Hayes St #1, Neutral Bay, NSW, 20891, AUSTRALIA

Farriss, Tim *Music Group, Musician*
8 Hayes St #1, Neutral Bay, NSW, 20891, AUSTRALIA

Farrow, Mallory *Actor*
Hervey/Grimes, PO Box 64249, Los Angeles, CA 90064 USA

Farrow, Mia *Actor*
124 Henry Sanford Road, Bridgewater, CT 06752- USA

Farulli, Piero *Musician*
Via G D'Annunzio 153, Florence, ITALY

Fasman, Gerald D *Biologist*
69 Kingswood Road, Newton, MA 02166 USA

Fass, Horst *Photographer, Journalist*
12 Norwich St, London, EC4A, UNITED KINGDOM (UK)

Fassbaender, Brigitte *Opera Singer*
Am Theater, Braunschweig, 38100, GERMANY

Fassell, Jim *Football Coach*
Baltimore Ravens, Ravens Stadium, 11001 Russell St, Baltimore, MD 21230 USA

Fast, Darrell *Religious Leader*
Mennonite Church General Conference, P O Box 347, Newton, KS 67114 USA

Fast, Larry *Composer, Musician*
Polydor Records, 70 Universal City Plaza, Universal City, CA 91608 USA

Fatboy Slim
1776 Broadway #1500, New York, NY 10019

Fath, Farah *Actor*
LINK Talent Group, 4741 Laurel Canyon
Blvd #106, Valley Village, CA 90607 USA

Fatone, Joey *Musician*
William Morris Agency (WMA-LA), 1
William Morris Pl, Beverly Hills, CA
90212 USA

Fatone, Joey Jr *Music Group*
Wright Entertainment, 7680 Universal
Blvd #500, Orlando, FL 32819 USA

Fauci, Anthony S *Doctor*
3012 43rd St NW, Washington, DC
20016 USA

Faucon, Bernard *Photographer*
6 Rue Barbanegre, Paris, 75019, FRANCE

Faulk, Marshall *Football Player*
6430 Clayton Road #305, Saint Louis, MO
63117 USA

Faulkner, Eric *Music Group, Musician*
27 Preston Grange, Preston Pans E,
Lothian, SCOTLAND

Faulkner, John *Scientist*
Scripps Institution of Oceanography, La
Jolla, CA 92093 USA

Faure, Maurice H *Government Official*
28 Blvd Raspail, Paris, 75007, FRANCE

Fauser, Mark *Writer*
United Talent Agency (UTA), 9560
Wilshire Blvd, Beverly Hills, CA 90212
USA

Faustino, David *Actor*
Innovative Artists (LA), 1505 Tenth St,
Santa Monica, CA 90401 USA

Fauts, Dan
4020 Murphy Canyon Rd., San Diego, CA
92123-4407

Fauza, Dario *Doctor, Misc*
Harvard Medical School, 25 Shattuck St,
Boston, MA 02115 USA

Favier, Jean-Jacques *Misc*
Technologies Avances, 17 Ave des
Martys, Grenoble Cedex, 38054, FRANCE

Favor-Hamilton, Suzy
PO Box 120, Indianapolis, IN 46206-0120

Favre, Brett L *Football Player*
3071 Gothic Court, Green Bay, WI,
54313 USA

Favreau, Jon *Actor, Writer*
United Talent Agency, 9560 Wilshire Blvd
#500, Beverly Hills, CA 90212 USA

Fawcett, Don W *Doctor, Misc*
1224 Lincoln Road, Missoula, MT 59802
USA

Fawcett, Farrah *Actor, Model*
10580 Wilshire Blvd #14NE, Los Angeles,
CA 90024 USA

Fawcett, Sherwood L *Physicist, Scientist*
1852 Riverside Dr #A, Columbus, OH
43212 USA

Faxon, Brad *Golfer*
77 Rumstick Road, Barrington, RI 02806
USA

Fay, David B *Golfer*
US Golf Assn, Golf House, Liberty Corner
Road, Far Hills, NJ 07931 USA

Fay, Martin *Music Group, Musician*
Macklam Feldman Mgmt, 1505 W 2nd
Ave #200, Vancouver, BC V6H 3Y4,
CANADA

Fay, Meagan *Actor*
Paradigm (LA), 10100 Santa Monica Blvd,
Fl 25, Los Angeles, CA 90067 USA

Fay, Meagen *Actor*
Main Title Entertainment, 5225 Wilshire
Blvd #500, Los Angeles, CA 90036 USA

Fay, Peter T *Judge*
US Court of Appeals, 99 NE 4th St,
Miami, FL 33132 USA

Faydoedeelay *Musician, Music Group*
Q Prime, 729 7th Ave #1600, New York,
NY 10019 USA

Fayed, Mohamed al- *Business Person*
Craven Cottage Stevenage Road, Fulham,
London, SW6 6HH, UNITED KINGDOM
(UK)

Fazio, Ernie
2310 Royal Oaks Dr., Alamo, CA 94507

Fazio, Tom *Architect, Golfer*
Fazio Golf Course Designers, 401 N Main
St #400, Hendersonville, NV 28792 USA

Fazzini, Enrico *Doctor*
New York University, Medical Center,
550 1st Ave, New York, NY 10016 USA

Fearnley-Whittingstall, Hugh *Chef*
BBC Artist Mail, PO Box 1116, Belfast,
BT2 7AJ, United Kingdom

Fearon, Douglas T *Doctor, Misc*
Wellcome Trust Immunology Unit, Hills
Road, Cambridge, CB2 2SP, UNITED
KINGDOM (UK)

Feaster, Allison *Basketball Player*
Charlotte Sting, 100 Hive Dr, Charlotte,
NC 28217 USA

Feck, Luke M *Editor*
6880 Worthington Road, Westerville, OH
43082 USA

Federer, Roger *Tennis Player*
Int'l Mgmt Group, 1 Erieview Plaza, 1360
E 9th St #1300, Cleveland, OH 44114
USA

Federko, Bernie *Hockey Player*
2219 Devonsbrook Dr, Chesterfield, MO
63005 USA

Federov, Sergei *Hockey Player*
1966 Tiverton Rd, Boomfield Hills, MI
48304 USA

Fedewa, Tim *Race Car Driver*
1737 Onondaga Road, Holt, MI 48842
USA

Fedorov, Sergei *Hockey Player*
1966 Tiverton Road, Bloomfield Hills, MI
48304 USA

Fedoseyev, Vladimir I
Moscow House of Recording, Kachalova
24, Moscow, 121069, RUSSIA

Fedotov, Maxim V *Musician*
Tolbukhin Str 8 #6, Moscow, 121596,
RUSSIA

Fee, Melinda *Actor*
145 S Fairfax Ave #310, Los Angeles, CA
90036 USA

Feehily, Mark
Westlife, 8750 Wilshire Blvd, Beverly
Hills, CA 90211

Feeney, Joe
32630 Concord Dr., Madison Heights, MI
48071

Fegley, Richard *Photographer*
Playboy Magazine, Reader Services 680 N
Lake Shore Dr, Chicago, IL 60611 USA

Feher, George *Physicist*
University of California, Physics Dept
9500 Gilman Dr, La Jolla, CA 92093 USA

Fehr, Brendan *Actor*
Look Mgmt, 1529 W 6th Ave #110,
Vancouver, BC V5J 1R1, CANADA

Fehr, Donald M *Misc*
Major League Baseball Players Assn, 805
3rd Ave, New York, NY 10022 USA

Fehr, Oded *Actor*
I FA Talent Agency, 8730 Sunset Blvd
#490, Los Angeles, CA 90069 USA

Fehr, Rick *Golfer*
2731 223rd Ave NE, Sammamish, WA
98074 USA

Fehr, Steve *Bowler*
6216 Highceder Court, Cincinnati, OH
45233 USA

Fehrenbach, Charles M *Astronomer*
Les Magnanarelles, Lourmarin, 84160,
FRANCE

Feiffer, Jules *Cartoonist*
325 W End Ave #12A, New York, NY
10023 USA

Feigenbaum, Armand V *Business Person,
Engineer*
General Systems, 23 South St #250,
Pittsfield, MA 01201 USA

Feigenbaum, Edward A *Scientist*
1017 Cathcart Way, Stanford, CA 94305
USA

Feilden, Bernard M *Architect*
Stiffkey Old Hall, Wells-next-to-the-Sea,
Norfolk, NR23 1QJ, UNITED KINGDOM
(UK)

Feinberg, Alan *Musician*
Cramer/Marder Artists, 3436 Springhill
Road, Lafayette, CA 94549 USA

Feinberg, Wilfred *Judge*
US Court of Appeals, US Courthouse
Foley Square, New York, NY 10007 USA

Feingold, Russell *Senator*
7114 Donna Dr, Middleton, WI 53562-
1709 USA

Feinstein, A Richard *Physicist, Doctor*
1760 2nd Ave #32C, New York, NY
10128 USA

Feinstein, Alan *Actor*
Badgley Connor Talent, 9229 Sunset Blvd
#311, Los Angeles, CA 90069 USA

Feinstein, Dianne *Politician*
United States Senate (Hart Office), 316
Hart Senate Office Building, Washington,
DC 20510 USA

Feinstein, John *Sportscaster,
Commentator, Writer*
22 Tuthill Dr, Shelter Island, NY 11964
USA

Feinstein, Michael *Music Group, Musician*
4647 Kingswell Ave #110, Los Angeles,
CA 90027 USA

Feist, Raymond E(lias) *Writer*
Doubleday, 1540 Broadway, New York,
NY 10036

Felashia
PO Box 31734, Tucson, AZ 87571

Felber, Dean *Music Group, Musician*
FishCo Mgmt, P O Box 5456, Columbia,
SC 29250 USA

Felch, William C *Physicist, Doctor*
8545 Carmel Valley Road, Carmel, CA
93923 USA

Feld, Eliot *Dancer, Choreographer*
Feld Ballet, 890 Broadway #800, New
York, NY 10003 USA

Feldenkrais, Moshe *Doctor, Misc*
University of Tel-Aviv, Psychology Dept,
Tel-Aviv, ISRAEL

Felder, Don *Musician, Music Group*
PO Box 6051, Malibu, CA 90264 USA

Felder, Raoul Lionel *Attorney General*
437 Madison Ave, New York, NY 10022
USA

Feldman, Bella *Artist*
12 Summit Lane, Berkeley, CA 94708
USA

Feldman, Corey *Actor*
Baker/Winokur/Ryder, 9100 Wilshire Blvd
#600, Beverly Hills, CA 90212 USA

Feldman, Ed
7700 Wisconsin Ave, Bethesda, MD
20814

Feldman, Jerome M *Doctor, Physicist*
2744 Sevier St, Durham, NC 27705 USA

Feldman, Michelle *Bowler*
Gary Feldman, P O Box 713, Skaneateles,
NY 13152 USA

Feldman, Myer *Government Official*
Ginsberg Feldman Bress, 1250
Connecticut Ave NW, Washington, DC
20036 USA

Feldman, Sandra *Misc*
American Federation of Teachers, 555
New Jersey Ave NW, Washington, DC
20001 USA

Feldmann, Marc *Doctor, Misc*
Charing Cross Hospital, Saint Dunstan's
Road, London, W6 8RP, UNITED
KINGDOM (UK)

Feldon, Barbara *Actor, Model*
14 E 74th St, New York, NY 10021 USA

Feldshuh, Tovah S *Actor*
322 Central Park W #11B, New York, NY
10025 USA

Feldstein, Martin *Government Official,
Economist*
147 Clifton St, Belmont, MA 02478 USA

Felici, Angelo Cardinal *Religious Leader*
Piazza della Citta Leonina 9, Rome,
00193, ITALY

Feliciano, Jose *Musician, Music Group*
World Entertainment Assoc, 297101
Kinderkamack Road #128, Oradell, NJ
07649 USA

Felipe *Prince*
Palacio de la Zarzuela, Madrid, 28080,
SPAIN

Felix the Cat
12020 Chandler Blvd. #200, No.
Hollywood, CA 91607

Felke, Petra *Track Athlete*
SC Motor Jena, Wollnitzevstr 42, Jena,
07749, GERMANY

Felker, Clay *Editor*
322 E 57th St, New York, NY 10022 USA

Fell, Ray
1555 E. Flamingo Rd. #252, Las Vegas,
NV 89119

Feller, Bob
Box 170, Novelty, OH 44072

Feller, Robert W A (Bob) *Baseball Player*
PO Box 157, Gates Mills, OH 44040 USA

Fellowes, Julian *Actor*
International Creative Mgmt, 76 Oxford
St, London, W1N 0AX, UNITED
KINGDOM (UK)

Fellows, Edith *Actor*
2016 1/2 N Vista Del Mar, Los Angeles,
CA 90068 USA

Felmy, Hansjorg
Berghofen, Eching, GERMANY, D-84174

Felsenstein, Lee *Inventor*
2490 Greer Road, Palo Alto, CA 94303
USA

Felton, Dennis *Basketball Player*
University of Georgia, Athletic Dept,
Athens, GA 30602 USA

Felton, John *Musician*
GMS, PO Box 1031, Montrose, CA 91021
USA

Felton, Tom *Actor*
Harry Potter Production, Leavesden
Studios, PO Box 3000, Leavesden,
Hertfordshire, WD2 7LT, United Kingdom

Felts, Narvel *Musician, Songwriter*
2005 Narvel Felts Way, Malden, MO
63863 USA

Feltsman, Vladimir *Musician*
Columbia Artists Mgmt Inc, 165 W 57th
St, New York, NY 10019 USA

Feltus, Alan E *Artist*
Porziano 68, Assisi PG, 06081, ITALY

Feltz, Vanessa *Actor*
XS Promotions, 57 Fonthill Rd, Aberdeen,
AB11 6UQ, UNITED KINGDOM (UK)

Fem 2 Fem
1122 B St. #308, Hayward, CA 94541-
4272

Femia, John
1650 Broadway #714, New York, NY
10019

Fencik, J Gary *Football Player*
1134 W Schubert Ave, Chicago, IL 60614
USA

Fender, Freddy *Musician, Songwriter*
6438 Revolution Dr, Corpus Christi, TX
78413 USA

Fenech, Edwige *Actor*
Carol Levi Co, Via Giuseppe Pisanelli,
Rome, 00196, ITALY

Fenech, Jeff *Boxer*
PO Box 21, Hardys Bay, NSW, 2257,
AUSTRALIA

Fenech-Adami, Edward *Prime Minister*
176 Main St, Birkikara, MALTA

Feng, Ying *Ballerina*
Central Ballet of China, 3 Taiping St,
Beijing, 100050, CHINA

Feng-HslungHsu *Engineer*
IBM T J Watson Research Center, PO Box
218, Yorktown Heights, NY 10598 USA

Fenimore, Robert D (Bob) *Football Player*
1214 Fairway Dr, Stillwater, OK 74074
USA

Fenley, Molissa *Dancer, Choreographer*
59 Walder St #4, New York, NY 10013
USA

Fenn, John B *Nobel Prize Laureate*
4909 Cary Street Road, Richmond, VA
23226 USA

Fenn, Sherilyn *Actor*
16501 Ventura Blvd, #304, Encino, CA
91436 USA

Fennell, Jan *Writer*
Harper Collins Publishers, 10 E 53rd St,
New York, NY 10022 USA

Fenske, Chuck
3 Tattnall Pl., Hilton Head, SC 29928

Fenton, James *Writer*
P F D Drury House, 34-43 Russell St,
London, WC2B 5HA, UNITED KINGDOM
(UK)

Fenton, Paul *Hockey Player*
524 Laurel St, Longmeadows, MA 01106

Feoktistov, Konstantin P *Cosmonaut*
Potcha Kosmonavtov, Moskovskoi Oblasti,
Syvisdny Goroduk, 141160, RUSSIA

Feore, Colm *Actor*
Endeavor Agency LLC (LA), 9601 Wilshire
Blvd Fl 3, Beverly Hills, CA 90210 USA

Ferarone, Jessica *Actor*
Evolution Entertainment, 901 N Highland
Ave, Los Angeles, CA 90038 USA

Feraud, Gianfranco *Fashion Designer*
25 Rue Saint Honore, Paris, 75001,
FRANCE

Ferdin, Pamela *Actor*
15000 Ventura Blvd #340, Sherman Oaks,
CA 91403 USA

Ferdinand, Marie *Basketball Player*
San Antonio Silver Stars, 1 SBC Center,
San Antonio, TX 78219 USA

Ferdinand, Ron
PO Box 1997, Monterey, CA 93942

Ferentz, Kirk *Football Coach*
University of Iowa, Ath

Ferentz, Kirk *Football Coach*
University of Iowa, Athletic Dept, Iowa
City, IA 52242 USA

Fergason, James L (Jim) *Inventor*
145 Gartland Dr, Menlo Park, CA 94025
USA

Fergus, Keith *Golfer*
Advantage International, 1751 Pinnacle
Dr, #1500, McLean, VA 22102 USA

Fergus-Thompson, Gordo *Musician*
150 Audley Road, Hendon, London, NW4
3EG, UNITED KINGDOM (UK)

Ferguson, Alexander C (Alex) *Soccer Player*
Manchester United FC, Old Trafford, Manchester, M16 0RA, UNITED KINGDOM (UK)

Ferguson, Charles A *Editor*
1448 Joseph St, New Orleans, LA 70115 USA

Ferguson, Christopher J *Astronaut*
16111 park Center Way, Houston, TX 77059 USA

Ferguson, Clarence C Jr *Diplomat, Attorney General*
Harvard University, Law School, Cambridge, MA 02138 USA

Ferguson, Craig *Actor, Comedian*
Creative Artists Agency, 9830 Wilshire Blvd, Beverly Hills, CA 90212 USA

Ferguson, Cullum Cathy *Swimmer*
21861 Oceanview Lane, Huntington Beach, CA 92646 USA

Ferguson, Frederick E *War Hero*
106 E Stellar Parkway, Chandler, AZ 85226 USA

Ferguson, James (Jim) *Misc*
26931 Whitehouse Road, Santa Clarita, CA 91351 USA

Ferguson, James L *Business Person*
General Foods Corp, 800 Westchester Ave, Rye Brook, NY 10573 USA

Ferguson, Jay *Actor*
560 N St SW, #304, Washington, DC 20024 USA

Ferguson, Joe C Jr *Football Player, Football Coach*
10457 Ervin McGarrah Road, Lowell, AR 72745 USA

Ferguson, Lynda *Actor*
606 N Larchmont Blvd, #309, Los Angeles, CA 90004 USA

Ferguson, Maynard *Musician*
PO Box 716, Ojai, CA 93024 USA

Ferguson, Roger W Jr *Government Official, Economist*
Federal Reserve Board, 20th & Constitution Ave NW, Washington, DC 20551 USA

Ferguson, Sarah *Royalty*
Birchchall, Windlesham, Surrey, GU20 6BN, UNITED KINGDOM (UK)

Ferguson, Stacy *Actor, Musician*
DAS Communications, 83 Riverside Dr, New York, NY 10024 USA

Ferguson, Thomas A Jr *Business Person*
Newell Rubbermaid Inc, Newell Center, 29 E Stephenson St, Freeport, IL 61032 USA

Ferguson, Tom *Rodeo Rider*
General Delivery, Miami, OK 74354 USA

Ferguson, Vasquero D (Vagas) *Football Player*
805 N 13th St, Richmond, IN 47374 USA

Ferguson, Warren J *Judge*
US Courts of Appeals, 34 Civic Center Plaza, Santa Ana, CA 92701 USA

Ferguson-Winn, Mabel *Track Athlete*
2575 S Steele Road, #206, San Bernardino, CA 92408 USA

Fergusson, Frances D *Educator*
Vassar College, President's Office, Poughkeepsie, NY 12603 USA

Ferigno, Lou *Actor*
Criag Mgmt, 125 S Sycamore Ave, Los Angeles, CA 90036 USA

Ferland, E James *Business Person*
Public Service Enterprise, 80 Park Plaza, PO Box 1171, Newark, NJ 07101 USA

Ferlinghetti, Lawrence *Writer, Publisher*
City Lights Booksellers, 261 Columbus Ave, San Francisco, CA 94133 USA

Ferlito, Vanessa *Actor*
3 Arts Entertainment Inc, 9460 Wilshire Blvd Fl 7, Beverly Hills, CA 90212 USA

Fernandez, Adrian *Race Car Driver*
7140 E Bronco Dr, Paradise Valley, AZ 85253 USA

Fernandez, Alejandro *Musician*
Hauser Entertainment, 11003 Rocks Road, Whittier, CA 90601 USA

Fernandez, C Sidney (Sid) *Baseball Player*
543 Punaa St, Kailua, HI 96734 USA

Fernandez, Chico
3322 24th St., Detroit, MI 48208

Fernandez, Craig *Writer, Director*
Gotham Group Inc, The, 9255 Sunset Blvd #515, Los Angeles, CA 90069 USA

Fernandez, Ester
Mitla 112 esq. Xola Colonia Narvarte, Mexico DF, MEXICO

Fernandez, Evalina
5911 Allison St., Los Angeles, CA 90022

Fernandez, Ferdinand F *Judge*
US Courts of Appeals, 125 S Grand Ave, Pasadena, CA 91105 USA

Fernandez, Gigi *Tennis Player*
Gigi Tennis Camp, 4202 E Fowler Ave #214, Tampa, FL 33620 USA

Fernandez, Giselle *Television Host*
3000 W Alameda Ave, Burbank, CA 91523 USA

Fernandez, Juan *Actor*
Don Buchwald, 6500 Wilshire Blvd, #2200, Los Angeles, CA 90048 USA

Fernandez, Lisa *Misc*
PO Box 3063, Lakewood, CA 90711 USA

Fernandez, Lujan *Actor*
Innovative Artists (LA), 1505 Tenth St, Santa Monica, CA 90401 USA

Fernandez, Mary Jo
133 1st St. NE, St. Petersburg, FL 33701

Fernandez, Mary Joe *Tennis Player*
6040 SW 104th St, Miami, FL 33156 USA

Fernandez, O Antonio (Tony) *Baseball Player*
3200 N Military Trail, #201, Boca Raton, FL 33431 USA

Fernandez, Pedro *Musician, Songwriter*
Exclusive Artists Productions, PO Box 65948, Los Angeles, CA 90065 USA

Fernandez, Vicente *Musician*
Hauser Entertainment, 11003 Rocks Road, Whittier, CA 90601 USA

Ferneyhough, Brian J P *Composer*
848 Allardice Way, Stanford, CA 94305 USA

Ferragamo, Vince *Football Player*
Touchdown Real Estate, 6200 E Canyon Rim Road, Anaheim, CA 92807 USA

Ferrante, Art *Musician*
Scott Smith, 12224 Avila Dr, Kansas City, MO 64145 USA

Ferrante, Jack *Football Player*
3712 Pembroke Lane, Ocean City, NJ 08226 USA

Ferrara, Abel *Director*
International Creative Mgmt, 8942 Wilshire Blvd, #219, Beverly Hills, CA 90211 USA

Ferrara, Adam *Actor*
Conversation Co, 697 Middle Neck Road, Great Neck, NY 11023 USA

Ferrare, Cristina *Model, Entertainer*
10727 Wilshire Blvd, #1602, Los Angeles, CA 90024 USA

Ferrari, Gianantonio *Business Person*
Honeywell Inc, Honeywell Plaza, Minneapolis, MN 55408 USA

Ferrari, Michael R Jr *Educator*
570 Greenway Dr, Lake Forest, IL 60045 USA

Ferrari, Tina *Dancer, Wrestler*
2901 S Las Vegas Blvd, Las Vegas, NV 89109 USA

Ferraro, Dave *Bowler*
672 E Chester St, Kingston, NY 12401 USA

Ferraro, Geraldine *Politician, Writer*
575 Park Avenue, New York, NY 10021 USA

Ferratti, Rebecca *Model, Actor*
10061 Riverside Dr, #721, Toluca Lake, CA 91602 USA

Ferrazzi, Ferruccio *Artist*
Piazza delle Muse, Via G G Porro 27, Rome, 00197, ITALY

Ferrazzi, Pierpaolo *Athlete*
EuroGrafica, Via del Progresso, Marano Vicenza, 36035, ITALY

Ferre, Gianfranco *Fashion Designer*
Villa Della Spiga 19/A, Milan, 20121, ITALY

Ferreira, Wayne *Tennis Player*
Int'l Mgmt Group, 1 Erieview Plaza, 1360 E 9th St #1300, Cleveland, OH 44114 USA

Ferrell, Conchata *Actor*
1335 N Seward St, Los Angeles, CA 90028 USA

Ferrell, Rachel *Musician*
Vida Music Group, 19800 Cornerstone Sq #415, Ashburn, VA 20147 USA

Ferrell, Rachelle *Musician*
Vida Music Group, 19800 Cornerstone Square, #415, Ashbum, VA 20147 USA

Ferrell, Tyra *Actor*
Gersh Agency, 232 N Canon Dr, Beverly Hills, CA 90210 USA

Ferrell, Will *Actor, Comedian*
Mosaic Media Group, 9200 Sunset Blvd Fl 10, Los Angeles, CA 90069 USA

Ferrell Edmonson, Barbara A *Track Athlete*
University of Newada, Athletic Dept, Las Vegas, NV 89154 USA

Ferreol, Andrea
10 Ave. George V, Paris, FRANCE, F-75008

Ferrer, Danay *Musician*
Evolution Talent, 1776 Broadway, #1500, New York, NY 10019 USA

Ferrer, Lupita
861 Stone Canyon Rd., Los Angeles, CA 90077

Ferrer, Mel *Actor*
6590 Camino Carreta, Carpinteria, CA 93013 USA

Ferrer, Miguel *Actor*
1007 Maybrook Dr, Beverly Hills, CA 90210 USA

Ferrera, America *Actor*
Endeavor Agency LLC (LA), 9601 Wilshire Blvd Fl 3, Beverly Hills, CA 90210 USA

Ferreras, Francisco (Pipin) *Misc*
7548 W Treasure Dr, North Bay Village, FL 33141 USA

Ferrero, Louis P *Business Person*
PO Box 675744, Rancho Santa Fe, CA 92067 USA

Ferrigno, Lou *Actor*
Carla Ferrigno Management, 621 17th Street, Santa Monica, CA 90402 USA

Ferrin, Arnie *Basketball Player*
910 Donner Way, #301, Salt Lake City, UT 84108 USA

Ferris, John *Swimmer*
1961 Klamath River Dr, Rancho Cordova, CA 95670 USA

Ferris, Michael (Mike) *Writer, Producer*
Broder Webb Chervin Silbermann Agency, The (BWCS), 9242 Beverly Blvd #200, Beverly Hills, CA 90210 USA

Ferris, Pamela
16601 Marques Ave. #405, Pacific Palisades, CA 90272

Ferriss, David M (Boo) *Baseball Player*
510 Robinson Dr, Cleveland, MS 38732 USA

Ferritor, Daniel E *Educator*
University of Arkansas, Chancellor's Office, Fayetteville, AR 72701 USA

Ferro, Talya
303 S. Crescent Heights, Los Angeles, CA 90048

Ferron *Musician, Songwriter*
JR Productions, 4930 Paradise Dr, Tiburon, CA 94920 USA

Ferry, Bryan *Musician, Songwriter*
IE Mgmt, 59-A Chesson Rd, London, W14 9QS, UNITED KINGDOM (UK)

Ferry, Daniel J W (Danny) *Basketball Player*
San Antonio Spurs, Alamodome, 1 SBC Center, San Antonio, TX 78219 USA

Ferry, David R *Writer*
Wellesley College, English Dept, Wellesley, MA 02181 USA

Ferry, John D *Misc*
6175 Mineral Point Road, Madison, WI 53705 USA

Ferry, Robert (Bob) *Basketball Player*
2129 Beach haven Road, Annapolis, MD 21401 USA

Fersht, Alan R *Misc*
2 Barrow Close, Cambridge, CB2 2AT, UNITED KINGDOM (UK)

Fesperman, John E *Business Person*
J C Penney Co, 6501 Legacy Dr, Plano, TX 75024 USA

Festinger, Leon *Misc*
37 W 12th St, New York, NY 10011 USA

Fetisov, Viachesiav (Slava) *Hockey Player*
65 Avon Dr, Essex Fells, NJ 07021 USA

Fetter, Trevor *Business Person*
Tenet Healthcare Corp, 3820 State St, Santa Barbara, CA 93105 USA

Fetterhoff, Robert *Religious Leader*
Fellowship of Grace Brethem, PO Box 386, Winona Lake, IN 46590 USA

Fettig, Jeff M *Business Person*
Whirlpool Corp, 2000 N State St, RR 63, Benton Harbor, MI 49022 USA

Fetting, Katie *Actor*
Niad Literary & Talent Management, 3465 Coy Dr, Sherman Oaks, CA 91423 USA

Fetting, Ralner *Artist*
Hasenhelde 61, Berlin, 61, GERMANY

Fettman, Martin J *Astronaut*
5468 Tiller Court, Fprt Collins, CO 80528 USA

Feuer, Cy *Producer*
Feuer & Martin, 630 Park Ave, New York, NY 10021 USA

Feuer, Debra
9560 Wilshire Blvd. #500, Beverly Hills, CA 90212

Feuerstein, Mark *Actor*
Innovative Artists, 1505 10th St., Santa Monica, CA 90401 USA

Feulner, Edvin J Jr *Misc*
Heritage Foundation, 214 Massachusetts Ave NE, Washington, DC 20002 USA

Feustel, Andrew J *Astronaut*
4003 Elm Crest, Houston, TX 77059 USA

Fewx, Gene *Misc*
666 15th St NE, Salem, OR 97301 USA

Fey *Musician*
RAC Paseo Palmas 1005, #1, Chapultapec Lomas, Mexico City, 11000, MEXICO

Fey, Michael *Cartoonist*
United Feature Syndicate, 200 Madison Ave, New York, NY 10016 USA

Fey, Tina *Comedian, Writer*
3 Arts Entertainment Inc, 9460 Wilshire Blvd Fl 7, Beverly Hills, CA 90212 USA

Fforde, Jasper *Writer*
Viking Press, 375 Hudson St, New York, NY 10014 USA

Fialkowska, Janina *Musician*
ICM Artists, 40 W 57th St, New York, NY 10019 USA

Fichtel, Anja
Stauferring 104, Tauberbischofsheim, GERMANY, D-97941

Fichter, Rick T *Cinematographer*
7 Kramer Place, San Francisco, CA 94133 USA

Fichtner, Hans J *Scientist*
612 Cleemont Dr SE, Huntsville, AL 35801 USA

Fichtner, William *Actor*
Endeavor Talent Agency, 9701 Wilshire Blvd, #1000, Beverly Hills, CA 90212 USA

Fidrych, Mark *Baseball Player*
260 West St., Northborough, MA 01532 USA

Fiedel, Brad *Composer*
Gortaine/Schwartz, 13245 Riverside Dr, #430, Sherman Oaks, CA 91423 USA

Fiedler, Jens
Bruno-Granz-Str. 48, Chemnitz, GERMANY, D-09122

Fiedler, John *Actor*
225 Adams St, #10B, Brooklyn, NY 11201 USA

Fieger, Geoffrey *Attorney General*
Fieger Fieger Schwartz, 19390 W Ten Mile Road, Southfield, MI 48075 USA

Field, Arabella *Actor*
S M S Talent, 8730 Sunset Blvd, #440, Los Angeles, CA 90069 USA

Field, Ayda *Actor*
Brillstein-Grey Entertainment, 9150 Wilshire Blvd #350, Beverly Hills, CA 90212 USA

Field, Chelsea *Actor*
Troxell, 15263 Mulholland Dr, Los Angeles, CA 90077 USA

Field, Helen *Opera Singer*
Athole Still, Foresters Hall, 25-27 Westow St, London, SE19 3RY, UNITED KINGDOM (UK)

Field, Sally *Actor*
Creative Artists Agency LCC (CAA-LA), 9830 Wilshire Blvd, Beverly Hills, CA 90212 USA

Field, Shirley Ann
2-4 Noel St., London, ENGLAND, W1V 2RB

Field, Shirley Arin *Actor*
London Mgmt, 2-4 Noel St, London, W1V 3RB, UNITED KINGDOM (UK)

Field, Todd *Actor*
Three Arts Entertainment, 9460 Wilshire Blvd, #700, Beverly Hills, CA 90212 USA

Fielder, Cecil G *Baseball Player*
4150 Dow Road, #103, Melbourne, FL 32934 USA

Fielding, Fred F *Attorney General, Government Official*
Wiley Rein Fielding, 7925 Jones Branch Dr, #6200, McLean, VA 22102 USA

Fielding, Helen *Writer*
Viking Press, 375 Hudson St, New York, NY 10014 USA

Fielding, Joy *Writer*
Atria Books, 1230 Ave of Americas, New York, NY 10020 USA

Fields, Debbi *Business Person*
Mrs Fields Cookies, 462 Bearcat Dr, Salt Lake City, UT 84115 USA

Fields, Freddie
8899 Beverly Blvd. #918, Los Angeles, CA
90048-2412

Fields, Harold T Jr *General*
126 Dear Run Strut, Enterprise, AL 36330
USA

Fields, Holly *Actor*
Don Buchwald, 6500 Wilshire Blvd,
#2200, Los Angeles, CA 90048 USA

Fields, Joseph C (Joe) Jr *Football Player*
Widener University, Alumni Association,
1 University Place, Chester, PA 191013
USA

Fields, Kim *Actor*
All Talent Agency, 72624 El Paseo, #83,
Palm Desert, CA 92260 USA

Fields, Valerie
PO Box 4025, Niagara Falls, NY 14304

Fieldstad, Oivin
Damfaret 59, Bryn-Oslo, 6, NORWAY

Fiennes, Joseph *Actor*
Creative Artists Agency LCC (CAA-LA),
9830 Wilshire Blvd, Beverly Hills, CA
90212 USA

Fiennes, Joseph *Actor*
Ken McReddie, 91 Regent St, London,
W1R 7TB, UNITED KINGDOM (UK)

Fiennes, Ralph *Actor*
PMK/HBH Public Relations (PMK-LA),
8500 Wilshire Blvd #700, Beverly Hills,
CA 90211 USA

Fiennes, Ralph N *Actor*
Ken McReddie, 91 Regent St, London,
W1R 7TB, UNITED KINGDOM (UK)

Fierek, Wolfgang
Ottobrunner Str. 15, Brunnthal,
GERMANY, D-85649

Fierstein, Harvey *Actor, Writer, Musician*
1479 Carla Ridge Dr, Beverly Hills, CA
90210 USA

Fieser, Louis *Inventor*
58 Medford St, Arlington, MA 02474 USA

Figg-Currier, Cindy *Golfer*
109 Blue Jay Dr, Lakeway, TX 78734 USA

Figgis, Michael (Mike) *Director*
Steven R Pines, 520 Broadway, #600,
Santa Monica, CA 90401 USA

Figgis, Mike *Director*
Steven Pines, 520 Broadway #600, Santa
Monica, CA 90401

Figini, Luigi *Architect*
Via Perone di S Martino 8, Milan, ITALY

Figini, Michela *Skier*
Ariolo, Prato Lavenina, 6799,
SWITZERLAND

Figo, Luis *Soccer Player*
Real Madrid FC, Avda Cincha Espina 1,
Madrid, 28036, SPAIN

Figueroa, Efrain *Actor*
Mitchell K Stubbs & Assoc (MKS), 8675 W
Washington Blvd #203, Culver City, CA
90232 USA

Figura, Maria Louisa *Actor*
Select Artists Ltd (CA-Westside Office),
1138 12th Street, Suite 1, Santa Monica,
CA 90403 USA

Fikrig, Erol *Doctor*
Yale University, Medical Center,
Infectious Disease Dept, New Haven, CT
06510 USA

Filatova, Ludmila P *Opera Singer*
Ryleyevastr 6, #13, Saint Petersburg,
RUSSIA

Filicia, Thom *Television Host*
Queer Eye for the Straight Guy, 119
Braintree St, Boston, MA 02134

Filiol, Jalme *Tennis Player*
Advantage International, 1025 Thomas
Jefferson NW, #430, Washington, DC
20007 USA

Filion, Herve *Race Car Driver*
18 Evans Ave, Alberston, NY 11507 USA

Filipacchi, Daniel *Publisher*
Hachette Filipacchi, 149-51 Rue Anatole-
France, Levallois, 92534, FRANCE

Filipchenko, Anatoli N *Cosmonaut,
General*
Potcha Kosmonavtov Moskovskoi Oblasti,
Syvisdny Goroduk, 141160, RUSSIA

Filippo, Lou
7826 Botany St., Downey, CA 90240-
2624

Filippo (Fillipo/Filippo), Fabrizio (Fab)
Actor
IFA Talent Agency, 8730 Sunset Blvd
#490, Los Angeles, CA 90069 USA

Filipski, Gene *Football Player*
1285 Caribou Lane, Hoffman Estates, IL
60192 USA

Fill, Shannon *Actor*
260 S Beverly Dr #200, Beverly Hills, CA
90212 USA

Fillion, Nathan *Actor*
3 Arts Entertainment Inc, 9460 Wilshire
Blvd Fl 7, Beverly Hills, CA 90212 USA

Fimmel, Travis *Model, Actor*
Management 360, 9111 Wilshire Blvd,
Beverly Hills, CA 90210 USA

Fimple, Dennis
3518 Cahuenga Blvd. W. #306, Los
Angeles, CA 90068

Finch, Jon *Actor*
London Mgmt, 2-4 Noel St, London, W1V
3RB, UNITED KINGDOM (UK)

Finch, Larry *Basketball Player, Coach*
5962 lake Tide Cove, Memphis, TN
38120 USA

Finch, Linda *Misc*
World Flight, 211 Switch Oaks, San
Antonio, TX 78230 USA

Finch, Tyrone *Comedian*
United Talent Agency (UTA), 9560
Wilshire Blvd, Beverly Hills, CA 90212
USA

Finchem, Timothy W *Golfer*
Professional Golfer's Assn, Sawgrass,
Ponte Vedra Beach, FL 32082 USA

Fincher, David *Director*
Creative Artists Agency, 9830 Wilshire
Blvd, Beverly Hills, CA 90212 USA

Finck, George C *War Hero*
143 Beaver Lane, Benton, LA 71006 USA

Fincke, E Michael (Mike) *Astronaut*
11923 Mighty Redwood Dr, Houston, TX
77059 USA

Finckel, David *Musician*
I M G Artists, 3 Burlington Lane, London,
W4 2TH, UNITED KINGDOM (UK)

Finder, Joseph *Writer*
Avon William Morrow, 1350 Ave of
Americas, New York, NY 10019 USA

Findlay, Conn F *Athlete, Yachtsman*
1920 Oak Knoll, Belmont, CA 94002 USA

Fine, David *Writer*
Endeavor Agency LLC (LA), 9601 Wilshire
Blvd Fl 3, Beverly Hills, CA 90210 USA

Fine, Jeanna
19 Hanover Pl. PMB 313, Hicksville, NY
11801-5103

Fine, Travis *Actor*
Vaughn D Hart, 200 N Robertson Blvd
#219, Beverly Hills, CA 90211 USA

Finfera, Joe *Actor*
Select Artists Ltd (CA-Westside Office),
1138 12th Street, Suite 1, Santa Monica,
CA 90403 USA

Finger Eleven *Music Group*
Wind-up Records, 72 Madison Ave, New
York, NY 10016 USA

Fingers, Roland G (Rollie) *Baseball Player*
10675 Fairfield Ave, Las Vegas, NV 89123
USA

Fingers, Rollie
PO Box 230729, Las Vegas, NV 89123

Fink, Gerald R *Scientist, Doctor*
40 Alston Road, West Newton, MA 02465
USA

Fink, John
1680 N. Vine St. #614, Hollywood, CA
90028

Fink, Mitchell
1835 E. Michelle St., West Covina, CA
91791

Finkel, Fyvush *Actor*
155 E 50th St, #6E, New York, NY 10022
USA

Finkel, Henry (Hank) *Basketball Player*
2 Pocahontas Way, Lynnfield, MA 01940
USA

Finkel, Shelly
310 Madison Ave, #804, New York, NY
10017 USA

Finlay, Frank *Actor*
Ken McReddie, 91 Regent St, London,
W1R 7TB, UNITED KINGDOM (UK)

Finley, Charles E (Chuck) *Baseball Player*
22 Old Course Dr, Newport Beach, CA
92660 USA

Finley, David *Opera Singer*
1642 Milvia St, #3S, Berkeley, CA 94709
USA

Finley, Gerald H *Opera Singer*
I M G Artists, 3 Burlington Lane,
Chiswick, London, W4 2TH, UNITED
KINGDOM (UK)

Finley, John L *Astronaut*
1894 Woodchase Glen Dr, Cordova, TN
38016 USA

Finley, Karen *Artist*
Creative Time, 307 7th Ave, #1904, New York, NY 10001 USA

Finley, Margot *Actor*
Pacific Artists Management, 1404-510 W Hastings St, Vancouver, BC V6B 1L, CANADA

Finley, Michael *Basketball Player*
Dallas Mavericks, 2909 Taylor St, Dallas, TX 75226 USA

Finley, Steven A (Steve) *Baseball Player*
2502 Ocean Front, Del Mar, CA 92014 USA

Finn, John *Actor*
Metropolitan Talent Agency (MTA), 4526 Wilshire Blvd, Los Angeles, CA 90010 USA

Finn, John W *War Hero*
36585 Old Highway 80, Pine Valley, CA 91962 USA

Finn, Neil *Musician, Songwriter*
William Morris Agency (WMA-LA), 1 William Morris Pl, Beverly Hills, CA 90212 USA

Finn, Patrick *Actor*
Brillstein/Grey, 9150 Wilshire Blvd, #350, Beverly Hills, CA 90212 USA

Finn, Tim *Musician*
Grant Thomas Mgmt, 98 Surrey St, Darlinghurst, NSW, 2010, AUSTRALIA

Finn, Veronica *Musician*
Evolution Talent, 1776 Broadway, #1500, New York, NY 10019 USA

Finn, William *Composer, Songwriter*
New York University, Music Dept, New York, NY 10012 USA

Finneran, John G *Admiral*
2904 N Leisure World Blvd, #404, Silver Spring, MD 20906 USA

Finneran, Rittenhouse Sharon *Swimmer*
212 Harbor Dr, Santa Cruz, CA 95062 USA

Finnerty, Dan *Actor, Musician*
William Morris Agency (WMA-LA), 1 William Morris Pl, Beverly Hills, CA 90212 USA

Finney, Albert *Actor*
Michael Simkins, 45/51 Whitfield St, London, W1P 6AA, UNITED KINGDOM (UK)

Finney, Allison *Golfer*
78160 Desert Mountain Circle, Indio, CA 92201 USA

Finney, Tom *Soccer Player*
Preston North End FC, Deepdale, Sir Finney Way, Preston, PR1 6RU, UNITED KINGDOM (UK)

Finnie, Linda A *Musician*
16 Golf Course Girvan, Ayrshire, KA26 9HW, UNITED KINGDOM (UK)

Finnigan, Jennifer *Actor*
Foundation Management, 100 N Crescent Dr #300, Beverly Hills, CA 90212 USA

Finsterwald, Dow *Golfer*
Broadmoor Golf Club, 1 Lake Circle, Colorado Springs, CO 80906 USA

Fiore, Kathryn *Actor*
Levine Management, 9028 W Sunset Blvd #PH1, Los Angeles, CA 90069 USA

Fiorentino, Linda *Actor*
United Talent Agency (UTA), 9560 Wilshire Blvd, Beverly Hills, CA 90212 USA

Fiorentino, Linda *Actor*
United Talent Agency, 9560 Wilshire Agency Blvd, #500, Beverly Hills, CA 90212 USA

Fiori, Fernando *Actor*
Latin World Entertainment Agency (WEA), 2800 Biscayne Blvd PH, Miami, FL 33137

Fiorillo, Elisbatta *Opera Singer*
Columbia Artists Mgmt Inc, 165 W 57th St, New York, NY 10019 USA

Fiorina, Carleton S (Carly) *Business Person*
Hewlett-Packard Co, 19111 Pruneridge Ave, Cupertino, CA 95014 USA

Firbank, Ann
76 Oxford St., London, ENGLAND, W1N OAX

Firefall
6400 Pleasant Park Dr, Chanhassen, MN 55317

Fireman, Paul B *Business Person*
Reebok International, 1895 J W Foster Blvd, Canton, MA 02021 USA

Fires, Earlie S *Jockey*
16337 Rivervale Lane, Rivervale, AR 72377 USA

Firestone, Eddie
303 S. Crescent Heights, Los Angeles, CA 90048

Firestone, Roy *Sportscaster*
Seizen/Wallach Productions, 257 S Rodeo Dr, Beverly Hills, CA 90212 USA

Firm, The
57A Great Titchfield St., London, ENGLAND, W1P 7FL

First, Neal L *Misc*
9437 W Garnette Dr, Sun City, AZ 85373 USA

Firth, Colin *Actor*
International Creative Mgmt, 76 Oxford St, London, W1N 0AX, UNITED KINGDOM (UK)

Firth, Peter *Actor*
Markham & Froggatt, Julian House, 4 Windmill St, London, W1P 1HF, UNITED KINGDOM (UK)

Fischbach, Ephraim *Physicist*
5821 Farm Ridge Road, West Lafayette, IN 47906 USA

Fischer, Adam
Askonas Holt Ltd, 27 Chancery Lane, London, WC2A 1PF, UNITED KINGDOM (UK)

Fischer, Bernard
208 King Rd., Kuna, ID 83634

Fischer, Bobby
186 Rt. 9-W, New Windsor, NY 12550

Fischer, Edmond H *Nobel Prize Laureate*
5540 N Windermere Road, Seattle, WA 98105 USA

Fischer, Ernst Otto *Nobel Prize Laureate*
Sohnckestr 16, Munich, 81479, GERMANY

Fischer, Heinz *President*
Prasidentschaftskanzlei, Hofburg, Alderstiege, Vienna, 1010, AUSTRIA

Fischer, Helmut
Kaiserplatz 5, Munich, GERMANY, D-80803

Fischer, Ivan
1 Andrassy Utca 27, Budapest, 1061, HUNGARY

Fischer, Jenna *Actor*

Fischer, Kate *Actor*
Current Entertainment, 1411 Fifth St #405, Santa Monica, CA 90401 USA

Fischer, Lisa *Musician*
Alive Enterprices, 3264 S Kihei Road, Kihei, HI 96753 USA

Fischer, Michael L *Misc*
California Coastal Conservancy, 1330 Broadway #1100, Oakland, CA 94612 USA

Fischer, Patrick (Pat) *Football Player*
PO Box 4289, Leesburg, VA 20177 USA

Fischer, Schmidt Birgit *Athlete*
Kuckuckswald 11, Kleinmachnow, 14532, GERMANY

Fischer, Stanley *Economist*
181 E 65th St, #23A, New York, NY 10021 USA

Fischer, Sven *Athlete*
Schillerhoehe 7, Schmalkalden, 98574, GERMANY

Fischer, Van *Director*
Gersh Agency, 232 N Canon Dr, Beverly Hills, CA 90210 USA

Fischer, Veronika
Glockengiesserwall 3, Hamburg, GERMANY, D-20095

Fischer, William A (Moose) *Football Player*
1790 Pinnacle Ridge Lane, Colorado Springs, CO 80919 USA

Fischer-Dieskau, Dietrich *Opera Singer*
Lindenallee 22, Berlin, 12587, GERMANY

Fischer-Diskau, Dietrich
Lindenallee 22, Berlin, GERMANY, D-14050

Fischetti, Brad *Musician*
Evolution Talent Agency LLC, 1776 Broadway Fl 15, New York, NY 10019 USA

Fischetti, Vincent *Biologist*
Rockefeller University, Medical Center, 1230 York Ave, New York, NY 10021 USA

Fischler, Patrick *Actor*
Peter Strain & Associates Inc (LA), 5724 W 3rd St #302, Los Angeles, CA 90036 USA

Fish, Ginger *Musician*
Mitch Schneider Organization, 14724 Ventura Blvd, #410, Sherman Oaks, CA 91403 USA

Fish, Howard M *General*
1223 Capilano Dr, Shreveport, LA 71106 USA

Fishbacher, Siegfried *Magician*
Mirage Hotel & Casino, 3400 Las Vegas
Blvd S, Las Vegas, NV 89109 USA

Fishbone
PO Box 4450, New York, NY 10101

Fishburne, Laurence *Actor*
Lanmark Entertainment, 4116 W Magnolia
Blvd, #101, Burbank, CA 91505 USA

Fishel, Danielle *Actor*
Innovative Artists (LA), 1505 Tenth St,
Santa Monica, CA 90401 USA

Fisher, Allison *Billiards Player*
Alfie Inc, 9021 Hwy 105, South Boone,
NC 28607

Fisher, Anna L *Astronaut*
1912 Elmen St, Houston, TX 77019 USA

Fisher, Antwone *Writer*
William Morris Agency (WMA-LA), 1
William Morris Pl, Beverly Hills, CA
90212 USA

Fisher, Bernard *Doctor*
5636 Aylesboro Ave, Pittsburgh, PA
15217 USA

Fisher, Bernard F *War Hero*
4200 W king Road, Kuna, ID 83634 USA

Fisher, Carrie *Actor*
1700 Coldwater Canyon Rd, Beverly Hills,
CA 90210 USA

Fisher, Climie
30 Bridstow Pl., London, ENGLAND, W2
5AE

Fisher, Derek *Basketball Player*
Los Angeles Lakers, Staples Center, 1111 S
Figueroa St, Los Angeles, CA 90015 USA

Fisher, Eddie *Actor, Musician*
1000 N Point St, #1802, San Francisco,
CA 94109 USA

Fisher, Eddie G *Baseball Player*
408 Cardinal Circle S, Altus, OK 73521
USA

Fisher, Elder A (Bud) *Bowler*
7551 Brackenwood Circle N,
Indianapolis, IN 46260 USA

Fisher, Evan *Musician*
GEMS, PO Box 1031, Montrose, CA
91021 USA

Fisher, Frances *Actor*
I F A Talent Agency, 8730 Sunset Blvd,
#490, Los Angeles, CA 90069 USA

Fisher, Gerry
River Bank Hartsfield Rd., W. Molesey
Surrey, ENGLAND

Fisher, Isla *Actor*
Mosaic Media Group, 9200 Sunset Blvd Fl
10, Los Angeles, CA 90069 USA

Fisher, Jeff *Football Coach*
Tennessee Titans, 460 Great Circle Road,
Nashville, TN 37228 USA

Fisher, Joel *Artist*
99 Commercial St, Brooklyn, NY 11222
USA

Fisher, Joely *Actor*
Foundation Management, 100 N Crescent
Dr #300, Beverly Hills, CA 90212 USA

Fisher, Jules E *Designer*
Jules Fisher Enterprises, 126 5th Ave, New
York, NY 10011 USA

Fisher, Kimberly *Model*
PO Box 69330 #703, West Hollywood,
CA 90069

Fisher, Mary *Misc*
Charles Scribner's Sons, 866 3rd Ave,
New York, NY 10022 USA

Fisher, Matthew *Misc*
39 Croham Road, South Croydon, CR2
7HD, UNITED KINGDOM (UK)

Fisher, Raymond C *Judge*
US Courts of Appeals, 125 S Grand Ave,
Pasadena, CA 91105 USA

Fisher, Red *Writer*
Montreal Gazette, 250 Saint Antoine W,
Montreal, QC, H2Y 3R7, CANADA

Fisher, Rob
45 Montague Rd., Richmond Surrey,
ENGLAND

Fisher, Robert *Business Person*
Gap Inc, 2 Folsom St, San Francisco, CA
94105 USA

Fisher, Roger *Musician*
Borman Entertainment, 1250 6th St, #401,
Santa Monica, CA 90401 USA

Fisher, Sarah *Race Car Driver*
PO Box 533189, Indianapolis, IN 46253
USA

Fisher, Steve *Coach*
San Diego State University, Athletic Dept,
San Diego, CA 92182 USA

Fisher, Terry Louise
5314 Pacific Ave., Marina del Rey, CA
90292-7118

Fisher, Thomas L
Nicor Inc, 1844 Ferry Road, Naperville, IL
60563 USA

Fisher, Trisha Leigh
243 Delfern Dr., Los Angeles, CA 90077

Fisher, William F *Astronaut*
1119 Woodland Dr, Seabrook, TX 77586
USA

Fishman, Jerald G *Business Person*
Analog Devices Inc, 1 Technology Way,
Norwood, MA 02062 USA

Fishman, Jon *Musician*
Dionyslan Productions, 431 Pine St,
Burlington, VT 05401 USA

Fishman, Michael
Box 133226, Big Bear Lake, CA 92315-
8918

Fishman, Michael *Actor*
1530 Bainum Dr, Topanga, CA 90290
USA

Fisk, Carlton E *Baseball Player*
16612 S Catawba Road, Horner Glenn, IL
60441 USA

Fisk, Pliny III *Architect*
Maximum Potential Building Systems
Center, 8604 FM 969, Austin, TX 78724
USA

Fiske, Robert B Jr *Attorney General*
19 Juniper Road, Darien, CT 06820 USA

Fisker, Bruce L *General*
9001 S Jimson Weed Way, Highlands
Ranch, CO 80126 USA

Fitch, Val L *Nobel Prize Laureate*
292 Hartley Ave, Princeton, NJ 08540
USA

Fites, Donald V *Business Person*
Caterpillar Inc, 100 NE Adams St, Peoria,
IL 61629 USA

Fitt of Bell's Hill, Gerald *Government
Official*
irish Club, 82 Eaton Square, London,
SW1, UNITED KINGDOM (UK)

Fittipaldi, Christian *Race Car Driver*
282 Alphaville Barueri, Sao Paulo,
064500, BRAZIL

Fittipaldi, Emerson *Race Car Driver*
735 Crandon Blvd, #503, Miami, FL
33149 USA

Fitts, Rick
1903 Dracena Dr., Los Angeles, CA
90068

Fitz, Raymond L *Educator*
University of Dayton, President's Office,
Dayton, OH 45469 USA

Fitzgerald, A Ernest *Government Official,
Lawyer*
Air Force Management Systems, Pentagon,
Washington, DC 20330 USA

FitzGerald, Frances *Writer*
Simon & Schuster, 1230 Ave of Americas,
New York, NY 10020 USA

FitzGerald, Garret *Prime Minister*
30 Palmerston Road, Dublin, 6, IRELAND

Fitzgerald, Geraldine *Actor*
Lip Service, 4 Kingly St, London, W1R
3RB, UNITED KINGDOM (UK)

Fitzgerald, Glenn *Actor*
Endeavor NY, 23 Watts St Fl 6, New York,
NY 10013 USA

FitzGerald, Helen *Actor*
Paul Lohner, 9300 Wilshire Blvd, #555,
Beverly Hills, CA 90212 USA

Fitzgerald, Jack *Actor*
William Kerwin Agency, 1605 N
Cahuenga, #202, Los Angeles, CA 90028
USA

Fitzgerald, James F *Misc*
Golden State Warriors, 1001 Broadway,
Oakland, CA 94607 USA

Fitzgerald, Larry *Football Player*
Arizona Cardinals, PO Box 888, Phoenix,
AZ 85001 USA

Fitzgerald, Melissa *Actor*
Geddes Agency, The, 8430 Santa Monica
Blvd #200, Los Angeles, CA 90069

Fitzgerald, Mosley Benita *Athlete*
Women in Cable/Telecommunications,
14555 Avion Parkway, Chantilly, VA
20151 USA

FitzGerald, Niali W A *Business Person*
Unilever NV, Weena 455, Rotterdam, DK,
3000, NETHERLANDS

Fitzgerald, Tac *Actor*
Iris Burton Agency, 8916 Ashcroft Ave,
Los Angeles, CA 90048 USA

Fitzgerald, Tara *Actor*
Caroline Dawson, 125 Gloucester Road,
London, SW7 4IE, UNITED KINGDOM
(UK)

Fitzmaurice, David J *Misc*
Electrical Radio & Machinists Union,
11256 156th St NW, Washington, DC
20005 USA

Fitzmaurice, Michael J *War Hero*
PO Box 178, Hartford, SD 57033 USA

Fitzpatrick, Leo *Actor*
9350 Wilshire Blvd, #328, Beverly Hills, CA 90212 USA

Fitzpatrick, Sonya *Psychic, Writer*
Animals Are Forever LLC, 12121 Wilshire Blvd, Suite 301, Los Angeles, CA 90025 USA

Fitzsimmons, Lowell (Cotton) *Coach*
Phoenix Suns, 201 E Jefferson St, Phoenix, AZ 85004 USA

Fitzsimmons, Lowell Cotton
201 E. Jefferson St, Phoenix, AZ 85004

Fitzsimonds, Roger L *Financier*
Firstar Corp, 777 E Wisconsin Ave, Milwaukee, WI 53202 USA

Fitzwater, Marlin *Government Official*
851 Cedar Drive, Deale, MD 20751 USA

Fix, Oliver *Athlete*
Ringstr 6, Stadtbergen, GERMANY

Fixman, Marshall *Misc*
Colorado State University, Chemistry Dept, Fort Collins, CO 80523 USA

Fizer, Marcus *Basketball Player*
Charlotte Bobcats, 129 W Trade St #700, Charlotte, NC 28202 USA

Flach, Ken *Tennis Player, Coach*
Vanderbilt University, Athletic Dept, Nashville, TN 37240 USA

Flach, Thomas *Yachtsman*
Johanna-Resch-Str 13, Berlin, 12439, GERMANY

Flack, Enya *Actor*
House of Representatives, 400 S Beverly Dr #101, Beverly Hills, CA 90212 USA

Flade, H Kiaus-Dietrich *Cosmonaut*
Airbus Industries, 1 Rond Point M Bellonte, Blagnac Cedex, 31707, FRANCE

Flagg, Fannie *Actor, Comedian*
1569 Miramar Lane, Santa Barbara, CA 93108 USA

Flaherty, Joe
530 Gretna Green, Los Angeles, CA 90049

Flaherty, John T *Baseball Player*
43981 Needmore Court, Ashburn, VA 20147 USA

Flaherty, Maureen
PO Box 65539, Tucson, AZ 85724-5539

Flaherty, Stephen *Composer*
William Morris Agency, 151 El Camino Dr, Beverly Hills, CA 90212 USA

Flaim, Eric *Speed Skater*
116 Bellvue Ave, Rutland, VT 05701 USA

Flair, Rick *Wrestler*
7205 Piper Point Ln, Charlotte, NC 27277-0379 USA

Flaman, Ferdinand C (Fernle) *Hockey Player*
29 Church St, Westwood, MA 02090 USA

Flamingos, The
2375 E. Tropicana Ave. #304, Las Vegas, NV 89119

Flanagan, Barry *Artist*
5E Fawe St, London, E14 6PD, UNITED KINGDOM (UK)

Flanagan, Ed *Football Player*
10981 Clayton St, Northglenn, CO 80233 USA

Flanagan, Edward M Jr *General*
Parade Rest, 12 Oyster Catcher Road, Beaufort, SC 29907 USA

Flanagan, Fionnula *Actor*
Guttman Associates, 118 S Beverly Dr #201, Beverly Hills, CA 90212 USA

Flanagan, Flonnula *Actor*
Guttman, 118 S Beverly Dr, Beverly Hills, CA 90212 USA

Flanagan, James L *Engineer*
Rulgers University, Computer Aids for Industry Center, Piscataway, NJ 08855 USA

Flanagan, Michael K (Mike) *Baseball Player*
15010 York Road, Sparks, MD 21152 USA

Flanagan, Tommy *Actor*
P F D, Drury House, 34-43 Russell St, London, WC2B 5HA, UNITED KINGDOM (UK)

Flanery, Bridget
8428-C Melrose Pl., Los Angeles, CA 90069

Flanery, Sean Patrick *Actor*
6351 Bryn Mawr Dr, Los Angeles, CA 90068 USA

Flanigan, Joe *Actor*
Foundation Management, 100 N Crescent Dr #300, Beverly Hills, CA 90212 USA

Flanigan, Lauren *Opera Singer*
Robert Lombardo, Harkness Plaza, 61 W 62nd St #6F, New York, NY 10023 USA

Flannery, Susan *Actor*
Flannery-Daedy-Leona, 6977 Shepard Mesa, Carpinteria, CA 93013 USA

Flannery, Thomas *Editor, Cartoonist*
911 Dartmouth Gien Way, Baltimore, MD 21212 USA

Flannigan, Maureen *Actor*
Gold Marshak Liedtke, 3500 W olive Ave, #1400, Burbank, CA 91505 USA

Flatley, Michael *Dancer*
Creative Artists Agency, 9830 Wilshire Blvd, Beverly Hills, CA 90212 USA

Flatley, Patrick (Pat) *Hockey Player*
69 Cherrylawn Ave, North York, ON M9L 2B3, CANADA

Flatley, Paul R *Football Player*
3600 W 80th St, #535, Minneapolis, MN 55431 USA

Flatt, Lester
PO Box 647, Hendersonville, TN 37215

Flaum, Joel M *Judge*
US District Court, 219 S Dearborn St, Chicago, IL 60604 USA

Flavell, Richard A *Misc*
Yale University, Medical Center, Immunology Dept, New Haven, CT 06520 USA

Flavin, Jennifer *Model*
30 Beverly Park, Beverly Hills, CA 90210 USA

Flavor, Flav *Artist, Actor, Comedian*
William Morris Agency, 151 El Camino Dr, Beverly Hills, CA 90212 USA

Flay, Bobby *Chef*
Food Network, 1180 Ave of Americas, #1200, New York, NY 10036 USA

Flea *Musician*
Q Prime, 729 7th Ave, #1600, New York, NY 10019 USA

Fleck, Bela *Musician, Composer*
Agency for Performing Arts, 9200 Sunset Blvd, #900, Los Angeles, CA 90069 USA

Fleck, Jack *Golfer*
12006 Edgewater Road, Fort Smith, AR 72903 USA

Fleder, Gary R *Director*
ACTW Filmworks, 624 Sunset Ave, Venice, CA 90291 USA

Fleeshman, Richard *Actor*
Granada Television, Quay Street, Manchester, M60 9EA, UNITED KINGDOM (UK)

Fleetwood, Ken *Fashion Designer*
14 Savile Row, London, SW1, UNITED KINGDOM (UK)

Fleetwood, Mick *Musician*
Courage Mgmt, 2899 Agoura Rd, #582, Westlake Village, CA 91361 USA

Fleischer, Arthur Jr *Attorney General*
Fried Frank Harris Shriver Jacobson, 1 New York Plaza, New York, NY 10004 USA

Fleischer, Charles
749 N. Crescent Heights, Los Angeles, CA 90038

Fleischer, Daniel *Religious Leader*
201 Princess Dr, Corpus Christi, TX 78410 USA

Fleischer, Richard O *Director*
Gersh Agency, 232 N Canon Dr, Beverly Hills, CA 90210 USA

Fleischman, Paul *Writer*
PO Box 646, Aromas, CA 95004 USA

Fleischmann, Peter *Director, Producer*
Filmzentrum Babelsberg, August-Bebel-Str 26-53, Potsdam, 14482, GERMANY

Fleisher, Bruce *Golfer*
207 Grand Pointe Dr, West Palm Beach, FL 33418 USA

Fleisher, Leon *Musician*
20 Merrymount Road, Baltimore, MD 21210 USA

Fleiss, Heidi *Business Person*
Jesse Fleiss, PO Box 291831, Los Angeles, CA 90027 USA

Fleiss, Michael (Mike) *Producer, Writer, Director*
Next Entertainment, 15301 Ventura Blvd, Bldg E, Sherman Oaks, CA 91403 USA

Fleiss, Noah *Actor*
3 Arts Entertainment (NY), 451 Greenwich St Fl 7, New York, NY 10013 USA

Fleming, Ed
RD #3Box 261K, Greensbury, PA 15601

Fleming, James P *War Hero*
PO Box 703, Longview, WA 98632 USA

Fleming, Mac A *Misc*
Maintenance of Ways Brotherhood, 26555
Evergreen Road, Southfield, MI 48076
USA

Fleming, Marvin (Marv) *Football Player*
909 Howard St, Marina del Rey, CA
90292 USA

Fleming, Peggy *Figure Skater*
1122 South Robertson Blvd #15, Los
Angeles, CA 90035 USA

Fleming, Peter E Jr *Attorney General*
Curtis Mallet-Prevost Colt Mosle, 101 Park
Ave, New York, NY 10178 USA

Fleming, Reginald S (Reggie) *Hockey
Player*
1605 E Central Road, #406A, Arlington
Heights, IL 60005 USA

Fleming, Renee *Opera Singer*
M L Falcone, 155 W 68th St, #1104, New
York, NY 10023 USA

Fleming, Rhonda *Actor*
10281 Century Woods Dr, Los Angeles,
CA 90067 USA

Fleming, Richard C D *Engineer*
Greater Denver Chamber of Commerce,
1445 Market ST, Denver, CO 80202 USA

Fleming, Scott *Government Official*
2750 Shasta Road, Berkeley, CA 94708
USA

Fleming, Vern *Basketball Player*
10713 Brixton Lane, Fishers, IN 46038
USA

Fleming, Wendell H *Mathematician*
9 Dolly Dr, Bristol, RI 02809 USA

Fleming Jenkins, Peggy *Figure Skater*
16387 Aztec Ridge Dr, Los Gatos, CA
95030 USA

Flemming, Catherine
Goethestr. 17, Munich, GERMANY,
D-80336

Flemming, John *Artist*
1409 Cambronne St, New Orleans, LA
70118 USA

Flemming, William N (Bill) *Sportscaster*
ABC-TV Sports Dept, 77 W 66th St, New
York, NY 10023 USA

Flemyng, Gordon *Director*
1 Albert Road, Wilmslow, Cheshire, SK9
5HT, UNITED KINGDOM (UK)

Flemyng, Jason *Actor*
Conway Van Gelder Robinson, 18-21
Jermyn St, London, SW1Y 6NB, UNITED
KINGDOM (UK)

Flemyng, Robert *Actor*
4 Netherbourne Road, London, SW4,
UNITED KINGDOM (UK)

Flennes, Ranulph T-W *Misc*
Greenlands Exford, Minehead, West
Sussex, UNITED KINGDOM (UK)

Flerstein, Harvey F *Writer, Actor,
Musician*
1479 Carla Ridge Dr, Beverly Hills, CA
90210 USA

Flessel, Craig *Cartoonist*
40 Camino Alto, #2306, Mill Valley, CA
94941 USA

Fletcher, Andy *Musician*
Reach Media, 295 Greenwich St, #109,
New York, NY 10007 USA

Fletcher, Arthur A *Government Official*
Commission on Civil Rights, 1121
Vermont Ave NW, Washington, DC
20005 USA

Fletcher, Betty Binns *Judge*
US Court of Appeals, US Courthouse,
1010 5th St, Seattle, WA 98104 USA

Fletcher, Brendan *Actor*
Seven Summits Mgmt, 8447 Wilshire
Blvd, #200, Beverly Hills, CA 90211 USA

Fletcher, Charles M *Physicist, Scientist*
2 Coastguard Cottages, Newtown, PO30
4PA, UNITED KINGDOM (UK)

Fletcher, Colin *Writer*
Brandt & Brandt, 1501 Broadway, New
York, NY 10036 USA

Fletcher, Dexter
1 Kingsway House Albion Rd., London,
ENGLAND, N16

Fletcher, Diane *Actor*
Ken McReddie, 91 regent St, London,
W1R 7TB, UNITED KINGDOM (UK)

Fletcher, Guy *Musician*
Damage Mgmt, 16 Lambton Place,
London, W11 2SH, UNITED KINGDOM
(UK)

Fletcher, Jamar *Football Player*
Miami Dolphins, 7500 SW 30th St, Davie,
FL 33314 USA

Fletcher, Louise *Actor*
1520 Camden Ave, #105, Los Angeles,
CA 90025 USA

Fletcher, Martin *Commentator*
NBC-TV, News Dept, 4001 Nebraska Ave
NW, Washington, DC 20016 USA

Fletcher, Scott B *Baseball Player*
300 Birkdale Dr, Favetteville, GA 30215
USA

Fletcher, William A *Judge*
US Court of Appeals, Courts Building, 95
7th St, San Francisco, CA 94103 USA

Fleury, Theoren *Hockey Player*
Chicago Blackhawks, United Center, 1901
W Madison St, Chicago, IL 60612 USA

Flick, Bob *Misc*
Bob Flick Productions, 300 Vine, #14,
Seattle, WA 98121 USA

Flick, Mick
Sherry Netherlands 5th & 59th, New York,
NY 10003

Flicker, John *Misc*
National Audubon Society, President's
Office, 700 Broadway, New York, NY
10003 USA

Flinelt, Flemming O *Choreographer,
Dancer*
Christiansholms Parkv 24, Klampenborg,
2930, DENMARK

Flint, Keith *Musician, Dancer*
Midi Mgmt, Jenkins Lane, Great
Hallinsbury, Essex, CM22 7QL, UNITED
KINGDOM (UK)

Flippin, Lucy Lee
1753 Canfield Ave., Los Angeles, CA
90035

Flock of Seagulls
526 Nicolett Mall, Minneapolis, MN
55402

Flockhart, Calista *Actor*
Talent Mgmt, 9100 Wilshire Blvd, #725E,
Beverly Hills, CA 90212 USA

Floetry *Music Group*
William Morris Agency (WMA-LA), 1
William Morris Pl, Beverly Hills, CA
90212 USA

Flom, Joseph H *Attorney General*
Skadden Arps State Meagher Flom, 4
Times Square, New York, NY 10036 USA

Flood, Ann *Actor*
15 E 91st St, New York, NY 10128 USA

Flor, Claus Peter *Conductor*
Intermusica Artists, 16 Duncan Terrace,
London, N1 8BZ, UNITED KINGDOM
(UK)

Florance, Sheila *Actor*
Melbourne Artists, 643 Saint Kikla Road,
Melbourne, VIC, 3004, AUSTRALIA

Florek, Dann *Actor*
145 W 45th St, #1204, New York, NY
10036 USA

Floren, Myron *Musician*
26 Georgeff Road, Rolling Hills, CA
90274 USA

Flores, Facusse Carlos *President*
Casa Presidencial, Blvd Juan Pablo II,
Tegucigalpa, HONDURAS

Flores, Francisco *President*
President's Office, Casa Presidencial, San
Salvador, EI SALVADOR

Flores, Patrick F *Religious Leader*
Archbishop's Residence, 2600 Woodlawn
Ave, San Antonio, TX 78228 USA

Flores, Thomas R (Tom) *Football Player,
Football Executive, Football Coach*
77741 Cove Point Circle, Indian Wells,
CA 92210 USA

Flores, Tom
11220 NE 53rd St., Kirkland, WA 98033

Floria, Holly *Actor*
Epstein-Wyckoff, 280 S Beverly Dr, #400,
Beverly Hills, CA 90212 USA

Floria, James J (Jim) *Governor*
Mudge Rose Guthrie, Coporate Center 2,
1673 E 16th St #16, Brooklyn, NY 11229
USA

Florin, Krista *Stylist*
Bulgari (NY), 730 5th Ave, New York, NY
10019 USA

Florio, Steven T *Publisher*
Conde Nast Publications, Publisher's
Office, 4 Times Square, New York, NY
10036 USA

Florio, Thomas A *Actor*
New Yorker Magazine, Publisher's Office,
4 Times Square, New York, NY 10036
USA

Flory, Med *Actor*
6044 Ensign Ave, North Hollywood, CA
91606 USA

Flournoy, Craig *Journalist*
Dallas News, Editorial Dept,
Communications Center, Dallas, TX
75265 USA

Flower, Joseph R *Religious Leader*
Assemblies of God, 1445 N Boonville
Ave, Springfield, MO 65802 USA

Flowers, Charles (Charlie) *Football Player*
6170 Mount Brook Way NW, Atlanta, GA
30342 USA

Flowers, Frank E *Writer, Director*
Firm, The, 9465 Wilshire Blvd, Beverly
Hills, CA 90212 USA

Flowers, Gennifer
4859 Cedar Springs #241, Dallas, TX
75219

Flowers of Queen's Gate, Brian H
Physicist
53 Athenaeum Road, London, N2O 9AL,
UNITED KINGDOM (UK)

Floyd, C Clifford (Cliff) *Baseball Player*
3804 Edgewater Dr, Hazel Crest, IL 60429
USA

Floyd, Carlisie *Composer*
4491 Yoakum Blvd, Houston, TX 77006
USA

Floyd, Eddie *Musician, Songwriter*
Jason West, Gables House, Saddlebow
Kings Lynn, PE34 3AR, UNITED
KINGDOM (UK)

Floyd, Eric (Sleepy) *Basketball Player*
22136 Westheimer Parkway, #201, Katy,
TX 77450 USA

Floyd, George *Football Player*
8621 Heritage Dr, Florence, KY 41042
USA

Floyd, Heather *Musician*
TBA Artists Mgmt, 300 10th Ave S,
Nashville, TN 37203 USA

Floyd, Marlene *Golfer*
Marlene Floyd Golf School, 5350 Club
House Lane, Hope Mills, NC 28348 USA

Floyd, Pink
370 City Rd. Islington, London,
ENGLAND, EC1V 2QA

Floyd, Ray
PO Box 545957, Surfside, FL 33154-5957

Floyd, Raymond (Ray) *Golfer*
PO Box 2163, Palm Beach, FL 33480
USA

Floyd, Susan
PO Box 5617, Beverly Hills, CA 90210

Floyd, Tim *Coach*
New Orleans Hornets, New Orleans
Arena, 1501 Girod St, New Orleans, LA
70113 USA

Fluckey, Eugene B *War Hero, Admiral*
1016 Sandpiper Lane, Annapolis, MD
21403 USA

Fluegel, Darlanne *Actor*
Shelter Entertainment, 9255 Sunset Blvd,
#1010, Los Angeles, CA 90069 USA

Fluno, Jere D *Business Person*
W W Grainger Inc, 5500 W Howard St,
Skokie, IL 60077 USA

Flutie, Doug *Football Player*
Provident Financial Mgmt, 10345 W
Olympic Blvd, Los Angeles, CA 90064
USA

Flynn, Barbara *Actor*
Markham & Froggatt, Julian House, 4
Windmill St, London, W1P 1HF, UNITED
KINGDOM (UK)

Flynn, Colleen *Actor*
LGM, 10390 Santa Monica Blvd, #300,
Los Angeles, CA 90025 USA

Flynn, George W *Misc*
382 Summit Ave, Leonia, NJ 07605 USA

Flynn, Jackie *Comedian*
Don Buchwald & Associates Inc (LA),
6500 Wilshire Blvd #2200, Los Angeles,
CA 90048 USA

Flynn, Neil *Actor*
Christopher Wright Management, 3340
Barham Blvd, Los Angeles, CA 90068

Flynn, Raymond L *Politician, Diplomat*
Catholic Alliance, Via CatholICity, PO
Box 1872, Chesapeake, VA 23327 USA

Flynt, Larry *Publisher*
Hustler Magazine, 9171 Wilshire Blvd,
#300, Beverly Hills, CA 90210 USA

Fo, Dario *Nobel Prize Laureate*
Pietro Sclotta, Via Alessandria 4, Milan,
20144, ITALY

Foale, C Michael *Doctor*
2101 Todville Rd #11, Seabrook, TX
77586 USA

Foale, C Michael (Mike) *Astronaut*
2101 Todville Road, #11, Seabrook, TX
77586 USA

Foch, Nina *Actor*
PO Box 1884, Beverly Hills, CA 90213
USA

Fodor, Eugene *Musician*
22314 N Turkey Creek Road, Morrison,
CO 80465 USA

Foege, William H *Misc*
10610 SW Cowan Road, Vashan, WA
98070 USA

Foeger, Luggi *Skier*
Christopher Foeger, 230 S Balsamina
Way, Portola Valley, CA 94028 USA

Foer, Jonathan Safron *Writer*
Houghton Mifflin, 222 Berkeley St, #700,
Boston, MA 02116 USA

Fogdoe, Tomas *Skier*
Skogsvagen 18, Gallvare, 970 02,
SWEDEN

Fogel, Robert W *Nobel Prize Laureate*
5321 S University Ave, Chicago, IL 60615
USA

Fogelberg, Dan *Musician, Songwriter*
H K Mgmt, 9200 W Sunset Blvd, #530,
Los Angeles, CA 90069 USA

Fogerty, John *Musician, Songwriter*
4570 Van Nuys Blvd, #3517, Sherman
Oaks, CA 91403 USA

Fogg, Kirk *Actor*
Brady Brannon & Rich/ VOX, 6300
Wilshire Blvd, Suite 900, Los Angeles, CA
90048 USA

Foggs, Edward L *Religious Leader*
Church of God, PO Box 2420, Anderson,
IN 46018 USA

Fogleman, Ronald R (Ron) *General*
406 Snowshoe Lane, Durango, CO 81301
USA

Fogler, Eddie *Basketball Player*
University of South Carolina, Athletic
Dept, Columbia, SC 53233 USA

Foglesong, Robert H (Doc) *General*
Vice Chief of Staff, HqUSAF Pentagon,
Washington, DC 20330 USA

Fokin, Vitold P *Prime Minister*
Cabinet of Ministers, Government
Building, Klev, UKRAINE

Foldberg, Henry C (Hank) *Football Player*
1204 S 12th St, Rogers, AR 72756 USA

Folds, Ben *Musician, Songwriter*
CEC, 1123 Broadway, #317, New York,
NY 10010 USA

Foley, Dave *Comedian*
Baker/Winokur/Ryder, 9100 Wilshire Blvd,
#600, Beverly Hills, CA 90212 USA

Foley, ex-Speaker Tom
601 W. 1st Ave. #2W, Spokane, WA
99204-0317

Foley, Jeremy *Actor*
Academy Kids Mgmt, 4942 Vineland Ave
#103, North Hollywood, CA 91601 USA

Foley, Linda *Misc*
Newspaper Guild, 8611 2nd Ave, Silver
Spring, MD 20910 USA

Foley, Maurice B *Judge*
US Tax Court, 400 2nd St NW,
Washington, DC 20217 USA

Foley, Mick *Wrestler*
World Wrestling Entertainment (WWE),
1241 E Main St, Stamford, CT 06905 USA

Foley, Robert F *War Hero, General*
110 Walkerson Dr, Marion, AL 36756
USA

Foley, Scott *Actor*
Handprint Entertainment, 1100 Glendon
Ave, Los Angeles, CA 90024 USA

Foley, Steve
8942 Wilshire Blvd., Beverly Hills, CA
90211

Foley, Sylvester R Jr *Admiral*
50 Apple Hill Dr, Tewksbury, MA 01876
USA

Foley, Thomas S *Diplomat*
PO Box 1047, Medical Lake, WA 99022
USA

Foley, Tim J *Football Player*
2851 Old Clifton ROad, Springfield, OH
45502 USA

Folger, Franklin *Cartoonist*
King Features Syndicate, 888 7th Ave,
New York, NY 10106 USA

Foligno, Mike *Hockey Player*
1179 Jill Dr, Hummelstown, PA 17036
USA

Folkenberg, Robert S *Religious Leader*
Seventh-Day Adventists, 12501 Old
Columbia Pike, Silver Spring, MD 20904
USA

Folkman, M Judah *Doctor*
18 Chatham Circle, Brookline, MA 02446
USA

Follesdal, Dagfinn K *Misc*
Staverhagen 7, Slepemdem, 1312,
NORWAY

Follett, Ken *Writer*
Box 4, Knebworth, SG3 6UT, UNITED KINGDOM (UK)

Follows, Megan *Actor*
Susan Smith, 121A N San Vicente Blvd, Beverly Hills, CA 90211 USA

Folon, Jean-Michel *Artist*
Burcy, Beaumont-du-Gatinais, 77890, FRANCE

Folsom, Allan R *Writer*
Little Brown, 3 Center Plaza, Boston, MA 02108 USA

Folsom, James E (Jim) Jr *Governor*
1482 Orchard Dr NE, Cullman, AL 35055 USA

Folsome, Claire *Biologist*
University of Hawaii, Microbiology Dept, 2600 Campus Road, Honolulu, HI 96822 USA

Fonda, Bridget *Actor*
United Talent Agency, 9560 Wilshire Blvd, #500, Beverly Hills, CA 90212 USA

Fonda, Jane *Actor*
Fonda Inc, PO Box 5840, Atlanta, GA 31107 USA

Fonda, Peter *Actor*
21 Foothills Dr, Bozeman, MT 59718 USA

Fondren, Debra Jo *Model, Actor*
PO Box 4351-856, Los Angeles, CA 90078 USA

Foner, Eric *Historian*
606 W 116th St, New York, NY 10027 USA

Fong, Darryl
247 S. Beverly Dr. #102, Beverly Hills, CA 90212

Fong, Hiram L *Senator*
1102 Alewa Dr, Honolulu, HI 96817 USA

Fonseca, Adriana *Actor*
Televisa, Blvd Adolfo Lopez Mateos 232, Colonia San Angel INN, DF, CP 01060, MEXICO

Fonseca, Lyndsy *Actor*
Sager Management, 260 South Bevely Drive, Suite 205, Beverly Hills, CA 90210 USA

Fontaine, Frank *Musician*
Suffolk Marketing, 475 5th Ave, New York, NY 10017 USA

Fontaine, Joan *Actor*
PO Box 222600, Carmel, CA 93922 USA

Fontaine, Lucien *Jockey*
1226 NW 11th Way, Pompano Beach, FL 33071 USA

Fontaine, Maurice A *Misc*
25 Rue Pierre Nicole, Paris, 75005, FRANCE

Fontana, D J
PO Box 262, Carteret, NJ 07008 USA

Fontana, Isabeli *Model*
Women Model Mgmt, 107 Greene St, #200, New York, NY 10012 USA

Fontana, Wayne *Musician*
Brian Gannon Mgmt, PO Box 106, Rochdale, OL16 4HW, UNITED KINGDOM (UK)

Fontes, Wayne H *Football Player, Football Coach*
2043 Harbour Watch Circle, Tarpon Springs, FL 34689 USA

Fonville, Charles *Track Athlete*
1845 Wintergreen Court, Ann Arbor, MI 48103 USA

Foo Fighters *Music Group*
Creative Artists Agency LCC (CAA-LA), 9830 Wilshire Blvd, Beverly Hills, CA 90212 USA

Foot, Michael M *Government Official*
308 Gray's Inn Road, London, WC1X 8DY, UNITED KINGDOM (UK)

Foote, Adam *Hockey Player*
11 Mountain Laurel Dr, Littleton, CO 80127 USA

Foote, Dan *Editor, Cartoonist*
Dallas Times Herald, Editorial Dept, Herald Square, Dallas, TX 75202 USA

Foote, Horton *Writer*
95 Horatio St, #322, New York, NY 10014 USA

Foote, Shelby *Writer*
542 East Parkway S, Memphis, TN 38104 USA

Foote II, Edward T *Educator*
University of Miami, President's Office, Coral Gables, FL 33124 USA

Foray, June *Actor*
22745 Erwin St, Woodland Hills, CA 91367 USA

Forbert, Steve *Musician, Songwriter*
Mongrel Music, 743 Center Blvd, Fairfax, CA 94930 USA

Forbes, Brian
Seven Pines Wentworth, Surrey, ENGLAND

Forbes, Bryan *Director, Writer*
Bookshop, Virginia Water, Surrey, UNITED KINGDOM (UK)

Forbes, Kristin *Government Official, Economist*
Council of Economic Advisers, Old Executive Office Bldg, Washington, DC 20500 USA

Forbes, Malcolm S (Steve) Jr *Editor*
Forbes Magazine, Editorial Dept, 60 5th Ave, New York, NY 10011 USA

Forbes, Michelle *Actor*
I F A Talent Agency, 8730 Sunset Blvd, #490, Los Angeles, CA 90069 USA

Forbes, West *Musician*
Paramount Entertainment, PO Box 12, Far Hills, NJ 07931 USA

Force, John *Race Car Driver*
John Force Racing, 22722 Old Canal Road, Yorba Linda, CA 92887 USA

Ford, Bette
1801 Ave. of the Stars #902, Los Angeles, XA, 90067

Ford, Betty
40365 San Dune Road, Rancho Mirage, CA 92270

Ford, Charlotte
25 Sutton Pl., New York, NY 10023

Ford, Cheryl *Basketball Player*
Detroit Shock Palace, 2 Championship Dr, Aubum Hills, MI 48326 USA

Ford, Chris *Coach, Basketball Player*
2 Melody Lane, Lynnfield, MA 01940 USA

Ford, Diane
201 San Vicente Blvd. #6, Santa Monica, XA, 90402

Ford, Doug *Golfer*
6128 Bear Creek Circle, Lake Worth, FL 33467 USA

Ford, Edward C (Whitey) *Baseball Player*
3750 Galt Ocean Dr, #1411, Fort Lauderdale, FL 33308 USA

Ford, Eileen
344 E. 59th St., New York, NY 10022

Ford, Elizabeth B (Betty) *Ex-First Lady*
40365 Sand Dune Road, Rancho Mirage, CA 92270 USA

Ford, Elleen O *Misc*
Ford Model Agency, 142 Greene St, #400, New York, NY 10012 USA

Ford, Faith *Actor*
9460 Wilshire Blvd, #7, Beverly Hills, CA 90212 USA

Ford, Frankie *Musician, Songwriter*
Ken Keane Artists, PO Box 1875, Gretna, LA 70054 USA

Ford, Gerald W *Misc*
Ford Model Agency, 142 Greene St, #400, New York, NY 10012 USA

Ford, Gilbert (Gib) *Basketball Player, Coach*
264 Edgemere Way E, Naples, FL 34105 USA

Ford, Glenn *Actor*
Peter Ford, 911 Oxford Way, Beverly Hills, CA 90210 USA

Ford, Harrison *Actor*
Pat McQueeney Mgmt, 10279 Century Woods Dr, Los Angeles, CA 90067 USA

Ford, Henry *Football Player*
3729 Brett Dr, Fort Worth, TX 76123 USA

Ford, Jack *Commentator*
CBS-TV, News Dept, 51 W 52nd St, New York, NY 10019 USA

Ford, Katie *Misc*
Ford Model Agency, 142 Greene St, #400, New York, NY 10012 USA

Ford, Kevin A *Astronaut*
1002 Oak Park Lane, Friendswood, TX 77546 USA

Ford, Lita *Musician*
RCA Records, 1540 Broadway #3500, New York, NY 10036 USA

Ford, Maria *Actor*
8281 Melrose Ave, #200, Los Angeles, CA 90046 USA

Ford, Mick
47 Courtfield Rd. #9, London, ENGLAND, SW7 4DB

Ford, Phil J Jr *Basketball Player*
12004 Iredell Dr, Chapel Hill, NC 27517 USA

Ford, Richard *Writer*
International Creative Mgmt, 40 W 57th St, #1800, New York, NY 10019 USA

Ford, Ruth *Actor*
Dakota Hotel, 1 W 72nd St, New York, NY 10023 USA

Ford, Scott *Business Person*
Alltel Corp, PO Box 94255, Palatine, IL 60094 USA

Ford, T J *Basketball Player*
Milwaukee Bucks, Bradley Center, 1001 N 4th St, Milwaukee, WI 53203 USA

Ford, Thomas Mikal *Actor*
Catch 23 Management, 301 N Canon Dr #207, Beverly Hills, CA 90210 USA

Ford, Tom *Fashion Designer*
Gucci Inc, 50 Hartz Way, Secaucus, NJ 07094 USA

Ford, Trent *Actor*
Paradigm (LA), 10100 Santa Monica Blvd, Fl 25, Los Angeles, CA 90067 USA

Ford, Wendell H *Governor, Senator*
423 Frederica St, #314, Owensboro, KY 42301 USA

Ford, Whitey
38 Schoolhouse Lane, Lake Success, NY 11020

Ford, Willa *Musician*
Atlantic Records (LA), 9229 Sunset Blvd, Los Angeles, CA 90069

Ford, William C Jr *Business Person*
Ford Motor Co, American Road, Dearborn, MI 48121 USA

Ford Jr, Gerald R *Politician, Ex-President*
40365 San Dune Road, Rancho Mirage, CA 92270 USA

Fordham, Julia *Musician, Songwriter*
Vanguard Records, 2700 Pennsylvania Ave, Santa Monica, CA 90404 USA

Foreigner *Music Group*
Creative Artists Agency LCC (CAA-LA), 9830 Wilshire Blvd, Beverly Hills, CA 90212 USA

Foreman, Amanda *Actor*
Lloyd and Kass Entertainment, 10202 W Washington Blvd, Bldg Astaire 2210, Culver City, CA 90232 USA

Foreman, Carol L T *Government Official*
5408 Trent St, Chevy Chase, MD 20815 USA

Foreman, Chuck
574 Prairie Center Dr. #156, Eden Prairie, MN 55344

Foreman, Deborah
9014 Melrose Ave, W. Hollywood, CA 90069-6710

Foreman, George *Boxer*
4402 Walham Court, Kingwood, TX 77345 USA

Foreman, Walter E (Chuck) *Football Player*
9716 Mill Creek Dr, Eden Prairie, MN 55347 USA

Forest, Michael
PO Box 69590, Los Angeles, CA 90069

Forester, Nicole *Actor*
Gage Group, 14724 Ventura Blvd, #505, Sherman Oaks, CA 91403 USA

Forester Sisters
3322 West End Ave, Nashville, TN 37203

Forget, Guy *Tennis Player*
Rue des Pacs 2, Neuchatel, 2000, SWITZERLAND

Forlani, Arnaldo *Prime Minister*
Piazzale Schumann 15, Rome, ITALY

Forlani, Claire *Actor*
Creative Artists Agency, 9830 Wilshire Blvd, Beverly Hills, CA 90212 USA

Forman, Milos *Director*
Lantz, 200 W 57th St, New York, NY 10019 USA

Forman, Stanley *Photographer, Journalist*
17 Cherry Road, Beverly, MA 01915 USA

Forman, Tom *Cartoonist*
10544 James Road, Celina, TX 75009 USA

Formesa, Fern
5018 N. 61st Ave., Glendale, AZ 85301

Formia, Osvaldo *Horse Racer*
6501 Winfield Blvd #A10, Margate, FL 33063 USA

Forney, G David Jr *Scientist*
6 Coolidge Hill Road, Cambridge, MA 02138 USA

Foronly, Richard *Actor*
House of Representatives, 400 S Beverly Dr, #101, Beverly Hills, CA 90212 USA

Forrest, Frederic *Actor*
11300 W Olympic Blvd, #610, Los Angeles, CA 90064 USA

Forrest, Katherine Virginia *Writer*
PO Box 31613, San Francisco, CA 94131

Forrest, Mark
13266 Bracken St., Arleta, CA 91331

Forrest, Sally *Actor*
1125 Angelo Dr, Beverly Hills, CA 90210 USA

Forrest, Steve *Actor*
1605 Michael Lane, Pacific Palisades, CA 90272 USA

Forrestal, Robert P *Financier, Government Official*
3949 Vermont Road NE, Atlanta, GA 30319 USA

Forrester, James *Scientist*
Cedars-Sinai Medical Center, 8700 Beverly Blvd, West Hollywood, CA 90048 USA

Forrester, Jay W *Inventor*
Massachusetts Institute of Technology, Management School, Cambridge, MA 02139 USA

Forrester, Patrick G *Astronaut*
3923 park Circle Way, Houston, TX 77059 USA

Forsberg, Peter *Hockey Player*
475 W 12th Ave, #16C, Denver, CO 80204 USA

Forsch, Kenneth R (Ken) *Baseball Player*
881 S Country Glen Way, Anaheim, CA 92808 USA

Forsch, Robert H (Bob) *Baseball Player*
9 Westmeade Court, Chesterfield, MO 63005 USA

Forslund, Constance *Actor*
165 W 46th St, #1109, New York, NY 10036 USA

Forsman, Dan *Golfer*
88 W 4500 N, Provo, UT 84604 USA

Forst, Bill *Cartoonist*
2320 Byer Road, Santa Cruz, CA 95062 USA

Forster, Brian
16172 Flamstead Dr., Hacienda Heights, CA 91745

Forster, Marc *Producer*
William Morris Agency (WMA-LA), 1 William Morris Pl, Beverly Hills, CA 90212 USA

Forster, Robert *Actor*
1115 Pine St, Santa Monica, CA 90405 USA

Forster, William H *General*
10245 Fairfax Dr, Fort Belvoir, VA 22060 USA

Forsyth, Bill *Director*
P F D, Drury House, 34-43 Russell St, London, WC2B 5HA, UNITED KINGDOM (UK)

Forsyth, Bruce *Actor, Comedian*
Kent House, Upper Ground, London, SE1, UNITED KINGDOM (UK)

Forsyth, Frederick *Writer*
Trans World Publishers, 61-63 Oxbridge Rd, Ealing, London, W5 5SA, UNITED KINGDOM (UK)

Forsythe, Bill
20 Winton Dr., Glasgow, SCOTLAND, G12 0QA

Forsythe, Gerald (Gary) *Motorcycle Racer*
Forsythe Racing, 7231 Georgetown Road, Indianapolis, IN 46268 USA

Forsythe, Gerry
9350 Castlegate Dr, Indianapolis, IN 46256

Forsythe, Henderson *Actor*
3002 Willow Spring Court, Williamsburg, VA 23185 USA

Forsythe, John *Actor*
3849 Roblar Ave, Santa Ynez, CA 93460 USA

Forsythe, Rosemary *Actor*
1591 Benedict Canyon, Beverly Hills, CA 90210 USA

Forsythe, William *Actor*
7532 Melba Ave, Canoga Park, CA 91304 USA

Forsythe, William *Choreographer*
Frankfurt Ballet, Untermainanlage 11, Frankfurt, 60311, GERMANY

Fort, Edward B *Educator*
North Carolina A&T State University, Chancellor's Office, Greensboro, NC 27411 USA

Fort-Brescia, Bernardo *Architect*
Arguitectonica International, 550 Brickell Ave, #200, Miami, FL 33131 USA

Forte, Fabian
6671 Sunset Blvd. #1502, Los Angeles, DA, 90028

Forte, Joseph *Basketball Player*
355 Elm Croft Blvd, #621, Rockville, MD 20850 USA

Fortier, Claude *Misc*
1014 De Grenoble, Sainte-Foy, Quebec,
QC, G1V 2Z9, CANADA

Fortier, Laurie *Actor*
Kritzer Entertainment, 12200 W Olympic
Blvd, #400, Los Angeles, CA 90064 USA

Fortner, Nell *Coach*
Aubum University, Athletic Dept, Aubum,
AL 36849 USA

Fortunato, Joseph F (Joe) *Football Player*
PO Box 934, Natchez, MS 39121 USA

Fortune, Jimmy *Musician*
American Major Talent, 8747 Highway
304, Hernando, MS 38632 USA

Fosbury, Dick
709 Canyon Run Box 1791, Ketchum, ID
83340

Fosbury, Richard D (Dick) *Track Athlete*
708 Canyon Run Blvd, Ketchum, ID
83340 USA

Foss, John W II *General*
16 Hampton Key, Williamsburg, VA
23185 USA

Foss, Lukas *Composer, Musician*
1140 5th Ave, #4B, New York, NY 10128
USA

Fossey, Brigitte *Actor*
18 Rue Troyon, Paris, 75017, FRANCE

Fossum, Michael E *Astronaut*
822 Rolling Run Court, Houston, TX
77062 USA

Foster, Barry *Football Player*
4604 Mill Springs Court, Colleyville, TX
76034 USA

Foster, Ben *Actor*
James/Levy/Jacobson Management, 3500
W Olive Ave #1470, Burbank, CA 91505
USA

Foster, Bill *Basketball Player*
Virginia Polytechnic Institute, Athletic
Dept, Blacksburg, VA 24061 USA

Foster, Brendan *Track Athlete*
Whitegates, 31 Meadowfield Road,
Stocksfield, Northumberland, UNITED
KINGDOM (UK)

Foster, Coy *Misc*
5486 Glen Lakes Dr, Dallas, TX 75231
USA

Foster, David *Songwriter, Musician*
3469 Cross Creek Road, Malibu, CA
90265 USA

Foster, Frank B III *Composer, Musician*
Joel Chriss, 300 Mercer St, #3J, New York,
NY 10003 USA

Foster, George A *Baseball Player*
Pro-Concepts, 2046 Treasure Coast Plaza,
#341, Vero Beach, FL 32960 USA

Foster, Jodie *Actor, Director*
P M K Public Relations, 8500 Wilshire
Blvd, #700, Beverly Hills, CA 90211 USA

Foster, Jon *Actor*
James/Levy/Jacobson Management, 3500
W Olive Ave #1470, Burbank, CA 91505
USA

Foster, Lawrence T *Conductor*
International Creative Mgmt, 40 W 57th
St, #1800, New York, NY 10019 USA

Foster, Meg *Actor*
Judy Schoen, 606 N Larchmont Blvd,
#309, Los Angeles, CA 90004 USA

Foster, Norman R *Architect*
Foster Assoc, Riverside 3, 22 Hester Road,
London, SW11 4AN, UNITED KINGDOM
(UK)

Foster, Radney *Musician, Songwriter*
PO Box 121452, Nashville, TN 37212
USA

Foster, Robert W (Bob) *Boxer*
913 Valencia Dr NE, Albuquerque, NM
87108 USA

Foster, Roy A *Football Player*
11522 W State Road 84, #267, Davie, FL
33325 USA

Foster, Sara *Actor*
Media Talent Group, 9200 Sunset Blvd
#810, W Hollywood, CA 90069 USA

Foster, Susanna
11255 W. Morrison St. #F, No.
Hollywood, CA 91601

Foster, Susannah *Actor, Musician*
11255 W Morrison St, #F, North
Hollywood, CA 91601 USA

Foster, Todd *Boxer*
249 21st Ave NW, Great Falls, MT 59404
USA

Foster, William E (Bill) *Coach*
152 Hollywood Dr, Coppell, TX 75019
USA

Foster Jr, John S *Physicist*
TRW Inc, 1 Space Parkway, Redondo
Beach, CA 90278 USA

Fou, Ts'ong *Musician*
62 Aberdeen Park, London, N5 2BL,
UNITED KINGDOM (UK)

Foudy, Judy (Julie) *Soccer Player, Model*
US Soccer Federation, 1801 S Prairie Ave,
Chicago, IL 60616 USA

Foudy, Julie
1801 S. Prairie Ave., Chicago, IL 60616

Foulke, Keith C *Baseball Player*
3506 Dryburgh Court, Huffman, TX
77336 USA

Foulkes, Llyn *Artist*
6010 Eucalyptus Lane, Los Angeles, CA
90042 USA

Fountain, Pete
237 N. Peters St. #400, New Orleans, Los
Angeles, 71030

Fountain, Peter D (Pete) Jr *Musician*
Paradise Artists, 108 E Matilija St, Ojai,
CA 93023 USA

Fountain, Rex
10475 Bellagio Rd., Los Angeles, CA
90077

Fountains of Wayne *Music Group*
Big Hassle, 157 Chambers St Fl 12, New
York, NY 10007 USA

Four Aces, The
11761 E. Speedway Blvd, Tucson, AZ
85748-2017

Four Freshman, The
PO Box 93534, Las Vegas, NV 89193-
3534

Four Lads, The
11761 E. Speedway Blvd., Tucson, AZ
85748-2017

Four Non Blondes
PO Box 170545, San Francisco, CA
94117

Four Tops *Music Group*
Famous Artists Agency, 555 Eighth Ave
#1803, New York, NY 10018 USA

Fournier, Brigitte *Opera Singer*
EMI America Records, 1370 Ave of
Americas, New York, NY 10019 USA

Fouts, Dan
4020 Murphy Canyon Rd., San Diego, CA
92123

Fouts, Daniel F (Dan) *Football Player,
Sportscaster*
ABC-TV, Sports Dept, 77 W 66th St, New
York, NY 10023 USA

Fowler, E Michael C *Architect*
Branches Giffords Road, Bienheim, RD 3,
NEW ZEALAND

Fowler, Earlene *Writer*
Berkley Publishing Group, 375 Hudson St,
New York, NY 10014 USA

Fowler, J Arthur (Art) *Baseball Player*
3046 E Main Street Extension,
Spartanburg, SC 29307 USA

Fowler, Jaimie *Race Car Driver*
Agency for the Performing Arts (APA-LA),
9200 Sunset Blvd #900, Los Angeles, CA
90069 USA

Fowler, Jim *Actor*
Wild Kingdom, Mutual of Omaha, Mutual
of Omaha Plaza, Omaha, NE 68175 USA

Fowler, Peggy Y *Business Person*
Portland General Electric, 121 SW Salmon
St, Portland, OR 97204 USA

Fowler, W Wyche Jr *Senator, Diplomat*
701 A St NE, Washington, DC 20002 USA

Fowles, John *Writer*
Sheil Kand Assoc, 43 Dougherty St,
London, WC1N 2LF, UNITED KINGDOM
(UK)

Fox, Allen *Tennis Player, Coach*
Pepperdine University, Athletic Dept,
Malibu, CA 90265 USA

Fox, Bernard *Actor*
6601 Burnet Ave, Van Nuys, CA 91405
USA

Fox, Charles I *Composer, Conductor*
American Int'l Artists, 356 Pine Valley
Road, Hoosick Falls, NY 12090 USA

Fox, Crystal *Actor*
Writers & Artists, 8383 Wilshire Blvd,
#550, Beverly Hills, CA 90211 USA

Fox, Edward *Actor*
25 Maida Ave, London, W2, UNITED
KINGDOM (UK)

Fox, Emilia
125 Glouster Rd., London, ENGLAND,
SW7 4TE

Fox, Everett *Misc*
Clark University, Jewish Studies Program,
Worcester, MA 01610 USA

Fox, George
4950 Yonge St. #2400, Toronto, .
CANADA, Ont M2N 6K

Fox, Jackie
23368 Ostronic Dr., Woodland Hills, CA 91367

Fox, James *Actor*
International Creative Mgmt, 76 Oxford St, London, W1N 0AX, UNITED KINGDOM (UK)

Fox, John *Football Coach*
Carolina Panthers, Ericsson Stadium, 800 S Mint St, Charlotte, NC 28202 USA

Fox, Jorja *Actor*
Flick East-West, 9057 Nemo St, #A, West Hollywood, CA 90069 USA

Fox, Marye Anne *Misc*
1903 Hillsborough St, Raleigh, NC 27607 USA

Fox, Matthew *Religious Leader*
Grace Episcopal Cathedral, 1 Nob Hill Circle, San Francisco, CA 94108 USA

Fox, Maurice S *Biologist*
983 Memorial Dr, #401, Cambridge, MA 02138 USA

Fox, Megan *Actor*
Stone Manners Talent Agency, 6500 Wilshire Blvd, Ste 550, Los Angeles, CA 90048 USA

Fox, Michael J *Actor*
Creative Artists Agency, 9830 Wilshire Blvd, Beverly Hills, CA 90212 USA

Fox, Neil *Actor*
Pop Idol (Fremantle Media), 2700 Colorado Ave #450, Santa Monica, CA 90404 USA

Fox, Paula *Writer*
Robert Lescher, 47 E 19th St, New York, NY 10003 USA

Fox, Rick *Basketball Player, Actor*
Healthsouth Training Center, 555 N Nash St, El Segundo, CA 90245 USA

Fox, Samantha *Musician, Model*
Session Connection, 110-112 Disraeli Road, London, SW15 2DX, UNITED KINGDOM (UK)

Fox, Shayna
6212 Banner Ave., Los Angeles, CA 90038

Fox, Sheldon *Architect*
Kohn Pederson Fox Assoc, 111 W 57th St, New York, NY 10019 USA

Fox, Tim *Football Player*
10 Longmeadow Dr, Westwood, MA 02090 USA

Fox, Vicente *Politician, President*
Patacio Nacional, Patio de Honor, 2 Piso, Mexico City, DF 06067, MEXICO

Fox, Vivica A *Actor*
PO Box 3538, Granada Hills, CA 91394 USA

Fox, Wesley L *War Hero*
855 Deercraft Dr, Blacksburg, VA 24060 USA

Fox Brothers
Rt. 6 Bending Chestnut, Franklin, TN 37064

Foxworth, Robert *Actor*
Paradigm (LA), 10100 Santa Monica Blvd, Fl 25, Los Angeles, CA 90067 USA

Foxworthy, Jeff *Comedian, Actor*
Parallel Entertainment, 8380 Melrose Ave #310, Los Angeles, CA 90069 USA

Foxx, Jamie *Actor, Comedian*
Nationwide Entertainment, 2756 N Green Valley Parkway, Henderson, NV 89014 USA

Foxx, Shyla *Adult Film Star*
Atlas Multimedia Inc, 22940 Burbank Blvd, Woodland Hills, CA 91367 USA

Foxx, Tanya
901-G Victoria St., Compton, CA 90220

Foy, Eddie III *Actor*
3003 W Olive Ave, Burbank, CA 91505 USA

Foyt, Anthony (A J) Jr *Race Car Driver*
19480 Stokes Road, Waller, TX 77484 USA

Frabotta, Don
5036 Riverton Ave. #2, No. Hollywood, CA 91601

Fradkov, Mikhail *Prime Minister*
Prime Minister's Office, Kremlin, Staraya Pl 4, Moscow, 103132, RUSSIA

Fradon, Dana *Cartoonist*
2 Brushy Hill Road, Newtown, CT 06470 USA

Fradon, Ramona *Cartoonist*
Tribune Media Services, 435 N Michigan Ave, #1500, Chicago, IL 60611 USA

Frain, James *Actor*
PFD, Drury House, 34-43 Russell St, London, WC2B 5HA, UNITED KINGDOM (UK)

Fraiture, Nikolai *Musician*
MVO Ltd, 370 7th Ave, #807, New York, NY 10001 USA

Fraker, William A *Cinematographer*
337 Lorraine Blvd, Los Angeles, CA 90020 USA

Frakes, Jonathan *Actor, Director*
10990 Wilshire Blvd, #1600, Los Angeles, CA 90024 USA

Fralic, William (Bill) *Football Player*
Fralic Insurance, 1145 Sanctuary Parkway, #150, Alpharetta, GA 30004 USA

Frampton, Peter *Musician, Songwriter*
1016 17th Ave S, #1, Nashville, TN 37212 USA

Franca, Celia *Ballerina, Choreographer*
157 King St E, Toronto, ON M5C 1G9, CANADA

France, Brian *Misc*
National Assn of Stock Car Racing, 1801 Speedway Blvd, Daytona Beach, FL 32114 USA

France, F Douglas (Doug) Jr *Football Player*
25993 Atherton Ave, Laguna Hills, CA 92653 USA

Franchione, Dennis *Football Coach*
Texas A&M University, Athletic Dept, College Station, TX 77843 USA

Franchitti, Dario *Race Car Driver*
7615 Zionsville Road, Indianapolis, IN 46268 USA

Franciosa, Anthony (Tony) *Actor*
567 N Tigertail Road, Los Angeles, CA 90049 USA

Franciosa, Tony
567 N. Tigertail Rd., Los Angeles, CA 90049-2310

Francis, Anne *Actor*
PO Box 5608, Santa Barbara, CA 93105 USA

Francis, Bob *Hockey Player, Coach*
7510 E Monterra Way, Scottsdale, AZ 85262 USA

Francis, Clarence (Bevo) *Basketball Player*
18340 Steubenyille Pike Road, Salineville, OH 43945 USA

Francis, Cleve *Musician*
Big Time Small Time Mgmt, 1227 17th Ave S, #A, Nashville, TN 37212 USA

Francis, Connie *Actor, Musician*
6413 NW 102nd Terr, Parkland, FL 33076 USA

Francis, Dick *Writer*
John Johnson Ltd, 45/47 Clerkenwell Green, London, EC1R 0HT, UNITED KINGDOM (UK)

Francis, Don *Scientist*
Genentech Inc, 460 Point San Bruno Blvd, South San Francisco, CA 94080 USA

Francis, Emile P *Coach*
7220 Crystal Lake Dr, West Palm Beach, FL 33411 USA

Francis, Fred *Commentator*
NBC-TV, News Dept, 4001 Nebraska Ave NW, Washington, DC 20016 USA

Francis, Freddie *Cinematographer*
12 Ashley Dr, Jersey Road, Osterley, Middlx, TW7 5QA, UNITED KINGDOM (UK)

Francis, Genie *Actor*
10990 Wilshire Blvd, #1600, Los Angeles, CA 90024 USA

Francis, James *Football Player*
2903 Main St, La Marque, TX 77568 USA

Francis, Joe *Producer*
Mantra Films, PO Box 150, Hollywood, CA 90078 USA

Francis, Paul *Actor*
Gilbertson-Kincaid Management, 1330 Fourth St, Santa Monica, CA 90401 USA

Francis, Richard S (Dick) *Writer*
PO Box 30866, Seven Mile Beach, Grand Cayman, WEST INDIES

Francis, Ron *Hockey Player*
12312 Birchfalls Dr, Raleigh, NC 27614 USA

Francis, Steve *Basketball Player*
Houston Rockets, Toyota Center, 2 E Greenway Plaza, Houston, TX 77046 USA

Francis, William (Bill) *Musician*
Artists International, 9850 Sandalwood Blvd, #458, Boca Raton, FL 33428 USA

Francisco, Don *Television Host*
Univision, 314 Main St, Chico, CA 95928 USA

Francisco, George J *Misc*
Fireman & Oilers Union, 1100 Circle 75 Parkway, Atlanta, GA 30339 USA

Franck, George H (Sonny) *Football Player*
2714 29th Ave, Rock Island, IL 61201
USA

Franco, James *Actor*
James/Levy/Jacobson Management, 3500
W Olive Ave #1470, Burbank, CA 91505
USA

Franco, John A *Baseball Player*
111 Helena Road, Staten Island, NY
10304 USA

Franco, Julio C *Baseball Player*
651 NE 23rd Court, Pompano Beach, FL
33064 USA

Francois-Poncet, Jean A *Financier,*
Government Official
6 Blvd Suchet, Paris, 75116, FRANCE

Francona, John P (Tito) *Baseball Player*
1109 Penn Ave, New Brighton, PA 15066
USA

Francona, Terry J *Baseball Player*
958 Hunt Dr, Yardley, PA 19067 USA

Frangione, Nancy
280 S. Beverly Dr. #400, Beverly Hills,
CA 90212

Frank, Anthony M *Government Official,*
Financier
Independent Bancorp, 3800 N Central,
Phoenix, AZ 85012 USA

Frank, Barney *Politician*
Congressman Barney Frank, 2252 Rayburn
HOB, Washington, DC 20515 USA

Frank, Charles *Actor*
S D B Partners, 1801 Ave of Stars, #902,
Los Angeles, CA 90067 USA

Frank, Claude *Musician*
Columbia Artists Mgmt Inc, 165 W 57th
St, New York, NY 10019 USA

Frank, Diana *Actor*
The Agency, 1800 Ave of Stars, #400, Los
Angeles, CA 90067 USA

Frank, Gary *Actor*
1401 S Bentley Ave, #202, Los Angeles,
CA 90025 USA

Frank, Howard *Business Person*
Carnival Corp, 3655 NW 87th Ave,
Miami, FL 33178 USA

Frank, Jason David *Actor, Comedian*
Richard Stone, 2 Henrietta St, London,
WC2E 8PS, UNITED KINGDOM (UK)

Frank, Jerome D *Educator*
818 W 40th St, #K, Baltimore, MD 21211
USA

Frank, Joanna *Actor*
1274 Capri Dr, Pacific Palisades, CA
90272 USA

Frank, Joe *Entertainer*
KCRW-FM, 1900 Pico Blvd, Santa
Monica, CA 90405 USA

Frank, Larry *Race Car Driver*
Larry Frank Auto Body Works, 832 Fork
Shoals Road, Greenville, SC 29605 USA

Frank, Louis A *Astronomer*
University of Iowa, Astronomy Dept, Iowa
City, IA 52242 USA

Frank, Neil L *Misc*
National Hurricane Center, 1320 S Dixie
Highway, Coral Gables, FL 33146 USA

Frank, Phil *Cartoonist*
500 Turley St, Sausalito, CA 94965 USA

Frankel, Felice *Artist, Photographer*
Massachusetts Institute of Technology,
Edgerton Center, Cambridge, MA 02139
USA

Frankel, Max *Editor*
New York Times, Editorial Dept, 229 W
43rd St, New York, NY 10036 USA

Franken, Al *Writer, Actor, Comedian*
Special Artists, 345 N Maple Dr, #302,
Beverly Hills, CA 90210 USA

Franken, Steve *Actor*
Acme Talent, 4727 Wilshire Blvd, #333,
Los Angeles, CA 90010 USA

Frankenthaler, Helen *Artist*
19 Contentment Island Road, Darien, CT
06820 USA

Frankl, Peter *Musician*
5 Gresham Gardens, London, NW11
8NX, UNITED KINGDOM (UK)

Franklin, Allen *Business Person*
Southern Co, 270 Peachtree St NW,
Atlanta, CA 30303 USA

Franklin, Anthony R (Tony) *Football*
Player
117 Shady Trail St, San Antonio, TX
78232 USA

Franklin, Aretha *Musician*
8450 Linwood St, Detroit, MI 48206 USA

Franklin, Barbara Hackman *Secretary*
1875 Perkins St, Bristol, CT 06010 USA

Franklin, Bonnie *Actor*
175 E 72nd St, #20A, New York, NY
10021 USA

Franklin, Carl M *Director*
Broder Kurland Webb Uffner, 9242
Beverly Blvd, #200, Beverly Hills, CA
90210 USA

Franklin, Diane *Actor*
Third Hill Entertainment, 195 S Beverly
Dr, #400, Beverly Hills, CA 90212 USA

Franklin, Don
10101 Santa Monica Blvd. #2500, Los
Angeles, CA 90067

Franklin, Don *Actor*
Paradigm Agency, 10100 Santa Monica
Blvd, #2500, Los Angeles, CA 90067 USA

Franklin, Farrah *Musician*
Supreme Entertainment, 262 Chestnut Hill
Avenue, Boston, MA 02135

Franklin, Gary
7610 Beverly Blvd. #480820, Los Angeles,
CA 90048-9998

Franklin, Howard *Director, Writer*
Creative Artists Agency, 9830 Wilshire
Blvd, Beverly Hills, CA 90212 USA

Franklin, Joe
Box 1, Lynbrook, NY 11563

Franklin, John *Actor*
Gilla Roos, 9744 Wilshire Blvd, #203,
Beverly Hills, CA 90212 USA

Franklin, John Hope *Historian, Judge*
208 Pineview Road, Durham, NC 27707
USA

Franklin, Jon D *Journalist*
9650 Strickland Road, Raleigh, NC 27615
USA

Franklin, Kirk *Musician, Songwriter*
Covenant Agency, 1011 4th St, #315,
Santa Monica, CA 90403 USA

Franklin, Melissa *Physicist*
Harvard University, Physics Dept,
Cambridge, MA 02138 USA

Franklin, Richard
8383 Wilshire Blvd. #550, Beverly Hills,
CA 90211-2404

Franklin, Robert *Business Person*
Placer Dome Inc, 1600-1055 Dunsmuir
St, Vancouver, BC V7X 1P1, CANADA

Franklin, Roshawn *Actor*
Braverman/Bloom Company, 6399
Wilshire Blvd #901, Los Angeles, CA
90048 USA

Franklin, Ryan *Baseball Player*
PO Box 321, Shawnee, OK 74802 USA

Franklin, Shirley *Politician*
Mayor's Office, City Hall, 55 Trinity Ave
S, Atlanta, GA 30303 USA

Franklin, William *Boxer, Misc*
920 La Sombra Dr, San Marcos, CA
92069 USA

Franklyn, Sabina *Actor*
CCA Mgmt, 4 Court Lodge, 48 Sloane
Square, London, SW1W 8AT, UNITED
KINGDOM (UK)

Franks, Frederick M Jr *General*
6364 Brampton Court, Alexandria, VA
22304 USA

Franks, Gerold
1745 Camino Palmero, Los Angeles, CA
90046

Franks, Michael *Musician, Songwriter*
Agency of Performing Arts, 9200 Sunset
Blvd, #900, Los Angeles, CA 90069 USA

Franks, Tommy R (Tom) *General*
Washington Speakers Bureau, 1660 Prince
St, Arlington, VA 22014 USA

Frankston, Robert M (Bob) *Designer*
State Corp, 15035 N 73rd St, Scottsdale,
AZ 85260 USA

Fransioli, Thomas A *Artist*
55 Dodges Row, Wenham, MA 01984
USA

Franti, Michael *Musician*
William Morris Agency, 151 El Camino
Dr, Beverly Hills, CA 90212 USA

Frantz, Adrienne *Actor*
Acme Talent, 4727 Wilshire Blvd, #333,
Los Angeles, CA 90010 USA

Frantz, Chris *Musician*
Premier Talent, 3 E 54th St, #1100, New
York, NY 10022 USA

Franz, Arthur *Actor*
1736 Talon Ave, Henderson, NV 89074
USA

Franz, Dennis *Actor*
2300 Century Hill, #75, Los Angeles, CA
90067 USA

Franz, Frederick W *Religious Leader*
Jehovah's Witnesses, 25 Columbia
Heights, Brooklyn, NY 11201 USA

Franz, Judy R *Physicist*
American Physical Society, 1 Physics
Eclipse, College Park, MD 20740 USA

Franz, Rodney T (Rod) *Football Player*
1448 Engberg Court, Carmichael, CA
95608 USA

Franzen, Jonathan *Writer*
Farrar Straus Giroux, 19 Union Square W,
New York, NY 10003 USA

Franzen, Ulrich J *Architect*
975 Park Ave, New York, NY 10028 USA

Frasca, Robert J *Architect*
Zimmer Gunsul Frasca, 320 SW Oak St,
#500, Portland, OR 97204 USA

Frasconi, Antonio *Artist*
26 Dock Road, Norwalk, CT 06854 USA

Fraser, Antonia *Writer*
Curtis Brown, Haymarket House, 28/29
Haymarket, London, SW1Y 4SP, UNITED
KINGDOM (UK)

Fraser, Brad *Writer*
Great North Artists Mgmt, 350 Dupont
Ave, Toronto, ON M5R 1V9, CANADA

Fraser, Brendan *Actor*
2118 Wilshire Blvd #513, Santa Monica,
CA 90403 USA

Fraser, Dawn *Athlete, Swimmer*
87 Birchgrove Road, Balmain, NSW,
Australia

Fraser, Douglas *Misc*
United Auto Workers, 8000 E Jefferson
Ave, Detroit, MI 48214 USA

Fraser, Elisabeth *Musician*
Int'l Talent Booking, 27A Floral St, #300,
London, SW1Y 4SP, UNITED KINGDOM
(UK)

Fraser, George MacDonald *Writer*
Curtis Brown, 28/29 Haymarket, London,
SW1Y 4SP, UNITED KINGDOM (UK)

Fraser, Gretchen
5023 236th Pl. SE, Woodinville, WA
98072-8610

Fraser, Hon
MalcolmThurulgoona, Redhill,
AUSTRALIA, Vic. 3937, AUSTRALIA

Fraser, Honor *Model*
Select Model Mgmt, Archer House, 43
King St, London, WC2E 8RJ, UNITED
KINGDOM (UK)

Fraser, Hugh *Actor*
Jonathan Altaras, 13 Shorts Gardens,
London, WC2H 9AT, UNITED KINGDOM
(UK)

Fraser, Ian E *War Hero*
Innisfallen, 47 Warren Dr, Wallasey,
Merseyside, UNITED KINGDOM (UK)

Fraser, Laura *Actor*
International Creative Management
(ICM-LA), 8942 Wilshire Blvd, Beverly
Hills, CA 90211 USA

Fraser, Malcolm *Prime Minister*
Thurulgoona, Redhill, VIC, 3937,
AUSTRALIA

Fraser, Neale *Tennis Player*
21 Bolton Ave, Hampton, VIC, 3188,
AUSTRALIA

Fraser, Ware Dawn *Swimmer*
403 Darling St, Balmain, NSW, 2041,
AUSTRALIA

Frashilla, Fran *Coach*
New Mexico University, Athletic Dept,
Albuquerque, NM 87131 USA

Fratangelo, Dawn *Journalist*
William Morris Agency (WMA-LA), 1
William Morris Pl, Beverly Hills, CA
90212 USA

Fratello, Michael R (Mike) *Coach,
Sportscaster*
NBC-TV, Sports Dept, 30 Rockefeller
Plaza, New York, NY 10112 USA

Fratianne, Linda S *Figure Skater*
15691 Borgas Court, Moorpark, CA 93021
USA

Fraumeni, Joseph F Jr *Inventor*
National Cancer Institute, Cancer Etiology
Division, Bethesda, MD 20892 USA

Frayn, Michael *Writer*
Greene & Heaton, 37A Goldhawk Road,
London, W12 8QQ, UNITED KINGDOM
(UK)

Frazer, Liz *Actor*
Peter Charlesworth, 68 Old Brompton
Road, #200, London, SW7 3LQ, UNITED
KINGDOM (UK)

Frazetta, Frank *Artist*
Frazetta Art Museum, 82 S Courtland St,
East Stroudsburg, PA 18301 USA

Frazier, Charles *Writer*
Atlantic Monthly Press, 841 Broadway,
New York, NY 10003 USA

Frazier, Dallas *Musician, Songwriter*
RR 5 Box 133, Longhollow Pike, Gallatin,
TN 37066 USA

Frazier, Herman *Track Athlete*
1777 Ala Moana Blvd, Honolulu, HI
96815 USA

Frazier, Ian *Writer*
Farrar Straus Giroux, 19 Union Square W,
New York, NY 10003 USA

Frazier, Joe *Athlete*
2917 North Broad Street, Philadelphia, PA
19132 USA

Frazier, Joseph (Smokin' Joe) *Boxer*
2917 N Broad St, Philadelphia, PA 19132
USA

Frazier, Kevin *Actor*
3731 Monteith Drive, Los Angeles, CA
90043 USA

Frazier, Mavis *Boxer*
2917 N Broad St, Philadelphia, PA 19132
USA

Frazier, Owsley B *Business Person*
Brown-Forman Corp, 850 Dixie Highway,
Louisville, KY 40210 USA

Frazier, Sheila
1179 S. Highland Ave, Los Angeles, CA
90019

Frazier, Walt
675 Flamingo Dr .SW, Atlanta, GA 30311

Frazier, Walter (Clyde) II *Basketball
Player*
WFAN-AM, 3412 36th St, Long Island
City, NY 11106 USA

Frears, Stephen A *Director*
93 Talbot Road, London, W2, UNITED
KINGDOM (UK)

Freberg, Stanley V (Stan) *Actor,
Comedian*
Radio Spirits, PO Box 3107, Wallingford,
CT 06492 USA

Freddie & The Dreamers
9 Ridge Rd., Emerson, NJ 07630

Fredericks, Frank (Frankie) *Track Athlete*
4497 Wimbledon Dr, Provo, UT 84604
USA

Fredericks, Fred *Cartoonist*
PO Box 475, Eastham, MA 02642 USA

Frederickson, Ivan C (Tucker) *Football
Player*
12414 Indian Road, North Palm Beach, FL
33408 USA

Fredrickson, George M *Historian*
741 Esplanada Way, Palo Alto, CA 94305
USA

Fredriksson, Gert *Athlete*
Bruunsgat 13, Nykoping, 61122, SWEDEN

Fredriksson, Marie *Musician, Songwriter*
D &D Mgmt, Lilla Nygatan 19,
Stockholm, 11128, SWEDEN

Free, Helen M *Inventor*
3752 E Jackson Blvd, Elkhart, IN 46516
USA

Free, World B *Baseball Player, Coach*
Philadelphia 76ers, 1st Union Center,
3601 S Broad St, Philadelphia, PA 19148
USA

Freebo
740 N. Hayworth Ave., Los Angeles, CA
90046

Freed, Audley *Musician*
Mitch Schneider Organization, 14724
Ventura Blvd, #410, Sherman Oaks, CA
91403 USA

Freed, Curt R *Biologist*
University of Colorado, Health Science
Center, 4200 E 9th Ave, Denver, CO
80220 USA

Freed, Jack H *Misc*
108 Homestead Circle, Ithaca, NY 14850
USA

Freed, James Ingo *Architect*
Pel Cobb Freed Partners, 88 Pine St, New
York, NY 10005 USA

Freedman, Alix M *Journalist*
Wall Street Journal, Editorial Dept, 200
Liberty St, New York, NY 10281 USA

Freedman, David A *Mathematician*
901 Alvarado Road, Berkeley, CA 94705
USA

Freedman, Eric *Journalist*
Detroit News, Editorial Dept, 615 W
Lafayette Blvd, Detroit, MI 48226 USA

Freedman, Gerald A *Director, Opera
Singer*
Theatre Julliard School, Lincoln Center
Plaza, New York, NY 10023 USA

Freedman, James O *Educator*
Dartmouth College, President's Office,
Hanover, NH 03755 USA

Freedman, Ronald *Social Activist*
1200 Earhart Road, #228, Ann Arbor, MI
48105 USA

Freedman, Wendy L *Astronomer*
Camegie Observatories, 813 Santa
Barbara St, Pasadena, CA 91101 USA

Freeh, Louis *FBI*
9th & Pennsylvania Ave. NW,
Washington, DC 20035

Freehan, William A (Bill) *Baseball Player*
6999 Indian Garden Road, Petoskey, MI
49770 USA

Freelon, Nnenna *Musician*
Ted Kurland, 173 Brighton Ave, Boston,
MA 02134 USA

Freeman, Bobby *Musician*
Lustig Talent, PO Box 770850, Orlando,
FL 32877 USA

Freeman, Cathy *Track Athlete*
PO Box 700, South Melbourne, VIC,
3205, AUSTRALIA

Freeman, Charles W Jr *Diplomat*
Project International, 1800 K St NW,
#1010, Washington, DC 20006 USA

Freeman, Isaac *Musician*
Keith Case Assoc, 1025 17th Ave S, #200,
Nashville, TN 37212 USA

Freeman, J E *Actor*
Gersh Agency, 232 N Canon Dr, Beverly
Hills, CA 90210 USA

Freeman, Mona *Actor*
608 N Alpine Dr, Beverly Hills, CA 90210
USA

Freeman, Morgan *Actor*
2472 Broadway, #227, New York, NY
10025 USA

Freeman, Orville *Ex-Governor*
3701 Bryant Ave So #802, Minneapolis,
MN 55409-1091 USA

Freeman, Russell *Writer*
280 Riverside Dr, New York, NY 10025
USA

Freeman, Sandi *Commentator*
Cable News Network, News Dept, 820 1st
ST NE, Washington, DC 20002 USA

Freeman, Yvette *Actor, Musician*
Stone Manners, 6500 Wilshire Blvd, #550,
Los Angeles, CA 90048 USA

Freeman Jr, Al *Actor*
Artists Agency, 1180 S Beverly Dr, #301,
Los Angeles, CA 90035 USA

Freeney, Dwight *Football Player*
Indianapolis Colts, 7001 W 56th St,
Indianapolis, IN 46254 USA

Fregosi, James L (Jim) *Baseball Player*
1092 Copeland Court, Tarpon Springs, FL
34688 USA

Fregosi, Jim
1092 Copeland Ct., Tarpon Springs, FL
34689

Fregoso, Ramon *Actor*
TV Azteca, Periferico Sur 4121, Colonia
Fuentes del Pedregal, DF, CP 14141,
Mexico

Frehley, Ace *Musician*
McGhee Entertainment, 8730 Sunset Blvd,
#195, West Hollywood, CA 90069 USA

Frei, Emil III *Misc*
Dana-Farber Cancer Institute, 44 Binney
St, Boston, MA 02115 USA

Frei Ruiz-Tagle, Eduardo *President*
President's Office, Palacio de la Monedo,
Santiago, CHILE

Freiberger, Marcus *Basketball Player*
14100 Hickory Marsh Lane, #95, Fort
Myers, FL 33912 USA

Freidheim, Cyrus *Business Person*
Chiquita Brands International, 250 E 5th
St, Cincinnati, OH 45202 USA

Freigang, Stephan
Strasse der Jugend 58, Cottbus,
GERMANY, D-03050

Freilicher, Jane *Artist*
Fishbach Gallery, 210 11th Ave, #801,
New York, NY 10001 USA

Freire, Nelson *Musician*
Columbia Artists Mgmt Inc, 165 W 57th
St, New York, NY 10019 USA

Freireich, Emil J *Doctor*
M D Anderson Medical Center, 1515
Holcombe Blvd, Houston, TX 77030 USA

Freis, Edward DJ *Doctor*
4515 Willard Ave, Chevy Chase, MD
20815 USA

Frelich, Phyllis *Actor*
Artists Group, 10100 Santa Monica Blvd,
#2490, Los Angeles, CA 90067 USA

French, Dawn *Actor, Comedian*
P F D Drury House, 34-43 Russell St,
London, WC2B 5HA, UNITED KINGDOM
(UK)

French, Heather
567 Circle Dr., Maysville, KY 41056-9124

French, Leigh *Actor*
1850 N Vista St, Los Angeles, CA 90046
USA

French, Marilyn *Writer*
Charlotte Sheedy Agency, 65 Bleecker St,
#1200, New York, NY 10012 USA

French, Niki *Musician*
Mega Artists Mgmt, PO Box 89, Edam, ZJ,
1135, NETHERLANDS

French, Paige *Actor*
Gersh Agency, 232 N Canon Dr, Beverly
Hills, CA 90210 USA

French, Rufus *Football Player*
Green Bay Packers, PO Box 10628, Green
Bay, WI 54307 USA

French, Susan
110 E. 9th St. #C-1005, Los Angeles, CA
90079

Freni, Mirelia *Opera Singer*
John Coast Mgmt, 31 Sinclair Road,
London, W14 0NS, UNITED KINGDOM
(UK)

Freni, Mirella *Opera Singer*
Decca/Universal Classics Records, 825
8th Ave, New York, NY 10019 USA

Frenkiel, Richard H *Engineer, Inventor*
Rutgers University, WINLAB, PO Box 909,
Piscataway, NJ 08855 USA

Frentzen, Heinz-Harald *Race Car Driver*
Formula One Ltd, Silverstone Circuit,
Northamptonshire, NN12 8TN, UNITED
KINGDOM (UK)

Frerotte, Gus *Football Player*
1360 Herschel Ave, Cincinnati, OH
45208 USA

Fresco, Paolo *Business Person*
Fiat SpA, Corso Marconi 10/20, Turin,
10125, ITALY

Fresh, Doug E *Musician*
Agency Group Ltd, 1775 Broadway, #430,
New York, NY 10019 USA

Fresno Larrain, Juan Cardinal *Religious Leader*
Erasmo Escala, Santiago 30D, 1822,
CHILE

Freud, Bella *Fashion Designer*
48 Rawstorne St, London, EC1V 7ND,
UNITED KINGDOM (UK)

Freud, Lucian *Artist*
Rawstron-Derrick, 90 Fetter Lane, London,
EC4A 1EQ, UNITED KINGDOM (UK)

Freund, Lambert B *Engineer*
3 Palisade Lane, Barrington, RI 02806
USA

Frewer, Matt *Actor*
International Creative Mgmt, 8942
Wilshire Blvd, #219, Beverly Hills, CA
90211 USA

Frey, Christopher
The Toft E. Dean nr. Chichester, Sussex,
ENGLAND

Frey, Donald N *Business Person, Engineer*
2758 Sheridan Road, Evanston, IL 60201
USA

Frey, Glenn *Musician, Songwriter, Actor*
5020 Brent Knoll Lane, Suwanee, GA
30024 USA

Frey, James G (Jim) *Baseball Player*
12101 Tullamore Court, #406, Timonium,
MD 21093 USA

Frey, Sami
21 Place des Vosges, Paris, FRANCE,
F-75003

Freyndlikh, Alisa B *Actor*
Rubinstein Str 11, #7, Saint Petersburg,
191002, RUSSIA

Freytag, Arny *Photographer*
22735 MacFarlane Dr, Woodland Hills,
CA 91364 USA

Frick, Gottlob *Opera Singer*
Eichelberg-Haus Waldfrieden, Olbronn-
Durrn, 75248, GERMANY

Frick, Stephen N *Astronaut*
4322 Towering Oak Court, Houston, TX
77059 USA

Fricke, Janie *Musician*
Janie Fricke Concerts, PO Box 798,
Lancaster, TX 75146 USA

Fricker, Brenda *Actor*
Meyer & Eden, 34 Kingly Court, London,
W1R 5LE, UNITED KINGDOM (UK)

Frid, Jonathan *Actor*
PO Box 2429, New York, NY 10108 USA

Friday, Nancy *Writer*
Harper Collins Publishers, 10 E 53rd St,
New York, NY 10022 USA

Friday Jr, Elbert W *Government Official*
US National Weather Service, 1125 East-
West Highway, Silver Spring, MD 20910
USA

Fridell, Squire
13563 Ventura Blvd. #200, Sherman
Oaks, CA 91403

Fridovich, Irwin *Misc*
3517 Courtland Dr, Durham, NC 27707
USA

Fridriksson, Fridrik T *Director*
Bjarkgata 8, Reykjavik, 101, ICELAND

Friebe, Anika
111 E. 22nd St. #200, New York, NY
10010

Fried, Charles *Government Official,*
Educator
Harvard University, Law School,
Cambridge, MA 02138 USA

Friedan, Betty *Writer, Social Activist*
2022 Columbia Road NW, #414,
Washington, DC 20009 USA

Friedel, Jacques *Physicist*
2 Rue Jean-Francois Gerbillon, Paris,
75006, FRANCE

Friedgen, Ralph *Football Coach*
University of Maryland, Athletic Dept,
College Park, MD 20742 USA

Friedkin, William *Director*
10451 Bellagio Road, Los Angeles, CA
90077 USA

Friedlander, Lee *Artist, Photographer*
44 S Mountain Road, New City, NY
10956 USA

Friedle, Will *Actor*
Diverse Talent Group, 1875 Century Park
E #2250, Los Angeles, CA 90067 USA

Friedman, Daniel M *Judge*
US Court of Appeals, 717 Madison Place
NW, Washington, DC 20439 USA

Friedman, Emanuel A *Educator*
Beth-Israel Hospital, 330 Brookline Ave,
Boston, MA 02215 USA

Friedman, Jeffrey *Misc*
Rockefeller University, Hughes Medical
Institute, New York, NY 10021 USA

Friedman, Jerome I *Nobel Prize Laureate*
75 Greenough St, Brookline, MA 02445
USA

Friedman, Lawrence M *Lawyer, Educator*
724 Frenchmans Road, Palo Alto, CA
94305 USA

Friedman, Milton *Nobel Prize Laureate*
Stanford University, Hoover Institution,
Stanford, CA 94305 USA

Friedman, Peter *Actor, Musician*
J Michael Bloom, 233 Park Ave S, #1000,
New York, NY 10003 USA

Friedman, Philip *Writer*
Ivy Books/Random House Inc, 1745
Broadway, #B1, New York, NY 10019
USA

Friedman, Sonya
208 Harristown Rd, Glen Rock, NJ 07452

Friedman, Stephen *Government Official,*
Financier
White House, 1600 Pennsylvania Ave
NW, Washington, DC 20500 USA

Friedman, Thomas L *Journalist*
New York Times, Editorial Dept, 229 W
43rd St, New York, NY 10036 USA

Friedman, Tom *Artist*
Artists on the Corner, 802 DeMun,
Clayton, MO 63105 USA

Friedman, Yona *Architect*
33 Blvd Garibaldi, Paris, 75015, FRANCE

Friedmann, Phil *Musician*
Overland Productions, 156 W 56th St,
#500, New York, NY 10019 USA

Friel, Anna *Actor*
Conway Van Gelder Robinson, 18-21
Jermyn St, London, CA SW1Y 6NB,
UNITED KINGDOM (UK)

Friel, Brian *Writer*
Drumaweir House, Greencastle, County
Donegal, IRELAND

Friels, Colin *Actor*
129 Brooke St, Woollomooloo, Sydney,
NSW, 2011, AUSTRALIA

Friend, Lionel *Conductor*
136 Rosendale Road, London, SE21 8LG,
UNITED KINGDOM (UK)

Friend, Patricia A *Misc*
1275 K St NW, #5, Washington, DC
20005 USA

Friend, Richard H *Misc*
Cavendish Laboratory, Chemistry Dept,
Cambridge, UNITED KINGDOM (UK)

Friend, Robert B (Bob) *Baseball Player*
4 Salem Circle, Pittsburgh, PA 15238 USA

Frier, Mike
265 140th Ave. NE, Bellevue, WA 98005

Fries, Chuck
6922 Hollywood Blvd., Los Angeles, CA
90028

Fries, Donald B *Publisher*
Life Magazine, Time-Life Building, New
York, NY 10020 USA

Friesen, David *Musician*
Thomas Cassidy, 11761 E Speedway Blvd,
Tucson, AZ 85748 USA

Friesen, Gil
770 Bonhill Rd., Los Angeles, CA 90049

Friesinger, Anni *Speed Skater*
WIGE Media AG, Geilbelweg 24,
Fellbach, 70736, GERMANY

Friesz, John *Football Player*
19116 NE 48th St, Redmond, WA 98074
USA

Frigid Pink
32885 Northampton, Warren, MI 48093

Frimout, Dirk D *Astronaut*
D-1/Nieuwe Ontwikkelingen, BD E
Jacqmainlaan 151, Brussels, 1210,
BELGIUM

Frisbee, Rob *Athlete*
Jerry Shandrew PR, 1050 South Stanley
Avenue, Los Angeles, CA 90019-6634
USA

Frischman, Daniel
145 S. Fairfax Ave. #310, Los Angeles, CA
90036

Frischmann, Justine *Musician*
CMO Mgmt, Ransomes Dock, 357-37
Parkgate Road, London, SW11 4NP,
UNITED KINGDOM (UK)

Frisell, William R (Bill) *Musician*
Nonesuch Records, 75 Rockefeller Plaza,
New York, NY 10019 USA

Frishberg, David L *Composer, Musician*
Irvin Arthur Assoc, PO Box 1358, New
York, NY 10028 USA

Frishman, Rick

Fritsch, Ted Jr *Football Player*
5014 Odins Way, Marietta, GA 30068
USA

Fritz, Harold A *War Hero*
1017 W Scottwood Dr, Peoria, IL 61615
USA

Fritz, Nikki *Actor*
PO Box 57764, Sherman Oaks, CA 91413
USA

Frizzell, David *Musician*
4694 E Robertson Road, Cross Plains, TN
37049 USA

Frizzell, John *Composer*
B M I, 8730 Sunset Blvd, #300, Los
Angeles, CA 90069 USA

Froboess, Cornelia
Rinklhof Kleinholzhausen, Raubling,
GERMANY, D-83064

Froemming, Bruce N *Referee*
702 W Haddonstone Place, Thiensville,
WI 53092 USA

Froese, Bob *Hockey Player*
5140 Stricker Road, Clarence, NY 14031
USA

Frohnmayer, David B (Dave) *Educator*
University of Oregon, President's Office,
Eugene, OR 97403 USA

Frohnmayer, John E *Government Official*
14080 Lone Bear Road, Bozeman, MT
59715 USA

Froines, John *Social Activist, Educator*
University of California, Public Health
School, Los Angeles, CA 90024 USA

Fromherz, Peter *Physicist*
Max Pianck Biochemistry Institute,
Biophysics Dept, Martinsried, GERMANY

Fromm, Fritz *Misc*
An der Bismarckschule 64, Hannover,
30173, GERMANY

Frommelt, Paul *Skier*
Liechtenstein Ski Federation, Vaduz,
LIECHTENSTEIN

Frondel, Clifford *Misc*
299 Cambridge St, #413, Winchester, MA
01890 USA

Fronius, Hans *Artist*
Guggenberggasse 18, Perchtoldadorf bel
Vienna, 2380, AUSTRIA

Frontiere, Dominic
280 S. Beverly Dr. #411, Beverly Hills,
CA 90212

Frontiere, Georgia *Misc*
Saint Louis Rams, 901 E Broadway, Saint
Louis, MO 63101 USA

Froom, Mitchell *Misc*
Gary Stamler Mgmt, 3055 Overland Ave,
#200, Los Angeles, CA 90034 USA

Frosch, Robert A *Government Official*
1 Heritage Hills Dr, #42 A, Somers, NY
10589 USA

Frost, Craig *Misc*
Lustig Talent, PO Box 770850, Orlando,
FL 32877 USA

Frost, David *Golfer*
Professional Golfer's Assn, PO Box
109601, Palm Beach Gardens, FL 33410
USA

Frost, David P *Entertainer*
13355 Noel Road, #1600, Dallas, TX
75240 USA

Frost, Lindsay *Actor*
William Morris Agency, 151 El Camino
Dr, Beverly Hills, CA 90212 USA

Frost, Mark *Writer*
Mark Frost Productions, PO Box 1723,
North Hollywood, CA 91614 USA

Frost, Sadie *Actor*
Julian Belfarge, 46 Albermarle St, London,
W1X 4PP, UNITED KINGDOM (UK)

Frost, Sir David
BBC Centre Wood Lane, London,
ENGLAND, W12 7RJ

Fruedek, Jacques *Physicist*
2 Rue Jean-Francois Gerbillon, Paris,
70006, FRANCE

Fruh, Eugen *Artist*
Romergasse 9, Zurich, 8001,
SWITZERLAND

Fruhbeck de Burgos, Rafael *Conductor*
Avenida dek Mediterraneo 21, Madrid,
28007, SPAIN

Frusciante, John *Musician*
10345 Olympic Blvd, #200, Los Angeles,
CA 90064 USA

Frutig, Ed *Football Player*
8343 Sego Court, Vero Beach, FL 32963
USA

Fruton, Joseph S *Misc*
123 York St, New Haven, CT 06511 USA

Fry, Arthur L *Inventor*
Minnesota Mining & Manufacturing, 3M
Center, Bldg 230-2S, Saint Paul, MN
55144 USA

Fry, Christopher *Writer*
Tott, East Dean near Chichester, Sussex,
UNITED KINGDOM (UK)

Fry, Michael *Cartoonist*
United Feature Syndicate, 200 Madison
Ave, New York, NY 10016 USA

Fry, Scott A *Admiral*
Director Joint Staff Operations, Pentagon,
Washington, DC 20318 USA

Fry, Stephen *Actor*
William Morris Agency (WMA-LA), 1
William Morris Pl, Beverly Hills, CA
90212 USA

Fry, Stephen J *Actor, Comedian, Writer*
Lorraine Hamilton Asper, 76 Oxford St,
London, W1N 0AT, UNITED KINGDOM
(UK)

Fry, Thornton C *Mathematician*
500 Mohawk Dr, Boulder, CO 80303
USA

Fry-Irvin, Shirley *Tennis Player*
1970 Asylum Ave, West Hartford, CT
06117 USA

Fryar, Irving D *Football Player,
Sportscaster*
51 Applegate Road, Jobstown, NJ 08041
USA

Frye, Meno
2713 N. Keystone, Burbank, CA 91504

Frye, Shawn
2713 N. Keystone, Burban, CA 91504

Frye, Soleil Moon *Actor*
PO Box 3743, Glendale, CA 91221 USA

Fryling, Victor J *Business Person*
CMS Energy Fairlane Plaza South, 330
Town Center Dr, Dearborn, MI 48126
USA

Fryman, D Travis *Baseball Player*
2600 Highway 196, Molino, FL 32577
USA

Fryman, Woodrow T (Woodie) *Baseball
Player*
RR 1 Box 21, Ewing, KY 41039 USA

Ftorek, Robert B (Robbie) *Hockey Player,
Coach*
79 Sunset Point Road, Wolfeboro, NH
03894 USA

Fu, Mingxia *Swimmer*
General Physical Culture Bureau, 9
Tiyuguan Road, Bejing, CHINA

Fuchs, Ann Sutherland *Publisher*
Vogue Magazine, 350 Madison Ave, New
York, NY 10017 USA

Fuchs, Joseph L *Publisher*
Mademoiselle Magazine, 350 Madison
Ave, New York, NY 10017 USA

Fuchs, Leo
609 N. Kilkea Dr., Los Angeles, CA 90048

Fuchs, Michael J *Television Host*
Home Box Office, 1100 Ave of
Americans, New York, NY 10036 USA

Fuchs, Victor R *Economist*
796 Cedro Way, Stanford, CA 94305 USA

Fuchsberger, Joachim *Actor*
Hubertusstr 62, Grunwald, 82031,
GERMANY

Fuchsberger, Joachin
Hubertusstr. 62, Grunwald, GERMANY,
D-82031

Fudge, Alan *Actor*
355 S Rexford Dr, Beverly Hills, CA
90212 USA

Fuel *Music Group*
Monterey Peninsula Artists (Monterey),
509 Hartnell St, Monterey, CA 93940 USA

Fuente, David I *Business Person*
Office Depot Inc, 2200 Old Germantown
Road, Delray Beach, FL 33445 USA

Fuente, Luis *Dancer*
98 Rue Lepic, Paris, 75018, FRANCE

Fuentealba, Victor W *Misc*
4501 Arabia Ave, Baltimore, MD 21214
USA

Fuentes, Carlos *Writer*
Harvard University, Latin American
Studies Dept, Cambridge, MA 02138 USA

Fuentes, Daisy *Entertainer, Model*
William Morris Agency (WMA-LA), 1
William Morris Pl, Beverly Hills, CA
90212 USA

Fuentes, Julio M *Judge*
US Court of Appeals, US Courthouse, 50
Walnut St, Newark, NJ 07102 USA

Fuentes, Tito
61 S. Maddux Dr., Reno, NV 89512

Fugard, Athol H *Writer*
PO Box 5090, Walmer, Port Elizabeth,
6065, SOUTH AFRICA

Fugate, Judith *Ballerina*
New York City Ballet, Lincoln Center
Plaza, New York, NY 10023 USA

Fugees, The
83 Riverside Dr., New York, NY 10024

Fugelsang, John *Comedian, Actor*
William Morris Agency, 151 El Camino
Dr, Beverly Hills, CA 90212 USA

Fugett, Jean *Football Player*
4801 Westparkway, Baltimore, MD 21229
USA

Fugger, Edward *Biologist*
305 Island View Dr, Penhook, VA 24137
USA

Fugit, David *Actor*
Gersh Agency, The (LA), 232 N Canon Dr,
Beverly Hills, CA 90210 USA

Fugit, Patrick *Actor*
Gersh Agency, 232 N Canon Dr, Beverly
Hills, CA 90210 USA

Fuglesang, Christer *Astronaut*
108 Englewood St, Bellaire, TX 77401
USA

Fuhr, Grant *Hockey Player*
80 Oswald Dr, Spruce Grove, AB T7X
3A1, CANADA

Fuhrman, Mark
PO Box 141, Sandpoint, ID 83864-0141

Fujimoto, Tak *Cinematographer*
The Skouras Agency, 631 Wilshire Blvd,
2nd Floor Suite C, Santa Monica, CA
90401 USA

Fujisaki, Judge Hiroshi
1705 Main St. #Q, Santa Monica, CA
90401

Fujita, Hiroyuki *Engineer*
1-9-14 Senkawa, Toshimaku, Tokyo, 171,
JAPAN

Fujita, Yoshio *Astronomer*
6-21-7 Renkoji, Tamashi, 206, JAPAN

Fukuto, Maru *Director*
Jim Preminger Agency, 450 N Roxbury
Dr, #1050, Beverly Hills, CA 90210 USA

Fukuyarna, Francis *Social Activist*
George Mason University, Public Policy
Dept, Fairfax, VA 22030 USA

Fuld, Richard S Jr *Financier*
Lehman Bros, 745 7th Ave, New York, NY
10019 USA

Fulford, Cariton W Jr *General*
Deputy CinC, US European Command
Stuttgart-Vaihingen Germany, APO, AE,
09128 USA

Fulgham, Robert *Writer*
Random House, 299 Park Ave, New York,
NY 10171

Fulghum, Robert *Writer*
Random House, 1745 Broadway, #B1,
New York, NY 10019 USA

Fulhage, Scott *Football Player*
RR 3 Box 95, Beloit, KS 67430 USA

Fulks, Robbie *Musician, Songwriter*
Mongrel Music, 743 Center Blvd, Fairfax,
CA 94930 USA

Fuller, Bob B *Writer*
37 Langton Way, London, 5E3, UNITED
KINGDOM (UK)

Fuller, Bonnie *Editor*
Glamour Magazine, Editorial Dept, 350
Madison Ave, New York, NY 10017 USA

Fuller, Charles *Writer*
William Morris Agency, 1325 Ave of
Americans, New York, NY 10019 USA

Fuller, Curtis D *Musician*
Denon Records, 135 W 50th St, #1915,
New York, NY 10020 USA

Fuller, Deiores *Actor, Songwriter*
3628 Ottawa Circle, Las Vegas, NV 89109
USA

Fuller, Dolores
3628 Ottawa Circle, Las Vegas, NV
89109-3301

Fuller, Drew *Actor*
Untitled Entertainment (LA), 8436 W 3rd
St #650, Los Angeles, CA 90048 USA

Fuller, Jack W *Editor, Publisher*
Chicago Tribune, Editorial Dept, 435 N
Michigan, Chicago, IL 60611 USA

Fuller, Kathryn S *Misc*
World Wildlift Fund, 1250 24th St NW,
Washington, DC 20037 USA

Fuller, Kurt *Actor*
Brady Brannon & Rich/ VOX, 6300
Wilshire Blvd, Suite 900, Los Angeles, CA
90048 USA

Fuller, Lance
1900 Longwood Ave., Los Angeles, CA
90016

Fuller, Linda *Social Activist*
Habitat for Humanity, 121 Habitat St,
Americus, GA 31709 USA

Fuller, Mark *Artist*
Wet Design, 90 Universal City Plaza,
Universal City, CA 91608 USA

Fuller, Marvin D *General*
6799 Patton Dr, Fort Hood, TX 76544
USA

Fuller, Millard *Social Activist*
Habitat for Humanity, 121 Habitat St,
Americus, GA 31709 USA

Fuller, Penny *Actor*
12428 Hesby St, North Hollywood, CA
91601 USA

Fuller, Randy
3718 Cambral St. #B, Fort Irwin, CA
92310

Fuller, Robert (Bob) *Actor*
5012 Auckland Ave, North Hollywood,
CA 91601 USA

Fuller, Simon *Producer, Writer*
19 Management Ltd, 33 Ransomes Dock,
35-37 Parkgate Rd, London, SW11 4NP,
UNITED KINGDOM (UK)

Fuller, Todd *Basketball Player*
Miami Heat, American Airlines Arena,
601 Biscayne Blvd, Miami, FL 33132 USA

Fuller, William H Jr *Football Player*
1424 Blue Heron Road, Virgini Beacha,
VA 23454 USA

Fullerton, C Gordon *Astronaut*
44046 28th St W, Bldg 4800D, Lancaster,
CA 93536 USA

Fullerton, Fiona *Actor*
London Mgmt, 2-4 Noel St, London, W1V
3RB, UNITED KINGDOM (UK)

Fullerton, Larry *Inventor*
Time Domain, 6700 Odyssey Dr NW,
Huntsville, AL 35806 USA

Fullmer, Gene *Boxer*
9250 S 2200 West, West Jordan, UT
84088 USA

Fulmer, Phillip *Football Coach*
University of Tennessee, Athletic Dept,
Knoxville, TN 37996 USA

Fulton, Eileen *Actor, Musician*
"As the World Turns Show" CBS-TV, 524
W 57nd St, New York, NY 10019 USA

Fulton, Fitz
1023 E Ave J-5, Lancaster, CA 93535 USA

Fulton, Fitzhugh Jr *Misc*
1023 e aVE j, #5, lANCASTER, CA 93535
USA

Fulton, Len
1900 Longwood Ave., Los Angeles, CA

Fulton, Soren *Actor*
Savage Agency, 6212 Banner Ave, Los
Angeles, CA 90038 USA

Fumero, David *Actor*
Latin World Entertainment Agency (WEA),
2800 Biscayne Blvd PH, Miami, FL 33137

Fumusa, Dominic *Actor*
Don Buchwald & Associates Inc (LA),
6500 Wilshire Blvd #2200, Los Angeles,
CA 90048 USA

Fun Affairs
Flossergasse 7, Munich, GERMANY,
D-81369

Funaki, Kazuyoshi *Skier*
Japanese Olympic Committee, 1-1-1 Jinan
Shilbuya-Ku, Tokyo, 150, JAPAN

Func, Eric *Composer*
PO Box 1073, Helena, MT 59624 USA

Func, Fred *Golfer*
24711 Harbour View Dr, Ponte Vedra, FL
32082 USA

Funderburk, Leonard J *War Hero*
2311 Lathan Road, Monroe, NC 28112
USA

Funicello, Annette *Actor, Musician*
16102 Sandy Lane, Encino, CA 91436
USA

Funk, Caribbean *Music Group*
Sony Music Miami, 605 Lincoln Rd,
Miami Beach, FL 33138 USA

Funke, Alex *Cinematographer*
1176 Fiske St, Pacific Palisades, CA 90272
USA

Funt, Peter
PO Box 827, Monterey, CA 93942

Fuqua, Antoine *Director*
International Creative Mgmt, 8942
Wilshire Blvd, #219, Beverly Hills, CA
90211 USA

Furay, Richie *Musician*
Agency Group, The (NY), 1775 Broadway
#430, New York, NY 10019 USA

Furcal, Rafael *Baseball Player, Athlete*
Atlanta Braves, Turner Field, PO Box
4064, Atlanta, GA 30302 USA

Furchgott, Robert F *Nobel Prize Laureate*
State University of New York, Health
Science Center, Brooklyn, NY 11203 USA

Furey, John *Actor*
House of Representatives, 400 S Beverly
Dr, #101, Beverly Hills, CA 90212 USA

Furgler, Kurt *President*
Dufourstr 34, Saint-Gail, 9000,
SWITZERLAND

Furian, Mira *Actor*
6410 Blarney Stone Court, Springfield, VA
22152 USA

Furianetto, Ferruccio *Opera Singer*
Metropolitan Opera Assn, Lincoln Center
Plaza, New York, NY 10023 USA

Furlan, Mira
247 S. Beverly Dr. #102, Beverly Hills,
CA 90212

Furlong, Edward *Actor*
New Wave Entertainment (LA), 2660 W
Olive Blvd, Burbank, CA 91505 USA

Furmann, Benno *Actor*
Artists Independent Network (UK), 32
Tavistock St, London, WC2E 7PB,
UNITED KINGDOM (UK)

Furniss, Bruce *Swimmer*
655 S Westford St, Anaheim, CA 92807
USA

Furno, Carlo Cardinal *Religious Leader*
Piazza Della Citta Leonina, Rome, 92807,
ITALY

Furst, Janos K *Conductor*
I M G Artists, 3 Burlington Lane,
Chiswick, London, W4 2TH, UNITED
KINGDOM (UK)

Furst, Nathan *Musician*
Working Artists Agency, 13525 Ventura
Blvd, Sherman Oaks, CA

Furst, Stephen *Actor, Comedian*
Gold Marshak Liedtke, 3500 W Olive
Ave, #1400, Burbank, CA 91505 USA

Furstenfeld, Jeremy *Musician*
Ashley Talent, 2002 Hogback Road, #20,
Ann Arbor, MI 48105 USA

Furstenfeld, Justin *Musician*
Ashley Talent, 2002 Hogback Road, #20,
Ann Arbor, MI 48105 USA

Furtado, Nelly *Musician, Songwriter*
Little Big Man Booking, Little Big Man
Bldg, 155 6th Avenue, 6th Floor, New
York, NY 10013 USA

Furth, George *Actor, Writer*
Bresler Kelly Assoc, 11500 W Olympic
Blvd, #510, Los Angeles, CA 90064 USA

Furuhashi, Hironshin *Swimmer*
3-9-11 Nozawa, Setagayaku, Tokyo,
JAPAN

Furukawa, Masaru *Swimmer*
5-5-12 Shinohara Honmachi, Nadaku,
Kobe, JAPAN

Furukawa, Satoshi *Astronaut*
NASDA, Tsukuba Space Center, 2-1-1
Sengen, Tukuhashi, Ibaraka, 305, JAPAN

Furuseth, Ole Christian *Skier*
John Colletts Alle 74, Oslo, 0854,
NORWAY

Fury, Ed
17957 Cohasset St., Reseda, CA 91335

Furyk, Jim *Golfer*
29 Loggerhard Lane, Ponte Vedra, FL
32082 USA

Fusina, Chuck A *Football Player*
1548 King James St, Pittsburgh, PA 15237
USA

Futey, Bohdan A *Judge*
US Claims Court, 717 Madison Place NW,
Washington, DC 20439 USA

Futral, Elizabeth *Opera Singer*
Neil Funkhouser Mgmt, 105 Arden St,
#5G, New York, NY 10040 USA

Futrell, Mary H *Misc*
George Washington University, Education
School, Washington, DC 20052 USA

Futter, Ellen V *Educator*
American Natural History Museum, Park
Ave West & 79th St, New York, NY
10034 USA

Futterman, Dan *Actor*
Gersh Agency, 232 N Canon Dr, Beverly
Hills, CA 90210 USA

Fuzz *Musician*
Mitch Schneider Organization, 14724
Ventura Blvd, #410, Sherman Oaks, CA
91403 USA

Fylstra, Daniel *Engineer*
Visicorp, 2895 Zanken Road, San Jose, CA
95134 USA

G

G, Franky *Actor*
Creative Artists Agency LCC (CAA-LA),
9830 Wilshire Blvd, Beverly Hills, CA
90212 USA

G, Kenny *Musician*
Creative Artists Agency LCC (CAA-LA),
9830 Wilshire Blvd, Beverly Hills, CA
90212 USA

G K *Actor*
11 Shyamala Vadana Street, Koyathoppu,
Chennai, TN 600 024, INDIA

G Love & Special Sauce *Music Group*
Asgard Promotions, 125 Pkwy, Regents
Park, London, NW1 7PS, United Kingdom

G Ponnambalam *Actor*
10 Dr Subbarray Nagar, II Street
Kodambakkam, Chennai, TN 600 024,
INDIA

Gaarder, Jostein *Misc*
Gullkroken 22A, Oslo, 0377, NORWAY

Gabaldon, Diana *Writer*
Delacorte Press, 1540 Broadway, New
York, NY 10036 USA

Gabbaja, Stefano
via Santa Cecilia 7, Milan, ITALY, 20122

Gabbana, Stefano *Fashion Designer*
Doice & Gabbana, Via Santa Cecilia 7,
Milan, 20122, ITALY

Gable, Brian *Cartoonist*
67 Riverside Dr, #1D, New York, NY
10024 USA

Gable, Daniel M (Danny) *Wrestler, Coach*
RR 2 Box 55, Iowa City, IA 52240 USA

Gable, John Clark
28855 Bison Ct., Malibu, CA 90265

Gabor, Zsa Zsa *Actor*
1001 Bel Air Road, Los Angeles, CA
90077 USA

Gaborik, Marian *Hockey Player*
Minnesota Wild, XCel Energy Arena, 175
Kellogg Blvd W, Saint Paul, MN 55102
USA

Gabriel, Ana *Musician*
AG Ediciones Musicales, Peten 117 Col
Narvarte, Mexico City, 03020, MEXICO

Gabriel, Charles A *General*
Flight International, International Airport,
Newport News, VA 23602 USA

Gabriel, Gunter
Vorhelmer Str. 63, Ennigerloh-Enniger,
GERMANY, D-59320

Gabriel, John *Actor*
130 W 42nd St, #1804, New York, NY
10036 USA

Gabriel, Juan *Musician, Songwriter*
Hauser Entertainment, 11003 Rooks Road,
Whittier, CA 90601 USA

Gabriel, Michael *Artist*
Dlouha 32, Prague 1, 110 00, CZECH
REPUBLIC

Gabriel, Peter *Musician, Songwriter*
PO Box 35, Corsham Wiltshire, London,
SW 13 8SZ, UNITED KINGDOM (UK)

Gabriel, Roman
16817 McKee Rd., Charlotte, NC 28278

Gabriel, Roman I Jr *Football Player*
PO Box 1676, Little River, SC 29566 USA

Gabrielle, Josefina *Actor*
Stone Manners Talent Agency, 6500
Wilshire Blvd, Ste 550, Los Angeles, CA
90048 USA

Gabrielle, Monique *Actor, Model*
Purrfect Productions, PO Box 1771,
Pompano Beach, FL 33061 USA

Gacy, Madonna Wayne *Musician*
Artists & Audience Entertainment, PO Box
35, Pawling, NY 12564 USA

Gaddafi, Muammar Muhammad al
President
President's Office, Bab el Aziziya
Barracks, Tripoli, LIBYA

Gaddis, John L *Historian*
Ohio University, Contemporary History
Institute, Brown House, Athens, OH
45701 USA

Gadinsky, Brian *Producer*
William Morris Agency (WMA-LA), 1
William Morris Pl, Beverly Hills, CA
90212 USA

Gadsby, William A (Bill) *Hockey Player*
28765 E Kalong Circle, Southfield, MI
48034 USA

Gadzhiev, Raul S O *Composer*
Azerbaijan State Popular Orchestra, Baku,
AZERBAIJAN

Gaeta, John *Special Effects Designer*
International Creative Management
(ICM-LA), 8942 Wilshire Blvd, Beverly
Hills, CA 90211 USA

Gaetano, Cortesi *Business Person*
Alfa Romeo SpA, Via Gatternelata 45,
Milan, 20149, ITALY

Gaetti, Gary J *Baseball Player*
14200 Allison Dr, Raleigh, NC 27615
USA

Gaffney, Derrick T *Football Player*
11750 Cherry Bark Dr E, Jacksonville, FL
32218 USA

Gaffney, F Andrew (Drew) *Astronaut*
6613 Chatsworth Place, Nashville, TN
37205 USA

Gaffney, Mo *Actor*
Stone Manners, 8436 W Third St #740,
Los Angeles, CA 90048

Gaffney, Paul F *Admiral*
President National Defense University,
Fort Lesley McNair, Washington, DC
20319 USA

Gage, Fred H *Misc*
Salk Biological Study Institute, 10110 N
Torrey Pines Road, La Jolla, CA 92037
USA

Gage, Nathaniel L *Educator*
85 Peter Courts Circle, Palo Alto, CA
94305 USA

Gage, Nicholas *Journalist*
37 Nelson St, North Grafton, MA 01536
USA

Gage, Paul *Inventor*
Craig Research, Highway 178 N,
Chippewa Falls, WI 55402 USA

Gagliano, Robert F (Bob) *Football Player*
1560 Newbury Road, Newbury Park, CA
91320 USA

Gagliardi, John *Football Coach*
Saint John's University, Athletic Dept,
Collegeville, MN 56321 USA

Gagne, Eric S *Baseball Player*
Los Angeles Dodgers, Stadium, 1000
Elysian Park Ave, Los Angeles, CA 90012
USA

Gagne, Greg C *Baseball Player*
746 Whetstone Hill Road, Somerset, MA
02726 USA

Gagne, Simon *Hockey Player*
Philadelphia Flyers, 1st Union Center,
3601 S Broad St, Philadelphia, PA 19148
USA

Gagner, Dave *Hockey Player*
Custon Ice, 404179 Harvester Road,
Burlington, ON L7L 5M4, CANADA

Gagnier, Holly *Actor*
Stone Manners, 6500 Wilshire Blvd, #550,
Los Angeles, CA 90048 USA

Gagnon, Andre Philippe
89 Rue Alexandra, Granby, CANADA, PQ
J2C 2P4

Gagnon, Edouard Cardinal *Religious Leader*
Pontifical Family Council, Palazzo S
Calisto, 00120, VATICAN CITY

Gago, Jenny *Actor*
Metropolitan Talent Agency, 4526
Wilshire Blvd, Los Angeles, CA 90010
USA

Gagosian, Larry *Business Person*
Gagosian Gallery, 980 Madison Ave,
#PH, New York, NY 10021 USA

Gahan, David *Musician*
Reach Media, 295 Greenwich St, #109,
New York, NY 10007 USA

Gahan, David (Dave) *Musician*
Creative Artists Agency LCC (CAA-LA), 9830 Wilshire Blvd, Beverly Hills, CA 90212 USA

Gaidar, Yegor T *Prime Minister*
Gazetny Per 5, Moscow, 111024, RUSSIA

Gail, David
Henze Management, 1925 Century Park E #2320, Los Angeles, CA 90067 USA

Gail, Joseph G *Biologist*
107 Bellemore Road, Baltimore, MD 21210 USA

Gail, Max *Actor*
28198 Rey de Copas Lane, Malibu, CA 90265 USA

Gaile, Jeri
880 Hilldale Ave. #3, Los Angeles, CA 90069

Gailey, T Chandler (Chan) *Football Player, Football Coach*
3497 Paces Valley Road NW, Atlanta, GA 30327 USA

Gaillard, Bob *Coach*
50 Bonnie Brae Dr, Novato, CA 94949 USA

Gaillard, Charles *Business Person*
General Mills Inc, 1 General Mills Blvd, PO Box 1113, Minneapolis, MN 55440 USA

Gaillard, Mary Katharine *Physicist*
University of California, Physics Dept, Berkeley, CA 94720 USA

Gaiman, Neil *Writer*
Creative Artists Agency LCC (CAA-LA), 9830 Wilshire Blvd, Beverly Hills, CA 90212 USA

Gain, Robert (Bob) *Football Player*
11 Nokomis Dr, Eastlake, OH 44095 USA

Gaines, Ambrose (Rowdy) IV *Swimmer*
6800 Hawaii Kai Dr, Honolulu, HI 96825 USA

Gaines, Boyd *Actor, Musician*
Duva/Flack, 200 W 57th St, #1407, New York, NY 10019 USA

Gaines, Clarence E (Big House) *Coach*
2015 E End Blvd, Winston Salem, NC 27101 USA

Gaines, Davis
315 W. 57th St. #4H, New York, NY 10019

Gaines, Ernest J *Writer*
128 Buena Vista Blvd, Lafayette, LA 70503 USA

Gaines, James R *Editor, Publisher*
Time Warner Inc, Time Magazine, Rockefeller Center, New York, NY 10020 USA

Gaines, Reese *Baseball Player*
Houston Rockets, Toyota Center, 2 E Greenway Plaza, Houston, TX 77046 USA

Gaines, Rowdy
6800 Hawaii Kai Dr, Honolulu, HI 96825

Gaines, William C *Journalist*
Chicago Tribune, Editorial Dept, 435 N Michigan Ave, Chicago, IL 60611 USA

Gainey, Robert M (Bob) *Hockey Player, Coach*
PO Box 829, Coppell, TX 75019 USA

Gainsbourg, Charlotte *Actor*
Artmedia, 20 Ave Rapp, Paris, 75007, FRANCE

Gaither, Bill *Musician, Songwriter*
Gaither Music Co, PO Box 737, Alexandria, IN 46001 USA

Gajarsa, Arthur J *Judge*
Us Court of Appeals, 717 Madison Place NW, Washington, DC 20439 USA

Gajdusek, D Carieton *Nobel Prize Laureate*
Human Virology Institute, 725 W Lombard St, #N460, Baltimore, MD 21201 USA

Galabru, Michael
11 rue Boissiere, Paris, FRANCE, F-75116

Galambos, Robert *Misc*
8826 La Jolla Scenic Dr, La Jolla, CA 92037 USA

Galanos, James *Fashion Designer*
1316 Sunset Plaza Dr, Los Angeles, CA 90069 USA

Galarraga, Andres *Baseball Player*
San Francisco Giants, Pacific Bell Park, 24 Willie Mays Plaza, San Francisco, CA 94114 USA

Galarrage, Andres J P *Baseball Player*
Barrio Nuevo Chapellin, Clejon Soledad #5, Caracas, VENEZUELA

Galati, Frank J *Director*
1144 Michigan Ave, Evanston, IL 60202 USA

Galbraith, Clint *Race Car Driver*
PO Box 902, Edwardsville, IL 62025 USA

Galbraith, Evan G *Diplomat, Financier*
133 E 64th St, New York, NY 10021 USA

Galbraith, John Kenneth *Government Official*
30 Francis Ave, Cambridge, MA 02138 USA

Galdikas, Birute M F *Misc*
Orangutan Foundation International, 822 Wellesley Ave, Los Angeles, CA 90049 USA

Gale, Ed *Actor*
Osbrink Talent Agency, 4343 Lankershim Blvd #100, Universal City, CA 91602 USA

Gale, Joseph H *Judge*
US Tax Court, 400 2nd St NW, Washington, DC 20217 USA

Gale, Robert P *Inventor*
980 Bluegrass Lane, Los Angeles, CA 90049 USA

Galecki, Johnny *Actor*
Industry Entertainment, 955 S Carrillo Dr #300, Los Angeles, CA 90048 USA

Galella, Ronald E (Ron) *Photographer*
Ron Galella Ltd, 12 Nelson Lane, Montville, NJ 07045 USA

Galer, Robert E *General*
3131 Maple Ave, #6D, Dallas, TX 75201 USA

Galiena, Anna *Actor*
ArtMedia, 20 Ave Rapp, Paris, 75007, FRANCE

Galifinakis, Zach *Comedian*
William Morris Agency (WMA-LA), 1 William Morris Pl, Beverly Hills, CA 90212 USA

Galigher, Ed *Football Player*
862 E Angela St, Pleasanton, CA 94566 USA

Galik, Denise *Actor*
Badgley Connor Talent, 9229 Sunset Blvd, #311, Los Angeles, CA 90069 USA

Galina, Stacy *Actor*
Alan Siegel Entertainment, 345 N Maple Dr #375, Beverly Hills, CA 90210 USA

Galindo, Rudy *Figure Skater*
1115 E Haley St, Santa Barbara, CA 93103 USA

Gall, Hugues *Opera Singer*
Grand Theatre de Geneva, 11 Blvd du Theatre, Geneva, 1211, SWITZERLAND

Gallacher, Kevin *Soccer Player*
Blackbum Rovers, Ewood Park, Blackbum, Lancashire, BB2 4JF, UNITED KINGDOM (UK)

Gallagher *Misc*
14984 Roan Court, Wellington, FL 33414 USA

Gallagher, Brian *Misc*
United Way of America, 701 N Fairfax Ave, Alexandria, VA 22314 USA

Gallagher, Bronagh *Actor*
Marmont Mgmt, Langham House, 302/8 Regent St, London, W1R 5AL, UNITED KINGDOM (UK)

Gallagher, David *Actor*
Strong/Morrone Entertainment, 9100 Wilshire Blvd #503E, Beverly Hills, CA 90212 USA

Gallagher, Helen *Actor, Musician*
260 W End Ave, New York, NY 10023 USA

Gallagher, John *Religious Leader*
Advent Christian Church, PO Box 551, Presque Isle, ME 04769 USA

Gallagher, Liam *Musician*
Ignition Mgmt, 54 Linhope St, London, NW1 6HL, UNITED KINGDOM (UK)

Gallagher, Mary *Actor*
Full Circle Management, 8961 Sunset Blvd, Los Angeles, CA 90069 USA

Gallagher, Megan *Actor*
Don Buchwald, 6500 Wilshire Blvd, #2200, Los Angeles, CA 90048 USA

Gallagher, Noel *Musician, Songwriter*
Ignition Management, 54 Linhope St, London, NW1 6HL, England

Gallagher, Peter *Actor*
Anonymous Content, 8522 National Blvd #101, Culver City, CA 90232 USA

Gallagher Jr, Jim *Golfer*
PO Box 507, Greenwood, MS 38935 USA

Gallagher-Smith, Jackie *Golfer*
Int'l Golf Partners, 3300 PGA Blvd, #909, West Palm Beach, FL 33410 USA

Gallant, Gerard *Hockey Player, Coach*
7322 Winnipeg Dr, Dublin, OH 43016 USA

Gallant, Mavis *Writer*
14 Rue Jean Ferrandi, Paris, 75006,
FRANCE

Gallardo, Camillio *Actor*
Innovative Artists, 1505 10th St, Santa
Monica, CA 90401 USA

Gallardo, Camilo
1505 10th St., Santa Monica, CA 90401

Gallardo, Silvana
10637 Burbank Blvd, No. Hollywood, CA
91601

Gallatin, Harry J *Basketball Player, Coach*
2010 Madison Ave, Edwardsville, IL
62025 USA

Gallego, Gina *Actor*
The Agency, 1800 Ave of Stars, #400, Los
Angeles, CA 90067 USA

Gallegos, Gilbert G *Misc*
Fraternal Order of Police, 1410
Donaldson Pike, Nashville, TN 37217
USA

Gallery, Robert *Football Player*
Oakland Raiders, 1220 Harbor Bay
Parkway, Alameda, CA 94502 USA

Galles, John *Misc*
National Small Business United, 1156
15th St NW, #1100, Washington, DC
20005 USA

Galletti, Carl *Business Person*

Galliano, John C *Fashion Designer*
House of Dior, 60 Rue D'Avron, Paris,
75020 USA

Galliano, John C *Fashion Designer*
House of Dior, 60 Rue D'Avron, Paris,
75020, FRANCE

Gallico, Gregory III *Doctor, Inventor*
Massachusetts General Hospital, 275
Cambridge St, Boston, MA 02114 USA

Galligan, Zach
151 El Camino Dr., Beverly Hills, CA
90212

Gallison, Joe *Actor*
PO Box 10187, Wilmington, NC 28404
USA

Gallo, Ernest *Business Person*
E & J Gallo Winery, 600 Yosemite Blvd,
Modesto, CA 95354 USA

Gallo, Frank *Artist*
University of Illinios, Art Dept, Urbana, IL
61801 USA

Gallo, Robert C *Scientist*
University of Maryland, Study of Viruses
Institute, Baltimore, MD 21228 USA

Gallo, Vincent *Actor, Director*
432 La Guardia Place, #600, New York,
NY 10012 USA

Gallo, William V (Bill) *Cartoonist, Boxer*
1 Mayflower Dr, Yonkers, NY 10710 USA

Gallop, Tom *Actor*
Metropolitan Talent Agency (MTA), 4526
Wilshire Blvd, Los Angeles, CA 90010
USA

Galloway, Don *Actor*
2501 Colorado Ave, #350, Santa Monica,
CA 90404 USA

Galloway, Jean *Religious Leader*
Volunteers of America, 1660 Duke St,
Alexandria, VA 22314 USA

Galloway, Joey *Football Player*
507 Lilly Court, Irving, TX 75063 USA

Gallup II, George H *Mathematician*
Great Road, Princeton, NJ 08540 USA

Galotti, Donna *Publisher*
Ladies Home Journal, 100 Park Ave, New
York, NY 10017 USA

Galotti, Ronald A *Publisher*
Conde Nast Publications, Publisher's
Office, 4 Times Square, New York, NY
10036 USA

Galston, Arthur W *Biologist*
307 Manley Heights Road, Orange, CT
06477 USA

Galvin, James *Writer*
University of Iowa, Writer's Workshop,
Iowa City, IA 52242 USA

Galvin, John R *General*
2714 Jodeco Circle, Jonesboro, GA 30236
USA

Galvin, Robert W *Business Person*
Motorola Corporate Office, 1303 East
Algonquin Road, Schaumberg, IL 60196

Galway, James *Musician*
Benzeholzstr 11, Meggen, 6045,
SWITZERLAND

Gam, Rita *Actor*
180 W 58th St, #8B, New York, NY
10019 USA

Gam, Stefan *Race Car Driver*
Indy Regency Racing, 5811 W 73rd St,
Indianapolis, IN 46278 USA

Gamache, Joey *Boxer*
66 Oak St, Lewiston, ME 04240 USA

Gamar, Charles D
7660 N 159th St E, Benton, KS 67017
USA

Gambee, Dave *Basketball Player*
PO Box 3070, Portland, OR 97208 USA

Gamble, Ed *Cartoonist*
Florida Times-Union, Editorial Dept, 1
Riverside Ave, Jacksonville, FL 32202
USA

Gamble, Kenny (Ken) *Football Player*
194 Haverford St, Hamden, CT 06517
USA

Gamble, Kevin *Basketball Player*
41 Forest Ridge, Springfield, IL 62707
USA

Gamble, Mason *Actor*
United Talent Agency, 9560 Wilshire
Blvd, #500, Beverly Hills, CA 90212 USA

Gamboa, Juan Pablo *Actor*
Televisa, Blvd Adolfo Lopez Mateos 232,
Colonia San Angel INN, DF, CP 01060,
MEXICO

Gambon, Michael *Actor*
Paradigm (LA), 10100 Santa Monica Blvd,
Fl 25, Los Angeles, CA 90067 USA

Gambon, Michael J *Actor*
International Creative Mgmt, 40 W 57th
St, #1800, New York, NY 10019 USA

Gambon, Sir Michael *Actor*
International Creative Management
(ICM-LA), 8942 Wilshire Blvd, Beverly
Hills, CA 90211 USA

Gambrell, David H *Senator*
3205 Arden Road NW, Atlanta, GA 30305
USA

Gambril, Don *Coach*
2 Old North River Point, Tuscaloosa, AL
35406 USA

Gambucci, Andre *Hockey Player, Coach*
660 Southpointe Court, Colorado Springs,
CO 80906 USA

Gammon, James *Actor*
414 N Sycamore Ave, #3, Los Angeles,
CA 90036 USA

Gammons, Peter *Writer*
Boston Globe, Editorial Dept, PO Box
2378, Boston, MA 02107 USA

Ganassi, Chip *Race Car Driver*
Chip Ganassi Racing, 11901 W Baseline
Road, Avondale, AZ 85323 USA

Ganassi, Sonia *Opera Singer*
Columbia Artists Mgmt Inc, 165 W 57th
St, New York, NY 10019 USA

Ganatra, Nisha *Director*
Cowan, DeBaets, Abrahams & Sheppard
LLP, 40 West 57th Street, Suite 2104,
New York, NY 10019 USA

Gand, Gale *Chef, Television Host*
Sweet Dreams, 1180 6th Ave Fl 12, New
York, NY 10036 USA

Gandhi, Sonia *Government Official,
Politician*
All India Congress Party, 24 Akbar Road,
New Delhi, New Delhi, 110011, INDIA

Gandhimathi *Actor, Bollywood*
59 Saidapet Road, Chennai, TN 600026,
INDIA

Gandler, Markus *Skier*
Sinwell 22, Kitzbuhel, 6370, AUSTRIA

Gandolfini, James *Actor*
Sanders/Armstrong Management, 2120
Colorado Blvd #120, Santa Monica, CA
90404 USA

Gandy, Wayne L *Football Player*
130 Sand Pine Lane, Davenport, FL 33837
USA

Ganellin, C Robin *Inventor*
University College, Chemistry Dept, 20
Gordon, London, WC1H OAJ, UNITED
KINGDOM (UK)

Ganesh, Gemini *Actor*
6 Nungambakkam High Road, Chennai,
TN 600 034, INDIA

Ganev, Tzetzi
1751 N. Berendo St. #21, Los Angeles, CA
90027

Ganga *Actor*
6 South Mada Street, Mylapore, Chennai,
TN 600 004, INDIA

Gangel, Jamie *Commentator*
NBC-TV News Dept, 30 Rockefeller
Plaza, New York, NY 10112 USA

Gannon, Richard J (Rich) *Football Player*
Oakland Raiders, 1220 Harbor Bay
Parkway, Alameda, CA 94502 USA

Gans, Danny *Entertainer*
Chip Lightman Management, 3400 Las
Vegas Blvd, Las Vegas, NV 89109 USA

Gansler, Bob *Soccer Player, Coach*
Kansas City Wizards, 2 Arrowhead Dr,
Kansas City, MO 64129 USA

Ganson, Arthur *Artist*
Massachusetts Institute of Technology,
Compton Gallery, Cambridge, MA 02139
USA

Gant, Harry *Race Car Driver*
RR3 Box 587, Taylorsville, NC 28681
USA

Gant, Robert *Actor*
Don Buchwald & Associates Inc (LA),
6500 Wilshire Blvd #2200, Los Angeles,
CA 90048 USA

Gant, Ronald E (Ron) *Baseball Player*
2005 Kings Cross Road, Alpharetta, GA
30022 USA

Gantin, Bernardin Cardinal *Religious
Leader*
Congregation for Bishops, Plazza Pio XII
10, Rome, 00193, ITALY

Gantos, Jack *Writer*
Farrar Straus Giroux, 19 Union Square W,
New York, NY 10003 USA

Gantt, Harvey
Rt. #1 Box 587, Taylorsville, NC 28681

Ganz, Bruno *Actor*
Mgmt Ema Baumbauer, Keplestr 2,
Munich, 81679, GERMANY

Ganzel, Teresa *Actor*
Irv Schechter, 9300 Wilshire Blvd, #410,
Beverly Hills, CA 90212 USA

Gao, Xiang *Musician*
Columbia Artists Mgmt Inc, 165 W 57th
St, New York, NY 10019 USA

Gao, Xingjian *Nobel Prize Laureate*
Chinese University of Hong Kong Press,
Shatin, Hong Kong, CHINA

Gaona, Jessica *Actor*
Abrams Artists Agency (LA), 9200 Sunset
Blvd Fl 11, Los Angeles, CA 90069 USA

Gap Band, The
89 Fifth Ave. #700, New York, NY 10003

Garabaldi, Bob
2143 Oregon Ave., Stockton, CA 95204

Garabedian, Paul R *Mathematician*
110 Bleekcker St, New York, NY 10012
USA

Garagiola, Joe *Baseball Player,
Sportscaster*
7433 E Tuckey Lane, Scottsdale, AZ
85250 USA

Garai, Romola *Actor*
Creative Artists Agency LCC (CAA-LA),
9830 Wilshire Blvd, Beverly Hills, CA
90212 USA

Garan, Ronald J Jr *Astronaut*
2002 Sea Cove Court, Houston, TX 77058
USA

Garas, Kaz *Actor*
10145 N Buchanan Ave, Portland, OR
97203 USA

Garavito, R Michael *Misc*
Michigan State University, Biochemistry
Dept, East Lansing, MI 48824 USA

Garbage *Music Group*
Creative Artists Agency LCC (CAA-LA),
9830 Wilshire Blvd, Beverly Hills, CA
90212 USA

Garbarek, Jan *Musician*
Niels Juels Gate 42, Oslo, 0257,
NORWAY

Garber, H Eugene (Gene) *Baseball Player*
771 Stonemill Dr, Elizabethtown, PA
17022 USA

Garber, Terri *Actor*
Metropolitan Talent Agency, 4526
Wilshire Blvd, Los Angeles, CA 90010
USA

Garber, Victor *Actor*
Gersh Agency, 232 N Canon Dr, Beverly
Hills, CA 90210 USA

Garces, Paula *Actor*
Untitled Entertainment (NY), 23 E 22nd St
Fl 3, New York, NY 10010 USA

Garcetti, Gil
139 N Cliffwood, Los Angeles, CA 90049
USA

Garci, Jose Luis *Director*
Direccion General del Libro, Paseo de la
Castellana 109, Madrid, 16, SPAIN

Garcia, Adam *Actor*
Brillstein-Grey Entertainment, 9150
Wilshire Blvd #350, Beverly Hills, CA
90212 USA

Garcia, Aimee *Actor*
Essential Talent Management, 6399
Wilshire Blvd #400, Los Angeles, CA
90048 USA

Garcia, Andy *Actor*
CineSon Productions Inc, 4519 Varna
Ave, Sherman Oaks, CA 91423 USA

Garcia, Armand *Actor*
Identity Talent Agency (ID), 2050 Bundy
Dr #200, Los Angeles, CA 90025 USA

Garcia, Danna *Actor*
Telemundo, 2470 West 8th Avenue,
Hialeah, FL 33010 USA

Garcia, David (Dave) *Baseball Player*
15420 Olde Highway 80, #19, El Cajon,
CA 92021 USA

Garcia, Freddy A *Baseball Player*
Quisquella Qta, Etapa M22 #52, La
Romana, DOMINICAN REPUBLIC

Garcia, Jesus *Actor*
Columbia Artists Mgmt Inc, 165 W 57th
St, New York, NY 10019 USA

Garcia, JoAnna *Actor*
Gold Marshak Liedtke, 3500 W Olive
Ave, #1400, Burbank, CA 91505 USA

Garcia, Jsu *Actor*
Carlyle Productions & Management, 2050
Laurel Canyon Blvd, Los Angeles, CA
90046

Garcia, Juan Carlos *Actor*
Gabriel Blanco Iglesias (Mexico), Rio
Balsas 35-32, Colonia Cuauhtemoc, DF,
06500, Mexico

Garcia, Karim *Baseball Player, Athlete*
Cleveland Indians, Jacobs Field, 2401
Ontario Street, Cleveland, OH 44115 USA

Garcia, Leonardo *Actor*
TV Azteca, Periferico Sur 4121, Colonia
Fuentes del Pedregal, DF, CP 14141,
Mexico

Garcia, Odalys *Actor*
Univision, 314 Main St, Chico, CA 95928
USA

Garcia, Pedro
1973 Parque del Condaro L4, Irb. Bairos
Park Caguas, PR 00725

Garcia, Rodrigo *Director*
Endeavor Agency LLC (LA), 9601 Wilshire
Blvd Fl 3, Beverly Hills, CA 90210 USA

Garcia, Russ
7920 Sunset Blvd. #300, Los Angeles, CA
90046

Garcia, Sergio *Golfer*
Strategies & Solutions, 2655 La Luene
Road, #605, Coral Gables, FL 33134 USA

Garcia Marquez, Gabriel *Nobel Prize
Laureate*
Fuego 144, Pedregal de San Angel,
Mexico City, DF, MEXICO

Garcia Posey, Tyler *Actor*
SDB Partners Inc, 1801 Ave of the Stars
#902, Los Angeles, CA 90067 USA

Garciaparra, Nomar *Baseball Player*
44 Pier 7, Charleston, MA 02129 USA

Gardeazabal, Marcela *Actor*
TV Caracol, Calle 76 #11 - 35, Piso
10AA, Bogota DC, 26484, COLOMBIA

Gardell, Billy *Actor*
Agency for the Performing Arts (APA-LA),
9200 Sunset Blvd #900, Los Angeles, CA
90069 USA

Gardener, Daryl *Football Player*
789 International Isle Dr, Castle Rock, CO
80108 USA

Gardenhire, Ronald C (Ron) *Baseball
Player*
668 Country Road B2E, Little Canada, MN
55117 USA

Gardiner, John Eliot *Conductor*
Gore Farm, Ashmore, Salisbury, Wilts,
SP5 5AR, UNITED KINGDOM (UK)

Gardiner, Robert K A *Misc*
PO Box 9274, The Airport, Accra,
GHANA

Gardner, Ashley *Actor*
S M S Talent, 8730 Sunset Blvd, #440, Los
Angeles, CA 90069 USA

Gardner, Calvin P (Cal) *Hockey Player*
1979 Remo Dr, Brights Grove, ON N0N
1C0, CANADA

Gardner, Carl *Musician*
Veta Gardner, 1789 SW McAllister Lane,
Port Saint Lucie, FL 34953 USA

Gardner, Dale *Astronaut*
4735 Broadmoor Bluffs Dr, Colorado
Springs, CO 80906 USA

Gardner, David P *Educator*
Hewlett Foundation, 2121 Sand Hill
Road, Menlo Park, CA 94025 USA

Gardner, Guy S *Astronaut*
316 S Taylor St, Arlington, VA 22204 USA

Gardner, Howard E *Physicist*
Harvard University, Graduate Education
School, Cambridge, MA 02138 USA

Gardner, James H *Basketball Player, Coach*
5465 Bromely Dr, Oak Park, CA 91377 USA

Gardner, John *Dancer*
American Ballet Theatre, 890 Broadway, New York, NY 10003 USA

Gardner, Moe *Football Player*
240 May Apple Lane, Alpharetta, GA 30005 USA

Gardner, Randy *Figure Skater*
4640 Glencove Ave, #6, Marina del Rey, CA 90291 USA

Gardner, Rulon *Wrestler*
PO Box 1242, Laramie, WY 82073 USA

Gardner, W Booth *Governor*
Norton Building, 801 2nd Ave #1300, Seattle, WA 98104 USA

Gardner, Wee Willie
400 E. Van Buren #300, Phoenix, AZ 85004

Gardner, Wilford R *Physicist*
University of California, Natural Resources College, Berkeley, CA 94720 USA

Gardner, William F (Billy) *Baseball Player*
35 Dayton Road, Waterford, CT 06385 USA

Gardocki, Christopher A (Chris) *Football Player*
Pittsburgh Steelers, 3400 S Water St, Pittsburgh, PA 15203 USA

Gare, Danny *Hockey Player*
4542 Lake Shore Road, Hamburg, NY 14075 USA

Garelick, Jeremy *Producer*
Principato/Young Management, 9665 Wilshire Blvd #500, Beverly Hills, CA 90212 USA

Garewal, Simi *Actor, Bollywood*
Paviova 6th Floor Little Gibb's Road, Malabar Hill, Bombay, MS 400 006, INDIA

Garfat, Jance *Musician*
Artists Int'l Mgmt, 9850 Sandalwood Blvd, #458, Boca Raton, FL 33428 USA

Garfield, Allen
8271 Melrose Ave. #202, Los Angeles, CA 90046

Garfield, Brian W *Writer*
345 N Maple Dr, #395, Beverly Hills, CA 90210 USA

Garfinkle, David *Producer*
Renegade 83 Entertainment, 5700 Wilshire Blvd, 6th Floor, Los Angeles, CA 90036 USA

Garfunkel, Art *Actor, Musician*
83 Hyacinth Road, Levittown, NY 11756 USA

Garity, Troy *Actor*
Pinnacle PR, 8265 Sunset Blvd #201, Los Angeles, CA 90046 USA

Garland, Beverly *Actor*
8014 Briar Summit Dr, Los Angeles, CA 90046 USA

Garland, Carrington
8014 Briar Summit Dr, Los Angeles, CA 90046

Garland, George D *Physicist*
5 Mawhiney Court, Huntsville, ON P0A 1K0, CANADA

Garland, Merrick B *Judge*
US Court of Appeals, 333 Constitution Ave NW, Washington, DC 20001 USA

Garlick, Jessica *Musician*
Pop Idol (Fremantle Media), 2700 Colorado Ave #450, Santa Monica, CA 90404 USA

Garlick, Scott *Soccer Player*
Colorado Rapids, 555 17th St, #3350, Denver, CO 80202 USA

Garlin, Jeff *Producer, Actor*
3 Arts Entertainment Inc, 9460 Wilshire Blvd Fl 7, Beverly Hills, CA 90212 USA

Garlits, Donald G (Big Daddy) *Race Car Driver*
Garlits Racing Museum, 13700 SW 16th Ave, Ocala, FL 34473 USA

Garmaker, Dick *Basketball Player*
5824 E 11th St, Tulsa, OK 74137 USA

Garmann, Greg *Actor*
8383 Wilshire Blvd, #550, Beverly Hills, CA 90211 USA

Garn, E Jacob (Jake) *Senator, Astronaut*
1626 Yale Ave, Salt Lake City, UT 84105 USA

Garn, Jake *Ex-Senator*
500 Huntsman Way, Salt Lake City, UT 84108-l235 USA

Garn, Stanley M *Misc*
1200 Earhart Road, #223, Ann Arbor, MI 48105 USA

Garneau, Marc *Astronaut*
Space Agency, 6767 Route de Aeroport, Sainte-Hubert, QC, J3Y 8Y9, CANADA

Garner, Charlie *Football Player*
Oakland Raiders, 1220 Harbor Bay Parkway, Alameda, CA 94502 USA

Garner, James *Actor*
33 Oakmont Dr, Los Angeles, CA 90049 USA

Garner, Jennifer *Actor*
Alias, 500 S Buena Vista St, Bldg 23 Rm 26, Burbank, CA 91521 USA

Garner, Philip M (Phil) *Baseball Player*
7503 Prairie Oak Trail, Humble, TX 77346 USA

Garner, Wendell R *Physicist*
PO Box 650, Branford, CT 06405 USA

Garner, William S *Cartoonist*
Memphis Commercial Appeal, Editorial Dept, 495 Union Ave, Memphis, TN 38103 USA

Garnett, Kevin *Basketball Player*
Minnesota Timberwolves, Target Center, 600 1st Ave N, Minneapolis, MN 55403 USA

Garofalo, Janeane *Actor*
Messina-Baker Entertainment, 955 Carillo Dr 100, Los Angeles, CA 90048 USA

Garouste, Gerard *Artist*
La Mesangere, Marcilly-sur-Eure, 27810, FRANCE

Garr, Ralph A *Baseball Player*
7819 Chaseway Dr, Missouri City, TX 77489 USA

Garr, Teri (Terri/Terry) *Actor*
Brillstein-Grey Entertainment, 9150 Wilshire Blvd #350, Beverly Hills, CA 90212 USA

Garrahy, J Joseph *Governor*
988 Centerville Road, Warwick, RI 02886 USA

Garrard, Rose *Artist*
105 Carpenters Road, #21, London, E18, UNITED KINGDOM (UK)

Garreis, Robert M *Geophysicist*
South Florida University, Marine Science Dept, Saint Petersburg, FL 33701 USA

Garrett, Betty *Actor, Musician*
3231 Oakdell Road, Studio City, CA 91604 USA

Garrett, Brad *Actor, Comedian*
Raw Talent, 9615 Brighton Way, #300, Beverly Hills, CA 90210 USA

Garrett, Carl *Football Player*
314 Teal St, Pittsburg, TX 75686 USA

Garrett, Cynthia *Entertainer*
NBC-TV, News Dept, 30 Rockefeller Plaza, New York, NY 10112 USA

Garrett, George P Jr *Writer*
1845 Wayside Place, Charlottesville, VA 22903 USA

Garrett, Jeremy *Actor*
William Morris Agency (WMA-LA), 1 William Morris Pl, Beverly Hills, CA 90212 USA

Garrett, Kathleen *Actor*
The Agency, 1800 Ave of Stars, #400, Los Angeles, CA 90067 USA

Garrett, Kenneth *Photographer*
National Geographic Magazine, 1145 17th St NW, Washington, DC 20036 USA

Garrett, Kenny *Musician*
Von Productions, 1915 Cullen Ave, Austin, TX 78757 USA

Garrett, Leif *Musician, Actor*
Artists Int'l Mgmt, 9850 Sandalwood Blvd, #458, Boca Raton, FL 33428 USA

Garrett, Lesley *Opera Singer*
PV Productions, Park Offices, 121 Dora Road, London, SW19 7JT, UNITED KINGDOM (UK)

Garrett, Lila *Director*
1245 Laurel Way, Beverly Hills, CA 90210 USA

Garrett, Michael L (Mike) *Football Player*
University of Southern California, Heritage Hall, Los Angeles, CA 90089 USA

Garrett, Pat *Musician, Songwriter*
Patrick Sickafus, PO Box 84, Strausstown, PA 19559 USA

Garrett, Wilbur E *Editor*
National Geographic Magazine, 17th & M Sts, Washington, DC 20036 USA

Garrett, William E *Photographer*
209 Seneca Road, Great Falls, VA 22066 USA

Garrett III, H Lawrence *Government Official*
RR1 Box 136-18, Boyce, VA 22620 USA

Garriott, Owen E *Doctor*
111 Lost Tree Dr SW, Huntsville, AL 35824-1313 USA

Garriott, Owen K *Astronaut*
111 Lost Tree Dr SW, Huntsville, AL
35824 USA

Garrison, David *Actor*
630 Estrada Redona, Santa Fe, NM 87501
USA

Garrison, Greg
1655 Hidden Valley Rd, Thousand Oaks,
CA 91361-5051

Garrison, John *Hockey Player*
Old Concord Road, Lincoln, MA 01773
USA

Garrison, Walt *Football Player*
187 E Hickory Hill Road, Argyle, TX
76226 USA

Garrison-Jackson, Zina *Tennis Player*
1701 Hermann Dr, #705, Houston, TX
77004 USA

Garrity, Freddie *Musician*
16 Ascot Close, Congleton, Cheshire,
CW1Z 1LL, UNITED KINGDOM (UK)

Garrum, Larry *Hockey Player*
987 Pleasant St, Framingham, MA 01701
USA

Garson, Willie *Actor*
Writers & Artists, 8383 Wilshire Blvd,
#550, Beverly Hills, CA 90211 USA

Garth, Jennie *Actor*
PO Box 1944, Studio City, CA 91614 USA

Garth, Leonard I *Judge*
US Court of Appeals, US Courthouse, 50
Walnut St, Newark, NJ 07102 USA

Gartner, Claus-Theo
Postfach 230313, Essen, GERMANY,
45071

Gartner, Michael G *Business Person,*
Publisher, Editor
366 W 11th St, New York, NY 10014
USA

Gartner, Mike *Hockey Player*
NHL Players Association, 2400-777 Bay
St, Toronto, ON M5G 2C8, CANADA

Garver, Cathy *Actor*
550 Mountain Home Road, Woodside,
CA 94062 USA

Garver, Kathy *Actor*
April Cheeseman, 620 Country Club Lane,
Coronado, CA 92118 USA

Garver, Ned F *Baseball Player*
1121 Town Line Road, #164, Bryan, OH
43506 USA

Garvey, Steve
11718 Barrington Ct. #6, Los Angeles, CA
90049-2930

Garvey, Steven P (Steve) *Baseball Player*
11718 Barrington Court, #6, Los Angeles,
CA 90049 USA

Garvey-Truhan, Cyndy
13924 Panay Way #309, Marina del Rey,
CA 90292-6102

Garwin, Richard L *Physicist*
16 Ridgecrest E, Scarsdale, NY 10583
USA

Garwood, Julie *Writer*
Pocket Books, 1230 Ave of Americas,
New York, NY 10020 USA

Garwood, William L (Will) *Judge*
US Court of Appeals, 903 San Jacinto
Blvd, Austin, TX 78701 USA

Gary, Cleveland E *Football Player*
1446 SW 169th Ave, Indiantown, FL
37956 USA

Gary, Lorraine *Actor*
1158 Tower Dr, Beverly Hills, CA 90210
USA

Garza, David *Musician*
Partisan Arts, PO Box 5085, Larkspur, CA
94977 USA

Garza, Emilio M *Judge*
US Court of Appeals, US Courthouse,
8200 1-10 W, San Antonio, TX 78230
USA

Garza, Nicole *Actor*
Agency for the Performing Arts (APA-LA),
9200 Sunset Blvd #900, Los Angeles, CA
90069 USA

Gascoigne, Paul J *Soccer Player*
Arran Gardner, Holborn Hall, 10 Grays
Inn Road, London, WC1X 8BY, UNITED
KINGDOM (UK)

Gascoine, Jill *Actor*
Marina Martin, 12/13 Poland St, London,
W1V 3DE, UNITED KINGDOM (UK)

Gascolgne, Sheryl
Stanstead Abbots, Hertfordshire,
ENGLAND

Gash, Samuel L (Sam) *Football Player*
53 Michael Anthony Lane, Depew, NY
14043 USA

Gaskill, Brian *Actor*
Agency for the Performing Arts (APA-LA),
9200 Sunset Blvd #900, Los Angeles, CA
90069 USA

Gasol, Pau *Basketball Player*
Memphis Grizzlies, 175 Toyota Plaza,
#150, Memphis, TN 38103 USA

Gaspari, Rich *Misc*
PO Box 29, Milltown, NJ 08850 USA

Gass, William H *Writer*
6304 Westminster Place, Saint Louis, MO
63130 USA

Gasslyev, Nikolal T *Opera Singer*
Mariinsky Theater, Teartainaya Pl 1, Saint
Petersburg, RUSSIA

Gassman, Alessandro *Actor*
Christian Cucchini Mgmt, Lungotevere del
Mellini 10, Rome, 00193, ITALY

Gast, Leon *Director*
William Morris Agency, 151 El Camino
Dr, Beverly Hills, CA 90212 USA

Gasteyer, Ana *Actor, Comedian*
William Morris Agency, 151 El Camino
Dr, Beverly Hills, CA 90212 USA

Gastineau, Marcus D (Mark) *Football*
Player
1717 S Dorsey Lane, Tempe, AZ 85281
USA

Gaston, Clarence E (Cito) *Baseball Player*
2 Blyth Dale Road, Toronto, ON M4N
3M2, CANADA

Gately, Stephen *Musician*
Carol Assoc-War Mgmt, Bushy Park Road,
57 Meadowbanl, Dublin, IRELAND

Gates, Bill *Business Person*
Microsoft Corporation, 1 Microsoft Way,
Redmond, WA 98052-8300 USA

Gates, Daryl
24962 Sea Crest Dr, Dana Point, CA
92629

Gates, Daryl F *Lawyer*
24962 Sea Crest Dr, Dana Point, CA
92629 USA

Gates, David *Musician, Songwriter*
Paradise Artists, 108 E Matilija St, Ojai,
CA 93023 USA

Gates, Gareth *Musician*
Pop Idol (Fremantle Media), 2700
Colorado Ave #450, Santa Monica, CA
90404 USA

Gates, Henry Lewis Jr *Educator*
Harvard University, Afro-American Studies
Dept, Cambridge, MA 02138 USA

Gates, Robert M *Government Official,*
Educator
Texas A&M University, President's Office,
College Station, TX 77843 USA

Gates III, William H *Designer, Business*
Person
Microsoft Corp, 1 Microsoft Way,
Redmond, WA 98052 USA

Gatlin, Larry
5100 Harris Ave., Kansas City, MO
64133-2331

Gatlin, Larry W *Musician, Songwriter*
McLachlan-Scruggs, 2821 Bransford Ave,
Nashville, TN 37204 USA

Gatski, Frank *Football Player*
PO Box 677, Grafton, WV 26354 USA

Gatti, Arturo *Boxer*
3208 Bergen Line Ave, Union City, NJ
07087 USA

Gatti, Jennifer *Actor*
S D B Partners, 1801 Ave of Stars, #902,
Los Angeles, CA 90067 USA

Gatting, Michael W *Cricketer*
Middlesex Cricket Club, Saint John's
Wood Road, London, NW8 8QN,
UNITED KINGDOM (UK)

Gattorno, Francisco *Actor*
Gabriel Blanco Iglesias (Mexico), Rio
Balsas 35-32, Colonia Cuauhtemoc, DF,
06500, Mexico

Gauci, Miriam *Opera Singer*
Kunstleragentur Raab & Bohm,
Plankengasse 7, Vienna, 1010, AUSTRIA

Gaudiani, Claire L *Educator*
53 Neptune Dr, Groton, CT 06340 USA

Gaul, Gilbert M *Journalist*
Philadelphia Inquirer, Editorial Dept, 400
N Broad St, Philadelphia, PA 19130 USA

Gault, William Campbell *Writer*
481 Mountain Dr, Santa Barbara, CA
93103 USA

Gault, Willie *Football Player*
PO Box 10759, Marina del Rey, CA
90295

Gault, Willie J *Football Player*
PO Box 10759, Marina del Rey, CA
90295 USA

Gaurav, Kumar *Actor*
Dimple 7 Pali Hill, Bandra, Bombay, MS
400 050, INDIA

Gauthier, Daniel *Business Person, Misc*
Cirque du Soleil, 8400 2nd Ave, Montreal,
QC, H1Z 4M6, CANADA

Gautier, Dick *Actor*
11333 Moorpark St #59, N Hollywood,
CA 91602 USA

Gava, Cassandra *Actor*
1745 Camino Palmero #210, Los Angeles,
CA 90046 USA

Gavaskar, Sunil M *Cricketer*
40 Bhalchandra Road #A Dadar, Bombay,
MS 400014, INDIA

Gavilan, Kid
1 Hall of Fame Dr., Canastota, NY 13032

Gavin, John *Actor, Diplomat*
2100 Century Park W #10263, Los
Angeles, CA 90067 USA

Gaviria, Trujillo Cesar *President*
Organization of American States, 17th &
Constitution NW, Washington, DC 20006
USA

Gavitt, Dave *Basketball Player, Misc*
Boston Celtics, 151 Merrimac St #1,
Boston, MA 02114 USA

Gavrilov, Andrei V *Music Group,
Musician*
Konzertdirektion Schlote, Danreitergasse
4, Salzburg, 5020 USA

Gavrilov, Andrei V *Music Group,
Musician*
Konzertdirektion Schlote, Danreitergasse
4, Salzburg, 5020, AUSTRIA

Gay, Don
1818 Rodeo Dr., Mesquite, TX 75149

Gay, George
588 Charlton Ct. NW, Marietta, GA
30064

Gay, Gerald H (Jerry) *Photographer,
Journalist*
P O Box 938, Blaine, WA 98231 USA

Gay, Peter J *Historian*
760 W End Ave #15A, New York, NY
10025 USA

Gaydos, Joey *Actor*
Cunningham-Escott-Dipene & Associates
Inc (CED-LA), 10635 Santa Monica Blvd
#130, Los Angeles, CA 90025 USA

Gaydukov, Sergei N *Astronaut, Misc*
Potchta Kosmonavtov, Moskovskoi
Oblasti, Syvisdny Goroduk, 141160,
RUSSIA

Gaye, Nona *Actor, Musician*
Creative Artists Agency LCC (CAA-LA),
9830 Wilshire Blvd, Beverly Hills, CA
90212 USA

Gayheart, Rebecca *Actor, Model*
BTA Mgmt, 853 7th Ave #9A, New York,
NY 10019 USA

Gayle, Crystal *Music Group, Musician*
51 Music Square E, Nashville, TN 37203
USA

Gaylor, Noel *Admiral*
2111 Mason Hill Dr, Alexandria, VA
22306 USA

Gaylord, Mitchell J (Mitch) *Gymnast,
Actor*
1593 Little Lake Dr, Park City, UT 84098
USA

Gaylord, Scott
1451 Depen, Lakewood, CO 80214

Gaylords, The
32630 Concord Dr., Madison Heights, MI
48071

Gaynes, George *Actor*
3344 Campanil Dr, Santa Barbara, CA
93109 USA

Gaynor, Gloria *Musician, Music Group*
Cliffside Music, P O Box 7172, Warren,
NJ 07069 USA

Gaynor, Mitzi *Actor, Dancer, Musician,
Music Group*
610 N Arden Dr, Beverly Hills, CA 90210
USA

Gayoom, Maumoon Abdul *President*
Presidential Palace, Orchid Magu, Male,
20-05, MALDIVES

Gayson, Eunice *Actor*
Spotlight, 7 Leicester Place, London,
WC2H 7BP, UNITED KINGDOM (UK)

Gayton, Joe *Writer*
Agency for the Performing Arts (APA-LA),
9200 Sunset Blvd #900, Los Angeles, CA
90069 USA

Gayton, Tony *Writer*
Agency for the Performing Arts (APA-LA),
9200 Sunset Blvd #900, Los Angeles, CA
90069 USA

Gazit, Doron *Artist*
Air Dimensional Inc, 14141 Covello St
Building 1, Van Nuys, CA 91405 USA

Gazzara, Ben *Actor*
Stone Manners Talent Agency, 6500
Wilshire Blvd, Ste 550, Los Angeles, CA
90048 USA

Gbagbo, Laurent *President*
President's Office, Boulevard Clozel,
Abidijan, IVORY COAST

Gearan, Mark *Government Official,
Educator*
Hobart & William Smith College,
President's Office, Geneva, NY 14456
USA

Gearhart, John *Doctor, Biologist*
Johns Hopkins Univesity, Medical Center,
Baltimore, MD 21218 USA

Geary, Anthony (Tony) *Actor*
7010 Pacific View Dr, Los Angeles, CA
90068 USA

Geary, Cynthia *Actor*
Baumgarten/Prophet, 1041 N Formosa
Ave #200, West Hollywood, CA 90046
USA

Geary, Tony
7010 Pacific View Dr., Los Angeles, CA
90068

Gebo, Daniel *Scientist*
Northern Illinois University, Paleontology
Dept, De Kalb, IL 60115 USA

Gebrselassie, Haile *Track Athlete*
Ethiopian Athletic Federation, P O Box
3241, Addis Ababa, ETHIOPIA

Gedda, Nicolai *Opera Singer*
Valhallavagen 128, Stockholm, 11441,
SWEDEN

Geddes, Jane *Golfer*
1139 Abbeys Way, Tampa, FL 33602 USA

Gedrick, Jason *Actor*
I F A Talent Agency, 8730 Sunset Blvd
#490, Los Angeles, CA 90069 USA

Gee, E Gordon *Educator*
Vanderbilt University, Chancellor's Office,
Nashville, TN 37240 USA

Gee, James D *Religious Leader*
Penecostal Church of God, 4901
Pennsylvania, Joplin, MO 64804 USA

Gee, Kim *Musician*
Pop Idol (Fremantle Media), 2700
Colorado Ave #450, Santa Monica, CA
90404 USA

Gee, Prunella *Actor*
Michael Ladkin Mgmt, 1Duchess St #1,
London, W1N 3DE, UNITED KINGDOM
(UK)

Geer, Dennis *Financier*
Federal Deposit Insurance, 550 17th St
NW, Washington, DC 20429 USA

Geer, Ellen *Actor*
21418 W Entrada Road, Topanga, CA
90290 USA

Geertz, Clifford J *Misc*
Institute for Advanced Study, Social
Science Dept, Princeton, NJ 08540 USA

Gees, Bee, The *Musician*
William Morris Agency (WMA-LA), 1
William Morris Pl, Beverly Hills, CA
90212 USA

Geeson, Judy *Actor*
Media Artists Group, 6300 Wilshire Blvd,
#1470, Los Angeles, CA 90048 USA

Geffen, Aviv
Bugroashov 26, Tel Aviv, ISRAEL, 63342

Geffen, David *Producer, Business Person*
DreamWorks SKG, 100 Universal Plaza,
Universal City, CA 91608 USA

Gegenhuber, John
9171 Wilshire Blvd. #441, Beverly Hills,
CA 90210

Gehman, Martha
2488 Cheremoya Ave, Los Angeles, CA
90068

Gehring, Frederick W *Mathematician*
2139 Melrose Ave, Ann Arbor, MI 48104
USA

Gehring, Walter J *Doctor, Scientist, Misc*
Hochfeldstr 32, Therwill, 4106,
SWITZERLAND

Gehry, Franko O *Architect*
Gehry Partners, 12541 Beatrice St, Los
Angeles, CA 90066 USA

Geiberger, Al *Golfer*
Professional Golfer's Assn, P O Box
109601, Palm Beach Gardens, FL 33410
USA

Geiberger, Brent *Golfer*
Cross Consulting, 5 Cathy Place, Menlo
Park, CA 94025 USA

Geiduschek, E Peter *Biologist*
University of California, Biology Dept
9500 Gilman Dr, La Jolla, CA 92093 USA

Geier, Philip H Jr *Business Person*
Interpublic Group, 1271 Ave of Americas, New York, NY 10020 USA

Geiger, Ken *Photographer, Journalist*
Dallas Mornig News, Communications Center, Dallas, TX 75265 USA

Geiger, Matt *Basketball Player*
5317 Boardwalk St, Holiday, FL 34690 USA

Geimer, Samantha
4245 Waipua, Kilauea, HI 96754

Geingob, Hage G *Prime Minister*
Prime Minister's Office, Private Bag 13338, Windhoek, 9000, NAMIBIA

Geismar, Thomas H *Architect*
Cambridge Seven Assoc, 1050 Massachusetts Ave, Cambridge, MA 02138 USA

Geiss, Johannes *Physicist*
University of Beme, Physics Instit Sidlerstr 5, Beme, 3012, SWITZERLAND

Geissendorfer, Hans
An den Herrenbergen 21a, Neustadt/ Aisch, GERMANY, D-91413

Geithner, Timothy *Financier*
Federal Reserve Bank, 33 Liberty St, New York, NY 10045 USA

Gelb, Leslie H *Educator*
Council of Foreign Relations, 58 E 68th St, New York, NY 10021 USA

Gelbart, Larry *Producer, Writer*
807 N Alpine Dr, Beverly Hills, CA 90210 USA

Geldof, Bob *Music Group*
14 Clifford St, Bond St House, London, W1X 2JD, UNITED KINGDOM (UK)

Gelfand, Izrael M *Mathematician*
118 N 5th Ave, Highland Park, NJ 18904 USA

Gelfant, Alan *Actor*
Peter Strain, 5724 W 3rd #302, Los Angeles, CA 90036 USA

Gelinas, Gratien *Actor, Writer*
316 Girouard St #207, Oka, QC, J0N 1E0, CANADA

Gell-Mann, Murray *Nobel Prize Laureate*
Santa Fe Institute, 1399 Hyde Park Road, Santa Fe, NM 87501 USA

Gellar, Sarah Michelle *Actor*
William Morris Agency (WMA-LA), 1 William Morris Pl, Beverly Hills, CA 90212 USA

Geller, Margaret J *Astronomer*
Harvard University, Astronomy Dept 60 Garden St, Cambridge, MA 02138 USA

Geller, Uri *Actor*
Celeb Agents, 77 Oxford St, London ON, W1D 2ES, UNITED KINGDOM (UK)

Gelman, Larry *Actor*
5121 Greenbush Ave, Sherman Oaks, CA 91423 USA

Gelman, Michael
7 Lincoln Sq., New York, NY 10023

Gemar, Charles D *Astronaut*
7660 N 159th St Court E, Benton, KS 67017 USA

Gemma, Giuliano
Via dei Riari 66, Rome, ITALY, 00165

Gems, Pam *Writer*
Cassarotto, 60/66 Wardour St, London, W1V 4ND, UNITED KINGDOM (UK)

Genaux, Vivicia *Opera Singer*
Robert Lombardo, Harkness Plaza 61 W 62nd St #6F, New York, NY 10023 USA

Gendron, George *Editor*
Inc Magazine, Editorial Dept 77 N Washington St, Boston, MA 02114 USA

Generation, The X
184 Glochester Pl., London, ENGLAND, NW1

Genesis *Music Group*
Hit and Run Music Ltd, 25 Ives Street, South Kensington, London, SW3 2ND, United Kingdom

Genet, Sabryn
7800 Beverly Blvd. #3305, Los Angeles, CA 90036

Genitallica *Music Group*
Sony Music Miami, 605 Lincoln Rd, Miami Beach, FL 33138 USA

Genovese, Eugene D *Historian*
1487 Shendan Walk NE, Atlanta, GA 30324 USA

Genscher, Hans-Dietrich
Am Kottenforst 16, Wachtberg 3, 5307, GERMANY

Gensler, M Arthur Jr *Architect*
Gensler & Assoc Architects, 550 Keamy St, San Francisco, CA 94108 USA

Gent, Peter *Writer*
208 N Center St, South Haven, MI 49090 USA

Gentry, Alvin *Basketball Player, Coach, Misc*
New Orleans Homets, New Orleans Arena 1501 Girod St, New Orleans, LA 70113 USA

Gentry, Bobbie *Music Group*
269 S Beverly Dr #368, Beverly Hills, CA 90212 USA

Gentry, Montgomery *Musician*
Monterey Peninsula Artists (Nashville), 124 12th Ave S #410, Nashville, TN 37203 USA

Gentry, Race
2379 Mountain View Dr, Escondido, CA 92116

Gentry, Teddy W *Music Group, Musician*
P O Box 529, Fort Payne, AL 35968 USA

Gentry, Troy *Music Group*
Hallmark Direction, 15 Music Square W, Nashville, TN 37203 USA

Genzel, Carrie *Actor*
Pakula/King, 9229 Sunset Blvd #315, Los Angeles, CA 90069 USA

Genzmer, Harald *Composer*
Eisensteinstr 10, Munich, 81679, GERMANY

Geoffrin, Bernard (Boom Boom) *Hockey Player*
4431 Dobbs Ferry Crossing Dr, Marietta, GA 30068 USA

Geoffripn, Scott *Race Car Driver*
592 Explorer St #B, Brea, CA 92821 USA

George, Boy *Music Group*
Concorde Int'l Artists, 101 Shepherds Bush Road, London, W6 9LP, UNITED KINGDOM (UK)

George, Christopher S (Chris) *Baseball Player*
121 E Maranta Road, Mooresville, NC 28117 USA

George, Eddie *Football Player*
4708 Stuart Glen Dr, Nashville, TN 37215 USA

George, Eddie *Actor*
United Talent Agency (UTA), 9560 Wilshire Blvd, Beverly Hills, CA 90212 USA

George, Edward A J *Financier*
Bank of England, Threadneedle St, London, EC2R 8AH, UNITED KINGDOM (UK)

George, Elizabeth *Writer*
William Morris Agency, 151 El Camino Dr, Beverly Hills, CA 90212 USA

George, Eric *Actor*
Lasher McManus Robinson, 1964 Westwood Blvd #400, Los Angeles, CA 90025 USA

George, Francis E Cardinal *Religious Leader*
Chicago Archidiocese, 1555 N State Parkway, Chaicago, IL 60610 USA

George, Gotz
Terrassenstr. 32, Berlin, GERMANY, D-14129

George, Jason *Actor*
Artists Group (LA), 10100 Santa Monica Blvd #2490, Los Angeles, CA 90067 USA

George, Jeffrey S (Jeff) *Football Player*
1980 Schwier Court, Indianapolis, IN 46229 USA

George, Lynda Day
10310 Riverside Dr. #104, Toluca Lake, CA 91602-2457

George, Melissa *Actor*
The Firm, 9100 Wilshire Blvd #100W, Beverly Hills, CA 90210 USA

George, Phyllis *Television Host, Misc, Beauty Pageant Winner*
Miss America Organization, 2 Miss America Way #1000, Atlantic City, NJ 08401 USA

George, Susan *Actor*
McKorkindale & Holton, 1-2 Langham Place, London, W1A 3DD, UNITED KINGDOM (UK)

George, Tony *Race Car Driver*
Indianapolis Motor Speedway, 4790 W 16th St, Indianapolis, IN 46222 USA

George, William W *Business Person*
Medtronic Inc, 7000 Central Ave NE, Minneapolis, MN 55432 USA

Georgel, Pierre *Misc*
24 Rue Richer, Paris, 76009, FRANCE

Georgi, Howard *Physicist*
Harvard University, Physics Dept Lyman Laboratory, Cambridge, MA 02138 USA

Georgian, Theodore J *Religious Leader*
Orthodox Presbyterian Church, P O Box P, Willow Grove, PA 19090 USA

Georgievski, Ljubisa (Ljupco) *Prime Minister*
Prime Minister's Office, Dame Grueva 6, Skopje, 91000, MACEDONIA

Georgije, Bishop *Religious Leader*
Serbian Orthodox Church, Sava Monastery P O Box 519, Libertyville, IL 60048 USA

Gephardt, Richard *Politician, Congressman*
Office of Congressman Richard Gehhardt, 1236 Longworth House Office Building, Washington, DC 20515 USA

Geraci, Sonny *Music Group*
Mars Talent, 27 L'Ambiance Court, Bardonia, NY 10954 USA

Gerard, Gil *Actor*
23679 Calabasas Road #325, Calabasas, CA 91302 USA

Gerard, Jean Shevlin *Diplomat*
American Embassy, 22 Blvd Emannanuel Servais, 2535, LUXEMBOURG

Gerardo (Mejia) *Artist, Music Group*
Tapestry Artists, 17337 Ventura Blvd #208, Encino, CA 91316 USA

Gerber, David
10800 Chalon Rd., Los Angeles, CA 90077

Gerber, H Joseph *Business Person*
Gerber Scientific Inc, 83 Gerber Road W, South Windsor, CT 06074 USA

Gerber, Joel *Judge*
US Tax Court, 400 2nd St NW, Washington, DC 20217 USA

Gerberding, Julie *Government Official, Physicist, Doctor*
Centers for Disease Control, 1600 Clifton Road NE, Atlanta, GA 30329 USA

Gere, Richard *Actor*
14 E 4th St #509, New York, NY 10012 USA

Gerela, Roy *Football Player*
P O Box 30001, Las Cruces, NM 88003 USA

Gerety, Tom Jr *Educator*
Amherst College, President's Office, Amherst, MA 01002 USA

Gerg, Hilde *Skier*
Brauneck Tolzer Hutte, Lenggries, 83661, GERMANY

Gerg-Leitner, Michaela *Skier*
Jachenauer Str 26, Lenggries, 83661, GERMANY

Gergen, David R *Editor*
31 Ash St, Cambridge, MA 02138 USA

Gergiev, Valery A
Kunstleragentur Raab & Bohm, Plankengasse 7, Vienna, 1010, AUSTRIA

Gerhardt, Alben *Musician*
Columbia Artists Mgmt Inc, 165 W 57th St, New York, NY 10019 USA

Gerhart, Ann *Writer*
Simon & Schuster, 1230 6th Ave, New York, NY 10020 USA

Gering, Galen *Actor*
Passions, 4024 Radford Ave, Studio City, CA 91604 USA

Gering, Jenna *Actor*
Paradigm (LA), 10100 Santa Monica Blvd, Fl 25, Los Angeles, CA 90067 USA

Gerlach, Gary *Publisher*
Des Moines Register & Tribune, 715 Locust St, Des Moines, IA 50309 USA

Germain, Paul M *Engineer*
3 Ave de Xhampaubert, Paris, 75015, FRANCE

German, Aleksei G *Director*
Marsovo Pole 7 #37, Saint Petersburg, 191041, RUSSIA

German, Jammi *Athlete, Football Player*
Cleveland Browns, 76 Lou Groza Blvd, Berea, OH 44017

German, William *Editor*
San Francisco Chronicle, Editorial Dept 901 Mission, San Francisco, CA 94103 USA

Germane, Geoffrey J *Engineer*
Brigham Young University, Mechanical Engineering Dept, Provo, UT 84602 USA

Germani, Fernando *Music Group, Musician*
Via Delle Terme Decians 11, Rome, ITALY

Germann, Greg *Actor, Director*
Writers & Artists, 8383 Wilshire Blvd #550, Beverly Hills, CA 90211 USA

Germano, Lisa *Music Group, Musician*
Artists & Audience Entertainment, P O Box 35, Pawling, NY 12564 USA

Germar, Manfred *Track Athlete*
DLV, Alsfelder Str 27, Darmstadt, 642889, GERMANY

Germeshausen, Bernhard *Athlete*
Hinter Dem Salon 39, Schwansee, 99195, GERMANY

Germond, Jack
1627 K St NW #1100, Washington, DC 20006

Gernander, Ken *Hockey Player*
311 Lakeview Dr, Grand Rapids, MN 55744 USA

Gerner, Robert *Doctor, Misc*
University of California, Neuropsychiatric Institute, Los Angeles, CA 90024 USA

Gernhardt, Michael L *Astronaut*
2705 Lighthouse Dr, Houston, TX 77058 USA

Gero, Gary D *Cinematographer*
2 McLaren #A, Irvine, CA 92618 USA

Geronimo, Cesar F *Baseball Player*
Tefeda Flo #46, Santo Domingo, DOMINICAN REPUBLIC

Gerring, Cathy *Golfer*
Tarrant Springs Trail, Fort Wayne, IN 46804 USA

Gershon, Gina *Actor*
200 Park Ave S #800, New York, NY 10003 USA

Gerson, Mark *Photographer*
3 Regal Lane Regent's Park, London, NW1 7TH, UNITED KINGDOM (UK)

Gerstell, A Frederick *Business Person*
CalMat Co, 3200 San Fernando Road, Los Angeles, CA 90065 USA

Gerstner V, Jr, Louis *Business Person*
IBM Corp, 1 North Castle Drive, Armonk, NY 10504 USA

Gerth, Jeff *Journalist*
New York Times, Editorial Dept 229 W 43rd St, New York, NY 10036 USA

Gertz, Jami *Actor*
International Creative Mgmt, 8942 Wilshire Blvd #219, Beverly Hills, CA 90211 USA

Gervin, George *Basketball Player, Coach*
San Antonio Spurs, Alamodome 1SBC Center, San Antonio, TX 78219 USA

Gerwick, Ben C Jr *Architect, Engineer*
5727 Country Club Dr, Oakland, CA 94618 USA

Geschke, Charles *Business Person*
Adobe Systems, 345 Park Ave, San Jose, CA 95110 USA

Gesinger, Michael *Photographer*
1136 Umatilla Ave, Port Townsend, WA 98368 USA

Gesner, Zen *Actor*
Innovative Artists, 1505 10th St, Santa Monica, CA 90401 USA

Gessendorf, Mechthild *Opera Singer*
Columbia Artists Mgmt Inc, 165 W 57th St, New York, NY 10019 USA

Gessle, Per *Music Group, Musician*
D&D Mgmt, Lilla Nygatan 19, Stockholm, 111 28, SWEDEN

Get Up Kids *Music Group*
Creative Artists Agency LCC (CAA-LA), 9830 Wilshire Blvd, Beverly Hills, CA 90212 USA

Gethers, Peter *Writer*
International Creative Management (ICM-LA), 8942 Wilshire Blvd, Beverly Hills, CA 90211 USA

Gets, Malcolm *Actor*
Baker Winokur Ryder (BWR-NY), 909 3rd Ave Fl 9, New York, NY 10022 USA

Gettelfinger, Ron *Misc*
United Auto Workers, 800 E Jefferson Ave, Detroit, MI 48214 USA

Getty, Andrew
2936 Montcalm Ave., W. Hollywood, CA 90046

Getty, Balthazar *Actor*
Three Arts Entertainment, 9460 Wilshire Blvd #700, Beverly Hills, CA 90212 USA

Getty, Estelle *Actor*
Goldman Litchenberg Assoc, 10960 Wilshire Blvd #2050, Los Angeles, CA 90024 USA

Getty, Gordon
2880 Broadway, San Francisco, CA 94115

Getty, Jeff *Misc*
ACT-UP Golden Gate, 519 Castro St, San Francisco, CA 94114 USA

Getz, John *Actor*
4124 Wade St, Los Angeles, CA 90066 USA

Geyer, Georgie Anne *Editor, Misc*
Plaza, 800 25th St NW, Washington, DC 20037 USA

Geyer, Hugh *Music Group*
2218 Ridge Road, McKeesport, PA 15135
USA

Ghai, Subhash *Director, Bollywood, Producer, Filmmaker*
12 Cliff Tower, Mount Mary Church Road
Bandra (W), Mumbai, MS 400050, INDIA

Ghannouchi, Mohamed *Prime Minister*
Prime Minister's Office, Place du
Gouvernement, Tunis, TUNISIA

Ghattas, Stephenos II Cardinal *Religious Leader*
Patriarcat Copte Catholique, BP 69 Rue
Ibn Sandar, Cairo, 11712, EGYPT

Ghauri, Yasmine *Model*
Next Model Mgmt, 23 Watts St, New
York, NY 10013 USA

Gheorghiu, Angela *Opera Singer*
Levon Sayan, 2 Rue du Prieure, Nyon,
1260, SWITZERLAND

Gheorghiu, Ion A *Artist*
27-29 Emil Pangratti St, Bucharest,
ROMANIA

Ghiardi, John F L *Economist, Government Official*
12 Park Overlook Court, Bathesda, MD
20817 USA

Ghiaurov, Nicolai *Opera Singer*
Mastroianni Assoc, 161 W 61st St #17E,
New York, NY 10023 USA

Ghiglia, Oscar A *Music Group, Musician*
Helfembergstr 14, Basel, 4059,
SWITZERLAND

Ghiorso, Albert *Scientist, Misc*
Lawrence Berkeley Laboratory, 1
Cyclotron Road, Berkeley, CA 94720 USA

Ghiuselev, Nicola *Opera Singer*
Villa della Pisana 370/B-2, Rome, 00163,
ITALY

Ghizikis, Phaidon *President, General*
25 Kountouriotou, Pefki, 151 21, GREECE

Ghosh, Gautam *Director*
28/1-A Gariahat Road Block 5 #50,
Calcutta, WB, 700029, INDIA

Ghosh, Partho *Director, Filmmaker, Producer, Bollywood*
D1 Hawa Apartments Opp Holy Spirit
Hospital, Mahakali Caves Road Andheri
(E), Bombay, MS 400 093, INDIA

Ghostface, Killa *Music Group, Musician*
Famous Artists Agency, 250 W 57th St,
New York, NY 10107 USA

Ghostley, Alice *Actor*
3800 Reklaw Dr, Studio City, CA 91604
USA

Ghuman Jr, JB *Actor*
Firm, The, 9465 Wilshire Blvd, Beverly
Hills, CA 90212 USA

Giacconi, Riccardo *Nobel Prize Laureate*
Associated Universities Inc, 1440 16th St
NW #730, Washington, DC 20036 USA

Giacomin, Edward (Ed) *Hockey Player*
3427 S Bloomington Dr W, Saint George,
UT 84790 USA

Giaever, Ivar *Nobel Prize Laureate*
2080 Van Antwerp Road, Schenectady,
NY 12309 USA

Giamatti, Marcus
9200 Sunset Blvd. #900, Los Angeles, CA
90069

Giamatti, Paul *Actor*
Endeavor Talent Agency, 9701 Wilshire
Blvd #1000, Beverly Hills, CA 90212 USA

Giambalvo, Louis *Actor*
Judy Schoen & Associates, 606 N
Larchmont Blvd #309, Los Angeles, CA
90004 USA

Giambastiani, Edmund P Jr *Admiral*
Deputy CNO for Resources/Warfare
Requirements, HqUSN, Washington, DC
20350 USA

Giambi, Jason G *Baseball Player*
1034 E Belmont Abbey Lane, Claremont,
CA 91711 USA

Giambra, Joey *Boxer*
7950 W Flamingo Road #1188, Las
Vegas, NV 89147 USA

Gian, Joseph
8271 Melrose Ave. #110, Los Angeles, CA
90046

Gianelli, John *Basketball Player*
P O Box 1097, Pinecrest, CA 95364 USA

Giannini, Andriano *Actor*
Peters Fraser & Dunlop (PFD - UK), Drury
House, 34-43 Russell St, London, WC2
B5, UNITED KINGDOM (UK)

Giannini, Giancario *Actor*
Via Salaria 292, Rome, 00199, ITALY

Giannini, Giancarlo
Via della Giuliana 101, Rome, ITALY,
I-00195

Giannulli, Mossimo *Fashion Designer*
Mossimo Supply, 2450 White Road #200,
Irvine, CA 92614 USA

Gianopoulos, David *Actor*
GVA Talent Agency Inc, 9229 Sunset Blvd
#320, Los Angeles, CA 90069 USA

Gianulias, Nicole (Nikki) *Bowler*
Ladies Professional Bowling Tour, 7200
Harrison Ave #7171, Rockford, IL 61112
USA

Giardello, Joey *Boxer*
1214 Severn Ave, Cherry Hill, NJ 08002
USA

Gibara, Samir *Business Person*
Goodyear Tire & Rubber, 1144 W Market
St, Akron, OH 44316 USA

Gibb, Barry *Musician, Music Group, Songwriter*
United Talent Agency (UTA), 9560
Wilshire Blvd, Beverly Hills, CA 90212
USA

Gibb, Cynthia *Actor*
1139 S Hill St #177, Los Angeles, CA
90015 USA

Gibb, Robin *Musician, Music Group, Songwriter*
Middle Ear, 1801 Bay Road, Miami
Beach, FL 33139 USA

Gibberd, Frederick *Architect*
House Marsh Lane Old Harlow, Essex,
CM17 0NA, UNITED KINGDOM (UK)

Gibbons, Beth *Music Group, Songwriter*
Fruit, Saga Center 326 Kensal Road,
London, W10 5BZ, UNITED KINGDOM
(UK)

Gibbons, Billy *Music Group, Musician*
Lone Wolf Mgmt, P O Box 16390, Austin,
TX 78761 USA

Gibbons, James F *Engineer*
320 Tennyson Ave, Palo Alto, CA 94301
USA

Gibbons, John D *Prime Minister*
Leeward 5 Leeside Dr, Pembroke, HM 05,
BERMUDA

Gibbons, Leeza *Entertainer*
Leeza Gibbons Enterprises (LGE), 3500 W
Olive Ave #980, Burbank, CA 91505

Gibbons, Tim *Producer*
International Creative Management
(ICM-LA), 8942 Wilshire Blvd, Beverly
Hills, CA 90211 USA

Gibbs, Georgia *Music Group*
Frank Gervasi, 965 5th Ave, New York,
NY 10021 USA

Gibbs, H Jarrell *Business Person*
Texas Utilities Co, Energy Plaza 1601
Bryan St, Dallas, TX 75201 USA

Gibbs, Jerry D (Jake) *Baseball Player, Football Player*
223 Saint Andres Circle, Oxford, MS
38655 USA

Gibbs, Joe J *Football Coach, Race Car Driver*
Washington Redskins, 21300 Redskin Park
Dr, Ashbum, VA 20147 USA

Gibbs, L Richard *Cricketer*
276 Republic Park, Peter's Hall EBD,
GUYANA

Gibbs, Lawrence B *Government Official*
Miller & Chevaliar, 655 15th St NW #900,
Washington, DC 20005 USA

Gibbs, Marla *Actor, Music Group*
3500 W Manchester Blvd #267,
Inglewood, CA 90305 USA

Gibbs, Martin *Biologist*
32 Slucom Road, Lexington, MA 02421
USA

Gibbs, Patt *Misc*
Flght Attendants Assn, 1275 K St NW
#500, Washington, DC 20005 USA

Gibbs, Roland C *Misc*
Palney Rectory, Devizes, Wills, SN10
3QZ, UNITED KINGDOM (UK)

Gibbs, Terri *Music Group, Songwriter*
312 Crawford Mill Lane, Grovetown, GA
30913 USA

Gibbs, Terry *Music Group, Musician*
Thomas Cassidy, 11761 E Speedway Blvd,
Tucson, AZ 85748 USA

Gibbs, Timothy *Actor*
P O Box 8764, Calabasas, CA 91372 USA

Giblett, Eloise R *Doctor, Misc*
6533 53rd St NE, Seattle, WA 98115 USA

Gibney, Rebecca
128 Rupert St., Collingwood, AUSTRALIA,
Vic. 3066

Gibney, Susan *Actor*
Lesher Entertainment Inc, 800 S Robertson
Blvd #8, Los Angeles, CA 90035 USA

Gibran, Kahill *Artist, Misc*
160 W Canton St, Boston, MA 02118 USA

Gibson, Bob
215 Bellevue Rd., Belleview, NE 68005-2442

Gibson, Charles *Commentator*
Good Morning America, 147 Columbus Ave Fl 6, New York, NY 10023 USA

Gibson, Deborah *Actor, Music Group*
GMI Entertainment, 656 5th Ave #302, New York, NY 10103 USA

Gibson, Derrick *Football Player*
Oakland Raiders, 1220 Harbor Bay Parkway, Alameda, CA 94502 USA

Gibson, Edward G *Astronaut*
Aviation Management Services, 1658 S Litchfield Road, Goodyear, AZ 85338 USA

Gibson, Everett K Jr *Geophysicist, Misc*
1015 Trowbridge Dr, Houston, TX 77062 USA

Gibson, Henry *Actor*
26740 Latigo Shore Dr, Malibu, CA 90265 USA

Gibson, Kirk H *Baseball Player, Football Player*
Detroit Tigers, Comerica Park 2100 Woodward Ave, Detroit, MI 48201 USA

Gibson, Mel *Actor, Producer, Director*
ICON Productions Inc, 808 Wilshire Blvd Fl 4, Santa Monica, CA 90401 USA

Gibson, Quentin H *Biologist, Misc*
3 Woods End Road, Etna, NH 03750 USA

Gibson, Ralph H *Photographer*
331 W Broadway, New York, NY 10013 USA

Gibson, Reginald W *Judge*
US Claims Court, 717 Madison Place NW, Washington, DC 20439 USA

Gibson, Robert (Bob) *Baseball Player*
215 Bellevue Blvd S, Bellevue, NE 68005 USA

Gibson, Robert L
1709 Shagbark Trail, Murfreesboro, TN 37130 USA

Gibson, Robert L (Hoot) *Astronaut*
1709 Shagbark Trail, Murfreesboro, TN 37130 USA

Gibson, Thomas *Actor*
Alliance Talent, 9171 Wilshire Blvd #441, Beverly Hills, CA 90210 USA

Gibson, Tyrese *Actor, Musician, Producer, Writer*
William Morris Agency, 151 El Camino Dr, Beverly Hills, CA 90212 USA

Gibson, William *Writer, Photographer*
Berkeley Publishing Group, 375 Hudson St, New York, NY 10014 USA

Gidada, Negasso *President*
President's Office, P O Box 5707, Addis Ababa, ETHIOPIA

Gideon, Raynold *Actor, Writer*
3524 Multiview Dr, Los Angeles, CA 90068 USA

Gidley, Pamela *Actor*
65 Hernando Dr, Marco Island, FL 34145 USA

Gidzenko, Yuri P *Astronaut, Misc*
Potchta Kosmonavtov, Moskovskoi Oblasti, Syvisdny Goroduk, 141160, RUSSIA

Giel, Paul
13400 E. McGinty Rd., Minnetonka, MN 55343

Gielen, Michael A *Composer, Conductor*
Hans Ulrich Schmid, Postfach 1617, Hanover, 30016, GERMANY

Giella, Joseph *Cartoonist*
191 Morris Dr, East Meadow, NY 11554 USA

Gienger, Eberhard
Friedrich-Schaal-Str. 53, Tubingen, GERMANY, D-72074

Gierasch, Stefan *Actor*
Brandon's Commercials Unlimited, 8383 Wilshire Blvd, Suite 850, Beverly Hills, CA 90211 USA

Gierer, Vincent A Jr *Business Person*
UST Inc, 100 W Putnam Ave, Greenwich, CT 06830 USA

Gierowski, Stefan *Artist*
UI Gagarina 15 m 97, Warsaw, 00-753, POLAND

Gifford, Frank N *Football Player, Sportscaster*
William Morris Agency (WMA-LA), 1 William Morris Pl, Beverly Hills, CA 90212 USA

Gifford, Gloria *Actor*
Schiowitz/Clay/Rose, 1680 N Vine St #1016, Los Angeles, CA 90028 USA

Gifford, Kathie Lee *Entertainer*
108 Cedar Cliff Road, Riverside, CT 06878 USA

Gift, Roland *Actor, Music Group*
Primary Talent Int'l, 1-12 Petonville Road, London, N1 9PL, UNITED KINGDOM (UK)

Gigli, Romeo *Fashion Designer*
37 W 57th St #900, New York, NY 10019 USA

Gigot, Paul *Journalist*
Wall Street Journal, Editorial Dept 200 Liberty St, New York, NY 10281 USA

Giguere, Russ *Music Group, Musician*
Variety Artists, 1924 Spring St, Paso Robles, CA 93446 USA

Giheno, John *President*
Prime Minister's Office, Marera Hau, Port Moresby, PAPUA NEW GUINEA

Gil, Ariadna *Actor*
Cineart, 36 Rue de Ponthieu, Paris, 75008, FRANCE

Gil, Geronimo *Baseball Player, Athlete*
Baltimore Orioles, Oriole Park, 333 W Camden St, Baltimore, MD 21201 USA

Gil, Gilberto *Music Group, Songwriter*
BPR, 36 Como St Ramford, Essex, RM 7 7DR, UNITED KINGDOM (UK)

Gil, R Benjamin (Benji) *Baseball Player*
417 Marshall Road, South Lake, TX 76092 USA

Gilbert, Brad
888 17th St. NW #1200, Washington, DC 20006

Gilbert, Bradley (Brad) *Tennis Player*
ProServe, 1101 Woodrow Wilson Blvd #1800, Arlington, VA 22209 USA

Gilbert, Chris *Football Player*
Greenbriar Mgmt, 4422 FM 1960 Road W, Houston, TX 77068 USA

Gilbert, David *Cartoonist*
King Features Syndicate, 888 7th Ave, New York, NY 10106 USA

Gilbert, Elsie
1016 N. Orange Grove #4, Los Angeles, CA 90046

Gilbert, Felix *Historian*
918 Bluffwood Dr, Iowa City, IA 52245 USA

Gilbert, Greg *Hockey Player, Coach*
303 Main St, Worcester, MA 01608 USA

Gilbert, J Freeman *Geophysicist*
780 Kalamath Dr, Del Mar, CA 92014 USA

Gilbert, Kenneth A *Music Group, Musician*
23 Cloitre Notre-Dame, Chartres, 28000, FRANCE

Gilbert, Lawrence I *Biologist*
1105 Phils Creek Road, Chapel Hill, NC 27516 USA

Gilbert, Lewis *Director, Producer*
19 Blvd de Suisse, Monte Carlo, MONACO

Gilbert, Martin J *Historian*
Merton College, Oxford, OX1 4JD, UNITED KINGDOM (UK)

Gilbert, Melissa *Actor*
25717 Mulholland Highway, Calabasas, CA 91302 USA

Gilbert, Peter *Director*
Innovative Artists, 1505 10th St, Santa Monica, CA 90401 USA

Gilbert, Richard W *Publisher*
Des Moines Register & Tribune, 715 Locust St, Des Moines, IA 50309 USA

Gilbert, Rodrique G (Rod) *Hockey Player*
344 Pacific Ave, Cedarhurst, NY 11516 USA

Gilbert, Ronnie *Music Group*
Donna Korones Mgmt, P O Box 8388, Berkeley, CA 94707 USA

Gilbert, S J Sr *Religious Leader*
Baptist Convention of America, 6717 Centennial Blvd, Nashville, TN 37209 USA

Gilbert, Sara *Actor*
16254 High Valley Dr, Encino, CA 91346 USA

Gilbert, Sean *Football Player*
7912 Baltusrol Lane, Charlotte, NC 28210 USA

Gilbert, Simon *Music Group, Musician*
Interceptor Enterprises, 98 White Lion St, London, N1 9PF, UNITED KINGDOM (UK)

Gilbert, Walter *Nobel Prize Laureate*
15 Gray Gardens W, Cambridge, MA 02138 USA

Gilberto, Astrud *Music Group*
Absolute Artists, 530 Howard Ave #200, San Francisco, CA 94105 USA

Gilberto, Bebel *Music Group*
Miracle Prestige, 1 Water Lane Camden Town, London, NW1 8NZ, UNITED KINGDOM (UK)

Gilbertson, Keith *Football Coach*
University of Washington, Athletic Dept, Seattle, WA 98195 USA

Gilbreth, David *Writer*
Jim Preminger Agency, 450 N Roxbury Dr #PH-1050, Beverly Hills, CA 90210 USA

Gilbride, Kevin *Football Player, Coach*
Pittsburgh Steelers, 3400 S Water St, Pittsburgh, PA 15203 USA

Gilchrist, Brent *Hockey Player*
204 Olive Branch Road, Nashville, TN 37205 USA

Gilchrist, Cookie *Football Player*
P O Box 5109, Wilmington, DE 19808 USA

Gilchrist, Pual R *Religious Leader*
Presbyterian Church in America, 1862 Century Place, Atlanta, GA 30345 USA

Gilder, Bob *Golfer*
1977 NW Bonney Dr, Corvallis, OR 97330 USA

Gilder, George F *Writer, Economist*
Main Road, Tyringham, MA 01264 USA

Giles, Brian J *Baseball Player*
444 Graves Ave, El Cajon, CA 92020 USA

Giles, Jimmie *Football Player*
10429 Greenmont Dr, Tampa, FL 33626 USA

Giles, Marcus *Baseball Player, Athlete*
Atlanta Braves, Turner Field, PO Box 4064, Atlanta, GA 30302 USA

Giles, Nancy *Actor*
12047 178th St, Jamaica, NY 11434 USA

Giles, Sandra
350 N. Crescent Dr., Beverly Hills, CA 90210-4847

Giletti, Alain *Figure Skater*
103 Place de L'Eglise, Chamonix, 74400, FRANCE

Gilfry, Rodney *Opera Singer*
Columbia Artists Mgmt Inc, 165 W 57th St, New York, NY 10019 USA

Gilgorov, Kiro *President*
President's Office, Skopje, MACEDONIA

Gill, AJ *Musician*
Fox Television Studios, 10201 W Pico Blvd, Bldg 41, Los Angeles, CA 90035

Gill, George N *Publisher*
Louisville Courier-Journal & Times, 525 W Broadway, Louisville, KY 40202 USA

Gill, Janis *Music Group*
Monty Hitchcock Mgmt, 5101 Overton Road, Nashville, TN 37220 USA

Gill, Johnny *Musician, Music Group, Songwriter*
4924 Balboa Blvd #366, Encino, CA 91316 USA

Gill, Kendall *Basketball Player*
Miami Heat, American Airlines Arena, 601 Biscayne Blvd, Miami, FL 33132 USA

Gill, Priya *Actor, Bollywood*
606 Nestle - B 4th Cross Road, Lokhandwala Complex Andheri (W), Mumbai, MS 400058, INDIA

Gill, Tim *Designer, Engineer, Misc*
Gill Foundation, 2215 Market St, Denver, CO 80205 USA

Gill, Vince *Musician, Music Group, Songwriter*
PO Box 700, Grover, MO 63040 USA

Gill, William A Jr *Government Official, Misc*
15975 Cove Lane, Dumfries, VA 22026 USA

Gillan, Ian *Musician*
Miracle Prestige, 1 Water Lane, Camden Town, London, NW1 8N2, UNITED KINGDOM (UK)

Gillen, Aidan *Actor*
International Creative Management (ICM-UK), Oxford House, 76 Oxford St, London, W1N OAX, UNITED KINGDOM (UK)

Giller, Walter
Via Tamporiva 26, Castagnola, SWITZERLAND, CH-6976

Gilles, Daniel *Writer*
161 Ave Churchill, Brussels, 1180, BELGIUM

Gillespie, Ann *Actor*
Greene Assoc, 7080 Hollywood Blvd #1017, Los Angeles, CA 90028 USA

Gillespie, Charles A Jr *Diplomat*
Scowcroft Group, 900 17th St #500, Washington, DC 20006 USA

Gillespie, Rhondda *Music Group, Musician*
2 Princess Road, Saint Leonards-on-Sea, East Sussex, TN37 6EL, UNITED KINGDOM (UK)

Gillespie, Robert *Financier*
KeyCorp, 127 Public Square, Cleveland, OH 44114 USA

Gillespie, Ronald J *Doctor, Misc*
McMaster University, Chemistry Dept, Hamilton, ON L8S 4M1, CANADA

Gillette, Anita *Actor*
501 S Beverly Dr #3, Beverly Hills, CA 90212 USA

Gilley, J Wade *Educator*
University of Tennessee, President's Office, Knoxville, TN 37996 USA

Gilley, Mickey *Music Group, Songwriter*
Gilley's Interests, PO Box 1242, Pasadena, TX 77501 USA

Gilliam, Armon *Basketball Player*
Pennsylvania State University, Athletic Dept, M,Keesport, PA 15131 USA

Gilliam, Burton
1427 Tascosa Ct., Allen, TX 75013

Gilliam, Herm *Basketball Player*
2701 Bon Air Ave, Winston Salem, NC 27105 USA

Gilliam, Terry *Actor, Writer, Animator*
Old Hall South Grove, Highgate, London, N6 6BP, UNITED KINGDOM (UK)

Gilliatt, Penelope
31 Chester Sq., London, ENGLAND, SW1W 9HT

Gillie, Nick *Producer*
Metropolitan Talent Agency (MTA), 4526 Wilshire Blvd, Los Angeles, CA 90010 USA

Gillies, Ben *Music Group, Musician*
John Watson Mgmt, P O Box 281, Sunny Hills, NSW, 2010, AUSTRALIA

Gillies, Clark *Hockey Player*
225 Old Country Road, Melville, NY 11747 USA

Gillies, Daniel *Actor*
Evolution Entertainment, 901 N Highland Ave, Los Angeles, CA 90038 USA

Gilligan, Carol *Educator*
Harvard University, Gender Studies Dept, Cambridge, MA 02138 USA

Gillilan, William J III *Business Person*
Centex Corp, P O Box 199000, Dallas, TX 75219 USA

Gilliland, Richard *Actor*
Metropolitan Talent Agency, 4526 Wilshire Blvd, Los Angeles, CA 90010 USA

Gilliland, Robert J *Misc*
P O Box 6367, Burbank, CA 91510 USA

Gillingham, Gale *Football Player*
1605 W River Road, Little Falls, MN 56345 USA

Gillingwater, Leah *Reality TV Star*
Real World, The, 6007 Sepulveda Blvd, Van Nuys, CA 91411 USA

Gillis, Malcolm *Educator*
Rice University, President's Office, Houston, TX 77251 USA

Gillman, Sid
2968 Playa Rd., Carlsbad, CA 92009

Gillom, Jennifer *Basketball Player*
LA Sparks, 555 N Nash Street, El Segundo, CA 90245 USA

Gillooly (Stone), Jeff
10408 SE 82nd Ave., Portland, OR 97266

Gilman, Alfred G *Nobel Prize Laureate*
10996 Crooked Creek Dr, Dallas, TX 75229 USA

Gilman, Billy *Music Group*
RPM Mgmt, 209 10th Ave S #9D, Nashville, TN 37203 USA

Gilman, Dorothy *Writer*
321 N Highland Ave, Ossining, NY 10562 USA

Gilman, Kenneth B *Business Person*
Limited Inc, 3 Limited Parkway, P O Box 1600, Columbus, OH 43216 USA

Gilman, Richard H *Publisher*
Boston Globe, Publisher's Office, 135 W T Morrissey Blvd, Dorchester, MA 02125 USA

Gilman, Sid *Doctor, Misc*
3441 Geddes Road, Ann Arbor, MI 48105 USA

Gilmartin, Raymond V *Business Person*
Merck Co, 1 Merck Dr P O Box 100, Whitehouse Station, NJ 08889 USA

Gilmer, Harry
7467 Highway No, O'Fallon, MO 63366

Gilmer, Harry V *Football Player*
7467 Highway N, O Fallon, MO 63366 USA

Gilmore, Artis *Basketball Player*
11043 Turnbridge Dr, Jacksonville, FL
32256 USA

Gilmore, Clarence P *Editor*
19725 Creekround Ave, Baton Rouge, LA
70817 USA

Gilmore, Jimmie Dale *Music Group,*
Songwriter
Crowley Artists Mgmt, 602 Wayside Dr,
Wimberley, TX 78676 USA

Gilmore, Kenneth O *Editor*
Charles Road, Mount Kisco, NY 10549
USA

Gilmour, Buddy *Race Car Driver*
P O Box 812, Bellmore, NY 11710 USA

Gilmour, David *Music Group, Musician*
P O Box 62 Heathfield, East Sussex, TN21
8ZE, UNITED KINGDOM (UK)

Gilmour, Doug *Hockey Player*
Octagon, 1751 Pinnacle Dr #1500,
McLean, VA 22102 USA

Gilmour of Craigmillar, Ian *Government*
Official
Ferry House Old Isleworth, Middx,
UNITED KINGDOM (UK)

Gilpin, Peri *Actor*
William Morris Agency, 151 El Camino
Dr, Beverly Hills, CA 90212 USA

Gilroy, Frank D *Writer*
6 Magnin Rd, Monroe, NY 10950 USA

Gilroy, Tom *Actor, Writer, Producer,*
Director
William Morris Agency (WMA-LA), 1
William Morris Pl, Beverly Hills, CA
90212 USA

Gilsig, Jessalyn *Actor*
Innovative Artists (LA), 1505 Tenth St,
Santa Monica, CA 90401 USA

Gilyard Jr, Clarence *Actor*
24040 Camino Del Avion #A239,
Monarch Bay, CA 92629 USA

Gimbel, Norman *Songwriter*
P O Box 50013, Santa Barbara, CA 93150
USA

Gimbrone, Michael A Jr *Doctor, Misc*
Brigham & Women's Hospital, Vascular
Pathology Dept, Boston, MA 02115 USA

Gimeno, Andres *Tennis Player*
Paseo de la Bnanova 38, Barcelona 6,
SPAIN

Gimpel, Erica
939 8th Ave. #400, New York, NY 10019-
2464

Gin Blossoms
PO Box 429094, San Francisco, CA
94142

Gina G *Music Group*
What Mgmt, P O Box 1463, Culver City,
CA 90232 USA

Ging, Jack *Actor*
48701 San Pedro St, La Quinta, CA 92253
USA

Gingerich, Philip D *Scientist, Misc*
University of Michigan, Paleontology
Dept, Ann Arbor, MI 48109 USA

Gingrich, Newton L (Newt) *Politician*
1301 K St NW #800W, Washington, DC
20005 USA

Ginibre, Jean-Louis *Editor*
Hachett Filipacchi, 1633 Broadway, New
York, NY 10019 USA

Ginn, William H Jr *General*
1002 Priscilla Lane, Alexandria, VA
22308 USA

Ginobili, Emanuel *Basketball Player*
San Antonio Spurs, Alamodome, 100
Montana Street, San Antonio, TX 78203
USA

Ginsberg, Justice Ruth Bader
700 New Hampshire Ave. NW,
Washington, DC 20037

Ginsburg, Art *Television Host*

Ginsburg, Douglas H *Judge*
US Court of Appeals, 333 Constitution
Ave NW, Washington, DC 20001 USA

Ginsburg, Ruth Bader *Judge, Lawyer,*
Misc
US Supreme Court, 1 1st St NE,
Washington, DC 20543 USA

Ginsburg, William
10100 Santa Monica Blvd #800, Los
Angeles, CA 90067 USA

Ginty, Robert *Actor*
Introvision, 1011 N Fuller Ave, North
Hollywood, CA 90046 USA

Ginuwine *Music Group*
International Creative Mgmt, 8942
Wilshire Blvd #219, Beverly Hills, CA
90211 USA

Ginzburg, Vitaly L *Nobel Prize Laureate*
Lebedev Physical Institute, Leninsky
Prospect 53, Moscow, 117924, RUSSIA

Ginzton, Edward L *Engineer, Business*
Person
Varian Assoc, 3100 Hansen Way, Palo
Alto, CA 94304 USA

Giofriddo, Al
64 Bristol Pl., Goleta, CA 93117

Giola, Dana *Government Official, Writer*
National Endowment for Arts, 1100
Pennsylvania Ave NW, Washington, DC
20506 USA

Giordano, Michele Cardinal *Religious*
Leader
Arcivescovado di Napoli, Largo
Donnaregina 22, Naples, 80138, ITALY

Giovanni, Aria *Adult Film Star*

Giovanni, Joseph *Architect*
Giovanni Assoc, 140 E 40th St, New York,
NY 10016 USA

Giovanni, Nikki E *Writer*
Virginia Polytechnic Institute, English
Dept, Blacksburg, VA 24061 USA

Giovinazzo, Carmine *Actor*
Saffron Management, 1701 N Beverly Dr,
Beverly Hills, CA 90210 USA

Gipsy Kings *Music Group*
350 Lincoln Rd #415, Miami Beach, FL
33139

Giradeau, Bernard
37 rue Froidevaux, Paris, FRANCE, 75014

GiradelII, Marc *Skier*
9413 Oberegg-Sulzbach, SWITZERLAND

Giradelli, Marc
Obererg-, Sulzbach, SWITZERLAND, CH-
9413

Giraldi, Robert N (Bob) *Director*
Giraldi Saurez, 581 Ave of Americas, New
York, NY 10011 USA

Giraldo, Greg *Actor, Comedian*
William Morris Agency (WMA-LA), 1
William Morris Pl, Beverly Hills, CA
90212 USA

Giraldo, Neil *Producer, Musician*
William Morris Agency (WMA-LA), 1
William Morris Pl, Beverly Hills, CA
90212 USA

Girardi, Joseph E (Joe) *Baseball Player*
1845 S James Court N, Lake Forest, IL
60045 USA

Girardot, Annie *Actor*
Artmedia, 20 Ave Rapp, Paris, 75007,
FRANCE

Giraudeau, Bernard *Actor*
Cineart, 36 Rue de Ponthieu, Paris,
75008, FRANCE

Giri, Tulsi *Prime Minister*
Jawakpurdham, District Dhanuka, NEPAL

Girls Aloud
Concorde Intl Artists Ltd, 101 Shepherds
Bush Rd, London, W6 7LP, UNITED
KINGDOM (UK)

Girone, Remo *Actor*
Cineart, 36 Rue de Ponthieu, Paris,
75008, FRANCE

Giroux, Robert *Publisher*
Farrar Straus Giroux, 19 Union Square W,
New York, NY 10003 USA

Giscard, d'Estaing Valery *President*
199 Blvd Saint-Germain, Paris, 75007,
FRANCE

Gish, Annabeth *Actor*
2104 E Main St #841, Ventura, CA 93001
USA

Gismonti, Egberto *Music Group, Musician*
International Music Network, 278 S Main
St #400, Gloucester, MA 01930 USA

Gitlin, Todd *Historian*
New York University, Culture &
Communications Dept, New York, NY
10012 USA

Gitomer, Jeffrey

Giuffre, Carlo
Via Massimi 45, Rome, ITALY, I-00136

Giuffre, James P (Jimmy) *Music Group,*
Musician
Legacy Records, 550 Madison Ave #1700,
New York, NY 10022 USA

Giuliani, Rudolph (Rudy) *Politician*
Giuliani Partners, 5 Times Square, New
York, NY 10036 USA

Giuliano, Louis J *Business Person*
ITT Industries, 4 W Red Oak Lane, White
Plains, NY 10604 USA

Giuliano, Tom *Music Group*
6929 N Hayden Road, Scottsdale, AZ
85250 USA

Giulini, Carlo Maria
Francesco Giulini, Via Bonnet 7, Milan,
20121, ITALY

Giullani, Rudolph W *Politician, Misc*
Guiliani Partners, 5 Times Square, New
York, NY 10036 USA

Giuranna, Bruno *Music Group, Musician*
Via Bembo 96, Asolo TV, 31011, ITALY

Giusti, David J (Dave) *Baseball Player*
524 Clair Dr, Pittsburgh, PA 15241 USA

Givenchy, Hubert
3 Ave. George V, Paris, FRANCE, 75008

Givens, Adele
William Morris Agency (WMA-LA), 1
William Morris Pl, Beverly Hills, CA
90212 USA

Givens, Jack *Basketball Player, Misc*
1536 Frazier Ave, Orlando, FL 32811
USA

Givens, Robin *Actor*
Gold/Liedtke & Associates Talent Agency,
3500 West Olive Ave, Ste 1400, Burbank,
CA 91505

Givins, Ernest P Jr *Football Player*
1447 Manor Way S, Saint Petersburg, FL
33705 USA

Gizzi, Claudio *Composer*
SIAE, Viaile dell Letteratura 30, Rome,
00100, ITALY

Gladden, Danny (Dan) *Baseball Player*
888 Brookgrove Ln, Cupertino, CA 95014
USA

Glamack, George *Basketball Player*
50 Pleasant Way, Rochester, NY 14622
USA

Glance, Harvey *Track Athlete*
2408 Old Creek Road, Montgomery, AL
36117 USA

Glanville, Jerry *Football Coach,
Sportscaster*
CBS-TV, Sports Dept 51 W 52nd St, New
York, NY 10019 USA

Glasbergen, Randy *Cartoonist*
King Features Syndicate, 888 7th Ave,
New York, NY 10106 USA

Glaser, Donald A *Nobel Prize Laureate*
University of California, Molecular
Biology Laboratory, Berkeley, CA 94720
USA

Glaser, Gabrielle (Gabby) *Music Group,
Musician*
Metropolitan Entertainment, 2 Penn Plaza
#2600, New York, NY 10121 USA

Glaser, Jim *Music Group*
Joe Taylor Artist Agency, 2802 Columbine
Place, Nashville, TN 37204 USA

Glaser, Jon *Actor, Writer*
3 Arts Entertainment Inc, 9460 Wilshire
Blvd Fl 7, Beverly Hills, CA 90212 USA

Glaser, Jonathan *Writer*
International Creative Management
(ICM-LA), 8942 Wilshire Blvd, Beverly
Hills, CA 90211 USA

Glaser, Milton *Artist, Misc*
Milton Glaser Assoc, 207 E 32nd St, New
York, NY 10016 USA

Glaser, Paul Michael *Actor, Director*
1221 Ocean Ave #1601, Santa Monica,
CA 90401 USA

Glaser, Robert *Doctor, Misc*
University of Pittsburgh, Psychology Dept,
Pittsburgh, PA 15260 USA

Glaser, Robert J *Misc*
555 Byron St #305, Palo Alto, CA 94301
USA

Glaser Brothers
91619th Ave, Nashville, TN 37212, US

Glasgow, W Victor (Vic) *Basketball Player*
6312 King Dr, Bartlesville, OK 74006
USA

Glashow, Sheldon Lee *Nobel Prize
Laureate*
30 Prescott St, Brookline, MA 02446 USA

Glaspie, April *Diplomat*
State Department, 2201 C St NW,
Washington, DC 20520 USA

Glass, David D *Business Person*
Wal-Mart Stores, 702 SW 8th St,
Bentonville, AK 72712 USA

Glass, H Bentley *Biologist*
P O Box 65, East Setauket, NY 11733
USA

Glass, Nancy *Journalist*
Glass DiFede Productions, 345
Montgomery Ave, Bala Cynwyd, PN,
19004

Glass, Philip *Composer*
IPA, 584 Broadway #108, New York, NY
10012 USA

Glass, Ron *Actor*
2485 Wild Oak Dr, Los Angeles, CA
90068 USA

Glass, William S (Bill) *Football Player*
Bill Glass Ministries, P O Box 761101,
Dallas, TX 75376 USA

Glass Tiger
238 Davenport #126, Toronto, CANADA,
Ont.M5R 1J

Glasser, Erika *Actor*
Gabriel Blanco Iglesias (Mexico), Rio
Balsas 35-32, Colonia Cuauhtemoc, DF,
06500, Mexico

Glasser, Ira S *Attorney General, Social
Activist, Lawyer, Misc*
American Civil Liberties Union, 132 W
43rd St, New York, NY 10036 USA

Glasser, William *Doctor, Misc*
11633 San Vincente Blvd, Los Angeles,
CA 90049 USA

Glatter, Lesli L *Director*
United Talent Agency, 9560 Wilshire Blvd
#500, Beverly Hills, CA 90212 USA

Glattes, Wolfgang *Producer*
Mirisch Agency, 1801 Century Park E
#1801, Los Angeles, CA 90067 USA

Glatzeder, Winfried
Gosslerstrasse 24, Berlin, GERMANY,
D-12161

Glau, Summer *Actor*
Kohner Agency, The, 9300 Wilshire Blvd
#555, Beverly Hills, CA 90212 USA

Glave, Matthew *Actor*
Innovative Artists (LA), 1505 Tenth St,
Santa Monica, CA 90401 USA

Glavin, Denis Joseph *Misc*
Electrical Radio & Machine Worders
Union, 11 E 1st St, New York, NY 10003
USA

Glavine, Thomas M (Tom) *Baseball Player*
8925 Old Southwick Pass, Alpharetta, GA
30022 USA

Glavine, Tom *Athlete*
8925 Old Southwick Pass, Alpharetta, GA
30022

Glazer, Jay *Sportscaster*
CBS-TV, Sports Dept 51 W 52nd St, New
York, NY 10019 USA

Glazer, Mitch *Producer*
Creative Artists Agency LCC (CAA-LA),
9830 Wilshire Blvd, Beverly Hills, CA
90212 USA

Glazer, Nathan *Social Activist, Misc*
12 Scott St, Cambridge, MA 02138 USA

Glazkov, Yuri N *Astronaut, General, Misc*
Potchta Kosmonavtov, Moskovskoi
Oblasti, Syvisdny Goroduk, 141160,
RUSSIA

Glazunov, Ilya S *Artist*
Razhviz Academy, Kamergersky Per 2,
Moscow, 103009, RUSSIA

Gleason, Andrew M *Mathematician*
110 Larchwood Dr, Cambridge, MA
02138 USA

Gleason, Joanna *Actor*
United Talent Agency, 9560 Wilshire Blvd
#516, Beverly Hills, CA 90212 USA

Gleason, Mary Pat *Actor, Writer*
Stone Manners Talent Agency, 6500
Wilshire Blvd, Ste 550, Los Angeles, CA
90048 USA

Gleason, Paul *Actor*
Stone Manners, 6500 Wilshire Blvd #550,
Los Angeles, CA 90048 USA

Gleeson, Brendan *Actor*
Keylight Entertainment (Joan Scott
Management), 888 7th Avenue, 35th
Floor, New York, NY 10106 USA

Gleicher, Jamie *Reality TV Star, Heir/
Heiress*
MTV Networks (NY), 1515 Broadway,
New York, NY 10036 USA

Glemp, Jozef Cardinal *Religious Leader*
Sekretariat Prymasa Kolski, Ul Miodowa
17, Warsaw, 00 246, POLAND

Glen, John *Director*
Spyros Skouras, 1015 Gayley Ave #300,
Los Angeles, CA 90024 USA

Glenn, Scott *Actor*
126 E De Vargas St #1902, Santa Fe, NM
87501 USA

Glenn, Terry *Football Player*
Dallas Cowboys, 1 Cowboys Parkway,
Irving, TX 75063 USA

Glenn, Wayne E *Misc*
United Paperworkers Int'l Union, 3340
Perimeter Hill Dr, Nashville, TN 37211
USA

Glenn Jr, John H *Astronaut, Senator*
Ohio State University, Stillman Hall 1947
College Road, Columbus, OH 43210 USA

Glennan, Robert E Jr *Educator*
Emporia State University, President's
Office, Emporia, KS 66801 USA

Glennie, Brian *Hockey Player*
Mortimer's Point Road, Port Carling, ON
P0B 1J0, CANADA

Glennie, Evelyn E A *Music Group, Musician*
P O Box 6 Sawtry Huntingdon, Cambs, PE17 5WE, UNITED KINGDOM (UK)

Glennie-Smith, Nick *Composer*
Vangelos Mgmt, 15233 Ventura Blvd #200, Sherman Oaks, CA 91403 USA

Gless, Sharon *Actor*
Rosenzweig Productions, P O Box 48005, Los Angeles, CA 90048 USA

Glick, Frederick (Freddie) *Football Player*
4226 Antlers Court, Fort Collins, CO 80526 USA

Glickman, Daniel R *Secretary, Misc*
Harvard University, Kennedy Government School, Cambridge, MA 02138 USA

Glidden, Bob *Race Car Driver*
P O Box 183, Whiteland, IN 46184 USA

Glidden, Robert *Educator*
Ohio University, President's Office, Athens, OH 45701 USA

Glidewell, Iain *Judge*
Rough Heys Farm Macclesfield, Cheshire, SK11 9PF, UNITED KINGDOM (UK)

Glimcher, Arnold O (Arne) *Artist, Misc*
Pace Gallery, 32 E 57th St, New York, NY 10022 USA

Glimm, James G *Mathematician*
State University of New York, Applied Math Dept, Stony Brook, NY 11794 USA

Glitman, Maynard W *Diplomat*
P O Box 438, Jeffersonville, VT 05464 USA

Glitter, Gary *Music Group, Songwriter*
Jef Hanlon Mgmt, 1 York St, London, W1H 1PZ, UNITED KINGDOM (UK)

Glmble, Johnny *Misc*
Nancy Fly Agency, 6618 Wolfcreek Pall, Austin, TX 78749 USA

Globus, Yoram *Producer*
Pathe International, 8670 Wilshire Blvd, Beverly Hills, CA 90211 USA

Glockner, Michael
Kaiserslautener Str. 54, Saarbrucken, GERMANY, D-66123

Glory, New Found *Music Group*
Ellis Industries Inc, 234 Shoreward Drive, Great Neck, NY 11021 USA

Glossop, Peter *Opera Singer*
End Cottage 7 Gate Close, Hawkchurch near Axminster, Devon, UNITED KINGDOM (UK)

Glouberman, Michael *Producer*
United Talent Agency (UTA), 9560 Wilshire Blvd, Beverly Hills, CA 90212 USA

Glover, Bloc *Motorcycle Racer*
American Motorcycle Assn, 13515 Yormouth Dr, Pickerington, OH 43147 USA

Glover, Brian *Actor*
DeWolfe, Manfield House 376/378 Strand, London, WC2R OLR, UNITED KINGDOM (UK)

Glover, Bruce *Actor*
11449 Woodbine St, Los Angeles, CA 90066 USA

Glover, Crispin *Actor*
3573 Carnation Ave, Los Angeles, CA 90026 USA

Glover, Danny *Actor*
P O Box 170069, San Francisco, CA 94117 USA

Glover, Jane A
Kaylor Mgmt, 130 W 57thSt #8G, New York, NY 10019 USA

Glover, John *Actor*
130 W 42ndSt #2400, New York, NY 10036 USA

Glover, Julian *Actor*
200 Fulham Road, London, SW10 9PN, United Kingdom

Glover, Kevin B *Football Player*
11553 Manor Stone Lane, Columbia, MD 21044 USA

Glover, La'Roi *Football Player*
841 49th St, San Diego, CA 92102 USA

Glover, Richard E (Rich) *Football Player*
4636 Nogal Canyon Road, Las Cruces, NM 88011 USA

Glowacki, Janusz *Writer*
845 W End Ave #4B, New York, NY 10025 USA

Gluck, Carol *Historian*
440 Riverside Dr, New York, NY 10027 USA

Gluck, Louise E *Writer*
Williams College, English Dept, Williamstown, MA 02167 USA

Glushchenko, Fedor I
1st Prydilnaya Str 11 #5, Moscow, 105037, RUSSIA

Glynn, Carlin *Actor*
1165 5th Ave, New York, NY 10029 USA

Glynn, Ian M *Physicist, Misc*
Daylesford Conduit Head Road, Cambridge, CB3 0EY, UNITED KINGDOM (UK)

Glynn, Robert D Jr *Business Person*
PG&E Corp, Spear Tower 1 Market St, San Francisco, CA 94105 USA

Gminski, Mike *Basketball Player, Sportscaster*
1309 Canterbury Hill Circle, Charlotte, NC 28211 USA

Gnedovsky, Yuri P *Architect*
Union of Architects, Granatny Per 22, Moscow, 103001, RUSSIA

Go-Go's, The *Musician*
Agency for the Performing Arts (APA-LA), 9200 Sunset Blvd #900, Los Angeles, CA 90069 USA

Goad, Jim *Journalist, Writer*
Simon & Schuster Books, 1230 Ave of Americas, New York, NY 10020 USA

Goalby, Bob *Golfer*
5950 Town Hall Road, Belleville, IL 62223 USA

Gocke, Justin
6763 Pistachio Pl., Palmdale, CA 93551-1622

Godard, Jean-Luc *Director*
15 Rue du Nord, Roulle, 1180, SWITZERLAND

Godbold, John C *Judge*
US Court of Appeals, P O Box 1589, Montgomery, AL 36102 USA

Godboldo, Dale *Actor*
Burstein Company, The, 15304 Sunset Blvd #208, Pacific Palisades, CA 90272 USA

Godchaux, Stephen *Producer*
William Morris Agency (WMA-LA), 1 William Morris Pl, Beverly Hills, CA 90212 USA

Goddard, Anna Marie
2112 Broadway, Santa Monica, CA 90404-2912

Goddard, Anna-Marie *Model*
Po Box 7028, Capistrano Beach, CA 92624 USA

Goddard, Daniel *Actor*
Mosaic Media Group, 9200 Sunset Blvd Fl 10, Los Angeles, CA 90069 USA

Goddard, John *Scientist, Misc*
4224 Beulah Dr, La Canada, CA 91011 USA

Goddard, Mark *Actor*
P O Box 778, Middleboro, MA 02346 USA

Goddard, Samuel P (Sam) Jr *Governor*
4724 E Camelback Canyon Dr, Phoenix, AZ 85018 USA

Godecki, Marzena *Actor*
Jonethan M. Shiff Productions, 373 Bay Street, Port Melbourne, Victoria, Australia, 3207

Godfrey, Paul V *Publisher*
Toronto Sun, 333 King St E, Toronto, ON M5A 3X5, CANADA

Godfrey, Randall *Football Player*
512 Cason St, Valdosta, GA 31601 USA

Godina, John
PO Box 120, Indianapolis, IN 46204-0120

Godley, Georgina *Fashion Designer*
42 Bassett Road, London, W10 6UL, UNITED KINGDOM (UK)

Godley, Kevin *Music Group, Musician*
Heronden Hall Tenterden, Kent, UNITED KINGDOM (UK)

Godmanis, Ivars *Misc, Politician*
Palasta St 1, Riga, 1954, LATVIA

Godreche, Judith *Actor*
William Morris Agency, 151 El Camino Dr, Beverly Hills, CA 90212 USA

Godsmack *Music Group*
Global Artists Management, 92 High St Unit T41, Medford, MA 02155

Godwin, Fay S *Photographer*
Fay Godwin Network, 3-4 Kerby St, London, E4N 8TS, UNITED KINGDOM (UK)

Godwin, Gail K *Writer*
P O Box 946, Woodstock, NY 12498 USA

Godwin, Linda M *Astronaut, Physicist*
16923 Cottonwood Way, Houston, TX 77059 USA

Godynyuk, Alexander *Hockey Player*
VIP Sports International, 110 E 59th St, New York, NY 10022 USA

Goebel, Timothy *Figure Skater*
Healthsouth Training Center, 555 N Nash St, El Segundo, CA 90245 USA

Goehr, Alexander
11 West Rd., Cambridge, ENGLAND

Goehr, P Alexander *Composer*
University of Cambridge, Music Faculty 11 West Road, Cambridge, UNITED KINGDOM (UK)

Goel, Jyotin *Actor, Bollywood*
258 Famous Cine Building, Mahalaxmi, Bombay, MS 400 011, INDIA

Goellner, Marc-Kevin *Tennis Player, Athlete*
Blau-Weiss Neuss, Tennishall Jahnstrasse, Neuss, 41464, GERMANY

Goelz, Dave (Gonzo) *Artist, Misc*
Jim Henson Productions, 117 E 69th St, New York, NY 10021 USA

Goen, Bob *Entertainer*
21767 Plainwood Dr, Woodland Hills, CA 91364 USA

Goerke, Glenn A *Educator*
University of Houston, President's Office, Houston, TX 77204 USA

Goestenkors, Gail *Basketball Player, Coach*
Duke University, Athletic Dept, Durham, NC 27708 USA

Goestschi, Renate *Skier*
Schwarzenbach 3, Obdach, 8742, AUSTRIA

Goettmann, Georgia
344 E. 59th St., New York, NY 10022

Goetz, Bernhard
55 W. 14th St., New York, NY 10011

Goetz, Eric *Yachtsman, Misc*
Eric Goetz Marine & Technology, 15 Broad Common Road, Bristol, RI 02809 USA

Goetz, Peter Michael *Actor*
Silver Massetti & Szatmary (SMS-LA), 8730 Sunset Blvd #440, Los Angeles, CA 90069 USA

Goetzman, Gary *Producer*
Creative Artists Agency LCC (CAA-LA), 9830 Wilshire Blvd, Beverly Hills, CA 90212 USA

Goffin, David *Producer*
International Creative Management (ICM-LA), 8942 Wilshire Blvd, Beverly Hills, CA 90211 USA

Goffin, Gerry *Songwriter, Misc*
9171 Hazen Dr, Beverly Hills, CA 90210 USA

Goggins, Walton *Actor*
Abrams Artists Agency (LA), 9200 Sunset Blvd Fl 11, Los Angeles, CA 90069 USA

Gogolak, Charles P (Charlie) *Football Player*
47 Village Ave #211, Dedham, MA 02026 USA

Gogolak, Peter (Pete) *Football Player*
R R Donnelley Financial, 75 Park Ave #300, New York, NY 10007 USA

Goh, Kun *Prime Minister*
Prime Minister's Office, 77 Sejonh-no, Chongnoku, Seoul, SOUTH KOREA

Goh, Rex *Music Group, Musician*
Agency for Performing Arts, 9200 Sunset Blvd #900, Los Angeles, CA 90069 USA

Goh Chok Tong *Prime Minister*
Prime Minister's Office, Istana Annexe, Singapore, 0923, SINGAPORE

Goheen, Robert F *Educator, Diplomat*
1 Orchard Circle, Princeton, NJ 08540 USA

Going, Joanna *Actor*
Cunningham-Escott-Dipene & Associates Inc (CED-LA), 10635 Santa Monica Blvd #130, Los Angeles, CA 90025 USA

Goings, E V *Business Person*
Tupperware Corp, P O Box 2353, Orlando, FL 32802 USA

Goings, Nick *Athlete*
Carolina Panthers, Ericsson Stadium, 800 S Mint St, Charlotte, NC 28202 USA

Goitschel-Beranger, Marielle *Skier*
Val Thorens, Saint-Martin de Belleville, 73440, FRANCE

Gola, Thomas J (Tom) *Basketball Player*
40 Governors Court, West Palm Beach, FL 33418 USA

Gola, Tom
15 King's Oak Lane, Philadelphia, PA 19115-4008

Gold, Andrew *Music Group, Songwriter*
Store, 22207 Summit Vue Dr, Woodland Hills, CA 91367 USA

Gold, Brandy *Actor*
Gold Marshak Liedtke, 3500 W Oliva Ave #1400, Burbank, CA 91505 USA

Gold, Elon *Actor, Comedian*
United Talent Agency, 9560 Wilshire Blvd #500, Beverly Hills, CA 90212 USA

Gold, Herbert *Writer*
1051 Broadway #A, San Francisco, CA 94133 USA

Gold, Jack *Director*
24 Wood Vale, London, N1O 3DP, UNITED KINGDOM (UK)

Gold, Jimmy
11990 San Vicente Blvd. #340, Los Angeles, CA 90049

Gold, Judy *Comedian*
Rick Dorfman Management, 450 W 15th St #500, New York, NY 10011 USA

Gold, Missy
3500 W. Olive Ave. #1400, Burbank, CA 91505

Gold, Todd
Trident Media Group LLC, 41 Madison Ave Fl 33, New York, NY 10010 USA

Gold, Tracey *Actor*
3500 W Olive Ave #1190, Burbank, CA 91505 USA

Goldberg, Adam *Actor*
Innovative Artists, 1505 10th St, Santa Monica, CA 90401 USA

Goldberg, Bernard R *Commentator*
CBS-TV, News Dept 51 W 52nd St, New York, NY 10019 USA

Goldberg, Bill *Actor*
Nicole Nassar PR, 521 Spoleto Dr, Pacific Palisades, CA 90272 USA

Goldberg, Bill *Wrestler, Football Player*
167 New Hope Road, Dawsonville, GA 30534 USA

Goldberg, Edward D *Geophysicist, Misc*
750 Val Sereno Dr, Encinitas, CA 92024 USA

Goldberg, Eric *Animator*
Walt Disney Studios, Animation Dept 500 S Buena Vista St, Burbank, CA 91521 USA

Goldberg, Gary David *Writer, Actor, Producer, Director*
UBU Productions, 4024 Radford Ave, Bungalow 14, Studio City, CA 91604 USA

Goldberg, Leonard *Producer*
Spectradyne Inc, 1198 Commerce Dr, Richardson, TX 75081 USA

Goldberg, Lucianne
255 W. 84th St. #6A, New York, NY 10024-4321

Goldberg, Luella G *Educator*
7019 Tupa Dr, Minneapolis, MN 55439 USA

Goldberg, Marshall (Biggie) *Artist*
222 Bowery Place, New York, NY 10012 USA

Goldberg, Richard W *Judge*
US International Trade Court, 1 Federal Plaza, New York, NY 10278 USA

Goldberg, Stan *Cartoonist*
8 White Birch Lane, Scarsdale, NY 10583 USA

Goldberg, Whoopi *Actor, Comedian*
One Ho Productions, 375 Greenwich St, Tribeca Film Center, New York, NY 10013 USA

Goldberger, Andi
Bleckenwegen 4, Waldzell, AUSTRIA, 4924

Goldberger, Andreas *Skier*
Bleckenwegen 4, Waldzell, 4924, AUSTRIA

Goldberger, Marvin L *Physicist, Educator*
621 Mira Monte, La Jolla, CA 92037 USA

Goldberger, Paul J *Journalist, Critic*
New York Times, Editorial Dept 229 W 43rd St, New York, NY 10036 USA

Goldblatt, Stephen L *Cinematographer*
Spyros Skouras, 631 Wilshire Blvd #2C, Santa Monica, CA 90401 USA

Goldblum, Jeff *Actor*
Industry Entertainment, 955 S Carrillo Dr #300, Los Angeles, CA 90048 USA

Golden, Arthur *Writer*
Vintage Press, 1111 Rancho Conejo Blvd, Newbury Park, CA 91320 USA

Golden, Harry *Bowler, Misc*
Professional Bowlers Assn, 719 2nd Ave #701, Seattle, WA 98104 USA

Golden, Kit *Producer*
Manhattan Project, 1775 Broadway, Suite 410, New York, NY 10019 USA

Golden, Michael *Business Person*
New York Times Co, 229 W 43rd St, New York, NY 10036 USA

Golden, William Lee *Music Group, Songwriter*
329 Rockland Road, Hendersonville, TN 37075 USA

Goldens, The
Box 1795, Hendersonville, TN 37077

Goldenthal, Elliot *Composer*
Gorfaine/Schwartz, 13245 Riverside Dr #450, Sherman Oaks, CA 91423 USA

Goldfinger, Sarah *Actor*
Creative Artists Agency LCC (CAA-LA), 9830 Wilshire Blvd, Beverly Hills, CA 90212 USA

Goldhaber, Maurice *Physicist*
91 S Gillette Ave, Bayport, NY 11705 USA

Goldin, Claudia D *Economist*
Harvard University, Economics Dept, Cambridge, MA 02138 USA

Goldin, Judah *Educator*
3300 Darby Road, Haverford, PA 19041 USA

Goldin, Nan *Photographer*
334 Bowry, New York, NY 10012 USA

Goldin, Ricky Paull *Actor*
365 W 52nd St #LE, New York, NY 10019 USA

Goldin, Ricky Paull *Actor*
Metropolitan Talent Agency, 4526 Wilshire Blvd, Beverly Hills, CA 90010 USA

Goldman, Bo *Writer*
Creative Artists Agency, 9830 Wilshire Blvd, Beverly Hills, CA 90212 USA

Goldman, Matt *Entertainer*
Blue Man Group, Luxor Hotel 3900 Las Vegas Blvd S, Las Vegas, NV 89119 USA

Goldman, William *Writer*
Janklow & Nesbit, 445 Park Ave #1300, New York, NY 10022 USA

Goldoni, Lelia
15459 Wyandotte St., Van Nuys, CA 91405

Goldreich, Peter M *Astronomer*
471 S Catalina Ave, Pasadena, CA 91106 USA

Goldrup, Ray
2383 Broderick, West Jordan, UT 84084

Goldsboro, Bobby *Music Group, Songwriter*
La Rana Productions, P O Box 4979, Ocala, FL 34478 USA

Goldschmidt, Neil E *Governor, Secretary, Misc*
222 SW Columbia St, Portland, OR 97201 USA

Goldsman, Akiva *Director*
Creative Artists Agency LCC (CAA-LA), 9830 Wilshire Blvd, Beverly Hills, CA 90212 USA

Goldsmith, Barbara *Writer*
Janklow Nesbit Assocs, 445 Park Ave #1300, New York, NY 10022 USA

Goldsmith, Judy *Social Activist*
National Organization for Women, 425 13th St NW, Washington, DC 20002 USA

Goldsmith, Kelly *Actor*
Defining Artists, 4342 Lankershim Blvd, Universal City, CA 91602 USA

Goldsmith, Olivia *Writer*
Metropolitan Talent Agency, 4526 Wilshire Blvd, Los Angeles, CA 90010 USA

Goldsmith, Paul
1148 Vivian Lane, Munster, IN 46321

Goldsmith, Stephen *Politician, Misc*
Governor's Office, State House, Indianapolis, IN 46204 USA

Goldsmith-Thomas, Elaine *Producer*
Red Om Films Inc, 16 W 19th St Fl 12, New York, NY 10011 USA

Goldstein, Allan L *Scientist, Biologist, Misc*
800 25th St NW #1005, Washington, DC 20037 USA

Goldstein, Avram *Misc*
735 Dolores St, Stanford, CA 94305 USA

Goldstein, Jenette
3932 Marathon St., Los Angeles, CA 90029

Goldstein, Joseph L *Nobel Prize Laureate*
3831 Turtle Creek Blvd #22B, Dallas, TX 75219 USA

Goldstein, Michael *Business Person*
Toy R Us Inc, 461 From Road, Paramus, NJ 07652 USA

Goldstein, Murray *Physicist, Misc*
United Cerebral Palsey Foundation, 1660 L St NW #700, Washington, DC 20036 USA

Goldstine, Herman H *Mathematician, Scientist*
56 Pasture Lane, Bryn Mawr, PA 19010 USA

Goldstone, Jeffrey *Physicist*
77 Massachusetts Ave #6-313, Cambridge, MA 02139 USA

Goldstone, Richard J *Judge*
Constitutional Court Private Bag X32, Braamfontein, 2017, SOUTH AFRICA

Goldstone, Steven F *Business Person*
Nabisco Group Holdings, 1301 Ave of Americas, New York, NY 10019 USA

Goldsworthy, Andrew C (Andy) *Artist, Photographer*
Hue-Williams Fine Art, 21 Cork St, London, W1X 1HB, UNITED KINGDOM (UK)

Goldthwait, Bob (Bobcat) *Actor, Comedian*
Gersh Agency, The (LA), 232 N Canon Dr, Beverly Hills, CA 90210 USA

Goldwasser, Eugene *Biologist, Misc*
5656 S Dorchester Ave, Chicago, IL 60637 USA

Goldwater Jr, Barry
4401 Connecticut Ave NW PMB 850, Washington, DC 20077-3548 USA

Goldwyn, Tony *Actor, Director*
Creative Artists Agency, 9830 Wilshire Blvd, Beverly Hills, CA 90212 USA

Goldwyn Jr, Samuel *Producer*
Samuel Goldwyn Company, 9570 W Pico Blvd #400, Los Angeles, CA 90035 USA

Goleman, Ph D, Daniel *Writer*
Bantam Books, 6 Commercial Street, Hicksville, NY 11801

Golembiewski, Billy *Bowler*
4966 N Wise Road, Coleman, MI 48618 USA

Golic, Robert P (Bob) *Football Player, Sportscaster*
1817 6th St, Manhattan Beach, CA 90266 USA

Golimowski, David A *Astronomer*
515 Holden Road, Towson, MD 21286 USA

Golina, Stacy
325 S. Swall Dr. #502, Los Angeles, CA 90048-3078

Golino, Valeria *Actor*
Creative Artists Agency, 9830 Wilshire Blvd, Beverly Hills, CA 90212 USA

Golisano, B Thomas *Business Person*
Paychex Inc, 911 Panorama Trail S, Rochester, NY 14625 USA

Golonka, Arlene *Actor*
Silver/Kass/Massetti, 8730 Sunset Blvd #480, Los Angeles, CA 90069 USA

Golson, Benny *Music Group, Musician, Composer*
Abby Hoffer, 223 1/2 E 48th St, New York, NY 10017 USA

Golub, Leon A *Artist*
530 LaGuardia Place, New York, NY 10012 USA

Golub, Richard
42 E. 64th St., New York, NY 10021

Gomez, Andres *Tennis Player*
ProServe, 1101 Woodrow Wilson Blvd #1800, Arlington, VA 22209 USA

Gomez, Carlos *Actor*
Michael Slessinger & Assoc, 8730 Sunset Blvd #270, Los Angeles, CA 90069 USA

Gomez, Edgar (Eddie) *Music Group, Musician*
Integrity Talent, P O Box 961, Burlington, MA 01803 USA

Gomez, Hector *Actor*
Televisa, Blvd Adolfo Lopez Mateos 232, Colonia San Angel INN, DF, CP 01060, MEXICO

Gomez, Ian *Actor*
Metropolitan Talent Agency (MTA), 4526 Wilshire Blvd, Los Angeles, CA 90010 USA

Gomez, Javier *Actor*
Gabriel Blanco Iglesias (Mexico), Rio Balsas 35-32, Colonia Cuauhtemoc, DF, 06500, Mexico

Gomez, Jill *Opera Singer*
16 Milton Park, London, N6 5QA, UNITED KINGDOM (UK)

Gomez, Panchito
PO Box 7016, Burbank, CA 91510

Gomez, Ralph E *Mathematician, Misc*
Alfred P Sloan Foundation, President's Office 630 5th Ave, New York, NY 10111 USA

Gomez, Rick *Actor*
Pop Art Management, 9615 Brighton Way #426, Beverly Hills, CA 90210

Gomez, Ruben *Baseball Player*
N43 Calle Luise E, Toa Baja, PR 00949 USA

Gomez, Scott *Hockey Player*
1812 Toklat St, Anchorage, AK 99508
USA

Gomez-Preston, Reagen *Actor*
Anonymous Content, 8522 National Blvd
#101, Culver City, CA 90232 USA

Gompf, Thomas (Tom) *Swimmer, Misc*
2716 Barrel Ave, Plant City, FL 33566
USA

Goncalves, Vascos dos Santos *Prime
Minister, General*
Ave Estados Unidos da America 86, 5 Esq,
Lisbon, 1700, PORTUGAL

Gonchar, Sergei *Hockey Player*
Int'l Management Group, 801 6th St SW
#235, Calgary, AB T2P 3V8, CANADA

Gondry, Michel *Director, Writer*
United Talent Agency (UTA), 9560
Wilshire Blvd, Beverly Hills, CA 90212
USA

Gonick, Larry *Cartoonist*
247 Missouri St, San Francisco, CA 94107
USA

Gonnenwein, Wolfgang
Opera et Concert, Maximilianstr 22,
Munich, 80539, GERMANY

Gonshaw, Francesca *Actor*
Greg Mellard, 12 D'Arblay St #200,
London, W1V 3FP, UNITED KINGDOM
(UK)

Gonsoulin, Austin (Goose) *Football Player*
5966 Reeves Dr, Silsbee, TX 77656 USA

Gonzales, Alberto *Judge, Government
Official*
White House, 1600 Pennsylvania Ave
NW, Washington, DC 20500 USA

Gonzales, Carlos *Cinematographer*
1549 1/2 N Commonwealth Ave, Los
Angeles, CA 90027 USA

Gonzalez, Alex *Baseball Player, Athlete*
Florida Marlins, 2269 Dan Marino Blvd,
Miami, FL 33056 USA

Gonzalez, Alexander S (Alex) *Baseball
Player*
8620 SW 102nd Ave, Miami, FL 33173
USA

Gonzalez, Araceli *Actor*
Telefe - Argentina, Pavon 2444
(C1248AAT), Buenos Aires, ARGENTINA

Gonzalez, Arthur *Judge*
US Bankruptcy Court, 1 Bowling Green,
New York, NY 10004 USA

Gonzalez, Clifton
955 S. Carrillo Dr. #300, Los Angeles, CA
90048

Gonzalez, Edith *Actor*
Televisa, Blvd Adolfo Lopez Mateos 232,
Colonia San Angel INN, DF, CP 01060,
MEXICO

Gonzalez, Hector *Religious Leader*
Baptist Churches USA, P O Box 851,
Valley Forge, PA 19482 USA

Gonzalez, Juan *Baseball Player, Athlete*
Texas Rangers, 1000 Ballpark Way,
Arlington, TX 76011 USA

Gonzalez, Juan A *Baseball Player*
Ext Catoni A9, Vega Baja, PR 00693 USA

Gonzalez, Juan Miguel & Elian
Marcelo Salado, Cardenas, CUBA

Gonzalez, Lazaro & Marisleysis
2319 NW 2nd St., Miami, FL 33125

Gonzalez, Luis E *Baseball Player*
6026 E Jenan Dr, Scottsdale, AZ 85254
USA

Gonzalez, Macchi Luis *President*
Palacio de Gobiemo, Ave Marisol Lopez,
Asuncion, PARAGUAY

Gonzalez, Marquez Felipe *Prime Minister*
Foudacion Socialismo XXI, Gobefas 31,
Madrid, 28023, SPAIN

Gonzalez, Miriam *Actor, Model*
Playboy Entertainment Group Inc, 2706
Media Center Dr, Los Angeles, CA 90065

Gonzalez, Phoenix *Actor*
Select Artists Ltd (CA-Westside Office),
1138 12th Street, Suite 1, Santa Monica,
CA 90403 USA

Gonzalez, Raul *Soccer Player*
Real Madrid FC, Avda Concha Espina 1,
Madrid, 28036, SPAIN

Gonzalez, Rick *Actor*
Paradigm (LA), 10100 Santa Monica Blvd,
Fl 25, Los Angeles, CA 90067 USA

Gonzalez, Susana *Actor*
Televisa, Blvd Adolfo Lopez Mateos 232,
Colonia San Angel INN, DF, CP 01060,
MEXICO

Gonzalez, Tony *Football Player*
Kansas City Chiefs, 1 Arrowhead Dr,
Kansas City, KS 64129 USA

Gonzalez, Victor *Actor*
Gabriel Blanco Iglesias (Mexico), Rio
Balsas 35-32, Colonia Cuauhtemoc, DF,
06500, Mexico

Gonzalez Martin, Marcelo Cardinal
Religious Leader
Arco de Palacio 1, Toledo, 45002, SPAIN

Gonzalez Zumarraga, Antonio J Cardinal
Religious Leader
Arzobispado, Apartado 17-01-00106,
Called Chile, Quito, 1140, ECUADOR

Gonzalez-Gonzalez, Pedro
4154 Charles Ave., Culver City, CA 90230

Gonzalo, Julie *Actor*
Lane Management Group, 13331
Moorpark St, #118, Sherman Oaks, CA
91423 USA

Good, Hugh W *Religious Leader*
Primitive Advent Christian Church, 273
Frame Road, Elkview, WV 25071 USA

Good, Meagan *Actor*
Lighthouse Entertainment, 409 North
Camden Drive #202, Beverly Hills, CA
90210 USA

Good, Meagan *Actor*
Coast to Coast Talent Group, 3350
Barham Blvd, Los Angeles, CA 90068
USA

Good, Melanie *Actor*
11288 Ventura Blvd #175, Studio City, CA
91604 USA

Good, Michael T *Astronaut*
2617 Broussard Court, Seabrook, TX
77586 USA

Good Charlotte *Music Group*
Creative Artists Agency LCC (CAA-LA),
9830 Wilshire Blvd, Beverly Hills, CA
90212 USA

Goodacre, Connick Jill *Model*
Harry Connick, Wilkins Mgmt 323
Broadway, Cambridge, MA 02139 USA

Goodacre, Glenna *Artist, Misc*
National Academy Museum, 1083 5th
Ave, New York, NY 10126 USA

Goodall, Caroline *Actor*
P F D Drury House, 34-43 Russell St,
London, WC2B 5HA, UNITED KINGDOM
(UK)

Goodall, Jane *Scientist, Misc*
Jane Goodall Institute, PO Box 14890,
Silver Spring, MD 20911 USA

Goode, David R *Business Person*
Norfolk Southern Corp, 3 Commercial
Place, Norfolk, VA 23510 USA

Goode, Joe *Artist*
1645 Electric Ave, Venice, CA 90291 USA

Goode, Matthew *Actor*
Dalzell & Beresford Ltd, 26 Astwood
Mews, London, SW7 4DE, UNITED
KINGDOM (UK)

Goode, Richard S *Music Group, Musician*
Frank Salonon, 201 W 54th St #1C, New
York, NY 10019 USA

Goodell, Brian S *Swimmer*
27040 S Ridge Dr, Mission Viejo, CA
92692 USA

Gooden, Drew *Basketball Player*
Orlando Magic, Waterhouse Center, 8701
Maitland Summit Blvd, Orlando, FL
32810 USA

Gooden, Dwight *Baseball Player*
8380 Golden Praire Dr, Tampa, FL 33647
USA

Goodenough, Ward H *Misc*
3300 Darby Road #5306, Haverford, PA
19041 USA

Goodeve, Charles P *Misc*
38 Middleway, London, NW11, UNITED
KINGDOM (UK)

Goodeve, Grant *Actor*
21416 NE 68th Court, Redmond, WA
98053 USA

Goodfellow, Peter N *Scientist, Misc*
Cancer Research Fund, Lincoln Inn Fields,
London, WC2A 3PX, UNITED KINGDOM
(UK)

Goodfriend, Linda
338 S. Beachwood Dr., Burbank, CA
91505-2713

Goodfriend, Lynda *Actor*
338 S Beachwood Dr, Burbank, CA 91506
USA

Gooding, Cuba Jr *Actor*
Rogers & Cowan, 1888 Century Park E,
#500, Los Angeles, CA 90067 USA

Gooding, Cuba Sr *Music Group*
Winston Collection, 630 9th Ave #908,
New York, NY 10036 USA

Gooding, Omar
3500 W. Olive Ave. #1400, Burbank, CA
91505

Goodlin, Chalmers *Misc*
7620 Red River Road, West Palm Beach, FL 33411 USA

Goodman, Alfred *Composer*
Bodenstedtstr 31, Munich, 81241, GERMANY

Goodman, Allegra *Writer*
Dial Press, 375 Hudson St, New York, NY 10014 USA

Goodman, Brian *Actor*
Agency for the Performing Arts (APA-LA), 9200 Sunset Blvd #900, Los Angeles, CA 90069 USA

Goodman, Corey S *Biologist, Misc*
Howard Hughes Medical Institute, Molecular/Cell Biology Dept, Berkeley, CA 94720 USA

Goodman, Dody
Scott Stander, 13701 Riverside Dr #201, Sherman Oaks, CA 91423 USA

Goodman, Ellen H *Editor, Misc*
Boston Globe, Editorial Dept 135 W T Morrissey Blvd, Dorchester, MA 02125 USA

Goodman, John *Actor*
619 Amalfi Dr, Pacific Palisades, CA 90272 USA

Goodman, Joseph W *Engineer*
570 University Terrace, Los Altos, CA 94022 USA

Goodman, Oscar *Attorney General*
520 S 4th St, Las Vegas, NV 89101 USA

Goodman, Richard *Producer*
Endeavor Agency LLC (LA), 9601 Wilshire Blvd Fl 3, Beverly Hills, CA 90210 USA

Goodnoff, Irvin *Cinematographer*
29997 Mulholland Highway, Agoura Hills, CA 91301 USA

Goodpaster, Andrew J *General, Educator*
6200 Oregon Ave NW #345, Washington, DC 20015 USA

Goodreault, Gene J *Football Player*
95 Colby St, Bradford, MA 01835 USA

Goodrem, Delta *Musician*
Sony Music Entertainment (Australia), 11-19 Hargrave St, E Sydney, NSW, 2010, AUSTRALIA

Goodrich, Gail
147 Byram Shore Rd, Greenwich, CT 06830-6907

Goodrich, Gail C Jr *Basketball Player*
270 Oceano Dr, Los Angeles, CA 90049 USA

Goodson, James A *War Hero*
37 Carolina Trail, Marshfield, MA 02050 USA

Goodwin, Doris Kearns *Historian*
General Delivery, 1649 Monument Lane, Concord, MA 01742 USA

Goodwin, Michael *Actor*
8271 Melrose Ave #110, Los Angeles, CA 90046 USA

Goodwin, Ron
Black Nest Cottage Hackford Lane, Brimpton Common, ENGLAND, RG7 4RP

Goodwin, Trudie *Actor*
Bosun House, 1 Deer Park Rd, Merton, London, SW19 3TL, ENGLAND

Goody, Joan E *Architect*
Goody Clancy Assoc, 334 Boylston St, Boston, MA 02116 USA

Goodyear, Scott *Race Car Driver*
Scott Goodyear Racing, PO Box 589, Carmel, IN 46082 USA

Goolagong Cawley, Evonne F *Tennis Player*
Private Bag 6060, Richmond, SV, 3121, AUSTRALIA

Goorjian, Michael *Actor*
Evolution Entertainment, 901 N Highland Ave, Los Angeles, CA 90038 USA

Goosen, Don *Boxer, Misc*
6320 Van Nuys Blvd, Van Nuys, CA 91401 USA

Gopi *Actor*
M3/F Anugraha Colony 3rd Avenue, Ashok Nagar, c, TN 600 083, INDIA

Gopi Krishna, B M *Actor*
14 Soundara Rajan Street, T Nagar, Chennai, TN 600 017, INDIA

Goranson, Alicia *Actor*
Paradigm (LA), 10100 Santa Monica Blvd, Fl 25, Los Angeles, CA 90067 USA

Gorbachev, Mikhail S *Politician, General, Secretary, Nobel Prize Laureate*
Leningradsky Prospekt 49, Moscow, 125468, RUSSIA

Gorbachev, Yuri *Artist*
Adrienne Editions, 377 Geary St, San Francisco, CA 94102 USA

Gorbatko, Viktor V *Astronaut, General, Misc*
Potchta Kosmonavtov, Moskovskoi Oblasti, Svyisdny Goroduk, 141160, RUSSIA

Gorchakova, Galina *Opera Singer*
Askonas Holt Ltd, 27 Chancery Lane, London, WC2A 1PF, UNITED KINGDOM (UK)

Gordeeva, Ekaterina *Figure Skater*
International Skating Center, PO Box 577, Simsbury, CT 06070 USA

Gordeyev, Vyacheslav M *Ballerina, Dancer, Choreographer*
Tverskaya Str 9 #78, Moscow, 103009, RUSSIA

Gordimer, Nadine *Nobel Prize Laureate*
7 Frere Road Parktown, Johannesburg, 2193, SOUTH AFRICA

Gordin, Charles *Actor*
187 Chestnut Hill Road, Wilton, CT 06897 USA

Gordon, Barry *Actor, Music Group*
1912 Kaweah Dr, Pasadena, CA 91105 USA

Gordon, Bert I *Director*
9640 Arby Dr, Beverly Hills, CA 90210 USA

Gordon, Bridgette *Basketball Player*
421 E Chelsea St, Deland, FL 32724 USA

Gordon, Bruce *Actor*
231 Tano Road #C, Santa Fe, NM 87506 USA

Gordon, Carl
8661 Pine Tree Pl., Los Angeles, CA 90069

Gordon, Danso *Actor*
Evolution Entertainment, 901 N Highland Ave, Los Angeles, CA 90038 USA

Gordon, David *Choreographer*
47 Great Jones St #2, New York, NY 10012 USA

Gordon, Don
6853 Pacific View Dr, Los Angeles, CA 90068

Gordon, Don *Actor*
Acme Talent, 4727 Wilshire Blvd #333, Los Angeles, CA 90010 USA

Gordon, Ed *Commentator*
NBC-TV, News Dept 30 Rockefeller Plaza, New York, NY 10112 USA

Gordon, Eve
10100 Santa Monica Blvd. #2500, Los Angeles, CA 90067

Gordon, Hannah Taylor *Actor*
Hutton Mgmt, 4 Old Manor Close Askett, Buckinghamshire, HP27 9NA, UNITED KINGDOM (UK)

Gordon, Harold P *Business Person*
Hasbro Inc, 1027 Newport Ave, Pawtucket, RI 02861 USA

Gordon, Howard *Writer, Producer*
Endeavor Agency LLC (LA), 9601 Wilshire Blvd Fl 3, Beverly Hills, CA 90210 USA

Gordon, Jeff *Race Car Driver*
1730 S Federal Highway, Delray Beach, FL 33483 USA

Gordon, John *Football Player*
40 Calle Fresno, San Clemente, CA 92672 USA

Gordon, Keith *Actor, Director, Writer*
United Talent Agency (UTA), 9560 Wilshire Blvd, Beverly Hills, CA 90212 USA

Gordon, Lancaster *Basketball Player*
2022 Murray Ave #1, Louisville, KY 40205 USA

Gordon, Lawrence *Business Person*
Largo Entertainment, 20th Century Fox 10201 W Pico Blvd, Los Angeles, CA 90064 USA

Gordon, Leo
9977 Wornon Ave., Sunland, CA 91040

Gordon, Lincoln *Economist, Diplomat*
3069 University Terrace NW, Washington, DC 20016 USA

Gordon, Mark *Actor*
Fifi Oscard Agency, 24 W 40th St, #1700, New York, NY 10018 USA

Gordon, Mary C *Writer*
Viking Penguin Press, 375 Sudson St, New York, NY 10014 USA

Gordon, Mike *Musician*
Dionysian Productions, 431 Pine St, Burlington, VT 05401 USA

Gordon, Milton A *Educator*
California State University, President's Office, Fullerton, CA 99264 USA

Gordon, Mita *Governor*
Belize House, Belnopan, BELIZE

Gordon, Nathan G *War Hero*
606 Green St, Morrilton, AZ 72110 USA

Gordon, Nina *Musician*
Q Prime, 729 7th Ave, #1600, New York, NY 10019 USA

Gordon, Pamela *Prime Minister*
United Bermuda Party, Burrows Bldg, Hamilton HM, CX, BERMUDA

Gordon, Richard
1 Craven Hill, London, ENGLAND, W2 3EN

Gordon, Richard F Jr *Astronaut*
65 Woodside Drive, Prescott, AZ 86305 USA

Gordon, Robby *Race Car Driver*
201 Rollings Hills Road, Mooresville, NC 28117 USA

Gordon, William E *Physicist*
Rice University, Space Physics Dept, PO Box 1892, Houston, TX 77251 USA

Gordon-Levitt, Joey
4024 Radford Ave Bldg. 3, Studio City, CA 91604

Gordon-Levitt, Joseph *Actor*
Gersh Agency, 232 N Canon Dr, Beverly Hills, CA 90210 USA

Gordy, Berry
878 Stradella Rd., Los Angeles, CA 90077

Gordy, Walter *Physicist*
2521 Perkins Road, Durham, NC 27705 USA

Gore, Al *Politician, Vice President*
1201 26th Street South, Arlington, VA 22202 USA

Gore, Lesley *Musician, Songwriter*
World Entertainment Assoc, 297101 Kinderkamack Road, #128, Oradell, NJ 07649 USA

Gore, Martin *Musician*
Reach Media, 295 Greenwich St, #109, New York, NY 10007 USA

Gore, Michael
15622 Royal Oak Rd, Encino, CA 91436

Gore, Tipper *Politician*
1201 26th Street South, Arlington, VA 22202 USA

Gore Jr, Albert A *Vice President*
312 Lunnwood Blvd, Nashville, TN 37205 USA

Gorecki, Henryk M *Composer*
UI HA Gornika 4 m 1, Katowice, 40-133, POLAND

Goren, Shlomo *Religious Leader, General*
Chief Rabbinate, Hechal Shlomo, Jerusalem, ISRAEL

Gorenstein, Mark B *Conductor*
Rublevskoye Shosses 28, #25, Moscow, 121609, RUSSIA

Goretta, Claude *Director*
10 Tour de Boel, Geneva, 1204, SWITZERLAND

Gorham, Christopher *Actor*
S M S Talent, 8730 Sunset Blvd, #440, Los Angeles, CA 90069 USA

Gorham, Eville *Misc*
1933 E River Terrace, Minneapolis, MN 55414 USA

Gorie, Dominic L *Astronaut*
16522 Craighurst Dr, Houston, TX 77059 USA

Gorillaz *Musician*
Virgin Records, 338 N Foothill Rd, Beverly Hills, CA 90210

Gorin, Charles
2617 First Dr., Austin, TX 78731

Goring, Robert T (Butch) *Hockey Player*
245 W 5th Ave, #108, Anchorage, AK 99501 USA

Goris, Eva *Actor*
International Creative Mgmt, 8942 Wilshire Blvd, #219, Beverly Hills, CA 90211 USA

Gorlin, Alexander *Architect*
Alexander Gorlin Architect, 137 Varick St, New York, NY 10013 USA

Gorman, Cliff
333 W. 57th St., New York, NY 10019

Gorman, Joseph T *Business Person*
TRW Inc, 1900 Richmond Road, Cleveland, OH 44124 USA

Gorman, Paul F Jr *General*
9175 Batesville Road, Alton, VA 22920 USA

Gorman, R C *Artist*
PO Box 1258, El Prado, NM 87529 USA

Gorman, Steve *Musician*
Mitch Schneider Organization, 14724 Ventura Blvd, #410, Sherman Oaks, CA 91403 USA

Gorman, Tom *Tennis Player*
ProServe, 1101 Woodrow Wilson Blvd, #1800, Arlington, VA 22209 USA

Gorman-Cahill, Margaret
4216 38th St. NW, Washington, DC 20016-2258

Gorme, Eydie *Musician*
944 Pinehurst Dr, Las Vegas, NV 89109 USA

Gormley, Antony *Artist*
13 South Villas, London, NW1 9BS, UNITED KINGDOM (UK)

Gorney, Karen Lynn *Actor*
Karen Company, Po Box 23-1060, New York, NY 10023 USA

Gorouuch, Edward Lee *Educator*
University of Alaska, President's Office, Anchorage, AK 99508 USA

Gorrell, Bob *Cartoonist*
Creators Syndicate, 5777 W Century Blvd, #700, Los Angeles, CA 90045 USA

Gorrell, Fred *Misc*
501 E Port au Prince Lane, Phoenix, AZ 85022 USA

Gorshin, Frank *Actor*
Scott Stander & Associates, 13701 Riverside Dr #201, Sherman Oaks, CA 91423 USA

Gorter, Cornelis J *Physicist*
Klobeniersburgwal 29, Amsterdam, NETHERLANDS

Gortman, Shaunzinski *Basketball Player*
Charlotte Sting, 100 Hive Dr, Charlotte, NC 28217 USA

Gosdin, Vern *Musician, Songwriter*
Rising Star, 1415 River Landing Way, Woodstock, GA 30188 USA

Goslin, Thomas B Jr *General*
Deputy CinC, US Strategic Command, Offutt Air Force Base, NE 68113 USA

Gosling, James *Designer*
Sun Microsystems, 2550 Garcia Ave, Mountain View, CA 94043 USA

Gosling, Ryan *Actor*
Artist Management, 1118 15th St #1, Santa Monica, CA 90403

Gosnell, Raja *Director*
United Talent Agency (UTA), 9560 Wilshire Blvd, Beverly Hills, CA 90212 USA

Goss, Luke *Actor*
Untitled Entertainment (LA), 8436 W 3rd St #650, Los Angeles, CA 90048 USA

Goss, Robert F *Misc*
Oil Chemical & Atomic International, 1636 Champa St, Denver, CO 80202 USA

Gossage, Goose
35 Marland Rd., Colorado Springs, CO 80906

Gossage, Richard M (Goose) *Baseball Player*
35 Marland Dr, Colorado Springs, CO 80906 USA

Gossard, Stone *Musician*
Annie Ohayon Media Relations, 525 Broadway, #600, New York, NY 10012 USA

Gosselaar, Mark-Paul *Actor*
30853 Romero Canyon Road, Castaic, CA 91384 USA

Gosselin, Mario *Hockey Player*
3225 NE 16th St, Pompano Beach, FL 33062 USA

Gossett, D Bruce *Football Player*
6109 Puerto Dr, Rancho Murieta, CA 95683 USA

Gossett, Lou
8383 Wilshire Blvd. #550, Beverly Hills, CA 90211

Gossett, Robert *Actor*
8306 Wilshire Blvd, #438, Beverly Hills, CA 90211 USA

Gossett Jr, Louis *Actor*
Writers & Artists, 8383 Wilshire Blvd, #550, Beverly Hills, CA 90211 USA

Gossick Crockatt, Sue *Swimmer*
13768 Christian Barrett Dr, Moorpark, CA 93021 USA

Goswami, Kunal *Director*
47 Jaihind Society 11th N S Road, JVPD Scheme, Bombay, MS 400 049, INDIA

Gotch, Karl
18530 Wayne Rd., Odessa, FL 33556-4739

Gothard, Michael
18 Shirlock Rd., London, ENGLAND, NW3 2HS

Gott, Karel *Musician*
Nad Bertramkou 18, Prague, 160 00, CZECH REPUBLIC

Gottfried, Brian *Tennis Player*
129 Teal Pointe Lane, Ponte Vedra Beach, FL 32082 USA

Gottfried, Gilbert *Actor, Comedian*
William Morris Agency, 151 El Camino
Dr, Beverly Hills, CA 90212 USA

Gotti, Victoria *Actor, Producer*
Growing Up Gotti, 13400 Riverside Dr
#300, Sherman Oaks, CA 91423 USA

Gottlieb, Michael *Director*
2436 Washington Ave, Santa Monica, CA
90403 USA

Gottlieb, Robert A *Editor, Publisher*
237 E 48th St, New York, NY 10017 USA

Gougeon, Donni *Misc*
Variety Artists, 1924 Spring St, Paso
Robles, CA 93446 USA

Gough, Alfred *Writer*
Millar/Gough Ink, 3800 Barham Blvd,
Suite 503, Los Angeles, CA 90068 USA

Gough, Michael *Actor*
Torleigh Green Lane, Ashmore, Salisbury,
Wills, SP5 5AO, UNITED KINGDOM
(UK)

Gough, Tommy *Musician*
Brothers Mgmt, 141 Dunbar Ave, Fords,
NJ 08863 USA

Gould, Alexander *Actor*
Stein Entertainment Group, 11271 Ventura
Blvd #477, Studio City, CA 91604 USA

Gould, Elizabeth *Doctor*
Princeton University, Medical Center,
Neurosciences Dept, Princeton, NJ 08544
USA

Gould, Elliott *Actor*
21250 Califa St, #201, Woodland Hills,
CA 91367 USA

Gould, Gordon *Inventor*
105 Buckeye Court, Sterling, VA 20164
USA

Gould, Harold *Actor*
603 Ocean Ave, #$E, Santa Monica, CA
90402 USA

Gould, Lawrence M *Misc*
201 E Rudasill Road, Tucson, AZ 85704
USA

Gould, Ronald M *Judge*
US Court of Appeals, US Courthouse,
1010 5th Ave, Seattle, WA 98104 USA

Gould, Shane
207 Kent St.Level 18, Sydney,
AUSTRALIA, NSW 2000

Gould, Terry *Producer*
Lenhoff & Lenhoff, 830 Palm Ave, West
Hollywood, CA 90069

Gould Innes, Shane *Swimmer*
207 Kent St, Level 18, Sydney, NSW,
2000, AUSTRALIA

Goulet, Michael *Hockey Player*
817 Fairchild Dr, Highlands Ranch, CO
80126 USA

Goulet, Robert *Actor, Musician*
3110 Monte Rosa Ave, Las Vegas, NV
89120 USA

Goundamani *Actor*
7 Cenatop Ist Cross Street, Teynampet,
Chennai, TN 600 018, INDIA

Gourley, Roark *Artist*
Roark Gourley Art Gallery, 33151 Paso
Dr, South Laguna Beach, CA 92677 USA

Gov't Mule *Music Group*
Monterey Peninsula Artists (Monterey),
509 Hartnell St, Monterey, CA 93940 USA

Govinda *Actor, Bollywood*
105 Jal Darshan, "A" Wing Ruia Park Juhu,
Mumbai, MS 400049, INDIA

Gowan, James *Architect*
2 Linden Gardens, London, W2 4ES,
UNITED KINGDOM (UK)

Gowdy, Curt *Sportscaster*
28 Graham St, Leominster, MA 01453
USA

Gower, David I *Cricketer*
David Gower Promotions, 6 George St,
Nottingham, NG1 3BE, UNITED
KINGDOM (UK)

Gowers, W Timothy *Mathematician*
Cambridge University, 16 Mill Lane,
Cambridge, CB2 1SB, UNITED
KINGDOM (UK)

Gowon, Yakub *General, President*
National Oil/Chemical Marketing Co,
38-39 Marina, Lagos, 2052, NIGERIA

Gowrie, Earl of *Government Official*
Government Securities, Stag Place,
London, SW1E 5DS, UNITED KINGDOM
(UK)

Gowtham *Actor*
9 Pooram prakash Rao Road, Balaji
Nagar, Chennai, TN 600 014, INDIA

Gowthami *Actor, Bollywood*
2-B, Syamvilla 2nd Main Road,
C.I.T.Colony Mylapore, Chennai, TN
600004, INDIA

Goycoechea, Sergio *Soccer Player*
Argentine Football Assn, Via Monte
1366-76, Buenos Aires, 1053,
ARGENTINA

Goyette, J G Philippe (Phil) *Hockey
Player*
815 38-E Ave, Lachine, QC, H8T 2C4,
CANADA

Goyri, Sergio *Actor*
Televisa, Blvd Adolfo Lopez Mateos 232,
Colonia San Angel INN, DF, CP 01060,
MEXICO

GQ
1560 Broadway #1308, New York, NY
10036

Grabe, Ronald J *Astronaut*
13302 E Country Shadows Road,
Chandler, AZ 85249 USA

Graber, Bill *Track Athlete*
PO Box 5019, Upland, CA 91785 USA

Graber, Susan P *Judge*
US Courts of Appeals, Pioneer
Courthouse, 555 SW Yamhill St, Portland,
OR 97204 USA

Grabois, Neil R *Educator*
Colgate University, President's Office,
Hamilton, NY 13346 USA

Grabow, John *Baseball Player*
534 Chestnut Rd, Dawsonville, GA 30434

Grabowski, James S (Jim) *Football Player*
1523 W Withom Lane, Palatine, IL 60067
USA

Grabowski, Jim
1523 W. Withorn Lane, Palatine, IL 60067

Grace, April *Actor*
Liberman/Zerman, 252 N Larchmont,
#200, Los Angeles, CA 90004 USA

Grace, Bud *Cartoonist*
PO Box 66, Oakton, VA 22124 USA

Grace, Maggie *Actor*
Darren Goldberg Management, 5225
Wilshire Blvd #419, Los Angeles, CA
90036

Grace, Nancy *Lawyer, Television Host*
Court TV, 600 Third Ave Fl 2, New York,
NY 10016 USA

Grace, Topher *Actor*
Baker Winokur Ryder (BWR-LA), 9100
Wilshire Blvd Fl 6, W Tower, Beverly
Hills, CA 90212 USA

Graceland
3765 Elvis Presley Blvd, Memphis, TN
38116

Gracen, Elizabeth *Actor, Beauty Pageant
Winner*
Metropolitan Talent Agency, 4526
Wilshire Blvd, Los Angeles, CA 90010
USA

Gracey, James S *Admiral, Business Person*
1 Westin Center, 2445 M St NW #260,
Washington, DC 20037 USA

Grach, Eduard D *Musician*
1st Smolensky Per 9, #98, Moscow,
113324, RUSSIA

Grachev, Pavel S *General*
Ovchinnikovskaya Nab 18/1, Moscow,
113324, RUSSIA

Gracheva, Nadezhda A *Ballerina*
1st Truzhennikov Per 17, #49, Moscow,
119121, RUSSIA

Grachvogel, Maria *Fashion Designer*
Maria Grachvogel, 5 South Molton Street,
London, England, W11 1LT, United
Kingdom

Gracie, Charlie *Musician*
Jeff Hubbard Productions, PO Box 53664,
Indianapolis, IN 46253 USA

Gracin, Joshua *Musician*
American Idol, 7800 Beverly Blvd #251,
Los Angeles, CA 90036 USA

Grad, Harold *Mathematician*
248 Overlook Road, New Rochelle, NY
10804 USA

Gradishar, Randy C *Football Player*
6441 S Southwood Dr, Centennial, CO
80121 USA

Grady, Don *Actor, Songwriter*
4444 Lankershim Blvd, #207, North
Hollywood, CA 91602 USA

Grady, Ellen
150 E. Olive #111, Burbank, CA 91502

Grady, James T *Politician*
International Teamsters Brotherhood, 25
Louisiana Ave NW, Washington, DC
20001 USA

Grady, Wayne *Golfer*
Advantage International, 1751 Pinnacle
Dr, #1500, McLean, VA 22102 USA

Graeber, Clark *Tennis Player*
411 Harbor Road, Fairfield, CT 06431
USA

Graelis, Francisco (Pancho) *Editor, Cartoonist*
Le Monde, Editorial Dept, 21 Bis Rue Claude Bernard, Paris, 75005, FRANCE

Graf, Bianca
Oppenheimstr. 6b, Wolfen, GERMANY, D-06766

Graf, Hans
Houston Symphony, Jesse Jones Hall, 615 Louisiana St, Houston, TX 77002 USA

Graf, Stefanie M (Steffi) *Tennis Player*
8921 Andre Dr, Las Vegas, NV 89148 USA

Graff, Ilena *Actor*
11455 Sunshine Terrace, Studio City, CA 91604 USA

Graff, Ilene
11455 Sunshine Terrace, Studio City, CA 91604

Graff, Randy *Actor*
Peter Strawn Assoc, 1501 Broadway, #2900, New York, NY 10036 USA

Graff, Todd
547 Hudson St., New York, NY 10014

Graffin, Guillaume *Ballerina*
American Ballet Theatre, 890 Broadway, New York, NY 10003 USA

Graffman, Gary *Musician*
Curtis Institute of Music, 1726 Locust St, Philadelphia, PA 19103 USA

Grafstein, Bernice *Physicist, Scientist*
Weill Medical College, Physiology Dept, 1300 York Ave, New York, NY 10021 USA

Grafton, Sue *Writer*
PO Box 41446, Santa Barbara, CA 93140 USA

Graham, Alex *Cartoonist*
Tribune Media Services, 435 N Michigan Ave, #1500, Chicago, IL 60611 USA

Graham, Aubrey *Actor*
Noble Caplan Agency, 1260 Yonge St Fl 2, Toronto ON, M4T 1W6, CANADA

Graham, Bob *Senator*
14814 Breckness Pl, Miami Lakes, FL 33016-1458 USA

Graham, Bruce J *Architect*
Graham & Graham, PO Box 8589, Hobe Sound, FL 33475 USA

Graham, Charles P *General*
134 Wabler Way, Georgetown, TX 78628 USA

Graham, Currie
9171 Wilshire Blvd. #406, Beverly Hills, CA 90210-5516

Graham, Daniel *Football Player*
New England Patriots, Gillete Stadium RR 1, 60 Washington, Foxboro, MA 02035 USA

Graham, David *Golfer*
PO Box 4997, Whitfish, MT 59937 USA

Graham, Dirk *Hockey Player, Coach*
7238 E Tyndall St, Mesa, AZ 85207 USA

Graham, Donald E *Publisher*
Washington Post Co, 1150 15th St NW, Washington, DC 20071 USA

Graham, Franklin *Religious Leader*
Samantan's Purse, PO Box 3000, Boone, NC 28607 USA

Graham, Gerrit *Actor*
S M S Talent, 8730 Sunset Blvd, #440, Los Angeles, CA 90069 USA

Graham, Glen *Musician*
Shapiro Co, 9229 Sunset Blvd, #607, Los Angeles, CA 90069 USA

Graham, Heather *Actor*
Creative Artists Agency, 9830 Wilshire Blvd, Beverly Hills, CA 90212 USA

Graham, John R *Writer*
University of California, Astronomy Dept, Berkeley, CA 94720 USA

Graham, Jorie *Writer*
General Delivery, West Tisbury, MA 02575 USA

Graham, Katherine
2920 R St. NW, Washington, DC 20007

Graham, Larry *Musician*
Groove Entertainment, 1005 N Alfred St, #2, West Hollywood, CA 90069 USA

Graham, Lauren *Actor*
Writers & Artists, 8383 Wilshire Blvd, #550, Beverly Hills, CA 90211 USA

Graham, Linda *Bowler*
4147 E Seneca Ave, Des Moines, IA 50317 USA

Graham, Loren R *Historian*
7 Francis Ave, Cambridge, MA 02138 USA

Graham, Lou *Golfer*
85 Concord Park W, Nashville, TN 37205 USA

Graham, Mikey *Musician*
JC Music, 84A Strand on the Green, London, W43 PU, UNITED KINGDOM (UK)

Graham, Otto
2216 Riviera Dr., Saratoga, FL 34232

Graham, Parker *Musician*
Performers of the World, 8901 Melrose Ave, #200, West Hollywood, CA 90069 USA

Graham, Ruth Bell
PO Box 937, Montreat, NC 28757

Graham, Samaria
Independent Management Group (IMG), 717 N Alta Vista Blvd, Los Angeles, CA 90046 USA

Graham, Susan *Opera Singer*
Columbia Artists Mgmt Inc, 165 W 57th St, New York, NY 10019 USA

Graham, William B *Business Person*
40 Devonshire Lane, Kenilworth, IL 60043 USA

Graham, William F (Billy) *Misc*
Billy Graham Evangelistic Assoc, PO Box 1270, Charlotte, NC 28201-1270 USA

Graham, William R *Government Official*
Xsirius Inc, 1110 N Glebe Road, #620, Arlington, VA 22201 USA

Graham-Smith, Francis *Astronomer*
Old School House, Henbury, Macclesfield, Cheshire, SK11 9PH, UNITED KINGDOM (UK)

Grahn, Nancy
4910 Agnes Ave., No. Hollywood, CA 91607

Grahn, Nancy Lee *Actor*
4910 Agnes Ave, North Hollywood, CA 91607 USA

Grainger, David W *Business Person*
WW Grainger Inc, 100 Grainger Parkway, Lake Forest, IL 60045 USA

Gralish, Tom *Photographer, Journalist*
203 E Cottage Ave, Haddonfield, NJ 08033 USA

Gralla, Lawrence *Publisher*
Gralla Publications, 1515 Broadway, New York, NY 10036 USA

Gralla, Milton *Publisher*
Gralla Publications, 1515 Broadway, New York, NY 10036 USA

Gramatica, Martin *Football Player*
PO Box 2291, Labelle, FL 33975 USA

Gramlich, Edward M *Economist, Government Official*
Federal Reserve Board, 20th & Constitution Aves NW, Washington, DC 20551 USA

Gramm, Lou *Musician*
Hard to Handle Mgmt, 16501 Ventura Blvd, #602, Encino, CA 91436 USA

Gramm, W Philip (Phil) *Senator*
UBS Warburg, 299 Park Ave, New York, NY 10171 USA

Gramm, Wendy L *Government Official*
Commodity Futures Trading Commission, 2033 K St NW, Washington, DC 20006 USA

Grammer, Kathy *Actor*
Artists Agency, 1180 S Beverly Dr, #301, Los Angeles, CA 90035 USA

Grammer, Kelsey *Actor*
Grammnet Productions, 5555 Melrose Ave, Lucy Bungalow 206 (TV), Los Angeles, CA 90038-3197

Gran, Phyllis
Penguin/Pitnam Publishing, 200 Madison Ave, New York, NY 10016

Granatelli, Andy *Misc*
1469 Edgecliff Lane, Montecito, CA 93108 USA

Granato, Catherine (Cammi) *Hockey Player*
13454 Wood Duck Dr, Plainfield, IL 60544 USA

Granato, Tony *Hockey Player, Coach*
11657 E Berry Dr, Eaglewood, CO 80111 USA

Grand Funk Railroad
1229 17th Ave. So., Nashville, TN 37212

Grand Ole Opry
2804 Opryland Dr, Nashville, TN 37214

Grandberry, Omari *Actor*
Ultimate Group, The, 848 N La Cienega Blvd #201, W Hollywood, CA 90069 USA

Grandin, Temple *Scientist*
2918 Silver Plume Dr, #C3, Fort Collins, CO 80526 USA

Grandmaster, Mele-Mel *Musician*
Groove Entertainment, 1005 N Alfred St, #2, West Hollywood, CA 90069 USA

Grandmont, Jean-Michel *Economist*
55 Blvd de Charonne, Les Doukas 23, Paris, 75011, FRANCE

Grandpre, Mary *Designer*
Scholastic Press, 555 Broadway, New York, NY 10012 USA

Grandy, Fred *Actor*
9417 Spruce Tree Circle, Bethesda, MD 20814 USA

Granger, Clive W J *Nobel Prize Laureate*
University of California, Economics Dept, 9500 Gilman Dr, La Jolla, CA 92093 USA

Granger, David *Athlete*
Ingalls & Snyder, 61 Broadway, #3100, New York, NY 10006 USA

Granger, Farley *Actor*
Dakota Hotel, 1 W 72nd St, #25D, New York, NY 10023 USA

Grannis, Paul D *Physicist*
Fermi Nat Accelerator Lab, CDF Collaboration, PO Box 500, Batavia, IL 60510 USA

Grant, Amy *Musician, Songwriter*
Po Box 2530, Nashville, TN 37202 USA

Grant, Beth
2852 Hollyridge Dr., Los Angeles, CA 90068

Grant, Boyd *Coach*
Colorado State University, Athletic Dept, Fort Collins, CO 80523 USA

Grant, Brian *Basketball Player*
145 Solano Prado, Coral Gables, FL 33156 USA

Grant, Bud
8134 Oakmere Rd, Bloomington, MN 55438-1333

Grant, Charles *Actor*
Media Artists Group, 6300 Wilshire Blvd, #1470, Los Angeles, CA 90048 USA

Grant, David Marshall *Actor*
International Creative Management (ICM-LA), 8942 Wilshire Blvd, Beverly Hills, CA 90211 USA

Grant, Deborah *Actor*
Larry Datzall, 17 Broad Court, #12, London, WC2B 5QN, UNITED KINGDOM (UK)

Grant, Edmond (Eddy) *Musician, Songwriter*
Consolidated Ale, PO Box 87, Tarporley, CW6 9FN, UNITED KINGDOM (UK)

Grant, Faye *Actor*
B & B Entertainment, 1640 S Sepulveda Blvd, #530, Los Angeles, CA 90025 USA

Grant, Gil *Producer*
Principal Entertainment (LA), 1964 Westwood Blvd #400, Los Angeles, CA 90025 USA

Grant, Gogi *Musician*
10323 Alamo Ave, #202, Los Angeles, CA 90064 USA

Grant, Harold P (Bud) *Football Player, Basketball Player, Coach*
8134 Oakmere Road, Bloomington, MN 55438 USA

Grant, Horace *Basketball Player*
719 N Eucalyptus Ave, #25B, Inglewood, CA 90302 USA

Grant, Hugh *Actor*
Redcliffe Road, #36, London, SW10 JNJ, UNITED KINGDOM (UK)

Grant, Hugh Jr *Misc*
414 E 75th St, #4, Gainesville, FL 32604 USA

Grant, James T (Mudcat) *Baseball Player*
1020 S Dunsmuir Ave, Los Angeles, CA 90019 USA

Grant, Jennifer *Actor*
Propaganda Films Mgmt, 1741 Ivar Ave, Los Angeles, CA 90028 USA

Grant, Johnny
7000 Hollywood Blvd, PH, Hollywood, 90028

Grant, Lee *Actor, Director*
Artists Agency, 10100 Santa Monica Blvd, #2490, Los Angeles, CA 90067 USA

Grant, Mickie *Actor*
250 W 94th St, #6G, New York, NY 10025 USA

Grant, Paul *Basketball Player*
Milwaukee Bucks, Bradley Center, 1001 N 4th St, Milwaukee, WI 53203 USA

Grant, Richard E *Actor*
International Creative Mgmt, 76 Oxford St, London, W1N 0AX, UNITED KINGDOM (UK)

Grant, Robert M *Educator*
RR 1 Box 1423, Berlin, NH 03570 USA

Grant, Rodney A *Actor*
Omar, 526 N Larchmont Blvd, Los Angeles, CA 90004 USA

Grant, Susannah *Writer, Director*
Creative Artists Agency LCC (CAA-LA), 9830 Wilshire Blvd, Beverly Hills, CA 90212 USA

Grant, Tom *Musician*
Brad Simon Organization, 122 E 57th St, #300, New York, NY 10022 USA

Grant, Toni *Misc*
610 S Ardmore Ave, Los Angeles, CA 90005 USA

Granville, Joseph *Financier, Writer*
Granville Market Letter, 2525 Market St, Kansas City, MO 64108 USA

Grass, Gunter *Nobel Prize Laureate*
Sekfretariat Glockengiesserstr 21, Lubeck, 23552, GERMANY

Grass, Gunther
Glockengiesserstr. 21, Lubeck, D-23552, GERMANY

Grassie, Karen *Actor*
PO Box 913, Pacific Palisades, CA 900272 USA

Grassle, Karen
PO Box 913, Pacific Palisades, CA 90272-0913

Grasso, Richard A *Financier*
New York Stock Exchange, 11 Wall St, New York, NY 10005 USA

Grassroots, The
108 E. Matilija St., Ojai, CA 93023

Grata, Enrique *Actor*
Univision, 314 Main St, Chico, CA 95928 USA

Grateful Dead
PO Box 1073-C, San Rafael, CA 94915

Grau, Shirley Ann *Writer*
12 Nassau Dr, Metairie, LA 70005 USA

Grauer, Ona *Actor*
Performers Management, 258 E 3rd St #B, Vancouver BC, V7W 1E7, CANADA

Grausman, Philip *Artist*
21 Barnes Road, Washington, CT 06793 USA

Gravel, Maurice R (Mike) *Senator*
1600 N Oak St, #1412, Arlington, VA 22209 USA

Graveline, Duane E *Astronaut*
494 Pleasant St, Island Pond, VT 05846 USA

Graves, Adam *Hockey Player*
574 Lis Crescent, Windsor, ON N9G 2M5, CANADA

Graves, Alex *Producer*
International Creative Management (ICM-LA), 8942 Wilshire Blvd, Beverly Hills, CA 90211 USA

Graves, Denyce *Actor*
Don Buchwald & Associates Inc (LA), 6500 Wilshire Blvd #2200, Los Angeles, CA 90048 USA

Graves, Denyce *Opera Singer*
Columbia Artists Mgmt Inc, 165 W 57th St, New York, NY 10019 USA

Graves, Earl G *Publisher*
Black Enterprise Magazine, 130 5th Ave, New York, NY 10011 USA

Graves, Ernest Jr *General*
2328 S Nash St, Arlington, VA 22202 USA

Graves, Harold N Jr *Journalist, Government Official*
4816 Grantham Ave, Chevy Chase, MD 20815 USA

Graves, Michael *Architect*
341 Nassau St, Princeton, NJ 08540 USA

Graves, Peter *Actor*
William Morris Agency (WMA-LA), 1 William Morris Pl, Beverly Hills, CA 90212 USA

Graves, Ray *Football Coach*
4230 Hartwood Lane, Tampa, FL 33624 USA

Graves, Richard G *General*
3107 Iron Stone Lane, San Antonio, TX 78230 USA

Graves, Rupert *Actor*
P F D, Drury House, 34-43 Russell St, London, WC2B 5HA, UNITED KINGDOM (UK)

Gravitte, Beau *Actor*
Paradigm Agency, 10100 Santa Monica Blvd, #2500, Los Angeles, CA 90067 USA

Gray, Alasdair J *Writer*
McAlpine, 2 Marchmont Terrace, Glasgow, G12 9LT, SCOTLAND

Gray, Alfred M Jr *General*
6317 Chaucer View Circle, Alexandria, VA 22304 USA

Gray, Billy *Actor*
19612 Grandview Dr, Topanga Canyon, CA 90290 USA

Gray, C Boyden *Government Official*
Wilmer Cutler Pickering, 2445 M St NW, Washington, DC 20037 USA

Gray, Coleen *Actor*
2337 Roscomare Road, #2-112, Los Angeles, CA 90077 USA

Gray, Colleen
2337 Roscomare Rd. #2-112, Los Angeles, CA 90077-1851

Gray, D'Wayne *General*
3423 Barger Dr, Falls Church, VA 22044 USA

Gray, David *Musician, Songwriter*
Helter Skelter, Plaza, 535 Kings Road, London, SW10 0S, UNITED KINGDOM (UK)

Gray, Dobie *Musician*
2211 Elliott Ave, Nashville, T N, 37204 USA

Gray, Doug *Musician*
Ron Rainey Mgmt, 315 S Beverly Dr, #407, Beverly Hills, CA 90212 USA

Gray, Duicie *Actor*
Barry Burnett, 31 Coventry St, London, W1V 8AS, UNITED KINGDOM (UK)

Gray, Dulcie
44 Brunswick Gardens #2, London, W8 4AN, ENGLAND

Gray, Ed *Basketball Player*
Houston Rockets, Toyota Center, 2 E Greenway Plaza, Houston, TX 77046 USA

Gray, Erin *Actor, Model*
10921 Alta View Dr, Studio City, CA 91604 USA

Gray, F Gary *Director*
H S I Productions, 3630 Eastham Dr, Culver City, CA 90232 USA

Gray, Fred Sr *Attorney General*
1005 Lakeshore Dr, Tuskegee, AL 36083 USA

Gray, George W *Misc*
Juniper House, Furzehill, Wimborne, Dorset, BH21 4HD, UNITED KINGDOM (UK)

Gray, Harry B *Misc*
1415 E California Blvd, Pasadena, CA 91106 USA

Gray, James *Director, Writer*
United Talent Agency, 9560 Wilshire Blvd, #500, Beverly Hills, CA 90212 USA

Gray, Jerry *Football Player*
27 Birdsong Parkway, Orchard Park, NY 14127 USA

Gray, Jim *Actor*
3325 Blair Drive, Los Angeles, CA 90068 USA

Gray, John *Writer*
Relationship Speakers Network, PO Box 12695, Scottsdale, AZ 85267 USA

Gray, Ken *Football Player*
356 Camoa Pajama Lane, Kingsland, TX 78639 USA

Gray, L Patrick III *Lawyer*
PO Box 1591, New London, CT 06320 USA

Gray, Linda *Actor*
PO Box 5064, Sherman Oaks, CA 91403 USA

Gray, Macy *Musician, Songwriter*
H K Mgmt, 9200 W Sunset Blvd, #530, Los Angeles, CA 90069 USA

Gray, Mel *Football Player*
2415 S Perryville Road, Rockford, IL 61108 USA

Gray, Michael
9294 Civic Center Dr., Beverly Hills, CA 90210

Gray, Simon J H *Writer*
Judy Daish, 2 Saint Charles Place, London, W10 6EG, UNITED KINGDOM (UK)

Gray, Spaiding *Artist, Writer*
22 Wooster St, New York, NY 10013 USA

Gray, Tamyra *Musician*
Fox Television Studios, 10201 W Pico Blvd, Bldg 41, Los Angeles, CA 90035

Gray, Theordore G (Ted) *Baseball Player*
2917 S Ocean Blvd, #1005, Highland Beach, FL 33487 USA

Gray, William H III *Misc*
United Negro College Fund, 500 E 62nd St, New York, NY 10021 USA

Graybeal, Mike *Actor*
Stein Entertainment Group, 11271 Ventura Blvd #477, Studio City, CA 91604 USA

Graybiel, Ann M *Scientist*
Massachusetts Institute of Technology, Cognitive Sci Dept, Cambridge, MA 02139 USA

Grayden, Sprague *Actor*
Abrams Artists Agency (LA), 9200 Sunset Blvd Fl 11, Los Angeles, CA 90069 USA

Graydon, Joe
1870 Caminito Del Cielo, Glendale, CA 91208

Grayhm, Steven *Actor*
Evolution Entertainment, 901 N Highland Ave, Los Angeles, CA 90038 USA

Graysmith, Robert *Editor, Cartoonist*
San Francisco Chronicle, 901 Mission St, San Francisco, CA 94103 USA

Grayson, C Jackson Jr *Government Official, Educator*
123 N Post Oak Lane, Houston, TX 77024 USA

Grayson, Kathryn *Actor, Musician*
Ruth Webb, 10580 Des Moines Ave, Northridge, CA 91326 USA

Grazer, Brian *Producer*
Imagine Entertainment, 9465 Wilshire Blvd Fl 7, Beverly Hills, CA 90212 USA

Grazia, Eugene *Hockey Player*
2421 NE 49th St, Fort Lauderdale, FL 33308 USA

Graziani, Ariel *Soccer Player*
San Jose Earthquakes, 3550 Stevens Creek Blvd, #200, San Jose, CA 95117 USA

Grazioso, Claudia *Writer, Producer*
International Creative Management (ICM-LA), 8942 Wilshire Blvd, Beverly Hills, CA 90211 USA

Grazzola, Kenneth E *Publisher*
Aviation Week Magazine, 1221 Ave of Americas, New York, NY 10020 USA

Greason, Staci
8831 Sunset Blvd. #304, Los Angeles, CA 90069

Great Big Sea *Musician*
Fleming & Associates, 733-735 North Main, Ann Arbor, MI 48104-1030

Greatbatch, Wilson *Inventor*
10000 Wehrie Dr, Clarence, NY 14031 USA

Grebenshchikov, Boris *Musician*
2 Marata St, #3, Saint Petersburg, RUSSIA

Grechko, Georgi M *Cosmonaut*
Potcha Kosmonavtov, Moskovskoi Oblasti, Syvisdny Goroduk, 141160, RUSSIA

Greco, Buddy *Musician*
Zane Mgmt, 1301 Yarmouth Road, Wynnewood, PA 19096 USA

Greco, Emilio *Artist*
Viale Cortina d'Ampezzo 132, Rome, 00135, ITALY

Greco, Juliette *Actor, Musician*
Maurice Maraouani, 37 Rue Marbeuf, Paris, 75008, FRANCE

Greco, Michael *Actor*
EastEnders, BBC Elstree Centre, Clarendon Road, Borehamwood, Herts, UNITED KINGDOM

Greeley, Andrew
6030 S. Ellis, Chicago, IL 60637

Greeley, Andrew M (Andy) *Writer*
6030 S Ellis Ave, Chicago, IL 60637 USA

Green, A C *Basketball Player*
201 E Jefferson St, Phoenix, AZ 85004 USA

Green, Adolph
211 Central Park W. #19E, New York, NY 10024

Green, Ahman *Football Player*
Green Bay Packers, PO Box 10628, Green Bay, WI 54307 USA

Green, Al *Musician*
William Morris Agency (WMA-NY), 1325 Ave of the Americas, New York, NY 10019 USA

Green, Al *Musician, Songwriter*
PO Box 456, Millington, TN 38083 USA

Green, B Eric *Football Player*
13131 Luntz Point Lane, Windermere, FL 34786 USA

Green, Barry *Misc*
Team Green, 7615 Zionsville Road, Indianapolis, IN 46268 USA

Green, Benny *Musician*
Jazz Tree, 211 Thompson St, #1D, New York, NY 10012 USA

Green, Brian Austin *Actor*
Interlink Management, 5061 Bluebell Ave, N Hollywood, CA 91607-2937 USA

Green, Charlie *Stylist*
Bryan Bantry, 4 W 58th St #PH, New York, NY 10019 USA

Green, Dallas *Baseball Player*
548 S Guernsey Rd, West Grove, PA 19390 USA

Green, Darrell *Football Player*
PO Box 30003, Alexandria, VA 22310 USA

Green, David *Director*
International Creative Mgmt, 76 Oxford St, London, W1N 0AX, UNITED KINGDOM (UK)

Green, David E *Misc*
5339 Brody Dr, Madison, WI 53705 USA

Green, David Gordon *Director, Producer, Writer*
International Creative Management (ICM-LA), 8942 Wilshire Blvd, Beverly Hills, CA 90211 USA

Green, David T *Inventor*
US Surgical Corp, 150 Glover Ave, Norwalk, CT 06850 USA

Green, Debbie *Volleyball Player*
239 5th St, Seal Beach, CA 90740 USA

Green, Dennis *Football Coach*
FLW Outdoors, Pax-TV, 601 Cleanwater Park Road, West Palm Beach, FL 33401 USA

Green, Gary F *Football Player*
16330 Walnut Creek Dr, San Antonio, TX 78247 USA

Green, Gerald *Writer*
88 Arrowhead Trail, New Canaan, CT 06840 USA

Green, Guy M *Cinematographer, Director*
Gersh Agency, 232 N Canon Dr, Beverly Hills, CA 90210 USA

Green, Hamilton *Prime Minister*
Plot D Lodge, Georgetown, GUYANA

Green, Howard *Physicist*
Harvard Medical School, Physiology & Biophysics Dept, Boston, MA 02115 USA

Green, Hubert *Golfer*
PO Box 142, Bay Point, Panama City, FL 32402 USA

Green, Janine *Actor*
Sweeney Management, 8755 Lookout Mountain Avenue, Los Angeles, CA 90046 USA

Green, Jeff *Race Car Driver*
Continental, 5909 Peachtree Dunwoody Road NE, Atlanta, GA 30328 USA

Green, John M (Johnny) *Basketball Player*
9 Susan Lane, Dix Hills, NY 11746 USA

Green, John N (Jack) Jr *Cinematographer*
516 Esplanade, #E, Redondo Beach, CA 90277 USA

Green, Kate *Writer*
Bantam/Delacorte/Dell/Doubleday Press, 1540 Broadway, New York, NY 10036 USA

Green, Ken *Golfer*
2875 Antietam Lane, West Palm Beach, FL 33409 USA

Green, Leonard I *Business Person*
Rite Aid Corp, 30 Hunter Lane, Camp Hill, PA 17011 USA

Green, Lucinda *Misc*
Appleshaw House, Andover, Hants, UNITED KINGDOM (UK)

Green, Mark J *Social Activist, Attorney General, Writer*
Democracy Project, 530 E 90th St, #6K, New York, NY 10128 USA

Green, Maurice Spurgeon *Editor*
Hermitage, Twyford House, Hants, UNITED KINGDOM (UK)

Green, Michael *Cinematographer*
11 Stevenson Lane, Upper Saddle River, NJ 07458 USA

Green, Mike *Football Player*
15271 Peach St, Chino Hills, CA 91709 USA

Green, Pat *Musician, Songwriter*
William Morris Agency, 2100 W End Ave, #1000, Nashville, TN 37203 USA

Green, Patricia *Producer, Writer*
Endeavor Agency LLC (LA), 9601 Wilshire Blvd Fl 3, Beverly Hills, CA 90210 USA

Green, Rick *Hockey Player*
RR 1, Peterborough, ON K9J 6X2, CANADA

Green, Robin *Writer*
Broder Webb Chervin Silbermann Agency, The (BWCS), 9242 Beverly Blvd #200, Beverly Hills, CA 90210 USA

Green, Robson *Actor*
Coastal Productions, 25B Broadchare, The Quayside, Newcastle-Upon-Tyne, NE1 3DQ, UNITED KINGDOM (UK)

Green, Sarah *Producer*
International Creative Management (ICM-LA), 8942 Wilshire Blvd, Beverly Hills, CA 90211 USA

Green, Seth *Actor, Comedian*
851 Oreo Place, Pacific Palisades, CA 90272 USA

Green, Shawn D *Baseball Player*
1831 Overview Circle, Santa Ana, CA 92705 USA

Green, Sidney *Basketball Player, Coach*
Florida Atlantic University, Athletic Dept, Boca Raton, FL 33431 USA

Green, Tammie *Golfer*
Ladies Pro Golf Assn, 100 International Golf Dr, Daytona Beach, FL 32124 USA

Green, Timothy J (Tim) *Football Player, Sportscaster*
1194 Breenfield Lane, Skaneateles, NY 13152 USA

Green, Tom *Actor, Comedian*
William Morris Agency, 151 El Camino Dr, Beverly Hills, CA 90212 USA

Green, Travis *Hockey Player*
4-810 Marine Dr, Gibsons, BC 1V0N 1V0, CANADA

Green, Trent *Football Player*
Kansas City Chiefs, 1 Arrowhead Dr, Kansas City, KS 64129 USA

Greenaway, Peter *Director*
Allarts Ltd, 387B King St, London, W6 9NH, UNITED KINGDOM (UK)

Greenberg, Adam *Cinematographer*
Gersh Agency, 232 N Canon Dr, Beverly Hills, CA 90210 USA

Greenberg, Alan C *Financier*
Bear Steams Co, 383 Madison Ave, New York, NY 10017 USA

Greenberg, Bernard *Biologist, Scientist*
1463 E 55th Place, Chicago, IL 60637 USA

Greenberg, Carl *Journalist*
6001 Canterbury Dr, Culver City, CA 90230 USA

Greenberg, Evan *Business Person*
American International Group, 70 Pine St, New York, NY 10270 USA

Greenberg, Jack *Attorney General, Educator*
118 Riverside Dr, New York, NY 10024 USA

Greenberg, Kathy *Writer*
Lloyd and Kass Entertainment, 10202 W Washington Blvd, Bldg Astaire 2210, Culver City, CA 90232 USA

Greenberg, Maurice R *Business Person*
American International Group, 70 Pine St, New York, NY 10270 USA

Greenberg, Morton I *Judge*
US Court of Appeals, Judicial Complex, 402 E State St, Trenton, NJ 08608 USA

Greenberg, Peter *Television Host*
The Today Show, 30 Rockefeller Plaza, Room 347E, New York, NY 10112 USA

Greenberg, Robbie S *Cinematographer*
11 Reef St, Marina del Rey, CA 90292 USA

Greenblatt, Stephen J *Writer*
Harvard University, English Dept, Cambridge, MA 02138 USA

Greenblatt, William
30710 Monte Lado Dr., Malibu, CA 90265

Greenburg, Dan *Writer*
323 E 50th St, New York, NY 10022 USA

Greenburg, Paul *Journalist*
5900 Scenic Dr, Little Rock, AR 72207 USA

Greenbush, Rachel Lindsay *Actor*
Gold Marshak Liedtke, 3500 W Olive Ave, #1400, Burbank, CA 91505 USA

Greenbush, Sidney Robin *Actor*
Gold Marshak Liedtke, 3500 W Olive Ave, #1400, Burbank, CA 91505 USA

Greene, Brian *Physicist, Mathematician*
Columbia University, Physics Dept, New York, NY 10027 USA

Greene, Charles E (Charlie) *Track Athlete*
5650 Hickory Crest Road, Lincoln, NE 68516 USA

Greene, Ellen *Musician*
Innovative Artists, 1505 10th St., Santa Monica, CA 90401 USA

Greene, Graham *Actor*
Susan Smith, 121A N San Vicente Blvd, Beverly Hills, CA 90211 USA

Greene, Jack *Musician*
Ace Productions, PO Box 428, Portland, TN 37148 USA

Greene, Jack P *Historian*
1974 Division Road, East Greenwich, RI 02818 USA

Greene, James
60 Pope's Grove Twickenham, Middlesex, ENGLAND

Greene, Joseph E (Mean Joe) *Football Player, Coach*
3380 S Horizon Place, Chandler, AZ 85248 USA

Greene, Leonard M *Inventor*
6 Hickory Road, Scarsdale, NY 10583 USA

Greene, Maurice *Track Athlete*
HSI Sports Mgmt, 2600 Michelson Dr #680, Irvine, CA 92612 USA

Greene, Mean Joe
2121 George Halas Dr. NW, Canton, OH 44708

Greene, Michele *Actor, Musician*
PO Box 29117, Los Angeles, CA 90029 USA

Greene, Michelle
PO Box 29117, Los Angeles, CA 90029-0117

Greene, Pat *Actor*
GVA Talent Agency Inc, 9229 Sunset Blvd #320, Los Angeles, CA 90069 USA

Greene, Robert B (Bob) Jr *Writer*
Chicago Tribune, Editorial Dept, 435 N Michigan Ave, Chicago, IL 60611 USA

Greene, Shecky *Comedian, Actor*
1642 S La Verne Way, Palm Springs, CA 92264 USA

Greene, Tony *Football Player*
Southeast Recycling, 9001 Brookville Road, Silver Spring, MD 20910 USA

Greenfield, James L *Journalist*
470 Park Ave, #9A, New York, NY 10022 USA

Greenfield, Jeff *Commentator*
Cable News Network, News Dept, 820 1st St NE, Washington, DC 20002 USA

Greengard, Paul *Nobel Prize Laureate*
362 E 69th St, New York, NY 10021 USA

Greengrass, Jim *Athlete*
232 Talking Creek Pro Rd, Chatsworth, GA 30705

Greenhouse, Linda *Journalist*
New York Times, Editorial Dept, 229 W 43rd St, New York, NY 10036 USA

Greenlee, David *Actor*
1811 N Whitley, #800, Los Angeles, CA 90028 USA

Greenspan, Alan *Business Person*
International Arts Entertainment, 8899 Beverly Blvd #800, Los Angeles, CA 90048

Greenspan, Alan *Financier, Government Official*
Federal Reserve Board, 20th St & Constitution Ave NW, Washington, DC 20551 USA

Greenspan, Bud *Producer, Director*
118 E 57th St, New York, NY 10022 USA

Greenspan, Melissa *Actor*
International Creative Management (ICM-LA), 8942 Wilshire Blvd, Beverly Hills, CA 90211 USA

Greenspoon, Jimmy *Musician*
McKenzie Accountancy, 5171 Caliente St, #134, Las Vegas, NV 89119 USA

Greenstein, Jeff *Producer*
Broder Webb Chervin Silbermann Agency, The (BWCS), 9242 Beverly Blvd #200, Beverly Hills, CA 90210 USA

Greenville, Georgina *Model*
Next Model Mgmt, 188 Rue de Rivoli, Paris, 75001, FRANCE

Greenwald, Milton *Misc*
University of California, Museum of Paleontology, Berkeley, CA 94720 USA

Greenwalt, T Jack *Misc*
2444 Madison Road, #1501, Cincinnati, OH 45208 USA

Greenwell, Michael L (Mike) *Baseball Player*
Family Fun Park, 35 NE Pine Island Road, Cape Coral, FL 33909 USA

Greenwich, Ellie *Musician*
203 SW 3rd Ave, Gainesville, FL 32601 USA

Greenwood, Bruce *Actor*
1465 Lindacrest Dr, Beverly Hills, CA 90210 USA

Greenwood, Colin *Musician*
Nasty Little Man, 72 Spring St, #1100, New York, NY 10012 USA

Greenwood, Jonny *Musician*
Nasty Little Man, 72 Spring St, #1100, New York, NY 10012 USA

Greenwood, L C H (L C) *Football Player*
329 S Dallas Ave, Pittsburg, PA 15208 USA

Greenwood, Lee *Musician, Songwriter*
Lee Greenwood Inc, 1025 16th Ave S, #301, Nashville, TN 37212 USA

Greenwood, Michael
Princes Gate1 4 Kingston House E, London, ENGLAND, SW7

Greenwood, Norman *Misc*
University of Leeds, Chemistry Dept, Leeds, LS2 9JT, UNITED KINGDOM (UK)

Greer, Brodie
300 S. Raymond Ave. #II, Pasadena, CA 91105

Greer, Dabbs *Actor*
284 S Madison, #102, Pasadena, CA 91101 USA

Greer, David S *Misc*
Brown University, PO Box G, Providence, RI 02912 USA

Greer, Germaine *Writer*
Atkin & Stone, 29 Fernshaw Road, London, SW10 0TG, UNITED KINGDOM (UK)

Greer, Gordon G *Editor*
Better Homes & Gardens Magazine, 1716 Locust St, Des Moines, IA 50309 USA

Greer, Harold E (Hal) *Basketball Player*
7900 E Princess Dr, #1021, Scottsdale, AZ 85255 USA

Greer, Howard *Admiral*
8539 Prestwick Dr, La Jolia, CA 92037 USA

Greer, Judy *Actor*
Creative Artists Agency, 9830 Wilshire Blvd, Beverly Hills, CA 90212 USA

Greevy, Bernadette *Musician*
Melrose, 672 Howth Road, Dublin, 5, IRELAND

Gregg, A Forrest *Football Player, Football Coach, Football Executive*
2985 Plaza Azul, Santa Fe, NM 87507 USA

Gregg, Clark *Actor*
United Talent Agency, 9560 Wilshire Blvd, #500, Beverly Hills, CA 90212 USA

Gregg, Eric E *Baseball Player*
34 S Merion Ave, Bryn Mawr, PA 19010 USA

Gregg, John
1/1 Punch St., Mosman, AUSTRALIA, NSW 2088

Gregg, Ricky Lynn *Musician*
ER Rimes Mgmt, 1103 Bell Grimes Lane, Nashville, TN 37207 USA

Gregg, Stephen *Writer*
Creative Artists Agency LCC (CAA-LA), 9830 Wilshire Blvd, Beverly Hills, CA 90212 USA

Gregg, Stephen R *War Hero*
130 Lexington Ave, Bayonne, NJ 07002 USA

Gregorian, Vartan *Educator*
Camegie Corp, President's Office, 437 Madison Ave, New York, NY 10022 USA

Gregorio, Rose *Actor*
Don Buchwald, 6500 Wilshire Blvd, #2200, Los Angeles, CA 90048 USA

Gregorios, Metropolitan Paulos M *Religious Leader*
Orthodox Seminary, PO Box 98, Kottayam, Kerala, 686001, INDIA

Gregory, Adam *Musician*
SL Feldman & Associates, 1505 W 2nd Ave #200, Vancouver BC, V6H 3Y, CANADA

Gregory, Andre *Actor*
William Morris Agency (WMA-NY), 1325 Ave of the Americas, New York, NY 10019 USA

Gregory, Bettina L *Commentator*
ABC-TV, News Dept, 5010 Creston St, Hyattsville, MD 20781 USA

Gregory, Cynthia *Ballerina*
American Ballet Theatre, 890 Broadway, New York, NY 10003 USA

Gregory, David
2200 Fletcher Ave., Ft. Lee, NJ 07024

Gregory, Dick *Actor, Comedian, Social Activist*
Dick Gregory Health Enterprise, PO Box 3270, Plymouth, MA 02361 USA

Gregory, Dorian *Actor, Television Host*
Compass Entertainment Group, 9255 Sunset Blvd #727, Los Angeles, CA 90069 USA

Gregory, Frederick D *Astronaut*
506 Tulip Road, Annapolis, MD 21403 USA

Gregory, Kathy *Cartoonist*
Playboy Magazine, Reader Services, 680 N Lake Shore Dr, Chicago, IL 60611 USA

Gregory, Nick *Actor*
Writers & Artists, 8383 Wilshire Blvd, #550, Beverly Hills, CA 90211 USA

Gregory, Paul
PO Box 38, Palm Springs, CA 92262

Gregory, Richard *Religious Leader*
Independent Fundamental Churches, 2684 Meadow Ridge, Byron Center, MI 49315 USA

Gregory, Roberta *Artist*
Fantagraphics Books, 7563 Lake City Way, Seattle, WA 98115 USA

Gregory, Stephen *Actor*
Carey, 64 Thornton Ave, London, W4 1QQ, UNITED KINGDOM (UK)

Gregory, William G *Astronaut*
2027 E Freeport Lane, Gilbert, AZ 85234 USA

Gregory, William H *Editor*
Aviation Week Magazine, 1221 Ave of Americas, New York, NY 10020 USA

Gregory, Wilton D *Religious Leader*
Illinois Diocese, Chancery Office, 222 S 3rd St, Belleville, IL 62220 USA

Gregory Moss, Shad (Lil Bow Wow)
Musician, Actor
Creative Artists Agency LCC (CAA-LA), 9830 Wilshire Blvd, Beverly Hills, CA 90212 USA

Gregory-Paul, Zoe *Actor*
Gordon Rael Agency LLC (GRA), 9242 Beverly Blvd, 3rd Floor, Beverly Hills, CA 90210 USA

Gregson, Wallace C *General*
Commanding General, Marine Forces Pacific, Camp HM Smith, HI 96861 USA

Gregson Wagner, Natasha *Actor*
Writers & Artists, 8383 Wilshire Blvd, #550, Beverly Hills, CA 90211 USA

Gregson-Williams, Harry *Composer*
Gorfaine/Schwartz, 13245 Riverside Dr, #450, Sherman Oaks, CA 91423 USA

Grehl, Michael *Editor*
Memphis Commercial Appeal, Editorial Dept, 495 Union Ave, Memphis, TN 38103 USA

Greiner, William R *Educator*
State University of New York, President's Office, Buffalo, NY 14221 USA

Greiner-Petter-Memm, Simone *Athlete*
Am Sportplatz 14, Waldau, 98667, GERMANY

Greise, Bob *Athlete*
3195 Ponce de Leon Blvd #412, Coral Gables, FL 33134

Greist, Kim *Actor*
Innovative Artists, 1505 10th St, Santa Monica, CA 90401 USA

Grelf, Michael *Director*
La Jolla Playhouse, PO Box 12039, La Jolla, CA 92039 USA

Grenier, Adrian *Actor*
1610 Broadway, Santa Monica, CA 90404 USA

Grenier, Sylvain *Wrestler*
World Wrestling Entertainment (WWE), 1241 E Main St, Stamford, CT 06905 USA

Grenier, Zach *Actor*
Essential Talent Management, 6399 Wilshire Blvd #400, Los Angeles, CA 90048 USA

Grentz, Theresa Shank *Coach*
University of Illinois, Athletic Dept, Champaign, IL 61820 USA

Gretzky, Wayne *Hockey Player*
Goldman Grant Tani, 9100 Wilshire Blvd, #1000W, Beverly Hills, CA 90212 USA

Grevey, Kevin *Basketball Player*
528 River Bend Road, Great Falls, VA 22066 USA

Grey, Beryl E *Ballerina*
Fernhill Priory Road, Forest Row, East Sussex, RH18 5JE, UNITED KINGDOM (UK)

Grey, Jennifer *Actor*
Jason Weinberg Mgmt, 122 E 25th St, #124, New York, NY 10010 USA

Grey, Joel *Actor*
Park Ave Talent Network, 404 Park Ave S, #1000, New York, NY 10016 USA

Greyeyes, Michael
3500 W. Olive Ave. #1400, Burbank, CA 91505

Gribow, Patti
3303 Clarendon Rd., Beverly Hills, CA 90210

Grich, Robert A (Bobby) *Baseball Player*
31 Madison Lane, Coto de Caze, CA 92679 USA

Grieco, Richard *Actor*
CR&G Enterprises, 95 Public Square, #304, Watertown, NY 13601 USA

Grieder, William *Journalist*
Simon & Schuster, 1230 Ave of Americas, New York, NY 10020 USA

Griem, Helmut *Actor*
Mgmt Erna Baumbauer, Keplerstr 2, Munich, 81679, GERMANY

Grier, David Alan *Actor, Comedian*
Endeavor Talent Agency, 9701 Wilshire Blvd, #1000, Beverly Hills, CA 90212 USA

Grier, Herbert E *Engineer*
9648 Blackgold Road, La Jolla, CA 92037 USA

Grier, Pam *Actor*
PO Box 370958, Denver, CO 80237 USA

Grier, Roosevelt (Rosey) *Football Player, Actor*
1250 4th St, #600, Santa Monica, CA 90401 USA

Gries, Jonathan *Actor*
Diverse Talent Group, 1875 Century Park E #2250, Los Angeles, CA 90067 USA

Griese, Robert A (Bob) *Football Player, Sportscaster*
3195 Ponce de Leon Blvd, #412, Coral Gables, FL 33134 USA

Griesemer, John N *Government Official*
RR 2 Box 204B, Springfield, MO 65802 USA

Grieve, Pierson M *Business Person*
Ecolab Inc, Ecolab Center, 370 Wabasha St N, Saint Paul, MN 55102 USA

Griffey, G Kenneth (Ken) *Baseball Player*
24606 SE Old Black Nugget Road, Issaquah, WA 98029 USA

Griffey Ken Sr *Athlete*
8216 Princeton Glendale Rd #103, Westchester, OH 45069, US

Griffey Sr, G Kenneth (Ken) *Athlete, Baseball Player*
6233 Foxfield Court, Windermere, FL 34786 USA

Griffin, Adrian *Basketball Player*
Dallas Marvericks, 2909 Taylor St, Dallas, TX 75226 USA

Griffin, Archie
4965 St. Andrews Dr., Westerville, OH 43082-8743

Griffin, Archie M *Football Player*
6845 Temperance Point Place, Westerville, OH 43082 USA

Griffin, David
13 Spencer Gardens, London, ENGLAND, SW14 7AH

Griffin, Eddie *Actor, Comedian*
Brillstein-Grey Entertainment, 9150 Wilshire Blvd #350, Beverly Hills, CA 90212 USA

Griffin, Eddie *Basketball Player*
Houston Rockets, Toyota Center, 2 E Greenway Plaza, Houston, TX 77046 USA

Griffin, Eric *Boxer*
PO Box 964, Jasper, TN 37347 USA

Griffin, James
25 Paulson Dr., Burlington, MA 01803

Griffin, James Bennett *Misc*
5023 Wyandot Court, Bethesda, MD 20816 USA

Griffin, Johnny *Musician*
Joel Chriss, 300 Mercer St, #3J, New York, NY 10003 USA

Griffin, Kathy *Actor*
United Talent Agency, 9560 Wilshire Blvd, #500, Beverly Hills, CA 90212 USA

Griffin, Merv *Entertainer*
Merv Griffin Enterprises, 9860 Wilshire Blvd, Beverly Hills, CA 90210 USA

Griffin, Patty *Musician, Songwriter*
Monterey Peninsula Artists, 509 Hartnell St, Monterey, CA 93940 USA

Griffin, Robert P *Senator, Judge*
Michigan Supreme Court, PO Box 30052, Lansing, MI 48909 USA

Griffin, Rod L *Writer*
$olvency International Inc, PO Box 17802, Clearwater, FL 33762 USA

Griffin, Thomas N Jr *General*
9749 Park Circle, Fairfax Station, VA 22039 USA

Griffith, Alan R *Financier*
Bank of New York, 1 Wall St, New York, NY 10286 USA

Griffith, Andy *Actor, Musician*
William Morris Agency (WMA-LA), 1 William Morris Pl, Beverly Hills, CA 90212 USA

Griffith, Anthony *Actor*
Spivak Sobol Entertainment, 11845 W Olympic Blvd #1125, Los Angeles, CA 90064 USA

Griffith, Bill *Cartoonist*
Pinhead Productions, PO Box 88, Hadlyme, CT 06439 USA

Griffith, Darrell *Basketball Player*
1300 Leighton Circle, Louisville, KY 40222 USA

Griffith, Emile A *Boxer*
150 Washington St, #6J, Hempstead, NY 11550 USA

Griffith, James *Business Person*
Timken Co, 1835 Dueber Ave SW, Canton, OH 44706 USA

Griffith, Melanie *Actor, Producer*
William Morris Agency (WMA-LA), 1 William Morris Pl, Beverly Hills, CA 90212 USA

Griffith, Nanci *Musician, Songwriter*
Gold Mountain, 2 Music Circle S, #212, Nashville, TN 37203 USA

Griffith, Robert *Football Player*
Cleveland Browns, 76 Lou Groza Blvd, Berea, OH 44017 USA

Griffith, Thomas Ian *Actor*
Endeavor Talent Agency, 9701 Wilshire Blvd, #1000, Beverly Hills, CA 90212 USA

Griffith, Tom W *Misc*
Rural Letter Carriers Assn, 1448 Duke St, #100, Alexandria, VA 22314 USA

Griffith, Wendy *Television Host, Religious Leader*
CBN Newswatch, 977 Centerville Tpke, Virginia Beach, VA 23464 USA

Griffith, Yolanda *Basketball Player*
Sacramento Monarchs, Arco Arena, 1 Sports Parkway, Sacramento, CA 95834 USA

Griffiths, Phillip A *Mathematician*
Advanced Study Institute, Director's Office, Olden Lane, Princeton, NJ 08540 USA

Griffiths, Rachel *Actor*
United Talent Agency, 9560 Wilshire Blvd, #500, Beverly Hills, CA 90212 USA

Griffiths, Richard *Actor*
BBC Television Centre, Incoming Mail, Wood Lane, London, W12 7RJ, UNITED KINGDOM (UK)

Griffiths, Susan
9300 Wilshire Blvd. #410, Beverly Hills, CA 90212

Griggs, Andy *Musician*
PO Box 120835, Nashville, TN 37212 USA

Grijalva, Lucy *Writer*
PO Box 1634, Benicia, CA 94510

Grijalva, Victor E *Business Person*
Schlumberger Ltd, 277 Park Ave, New York, NY 10172 USA

Grill, Rob *Musician*
Paradise Artists, 108 E Matilija St, Ojai, CA 93023 USA

Grim, Robert (Bob) *Football Player*
18 NW Saginaw Ave, Bend, OR 97701 USA

Grimaldi, Dan *Actor*
Sopranos, The, 42-22 22nd St Fl 3, Long Island City, NY 11101 USA

Grimaud, Helene *Musician*
I C M Artists, 40 W 57th St, New York, NY 10019 USA

Grimes, Gary
4578 W. 165th St., Lawndale, CA 90260

Grimes, Karolyn
PO Box 145, Carnation, WA 98014

Grimes, Martha *Writer*
115 D St SE, #G-6, Washington, DC 20003 USA

Grimes, Scott *Actor*
12019 Moccasin Court, Orlando, FL 32828 USA

Grimes, Tammy *Actor, Musician*
Don Buchwald, 10 E 44th St, New York, NY 10017 USA

Grimes, Tinsley *Actor*
Innovative Artists (LA), 1505 Tenth St, Santa Monica, CA 90401 USA

Griminelli, Andrea *Musician*
Columbia Artists Mgmt Inc, 165 W 57th St, New York, NY 10019 USA

Grimm, Russ *Football Player, Football Coach*
12177 Hickory Knoll Place, Fairfax, VA 22033 USA

Grimm, Tim *Actor*
Abrams Artists, 9200 Sunset Blvd, #1125, Los Angeles, CA 90069 USA

Grimshaw, Nicholas T *Architect*
1 Conway St, Fitzroy Square, London, W1P 5HA, UNITED KINGDOM (UK)

Grimsley, Ross A *Baseball Player*
PO Box 4587, Timonium, MD 21094 USA

Grimsson, Olafur Ragnar *President*
President's Office, Sto'marradshusini v/Lackjartog, Reykjavik, ICELAND

Grinberg, Anouk *Actor*
Artmedia, 20 Ave Rapp, Paris, 75007, FRANCE

Grindenko, Tatyana T *Musician*
Moscow State Philharmonic, Tverskaya Str 31, Moscow, 103050, RUSSIA

Grindlay, Annie *Actor*
Lichtman/Salners, 12216 Moorpark St, Studio City, CA 91604 USA

Griner, Paul *Writer*
Random House, 1745 Broadway, #B1, New York, NY 10019 USA

Grinham, Rawley Judy *Swimmer*
103 Green Lane Northwood, Middx, HA6 1AP, UNITED KINGDOM (UK)

Grinnell, Alan D *Physicist*
University of California, Medical School, Lewis Center, Los Angeles, CA 90024 USA

Grinstead, Irish *Musician*
Creative Artists Agency, 9830 Wilshire Blvd, Beverly Hills, CA 90212 USA

Grinstead, LeMisha *Musician*
Creative Artists Agency, 9830 Wilshire Blvd, Beverly Hills, CA 90212 USA

Grinstein, Gerald *Business Person*
Delta Airlines, Hartsfield International Airport, Atlanta, GA 30320 USA

Grint, Rupert *Actor*
Studio, 63A Ladbroke Road, London, W11 3PD, UNITED KINGDOM (UK)

Grinville, Patrick *Writer*
Academie Goncourt, 38 Rue du Faubourg Saint Jacques, Paris, 75014, FRANCE

Grisanti, Eugene P *Business Person*
International Flavors, 521 W 57th St, New York, NY 10019 USA

Grisez, Germain *Misc*
Mount Saint Mary's College, Christain Ethics Dept, Emmitsburg, MD 21727 USA

Grisham, John *Writer*
Gernert Company, 136 E 57th St, New York, NY 10022 USA

Grishin, Evgenil *Speed Skater*
Committee of Physical Culture, Skatertny Pl 4, Moscow, RUSSIA

Grishuk, Okasana (Pasha) *Dancer*
Int'l Mgmt Group, 22 E 71st St, New York, NY 10021 USA

Grishuk, Pasha
Luzhnetskaia nab. 8, Moscow, RUSSIA, 119871

Grisman, David *Composer, Musician*
CM Mgmt, 5749 Larryan Dr, Woodland Hills, CA 91367 USA

Grissom, Marguis D *Baseball Player*
PO Box 741810, Riverdale, GA 30274 USA

Grissom, Steve *Race Car Driver*
Source International, 3475 Myer Lee Dr, Winston Salem, NC 27101 USA

Grist, Reri *Opera Singer*
Columbia Artists Mgmt Inc, 165 W 57th St, New York, NY 10019 USA

Grizzard, George *Actor*
400 E 54th St, New York, NY 10022 USA

Grizzard, George *Baseball Player, Basketball Player*
Champion Lakes, PO Box 288, Bolivar, PA 15923 USA

Groat, Dick
320 Beach St., Pittsburgh, PA 15218

Groban, Josh *Musician, Songwriter*
Avnet Mgmt, PO Box 570607, Tarzana, CA 91357 USA

Grobell, Werner (Mr Frick) *Misc*
PO Box 7886, Incline Village, NV 89452 USA

Grocholewski, Zenon Cardinal *Religious Leader*
Palazzo della Congregazioni, Piazzo Pio XII #3, Rome, 00193, ITALY

Grodin, Charles
187 Chestnut Hill Rd., Wilton, CT 06897-4106

Groener, Harry *Actor*
Susan Smith, 121A N San Vicente Blvd, Beverly Hills, CA 90211 USA

Groening, Matt *Writer, Director, Animator*
1420 20th St, Santa Monica, CA 90404 USA

Groening, Matthew (Matt) *Cartoonist*
1420 20th St, Santa Monica, CA 90404 USA

Groetzinger Jr, Jon *Business Person*
American Greetings Corp, 1 American Road, Cleveland, OH 44144 USA

Grofe Jr, Ferde
18139 W Coastline, Malibu, CA 90265 USA

Grogan, Steve
8 Country Club Dr., Foxboro, MA 02035

Grogan, Steven J (Steve) *Football Player*
6 Country Club Lane, Foxborough, MA 02035 USA

Groh, Al *Football Coach*
University of Virginia, Athletic Dept, Charlottesburg, VA 22903 USA

Groh, David *Actor*
Sharp/Karrys, 117 N Orlando Ave, Los
Angeles, CA 90048 USA

Groh, Gary *Golfer*
Int'l Mgmt Group, 1 Erieview Plaza, 1360
E 9th St #1300, Cleveland, OH 44144
USA

Grohl, David *Musician, Songwriter*
Nasty Little Man, 72 Spring St, #1100,
New York, NY 10012 USA

Gromov, Mikhael L *Mathematician*
91 Rue de la Sante, Paris, 75013, FRANCE

Gronemeyer, Herbert
Leopoldstr. 19, Munich, GERMANY,
D-80802

Gronk *Artist*
Saxon-Lee Gallery, 7525 Beverly Blvd,
Los Angeles, CA 90036 USA

Gronman, Tuomas *Hockey Player*
Pittsburgh Penguins, Mellon Arena, 66
Mario Lemieux Place, Pittsburgh, PA
15219 USA

Groom, Jerome P (Jerry) *Football Player*
625 Beach Road, #201, Sarasota, FL
34242 USA

Groom, Sam *Actor*
8730 Sunset Blvd, #440, Los Angeles, CA
90069 USA

Gropp, Louis Oliver *Editor*
140 Riverside Dr, #6G, New York, NY
10024 USA

Gros, Francois *Misc*
102 Rue de la Tour, Paris, 75116,
FRANCE

Gros Louis, Kenneth R R *Educator*
Indiana University, President's Office,
Bloomington, IN 47405 USA

Grosbard, Ulu *Director*
29 W 10th St, New York, NY 10011 USA

Gross, Arye
112 So. Almont Dr., Los Angeles, CA
90048

Gross, Charles G *Psychic*
45 Woodside Lane, Princeton, NJ 08540
USA

Gross, David *Comedian*
United Talent Agency (UTA), 9560
Wilshire Blvd, Beverly Hills, CA 90212
USA

Gross, Henry *Musician*
Zelda Mgmt, PO Box 150163, Nashville,
TN 37215, us

Gross, Henry *Musician*
Zelda Mgmt, PO Box 150163, Nashville,
TN 37215 USA

Gross, Jordan *Football Player*
Carolina Panthers, Ericsson Stadium, 800
S Mint St, Charlotte, NC 28202 USA

Gross, Mary *Actor, Comedian*
9100 Sunset Blvd, #300, Los Angeles, CA
90069 USA

Gross, Michael *Swimmer*
Paul-Ehrlich-Str 6, Frankfurt/Main, 60596,
GERMANY

Gross, Michael *Actor*
4431 Woodleigh Ln, La Canada Flintridge,
CA 91011 USA

Gross, Paul *Actor*
Alliance Communications, 121 Bloor E,
#1400, Toronto, ON M4M 3M5,
CANADA

Gross, Ricco *Athlete*
Waldbahnstr 34A, Ruhpolding, 83324,
GERMANY

Gross, Robert (Bob) *Basketball Player*
13466 SE Red Rose Lane, Portland, OR
97236 USA

Gross, Robert A *Physicist*
14 Sunnyside Way, New Rochelle, NY
10804 USA

Gross, Terry R *Commentator*
WHYY-Radio, News Dept, Independence
Mall W, Philadelphia, PA 19104 USA

Grosscup, Lee *Football Player*
330 Westline Dr, #B227, Alameda, CA
94501 USA

Grossfeld, Stanley *Journalist*
Boston Globe, Editorial Dept, 135 W T
Morrissey Blvd, Dorchester, MA 02125
USA

Grossman, Allen R *Writer*
100 W University Parkway, #8A,
Baltimore, MD 21210 USA

Grossman, Judith *Writer*
Warren Wilson College, English Dept,
Swannanoa, NC 28778 USA

Grossman, Judith *Football Player*
Chicago Bears, 1000 Football Dr, Lake
Forest, IL 60045 USA

Grossman, Leslie *Actor*
Metropolitan Talent Agency (MTA), 4526
Wilshire Blvd, Los Angeles, CA 90010
USA

Grossman, Robert *Misc*
19 Crosby St, New York, NY 10013 USA

Grosvenor, Gilbert M *Publisher*
National Geographic Society, 17th & M
NW, Washington, DC 20036 USA

Grotenfelt, Georg E J *Architect*
Kapteeninkatu 20D, Helsinki, 00140,
FINLAND

Grouch, Roger K *Astronaut*
Life/Microgravity Sciences Office, NASA
Headquarters, Washington, DC 20546
USA

Grove, Andrew S *Business Person*
Intel Corp, 2200 Mission College Blvd,
Santa Clara, CA 95054 USA

Grover, Gulshan *Actor, Bollywood*
501/601 Woodstock JP Road, 7
Bungalows Versova Andheri (W),
Mumbai, MS 400061, INDIA

Grover, Gushan *Actor*
501/601 Woodstock J P Road, 7
Bangalows Versova Andheri (W), Bombay,
MS 400 061, INDIA

Groves, Richard H *General*
400 Madison St, #1302, Alexandria, VA
22314 USA

Growney, Robert L *Business Person*
Motorola Inc, 1303 E, Schaumburg, IL
60196 USA

Groza, Louis R (Lou) *Football Player*
287 Parkway Dr, Berea, OH 44017 USA

Grroms, Charles R (Red) *Artist*
85 Walker St, New York, NY 10013 USA

Grubb, Robert
129 Bourke St., Woolloomooloo,
AUSTRALIA, NSW 2011

Grubbs, Gary *Actor*
Parasigm Agency, 10100 Santa Monica
Blvd, #2500, Los Angeles, CA 90067 USA

Grubbs, Robert H *Misc*
California Institute of Technology,
Chemistry Dept, Pasadena, CA 91125
USA

Gruber, Kelly W *Baseball Player*
3300 Bee Cave Road, #650-227, Austin,
TX 78746 USA

Gruberova, Edita *Opera Singer*
Opera et Concert, Maximillianstr 22,
Munich, 80539, GERMANY

Grubman, Allen J *Lawyer*
Grubman Indursky Schindler Goldstein,
152 W 57th St, New York, NY 10019
USA

Gruden, Jon *Coach*
Tampa Bay Buccaneers, 1 W Buccaneer
Place, Tampa, FL 33607 USA

Grudens, Richard
Box 344 Main St., Stony Brook, NY 11790

Grudzlelanek, Mark J *Baseball Player*
Tom Grudzielanek, 550 E Mona Dr, Oak
Creek, WI 53154 USA

Gruenberg, Erich *Musician*
80 Northway, Hampstead Garden Suburb,
London, NW11 6PA, UNITED KINGDOM
(UK)

Gruffudd, Ioan *Actor*
Firm, The, 9465 Wilshire Blvd, Beverly
Hills, CA 90212 USA

Gruffudd, Ioan *Actor*
Hamilton Hodell, 24 Hanway St, London,
W1T 1UH, UNITED KINGDOM (UK)

Grum, Clifford J *Business Person*
Temple-Inland Inc, 303 S Temple Dr,
Diboll, TX 75941 USA

Grumman, Cornelia *Journalist*
Chicago Tribune, Editorial Dept, 435 N
Michigan Ave, Chicago, IL 60611 USA

Grummer, Elisabeth *Opera Singer*
Am Schlachtensee 104, Berlin, 14163,
GERMANY

Grunberg, Greg *Actor*
Greene Assoc, 7080 Hollywood Blvd,
#1017, Los Angeles, CA 90028 USA

Grunberg-Manago, Marianne *Misc*
80 Boulevard Pasteur, Paris, 75015,
FRANCE

Grundfest, Joseph A *Government Official*
Stanford University, Law School, Stanford,
CA 94305 USA

Grundhofer, Jerry A *Financier*
Firstar Corp, 777 E Wisconsin Ave,
Milwaukee, WI 53202 USA

Grundhofer, John F *Financier*
US Bancorp, US Bank Place, 601 2nd Ave
S, Minneapolis, MN 55402 USA

Grundy, Hugh *Musician*
Lustig Talent, PO Box 770850, Orlando,
FL 32877 USA

Grune, George V *Publisher*
PO Box 2348, Ponte Vedra Beach, FL
32004 USA

Grunfeld, Ernie *Basketball Player*
1950 W Dean Road, Milwaukee, WI
53217 USA

Grunsfeld, John M *Astronaut*
4202 Lake Grove Dr, Seabrook, TX 77586
USA

Grunwald, Ernie *Actor*
TalentWorks (LA), 3500 W Olive Ave
#1400, Burbank, CA 91505 USA

Grunwald, Henry A *Editor, Diplomat*
654 Madison Ave, #1605, New York, NY
10021 USA

Grunwald, Norten
Nyborggade Strandboulevarden 160-162
DK-2100, Copenhagen, DENMARK

Grupo Mania *Music Group*
Sony Music Miami, 605 Lincoln Rd,
Miami Beach, FL 33138 USA

Grushin, Dave
200 W. Superior #202, Chicago, IL 60710

Grushin, Pyotr D *Engineer*
Academy of Sciences, 14 Lenisky
Prospekt, Moscow, RUSSIA

Grusin, Dave *Musician, Composer*
Monterey International, 200 W Superior,
#202, Chicago, IL 60610 USA

Grutman, N Roy *Lawyer*
Grutman Miller Greenspoon Hendler, 505
Park Ave, New York, NY 10022 USA

Guadagnino, Kathy Baker *Golfer*
Int'l Mgmt Group, 1 Erieview Plaza, 1360
E 9th St #1300, Cleveland, OH 44114
USA

Guard, Christopher
76 Oxford St., London, ENGLAND, W1N
OAX

Guardado, Edward A (Eddie) *Baseball
Player*
10715 Plumas Way, Tustin, CA 92782
USA

Guardino, Harry *Actor*
2949 E Via Vaquero Road, Palm Springs,
CA 92262 USA

Guare, John *Writer*
R Andrew Boose, 1 Dag Hammarskjold
Plaza, New York, NY 10017 USA

Guarini, Justin *Musician*
Handprint Entertainment, 1100 Glendon
Ave #1000, Los Angeles, CA 90024 USA

Guarrera, Frank *Opera Singer*
4514 Latona Ave NE, Seattle, WA 98105
USA

Guaty, Camille *Actor*
Innovative Artists (LA), 1505 Tenth St,
Santa Monica, CA 90401 USA

Gubaidulina, Sofia A *Composer*
2D Pugachevskaya 8, Korp 5 #130,
Moscow, 107061, RUSSIA

Gubarev, Aleksei A *Cosmonaut, General*
Potchta Kosmonavtov, Moskovskoi
Oblasti, Syvisdny Goroduk, 141160,
RUSSIA

Guber, Peter *Producer*
Mandaly Entertainment, 10202 W
Washington Blvd, #1070, Culver City, CA
90232 USA

Gubert, Walter A *Financier*
J P Morgan Chase, 270 Park Ave, New
York, NY 10017 USA

Guccione, Bob
11 Penn. Plaza. 12th Flr, New York, NY
10001

Guccione, Robert (Bob) *Publisher*
11 Penn Plaza, #1200, New York, NY
10001 USA

Guckel, Henry *Engineer*
University of Wisconsin, Engineering
Dept, Madison, WI 53706 USA

Guelleh, Ismail Omar *President*
President's Office, 8-10 Ahmed Nessim St,
Djibouti, DJIBOUTI

Guennel, Joe *Soccer Player*
835 Front Range Road, Littleton, CO
80120 USA

Guenther, Johnny *Bowler*
23826 115th Place W, Woodway, WA
98020 USA

Guerard, Michael E *Chef*
Les Pres d'Eugenie, Eugenie les Bains,
40320, FRANCE

Guerin, Bill *Hockey Player*
39 W Colonial Road, Wilbraham, MA
01905 Usa

Guerin, Richie *Basketball Player*
1355 Bear Island Dr, West Palm Beach,
FL 33409 USA

Guerra, Blanca *Actor*
Televisa, Blvd Adolfo Lopez Mateos 232,
Colonia San Angel INN, DF, CP 01060,
MEXICO

Guerra, Eddie *Actor*
Creative Artists Agency LCC (CAA-LA),
9830 Wilshire Blvd, Beverly Hills, CA
90212 USA

Guerra, Jackie *Comedian*
Brillstein-Grey Entertainment, 9150
Wilshire Blvd #350, Beverly Hills, CA
90212 USA

Guerra, Saverio *Actor*
Writers & Artists, 8383 Wilshire Blvd,
#550, Beverly Hills, CA 90211 USA

Guerrero, Julen *Soccer Player*
AC Bilbao, Alameda Mazarredo 23,
Bilbao, 48009, SPAIN

Guerrero, Lisa *Talk Show Host*
Jerry Shandrew PR, 1050 South Stanley
Avenue, Los Angeles, CA 90019-6634
USA

Guerrero, Pedro *Baseball Player*
4004 Saint Andrews Drive SE, Rio
Rancho, NM 87124 USA

Guerrero, Roberto *Race Car Driver*
31642 Via Cervantes, San Juan
Capistrano, CA 92675 USA

Guerrero, Viadmir *Baseball Player*
Montreal Expos, Plympic Stadium,
Montreal, QC, H1V 3N7, CANADA

Guerrero, Vladimir *Baseball Player,
Athlete*
Montreal Expos, PO Box 500, Station M,
Montreal, H1V 3P, Canada

Guerrero Coles, Lisa *Actor, Sportscaster*
ABC-TV, Sports Dept, 77 W 66th St, New
York, NY 10023 USA

Guers, Paul
40 rue de Buci, Paris, FRANCE, 75006

Guess Who
31 Hemlock Pl. Winnepeg, Man.,
CANADA, R2H 1L8

Guest, Christopher H *Actor, Director*
Creative Artists Agency, 9830 Wilshire
Blvd, Beverly Hills, CA 90212 USA

Guest, Cornelia *Model*
1419 Donhill Dr, Beverly Hills, CA 90210
USA

Guest, Douglas *Misc*
Gables, Minchinhampton, Gloscester, GL6
9JE, UNITED KINGDOM (UK)

Guest, Lance
2269 La Granada Dr., Los Angeles, CA
90068

Guetary, Francois *Actor*
Cineart, 36 Rue de Ponthieu, Paris,
75008, FRANCE

Guffey Jr, John W *Business Person*
Coltec Industries, 2550 W Tyvola Road,
Charlotte, NC 28217 USA

Gugelmin, Mauricio *Race Car Driver*
PacWest Reacing Group, PO Box 1607,
Bellevue, WA 98009 USA

Guggenheim, Alan *Inventor*
Northwest Power Systems, PO Box 5339,
Bend, OR 97708 USA

Guggenheim, Marc *Actor*
United Talent Agency (UTA), 9560
Wilshire Blvd, Beverly Hills, CA 90212
USA

Gugino, Carla *Actor*
Three Arts Entertainment, 9460 Wilshire
Blvd, #700, Beverly Hills, CA 90212 USA

Guglielmi, Ralph *Football Player*
8501 White Pass Court, Potomac, MD
20854 USA

Gugloitta, Tom *Basketball Player*
27 W Sierra Vista Dr, Phoenix, AZ 85013
USA

Guice, Jackson *Cartoonist*
DC Comics, 1700 Broadway, New York,
NY 10019 USA

Guida, Gloria
Via Francesco Denza 48, Rome, ITALY,
I-00197

Guida, Lou *Misc*
4800 N Highway A1A, #505, Vero Beach,
FL 32963 USA

Guidi, Osvaldo *Actor*
Telefe - Argentina, Pavon 2444
(C1248AAT), Buenos Aires, ARGENTINA

Guidoni, Umberto *Astronaut*
15010 Cobre Valley Dr, Houston, TX
77062 USA

Guidry, Mark
1264 Camelot Lane, Lemont, IL 60439

Guidry, N T *Engineer*
23971 Coral Springs Lane, Tehachapi, CA
93561 USA

Guidry, Ron
PO Box 666, Scott, Los Angeles, 70583

Guidry, Ronald A (Ron) *Baseball Player*
PO Box 278, Scott, LA 70583 USA

Guilland, Richard
4526 Wilshire Blvd., Los Angeles, CA
90010

Guilbert, Ann *Actor*
550 Erskine Dr, Pacific Palisades, CA
90272 USA

Guilfoyle, Paul *Actor*
S M S Talent, 8730 Sunset Blvd, #440, Los
Angeles, CA 90069 USA

Guillaume, Robert *Actor*
4709 Noeline Ave, Encino, CA 91436
USA

Guillem, Sylvie *Ballerina*
Royal Ballet, Convent Garden, Bow St,
London, WC2E 9DD, UNITED KINGDOM
(UK)

Guillemin, Roger C L *Nobel Prize
Laureate*
7316 Encelia Ave, La Jolla, CA 92037
USA

Guillen, Francesca *Actor*
Televisa, Blvd Adolfo Lopez Mateos 232,
Colonia San Angel INN, DF, CP 01060,
MEXICO

Guillen, Michael *Doctor, Correspondent*
20/20, 147 Columbus Ave, New York, NY
10023, US

Guillen, Oswaldo J (Ozzie) *Baseball
Player*
21218 Saint Andrews Blvd, #305, Boca
Raton, FL 33433 USA

Guillerman, John *Director*
309 S Rockingham Ave, Los Angeles, CA
90049 USA

Guillermin, John
309 S. Rockingham Ave., Los Angeles, CA
90049

Guillo, Dominque *Actor*
Cineart, 36 Rue de Ponthieu, Paris,
75008, FRANCE

Guillory, Bennet
1519 Galaxy Ct., Rohnert Park, CA
94928-5611

Guillory, Sienna *Actor*
William Morris Agency (WMA-LA), 1
William Morris Pl, Beverly Hills, CA
90212 USA

Guinan, Francis
606 N. Larchmont Blvd. #309LA, CA
90004

Guindon, Richard G *Cartoonist*
321 W Lafayette Blvd, Detroit, MI 48226
USA

Guinee, Tim *Actor*
Lighthouse, 409 N Camden Dr, #202,
Beverly Hills, CA 90210 USA

Guinier, Lani *Lawyer, Educator*
University of Pennsylvania, Law School,
3400 Chestnut, Philadelphia, PA 19104
USA

Guinney, Bob *Reality TV Star*
Bachelor, The, 15301 Ventura Blvd, Bldg
E, Sherman Oaks, CA 91403 USA

Guirgis, Stephen Adly *Comedian*
Gersh Agency, The (LA), 232 N Canon Dr,
Beverly Hills, CA 90210 USA

Guisewite, Cathy L *Cartoonist*
4039 Camellia Ave, Studio City, CA
91604 USA

Gujral, Inder Kumar *Prime Minister*
5 Janpath, New Delhi, Delhi, 110011,
INDIA

Gulager, Clu *Actor*
Clu Gulager Acting, 320 Wilshire Blvd,
Santa Monica, CA 90401 USA

Gulbinowicx, Henryk Roman Cardinal
Religious Leader
Metropolita Wroclawski, UL Katedraina
11, Wroclaw, 50-328, POLAND

Guldelli, Giovanni *Actor*
Carol Levi Co, Via Giuseppe Pisanelli,
Rome, 00196, ITALY

Guleghina, Maria *Opera Singer*
Askonas Holt Ltd, 27 Chancery Lane,
London, WC2A 1PF, UNITED KINGDOM
(UK)

Gullett, Donald E (Don) *Baseball Player*
RR1 Box 615N, South Shore, KY 41175
USA

Gulli, Franco *Musician*
Columbia Artists Mgmt Inc, 165 W 57th
St, New York, NY 10019 USA

Gullickson, William L (Bill) *Baseball
Player*
3 Banchory Court, Palm Beach Gardens,
FL 33418 USA

Gullikson, Tom *Athlete*
Tim & Tom Gullikson Foundation, 8000
Sears Tower, Chicago, IL 60606

Gullit, Ruud *Soccer Player*
FC Chelsea, Stamford Bridge, Fulham
Road, London, SW6 1HS, UNITED
KINGDOM (UK)

Gulliver, Dorothy
28792 Lajos Lane, Valley Center, A,
92082

Gulliver, Harold *Editor*
Atlanta Constitution, Editorial Dept, 72
Marieta St NW, Atlanta, GA 30303 USA

Gulyas, Denes *Opera Singer*
Hungarian State Opera, Andrassy Utca 22,
Budapest, 1062, HUNGARY

Gulzar *Bollywood, Songwriter*
Boskiyana Pali Hill, Bandra (W), Mumbai,
MS 400050, INDIA

Guman, Michael D (Mike) *Football Player*
3913 Pleasant Ave, Allentown, PA 18103
USA

Gumbel, Bryant C *Commentator,
Television Host*
Real Sports with Bryant Gumbel, 1100
Ave of the Americas, New York, NY
10036 USA

Gumbel, Greg *Sportscaster*
220 Heatherwood Court, Winter Springs,
FL 32708 USA

Gund, Agnes *Misc*
Museum of Modern Art, 11 W 53rd St,
New York, NY 10019 USA

Gundi *Actor*
RR1, Roseneath, ON KOK 2XO, CANADA

Gundling, Beulah *Swimmer*
Coral Ridge South, 3333 NE 34th St,
#1517, Fort Lauderdale, FL 33308 USA

Gundu, Kalyanam *Actor*
D-1 Block Lloyds Colony, Royapettah,
Chennai, TN 600 014, INDIA

Gunn, Anna
10100 Santa Monica Blvd. #2500, Los
Angeles, CA 90067

Gunn, James P *Astronomer*
Princeton University, Astrophysics Dept,
Princeton, NJ 08544 USA

Gunn, Janet *Actor*
David Shapira & Associates, 15821
Ventura Blvd #235, Encino, CA 91436
USA

Gunn, Nathan *Opera Singer*
ICM Artists, 40 W 57th St, New York, NY
10019 USA

Gunn, Richard
12216 Moorpark St., Studio City, CA
91604

Gunn, Sean *Actor*
1421 Shenandosh, Suite 1, Los Angeles,
CA 90035 USA

Gunnell, Sally *Track Athlete*
18 Shepherd's Croft, Brighton, East Sussex,
UNITED KINGDOM (UK)

Guns N' Roses *Music Group*
Sanctuary Music Management (LA), 301
Arizona Ave #200, Santa Monica, CA
90401

Gunsalus, Irwin C *Writer*
3407 Cherry Hills Dr, Champaign, IL
61822 USA

Gunter, Dan *Actor*
Century Artists, PO Box 59747, Santa
Barbara, CA 93150 USA

Gunter, Sue *Coach*
9275 Highway 71, Longville, LA 70652
USA

Guokas Jr, Matt *Basketball Player, Coach*
458 Devon Place, Heathrow, FL 32746
USA

Gupta, Neena *Actor*
129 Aram Nagar II Versova Road,
Andheri, Bombay, MS 400 061, INDIA

Gupta, Raj *Business Person*
Rohm & Haas Co, 100 S Independence
Mall W, #1A, Philadelphia, PA 19106
USA

Gupta, Sudhir *Misc*
University of California, Medicine Dept,
Irvine, CA 92717 USA

Gur, Mordechai *General*
25 Mishmeret St, Afeka, Tel-Aviv, 69694,
ISRAEL

Gura, Larry C *Baseball Player*
205 Serrana Dr, Litchfield Park, AZ 85340
USA

Gurchenko, Ludmilla M *Actor*
Trekjprudny Per 5/15, #22, Moscow,
103001, RUSSIA

Gurdon, John B *Misc*
Magdalene College, Master's Cottage, Cambridge, CB3 0AG, UNITED KINGDOM (UK)

Guren, Peter *Cartoonist*
Creators Syndicate, 5777 W Century Blvd, #700, Los Angeles, CA 90045 USA

Gurewitz, Brett *Musician*
William Morris Agency, 151 El Camino Dr, Beverly Hills, CA 90212 USA

Gurian, Michael *Writer*
417 W 32nd Ave, Spokane, WA 99203 USA

Gurney, Dan
2334 S. Broadway, Santa Ana, CA 92707-0186

Gurney, Daniel S (Dan) *Race Car Driver*
All-American Racers Inc, 2334 S Broadway, Santa Ana, CA 92707 USA

Gurney, Hilda *Horse Racer*
8430 Waters Road, Moorpark, CA 93021 USA

Gurney, Scott *Actor*
Guttman Associates, 118 S Beverly Dr #201, Beverly Hills, CA 90212 USA

Gurney Jr, Albert R (A R) *Writer*
40 Wellers Bridge Road, Roxbury, CT 06783 USA

Gurraggchaa, Jugderdemidijn *Cosmonaut, General*
Lyotchik Kosmonavt, MNR Central Post Office Box 378, Ulan Bator, Mongolia

Gurraggchaa, Jugderdemidijn *Cosmonaut, General*
Lyotchik Kosmonavt, MNR Central Post Office Box 378, Ulan Bator, MONGOLIA

Gurry, Kick *Actor*
Himber Entertainment Inc, 211 S Beverly Dr #208, Beverly Hills, CA 90212 USA

Guru *Musician*
William Morris Agency, 151 El Camino Dr, Beverly Hills, CA 90212 USA

Gurwitch, Annabelle *Actor*
Don Buchwald, 6500 Wilshire Blvd, #2200, Los Angeles, CA 90048 USA

Gus Gus
PO Box 1141 121 Reykjavik, ICELAND

Gusarov, Alexei *Hockey Player*
Saint Louis Blues, Sawis Center, 1401 Clark Ave, Saint Louis, MO 63103 USA

Gusella, James *Inventor*
Harvard Medical School, 25 Shattuck St, Boston, MA 02115 USA

Gushiken, Koji *Gymnast*
Nippon Physical Education College, Judo School, Tokyo, JAPAN

Gusmao, Jose Alexandre (Xanana) *President*
President's Office, Dili, EAST TIMOR

Guss, Louis *Actor*
Amset Eisenstadt Frazier, 5757 Wilshire Blvd, #510, Los Angeles, CA 90036 USA

Gustafson, Kathryn *Architect*
Gustafson Guthrie Nichol, Pier 55, #31101 Alaskan Way, Seattle, WA 98101 USA

Gustafson, Steven *Musician*
Agency for Performing Arts, 9200 Sunset Blvd, #900, Los Angeles, CA 90069 USA

Gustav, King Carl XVI HM
Kungliga Slottet, Stockholm, SWEDEN, 11130

Guster *Music Group*
Nettwerk Management (NY), 345 Seventh Ave Fl 24, New York, NY 10001 USA

Gutensohn-Knopf, Katrin *Skier*
Oberfeldweg 12, Oberaudorf, 83080, GERMANY

Guterman, Lawrence M *Director*
Endeavor Agency LLC (LA), 9601 Wilshire Blvd Fl 3, Beverly Hills, CA 90210 USA

Guterson, David *Writer*
Georges Borchardt, 136 E 57th St, New York, NY 10022 USA

Guth, Alan H *Physicist*
Massachusetts Institute of Technology, Physics Dept, Cambridge, MA 02139 USA

Guthe, Manfred *Cinematographer*
122 Collier St, Toronto, ON M4W 1M3, CANADA

Guthman, Edwin O *Editor*
Philadelphia Inquirer, Editorial Dept 400 N Broad St, Philadelphia, PA 19130 USA

Guthrie, Arlo *Music Group, Songwriter*
The Farm, Washington, MA 01223 USA

Guthrie, Janet *Race Car Driver*
PO Box 505, Aspen, CO 81612 USA

Guthrie, Jennifer *Actor*
Don Buchwald, 6500 Wilshire Blvd #2200, Los Angeles, CA 90048 USA

Gutierrez, Carlos M *Business Person*
Kellogg Co, 1 Kellogg Square, PO Box 3599, Battle Creek, MI 49016 USA

Gutierrez, Diego *Actor*
Creative Artists Agency LCC (CAA-LA), 9830 Wilshire Blvd, Beverly Hills, CA 90212 USA

Gutierrez, Gustavo *Misc*
Instituto Bartolome Las Casas-Rimac, Apartado 3090, Lima, 100, PERU

Gutierrez, Horacio *Music Group, Musician*
I C M Artists, 40 W 57th St, New York, NY 10019 USA

Gutierrez, Luclo *President*
Palacio de Gobiemo, Garcia Moreno, Quito, 1043, ECUADOR

Gutierrez, Sidney M *Astronaut*
324 Sarah Lane NW, Albuquerque, NM 87114 USA

Gutman, Natalia G *Music Group, Musician*
Askonas Holt Ltd, 27 Chancery Lane, London, WC2A 1PF, UNITED KINGDOM (UK)

Gutman, Roy W *Journalist*
13132 Curved Iron Road, Hemdon, VA 20171 USA

Gutmann, Amy *Educator*
Princeton University, President's Office, Princeton, NJ 08544 USA

Gutsche, TorstenHans- *Athlete*
Hans-Marchwitza-Ring 51, Potsdam, 14473, GERMANY

Guttenberg, Steve *Actor*
Untitled Entertainment (LA), 8436 W 3rd St #650, Los Angeles, CA 90048 USA

Gutteridge, Lucy
76 Oxford St., London, ENGLAND, W1N 0AX

Guy, Buddy *Music Group, Musician*
Monterey International, 200 W Superior #202, Chicago, IL 60610 USA

Guy, Fabrice
50 rue de Marquisats F-74011, Annecy Cedex, FRANCE

Guy, Francois-Frederic *Music Group, Musician*
Van Walsum Mgmt, 4 Addison Bridge Place, London, W14 8XP, UNITED KINGDOM (UK)

Guy, Jasmine *Actor*
Pantich, 21243 Ventura Blvd #101, Woodland Hills, CA 91364 USA

Guy, Ray *Football Player*
1389 Wrightsboro Road NW, Thomson, GA 30824 USA

Guy, Sebastien *Actor*
Acme Talent & Literary Agency (LA), 4727 Wilshire Blvd #333, Los Angeles, CA 90010 USA

Guy, William L *Governor*
5210 12th St S #105, Fargo, ND 58104 USA

Guyer, Cindy
2 Lincoln Sq. Plaza, New York, NY 10023

Guyer, David B *Misc*
Save the Children Foundation, 514 2nd St, Owyhee, NV 89832 USA

Guynn, Jack *Government Official, Financier*
Federal Reserve Bank, 1000 Peachtree St NE, Atlanta, GA 30309 USA

Guyon, John C *Educator*
Southern Illinois Univesity, President's Office, Carbondale, IL 62901 USA

Guyot, Paul *Actor, Writer, Producer*
Creative Artists Agency LCC (CAA-LA), 9830 Wilshire Blvd, Beverly Hills, CA 90212 USA

Guzman, Alejandra *Musician*
BMG, 1540 Broadway, New York, NY 10036 USA

Guzman, Andrea *Actor*
TV Caracol, Calle 76 #11 - 35, Piso 10AA, Bogota DC, 26484, COLOMBIA

Guzman, Luis *Actor*
Gersh Agency, 232 N Canon Dr, Beverly Hills, CA 90210 USA

Guzy, Carol *Photographer, Journalist*
2145 Fort Scott Dr, Arlington, VA 22202 USA

Gwathmey, Charles *Architect*
Gwathmey Siegel Architects, 475 10th Ave, New York, NY 10018 USA

Gwinn, Mary Ann *Journalist*
Seattle Times, Editorial Dept, 1120 John St, Seattle, WA 98109 USA

Gwynn, Anthony K (Tony) *Baseball Player, Coach*
15643 Boulder Ridge Lane, Poway, CA 92064 USA

Gwynn, Darrell *Race Car Driver*
4850 SW 52nd St, Davie, FL 33314 USA

Gwynn, Tony
15643 Boulder Ridge Lane, Poway, CA
92064

Gwynne, A Patrick *Architect*
Homewood Esher, Surrey, KT10 9JL,
UNITED KINGDOM (UK)

Gyanendra *King*
Royal Palace, Narayanhiti Durbag Marg,
Kathmandu, NEPAL

Gyll, J Soren *Business Person*
Volvo AB, Goteborg, 405 08, SWEDEN

Gyllenhaal, Jake *Actor*
Creative Artists Agency, 9830 Wilshire
Blvd, Beverly Hills, CA 90212 USA

Gyllenhaal, Maggie *Actor*
Creative Artists Agency, 9830 Wilshire
Blvd, Beverly Hills, CA 90212 USA

Gyllenhaal, Stephen G *Director, Writer,
Producer*
William Morris Agency (WMA-LA), 1
William Morris Pl, Beverly Hills, CA
90212 USA

Gyllenhammer, Pehr G *Business Person*
CHU PLC Saint Helen's 1 Undershaft,
London, EC3P 3DQ, UNITED KINGDOM
(UK)

GZA *Music Group, Musician*
Agency Group Ltd, 1775 Broadway #430,
New York, NY 10019 USA

H

Ha Jin *Writer*
Emory University, English Dept, Atlanta,
GA 30332 USA

Haag, Rudolf *Physicist*
Waldschmidt Str 4B, Schliersee-Neuhaus,
83727, GERMANY

Haake, James
1256 N. Flores #l, Los Angeles, CA 90069

Haakon *Prince*
Det Kongeligel Slottet, Drammensveien 1,
Oslo, 0010, NORWAY

Haas, Andrew T *Misc*
Auto Aero & Agricultural Union, 1300
Connecticut NW, Washington, DC 20036
USA

Haas, Carl
500 Tower Parkway, Lincolnshire, IL
60069

Haas, Ernest *Photographer*
853 7th Ave, New York, NY 10019 USA

Haas, Freddie *Golfer*
147 E Oakridge Park, Metairie, LA 70005
USA

Haas, Jay
4 Tuscany Ct, Greer, SC 29650 USA

Haas, Lucas *Actor*
Lighthouse, 409 N Camden Dr #202,
Beverly Hills, CA 90210 USA

Haas, Lukas *Actor*
Untitled Entertainment (LA), 8436 W 3rd
St #650, Los Angeles, CA 90048 USA

Haas, Philip *Actor*
Gersh Agency, The (LA), 232 N Canon Dr,
Beverly Hills, CA 90210 USA

Haas, Richard J *Artist*
29 Overcliff St, Yonders, NY 10705 USA

Haas, Robert D *Business Person*
Levi Strauss Assoc, 1155 Battery St, San
Francisco, CA 94111 USA

Haas, Thomas (Tommy) *Tennis Player*
TC Weiden am Postkeller, Schmiritzer
Weg, Weiden, 92637, GERMANY

Haas, Waltraud
Kuniglberggasse 45, Vienna, AUSTRIA,
A-1130

Habash, George *Politician*
Popular Front for Palestine Liberation, PO
Box 12144, Damascus, SYRIA

Habel, Karl *Scientist, Misc*
Reading Institute of Rehabilitation, RR 1
Box 252, Reading, PA 19607 USA

Haber, Norman *Inventor*
Haber Inc, 470 Main Road, Towaco, NJ
07082 USA

Habermann, Eva
Kuckuchsberg 9, Lutiansee, GERMANY,
D-22952

Habermas, Jurgen *Misc*
Ringstr 8B, Stamberg, 82319, GERMANY

Habib, Munir *Astronaut, Misc*
Potchta Kosmonavtov, Moskovskoi
Oblasti, Syvisdny Goroduk, 141160,
RUSSIA

Habibie, Baharuddin Jusuf *President*
President's Office, 15 Jalan Merdeka
Utara, Jakarta, INDONESIA

Habiger, Eugene E (Gene) *General*
Energy Department, Security Ops 1000
Independence NW, Washington, DC
20585 USA

Habraken, Nicolaas J *Architect*
63 Wildemislaan, Apeldoom, 7313 BD,
NETHERLAND

Hachette, Jean-Louis *Publisher*
Hachette Livre, 83 Ave Marceau, Paris,
75116, FRANCE

Hack, Olivia *Actor*
Gilbertson-Kincaid Management, 1330
Fourth St, Santa Monica, CA 90401 USA

Hack, Shelley *Actor, Model*
1208 Georgina, Santa Monica, CA 90402
USA

Hackerman, Norman *Misc*
3 Woodstone Square, Austin, TX 78703
USA

Hackett, Grant *Swimmer*
PO Box 940, Dickson, ACT, 2602,
AUSTRALIA

Hackett, Martha *Actor*
Vaughn D Hart, 8899 Beverly Blvd #815,
Los Angeles, CA 90048 USA

Hackford, Taylor *Director, Producer*
2003 La Brea Terrace, Los Angeles, CA
90046 USA

Hackl, Georg *Athlete*
Caftehaus Soamatl Ramsauerstr 100,
Berchtesgaden-Engedey, 83471,
GERMANY

Hackman, Gene *Actor*
Dick Guttman, 118 S Beverly Dr #201,
Beverly Hills, CA 90212 USA

Hackney, Lisa *Golfer*
Signature Sports Group, 4150 Olson
Memorial Highway, Minneapolis, MN
55422 USA

Hackney, Roderick P *Architect*
Saint Peter's House, Windmill St
Macclesfield, Cheshire, SK11 7HS,
UNITED KINGDOM (UK)

Hackwith, Scott *Music Group, Musician,
Songwriter*
Overland Productions, 156 W 56th St
#500, New York, NY 10019 USA

Hackworth, David H *War Hero*
PO Box 11179, Greenwich, CT 06831
USA

Hadas, Rachel C *Writer, Educator*
838 W End Ave #3A, New York, NY
10025 USA

Haddon, Dayle *Model, Actor*
Hyperion Books, 114 5th Ave, New York,
NY 10011 USA

Haddon, Lawrence *Actor*
14950 Sutton St, Sherman Oaks, CA
91403 USA

Haden, Charles E (Charlie) *Music Group,
Musician, Composer*
Merlin Co, 17609 Ventura Blvd #212,
Encino, CA 91316 USA

Haden, Pat *Football Player*
1525 Wilson Ave, San Marino, CA 91108

Haden, Patrick C (Pat) *Football Player,
Sportscaster*
1525 Wilson Ave, San Marino, CA 91108
USA

Hadfield, Chris A *Astronaut*
638 Shorewood Dr, Kemah, TX 77565
USA

Hadid, Zaha *Architect*
Studio 9, 10 Bowling Green Lane,
London, WC1R 0BD, UNITED KINGDOM
(UK)

Hadl, John W *Football Player*
Kansas University, Allen Field House,
Lawrence, KS 66045 USA

Hadlee, Richard J *Cricketer*
PO Box 29186, Christchurch, NEW
ZEALAND

Hadley, Brett *Actor*
5070 Woodley Ave, Encino, CA 91436
USA

Hadley, Jerry *Opera Singer*
George M Martynuk, 352 7th Ave, New
York, NY 10001 USA

Hadley, Lisa Ann
270 N. Canon Dr. #1064, Beverly Hills,
CA 90210

Hadley, Tony *Music Group*
Mission Control, Business Center Lower
Road, London, SE16 2XB, UNITED
KINGDOM (UK)

Haebler, Ingrid *Music Group, Musician*
Ibbs & Tillett, 420-452 Edgware Road,
London, W2 1EG, UNITED KINGDOM (
UK)

Haechen, Hartmut *Conductor*
Organisation Int'l Artistique, 16 Ave F D
Roosevelt, Paris, 75008, FRANCE

Haegele, Patricia *Publisher*
Good Housekeeping Magazine, 959 8th Ave, New York, NY 10019 USA

Haegg, Gunder *Track Athlete*
Swedish Olympic Committee, Idrottens Hus, Farsta, 12387, SWEDEN

Haendel, Ida *Music Group, Musician*
Harlod Holt, 31 Sinclair Road, London, W14 0NS, UNITED KINGDOM (UK)

Haenicke, Diether H *Educator*
Western Michigan University, President's Office, Kalamazoo, MI 49008 USA

Hafer, Fred D *Business Person*
GPU Inc, 300 Madison Ave, Morristown, NJ 07960 USA

Hafner, Dudley H *Misc*
140 Estrada Maya, Santa Fe, NM 87506 USA

Hafstein, Johann *Prime Minister*
Sjalfstaedisflokkurinn Laufasvegi 46, Reykjavik, ICELAND

Hagan, Cliff O *Basketball Player*
3637 Castlegate West Wynd, Lexington, KY 40502

Hagan, Clifford O (Cliff) *Basketball Player, Coach*
3637 Castlegate West Wynd, Lexington, KY 40502 USA

Hagan, Molly *Actor*
210 S Amaz Dr #3, Beverly Hills, CA 90211 USA

Hagan, Sarah *Actor*
Mark Robert Management, 14014 Moorpark St #316, Sherman Oaks, CA 91423 USA

Hagar, Sammy *Music Group, Musician, Songwriter*
Rogers & Cowan, 6340 Breckenridge Run, Rex, GA 30273 USA

Hagee, Michael W *General*
Commandant HqUSMC, 2 Navy Annex, Washington, DC 20380 USA

Hagegard, Hakan *Opera Singer*
Gunnarsbyn, Edane, 670 30, SWEDEN

Hagemeister, Charles C *War Hero*
1908 Canterbury Court, Leavenworth, KS 66048 USA

Hagen, Alexander
Mittelweg 58, Hamburg, GERMANY, D-20149

Hagen, Kevin *Actor*
PO Box 1862, Grants Pass, OR 97528 USA

Hagen, Nina *Music Group*
Performers of the World, 8901 Melrose Ave #200, West Hollywood, CA 90069 USA

Hager, Bob
4001 Nebraska Ave. NW, Washington, DC 20016

Hager, Robert *Commentator*
NBC-TV, News Dept 4001 Nebraska Ave NW, Washington, DC 20016 USA

Hager Twins
PO Box 1516, Champaign, IL 61824

Hagerty, Julie *Actor*
The Firm, 9100 Wilshire Blvd #100W, Beverly Hills, CA 90210 USA

Hagerty, Michael *Actor*
Greene & Associates, 526 N Larchmont Blvd #201, Los Angeles, CA 90004 USA

Haggard, Merle *Music Group, Songwriter*
235 Murrell Meadows Dr #72, Sevierville, TN 37876 USA

Hagge, Marlene Bauer *Golfer*
PO Box 570, La Quinta, CA 92253 USA

Haggerty, Dan *Actor*
404 East 1st St #1287, Long Beach, CA 90802 USA

Haggerty, Julie *Actor*
Framework Entertainment (LA), 9057 Nemo St #C, W Hollywood, CA 90069 USA

Haggerty, Tim *Cartoonist*
United Feature Syndicate, 200 Madison Ave, New York, NY 10016 USA

Hagler, Marvin *Boxer*
Peter Devener, 75 Presidential Dr #4, Quincy, MA 02169 USA

Hagman, Larry *Actor*
9950 Sulphur Mountain Road, Ojai, CA 93023 USA

Hagn, Johanna *Athlete*
ASG Elsdorf, Behrgasse 6, Elsdorf, 50198, GERMANY

Hague, William MP *Government Official*
House of Commons, Westminster, London, SW1A 0AA, UNITED KINGDOM (UK)

Hahn, Beatrice H *Biologist*
University of Alabama, Medical School Microbiology Dept, Bermingham, AL 35294 USA

Hahn, Erwin L *Physicist*
69 Stevenson Ave, Berkeley, CA 94708 USA

Hahn, Frank H *Economist*
61 Adams Road, Cambridge, CB3 9AD, UNITED KINGDOM (UK)

Hahn, Hilary *Musician, Music Group*
Hans Ulrich Schmid, Postfach 1617, Hanover, 30016, GERMANY

Hahn, James *Politician*
Mayor's Office, City Hall 200 N Spring St, Los Angeles, CA 90012 USA

Hahn, Jessica *Actor, Model*
6345 Balboa Blvd #375, Encino, CA 91316 USA

Hahn, Joseph *Music Group*
Artist Group International, 9560 Wilshire Blvd #400, Beverly Hills, CA 90212 USA

Hai, Do Thi *Actor*
Agency for the Performing Arts (APA-LA), 9200 Sunset Blvd #900, Los Angeles, CA 90069 USA

Haid, Charles *Actor*
4376 Forman Ave, Toluca Lake, CA 91602 USA

Haider, Jorg *Government Official*
Freedom Party, Kamtnerstr 28, Vienna, 1010, AUSTRIA

Haig, Alexander M Jr *Secretary, General*
685 Island Dr, Palm Beach, FL 33480 USA

Haignere, Jean-Pierre *Misc*
CNES, 2Place Maurice Quentin, Paris Cedeux, 75039, FRANCE

Hailey, Arthur *Writer*
Lyford Cay PO Box N7776, Nassau, BAHAMAS

Hailey, Joel *Actor, Musician*
Creative Artists Agency LCC (CAA-LA), 9830 Wilshire Blvd, Beverly Hills, CA 90212 USA

Hailey, Leisha *Music Group, Songwriter*
Evolution Talent, 1776 Broadway #1500, New York, NY 10019 USA

Hailey, Oliver
11747 Canton Pl., Studio City, CA 91604

Hailston, Earl B *General*
Commanding General, Marine Corps Forces Pacific, Camp H M Smith, HI 96861 USA

Haim, Corey *Actor*
Innovative Artists (LA), 1505 Tenth St, Santa Monica, CA 90401 USA

Haimovitz, Jules *Business Person*
King Worls Productions, 12400 Wilshire Blvd, Los Angeles, CA 90025 USA

Haimovitz, Matt *Music Group, Musician*
Columbia Artists Mgmt Inc, 165 W 57th St, New York, NY 10019 USA

Haines, Connie *Music Group*
880 Mandalay Ave #3-109, Clearwater, FL 33767 USA

Haines, George *Swimmer, Coach*
1033 Tioga Court, Lincoln, CA 95648 USA

Haines, Lee M *Religious Leader*
Wesleyan Church, PO Box 50434, Indianapolis, IN 46250 USA

Haines, Randa *Director*
1429 Avon Park Terrace, Los Angeles, CA 90026 USA

Haire, John E *Publisher*
Time Magazine, Rockefeller Center, New York, NY 10020 USA

Hairi, Gisue *Architect*
Hairi & Hairi, 18 E 12th St, New York, NY 10003 USA

Hairi, Moigan *Architect*
Hairi & Hairi, 18 E 12th St, New York, NY 10003 USA

Haise, Fred W
14316 FM 2354 Rd, Baytown, TX 77520 USA

Haise, Fred W Jr *Astronaut, Misc*
9038 N Point Dr, Baytown, TX 77520 USA

Haislip, Marcus *Basketball Player*
Milwaukee Bucks, Bradley Center 1001 N 4th St, Milwaukee, WI 53203 USA

Haitink, Bernard J H *Conductor*
Harold Holt, 31 Sinclair Road, London, W14 0NS, UNITED KINGDOM (UK)

Hajak, Ron
17420 Ventura Blvd. #4, Encino, CA 91316

Haje, Khrystyne *Actor*
PO Box 8750, Universal City, CA 91618 USA

Hajek, Andreas *Athlete*
Weissbundenweg 18, Halle/Saale, 06128, GERMANY

Hajiro, Barney *War Hero*
94-535 Awamoi St, Walpahu, HI 96797 USA

Hakkinen, Mikka *Race Car Driver*
McLaren International, Albert Dr, Woking, Surrey, GU21 5JY, UNITED KINGDOM (UK)

Haland, Bjoro
Sor-Audnedal, NORWAY, N-4520

Halas, John *Animator*
Educational Film Center, 5-7 Kean St, London, WC2B 4AT, UNITED KINGDOM (UK)

Halberstam, David *Writer*
William Morrow, 1350 Ave of Americas, New York, NY 10019 USA

Halbert, David *Business Person*
Advance PCS, 750 W John Carpenter Fwy #1200, Irving, TX 75039-2507

Halbert, Gary

Halbreich, Kathy *Director, Misc*
Walker Art Center, 725 Vineland Place, Minneapolis, MN 55403 USA

Haldeman, Charles (Ed) *Financier*
Putnam Investments, 1 Post Office Square, Boston, MA 02109 USA

Haldorson, Burdette (Burdie) *Basketball Player*
2422 Zane Place, Colorado Springs, CO 80909 USA

Hale, Alan *Astronomer*
Southwest Space Research Institute, 15 E Spur Road, Cloudcraft, NM 88317 USA

Hale, Alan Spencer
5476 St. Paul Rd, Morristown, NJ 07813

Hale, Barbara *Actor*
PO Box 6061-261, Sherman Oaks, CA 91413 USA

Hale, Georgina *Actor*
74A St John's Wood High St, London, NW8, UNITED KINGDOM (UK)

Hale, Monte *Actor, Music Group*
11732 Moorpark St #B, Studio City, CA 91604 USA

Haley, Charles J *Football Player*
1502 Estates Way, Carrollton, TX 75006 USA

Haley, Maria *Financier*
Export-Import Bank, 811 Vermont Ave NW, Washington, DC 20571 USA

Halffter, Cristobal J *Composer, Conductor*
Jurgen Erlebach, Grillparsestr 24, Hamburg, 22085, GERMANY

Halford, Rob *Music Group*
International Creative Mgmt, 40 W 57th St #1800, New York, NY 10019 USA

Halfvarson, Eric *Opera Singer*
Munro Artist Mgmt, 786 Darthmouth St, South Darthmouth, MA 02748 USA

Hall, Alaina Reed *Actor*
10636 Rathburn, Northridge, CA 91326 USA

Hall, Anthony Michael *Actor*
International Creative Management (ICM-LA), 8942 Wilshire Blvd, Beverly Hills, CA 90211 USA

Hall, Arsenio *Entertainer*
Endeavor Talent Agency, 9701 Wilshire Blvd #1000, Beverly Hills, CA 90212 USA

Hall, Barbara *Writer, Producer*
Creative Artists Agency LCC (CAA-LA), 9830 Wilshire Blvd, Beverly Hills, CA 90212 USA

Hall, Bobby
20122 Hall Dr., Brooksville, FL 34601

Hall, Bridget *Model*
I M G Models, 304 Park Ave S #1200, New York, NY 10010 USA

Hall, Bruce Michael *Actor*
Jerry Shandrew PR, 1050 South Stanley Avenue, Los Angeles, CA 90019-6634 USA

Hall, Bug *Actor*
Relativity Management, 8899 Beverly Blvd #510, Los Angeles, CA 90048 USA

Hall, Charles *Inventor*
Basic Designs, 5815 Bennett Valley Road, Santa Rosa, CA 95404 USA

Hall, Cynthia Holcomb *Judge*
US Court of Appeals, 125 S Grand Ave, Pasadena, CA 91105 USA

Hall, Dante *Athlete*
Kansas City Chiefs, 1 Arrowhead Dr, Kansas City, MO 64129 USA

Hall, Daryl *Music Group, Songwriter*
Creative Artists Agency, 9830 Wilshire Blvd, Beverly Hills, CA 90212 USA

Hall, Deidre *Actor*
11041 Santa Monica Blvd, PO Box 715, Los Angeles, CA 90078 USA

Hall, Delores *Actor, Music Group*
Agency for Performing Arts, 485 Madison Ave, New York, NY 10022 USA

Hall, Donald *Writer*
Eagle Point Farm, Wilmot, NH 03287 USA

Hall, Donald J *Business Person*
Hallmark Cards, 2501 McGee St, Kansas City, MO 64108 USA

Hall, Edward T *Doctor, Writer*
8 Calle Jacinta, Santa Fe, NM 87508 USA

Hall, Ervin (Erv) *Track Athlete*
Citicorp Mortgage, 670 Mason Ridge Center Dr, Saint Louis, MO 63141 USA

Hall, Fawn -
1568 Viewsite Dr, Los Angeles, CA 90069

Hall, Galen *Football Coach, Football Player*
Pennsylvania State University, Greenberg Complex, University Park, PA 16802 USA

Hall, Gary C *Engineer*
PO Box 715, Rosamond, CA 93560 USA

Hall, Glenn H *Hockey Player*
CSAS, PO Box 60036, RPO Glen Abbey, Oakville, ON L6M 3H2, CANADA

Hall, Greff Kaye *Swimmer*
906 3rd St, Mukilteo, WA 98275 USA

Hall, James E (Jim) *Race Car Driver, Misc*
RR 7 Box 640, Midland, TX 79706 USA

Hall, James S (Jim) *Music Group, Musician*
Jazz Tree, 211 Thompson St #LD, New York, NY 10012 USA

Hall, Jerry *Actor, Model*
471-473 Kings Road, London, SW10 0LU, UNITED KINGDOM (UK)

Hall, Jerry *Doctor, Misc*
George Washington University, Med Center 2300 St NW, Washington, DC 20037 USA

Hall, Joe B *Basketball Player, Coach*
Central Bank & Trust Co, 300 W Vine St, Lexington, KY 40507 USA

Hall, Karen *Writer*
9242 Beverly Dr, #200, Beverly Hills, CA 90210 USA

Hall, Kevan *Fashion Designer*
Kevan Hall Studio, 756 S Spring St #11E, Los Angeles, CA 90014 USA

Hall, L Parker *Football Player*
4712 Cole Road, Memphis, TN 38117 USA

Hall, Lani *Music Group*
31930 Pacific Coast Highway, Malibu, CA 90265 USA

Hall, Lanny *Educator*
Hardin-Simmons University, President's Office, Abilene, TX 79698 USA

Hall, Lloyd M Jr *Religious Leader*
Congregation Christian Church Assn, PO Box 1620, Oak Creek, MI 53154 USA

Hall, Michael C *Actor*
Gersh Agency, The (LA), 232 N Canon Dr, Beverly Hills, CA 90210 USA

Hall, Monty
519 N. Arden Dr., Beverly Hills, CA 90210

Hall, Nigel J *Artist*
11 Kensington Park Gardens, London, W11 3HD, UNITED KINGDOM (UK)

Hall, Peter R F *Director*
Peter Hall Co, 18 Exeter St, London, WC2E 7DU, UNITED KINGDOM (UK)

Hall, Philip Baker *Actor*
Writers & Artists, 8383 Wilshire Blvd #550, Beverly Hills, CA 90211 USA

Hall, Reamy *Actor*
Irv Schechter Company, 9460 Wilshire Blvd, Suite 300, Beverly Hills, CA 90212 USA

Hall, Regina *Actor*
100 N Clark Dr #205, West Hollywood, CA 90048 USA

Hall, Robert N *Inventor*
2315 Gurenson Lane, Niskayuna, NY 12309 USA

Hall, Samuel (Sam) *Swimmer, Misc*
5759 Wilcke Way, Dayton, OH 45459 USA

Hall, Sonny *Misc*
Transport Workers Union, 80 W End Ave, New York, NY 10023 USA

Hall, Tom T *Music Group, Songwriter*
Tom T Hall Enterprises, PO Box 1246, Franklin, TN 37065 USA

Hall, William Sr *Bowler*
5108 N 126th Ave, Omaha, NE 68164
USA

Hall & Oates *Music Group*
Doyle-Kos Entertainment, 494 Eighth Ave,
Floor 24, New York, NY 10001 USA

Hall Jr, Gary *Swimmer*
2501 N 32nd St, Phoenix, AZ 85005 USA

Hall-Garmes, Ruth *Actor*
432 Alandele Ave, Los Angeles, CA 90036
USA

Halla, Brian L *Business Person*
National Semiconductor, 2900
Semiconductor Dr, Santa Clara, CA 95051
USA

Halladay, H Leroy (Roy) *Baseball Player*
4537 Rutledge Dr, Palm Harbor, FL 34685
USA

Hallam, John
51 Lansdowne Gardens, London,
ENGLAND, SW8 2EL

Haller, Gordon *Athlete*
20514 E Caley Dr, Centennial, CO 80016
USA

Haller, Kevin *Hockey Player*
113-276 Midpark Way SE, Calgary, AB
T2X 1J6, CANADA

Hallervorden, Dieter
Nurnberger Str. 33, Berlin, GERMANY,
D-10777

Hallet, Jim *Golfer*
232 Shell Bluff Court, Ponte Vedra, FL
32082 USA

Hallick, Tom
13900 Tahiti Way #108, Marina del Rey,
CA 90292

Hallier, Lori *Actor*
Epstein-Wyckoff, 280 S Beverly Dr #400,
Beverly Hills, CA 90212 USA

Hallinan, Joseph T *Journalist*
Random House, 1745 Broadway #B1,
New York, NY 10019 USA

Halliwell, Geri *Music Group*
Andy Stephens, 60A Highgate High St,
London, N6 5HX, UNITED KINGDOM
(UK)

Hallman, Tom Jr *Journalist*
Portland Oregonian, Editorial Dept, 1320
SW Broadway, Portland, OR 97201 USA

Hallstrom, Holly *Model, Entertainer*
5757 Wilshire Blvd #206, Los Angeles,
CA 90036 USA

Hallstrom, Lasse *Director*
United Talent Agency, 9560 Wilshire Blvd
#500, Beverly Hills, CA 90212 USA

Hallwachs, Hans-Peter
Lindenstr. 9a, Grunwald, GERMANY,
83021

Hallyday, Johnny *Actor, Music Group*
CC Productions, 6 Rue Daubigny, Paris,
75017, FRANCE

Halonen Tarja, Kaarina *President*
Presidential Palace, Pohjoisesplandi 1,
Helsinki 17, 00170, FINLAND

Halperin, Bertrand I *Physicist*
Harvard University, Physics Dept,
Cambridge, MA 02138 USA

Halpern, Daniel *Writer*
9 Mercer St, Princeton, NJ 08540 USA

Halpern, Jack *Misc*
5801 S Dorchester Ave #4A, Chicago, IL
60637 USA

Halpern, James S *Judge*
US Tax Court, 400 2nd St NW,
Washington, DC 20217 USA

Halpin, Luke
PO Box 391233, Deltona, FL 32739-1233

Halprin, Lawrence *Architect, Misc*
1160 Battery St #50, San Francisco, CA
94111 USA

Halsell, James D Jr *Astronaut*
1617 Stoney Lake Dr, Friendswood, TX
77546 USA

Ham, Jack R *Football Player*
Ham Enterprises, 540 Lindergh Dr, Moon
Township, PA 15108 USA

Ham, Kenneth T *Astronaut*
904 W Viejo Dr, Friendswood, TX 77546
USA

Hamao, Stephen Fumio Cardinal
Religious Leader
Pastoral Care of Migrants, Piazza S Calisto
16, 00120, VATICAN CITY

Hamari, Julia *Opera Singer*
Max Brod-Weg 14, Stuttgart, 70437,
GERMANY

Hambling, Maggi *Artist*
Morley College, Westminster Bridge Road,
London, SE1 7HT, UNITED KINGDOM
(UK)

Hambro, Leonid *Music Group, Musician*
California Institute of Arts, Music Dept,
Valencia, CA 91355 USA

Hamburger, Michael P L *Writer*
John Johnson, 45/47 Clerkenwell Green,
London, EC1R 0HT, UNITED KINGDOM
(UK)

Hamed, Nihad *Religious Leader*
Islamic Assn in US/Canada, 25351 Five
Mile Road, Redford Township, MI 48239
USA

Hamed, Prince Naseem *Athlete, Boxer*
26 Newman Rd, Wincobank, Sheffield, S9
1LP, UNITED KINGDOM (UK)

Hamel, Alan
PO Box 827, Monterey, CA 93942

Hamel, Michael A *Astronaut*
HQ AFSPC/DR, 150 Vandenburg St#1105,
Colorado Springs, CO 80914 USA

Hamel, Veronica *Actor, Model*
Gersh Agency, The (LA), 232 N Canon Dr,
Beverly Hills, CA 90210 USA

Hamel, William *Religious Leader*
Evangelical Free Church, 901 E 78th St,
Minneapolis, MN 55420 USA

Hamill, Dorothy *Figure Skater*
Int'l Mgmt Group, 1 Erieview Plaza, 1360
E 9th St #1300, Cleveland, OH 44114
USA

Hamill, Mark *Actor*
1101 Holly Spring Lane, Grand Blanc, MI
48439 USA

Hamill, W Pete *Writer, Editor*
8 Whiskey Hill Road, Wallkitt, NY 12589
USA

Hamilton, Allan G (Al) *Hockey Player*
2452 11th St, Edmonton, AB T6J 3S1,
CANADA

Hamilton, Ashley *Actor*
9255 Doheny Rd #2302, Los Angeles, CA
90069 USA

Hamilton, Bobby Jr *Race Car Driver*
Motorsports Decisions, 1435 W Morehead
St #190, Charlotte, NC 28208 USA

Hamilton, David *Photographer*
41 Blvd du Montpamasse, Paris, 75006,
FRANCE

Hamilton, Forestom (Chico) *Music
Group, Musician*
Chico Hamilton Productions, 321 E 45th
St #PH, New York, NY 10017 USA

Hamilton, George *Actor*
Agency for Performing Arts, 9200 Sunset
Blvd #900, Los Angeles, CA 90069 USA

Hamilton, George IV *Music Group,
Musician, Songwriter*
Blade Agency, 203 SW 3rd Ave,
Gainesville, FL 32601 USA

Hamilton, Guy *Director*
Puerto de Andraitz, Apartado III, Palma de
Mallorca, SPAIN

Hamilton, Joe Frank & Reynolds
1629 E. Sahara Ave., Las Vegas, NV
89104

Hamilton, Josh *Actor*
William Morris Agency, 151 El Camino
Dr, Beverly Hills, CA 90212 USA

Hamilton, Lee H *Politician, Misc*
Wilson Int'l Schorlars Center, 1300
Pennsylvania Ave NW, Washington, DC
20004 USA

Hamilton, Leonard *Basketball Player,
Coach*
Florida State University, Athletic Dept,
Tallahassee, FL 32306 USA

Hamilton, Linda *Actor*
Edrick/Rich Mgmt, 8955 Norma Place, Los
Angeles, CA 90069 USA

Hamilton, Lisa Gay *Actor*
Writers & Artists, 8383 Wilshire Blvd
#550, Beverly Hills, CA 90211 USA

Hamilton, Lynn
1042 S. Burnside Ave., Los Angeles, CA
90019

Hamilton, Marcus
12225 Ranburne Rd., Charlotte, NC
28227

Hamilton, Michael *Artist*
2012 N 19th St, Boise, ID 83702 USA

Hamilton, Natasha *Musician*
Concorde Intl Artists Ltd, 101 Shepherds
Bush Rd, London, W6 7LP, UNITED
KINGDOM (UK)

Hamilton, Paula *Actor*
PFD Drury House, 34-43 Russell St,
London, WC2B 5HA, UNITED KINGDOM
(UK)

Hamilton, Richard *Artist*
Northend Form, Northend, Oxon, RG9
6LQ, UNITED KINGDOM (UK)

Hamilton, Richard *Basketball Player*
Detroit Pistons, Palace 2 Championship
Dr, Auburn Hills, MI 48326 USA

Hamilton, Scott S *Figure Skater*
Berkeley Agency, 2608 9th St, Berkeley,
CA 94710 USA

Hamilton, Suzanna *Actor*
Julian Belfarge, 46 Albermarie St, London,
W1X 4PP, UNITED KINGDOM (UK)

Hamilton, Suzy
PO Box 655, New Glarus, WI 53574

Hamilton, Tom *Music Group, Musician*
PO Box 67039, Newton, MA 02167 USA

Hamilton, Victoria *Actor*
Paradigm (LA), 10100 Santa Monica Blvd,
Fl 25, Los Angeles, CA 90067 USA

Hamilton, William *Cartoonist, Writer*
17 E 95th St #3F, New York, NY 10128
USA

Hamilton-Klemperer, Kim
44 W. 62nd St.10th Flr., New York, NY
10023

Hamlin, Brooke *Actor*
Coast to Coast Talent Group, 3350
Barham Blvd, Los Angeles, CA 90068
USA

Hamlin, Harry *Actor*
PO Box 25578, Los Angeles, CA 90025
USA

Hamlisch, Marvin *Composer, Conductor*
970 Park Ave #501, New York, NY 10028
USA

Hamm, Jon *Actor*
International Creative Management
(ICM-LA), 8942 Wilshire Blvd, Beverly
Hills, CA 90211 USA

Hamm, Mia *Soccer Player, Model*
US Soccer Federation, 1801 S Prairie Ave,
Chicago, IL 60616 USA

Hamm, Nick *Director*
International Creative Mgmt, 8942
Wilshire Blvd #219, Beverly Hills, CA
90211 USA

Hamm, Richard L *Religious Leader*
Christian Church Disciples of Christ, PO
Box 1986, Indianapolis, IN 46206 USA

Hammad al-Bassam, Abd al-Mohsin
Cosmonaut
Royal Embassy of Saudi Arabia, 22
Holland Park, London, W11, UNITED
KINGDOM (UK)

Hammel, Eugene A *Misc*
2332 Piedmont Ave, Berkeley, CA 94720
USA

Hammer *Musician, Music Group*
Terrie Williams Agency, 1500 Broadway
Front, #7, New York, NY 10036 USA

Hammer, Victor S *Cinematographer*
PO Box 10788, Marina del Rey, CA
90295 USA

Hammer Jr, Jan *Composer, Musician*
2 W 45th St, #1102, New York, NY
10036 USA

Hammergren, John H *Business Person*
McKesson HBOC Inc, 1 Post St, San
Francisco, CA 94104 USA

Hammerman, Stephen *Financier*
Merrill Lynch Co, World Financial Center,
2 Vesey St, New York, NY 10007 USA

Hammes, Gordon G *Misc*
11 Staley Place, Durham, NC 27705 USA

Hammett, Kirk *Musician, Music Group*
2505 Divisadero St, San Francisco, CA
94115 USA

Hammon, Becky *Basketball Player*
New York Liberty, Madison Square
Garden, 2 Penn Plaza, New York, NY
10121 USA

Hammon, Jennifer
270 N. Canon Dr. #1064, Beverly Hills,
CA 90210

Hammond, Albert Jr *Music Group,
Musician*
MVO Ltd, 370 7th Ave #807, New York,
NY 10001 USA

Hammond, Caleb D Jr *Publisher, Misc*
61 Woodland Road, Maplewood, NJ
07040 USA

Hammond, Darrell *Actor, Comedian*
International Creative Mgmt, 8942
Wilshire Blvd #219, Beverly Hills, CA
90211 USA

Hammond, Fred *Music Group*
Face to Face, 21421 Hilltop St Blvd 20,
Southfield, MI 48034 USA

Hammond, James T *Religious Leader*
Pentecostal Free Will Baptist Church, PO
Box 1568, Dunn, NC 28335 USA

Hammond, Jay S *Governor*
Lake Charles Lodge, Port Alsworth, AK
99652 USA

Hammond, Joan H *Opera Singer*
Private Bag 101, Geelong Mail Center,
VIC, 3221, AUSTRALIA

Hammond, John *Musician, Music Group*
Rosebud Agency, PO Box 170429, San
Francisco, CA 94117 USA

Hammond, L Blaine Jr *Astronaut*
Gulfstream Aircraft, 4150 E Donald
Douglas Dr #926, Long Beach, CA 90808
USA

Hammond, Robert D *General*
PO Box 222032, Carmel, CA 93922 USA

Hammond, Tom *Sportscaster*
NBC-TV, Sprots Dept 30 Rockefeller
Plaza, New York, NY 10112 USA

Hammons, David *Artist*
Studio Museum in Harlem, 144 W 125th
St, New York, NY 10027 USA

Hammons, Roger *Religious Leader*
Primitive Advent Christian Church, 273
Frame Road, Elkview, WV 25071 USA

Hamner, Earl
11575 Amanda Dr., Studio City, CA
91604

Hamnett, Katharine *Fashion Designer*
Katharine Hamnett Ltd, 202 New North
Road, London, N1, UNITED KINGDOM
(UK)

Hampel, Olaf *Athlete*
Pommenweg 2, Bielefeld, 33689,
GERMANY

Hampshire, Susan *Actor*
Chatto & Linnit, Prince of Wales Coventry
St, London, W1V 7FE, UNITED
KINGDOM (UK)

Hampson, Thomas *Opera Singer*
Starkfriedgasse 53, Vienna, 1180,
AUSTRIA

Hampton, Brenda *Producer*
Ziffren Brittenham Branca Fischer Gilbert-
Lurie & Stiffman LLP, 1801 Century Park
W, Los Angeles, CA 90067 USA

Hampton, Christopher J *Writer*
2 Kensington Park Gardens, London,
W11, UNITED KINGDOM (UK)

Hampton, Daniel O (Dan) *Football Player*
8641 Oak Park Ave, Burbank, IL 60459
USA

Hampton, James *Actor*
102 Forest Hill Dr, Roanoke, TX 76262
USA

Hampton, Locksley (Slide) *Music Group,
Musician*
Charismic Productions, 2604 Mozart
Place NW, Washington, DC 20009 USA

Hampton, Michael W (Mike) *Baseball
Player*
YSA, 2001 Blake St, Denver, CO 80205
USA

Hampton, Millard *Track Athlete*
201 W Mission St, San Jose, CA 95110
USA

Hampton, Ralph C Jr *Religious Leader*
Free Will Baptist Bible College, 3606 W
End Ave, Nashville, TN 37205 USA

Hamrlik, Roman *Hockey Player*
New York Islanders, Nassau Coliseum,
Hempstead Turnpike, Uniondale, NY
11553 USA

Hamzah *Prince*
Crown Prince's Office, Royal Palace,
Amman, JORDAN

Han, Suyin *Writer*
37 Montoie, Lausanne, 1007,
SWITZERLAND

Hanafusa, Hidesaburo *Biologist*
Rockefeller University, 1230 York Ave,
New York, NY 10021 USA

Hanauer, Chip *Yachtsman*
Hanauer Enterprises, 2702 NE 88th St,
Seattle, WA 98115 USA

Hanauer, Terri
8271 Melrose Ave. #110, Los Angeles, CA
90046

Hanburger, Christian (Chris) Jr *Football
Player*
708 Winter Hill Dr, Apex, NC 27502 USA

Hanbury-Tension, Robin *Scientist*
Maidenwell, Cardinham Bodmin,
Comwall, PL3O 4DW, UNITED
KINGDOM (UK)

Hance Jr, James H *Financier*
Bank of America Corp, 100 N Tyron St,
Charlotte, NC 28255 USA

Hancock, Butch *Songwriter, Musician*
Valdenn Agency, 13801 RR 12, #202,
Wimberley, TX 78676 USA

Hancock, Herbert J (Herbie) *Musician,
Composer*
DL Media, PO Box 2728, Bela Cynwyd,
PA 19004 USA

Hancock, John D *Director*
7355 N Fail Road, La Porte, IN 46350
USA

Hancock, John Lee *Writer, Director, Producer*
Creative Artists Agency LCC (CAA-LA), 9830 Wilshire Blvd, Beverly Hills, CA 90212 USA

Hand, Jon T *Football Player*
13013 Broad St, Carmel, IN 46032 USA

Handelsman, J B *Cartoonist*
New Yorker Magazine, Editorial Dept 4 Times Square, New York, NY 10036 USA

Handelsman, Walt *Editor, Cartoonist*
Newsday, Editorial Dept 235 Pinelawn Road, Melville, NY 11747 USA

Handford, Martin *Cartoonist*
Walker Books, 87 Vauxhall Walk, London, SE11 5HU, UNITED KINGDOM (UK)

Handke, Peter *Writer*
Farrar Straus Giroux, 19 Union Square W, New York, NY 10003 USA

Handler, Evan *Actor*
Liberman/Zerman, 252 N Larchmont #200, Los Angeles, CA 90004 USA

Handley, Taylor *Actor*
Booh Schut Company, 11350 Ventura Blvd #200, Studio City, CA 91604 USA

Handley, Vernon G *Conductor*
Cwm Cottage, Bettws Abergavenny, Monmouhshire, NP7 7LG, WALES

Handlin, Oscar *Historian*
18 Agassiz St, Cambridge, MA 02140 USA

Hands, Terence *Director*
Clwyd Theater Cymru, Mold, Flintshire, NORTH WALES

Hands, William A (Bill) *Baseball Player*
PO Box 334, Orient, NY 11957 USA

Handsome
9255 Sunset Blvd. #200, Los Angeles, CA 90069-3309

Handy, John *Music Group, Musician*
Integrity Talent, PO Box 961, Burlington, MA 01803 USA

Handy, John W *General*
Commander-in-Chief, Transportation Command, Scott Air Force Base, IL 62225 USA

Hanes, Ken
8281 Melrose Ave #200, Los Angeles, CA 90046

Haney, Lee *Writer*
Lee Haney Enterprises, 105 Trail Point Circle, Fairburn, GA 30213 USA

Hanfmann, George M A *Archaeologist*
Harvard University, Fogg Art Museum, 32 Quincy St, Cambridge, MA 02138 USA

Hanft, Ruth S *Scientist*
3340 Brookside Dr, Charlottesville, VA 22901 USA

Hanin, Roger *Actor*
9 rue du Boccador, Paris, 75008, FRANCE

Hankinson, Tim *Soccer Player, Coach*
Columbus Crew, 2121 Velman Ave, Columbus, OH 43211 USA

Hanks, Colin *Actor*
Creative Artists Agency, 9830 Wilshire Blvd, Beverly Hills, CA 90212 USA

Hanks, Merton *Football Player*
855 E Davisburg Road, Holly, MI 48442 USA

Hanks, Tom *Actor*
Playtone Productions, PO Box 7340, Santa Monica, CA 90406 USA

Hanley, Bridget
12021 Hesby St., Valley Village, CA 91607-3115

Hanley, Charles *Journalist*
Associated Press, 50 Rockefeller Plaza, New York, NY 10020 USA

Hanley, Frank *Misc*
Int'l Union of Operating Engineers, 1125 17th St NW, Washington, DC 20036 USA

Hanley, Jenny *Actor*
MGA, Southbank House, Black Prince Road, London, SE1 7SJ, UNITED KINGDOM (UK)

Hanley, Kay *Music Group*
Little Big Man, 155 Ave of Americas #700, New York, NY 10013 USA

Hanley, Richard *Swimmer*
E266 Lake Road, Ironwood, MI 49938 USA

Hanlon, Edward Jr *General*
Commanding General, Marine Combat Development Command, Quantico, VA 22134 USA

Hanlon, Glen *Hockey Player*
8781 Piney Orchard Parkway, Odenton, MD 21113 USA

Hann, Judith
56 Wood Lane, London, ENGLAND, W12 7RJ

Hanna, Jack
PO Box 400, Powell, OH 43065

Hanna, Jerome *Music Group*
Paramount Entertainment, PO Box 12, Far Hills, NJ 07931 USA

Hannah, Bob *Motorcycle Racer*
American Motorcycle Assn, 13515 Yarmouth Dr, Pickerington, OH 43147 USA

Hannah, Bob *Baseball Player, Coach*
University of Delaware, Athletic Dept, Newark, DE 19716 USA

Hannah, Charles A (Charley) *Football Player*
PO Box 2671, Lutz, FL 33548 USA

Hannah, Daryl *Actor*
Binder & Associates, 1465 Lindacrest Dr, Beverly Hills, CA 90210 USA

Hannah, John *Actor*
William Morris Agency, 52/53 Poland Place, London, W1F 7LX, UNITED KINGDOM (UK)

Hannah, John A *Football Player*
26 Barletts Beach, Amesbury, MA 01913 USA

Hannah, Wayne *Religious Leader*
Fellowship of Grace Brethren Churches, PO Box 386, Winona Lake, IN 46590 USA

Hannawald, Sven *Skier*
WH Sport Int'l GmbH, Im Sabel 4, Trier, 54294, GERMANY

Hanneman, Steve *Actor*
Abrams Artists Agency (LA), 9200 Sunset Blvd Fl 11, Los Angeles, CA 90069 USA

Hannigan, Alyson *Actor*
Innovative Artists, 1505 10th St, Santa Monica, CA 90401 USA

Hannity, Sean *Commentator*
Fox-TV, News Dept 205 E 67th St, New York, NY 10021 USA

Hannuia, Dick *Swimmer, Coach*
1021 Westley Dr, Tacoma, WA 98465 USA

Hanratty, Terrance R (Terry) *Football Player*
22 Hunters Creek Lane, New Canaan, CT 06840 USA

Hans-Adam II *Prince*
Schloss Vaduz, 9490 Vaduz, LIECHTENSTEIN

Hansen, Alfred G *General, Business Person*
Lockheed Aero Systems, 86 S Cobb Dr, Marietta, GA 30063 USA

Hansen, Clifford P *Governor, Senator*
PO Box 448, Jackson, WY 83001 USA

Hansen, Frederick M (Fred) *Track Athlete*
201 Vanderpool Lane #12, Houston, TX 77024 USA

Hansen, Gale *Actor*
721 SE 29th Ave, Portland, OR 97214 USA

Hansen, Gunnar *Actor*
PO Box 368, North East Harbor, ME 04662 USA

Hansen, Jacqueline *Track Athlete*
1133 9th St, Santa Monica, CA 90403 USA

Hansen, James E *Scientist, Physicist*
Goddard Institute for Space Studies, 2880 Broadway, New York, NY 10025 USA

Hansen, Jed *Baseball Player*
PO Box 3665, Omaha, NE 68103

Hansen, Mark Victor *Business Person*
PO Box 7665, Newport Beach, CA 92658

Hansen, Patti *Model*
Redlands W Wittering, Chichester, Sussex, UNITED KINGDOM (UK)

Hansen, Peter *Actor*
Stone Manners, 6500 Wilshire Blvd, #550, Los Angeles, CA 90048 USA

Hanson *Music Group*
Creative Artists Agency LCC (CAA-LA), 9830 Wilshire Blvd, Beverly Hills, CA 90212 USA

Hanson, Carl T *Admiral*
900 Birdseye Road, Orient, NY 11967 USA

Hanson, Curtis *Director, Writer*
United Talent Agency, 9560 Wilshire Blvd #500, Beverly Hills, CA 90212 USA

Hanson, Isaac *Music Group, Musician, Songwriter*
1045 W 78th St, Tulsa, OK 74132 USA

Hanson, Jason D *Football Player*
3165 Midvale Dr, Rochester Hills, MI 48309 USA

Hanson, Jennifer *Musician*
Creative Artists Agency (CAA-Nashville), 3310 West End Ave Fl 5, Nashville, TN 37203 USA

Hanson, Sir James
180 Brompton Rd., ENGLAND, London, SW3 1HQ

Hanson, Stan
PO Box 970, Hotchkiss, CO 81419-0970

Hanson, Taylor *Music Group, Musician, Songwriter*
1045 W 78th St, Tulsa, OK 74132 USA

Hanson, William R *Artist*
78 W Notre Dame St, Glens Falls, NY 12801 USA

Hanson, Zachary *Music Group, Musician, Songwriter*
1045 W 78th St, Tulsa, OK 74132 USA

Hansraj, Jugal *Actor, Bollywood*
14-A Queens Apt, Pali Hill Bandra (W), Mumbai, MS 400050, INDIA

Hanss, Ted *Scientist*
Information Technology Intergration Center, 3025 Boardwalk, Ann Arbor, MI 48108 USA

Hanuja *Actor, Bollywood*
No 20 Periyar Street, Gandhi Nagar, Chennai, TN INDIA

Hanzlik, Bill *Basketball Player, Coach*
5701 Green Oaks Dr, Greenwood Village, CO 80121 USA

Hapke, Bruce *Misc*
1702 Georgetown Place, Pittsburgh, PA 15235 USA

Harad, George J *Business Person*
Boise Cascade Corp, 1111 W Jefferson St, Boise, ID 83728 USA

Harada, Masahiko (Fighting) *Boxer*
2-21-5 Azabu-Juban, Minatoku, Tokyo, 106, JAPAN

Harald V *King*
Det Kongelige Slott, Drammensvelen 1, Oslo, 0010, NORWAY

Harbach, Otto
3455 Congress St, Fairfield, CT 06430-2036

Harbaugh, Gregory J *Astronaut*
2434 Hollingsworth Hill Ave, Lakeland, FL 33803 USA

Harbaugh, James J (Jim) *Football Player*
7051 Broadway Terrace, Oakland, CA 94611 USA

Harbaugh, Robert E *Doctor*
Dartmouth-Hitchcock Medical Center, Surgery Dept, Hanover, NH 03756 USA

Harbison, John H *Composer*
479 Franklin St, Cambridge, MA 02139 USA

Hard, Darlene R *Tennis Player*
22924 Erwin St, Woodland Hills, CA 91367 USA

Hardaway, Anfemee (Penny) *Basketball Player*
PO Box 2132, Farmington Hills, MI 48333 USA

Hardaway, Anfernee (Penny) *Basketball Player*
6516 N 64th Pl, Paradise Valley, AZ 85253 USA

Hardaway, Timothy D (Tim) *Basketball Player*
10050 SW 62nd Ave, Miami, FL 33156 USA

Harden, Marcia Gay *Actor*
Framework Entertainment (LA), 9057 Nemo St #C, W Hollywood, CA 90069 USA

Hardenberger, Hahan *Music Group, Musician*
Columbia Artists Mgmt Inc, 165 W 57th St, New York, NY 10019 USA

Hardesty Jr, David C *Educator*
West Virginia University, President's Office, Morgantown, WV 26506 USA

Hardie, Kate *Actor*
Jonathan Altaras, 13 Shorts Gardens, London, WC2H 9AT, UNITED KINGDOM (UK)

Hardin, Clifford M *Secretary*
10 Road Lane, Saint Louis, MO 63124 USA

Hardin, Jerry
3033 Vista Crest Dr., Los Angeles, CA 90068

Hardin, Melora *Actor*
3256 Hilloak Dr, Los Angeles, CA 90068 USA

Hardin, Paul III *Educator*
University of North Carolina, Chancellor's Office, Chapel Hill, NC 27599 USA

Hardin, Ty *Actor*
PO Box 1821, Gig Harbor, WA 98335 USA

Harding, Daniel *Musician*
International Creative Management (ICM-LA), 8942 Wilshire Blvd, Beverly Hills, CA 90211 USA

Harding, John Wesley *Music Group, Songwriter*
Sincere Mgmt, 6 Bravington Road #6, London, W9 3AH, UNITED KINGDOM (UK)

Harding, Tonya *Athlete*
PO Box 6132, Vancouver, WA 98668, CANADA

Harding, Tonya M *Figure Skater, Actor*
PO Box 6132, Vancouver, WA 98668 USA

Hardis, Stephen R *Business Person*
Eaton Corp, Eaton Center 1111 Superior Ave, Cleveland, OH 44114 USA

Hardison, Kadeem *Actor*
19743 Valleyview Dr, Topanga, CA 90290 USA

Hardisty, Huntington *Admiral*
Lexington Institute, 1600 Wilson Blvd #900, Arlington, VA 22209 USA

Hardman, Earl
1400 E. Carson, Pittsburgh, PA 15302

Hardnett, Charles (Charlie) *Basketball Player, Coach*
1906 Swainsboro Dr, Louisville, KY 40218 USA

Hardt, Eloise *Actor*
Daje Garrick, 8831 Sunset Blvd, #402, Los Angeles, CA 90069 USA

Hardt, Michael *Educator*
Duke Univesity, English Dept, Durham, NC 27708 USA

Hardwick, Billy
1576 S. White Station, Memphis, TN 38117

Hardwick, Catherine *Director*
International Creative Management (ICM-LA), 8942 Wilshire Blvd, Beverly Hills, CA 90211 USA

Hardwick, Chris *Actor*
Platform Public Relations, 2133 Holly Drive, Los Angeles, CA 90068 USA

Hardwick, Elizabeth *Writer*
15 W 67th St, New York, NY 10023 USA

Hardwick, Gary C *Producer, Writer, Director*
Broder Webb Chervin Silbermann Agency, The (BWCS), 9242 Beverly Blvd #200, Beverly Hills, CA 90210 USA

Hardwick, Johnny *Writer, Voice Over Artist*
Creative Artists Agency LCC (CAA-LA), 9830 Wilshire Blvd, Beverly Hills, CA 90212 USA

Hardwick, William B (Billy) *Bowler*
10266 Waterford Road, Collierville, TN 38017 USA

Hardy, Bruce A *Football Player*
5150 SW 20th St, Plantation, FL 33317 USA

Hardy, Carroll *Football Player, Baseball Player*
27875 E Whitewood Dr, Steamboat Springs, CO 80487 USA

Hardy, Hagood *Musician, Composer*
SOCAN, 41 Valleybrook Dr, Don Mills, ON M3B 2S6, CANADA

Hardy, Hugh *Architect*
Hardy Holzman Pfeiffer, 902 Broadway, New York, NY 10010 USA

Hardy, Jeff *Wrestler*
HarperCollins Publishers, 10 East 53rd Street, New York, NY 10022 USA

Hardy, Kevin *Football Player*
2118 College St, Jacksonville, FL 32204 USA

Hardy, Mark *Hockey Player*
220 21st St, #B, Manhattan Beach, CA 90266 USA

Hardy, Matt *Wrestler*
World Wrestling Entertainment (WWE), 1241 E Main St, Stamford, CT 06905 USA

Hardy, Robert *Actor*
Chatto & Linnit, Prince of Wales, Coventry St, London, W1V 7FE, UNITED KINGDOM (UK)

Hardy, Sophie *Doctor*
332 Ave du Marechal Juin, Boulogne, FRANCE, 92100, FRANCE

Hare, David *Writer*
95 Linden Gardens, London, WC2, UNITED KINGDOM (UK)

Harewood, Dorian *Actor*
2 Bearwood Dr, Toronto, ON M9A 4A4,
CANADA

Harewood, Dorien
2 Bearwood Dr, Toronto, CANADA, Ont.
M9A 4

Harewood, Nancy *Actor*
Metropolitan Talent Agency, 4526
Wilshire Blvd, Los Angeles, CA 90010
USA

Hargis, Billy James *Religious Leader*
Rose of Sharon Farm, Neosho, MO 64850
USA

Hargitay, Mariska *Actor*
William Morris Agency (WMA-LA), 1
William Morris Pl, Beverly Hills, CA
90212 USA

Hargitay, Mickey
1255 N. Sycamore Ave., Los Angeles, CA
90038

Hargrove, D Michael (Mike) *Baseball
Player, Misc*
3925 Ramblewood Drive, Richfield, OH
44286 USA

Hargrove, Linda *Coach*
Washington Mystics, MCI Center, 601 E St
NW, Washington, DC 20004 USA

Hargrove, Marion
401 Montana Ave. #6, Santa Monica, A,
90403-1303

Harker, Al *Soccer Player*
620 Wigard Ave, Philadelphia, PA 19128
USA

Harker, Susannah
55 Ashburnham Grove Greenwich,
London, ENGLAND, SW10 8UJ

Harket, Morten *Music Group*
Bandana Mgmt, 11 Elvaston Place #300,
London, SW7 5QC, UNITED KINGDOM
(UK)

Harkin, Tom *Senator*
880 Locust St #125, Dubuque, IA 52001
USA

Harkness, Ned *Hockey Player, Coach*
12 Flower Ave, Glens Falls, NY 12801
USA

Harlan, Jack R *Scientist*
University of Illinois, Agronomy Dept,
Urbana, IL 61801 USA

Harlan, Kevin *Sportscaster*
CBS-TV, Sprots Dept, 51 W 52nd St, New
York, NY 10019 USA

Harlem Globetrotters
400 E. Van Buren #300, Phoenix, AZ
85004

Harley, Steve *Music Group*
Work Hard, 19D Pinfold Road, London,
SW16 2SL, UNITED KINGDOM (UK)

Harlin, Renny *Director, Producer*
Midnight Sun Pictures, 8800 Sunset Blvd
#400, Los Angeles, CA 90069 USA

Harlow, Bill *Writer*
Charles Scribner's Sons, 866 3rd Ave,
New York, NY 10022 USA

Harlow, Shalom *Model*
38 Stephen Ave, Courtice, ON L1E 1Z1,
CANADA

Harman, Denham *Biologist*
9817 Hamey Parkway S, Omaha, NE
68114 USA

Harman, Katie *Beauty Pageant Winner*
The Miss America Organization, Two Miss
America Way, Suite 1000, Atlantic City,
NJ 08401 USA

Harman, Nigel *Actor*
EastEnders, BBC Elstree Centre, Clarendon
Road, Borehamwood, Herts, UNITED
KINGDOM

Harmon, Debbie
13243 Valley Heart, Sherman Oaks, CA
91423

Harmon, Joy *Actor*
9901 Poole Ave, Sunland, CA 91040 USA

Harmon, Kelly *Actor, Model*
13224 Old Oak Lane, Los Angeles, CA
90049 USA

Harmon, Larry
10590 Wilshire Blvd. #1604, Los Angeles,
CA 90024-4353

Harmon, Manny -
8350 Santa Monica Blvd, Los Angeles, CA
90069

Harmon, Mark *Actor*
Paradigm (LA), 10100 Santa Monica Blvd,
Fl 25, Los Angeles, CA 90067 USA

Harmon, Merle *Sportscaster*
424 E Lamar Blvd #210, Arlington, TX
76011 USA

Harmon, Nigel *Astronaut*
Church Crookham, Aldershot, UNITED
KINGDOM (UK)

Harmon, Ronnie K *Football Player*
13022 218th St, Lauretton, NY 11413
USA

Harmon, Winsor
Jerry Shandrew PR, 1050 South Stanley
Avenue, Los Angeles, CA 90019-6634
USA

Harmon-Sehorn, Angie *Actor*
Creative Artists Agency LCC (CAA-LA),
9830 Wilshire Blvd, Beverly Hills, CA
90212 USA

Harmonica Rascals, The
4585 N. River Rd., E. Zanesville, OH
43701-8174

Harms, Alfred G Jr *Admiral*
Chief Education/Training, Naval Air
Station, Pensacola, FL 32508 USA

Harms, Joni *Music Group, Songwriter*
David Skepner/Buckskin Co, PO Box
158488, Nashville, TN 37215 USA

Harms, Kristin *Producer*
West Wing, The, 4000 Warner Blvd,
Trailer 8, Burbank, CA 91522

Harnden, Arthur (Art) *Track Athlete*
7218 Pepper Ridge, Corpus Christi, TX
78413 USA

Harnell, Joe *Composer, Conductor*
41616 Weslin Ave, Sherman Oaks, CA
91423 USA

Harner, Levi *Horse Racer*
RR 1, Millville, PA 17846 USA

Harness, William E *Opera Singer*
PO Box 328, Washougal, WA 98671 USA

Harney, Paul *Golfer*
72 Club Valley Dr, East Falmouth, MA
02536 USA

Harnick, Sheldon M *Songwriter*
Deutsch & Blasband, 800 3rd Ave, New
York, NY 10022 USA

Harnisch, Peter T (Pete) *Baseball Player*
2 Cornfield Lane, Commack, NY 11725
USA

Harnoncourt, Nikolaus
38 Piaristangasse, Vienna, 1080, AUSTRIA

Harnos, Christine *Actor*
Gersh Agency, 232 N Canon Dr, Beverly
Hills, CA 90210 USA

Harnoy, Ofra *Musician*
437 Spadina Road, PO Box 23046,
Toronto, ON M5P 2W0, CANADA

Harold, Erika *Beauty Pageant Winner*
The Miss America Organization, Two Miss
America Way, Suite 1000, Atlantic City,
NJ 08401 USA

Harold, Gale *Actor*
Queer As Folk, 20 Butterick Rd, Toronto,
M8W 3Z, CANADA

Harout, Magda *Actor*
13452 Vose St, Van Nuys, CA 91405 USA

Harper, Alvin C *Football Player*
1304 Split Rock Lane, Fort Washington,
MD 20744 USA

Harper, Ben *Musician, Music Group,
Songwriter*
Nasty Little Man, 15 Maiden Ave #800,
New York, NY 10038 USA

Harper, Chandler *Golfer*
4412 Gannon Road, Portsmouth, VA
23703 USA

Harper, Charles M *Business Person*
6625 State St, Omaha, NE 68152 USA

Harper, Derek *Basketball Player*
2215 Highpoint Circle, Carrollton, TX
75007 USA

Harper, Donald D W (Don) *Swimmer*
1765 Lynnhaven Dr, Columbus, OH
43221 USA

Harper, Edward J *Composer*
7 Morningside Park, Edinburgh, EH10
5HD, SCOTLAND

Harper, Heather M *Opera Singer*
20 Milverton Road, London, NW6 7AS,
UNITED KINGDOM (UK)

Harper, Heck
13647 Gaffney #17, Oregon City, OR
97045

Harper, Hill *Actor*
Gersh Agency, The (LA), 232 N Canon Dr,
Beverly Hills, CA 90210 USA

Harper, Jessica *Actor, Music Group*
15430 Brownwood Place, Los Angeles,
CA 90077 USA

Harper, John
9700 Kessler Ave., Chatsworth, CA 91311

Harper, Judson M *Engineer*
1818 Westview Road, Fort Collins, CO
80524 USA

Harper, Robert *Actor*
Karg/Weissenbach, 329 N Wetherly Dr,
#101, Beverly Hills, CA 90211 USA

Harper, Ron *Actor*
13317 Ventura Blvd #1, Sherman Oaks, CA 91423 USA

Harper, Ron *Basketball Player*
8934 Brecksville Rd #417, Cleveland, OH 44141 USA

Harper, Tess *Actor*
2271 Betty Lane, Beverly Hills, CA 90210 USA

Harper, Valarie *Actor*
David Shapira, 15821 Ventura Blvd #235, Encino, CA 91436 USA

Harper, Valerie
PO Box 7187, Beverly Hills, CA 90212-7187 USA

Harper, Willie M *Football Player*
777 Hollenbeck Ave #7G, Sunnyvale, CA 94087 USA

Harptones, The
55 W. 119th St., New York, NY 10026

Harrah, Colbert D (Toby) *Baseball Player*
316 Leewood Circle, Azle, TX 76020 USA

Harrah, Dennis W *Football Player*
1509 Oak Ave, Panama City, FL 32405 USA

Harrar, J George *Misc*
125 Puritan Dr, Scarsdale, NY 10583 USA

Harrell, James A *Geophysicist*
University of Toledo, Geology Dept, Toledo, OH 43606 USA

Harrell, Lynn M *Musician*
I M G Artists, 420 W 45th St, New York, NY 10036 USA

Harrell, Tom *Music Group, Musician*
Joel Chriss, 300 Mercer St #3J, New York, NY 10003 USA

Harrelson, Brett *Actor*
Agency for Performing Arts, 9200 Sunset Blvd #900, Los Angeles, CA 90069 USA

Harrelson, Derrell M (Bud) *Baseball Player*
357 Ridgefield Road, Hauppauge, NY 11788 USA

Harrelson, Kenneth S (Ken) *Baseball Player*
90006 Shawn Park Place, Orlando, FL 32819 USA

Harrelson, Woody *Actor*
Creative Artists Agency, 9830 Wilshire Blvd, Beverly Hills, CA 90212 USA

Harrick, Jim *Basketball Player, Coach*
Denver Nuggets, Pepsi Center, 1000 Chopper Circle, Denver, CO 80204 USA

Harring, Laura Elena *Actor, Beauty Pageant Winner*
12335 Santa Monica Blvd #302, Los Angeles, CA 90025 USA

Harrington, Curtis *Director*
6286 Vine Way, Los Angeles, CA 90068 USA

Harrington, David *Music Group, Musician*
Kronos Quartet, 1235 9th Ave, San Francisco, CA 94122 USA

Harrington, Desmond *Actor*
Untitled Entertainment (LA), 8436 W 3rd St #650, Los Angeles, CA 90048 USA

Harrington, Donald J *Educator*
Saint John's Univesity, President's Office, Jamaica, NY 11439 USA

Harrington, Joey *Football Player*
Detroit Lions, 222 Republic Dr, Allen Park, MI 48101 USA

Harrington, John *Hockey Player, Coach*
Saint John's Univesity, Athletic Dept, PO Box 7277, Collegeville, MN 56321 USA

Harrington, Pat
730 Marzella Ave., Los Angeles, A, 90049

Harrington, Pat Jr *Actor*
730 Marzella Ave, Los Angeles, CA 90049 USA

Harrington, Robert *Race Car Driver*
2609 Woodshade Ave, Kannapolis, NC 28127 USA

Harriott, Ainsley
12 Ogle St., London, ENGLAND, W1P 7LG

Harris, Barbara
159 W. 53rd St. #12-D, New York, NY 10019-6005

Harris, Barbara C *Religious Leader, Social Activist*
Episcopal Diocese of Massachusetts, 138 Tremont St, Boston, MA 02111 USA

Harris, Barry *Music Group, Musician*
Brad Simon Organization, 122 E 57th St #300, New York, NY 10022 USA

Harris, Bernard A Jr *Astronaut*
3411 Erin Knoll Court, Houston, TX 77059 USA

Harris, Bill *Critic*
12747 Riverside Dr, #208, Valley Village, CA 91607 USA

Harris, Bishop Barbara
138 Tremont St., Boston, MA 02111

Harris, Cliff *Football Player*
722 Kentwood Dr, Rockwall, TX 75032 USA

Harris, Cristi Ellen
PO Box 1471, Studio City, CA 91604

Harris, Damian *Director*
International Creative Mgmt, 8942 Wilshire Blvd #219, Beverly Hills, CA 90211 USA

Harris, Danielle *Actor*
Metropolitan Talent Agency (MTA), 4526 Wilshire Blvd, Los Angeles, CA 90010 USA

Harris, E Lynn *Actor*

Harris, Ed *Actor*
Creative Artists Agency, 9830 Wilshire Blvd, Beverly Hills, CA 90212 USA

Harris, Emmylou *Music Group, Songwriter*
Vector Management, 1607 17th Ave S, Nashville, TN 37212 USA

Harris, Estelle *Actor*
Agy for Performing Arts, 9200 Sunset Blvd #900, Los Angeles, CA 90069 USA

Harris, Franco
200 Chauser Ct. So., Sewickley, PA 15143-8726

Harris, Franko *Football Player*
200 Chaucer Court S, Sewickley, PA 15143 USA

Harris, Gail Robyn *Actor*
Don Gerler, 3349 Cahuenga Blvd W #1, Los Angeles, CA 90068 USA

Harris, Henry *Biologist*
William Dunn Pathology School, South Parks Road, Oxford, OX1 3RE, UNITED KINGDOM (UK)

Harris, James L *Football Player*
9722 Groffs Mill Dr #106, Owings Mill, MD 21117 USA

Harris, Jared *Actor*
Artists Independent Network (NY), 270 La Fayette St #402, New York, NY 10012 USA

Harris, Jay *Cartoonist*
King Features Syndicate, 888 7th Ave, New York, NY 10106 USA

Harris, Joanne *Writer*
E P Dutton Books, 375 Hudson St, New York, NY 10014 USA

Harris, Joe Frank *Governor*
712 West Ave, Cartersville, GA 30120 USA

Harris, John R *Architect*
24 Devonshire Place, London, W1N 2BX, UNITED KINGDOM (UK)

Harris, Joshua *Actor*
1800 Vine St #305, Los Angeles, CA 90028 USA

Harris, Julie *Actor*
132 Barn Hill Road #1267, West Chatham, MA 02669 USA

Harris, Katherine
Trident Media Group LLC, 41 Madison Ave Fl 33, New York, NY 10010 USA

Harris, Kwame *Football Player*
San Francisco 49ers, 4949 Centennial Blvd, Santa Clara, CA 95054 USA

Harris, Lara
400 S. Beverly Dr. #101, Beverly Hills, CA 90212

Harris, Laura *Actor*
Gersh Agency, The (LA), 232 N Canon Dr, Beverly Hills, CA 90210 USA

Harris, Leon *Commentator*
Cable News Network, News Dept, 1050 Techwood Dr NW, Atlanta, GA 30318 USA

Harris, Louis *Mathematician*
200 E 66th St, #2004, New York, NY 10021 USA

Harris, Marilyn
217 N. San Marino Ave., San Gabriel, CA 91775

Harris, Mark
1153 Roscomare Rd., Los Angeles, CA 90077

Harris, Mark Jonathan *Writer*
Principato/Young Management, 9665 Wilshire Blvd #500, Beverly Hills, CA 90212 USA

Harris, Mel *Actor*
VOX, 5670 Wilshire Blvd #820, Los Angeles, CA 90036 USA

Harris, Moira *Actor*
Writers & Artists, 8383 Wilshire Blvd #550, Beverly Hills, CA 90211 USA

Harris, Naomie *Actor*
Artists Rights Group (ARG London), 4 Great Portland St, London, W1W 8PA, UNITED KINGDOM (UK)

Harris, Neil *Historian*
5555 S Everett Ave, Chicago, IL 60637 USA

Harris, Neil Patrick *Actor*
Booh Schut, 11350 Ventura Blvd #206, Studio City, CA 91604 USA

Harris, Odie L Jr *Football Player*
1404 Knob Hill Dr, Desoto, TX 75115 USA

Harris, Rachael *Comedian*
Principato/Young Management, 9665 Wilshire Blvd #500, Beverly Hills, CA 90212 USA

Harris, Rene *President*
President's Office, Government Offices, Yaren, NAURU

Harris, Richard *Music Group*
Paramount Entertainment, PO Box 12, Far Hills, NJ 07931 USA

Harris, Rolf *Entertainer*
Billy Marsh Assoc, 174-178 N Gower St, London, NW1 2NB, UNITED KINGDOM (UK)

Harris, Ronald W (Ronnie) *Boxer*
1365 Glenview St NE, Canton, OH 44721 USA

Harris, Rosemary *Actor*
International Creative Mgmt, 76 Oxford St, London, W1N 0AX, UNITED KINGDOM (UK)

Harris, Ross
6542 Fulcher Ave., No. Hollywood, CA 91606

Harris, Sam *Music Group*
Scott Stander, 13701 Riverside Dr #201, Sherman Oaks, CA 91423 USA

Harris, Samantha *Actor*
Visionary Entertainment, 8265 Sunset Blvd #104, Los Angeles, CA 90046 USA

Harris, Sidney *Cartoonist*
302 W 86th St #9A, New York, NY 10024 USA

Harris, Stefon *Misc*
Joel Chriss, 300 Mercer St, #3J, New York, NY 10003 USA

Harris, Steve *Musician*
Sanctuary Music Mgmt, 82 Bishop's Bridge Road, London, W2 6BB, UNITED KINGDOM (UK)

Harris, Steve *Actor*
Writers & Artists, 8383 Wilshire Blvd #550, Beverly Hills, CA 90211 USA

Harris, Susan *Producer*
11828 La Grange Ave #200, Los Angeles, CA 90025 USA

Harris, Thomas *Writer*
Saint Martin's Press, 175 5th Ave, New York, NY 10010 USA

Harris, Timothy D (Tim) *Football Player*
San Francisco 49ers, 4949 Centennial Blvd, Santa Clara, CA 95054 USA

Harris, Tomas *Writer*
Creative Artists Agency LCC (CAA-LA), 9830 Wilshire Blvd, Beverly Hills, CA 90212 USA

Harris, Tommie *Football Player*
Chicago Bears, 1000 Football Dr, Lake Forest, IL 60045 USA

Harris, Walt *Football Player*
1873 Blore Heath, Carmel, IN 46032 USA

Harris, Wood *Actor*
Gersh Agency, 232 North Canon Drive, Beverly Hills, CA 90210 USA

Harris-Stewart, Lusia M (Lucy) *Basketball Player*
1002 Cherry St, Greenwood, MS 38930 USA

Harrison, Alvin *Track Athlete*
Octagon, 1751 Pinnacle Dr #1500, McLean, VA 22102 USA

Harrison, Bertram C *General*
749 Dragon Dr, Mount Pleasant, SC 29464 USA

Harrison, Bret *Actor*
United Talent Agency (UTA), 9560 Wilshire Blvd, Beverly Hills, CA 90212 USA

Harrison, C Richard *Business Person*
Parametric Technology, 140 Kendrick St, Needham Heights, MA 02494 USA

Harrison, Granville *Football Player*
200 S High St, Franklin, VA 23851 USA

Harrison, Gregory *Actor*
Stone Manners Talent Agency, 6500 Wilshire Blvd, Ste 550, Los Angeles, CA 90048 USA

Harrison, Jenilee *Actor*
DDK Talent, 3800 Barham Blvd #303, Los Angeles, CA 90068 USA

Harrison, Jerry *Musician*
Sire/Warner Bros Records, 3300 Warner Blvd, Burbank, CA 91505 USA

Harrison, Jim *Writer*
Longstreet Press, 2974 Hardman Court NE, Atlanta, GA 30305 USA

Harrison, Kathryn *Writer*
Random House, 1745 Broadway #B1, New York, NY 10019 USA

Harrison, Linda *Actor*
211A N Main St, Berlin, MD 21811 USA

Harrison, Mark *Editor*
The Gazette, 250 Saint Antoine St W, Montreal, QC, H2Y 2R7, CANADA

Harrison, Marvin *Football Player*
5519 Nighthawk Dr, Indianapolis, IN 46254 USA

Harrison, Matthew *Director*
Rigberg Roberts Rugolo, 1180 S Beverly Dr #601, Los Angeles, CA 90035 USA

Harrison, Michael Allen *Composer, Musician*
MAH Records, 1610 NE Tillamook St, #1, Portland, OR 97212 USA

Harrison, Nolan *Football Player*
20245 Augusta Dr, Olympia Fields, IL 60461 USA

Harrison, Randy *Actor*
Queer As Folk, 20 Butterick Rd, Toronto, M8W 3Z, CANADA

Harrison, Schae
7800 Beverly Blvd. #3371, Los Angeles, CA 90036

Harrison, Tony *Writer*
Gordon Dickinson, 2 Crescent Grove, London, SW4 7AH, UNITED KINGDOM (UK)

Harrison, William B Jr *Financier*
JP Morgan Chase Corp, 270 Park Ave, New York, NY 10017 USA

Harrison, William H *General*
7302 Amber Lane SW, Tacoma, WA 98498 USA

Harrison Breetzke, Joan *Swimmer*
16 Clevedon Road, East London, 5201, SOUTH AFRICA

Harrold, Kathryn *Actor*
9255 Sunset Blvd #901, Los Angeles, CA 90069 USA

Harron, Mary *Director*
William Morris Agency, 151 El Camino Dr, Beverly Hills, CA 90212 USA

Harrow, Lisa
46 Albermarle St, London, ENGLAND, W1X 4PP

Harry *Prince*
Clarence House, Stable Yard Gate, London, SW1, UNITED KINGDOM (UK)

Harry, Deborah *Actor*
Untitled Entertainment (LA), 8436 W 3rd St #650, Los Angeles, CA 90048 USA

Harry, Deborah A (Debbie) *Actor, Music Group, Songwriter*
T-Best Talent Agency, 508 Honey Lake Court, Danville, CA 94506 USA

Harry, HRH Prince
Highgrove House, Gloucestershire, ENGLAND

Harryhausen, Ray
2 Ilchester Pl, London, ENGLAND, W14 8AA

Harryhausen, Ray F *Director*
2 Ilchester Place, West Kensington, London, W14 8AA, UNITED KINGDOM (UK)

Harsch, Eddie *Musician, Music Group*
Mitch Schneider Organization, 14724 Ventura Blvd #410, Sherman Oaks, CA 91403 USA

Harshman, John E (Jack) *Baseball Player*
2003 Bayview Hieghts Dr #12, San Diego, CA 92105 USA

Harshman, Marvel K (Marv) *Basketball Player, Coach*
19221 90th Place NE, Bothell, WA 98011 USA

Hart, Bob *Bowler*
5740 Laurel Oak Dr, Suwanee, GA 30024 USA

Hart, Bret
435 Patina Place SE, Calgary, CANADA, Alb T3H 2P

Hart, Christopher
1423 N. Martel Ave. #4, Los Angeles, CA 90046-4204

Hart, Corey
1445 Lambert Close #300, Montreal, CANADA, PQ H3H 1Z5

Hart, Dolores (Mother Dolores) *Actor*
Regina Laudis Abbey, 275 Flanders Road, Bethlehem, CT 06751 USA

Hart, Doris *Tennis Player*
600 Biltmore Way #306, Coral Gables, FL 33134 USA

Hart, Dorothy
43 Martindale Rd., Asheville, NC 28804

Hart, Dudley *Golfer*
10401 Golden Eagle Court, Plantation, FL 33324 USA

Hart, Freddie *Music Group, Musician, Songwriter*
317 N Kenwood, Burbank, CA 91505 USA

Hart, Gary *Ex-Senator*
950 17th St #2050, Denver, CO 80202-2820 USA

Hart, Gary W *Senator*
950 17th St #1800, Denver, CO 80202 USA

Hart, Herbert L A *Lawyer, Misc*
11 Manor Place, Oxford, UNITED KINGDOM (UK)

Hart, Ian *Actor*
P F D, Drury House 34-43 Russell St, London, WC2B 5HA, UNITED KINGDOM (UK)

Hart, James V *Writer, Director, Producer*
Creative Artists Agency LCC (CAA-LA), 9830 Wilshire Blvd, Beverly Hills, CA 90212 USA

Hart, James W (Jim) *Football Player, Misc*
3141 Dominica Way, Naples, FL 34119 USA

Hart, Jim
207 Anthony Hall-SIUC, Carbondale, IL 62901-4312

Hart, John *Actor*
35109 Highway 79 #134, Warner Springs, CA 92086 USA

Hart, John L (Johnny) *Cartoonist*
Creators Syndicate, 5777 W Century Blvd #700, Los Angeles, CA 90045 USA

Hart, John R *Commentator*
International Creative Mgmt, 40 W 57th St #1800, New York, NY 10019 USA

Hart, Johnny
5777 W. Century Blvd. #700, Los Angeles, CA 90045

Hart, Leon
3904 Cottontail Lane, Bloomfield, MI 48301-1908

Hart, Margie
228 S. Hudson Ave., Los Angeles, CA 90004

Hart, Mary *Entertainer*
Brokaw Co, 9255 Sunset Blvd #804, Los Angeles, CA 90069 USA

Hart, Melissa Joan *Actor*
Creative Artists Agency LCC (CAA-LA), 9830 Wilshire Blvd, Beverly Hills, CA 90212 USA

Hart, Mickey *Musician, Music Group*
PO Box 1073, San Rafael, CA 94915 USA

Hart, Parker T *Diplomat*
4705 Berkeley Terrace NW, Washington, DC 20007 USA

Hart, Roxanne
Agency for Performing Arts, 9200 Sunset Blvd. #900, - Los Angeles, CA 90069

Hart, Stanley R *Geophysicist*
53 Quonset Road, Falmouth, MA 02540 USA

Hart, Terry J *Astronaut*
PO Box V, Hellertown, PA 18055 USA

Hartack, Bill
PO Box 250, Lexington, KY 40588-0250

Hartack, William J (Bill) *Jockey*
Jockey's Guild, PO Box 150, Monrvia, CA 91017 USA

Harte, Houston H *Publisher*
Harte-Hanks Communications, 200 Concord Plaza Dr, San Antonio, TX 78216 USA

Hartenstine, Michael A (Mike) *Football Player*
322 Winchester Court, Lake Bluff, IL 60044 USA

Harter, Dick *Basketball Player, Coach*
Philadelphia 76ers, 1st Union Center, 3601 S Broad St, Philadelphia, PA 19148 USA

Harth, Sidney *Musician*
135 Westland Dr, Pittsburgh, PA 15217 USA

Hartigan, Grace *Artist*
1701 1/2 Eastern Ave, Baltimore, MD 21231 USA

Hartings, Jeff *Football Player*
Pittsburgh Steelers, 3400 S Water St, Pittsburgh, PA 15203 USA

Hartley, Bob *Hockey Player, Coach*
Atlanta Thrashers, Philips Arena, 13 South Ave Se, Atlanta, GA 30315 USA

Hartley, Hal *Director*
True Fiction Pictures, 39 W 14th St #406, New York, NY 10011 USA

Hartley, Harry J *Educator*
University of Connecticut, President's Office, Storrs, CT 06269 USA

Hartley, Mariette *Actor*
J Michael Bloom, 9255 Sunset Blvd, #710, Los Angeles, CA 90069 USA

Hartley, Ted
524 N. Rockingham Ave., Los Angeles, CA 90049

Hartline, Mary *Actor*
Pierce & Shelly, 13775-A Mono Way #220, Sonora, CA 95370 USA

Hartman, Arthur A *Diplomat*
APCO Consulting Group, 1615 L St NW, Washington, DC 20036 USA

Hartman, David
16-00 Rt. 208 Box 770, Fair Lawn, NJ 07410

Hartman, George E *Architect*
3525 Hamlet Place, Bethesda, MD 20815 USA

Hartman, Kevin *Soccer Player*
Los Angeles Galaxy, 1010 Rose Bowl Dr, Pasadena, CA 91103 USA

Hartman, William C (Bill) Jr *Football Player*
149 Lucy Lane, Athens, GA 30606 USA

Hartman, William K (Bill) *Misc*
Planetary Science Institute, 1700 E Fort Lowell Road #106, Tucson, AZ 85719 USA

Hartmann, Frederick W *Editor*
Florida Times-Union, Editorial Dept, 1 Riverside Ave, Jacksonville, FL 32202 USA

Hartmann, Robert T *Government Official*
4129 Estate La Grande Princess #C, Christiansted, VI 00820 USA

Hartnett, Josh *Actor*
8916 Ashcroft Ave, West Hollywood, CA 90048 USA

Hartog, Jan de *Writer*
Andrew Nurnberg Assoc, 45/47 Clerkenwell Green, London, EC1R 0HT, UNITED KINGDOM (UK)

Hartsfield, Henry W
422 Willow Vista Dr, Seabrook, TX 77586-7338 USA

Hartsfield, Henry W (Hank) Jr *Astronaut*
422 Willow Vista Dr, Seabrook, TX 77586 USA

Hartung, Clint
1018 E. Fulton, Sinton, TX

Hartung, James *Gymnast*
3621 Portia St, Lincoln, NE 68521 USA

Hartunian, Paul *Business Person*

Hartwell, Leland H (Lee) *Nobel Prize Laureate*
Hutchinson Cancer Research Center, PO Box 19024, Seattle, WA 98109 USA

Hartzog, George B Jr *Government Official*
1643 Chain Bridge Road, McLean, VA 22101 USA

Haruf, Kent *Writer*
Southern Illinois University, English Dept, Carbondale, IL 62901 USA

Harvey, Anthony *Director*
Arthur Greene, 101 Park Ave #4300, New York, NY 10178 USA

Harvey, Cynthia T *Ballerina*
American Ballet Theater, 890 Broadway, New York, NY 10003 USA

Harvey, David R *Business Person*
Sigme-Aldrich Corp, 3050 Spruce St, Saint Louis, MO 63103 USA

Harvey, Don
6310 San Vicente Blvd. #520, Los Angeles, CA 90048

Harvey, Donnell *Basketball Player*
Orlando Magic, Waterhouse Center, 8701 Maitland Summit Blvd, Orlando, FL 32810 USA

Harvey, Fred
397 Parkhurst Dr, Fredericton, CANADA, NB E3B 2K2

Harvey, H Douglas (Doug) *Baseball Player*
16081 Mustang Dr, Springville, CA 93265 USA

Harvey, Harry *Horse Racer, Educator*
34 Deep Hollow Lane N, Columbus, NJ 08022 USA

Harvey, Jan
169 Queensgate #8A, London, ENGLAND, SW7 5EH

Harvey, Jonathan D *Composer*
Faber Music, 3 Queen Square, London, WC1N 3AU, UNITED KINGDOM (UK)

Harvey, Paul *Commentator*
Paulyanne, 1035 Park Ave, River Forest, IL 60305 USA

Harvey, PJ *Musician*
Creative Artists Agency LCC (CAA-LA), 9830 Wilshire Blvd, Beverly Hills, CA 90212 USA

Harvey, Polly Jean (P J) *Music Group, Musician, Songwriter*
Helter Skelter, Plaza 535 Kings Road, London, SW10 0S, UNITED KINGDOM (UK)

Harvey, Steve *Comedian, Actor*
9465 Wilshire Blvd #517, Beverly Hills, CA 90212 USA

Harvick, Kevin *Race Car Driver*
Richard Childress Racing, PO Box 1189, Industrial Dr, Welcome, NC 27374 USA

Harwell, Ernie
2121 Trumbull Ave., Detroit, MI 48216

Harwell, Steve *Music Group*
Creative Artists Agency, 9830 Wilshire Blvd, Beverly Hills, CA 90212 USA

Harwell, W Ernest (Ernie) *Sportscaster*
141 Fernery Road #A6, Lakeland, FL 33809 USA

Harwood, Ronald *Writer*
International Creative Management (ICM-LA), 8942 Wilshire Blvd, Beverly Hills, CA 90211 USA

Hary, Armin *Track Athlete*
Schloss, Diessen/Ammersee, 86911, GERMANY

Hase, Dagmar *Swimmer*
Niederndodeleber Str 14, Magdeburg, 29110, GERMANY

Hasek, Dominik *Hockey Player*
Ottawa Senators, 1000 Palladium Dr, Kanata, ON K2V 1A4, CANADA

Haselkorn, Robert *Scientist*
5834 S Stony Island Ave, Chicago, IL 60637 USA

Haseltine, Dan *Music Group*
Flood Bumstead McCarthy, 1700 Hayes St #304, Nashville, TN 37203 USA

Haseltine, William A *Biologist*
Human Genome Sciences, 9410 Key West Ave, Rockville, MD 20850 USA

Hasen, Irvin H *Cartoonist*
68 E 79th St, New York, NY 10021 USA

Hashimoto, Ryutaro *Prime Minister*
Liberal Democratic Party, 1-11-23 Nagatocho, Chiyodaku, Tokyo, 100, JAPAN

Haskell, Colleen Marie *Actor*
International Creative Management (ICM-LA), 8942 Wilshire Blvd, Beverly Hills, CA 90211 USA

Haskell, Jimmie
11800 Laughton Way, Northridge, CA 91326

Haskell, Peter *Actor*
19924 Acre St, Northridge, CA 91324 USA

Haskins, Clem *Basketball Player, Coach*
2632 Roberts Road, Campbellsville, KY 42718 USA

Haskins, Dennis *Actor*
345 N Maple Dr #302, Beverly Hills, CA 90210 USA

Haskins, Don *Basketball Player*
Chicago Bulls, United Center, 1901 W Madison St, Chicago, IL 60612 USA

Haskins, Michael D *Admiral*
Inspector General HqUSN, Pentagon, Washington, DC 20350 USA

Haskins, Samuel J (Sam) *Photographer*
PO Box 59, Wimbledon, London, SW19, UNITED KINGDOM (UK)

Hasler, Otmar *Prime Minister*
Primier's Office, Regierungsgebaude, Vaduz, 9490 USA

Haslett, James D (Jim) *Football Player, Coach*
PO Box 190, Destrehan, LA 70047 USA

Hasluck, Paul M C *Government Official*
2 Adams Road, Dalkeith, WA 6009, AUSTRALIA

Hass, Robert *Writer*
University of California, English Dept, Berkeley, CA 94720 USA

Hassan, Fred *Business Person*
Schering-Plough Corp, 1 Giralda Farms, Madison, NJ 07940 USA

Hassan, Kamal *Actor, Filmmaker, Director, Producer*
63 Luz Church Road, Chennai, TN 600 004, i

Hassan, Kamal *Actor, Filmmaker, Director, Producer*
63 Luz Church Road, Chennai, TN 600 004, INDIA

Hassan Ibn Talal *Prince*
Deputy King's Office, Royal Palace, Amman, JORDAN

Hassel, Gerald L *Financier*
Bank of New York, 1 Wall St, New York, NY 10286 USA

Hasselbeck, Donald W (Don) *Football Player*
38 Noon Hill Ave, Norfolk, VA 02056 USA

Hasselbeck, Elisabeth *Reality TV Star, Television Host*
The View, 320 W 66th St, New York, NY 10023 USA

Hasselhoff, David *Actor, Music Group*
5180 Louise Ave, Encino, CA 90316 USA

Hasselmo, Nils *Educator*
Assn of American Universities, 1200 New York Ave #1200, Washington, DC 20005 USA

Hassenfeld, Alan G *Business Person*
Hasbro Inc, 1027 Newport Ave, Pawtucket, RI 02861 USA

Hassett, Marilyn *Actor*
8905 Rosewood Ave, West Hollywood, CA 90048 USA

Hasson, Maurice *Musician*
18 West Heath Court, North End Road, London, NW11, UNITED KINGDOM (UK)

Hast, Adele *Editor*
Newberry Library, 60 W Walton St, Chicago, IL 60610 USA

Hastert, Speaker Dennis
2438 Rayburn HOB, Washington, DC 20515

Hastings, Barry G *Financier*
Northern Trust Corp, 50 S La Salle St, Chicago, IL 60603 USA

Hastings, Bob
620 S. Sparks St., Burbank, CA 91505

Hastings, Don *Actor*
524 W 57th St #5330, New York, NY 10019 USA

Haston, Kirk *Basketball Player*
382 E Mill St, Henderson, TN 38340 USA

Hatch, Harold A *General*
8655 White Beach Way, Vienna, VA 22182 USA

Hatch, Henry J *General*
2715 Silkwood Court, Oakton, VA 22124 USA

Hatch, Monroe W Jr *General*
8210 Thomas Ashleigh Lane, Clifton, VA 20124 USA

Hatch, Orrin *Senator*
2127 Galloping Way, Vienna, VA 22180 USA

Hatch, Richard *Actor*
10977 Bluffside Dr, #1403, Studio City, CA 91604 USA

Hatchell, Sylvia *Basketball Player*
University of North Carolina, Athletic Dept, Chapell Hill, NC 27515 USA

Hatcher, Kevin *Hockey Player*
1225 S Water St, Marine City, MI 48039 USA

Hatcher, R Dale *Football Player*
906 White Plains Road, Gaffney, SC 29340 USA

Hatcher, Teri *Actor*
Jorgensen & Rogers, 10100 Santa Monica Blvd #410, Los Angeles, CA 90067 USA

Hatchett, Joseph W *Judge*
US Court of Appeals, 810 Lewis State Bank Building, Tallahassee, FL 32302 USA

Hatfield, Juliana *Music Group, Songwriter*
Fort Apache Mgmt, 1 Camp St, Cambridge, MA 02140 USA

Hatfield, Mark *Politician, Ex-Governor, Ex-Senator, Philanthropist*
Natl Institute of Health, 6100 Executive Blvd #3C01, MSC 7511, Bethesda, MD 20892-7511 USA

Hatfield, Mark O *Governor, Senator*
17400 Holy Names Dr #E306, Lake Oswego, OR 97034 USA

Hathaway, Amy
4526 Wilshire Blvd., Los Angeles, CA 90010

Hathaway, Anne *Actor*
William Morris Agency, 151 El Camino Dr, Beverly Hills, CA 90212 USA

Hathaway, William D *Senator*
Federal Maritime Commission, 800 N
Capitol St NW, Washington, DC 20002
USA

Hatori, Miho *Music Group*
Billions Corp, 833 W Chicago Ave #101,
Chicago, IL 60622 USA

Hatosy, Shawn *Actor*
853 7th Ave #9A, New York, NY 10019
USA

Hatsopoulos, George N *Business Person,
Engineer*
Thermo Electron Corp, 81 Wyman St, PO
Box 9046, Waltham, MA 02454 USA

Hatten, Tom *Actor*
1759 Sunset Plaza Dr, Los Angeles, CA
90069 USA

Hattersley, Roy S G *Government Official*
House of Lords, Westminster, London,
SW1A 0PW, UNITED KINGDOM (UK)

Hattestad, Stine Lise *Skier*
Sundlia 1B, Nesoya, 1315, NORWAY

Hatton, Vernon *Basketball Player*
PO Box 8405, Lexington, KY 40533 USA

Hau, Lene Vestergaard *Physicist*
Harvard University, Applied Physics Dept,
Cambridge, MA 01238 USA

Hauck, Frederick H (Rick) *Astronaut*
7918 Turncrest Dr, Potomac, MD 20854
USA

Hauck, Silke 16
Mt. Bundt Verlag K2, Mannheim,
GERMANY, 69159

Hauer, Rutger *Actor*
1601 Cloverfield Blvd #5000N, Santa
Monica, CA 90404 USA

Hauerwas, Stanley *Religious Leader, Misc*
Duke University, Divinity School,
Durham, NC 27706 USA

Haughey, Charles J *Prime Minister*
Abbeville, Kinsakey, Malahide County
Dublin, IRELAND

Hauk, A Andrew *Judge, Skier*
US Court House, 312 N Spring St, Los
Angeles, CA 90012 USA

Haun, Darla
300 S. Raymond Ave. #11, Pasadena, CA
91105

Haun, Lindsey *Actor*
Kazarian/Spencer & Assoc, 11365 Ventura
Blvd #100, Box 7403, Studio City, CA
91604 USA

Hauptman, Herbert A *Nobel Prize
Laureate*
121 Woodbury Dr, Buffalo, NY 14226
USA

Haus, Herman A *Engineer, Scientist*
38 Jeffrey Terrace, Lexington, MA 02420
USA

Hauser, Cole *Actor*
2133 Holly Dr, Los Angeles, CA 90068
USA

Hauser, Erich *Artist*
Saline 36, Rottweil, 78628, GERMANY

Hauser, Tim *Music Group*
3855 Landershim Blvd #214, North
Hollywood, CA 91604 USA

Hauser, Wings *Actor*
9450 Chivers Ave, Sun Valley, CA 91352
USA

Hausman, Jerry A *Economist*
Massachussetts Institute of Technology,
Economics Dept, Cambridge, MA 02139
USA

Hauss, Lenard M (Len) *Football Player*
PO Box 1808, Reidsville, GA 30453 USA

Havel, Vaclav *President, Writer*
Kancelar Prezidenta Republiky, Hradecek,
Prague, 119 08, CZECH REPUBLIC

Havelange, Jean M F G (Joao) *Soccer
Player*
Ave Rio Branco 89B, Conj 602 Centro,
Rio de Janiero, 20040-004, BRAZIL

Havelange, JoaoRua
Prudente de Marosa 1700 Apto. 1001, Rio
de Janeiro, BRAZIL, BR 20420-0

Havelid, Niclas *Hockey Player*
Anaheim Mighty Ducks, 2000 E Gene
Autry Way, Anaheim, CA 92806 USA

Haven, Annette
PO Box 1244, Sausalito, CA 94966

Havens, Frank B *Athlete*
PO Box 55, Harborton, VA 23389 USA

Havens, Richie *Music Group, Musician,
Songwriter*
177 Woodland Ave, Westwood, NJ 07675
USA

Haver, June *Actor*
485 Halvern Dr, Los Angeles, CA 90049
USA

Havers, Nigel *Actor*
Michael Whitehall, 125 Gloucester Road,
London, SW7 4TE, UNITED KINGDOM
(UK)

Havlat, Martin *Hockey Player*
Ottawa Senators, 1000 Palladium Dr,
Kanata, ON K2V 1A4, CANADA

Havlish, Jean *Bowler*
1277 Kent St, Saint Paul, MN 55117 USA

Havoc, June *Actor*
405 Old Long Ridge Road, Stamford, CT
06903 USA

Havrilla, Jo Ann
9751 Old Route 99, McKean, PA 16426-
1725

Hawerchuck, Dale *Hockey Player*
Grand Farms, 95404 7th Line EHS, RR 5,
Orangeville, ON L9W 2Z2, CANADA

Hawk, John D *War Hero*
3243 Solie Ave, Bremerton, WA 98310
USA

Hawk, Tony *Actor, Skateboarder*
31878 Del Obispo, #118-602, San Juan
Capistranl, CA 92675 USA

Hawke, Bob
GPO Box 36, Sydney, AUSTRALIA, NSW
2001, AUSTRALIA

Hawke, Ethan *Actor*
Three Arts Entertainment, 9460 Wilshire
Blve #700, Beverly Hills, CA 90212 USA

Hawke, Robert J L *Prime Minister*
GPO Box 36, Sydney, NSW, 2001,
AUSTRALIA

Hawkes, Christopher *Archaeologist*
19 Walton St, Oxford, OX1 2HQ,
UNITED KINGDOM (UK)

Hawkes, John *Artist*
Rigberg-Rugolo Entertainment, 1180 S
Beverly Dr #601, Los Angeles, CA 90035
USA

Hawking, Stephen *Physicist*
University of Cambridge, Applied Math
Dept, Cambridge, CB3 9EW, UNITED
KINGDOM (UK)

Hawkins, Arthur R *War Hero*
28496 Perdido Pass Dr, Orange Beach, AL
36561 USA

Hawkins, Barbara *Music Group*
Superstars Unlimited, PO Box 371371,
Las Vegas, NV 89137 USA

Hawkins, Benjamin C (Ben) *Football
Player*
104 Deforest St, Roslindale, MA 02131
USA

Hawkins, Brad
47 Music Sq. E., Nashville, TN 37203

Hawkins, Cornelius (Connie) *Basketball
Player*
Phoenix Suns, 201 E Jefferson St, Phoenix,
AZ 85004 USA

Hawkins, Dale *Musician, Music Group,
Songwriter*
4618 John F Kennedy Blvd #107, North
Little Rock, AR 72116 USA

Hawkins, Edwin *Music Group*
PAZ Entertainment, 2041 Locust St,
Philadelphia, PA 19103 USA

Hawkins, Frank *Football Player*
2300 Alta Dr, Las Vegas, NV 89107 USA

Hawkins, Hersey R Jr *Basketball Player*
New Orleans Hornets, New Orleans
Arena, 1501 Girod St, New Orleans, LA
70113 USA

Hawkins, M Andrew (Andy) *Baseball
Player*
RR 1, Dawson, TX 76639 USA

Hawkins, Michael Daly *Judge*
US Court of Appeals, 230 N 1St, Phoenix,
AZ 85025 USA

Hawkins, Paula *Senator*
1214 Park Ave N, Winter Park, FL 32789
USA

Hawkins, Ronnie *Music Group*
Agency Group Ltd, 59 Berkeley St,
Toronto, ON M5A 2W5, UNITED
KINGDOM (UK)

Hawkins, Rosa *Music Group*
Superstars Unlimited, PO Box 371371,
Las Vegas, NV 89137 USA

Hawkins, Rowena
PO Box 15277, Chattanooga, TN 37415-
0277

Hawkins, Sophie B *Musician, Music
Group, Songwriter*
Trumpet Swan Productions, 520
Washington Blvd #337, Marina del Rey,
CA 90292 USA

Hawkins, Tommy *Basketball Player*
1745 Manzanita Park Ave, Malibu, CA
90265 USA

Hawkins, Willis M *Scientist*
Marshall Institute, 1625 K St NW, #1050, Washington, DC 20006 USA

Hawkinson, Tim *Artist*
Ace Gallery, 5514 Wilshire Blvd, Los Angeles, CA 90036 USA

Hawks, Steve *Artist*
Hadley House, 1101 Hampshire Road S, Bloomington, MN 55438 USA

Hawksworth, John
24 Cottesmore Gardens #2, London, ENGLAND, W8 5PR

Hawlata, Franz *Opera Singer*
I M G Artists, 3 Burlington Lane, Chiswick, London, W4 2TH, UNITED KINGDOM (UK)

Hawley, Frank *Race Car Driver*
Frank Hawley Drag Racing School, County Road 225, Gainesville, FL 32609 USA

Hawley, Sandy *Jockey*
9625 Merrill Road, Silverwood, MI 48760 USA

Hawley, Steven A *Astronaut*
3929 Walnut Pond Dr, Houston, TX 77059 USA

Hawn, Goldie *Actor*
Clearlight Productions, 9255 Sunset Blvd #1010, West Hollywood, CA 90069 USA

Haworth, Jill *Actor*
300 E 51st St, New York, NY 10022 USA

Hawpe, David V *Editor*
Louisville Courier-Journal, Editorial Dept, 525 Broadway, Louisville, KY 40202 USA

Hawthorne, Sir Nigel
Febdens Park Cold Christmas Lane, Thundridge Herts, ENGLAND, SG12 QUE

Hawthorne, William R *Engineer*
Churchill College, Engineering School, Cambridge, CB2 0DS, UNITED KINGDOM (UK)

Hax, Carolyn *Writer*
Washington Post, Editorial Dept, 1150 15th St NW, Washington, DC 20071 USA

Hay, Colin *Music Group*
TPA, PO Box 125, Round Corner, NSW, 2158, AUSTRALIA

Hay, Louise

Hay, Louise L *Writer*
Hay House, PO Box 5100, Carlsbad, CA 92018-5100

Hayaishi, Osamu *Biologist*
1-29 Izumigawacho, Shimogamo Sakyoku, Kyoto, 606-0807, JAPAN

Hayareet, Haya
Herons Flight Marlow, Buckinghamshire, ENGLAND

Hayashi, Henry
5127 Klump Ave, No. Hollywood, CA 91601-3725

Hayashi, Izuo *Engineer*
OptoElectrics Research Lab, 5-5 Tohkodai, Tsukuba, Ibaraki, 300-26, JAPAN

Hayashi, Shizuya *War Hero*
1331 Hoowai St, Pearl City, HI 96782 USA

Haydee, Marcia *Ballerina*
Stuttgart Ballet, Oberer Schlossgarten 6, Stuttgart, 70173 USA

Hayden
431-67 Mowat Ave, Toronto, CANADA, Ont. M6K 3

Hayden, Frederick *Biologist*
University of Virginia, Med Ctr, Microbiology Dept, Charlottesville, VA 22903 USA

Hayden, J Michael (Mike) *Governor*
5809 Sagamore Court, Lawrence, KS 66047 USA

Hayden, Jim *Publisher*
Philadelphia Inquirer, 400 N Broad St, Philadelphia, PA 19130 USA

Hayden, Linda *Actor*
Michael Ladkin Mgmt, 1 Duchess St #1, London, W1N 3DE, UNITED KINGDOM (UK)

Hayden, Michael *Actor*
H W A Talent, 3500 W Olive Ave #1400, Burbank, CA 91505 USA

Hayden, Michael V *General*
Director National Security Agency, Fort George C Meade, MD 20755 USA

Hayden, Neil Steven *Publisher*
1755 York Ave #19A, New York, NY 10128 USA

Hayden, Tom *Politician*
152 Wadsworth Ave, Santa Monica, CA 90405 USA

Hayden, William G *Governor, General*
GPO Box 7829, Waterfront Place, Brisbane, QLD, 4001, AUSTRALIA

Haydon, Jones Ann *Tennis Player*
85 Westerfield Road, Edgloaston, Birmingham 15, UNITED KINGDOM (UK)

Hayek, Julie
5645 Burning Tree Dr., La Canada, CA 91011

Hayek, Nicolas G *Designer*
SMH, Seevorstadt 6, Biel, 2502, SWITZERLAND

Hayek, Salma *Actor, Model*
Talent Entertainment Group, 9111 Wilshire Blvd, Beverly Hills, CA 90210 USA

Hayers, Sidney A *Director*
John Redway, 5 Denmark St, London, WC2H 8LP, UNITED KINGDOM (UK)

Hayes, Amy *Model, Sportscaster*
641 N Hardin Heights, Harrodsburg, KY 40330 USA

Hayes, Bill *Actor, Music Group*
4528 Beck Ave, North Hollywood, CA 91602 USA

Hayes, Billie
PO Box 69493, Los Angeles, CA 90069

Hayes, Bob
2717 King Cole Dr., Dallas, TX 75216-3430

Hayes, Brian
60 Charlotte St., London, ENGLAND, W1P 1LS

Hayes, Dade
Trident Media Group LLC, 41 Madison Ave Fl 33, New York, NY 10010 USA

Hayes, Darren *Musician, Music Group*
PO Box 2758, Sausalito, CA 94966 USA

Hayes, Denis A *Geophysicist, Misc*
Green Seal, PO Box 18237, Washington, DC 20036 USA

Hayes, Dennis C *Engineer, Inventor*
Hayes Microcomputer Products, 945 E Paces Ferry Road NE, Atlanta, GA 30326 USA

Hayes, Elvin E *Basketball Player*
252 Piney Point Road, Houston, TX 77024 USA

Hayes, Isaac *Actor*
Saffron Management, 1701 N Beverly Dr, Beverly Hills, CA 90210 USA

Hayes, Jarvis *Basketball Player*
Washington Wizards, MCI Center 601 F St NW, Washington, DC 20004 USA

Hayes, Julia
7227 Winchester #266, Memphis, TN 38125

Hayes, Louis S *Music Group, Musician*
Abby Hoffer, 223 1/2 E 48th St, New York, NY 10017 USA

Hayes, Mark *Golfer*
1014 Saint Andrews Dr, Edmond, OK 73003 USA

Hayes, Reggie *Actor*
TalentWorks (LA), 3500 W Olive Ave #1400, Burbank, CA 91505 USA

Hayes, Robert M *Social Activist*
National Coalition for the Homeless, 105 E 22nd St, New York, NY 10010 USA

Hayes, Sean *Actor*
Will & Grace, 4024 Radford Ave, Bungalow 3, Studio City, CA 91604 USA

Hayes, Sean P *Actor*
William Morris Agency, 151 El Camino Dr, Beverly Hills, CA 90212 USA

Hayes, Susan Seaforth
4528 Beck Ave., No. Hollywood, CA 91602

Hayes, Wade *Music Group*
Trey Turner Assoc, 40 Music Square W, Nashville, TN 37203 USA

Hayman, David T *Actor, Director*
International Creative Management (ICM-UK), Oxford House, 76 Oxford St, London, W1N OAX, UNITED KINGDOM (UK)

Hayman, Fred *Fashion Designer*
6946 Wildlife Road, Malibu, CA 90265 USA

Hayman, Gorgon I *Cinematographer*
54 Lakes Lane, Beaconsfield, London, HP9 2LB, UNITED KINGDOM (UK)

Hayman, James *Director*
Creative Artists Agency LCC (CAA-LA), 9830 Wilshire Blvd, Beverly Hills, CA 90212 USA

Haynes, Al *Misc*
4410 S 182nd St, Seatac, WA 98188 USA

Haynes, Betsy *Writer*
212 Windbrook Court, Marco Island, FL 34145 USA

Haynes, Haynes
7200 Sandering Ct., Carlsbad, CA 92009-5173

Haynes, Mark *Football Player*
Shaka Franklin Foundation, 8101 E
Dartmouth Ave #11, Denver, CO 80231
USA

Haynes, Marques O *Basketball Player,*
Coach
PO Box 191, Dallas, TX 75221 USA

Haynes, Michael *Football Player*
Chicago Bears, 1000 Football Dr, Lake
Forest, IL 60045 USA

Haynes, Richard *Attorney General*
2701 Fannin St, Houston, TX 77002 USA

Haynes, Roy O *Musician*
Ted Kurland, 173 Brighton Ave, Boston,
MA 02134 USA

Haynes, Todd *Director*
Creative Artists Agency LCC (CAA-LA),
9830 Wilshire Blvd, Beverly Hills, CA
90212 USA

Haynes Jr, Cornell "Nelly" *Musician*
United Talent Agency (UTA), 9560
Wilshire Blvd, Beverly Hills, CA 90212
USA

Haynesworth, Albert *Football Player*
Tennessee Titans, 460 Great Circle Road,
Nashville, TN 37228 USA

Haynie, Jim
10100 Santa Monica Blvd. #2500, Los
Angeles, CA 90067

Haynie, Sandra J *Golfer*
PO Box 1111, Keller, TX 76244 USA

Hays, Robert *Actor*
919 Victoria Ave, Venice, CA 90291 USA

Hays, Ronald J *Admiral*
869 Kamoi Place, Honolulu, HI 96825
USA

Hays, Thomas C *Business Person*
Fortune Brands Inc, 300 Tower Parkway,
Lincolnshire, IL 60069 USA

Haysbert, Dennis *Actor*
1155 Winston Ave, San Marino, CA
91108 USA

Hayter, David *Writer*
Kaplan/Perrone Entertainment, 10202
West Washington Blvd, Astaire Bldg, Suite
#3003, Culver City, CA 90232 USA

Hayward, Brooke
305 Madison Ave. #956, New York, NY
10165-1001

Hayward, Charles E *Publisher*
Little Brown Co, Time-Life Building,
Rockefeller Center, New York, NY 10020
USA

Hayward, Justin *Music Group, Musician*
Bright Music, PO Box 4536, Henley-on-
Thames, Berkshire, RG9 3YD, UNITED
KINGDOM (UK)

Hayward, Thomas B *Admiral*
2200 Ross Ave #3800, Dallas, TX 75201
USA

Haywood, Spencer *Basketball Player*
46866 Mornington Road, Canton, MI
48188 USA

Hazard, Geoffrey C Jr *Attorney General,*
Educator
200 W Willow Grove Ave, Philadelphia,
PA 19118 USA

Haze, Jonathan
3636 Woodhill Canyon, Studio City, CA
91604

Haziza, Shlomi *Artist*
H Studio, 8640 Tamarack Ave, Sun
Valley, CA 91352 USA

Hazzard, Shirley *Writer*
200 E 66th St, New York, NY 10021 USA

Heacock, Raymond L *Engineer*
Jet Production Laboratory, 4800 Oak
Grove Dr, Pasadena, CA 91109 USA

Head, Anthony *Actor*
Gordon & French, 12-13 Poland St,
London, W1F 8QB, ENGLAND

Head, Anthony Stewart *Actor*
710 Ocean Park Blve #3, Santa Monica,
CA 90405 USA

Head, James W *Scientist*
Brown University, Geological Sciences
Dept, Providence, RI 02912 USA

Head, Roy *Musician*
Texas Sounds Entertainment, 2317 Pecan,
Dickinson, TX 77539 USA

Headden, Susan M *Journalist*
Indianapolis Star, Editorial Dept, 307 N
Pennsylvania, Indianapolis, IN 46204 USA

Headey, Lena *Actor*
Lou Coulson, 37 Berwick St, London,
W1V 3RF, UNITED KINGDOM (UK)

Headley, Glenne
8942 Wilshire Blvd., Beverly Hills, CA
90211

Headley, Heather *Actor, Musician*
Paradigm Agency, 10100 Santa Monica
Blvd #2500, Los Angeles, CA 90067 USA

Headley, Shari
112-26 178th St., Jamaica, NY 11433

Headly, Glenne *Actor*
7929 Hollywood Blvd, Los Angeles, CA
90046 USA

Heald, Anthony *Actor*
Endeavor Talent Agency, 9701 Wilshire
Blvd #1000, Beverly Hills, CA 90212 USA

Healey, Danis W *Government Official*
Pingles Place, Alfriston, East Sussex, BN26
5TT, UNITED KINGDOM (UK)

Healey, Derek E *Composer*
29 Stafford Road, Ruislip Gardens, Middx,
H4A 6PB, UNITED KINGDOM (UK)

Healey, James
415 S. Spalding Dr. #306, Beverly Hills,
CA 90212

Healey, John G *Misc*
Amnesty International USA, 322 8th Ave,
New York, NY 10001 USA

Healy, Bernadine *Doctor*
430 17th St NW, Washington, DC 20006
USA

Healy, Cornelius T *Misc*
Plate Die Engravers Union, 228 S
Swarthmore Ave, Ridley Park, PA 19078
USA

Healy, Fran *Music Group*
Wildlife Entertainment, 21 Heathmans
Road, London, SW6 4TJ, UNITED
KINGDOM (UK)

Healy, Jane E *Journalist*
Orlando Sentinel, Editrial Dept, 633 N
Orange Ave, Orlando, FL 32801 USA

Healy, Jeremiah *Writer*
186 Commonwealth Ave, #31, Boston,
MA 02116 USA

Healy, Mary *Actor*
8641 Robinson Ridge Dr, Las Vegas, NV
89117 USA

Healy, Patricia *Actor*
Shelter Entertainment, 9255 Sunset Blvd
#1010, Los Angeles, CA 90069 USA

Heaney, Gerald W *Judge*
US Court of Appeals, Federal Building,
Duluth, MN 55802 USA

Heaney, Seamus
3 Queens Sq., London, ENGLAND,
WC1N 3AU

Heaney, Seamus J *Nobel Prize Laureate*
191 Strand Road, Dublin 4, IRELAND

Heard, G Alexander *Educator, Politician,*
Scientist
2100 Golf Club Lane, Nashville, TN
37215 USA

Heard, John *Actor*
853 7th Ave #9A, New York, NY 10019
USA

Hearn, Chick
16053 Sabana Lane, Encino, CA 91316

Hearn, George *Actor, Music Group*
211 S Beverly Dr #211, Beverly Hills, CA
90212 USA

Hearn, J Woodrow *Religious Leader*
United Methodist Church, PO Box 320,
Nashville, TN 37202 USA

Hearn, Kevin *Musician*
Nettwerk Mgmt, 8730 Wilshire Blvd
#304, Beverly Hills, CA 90211 USA

Hearn, Thomas K Jr *Educator*
Wake Forest University, President's Office,
Winston Salem, NC 27109 USA

Hearne, Bill *Music Group, Musician*
Class Act Entertainment, PO Box 160236,
Nashville, TN 37216 USA

Hearnes, Warren E *Governor*
118 N Main St, Charleston, MO 63834
USA

Hearns, Thomas (Tommy) *Boxer*
3165 Castle Canyon Ave, Henderson, NV
89052 USA

Hearst, Donald P *Engineer*
Langley Research Center, NASA,
Hampton, VA 23665 USA

Hearst, G Garrison *Football Player*
3753 Augusta Road, Lincolnton, GA
30817 USA

Hearst, Rick *Actor*
Stone Manners, 6500 Wilshire Blvd #550,
Los Angeles, CA 90048 USA

Hearst, Victoria
865 Comstock Ave., Los Angeles, CA
90024

Hearst Shaw, Patricia C (Patty) *Actor*
110 5th St, San Francisco, CA 94103 USA

Heart *Musician*
Creative Artists Agency LCC (CAA-LA),
9830 Wilshire Blvd, Beverly Hills, CA
90212 USA

Heaslip, Mark *Hockey Player*
11 Leland Court, Chevy Chase, MD
20815 USA

Heath, Albert (Tootie) *Music Group,
Musician*
Ted Kurland, 173 Brighton Ave, Boston,
MA 02134 USA

Heath, ex-PM Edward *Prime Minister*
House of Commons, Westminster,
London, SW1A 0AA, UNITED KINGDOM
(UK)

Heath, James E (Jimmy) *Music Group,
Musician, Composer*
Ted Kurland, 173 Brighton Ave, Boston,
MA 02134 USA

Heath, Percy *Music Group, Musician*
Atlantic Records, 1290 Ave of Americas,
New York, NY 10104 USA

Heath-Stubbs, John F A *Writer*
22 Artesian Road, London, W2 5AR,
UNITED KINGDOM (UK)

Heathcock, Clayton H *Misc*
5235 Alhambra Valley Road, Martinez,
CA 94553 USA

Heathcote, Jud *Basketball Player, Coach*
5418 S Quail Ridge Circle, Spokane, WA
99223 USA

Heatherly, Eric
PO Box 24895, Chattanooga, TN 37422-
4895

Heaton, Patricia *Actor*
FourBoys Films, 200 Larchmont Dr Fl 2,
Los Angeles, CA 90004 USA

Heatwave
6464 Sunset Blvd. #1010, Hollywood, CA
90028

Heavy D *Artist, Music Group*
Soul On Soul, PO Box 1009, Pelham, NY
10803 USA

Hebert, Johnny *Race Car Driver*
Team Lotus, Kettering Hamm Hall,
Wymondham, Norfolk, NR18 7HW,
UNITED KINGDOM (UK)

Heche, Anne *Actor*
Untitled Entertainment (NY), 23 E 22nd St
Fl 3, New York, NY 10010 USA

Hecht, Albie *Writer, Producer*
Spike TV, 1515 Broadway, New York, NY
10036 USA

Hecht, Anthony E *Writer*
4256 Nebraska Ave NW, Washington, DC
20016 USA

Hecht, Duvall *Misc*
2910 W Garry Ave, Santa Ana, CA 92704
USA

Hecht, Jessica *Actor*
Innovative Artists (LA), 1505 Tenth St,
Santa Monica, CA 90401 USA

Hecht-Herskowitz, Gina *Actor*
5930 Foothill Dr, Los Angeles, CA 90068
USA

Hechter, Daniel *Fashion Designer*
4 Ave Ter Hoche, Paris, 75008, FRANCE

Hecker, Zvi *Architect*
19 Elzar St, Tel Aviv, 65157, ISRAEL

Heckerling, Amy *Director, Producer*
1330 Schuyler Road, Beverly Hills, CA
90210 USA

Heckler, Margaret M *Secretary*
1401 N Oak St, Arlington, VA 22209 USA

Heckman, James J *Nobel Prize Laureate*
4807 S Greenwood Ave, Chicago, IL
60615 USA

Heckscher, August *Writer*
333 E 68th St, New York, NY 10021 USA

Hedaya, Dan *Actor*
Gersh Agency, 232 North Canon Dr,
Beverly Hills, CA 90210 USA

Hedberg, Mitch *Comedian*
William Morris Agency (WMA-LA), 1
William Morris Pl, Beverly Hills, CA
90212 USA

Hedeman, Richard (Tuff) *Misc*
PO Box 224, Morgan Mill, TX 76465 USA

Hedford, Eric *Music Group, Musician*
Monqui Mgmt, PO Box 5908, Portland,
OR 97228 USA

Hedges, Clifton
10475 Crosspoint Blvd., Indianapolis, IN
46256-3323

Hedges, Peter *Director, Writer*
Hyperion Books, 114 5th Ave, New York,
NY 10011 USA

Hedican, Bret *Hockey Player*
2500 E Las Olas Blvd #502, Fort
Lauderdale, FL 33301 USA

Hedison, Alexandra *Actor*
Neuman & Associates CPA, 16255
Ventura Blvd #920, Encino, CA 91436
USA

Hedison, David *Actor*
PO Box 1470, Beverly Hills, CA 90213
USA

Hedren, Tippi *Actor*
6867 Soledad Canyon Road, Acton, CA
93510 USA

Hedrick, Jerry L *Misc*
25280 Cartsbad Ave, Davis, CA 95616
USA

Hedrick, Joan D *Writer*
Trinity College, Women's Studies
Program, 300 Summit St, Hartford, CT
06106 USA

Hedrick, Larry
PO Box 749, Stateville, NC 28677

Heeger, Alan J *Nobel Prize Laureate*
1042 Las Alturas Road, Santa Barbara, CA
93103 USA

Heera *Actor, Bollywood*
Nungambakkam, Chennai, TN 600034,
INDIA

Heeschen, David S *Astronomer*
702 Copa D'Oro, Marathon, FL 33050
USA

Heesters, Johannes
Heimgartenstr. 21, Starnberg, GERMANY,
D-82319

Heeter, Carrie *Inventor*
Michigan State Univesity, Communication
Technology Lab, East Lansing, MI 48824
USA

Heffernan, Kevin *Comedian*
United Talent Agency (UTA), 9560
Wilshire Blvd, Beverly Hills, CA 90212
USA

Heffner, Kyle *Actor*
Sharp/Karrys, 117 N Orlando Ave, Los
Angeles, CA 90048 USA

Heffron, Richard T *Director*
Shapiro-Lichtman Talent Agency, 8827
Beverly Blvd, Los Angeles, CA 90048 USA

Heflin, Howell *Senator*
311 E 6th St, Tuscumbia, AL 35674 USA

Hefner, Christie *Publisher*
Playboy Enterprises, 680 N Lake Shore Dr,
Chicago, IL 60611 USA

Hefner, Hugh *Producer, Publisher*
Playboy Enterprises Inc, 680 North Lake
Shore Drive, Chicago, CA 60611 USA

Hefner, Hugh M *Publisher, Editor*
10236 Channg Cross Road, Los Angeles,
CA 90024 USA

Hefner, Lene
15127 Califa St., Van Nuys, CA 91411

Heft, Bob
4098 Green St., Saginaw, MI 48603-6618

Heft, Robert (Bob) *Designer*
PO Box 20404, Saginaw, MI 48602 USA

Hefti, Neal *Composer*
Encino Music, 9454 Wilshire Blvd #405,
Beverly Hills, CA 90212 USA

Heger, Rene *Actor*
Jerry Shandrew PR, 1050 South Stanley
Avenue, Los Angeles, CA 90019-6634
USA

Hegerland, Anita
1315 Nesoya, NORWAY

Heggtveit, Ann Hamilton *Skier*
General Delivery, Grand Isle, VT 05458
USA

Hegyes, Robert *Actor*
2404 Pacific Ave, Venice, CA 90291 USA

Hehn, Sascha
Postfach 100823, Munich, GERMANY,
D-80082

Heidelberger, Charles *Misc*
1495 Poppy Peak Dr, Pasadena, CA
91105 USA

Heiden, Beth
PO Box 110, Dollar Bay, MI 49922-0110

Heiden, Elizabeth L (Beth) *Speed Skater*
PO Box 110, Dollar Bay, MI 49922 USA

Heiden, Eric *Speed Skater, Misc*
240 Sandburg Dr, Sacramento, CA 95819
USA

Heidmann, Manfred
Borbecker Str. 237, Essen, GERMANY,
D-45355

Heidt Jr, Horace
4155 Witzel Dr, Sherman Oaks, CA
91423 USA

Height, Dorothy I *Social Activist*
Duane Morris Heckscher, 1667 K St NW,
Washington, DC 20006 USA

Heigl, Jennifer *Actor*
Writers & Artists, 8383 Wilshire Blvd
#550, Beverly Hills, CA 90211 USA

Heigl, Katherine *Actor, Model*
8436 W 3rd St #650, Los Angeles, CA
90048 USA

Heilbron, Lorna *Actor*
Brunskill, 169 Queen's Gate, London,
SW7 5HE, UNITED KINGDOM (UK)

Heilbroner, Robert L *Economist*
435 E 57th St, New York, NY 10022 USA

Heilmeier, George H *Inventor*
Telecordia Technologies, 445 South St,
Morristown, NJ 07960 USA

Heimbold, Charles A Jr *Business Person*
Bristol-Myers Squibb, 345 Park Ave, New
York, NY 10154 USA

Heimel, Cynthia *Writer*
Simon & Schuster, 1230 Ave of Americas,
New York, NY 10020 USA

Heimlich, Henry J *Doctor, Physicist*
17 Elmhurst St, Cincinnati, OH 45208
USA

Heine, Jutta *Track Athlete*
Blaue Muhle, Burglahr, 57614,
GERMANY

Heinle, Amelia *Actor*
Gallin Morey, 335 N Maple Dr #351,
Beverly Hills, CA 90210 USA

Heinsohn, Thomas W (Tom) *Basketball
Player, Coach*
PO Box 422, Newton Upper Falls, MA
02464 USA

Heinz, W C *Sportscaster, Writer*
1150 Nichols Hill Road, Dorset, VT
05251 USA

Heinzer, Franz *Skier*
Lauenen, Rickenbach/Schwyz, 6432,
SWITZERLAND

Heiss Jenkins, Carol *Figure Skater*
3183 Regency Place, Westlake, OH
44145 USA

Heitmeyer, Jayne
4450 Lakeside Dr. #350, Burbank, CA
91505

Hejduk, Milan *Hockey Player*
3155 Rockbridge Dr, Littleton, CO 80129
USA

Held, Al *Artist*
Andre Emmerich Gallery, 41 E 57th St,
New York, NY 10022 USA

Held, Archie *Artist, Misc*
A New Leaf Garden, 1286 Gilman St,
Berkeley, CA 94706 USA

Held, Carl
1817 Hillcrest Rd. #51, Los Angeles, CA
90068

Held, Franklin (Bud) *Track Athlete*
13367 Caminito Mar Villa, Del Mar, CA
92014 USA

Held, Richard M *Doctor*
Massachusetts Institute of Technology,
Psychology Dept, Cambridge, MA 02139
USA

Helde, Annette
8430 Santa Monica Blvd. #200, Los
Angeles, CA 90036

Helfand, David *Astronomer*
Columbia Univesity, Astronomer Dept,
New York, NY 10027 USA

Helfer, Ricki Tigert *Financier*
Federal Deposit Insurance, 550 17th St
NW, Washington, DC 20429 USA

Helford, Bruce *Producer, Writer*
United Talent Agency (UTA), 9560
Wilshire Blvd, Beverly Hills, CA 90212
USA

Helgeland, Brian *Director*
United Talent Agency, 9650 Wilshire Blvd
#500, Beverly Hills, CA 90212 USA

Helgenberger, Marg *Actor*
International Creative Mgmt, 8942
Wilshire Blve #219, Beverly Hills, CA
90211 USA

Helinski, Donald R *Biologist*
University of California, Molecular
Genetics Center, La Jolla, CA 92093 USA

Helix
1505 W. 2nd Ave. #200, Vancouver,
CANADA, BC V6H 3Y4

Hellawell, Keith *Lawyer, Government
Official*
Government Offices, Great George St,
London, SW1A 2AL, UNITED KINGDOM
(UK)

Heller, Andre
Singerstr. 8, Vienna, AUSTRIA, A-1010

Heller, Daniel M *Attorney General*
Israel Discount Bank Building, 14 NE 1st
Ave, Miami, FL 33132 USA

Heller, Jane *Writer*
208 S Spalding Dr, Beverly Hills, CA
90212 USA

Heller, Jeffrey M *Business Person*
Electronic Data Systems, 5400 Legacy Dr,
Plano, TX 75024 USA

Heller, John H *Scientist*
74 Horsehoe Road, Wilton, CT 06897
USA

Hellerman, Fred *Music Group, Songwriter*
83 Goodhill Road, Weston, CT 06883
USA

Hellickson, Russell (Russ) *Wrestler*
6893 Lauren Place, Columbus, OH 43235
USA

Helling, Ricky A (Rick) *Baseball Player*
2706 Henry, Irving, TX 75062 USA

Hellion
18653 Ventura Blvd. #307, Tarzana, CA
91356

Helliwell, Robert A *Scientist*
2240 Page Mill Road, Palo Alto, CA
94304 USA

Hellman, Bonnie
1680 N. Vine St. #614, Hollywood, CA
90028

Hellman, Martin E *Inventor*
855 Serra St, Stanford, CA 94305 USA

Hellman, Monte *Director*
8588 Appian Way, Los Angeles, CA
90046 USA

Hellmann, Martina *Track Athlete*
Neue Leipziger Str 14, Leipzig, 04205,
GERMANY

Hellmuth, George F *Architect*
10111 Ingleside Dr, Saint Louis, MO
63124 USA

Hellstrand, Kristoffer *Biologist*
Goteborg University, Virology Dept,
Goteborg, 405 30, SWEDEN

Hellyer, Paul T *Government Official*
65 Harbour Square #506, Toronto, ON
M5J 2L4, CANADA

Helm, Levon *Music Group, Musician,
Actor*
160 Plochmann Lane, Woodstock, NY
12498 USA

Helm, Peter
1480 S. Wild Oaks Dr., Nixa, MO 65714

Helmberger, Don V *Misc*
California Institute of Technology,
Seismology Dept, Pasadena, CA 91125
USA

Helmerich, Hans C *Business Person*
Helmerich & Payne Inc, Utica & 21st St,
Tulsa, OK 74114 USA

Helmerich, Walter H III *Business Person*
Helmerich & Payne Inc, Utica & 21st St,
Tulsa, OK 74114 USA

Helmerson, Frans *Music Group, Musician*
Columbia Artists Mgmt Inc, 165 W 57th
St, New York, NY 10019 USA

Helmly, James R *General*
Commander, US Army Reserves, HqUSA
Pentagon, Washington, DC 20310 USA

Helmond, Katherine *Actor*
14170 Montecito Place, Victorville, CA
92392 USA

Helmreich, Ernst J M *Misc*
University of Wurzburg Biozentrum, Am
Hubland, Wurzburg, 97074, GERMANY

Helms, Jesse *Senator*
403 Dirksen Bldg, Washington, DC 20510
USA

Helms, L S *Financier*
KeyCorp, 127 Public Square, Cleveland,
OH 44114 USA

Helms, Susan J *Astronaut*
NASA, Johnson Space Center, 2101 NASA
Road, Houston, TX 77058 USA

Helmsley, Leona M *Business Person*
36 Central Park South, New York, NY
10019 USA

Helmstetter, Shad *Writer, Motivational
Speaker*
Goals-On-Line.com Corporate Offices,
362 Gulf Breeze Parkway, Suite 104, Gulf
Breeze, FL 32561 USA

Helmut
1775 Broadway #433, New York, NY
10019

Helnwein, Gottfried *Artist*
Aul der Burg 2, Burgbrol, 56659,
GERMANY

Heloise
PO Box 795000, San Antonio, TX 78279

Heloise *Journalist*
PO Box 795000, San Antonio, TX 78279
USA

Helpern, Joan G *Fashion Designer*
Joan & David Helpern Inc, 46 W 56th St
#200, New York, NY 10019 USA

Heltau, Michael *Actor, Music Group*
Sulzweg 11, Vienna, 1190, AUSTRIA

Helton, Bill D *Business Person*
New Century Energies, 1225 17th St,
Denver, CO 80202 USA

Helton, RJ *Musician*
American Idol, 7800 Beverly Blvd #251,
Los Angeles, CA 90036 USA

Helton, Todd L *Baseball Player*
1 White Pelican Circle, Denver, CO
80241 USA

Helvin, Marie *Model*
IMG Models, 23 Eyot Gardens, London,
W6 9TN, UNITED KINGDOM (UK)

Helwig, David G *Writer*
Belfast Prince Edward Island, C0A 1A0,
CANADA

Hely, Steve *Actor*
William Morris Agency (WMA-LA), 1
William Morris Pl, Beverly Hills, CA
90212 USA

Hemenway, Robert E *Educator*
University of Kansas, President's Office,
Lawrence, KS 66045 USA

Hemingway, Gerardine *Fashion Designer*
Red or Dead Ltd, Courtney Road Bldg
201, Wembley, Middx, HA9 7PP,
UNITED KINGDOM (UK)

Hemingway, Mariel *Actor, Model*
PO Box 2249, Ketchum, ID 83340 USA

Hemingway, Wayne *Fashion Designer*
Red or Dead Ltd, Courtney Road Bldg
201, Wembley, Middx, HA9 7PP,
UNITED KINGDOM (UK)

Hemmer, Bill *Commentator*
Cable News Network, News Dept, 1050
Techwood Dr NW, Atlanta, GA 30318
USA

Hemmi, Heini *Skier*
Chalet Bel-Lia, Valbella, 7077,
SWITZERLAND

Hempel, Amy *Writer*
Charles Scribner's Sons, 866 3rd Ave,
New York, NY 10022 USA

Hemphill, Joel *Music Group*
Harper Agency, PO Box 144,
Goodlettsville, TN 37070 USA

Hemphill, Labreeska *Music Group*
Harper Agency, PO Box 144,
Goodlettsville, TN 37070 USA

Hempstone, Smith Jr *Writer, Diplomat*
7611 Fairfax Road, Bethesda, MD 20814
USA

Hemsley, Sherman *Actor*
Kenny Johnston, PO Box 5344, Sherman
Oaks, CA 91413 USA

Hemsley, Stephen J *Business Person*
United HealthCare Corp, Opus Center,
9900 Bren Road E, Minnetonka, MN
55343 USA

Hemus, Solly
6565 W. Loop South #555, Bellaire, TX
77401

Hencken, John F *Swimmer*
10532 Tujunga Canyon Blvd, Tujunga, CA
91042 USA

Henderson, Alan *Basketball Player*
Atlanta Hawks, 190 Marieta St SW,
Atlanta, GA 30303 USA

Henderson, Biff *Misc*
Late Show with David Letterman, 1697
Broadway, 11th Floor, New York, NY
10019 USA

Henderson, Billy *Music Group*
Buddy Allen Mgmt, 3750 Hudson Manor
Terrace, #3AG, Bronx, NY 10463 USA

Henderson, Bruce *Music Group,
Songwriter*
Fitch Thomas Mgmt, 75 E End Ave #4C,
New York, NY 10028 USA

Henderson, Chris *Soccer Player*
Columbus Crew, 2121 Velman Ave,
Columbus, OH 43211 USA

Henderson, Dave
6004 142nd Ct. SE, Bellevue, WA 98006

Henderson, David L (Dave) *Baseball
Player*
6004 142nd Court SE, Bellevue, WA
98006 USA

Henderson, Donald A *Educator, Misc*
3802 Greenway, Baltimore, MD 21218
USA

Henderson, Felicia *Writer*
Vision Art Management, 9200 Sunset
Blvd, Penthouse 1, Los Angeles, CA
90069 USA

Henderson, Florence *Actor, Music Group*
Cliff Ayers Enterprises, PO Box 17059,
Nashville, TN 37217 USA

Henderson, Gordon *Fashion Designer*
World Hong Kong, 80 W 40th St, New
York, NY 10018 USA

Henderson, James A *Business Person*
Cummins Engine Co, PO Box 3005, 500
Jackson St, Columbus, IN 47201 USA

Henderson, John *Football Player*
Jacksonville Jaguars, 1 AllTel Stadium
Place, Jacksonville, FL 32202 USA

Henderson, Karen LeCraft *Judge*
US Court of Appeals, 333 Constitution
Ave NW, Washington, DC 20001 USA

Henderson, Lyle (Skitch) *Musician,
Composer, Conductor*
Hunt Hill Farm, 44 Upland Road, New
Milford, CT 06776 USA

Henderson, Martin *Actor*
Management 360, 9111 Wilshire Blvd,
Beverly Hills, CA 90210 USA

Henderson, Mike *Music Group, Musician,
Songwriter*
Press Network, PO Box 90528, Nashville,
TN 37209 USA

Henderson, Paul III *Journalist*
Seattle Times, Editorial Dept, 1120 John
St, Seattle, WA 98109 USA

Henderson, Richard *Biologist*
MRC Molecular Biology Laboratory, Hills
Road, Cambridge, CB2 2QH, UNITED
KINGDOM (UK)

Henderson, Rickey *Baseball Player*
10561 Englewood Dr, Oakland, CA
94605 USA

Henderson, Shirley *Actor*
Hamilton Hodell, 24 Hanway St, London,
W1T 1UH, UNITED KINGDOM (UK)

Henderson, Skitch
Upland Rd RFD #3, New Milford, CT
06776

Henderson, Tareva
PO Box 17303, Nashville, TN 37217

Henderson, Thomas
7 Seafield Lane, Westhampton Beach, NY
11978

Henderson, Thomas (Tom) *Basketball
Player*
14003 Piney Run Court, Houston, TX
77066 USA

Hendler, Lauri
4034 Stone Canyon, Sherman Oaks, CA
91403

Hendricks, Barbara *Opera Singer*
I M G Artists, 420 W 45th St, New York,
NY 10036 USA

Hendricks, Jon *Music Group*
Virginia Wicks, 2737 Edwin Place, Los
Angeles, CA 90046 USA

Hendricks, Theodore P (Ted) *Football
Player*
1232 W Weston Dr, Arlington Heights, IL
60004 USA

Hendrix, Elaine *Actor*
Rigberg Roberts Rugolo, 1180 S Beverly
Dr #601, Los Angeles, CA 90035 USA

Hendrix, John W *General*
Commanding General, Army Forces
Command, Fort McPherson, GA 30330
USA

Hendry, Gloria *Actor*
H David Moss, 733 N Seward St #PH, Los
Angeles, CA 90038 USA

Hendryx, Nona *Musician*
Black Rock, 6201 Sunset Blvd #329,
Hollywood, CA 90028 USA

Henenlotter, Frank *Director*
81 Bedford St #6E, New York, NY 10014
USA

Henin-Hardenne, Justine *Tennis Player*
Octagon, 1751 Pinnacle Dr, #1500,
McLean, VA 22102 USA

Henke, Brad *Actor*
Atlas Entertainment, 6100 Wilshire Blvd
#1170, Los Angeles, CA 90048 USA

Henke, Nolan *Golfer*
19662 Lost Creek Dr, Fort Myers, FL
33912 USA

Henkel, Andrea *Athlete*
TKW Sport-Promotion, Lerchenstr 39,
Memmingen, 87700, GERMANY

Henkel, Heike *Track Athlete*
Tannenbergstr 57, Leverkusen, 51373,
GERMANY

Henkel, Herbert L *Business Person*
Ingersoll-Rand Co, 200 Chestnut Ridge
Road, Woodcliff Lake, NJ 07677 USA

Henkin, Louis *Attorney General, Educator*
460 Riverside Dr, New York, NY 10027
USA

Henle, Gertrude *Scientist*
533 Ott Road, Bala Cynwyd, PA 19004
USA

Henley, Beth *Writer*
William Morris Agency, 1325 Ave of
Americas, New York, NY 10019 USA

Henley, Don *Music Group, Songwriter*
H K Mgmt, 9200 W Sunset Blvd #530,
Los Angeles, CA 90069 USA

Henley, Edward T *Misc*
Hotel & Restaurant Employees Union, 1219 28th St NW, Washington, DC 20007 USA

Henley, Elizabeth B (Beth) *Writer*
William Morris Agency, 1325 Ave of Americas, New York, NY 10019 USA

Henley, J Smith *Judge*
US Court of Appeals, 200 Federal Building, Harrison, AR 72601 USA

Henley, Larry *Composer*
Creative Directions, PO Box 335, Brentwood, TN 37024 USA

Henley, Patricia
PO Box 259, Battle Ground, IN 47920

Henley, Virginia *Writer*
Penguin Putnam Press, 375 Hudson St, New York, NY 10014 USA

Henman, Graham *Director*
Agency for Performing Arts, 9200 Sunset Blvd #900, Los Angeles, CA 90069 USA

Henn, Mark *Animator*
Walt Disney Animation, PO Box 10200, Lake Buena Vista, FL 32830 USA

Henn, Walter *Architect*
Ramsachleite 13, Mumau, 82418, GERMANY

Henneman, Brian *Music Group*
Hard Head Productions, 180 Varick St #800, New York, NY 10014 USA

Hennen, Thomas J *Astronaut*
522 Villa Dr, Seabrook, TX 77586 USA

Henner, Marilu *Actor*
2101 Castilian Dr, Los Angeles, CA 90068 USA

Hennessey, Tom *Bowler*
157 Forest Brook Lane, Saint Louis, MO 63146 USA

Hennessy, Jill *Actor*
Creative Artists Agency, 9830 Wilshire Blvd, Beverly Hills, CA 90212 USA

Hennessy, John *Educator*
Stanford University, President's Office, Stanford, CA 94305 USA

Hennessy, John B *Archaeologist*
497 Old Windsor Road, Kellyville, NSW, 2153, AUSTRALIA

Henney, Jane *Government Official*
Food & Drug Administration, 5600 Fishers Lane, Rockville, MD 20852 USA

Henning, Anne *Speed Skater*
5001 W Portland Dr, Littleton, CO 80128 USA

Henning, John F Jr *Publisher*
Sunset Magazine, 80 Willow Road, Menlo Park, CA 94025 USA

Henning, Larry
7426 43rd Ave. SE., St. Cloud, MN 53704-9579

Henning, Linda *Actor*
843 N Sycamore Ave, Los Angeles, CA 90038 USA

Henning, Lorne E *Hockey Player, Coach*
59 Bankside Dr, Centerport, NY 11721 USA

Henning, Paul
4250 Navajo St., Toluca, CA Lake 91602

Henning-Walker, Anne *Speed Skater*
5001 W Portland Dr, Littleton, CO 80128 USA

Hennings, Chad W *Football Player*
6101 Bay Valley Court, Flower Mound, TX 75022 USA

Hennings, Sam *Actor*
Artist's Agency, The (LA), 1180 S Beverly Dr #301, Los Angeles, CA 90035 USA

Henrich, Dieter *Misc*
Gerlichstr 7A, Munich, 81245, GERMANY

Henrich, Thomas D (Tommy) *Baseball Player*
3801 Woodbine Ave, Dayton, OH 45420 USA

Henrich, Tom
1547 Albino Trail, Dewey, AZ 86327

Henricks, Jon N *Swimmer*
254 Laurel Ave, Des Plaines, IL 60016 USA

Henricks, Terence T (Tom) *Astronaut*
Timken Aerospace, PO Box 547, Keene, NH 03431 USA

Henrie, David *Actor*
Noble Media Group Inc, 53 Sunrise Creek Rd, Superior, MT 59872

Henrik *Prince*
Amalienborg Palace, Copenhagen K, 1257, DENMARK

Henriksen, Lance *Actor*
Innovative Artists, 1505 10th St, Santa Monica, CA 90401 USA

Henriquez, Ron *Actor*
PO Box 38027, Los Angeles, CA 90038 USA

Henry, Buck *Actor, Writer*
117 E 57th St, New York, NY 10022 USA

Henry, Clarence
3309 Lawrence St, New Orleans, LA 70114-3230

Henry, Clarence (Forgman) *Music Group, Songwriter*
3309 Lawrence St, New Orleans, LA 70114 USA

Henry, David *Actor*
Peters Fraser & Dunlop (PFD - UK), Drury House, 34-43 Russell St, London, WC2 B5, UNITED KINGDOM (UK)

Henry, Geoffrey A *Prime Minister*
PO Box 281, Rarotonga, COOK ISLANDS

Henry, Gloria *Actor*
849 N Harper Ave, Los Angeles, CA 90046 USA

Henry, Gregg *Actor*
8956 Appian Way, Los Angeles, CA 90046 USA

Henry, Joe *Music Group, Songwriter*
Monterey Peninsula Artists, 509 Hartnell St, Monterey, CA 93940 USA

Henry, Joseph L *Doctor*
60 Marinita Ave, San Rafael, CA 94901 USA

Henry, Justin *Actor*
Slamdunk Films, 202 Main St #14, Venice, CA 90291 USA

Henry, Lenny *Actor*
William Morris Agency (WMA-LA), 1 William Morris Pl, Beverly Hills, CA 90212 USA

Henry, Mike *Actor*
Endeavor Agency LLC (LA), 9601 Wilshire Blvd Fl 3, Beverly Hills, CA 90210 USA

Henry, Pierre *Composer*
32 Rue Toul, Paris, 75012, FRANCE

Henry, Piper
1680 N. Vine St. #614, Hollywood, CA 90028

Henry, Robert H *Judge*
US Court of Appeals, PO Box 1767, Oklahoma City, OK 73101 USA

Henry, Thierry (Titi) *Soccer Player*
Arsenal FC, Arsenal Stadium, Avenell Rd Highbury, London, N5 1BU, UNITED KINGDOM (UK)

Henry, William H Jr *Producer*
Time-Life Books, Rockefeller Center, New York, NY 10020 USA

Hensel, Bruce *Doctor*
17526 Tramanto Dr, Pacific Palisades, CA 90272 USA

Hensel, Robert M *World Record Holder*
wheelierecord@yahoo.com, 215 East 8th Street, Back Apartment, Oswego, NY 13126 USA

Hensel, Witold *Archaeologist*
Ul Marszalkowska 84/92M, Warsaw, 109 00-514, POLAND

Hensilwood, Christopher *Scientist, Misc*
Iziko Museum, 25 Queen Victoria St, Cape Town, SOUTH AFRICA

Hensley, John *Actor*
Innovative Artists (LA), 1505 Tenth St, Santa Monica, CA 90401 USA

Hensley, Jon
1505 10th St., Santa Monica, CA 90401

Hensley, Kirby J *Religious Leader*
Universal Life Church, 601 3rd St, Modesto, CA 95351 USA

Hensley, Pamela *Actor*
9526 Dalegrove Dr, Beverly Hills, CA 90210 USA

Henson, Darrin *Actor*
Don Buchwald & Associates Inc (LA), 6500 Wilshire Blvd #2200, Los Angeles, CA 90048 USA

Henson, Elden *Actor*
Binder & Associates, 1465 Lindacrest Dr, Beverly Hills, CA 90210 USA

Henson, John *Comedian, Actor*
Conversation Co, 1044 Northem Blvd, #304, Roslyn, NY 11576 USA

Henson, Lisa *Producer*
Columbia Pictures, 2400 Riverside Dr, Burbank, CA 91505 USA

Henson, Lou *Basketball Player, Coach*
New Mexico State University, Athletic Dept, Las Cruces, NM 88033 USA

Henson, Taraji P *Actor*
Vincent Cirrincione Associates, 8721 Sunset Blvd #205, Los Angeles, CA 90069 USA

Henstridge, Natasha *Model, Actor*
345 N Maple Dr #397, Beverly Hills, CA
90210 USA

Hentgen, Patrick G (Pat) *Baseball Player*
14451 Knightsbridge Dr, Shelby
Township, MI 48315 USA

Hentoff, Nathan I (Nat) *Musician, Critic*
Village Voice, Editorial Dept, 36 Cooper
Square, New York, NY 10003 USA

Henton, John *Actor*
Gersh Agency, The (LA), 232 N Canon Dr,
Beverly Hills, CA 90210 USA

Hentrich, Helmut *Architect*
Dusseldorfer Str 67, Dusseldorf-
Oberkassel, 40545, GERMANY

Henze, Hans Werner *Composer,
Conductor*
Weihergarten 1-5, Mainz, 55116,
GERMANY

Heppel, Leon A *Biologist*
Cornell University, Biochemistry Dept,
Ithaca, NY 14850 USA

Heppner, Ben *Opera Singer*
Columbia Artists Mgmt Inc, 165 W 57th
St, New York, NY 10019 USA

Her Majesty The Queen, Elizabeth II
Royalty
Buckingham Palace, London, SW1A 1AA,
UNITED KINGDOM (UK)

Herb, Marvin *Business Person*
Coca-Cola Bottling Company of Chicago,
7400 North Oak Park Avenue, Niles, IL
60714

Herbert, Bob *Writer*
New York Times, Editorial Dept, 229 W
43rd St, New York, NY 10036 USA

Herbert, Don (Mr Wizard) *Educator*
PO Box 83, Canoga Park, CA 91305 USA

Herbert, Holly *Journalist*
Celebrity Justice c/o Warner Bros, 4000
Warner Blvd, Burbank, CA 91522 USA

Herbert, James *Writer*
David Higham Associates, 5-8 Lower John
St, London, W1R 4HA, UNITED
KINGDOM (UK)

Herbert, Johnny *Race Car Driver*
PP Sayber AG, Wildbachstr 9, Hinwil,
8340, SWITZERLAND

Herbert, Michael K *Editor*
990 Grove St, Evanston, IL 60201 USA

Herbert, Raymond E (Ray) *Baseball Player*
9360 Taylors Turn, Stanwood, AL 35901
USA

Herbert, Walter W (Wally) *Scientist*
Rowan Cottage, Catlodge, Laggan,
Inverness-shire, PH20 1AH, UNITED
KINGDOM (UK)

Herbert of Hemingford, D Nicholas
Publisher
Old Rectory, Hemingford Abbots,
Huntington Cambs, PE18 9AN, UNITED
KINGDOM (UK)

Herbig, George H *Astronomer*
University of Hawaii, Astronomy Institute,
2680 Woodlawn Dr, Honolulu, HI 96822
USA

Herbig, Gunther
Toronto Symphony, 60 Simcoe St #C116,
Toronto, ON MJ5 2H5, CANADA

Herbst, William *Astronomer*
Wesleyan Univesity, Astronomy Dept,
Middletown, CT 06459 USA

Herczegh, Gezar G *Judge*
Int'l Court of Justice, Camegieplein 2, KJ
Hague, 2517, NETHERLANDS

Herd, Carla
8281 Melrose Ave. #200, Los Angeles, CA
90046

Herd, Richard *Actor*
PO Box 56297, Sherman Oaks, CA 91413
USA

Herda, Frank A *War Hero*
PO Box 34239, Cleveland, OH 44134
USA

Herek, Stephen R *Director*
Endeavor Talent Agency, 9701 Wilshire
Blvd#1000, Beverly Hills, CA 90212 USA

Herincx, Raimund *Opera Singer*
Monk's Vineyard, Larkbarrow, Shepton
Mallet, Somerset, BA4 4NR, UNITED
KINGDOM (UK)

Herman, David J *Business Person*
Adam Opel AG, Bahnhofplatz 1,
Russelsheim, 65429, GERMANY

Herman, George E *Commentator*
4500 Q Lane NW, Washington, DC
20007 USA

Herman, Jerry *Composer, Songwriter*
1196 Cabrillo Dr, Beverly Hills, CA 90210
USA

Herman, Pee Wee
PO Box 29373, Los Angeles, CA 90029

Herman, Pee Wee (Paul Reubens) *Actor,
Comedian*
PO Box 29373, Los Angeles, CA 90029
USA

Hermann, Allen M *Physicist*
2704 Lookout View Dr, Golden, CO
80401 USA

Hermannson, Dustin M *Baseball Player*
9002 E Rimrock Dr, Scottsdale, AZ 85255
USA

Hermannsson, Steingrimur *Prime Minister*
Mavanes 19, Gardaba, 210, ICELAND

Hermaszewski, Miroslav *Astronaut,
General*
Ul Czeczota 25, Warsaw, 02-650,
POLAND

Hermits s/ Peter Noone, Herman's
Musician
Paradise Artists, PO Box 1821, Ojai, CA
93024 USA

Hermlin, Stephan *Writer*
Hermann-Hesse-Str 39, Berlin, 13156,
GERMANY

Hermon, John C *Lawyer, Government
Official*
Warren Road, Donaghadee, County
Down, NORTHERN IRELAND

Herms, George *Artist*
Jack Rutberg Fine Arts, 357 N La Brea
Ave, Los Angeles, CA 90036 USA

Hernandez, Genaro *Boxer*
24442 Ferrocarril, Mission Viejo, CA
92691 USA

Hernandez, Guillermo (Willie) *Baseball
Player*
PO Box 125 Bo Espina, Calle C Buzon,
Aguada, PR 00602 USA

Hernandez, Jay *Actor*
United Talent Agency, 9560 Wilshire Blvd
#500, Beverly Hills, CA 90212 USA

Hernandez, Jose A *Baseball Player*
22 Calle Sur, Vega Alta, PR 00692 USA

Hernandez, Keith *Baseball Player*
255 E 49th St #28D, New York, NY
10017 USA

Hernandez, Los Bros *Artist*
Fantagraphics Books, 7563 Lake City
Way, Seattle, WA 98115 USA

Hernandez, Orlando *Baseball Player,
Athlete*
Montreal Expos, PO Box 500, Station M,
Montreal, H1V 3P, Canada

Hernandez, Robert J *Business Person*
USX Corp, 600 Grant St, Pittsburgh, PA
15219 USA

Hernandez, Rodolfo P *War Hero*
5328 Bluewater Place, College Lakes,
Fayetteville, NC 28311 USA

Hernandez Colon, Rafael *Governor*
PO Box 5788, Puerta de Tierra, San Juan,
PR 00906 USA

Herndon, Mark J *Music Group, Musician*
RR 1 Box 239A, Mentone, AL 35984 USA

Herndon, Ty *Music Group*
PO Box 121858, Nashville, TN 37212
USA

Herr, John C *Scientist*
University of Virginia, Med Center,
Immunology Dept, Charlottesville, VA
22903 USA

Herr, Thomas M (Tommy) *Baseball Player*
1077 Olde Forge Crossing, Lancaster, PA
17601 USA

Herranz Casado, Julian Cardinal *Religious
Leader*
Legislative Texts Curia, Piazza Pio XII #10,
Rome, 00193, ITALY

Herrera, Carolina *Fashion Designer*
Carolina Herrera Ltd, 501 Fashion Ave,
#1700, New York, NY 10018 USA

Herrera, Caroline *Fashion Designer*
501 Seventh Ave Fl 17, New York, NY
10018 USA

Herrera, Efren *Football Player*
2437 E Parkside Ave, Orange, CA 92867
USA

Herrera, Pamela *Ballerina*
American Ballet Theatre, 890 Broadway,
New York, NY 10003 USA

Herrera, Silvestre S *War Hero*
7222 W Windsor Blvd, Glendale, AZ
85303 USA

Herres, Robert T *General, Business
Person*
United Services Automobile Assn, USAA
Building, San Antonio, TX 78288 USA

Herring, Laura
4702 N. 36th St., Phoenix, AZ 85018-3423

Herring, Lynn *Actor*
37900 Road 800, Raymond, CA 93653 USA

Herring, Vincent *Musician, Composer*
Fat City Artists, 1906 Chet Atkins Place #502, Nashville, TN 37212 USA

Herrington, John B *Astronaut*
16411 Clearcrest Dr, Houston, TX 77059 USA

Herrington, John S *Secretary, Business Person*
Harcourt Brace, 525 B St, San Diego, CA 92101 USA

Herrmann, Edward (Ed) *Actor*
220 E 23rd St #400, New York, NY 10010 USA

Herrmann, Mark *Football Player*
8525 Tidewater Dr W, Indianapolis, IN 46236 USA

Herron, Cindy *Music Group*
East West Records, 75 Rockefeller Plaza #1200, New York, NY 10019 USA

Herron, Denis *Hockey Player*
12841 Marsh Point Way, West Palm Beach, FL 33418 USA

Herron, Robert J *Architect*
Herron Assoc, 28-30 Rivington St, London, EC2A 3DU, UNITED KINGDOM (UK)

Herron, Tim *Golfer*
3630 Archer Lane N, Plymouth, MN 55446 USA

Hersch, Fred *Music Group, Musician*
SRO Artists, PO Box 9532, Madison, WI 53715 USA

Hersch, Michael *Composer*
21C Music Publishing, 30 W 63rd St #15S, New York, NY 10023 USA

Herschler, E David *Artist*
PO Box 5859, Santa Barbara, CA 92150 USA

Hersh, Kristin *Music Group, Songwriter*
Throwing Mgmt, PO Box 284, Batesville, VA 22924 USA

Hersh, Seymour *Writer, Journalist*
1211 Connecticut Ave NW, Washington, DC 20036 USA

Hershey, Barbara *Actor*
Talent Entertainment Group, 9111 Wilshire Blvd, Beverly Hills, CA 90210 USA

Hershey, Erin *Actor*
PO Box 16212, Irvine, CA 92623 USA

Hershey, Maralyn
37337 Green Level Rd., Wakefield, VA 23888

Hershiser, Orel *Athlete, Baseball Player, Sportscaster*
5277 Isleworth Country Club Drive, Windermere, FL 34786 USA

Hershiser, Orel L Q *Baseball Player, Sportscaster*
6230 Stefani Dr, Dallas, TX 75225 USA

Herta, Bryan *Race Car Driver*
5449 Briardale Lane, Dublin, OH 43016 USA

Hertz, C Hellmuth *Physicist*
Lund INstitute of Technology, Physics School, Lund, SWEDEN

Hertzberg, Arthur *Religious Leader*
83 Glenwood Road, Englewood, NJ 07631 USA

Hertzberg, Daniel *Journalist*
Wall Street Journal, Editorial Dept, 200 Liberty St, New York, NY 10281 USA

Hertzberg, Sidney (Sonny) *Basketball Player*
535 Hazel Dr, Woodmere, NY 11598 USA

Hertzberger, Herman *Architect*
Architectourstudio, Box 74665, Amsterdam, BR, 1070, NETHERLANDS

Hervey, Jason *Actor*
2049 Century Park E #2500, Los Angeles, CA 90067 USA

Herzenberg, Caroline Littlejohn *Physicist*
1700 E 56th St #2707, Chicago, IL 60637 USA

Herzfeld, John *Director*
Endeavor Agency LLC (LA), 9601 Wilshire Blvd Fl 3, Beverly Hills, CA 90210 USA

Herzfeld, John M *Director*
Industry Entertainment, 955 Carillo Dr #300, Los Angeles, CA 90048 USA

Herzigova, Eva *Model*
Men/Women Model Inc, 199 Lafayette St #700, New York, NY 10012 USA

Herzog, Arthur III *Writer*
4 E 81st St, New York, NY 10028 USA

Herzog, Dorrel N E (Whitey) *Baseball Player, Misc*
9426 Sappington Estates Dr, Saint Louis, MO 63127 USA

Herzog, Jacques *Architect, Misc*
Herzog & De Meuron Architekten, Rheinschanze 6, Basel, 4056, SWITZERLAND

Herzog, Maurice *Mountaineer*
84 Chernin De La Tournette, Chamoinix-Mont-Blanc, 74400, FRANCE

Herzog, Roman *Politician, Ex-President*
Schloss Bellevue, Spreeweg 1, Berlin, 10557, GERMANY

Herzog, Werner *Director*
Herzog Film Productions, Turkenstr 91, Munich, 80799 USA

Herzog, Whitey
9426 Sappington Estates Dr., St. Louis, MO 63127

Hesburgh, Father Theodore
1320 Hesburgh Library, South Bend, IN 46566

Hesburgh, Theodore M *Educator*
University of Natre Dame, 1301 Hesburgh Library, Notre Dame, IN 46556 USA

Heseltine, Michael R D *Government Official*
Thenford House near Banbury, Oxon, OX17 2BX, UNITED KINGDOM (UK)

Heslov, Grant *Actor*
Gold Coast Management, 1023-1/2 Abbott Kinney Blvd, Venice, CA 90291

Hess, Erika *Skier*
Aeschi, Gratenort, 6388, SWITZERLAND

Hess, Ilse
Gailenberg 22, Hindelang/Allgau, GERMANY, D-87541

Hess, John B *Business Person*
Amerada Hess Corp, 1185 Ave of Americas, New York, NY 10036 USA

Hesseman, Howard *Actor*
Innovative Artists, 1505 10th St, Santa Monica, CA 90401 USA

Hessenland, Dagmar
Amsterdamer Str. 3, Munich, GERMANY, D-80805

Hessler, Curtis A *Publisher*
Times-Mirror Co, Times-Mirror Square, Los Angeles, CA 90053 USA

Hessler, Gordon *Director*
8910 Holly Place, Los Angeles, CA 90046 USA

Hessler, Robert R *Oceanographer*
Scripps Institute of Oceanography, Biodiversity Dept, La Jolla, CA 92037 USA

Hester, Jessie L *Football Player*
12813 Pine Acre Court, Wellington, FL 33414 USA

Hester, Paul V *General*
Commander, Special Operations Command, Hurlburt Field, FL 32544 USA

Heston, Charlton *Actor*
2859 Coldwater Canyon, Beverly Hills, CA 90210 USA

Hetfield, James *Music Group, Musician*
2020 Union St, San Francisco, CA 94123 USA

Hetherington, Eileen M *Doctor*
University of Virginia, Psychology Dept, Gilmer Hall, Charlottesville, VA USA

Hetrick, Jennifer *Actor*
Borinstein Oreck Bogart, 3172 Dona Susana, Studio City, CA 91604 USA

Hettich, Arthur M *Editor*
606 Shore Acres Dr, Mamaroneck, NY 10543 USA

Hetzel, Fred *Basketball Player*
218 Corwall St NW, Leesburg, VA 20176 USA

Heuga, Jimmie *Skier*
111 Rawhide, PO Box 686, Avon, CO 81620 USA

Heuring, Lori *Actor*
Mosaic Media Group, 9200 Sunset Blvd Fl 10, Los Angeles, CA 90069 USA

Hewett, Christopher
1422 N. Sweetzer #110, Los Angeles, CA 90069

Hewett, Howard *Music Group*
GHR Entertainment, 6014 N Pointe Place, Woodland Hills, CA 91367 USA

Hewish, Anthony *Nobel Prize Laureate*
Pryor's Cottage, Kingston, Cambridge, CB3 7NQ, UNITED KINGDOM (UK)

Hewitt, Angela *Musician*
Cramer/Marder Artists, 3436 Springhill Road, Lafayette, CA 94549 USA

Hewitt, Bob *Tennis Player*
822 Boylston St #203, Chestnut Hill, MA 02467 USA

Hewitt, Christopher *Actor*
154 E 66th St, New York, NY 10021 USA

Hewitt, Don *Producer*
CBS-TV, News Dept, 51 W 52nd St, New York, NY 10019 USA

Hewitt, Heather
6324 Tahoe Dr., Los Angeles, CA 90068

Hewitt, Jennifer Love *Actor, Music Group*
Handprint Entertainment, 1100 Glendon Ave #1000, Los Angeles, CA 90024 USA

Hewitt, Lleyton *Tennis Player*
PO Box 1235, North Sydney, NSW, 2059, AUSTRALIA

Hewitt, Martin *Actor*
1147 Horn Ave #3, Los Angeles, CA 90069 USA

Hewitt, Paul *Basketball Player, Coach*
Georgia Institute of Technology, Athletic Dept, Atlanta, GA 30332 USA

Hewitt, Peter *Director*
Creative Artists Agency, 9830 Wilshire Blvd, Beverly Hills, CA 90212 USA

Hewlett, Donald
King's Head House Island Wall Whitstable, Kent, ENGLAND, CT5 1EP

Hewlett, Howard *Music Group*
Green Light Talent Agency, PO Box 3172, Beverly Hills, CA 90212 USA

Hewlett, Mark *Reality TV Star*
Jerry Shandrew PR, 1050 South Stanley Avenue, Los Angeles, CA 90019-6634 USA

Hewson, John *Government Official*
ABN Amro Australia, 10 Spring St #14, Sydney, NSW, 2000, AUSTRALIA

Hextall, Dennis H *Hockey Player*
2631 Harvest Hills Dr, Brighton, MI 48114 USA

Hextall, Ronald (Ron) *Hockey Player*
Philadelphia Flyers, 1st Union Center, 3601 S Broad St, Philadelphia, PA 19148 USA

Hey, John D *Economist, Mathematician*
University of York, Economics Dept, Heslington, York, YO1 5DD, UNITED KINGDOM (UK)

Hey, Virginia *Actor*
Anthony Williams Mgmt, 50 Oxford St, Paddington, NSW, 2021, AUSTRALIA

Heyland, Rob
The Manor Middle Lyttleton, Worcestershire, ENGLAND

Heyliger, Vic *Hockey Player, Coach*
2122 Hercules Dr, Colorado Springs, CO 80906 USA

Heyman, Arthur B (Art) *Basketball Player*
321 Lincoln Ave, Rockville Center, NY 11570 USA

Heyman, Richard *Biologist*
Ligand Pharmaceuticals, 9393 Town Center Dr #100, San Diego, CA 92121 USA

Heywood, Anne *Actor*
9966 Liebe Dr, Beverly Hills, CA 90210 USA

Heywood, Joanne
122 Wardour St., London, ENGLAND, W1V 3LA

Hi-Five
PO Box 3030, Jamaica, NY 11431

Hiassen, Carl *Writer*
Knopf Publishers, 201 E 50th St, New York, NY 10022 USA

Hiatt, Andrew *Biologist*
Scripps Research Foundation, 10666 N Torrey Pines Road, La Jolla, CA 92037 USA

Hiatt, John *Music Group, Musician, Songwriter*
Metropolitan Entertainment, 363 US Highway 46 #300F, Fairfield, NJ 07004 USA

Hibbert, Edward *Actor*
Gage Group, 14724 Ventura Blvd #505, Sherman Oaks, CA 91403 USA

Hick, Graeme A *Cricketer*
Worcestershire County Cricket Club, New Road, Worcester, UNITED KINGDOM (UK)

Hick, John H *Religious Leader*
144 Oak Tree Lane, Selly Oak, Birmingham, B29 6HU, UNITED KINGDOM (UK)

Hickam, Homer H Jr *Writer*
9532 Hemlok Dr SE, Huntsville, AL 35803 USA

Hickcox, Charles B (Charlie) *Swimmer*
8315 Redfield Road, Scottsdale, AZ 85260 USA

Hicke, William A (Bill) *Hockey Player*
61 Dogwood Place, Regina, SK S4S 5A1, CANADA

Hickel, Walter J *Secretary, Governor*
1905 Loussac Dr, Anchorage, AK 99517 USA

Hickenbottom, Michael *Wrestler*
World Wrestling Entertainment (WWE), 1241 E Main St, Stamford, CT 06905 USA

Hickerson, R Gene *Football Player*
4471 Nagle Road, Avon, CO 44011 USA

Hickey, James A Cardinal *Religious Leader*
Archdiocesan Pastoral Center, 5002 Eastern Ave, Washington, DC 20017 USA

Hickey, John Benjamin *Actor*
TalentWorks (LA), 3500 W Olive Ave #1400, Burbank, CA 91505 USA

Hickey, Maurice *Publisher*
Denver Post, 65015th St, Denver, CO 80202 USA

Hickey, Thomas J *General*
2127 Bobbyber Dr, Vienna, VA 22182 USA

Hickey, William V *Business Person*
Sealed Air Corp, Park 80 E, Saddle Brook, NJ 07663 USA

Hickland, Catherine *Actor*
255 W 84th St #2A, New York, NY 10024 USA

Hickman, Darryl *Actor*
171 Hermosillo Road, Santa Barbara, CA 93108 USA

Hickman, Dwayne *Actor*
PO Box 17226, Encino, CA 91416 USA

Hickman, Fred *Sportscaster*
Cable News Network, Sports Dept, 1050 Techwood Dr NW, Atlanta, GA 30318 USA

Hickman, Sara *Music Group, Songwriter*
Valdenn, 13801 RR 12 #202, Wimberley, TX 78676 USA

Hickox, Marc
10 St. Mary St. #308, Toronto, CANADA, Ont. M4Y 1

Hickox, Richard S *Conductor*
35 Ellington St, London, N7 8PN, UNITED KINGDOM (UK)

Hicks, Catherine *Actor*
Gersh Agency, 232 N Canon Dr, Beverly Hills, CA 90210 USA

Hicks, Dan *Music Group*
Leslie Wiener, PO Box 245, Sausalito, CA 94966 USA

Hicks, Dan *Sportscaster*
NBC-TV, Sports Dept, 30 Rockefeller Plaza, New York, NY 10112 USA

Hicks, Dwight
4949 Centennial Blvd, Santa Clara, CA 95054

Hicks, John *Music Group, Musician*
John Penny Enterprises, 484 Lexington St, Waltham, MA 02452 USA

Hicks, John C Jr *Football Player*
3287 Green Cook Road, Johnstown, OH 43031 USA

Hicks, Michael *Actor*
Innovative Artists (LA), 1505 Tenth St, Santa Monica, CA 90401 USA

Hicks, Michael *Basketball Player*
New York Knicks, Madison Square Garden, 4 Penn Plaza, New York, NY 10121 USA

Hicks, Michelle *Actor*
Innovative Artists (LA), 1505 Tenth St, Santa Monica, CA 90401 USA

Hicks, Scott *Director*
PO Box 824, Kent Town, 5071, SOUTH AFRICA

Hidalgo, David *Music Group, Songwriter*
Gold Mountain, 3575 Cahuenga Blvd W #450, Los Angeles, CA 90068 USA

Hidalgo, John *Government Official*
May's Valentine Davenport Moore, 1899 L St NW, Washington, DC 20036 USA

Hide, Chris *Musician*
Pop Idol (Fremantle Media), 2700 Colorado Ave #450, Santa Monica, CA 90404 USA

Hide, Herbie *Boxer*
Matchroom, 10 Western Road, Romford, Essex, RM1 3JT, UNITED KINGDOM (UK)

Hide, Raymond *Geophysicist*
University of Oxford, Jesus College, Oxford, OX1 3DW, UNITED KINGDOM (UK)

Hieb, Richard J *Astronaut*
Allied Signal Tech Services, 7515 Mission Dr, Lanham Seabrook, MD 20706 USA

Hiebert, Erwin N *Historian*
40 Payson Road, Belmont, MA 02478
USA

Hier, Marvin *Religious Leader, Social Activist*
Simon Wiesenthal Holocaust Center, 9766 W Pico Blvd, Los Angeles, CA 90035 USA

Hieronymus, Clara W *Journalist*
50 Spring St, Sevannah, TN 38372 USA

Higdon, Bruce *Cartoonist*
210 Canvasback Court, Murfreesboro, TN 37130 USA

Higginbotham, Joan E *Astronaut*
1409 Mija Lane, Seabrook, TX 77586 USA

Higginbotham, Patrick E *Judge*
US Court of Appeals, US Courthouse, 1100 Commerce St, Dallas, TX 75242 USA

Higgins, Al *Producer*
Creative Artists Agency LCC (CAA-LA), 9830 Wilshire Blvd, Beverly Hills, CA 90212 USA

Higgins, Bertie *Music Group, Songwriter*
5775 Peachtree Dunwoody, Atlanta, GA 30342 USA

Higgins, Chester Jr *Photographer*
New York Times, Editorial Dept, 229 W 43rd St, New York, NY 10036 USA

Higgins, J Kenneth *Misc*
Boeing Commercial Airplane Group, PO Box 3707, Seattle, WA 98124 USA

Higgins, Jack *Writer*
September Tide, Mont de la Rocque Jersey, Channel Island, UNITED KINGDOM (UK)

Higgins, Jack *Editor, Cartoonist*
59 Waverly Ave, Clarendon Hills, IL 60514 USA

Higgins, Joel *Actor*
3 Devon Road, Westport, CT 06880 USA

Higgins, John *Swimmer, Coach*
40 Williams Dr, Annapolis, MD 21401 USA

Higgins, John Michael *Actor*
Metropolitan Talent Agency (MTA), 4526 Wilshire Blvd, Los Angeles, CA 90010 USA

Higgins, Michael *Actor*
Michael Hartig Agency, 156 5th Ave #820, New York, NY 10010 USA

Higgins, Robert *Business Person*
Fleet Boston Corp, 1 Federal St, Boston, MA 02110 USA

Higgins, Rosalyn *Judge*
International Court of Justice, Peace Palace, Hague, KJ, 2517, NETHERLANDS

Higginson, John *Doctor*
16 Sundew Road, Savannah, GA 31411 USA

Higham, Scott *Journalist*
Washington Post, Editorial Dept, 1150 15th St NW, Washington, DC 20071 USA

Highman, Charles
4027 Farmouth Dr., Los Angeles, CA 90027

Hightower, John B *Director*
101 Museum Parkway, Newport News, VA 23606 USA

Hightower, Rosella *Ballerina, Dancer, Choreographer*
Villa Piege Luiere, Parc Florentina Ave Vallauris, Cannes, 06400, FRANCE

Highway 101
PO Box 1547, Goodlettsville, TN 37050-1547

Hijuelos, Oscar *Writer*
Hofstra University, English Dept, 10000 Fulton Ave, Hempstead, NY 11550 USA

Hiken, Gerald
910 Moreno Ave., Palo Alto, CA 94303

Hilario, Maybyner (Nene) *Basketball Player*
Denver Nuggets, Pepsi Center, 1000 Chopper Circle, Denver, CO 80204 USA

Hilario, Nene *Basketball Player*
Denver Nuggets, Pepsi Center, 1000 Chopper Cir, Denver, CO 80204 USA

Hilbe, Alfred J *Government Official*
9494 Schaan, Garsill 11, LIECHTENSTEIN

Hildebrand, John G *Biologist*
629 N Olsen Ave, Tucson, AZ 85719 USA

Hildebrandt, Dieter
Rollenhagenstr. 3a, Munich, GERMANY, D-81739

Hildebrandt, Greg *Cartoonist*
Dark Horse, 10956 SE Main St, Milwaukie, OR 97222 USA

Hildegarde *Music Group*
230 E 48th St, New York, NY 10017 USA

Hildreth, Eugene A *Doctor*
5285 Sweitzer Road, Mohnton, PA 19540 USA

Hilfiger, Ally *Heir/Heiress, Reality TV Star*
Tommy Hilfiger, 25 W 39th St, New York, NY 10018 USA

Hilfiger, Tommy *Fashion Designer*
Tommy Hilfiger USA, 485 5th Ave, New York, NY 10017 USA

Hilgenberg, Jay W *Football Player*
1296 Kimmer Court, Lake Forest, IL 60045 USA

Hilger, Rusty *Football Player*
1145 SW 78th Terrace, Oklahoma City, OK 73139 USA

Hill, Andrew (Drew) *Football Player*
37 Westgate Park Lane, Newnan, GA 30263 USA

Hill, A Derek *Artist*
National Art Collections Fund, 20 John Islip St, London, SW1, UNITED KINGDOM (UK)

Hill, Anita *Educator*
600 Third Ave #200, New York, NY 10016 USA

Hill, Arthur *Actor*
2220 Ave of Stars #605, Los Angeles, CA 90067 USA

Hill, Bernard *Actor*
Julian Belfarge, 46 Albermarle St, London, W1X 4PP, UNITED KINGDOM (UK)

Hill, Brendan *Music Group, Musician*
ArtistDirect, 10900 Wilshire Blvd #1400, Los Angeles, CA 90024 USA

Hill, Calvin *Football Player*
10300 Walker Lake Dr, Great Falls, VA 22066 USA

Hill, Damon G D *Race Car Driver*
PO Box 100, Nelson, Lanscashire, BB9 8AQ, UNITED KINGDOM (UK)

Hill, Dan
1407 Mt. Pleasant Rd., Toronto, CANADA, Ont. M4N 2

Hill, Dan *Music Group, Songwriter*
Paquin Entertainment, 1067 Sherwin Road, Winnipeg, MB R3H 0TB, CANADA

Hill, Daniel W (Dan) *Football Player*
171 Montrose Dr, Dunbarton, Durham, NC 27707 USA

Hill, Dave *Golfer*
Eddie Elias Enterprises, PO Box 5118, Akron, OH 44334 USA

Hill, David L (Tex) *War Hero*
317 Elizabeth Road, San Antonio, TX 78209 USA

Hill, Draper *Editor, Cartoonist*
368 Washington Road, Grosse Pointe Woods, MI 48230 USA

Hill, Dule *Actor*
Innovative Artists (LA), 1505 Tenth St, Santa Monica, CA 90401 USA

Hill, Dusty *Music Group, Musician*
Lone Wolf Mgmt, PO Box 163690, Austin, TX 78716 USA

Hill, Faith *Musician, Music Group*
Borman Entertainment, 1250 6th St #401, Santa Monica, CA 90401 USA

Hill, Gary *Artist*
Comish College of the Arts Galleries, 1000 Lenora St, Seattle, WA 98121 USA

Hill, Geoffrey W *Writer*
Boston University, University Professors, 745 Commonwealth St, Boston, MA 02215 USA

Hill, George Roy
59 E. 54th St. #73, New York, NY 10022

Hill, Grant *Basketball Player*
9113 Southern Breeze Dr, Orlando, FL 32836 USA

Hill, Greg L *Football Player*
301 N Joe Wilson Road #1726, Cedar Hill, TX 75104 USA

Hill, Harlon *Football Player*
400 Country Road 388, Killen, AL 35645 USA

Hill, Jack *Director, Producer*
1445 N Fairfax Ave #105, West Hollywood, CA 90046 USA

Hill, James C *Judge*
US Court of Appeals, 56 Forsyth St NW, Atlanta, GA 30303 USA

Hill, James T *General*
Commanding General, Army Forces Command, Fort McPherson, GA 30330 USA

Hill, Jessie *Music Group, Musician*
1210 Caffin Ave, New Orleans, LA 70117 USA

Hill, Jim *Sportscaster*
ABC-TV, Sprots Dept, 77 W 66th St, New York, NY 10023 USA

Hill, Julia Butterfly *Misc*
Circle of Life Foundation, PO Box 3764, Oakland, CA 94609 USA

Hill, Kent A *Football Player*
630 Hawthorne Place, Fayetteville, GA
30214 USA

Hill, Kim *Music Group*
Ambassador Artist Agency, PO Box
50358, Nashville, TN 37205 USA

Hill, Lauryn *Musician, Actor*
Columbia Records, 2100 Colorado Ave,
Santa Monica, CA 90404 USA

Hill, Pat *Football Player*
California State University, Athletic Dept,
Fresno, CA 93740 USA

Hill, Phil *Race Car Driver*
PO Box 3008, Santa Monica, CA 90408
USA

Hill, Ron *Track Athlete*
PO Box 11, Hyde, Cheshire, SK14 1RD,
UNITED KINGDOM (UK)

Hill, Sean *Hockey Player*
12441 Bagleaf Church Road, Raleigh, NC
27614 USA

Hill, Steven *Actor*
18 Jill Lane, Monsey, NY 10952 USA

Hill, Susan E *Writer*
Longmoor Farmhouse Ebrington, Chipping
Campden, Glos, GL55 6NW, UNITED
KINGDOM (UK)

Hill, Terence *Actor*
3 Los Pinos Road, Santa Fe, NM 87505
USA

Hill, Terrell L *Biologist, Physicist*
3400 Paul Sweet Road #C220, Santa
Cruz, CA 95065 USA

Hill, Thomas (Tom) *Track Athlete*
428 Elmcrest Dr, Norman, OK 73071 USA

Hill, Virgil *Boxer*
1618 Santa Gertrudis Loop, Bismarck, ND
58503 USA

Hill, Virgil L Jr *Admiral*
1000 Glendon Court, Ambler, PA 19002
USA

Hill, Walter *Director*
836 Greenway Dr, Beverly Hills, CA
90210 USA

Hill Hearth, Amy
Trident Media Group LLC, 41 Madison
Ave Fl 33, New York, NY 10010 USA

Hill Smith, Marilyn *Opera Singer*
Music International, 13 Ardilaun Road,
Highbury, London, N5 2QR, UNITED
KINGDOM (UK)

Hillaby, John *Writer*
Constable Co, Lanchesters, 102 Fulham
Palace Road, London, W6 9ER, UNITED
KINGDOM (UK)

Hillaker, Harry *Engineer*
1802 Palace Dr, Grand Prairie, TX 75050
USA

Hillan, Patrick *Actor*
11005 Morrison St #206, N Hollywood,
CA 91601

Hillary, Edmund P *Mountaineer, Scientist*
278A Remuera Road, Auckland, SE2,
NEW ZEALAND

Hillary, Sir Edmund
278A Remuera Rd., Auckland, NEW
ZEALAND, SE 2

Hille, Bertil *Doctor*
10630 Lakeside Ave NE, Seattle, WA
98125 USA

Hille, Einar *Mathematician*
8862 La Jolla Scenic Dr N, La Jolla, CA
92037 USA

Hillebrecht, Rudolf F H *Architect*
Gneiststr 7, Hanover, 30169, GERMANY

Hillel, Shlomo *Government Official*
14 Gelber St, Jerusalem, 96755, ISRAEL

Hilleman, Maurice R *Scientist*
Merck Therapeutic Research Institute,
WP53C 350, West Point, PA 19118 USA

Hillen, Bobby *Race Car Driver*
Donlavey Racing, 5011 Midlothian
Turnpike, Richmond, VA 23225 USA

Hillenbrand, Daniel A *Business Person*
Hillenbrand Industries, 700 State RR 46 E,
Batesville, IN 47006 USA

Hillenbrand, Laura *Writer*
Random House, 1745 Broadway #B1,
New York, NY 10019 USA

Hillenbrand, Martin J *Diplomat*
University of Georgia, International Trade/
Security Center, Athens, GA 30602 USA

Hillenbrand, Shea *Baseball Player*
16208 E Via De Palmas, Gilbert, AZ
85297 USA

Hiller, Arthur *Director*
1218 Benedict Canyon, Beverly Hills, CA
90210 USA

Hiller, Susan *Artist*
83 Loudoun Road, London, NW8 0DL,
UNITED KINGDOM (UK)

Hillerman, John *Actor*
1110 Bade St, Houston, TX 77055 USA

Hillerman, Tony *Writer*
1632 Francisca Road NW, Albuquerque,
NM 87107 USA

Hillery, Patrick J *President*
Grasmere Greenfield Road, Sutton, Dublin
13, IRELAND

Hilliard, Ike *Football Player*
New York Giants, Giants Stadium, East
Rutherford, NJ 07073 USA

Hillier, James *Inventor*
22 Arreton Road #CR31, Princeton, NJ
08540 USA

Hillier, Steve *Music Group, Musician*
Primary Talent Int'l, 2-12 Petonville Road,
London, N1 9PL, UNITED KINGDOM
(UK)

Hillis, Ali *Actor*
4460 Stern Ave, Back Guest House,
Sherman Oaks, CA 91423 USA

Hillis, W Daniel (Danny) *Scientist*
Applied Minds, 1209 Grand Central Ave,
Glendale, CA 91201 USA

Hillman, Chris *Music Group, Musician,
Songwriter*
McMullen Co, 433 N Camden Dr #400,
Beverly Hills, CA 90210 USA

Hills, Carla *Secretary*
3125 Chain Bridge Road NW,
Washington, DC 20016 USA

Hills, Roderick M *Business Person,
Government Official*
Mudge Rose Guthrie Alexander Ferdon,
1200 19th St NW, Washington, DC 20036
USA

Hilmers, David C *Astronaut*
18502 Point Lookout Dr, Houston, TX
77058 USA

Hilmes, Jerome B *General*
4900 Windsor Park, Sarasota, FL 34235
USA

Hilton, Barron *Business Person*
Hilton Hotels Corp, 9336 Civic Center Dr,
Beverly Hills, CA 90210 USA

Hilton, Janet *Music Group, Musician*
Holly House E Downs Road, Bowdon
Altrincham, Cheshire, WA14 2LH,
UNITED KINGDOM (UK)

Hilton, Nikki *Heir/Heiress*
Hilton Hotels Corp, 9336 Civic Center Dr,
Beverly Hills, CA 90210 USA

Hilton, Paris *Heir/Heiress, Reality TV Star*
Untitled Entertainment (LA), 8436 W 3rd
St #650, Los Angeles, CA 90048 USA

Hiltz, Nichole *Actor*
Metropolitan Talent Agency (MTA), 4526
Wilshire Blvd, Los Angeles, CA 90010
USA

Hiltzik, Michael A *Journalist*
Los Angeles Times, Editorial Dept, 202 W
1st, Los Angeles, CA 90012 USA

Himelstein, Aaron *Actor*
Stewart Talent, 58 West Huron, Chicago,
IL 60610

Himmelfarb, Gertrude *Historian*
2510 Virginia Ave NW, Washington, DC
20037 USA

Hinault, Bernard
7 rue de la Sauvaie 21 Sud-Est., Rennes,
FRANCE, F-35000

Hinckley, Gordon B *Religious Leader*
Church of Latter Day Saints, 50 E North
Temple, Salt Lake City, UT 84150 USA

Hinckley Jr, John
2700 Martin Luther King Ave,
Washington, DC 20005 USA

Hindle, Art *Actor*
3005 Main St, Santa Monica, CA 90405
USA

Hinds, Ciaran *Actor*
Larry Dalzell, 91 Regent St, London, W1R
7TB, UNITED KINGDOM (UK)

Hinds, Cirian *Actor*
Endeavor Agency LLC (LA), 9601 Wilshire
Blvd Fl 3, Beverly Hills, CA 90210 USA

Hinds, Samuel A A *Prime Minister*
Prime Minister's Office, Public Buildings,
Georgetown, GUYANA

Hinds, William E *Cartoonist*
1301 Spring Oaks Circle, Houston, TX
77055 USA

Hine, Maynard K *Doctor*
1121 W Michigan St, Indianapolis, IN
46202 USA

Hine, Patrick *Misc*
Lloyd's Bank, Cox's & Kings, 7 Pall Mall,
London, SW1 5NA, UNITED KINGDOM
(UK)

Hiner, Glen H *Business Person*
Owens-Coming, 1 Owens Coming Parkway, Toledo, OH 43659 USA

Hines, Cheryl *Actor*
International Creative Management (ICM-LA), 8942 Wilshire Blvd, Beverly Hills, CA 90211 USA

Hines, Deni *Music Group*
Peter Rix Mgmt, 49 Hume St #200, Crows Nest, NSW, 2065, AUSTRALIA

Hines, Mimi
1605 S. 11th St., Las Vegas, NV 89109-1611

Hingis, Martina *Tennis Player*
30165 Fairway Dr, Wesley Chapel, FL 33543 USA

Hingle, Pat *Actor*
PO Box 2228, Carolina Beach, NC 28428 USA

Hingorani, Narain G *Engineer*
1286 Lexington Lane, Lake Zurich, IL 60047 USA

Hings, Donald L *Inventor*
281 Howard Ave, North Burnaby, BC V5B 4Y7, CANADA

Hingsen, Jurgen *Track Athlete*
655 Circle Dr, Santa Barbara, CA 93108 USA

Hinkle, Marin *Actor*
Innovative Artists (LA), 1505 Tenth St, Santa Monica, CA 90401 USA

Hinkle, Robert
5225 Agnes Ave. #102, No. Hollywood, CA 91607

Hinkley, Brent *Actor*
Gage Group, The (LA), 14724 Ventura Blvd #505, Los Angeles, CA 91403 USA

Hinners, Noel *Government Official*
7 Greyswood Court, Rockville, MD 20854 USA

Hino, Kazuyoshi *Fashion Designer*
Hino & Malee Inc, 3701 N Ravenswood Ave, Chicago, IL 60613 USA

Hinojosa, Ricardo H *Judge*
US District Court, PO Box 5007, McAllen, TX 78502 USA

Hinojosa, Tish *Music Group, Songwriter*
PO Box 3304, Austin, TX 78764 USA

Hinrich, Kurt *Basketball Player*
Chicago Bulls, United Center, 1901 W Madison St, Chicago, IL 60612 USA

Hinsche, Billy
2588-F El Camino Real PMB 101, Carlsbad, CA 92008

Hinske, Eric *Baseball Player*
Toronto Blue Jays, Skydome, 1 Blue Jay Way, Toronto, ON M5V 1J1, CANADA

Hinson, Larry *Golfer*
3179 Highway 32 E, Douglas, GA 31533 USA

Hinson, Roy *Basketball Player*
4272 State Highway 27, Monmouth Junction, NJ 08852 USA

Hinterseer, Ernst *Skier*
Hahnenkammstr, Kitzbuhel, 6370, AUSTRIA

Hintikka, Jaakko J *Misc*
University of Helsinki, PO Box 24, Helsinki, 00014, FINLAND

Hinton, Christopher J (Chris) *Football Player*
5136 Falcon Chase Lane, Atlanta, GA 30342 USA

Hinton, Darby *Actor*
1267 Bel Air Road, Los Angeles, CA 90077 USA

Hinton, Eddie *Football Player*
12109 Poulson Dr, Houston, TX 77031 USA

Hinton, James David
2806 Oak Point Dr, Los Angeles, CA 90068

Hinton, S E
8955 Beverly Blvd, Los Angeles, CA 90048 USA

Hinton, Sam *Music Group, Songwriter*
9420 La Jolla Shores Dr, La Jolla, CA 92037 USA

Hinton, Susan Eloise (S E) *Writer*
Delacorte Press, 1540 Broadway, New York, NY 10036 USA

Hinton of Bankside, Christopher *Government Official, Engineer*
Tiverton Lodge, Dulwich Common, London, SG2 7EW, UNITED KINGDOM (UK)

Hintz, Donald C *Business Person*
Entergy Corp, 10055 Grogans Mill Road #5A, The Woodlands, TX 77380 USA

Hiort, Esbjonm *Architect*
Bel Colles Farm, Parkvej 6, Rungsted Kyst, 2960, DENMARK

Hipp, Paul
8383 Wilshire Blvd. #550, Beverly Hills, CA 90211-2404

Hipwell, Elizabeth
18 Gramercy Park So, New York, NY 10003-1724

Hird, Thora
21 Leinster Mews, London, ENGLAND, W2 3EY

Hire, Kathryn P (Kay) *Astronaut*
PO Box 580146, Houston, TX 77258 USA

Hiroshima
1460 4th St. #205, Santa Monica, CA 90401

Hirosue, Ryoyo *Actor*
OmniotComp, Sowinskiego 27A, Grodzisk, Mazowiecki, POLAND

Hirsch, David
6255 Sunset Blvd. #627, Los Angeles, CA 90028

Hirsch, E D Jr *Educator*
University of Virginia, Education Dept, Charlottesville, VA 22906 USA

Hirsch, Elroy
50 Oak Creek Trail, Madison, WI 53717

Hirsch, Emile *Actor*
9615 Brighton Way #426, Beverly Hills, CA 90210 USA

Hirsch, Hallee *Actor, Musician*
Innovative Artists (LA), 1505 Tenth St, Santa Monica, CA 90401 USA

Hirsch, Judd *Actor*
137 W 12th St, New York, NY 10011 USA

Hirsch, Laurence E *Business Person*
Centex Corp, 2728 N Harwood, Dallas, TX 75201 USA

Hirsch, Leon C *Inventor*
150 Glover Ave, Norwalk, CT 06850 USA

Hirsch, Robert P *Actor*
1 Pl du Palais Bourbon, Paris, 75007, FRANCE

Hirsch, Stan
16027 Ventura Blvd. #206, Encino, CA 91436-2733

Hirschfeld, Gerald *Cinematographer*
425 Ashland St, Ashland, OR 97520 USA

Hirschfelder, David *Composer*
APRA, PO Box 567, Crows Nest, NSW, 2065 USA

Hirschfielder, Gerald J *Cinematographer*
425 Ashland St, Ashland, OR 97520 USA

Hirschman, Albert O *Economist*
16 Newlin Road, Princeton, NJ 08540 USA

Hirschmann, Ralph F *Misc*
740 Palmer Place, Blue Bell, PA 19422 USA

Hirson, Alice *Actor*
Halpem Assoc, PO Box 5597, Santa Monica, CA 90409 USA

Hirst, Damien *Artist*
White Cube Gallery, Saint James's, 44 Duke St, London, SW1Y 6DD, UNITED KINGDOM (UK)

Hirtz, Dagmar
Jollystr. 14, Munich, GERMANY, D-81545

Hirzebruch, Friedrich E P *Mathematician*
Thuringer Allee 127, Saint Augustin, 53757, GERMANY

Hisle, Larry E *Baseball Player*
312 W Saddleworth Court W, Mequon, WI 53092 USA

Hitchcock, Ken *Hockey Player*
14820 Bellbrook Dr, Dallas, TX 75254 USA

Hitchcock, Michael *Actor*

Hitchcock, Patricia
3835 E. Thousand Oaks Blvd. #435, Westlake Village, CA 91362

Hitchcock, Robyn *Music Group, Songwriter*
Agency Group Ltd, 1775 Broadway #430, New York, NY 10019 USA

Hitchcock, Russell *Musician*
Agency for Performing Arts, 9200 Sunset Blvd #900, Los Angeles, CA 90069 USA

Hitchins, Christopher
2022 Columbia Rd. NW, Washington, DC 20009

Hite, Shere
PO Box 1037, New York, NY 10028

Hite, Shere D *Writer*
75 Haywood St #312, Asheville, NC 28801 USA

Hitt, John C *Educator*
1000 Central Florida Blvd, Orlando, FL 32826 USA

Hix, Charles *Fashion Designer, Writer*
Simon & Schuster, 1230 Ave of Americas, New York, NY 10020 USA

Hjejle, Iben *Actor*
William Morris Agency, 151 El Camino Dr, Beverly Hills, CA 90212 USA

Hlass, I Jerry *Engineer*
National Space Technology Laboratories, NSTL Station, MS 39529 USA

Hlinka, Nichol *Ballerina*
New York City Ballet, Lincoln Center Plaza, New York, NY 10023 USA

Hnilicka, Milan *Hockey Player*
Los Angeles Kings, Staples Center, 1111 S Figueroa St, Los Angeles, CA 90015 USA

Ho, David *Scientist*
Aaron Diamond AIDS Research Center, 455 1st Ave, New York, NY 10016 USA

Ho, Don
PO Box 90039, Honolulu, HI 96825-0039

Ho, Donald T (Don) *Music Group*
277 Lewers St, Honolulu, HI 96815 USA

Ho, Tao *Architect*
Upper Deck North Point West, Passenger Ferry Pier, North Point, HONG KONG

Hoag, Charles *Basketball Player*
2927 SW Foxcroft Court #2, Topeka, KS 66614 USA

Hoag, Jan
855 N. Martel Ave., Los Angeles, CA 90046

Hoag, Judith W *Actor*
HWA Talent, 3500 W Olive Ave, #1400, Burbank, CA 91505 USA

Hoag, Peter C *Misc*
3566 Little Rock Dr, Provo, UT 84604 USA

Hoag, Tami *Writer*
Delacorte Press, 1540 Broadway, New York, NY 10036 USA

Hoage, Terrell L (Terry) *Football Player*
11 Meadow Road, Rosemont, PA 19010 USA

Hoagland, Edward *Writer*
85 Red Pine Road, Bennington, VT 05201 USA

Hoagland, Jaheim *Musician*
JL Entertainment Inc, 18653 Ventura Blvd, #340, Tarzana, CA 91356

Hoagland, Jimmie L (Jim) *Journalist*
Washington Post, Editorial Dept, 1150 15th St NW, Washington, DC 20071 USA

Hoaglin, Fred *Football Player, Football Coach*
7 Governors Road, Hilton Head, SC 29928 USA

Hoar, Joseph P *General*
386 13th St, Del Mar, CA 92014 USA

Hoare, C Antony R *Engineer*
Oxford University, Computing Lab, Parks Road, Oxford, OX1 3QD, UNITED KINGDOM (UK)

Hoare, Tony
430 Edgware Rd, London, ENGLAND, W2 1EG

Hoban, Russell C *Writer*
6 Musgrave Crescent, London, SW6 4PT, UNITED KINGDOM (UK)

Hobart, Nick *Cartoonist*
5632 Indiana Ave, New Port Richey, FL 34652 USA

Hobaugh, Charles O *Astronaut*
NASA, Johnson Space Center, 2101 NASA Road, Houston, TX 77058 USA

Hobault, John *Scientist*
51 Winster Fax, Williamsburg, VA 23185 USA

Hobbs, Becky *Musician*
Entertainment Artists, 2409 21st Ave S, #100, Nashville, TN 37212 USA

Hobbs, Franklin (Fritz) *Misc*
151 E 79th St, New York, NY 10021 USA

Hobbs, Rebecca *Actor*
Kathryn Rawlings Actors Agency, PO Box 105, Auckland Central, 657, NEW ZEALAND

Hobson, Clell L (Butch) *Baseball Player*
3705 Dearing Downs Dr, Tuscaloosa, AL 35405 USA

Hobson, J Allan *Scientist*
Harvard University, Sleep Laboratory, Cambridge, MA 02138 USA

Hobson, Jeff *Misc*
Jack Grenier Productions, 32630 Concord Dr, Madison Heights, MI 48071 USA

Hoch, Danny *Artist*
Columbia Artists Mgmt Inc, 165 W 57th St, New York, NY 10019 USA

Hoch, Scott *Golfer*
9329 Cypress Cove, Orlando, FL 32819 USA

Hochhuth, Rolf *Writer*
PO Box 661, Basel, 4002, SWITZERLAND

Hochstrasser, Robin M *Misc*
University of Pennsylvania, Chemistry Dept, Philadelphia, PA 19104 USA

Hochwald, Bari *Actor*
Herb Tannen, 10801 National Blvd #101, Los Angeles, CA 90064 USA

Hock, Dee Ward *Business Person*
Visa International, 900 Metro Center Blvd, Foster City, CA 94404 USA

Hocke, Stefan *Skier*
Sportgymnasium, Am Harzwald 3, Oberhof, 98558, GERMANY

Hockenberry, John *Commentator*
ABC-TV, News Dept, 77 W 66th St, New York, NY 10023 USA

Hockney, David *Artist*
7508 Santa Monica Blvd, Los Angeles, CA 90046 USA

Hodder, Kane *Actor*
3701 Senda Calma, Calabasas, CA 91302 USA

Hodder, Kenneth *Religious Leader*
Salvation Army, 615 Slaters Lane, Alexandria, VA 22314 USA

Hoddinott, Alun *Composer*
64 Gowerton Road, Three Crosses, Swansea, SA4 3PX, WALES

Hoddle, Glenn *Soccer Player*
Football Assn, 16 Lancaster Gate, London, W2 3LW, UNITED KINGDOM (UK)

Hodel, Donald P *Secretary*
1801 Sara Dr, #L, Chesapeake, VA 23320 USA

Hodge, Charles E (Charlie) *Hockey Player*
21356 86A Crescent, Langley, BC V1M 2A2, CANADA

Hodge, Daniel A (Dan) *Wrestler*
General Delivery, Perry, OK 73077 USA

Hodge, Douglas *Actor*
Peters Fraser & Dunlop (PFD - UK), Drury House, 34-43 Russell St, London, WC2 B5, UNITED KINGDOM (UK)

Hodge, Kenneth R (Ken) Sr *Hockey Player*
1115 Main St, Lynnfield, MA 01940 USA

Hodge, Patricia *Actor*
International Creative Mgmt, 76 Oxford St, London, W1N 0AX, UNITED KINGDOM (UK)

Hodge, Stephanie *Actor*
Gersh Agency, 232 N Canon Dr, Beverly Hills, CA 90210 USA

Hodge, Sue
82 Constance Rd. Twickenham, Middlesex A, ENGLAND, TW2 7J

Hodges, Bill *Basketball Player, Coach*
Georgia College, Athletic Dept, Milledgeville, GA 31061 USA

Hodges, Eric *Actor*
3800 West Alameda Ave, Burbank, CA 91505

Hodges, Louise
31A St. George's Rd Leyton, London, ENGLAND, EIO 5RH

Hodges, Mike *Director*
Wesley Farm Durweston, Blanford Forum, Dorset, DT11 0QG, UNITED KINGDOM (UK)

Hodges, Trey *Baseball Player, Athlete*
Atlanta Braves, Turner Field, PO Box 4064, Atlanta, GA 30302 USA

Hodgkin, Howard *Artist*
Anthony D'Offay Gallery, 9/24 Dering St, London, W1R 9AA, UNITED KINGDOM (UK)

Hodgson, James D *Secretary*
10132 Hillgrove Dr, Beverly Hills, CA 90210 USA

Hodler, Marc *Skier*
Int'l Ski Federation, Worbstr 210, Gumligen B Bem, 3073, SWITZERLAND

Hodo, David *Music Group*
8255 Sunset Blvd, West Hollywood, CA 90046 USA

Hoechlin, Tyler *Actor*
Blue Train Entertainment, 9100 Wilshire Blvd #340W, Beverly Hills, CA 90212 USA

Hoeft, William F (Billy) *Baseball Player*
Canadian Lakes, 9965 Lost Canyon Dr, Stanwood, MI 49346 USA

Hoenig, Michael *Composer*
Gorfaine/Schwartz, 13245 Riverside Dr #450, Sherman Oaks, CA 91423 USA

Hoenig, Thomas M *Financier, Government Official*
615 W Meyer Blvd, Kansas City, MO 64113 USA

Hoest, Bunny *Cartoonist*
William Hoest Enterprises, 27 Watch Way, Lloyd Neck, Huntington, NY 11743 USA

Hoff, Marcian E (Ted) Jr *Inventor*
12226 Colina Dr, Los Altos Hills, CA
94024 USA

Hoff, Philip H *Governor*
Hoff Wilson Powell Lang, PO Box 567,
Burlington, VT 05402 USA

Hoff, Syd
PO Box 2463, Miami Beach, FL 33140

Hoffa, James P *Misc*
2593 Hounds Chase Dr, Troy, MI 48098
USA

Hoffman, Alan J *Mathematician*
IBM Research Center, PO Box 218,
Yorktown Heights, NY 10598 USA

Hoffman, Alice *Writer*
3 Hurlbut St, Cambridge, MA 02138 USA

Hoffman, Basil *Actor*
26 Aller Court, Glendale, CA 91206 USA

Hoffman, Darleane C *Physicist*
Lawrence Berkeley Laboratory, 1
Cyctotron Road, Berkeley, CA 94720 USA

Hoffman, Dustin *Actor, Producer,
Director*
Punch Productions, 11661 San Vicente
Blvd #222, Los Angeles, CA 90049

Hoffman, Dustine L *Actor*
Punch Productions, 11661 San Vicente
Blvd #222, Los Angeles, CA 90049 USA

Hoffman, Elizabeth *Actor*
Bauman Assoc, 5750 Wilshire Blvd, #473,
Los Angeles, CA 90036 USA

Hoffman, Elizabeth *Educator*
University of Colorado, President's Office,
Boulder, CO 80309 USA

Hoffman, Glenn E *Baseball Player*
201 S Old Bridge Road, Anaheim, CA
92808 USA

Hoffman, Jackie *Actor*
International Creative Management
(ICM-LA), 8942 Wilshire Blvd, Beverly
Hills, CA 90211 USA

Hoffman, Jeffrey A *Astronaut*
US Embassy, 2 Ave Gabriel, PSC 116/
NASA, Paris Cedex, 75382, FRANCE

Hoffman, John Robert *Writer*
Industry Entertainment, 955 S Carrillo Dr
#300, Los Angeles, CA 90048 USA

Hoffman, Jorg *Swimmer*
Saarmunder Str 74, Potsdam, 14478,
GERMANY

Hoffman, Matt *Actor*
DDK Talent, 3800 Barham Blvd #303, Los
Angeles, CA 90068 USA

Hoffman, Michael *Director*
International Creative Management
(ICM-LA), 8942 Wilshire Blvd, Beverly
Hills, CA 90211 USA

Hoffman, Paul Felix *Geophysicist*
162 Cypress St, Brookline, MA 02445
USA

Hoffman, Philip Seymour *Actor*
Hedges Hoffman, 1008 Harry St,
Conshohocken, PA 19428 USA

Hoffman, Rick *Actor*
Anonymous Content, 8522 National Blvd
#101, Culver City, CA 90232 USA

Hoffman, Ted Jr *Bowler*
1568 Partarian Way, San Jose, CA 95129
USA

Hoffman, Toby *Music Group, Musician*
Columbia Artists Mgmt Inc, 165 W 57th
St, New York, NY 10019 USA

Hoffman, William M *Writer, Songwriter*
190 Prince St, New York, NY 10012 USA

Hoffmann, Christian *Skier*
Frunwald 7, Aigen, 4160, AUSTRIA

Hoffmann, Frank N (Nordy) *Football
Player*
400 N Capitol St NW #327, Washington,
DC 20001 USA

Hoffmann, Gaby
8942 Wilshire Blvd, Beverly Hills, CA
90211

Hoffmann, Isabella
6500 Wilshire Blvd. #2200, Los Angeles,
CA 90048

Hoffmann, Roald *Nobel Prize Laureate*
4 Sugarbush Lane, Ithaca, NY 14850 USA

Hoffmann, Robert
Rehling Westenriederstr. 8, Munich,
GERMANY, D-80331

Hoffs, Susanna *Musician*
Bangles Mall, 1341W Fullerton Ave, Box
180, Chicago, IL 60614 USA

Hofheimer, Charlie *Actor*
Innovative Artists (LA), 1505 Tenth St,
Santa Monica, CA 90401 USA

Hofmann, Al *Race Car Driver*
PO Box 346, Umatilla, FL 32784 USA

Hofmann, Detief *Athlete*
Saarlandstr 164, Karlsruhe, 76187,
GERMANY

Hofmann, Douglas *Artist*
8602 Saxon Circle, Baltimore, MD 21236
USA

Hofmann, Isabella *Actor*
Don Buchwald, 6500 Wilshire Blvd
#2200, Los Angeles, CA 90048 USA

Hofmann, Peter *Opera Singer*
Postfach 127, Kemnath, 95474,
GERMANY

Hofschneider, Marco *Actor*
Progressive Artists Agency, 400 S Beverly
Dr #216, Beverly Hills, CA 90212 USA

Hofstatter, Peter R *Psychic, Doctor*
Lehmkuhleweg 16, Buxtehude, 21614,
GERMANY

Hogan, Chris *Actor*
Rigberg-Rugolo Entertainment, 1180 S
Beverly Dr #601, Los Angeles, CA 90035
USA

Hogan, Craig *Astronomer*
University of Washington, Astronomy
Dept, Seattle, WA 98195 USA

Hogan, Hulk *Actor, Wrestler*
130 Willadel Dr, Belleair, FL 33756 USA

Hogan, Linda *Writer*
University of Colorado, English Dept,
Boulder, CO 80309 USA

Hogan, Paul *Reality TV Star*
Acme Talent & Literary Agency (LA), 4727
Wilshire Blvd #333, Los Angeles, CA
90010 USA

Hogan, Paul *Actor*
Silver Lion Films, 701 Santa Monica Blvd,
Santa Monica, CA 90401

Hogan, Paul *Actor*
18 Marshall Crescent, Beacon Hill, NSW,
2060, AUSTRALIA

Hogan, Paul (PJ) *Director, Writer,
Producer*
Creative Artists Agency LCC (CAA-LA),
9830 Wilshire Blvd, Beverly Hills, CA
90212 USA

Hogan, Robert *Actor*
344 W 89th St #1B, New York, NY 10024
USA

Hogan, Terry
130 Willadel Dr., Belleair, FL 34616

Hogarth, Freddie
69 St. Quentin Ave. #1, London,
ENGLAND, W10 6PA

Hogestyn, Drake *Actor*
6080 Cavalleri Road, Malibu, CA 90265
USA

Hogg, Christopher A *Business Person*
Courtaulds, 18 Hanover Square, London,
W1A 2BB, UNITED KINGDOM (UK)

Hogg, James R *Admiral*
Prescott Farm, 2556 W Main Road,
Portsmouth, RI 02871 USA

Hoggard, Jay *Music Group, Musician*
Creative Music Consultants, 181 Christie
St #300, New York, NY 10002 USA

Hogue, Stacey
10474 Santa Monica Blvd. #380, Los
Angeles, CA 90025

Hogwood, Christopher J H *Musician,
Conductor*
10 Brookside, Cambridge, CB2 1JE,
UNITED KINGDOM (UK)

Hohmann, John *Misc*
Louis Berger Assoc, 1110 E Missouri Ave,
#200, Phoenix, AZ 85014 USA

Hohne, Claus
An der Kiesgrube 3, Holzkirchen,
GERMANY, D-83607

Hoiby, Lee *Composer, Musician*
9807 County Highway 28, Long Eddy, NY
12760 USA

Hoku *Musician*
Evolution Talent, 1776 Broadway, #1500,
New York, NY 10019 USA

Holahan, Dennis
9250 Wilshire Blvd. #208, Beverly Hills,
CA 90212

Holbert, Jerry *Editor, Cartoonist*
Boston Herald, Editorial Dept, 1 Herald St,
Roxbury, MA 02118 USA

Holbrook, Bill *Cartoonist*
King Features Syndicate, 888 7th Ave,
New York, NY 10106 USA

Holbrook, Hal *Actor*
PO Box 1980, Studio City, CA 91614 USA

Holbrook, Karen *Educator*
Presidint's Office, Ohio State University,
Columbus, OH 43210 USA

Holbrook, Terry *Hockey Player*
8799 Arrowood Dr, Mentor, OH 44060
USA

Holcomb, Corey *Comedian*
William Morris Agency (WMA-LA), 1
William Morris Pl, Beverly Hills, CA
90212 USA

Holden, Alexandra *Actor*
United Talent Agency (UTA), 9560
Wilshire Blvd, Beverly Hills, CA 90212
USA

Holden, Amanda *Actor*
Amanda Howard, 21 Berwick St, London,
W1F 0PZ, UNITED KINGDOM (UK)

Holden, Jennifer
115 S. Topanga Canyon #153, Topanga,
CA 90290

Holden, Joyce
444 N. El Camino Real #89, Encinitas, CA
92024-1313

Holden, Laurie *Actor*
Untitled Entertainment (LA), 8436 W 3rd
St #650, Los Angeles, CA 90048 USA

Holden, Mariean *Actor*
L A Talent, 8335 Sunset Blvd #200, Los
Angeles, CA 90069 USA

Holden, Rebecca *Actor, Music Group*
Box Office, 5207 Rustic Way, Old
Hickory, TN 37138 USA

Holden, William Wildlife Foundation
PO Box 67981, Los Angeles, CA 90067

Holden-Reid, Kristen *Actor*
Paradigm (LA), 10100 Santa Monica Blvd,
Fl 25, Los Angeles, CA 90067 USA

Holder, Christopher *Actor*
H David Moss, 733 Seward St #PH, Los
Angeles, CA 90038 USA

Holder, Geoffrey *Actor, Dancer*
565 Broadway, New York, NY 10012
USA

Holderness, Sue
10 Rectory Close Windsor, Berks.,
ENGLAND, SL4 5ER

Holding, John Simon
15060 Ventura Blvd. #360, Sherman
Oaks, CA 91403

Holdorf, Willi *Track Athlete*
Adidas KG, Herzogenaurach, 91074,
GERMANY

Holdsclaw, Chamique *Basketball Player*
Washington Mystics, MCI Center, 601 F St
NW, Washington, DC 20004 USA

Hole
150 E. 58th St. #1900, New York, NY
10155-0002

Holgren, Paul H
724 Southwick Cir, Somerdale, NJ 08083
USA

Holl, Steven M *Architect*
Steven Holl Architects, 435 Hudson St
#400, New York, NY 10014 USA

Holladay, Wilhelmina Cole *Misc*
National Museum of Women in Arts,
1250 New York NW, Washington, DC
20005 USA

Holland, Agnieszka *Director, Writer*
Agence Nicole Cann, 1 Rue Alfred de
Vigny, Paris, 75008, FRANCE

Holland, Dave *Music Group, Musician*
DL Media, PO Box 2728, Bala Cynwyd,
PA 19004 USA

Holland, Dexter *Musician*
Rebel Waltz, 31652 2nd Ave, Laguna
Beach, CA 92651 USA

Holland, Heinrich D *Geophysicist*
14 Rangely Road, Winchester, MA 01890
USA

Holland, John R *Religious Leader*
Foursquare Gospel Int'l Church, 1910 W
Sunset Blvd, Los Angeles, CA 90026 USA

Holland, Jools *Music Group*
Miracle Artists, 1 York Street, London,
England, W1U 6PA, United Kingdom

Holland, Josh
4533 Willis Ave., Sherman Oaks, CA
91403-2710

Holland, Juliam M (Jools) *Musician*
One Fifteen, Gallery 28 Wood Wharf,
Horseferry, London, SE10 9BT, UNITED
KINGDOM (UK)

Holland, Paul *Musician*
Variety Artists, 1924 Spring St, Paso
Robles, CA 93446 USA

Holland, Richard
9019 Wonderland Park Ave., Los Angeles,
CA 90046

Holland, Todd *Director*
Endeavor Agency LLC (LA), 9601 Wilshire
Blvd Fl 3, Beverly Hills, CA 90210 USA

Holland, Willard R Jr *Business Person*
FirstEnergy Corp, 76 S Main St, Akron,
OH 44308 USA

Hollander, John *Writer*
Yale University, English Dept, New
Haven, CT 06520 USA

Hollander, Lorin *Musician*
I C M Artists, 40 W 57th St, New York,
NY 10019 USA

Hollander, Nicole *Cartoonist*
Sylvia Syndicate, 1440 N Dayton St,
Chicago, IL 60622 USA

Hollander, Xaviera
Stadionweg 17, Amsterdam, HOLLAND,
1077 RU

Hollander, Zander *Writer*
1018 N Carolina Ave SE, Washington, DC
20003 USA

Hollandsworth, Todd M *Baseball Player*
4020 Ghiotti Court, Pleasonton, CA
94588 USA

Holldobler, Berthold K *Writer, Biologist*
University of Wurzburg, Zoologie II, Am
Nubland, Wurzburg, 97074, GERMANY

Hollein, Hans *Architect, Misc*
Eiskellerstr 1, Dusseldorf, 40213,
GERMANY

Holleran, Leslie *Producer*
Laha Films, 115 East 92nd Street, 7C,
New York, NY 10128 USA

Hollerer, Walter F *Writer*
Heerstr 99, Berlin, 14055, GERMANY

Holliday, Charles O *Business Person*
E I DuPont de Nemours, 1007 Market St,
Wilmington, DE 19801 USA

Holliday, Cheryl *Writer*
United Talent Agency (UTA), 9560
Wilshire Blvd, Beverly Hills, CA 90212
USA

Holliday, Fred *Actor*
4610 Forman Ave, Toluca Lake, CA
91602 USA

Holliday, Jennifer *Actor, Music Group*
Evolution Talent, 1776 Broadway #1500,
New York, NY 10019 USA

Holliday, Kathy
345 N. Maple Dr. #397, Beverly Hills, CA
90210

Holliday, Kene
9300 Wilshire Blvd. #400, Beverly Hills,
CA 90212

Holliday, Polly D *Actor, Music Group*
201 E 17th St #23H, New York, NY
10003 USA

Hollies, The
Hill Farm Hackleton, Northants.,
ENGLAND, NN7 2DH

Holliger, Heinz *Musician, Composer*
Konzertgellschaft, Hochstr 51, Basel,
4002, SWITZERLAND

Holliman, Earl *Actor*
PO Box 1969, Studio City, CA 91614 USA

Hollings, Ernest *Senator*
200 E Bay St. #112, Charleston, SC

Hollings, Michael R *Religious Leader*
Saint Mary of Angels, Moorhouse Road
Bayswater, London, W2 5DJ, UNITED
KINGDOM (UK)

Hollins, Lionel *Basketball Player, Coach*
7594 Tagg Dr, Germantown, TN 38138
USA

Hollister, Dave *Music Group*
Creative Artists Agency, 9830 Wilshire
Blvd, Beverly Hills, CA 90212 USA

Hollit, Raye (Zapp)
2554 Lincoln Blvd. #638, Marina del Rey,
CA 90292

Holloman, Laurel *Actor*
Pinnacle PR, 8265 Sunset Blvd #201, Los
Angeles, CA 90046 USA

Holloway, Brenda *Musician*
Universal Attractions, 145 W 57th St,
#1500, New York, NY 10019 USA

Holloway, Brian *Football Player*
742 New York Route 43, Stephentown,
NY 12168 USA

Holloway, James L III *Admiral*
4800 Fillmore Ave #1058, Alexandria, VA
22311 USA

Holloway, Ken *Music Group*
World Class/Berry Mgmt, 1848 Tyne Blvd,
Nashville, TN 37215 USA

Holloway, Loleatta *Music Group*
Atlantic Entertainment Group, 2922
Atlantic Ave #200, Atlantic City, NJ 08401
USA

Holloway, Matt *Writer*
9 Yards Entertainment, 8530 Wilshire Blvd
Fl 5, Beverly Hills, CA 90211 USA

Holloway, Robin G *Composer*
Gonville & Caius College, Music Dept,
Cambridge, CB2 1TA, UNITED
KINGDOM (UK)

Holloway, William J Jr *Judge*
US Court of Appeals, PO Box 1767,
Oklahoma City, OK 73101 USA

Holly, Buddy Memorial Society
PO Box 6123, Lubbock, TX 79413

Holly, Lauren *Actor*
9 Yards Entertainment, 8530 Wilshire Blvd
Fl 5, Beverly Hills, CA 90211 USA

Holly, Molly *Wrestler*
World Wrestling Entertainment (WWE),
1241 E Main St, Stamford, CT 06905 USA

Hollyday, Christopher *Musician*
Ted Kurland, 173 Brighton Ave, Boston,
MA 02134 USA

Holm, Celeste *Actor*
88 Central Park West, New York, NY
10023 USA

Holm, Ian *Actor*
Markham & Froggatt, Julian House, 4
Windmill St, London, W1P 1HF, UNITED
KINGDOM (UK)

Holm, Jeanne M *General*
2707 Thyme Dr, Edgewater, MD 21037
USA

Holm, Joan *Bowler*
5829 N Magnolia Ave, Chicago, IL 60660
USA

Holm, Peter
1 rue de Fer Achevel Port Grimaud,
Cogolin, FRANCE, F- 83310

Holm, Richard H *Misc*
483 Pleasant St #10, Belmont, MA 02478
USA

Holm, Sir Ian
46 Albermarle St., London, ENGLAND,
W1X 4PP

Holman, C Ray *Business Person*
Mallinckrodt Inc, 675 McDonell Blvd,
Saint Louis, MO 63134 USA

Holman, Marshall *Bowler*
1610 Thrasher Lane, Medford, OR 97504
USA

Holman, Ralph T *Biologist*
1403 2nd Ave SW, Austin, MN 55912
USA

Holmberg, Mark *Musician*
MOB Agency, 6404 Wilshire Blvd #505,
Los Angeles, CA 90048 USA

Holmes, A M *Writer*
Columbia Univesity, English Dept, New
York, NY 10027 USA

Holmes, Clint *Music Group*
Conversation Co, 697 Middle Neck Road,
Great Neck, NY 11023 USA

Holmes, D Brainerd *Engineer, Business
Person*
Bay Colony Corp Center, 950 Winter St
#4350, Waltham, MA 02451 USA

Holmes, Ernie *Football Player*
PO Box 299, Wiergate, TX 75977 USA

Holmes, Jennifer *Actor*
PO Box 6303, Carmel, CA 93921 USA

Holmes, Katie *Actor*
17430 Miranda St, Encino, CA 91316
USA

Holmes, Larry *Boxer*
91 Larry Holmes Dr #200, Easton, PA
18042 USA

Holmes, Priest *Football Player*
Kansas City Chiefs, 1 Arrowhead Dr,
Kansas City, KS 64 129 USA

Holmes, Rupert *Music Group, Songwriter*
Mars Talent, 27 L'Ambiance Court,
Bardonia, NY 10954 USA

Holmes, Sherlock Society
221B Baker St., London, ENGLAND, W1

Holmes, Thomas F (Tommy) *Baseball
Player*
1 Pine Dr, Woodbury, NY 11797 USA

Holmgren, Janet L *Educator*
Mills College, President's Office, Oakland,
CA 94613 USA

Holmgren, Michael G (Mike) *Football
Coach*
Seattle Seahawks, 11220 NE 53rd,
Kirkland, WA 98033 USA

Holmgren, Paul H *Hockey Player, Coach*
724 Southwick Circle, Somerdale, NJ
08083 USA

Holmquest, Donald L *Astronaut*
229 Princeton Road, Menlo Park, CA
94025 USA

Holmstrom, Carl *Skier*
1703 E 3rd St #101, Duluth, MN 55812
USA

Holmstrom, Peter *Musician*
Monqui Mgmt, PO Box 5908, Portland,
OR 97228 USA

Holovak, Michael J (Mike) *Football
Player, Coach*
3432 Highlands Bridge Road, Sarasota, FL
34235 USA

Holroyd, Michael *Writer*
85 Saint Marks Road, London, W10 6JS,
UNITED KINGDOM (UK)

Holst, Per *Producer*
Per Holst Film A/S, Rentemestervej 69A,
Copenhagen, NV 2400, DENMARK

Holt, David Lee *Musician*
AristoMedia, 1620 16th Ave S, Nashville,
TN 34212 USA

Holt, Glenn L *Misc*
PO Box 4055, Kokomo, IN 46904 USA

Holt, Lester *Commentator*
NBC-TV, News Dept, 30 Rockefeller
Plaza, New York, NY 10112 USA

Holt, Sandrine *Actor*
Somers Teitelbaum David, 8840 Wilshire
Blvd #200, Beverly Hills, CA 90211 USA

Holt Jr, Jack
504 Temple Dr, Harrah, OK 73045 USA

Holt-Kramer, Toni
1229 Santa Monica Blvd, Santa Monica,
CA 90404

Holtermann, E Louis Jr *Publisher*
Glamour Magazine, 350 Madison Ave,
New York, NY 10017 USA

Holton, A Linwood Jr *Physicist*
64 Francis Ave, Cambridge, MA 02138
USA

Holton, Michael *Basketball Player, Coach*
10657 SW Adele Dr, Portland, OR 97225
USA

Holtz, Louis L (Lou) *Football Coach*
1300 Rosewood Dr, Columbia, SC 29208
USA

Holtzman, Elizabeth (Liz) *Misc*
2 Park Ave #2100, New York, NY 10016
USA

Holtzman, Jerome *Writer*
1225 Forest Ave, Evanston, IL 60202 USA

Holtzman, Kenneth D (Ken) *Baseball
Player*
256 Waterside Dr, Grover, MO 63040
USA

Holtzman, Wayne H *Doctor*
3300 Foothill Dr, Austin, TX 78731 USA

Holub, E J *Football Player*
2311 S County Road 1120, Midland, TX
79706 USA

Holum, Dianne *Speed Skater*
1344 McIntosh Ave, Broomfield, CO
80020 USA

Holum, Kristin *Speed Skater*
10596 Steele St, Northglenn, CO 80233
USA

Holway, Jerome F *Cinematographer*
448 Spruce Dr, Exton, PA 19341 USA

Holy, Steve *Musician*
Monterey Peninsula Artists (Nashville),
124 12th Ave S #410, Nashville, TN
37203 USA

Holyfield, Evander *Boxer*
794 Evander Holyfield Highway, Fairburn,
GA 30213 USA

Holzer, Helmut *Scientist*
2103 Greenwood Place SW, Huntsville,
AL 35802 USA

Holzer, Jenny *Artist*
80 Hewitts Road, Hoosick Falls, NY
12090 USA

Holzier, James *Actor*
Agency for the Performing Arts (APA-LA),
9200 Sunset Blvd #900, Los Angeles, CA
90069 USA

Holzman, Malcolm *Architect*
Hardy Holzman Pfeiffer, 902 Broadway,
New York, NY 10010 USA

Homeier, Skip
247 N. Castellana, Palm Desert, CA
92260

Homes, A M *Writer*
Charles Scribner's Sons, 866 3rd Ave,
New York, NY 10022 USA

Homfeld, Conrad *Horse Racer*
Sandron, 11744 Marblestone Court,
Wellington, FL 33414 USA

Honda, Yuka *Music Group*
Billions Corp, 833 W Chicago Ave #101,
Chicago, IL 60622 USA

Honderich, Beland H *Publisher*
Toronto Star, 1 Yonge St, Toronto, ON
M5E 1E6, CANADA

Honderich, John H *Editor*
Toronto Star, Editorial Dept, 1 Yonge St,
Toronto, ON M5E 1E6, CANADA

Honegger, Fritz *President*
Schloss-Str 29, Ruschlidon, 8803,
SWITZERLAND

Honeycutt, Frederick W (Rick) *Baseball
Player*
207 Forrest Road, Fort Oglethorpe, GA
30742 USA

Honeycutt, Rick
207 Forrest Rd., Fort Oglethorpe, GA
30742

Honeycutt, Van B *Business Person*
Computer Sciences Corp, 2100 E Grand Ave, El Segundo, CA 90245 USA

Honeyghan, Lloyd *Boxer*
50 Barnfield Wood Road, Park Langley Beckenham, Kent, UNITED KINGDOM (UK)

Honeymoon Suite
1505 W. 2nd Ave. #200, Vancouver, CANADA, BC V6H 3Y4

Hong, James *Actor*
8235 Sunset Blvd #202, West Hollywood, CA 90046 USA

Hong Song Nam *Prime Minister*
Premier's Office, Pyongyong, NORTH KOREA

Honig, Edwin *Writer*
229 Medway St #305, Providence, RI 02906 USA

Honore, Jean Cardinal *Religious Leader*
Archeveche, BP 1117, 27 Rue Jules-Simon, Tours Cedex, 37011, FRANCE

Hood, Kenneth *Religious Leader*
5799 Bloomfield Ave, Verona, NJ 07044 USA

Hood, Leroy E *Inventor, Scientist*
1441 N 34th St, Seattle, WA 98103 USA

Hood, Robert
Boys Life Magazine, Editorial Dept, 1325 Walnut Hill Lane, Irving, TX 75038 USA

Hood, Robin *Golfer*
6705 Shoal Creek Dr, Arlington, TX 76001 USA

Hoogstratten, Louise
12451 Mulholland Dr., Beverly Hills, CA 90210

Hooker, Charles R *Artist*
28 Whippingham Road, Brighton, Sussex, BN2 3PG, UNITED KINGDOM (UK)

Hooks, Bell *Writer*
291 W 12th St, New York, NY 10014 USA

Hooks, Benjamin L *Social Activist*
200 Wagner Pl #407-8, Memphis, TN 38103 USA

Hooks, Jan *Actor*
Innovative Artists (LA), 1505 Tenth St, Santa Monica, CA 90401 USA

Hooks, Kevin *Director*
International Creative Mgmt, 8942 Wilshire Blvd #219, Beverly Hills, CA 90211 USA

Hooks, Robert *Actor*
145 N Valley St, Burbank, CA 91505 USA

Hookstratten, Edward G *Attorney General*
Ed Hookstratten Mgmt, 9536 Wilshire Blvd #500, Beverly Hills, CA 90212 USA

Hooper, Brandon
3003 3rd St. #4, Santa Monica, CA 90405-5488

Hooper, C Darrow *Track Athlete*
10909 Strait Lane, Dallas, TX 75229 USA

Hooper, Kay *Writer*
Bantam Books, 1540 Broadway, New York, NY 10036 USA

Hooper, Tobe
PO Box 5617, Beverly Hills, CA 90210

Hooten, Burt
3619 Grandby Ct., San Antonio, TX 78217

Hootie & The Blowfish *Music Group*
Monterey Peninsula Artists (Monterey), 509 Hartnell St, Monterey, CA 93940 USA

Hooton, Burt C *Baseball Player*
3619 Granby Court, San Antonio, TX 78217 USA

Hoover, Dick *Bowler*
112 Melody Dr, Copley, OH 44321 USA

Hoover, Herbert III
200 S. Los Robles Ave. #520, Pasadena, CA 91101-2431

Hoover, Robert A (Bob) *Misc*
Bob Hoover Airshows, 1100 E Imperial Ave, El Segundo, CA 90245 USA

Hope, Alec D *Writer*
PO Box 7949, Alice Springs, NT, 0871, AUSTRALIA

Hope, Jim *Producer*
Endeavor Agency LLC (LA), 9601 Wilshire Blvd Fl 3, Beverly Hills, CA 90210 USA

Hope, Leslie *Actor*
Kritzer, 12200 W Olympic Blvd #400, Los Angeles, CA 90064 USA

Hope, Maurice *Boxer*
582 Kingsland Road, London, E8, UNITED KINGDOM (UK)

Hope, Tamara *Actor*
Atlas Entertainment, 6100 Wilshire Blvd #1170, Los Angeles, CA 90048 USA

Hopkins, Anthony *Actor*
Global Business Mgmt, 15250 Ventrua Blvd #710, Sherman Oaks, CA 91403 USA

Hopkins, Antony *Composer, Writer*
Woodyard Cottage Ashridge, Berkhamsted, Herts, HP4 1PS, UNITED KINGDOM (UK)

Hopkins, Bo *Actor*
6628 Ethel Ave, North Hollywood, CA 91606 USA

Hopkins, Gareth *Business Person*
EMI Recorded Music (London), 4 Tenterden St, Hanover Square, London, W1A 2AY, UNITED KINGDOM

Hopkins, Godfrey T *Photographer*
Wilmington Cottage Wilmington Road, Seaford, E Sussex, BN25 2EH, UNITED KINGDOM (UK)

Hopkins, Jan *Commentator*
Cable News Network, News Dept, 1050 Techwood Dr NW, Atlanta, GA 30318 USA

Hopkins, Josh *Actor*
Gersh Agency, 232 N Canon Dr, Beverly Hills, CA 90210 USA

Hopkins, Kaitlin *Actor*
19528 Ventura Blvd #559, Tarzana, CA 91356 USA

Hopkins, Katherine
215 S. La Cienega Blvd. PH, Beverly Hills, CA 90211

Hopkins, Linda *Music Group*
2055 N Ivar St #PH, Los Angeles, CA 90068 USA

Hopkins, Michael J *Architect*
27 Broadley Terrace, London, NW1 6LG, UNITED KINGDOM (UK)

Hopkins, Paul
10100 Santa Monica Blvd. #2500, Los Angeles, CA 90067

Hopkins, Stephen
8942 Wilshire Blvd., Beverly Hills, CA 90211

Hopkins, Stephen J *Director*
International Creative Mgmt, 8942 Wilshire Blvd #219, Beverly Hills, CA 90211 USA

Hopkins, Sy *Music Group*
Paramount Entertainment, PO Box 12, Far Hills, NJ 07931 USA

Hopkins, Telma *Actor, Music Group*
4122 Don Luis Dr, Los Angeles, CA 90008 USA

Hoppe, Fred *Artist*
7401NW 105th St, Malcolm, NE 68402 USA

Hoppe, Wolfgang *Athlete*
Dieterstedter Str 11, Apolda, 99510, GERMANY

Hopper, Dennis *Actor, Director*
330 Indiana Ave, Venice, CA 90291 USA

Hopper, Heather *Actor*
Baron Entertainment, 5757 Wilshire Blvd #659, Los Angeles, CA 90036

Hopper, John D Jr *General*
Commander, Air Education/Training Command, Randolph Air Force Base, TX 78155 USA

Hoppus, Mark *Musician*
Creative Artists Agency, 9830 Wilshire Blvd, Beverly Hills, CA 90212 USA

Hopson, Dennis *Basketball Player*
5608 Brickstone Place, Hilliard, OH 43026 USA

Horan, Machael W (Mike) *Football Player*
5440 Lakeshore Dr, Littleton, CO 80123 USA

Horbiger, Christiane
Frankengasse 28, Zurich, SWITZERLAND, CH-8001

Horecker, Bernard L *Biologist*
16517 Cypress Villa Lane, Fort Myers, FL 33908 USA

Horgan, Patrick *Actor*
201 E 89th St, New York, NY 10128 USA

Horinek, Ramon A *War Hero*
181 National Blvd, Universal City, TX 78148 USA

Horlock, John H *Engineer, Educator*
2 The Avenue, Ampthill, Bedford, MK45 2NR, UNITED KINGDOM (UK)

Horn, Gyula *Prime Minister*
Parliament, Kossuth Lajor Ter 1/3, Budepest, 1055, HUNGARY

Horn, Marian Blank *Judge*
US Claims Court, 717 Madison Place NW, Washington, DC 20439 USA

Horn, Paul J *Musician*
4601 Leyns Road, Victoria, BC V8N 3A1, CANADA

Horn, Roy *Magician*
Mirage Hotel & Casino, 3400 Las Vegas Blvd S, Las Vegas, NV 89109

Horn, Shirley
473 Four Seasons Dr, Charlottesville, VA 22901-1359

Horn, Shriley *Music Group*
1007 Towne Lane, Charlottesville, VA 22901 USA

Hornaday, Ron *Race Car Driver*
PO Box 229, Mooresville, NC 28115 USA

Hornburg, Hal M *General*
Commander, Air Combat Command, Langley Air Force Base, VA 23665 USA

Hornby, Nick *Writer*
Cassarotto, 60/66 Wardour St, London, W1V 4ND, UNITED KINGDOM (UK)

Horne, Donald R *Writer*
53 Grosvenor St, Woollahra, Sydney, NSW, 2025, AUSTRALIA

Horne, Jimmy Bo *Dancer, Musician, Music Group*
Talent Consultants International, 1560 Broadway #1308, New York, NY 10036 USA

Horne, John R *Business Person*
Navistar International, PO Box 1488, Warrenville, IL 60555 USA

Horne, Lena *Musician, Actor*
Volney Apartments, 23 E 74th St, New York, NY 10021 USA

Horne, Marilyn *Opera Singer*
Columbia Artists Mgmt, 165 W 57th St, New York, NY 10019 USA

Horne, Steve *Race Car Driver*
Tasman Motor Sports Group, 4192 Weaver Court, Hilliard, OH 43026 USA

Horneber, Petra *Misc*
Ringstr 77, Kranzberg, 85402, GERMANY

Horneff, Wil *Actor*
Creative Artists Agency LCC (CAA-LA), 9830 Wilshire Blvd, Beverly Hills, CA 90212 USA

Horner, Charles A *General*
2824 Jack Nicklaus Way, Shalimar, FL 32579 USA

Horner, Freeman V *War Hero*
1501 Doubletree Dr, Columbus, GA 31904 USA

Horner, George R (Red) *Hockey Player*
CSAS PO Box 60036, RPO Glen Abbey, Oakville, ON L6M 3H2, CANADA

Horner, James *Composer*
13245 Riverside Dr #450, Sherman Oaks, CA 91423 USA

Horner, John R (Jack) *Scientist*
70 Cougar Dr, Bozeman, MT 59718 USA

Horner, Martina S *Educator, Business Person*
TIAA-CREF, 730 3rd Ave, New York, NY 10017 USA

Horner, Red
20 Avoca Ave. #1404, Toronto, CANADA, Ont. M4T 2

Hornig, Donald F *Misc*
1 Little Pond Cove Road, Little Compton, RI 02837 USA

Hornsby, Bruce *Musician, Music Group*
PO Box 3545, Williamsburg, VA 23187 USA

Hornung, Paul V *Actor*
3700 Kemen Court, Louisville, KY 40241 USA

Horovitz, Adam (King Ad-Rock) *Artist, Musician, Music Group*
GAS Entertainment, 8935 Lindblade St, Culver City, CA 90232 USA

Horovitz, Israel A *Writer*
146 W 11th St, New York, NY 10011 USA

Horovitz, Joseph *Composer*
Royal College of Music, Prince Consort Road, London, SW7 2BS, UNITED KINGDOM (UK)

Horowitz, Amy *Stylist*

Horowitz, David C *Commentator*
4267 Marina City Dr #810, Marina del Rey, CA 90292 USA

Horowitz, Jerome P *Scientist*
Michigan Cancer Foundation, 110 E Warren Ave, Detroit, MI 48201 USA

Horowitz, Norman H *Biologist*
2495 Brighton Road, Pasadena, CA 91104 USA

Horowitz, Paul *Physicist, Doctor*
111 Chilton St, Cambridge, MA 02138 USA

Horowitz, Sari *Journalist*
Washington Post, Editorial Dept, 1150 15th St NW, Washington, DC 20071 USA

Horowitz, Scott J *Astronaut*
16819 Whitewater Falls Court, Houston, TX 77059 USA

Horowitz, Shel

Horrocks, Jane *Actor, Music Group*
P F D, Drury House, 34-43 Russell St, London, WC2B 5HA, UNITED KINGDOM (UK)

Horry, Robert *Basketball Player*
9 E Rivercrest Dr, Houston, TX 77042 USA

Horsey, David *Editor, Cartoonist*
Kings Features Syndicate, 888 7th Ave, New York, NY 10106 USA

Horsford, Anna Maria *Actor*
PO Box 48082, Los Angeles, CA 90048 USA

Horsley, Lee A *Actor*
9350 E Caley Ave #200, Englewood, CO 80111 USA

Horsley, Richard D *Financier*
Regions Financial Corp, 417 20th St N, Birmingham, AL 35203 USA

Horst, Lisa Ann
PO Box 8633, Lancaster CO, PA 17604

Horton, Ethan S *Football Player*
WFNZ-Radio, PO Box 30247, Charlotte, NC 28230 USA

Horton, Frank E *Educator*
288 River Ranch Circle, Bayfield, CO 81122 USA

Horton, Michael *Editor*
Mirisch Agency, 1801 Century Park E #1801, Los Angeles, CA 90067 USA

Horton, Peter *Actor*
409 Santa Monica Blvd #PH, Santa Monica, CA 90401 USA

Horton, Robert *Actor*
5317 Andasol Ave, Encino, CA 91316 USA

Horton, William W (Willie) *Baseball Player*
Reid, 15124 Warwick, Detroit, MI 48223 USA

Horton, Willie(baseball)
15124 Warwick St., Detroit, MI 48223

Horvath, Bronco J *Hockey Player*
27 Oliver St, South Yarmouth, MA 02664 USA

Horvitz, H Robert *Nobel Prize Laureate*
Massachusetts Institute of Technology, Biology Dept, Cambridge, MA 02139 USA

Horvitz, Louis J *Director*
Gersh Agency, The (LA), 232 N Canon Dr, Beverly Hills, CA 90210 USA

Horwitz, Tony *Journalist*
Wall Street Journal, Editorial Dept, 200 Liberty St, New York, NY 10281 USA

Hosea, Bobby
4526 Wilshire Blvd., Los Angeles, CA 90010

Hosket, William (Bill) *Basketball Player*
7461 Worthington Galena Road, Worthington, OH 43085 USA

Hoskins, Bob *Actor*
Cassarotto, 60/66 Wardour St, London, W1V 4ND, UNITED KINGDOM (UK)

Hosmer, Bradley C (Brad) *General*
PO Box 1128, Cedar Crest, NM 87008 USA

Hossein, Robert *Actor, Director*
Ghislaine de Wing, 10 Rue du Docteur Roux, Paris, 75015, FRANCE

Hostak, Al *Boxer*
11501 161st Ave SE, Renton, WA 98059 USA

Hostetler, David L *Artist*
PO Box 989, Athens, OH 45701 USA

Hostetter, G Richard *Religious Leader*
Presbyterian Church in America, 1852 Century Plaza, Atlanta, GA 30345 USA

Hotani, Hirokazu *Engineer*
Teikyo University, Biosciences Dept, Toyosatodai, Utsunomiya, 320, JAPAN

Hotchkiss, Rob *Musician*
Jon Landau, 80 Mason St, Greenwich, CT 06830 USA

Hotchkiss, Rollin D *Scientist, Doctor*
2-4 Rolling Hills, Lenox, MA 01240 USA

Hotchner, Aaron
14 Hillandale Rd., Westport, CT 06880

Hottelet, Richard C *Commentator*
120 Chestnut Hill Road, Wilton, CT 06897 USA

Hoty, Dee
333 W. 56th St., New York, NY 10019

Hou, Ya-Ming *Biologist*
Massachusetts Institute of Technology, Biology Dept, Cambridge, MA 02139 USA

Houbregs, Robert J (Bob) *Basketball Player*
6042 Troon Lane SE, Olympia, WA 98501 USA

Houcke, Sara *Misc*
Feld Enterprises, 1313 17th St E, Palmetto, FL 34221 USA

Hough, Charles O (Charlie) *Baseball Player*
2266 Shade Tree Circle, Brea, CA 92821 USA

Hough, Charlie *Athlete*
2266 Shade Tree Cir, Brea, CA 92621

Hough, John *Director*
Associated International Mgmt, 5 Denmark St, London, WC2H 8LP, UNITED KINGDOM (UK)

Hough, Joseph C Jr *Educator*
Union Theological Seminary, President's Office, New York, NY 10027 USA

Hough, Michael A *General*
Deputy Cofs Aviation, HqUSMC 2 Navy St, Washington, DC 20380 USA

Hough, Stephen A G *Musician*
Harrison/Parrott, 12 Penzance Place, London, W11 4PA, UNITED KINGDOM (UK)

Houghton, Charles N *Director*
11 E 9th St, New York, NY 10003 USA

Houghton, James *Business Person*
Field 36 Spencer Hill Road, Corning, NY 14830 USA

Houghton, John *Physicist*
Rutherford Appleton Laboratory, Chilton, Didcot Oxon, OX11 0QX, UNITED KINGDOM (UK)

Houghton, Katherine *Actor*
Ambrosio/Mortimer, 165 W 46th St, New York, NY 10036 USA

Houghton of Sowerby, Douglas *Government Official*
110 Marsham Court, London, SW1, UNITED KINGDOM (UK)

Hougland, William (Bill) *Basketball Player*
PO Box 2629, Edwards, CO 81632 USA

Houk, Ralph G *Baseball Player, Misc*
3000 Plantation Road, Winter Haven, FL 33884 USA

Houle, Rejean *Hockey Player*
7941 Boul Lasalle, Lasalle, QC, H8P 3R1, CANADA

Hounsfield, Godfrey N *Nobel Prize Laureate*
15 Crane Park Road, Whitton Twickenham, Middx, TW2 6DF, UNITED KINGDOM (UK)

Hounsou, Djimon *Actor, Model*
Brillstein/Grey, 9150 Wilshire Blvd #350, Beverly Hills, CA 90212 USA

House, David (Dave) *Business Person*
Nortel Networks Corp, 8200 Dixie Road, Brampton, ON L6T 5P6, CANADA

House, H Franklin (Frank) *Baseball Player*
875 Calellmium Way, Birmingham, AL 35242 USA

House, James
1313 16th Ave. So., Nashville, TN 37212

House, Karen Ellot *Journalist*
58 Cleveland Lane, Princeton, NJ 08540 USA

House, Stormy
12334 Gorham Ave., Los Angeles, CA 90049

House, Yoanna *Reality TV Star*
Ty Ty Baby Productions, 8346 W Third St #650, Los Angeles, CA 90048 USA

House of Pain *Music Group*
William Morris Agency (WMA-LA), 1 William Morris Pl, Beverly Hills, CA 90212 USA

Houseley, Phil *Hockey Player*
Chicago Blackhawks, United Center, 1901 W Madison St, Chicago, IL 60612 USA

Houser, Huell
450 N. Rossmore Ave. #602, Los Angeles, CA 90004

Houser, Jerry *Actor*
8325 Skyline Dr, Los Angeles, CA 90046 USA

Housner, George W *Engineer, Misc*
California Institute of Technology, Engineering Dept, Pasadena, CA 91125 USA

Houston *Adult Film Star*
Atlas Multimedia Inc, 22940 Burbank Blvd, Woodland Hills, CA 91367 USA

Houston, Allan *Basketball Player*
New York Knicks, Madison Square Garden, 2 Penn Plaza, New York, NY 10121 USA

Houston, Byron *Basketball Player*
1732 Lionsgate Circle, Bethany, OK 73008 USA

Houston, Cissy *Musician, Music Group*
2160 N Central Road, Fort Lee, NJ 07024 USA

Houston, Edwin A *Business Person*
Ryder System Inc, 3600 NW 82nd Ave, Miami, FL 33166 USA

Houston, James A *Writer*
24 Main St, Stonington, CT 06378 USA

Houston, Kenneth R (Ken) *Football Player*
3603 Forest Village Dr, Kingwood, TX 77339 USA

Houston, Marques (Batman) *Musician, Actor*
Ultimate Group, The, 848 N La Cienega Blvd #201, W Hollywood, CA 90069 USA

Houston, Penelope *Music Group*
Absolute Artists, 8490 W Sunset Blvd #403, West Hollywood, CA 90069 USA

Houston, Russell *Artist*
General Delivery, Eagar, AZ 85925 USA

Houston, Thelma *Musician*
4296 Mount Vernon Dr, Los Angeles, CA 90008 USA

Houston, Wade *Basketball Player, Coach*
University of Tennessee, Athletic Dept, Knoxville, TN 37901 USA

Houston, Whitney *Musician*
Nippy Inc, 60 Park Pl Fl 18, Newark, NJ 07102 USA

Houthakker, Hendrik S *Economist*
1 Ivy Pointe Way, Hanover, NH 03755 USA

Hovan, Chris *Football Player*
Minnesota Vikings, 9520 Viking Dr, Eden Prairie, MN 55344 USA

Hove, Andrew C Jr *Financier*
Federal Deposit Insurance, 550 17th St NW, Washington, DC 20429 USA

Hovind, David J *Business Person*
PACCAR Inc, 777 106th Ave NE, Bellevue, WA 98004 USA

Hoving, Thomas *Director, Editor*
Hoving Assoc, 150 E 73rd St, New York, NY 10021 USA

Hovland, Tim *Volleyball Player*
Assn of Volleyball Pros, 330 Washington Blvd #400, Marina del Rey, CA 90292 USA

Hovsepian, Vatche *Religious Leader*
Armenian Church of America West, 1201 N Vine St, Los Angeles, CA 90038 USA

Howard, Adina *Musician*
International Creative Mgmt, 40 W 57th St #1800, New York, NY 10019 USA

Howard, Alan *Actor*
Julian Belfrage, 46 Albermarle St, London, W1X 4PP, UNITED KINGDOM (UK)

Howard, Ann *Opera Singer*
Stafford Law Assoc, 6 Barham Close, Weybridge, Surrey, KT13 9PR, UNITED KINGDOM (UK)

Howard, Arliss *Actor, Director*
William Morris Agency, 151 El Camino Dr, Beverly Hills, CA 90212 USA

Howard, Barbara *Actor*
Artists Group, 10100 Santa Monica Blvd #2490, Los Angeles, CA 90067 USA

Howard, Bryce Dallas *Actor*
Management 360, 9111 Wilshire Blvd, Beverly Hills, CA 90210 USA

Howard, Clint *Actor*
4286 Clybourn Ave, Burbank, CA 91505 USA

Howard, Desmond *Football Player*
7459 Winding Way, Tampa, FL 33625 USA

Howard, Dwight *Basketball Player*
Orlando Magic, Waterhouse Center, 8701 Maitland Summit Blvd, Orlando, FL 32810 USA

Howard, Frank O *Baseball Player*
20784 Iris Drive, Sterling, VA 20165 USA

Howard, George *Bowler*
8415 Brookwood Dr, Portage, MI 49024 USA

Howard, George *Musician*
David Rubinson, PO Box 411197, San Francisco, CA 94141 USA

Howard, Greg *Cartoonist*
3403 W 28th St, Minneapolis, MN 55416 USA

Howard, Harry N *Historian*
6508 Greentree Road, Bradley Hills Grove, Bethesda, MD 20817 USA

Howard, Hobie *Music Group*
Sawyer Brown Inc, 5200 Old Harding Road, Franklin, TN 37064 USA

Howard, James J III *Business Person*
Northern States Power, 414 Nicollett Mall, Minneapolis, MN 55401 USA

Howard, James Newton *Composer*
Gorfaine/Schwartz, 13245 Riverside Dr #450, Sherman Oaks, CA 91423 USA

Howard, Jan *Music Group*
Tessier-Marsh Talent, 2825 Blue Brick Dr, Nashville, TN 37214 USA

Howard, Jeffrey R *Judge*
US Court of Appeals, US Courthouse, 55 Pleasant St, Concord, NH 03301 USA

Howard, John W *Prime Minister*
Prime Minister's Office, Parliament House, Canbera, ACT, 2600, AUSTRALIA

Howard, Josh *Basketball Player*
Dallas Mavericks, 2909 Taylor St, Dallas, TX 75226 USA

Howard, Joyce
147 Ocean Ave., Santa Monica, CA 90403

Howard, Juwan *Basketball Player*
Houston Rockets, Toyota Center, 2 E Greenway Plaza, Houston, TX 77046 USA

Howard, Ken *Actor*
Ken Howard Productions, 59 E 49th St #22, New York, NY 10022 USA

Howard, Kyle
6212 Banner Ave., Los Angeles, CA 90038

Howard, Lisa
247 S. Beverly Dr. #102, Beverly Hills, CA 90212

Howard, Michael *Government Official*
House of Commons, Westminster, London, SW1A 0AA, UNITED KINGDOM (UK)

Howard, Miki *Musician*
GHR Entertainment, 6014 N Pointe Place, Woodland Hills, CA 91367 USA

Howard, ohn
GPO Box 59, Sydney, AUSTRALIA, NSW 2001, AUSTRALIA

Howard, Rance *Actor*
4286 Clybourne Ave, Burbank, CA 91505 USA

Howard, Rebecca Lynn *Musician*
William Morris Agency, 2100 W End Ave #1000, Nashville, TN 37203 USA

Howard, Richard *Writer*
23 Waverly Place #5X, New York, NY 10003 USA

Howard, Robert (Hardcore Holly) *Wrestler*
World Wrestling Entertainment (WWE), 1241 E Main St, Stamford, CT 06905 USA

Howard, Ron *Director, Actor*
Creative Artists Agency LCC (CAA-LA), 9830 Wilshire Blvd, Beverly Hills, CA 90212 USA

Howard, Sherri *Track Athlete*
14059 Bridle Ridge Road, Sylmar, CA 91342 USA

Howard, Sherry
14059 Bridle Ridge Rd., Sylmar, CA 91342

Howard, Susan *Actor*
PO Box 1456, Boerne, TX 78006 USA

Howard, Terrence *Actor*
Endeavor Agency LLC (LA), 9601 Wilshire Blvd Fl 3, Beverly Hills, CA 90210 USA

Howard, Tim *Soccer Player*
Manchester United FC, Sir Matt Busby Way, Old Trafford, Manchester, M16 0RA, ENGLAND

Howard, Traylor *Actor*
9560 Wilshire Blvd #500, Beverly Hills, CA 90212 USA

Howard, William W Jr *Misc*
National Wildlife Federation, 11100 Wildlife Center Dr, Reston, VA 20190 USA

Howarth, Elgar *Composer*
27 Cromwell Ave, London, N6 5HN, UNITED KINGDOM (UK)

Howarth, Judith *Opera Singer*
Lies Askonas, 6 Henrietta St, London, WC2E 8LA, UNITED KINGDOM (UK)

Howarth, Roger *Actor*
K&H, 1212 Ave of the Americas #3, New York, NY 10036 USA

Howarth, Thomas *Architect*
University of Toronto, 230 College St, Toronto, ON M5S 1R1, CANADA

Howatch, Susan *Writer*
Atiken & Stone, 29 Femshaw Road, London, SW10 0TG, UNITED KINGDOM (UK)

Howe, Arthur *Journalist*
Philadelphia Inquirer, Editorial Dept, 400 N Broad St, Philadelphia, PA 19130 USA

Howe, Arthur H (Art) Jr *Baseball Player*
711 Kahldon Court, Houston, TX 77079 USA

Howe, Brian *Musician, Music Group*
Union Entertainment, 31225 La Baya Dr #213, Westlake Village, CA 91362 USA

Howe, G Woodson *Editor*
Omaha World-Herald, Editorial Dept, World-Herald Square, Omaha, NE 68102 USA

Howe, Gordie
1008 Glenwood Ct., Bloomfield Hills, MI 48302-1453

Howe, Gordon (Gordie) *Hockey Player*
2000 Easy St, Commerce Township, MI 48390 USA

Howe, Jonathan T *Admiral*
Arthur Vining Davis Foundation, 225 Water St #1510, Jacksonville, FL 32202 USA

Howe, Mark S *Hockey Player*
1120 Jefferson Lane, Huntingdon Valley, PA 19006 USA

Howe, Oscar *Artist*
5900 S Prairie View Court, Sioux Falls, SD 57108 USA

Howe, Steve
PO Box 1355, Warsaw, IN 46581

Howe, Steven R (Steve) *Baseball Player*
PO Box 1355, Warsaw, IN 46581 USA

Howe, Tina *Writer*
333 W End Ave, New York, NY 10023 USA

Howe of Aberavon, R E Geoffrey *Government Official*
Barclays Bank, Cavendish Square Branch, 4 Vere St, London, W1, UNITED KINGDOM (UK)

Howell, Alex *Cartoonist*
King Features Syndicate, 888 7th Ave, New York, NY 10106 USA

Howell, Bailey *Basketball Player*
1989 S Montgomery St, Starkville, MS 19759 USA

Howell, Brad
Gunterring 21, Hattersheim, GERMANY, D-65795

Howell, C Thomas *Actor*
3960 Laurel Canyon Dr #297, Studio City, CA 91604 USA

Howell, Francis C *Misc*
1994 San Antonio Ave, Berkeley, CA 94707 USA

Howell, Harry
21 Bruce St., Hamilton, CANADA, Ont. L8P 3

Howell, Henry V (Harry) *Hockey Player*
21 Bruce St, Hamilton, ON L8P 3M5, CANADA

Howell, Jay C *Baseball Player*
4920 Highway 9 N #329, Alpharetta, GA 30004 USA

Howell, Kathleen *Engineer*
Purdue University, Aeronautical Engineering Dept, West Lafayette, IN 47907 USA

Howell, Ken *Baseball Player*
PO Box 2887, Vero Beach, FL 32961

Howell, Margaret *Fashion Designer*
5 Garden House, 8 Battersea Park Road, London, SW8, UNITED KINGDOM (UK)

Howell, Margaret *Actor*
Chateau/Billings Agency, 5657 Wilshire Blvd #200, Los Angeles, CA 90036 USA

Howell, William R *Business Person*
JC Penney Co, PO Box 10001, Dallas, TX 75301 USA

Howells, Anne *Opera Singer*
Milestone Broom Close, Esher Surrey, UNITED KINGDOM (UK)

Howells, William W *Misc*
11 Lawrence Lane, Kittery Point, ME 03905 USA

Howes, Sally Ann *Actor, Music Group, Musician*
Saraband, 265 Liverpool Road, London, N1 1LX, UNITED KINGDOM (UK)

Howey, Steve *Actor*
Endeavor Agency LLC (LA), 9601 Wilshire Blvd Fl 3, Beverly Hills, CA 90210 USA

Howitt, Peter *Director*
Industry Entertainment, 955 Carillo Dr #300, Los Angeles, CA 90048 USA

Howland, Ben *Basketball Player, Coach*
University of California, Athletic Dept, Los Angeles, CA 90024 USA

Howland, Beth *Actor*
255 Amalfi Dr, Santa Monica, CA 90402 USA

Howland, Chris
Vordersten Buchel 11, Rosrath, GERMANY, D-51503

Howle, Paul *Cartoonist*
United Feature Syndicate, 200 Madison Ave, New York, NY 10016 USA

Howlett, Liam *Musician, Composer*
Midi Mgmt, Jenkins Lane, Great Hallinsbury, Essex, CM22 7QL, UNITED KINGDOM (UK)

Howze, Leonard Earl *Actor*
Platform Public Relations, 2133 Holly Drive, Los Angeles, CA 90068 USA

Hoyland, John *Artist*
41 Charterhouse Square, London, EC1M 6EA, UNITED KINGDOM (UK)

Hoyos, Luis Fernando *Actor*
Gabriel Blanco Iglesias (Mexico), Rio Balsas 35-32, Colonia Cuauhtemoc, DF, 06500, Mexico

Hoyt, D LaMarr *Baseball Player*
1012 Belfair Way, Irmo, SC 29063 USA

Hrabosky, Alan T (Al) *Baseball Player, Sportscaster*
9 Frontenac Estates Dr, Saint Louis, MO 63131 USA

Hrbek, Kent A *Baseball Player*
2611 W 112th St, Bloomington, MN 55431 USA

Hrdy, Sarah Blaffer *Misc*
University of California, Anthropology Dept, Davis, CA 95616 USA

Hrkac, Tony *Hockey Player*
9 Dunleith Dr, Saint Louis, MO 63124 USA

Hrudey, Kelly *Hockey Player*
Hockey Night, PO Box 500 Station A, Toronto, ON M5W 1E6, CANADA

Hu, Jintao *President*
Communist Party Central Committee, 1 Zhong Nan Hai, Beijing, CHINA

Hu, Kelly *Actor*
Innovative Artists, 1505 10th St, Santa Monica, CA 90401 USA

Hu, Qili *Government Official*
Consultative Conference, 23 Taipingqiao St, Beijing, 100283, CHINA

Huang, Helen *Musician*
I C M Artists, 40 W 57th St, New York, NY 10019 USA

Huang, Henry *Inventor, Biologist*
Washington Universtiy, Biology Dept, Saint Louis, MO 63130 USA

Huang, James *Actor*
Cunningham-Escott-Dipene & Associates Inc (CED-LA), 10635 Santa Monica Blvd #130, Los Angeles, CA 90025 USA

Huang, Nina
8007 Highland Terr., Los Angeles, CA 90046

Huarte, John G *Football Player*
Arizona Tile Supply, 8829 S Priest Dr, Tempe, AZ 85284 USA

Hub *Musician*
William Morris Agency, 1325 Ave of Americas, New York, NY 10019 USA

Hubbard, Elizabeth
1505 10th Street, Santa Monica, CA 90401

Hubbard, Frederick D (Freddie) *Musician, Composer*
Thomas Cassidy, 11761 E Speedway Blvd, Tucson, AZ 85748 USA

Hubbard, Gregg (Hobbie) *Music Group, Musician*
Sawyer Brown Inc, 5200 Old Harding Road, Franklin, TN 37064 USA

Hubbard, John *Artist*
Chilcombe House, Chilcombe near Bridport, Dorset, UNITED KINGDOM (UK)

Hubbard, Marvin R (Marv) *Football Player*
5804 Dawn View Court, Castro Valley, CA 94552 USA

Hubbard, Philip (Phil) *Basketball Player, Coach*
Washington Wizards, MCI Center, 601 F St NW, Washington, DC 20004 USA

Hubcaps
PO Box 1388, Dover, DE 19003

Hubel, David H *Nobel Prize Laureate*
98 Collins Road, Waban, MA 02468 USA

Hubenthal, Karl *Editor, Cartoonist*
5536 Via La Mesa #A, Laguna Hills, CA 92653 USA

Huber, Anke *Tennis Player*
Dieselstr 10, Karlsdorf-Neuthard, 76689, GERMANY

Huber, Robert *Nobel Prize Laureate*
Planck Biochemie Instiut, Am Kiopferspitz, Manrinsried, 82152, GERMANY

Hubert-Whitten, Janet
10061 Riverside Dr. #204, Toluca Lake, CA 91602-2515

Hubley, Season *Actor*
31 Mansfield Ave, Essex Junction, VT 05452 USA

Huchra, John P *Astronomer*
Harvard University, Astronomy Dept, Cambridge, MA 02138 USA

Huckabee, Cooper *Actor*
1800 El Cerrito Place #34, Los Angeles, CA 90068 USA

Hucknall, Mick
Box 334, Manchester, ENGLAND, M60 3RJ

Hucknall, Mick *Musician*
So What Arts, Lock Keeper's College, Manchester, M3 4QL, UNITED KINGDOM (UK)

Huckstep, Ronald L *Doctor*
108 Sugarloaf Crescent, Castlecrag, Syndey, NSW, 2068, AUSTRALIA

Hudd, Roy
652 Finchley Rd., London, ENGLAND, NW11 7NT

Huddleston, David *Actor*
9200 Sunset Blvd #612, Los Angeles, CA 90069 USA

Hudecek, Vaclav *Musician*
Londynska 25, Prague 2, 120 00, CZECH REPUBLIC

Hudlin, Reginald *Director, Writer, Producer, Actor*
Writers and Artists Group Intl (LA), 8383 Wilshire Blvd #550, Beverly Hills, CA 90211 USA

Hudner, Thomas J Jr *War Hero*
31 Allen Farm Lane, Concord, MA 01742 USA

Hudson, Bill
7023 Birdview, Malibu, CA 90265-4106

Hudson, Brett
151 El Camino Dr., Beverly Hills, CA 90212

Hudson, C B Jr *Business Person*
Torchmark Corp, 2001 3rd Ave S, Birmingham, AL 35233 USA

Hudson, Clifford G *Financier*
Securities Investor Protection, 805 15th St NW, Washington, DC 20005 USA

Hudson, Emie *Actor*
5711 Hoback Glen Road, Hidden Hills, CA 91302 USA

Hudson, Ernie *Actor*
Marshak/Zachary Company, The, 8840 Wilshire Blvd Fl 1, Beverly Hills, CA 90211 USA

Hudson, Garth *Musician, Music Group*
Skyline Music, 32 Clayton St, Portland, ME 04103 USA

Hudson, Gary *Actor*
Origin Talent, 3393 Barham Blvd, Los Angeles, CA 90068 USA

Hudson, Hugh *Director*
Jenks & Partners, 37 W 28th St #7, New York, NY 10001 USA

Hudson, James *Doctor*
Harvard Medical School, Psychiatry Dept, 25 Shattuck St, Boston, MA 02115 USA

Hudson, Jennifer *Reality TV Star, Musician*
American Idol, 7800 Beverly Blvd #251, Los Angeles, CA 90036 USA

Hudson, Kate *Actor*
Creative Artists Agency LCC (CAA-LA), 9830 Wilshire Blvd, Beverly Hills, CA 90212 USA

Hudson, Lou *Basketball Player*
1589 Little Kate Road, Park City, UT 84060 USA

Hudson, Lucy-Jo *Actor*
Granada Television, Quay St, Manchester, M60 9EA, ENGLAND

Hudson, Oliver *Actor, Producer*
Workshed Entertainment, 9255 Sunset Blvd #1010, West Hollywood, CA 90069 USA

Hudson, Ray *Soccer Player, Coach*
DC United, 14120 Newbrook Dr, Chantilly, VA 20151 USA

Hudson, Sally *Skier*
PO Box 2343, Olympic Valley, CA 96146 USA

Hudson, Timothy A (Tim) *Baseball Player*
705 Watson Canyon Court #202, San Ramon, CA 94583 USA

Hudson Brothers
151 El Camino Dr, Beverly Hills, CA 90212, US

Huertas, Jon *Actor*
Cirrincione Assoc, 300 W 5th St, New York, NY 10019 USA

Hues, Frankie
2640 NE 135th St. #302, Miami Beach, FL 33181

Hues Corporation
1560 Broadway #1308, New York, NY 10036

Huff, Brent *Actor*
Artists Group, 10100 Santa Monica Blvd
#2490, Los Angeles, CA 90067 USA

Huff, Gary E *Football Player*
5648 Braveheart Way, Tallahassee, FL
32317 USA

Huff, Kenneth W (Ken) *Football Player*
105 Blackford Court, Durham, NC 27712
USA

Huff, Robert L (Sam) *Football Player*
Middleburg Broadcasting Network, 8 N
Jay St, Middleburg, VA 20118 USA

Huff, Shawn
1505 10th St., Santa Monica, CA 90401

Huffington, Arianna *Writer*
3299 K St NW #402, Washington, DC
20007 USA

Huffington, Michael *Politician, Ex-Congressman*
3005 45th Street NW, Washington, DC
20016 USA

Huffins, Chris *Track Athlete*
Georgia Institute of Technology, Athletic
Dept, Atlanta, GA 30332 USA

Huffman, Felicity *Actor*
International Creative Management
(ICM-LA), 8942 Wilshire Blvd, Beverly
Hills, CA 90211 USA

Hufsey, Billy *Actor*
15415 Muskingam, Brook Park, OH
44142 USA

Hufstedler, Shirley M *Secretary, Educator*
720 Iverness Dr, La Canada-Flintridge, CA
91011 USA

Hug, Procter R Jr *Judge*
US Court of Appeals, 400 S Virginia St,
Reno, NV 89501 USA

Huggins, Bob *Basketball Player, Coach*
207 Beecher Hall, Cincinnati, OH 45221
USA

Hughes, Albert *Director*
Creative Artists Agency, 9830 Wilshire
Blvd, Beverly Hills, CA 90212 USA

Hughes, Allen *Director*
Creative Artists Agency, 9830 Wilshire
Blvd, Beverly Hills, CA 90212 USA

Hughes, Barnard *Actor*
J Michael Bloom, 9255 Sunset Blvd, #710,
Los Angeles, CA 90069 USA

Hughes, Edward Z *Publisher*
American Heritage Magazine, Forbes
Building, 60 5th Ave, New York, NY
10011 USA

Hughes, Finola *Actor*
Metropolitan Talent Agency, 4526
Wilshire Blvd, Los Angeles, CA 90010
USA

Hughes, Frank John *Actor*
Nicole Nassar PR, 521 Spoleto Dr, Pacific
Palisades, CA 90272 USA

Hughes, H Richard *Architect*
47 Chiswick Quay, London, W4 3UR,
UNITED KINGDOM (UK)

Hughes, Harold R (Harry) *Governor*
Patton Boggs Blow, 2550 M St NW #500,
Washington, DC 20037 USA

Hughes, Irene
500 N. Michigan Ave. #1039, Chicago, IL
60611

Hughes, John *Director*
Bloom Hergott & Diemer LLP, 150 S
Rodeo Dr Fl 3, Beverly Hills, CA 90212
USA

Hughes, John *Hockey Player*
73 Lowell St, Somerville, MA 02143 USA

Hughes, John W *Director, Writer*
Hughes Entertainment, 1 Westminster
Place, Lake Forest, IL 60045 USA

Hughes, Karen *Government Official*
White House, 1600 Pennsylvania Ave
NW, Washington, DC 20500 USA

Hughes, Kathleen *Actor*
8818 Rising Glen Place, Los Angeles, CA
90069 USA

Hughes, Keith W *Financier*
Associates First Capital, 250 E John
Carpenter Freeway, Irving, TX 75062 USA

Hughes, Larry *Basketball Player*
Washington Wizards, MCI Centre, 601 F
St NW, Washington, DC 20004 USA

Hughes, Mervyn G *Cricketer*
Australian Cricket Board, 90 Jollimant St,
Melbourne, VIC, 3002, AUSTRALIA

Hughes, Miko *Actor*
Jamieson Assoc, 53 Sunrise Road,
Superior, MT 59872 USA

Hughes, Richard H (Dick) *Baseball Player*
PO Box 598, Stephens, AR 71764 USA

Hughes, Robert S F *Critic*
143 Prince St, New York, NY 10012 USA

Hughes, Sarah *Figure Skater*
John Hughes, 12 Channel Dr, Great Neck,
NY 11024 USA

Hughes, Thomas J Jr *Admiral*
400 Mar Vista Dr #4, Monterey, CA
93940 USA

Hughes, Tyrone C *Football Player*
7340 Crestmont Road, New Orleans, LA
70126 USA

Hughes, Wendy *Actor*
129 Bourke St Woolloomooloo, Sydney,
NSW, 2011, AUSTRALIA

Hughes-Fulford, Millie *Astronaut*
Veterans Affairs Dept, Medical Center,
4150 Clement St, San Francisco, CA
94121 USA

Hughley, D L *Actor, Comedian*
3 Arts Entertainment Inc, 9460 Wilshire
Blvd Fl 7, Beverly Hills, CA 90212 USA

Hugstedt, Petter *Skier*
Kongsberg, 3600, NORWAY

Huguenin, G Richard *Inventor*
Millitech Corp, South Deerfield, MA
01373 USA

Huisgen, Rolf *Misc*
Kaulbachstr 10, Munich, 80539,
GERMANY

Huizenga, H Wayne *Business Person*
Huizenga Holdings, 200 S Andrews Ave,
Fort Lauderdale, FL 33301 USA

Huizenga, John R *Scientist*
43 McMichael Dr, Pinehurst, NC 28374
USA

Hulce, Tom *Actor*
2305 Stanley Hills Dr, Los Angeles, CA
90046 USA

Hulcher, Janet
Arnold Palmer Enterprises, 9000 Bay Hill
Blvd, Orlando, FL 32819-4999 USA

Hull, Bobby *Actor*
48 Huntington Chase Dr, Asheville, NC
28805-1183 USA

Hull, Brett A *Hockey Player*
3520 Eben Way, Stillwater, MN 55082
USA

Hull, Dennis
115 E. Maple St., Hinsdale, IL 60521

Hull, Dennis W *Hockey Player*
Rose City Dodge, 435 West Side,
Welland, ON L3B 5X1, CANADA

Hull, Don *Misc*
US Olympic Committe, 1 Olympia Plaza,
Colorado Springs, CO 80909 USA

Hull, J Kent *Football Player*
RR 1 Box 5748, Greenwood, MS 38930
USA

Hull, James D *Admiral*
Commander US Coast Guard Atlantic,
4131 Crawford St, Portsmouth, VA 23704
USA

Hull, Robert M (Bobby) *Hockey Player*
48 Huntington Chase Dr, Ashville, NC
28805 USA

Hull, Roger H *Educator*
Union College, Chancellor's Office,
Schenectady, NY 12308 USA

Hullar, Theodore L *Educator*
3 Lowell Place, Ithaca, NY 14850 USA

Hulme, Denis *Race Car Driver*
CI-6, RDTE Puke, Bay of Plenny, NEW
ZEALAND

Hulme, Etta *Editor, Cartoonist*
Fort Worth Star-Telegram, Editorial Dept,
400 W 7th St, Fort Worth, TX 76102 USA

Hulme, Keri *Writer*
Hodder & Stoughton, 338 Euston Road,
London, NW1 3BH, UNITED KINGDOM
(UK)

Hulse, Russell A *Nobel Prize Laureate*
PO Box 451, Princeton, NJ 08543 USA

Huly, Jan C *General*
Deputy CofS Plans Policies & Ops,
HqUSMC 2 Navy St, Washington, DC
20380 USA

Human League *Music Group*
Performers Of the World/ Management
Interests Associates (POW/MIA), 8901
Melrose Avenue, 2nd Floor, West
Hollywood, CA 90069 USA

Humann, L Philip *Financier*
Sun Trust Banks, 303 Peachtree St NE,
Atlanta, GA 30308 USA

Humayan, Mark S *Doctor*
Johns Hopkins University, Wilmer
Ophthalmology Institute, Baltimore, MD
21218 USA

Humbert, John O *Religious Leader*
Christian Church Disciples of Christ, 130
E Washington, Indianapolis, IN 46204
USA

Hume, A Britton (Brit) *Commentator*
3100 N St NW #9, Washington, DC
20007 USA

Hume, Alan
Deanrise Deanwood Rd., Jordans Bucks.,
ENGLAND

Hume, Britt *Television Host*
Special Report with Brit Hume, 400 N
Capitol St NW #550, Washington, DC
20001 USA

Hume, John *Nobel Prize Laureate*
5 Bayview Terrace, Derry, BT48 7EE,
NORTHERN IRELAND

Hume, Kirsty *Model*
Elite Model Mgmt, 111 E 22nd St, #200,
New York, NY 10010 USA

Hume, Roger
9 Blenheim St., London, ENGLAND, W1Y
9LE

Hume, Stephen *Editor*
Vancouver Sun, 2250 Granville St,
Vancouver, BC V6H 3G2, CANADA

Humes, Edward *Journalist*
Simon & Schuster, 1230 Ave of Americas,
New York, NY 10020 USA

Humes, John P *Diplomat*
Forest Mill Road, Mill Neck, NY 11765
USA

Humes, Mary Margaret
PO Box 1168-714, Studio City, CA 91604

Humes, Mary-Margaret *Actor, Model*
Stone Manners, 6500 Wilshire Blvd #550,
Los Angeles, CA 90048 USA

Hummes, Claudio Hummes Cardinal
Religious Leader
Avenida Higienopolis 890, CP 1670, Sao
Paulo, 01238-908, BRAZIL

Humperdinck, Engelbert *Musician*
14724 Ventura Blvd #507, Sherman Oaks,
CA 91403 USA

Humphrey, Gordon J *Senator*
78 Garvin Hill Road, Chichester, NH
03258 USA

Humphrey, Jackie *Track Athlete*
616 Powder Horn Road, Richmond, KY
40475 USA

Humphrey, Renee
9300 Wilshire Blvd. #555, Beverly Hills,
CA 90212

Humphrey, Ryan *Basketball Player*
Memphis Grizzlies, 175 Toyota Plaza
#150, Memphis, TN 38103 USA

Humphries, Barry *Actor*
5 Soho Square, London, W1V 5DE,
UNITED KINGDOM (UK)

Humphries, Jay *Basketball Player*
PO Box 1810, Parker, CO 80134 USA

Humphries, Stan *Football Player*
Northeast Louisiana Univ, Alumni Assn,
700 University Ave, Monroe, LA 71209
USA

Humphry, Derek *Social Activist*
ERGO, 24828 Norris Lane, Junction City,
OR 97448 USA

Hun, Sen *Prime Minister*
Prime Minister's Office, Supreme National
Council, Phnom Penh, COMBODIA

Hundertwasser, FriedensreichMu
hle Odissenbach, Rapottenstein,
AUSTRIA, 3911

Hundley, Randy (C Randolph) *Baseball
Player*
122 E Forest Lane, Palatine, IL 60067 USA

Hundley, Rod (Hot Rod) *Basketball
Player, Sportscaster*
1860 E Siggard Dr, Salt Lake City, UT
84106 USA

Hundt, Reed E *Government Official*
6416 Brookside Dr, Bethesda, MD 20815
USA

Hung, Sammo *Actor*
PO Box 1566, Los Angeles, CA 90078
USA

Hunger, Daniela *Swimmer*
SV Preussen, Hansastr 190, Berlin, 13088,
GERMANY

Huniford, James *Designer, Architect*
Sills Hunifor Assoc, 30 E 67th St, New
York, NY 10021 USA

Hunkapiller, Michael *Inventor, Biologist*
Applied Biosystems, 850 Lincoln Center
Dr, Foster City, CA 94404 USA

Hunley, Leann *Actor*
Susan Smith, 121A N San Vincente Blvd,
Beverly Hills, CA 90211 USA

Hunley, Ricky C *Football Player*
9617 Stonemasters Dr, Loveland, OH
45140 USA

Hunnam, Charlie *Actor*
I/D PR (LA), 8409 Santa Monica Blvd,
West Hollywood, CA 90069 USA

Hunnan, Charlie *Actor*
I/D PR (LA), 8409 Santa Monica Blvd,
West Hollywood, CA 90069 USA

Hunnicutt, Gayle *Actor*
174 Regents Park Road, London, NW1,
UNITED KINGDOM (UK)

Hunt, Bonnie *Actor, Director*
International Creative Mgmt, 8942
Wilshire Blvd #219, Beverly Hills, CA
90211 USA

Hunt, Bryan *Artist*
31 Great Jones St, New York, NY 10012
USA

Hunt, Gareth
4 Court Lodge 48 Sloane Sq., London,
ENGLAND, SW1W 8AT

Hunt, Helen *Actor*
Creative Artists Agency, 9830 Wilshire
Blvd, Suite 700, Beverly Hills, CA 90212
USA

Hunt, Jimmy *Actor*
2279 Lansdale Court, Simi Valley, CA
93065 USA

Hunt, John R *Religious Leader*
Evangelical Covenant Church, 5101 N
Francisco Ave, Chicago, IL 60625 USA

Hunt, Lamar *Football Executive, Tennis
Player, Soccer Player*
Thanksgiving Tower, 1601 Elm St #2800,
Dallas, TX 75201 USA

Hunt, Linda *Actor*
1409 N Genesee Ave, Los Angeles, CA
90046 USA

Hunt, Marsha *Actor*
13131 Magnolia Blvd, Van Nuys, CA
91423 USA

Hunt, Nelson Bunker *Business Person*
Hunt Resources Corp, 1st International
Building #3600, Dallas, TX 75270 USA

Hunt, Peter
2337 Roscomare Rd. #2, Los Angeles, CA
90077

Hunt, R Timothy *Nobel Prize Laureate*
Imperial Cancer Research Fund, PO Box
123, London, WC2A 3PX, UNITED
KINGDOM (UK)

Hunt, Randy *Baseball Player*
St Louis Cardinals, 324 Holly Ridge Dr,
Montgomery, AL 36109-3904 USA

Hunt, Ray
1401 Elm St, Dallas, TX 75202

Hunt, Richard
1017 W Lill Ave, Chicago, IL 60614 USA

Hunt, Robert M *Publisher*
New York Daily News, 220 E 42nd St,
New York, NY 10017 USA

Hunt, Ronald K (Ron) *Baseball Player*
2806 Jackson Road, Wentzville, MO
63385 USA

Hunten, Donald M *Astronomer*
10 E Calle Corts, Tucson, AZ 85716 USA

Hunter, Anthony R (Tony) *Biologist*
Salk Institute, 10100 N Torrey Pines Road,
La Jolla, CA 92037 USA

Hunter, Arthur (Art) *Football Player*
12521 Wedgewood Circle, Tustin, CA
92780 USA

Hunter, Bill
Box 478, King's Cross, AUSTRALIA, NSW
1340

Hunter, Billy *Baseball Player*
St Louis Browns, 104 E Seminary Ave,
Lutherville, MD 21093-6127 USA

Hunter, Brian *Baseball Player*
Houston Astros, 1300 SE 181st Ave,
Vancouver, WA 98683-7208 USA

Hunter, Brian *Baseball Player*
Atlanta Braves, 47 Vista Toscana, Lake
Elsinore, CA 92532-0215 USA

Hunter, Buddy
Boston Red Sox, 14616 Fir Cir,
Plattsmouth, NE 68048-5112 USA

Hunter, Charlie *Musician, Music Group*
Figurehead Mgmt, 3470 19th St, San
Francisco, CA 94110 USA

Hunter, Evan (Ed McBaln) *Writer*
324 Main Ave #339, Norwalk, CT 06851
USA

Hunter, Holly *Actor*
23801 Calabasas Road #2004, Calabasas,
CA 91302 USA

Hunter, Ian *Music Group, Musician,
Songwriter*
Helter Skelter, Plaza, 535 Kings Road,
London, SW10 0S, UNITED KINGDOM
(UK)

Hunter, Jack D
22 Hypolita St, St. Augustine, FL 32084
USA

Hunter, James E *Football Player*
5846 Prado Court, Orchard Lake, MI 48324 USA

Hunter, Jesse *Music Group, Musician*
Friedman & LaRosa, 1334 Lexington Ave, New York, NY 10128 USA

Hunter, Jim *Baseball Player*
Milwaukee Brewers, 108 Tindall Rd, Middletown, NJ 07748-2323 USA

Hunter, Jim *Skier*
Jungle Jim Hunter Mgmt, 864 Woodpark Way SW, Calgary, AB T2W 2V8, CANADA

Hunter, John *Engineer*
Lawrence Livermore Laboratory, 7000 East St, Livermore, CA 94550 USA

Hunter, Les *Basketball Player*
8712 W 92nd St, Overland Park, KS 66212 USA

Hunter, Paul *Director, Editor, Writer*
William Morris Agency (WMA-LA), 1 William Morris Pl, Beverly Hills, CA 90212 USA

Hunter, Rachel *Model, Actor*
23 Beverly Park Terrace, Beverly Hills, CA 90210 USA

Hunter, Rich *Baseball Player*
Philadelphia Phillies, 23675 Iride Cir, Murrieta, CA 92562-2092 USA

Hunter, Ronald
8730 Sunset Blvd. #480, Los Angeles, CA 90069

Hunter, Stephen *Writer*
Washington Post, Editorial Dept, 1150 15th St NW, Washington, DC 20071 USA

Hunter, Steven *Basketball Player*
Orlando Magic, Waterhouse Center, 8701 Maitland Summit Blvd, Orlando, FL 32810 USA

Hunter, Tab *Actor, Music Group, Musician*
PO Box 1048, Santa Fe, NM 87504 USA

Hunter, Torii K *Baseball Player*
2408 Belmoor Dr, Pine Bluff, AR 71601 USA

Hunter, Torll *Baseball Player*
Minnesota Twins, 5716 Big River Dr, The Colony, TX 75056-3720 USA

Hunter, Willard *Baseball Player*
Los Angeles Dodgers, 2562 Poppleton Ave, Omaha, NE 68105-2303 USA

Hunter Tommy
2806 Opryland Dr., Nashville, TN 37214

Hunter-Gault, Charlayne *Commentator*
News Hour Show, 2700 S Quincy St #250, Arlington, VA 22206 USA

Hunthausen, Raymond G *Religious Leader*
Catholic Archdiocese of Seattle, 910 Marion, Seattle, WA 98104 USA

Huntington, Sam *Actor*
Innovative Artists (LA), 1505 Tenth St, Santa Monica, CA 90401 USA

Huntington, Samuel P *Politician*
Harvard University, Olin Institute, Political Science Dept, Cambridge, MA 02138 USA

Huntley, Noah *Actor*
Peters Fraser & Dunlop (PFD - UK), Drury House, 34-43 Russell St, London, WC2 B5, UNITED KINGDOM (UK)

Huntsman, Stanley H *Coach*
5532 Timbercrest Trail, Knoxville, TN 37909 USA

Huntz, Steve *Baseball Player*
St Louis Cardinals, 22495 Haber Dr, Cleveland, OH 44126-2923 USA

Hunyadfi, Steven *Swimmer, Coach*
838 Ridgewood Dr #12, Fort Wayne, IN 46805 USA

Hunyady, Emese *Speed Skater*
Beim Spitzriegel 1/2/9, Baden, 2500, AUSTRIA

Hunziker, Terry *Designer*
208 3rd Ave S, Seattle, WA 98104 USA

Huo, Yaobang *General, Secretary*
Communist Party Central Committee, Zhongguo Gongchan Dang, Beijing, CHINA

Huot, Raymond P *General*
Inspector General HqUSAF, Pentagon, Washington, DC 20330 USA

Hupp, Jana Marie *Actor*
Metropolitan Talent Agency, 4526 Wilshire Blvd, Los Angeles, CA 90010 USA

Huppert, Dave *Baseball Player*
Baltimore Orioles, 6732 Stephens Path, Zephyrhills, FL 33542-0652 USA

Huppert, Isabelle *Actor*
VMA, 20 Ave Rapp, Paris, 75007 USA

Hurd, Douglas R *Government Official*
Hawkpoint, Crosby Court, 4 Great Saint Helens, London, EC3A 6HA, UNITED KINGDOM (UK)

Hurd, Gale Ann
270 No. Canon Dr. #1195, Beverly Hills, CA 90210

Hurd, Gale Anne *Producer*
Pacific Western Productions, 270 N Canon Dr #1195, Beverly Hills, CA 90210 USA

Hurd, Michelle *Actor*
TMT Entertainment Group, 648 Broadway #1002, New York, NY 10022 USA

Hurdle, Clinton M (Clint) *Baseball Player*
Kansas City Royals, 9068 Strubridge Place, Littleton, CO 80129-2238 USA

Hurford, Peter J *Musician*
Broom House Saint Bernard's Road, Saint Albans, Herts, AL3 5RA, UNITED KINGDOM (UK)

Hurley, Alfred F *Historian*
University of North Texas, President's Office, Denton, TX 76203 USA

Hurley, Bobby *Basketball Player*
6 Orchard Lane, Colts Neck, NJ 07722 USA

Hurley, Craig
9255 Sunset Blvd. #515, Los Angeles, CA 90069

Hurley, Douglas G *Astronaut*
700 Thomwood Dr, Friendswood, TX 77546 USA

Hurley, Elizabeth *Actor, Model*
36 Redcliff Road, London, SW10 9NJ, UNITED KINGDOM (UK)

Hurn, David *Photographer*
Prospect Cottage, Tintem, Gwent, WALES

Hurnick, Ilja *Musician, Composer*
Narodni Trida 35, Prague 1, 11000, CZECH REPUBLIC

Hurst, Bill *Baseball Player*
Florida Marlins, 9331 SW 192nd Dr, Miami, FL 33157-7973 USA

Hurst, Bruce *Baseball Player*
Boston Red Sox, 1080 N Riata St, Gilbert, AZ 85234-3466 USA

Hurst, James *Baseball Player*
Texas Rangers, 1413 Van Pelt Rd, Sebring, FL 33870-9567 USA

Hurst, Jimmy *Baseball Player*
Detroit Tigers, 1310 37th St E, Tuscaloosa, AL 35405-2544 USA

Hurst, Jonathan *Baseball Player*
Montreal Expos, 308 Woodbum Creek Rd, Spartanburg, SC 29302-4279 USA

Hurst, Michael *Actor*
Bruce Ugly Agency, 218 Richmond Road, Grey Lynn, Auckland 2, NEW ZEALAND

Hurst, Pat *Golfer*
Ladies Pro Golf Association (LPGA), 100 International Golf Drive, Daytona Beach, FL 32124 USA

Hurst, Rick *Actor*
Badgley-Connor Agency, 9229 Sunset Blvd #311, Los Angeles, CA 90069

Hurst, Ryan *Actor*
Endeavor Talent Agency, 9701 Wilshire Blve #1000, Beverly Hills, CA 90212 USA

Hurt, Frank *Misc*
Bakery Confectionery Tobacco Union, 10401 Connecticut, Kensington, MD 20895 USA

Hurt, John *Actor*
Julian Belfarge, 46 Albermarle St, London, W1X 4PP, UNITED KINGDOM (UK)

Hurt, Mary Beth *Actor*
1619 Broadway #900, New York, NY 10019 USA

Hurt, William *Actor*
Wolf/Kasteller, 335 N Maple Dr #351, Beverly Hills, CA 90210 USA

Hurtado, Edwin *Baseball Player*
Toronto Blue Jays, 1202 15th Ave N, Lake Worth, FL 33460-1725 USA

Hurtado Larrea, Oswaldo *President*
Suecia 277 y Av Los Shyris, Quito, ECUADOR

Hurwich, Leo M *Doctor*
University of Pennsylvania, Psychology Dept, Philadelphia, PA 19104 USA

Hurwicz, Leonid *Economist*
3318 Edmund Blvd, Minneapolis, MN 55406 USA

Hurwit, Bruce *Director*
MBST Entertainment, 345 N Maple D #200, Suite 200, Beverly Hills, CA 90210 USA

Hurwitz, Emanuel H *Musician*
25 Dollis Ave, London, N3 1DA, UNITED KINGDOM (UK)

Hurwitz, Jerard *Biologist*
Memorial Sioan Kettering Cancer Center, 1275 York Ave, New York, NY 10021 USA

Husa, Karel J *Composer*
1 Bellwood Lane, Ithaca, NY 14850 USA

Husain, Mishal *Journalist*
BBC Artist Mail, PO Box 1116, Belfast, BT2 7AJ, United Kingdom

Husaini *Actor*
T 16/2 Kalasethra Colony, Besant Nagar, Chennai, TN 600 090, INDIA

Husar, Lubomyr Cardinal *Religious Leader*
Ploscha Sviatoho Jura 5, Lviv, 290000, UKRAINE

Husbands, Clifford *General, Governor*
Governor General's Office, Bay St, Saint Michael, Bridgetown, BARBADOS

Huselius, Kristian *Hockey Player*
Florida Panthers, 1 Panthers Parkway, Sunrise, FL 33323 USA

Husen, Torsten *Educator*
Int'l Educational Institute, Armfeltsgatan 10, Stockholm, 115 34, SWEDEN

Husenov, Surat *Prime Minister*
Prime Minister's Office, Baku, AZERBAIJAN

Hush, Lizabeth
4512 Gentry Ave., No. Hollywood, CA 91607

Huskey, Robert L *Baseball Player*
New York Mets, PO Box 996, Apache, OK 73006-0996 USA

Husky, Ferlin *Musician, Music Group, Songwriter*
Richard Davis Mgmt, 1030 N Woodland Dr, Kansas City, MO 64118 USA

Husky, Rick
13565 Lucca Dr., Pacific Palisades, CA 90272

Huson, Jeff *Baseball Player*
Montreal Expos, PO Box 4296, Sedona, AZ 86340-4296 USA

Hussain, Nasir *Filmmaker, Director, Producer*
24 Pali Hill, Bandra, Bombay, MS 400 050, INDIA

Hussey, Olivia *Actor*
Richard Schwartz Management, 2934-1/2 Beverly Glen Cir #107, Los Angeles, CA 90077

Hussey, Ruth
3361 Don Pablo Dr., Carlsbad, CA 92008

Husted, Dave *Bowler*
8880 SE Manfield Court, Clackamas, OR 97015 USA

Husted, Wayne D *Artist*
Keep Homestead Museum, Ely Road, Monson, MA 01057 USA

Huston, Anjelica *Actor, Director*
57 Windward Ave, Venice, CA 90291 USA

Huston, Carol
10100 Santa Monica Blvd. #2500, Los Angeles, CA 90067

Huston, Daniel (Danny) *Director*
William Morris Agency, 151 El Camino Dr, Beverly Hills, CA 90212 USA

Huston, John *Golfer*
307 Lakeview Dr, Tarpon Springs, FL 34689 USA

Hutch, Jesse *Actor*
Pacific Artists Management, 1404-510 W Hastings St, Vancouver, BC V6B 1L, CANADA

Hutcherson, Josh *Actor*
Beddingfield Company, The, 9255 Sunset Blvd #920, Los Angeles, CA 90069 USA

Hutcherson, Robert (Bobby) *Musician*
Abby Hoffer, 223 1/2 E 48th St, New York, NY 10017 USA

Hutchins, Mel *Basketball Player*
1211 S Pacific St #B, Oceanside, CA 92054 USA

Hutchins, Will *Actor*
PO Box 371, Glen Head, NY 11545 USA

Hutchinson, Barbara *Misc*
American Federation of Labor, 815 15th St NW, Washington, DC 20005 USA

Hutchinson, Chad *Baseball Player*
St Louis Cardinals, 110 Blue Ravine Rd Ste 105, Folsom, CA 95630-4712 USA

Hutchinson, Clyde A Jr *Misc*
University of Chicago, Searle Laboratory, Chimestry Dept, Chicago, IL 60637 USA

Hutchinson, Doug *Actor*
United Talent Agency, 9560 Wilshire Blvd, #500, Beverly Hills, CA 90212 USA

Hutchinson, Doug *Actor*
Agency for the Performing Arts (APA-LA), 9200 Sunset Blvd #900, Los Angeles, CA 90069 USA

Hutchinson, Frederick E *Educator*
University of Maine, President's Office, Orono, ME 04469 USA

Hutchinson, J Maxwell *Architect*
Cavendish Mansions, #61 Clerkenwell Road, London, EC1R 5DH, UNITED KINGDOM (UK)

Hutchinson, Kay Bailey *Senator*
703 Hart Bldg, Washington, DC 20510 USA

Huth, Edward J *Editor, Doctor*
1124 Morris Ave, Bryn Mawr, PA 19010 USA

Hutson, Candace
3500 W. Olive Ave. #920, Burbank, CA 91505

Hutson, Herb *Baseball Player*
Chicago Cubs, 7203 W Suger Tree Ct, Savannah, GA 31410-2414 USA

Hutt, Peter B *Attorney General*
Covington & Berlin, 1201 Pennsylvania Ave NW, Washington, DC 20004 USA

Hutto, Jim *Baseball Player*
Philadelphia Phillies, 1317 John Carroll Dr, Pensacola, FL 32504-7114 USA

Hutton, Betty *Actor, Musician, Music Group*
Lloyd, 931 Blair Ridge Road, West Des Moines, IA 50265 USA

Hutton, Danny *Musician, Music Group*
2437 Horseshoe Canyon Road, Los Angeles, CA 90046 USA

Hutton, Lauren *Actor, Model*
382 Lafayette St #6, New York, NY 10003 USA

Hutton, Mark *Baseball Player*
New York Yankees, 6 Corfu Court, Westlakes Adelaide, 5021, AUSTRALIA

Hutton, Ralph *Swimmer*
Vancouver Police Department, 312 Main St, Vancouver, BC CANADA

Hutton, Rif
10100 Santa Monica Blvd. #2490, Los Angeles, CA 90067

Hutton, Timothy *Actor*
Creative Artists Agency, 9830 Wilshire Blvd, Beverly Hills, CA 90212 USA

Hutton, Tommy
Los Angeles Dodgers, 18 Huntly Dr, Palm Beach Gardens, FL 33418-6812 USA

Hutzler, Brody *Actor*
Young and the Restless, The, 7800 Beverly Blvd, Ste 3305, Los Angeles, CA 90036 USA

Huxley, Andrew F *Nobel Prize Laureate*
Manor Field, 1 Vicarage Dr Grantchester, Cambridge, CB3 9NG, UNITED KINGDOM (UK)

Huxley, Hugh E *Biologist*
349 Nashawtuc Road, Concord, MA 01742 USA

Huxley, Laura *Writer, Doctor*
6233 Mulholland Dr, Los Angeles, CA 90068 USA

Huxtable, Ada Louise *Critic*
969 Park Ave, New York, NY 10028 USA

Huyck, Willard *Director*
39 Oakmont Dr, Los Angeles, CA 90049 USA

Hvorostovsky, Dmitri *Opera Singer*
Lies Askonas, 6 Henrietta St, London, WC2E 8LA, UNITED KINGDOM (UK)

Hwang, David Henry *Writer*
70 W 36th St #501, New York, NY 10018 USA

Hyams, Joe
10375 Wilshire Blvd. #4D, Los Angeles, CA 90024-4722

Hyams, Joseph I (Joe) Jr *Writer*
10375 Wilshire Blvd #4D, Los Angeles, CA 90024 USA

Hyams, Peter *Director*
PO Box 10, Basking Ridge, NJ 07920 USA

Hyatt, Joel Z *Attorney General, Business Person*
Haytt Legal Services, 1215 Superior Ave E, Cleveland, OH 44114 USA

Hybl, William J *Misc*
US Olympic Committe, 1 Olympia Plaza, Colorado Springs, CO 80909 USA

Hyche, Heath *Comedian*
Brillstein-Grey Entertainment, 9150 Wilshire Blvd #350, Beverly Hills, CA 90212 USA

Hyde, Christopher *Writer*
Onyx Penguin Putnam, 375 Hudson St, New York, NY 10014 USA

Hyde, Dick *Baseball Player*
Washington Senators, 1506 Cambridge Dr, Champaign, IL 61821-4957 USA

Hyde, Harry
PO Box 291, Harrisburg, NC 28075

Hyde, Jonathan *Actor*
William Morris Agency, 52/53 Poland Place, London, W1F 7LX, UNITED KINGDOM (UK)

Hyde-White, Alex *Actor*
Borinstein Oreck Bogart, 3172 Dona Susana Dr, Studio City, CA 91604 USA

Hyers, Tim *Baseball Player*
San Diego Padres, 241 Ridge Rd, Covington, GA 30016-5138 USA

Hyland, Brian *Musician*
Stone Buffalo, PO Box 101, Helendale, CA 92342 USA

Hylton, Thomas J *Journalist*
Pottstown Mercury, Editorial Dept, Hanover & Kings Sts, Pottstown, PA 19464 USA

Hyman, B D
PO Box 7107, Charlottesville, VA 22906 USA

Hyman, Dick
223 1/2 E. 48th St., New York, NY 10017

Hyman, Dorothy
7 Norman Close Barnsley, So. Yorks, ENGLAND, S71 244

Hyman, Earle *Actor*
Manhattan Towers, 484 W 43rd St #33E, New York, NY 10036 USA

Hyman, Fracaswell *Producer*
William Morris Agency (WMA-LA), 1 William Morris Pl, Beverly Hills, CA 90212 USA

Hyman, Kenneth
Sherwood House Tilehouse Lane Denham, Bucks, ENGLAND.

Hyman, Misty *Swimmer*
3826 E Lupine Ave, Phoenix, AZ 85028 USA

Hyman, Richard R (Dick) *Musician, Composer*
Abby Hoffer, 223 1/2 E 48th St, New York, NY 10017 USA

Hynd, Ronald *Ballerina, Choreographer*
Fern Cottage Up Somerton, Bury Saint Edmonds, Suffolk, IP29 4ND, UNITED KINGDOM (UK)

Hynde, Chrissie *Musician, Music Group, Songwriter*
Premier Talent, 3 E 54th St #1100, New York, NY 10022 USA

Hynes, Garry *Director*
Druid Theater Co, Chapel Lane, Galway, IRELAND

Hynes, Samuel *Writer*
130 Moore St, Princeton, NJ 08540 USA

Hynes, Tyler *Actor*
201 Laurier Ave E #202, Ottawa, ON K1N 6P1, CANADA

Hyser, Joyce *Actor*
Artists Agency, 1180 S Beverly Dr #301, Los Angeles, CA 90035 USA

Hysong, Nick *Track Athlete*
2822 E Cholla St, Phoenix, AZ 85028 USA

Hytner, Nicholas R *Director*
National Theatre, South Bank, London, SE1 9PX, UNITED KINGDOM (UK)

Hyzdu, Adam *Baseball Player*
Pittsburgh Pirates, 7823 E Red Hawk Cir, Mesa, AZ 85207-1167 USA

I

Iacocca, Lee
10614 Chalon Rd., Los Angeles, 90077

Iacocca, Lido A (Lee) *Business Person*
EV Global Motors, 10900 Wilshire Blvd #520, Los Angeles, CA 90024 USA

Iaconio, Frank *Race Car Driver*
250 US Highway 206, Flanders, NJ 07836 USA

Iafrate, Al A *Hockey Player*
27480 Five Mile Road, Livonia, MI 48154 USA

Iakovas, Primate Archbishop *Religious Leader*
31 Park Dr, South Rye, NY 10021 USA

Ian, Janis *Musician, Music Group, Songwriter*
Senior Mgmt, 56 Lindsley Ave, Nashville, TN 37210 USA

Ibanez, Raul *Baseball Player*
Seattle Mariners, 7497 SW 109th Pl, Miami, FL 33173-2744 USA

Ibbetson, Arthur *Cinematographer*
Tanglewood Chalfont Lane, Chorley Wood, Herts, UNITED KINGDOM (UK)

Ibers, James A *Misc*
2657 Orrington Ave, Evanston, IL 60201 USA

Ibiam, Francis A *Religious Leader*
Ganymede Unwana, PO Box 240 Afikpo, Imo State, NIGERIA

Ibn Salman Ibn ' Abd Al-' Aziz Al-Saud *Astronaut, Misc*
PO Box 18368, Riyadh, 11415, SAUDI ARABIA

Ibrahim, Abdullah (Dollar Brand) *Musician, Composer*
Brad Simon Organization, 122 E 57th St #300, New York, NY 10022 USA

Ibrahim, Barre Mainassara *Misc*
Head of State's Office, Presidential Palace, Niamey, NIGER

Ibuka, Yaeko *Social Activist*
Fukusei Byoin, Leprosarium, Mount Fuji, JAPAN

Icahn, Carl C *Business Person*
Ichan Co, 100 S Bedford Road, Mount Kisco, NY 10549 USA

Ice
11500 W. Olympic Blvd. #655, Los Angeles, CA 90064

Ice, Vanilla *Musician*
SBK Records, 1290 Ave of the Americas #4200, New York, NY 10104

Ice Cube *Musician, Actor, Director*
5420 Lindley Ave #4, Encino, CA 91316 USA

Ice T *Actor, Artist*
Coast II Coast, 3350 Wilshire Blvd #1200, Los Angeles, CA 90010 USA

Ice-T *Musician, Actor*
Coast II Coast Entertainment (LA), 3350 Wilshire Blvd, Suite 1200, Los Angeles, CA 90010 USA

Icehouse
Box KX-300 Kings Cross, Sydney, AUSTRALIA, 2011

Ichaco, Leon *Director*
Creative Artists Agency, 9830 Wilshire Blvd, Beverly Hills, CA 90212 USA

Ichaso, Leon *Director*
Innovative Artists (LA), 1505 Tenth St, Santa Monica, CA 90401 USA

Ickx, Jacky *Race Car Driver*
171 Chaussee de la Hulpe, Brussels, 1170, BELGIUM

Idle, Eric *Actor, Comedian*
Mayday Mgmt, 68A Delancey St, Camden Town, London, NW1 7RY, UNITED KINGDOM (UK)

Idol, Billy *Musician, Songwriter*
East End Mgmt, 8209 Melrose Ave #200, Los Angeles, CA 90046 USA

Iduarte Foucher, Andres *Writer*
Calle Edimburgo 3, Colonia del Valle, Mexico City, DF, 12, MEXICO

Idzlak, Slawomir *Cinematographer*
Ul Wazow 1-Z, Warsaw, 01-986, POLAND

Ifans, Rhys *Actor*
Endeavor Talent Agency, 9701 Wilshire Blve #1000, Beverly Hills, CA 90212 USA

Ifukube, Akira *Composer*
7-13-1 Nishishimbashi, Minatoku, Tokyo, 105, JAPAN

Iger, Robert A *Business Person*
Walt Disney Co, 500 S Buena Vista St, Burbank, CA 91521 USA

Iginla, Jarome *Hockey Player*
Newport Mgmt, 601-201 City Centre Dr, Mississauga, ON L58 2T4, CANADA

Iginla, Jerome *Hockey Player*
Newport Management, 601-201 City Centre Dr, Mississauga ON, L58 2T4, CANADA

Iglesias, Enrique *Musician*
Creative Artists Agency LCC (CAA-LA), 9830 Wilshire Blvd, Beverly Hills, CA 90212 USA

Iglesias, Enrique V *Financier, Government Official*
Inter-American Development Bank, 1300 New York Ave NW, Washington, DC 20577 USA

Iglesias, Julio *Musician*
1177 Kane Concourse, Bay Harbor Islands, FL 33154 USA

Iglesias, Julio Jr *Musician, Music Group, Songwriter*
Creative Artists Agency, 9830 Wilshire Blvd, Beverly Hills, CA 90212 USA

Ignarro, Louis J *Nobel Prize Laureate*
University of California, Medical School, 10833 LeConte, Los Angeles, CA 90095 USA

Ignasiak, Gary *Baseball Player*
Detroit Tigers, 3084 Angelus Dr, Waterford, MI 48329-2506 USA

Ignasiak, Mike *Baseball Player*
Milwaukee Brewers, 5821 Saline Ann Arbor Rd, Saline, MI 48176-9566 USA

Ignatius, Paul R *Government Official*
3650 Fordham Road, Washington, DC 20016 USA

Ignatius Zakka I Iwas, Patriarch *Religious Leader*
Syrian Orthodox Patriarchate, Bab Toma, PB 22260, Damascus, SYRIA

Ignizo, Mildred *Bowler*
241 Shore Acres Dr, Rochester, NY 14612 USA

Iha, James *Musician, Music Group*
1245 W Glenlake, Chicago, IL 60660 USA

Ihara, Michio *Artist*
63 Wood St, Concord, MA 01742 USA

Ihnatowicz, Zbigniew *Architect*
UI Mokotowska 31 M 15, Warsaw, 00-560, POLAND

Ike, Reverend *Religious Leader*
4140 Broadway, New York, NY 10033 USA

Ikeda, Daisaku *Religious Leader, Misc*
Soka Gokkai, 32 Shinanomachi, Shinjuku, Tokyo, 160-8583, JAPAN

Iken, Monica
William Morris Agency (WMA-LA), 1 William Morris Pl, Beverly Hills, CA 90212 USA

Ikenberry, Stanley O *Educator*
American Council on Education, 1 Dupont Circle NW, Washington, DC 20036 USA

Ikle, Fred C *Scientist*
7010 Glenbrook Road, Washington, DC 20014 USA

Ikola, Willard *Hockey Player, Coach*
5697 Green Circle Drive #316, Minnetonka, MN 55343 USA

Ilavarasi *Actor, Bollywood*
69 Vedawali Street, Kannbiran Colony, Chennai, TN 600093, INDIA

Iler, Robert *Actor*
Innovative Artists (LA), 1505 Tenth St, Santa Monica, CA 90401 USA

Iley, Barbara *Actor*
Paradigm Agency, 10100 Santa Monica Blvd #2500, Los Angeles, CA 90067 USA

Ilg, Raymond P *Admiral*
5504 Teak Court, Alexandria, VA 22309 USA

Ilgauskas, Zydrunas *Basketball Player*
Cleveland Cavaliers, Gund Arena, 1 Center Court, Cleveland, OH 44115 USA

Iliescu, Ion *President*
President's Office, Calea Victoriei 59-53, Bucharest, ROMANIA

Ilitch, Michael *Hockey Player, Baseball Player*
Detroit Red Wings, Joe Louis Arena, 600 Civic Center Dr, Detroit, MI 48226 USA

Illmann, Margaret *Ballerina*
National Ballet of Canada, 157 E King St, Toronto, ON M5C 1G9, CANADA

Illsley, John *Musician*
Damage Mgmt, 16 Lambton Place, London, W11 2SH, UNITED KINGDOM (UK)

Iloilo, Ratu Josefa *President*
President's Office, PO Box 2513, Suva, Viti Levu, FIJI

Ilsley, Blaise *Baseball Player*
Chicago Cubs, 127 E Lincoln St, Alpena, MI 49707-3710 USA

Ilyenko, Yuriy G *Cinematographer*
9 Michail Koyzybinksy Str #22, Kiev, 252030, UKRAINE

Imai, Kenji *Architect*
4-12-28 Kitazawa, Setagayaku, Tokyo, JAPAN

Imai, Nobuko *Musician*
Irene Witmer Mgmt, Kerkstrat 97, Amsterdam, GD, 1017, NETHERLANDS

Imamura, Shohei *Director*
Toei Co, 3-2-17 Ginza, Chuoku, Tokyo, JAPAN

Iman *Model, Actor*
Elite Model Management (UK), 40-42 Parker St, London, WC2B 5PQ, United Kingdom

Imbert, Bertrand S M *Engineer, Scientist*
50 Rue de Turenne, Paris, 75003, FRANCE

Imbert, Peter M *Lawyer*
Lieutenancy Office, City Hall, Victoria St, London, S1E 6QP, UNITED KINGDOM (UK)

Imbrie, Andrew W *Composer*
2625 Rose St, Berkeley, CA 94708 USA

Imbruglia, Natalie *Musician, Actor*
Russells, Regency House, 1-4 Warwick St, London, W1R 6LJ, UNITED KINGDOM (UK)

Imes Jackson, Monique (Mo'Nique) *Actor, Comedian, Television Host*
William Morris Agency (WMA-LA), 1 William Morris Pl, Beverly Hills, CA 90212 USA

Imhoff, Darrall *Basketball Player*
3637 Sterling Wood Dr, Eugene, OR 97408 USA

Imhoff, Darrell *Athlete*
3637 Sterling Wood Dr, Eugene, OR 97408

Imhoff, Gary *Actor*
Samantha Group, 300 S Raymond Ave, Pasadena, CA 91105 USA

Imle, John F Jr *Business Person*
Unocal Corp, 2141 Rosecrans Ave, El Segundo, CA 90245 USA

Immelt, Jeffrey (Jeff) *Business Person*
General Electric Co, 3135 Easton Turnpike, Fairfield, CT 06828 USA

Immerfall, Daniel (Dan) *Speed Skater*
5421 Trempeleau Trail, Madison, WI 53705 USA

Imperato, Carlo
6120 Cartwright, No. Hollywood, CA 91606

Imperioli, Michael *Actor*
3141 Baisley Ave, Bronx, NY 10465 USA

Imus, Don *Entertainer*
WFAN-Radio, 3412 36th St, Astoria, NY 11106 USA

IMX *Music Group*
Pyramid Entertainment Group, 89 Fifth Ave Fl 7, New York, NY 10003 USA

Inamori, Kazuo *Business Person*
KDDI Corp, 3-22 Nishi-Shinjuku, Shinjuku, Tokyo, 163-8003, JAPAN

Inbal, Eliahu *Conductor*
Heissischer Rundfunk, Bertramstr 8, Frankfurt/Main, 60320, GERMANY

Incandella, Sal *Race Car Driver*
Indy Racing Regency, 5811 W 73rd St, Indianapolis, IN 46278 USA

Incavglia, Peter J (Pete) *Baseball Player*
PO Box 526, Pebble Beach, CA 93953 USA

Incaviglia, Pete *Baseball Player*
Texas Rangers, PO

Incaviglia, Pete *Baseball Player*
Texas Rangers, PO Box 526, Pebble Beach, CA 93953-0526 USA

Inclan, Rafael *Actor*
Televisa, Blvd Adolfo Lopez Mateos 232, Colonia San Angel INN, DF, CP 01060, MEXICO

Incubus *Music Group*
Creative Artists Agency LCC (CAA-LA), 9830 Wilshire Blvd, Beverly Hills, CA 90212 USA

Indhu *Actor, Bollywood*
D/o G.K.Ram Kumar, 2 Circular Road United India Colony, Chennai, TN 600024, INDIA

Indiana, Robert *Artist*
Press Box 464, Vinalhaven, ME 04863 USA

Indigo Girls *Music Group*
Russell Carter Artist Management, 315 West Ponce De Leon Avenue, Suite 755, Decatur, GA 30030 USA

Indraja *Actor, Bollywood*
89 Krishna Nagar, Virugambakkam, Chennai, TN 600092, INDIA

Indurain, Miguel
Avendia Villava, Pamplona (Navarra), SPAIN, E-31013

Infante, Guillermo Cabrera
53 Gloucester Rd., London, ENGLAND, SW7 4QT

Infante, Lindy *Football Coach*
6870 A1AS, Saint Augustine, FL 32080 USA

Infante, Topo *Actor*
Televisa, Blvd Adolfo Lopez Mateos 232, Colonia San Angel INN, DF, CP 01060, MEXICO

Infill, O Urcille Jr *Religious Leader*
African Methodist Church, PO Box 19039, Philadelphia, PA 19138 USA

Ing, Hout *Government Official*
Foreign Affairs Ministry, Phnom Penh, COMBODIA

Inge, Brandon *Baseball Player*
Detroit Tigers, 525 Erikas Woods Ct, Ann
Arbor, MI 48103-9030 USA

Inge, Peter A *Misc*
House of Lords, Westminster, London,
SW1A 0PW, UNITED KINGDOM (UK)

Ingels, Marty *Actor, Comedian*
16400 Ventura Blvd, Encino, CA 91436
USA

Ingersoll, Ralph II *Publisher*
Ingersoll Publications, PO Box 1869,
Lakeville, CT 06039 USA

Inghram, Mark G *Physicist*
13837 W Casa Linda Dr, Sun City West,
AZ 85375 USA

Ingle, Doug *Musician, Music Group*
Entertainment Services Int'l, 6400 Pleasant
Park Dr, Chanhassen, MN 55317 USA

Ingle, John *Actor*
Artists Group, 10100 Santa Monica Blvd
#2490, Los Angeles, CA 90067 USA

Ingle, Robert D *Editor*
San Jose Mercury News, Editorial Dept,
750 Ridder Park Dr, San Jose, CA 95131
USA

Ingman, Elnar H Jr *War Hero*
W4053 N Silver Lake Road, Irma, WI
54442 USA

Ingraham, Hubert A *Prime Minister*
Prime Minister's Office, Whitfield Center,
Box CB10980, Nassau, BAHAMAS

Ingram, A John *Doctor*
4940 Sullivan Woods Cove, Memphis, TN
38117 USA

Ingram, Garey *Baseball Player*
Los Angeles Dodgers, 5237 Orange Dr,
Columbus, GA 31907-2832 USA

Ingram, James *Musician, Music Group,
Songwriter*
867 Muirfield Road, Los Angeles, CA
90005 USA

Ingram, Lonnie *Biologist*
University of Florida, Microbiology/Cell
Science Dept, Gainesville, FL 32611 USA

Ingram, Riccardo *Baseball Player*
Detroit Tigers, 1571 Twin Oaks Dr,
Toledo, OH 43615-4036 USA

Ingram, Vernon M *Biologist*
Massachusetts Institute of Technology,
Biochemistry Dept, Cambridge, MA
02139 USA

Ingrao, Pietro *Government Official*
Centro Studie Iniziative Per La Reforma,
Via Della Vite 13, Rome, ITALY

Ingrassia, Paul J *Journalist*
111 Division Ave, New Providence, NJ
07974 USA

Ink Spots, The
5100 DuPont Blvd. #10A, Ft. Lauderdale,
FL 33308

Inkeles, Alex *Social Activist*
1001 Hamilton Ave, Palo Alto, CA 94301
USA

Inkster, Jull Simpson *Golfer*
23140 Mora Glen Dr, Los Altos Hills, CA
94024 USA

Inman, Bobby Ray *Admiral, Government
Official*
701 Brazos St #500, Austin, TX 78701
USA

Inman, Jerry *Football Player*
PO Box 1113, Battle Ground, WA 98604
USA

Inman, John *Actor*
AMG Ltd, 8 King St, London, WC2E 8HN,
UNITED KINGDOM (UK)

Inman, John *Golfer*
2210 Chase St, Durham, NC 27707 USA

Innauer, Anton (Toni) *Skier, Coach*
Steinbruckstr 8/11, Innsbruck, 6024,
AUSTRIA

Innaurato, Albert F *Writer*
325 W 22nd St, New York, NY 10011
USA

Innes, Laura *Actor*
Paradigm Agency, 10100 Santa Monica
Blvd #2500, Los Angeles, CA 90067 USA

Innis *Musician*
Paradigm (LA), 10100 Santa Monica Blvd,
Fl 25, Los Angeles, CA 90067 USA

Innis, Jeff *Baseball Player*
New York Mets, 4920 Woodlong Ln,
Cumming, GA 30040-5275 USA

Innis, Roy
800 Riverside Dr. #6E, New York, NY
10032

Innis, Roy E A *Social Activist*
817 Broadway, New York, NY 10003
USA

Innocenti, Antonio Cardinal *Religious
Leader*
Piazza della Citta Lemonia 9, Rome,
00193 USA

Inogradov, Pavel *Astronaut, Misc*
Potchta Kosmonavtov, Moskovskol
Oblasti, Syvisdny Goroduk, 141160,
RUSSIA

Inoue, Shinya *Biologist, Photographer*
Marine Biological Laboratory, 167 Water
St, Woods Hole, MA 02543 USA

Inoue, Yuichi *Artist*
Ohkamiyashiki 2475-2 Kurami,
Samakawamachi 253-01 Kozagun, Kam,
JAPAN

Inouye, Daniel K *Senator, War Hero*
300 Ala Moana Blvd #7-212, Honolulu,
HI 96850 USA

Inouye, Lisa *Actor*
Media Artists Group, 6300 Wilshire Blvd
#1470, Los Angeles, CA 90048 USA

Insane Clown Posse *Music Group*
William Morris Agency (WMA-LA), 1
William Morris Pl, Beverly Hills, CA
90212 USA

Insko, Delmer M (Del) *Horse Racer*
2360 Fischer Road, South Beloit, IL 61080
USA

Insley, Will *Artist*
231 Bowery, New York, NY 10002 USA

Insolla, Anthony *Editor*
Newsday, Editorial Dept, 235 Pinelawn,
Melville, NY 11747 USA

Inspectah, Deck *Artist*
Famous Artists Agency, 250 W 57th St,
New York, NY 10107 USA

INXS
8 Hayes St. #1, Neutray Bay, AUSTRALIA,
NSW 20891

Inzaghi, Filippo *Soccer Player*
AC Milan, Via Turati 3, Milan, 20221,
Italy

Ionatana, Ionatana *Prime Minister*
Prime Minister's Office, Vaiaku, Funafuti,
TUVALU

Iorg, Dane *Baseball Player*
Philadelphia Phillies, 928 Sage Dr,
Pleasant Grove, UT 84062-2021 USA

Iorg, Garth *Baseball Player*
Toronto Blue Jays, 1446 Davis Ln Apt J,
Knoxville, TN 37923-6707 USA

Ioss, Walter *Photographer*
152 De Forrest Road, Montauk, NY 11954
USA

Irabu, Hideki *Baseball Player*
New York Yankees, 140 Ocean Park Blvd
Apt 629, Santa Monica, CA 90405-3578
USA

Irani, Aruna *Actor, Bollywood*
603 B Gazdar Apartments, Near Juhu
Hotel Juhu, Mumbai, MS 400049, INDIA

Irani, Ray R *Business Person*
Occidental Petroleum, 10889 Wilshire
Blvd, Los Angeles, CA 90024 USA

Irbe, Arturs *Hockey Player*
10733 Trego Trail, Raleigh, NC 27614
USA

Iredale, Randle W *Architect*
1151 W 8th Ave, Vancouver, BC V6H
1C5, CANADA

Ireland, Dan *Director, Writer, Producer*
Gersh Agency, The (LA), 232 N Canon Dr,
Beverly Hills, CA 90210 USA

Ireland, Kathy *Model, Actor*
Sterling Winners, 10877 Wilshire Blvd
#15, Los Angeles, CA 90024 USA

Ireland, Patricia *Misc*
Katz Kutler Haigler Assoc, 801
Pennsylvania Ave NW #750, Washington,
DC 20004 USA

Ireland, Tim *Baseball Player*
Kansas City Royals, 20932 Times Ave,
Hayward, CA 94541-3754 USA

Iris, Donnie *Musician, Music Group,
Songwriter*
807 Darlington Road, Beaver Falls, PA
15010 USA

Irish Rovers, The
1505 W. 2nd Ave. #200, Vancouver,
CANADA, BC V6H 3Y4

Irizarry, Vincent *Actor*
David Shapira, 15821 Ventura Blvd #235,
Encino, CA 91436 USA

Irobe, Yoshiaki *Financier*
26-6-6 Saginomiya, Nakanoku, Tokyo,
JAPAN

Iron Butterfly
PO Box 770850, Orlando, FL 32877

Iron Maiden *Music Group*
Creative Artists Agency LCC (CAA-LA),
9830 Wilshire Blvd, Beverly Hills, CA
90212 USA

Irons, Jeremy *Actor*
Hutton Mgmt, 4 Old Manor Close, Askett,
Buckinghamshire, HP27 9NA, UNITED
KINGDOM (UK)

Ironside, Michael *Actor, Producer, Writer*
Innovative Artists (LA), 1505 Tenth St,
Santa Monica, CA 90401 USA

Irrera, Dom *Actor, Comedian*
Irvin Arthur Assoc, PO Box 1358, New
York, NY 10028 USA

Irvan, Ernie *Race Car Driver*
629 El Cardinal Lane, Mooresville, NC
28115 USA

Irvin, Anthony
One Olympic Plaza, Colorado Springs,
CO 80909-5770

Irvin, Daryl *Baseball Player*
Boston Red Sox, 2704 Hopkins Dr,
McGaheysville, VA 22840-2150 USA

Irvin, John *Director*
6 Lower Common South, London, SW15
1BP, UNITED KINGDOM (UK)

Irvin, LeRoy Jr *Football Player*
2905 Ruby Dr #C, Fullerton, CA 92831
USA

Irvin, Michael
1280 S. Main St. #103, Grapevine, TX
76051-7509

Irvin, Michael J *Football Player*
1221 Brickell Ave #200, Miami, FL 33131
USA

Irvin, Monford M (Monte) *Baseball Player*
New York Giants, 11 Douglas Court S,
Homosassa, FL 34446-3830 USA

Irvine, Eddie *Race Car Driver*
Ferrari SpA, Casella Postale 589, Modena,
41100, ITALY

Irvine, Paula
23852 Pacific Coast Hwy. PMB 195,
Malibu, CA 90265

Irving, Amy *Actor*
Rigberg Roberts Rugolo, 1180 S Beverly
Dr #601, Los Angeles, CA 90035 USA

Irving, John *Writer*
Creative Artists Agency LCC (CAA-LA),
9830 Wilshire Blvd, Beverly Hills, CA
90212 USA

Irving, John W *Writer*
Tumbull Agency, PO Box 757, Dorset, VT
05251 USA

Irving, Paul H *Attorney General*
Manatt Phelps Phillips, 11355 W Olympic
Blvd, Los Angeles, CA 90064 USA

Irving, Stu *Hockey Player*
93 Hart St, Beverly Farms, MA 01915
USA

Irwin, Bill *Entertainer*
20 1st Ave, Nyack, NY 10960 USA

Irwin, Hale S *Golfer*
10726 Manchester Road #212, Saint
Louis, MO 63122 USA

Irwin, Jennifer *Actor*
New Wave Entertainment (LA), 2660 W
Olive Blvd, Burbank, CA 91505 USA

Irwin, Malcolm R *Biologist*
4720 Regent St, Madison, WI 53705 USA

Irwin, Mark *Cinematographer*
1522 Olive St, Santa Barbara, CA 93101
USA

Irwin, Paul G *Misc*
Humane Society of the United States,
2100 L St NW, Washington, DC 20037
USA

Irwin, Robert W *Artist*
Pace Gallery, 32 E 57th St, New York, NY
10022 USA

Irwin, Steve *Actor*
Australia Zoo, Goasshouse Mountains
Route, Beerwah, QLD, AUSTRALIA

Irwin, Tom
PO Box 5617, Beverly Hills, CA 90210

Irwin-Mellencamp, Elaine *Model*
John Caugar Mellencamp, 5072 W
Stevens Road, Nashville, IN 47448 USA

Isaac, Victor *Actor*
Epstein Wyckoff Corsa Ross & Assoc (LA),
280 S Beverly Dr #400, Beverly Hills, CA
90212 USA

Isaacks, Levie C *Cinematographer*
6634 Sunnyslope Ave, Van Nuys, CA
91401 USA

Isaacksen, Peter
4635 Placidia Ave, No. Hollywood, CA
91602

Isaacs, Gregory *Musician*
Famous Artists Agency, 250 W 57th St,
New York, NY 10107 USA

Isaacs, Jason *Actor*
International Creative Mgmt, 76 Oxford
St, London, CA W1N 0AX, UNITED
KINGDOM (UK)

Isaacs, Jeremy I *Director*
Royal Opera House, Covent Garden Bow
St, London, WC1 7Q4, UNITED
KINGDOM (UK)

Isaacs, John (Speed) *Basketball Player*
1412 Crotona Ave, Bronx, NY 10456 USA

Isaacs, Susan *Writer*
Harper Collins Publishers, 10 E 53rd St,
New York, NY 10022 USA

Isaacson, Julius *Misc*
Novelty & Production Workers Union,
1815 Franklin Ave, Valley Stream, NY
11581 USA

Isaacson, Walter S *Journalist*
Simon & Schuste, 1230 Ave of Americas,
New York, NY 10020 USA

Isaak, Chris *Actor, Musician, Songwriter*
PO Box 547, Larkspur, CA 94977 USA

Isaak, Russell *Business Person*
CPI Corp, 1706 Washington Ave, Saint
Louis, MO 63103 USA

Isabel, Margarita *Actor*
TV Azteca, Periferico Sur 4121, Colonia
Fuentes del Pedregal, DF, CP 14141,
Mexico

Isabelle, Katharine *Actor*
IFA Talent Agency, 8730 Sunset Blvd
#490, Los Angeles, CA 90069 USA

Isabelle, Katherine *Actor*
IFA Talent Agency, 8730 Sunset Blvd
#490, Los Angeles, CA 90069 USA

Isacksen, Peter *Actor*
4635 Placidia Ave, Toluca Lake, CA
91602 USA

Isaksson, Irma Sara *Musician, Songwriter*
United Stage Artists, PO Box 11026,
Stockholm, 100 61, SWEDEN

Isales, Orlando *Baseball Player*
Philadelphia Phillies, 14710 SW 106th
Ave, Miami, FL 33176-7791 USA

Isard, Walter *Economist*
3218 Garrett Road, Drexel Hill, PA 19026
USA

Isbin, Sharon *Musician*
Columbia Artists Mgmt Inc, 165 W 57th
St, New York, NY 10019 USA

Iscove, Robert (Rob) *Director*
16045 Royal Oak Road, Encino, CA
91436 USA

Isdell, E Neville *Business Person*
Coca-Cola Co, 1 Coca-Cola Plaza, 310
North Ave NW, Atlanta, GA 30313 USA

Isenburger, Eric *Artist*
140 E 56th St, New York, NY 10022 USA

Isham, Mark *Composer*
Ron Moss Mgmt, 2635 Griffith Park Blvd,
Los Angeles, CA 90039 USA

Ishara, B R *Actor, Bollywood*
C36 North Bombay Housing Society, Juhu
Tara Road, Mumbai, MS 400049, INDIA

Ishibashi, Kanichiro *Business Person*
1 Nagasakacho Azabu, Minatoku, Tokyo,
JAPAN

Ishida, Jim *Actor*
871 N Vail Ave, Montebello, CA 90640
USA

Ishiguro, Kazuo *Writer*
Rogers Coleridge White, 20 Powis Mews,
London, W11 1JN, UNITED KINGDOM
(UK)

Ishihara, Shintaro *Government Official*
Sanno Grand Building, #606 2-14-2
Nagatocho Chiyodaku, Tokyo, JAPAN

Ishii, Kazuhiro *Architect*
4-14-27 Akasaka, Minatoku, Tokyo, 107,
JAPAN

Ishikawa, Sigeru *Economist*
19-8-4 Chome Kugayama, Suginamiku,
Tokyo, 168-0082, JAPAN

Ishimaru, Akira *Engineer*
2913 165th Place NE, Bellevue, WA
98008 USA

Ishizaka, Kimishiga *Doctor*
Allergy/Immunology Institute, 11149 N
Torrey Pines Road, La Jolla, CA 92037
USA

Ishizaka, Teruko *Doctor*
Good Samaritan Hospital, 5601 Loch
Raven Blvd, Baltimore, MD 21239 USA

Iskander, Fazil A *Writer*
Krasnoarmeiskaya Str 23 #104, Moscow,
125319, RUSSIA

Islas, Claudia *Actor*
TV Azteca, Periferico Sur 4121, Colonia
Fuentes del Pedregal, DF, CP 14141,
Mexico

Islas, Mauricio *Actor*
Televisa, Blvd Adolfo Lopez Mateos 232, Colonia San Angel INN, DF, CP 01060, MEXICO

Isley, Ronald (Ron) *Musician*
Ron Weisner Mgmt, PO Box 261640, Encino, CA 91426 USA

Isley Brothers *Music Group*
Keith Sherman & Associates, 1776 Broadway #1200, New York, NY 10019 USA

Ismail, Ahmed Sultan *Engineer*
43 Ahmed Abdel Aziz St, Dokki, Cairo, EGYPT

Ismail, Raghib R (Rocket) *Football Player*
7423 Marigold Dr, Irving, TX 75063 USA

Ison, Christopher J *Journalist*
Minneapolis-Saint Paul Star Tribune, 425 Portland Ave, Minneapolis, MN 55488 USA

Isozaki, Arata *Architect*
Arata Assoc, 6-17-9 Adasaka, Minatoku, Tokyo, 107, JAPAN

Israel, Werner *Physicist*
5189 Polson Terrace, Victoria, BC V8Y 2C5, CANADA

Isringhausen, Jason *Baseball Player*
New York Mets, 550 E Lake Dr, Tarpon Springs, FL 34688-8628 USA

Issel, Daniel P (Dan) *Basketball Player, Coach*
10163 E Fair Circle, Englewood, CO 80111 USA

Isselbacher, Kurt J *Doctor*
20 Nobscot Road, Newton Center, MA 02459 USA

Isserlis, Steven *Musician*
Harrison/Parrott, 12 Penzance Place, London, W11 4PA, UNITED KINGDOM (UK)

Ito, Lance *Judge*
Los Angeles Superior Court, 210 W Temple St, Los Angeles, CA 90012 USA

Ito, Masayoshi *Government Official*
1-28-3 Chitose-Dai, Setagayaku, Tokyo, 157, JAPAN

Ito, Midori *Figure Skater*
Skating Federation, Kryshi Taaikukan 1-1-1, Shibuyaku, Tokyo, 10, JAPAN

Ito, Robert *Actor*
843 N Sycamore Ave, Los Angeles, CA 90038 USA

Itzin, Gregory *Actor*
Borinstein Oreck Bogart, 3172 Dona Susana Dr, Studio City, CA 91604 USA

Ivanchenkov, Aleksandr S *Astronaut, Misc*
Potchta Kosmonavtov, Moskovskoi Oblasti, Syvisdny Goroduk, 141160, RUSSIA

Ivanchenkov, Alexander
141 160 Zvezdny Gorodok, Moscow Obl., RUSSIA

Ivanek, Zeljko
145 W. 45th St. #1204, New York, NY 10036

Ivanisevic, Goran *Tennis Player*
Alijnoviceva 28, Split, 58000, SERBIA & MONTENEGRO

Ivanov, Igor S *Government Official*
Foreign Affairs Ministry, Smolenskaya-Sennaya 32/34, Moscow, RUSSIA

Ivens, Terri *Actor*
Kohner Agency, The, 9300 Wilshire Blvd #555, Beverly Hills, CA 90212 USA

Ivers, Eileen *Misc, Athlete*
Sony Records, 2100 Colorado Ave, Santa Monica, CA 90404 USA

Iverson, Allen *Basketball Player*
PO Box 901, Conshohocken, PA 19428 USA

Iverson, Portia *Religious Leader*
4511 Pacific Ave, Wildwood, NJ 08260 USA

Ivery, Eddie Lee *Football Player*
49 Rocky Ford Road, Atlanta, GA 30317 USA

Ives, J Atwood *Business Person*
Eastern Enterprises, 201 Rivermoor St, West Roxbury, MA 02132 USA

Ivey, Dana *Actor*
Paradigm Agency, 10100 Santa Monica Blvd #2500, Los Angeles, CA 90067 USA

Ivey, James
5856 Dahlia Dr. #7, Orlando, FL 32807-3267

Ivey, James B (Jim) *Editor, Cartoonist*
5840 Dahlia Dr #7, Orlando, FL 32807 USA

Ivey, Judith *Actor*
53 W 87th St #2, New York, NY 10024 USA

Ivie, Mike *Baseball Player*
San Diego Padres, 894 Rocker Rd, Crawfordville, GA 30631-1339 USA

Ivins, Marsha S *Astronaut*
2811 Timber Briar Circle, Houston, TX 77059 USA

Ivins, Molly *Commentator, Writer*
CBS-TV, News Dept, 51 W 52nd St, New York, NY 10019 USA

Ivo, Tommy
247 S. Orchard Dr, Burbank, CA 91506

Ivory, Horace O *Football Player*
5321 Diaz Ave, Fort Worth, TX 76107 USA

Ivory, James *Producer*
18 Patroon St, Claverack, NY 12513

Ivory, James F *Director, Producer, Filmmaker*
18 Patroon St, Claverach, NY 12513 USA

Ivosev, Aleksandra *Misc*
Sluzbeni put Zavoda 5, Careva Cuprija, Belgrad, 11030, SERBIA & MONTENEGRO

Iwago, Mitsuaki *Photographer*
Edelhof Daichi Building #2F, 8 Honsio-cho Shinjukaku, Tokyo, 160, JAPAN

Iwerks, Donald W *Business Person*
Iwerks Entertainment, 4520 W Valerio St, Burbank, CA 91505 USA

Iyanaga, Shokichi *Mathematician*
12-4 Otsuka 6-Chome, Bunkyoku, Tokyo, 112-0012, JAPAN

Iyer, Kalpana *Actor, Dancer*
E 43 Geeta Kiran Society J P Road Four Bangalows, Andheri, Bombay, MS 400 058, INDIA

Izquierdo, Hank *Baseball Player*
Minnesota Twins, 12458 71st Pl N, West Palm Beach, FL 33412-1438 USA

Izturis, Cesar *Baseball Player, Athlete*
Toronto Blue Jays, 375 Douglas Avenue, Clearwater, FL 33755 USA

Izzard, Eddie *Comedian, Actor*
Mitch Schneider Organization, 14724 Ventura Blvd #410, Sherman Oaks, CA 91403 USA

Izzo, Tom *Basketball Player, Coach*
Michigan State University, Athletic Dept, East Lansing, MI 48824 USA

J

J-Bolt *Producer*
Lightning Bolt Entertainment, 3342 S Sandhill Rd, Suite 9-424, Las Vegas, NV 89121 USA

Ja Rule *Musician, Actor, Artist*
Violator Mgmt, 205 Lexington Ave #400, New York, NY 10016 USA

Jablonski, Henryk *President*
Ul Filtrowa 61 m 4, Warsaw, 02-056, POLAND

Jack, Beau
1 Hall of Fame Dr., Canastota, NY 13032

Jack, Lind *Baseball Player*
Milwaukee Brewers, 6132 E Redmont Dr, Mesa, AZ 85215-0878 USA

Jacke, Christoper L (Chris) *Football Player*
Arizona Cardinals, PO Box 888, Phoenix, AZ 85001 USA

Jackee *Actor*
7250 Franklin Ave, #814, Los Angeles, CA 90046 USA

Jacklin, Tony *Golfer, Sportscaster*
1175 51st Street West, Bradenton, FL 34209 USA

Jackman, Hugh *Actor*
Endeavor Agency LLC (LA), 9601 Wilshire Blvd Fl 3, Beverly Hills, CA 90210 USA

Jackson, Alfred *Football Player*
1811 Kirby Dr, Houston, TX 77019 USA

Jackson, Al *Baseball Player*
Pittsburgh Pirates, 3321 SE Morningside Blvd, Port Saint Lucie, FL 34952-5906 USA

Jackson, Alan *Musician, Songwriter*
Force Inc, 1505 16th Ave S, Nashville, TN 37212 USA

Jackson, Alphonso *Secretary*
Housing & Urban Development Department, 451 7th SW, Washington, DC 20410 USA

Jackson, Alvin N (Al) *Baseball Player*
3321 SE Morningside Blvd, Port Saint Lucie, FL 34952 USA

Jackson, Anne *Actor*
90 Riverside Dr, New York, NY 10024 USA

Jackson, Arthur J *War Hero*
1290 E Spring Court, Boise, ID 83712 USA

Jackson, Barry
29 Rathcoole Ave., London, ENGLAND, N8 9LY

Jackson, Betty *Fashion Designer*
Betty Jackson Ltd, 1 Netherwood Place, London, W14 0BW, UNITED KINGDOM (UK)

Jackson, Bo
PO Box 158, Mobile, AL 36601-8313

Jackson, Bobby *Basketball Player*
Sacramento Kings, Arco Arena, 1 Sports Parkway, Sacramento, CA 95834 USA

Jackson, Chuck *Musician*
Universal Attractions, 225 W 57th St #500, New York, NY 10019 USA

Jackson, Curtis (50 Cent) *Musician*
Interscope Records (LA) - Main, 2220 Colorado Ave, Santa Monica, CA 90404 USA

Jackson, Danny L *Baseball Player*
Philadelphia Phillies, Veterans Stadium, 3501 S Broad, Philadelphia, PA 19148 USA

Jackson, Daryl S *Architect*
161 Hotham St, East Melbourne, VIC, 3002, AUSTRALIA

Jackson, Deanna *Basketball Player*
Indiana Fever, Conseco Fieldhouse, 125 S Pennsylvania, Indianapolis, IN 46204 USA

Jackson, Donald
1080 Brocks, South Pickering ON, CANADA

Jackson, Doris *Musician*
Nationwide Entertainment, 2756 N Green Valley Parkway, Henderson, NV 89014 USA

Jackson, Eddie *Bowler*
3961 Glenmore Ave, Cincinnati, OH 45211 USA

Jackson, Francis A *Musician, Composer*
Nether Garth, East Acklam, Malton North Yorkshire, YO17 9RG, UNITED KINGDOM (UK)

Jackson, Freddie *Musician, Songwriter*
Associated Booking Corp, 1995 Broadway #501, New York, NY 10023 USA

Jackson, Gildart *Actor*
Binder & Associates, 1465 Lindacrest Dr, Beverly Hills, CA 90210 USA

Jackson, Glenda *Actor*
Crouch Assoc, 9-15 Neal St, London, WC2H 9PF, UNITED KINGDOM (UK)

Jackson, Harold *Football Player, Coach*
6144 Flight Ave, Los Angeles, CA 90056 USA

Jackson, Harold *Journalist*
Birmingham News, Editorial Dept, 2200 N 4th Ave N, Birmingham, AL 35203 USA

Jackson, Harry A *Artist*
PO Box 2836, Cody, WY 82414 USA

Jackson, Huson *Architect*
Sert Jackson Assoc, 442 Marrett Road #101, Lexington, MA 02421 USA

Jackson, James A (Jim) *Basketball Player*
17827 Windflower Way, Dallas, TX 75252 USA

Jackson, Janet *Musician, Actor, Dancer*
United Talent Agency, 9560 Wilshire Blvd #500, Beverly Hills, CA 90212 USA

Jackson, Jeff *Athlete*
5094 Panola Mill Dr, Lithonia, GA 30038-2349

Jackson, Jermaine *Musician, Music Group, Songwriter*
4641 Hayvenhurst Dr, Encino, CA 91436 USA

Jackson, Jermaine *Basketball Player*
Atlanta Hawks, 190 Marietta St SW, Atlanta, GA 30303 USA

Jackson, Jesse L *Politician, Social Activist, Religious Leader*
400 T Street NW, Washington, DC 20001 USA

Jackson, Joe *Musician, Songwriter*
Primary Talent Int'l, 2-12 Pentonville Road, London, N1 9PL, UNITED KINGDOM (UK)

Jackson, Joe M *War Hero*
25320 38th Ave S, Kent, WA 98032 USA

Jackson, John David *Boxer*
1022 S State St, Tacoma, WA 98405 USA

Jackson, John M *Actor*
JAG, 5555 Melrose Ave, Clara Bow #204, Los Angeles, CA 90038 USA

Jackson, Jonathan *Actor*
1815 Butler Ave #120, Los Angeles, CA 90025 USA

Jackson, Joshua *Actor*
Johansmeier, 326 Columbus Ave #5G, New York, NY 10023 USA

Jackson, Kate *Actor*
1628 Martay Dr, Los Angeles, CA 90069 USA

Jackson, Keith J *Football Player*
1801 Champlin Dr #1707, Little Rock, AR 72223 USA

Jackson, Keith M *Sportscaster*
ABC-TV, Sports Dept, 77 W 66th St, New York, NY 10023 USA

Jackson, Kevin *Wrestler*
7215 Montarbor Dr, Colorado Springs, CO 80918 USA

Jackson, Kwame *Business Person, Reality TV Star*
Mark Burnett Productions, 1661 Lincoln Blvd #200, Santa Monica, CA 90404 USA

Jackson, Larry R *Misc*
Grain Millers Federation, 4949 Oslon Memorial Parkway, Minneapolis, MN 55422 USA

Jackson, LaToya *Musician, Model*
14126 Rosecrans Ave, Santa Fe Springs, CA 90670 USA

Jackson, Lauren *Basketball Player*
Seattle Storm, Key Arena, 351 Elliott Ave W #500, Seattle, WA 98119 USA

Jackson, Lucious (Luke) *Basketball Player*
Cleveland Cavaliers, Gund Arena, 1 Center Court, Cleveland, OH 44115 USA

Jackson, Mark A *Basketball Player*
628 Main St, Windsor, CO 80550 USA

Jackson, Marlon
4641 Hayvenhurst Ave., Encino, CA 91316

Jackson, Mary *Actor*
2055 Grace Ave, Los Angeles, CA 90068 USA

Jackson, Mary Ann *Actor*
1242 Alessandro Dr, Newbury Park, CA 91320 USA

Jackson, Mayor Maynard
68 Mitchell, Atlanta, GA 30303

Jackson, Mel *Actor*
Stone Manners Talent Agency, 6500 Wilshire Blvd, Ste 550, Los Angeles, CA 90048 USA

Jackson, Michael J *Musician*
Ziffren Brittenham Branca Fischer Gilbert-Lurie & Stiffman LLP, 1801 Century Park W, Los Angeles, CA 90067 USA

Jackson, Mick *Director*
1349 Berea Place, Pacific Palisades, CA 90272 USA

Jackson, Millie *Musician, Songwriter*
Associated Booking Corp, 1995 Broadway #501, New York, NY 10023 USA

Jackson, Monte C *Football Player*
7646 Westbrook Ave, San Deigo, CA 92139 USA

Jackson, Pervis *Musician*
Buddy Allen Mgmt, 3750 Hudson Manor Terrace #3AG, Bronx, NY 10463 USA

Jackson, Peter *Director*
Wing Nut Films, PO Box 15208, Miramar, Wellington, NEW ZEALAND

Jackson, Phil *Coach*
Original Film, 2045 S Barrington Ave, Los Angeles, CA 90025 USA

Jackson, Philip *Actor*
Markham & Froggatt, Julian House, 4 Windmill St, London, W1P 1HF, UNITED KINGDOM (UK)

Jackson, Philip D (Phil) *Basketball Player, Coach*
Los Angeles Lakers, Staples Center, 1111 S Figueroa St, Los Angeles, CA 90015 USA

Jackson, R Graham *Architect*
Calhoun Tungate Jackson Dill Architects, 6200 Savoy Dr, Houston, TX 77036 USA

Jackson, Randy *Musician*
Big J Productions, PO Box 24455, New Orleans, LA 70184 USA

Jackson, Rebbie *Musician, Music Group, Songwriter*
4641 Hayvenhurst Dr, Encino, CA 91436 USA

Jackson, Reginald M (Reggie) *Baseball Player*
305 Amador Ave, Seaside, CA 93955 USA

Jackson, Richard A *Religious Leader*
North Phoenix Baptist Church, 5757 N Central Ave, Phoenix, AZ 85012 USA

Jackson, Richard Lee
1815 Butler Avenue, #120, Los Angeles, CA 90025-5644

Jackson, Richard S (Richie) *Football Player*
All Pro Inc, 6000 Kingston Court, New Orleans, LA 70131 USA

Jackson, Rickey A *Football Player*
325 S Barfield Highway, Pahokee, FL 33476 USA

Jackson, Ronald Shannon *Musician*
Worldwide Jazz, 1128 Broadway #425,
New York, NY 10010 USA

Jackson, Samuel L *Actor*
P M K Public Relations, 8500 Wilshire
Blvd #700, Beverly Hills, CA 90211 USA

Jackson, Sherry *Actor*
4933 Encino Ave, Encino, CA 91316 USA

Jackson, Shirley Ann *Physicist, Educator*
Rensselaer Polytechnic Institute,
President's Office, Troy, NY 12180 USA

Jackson, Stonewall *Musician, Music
Group, Songwriter*
6007 Cloverland Dr, Brentwood, TN
37027 USA

Jackson, Stoney *Actor*
3151 Cahuenga Blvd W #310, Los
Angeles, CA 90068 USA

Jackson, Thomas (Tom) *Football Player,
Sportscaster*
ESPN-TV, Sports Dept ESPN Plaza, 935
Middle St, Bristol, CT 06010 USA

Jackson, Thomas Penfield *Judge*
US District Court, 333 Constitution Ave
NW, Washington, DC 20001 USA

Jackson, Tito *Musician, Music Group*
4301 Willow Glen St, Calabasas, CA
91302 USA

Jackson, Tracey *Writer*
Endeavor Agency LLC (LA), 9601 Wilshire
Blvd Fl 3, Beverly Hills, CA 90210 USA

Jackson, Trina *Swimmer*
8727 Hunters Creek Dr S, Jacksonville, FL
32256 USA

Jackson, Victoria *Actor, Comedian*
Agency for Performing Arts, 9200 Sunset
Blvd, #900, Los Angeles, CA 90069 USA

Jackson, Vincent E (Bo) *Baseball Player,
Football Player*
PO Box 158, Mobile, AL 36601 USA

Jackson, Wanda *Musician, Music Group*
Wanda Jackson Enterprises, 8200 S
Pennsylvania Ave, Oklahoma City, OK
73159 USA

Jackson Hoye, Rose *Actor*
Haldeman Business Management, 1137
2nd Street, Santa Monica, CA 90403 USA

Jacob, Francois *Nobel Prize Laureate*
15 Rue de Conde, Paris, 75006, FRANCE

Jacob, Irene *Actor*
Nicole Cann, 1 Rue Alfred du Vigny,
Paris, 75008, FRANCE

Jacob, John E *Social Activist*
National Urban League, 120 Wall St
#700, New York, NY 10005 USA

Jacob, Katerina *Actor*
Agentur Doris Mattes, Merzstr 14,
Munich, 81679 USA

Jacob, Stanley W *Doctor*
1055 SW Westwood Court, Portland, OR
97239 USA

Jacobi, Derek G *Actor*
International Creative Mgmt, 76 Oxford
St, London, W1N OAX, UNITED
KINGDOM (UK)

Jacobi, Lou *Actor*
240 Central Park South, New York, NY
10019 USA

Jacobs, Glenn *Wrestler*
World Wrestling Entertainment (WWE),
1241 E Main St, Stamford, CT 06905 USA

Jacobs, Irwin M *Business Person*
Qualcomm Inc, 5775 Morehouse Dr, San
Deigo, CA 92121 USA

Jacobs, Jack H *War Hero*
Bankers Trust Co, 1 Appold St, London,
EC2A 2HE, UNITED KINGDOM (UK)

Jacobs, Jane *Writer*
Random House, 1745 Broadway #B1,
New York, NY 10019 USA

Jacobs, Jim *Writer*
International Creative Mgmt, 40 W 57th St
#1800, New York, NY 10019 USA

Jacobs, Julien I *Judge*
US Tax Court, 400 2nd St NW,
Washington, DC 20217 USA

Jacobs, Lawrence-Hilton *Actor*
PO Box 67905, Los Angeles, CA 90067
USA

Jacobs, Marc *Fashion Designer*
403 Bleeker St, New York, NY 10014
USA

Jacobs, Norman J *Publisher*
Century Publishing Co, 990 Grove St,
Evanston, IL 60201 USA

Jacobs, Wilfred E *General, Governor*
Government House, Saint John's, Antigua,
ANTIGUA & BARBUDA

Jacobsen, Casey *Basketball Player*
Phoenix Suns, 201 E Jefferson St, Phoenix,
AZ 85004 USA

Jacobsen, Peter *Golfer*
16 Dover Way, Lake Oswego, OR 97034
USA

Jacobsen, Steven C *Engineer*
University of Utah, Engineering Design
Center, Salt Lake City, UT 84112 USA

Jacobson, A Thurl *Geophysicist*
8101 W Silkwood Court, Boise, ID 83704
USA

Jacobson, D D *Bowler*
8261 Rees St, Playa del Rey, CA 90293
USA

Jacobson, Herbert L *Diplomat, Journalist*
Apartado 160, Escazu, COSTA RICA

Jacobson, Nina
Creative Artists Agency LCC (CAA-LA),
9830 Wilshire Blvd, Beverly Hills, CA
90212 USA

Jacobson, Peter *Actor*
Innovative Artists (LA), 1505 Tenth St,
Santa Monica, CA 90401 USA

Jacobson, Scott *Actor*
Creative Artists Agency LCC (CAA-LA),
9830 Wilshire Blvd, Beverly Hills, CA
90212 USA

Jacoby, Billy
PO Box 46324, Los Angeles, CA 90046

Jacoby, Laura
PO Box 46324, Los Angeles, CA 90046

Jacoby, Lowell E *Admiral*
Director Defense Intelligence Agency,
Washington, DC 20340 USA

Jacoby, Scott *Actor*
PO Box 461100, Los Angeles, CA 90046
USA

Jacot, Christopher *Actor*
Schachter Entertainment, 1157 S Beverly
Dr Fl 3, Los Angeles, CA 90035 USA

Jacot, Michele *Skier*
Residence du Brevent, 74 Chamonix,
FRANCE

Jacques, Russell *Artist*
73005 Haystack Road, Palm Desert, CA
92260 USA

Jacuzzi, Roy *Business Person*
Jacuzzi Whirlpool Bath, 2121 N California
Blvd, Walnut Creek, CA 94596 USA

Jadakiss *Music Group, Artist, Musician*
International Creative Mgmt, 8942
Wilshire Blvd, #219, Beverly Hills, CA
90211 USA

Jade
3380 Parkland St., Titusville, FL 32796-
4226

Jadot, Jean L O *Religious Leader*
Ave de l'Atlantique 71-B-12, Brussels,
1150, BELGIUM

Jae, Jana
PO Box 35736, Tulsa, OK 74153

Jaeckin, Just *Director*
8 Villa Mequillet, Neuilly/Seine, 92200,
FRANCE

Jaeger, Andrea *Tennis Player*
Kids Stuff Foundation, Silver Lining Ranch,
1490 S Ute Ave, Aspen, CO 81611 USA

Jaeger, Jeff T *Football Player*
3026 Sahalee Dr W, Sammamish, WA
98074 USA

Jaenicke, Hannes
Goetherstr. 17, Munich, GERMANY,
D-80336

Jaffe, Arthur M *Mathematician*
27 Lancaster St, Cambridge, MA 02140
USA

Jaffe, Herold W *Doctor*
Centers for Disease Control, 1600 Clifton
Road, Atlanta, GA 30333 USA

Jaffe, Robert L *Physicist*
Massachusetts Institute of Technology,
Physics Dept, Cambridge, MA 02139 USA

Jaffe, Rona *Writer*
Janklow & Nesbitt, 445 Park Ave #1300,
New York, NY 10022 USA

Jaffe, Stanley R *Producer, Director*
Lean Building, 10202 Washington Blvd,
Culver City, CA 90232 USA

Jaffe, Susan *Ballerina*
American Ballet Theatre, 890 Broadway,
New York, NY 10003 USA

Jaffrey, Saeed *Actor, Bollywood,
Comedian*
503 Sejal New Link Road, Andheri,
Bombay, MS 400 058, INDIA

Jagan, Janet *President*
65 Plantation Bel Air, East Coast
Demerara, Georgetown, GUYANA

Jagdeo, Bharrat *Prime Minister*
President's Office, Brickham, New Garden
& South Sts, Georgetown, GUYANA

Jagendort, Andre T *Doctor*
455 Savage Farm Dr, Ithaca, NY 14850
USA

Jager, Thomas (Tom) *Swimmer*
745 4th Ave E, Kalispell, MT 59901 USA

Jager, Tom
64 Ramble Wood Blvd., Tijeras, NM 87059

Jagge, Finn Christian *Skier*
Michelets Vei 108, Stabekk, 1320, NORWAY

Jagged Edge *Music Group*
Family Tree Entertainment, 135 E 57th St Fl 26, New York, NY 10022 USA

Jagger, Bianca *Actor, Model*
530 Park Ave #18D, New York, NY 10021 USA

Jagger, Blanca *Actor, Model*
530 Park Ave #18D, New York, NY 10021 USA

Jagger, Mick *Musician*
Marathon Music, 5 Church Row, Wandsworth Plain, London, SW18 1ES, UNITED KINGDOM (UK)

Jagland, Thorbjoern *Prime Minister*
Stortinget, Karl Johans Gate 22, Oslo, 0026, NORWAY

Jaglom, Henry *Director*
9165 W Sunset Blvd #300, Los Angeles, CA 90069 USA

Jagr, Jaromir *Hockey Player*
2548 Appletree Dr, Pittsburgh, PA 15241 USA

Jaguares *Music Group*
BMG, 1540 Broadway, New York, NY 10036 USA

Jahan, Marine *Actor, Dancer*
Media Artists Group, 6300 Wilshire Blvd #1470, Los Angeles, CA 90048 USA

Jaheim *Musician*
Diane Mill, 100 Evergreen Point #402, East Orange, NJ 07018 USA

Jahn, Helmut *Architect*
Murphy/Jahn, 35 E Wacker Dr, Chicago, IL 60601 USA

Jahn, Robert G *Engineer*
Princeton University, Aerospace Sciences Dept, Princeton, NJ 08544 USA

Jahn, Sigmund *Astronaut, General, Misc*
Fontanestr 35, Strausberg, 15344, GERMANY

Jai *Musician, Music Group, Songwriter*
Evolution Talent, 1776 Broadway #1500, New York, NY 10019 USA

Jaidah, Ali Mohammed *Government Official*
Qatar Petroleum Corp, PO Box 3212, Doha, QATAR

Jaime, Bergman
8383 Wilshire Blvd #550, Beverly Hills, CA 90211

Jaitley, Celina *Beauty Pageant Winner*
Miss Universe Organization, The, 1370 Ave of the Americas Fl 16, New York, NY 10019 USA

Jakel, Bernd *Yachtsman*
Salvador-Allende-Str 48, Berlin, 12559, GERMANY

Jakes, Bishop T D *Musician*
Creative Artists Agency LCC (CAA-LA), 9830 Wilshire Blvd, Beverly Hills, CA 90212 USA

Jakes, T D *Religious Leader*
Potter's House, 6777 W Kiest Blvd, Dallas, TX 75211 USA

Jaki, Stanley L *Physicist, Misc*
PO Box 167, Princeton, NJ 08542 USA

Jakobs, Marco *Athlete*
Oststr 1B, Unna, 59427, GERMANY

Jakobson, Maggie *Actor*
Writers & Artists, 8383 Wilshire Blvd #550, Beverly Hills, CA 90211 USA

Jakobson, Max *Journalist, Government Official*
Rahapajankatu 3B 17, Helsinki 16, 00160, FINLAND

Jakosits, Michael *Misc*
Karlsbergstr 140, Homburg/Saar, 66424, GERMANY

Jakub, Lisa *Actor*
Metropolitan Talent Agency, 4526 Wilshire Blvd, Los Angeles, CA 90010 USA

Jalal, Farida *Actor, Bollywood*
3B Nandini Unik Housing Society, Opp Bon Bon J P Road Andheri, Mumbai, MS 400058, INDIA

Jalbert, Pierre
2642 N. Beverly Glen Blvd, Los Angeles, CA 90077

Jamail, Joseph D Jr *Attorney General*
Jamail & Kolius, 500 Dallas St #3434, Houston, TX 77002 USA

Jamal, Ahmad *Musician, Music Group*
Brad Simon Organization, 122 E 57th St #300, New York, NY 10022 USA

Jambor, Agi *Musician, Music Group*
1616 Bolton St, Baltimore, MD 21217 USA

James, Anthony *Actor*
CNA Assoc, 1875 Century Park East, #2250, Los Angeles, CA 90067 USA

James, Boney *Musician*
Monterey Peninsula Artists (Monterey), 509 Hartnell St, Monterey, CA 93940 USA

James, Charmayne *Misc*
Gold Buckle Ranch, 2100 N Highway 360 #1207, Grand Prairie, TX 75050 USA

James, Cheryl (Salt) *Musician, Music Group, Artist*
Famous Artists Agency, 250 W 57th St, New York, NY 10107 USA

James, Clifton *Actor*
500 W 43rd St #25D, New York, NY 10036 USA

James, Clive V L *Journalist, Misc*
P F D, Drury House, 34-43 Russell St, London, WC2B 5HA, UNITED KINGDOM (UK)

James, Craig *Football Player*
12714 W FM 455, Celina, TX 75009 USA

James, D Clayton *Historian*
106 Wagon Wheel Trail, Moneta, VA 24121 USA

James, Dalton
303 N. Buena Vista #209, Burbank, CA 91505-3686

James, Don *Football Coach*
7047 Chanticleer Ave SE, Snoqualmie, WA 98065 USA

James, Donald M *Business Person*
Vulcan Materials Co, 1200 Urban Center Dr, Birmingham, AL 35242 USA

James, Duncan *Musician*
Concorde Intl Artists Ltd, 101 Shepherds Bush Rd, London, W6 7LP, UNITED KINGDOM (UK)

James, Edgerrin *Football Player*
709 Hendry St, Immokalee, FL 34142 USA

James, Etta *Musician, Music Group*
16409 Sally Lane, Riverside, CA 92504 USA

James, Forrest H (Fob) Jr *Governor*
39 Alabama Road, Lehigh Acres, FL 33936 USA

James, G Larry *Track Athlete*
Stockton State College, Athletic Dept, Pomona, NJ 08240 USA

James, Geraldine *Actor*
Julian Belfarge, 46 Albermarle St, London, W1X 4PP, UNITED KINGDOM (UK)

James, Godfrey
The Shack Western Rd. Pevensey Bay, E. Sussex, ENGLAND

James, Jesse *Actor*
Coast to Coast Talent, 3350 Barham Blvd, Los Angeles, CA 90068 USA

James, Jessie
Box 1271, Lutz, FL 33549

James, John *Actor*
PO Box 9, Cambridge, NY 12816 USA

James, Joni *Musician, Music Group*
PO Box 7027, Westchester, IL 60154 USA

James, Kate *Model*
Men/Women Model Inc, 199 Lafayette St, New York, NY 10012 USA

James, Kevin *Actor, Comedian*
1471 E Mosherville Road, Jonesville, MI 49250 USA

James, Larry D *Astronaut*
AFELM, USS Space Command, Peterson Air Force Base, CP, 80914 USA

James, LeBron *Basketball Player*
GAP Communications, 5000 Euclid Ave #400, Cleveland, OH 44103 USA

James, Oliver *Actor, Musician*
Firm, The, 9465 Wilshire Blvd, Beverly Hills, CA 90212 USA

James, Oscar *Stylist*
Ken Barboza Associates, 853 Broadway #1603, New York, NY 10003 USA

James, P D *Writer*
Elaine Greene Ltd, 37A Goldhawk Road, London, W12 8QQ, UNITED KINGDOM (UK)

James, Ralph
205 S. Arnaz Dr. #4, Beverly Hills, CA 90211

James, Robert (Bob) *Musician, Music Group, Songwriter*
Monterey International, 200 W Superior #202, Chicago, IL 60610 USA

James, Ryan *Actor*
Stein Entertainment Group, 11271 Ventura Blvd #477, Studio City, CA 91604 USA

James, Sheila *Actor*
3201 Pearl St, Santa Monica, CA 90405 USA

James, Sheryl *Journalist*
Saint Petersburg Times, Editorial Dept, 490 1st Ave, Saint Petersburg, FL 33701 USA

James, Sonny *Musician, Music Group, Songwriter*
McFadden Artists, 818 18th Ave S, Nashville, TN 37203 USA

James, Stanislaus A *Governor, General*
Government House, Morue, Castries, SAINT LUCIA

James, Tommy *Musician, Music Group*
Aura Entertainment, PO Box 4354, Clifton, NJ 07012 USA

James of Holland Park, Phyllis D *Writer*
Elaine Green Ltd, 37A Goldhawk Road, London, W12 SQQ, UNITED KINGDOM (UK)

James-Roadman, Charmayne *Misc*
General Delivery, Clayton, NM 88415 USA

Jameson, Elizabeth M (Betty) *Golfer*
514 SW 20th St, Boynton Beach, FL 33426 USA

Jameson, Jenna *Adult Film Star*
Alley Katz Enterprises, 9899 Santa Monica Blvd #606, Beverly Hills, CA 90212

Jameson, Louise
18-21 Jermyn St., London, ENGLAND, SW1Y 6HP

Jameson, Paulene
7 Warrington Gardens, London, ENGLAND, W9 2QB

Jamieson, John K *Business Person*
10313 Stanley Circle, Minneapolis, MN 55437 USA

Jamiroquai
151 El Camino Dr., Beverly Hills, CA 90212

Jamison, Antawn *Basketball Player*
Dallas Mavericks, 2909 Taylor St, Dallas, TX 75226 USA

Jamison, Jayne *Publisher*
Redbook Magazine, 224 W 57th St, New York, NY 10019 USA

Jamison, Judith *Dancer, Choreographer*
Alvin Ailey American Dance Foundation, 211 W 61st St #300, New York, NY 10023 USA

Jamison, Mae
PO Box 580317, Houston, TX 77258-0317

Jamison, Milo
1231 Tennyson St, Manhattan Beach, CA 90266

Jammeh, Yahya A J J *Misc*
President's Office, State House, Banjul, GAMBIA

Jammer, Quentin *Football Player*
San Diego Chargers, 4020 Murphy Canyon Road, San Diego, CA 92123 USA

Jampolsky, Gerald *Writer*
Celestial Arts, PO Box 7123, Berkeley, CA 94707

Jan & Dean
221 Main St. #P, Huntington Beach, CA 92648

Janakaraj *Actor*
8 H D Raja Street, Teynampet, Chennai, TN 600 018, INDIA

Janaki, Sowcar *Actor, Bollywood*
13 Cenetop Road, 2nd Street, Chennai, TN 600018, INDIA

Jance, J A *Writer*
Avon/William Morrow, 1350 Ave of Americas, New York, NY 10019 USA

Jancso, Miklos *Director*
Solyom Laszio Utca 17, Budapest II, 1022, HUNGARY

Janda, Krystyna *Actor*
Teatr Powszechny, UI Zamoyskiego 20, Warsaw, POLAND

Jande, Marine *Actor*
Gilla Roos, 16 West 22nd Street, 3rd Floor, New York, NY 10010

Jane, Thomas *Actor*
Kelly Bush, 3859 Cardiff Ave #200, Culver City, CA 90232 USA

Janeway, Elizabeth H *Writer*
350 E 79th St, New York, NY 10021 USA

Janeway, Michael C *Editor*
Northwestern University, Fisk Hall, Evanston, IL 60201 USA

Janeway, Richard *Doctor*
PO Box 188, Blowing Rock, NC 28605 USA

Janikowski, Sebastian *Football Player*
Oakland Raiders, 1220 Harbor Bay Parkway, Alameda, CA 94502 USA

Janis, Byron *Musician, Music Group*
Columbia Artists Mgmt Inc, 165 W 57th St, New York, NY 10019 USA

Janis, Conrad *Actor, Musician, Music Group*
1434 N Genesee Ave, Los Angeles, CA 90046 USA

Janis, Ryan *Actor*
Stein Entertainment Group, 11271 Ventura Blvd #477, Studio City, CA 91604 USA

Janitz, John A *Business Person*
Textron Inc, 40 Westminster St, Providence, RI 02903 USA

Jankowska-Cieslak, Jadwiga *Actor*
Film Polski, UI Mazewiecka 6/8, Warsaw, 00-950, POLAND

Jankowski, Gene F *Television Host*
American Film Institute, 901 15th St NW #700, Washington, DC 20005 USA

Jannazzo, Izzy *Boxer*
6924 62nd Ave, Flushing, NY 11379 USA

Janney, Allison *Actor*
Paradigm Agency, 10100 Santa Monica Blvd #2500, Los Angeles, CA 90067 USA

Janney, Craig H *Hockey Player*
3 Overhill Road, Enfield, CT 06082 USA

Janov, Arthur *Philanthropist, Psychic*
1205 Abbot Kinney Blvd, Venice, CA 90291 USA

Janowicz, Josh *Actor*
Darren Goldberg Management, 5225 Wilshire Blvd #419, Los Angeles, CA 90036

Janowitz, Gundula *Opera Singer*
3072 Kasten, 75, AUSTRIA

Janowitz, Tama *Writer*
Doubleday Press, 1540 Broadway, New York, NY 10036 USA

Janowski, Marek *Conductor*
I M G Artists, 3 Burlington Lane, Chiswick, London, W4 2TH, UNITED KINGDOM (UK)

Janseen, Daniel *Business Person*
Solvay & Cie, 33 Rue du Prince Albert, Brussels, 1050, BELGIUM

Janseen, Famke *Actor, Model*
Creative Artists Agency, 9830 Wilshire Blvd, Beverly Hills, CA 90212 USA

Jansen, Daniel E (Dan) *Speed Skater*
PO Box 567, Greendale, WI 53129 USA

Jansen, Lawrence J (Larry) *Baseball Player*
3207 NW Highway 47, Forest Grove, OR 97116 USA

Jansen, Raymond A *Publisher*
Newsday Inc, 235 Pinelawn Road, Melville, NY 11747 USA

Jansons, Mariss *Conductor*
I M G Artists, 3 Burlington Lane, Chiswick, London, W4 2TH, UNITED KINGDOM (UK)

Janssen, Dani
2220 Avenue of the Stars #2803, Los Angeles, CA 90067

Janssen, Famke *Actor, Model*
Industry Entertainment, 955 Carillo Dr, #300, Los Angeles, CA 90048 USA

Jantz, Richard *Misc*
University of Tennessee, Anthropology Dept, Knoxville, TN 37996 USA

January, Don *Golfer*
14316 Hughes Lane, Dallas, TX 75254 USA

January, Lois *Actor*
PO Box 1233, Beverly Hills, CA 90213 USA

Jany, Alexandre (Alex) *Swimmer*
104 Blvd Livon, Marseille, 13007, FRANCE

Janzen, Daniel H *Biologist*
University of Pennsylvania, Biology Dept, Philadelphia, PA 19104 USA

Janzen, Edmund *Religious Leader*
General Conference of Mennonite Brethren, 8000 W 21st St, Wichita, KS 67205 USA

Janzen, Lee *Golfer*
9088 Point Cypress Dr, Orlando, FL 32836 USA

Jardine, Al
Box 36, Big Sur, CA 93920

Jardine, Alan C (Al) *Musician*
PO Box 36, Big Sur, CA 93920 USA

Jarecki, Andrew *Director, Producer, Musician*
Hit the Ground Running Films, 200 W 57th St #1304, New York, NY 10019 USA

Jarman Jr, Claude *Actor*
11 Dos Encinas, Orinda, CA 94563 USA

Jarmusch, Jim *Director*
Exoskeleton Inc, 208 E 6th St, New York, NY 10003 USA

Jarre, Maurice A *Musician, Composer*
27011 Sea Vista Dr, Malibu, CA 90265 USA

Jarreau, Al *Musician*
Patrick Rains, 29161 Grayfox St, Malibu, CA 90265 USA

Jarrell, Tom
77 W. 66th St., New York, NY 10023

Jarrett, Dale *Race Car Driver*
1510 46th Ave NE, Hickory, NC 28601 USA

Jarrett, Keith *Musician, Composer*
Stephen Cloud, PO Box 4774, Santa Barbara, CA 93140 USA

Jarrett, Ned
3182 Ninth Tee Dr., Newton, NC 28658

Jarrett, Ned M *Race Car Driver*
Ned Jarrett Enterprises, RR 1 Box 160, Newton, NC 28658 USA

Jarrett, Will *Editor*
Dallas Times Herald, Editorial Dept, Herald Square, Dallas, TX 75202 USA

Jarriel, Thomas E (Tom) *Commentator*
ABC-TV, News Dept, 77 W 66th St, New York, NY 10023 USA

Jarrier, Jean-Pierre
17 bd. Larvotto, Monte Carlo, MONACO

Jarrott, Charles *Director*
4314 Marina City Dr, #418, Marina del Rey, CA 90292 USA

Jarryd, Anders *Tennis Player*
Maaneskoldsgatan 37, Lidkoping, 531 00, SWEDEN

Jars of Clay *Music Group*
Creative Artists Agency LCC (CAA-LA), 9830 Wilshire Blvd, Beverly Hills, CA 90212 USA

Jaru the Damaja *Musician*
William Morris Agency, 1325 Ave of Americas, New York, NY 10019 USA

Jaruzelski, Wojciech *President, General*
Biuro Bylego, Al Jerozolimskie 91, Warsaw, 02-001, POLAND

Jarvi, Neeme *Conductor*
PO Box 305, Sea Bright, NJ 07760 USA

Jarvi, Paavo *Conductor*
Cincinnati Symphony, Music Hall, 1241 Elm St, Cincinnati, OH 45202 USA

Jarvis, Doug *Hockey Player*
812 Crane Dr, Coppell, TX 75019 USA

Jarvis, Graham
15351 Via De Las Olas, Pacific Palisades, CA 90272

Jarvis, Lucy
171 W. 57th St., New York, NY 10019

Jarvis, Martin
2-4 Noel St., London, ENGLAND, W1V 3RB

Jason, Harvey
1280 Sunset Plaza Dr, Los Angeles, CA 90069

Jason, Sybil *Actor*
PO Box 40024, Studio City, CA 91614 USA

Jason Shane, Scott
Agency for the Performing Arts, 9200 Sunset Blvd #900, Los Angeles, CA 90069

Jasrai, Puntsagiin *Prime Minister*
Prime Minister's Office, Ulan Bator, MONGOLIA

Jastremski, Chet *Swimmer*
1920 E 3rd St, Bloomington, IN 47401 USA

Jastrow, Robert *Physicist, Writer*
Mount Wilson Observatory, 740 Holladay Road, Pasadena, CA 91106 USA

Jastrow, Terry L *Director*
13201 Old Oak Lane, Los Angeles, CA 90049 USA

Jastrow II, Kenneth M *Business Person*
Temple-Inland Inc, 303 S Temple Dr, Diboll, TX 75941 USA

Jathar, Anjali *Actor, Bollywood*
Anand Ashram 1st Floor Building 22, Pandita Rambai Road Gamdevi, Mumbai, MS 400007, INDIA

Jatoi, Ghulan Mustafa *Prime Minister*
Jatoi House, 18 Khayaban-E-Shamsheer Housing, #V, Karachi, PAKISTAN

Jaumotte, Andre *Engineer*
33 Ave jeanne Bte 17, Brussels, 1050, BELGIUM

Jauron, Dick M *Football Player, Football Coach*
1921 W Salisbury Lane, Lake Forest, IL 60045 USA

Javan, Ali *Physicist*
12 Hawthome St, Cambridge, MA 02138 USA

Javed, Miandad Khan *Cricketer*
Pakistani Crciket Control Board, Gaddafi Stadium, Lahore, PAKISTAN

Javerbaum, David *Writer*
3 Arts Entertainment Inc, 9460 Wilshire Blvd Fl 7, Beverly Hills, CA 90212 USA

Javier Galvan Y Fama *Music Group*
Sony Music Miami, 605 Lincoln Rd, Miami Beach, FL 33138 USA

Javierre Ortas, Antonio M Cardinal *Religious Leader*
Via Rusticucci 13, Rome, 00193, ITALY

Jaworski, Marian Cardinal *Religious Leader*
Mytropolycha Kuria Latynskoho, Ploscha Katedraina 1, 29008, UKRAINE

Jaworski, Ron
8 Silver Hill Lane, West Berlin, NJ 08043

Jaworski, Ronald V (Ron) *Football Player, Sportscaster*
200 Golfview Dr, Blackwood, NJ 08012 USA

Jay, Joseph R (Joey) *Baseball Player*
7209 Battenwood Court, Tampa, FL 33615 USA

Jay, Ken *Musician*
Andy Gould Mgmt, 9100 Wilshire Blvd, #400W, Beverly Hills, CA 90212 USA

Jay, Natalie
6230 Wilshire Blvd. #153, Los Angeles, CA 90048

Jay, Peter *Government Official*
Hensington Farmhouse, Woodstock, Oxon, OX20 1LH, UNITED KINGDOM (UK)

Jay, Ricky *Actor*
Simone, 1790 Broadway, #1000, New York, NY 10019 USA

Jay, Tony *Actor*
Pakula/King & Associates, 9229 Sunset Blvd #315, Los Angeles, CA 90069 USA

Jay & The Americans
1045 Pomme De Pin Dr, New Port Ritchey, FL 34655

Jay & The Techniques
4250 AIA South #D-11, St. Augustine, FL 32080-7431

Jay-Z *Musician*
Ujaama Entertainment Inc, 261 West 35th Street, Suite 801, New York, NY 10001 USA

Jay-Z *Musician, Songwriter*
Diaama Ent, 261 W 35th St, #801, New York, NY 10001 USA

Jaya Pradha *Actor, Bollywood*
202 Juhu Princes Juhu Beach, Juhu, Bombay, MS 400 049, INDIA

Jayabharathi *Actor, Bollywood*
75 4th Cross Street, Loghia Colony Saligramam, Chennai, TN 600093, INDIA

Jayachitra *Actor, Bollywood*
Lynwood Avenue 9 Lady Madhavan Nair Road, Mahalingapuram Gandhi Nagar, Chennai, TN 600093, INDIA

Jayamalini *Actor, Bollywood*
1 1st Mail Road, Thirunagar, Chennai, TN 600026, INDIA

Jayanthi *Actor, Bollywood*
873 19th Main Bana Shankari, II Stage, Bangalore, KA, 500070, INDIA

Jayapradha *Actor, Bollywood*
1 Hindi Prachara Sabha Road, T Nagar, Chennai, TN 600017, INDIA

Jayasudha *Actor, Bollywood*
Veenas Colony, 9-13 II Street, Chennai, TN 600018, INDIA

Jayne, Billy
8521 Nash Dr., Los Angeles, CA 90046

Jayston, Michael *Actor*
Michael Whitehall, 125 Gloucester Road, London, SW7 4TE, UNITED KINGDOM (UK)

Jazz Crusaders, The *Music Group*
Universal, 225 W 57th St, Floor 5, New York, NY 10019

Jbara, Gregory *Actor*
Silver Massetti & Szatmary (SMS-LA), 8730 Sunset Blvd #440, Los Angeles, CA 90069 USA

JBJ *Musician*
Q Prime, 729 7th Ave, #1600, New York, NY 10019 USA

Jean *Royalty*
Grand Ducal Palace, PB 331, 2013, LUXEMBOURG

Jean, Gloria *Actor, Musician*
3844 W Channel Islands Blvd, #166, Oxnard, CA 93035 USA

Jean, Wyclef *Musician*
William Morris Agency, 1325 Ave of Americas, New York, NY 10019 USA

Jean-Baptiste, Marianne *Actor*
Innovative Artists, 1505 10th St, Santa Monica, CA 90401 USA

Jean-Paul, Gaultier *Fashion Designer*
Jean-Paul Gaultier SA, 70 Galerie Vivienne, Paris, 75002, FRANCE

Jeangerard, Robert (Bob) *Basketball Player*
1930 Belmont Ave, San Carlos, CA 94070 USA

Jeanmaire, ZiZi *Actor, Ballerina*
Ballets Roland Petit, 20 Blvd Gabes, Marseilles, 13008, FRANCE

Jeanrenaud, Joan *Musician*
Kronos Quartet, 1235 9th Ave, San Francisco, CA 94122 USA

Jeantot, Philippe *Yachtsman*
Jeantot Organization, Siege: BP 01, Les Sables D'Olonne, 85100, FRANCE

Jee, Elizabeth *Actor*
Commercials Unlimited, 8383 Wilshire Blvd, #850, Beverly Hills, CA 90211 USA

Jee, Rupert *Business Person*
Hello Deli, 213 West 53rd Street, New York, NY 10019

Jeetendra *Actor, Bollywood*
Plot No 26 Greater Bombay Co-Op Society, Gulmohar Cross Road No 5 JVPD Scheme, Mumbai, MS 400049, INDIA

Jeffcoat, Don *Actor*
House of Representatives, 400 S Beverly Dr #101, Beverly Hills, CA 90212 USA

Jeffcoat, James W (Jim) *Football Player*
5135 Summit Hill Dr, Dallas, TX 75287 USA

Jeffers, Eve Jihan *Actor*
William Morris Agency (WMA-LA), 1 William Morris Pl, Beverly Hills, CA 90212 USA

Jeffers, Rusty *Athlete*
PO Box 30081, Phoenix, AZ 85024

Jefferson, George *Track Athlete*
9414 Petit Circle, Ventura, CA 93004 USA

Jefferson, John L *Football Player*
21272 Victorias Cross Terrace, Ashbum, VA 20147 USA

Jefferson, Margo *Journalist*
New York Times, Editorial Dept, 229 W 43rd St, New York, NY 10036 USA

Jefferson, Reggie *Baseball Player*
Cincinnati Reds, 2693 Miccosukee Rd, Tallahassee, FL 32308-5412 USA

Jefferson, Richard *Basketball Player*
New Jersey Nets, 390 Murray Hill Parkway, East Rutherford, NJ 07073 USA

Jefferson, Stan *Baseball Player*
New York Mets, 2420 Hunter Ave Apt 3E, Bronx, NY 10475-5644 USA

Jefferson Starship *Music Group*
Mission Control, 15030 Ventura Blvd #541, Sherman Oaks, CA 91403 USA

Jeffre, Justin *Musician*
DAS Communications, 83 Riverside Dr, New York, NY 10024 USA

Jeffrey, Arthur F *War Hero*
752 Juniper Glen Court, Ballwin, MO 08540 USA

Jeffrey, Richard C *Misc*
55 Patton Ave, Princeton, NJ 08540 USA

Jeffreys, Anne *Actor*
18915 Nordhoff St, #5, Northridge, CA 91324 USA

Jeffreys, Harold *Astronomer*
160 Huntingdon Road, Cambridge, CB3 0LB, UNITED KINGDOM (UK)

Jeffries, Chris *Basketball Player*
Toronto Raptors, Air Canada Center, 40 Bay St, Toronto, ON M5J 2NB, CANADA

Jeffries, Herb *Musician*
Flaming-O Productions, 44489 Town Center Way, Palm Desert, CA 92260 USA

Jeffries, Jared *Basketball Player*
Washington Wizards, MCI Centre, 601 F St NW, Washington, DC 20004 USA

Jeffries, John T *Astronomer*
1652 E Camino Cieto, Tucson, AZ 85718 USA

Jeffries, Lionel *Actor, Director*
International Creative Mgmt, 76 Oxford St, London, ENGLAND, W1N 0AX, UNITED KINGDOM (UK)

Jelic, Chris *Baseball Player*
New York Mets, 88 Forest Glen Dr, Imperial, PA 15126-9673 USA

Jelks, Greg
Philadelphia Phillies, 615 Bay Springs Rd, Centre, AL 35960-1212 USA

Jellicoe, George P J R *Government Official*
Tidcombe Manor, Tidcombe near Marlborough, Wilts, SN8 2SL, UNITED KINGDOM (UK)

Jeltz, Steve *Baseball Player*
Philadelphia Phillies, 10211 Ura Ln, Denver, CO 80260-6360 USA

Jemison, Antawn *Basketball Player*
Washington Wizards, MCI Centre, 601 F St NW, Washington, DC 20004 USA

Jemison, Eddie *Actor*
Schachter Entertainment, 1157 S Beverly Dr Fl 3, Los Angeles, CA 90035 USA

Jemison, Mae C *Astronaut*
Dartmouth College, Environment Studies Dept, Hanover, NH 03755 USA

Jemison, Theodore J *Religious Leader*
National Bapist Convention USA, 1620 White's Creek Pike, Nashville, TN 37207 USA

Jencks, William P *Misc*
11 Revere St, Lexington, MA 02420 USA

Jendresen, Erik *Writer*
CAA, 9830 Wilshire Blvd, Beverly Hills, CA 90212

Jenes Jr, Theodore G *General*
809 169th Place SW, Lynnwood, WA 98037 USA

Jeni, Richard *Comedian*
Agency for the Performing Arts (APA-LA), 9200 Sunset Blvd #900, Los Angeles, CA 90069 USA

Jenifer, Franklyn G *Educator*
University of Texas at Dallas, President's Office, Richardson, TX 75083 USA

Jenkin of Roding, Patrick F *Government Official*
703 Howard House, Dolphin Square, London, SW1V 3PQ, UNITED KINGDOM (UK)

Jenkins, Alfred *Football Player*
2993 Cascade Road SW, Atlanta, GA 30311 USA

Jenkins, Alfred le Sesne *Diplomat*
Stalsama High Knob, PO Box 586, Front Royal, VA 22630 USA

Jenkins, Bill *Race Car Driver*
Jenkins Competition, 153 Pennsylvania Ave, Malvern, PA 19335-2419

Jenkins, Bill (Grumpy) *Misc*
Jenkins Competition, 153 Pennsylvania Ave, Malvern, PA 19355 USA

Jenkins, Charlie *Track Athlete*
Once RCA Dome, Indianapolis, IN 46225

Jenkins, Daniel *Actor*
S M S Talent, 8730 Sunset Blvd, #440, Los Angeles, CA 90069 USA

Jenkins, David W *Figure Skater*
5947 S Atlanta Ave, Tulsa, OK 74105 USA

Jenkins, Dean *Hockey Player*
405 Great Rd #10, Acton, MA 01720

Jenkins, Don J *War Hero*
3783 Bowling Green Road, Morgantown, KY 42261 USA

Jenkins, Ferguson *Baseball Player*
Philadelphia Phillies, 41913 N Signal Hill Ct, Phoenix, AZ 85086-1919 USA

Jenkins, Geoff *Baseball Player*
Colorado Rockies, 3637 E Marlette Ave, Paradise Valley, AZ 85253-3829 USA

Jenkins, George *Designer, Director*
740 Kingman Ave, Santa Monica, CA 90402 USA

Jenkins, Hayes Alan *Figure Skater*
3183 Regency Place, Westlake, OH 44145 USA

Jenkins, Jackie
Rt. #6 Box 541-G, Fairview, NC 28730

Jenkins, Jerry B *Writer*
Tyndale House Publishers, 351 Executive Dr, PO Box 80, Wheaton, IL 60189 USA

Jenkins, Kackie (Butch) *Actor*
PO Box 541G, Fairview, NC 28730 USA

Jenkins, Ken *Actor*
NBC Entertainment Publicity, 3000 West Alameda Avenue, #350, Burbank, CA

Jenkins, Kris *Football Player*
Carolina Panthers, Ericsson Stadium, 800 S Mint St, Charlotte, NC 28202 USA

Jenkins, Loren *Journalist*
Washington Post, Editorial Dept, 1150 15th St NW, Washington, DC 20071 USA

Jenkins, Patty *Director, Writer*
Junction Films, 415 N Camden Dr, Beverly Hills, CA 90210 USA

Jenkins, Paul *Artist*
Image Terrae, PO Box 6833, Yorkville Station, New York, NY 10128 USA

Jenkins, Richard *Actor*
Gersh Agency, The (LA), 232 N Canon Dr, Beverly Hills, CA 90210 USA

Jenkins, Stephan *Musician*
Eric Godtland Mgmt, 5715 Claremont Ave, #C, Oakland, CA 94618 USA

Jenner, Bruce *Actor, Track Athlete*
2345 Elbury Court, Thousand Oaks, CA 91361 USA

Jenney, Lucinda
1505 10th Street, Santa Monica, CA 90401

Jennings, Bill *Baseball Player*
St Louis Browns, 7065 Foxcroft Dr, Affton, MO 63123-1648 USA

Jennings, Dave *Football Player*
1 Briarcliffe Rd, Upper Saddle River, NJ 07458-9434

Jennings, David T (Dave) *Football Player*
1 Briarcliff Road, Upper Saddle River, NJ 07458 USA

Jennings, Delbert O *War Hero*
3701 25th Way SE, Olympia, WA 98501 USA

Jennings, Doug
Oakland A's, 3030 Canterbury Dr, Boca Raton, FL 33434-3348 USA

Jennings, Jason *Baseball Player*
Colorado Rockies, 9284 S Cedar Hill Way, Lone Tree, CO 80124-5403 USA

Jennings, Lynn *Track Athlete*
17 Cushing Road, Newmarket, NH 03857 USA

Jennings, Paul C *Engineer*
640 S Grand Ave, Pasadena, CA 91105 USA

Jennings, Peter *Journalist*
World News Tonight with Peter Jennings, 47 W 66th St Fl 2, New York, NY 10023-6201 USA

Jennings, Peter C *Commentator*
ABC-TV, News Dept, 47 W 66th St, New York, NY 10023 USA

Jennings, Robert B *Doctor*
Duke University, Medical Center, Pathology Dept, Durham, NC 27710 USA

Jennings, Robert Y *Judge*
61 Bridle Way, Grantchester, Cambridge, CB3 9NY, UNITED KINGDOM (UK)

Jennings, Robin *Baseball Player*
Chicago Cubs, 7773 Shootingstar Drive, Sprinfield, VA 22152 USA

Jennings, Shooter
824 Old Hickory Blvd., Brentwood, TN 37027

Jennings, Will *Songwriter*
Gorfaine/Schwartz, 13245 Riverside Dr, #450, Sherman Oaks, CA 91423 USA

Jenrette, Richard H *Business Person*
67 E 93rd St, New York, NY 10128 USA

Jens, Salome *Actor*
Badgley Connor Talent, 9229 Sunset Blvd #311, Los Angeles, CA 90069 USA

Jens, Walter *Writer*
Sonnenstr 5, Tubingen, GERMANY

Jensen, Arthur R *Misc*
30 Canyon View Dr, Orinda, CA 94563 USA

Jensen, Dan
PO Box 567, Greendale, WI 53129

Jensen, Debra *Model*
31441 Santa Margarita Pkwy #322, Rancho Santa Margarita, CA 92688

Jensen, Elwood V *Misc*
Karolinska Institute, Medical Nutrition Dept, Huddinge, 141 86, SWEDEN

Jensen, James *Misc*
Brigham Young University, Geology Dept, Provo, UT 84602 USA

Jensen, Karen *Actor*
9363 Wilshire Blvd, #212, Beverly Hills, CA 90210 USA

Jensen, Luke *Tennis Player*
370 Ferry Landing NW, Atlanta, GA 30328

Jensen, Marcus *Baseball Player*
San Francisco Giants, 19550 N Grayhawk Dr Unit 1134, Scottsdale, AZ 85255-3987 USA

Jensen, Maren *Actor*
Kessler & Schneider Co, 15260 Ventura Blvd, Suite 1040, Somerset, CA 91403

Jensen, Roger W *Senator*
3542 Pennyroyal Road, Port Charlotte, FL 33953 USA

Jensen, Ryan *Baseball Player*
San Francisco Giants, 4070 Petersen Ln, West Valley, UT 84120-3256 USA

Jensen Jr, James W *Cinematographer*
28853 Garnet Hill Court, Agoura Hills, CA 91301 USA

Jeremiah, David E *Admiral*
2898 Melanie Lane, Oakton, VA 22124 USA

Jeremy, Ron *Adult Film Star*
Coast II Coast Entertainment (LA), 3350 Wilshire Blvd, Suite 1200, Los Angeles, CA 90010 USA

Jericho, Chris (Y2J) *Wrestler*
World Wrestling Entertainment (WWE), 1241 E Main St, Stamford, CT 06905 USA

Jerkens, H Allen *Horse Racer*
9509 242nd St, Floral Park, NY 11001 USA

Jermann, David *Artist*
2 Union St, Sparkill, NY 10976

Jernberg, Sixten *Skier*
Fritidsby 780, Lima, 7806, SWEDEN

Jernigan, Tamara E (Tammy) *Astronaut*
4268 Brindisi Place, Pleasanton, CA 94566 USA

Jerusalem, Siegfried *Opera Singer*
Sudring 9, Eckental, 90542, GERMANY

Jeruzelski, Wojciech *President*
Bluro Bylego, Al Jerozolimskie 91, Warsaw, 02-001, POLAND

Jerzembeck, Mike *Baseball Player*
New York Yankees, 22011 Hartland Ave, Queens Village, NY 11427-1227 USA

Jessee, Michael A *Financier*
Federal Home Loan Bank, 1 Financial Center, Boston, MA 02111 USA

Jestadt, Garry *Baseball Player*
Montreal Expos, 9495 E San Salvador Dr Ste 100, Scottsdale, AZ 85258-5553 USA

Jester, Virgil *Baseball Player*
Boston Braves, 8130 Raleigh Pl, Westminster, CO 80031-4317 USA

Jester, Virgil *Baseball Player*
Boston Braves, 8130 Raleigh Pl, Westminster, CO 80031-4317, u

Jeter, Derek *Baseball Player*
New York Yankees, 17005 Candeleda De Avila, Tampa, FL 33613-5213 USA

Jeter, Gary M *Football Player*
32725 Shadowbrook Dr, Solon, OH 44139 USA

Jeter, John *Baseball Player*
Pittsburgh Pirates, 4717 Murdock Ave, Bronx, NY 10466-1011 USA

Jeter, Robert D (Bob) *Football Player*
7147 S Paxton Ave, Chicago, IL 60649 USA

Jeter, Shawn *Baseball Player*
Chicago White Sox, 4287 Walford St, Columbus, OH 43224-2342 USA

Jethro Tull *Music Group*
William Morris Agency (WMA-LA), 1 William Morris Pl, Beverly Hills, CA 90212 USA

Jets, The *Music Group*
Lustig Talent Enterprises, PO Box 770850, Orlando, FL 32877

Jetsons *Music Group*
Signature Entertainment, Suite 3, 5727 Topanga Canyon, Woodland Hills, CA 91367

Jett, Brent W *Astronaut*
1120 Texas St, #4C, Houston, TX 77002 USA

Jeunet, Jean-Pierre *Director*
International Creative Mgmt, 8942 Wilshire Blvd, #219, Beverly Hills, CA 90211 USA

Jevanord, Oystein *Musician*
Bandana Mgmt, 11 Elvaston Place, #300, London, SW7 5QC, UNITED KINGDOM (UK)

Jewel *Songwriter, Musician, Actor*
PO Box 1388, Brea, CA 92822 USA

Jewell, Buddy *Musician*
William Morris Agency (WMA-TN), 2100 W End Ave #1000, Nashville, TN 37203 USA

Jewison, Norman F *Director, Producer, Actor, Writer*
Yorktown Productions Ltd, 18 Gloucester Ln, Floor 5, Toronto ON, M4Y 1L5, CANADA

Jhabvala, Ruth Prawer *Writer*
400 E 52nd St, New York, NY 10022 USA

Jhene *Musician*
Ultimate Group, The, 848 N La Cienega Blvd #201, W Hollywood, CA 90069 USA

Jhulka, Ayesha *Actor, Bollywood*
102 Tirupati Apartments, 7 Bungalows Versova Andheri (W), Mumbai, MS 400061, INDIA

Jia, Li *Misc*
Duke University, Medical Center,
Hematology Dept, Durham, NC 27708
USA

Jiahua, Zou *Government Official*
Communist Party Central Committee,
Jhong Nan Hai, Beijing, CHINA

Jiang, Tian *Musician*
Columbia Artists Mgmt Inc, 165 W 57th
St, New York, NY 10019 USA

Jiang, Tiefeng *Artist*
Fingerhut Gallery, 690 Bridgeway,
Sausalito, CA 94965 USA

Jiang, Zemin *President*
Central Military Commitee, Zhonganahai,
Beijing, CHINA

Jiles, Pam *Track Athlete*
2623 Wisteria St, New Orleans, LA 70122

Jiles, Pamela (Pam) *Track Athlete*
2623 Wisteria St, New Orleans, LA 70122
USA

Jillian, Ann *Actor*
PO Box 57739, Sherman Oaks, CA 91413
USA

Jim & Jesse
PO Box 27 Gallatin, TN CA 37066

Jimenez, Carlos *Architect*
Jimenez Architectural Design Studio, 1116
Willard St, Houston, TX 77006 USA

Jimenez, Flaco *Misc*
DeLeon Artists, 4031 Panama Court,
Piedmont, CA 94611 USA

Jimenez, Manny *Baseball Player*
Kansas City A's, 24003 Colmar Ln,
Murrieta, CA 92562-1978 USA

Jimenez, Nicario *Artist*
5531 Teak Wood Dr NW, Naples, FL
34119 USA

Jimenez Pons, Eduardo *Writer*
Gabriel Blanco Iglesias (Mexico), Rio
Balsas 35-32, Colonia Cuauhtemoc, DF,
06500, Mexico

Jiminez, Joe *Golfer*
29243 Enchanted Glen, Boeme, TX 78015
USA

Jiminez, Miguel *Baseball Player*
Oakland A's, 128 Post Ave, New York,
NY 10034-3432 USA

Jimmy, Jimmy
44 Harton Way Kings Heath, Birmingham,
ENGLAND, 146 PF

Jimmy Eat World *Music Group*
GAS, 722 Seward St, Los Angeles, CA
90038

Jimmy Jam
9830 Wilshire Blvd., Beverly Hills, CA
90212

Jin, Svoboda *Director*
Na Balkane 120, Prague 3, CZECH
REPUBLIC

Jindrak, Mark *Wrestler*
2355 Reyer Rd, Auburn, NY 13021

Jirsa, Ron *Coach*
University of Georgia, Athletic Dept,
Athens, GA 30613 USA

Jiscke, Martin C *Educator*
Iowa State University, President's Office,
Ames, IA 50011 USA

Jive Bunny
5-7 Sixth Williams St Parthgate, So.
Yorkshire, ENGLAND, S62 6EP

JIVEjones *Musician*
Evolution Talent Agency LLC, 1776
Broadway Fl 15, New York, NY 10019
USA

Joan, Jett *Musician, Songwriter*
Jet Lagg/Blackheart Records, 636
Broadway #1218, New York, NY 10012
USA

Joanou, Phil *Director*
Creative Artists Agency, 9830 Wilshire
Blvd, Beverly Hills, CA 90212 USA

Job, Brian *Swimmer*
PO Box 70427, Sunnyvale, CA 94086
USA

Jobe, Frank W *Doctor*
Kerlan-Jobe Orthopedic Clinic, 501 E
Hardy St, #200, Inglewood, CA 90301
USA

Jobert, Marlene
8-10 blvd. de Courcelles, Paris, FRANCE,
75008

Jobrani, Maz *Actor*
Mitchell K Stubbs & Assoc (MKS), 8675 W
Washington Blvd #203, Culver City, CA
90232 USA

Jobs, Steven P *Business Person, Producer*
Apple Computer, 1 Infinite Loop,
Cupertino, CA 95014 USA

Jodie, Brett *Baseball Player*
New York Yankees, 1359 Corley Mill Rd,
Lexington, SC 29072-7635 USA

Joe *Musician*
International Creative Management
(ICM-LA), 8942 Wilshire Blvd, Beverly
Hills, CA 90211 USA

Joe, Billy *Football Player*
3150 Shamrock East, Tallahassee, FL
32309

Joe, Fat *Actor, Artist, Music Group*
Famous Artists Agency, 250 W 57th St,
New York, NY 10107 USA

Joe, William (Billy) *Football Player*
Florida A&M University, Athletic Dept,
Tallahassee, FL 32307 USA

Joel, Billy *Musician, Songwriter*
Paradigm (LA), 10100 Santa Monica Blvd,
Fl 25, Los Angeles, CA 90067 USA

Joel, Richard M *Educator*
Yeshiva University, President's Office, 500
W 185th St, New York, NY 10033 USA

Joelson, Tsianina *Actor*
Sandra Marsh Management, 9150
Wilshire Blvd #220, Beverly Hills, CA
90212 USA

Joens, Michael *Writer*
Natasha Kern Literary Agency, PO Box
2908, Portland, OR 97208-2908 USA

Joey Z *Musician*
Agency Group Ltd, 1775 Broadway, #430,
New York, NY 10019 USA

Joffee, Roland V *Director, Producer*
Nomad, 10351 Santa Monica Blvd, #402,
Los Angeles, CA 90025 USA

Jofre, Eder *Boxer*
Alamo de Ministero Rocha, Azevedo 373
C Cesar 21-15, Sao Paulo, BRAZIL

Jogis, Chris *Athlete*
7 Birch Rd, Larchmont, NY 10538

Johannesen, Lena *Athlete*
PO Box 325, Studio City, CA 90232

Johannsen, Jake *Comedian, Actor*
Ellis Talent Group, 4705 Laurel Canyon
Blvd, Suite 300, Valley Village, CA 91607
USA

Johannsson, Kristian *Opera Singer*
Herbert Breslin, 119 W 57th St, #1505,
New York, NY 10019 USA

Johanos, Donald *Conductor*
Honolulu Symphony, 650 Iwilei Road,
#202, Honolulu, HI 96817 USA

Johansen, David *Musician*
Agency Group Ltd, 1775 Broadway, #430,
New York, NY 10019 USA

Johansen, Iris *Writer*
Bantam Books, 1540 Broadway, New
York, NY 10036

Johansen, John M *Architect*
Johansen & Bhavnani, 821 Broadway,
New York, NY 10003 USA

Johanson, Donald C *Misc*
Arizona State University, Human Origins
Institute, Tempe, AZ 85287 USA

Johanson, Erika *Writer*
Gabriel Blanco Iglesias (Mexico), Rio
Balsas 35-32, Colonia Cuauhtemoc, DF,
06500, Mexico

Johanssen, David
9200 Sunset Blvd. #900, Los Angeles, CA
90069

Johansson, Ingemar *Boxer*
PO Box 134, Stockholm, S-13054,
SWEDEN

Johansson, Kathy *Model*
PO Box 13923, Tucson, AZ 85732-3923

Johansson, Paul *Actor*
Gilbertson & Kincaid Mgmt, 1330 4th St,
Santa Monica, CA 90401 USA

Johansson, Scarlett *Actor*
Melanie Johansson, 7135 Hollywood
Blvd, #804, Los Angeles, CA 90046 USA

John, Caspar *Admiral*
Trethewey, Mousehole Penzance,
Cornwall, UNITED KINGDOM (UK)

John, David D *Misc*
7 Cyncoed Ave, Cardiff, CF2 6ST, WALES

John, Elton *Musician, Songwriter*
John Reid, Singers House, 32 Galena
Road, London, W6 0LT, UNITED
KINGDOM (UK)

John, Elton *Songwriter, Musician*
Outside Organization, 180 Tottenham
Court Road, London, W1P 9LE, UNITED
KINGDOM (UK)

John, Gottfried *Actor*
Elisabethweg 4, Utting, GERMANY,
D-86919

John, Tommy *Baseball Player*
Cleveland Indians, 6202 Seton House Ln,
Charlotte, NC 28277-4524 USA

John, Tylyn *Model*
813 Harbor Blvd #133, W Sacramento, CA 95691

John Paul II, Pope *Religious Leader*
Palazzo Apostolico Vaticano, Citta del Vaticano, ITALY, I-00120, VATICAN CITY

Johncock, Gordon *Race Car Driver*
931 Bedtelyon Road, West Branch, MI 48661 USA

Johnny & The Hurricanes
195 Hannum Ave., Rossford, OH 43460

Johns, Bibi
D-82049, Pullach, GERMANY

Johns, Cindy *Actor*
PO Box 369, Arlington, TX 76004

Johns, Daniel *Musician*
John Watson Mgmt, PO Box 281, Sunny Hills, NSW, 2010, AUSTRALIA

Johns, Doug *Baseball Player*
Oakland A's, 1131 SW 72nd Ave, Plantation, FL 33317-4125 USA

Johns, Glynis *Actor*
10701 Wilshire Blvd., #2201, Los Angeles, CA 90024 USA

Johns, Jasper *Artist*
97 Low Rd., #642, Sharon, CT 06069 USA

Johns, Lori *Race Car Driver*
4418 Congressional Dr, Corpus Christi, TX 78413 USA

Johns, Marcus *Actor*
Lane Management Group, 13331 Moorpark St, #118, Sherman Oaks, CA 91423 USA

Johns, Milton *Actor*
78 Temple Sheen Rd, London, SW14 7RJ, ENGLAND

Johns, Stratford
29 Mostyn Rd. Merton Park, London, ENGLAND, SW19 3LL

Johnson, Adam *Baseball Player*
Minnesota Twins, 3923 Montefrio Ct, San Diego, CA 92130-2280 USA

Johnson, Addison *Cartoonist*
King Features Syndicate, 888 7th Ave, New York, NY 10106 USA

Johnson, Alex *Baseball Player*
Philadelphia Phillies, 18425 Bretton Dr, Detroit, MI 48223-1311 USA

Johnson, Alexz *Actor*
William Morris Agency (WMA-LA), 1 William Morris Pl, Beverly Hills, CA 90212 USA

Johnson, Allen *Track Athlete*
Octagon, 1751 Pinnacle Dr, #1500, McLean, VA 22102 USA

Johnson, Amy Jo *Actor*
3940 Laurel Canyon Blvd, #463, Studio City, CA 91604 USA

Johnson, Andreas *Musician*
United Stage Artist, PO Box 11029, Stockholm, S-10061, SWEDEN

Johnson, Anne Marie *Actor*
2606 Ivan Hill Terrace, Los Angeles, CA 90039

Johnson, Anne-Marie *Actor*
2522 Silver Lake Terrace, Los Angeles, CA 90039 USA

Johnson, Art *Baseball Player*
Boston Bees, 23 Hemlock Dr, Holden, MA 01520-1617 USA

Johnson, Arte *Actor, Comedian*
2725 Bottlebrush Dr, Los Angeles, CA 90077 USA

Johnson, Ashley *Actor*
Untitled Entertainment, 8436 W 3rd St, #650, Los Angeles, CA 90048 USA

Johnson, Bart *Baseball Player*
Chicago White Sox, 904 Indian Boundary Dr, Westmont, IL 60559-1079 USA

Johnson, Batsey L *Fashion Designer*
Betsey Johnson Co, 127 E 9th St, #703, Los Angeles, CA 90015 USA

Johnson, Ben *Baseball Player*
Chicago Cubs, 112 Locksley Dr, Greenwood, SC 29649-9185 USA

Johnson, Betsey *Fashion Designer*
Betsey Johnson, 498 Seventh Ave Fl 21, New York, NY 10018 USA

Johnson, Beverly *Model, Actor*
2711 Angelo Dr, Los Angeles, CA 90077 USA

Johnson, Bill *Actor*
Actors Clearinghouse, 501 N 1H35, Austin, TX 78702 USA

Johnson, Bill *Baseball Player*
Chicago Cubs, 14 Rankin Rd, Newark, DE 19711-4851 USA

Johnson, Billy *Baseball Player*
New York Yankees, 2903 Lake Forest Dr, Augusta, GA 30909-3025 USA

Johnson, Bob *Baseball Player*
Texas Rangers, 265 Quari St, Aurora, CO 80011-8339 USA

Johnson, Bob D *Baseball Player*
New York Mets, 255 Nunan St, Jacksonville, OR 97530-9699 USA

Johnson, Bob W *Baseball Player*
Kansas City A's, 1474 Barcley St, Saint Paul, MN 55106-1408 USA

Johnson, Brian *Baseball Player*
San Diego Padres, 11306 Portobelo Dr Unit 4, San Diego, CA 92124-4018 USA

Johnson, Brian *Musician*
11 Leominster Road, Morden, Surrey, SA4 6HN, UNITED KINGDOM (UK)

Johnson, Brooks *Coach*
Stanford University, Athletic Dept, Stanford, CA 94305 USA

Johnson, Bryce *Actor*
Jerry Shandrew PR, 1050 South Stanley Avenue, Los Angeles, CA 90019-6634 USA

Johnson, Butch *Football Player*
9719 S Red Oakes Dr, Highlands Ranch, CO 80126 USA

Johnson, Carolyn Dawn *Songwriter, Musician*
RPM Mgmt, 209 10th Ave S, #229, Nashville, TN 37203 USA

Johnson, Charles *Baseball Player*
Florida Marlins, 12301 NW 7th St, Plantation, FL 33325-1729 USA

Johnson, Charles L (Charley) *Football Player*
PO Box 1312, Mesilla, NM 88046 USA

Johnson, Charles R *Writer*
University of Washington, English Dept, Seattle, WA 98105 USA

Johnson, Chris *Golfer*
W K Shearman Co, 7925 N Oracle Road, #388, Tucson, AZ 85704 USA

Johnson, Clark
9560 Wilshire Blvd. #516, Beverly Hills, CA 90212

Johnson, Claude (Juan) *Musician*
Mars Talent, 27 L'Ambiance Court, Bardonia, NY 10954 USA

Johnson, Claude A (Lady Bird) *Ex-First Lady*
LBJ Ranch, Stonewall, TX 78671 USA

Johnson, Cliff *Baseball Player*
Houston Astros, RR 1 Box 226J, Converse, TX 78109-9801 USA

Johnson, Connie *Baseball Player*
Chicago White Sox, 1900 E 54th St, Kansas City, MO 64130-3301 USA

Johnson, Courtney *Misc*
8472 W Granite Dr, Granite Bay, CA 95746 USA

Johnson, Curt *Writer, Producer*
Abrams Artists Agency (LA), 9200 Sunset Blvd Fl 11, Los Angeles, CA 90069 USA

Johnson, Dale *Actor*
LA Models, 7700 Sunset Blvd, Los Angeles, CA 90046 USA

Johnson, Dane *Baseball Player*
Chicago White Sox, PO Box 465 Stn Main, Medicine Hat, AB T1A 7G2, CANADA

Johnson, Darrell *Baseball Player*
St Louis Browns, 65 Willotta Dr, Sulsun City, CA 94534-1452 USA

Johnson, Dave *Baseball Player*
Baltimore Orioles, 3202 Woodhollow Cir, Abllene, TX 79606-4211 USA

Johnson, Dave *Misc*
United Garment Workers, 4207 Lebanon Road, Hermitage, TN 37076 USA

Johnson, Dave *Baseball Player*
Pittsburgh Pirates, 7101 Mount Vista Rd, Kingsville, MD 21087-1728 USA

Johnson, Davey *Baseball Player*
Baltimore Orioles, 1064 Howell Branch Road, Winter Park, FL 32789-1004 USA

Johnson, David (Dave) *Track Athlete*
Azusa Pacific University, PO Box 2713, Azusa, CA 91702 USA

Johnson, David Cay *Journalist*
New York Times, Editorial Dept, 229 W 43rd St, New York, NY 10036 USA

Johnson, David G *Economist*
1700 E 56th St, #1306, Chicago, IL 60637 USA

Johnson, David W *Business Person*
Campbell Soup Co, 1 Campbell Place, Camden, NJ 08103 USA

Johnson, Dennis W *Basketball Player*
15003 Chuparosa St, Victorville, CA 92394 USA

Johnson, DerMarr *Basketball Player*
Phoenix Suns, 201 E Jefferson St, Phoenix, AZ 85004 USA

Johnson, Dick *Baseball Player*
Chicago Cubs, 717 N Matterhorn Rd, Payson, AZ 85541-3926 USA

Johnson, Don *Actor*
William Morris Agency, 151 El Camino Dr, Beverly Hills, CA 90212 USA

Johnson, Dwayne *Actor*
Endeavor Agency LLC (LA), 9601 Wilshire Blvd Fl 3, Beverly Hills, CA 90210 USA

Johnson, Earl *Bowler*
3625 Woody Lane, Minnetonka, MN 55305 USA

Johnson, Earvin
9100 Wilshire Blvd. #1060 W. Tower, Beverly Hills, CA 90212

Johnson, Edward (Eddie) *Basketball Player*
6133 N 61st Place, Paradise Valley, AZ 85253 USA

Johnson, Emma *Misc*
Columbia Artists Mgmt Inc, 165 W 57th St, New York, NY 10019 USA

Johnson, Eric *Actor*
Smallville, 4000 Warner Blvd, Bldg 160 #200, Burbank, CA 91522 USA

Johnson, Eric *Musician*
Joe Priesnitz Artist Mgmt, PO Box 5249, Austin, TX 78763 USA

Johnson, Erik *Baseball Player*
San Francisco Giants, PO Box 2989, San Ramon, CA 94583-7989 USA

Johnson, Ernie *Baseball Player*
Boston Braves, 500 Dorris Rd, Alpharetta, GA 30004-3433 USA

Johnson, Ervin *Basketball Player*
Minnesota Timberwolves, Target Center, 600 1st Ave N, Minneapolis, MN 55403 USA

Johnson, Frank *Baseball Player*
San Francisco Giants, 1151 Cypress Hill Ln, Stockton, CA 95206-6245 USA

Johnson, Frank *Basketball Player, Coach*
10929 Pebble Run Dr, Silver Spring, MD 20902 USA

Johnson, Gandia *Reality TV Star*
Survivor, 1661 Lincoln Blvd, Ste 200, Santa Monica, CA 90404

Johnson, Gary *Baseball Player*
Anaheim Angels, 485 Canyon Oaks Dr Apt F, Oakland, CA 94605-3859 USA

Johnson, Gary L *Football Player*
450 Oliver Road, Haughton, LA 71037 USA

Johnson, Georgann *Actor*
218 N Glenroy Place, Los Angeles, CA 90049 USA

Johnson, George *Golfer*
T & J Ventures, PO Box 1038, Lewisville, NC 27023 USA

Johnson, Graham R *Musician*
83 Fordwych Road, London, NW2 3TL, UNITED KINGDOM (UK)

Johnson, Gregory C *Astronaut*
1002 Applewood Dr, Friendswood, TX 77456 USA

Johnson, Hansford T *General*
USAA Capital Corp, 9800 Fredericksburg Road, San Antonio, TX 78284 USA

Johnson, Harold *Boxer*
6101 Morris St, Philadelphia, PA 19144 USA

Johnson, Haynes B *Journalist*
George Washington University, Communications Studies Ctr, Washington, DC 20052 USA

Johnson, Holly *Musician*
Lustig Talent, PO Box 770850, Orlando, FL 32877 USA

Johnson, Howard *Baseball Player*
Detroit Tigers, 8597 SE Coconut St, Hobe Sound, FL 33455-2914 USA

Johnson, I Birger *Engineer*
1508 Barclay Place, Niskayuna, NY 12309 USA

Johnson, Ian *Journalist*
Wall Street Journal, Editorial Dept, 200 Liberty St, New York, NY 10281 USA

Johnson, J Bradley (Brad) *Football Player*
PO Box 732, Black Mountain, NC 28711 USA

Johnson, J J
648 Broadway #703, New York, NY 10012 USA

Johnson, J Seward *Artist*
Sculpture Foundation, 2525 Michigan Ave, #A6, Santa Monica, CA 90404 USA

Johnson, James A *Financier*
Federal National Mortgage Assn, 3900 Wisconsin Ave NW, Washington, DC 20016 USA

Johnson, James E (Johnnie) *War Hero*
Stables, Hargate Hall Buxton, Derbyshire, SK17 8TA, UNITED KINGDOM (UK)

Johnson, Jannette *Skier*
PO Box 901, Sun Valley, ID 83353 USA

Johnson, Jason *Baseball Player*
Pittsburgh Pirates, PO Box 238, Santa Clara, UT 84765-0238 USA

Johnson, Jay *Actor, Comedian*
William Morris Agency (WMA-LA), 1 William Morris Pl, Beverly Hills, CA 90212 USA

Johnson, Jay Kenneth *Actor*
Strong/Morrone Entertainment, 9100 Wilshire Blvd #503E, Beverly Hills, CA 90212 USA

Johnson, Jenna *Swimmer, Coach*
University of Tennessee, Athletic Dept, PO Box 15016, Knoxville, TN 37901 USA

Johnson, Jerald Penny *Actor*
Susan Smith, 121A N San Vicente Blvd, Beverly Hills, CA 90211 USA

Johnson, Jerome L *Admiral*
Navy-Marine Corps Releif Society, 801 N Randolph St, Arlington, VA 22203 USA

Johnson, Jimmie *Race Car Driver*
Jimmie Johnson Racing, PO Box 4283, Morresville, NC 28117 USA

Johnson, Jimmy *Football Player*
656 Amaranth Blvd, Mill Valley, CA 94941 USA

Johnson, Jimmy *Cartoonist*
United Feature Syndicate, 200 Madison Ave, New York, NY 10016 USA

Johnson, Joanna *Actor*
William Morris Agency (WMA-LA), 1 William Morris Pl, Beverly Hills, CA 90212 USA

Johnson, Joe *Basketball Player*
Phoenix Suns, 201 E Jefferson St, Phoenix, AZ 85004 USA

Johnson, Johari *Actor*
H W A Talent, 3500 W Olive Ave, #1400, Burbank, CA 91505 USA

Johnson, John H *Publisher*
Johnson Publishing Co, 1750 Pennsylvania Ave NW, Washington, DC 20006 USA

Johnson, Johnnie *Songwriter, Musician*
Talent Source, 1560 Broadway, #1308, New York, NY 10036 USA

Johnson, Judge S *Misc*
39 S La Salle St, #825, Chicago, IL 60603 USA

Johnson, Junior *Race Car Driver*
1100 Glen Oaks Dr, Hamptonville, NC 27020 USA

Johnson, Keith *Misc*
Woodworkers of America Union, 1622 N Lombard St, Portland, OR 97217 USA

Johnson, Kermit *Football Player*
3259 Lincoin Ave, Altadena, CA 91001 USA

Johnson, Kevin
201 E. Jefferson St., Phoenix, AZ 85004-2400

Johnson, Kevin *Baseball Player, Sportscaster*
NBC-TV, Sports Dept, 30 Rockefeller Plaza, New York, NY 10112 USA

Johnson, Keyshawn *Football Player*
Reign, 180 N Robertson Blvd, Beverly Hills, CA 90211 USA

Johnson, Lamont *Director*
935 Mesa Road, Monterey, CA 93940 USA

Johnson, Lance *Baseball Player*
5712 Foxfire Rd, Mobile, AL 36618

Johnson, Larry *Football Player*
Kansas City Chiefs, 1 Arrowhead Dr, Kansas City, KS 64129 USA

Johnson, Larry D *Basketball Player*
310 N Kings Dr, Charlotte, NC 28204 USA

Johnson, Laura
1917 Weepah Way, Los Angeles, CA 90046

Johnson, Laurie *Composer*
Priority House, Camp Hill Stanmore, Middx, HA7 3JQ, UNITED KINGDOM (UK)

Johnson, Luci Baines
LBJ Ranch, Stonewall, TX 78701

Johnson, Lynn-Holly *Actor*
Cavaleri, 178 S Victory Blvd, #205, Burbank, CA 91502 USA

Johnson, Marc *Musician*
A Train Mgmt, PO Box 29242, Oakland, CA 94604 USA

Johnson, Mark *Boxer*
1204 Howison Place SW, Washington, DC 20024 USA

Johnson, Mark E *Hockey Player, Coach*
5901 Hempstead Road, Madison, WI
53711 USA

Johnson, Mark Steven *Actor, Writer, Director*
Creative Artists Agency LCC (CAA-LA),
9830 Wilshire Blvd, Beverly Hills, CA
90212 USA

Johnson, Marvin *Boxer*
5452 Turfway Circle, Indianapolis, IN
46228 USA

Johnson, Marvin M *Engineer*
4413 Woodland Road, Bartlesville, OK
74006 USA

Johnson, Michael *Musician*
Buddy Lee, 38 Music Square East, #300,
Nashville, TN 37203 USA

Johnson, Michael D *Track Athlete*
Gold Medal Mgmt, 1750 14th St, Boulder,
CO 80302 USA

Johnson, Michelle *Actor, Model*
Agency for performing Arts, 9200 Sunset
Blvd, #900, Los Angeles, CA 90069 USA

Johnson, Monica *Writer*
Innovative Artists, 1505 10th St, Santa
Monica, CA 90401 USA

Johnson, Neil *Basketball Player*
821 Plymouth Lane, Virginia Beach, VA
23451 USA

Johnson, Nicholas *Lawyer, Writer*
PO Box 1876, Iowa City, IA 52244 USA

Johnson, Norm *Football Player*
400 Peachtree Industrial Blvd, #1615,
Suwanee, GA 30024 USA

Johnson, Norma Holloway *Judge*
US District Court, 333 Constitution Ave
NW, Washington, DC 20001 USA

Johnson, Norman *Musician*
Paramount Entertainment, PO Box 12, Far
Hills, NJ 07931 USA

Johnson, Ora J *Religious Leader*
General Assn of General Baptists, 100
Stinson Dr, Poplar Bluff, MO 63901 USA

Johnson, Paul *Hockey Player*
1719 Yale Ave, Nurley, ID 83318 USA

Johnson, Paul B *Historian*
Coach House, Over Stowey near
Bridgewater, Somerset, TA5 1HA,
UNITED KINGDOM (UK)

Johnson, Penny
121 N. San Vicente Blvd., Beverly Hills,
CA 90211

Johnson, Philip C *Architect*
John Burgee Architects, 4 Columbus
Circle, New York, NY 10013 USA

Johnson, R E *Misc*
Train Dispatchers Assn, 1370 Ontario St,
#1040, Cleveland, OH 44113 USA

Johnson, Rafer L *Actor, Track Athlete*
4217 Woodcliff Road, Sherman Oaks, CA
91403 USA

Johnson, Ralph E *Architect*
Perkins & Will, 330 N Wabash Ave,
#3600, Chicago, IL 60611 USA

Johnson, Randall D (Randy) *Baseball
Player*
Arizona Diamondbacks, Bank One
Ballpark, 401 E Jefferson, Phoenix, AZ
85004 USA

Johnson, Raymond Edward
167 Grieb Rd., Wallingford, CT 06492

Johnson, Richard
18-21 Jermyn St., London, ENGLAND,
SW1Y 6NB

Johnson, Richard K *Actor*
Conway Van Gelder Robinson, 18-21
Jermyn St, London, SW1Y 6NB, UNITED
KINGDOM (UK)

Johnson, Rob *Football Player*
26635 Aracena Dr, Mission Viejo, CA
92691 USA

Johnson, Robert *Business Person*
BET - Black EntertainmentTelevision (DC),
1235 W Place NE, Washington, DC
20018-1211 USA

Johnson, Robert D (Bob) *Football Player*
2 Ault Lane, Cincinnati, OH 45246 USA

Johnson, Robert L *Business Person*
Black Entertainment TV, 1900 W Place
NE, Washington, DC 20018 USA

Johnson, Ronald A (Ron) *Football Player*
226 Summit Ave, Summit, NJ 07901 USA

Johnson, Roy *Misc*
Roofers & Waterproofers Union, 1125
17th St NW, Washington, DC 20036 USA

Johnson, Russell *Actor*
Professor's Place, PO Box 1198,
Bainbridge Island, WA 98110 USA

Johnson, Shannon *Basketball Player*
Connecticut Sun, Mohegan Sun Arena,
Uncasville, CT 06382 USA

Johnson, Shelly W *Cinematographer*
970 Jimeno Road, Santa Barbara, CA
93103 USA

Johnson, Sonia *Social Activist*
3318 2nd St S, Arlington, VA 22204 USA

Johnson, Spencer *Writer*
G P Putnam's Sons, 375 Hudson St, New
York, NY 10014 USA

Johnson, Steve *Basketball Player*
9715 SW Quail Post Road, Portland, OR
97219 USA

Johnson, Syl *Songwriter, Musician*
Blue Sky Artists, 761 Washington Ave N,
Minneapolis, MN 55401 USA

Johnson, Taj
170 N. Rexford Dr., Beverly Hills, CA
90210

Johnson, Thomas C (Tom) *Hockey Player*
16 Spartina Place, West Falmouth, MA
02574 USA

Johnson, Tim *Football Player*
Washington Redskins, 21300 Redskin Park
Dr, Ashburn, VA 20147 USA

Johnson, Timothy *Doctor, Correspondent*
20/20, 147 Columbus Ave, New York, NY
10023, US

Johnson, Tom *Hockey Player*
80 Holden Rd, Sterling, MA 01564-2424

Johnson, Torrence V *Astronomer*
Jet Propulsion Laboratory, 4800 Oak
Grove Dr, Pasadena, CA 91109 USA

Johnson, Van *Actor*
Studio Artists, 305 West 52nd Street, #1H,
New York, NY 10019 USA

Johnson, Vaughan M *Football Player*
New Orleans Saints, 5800 Airline
Highway, Metairie, LA 70003 USA

Johnson, Vickie *Basketball Player*
New York Liberty, 2 Penn Plz Fl 14, New
York, NY 10121 USA

Johnson, Vinnie *Basketball Player*
5236 Elmsgate Dr, Orchard Lake, MI
48324 USA

Johnson, Virginia *Ballerina*
133 W 71st St, New York, NY 10023 USA

Johnson, Virginia E *Doctor*
Johnson Assoc, 800 Holland Road,
Ballwin, MO 63021 USA

Johnson, Warren *Race Car Driver*
PO Box 1357, Buford, GA 30515 USA

Johnson, Warren C *Misc*
946 Bellclair Road SE, Grand Rapids, MI
49506 USA

Johnson, Wendy *Race Car Driver*
126 Red Brook Lane, Mooresville, NC
28117 USA

Johnson, William A (Billy White Shoes)
Football Player
3701 Whitney Place, Duluth, GA 30096
USA

Johnson, William B *Business Person*
Ritz-Carlton Hotels, 4445 Willard Ave,
#800, Chevy Chase, MD 20815 USA

Johnson, William R *Business Person*
H J Heinz Co, PO Box 57, Pittsburgh, PA
15230 USA

Johnson III, Joseph E *Physicist, Doctor*
Philadelphian, 2401 Pennsylvania Ave,
#15C44, Philadelphia, PA 19130 USA

Johnson Jr, Benjamin S (ben) *Track
Athlete*
Ed Futerman, 2 Saint Clair Ave E, #1500,
Toronto, ON M4T 2R1, CANADA

Johnson Jr, Earvin (Magic) *Basketball
Player, Coach*
Magic Johnson Enterprises Inc, 9100
Wilshire Blvd #700, East Tower, Beverly
Hills, CA 90212 USA

Johnson Jr, Ernie *Sportscaster*
TNT-TV, Sports Department, 1050
Techwood Dr, Atlanta, GA 30318 USA

Johnson Jr, G Griffith *Government
Official*
300 Locust Ave, Annapolis, MD 21401
USA

Johnson Jr, Johnnie *Football Player*
PO Box 114, La Grange, TX 78945 USA

Johnson Jr, Manuel H *Economist,
Government Official*
Johnson Smick Int'l, 2099 Pennsylvania
Ave NW, #950, Washington, DC 20006
USA

Johnson Pucci, Gail *Swimmer*
2132 Ward Dr, Walnut Creek, CA 94596
USA

Johnston, Alastair *Misc*
International Mgmt Group, 75490 Fairway
Dr, Indian Wells, CA 92210 USA

Johnston, Allen H *Religious Leader*
Bishop's House, 3 Wymer Terrace, PO Box 21, Hamilton, NEW ZELAND

Johnston, Bruce *Musician*
International Creative Mgmt, 8942 Wilshire Blvd, #219, Beverly Hills, CA 90211 USA

Johnston, Daryl (Moose) *Football Player*
5520 Roland Dr, Plano, TX 75093 USA

Johnston, Freedy *Songwriter, Musician*
Morebarn Music, 30 Hilcrest Ave, Morristown, NJ 07960 USA

Johnston, Gerald A *Business Person*
McDonnell Douglas Corp, PO Box 516, Saint Louis, MO 63166 USA

Johnston, Gerald E *Business Person*
Clorox Co, 1221 Broadway, Oakland, CA 94612 USA

Johnston, Harold S *Misc*
285 Franklin St, Harrisonburg, VA 22801 USA

Johnston, J Bennett Jr *Senator*
Johnston Assoc, 2099 Pennsylvania Ave NW, #1000, Washington, DC 20006 USA

Johnston, John Dennis *Actor*
S D B Partners, 1801 Ave of Stars, #902, Los Angeles, CA 90067 USA

Johnston, Ken
6300 Wilshire Blvd. #2110, Los Angeles, CA 90048

Johnston, Kristen *Actor*
Anonymous Content, 8522 National Blvd #101, Culver City, CA 90232 USA

Johnston, Lynn *Cartoonist*
Universal Press Syndicate, 4520 Main St, Kansas City, MO 64111 USA

Johnston, Rex D *Football Player, Baseball Player*
11372 Weatherby Road, Los Alamitos, CA 90720 USA

Johnston, Tom *Musician*
PO Box 359, Sonoma, CA 95476

Johnston Jr, S K *Business Person*
Coca-Cola Enterprises, 2500 Windy Ridge Parkway, Atlanta, GA 30339 USA

Johnston McKay, Marry H *Astronaut*
University of Tennessee, Space Institute, Tullahoma, TN 37388 USA

Johnston-Forbes, Cathy *Golfer*
Ladies Pro Golf Assn, 100 International Golf Dr, Daytona Beach, FL 32124 USA

Johnstone, Jay
9560 Wilshire Blvd. #516, Beverly Hills, CA 90211

Johnstone Jr, John W *Business Person*
467 Carter St, New Canaan, CT 06840 USA

Joiner, Charlie
2254 Moore St., San Diego, CA 92110

Joiner, Rusty *Actor, Model, Athlete*
Origin Talent, 3393 Barham Blvd, Los Angeles, CA 90068 USA

Joiner Jr, Charles (Charlie) *Football Player, Football Coach*
2254 Moore St, San Diego, CA 92110 USA

Jolas, Betsy M *Composer*
Nat Superieur Musique Conservatoire, 209 Ave Jaures, Paris, 75019, FRANCE

Joli, France *Musician*
Brothers Mgmt, 141 Dunbar Ave, Fords, NJ 08863 USA

Joliceur, David *Musician*
Famous Artists Agency, 250 W 57th St, New York, NY 10107 USA

Jolie, Angelina *Actor, Model*
Industry Entertainment, 955 Carillo Dr, #300, Los Angeles, CA 90048 USA

Joliot, Pierre A *Biologist*
16 Rue de la Glaciere, Paris, 75013, FRANCE

Jolly, Allison *Yachtsman*
1275 Seville Lane NE, Saint Petersburg, FL 33704 USA

Jolly, E Grady *Judge*
US Court of Appeals, Eastland Courthouse, 245 E Capitol St, Jackson, MS 39201 USA

Jolovitz, Jenna *Writer, Actor*
Creative Artists Agency LCC (CAA-LA), 9830 Wilshire Blvd, Beverly Hills, CA 90212 USA

Joltz, Joachim *Engineer*
AM Forsthof 16, Wuppertal, 42119, GERMANY

Jomdt, L daniel *Business Person*
Walgreen Co, 200 Wilmot Road, Deerfield, IL 60015 USA

Jon-Jules, Danny *Actor*
BBC Information - Artist Mail, PO Box 1116, Belfast, B3Z 7AJ, UK

Jonathan, Wesley *Actor*
Sanders/Armstrong Management, 2120 Colorado Blvd #120, Santa Monica, CA 90404 USA

Jones, Alex S *Journalist*
1 Waterhouse St, #61, Cambridge, MA 02138 USA

Jones, Alfred *Boxer*
19303 Patton St, Detroit, MI 48219 USA

Jones, Allen *Artist*
41 Charterhouse Square, London, EC1M 6EA, UNITED KINGDOM (UK)

Jones, Andruw R *Athlete*
Atlanta Braves, Turner Field, PO Box 4064, Altanta, GA 30302

Jones, Angus T *Actor*
Abrams Artists Agency (LA), 9200 Sunset Blvd Fl 11, Los Angeles, CA 90069 USA

Jones, Antonia *Actor*
Buzz Halliday, 8899 Beverly Blvd, #620, Los Angeles, CA 90048 USA

Jones, Arthur *Inventor*
MedX, 1155 NE 77th St, Ocala, FL 34479 USA

Jones, Asjha *Basketball Player*
Connecticut Sun, Mohegan Sun Arena, Uncasville, CT 06382 USA

Jones, Ben J *Prime Minister*
Victoria St, Greenville, Saint Andrew's, GRENADA

Jones, Bertram H (Bert) *Football Player*
Mid-States Wood Preservers, PO Box 248, Simsboro, LA 71275 USA

Jones, Bill T *Choreographer*
Bill T Jones/Amie Zane Dance Co, 853 Broadway, #1706, New York, NY 10003 USA

Jones, Bobby *Basketball Player*
7413 Valleybrook Road, Charlotte, NC 28270 USA

Jones, Booker T *Musician*
Rosebud Agency, PO Box 170429, San Francisco, CA 94117 USA

Jones, Brent M *Football Player, Sportscaster*
5483 Blackhawk Dr, Danville, CA 94506 USA

Jones, Bryn Terfel *Opera Singer*
Harlequin Agency, 203 Fidlas Road, Cardiff, CF4 5NA, WALES

Jones, Carnetta *Actor*
CunninghamEscottDipene, 10635 Santa Monica Blvd, #130, Los Angeles, CA 90025 USA

Jones, Charles W *Misc*
Brotherhood of Boilermakers, 753 S 8th Ave, Kansas City, KS 66105 USA

Jones, Charlie *Sportscaster*
8080 El Paseo Grande, La Jolla, CA 92037 USA

Jones, Cherry *Actor*
William Morris Agency, 151 El Camino Dr, Beverly Hills, CA 90212 USA

Jones, Chipper *Baseball Player, Athlete*
Atlanta Braves, Turner Field, PO Box 4064, Atlanta, GA 30302 USA

Jones, Christopher *Actor*
4057 Sapphire Dr, Encino, CA 91436 USA

Jones, Claude Earl *Actor*
Henderson/Hogan, 8285 W Sunset Blvd, #1, West Hollywood, CA 90046 USA

Jones, Cobi *Soccer Player*
501 N Edinburgh Ave, Los Angeles, CA 90048 USA

Jones, Courtney J L *Figure Skater*
National Skating Assn, 15-27 Gee St, London, EC1V 3RE, UNITED KINGDOM (UK)

Jones, Darryl *Musician*
Rascoff/Zysblat, 110 W 57th St, #300, New York, NY 10019 USA

Jones, David (Davy) *Musician*
Paradise Artists, 108 E Matilija St, Ojai, CA 93023 USA

Jones, David (Deacon) *Football Player*
715 S Canyon Mist Lane, Anaheim, CA 92808 USA

Jones, David A *Business Person*
Humana Corp, 500 W Main St, Louisville, KY 40202 USA

Jones, Davy *Race Car Driver*
TRW Racing, 2000 Jaguar Dr, Valparaiso, IN 46383 USA

Jones, Dean *Actor, Musician*
PO Box 570276, Tarzana, CA 91357 USA

Jones, Denise *Musician*
TBA Artists Mgmt, 300 10th Ave S, Nashville, TN 37203 USA

Jones, Dick *Actor*
PO Box 7716, Northridge, CA 91322

Jones, Donell *Musician*
Pyramid Entertainment Group, 89 Fifth Ave Fl 7, New York, NY 10003 USA

Jones, Doug *Actor*
OmniPop Inc (LA), 10700 Ventura Blvd Fl 2, Studio City, CA 91604 USA

Jones, Dub
223 Glendale, Rusten, LA 71270

Jones, Dwight *Basketball Player*
17122 Silyerthome Lane, Spring, TX 77379 USA

Jones, E Edward *Religious Leader*
Baptist Convention of America, 777 S R L Thornton Freeway, Dallas, TX 75203 USA

Jones, E Fay *Architect*
Fay Jones/Maurice Jennings Architects, 619 W Dickson, Fayetteville, AR 72701 USA

Jones, Earl *Track Athlete*
15114 Petroskey Ave, Detroit, MI 48238 USA

Jones, Ed
1 Lost Valley Dr., Dallas, TX 75234

Jones, Eddie *Basketball Player*
3400 Paddock Road, Weston, FL 33331 USA

Jones, Eddie *Actor*
Gage Group, 14724 Ventura Blvd, #505, Sherman Oaks, CA 91403 USA

Jones, Edith H *Judge*
US Court of Appeals, 515 Rusk Ave, Houston, TX 77002 USA

Jones, Elvin R *Musician*
DL Media, PO Box 2728, Bala Cynwyd, PA 19004 USA

Jones, Etta
160 Goldsmith Ave., Newark, NJ 07112

Jones, Evan *Actor*
Curtis Talent Management, 9607 Arby Dr, Beverly Hills, CA 90210 USA

Jones, Gemma *Actor*
Conway Van Gelder Robinson, 18-21 Jermyn St, London, SW1Y 6NB, UNITED KINGDOM (UK)

Jones, George *Musician, Songwriter*
George Jones Enterprises, 500 Wilson Pike Cir, #200, Brentwood, TN 37027 USA

Jones, Glenn *Musician*
Universal Attractions, 145 W 57th St, #1500, New York, NY 10019 USA

Jones, Grace *Model, Actor, Musician*
Denis Vaughan Mgmt, PO Box 28286, #700, London, NY N21 3WT, UNITED KINGDOM (UK)

Jones, Greg *Skier*
PO Box 500, Tahoe City, CA 96145 USA

Jones, Griff Rhys *Actor, Writer, Producer*
TalkBack Productions, 20-21 Newman St, London, W1T 1PG, UNITED KINGDOM (UK)

Jones, Gwyneth *Opera Singer*
PO Box 556, Zurich, 8037, SWITZERLAND

Jones, Hal *Baseball Player*
Cleveland Indians, 4125 Palmyra Rd, Los Angeles, CA 90008-2445 USA

Jones, Hayes W *Track Athlete*
1040 James K Blvd, Pontiac, MI 48341 USA

Jones, Henry (Hank) *Musician*
Joel Chriss, 300 Mercer St, #3J, New York, NY 10003 USA

Jones, Homer C *Football Player*
408 S Texas St, Pittsburg, TX 75686 USA

Jones, Howard *Musician, Songwriter*
FML, 33 Alexander Road, Aylesbury, HP20 2NR, UNITED KINGDOM (UK)

Jones, Jack *Musician*
75-825 Osage Trail, Indian Wells, CA 92210 USA

Jones, Jacques *Baseball Player*
Minnesota Twins, 347 Saint Rita Ct, San Diego, CA 92113-2092 USA

Jones, James Earl *Actor*
226 W 46th St, New York, NY 10036 USA

Jones, James L (Jack) *Misc*
74 Ruskin Park House, Champion Hill, London, SE5, UNITED KINGDOM (UK)

Jones, Jamie *Musician*
MPI Talent, 9255 Sunset Blvd, #407, Los Angeles, CA 90069 USA

Jones, Janet *Actor*
9100 Wilshire Blvd, #1000W, Beverly Hills, CA 90212 USA

Jones, January *Actor*
Mosaic Media Group, 9200 Sunset Blvd Fl 10, Los Angeles, CA 90069 USA

Jones, Jason *Baseball Player*
Texas Rangers, 1205 Mountain Springs Pl NW, Kennesaw, GA 30144-5617 USA

Jones, Jeff *Coach*
University of Virginia, Athletic Dept, Charlottesville, VA 22903 USA

Jones, Jeff *Baseball Player*
Oakland A's, 51 Emmons Ct, Wyandotte, MI 48192-253 USA

Jones, Jeff *Baseball Player*
Cincinnati Reds, 311 White Horse Pike, Haddon Heights, NJ 08035-1704 USA

Jones, Jeffrey *Actor*
7336 Santa Monica Blvd, #691, West Hollywood, CA 90046 USA

Jones, Jennifer *Actor*
22400 Pacific Coast Highway, Malibu, CA 90265 USA

Jones, Jenny *Comedian*
600 Plum Tree Road, Barrington, IL 60010 USA

Jones, Jerrauld C (Jerry) *Misc*
Dallas Cowboys, 1 Cowboys Parkway, Irving, TX 75063 USA

Jones, Jill Marie *Actor*
Identity Talent Agency (ID), 2050 Bundy Dr #200, Los Angeles, CA 90025 USA

Jones, Jimmy *Baseball Player*
San Diego Padres, 3054 Newcastle Dr, Dallas, TX 75220-1636 USA

Jones, John Marshall
1801 Ave. of the Stars #307, Los Angeles, CA 90067

Jones, John Paul *Musician*
Opium Arts, 49 Portland Road, London, W11 4LJ, UNITED KINGDOM (UK)

Jones, Johnny (Lam) *Football Player, Track Athlete*
4748 Old Bent Tree Lane, Dallas, TX 75287 USA

Jones, Kelly *Musician*
Marsupial Mgmt, Home Farm, Welfor Newbury, Berkshire, RG20 8HR, UNITED KINGDOM (UK)

Jones, Kenneth V *Actor*
PRS, 29/33 Berners St, London, W1P 4AA, ENGLAND

Jones, L Q *Actor*
2144 1/2 N Cahuenga Blvd, Los Angeles, CA 90068 USA

Jones, Larry *Basketball Player*
1442 Cottingham Court, Columbus, OH 43209 USA

Jones, Larry W (Chipper) *Baseball Player*
63 W Wieuca Road NE, #2, Atlanta, GA 30342 USA

Jones, Leilani *Actor*
Writers & Artists, 8383 Wilshire Blvd, #550, Beverly Hills, CA 90211 USA

Jones, LeRoi (Imamu Amiri Baraka) *Writer*
State University of New York, Afro American Studies Dept, Stony Brook, NY 11794 USA

Jones, Lou *Track Athlete*
14 Winyah Terrace, New Rochelle, NY 10801 USA

Jones, Lyle V *Misc*
RR 7, Pittsboro, NC 27312 USA

Jones, Lynn *Baseball Player*
Detroit Tigers, 9959 Dicksonburg Rd, Conneautville, PA 16406-1817 USA

Jones, Mack *Baseball Player*
Milwaukee Braves, PO Box 1578, Mableton, GA 30126-1009 USA

Jones, Mandana *Actor*
CAM, 19 Denmark Street, London, WC2H 8NA, England

Jones, Marcia Mae *Actor*
4541 Hazeltine Ave, #4, Sherman Oaks, CA 91423 USA

Jones, Marcus *Football Player*
18701 Pepper Pike, Lutz, FL 33558 USA

Jones, Marcus *Baseball Player*
Oakland A's, 20375 Longbay Dr, Yorba Linda, CA 92887 USA

Jones, Marilyn *Actor*
Kaplan-Stahler Agency, 8383 Wilshire Blvd, #923, Beverly Hills, CA 90211 USA

Jones, Marion *Track Athlete*
PO Box 3065, Cary, NC 27519 USA

Jones, Marvin M *Football Player*
8891 NW 193rd St, Miami, FL 33157 USA

Jones, Maxine *Musician*
East West Records, 75 Rockefeller Plaza, #1200, New York, NY 10019 USA

Jones, Merlakia *Basketball Player*
Cleveland Rockers, Gund Arena, 1 Center Court, Cleveland, OH 44115 USA

Jones, Mick *Musician*
Hard to Handle Mgmt, 16501 Ventura Blvd, #602, Encino, CA 91436 USA

Jones, Mickey *Actor, Musician*
Lichtman/Salners, 12216 Moorpark St, Studio City, CA 91604 USA

Jones, Mike *Baseball Player*
Kansas City Royals, 44 Almeria Ave, Jacksonville, FL 32211-7601 USA

Jones, Nasir (Nas) *Musician, Actor, Producer, Writer*
International Creative Management (ICM-LA), 8942 Wilshire Blvd, Beverly Hills, CA 90211 USA

Jones, Nathaniel R *Judge*
US Court of Appeals, US Courthouse, 425 Walnut St, Cincinnati, OH 45202 USA

Jones, Norah *Musician*
Creative Artists Agency LCC (CAA-LA), 9830 Wilshire Blvd, Beverly Hills, CA 90212 USA

Jones, Odell *Baseball Player*
Pittsburgh Pirates, 5831 Opal Ave, Palmdale, CA 93552-3967 USA

Jones, Orlando *Actor*
Creative Artists Agency, 9830 Wilshire Blvd, Beverly Hills, CA 90212 USA

Jones, P J *Race Car Driver*
Patrick Racing, 8431 Georgetown Road, Indianapolis, IN 46268 USA

Jones, Parnelli *Race Car Driver*
20550 Earl St, Torrance, CA 90503 USA

Jones, Quincy *Producer, Actor, Musician*
Quincy Jones Media Group, 3800 Barham Blvd Fl 5, Los Angeles, CA 90068 USA

Jones, Randy *Baseball Player*
San Diego Padres, 2638 Cranston Dr, Escondido, CA 92025-7338 USA

Jones, Rashida *Actor, Musician*
1606 Rosecrans Ave, Bldg 4A Fl 3, Manhattan Beach, CA 90266

Jones, Rebecca *Actor*
Gabriel Blanco Iglesias (Mexico), Rio Balsas 35-32, Colonia Cuauhtemoc, DF, 06500, Mexico

Jones, Rebinhak *Actor*
Writers & Artists, 8383 Wilshire Blvd, #550, Beverly Hills, CA 90211 USA

Jones, Reginald V *Physicist*
8 Queen's Terrace, Aberdeen, AB1 1XL, SCOTLAND

Jones, Renee *Actor*
256 S Robertson Blvd, #700, Beverly Hills, CA 90211 USA

Jones, Richard T *Actor*
Endeavor Talent Agency, 9701 Wilshire Blvd, #1000, Beverly Hills, CA 90212 USA

Jones, Richard Timothy
584 Broadway #1009, New York, NY 10012

Jones, Rick *Baseball Player*
Boston Red Sox, 1834 Weston Cir, Orange Park, FL 32003-8045 USA

Jones, Rickie Lee *Songwriter, Musician*
476 Broome St, #6A, New York, NY 10013 USA

Jones, Ricky *Baseball Player*
Baltimore Orioles, 1834 Weston Cir, Orange Park, FL 32003-8045 USA

Jones, Robert (K C) *Basketball Player, Coach*
6734 Cortez Place NW, Bremerton, WA 98311 USA

Jones, Ron *Baseball Player*
Philadelphia Phillies, 2316 Chapman St, Seguin, TX 78155-1612 USA

Jones, Rosie *Golfer*
4895 High Point Road, Atlanta, GA 30342 USA

Jones, Ross *Baseball Player*
New York Mets, 5737 NE 17th Ter, Fort Lauderdale, FL 33334-5984 USA

Jones, Rulon *Football Player*
3985 North 3775 East, Liberty, UT 84310 USA

Jones, Rulon K *Football Player*
3985 N 3775 E, Eden, UT 84310 USA

Jones, Ruppert *Baseball Player*
Kansas City Royals, 18766 Bernardo Center Dr Ste 114-A, San Diego, CA 92128-2545 USA

Jones, Sam J *Actor*
Artists Group, 10100 Santa Monica Blvd, #2490, Los Angeles, CA 90067 USA

Jones, Samuel (Sam) *Basketball Player*
15417 Tierra Dr, Silver Spring, MD 20906 USA

Jones, Sherman *Baseball Player*
San Francisco Giants, 3736 Weaver Dr, Kansas City, KS 66104-3763 USA

Jones, Shirley *Musician, Actor*
4531 Noeline Way, Encino, CA 91436 USA

Jones, Simon *Actor*
Innovative Artists, 1505 10th St, Santa Monica, CA 90401 USA

Jones, Stacy *Baseball Player*
Baltimore Orioles, 1777 Ponderosa Rd, Attalia, AL 35954-5653 USA

Jones, Stan
PO Box 813, Fraser, CO 80442

Jones, Star *Commentator*
William Morris Agency, 151 El Camino Dr, Beverly Hills, CA 90212 USA

Jones, Stephen *Lawyer*
Jones & Wyatt, PO Box 472, Enid, OK 73702 USA

Jones, Stephen J M *Fashion Designer*
36 Great Queen St, London, WC1E 6BT, UNITED KINGDOM (UK)

Jones, Steve *Golfer*
3150 Graf St, #5, Bozeman, MT 59715 USA

Jones, Steve *Musician*
Solo Agency, 55 Fulham High St, London, SW6 3JJ, UNITED KINGDOM (UK)

Jones, Steve *Basketball Player*
2871 NE Alameda St, Portland, OR 97212 USA

Jones, Steve *Baseball Player*
Chicago White Sox, 8116 Kingsdale Dr, Knoxville, TN 37919-7005 USA

Jones, Steven *Physicist*
Brigham Young University, Physics Dept, Provo, UT 84602 USA

Jones, Tamala *Actor*
Roklin Management, 8265 Sunset Blvd #101, Los Angeles, CA 90046 USA

Jones, Taylor *Cartoonist*
Times-Mirror Syndicate, Times-Mirror Square, Los Angeles, CA 90053 USA

Jones, Terry *Animator, Director*
Python Pictures, 34 Thistlewaite Road, London, E5 QQQ, UNITED KINGDOM (UK)

Jones, Terry *Musician*
TBA Artists Mgmt, 300 10th Ave S, Nashville, TN 37203 USA

Jones, Thomas D *Astronaut*
3105 Windsong Dr, Oakton, VA 22124 USA

Jones, Thomas V *Business Person*
1050 Moraga Dr, Los Angeles, CA 90049 USA

Jones, Tim *Baseball Player*
Saint Louis Cardinals, 4 Rickledge Pl, Maumelle, AR 72113-6005 USA

Jones, Tim *Baseball Player*
Pittsburgh Pirates, 6204 Green Eyes Way, Orangevale, CA 95662-4115 USA

Jones, Todd B G *Baseball Player*
4205 Mays Bend Road, Pell City, AL 35128 USA

Jones, Tom *Musician*
13976 Aubrey Road, Beverly Hills, CA 90210 USA

Jones, Tommy Lee *Actor*
Michael Black Mgmt, 5750 Wilshire Blvd, #640, Los Angeles, CA 90036 USA

Jones, Tracy *Baseball Player*
Cincinnati Reds, 4863 Bridge Ln Apt 11, Mason, OH 45040-6945 USA

Jones, Trevor *Composer*
46 Ave Road Highgate, London, N6 5DR, UNITED KINGDOM (UK)

Jones, Tyler Patrick *Actor*

Jones, Vaughan F R *Mathematician*
University of California, Mathematics Dept, Berkeley, CA 94720 USA

Jones, Vinnie *Actor*
Creative Artists Agency LCC (CAA-LA), 9830 Wilshire Blvd, Beverly Hills, CA 90212 USA

Jones, Volus
625 S. Griffith Park Dr, Burbank, CA 91506

Jones, Wali *Basketball Player*
PO Box 3642, Winter Haven, FL 33885 USA

Jones, Wallace (Wah-Wah) *Basketball Player*
512 Chinoe Road, Lexington, KY 40502 USA

Jones, Walter *Football Player*
RR 1 Box 128, Carrolton, AL 35447 USA

Jones, Walter Emanuel *Actor*
K & K Entertainment, 1498 W Sunset Blvd, Los Angeles, CA 90026 USA

Jones, Wayne *Actor, Comedian*
Smooth Man Productions, 206 Belmont Dr, Palatka, FL 32177 USA

Jones, Wesley *Architect*
Holt Hinshaw Jones, 320 Florida St, San Francisco, CA 94110 USA

Jones, William A (Dub) *Football Player*
904 Glendale Dr, Ruston, LA 71270 USA

Jones Girls, The
PO Box 6010 #761, Sherman Oaks, CA 91413-6010

Jones III, June S *Football Coach, Football Player*
University of Hawaii, Athletic Dept, 2600 Campus Road, Honolulu, HI 96822 USA

Jones Jr, James L *General*
Supreme Allied Commander, Supreme Headquarters, APO, AE, 09705 USA

Jones Jr, Roy *Boxer*
Square Ring, 200 W LaRue St, Pensacola, FL 32501 USA

Jong, Erica
121 Davis Hill Rd., Weston, CT 06883

Jong, Erica M *Writer*
PO Box 1434, New York, NY 10021 USA

Jonrowe, Dee Dee *Athlete*
PO Box 272, Willow, AK 99688 USA

Jonsen, Albert R *Doctor*
University of Washington, Med School, Medical Ethics Dept, Seattle, WA 98195 USA

Jonson, Johnny *Football Player*
PO Box 4283, Mooresville, NC 28117

Jonsson, Jorgen *Hockey Player*
Anaheim Mighty Ducks, 2000 E Gene Autry Way, Anaheim, CA 92806 USA

Jonsson, Kenny *Hockey Player*
37 Midway Ave, Locust Valley, NY 11560 USA

Jonze, Spike *Director, Actor*
1741 Ivar Ave, Los Angeles, CA 90028 USA

Joop, Wolfgang *Fashion Designer*
Joop, Harvestehuder Weg 22, Hamburg, 20149, GERMANY

Joos, Gustaaf Cardinal *Religious Leader*
Dioceseof Ghent, Bisdomplein 1, Ghent, 9000, BELGUIM

Joost, Edwin D (Eddie) *Baseball Player*
Cincinnati Reds, 303 Belhaven Circle, Santa Rosa, CA 95409-6004 USA

Joosten, Kathryn *Actor*
Schiowitz/Clay/Rose, 1680 N Vine St, #614, Los Angeles, CA 90028 USA

Jopling, T Michael *Government Official*
Ainderby Hall, Thirsk, North Yorks, YO7 4HZ, UNITED KINGDOM (UK)

Jordan, Brian *Baseball Player*
St Louis Cardinals, 1050 Bedford Gardens Dr, Alpharetta, GA 30022-6276 USA

Jordan, Charles M *Designer*
PO Box 8330, Rancho Santa Fe, CA 92067 USA

Jordan, Don *Boxer*
5100 2nd Ave, Los Angeles, CA 90043 USA

Jordan, Don D *Business Person*
Reliant Energy, 1111 Louisiana Ave, Houston, TX 77002 USA

Jordan, Eddie *Basketball Player, Coach*
Washington Wizards, MCI Centre, 601 F St NW, Washington, DC 20004 USA

Jordan, Glenn *Director*
9401 Wilshire Blvd, #700, Beverly Hills, CA 90212 USA

Jordan, I King *Educator*
Gallaudet University, President's Office, 800 Florida NW, Washington, DC 20001 USA

Jordan, Kathy *Tennis Player*
114 Walter Hays Dr, Palo Alto, CA 94303 USA

Jordan, Kevin *Baseball Player*
Philadelphia Phillies, 1018 Bowdoin St, San Francisco, CA 94134-1802 USA

Jordan, Larry R *General*
Deputy Commander in Chief, US Army Europe/7th Army, APO, AE, 09014 USA

Jordan, Le Roy
2425 Burbank St., Dallas, TX 75235-3196

Jordan, Lee Roy *Football Player*
7710 Caruth Blvd, Dallas, TX 75225 USA

Jordan, Mary *Journalist*
Washington Post, Editorial Dept, 1150 15th St NW, Washington, DC 20071 USA

Jordan, Michael J *Basketball Player*
Jump Inc, 676 N Michigan Ave #293, Chicago, IL 60611 USA

Jordan, Montell *Musician*
Mitch Schneider Organization, 14724 Ventura Blvd, #410, Sherman Oaks, CA 91403 USA

Jordan, Neil *Director, Writer*
William Morris Agency (WMA-LA), 1 William Morris Pl, Beverly Hills, CA 90212 USA

Jordan, Neil P *Director*
6 Sorrento Terrace, Dalkey, County Dublin, IRELAND

Jordan, Niles *Baseball Player*
Philadelphia Phillies, 1114 Metcalf St, Sedro Woolley, WA 98284 USA

Jordan, Payton *Coach*
3775 Modoc Road, #264, Santa Barbara, CA 93105 USA

Jordan, Ricardo *Baseball Player*
Toronto Blue Jays, 722 N Highland Ave, Tarpon Springs, FL 34688-8944 USA

Jordan, Ricky *Baseball Player*
Cleveland Indians, 11472 Ghirardelli Ct, Gold River, CA 95670-7864 USA

Jordan, Scott *Baseball Player*
Cleveland Indians, 300 Piedmont Ct Ste E, Atlanta, GA 30340-3149 USA

Jordan, Stanley *Musician*
SJ Productions, 16845 N 29th Ave, #2000, Phoenix, AZ 85053 USA

Jordan, Steve *Football Player*
581 W San Marcos Dr, Chandler, AZ 85225 USA

Jordan, Tom *Baseball Player*
Chicago White Sox, 2909 S Wyoming Ave, Roswell, NM 88203-2374 USA

Jordan Jr, Vernon E *Civil Rights Activist*
Lazard Freres, 30 Rockefeller Plz, #400, New York, NY 10112 USA

Jordanaires, The
46-19 220th Pl., Bayside, NY 11361-3654

Jordensen, Anker *Prime Minister*
Borgbjergvej 1, Copenhagen, SV, 2450, DENMARK

Jordenson, Dale W *Economist*
1010 Memorial Dr, #14C, Cambridge, MA 02138 USA

Jorgensen, Mike *Baseball Player*
New York Mets, 3543 Halliday Ave, Saint Louis, MO 63118-1124 USA

Jorgensen, Terry *Baseball Player*
Minnesota Twins, 1493 S Sugar Bush Rd, Luxemburg, WI 54217-9311 USA

Jorginho *Soccer Player*
Rua Levi Carreiro 420, Barra de Tijuca, BRAZIL

Jose, Felix *Baseball Player*
Oakland A's, 11 Broadway Apt 2, Bayonne, NJ 07002-3430 USA

Jose, Jose *Musician*
Fanny Schatz Mgmt, Melchor Ocampo 309, Mexico City, DF CP, 11590, MEXICO

Jose, Lind *Baseball Player*
Pittsburgh Pirates, 18 Villa Santa, Dorado, PR 00646-5770 USA

Josefowicz, Leila *Musician*
I M G Artists, 420 W 45th St, New York, NY 10036 USA

Joseph, Curtis *Hockey Player*
Newport Sports Mgmt, 601-201 City Centre, Mississauga, ON L5B 2T4, CANADA

Joseph, Daryl J *Astronaut*
1657 Luika Place, Campbell, CA 95008 USA

Joseph, Jeffrey
400 S. Beverly Dr. #102, Beverly Hills, CA 90212

Joseph, Stephen *Doctor*
New York City Health Department, 125 Worth St, New York, NY 10013 USA

Joseph, William *Football Player*
New York Giants, Giants Stadium, East Rutherford, NJ 07073 USA

Joseph III, Joseph E *Doctor*
University of Michigan, Taubman Center, Ann Arbor, MI 48109 USA

Josephine, Charlotte *Royalty*
Grand Ducal Palace, Luxembourg, LUXEMBOURG

Josephs, Wilfred *Composer*
4 Grand Union Walk, Kentish Town Rd Camden Town, London, NW1 9LP, UNITED KINGDOM (UK)

Josephson, Brian D *Nobel Prize Laureate*
Cavendish Laboratory, Madingley Road, Cambridge, CB3 0HE, UNITED KINGDOM (UK)

Josephson, Eriand *Actor*
Royal Dramatic Theater, Nybroplan, Box 5037, Stockholm, 10241, SWEDEN

Josephson, Erland *Actor*
Royal Dramatic Theater, Nybroplan, Box 5037, Stockholm, SWEDEN, 102 41

Josephson, Karen *Swimmer*
1923 Junction Dr, Concord, CA 94518
USA

Josephson, Lester (Josey) *Football Player*
5388 N Genernatas Dr, Tucson, AZ
85704 USA

Josephson, Sarah *Swimmer*
1923 Junction Dr, Concord, CA 94518
USA

Joshi, Pallavi *Actor, Talk Show Host,
Bollywood*
23 Shefalee Makrand Soc, Veer Savarkar
Rd Mahim, Bombay, MS 400016, INDIA

Joshua, Von *Baseball Player*
Los Angeles Dodgers, 1055 W 48th St,
San Bernardino, CA 92407-3425 USA

Jospin, Lionel R *Prime Minister*
Haute-Garonne Conseil, Place Saint
Etienne, Toulouse Cedex, 31090, FRANCE

Jothilakshmi *Actor, Bollywood*
32 Sarangapani Street, T Nagar, Chennai,
TN 600017, INDIA

Jothimeena *Actor, Bollywood*
32 Sarangapani Street, T Nagar, Chennai,
TN 600017, INDIA

Joubert, Beverly *Photographer*
National Geographic Magazine, 17th & M
Sts NW, Washington, DC 20036 USA

Joubert, Dereck *Photographer*
National Geographic Magazine, 17th & M
Sts NW, Washington, DC 20036 USA

Joulwan, George A *General*
1348 S 19th St, Arlington, VA 22202 USA

Jourdain Jr, Michel *Race Car Driver*
Team Rahal, 4601 Lyman Dr, Hillard, OH
43026 USA

Jourdan, Louis *Actor*
1139 Maybrook Dr, Beverly Hills, CA
90210 USA

Journell, Jimmy *Baseball Player*
Saint Louis Cardinals, 40 S 4th St Apt 318,
Memphis, TN 38103-5234 USA

Journey *Music Group*
azoffmusic management, 1100 Glendon
Ave #200, Los Angeles, CA 90024 USA

Jovanovich, Peter W *Publisher*
MacMillan, 1177 Ave of Americas,
#1965, New York, NY 10036 USA

Jovanovski, Ed *Hockey Player*
2382 NW 49th Lane, Boca Raton, FL
33431 USA

Jovovich, Milla *Actor, Musician, Model*
Creature Entertainment, 11766 Wilshire
Blvd #1610, Los Angeles, CA 90025 USA

Joyce, Andrea *Sportscaster, Commentator*
Arts & Entertainment, 235 E 45th St, New
York, NY 10017 USA

Joyce, Dick *Baseball Player*
Kansas City A's, 406 Versallies Dr, Cary,
NC 27511-6013 USA

Joyce, Elaine *Actor*
10745 Chalon Road, Los Angeles, CA
90077 USA

Joyce, Joan *Golfer*
22856 Marbella Circle, Boca Raton, FL
33433 USA

Joyce, John T *Misc*
Bricklayers & Allied Craftsmen, 815 15th
St NW, Washington, DC 20005 USA

Joyce, Mike *Baseball Player*
Chicago White Sox, 1609 Whitman Ln,
Wheaton, IL 60187-7445 USA

Joyce, Tom *Artist*
21 Likely Road, Santa Fe, NM 87508 USA

Joyce, William *Artist, Writer*
3302 Centenary Blvd, Shreveport, LA
71104 USA

Joyce, William H *Business Person*
Union Carbide, 39 Old Ridgebury Road,
Danbury, CT 06810 USA

Joyeux, Odette
1 rue Seguier, Paris, FRANCE, 75006

Joyner, Alrederick (Al) *Track Athlete*
JJK Assoc, PO Box 69047, Saint Louis,
MO 63169 USA

Joyner, Michelle *Actor*
Paradigm Agency, 10100 Santa Monica
Blvd, #2500, Los Angeles, CA 90067 USA

Joyner, Tom *Radio Personality*
PO Box 630495, Irving, TX 75063

Joyner, Wally *Baseball Player*
California Angels, 856 Hawks Rest Drive,
Mapleton, UT 84664-5039 USA

Joyner-Kersee, Jacqueline (Jackie) *Track
Athlete*
JJK Assoc, PO Box 69047, Saint Louis,
MO 63169 USA

Jozwiak, Brian J *Football Player, Football
Coach*
51 Rohor Ave, Buckhannon, WV 26201
USA

Ju, Ming *Artist*
28 Lane 460, Chih Shan Road Section 2,
Taipei, TAIWAN

Ju-Ju *Musician*
Agency Group Ltd, 1775 Broadway, #430,
New York, NY 10019 USA

Juanes *Musician*
William Morris Agency, 151 El Camino
Dr, Beverly Hills, CA 90212 USA

Juantorena Danger, Alberto *Track Athlete*
National Institute for Sports, Sports City,
Havana, CUBA

Juby, Marcus L *Religious Leader*
Reformed Church of Latter-Day Saints,
801 W 23rd St, Independence, MO 64055
USA

Juckes, Gordon W *Misc*
1475 Avenue B, Big Pine Key, FL 33043
USA

Jud, Brian *Business Person*

Judd, Ashley *Actor*
PO Box 1569, Franklin, TN 37065 USA

Judd, Bob *Writer*
Harper Collins Publishers, 10 E 53rd St,
New York, NY 10022 USA

Judd, Cledus T
707 18th Ave So, Nashville, TN 37203
USA

Judd, Cris *Choreographer, Actor*
Creative Management Group (CMG),
9465 Wilshire Blvd #335, Beverly Hills,
CA 90212 USA

Judd, Howard L *Misc*
University of California, Medical Center,
Ob-Gyn Dept, Los Angeles, CA 90024
USA

Judd, Jackie *Commentator*
ABC-TV, News Dept, 77 W 66th St, New
York, NY 10023 USA

Judd, Mike *Baseball Player*
Los Angeles Dodgers, 9805 Shadow Rd,
La Mesa, CA 91941-4154 USA

Judd, Naomi *Musician, Songwriter*
Wynonna Inc, PO Box 128229, Nashville,
TN 37212 USA

Judd, Wynonna *Musician*
William Morris Agency, 151 El Camino
Dr, Beverly Hills, CA 90212 USA

Juden, Jeff *Baseball Player*
Houston Astros, 2940 Tohopekaliga Dr,
Saint Cloud, FL 34772-7646 USA

Judge, Christopher *Actor*
Cunningham-Escott-Dipene & Associates
Inc (CED-LA), 10635 Santa Monica Blvd
#130, Los Angeles, CA 90025 USA

Judge, George *Economist*
University of California, Economics Dept,
Berkeley, CA 94720 USA

Judge, Mike *Animator*
Three Arts Entertainment, 9460 Wilshire
Blvd, #700, Beverly Hills, CA 90212 USA

Judkins, Jeff *Basketball Player, Coach*
3471 S 3570 E, Salt Lake City, UT 84109
USA

Judson, Howie *Baseball Player*
Chicago White Sox, 239 Fairway Cir,
Winter Haven, FL 33881-8742 USA

Juergensen, Heather *Actor*
Framework Entertainment (LA), 9057
Nemo St #C, W Hollywood, CA 90069
USA

Jugnauth, Aneerod *Prime Minister*
La Caverne 1, Vacoas, MAURITIUS

Juhl, Finn *Designer*
Kratvaenget 15, Chartottenlund, 2920,
DENMARK

Julavits, Heidi *Writer*
G P Putnam's Sons, 375 Hudson St, New
York, NY 10014 USA

Julian, Janet *Actor*
Borinstein Oreck Bogart, 3172 Dona
Susana Dr, Studio City, CA 91604 USA

Julian II, Alexander *Fashion Designer*
Alexander Julian Inc, PO Box 60,
Georgetown, CT 06829 USA

Julien, Max *Actor*
3580 Avenida del Sol, Studio City, CA
91604 USA

Julius, DeAnne *Economist*
Bank of England, Threadneedle St,
London, EC2R 8AH, UNITED KINGDOM
(UK)

Jullen, Claude *Coach*
Montreal Canadiens, 1260 de la
Gauchetiere W, Montreal, QC, H3B 5E8,
CANADA

Jump 5 *Music Group*
Jeff Roberts & Associates, 206 Bluebird
Drive, Goodlettsville, TN 37072 USA

Jumper, John P *General*
Chief of Staff, HqUSAF Pentagon, Washington, DC 20330 USA

Junck, Mary *Publisher*
Baltimore Sun, 501 N Calvert St, Baltimore, MD 21202 USA

Juncker, Jean-Claude *Prime Minister*
Hotel de Bourgogne, 4 Rue de la Congregation, 2910, LUXEMBOURG

Jung, Ernst *Writer*
8815 Lagenensligen/Wiltingen, GERMANY

Jung, Richard *Misc*
Waldhofstr 42, Freiburg, 71691, GERMANY

Junge, Eric *Baseball Player*
Philadelphia Phillies, 27 Claremont Ave, Rye, NY 10580-2503 USA

Junger, Gil *Director*
Creative Artists Agency, 9830 Wilshire Blvd, Beverly Hills, CA 90212 USA

Junger, Sebastian *Writer*
United Talent Agency, 9560 Wilshire Blvd, #500, Beverly Hills, CA 90212 USA

Junger Witt, Paul *Producer*
Witt/ Thomas Films, 4000 Warner Blvd, Producers 3, Room 20, Burbank, CA 91522 USA

Jungueira, Bruno *Race Car Driver*
2127 Brickell Ave, #3105, Miami, FL 33129 USA

Junior, Ester J (E J) *Football Player*
1001 NW 78th Terrace, Plantation, FL 33322 USA

Junior Balaiya *Actor*
3 Melgai Vaniyagar Street, Vadapalani, Chennai, TN 600 026, INDIA

Juppe, Alain
57 rue de Varenne, Paris, FRANCE, F-75007

Juppe, Alain M *Prime Minister*
Mairie, Place Pey-Berland, Bordeaux Cedex, 33077, FRANCE

Jur, Jeffrey *Cinematographer*
10615 Northvale Road, Los Angeles, CA 90064 USA

Jurak, Ed *Baseball Player*
Boston Red Sox, 3650 S Walker Ave, San Pedro, CA 90731-6046 USA

Juran, Joseph M *Engineer*
Juran Institute, 11 River Road, Wilton, CT 06897 USA

Juran, Nathan
623 Via Horquilla, Palos Verdes, CA 90274

Jurasik, Peter *Actor*
969 1/2 Manzanita Street, Los Angeles, CA 90029 USA

Jurewicz, Mike *Baseball Player*
New York Yankees, 13804 Evergreen Ct, Apple Valley, MN 55124-9257 USA

Jurgens, Dan
5033 Green Farms Rd., Edina, MN 55436-1091

Jurgens, Udo
Carmenstr. 25, Zurich, SWITZERLAND, CH-8032

Jurgensen, Karen *Editor*
USA Today, Editorial Dept, 1000 Wilson Blvd, Arlington, VA 22229 USA

Jurgensen III, Christian A (Sonny)
Football Player
PO Box 53, Mount Vernon, VA 22121 USA

Jurich, Tom *Football Player*
Northern Arizona University, Athletic Dept, Flagstaff, AZ 86011 USA

Juriga, Jim *Football Player*
3001 Easton Place, Saint Charles, IL 60175 USA

Jurinac, Sena *Opera Singer*
State Opera House, Opernring 2, Vienna, 1010, AUSTRIA

Jurow, Martin
5833 Berkshire Lane, Dallas, TX 75209

Just, Joe *Baseball Player*
Cincinnati Reds, 7001 W Rawson Ave, Franklin, WI 53132-8113 USA

Just, Walter *Publisher*
Milwaukee Journal, 333 W State St, Milwaukee, WI 53203 USA

Just, Ward S *Writer*
36 Ave Junot, Paris, FRANCE

Justice, Charlie
315 E. Main St., Cherryville, NC 28021

Justice, David *Baseball Player*
Atlanta Braves, 15260 Ventura Blvd Ste 2100, Sherman Oaks, CA 91403-5360 USA

Justice, Donald R *Writer*
338 Rocky Shore Dr, Iowa City, IA 52246 USA

Justice, William
3832 Chanson Dr., Los Angeles, CA 90043

Justman, Seth *Musician*
Nick Ben-Meir, 652 N Doheny Dr, Los Angeles, CA 90069 USA

Jutze, Skip *Baseball Player*
St Louis Cardinals, 3395 Zephyr Ct, Wheat Ridge, CO 80033-5967 USA

Juvenile *Musician*
International Creative Management (ICM-LA), 8942 Wilshire Blvd, Beverly Hills, CA 90211 USA

K

K Bagyaraj *Actor*
Off 1 Kuppusamy Street, T Nagar, Chennai, TN 600 017, INDIA

K Balaji *Actor*
58 Pantheon Road, Egmore, Chennai, TN 600 008, INDIA

K Balasing *Actor*
86/2 Maddox Street Choolai, Chennai, TN 600 112, INDIA

K Bapaiah *Director, Bollywood*
15 Seethamma Colony 3rd Cross Road, Alwarpet, Madras, TN 600 017, INDIA

K Prabakaran *Actor*
23-C North Boag Road, T Nagar, Chennai, TN 600 017, INDIA

K-Ci & JoJo *Music Group*
Creative Artists Agency LCC (CAA-LA), 9830 Wilshire Blvd, Beverly Hills, CA 90212 USA

Kaake, Jeff *Actor*
2533 N Carson St, #3105, Carson City, NV 89706 USA

Kaas, Carmen *Model*
Men/Women Model Inc, 199 Lafayette St, #700, New York, NY 10012 USA

Kaas, Jon H *Psychic*
Vanderbilt University, Psychology Dept, Nashville, TN 37240 USA

Kaas, Patrica *Musician*
Talent Sorcier, 3 Rue des Petites-Ecuries, Paris, 75010, FRANCE

Kaat, Jim *Baseball Player*
Washington Senators, PO Box 1130, Port Salerno, FL 34992-1130 USA

Kabakov, Ilya *Artist*
Gladstone Gallery, 525 W 52nd St, New York, NY 10019 USA

Kabbah, Ahmad Tejan *President*
President's Office, State House, Independence Ave, Freetown, SIERRA LEONE

Kabila, Joseph *President, General*
President's Office, Mont Ngaliema, Kinshaha, CONGO DEMOCRATIC REPUBLIC

Kabua, Imata *President*
President's Office, Cabinet Building, PO Box 2, Majuro, MARSHALL ISLANDS

Kaci *Musician*
Curb Records, 47 Music Square East, Nashville, TN 37203 USA

Kaczmarek, Jane *Actor*
Innovative Artists, 1505 10th St, Santa Monica, CA 90401 USA

Kadafi, Moammar
Bab el Aziziya, Tripoli, LIBYA

Kadanoff, Leo P *Physicist*
5421 S Cornell Ave, Chicago, IL 60615 USA

Kadare, Ismael *Writer*
63 Blvd Saint-Michel, Paris, 75005, FRANCE

Kadenyuk, Leonld K *Cosmonaut*
Potchta Kosmonavtov, Moskovskoi Oblasti, Syvisdny Goroduk, 141160, RUSSIA

Kadher, Pakkoda *Actor*
9 Ponmana Semmal Street, M G R Nagar, Chennai, TN 600 078, INDIA

Kadish, Michael S (Mike) *Football Player*
7941 Sudbury Lane SE, Ada, MI 49301 USA

Kadish, Ronald T (Ron) *General*
Director, Missile Defense Agency, Washington, DC 20301 USA

Kadison, Joshua *Songwriter, Musician*
Nick Bode, 1265 Electric Ave, Venice, CA 90291 USA

Kaelin, Kato
6404 Wilshire Blvd. #950, Los Angeles, CA 90048-5529

Kaestle, Carl F *Historian*
35 Charlesfield St, Providence, RI 02906
USA

Kafelnikov, Yevgeny A *Tennis Player*
Int'l Mgmt Group, 26 Riverside Dr,
Rumson, NJ 07760 USA

Kaftan, George *Basketball Player*
2591 Lantern Light Way, Manasquan, NJ
08736 USA

Kagan, Daryn *Commentator*
Cable News Network, News Dept, 1050
Techwood Dr NW, Atlanta, GA 30318
USA

Kagan, Elaine *Actor, Writer*
Avon/William Morrow, 1350 Ave of
Americas, New York, NY 10019 USA

Kagan, Henri Boris *Misc*
University Paris-Sud, Institut de Chimie
Moleculaire, Orsay, 91405, FRANCE

Kagan, Jeremy Paul *Director*
2024 N Curson Ave, Los Angeles, CA
90046 USA

Kagen, David *Actor*
6457 Firmament Ave, Van Nuys, CA
91406 USA

Kagge, Erling *Skier*
Munkedamsveien 86, Oslo, 0270,
NORWAY

Kahane, Jeffrey *Musician*
I M G Artists, 420 W 45th St, New York,
NY 10036 USA

Kahin, Brian *Educator*
Harvard University, Information
Infrastructure Project, Cambridge, MA
02138 USA

Kahlil, Aisha *Musician*
Sweet Honey Agency, PO Box 600099,
Newtonville, MA 02460 USA

Kahn, Alfred E *Government Official,
Economist*
308 N Cayuga St, Ithaca, NY 14850 USA

Kahn, David R *Publisher*
New Yorker Magazine, Publisher's Office,
4 Times Square, New York, NY 10036
USA

Kahn, Harold *Business Person*
Montgomery Ward Co, PO Box 5238,
Elgin, IL 60121 USA

Kahn, Joseph *Director, Writer*
HSI Entertainment, 3630 E Ham Dr,
Culver City, CA 90232 USA

Kahn, Robert E *Scientist*
909 Lynton Place, Mclean, VA 22102
USA

Kahn, Roger *Writer*
280 Marcotte Road, Kingston, NY 12401
USA

Kahneman, Daniel *Nobel Prize Laureate*
41 Adams Dr, Princeton, NJ 08540 USA

Kai, Teanna *Adult Film Star*
Atlas Multimedia Inc, 22940 Burbank
Blvd, Woodland Hills, CA 91367 USA

Kaifu, Toshiki *Prime Minister*
House of Representatives, Diet, Tokyo,
100, JAPAN

Kain, Karin A *Dancer*
National Ballet of Canada, 470 Queens
Quay, Toronto, ON M5V 3K4, CANADA

Kain, Khalil *Actor*
Envision Entertainment, 9255 Sunset Blvd
#300, Los Angeles, CA 90069 USA

Kainer, Don *Baseball Player*
Texas Rangers, 1923 Sieber Dr, Houston,
TX 77017-6201 USA

Kaiser, A Dale *Misc*
832 Santa Fe Ave, Stanford, CA 94305
USA

Kaiser, George B *Financier*
Bank of Oklahoma, Bank of Oklahoma
Tower, PO Box 2300, Tulsa, OK 74102
USA

Kaiser, Michael *Misc*
Kennedy Center for Performing Arts,
Washington, DC 20011 USA

Kaiser, Natasha *Track Athlete*
2601 Hickman Road, Des Moines, IA
50310 USA

Kaiser, Tim *Producer*
Vision Art Management, 9200 Sunset
Blvd, Penthouse 1, Los Angeles, CA
90069 USA

Kaiserman, William *Fashion Designer*
29 W 56th St, New York, NY 10019 USA

Kaji, Gautam S *Financier*
World Bank Group, 1818 H St NW,
Washington, DC 20433 USA

Kajol *Actor*
Usha Kiran, Altamount Road, Mumbai,
MS 400026, INDIA

Kakhidze, Djansug I *Conductor*
Leselidze St 18, Tbilisi, 380005,
GEORGIA

Kakutani, Michiko *Journalist*
New York Times, Editorial Dept, 229 W
43rd St, New York, NY 10036 USA

Kalafat, Ed *Basketball Player*
1814 Pinehurst Ave, Saint Paul, MN
55116 USA

Kalam, A P J Abdul *President*
President's Office, Bharat ka Rashtrapati
Bhavan, New Delhi, New Delhi, 110004,
INDIA

Kalangis, Ike *Financier*
Boafmen's Sunwest, 303 Roma Ave NW,
Albuquerque, NM 87102 USA

Kalas, Harry *Sportscaster*
Philadelphia Philies, Veterans Stadium,
3501 S Broad, Philadelphia, PA 19148
USA

Kalashnikov, Mikhail T *Designer, General*
A O Izhmash, 426006 Izhevsk, Udmurtia
Republic, RUSSIA

Kalb, Marvin *Commentator, Educator*
Harvard University, Shorenstein Center,
79 JF Kennedy St, Cambridge, MA 02138
USA

Kalem, Toni *Actor*
House of Representatives, 400 S Beverly
Dr, #101, Beverly Hills, CA 90212 USA

Kalember, Patricia *Actor*
Innovative Artists, 1505 10th St, Santa
Monica, CA 90401 USA

Kalen, Herbert D *War Hero*
General Delivery, Angel Fire, NM 87710
USA

Kaler, Jamie *Actor*
Innovative Artists (LA), 1505 Tenth St,
Santa Monica, CA 90401 USA

Kalichstein, Joseph *Musician*
I C M Artists, 40 W 57th St, New York,
NY 10019 USA

Kalikow, Peter S *Publisher*
H J Kalikow Co, 101 Park Ave, New York,
NY 10178 USA

kalina, Mike *Chef*
Travelin Gourmet Show, PBS-TV, 1320
Braddock Place, Alexandira, VA 22314
USA

kalina, Richard *Artist*
44 King St, New York, NY 10014 USA

Kaline, Albert W (Al) *Baseball Player*
Detroit Tigers, Comercia Park, 2100
Woodward Ave, Detroit, MI 48201 USA

Kalis, Todd A *Football Player*
172 Woodhaven Dr, Mars, PA 16046 USA

Kalish, Martin *Misc*
School Administrators Federation, 853
Broadway, New York, NY 10003 USA

Kalitta, Connie *Race Car Driver*
American International Airways, 804
Willow Run Airport, Ypsilanti, MI 48198
USA

Kallaugher, Kevin (Kall) *Cartoonist*
Baltimore Sun, Editorial Dept, 501 N
Calvert St, Baltimore, MD 21202 USA

Kallen, Jackie
Trident Media Group LLC, 41 Madison
Ave Fl 33, New York, NY 10010 USA

Kallen, Kitty *Musician*
35 Winthrop Place, Englewood, NJ 07631
USA

Kallir, Lilian *Musician*
Columbia Artists Mgmt Inc, 165 W 57th
St, New York, NY 10019 USA

Kallman, Gerhard M *Architect*
Kallman McKinnell Wood, 939 Boylston
St, Boston, MA 02115 USA

Kalman, Rudolf E *Mathematician*
ETH Zentrum, Zurich, 8092,
SWITZERLAND

Kalmbach, Herbert
1056 Santiago Dr., Newport Beach, CA
92660

Kalplan, Deborah *Writer, Director*
Benderspink, 6735 Yucca St, Hollywood,
CA 90028

Kalpokas, Donald *Prime Minister*
Prime Minister's Office, PO Box 110, Port
Vila, VANUTA

Kalule, Ayub *Boxer*
Palle Skjulet, Bagsvaert 12, Copenhagen,
2880, DENMARK

Kalyagin, Aleksander A *Actor*
1905 Goda Str 3, #91, Moscow, 123100,
RUSSIA

Kamal, Gray *Musician*
William Morris Agency, 1325 Ave of
Americas, New York, NY 10019 USA

Kamali, Norma *Fashion Designer*
OMO Norma Kamali, 11 W 56th St, New
York, NY 10019 USA

Kamano, Stacy *Actor*
Amsel Eisenstadt & Frazier Inc, 5757 Wilshire Blvd #510, Los Angeles, CA 90036 USA

Kamarck, Martin A *Financier*
Export-Import Bank, 811 Vermont Ave NW, Washington, DC 20571 USA

Kamb, Alexander *Misc*
202 Katahdin Dr, Lexington, MA 02421 USA

Kamel, Stanley *Actor*
Irv Schechter, 9300 Wilshire Blvd, #410, Beverly Hills, CA 90212 USA

Kamen, Dean *Inventor*
15 W Wind Dr, Bedford, NH 03110 USA

Kamensky, Valeri *Hockey Player*
4 Bermuda Lake Dr, West Palm Beach, FL 33418 USA

Kamesh, Kamala *Actor, Bollywood*
4F 3rd Block, Shanthi Towers 88 ArcotRoad Vadapalani, Chennai, TN 600026, INDIA

Kamin, Blair *Critic*
Chicago Tribune, Editorial Dept, 435 N Michigan Ave, Chicago, IL 60611 USA

Kaminir, Lisa *Actor*
Ellis Talent Group, 14241 N Maple Dr, #207, Sherman Oaks, CA 01423 USA

Kaminski, Janusz Z *Cinematographer*
23801 Catabasas Road, #2004, Catabasas, CA 91302 USA

Kaminski, Marek *Misc*
Ul Dickmana 14/15, Gdansk, 80-339, POLAND

Kaminsky, Arthur C *Lawyer*
Athletes & Artists, 888 7th Ave, #3700, New York, NY 10106 USA

Kaminsky, Walter *Misc*
Hamburg University, Martin-Luther-King Platz 6, Hamburg, 20146, GERMANY

Kamisar, Yale *Lawyer, Educator*
2910 Daleview Dr, Ann Arbor, MI 48105 USA

Kamm, Henry *Journalist*
New York Times, Editorial Dept, 229 W 43rd St, New York, NY 10036 USA

Kammen, Michael G *Historian*
Comell University, History Dept, McGraw Hall, Ithaca, NY 14853 USA

Kamoze, Ini *Musician*
Famous Artists Agency, 250 W 57th St, New York, NY 10107 USA

Kampelman, Max M *Government Official, Diplomat*
3154 Highland Place NW, Washington, DC 20008 USA

Kamu, Okko T
Calle Mozart 7, Rancho Domingo, Benalmedina Pueblo, 29369, SPAIN

Kan, Yuet Wai *Misc*
20 Yerba Buena Ave, San Francisco, CA 94127 USA

Kanaga *Actor*
33 1st Mall Road, R A Puram, Chennai, TN 600028, INDIA

Kanakaredes, Melina *Actor*
Gersh Agency, The (LA), 232 N Canon Dr, Beverly Hills, CA 90210 USA

Kanal, Tony *Songwriter, Musician*
Rebel Waltz Inc, 31652 2nd Ave, Laguna Beach, CA 92651 USA

Kanaly, Steve *Actor*
4663 Grand Ave, Ojai, CA 93023 USA

Kanamori, Hiroo *Physicist*
California Institute of Technology, Geophysics Dept, Pasadena, CA 91125 USA

Kanan, Sean
4526 Wilshire Blvd., Los Angeles, CA 90010

Kanan, Tony *Race Car Driver*
Mo Nunn Racing, 2920 Fortune Circle W, #E, Indianapolis, IN 46241 USA

Kananln, Roman G *Architect*
Join-Stock Mosprojekt, 13/14 1 Brestkaya Str, Moscow, 125190, RUSSIA

Kancheli, Giya A (Georgy) *Composer*
Tovstonogov Str 6, Tbilisi, 380064, GEORGIA

Kandel, Eric R *Nobel Prize Laureate*
9 Sigma Place, Bronx, NY 10471 USA

Kander, John H *Composer*
B M I, 8730 Sunset Blvd, #300, Los Angeles, CA 90069 USA

Kane, Big Daddy *Musician*
Tough Guy Mgmt, 53 W 23rd St, #1100, New York, NY 10010 USA

Kane, Carol *Actor*
Slater, PO Box 8002, Universal City, CA 95409 USA

Kane, Christian *Actor*
Blue Train Entertainment, 9333 Wilshire Blvd, G Level, Beverly Hills, CA 90210 USA

Kane, John C *Business Person*
Cardinal Health, 7000 Cardinal Place, Dublin, OH 43017 USA

Kane, Kelly *Actor*
D H Talent, 1800 N Highland Ave, #300, Los Angeles, CA 90028 USA

Kane, Khalil *Actor*
Envision Entertainment, 9255 Sunset Blvd #300, Los Angeles, CA 90069 USA

Kane, Nick *Musician*
AstroMedia, 1620 16th Ave S, Nashville, TN 37212 USA

Kane Elson, Marion *Swimmer*
4669 Badger Road, Santa Rosa, CA 95409 USA

Kanell, Danny *Football Player*
5340 NE 33rd Ave, Fort Lauderdale, FL 33308 USA

Kanew, Jeffery R *Director*
Gersh Agency, 232 N Canon Dr, Beverly Hills, CA 90210 USA

Kang, Dong-Suk *Musician*
Clarion/Seven Muses, 47 Whitehall Park, London, N19 3TW, UNITED KINGDOM (UK)

Kango, Mayuri *Actor, Bollywood*
21 Kala Pathar Gokul Paradise, Thakur Complex Kandivili (E), Mumbai, MS 400101, INDIA

Kanievska, Marek *Director*
International Creative Mgmt, 8942 Wilshire Blvd, #219, Beverly Hills, CA 90211 USA

Kanin, Fay *Writer*
653 Palisades Beach Road, Santa Monica, CA 90402 USA

Kann, Peter R *Business Person, Publisher, Journalist*
Dow Jones Co, 200 Liberty St, New York, NY 10281 USA

Kann, Stan
570 N. Rossmore Ave., Los Angeles, CA 90004

Kannadasan, Vishali *Actor, Bollywood*
29/1 1st Cross Street, Chinmaya Nagar, Chennai, TN 600011, INDIA

Kannaiah, Ennathe *Actor*
RP Block No8 Llyods Colony, Royapet, Chennai, TN 600 014, INDIA

Kanne, Michael S *Judge*
US Court of Appeals, PO Box 1340, Lafayette, IN 47902 USA

Kannenberg, Bernd *Track Athlete*
Sportschule, Sonthofen/Aligau, 87527, GERMANY

Kanouse, Lyle *Actor*
Gage Group, The (LA), 14724 Ventura Blvd #505, Los Angeles, CA 91403 USA

Kanovitz, Howard *Artist*
361 N Sea Mecox Road, Southampton, NY 11968 USA

Kansas *Musician*
Creative Artists Agency LCC (CAA-LA), 9830 Wilshire Blvd, Beverly Hills, CA 90212 USA

Kansch, Heather *Artist*
Knowle, Rundlerohy Newton Abbot, Devon, TQ12 2PJ, UNITED KINGDOM (UK)

Kanter, Hal *Producer, Writer*
Hecox Horn Wheeler, 4730 Woodman Ave, Sherman Oaks, CA 91423 USA

Kanter, Paul *Musician*
Ron Rainey Mgmt, 315 S Beverly Dr, #407, Beverly Hills, CA 90212 USA

Kantor, Michael (Mickey) *Secretary*
4436 Edmunds St NW, Washington, DC 20007 USA

Kantor, Secy
Mickey 5019 Klingle St NW, Washington, DC 20016 USA

Kantrowitz, Adrian *Doctor*
70 Gallogly Road, Lake Angelus, MI 48326 USA

Kantrowitz, Arthur R *Physicist*
4 Downing Road, Hanover, NH 03755 USA

Kanwaljit *Actor, Bollywood*
B-1001 Abhishek Apts, Juhu Versova Link Road 4 Bungalows Andheri (W), Mumbai, MS 400053, INDIA

Kanwar, Anita *Actor, Bollywood*
501A Anisha Apartments Yari Road, Versova Andheri, Mumbai, MS 400061, INDIA

Kanwar, Raj *Director, Filmmaker, Bollywood, Producer*
6 Mewawala Building Haidery House, Next To Arrow Studio Vakola Masjid Santacruz (E), Bombay, MS 400 055, INDIA

Kao, Archie *Actor*
Gold Marshak Liedtke, 3500 W Olive Ave, #1400, Burbank, CA 91505 USA

Kao, Charles K *Engineer*
Transtech Services, 3 Gloucester Road, Wanchai, Hong Kong, CHINA

Kapadia, Dimple *Actor, Bollywood*
201-A Vastu Bldg, Military Rd Juhu, Mumbai, MS 400049, INDIA

Kapanen, Sami *Hockey Player*
104 Royal Pine Court, Cary, NC 27511 USA

Kapelos, John *Actor*
Axiom Management, 10701 Wilshire Blvd #1202, Los Angeles, CA 90024

Kapioitas, John *Business Person*
ITT Sheraton Corp, 1111 Westchester Ave, West Harrison, NY 10604 USA

Kaplan, Gabe *Actor, Comedian*
9551 Hidden Valley Road, Beverly Hills, CA 90210 USA

Kaplan, Gabriel
9551 Hidden Valley Rd., Beverly Hills, CA 90210

Kaplan, Jonathan S *Director*
4323 Ben Ave, Studio City, CA 91604 USA

Kaplan, Justin *Writer*
PO Box 219, Truro, MA 02666 USA

Kaplan, Marvin *Actor*
PO Box 1522, Burbank, CA 91507 USA

Kaplan, Nathan O *Misc*
8587 La Jolla Scenic Dr, La Jolla, CA 92037 USA

Kaplon, Al *Actor*
2899 Agoura Road, Suite 172, Westlake Village, CA 91361 USA

Kaplow, Herbert E *Commentator*
211 N Van Buren St, Falls Church, VA 22046 USA

Kapnek, Emily *Actor*
Creative Artists Agency LCC (CAA-LA), 9830 Wilshire Blvd, Beverly Hills, CA 90212 USA

Kapoor, Anil *Actor, Bollywood*
31 Shringar, Presidency Society, 7th Road JVPD Scheme, Mumbai, MS 400049, INDIA

Kapoor, Anish *Artist*
33 Coleherne Road, London, SW10, UNITED KINGDOM (UK)

Kapoor, Kareena *Actor, Bollywood*
2-B/110/1201 Excellency 4th Cross Road, Lokhandwala Complex Andheri(W), Mumbai, MS 400058, INDIA

Kapoor, Karishma *Actor, Bollywood*
2B Excellency 1101/1201, 4th Cross Road, Lokhandwala Complex Andheri (W), Mumbai, MS 400048, INDIA

Kapoor, Karisma *Actor, Bollywood*
2B Excellency 1101 1201 4th Cross Road, Lokhandwala Complex, Bombay, MS 400 058, INDIA

Kapoor, Rajiv *Director, Actor, Filmmaker, Producer, Bollywood*
R K Studios, Chembur, Bombay, MS 400 071, INDIA

Kapoor, Randhir *Actor, Director, Producer, Bollywood*
R K Studios, Chembur, Bombay, MS 400 071, INDIA

Kapoor, Rishi *Actor, Bollywood*
27 Krishna Raj, Pali Hill Bandra, Mumbai, MS 400058, INDIA

Kapoor, Sanjay *Actor, Bollywood*
18 Arjun Magnum Bungalows, Lokhandwala Complex Andheri (W), Mumbai, MS 400053, INDIA

Kapoor, Shakti *Actor, Bollywood, Comedian*
Palm Beach 7th Floor Gandhigram Road, Juhu, Bombay, MS 400 049, INDIA

Kapoor, Shammi *Actor, Bollywood*
2 Blue Heaven Malabar Hill, Mt Pleasant Rd, Mumbai, MS 400006, INDIA

Kapoor, Shashi *Actor, Bollywood*
112 Atlas Apartments, Harkness Road, Bombay, MS 400 006, INDIA

Kapor, Mitchell D *Engineer*
Open Source Application Foundation, 177 Post St, #900, San Francisco, CA 94108 USA

Kapp, Joseph (Joe) *Football Player, Football Coach*
233 Edelen Ave, Los Gatos, CA 95030 USA

Kappu, Satyen *Actor, Bollywood*
201 Canvera J P Road, Versova Andheri, Bombay, MS 400 061, INDIA

Kapriski, Valerie
10 Ave. George V, Paris, FRANCE, F-75008

Kaprisky, Valerie *Actor*
Artmedia, 20 Ave Rapp, Paris, 75007, FRANCE

Kapture, Mitzi *Actor*
Bradley-Kapture, 3605 Sandy Plains Road, #240-116, Marietta, GA 30066 USA

Kapur, Shekhar *Actor, Bollywood, Director, Filmmaker, Producer*
42 Sheetal A B Nair Road, Juhu, Bombay, MS 400 049, INDIA

kar-Wai, Wong *Director*
Anonymous Content, 8522 National Blvd #101, Culver City, CA 90232 USA

Karageorghis, Vassos *Misc*
Foundation Anastasios Leventis, 28 Sofoulis St, Nicosia, CYPRUS

Karamanov, Alemdar S *Composer*
Voykova Str 2, #4, Simferopol, Crimea, UKRAINE

Karan, Donna *Fashion Designer*
Donna Karan Co, 361 Newbury St, Suite 1500, Boston, MA 02115 USA

Karapati, Gyorgy *Misc*
II Liva Utca 1, Budapest, 1025, HUNGARY

Karath, Kym
2267 Roscomare Rd., Los Angeles, CA 90077

Karathanasis, Sotirios K *Scientist*
Harvard Medical School, 25 Shattuck St, Boston, MA 02115 USA

Karatz, Bruce E *Business Person*
Kaufman & Broad Home, 10990 Wilshire Blvd, Los Angeles, CA 90024 USA

Karbacher, Bernd
Hufnagelstrasse 13, Munich, GERMANY, D-80686

Kardashian, Robert
18056 Lake Encino Dr., Encino, CA 91316

Karelskaya, Rimma K *Ballerina*
Bolshol Theater, Teatralnaya Pi 1, Moscow, 103009, RUSSIA

Karen, James
4455 Los Feliz Blvd. #807, Los Angeles, CA 90027

Karieva, Bernara *Ballerina*
Navoi Opera Theater, 28 M K Otaturk St, Tashkent, 700029, UZBEKISTAN

Karim, Reef *Actor*
Select Artists Ltd (CA-Westside Office), 1138 12th Street, Suite 1, Santa Monica, CA 90403 USA

Karim-Lamrani, Mohammed *Prime Minister*
Rue du Mont Saint Michel, Anfa Superieur, Casablanca, 21300, MOROCCO

Karimov, Islam M *President*
President's Office, Uzbekistansky Prosp 45, Tashkent, UZBEKISTAN

Karin, Anna *Actor*
Greene Assoc, 7080 Hollywood Blvd, #1017, Los Angeles, CA 90028 USA

Karina, Anna *Actor*
Artmedia, 20 Ave Rapp, Paris, 75007, FRANCE

Kariya, Paul *Hockey Player*
2493 Aquasanta, Tustin, CA 92782 USA

Karl, George *Coach*
10936 N Port Washington Road, Mequon, WI 53092 USA

Karl, Jan
5555 Melrose Ave. L, Los Angeles, CA 90038

Karle, Isabelia *Misc*
6304 Lakeview Dr, Falls Church, VA 22041 USA

Karle, Jerome *Nobel Prize Laureate*
6304 Lakeview Dr, Falls Church, VA 22041 USA

Karlen, John *Actor*
PO Box 1195, Santa Monica, CA 90406 USA

Karlin, Ben *Writer, Producer*
3 Arts Entertainment Inc, 9460 Wilshire Blvd Fl 7, Beverly Hills, CA 90212 USA

Karlin, Fred
1187 Coast Village Rd. #1-339, Montecito, CA 93108

Karlin, Samuel *Mathematician*
Stanford University, Mathematics Dept, Stanford, CA 94305 USA

Karling, John S *Misc*
1219 Tuckahoe Lane, West Lafayette, IN 47906 USA

Karloff, Sara
PO Box 2424, Rancho Mirage, CA 92270

Karlson, Phil
3094 Patricia Ave., Los Angeles, CA 90064

Karlsson, Lena *Musician*
MOB Agency, 6404 Wilshire Blvd, #807, Los Angeles, CA 90048 USA

Karlstad, Geir *Speed Skater*
Hamarveien 5A, Fjellhamar, 1472, NORWAY

Karlzen, Mary *Songwriter, Musician*
Little Big Man, 155 Ave of Americas, #700, New York, NY 10013 USA

Karmanos Jr, Peter *Business Person*
Compuware Corp, 1 Campus Martius, Detroit, MI 48226 USA

Karmi, Ram *Architect*
Karmi Architects, 17 Kaplan St, Tel Aviv, 64734, ISRAEL

Karmi-Melamede, Ada *Architect*
Karmi Architects, 17 Kaplan St, Tel Aviv, 64734, ISRAEL

Karn, Richard *Actor*
Special Artists Agency, 345 N Maple Dr, #302, Beverly Hills, CA 90210 USA

Karnad, Girish *Actor*
Silver Cascade Mount Mary Road, Bandra, Bombay, MS 400 050, INDIA

Karnes, David K *Senator*
Kutak Rock, Omaha Building, 1650 Farnam St, Omaha, NE 68102, us

Karnes, David K *Senator*
Kutak Rock, Omaha Building, 1650 Farnam St, Omaha, NE 68102 USA

Karnow, Stanley *Historian*
10850 Spring Knolls Dr, Potomac, MD 20854 USA

Karolyi, Bela *Coach*
478 Forest Service 200 Road, Huntsville, TX 77340 USA

Karon, Jan *Writer*
7060 Esmont Farm, Esmont, VA 22937 USA

Karp, Richard M *Scientist*
University of Washington, Computer Science Dept, Seattle, WA 98195 USA

Karpatkin, Rhonda H *Publisher*
Consumer Reports Magazine, 101 Truman Ave, Yonkers, NY 10703 USA

Karplus, Martin *Misc*
Harvard University, Chemistry Dept, Cambridge, MA 02138 USA

Karpov, Anatoly *Misc*
International Peace Fund, Prechistenka 10, Moscow, RUSSIA

Karr, Mary *Writer*
Syracuse University, English Dept, Syracuse, NY 13244 USA

Karras, Alex
7943 Woodrow Wilson Dr., Los Angeles, CA 90046

Karras, Alexander G (Alex) *Actor, Football Player*
7943 Woodrow Wilson Dr, Los Angeles, CA 90046 USA

Karras, Chester L *Writer*
1633 Stanford St, Santa Monica, CA 90404 USA

Karros, Eric P *Baseball Player*
6612 Madra Ave, San Diego, CA 92120 USA

Kartheiser, Vincent *Actor*
International Creative Management (ICM-LA), 8942 Wilshire Blvd, Beverly Hills, CA 90211 USA

Karusseit, Ursula *Actor*
Volksbunne, Rasa Luxemburg Platz, Berlin, 10178, GERMANY

Karyo, Tcheky *Actor*
Current Entertainment, 1411 Fifth St #405, Santa Monica, CA 90401 USA

Karzai, Hamid *Prime Minister*
Prime Minister's Office, Shar Rahi Sedarat, Kabul, AFGHANISTAN

Kasaks, Sally Frame *Business Person*
Ann Taylor Stores, 142 W 57th St, New York, NY 10019 USA

Kasaronov, Alexei *Hockey Player*
153 Eagle Rock Way, Montclair, NJ 07042 USA

Kasarova, Vesselina *Opera Singer*
Columbia Artists Mgmt Inc, 165 W 57th St, New York, NY 10019 USA

Kasatkina, Natalya R *Ballerina, Choreographer*
Saint Karietny Riad, H 5/10 B 37, Moscow, 103006, RUSSIA

Kasay, John *Football Player*
12707 NE 101st Place, Kirkland, WA 98033 USA

Kasch, Max *Actor*
Abrams Artists Agency (LA), 9200 Sunset Blvd Fl 11, Los Angeles, CA 90069 USA

Kasdan, Lawrence E *Director, Writer*
Creative Artists Agency, 9830 Wilshire Blvd, Beverly Hills, CA 90212 USA

Kasem, Casey *Entertainer, Actor*
138 N Mapleton Dr, Los Angeles, CA 90077 USA

Kasem, Jean *Actor*
138 N Mapleton Dr, Los Angeles, CA 90077 USA

Kaser, Helmut A *Misc*
Hitzigweg 11, Zurich, 8032, SWITZERLAND

Kasha, Al *Composer, Musician*
458 N Oakhurst Dr, #102, Beverly Hills, CA 90210 USA

Kashkashian, Kim *Musician*
Musicians Corporate Mgmt, PO Box 589, Millbrook, NY 12545 USA

Kashthuri *Actor, Bollywood*
4 Kashthuri Ranga Road, Chennai, TN 600018, INDIA

Kaskey, Raymond J *Artist*
Portlandia Productions, PO Box 25658, Portland, OR 97298 USA

Kason, Corinne *Actor*
Lovell Assoc, 7095 Hollywood Blvd, #1006, Los Angeles, CA 90028 USA

Kasovitz, Mathieu *Actor*
Cineart, 36 Rue de Ponthieu, Paris, FRANCE, 75008

Kasparaitis, Darius *Hockey Player*
48 Steers Ave, Northport, NY 11768 USA

Kasparaltis, Darius
170 Fairway Landings Dr., Canonsburg, PA 15317-9567

Kasparov, Garri *Misc*
Russian Chess Federation, Luzhnetskaya 8, Moscow, 119270, RUSSIA

Kasper, Steve *Hockey Player, Coach*
156 Lancaster Road, North Andover, MA 01845 USA

Kasper, Walter Cardinal *Religious Leader*
Via dell Erba 1, Rome, 00193, ITALY

Kaspszyk, Jacek *Conductor*
Teatr Wielu, Pl Teatrainy 1, Warsaw, 00-077, POLAND

Kasrashvili, Makvala *Opera Singer*
Bolshoi Theater, Teatralnaya Pl 1, Moscow, 103009, RUSSIA

Kass, Carmen *Model*
City Models, Rue Jean Mermoz, Paris, 75008, FRANCE

Kass, Danny *Skier*
PO Box 8549, Mammoth Lakes, CA 93546 USA

Kass, Leon R *Misc*
1150 17th St NW, #AE1, Washington, DC 20036 USA

Kass, Patricia
B.P. 203, Illkirch, FRANCE, F-06700

Kassebaum, Nancy Landon *Senator*
US Embassy, Tokyo, Unit 45004 Box 200, APO, AP, 96337 USA

Kassebaum-Baker, Nancy *Ex-Senator*
PO Box 8, Huntsville, TN 37756-0008 USA

Kassell, Carl *Commentator*
National Public Radio, 635 Massachusetts Ave, Washington, DC 20001 USA

Kassir, John *Actor, Writer, Producer*
8436 West 3rd Street #740, Los Angeles, CA 90048 USA

Kassorla, Irene C *Doctor*
908 N Roxbury Dr, Beverly Hills, CA 90210 USA

Kassulke, Karl O *Football Player*
3030 McCarthy Ridge, Saint Paul, MN 55121 USA

Kastner, Elliott *Producer*
Winkast Films, Pinewood Studios, Iver Heath, Iver, SL0 0NH, UNITED KINGDOM (UK)

Kastner, Peter *Actor*
459 Broadway, Cambridge, MA 02138

Kasyanov, Mikhail M *Prime Minister*
Prime Minister's Office, Kremlin, Staraya Pl 4, Moscow, 103132, RUSSIA

Katchor, Ben *Cartoonist*
Little Brown, 3 Center Plaza, Boston, MA 02108 USA

Kates, Kimberley *Actor*
David Talent, 116 S Gardner St, Los
Angeles, CA 90036 USA

Kates, Kimberly
3500 W. Olive Ave. #1400, Burbank, CA
91505

Kates, Robert W *Misc*
1081 Bar Harbor Road, Trenton, ME
04605 USA

Kathadi, Ramamurthi *Actor*
4 Krishna Avenue, C V Raman Road,
Chennai, TN 600 006, INDIA

Katims, Jason *Producer*
Creative Artists Agency LCC (CAA-LA),
9830 Wilshire Blvd, Beverly Hills, CA
90212 USA

Katims, Milton *Musician, Conductor*
Fairway Estales, 8001 Sand Point Way NE,
Seattle, WA 98115 USA

Katin, Peter R *Musician*
Maureen Lunn, Top Farm Parish Lane,
Hedgerley, Bucks, SL2 3JH, UNITED
KINGDOM (UK)

Katrina & The Waves
45 Belvoir Rd. Cambridge,
Cambridgeshire, ENGLAND, CB4 1JH

Katritzky, Alan R *Misc*
1221 SW 21st Ave, Gainesville, FL 32601
USA

Katsav, Moshe *President*
President's Office, 3 Hanassi, Jerusalem,
92188, ISRAEL

Katsoudas, Stella *Songwriter, Musician*
Ashley Talent, 2002 Hogback Road, #20,
Ann Arbor, MI 48105 USA

Katsulas, Andreas *Actor*
Innovative Artists, 1505 10th St, Santa
Monica, CA 90401 USA

Katt, Nicky *Actor*
Baker/Winokur/Ryder, 9100 Wilshire Blvd,
#600, Beverly Hills, CA 90212 USA

Katt, William *Actor*
5860 Le Sage Ave, Woodland Hills, CA
91367 USA

Kattan, Chris *Comedian*
Endeavor Agency LLC (LA), 9601 Wilshire
Blvd Fl 3, Beverly Hills, CA 90210 USA

Kattan, Mohammed Imad *Architect*
PO Box 950846, Amman, 11195,
JORDAN

Katz, Abraham *Diplomat*
US Council for International Business,
1212 Ave of Americas, New York, NY
10036 USA

Katz, Alex *Artist*
435 W Broadway, New York, NY 10012
USA

Katz, Cindy
8370 Wilshire Blvd. #209, Beverly Hills,
CA 90211

Katz, Donald L *Engineer*
2011 Washtenaw Ave, Ann Arbor, MI
48104 USA

Katz, Douglas J (Doug) *Admiral*
1530 Gordon Cove Dr, Annapolis, MD
21403 USA

Katz, Harold *Misc*
Philadelphia 76ers, 1st Union Center,
3601 S Broad St, Philadelphia, PA 19148
USA

Katz, Hilda *Artist*
915 W End Ave, #5D, New York, NY
10025 USA

Katz, Jonathan *Actor, Comedian,
Animator*
Creative Artists Agency, 9830 Wilshire
Blvd, Beverly Hills, CA 90212 USA

Katz, Mark

Katz, Michael *Misc*
1 Griggs Lane, Chappaqua, NY 10514
USA

Katz, Omri *Actor*
JH Productions, 23679 Calabasas Road,
#333, Calabasas, CA 91302 USA

Katz, Ross *Producer*
United Talent Agency (UTA), 9560
Wilshire Blvd, Beverly Hills, CA 90212
USA

Katz, Samuel L *Misc*
1917 Wildcat Creek Road, Chapel Hill,
NC 27516 USA

Katz, Simon *Musician*
Searles, Chapel, 26A Munster St, London,
SW6 4EN, UNITED KINGDOM (UK)

Katz, Stephen M *Cinematographer*
8581 Santa Monica Blvd, PO Box 453,
West Hollywood, CA 90069 USA

Katz, Tonnie L *Editor*
Orange Country Register, Editorial Dept,
625 N Grand Ave, Santa Ana, CA 92701
USA

katz, Vera *Politician*
Mayor's Office, City Hall, 1221 SW 4th
Ave #340, Portland, OR 97204 USA

Katzenbach, John *Writer*
Knopf/Ballatine/Fawcett Publishers, 201 E
50th St, New York, NY 10022 USA

Katzenbach, Nicholas deB *Attorney
General*
33 Greenhouse Dr, Princeton, NJ 08540
USA

Katzenbach, Nicolas
33 Greenhouse Dr., Princeton, NJ 08540

Katzenberg, Jeffrey *Business Person*
DreamWorks SKG, 100 Universal City
Plaza, Universal City, CA 91608 USA

Katzenmoyer, Andy *Football Player*
859 W Main St, Westville, OH 43081
USA

Katzir, Ephraim *President*
Weizmann Institute of Science, PO Box
26, Rehovot, ISRAEL

Katzur, Klaus *Swimmer*
Robert-Siewart-Str 76, Chemnitz, 0912,
GERMANY

Kauffman, Marta *Writer, Producer*
Bright Kauffman Crane Productions, 4000
Warner Blvd, Bldg 160 #750, Burbank,
CA 91522

Kaufman, Adam *Actor*
Endeavor Agency LLC (LA), 9601 Wilshire
Blvd Fl 3, Beverly Hills, CA 90210 USA

Kaufman, Bob (Ajax) *Basketball Player*
1677 Rivermist Dr SW, Lilbum, GA 30047
USA

Kaufman, Charlie *Writer*
United Talent Agency (UTA), 9560
Wilshire Blvd, Beverly Hills, CA 90212
USA

Kaufman, Dan S *Misc*
University of Wisconsin, Medical School,
Hematology Dept, Madison, WI 53706
USA

Kaufman, Donald *Writer*
United Talent Agency (UTA), 9560
Wilshire Blvd, Beverly Hills, CA 90212
USA

Kaufman, Henry *Financier*
Henry Kaufman Co, 65 E 55th St, New
York, NY 10022 USA

Kaufman, Moises *Director*
International Creative Management
(ICM-LA), 8942 Wilshire Blvd, Beverly
Hills, CA 90211 USA

Kaufman, Napoleon *Football Player*
72 Incline Green Lane, Alamo, CA 94507
USA

Kaukonen, Jorma *Misc*
Agency Group Ltd, 1775 Broadway, #430,
New York, NY 10019 USA

Kausalya *Actor*
15 A-2 Akshar, Palace Road, Bangalore,
KA, 52, INDIA

Kaushal, Kamini *Actor, Dancer,
Bollywood*
B2 Anita Mt Pleasant Road, Malabar Hill,
Bombay, MS 400 006, INDIA

Kaushik, Satish *Actor, Bollywood,
Comedian, Director, Filmmaker, Produc*
1/124 Park View Zakaria Agadi Nagar,
Yari Road Versova Andheri, Bombay, MS
400 061, INDIA

Kavana *Musician*
Tony Denton Promotions, 19 S Molton Ln,
Mayfair, London, England, W1K 5LE

kavanaugh, Kenneth W (Ken) *Football
Player*
4907 Palm Aire Dr, Sarasota, FL 34243
USA

Kavandi, Janet L *Astronaut*
3907 Park Circle Way, Houston, TX
77059 USA

Kaveri *Actor, Bollywood*
114 4th Street, New Britania Nagar,
Chennai, TN 600087, INDIA

Kaviya *Actor, Bollywood*
Santhi Apts, Kumaran Colony 9th Street,
Chennai, TN 600026, INDIA

Kavner, Julie *Actor*
25154 Malibu Road, #2, Malibu, CA
90265 USA

Kavovit, Andrew *Actor*
TalentWorks (LA), 3500 W Olive Ave
#1400, Burbank, CA 91505 USA

Kawakubo, Rei *Fashion Designer*
Comme des Garcons, 5-11-5
Minamiaoyana, Minatoku, Tokyo, JAPAN

Kawalerowicz, Jersy *Director, Writer*
Ul Marconich 5m 21, Warsaw, 02-954,
POLAND

Kawawa, Rashidi M *Prime Minister*
Ministry of Defense, Dar es Salaam, TANZANIA

Kay, Alan C *Engineer*
Viewpoints Research Institute, 1209 Grand Capital Ave, Glendale, CA 91201 USA

Kay, Charles
18 Epple Rd., London, ENGLAND, SW6

Kay, Dianne *Actor*
1559 Palisades Dr, Pacific Palisades, CA 90272 USA

Kay, Jason (Jay) *Musician*
Searles, Chapel, 26A Munster St, London, SW6 4EN, UNITED KINGDOM (UK)

Kay, John *Musician*
Elite Management Corp, 2211 Norfolk St, #760, Houston, TX 77098 USA

Kay, Vanessa *Actor*
Comedy Central (LA), 2049 Century Park E #4170, Los Angeles, CA 90067 USA

Kaye, Davie A
1044 Ironwork Pass, Vancouver, BC V6H 3P1, CANADA

Kaye, Judy *Actor, Musician*
Bret Adams, 448 W 44th St, New York, NY 10036 USA

Kaye, Lila
47 Courtfield Rd. #9, London, ENGLAND, SW7 4DB

Kaye, Melvina
PO Box 6085, Burbank, CA 91510

Kaye, Thorsten *Actor*
International Creative Management (ICM-LA), 8942 Wilshire Blvd, Beverly Hills, CA 90211 USA

Kaye, Tony *Misc*
Sun Artists, 9 Hillgate St, London, W8 7SP, UNITED KINGDOM (UK)

Kaysen, Carl *Economist*
41 Holden St, Cambridge, MA 02138 USA

Kayser, Elmer L *Historian*
2921 34th St NW, Washington, DC 20008 USA

Kaz *Artist*
Fantagraphics Books, 7563 Lake City Way, Seattle, WA 98115 USA

Kazan, Lainie *Actor, Musician*
9903 Santa Monica Blvd, #283, Beverly Hills, CA 90212 USA

Kazankina, Tatyana *Track Athlete*
Hoshimina St, 111211, Saint Petersburg, RUSSIA

Kazarnovskaya, Lubov Y *Opera Singer*
Hohenbergstr 50, Vienna, 1120, AUSTRIA

Kazer, Beau
139-A N. San Fernando Rd, Burbank, CA 91502

Kazmaier, Dick
261 Park Lane, Concord, MA 01742

Kazmaier Jr, Richard W (Dick) *Football Player*
24 Dockside Lane, Box 29, Key Largo, FL 33037 USA

KC & The Sunshine Band *Music Group*
William Morris Agency (WMA-LA), 1 William Morris Pl, Beverly Hills, CA 90212 USA

Keach, James *Actor*
Metropolitan Talent Agency, 4526 Wilshire Blvd, Los Angeles, CA 90010 USA

Keach, Stacy *Actor*
27525 Winding Way, Malibu, CA 90265 USA

Keady, Gene *Coach*
Purdue University, Mackey Arena, West Lafayette, IN 47907 USA

Kean, Jane
Pierce & Shelly, 13775-A Mono Way #220, Sonora, CA 95370 USA

Kean, Thomas H *Governor, Educator*
Drew University, President's Office, 36 Madison Ave, Madison, NJ 07940 USA

Keanan, Staci *Actor*
Metropolitan Talent Agency, 4526 Wilshire Blvd, Los Angeles, CA 90010 USA

Keane, Bill *Cartoonist*
5815 E Joshua Tree Lane, Paradise Valley, AZ 85253 USA

Keane, Glen *Animator*
Walt Disney Studios, Animation Dept, 500 S Buena Vista St, Burbank, CA 91521 USA

Keane, James
612 Lighthouse Ave #220, Pacific Grove, CA 93951

Keane, John B
37 William St, Listowel County Kerry, IRELAND

Keane, John M (Jack) *General*
Vice Chief of Staff HqUSA, Pentagon, Washington, DC 20310 USA

Keane, Kerrie *Actor*
S D B Partners, 1801 Ave of Stars, #902, Los Angeles, CA 90067 USA

Keane, Roy M *Soccer Player*
Manchester United, Busby Way, Old Trafford, Manchester, M16 0RA, UNITED KINGDOM (UK)

Keane, Sean *Misc*
Macklam Feldman Mgmt, 1505 W 2nd Ave, #200, Vancouver, BC V6H 3Y4, CANADA

Keane, William
4526 Wilshire Blvd., Los Angeles, CA 90010

Kear, David *Misc*
34 W End, Ohope, NEW ZELAND

Kearns, Austin *Athlete*
Cinergy Field, 100 Cinergy Field, Cincinatti, OH 45202

Kearns, Dennis M *Hockey Player*
605 King Georges Way, West Vancouver, BC V7S 1S2, CANADA

Kearse, Amalya L *Judge*
US Court of Appeals, US Courthouse, Foley Square, New York, NY 10007 USA

Kearse, Jevon *Football Player*
3750 Madison Ave, Fort Myers, FL 33916 USA

Keathley, George *Director*
Missouri Repertory Theater, 4949 Cherry St, Kensas City, MO 64110 USA

Keating, Charles *Actor*
Don Buchwald, 10 E 44th St, New York, NY 10017 USA

Keating, Dominic *Actor*
Integrated Films & Management, 1041 N Formosa Ave, Santa Monica Bldg W #17, W Hollywood, CA 90046 USA

Keating, Edward *Photographer*
New York Times, Editorial Dept, 229 W 43rd St, New York, NY 10036 USA

Keating, Henry (H R F) *Writer*
35 Northumberland Place, London, W2 5AS, UNITED KINGDOM (UK)

Keating, Paul *Royalty*
31 Bligh St Level 2, Sydney, 2000, AUSTRALIA

Keating, Paul J *Prime Minister*
Keating Assoc-War Mgmt, Bushy Park Road, 57 Meadowbank, Dublin, IRELAND

Keating, Ronan *Musician*
Carol Assoc-War Mgmt, Bushy Park Rd, 57 Meadowbank, Dublin, IRELAND

Keating II, Francis A (Frank) *Governor*
American Life Insurers Council, 101 Constitution Ave NW, Washington, DC 20001 USA

Keaton, Diane *Actor, Director*
International Creative Management (ICM-LA), 8942 Wilshire Blvd, Beverly Hills, CA 90211 USA

Keaton, Joshua (Josh) *Actor*
Evolution Entertainment, 901 N Highland Ave, Los Angeles, CA 90038 USA

Keaton, Michael *Actor*
11901 Santa Monica Blvd, #547, Los Angeles, CA 90025 USA

Keats, Donald H *Composer*
University of Denver, Music School, Denver, CO 80208 USA

Keats, Ele *Actor*
Identity Talent Agency (ID), 2050 Bundy Dr #200, Los Angeles, CA 90025 USA

Keb Mo *Songwriter, Musician*
Monterey International, 200 W Superior, #202, Chicago, IL 60610 USA

Kebble (Kebbel), Arielle *Actor*
Himber Entertainment Inc, 211 S Beverly Dr #208, Beverly Hills, CA 90212 USA

Kebede, Liya *Model*
IMG Models, 304 Park Ave S, #1200, New York, NY 10010 USA

Kebich, Vyacheslau F *Prime Minister*
National Assembly, K Marksa Str 38, Dom Urada, Minsk, 220016, BELARUS

Keck, Donald B *Inventor*
2877 Chequers Circle, Big Flats, NY 14814 USA

Keck, Howard B *Philanthropist*
600 Wilshire Blvd, #17, Los Angeles, CA 90017 USA

Keck Jr, Herman *Religious Leader*
Calvary Grace Christian Church of Faith, US Box 4266, Norton AFB, CA 92409 USA

Kedah *King*
Istana Anak Bukit, Alor Setar, Kedah, Darul Aman, MALAYSIA

Kedes, Maureen *Actor*
Tisherman Agency, 6767 Forest Lawn Dr, #101, Los Angeles, CA 90403 USA

Kee, John P *Musician*
Covenant Agency, 1011 4th St, #315, Santa Monica, CA 90403 USA

Keeble, John *Musician*
International Talent Group, 729 7th Ave, #1600, New York, NY 10019 USA

Keefe, Adam *Basketball Player*
15933 Alcima Ave, Pacific Palisades, CA 90272 USA

Keefe, Mike *Cartoonist*
Denver Post, Editorial Dept, PO Box 1709, Denver, CO 80201 USA

Keefer, Don *Actor*
4146 Allot Ave, Sherman Oaks, CA 91423 USA

Keeffe, Bernard *Conductor*
153 Honor Oak Road, London, SE23 3RN, UNITED KINGDOM (UK)

Keegan, Andrew *Actor*
Scott Appel, 13601 Ventura Blvd, #203, Sherman Oaks, CA 91423 USA

Keegan, John *Historian*
Manor House, Kilmington near Warminster, Wilts, BA12 6RD, UNITED KINGDOM (UK)

Keehne, Virginya *Actor*
Craig Mgmt, 125 S Sycamore Ave, Los Angeles, CA 90036 USA

Keel, Howard *Actor, Musician*
Clifford Productions, 394 Red River Rd, Palm Desert, CA 92211 USA

Keel Jr, Alton G *Diplomat, Business Person*
Atlantic Partners, 2891 S River Road, Stanardsville, VA 22973 USA

Keeler, Don
24000 Jensen Dr., West Hills, CA 91304

Keeler, William H Cardinal *Religious Leader*
National Conference of Catholic Bishops, 3211 4th St, Washington, DC 20017 USA

Keeley, Robert V *Diplomat*
3814 Livingston St NW, Washington, DC 20015 USA

Keeling, Charles D *Musician*
Scripps Oceanography Institute, Ritler Hall, 9500 Gilman Dr, La Jolla, CA 92093 USA

Keelor, Greg *Musician*
ArtisDirect, 10900 Wilshire Blvd, #1400, Los Angeles, CA 90024 USA

Keen, Geoffrey *Actor*
50 Lock Road, Ham Richmond, Surrey, TW10 7LN, UNITED KINGDOM (UK)

Keen, Robert Earl *Songwriter, Musician*
Rosetta, PO Box 2186, Bandera, TX 78003 USA

Keen, Sam *Writer, Misc*
16331 Norrbom Road, Sonoma, CA 95476 USA

Keena, Monica *Actor*
Gersh Agency, The (LA), 232 N Canon Dr, Beverly Hills, CA 90210 USA

Keenan, Joseph D *Misc*
2727 29th St NW, Washington, DC 20008 USA

Keenan, Maynard James *Musician*
Spivak Entertainment, 11845 W Olympic Blvd, #1125, Los Angeles, CA 90064 USA

Keenan, Mike *Misc*
550 NE 21st Ave, #13, Deerfield Beach, FL 33441 USA

Keene, Donald L *Educator*
Columbia University, Language Dept, Kent Hall, New York, NY 10027 USA

Keene, Tommy *Songwriter, Musician*
Black Park Mgmt, PO Box 107, Sunbury, NC 27979 USA

Keene Cherot, Kyera *Actor*
Creative Artists Agency LCC (CAA-LA), 9830 Wilshire Blvd, Beverly Hills, CA 90212 USA

Keenen, Mary Jo
9200 Sunset Blvd. #1130, Los Angeles, CA 90069

Keener, Catherine *Actor*
More/Medavoy, 7920 W Sunset Blvd, #400, Los Angeles, CA 90046 USA

Keenlyside, Simon *Opera Singer*
Columbia Artists Mgmt Inc, 165 W 57th St, New York, NY 10019 USA

Keeny Jr, Spurgeon M *Misc*
3600 Albernarle St NW, Washington, DC 20008 USA

Keerthana, K *Actor, Bollywood*
71 A Kamarajar Salai, R A Puram, Chennai, TN 600028, INDIA

Keeshan, Bob *Actor*
Robert Keeshan Assoc, 40 W 57th St, #1600, New York, NY 10019 USA

Keeslar, Matt *Actor*
Stone Manners Talent Agency, 6500 Wilshire Blvd, Ste 550, Los Angeles, CA 90048 USA

Keezer, Geoff *Misc*
DL Media, PO Box 2728, Bala Cynwyd, PA 19004 USA

Kegel, Oliver *Athlete*
Am Bogen 23, Berlin, 13589, GERMANY

Kehoe, Rick *Hockey Player, Coach*
1027 Highland Dr, Cincinnati, OH 45211 USA

Keibler, Stacy *Wrestler*
World Wrestling Entertainment (WWE), 1241 E Main St, Stamford, CT 06905 USA

Keightley, David N *Historian*
University of California, History Dept, Berkeley, CA 94720 USA

Keillor, Garrison E *Commentator, Writer*
A Prairie Home Companion, 611 Frontenac Place, Saint Paul, MN 55104 USA

Keim, Betty Lou
10642 Arnel Pl., Chatsworth, CA 91311

Keim, Jenny *Swimmer*
R O'Brien, Swimming Hall of Fame, 1 Hall of Fame Dr, Fort Lauderdale, FL 33316 USA

Keita, Ibrahaim Boubakar *Prime Minister*
Prime Minister's Office, BP97, Bamako, MALI

Keita, Salif *Musician, Composer*
International Music Network, 278 S Main St, #400, Gloucester, MA 01930 USA

Keitel, Harvey *Actor*
25 N Moore St, #2A, New York, NY 10013 USA

Keith, David *Actor*
Writers and Artists Group Intl (LA), 8383 Wilshire Blvd #550, Beverly Hills, CA 90211 USA

Keith, Louis *Doctor*
333 E Superior St, #476, Chicago, IL 60611 USA

Keith, Penelope *Actor*
66 Berkeley House, Hay Hill, London, SW3, UNITED KINGDOM (UK)

Keith, Toby *Musician*
TKO Artist Mgmt, 1107 17th Ave S, Nashville, TN 37212 USA

Keith Rennie, Callum *Actor*
Agency for the Performing Arts (APA-LA), 9200 Sunset Blvd #900, Los Angeles, CA 90069 USA

Kekalainen, Jarmo *Hockey Player*
145 Hillcrest Road, Needham, MA 02492 USA

Kelcher, Louie J *Football Player*
10204 Carlotta Cove, Austin, TX 78733 USA

Keleti, Agnes *Misc*
Wingate Institute for Physical Education & Sport, Matanya, 42902, ISRAEL

Kelis *Musician*
Solo Agency Ltd (UK), 55 Fulham High St, London, SW6 3JJ, United Kingdom

Kelis, Kid 'N Play *Music Group*
1650 Broadway #508, New York, NY 10019

Kelker-Kelly, Robert
5 Tate Ave. #15, Piermont, NY 10968

Kell, George
PO Box 70, Swifton, AR 72471

Kell, George C *Baseball Player*
PO Box 158, Swifton, AR 72471 USA

Kellaway, Roger *Composer*
Pat Phillips Mgmt, 520 E 81st St, #PH C, New York, NY 10028 USA

Kelleher, Bill *Journalist*
New York Times, Editorial Dept, 229 W 43rd St, New York, NY 10036 USA

Kelleher, Erhard *Misc*
Sudliche Munchneustr 6A, Grunwald, 82031, GERMANY

Kelleher, Herbert D *Business Person*
144 Thelma Dr, San Antonio, TX 78212 USA

Keller, Cord *Producer*
Innovative Artists (LA), 1505 Tenth St, Santa Monica, CA 90401 USA

Keller, Jason *Race Car Driver*
Progressive Motorsports, 177 Knob Hill Road, Mooresville, NC 28117 USA

Keller, John *Basketball Player*
2100 24th St, Great Bend, KS 67530 USA

Keller, Joseph B *Mathematician*
820 Sonoma Terrace, Stanford, CA 94305 USA

Keller, Leonard B *War Hero*
6350 Majzun Road, Milton, FL 32570 USA

Keller, Martha *Actor*
Lemonstr 9, Munich, 81679, GERMANY

Keller, Marthe
5 rue St. Dominique, Paris, FRANCE, 75007

Keller, Mary Page *Actor*
William Morris Agency, 151El Camino Dr, Beverly Hills, CA 90212 USA

Keller, Thomas *Chef*
French Laundry, 6540 Washington St, Yountville, CA 94599 USA

Kellerman, Faye *Writer*
Karpfinger Agency, 357 W 20th St, New York, NY 10011 USA

Kellerman, Jonathan S *Writer*
Karpfinger Agency, 357 W 20th St, New York, NY 10011 USA

Kellerman, Sally *Actor*
7944 Woodrow Wilson Dr, Los Angeles, CA 90046 USA

Kelley, Allen (Al) *Basketball Player*
5900 Longleaf Dr, Lawrence, KS 66049 USA

Kelley, Bill *Writer*

Kelley, David E *Writer, Producer*
David Kelley Productions, 10201 W Pico Blvd, Los Angeles, CA 90064 USA

Kelley, Dean *Basketball Player*
5900 Longleaf Dr, Lawrence, KS 66049 USA

Kelley, Donald R *Historian*
45 Jefferson Ave, New Brunswick, NJ 08901 USA

Kelley, Earl A *Basketball Player*
21430 Windmere Lane, Tremont, IL 61566 USA

Kelley, Gaynor N *Business Person*
Perkin-Elmer Corp, 710 Bridgeport Ave, Shelton, CT 06484 USA

Kelley, Harold H *Psychic*
21634 Rambla Vista St, Maliby, CA 90265 USA

Kelley, John A (Marathon) *Track Athlete*
136 Cedar Hill Road, East Dennis, MA 02641 USA

Kelley, Jon *Television Host*
Extra (LA), 1840 Victory Blvd, Glendale, CA 91201 USA

Kelley, Kitty *Writer*
1228 Eton Court NW, Washington, DC 20007 USA

Kelley, Manon
PO Box 315, Bellmore, NY 11710

Kelley, Mike *Artist*
2472 Eastman Ave, #35-36, Ventura, CA 93003 USA

Kelley, Paul X *General*
1600 N Oak St, #1619, Arlington, VA 22209 USA

Kelley, Rich *Basketball Player*
314 Raymundo Dr, Woodside, CA 94062 USA

Kelley, Sheila *Actor*
537 N June St, Los Angeles, CA 90004 USA

Kelley, Steve *Cartoonist*
San Diego Union, Editorial Dept, 350 Camino de la Reina, San Diego, CA 92108 USA

Kelley, Thomas G *War Hero*
693 E 8th St, Boston, MA 02127 USA

Kelley, William G *Business Person*
Consolidated Stores, 1105 N Market St, Wilmington, DE 19801 USA

Kellman, Barnet *Director*
Jackoway Tyerman Wertheimer Austen Mandelbaum & Morris, 1888 Century Park E Fl 18, Los Angeles, CA 90067 USA

Kellner, Catherine *Actor*
Paradigm (LA), 10100 Santa Monica Blvd, Fl 25, Los Angeles, CA 90067 USA

Kellner, Deborah *Actor*
International Creative Management (ICM-LA), 8942 Wilshire Blvd, Beverly Hills, CA 90211 USA

Kellogg, Clark *Basketball Player, Sportscaster*
5423 Medallion Dr E, Westerville, OH 43082 USA

Kellogg, William S *Business Person*
Kohl's Corp, N56W17000 Ridgewood Dr, Menomonee Falls, WI 53051 USA

Kellogg Jr, Allan J *War Hero*
250 Ilihau St, Kailua, HI 96734 USA

Kelly, Annesse *Bowler*
2912 Cape Verde Lane, Las Vegas, NV 89128 USA

Kelly, Barbara
5 Kidderpore Ave., London, ENGLAND, NW3 7SX

Kelly, Brendon John *Actor*

Kelly, Chris
21/22 Poland St., London, ENGLAND, W1V 3DD

Kelly, Daniel-Hugh *Actor*
Innovative Artists, 1505 10th St, Santa Monica, CA 90401 USA

Kelly, David *Actor*
535 King St. #219, The Plaza, London, ENGLAND, SW10 0SZ

Kelly, Donald P *Business Person*
DP Kelly Assoc, 701 Harger Road, #190, Oak Brook, IL 60523 USA

Kelly, Eamon M *Educator*
3122 Octavia St, New Orleans, LA 70125 USA

Kelly, Elisworth *Artist*
PO Box 1708, Chatham, NY 12037 USA

Kelly, Henry
10 Clorane Gardens, London, ENGLAND, NW3 7PR

Kelly, J Thomas (Tom) *Baseball Player*
1643 Carrie St, Maplewood, MN 55119 USA

Kelly, James E (Jim) *Football Player*
44 Hillsboro Dr, Orcahrd Park, NY 14127 USA

Kelly, James M (Jim) *Astronaut*
14634 Graywood Groove Lane, Houston, TX 77062 USA

Kelly, Jean Louisa *Actor*
Gersh Agency, The (LA), 232 N Canon Dr, Beverly Hills, CA 90210 USA

Kelly, Jim *Actor*
Castle-Hill Talent Agency, 1101 S Orlando Ave, Los Angeles, CA 90035 USA

Kelly, Joanne *Actor*
Burstein Company, The, 15304 Sunset Blvd #208, Pacific Palisades, CA 90272 USA

Kelly, John *Musician*
EMI America Records, 6920 Sunset Blvd, Los Angeles, CA 90028 USA

Kelly, John H *Diplomat*
International Equity Partners, 1808 Overlake Dr SE, #D, Conyers, GA 30013 USA

Kelly, Leonard P (Red) *Hockey Player*
30 Dunvegan, Toronto, ON M4V 2P6, CANADA

Kelly, Leroy *Football Player*
115 Eastbrook Lane, Willingboro, NJ 08046 USA

Kelly, Lisa Robin *Actor*
Metropolitan Talent Agency (MTA), 4526 Wilshire Blvd, Los Angeles, CA 90010 USA

Kelly, Mark E *Astronaut*
2121 Barrington Dr, League City, TX 77573 USA

Kelly, Moira *Actor*
2329 Rodeo Dr, Austin, TX 78727 USA

Kelly, Paul *Songwriter, Musician*
Robert Bamham Mgmt, 432 Tyagarah Road, Myocum, NSW, 2038, AUSTRALIA

Kelly, R *Songwriter, Musician, Artist*
Creative Artists Agency, 9830 Wilshire Blvd, Beverly Hills, CA 90212 USA

Kelly, Raymond *Misc*
Police Commissioner's Office, 1 Police Plaza, New York, NY 10038 USA

Kelly, Richard (Rich) *Writer, Director*
Creative Artists Agency LCC (CAA-LA), 9830 Wilshire Blvd, Beverly Hills, CA 90212 USA

Kelly, Roz
5161 Riverton Ave. #105, No. Hollywood, CA 91601-3943

Kelly, Scott J *Astronaut*
2121 Barrington Dr, League City, TX 77573 USA

Kelly, Tom *Baseball Player*
1643 Currie St N, Maplewood, MN 55119

Kelly III, Thomas J *Journalist*
PO Box 2208, Sanatoga Branch, Pottstown, PA 19464 USA

Kelly Jr, Thomas J *Biologist*
Memorial Stolan Kettering Cancer Center, 1275 York Ave, New York, NY 10021 USA

Kelman, Arthur *Misc*
1406 Springmoor Circle, Raleigh, NC 27615 USA

Kelman, James *Writer*
Weidenfeld-Nicolson, Upper Saint Martin's Lane, London, WC2H 9EA, UNITED KINGDOM (UK)

Kelsey, David *Actor*
Select Artists Ltd (CA-Westside Office),
1138 12th Street, Suite 1, Santa Monica,
CA 90403 USA

Kelsey, Frances O *Misc*
Federal Drug Administration, 5600 Fishers
Lane, Rockville, MD 20852 USA

Kelsey, Linda *Actor*
400 S Beverly Dr, #101, Beverly Hills, CA
90212 USA

Kelso II, Frank B *Admiral*
7794 Turlock Road, Springfield, VA
22153 USA

Kemal, Yashar *Writer*
PK14 Basinkoy, Istanbul, TURKEY

Kemmer, Ed *Actor*
11 Riverside Dr, #17PE, New York, NY
10023 USA

Kemp, Gary *Musician*
International Talent Group, 729 7th Ave,
#1600, New York, NY 10019 USA

Kemp, Jack
1776 I St. NW #800, Washington, DC
20006

Kemp, Jeff
12220 NE 53rd St., Kirkland, WA 98033

Kemp, Jeremy *Actor*
Marina Martin, 12/13 Poland St, London,
W1V 3DE, UNITED KINGDOM (UK)

Kemp, John F (Jack) *Secretary*
7904 Greentree Road, Bethesda, MD
20817 USA

Kemp, Martin *Musician*
Mission Control, Business Center, Lower
Road, London, SE16 2XB, UNITED
KINGDOM (UK)

Kemp, Ross *Actor*
EastEnders, BBC Elstree Centre, Clarendon
Road, Borehamwood, Herts, UNITED
KINGDOM

Kemp, Shawn T *Basketball Player*
1700 E 13th St, #12T, Cleveland, OH
44114 USA

Kemp, Steve *Baseball Player*
Detroit Tigers, 4208 City Lights Dr, Aliso
Viego, CA 92656-2638 USA

Kemper, Randolph E (Randy) *Fashion
Designer*
Randy Kemper Corp, 530 Fashion Ave,
#1400, New York, NY 10018 USA

Kemper, Victor J *Cinematographer*
Gersh Agency, 232 N Canon Dr, Beverly
Hills, CA 90210 USA

Kemper II, David W *Financier*
Commerce Bancshares, 1000 Walnut St,
Kansas City, MO 64106 USA

Kempf, Cecil J *Admiral*
831 Olive Ave, Coronado, CA 92118 USA

Kempner, Walter *Misc*
1505 Virginia Ave, Durham, NC 27705
USA

Kenan, Sean
77 W. 66th St., New York., NY 10033

Kendal, Felicity *Actor*
Chatto & Linnit, Prince of Wales Coventry
St, London, W1V 7FE, UNITED
KINGDOM (UK)

Kendall, A Bruce *Yachtsman*
6 Pedersen Place, Bucklands Beach,
Auckland, NEW ZELAND

Kendall, Barbara *Yachtsman*
Kendall Distributing, 82B Great South
Road, Auckland, NEW ZELAND

Kendall, Donald M *Business Person*
PepsiCo Inc, Anderson Hill Road,
Purchase, NY 10577 USA

Kendall, Fred *Baseball Player*
San Diego Padres, 612 John St, Manhattan
Beach, CA 90266-5837 USA

Kendall, Jason *Baseball Player*
Pittsburgh Pirates, 612 John St, Manhattan
Beach, CA 90266-5837 USA

Kendall, Jeannie *Musician*
Joe Taylor Artist Agency, 2802 Columbine
Place, Nashville, TN 37204 USA

Kendall, Pete *Football Player*
Arizona Cardinals, PO Box 888, Phoenix,
AZ 85001 USA

Kendall, Tom *Race Car Driver*
International Motor Sports Assn, 1394
Broadway Ave, Braselton, GA 30517 USA

Kendall, Tony
Via G. Talombini 12, Rome, ITALY,
00156

Kenders, Al *Baseball Player*
Philadelphia Phillies, 8744 Matilija Ave,
Van Nuys, CA 91402-3320 USA

Kendler, Bob *Misc*
US Handball Assn, 4101 Dempster St,
Skokie, IL 60076 USA

Kendrick, Anna *Actor*
Endeavor Agency LLC (LA), 9601 Wilshire
Blvd Fl 3, Beverly Hills, CA 90210 USA

Kendrick, Rodney *Composer, Musician*
Carolyn McClair, 410 W 53rd St, #128C,
New York, NY 10019 USA

Keneally, Thomas M *Writer*
24 Serpentine, Bilgola Beach, NSW, 2107,
AUSTRALIA

Kenilorea, Peter *Prime Minister*
Kalala House, PO Box 535 Honiara,
Guadacanal, SOLOMON ISLANDS

Kenn, Michael L (Mike) *Football Player*
360 Bardolier, Alpharetta, GA 30022 USA

Kenna, E Douglas (Doug) *Business Person,
Football Player*
11450 Turtle Beach Road, North Palm
Beach, FL 33408 USA

Kenna, Edward *War Hero*
121 Coleraine Road, Hamilton, VIC,
3300, AUSTRALIA

Kennan, Brian *Musician*
Lustig Talent, PO Box 770850, Orlando,
FL 32877 USA

Kennan, George F *Diplomat, Writer*
Institute for Advanced Study, Olden Lane,
Princeton, NJ 08540 USA

Kennard, William (Bill) *Government
Official*
Carlyie Group, 1001 Pennsylvania Ave
NW, Washington, DC 20004 USA

Kenne, Leslie F *General*
Deputy CofS for Warfighting Integration,
HqUSA Pentagon, Washington, DC 20310
USA

Kennedy, Adam *Baseball Player*
Anaheim Angels, 23996 Sanctuary Pkwy,
Yorba Linda, CA 92887-5647 USA

Kennedy, Alan D *Business Person*
Tupperware Corp, PO Box 2353,
Orlando, FL 32802 USA

Kennedy, Anthony M *Judge*
US Supreme Court, 1 1st St NE,
Washington, DC 20543 USA

Kennedy, Bob *Baseball Player*
Chicago White Sox, 5505 E McLellan Rd
Unit 103, Mesa, AZ 85205-3408 USA

Kennedy, Claudia J *General*
William Morris Agency, 151 El Camino
Dr, Beverly Hills, CA 90212 USA

Kennedy, Coenelia G *Judge*
US Court of Appeals, US Courthouse, 231
W Lafayette Blvd, Detroit, MI 48226 USA

Kennedy, Cortez *Football Player*
3005 122nd Place NE, Bellevue, WA
98005 USA

Kennedy, D James *Religious Leader*
Coral Ridge Presbyterian Church, 5554 N
Federal Hwy, Fort Lauderdale, FL 33308
USA

Kennedy, David M *Secretary*
3838 Ruth Dr, Salt Lake City, UT 84124
USA

Kennedy, David M *Historian*
Stanford University, History Dept,
Stanford, CA 94305 USA

Kennedy, Donald *Educator*
Stanford University, International Studies
Institute, Stanford, CA 94305 USA

Kennedy, Dwayne *Comedian*
International Creative Management
(ICM-LA), 8942 Wilshire Blvd, Beverly
Hills, CA 90211 USA

Kennedy, Forbes T *Hockey Player*
9 Birchwood St, Charlottetown, PE C1A
5B4, CANADA

Kennedy, George *Actor*
1617 N Dunsmurr Way, Eagle, ID 83616
USA

Kennedy, James C *Business Person*
Cox Enterprises, 1400 Lake Hearn Dr NE,
Atlanta, GA 30319 USA

Kennedy, Jamie *Actor*
Jamie Kennedy Experiment, The, 1149 N
Gower St #294, Hollywood, CA 90038
USA

Kennedy, Jim *Baseball Player*
St Louis Cardinals, 17035 NW Brugger
Rd, Portland, OR 97229-1413 USA

Kennedy, Jimmy *Football Player*
Saint Louis Rams, 901 N Broadway, Saint
Louis, MO 63101 USA

Kennedy, John *Baseball Player*
Washington Senators, 2 Rodney Rd,
Peabody, MA 01960-3517 USA

Kennedy, John Milton *Actor*
5711 Reseda Blvd, #204, Tarzana, CA
91356 USA

Kennedy, Junior *Baseball Player*
Cincinnati Reds, 6601 Eucalyptus Dr Spc
215, Bakersfield, CA 93306-6844 USA

Kennedy, Kathleen *Producer*
Kennedy-Marshall Co, 650 N Bronson Ave, #100W, Los Angeles, CA 90004 USA

Kennedy, Kevin *Television Host*
Best Damned Sports Show Period, The, 10201 W Pico Blvd, Trailer 103, Los Angeles, CA 90035 USA

Kennedy, Lee *Business Person*
Equifax Inc, 1550 Peachtree St NE, Atlanta, GA 30309 USA

Kennedy, Leon Isaac *Actor*
859 N Hollywood Way, #384, Burbank, CA 91505 USA

kennedy, M Peter *Figure Skater*
7650 SE 41st, Mercer Island, WA 98040 USA

Kennedy, Mimi *Actor*
Agency for Performing Arts, 9200 Sunset Blvd, #900, Los Angeles, CA 90069 USA

Kennedy, Nigel *Musician*
Russels, Regency House, 1-4 Warwick St, London, W1R 5WB, UNITED KINGDOM (UK)

Kennedy, Page *Actor*
Mitchell K Stubbs & Assoc (MKS), 8675 W Washington Blvd #203, Culver City, CA 90232 USA

Kennedy, Paul M *Historian*
409Humphrey St, New Haven, CT 06511 USA

Kennedy, Randall L *Lawyer, Educator*
Harvard University, Law School, Cambridge, MA 02138 USA

Kennedy, Ray F *Business Person*
Masco Corp, 21001Van Born Road, Taylor, MI 48180 USA

Kennedy, T Lincoln *Football Player*
3917 Spring Garden Place, #1, Spring Valley, CA 91977 USA

Kennedy, Terrence E *Baseball Player*
PO Box 6670, Chandler, AZ 85246

Kennedy, Terrence E (Terry) *Baseball Player*
St Louis Cardinals, 333 N Pennington Dr Unit 23, Chandler, AZ 85224-8266 USA

Kennedy, Theodore S (Teeder) *Hockey Player*
22 Lakeside Place W, Port Colbome, ON L3K 6B1, CANADA

Kennedy, William J *Writer*
New York State Writers Institute, Washington Ave, Albany, NY 12222 USA

Kennedy, X Joseph (X J) *Writer*
22 Revere St, Lexington, MA 02420 USA

Kennedy Jr, Joey D (Joe) *Journalist*
1635 11th Place S, Birmingham, AL 35205 USA

Kennedy-Powell, Kathleen *Judge*
Los Angeles Municipal Court, 110 N Grand Ave, Los Angeles, CA 90012 USA

kenner, Kevin *Musician*
Columbia Artists Mgmt Inc, 165 W 57th St, New York, NY 10019 USA

Kennerly, David Hume *Journalist*
1015 18th St, Santa Monica, CA 90403 USA

Kenney, Art *Baseball Player*
Boston Bees, 3 Timber Ln, North Reading, MA 01864-3016 USA

Kenney, Jerry *Baseball Player*
New York Yankees, 1980 Harrison Ave, Beloit, WI 53511-3048 USA

Kenney, Stephen F (Steve) *Football Player*
1105 Silver Oaks Court, Raleigh, NC 27614 USA

Kennibrew, Dee Dee *Musician*
Superstars Unlimited, PO Box 371371, Las Vegas, NV 89137 USA

Kenniff, Sean *Doctor*
6 Madison Lane #2, Carle Place, NY 11514 USA

Kennison, Eddie *Football Player*
Kansas City Chiefs, 1 Arrowhead Dr, Kansas City, KS 64129 USA

Kenny, Shannon *Actor*
Burstein Company, The, 15304 Sunset Blvd #208, Pacific Palisades, CA 90272 USA

Kenny, Shirley Strum *Educator*
State University of New York, President's Office, Stony Brook, NY 11794 USA

Kenny, Yvonne *Opera Singer*
I M G Artists, 3 Burlington Lane, Chiswick, London, W4 2TH, UNITED KINGDOM (UK)

Kenny G *Musician*
Turner Management Group, 374 Poli St, #205, Ventura, CA 93001 USA

Kensit, Patsy *Actor, Musician*
14 Lambton Place Nottinghill, London, W11 2SH, UNITED KINGDOM (UK)

Kent *Misc*
York House, Saint James's Place, London, SW1, UNITED KINGDOM (UK)

Kent, Allegra *Ballerina*
New York City Ballet, Lincoln Center Plaza, New York, NY 10023 USA

Kent, Arthur *Commentator*
2184 Torringford St, Torrington, CT 06790 USA

Kent, Heather Paige
Untitled Entertainment (LA), 8436 W 3rd St #650, Los Angeles, CA 90048 USA

Kent, Jean *Actor*
London Mgmt, 2-4 Noel St, London, W1V 3RB, UNITED KINGDOM (UK)

Kent, Jeff *Baseball Player*
Toronto Blue Jays, 1507 Resaca Blvd, Austin, TX 78738-5508 USA

Kent, Jonathan *Director*
International Creative Mgmt, 76 Oxford St, London, W1N 0AX, UNITED KINGDOM (UK)

Kent, Julie *Ballerina*
American Ballet Theatre, 890 Broadway, New York, NY 10003 USA

Kent, Marjorie
1169 Mary Circle, LaVerne, CA 91750

Kent, Peter *Misc*
43 Trinity Court Gray's Inn Road, London, WC1, UNITED KINGDOM (UK)

Kent, Steve *Baseball Player*
Tampa Bay Devil Rays, 10750 SW 11th St Apt 6, Miami, FL 33174-2511 USA

Kentner, Louis *Musician*
1 Mallord St, London, SW3, UNITED KINGDOM (UK)

Kentucky Headhunters
209 10th Ave. So. #322, Nashville, TN 37203-0744

Kenty, Hilmer *Boxer*
Escot Boxing, 19260 Bretton Dr, Detroit, MI 48223 USA

Kenworthy, Dick *Baseball Player*
Chicago White Sox, 5551 Rue Royale Apt D, Indianapolis, IN 46227-1960 USA

Kenyon, Mel *Race Car Driver*
2645 S 25th West, Lebanon, IN 46052 USA

Kenzie, Leila
151 El Camino Dr., Beverly Hills, CA 90212

Kenzle, Leila *Actor*
William Morris Agency, 151 El Camino Dr, Beverly Hills, CA 90212 USA

Kenzo *Fashion Designer*
3 Place des Victories, Paris, 75001, FRANCE

Keobouphan, Sisavat *Prime Minister*
Premier's Office, Vientiane, LAOS

Keogh, James *Government Official*
Byram Dr, Belle Haven, Greenwich, CT 06830 USA

Keoghan, Phil *Television Host*
International Creative Management (ICM-LA), 8942 Wilshire Blvd, Beverly Hills, CA 90211 USA

Keohane, Nannerl O *Educator*
Duke University, President's Office, Durham, NC 27706 USA

Keoke, Kimo *Actor*
612 1/2 N Spaulding Avenue, Los Angeles, CA 90036 USA

Keon, Dave
115 Brackenwood Rd, Palm Beach Gardens, FL 33418

Keon, David M (Dave) *Hockey Player*
115 Brackenwood Road, Palm Beach Gardens, FL 33418 USA

Keough, Donald R *Financier*
200 Galleria Parkway, #970, Atlanta, GA 30339 USA

Keough, Harry J *Soccer Player, Coach*
7325 Rainor Court, Saint Louis, MO 63116 USA

Keough, Joe *Baseball Player*
Oakland A's, 24245 Wilderness Oak Apt 811, San Antonio, TX 78258 USA

Keough, Lainey *Fashion Designer*
42 Dawson St, Dublin, 2, IRELAND

Keough, Marty *Baseball Player*
Boston Red Sox, 6874 E Nightingale Star Cir, Scottsdale, AZ 85262 USA

Keough, Matt *Baseball Player*
Oakland A's, 6281 Southfrond Rd, Livermore, CA 94551-8215 USA

Kepshire, Kurt *Baseball Player*
St Louis Cardinals, 141 Folino Dr, Bridgeport, CT 06606-1013 USA

Kercheval, Ken *Actor*
PO Box 4844, Louisville, KY 40204 USA

Kerekorian, Kirk *Business Person*
MGM/UA Communications, 2500
Broadway St, Santa Monica, CA 90404
USA

Kerekou, Mathieu A *President, General*
President's Office, Boite Postale, Cotonou,
2020, BENIN

Keresztes, K Sandor *Architect*
Fo Utca 44/50, Budapest, 1011,
HUNGARY

Kerfeld, Charlie *Baseball Player*
Houston Astros, 250 Vallombrosa Ave Ste
200, Chico, CA 95926-3976 USA

Kern, Bill *Baseball Player*
Kansas City A's, 625 W Green St,
Allentown, PA 18102-1601 USA

Kern, Ericca
3972 Barranca Parkway #J-321, Irvine, CA
92714

Kern, Geof *Photographer*
1355 Conant St, Dallas, TX 75207 USA

Kern, Jim *Baseball Player*
Cleveland Indians, 6009 Amberwood Ct,
Arlington, TX 76016-1001 USA

Kern, Joey *Actor*
Paradigm (LA), 10100 Santa Monica Blvd,
Fl 25, Los Angeles, CA 90067 USA

Kern, Rex W *Football Player*
2816 Avenida de Autlan, Camarillo, CA
93010 USA

Kernek, George *Baseball Player*
St Louis Cardinals, 16423 Cooton Gin
Ave, Wayne, OK 73095-3172 USA

Kerns, Joanna *Actor*
PO Box 49216, Los Angeles, CA 90049
USA

Kerns, Sandra
620 Resolano Dr., Pacific Palisades, CA
90272

Kerns Jr, David V *Engineer*
Vanderbilt University, Electrical
Engineering Dept, Nashville, TN 37235
USA

Kerr, Allen *Musician*
419 Carrington St, Adelaide, SA, 5000,
AUSTRALIA

Kerr, Brooke *Actor*
Innovative Artists (LA), 1505 Tenth St,
Santa Monica, CA 90401 USA

Kerr, Buddy *Baseball Player*
New York Giants, 341 Grove St, Oradell,
NJ 07649-2229 USA

Kerr, Deborah *Actor*
Wyhergut, Klosters, Grisons, 7250,
SWITZERLAND

Kerr, Edward
9701 Wilshire Blvd.10th Flr., Beverly
Hills, CA 90212

Kerr, Graham *Writer*
Kerr Corp, 1020 N Sunset Dr, Camano
Island, WA 98282 USA

Kerr, John
16130 Ventura Blvd. #650, Encino, CA
91436

Kerr, John G *Actor*
2975 Monterey Road, San Marino, CA
91108 USA

Kerr, John G (Red) *Basketball Player,
Coach, Sportscaster*
8700 W Bryn Mawr Ave, #600SO,
Chicago, IL 60631 USA

Kerr, Judy *Actor*
4139 Tujunga Ave, Studio City, CA 91604
USA

Kerr, Pat *Fashion Designer*
Pat Kerr Inc, 200 Wagner Place, Memphis,
TN 38103 USA

Kerr, Philip *Writer*
AP Watts Agents, 20 John St, London,
WC1N 2DR, UNITED KINGDOM (UK)

Kerr, Steve *Basketball Player*
789 Grandview, San Antonio, TX 78209
USA

Kerr, Tim *Hockey Player, Coach*
Power Play Really, 2528 Dune Dr,
Avalon, NJ 08202 USA

Kerr, William T *Business Person*
Meredith Corp, 1716 Locust St, Das
Moines, IA 50309 USA

Kerr Jr, Donald M *Physicist*
Science Applications International, 1241
Cave St, La Jolla, CA 92037 USA

Kerrey, J Robert (Bob) *Governor*
New School University, President's Office,
66W 12th St, New York, NY 10011 USA

Kerrick, Donald L *General*
Deputy Assistant National Security
Agency, Fort George C Meade, MD 20755
USA

Kerrigan, Joseph T (Joe) *Baseball Player*
Montreal Expos, 450 Forest Lane, North
Wales, PA 19454-2478 USA

Kerrigan, Nancy *Figure Skater*
11 Cedar Ave, Stoneham, MA 02180 USA

Kerry, Alexandra *Actor*
TalentWorks (LA), 3500 W Olive Ave
#1400, Burbank, CA 91505 USA

Kerry, Bob *Ex-Senator*
7602 Pacific St, Omaha, NE 78114 USA

Kersee, Bob
1034 S. Brentwood Blvd. #1530, St. Louis,
MO 63117-1215

Kersee, Jackie Joyner *Track Athlete*
JJK Assoc, PO Box 69047, St. Louis, MO
63169 USA

Kersey, Jerome *Basketball Player*
Milwaukee Bucks, Bradley Center, 1001
N 4th St, Milwaukee, WI 53203 USA

Kersey, Paul *Actor*
TalentWorks (LA), 3500 W Olive Ave
#1400, Burbank, CA 91505 USA

Kersh, David *Musician*
Mark Hybner Entertainment, PO Box 223,
Shiner, TX 77984 USA

Kershaw, Doug *Musician*
RR 1 Box 34285, Weld County Road 47,
Eaton, CO 80615 USA

Kershaw, Sammy *Musician*
Go Tell Mgmt, 4773 Lickton Park, Whites
Creek, TN 37189 USA

Kershner, Irvin *Director*
Somers Teitelbaum David, 8840 Wilshire
Blvd, #200, Beverly Hills, CA 90211 USA

Kertesz, Imre *Nobel Prize Laureate*
Northwestern University Press, 625 Colfax
St, Evanston, IL 60208 USA

Kerwin, Brian *Actor*
Paradigm Agency, 200 W 57th St, #900,
New York, NY 10019 USA

Kerwin, Joseph P *Astronaut*
1802 Royal Fern Court, Houston, TX
77062 USA

Kerwin, Lance *Actor*
PO Box 101, Temecula, CA 92593 USA

Kerwin, Larkin *Physicist*
2166 Bourboniere Park, Sillery, QC, G1T
1B4, CANADA

Keshishian, Alek
450 N. Rossmore Ave. #608, Los Angeles,
CA 90004

Kesner, Jillian *Actor*
William Carroll Agency, 11360 Brill Dr,
Studio City, CA 91604 USA

Kessinger, Donald E (Don) *Baseball Player*
Chicago Cubs, 2200 Longspur Point,
Oxford, MS 38655-5958 USA

Kessinger, Keith *Baseball Player*
Cincinnati Reds, 4017 Sage Meadows
Blvd, Jonesboro, AR 72401-8028 USA

Kessler, Alice & Ellen
Nymphenburger Str. 86, Munich,
GERMANY, D-80636

Kessler, David A *Government Official,
Doctor*
University of California, Med School,
Dean's Office, San Francisco, CA 94143
USA

Kessler, Glenn *Producer, Writer*
Creative Artists Agency LCC (CAA-LA),
9830 Wilshire Blvd, Beverly Hills, CA
90212 USA

Kessler, Robert (Bob) *Basketball Player*
14 Twin Pines Road, Hilton Head, SC
29928 USA

Kessler, Ron *Writer*
William Morris Agency, 151 El Camino
Dr, Beverly Hills, CA 90212 USA

Kessler, Stephen
1120 S. Ridgley Dr., Los Angeles, CA
90019-2528

Kessler, Todd *Writer, Producer*
Creative Artists Agency LCC (CAA-LA),
9830 Wilshire Blvd, Beverly Hills, CA
90212 USA

Kester, Rick *Baseball Player*
Atlanta Braves, PO Box 623, Gardnerville,
NV 89410-0623 USA

Kestner, Boyd *Actor*
Mirisch Agency, 1801 Century Park E,
#1801, Los Angeles, CA 90067 USA

Ketchum, Dave
2318 Waterby St., Westlake Village, CA
91361-1834

Ketchum, Hal *Musician*
The Bobby Roberts Company Inc, PO Box
1547, Goodlettsville, TN 37070-1547
USA

Ketchum, Howard *Engineer*
3800 Washington Road, West Palm
Beach, FL 33405 USA

Ketchum, Rai *Songwriter, Musician*
602 Wayside Dr, Wimberley, TX 78676 USA

Ketterle, Wolfgang *Nobel Prize Laureate*
25 Bellingham Dr, Brookline, MA 02446 USA

Kettle, Roger *Cartoonist*
King Features Syndicate, 888 7th Ave, New York, NY 10106 USA

Keves, Gyorgy *Architect*
Keves es Epitesztarsai Rt, Melinda Utca 21, Budapest, 1121, HUNGARY

Kevorkian, Jack *Doctor*
4870 Lockhart St, West Bloomfield, MI 48323-2533 USA

Key, James E (Jimmy) *Baseball Player*
Toronto Blue Jays, 30 June Road, North Salem, NY 10560-2318 USA

Key, Ted *Cartoonist*
1694 Glenhardie Road, Wayne, PA 19087 USA

Keyes, Daniel *Writer*
222 NW 69th St, Boca Raton, FL 33487 USA

Keyes, Evelyn *Actor*
999 N Doheny Dr, #509, Los Angeles, CA 90069 USA

Keyes, Leroy *Football Player*
6156 Pleasant Ave, Pennsauken, NJ 08110 USA

Keyes, Robert W *Engineer*
IBM Research Division, PO Box 218, Yorktown Heights, NY 10598 USA

Keyfitz, Nathan *Mathematician*
61 Mill Road, North Hampton, NH 03862 USA

Keymah, T'Keyah Crystal *Actor*
121 N San Vicente Blvd, Beverly Hills, CA 90211 USA

Keys, Alicia *Musician, Songwriter*
MBK Ent, 156 W 56th St, #400, New York, NY 10019 USA

Keys, Ronald E *General*
Commander in Chief Allied Forces South Europe, Box 1 PSC 813, FPO, AE, 09620 USA

Keys, Tyrone *Athlete, Football Player, Coach, Football Coach*
All Sports Community Service, 4732 North Dale Mabry, Suite 405, Tampa, FL 33614 USA

Keyser, Brian *Baseball Player*
Chicago White Sox, 233 Summer Glenn Way, Central Point, OR 97502-8617 USA

Keyser, Richard L *Business Person*
WW Grainger Inc, 100 Grainger Parkway, Lake Forest, IL 60045 USA

Keyser Jr, F Ray *Governor*
64 Warner Ave, Proctor, VT 05765 USA

Keysey, Ken
Rt. 8 Box 477, Pleasant Hill, OR 97401

Khabibulin, Nikolai *Hockey Player*
11424 E Palomino Road, Scottsdale, AZ 85259 USA

Khajag, Barsamian *Religious Leader*
Armenian Church of America, Eastern Diocese, 630 2nd Ave, New York, NY 10016 USA

Khaled *Musician*
Firstars Mgmt, 14724 Ventura Blvd, #PH, Sherman Oaks, CA 91403 USA

Khali, Simbi *Actor*
Innovative Artists, 1505 10th St, Santa Monica, CA 90401 USA

Khalifa, Sam *Baseball Player*
Pittsburgh Pirates, 741 E 6th St, Tucson, AZ 85719-5003 USA

Khalifa, Sheikh Hamad bin Isa al *Misc*
Rifa's Palace, Manama, BAHARIN

Khalifa, Sheikh Khalifa bin Sulman al *Prime Minister*
Prime Minister's Office, Government House, Manama, BAHARIN

Khalifa-al-Thani, Hamad Bin *Prime Minister, Prince*
Royal Palace, PO Box 923, Doha, QATAR

Khalil, Cristel *Actor*
Young and the Restless, The, 7800 Beverly Blvd, Ste 3305, Los Angeles, CA 90036 USA

Khalil, Mustafa *Prime Minister*
9A El Maahad El Swisry St, Zamalek, Cairo, EGYPT

Khamenei, Hojatolislam Sayyed Ali *President*
Religious Leader's Office, Teheran, IRAN

Khamtai, Siphandon *Prime Minister*
Prime Minister's Office, Council of Ministers, Vientiane, LAOS

Khan, Aamir *Actor, Bollywood*
11 Bela Vista Apts, Pali Hill Bandra (W), Mumbai, MS 400050, INDIA

Khan, Abdulla *Actor*
20/1 Arch Bishop Avenue, Boat Club Road, Chennai, TN 600 018, INDIA

Khan, Ali Akbar *Composer*
Gregory DiGiovine Mgmt, 121 Jordan St, San Rafael, CA 94901 USA

Khan, Amjad Ali *Composer*
3 Sadhna Enclave, Panchsheel Park, New Delhi, New Delhi, 110 017, INDIA

Khan, Arbaaz *Actor, Bollywood*
3 Galaxy Apts BJ Road, Band Stand Bandra, Mumbai, MS 400050, INDIA

Khan, Ayub *Actor, Bollywood*
Xavier House 2nd Floor, St Peter Colony Bandra (W), Mumbai, MS 400050, INDIA

Khan, Chaka *Musician, Actor*
Earthsong, 12431 Oxnard St, #B, North Hollywood, CA 91606 USA

Khan, Fardeen *Actor, Bollywood*
Sunshine Jassawala Wadi, Juhu Road Juhu, Mumbai, MS 400049, INDIA

Khan, Feroz *Actor, Bollywood, Filmmaker, Director, Producer*
Sunshine Jussawala Wadi, Juhu Church Road, Mumbai, MS 400049, INDIA

Khan, Gulam Ishaq *Ex-President*
3B University Town, Jamrud Road, Peshawar, PAKISTAN

Khan, Inamullah *Religious Leader*
Muslim Congress, D26 Block 8, Gulshan-E_Iqbal, Karachi, 75300, PAKISTAN

Khan, Kader *Actor, Bollywood*
102 Raj Kamal, 2nd Hasnabad Lane Santacruz, Mumbai, MS 400054, INDIA

Khan, Niazi Imran *Cricketer*
Shankat Khanum Memorial Trust, 29 Shah Jamai, Lahore, 546000, PAKISTAN

Khan, Prince Sadruddin Aga
Collonge-Bellerive, SWITZERLAND, CH-1245

Khan, Princess Yasmin
146 Central Park W, New York, NY 10023

Khan, Salman *Actor, Bollywood*
3 Galaxy Apartments BJ Road, Band Stand Bandra, Mumbai, MS 400050, INDIA

Khan, Sanjay *Actor, Director, Bollywood, Producer*
Sanjay House 11 Silver Beach A B Nair Road, Juhu, Bombay, MS 400 049, INDIA

Khan, Shahbaaz *Actor, Bollywood*
GB6 Agha Khan Baug, Versova Andheri, Bombay, MS 400 061, INDIA

Khan, Shahrukh *Actor, Bollywood*
7th Floor Amrit Apt, 15th Carter Road Bandra, Mumbai, MS 400050, INDIA

Khan, Sohail *Actor, Bollywood, Producer, Director*
4 Coral Reef 55 Chimbai Road, Bandra (W), Mumbai, MS 400050, INDIA

Khan, The Aga IV
Aiglemont, Gouvieux, FRANCE, F-60270

Khanh, Emanuelle *Fashion Designer*
Emanuelle Khanh International, 45 Ave Victor Hugo, Paris, 75116, FRANCE

Khanna, Akshaye *Actor, Bollywood*
13/C Elplaza, Little Gibs Road Malabar Hill, Mumbai, MS 400026, INDIA

Khanna, Amit *Actor, Bollywood*
301 Sea Star Near Holiday Inn, Balraj Sahni Marg, Mumbai, MS 400049, INDIA

Khanna, Mukesh *Actor, Bollywood, Director*
3 Parijat 95, Marine Drive, Bombay, MS 400 002, INDIA

Khanna, Rahul *Actor, Bollywood*
12/18 V.P. Road, C.P. Tank Mumbai 4, Mumbai, MS 400004, INDIA

Khanna, Rajesh *Actor, Bollywood*
Ashirwad 2 Carter Road, Bandra, Bombay, MS 400 050, INDIA

Khanna, Rinke *Actor, Bollywood*
201-A Vastu Bldg, Military Rd Juhu, Mumbai, MS 400049, INDIA

khanna, Twinkle *Actor, Bollywood*
Samudra Mahal Birla Lane, Juhu, Mumbai, MS 400049, INDIA

Khanna, Vinod *Actor, Bollywood*
11 Palazo 13th Flr Behind WIAA, Malabar Hill, Mumbai, MS 400006, INDIA

Khanzadian, Vahan *Opera Singer*
3604 Broadway, #2N, New York, NY 10031 USA

Kharbanda, Kulbhushan *Actor*
501 Silver Cascade Mount Mary Road, Bandra, Bombay, MS 400 050, INDIA

Khariton, Yuli B *Physicist*
Nuclear Energy Center, Arsamas 16, Nizhy Novgorog Region, RUSSIA

Khashoggi, Adnan
Box 6, Riyadh, SAUDI ARABIA

Khashoggi, Adnan M *Business Person*
La Baraka, Marbella, SPAIN

Khatami, Mohammad *Politician, President*
President's Office, Dr Ali Shariati Ave,
Teheran, IRAN

Khavin, Vladimir Y *Architect*
Glavmosarchitectura, Mayakovsky Square
1, Moscow, 103001, RUSSIA

Khayat, Edward (Eddie) *Football Player,*
Football Coach
7813 Haydenberry Cove, Nashville, TN
37221 USA

Khayat, Robert *Educator*
University of Mississippi, Chancellor's
Office, University, MS 38677 USA

Kheel, Theodore W *Misc*
280 Park Ave, New York, NY 10017 USA

Kher, Anupam *Actor, Bollywood*
402 Marina, Juhu Tara Road Juhu Beach,
Mumbai, MS 400049, INDIA

Khitty *Actor*
E3 Sea Brook Apartments 4th C'Ward
Road, Valmigi Nagar Thiruvanmiyur,
Chennai, TN 600 041, INDIA

Khokhlov, Boris *Dancer*
Myaskovsky St 11-13, #102, Moscow,
121019 USA

Khondji, Darius *Cinematographer*
International Creative Mgmt, 8942
Wilshire Blvd, #219, Beverly Hills, CA
90211 USA

Khorana, Har Gobind *Nobel Prize*
Laureate
39 Amherst Road, Belmont, MA 02478
USA

Khotan *Musician*
Gabriel Blanco Iglesias (Mexico), Rio
Balsas 35-32, Colonia Cuauhtemoc, DF,
06500, Mexico

Khouna, Sheikh El Afia Quid Mohamed
Prime Minister
Prime Minister's Office, Nouakchott,
MAURITANIA

Khourl, Callie *Director*
International Creative Mgmt, 8942
Wilshire Blvd, #219, Beverly Hills, CA
90211 USA

Khrennikov, Tikhon N *Composer*
Plotnikov Per 10/28, #19, Moscow,
121200, RUSSIA

Khristenko, Viktor *Prime Minister*
Prime Minister's Office, Kremlin, Staraya
Pl 4, Moscow, 103132, RUSSIA

Khruschev, Sergei
PO Box 1948, Providence, RI 02912

Khush, Gurdev S *Scientist*
Int'l Rice Research Institute, PO Box 933,
Manila, 1099, PHILLIPINES

Khvorostovsky, Dimitri A *Opera Singer*
Elen Victorova, Mosfilmovskaya 26, #5,
Moscow, RUSSIA

Kiana *Talk Show Host*
ESPN 2, 935 Middle St, Bristol, CT 06010

Kiarostaml, Abbas *Director*
Zeitgeist Films, 247 Center St, #200, New
York, NY 10013 USA

Kibaki, Mwai *President*
President's Office, Harambee House,
Harambee Ave, Nairobi, KENYA

Kibrick, Anne *Educator*
130 Seminary Ave, #312, Auburndale,
MA 02466 USA

Kibrick, Sidney
10490 Wilshire Blvd. #1901, Los Angeles,
CA 90024-4649

Kichel III, Walter *Editor*
Fortune Magazine, Editorial Dept, 1291
Ave of Americas, New York, NY 10020
USA

Kid Rock *Musician*
Pinnacle Entertainment, 30 Glenn St,
White Plains, NY 10603 USA

Kidd, Billy
2305 Mt. Werner Circle, Steamboat
Springs, CO 80487

Kidd, Dylan *Director*
Creative Artists Agency LCC (CAA-LA),
9830 Wilshire Blvd, Beverly Hills, CA
90212 USA

Kidd, Jason *Basketball Player*
New Jersey Nets, 390 Murray Hill Pkwy, E
Rutherford, NJ 07073 USA

Kidd, Jodie *Model*
IMG Models, 13-16 Jacob's Well Mews,
George St, London, W1H 5PD, UNITED
KINGDOM (UK)

Kidd, Michael *Choreographer, Dancer*
1614 Old Oak Road, Los Angeles, CA
90049 USA

Kidd, William W (Billy) *Skier*
Billy Kidd Racing, 2305 Mount Werner
Circle, Steamboat Springs, CO 80487 USA

Kidder, Margot *Actor*
315 W Lewis St, Livingston, MT 58047
USA

Kidder, Tracy *Writer*
George Borchardt, 136 E 57th St, New
York, NY 10022 USA

Kidder Lee, Barbara *Skier*
1308 W Highland, Phoenix, AZ 85013
USA

Kidjo, Angelique *Musician*
Primary Talent, 2-12 Petonville Road,
London, N1 9PL, UNITED KINGDOM
(UK)

Kidman, Nicole *Actor, Model*
PMK/HBH Public Relations (PMK-LA),
8500 Wilshire Blvd #700, Beverly Hills,
CA 90211 USA

Kiecker, Dana *Baseball Player*
Boston Red Sox, 4104 Prairie Ridge Rd,
Saint Paul, MN 55123-1625 USA

Kiedis, Anthony *Musician*
Q Prime, 729 7th Ave, #1600, New York,
NY 10019 USA

Kiefer, Adolph G *Swimmer, Coach*
42125 N Hunt Club Road, Wadsworth, IL
60083 USA

Kiefer, Mark *Baseball Player*
Milwaukee Brewers, 1182 Old Fashion
Way, Garden Grove, CA 92840-2117
USA

Kiefer, Steve *Baseball Player*
Oakland A's, 1182 Old Fashion Way,
Garden Grove, CA 92840-2117 USA

Kiehl, Marina *Skier*
Hermie-Bland Str 11, Munich, 81545,
GERMANY

Kiehl, Stuart *Cinematographer*
4193 Concord Ave, Santa Rosa, CA 95407
USA

Kiel, Richard *Actor*
327 Adler Ave, Clovis, CA 93612 USA

Kielty, Bob *Baseball Player*
Minnesota Twins, 29287 Stampede Way,
Canyon Lake, CA 92587-7634 USA

Kiely, John *Baseball Player*
Detroit Tigers, 545 Main St, Wareham,
MA 02571-1030 USA

Kiely, Mark
9255 Sunset Blvd. #620, Los Angeles, CA
90069

Kier, Udo *Actor*
Agentur Players, Sophienstr 21, Berlin,
10178, GERMANY

Kiermayer, Susanne *Misc*
Amthofplatz 5, Kirchberg, 94259,
GERMANY

Kieschnick, Brook *Baseball Player*
Chicago Cubs, 201 Evans Ave, San
Antonio, TX 78209-3721 USA

Kiesel, Theresia *Track Athlete*
Stifterstr 24, Truan, 4050, AUSTRIA

Kihn, Greg *Musician*
Riot Mgmt, 55 Santa Clara Ave, #120,
oakland, CA 94610 USA

Kiick, James F (Jim) *Football Player*
4001 E Lake Estates Dr, Davie, FL 33328
USA

Kikutake, Kiyonori *Architect*
1-11-15 Otsuka, Bunkyoku, Tokyo, JAPAN

Kilar, Wojciech *Composer*
Ul Ksciuszki 165, Katowice, 40-524,
POLAND

Kilbey, Steve *Musician*
Globeshine, 101 Chamberlayne Road,
London, NW10 3ND, UNITED
KINGDOM (UK)

Kilbey, Steven *Musician*
Globeshine, 101 Chamberlayne Road,
London, NW10 3ND, UNITED
KINGDOM (UK)

Kilborn, Craig *Talk Show Host*
Late Late Show with Craig Kilborn, 1697
Broadway, New York, NY 10019

Kilbourne, Wendy *Actor*
9300 Wilshire Blvd, #410, Beverly Hills,
CA 90212 USA

Kilburn, Terry *Actor*
Meadowbrook Theatre, Oakland
University, Walton & Squirrel, Rochester,
MI 48063 USA

Kilby, Jack S *Nobel Prize Laureate*
7723 Midbury St, Dallas, TX 75230 USA

Kilcher, Jewel *Musician*
PO Box 1388, Brea, CA 92822 USA

Kiley, Ariel *Actor*
Untitled Entertainment (NY), 23 E 22nd St
Fl 3, New York, NY 10010 USA

Kilgallon, Robert D *Scientist*
662 Park Ave, Meadville, PA 16335 USA

Kilgore, Al *Cartoonist*
21655 113th Dr, Queens Village, NY 11429 USA

Kilgore, Jerry *Songwriter, Musician*
TBA Artist Mgmt, 300 10th Ave S, Nashville, TN 37203 USA

Kilgore, Merle
Box 850, Paris, TN 38242

Kilgus, Paul *Baseball Player*
Texas Rangers, 2102 Smallhouse Rd, Bowling Green, KY 42104-3266 USA

Kilian, Thomas J *Business Person*
Conseco Inc, PO Box 1957, Carmel, IN 46082 USA

Kilius, Marika *Figure Skater*
Postfach 201151, Dreieich, 63271, GERMANY

Kilkenny, Mike *Baseball Player*
Detroit Tigers, 274 Holland St W, Bradford, ON L3Z 1J1, CANADA

Killebrew, Harmon *Baseball Player*
Washington Senators, PO Box 14550, Scottsdale, AZ 85267-4550 USA

Killeen, Evans *Baseball Player*
Kansas City A's, 208 Collins Ave Apt 2-C, Mount Vernon, NY 10552-1701 USA

Killinger, Kerry K *Financier*
Washington Mutual Inc, 1201 3rd Ave, Seattle, WA 98101 USA

Killip, Christopher D *Photographer*
Harvard University, Visual Studies Dept, 24 Quincy St, Cambridge, MA 02138 USA

Killy, Jean-Claude *Skier*
Villa Les 13 Chemin Bellefontaine, Cologny-GE, 1223, SWITZERLAND

Kilmer, Billy
111 S St Joseph St, S Bend, IN 46601-1901

Kilmer, Val *Actor*
International Creative Management (ICM-LA), 8942 Wilshire Blvd, Beverly Hills, CA 90211 USA

Kilmer, William O (Billy) *Football Player*
1853 Monte Carto Way, #36, Coral Springs, FL 33071 USA

Kilmore, Chris *Musician*
ArtistDirect, 10900 Wilshire Blvd, #1400, Los Angeles, CA 90024 USA

Kilner, Kevin *Actor*
Innovative Artists, 1505 10th St, Santa Monica, CA 90401 USA

Kilpatrick, Eric
6330 Simpson Ave. #3, No. Hollywood, CA 91606

Kilpatrick, Kwame *Politician*
Mayor's Office, City-County Building, 2 Woodward Ave, Detroit, MI 48226 USA

Kilpatrick Jr, James J *Writer*
White Walnut Hill, Woodville, VA 22749 USA

Kilrain, Susan L *Astronaut*
PO Box 420201, Roosevelt Roads, PR 00742 USA

Kilrea, Brian *Hockey Player, Coach*
2192 Saunderson Dr, Ottawa, ON K1G 2G4, CANADA

Kilts, James M *Business Person*
Gillette Co, Prudential Tower Building, Boston, MA 02199 USA

Kilzer, Louis C (Lon) *Journalist*
Minneapolis-Saint Paul Star-Tribune, 425 Portland Ave, Minneapolis, MN 55488 USA

Kim, Byung Hyun *Baseball Player*
Arizona Diamondbacks, 2037 N Chestnut, Mesa, AZ 85213-2274 USA

Kim, Jacqueline *Actor*
Innovative Artists, 1505 10th St, Santa Monica, CA 90401 USA

Kim, Jaegwon *Misc*
Brown University, Philosophy Dept, Providence, RI 02912 USA

Kim, Nelli V *Gymnast*
2480 Cobblehill, #A Alocove, Woodbury, MN 55125 USA

Kim, Peter S *Misc*
Whitehead Institute, 9 Cambridge Center, Cambridge, MA 02142 USA

Kim, Stephan Sou-hwan Cardinal *Religious Leader*
Archbishop's House, 2 Ka 1 Myong Dong Chungku, Seoul, 100, SOUTH KOREA

Kim, Susan *Writer*
Writers and Artists Group Intl (LA), 8383 Wilshire Blvd #550, Beverly Hills, CA 90211 USA

Kim, Young Sam *President*
Sangdo-dong 7-6, Tongjakku, Seoul, SOUTH KOREA

Kim, Young Uck *Musician*
Columbia Artists Mgmt Inc, 165 W 57th St, New York, NY 10019 USA

Kim Il, Jong *President*
President's Office, Central Committee, Pyongyang, NORTH KOREA

kim Il, Jong P *Prime Minister*
Prime Minister's Office, 77 Sejong-no, Chongnoku, Seoul, SOUTH KOREA

Kimball, Bobby *Musician*
World Entertainment Assoc, 297101 Kinderkamack Road, #128, Oradell, NJ 07649 USA

Kimball, Christopher *Chef*
Public Broadcasting SYstem, 1320 Braddock Place, Alexandria, VA 22314 USA

Kimball, Dick *Coach*
1540 Waltham Dr, Ann Arbor, MI 48103 USA

Kimball, Ward
8910 Ardendale Ave., San Gabriel, CA 91775

Kimball, Warren F *Historian*
2540 Otter Lane, Johns Island, SC 29455 USA

Kimble, Warren *Artist*
RR 3Box 1038, Brandon, VT 05733 USA

Kimbrough, Charles *Actor, Musician*
255 Amalfi Dr, Santa Monica, CA 90402 USA

Kimbrough, John A *Football Player*
801 N Ave L, Haskell, TX 79521 USA

Kimery, James L *Misc*
Veterans of Foreign Wars, 405 W 34th St, Kansas City, MO 64111 USA

Kimm, Bruce *Baseball Player*
Detroit Tigers, 3168 121st St, Amana, IA 52203-8046 USA

Kimmel, Jimmy *Writer, Comedian, Television Host*
Jimmy Kimmel Live, 6834 Hollywood Blvd, Hollywood, CA 90028 USA

Kimmelman, Michael *Critic*
New York Times, Editorial Dept, 229 W 43rd St, New York, NY 10036 USA

Kimmins, Kenneth *Actor*
J Michael Bloom, 9255 Sunset Blvd, #710, Los Angeles, CA 90069 USA

Kimura, Doreen *Psychic*
211 Madison Ave, Toronto, ON M5R 2S6, CANADA

Kimura, Kazuo *Designer*
Japan Design Foundation, 2-2 Cenba Chuo, Higashiku, Osaka, 541, JAPAN

Kimura, Motoo *Biologist*
Institute of Genetics, Yata 1, 111 Mishima, Shizuokaken, 411, JAPAN

Kinard, Terry *Football Player*
19 English St, Sumter, SC 29150 USA

Kincaid, Aron *Actor*
Coast to Coast Talent, 3350 Barham Blvd, Los Angeles, CA 90068 USA

Kincaid, Jamaica *Writer*
College Road, North Bennington, VT 05257 USA

Kinchen, Todd W *Football Player*
1010 S Acadian Thruway, Building F, Baton Rouge, LA 70806 USA

Kinchla, Chan *Musician*
ArtistDirect, 10900 Wilshire Blvd, #1400, Los Angeles, CA 90024 USA

Kincses, Veronika *Opera Singer*
Hungarian State Opera, Andrassy Ulca 22, Budapest, 1061, HUNGARY

Kind, Richard *Actor*
144 W 82nd St, New York, NY 10024 USA

Kind, Roslyn *Actor, Musician*
Scott Stander, 13707 Riverside Dr, #201, Sherman Oaks, CA 91423 USA

Kindall, Jerry *Baseball Player*
Chicago Cubs, 7220 E Grey Fox Ln, Tucson, AZ 85750-1377 USA

Kinder, Melvyn *Psychic*
1951 San Ysidro Dr, Beverly Hills, CA 90210 USA

Kinder, Richard D *Business Person*
Enron Corp, PO Box 1188, Houston, TX 77251 USA

Kindler, Klaus
Am Berg 6, Schwietenkirchen, GERMANY, D-85301

Kindred, David A *Writer*
Atlanta Constitution, Editorial Dept, 72 Marietta St, Atlanta, GA 30303 USA

Kiner, Ralph M *Baseball Player, Sportscaster*
Pittsburgh Pirates, 70346 Calico Road, Rancho Mirage, CA 92270-3410 USA

Kiner, Steve *Football Player*
112 N Ole Hickory Trail, Carrollton, GA 30117 USA

King, Alan *Actor, Comedian*
William Morris Agency, 151 El Camino Dr, Beverly Hills, CA 90212 USA

King, Albert *Basketball Player*
88 Sturbridge Circle, Wayne, NJ 07470 USA

King, B B *Musician*
PO Box 1984, Teaneck, NJ 07666 USA

King, BB *Musician*
Entertainment Consultants Inc, 164 Woodstone Dr, Buffalo Grove, IL 60089

King, Ben E *Musician*
Smiling Clown Music, PO Box 1097, Teaneck, NJ 07666 USA

King, Benjamin *Actor*
Relativity Management, 8899 Beverly Blvd #510, Los Angeles, CA 90048 USA

King, Bernard *Basketball Player*
307 Jupiter Hills Dr, Dututh, GA 30097 USA

King, Betsy *Golfer*
Ladies Pro Golf Association (LPGA), 100 International Golf Drive, Daytona Beach, FL 32124 USA

King, Billie Jean *Tennis Player*
World Team Tennis, 250 Park Ave S, #900, New York, NY 10003 USA

King, Bruce *Governor*
4264 Indian Springs Dr NE, Albuquerque, NM 87109 USA

King, Cammie *Actor*
511 Cypress St, Fort Bragg, CA 95437 USA

King, Cammie Conlon
Pierce & Shelly, 13775-A Mono Way #220, Sonora, CA 95370 USA

King, Carole *Musician, Composer*
Manatt Phelps & Phillips LLP, 11355 W Olympic Blvd, Los Angeles, CA 90064 USA

King, Carolyn Dineen *Judge*
US Court of Appeals, US Courthouse, 515 Rusk Ave, Houston, TX 77002 USA

King, Cheryl *Actor*
CLInc Talent, 843 N Sycamore Ave, Los Angeles, CA 90038 USA

King, Chick *Baseball Player*
Detroit Tigers, 4036 Highway 54, Paris, TN 38242-6335 USA

King, Claude *Musician*
House of Talent, 9 Lucy Lane, Sherwood, AR 72120 USA

King, Clyde E *Baseball Player*
Brooklyn Dodgers, 103 Stratford Road, Goldsboro, NC 27534-8971 USA

King, Colbert *Journalist*
Washington Post, Editorial Dept, 1150 15th St NW, Washington, DC 20071 USA

King, Coretta Scott *Social Activist*
M L King Nonviolent Social Change Center, 449 Aubum Ave NE, Atlanta, GA 30312 USA

King, Dana *Commentator*
CBS-TV, News Dept, 524 W 57th St, New York, NY 10019 USA

King, David A *Misc*
Masters Lodge, Downing College, Cambridge, CB2 1DQ, UNITED KINGDOM (UK)

King, Dennis *Artist*
3857 26th St, San Francisco, CA 94131 USA

King, Derek *Hockey Player*
8 Indian Club Road, Northport, NY 11768 USA

King, Dexter Scott *Misc*
M L King Nonviolent Social Change Center, 449 Aubum Ave NE, Atlanta, GA 30312 USA

King, Don
Don King Productions, 968 Pinehurst Drive, Las Vegas, NV 89109 USA

King, Don *Misc*
Don King Productions, 968 Pinehurst Dr, Las Vegas, NV 89109 USA

King, Edward J *Governor*
A J Lane Co, 1500 Worcester Road, Framingham, MA 01702 USA

King, Elizabeth (Betsy) *Golfer*
General Delivery, Limekiln, PA 19535 USA

King, Eric *Baseball Player*
Detroit Tigers, 1063 Stanford Dr, Simi Valley, CA 93065-4952 USA

King, Erik *Actor*
Burstein Company, The, 15304 Sunset Blvd #208, Pacific Palisades, CA 90272 USA

King, Evelyn
1560 Broadway #1308, New York, NY 10036

King, Evelyn (Champagne) *Musician*
Nationwide Entertainment, 2756 N Green Valley Parkway, Henderson, NV 89014 USA

King, Francis H *Writer*
19 Gordon Place, London, W8 4JE, UNITED KINGDOM (UK)

King, George *Basketball Player*
109 Clubhouse Lane, #295, Naples, FL 34105 USA

King, Gordon D *Football Player*
2641 Highwood Dr, Roseville, CA 95661 USA

King, Hall *Baseball Player*
Houston Astros, 828 Geneva Dr, Oviedo, FL 32765-9503 USA

King, Hogue Maxine (Mick) *Swimmer*
US Air Force Academy, PO Box 155, USAF Academy, CO 80840 USA

King, Jaime *Actor, Model*
International Creative Mgmt, 8942 Wilshire Blvd, #219, Beverly Hills, CA 90211 USA

King, James (Jaime) *Actor*
Creative Artists Agency LCC (CAA-LA), 9830 Wilshire Blvd, Beverly Hills, CA 90212 USA

King, James A *Opera Singer*
Columbia Artists Mgmt Inc, 165 W 57th St, New York, NY 10019 USA

King, James B *Editor*
Seattle Times, Editorial Dept, 1120 John St, Seattle, WA 98109 USA

King, James C *General*
Director, National Imagery/Mapping Agency, Chantilly, VA 22021 USA

King, Jean
5510 Cahuenga Blvd, No. Hollywood, CA 91601

King, Jeff *Misc*
PO Box 48, Denali National Park, AK 99755 USA

King, Jonathan
1 Wyndham Yard, London, ENGLAND, W1H 1AR

King, Kathryn (Katie) *Hockey Player*
6 Birchwood Road, Salem, NH 03079 USA

King, Kent Masters *Actor*
Richard Schwartz Management, 2934-1/2 Beverly Glen Cir #107, Los Angeles, CA 90077

King, Lamnar *Football Player*
1453 Browning Dr, Essex, MD 21221 USA

King, Larry *Commentator*
13607 Hatteras St, Van Nuys, CA 91401 USA

King, Mary-Claire *Misc*
University of Washington, Medical School, Genetics Dept, Seattle, WA 98195 USA

King, Mervyn A *Economist*
Bank of England, Threadneedle St, London, EC2R 8AH, UNITED KINGDOM (UK)

King, Michael *Business Person*
King World Productions Inc (LA), 2401 Colorado Ave #110, Santa Monica, CA 90404

King, Michael *Business Person*
King World Productions, 12400 Wilshire Blvd, Los Angeles, CA 90025 USA

King, Michael Patrick *Producer, Writer*
Jackoway Tyerman Wertheimer Austen Mandelbaum & Morris, 1888 Century Park E Fl 18, Los Angeles, CA 90067 USA

King, Morgana *Actor, Musician*
Subrena Artists, 330 W 56th St #18M, New York, NY 10019 USA

King, Patsy
6/70 Hawksburn Rd South Yarra, Victoria, AUSTRALIA, 3141

King, Perry *Actor*
3647 Wrightwood Dr, Studio City, CA 91604 USA

King, Phillip *Artist*
Bernard Jackson Gallery, 14A Clifford St, London, W1X 1RF, UNITED KINGDOM (UK)

King, R Stacey *Basketball Player*
5340 Prairie Crossing, Long Grove, IL 60047 USA

King, Regina *Actor*
Gersh Agency, 232 N Canon Dr, Beverly Hills, CA 90210 USA

King, Richard L *Business Person*
Albertson's Inc, 250 Parkcenter Blvd,
Boise, ID 83726 USA

King, Roger *Business Person*
King World Productions, 12400 Wilshire
Blvd, Los Angeles, CA 90025 USA

King, Shaun *Athlete, Football Player*
Tampa Bay Buccaneers, 1 Bucaneer
Place, Tampa, FL 33607 USA

King, Stephen *Writer*
Juliann Eugley, 49 Florida Ave, Bangor,
ME 04401 USA

King, Stephen E *Writer*
Juliann Eugley, 49 Florida Ave, Bangor,
ME 04401 USA

King, Ted *Actor, Musician*
Paradigm (LA), 10100 Santa Monica Blvd,
Fl 25, Los Angeles, CA 90067 USA

King, Thea *Musician*
16 Milverton Road, London, NW6 7AS,
UNITED KINGDOM (UK)

King, Thomas J (Tom) *Government
Official*
House of Commons, Westminster,
London, SW1A 0AA, UNITED KINGDOM
(UK)

King, W David *Coach*
Calgary Flames, PO Box 1540, Station M,
Calgary, AB T2P 3B9, CANADA

King, William (Bill) *Misc*
Management Assoc, 1920 Benson Ave,
Saint Paul, MN 55116 USA

King, Yolanda *Producer, Motivational
Speaker, Actor*
Higher Ground Productions, 10736
Jefferson Blvd, #233, Culver City, CA
90230 USA

King, Zalman *Director*
308 Alta Ave, Santa Monica, CA 90402
USA

King III, Martin Luther *Social Activist*
Southern Christian Leadership, 591
Edgewood Ave SE, #A, Atlanta, GA 30312
USA

King Jr, Woodie *Producer*
417 Convent Ave, New York, NY 10031
USA

King Kong *Actor*
77 Sastri Street, Kaveri Nagar Saidapet,
Chennai, TN 600 015, INDIA

King Sisters
10275 S. 2505 E., Sandy, UT 84092-4464

Kingdom, Roger *Track Athlete*
146 S Fairmont St, #1, Pittsburgh, PA
15206 USA

Kinglsey, Ben *Actor*
International Creative Mgmt, 76 Oxford
St, London, W1N 0AX, UNITED
KINGDOM (UK)

Kings Norton *Scientist, Engineer*
Westcote House, Chipping Campden,
Glos, UNITED KINGDOM (UK)

Kingsley, Ben *Actor*
International Creative Management
(ICM-LA), 8942 Wilshire Blvd, Beverly
Hills, CA 90211 USA

Kingsley, Ben *Actor*
New Penworth House, Strafford upon
Avon, Warwickshire, 0V3 7QX, UNITED
KINGDOM (UK)

Kingsley, Patricia
371 Alma Real Dr., Pacific Palisades, CA
90272

Kingsmen, The
1720 N. Ross Ave., Santa Ana, CA 92706

Kingston, Alex *Actor*
3400 Floyd Terrace, Los Angeles, CA
90068 USA

Kingston, Kenny
11561 Dona Dorotea Dr., Studio City, CA
91604

Kingston, Mark
47 Courtfield Rd. #9, London, ENGLAND,
SW7 4DB

Kingston, Maxine Hong *Writer*
University of California, English Dept,
Berkeley, CA 94720 USA

Kingston Trio, The
9410 S. 46th St., Phoenix, AZ 85044

Kinkade, Thomas *Artist*
Media Arts Group, 900 Lightpost Way,
Morgan Hill, CA 95037, US

Kinkel, Klaus *Government Official*
Auswartigen Amt, Adenauerallee 101,
Bonn, 53113, GERMANY

Kinks, The
29 Ruston Mews, London, ENGLAND,
W11 1RB

Kinley, Heather *Musician*
Epic Records, 1211 S Highland Ave, Los
Angeles, CA 90019 USA

Kinley, Jennifer *Musician*
Epic Records, 1211 S Highland Ave, Los
Angeles, CA 90019 USA

Kinley's, The
PO Box 128501, Nashville, TN 37212

Kinmont, Boothe Jill *Skier*
310 SUnland Dr, RR1 Box 11, Bishop, CA
93514 USA

Kinmont, Jill
310 Sunland Ave., Bishop, CA 93514

Kinmont, Kathleen *Actor*
9929 Sunset Blvd, #310, Los Angeles, CA
90069 USA

Kinnan, Timothy A *General*
US Military Representative, NATO Blvd
Leopold III, Brussels, 1110, BELGIUM

Kinnear, Dominic *Coach*
San Jose Earthquakes, 3550 Stevens Creek
Blvd, #200, San Jose, CA 95117 USA

Kinnear, Greg *Actor, Comedian*
2280 Mandeville Canyon Road, Los
Angeles, CA 90049 USA

Kinnear III, James W *Business Person*
Ten Standard Forum, PO Box 120,
Stamford, CT 06904 USA

Kinnell, Galway *Writer*
110 Bleecker St, #6D, New York, NY
10012 USA

Kinney, Dallas *Journalist*
484 Egret Circle, Sebastian, FL 32976 USA

Kinney, Kathy *Actor*
10061 Riverside Dr, #777, Toluca Lake,
CA 91602 USA

Kinney, Matt *Athlete*
23 Fieldstone Dr, Bangor, ME 04401-3279

Kinney, Terry *Actor*
Gersh Agency, 232 N Canon Dr, Beverly
Hills, CA 90210 USA

Kinnock, Neil G *Government Official*
European Communities Commission, 200
Rue de Loi, Brussels, 1049, BELGIUM

Kinsella, Brooke *Actor*
EastEnders, BBC Elstree Centre, Clarendon
Road, Borehamwood, Herts, UNITED
KINGDOM

Kinsella, John P *Swimmer*
PO Box 3067, Sumas, WA 98295 USA

Kinsella, Thomas *Writer*
Killalane, Laragh, County Wicklow,
IRELAND

Kinsella, W P
PO Box 3067, Sumas, WA 98295 USA

Kinsella, William Patrick (W P) *Writer*
1952-152A St, #216, Surrey, BC V4A 9T2,
CANADA

Kinser, Steve *Race Car Driver*
King Racing, PO Box 2115, Allen, TX
75013 USA

Kinsey, James L *Misc*
Rice University, Natural Sciences School,
Houston, TX 77005 USA

Kinshofer-Guthlein, Christa *Skier*
Munchnerstr 44, Rosenheim, 83026,
GERMANY

Kinski, Nastassja *Actor, Model*
1000 Bel Air Place, Los Angeles, CA
90077 USA

Kinsley, Michael E *Editor, Commentator*
14150 NE 20th St, #527, Bellevue, WA
98007 USA

Kinsman, Brent *Actor*
AKA Talent Agency, 6310 San Vicente
Blvd #200, Los Angeles, CA 90048 USA

Kinsman, Shane *Actor*
AKA Talent Agency, 6310 San Vicente
Blvd #200, Los Angeles, CA 90048 USA

Kinsman, T James (Jim) *War Hero*
111 Howe Road E, Winlock, WA 98596
USA

Kintner, William R *Scientist*
Foreign Policy Research Institute, 3508
Market St, Philadelphia, PA 19104 USA

Kiper Jr, Mel *Sportscaster*
ESPN-TV, Sports Dept ESPN Plaza, 935
Middle St, Bristol, CT 06010 USA

Kipketer, Wilson *Track Athlete*
Atletik Forbund Idraettens Hus, Brondby
Stadion 20, Brondby, 2605, DENMARK

Kiplinger, Austin H *Publisher*
Montevideo, 1680 River Road,
Poolesville, MD 20837 USA

Kiraly, Charles F (Karch) *Volleyball
Player, Coach*
Assn of Volleyball Pros, 330 Washington
Blvd, #400, Marina del Rey, CA 90292
USA

Kirby, Bruce *Actor*
629 N Orlando Ave, #3, West Hollywood,
CA 90048 USA

Kirby, Durwood *Writer*
PO Box 3454, Fort Myers, FL 33918 USA

Kirby, Luke *Actor*
Creative Artists Agency LCC (CAA-LA), 9830 Wilshire Blvd, Beverly Hills, CA 90212 USA

Kirby, Pete
PO Box 1734, Madison, TN 37116

Kirby, Ronald H *Architect*
PO Box 337, Melville, Johannesburg, 2109, SOUTH AFRICA

Kirby, Will *Reality TV Star*
William Morris Agency (WMA-LA), 1 William Morris Pl, Beverly Hills, CA 90212 USA

Kirchbach, Gunar *Athlete*
Georgi-Dobrowoiski-Ste 10, Furstenwalde, 15517, GERMANY

Kirchenbauer, Bill
3800 Barham Blvd., Los Angeles, CA 90068-1042

Kirchhoff, Ulrich *Misc*
Hoven 258, Rosendahl, 48720, GERMANY

Kirchner, Leon *Composer, Conductor*
Harvard University, Music Dept, Cambridge, MA 02138 USA

Kirchner, Mark *Athlete*
Haruptstr 74A, Scheibe-Alsbach, 98749, GERMANY

Kirchner, Nestor *President*
Casa de Gobiemo, Balcarce 50, Buenos Aires, 1064, ARGENTINA

Kirchschlager, Angelika *Opera Singer*
Mastrioanni Assoc, 161 W 61st St, #17E, New York, NY 10023 USA

Kirgo, George *Actor, Writer*
178 N Carmelina Ave, Los Angeles, CA 90049 USA

Kirk, Claude R Jr *Governor*
Kirk Co, 1180 Gator Trail, West Palm Beach, FL 33409 USA

Kirk, Justin *Actor*
Gersh Agency, The (NY), 41 Madison Ave Fl 33, New York, NY 10010 USA

Kirk, Phyllis *Actor*
321 S Beverly Dr, #M, Beverly Hills, CA 90212 USA

Kirk, Rahsaan Roland *Musician*
Atlantic Records, 9229 Sunset Blvd, #900, Los Angeles, CA 90069 USA

Kirk, Thomas B *Physicist*
Brookhaven National Laboratory, Physics Dept, 2 Center St, Upton, NY 11973 USA

Kirk Jr, Walton (Walt) *Basketball Player*
2355 Coventry Parkway, #B202, Dubuque, IA 52001 USA

Kirkby, Emma *Musician*
Consort of Music, 54A Leamington Road Villas, London, W11 1HT, UNITED KINGDOM (UK)

Kirkconnell, Clare
Box 63, Rutherford, CA 94573-0063

Kirkeby, Per *Artist*
Margarete Roeder Gallery, 545 Broadway, New York, NY 10012 USA

Kirkland, Gelsey *Ballerina*
500 Mount Tailac Court, Roseville, CA 95747 USA

Kirkland, Lori *Producer*
Roklin Management, 8265 Sunset Blvd #101, Los Angeles, CA 90046 USA

Kirkland, Mike *Musician*
Bob Flick Productions, 300 Vine, #14, Seattle, WA 98121 USA

Kirkland, Sally *Actor*
11300 W Olympic Blvd, #610, Los Angeles, CA 90064 USA

Kirkman, Rick *Cartoonist*
King Features Syndicate, 888 7th Ave, New York, NY 10106 USA

Kirkpatrick, Chris *Musician*
Wright Entertainment, 7680 Universal Blvd, #500, Orlando, FL 32819 USA

Kirkpatrick, Jeane D J *Government Official*
American Enterprise Institute, 1150 17th St NW, Washington, DC 20036 USA

Kirkpatrick, Maggie *Actor*
Shanahan Mgmt, PO Box 1509, Darlinghurst, NSW, 1300, AUSTRALIA

Kirkpatrick, Ralph *Musician*
Old Quarry, Guilford, CT 06437 USA

Kirkup, James *Writer*
British Monomarks, BM-Box 2780, London, WC1V 6XX, UNITED KINGDOM (UK)

Kirkwood, Craig *Actor*
Michael Slessinger & Assoc, 8730 Sunset Blvd #270, Los Angeles, CA 90069 USA

Kirllenko, Andrei *Basketball Player*
Utah Jazz, Delta Center, 301 W South Temple, Salt Lake City, UT 84101 USA

Kirrane, John (Jack) *Hockey Player*
3 Centre St, Brookline, MA 02446 USA

Kirsch, Stan
275 S. Beverly Dr. #215, Beverly Hills, CA 90212

Kirschner, Carl *Educator*
Rutgers State University College, President's Office, New Brunswick, NJ 08093 USA

Kirschstein, Ruth L *Doctor*
National Institute of Health, 9000 Rockville Pike, Bethesda, MD 20892 USA

Kirsebom, Vendela *Model, Actor*
William Morris Agency (WMA-LA), 1 William Morris Pl, Beverly Hills, CA 90212 USA

Kirsh, Stan *Actor*
Kritzer, 12200 W Olympic Blvd, #400, Los Angeles, CA 90064 USA

Kirshbaum, Laurence J *Publisher*
Warner Books, Time-Life Building, Rockefeller Center, New York, NY 10020 USA

Kirshbaum, Ralph *Musician*
Columbia Artists Mgmt Inc, 165 W 57th St, New York, NY 10019 USA

Kirshner, Irwin
9200 Sunset Blvd. #401, Los Angeles, CA 90069

Kirshner, Mia *Actor*
Brillstein-Grey Entertainment, 9150 Wilshire Blvd #350, Beverly Hills, CA 90212 USA

Kirszenstein, Szewinska Irena *Track Athlete*
Ul Bagno 5m 80, Warsaw, 00-112, POLAND

Kisabaka, Lisa *Track Athlete*
Franz-Hitze-Str 22, Leverkusen, 51372, GERMANY

Kiser, Terry *Actor*
Innovative Artists, 1505 10th St, Santa Monica, CA 90401 USA

Kishida, Kyoko
7-5-34-801 Akasada Miatuku, Tokyo, JAPAN

Kishlansky, Mark A *Historian*
Harvard University, History Dept, Cambridge, MA 02138 USA

Kisio, Kelly *Hockey Player*
Birch Cliff, Bentley, AB T0C 0J0, CANADA

Kisner, Jacob *Writer*
245 Park Ave S, #PH F, New York, NY 10003 USA

Kison, Bruce E *Baseball Player*
1403 Riverside Circle, Bradenton, FL 33529 USA

KISS *Music Group*
McGhee Entertainment, 8730 Sunset Blvd #175, Los Angeles, CA 90069

Kissin, Evgeni I *Musician*
Harold Holt, 31 Sinclair Rd, London, W14 0NS, UNITED KINGDOM (UK)

Kissinger, Henry A *Secretary, Nobel Prize Laureate*
350 Park Ave, New York, NY 10022 USA

Kissling, Conny *Skier*
Hubel, Messen, 3254, SWITZERLAND

Kistler, Darci *Ballerina*
New York City Ballet, Lincoln Center Plaza, New York, NY 10023 USA

Kitaen, Tawny *Actor*
Talent Group, 5670 Wilshire Blvd #820, Los Angeles, CA 90036 USA

Kitaj, R B *Artist*
Mariborough Fine Art, 6 Albermarle St, London, W1, UNITED KINGDOM (UK)

Kitano, Takeshi *Actor, Director*
Office Kitano, 5-4-14 Akasaka Minataku, Tokyo, 107-0052, JAPAN

Kitaro *Musician, Composer*
GLP Huetteldorferstra 259, Vienna, 1140, AUSTRIA

Kitayenko, Dmitri G *Conductor*
Chalet Kalimor, Botterens, 1652, SWITZERLAND

Kitbunchu, M Michael Cardinal *Religious Leader*
122 Soi Naaksuwan, Thanon Nonsi Yannawa, Bangkok, 10120, THAILAND

Kitchen, Michael *Actor*
International Creative Mgmt, 76 Oxford St, London, W1N 0AX, UNITED KINGDOM (UK)

Kite, Greg *Basketball Player*
3060 Seigneury Dr, Windermere, FL 34786 USA

Kite, Thomas O (Tom) Jr *Golfer*
Pros Inc, 7100 Forest Ave, #201, Richmond, VA 23226 USA

Kithune, Robert K U *Admiral*
1597 Haloloke St, Hilo, HI 96720 USA

Kitna, John *Football Player*
11317 Madera Circle SW, Lakewood, WA 98499 USA

Kitt, A J *Skier*
2437 Franklin Ave, Louisville, CO 80027 USA

Kitt, Eartha *Musician, Actor*
Cunningham-Escott-Dipene & Associates Inc (CED-LA), 10635 Santa Monica Blvd #130, Los Angeles, CA 90025 USA

Kittel, Charles *Physicist*
University of California, Physics Dept, Berkeley, CA 94720 USA

Kittinger Jr, Joseph W (Joe) *Misc*
608 Mariner Way, Altamonte Springs, FL 32701 USA

Kittle, Ronald D (Ron) *Baseball Player*
68 Ridge Ave, Greendale, IN 47025 USA

Kittles, Kerry *Basketball Player*
New Jersey Nets, 390 Murray Hill Parkway, East Rutherford, NJ 07073 USA

Kittles, Tory *Actor*
9 Yards Entertainment, 8530 Wilshire Blvd Fl 5, Beverly Hills, CA 90211 USA

Kitzhaber, John A *Governor*
Oregon Health & Science University, Evidence Based Policy, Portland, OR 97201 USA

Kiyosaki, Robert T *Writer*
Cashflow of Arizona, 4330 N Civic Center Plaza, Scottsdale, AZ 85251 USA

Kizer, Carolyn A *Writer*
University of Arizona, English Dept, Tucson, AZ 85271 USA

Kizim, Leonid D *Cosmonaut*
Mojaysky Military School, Russian Space Forces, Saint Petersburg, RUSSIA

Kjer, Bodil *Actor*
Vestre Pavilion Frydenlund, Frydenlund Alle 19, Vedbaek, 2950, DENMARK

Kjus, Lasse *Skier*
Rugdeveien 2C, Siggerud, 1404, NORWAY

Klabunde, Charles S *Artist*
68 W 3rd St, New York, NY 10012 USA

Klammer, Franz *Skier*
Mooswald 22, Fresach/Ktn, 9712, AUSTRIA

Klaplisch, Cedric *Director*
Cineart, 36 Rue de Ponthieu, Paris, 75008, FRANCE

Klares, John *Bowler*
1760 N Decatur Blvd, #10, Las Vegas, NV 89108 USA

Klas, Eri *Conductor*
Nurme 54, Tallinn, 0016, ESTONIA

Klaus, Deita *Actor*
Digigraphics/Dream Girl World, 4650 Libbit Ave, Encino, CA 91436 USA

Klaus, Vaclav *President, Politician*
Kancelar Prezidenta Republiky (Czech Republic), Hradecek, Prague 1, 119 08, Czech Republic

Klausing, Chuck *Football Coach*
2115 Lazor St, Indiana, PA 15701 USA

Klausner, Richard D *Biologist*
National Cancer Institute, 31 Center Dr, Bethesda, MD 20892 USA

Klebba, Martin *Actor*
Stevens Group, The, 14011 Ventura Blvd #201, Sherman Oaks, CA 91423 USA

Klebe, Giselher *Composer*
Bruchstr 16, Detmold, 32756, GERMANY

Klecko, Joseph E (Joe) *Football Player*
105 Stella Lane, Aston, PA 19014 USA

Klees, Christian *Misc*
Eutiner Sportschutzen, Schutzenweg 26, Eutin, 23701, GERMANY

Kleihues, Josef P *Architect*
Schlickweg 4, Berlin, 14129, GERMANY

Klein, Alex *Misc*
Columbia Artists Mgmt Inc, 165 W 57th St, New York, NY 10019 USA

Klein, Calvin R *Fashion Designer*
Calvin Klein Industries, 205 W 39th St, New York, NY 10018 USA

Klein, Chris *Actor*
Brillstein-Grey Entertainment, 9150 Wilshire Blvd #350, Beverly Hills, CA 90212 USA

Klein, Danny *Musician*
Nick Ben-Meir, 652 N Doheny Dr, Los Angeles, CA 90069 USA

Klein, David *Misc*
National Child Health Institute, 9000 Rockville Pike, Bethesda, MD 20892 USA

Klein, Edward
Trident Media Group LLC, 41 Madison Ave Fl 33, New York, NY 10010 USA

Klein, Emilee *Golfer*
Int'l Mgmt Group, 1 Erieview Plaza, 1360 E 9th St #1300, Cleveland, OH 44114 USA

Klein, George *Biologist*
Kottlavagen 10, Lidingo, 181 61, SWEDEN

Klein, Herbert G *Government Official, Publisher*
Copley Press, 350 Camino de Reina, San Diego, CA 92108 USA

Klein, Jennifer *Producer*
Lichter Grossman Nichols Adler & Goodman, 9200 Sunset Blvd #1200, Los Angeles, CA 90069 USA

Klein, Jenny
201 S. Capitol Ave. #430, Indianapolis, IN 46225

Klein, Jess *Songwriter, Musician*
Drake Assoc, 177 Woodland Ave, Westwood, NJ 07675 USA

Klein, Joe *Journalist, Writer*
Newsweek Magazine, Editorial Dept, 251 W 57th St, New York, NY 10019 USA

Klein, Joel *Lawyer, Government Official, Educator*
NY City Schools, Chancellor's Office, 110 Livingston St, Brooklyn, NY 11201 USA

Klein, Lawrence R *Nobel Prize Laureate*
101 Cheswold Lane, #4C, Haverford, PA 19041 USA

Klein, Lester A *Doctor*
Scripps Clinic, Urology Dept, 10666 N Torrey Pines Road, La Jolla, CA 92037 USA

Klein, Robert *Entertainer*
67 Ridgecrest Road, Briarcliff Manor, NY 10510 USA

Klein, Robert O (Bob) *Football Player*
15933 Alcima Ave, Pacific Palisades, CA 90272 USA

Klein Borkow, Dana *Producer*
William Morris Agency (WMA-LA), 1 William Morris Pl, Beverly Hills, CA 90212 USA

Kleindienst, Richard
3103 Crestview Dr., Prescott, AZ 86301-5001

Kleine, Joseph (Joe) *Baseball Player*
4819 Stony Ford Dr, Dallas, TX 75287 USA

Kleinert, Harold E *Doctor*
225 Abraham Flexner Way, Louisville, KY 40202 USA

Kleinfeld, Andrew J *Judge*
US Court of Appeals, Courthouse Square, 250 Cushman St, Fairbanks, AK 99701 USA

Kleinman, Arthur M *Psychic*
Harvard University, Anthropology Dept, Cambridge, MA 02138 USA

Kleinrock, Leonard *Scientist*
318 N Rockingham Ave, Los Angeles, CA 90049 USA

Kleinsmith, Bruce *Cartoonist*
PO Box 325, Aromas, CA 95004 USA

Kleiser, Randal *Director*
3050 Runyan Canyon Road, Los Angeles, CA 90046 USA

Klemmer, John *Musician*
Boardman, 10548 Clearwood Court, Los Angeles, CA 90077 USA

Klemp, Cardinal Jozef
Kolski U1Miodowa 17, Warsaw, POLAND, PL-00-583

Klemperer, William *Misc*
53 Shattuck Road, Watertown, MA 02472 USA

Klemt, Becky *Lawyer*
Pence & MacMilan, PO Box 1285, Laramie, WY 82073 USA

Klensch, Elsa
1050 Techwood Dr. NW, Atlanta, GA 30318

Kleppe, Thomas S *Secretary*
7100 Darby Road, Bethesda, MD 20817 USA

Klesko, Ryan A *Baseball Player*
9219 Nickles Blvd, Boynton Beach, FL 33436 USA

Klesla, Rotislav *Hockey Player*
Columbus Blue Jackts, Arena, 200 W Nationwide Blvd, Columbus, OH 43215 USA

Klett, Peter *Musician*
11410 NE 124th St, #627, Kirkland, WA 98034 USA

Kley Minnis, Chaney *Actor*
International Creative Management (ICM-LA), 8942 Wilshire Blvd, Beverly Hills, CA 90211 USA

Kliendienst, Richard
3103 Crestview Dr., Prescott, AZ 86301-5001

Kliks, Rudolf R *Architect*
Russian Chamber of Commerce, UI Kuibysheva 6, Moscow, RUSSIA

Klim, Michael *Swimmer*
177 Bridge Road, Richmond, VIC, 3121, AUSTRALIA

Klima, Petr *Hockey Player*
5002 Avenue Avignon, Lutz, FL 33558 USA

Klimke, Reiner *Misc*
Krumme Str 3, Munster, 48143, GERMANY

Klimuk, Pyotr I *Cosmonaut*
Potchta Kosmonavtov, Moskovskoi Oblasti, Syvisdny Goroduk, 141160, RUSSIA

Kline, Jeff *Writer, Producer*
Endeavor Agency LLC (LA), 9601 Wilshire Blvd Fl 3, Beverly Hills, CA 90210 USA

Kline, Kevin D *Actor*
1636 3rd Ave, #309, New York, NY 10128 USA

Kline, Richard *Actor*
TalentWorks (LA), 3500 W Olive Ave #1400, Burbank, CA 91505 USA

Klingensmith, Michael J *Publisher*
Entertainment Weekly Magazine, Rockefeller Center, New York, NY 10020 USA

Klingman, Lynzee *Actor*
United Talent Agency (UTA), 9560 Wilshire Blvd, Beverly Hills, CA 90212 USA

Klinsmann, Jurgen *Soccer Player*
3419 Via Lido, #600, Newport Beach, CA 92663 USA

Klippstein, John C (Johnny) *Baseball Player*
12500 Elmwood Court, Huntley, IL 60142 USA

Klitbo, Cynthia *Actor*
Televisa, Blvd Adolfo Lopez Mateos 232, Colonia San Angel INN, DF, CP 01060, MEXICO

Klitschko, Wladimir *Boxer*
Am Stradtrand 2, Hamburg, 22047, GERMANY

Kllesmet, Robert B *Misc*
Union of Police Assns, 815 16th St NW, #307, Washington, DC 20006 USA

Klotz, H Louis (Red) *Basketball Player, Coach*
114 S Osbourne Ave, Margate City, NJ 08402 USA

Klotz, Irving M *Misc*
1500 Sheridan Road, #7D, Wilmette, IL 60091 USA

Klous, Patricia *Actor*
2539 Benedict Canyon Dr, Beverly Hills, CA 90210 USA

Kluer, Duane *Basketball Player, Coach*
252 Francis Avenue Court, Terre Haute, IN 47804 USA

Klug, Aaron *Nobel Prize Laureate*
70 Cavendish Ave, Cambridge, CB1 40T, UNITED KINGDOM (UK)

Kluge, John W *Business Person*
Metromedia Co, 1 Meadowlands Plaza, #300, East Rutherford, NJ 07073 USA

Kluger, Richard *Writer*
William Morris Agency, 151 El Camino Dr, Beverly Hills, CA 90212 USA

Klugh, Earl *Musician*
International Creative Mgmt, 8942 Wilshire Blvd, #219, Beverly Hills, CA 90211 USA

Klugman, Jack *Actor*
22548 W Pacific Coast Highway, #110, Malibu, CA 90265 USA

Klum, Heidi *Model, Actor*
Elite Model Mgmt, 111 E 22nd St, #200, New York, NY 10010 USA

Klvan, Andrew *Writer*
Dell Publishing, 1540 Broadway, New York, NY 10036 USA

Klyn, Vincent
4200 Ocean View Dr, Malibu, CA 90265

Klyszewski, Waclaw *Architect*
UI Gomoslaska 16m 15A, Warsaw, 00-432, POLAND

Kmetko, Steve
5670 Wilshire Blvd. #200, Los Angeles, CA 90036

Knape, Lindberg Ulrike *Swimmer*
Drostvagen 7, Karlskoga, 691 33, SWEDEN

Knapp, Charles B *Educator*
Aspen Institute, 1333 New Hampshire Ave NW, Washington, DC 20036 USA

Knapp, Cleon T *Publisher*
Talewood Corp, 10100 Santa Monica Blvd, #2000, Los Angeles, CA 90067 USA

Knapp, Jennifer *Musician*
Creative Artists Agency, 9830 Wilshire Blvd, Beverly Hills, CA 90212 USA

Knapp, John W *Educator, General*
Virginia Military Institute, Superintendent's Office, Lexington, VA 24450 USA

Knapp, Stefan *Artist*
Sandhills, Godalming, Surrey, UNITED KINGDOM (UK)

Knappenberger, Alton W *War Hero*
PO Box 364, Main St, Schwenksville, PA 19473 USA

Knaus, William *Doctor*
George Washington University, Medical Center, Washington, DC 20052 USA

Knauss, Hans *Skier*
Fastenberg 60, Schladming, 8970, AUSTRIA

Knauss, Melania *Model*
T Mgmt, 91 5th Ave, New York, NY 10003 USA

Kneale, R Bryan C *Artist*
10A Muswell Road, London, N10 2BG, UNITED KINGDOM (UK)

Knebel, John A *Secretary*
1418 Labumum St, McLean, VA 22101 USA

Knepper, Robert *Actor*
Stone Manners Talent Agency, 6500 Wilshire Blvd, Ste 550, Los Angeles, CA 90048 USA

Knepper, Robert W (Bob) *Baseball Player*
627 Forest View Way, Monument, CO 80132 USA

Kness, Richard M *Opera Singer*
240 Central Park South, #16M, New York, NY 10019 USA

Kneuer, Cameo *Misc*
Starshape by Cameo, 2554 Lincoln Blvd, #640, Venice, CA 90291 USA

Knight, Andrew S B *Editor, Publisher*
News International, PO Box 495, Virginia St, London, W1 9XY, UNITED KINGDOM (UK)

Knight, Beverley *Musician*
International Talent Booking (ITB - UK), 27A Floral Street, Third Floor, Covent Garden, London, WC2E 9, United Kingdom

Knight, Billy *Basketball Player*
6375 W Massey Manor Lane, Memphis, TN 38120 USA

Knight, C Ray *Baseball Player*
2308 Tara Dr, Albany, GA 31721 USA

Knight, Charles F *Business Person*
Emerson Electric Co, 8000 W Florissant Ave, Box 41000, Saint Louis, MO 63136 USA

Knight, Chris *Songwriter, Musician*
Rick Alter Mgmt, 1018 17th Ave S, #12, Nashville, TN 37212 USA

Knight, Douglas M *Educator*
68 Upper Creek Road, Stockton, NJ 08559 USA

Knight, Gladys *Musician*
Entertainment Consultants, 184 Woodstone Dr, Buffalo Grove, IL 60089 USA

Knight, Jean *Musician*
Ken Keene Artists, PO Box 1875, Gretna, LA 70054 USA

Knight, Jonathan *Musician*
90 Apple Street, Essex, MA 01929 USA

Knight, Jordan *Musician*
Evolution Talent, 1776 Broadway Dr, #1500, New York, NY 10019 USA

Knight, Michael E
1344 Lexington Ave, New York, NY 10120-1307 USA

Knight, Philip H *Business Person*
Nike Inc, 1 SW Bowerman Dr, Beaverton, OR 97005 USA

Knight, Robert M (Bobby) *Basketball Player, Coach*
Texas Tech University, Athletic Dept, Lubbock, TX 79409 USA

Knight, Shirley *Actor*
1548 N Orange Ave, Los Angeles, CA 90028 USA

Knight, Steve *Writer*
Creative Artists Agency LCC (CAA-LA), 9830 Wilshire Blvd, Beverly Hills, CA 90212 USA

Knight, Summer
PO Box 9786, Marina del Rey, CA 90295

Knight, Tom *Football Player*
Anzona Cardinals, PO Box 888, Phoenix, AZ 85001 USA

Knight, Wayne *Actor*
Agency for the Performing Arts (APA-LA), 9200 Sunset Blvd #900, Los Angeles, CA 90069 USA

Knight, Wendi *Adult Film Star*
Atlas Multimedia Inc, 22940 Burbank Blvd, Woodland Hills, CA 91367 USA

Knight-Pulliam, Keshla *Actor*
PO Box 866, Teaneck, NJ 07666 USA

Knightley, Keira *Actor*
P F D, Drury House, 34-43 Russell St, London, WC2B 5HA, UNITED KINGDOM (UK)

Knightlinger, Lauren *Actor*
Principato/Young Management, 9665 Wilshire Blvd #500, Beverly Hills, CA 90212 USA

Knights, Dave *Musician*
195 Sandycombe Road, Kew, TW9 2EW, UNITED KINGDOM (UK)

Knobbs, Brian
14804 58th St., North Clearwater, FL 34620

Knoblauch, E Charles (Chuck) *Baseball Player*
101 Westcott St, #1105, Houston, TX 77007 USA

Knoll, Andrew H *Misc*
Harvard University, Botanical Museum, 26 Oxford St, Cambridge, MA 02138 USA

Knoll, Jozsef *Misc*
Semmelweis Medical University, Pharmacology Dept, Budapest, 1089, HUNGARY

Knopf, Sascha *Actor, Model*
Creative Management Group (CMG), 9465 Wilshire Blvd #335, Beverly Hills, CA 90212 USA

Knopfler, David *Musician*
Damage Mgmt, 16 Lambton Place, London, W11 2SH, UNITED KINGDOM (UK)

Knopfler, Mark *Musician*
Paul Crockford Mgmt, 37 Ruston Mews, London, W11 1RB, UNITED KINGDOM (UK)

Knopoff, Leon *Physicist*
University of California, Geophysics Institute, Los Angeles, CA 90024 USA

Knorr, Randy *Baseball Player*
Toronto Blue Jays, 12134 Bishopsford Dr, Tampa, FL 33626-1319 USA

Knostman, Richard (Dick) *Basketball Player*
3960 Schooner Ridge, Alpharetta, GA 30005 USA

Knott, Eric *Baseball Player*
Arizona Diamondbacks, 1717 Hyacinth Ave, Sebring, FL 33875-6062 USA

Knotts, Don *Actor, Comedian*
Barry Freed Company, The, 468 N Camden Ave #201, Beverly Hills, CA 90210 USA

Knotts, Gary *Baseball Player*
Florida Marlins, 18 Covey Rd, Decatur, AL 35603-6021 USA

Knowles, Beyonce *Musician, Actor*
Music World, PO Box 53208, Houston, TX 77052 USA

Knowles, Darold *Baseball Player*
Baltimore Orioles, 2322 Dora Dr, Clearwater, FL 33765-2719 USA

Knowles, Jeremy R *Misc*
67 Francis Ave, Cambridge, MA 02138 USA

Knowles, Solange *Musician, Actor*
Creative Artists Agency LCC (CAA-LA), 9830 Wilshire Blvd, Beverly Hills, CA 90212 USA

Knowles, William S *Nobel Prize Laureate*
PO Box 71, Kelly, WY 83011 USA

Knowlton, Steve R *Skier*
Palmer Yeager Assoc, 6600 E Hampden Ave, #210, Denver, CO 80224 USA

Knowlton, William A *General*
4520 4th Road North, Arlington, VA 22203 USA

Knox, Chuck
11220 NE 53rd St., Kirkland, WA 98033

Knox, John *Baseball Player*
Detroit Tigers, 1413 Thames Dr, Plano, TX 75075-2734 USA

Knox, Terence *Actor*
House of Representatives, 400 S Beverly Dr #101, Beverly Hills, CA 90212 USA

Knox-Johnson, Robin *Yachtsman*
26 Sefton St, Putney, London, SW15, UNITED KINGDOM (UK)

Knoxville, Johnny *Actor*
Handprint Entertainment, 1100 Glendon Ave, #1000, Los Angeles, CA 90024 USA

Knudsen, Arthur G *Skier*
5111 Wright Ave, #104, Racine, WI 53406 USA

Knudsen, Keith *Musician*
Monterey Peninsula Artists, 509 Hartnell St, Monterey, CA 93940 USA

Knudsen, Kurt *Baseball Player*
Detroit Tigers, 5155 Patti Jo Dr, Carmichael, CA 95608-0968 USA

Knudson, Mark *Baseball Player*
Houston Astros, 881 W 100th Ave, Northglenn, CO 80260-6255 USA

Knudson, Thomas J *Journalist*
Sacramento Bee, Editorial Dept, 21st & Q Sts, Sacramento, CA 95852 USA

Knudson Jr, Alfred G *Misc*
Institute for Cancer Research, 7701 Burholme Ave, Philadelphia, PA 19111 USA

Knussen, S Oliver *Composer*
Harrison/Parrott, 12 Penzance Place, London, W11 4PA, UNITED KINGDOM (UK)

Knuth, Donald E *Scientist*
Stanford University, Computer Sciences Dept, Gates Building, Stanford, CA 94305 USA

Knutson, Ronald *Religious Leader*
Free Lutheran Congregations Assn, 402 W 11th St, Canton, SD 57013 USA

Koba, Jeff
8899 Beverly Blvd. #705, Los Angeles, CA 90048

Koback, Nick *Baseball Player*
Pittsburgh Pirates, 71 Hopmeadow St Apt 9A-1, Weatogue, CT 06089-9635 USA

Kobashigawa, Yeiki *War Hero*
85-120 Mill St, Waianae, HI 96793 USA

Kobel, Kevin *Baseball Player*
Milwaukee Brewers, 2415 S Hillcrest Dr, Camp Verde, AZ 8632-6904 USA

Kober, Jeff *Actor*
4544 Ethel Ave, Studio City, CA 91604 USA

Koblik, Steven *Educator*
Huntington Library & Art Gallery, 1151 Oxford Road, San Marino, CA 91108 USA

Koch, Alan *Baseball Player*
Detroit Tigers, 1714 Pebble Creek Dr, Prattville, AL 3606-7206 USA

Koch, Bill
PO Box 1011, Kula, HI 96790-1011

Koch, Billy *Baseball Player*
Toronto Blue Jays, 310 Signature Ct, Safety Harbor, FL 34695-5436 USA

Koch, David
1040 Fifth Ave., New York, NY 10028

Koch, Desmond (Des) *Track Athlete, Football Player*
23296 Gilmore St, Canoga Park, CA 91307 USA

Koch, Ed *Artist*
1211 NW Ogden Ave, Bend, OR 97701 USA

Koch, Edward I *Politician*
Robinson Silverman Pearce, 1290 Ave of the Americas, New York, NY 10104 USA

Koch, Gregory M (Greg) *Football Player*
4412 Darsey St, Bellaire, TX 77401 USA

Koch, James V *Educator*
Old Dominion University, President's Office, Norfolk, VA 23529 USA

Koch, Marianne
Am Hohenberg 27, Tutzing, GERMANY, D-82327

Koch, Peter *Actor*
Fly Trap, The, 900 E 1st St, Los Angeles, CA 90012 USA

Koch, William (Bill) *Skier*
PO Box 115, Ashland, OR 97520 USA

Koch, William I (Bill) *Yachtsman, Business Person*
Oxbow Corp, 1601 Forum Place, West Palm Beach, FL 33401 USA

Kocharian, Robert *President, Prime Minister*
President's Office, Marshal Bagramian Prosp 19, Yerevan, 375010, ARMENIA

Kocherga, Anatoli I *Opera Singer*
Gogolevskaya 37/2/47, Kiev, 254053, RUSSIA

Kochi, Jay K *Misc*
4372 Faculty Lane, Houston, TX 77004
USA

Kocsis, Zoltan *Composer, Musician*
Narcisa Ulca 29, Budapest, 1126,
HUNGARY

Kodes, Jan *Tennis Player*
Na Berance 18, Prague 6/Dejvioe, 160 00,
CZECH REPUBLIC

Kodjoe, Boris *Actor, Model*
9100 Wilshire Blvd #503E, Beverly Hills,
CA 90212 USA

Koecher, Dick *Baseball Player*
Philadelphia Phillies, 11380 Quall Village
Way #104, Naples, FL 34119-8949 USA

Koegel, Pete *Baseball Player*
Milwaukee Brewers, 33 Barclay St #9,
Saugerties, NY 12477-1905 USA

Koehler, Horst *Financier*
International Monetary Fund, 700 19th St
NW, Washington, DC 20431 USA

Koehler, Horst *President*
Bundeskanzlerant, Schlossplatz 1, Berlin,
10178, GERMANY

Koelle, George B *Misc*
3300 Darby Road, #3310, Haverford, PA
19041 USA

Koelling, Brian *Baseball Player*
Cincinnati Reds, 522 Laurelwood Dr,
Cleves, OH 45002-1395 USA

Koen, Karleen *Writer*
Random House, 1745 Broadway, #B1,
New York, NY 10019 USA

Koenekamp, Fred *Cinematographer*
9756 Shoshine Ave, Northridge, CA
91325 USA

Koenig, Walter *Actor*
PO Box 4395, North Hollywood, CA
91617 USA

Koepke, Andreas
441 av. du Prado B.P. 124, Marseilles
Cedex 08, FRANCE, F-13267

Koepp, David *Writer, Director*
Hofflund-Polone, 9465 Wilshire Blvd,
#820, Beverly Hills, CA 90212 USA

Koester, Helmut H K E *Misc*
12 Flintlock Road, Lexington, MA 02420
USA

Koetter, Dirk *Football Coach*
Arizona State University, Athletic Dept,
Tempe, AZ 85287 USA

Kogan, Pavel L *Musician, Conductor*
Bryusov Per 8/10, Moscow, 103009,
RUSSIA

Kogan, Theo *Musician, Actor*
Wilhelmina Creative Mgmt, 300 Park Ave
S, #200, New York, NY 10010 USA

Kogen, Jay *Producer*
Endeavor Agency LLC (LA), 9601 Wilshire
Blvd Fl 3, Beverly Hills, CA 90210 USA

Kohan, David *Producer*
Will & Grace, 4024 Radford Ave,
Bungalow 3, Studio City, CA 91604 USA

Kohde-Kilsch, Claudia *Tennis Player*
Elsa-Brandstrom-Str 22, Saarbrucken,
66119, GERMANY

Kohl, Helmut *Politician*
CDU/CSU, Maurestr 85, Berlin, 10117,
GERMANY

Kohler, Jurgen *Soccer Player*
Borussia Dortmund, Postfach 100509,
Dortmund, 44005, GERMANY

Kohli, Armaan *Actor, Bollywood*
44 Union Park Chembur, Mumbai, MS
400071, INDIA

Kohli, Raj Kumar *Director, Filmmaker,
Producer, Bollywood*
Behind Lido Cinema, Juhu Road, Bombay,
MS 400 049, INDIA

Kohlmeier, Ryan *Baseball Player*
Baltimore Orioles, 301 Vine Street,
Cottonwood Falls, KS 66845 USA

Kohlsaat, Peter *Cartoonist*
420 N 5th St, #707, Minneapolis, MN
55401 USA

Kohn, A Eugene *Architect*
Kohn Pedersen Fox Assoc, 111 W 57th St,
New York, NY 10019 USA

Kohn, Joseph J *Mathematician*
32 Sturges Way, Princeton, NJ 08540 USA

Kohn, Walter *Nobel Prize Laureate*
236 La Vista Grande, Santa Barbara, CA
93103 USA

Kohoutek, Lubos *Astronomer*
Corthumstr 5, Hamburg, 21029,
GERMANY

Koib, Thomas Claudia A *Swimmer, Coach*
Stanford University, Athletic Dept,
Stanford, CA 94305 USA

Koirala, manicha *Actor, Bollywood*
302 Beachwood Towers, Yari Road,
Versova, Andheri (W), Mumbai, 400061,
India

Koivu, Saku *Hockey Player*
2200-201 Portage Ave, Winnipeg, MB
R3B 3L3, CANADA

Koizumi, Junichiro *Prime Minister*
Prime Minister's Office, 1-6-1 Negatoicho,
Chiyodaku, Tokyo, 100, JAPAN

Kojac, George *Swimmer*
33 Arboles del Norte, Fort Pierce, FL
34951 USA

Kojis, Don *Basketball Player*
7652 Stevenson Way, San Diego, CA
92120 USA

Kok Oudegeest, Mary *Swimmer*
Escuela Nacional de Natacion, Izarra,
Alava, SPAIN

Kokkonen, Elissa Lee *Musician*
Columbia Artists Mgmt Inc, 165 W 57th
St, New York, NY 10019 USA

Kokonin, Vladimir *Opera Singer*
Bolshoi Theater, Teatralnaya Pl 1,
Moscow, 103009, RUSSIA

Kokosalaki, Sophia *Fashion Designer*
Sophia Kokosalaki, 3/138 Long Acre,
Convent Garden, London, England,
United Kingdom

Kokotakis, Nick
9229 Sunset Blvd. #315, Los Angeles, CA
90069

Kola, Joey *Comedian*
William Morris Agency (WMA-LA), 1
William Morris Pl, Beverly Hills, CA
90212 USA

Kolakowski, Leszek *Misc*
77 Hamilton Road, Oxford, OX2 7QA,
UNITED KINGDOM (UK)

Kolb, Brandon *Baseball Player*
Cincinnati Reds, 6895 Carnation Dr,
Carlsbad, CA 92009-3809 USA

Kolb, Danny *Baseball Player*
Texas Rangers, 205 S Main St, Walnut, IL
61376-9370 USA

Kolb, Gary *Baseball Player*
St Louis Cardinals, 5143 Hopewell Dr,
Cross Lanes, WV 25313-1784 USA

Kolber, Suzy *Sportscaster*
ESPN-TV, Sports Dept, ESPN Plaza 935
Middle St, Bristol, CT 06010 USA

Kolbert, Kathryn *Lawyer*
Center for Reproductive Law & Policy,
120 Wall St, New York, NY 10005 USA

Kolden, Scott
8743 Quakertown Ave, Northridge, CA
91324

Kolehmainen, Mikko *Athlete*
Poppelitie 18, Mikkeli, 50130, FINLAND

Kolff, Willem J *Inventor*
510 35th St, Port Townsend, WA 98368
USA

Kolinsky, Sue *Producer*
Innovative Artists (LA), 1505 Tenth St,
Santa Monica, CA 90401 USA

Kollas, Konstantinos V *Prime Minister*
124 Vassil Sophias St, Ampelokipi,
Athens, GREECE

Kollek, Mayor Teddy
22 Jaffa Rd., Jerusalem, ISRAEL

Koller, Dagmar
Naglergasse 2, Vienna, AUSTRIA, A-1010

Koller, William C *Misc*
University of Kansas, Medical School,
Neurology Dept, Kansas City, KS 66160
USA

Kollner, Eberhard *Cosmonaut*
An der Trainierbahn 7, Neuenhagen,
115366, GERMANY

Kollo, Rene *Opera Singer*
Opera et Concert, Maximillianstr 22,
Munich, 80539, GERMANY

Kolm, Henry V *Engineer*
Weir Meadow Road, Wayland, MA 01778
USA

Kolodner, Richard D *Scientist*
Dana-Forber Cancer Institute, 44 Binnery
St, Boston, MA 02115 USA

Kolpakova, Irina A *Ballerina*
American Ballet Theatre, 890 Broadway,
New York, NY 10003 USA

Kolstad, Hal *Baseball Player*
Boston Red Sox, 15149 Bel Escou Dr, San
Jose, CA 95124-5032 USA

Kolsti, Paul *Cartoonist*
Dallas News, Editorial Dept,
Communications Center, Dallas, TX
75265 USA

Kolvenbach, Peter-Hans *Religious Leader*
Borgo Santo Spirito 5, CP 6139, Rome, 00195, ITALY

Kolzig, Olaf *Hockey Player*
10931 E Bahia Dr, Scottsdale, AZ 85255 USA

Komal *Royalty*
Royal Palace, Narayanhiti, Durbag Marg, Kathmandu, NEPAL

Koman, Michael *Writer*
International Creative Management (ICM-LA), 8942 Wilshire Blvd, Beverly Hills, CA 90211 USA

Komarkova, Vera *Misc*
University of Colorado, INSTAAR, Boulder, CO 80302 USA

Komenich, Kim *Journalist*
111 Cornelia Ave, Mill Valley, CA 94941 USA

Kominsky, Cheryl *Bowler*
Ladies Professional Bowling Tour, 7200 Harrison Ave, #7171, Rockford, IL 61112 USA

Komleva, Gabriela T *Ballerina*
Fontanka River 116, #34, Saint Petersburg, 198005, RUSSIA

Komlos, Peter *Musician*
Torokvesz Ulca 94, Budapest, 1025, HUNGARY

Komminsk, Brad *Baseball Player*
Atlanta Braves, 688 Fallside Ln, Westerville, OH 43081-5003 USA

Komunyakaa, Yusef *Writer*
526 N Washington St, Bloomington, IN 47408 USA

Konare, Alpha Oumar *President*
President's Office, BP, Bamako, MALI

Koncak, Jon *Basketball Player*
2575 Red House Road, Jackson, WY 83001 USA

Koncar, Mark *Football Player*
447 N Alpine Blvd, Alpine, UT 84004 USA

Konchalovsky, Andrei *Director*
Creative Artists Agency, 9830 Wilshire Blvd, Beverly Hills, CA 90212 USA

Kondakova, Elena V *Cosmonaut*
Scientific Industrial Assn, Ulica Lenina 4A, Kallningrad, 141070 USA

Kondratiyeva, Maria V *Ballerina*
Bolshoi Theater, Teatralnaya Pt1, Moscow, 103009, RUSSIA

Konerko, Paul *Baseball Player*
Los Angeles Dodgers, 11623 E Bloomfield Dr, Scottsdale, AZ 85259-2749 USA

Konieczny, Doug *Baseball Player*
Houston Astros, 9503 Dundalk St, Spring, TX 77379-4314 USA

Konig, Franz Cardinal *Religious Leader*
Wollzeile 2, Vienna, 1010, AUSTRIA

Konik, George *Hockey Player*
1027 Savannah Road, Eagan, MN 55123 USA

Konitz, Lee *Musician*
Bennett Morgan, 1282 RR 376, Wappingers Falls, NY 12590 USA

Konner, Lawrence (Larry) *Writer*
Endeavor Agency LLC (LA), 9601 Wilshire Blvd Fl 3, Beverly Hills, CA 90210 USA

Kononenko, Oleg D *Cosmonaut*
Potchta Kosmoriavtov, Moskovskoi Oblasti, Syvisdny Goroduk, 141160, RUSSIA

Konrad, Dorothy
10650 Missouri Ave. #2, Los Angeles, CA 90025

Konrad, John H *Astronaut*
Hughes Space-Communications Group, PO Box 92919, Los Angeles, CA 90009 USA

Konsalik, Heinz
Aegidienberg, Bad Honnef, GERMANY, D-53604

Konstantinidis, Aris *Architect*
4 Vasilissis Sofias Blvd, Athens, 106 74, GREECE

Konstantinov, Vladimir *Hockey Player*
15 Windsor Place, Essex Fells, NJ 07021 USA

Konuszewski, Dennis *Baseball Player*
Pittsburgh Pirates, 3054 Yorkshire Dr, Bay City, MI 48706-9244 USA

Konyukhov, Fedor F *Misc*
Tourism/Sports Union, Studeniy Proyezd 7, Moscow, 129282, RUSSIA

Kool & The Gang *Music Group*
J Bird Entertainment Agency, 4905 S Atlantic Ave, Daytona Beach, FL 32127 USA

Kool Moe Dee
151 El Camino Dr., Beverly Hills, CA 90212

Koolhaas, Rem *Architect*
Metropolitan Architecture, Heer Bokelweg 149, Rotterdam, 3032, NETHERLANDS

Koolman, Olindo *Governor*
Governor's Office, Oranjestad, ARUBA

Koonce, Graham *Baseball Player*
Oakland A's, 1833 Whispering Pines Dr, Julian, CA 92036-9409 USA

Koons, Jeff *Artist*
600 Broadway, New York, NY 10012 USA

Koontz, Dean R *Writer*
PO Box 9529, Newport Beach, CA 92658 USA

Koop, C Everett *Doctor*
3 Ivy Pointe Way, Hanover, NH 03755 USA

Kooper, Al *Musician*
Legacy Records, 550 Madison Ave, #1700, New York, NY 10022 USA

Koopman, A Ton G M *Conductor*
Meerweg 23, BC Bussu, 1405, NETHERLANDS

Koopmans-Kint, Cor *Swimmer*
Pacific Sands C'Van Park, Nambucca Heads, NSW, 2448, AUSTRALIA

Koosman, Jerry *Baseball Player*
New York Mets, 2483 State Road 35, Osceola, WI, 54020-4216 USA

Kopacz, George *Baseball Player*
Atlanta Braves, 14150 Somerset Ct, Orland Park, IL 60467-1142 USA

Kopell, Bernie *Actor*
19413 Olivos Dr, Tarzana, CA 91356 USA

Kopeloff, Eric *Director*
William Morris Agency (WMA-LA), 1 William Morris Pl, Beverly Hills, CA 90212 USA

Kopelson, Arnold *Producer*
901 N Roxbury Dr, Beverly Hills, CA 90210 USA

Kopervas, Gary *Cartoonist*
King Features Syndicate, 888 7th Ave, New York, NY 10106 USA

Kopins, Karen *Actor*
Sutton Barth Vennari, 145 S Fairfax Ave, #310, Los Angeles, CA 90036 USA

Kopit, Arthur *Writer*
240 W 98th St, #11B, New York, NY 10025 USA

Koplan, Jeffrey *Misc*
Emory University, Academic Health Affairs Dept, Atlanta, GA 30322 USA

Koplitz, Howie *Baseball Player*
Detroit Tigers, 623 Boyd St, Oshkosh, WI 54901-4634 USA

Koplitz, Lynne *Actor*
NS Bienstock, 1740 Broadway Fl 24, New York, NY 10019 USA

Koplove, Mike *Baseball Player*
Arizona Diamondbacks, 39 Festival Dr, Voorhees, NJ 08043-4325 USA

Kopolsky, Ken
151 El Camino Dr., Beverly Hills, CA 90212

Kopp, Jeff *Athlete*
9409 Hannahs Mill Dr #403, Owings Mills, MD 21117

Kopp, Wendy *Misc*
Teach for America Foundation, 315 W 36th St, #6, New York, NY 10018 USA

Koppe, Joe *Baseball Player*
Milwaukee Braves, 7887 Beatrice, Westland, MI 48185-2507 USA

Koppel, Ted *Commentator*
Nightline, 1717 Desales St NW, Washington, DC 20036-4401 USA

Koppelman, Chaim *Artist*
498 Broome St, New York, NY 10013 USA

Kopper, Hilmar *Financier*
Deutsche Bank AG, Taunusanlage 12, Frankfurt/Main, 60325, GERMANY

Koppes, Peter *Musician*
Globeshine, 101 Chamberlayne Road, London, NW10 3ND, UNITED KINGDOM (UK)

Kopple, Barbara J *Director*
Cabin Creek Films, 155 Ave of Americas, New York, NY 10013 USA

Kopra, Timothy L *Astronaut*
2518 Lakeside Dr, Seabrook, TX 77586 USA

Koprowski, Hilary *Biologist*
334 Fairhill Road, Wynnewood, PA 19096 USA

Koptchak, Sergei *Opera Singer*
Robert Lombardo, Harkness Plaza, 61 W 62nd St #6F, New York, NY 10023 USA

Koralek, Paul G *Architect*
7 Chalcot Road, #1, London, NW1 8LH,
UNITED KINGDOM (UK)

Korben *Musician*
Pop Idol (Fremantle Media), 2700
Colorado Ave #450, Santa Monica, CA
90404 USA

Korbut, Olga V *Gymnast*
8250 N Via Paseo Del Norte, #E106,
Scottsdale, AZ 85258 USA

Korcheck, Steve *Baseball Player*
Washington Senators, 6424 98th St E,
Bradenton, FL 34202-9769 USA

Kord, Kazimierz *Conductor*
Filharmonia Narodowa, Ul Jasna 5,
Warsaw, 00-950, POLAND

Korda, Maria
304 N. Screenland Dr., Burbank, CA
91505

Korda, Michael V *Writer*
Simon & Schuster/Pocket/Summit, 1230
Ave of the Americas, New York, NY
10020 USA

Korda, Petr *Tennis Player*
4909 61st Ave Dr W, Bradenton, FL
34210 USA

Korec Jan, Chryzostom Cardinal *Religious Leader*
Biskupstvo Nitra, PP 46A, Nitra, 95050,
SLOVAKIA

Koren, Edward B *Cartoonist*
New Yorker Magazine, Editorial Dept, 4
Times Square, New York, NY 10036 USA

Koren, Steve *Writer, Producer*
Creative Artists Agency LCC (CAA-LA),
9830 Wilshire Blvd, Beverly Hills, CA
90212 USA

Korf, Mia *Actor*
Paradigm Agency, 10100 Santa Monica
Blvd, #2500, Los Angeles, CA 90067 USA

Korince, George *Baseball Player*
Detroit Tigers, 50 Lakeshore Rd, St
Catharines, ON L2N 6P8, CANADA

Korjus, Tapio *Track Athlete*
General Delivery, Lapua, FINLAND

Korman, Harvey *Actor, Comedian*
1136 Stradella Road, Los Angeles, CA
90077 USA

Korman, Maxime Carlot *Prime Minister*
Prime Minister's Office, PO Box 110, Port
Vila, VANUATU

Kormann, Peter *Gymnast*
US Olympic Committee, 1 Olympia
Plaza, Colorado Springs, CO 80909 USA

Korn *Music Group*
William Morris Agency (WMA-LA), 1
William Morris Pl, Beverly Hills, CA
90212 USA

Kornberg, Arthur *Nobel Prize Laureate*
365 Golden Oak Dr, Portola Valley, CA
94028 USA

Kornberg, Hannah *Actor*
Williams Unlimited, 5010 Buffalo Ave,
Sherman Oaks, CA 91423

Kornheiser, Tony *Sportscaster, Writer*
Washington Post, Editorial Dept, 1150
15th St NW, Washington, DC 20071 USA

Korowi, Wiwa *Governor*
Government House, Konedobu, Box 79,
Port Moresby, Boroko, PAPUA NEW
GUINEA

Korpan, Richard *Business Person*
Florida Progress Corp, 100 Central Ave,
Saint Petersburg, FL 33701 USA

Kors, Michael *Fashion Designer*
550 Fashion Ave Fl 7, New York, NY
10018 USA

Korsantiya, Alexander *Musician*
Columbia Artists Mgmt Inc, 165 W 57th
St, New York, NY 10019 USA

Korvald, Lars *Prime Minister*
Vinkelgaten 6, Mjondalen, 3050,
NORWAY

Korzun, Valery G *Cosmonaut*
Potchta Kosmoriavtov, Moskovskoi
Oblasti, Syvisdny Goroduk, 14

Korzun, Valery G *Cosmonaut*
Potchta Kosmoriavtov, Moskovskoi
Oblasti, Syvisdny Goroduk, 141160,
RUSSIA

Kosar, Bernie
6969 Ron Park Pl., Youngstown, OH
44512

Kosar Jr, Bernie J *Football Player*
2672 Rivera Manor, Weston, FL 33332
USA

Kosco, Andy *Baseball Player*
Minnesota Twins, 3166 Howell Dr,
Youngstown, OH 44514-2459 USA

Koshalek, Richard *Director*
Museum of Contemporary Art, 250 S
Grand Ave, Los Angeles, CA 90012 USA

Koshiba, Masatoshi *Nobel Prize Laureate*
University of Tokyo, 7-3-1 Hongo,
Nunkyoku, Tokyo, 113-8654, JAPAN

Koshiro IV, Matsumoto *Actor, Dancer*
Kabukiza Theatre, 12-15-4 Ginza,
Chuoku, Tokyo, 104, JAPAN

Koshland Jr, Daniel E *Misc*
3991 Happy Valley Road, Lafayette, CA
94549 USA

Koski, Bill *Baseball Player*
Pittsburgh Pirates, 1120 Valencia Ct,
Modesto, CA 95350-4665 USA

Koskie, Corey *Baseball Player*
Minnesota Twins, 6284 Niagara Ln N,
Osseo, MN 55311-4160 USA

Koskoff, Sarah *Actor*
Mitchell K Stubbs & Assoc (MKS), 8675 W
Washington Blvd #203, Culver City, CA
90232 USA

Koslo, Paul
Box 407, Lake Hughes, CA 93532

Koslofski, Kevin *Baseball Player*
Kansas City Royals, 521 E Washington St,
Maroa, IL 61756-9239 USA

Koslow, Lauren *Actor*
Michael Bruno, 13576 Cheltenham Dr,
Sherman Oaks, CA 91423 USA

Kosner, Edward A *Editor*
Esquire Magazine, Editorial Dept, 1790
Broadway #1300, New York, NY 10019
USA

Koss, Amy Goldman *Writer*
Puffin Publicity, 375 Hudson St, New
York, NY 10014

Koss, Johann Olav *Speed Skater*
Dagaliveien 21, Oslo, 0387, NORWAY

Koss, John C *Inventor*
Koss Corp, 4129 N Port Washington Ave,
Milwaukee, WI 53212 USA

Kossoff, David
45 Roe Green Close College Lane,
Hatfield Herts., ENGLAND

Kostadinova, Stefka *Track Athlete*
Rue Anghel Kantchev 4, Sofia, 1000,
BULGARIA

Kostal, Irwin
3149 Dona Susana Dr., Studio City, CA
91604

Kostelic, Janica *Skier*
Ski Association, Trg Sportova 11, Zagreb,
1000, CROATIA

Koster, Steven J *Cinematographer*
26881 Goya Circle, Mission Viejo, CA
92691 USA

Kostner, Isolde *Skier*
General Delivery, Hortisei BZ, ITALY

Kostro, Frank *Baseball Player*
Detroit Tigers, 36 Steele St Ste 20,
Denver, CO 80206-5711 USA

Kosuth, Joseph *Artist*
591 Broadway, New York, NY 10012
USA

Kotcheff, W Theodore (Ted) *Director*
Ted Kotcheff Productions, 13451 Firth Dr,
Beverly Hills, CA 90210 USA

Koteas, Elias *Actor*
Endeavor Agency LLC (LA), 9601 Wilshire
Blvd Fl 3, Beverly Hills, CA 90210 USA

Koterba, Jeff *Cartoonist*
Omaha World Herald, Editorial Dept,
14th & Dodge St Wichita, Omaha, NE
68102 USA

Kotite, Rich *Football Player*
241 Fanning St, Staten Island, NY 10314
USA

Kotite, Richard E (Rich) *Football Player, Football Coach*
241 Fanning St, Staten Island, NY 10314
USA

Kotlarek, Gene *Skier*
4910 Walking Horse Point, Colorado
Springs, CO 80917 USA

Kotlarek, George *Skier*
330 N Arlington Ave, #512, Duluth, MN
55811 USA

Kotlayakov, Vladimir M *Geophysicist*
Geography Institute, Staromonetny per 29,
Moscow, 109017, RUSSIA

Kotsay, Mark *Baseball Player*
Florida Marlins, 2947 Flint Ridge Ct,
Reno, NV 89511-5327 USA

Kotsonis, Ieronymous *Religious Leader*
Archdiocese of Athens, Hatzichristou 8,
Athens 402, Greece, 53212 USA

Kottke, Leo *Songwriter, Musician*
Chuck Morris Entertainment, 1658 York
St, Denver, CO 80206 USA

Kotto, Yaphet *Actor, Writer, Director, Producer*
Diverse Talent Group, 1875 Century Park E #2250, Los Angeles, CA 90067 USA

Kotto, Yaphet F *Actor*
Artists Group, 10100 Santa Monica Blvd, #2490, Los Angeles, CA 90067 USA

Kotulak, Ronald *Editor*
Chicago Tribune, Editorial Dept, 435 N Michigan Ave, Chicago, IL 60611 USA

Kotz, John *Basketball Player*
PO Box 7900, Madison, WI 53707 USA

Kotzky, Alex S *Cartoonist*
20317 56th Sve, Oakland Gardens, NY 11364 USA

Kouchner, Bernard *Doctor*
L'Action d'Humanitaire, 8 Ave de Segur, Paris, 75350 USA

Koudelka, Josef *Photographer*
Magnum Photos, Moreland Bldgs, 23 Old St, London, EC1V 9HL, UNITED KINGDOM (UK)

Koufax, Sandy *Baseball Player*
Brooklyn Dodgers, PO Box 8306, Vero Beach, FL 32963-8306 USA

Kournikova, Anna *Tennis Player*
300 S Pointe Dr, #PH 3, Miami Beach, FL 33139 USA

Kovacevich, Richard M *Financier*
Wells Fargo Co, 420 Montgomery St, San Francisco, CA 94163 USA

Kovacevich, Stephen *Musician, Conductor*
Van Walsum Mgmt, 4 Addison Bridge Place, London, W14 8XP, UNITED KINGDOM (UK)

Kovach, Bill *Editor*
Harvard University, Nieman Fellows Program, Cambridge, MA 02138 USA

Kovacic, Ernst *Musician*
Ingpen & Williams, 14 Kensington Court, London, W8 5DN, UNITED KINGDOM (UK)

Kovacic-Ciro, Zdravko *Misc*
JP Kamova 57, Rijeka, 51000, SERBIA & MONTENEGRO

Kovack, Nancy
27 Oakmont Dr., Los Angeles, CA 90049

Kovacs, Andras *Director*
Magyar Jakobinusok Ter 2/3, Budapest, 1122, HUNGARY

Kovacs, Denes *Musician*
Iranyi Utca 12, Budapest V, HUNGARY

Kovacs, Laszlo *Cinematographer*
Feinstein & Berson, 16255 Ventura Blvd, #625, Encino, CA 91436 USA

Kovacs, Mijou
Sieberinger-Str. 92, Vienna, AUSTRIA, 1030

Kovai, Anuradha *Actor*
2 23rd Street Amirtha Apartments, Nanganallur, Chennai, TN 600 061, INDIA

Kovai, Sarala *Actor, Bollywood*
80 Nevkatesh Nagar I Street, Dhasaratha Puram, Chennai, TN 600093, INDIA

Kovalchuk, Ilya *Hockey Player*
SFX Sports, 220 W 42nd St, New York, NY 10036 USA

Kovalenko, Alexei *Hockey Player*
1 Trimont Lane, #2000A, Pittsburg, PA 15211 USA

Kovalenok, Vladimir S *Cosmonaut, General*
3 Ap 22, Hovanskaya St, Moscow, 129515, RUSSIA

Kovalev, Alexei *Hockey Player*
4 Kassel Court, Mamaroneck, NY 10543 USA

Kovalevsky, Jean *Astronomer*
Villa La Padovane, 8 Rue Saint Michael, Saint-Antoine, Grasse, 06130, FRANCE

Kove, Martin *Actor*
11595 Huston St, North Hollywood, CA 91601 USA

Kowal, Charles T *Astronomer*
Space Telescope Science Institute, Homewood Campus, Baltimore, MD 21218 USA

Kowalczyk, Ed *Musician*
Freedman & Smith, 350 W End Ave, #1, New York, NY 10024 USA

Kowalczyk, Jozef *Religious Leader*
Nuncjatura Apostolska, Al Ch Szucha 12, #163, Warsaw, 00-582, POLAND

Kowalski, Ted *Musician*
GEMS, PO Box 1031, Montrose, CA 91021 USA

Kowalski, Walter
PO Box 67, Reading, MA 01867 USA

Kowitz, Brian *Baseball Player*
Atlanta Braves, 7218 Park Heights Ave, Pikesville, MD 21208-5474 USA

Koy, Ernie *Baseball Player*
Brooklyn Dodgers, 1047 S Oak St, Bellville, TX 77418-2732 USA

Koz, Dave *Musician*
5850 W 3rd St, #307, Los Angeles, CA 90036 USA

Kozak, Harley Jane *Actor*
21336 Colina Dr, Topanga, CA 90290 USA

Kozak, Julie *Journalist*
Extra c/o Warner Bros, 4000 Warner Blvd, Burbank, CA 91522 USA

Kozakov, Mikhail M *Actor, Director*
Mayakovsky Theater, B Nikitskaya Str 17, Moscow, 103009, RUSSIA

Kozar, Al *Baseball Player*
Washington Senators, 5966 Bay Hill Cir, Lake Worth, FL 33463-6569 USA

Kozar, Heather *Actor*
PO Box 480872, Los Angeles, CA 90048-9472

Kozeev, Konstantin *Cosmonaut*
Potchta Kosmonavtov, Moskovskoi Oblasti, Syvisdny Goroduk, 141160, RUSSIA

Kozena, Magdalena *Opera Singer*
Narodni Divadio, Dvorakova 11, Brno, 60000, CZECH REPUBLIC

Kozinski, Alex *Judge*
US Court of Appeals, 125 S Grand Ave, Pasadena, CA 91105 USA

Kozlova, Anna *Swimmer*
Premier Management Group, 200 Merry Hill Dr, Cary, NC 27511 USA

Kozlova, Valentina *Ballerina*
New York City Ballet, Lincoln Center Plaza, New York, NY 10023 USA

Kozlowiecki, Adam Cardinal *Religious Leader*
PO Box 50003, Ridgeway, 15101, ZAMBIA

Kozlowski, Ben *Baseball Player*
Texas Rangers, 10701 59th Ave, Seminole, FL 33772-7306 USA

Kozlowski, Linda *Actor*
18 Marshall Crescent, Beacon Hill, NSW, 2060, AUSTRALIA

Kozol, Jonathan *Writer*
PO Box 145, Byfield, MA 01922 USA

Kraatz, Victor *Figure Skater*
Connecticut Skating Center, 300 Alumni Road, Newington, CT 06111 USA

Krabbe, Jeroen *Actor*
Van Eeghaustraat 107, Amsterdam, EZ, 1071, NETHERLANDS

Krabbe, Katrin
Jahnstadion Schwedenstr. 25, Neubrandenburg, GERMANY, D-17033

Krabbe-Zimmermann, Katrin *Track Athlete*
Dorfstr 9, Pinnow, 17091, GERMANY

Krackow, Jurgen *Business Person*
Schumannstr 100, Dusseldorf, 40237, GERMANY

Kraemer, Harry J *Business Person*
Baxter International, 1 Baxter Parkway, Deerfield, IL 60015 USA

Kraemer, Joe *Baseball Player*
Chicago Cubs, 3212 NE 401st Cir, La Center, WA 98629-5241 USA

Kraft, Chris
14919 Village Elm St, Houston, TX 77062-2914

Kraft, Christopher C (Chris) Jr *Misc*
14919 Village Elm St, Houston, TX 77062 USA

Kraft, Craig A *Artist*
931 R St NW, Washington, DC 20001 USA

Kraft, Greg *Golfer*
14820 Rue De Bayonne, #302, Clearwater, FL 33762 USA

Kraft, Leo A *Composer*
9 Dunster Road, Great Neck, NY 11021 USA

Kraft, Robert *Composer*
4722 Noeline Ave, Encino, CA 91436 USA

Kraft, Robert P *Physicist*
University of California, Lick Observatory, Santa Cruz, CA 95064 USA

Kragen, Ken
240 Baroda, Los Angeles, CA 90077

Krainev, Vladimir V *Musician*
Staatiche Hochschule fur Musik, Walderseestr 100, Hanover, GERMANY

Krajicek, Richard *Tennis Player*
Octagon, 1751 Pinnacle Dr, #1500, McLean, VA 22102 USA

Krakowski, Jane *Actor, Musician*
Borinstein Oreck Bogart, 3172 Dona Susana Dr, Studio City, CA 91604 USA

Krall, Diana *Musician*
Macklam Feldman Mgmt, 1505 W 2nd Ave, #200, Vancouver, BC V6H 3Y4, CANADA

Kraly, Steve *Baseball Player*
New York Yankees, 12 Davis Ave, Johnson City, NY 13790-3007 USA

Kramarsky, David *Director*
1336 Havenhurst Dr, West Hollywood, CA 90046 USA

Kramer, Billy J *Musician*
Mars Talent, 27 L'Ambiance Court, Bardonia, NY 10954 USA

Kramer, Clare *Actor*
Darren Goldberg Management, 5225 Wilshire Blvd #419, Los Angeles, CA 90036

Kramer, Eric Allan *Actor*
Artists Group (LA), 10100 Santa Monica Blvd #2490, Los Angeles, CA 90067 USA

Kramer, Gerald L (Jerry) *Football Player*
11768 Chinden Blvd, Boise, ID 83714 USA

Kramer, Jack
231 N. Glenroy Pl, Los Angeles, CA 90049

Kramer, Jim *Writer*
3 Arts Entertainment Inc, 9460 Wilshire Blvd Fl 7, Beverly Hills, CA 90212 USA

Kramer, Joel R *Editor*
Minneapolis Star Tribune, 425 Portland Ave, Minneapolis, MN 55488 USA

Kramer, Joey *Musician*
282 Pudding Hill Road, Marshfield, MA 02050 USA

Kramer, John A (Jack) *Tennis Player*
231 Glenroy Place, Los Angeles, CA 90049 USA

Kramer, Larry *Writer, Social Activist*
Gay Men's Health Crisis, 119 W 24th St, New York, NY 10011 USA

Kramer, Paul
20023 Bernist Ave., Torrance, CA 90503-2103

Kramer, Randy *Baseball Player*
Pittsburgh Pirates, PO Box 2001, Cedar Rapids, IA 52406-2001 USA

Kramer, Ron *Athlete*
PO Box 473, Fenton, MI 48430

Kramer, Ronald J (Ron) *Football Player*
Ron Kramer Industries, PO Box 473, Fenton, MI 48430 USA

Kramer, Stepfanie *Actor*
Don Buchwald, 6500 Wilshire Blvd, #2200, Los Angeles, CA 90048 USA

Kramer, Steve
1126 Hollywood Way #203-A, Burbank, CA 91505

Kramer, Thomas (Tommy) *Football Player*
6381 Stable Farm, San Antonio, TX 78249 USA

Kramer, Tom *Baseball Player*
Cleveland Indians, 1065 Hamilton Ave, Cincinnati, OH 45231-1703 USA

Kramer, W Erik *Football Player*
3150 Fallen Oaks Court, Rochester Hills, MI 48309 USA

Kramer, Wayne *Musician*
Performers of the World, 8901 Melrose Ave, #200, West Hollywood, CA 90069 USA

Kramnik, Vladmir *Misc*
Russian Chess Federation, Luchnetskaya 8, Moscow, 119270, RUSSIA

Kranek, Ernst
623 Chino Canyon Rd., Palm Springs, CA 92262

Kranepool, Ed *Baseball Player*
New York Mets, 177 High Pond Dr, Jericho, NY 11753-2806 USA

Krantz, Judith *Writer*
166 Groverton Place, Los Angeles, CA 90077 USA

Krantz, Steve
166 Groverton Pl., Los Angeles, CA 90077

Kranz, Eugene (Gene) *Scientist*
1108 Shady Oak Lane, Dickinson, TX 77539 USA

Kranz, Fran *Actor*
Hofflund/Polone, 9465 Wilshire Blvd #820, Beverly Hills, CA 90212 USA

Krapek, Karl *Business Person*
United Technologies Corp, United Technologies Building, Hartford, CT 06101 USA

Krasniqi, Luan *Boxer*
Oschlewg 10, Rottweil, 78628, GERMANY

Krasnoff, Eric *Business Person*
Pall Corp, 2200 Northem Blvd, Greenvale, NY 11548 USA

Krasny, Yuri *Artist*
Sloane Gallery, Oxford Office Building, 1612 17th St, Denver, CO 80202 USA

Kratochvilova, Jarmila *Track Athlete*
Goleuv Jenikov, 582 82, CZECH REPUBLIC

Kratzert, Bill *Golfer*
7470 Founders Way, Ponte Vedra, FL 32082 USA

Kraus, Peter
Kaiserplatz 7, Munich, GERMANY, D-80803

Krause, Brian *Actor*
Jonas PR, 240 26th St #3, Santa Monica, CA 90402 USA

Krause, Chester L *Publisher*
Krause Publications, 700 E State St, Iola, WI 54990 USA

Krause, Dieter *Athlete*
Karl-Marx-Allee 21, Berlin, 1017, GERMANY

Krause, Paul J *Football Player*
18099 Judicial Way N, Lakeville, MN 55044 USA

Krause, Peter *Actor*
Creative Artists Agency LCC (CAA-LA), 9830 Wilshire Blvd, Beverly Hills, CA 90212 USA

Krause, Richard M *Misc*
4000 Cathedral Ave NW, #413B, Washington, DC 20016 USA

Kraushaar, Sitke *Athlete*
Friedr-Ludwig-Jahn-Str 34, Sonneberg, 02692, GERMANY

Kraushaar, William L *Physicist*
27 Stoney Creek Road, Scarborough, ME 04074 USA

Krauss, Alison *Musician*
Keith Case Assoc, 1025 17th Ave S, #200, Nashville, TN 37212 USA

Krauss, Lawrence M *Physicist*
Case Western Reserve University, Physics Dept, Cleveland, OH 44106 USA

Krausse, Lew *Baseball Player*
Kansas City A's, 12811 NE 186th St, Holt, MO 64048-8956 USA

Krausse, Stefan *Athlete*
Kart-Zink-Str 2, Ilmenau, 96883, GERMANY

Krauthammer, Charles *Writer*
Washington Post Writers Group, 1150 15th St NW, Washington, DC 20071 USA

Kravchuk, Igor *Hockey Player*
Florida Partners, 1 Panthers Parkway, Sunrise, FL 33323 USA

Kravec, Ken *Baseball Player*
Chicago White Sox, 6752 Taeda Dr, Sarasota, FL 34241-9152 USA

Kravitch, Phyllis A *Judge*
US Court of Appeals, 56 Forsyth St NW, Atlanta, GA 30303 USA

Kravits, Jason
6310 San Vicente Blvd. #520, Los Angeles, CA 90048

Kravitz, Danny *Baseball Player*
Pittsburgh Pirates, RR 1 Box 1119, Dushore, PA 18614-9353 USA

Kravitz, Lenny *Musician, Songwriter*
14681 Harrison St, Miami, FL 33176 USA

Krayer, Otto H *Misc*
4140 E Cooper St, Tucson, AZ 85711 USA

Krayzelburg, Lenny *Swimmer*
Octagon, 1751 Pinnacle Dr, #1500, McLean, VA 22102 USA

Krayzle, Bone *Musician*
Creative Artists Agency, 9830 Wilshire Blvd, Beverly Hills, CA 90212 USA

Krebbs, John *Race Car Driver*
Diamond Ridge, 3232 Amoruso Way, Roseville, CA 95747 USA

Krebs, Edwin G *Nobel Prize Laureate*
1819 41st Ave E, Seattle, WA 98112 USA

Krebs, Robert D *Business Person*
Burlington North/Santa Fe, 2650 Lou Menk Dr, Fort Worth, TX 76131 USA

Krebs, Susan *Actor*
4704 Tobias Ave, Sherman Oaks, CA 91403 USA

Kredel, Elmar Maria *Religious Leader*
Obere Karolinenstra 5, Bamber, 96033, GERMANY

Kregel, Kevin R *Astronaut*
858 Shadwell Dr, Houston, TX 77062 USA

Krehbiel, Frederick A *Business Person*
Molex Inc, 2222 Wellington Court, Lisle, IL 60532-1682

Krehbiel, John Hammond *Business Person*
Molex Inc., 2222 Wellington Court, Lisle, IL 60532-1682

Krejc, Otomar
Kubisova 26, Praha 8, CZ-18200, Czech Republic

krels, Jason *Soccer Player*
Dallas Burn, 14800 Quorum Dr, #300, Dallas, TX 75254 USA

Krementz, Jill *Photographer*
620 Sagaponack Main St, Southampton, NY 11968 USA

Kremer, Andrea *Sportscaster*
ESPN-TV, Sports Dept, ESPN Plaza 935 Middle St, Bristol, CT 06010 USA

Kremer, Gidon *Musician*
I C M Artists, 40 W 57th St, New York, NY 10019 USA

Kremer, Howard *Comedian*
International Creative Management (ICM-LA), 8942 Wilshire Blvd, Beverly Hills, CA 90211 USA

Kremer, John *Business Person*

Krens, Thomas *Misc*
Solomon R Guggenheim Museum, 1071 5th Ave, New York, NY 10128 USA

Krentz, Jayne Ann (Amanda Quick) *Writer*
Axelrod Agency, 66 Church St, Lenox, MA 01240 USA

Krenwinkel, Patricia
#W8314 Bed #MA11U CA Inst. for Women16756 Chino Corona, Frontera, CA 91720

Krenz, Jan *Composer, Conductor*
Filharmonia Narodowa, Ul Jasna 5, Warsaw, POLAND

Kreppel, Paul
14300 Killion St., Van Nuys, CA 91401

Kreps, David M *Economist*
Stanford University, Graduate Business School, Stanford, CA 94305 USA

Kreps, Juanita M *Secretary*
1407 W Pettigrew St, Durham, NC 27705 USA

Kresa, Kent *Business Person*
Northrop Grumman Corp, 1840 Century Park East, Los Angeles, CA 90067 USA

Kreskin *Misc*
444 2nd St, Pitcaim, PA 15140 USA

Kressley, Carson *Television Host*
Queer Eye for the Straight Guy, 119 Braintree St, Boston, MA 02134

Kretchmer, Arthur *Editor*
Playboy Magazine, Editorial Dept, 680 N Lake Shore Dr, Chicago, IL 60611 USA

Kretschmann, Thomas *Director*
United Talent Agency (UTA), 9560 Wilshire Blvd, Beverly Hills, CA 90212 USA

Kreuk, Kristin *Actor*
Pacific Artists Mgmt, 1404-510 W Hastings, Vancouver, BC V6B 1L8, CANADA

Kreutzmann, Bill *Musician*
PO Box 1073, San Rafael, CA 94915 USA

Kreuzer, Lisa
Bavariaring 32, Munich, GERMANY, D-80336

Kreviazuk, Chantal *Musician, Songwriter*
Macklam Feldman Mgmt, 1505 W 2nd Ave, #200, Vancouver, BC V6H 3Y4, CANADA

Krevlazuk, Chantel
1505 W. 2nd Ave. #200, Vancouver, CANADA, BC V6H 3Y4

Kricfalusi (Kricfaluci), John K *Writer, Director, Actor*
Endeavor Agency LLC (LA), 9601 Wilshire Blvd Fl 3, Beverly Hills, CA 90210 USA

Krickstein, Aaron *Tennis Player*
7559 Fairmont Court, Boca Raton, FL 33496 USA

Krieg, Arthur M *Misc*
University of Iowa, Medical College, Immunology Dept, Iowa City, IA 52242 USA

Krieg, David M (Dave) *Football Player*
2439 E Desert Willow Dr, Phoenix, AZ 85048 USA

Krieger, Robbie *Songwriter, Musician*
3011 Ledgewood Dr, Los Angeles, CA 90068 USA

Krier, Leon *Architect*
16 Belsize Park, London, NW3, UNITED KINGDOM (UK)

Krige, Alice *Actor*
2875 Barrymore Dr, Malibu, CA 90265 USA

Krikalev, Sergei K *Cosmonaut*
Potchta Kosmonavtov, Moskovskoi Oblasti, Syvisdny Goroduk, 141160, RUSSIA

Krim, Mathilde *Musician*
Amer Foundation for AIDS Research, 5900 Wilshire Blvd, Los Angeles, CA 90036 USA

Kripke, Saul A *Misc*
Princeton University, Philosophy Dept, Princeton, NJ 08544 USA

Kris Kross
9380 SW 72nd St. #B220, Miami, FL 33173

Krishnamurthy, Suchithra *Actor, Bollywood*
402A Leela Apartments, Cuerpark Co-op Society Yari Road Andheri (W), Mumbai, MS 400061, INDIA

Krishnan, Ramya *Actor, Bollywood*
7 Lakshmi Sri Street, Janaki Nagar, Chennai, TN 600087, INDIA

Kriss, Gerard A *Astronomer*
Johns Hopkins University, Astronomy Dept, Baltimore, MD 21218 USA

Kristel, Sylvia *Actor*
Edrick/Rich Mgmt, 2400 Whitman Place, Los Angeles, CA 90068 USA

Kristen, Marta *Actor*
475 Mesa Dr, Santa Monica, CA 90402 USA

Kristiansen, Ingrid *Track Athlete*
Nils Collett Vogts Vei 51B, Oslo, 0765, NORWAY

Kristiansen, Kjeld Kirk *Business Person, Educator*
Lego Group, Billund, 7190, DENMARK

Kristien, Dale
691 Country Club Dr., Burbank, CA 91501

Kristine, W *Musician*
PO Box 71311, Las Vegas, NV 89170 USA

Kristof, Kathy M *Writer*
Los Angeles Times, Editorial Dept, 202 W 1st St, Los Angeles, CA 90012 USA

Kristof, Nicholas D *Journalist*
New York Times, Editorial Dept, 229 W 43rd St, New York, NY 10036 USA

Kristoff, Joe *Bowler*
4290 Meadowview Court, Columbus, OH 43224 USA

Kristofferson, Kris *Actor, Songwriter, Musician*
Current Entertainment, 1411 5th St, #405, Santa Monica, CA 90401 USA

Kristol, Irving *Scientist, Editor*
Public Interest Magazine, 1112 16th St NW, Washington, DC 20036 USA

Kristol, William
6625 Jill Ct., McLean, VA 22101

Kriwet, Heinz *Business Person*
Thyssen AG, August-Thyssen-Str 1, Dusseldorf, 40211, GERMANY

Kroeger, Chad *Musician, Songwriter*
Union Entertainment Group, 31225 La Baya Dr, #213, Westlake Village, CA 91362 USA

Kroeger, Gary *Actor, Comedian*
10474 Santa Monica Blvd, #380, Los Angeles, CA 90025 USA

Kroemer, Herbert *Nobel Prize Laureate*
University of California, Electrical/Computer Eng Dept, Santa Barbara, CA 93106 USA

Krofft, Marty *Misc*
700 Greentree Road, Pacific Palisades, CA 90272 USA

Krofft, Sid *Misc*
7710 Woodrow Wilson Dr, Los Angeles, CA 90046 USA

Kroft, Steve *Commentator*
CBS-TV, News Dept, 51 W 52nd St, New York, NY 10019 USA

Krol, John Cardinal
222 N. 17th St., Philadelphia, PA 19103

Kroll, Alexander S (Alex) *Football Player, Business Person*
Young & Rubicam, 285 Madison Ave, New York, NY 10017 USA

Kroll, Lucien *Architect*
Ave Louis Berlaimont 20, Boite 9, Brussels, 1160, BELGIUM

Kroll, Sylvio
Tranitzer Str. 8, Cottbus, GERMANY, D-03048

Kromm, Bob *Coach*
Detroit Red Wings, Joe Louis Arena, 600 Civic Center Dr, Detroit, MI 48226 USA

Kromm, Richard (Rich) *Hockey Player, Coach*
35469 Banbry St, Livonia, MI 48152 USA

Kronberger, Petra *Skier*
Ellmautal 37, Pfarrwerfen, 5452, AUSTRIA

Krone, Julie
250 W. Main St. #1820, Lexington, KY 40507

Krone, Julie *Jockey*
Jay Hovdey, Daily Racing Form, 100 Broadway #700, New York, NY 10005 USA

Kropfeld, Jim *Race Car Driver*
Hydroplanes Inc, 9117 Zoellner Dr, Cincinnati, OH 45251 USA

Kropfelder, Nicholas *Soccer Player*
13803 Lighthouse Ave, Ocean City, IN 21842 USA

Kroto, Harold W *Nobel Prize Laureate*
Sussex University, Chemistry Dept, Falmer, Brighton, BN1 9QJ, UNITED KINGDOM (UK)

KRS-One *Musician*
Famous Artists Agency, 250 W 57th St, New York, NY 10107 USA

Krstic, Nenad *Basketball Player*
New Jersy Nets, 390 Murray Hill Parkway, East Rutherford, NJ 07073 USA

Krueger, Anne O *Economist*
Stanford University, Economics Dept, Stanford, CA 94305 USA

Krueger, Charles A (Charlie) *Football Player*
44 Regency Dr, Clayton, CA 94517 USA

Krueger, Charlie
44 Regency Dr., Clayton, CA 94617

Krueger, James G *Misc*
Rockefeller University, Medical Center, 1230 York Ave, New York, NY 10021 USA

Krueger, Kurt
1221 La Collina Dr., Beverly Hills, CA 90210

Krueger, Robert C (Bob) *Senator, Diplomat*
US Embassy-Burundl, State Department, 2201 C St NW, Washington, DC 20522 USA

Krug, Manfred
Rankestr. 9, Berlin, GERMANY, D-10789

Kruger, Christiane
Waldschmidtstr. 16, Starnberg, GERMANY, 82319

Kruger, Diane *Actor, Model*
Artists Independent Network, 32 Tavistock St, London, WC2E 7PB, UNITED KINGDOM (UK)

Kruger, Hardy
Box 726, Crestline, CA 92325

Kruger, Hardy *Actor*
L Von dem Knesebeck, Maximilianstr 23, Munich, 80539, GERMANY

Kruger, Mike
Gorch-Fock-Kehre 9, Quickborn, GERMANY, D-25451

Kruger, Pit *Actor*
Geleitstr 10, Frankfurt/Main, 60599, GERMANY

Krugman, Paul R *Economist*
70 Lambert Dr, Princeton, NJ 08540 USA

Krulwich, Robert *Commentator*
CBS-TV, News Dept, 524 W 57th St, New York, NY 10019 USA

Krumholtz, David *Actor*
8809 Appian Way, Los Angeles, CA 90046 USA

Krumrie, Tim *Football Player*
Cincinnati Bengals, 1 Paul Brown Stadium, Cincinnati, OH 45202 USA

Krupin, Paul *Writer*

Kruschen, Jack
PO Box 10143, Canoga Park, CA 91309-1143

Kruse, Earl J *Misc*
Roofers/Waterproofers/Allied Workers, 1125 17th St NW, Washington, DC 20036 USA

Kruse, Martin *Religious Leader*
Prinz-Friedrrich-Leopold-Str 14, Berlin, 14219, GERMANY

Krusiec, Michelle *Actor*
Himber Entertainment Inc, 211 S Beverly Dr #208, Beverly Hills, CA 90212 USA

Kruskal, Martin D *Mathematician*
60 Littlebrook Road N, Princeton, NJ 08540 USA

Krypreos, Nick *Hockey Player*
9209 Copenhaven Dr, Potomac, MD 20854 USA

Krzyzewski, Michael W (Mike) *Coach*
Duke University, Cameron Indoor Stadium, Athletic Dept, Durham, NC 27706 USA

Kuban, Bob *Musician*
17626 Lasiandra Dr, Chesterfield, MO 63005 USA

Kubasov, Valeri N *Cosmonaut*
Potchta Kosmonavtov, Moskovskoi Oblasti, Syvisdny Goroduk, 141160, RUSSIA

Kubasov, Valery
141-160 Svyossdy Gorodok, Potchta Kosmonavtov, RUSSIA

Kubek, Anthony C (Tony) *Baseball Player, Sportscaster*
W6129 Pilgrim St, Appleton, WI 54914 USA

Kubiak, Gary *Football Player, Football Coach*
4330 Preserve Parkway S, Littleton, CO 80121 USA

Kubler-Ross, Elisabeth *Writer*
PO Box 6168, Scottsdale, AZ 85261 USA

Kucan, Milan *President*
President's Office, Erjavcera 17, Ljublijana, 61000, SOLVENIA

Kucera, Frantisek *Hockey Player*
Pittsburg Penguins, Mellon Arena, 66 Mario Lemieux Place, Pittsburgh, PA 15219 USA

Kuchma, Leonid D *President*
President's Office, Bankova Str 11, Kiev, 252011, UKRAINE

Kucinich, Dennis
12217 Milan, Cleveland, OH 44111

Kucinich, Dennis J *Misc*
14518 Drake Road, Cleveland, OH 44136 USA

Kuczynski, Betty *Bowler*
4515 Prescott Ave, Lyons, IL 60534 USA

Kud *Musician*
Agency Group Ltd, 1775 Broadway, #430, New York, NY 10019 USA

Kudelka, James A *Dancer, Choreographer*
National Ballet of Canada, 470 Queens Quay W, Toronto, ON M5V 3K4, CANADA

Kudelski, Bob *Hockey Player*
64 Diamond Basin Road, Cody, WY 82414 USA

Kuder, Mary *Artist*
Kuder Art Studio, 539 Navahopi Road, Sedona, AZ 86336 USA

Kudlow, Lawrence *Television Host*
Kudlow & Cramer, 900 Sylvan Ave, Englewood Cliffs, NJ 07632 USA

Kudrna, Julius *Athlete*
Sekaninova 36, Prague 2, 120 00, CZECH REPUBLIC

Kudrow, Lisa *Actor*
Po Box 691900, Los Angeles, CA 90069 USA

Kuebler, David *Opera Singer*
Haydn Rawstron, 36 Station Road, London, SE20 7BQ, UNITED KINGDOM (UK)

Kuechenberg, Robert J (Bob) *Football Player*
2519 SW 30th Terrace, Fort Lauderdale, FL 33312 USA

Kuehn, Enrico *Athlete*
BSD, An der Schiessstatte 4, Berchtesgaden, 83471, GERMANY

Kuehne, Kelli *Golfer*
Gaylord Sports Mgmt, 14646 N Kierland Blvd, #230, Scottsdale, AZ 85254 USA

Kuerten, Gustavo *Tennis Player*
Octagon, 1751 Pinnacle Drive, #1500, McLean, VA 22102 USA

Kufeldt, James *Business Person*
Winn-Dixie Stores, 5050 Edgewood Court, Jacksonville, FL 32254 USA

Kufuor, John Agyekum *President*
Chairman's Office, Castle, PO Box 1627, Accra, GHANA

Kuhaulua, Jesse *Wrestler*
Azumazeki Stable, 4-6-4 Higashi Komagata, Ryogoku, Tokyo, JAPAN

Kuhlman, Ron *Actor*
5738 Willis Ave, Van Nuys, CA 91411 USA

Kuhlmann, Kathleen M *Opera Singer*
Int'l Management Group, G Paris, 54 Ave Marceau, Paris, 75008, FRANCE

Kuhlmann-Wilsdorf, Doris *Physicist*
University of Virginia, Materials Science Dept, Charlottesville, VA 22901 USA

Kuhn, Gustav *Conductor*
6343 Ere, AUSTRIA

Kuhn, Stephen L (Steve) *Musician, Composer*
Berkeley Agency, 2608 9th St, Berkeley, CA 94710 USA

Kuhweide, Wilhelm
10031 E. Buckskin Trail, Scottsdale, AZ 85255

Kukoc, Toni *Basketball Player*
1850 Hybernia Dr, Highland Park, IL
60035 USA

Kuleshov, Valery *Musician*
Musicians Corporate Mgmt, PO Box 589,
Millbrook, NY 12545 USA

Kulich, Vladimir *Actor*
Jeff Goldberg Management, 817 Monte
Leon Dr, Beverly Hills, CA 90210 USA

Kulikov, Viktor G *Misc*
Ministry of Defense, Myasnitskaya Str 37,
Moscow, 10100, RUSSIA

Kulka, Konstanty A *Musician*
Filharmonia Narodowa, Ul Jasna 5,
Warsaw, 00-007, POLAND

Kulkarni, Mamta *Actor, Bollywood*
D Wing 7th Floor 701 RC Complex,
Versova Yari Road, Mumbai, MS 400061,
INDIA

Kulkarni, Shrinivas R *Astronomer*
California Institute of Technology,
Astronomy Dept, Pasadena, CA 91125
USA

Kumanyika, Shiriki K *Misc*
University of Illinois, Nutrition/Dietetics
Dept, Chicago, IL 60607 USA

Kumar, Akshay *Actor, Bollywood*
203 A Wing Benzer, Lokhandwala
Complex Andheri (W), Mumbai, MS
400053, INDIA

Kumar, Ashok *Actor, Bollywood*
47 Union Park Chembur, Mumbai, MS
400071, INDIA

Kumar, Dilip *Actor, Bollywood*
34/B Palli Hill, Nargis Dutt Road Bandra
(W), Mumbai, MS 400050, INDIA

Kumar, Kiran *Actor*
Jeevan Kiran S V Road, Bandra, Bombay,
MS 400 050, INDIA

Kumar, Manoj *Actor, Director, Filmmaker,
Producer*
Lakshmi Villa Grount Floor-45, Tagore
Road Santacruz (W), Bombay, MS 400
054, INDIA

Kumar, Mehul *Director, Bollywood,
Producer, Filmmaker*
302 Atlantic J P Road, Seven Bangalows
Andheri, Bombay, MS 400 061, INDIA

Kumar, Mohan *Director, Filmmaker,
Bollywood*
Prem Sagar 'B' Linking Road, Khar,
Bombay, MS 400 052, INDIA

Kumar, Rajendra *Actor, Director,
Filmmaker, Producer, Bollywood*
Dimple 7 Pali Hill, Bandra, Bombay, MS
400 050, INDIA

Kumar, Sanjay *Business Person*
Computer Associates Int'l, 1 Computer
Associates Plaza, Islandia, NY 11749 USA

Kumar, Sarath *Actor*
16 Rajamannaar Saalai, Thyagaraya
Nagar, Chennai, TN 600 017, INDIA

Kumaratunga, Chandrika B *President*
President's Office, Republic Square, Sri
Jayewardenepura Kotte, SRI LANKA

Kumbernuss, Astrid *Track Athlete*
Neubrandenburg Jahnstadion,
Schwedenstr 25, Neubrandenburg, 17033,
GERMANY

Kumble, Roger *Director, Actor, Writer*
United Talent Agency (UTA), 9560
Wilshire Blvd, Beverly Hills, CA 90212
USA

Kumin, Maxine W *Writer*
Joppa Road, Warner, NH 03278 USA

Kummer, Glenn F *Business Person*
Fleetwood Enterprises, 3125 Myers St,
Riverside, CA 92503 USA

Kump, Ernest J *Architect*
Villa Boecklin, Jupiterstr 15, Zurich, 8032,
SWITZERLAND

Kundera, Milan *Writer*
Gallimard, 5 Rue Sebastien-Bottin, Paris,
75007, FRANCE

Kundla, John A *Basketball Player, Coach*
4519 Zenith Ave N, Minneapolis, MN
55422 USA

Kunerth, Mark J *Writer, Producer*
Broder Webb Chervin Silbermann Agency,
The (BWCS), 9242 Beverly Blvd #200,
Beverly Hills, CA 90210 USA

Kunes, Ellen *Editor*
Oprah Magazine, 224 W 57th St, #900,
New York, NY 10019 USA

Kung, Hans *Misc*
Waldhauserstr 23, Tubingen, 72076,
GERMANY

Kung, Patrick C *Misc*
T Cell Sciences, 119 4th Ave, Needham,
MA 02494 USA

Kunis, Mila *Actor*
PMK/HBH Public Relations (PMK-LA),
8500 Wilshire Blvd #700, Beverly Hills,
CA 90211 USA

Kunitz, Matt *Producer*
William Morris Agency (WMA-LA), 1
William Morris Pl, Beverly Hills, CA
90212 USA

Kunitz, Stanley J *Writer*
37 W 12th St, New York, NY 10011 USA

Kunkel, Louis M *Misc*
Children's Hospital, 300 Longwood Ave,
Boston, MA 02115 USA

Kunkle, John F *Religious Leader*
Evangelical Methodist Church, 3000 W
Kellogg Dr, Wichita, KS 67213 USA

Kunnert, Kevin *Basketball Player*
8286 SW Qilderland Court, Tigard, OR
97224 USA

Kunstmann, Doris
Alexander Lamonstrasse 9, Munich,
GERMANY, D-81679

Kunz, George J *Football Player*
8215 S Bermuda Road, Las Vegas, NV
89123 USA

Kunzel, Erich Jr *Conductor*
TRM Mgmt, 825 S Lazelle St, Columbus,
OH 43206 USA

Kunzu, Hari *Writer*
EP Dutton, 375 Hudson St, New York, NY
10014 USA

Kupchak, Mitch
156 N. Gunston Dr., Los Angeles, CA
90049-2013

Kupchak, Mitchell (Mitch) *Basketball
Player*
156 N Gunston Dr, Los Angeles, CA
90049 USA

Kupcinet, Kari *Actor*
1931 W Roscoe St, Chicago, IL 60657
USA

Kupetsky, Allen I *Director*

Kupfer, Carl *Misc*
National Eye Institute, 9000 Rockville
Pike, Bethesda, MD 20892 USA

Kupfer, Harry *Director*
Komische Oper, Behrenstr 55-57, Berlin,
10117, GERMANY

Kupferberg, Sabine *Ballerina*
Dans Theater 3, Scheldoldoekshaven 60,
Gravenhage, EN, 2511, NETHERLANDS

Kupp, Jacob (Jake) *Football Player*
4801 Snowmountain Road, Yakima, WA
98908 USA

Kupper, William P Jr *Publisher*
Business Week, 1221 Ave of Americas,
New York, NY 10020 USA

Kupperman, Joel
577 Wormwood Hill Rd, Mansfield
Center, CT 06250

Kuranari, Tadashi *Government Official*
2-18-12 Daita, Setangayaku, Tokyo, 155,
JAPAN

Kurant, Willy *Cinematographer*
Lyons Sheldon Agency, 800 S Robertson
Blvd, #6, Los Angeles, CA 90035 USA

Kuras, Ellen M *Cinematographer*
54 Summit St, Nyack, NY 10960 USA

Kurasov, Georgy *Artist*
4/2 Inzenernaja St, Saint Petersburg,
191011, RUSSIA

Kureishi, Hanif *Writer*
81 Comeragh Road, London, W14 9HS,
UNITED KINGDOM (UK)

Kurkova, Karolina *Model*
DNA Model Mgmt, 520 Broadway, New
York, NY 10012 USA

Kurland, Robert A (Bob) *Basketball Player*
1024 Kings Crown Dr, Sanibel, FL 33957
USA

Kurlander, Tom
1801 Avenue of the Stars #902, Los
Angeles, CA 90067

Kurokawa, Kisho *Architect*
Aoyama Building, #11F 1-2-3 Kita
Aoyama, Minatoku, Tokyo, JAPAN

Kurrat, Kiaus-Dieter *Track Athlete*
Am Hochwald 30, 28460, Klemmachow,
1453, GERMANY

Kurri, Jarri *Hockey Player*
Colorado Avalanche, Pepsi Center, 1000
Chopper Circle, Denver, CO 80204 USA

Kurtag, Gyorgy *Composer*
Lihego V3, Veroce, 2621, HUNGARY

Kurtenbach, Orland J *Hockey Player*
119-15500 Rosemary Heights Crescent,
Surrey, BC V3S 0K1, CANADA

Kurth, Wallace (Wally) *Actor, Musician*
2143 N Valley Dr, Manhattan Beach, CA
90266 USA

Kurtis, Bill *Television Host*
Kurtis Productions, 400 W Erie St #500,
Chicago, IL 60610 USA

Kurtis, Dalene *Actor*
It Girl Public Relations, 3763 Eddingham
Ave, Calabasas, CA 91302 USA

Kurtz, Swoosie *Actor*
320 Central Park West, New York, NY
10025 USA

Kurtzberg, Joanne *Physicist*
Duke University, Medical Center,
Durham, NC 27708 USA

Kurtze, Andrew *Business Person*
Sprint PCS Group, PO Box 11315, Kansas
City, MO 64112 USA

Kurtzman, Katy *Actor, Director*
Lynn Production & Mgmt, 20411 Chapter
Dr, Woodland Hills, CA 91364 USA

Kurupt *Musician*
William Morris Agency, 151 El Camino
Dr, Beverly Hills, CA 90212 USA

Kurzweil, Raymond *Inventor*
Kurzwell Applied Intelligence, 411
Waverly Oaks Road, Waltham, MA 02452
USA

Kusama, Karyn *Director*
Endeavor Talent Agency, 9701 Wilshire
Blvd, #1000, Beverly Hills, CA 90212
USA

Kusatsu, Clyde *Actor*
Paradign Agency, 10100 Santa Monica
Blvd, #2500, Los Angeles, CA 90067 USA

Kuschak, Metropolitan Andrei *Religious
Leader*
Ukranian Orthodox Church in America, 3
Davenport Ave, New Rochelle, NY 10805
USA

Kushboo *Actor, Bollywood*
20/1 Arch Bshap, Mithyas Ave Boat Club
Road, Chennai, TN 600018, INDIA

Kushell, Lisa *Actor*
Abrams Artists Agency (LA), 9200 Sunset
Blvd Fl 11, Los Angeles, CA 90069 USA

Kushner, Harold S *Writer*
145 Hartford St, Natick, MA 01760

Kushner, Robert E *Artist*
DC Moore Gallery, 724 5th Ave, New
York, NY 10019 USA

Kushner, Tony *Writer*
Joyce Ketay Agency, 1501 Broadway,
#1910, New York, NY 10036 USA

Kuske, Kevin *Athlete*
BSD, An der Schlessstatte 4,
Berchtesgaden, 83471, GERMANY

Kutcher, Ashton *Actor, Producer*
Katalyst Films, 8436 W Third St #650, Los
Angeles, CA 90048

Kuti, Fela *Musician*
Rosebud Agency, PO Box 170429, San
Francisco, CA 94117 USA

Kutner, Malcom J (Mal) *Football Player*
6502 Ashmore Lane, Tyler, TX 75703
USA

Kutner, Rob *Writer*
Kaplan-Stahler-Gumer Agency, 8383
Wilshire Blvd #923, Beverly Hills, CA
90211 USA

Kuttner, Stephan G *Historian*
2270 Le Conte Ave, #601, Berkeley, CA
94709 USA

Kutty, Padmini *Actor, Bollywood*
33 1st Street Kamdar Nagar,
Nungambakkam, Chennai, TN 600034,
INDIA

Kutyna, Donald J *General*
4818 Kenyon Court, Colorado Springs,
CO 80917 USA

Kutz, Mae
140 Buckingham Ct, Goodlettsville, TN
37072

Kuykendall, John W *Educator*
Davidson College, President's Office,
Davidson, NC 28036 USA

Kuznetsoff, Alexel *Musician*
Columbia Artists Mgmt Inc, 165 W 57th
St, New York, NY 10019 USA

Kuzyk, Mimi *Actor*
Artists Agency, 1180 S Beverly Dr, #301,
Los Angeles, CA 90035 USA

Kwalick, Thaddeus J (Ted) *Football Player*
755 Purdue Court, Santa Clara, CA 95051
USA

Kwan, Jennie *Actor*
Innovative Artists, 1505 10th St, Santa
Monica, CA 90401 USA

Kwan, Michelle *Figure Skater*
Ice Skating Castle, 27307 Highway 189,
Blue Jay, CA 92317 USA

Kwan, Nancy *Actor*
Contemporary Artists, 610 Santa Monica
Blvd, #202, Santa Monica, CA 90401 USA

Kwapis, Ken *Comedian*
Writers and Artists Group Intl (LA), 8383
Wilshire Blvd #550, Beverly Hills, CA
90211 USA

Kwasniewski, Aleksander *President*
Kancelaria Prezydenta RP, Ul Wiejska 4/8,
Warsaw, 00-902, POLAND

Kwoh, Yik San *Engineer*
Memorial Medical Center, PO Box 1428,
Long Beach, CA 90801 USA

Kwolek, Stephanie L *Inventor*
312 Spalding Road, Wilmington, DE
19803 USA

Kwouk, Burt *Actor*
Diamond Mgmt, 31 Percey St, London,
W1T 2DD, UNITED KINGDOM (UK)

Kyle, David L *Business Person*
ONEOK Inc, 100 W 5th St, PO Box 871,
Tulsa, OK 74102 USA

Kylian, Jiri *Dancer*
Dance Theatre, Scheldeldoekshaven 60,
Gravenhage, EN, 2511, NETHERLANDS

Kyo, Machiko *Actor*
Olimpia Copu, 6-35 JinguMae, Shibuyaku,
Tokyo, JAPAN

L

L *Musician*
Writers & Artists, 8383 Wilshire Blvd,
#550, Beverly Hills, CA 90211 USA

L'Engle, Madeleine *Writer*
924 W End Ave, New York, NY 10025
USA

L'Erario, Joe
7700 Wisconsin Ave, Bethesda, MD
20814

L'Hermitte, Thierry *Actor*
ICE 3, 13 Rue Yves-Toudic, Paris, 75010,
France

La Costeþa, Banda *Music Group*
BMG, 1540 Broadway, New York, NY
10036 USA

La Fong, Michelle
3855 Shore Parkway #1D, Brooklyn, NY
11235

La Lanne, Jack *Athlete*
430 Quitana Rd, Morro Bay, CA 93442
USA

La Lanne, Jack
430 Quintana Rd. #151, Morro Bay, CA
93442-1948

La Ley *Music Group*
United Talent Agency (UTA), 9560
Wilshire Blvd, Beverly Hills, CA 90212
USA

La Mura, Mark
6399 Wilshire Blvd. #414, Los Angeles,
CA 90048

La Oreja de Van Gogh *Music Group*
Sony Music Miami, 605 Lincoln Rd,
Miami Beach, FL 33138 USA

La Placa, Alison
4526 Wilshire Blvd., Los Angeles, CA
90010

La Rue, Danny
57 Gr. Cumberland Pl, London,
ENGLAND, W1M 7LJ

La Rue, Florence
4300 Louise Ave., Encino, CA 91316

Laatasi, Kamuta *Prime Minister*
Prime Minister's Office, Vaiaku, Funafuti,
TUVALU

Labaff, Ernie *Misc*
Aluminum Brick Glass Workers Union,
3362 Hollenberg, Bridgeton, MO 63044
USA

LaBeef, Sleepy *Musician*
14469 E Highway 264, Lowell, AR 72745
USA

LaBelle, Patti *Musician*
Direct Management, 947 N La Clenega
Blvd, #G, Los Angeles, CA 90069 USA

LaBeouf (LeBeouf), Shia *Actor*
John Crosby Management, 1729 N
Sycamore Ave, Los Angeles, CA 90028
USA

Labeque, Katia *Musician*
Columbia Artists Mgmt Inc, 165 W 57th
St, New York, NY 10019 USA

Labeque, Marielle *Musician*
Columbia Artists Mgmt Inc, 165 W 57th
St, New York, NY 10019 USA

Labeyrie, Antoine *Astronomer*
Haute-Provence Observatoire, Saint-
Michael Observatolre, FRANCE

Labine, Clem
311 N. Grove Isle Circle, Vero Beach, FL
32962

Labine, Clement W (Clem) *Baseball Player*
311 N Grove Isle Circle, #311, Vero Beach, FL 32962 USA

Labine, Tyler *Actor*
United Talent Agency (UTA), 9560 Wilshire Blvd, Beverly Hills, CA 90212 USA

Labiosa, David *Actor*
Artist's Agency, The (LA), 1180 S Beverly Dr #301, Los Angeles, CA 90035 USA

Labonte, Bobby *Race Car Driver*
403 Interstate Dr, Archdale, NC 27263 USA

Labonte, Terry *Race Car Driver*
Melanie Trader, 5740 Hopewell Church Road, Trinity, NC 27370 USA

Laborde, Alden J *Business Person*
63 Oriole St, New Orleans, LA 70124 USA

Labre, Yvon *Hockey Player*
PO Box 3994, Crofton, MD 21114 USA

LaBute, Neil *Director, Writer*
Sanford Gross, 6715 Hollywood Blvd, #236, Los Angeles, CA 90028 USA

Labyorteaux, Matthew *Actor*
167 W 72nd St, #3F, New York, NY 10023 USA

Labyorteaux, Patrick *Actor*
8447 Wilshire Blvd, #206, Beverly Hills, CA 90211 USA

Lacey, Deborah *Actor*
1801 Ave of Stars, #1250, Los Angeles, CA 90067 USA

Lach, Elmer J *Hockey Player*
89 Bayview Ave, Pointe Claire, QC, M9S 5C4, CANADA

Lachance, Michael (Mike) *Race Car Driver*
183 Sweetmans Lane, Englishtown, NJ 07726 USA

LaChapelle, David *Photographer*
Simon & Schuster/Pocket/Summit, 1230 Ave of the Americas, New York, NY 10020 USA

LaChappelle, Sean P *Football Player*
8724 Lodestone Circle, Elk Grove, CA 95624 USA

Lachemann, Marcel E *Baseball Player*
PO Box 587, Penryn, CA 95663 USA

Lachemann, Rene G *Baseball Player*
7500 E Boulders Parkway, #68, Scottsdale, AZ 85262 USA

Lachey, Drew *Musician*
DAS Communications, 83 Riverside Dr, New York, NY 10024 USA

Lachey, James M (Jim) *Football Player*
1445 Roxbury Road, Columbus, OH 43212 USA

Lachey, Nick *Musician*
DAS Communications, 83 Riverside Dr, New York, NY 10024 USA

Lachhiman, Gurung *War Hero*
Village Dahakhani, Village Development Conmelle, Ward 4, Chitwan, NEPAL

Lackey, Brad *Race Car Driver*
Badco, 35 Monument Plaza, Pleasant Hill, CA 94523 USA

Lackey, Elizabeth *Actor*
Don Buchwald & Associates Inc (LA), 6500 Wilshire Blvd #2200, Los Angeles, CA 90048 USA

Laclavere, Georges *Physicist*
53 Ave de Breteuil, Paris, 75007, FRANCE

Laclotte, Michel R *Director*
10 Bis Rue du Pre-aux-Clerc, Paris, 75007, FRANCE

Lacombe, Henri *Oceanographer*
20 Bis Ave de Lattre de Tassigny, Bourg-la-Reine, 92340, FRANCE

Lacombe, Henrt *Oceanographer*
20 Bis Ave de Lattre de Tassigny, Bourg-la-Reine, FRANCE

Lacoste, Catherine *Golfer*
Calle B6, #4 El Soto de la Moraleja Alcobendas, Madrid, SPAIN

Lacroix, Andre J *Hockey Player*
6770 Oakwood Dr, Oakland, CA 94611 USA

LaCroix, Christian
73 rue du Faubourg-St.-Honore, Paris, FRANCE, F-75008

Lacroix, Christian M M *Fashion Designer*
73 Rue du Faubourg Saint Honore, Paris, 75008, FRANCE

Lacy, Alan *Business Person*
Sears Roebuck Co, 3333 Beverly Blvd, Hoffman Estates, IL 60179 USA

Lacy, Kerry *Baseball Player*
Boston Red Sox, 124 County Road 713, Higdon, AL 35979-6123 USA

Lacy, Lee *Baseball Player*
Los Angeles Dodgers, 4424 Webster St, Oakland, CA 94609-2131 USA

Ladd, Alana
1420 Moraga Dr, Los Angeles, CA 90049

Ladd, Cheryl *Actor*
International Creative Mgmt, 8942 Wilshire Blvd, #219, Beverly Hills, CA 90211 USA

Ladd, David *Actor*
9212 Hazen Dr, Beverly Hills, CA 90210 USA

Ladd, Diane *Actor*
3860 Grand Ave, Ojai, CA 93023 USA

Ladd, Jordan *Actor*
Anonymous Content, 8522 National Blvd #101, Culver City, CA 90232 USA

Ladd, Margaret *Actor*
444 21st St, Santa Monica, CA 90402 USA

Ladd, Pete *Baseball Player*
Houston Astros, 3100 W Lynne Pl, Tucson, AZ 85742-9510 USA

Ladd Jr, Alan
1005 Benedict Canyon Dr, Beverly Hills, CA 90210 USA

Ladd Jr, Alan W *Producer*
1005 Benedict Canyon Dr, Beverly Hills, CA 90210 USA

Laden, Nina B
6750 26th Ave NW, Seattle, WA 98117-5828 USA

Laderman, Exra *Composer*
Yale University, Music School, New Haven, CT 06520 USA

Ladewig, Marion *Bowler*
Ladies Professional Bowling Tour, 7200 Harrison Ave, #7171, Rockford, IL 61112 USA

Ladin, Eric *Actor*
Halpern & Associates, 12304 Santa Monica Blvd #104, Los Angeles, CA 90025 USA

Laettner, Christian *Basketball Player*
Washington Wizards, MCI Center, 601 F Street NW, Washington DC, 20004 USA

Laettnew, Christian D *Basketball Player*
1225 Church Road, Angola, NY 14006 USA

Lafata, Joe *Baseball Player*
New York Giants, 29321 W Brittany Ct, Roseville, MI 4806-2005 USA

Laffer, Arthur *Doctor*
5375 Exec Sq #330, La Jolla, CA 92037 USA

Laffer, Arthur B *Economist*
24255 Pacific Coast Highway, Malibu, CA 90263 USA

Lafferty, James *Actor*
United Talent Agency (UTA), 9560 Wilshire Blvd, Beverly Hills, CA 90212 USA

Laffite, Jacques
Technopole de la Nievre, Magny Cours, FRANCE, F-58470

Lafforgue, Laurent *Mathematician*
IHES, Mathematics Dept, Bures-sur-Yvette, 91440, FRANCE

Lafleur, Guy D *Hockey Player*
14 Place du Molin, L'Ile-Bizard, QC, H9E 1N2, CANADA

Lafley, Alan G *Business Person*
Procter & Gamble Co, 1 Procter & Gamble Plaza, Cincinnati, OH 45202 USA

Lafontaine, Oskar *Government Official*
Landtag Saarland, Postfach 101833, Saarbrucken, 66018, GERMANY

LaFontaine, Patrick (Pat) *Hockey Player*
3 Beach Dr, Lloyd Harbor, NY 11743 USA

LaFosse, Robert *Choreographer*
New York City Ballet, Lincoln Center Plaza, New York, NY 10023 USA

Lafrancois, Roger *Baseball Player*
Boston Red Sox, 64 Aspinook St, Jewett City, CT 06351-1802 USA

LaFrentz, Raef *Basketball Player*
1100 La Paloma Court, Southlake, TX 76092 USA

Lafton, James D *Football Player*
15487 Mesquite Tree Trail, Poway, CA 92064 USA

Laga, Mike *Baseball Player*
Detroit Tigers, 838 Route 6, Shohola, PA 18458-3507 USA

Lagarde, Tom *Basketball Player*
135 Rivington St, New York, NY 10002 USA

Lagasse, Emeril *Chef*
829 Saint Charles Ave, New Orleans, LA 70130 USA

Lagattuta, Bill *Commentator*
CBS-TV, News Dept, 7800 Beverly Blvd,
Los Angeles, CA 90036 USA

Lagerberg, Bengt *Musician*
Motor SE, Gotabergs Gatan 2,
Gothenburg, 400 14, SWEDEN

Lagerfeld, Karl *Fashion Designer*
14 Blvd de la Madeleine, Paris, 75008,
FRANCE

Lagerfelt, Caroline *Actor*
8730 Sunset Blvd, #480, Los Angeles, CA
90069 USA

Laghi, Pio Cardinal *Religious Leader*
Catholic Education Congregation, Piazza
Pio XII 3, Rome, 00193, ITALY

Lago, David *Actor*
Young and the Restless, The, 7800 Beverly
Blvd, Ste 3305, Los Angeles, CA 90036
USA

Lagoo, Shreeram *Actor, Bollywood*
3 Gold Mist 36 Carter Road, Bandra,
Bombay, MS 400 050, INDIA

Lagos, Richard *President*
President's Office, Palacio de la Monedo,
Santiago, CHILE

Lagrow, Lerrin *Baseball Player*
Detroit Tigers, 12271 E Turquoise Ave,
Scottsdale, AZ 85259-5105 USA

Laguardia, Ernesto *Actor*
Gabriel Blanco Iglesias (Mexico), Rio
Balsas 35-32, Colonia Cuauhtemoc, DF,
06500, Mexico

Laguna, Frederica de *Misc*
Quadrangle, 3300 Darby Road #1310,
Haverford, PA 19041 USA

Laguna, Ismael *Boxer*
Panama Zona 6, Entrega General,
PANAMA

LaHaye, Tim *Writer*
Tyndale House Publishers, 351 Executive
Dr, PO Box 80, Wheaton, IL 60189 USA

Lahbib, Simone *Actor*
Ken McReddie Ltd, Paurelle House, 91
Regent St, London, W1R7TB, UNITED
KINGDOM (UK)

Lahiri, Jhumpa *Writer*
Houghton Mifflin, 222 Berkeley St, #700,
Boston, MA 02116 USA

Lahoud, Joe *Baseball Player*
Boston Red Sox, PO Box 2503, New
Preston, CT 06777-0503 USA

Lahould, Emile *President*
Presidential Palace, Baabda, Beirut,
LEBANON

Lahti, Christine *Actor, Director*
237 S Burlingame Ave, Los Angeles, CA
90049 USA

Lahti, Jeff *Baseball Player*
St Louis Cardinals, 4632 Tyler Dr, Hood
River, OR 97031-9742 USA

Lai, Francis *Composer*
23 Rue Franklin, Paris, 75016, FRANCE

Lail, Leah *Actor*
Diverse Talent Group, 1875 Century Park
E #2250, Los Angeles, CA 90067 USA

Laimbeer, Bill *Basketball Player*
4310 S Bay Dr, Orchard Lake, WI 48323
USA

Laine, Cleo *Musician*
Acker's Int'l Jazz, 53 Cambridge
Mansions, London, SW11 4RX, UNITED
KINGDOM (UK)

Laine, Dame Cleo
The Old Rectory Wavendon, Milton
Keynes, ENGLAND, MK17 8LT

Laine, Frankie *Musician, Songwriter*
352 San Gorgonio St, San Diego, CA
92106 USA

Laingen, L Bruce *Diplomat*
5627 Old Chester Road, Bethesda, MD
20814 USA

Laird, Gerald *Baseball Player*
Texas Rangers, 8891 Mac Alpine Rd,
Garden Grove, CA 92841-2321 USA

Laird, Melvin R *Secretary, Business Person*
1730 Rhode Island Ave NW, #406,
Washington, DC 20036 USA

Laird, Peter *Cartoonist*
Teenage Mutant Ninja Turtles, PO Box
417, Haydenville, MA 01039 USA

Laird, Ron
4706 Diane Dr., Ashtabula, OH 44004

Laird, Ronald (Ron) *Track Athlete*
4706 Diane Dr, Ashtabuta, OH 44004
USA

Laithwaite, Eric R *Engineer*
Imperial College, Electrical Engineering
Dept, London, SW7 2BT, UNITED
KINGDOM (UK)

Laitman, Jeffrey *Misc*
Mount Sinai Medical Center, Anatomy
Dept, 1 Lavy Place, New York, NY 10029
USA

LaJoie, Randy *Race Car Driver*
Phoenix Racing, 195 Jones Road,
Spartanburg, SC 29307 USA

Lake, Carnell A *Football Player*
Baltimore Ravens, Ravens Stadium, 11001
Russell St, Baltimore, MD 21230 USA

Lake, Don *Actor, Writer*
Divine Management, 3822 Latrobe St, Los
Angeles, CA 90031

Lake, Greg *Musician*
Asia, 9 Hillgate St, London, W8 7SP,
UNITED KINGDOM (UK)

Lake, James A *Biologist*
University of California, Molecular
Biology Institute, Los Angeles, CA 90024
USA

Lake, Oliver E *Musician*
DL Media, PO Box 2728, Bala Cynwyd,
PA 19004 USA

Lake, Sanoe *Actor*
Jet Set Talent Agency, 2160 Alzanida de
la Playa, La Jolla, CA 92037

Lake, Steve *Baseball Player*
Chicago Cubs, 7402 N 177th Ave,
Waddell, AZ 85355-9320 USA

Laker, Fredrick A *Business Person*
Princess Tower West Sunrise, Box F207
Freeport, Grand Bahamas, BAHAMAS

Laker, Jim *Cricketer*
Oak End, 9 Portlinscale Road Putney,
London, SW15, UNITED KINGDOM (UK)

Laker, Sir Freddie
138 Cheapside, London, ENGLAND,
EC2V 6BL

Laker, Tim *Baseball Player*
Montreal Expos, 673 Azure Hills Dr, Simi
Valley, CA 93065-5518 USA

Lakes, Gary *Opera Singer*
I C M Artists, 40 W 57th St, New York,
NY 10019 USA

Lakin, Christine *Actor*
Platform Public Relations, 2133 Holly
Drive, Los Angeles, CA 90068 USA

Lakner, Yehoshua *Composer*
Postfach 7851, Luceme 7, 6000,
SWITZERLAND

Lakoue, Enoch Devant *Prime Minister*
Prime Minister's Office, Bangui, CENTRAL
AFRICAN REPUBLIC

Lakshmi, Padma *Actor*
Writers and Artists Group Intl (LA), 8383
Wilshire Blvd #550, Beverly Hills, CA
90211 USA

Lalaine *Actor*
Anonymous Content, 8522 National Blvd
#101, Culver City, CA 90232 USA

LaLanne, Jack *Misc*
430 Quitana Road, Morro Bay, CA 93442
USA

Laliberte, Guy *Misc*
Cirque de Soleil, 8400 2nd Ave, Montreal,
QC, H1Z 4M6, CANADA

Laliberte-Bourque, Andree *Director*
Musee du Quebec, 1 Ave Wolfe-
Montcalm, Quebec, QC, G1R 5H3,
CANADA

Lalime, Patrick *Hockey Player*
Saint Louis Blues, Sawis Center, 1401
Clark Ave, Saint Louis, MO 63103 USA

Lalitha, Devi *Actor, Bollywood*
23 Karaneeswar Koil Street, Saidapet,
Chennai, TN 600015, INDIA

Lall, Leah *Actor*
Writers & Artists, 8383 Wilshire Blvd,
#550, Beverly Hills, CA 90211 USA

Lalli, Frank *Editor*
Money Magazine, Editorial Dept,
Rockefeller Center, New York, NY 10020
USA

Lalonde, Donny
2554 Lincoln Blvd. #729, Venice, CA
90291

Lalonde, Larry *Musician*
Figurehead Mgmt, 3470 19th St, San
Francisco, CA 94110 USA

Lama, Dalai *Religious Leader, Nobel Prize
Laureate*
Office of His Holiness the Dalai Lama,
Thekchen Choeling, McLeod Ganj,
Dharamsala, H P, 176219, INDIA

Lamabe, Jack *Baseball Player*
Pittsburgh Pirates, 16224 Antietam Ave,
Baton Rouge, LA 70817-3148 USA

Lamacchia, Al *Baseball Player*
St Louis Browns, 13515 Vista Bonita, San
Antonio, TX 78216-2203 USA

Lamar, Dwight (Bo) *Basketball Player*
103 Claire St, Lafayette, LA 70507 USA

Lamas, Lorenzo *Actor*
2149 E Live Oak Dr, Los Angeles, CA
90068 USA

Lamb, Allan J *Cricketer*
Lamb Assoc, 4 Saint Giles St, #400,
Northampton, NN1 1JB, UNITED
KINGDOM (UK)

Lamb, David *Baseball Player*
Tampa Bay Devil Rays, 821 Jensen St,
Livemore, CA 94550-3630 USA

Lamb, Dennis *Diplomat*
19 Rue de Franqueville, Paris, 75016,
FRANCE

Lamb, John *Baseball Player*
Pittsburgh Pirates, Sharon Valley Road,
Sharon, CT 06069 USA

Lamb, Ray *Baseball Player*
Los Angeles Dodgers, 3 Corte Tallista, San
Clemente, CA 92673-6863 USA

Lamb Jr, Willis E *Nobel Prize Laureate*
315 Red Rock Dr, Sedona, AZ 86351 USA

Lamberg, Adam *Actor*
Firm, The, 9465 Wilshire Blvd, Beverly
Hills, CA 90212 USA

Lambert, Christophe *Actor*
9 Ave Trempley, C/Lui, Geneva, 1209,
SWITZERLAND

Lambert, Christopher *Actor, Producer,
Writer*
Brillstein-Grey Entertainment, 9150
Wilshire Blvd #350, Beverly Hills, CA
90212 USA

Lambert, Jack
2121 George Halas Dr. NW, Canton, OH
44708-2699

Lambert, Jerry
PO Box 25371, Charlotte, NC 28212

Lambert, John H (Jack) *Football Player*
RR 2 Box, 101A, Worthington, PA 16262
USA

Lambert, L W
Rt. #1, Olin, NC 28860 USA

Lambert, Mary M *Director*
International Creative Mgmt, 8942
Wilshire Blvd, #219, Beverly Hills, CA
90211 USA

Lambert, Phyllis *Architect*
Centre d'Architecture, 1920 Rue Baile,
Montreal, QC, H3H 2S6, CANADA

Lambert, Sheila *Basketball Player*
Charlotte Sting, 100 Hive Dr, Charlotte,
NC 28217 USA

Lambrecht, Dietrich R *Engineer*
Rathenaustr 11, Mulheim an der Ruhr,
45470, GERMANY

Lambro, Phillip *Composer*
Trigram Music, 1888 Century Park East,
#10, Los Angeles, CA 90067 USA

Lambros, Andy
9310 Topanga Canyon Blvd. #125,
Chatsworth, CA 91311

Lambsdorff, Otto *Government Official*
Strasschensweg 7, Bon, 53113,
GERMANY

Lamelin, Stephanie *Actor*
Writers and Artists Group Intl (LA), 8383
Wilshire Blvd #550, Beverly Hills, CA
90211 USA

Lamm, Julie
Box B, Aspen, CO 81612-7402

Lamm, Richard D *Ex-Governor*
University of Denver, Public Policy
Center, Denver, CO 80208 USA

Lamm, Robert *Musician*
Air Tight Mgmt, 115 West Road,
Winchester Center, CT 06098 USA

Lammers, Esmee *Director, Writer*
Features Creative Mgmt, Entrepotdok 76A,
Amsterdam, AD, 101, NETHERLANDS

Lamonica, Darryl
8796 N. 6th St., Fresno, CA 93720

Lamonica, Darryl P *Football Player*
Mad Bomber Fishing Lures, 8796 N 6th
St, Fresno, CA 93720 USA

Lamonica, Roberto de *Artist*
Rua Anibal de Mendanca 180, AP 202,
Rio de Janeiro, RJ, ZC-37, BRAZIL

Lamont, Gene W *Baseball Player*
Detroit Tigers, 5194 Siesta Woods Dr,
Sarasota, FL 34242-1457 USA

Lamont, Norman S H *Government
Official*
Balli Group PLC, 5 Stanhope Gate,
London, W1Y 5LA, UNITED KINGDOM
(UK)

Lamontagne, Donald A *General*
Commander, Air University, Maxwell Air
Force Base, AL 36112 USA

LaMorte, Robia *Actor*
Identity Talent Agency (ID), 2050 Bundy
Dr #200, Los Angeles, CA 90025 USA

LaMotta, Jake *Boxer*
400 E 57th St, New York, NY 10022 USA

LaMotta, Vikki *Model*
PO Box 152, Deerfield Beach, FL 33443
USA

Lamoureux, Robert
29 Bd. d'Aulteuil, Bologne, FRANCE,
92100

Lamp, Dennis *Baseball Player*
Chicago Cubs, 22751 El Prado Apt 4303,
Rancho Santa Margarita, CA 92688-3829
USA

Lamp, Jeff *Basketball Player*
4971 Credit River Dr, Savage, MN 55378
USA

Lampa, Rachael
25 Music Sq. W., Nashville, TN 37203

Lampard, Keith *Baseball Player*
Houston Astros, 842 NE 74th Ave,
Portland, OR 97213-6233 USA

Lamparski, Richard *Writer*
216 N Milpas St, #G, Santa Barbara, CA
93103 USA

Lampert, Zohra *Actor*
Don Buchwald, 6500 Wilshire Blvd,
#2200, Los Angeles, CA 90048 USA

Lampkin, Tom *Baseball Player*
Cleveland Indians, 3810 SE 153rd Ct,
Vancouver, WA 98683-5313 USA

Lampley, Jim *Sportscaster*
PO Box 763, Rancho Santa Fe, CA 92067
USA

Lampson, Butler W *Engineer*
Microsoft Research Corp, 16011 NE 36th
Way, Redmond, WA 98073 USA

Lampton, Michael *Astronaut*
University of California, Space Science
Laboratory, Berkeley, CA 94720 USA

Lanbros, Andy
9040 Topanga Canyon Blvd. #200, West
Hills, CA 91304-1435

Lancaster, Les *Baseball Player*
Chicago Cubs, 22116 Saratoga Dr,
Athens, AL 35613-2318 USA

Lance, Bert
PO Box 637, Calhoun, GA 30701

Lance, Dirk *Musician*
ArtistDirect, 10900 Wilshire Blvd, #1400,
Los Angeles, CA 90024 USA

Lance, Gary *Baseball Player*
Kansas City Royals, 212 Sunset Cir,
Prosperity, SC 29127-8426 USA

Lancelotti, Rick *Baseball Player*
San Diego Padres, 5190 Thompson Rd,
Clarence, NY 14031-1127 USA

Landau, Irvin *Editor*
Consumer Reports Magazine, Editorial
Dept, 101 Truman Ave, Yonkers, NY
10703 USA

Landau, Jacob *Artist*
2 Pine Dr, Roosevelt, NJ 08555 USA

Landau, Juliet *Actor*
Sweeney Management, 8755 Lookout
Mountain Avenue, Los Angeles, CA 90046
USA

Landau, Martin *Actor*
PO Box 10959, Beverly Hills, CA 90213
USA

Landau, Saul *Writer*
Institute for Policy Studies, 1601
Connecticut Ave NW, Washington, DC
20009 USA

Landeau, Aleksia *Actor*
Metropolitan Talent Agency (MTA), 4526
Wilshire Blvd, Los Angeles, CA 90010
USA

Landecker, John Records
MAGIC 104.3 WJMK, 180 N. Stetson
Suite 900, Prudential 2 Building, Chicago,
IL 60601

Lander, Benjamin *Educator*
American University, President's Office,
Washington, DC 20016 USA

Lander, David L *Actor*
5819 Saint Laurent Dr, Agoura Hills, CA
90301 USA

Landers, Andy *Coach*
University of Georgia, Athletic Dept,
Athens, GA 30602 USA

Landers, Audrey *Actor, Musician*
4048 Las Palmas Dr, Sarasota, FL 34238
USA

Landers, Judy *Actor*
Media Artists Group, 6300 Wilshire Blvd,
#1470, Los Angeles, CA 90048 USA

Landes, David S *Historian*
24 Highland St, Cambridge, MA 02138
USA

Landes, Michael
10100 Santa Monica Blvd. #2500, Los
Angeles, CA 90067

Landesberg, Steve *Actor*
Mucci & Lagnese Inc, 6300 Wilshire Blvd, #1190, Los Angeles, CA 90048 USA

Landestoy, Rafael *Baseball Player*
Los Angeles Dodgers, 3121 SW 140th Avenue, Miami, FL 33175 USA

Landey, Nina *Actor*
Bauman Redanty & Shaul Agency, 5757 Wilshire Blvd #473, Los Angeles, CA 90036 USA

Landgrebe, Ludrun
Goethstr. 17, Munich, GERMANY, D-80336

Landi, Sal *Actor*
AKA Talent Agency, 6310 San Vicente Blvd #200, Los Angeles, CA 90048 USA

Landis, Bill *Baseball Player*
Kansas City A's, 625 E Sycamore Dr, Hanford, CA 93230-1443 USA

Landis, Jim *Baseball Player*
Chicago White Sox, 203 Alchemy Way, Napa, CA 94558-7214 USA

Landis, John D *Director*
1168 San Ysidre Dr, Beverly Hills, CA 90210 USA

Landon, Howard C R *Writer*
Chateau de Foncoussieres, Rabastens, Tarn, 81800, FRANCE

Landreaux, Ken *Baseball Player*
California Angeles, 608 Leonard St, Montebello, CA 90640-1514 USA

Landres, Paul
5343 Amestoy Ave, Encino, CA 91316

Landreth, Larry *Baseball Player*
Montreal Expos, 116 W 66th St Apt 39H, Stratford, ON N5A 2W8, CANADA

Landrieu, Mary *Senator*
7523 N Jefferson Pl Cir, Baton Rouge, LA 70809-7644 USA

Landrieu, Moon *Secretary*
4301 S Prieur St, New Orleans, LA 70125 USA

Landrith, Hobie *Baseball Player*
Cincinnati Reds, 1462 Nome Ct, Sunnyvale, CA 94087-4264 USA

Landrum, Bill *Baseball Player*
Cincinnati Reds, 715 Sharpe Rd, Columbia, SC 29203-9347 USA

Landrum, Ced *Baseball Player*
Chicago Cubs, 2412 Hillview Dr, Fort Worth, TX 76119-2723 USA

Landrum, Joe *Baseball Player*
Brooklyn Dodgers, 715 Sharpe Rd, Columbia, SC 29203-9347 USA

Landrum, Tito *Baseball Player*
St Louis Cardinals, 160 W 66th St Apt 39H, New York, NY 10023-6564 USA

Landry, Ali *Actor, Model*
United Talent Agency, 9560 Wilshire Blvd, #500, Beverly Hills, CA 90212 USA

Landry, Gregory P (Greg) *Football Player, Football Coach*
133 Melanie Lane, Troy, MI 48098 USA

Landsburg, Valerie *Actor*
22745 Chamera Lane, Topanga Canyon, CA 90290 USA

Landy, Bernard *Government Official*
Government du Quebec, 885 Grand Allee Est, Quebec, QC, GLA 1A2, CANADA

Landzaat, Andre
7500 Devista Dr, Los Angeles, CA 90046

Lane, Abbe *Actor, Musician*
444 N Faring Road, Los Angeles, CA 90077 USA

Lane, Charles
321 Gretna Green Way, Los Angeles, CA 90049

Lane, Cristy *Musician*
PO Box 654, Madison, TN 37116 USA

Lane, Diane *Actor*
Hyler Management, 20 Ocean Park Blvd #25, Santa Monica, CA 90405 USA

Lane, Dick *Baseball Player*
Chicago White Sox, 8824 Faircrest Dr, Las Vegas, NV 89134-8574 USA

Lane, John R (Jack) *Misc*
San Francisco Museum of Modem Art, 151 3rd St, San Francisco, CA 94103 USA

Lane, Johnny
5048 Casa Dr., Tarzana, CA 91356-4422

Lane, Kenneth Jay *Fashion Designer*
Kenneth Jay Lane Inc, 20 W 37th St, New York, NY 10018 USA

Lane, Lilas *Actor*
Impact Artists Group LLC, 10508 La Maida St, Toluca Woods, CA 91601 USA

Lane, MacArthur *Football Player*
3238 Knowland Ave, Oakland, CA 94619 USA

Lane, Malcolm D *Misc*
5607 Roxbuy Place, Baltimore, MD 21209 USA

Lane, Marv *Baseball Player*
Detroit Tigers, 40164 Gulliver Dr, Sterling Heights, MI 48310-1729 USA

Lane, Melvin B *Publisher*
99 Tallwood Court, Menlo Park, CA 94027 USA

Lane, Mike *Cartoonist*
Baltimore Sun, Editorial Dept, 501 N Calvert St, Baltimore, MD 21202 USA

Lane, Nathan *Actor, Musician*
Creative Artists Agency, 9830 Wilshire Blvd, Beverly Hills, CA 90212 USA

Lane Jr, Lawrence W *Diplomat, Publisher*
3000 Sandhill Road, #215, Menlo Park, CA 94025 USA

Lane of St Ippollitts, Geoffrey D *Judge*
Royal Courts of Justice, Strand, London, WC2A 2LL, UNITED KINGDOM (UK)

Lanegan, Mark *Musician*
Helter Skelter Plaza, 535 Kings Road, London, SW1O 0S, UNITED KINGDOM (UK)

Laneuville, Eric *Actor*
5138 W Slauson Ave, Los Angeles, CA 90056 USA

Laney, James T *Educator, Diplomat*
2015 Grand Prix Dr NE, Atlanta, GA 30345 USA

Lang, Belinda *Actor*
Ken McReddie, 91 Regent St, London, W1R 7TB, UNITED KINGDOM (UK)

Lang, Chip *Baseball Player*
Montreal Expos, 985 Homer Ave, Pittsburgh, PA 15237-2208 USA

Lang, Don *Baseball Player*
Cincinnati Reds, 5700 Kirkside Dr Apt F, Bakersfield, CA 93309-3669 USA

Lang, Ed *Photographer*
Elysium Growth Press, 16255 Ventura Blvd, #515, Encino, CA 91436 USA

Lang, George C *War Hero*
3786 Clark St, Seaford, NY 11783 USA

Lang, Helmut *Fashion Designer*
Michele Morgan, 184 Rue Saint-Maur, Paris, 75010, FRANCE

Lang, Jack *Government Official*
Mairie, Blois, 41000, FRANCE

Lang, Jack *Writer*
Baseball Writers Assn, 36 Brookfield Road, Northport, NY 11768 USA

Lang, Jonny *Musician*
Blue Sky Artists, 761 Washington Ave N, Minneapolis, MN 55401 USA

Lang, June *Actor*
12756 Kahlenberg Lane, North Hollywood, CA 91607 USA

Lang, Katherine Kelly *Actor, Model*
Agency for Performing Arts, 9200 Sunset Blvd, #900, Los Angeles, CA 90069 USA

Lang, KD *Musician, Actor*
Direct Management Group, 947 N La Cienega Blvd #G, Los Angeles, CA 90064 USA

Lang, Pearl *Dancer, Choreographer*
382 Central Park West, New York, NY 10025 USA

Lang, Robert *Hockey Player*
PO Box 663, Diablo, CA 94528 USA

Lang, Stephen *Actor*
Brillstein-Grey Entertainment, 9150 Wilshire Blvd #350, Beverly Hills, CA 90212 USA

Langbo, Arnold G *Business Person*
Kellogg Co, 1 Kellogg Square, PO Box 3599, Battle Creek, MI 49016 USA

Langdon, Brooke
1180 S. Beverly Dr. #608, Los Angeles, CA 90035

Langdon, Harry *Photographer*
PO Box 16816, Beverly Hills, CA 90209 USA

Langdon, Michael
34 Arnham Ct. Grand Ave., Hove E. Sussex, ENGLAND

Langdon, Sue Ane *Actor*
24115 Long Valley Road, Hidden Hills, CA 91302 USA

Lange, Allison
3500 W. Olive Ave. #1400, Burbank, CA 91505

Lange, Andre *Athlete*
BSD, An der Schiessstatte 4, Berchtesgaden, 83471, GERMANY

Lange, Andrew *Astronomer*
University of California, Astronomy Dept, Berkeley, CA 94720 USA

Lange, Bonnie
PO Box 3827, Beverly Hills, CA 90212

Lange, David R *Prime Minister*
14 Ambury Road, Mangere Bridge, Auckland, NEW ZEALAND

Lange, Detective Tom
12021 Wilshire Blvd. #846, Los Angeles, CA 90025

Lange, Dick *Baseball Player*
California Angels, 39744 Salvatore Dr, Sterling Heights, MI 48313-5165 USA

Lange, Hope *Actor*
10601 Wilshire Blvd, #301, Los Angeles, CA 90024 USA

Lange, Jessica *Actor*
Creative Artists Agency LCC (CAA-LA), 9830 Wilshire Blvd, Beverly Hills, CA 90212 USA

Lange, Niklaus
4526 Wilshire Blvd., Los Angeles, CA 90010

Lange, Stephan *Actor*

Lange, Ted *Actor*
6950 McLennan Ave, Van Nuys, CA 91406 USA

Lange, Thomas *Athlete*
ratzeburger Ruderclub, Domhof 57, Ratzburg, 23909, GERMANY

Langella, Frank *Actor*
108 Sunlit Dr W, Santa Fe, NM 87508 USA

Langen, Christoph *Athlete*
BC Onterhaching, Ottobrunner Str 16, Unterhaching, 82008, GERMANY

Langencamp, Reather *Actor*
156 F St SE, Washington, DC 20003 USA

Langenkamp, Heather *Actor*
Harrison Cheung & Associates, 12540 Braddock Drive, Suite 121, Los Angeles, CA 90066 USA

Langer, A J *Actor*
Gersh Agency, 232 N Canon Dr, Beverly Hills, CA 90210 USA

Langer, Alois A *Inventor*
111 Saddlebrook Dr, Harrison City, PA 15636 USA

Langer, Bernhard *Golfer*
1120 SW 21st Lane, Boca Raton, FL 33486 USA

Langer, James J (Jim) *Football Player*
14280 Wolfram St NW, Ramsey, MN 55303 USA

Langer, James S *Physicist*
1130 Las Canoas Lane, Santa Barbara, CA 93105 USA

Langer, Robert *Doctor*
Massachusetts Institute of Technology, Chem Engineer Dept, Cambridge, MA 02139 USA

Langer, Robert S *Engineer, Inventor*
Massachusetts Institute of Technology, Engineering Dept, Cambridge, MA 02139 USA

Langerhans, Ryan *Baseball Player*
Atlanta Braves, 2311 Falcon Dr, Round Rock, TX 78681-2718 USA

Langevin, Dave *Hockey Player*
2224 Copperfield Dr, Saint Paul, MN 55120 USA

Langford, Frances *Actor, Musician*
PO Box 96, Jensen Beach, FL 34958 USA

Langford, John *Engineer*
Aurora Flight Sciences, 9950 Wakerman Dr, Manassas, VA 20110 USA

Langford, Rick *Baseball Player*
Pittsburgh Pirates, 8330 9th Avenue Ter NW, Bradenton, FL 34209-9678 USA

Langham, C Antonio *Football Player*
PO Box 232, Town Creek, AL 35672 USA

Langham, Michael *Director*
Julliard School, Drama Division, 144 W 66th St, New York, NY 10023 USA

Langham, Wallace *Actor*
10264 Rochester Ave, Los Angeles, CA 90024 USA

Langham, Wally *Actor*
United Talent Agency (UTA), 9560 Wilshire Blvd, Beverly Hills, CA 90212 USA

Langkow, Daymond *Hockey Player*
7940 E Quill Lane, Scottsdale, AZ 85255 USA

Langley, H Desmond A *Governor, General*
Governor's Office, 11 Langton Hill, Pembroke, Hamilton, HM 13, BERMUDA

Langley, Roger *Skier*
Broad St, Barre, MA 01005 USA

Langlois, Lisa *Actor*
House of Representatives, 400 S Beverly Dr, #101, Beverly Hills, CA 90212 USA

Langlois, Paul *Musician*
Management Trust, 219 Dufferin St, #309B, Toronto, ON M5K 3J1, CANADA

Langlois Jr, Albert *Hockey Player*
2473 Crest View Dr, Los Angeles, CA 90046 USA

Langston, J William *Doctor*
Parkinson's Foundation, 2444 Moorpark Ave, San Jose, CA 95128 USA

Langston, Mark E *Baseball Player*
Seattle Mariners, 2511 N Skytop Court, Orange, CA 92867-6492 USA

Langston, Murray *Actor, Comedian*
Entertainment Alliance, PO Box 4734, Santa Rosa, CA 95402 USA

Langton, Brooke *Actor*
United Talent Agency (UTA), 9560 Wilshire Blvd, Beverly Hills, CA 90212 USA

Langton, Brooke *Actor*
Rigberg Roberts Rugolo, 1180 S Beverly Dr, #601, Los Angeles, CA 90035 USA

Langway, Rod C *Hockey Player*
3613 Brook Road, Richmond, VA 23227 USA

Lanier, Chris *Artist*
Fantagraphics Books, 7563 Lake City Way, Seattle, WA 98115 USA

Lanier, H Max *Baseball Player*
St Louis Cardinals, 11250 SW 186th Cir, Dunnellon, FL 34432-4528 USA

Lanier, Hal *Baseball Player*
San Francisco Giants, 3270 Countryside View Drive, Saint Cloud, FL 34772 USA

Lanier, Harold C (Hal) *Misc*
19380 SW 90th Lane Road, Dunnellon, FL 34432 USA

Lanier, Jaron *Engineer*
Advanced Network Services, 200 Business Park Dr, Armonk, NY 10504 USA

Lanier, Rimp *Baseball Player*
Cleveland Indians, 4515 E Frontenac Dr, Cleveland, OH 44128-5004 USA

Lanier, Willie E *Football Player*
2911 E Brigstock Road, Midlothian, VA 23113 USA

Lanier Jr, Robert J (Bob) *Basketball Player, Coach*
National Basketball Assn, TeamUp Program, 645 5th Ave, New York, NY 10022 USA

Lanin, Lester *Musician*
Ted Schmidt Assoc, 901 Winding River Road, Vero Beach, FL 32963 USA

Lanker, Brian *Journalist*
1993 Kimberly Dr, Eugene, OR 97405 USA

Lankford, Frank *Baseball Player*
Los Angeles Dodgers, 104 Lakeview Ave NE, Atlanta, GA 30305-3725 USA

Lankford, Kim *Actor*
House of Representatives, 400 S Beverly Dr, #101, Beverly Hills, CA 90212 USA

Lankford, Ray *Baseball Player*
St Louis Cardinals, 15 Terry Hill Ln, Saint Louis, MO 63131 USA

Lanois, Daniel *Musician, Actor*
Monterey Peninsula Artists (Monterey), 509 Hartnell St, Monterey, CA 93940 USA

LanSala, James *Misc*
Amalgamated Transit Union, 5025 Wisconsin Ave NW, Washington, DC 20016 USA

Lansbury, Angela *Actor, Musician*
635 N Bonhill Rd, Los Angeles, CA 90049 USA

Lansbury, David *Actor*
Don Buchwald, 6500 Wilshire Blvd, #2200, Los Angeles, CA 90048 USA

Lansdale, Joe R
113 Timberridge St, Nacogdoches, TX 75961 USA

Lansdowne, J Fenwick *Artist*
941 Victoria Ave, Victoria, BC V8S 4N6, CANADA

Lansford, Camey *Baseball Player*
California Angels, 1701 Homestead Rd, Santa Clara, CA 95050-5257 USA

Lansford, Jody *Baseball Player*
San Diego Padres, 5730 San Lorenzo Dr, San Jose, CA 95123-2967 USA

Lansing, Mike *Baseball Player*
Montreal Expos, 9691 Sun Meadow St, Highlands Ranch, CO 80129-6925 USA

Lansing, Sherry L *Producer*
10451 Bellagio Road, Los Angeles, CA 90077 USA

Lant, Jeffrey *Business Person*

Lanvin, Bernard *Fashion Designer*
22 Rue du Faubourg Saint Honore, Paris, 70008, FRANCE

Lanz, David *Musician*
Siddons Assoc, 14930 Ventura Blvd,
#205, Sherman Oaks, CA 91403 USA

Lanza, Suzanne
345 N. Maple Dr. #397, Beverly Hills, CA
90210

Laoretti, Larry *Golfer*
10567 Whooping Crane Way, Palm City,
FL 34990 USA

LaPaglia, Anthony *Actor*
International Creative Mgmt, 8942
Wilshire Blvd, #219, Beverly Hills, CA
90211 USA

LaPaglia, Jonathan
1505 10th St., Santa Monica, CA 90401

Lapaine, Daniel *Actor*
Envision Entertainment, 409 Santa Monica
Blvd, Santa Monica, CA 90401 USA

Laperriere, J Jacques H *Hockey Player,
Coach*
1983 Nice Chomedey Estate, Laval, QC,
H7S 1G5, CANADA

Lapham, Lewis H *Editor*
Harper's Magazine, Editorial Dept, 666
Broadway, New York, NY 10012 USA

Lapidus, Alan *Architect*
Lapidus Assoc, 43 W 61st St, New York,
NY 10023 USA

Lapidus, Edmond (Ted) *Fashion Designer*
66 Blvd Maurice-Barres, Neuilly-sur-Seine,
92200, FRANCE

Lapierre, Dominique *Historian*
Les Bignoles, Ramatuelle, 83350, FRANCE

Lapine, James E *Writer, Director*
85 Mill River Road, South Salem, NY
10590 USA

LaPlaca, Alison *Actor*
1614 N Argyle Ave, Hollywood, CA
90028 USA

LaPlanche, Rosemary *Actor*
13914 Hartsook St, Sherman Oaks, CA
91423 USA

LaPlante, Lynda *Writer*
Random House, 1745 Broadway, #B1,
New York, NY 10019 USA

Lapli, John *General*
Governor General's House, Box 252,
Honiara, GUADACANAL SOLOMON
ISLANDS

Lapointe, Guy
4568 E. des Bousquets, Augustin,
CANADA, PQ 6A3 1C4

Laport, Osvaldo *Actor*
Telefe - Argentina, Pavon 2444
(C1248AAT), Buenos Aires, ARGENTINA

LaPorte, Danny *Race Car Driver*
949 Via Del Monte, Palos Verdes Estates,
CA 90274 USA

Laposata, Joseph S *General*
Battle Monuments Commission, 20
Massachusetts, Washington, DC 20314
USA

Lapotaire, Jane *Actor*
92 Oxford Gardens, #C, London, W10,
UNITED KINGDOM (UK)

Lappalainen, Markku *Musician*
Island Def Jam Records, 8920 Sunset Blvd,
#200, Los Angeles, CA 90069 USA

Lappas, Steve *Coach*
Villanova University, Athletic Dept,
Villanova, PA 19085 USA

Laprade, Edgar *Hockey Player*
12 Shuniah St., Thunder Bay, ON P7A
2Y8, CANADA

LaPraed, Ronald (Ron) *Musician*
Management Assoc, 1920 Benson Ave,
Saint Paul, MN 55116 USA

Laquer, Walter *Historian*
Georgetown University, Strategic Studies,
1800 K St NW, Washington, DC 20006
USA

Lara, Brian C *Cricketer*
West Indies Cricket Club, PO Box 616,
Saint John's, ANTIGUA

Lara, Claude Autant
66 rue Lepic, Paris, FRANCE, 75018

Lara, Joe *Actor*
Peter Giagni Management, 8981 Sunset
Blvd #103, West Hollywood, CA 90069

Laragh, John H *Educator, Doctor*
435 E 70th St, New York, NY 10021 USA

Laraki, Azeddine *Prime Minister*
Islamic Conference, Kilo 6, Mecca Road,
Jeddah, 21411, SAUDI ARABIA

Larch, John *Actor*
4506 Varna Ave, Sherman Oaks, CA
91423 USA

Lardner Jr, George *Journalist*
Washington Post, Editorial Dept, 1150
15th St NW, Washington, DC 20071 USA

Lardy, Henry A *Misc*
1829 Thorstrand Road, Madison, WI
53705 USA

Laredo, Jaime *Musician*
Harold Holt, 31 Sinclair Road, London,
W14 0NS, UNITED KINGDOM (UK)

Laredo, Ruth *Musician*
I C M Artists, 40 W 57th St, New York,
NY 10019 USA

Larena, John *Designer*
Mirisch Agency, 1801 Century Park E
#1801, Los Angeles, CA 90067 USA

Laresca, Vincent *Actor*
Writers and Artists Group Intl (LA), 8383
Wilshire Blvd #550, Beverly Hills, CA
90211 USA

Largent, Steve M *Football Player*
Wireless Trade Assn, 1250 Connecticut
Ave NW, Washington, DC 20036 USA

Larionov, Igor *Hockey Player*
Detroit Red Wings, Joe Louis Arena, 600
Civic Center Dr, Detroit, MI 48226 USA

Lark, Maria *Actor*
Frontier Booking International, 1560
Broadway #1110, New York, NY 10036
USA

Larkin, Barry L *Baseball Player*
3348 Brinton Trail, Cincinnati, OH 45241
USA

Larkin, Gene *Baseball Player*
9496 Abbott Ct, Eden Prairie, MN 55347
USA

Larkin, Patty *Musician, Songwriter*
SRO Artists, 6629 University Ave, #206,
Middleton, WI 53562 USA

Larkin, Sheila
9229 Sunset Blvd. #311, Los Angeles, CA
90069

Larmore, Jennifer *Opera Singer*
I C M Artists, 40 W 57th St, New York,
NY 10019 USA

Larner, Stevan *Cinematographer*
1209 Ballard Canyon Road, Solvang, CA
93463 USA

Laro, David *Judge*
US Tax Court, 400 2nd St NW,
Washington, DC 20217 USA

LaRoche, Philippe *Skier*
Club de Ski Acrobatique, Lac Beauport,
QC, G0A 20Q, CANADA

LaRocque, Gene R *Government Official*
5015 Macomb St NW, Washington, DC
20016 USA

Laroque, Michele *Actor*
Artmedia, 20 Ave Rapp, Paris, 75007,
FRANCE

LaRosa, Julius *Musician*
67 Sycamore Lane, Irvington, NY 10533
USA

Larose, Claude D *Hockey Player*
5060 NW 54th St, Coconut Creek, FL
33073 USA

Larouch, Pierre
116 Lancaster Ave., Pittsburgh, PA 15228-
2354

LaRouche, Lyndon
15820 Round Top Lane, Round Hill, VA
20141-2052

Larouche, Pierre *Hockey Player*
112 Vanderbilt Dr, Pittsburgh, PA 15243
USA

LaRouche Jr, Lyndon H *Politician*
18520 Round Top Lane, Round Hill, VA
20141 USA

Larroquette, John *Actor*
Port Street Films, 15332 Antioch St, PO
Box 318, Pacific Palisades, CA 90272
USA

Larry, Wendy *Coach*
Old Dominion University, Athletic Dept,
Norfolk, VA 23529 USA

Larsen, Art *Tennis Player*
203 Lorraine Blvd, San Leandro, CA
94577 USA

Larsen, Bruce *Editor*
Vancouver Sun, 2250 Granville St,
Vancouver, BC V6H 3G2, CANADA

Larsen, Don
Box 2863, Hayden Lake, ID 83835-2863

Larsen, Don J *Baseball Player*
PO Box 2863, Hayden Lake, ID 83835
USA

Larsen, Gary L *Football Player*
4612 14 1st Court SE, Bellevue, WA
98006 USA

Larsen, Libby *Composer*
2205 Kenwood Parkway, Minneapolis,
MN 55405 USA

Larsen, Paul E *Religious Leader*
Evangelical Convenant Church, 5101 N
Francisco Ave, Chicago, IL 60625 USA

Larsen, Ralph S *Business Person*
Johnson & Johnson, 1 Johnson & Johnson Plaza, New Brunswick, NJ 08933 USA

Larson, April U *Religious Leader*
Evangelical Lutheran Church, PO Box 4900, Rochester, MN 55903 USA

Larson, Brie *Actor*
Saffron Management, 1701 N Beverly Dr, Beverly Hills, CA 90210 USA

Larson, Charles R (Chuck) *Admiral*
591 Coover Road, Annapolis, MD 21401 USA

Larson, Darrell
8380 Melrose Ave. #207, Los Angeles, CA 90069

Larson, Eric *Publisher*
TV Guide Magazine, 100 Matsonford Road, Radnor, PA 19080 USA

Larson, Erik *Writer*
Crown Publishers, 225 Park Ave S, New York, NY 10003 USA

Larson, Gary *Cartoonist*
Universal Press Syndicate, 4520 Main St, Kansas City, MO 64111 USA

Larson, Gerald (Jerry Lacy) *Actor*
Sutton Barth & Vennari Inc, 145 S Fairfax #310, Los Angeles, CA 90036 USA

Larson, Jack *Actor*
449 N Skyewiay Road, Los Angeles, CA 90049 USA

Larson, Jill *Actor*
Innovative Artists, 1505 10th St, Santa Monica, CA 90401 USA

Larson, Lance *Swimmer*
41 Balboa Coves, Newport Beach, CA 92663 USA

Larson, Peter N *Business Person*
Brunswick Corp, 1 N Field Court, Lake Forest, IL 60045 USA

Larson, Reed
14334 Fairway Dr., Eden Prairie, MN 55344-1956

Larson, Wolf *Actor*
10600 Holman Ave, # 1, Los Angeles, CA 90024 USA

Larsson, Lars-Eric
Master Ernsts gata 6A, Helsingborg, SWEDEN, S-25435

Larsson, Magnus
Pier House Strand on the Green Chiswick, London, ENGLAND, W4

Larter, Al
6100 Wilshire Blvd. #1170, Los Angeles, CA 90048

Larter, Ali *Actor*
Water Street Management, 5225 Wilshire Blvd #615, Los Angeles, CA 90036 USA

LaRue, Florence *Actor, Musician*
Sterling Winters, 10877 Wilshire Blvd, #15, Los Angeles, CA 90024 USA

Larue, Renee *Adult Film Star*
Atlas Multimedia Inc, 22940 Burbank Blvd, Woodland Hills, CA 91367 USA

LaRue Callahan, Eva *Actor*
11661 San Vicente Blvd, #307, Los Angeles, CA 90049 USA

LaRussa, Tony
338 Golden Meadow Pl., Alamo, CA 94507

LaRusso, Vincent
419 Park Ave. So. #1009, New York, NY 10016

Lary, Frank S *Baseball Player*
11813 Baseball Dr, Northport, AL 35475 USA

Lary, R Yale *Football Player*
6366 Lansdale Road, Fort Worth, TX 76116 USA

Las Ketchup *Music Group*
Sony Music Miami, 605 Lincoln Rd, Miami Beach, FL 33138 USA

LaSalle, Denise *Musician*
CAI Entertainment Agency, PO Box 9267, Jackson, MS 39286 USA

LaSalle, Eriq *Actor, Director*
PO Box 2369, Beverly Hills, CA 90213 USA

Lascher, David *Actor*
Untitled Entertainment (LA), 8436 W 3rd St #650, Los Angeles, CA 90048 USA

LaScola, Judith *Artist*
Compositions Gallery, 317 Sutter St, San Francisco, CA 94108 USA

Lash, Bill *Skier*
17438 Bothell Way NE, #C305, Bothell, WA 98011 USA

Lasker, Dee Dee *Golfer*
1665 Chamisal Court, Carlsbad, CA 92009 USA

Lasorda, Thomas C (Tommy) *Baseball Player*
1473 W Maxzim Ave, Fullerton, CA 92833 USA

Lasorda, Tommy
1473 West Maxzim Avenue, Fullerton, CA 92633 USA

Lassally, Walter *Cinematographer*
6 Ladbroke Gardens, London, W11 2PT, UNITED KINGDOM (UK)

Lasser, Louise *Actor, Comedian*
200 E 71st St, #20C, New York, NY 10021 USA

Lasseter, John *Director, Animator*
Pixar, 1200 Park Ave, Emeryville, CA 94608 USA

Lassez, Sarah *Actor*
Innovative Artists, 1505 10th St, Santa Monica, CA 90401 USA

Lassick, Sydney
2734 Bellevue, Los Angeles, CA 90026

Lassie
16133 Soledad Canyon Rd, Canyon Country, CA 91351

Lassiter, Amanda *Basketball Player*
Minnesota Lunx, Target Center, 600 1st Ave N, Minneapolis, MN 55403 USA

Last, James *Musician*
Schone Aussicht 16, Hamburg, 22085, GERMANY

Laster, Danny B *Scientist*
Hruska Meal Animal Research Center, PO Box 166, Clay Center, NE 68933 USA

Laszlo, Andrew *Cinematographer*
15838 Magnolia Blvd, Encino, CA 91436 USA

Lateef, Yusef *Composer, Musician*
Rhino Records, 10635 Santa Monica Blvd, Los Angeles, CA 90025 USA

Latham, David *Astronomer*
Harvard University, Astronomy Dept, Cambridge, MA 02138 USA

Latham, Louise *Actor*
2125 Piedras Dr, Santa Barbara, CA 93108 USA

Lathan, Sanaa *Actor*
Brookside Artists Management (NY), 250 W 57th St #2303, New York, NY 10107 USA

Lathan, Stan *Director, Writer, Producer*
Simmons Lathan Media Group, 6100 Wilshire Blvd #1111, Los Angeles, CA 90048 USA

Lathiere, Bernard *Business Person*
Airbus Industries, 5 Ave de Villiers, Paris, 75017, FRANCE

Lathon, Lamar L *Football Player*
14803 Via del Norte, Houston, TX 77083 USA

Latifah, Queen *Musician, Actor*

Latimore *Musician*
Rodgers Redding, 1048 Tatnall St, Macon, GA 31201 USA

Latimore, Joseph
1505 10th St., Santa Monica, CA 90401

Latortue, Gerard *Prime Minister*
Prime Minister's Office, Palais Ministeres, Port-au-Prince, HAITI

LaTourette, John E *Educator*
218 S Deerview Circle, Prescott, AZ 86303 USA

Lattimore, Kenny
151 El Camino Dr., Beverly Hills, CA 90212

Lattisaw, Stacy *Musician*
Walter Reeder Productions, PO Box 27641, Philadelphia, PA 19118 USA

Lattlmore, Kenny *Musician*
Rhythm Jazz Entertainment Group, 4465 Don Milagro Dr, Los Angeles, CA 90008 USA

Lattner, John J (Johnny) *Football Player*
1700 Riverwoods Dr, #503, Melrose Park, IL 60160 USA

Lattner, Johnny
933 Wenonah Ave., Oak Park, IL 60304-1818

Lattuada, Alberto
via N. Paganini, Rome, ITALY, 00198

Lauda, Andreas-Nikolaus (Niki) *Race Car Driver*
San Costa de Baix, Santa Eulalia, Ibiza, SPAIN

Lauda, Niki
San Costa de Baix, Santa Eularia des Riu (Ibiza), SPAIN, E-07840

Lauder, Leonard A *Business Person*
Estee Lauder Companies, 767 5th Ave, New York, NY 10153 USA

Lauderdale, Jim *Musician, Songwriter*
Press Network, 1035 16th Ave S, #200, Nashville, TN 37212 USA

Lauer, Andrew *Actor*
3018 3rd St, Santa Monica, CA 90405 USA

Lauer, Andy *Actor*
Jerry Shandrew PR, 1050 South Stanley Avenue, Los Angeles, CA 90019-6634 USA

Lauer, Martin *Track Athlete*
Hardstr 41, Lauf, 77886, GERMANY

Lauer, Matt *Commentator*
NBC-TV, News Dept, 30 Rockefeller Plaza, New York, NY 10112 USA

Lauer, Tod R *Astronomer*
6471 N Tierra de Las Catalina, Tucson, AZ 85718 USA

Laughlin, John *Actor*
Laughlin Enterprises, 13116 Albers St, Sherman Oaks, CA 91401 USA

Laughlin, Lori *Actor*
General Hospital, 4151 Prospect Ave, Los Angeles, CA 90027 USA

Laughlin, Robert B *Nobel Prize Laureate*
Stanford University, Physics Dept, Stanford, CA 94305 USA

Laughlin, Thomas R (Tom) *Actor, Director*
PO Box 840, Moorpark, CA 93020 USA

Laughlin, Tom
PO Box 840, Moorpark, CA 93020-0840

Laukkanen, Janne *Hockey Player*
Tampa Bay Lightning, Ice Palace, 401 Channelside Dr, Tampa, FL 33602 USA

Laumer, Keith
PO Box 972, Brookside, FL 33512

Lauper, Cyndi *Musician, Songwriter*
William Morris Agency, 1325 Ave of Americas, New York, NY 10019 USA

Laurance, Dale *Business Person*
Occidental Petroleum, 10889 Wilshire Blvd, Los Angeles, CA 90024 USA

Laurance, Matthew *Actor*
1951 Hillcrest Road, Los Angeles, CA 90068 USA

Laure, Carole *Actor, Musician*
Cineart, 36 Rue de Ponthieu, Paris, 75008, FRANCE

Lauren, Ralph *Fashion Designer*
Polo Ralph Lauren Corp, 650 Madison Ave, #C1, New York, NY 10022 USA

Lauren, Tammy *Actor*
Gage Group, 14724 Ventura Blvd, #505, Sherman Oaks, CA 91403 USA

Laurents, Arthur *Writer*
PO Box 582, Quoque, NY 11959 USA

Laurer, Joanie (Chyna) *Wrestler*
World Wrestling Entertainment (WWE), 1241 E Main St, Stamford, CT 06905 USA

Lauria, Dan *Actor*
3960 Carpenter Ave, #5, Studio City, CA 91604 USA

Lauricella, Francis E (Hank) *Football Player*
1200 S Clearview Parkway, #1166, Harahan, LA 70123 USA

Lauridsen, Morten *Composer, Musician*
University of Southern California, Music Dept, Los Angeles, CA 90089 USA

Laurie, Greg *Religious Leader*
Harvest Christian Fellowship Church, 6115 Arlington Ave, Riverside, CA 92504 USA

Laurie, Hugh *Actor, Comedian, Writer*
Gersh Agency, The (LA), 232 N Canon Dr, Beverly Hills, CA 90210 USA

Laurie, Piper *Actor*
2118 Wilshire Blvd, #931, Santa Monica, CA 90403 USA

Lautenberg, Frank *Senator*
506 Hart Senate Office Bldg., Washington, DC 20510 USA

Lauter, Ed *Actor*
9165 Sunset Blvd, #202, Los Angeles, CA 90069 USA

Lauterbur, Paul C *Nobel Prize Laureate*
2702 Holcomb Dr, Urbana, IL 61802 USA

Lautner, Georges C *Director*
9 Chemin des Basses Ribes, Grasse, 06130, FRANCE

Lave, Lester B *Economist*
1008 Devonshire Road, Pittsburgh, PA 15213 USA

Laveikin, Aleksandr I *Cosmonaut*
Potchta Kosmonavtov, Moskovskoi Oblasti, Syvisdny Goroduk, 141160, RUSSIA

Lavelli, Dante B J *Football Player*
23273 Pheasant Lane, #11, Cleveland, OH 44145 USA

Lavender, Jay *Producer*
Principato/Young Management, 9665 Wilshire Blvd #500, Beverly Hills, CA 90212 USA

Laventhol, Henry L (Hank) *Artist*
445 Heritage Hills, #F, Somers, NY 10589 USA

Laver, Rod
Box 4798, Hilton Head Island, SC 29928

Laver, Rodney G (Rod) *Tennis Player*
PO Box 4798, Hilton Head Island, SC 29938 USA

Lavery, Sean *Dancer*
New York City Ballet, Lincoin Center Plaza, New York, NY 10023 USA

Lavi, Daliah *Actor*
Dahlienweg 2, Herdecke, 58313, GERMANY

Lavigne, Avril *Musician, Songwriter*
Arista Records, 888 7th Ave, #3800, New York, NY 10106 USA

Lavin, Bernice E *Business Person*
Alberto-Culver, 2525 Armitage Ave, Melrose Park, IL 60160 USA

Lavin, Leonard H *Business Person*
Alberto-Culver, 2525 Armitage Ave, Melrose Park, IL 60160 USA

Lavin, Linda *Actor, Musician*
321 N Front St, Wilmington, NC 28401 USA

Laviolette, Peter *Hockey Player, Coach*
233 Huntington Bay Road, Halesite, NY 11743 USA

Lavoine, Marc *Actor*
ArtMedia, 20 Ave Rapp, Paris, 75007, FRANCE

Lavoir, Jennifer
PO Box 846, Merrimack, NH 03054

LaVorgna, Adam *Actor*
Anonymous Content, 8522 National Blvd #101, Culver City, CA 90232 USA

Lavrosky, Mikhail L *Ballerina*
Voznesesenky Per 16/4, #7, Moscow, 103009, RUSSIA

Lavrov, Kyrill Y *Actor*
Michurinskaya 1, #36, Saint Petersburg, 197046, RUSSIA

Law, Bernard F Cardinal *Religious Leader*
Saint Mary Major Basilica, 00120, VATICAN CITY

Law, John Philip *Actor*
1339 Miller Dr, Los Angeles, CA 90069 USA

Law, John Phillip
1339 Miller Dr., Los Angeles, CA 90069

Law, Jude *Actor*
Julian Belfarge, 46 Albermarie St, London, W1X 4PP, UNITED KINGDOM (UK)

Law, Vernon S *Baseball Player*
1718 N 1050 West, Provo, UT 84604 USA

Lawford, Christopher
1 Sutton Pl. So., New York, NY 10021

Lawler, Jerry
5190 Walnut Grove Rd, Memphis, TN 37117-2876

Lawler, Kate *Reality TV Star*
Channel 4 Television Corporation, 124 Horseferry Road, London, SW1P 2

Lawless, Lucy *Actor*
Original Film, 2045 S Barrington Ave, Los Angeles, CA 90025 USA

Lawless, Robert W *Educator*
University of Tulsa, President's Office, Tulsa, OK 74104 USA

Lawn, John C *Lawyer*
New York Yankees, Yankee Stadium, 161st St & River Ave, Bronx, NY 10451 USA

Lawrence, Andrea Mead
Box 43, Mammoth Lakes, CA 93546

Lawrence, Andrea Meade *Skier*
PO Box 43, Mammoth Lakes, CA 93546 USA

Lawrence, Andrew *Actor*
Firm, The, 9465 Wilshire Blvd, Beverly Hills, CA 90212 USA

Lawrence, Bill *Writer*
Broder Webb Chervin Silbermann Agency, The (BWCS), 9242 Beverly Blvd #200, Beverly Hills, CA 90210 USA

Lawrence, Braxton Janice *Basketball Player*
Cleveland Rockers, Gund Arena, 1 Center Court, Cleveland, OH 44115 USA

Lawrence, Carol *Actor*
12337 Ridge Circle, Los Angeles, CA 90049 USA

Lawrence, Cynthia *Opera Singer*
Herbert Breslin, 119 W 57th St, #1505, New York, NY 10019 USA

Lawrence, David Jr *Publisher*
Miami Herald, 1 Herald Plaza, Miami, FL
33132 USA

Lawrence, Francis *Actor*
Hansen Jacobson Teller & Hoberman, 450
N Roxbury Dr Fl 8, Beverly Hills, CA
90210 USA

Lawrence, Francis *Director*
David Naylor & Associates, 6535 Santa
Monica Blvd, Hollywood, CA 90038 USA

Lawrence, Francis L *Educator*
Rutgers University, President's Office,
New Brunswick, NJ 08903 USA

Lawrence, Henry *Football Player*
2110 2nd Ave E, Palmetto, FL 34221 USA

Lawrence, James (Loz) *Musician*
PO Box 33, Pontypool, Gwent, NP4 6YU,
UNITED KINGDOM (UK)

Lawrence, Jerome *Writer*
PO Box 2770, Malibu, CA 90265 USA

Lawrence, Joseph (Joey) *Actor*
Paradigm (LA), 10100 Santa Monica Blvd,
Fl 25, Los Angeles, CA 90067 USA

Lawrence, Linda
4926 Commonwealth, La Canada, CA
91011

Lawrence, Marc *Actor*
2200 N Vista Grande Ave, Palm Springs,
CA 92262 USA

Lawrence, Marjie
13 Glenhurst Ave., London, ENGLAND,
NW5

Lawrence, Martin *Actor, Comedian*
The Firm, 9100 Wilshire Blvd, #400W,
Beverly Hills, CA 90210 USA

Lawrence, Matthew *Actor*
William Morris Agency, 151 El Camino
Dr, Beverly Hills, CA 90212 USA

Lawrence, Patricia
33 St. Luke's St., London, ENGLAND,
SW3

Lawrence, Richard D *General*
7301 Valbum Dr, Austin, TX 78731 USA

Lawrence, Robert S *Physicist*
Highfield House, 4000 Charles St #1112,
Baltimore, MD 21218 USA

Lawrence, Russell
7800 Beverly Blvd. #3305, Los Angeles,
CA 90036

Lawrence, Sharon *Actor*
PO Box 462048, Los Angeles, CA 90046
USA

Lawrence, Steve *Musician*
944 Pinehurst Dr, Las Vegas, NV 89109
USA

Lawrence, Tracy *Musician, Songwriter*
Holley, 3415 W End Ave, #101D,
Nashville, TN 37203 USA

Lawrence, Vicki *Actor, Musician*
6000 Lido Ave, Long Beach, CA 90803
USA

Lawrence, Wendy B *Astronaut*
National Reconnaissance Office, 14675
Lee Road, Chantilly, VA 20151 USA

Lawrence, William P *Admiral*
303 Kyle Road, Crownsville, MD 21032
USA

Laws, Hubert
1078 S. Ogden Dr., Los Angeles, CA
90019

Laws, Ronnie *Musician*
Pyramid Entertainment, 89 5th Ave, #700,
New York, NY 10003 USA

Lawson, Bianca *Actor*
Tencer & Associates PR, 9777 Wilshire
Blvd, #504, Beverly Hills, CA 90212 USA

Lawson, Chene *Actor*
Michael Slessinger & Assoc, 8730 Sunset
Blvd #270, Los Angeles, CA 90069 USA

Lawson, Ken (Ken L) *Actor*
Agency West Entertainment, 6255 West
Sunset Blvd, Suite 908, Hollywood, CA
90028 USA

Lawson, Leigh *Actor*
P F D Drury House, 34-43 Russell St,
London, WC2B 5HA, UNITED KINGDOM
(UK)

Lawson, Maggie *Actor*
Ellen Meyer Entertainment, 8899 Beverly
Blvd #616, Los Angeles, CA 90048 USA

Lawson, Nigella *Chef, Writer*
El Television, 5750 Wilshire Blvd, Los
Angeles, CA 90036 USA

Lawson, Richard *Actor*
8840 Wilshire Blvd, #200, Beverly Hills,
CA 90211 USA

Lawson, Richard L *General*
6910 Clifton Road, Clifton, VA 20124
USA

Lawson, Twiggy *Actor, Model, Writer*
Peters Fraser & Dunlop (PFD - UK), Drury
House, 34-43 Russell St, London, WC2
B5, UNITED KINGDOM (UK)

Lawson of Blaby, Nigel *Government
Official*
32 Sutherland Walk, London, SE17,
UNITED KINGDOM (UK)

Lawton, Mary *Cartoonist*
Chronicle Features, 901 Mission St, San
Francisco, CA 94103 USA

Lawton, Matthew (Matt) *Baseball Player*
27264 Highway 67, Saucier, MS 39574
USA

Lawton, Robert B *Educator*
Loyola Marymount University, President's
Office, Los Angeles, CA 90045 USA

Lawwill, Theodore *Misc*
7609 Tallwood Road, Prospect, KY 40059
USA

Lax, John *Hockey Player*
3 Greendale Lane, Harwich, MA 02645
USA

Lax, Melvin *Physicist*
12 High St, Summit, NJ 07901 USA

Lax, Peter D *Mathematician*
251 Mercer St, New York, NY 10012 USA

Laxalt, Paul D *Ex-Senator, Ex-Governor*
801 Pennsylvania Ave NW, #750,
Washington, DC 20004 USA

Laxmikant, Berde *Actor, Bollywood*
105 Nirakar B-Wing, 1st Floor Kalyan
Complex Yari Road Versova Andheri,
Bombay, MS 400061, INDIA

Lay, Donald P *Judge*
US Court of Appeals, 316 Robert St N,
Saint Paul, MN 55101 USA

Layevska, Anna *Actor*
Televisa, Blvd Adolfo Lopez Mateos 232,
Colonia San Angel INN, DF, CP 01060,
MEXICO

Layzie, Bone *Musician*
Creative Artists Agency, 9830 Wilshire
Blvd, Beverly Hills, CA 90212 USA

Lazar, Laurence *Religious Leader*
Romanian Orthodox Episcopate, 2522
Grey Tower Road, Jackson, MI 49201
USA

Lazard, Justin
9350 Wilshire Blvd. #324, Beverly Hills,
CA 90212

Lazarev, Alexander N
Christopher Tennant Artists, 39 Taderna
ROad, #2, London, SW10 0PY, UNITED
KINGDOM (UK)

Lazaroff, Barbara
805 N. Sierra Dr., Beverly Hills, CA
90210

Lazarus, Mell *Cartoonist*
Creators Syndicate, 5777 W Century Blvd,
#700, Los Angeles, CA 90045 USA

Lazarus, Shelly *Business Person*
Ogilvy & Mather Worldwide, 309 W 49th
St, New York, NY 10019 USA

Lazear, Edward P *Economist*
277 Old Spanish Trail, Portola Valley, CA
94028 USA

Lazenby, George *Actor*
PO Box 55306, Sherman Oaks, CA 91413
USA

Lazier, Buddy *Race Car Driver*
Performance Marketing, 1545 W 4th Ave,
Vancouver, BC V6U 1L6, CANADA

Lazlo, Viktor
56 rue de Lisbonne, Paris, FRANCE,
F-75008

Lazuktin, Alexander I *Cosmonaut*
Potcha Kosmonavtov, Moskovskoi Oblasti,
Syvisdny Goroduk, 141160, RUSSIA

Lazure, Gabrielle *Actor*
Cineart, 36 Rue de Ponthieu, Paris,
75008, FRANCE

Le Duc, Anh *President, General*
President's Office, Hoang Hoa Tham,
Hanoi, VIETNAM

Le Mat, Paul
1100 N. Alta Loma #805, Los Angeles, CA
90069

Le Prevost, Nicholas
43A Princess Rd. Regents Park, London,
ENGLAND, NW1 8JS

Le Prevost, Nigel
43A Princess Rd., London, ENGLAND,
W1

Le Vert
110-112 Lantoga Rd. #D, Wayne, PA
19087

Lea, Charles W (Charlie) *Baseball Player*
521 Old Collierville Arlin Road,
Collierville, TN 38017 USA

Lea, Nicholas *Actor*
Gersh Agency, The (LA), 232 N Canon Dr, Beverly Hills, CA 90210 USA

Leach, Henry C *Admiral*
Wonston Lea, Winchester, Hants, SO21 3LS, UNITED KINGDOM (UK)

Leach, Penelope *Misc*
3 Tanza Lane, London, NW3 2UA, UNITED KINGDOM (UK)

Leach, Robin *Television Host, Producer, Entertainer*
1 Dag Hammarskjold Plaza, #2100, New York, NY 10017 USA

Leach, Rosemary *Actor*
Felix de Wolfe, 51 Maida Vale, London, W9 1SD, UNITED KINGDOM (UK)

Leach, Sheryl *Animator*
Lyons Group, 300 E Bethany Road, Allen, TX 75002 USA

Leach, Terry *Baseball Player*
New York Mets, 2135 SW Locks Rd, Stuart, FL 34997-7011 USA

Leachman, Cloris *Actor*
410 S Barrington Ave, #307, Los Angeles, CA 90049 USA

Leader, George M *Governor*
Country Meadows, 830 Cherry Dr, Hershey, PA 17033 USA

Leader, Tom *Architect*
1212 Nelson St, Albany, CA 94706 USA

Leadon, Bernie *Musician*
Joe's Garage, 4405 Belmont Park Terrace, Nashville, TN 37215 USA

Leaf, Alexander *Physicist*
5 Sussex Road, Winchester, MA 01890 USA

Leahy, Patrick *Senator*
433 Russell Senate Office Bldg, Washington, DC 20510 USA

Leahy, Patrick J (Pat) *Football Player*
717 Chamblee Lane, Saint Louis, MO 63141 USA

Leak, Jennifer *Actor*
James D'Auria Associates, PO Box 2219, Amagansett, NY 11930 USA

Leakey, Meave G *Biologist*
PO Box 24926, Nairobi, KENYA

Leakey, Richard E F *Biologist*
PO Box 24926, Nairobi, KENYA

Leaks, Roosevelt Jr *Football Player*
Roosevelt Leaks Properties, 8907 N Plaza Court, Austin, TX 78753 USA

Leal, Sharon *Actor, Musician*
Edmonds Management, 1635 N Cahuenga Blvd Fl 5, Los Angeles, CA 90028 USA

Leandros, Vicky
Postfach 31 28, Kiel, GERMANY, D-24030

Lear, Evelyn *Opera Singer*
414 Sailboat Circle, Weston, FL 33326 USA

Lear, Norman M *Producer, Writer, Director*
100 N Crescent Dr, #250, Beverly Hills, CA 90210 USA

Learned, Michael *Actor*
1600 N Beverly Dr, Beverly Hills, CA 90210 USA

Leary, Denis *Actor, Comedian*
Entertainment Travel, 9171 Wilshire Blvd, #406, Beverly Hills, CA 90210 USA

Leary, Tim *Baseball Player*
New York Mets, 17020 W Sunset Blvd Apt 8, Pacific Palisades, CA 90272-3216 USA

Leatherdale, Douglas W *Business Person*
Saint Paul Companies, 385 Washington St, Saint Paul, MN 55102 USA

Leaud, Jean-Pierre *Actor*
Artmedia, 20 Ave Rapp, Paris, 75007, FRANCE

Leavenworth, Scotty *Actor*
Curtis Talent Management, 9607 Arby Dr, Beverly Hills, CA 90210 USA

Leavitt, Michael O *Government Official, Governor*
Environmental Protection Agency, 401 M St SW, Washington, DC 20460 USA

Leavitt, Phil *Musician*
GEMS, PO Box 1031, Montrose, CA 91021 USA

Leavy, Edward *Judge*
US Court of Appeals, 555 SW Yamhill St, Portland, OR 97204 USA

Lebadang *Artist*
Circle Gallery, 303 E Wacker Dr, Chicago, IL 60601 USA

LeBaron, Eddie
400 Capitol Mall #1700, Sacramento, CA 95814

LeBaron, Edward W (Eddie) Jr *Football Player*
7524 Pineridge Lane, Fair Oaks, CA 95628 USA

LeBeau, Becky
9461 Charleville Blvd. #602, Beverly Hills, CA 90212

LeBeau, C Richard (Dick) *Football Player, Coach*
10405 Stone Court, Cincinnati, OH 45242 USA

LeBeauf, Sabrina *Actor*
735 Kappock St, #6F, Bronx, NY 10463 USA

Lebedev, Valentin V *Cosmonaut*
Potcha Kosmonavtov, Moskovskoi Oblasti, Syvisdny Goroduk, 141160, RUSSIA

LeBel, B Harper *Football Player*
3379 Scadlock Lane, Sherman Oaks, CA 91403 USA

LeBel, Robert (Bob) *Misc*
25 Rue Saint Pierre, Cite de Chambly, QC, J3L 1L7, CANADA

Lebis, Attilo *Dancer, Choreographer*
Opera de Paris, 120 Rue Lyon, Paris, 75012, FRANCE

LeBlanc, Christian
12840 Moorpark St. #106, Studio City, CA 91604-1363

LeBlanc, Matt *Actor*
United Talent Agency, 9560 Wilshire Blvd, #500, Beverly Hills, CA 90212 USA

LeBlanc, Sherri *Ballerina*
New York City Ballet, Lincoln Center Plaza, New York, NY 10023 USA

LeBoeuf, Raymond W *Business Person*
PPG Industries, 1 PPG Place, Pittsburg, PA 15272 USA

LeBon, Simon *Musician, Songwriter*
DD Productions, 93A Westbourne Park Villas, London, W2 5ED, UNITED KINGDOM (UK)

Lebovitz, Hall *Writer*
2380 Edgerton Road, Cleveland, OH 44118 USA

Lebowitz, Fran *Writer*
Random House, 1745 Broadway, #B1, New York, NY 10019 USA

Lebowitz, Joel L *Mathematician*
Rutgers University, Mathematics Dept, New Brunswick, NJ 08903 USA

Leboyer, Frederick *Physicist*
Georges Borchardt, 136 E 57th St, New York, NY 10022 USA

LeBrock, Kelly *Actor, Model*
Bartels Co, PO Box 57593, Sherman Oaks, CA 91413 USA

LeBrun, Christopher M *Artist*
Marlborough Fine Art, 6 Albermarle St, London, W1X 4BY, UNITED KINGDOM (UK)

LeCarre, John *Writer*
9 Gainsborough Gardens, London, NW3 1BJ, UNITED KINGDOM (UK)

LeCavalier, Vincent *Hockey Player*
Tampa Bay Lightning, Ice Palace, 401 Channelside Drive, Tampa, FL 33602 USA

Lechter, Sharon L *Writer*
Cashflow Technologies, 4330 N Civic Center Plaza, Scottsdale, AZ 85251 USA

LeClair, James M (Jim) *Football Player*
43 4th Ave NE, Mayville, ND 58257 USA

LeClair, John *Hockey Player*
715 Dodds Lane, Gladwyne, PA 19035 USA

LeClerc, Jean *Actor*
19 W 44th St, #1500, New York, NY 10036 USA

LeClere, Jennifer
5601 Navigation Blvd, Houston, TX 77011

LeClezio, Jean-Marie *Writer*
Editions Gallimard, 5 Rue Sebastien-Bottin, Paris, 75007 USA

Lecomte, Benoit *Swimmer*
Cross Atlantic Swimming Challenge, 3005 S Lamar, #D109-353, Austin, TX 78704 USA

Leconte, Henri *Tennis Player*
IMG, Pier House, Strand-on-Green, Chiswick, London, W4 3NN, UNITED KINGDOM (UK)

Leconte, Patrice *Director*
William Morris Agency, 151 El Camino Dr, Beverly Hills, CA 90212 USA

Lecroy, Matt *Baseball Player*
Minnesota Twins, 410 Brown Ave, Belton, SC 29627-1504 USA

Ledee, Ricky *Baseball Player*
New York Yankees, D29 Ext Carmen, Salinas, PR 00751-2208 USA

Leder, Mimi *Director*
Bauer Company, The, 9300 Wilshire Blvd
#PH, Beverly Hills, CA 90212 USA

Leder, Philip *Scientist*
Howard Hughes Med Institute, 4000 Jones
Bridge Road, Chevy Chase, MD 20815

Lederberg, Joshua *Nobel Prize Laureate*
Rockefeller University, President's Office,
1230 York Ave, New York, NY 10021
USA

Lederer, Jerome *Engineer*
468 Calle Cadiz, #D, Laguna Beach, CA
92653 USA

Lederman, Leon M *Nobel Prize Laureate*
3101 S Dearborn St, Chicago, IL 60616
USA

Ledesma, Aaron *Baseball Player*
New York Mets, 2446 Douglas St, Union
City, CA 94587-1865 USA

Ledford, Brandy *Actor*
Marshak/Zachary Company, The, 8840
Wilshire Blvd Fl 1, Beverly Hills, CA
90211 USA

Ledford, Frank F Jr *General*
Southwest Biomed Research Foundation,
PO Box 760549, San Antonio, TX 78245
USA

Ledford, Judith
11365 Ventura Blvd. #100, Studio City,
CA 91604

Ledger, Heath *Actor*
Creative Artists Agency LCC (CAA-LA),
9830 Wilshire Blvd, Beverly Hills, CA
90212 USA

Ledley, Robert S *Inventor*
17000 Melbourne Dr, Laurel, MD 20707
USA

Ledoux, Chris *Musician, Songwriter,
Rodeo Rider*
PO Box 253, Sumner, IA 50674 USA

Ledoyen, Virginie *Actor, Model*
80 Ave Gen Charles de Gaulle, Neuilly,
92200, FRANCE

Lee, Alexandra *Actor*
Writers & Artists, 8383 Wilshire Blvd,
#550, Beverly Hills, CA 90211 USA

Lee, Amy *Musician*
Dennis Rider Management, 927 Hilldale
Avenue, West Hollywood, CA 90069 USA

Lee, Andy Scott *Musician*
Pop Idol (Fremantle Media), 2700
Colorado Ave #450, Santa Monica, CA
90404 USA

Lee, Ang *Director*
417 Canal St, #410, New York, NY 10013
USA

Lee, Anthonia W (Amp) *Football Player*
990 Brickyard Road, Chipley, FL 32428
USA

Lee, Bertram M *Misc*
Denver Nugglets, Pepsi Center, 1000
Chopper Circle, Denver, CO 80204 USA

Lee, Beverly
10100 Santa Monica Blvd. #2490, Los
Angeles, CA 90067

Lee, Beverly *Musician*
Bevi Corp, PO Box 100, Clifton, NJ 07015
USA

Lee, Bill *Baseball Player*
Boston Red Sox, 305 Common View Dr,
Craftsbury, VT 05826-9779 USA

Lee, Bob *Baseball Player*
Los Angeles Angels, 2110 Casper Dr, Lake
Havasu City, AZ 86406-8143 USA

Lee, Bobby *Actor*
Gersh Agency, The (LA), 232 N Canon Dr,
Beverly Hills, CA 90210 USA

Lee, Brenda *Musician*
Brenda Lee Productions, 2175 Carson St,
Nashville, TN 37211 USA

Lee, Butch *Basketball Player*
1322 Teller Ave, Bronx, NY 10456 USA

Lee, Catherine J *Artist*
2625 Harkness St, Sacramento, CA 95818
USA

Lee, Chang-Rae *Writer*
International Creative Mgmt, 40 W 57th
St, #1800, New York, NY 10019 USA

Lee, Charles R *Business Person*
GTE Corp, 1255 Corporate Dr, Irving, TX
75038 USA

Lee, Christopher *Actor*
L 2/4 Noel St, London, ENGLAND, W1V
3RB

Lee, Christopher F C *Actor*
5 Sandown House, Wheat Field Terrace,
London, W4, UNITED KINGDOM (UK)

Lee, Cliff *Baseball Player*
Cleveland Indians, 602 Nalley St, Benton,
AR 72015-2261 USA

Lee, Corey *Baseball Player*
Texas Rangers, 702 Joyner St, Clayton, NC
27520-2838 USA

Lee, Daniel
Columbia Artists Mgmt Inc, 165 W 57th
St, New York, NY 10019 USA

Lee, David *Director, Writer*
Jim Preminger Agency, 450 N Roxbury
Dr, #1050, Beverly Hills, CA 90210 USA

Lee, David *Baseball Player*
Colorado Rockies, 1429 Manley St,
Pittsburgh, PA 15205-3926 USA

Lee, David H *Astronomer, Writer*
Plenum Publishing Group, 233 Spring St,
New York, NY 10013 USA

Lee, David L *Business Person*
Global Crossing Ltd, Wessex House, 45
Reid St, Hamilton, HM, 12, Bermuda

Lee, David M *Nobel Prize Laureate*
Cornell University, Physics Dept, Clark
Hall, Ithaca, NY 14853 USA

Lee, Derek *Baseball Player*
Minnesota Twins, 932 E 44th St, Chicago,
IL 60653-3603 USA

Lee, Derrek *Baseball Player*
San Diego Padres, 3576 Brittany Way, El
Dorado Hills, CA 95762-3952 USA

Lee, Dickey *Musician*
Mars Talent, 27 L'Ambiance Court,
Bardonia, NY 10954 USA

Lee, Don *Baseball Player*
Detroit Tigers, 9101 E Palm Tree Dr,
Tucson, AZ 85710-8626 USA

Lee, Eunice *Musician*
Columbia Artists Mgmt Inc, 165 W 57th
St, New York, NY 10019 USA

Lee, Geddy *Musician*
Macklam Feldman Mgmt, 1505 W 2nd
Ave, #200, Vancouver, BC V6H 3Y4,
CANADA

Lee, Gordon
800 W. 65th St. #103, Richfield, MN
55423

Lee, Gordon (Porky) *Actor*
Dick Strand, 800 W 65th St, #103,
Richfield, MN 55423 USA

Lee, Grandma *Actor, Comedian*
Lee Strong, 626 Staffordshire Dr,
Jacksonville, FL 32225 USA

Lee, H Douglas *Educator*
Stetson University, President's Office,
Deland, FL 32720 USA

Lee, Harper *Writer*
McIntosh & Otis, 353 Lexington Ave,
#1500, New York, NY 10016 USA

Lee, Homer & The Braschler's
PO Box 1408, Branson, MO 65616

Lee, Howard V *War Hero*
529 King Arthur Dr, Virginia Beach, VA
23464 USA

Lee, Jared B *Cartoonist*
Jared B Lee Studio, 2942 Hamilton Road,
Lebanon, OH 45036 USA

Lee, Jason *Actor*
PO Box 1083, Pearl City, HI 96782 USA

Lee, Jason Scott *Actor*
United Talent Agency, 9560 Wilshire
Blvd, #500, Beverly Hills, CA 90212 USA

Lee, Jeahette *Billiards Player*
Octagon, 1751 Pinnacle Dr, #1500,
McLean, VA 22102 USA

Lee, Jeanette *Billiards Player*
1427 W 86th St, #183, Indianapolis, IN
46260 USA

Lee, Joe *Business Person*
Darden Restaurants, 5900 Lake Ellenor
Dr, Orlando, FL 32809 USA

Lee, Johnny *Musician, Songwriter*
WIFT Mgmt, 2317 Pecan, Dickinson, TX
77539 USA

Lee, Jong-Wook *Government Official*
World Health Organization, Ave Appia,
Geneva, 1211, SWITZERLAND

Lee, Jonna *Actor*
8721 Sunset Blvd, #103, Los Angeles, CA
90069 USA

Lee, Kathy
204 River Edge Lane, Seiverville, TN
37862

Lee, Keith *Basketball Player*
3617 Clearbrook St, Memphis, TN 38118
USA

Lee, Kuan Yew *Prime Minister*
Senoir Minister's Office, Istana Annexe,
Istana, Singapore, 0923, SINGAPORE

Lee, Laron *Baseball Player*
St Louis Cardinals, 8150 Warren Ct,
Granite Bay, CA 95746-9576 USA

Lee, Laura
155 N. Beverwyck PMB 245, Lake
Hiawatha, NJ 07034

Lee, Lela *Actor*
Artists Group (LA), 10100 Santa Monica
Blvd #2490, Los Angeles, CA 90067 USA

Lee, London
1650 Broadway #1410, New York, NY
10019

Lee, Mark *Baseball Player*
San Diego Padres, 130 N Rosemont St,
Amarillo, TX 79106-5214 USA

Lee, Mark *Baseball Player*
Kansas City Royals, 3580 Brunswick Dr,
Colorado Springs, CO 80920-7338 USA

Lee, Mark C *Astronaut*
6833 Phil Lewis Way, Middleton, WI
53562 USA

Lee, Michele
830 Birchwood, Los Angeles, CA 90024

Lee, Michelle *Actor*
830 Birchwood Dr, Los Angeles, CA
90024 USA

Lee, Mike *Baseball Player*
Cleveland Indians, 1790 Calmin Dr,
Fallbrook, CA 92028-4303 USA

Lee, Raphael C *Doctor*
Massachusetts Institute Technology,
Engineering Dept, Cambridge, MA 02139
USA

Lee, Ron *Basketball Player*
35788 Woodridge Court, Farmington, MI
48335 USA

Lee, Ruta *Actor*
2623 Laurel Canyon Road, Los Angeles,
CA 90046 USA

Lee, Sammy *Doctor*
16537 Harbour Ln, Huntington Beach, CA
92649 USA

Lee, Samuel (Sammy) *Coach*
16537 Harbour Lane, Huntington Beach,
CA 92649 USA

Lee, Shannon *Actor*
Innovative Artists (LA), 1505 Tenth St,
Santa Monica, CA 90401 USA

Lee, Sheryl *Actor*
William Morris Agency, 151 El Camino
Dr, Beverly Hills, CA 90212 USA

Lee, Spike *Director*
40 Acres & A Mule Filmworks Inc (NY),
124 DeKalb Ave, New York, NY 11217
USA

Lee, Stan *Publisher, Cartoonist*
Marvel Entertainment, 1440 S Sepulveda
Blvd, #114, Los Angeles, CA 90025 USA

Lee, Sung Hi *Actor*
TalentWorks (LA), 3500 W Olive Ave
#1400, Burbank, CA 91505 USA

Lee, Terry *Baseball Player*
Cincinnati Reds, 143 Wedgewood Dr,
Eugene, OR 97404-5909 USA

Lee, Tommy *Musician*
Immortal Entertainment, 12200 Olympic
Blvd, Suite 400, Los Angeles, CA 90064
USA

Lee, Tony *Actor*
Edmonds Management, 1635 N Cahuenga
Blvd Fl 5, Los Angeles, CA 90028 USA

Lee, Travis *Baseball Player*
Arizona Diamondbacks, 985 Via Colinas,
Westlake Village, CA 91362-5051 USA

Lee, Tsung-Dao *Nobel Prize Laureate*
25 Claremont Ave, New York, NY 10027
USA

Lee, Vernon R *Religious Leader*
Wyatt Baptist Church, 4621 W Hillsboro
St, El Dorado, AR 71730 USA

Lee, Wayne *Engineer*
Jet Propulsion Laboratory, 4800 Oak
Grove Dr, Pasadena, CA 91109 USA

Lee, William Gregory *Actor*
Agency for the Performing Arts (APA-LA),
9200 Sunset Blvd #900, Los Angeles, CA
90069 USA

Lee, Yuan T *Nobel Prize Laureate*
Academy Sinica, Nankang, Taipei, 11529,
TAIWAN

Leech, Beverly
9150 Wilshire Blvd. #175, Beverly Hills,
CA 90212

Leech, Richard *Opera Singer*
Thea Dispeker Artists, 59 E 54th St, New
York, NY 10022 USA

Leek, Gene *Baseball Player*
Cleveland Indians, 4055 Hamilton St Apt
5, San Diego, CA 92104-6108 USA

Leek, Sybil *Misc*
Prentice-Hall, RR 9W, Englewood Cliffs,
NJ 07632 USA

Leen, Bill *Musician*
William Morris Agency, 2100 W End Ave,
#1000, Nashville, TN 37203 USA

Leeper, Dave *Baseball Player*
Kansas City Royals, 7730 Briarglen Loop
Unit D, Stanton, CA 90680-4128 USA

Leerhsen, Erica *Actor*
Principal Entertainment (LA), 1964
Westwood Blvd #400, Los Angeles, CA
90025 USA

Leese, Howard *Musician*
219 2st Ave N, #333, Seattle, WA 98109
USA

Leestma, David C *Astronaut*
4314 Lake Grove Dr, Seabrook, TX 77586
USA

Leetch, Brian
29 Stratton Dr., Cheshire, CT 06410

Leetch, Brian J *Hockey Player*
225 W 83rd St, New York, NY 10024
USA

Leetsma, David C
2101 NASA Rd, Houston, TX 77058 USA

Leetzow, Max *Athlete*
7315 S Birch St, Littleton, CO 80122-2232

Leeves, Jane *Actor*
William Morris Agency, 151 El Camino
Dr, Beverly Hills, CA 90212 USA

Lefcourt, Peter *Actor*
Creative Artists Agency LCC (CAA-LA),
9830 Wilshire Blvd, Beverly Hills, CA
90212 USA

Lefebvre, Bill *Baseball Player*
Boston Red Sox, 7349 Ulmerton Rd Lot
1379, Largo, FL 33771-4859 USA

Lefebvre, Jim *Baseball Player*
Los Angeles Dodgers, 10160 E Whispering
Wind Dr, Scottsdale, AZ 85255-3007 USA

Lefebvre, Joe *Baseball Player*
New York Yankees, 10 Shore View Dr,
Bow, NH 03304-4116 USA

Lefferts, Craig *Baseball Player*
Chicago Cubs, 1818 Emerson Park Dr,
Knoxville, TN 37922-8541 USA

Leflore, Ron *Baseball Player*
Detroit Tigers, 6263 93rd Ter Apt 4206,
Pinellas Park, FL 33782-4640 USA

Leftwich, Byron *Football Player*
Jacksonville Jaguars, 1 AllTel Statium
Place, Jacksonville, FL 32202 USA

Leftwich, Phil *Baseball Player*
California Angels, 1443 Rainbow Forest
Dr, Lynchburg, VA 24502-3098 USA

Legace, Jean-Guy *Hockey Player*
126 Cassa Grande Lane, Santa Rosa
Beach, FL 32459 USA

LeGault, Lance *Actor*
16105-8H Victory Blvd, #382, Van Nuys,
CA 91406 USA

Legg, Greg *Baseball Player*
Philadelphia Phillies, 412 Jenna Kay Dr,
Archbald, PA 18403-1583 USA

Legge, Michael *Actor*
Hatton McEwan, PO Box 37385, London,
N1 7XF, UNITED KINGDOM (UK)

Leggett, Anthony J *Nobel Prize Laureate*
607 W Pennsylvania Ave, Urbana, IL
61801 USA

Legien, Waldemar *Athlete*
Ul Grottgera 10, Bytom, 41-902,
POLAND

Legorreta, Vilchis Ricardo *Architect*
Palacio de Versalles, #285A, C Lomas
Reforma, Mexico City, 11020, MEXICO

Legrand, Michel *Composer, Conductor,*
Musician
F Sharp Productions, PO Box 2040, New
York, NY 10101 USA

Legris, Manuel C *Ballerina*
National Theater of Paris Opera, 8 Rue
Scribe, Paris, 75009, FRANCE

LeGros, James *Actor*
I F A Talent Agency, 8730 Sunset Blvd,
#490, Los Angeles, CA 90069 USA

LeGuin, Ursula K *Writer*
3321 NW Thurman St, Portland, OR
97210 USA

Leguizamo, John *Actor, Comedian,*
Producer, Writer
3 Arts Entertainment Inc, 9460 Wilshire
Blvd Fl 7, Beverly Hills, CA 90212 USA

Leguizano, John *Actor*
I D Public Relations, 8409 Santa Monica
Blvd, West Hollywood, CA 90069 USA

Lehane, Dennis *Writer*
1412 Jackson Road, Kerrville, TX 78028
USA

Lehew, Jim *Baseball Player*
Baltimore Orioles, 3086 Fairview Rd,
Grantsville, MD 21536-2239 USA

Lehman, I Robert *Scientist*
895 Cedro Way, Palo Alto, CA 94305
USA

Lehman, Jeffrey *Educator*
Cornell University, President's Office,
Ithaca, NY 14853 USA

Lehman, Ken *Baseball Player*
Brooklyn Dodgers, 3463 Renee Dr, Sedro
Woolley, WA 98284-8812 USA

Lehman, Kristen *Actor*
Oscars Abrams Zimel & Associates, 438 Queen St E, Toronto ON, M5A 1T4, CANADA

Lehman, Tom *Golfer*
9820 E Thompson Peak Parkway, #704, Scottsdale, AZ 85255 USA

Lehmann, Edie *Actor*
24844 Malibu Road, Malibu, CA 90265 USA

Lehmann, Erich L *Misc*
Research Statistics Group, Education Testing Service, Princeton, NJ 08541 USA

Lehmann, Karl Cardinal *Religious Leader*
Bischofliches Ordinariat, PF 1560, Bischofsplatz 2, Mainz, 55116, GERMANY

Lehmann, Michael *Director*
Creative Artists Agency, 9830 Wilshire Blvd, Beverly Hills, CA 90212 USA

Lehmberg, Stanford E *Historian*
1005 Calle Largo, Santa Fe, NM 87501 USA

Lehn, Jean Marie
21 rue d'Oslo, Strasbourg, FRANCE, F-67000

Lehn, Jean-Marie P *Nobel Prize Laureate*
Louis Pasteur Universite, 4 Rue Blaise Pascal, Strasbourg, 67008, FRANCE

Lehninger, Albert L *Misc*
15020 Tanyard Road, Sparks, MD 21152 USA

Lehr, John *Actor, Writer, Producer*
William Morris Agency (WMA-LA), 1 William Morris Pl, Beverly Hills, CA 90212 USA

Lehrer, Jim *Journalist*
Newshour with Jim Lehrer, 2700 S Quincy St, Arlington, VA 22206

Lehrer, Robert I *Biologist*
University of California, Med Center, Hematology Dept, Los Angeles, CA 90024 USA

Lehrer, Thomas A (Tom) *Musician, Comedian*
University of California, Cowell College, Santa Cruz, CA 95064 USA

Lehrer, Tom
11 Sparks St., Cambridge, MA 02138

Lehtinen, Dexter *Attorney General, Government Official*
US Attorney's Office, Justice Dept, 155 Miami Ave, Miami, FL 33130 USA

Lehtinen, Jere *Hockey Player*
569 Indian Rock Dr, Coppell, TX 75019 USA

Leibel, Rudolph *Misc*
464 Riverside Dr, #95, New York, NY 10027 USA

Leiber, Jerry *Songwriter*
Leiber & Stoller Ent, 9000 W Sunset Blvd, West Hollywood, CA 90069 USA

Leibman, Ron *Actor*
27 W 87th St, #2, New York, NY 10024 USA

Leibovitz, Annie *Photographer*
547 W 26th St, New York, NY 10001 USA

Leibovitz, Mitchell G *Business Person*
Pep Boys-Manny Moe & Jack, 3111 W Allegheny Ave, Philadelphia, PA 19132 USA

Leick, Hudson *Actor*
Paradigm Agency, 200 W 57th St, #900, New York, NY 10019 USA

Leifer, Carol *Actor, Comedian*
Brillstein/Grey, 9150 Wilshire Blvd, #350, Beverly Hills, CA 90212 USA

Leiferkus, Sergei P *Opera Singer*
5 The Paddocks, Abberbury Road, Iffley, Oxford, OX4 4ET, UNITED KINGDOM (UK)

Leifheit, Sylvia *Model*
Agentur Reed, Treppendorfer Weg 13, Berlin, 12527, GERMANY

Leigh, Barbara
PO Box 246, Los Angeles, CA 90078-0246

Leigh, Chyler *Actor*
Lane Management Group, 13331 Moorpark St, #118, Sherman Oaks, CA 91423 USA

Leigh, Danni *Musician*
William Morris Agency, 151 El Camino Dr, Beverly Hills, CA 90212 USA

Leigh, Janet *Actor*
1625 Summitridge Dr, Beverly Hills, CA 90210 USA

Leigh, Jennifer Jason *Actor*
Edrick/Rich Mgmt, 2400 Whitman Place, Los Angeles, CA 90068 USA

Leigh, Mike *Director*
Thin Man Films, 9 Greek St, Soho, London, W1D 4DQ, UNITED KINGDOM (UK)

Leigh, Mitch *Composer*
29 W 57th St, #1000, New York, NY 10019 USA

Leigh, Regina *Musician*
Bobby Roberts, 909 Meadowlark Lane, Goodlettsville, TN 37072 USA

Leigh, Tara *Actor*
William Morris Agency (WMA-LA), 1 William Morris Pl, Beverly Hills, CA 90212 USA

Leighton, Laura *Actor*
PO Box 5617, Beverly Hills, CA 90210 USA

Leija, James (Jesse) *Boxer*
9735 Richey Otis Way, San Antonio, TX 78223 USA

Leimkuehler, Paul *Skier, Business Person*
351 Darbys Run, Bay Village, OH 44140 USA

Leiper, Dave *Baseball Player*
Oakland A's, 13082 N 103rd St, Scottsdale, AZ 85260-7272 USA

Leister, John *Baseball Player*
Boston Red Sox, 304 Devon Dr, Saint Louis, MI 48880-9427 USA

Leisure, David *Actor*
26358 Woodlark Lane, Valencia, CA 91355 USA

Leitch, Donovan
8794 Lookout Mountain Ave., Los Angeles, CA 90046-1859

Leitch, Matthew *Actor*
Innovative Artists (LA), 1505 Tenth St, Santa Monica, CA 90401 USA

Leitch, Megan *Actor*

Leiter, Alois T (Al) *Baseball Player*
New York Yankees, 2660 Riviera Manor, Weston, FL 33332-3422 USA

Leiter, Mark *Baseball Player*
New York Yankees, 110 Pine St, Tomes River, NJ 08753-6822 USA

Leith, Emmett N *Engineer*
51325 Murray Hill Dr, Canton, MI 48187 USA

Leitner, Patric-Fritz *Athlete*
BSD, An der Schiessstatte 4, Berchtesgaden, 83471, GERMANY

Leitzel, Joan *Educator*
University of Nebraska, President's Office, Lincoln, NE 68588 USA

Leius, Scott *Baseball Player*
Minnesota Twins, 12620 42nd Pl N, Minneapolis, MN 55442-2344 USA

Lejohn, Don *Baseball Player*
Los Angeles Dodgers, 154 Edwards St, Brownsville, PA 15417-9316 USA

Lekang, Anton *Skier*
47 Pratt St, Winsted, CT 06098 USA

Lelbrandt, Charlie *Baseball Player*
Cincinnati Reds, 1235 Stuart Rdg, Alpharetta, GA 30022-6364 USA

Lelliott, Jeremy *Actor*
Joan Green Management, 1836 Courtney Terr, Los Angeles, CA 90046 USA

Lelong, Pierre J *Mathematician*
9 Place de Rungis, Paris, 75013, FRANCE

LeLouch, Claude *Director*
15 Ave Hoche, Paris, 75008, FRANCE

Lelyveld, Joseph *Editor*
New York Times, Editorial Dept, 229 W 43rd St, New York, NY 10036 USA

Lem, Stanislaw *Writer*
Ul Narwik 66, Cracow, 30-437, POLAND

Lemaire, Jacques G *Hockey Player, Coach*
6667 Avenue B, Sarasota, FL 34231 USA

Lemanczyk, Dave *Baseball Player*
Detroit Tigers, 24 Lehigh Ct, Rockville Centre, NY 11570-2016 USA

Lemaster, Denny *Baseball Player*
Milwaukee Braves, 4833 Carlene Way SW, Lilbum, GA 30047-4705 USA

Lemaster, Johnnie *Baseball Player*
San Francisco Giants, 372 4th St, Paintsville, KY 41240-1135 USA

LeMat, Paul *Actor*
1100 N Alta Loma Road, #805, West Hollywood, CA 90069 USA

Lemay, Dick *Baseball Player*
San Francisco Giants, 4821 S Florence Ave, Tulsa, OK 74105-5332 USA

LeMay-Doan, Michelle *Speed Skater*
Landmark Sport Group, 277 Richmond St W, Toronto, ON M5V 1X1, CANADA

Lembeck, Michael *Director, Actor*
23852 Pacific Coast Highway, #355, Malibu, CA 90265 USA

Lemche, Kris *Actor*
Evolution Entertainment, 901 N Highland Ave, Los Angeles, CA 90038 USA

Lemelson, Jerome H *Inventor*
48 Parkside Dr, Princeton, NJ 08540 USA

LeMesurier, John *Actor*
56 Barron's Keep, London, W14, UNITED KINGDOM (UK)

Lemieux, Claude *Hockey Player*
6008 N Saguaro Place, Paradise Valley, AZ 85253 USA

Lemieux, Jocelyn *Hockey Player*
1123 Sandhurst Court, Buffalo Grove, IL 60089 USA

Lemieux, Joseph H *Business Person*
Owens-Illinois Inc, 1 Sea Gate, Toledo, OH 43666 USA

LeMieux, Kathryn *Cartoonist*
King Features Syndicate, 888 7th Ave, New York, NY 10106 USA

Lemieux, Mario *Hockey Player*
630 Academy St, Sewickley, PA 15143 USA

Lemieux, Raymond U *Misc*
7602 119th St, Edmonton, AB T6G 1W3, CANADA

Lemke, Mark A *Baseball Player*
Atlanta Braves, 3 Olena Dr, Whitesboro, NY 13492-2103 USA

Lemme, Steve *Comedian*
United Talent Agency (UTA), 9560 Wilshire Blvd, Beverly Hills, CA 90212 USA

Lemmon, Chris *Actor*
80 Murray Dr, South Glastonbury, CT 06073 USA

Lemmons, Kasi *Director, Writer*
8605 Appian Way, Los Angeles, CA 90046 USA

Lemon, Chester E (Chet) *Baseball Player*
Chicago White Sox, PO Box 951436, Lake Mary, FL 32795-1436 USA

Lemon, Jim *Baseball Player*
Cleveland Indians, 432 Lexington Dr, Sebring, FL 33876-6020 USA

Lemon, Lynn
4914 17th Pl., Lubbock, TX 79415

Lemon, Peter C *War Hero*
6245 Viewfield Heights, Colorado Springs, CO 80919 USA

Lemonds, Dave *Baseball Player*
Chicago Cubs, 5029 Jackson Dr, Charlotte, NC 28269-1910 USA

Lemongelio, Mark *Baseball Player*
Houston Astros, 13437 S 47th St, Phoenix, AZ 85044-4833 USA

Lemonheads
1775 Broadway #433, New York, NY 10019

Lemons, Abe
4314 St. Thomas, Oklahoma City, OK 73120

Lemos, Richie *Boxer*
18658 Klum Place, Rowland Heights, CA 91748 USA

Lemper, Ute *Musician, Actor, Dancer*
Les Visiteurs du Soir, 40 Rue de la Folie Regnault, Paris, 75011, FRANCE

Lenahan, Edward P *Publisher*
Fortune Magazine, Rockefeller Center, New York, NY 10020 USA

Lenard, Michael B *Misc*
US Olympic Committee, 1 Olympia Plaza, Colorado Springs, CO 80909 USA

Lenard, Voshon *Basketball Player*
Denver Nuggets, Pepsi Center, 1000 Chopper Circle, Denver, CO 80204 USA

Lendl, Ivan *Tennis Player*
400 5 1/2 Mile Road, Goshen, CT 06756 USA

Lenfant, Claude J M *Physicist*
PO Box 83027, Gaithersburg, MD 20883 USA

Lengies, Vanessa *Actor*
Brillstein-Grey Entertainment, 9150 Wilshire Blvd #350, Beverly Hills, CA 90212 USA

Lenhardt, Don *Baseball Player*
St Louis Browns, 13317 Woodlake Village Ct, Saint Louis, MO 63141-6071 USA

Lenihan, Brian J *Government Official*
24 Park View, Castleknock, County Dublin, IRELAND

Leningrad CowboysBMG Ariola
Steinhauser Str. 3, Munich, GERMANY, D-81677

Lenk, Maria *Swimmer*
Rua Cupertino Durao 16, Leblon, Rio de Janeiro, 22441, BRAZIL

Lenk, Thomas *Artist*
Gemeinde Braunsbach, Schloss Tierberg, 7176, GERMANY

Lenk, Tom *Actor*
Creative Management Group, 3815 Hughes Ave Fl 3, Culver City, CA 90232 USA

Lennie, Angus *Actor*
Jean Drysdale, 15 Pembroke Gardens, London, W8, UNITED KINGDOM (UK)

Lennix, Harry *Actor*
International Creative Management (ICM-LA), 8942 Wilshire Blvd, Beverly Hills, CA 90211 USA

Lennon, Bob *Baseball Player*
New York Giants, 8 Dudley Ln, Dix Hills, NY 11746-6504 USA

Lennon, Diane *Musician*
1984 State Highway 165, Branson, MO 65616 USA

Lennon, Janet *Musician*
1984 State Highway 165, Branson, MO 65616 USA

Lennon, Julian *Musician, Songwriter*
30 Ives St, London, SW3 2ND, UNITED KINGDOM (UK)

Lennon, Kathy *Musician*
Overlook Dr, #10, Branson, MO 65616 USA

Lennon, Patrick *Baseball Player*
Seattle Mariners, 716 Pinewood Dr, Whiteville, NC 28472-3828 USA

Lennon, Peggy *Musician*
1984 State Highway 165, Branson, MO 65616 USA

Lennon, Richard G *Religious Leader*
Archdiocese of Boston, 2121 Commonwealth Ave, Boston, MA 02135 USA

Lennon, Sean *Musician*
Dakota Hotel, 1 W 72nd St, New York, NY 10023 USA

Lennon, Thomas *Actor*
Principato/Young Management, 9665 Wilshire Blvd #500, Beverly Hills, CA 90212 USA

Lennon Sisters
1984 State Highway 165, Branson, MO 65616-8936

Lennox, Annie *Musician*
Nineteen Music Mgmt, 35-37 Parkgate Road, London, SW11 4NP, UNITED KINGDOM (UK)

Lennox, William Jr *General, Educator*
Superintendent, US Military Academy, West Point, NY 10996 USA

Leno, Jay *Actor, Comedian*
Big Dog Productions, PO Box 7885, Burbank, CA 91510 USA

Lenoir, William B *Astronaut*
Space Flight & Station Office, NASA Hq, Code M/S, Washington

Lenoir, William B *Astronaut*
Space Flight & Station Office, NASA Hq, Code M/S, Washington, DC 20546 USA

Lenska, Rula *Model, Actor*
David Daley Assoc, 586A Kings Road, London, SW6 2DX, UNITED KINGDOM (UK)

Lentine, Jim *Baseball Player*
St Louis Cardinals, 1066 Calle Del Cerro Unit 1411, San Clemente, CA 92672-6075 USA

Lenz, Bethany Joie *Actor*
Envoy Entertainment, 1640 S Sepulveda Blvd #530, Los Angeles, CA 90025 USA

Lenz, Kay *Actor*
5916 Filaree Heights, Malibu, CA 90265 USA

Lenz, Kim *Musician, Songwriter*
Mark Pucia Media, 5000 Oak Bluff Court, Atlanta, GA 30350 USA

Lenz, Rick *Actor*
12955 Calvert St, Van Nuys, CA 91401 USA

Lenzi, Mark *Misc*
117 Bay Meadow Lane, Benson, NC 27504 USA

Leo, Melissa *Actor*
Agency for Performing Arts, 9200 Sunset Blvd, #900, Los Angeles, CA 90069 USA

Leon
1180 S. Beverly Dr. #608, Los Angeles, CA 90035

Leon, Carlos
4519 Cockerham Dr., Los Angeles, CA 90027-1223

Leon, Melina *Musician*
Sony Music Miami, 605 Lincoln Rd, Miami Beach, FL 33138 USA

Leon, Valerie *Actor*
Essanay Ltd, 2 Conduit St, London, W1R 9TG, UNITED KINGDOM (UK)

Leonard, Bob (Slick) *Basketball Player, Coach*
1241 Hillcrest Dr, Carmel, IN 46033 USA

Leonard, Dennis P *Baseball Player*
4102 SW Evergreen Lane, Blue Springs, MO 64015 USA

Leonard, Elmore *Writer*
2192 Yarmouth Road, Bloomfield Village, MI 48301 USA

Leonard, Hugh *Writer*
6 Rossaun Pilot View, Dalkey, County Dublin, IRELAND

Leonard, Joanne *Photographer*
University of Michigan, Art Dept, Ann Arbor, MI 48109 USA

Leonard, Joe *Race Car Driver, Motorcycle Racer*
Motorsports Hall of Fame, PO Box 194, Novi, MI 48376 USA

Leonard, Joshua *Actor*
Innovative Artists (LA), 1505 Tenth St, Santa Monica, CA 90401 USA

Leonard, Justin *Golfer*
3304 Dartmouth Ave, Dallas, TX 75205 USA

Leonard, Ray C (Sugar Ray) *Boxer*
4401 East West Highway, #206B, Bethesda, MD 20814 USA

Leonard, Robert Sean *Actor*
14 Bergen Ave, Waldwick, NJ 07463 USA

Leonard, Wayne *Business Person*
Entergy Corp, 10055 Grogans Mill Road, #5A, The Woodlands, TX 77380 USA

Leonetti, John R *Cinematographer*
5251 Genesta Ave, Encino, CA 91316 USA

Leonetti, Matthew *Cinematographer*
1362 Bella Oceana Vista, Pacific Palisades, CA 90272 USA

Leong, Page *Actor*
C N A Assoc, 1925 Century Park East, #750, Los Angeles, CA 90067 USA

Leonhart, William *Diplomat*
2618 30th St NW, Washington, DC 20008 USA

Leoni, Tea *Actor*
PO Box 10459, Burbank, CA 91510 USA

Leonov, Aleksei A *Cosmonaut, General*
Alfa Capital, Acad Sakharov Prospect 12, Moscow, 107078, RUSSIA

Leonskaja, Elisabeth *Musician*
Columbia Artists Mgmt Inc, 165 W 57th St, New York, NY 10019 USA

Leopold, Luna B *Engineer*
PO Box 1040, Pinedale, WY 82941 USA

Leopold, Tom *Comedian*
Gersh Agency, The (LA), 232 N Canon Dr, Beverly Hills, CA 90210 USA

LePelley, Guernsey *Editor, Cartoonist*
35 Saint Germain St, Boston, MA 02115 USA

LePichon, Xavier *Geophysicist*
Ecole Normale Superieure, 24 Rue Lhomond, Paris, 75005, FRANCE

Leppard, Raymond J
Indianapolis Symphony, 32 E Washington St, #600, Indianapolis, IN 46204 USA

Lerach, William (Bill) *Attorney General*
Milberg Weiss Hynes Lerach, 1600 W Broadway, #1800, San Diego, CA 92101 USA

Lerman, Logan *Actor*
Abrams Artists Agency (LA), 9200 Sunset Blvd Fl 11, Los Angeles, CA 90069 USA

Lerner, Michael *Actor*
Innovative Artists, 1505 10th St, Santa Monica, CA 90401 USA

LeRoux, Francois *Opera Singer*
I M G Artists, 3 Burlington Lane, Chiswick, London, W4 2TH, UNITED KINGDOM (UK)

LeRoy, Gloria *Actor*
Shelly & Pierce, 13775A Mono Way, #220, Sonora, CA 95370 USA

Leroy, Philippe
77 rue Pigalle, Paris, FRANCE, F-75009

Lesar, David *Business Person*
Halliburton Co, Lincoln Plaza, 500 N Akard St, Dallas, TX 75201 USA

Leschin, Luisa *Writer, Producer*
William Morris Agency (WMA-LA), 1 William Morris Pl, Beverly Hills, CA 90212 USA

Lesco, Lisa *Actor*
1224 N Crescent Heights Blvd, #6, West Hollywood, CA 90046 USA

Lesh, Phil *Musician*
PO Box 1073, San Rafael, CA 94915 USA

Leshana, David C *Educator*
5737 Charles Circle, Lake Oswego, OR 97035 USA

Leslie, Aleen
1700 Lexington Rd., Beverly Hills, CA 90210

Leslie, Fred W *Astronaut*
2513 Clifton Dr SE, Huntsville, AL 35803 USA

Leslie, Joan *Actor*
2228 N Catalina, Los Angeles, CA 90027 USA

Leslie, Lisa *Basketball Player, Model*
5200 Shenandoah Ave, Los Angeles, CA 90056 USA

Lesnar, Brock *Wrestler*
World Wrestling Entertainment (WWE), 1241 E Main St, Stamford, CT 06905 USA

Lesnie, Andrew *Cinematographer*
United Talent Agency (UTA), 9560 Wilshire Blvd, Beverly Hills, CA 90212 USA

Lessard, Stefan *Musician, Songwriter*
Red Light Mgmt, 3302 Loban Place, Charlottesville, VA 22903 USA

Lesser, Len *Actor*
934 N Evergreen St, Burbank, CA 91505 USA

Lessing, Doris M *Writer*
11 Kingscroft Road, #3, London, NW2 3QE, UNITED KINGDOM (UK)

Lester, Darrell G *Football Player*
3103 Meadow Oaks Dr, Temple, TX 76502 USA

Lester, Ketty *Actor, Musician*
5931 Comey Ave, Los Angeles, CA 90034 USA

Lester, Mark *Actor*
Carlton Clinic, 1 Carlton St, Cheltenham, Glou, GLS2 6AG, UNITED KINGDOM (UK)

Lester, Mark L *Director*
17268 Camino Yatasto, Pacific Palisades, CA 90272 USA

Lester, Richard
River Lane Petersham, Surrey, ENGLAND

Lester, Richard (Dick) *Director*
River Lane, Petersham, Surrey, UNITED KINGDOM (UK)

Lester of Herne Hill, Anthony P *Attorney General*
Blackstone Chambers, Blackstone House, Temple, London, EC4Y 9BW, UNITED KINGDOM (UK)

Lesure, James *Actor*
Integrated Films & Management, 1041 N Formosa Ave, Santa Monica Bldg W #17, W Hollywood, CA 90046 USA

Letarte, Pierre *Cinematographer*
551 W Pinacle, Albercom, QC, J0E 1B0, CANADA

Letbetter, R Steve *Business Person*
Reliant Energy, 1111 Louisiana, Houston, TX 77002 USA

Lethem, Jonathan *Writer*
Doubleday Press, 1540 Broadway, New York, NY 10036 USA

Letlow, W R (Russ) *Football Player*
1876 Thelma Dr, San Luis Obispo, CA 93405 USA

Leto, Jared *Actor*
United Talent Agency, 9560 Wilshire Blvd, #500, Beverly Hills, CA 90212 USA

Letscher, Matt *Actor*
SLJ Management, 8336 De Longpre Ave, Los Angeles, CA 90069 USA

Letsie III *King*
Royal Palace, PO Box 524, Maseru, LESOTHO

Lett, Leon *Football Player*
4959 Cape Coral Dr, Dallas, TX 75287 USA

Letterle, Daniel *Actor*
Endeavor Agency LLC (LA), 9601 Wilshire Blvd Fl 3, Beverly Hills, CA 90210 USA

Letterman, David *Entertainer, Comedian*
Worldwide Pants, 1697 Broadway, 30th Floor, New York, NY 10019 USA

Lettermen, The
9255 Sunset Blvd. #407, Los Angeles, CA 90069

Letts, Billie *Writer*
Warner Books, 1271 Ave of Americas, New York, NY 10020 USA

Leung, Ken *Actor*
Anonymous Content, 8522 National Blvd #101, Culver City, CA 90232 USA

Leuwerik, Ruth
Zuccalistr. 31, Munich, GERMANY, D-80639

Levangie, Gigi *Writer*
William Morris Agency (WMA-LA), 1 William Morris Pl, Beverly Hills, CA 90212 USA

LeVay, Simon *Scientist*
970 Palm Ave, West Hollywood, CA 90069 USA

Levchenko, Alexander
141 Sryosdny Gorodok, Potchta Kosmonavtov, RUSSIA

Levellers *Music Group*
Little Big Man Booking, Little Big Man Bldg, 155 6th Avenue, 6th Floor, New York, NY 10013 USA

Levene, Ben *Artist*
Royal Academy of Arts, Piccadilly, London, W1V 2LP, UNITED KINGDOM (UK)

Levens, Dorsey *Football Player*
224 Primrose Ave, Syracuse, NY 13205 USA

Levenstein, John *Comedian*
International Creative Management (ICM-LA), 8942 Wilshire Blvd, Beverly Hills, CA 90211 USA

Leveque, Michel *Politician*
Minister of State's Office, BP 522, Monaco Cedex, 98015, MONACO

Lever, Johny *Actor, Comedian, Bollywood*
151/152 Oxford Tower Yamuna Nagar, Lokhandwala Complex Andheri, Bombay, MS 400 058, INDIA

Leverington, Shelby
1801 Ave. of the Stars #1250, Los Angeles, CA 90067

Levert, Eddie *Musician*
Associated Booking Corp, 1995 Broadway, #501, New York, NY 10023 USA

Levert, Gerald *Musician*
Associated Booking Corp, 1995 Broadway #501, New York, NY 10023 USA

Levesque, Paul Michael *Wrestler*
Endeavor Agency LLC (LA), 9601 Wilshire Blvd Fl 3, Beverly Hills, CA 90210 USA

Levi, Wayne *Golfer*
17 Ironwood Road, New Hartford, NY 13413 USA

Levi, Yoel
Askonas Holt Ltd, 27 Chancery Lane, London, WC2A 1PF, UNITED KINGDOM (UK)

Levi-Montalcini, Rita *Nobel Prize Laureate*
Cell Biology Institute, Piazzale Aldo Moro 7, Rome, 00185, ITALY

Levi-Strauss, Claude *Misc*
2 Rue des Marronniers, Paris, 75016, FRANCE

LeVias, Jerry *Football Player*
3322 Chris Dr, Houston, TX 77063 USA

Levin, Drake *Musician*
Paradise Artists, 108 E Matilija St, Ojai, CA 93023 USA

Levin, Harvey
6922 Hollywood Blvd. #415, Hollywood, CA 90028

Levin, Ira *Writer*
1172 Park Ave, New York, NY 10128 USA

Levin, Richard C *Educator*
Yale University, President's Office, New Heaven, CT 06520 USA

Levin, Tony *Musician*
Agency Group, The (NY), 1775 Broadway #430, New York, NY 10019 USA

Levine, Arnold *Biologist, Educator*
Rockefeller University, President's Office, 1230 York Ave, New York, NY 10021 USA

Levine, David *Artist*
161 Henry St, Brooklyn, NY 11201 USA

Levine, Ellen R *Editor*
Good Housekeeping Magazine, 959 8th Ave, New York, NY 10019 USA

Levine, Irving R *Commentator*
Lynn University, International Studies/ Economics Dept, Boca Raton, FL 33431 USA

Levine, Jack *Artist*
68 Morton St, New York, NY 10014 USA

Levine, James
Boston Symphony Orchestra, 301 Massachusetts Ave, Boston, MA 02115 USA

Levine, Jerry
1505 10th St., Santa Monica, CA 90401

Levine, Ken *Writer*
Broder Webb Chervin Silbermann Agency, The (BWCS), 9242 Beverly Blvd #200, Beverly Hills, CA 90210 USA

Levine, Michael
10333 Ashton Ave., Los Angeles, CA 90024

Levine, Philip *Writer*
4549 N Van Ness Blvd, Fresno, CA 93704 USA

Levine, Rachmiel *Misc*
614 Walnut St, Newton, 02460 USA

Levine, S Robert *Business Person*
Cabletron Systems, PO Box 5005, Rochester, NH 03866 USA

Levine, Samm *Actor*
3 Arts Entertainment Inc, 9460 Wilshire Blvd Fl 7, Beverly Hills, CA 90212 USA

Levine, Seymour *Biologist*
1512 Notre Dame Dr, Davis, CA 95616 USA

Levine, Sol *Social Activist*
30 Powell St, Brookline, MA 02446 USA

Levine, Ted *Actor*
Innovative Artists (LA), 1505 Tenth St, Santa Monica, CA 90401 USA

Levingston, Cliff *Basketball Player*
Denver Nuggets, Pepsi Center, 1000 Chopper Circle, Denver, CO 80204 USA

Levingstone, Ken *Government Official*
House of Commons, Westminster, London, SW1A 0AA, UNITED KINGDOM (UK)

Levinsohn, Gary *Producer*
Mutual Film Company, 650 Bronson Ave, Clinton Bldg, Los Angeles, CA 90004 USA

Levinson, Barry *Director, Producer, Writer, Actor*
Levinson/Fontana Company, The, 185 Broome St, New York, NY 10022

Levinson, Chris *Writer*
Endeavor Agency LLC (LA), 9601 Wilshire Blvd Fl 3, Beverly Hills, CA 90210 USA

Levinson, Sanford V *Attorney General, Educator*
3410 Windsor Road, Austin, TX 78703 USA

Levinthal, Cyrus *Biologist*
Columbia University, Biological Sciences Dept, New York, NY 10027 USA

Levis, Patrick *Actor*
TalentWorks (LA), 3500 W Olive Ave #1400, Burbank, CA 91505 USA

Levitas, Andrew *Actor*
Metropolitan Talent Agency, 4526 Wilshire Blvd, Los Angeles, CA 90010 USA

Levitch, Ashlee *Actor*
McConnell Management Group (MMG), 8671 Wilshire Blvd #501, Beverly Hills, CA 90211 USA

Levitt, Arthus Jr *Government Official, Financier*
Carlyle Group, 1001 Pennsylvania Ave NW, Washington, DC 20004 USA

Levitt, Gene
9200 Sunset Blvd. PH 25, Los Angeles, CA 90069

Levitt, George *Misc*
82 Via Del Corso, Palm Beach Gardens, FL 33418 USA

LeVox, Gary *Musician*
LBG Media, 1228 Pineview Lane, Nashville, TN 37211 USA

Levy, Clifford J *Journalist*
New York Times, Editorial Dept, 229 W 43rd St, New York, NY 10036 USA

Levy, David *Government Official*
New Way Party, Knesset, Kiryat Ben Gurion, Jerusalem, 91950, ISRAEL

Levy, David H *Astronomer*
Mount Palomar Observatory, Palomar Mountain, Mount Palomar, PA 92060 USA

Levy, Eugene *Actor, Director*
7481 Beverly Blvd, #301, Los Angeles, CA 90036 USA

Levy, Kenneth *Business Person*
KLA-Tencor Corp, 160 Rio Robles, San Jose, CA 95134 USA

Levy, Leonard W *Historian*
1025 Timberline Terrace, Ashland, OR 97520 USA

Levy, Mariana *Actor*
Televisa, Blvd Adolfo Lopez Mateos 232, Colonia San Angel INN, DF, CP 01060, MEXICO

Levy, Marvin David *Composer*
Sheldon Sofer Mgmt, 130 W 56th St, New York, NY 10019 USA

Levy, Michael R *Publisher*
Texas Monthly Magazine, PO Box 1569, Austin, TX 78767 USA

Levy, Peter *Cinematographer*
International Creative Mgmt, 8942 Wilshire Blvd, #219, Beverly Hills, CA 90211 USA

Levy, Shawn *Director, Actor*
Firm, The, 9465 Wilshire Blvd, Beverly
Hills, CA 90212 USA

Lewinsky, Monica *Fashion Designer*
Baker Winokur Ryder (BWR-LA), 9100
Wilshire Blvd Fl 6, W Tower, Beverly
Hills, CA 90212 USA

LeWinter, Nancy Nadler *Publisher*
Esquire Magazine, 1790 Broadway, 1300,
New York, NY 10019 USA

Lewis, Bernard *Historian*
Princeton University, Near Eastern Studies
Dept, Princeton, NJ 08544 USA

Lewis, Aaron *Musician*
Staind/Elektra Records, 75 Rockefeller Plz,
New York, NY 10019

Lewis, Al
Pierce & Shelly, 13775-A Mono Way
#220, Sonora, CA 95370 USA

Lewis, Al (Grandpa) *Actor*
PO Box 277, New York, NY 10044 USA

Lewis, Albert R *Football Player*
3532 Macedonia Road, Centreville, MS
39631 USA

Lewis, Allen *Government Official*
Beaver Lodge, Mom PO Box 1076,
Castries, Sanit Lucia, WEST INDIES

Lewis, Ananda *Talk Show Host*
Endeavor Agency LLC (LA), 9601 Wilshire
Blvd Fl 3, Beverly Hills, CA 90210 USA

Lewis, Andrew L (Drew) *Secretary,
Business Person*
PO Box 70, Lederach, PA 19450 USA

Lewis, Anthony *Writer*
New York Times, Editorial Dept, 2 Faneuil
Hall, Boston, MA 02109 USA

Lewis, Barbara *Musician*
Hello Stranger Productions, PO Box
300488, Fern Park, FL 32730 USA

Lewis, Bill *Football Coach*
Georgia Institute of Technology, Athletic
Dept, Atlanta, GA 30332 USA

Lewis, Bobby *Musician*
Lustig Talent, PO Box 770850, Orlando,
FL 32877 USA

Lewis, Carl *Actor*
William Morris Agency (WMA-LA), 1
William Morris Pl, Beverly Hills, CA
90212 USA

Lewis, Charlotte *Basketball Player*
2814 N Sheridan Road, Peoria, IL 61604
USA

Lewis, Clea *Actor*
1659 S Highland Ave, Los Angeles, CA
90019 USA

Lewis, Crystal *Musician*
Proper Mgmt, PO Box 150867, Nashville,
TN 37215 USA

Lewis, Cynthia R *Publisher*
Harper's Bazaar, 1770 Broadway, New
York, NY 10019 USA

Lewis, D D *Football Player*
PCS Sales, 1624 Northcrest Dr, Plano, TX
75075 USA

Lewis, Damian *Actor*
Markham & Froggalt, Julian House, 4
Windmill St, London, W1P 1HF, UNITED
KINGDOM (UK)

Lewis, Damione *Football Player*
Saint Louis Rams, 901 N Broadway, Saint
Louis, MO 63101 USA

Lewis, Darren *Football Player*
641 Seabeach Road, Dallas, TX 75232
USA

Lewis, Dave *Hockey Player, Coach*
22583 Heatherbridge Lane, Northville,
MN 48167 USA

Lewis, David Levering *Writer*
Rutgers University, History Dept, East
Rutherford, NJ 08903 USA

Lewis, David R *Football Player*
2363 Gallant Fox Court, Reston, VA
20191 USA

Lewis, Dawnn *Actor*
PO Box 56718, Sherman Oaks, CA 91413
USA

Lewis, Emmanuel (Manny) *Actor*
Orange Grove Group Inc, 12178 Ventura
Blvd #205, Studio City, CA 91604 USA

Lewis, F Carlton (Carl) *Track Athlete*
9777 Harwin, #307, Houston, TX 77036
USA

Lewis, Gary *Musician*
701 Balin Court, Nashville, TN 37221
USA

Lewis, Geoffrey *Actor*
William Morris Agency, 151 El Camino
Dr, Beverly Hills, CA 90212 USA

Lewis, Grady *Basketball Player*
8926 W Topeka Dr, Peoria, IL 61615 USA

Lewis, Huey *Musician, Actor*
Bob Brown Mgmt, PO Box 779, Mill
Valley, CA 94942 USA

Lewis, Jamal *Football Player*
Baltimore Ravens, Ravens Stadium, 11001
Russell St, Baltimore, MD 21230 USA

Lewis, Jason *Actor*
ROAR LLC, 2400 Broadway #350, Santa
Monica, CA 90404 USA

Lewis, Jazsmin
Evolution Entertainment, 901 N Highland
Ave, Los Angeles, CA 90038 USA

Lewis, Jenifer
PO Box 5617, Beverly Hills, CA 90210

Lewis, Jenna
777 Davis St., San Francisco, CA 94111

Lewis, Jennifer *Journalist*
NBC Television (NY), 30 Rockefeller
Plaza, New York, NY 10112 USA

Lewis, Jermaine *Football Player*
Octagon, 1751 Pinnacle Dr, #1500,
McLean, VA 22102 USA

Lewis, Jerry *Comedian, Actor, Director*
1701 Waldman Ave, Las Vegas, NV
89102 USA

Lewis, Jerry Lee *Musician, Composer*
JKL Enterprise, PO Box 384, Nesbit, MS
38651 USA

Lewis, Jon Peter *Reality TV Star, Musician*
American Idol, 7800 Beverly Blvd #251,
Los Angeles, CA 90036 USA

Lewis, Judy
71359 Cypress Dr., Rancho Mirage, CA
92270-3553

Lewis, Juliette *Actor*
8995 Elevado, Los Angeles, CA 90069
USA

Lewis, Karen *Writer*
Sarnoff Co, 10 Universal City Plz Fl 20,
Universal City, CA 91608 USA

Lewis, Kenneth D *Financier*
Bank of America Corp, 100 N Tryon St,
Charlotte, NC 28255 USA

Lewis, Lennox *Boxer*
Panix Promotions, 99 Middlesex St,
London, E1 7DA, UNITED KINGDOM
(UK)

Lewis, Marcia
700 New Hampshire Ave. NW,
Washington, DC 20037

Lewis, Marvin *Football Coach*
Cincinnati Bengals, 1 Paul Brown
Stadium, Cincinnati, OH 45202 USA

Lewis, Mary (Christianni Brand) *Writer*
88 Maida Vale, London, W9, UNITED
KINGDOM (UK)

Lewis, Matthew *Actor*
Curtis Brown Ltd, Hay Market House
28/29, Hay Market Fl 4, London, SW1
Y45, UNITED KINGDOM (UK)

Lewis, Michael *Writer*
W W Norton, 500 5th Ave, New York,
NY 10110 USA

Lewis, Mo *Football Player*
89 The Glen, Glen Head, NY 11545 USA

Lewis, Monica *Musician*
Lang, 1100 Alta Loma Road, #16A, Los
Angeles, CA 90069 USA

Lewis, Peter B *Business Person*
Progressive Corp, 6300 Wilson Mills
Road, Cleveland, OH 44143 USA

Lewis, Phill
10000 Santa Monica Blvd. #305, Los
Angeles, CA 90067

Lewis, Ramsey *Musician, Composer*
APA Talent and Literary Agency, 9200
Sunset Blvd, Los Angeles, CA 90069 USA

Lewis, Rashard *Basketball Player*
Seattle SuperSonics, 351 Elliott Ave W,
#500, Seattle, WA 98119 USA

Lewis, Ray *Football Player*
1421 Connestee Road, Lakeland, FL
33805 USA

Lewis, Richard *Comedian, Actor*
8001 Hemet Place, Los Angeles, CA
90046 USA

Lewis, Richard J *Producer*
Writers and Artists Group Intl (LA), 8383
Wilshire Blvd #550, Beverly Hills, CA
90211 USA

Lewis, Russell T *Business Person,
Publisher*
New York Times Co, 229 W 43rd St, New
York, NY 10036 USA

Lewis, Shaznay *Musician*
Concorde Intl Artists Ltd, 101 Shepherds
Bush Rd, London, W6 7LP, UNITED
KINGDOM (UK)

Lewis, Vaughan A *Prime Minister*
United Workers Party, 1 Riverside Road,
Castries, SAINT LUCIA

Lewis, Vicki *Actor, Comedian*
Special Artists Agency, 345 N Maple Dr, #302, Beverly Hills, CA 90210 USA

Lewis, Victor *Musician*
Joanne Klein, 130 W 28th St, New York, NY 10001 USA

Lewiston, Denis C *Cinematographer*
13700 Tahiti Way, #24, Marina del Rey, CA 90292 USA

Lewit-Nirenberg, Julie *Publisher*
Mademoiselle Magazine, 350 Madison Ave, New York, NY 10017 USA

LeWitt, Sol *Artist*
20 Pratt St, Chester, CT 06412 USA

Ley, La *Musician*
Creative Artists Agency LCC (CAA-LA), 9830 Wilshire Blvd, Beverly Hills, CA 90212 USA

Leyden, Paul *Actor*
Gersh Agency, The (NY), 41 Madison Ave Fl 33, New York, NY 10010 USA

Leygue, Louis Georges *Artist*
6 Rue de Docteur Blanche, Paris, 75016, FRANCE

Leyland, James R (Jim) *Baseball Player*
261 Tech Road, Pittsburgh, PA 15205 USA

Leyritz, James J (Jim) *Baseball Player*
495 Vinegarten Dr, Cincinnati, OH 45255 USA

Leyton, John *Actor, Musician*
53 Keyes House, Dolphin Square, London, SW1V 3NA, UNITED KINGDOM (UK)

Leyva, Nicholas T (Nick) *Baseball Player*
1098 Tilghman Road, Chesterbrook, PA 19087 USA

LFO *Musician*
Evolution Talent Agency LLC, 1776 Broadway Fl 15, New York, NY 10019 USA

Li, Frederick *Biologist*
Dana-Farber Cancer Institute, 44 Binney St, Boston, MA 02115 USA

Li, Gong *Actor, Model*
Xi'an Film Studio, Xi'an City, Shaanxi Province, CHINA

Li, Jet *Actor*
International Creative Mgmt, 8942 Wilshire Blvd, #219, Beverly Hills, CA 90211 USA

Li, Keyu *Fashion Designer*
21 Gong-Jian Hutong, Di An-Men, Beijing, 100009, CHINA

Li, Lanqing *Government Official*
Communist Party Central Committee, Zhong Nan Hai, Beijing, CHINA

Li, Peng *President*
Communist Party Central Committee, Zhong Nan Hai, Beijing, CHINA

Liacouras, Peter J *Educator*
Temple University, President's Office, Philadelphia, PA 19122 USA

Liaklev, Reidar *Speed Skater*
2770 Jaren, NORWAY

Libano Christo, Carlos A *Social Activist, Writer*
Rua Atibaia 420, Sao Paulo, 01235-010, BRAZIL

Liberace, Dora
1775 E. Tropicana, Las Vegas, NV 89119

Libertini, Richard *Actor*
2313 McKinley Ave, Venice, CA 90291 USA

Liberty, Richard
225 SW 6th St., Dania, FL 33004

Libeskind, Daniel *Architect*
Studio Daniel Libeskund, Windscheidstr 18, Berlin, 10627, GERMANY

Libutti, Frank *General, Misc*
New York City Deputy Commissioner's Office, Police Plaza, New York, NY 10038 USA

Licad, Cecile *Musician*
Columbia Artists Mgmt Inc, 165 W 57th St, New York, NY 10019 USA

Lichfield, Earl of *Photographer*
Lichfield Studios, 133 Oxford Gardens, London, W10 6NE, UNITED KINGDOM (UK)

Licht, Jeremy *Actor*
4355 Clybourn Ave, Toluca Lake, CA 91602 USA

Licht, Louis *Scientist*
Ecoltree, 3017 Valley View Lane NE, North Liberty, IA 52317 USA

Lichtenberg, Byron K *Astronaut*
5701 Impala South Road, Athens, TX 75752 USA

Lichtenberger, H W *Business Person*
Praxair Inc, 39 Old Ridgebury Road, Danbury, CT 06810 USA

Lichtenstein, Harvey *Music Group*
Brooklyn Academy of Music, 30 Lafayette Ave, Brooklyn, NY 11217 USA

Lick, Dennis A *Football Player*
6140 S Knox Ave, Chicago, IL 60629 USA

Licon, Jeffrey *Actor*
Paradigm (LA), 10100 Santa Monica Blvd, Fl 25, Los Angeles, CA 90067 USA

Lidback, Jenny *Golfer*
Ladies Pro Golf Assn, 100 International Golf Dr, Daytona Beach, FL 32124 USA

Liddy, Edward M *Business Person*
Allstate Corp, Allstate Plaza, 2775 Sanders Road, Northbrook, IL 60062 USA

Liddy, G Gordon *Actor*
9112 Riverside Dr, Fort Washington, MD 20744 USA

Lidov, Arthur *Artist*
Pleasant Ridge Road, Poughquag, NY 12570 USA

Lidstrom, Nicklas *Hockey Player*
21174 Dundee Dr, Novi, MI 48375 USA

Lieber, Jonathan R (Jon) *Baseball Player*
310 Main St, Springville, AL 35146 USA

Lieber, Larry *Cartoonist*
King Features Syndicate, 888 7th Ave, New York, NY 10106 USA

Lieber, Paul *Actor*
Margrit Polak Management, 1411 Carroll Ave, Los Angeles, CA 90026 USA

Lieber, Rob *Writer*
International Creative Management (ICM-LA), 8942 Wilshire Blvd, Beverly Hills, CA 90211 USA

Lieberman, Joseph I *Senator*
Senate Hart Office Bldg #SH-706, Washington, DC 20510 USA

Lieberman, Wendy
PO Box 5617, Beverly Hills, CA 90210

Lieberman, William S *Misc*
Metropolitan Museum of Art, 5th Ave & 82nd St, New York, NY 10028 USA

Lieberman-Cline, Nancy *Basketball Player*
6616 Dupper Court, Dallas, TX 75252 USA

Liebert, Ottmar *Musician*
Jones & O'Malley, 10123 Carmarillo St, Toluca Lake, CA 91602 USA

Lieberthal, Michael S (Mike) *Baseball Player*
1750 Larkfield Ave, Westlake Village, CA 91362 USA

Liebeskind, John *Doctor*
University of California Medical Center, Surgery Dept, Los Angeles, CA 90024 USA

Liebesman, Jonathan *Director*
Current Entertainment, 1411 Fifth St #405, Santa Monica, CA 90401 USA

Liebman, David *Musician*
2206 Brislin Road, Stroudsberg, PA 18360 USA

Liebowitz, Fran
205 W. 57th St., New York, NY 10019

Liefeld, Rob *Cartoonist*
Image Comics, 1071 N Batavia St, #A, Orange, CA 92867 USA

Lien, Chan *Prime Minister*
Prime Minister's Office, 1 Chunghsiano East Road, Sec 1, Taipei, TAIWAN

Lien, Jennifer *Actor*
1700 Varilla Dr, West Covina, CA 91792 USA

Lienas, Winston *Baseball Player*
California Angels, Apartado #92, Santiago Dominican Republic

Lienhard, William (Bill) *Basketball Player*
1320 Lawrence Ave, Lawrence, KS 66049 USA

Liepa, Andris *Ballerina*
Bryusov Per 17, #12, Moscow, 103009, RUSSIA

Liepa, Iisa *Ballerina*
Bryusov Per 17, #12, Moscow, 103009, RUSSIA

Liepmann, Hans W *Physicist, Engineer*
55 Haverstock Road, La Canada-Flintridge, CA 91011 USA

Lietzke, Bruce *Golfer*
5716 Arcady Place, Plano, TX 75093 USA

Lifehouse *Music Group*
Creative Artists Agency (CAA-Nashville), 3310 West End Ave Fl 5, Nashville, TN 37203 USA

Lifeson, Alex *Musician*
Macklam Feldman Mgmt, 1505 W 2nd Ave, #200, Vancouver, BC V6H 3Y4, CANADA

Lifford, Tina *Actor*
Sanders/Armstrong Management, 2120 Colorado Blvd #120, Santa Monica, CA 90404 USA

Lifvendahl, Harold R *Publisher*
Orlando Sentinel, 633 N Orange Ave, Orlando, FL 32801 USA

Ligarde, Sebastian *Actor*
Televisa, Blvd Adolfo Lopez Mateos 232, Colonia San Angel INN, DF, CP 01060, MEXICO

Ligeti, Gyorgy S *Composer*
Himmelhofgasse 34, Vienna, 1130, AUSTRIA

Light, John *Actor*
CAA, 9830 Wilshire Blvd, Beverly Hills, CA 90212

Light, Judith *Actor*
1888 Century Park East, #500, Los Angeles, CA 90067 USA

Lightfoot, Gordon *Musician, Songwriter*
That's Entertainment, 1711 Lawrence Road, #101, Franklin, TN 37069 USA

Lightfoot, Leonard
446 S. Orchard Dr., Burbank, CA 91506-2738

Lightner, Candy *Social Activist*
22653 Pacific Coast Highway, #289, Malibu, CA 90265 USA

Ligon, Tom
227 Waverly Pl., New York, NY 10014

Ligouri, James A *Educator*
Iona College, President's Office, New Rochelle, NY 10801 USA

Likens, Gerie E *Biologist*
Ecosystem Studies Institute, PO Box AB, Millbrook, NY 12545 USA

Likens, Peter W *Educator*
Lehigh University, President's Office, Bethlehem, PA 18015 USA

Lil Jon & the East Side Boys *Music Group*
TVT Records, 23 East 4th Street, New York, NY 10003 USA

Lil' Cease *Musician*
Famous Artists Agency, 250 W 57th St, New York, NY 10107 USA

Lil' J *Musician, Actor, Television Host*
Thruline Entertainment, 9250 Wilshire Blvd, Ground Floor, Beverly Hills, CA 90210 USA

Lil' Kim *Musician*
Entertainment Artists, 2409 21st Ave S, #100, Nashville, TN 37212 USA

Lilienfeld, Abraham M *Biologist*
3203 Old Post Dr, Pikesville, MD 21208 USA

Lill, John R *Musician*
Harold Holt, 31 Sinclair Road, London, W14 0NS, UNITED KINGDOM (UK)

Lillard, Bill *Bowler*
5418 Imogene St, Houston, TX 77096 USA

Lillard, Matthew *Actor*
Mosaic Media Group, 9200 Sunset Blvd Fl 10, Los Angeles, CA 90069 USA

Lillee, Dennis K *Cricketer*
Swan Sport, PO Box 158, Byron Bay, NSW, 2481, AUSTRALIA

Lilley, James R *Diplomat*
2801 New Mexico Ave NW, #407, Washington, DC 20007 USA

Lillis, Charles M *Business Person*
MediaOne Group, 188 Iverness Dr W, Englewood, CO 80112 USA

Lillix *Music Group*
SL Feldman & Associates, 1505 W 2nd Ave #200, Vancouver BC, V6H 3Y, CANADA

Lilly, Kristine *Athlete, Soccer Player*
Boston Breakers, 200 Highland Avenue, Suite 400, Needham, MA 02494 USA

Lilly, Robert L (Bob) *Football Player*
104 Aster Circle, Georgetown, TX 78628 USA

Lillywhite, Verl
PO Box 957, Inyokern, CA 93527-0597

Lim, Kwan Hi
1660 Piikoi St., Honolulu, HI 96822

Lima, Adriana *Actor*
DNA Model Management, 520 Broadway Fl 11, New York, NY 10012 USA

Lima, Devin
LFO/BMG Records, 8750 Wilshire Blvd, Beverly Hills, CA 90211

Lima, Jose *Baseball Player*
Carr Janico Km 12 1/2, #61, Santigo, DOMINICAN REPUBLIC

Lima, Luis *Opera Singer*
1950 Redondela Dr, Rancho Palos Verdes, CA 90275 USA

Limato, Ed
456 S. Plymouth Blvd, Los Angeles, CA 90020

Limbaugh, Rush *Entertainer*
PO Box 2182, Palm Beach, FL 33480 USA

Lime, Yvonne *Actor*
Fedderson, 6135 E McDonald Dr, Paradise Valley, AZ 85253 USA

Limelighters, The
11761 E. Speedway Blvd, Tucson, AZ 85748-2017

Limelights
11761 E. Speedway Blvd., Tucson, AZ 85748-2917

Limos, Tiffany *Actor*
Paradigm (LA), 10100 Santa Monica Blvd, Fl 25, Los Angeles, CA 90067 USA

Lin, Bridget *Actor*
8 Fei Ngo Shan Road, Kowloon, Hong Kong, CHINA

Lin, Ching-Hsia *Actor*
Taiwan Cinema-Drama Assn, 196 Chunghua Road, 10/F Sec 1, Taipei, TAIWAN

Lin, Cho-Laing
473 West End Ave. #15A, New York, NY 10024

Lin, Cho-Liang *Musician*
Hilliard School, 60 Lincoln Center Plaza, New York, NY 10023 USA

Lin, Maya Ying *Architect, Artist*
Sidney Janis Gallery, 120 E 75th St, #6A, New York, NY 10021 USA

Lin, Tsung-Yi *Misc*
6287 MacDonald St, Vancouver, BC V6N 1E7, CANADA

Lincoln, Abbey *Songwriter, Musician*
645 W End Ave, New York, NY 10025 USA

Lincoln, Andrew *Actor*
International Creative Management (ICM-UK), Oxford House, 76 Oxford St, London, W1N OAX, UNITED KINGDOM (UK)

Lincoln, Keith P *Football Player*
770 SE Ridgeview Court, Pullman, WA 99163 USA

Lincoln, Lar Park
8899 Beverly Blvd. #510, Los Angeles, CA 90048

Lind, DeDe
PO Box 1712, Boca Raton, FL 33429

Lind, Don L *Astronaut*
51 N 376 E, Smithfield, UT 84335 USA

Lind, Joan *Athlete*
240 Euclid Ave, Long Beach, CA 90803 USA

Lind, Juha *Hockey Player*
Montreal Canadiens, 1260 de la Gauchetiere W, Montreal, QC, H3B 5E8, CANADA

Lind, Marshall L *Educator*
University of Alaska Southeast, Chancellor's Office, Janeau, AK 99801 USA

Lindahl, George III *Business Person*
Union Pacific Resources, PO Box 1330, Houston, TX 77251 USA

Lindbeck, Assar *Economist*
50 Ostermalmsgatan, Stockholm, 114 26, SWEDEN

Lindbeck, Em *Baseball Player*
Detroit Tigers, 210 Hillcrest Dr, Kewanee, IL 61443-3424 USA

Lindberg, Chad *Actor*
Michael Black Management, 5750 Wilshire Blvd #640, Los Angeles, CA 90036 USA

Lindblad, Paul *Baseball Player*
Kansas City A's, 4802 Ashworth Ct, Arlington, TX 76017-1036 USA

Lindelind, Liv *Model*
PO Box 1029, Frazier Park, CA 93225 USA

Lindeman, Jim *Baseball Player*
St Louis Cardinals, 2278 S Scott St, Des Plaines, IL 60018-3147 USA

Linden, Hal *Actor*
Studio 54, 254 W 54th St, New York, NY 10019 USA

Linden, Todd *Baseball Player*
San Francisco Giants, 6918 208th St SW Unit 306, Lynnwood, WA 98036-5867 USA

Linden, Walt *Baseball Player*
Boston Braves, 4432 Harvey Ave, Western Springs, IL 60558-1645 USA

Lindenlaub, Karl W *Cinematographer*
3021 Nicholas Canyon Road, Los Angeles, CA 90046 USA

Lindenmann, Tony *Bowler*
35096 Jefferson Ave, #216, Harrison Township, MI 48045 USA

Linder, Kate *Actor*
9111 Wonderland Ave, Los Angeles, CA 90046 USA

Lindes, Hal *Musician*
Damage Mgmt, 16 Lambton Place, London, W11 2SH, UNITED KINGDOM (UK)

Lindh, Hilary *Skier*
PO Box 33036, Juneau, AK 99803 USA

Lindholm, Ingvar
Hringe Hages Vag 33, Ronninge, SWEDEN, 14400

Lindig, Bill M *Business Person*
Sysco Corp, 1390 Enclave Parkway, Houston, TX 77077 USA

Lindley, Christina *Model*
Lindley Enterprises, PO Box 712, Madison, TN 37116 USA

Lindley, John W *Cinematographer*
15332 Antioch St, PO Box 351, Pacific Palisades, CA 90272 USA

Lindner, William G *Misc*
Transport Workers Union, 80 W End Ave, New York, NY 10023 USA

Lindo, Delroy *Actor*
Rigberg-Rugolo Entertainment, 1180 S Beverly Dr #601, Los Angeles, CA 90035 USA

Lindon, Vincent *Actor*
Artmedia, 20 Ave Rapp, Paris, 75007, FRANCE

Lindquist, Susan L *Biologist*
Whitehead Institute, 9 Cambridge Circle, Cambridge, MA 02142 USA

Lindros, Eric *Hockey Player*
411 Glencaim Ave, Toronto, ON M5N 1V4, CANADA

Lindroth, Eric *Misc*
13151 Dufresne Place, San Diego, CA 92129 USA

Lindsay, Jack *Writer*
56 Maids Causeway, Cambridge, UNITED KINGDOM (UK)

Lindsay, Mark *Musician, Songwriter*
Mars Talent, 27 L'Ambiance Court, Bardonia, NY 10954 USA

Lindsay, Mort
6970 Fernhill Dr., Malibu, CA 90265

Lindsay, R B Theodore (Ted) *Hockey Player*
2598 Invitational Dr, Oakland, MI 48363 USA

Lindsay, Robert *Actor, Musician*
Felix de Wolfe, 1 Robert St, Adelphi, London, WC2N 6BH, UNITED KINGDOM (UK)

Lindsay, Robert V *Financier*
PO Box 1454, Millbrook, NY 12545 USA

Lindsey, Bill *Baseball Player*
Chicago White Sox, 3646 NE 5th Ter, Ocala, FL 34479-2331 USA

Lindsey, Doug *Baseball Player*
Philadelphia Phillies, 1909 Woodland Dr, Cedar Park, TX 78613-6737 USA

Lindsey, George (Goober) *Actor, Musician*
PO Box 12089, Nashville, TN 37212 USA

Lindsey, Johanna *Writer*
Avon William Morrow, 1350 Ave of Americas, New York, NY 10019 USA

Lindsey, Rodney *Baseball Player*
Detroit Tigers, 507 Comanchee Dr, Opelika, AL 36804-7773 USA

Lindsey, Steven W *Astronaut*
14702 Dawn Vale Dr, Houston, TX 77062 USA

Lindsey, Tracy
651 N. Kilkea Dr., Los Angeles, CA 90048

Lindsley, Blake *Actor*
Gold Marshak Liedtke, 3500 W Olive Ave, #1400, Burbank, CA 91505 USA

Lindsley, Donald B *Physicist*
517 11th St, Santa Monica, CA 90402 USA

Lindstrand, Per *Misc*
Thunder & Colt, Maesbury Road, Oswestry, Shropshire, SY10 8HA, UNITED KINGDOM (UK)

Lindstrom, Charlie *Baseball Player*
Chicago White Sox, PO Box 486, Atlanta, IL 61723-0486 USA

Lindstrom, Jack *Cartoonist*
United Feature Syndicate, 200 Madison Ave, New York, NY 10016 USA

Lindstrom, Jon *Actor*
Artists Group, 10100 Santa Monica Blvd, #2490, Los Angeles, CA 90067 USA

Lindvall, Olle *Doctor*
University of Lund, Medical Cell Research Dept, Lund, 23362, SWEDEN

Lindwall, Raymond R *Cricketer*
3 Wentworth Court, Endeavour St Mt Ommaney, Brisbane, QLD, 4074, AUSTRALIA

Linear
2139 University Dr. #348, Coral Springs, FL 33071

Linebrink, Scott *Baseball Player*
San Francisco Giants, PO Box 862, Taylor, TX 76574-0862 USA

Lineger, Jerry
2101 NASA Rd., Houston, TX 77058-3696

Lineker, Gary W *Soccer Player*
Markee UK, 6 Saint George St, Nottingham, NG1 3BE, UNITED KINGDOM (UK)

Linenger, Jerry M *Astronaut*
550 S Stoney Point Road, Suttons Bay, MI 49682 USA

Lines, Dick *Baseball Player*
Washington Senators, 46 Oceans Blvd, Naples, FL 34104-4123 USA

Liney, John *Cartoonist*
King features Syndicate, 888 7th Ave, New York, NY 10106 USA

Ling *Model*
I M G Models, 304 Park Ave S, #1200, New York, NY 10010 USA

Ling, Bai *Actor*
Innovative Artists, 1505 10th St, Santa Monica, CA 90401 USA

Ling, Lisa *Commentator*
William Morris Agency, 1325 Ave of Americas, New York, NY 10019 USA

Ling, Sergei S *Prime Minister*
Prime Minister's Office, Pl Nezavisimosti, Minsk, 220010, BELARUS

Linhart, Cart *Baseball Player*
Detroit Tigers, 2647 Delmar Ave, Granite City, IL 62040-3439 USA

Liniak, Cole *Baseball Player*
Chicago Cubs, 6973 Blue Orchid Ln, Carlsbad, CA 92009-5164 USA

Link, Arthur A *Governor*
2201 Grimsrud Dr, Bismarck, ND 58501 USA

Linke, Paul *Actor*
Zealous Artists, 139 S Beverly Dr, #225, Beverly Hills, CA 90212 USA

Linker, Amy *Actor*
Lemack & Company (Mgmt), 221 south Gale Drive, Suite 403, Beverly HIlls, CA 90211 USA

Linkert, Lo *Cartoonist*
Singer Media Corp, 23411 Summerfield, #16E, Aliso Viejo, CA 92656 USA

Linklater, Richard *Director, Writer*
Creative Artists Agency, 9830 Wilshire Blvd, Beverly Hills, CA 90212 USA

Linklatter, Hamish
800 S. Robertson Blvd., Los Angeles, CA 90035

Linkletter, Art *Entertainer*
1100 Bel Air Road, Los Angeles, CA 90077 USA

Linkletter, John A *Editor*
Popular Mechanics Magazine, Editorial Dept, 224 W 57th St, New York, NY 10019 USA

Linn, Richard *Judge*
US Court of Appeals, 717 Madison Place NW, Washington, DC 20439 USA

Linn, Teri Ann *Actor*
Sutton Barth Vennari, 145 S Fairfax Ave, #310, Los Angeles, CA 90036 USA

Linn-Baker, Mark *Actor*
27702 Fairweather St, Canyon Country, CA 91351 USA

Linnehan, Richard M *Astronaut*
16802 Hartwood Way, Houston, TX 77058 USA

Linney, Laura *Actor*
The Firm, 9100 Whilshire Blvd, #100W, Beverly Hills, CA 90210 USA

Linowitz, Sol M *Diplomat*
2230 California St NW, #4B, Washington, DC 20008 USA

Linseman, Ken *Hockey Player*
1070 Ocean Blvd, Hampton, NH 03842 USA

Linson, Art *Director, Producer*
Art Linson Productions, Warner Bros, 4000 Warner Blvd, Burbank, CA 91522 USA

Lint, Royce *Baseball Player*
St Louis Cardinals, 6814 SE Jack Rd, Milwaukie, OR 97222-2834 USA

Lintel, Michelle *Actor*
William Morris Agency (WMA-LA), 1 William Morris Pl, Beverly Hills, CA 90212 USA

Linteris, Gregory T *Astronaut*
US Commerce Dept, Fire Science Division, Gaithersburg, MD 20899 USA

Linton, Doug *Baseball Player*
Toronto Blue Jays, 201 Ellison St, Rochester, NY 14609-4047 USA

Lintz, Larry *Baseball Player*
Montreal Expos, PO Box 231854, Sacramento, CA 95823-0414 USA

Linville, Joanne *Actor*
345 N Maple Dr, #302, Beverly Hills, CA 90210 USA

Linz, Alex D *Actor*
Innovative Artists, 1505 10th St, Santa Monica, CA 90401 USA

Linz, Phil *Baseball Player*
New York Yankees, 20 Rocky Raplds Rd, Stamford, CT 06903-3131 USA

Linzy, Frank *Baseball Player*
San Francisco Giants, RR 2 Box 39-5, Coweta, OK 74429-9802 USA

Lioeanjie, Rene *Misc*
National Maritime Union, 1150 17th St NW, Washington, DC 20036 USA

Lionetti, Donald M *General*
7648 San Remo Place, Orlando, FL 32835 USA

Lions, Jacques-Louis *Mathematician*
7 Rue Paul Barruel, Paris, 75015 USA

Lions, Pierre-Louis *Mathematician*
Paris University, Place Marechal Lattre-de-Tessigny, Paris, 75775, FRANCE

Liotta, Ray *Actor*
16829 Monte Hermosa Dr, Pacific Palisades, CA 90272 USA

Lipa, Elisabeta *Athlete*
Str Reconstructiei 1, #78, Bucharest, ROMANIA

Lipetri, Angelo *Baseball Player*
Philadelphia Phillies, 150 Yoakum Ave, Farmingdale, NY 11732-5034 USA

Lipinski, Ann Marie *Journalist*
Chicago Tribune, Editorial Dept, 435 N Michigan Ave, Chicago, IL 60611 USA

Lipinski, Tara *Figure Skater, Actor*
PO Box 1487, Sugar Land, TX 77487-1487 USA

Lipovsek, Marjana *Opera Singer*
Artists Mgmt Zurich, Rutistr 52, Zurich-Gockhausen, 8044, SWITZERLAND

Lippard, Stephen J *Misc*
975 Memorial Dr, #602, Cambridge, MA 02138 USA

Lippincott, Philip E *Business Person*
Campbell Soup Co, Campbell Place, Cemden, NJ 08103 USA

Lipporien, Paavo Tapio *Prime Minister*
Premier's Office, Snellmaninkatu 1, Helsinki, 00170, FINLAND

Lipps, Lisa
2251 N. Rampart Blvd. #355, Las Vegas, NV 89128-7640

Lipps, Louis *Football Player*
276 Annex Dr, Reserve, LA 70084 USA

Lipscomb, William N Jr *Nobel Prize Laureate*
142 Garden St, Cambridge, MA 02138 USA

Lipset, Seymour M *Misc*
900 N Strafford St, #2131, Arlington, VA 22203 USA

Lipsett, Mortimer B *Physicist*
National Institute of Health, 9000 Rockville Pike, Bethesda, MD 20892 USA

Lipshutz, Bruce H *Misc*
University of California, Chemistry Dept, Santa Barbara, CA 93106 USA

Lipski, Bob *Baseball Player*
Cleveland Indians, 1 Snook St, Scranton, PA 18505-2865 USA

Lipson, D Herbert *Publisher*
Philadelphia Magazine, 1500 Walnut St, Philadelphia, PA 19102 USA

Lipton, Holly
1021 16th Ave. So., Nashville, TN 37212

Lipton, James *Television Host, Actor, Producer*
Actors Studio Drama School of NYU, 66 W 12th St, New York, NY 10011

Lipton, Martin *Attorney General*
Wachtell Lipton Rosen Katz, 51 W 52nd St, New York, NY 10019 USA

Lipton, Peggy
Innovative Artists, 1505 10th St, Santa Monica, CA 90401 USA

Lipton, Robert
9300 Wilshire Blvd. #410, Beverly Hills, CA 90212

Liquori, Martin (Marty) *Track Athlete, Sportscaster*
2915 NW 58th Blvd, Gainesville, FL 32606 USA

Liquori, Marty
2915 NW 58th Blvd., Gainesville, FL 32606

Lis, Joe *Baseball Player*
Philadelphia Phillies, 4055 Secretariat Dr, Newburgh, IN 47630-2215 USA

Lisa, Lisa *Musician*
Talent Consultants International, 1560 Broadway, #1308, New York, NY 10036 USA

Lisa, Mona
8860 Corbin #185, Northridge, CA 91324

Lisa Lisa
1560 Broadway #1308, New York, NY 10036

Lisbe, Mike *Writer*
Principato/Young Management, 9665 Wilshire Blvd #500, Beverly Hills, CA 90212 USA

Lisi, Virna *Actor*
Via di Filomarino 4, Rome, ITALY

Lisitsa, Valentina *Musician*
Columbia Artists Mgmt Inc, 165 W 57th St, New York, NY 10019 USA

Liska, Stephen
15050 Sherman Way #167, Van Nuys, CA 91405

Liskov, Barbara H *Engineer*
Massachusetts Institute of Technology, Computer Sci Lab, Cambridge, MA 02139 USA

Liss, Joe *Actor*
Howard Entertainment, 10850 Wilshire Blvd, Suite 1260, Los Angeles, CA 90024 USA

Lissner, Stephane *Opera Singer*
Theatre du Chatelet, 2 Rue Eduouard Colonne, Paris, 75001, FRANCE

List, Peyton *Actor*
As The World Turns, JC Studios, 1268 E 14th St, New York, NY 11230 USA

List, Robert F *Governor*
1660 Catalpa Lane, Reno, NV 89511 USA

Listach, Pat *Baseball Player*
Milwaukee Brewers, PO Box 2012, netchitoches, LA 71457-2012 USA

Lister, Alton *Basketball Player*
233 Hudson Bay, Alameda, CA 94502 USA

Lister Jr, Tommy (Tiny Zeus) *Actor*
Agency for the Performing Arts (APA-LA), 9200 Sunset Blvd #900, Los Angeles, CA 90069 USA

Listowel, Earl of (William F Hare) *Government Official*
10 Downshire Hill, London, NW3, UNITED KINGDOM (UK)

Lithgow, John *Actor*
1319 Warnall Ave, Los Angeles, CA 90024 USA

Littell, Mark *Baseball Player*
Kansas City Royals, 6730 E Hermosa Vista Dr Unit 42, Mesa, AZ 85215-2249 USA

Littell, Robert *Writer*
Penguin Books, 375 Hudson St, New York, NY 10014 USA

Littenberg, Barbara *Architect*
Peterson/Littenberg Achitecture, 13 E 66th St, New York, NY 10021 USA

Litterell, Brian *Musician*
The Firm, 9100 Wilshire Blvd, #100W, Beverly Hills, CA 90210 USA

Little, Milton *Musician*
Camil Productions, 6606 Solitary Ave, Las Vegas, NV 89110 USA

Little, Anthony (Gordine) *Musician*
Mars Talent, 27 L'Ambiance Court, Bardonia, NY 10954 USA

Little, Big Tiny
W. 3985 Taft Dr., Spokane, WA 99208

Little, Bryan *Baseball Player*
Montreal Expos, 4766 Tiffany Park Cir, Bryan, TX 77802-5822 USA

Little, Carole *Fashion Designer*
Carole Little Inc, PO Box 77917, Los Angeles, CA 90007 USA

Little, Chad *Race Car Driver*
5400 Little Parkway, Sherrills Ford, NC 28673 USA

Little, Charles L *Misc*
United Transportation Union, 14600 Detroit Ave, Cleveland, OH 44107 USA

Little, David L *Football Player*
4237 Nandina St, Lake Wales, FL 33898 USA

Little, Dwight H *Director*
Creative Artists Agency, 9830 Wilshire
Blvd, Beverly Hills

Little, Dwight H *Director*
Creative Artists Agency, 9830 Wilshire
Blvd, Beverly Hills, CA 90212 USA

Little, Floyd D *Football Player*
Pacific Coast Ford, 33207 Pacific
Highway S, Federal Way, WA 98003 USA

Little, Jeff *Baseball Player*
St Louis Cardinals, 5711 County Road
169, Genoa, OH 43430 USA

Little, Larry C *Football Player, Coach*
14761 SW 169th Lane, Miami, FL 33187
USA

Little, Mark *Baseball Player*
St Louis Cardinals, 518 Gilbert Dr,
Edwardsville, IL 62025-5300 USA

Little, Rich *Actor, Comedian*
David Martin Management, 13849
Riverside Dr, Sherman Oaks, CA 91423
USA

Little, Robert A *Chef*
49 Firth St, London, W1V 5TE, UNITED
KINGDOM (UK)

Little, Sally *Golfer*
Endicott Assoc, PO Box 10850, Palm
Desert, CA 92255 USA

Little, Scott *Baseball Player*
Pittsburgh Pirates, 1321 Rosebud Dr,
Kackson, MO 63755-1086 USA

Little, Steven *Musician*
Premier Talent, 3 E 54th St, #1100, New
York, NY 10022 USA

Little, Tasmin E *Musician*
harold Holt, 31 Sinclair Road, London,
W14 0NS, UNITED KINGDOM (UK)

Little, Tawny
5515 Melrose Ave., Los Angeles, CA
90038

Little, Tawny Godin *Entertainer, Beauty Pageant Winner*
17941 Sky Park Circle, #F, Irvine, CA
92614 USA

Little, W Grady *Misc*
1 Glen Abbey Trail, Pinehurst, NC 28374
USA

Little Anthony (Gourdine)
27 L'Ambiance Ct., Bardonia, NY 10954-
1421

Little Eva
1161 NW 76th Ave., Ft. Lauderdale, FL
33322

Little River Band
9850 Sandalfoot Blvd. #458, Boca Raton,
FL 33428

Littlefield, John *Baseball Player*
St Louis Cardinals, 1935 Ramar Rd,
Bullhead City, AZ 86442-6949 USA

Littlefield, Warren *Producer*
Littlefield Company, The, 5555 Melrose
Ave, Cooper #115, Hollywood, CA 90038

Littleford, Beth *Actor*
Metropolitan Talent Agency (MTA), 4526
Wilshire Blvd, Los Angeles, CA 90010
USA

Littlejohn, Dennis *Baseball Player*
San Francisco Giants, 6813 Klamath Way
Apt D, Bakersfield, CA 93309-7899 USA

Littler, Gene *Golfer*
PO Box 1949, Rancho Santa Fe, CA
92067 USA

Littles, Gene *Basketball Player*
Denver Nuggets, Pepsi Center, 1000
Chopper Circle, Denver, CO 80204 USA

Littleton, Harvey K *Artist*
RR 1 Box 843, Spruce Pine, NC 28777
USA

Littleton, Larry *Baseball Player*
Cleveland Indians, 107 Avery Dr NE,
Atlanta, GA 30309-2703 USA

Littman, Jonathan *Producer*
Creative Artists Agency LCC (CAA-LA),
9830 Wilshire Blvd, Beverly Hills, CA
90212 USA

Litton, Andrew
IMG Artists, Media House, 3 Burlington
Lane, London, W4 2TH, UNITED
KINGDOM (UK)

Litton, Drew *Editor, Cartoonist*
Rocky Mountain News, Editorial Dept,
400 W Colfax Ave, Denver, CO 80204
USA

Litton, Greg *Baseball Player*
San Francisco Giants, 4296 Brighton Dr,
Pensacola, FL 32504-4928 USA

Littrell, Brian *Musician*
Firm, The, 9465 Wilshire Blvd, Beverly
Hills, CA 90212 USA

Littrell, Gary L *War Hero*
4302 Belle Vista Dr, Saint Petersburg
Beach, FL 33706 USA

Littrell, Jack *Baseball Player*
Philadelphia Athletics, 7510 Floydsburg
Rd, Crestwood, KY 40014-9297 USA

Litwhiler, Danny *Baseball Player*
Philadelphia Phillies, 1411 Stroud Ct,
New Port Richey, FL 34655-4277 USA

Liu, Lucy *Actor*
Framework Entertainment (LA), 9057
Nemo St #C, W Hollywood, CA 90069
USA

Liu, Matthew Stephen
10635 Santa Monica Blvd. #130, Los
Angeles, CA 90025

Liu, Nancy
9057-C Nemo St., W. Hollywood, CA
90069

Liut, Mike *Hockey Player*
945 Wellsley Court, Bloomfield Hills, MI
48304 USA

Livage, Jacques *Misc*
College de France, 11 Place M Berthelot,
Paris Cedex 05, 75231, FRANCE

Lively, Bud *Baseball Player*
Cincinnati Reds, 8605 Esslinger Ct SE,
Huntsville, AL 35802-3640 USA

Lively, Eric *Actor*
Gersh Agency, 232 N Canon Dr, Beverly
Hills, CA 90210 USA

Lively, Penelope M *Writer*
Duck End, Great Rollright, Chipping,
North Oxfordshire, OX7 5SB, UNITED
KINGDOM (UK)

Lively, Robyn *Actor*
William Morris Agency, 151 El Camino
Dr, Beverly Hills, CA 90212 USA

Livermore, Ann *Business Person*
Hewlett-Packard Co, 300 Hanover St,
Palo Alto, CA 94304 USA

Living Colour
6201 Sunset Blvd. #329, Hollywood, CA
90028

Livingston, Barry *Actor*
11310 Blix St, North Hollywood, CA
91602 USA

Livingston, James E *War Hero, General*
3609 Red Oak Court, New Orleans, LA
70131 USA

Livingston, Robert L Jr *Politician*
Livingston Group, 499 S Capitol St SW,
#600, Washington, DC 20003 USA

Livingston, Ron *Actor*
Rigberg Roberts Rugolo, 1180 S Beverly
Dr, #601, Los Angeles, CA 90035 USA

Livingston, Shaun *Basketball Player*
Los Angeles Clippers, Staples Center,
1111 S Figueroa St, Los Angeles, CA
90015 USA

Livingston, Stanley *Actor*
PO Box 1782, Studio City, CA 91614 USA

Livingstone, Scott *Baseball Player*
Detroit Tigers, 1303 Pecos Dr, Southlake,
TX 76092-5915 USA

Livinston *Actor*
45 Thackers Street, Pursawakkam,
Chennai, TN 600 084, INDIA

Lizalde, Enrique *Actor*
Televisa, Blvd Adolfo Lopez Mateos 232,
Colonia San Angel INN, DF, CP 01060,
MEXICO

Lizarazo, Carolina *Actor*
Gabriel Blanco Iglesias (Mexico), Rio
Balsas 35-32, Colonia Cuauhtemoc, DF,
06500, Mexico

Lizaso, Saul *Actor*
Televisa, Blvd Adolfo Lopez Mateos 232,
Colonia San Angel INN, DF, CP 01060,
MEXICO

Lizer, Kari *Actor*
15260 Ventura Blvd, #1040, Sherman
Oaks, CA 91403 USA

Ljungberg, Freddie *Model, Soccer Player*
Calvin Klein Inc, 205 W 39th St Fl 15,
New York, NY 10018 USA

LL Cool J *Musician, Actor*
405 Park Ave #1500, New York, NY
10022 USA

Llaca, Patricia *Actor*
TV Azteca, Periferico Sur 4121, Colonia
Fuentes del Pedregal, DF, CP 14141,
Mexico

Llamosa, Carlos *Soccer Player*
New England Revolution, CMGI Field, 1
Patriot Place, Foxboro, MA 02035 USA

Llewellyn, John A *Astronaut*
University of South Florida, 4202 E Fowler
Ave, Tampa, FL 33620 USA

Llewellyn, Robert *Actor, Writer*
Peters Fraser & Dunlop (PFD - UK), Drury
House, 34-43 Russell St, London, WC2
B5, UNITED KINGDOM (UK)

Llewelyn, Doug
8075 W. 3rd St. #303, Los Angeles, CA 90048

Llosa, Mario Vargas *Writer*
Las Magnolias 295, 6 Piso, Barranco, Lima, 4, PERU

Lloyd, Arroyn *Actor*
Water Street Management, 5225 Wilshire Blvd #615, Los Angeles, CA 90036 USA

Lloyd, Charles *Musician, Composer*
Joel Chriss, 300 Mercer St, #3J, New York, NY 10003 USA

Lloyd, Christopher *Actor*
Managemint, PO Box 491246, Los Angeles, CA 90049 USA

Lloyd, Clive H *Cricketer*
Harefield, Harefield Dr, Wilmslow, Cheshire, SK9 1NJ, UNITED KINGDOM (UK)

Lloyd, Earl *Basketball Player, Coach*
PO Box 1976, Crossville, TN 38558 USA

Lloyd, Emily *Actor*
Malcolm Sheddon Mgmt, 1 Charlotte Square, London, W1P 1DH, UNITED KINGDOM (UK)

Lloyd, Eric *Actor*
Gersh Agency, The (LA), 232 N Canon Dr, Beverly Hills, CA 90210 USA

Lloyd, Geoffrey E R *Misc*
2 Prospect Row, Cambridge, CB1 1DU, UNITED KINGDOM (UK)

Lloyd, Georgina *Writer*
Bantam Books, 1540 Broadway, New York, NY 10036 USA

Lloyd, Graeme *Baseball Player*
Milwaukee Brewers, 1695 Barrabool Road RMB Gnarwarre, Victoria, 3221, AUSTRALIA

Lloyd, Greg
10 Holly Plaza #l33, Santa Claus, IN 47579

Lloyd, Jake *Actor*
Osbrink Talent, 4343 Lankershim Blvd, #100, North Hollywood, CA 91602 USA

Lloyd, Kathleen *Actor*
House of Representatives, 400 S Beverly Dr, #101, Beverly Hills, CA 90212 USA

Lloyd, Madison *Actor*
Osbrink Talent, 4343 Lankershim Blvd, #100, North Hollywood, CA 91602 USA

Lloyd, Norman *Actor*
1813 Old Ranch Road, Los Angeles, CA 90049 USA

Lloyd, Robert A *Opera Singer*
67B Fortis Green, London, SE1 9HL, UNITED KINGDOM (UK)

Lloyd, Sabrina *Actor*
Paradigm Agency, 10100 Santa Monica Blvd, #2500, Los Angeles, CA 90067 USA

Lloyd, Sam *Actor*
Stone Manners Talent Agency, 6500 Wilshire Blvd, Ste 550, Los Angeles, CA 90048 USA

Lloyd, Sue *Actor*
Barry Burnett, 31 Coventry St, London, W1V 8AS, UNITED KINGDOM (UK)

Lloyd, Walt *Cinematographer*
22287 Mulhotlland Highway, #393, Calabasas, CA 91302 USA

Lloyd Webber, Andrew *Composer*
Really Useful Group, 19/22 Tower St, London, WC2H 9NS, UNITED KINGDOM (UK)

Lo, Ismael *Musician*
Mad Minute Music, 5-7 Rue Paul Bert, Saint Ouen, 93400, FRANCE

Lo Bianco, Tony
Artists Only Management, 1901 Avenue of the Stars, Suite 605, Los Angeles, CA 90067 USA

Loach, Ken C *Director*
Sixteen Films, 187 Wardour St, Floor 2, London, W1F 8ZB, ENGLAND

Loach, Kenneth (Ken) *Director*
Parallax Pictures, 7 Denmark St, London, WC2H 8LS, UNITED KINGDOM (UK)

Loaiza, Esteban A *Baseball Player*
779 Florida St, Imperial Beach, CA 91932 USA

Loalza, Esteban *Baseball Player*
Pittsburgh Pirates, 1404 Lands End Ct, Southlake, TX 76092-4224 USA

Lobdell, Frank *Artist*
Pier 70, San Francisco, CA 94102 USA

Lobel, Anita *Writer*
Greenwillow Books/William Morrow, 1350 Ave of Americas, New York, NY 10019 USA

Lobel, Bruno
Ramering 4, Heldenstein, GERMANY, 84431

Lobkowicz, Nicholas *Misc*
Katholische Universitat, Eichstatt, 85071, GERMANY

Lobo
707 18th Ave. So., Nashville, TN 37203

Lobo, Rebecca *Basketball Player*
216 Klaus Anderson Road, Southwick, MA 01077 USA

Loc, Tone
7932 Hillside Ave., Los Angeles, CA 90046

Loc, Tone *Music Group*
Entertainment Artists Nashville, 2409 21st Avenue South, Suite 100, Nashville, TN 37212

Local, Ivars Godmanis *Prime Minister*
Brivibus Bluv 36, Riga, PDP, 226170, LATVIA

Locane, Amy *Actor*
Don Buchwald & Associates Inc (LA), 6500 Wilshire Blvd #2200, Los Angeles, CA 90048 USA

Locatelli, Paul L *Educator*
Santa Clara University, President's Office, Santa Clara, CA 95053 USA

Loceff, Michael *Producer*
Roklin Management, 8265 Sunset Blvd #101, Los Angeles, CA 90046 USA

Locher, Dick
435 N. Michigan Ave., Chicago, IL 60611

Locher, Richard (Dick) *Editor, Cartoonist*
Chicago Tribune, Editorial Dept, 435 N Michigan Ave, Chicago, IL 60611 USA

Lochhead, Kenneth C *Artist*
35 Wilton Crescent, Ottawa, ON K1S 2T4, CANADA

Lochner, Philip R Jr *Government Official, Business Person*
Time Warner Inc, 75 Rockfeller Plaza, New York, NY 10019 USA

Lochner, Rudi
Hofreitstr. 15, Schonau, GERMANY, D-83471

Lock, Don *Baseball Player*
Washington Senators, 1330 Walnut St, kingman, KS 67068-1061 USA

Lockbaum, Gordie *Football Player*
35 Brookshire Road, Worcester, MA 01609 USA

Locke, Bruce *Actor*
5670 Wilshire Blvd #820, Los Angeles, CA 90048

Locke, Charlie *Baseball Player*
Baltimore Orioles, 1560 Haven Hills Rd, Poplar Bluff, MO 63901-2749 USA

Locke, Larry *Baseball Player*
Cleveland Indians, 155 Eighty Acres Rd Apt 2, Dunbar, PA 15431-2275 USA

Locke, Ron *Baseball Player*
New York Mets, 15 Lewiston Ave, West Kingston, RI 02892-1131 USA

Locke, Sonda *Actor*
David Shapira & Associates, 15821 Ventura Blvd #235, Encino, CA 91436 USA

Locke, Sondra *Actor*
7465 Hillside Ave, Los Angeles, CA 90046 USA

Locke, Tembi *Actor*
McGowan Management, 8733 W Sunset Blvd #103, W Hollywood, CA 90069 USA

Locker, Bob *Baseball Player*
Chicago White Sox, 3408 Echo Springs Rd, Lafayette, CA 94549-2119 USA

Lockerman, Brad
300 S. Raymond Ave. #11, Pasadena, CA 91105

Lockhart, Anne *Actor*
191 Upper Lake Road, Lake Sherwood, CA 91361 USA

Lockhart, Eugene *Football Player*
2215 High Country Dr, Carrollton, TX 75007 USA

Lockhart, James
105 Woodcock Hill, Harrow, Middx, HA3 0JJ, UNITED KINGDOM (UK)

Lockhart, June *Actor*
12850 Marlboro St, Los Angeles, CA 90049 USA

Lockhart, Keith
Boston Pops Orchestra, Symphony Hall, 301 Massachusetts Ave, Boston, MA 02115 USA

Lockhart, Keith *Baseball Player*
San Diego Padres, 710 Woodbrook Way, Lawrenceville, GA 30043-6853 USA

Lockhart, Paul S *Astronaut*
3142 Pleasant Cove Court, Houston, TX 77059 USA

Lockington, David
Cramer/Marder Artists, 3436 Springhill
Road, Lafayette, CA 94549 USA

Locklear, Gene *Baseball Player*
Cincinnati Reds, 1811 Penasco Rd, El
Cajon, CA 92019-3708 USA

Locklear, Heather *Actor*
United Talent Agency, 9560 Wilshire
Blvd, #500, Beverly Hills, CA 90212 USA

Locklin, Hank
PO Box 117, Brewton, AL 36427

Locklin, Stu *Baseball Player*
Cleveland Indians, 224 Paseo Del Volcan
SW Trir 43, Albuquerque, NM 87121-
8727 USA

Lockman, Whitey *Baseball Player*
New York Giants, 8234 N 75th St,
Scottsdale, AZ 85258-2778 USA

Lockwood, Gary *Actor*
1065 E Loma Alta Dr, Altadena, CA
91001 USA

Lockwood, Skip *Baseball Player*
Kansas City A's, 47 John Druce Ln,
Wrentham, MA 02093-1390 USA

Locorriere, Dennis *Musician*
Artists International Mgmt, 9850
Sandalwood Blvd, #458, Boca Raton, FL
33428 USA

Loder, Kurt *Journalist*
MTV News, 1515 Broadway Fl 29, New
York, NY 10036 USA

Lodge, David
8 Sydney Rd., Richmond Surrey,
ENGLAND

Lodge, David John *Writer*
University of Birmingham, English Dept,
Birmingham, B15 2TT, UNITED
KINGDOM (UK)

Lodge, Roger *Actor, Television Host*
Rogers & Cowan PR, 1888 Century Park E
#500, Los Angeles, CA 90067 USA

Lodise, Peter
3227 Cardiff Ave., Los Angeles, CA 90034

Lodish, Harvey F *Biologist*
195 Fisher Ave, Brookline, MA 02445
USA

Loe, Harald A *Doctor*
National Dental Research Institute, 9000
Rockville Pike, Bathesda, MD 20892 USA

Loeb, Jerome T *Business Person*
May Department Stores, 611 Olive St,
Saint Louis, MO 63101 USA

Loeb, John L Jr *Diplomat, Financier*
1 Rockefeller Plaza, #2500, New York,
NY 10020 USA

Loeb, Lisa *Musician, Songwriter*
1028 3rd Ave, #A, New York, NY 10021
USA

Loeb, Marshall R *Editor*
31 Montrose Road, Scarsdale, NY 10583
USA

Loehr, Bret *Actor*
Coast to Coast Talent Group, 3350
Barham Blvd, Los Angeles, CA 90068
USA

Loengard, John *Photographer*
20 W 86th St, New York, NY 10024 USA

Loewen, James W *Historian*
Catholic University, History Dept,
Washington, DC 20064 USA

Lofgren, Nils *Musician, Songwriter*
Vision Music, 8012 Old Georgetown
Road, Bathesda, MD 20814 USA

Lofton, Cirroc *Actor*
Innovative Artists (LA), 1505 Tenth St,
Santa Monica, CA 90401 USA

Lofton, Fred C *Religious Leader*
Progressive National Baptist Convention,
601 50th St NE, Washington, DC 20019
USA

Lofton, James D *Football Player*
15487 Mesquite Tree Trail, Poway, CA
92064 USA

Lofton, Kenneth (Kenny) *Baseball Player*
PO Box 68473, Tucson, AZ 85737 USA

Lofton, Kenny *Athlete*
PO Box 68473, Tucson, AZ 85737

Logan, Don *Publisher*
Time Inc, Time-Life Building, Rockefeller
Center, New York, NY 10020 USA

Logan, Jack *Musician*
William Morris Agency, 1325 Ave of
Americas, New York, NY 10019 USA

Logan, James K *Judge*
US Court of Appeals, PO Box 790, 1
Patrons Plaza, Olathe, KS 66061 USA

Logan, Jerry *Football Player*
112 Guinevere Court, Weatherford, TX
76086 USA

Logan, John (Johnny) *Baseball Player*
6115 W Cleveland Ave, Milwaukee, WI
53519 USA

Logan, Johnny
6115 W. Cleveland Ave., Milwaukee, WI
53219

Logan, Melissa *Musician*
K Records, 924 Jefferson St SE, #101,
Olympia, WA 98501 USA

Logan, Phyllis
47 Courtfield Rd. #9, London, ENGLAND,
SW7 4DB

Logan, Rayford W *Historian*
3001 Veazey Terrace NW, Washington,
DC 20008 USA

Loges, Stephan *Opera Singer*
Van Walsum Mgmt, 4 Addison Bridge
Place, London, W14 8XP, UNITED
KINGDOM (UK)

Loggia, Robert *Actor*
544 Bellagio Terrace, Los Angeles, CA
90049 USA

Loggins, Kenny *Musician, Songwriter*
670 Oak Springs Lane, Santa Barbara, CA
93108 USA

Logue, Donal *Actor*
Lasher McManus Robinson, 1964
Westwood Blvd, #400, Los Angeles, CA
90025 USA

Loh, John M (Mike) *General*
125 Captain Graves, Williamsburg, VA
23185 USA

Lohan, Lindsay *Actor, Model*
Act IV Mgmt, 223 Wall St, #192,
Huntington, NY 11743 USA

Lohan, Sinead *Musician, Songwriter*
Pat Egan Sound, Merchant's Court, 24
Merchant's Quay, Dublin, IRELAND

Lohman, Alison *Actor*
Creative Artists Agency LCC (CAA-LA),
9830 Wilshire Blvd, Beverly Hills, CA
90212 USA

Lohmann, Katie *Actor*
Zanuck, Passon and Pace, Inc, 4717 Van
Nuys Blvd, Atrium #102, Sherman Oaks,
CA 91403

Lohr, Bob *Golfer*
8225 Breeze Cove Lane, Orlando, FL
32819 USA

Loiola, Jose *Volleyball Player*
3521 Maple Dr, Manhattan Beach, CA
90266 USA

Loisel, John S *War Hero*
2504 Overcreek Dr, Richardson, TX
75080 USA

Loken, Kristanna *Actor*
James/Levy/Jacobson Management, 3500
W Olive Ave #1470, Burbank, CA 91505
USA

Lokoloko, Tore *Governor*
PO Box 5622, Port Moresby, PAPUA
GUINEA

Lolich, Michael S (Mickey) *Baseball
Player*
6252 Robin Hill, Washington, MI 48094
USA

Lolita
Grossgmain, AUSTRIA, - A-5084

Lollobrigida, Gina *Actor*
Via Appia Antica 223, Rome, 00178,
ITALY

Lom, Herbert *Actor*
London Mgmt, 2-4 Noel St, London, W1V
3RB, UNITED KINGDOM (UK)

Lomax, Melanie
5900 Wilshire Blvd, Los Angeles, CA
90036

Lomax, Michael *Educator*
United Negro Fund, 500 E 62nd St, New
York, NY 10021 USA

Lomax, Neil V *Football Player*
6191 SW Wilhelm Road, Tualatin, OR
97062 USA

Lombard, Karina *Actor, Model*
McGowan Management, 8733 W Sunset
Blvd #103, W Hollywood, CA 90069 USA

Lombard, Louise
P F D Drury House, 34-43 Russell St,
London, WC2B 5HA, UNITED KINGDOM
(UK)

Lombardi, John V *Educator*
University of Florida, President's Office,
Gainesville, FL 32611 USA

Lombardi, Leigh *Actor*
Abrams Artists Agency (NY), 275 Seventh
Ave Fl 26, New York, NY 10001

Lombardo, John *Musician*
Agency for Performing Arts, 9200 Sunset
Blvd, #900, Los Angeles, CA 90069 USA

Lombreglio, Ralph *Writer*
Doubleday Press, 1540 Broadway, New
York, NY 10036 USA

Lomma, Jonathan
1120 S. Washington Ave, Scranton, PA 18505

Lonborg, James R (Jim) *Baseball Player*
498 First parish Road, Scituate, MA 02066 USA

Lonchakov, Yuri V *Cosmonaut*
Potcha Kosmonavtov, Moskovskoi Oblasti, Syvisdny Goroduk, 141160, RUSSIA

London, Irving M *Physicist*
Harvard-MIT Health Sciences, 77 Massachusetts Ave, Cambridge, MA 02139 USA

London, Jason *Actor*
Writers and Artists Group Intl (LA), 8383 Wilshire Blvd #550, Beverly Hills, CA 90211 USA

London, Jeremy *Actor*
Gersh Agency, 232 N Canon Dr, Beverly Hills, CA 90210 USA

London, Jonathan *Writer*
Chronicle Books, 85 2nd St, San Francisco, CA 94105 USA

London, Lisa *Actor, Model*
8949 Sunset Blvd, #201, Los Angeles, CA 90069 USA

London, Rick *Cartoonist*
503 W Main Ave, #B, Lumberton, MS 39455 USA

Lone, John *Actor*
Levine Thall Plotkin, 1740 Broadway, New York, NY 10019 USA

Lonergan, Kenneth *Writer*
William Morris Agency (WMA-LA), 1 William Morris Pl, Beverly Hills, CA 90212 USA

Lonestar *Music Group*
Borman Entertainment, 1250 6th St #401, Santa Monica, CA 90401 USA

Long, Anthony A *Educator*
1088 Telvin St, Albany, CA 94706 USA

Long, Charles F (Chuck) II *Football Player*
2425 N MacArthur Blvd, Oklahoma City, OK 73127 USA

Long, Dale W *Publisher*
Working Woman Magazine, 342 Madison Ave, New York, NY 10173 USA

Long, Dallas *Track Athlete*
1337 Galaxy Dr, Newport Beach, CA 92660 USA

Long, David L *Publisher*
Sports Illustrated Magazine, Rockefeller Center, New York, NY 10020 USA

Long, Dennis (Denny) *Soccer Player*
RR 5, Poplar Bluff, MO 63901 USA

Long, Elizabeth Valk *Publisher*
Time Magazine, Rockefeller Center, New York, NY 10020 USA

Long, Grant *Basketball Player*
3257 Belmont Glen Dr, Marietta, GA 30067 USA

Long, Howie *Football Player, Sportscaster, Actor*
International Creative Mgmt, 8942 Wilshire Blvd, #219, Beverly Hills, CA 90211 USA

Long, Joan D *Producer*
La Burrage Place, Lindfield, NSW, 2070, AUSTRALIA

Long, Justin *Actor*
Handprint Entertainment, 1100 Glendon Ave #1000, Los Angeles, CA 90024 USA

Long, Mark *Reality TV Star*
MTV Networks (LA), 2600 Colorado Blvd, Santa Monica, CA 90405

Long, Matthew (Matt) *Actor*
One Entertainment (LA), 9220 W Sunset Blvd #306, Los Angeles, CA 90069 USA

Long, Nia *Actor*
David Naylor & Associates, 6535 Santa Monica Blvd, Hollywood, CA 90038 USA

Long, Richard *Artist*
Old School, Lower Failand, Bristol, BS8 3SL, UNITED KINGDOM (UK)

Long, Rien *Football Player*
Tennessee Titans, 460 Great Circle Road, Nashville, TN 37228 USA

Long, Robert *Misc*
University of California, Paleontology Museum, Berkeley, CA 94720 USA

Long, Robert M *Business Person*
Longs Drug Stores, 141 N Civic Dr, Walnut Creek, CA 94596 USA

Long, Scott *Actor, Reality TV Star*
Big Brother, Arnold Shapiro Productions, 12925 Riverside Dr Fl 4, Sherman Oaks, CA 91423 USA

Long, Sharon R *Scientist*
Standard University, Biological Sciences Dept, Stanford, CA 94305 USA

Long, Sharon R *Scientist*
Standard University, Biological Sciences Dept, Stanford, CA 94305 USA

Long, Shelley *Actor*
15237 Sunset Blvd, Pacific Palisades, CA 90272 USA

Long, William Ivey *Designer*
International Creative Mgmt, 40 W 57th St, #1800, New York, NY 10019 USA

Longdon, Johnny
5401 Palmer Dr., Banning, CA 92220

Longet, Claudine *Actor*
Ronald D Austin, 6000 E Hopkins, Aspen, CO 81611 USA

Longfield, William *Business Person*
CR Bard Inc, 730 Central Ave, New Providence, NJ 07974 USA

Longley, Luc *Basketball Player*
New York Knicks, Madison Square Garden, 2 Penn Plaza, New York, NY 10121 USA

Longmuir, Alan *Musician*
27 Preston Grange, Preston Pans E, Lothian, SCOTLAND

Longmuir, Derek *Musician*
27 Preston Grange, Preston Pans E, Lothian, SCOTLAND

Longo, Lenny *Musician*
Texas Sounds, PO Box 1644, Dickinson, TX 77539 USA

Longo, Robert *Artist*
Longo Studio, 224 Center St, New York, NY 10013 USA

Longo, Tony
24 Westwind St., Marina del Rey, CA 90292

Longoria, Eva *Actor*
Linda Reitman Management, 820 N San Vicente Blvd, Los Angeles, CA 90069 USA

Longuet-Higgins, H Christopher *Misc*
Sussex University, Exper Psych Lab, Falmer, Brighton, BN1 9QG, UNITED KINGDOM (UK)

Lonneke *Model*
Pauline's Talent Corp, 379 W Broadway, #502, New York, NY 10012 USA

Lonow, Claudia *Comedian*
International Creative Management (ICM-LA), 8942 Wilshire Blvd, Beverly Hills, CA 90211 USA

Lonsbrough, Porter Anita *Swimmer*
6 Rivendell Gardens, Tettendall, Wolverhampton, WV6 8SY, UNITED KINGDOM (UK)

Lonsdale, Gordon C *Cinematographer*
532 W 740 N, Orem, UT 84057 USA

Lonsdale, Michael
25 rue de General-Foy, Paris, FRANCE, F-75008

Look, Dean Z *Baseball Player, Football Player*
4708 Okemos Road, Okemos, MI 48864 USA

Lookinland, Mike *Actor*
PO Box 9968, Salt Lake City, UT 84109 USA

Loomis, Rod
5114 Vineland Ave., Universal City, CA 91601

Looney, Donald L (Don) *Football Player*
PO Box 3103, Midland, TX 79702 USA

Looney, Shelley *Hockey Player*
31 Beaman Lane, North Falmouth, MA 02556 USA

Looney, William R III *General*
Commander, Electronic Systems Center, Hanscom Air Force Base, MA 01731 USA

Loose, A Mohan *Actor*
15A/4 Kesavaperumal East Street, Chennai, TN 600 004, INDIA

Loose, John W *Business Person*
Coming Corp, Houghton Park, Corning, NY 14831 USA

Looseleaf, Victoria
144 S. Doheny Dr. #304, Los Angeles, CA 90048

Lopardo, Frank *Opera Singer*
7 Suzanne B Court, Massapeque, NY 11758 USA

Lopert, Tanya *Actor*
Cineart, 36 Rue de Pnthieu, Paris, 75008, FRANCE

Lopes, David E (Davey) *Baseball Player*
17762 Vinceyard Lane, Poway, CA 92064 USA

Lopes, Lisa
1505 10th St., Santa Monica, CA 90401

Lopez, Adamari *Actor*
Telemundo, 2470 West 8th Avenue, Hialeah, FL 33010 USA

Lopez, Al
3601 Beach St, Tampa, FL 33609

Lopez, Alfonso R (Al) *Baseball Player*
3601 Beach Dr, Tampa, FL 33629 USA

Lopez, Areliano Oswaldo *President, General*
Servico Aereo de Honduras, Apdo 129, Tegucigalpa, DC HONDURAS

Lopez, Danny (Little Red) *Boxer*
16531 Aguamarine Court, Chino Hills, CA 91709 USA

Lopez, Felipe *Basketball Player*
Minnesota Timberwolves, Target Center, 600 1st Avenue North, Minneapolis, MN 55403 USA

Lopez, George *Comedian, Actor*
George Lopez Show, The, 4000 Warner Blvd, Bldg 19 Rm 229, Burbank, CA 91522 USA

Lopez, Hector *Athlete*
11415 Faldo Ct, Hudson, FL 34667

Lopez, Israel (Cachao) *Musician*
Estefan Enterprises, 6205 SW 40th St, Miami, FL 33155 USA

Lopez, Javy *Baseball Player*
Baltimore Orioles, Oriole Park, 333 W Camden St, Baltimore, MD 21201 USA

Lopez, Jennifer *Actor, Musician*
Endeavor Talent Agency, 9701 Wilshire Blvd, #1000, Beverly Hills, CA 90212 USA

Lopez, Jose M *War Hero*
1347 Lockhill Selma Road, San Antonio, TX 78213 USA

Lopez, Lourdes *Ballerina*
New York City Ballet, Lincoln Center Plaza, New York, NY 10023 USA

Lopez, Lynda *Television Host*
Style Network, 5750 Wilshire Blvd, Los Angeles, CA 90036 USA

Lopez, Marga *Actor*
Televisa, Blvd Adolfo Lopez Mateos 232, Colonia San Angel INN, DF, CP 01060, MEXICO

Lopez, Mario *Actor, Television Host*
Metropolitan Talent Agency (MTA), 4526 Wilshire Blvd, Los Angeles, CA 90010 USA

Lopez, Nancy *Golfer*
2308 Tara Dr, Albany, GA 31721 USA

Lopez, Perry
8520 Sherwood Dr., Los Angeles, CA 90069

Lopez, Priscilla *Actor*
Writers & Artists, 19 W 44th St, #1000, New York, NY 10036 USA

Lopez, Raul *Basketball Player*
Utah Jazz, Delta Center, 301 W South Temple, Salt Lake City, UT 84101 USA

Lopez, Robert S *Historian*
41 Richmond Ave, New Haven, CT 06515 USA

Lopez, Rodrigo *Baseball Player*
Baltimore Orioles, Oriole Park, 333 W Camden St, Baltimore, MD 21201 USA

Lopez, Sal *Actor, Musician*
Arenas Entertainment, 100 N Crescent Dr, Garden Level, Beverly Hills, CA 90210 USA

Lopez, Sergi *Actor*
International Creative Management (ICM-LA), 8942 Wilshire Blvd, Beverly Hills, CA 90211 USA

Lopez, Trini *Musician, Actor*
1139 Abrigo Road, Palm Springs, CA 92262 USA

Lopez Rodriguez, Nicolas de J Cardinal *Religious Leader*
Archdiocese of Santo Domingo, Santo Domingo, AP, 186, DOMINICAN REPUBLIC

Lopez Tarso, Ignacio *Actor*
Televisa, Blvd Adolfo Lopez Mateos 232, Colonia San Angel INN, DF, CP 01060, MEXICO

Lopez Trujillo, Alfonso Cardinal *Religious Leader*
Arzobispado, Calle 57 N 48-28, Medellin, COLUMBIA

Lopez-Alegria, Michael E *Astronaut*
1919 Tangle Press Court, Houston, TX 77062 USA

Lopez-Cobos, Jesus
Terry Harrison Mgmt, 1 Clarendon Court, Charlbury, Oxon, OX7 3PS, UNITED KINGDOM (UK)

Lopez-Garcia, Antonio *Artist*
Marlborough Fine Art, 6 Albermarle St, London, W1, UNITED KINGDOM (UK)

Loprieno, John
10647 Wilkins Ave. #306, Los Angeles, CA 90024

Loquasto, Santo *Designer*
Paradigm Agency, 10100 Santa Monica Blvd, #2500, Los Angeles, CA 90067 USA

Lorant, Stefan
215 W. Mountain Rd., Lenox, MA 01240

Lorca, Valeria *Actor*
Telefe - Argentina, Pavon 2444 (C1248AAT), Buenos Aires, ARGENTINA

Lorch, George A *Business Person*
Armstrong World, 313 W Liberty St, Lancaster, PA 17603 USA

Lord, Albert L *Business Person*
SLM Holding Corp, 11600 Sallie Mae Dr, Reston, VA 20193 USA

Lord, Lance W *General*
Commander, US Space Command, Peterson Air Force Base, CO 80914 USA

Lord, M G *Editor, Cartoonist*
Newsday, Editorial Dept, 235 Pinetawn Road, Melville, NY 11747 USA

Lord, Marjorie *Actor*
1110 Maytor Place, Beverly Hills, CA 90210 USA

Lord, Peter *Animator, Director*
Aardman Animations, Gas Ferry Road, Bristol, BS1 6UN, UNITED KINGDOM (UK)

Lord, Walter
116 E. 68th St., New York, NY 10021

Lord, Winston *Diplomat*
740 Park Ave, New York, NY 10021 USA

Lords, Traci
345 N. Maple Dr. #375, Beverly Hills, CA 90210

Loree, Brad *Actor*
TalentCo, 111 Water St #308, Vancouver BC, V6B 1A7, CANADA

Loren, Sophia *Actor*
La Concordia Ranch, 1151 Hidden Valley Road, Thousand Oaks, CA 91361 USA

Lorentz, Jim *Hockey Player*
2555 Staley ROad, Grand Island, NY 14072 USA

Lorenz, Edward N *Scientist*
Massachusetts Institute of Technology, Earth Sciences Dept, Cambridge, MA 02139 USA

Lorenz, Lee *Cartoonist*
PO Box 131, Easton, CT 06612 USA

Lorenzen, Fred *Race Car Driver*
906 Burr Oak Court, Oak Brook, IL 60523 USA

Lorenzo, Blas *Actor*
PO Box 2127, Los Angeles, CA 90078

Lorenzoni, Andrea *Astronaut*
Via B Vergine del Carmelo 168, Rome, 00144, ITALY

Loria, Christopher (Gus) *Astronaut*
102 Sea Mist Dr, League City, TX 77573 USA

Loring, Gloria *Actor, Musician*
PO Box 1243, Cedar Glen, CA 92321 USA

Loring, John R *Artist*
403 W 46th St, New York, NY 10036 USA

Loring, Lynn *Actor*
1232 Sunset Plaza Dr, Los Angeles, CA 90069 USA

Loriod, Yvonne *Musician*
Bureau de Concerts, 7 Rue de Richepanse, Paris, 75008, FRANCE

Lorius, Claude *Scientist*
Glaciologis Laboratoire, Rue Moliere, Saint-Martin d'Heres, 38402, FRANCE

Lorring, Joan
345 E. 68th St., New York, NY 10021

Lorscheider, Aloisio Cardinal *Religious Leader*
Guna Metropolitana, CP 05 Tone Basilica, Aparecida, SP, 12570-000, BRAZIL

Lortie, Louis *Musician*
Cramer/Marder Artists, 3436 Springhill Road, Lafayette, CA 94549 USA

Los, Marinus *Misc*
American Cyanamid Corp, 4201 Quakebridge Road, Princeton Junction, NJ 08550 USA

Los Lagos, Banda *Music Group*
Sony Music Miami, 605 Lincoln Rd, Miami Beach, FL 33138 USA

Los Lobos *Music Group*
Gold Mountain Entertainment, 3940 Laurel Canyon Blvd #444, Studio City, CA 91604-3709 USA

Los Mauricios *Writer*
Gabriel Blanco Iglesias (Colombia), Dg 127A #20-36, Conjunto Plenitud, Apto 132, Bogota, Colombia

Los Rabanes *Music Group*
Sony Music Miami, 605 Lincoln Rd,
Miami Beach, FL 33138 USA

Los Sementales de Nuevo Leon *Music Group*
Sony Music Miami, 605 Lincoln Rd,
Miami Beach, FL 33138 USA

Loscutoff, James (Jim) *Basketball Player, Coach*
166 Jenkins, Andover, MA 01810 USA

Lost Boys
1775 Broadway #433, New York, NY
10019

Lott, Felicity A *Opera Singer*
Kunstleragentur Raab & Bohm,
Plankengasse 7, Vienna, 1010, AUSTRIA

Lott, Ronald M (Ronnie) *Football Player, Sportscaster*
Fox-TV, Sports Dept, PO Box 900, Beverly
Hills, CA 90213 USA

Lott, Ronnie
11342 Canyon View Circle, Cupertino,
CA 95014

Lott, Trent *Senator*
3100 S Pascagoula St, Pascagoula, MS
39567 USA

Lotti, Helmut
Bevrijdingstraat 39, Turnhout, BELGIUM,
2300

Lotz, Anne Graham *Religious Leader*
AnGel Ministries, 3246 Lewis Farm Road,
Raleigh, NC 27607 USA

Lotz, Dick *Golfer*
6052 Southerness Dr, El Dorado Hills, CA
95762 USA

Loucks, Vernon R Jr *Business Person*
Baxter International, 1 Baxter Parkway,
Deerfield, IL 60015 USA

Loudon, Rodney *Physicist*
3 Gaston St, East Bergholt, Colchester,
Essex, CO7 6SD, UNITED KINGDOM
(UK)

Louganis, Greg
PO Box 4130, Malibu, CA 90264

Louganis, Gregory E (Greg) *Misc*
PO Box 4130, Malibu, CA 90264 USA

Loughery, Kevin *Basketball Player, Coach*
4474 Club Dr NE, Atlanta, GA 30319
USA

Loughlin, Lori *Actor, Musician*
Miller/Boyette, 10202 W Washington
Blvd, Culver City, CA 90232 USA

Loughlin, Mary Anne *Commentator*
WTBS-TV News Dept, 1050 Techwood Dr
NW, Atlanta, GA 30318 USA

Loughran, James
34 Cleveden Dr, Glasgow, G12 0RX,
SCOTLAND

Louis, Jin Luxian *Religious Leader*
Shesshan Catholic Seminary, Beijing,
CHINA

Louis, Murray *Dancer, Choreographer*
Nikolais/Louis Foundation, 375 W
Broadway, New York, NY 10012 USA

Louis-Dreyfus, Julia *Actor*
131 S Rodeo Dr, #300, Beverly Hills, CA
90212 USA

Louis-Dreyfus, Robert L M *Business Person*
Adidas AG, Adi Dassier Str 2,
Herzogenaurach, 91702, GERMANY

Louisa, Maria *Model*
Next Model Mgmt, 23 Watts St, New
York, NY 10013 USA

Louise, Tina *Actor, Musician*
310 E 46th St, #18T, New York, NY
10017 USA

Louiso, Todd *Actor*
S M S Talent, 8730 Sunset Blvd, #440, Los
Angeles, CA 90069 USA

Louisy, C Pearlette *Governor*
Governer General's House, Morne,
Castries, SAINT LUCIA

Lounge, John
555 Forge River Rd #150, Webster, TX
77590 USA

Lounge, John M (Mike) *Astronaut*
1304 Blue Heron St, Hitchcock, TX 77563
USA

Lourdusamy, D Simon Cardinal *Religious Leader*
Palazzo dei Convertendi, 64 Via della
Conciliazione, Rome, 00193, ITALY

Lourie, Alan D *Judge*
US Court of Appeals, 717 Madison Place
NW, Washington, DC 20439 USA

Louris, Gary *Musician, Songwriter*
Sussman Assoc, 1222 16th Ave S, #300,
Nashville, TN 37212 USA

Lousma, Jack R *Astronaut*
2722 Roseland St, Ann Arbor, MI 48103
USA

Loutty, All *Prime Minister*
29 Ahmed Hesmat St, Zamalek, Cairo,
EGYPT

Louvier, Alain *Composer*
53 Ave Victor Hugo, Boulogne-
Billancourt, 92100, FRANCE

Louvin, Charlie *Musician, Songwriter*
2851 Sainville Road, Manchester, TN
37355 USA

Lovano, Joe *Composer*
International Music Network, 278 S Main
St, #400, Gloucester, MA 01930 USA

Love, Alexis
PO Box 491205, Los Angeles, CA 90049

Love, Ben H *Misc*
Boy Scouts of America, 4407 Eaton Circle,
Colleyville, TX 76034 USA

Love, Courtney *Musician, Songwriter*
P M K Public Relations, 8500 Wilshire
Blvd, #700, Beverly Hills, CA 90211 USA

Love, Darlene *Musician, Actor*
Greater Talent, 437 5th Ave, New York,
NY 10016 USA

Love, Davis III *Golfer*
PO Box 30959, Sea Island, GA 31561
USA

Love, Faizon *Actor*
Power Entertainment, 12200 W Olympic
Blvd #499, Los Angeles, CA 90064 USA

Love, Gael *Editor*
Connoisseur Magazine, Editorial Dept,
1790 Broadway, New York, NY 10019
USA

Love, Loni *Actor, Comedian*
Power Entertainment, 12200 W Olympic
Blvd #499, Los Angeles, CA 90064 USA

Love, Michael D (Mike) *Musician*
PO Box 7800, Incline Village, NV 89452
USA

Love, Mike
24563 Ebelden Ave., Santa Clarita, CA
91321

Love, Stan *Basketball Player*
1950 Egan Way, Lake Oswego, OR 97034
USA

Love, Stanley G *Astronaut*
4315 Indian Sunrise Court, Houston, TX
77059 USA

Love & Rockets *Music Group*
4 The Lakes Bushey, Hertfordshire,
ENGLAND, WD2 1HS

Loveless, Patty *Musician, Songwriter*
1227 17th Ave S, Nashville, TN 37212
USA

Lovell, A C Bernard *Astronomer*
Quinta, Swettenham near Congleton,
Cheshire, UNITED KINGDOM (UK)

Lovell, Jacqueline
8707 Shirley Ave., Northridge, CA 91324-
3410

Lovell, James A, Jr *Astronaut*
Lovell Communications, PO Box 49, Lake
Forest, IL 60045 USA

Lovell, Marilyn
7840 Torreyson Dr, Los Angeles, CA
90046

Lovellette, Clyde E *Basketball Player*
319 Maple St, Munising, MI 49862 USA

Lovelock, James E *Scientist, Inventor*
Coombe Mill, Saint Giles-on-Heath,
Launceston, Cornwall, PL 15 9RY,
UNITED KINGDOM (UK)

Lover, Ed *Actor*
Artists Group (LA), 10100 Santa Monica
Blvd #2490, Los Angeles, CA 90067 USA

Lover, Seth *Inventor, Engineer*
4 Village Dr, Saint Louis, MO 63146 USA

Loverboy
1505 W. 2nd St. #200, Vancouver,
CANADA, BC V6H 3Y4

Lovett, Lyie *Musician, Songwriter*
Haber Corp, 1016 17th Ave S, #1,
Nashville, TN 37212 USA

Lovett, Lyle *Musician*
Monterey Peninsula Artists (Monterey),
509 Hartnell St, Monterey, CA 93940 USA

Lovett, Ruby *Musician*
Myers Media, PO Box 378, Canton, NY
13617 USA

Lovett, Steve *Actor*
Lovett Management, 1327 Brinkley Ave,
Los Angeles, CA 90049 USA

Lovin' Spoonful
1924 Spring St., Paso Robles, CA 93446

Lovine, Vicki
Trident Media Group LLC, 41 Madison
Ave Fl 33, New York, NY 10010 USA

Loving, Candy *Actor, Model*
Playboy Enterprises Inc, 680 North Lake
Shore Drive, Chicago, CA 60611 USA

Lovins, Amory B *Physicist*
Hypercar Inc, 220 Cody Lane, Basalt, CO 81621 USA

Lovitz, Jon *Actor, Comedian*
4774 Park Encino Lane, #305, Encino, CA 91436 USA

Lovrich, Pete *Baseball Player*
Kansas City A's, 19626 Beechnut Dr, Mokena, IL 60448-9333 USA

Lovullo, Torey *Baseball Player*
Detroit Tigers, 16825 Bajio Rd, Encino, CA 91436-3522 USA

Low, Francis E *Physicist*
28 Adams St, Belmont, MA 02478 USA

Low, G David *Astronaut*
Orbital Science Group, 21839 Atlantic Blvd, Sterling, VA 20166 USA

Low, Stephen *Diplomat*
2855 Tilden St NW, Washington, DC 20008 USA

Lowder, Kyle *Actor*
Michael Meltzer & Associates, 12207 Riverside Dr #208, Valley Village, CA 91607 USA

Lowdermilk, R Kirk *Football Player*
9475 Apollo Road NE, Kensington, OH 44427 USA

Lowe, Barry
31S. Audley St., London, ENGLAND, W1

Lowe, Chad *Actor*
Innovative Artists (LA), 1505 Tenth St, Santa Monica, CA 90401 USA

Lowe, Chan *Editor, Cartoonist*
Fort Lauderdale Sun-Sentinel, 200 E Olas Blvd, Fort Lauderdale, FL 33301 USA

Lowe, Derek *Baseball Player*
Boston Red Sox, 15401 Old Wedgewood Ct, Fort Myers, FL 33908-7207 USA

Lowe, Derek C *Baseball Player*
Boston Red Sox, Fenway Park, 4 Yawkey Way, Boston, MA 02215 USA

Lowe, Kevin *Hockey Player, Coach*
Edmonton Oilers, 11230 110th St, Edmonton, AB T5G 3H7, CANADA

Lowe, Nick *Musician, Songwriter*
MVO Ltd, 307 7th Ave, #807, New York, NY 10001 USA

Lowe, Rob *Actor*
Creative Artists Agency LCC (CAA-LA), 9830 Wilshire Blvd, Beverly Hills, CA 90212 USA

Lowe, Sean *Baseball Player*
St Louis Cardinals, 9948 County Road 2469, Royse City, TX 75189-5246 USA

Lowe, Sidney *Basketball Player, Coach*
2631 Wallingford Road, Winston Salem, NC 27101 USA

Lowe, Todd *Actor*
Liberman/Zerman Management, 252 N Larchmont Blvd #200, Los Angeles, CA 90004 USA

Lowe, Woodrow *Football Player, Coach*
282 Grande View Parkway, Maylene, AL 35114 USA

Lowell, Carey *Actor, Model*
International Creative Mgmt, 8942 Wilshire Blvd, #219, Beverly Hills, CA 90211 USA

Lowell, Charlie *Musician*
Flood Burnstead McCready McCarthy, 1700 Hayes St, #304, Nashville, TN 37203 USA

Lowell, Christopher *Television Host*
Christopher Lowell Show, The, 12121 Wilshire Blvd #750, Los Angeles, CA 90025 USA

Lowell, Elizabeth *Writer*
Avon Books, 1350 Ave of Americas, New York, NY 10019 USA

Lowell, Michael A (Mike) *Baseball Player*
New York Yankees, 620 Santurce Ave, Coral Gables, FL 33143 USA

Lowell, Scott
6500 Wilshire Blvd. #2200, Los Angeles, CA 90048

Lowenstein, John *Baseball Player*
Cleveland Indians, PO Box 750148, Las Vegas, NV 89136-0148 USA

Lowenstein, Louis *Attorney General, Educator*
5 Oak Lane, Larchmont, NY 10538 USA

Lowery, Corey *Musician*
Agency Group Ltd, 1775 Broadway, #430, New York, NY 10019 USA

Lowery, Terrell *Baseball Player*
Chicago Cubs, 3565 Antigua Pl, W Sacramento, CA 95691-5822 USA

Lowitsch, Klaus
Am Hochacker 51, Munich, GERMANY, D-81827

Lowman, Frank A *Financier*
Federal Home Loan Bank, 2 Townsite Plaza, Topeka, KS 66603 USA

Lown, Bernard *Doctor*
Lown Cardiovascular Group, 21 Longwood Ave, Brookline, MA 02446 USA

Lown, Turk *Baseball Player*
Chicago Cubs, 1106 Van Buren St, Pueblo, CO 81004-2832 USA

Lowry, Lois *Writer*
205 Brattle St, Cambridge, MA 02138 USA

Lowry, Noah *Baseball Player*
San Francisco Giants, 181 N Encinal Ave, Ojai, CA 93023-2119 USA

Loy, Frank E *Misc*
Marshall German Fund, 11 Dupont Circle NW, Washington, DC 20036 USA

Loy, James M *Admiral, Government Official*
Transportation Security Administration, 400 7th St SW, Washington, DC 20590 USA

Loynd, Mike *Baseball Player*
Texas Rangers, 19 Randall Dr, Short Hills, NJ 07078-1957 USA

Lozada, Johnny *Actor*
Televisa, Blvd Adolfo Lopez Mateos 232, Colonia San Angel INN, DF, CP 01060, MEXICO

Lozado, Willie *Baseball Player*
Milwaukee Brewers, 4407 Sunrise Ct, Sellersburg, IN 47172-9248 USA

Lozano, Conrad *Musician*
Gold Mountain, 3575 Cahuenga Blvd W, #450, Los Angeles, CA 90068 USA

Lozano, Ignacio E Jr *Editor*
La Opinion, 411 W 5th St, Los Angeles, CA 90013 USA

Lozano, Karyme *Actor*
Arenas Entertainment, 100 N Crescent Dr, Garden Level, Beverly Hills, CA 90210 USA

Lozano, Silvia *Choreographer*
Ballet Folklorico, 31 Esq Con Riva Palacio, Mexico City, DF, MEXICO

Lozano Barragan, Javier Cardinal *Religious Leader*
Health Care Workers Assistance, Via Conciliazione 3, Rome, 00193, ITALY

Lu, Edward T (Ed) *Astronaut*
18222 Bal Harbour Dr, Houston, TX 77058 USA

Lu, Lisa
1737 N. Orange Grove Ave, Los Angeles, CA 90046

Lu, Qihui *Artist*
100-301, 398 Xin-Pei Road, Xin-Zuan, Shanghai, CHINA

Lualdi, Antonella
via Cassia Antica 35, Rome, ITALY

Lubanski, Ed *Bowler*
5326 Christi Dr, Warren, MI 48091 USA

Lubbers, Ruud F M *Prime Minister*
Lambertweg 4, Rotterdam, RA, 3062, NETHERLANDS

Lubchenco, Jane *Biologist*
Oregon State University, Marine Biology Dept, Corvallis, OR 97331 USA

Lubezki, Emmanuel *Cinematographer*
Broder Kurland Webb Uffner, 9242 Beverly Blvd, #200, Beverly Hills, CA 90210 USA

Lubich, Bronko *Wrestler*
3146 Whitemarsh Circle, Dallas, TX 75234 USA

Lubich, Silvia Chiara *Misc*
Focolare Movement, 306 Via di Frascati, Rocca di Papa, RM, 00040, ITALY

Lubin, Arthur
5737 Newcastle Ave., Encino, CA 91316

Lubin, Steven *Musician*
State University of New York, School of Arts, Purchase, NY 10577 USA

Lubotsky, Mark *Musician*
Overtoom 329 III, Amsterdam, JM, 1054, NETHERLANDS

Lubovitch, Lar *Dancer, Choreographer*
Lar Lubovitch Dance Co, 229 W 42nd St, #8, New York, NY 10036 USA

Lubratich, Steve *Baseball Player*
California Angels, 24 Sackett Rd, Lee, NH 03824-6616 USA

Lubs, Herbert A *Scientist*
5133 SW 71st Place, Miami, FL 33155 USA

Lubys, Bronislovas *Prime Minister*
Prime Minister's Office, Tuo-Vaizganto 2, Vilnius, LITHUANIA

Luc, Tone *Musician, Actor*
Headline Talent, 1650 Broadway, #508, New York, NY 10019 USA

Lucado, Max
19595 W 1H 10, San Antonio, TX 78257-9506

Lucaro, Carlos *Judge*
US Court of Appeals, 1929 Stout St, Denver, CO 80294 USA

Lucas, Aubrey K *Educator*
University of Southern Mississippi, President's Office, Hattiesburg, MS 39406 USA

Lucas, Cornel *Photographer*
57 Addison Road, London, W148JJ, UNITED KINGDOM (UK)

Lucas, Criag *Songwriter, Writer*
William Morris Agency, 1325 Ave of Americas, New York, NY 10019 USA

Lucas, Gary *Baseball Player*
San Diego Padres, 1511 High St, Rice Lake, WI 54868-1874 USA

Lucas, George *Producer, Director*
LucasFilm, PO Box 2009, San Rafael, CA 94912 USA

Lucas, Jacklyn H (Jack) *War Hero*
75 Elks Lake Road, Hattiesburg, MS 39401 USA

Lucas, Jerry R *Basketball Player*
3904 Lori Dr, #A1, Erlanger, KY 41018 USA

Lucas, Josh *Actor*
International Creative Mgmt, 8942 Wilshire Blvd, #219, Beverly Hills, CA 90211 USA

Lucas, Maurice *Basketball Player, Coach*
5691 Bonita Road, Lake Oswego, OR 97035 USA

Lucas, Richard J (Richie) *Football Player*
1269 Estate Dr, West Chester, PA 19380 USA

Lucas, Robert E Jr *Nobel Prize Laureate*
5448 S East View Park, #3, Chicago, IL 60615 USA

Lucas, William *Government Official*
Justice Department, Constitution & 10th NW, Washington, DC 20530 USA

Lucca, Tony *Actor*
Burstein Company, The, 15304 Sunset Blvd #208, Pacific Palisades, CA 90272 USA

Lucchesi, Frank
3027 Glasgow Dr., Arlington, TX 76015-2258

Lucchesini, Andrea *Musician*
Arts Management Group, 1133 Broadway, #1025, New York, NY 10010 USA

Lucci, Susan *Actor*
16 Carteret Place, Garden City, NY 11530 USA

Lucci, Vince Sr *Bowler*
1182 Queens Way, West Chester, PA 19382 USA

Luce, Henry III *Publisher*
Mill Hill Road, Mill Neck, NY 11765 USA

Luce, R Duncan *Misc*
20 Whitman Court, Irvine, CA 92612 USA

Luce, Richard N *Governor*
Governor's Office, Convent, GIBRALTAR

Luce, William (Bill) *Writer*
PO Box 370, Depoe Bay, OR 97341 USA

Lucebert *Artist, Writer*
Boendermakerhof 10, Bergen N-H, TB, 1861, NETHERLANDS

Lucero *Musician*
Sony Music Miami, 605 Lincoln Rd, Miami Beach, FL 33138 USA

Luchko, Klara S *Actor*
Kotelmicheskaya Nab 1/15 Korp B, #308, Moscow, 109240, RUSSIA

Lucid, Shannon W *Astronaut, Physicist*
1622 Gunwale Road, Houston, TX 77062 USA

Lucien, Jon *Musician*
Maxine Harvard, 7942 W Bell Road, Glendale, AZ 85308 USA

Lucier, Lou *Baseball Player*
Boston Red Sox, 579 Highland St, Northbridge, MA 01534-1113 USA

Lucin, Arthur
5737 Newcastle Ave, Encino, CA 91316

Luck, Frank *Athlete*
Lerchenweg 9, Springstille, 98587, GERMANY

Luckenbill, Laurence
PO Box 636, Cross River, NY 10518

Luckinbill, Laurence *Actor*
RR 3 Flintlock Ridge Rd, Katonah, NY 10536 USA

Luckinbill, Lawrence *Actor*
PO Box 636, Cross River, NY 10518 USA

Luckinbill, Thad *Actor*
Young and the Restless, The, 7800 Beverly Blvd, Ste 3305, Los Angeles, CA 90036 USA

Lucking, William *Actor*
Twentieth Century Artists, 15760 Ventura Blvd, Ste 700, Encino, CA 91436 USA

Luckovich, Mike *Editor, Cartoonist*
Atlanta Constitution, Editorial Dept, 72 Marietta St, Atlanta, GA 30303 USA

Lucky, Robert W *Engineer*
48 Gillespie Ave, Fair Haven, NJ 07704 USA

Luczo, Stephen J *Business Person*
Seagate Technology, 920 Disc Dr, Scotts Valley, CA 95066 USA

Luddy, Barbara
119 Sultan Ave., Capitol Heights, MD 20743-1954

Luder, Owen H *Architect*
Communication in Construction, 2 Smith Square, London, SW1P 3H5, UNITED KINGDOM (UK)

Ludes, John T *Business Person*
Fortune Brands Inc, 300 Tower Parkway, Lincolnshire, IL 60069 USA

Luding-Rothenburger, Christa *Speed Skater*
Dresdener Eisspot-Club, Pieschener Allee 1, Dresden, 01067, GERMANY

Ludlum, Robert *Actor*
International Creative Management (ICM-LA), 8942 Wilshire Blvd, Beverly Hills, CA 90211 USA

Ludwick, Eric *Baseball Player*
St Louis Cardinals, 10183 Whispy willow Way, Las Vegas, NV 89135-2089 USA

Ludwick, Ryan *Baseball Player*
Texas Rangers, 10183 Whispy willow Way, Las Vegas, NV 89135-2089 USA

Ludwig, Christa *Opera Singer*
Calliopie, 162 Chemin du Santon, Mougins, 06250, FRANCE

Ludwig, George H *Physicist*
215 Aspen Trail, Winchester, VA 22602 USA

Ludwig, Ken *Writer*
Steptoe & Johnson, 4603 Harrison St, Chevy Chase, MD 20815 USA

Luebber, Steve *Baseball Player*
Minnesota Twins, 3302 Moorehead Dr, Joplin, MO 64804-5323 USA

Luebbers, Larry *Baseball Player*
Cincinnati Reds, 844 Issac Shelby Cir E, Frankfort, KY 40601-8806 USA

Luecken, Rick *Baseball Player*
Kansas City Royals, 2902 Fontena Dr, Houston, TX 77043-1305 USA

Luft, Joey
108 E. Matilija St, Ojai, CA 93023

Luft, Lorna *Actor, Musician*
Golden Goldberg, 9100 Wilshire Blvd, #455, Beverly Hills, CA 90212 USA

Luft, Sid
108 E. Matilija St., Ojai, CA 93023

Lugar, Richard *Senator*
7841 Old Dominion Dr, McLean, VA 22101 USA

Lugbill, Jon *Athlete*
American Cance Assn, 7432 Alban Station Blvd, #B232, Springfield, VA 22150 USA

Luger, Lex
52B49 uford Hwy., Atlanta, GA 30340

Lugo, Julio *Baseball Player*
Houston Astros, 440 Neptune Ave Apt 120, Brooklyn, NY 11224-4446 USA

Lugo, Richard *Actor*
Official International Fan Club, PO Box 6079, Bellingham, WA 98227 USA

Lugosi Jr, Bela
520 N Central Ave #800, Glendale, CA 91203 USA

Luhrmann, Baz *Director*
Hilary Linstead, 500 Oxford St, Bondi Junction, NSW, 2022, AUSTRALIA

Lui, Stephen
10635 Santa Monica Blvd. #130, Los Angeles, CA 90025

Luisetti, Hank
131 Winchester Ct, Foster City, CA 94404-3540

Luisi, James
22562 Seaver Ct., Santa Clarita, CA 91350-1389

Lujack, John C (Johnny) *Football Player*
3700 N Harrison St, Davenport, IA 52806 USA

Lujack, Johnny
6321 Crow Valley Dr., Bettendorf, IA 52722

Lujan, Fernando *Actor*
TV Azteca, Periferico Sur 4121, Colonia Fuentes del Pedregal, DF, CP 14141, Mexico

Lujan, Manuel Jr *Secretary*
Manuel Lujan Agencies, PO Box 3727, Albuquerque, NM 87190 USA

Lukachyk, Robert *Baseball Player*
Montreal Expos, 14706 Beacon Hill Ct, Midlothlan, VA 23112-2320 USA

Lukas, D Wayne *Coach*
5242 katella Ave, #103, Los Alamitos, CA 90720 USA

Lukashenko, Aleksandr *President*
President's Office, JK Marks St 38, Minsk, 220016, BELARUS

Lukasiewicz, Mark *Baseball Player*
Anahelm Angels, 8035 Fir Dr, Clay, NY 13041-8646 USA

Lukather, Steve *Musician*
Fitzgerald-Hartley, 34 N Palm St, Ventura, CA 93001 USA

Luke *Musician*
Richard Walters, 1800 Argyle Ave, #408, Los Angeles, CA 90028 USA

Luke, Derek *Actor*
651N Kilkea Dr, Los Angeles, CA 90048 USA

Luke, John A Jr *Business Person*
Westvaco Corp, 299 Park Ave, New York, NY 10171 USA

Luke, Matt *Baseball Player*
New York Yankees, 2467 Middlesex Pl, Fullerton, CA 92835-3121 USA

Lukens, Max L *Business Person*
Baker Hughes Inc, 3900 Essex Lane, Houston, TX 77027 USA

Luketic, Robert *Actor*
Mosaic Media Group, 9200 Sunset Blvd Fl 10, Los Angeles, CA 90069 USA

Lukin, Matt *Musician*
Legends of 21st Century, 7 Trinity Row, Florence, MA 01062 USA

Lukkarinen, Marjut *Skier*
Lohja Ski Team, Lohja, FINLAND

Lula da Silva, Luis Ignacio *President*
Palacio do Planotto, Praca dos 3 Poderas, Brasilia, DF, 70 150, BRAZIL

Lulabel & Scottie
PO Box 171132, Nashville, TN 37217

Lulu *Musician, Actor*
CIA, 101 Shepherds Bush, Concorde House, London, W6 7LP, UNITED KINGDOM (UK)

Lum, Mike *Baseball Player*
Atlanta Braves, 3476 Cochise Dr SE, Atlanta, GA 30339-4324 USA

Lumbly, Carl *Actor*
8721 Sunset Blvd, #205, Los Angeles, CA 90069 USA

Lumenti, Ralph *Baseball Player*
Washington Senators, 9 Tomaso Rd, Milford, MA 01757-2224 USA

Lumet, Sidney *Director*
Amjen Entertainment, 259 W 54th St, New York, NY 10019 USA

Lumley, Joanna *Actor*
International Creative Mgmt, 76 Oxford St, London, W1N 0AX, UNITED KINGDOM (UK)

Lumley, John L *Physicist*
743 Snyder Hill Road, Ithaca, NY 14850 USA

Lumme, Jyrki *Hockey Player*
Toronto Maple Leafs, 40 Bay St, Toronto, ON M5J 2K2, CANADA

Lumpe, Jerry *Baseball Player*
New York Yankees, 732 S Pearson Dr, Springfield, MO 65809 USA

Lumpp, Raymond (Ray) *Basketball Player*
21 Hewlett Dr, East Williston, NY 11596 USA

Lumsden, David J
Melton House, Soham, Cambridgeshire, UNITED KINGDOM (UK)

Luna, Barbara *Actor*
18026 Rodarte Way, Encino, CA 91316 USA

Luna, Denise *Rodeo Rider, Model*
PO Box 2462, Burleson, TX 76097 USA

Luna, Diego *Actor*
Endeavor Agency LLC (LA), 9601 Wilshire Blvd Fl 3, Beverly Hills, CA 90210 USA

Lunar, Fernando *Baseball Player*
Atlanta Braves, 1508 Campbell Pl, Alamogordo, NM 88310-4832 USA

Lunatics, St *Musician*
Team Lunatics (MO), 4246 Forest Park Avenue, Suite 2C, St Louis, MO 63108 USA

Lund, Bill
14 Ivy Bank Haworth nr. Keighley, W. Yorks, ENGLAND.

Lund, Don *Baseball Player*
Brooklyn Dodgers, 1000 S State St, Ann Arbor, MI 48109-2202 USA

Lund, Gordon *Baseball Player*
Cleveland Indians, 1602 S Harvard Ave, Arlington Heights, IL 60005-3517 USA

Lund, Katia *Director*
Gersh Agency, The (LA), 232 N Canon Dr, Beverly Hills, CA 90210 USA

Lundberg, Anders *Misc*
Goteberg University, Physiology Dept, Box 33033, Goteborg, 40 033, SWEDEN

Lundberg, Fred Borre *Skier*
Skogbrynet 11, Bardu, 9250, NORWAY

Lunden, Joan *Commentator*
Tekepictures Productions, 1271 Ave of Americas, #4332, New York, NY 10020 USA

Lundgren, Dolph *Actor*
William Morris Agency, 151 El Camino Dr, Beverly Hills, CA 90212 USA

Lundgren, Terry *Business Person*
Federated Department Stores, 151 W 34th St, New York, NY 10001 USA

Lundholm, Mark *Actor, Comedian*
William Morris Agency (WMA-LA), 1 William Morris Pl, Beverly Hills, CA 90212 USA

Lundi, Monika
Viktoriastr. 24, Munich, GERMANY, D-80803

Lundon, Joan
235 E. 45th St., New York, NY 10017

Lundquist, Dave *Baseball Player*
San Diego Padres, 6513 Emory Dr, Hickory, NC 28601-9467 USA

Lundquist, Gus *Misc*
100 Holley Ridge Road, Aiken, SC 29803 USA

Lundquist, Steve *Swimmer*
PO Box 1545, Stockbridge, GA 30281 USA

Lundquist, Verne *Sportscaster*
NBC-TV, Sports Dept, 30 Rockefeller Plaza, New York, NY 10112 USA

Lundsledt, Tom *Baseball Player*
Chicago Cubs, PO Box 409, Ephraim, WI 54211-0409 USA

Lundy, Carmen *Musician*
Abby Hoffer, 223 1/2 E 48th St, New York, NY 10017 USA

Lundy, Jessica *Actor*
280 S Beverly Dr, #400, Beverly Hills, CA 90212 USA

Lundy, Lamar
1109 S. A St., Richmond, IN 47374-5525

Lundy, Victor A *Architect*
Victor A Lundy Assoc, 701 Mulberry Lane, Bellaire, TX 77401 USA

Luner, Jaime *Actor*
Martin Hurwitz, 427 N Canon Dr, #215, Beverly Hills, CA 90210 USA

Luner, Jamie *Actor*
Himber Entertainment Inc, 211 S Beverly Dr #208, Beverly Hills, CA 90212 USA

Lunghi, Cherie *Actor*
Marion Rosenberg, PO Box 69826, West Hollywood, CA 90069 USA

Lunka, Zoltan *Boxer*
Weinheimer Str 2, Schriesheim, 69198, GERMANY

Lunn, Bob *Golfer*
PO Box 1495, Woodbridge, CA 95258 USA

Lunney, Glenn *Scientist*
United Space Alliance, 1150 Gemini Dr, Houston, TX 77058 USA

Lunsford, Trey *Baseball Player*
San Francisco Giants, 3955 Nall Rd, Southaven, MS 38672-6739 USA

Lupberger, Edwin A *Business Person*
Entergy Corp, 10055 Grogans Mill Road, #5A, The Woodlands, TX 77380 USA

Lupica, Mike *Writer*
55 Runningbrook Lane, New Canaan, CT 06840 USA

Luplen, Tony *Baseball Player*
Boston Red Sox, PO Box 351, Norwich, VT 05055-0351 USA

Luplow, Al *Baseball Player*
Cleveland Indians, 2450 Starlite Dr, Saginaw, MI 48603-2537 USA

Lupo, Benedetto *Musician*
Gerhild Baron Mgmt, Dombacher Str 41/III/3, Vienna, 1170, AUSTRIA

Lupo, Frank *Writer, Producer*
Evolution Entertainment, 901 N Highland Ave, Los Angeles, CA 90038 USA

LuPone, Patti *Musician, Actor*
Innovative Artists (NY), 235 Park Ave S Fl 7, New York, NY 10003 USA

Lupu, Radu *Musician*
Terry Harrison Mgmt, 3 Clarendon Court, Charlbury, Oxon, 0X7 3PS, UNITED KINGDOM (UK)

Lupus, Peter *Actor*
2401 S 24th St, #110, Phoenix, AZ 85034 USA

Lurie, Alison *Writer*
Cornell University, English Dept, Ithaca, NY 14850 USA

Lurie, Ranan R *Editor, Cartoonist*
Cartoonnews International, PO Box 698, Greenwich, CT 06836 USA

Lusader, Scott *Baseball Player*
Detroit Tigers, 4169 Bold Meadows, Oakland Township, MI 48306-4701 USA

Lusha, Masiela *Actor*
Anonymous Content, 8522 National Blvd #101, Culver City, CA 90232 USA

Lusis, Janis *Track Athlete*
Vesetas 8-3, Riga, 1013, LATVIA

Lustig, William
1441 No. Ogden Dr., Los Angeles, CA 90046

Lustiger, Jean-Marie Cardinal *Religious Leader*
Maison Dioceine, 8 Rue de la Ville-l'Eveque, Paris, 75008, FRANCE

Lusztig, George *Mathematician*
106 Grant Ave, Newton, MA 02459 USA

Lutcher, Nellie *Musician*
Alan Eichler, 6064 Selma Ave, Los Angeles, CA 90028 USA

Lutes, Eric *Actor*
Artists Group, 10100 Santa Monica Blvd, #2490, Los Angeles, CA 90067 USA

Lutt, Jorg-UweProf
Mensing-Str 17, Flensburg, D-24937, GERMANY

Luttig, J Michael *Judge*
US Appeals Court, 200 S Washington St, Alexandria, VA 22314 USA

Lutz, Bob *Tennis Player*
101 Via Ensueno, San Clemente, CA 92672 USA

Lutz, Joe *Baseball Player*
St Louis Browns, 1411 Quall Dr, Sarasota, FL 34231-3563 USA

Lutz, Joleen *Actor*
H David Moss, 733 Seward St, #PH, Los Angeles, CA 90038 USA

Lutz, Mark *Actor*
LeFeaver Talent Management Ltd, 2 College St #202, Toronto ON, M5G 1K3, CANADA

Lutz, Robert A *Business Person*
3600 Green Court, #720, Ann Arbor, MI 48105 USA

Luuloa, Kelth *Baseball Player*
Anaheim Angels, 29126 Old Wrangler Road, Riverside, CA 91790 USA

LuValle, James *Track Athlete*
1174 Los Altos Ave, #160, Los Altos, CA 94022 USA

Luxon, Benjamin M *Opera Singer*
Mazet, Relubbus Lane, Saint Hillary, Penzance, Cornwall, TR20 9DS, UNITED KINGDOM (UK)

Luyendyk, Arie *Race Car Driver*
12494 N 116th St, Scottsdale, AZ 85259 USA

Luyties, Ricci *Volleyball Player*
Assn of Volleyball Pros, 330 Washington Blvd, #400, Marina del Rey, CA 90292 USA

Luz, Franc
606 N. Larchmont Blvd. #309, Los Angeles, CA 90004

Luzhkov, Yuri M *Politician*
Government of Moscow, Tverskaya Str 13, Moscow, 103032, RUSSIA

Luzi, Mario *Writer*
Via Belle Riva 20, Florence, 50136, ITALY

Luzinski, Greg *Baseball Player*
Philadelphia Phillies, 25199 Ridge Oak Dr, Bonita Springs, FL 34134-1927 USA

Luzinski, Gregory M (Greg) *Baseball Player*
25680 Streamlet Court, Bonita Springs, FL 34135 USA

Lyakhov, Vladimir A *Cosmonaut*
Potcha Kosmonavtov, Moskovskoi Oblasti, Syvisdny, Goroduk, 141160, RUSSIA

Lyden, Mitch *Baseball Player*
Florida Marlins, 227 Shore Ct, Lauderdale By The SE, FL 33308-5037 USA

Lydon, James (Jimmy) *Actor*
3538 Lomacitas Lane, Bonita, CA 91902 USA

Lydon, John (Johnny Rotten) *Musician*
31962 Pacific Coast Highway, Malibu, CA 90265 USA

Lydon, Malcolm *Astronaut*
1429 Jaudon Road, Dover, FL 33527 USA

Lydy, Scott *Baseball Player*
Oakland A's, 3971 W Chicago St, Chandler, AZ 85226-3875 USA

Lyght, Todd W *Football Player*
2185 Lindsey Court, Tustin, CA 92782 USA

Lyle, Kami *Musician, Songwriter*
DS Mgmt, 2814 12th Ave S, #202, Nashville, TN 37204 USA

Lyle, Sandy *Golfer*
Advantage International, 1024 Thomas Jefferson NW, #450, Washington, DC 20007 USA

Lyle, Sparky *Baseball Player*
Boston Red Sox, 17 SIgnal Hill Dr, Voorhees, NJ 08043 USA

Lyles, A C
2115 Linda Flora, Los Angeles, CA 90024 USA

Lyles, Lester L (Les) *General*
Commander Air Material Command, Wright-Patterson Air Force Base, OH 45433 USA

Lyman, Arthur
508 Kaanini Circle, Hilo, HI 96720

Lyman, Dorothy
9200 Sunset Blvd. #900, Los Angeles, CA 90069

Lyman, Richard W *Educator*
Stanford University, Education School, Stanford, CA 94305 USA

Lymon, Frankie
1650 Broadway #508, New York, NY 10019

Lympany, Moura *Musician*
Transart, 8 Bristol Gardens, London, W9 2JG, UNITED KINGDOM (UK)

Lyn, Dawn *Actor*
PO Box 1527, Avalon, CA 90704 USA

Lyn, Mai
190 W. Kern St., McFarland, CA 93250

Lynch, Allen J *War Hero*
438 Belie Plaine Ave, Gurnee, IL 60031 USA

Lynch, Claire
1 Camp St, Cambridge, MA 02140

Lynch, Dan *Editor, Cartoonist*
Fort Wayne-Journal-Gazette, Editorial Dept, 600 W Main St, Fort Wayne, IN 46802 USA

Lynch, David *Director*
Creative Artists Agency LCC (CAA-LA), 9830 Wilshire Blvd, Beverly Hills, CA 90212 USA

Lynch, David K *Director*
PO Box 93624, Los Angeles, CA 90093 USA

Lynch, Ed *Baseball Player*
New York Mets, 5940 SW 120th St, Miami, FL 33156-5758 USA

Lynch, Edele *Musician*
Clintons, 55 Drury Lane, Covent Garden, London, WC2B 5SQ, UNITED KINGDOM (UK)

Lynch, James E (Jim) *Football Player*
1717 W 91st Place, Kansas City, MO 64114 USA

Lynch, Jane *Actor*
Halpern & Associates, 12304 Santa Monica Blvd #104, Los Angeles, CA 90025 USA

Lynch, Jennifer *Actor*
1894 El Cerrito Place, Los Angeles, CA 90068 USA

Lynch, Jerry *Baseball Player*
Pittsburgh Pirates, 4840 Chamblee Dunwoody Rd, Atlanta, GA 30338-5808 USA

Lynch, Jessica *War Hero*
Knopf, 1745 Broadway, New York, NY 10019 USA

Lynch, Jessica *Beauty Pageant Winner*
Miss New York City Scholarship Organization, 35 East 19th Street, 2nd Floor, New York, NY 10003 USA

Lynch, John *Football Player*
Tampa Bay Buccaneers, 1 W Buccaneer Place, Tampa, FL 33607 USA

Lynch, John Carroll *Actor*
James Suskin Management, 253 West 72nd Street, Suite 1014, New York, NY 10023 USA

Lynch, Keavy *Musician*
Clintons, 55 Drury Lane, Covent Garden, London, WC2B 5SQ, UNITED KINGDOM (UK)

Lynch, Kelly *Actor, Model*
2648 Mandeville CAnyon Road, Los
Angeles, CA 90049 USA

Lynch, Peg
304 11th St Box 339, Becket, MA 01223

Lynch, Peter S *Financier*
27 State St, Boston, MA 02109 USA

Lynch, Richard *Actor*
Richard Sindell, 1910 Holmby Ave, #1,
Los Angeles, CA 90025 USA

Lynch, Richard (Dick) *Football Player*
203 Manor Road, Douglaston, NY 11363
USA

Lynch, Sandra L *Judge*
US Appeals Court, McCormack Federal
Building, Boston, MA 02109 USA

Lynch, Shane *Musician*
Carol Assoc-War Mgmt, Bushy Park Road,
57 Meadowbank, Dublin, IRELAND

Lynch, Stephen *Comedian*
William Morris Agency (WMA-LA), 1
William Morris Pl, Beverly Hills, CA
90212 USA

Lynch, Thomas C *Admiral*
1236 Denbigh Lane, Radnor, PA 19087
USA

Lynde, Janice *Actor*
Artist's Agency, The (LA), 1180 S Beverly
Dr #301, Los Angeles, CA 90035 USA

Lynden-Bell, Donald *Astronomer*
Institute of Astronomy, MAdingley Road,
Cambridge, CB3 0HA, UNITED
KINGDOM (UK)

Lyndon, Frank *Musician*
Paramount Entertainment, PO Box 12, Far
Hills, NJ 07931 USA

Lynds, Roger *Astronomer*
Kitt Peak National Observatory, Tucson,
AZ 85726 USA

Lyne, Adrian
9876 Beverly Grove Dr., Beverly Hills, CA
90210

Lyngstad, Anni-Frida *Musician, Songwriter*
Mono Music, Sodra Brobaeken 41A,
Stockholm, 111 49, SWEDEN

Lynley, Carol *Actor*
Don gerler, 3349 Cahuenga Blvd, #1, Los
Angeles, CA 90068 USA

Lynn, Betty
10424 Tennessee Ave., Los Angeles, CA
90064

Lynn, Cheryl *Musician, Actor*
PO Box 667, Smithtown, NY 11787 USA

Lynn, Frederic M (Fred) *Baseball Player*
Boston Red Sox, 7336 El Fuerte St,
Carlsbad, CA 92009-6409 USA

Lynn, Ginger *Adult Film Star*
Atlas Multimedia Inc, 22940 Burbank
Blvd, Woodland Hills, CA 91367 USA

Lynn, Greg *Architect*
University of California, Architecture
School, Los Angeles, CA 90024 USA

Lynn, James T *Secretary*
6 Sunset Cay Road, Key Largo, FL 33037
USA

Lynn, Jonathan *Director*
Holflund/Polane, 9465 Wilshire Blvd,
#820, Beverly Hills, CA 90212 USA

Lynn, Loretta *Musician, Songwriter*
Loretta Lynn Enterprises, PO Box 120369,
Nashville, TN 37212 USA

Lynn, Meredith Scott *Actor*
Rigberg Roberts Rugolo, 1180 S Beverly
Dr, #601, Los Angeles, CA 90035 USA

Lynn, Salomon Janet *Figure Skater*
PO Box 1026, Haymarket, VA 20168 USA

Lynn, Therese
PO Box 6057, Hoboken, NJ 07030

Lynn, Vera *Actor, Musician*
Ditchling, Sussex, UNITED KINGDOM
(UK)

Lynn Spears, Jamie *Actor*
Creative Artists Agency LCC (CAA-LA),
9830 Wilshire Blvd, Beverly Hills, CA
90212 USA

Lynne, Bobbe
22732 Foothill Rd. #6, Hayward, CA
94541

Lynne, Gillian *Dancer, Choreographer*
Lean-2 Productions, 18 Rutland St,
Knightsbridge, London, SW7 1EF, UNITED
KINGDOM (UK)

Lynne, Gloria *Musician*
Subrena Artists, 330 W 56th St, #18M,
New York, NY 10019 USA

Lynne, Jeff *Musician, Songwriter*
PO Box 5850, Santa Barbara, CA 93150
USA

Lynne, Shelby *Musician, Songwriter*
William Morris Agency (WMA-LA), 1
William Morris Pl, Beverly Hills, CA
90212 USA

Lynskey, Melanie *Actor*
I/D PR (LA), 8409 Santa Monica Blvd,
West Hollywood, CA 90069 USA

Lynyrd Skynyrd *Music Group*
William Morris Agency (WMA-TN), 2100
W End Ave #1000, Nashville, TN 37203
USA

Lyon, Brandon *Baseball Player*
Toronto Blue Jays, 1244 Morning Sun Dr,
Salt Lake City, UT 84123-4862 USA

Lyon, Lisa *Actor, Athlete*
Jungle Gym, PO Box 585, Santa Monica,
CA 90406 USA

Lyon, Sue *Actor*
1244 N Havenhurst Dr, West Hollywood,
CA 90046 USA

Lyon, William *General, Business Person*
William Lyon Co, 4490 Von Karman Ave,
Newport Beach, CA 92660 USA

Lyonne, Natasha *Actor*
5255 Collins Ave, Miami, FL 33140 USA

Lyons, Barry *Baseball Player*
New York Mets, 1079 Frank P Corso St,
Biloxi, MS 39530-1922 USA

Lyons, Bill *Baseball Player*
St Louis Cardinals, 811 Tomahawk,
Heyworth, IL 61745-9309 USA

Lyons, Curt *Baseball Player*
Cincinnati Reds, 124 Virginia Dr,
Richmond, KY 40475-8631 USA

Lyons, Ed *Baseball Player*
Washington Senators, 1466 Ebert St,
Winston Salem, NC 27103-5002 USA

Lyons, Elena *Actor*
Sweeney Management, 8755 Lookout
Mountain Avenue, Los Angeles, CA 90046
USA

Lyons, Hersh *Baseball Player*
St Louis Cardinals, 7900 Dunbarton Ave,
Los Angeles, CA 90045-1035 USA

Lyons, James A Jr *Admiral*
9481 Piney Mountain Road, Warrenton,
VA 20186 USA

Lyons, Jeffrey
205 W. 57th St., New York, NY 10019

Lyons, Mitchell W (Mitch) *Football Player*
7355 Decosta Dr NE, Rockford, MI 49341
USA

Lyons, Phyllis
9171 Wilshire Blvd. #441, Beverly Hills,
CA 90210

Lyons, Robert F *Actor*
1801 Ave of Stars, #1250, Los Angeles,
CA 90067 USA

Lyons, Steve *Commentator*
Fox-TV, Sports Dept, 205 W 67th St, New
York, NY 10021 USA

Lysiak, Tom *Hockey Player*
13064 Highway 278 E, Social Circle, GA
30025 USA

Lyst, John H *Editor*
Indianapolis Star, Editorial Dept, 307 N
Pennsylvania, Indianapolis, IN 46204 USA

Lythgoe, Nigel *Producer*
Creative Artists Agency LCC (CAA-LA),
9830 Wilshire Blvd, Beverly Hills, CA
90212 USA

Lyubimov, Alexey B *Musician*
Klimentovskiy Per 9, #12, Moscow,
RUSSIA

Lyubimov, Yuri P *Director, Actor*
Tanganka Theater, Chkalova Str 76,
Moscow, RUSSIA

Lyubshin, Stanislav A *Actor*
Vernadskogo Prosp 123, #171, Moscow,
117571, RUSSIA

M

M, Banumathi *Actor, Bollywood*
15 Poes Road, 4th Street, Chennai, TN
600018, INDIA

M Karthik *Actor*
2 Kasthuri Ranga 1st Road, Teynampet,
Chennai, TN 600 018, INDIA

M'Bow, Amadou-Mahtar *Government Official*
BP 5276, Dakar-Fann, SENEGAL

M2M *Music Group*
Creative Artists Agency LCC (CAA-LA),
9830 Wilshire Blvd, Beverly Hills, CA
90212 USA

Ma, Tzi *Actor*
Greene & Associates, 526 North
Larchmont Blvd, #201, Los Angeles, CA
90004

Ma, Yo Yo *Musician*
International Creative Management
(ICM-LA), 8942 Wilshire Blvd, Beverly
Hills, CA 90211 USA

Ma, Yo-Yo *Musician*
Askonas Holt Ltd, 27 Chancery Lane, London, WC2A 1PF, UNITED KINGDOM (UK)

Maas, Alex
6962 Wildlife, Malibu, CA 90265-4309

Maas, William T (Bill) *Football Player*
PO Box 2175, Lees Summit, MO 64063 USA

Maathai, Wangari *Social Activist, Misc*
Green Belt Movement, PO Box 67545, Nairobi, KENYA

Maazel, Lorin V *Conductor, Musician*
New York Philharmonic, Avery Fisher Hall, 10 Lincoln Center, New York, NY 10023 USA

Mabe, Manabu *Artist*
Rua das Canjeranas 321, Jabaquara, Sao Paulo, SP, BRAZIL

Mabius, Eric *Actor*
Innovative Artists (LA), 1505 Tenth St, Santa Monica, CA 90401 USA

Mably, Luke *Actor*
Endeavor NY, 23 Watts St Fl 6, New York, NY 10013 USA

Mabrey, Sunny *Actor*
Paradigm (LA), 10100 Santa Monica Blvd, Fl 25, Los Angeles, CA 90067 USA

Mabrey, Vicki *Correspondent*
60 Minutes II, 524 W 57th St Fl 9, New York, NY 10019-2925 USA

Mabus, Raymond E Jr *Governor*
PO Box 200, Jackson, MS 39205 USA

Mac, Bernie *Comedian, Actor*
Associated Booking Corp, 1995 Broadway, #501, New York, NY 10023 USA

Mac, Fleetwood *Music Group*
Agency for the Performing Arts (APA-LA), 9200 Sunset Blvd #900, Los Angeles, CA 90069 USA

Mac, Robert
9242 Beverly Blvd. #200, Beverly Hills, CA 90210-3710

Mac Mohan *Actor*
Gulam Cottage Four Bungalows, Andheri, Bombay, MS 400 058, INDIA

MacAfee, Ken *Football Player*
8 Deerfield Dr, Medfield, MA 02052 USA

MacAfee, Kenneth A (Ken) *Football Player*
8 Deerfield Dr, Medfield, MA 02052 USA

Macapagal-Arroyo, Gloria *President*
Malacanang Palace, JP Laurel St, Metro Manila, 100, PHILIPPINES

MacArthur, James
74092 Covered Wagon Trail, Palm Desert, CA 92260-5604

MacArthur, James *Actor*
74092 Covered Wagon Trail, Palm Desert, CA 92260 USA

MacArthur, Robb *Reality TV Star*
Boy Meets Boy, 299 Queen Street West, Toronto ON, M5V 2Z5, Canada

Macat, Julio G *Cinematographer*
Gersh Agency, 232 N Canon Dr, Beverly Hills, CA 90210 USA

Macauley, Edward C (Easy Ed) *Basketball Player*
13277 Barrett Chase Circle, Baltwin, MO 63021 USA

MacAvoy, Paul W *Economist*
6 Mechanic St, Woodstock, VT 05091 USA

MacBeth, Lois
4095 Athenia Way, Los Angeles, CA 90043

Macchio, Ralph *Actor*
451 Deerpark Ave, Dix Hills, NY 11746 USA

MacCorkindale, Simon *Actor*
James Sharkey, 21 Golden Square, London, W1R 3PA, UNITED KINGDOM (UK)

MacCormac, Richard C *Architect*
9 Heneage St, London, E1 5LJ, UNITED KINGDOM (UK)

MacCormack, Jean F *Educator*
University of Massachusetts, President's Office, Boston, MA 02125 USA

MacCready, Paul B *Engineer*
AeroVironment Inc, 222 E Huntlington Dr, Monrovia, CA 91016 USA

MacDermid, Paul *Hockey Player*
81 Lakeland Dr, Sauble Beach, ON N0H 2G0, UNITED KINGDOM (UK)

MacDermot, Galt *Composer*
MacDermot Assoc, 12 Silver Lake Road, Staten Island, NY 10301 USA

MacDiarmid, Alan G *Nobel Prize Laureate*
635 Drexel Ave, Drexel Hill, PA 19026 USA

Macdissi, Peter *Actor*
Acme Talent & Literary Agency (LA), 4727 Wilshire Blvd #333, Los Angeles, CA 90010 USA

MacDonald, C Parker *Hockey Player*
3 Miller Road, Northford, CT 06472 USA

MacDonald, Charles *War Hero*
RR 5 Box C77, Definiak Springs, FL 32433 USA

MacDonald, Jeffrey *Doctor*
#00131-177 Fed Corr Inst 27072 Ballston, Sheridan, OR 97378 USA

MacDonald, Julien *Fashion Designer*
Julien MacDonald, Haydens Place, 247A Portobello Road, London, England, W11 1LT, United Kingdom

Macdonald, Norm *Comedian, Actor*
Brillstein-Grey Entertainment, 9150 Wilshire Blvd #350, Beverly Hills, CA 90212 USA

MacDonald, Ryan
5000 Delita Pl., Woodland Hills, CA 91364

MacDowell, Andie *Actor, Model*
Davien Littlefield Management, 939 Eighth Ave #609, New York, NY 10019 USA

MacFadyen, Angus *Actor*
International Creative Mgmt, 8942 Wilshire Blvd, #219, Beverly Hills, CA 90211 USA

MacFarlane, Seth *Actor, Writer, Director*
Endeavor Agency LLC (LA), 9601 Wilshire Blvd Fl 3, Beverly Hills, CA 90210 USA

MacGowan, Shane *Musician*
Free Trade Agency, Chapel Place, Rivington St, London, EC2A 3DQ, UNITED KINGDOM (UK)

MacGraw, Ali *Actor*
Agency for Performing Arts, 9200 Sunset Blvd, #900, Los Angeles, CA 90069 USA

MacGregor, Ian K *Government Official*
Castleton House, Lochgilphead, Argyll, SCOTTLAND

MacGregor, Jeff
151 El Camino Dr., Beverly Hills, CA 90212

MacGregor, Joanna C *Musician*
Columbia Artists Mgmt Inc, 165 W 57th St, New York, NY 10019 USA

MacGregor, Katherine *Actor*
1900 N Vine St #306, Los Angeles, CA 90068 USA

Macha, Kenneth H (Ken) *Baseball Player*
6934 Berkshire Dr, Export, PA 15632 USA

Machado, Justina *Actor*
Allman/Rea Management, 141 Barrington #E, Los Angeles, CA 90049 USA

Machado, Mario
5750 Briarcliff Rd., Los Angeles, CA 90068

Machado, Robert *Baseball Player, Athlete*
Oakland Athletics, 7000 Coliseum Way, Oakland, CA 94621 USA

Macharski, Franciszak Cardinal *Religious Leader*
Metropolita Krakowski, Ul Franciszkanska 3, Krakow, 31-004, POLAND

Machlis, Gail *Cartoonist*
Chronicle Features, 150 4th St, #695, San Francisco, CA 94103 USA

Machover, Tod *Composer*
Massachusetts Institute of Technology, Media Laboratory, Cambridge, MA 02139 USA

Macht, Gabriel *Actor*
Three Arts Entertainment, 9460 Wilshire Blvd, #700, Beverly Hills, CA 90212 USA

Macht, Stephen *Actor*
248 S Rodeo Dr, Beverly Hills, CA 90212 USA

Macias, Eduardo R *Director*
Gabriel Blanco Iglesias (Mexico), Rio Balsas 35-32, Colonia Cuauhtemoc, DF, 06500, Mexico

Macias, Jose *Baseball Player, Athlete*
Montreal Expos, PO Box 500, Station M, Montreal, H1V 3P, Canada

Macinnis, Allan (Al) *Hockey Player*
710 Hamptons Lane, Chesterfield, MO 63017 USA

MacIntosh, Craig *Cartoonist*
3403 W 28th St, Minneapolis, MN 55416 USA

MacIntosh, Sir Cameron
1 Bedford Sq., London, ENGLAND, WC1B 3RA

Macintyre, Marguerite *Actor*
Silver Massetti & Szatmary (SMS-LA),
8730 Sunset Blvd #440, Los Angeles, CA
90069 USA

Macionis, John *Swimmer*
25 Washington Lane, #607, Wyncote, PA
19095 USA

Mack, Allison *Actor*
Innovative Artists (LA), 1505 Tenth St,
Santa Monica, CA 90401 USA

Mack, J Kevin *Football Player*
7402 Greenwood Lake Dr, Sugar Land, TX
77479 USA

Mack, John E *Misc*
Harvard Medical School, 25 Shattuck St,
Boston, MA 02115 USA

Mack, Lonnie *Musician*
Concerted Efforts, 59 Parsons St, West
Newton, MA 02465 USA

Mack, Rodney *Wrestler*
World Wrestling Entertainment (WWE),
1241 E Main St, Stamford, CT 06905 USA

Mack, Thomas I (Tom) *Football Player*
Palo Verde Nuclear Generating Plant,
Palo Verde, AZ 85343 USA

Mack, Warner *Musician*
National Talent Agency, 2260 E Apple
Ave, Muskegon, MI 49442 USA

Mack 10 *Musician*
Famous Artists Agency, 555 Eighth Ave
#1803, New York, NY 10018 USA

Mackay, David *Director*
Gersh Agency, 232 N Canon Dr, Beverly
Hills, CA 90210 USA

Mackay, Harvey *Writer*
Mackay Envelope Corp, 2100 Elm St SE,
Minneapolis, MN 55414 USA

Macke, Richard C *Admiral*
1887 Alaweo St, Honolulu, HI 96821
USA

MacKenney, Tamara
4935 Parkers Mill Rd., Lexington, KY
40501

MacKenzie, J C
3500 W Olive Ave #1400, Burbank, CA
91505 USA

Mackenzie, Jeremy J G *General*
Royal Hospital, Chelsea, London, Sw3
4SR, UNITED KINGDOM (UK)

MacKenzie, John L *Director*
International Creative Mgmt, 8942
Wilshire Blvd, #219, Beverly Hills, CA
90211 USA

MacKenzie, Patch
3500 W. Olive #1400, Burbank, CA
91505

MacKenzie, Peter *Actor*
Greene & Associates, 526 N Larchmont
Blvd #201, Los Angeles, CA 90004 USA

Mackenzie, Warren *Artist*
8695 68th St N, Stillwater, MN 55082
USA

Mackerras, A Charles M
10 Hamilton Terrace, London, NW8 9UG,
UNITED KINGDOM (UK)

Mackey, George W *Mathematician*
25 Coolidge Hill Road, Cambridge, MA
02138 USA

Mackey, John *Football Player*
1198 Pacific Coast Highway, #D506, Seal
Beach, CA 90740 USA

Mackey, Rick *Misc*
5938 Four Mile Rd, Nanana, AK 99760
USA

Mackie, Bob
767 Fifth Ave. #400, New York, NY
10153

Mackie, Robert G (Bob) *Fashion Designer*
Bob Mackie Ltd, 530 Fashion Ave, New
York, NY 10018 USA

MacKinnon, Catherine *Lawyer*
University of Michigan, Law School, Ann
Arbor, MI 48109 USA

MacKinnon, Gillies *Director*
International Creative Management
(ICM-LA), 8942 Wilshire Blvd, Beverly
Hills, CA 90211 USA

MacKinnon, Roderick *Nobel Prize
Laureate*
545 W End Ave, New York, NY 10024
USA

Mackinnon, Simmone *Actor*
David Shapira & Associates, 15821
Ventura Blvd #235, Encino, CA 91436
USA

Mackintosh, Cameron A *Producer*
Cameron Mackintosh Ltd, 1 Bedford Sq,
London, WC1B 3RA, UNITED KINGDOM
(UK)

Macklin, David *Actor*
5410 Wilshire Blvd, #227, Los Angeles,
CA 90036 USA

Macknowski, Stephen *Athlete*
462 Kimball Ave, Yonkers, NY 10704
USA

MacLachian, Kyle *Actor*
Industry Entertainment, 955 Carillo Dr,
#300, Los Angeles, CA 90048 USA

MacLachlan, Janet
1919 N. Taft Ave., Los Angeles, CA 90068

MacLachlan, Kyle *Actor*
Management 360, 9111 Wilshire Blvd,
Beverly Hills, CA 90210 USA

MacLachlan, Patricia *Writer*
21 Unquomonk Road, Williamsburg, MA
01096 USA

MacLaine, Shirley *Actor*
Shirley MacLaine Enterprises, PO Box
46609, Los Angeles, CA 90046 USA

MacLane, Saunders *Mathematician*
42 Circle Dr, Chesterton, IN 46304 USA

MacLean, Don *Basketball Player*
216 Los Padres Dr, Thousand Oaks, CA
91361 USA

MacLean, Doug *Coach*
330 Tucker Dr, Worthington, OH 43085
USA

MacLean, Steven G *Astronaut*
Astronaut Program, 6767 Rt de Aeroport,
Saint-Hubert, QC, J3Y 8Y9, CANADA

MacLeish, Rick *Hockey Player*
5612 Bay Ave, Ocean City, NJ 08226
USA

Maclennan, Robert A R *Government
Official*
74 Abingdon Villas, London, W8 6XB,
UNITED KINGDOM (UK)

MacLeod, Gavin *Actor*
1877 Michael Lane, Pacific Palisades, CA
90272 USA

MacLeod, John *Coach*
4610 E Fanfol Dr, Phoenix, AZ 85028
USA

MacLeond, Lewis
BBC Scotland Queen Margaret Dr.,
Glasgow, SCOTLAND, G12 8DG

MacMahon, Brian *Misc*
89 Warren St, Needham, MA 02492 USA

MacMillan, Shannon *Soccer Player*
Portland University, Athletic Dept,
Portland, OR 97203 USA

MacMurray, William *Engineer*
200 Deer Run Road, Schaghticoke, NY
12154 USA

MacNabb, B Gordon *Engineer*
1406 Praine Ave, Cheyenne, WY 82009
USA

MacNamara, William
PO Box 25148, Farmington, NY 14425-
0148

Macnee, Patrick *Actor*
PO Box 1853, Rancho Mirage, CA 92270
USA

MacNeil, Cornell H *Opera Singer*
Columbia Artists Mgmt Inc, 165 W 57th
St, New York, NY 10019 USA

MacNeil, Rita
4950 Yonge St. #2400Toronto, Ont,
CANADA, M2N 6K1

Macneil, Robert
356 W. 58th St., New York, NY 10019

MacNichol, Peter *Actor*
International Creative Mgmt, 8942
Wilshire Blvd, #219, Beverly Hills, CA
90211 USA

Macomber, Debbie
PO Box 1458, Port Orchard, WA 98366-
0110

Macomber, Dick *Jockey*
6720 NW 28th Terrace, Fort Lauderdale,
FL 33309 USA

Macomber, George B H *Skier*
1 Design Center Place, #600, Boston, MA
02210 USA

MacPhail, Leland S (Lee) Jr *Misc*
1421 Meadow Ridge, Redding, CT 06896
USA

MacPherson, Duncan I *Editor, Cartoonist*
Toronto Star, Editorial Dept, 1 Yonge St,
Toronto, ON M5E 1E6, CANADA

Macpherson, Elle *Model*
Artists Mgmt Assn, 118 Lake Dr,
Bethlehem, CT 06751 USA

Macpherson, Wendy *Bowler*
PO Box 93433, Henderson, NV 89009
USA

MacQuitty, Jonathan *Inventor*
Abingworth Mgmt Inc, 2465 E Bayshore
Road, #348, Palo Alto, CA 94303 USA

MacRae, Sheila *Actor, Musician*
666 West End Ave, #10H, New York, NY
10025 USA

MacTavish, Craig *Hockey Player, Coach*
3 Quail Hollow Court, Voorhees, NJ
08043 USA

Maculan, Tim *Actor*
Opus Entertainment, 5225 Wilshire Blvd
#905, Los Angeles, CA 90036 USA

Macy, Bill
10130 Angelo Circle, Beverly Hills, CA
90210

Macy, Geoffrey W *Astronomer*
University of California, Integrative
Planetary Science Ctr, Berkeley, CA
94720 USA

Macy, Kyle *Basketball Player*
226 N Wilson Ave, Morehead, KY 40351
USA

Macy, William H *Actor*
Writers & Artists, 8383 Wilshire Blvd,
#550, Beverly Hills, CA 90211 USA

Madball
11-15 46th Rd. #4E, Long Island, NY
11101

Maddaloni, Martin J *Misc*
Plumbing & Pipe Fitting Union, 901
Massachusetts Ave NW, Washington, DC
20001 USA

Madden, Benji *Musician*
Creative Artists Agency LCC (CAA-LA),
9830 Wilshire Blvd, Beverly Hills, CA
90212 USA

Madden, D S *Religious Leader*
American Baptist Assn, 4605 N State Line,
Texarkana, TX 75503 USA

Madden, Dave *Actor*
9921 Belville Road, Miami, FL 33157
USA

Madden, David *Writer*
Louisiana State University, US Civil War
Center, Baton Rouge, LA 70803 USA

Madden, Diane *Dancer*
Trisha Brown Dance Co, 211 W 61st St,
New York, NY 10023 USA

Madden, John *Director*
Creative Artists Agency LCC (CAA-LA),
9830 Wilshire Blvd, Beverly Hills, CA
90212 USA

Madden, John E *Football Player, Football
Coach, Sportscaster*
5955 Coronado Blvd, Pleasanton, CA
94588 USA

Madden, John P *Director*
William Morris Agency, 52/53 Poland
Place, London, W1F 7LX, UNITED
KINGDOM (UK)

Maddox, Lester *Ex-Governor*
3155 Johnson Ferry NE, Marietta, GA
30062 USA

Maddux, Greg
8124 Desert Jewel Circle, Las Vegas, NV
89128

Maddux, Gregory A (Greg) *Baseball
Player*
4132 S Rainbow Blvd, Las Vegas, NV
89103 USA

Maddy, Penelope Jo *Misc*
University of California, Philosophy Dept,
Irvine, CA 92717 USA

Mader, Gunther *Skier*
Am Brenner 28, Gries, 6156, AUSTRIA

Madfai, Kahtan al *Architect*
22 Vassileos Constantinou, Athens,
11635, GREECE

Madhavi *Actor, Bollywood*
21/C Neha Ave, Juhu Tara Road, Mumbai,
MS 400049, INDIA

Madhoo *Actor, Bollywood*
Krishna Kutir, Sagarika Society Juhu Tara
Road, Bombay, MS 400049, INDIA

Madhubala *Actor, Bollywood*
Krishna Kutir, 1 Juhu Tara Road, Mumbai,
MS 400049, INDIA

Madi, Ferenc *President*
Egyetem Ter 1-3, Budapest, 1364,
HUNGARY

Madigan, Amy *Actor*
22031 Carbon Mesa Road, Malibu, CA
90265 USA

Madigan, John W *Business Person,
Publisher*
Tribune Co, 435 N Michigan Ave, #1800,
Chicago, IL 60611 USA

Madigan, Kathleen *Comedian*
Personal Publicity

Madigan, Martha *Photographer*
Tyler School of Art Beech & Penrose Aves,
Philadelphia, PA 19126 USA

Madigan, Sam *Football Player*
3685 Heron Ridge Lane, Weston, FL
33331 USA

Madison, Sarah Danielle *Actor*
Tavel Entertainment, 9171 Wilshire Blvd
#406, Beverly Hills, CA 90210 USA

Madlock, Bill *Baseball Player*
18 Meeting House Ln, Shelton, CT 06484
USA

Madonna *Musician, Actor, Dancer*
Caliente Entertainment, 9348 Civic Center
Dr, Mezzanine Level, Beverly Hills, CA
90210 USA

Madrazo, Ignacio N *Doctor*
Av Paseo de la Reforma, #476 1er Piso,
Col Juarez CP, DF, 6698, MEXICO

Madsen, Loren *Artist*
426 Broome St, New York, NY 10013
USA

Madsen, Michael *Actor*
Brillstein-Grey Entertainment, 9150
Wilshire Blvd #350, Beverly Hills, CA
90212 USA

Madsen, Virginia *Actor*
Untitled Entertainment (LA), 8436 W 3rd
St #650, Los Angeles, CA 90048 USA

Madson, Michael *Actor*
The Firm, 9100 Wilshire Blvd, #100W,
Beverly Hills, CA 90210 USA

Madura, Ricardo *President*
Casa Presidencial, Blvd Juan Pablo II,
Tegucigalpa, HONDURAS

Mae, Vanessa *Musician*
PO Box 363, Boumouth, Dorset, BH
76LA, UNITED KINGDOM (UK)

Maedizossian, Prefate Moushegh
Religious Leader
Armenian Apostolic Church, 4401 Russell
Ave, Los Angeles, CA 90027 USA

Maegte, Richard L (Dick) *Football Player*
4047 Aberdeen Way, Houston, TX 77025
USA

Maestro, Johnny *Musician*
PO Box 309M, Bay Shore, NY 11706 USA

Maestro, Mia *Actor*
3 Arts Entertainment Inc, 9460 Wilshire
Blvd Fl 7, Beverly Hills, CA 90212 USA

Maffay, Peter
Klenzestr. 1, Tutzing, GERMANY,
D-82327

Maffett, Debra
1525 McGavock St., Nashville, TN 37203

Maffett, Debra Sue (Debbie) *Beauty
Pageant Winner*
1525 McGavock St, Nashville, TN 37203
USA

Maffia, Roma *Actor*
Stone Manners Talent Agency, 6500
Wilshire Blvd, Ste 550, Los Angeles, CA
90048 USA

Magaw, John W *Lawyer, Government
Official*
Transportation Security Administration,
400 7th St SW, Washington, DC 20590
USA

Magaziner, Henry J *Architect*
1504 South St, Philadelphia, PA 19146
USA

Magee, Dave *Race Car Driver*
5S350 Deer Ridge Path, Big Rock, IL
60511 USA

Maggard, Dave *Track Athlete*
University of Houston, Athletic Dept,
Houston, TX 77204 USA

Maggart, Brandon *Actor*
8730 Sunset Blvd #480, Los Angeles, CA
90069

Maggart, Garett *Actor*
SDB Partners Inc, 1801 Ave of the Stars
#902, Los Angeles, CA 90067 USA

Maggert, Jeff *Golfer*
3 S Regent Oak, The Woodlands, TX
77381 USA

Maggette, Corey *Basketball Player*
Los Angeles Clippers, Staples Center,
1111 S Figueroa St, Los Angeles, CA
90015 USA

Magill, Frank J *Judge*
US Court of Appeals, Federal Building,
657 2nd Ave N, Fargo, ND 58102 USA

Magilton, Gerald E (Jerry) *Astronaut*
Marlin Marietta Astro Space, 100 Campus
Dr, Newtown, PA 18940 USA

Magistretti, Vico *Architect*
Via Conservatorio 20, Milan, ITALY

Magnus, Edie *Commentator*
NBC-TV, News Dept, 30 Rockefeller
Plaza, New York, NY 10112 USA

Magnus, Robert *General*
Deputy CofS Programs/Resources,
HqUSMC, 2 Navy St, Washington, DC
20380 USA

Magnus, Sandra H (Sandy) *Astronaut*
3477 Vinnings North Trail SE, Smyrna, GA 30080 USA

Magnuson, Ann
1317 Maltman Ave, Los Angeles, CA 90026

Magnussen, Karen
2852 Thorndiff Dr., N. Vancouver BC, CANADA, V7R 285

Magoon, Bob *Misc*
1688 Meridian Ave, Miami Beach, FL 33139 USA

Magri, Charles G (Charlie) *Boxer*
345 Bethnal Green Road, Bethnal Green, London, E2 6LG, UNITED KINGDOM (UK)

Magsamen, Sandra *Writer, Artist*
Orchard Books/Scholastic, 557 Broadway, New York, NY 10012 USA

Maguire, Adrian E *Jockey*
Jockey Club, 42 Portman Square, London, W1H 0EM, UNITED KINGDOM (UK)

Maguire, Les *Musician*
Barry Collins, 21A Cliftown Road, Southend-on-Sea, Essex, SS1 1AB, UNITED KINGDOM (UK)

Maguire, Michael *Actor*
Epstein-Wyckoff, 280 S Beverly Dr, #400, Beverly Hills, CA 90212 USA

Maguire, Paul L *Sportscaster, Football Player*
9063 Jennings Road, Eden, NY 14057 USA

Maguire, Richard W *Cinematographer*
26 Condesa Road, Santa Fe, NM 87508 USA

Maguire, Tobey *Actor*
Industry Entertainment, 955 Carillo Dr, #300, Los Angeles, CA 90048 USA

Maguson, Keith A *Hockey Player*
265 King Muir Road, Lake Forest, IL 60045 USA

Mahaffey, Arthur (Art) *Baseball Player*
PO Box 404, Newtown Square, PA 19073 USA

Mahaffey, John *Golfer*
29 Cokeberry St, The Woodlands, TX 77380 USA

Mahaffey, Valerie *Actor*
Kazarian/Spencer, 11365 Ventura Blvd, #100, Studio City, CA 91604 USA

Mahaffey, Valerio
121 N. San Vicente Blvd, Beverly Hills, CA 90211

Mahal, Taj *Musician, Songwriter*
Bill Graham Mgmt, PO Box 429094, San Francisco, CA 94142 USA

Mahalingam, Gemini *Actor*
47 Harrington Road, Chennai, TN 600 031, INDIA

Mahan, Larry
Box 41, Camp Verde, TX 78010

Mahan, Lawrence (Larry) *Rodeo Rider*
4771 Fruitland Road, Sunset, TX 76270 USA

Maharidge, Date D *Writer*
Stanford University, Communications Dept, Stanford, CA 94305 USA

Maharis, George *Actor*
13150 Mulholland Dr, Beverly Hills, CA 90210 USA

Maharishi Mahesh Yogi *Religious Leader*
Maharishi University, Institute of World Leadership, Fairfield, IA 52556 USA

Maher, Bill *Talk Show Host*
Brillstein-Grey Entertainment, 9150 Wilshire Blvd #350, Beverly Hills, CA 90212 USA

Maher, Sean
PO Box 5617, Beverly Hills, CA 90210

Maheswari *Actor, Bollywood*
9 North Ave, Sree Nagar Colony Saidapet, Chennai, TN 600015, INDIA

Maheu, Robert
3523 Cochise Lane, Las Vegas, NV 89109

Mahfouz, Naguib *Nobel Prize Laureate*
172 Nile St, Cairo, EGYPT

Mahlberg, Greg *Baseball Player*
Texas Rangers, 5100 N Placita Del Lazo, Tucson, AZ 85750-1535 USA

Mahler, Mickey *Baseball Player*
Atlanta Braves, 7911 Quirt St, San Antonio, TX 78227-2636 USA

Mahler, Rick *Baseball Player*
Atlanta Braves, 551 NW Waverly Cir, Port St Lucie, FL 34983-3409 USA

Mahogany, Kevin *Actor, Musician*
Ted Kurland, 173 Brighton Ave, Boston, MA 02134 USA

Mahomes, Patrick *Baseball Player*
Minnesota Twins, PO Box 1025, Lindale, TX 75771-1025 USA

Mahon, Sean *Actor*
McCabe/Justice, 247 S Beverly Dr #102, Beverly Hills, CA 90212 USA

Mahoney, David L *Business Person*
McKesson HBOX Inc, 1 Post St, San Francisco, CA 94104 USA

Mahoney, Jim *Baseball Player*
Boston Red Sox, 150 Sycamore Ter, Glen Rock, NJ 07452-1907 USA

Mahoney, John *Actor*
International Creative Management (ICM-NY), 40 W 57th St, New York, NY 10019 USA

Mahoney, Mike *Baseball Player*
Chicago Cubs, 4412 98th St, Urbandale, IA 50322-1362 USA

Mahony, Cardinal Roger
1531 W. 9th St., Los Angeles, CA 90012

Mahood, Beverly *Musician*
Paquin Entertainment Agency, 110 Bond St, Toronto ON, M5B 1X8, CANADA

Mahorn, Rick *Basketball Player*
3091 Mapleridge Court, Rochester Hills, MI 48309 USA

Mahovlich, Francis W (Frank) *Hockey Player*
2-954 Ave ROad, Toronto, ON M5P 2K8, CANADA

Mahre, Phil
70 Roza View Dr., Yakima, WA 98901-9390

Mahre, Phillip (Phil) *Skier*
70 Roza View Dr, Yakima, WA 98901 USA

Mahre, Steve *Skier*
100 McCormick Road, Yakima, WA 98908 USA

Maida, Adam J Cardinal *Religious Leader*
Archdiocese of Detroit, 1234 Washington Blvd, Detroit, MI 48226 USA

Maiden-Naccarato, Jeanne *Bowler*
1 N Stadium Way, #4, Tacoma, WA 98406 USA

Maier, Hermann *Skier*
Reitdorf 116, Flachau, 5542, AUSTRIA

Maier, Pauline R *Historian*
60 Larchwood Dr, Cambridge, MA 02138 USA

Maier, Sepp *Soccer Player*
Parkstr 62, Anzing, 84405, GERMANY

Mailer, Norman
142 Columbia Heights, Brooklyn, NY 11201

Mailer, Norman K (Norm) *Writer*
625 Commerical St, Provincetown, MA 02657 USA

Mailho, Emil *Baseball Player*
Philadelphia Athletics, 566 Scott St, Fremont, CA 94539-5208 USA

Mailinvaud, Edmond *Economist*
42 Ave de Saxe, Paris, 75007, FRANCE

Maillard, Carol *Musician*
Sweet Honey Agency, PO Box 600099, Newtonville, MA 02460 USA

Maiman, Theodore H (Ted) *Inventor*
15A Alberni St, Vancouver, BC V6G 3N7, CANADA

Maines, Natalie *Musician*
Senior Mgmt, 56 Lindsey Ave, Nashville, TN 37210 USA

Maisel, Jay *Photographer*
190 Bowery, New York, NY 10012 USA

Maisel, Sherman J *Economist*
2164 Hyde St, San Francisco, CA 94109 USA

Maisenberg, Olega *Musician*
In Der Gugl 9, Klostemeuburg, AUSTRIA

Maisky, Mischa M *Musician*
Columbia Artists Mgmt Inc, 165 W 57th St, New York, NY 10019 USA

Maisnik, Kathy
260 S. Beverly Dr. #308, Beverly Hills, CA 90212

Maisonneuve, Brian *Soccer Player*
Columbus Crew, 2121 Volman Ave, Columbus, OH 43211 USA

Maitland, Beth *Actor*
Epstein-Wyckoff, 280 S Beverly Dr, #400, Beverly Hills, CA 90212 USA

Majdarzavyn, Ganzorig *Cosmonaut*
Academy of Sciences, Peace Ave 54B, Ulan Bator, 51, MONGOLIA

Majerus, Rick *Basketball Player, Coach*
ESPN-TV Sports Dept, ESPN Plaza, 935 Middle St, Bristol, CT 06010 USA

Majoli, Iva *Tennis Player*
27 Framingham Lane, Pittsford, NY 14534 USA

Major, Clarence L *Writer*
University of California, English Dept, Voorhies Hall, Davis, CA 95616 USA

Major, John *Prime Minister*
8 Stuckley Road, Huntingdon, Cambs,
UNITED KINGDOM (UK)

Majoras, Deborah *Government Official*
Federal Trade Commission, Pennsylvania
Ave & 6th St NW, Washington, DC 20580
USA

Majorino, Tina *Actor*
Envoy Entertainment, 1640 S Sepulveda
Blvd #530, Los Angeles, CA 90025 USA

Majors, Austin
Major Minors, 3940 Lauren Canyon Blvd
#177, Studio City, CA 91604

Majors, John I (Johnny) *Football Player,*
Football Coach
4215 Bigelow Blvd, Pittsburgh, PA 15213
USA

Majors, Lee *Actor*
16030 Ventura Blvd #380, Encino, CA
91436-2778 USA

MajorSundararajan *Actor*
9 Pooram Prakash Rao Street, Balaji Nagar
Royapeta, Chennai, TN 600 014, INDIA

Makarov, Askold A *Dancer*
Plutalova Str 18-4, Saint Petersburg,
197136, RUSSIA

Makarov, Sergei *Hockey Player*
Professional Sports Services, 4072 Teale
Ave, San Jose, CA 95117 USA

Makarova, Inna V *Actor*
Ukrainian Blvd 11, Moscow, 121059,
RUSSIA

Makarova, Natalia R *Ballerina*
Herbert Breslin, 119 W 57th St, #1505,
New York, NY 10019 USA

Makeba, Miriam *Musician*
Sadiane Corp, 60 E 42nd St, #1201, New
York, NY 10169 USA

Makem, Tommy
2 Longmeadow Rd., Dover, NH 03820

Makhalina, Yufia *Ballerina*
Kirov Ballet Theater, 1 Pl Iskusstr, Saint
Petersburg, 190000, RUSSIA

Makinson, Jessica *Comedian*
OmniPop Inc (LA), 10700 Ventura Blvd Fl
2, Studio City, CA 91604 USA

Makk, Karoly *Director*
Hanoczy Jeno Utca 15, Budapest, 1022,
HUNGARY

Makkena, Wendy *Actor*
Blueprint Management, 5670 Wilshire
Blvd #2525, Los Angeles, CA 90036 USA

Mako *Actor*
6477 Pepper Tree Lane, Somis, CA 93066
USA

Mako, C Gene *Tennis Player*
430 S Burnside Ave, #MC, Los Angeles,
CA 90036 USA

Makowski, Tom *Baseball Player*
Detroit Tigers, 6686 Omphalius Rd # 2,
Colden, NY 14033-9763 USA

Maksimoya, Yekaterina S *Ballerina*
Bolshoi Theater, Teatrainsya Pl 1,
Moscow, 103009, RUSSIA

Maksudian, Mike *Baseball Player*
Toronto Blue Jays, 10042 E Karen Dr,
Scottsdale, AZ 85260-9203 USA

Maksymiuk, Jerzy
Hoza 5A m 13, Warsaw, 00-528,
POLAND

Maktoum, Shaikh Maktoum bin Rashid al-
Prime Minister
Royal Palace, PO Box 899, Abu Dhabi,
UNITED ARAB EMIRATES

Malahide, Patrick *Actor*
International Creative Mgmt, 76 Oxford
St, London, W1N 0AX, UNITED
KINGDOM (UK)

Malakhov, Vladimir *Hockey Player*
31 Mary Court, Melville, NY 11747 USA

Malakian, Daron *Musician*
Velvet Hammer, 9911 W Pico Blvd, #350,
Los Angeles, CA 90035 USA

Malandrino, Catherine *Fashion Designer*
468 Bromme St, New York, NY 10013
USA

Malandro, Kristina *Actor*
2518 Cardigan Court, Los Angeles, CA
90077 USA

Malaska, Mark *Baseball Player*
Tampa Bay Devil Rays, 612 Clearmount
Dr, Youngstown, OH 44511-3156 USA

Malavoy, Christopher
9 sq. de Montsouris, Paris, FRANCE,
F-75014

Malaysia Vasudevan *Actor*
5 Kaman Street SFI Apts, 6-B Samiyar
Matt, Chennai, TN 600 024, INDIA

Malchow, Tom
One Olympic Plaza, Colorado Springs,
CO 80909-5770

Malco, Romany *Actor*
Greene & Associates, 526 N Larchmont
Blvd #201, Los Angeles, CA 90004 USA

Malcolm, George J *Musician*
99 Wimbledon Hill Road, London, SW19
4BE, UNITED KINGDOM (UK)

Maldacena, Juan *Physicist*
Harvard University, Physics Dept,
Cambridge, MA 02138 USA

Malden, Karl *Actor*
1845 Mandeville Canyon Rd, Los Angeles,
CA 90049 USA

Maldini, Paolo *Soccer Player, Coach*
AC Milan, Via Turati 3, Milan, 20221,
ITALY

Maldonado, Candy *Baseball Player*
Los Angeles Dodgers, HC 2 Box 16800,
Arecibo, PR 00612-9396 USA

Malee, Chompoo *Fashion Designer*
Hino & Malee Inc, 3701 N Ravenswood
Ave, Chicago, IL 60613 USA

Maleeva, Katerina *Tennis Player*
Mladostr 1 #45, NH 14, Sofia, 1174,
BULGARIA

Maleeva-Fragniere, Manuela *Tennis*
Player
Bourg-Dessous 28, La Tour de Peitz,
1814, SWITZERLAND

Malenchenko, Yuri I *Cosmonaut*
Potcha Kosmonavtov, Moskovskoi Oblasti,
Syvisdny Goroduk, 141160, RUSSIA

Maler, Jim *Baseball Player*
Seattle Mariners, 2163 NE 122nd St,
North Miami, FL 33181-2908 USA

Malerba, Franco E *Astronaut*
Via Cantore 10, Genova, 16149, ITALY

Malerba, Luigi
Via Tro Millina 31, Rome, CA ITALY

Malfitano, Catherine *Opera Singer*
Columbia Artists Mgmt Inc, 165 W 57th
St, New York, NY 10019 USA

Malhotra, Harmesh *Director, Producer,*
Filmmaker, Bollywood
32A Sunset Heights 59 Pali Hill, Nargis
Dutt Road Bandra, Bombay, MS 400 050,
INDIA

Malice *Musician*
Star Trak/Arista Records, 888 7th Ave,
#3800, New York, NY 10106 USA

Malick, Terrence
7920 Sunset Blvd., Los Angeles, CA
90046

Malick, Wendie *Actor, Model*
Innovative Artists, 1505 10th St, Santa
Monica, CA 90401 USA

malicki-Sanchez, Keram *Actor*
Ramaker Management, 400 North
Gardner Street, Los Angeles, CA 90036
USA

Malicky, Neal *Educator*
Baldwin-Wallace College, President's
Office, Berea, OH 44017 USA

Malielegaoi, Tuilaepa Sailele *Prime*
Minister
Prime Minister's Office, PO Box L1861,
Vailima, Apia, SAMOA

Malik, Art *Actor*
18 Sydney Mews, London, SW3 6HL,
UNITED KINGDOM (UK)

Malina, Josh
2262 Cloverfield Blvd., Santa Monica, CA
90405

Malina, Joshua *Actor*
Innovative Artists (LA), 1505 Tenth St,
Santa Monica, CA 90401 USA

Malina, Judith
800 West End Ave., New York, NY 10025

Malinger, Ross
6212 Banner Ave., Los Angeles, CA
90038

Malini, Hema *Actor, Bollywood*
17 Jai Hind Society, 12th Road Juhu
Scheme, Mumbai, MS 400049, INDIA

Malinin, Mike *Musician*
Atlas/Third Rail Entertainment, 9200 W
Sunset Blvd, West Hollywood, CA 90069
USA

Malinosky, Tony *Baseball Player*
Brooklyn Dodgers, 5540 W 5th St Spc 60,
Oxnard, CA 93035-4872 USA

Maliozzi, Ray *Talk Show Host*
PBS, 1320 Braddock Pl, Alexandria, VA
22314

Maliozzi, Tom *Talk Show Host*
PBS, 1320 Braddock Pl, Alexandria, VA
22314

Maliponte, Adrianna *Opera Singer*
Gorlinsky Promotions, 35 Darer, London,
W1, UNITED KINGDOM (UK)

Malkan, Matthew A *Astronomer*
University of Arizona, Steward
Observatory, Tucson, AZ 85721 USA

Malkhov, Vladimir *Ballerina*
American Baliet Theatre, 890 Broadway, New York, NY 10003 USA

Malkin, Evgenl *Hockey Player*
Pittsburgh Penguins, Mellon Arena, 66 Mario Lemieux Place, Pittsburgh, PA 15219 USA

Malkin, Laurence *Writer*
Jericho Entertainment, 2121 Ave of the Stars #2900, Los Angeles, CA 90067

Malkin, Peter Z *Lawyer, Government Official*
135 W 74th St, #2R, New York, NY 10023 USA

Malkmus, Bobby *Baseball Player*
Milwaukee Braves, 400 Wallingford Ter, Union, NJ 07083-7328 USA

Malkovich, John *Actor*
PO Box 5106, Westport, CT 06881 USA

Mallary, Robert *Artist*
PO Box 97, Conway, MA 01341 USA

Mallea, Eduardo *Writer*
Posadas 1120, Buenos Aires, ARGENTINA

Mallet, W George *Governor*
Governor General's Office, Morne, Castries, SAINT LUCIA

Mallett, Jerry *Baseball Player*
Boston Red Sox, 7610 Forest Park Dr, Beaumont, TX 77707-1626 USA

Mallette, Alfred J *General*
681 Lambeth Dr, Evans, GA 30809 USA

Mallette, Brian *Baseball Player*
Milwaukee Brewers, 3012 Gilder Rd, Glenwood, GA 30428-2202 USA

Mallette, Mai *Baseball Player*
Brooklyn Dodgers, 15 Barratts Chapel Ct, Durham, NC 27705-1311 USA

Malley, Kenneth C *Admiral*
136 Riverside Road, Edgewater, MD 21037 USA

Mallick, Dan *Misc*
42045 N Tilton Dr, Quartz Hill, CA 93536 USA

Mallicoat, Rob *Baseball Player*
Houston Astros, 2050 SE Larson Ct, Hillsboro, OR 97123-5304 USA

Mallon, Meg *Golfer*
Pro's Inc, 7100 Forest Ave, #201, Richmond, VA 23226 USA

Mallory, Carole *Actor*
2300 5th Ave, New York, NY 10037 USA

Mallory, Glynn C Jr *General*
19221 Heather Forest, San Antonio, TX 78258 USA

Mallory, Sheldon *Baseball Player*
Oakland A's, 21353 Old North Church Rd, Frankfort, IL 60423-3016 USA

Malloy, Bob *Baseball Player*
Texas Rangers, 1904 San Carlos Ave, Allen, TX 75002-2626 USA

Malloy, Bob *Baseball Player*
Cincinnati Reds, 3850 Kirkup Ave, Cincinnati, OH 45213-1922 USA

Malloy, Edward A *Educator*
University of Notre Dame, President's Office, Notre Dame, IN 46556 USA

Malloy, Marty *Baseball Player*
Atlanta Braves, 2030 SW 100th St, Trenton, FL 32693-5530 USA

Malloy, Robert (Pete Hamil) *Writer, Actor*
International Creative Management (ICM-LA), 8942 Wilshire Blvd, Beverly Hills, CA 90211 USA

Malloy, Tommy
1687 Amsterdam Ave Merrick, LI, NY 11566

Malloys, The *Music Group*
Creative Artists Agency LCC (CAA-LA), 9830 Wilshire Blvd, Beverly Hills, CA 90212 USA

Malmuth, Bruce
9981 Robin Dr., Beverly Hills, CA 90210

Malo, Raul *Musician, Songwriter*
AristoMedia, 1620 16th Ave S, Nashville, TN 37212 USA

Maloff, Sam *Designer*
PO Box 51, Alta Lorna, CA 91701 USA

Malone, Arthur L (Art) *Football Player*
1619 E Carmen St, Tempe, AZ 85283 USA

Malone, Beverly L *Misc*
American Nurses Assn, Maryland Ave SW, Washington, DC 20002 USA

Malone, Brendan *Coach*
Indiana Pacers, Conseco Fieldhouse, 125 S Pennsylvania, Indianapolis, IN 46204 USA

Malone, Chuck *Baseball Player*
Philadelphia Phillies, 310 Liberty St, Marked Tree, AR 72365-2209 USA

Malone, Dorothy *Actor*
PO Box 7287, Dallas, TX 75209 USA

Malone, Eddie *Baseball Player*
Chicago White Sox, 224 Avenida Majorca Unit A, Laguna Woods, CA 92653-4133 USA

Malone, Jena *Actor*
United Talent Agency (UTA), 9560 Wilshire Blvd, Beverly Hills, CA 90212 USA

Malone, Karl
301 W. South Temple, Salt Lake City, UT 84101

Malone, Patricia *Business Person*
Gucci America, 50 Hartz Way, Secaucus, NJ 07094 USA

Malone, Shannon *Actor, Television Host*
Jerry Shandrew PR, 1050 South Stanley Avenue, Los Angeles, CA 90019-6634 USA

Maloney, Jim *Baseball Player*
Cincinnati Reds, 7027 N Teilman Ave #102, Fresno, CA 93711-0589 USA

Maloney, Patty
6767 Forest Lawn Dr. #101, Los Angeles, CA 90068

Maloney, Sean *Baseball Player*
Milwaukee Brewers, 4601 E Skyline Drive Apt 1205, Tucson, AZ 85718 USA

Malrena, Oswaldo *Baseball Player*
Chicago Cubs, 160 E 6th Pl, Mesa, AZ 85201-5068 USA

Maltin, Leonard *Correspondent*
Entertainment Tonight (ET), 5555 Melrose Ave, Mae West Bldg Fl 2, Hollywood, CA 90038 USA

Maly, Arturo *Actor*
Telefe - Argentina, Pavon 2444 (C1248AAT), Buenos Aires, ARGENTINA

Malzone, Frank *Baseball Player*
Boston Red Sox, 16 Aletha Rd, Needham, MA 02492-4302 USA

Mamas & The Papas, The
61 Purchase St. #2, Rye, NY 10580

Mambo, Kevin
3500 W. Olympic Blvd. #1400, Burbank, CA 91505

Mamet, David *Writer, Director, Producer, Actor*
8707 Skokie Blvd #400, Skokie, IL 60077-2283

Mana *Music Group*
Creative Artists Agency LCC (CAA-LA), 9830 Wilshire Blvd, Beverly Hills, CA 90212 USA

Manatt, Charles T
4814 Woodway Ln NW, Washington, DC 20016 USA

Manchester, Melissa
5440 Corbin Ave., Tarzana, CA 91356

Mancina, Mark *Actor*
Gorfaine/Schwartz Agency, The, 13245 Riverside Dr #450, Sherman Oaks, CA 91423 USA

Mancini, Ray
12524 Indianapolis St, Los Angeles, CA 90066-1512

Mancuso, Frank *Baseball Player*
St Louis Browns, 5126 Cripple Creek Dr, Houston, TX 77017-6005 USA

Mancuso, Nick *Actor*
Agency for the Performing Arts (APA-LA), 9200 Sunset Blvd #900, Los Angeles, CA 90069 USA

Mancuso Jr, Frank *Producer*
FGM Entertainment, 201 N Canon Dr #328, Beverly Hills, CA 90210

Mandan, Robert
247 S. Beverly Dr. #102, Beverly Hills, CA 90212

Mandel, Howie *Comedian*
3 Arts Entertainment Inc, 9460 Wilshire Blvd Fl 7, Beverly Hills, CA 90212 USA

Mandel, Johnny
28946 Cliffside Dr, Malibu, CA 90265

Mandel, Loring
555 W. 57th St. #1230, New York, NY 10019

Mandela, N Winnie Madikizela *Social Activist*
Orlando West, Soweto, Johannesburg, SOUTH AFRICA

Mandela, Nelson R *Politician*
Private Bag X70000, Houghton, 2041, SOUTH AFRICA

Manders, Hal *Baseball Player*
Detroit Tigers, PO Box 149, Dallas Center, IA 50063-0149 USA

Mandrell, Barbara *Musician*
Creative Artists Agency LCC (CAA-LA),
9830 Wilshire Blvd, Beverly Hills, CA
90212 USA

Mandrell, Erline
2046 Parkway, Pigeon Forge, TN 37863-
2959

Mandrell, Louise
2046 Parkway, Pigeon Forge, TN 37863-
2959

Mandylor, Costas *Actor*
Atlas Entertainment, 6100 Wilshire Blvd
#1170, Los Angeles, CA 90048 USA

Mandylor, Louis *Actor*
Metropolitan Talent Agency (MTA), 4526
Wilshire Blvd, Los Angeles, CA 90010
USA

Mane, Tyler *Actor*
Miller & Company Management, 427
North Canon Drive, #215, Beverly Hills,
CA 90210 USA

Manetti, Larry
4615 Winnetka, Woodland Hills, CA
91364

Mangan, Jlm *Baseball Player*
Pittsburgh Pirates, 6878 Trinidad Dr, San
Jose, CA 95120-2057 USA

Mangelsdorff, AlbertEmil-
Claar-Str. 23, Frankfurt/Main, GERMANY,
60322

Mangione, Chuck
476 Hampton Blvd., Rochester, NY 14612

Mangold, James Allen *Director, Writer,
Producer*
Tree Line Films, 10202 W Washington
Blvd, Tristar Bldg 222, Culver City, CA
90232 USA

Mangual, Angel *Baseball Player*
Pittsburgh Pirates, 1406 R Del Valle,
Ponce, PR 00728 USA

Mangual, Pepe *Baseball Player*
Montreal Expos, 2325 Calle Tabonuco,
Ponce, PR 00716-2712 USA

Mangum, Jonathan *Actor*
Shapiro/West & Associates, 141 El
Camino Dr #205, Beverly Hills, CA 90212

Manheim, Camryn *Actor, Producer,
Writer*
Framework Entertainment (LA), 9057
Nemo St #C, W Hollywood, CA 90069
USA

Manilow, Barry *Musician*
Stiletto Entertainment, 8295 S La Cienega,
Inglewood, CA 90301 USA

Manisha, Koirala *Actor, Bollywood*
302 Beachwood Towers, Yari Road
Versova Andher (W), Mumbai, MS
400061, INDIA

Mankiewicz, Frank
The Wyoming Columbia Rd. NW,
Washington, DC 20009

Mankiewicz, Tom
1609 Magnetic Terrace, Los Angeles, CA
90069

Mankiller, Wilma P *Social Activist*
Cherokee Nation, PO Box 948,
Tahlequah, OK 74465 USA

Mankowitz, Wolf
Ahakista County Cork, Kilcrohane,
IRELAND, 11

Mankowski, Phil *Baseball Player*
Detroit Tigers, PO Box 141, Orchard Park,
NY 14127-0141 USA

Manley, Elizabeth *Figure Skater*
Marco Enterprises, 74830 Velie Dr, #A,
Palm Desert, CA 92260 USA

Manlikova, Hana
Vymolova 8, Prague 5, 15000, Czech
Republic

Mann, Abby *Writer*
Writers & Artists, 8383 Wilshire Blvd,
#550, Beverly Hills, CA 90211 USA

Mann, Almee *Musician, Songwriter*
Michael Hausman Mgmt, 511 Ave of
Americas, #197, New York, NY 10011
USA

Mann, Barry *Composer*
1010 Laurel Way, Beverly Hills, CA
90210 USA

Mann, Carol *Golfer*
6 Cape Chestnut Dr, The Woodlands, TX
77381 USA

Mann, Catherine
9417 Spruce Tree Circle, Bethesda, MD
20814-1654

Mann, David W *Religious Leader*
10550 S 200 W, Columbia City, IN 46725
USA

Mann, Delbert *Director, Producer*
Caroline Productions, 556 S Ogden Dr,
Los Angeles, CA 90036 USA

Mann, Dick *Motorcycle Racer*
American Motorcycle Assn, 13515
Yarmouth Dr, Pickerington, OH 43147
USA

Mann, Gabriel *Actor*
IFA Talent Agency, 8730 Sunset Blvd
#490, Los Angeles, CA 90069 USA

Mann, Garbriel *Actor*
United Talent Agency, 9560 Wilshire
Blvd, #500, Beverly Hills, CA 90212 USA

Mann, H Thompson *Swimmer*
49 Water St, Newburyport, MA 01950
USA

Mann, Jim *Baseball Player*
New York Mets, 197 N Franklin St,
Holbrook, MA 02343-1111 USA

Mann, Johnny *Composer, Conductor*
78516 Gorman Lane, Indio, CA 92203
USA

Mann, Kelly *Baseball Player*
Atlanta Braves, 10761 Lawler St Apt 2,
Los Angeles, CA 90034-5474 USA

Mann, Leslie *Actor*
Endeavor Agency LLC (LA), 9601 Wilshire
Blvd Fl 3, Beverly Hills, CA 90210 USA

Mann, Manfred *Misc*
EMI Records, 43 Brook Green, London,
W6 7EF, UNITED KINGDOM (UK)

Mann, Marvin L *Business Person*
Lexmark International, 740 W New Circle
Road, Lexington, KY 40550 USA

Mann, Michael *Director, Producer*
Forward Pass Inc, 12233 W Olympic Blvd
#340, Los Angeles, CA 90064

Mann, Michael K *Producer, Director*
13746 Sunset Blvd, Pacific Palisades, CA
90272 USA

Mann, Monroe *Actor, Producer, Writer*
Monroe Mann, Inc, PO Box 3674, New
York, NY 10163 USA

Mann, Robert *Football Player*
1979 Orleans St, #252, Detroit, MI 48207
USA

Mann, Robert W *Engineer*
5 Pelham Road, Lexington, MA 02421
USA

Mann, Shelley I *Swimmer*
1301 S Scott St, #638S, Arlington, VA
22204 USA

Mann, Terrence V *Actor*
111 W 96th St, #1, New York, NY 10025
USA

Manners, Miss
1651 Harvard St. NW, Washington, DC
20009

Mannheim Steamroller *Music Group*
9120 Mormon Bridge Rd, Omaha, NE
68152 USA

Manning, E Archie III *Football Player,
Sportscaster*
WWL-TV, Sports Dept, 1024 N Rampart
St, New Orleans, LA 70116 USA

Manning, Eli *Football Player*
New York Giants, Giants Stadium, East
Rutherford, NJ 07073 USA

Manning, Jane *Opera Singer*
2 Wilton Square, London, N1, UNITED
KINGDOM (UK)

Manning, Jim *Baseball Player*
Minnesota Twins, 41 Fox Run Dr,
Weaverville, NC 28787-8307 USA

Manning, Peyton *Football Player*
1420 1st St, New Orleans, LA 70130 USA

Manning, Richard E (Rick) *Baseball Player*
Cleveland Indians, 12151 New Market,
Chesterland, OH 44026-2041 USA

Manning, Rob *Engineer*
Jet Propulsion Laboratory, 4800 Oak
Grove Dr, Pasadena, CA 91109 USA

Manning, Robert J *Editor*
191 Commonwealth Ave, Boston, MA
02116 USA

Manning, Susanne *Musician*
Pop Idol (Fremantle Media), 2700
Colorado Ave #450, Santa Monica, CA
90404 USA

Manning, Taryn *Actor, Musician*
Platform, 2666 N Beachwood Dr, Los
Angeles, CA 90068 USA

Manoff, Dinah *Actor*
Innovative Artists, 1505 10th St, Santa
Monica, CA 90401 USA

Manoogian, RIchard A *Business Person*
Masco Corp, 2100 Van Born Road,
Taylor, MI 48180 USA

Manorama *Actor, Bollywood*
5 Neelagandan Street, T Nagar, Chennai,
TN 600017, INDIA

Manrique, Fred *Baseball Player*
Toronto Blue Jays, 1775 SW 2nd Ave,
Boca Raton, FL 33432-7230 USA

Mansell, Kevin *Business Person*
Kohl's Corp, N56W17000 RIdgewood Dr, Menomonee Falls, WI 53051 USA

Mansell, Nigel *Race Car Driver*
Nigel Mansell Racing, Brands Hatch, Longfield, Kent, DA3 8NG, UNITED KINGDOM (UK)

Manser, Michael J *Architect*
Morton House, Chiswick Mall, London, W4 2PS, UNITED KINGDOM (UK)

Mansfield, Mike *Ex-Senator*
1101 Pennsylvania Ave NW #900, Washington, DC 20004-2514 USA

Mansfield, Peter *Nobel Prize Laureate*
Notingham University, Physics Dept, Nottingham, NG7 2RD, UNITED KINGDOM (UK)

Mansholt, Sicco L *Government Official*
Oosteinde 16, Wapserveen, HB, 8351, NETHERLANDS

Manson, Dave *Hockey Player*
Dallas Stars, StarCenter, 211 Cowboys Parkway, Irving, TX 75063 USA

Manson, Marilyn *Musician*
25935 Detroit Road, Westlake, OH 44145 USA

Manson, Shirley *Musician*
Borman Entertainment, 1250 6th St, #401, Santa Monica, CA 90401 USA

Mansouri, Lotfi *Actor*
San Francisco Opera House, 301 Van Ness Ave, San Francisco, CA 94102 USA

Mantee, Paul *Actor*
Flick East-West, 9057 Nemo St, #A, West Hollywood, CA 90069 USA

Mantegna, Joe *Actor*
PO Box 7304, #103, North Hollywood, CA 91603 USA

Mantei, Matt *Baseball Player*
Florida Marlins, 8509 E Krail St, Scottsdale, AZ 85250-4932 USA

Mantel, Hillary M *Writer*
AM Heath, 79 Saint Martin's Lane, London, WC2N 4AA, UNITED KINGDOM (UK)

Mantello, Joe *Director*
Writers & Artists, 19 W 44th St, #1000, New York, NY 10036 USA

Mantenuto, Michael *Actor*
Creative Artists Agency LCC (CAA-LA), 9830 Wilshire Blvd, Beverly Hills, CA 90212 USA

Mantha, Mo
8423 Tally Ho Rd., Lutherville, MD 20193

Mantha, Moe *Hockey Player*
1538 Scio Ridge ROad, Ann Arbor, MI 48103 USA

Manthra *Actor, Bollywood*
5-A Block 2 Vijay Shanti Apts, Arcot Road Vadapalani, Chennai, TN 600026, INDIA

Mantilla, Felix *Baseball Player*
Milwaukee Braves, 6973 N Tacoma St, Milwaukee, WI 53224-4759 USA

Mantley, John
4121 Longridge Ave., Sherman Oaks, CA 91423

Manto, Jeff *Baseball Player*
Cleveland Indians, 802 3rd Ave, Bristol, PA 19007-3222 USA

Mantooth, Randolph *Actor*
2830 Lambert Dr, Los Angeles, CA 90068 USA

Mantreola, Patricia
BMG, 1540 Broadway, New York, NY 10036 USA

Manuel, Barry *Baseball Player*
Texas Rangers, 805 Oak St, Mamou, LA 70554-2715 USA

Manuel, Charles F (Chuck) *Baseball Player*
2931 Plantation Road, Winter Haven, FL 33884 USA

Manuel, Charlie *Baseball Player*
Minnesota Twins, 2931 Plantation Rd, Winter Haven, FL 33884-1233 USA

Manuel, Jerry *Baseball Player*
Detroit Tigers, 4023 Greenview Dr, El Dorado Hills, CA 95762-7620 USA

Manuel, Robert *Actor*
La Maison du Buisson, 22-26 Rue Jules Regnier, Plaisir, 78370, FRANCE

Manuelidis, Laura *Misc*
Yale University Medical School, Neuropathology Dept, New Haven, CT 06520 USA

Manuelle, Victor *Musician*

Manulis, Martin
242 Copa de Oro Rd., Los Angeles, CA 90077

Manville, Dick *Baseball Player*
Boston Braves, 1436 Lake Francis Dr, Apopka, FL 32712-2007 USA

Manwaring, Kirt *Baseball Player*
San Francisco Giants, 20 Prospect Rdg, Horseheads, NY 14845-7988 USA

Manwaring, Kurt D *Baseball Player*
20 Prospect Ridge, Horseheads, NY 14845 USA

Manz, Wolfgang *Musician*
Pasteuralle 55, Hanover, 30655, GERMANY

Manza, Ralph
550 Hygeia Ave., Leucadia, CA 92024

Manzanero, Armando *Musician*
Pro Art, Paz Soidan 170, Of 903, San Isidro, Lima, 27, PERU

Manzanillo, Josias *Baseball Player*
Boston Red Sox, 274 Kennebec St, Mattapan, MA 02126-1106 USA

Manzarek, Ray *Musician*
Goldman & Knell, 1801 Century Park E, #2160, Los Angeles, CA 90067 USA

Manzi, Catello *Horse Racer*
1 Hickory Lane, Freehold, NJ 07728 USA

Manzoni, Giacomo *Composer*
Viale Papiniano 31, Milan, 20123, ITALY

Mapes, Cliff
PO Box 872, Pryor, OK 74362

Mapother, William *Actor*
Creative Artists Agency, 9830 Wilshire Blvd, Beverly Hills, CA 90212 USA

Mara, Adele *Actor, Dancer*
1928 Mandeville Canyon Road, Los Angeles, CA 90049 USA

Mara, Ratu Sir Kamisese K T *President*
11 Ballery Road, Suva, FIJI

Mara, Wellington T *Football Executive*
16 Park Dr S, Rye, NY 10580 USA

Marachuk, Steve
568 Hana Hwy., Pai Maui, HI 96779

Maradona, Diego
Brandsen 805, Capital Federal, ARGENTINA, 1161

Marak, Paul *Baseball Player*
Atlanta Braves, 1211 Comanche Trl, Alamogordo, NM 88310-4010 USA

Maramorosch, Karl *Scientist*
1050 George St, New Brunswick, NJ 08901 USA

Maran, Josie *Actor*
Darren Goldberg Management, 5225 Wilshire Blvd #419, Los Angeles, CA 90036

Maraniss, David *Journalist*
Washington Post, Editorial Dept, 1150 15th St NW, Washington, DC 20071 USA

Maratos, Terry *Actor*
The Cage Group, 14724 Ventura Blvd #505, Sherman Oaks, CA 91423

Maratos-Flier, Elfetheria *Doctor*
Joslin Diabetes Center, 1 Joslin Place, Boston, MA 02215 USA

Marber, Patrick *Writer*
Judy Daish, 2 Saint Charles Place, London, W10 6EG, UNITED KINGDOM (UK)

Marbury, Stephon *Basketball Player*
Phoenix Suns, 201 E Jefferson St, Phoenix, AZ 85004 USA

Marbut, Robert G *Publisher*
Argyle Communications, 100 NE Loop, #1400, San Antonio, TX 78216 USA

Marc, Alessandra *Opera Singer*
Columbia Artists Mgmt Inc, 165 W 57th St, New York, NY 10019 USA

Marceau, Sophie *Actor*
Artmedia, 20 Ave Rapp, Paris, 75007, FRANCE

Marcelino, Mario
1418 N. Highland Ave. #102, Los Angeles, CA 90028

March, Forbes *Actor*
Innovative Artists (LA), 1505 Tenth St, Santa Monica, CA 90401 USA

March, Jane *Actor, Model*
Storm Model Mgmt, 5 Jubilee Place, #100, London, SW3 3TD, UNITED KINGDOM (UK)

March, Joan
Whale Rock Ranch Rd., Ojai, CA 93023

March, Little Peggy *Musician*
Cape Entertainment, 1161 NW 76th Ave, Plantation, FL 33822 USA

March, Peggy
1161 NW 76th Ave., Ft. Lauderdale, FL 33322

March, Stephanie *Actor*
I/D PR (NY), 155 Spring St Fl 6, New York, NY 10013 USA

Marchand, Guy
40 rue Francois ler, Paris, FRANCE, F-75008

Marchette, Josh
6500 Wilshire Blvd. #2200, Los Angeles, CA 90048

Marchetti, Gino
1121 Charles St., Wilkes-Barre, PA 18702-6902

Marchetti, Gino J *Football Player*
324 Devon Way, West Chester, PA 19380 USA

Marchetti, Leo V *Misc*
Fraternal Order of Police, 5615 Belair Road, Baltimore, MD 21206 USA

Marchinko, Jhoni *Producer*
United Talent Agency (UTA), 9560 Wilshire Blvd, Beverly Hills, CA 90212 USA

Marchionne, Sergio *Business Person*
Fiat SpA, Via Nizza 250, Turin, 10126, ITALY

Marchisano, Francesco Cardinal *Religious Leader*
Cancelleria Apostolica Palazzo, Plazza Cancelleria 1, Rome, 00186, ITALY

Marchuk, Guri I *Mathematician*
Numerical Mathematics Institute, Gubkin Str 8, Mascow, 117333, RUSSIA

Marchuk, Yevhen K *Prime Minister*
Verkovna Rada, M Hrushevskoho Str 5, Kiev, 252008, UKRAINE

Marciano, David *Actor*
Don Buchwald & Associates Inc (LA), 6500 Wilshire Blvd #2200, Los Angeles, CA 90048 USA

Marcikic, Ivan *Physicist, Inventor*
Geneva University, 24 Rue du General Dufour, Geneva, 1211, SWITZERLAND

Marcil, Vanessa *Actor*
11110 Ohio Ave, #104, Los Angeles, CA 90025 USA

Marcinkevicius, Iustinus M *Writer*
Mildos Str 33, #6, Vilnius, 232055, LITHUANIA

Marcis, Dave *Race Car Driver*
71 Beadle Road, Arden, NC 28704 USA

Marco, Gian *Musician*
Creative Artists Agency LCC (CAA-LA), 9830 Wilshire Blvd, Beverly Hills, CA 90212 USA

Marcol, Czeslaw C (Chester) *Football Player*
PO Box 466, Dollar Bay, MI 49922 USA

Marcos *Musician*
East West America Records, 75 Rockefeller Plaza, New York, NY 10019 USA

Marcos, Imelda
Leyte Providencia Dept, Tolosa Leyte, PHILIPPINES

Marcotte, Don *Hockey Player*
12 Cote St, Amesbury, MA 1913 USA

Marcovicci, Andrea *Actor, Musician*
Donald Smith Promotions, 1640 E 48th St, #14U, New York, NY 10017 USA

Marcucci, Bob
10600 Holman Ave., Los Angeles, CA 90024

Marcum, Art *Writer*
9 Yards Entertainment, 8530 Wilshire Blvd Fl 5, Beverly Hills, CA 90211 USA

Marcus, Bernard *Business Person*
Home Depot Inc, 2455 Paces Ferry Road SE, Atlanta, GA 30339 USA

Marcus, Jurgen
Pestalozzistr. 23a, Munich, GERMANY, D-80469

Marcus, Ken *Photographer*
6916 Melrose Ave, Los Angeles, CA 90038 USA

Marcus, Rudolph A *Nobel Prize Laureate*
331 S Hill Ave, Pasadena, CA 91106 USA

Marcus, Ruth B *Misc*
311 Saint Roman St, New Haven, CT 06511 USA

Marcus, Trula M *Actor*
The Agency, 1800 Ave of the Stars, #400, Los Angeles, CA 90067 USA

Marcy, Geoffrey *Astronomer*
San Francisco State University, Astronomy Dept, San Francisco, CA 94132 USA

Mardall, Cyril L *Architect*
5 Boyne Terrace Mews, London, W11 3LR, UNITED KINGDOM (UK)

Marden, Brice *Artist*
6 Saint Lukes Place, New York, NY 10014 USA

Marder, Barry
Trident Media Group LLC, 41 Madison Ave Fl 33, New York, NY 10010 USA

Mardones, Benny *Musician*
Tony Cee, PO Box 410, Utica, NY 13503 USA

Mare, Olindo *Football Player*
2961 W Lake Circle, Davie, FL 33329 USA

Maree, Sydney *Track Athlete*
2 Braxton Road, Bryn Mawr, PA 19010 USA

Maren, Elizabeth *Actor*
3126 Oakcrest Dr, Los Angeles, CA 90068 USA

Maren, Jerry
3126 Oakcrest Dr., Los Angeles, CA 90068

Marentette, Leo *Baseball Player*
Detroit Tigers, 33606 Beechwood St, Westland, MI 48185-3002 USA

Margal, Albert M *Prime Minister*
8 Hornsey Rise Gardens, London, N19, UNITED KINGDOM (UK)

Margalit, Israela *Musician*
Columbia Artists Mgmt Inc, 165 W 57th St, New York, NY 10019 USA

Margeot, Jean Cardinal *Religious Leader*
Bonne Terre, Vacoas, MAURITIUS

Margera, Bam *Actor, Producer, Writer*
Writers and Artists Group Intl (LA), 8383 Wilshire Blvd #550, Beverly Hills, CA 90211 USA

Margison, Richard *Opera Singer*
George Martynuk, 352 7th Ave, New York, NY 10001 USA

Margo, Philip *Musician*
American Mgmt, 19948 Mayall St, Chatsworth, CA 91311 USA

Margoliash, Emmanuel *Scientist*
353 Madison Ave, Glencoe, IL 60022 USA

Margolin, Phillip *Writer*
Harper Collins Publishers, 10 E 53rd St, New York, NY 10022 USA

Margolin, Stuart *Actor*
Three Owl Productions, Box 478, Ganges, BC V0S 1E0, CANADA

Margolis, Cindy *Model, Actor*
Esterman Events, 220 Park Rd, Riva, MD 21140 USA

Margolis, Lawrence S *Judge*
US Claims Court, 717 Madison Place NW, Washington, DC 20439 USA

Margolyes, Miriam *Actor*
Peters Fraser & Dunlop (PFD - UK), Drury House, 34-43 Russell St, London, WC2 B5, UNITED KINGDOM (UK)

Margon, Bruce H *Astronomer*
University of Washington, Astronomy Dept, PO Box 351580, Seattle, WA 98195 USA

Margoyles, Miriam *Actor*
P F D Drury House, 34-43 Russell St, London, WC2B 5HA, UNITED KINGDOM (UK)

Margrave, John L *Misc*
4511 Vrone, Bellaire, TX 77401 USA

Margret, Ann (Ann-Margret) *Musician, Actor, Dancer*
International Creative Management (ICM-LA), 8942 Wilshire Blvd, Beverly Hills, CA 90211 USA

Margrethe II *Royalty*
Amalienborg Palace, Copenhgen K, 1257, DENMARK

Margulies, Donald *Writer*
Yale University, English Dept, New Haven, CT 06520 USA

Margulies, James H (Jimmy) *Editor, Cartoonist*
Hackensack Record, Editorial Dept, 150 River St, Hackensack, NJ 07601 USA

Margulies, Julianna *Actor*
The Firm, 9100 Wilshire Blvd, #100W, Beverly Hills, CA 90210 USA

Margulis, Lynn *Biologist*
2 Cummington St, Boston, MA 02215 USA

Mariago, Cesare
19 788 Citadel Dr.#120, Pt. Coquitlam, CANADA, BC V3C 6G

Mariam, Mengistu Haile *President*
PO Box 1536, Gunhill Enclave, Harare, ZIMBABWE

Mariategui, Sandro *Prime Minister*
Ave Ramirez Gaston 375, Miraflores, Lima, PERU

Marichal, Juan *Baseball Player*
9458 Doral Blvd, Miami, FL 33178 USA

Marie, Aurelius J B L *President*
Zicack, Portsmouth, DOMINICA

Marie, Constance *Actor*
Kass & Stokes Management, 9229 Sunset Blvd #504, Los Angeles, CA 90069 USA

Marie, Lisa *Actor, Model*
William Morris Agency (WMA-LA), 1
William Morris Pl, Beverly Hills, CA
90212 USA

Marie, Princess *Royalty*
Schloss Vaduz, Vaduz, 9490,
LIECHTENSTEIN

Marie, Teena *Musician*
1000 Laguna Road, Pasadena, CA 91105
USA

Marienthal, Eli *Actor*
International Creative Management
(ICM-LA), 8942 Wilshire Blvd, Beverly
Hills, CA 90211 USA

Marilyn
33-34 Cleveland St., London, ENGLAND,
W1

Marimow, William K *Journalist*
1025 Winding Way, Baltimore, MD
21210 USA

Marin, Christian
27 rue de Richelieu, Paris, FRANCE,
F-75001

Marin, Jack *Basketball Player*
3909 Regent Road, Durham, NC 27707
USA

Marin, Maguy *Choreographer*
Compagnie Maguy Marin, Place Salvador
Allende, Creteil, 94000, FRANCE

Marin, Richard A (Cheech) *Actor,
Comedian*
Paradigm (LA), 10100 Santa Monica Blvd,
Fl 25, Los Angeles, CA 90067 USA

Marinaro, Edward F (Ed) *Actor, Football
Player*
Innovative Artists, 1505 10th St, Santa
Monica, CA 90401 USA

Marino, Daniel C (Dan) Jr *Football Player*
300 SW 1st Ave, Fort Lauderdale, FL
33301 USA

Marino, Ken *Actor*
I F A Talent Agency, 8730 Sunset Blvd,
#490, Los Angeles, CA 90069 USA

Marinus, Martin
Postbus 724, AS Gouda, THE
NETHERLANDS, 2800

Mario, Ernest *Business Person*
ALZA Corp, 1950 Charleston Road,
Mountain View, CA 94043 USA

Marion, Brock E *Football Player*
13825 Luray Road SW, Ranches, FL
33330 USA

Marion, Martin W (Marty) *Baseball Player*
8 Forcee Lane, Saint Louis, MO 63124
USA

Marion, Marty
8 Forces Lane, St. Louis, MO 63124

Marion, Shawn *Basketball Player*
Phoenix Suns, 201 E Jefferson St, Phoenix,
AZ 85004 USA

Mariotti, Ray *Editor*
Austin American-Statesman, Editorial
Dept, 166 E Riverside, Austin, TX 78704
USA

Maris, Ada
10100 Santa Monica Blvd#2500, Los
Angeles, CA 90067

Marisol *Artist*
Marlborough Gallery, 40 W 57th St, New
York, NY 10019 USA

Mariucci, Steve *Football Coach*
Detroit Lions, 222 Republic Dr, Allen
Park, MI 48101 USA

Mariye, Lily *Director, Writer*
Bauman Redanty & Shaul Agency, 5757
Wilshire Blvd #473, Los Angeles, CA
90036 USA

Mark, Albert J *Beauty Pageant Winner*
Miss American Pageant, 1325 Broadway,
Atlantic City, NJ 08401 USA

Mark, Bruce *Ballerina, Artist, Director*
Boston Ballet Co, 19 Clarendon St,
Boston, MA 02116 USA

Mark, Hans M *Government Official,
Physicist, Educator*
1715 Scenic Dr, Austin, TX 78703 USA

Mark, Marky
63 Pilgrim Rd., Braintree, MA 02184-6003

Mark, Mary Ellen *Photographer*
143 Price St, New York, NY 10012 USA

Mark, Reuben *Business Person*
Colgate-Palmolive Co, 300 Park Ave, New
York, NY 10022 USA

Mark, Robert *Lawyer, Government
Official*
Esher, Surrey, KT10 8LU, UNITED
KINGDOM (UK)

Markaryants, Vladimir S *Government
Official*
Council of Ministers, Yerevan, ARMENIA

Marken, William R *Editor*
Sunset Magazine, Editorial Dept, 80
Willow Road, Mento Park, CA 94025 USA

Marker, Laurie *Biologist*
Cheetah Conservation Fund, PO Box
1380, Ojai, CA 93024 USA

Marker, Steve *Musician*
Borman Entertainment, 1250 6th St, #401,
Santa Monica, CA 90401 USA

Markey, Lucille P *Misc*
18 La Gorce Circle Lane, La Gorce Island,
Miami Beach, FL 33141 USA

Markham, Monte *Actor*
PO Box 607, Malibu, CA 90265 USA

Markie, Biz *Artist*
William Morris Agency, 151 El Camino
Dr, Beverly Hills, CA 90212 USA

Markle, C Wilson *Engineer*
Colorization Inc, 26 Scho St, Toronto, ON
M5T 1Z7, CANADA

Markle, Peter F *Director*
7510 W Sunset Blvd, #509, Los Angeles,
CA 90046 USA

Markova, Alicia *Ballerina*
Barclays Bank, PO Box 4599, London,
SW3 1KE, UNITED KINGDOM (UK)

Markowitz, Barry *Cinematographer*
225 W 83rd St, #20G, New York, NY
10024 USA

Markowitz, Harry M *Nobel Prize Laureate*
1010 Turquoise St, #245, San Diego, CA
92109 USA

Markowitz, Michael *Artist*
23rd Street Gallery, 3747 23rd St, San
Francisco, CA 94114 USA

Markowitz, Robert *Director, Producer*
11521 Amanda Dr, Studio City, CA 91604
USA

Marks, Chandler
PO Box 184, Franklin, TN 37065

Marks, Paul A *Biologist*
25680 Military Road, Watertown, NY
13601 USA

Markstein, Gary *Editor, Cartoonist*
Milwaukee Journal, Editorial Dept, 333 W
State St, Milwaukee, WI 53203 USA

Markwart, Nevin *Hockey Player*
210 Cushing Hill Road, Hanover, MA
02339 USA

Marlette, Douglas N (Doug) *Editor,
Cartoonist*
PO Box 32188, Charlotte, NC 28232 USA

Marley, Damian *Musician*
William Morris Agency (WMA-LA), 1
William Morris Pl, Beverly Hills, CA
90212 USA

Marley, Ziggy *Musician, Songwriter*
Jack's Hill, Kingston, JAMAICA

Marlin, Sterling *Race Car Driver*
995 Mahon Road, Columbia, TN 38401
USA

Marlow, Jean
32 Exeter Rd., London, ENGLAND, NW2

Marlowe, Scott
6399 Wilshire Blvd. #414, Los Angeles,
CA 90048

Marm, Walter J Jr *War Hero*
PO Box 2017, Fremont, NC 27830 USA

Marnie, Larry *Football Coach*
Arizona State University, Athletic Dept,
Tempe, AZ 85287 USA

Marohn, William D *Business Person*
Whirlpool Corp, 2000 N State St, RR 63,
Benton Harbor, MI 49022 USA

Maron, Marc *Comedian*
United Talent Agency (UTA), 9560
Wilshire Blvd, Beverly Hills, CA 90212
USA

Maroney, Daniel V Jr *Misc*
Amalgamated Transil Union, 5025
Wilconsin Ave NW, Washington, DC
20016 USA

Maroney, Kelli *Actor*
Peter Strain, 5724 W 3rd St, #302, Los
Angeles, CA 90036 USA

Marotte, Carl
438 Queen E, Toronto, CANADA, Ont.
M5A 1

Marotte, J Gilles *Hockey Player*
1759 Notre Dameo, Victoriaville, QC,
G6A 7M4, CANADA

Marquand, Christian
45 rue de Bellechasse, Paris, FRANCE,
F-75007

Marques, Gabriel Garcia
Fuego 144, Pedregal de San Angel Mexico
DF, MEXICO

Marques, Maria Elena
Nubes 723 Pedregal, Mexico DF,
MEXICO

Marquette, Chris *Actor*
Agency West Entertainment, 6255 West Sunset Blvd, Suite 908, Hollywood, CA 90028 USA

Marquette, Christopher *Actor*
Williams Unlimited, 5010 Buffalo Ave, Sherman Oaks, CA 91423

Marquez, Raul -
14611 Maisemore, Houston, TX 77015

Marriner, Neville
Academy Saint Martin in Fields, Raine St, London, E1 9RG, UNITED KINGDOM (UK)

Marriott, Evan *Reality TV Star*
Esterman Events, 220 Park Rd, Riva, MD 21140 USA

Marriott, J Willard Jr *Business Person*
Marriott International, 10400 Fernwood Road, Bethesda, MD 20817 USA

Marriott, Richard E *Business Person*
Host Marriott Corp, 10400 Fernwood Road, Bethesda, MD 20817 USA

Marro, Anthony J *Editor*
Newsday, Editorial Dept, 235 Pinelawn Road, Melville, NY 11747 USA

Marron, Donald B *Financier*
UBS PaineWebber, 1285 6th Ave, New York, NY 10019 USA

Marrow, Tracy (Ice T) *Musician*
United Talent Agency (UTA), 9560 Wilshire Blvd, Beverly Hills, CA 90212 USA

Mars, Kenneth *Actor*
International Creative Mgmt, 8942 Wilshire Blvd, #219, Beverly Hills, CA 90211 USA

Marsalis, Branford *Musician, Composer*
Wilkins Mgmt, 323 Broadway, Cambridge, MA 02139 USA

Marsalis, Ellis *Musician*
Management Ark, 116 Village Blvd, #200, Princeton, NJ 08540 USA

Marsalis, Wynton *Musician, Composer*
Management Ark, 116 Village Blvd, #200, Princeton, NJ 08540 USA

Marschall, Marita *Actor*
Agentur Alexander, Lamontstr 9, Munich, 81679, GERMANY

Marsden, Bernie *Musician*
Int'l Talent Booking, 27A Floral St, #300, London, WC2E 9DQ, UNITED KINGDOM (UK)

Marsden, Freddie *Musician*
Barry Collins, 21A Cliftown Road, Southend-on-Sea, Essex, SS1 1AB, UNITED KINGDOM (UK)

Marsden, Gerald (Gerry) *Musician*
Barry Collins, 21A Cliftown Rd, Southend-on-Sea, Essex, SS1 1AB, UNITED KINGDOM (UK)

Marsden, Gerard (Gerry) *Musician*
Barry Collins, 21A Cliftown Road, Southend-on-Sea, Essex, SS1 1AB, UNITED KINGDOM (UK)

Marsden, James *Actor*
Brillstein-Grey Entertainment, 9150 Wilshire Blvd #350, Beverly Hills, CA 90212 USA

Marsden, Jason *Actor*
Cunningham-Escott-Dipene & Associates Inc (CED-LA), 10635 Santa Monica Blvd #130, Los Angeles, CA 90025 USA

Marsden, Matthew *Actor*
Creative Artists Agency LCC (CAA-LA), 9830 Wilshire Blvd, Beverly Hills, CA 90212 USA

Marsden, Roy *Actor*
London Mgmt, 2-4 Noel St, London, W1V 3RB, UNITED KINGDOM (UK)

Marsh, Brad *Hockey Player*
Ottawa Senators, 1000 Palladium Dr, Kanata, ON K2V 1A4, CANADA

Marsh, Carol
7 Leicester Pl. #100, London, ENGLAND, WC2H 7B1

Marsh, Graham *Golfer*
PGA Tour, 112 PGA Tour Blvd, Ponte Vedra Beach, FL 32082 USA

Marsh, Henry *Track Athlete*
General Delivery, Bountiful, UT 84010 USA

Marsh, Jean *Actor*
London Management, 2-4 Noel St, London, W1V 3RB, UNITED KINGDOM (UK)

Marsh, Kym *Musician*
Safe Management, 111 Guildford Rd, Lightwater, Surrey, GU18 5RA, UNITED KINGDOM (UK)

Marsh, Linda *Actor*
170 W End Ave, 22P, New York, NY 10023 USA

Marsh, Little Peggy
8236 NW 9th St., Plantation, FL 33324

Marsh, Marian *Actor*
PO Box 1, Palm Desert, CA 92261 USA

Marsh, Michael (Mike) *Track Athlete*
2425 Holly Hall St, #152, Houston, TX 77054 USA

Marsh, Mike
2847 Indian Trail Dr., Missouri City, TX 77489

Marsh, Miles L *Business Person*
Fort James Corp, 1919 S Broadway, Green Bay, WI 54304 USA

Marsh, Robert T *General, Business Person*
6659 Avignon Blvd, Falls Church, VA 22043 USA

Marsh of Mannington, Richard W *Government Official*
House of Lords, Westminster, London, SW1A 0PW, UNITED KINGDOM (UK)

Marshall, Albert L (Ben) *Hockey Player*
9603 166th Street Court E, Puyullup, WA 98375 USA

Marshall, Amanda *Reality TV Star*
Bachelor, The, 15301 Ventura Blvd, Bldg E, Sherman Oaks, CA 91403 USA

Marshall, Amanda *Actor*
Macklam Feldman Mgmt, 1505 W 2nd Ave, #200, Vancouver, BC V6H 3Y4, CANADA

Marshall, Amanda *Musician*
Creative Artists Agency LCC (CAA-LA), 9830 Wilshire Blvd, Beverly Hills, CA 90212 USA

Marshall, Arthur *Athlete*
2918 Crosscreek Rd, Hephzibah, GA 30815-6547

Marshall, Barry J *Scientist*
Queen Elizabeth II Med Center, Nedlands, WA 6009, AUSTRALIA

Marshall, Brian *Musician*
Agency Group, 1776 Broadway, #430, New York, NY 10010 USA

Marshall, Carolyn M *Religious Leader*
United Methodist Church, 204 N Newlin St, Veedersburg, IN 47987 USA

Marshall, Dale Rogers *Educator*
Whealon COllege, President's Office, Norton, MA 02766 USA

Marshall, Donyell *Basketball Player*
12440 SE 27th St, Kent, WA 98030 USA

Marshall, F Ray *Secretary*
PO Box Y, Austin, TX 78713 USA

Marshall, Frank W *Producer, Filmmaker*
Kennedy/Marshall Co, 650 N Bronson Ave, #100, Los Angeles, CA 90004 USA

Marshall, Garry *Actor*
Creative Artists Agency LCC (CAA-LA), 9830 Wilshire Blvd, Beverly Hills, CA 90212 USA

Marshall, Garry K *Director, Actor*
22440 Pacific Coast Highway, Malibu, CA 90265 USA

Marshall, James *Actor*
1833 Rulgers Dr, Thousands Oaks, CA 91360 USA

Marshall, James L (Jim) *Football Player*
5608 Xerxes Ave S, Minneapolis, MN 55410 USA

Marshall, Ken *Actor*
Marshall Artists, 345 N Maple Dr, #302, Beverly Hills, CA 90210 USA

Marshall, Kris *Actor*
International Creative Management (ICM-UK), Oxford House, 76 Oxford St, London, W1N OAX, UNITED KINGDOM (UK)

Marshall, Margaret A *Opera Singer*
Woodside, Main St, Gargunnock, Stirling, FKS 3BP, SCOTLAND

Marshall, Michael A (Mike) *Baseball Player*
Albany-Colonie Diamond Dogs, Heritage Park, Albany, PA 12211 USA

Marshall, Michael G (Mike) *Baseball Player*
38313 Vinson Ave, Zephyhills, FL 33542 USA

Marshall, Mike
4436 Plum St., Zephyrhills, FL 33541

Marshall, Patricia
807 N. Alpine Dr., Beverly Hills, CA 90210

Marshall, Paula *Actor*
1505 10th St, Santa Monica, CA 90401 USA

Marshall, Penny *Actor, Director*
Parkway Productions, 100 Universal City Plaza, Bldg 1320, Suite 3B, Universal City, CA 91608 USA

Marshall, Peter *Television Host*
16714 Oak View Dr, Encino, CA 91436
USA

Marshall, Rob *Director*
PMK/HBH Public Relations (PMK-LA),
8500 Wilshire Blvd #700, Beverly Hills,
CA 90211 USA

Marshall, W W (Bones) *General, War Hero*
1517 Ehupua Place, Honolulu, HI 96821
USA

Marshall, Wilber B *Football Player*
PO Box 1072, Titusville, FL 32781 USA

Marshall, Willard
204 Main St., Forrt Lee, NJ 07024

Marshall of Knightsbridge, Colin M
Business Person
British Airways, Heathrow Airport,
Hounslow, Middx, TW6 2JA, UNITED
KINGDOM (UK)

Marshall Tucker Band
100 W. Putnam, Greenwich, CT 06830

Marsters, James *Actor*
Himber Entertainment Inc, 211 S Beverly
Dr #208, Beverly Hills, CA 90212 USA

Marston, Joshua *Director, Writer*
William Morris Agency (WMA-LA), 1
William Morris Pl, Beverly Hills, CA
90212 USA

Marston, Natalie Elizabeth *Actor*
Marshak/Zachary Company, The, 8840
Wilshire Blvd Fl 1, Beverly Hills, CA
90211 USA

Marston, Nathanial *Actor*
Donegan Entertainment, 129 W 27th St,
New York, NY 10001 USA

Marston, Nathaniel *Actor*
One Life to Live, 56 W 66th St, New
York, NY 10023 USA

Marta, Lynn
4342 Lankershim Blvd., Universal City,
CA 91608

Marte, Judy *Actor*
William Morris Agency (WMA-LA), 1
William Morris Pl, Beverly Hills, CA
90212 USA

Martel, Arlene *Actor*
2109 S Wilbur Ave, Walla Walla, WA
99362 USA

Martel, Yann *Writer*
Harcourt Brace, 525 B St, San Diego, CA
92101 USA

Martell, Donna
PO Box 3335, Granada Hills, CA 91394

Martens, Wilfried *Prime Minister*
Europese Volkspartij, 16 Rue de la
Victoire, Brussels, 1060, BELGIUM

Marti, Benita *Actor*
Select Artists Ltd (CA-Valley Office), PO
Box 4359, Burbank, CA 91503 USA

Martika *Musician*
Entertainment Artists, 2409 21st Ave S,
#100, Nashville, TN 37212 USA

Martin, Agnes B *Artist*
414 Placilas Road, Taos, NM 87571 USA

Martin, Alastair B *Misc*
Bessemer Trust Co, 630 5th Ave, New
York, NY 10111 USA

Martin, Albert C *Architect*
Albert C Martin Assoc, 811 W 7th St,
#800, Los Angeles, CA 90017 USA

Martin, Andrea *Actor*
Gilla Roos, 9744 Wilshire Blvd, #203,
Beverly Hills, CA 90212 USA

Martin, Ann *Commentator*
KCBS-TV, News Dept, 6121 Sunset Blvd,
Los Angeles, CA 90028 USA

Martin, Barney *Actor*
12838 Milbank St, Studio City, CA 91604
USA

Martin, Billy *Musician*
Creative Artists Agency LCC (CAA-LA),
9830 Wilshire Blvd, Beverly Hills, CA
90212 USA

Martin, Boyce F Jr *Judge*
US Court of Appeals, US Courthouse, 601
W Broadway, Louisville, KY 40202 USA

Martin, Brian *Athlete*
777 San Antonio, #132, Palo Alto, CA
94303 USA

Martin, Casey
PO Box 109601, Palm Beach Gardens, FL
33410

Martin, Chris *Musician*
Network Mgmt, 1650 W 2nd Ave,
Vancouver, BC V6J 4R3, CANADA

Martin, Christy *Boxer*
1203 Foxtree Trail, Apopka, FL 32712
USA

Martin, Curtis *Football Player*
New York Jets, 1000 Fullon Ave,
Hempstead, NY 11550 USA

Martin, David *Commentator*
CBS-TV, News Dept, 2020 M St NW,
Washington, DC 20036 USA

Martin, Demetri *Comedian*
International Creative Management
(ICM-LA), 8942 Wilshire Blvd, Beverly
Hills, CA 90211 USA

Martin, Denise B *Editor*
MOney Magazine, Editorial Dept, Time-
Life Building, New York, NY 10020 USA

Martin, Dewey
1371 E. Ave. De Los Arboles, Thousand
Oaks, CA 91360

Martin, Dick *Actor, Comedian*
30765 Pacific Coast Highway, #103,
Malibu, CA 90265 USA

Martin, Duane *Actor*
Paul Konner, 9300 Wilshire Blvd, #555,
Beverly Hills, CA 90212 USA

Martin, Ed F *Actor*
Talent Syndicate, LLC, The (LA), 1680
North Vine Street, Suite 614, Los Angeles,
CA 90028

Martin, Edward H *Admiral*
729 Guadalupe Ave, Coronado, CA
92118 USA

Martin, Eric *Football Player*
18 Carlsbad Dr, Kenner, LA 70065 USA

Martin, Eric Band
PO Box 5952, San Francisco, CA 94101

Martin, George C *Engineer*
900 University St, #5P, Seattle, WA 98101
USA

Martin, Greg *Musician*
Mitchell Fox Mgmt, 212 3rd Ave N, #301,
Nashville, TN 37201 USA

Martin, Gregory S *General*
Commander, US Air Forces Europe,
Ramstein Air Base, APO, AE, 09094 USA

Martin, Helen
1440 N. Fairfax Ave. #109, Los Angeles,
CA 90046

Martin, Henry R *Cartoonist*
1382 Newtown Langhorne Road, #G206,
Newtown, PA 18940 USA

Martin, Jacques *Coach*
Florida Panthers, 1 Panthers Parkway,
Sunrise, FL 33323 USA

Martin, James G *Governor*
Carolina Medical Center, PO Box 32861,
Charlotte, NC 28232 USA

Martin, Jeanne
613 N. Linden Dr., Beverly Hills, CA
90210

Martin, Jesse L *Actor*
Endeavor Talent Agency, 9701 Wilshire
Blvd, #1000, Beverly Hills, CA 90212
USA

Martin, Joe *Cartoonist*
King Features Syndicate, 888 7th Ave,
New York, NY 10106 USA

Martin, John H *Educator*
JHM Corp, 3930 RCA Blvd, #3240, Palm
Beach Gardens, FL 33410 USA

Martin, Judith (Miss Manners) *Journalist*
1651 harvard St NW, Washington, DC
20009 USA

Martin, Kellie *Actor*
5918 Van Nuys Blvd, Van Nuys, CA
91401 USA

Martin, Kenyon *Basketball Player*
Denver Nuggets, Pepsi Center, 1000
Chopper Circle, Denver, CO 80204 USA

Martin, LeRoy *Lawyer, Government Official*
Chicago Police Dept, Superintendent's
Office, Chicago, IL 60602 USA

Martin, Lynn M *Secretary*
171 Willabay Dr, Williams Bay, WI
53191 USA

Martin, Maria *Actor*
Select Artists Ltd (CA-Valley Office), PO
Box 4359, Burbank, CA 91503 USA

Martin, Marilyn *Musician*
422 Mgmt, 1808 W End Ave, #1100,
Nashville, TN 37203 USA

Martin, Mark *Race Car Driver*
1648 Taylor Road, #606, Port Orange, FL
32128 USA

Martin, Marsha P *Financier*
Farm Credit Administration, 1501 Farm
Credit Dr, McLean, VA 22102 USA

Martin, Max
Innovative Artists (LA), 1505 Tenth St,
Santa Monica, CA 90401 USA

Martin, Millicent *Actor, Musician*
London Mgmt, 2-4 Noel St, London, W1V
3RB, UNITED KINGDOM (UK)

Martin, Nan *Actor*
33604 Pacific Coast Highway, Malibu, CA
90265 USA

Martin, Pamela Sue *Actor*
Shelly & Pierce, 13775A Mono Way, #220, Sonora, CA 95370 USA

Martin, Paul *Government Official*
Finance Department, 140 O'Connor St, Ottawa, ON K1A 0G5, CANADA

Martin, Preston *Government Official, Financier*
1130 N Lake Shore Dr, #4E, Chicago, IL 60611 USA

Martin, R Bruce *Misc*
University of Virginia, Chemistry Dept, Charlottesville, VA 22903 USA

Martin, Ray *Billiards Player*
11-05 Cadmus Place, Fair Lawn, NJ 07410 USA

Martin, Renie *Baseball Player*
509 Little Eagle Ct, Valrico, FL 33594 USA

Martin, Ricky *Musician, Actor*
Angelo Medino Entertainment, 1406 Georgetti St, Santurce, PR 00909 USA

Martin, Ronald D *Editor*
Atlanta Journal-Constitution, Editorial Dept, 72 Marietta, Atlanta, GA 30303 USA

Martin, Rudolf *Actor*
Kohner Agency, The, 9300 Wilshire Blvd #555, Beverly Hills, CA 90212 USA

Martin, Sandy *Actor*
CNA Assoc, 1875 Century Park East, #2250, Los Angeles, CA 90067 USA

Martin, Sir George
Lynhurst Road Hampstead, London, ENGLAND, NW3 5NG

Martin, Stater N *Basketball Player*
4119 Placid St, Houston, TX 77022 USA

Martin, Steve *Actor, Comedian*
PO Box 929, Beverly Hills, CA 90213 USA

Martin, Sylvia Wene *Bowler*
3875 Cambridge St, #1003, Las Vegas, NV 89119 USA

Martin, Todd *Tennis Player*
24586 Harbour View Dr, Ponte Vedra Beach, FL 32082 USA

Martin, Tony *Actor, Musician*
10724 Wilshire Blvd, #1406, Los Angeles, CA 90024 USA

Martin, Victor Hugo *Actor*
TV Azteca, Periferico Sur 4121, Colonia Fuentes del Pedregal, DF, CP 14141, Mexico

Martin Chase, Deborah (Debra) *Producer*
William Morris Agency (WMA-LA), 1 William Morris Pl, Beverly Hills, CA 90212 USA

Martindale, Wink *Entertainer, Musician*
5744 Newcastle Lane, Calabasas, CA 91302 USA

Martineau, Ande

Martinez, A *Actor*
PO Box 6387, Malibu, CA 90264 USA

Martinez, Ana Maria *Opera Singer*
JF Mastroianni, 151 W 51st St, #17E, New York, NY 10023 USA

Martinez, Angela *Television Host*
Abrams Artists Agency (LA), 9200 Sunset Blvd Fl 11, Los Angeles, CA 90069 USA

Martinez, Angie *Musician*
WMA, 151 S El Camino Dr, Beverly Hills, CA 90212

Martinez, Conchita *Tennis Player*
511 Westminster Dr, Cardiff-by-the-Sea, CA 92007 USA

Martinez, Constantino (Tino) *Baseball Player*
324 Blanca Ave, Tampa, FL 33606 USA

Martinez, Daniel J *Artist*
University of California, Studio Art Dept, Irvine, CA 92717 USA

Martinez, Edgar *Baseball Player*
Bo Maguayo Buzon, 1295RR, Dorado, PR 00646 USA

Martinez, J Dennis *Baseball Player*
9400 SW 63rd Court, Miami, FL 33156 USA

Martinez, Jorge *Actor*
Telefe - Argentina, Pavon 2444 (C1248AAT), Buenos Aires, ARGENTINA

Martinez, Olivier *Actor*
Artmedia, 20 Ave Rapp, Paris, 75007, FRANCE

Martinez, Patrice *Actor*
Select Artists Ltd (CA-Valley Office), PO Box 4359, Burbank, CA 91503 USA

Martinez, Pedro A *Baseball Player*
186 Fairmont Ave, Hyde Park, MA 02136 USA

Martinez, Ramon J *Baseball Player*
3029 Birkdale Dr, Weston, FL 33332 USA

Martinez, Robert (Bob) *Government Official, Governor*
4647 W San Jose St, Tampa, FL 33629 USA

Martinez Somalo, Eduardo Cardinal *Religious Leader*
Palazzo delle Congregazioni, Piazza Pio XII 3, Rome, 00193, ITALY

Martini, Carlo Maria Cardinal *Religious Leader*
Palazzo Arcivescovile, Piazza Fontana 2, Milan, 20122, ITALY

Martini, Steven *Writer*
G P Putnam's Sons, 375 Hudson St, New York, NY 10014 USA

Martino, Al *Actor, Musician*
927 N Rexford Dr, Beverly Hills, CA 90210 USA

Martino, Donald J *Composer*
Harvard University, Music Dept, Cambridge, MA 02138 USA

Martino, Frank D *Misc*
Chemical Workers Union, 1655 W Market St, Akron, OH 44313 USA

Martino, Pat *Musician, Composer*
2318 S 16th St, Philadelphia, PA 19145 USA

Martino, Renato R Cardinal *Religious Leader*
Justice & Peace Curia, Piazzo S Calisto 16, Vatican City, 00120, VATICAN CITY

Martins, Joao Carlos *Musician*
Musicians Corporate Mgmt, PO Box 589, Millbrook, NY 12545 USA

Martins, Peter *Dancer, Ballerina, Director*
New York City Ballet, Lincoln Center Plaza, New York, NY 10023 USA

Martinson, Leslie
2288 Coldwater Canyon, Beverly Hills, CA 90210

Martinson, Lestie H *Director*
2288 Coldwater Canyon Dr, Beverly Hills, CA 90210 USA

Martlin, Marlee *Actor*
10340 Santa Monica Blvd, Los Angeles, CA 90025 USA

Marton, Eva *Opera Singer*
Opera et Concert, Maximilianstr 22, Munich, 80539, GERMANY

Martone, Lino *Musician*
Gabriel Blanco Iglesias (Mexico), Rio Balsas 35-32, Colonia Cuauhtemoc, DF, 06500, Mexico

Marty, Martin E *Misc*
239 Scottswood Road, Riverside, IL 60546 USA

Marty, Mike *Football Coach*
Saint Louis Rams, 901 N Broadway, Saint Louis, MO 63101 USA

Martzke, Rudy *Writer*
USA Today, Editorial Dept, 1000 Wilson Blvd, Arlington, VA 22209 USA

Marusha
Kaiser-Friedrich-Str. 41, Berlin, GERMANY, D-10627

Marusin, Yury M *Opera Singer*
Mariinsky Theater, Teatralnaya Pl 1, Saint Petersburg, RUSSIA

Maruyama, Karen *Actor*
Halpern & Associates, 12304 Santa Monica Blvd #104, Los Angeles, CA 90025 USA

Marvelettes, The *Music Group*
9936 Majorca Pl, Boca Raton, FL 33434 USA

Marx, Gilda *Fashion Designer*
Gilda Marx Industries, 11755 Exposition Blvd, Los Angeles, CA 90064 USA

Marx, Gyorgy *Physicist*
Fehervari Utca 119, Budapest, 1119, HUNGARY

Marx, Jeffrey A *Journalist*
Lexington Herald-Leader, Editorial Dept, Main & Midland, Lexington, KY 40507 USA

Marx, Richard *Musician, Songwriter*
Principal Artists, 9777 Wilshire Blvd, #1018, Beverly Hills, CA 90212 USA

Marx, Timothy *Producer*
International Creative Management (ICM-LA), 8942 Wilshire Blvd, Beverly Hills, CA 90211 USA

Mary Mary *Music Group*
Creative Artists Agency (CAA-Nashville), 3310 West End Ave Fl 5, Nashville, TN 37203 USA

Maryland, Russell *Football Player*
1330 Eagle Bend, Southlake, TX 76092 USA

Marzich, Andy Bowler
1421 Cravens Ave, #318, Torrance, CA 90501 USA

Marzio, Peter C Director
Houston Museum of Fine Arts, 1001 Bissonnet, PO Box 6826, Houston, TX 77265 USA

Marzoli, Andrea Misc
Berkeley Geochronolgoy Center, 2455 Ridge Road, Berkeley, CA 94709 USA

Mas, Adrian Actor
Gabriel Blanco Iglesias (Mexico), Rio Balsas 35-32, Colonia Cuauhtemoc, DF, 06500, Mexico

Masak, Ron Actor
5440 Shirley Ave, Tarzana, CA 91356 USA

Masakayan, Liz Volleyball Player
2864 Palomino Circle, La Jolla, CA 92037 USA

Masako, Princess Royalty
Imperial Palace, 1-1 Chiyoda-ku, Tokyo, JAPAN

Masaoka, Onan Baseball Player
Los Angeles Dodgers, 1323 Auwae Rd, Hilo, HI 96720-6906 USA

Mascaras, Mil
200 W. 16th St. #10, New York, NY 10011-6150

Masco, Judit
Paseo De Gracia 67 Pral. lA, Barcelona, SPAIN, 08008

Mascolo, Joseph
5460 White Oak Ave. #A-208, Encino, CA 91316

Mase Musician
International Creative Mgmt, 8942 Wilshire Blvd, #219, Beverly Hills, CA 90211 USA

Masefield, J Thorold Governor
Government House, 11 Langton Hill, Pembroke, HM13, BERMUDA

Masekela, Hugh Musician
Peformers of the World, 8901 Melrose Ave, #200, West Hollywood, CA 90069 USA

Mashburn, Jamal Basketball Player
5529 Saint Andrews Court, Plano, TX 75093 USA

Mashburn, Jesse Track Athlete
8520 S Pennsylvania Ave, Oklahoma City, OK 73159 USA

Mashkov, Vladimir L Actor
Oleg Tabakov Theater, Chaokygina Str 12A, Moscow, RUSSIA

Mashore, Clyde Baseball Player
Cincinnati Reds, PO Box 1023, Livingston, TX 77351-0018 USA

Mashore, Damon Baseball Player
Oakland A's, 1519 Heather Dr, Concord, CA 94521-3039 USA

Masiello, Tony Politician
Mayor's Office, City Hall, 65 Niagara Square, Buffalo, NY 14202 USA

Masire, Q Ketumile J President
PO Box 70, Gaborone, BOTSWANA

Maske, Henry Boxer
Sauerland Promotion, Hochstadenstr 1-3, Cologne, 50674, GERMANY

Maslansky, Paul Producer, Filmmaker, Director
Henry Barnberger, 10866 Wilshire Blvd, #1000, Los Angeles, CA 90024 USA

Masloff, Sophie Politician
Mayor's Office, City-County Building, 414 Grant St, Pittsburgh, PA 15219 USA

Mason, Anthony Basketball Player
7818 Sawyer Brown Road, Nashville, TN 37221 USA

Mason, B John Misc
64 Christchurch Road, East Sheen, London, SW14, UNITED KINGDOM (UK)

Mason, Birny Jr Engineer
6 Island Dr, Rye, NY 10580 USA

Mason, Bobbie Ann Writer
PO Box 518, Lawrenceburg, KY 40342 USA

Mason, Brent Musician
Mercury Records, 54 Music Square E, #300, Nashville, TN 37203 USA

Mason, Dave Musician, Songwriter
11205 McPherson Way, Ventura, CA 93001 USA

Mason, Desmond Basketball Player
Milwaukee Bucks, Bradley Center, 1001 N 4th St, Milwaukee, WI 53203 USA

Mason, Don Baseball Player
San Francisco Giants, 8 Fawn Rd, South Yarmouth, MA 02664-1808 USA

Mason, Glen Football Coach
University of Minnesota, Athletic Dept, Minneapolis, MN 55455 USA

Mason, Hank Baseball Player
Philadelphia Phillies, 3801 Brook Rd, Richmond, VA 23227-4101 USA

Mason, Jackie Comedian, Actor
World According to Me, 146 W 57th St, #68D, New York, NY 10019 USA

Mason, James Appreciation Society
PO Box 3552, London, ENGLAND, SWl9 3QH

Mason, Jim Baseball Player
Washington Senators, 11410 Queens Way, Theodore, AL 36582-8312 USA

Mason, Larry B War Hero
826 Cinebar Road, Cinebar, WA 98533 USA

Mason, Marilyn
27 Glen Oak, Medford, OR 97504

Mason, Marlyn Actor, Musician
27 Glen Oak Court, Medford, OR 97504 USA

Mason, Marsha Actor
528 Don Gaspar Ave, Santa Fe, NM 87505 USA

Mason, Mike Baseball Player
Texas Rangers, 2711 Piper Ridge Ln, Excelslor, MN 55331-7803 USA

Mason, Mila Musician
PO Box 24392, Louisville, KY 40224 USA

Mason, Monica Ballerina
Royal Opera House, Convent Garden, Bow St, London, WC2, UNITED KINGDOM (UK)

Mason, Nick Musician
Agency Group, 370 City Road, London, EC1V 2QA, UNITED KINGDOM (UK)

Mason, Roger Baseball Player
Detroit Tigers, 4467 Ritt Rd, Bellaire, MI 49615-9697 USA

Mason, Ron Coach
Michigan State University, Athletic Dept, East Lansing, MI 48224 USA

Mason, Stephen Musician, Songwriter
Evolution Talent, 1776 Broadway, #1500, New York, NY 10019 USA

Mason, Stephen Musician
Flood Bumstead McCready McCarthy, 1700 Hayes St, #304, Nashville, TN 37203 USA

Mason, Steve Musician
Agency Group Ltd, 370 City Road, London, EC1V 2QA, UNITED KINGDOM (UK)

Mason, Sully
4043 Irving Pl., Culver City, CA 90230

Mason, Thomas C (Tommy) Football Player
920 Heather Ave, La Habra, CA 90631 USA

Mason, Tom Actor
870 Heights Place, Oyster Bay, NY 11771 USA

Mason, Vince Musician
Famous Artists Agency, 250 W 57th St, New York, NY 10107 USA

Mason Dixon
PO Box 214 Flint, TX CA 75762

Mason of Barnsley, Roy Government Official
12 Victoria Ave, Barnsley, South Yorks, S7O 2BH, UNITED KINGDOM (UK)

Masri, Tahir Nashat Prime Minister
PO Box 5550, Amman, JORDAN

Mass, Jochen Race Car Driver
RTL-Sportredaktion, Cologne, 50570, GERMANY

Massa, Felipe Race Car Driver
Jaguar Racing Ltd, Bradbourne Drive, Tilbrook, Milton Keynes, MK7 8BJ, United Kingdom

Massa, Gordon Baseball Player
Chicago Cubs, 8255 Bonanza Ln, Cincinnati, OH 45255-2504 USA

Massari, Lea
Viale Parioli 59, Rome, ITALY, I-00197

Massen, Osa
10501 Wilshire Blvd. #704, Los Angeles, CA 90024

Massengale, Don Golfer
715 W Davis St, Conroe, TX 77301 USA

Masset, Andrew
11635 Huston, No. Hollywood, CA 91607

Massevitch, Alla G Astronomer
6 Pushkurev Per, #4, Moscow, 103045, RUSSIA

Massey, Anna Actor
Markham and Froggatt, Julian House, 4 Windmill St, London, W1P 1HF, UNITED KINGDOM (UK)

Massey, Athena
PO Box 6180, Beverly Hills, CA 90212

Massey, Debbie *Golfer*
PO Box 110, Cheboygan, MI 49721 USA

Massey, Vincent *Misc*
University of Michigan, Biochemistry
Dept, Ann Arbor, MI 48109 USA

Massey, Waiter E *Educator, Physicist*
Morehouse College, President's Office,
830 Westview Dr SW, Atlanta, GA 30314
USA

Massie, Robert K *Writer*
52 W Clinton Ave, Irvington, NY 10533
USA

Massimino, Michael J *Astronaut*
15814 Elk Park Lane, Houston, TX 77062
USA

Massimino, Rollie *Coach*
18578 ES Ferland Court, Jupiter, FL 33469
USA

Mast, Rick *Race Car Driver*
390 E Midland Trail, Lexington, VA 24450
USA

Masta, Killa *Musician*
Famous Artists Agency, 250 W 57th St,
New York, NY 10107 USA

Masteller, Dan *Baseball Player*
Minnesota Twins, 159111 Aldersyde Dr,
Shaker Heights, OH 44120 USA

Master, P *Music Group, Actor*
New No Limit Records, 1755 Broadway,
#700, New York, NY 10019 USA

Masterhoff, Joe *Writer*
2 Horalio St, New York, NY 10014 USA

Masters, Alfreda
1045 A. Cloverdale #2, Los Angeles, CA
90019

Masters, Ben
8730 Sunset Blvd. #480, Los Angeles, CA
90069

Masters, Geoff *Tennis Player*
De Lorain St, Wavell Heights, QLD, 4012,
AUSTRALIA

Masters, John *Writer*
McGraw-Hill, 1221 Ave of Americas,
New York, NY 10020 USA

Masters, Roy
8780 Venice Blvd.Box 34036, Los
Angeles, CA 90034

Masterson, Christopher (Chris) Kennedy
Actor
United Talent Agency (UTA), 9560
Wilshire Blvd, Beverly Hills, CA 90212
USA

Masterson, Danny *Actor*
6277 Holly Dr, Los Angeles, CA 90068
USA

Masterson, Fay
PO Box 5617, Beverly Hills, CA 90210

Masterson, Mary Stuart *Actor*
Constellation, PO Box 1249, White River
Junction, VT 05001 USA

Masterson, Peter *Writer, Director,*
Producer
1165 5th Ave, #15A, New York, NY
10029 USA

Masterson, Valerie *Opera Singer*
Music International, 13 Ardilaun Road,
London, N5 2QR, UNITED KINGDOM
(UK)

Masterson, Walt *Baseball Player*
Washington Senators, 4515 Carteret Dr,
Trent Woods, NC 28562-7209 USA

Mastracchio, Richard A
1910 Hillside Oak Ln, Houston, TX 77062
USA

Mastracchio, Richard A (Rick) *Astronaut*
4410 Pine Blossom Trail, Houston, TX
77059 USA

Mastrangelo, Carlo *Musician*
Paramount Entertainment, PO Box 12, Far
Hills, NJ 07931 USA

Mastrantonio, Mary Elizabeth *Actor,*
Musician
International Creative Mgmt, 8942
Wilshire Blvd, #219, Beverly Hills, CA
90211 USA

Mastrogiacomo, Gina *Actor*
Pakula/King, 9229 Sunset Blvd, #315, Los
Angeles, CA 90069 USA

Mastroianni, Chiara *Actor*
P F D Drury House, 34-43 Russell St,
London, WC2B 5HA, UNITED KINGDOM
(UK)

Masui, Yoshio *Biologist*
32 Iverton Crescent, North York, ON M3B
2V2, CANADA

Masur, Kurt
Leipzing Gweandhausorchester,
Augustusplatz 8, Leipzig, 04109,
GERMANY

Masur, Richard *Actor*
10340 Santa Monica Blvd, Los Angeles,
CA 90025 USA

Masurok, Yuri *Opera Singer*
Bolshoi Theater, Teatralnaya Pl 1,
Moscow, 103009, RUSSIA

Mata'aho *Royalty*
Royal Palace, PO Box 6, Nuku'alofa,
TONGA

Matarazza, Heather *Actor*
Agency for Performing Arts, 9200 Sunset
Blvd, #900, Los Angeles, CA 90069 USA

Matarazzo, Heather *Actor*
Gersh Agency, The (LA), 232 N Canon Dr,
Beverly Hills, CA 90210 USA

Matarazzo, Len *Baseball Player*
Philadelphia Athletics, 2715 Carlisle St,
New Castle, PA 16105-1714 USA

Matchbox 20 *Music Group*
Creative Artists Agency LCC (CAA-LA),
9830 Wilshire Blvd, Beverly Hills, CA
90212 USA

Matchetts, John *Hockey Player*
2415 Chelton Road, Colorado Springs,
CO 80909 USA

Matchick, Tom *Baseball Player*
Detroit Tigers, 7700 Pilliod Rd, Holland,
OH 43528-8077 USA

Mateo, Guillermo *Baseball Player, Athlete*
Montreal Expos, PO Box 500, Station M,
Montreal, H1V 3P, Canada

Matesa, Zlatko *Prime Minister*
Prime Minister's Office, Jordanovac 71,
Zagreb, 41000, CROATIA

Matheny, Mike *Baseball Player*
Milwaukee Brewers, 2034 Joes Way,
Chesterfield, MO 63005-6545 USA

Mather, John C *Misc*
Goddard Space Flight, G85 Code,
Greenbelt, MD 20771 USA

Mathers, Frank *Hockey Player*
32 Oakglade Dr, Hummelstown, PA
17036 USA

Mathers, Jerry *Actor*
30290 Rancho Viejo Rd, #122, San Juan
Capistrano, CA 92675 USA

Matherson, Tim *Actor, Director*
246 Miramar Ave, Montecito, CA 93108
USA

Matheson, Don
10275 1/2 Missouri Ave., Los Angeles, CA
90025

Matheson, Richard
PO Box 81, Woodland Hills, CA 91364

Matheson, Tim *Actor, Director*
246 Miramar Ave, Montecito, CA 93108
USA

Mathews, Eddie
13744 Recuerdo Dr., Del Mar, CA 92014

Mathews, F David *Secretary*
6050 Mad River Road, Dayton, OH
45459 USA

Mathews, Francine *Writer*
Doubleday Press, 1540 Broadway, New
York, NY 10036 USA

Mathews, Greg *Baseball Player*
St Louis Cardinals, 1752 Craig Rd, Saint
Louis, MO 63146-4710 USA

Mathews, Harlan *Senator*
420 Hunt Club Road, Nashville, TN
37221 USA

Mathews, Kerwin *Actor*
67A Buena Vista Terrace, #A, San
Francisco, CA 94117 USA

Mathews, Nelson *Baseball Player*
Chicago Cubs, 211 E Crestview Dr,
Columbia, IL 62236-1203 USA

Mathews, Sheila
21554 Pacific Coast Hwy, Malibu, CA
90265

Mathews, T J *Baseball Player*
St Louis Cardinals, 10802 Vemoa Dr, Las
Vegas, NV 89141-3836 USA

Mathews, Terry *Baseball Player*
Texas Rangers, 1132 Belgard Bnd, Boyce,
LA 71409-9216 USA

Mathias, Bob
7469 E. Pine Ave., Fresno, CA 93727

Mathias, Buster Jr *Boxer*
4409 Carol Ave SW, Wyoming, MI 49509
USA

Mathias, Carl *Baseball Player*
Cleveland Indians, 567 Long Ln, Oley, PA
19547-9009 USA

Mathias, Charles McC Jr *Senator,*
Financier
3808 Leland St, Chevy Chase, MD 20815
USA

Mathias, Robert B (Bob) *Track Athlete*
7469 E Pine Ave, Fresno, CA 93727 USA

Mathias, William *Composer*
Y Graigwen Cadnant Road, Menai Bridge, Anglesey, Gwynedd, LL59, WALES

Mathieu, Georges V A *Artist*
125 Ava de Makakoff, Paris, 75116, FRANCE

Mathieu, Mireille
12 rue du Bois de Boulogne, Neuilly, FRANCE, F-92200

Mathieu, Philip *Musician*
Lindy S MArtin Mgmt, 5 Lob Lolly Court, Executive Suite, Pinehurst, NC 28374 USA

Mathilde, Princess *Royalty*
Koninklijk Palace, Rue de Brederode, Brussels, 1000, BELGIUM

Mathis, Clint *Soccer Player*
New York/New Jersey MetroStars, 1 Harmon Plaza, #300, Secaucus, NJ 07094 USA

Mathis, Edith *Opera Singer*
Ingpen & Williams, 14 Kensington Court, London, W8 5DN, UNITED KINGDOM (UK)

Mathis, Johnny *Musician*
Rojon Productions, 1612 W Olive Ave #305, Burbank, CA 91506 USA

Mathis, Ron *Baseball Player*
Houston Astros, 2922 Kismet Ln, Houston, TX 77043-1322 USA

Mathis, Samantha *Actor*
7536 Sunnywood Lane, Los Angeles, CA 90046 USA

Mathis, Terance *Football Player*
Pittsburgh Steelers, 3400 S Water St, Pittsburgh, PA 15203 USA

Mathis Jr, Buster
4409 Carol SW, Wyoming, MI 49509 USA

Mathis-Eddy, Dariene *Writer*
1409 W Cardinal St, Muncie, IN 47303 USA

Mathison, Cameron *Actor*
Innovative Artists (LA), 1505 Tenth St, Santa Monica, CA 90401 USA

Mathison, Melissa *Writer*
655 MacCulloch Dr, Los Angeles, CA 90049 USA

Matias, John *Baseball Player*
Chicago White Sox, 98-1616 Hoolauae St, Alea, HI 96701-1801 USA

Matkevich, Mark *Actor*
Glasser/Black Management, 283 Cedarhurst Ave, Cedarhurst, NY 11516 USA

Matlack, Jon *Baseball Player*
New York Mets, 35 Yorkshire Dr, Queensbury, NY 12804-8620 USA

Matlin, Marlee *Actor, Producer*
Solo One Productions, 8205 Santa Monica Blvd #1279, Los Angeles, CA 90046-5912

Matlock, Glen *Musician*
Solo Agency, 55 Fulham High St, London, SW6 3JJ, UNITED KINGDOM (UK)

Matlock, Jack F Jr *Diplomat*
940 Princeton Kingston Road, Princeton, NJ 08540 USA

Matola, Sharon *Misc*
Belize Zoo & Tropical Education Center, PO Box 1787, Belize City, BELIZE

Matondkar, Urmila *Actor, Bollywood*
93/14 Sangam Lokhandwala Road, Andheri (W), Mumbai, MS 400058, INDIA

Matorin, Vladimir A *Opera Singer*
Ulansky Per 21 Korp 1, #53, Moscow, 103045, RUSSIA

Matranga, Dave *Baseball Player*
Houston Astros, 303 N Park Ln, Orange, CA 92867-7642 USA

Matricaria, Ronald *Business Person*
Saint Jude Medical Inc, 1 Lillehei Plaza, Saint Paul, MN 55117 USA

Matsch, Richard P *Judge*
US District Court, 1929 Stout St, Denver, CO 80294 USA

Matsik, George A *Business Person*
Ball Corp, 10 Longs Peak Dr, Broomfield, CO 80021 USA

Matson, J Randel (Randy) *Track Athlete*
1002 Park Place, College Station, TX 77840 USA

Matson, Oliver G (Ollie) *Football Player, Track Athlete*
1319 S Hudson Ave, Los Angeles, CA 90019 USA

Matson, Ollie
1319 S. Hudson, Los Angeles, CA 90019

Matson, Randy
1002 Park Pl., College Station, TX 77840

Matsuda, Seiko *Musician, Actor*
Propaganda Films Mgmt, 1741 Ivar Ave, Los Angeles, CA 90028 USA

Matsui, Keiko *Musician*
Ted Kurland, 173 Brighton Ave, Boston, MA 02134 USA

Matsui, Kosei *Artist*
Ibaraki-ken, Kasama-shi, Kasama, 350, JAPAN

Matsumoto, Shigeharu *Writer*
International House of Japan, 11-16 Roppongi, Minatuku, Tokyo, JAPAN

Matsushita, Hiro *Race Car Driver*
14772 Ridgeboro Place, Tustin, CA 92780 USA

Matt, Mike *Rodeo Rider*
111 S 24th St W, #9125, Billings, MT 59102 USA

Matta, del Meskin *Religious Leader*
Deir el Makarios Monastery, Cairo, EGYPT

Matte, Thomas R (Tom) *Football Player*
11309 Old Carriage Road, Glen Arm, MD 21057 USA

Mattea, Kathy *Musician*
TBA Artists Mgmt, 300 10th Ave S, Nashville, TN 37203 USA

Mattei, Frank *Musician*
Joe Taylor Mgmt, PO Box 1017, Turnersville, NJ 08012 USA

Mattes, Eva *Actor*
Agentur Carola Studlar, Neurieder Str, #1C, Planegg, 92152, GERMANY

Mattes, Troy *Baseball Player*
Montreal Expos, 2932 Lexington St, Sarasota, FL 34231-6118 USA

Mattesich, Rudi *Skier*
General Delivery, Troy, VT 05868 USA

Matthes, Roland *Swimmer*
Luitpoldstr 35A, Marktheidenfeld, 97828, GERMANY

Matthes, Ulrich *Actor*
Kuno-Fischer-Str 14, Berlin, 14057, GERMANY

Matthews, Bruce R *Football Player*
0423 Oilfield Road, Sugar Land, TX 77479 USA

Matthews, Carys *Musician*
MRM Productions, 5 Kirby St, London, EC1N 8TS, UNITED KINGDOM (UK)

Matthews, Cerys *Musician*
MRM Productions, 5 Kirby St, London, EC1N 8TS, UNITED KINGDOM (UK)

Matthews, Chris *Television Host*
Hardball with Chris Matthews, 400 N Capitol St NW #850, Washington, DC 20001-1555 USA

Matthews, Dakin *Actor*
McCabe/Justice, 247 S Beverly Dr #102, Beverly Hills, CA 90212 USA

Matthews, Dave *Music Group, Musician*
Red Light Mgmt, 3302 Lobban Place, Charlottesville, VA 22903 USA

Matthews, DeLane *Actor*
Don Buchwald, 5500 Wilshire Blvd, #2200, Los Angeles, CA 90048 USA

Matthews, Gary *Baseball Player*
San Diego Padres, 4653 Willens Ave, Woodland Hills, CA 91364-3812 USA

Matthews, Gary *Baseball Player*
San Francisco Giants, 1542 W Jackson Blvd, Chicago, IL 60607-5304 USA

Matthews, Gary N *Baseball Player*
1542 W Jackson Blvd, Chicago, IL 60607 USA

Matthews, Ian *Musician*
Geoffrey Blumenauer, 11846 Balboa Blvd, #204, Granada Hills, CA 91344 USA

Matthews, Keith *Astronomer*
California Institute of Technology, Astronomy Dept, Pasadena, CA 91125 USA

Matthews, Liesel *Actor*
Creative Artists Agency LCC (CAA-LA), 9830 Wilshire Blvd, Beverly Hills, CA 90212 USA

Matthews, Mike *Baseball Player*
St Louis Cardinals, 735 Pleasant Valley, Milford, MI 48430 USA

Matthews, Pat Stanley *Actor*
210 Stanton, Walla Walla, WA 99362 USA

Matthews, Robert C O *Economist*
Clare College, Cambridge, CB2 1TL, UNITED KINGDOM (UK)

Matthews, Vincent (Vince) *Track Athlete*
6755 193rd Lane, Fresh Meadows, NY 11365 USA

Matthews, W Clay Jr *Football Player*
6068 Canterbury Dr, Agoura Hills, CA 91301 USA

Matthies, Nina *Volleyball Player, Coach*
Pepperdine University, Athletic Dept, Malibu, CA 90265 USA

Matthiessen, Peter *Writer*
Bridge Lane, Sagaponack, NY 11962 USA

Mattick, Bobby *Baseball Player*
Chicago Cubs, 14500 N Frank Lloyd Wright Blvd, Scottsdale, AZ 85260-8822 USA

Mattila, Karita M *Opera Singer*
45B Croxley Road, London, W9 3HJ, UNITED KINGDOM (UK)

Mattingly, Donald A (Don) *Baseball Player*
New York Yankees, 11825 Darmstadt Rd, Evansville, IN 47725-9542 USA

Mattingly, Mack F *Senator*
4315 10th St, East Beach, Saint Simons Island, GA 31522 USA

Mattingly, Thomas K II *Astronaut, Admiral*
Rocket Development Co, 1501 Quail St, #102, Newport Beach, CA 92660 USA

Mattson, Robin *Actor*
Stan Kamens Mgmt, 7772 Torreyson Dr, Los Angeles, CA 90046 USA

Mattson, Walter E *Publisher*
New York Times Co, 229 W 43rd St, New York, NY 10036 USA

Matula, Rick *Baseball Player*
Atlanta Braves, 1817 Chapel Hts, Wharton, TX 77488-4459 USA

Matuszek, Len *Baseball Player*
Philadelphia Phillies, 10326 Deerfield Rd, Cincinnati, OH 45242-5105 USA

Matz, Johanna
Opernring 4, Vienna, AUSTRIA, 1010

Matzdorf, Pat *Track Athlete*
1252 Bainbridge Dr, Naperville, IL 60563 USA

Mauban, Maria
4 sq. Vitruve, Paris, FRANCE, 75020

Mauch, Billy & Bobby
538-C W. Northwest Hwy, Palatine, IL 60067

Mauch, Billy (Bill) *Actor*
538 W Northwest Highway, #C, Palatine, IL 60067 USA

Mauch, Gene *Baseball Player*
Brooklyn Dodgers, 71 Princeton Dr, Rancho Mirage, CA 92270-3651 USA

Mauer, Joe *Baseball Player*
Minnesota Twins, 10508 Washingtonia Palm Way Apt 4525, Fort Myers, FL 33912-6958 USA

Maugham, R H *Religious Leader*
Christian & Missionary Alliance, PO Box 35000, Colorado Springs, CO 80935 USA

Maughan, Deryck *Financier*
Citigroup Inc, 399 Park Ave, New York, NY 10022 USA

Mauinier, Thierry
3 rue Yves-Carriou, Marnes-la-Coquette, FRANCE, 92430

Maulden, Jerry L *Business Person*
Entergy Corp, 10055 Grogans Mill Road, #5A, The Woodlands, TX 77380 USA

Mauldin, William H *Cartoonist*
Loomis-Watkins Agency, 150 E 35th St, New York, NY 10016

Maule, Brad *Actor*
Jerry Shandrew PR, 1050 South Stanley Avenue, Los Angeles, CA 90019-6634 USA

Maulnier, Thierry *Writer*
3 Rue Yves-Carriou, Marnes-la-Coquette, 92430, FRANCE

Maumenee, Alfred E *Misc*
1700 Hillside Road, Stevenson, MD 21153 USA

Maupin, Armistead
8942 Wilshire Blvd., Beverly Hills, CAC, 90211

Maupin, Armistead J Jr *Writer*
584 Castro St, #528, San Francisco, CA 94114 USA

Maura, Carmen *Actor*
GRPC SL, Calle Fuencarral 17, Madrid, 28004, SPAIN

Maurer, Dave *Baseball Player*
San Diego Padres, 884 Saint Moritz, Victoria, MN 55386-3700 USA

Maurer, Gilbert C *Publisher*
Hearst Corp, 250 W 55th St, New York, NY 10019 USA

Maurer, Rob *Baseball Player*
Texas Rangers, 2332 E Powell Ave, Evansville, IN 47714-2328 USA

Maurer, Robert D *Inventor*
2572 W 28th Ave, Eugene, OR 97405 USA

Maurey, Nicole
21 chemin Vauillons, Marly-le-Roi, FRANCE, 78160

Mauriac, Claude *Writer*
24 Quai de Bethune, Paris, 75004, FRANCE

Maurice, Paul *Hockey Player*
205 Calm Winds Court, Cary, NC 27513 USA

Mauriello, Ralph *Baseball Player*
Los Angeles Dodgers, 4241 Persimmon St, Moorpark, CA 93021-3515 USA

Mauriello, Tammy *Boxer*
1148 E 81st St, Brooklyn, NY 11236 USA

Maurier, Claire
ll rue de la Montague-le-Breuil, Epinay Orge, FRANCE, 91360

Maurin, Laurence *Skier*
PO Box 1980, West Bend, WI 53095 USA

Mauro, Carmen *Baseball Player*
Chicago Cubs, 5545 Marconl Ave Apt 118, Carmichael, CA 95608-4436 USA

Mauroy, Pierre *Prime Minister*
17-19 Rue Voltaire, Lille, 59800, FRANCE

Maurstad, Toralv *Director, Actor*
National Theatre, Storlingsgt 15, Osto, 1, NORWAY

Mauser, Tim *Baseball Player*
Philadelphia Phillies, 1321 Saxony Rd, Fort Worth, TX 76116-1658 USA

Mauz, Henry H (Hank) Jr *Admiral*
1608 Viscaine Road, Pebble Beach, CA 93953 USA

Maven, Max
PO Box 3819, La Mesa, CA 91944-3819

Mavericks, The *Music Group*
Asgard Promotions, 125 Pkwy, Regents Park, London, NW1 7PS, United Kingdom

Mavis, Bob *Baseball Player*
Detroit Tigers, 300 Markwood Dr, Little Rock, AR 72205-2412 USA

Mawae, Kevin J *Football Player*
11220 NE 53rd St, Kirkland, WA 98033 USA

Mawby, Russell G *Misc*
WK Kellogg FOundation, 1 Michigan Ave E, Battle Creak, MI 49017 USA

Max, Peter *Artist*
118 Riverside Dr, New York, NY 10024 USA

Maxa, Rudy *Television Host*
Public Broadcasting Service (PBS), 1320 Braddock Pl, Alexandria, VA 22314 USA

Maxcy, Brian *Baseball Player*
Detroit Tigers, 8 Azalea Ln, Amory, MS 38821-8700 USA

Maxey, Virginia
16414 Pick Pl., Riverside, CA 92504

Maxi, Fumihiko *Architect*
5-16-22 Higashi Gotanda, Shinagawaku, Tokyo, JAPAN

Maxie, Larry *Baseball Player*
Atlanta Braves, 296 Verdugo Way, Upland, CA 91786-7138 USA

Maximova, Ekaterina *Ballerina*
Bolshoi Theater, Teatralnaya Pi 1, Moscow, 103009, RUSSIA

Maxson, Robert *Educator*
California State University, President's Office, Long Beach, CA 90840 USA

Maxvill, Dal *Baseball Player*
St Louis Cardinals, 1115 Eagle Creek Rd, Chesterfield, MO 63005-6606 USA

Maxwell *Musician*
Violator Mgmt, 205 Lexington Ave, #400, New York, NY 10016 USA

Maxwell, Arthur E *Oceanographer*
8115 Two Coves Dr, Austin, TX 78730 USA

Maxwell, Cedric (Cornbread) *Basketball Player*
WEEI Sports Radio, 116 Huntington Ave, Boston, MA 02116 USA

Maxwell, Charlie *Baseball Player*
Boston Red Sox, 730 Mapleview Dr, Paw Paw, MI 49079-1185 USA

Maxwell, Dobie *Comedian*
333 W North Ave #343, Chicago, IL 60610 USA

Maxwell, Frank *Politician*
Federation of TV-Radio Artists, 260 Madison Ave, New York, NY 10016 USA

Maxwell, Ian *Publisher*
Eaton Terrace, London, SW1, UNITED KINGDOM (UK)

Maxwell, Jacqui *Actor*
Untitled Entertainment (LA), 8436 W 3rd St #650, Los Angeles, CA 90048 USA

Maxwell, Jason *Baseball Player*
Chicago Cubs, 1821 Brockton Pi, Franklin, TN 37064-8918 USA

Maxwell, Kevin F H *Publisher*
Hill Burn, Hailey near Wallingford,
Oxford, OX10 6AD, UNITED KINGDOM
(UK)

Maxwell, Lois *Actor*
Artists Independent Network, 32 Tavistock
St, London, WC2E 7PB, UNITED
KINGDOM (UK)

Maxwell, Robert D *War Hero*
1001 SE 15th St, #44, Bend, OR 97702
USA

Maxwell, Ron *Director*
Firm, The, 9465 Wilshire Blvd, Beverly
Hills, CA 90212 USA

Maxwell, Ronald F (Ron) *Director, Writer*
5531 Bonneville Road, Hidden Hills, CA
91302 USA

May, Arthur *Architect*
Kohn Pedersen Fox Assoc, 111 W 57th St,
New York, NY 10019 USA

May, Briane *Musician, Songwriter*
Old Bakehouse, 16A High St Barnes,
London, SW13, UNITED KINGDOM (UK)

May, Carlos *Baseball Player*
Chicago White Sox, 22 S Arbor Trl, Park
Forest, IL 60466-2606 USA

May, Darrell *Baseball Player*
Atlanta Braves, 747 Minthome Rd, Rogue
River, OR 97537-9692 USA

May, Dave *Baseball Player*
Baltimore Orioles, 124 Madison Dr,
Newark, DE 19711-4406 USA

May, Deborah *Actor*
Artists Agency, 1180 S Beverly Dr, #301,
Los Angeles, CA 90035 USA

May, Derrick *Baseball Player*
Chicago Cubs, 2 Jaymar Blvd, Newark, DE
19702-2877 USA

May, Don *Basketball Player*
1128 Colwick Dr, Dayton, OH 45420
USA

May, Donald
733 N. Seward St, PH, LA 90038

May, Elaine *Actor, Director*
William Morris Agency, 151 El Camino
Dr, Beverly Hills, CA 90212 USA

May, Joe *Misc*
General Delivery, Thome Bay, AK 99919
USA

May, Lee *Baseball Player*
Cincinnati Reds, 2272 4th Place Cir NE #
NE, Birmingham, AL 35215-3808 USA

May, Lee A *Baseball Player*
5593 Hill Dale Dr, Cincinnati, OH 45213
USA

May, Mark E *Football Player, Sportscaster*
Mark May Salisbury Ford, 1902 N
Salisbury Blvd, Salisbury, MD 21801 USA

May, Mathilda *Actor*
Artmedia, 20 Ave Rapp, Paris, 75007,
FRANCE

May, Milt *Baseball Player*
Pittsburgh Pirates, 410 22nd St W,
Bradenton, FL 34205-5424 USA

May, Misty *Volleyball Player*
Assn of Volleyball Pros, 330 Washington
Blvd #400, Marina del Rey, CA 90292
USA

May, Scott G *Basketball Player*
2001 E Hillside Dr, Bloomington, IN
47401 USA

May, Torsten *Boxer*
Sauerland Promotion, Hans-Bockler-Str
163, Hurth, 50354, GERMANY

Mayaki, Ibrahim Hassane *Prime Minister*
Prime Minister's Office, State House,
Niamey, NIGER

Mayall, John *Musician, Composer*
Monterey International, 200 W Superior,
#202, Chicago, IL 60610 USA

Mayall, Rik *Actor, Comedian*
Brunskill Mgmt, 169 Queen's Gale,
London, SW7 5HE, UNITED KINGDOM
(UK)

Mayasich, John E *Hockey Player*
2250 Riverwood Place, Saint Paul, MN
55104 USA

Mayberry, John C *Baseball Player*
11115 W 121st Terrace, Overland Park,
KS 66213 USA

Maybury, John *Director*

Maydan, Dan *Business Person*
Applied Materials, 3050 Bowers Ave,
Santa Clara, CA 95054 USA

Mayer, Chip
15136 La Maida St., Sherman Oaks, CA
91403

Mayer, Christian *Skier*
Siedlerweg 18, Finkelstein, 9884,
AUSTRIA

Mayer, Gene *Tennis Player*
115 South St, Glen Dale, MD 20769 USA

Mayer, H Robert *Judge*
US Court of Appeals, 717 Madison Place
NW, Washington, DC 20439 USA

Mayer, John *Musician, Songwriter*
Columbia Records, 2100 Colorado Ave,
Santa Monica, CA 90404 USA

Mayer, Joseph E *Physicist*
2345 Via Siena, La Jolla, CA 92037 USA

Mayer, Martin J *Admiral*
Deputy CinC, Joint Forces Command, 116
Lake View Parkway, Suffolk, VA 23435
USA

Mayer, P Augustin Cardinal *Religious Leader*
Ecclesia Dei, Vatican City, 00120,
VATICAN CITY

Mayer, Phil
Rt. 9 Box 715-M, Yakima, WA 98901

Mayer, Travis *Skier*
37050 Williams St, Steamboat Springs,
CO 80487 USA

Mayes, Rueben *Football Player*
610 SE Edge Knoll Dr, Puliman, WA
99163 USA

Mayes, Wendell
1504 Bel Air Rd., Los Angeles, CA 90077

Mayfair, Billy *Golfer*
7666 E Camo Belio Dr, Scottsdale, AZ
85255 USA

Mayfield, Jeremy *Race Car Driver*
Everham Motorsports, 320 Aviation Dr,
Statesville, NC 28577 USA

Mayhew, Patrick B B *Government Official*
House of Lords, Westminster, London,
SW1A 0PW, UNITED KINGDOM (UK)

Mayle, Peter *Writer*
Knopf Publishers, 201 E 50th St, New
York, NY 10022 USA

Maynard, Andrew *Boxer*
Mike Trainer, 3922 Fairmont Ave,
Bethesda, MD 20814 USA

Maynard, Don
6545 Butterfield Dr, El Paso, TX 79932

Maynard, Donald R (Don) *Football Player*
6545 Butterfield Dr, El Paso, TX 79932
USA

Maynard, Mimi *Actor*
Badgley Connor Talent, 9229 Sunset Blvd,
#311, Los Angeles, CA 90069 USA

Mayne, D Roger *Photographer*
Colway Manor, Colway Lane, Lyme Regis,
Dorset, DT7 3HD, UNITED KINGDOM
(UK)

Mayne, Kenny *Sportscaster*
ESPN-TV, Sports Dept ESPN Plaza, 935
Middle St, Bristol, CT 06010 USA

Mayne, Thomas *Architect*
Morphosis Architects, 2041 Colorado Ave,
Santa Monica, CA 90404 USA

Mayne, William *Writer*
Harold Ober Assoc, 425 Madison Ave,
New York, NY 10017 USA

Maynor, Asa
PO Box 1641, Beverly Hills, CA 90213

Mayo, Virginia *Actor*
109 E Avenida de Los Aboles, Thousand
Oaks, CA 91360 USA

Mayor, Michel *Astronomer*
Univeristy of Geneva, Geneva
Observatory, Geneva, SWITZERLAND

Mayor, Zaragoza Federico *Government Official*
UNESCO, 7 Place de Fonteroy, Paris,
75352, FRANCE

Mayotte, Timothy S (Tim) *Tennis Player*
SFX Sports Group, 2665 S Bayshore Dr,
#602, Miami, FL 33133 USA

Mayr, Ernst *Biologist*
207 Badger Terrace, Bedford, MA 01730
USA

Mayron, Melanie *Actor, Director*
1435 N Ogden Dr, Los Angeles, CA
90046 USA

Mays, Lowry *Business Person*
Clear Channel Communications, 200
Concord Plaza, San Antonio, TX 78216
USA

Mays, Lyle *Musician*
Ted Kurland, 173 Brighton Ave, Boston,
MA 02134 USA

Mays, Mark P *Business Person*
Clear Channel Communications, 200
Concord Plaza, San Antonio, TX 78216
USA

Mays, Rueben
7306 172nd St. SW, Edmonds, WA
98026-5121

Mays, Willie
PO Box 2410, Menlo Park, CA 94026-
2410

Mays, Willie H *Baseball Player*
51 Mount Vernon Lane, Atherton, CA
94027 USA

Mayweather, Floyd Jr *Boxer*
4720 Laguna Vista St, Las Vegas, NV
89147 USA

Mazach, John J *Admiral*
5423 Grist Mills Woods Road, Alexandria,
VA 22309 USA

Mazar, Debi *Actor*
United Talent Agency, 9560 Wilshire
Blvd, #500, Beverly Hills, CA 90212 USA

Mazaroski, William S (Bill) *Baseball
Player*
RR 6 Box 130, Greensburg, PA 15601
USA

Mazeroski, Bill
RR #6 Box 130, Greensburg, PA 15601

Mazor, Stanley (Stan) *Inventor*
FTI/Teklicon, 3031 Tisch Way, San Jose,
CA 95128 USA

Mazowiecki, Tadeusz *Prime Minister*
Sejm RP Ul Qiekska 4/6/8, Warsaw, 00-
902, POLAND

Mazur, Jay J *Misc*
Industrial Textile Employees Needletrades,
1710 Broadway, New York, NY 10019
USA

Mazur, Monet *Actor*
Principal Entertainment (LA), 1964
Westwood Blvd #400, Los Angeles, CA
90025 USA

Mazurok, Yuri A *Opera Singer*
Boshoi State Theater, Teatralnaya Pl 1,
Moscow, 103009, RUSSIA

Mazursky, Paul *Director*
614 26th St, Santa Monica, CA 90402
USA

Mazza, Valeria *Model*
Riccardo Ga, 8/10 Via Revere, Milan,
20123, ITALY

Mazzara, Glen *Producer*
Creative Artists Agency LCC (CAA-LA),
9830 Wilshire Blvd, Beverly Hills, CA
90212 USA

Mazzarello, Marcelo *Actor*
Telefe - Argentina, Pavon 2444
(C1248AAT), Buenos Aires, ARGENTINA

Mazzello, Joseph *Actor*
46691 Mission Blvd #536, Fremont, CA
94539

Mazzie, Marin *Actor, Musician*
J Michael Bloom, 233 Park Ave S, #1000,
New York, NY 10003 USA

Mazzilli, Lee L *Baseball Player*
67 Stonehedhe Dr S, Greenwich, CT
06831 USA

Mazzo, Kay *Ballerina*
American Ballet School, 144 W 66th St,
New York, NY 10023 USA

Mazzola, Anthony T *Editor*
Town & Country Magazine, Editorial
Dept, 1790 Broadway, New York, NY
10019 USA

Mba, Casimir Oye *Prime Minister*
Prime Minister's Office, Boile Postale 546,
Libreville, GABON

Mbasogo, Teodoro Obiang Nguema
President
President's Office, Malabo, EQUATORIAL
GUINEA

Mbeki, Thabo *President*
President's Office, Union Buildings,
Pretoria, 0001, SOUTH AFRICA

McAdams, Rachel *Actor*
Magnolia Entertainment, 1620 26th St
#480, Santa Monica, CA 90404 USA

McAdoo, Robert A (Bob) *Basketball
Player, Coach*
16710 SW 82nd Ave, Village of Palmetto
Bay, FL 33157 USA

McAfee, George *Football Player*
2600 Croasdaile Farm Parkway, #D105,
Durham, NC 27705 USA

McAfee, Ken
8 Deerfield Rd., Medfield, MA 02052-
1318

McAleese, Mary P *President*
President's Office, Baile Athe Cliath 8,
Dublin, IRELAND

McAlister, James E *Football Player, Track
Athlete*
155 Glorietta St, Pasadena, CA 91103
USA

McAlpine, Donald M *Cinematographer*
377 Placer Creek Lane, Henderson, NV
89014 USA

McAnally, Mac *Songwriter, Musician*
TKO Artist Mgmt, 1107 17th Ave S,
Nashville, TN 37212 USA

McArdle, Andrea *Musician, Actor*
Edd Kalehoff, 14 Shady Glen Court, New
Rochelle, NY 10805 USA

McArthur, Alex *Actor*
10435 Wheatland Ave, Sunland, CA
91040 USA

McArthur, William S (Bill) Jr *Astronaut*
14503 Sycamore Lake Road, Houston, TX
77062 USA

McAuliffe, Dennis P *General*
9076 Belvoir Woods Parkway, Fort
Belvoir, VA 22060 USA

McAuliffe, Dick
2010 Prince Dr., Naples, FL 33942-1033

McAvoy, James *Actor*
Peters Fraser & Dunlop (PFD - UK), Drury
House, 34-43 Russell St, London, WC2
B5, UNITED KINGDOM (UK)

McBain, Diane *Actor*
20185 Canyon View Dr, #1, Canyon
Country, CA 91351 USA

McBain, Ed *Writer*
324 Main Ave, PO Box 339, Norwalk, CT
0686 USA

McBride, Chi *Actor*
United Talent Agency, 9560 Wilshire
Blvd, #500, Beverly Hills, CA 90212 USA

McBride, Jeff
4185 Paradise Rd. #2081, Las Vegas, NV
89109-6508

McBride, Jon A *Astronaut*
Image Development Group, 1018
Kanawha Blvd, #901, Charleston, WV
25301 USA

McBride, Martina *Musician*
Bruce Allen Talent, 406-68 Water St,
Vancouver, BC V6B 1A4, CANADA

McBride, Patricia *Ballerina*
Sharon Wagner Artists, 150 W End Ave,
New York, NY 10023 USA

McBride, William J *Misc*
Gorse Lodge, Ballyclare, County Antrim,
BT39 9DE, NORTHERN IRELAND

McBroom, Amanda *Musician, Songwriter*
167 Fairview Road, Ojai, CA 93023 USA

McCabe, Frank *Basketball Player*
6202 N Fairlane Dr, Peoria, IL 61614 USA

McCabe, John *Musician*
Novello Co, 8/9 Firth St, London, W1V
5TZ, UNITED KINGDOM (UK)

McCabe, Marcia
1990 Broadway Box 417 Ansonia Sta, .
New York, NY 10023

McCabe, Patrick *Writer*
Picador, Macmillan Books, 25 Ecckeston
Place, London, SW1W 9NF, UNITED
KINGDOM (UK)

McCabe, Zia *Musician*
Mongui Mgmt, PO Box 5908, Portland,
OR 97228 USA

McCafferty, Donald F (Don) Jr *Football
Coach*
167 E Shore Road, Halesite, NY 11743
USA

McCaffrey, Barry R *General*
506 Crown View Dr, Alexandria, VA
22314 USA

McCaig, Donald *Writer*
WW Norton, 500 5th Ave, New York, NY
10110 USA

McCain, Edwin *Songwriter*
Westwood Entertainment Group, 1031
Amboy Ave, #202, Edison, NJ 08837 USA

McCain, John *Politician*
U.S. Senate, 241 Russell, Senate Office
Bldg, Washington, DC 20510 USA

McCall, Mitzi *Actor*
Epstein-Wyckoff, 280 S Beverly Dr, #400,
Beverly Hills, CA 90212 USA

McCall, Robert T *Artist*
4816 E Moonlight Way, Paradise Valley,
AZ 85253 USA

McCallany, Holt *Actor*
Agency for Performing Arts, 9220 Sunset
Blvd, #900, Los Angeles, CA 90069 USA

McCallister, Lon *Actor*
PO Box 6030, Stateline, NV 89449 USA

McCallum, David *Actor*
Hilary Gagan, Caprice House, 3 New
Burlington St, London, W1X 1FE, UNITED
KINGDOM (UK)

McCallum, John
1740 Pittwater Rd., Bayview, AUSTRALIA,
NSW 2104

McCallum, Napoleon *Football Player*
314 Doe Run Circle, Henderson, NV
89012 USA

McCambridge, Mercedes *Astronaut*
210932 Pleasant Park Dr, Conifer, CO
80433 USA

McCandless, Bruce *Doctor*
21852 Pleasant Park Dr, Conifer, CO
80433 USA

McCann, Chuck *Actor, Comedian*
2941 Briar Knoll Dr, Los Angeles, CA
90046 USA

McCann, David A *Publisher*
Town & Country Magazine, 1700
Broadway, New York, NY 10019 USA

McCann, Les *Musician, Composer*
DeLeon Artists, 4031 Panama Court,
Piedmont, CA 94611 USA

McCann, Lila *Musician*
William Morris Agency, 2100 W End Ave,
#1000, Nashville, TN 37203 USA

McCann, Michelle
1200 Singer Dr., West Palm Beach, FL
33404

McCann, Terrence (Terry) *Wrestler*
PO Box 9052, Mission Viejo, CA 92690
USA

McCarrick, Theodore E Cardinal *Religious Leader*
Archdiocesan Pastoral Center, 5001
Eastern Ave, Washington, DC 20017 USA

McCarron, Chris
PO Box 861, Sierra Madre, CA 91025

McCarron, Christopher (Chris) *Jockey*
Dun Roamin, 318 N Terrace View Dr,
Monrovia, CA 91016 USA

McCarron, Douglas J *Misc*
Carpenters/Joiners Brotherhood, 101
Connecticut Ave NW, Washington, DC
20001 USA

McCarron, Scott *Golfer*
Cross Consulting, 4 Cathy Place, Menlo
Park, CA 94025 USA

McCarry, Charles *Writer*
Random House, 1745 Broadway, #B1,
New York, NY 10019 USA

McCartan, Jack *Hockey Player*
8818 Logan Ave S, Bloomington, MN
55431 USA

McCarter Sisters
PO Box 121551, Nashville, TN 37212

McCarthy, Andrew *Actor*
4708 Vesper Ave, Sherman Oaks, CA
91403 USA

McCarthy, Cormac *Writer*
1101 N Mesa, El Paso, TX 79002 USA

McCarthy, Dennis *Composer*
Vangelos Mgmt, 15233 Ventura Blvd,
#200, Sherman Oaks, CA 91403 USA

McCarthy, Dennis M *General*
Commander Forces Reserve, HqUSMC, 2
Navy St, Washington, DC 20380 USA

McCarthy, Donald W *Astronomer*
Stewart Observatory, University of
Arizona, Tucson, AZ 85721 USA

McCarthy, Eugene *Ex-Senator*
271 Hawlin Rd, Woodville, VA 22749
USA

McCarthy, Eugene J *Senator*
Harcoul Brace Jovanovich, 1666
Connecticut Ave NW, #300, Washington,
DC 20009 USA

McCarthy, Jenny *Actor*
International Creative Management
(ICM-LA), 8942 Wilshire Blvd, Beverly
Hills, CA 90211 USA

McCarthy, Jenny *Model, Actor*
8424A Santa Monica Blvd, #504, Los
Angeles, CA 90069 USA

McCarthy, John *Scientist*
Stanford University, Computer Science
Dept, Stanford, CA 94305 USA

McCarthy, Julianna *Actor*
Stone Manners, 6500 Wilshire Blvd, #550,
Los Angeles, CA 90048 USA

McCarthy, Kevin *Actor*
14854 Sutton St, Sherman Oaks, CA
91403 USA

McCarthy, Lin
233 N. Swall Dr., Beverly Hills, CA 90210

McCarthy, Mary Frances *Writer, Educator*
Trinity College, English Dept, Washington,
DC 20017 USA

McCarthy, Melissa *Actor*
Gilmore Girls, 4000 Warner Blvd,
Building 2222, Burbank, CA 91522

McCarthy, Nobu
9229 Sunset Blvd. #311, Los Angeles, CA
90069

McCarthy, Norma
818385 Mead Lane SLU Box 9063,
Victorville, CA 92392

McCarthy, Timothy
8686 Butterfield Lane, Orland Park, IL
60462

McCarthy, tom *Director*
Gersh Agency, The (LA), 232 N Canon Dr,
Beverly Hills, CA 90210 USA

McCarthy, Tony *Songwriter*
29/33 Berners Road, London, W1P 4AA,
UNITED KINGDOM (UK)

McCartney, Heather Mills *Social Activist*
MPL Communications Ltd, 1 Soho Square,
London, W1V 6BQ, ENGLAND

McCartney, Jesse *Actor*
Noble Media Group Inc, 53 Sunrise Creek
Rd, Superior, MT 59872 USA

McCartney, Paul *Musician, Songwriter*
MPL Communications Ltd, 1 Soho Square,
London, W1V 6BO, UNITED KINGDOM
(UK)

McCartney, Stella *Fashion Designer*
13 Rue Turbigo, Paris, 75002, FRANCE

McCarty, Chris
9105 Carmelita Ave. #101, Beverly Hills,
CA 90210-3543

McCarty, Darren *Athlete*
Detroit Red Wings, Joe Luis Arena, 600
Civic Center Drive, Detroit, MI 48226

McCarty, Maclyn *Biologist, Scientist*
Rockefeller University, 66th St & York
Ave, New York, NY 10021 USA

McCarver, J Timothy (Tim) *Baseball Player, Sportscaster*
118 County Line Road, Bryn Mawr, PA
19010 USA

McCarver, Shonna
13280 NW Fwy. F-252, Houston, TX
77040

McCarver, Tim *Athlete*
118 County Line Rd, Bryn Mawr, PA
19010

McCary, Michael *Musician*
Southpaw Entertainment, 10675 Santa
Monica, Los Angeles, CA 90025 USA

McCashin, Constance *Actor*
Po Box 452, Chatham, MA 02633 USA

McCaskill, Kirk E *Baseball Player*
PO Box 451, Rancho Santa Fe, CA 92067
USA

McCaughey Septuplets, The
615 N. First, Carlisle, IA 50047

McCauley, Barry *Opera Singer*
598 Ridgewood Road, Oradell, NJ 07649
USA

McCauley, Donald F (Don) Jr *Football Player*
36 Taylor Road, Halesite, NY 11743 USA

McCauley, William F *Admiral*
570 Margarita Ave, Coronado, CA 92118
USA

McCay, Peggy *Actor*
2714 Carmar Dr, Los Angeles, CA 90046
USA

McClain, Cady *Actor*
All My Children, 320 W 66th St, New
York, NY 10023

McClain, Charly *Musician*
John Lentz, PO Box 198888, Nashville,
TN 37219 USA

McClain, Katrina *Basketball Player*
155 Standing Oak Place, Fairburn, GA
30213 USA

McClairen, Jack (Cy) *Football Coach*
1337 Idlewild Dr, Daytona Beach, FL
32114 USA

McClanahan, Robert (Rob) *Hockey Player*
1462 Hunter Dr, Wayzala, MN 55391
USA

McClanahan, Rue *Actor*
Don Buchwald, 6500 Wilshire Blvd,
#2200, Los Angeles, CA 90048 USA

McClary, Thomas (Tom) *Musician*
Management Assoc, 1920 Benson Ave,
Saint Paul, MN 55116 USA

McCleery, Finnis D *War Hero*
828 Cactus Lane, #7, San Angelo, TX
76903 USA

McClellan, Scott *Government Official*
White House, 1600 Pennsylvania Ave
NW, Washington, DC 20500 USA

McClelland, David C *Psychic*
81 Washington Ave, Cambridge, MA
02140 USA

McClenathan, Cory *Race Car Driver*
MBNA Motorsports, 1198 Knollwood
Circle, Anaheim, CA 92801 USA

McClendon, Sarah
3133 Connecticut Ave. NW #215,
Washington, DC 20008

McClintock, Eddie *Actor*
Beddingfield Company, The, 9255 Sunset
Blvd #920, Los Angeles, CA 90069 USA

McClintock, Jessica *Fashion Designer*
Jessica McClintock Co, 1400 16th St, San
Francisco, CA 94103 USA

McCloskey, J Michael *Misc*
Sierra Club, 85 2ns St, #200, San Francisco, CA 94105 USA

McCloskey, Jack *Basketball Player*
Minnesota Timberwolves, Target Center, 600 1st Ave N, Minneapolis, MN 55403 USA

McCloskey, Jim *Social Activist*
221 Witherspoon St, Princeton, NJ 08542 USA

McCloskey, Leigh
6032 Philip Ave., Malibu, CA 90265

McCloskey, Leigh J *Actor*
6032 Philip Ave, Malibu, CA 90265 USA

McCloskey, Rep *Politician*
580 Mountain Home Rd, Woodside, CA 94062

McCloskey, Robert J *Diplomat*
111 Hesketh St, Chevy Chase, MD 20815 USA

McClure, Donald S *Misc*
23 Hemlock Circle, Princeton, NJ 08540 USA

McClure, Marc
1420 Beaudry Blvd., Glendale, CA 91208

McClure, Molly
12456 Ventura Blvd. #1, Studio City, CA 91604

McClure, Tane *Actor*
Don Gerler, 3349 Cahuenga Blvd W, #1, Los Angeles, CA 90068 USA

McClurg, Edie
9229 Sunset Blvd. #315, Los Angeles, CA 90069

McClurkin, Donnie *Musician*
The Covenant Agency, 1011 4th Street, Suite 315, Santa Monica, CA 90403 USA

McColm, Matt *Actor*
ReBar Management, 729 N Seward St #101, Los Angeles, CA 90038

McColms, Matt *Actor*
Agency for the Performing Arts (APA-LA), 9200 Sunset Blvd #900, Los Angeles, CA 90069 USA

McConaughey, Matthew *Actor*
J.K. Livin', 238 South Lasky Drive, Beverly Hills, CA 90212 USA

McConkey, Jim C *Cinematographer*
505 W 54th St, #PH-12, New York, NY 10019 USA

McConnell, Harden M *Misc*
Stanford University, Chemistry Dept, Stanford, CA 94305 USA

McConnell, John P *Business Person*
Worthington Industries, 1205 Dearborn Dr, Columbus, OH 43085 USA

McConnell, Robert M G (Rob) *Musician*
Thomas Cassidy, 11761 E Speedway Blvd, Tucson, AZ 85748 USA

McConville, Frank *Misc*
Union of Plant Guard Workers of America, 25510 Kelly Road, Roseville, MI 48066 USA

McCoo, Marilyn
2639 Lavery Ct. #5, Newbury Park, CA 91320

McCook, John *Actor*
10245 Briarwood, Los Angeles, CA 90077 USA

McCord, Bob *Hockey Player*
11540 Donley Dr, Parker, CO 80138 USA

McCord, Kent
6767 Forest Lawn Dr. #115, Los Angeles, CA 90068

McCormack, Catherine *Actor*
United Talent Agency (UTA), 9560 Wilshire Blvd, Beverly Hills, CA 90212 USA

McCormack, Eric *Actor*
Will & Grace, 4024 Radford Ave, Bungalow 3, Studio City, CA 91604 USA

McCormack, Mary *Actor*
PO Box 67335, Los Angeles, CA 90067-0035 USA

McCormack, Patty
4360 Tujunga Ave., Studio City, CA 91604

McCormack, Will *Actor*
Mosaic Media Group, 9200 Sunset Blvd Fl 10, Los Angeles, CA 90069 USA

McCormick, Carolyn *Actor*
Bresler Kelly Assoc, 11500 W Olympic Blvd, #510, Los Angeles, CA 90064 USA

McCormick, Kelly
Box 250, Seal Beach, CA 90740

McCormick, Maureen *Actor, Musician*
32118 Beach Lake Ln, Westlake Village, CA 91361-3606 USA

McCormick, Mike
532 Crawford Dr., Sunnyvale, CA 94087

McCormick, Pat (comedian-writer)
23388 Mulholland Dr., Woodland Hills, CA 91364-2733

McCormick, Pat (swimmer)
Box 250, Seal Beach, CA 90740

McCormick, Richard *Educator*
Rutgers State University, President's Office, East Rutherford, NJ 08903 USA

McCormick, Tim *Basketball Player*
2500 Leroy Lane, West Bloomfield, MI 48324 USA

McCorvey, Norma
12730 Thomas Sumpter St., San Antonio, TX 78223

McCouch, Grayson
9255 Sunset Blvd. #1010, W. Hollywood, CA 90069

McCourt, Frank
Charles Scribner's Sons, 866 3rd Ave, New York, NY 10022

McCowen, Sir Alec
3 Goodwin's Ct. St. Martin's Lane, London, ENGLAND, WG2

McCoy, Charlie *Musician*
PO Box 50455, Nashville, TN 37205 USA

McCoy, Dave *Misc*
Mammoth Mountain Chairlifts, PO Box 24, Mammoth Lakes, CA 93546 USA

McCoy, John B *Financier*
Corillian, 3400 NW John Olsen Place, Hillsboro, OR 97124 USA

McCoy, Mark
7120 Hawthorne #18, Los Angeles, CA 90046

McCoy, Matt *Actor*
Artists Agency, 1180 S Beverly Dr, #301, Los Angeles, CA 90035 USA

McCoy, Neal *Musician*
Cherry Miller Kane Entertainment, 2021 21st Ave S, #320, Nashville, TN 37212 USA

McCracken, Jeff
15760 Ventura Blvd. #1730, Encino, 91436

McCracken, Paul W *Economist, Government Official*
2564 Hawthome Road, Ann Arbor, MI 48104 USA

McCrane, Paul *Actor*
VOX, 5670 Wilshire Blvd, #820, Los Angeles, CA 90036 USA

McCrary, Darius *Actor*
Diverse Talent Group, 1875 Century Park E #2250, Los Angeles, CA 90067 USA

McCrary, Joel *Actor*
Stone Manners Talent Agency, 6500 Wilshire Blvd, Ste 550, Los Angeles, CA 90048 USA

McCray, Nikki *Basketball Player*
288 S Center St, #6, Collierville, TN 38017 USA

McCrea, Jody
Country Rd. 395 Box 195, Hondo, NM 89336

McCrea, John *Musician, Songwriter*
Absolute Artists, 8490 W Sunset Blvd, #403, West Hollywood, CA 90069 USA

McCready, Mike *Musician*
Annie Ohayon Media Relations, 525 Broadway, #600, New York, NY 10012 USA

McCready, Mindy *Musician*
Creative Artists Agency, 3310 W End Ave, #500, Nashville, TN 37203 USA

McCreary, Tex
PO Box 405, Mill Neck, NY 11765-0405

McCrills, John W *Writer*
McCrillis & Eldredge Insurance, 17 Depot St, Newport, NH 03773 USA

McCrimmon, Brad *Hockey Player*
Atlanta Thrashers Philips Arena, 13 South Ave SE, Atlanta, GA 30315 USA

McCrory, Glenn *Boxer*
Holborn 35 Station Road, County Durham, UNITED KINGDOM (UK)

McCrory, Milton (Milt) *Boxer*
Escot Boxing Enterprises, 19244 Bretton Dr, Detroit, MI 48223 USA

McCrudden, Ian *Actor*
Margrit Polak Management, 1411 Carroll Ave, Los Angeles, CA 90026 USA

McCulley, Michael J *Astronaut*
1112 Tall Pines Dr, Friendswood, TX 77546 USA

McCullin, Donald (Don) *Photographer*
Holly Hill House, Batcombe Shepton Mallet, Somerset, BA4 6BL, UNITED KINGDOM (UK)

McCulloch, Ed *Race Car Driver*
1397 Cherry Tree Road, Avon, IN 46123 USA

McCulloch, Frank W *Educator, Lawyer*
5604 Kirkside Dr, Chevy Chase, MD 20815 USA

McCulloch (McCullough), Bruce *Actor*
United Talent Agency (UTA), 9560 Wilshire Blvd, Beverly Hills, CA 90212 USA

McCullough, Colleen *Writer*
PO Box 333, Norfolk Island, NSW, 2899, AUSTRALIA

McCullough, David *Actor*
Creative Artists Agency LCC (CAA-LA), 9830 Wilshire Blvd, Beverly Hills, CA 90212 USA

McCullough, David *Writer*
Janklow & Nesbit Assoc, 445 Park Ave, #1300, New York, NY 10022 USA

McCullough, Earl *Football Player, Track Athlete*
2108 Santa Fe Ave, Long Beach, CA 90810 USA

McCullough, Julie *Model, Actor*
8033 Sunset Blvd, #353, West Hollywood, CA 90046 USA

McCullough, Kimberly
9229 Sunset Blvd. #315, Los Angeles, CA 90069

McCullough, Shanna
7920 Alabama Ave., Canoga Park, CA 91304

McCullough, Wayne *Boxer*
601 Hermosa Canyon Dr, Las Vegas, NV 89145 USA

McCully, Kilmer *Doctor*
Veteran Affairs Med Center, Pathology Dept, Davis Park, Providence, RI 02908 USA

McCumber, Mark *Golfer, Sportscaster*
53 Ponte Vedra Blvd, Ponte Vedra Beach, FL 32082 USA

McCurry, Margaret *Architect*
Tigerman McCurry Architects, 444 N Wells St, Chicago, IL 60610 USA

McCurry, Mike *Politician, Journalist*
Cable News Network, News Dept, 1050 Techwood Dr NW, Atlanta, GA 30318 USA

McCutcheon, Lawrence *Football Player*
19981 Weems Lane, Huntington Beach, CA 92646 USA

McCutcheon, Linda *Publisher*
AARP Publications, Director's Office, 601 E St NW, Washington, DC 20049 USA

McCutcheon, Martine *Musician*
P F D Drury House, 34-43 Russell St, London, WC2B 5HA, UNITED KINGDOM (UK)

McDaniel, James *Actor*
Innovative Artists, 1505 10th St, Santa Monica, CA 90401 USA

McDaniel, Lindy
Rt. #2 Box 353A, Hollis, OK 73550

McDaniel, Lyndail D (Lindy) *Baseball Player*
RR 2 Box 355, Hollis, OK 73550 USA

McDaniel, Mel *Musician, Songwriter*
106 Cranwell Dr, Hendersonville, TN 37075 USA

McDaniel, Randall C *Football Player*
2818 Safe Harbor Drive, Tampa, FL 33618 USA

McDaniel, Singleton Mildred *Track Athlete*
211 W Poppy Field Dr, Altadena, CA 91001 USA

McDaniel, Xavier *Basketball Player*
2 Oakmist Court, Blythewood, SC 29016 USA

McDaniels, Darryl (Darryl M) *Musician, Music Group*
Entertainment Artists, 2409 21st Ave S, #100, Nashville, TN 37212 USA

McDavid, Ray *Baseball Player*
San Diego Padres, 3819 Hemlock St, San Diego, CA 92113-2837 USA

McDermott, Alice *Writer*
Farrar Straus Giroux, 19 Union Square W, New York, NY 10003 USA

McDermott, Brian
27 Upper Berkeley St., London, ENGLAND, W1

McDermott, Dean *Actor*
Schachter Entertainment, 1157 S Beverly Dr Fl 3, Los Angeles, CA 90035 USA

McDermott, Dylan *Actor*
201 S Rockingham Ave, Los Angeles, CA 90049 USA

McDermott, Edward A *Government Official*
Lake House South, 875 E Camino Real, Boca Raton, FL 33432 USA

McDermott, R Terrance (Terry) *Speed Skater*
5078 Chainbridge, Bloomfield Hills, MI 48304 USA

McDermott, Shane
200 W. 57th St. #900, New York, NY 10106

McDermott, Terry *Baseball Player*
Los Angeles Dodgers, 7205 Sunlight Peak Dr NE, Rio Rancho, NM 87144-7508 USA

McDevitt, Danny *Baseball Player*
Brooklyn Dodgers, 2274 Salem Rd SE Ste 106, Conyers, GA 30013-2097 USA

McDiarmid, Ian *Actor*
Wood Lane, London, W12 7RJ, UNITED KINGDOM (UK)

McDill, Allen *Baseball Player*
Kansas City Royals, 397 Helms Rd, Arkadelphia, AR 71923-8000 USA

McDivitt, James
9146 Cherry Ave., Rapid City, MI 49676

McDivitt, James A (Jim) *Astronaut, General*
3530 E Calle Puerta den Acero, Tucson, AZ 85718 USA

McDonagh, Martin *Writer*
Creative Artists Agency, 9830 Wilshire Blvd, Beverly Hills, CA 90212 USA

McDonald, Alvin B (Ab) *Hockey Player*
419 Thompson Dr, Winnipeg, MB R3J 3E7, CANADA

McDonald, Audra *Actor, Musician*
Gersh Agency, 232 N Canon Dr, Beverly Hills, CA 90210 USA

McDonald, Ben *Baseball Player*
Baltimore Orioles, General Delivery, Denham Springs, LA 70726-9999 USA

McDonald, Christopher
151 El Camino Dr., Beverly Hills, CA 90212

McDonald, Country Joe *Musician*
PO Box 7054, Berkeley, CA 94707 USA

McDonald, Dave *Baseball Player*
New York Yankees, 2545 SE 3rd St, Pompano Beach, FL 33062-5401 USA

McDonald, David L *Admiral*
PO Box 45214, Jacksonville, FL 32232 USA

McDonald, Donzell *Baseball Player*
New York Yankees, 3353 W Monterey St, Chandler, AZ 85226-2337 USA

McDonald, Forrest *Historian*
Po Box 155, Coker, AL 35452 USA

McDonald, Gregory C *Writer*
Arthur Greene, 101 Park Ave, New York, NY 10178 USA

McDonald, Jiggs *Sportscaster*
5272 NW 106th Dr, Coral Springs, FL 33076 USA

McDonald, Jim *Baseball Player*
Boston Red Sox, 3767 Stirrup Dr, Kingman, AZ 86401-2943 USA

McDonald, Joe
17337 Ventura Blvd. #208, Encino, CA 91316-3058

McDonald, John *Baseball Player*
Cleveland Indians, 11 Nelson Dr, East Lyme, CT 06333-1146 USA

McDonald, Keith *Baseball Player*
St Louis Cardinals, 5158 E Greensboro Ln, Anaheim, CA 92807-4612 USA

McDonald, Kevin Hamilton *Actor, Writer*
Celebrity Connection, 4311 Wilshire Blvd, Suite 300, Los Angeles, CA 90010-371 USA

McDonald, Lanny *Hockey Player*
CHA, 2424 University NW, Calgary, AB T2N 3Y9, CANADA

McDonald, Michael *Musician, Songwriter*
Lippin Group, 369 Lexington Ave, #1100, New York, NY 10017 USA

McDonald, Paul *Football Player*
1815 Tradewinds Lane, Newport Beach, CA 92660 USA

McDonald, Richie *Musician*
PO Box 128648, Nashville, TN 37212 USA

McDonald, Thomas F (Tommy) *Football Player*
537 W Valley Forge Road, King of Prussia, PA 19406 USA

McDonell, R Terry *Editor*
US Weekly, Editorial Dept, 1290 Ave of Americas, New York, NY 10104 USA

McDonnell, John F *Business Person*
McDonnell Douglas Corp, PO Box 516, Saint Louis, MO 63166 USA

McDonnell, Mary *Actor*
PO Box 6010-540, Sherman Oaks, CA 91413 USA

McDonnell, Patrick *Cartoonist*
King Features Syndicate, 888 7th Ave, New York, NY 10106 USA

McDonough, Mary *Actor*
6858 Canteloupe Ave, Van Nuys, CA 91405 USA

McDonough, Neal *Actor*
Rigberg-Rugolo Entertainment, 1180 S Beverly Dr #601, Los Angeles, CA 90035 USA

McDonough, Neil *Actor*
Rigberg Robert Rugolo, 1180 S Beverly Dr, #601, Los Angeles, CA 90035 USA

McDonough, Sean *Sportscaster*
ABC-TV, Sports Dept, 77 W 66th St, New York, NY 10023 USA

McDonough, William *Architect*
410 E Water St, Charlottesville, VA 22902 USA

McDonough, William J *Financier*
Public Company Accounting Oversight Board, 1666 K NW, Washington, DC 20006 USA

McDormand, Frances *Actor*
Endeavor Talent Agency, 9701 Wilshire Blvd, #1000, Beverly Hills, CA 90212 USA

McDormond, Frances
333 West End Ave. #12C, New York, NY 10023

McDougal, Mike *Hockey Player*
3202 Poplar St, Port Huron, MI 48060 USA

McDougal, Susan
350 S. Grand Ave. #3900, Los Angeles, CA 90071-3460

McDougald, Gil
10 Warren Ave., Spring Lake, NJ 07762

McDougald, Gilbert J (Gil) *Baseball Player*
New York Yankees, 2005 Mill Pond Ct, Belmar, NJ 07719-3660 USA

McDougall, Charles *Writer*
Industry Entertainment, 955 S Carrillo Dr #300, Los Angeles, CA 90048 USA

McDougall, Ian *Producer*
Gersh Agency, The (LA), 232 N Canon Dr, Beverly Hills, CA 90210 USA

McDougall, Walter A *Historian*
University of Pennsylvania, History Dept, Philadelphia, PA 19104 USA

McDowell, Frank *Doctor*
100 N Kalaheo Place, #F, Kailua Kona, HI 96734 USA

McDowell, Jack *Baseball Player*
Chicago White Sox, 2530 Crawford Ave Ste 307, Evanston, IL 60201-4972 USA

McDowell, Malcolm *Actor*
Markham & Froggatt, Julian House, 4 Windmill St, London, W1P 1HF, UNITED KINGDOM (UK)

McDowell, Oddlbe *Baseball Player*
Texas Rangers, 5240 SW 18th St, Hollywood, FL 33023-3157 USA

McDowell, Roger *Baseball Player*
New York Mets, 58 Robinwood Pl, Jackson, MS 39211-2405 USA

McDowell, Ronnie *Musician*
PO Box 53, Portland, TN 37148 USA

McDowell, Samuel E (Sam) *Baseball Player*
Cleveland Indians, 12902 Brown Bark Trl, Clermont, FL 34711-7646 USA

McDuffie, Otis J (O J) *Football Player*
1333 NW 121st Ave, Plantation, FL 33323 USA

McDuffie, Robert *Musician*
Columbia Artists Mgmt Inc, 165 W 57th St, New York, NY 10019 USA

McDyess, Antonio *Basketball Player*
410 Thompson Ave, Quitman, MS 39355 USA

McEldowney, Brooke *Cartoonist*
United Feature Syndicate, 200 Madison Ave, New York, NY 10016 USA

McElhenny, Hugh *Football Player*
3013 Via Venezia, Henderson, NV 89052 USA

McElhone, Natascha *Actor*
Creative Artists Agency, 9830 Wilshire Blvd, Beverly Hills, CA 90212 USA

McElhorne, Natascha *Artist*
International Creative Management (ICM-LA), 8942 Wilshire Blvd, Beverly Hills, CA 90211 USA

McElligott, Sarah *Actor*
Chasin Agency, The, 8899 Beverly Blvd #716, Los Angeles, CA 90048 USA

McElmury, Jim *Hockey Player*
9122 78th Street S, Cottage Grove, MN 55016 USA

McElroy, Chuck *Baseball Player*
Philadelphia Phillies, 1049 Nederland Ave, Port Arthur, TX 77640-4338 USA

McElroy, Joseph P *Writer*
Georges Borchandt, 136 E 57th St, New York, NY 10022 USA

McEnaney, Will *Baseball Player*
Cincinnati Reds, 1055 SW 3rd St, Boca Raton, FL 33486-4553 USA

McEnery, Peter *Actor*
International Creative Agency, 76 Oxford St, London, W1N 0AX, UNITED KINGDOM (UK)

McEnroe, John *Tennis Player*
23712 Malibu Colony Rd, Malibu, CA 90265 USA

McEntee, Gerald W *Politician*
State County Municipal Employees Union, 1625 L St NW, Washington, DC 20036 USA

McEntire, Reba *Musician*
Starstruck Entertainment, 40 Music Square W, Nashville, TN 37203 USA

McEwan, Geraldine *Actor*
Marmont Mgmt, Langham House, 302/8 Regent St, London, W1R 5AL, UNITED KINGDOM (UK)

McEwan, Ian R *Writer*
15 Park Town, Oxford, OX2 6SN, UNITED KINGDOM (UK)

McEwen, Bruce S *Scientist*
Rockefeller University, Immunology Dept, 1230 York Ave, New York, NY 10021 USA

McEwen, Mark *Commentator*
CBS Television Network (NY), 1515 Broadway Fl 49, New York, NY 10036

McEwen, Tom *Writer*
Tampa Tribune, Editorial Dept, 202 S Parker St, Tampa, FL 33606 USA

McEwing, Joe *Baseball Player*
St Louis Cardinals, 104 Iron Horse Dr, Yardley, PA 19067-1633 USA

McFadden, Cynthia *Correspondent*
20/20, 147 Columbus Ave, New York, NY 10023, US

McFadden, Daniel L *Nobel Prize Laureate*
41 Southampton Ave, Berkeley, CA 94707 USA

McFadden, Gates *Actor*
2332 E Allview Terrace, Los Angeles, CA 90068 USA

McFadden, James (Banks) *Football Player, Basketball Player*
130 Whispering Pines, Lake Wylie, SC 29710 USA

McFadden, Leon *Baseball Player*
Houston Astros, 8617 S 10th Ave, Inglewood, CA 90305-2346 USA

McFadden, Mary J *Fashion Designer*
240 W 35th St, #700, New York, NY 10001 USA

McFadden, Robert D *Journalist*
New York Times, Editorial Dept, 229 W 43rd St, New York, NY 10036 USA

McFadin, Bud
1467 Albrecht Rd, Victoria, TX 77905-2613

McFadin, Lewis P (Bud) *Football Player*
647 Springwood, Victoria, TX 77905 USA

McFadyen, Angus *Actor*
Creative Artists Agency LCC (CAA-LA), 9830 Wilshire Blvd, Beverly Hills, CA 90212 USA

McFarland, Kirsten *Writer*
International Creative Management (ICM-LA), 8942 Wilshire Blvd, Beverly Hills, CA 90211 USA

McFarlane, Andrew *Actor*
Anonymous Content, 8522 National Blvd #101, Culver City, CA 90232 USA

McFarlane, Orlando *Baseball Player*
Pittsburgh Pirates, 2102 Lakeview Dr W # 2, Royal Palm Beach, FL 33411-8776 USA

McFarlane, Robert C *Government Official*
2010 Prospect St NW, Washington, DC 20037 USA

McFarlane, Todd *Cartoonist*
PO Box 12230, Tempe, AZ 85284 USA

McFayden, Brian *Actor*
William Morris Agency (WMA-LA), 1 William Morris Pl, Beverly Hills, CA 90212 USA

McFeeley, William S *Historian, Writer*
35 Mill Hill Road, Wellfleet, MA 02667 USA

McFerrin, Bobby *Actor, Songwriter*
Original Artists, 826 Broadway, #400, New York, NY 10003 USA

McGaffigan, Andy *Baseball Player*
New York Yankees, 6243Forestwood Dr E, Lakeland, FL 33811-2402 USA

McGahee, Willis *Football Player*
Buffalo Bills, 1 Bills Dr, Orchard Park, NY 14127 USA

McGahern, John *Writer*
Faber & Faber, 3 Queen Square, London, WC1N 3AU, UNITED KINGDOM (UK)

McGahey, James C *Misc*
Plant Guard Workers Union, 25510 Kelly Road, Roseville, MI 48066 USA

McGann, Michelle *Golfer*
1200 Singer Dr, Riviera Beach, FL 33404 USA

McGann, Paul *Actor*
Marina Martin, 12/13 Poland St, London, W1V 3DE, UNITED KINGDOM (UK)

McGarity, Vernon *War Hero*
6901 Andrews Road, Bartlett, TN 38135 USA

McGarrigle, Anne *Musician*
Concerted Efforts, 59 Parsons St, West Newton, MA 02465 USA

McGarrigle, Kate *Musician*
Concerted Efforts, 59 Parsons St, West Newton, MA 02465 USA

McGarry, Steve *Cartoonist*
United feature Syndicate, 200 Madison Ave, New York, NY 10016 USA

McGaugh, James L *Biologist*
2327 Aralia St, Newport Beach, CA 92660 USA

McGavin, Darren *Actor*
PO Box 2939, Beverly Hills, CA 90213 USA

McGaw, Patrick *Actor*
Banner Entertainment, 8265 W Sunset Blvd, #200, West Hollywood, CA 90046 USA

McGeady, Sister Mary Rose *Social Activist*
Covenant House, 460 W 41st St, New York, NY 10036 USA

McGee, Henry
19 Sydney Mews, London, ENGLAND, SW3 6HL

McGee, Kirk
PO Box 626, Franklin, TN 37064

McGee, Michael B (Mike) *Football Player*
University of South Carolina, Athletic Dept, Columbia, SC 29208 USA

McGee, Pamela (Pam) *Basketball Player*
Los Angeles Sparks, Staples Center, 1111 S Figueroa St, Los Angeles, CA 90015 USA

McGee, Vonetta
1801 Avenue of the Stars #902, Los Angeles, CA 90067

McGee, William M (Max) *Football Player*
5275 Edina Industrial Blvd, #211, Edina, MN 55439 USA

McGee, Willie D *Baseball Player*
St Louis Cardinals, 2081 Lupine Road, Hercules, CA 94547-1104 USA

McGegan, Nicholas *Conductor*
Schwalbe Partners, 170 E 61st St, #5N, New York, NY 10021 USA

McGehee, Kevin *Baseball Player*
Baltimore Orioles, 18 Melmoore Dr, Pineville, LA 71360-3108 USA

McGhee, George C *Government Official*
36276 Mountville Road, Middleburg, VA 20117 USA

McGhee-Anderson, Kathleen *Producer*
Creative Artists Agency LCC (CAA-LA), 9830 Wilshire Blvd, Beverly Hills, CA 90212 USA

McGilberry, Randy *Baseball Player*
Kansas City Royals, 7521 Creekwood Dr, Mobile, AL 36695-4061 USA

McGill, Billy *Basketball Player*
5129 W 58th Place, Los Angeles, CA 90056 USA

McGill, Bruce *Actor*
3920 East Blvd, Los Angeles, CA 90066 USA

McGill, Bryant *Writer*
11C Lower Dorset St, Dubline, 1, IRELAND

McGill, William J *Educator*
2624 Costebelle Dr, La Jolla, CA 92037 USA

McGillin, Howard
151 El Camino Dr., Beverly Hills, CA 90212

McGillis, Kelly *Actor*
Kelly's Caribbean Bar & Grill, 303 Whitehead St, Key West, FL 33040 USA

McGinest, Willie *Football Player*
2001 Marina Dr, #211, Quincy, MA 02171 USA

McGinley, John C *Actor*
Innovative Artists, 1505 10th St, Santa Monica, CA 90401 USA

McGinley, Ted *Actor*
14951 Alva Dr, Pacific Palisades, CA 90272 USA

McGinn, Bernard J *Misc*
5702 Kenwood Ave, Chicago, IL 60637 USA

McGinn, Dan *Baseball Player*
Cincinnati Reds, 1340 S 163rd St, Omaha, NE 68130-1417 USA

McGinnis, Dave *Football Coach*
Arizona Cardinals, PO Box 888, Phoenix, AZ 85001 USA

McGinnis, George *Basketball Player*
11245 Marlin Road, Indianapolis, IN 46239 USA

McGinnis, Joe *Writer*
Janklow & Nesbit, 445 Park Ave, #1300, New York, NY 10020 USA

McGinnis, Russ *Baseball Player*
Texas Rangers, 1110 N Judd Pl, Chandler, AZ 85226-8709 USA

McGinnis, Susan *Television Host*
CBS Morning News, 524 W 57th St, New York, NY 10019 USA

McGinty, John J III *War Hero*
51 Barbara Lane, Hudson, NH 03051 USA

McGirt, James (Buddy) *Boxer*
195 Suffolk Ave, Brentwood, NY 11717 USA

McGlinchy, Kevin *Baseball Player*
Atlanta Braves, 1927 Halifax Rd, Danville, VA 24540-5827 USA

McGlockin, Jon *Basketball Player*
5281 State Road, #83, Heartland, WI 53029 USA

McGlockton, Chester *Football Player*
6930 S Perth St, Aurora, CO 80016 USA

McGlothin, Pat *Baseball Player*
Brooklyn Dodgers, 1454 Kenesaw Ave, Knoxville, TN 37919-7749 USA

McGlynn, Dennis *Race Car Driver*
Dover Downs Speedway, PO Box 843, Dover, DE 19903 USA

McGlynn, Dick *Hockey Player*
17 Butternut Ave, Peabody, MA 01960 USA

McGlynn, Pat *Musician*
27 Preston Grange, Preston Pans E, Lothian, SCOTLAND

McGoohan, Patrick *Actor*
523 Chapala Dr, Pacific Palisades, CA 90272 USA

McGoon, Dwight C *Doctor*
211 2nd St NW, #2016, Rochester, MN 55901 USA

McGovern, Elizabeth *Actor*
17319 Magnolia Blvd, Encino, CA 91316 USA

McGovern, George S *Politician, Senator*
FAO, Via delle Terme di Carachkka, Rome, 00100, ITALY

McGovern, Jimmy *Golfer*
788 Schirra Dr, Oradell, NJ 07649 USA

McGovern, Maureen *Musician*
Agency for Performing Arts, 9200 Sunset Blvd, #900, Los Angeles, CA 90069 USA

McGowan, Charles E *Religious Leader*
Presbyterian Church in America, 1852 Century Place, Atlanta, GA 30345 USA

McGowan, Rose *Actor*
Pulton & Meyer, 17530 Ventura Blvd, #201, Encino, CA 91316 USA

McGrady, Michael *Actor*
SDB Partners Inc, 1801 Ave of the Stars #902, Los Angeles, CA 90067 USA

McGrady, Tracy *Basketball Player*
Orlando Magic, 8701 Maitland Summit Blvd, Orlando, FL 32810 USA

McGrath, Doug *Director*
International Creative Management (ICM-LA), 8942 Wilshire Blvd, Beverly Hills, CA 90211 USA

McGrath, Douglas *Actor, Writer, Director*
International Creative Management (ICM-LA), 8942 Wilshire Blvd, Beverly Hills, CA 90211 USA

McGrath, Eugene R *Business Person*
Consolidated Edison, 4 Irving Place, New York, NY 10003 USA

McGrath, James *Scientist*
Yale University, Genetics Dept, New Haven, CT 06520 USA

McGrath, Jeremy *Motorcycle Racer*
American Motorcycle Assn, 13515 Yarmouth Dr, Pickerington, OH 43147 USA

McGrath, Mark *Musician*
Pinnacle Ent, 30 Glenn St, White Plains, NY 10603 USA

McGrath, Mike *Bowler*
738 Colusa Ave, El Cerrito, 94530 USA

McGraw, Harold W Jr *Publisher*
McGraw-Hill Inc, 1221 Ave of Americas,
New York, NY 10020 USA

McGraw, Phil (Dr Phil) *Talk Show Host,
Doctor*
Dr Phil, 5555 Melrose Ave, Mae West
Bldg, Los Angeles, CA 90038 USA

McGraw, Phillip C *Entertainer*
PO Box 140143, Irving, TX 75014 USA

McGraw, Thurman *Football Player*
749 Sandpiper Court, Fort Collins, CO
80525 USA

McGraw, Tim *Musician*
RPM Mgmt, 209 10th Ave S, #229,
Nashville, TN 37203 USA

McGraw, Tom *Baseball Player*
St Louis Cardinals, 930 N Parkway Ave
Apt K, Battle Ground, WA 98604-8078
USA

McGraw, Tug *Baseball Player*
New York Mets, 910 Pinecroft Rd,
Berwyn, PA 19312-2124 USA

McGraw III, Harold W *Business Person,
Publisher*
McGraw-Hill Inc, 1221 Ave of Americas,
New York, NY 10020 USA

McGregor, Ewan *Actor*
Creative Artists Agency LCC (CAA-LA),
9830 Wilshire Blvd, Beverly Hills, CA
90212 USA

McGregor, Ewan *Actor*
P F D Drury House, 34-43 Russell St,
London, WC2B 5HA, UNITED KINGDOM
(UK)

McGregor, Maurice *Doctor*
Royal Victoria Hospital, 687 Pine Ave W,
Montreal, QC, H3A 1A1, CANADA

McGregor, Scott H *Baseball Player*
Baltimore Orioles, 1514 Providence Road,
#A, Towson, MD 21286-1523 USA

McGriff, Frederick S (Fred) *Baseball
Player*
Toronto Blue Jays, 16314 Milan de Avila,
Tampa, FL 33613-1089 USA

McGriff, Hershel *Race Car Driver*
General Delivery, Green Valley, AZ
85622 USA

McGriff, James H (Jimmy) Jr *Musician,
Music Group*
Maxine Harvard, 7942 W Bell Road,
Glendale, AZ 85308 USA

McGriff, Tery *Baseball Player*
Cincinnati Reds, 2905 Langston Dr, Fort
Pierce, FL 34946-1089 USA

McGruder, Aaron *Cartoonist*
Universal Press Syndicate, 4520 Main St,
Kansas City, MO 64111 USA

McGuane III, Thomas F *Writer*
410 S 3rd Ave, Bozeman, MT 59715 USA

McGuinn, Martin G *Financier*
Mellon Financial Corp, Mellon Bank
Center, 500 Grant St, Pittsburgh, PA
15258 USA

McGuinn, Roger *Musician, Songwriter*
Elizabeth Rush Agency, 100 Park St, #4,
Montclair, NJ 07042 USA

McGuire, Allie
4 Tanglewood Lane, Winchester, MA
01890

McGuire, Betty *Actor*
H David Moss, 733 Seward St, #PH, Los
Angeles, CA 90038 USA

McGuire, Bill *Baseball Player*
Seattle Mariners, 17209 I St, Omaha, NE
68135-3626 USA

McGuire, Christine *Musician*
100 Rancho Circle, Las Vegas, NV 89107
USA

McGuire, Dorothy *Musician*
100 Rancho Circle, Las Vegas, NV 89107
USA

McGuire, Kevin E *Basketball Player*
20 Blue Jay Lane, North Oaks, MN 55127
USA

McGuire, Mark D *Baseball Player*
18631 Carousel Lane, Huntington Beach,
CA 92649 USA

McGuire, Mickey *Baseball Player*
Baltimore Orioles, 67 Oxford Ave,
Dayton, OH 45407-2147 USA

McGuire, Patricia A *Educator*
Trinity College, President's Office,
Washington, DC 20017 USA

McGuire, Phyllis *Musician*
100 Rancho Circle, Las Vegas, NV 89107
USA

McGuire, Richard J (Dick) *Basketball
Player, Coach*
17 Redwood Dr, Dix Hills, NY 11746
USA

McGuire, Ryan *Baseball Player*
Montreal Expos, 2 Spoon Ln, Trabuco
Canyon, CA 92679-4924 USA

McGuire, Willard H *Misc*
National Education Assn, 1201 16th St
NW, Washington, DC 20036 USA

McGuire, William Biff *Actor*
McKenrick, 1443 Pandoza Ave, Los
Angeles, CA 90024 USA

McGuire, William W *Business Person*
United HealthCare Corp, Opus Center,
9900 Bren Road E, Minnetonka, MN
55343 USA

McGuire Sisters *Music Group*
Stan Scottland Entertainment, 157 E 57th
St #18-B, New York, NY 10022 USA

McGwire, Daniel S (Dan) *Football Player*
10755 Scripps Poway Parkway, #F465,
San Diego, CA 92131 USA

McGwire, Mark *Baseball Player*
Oakland A's, 750 S Hanley Rd Apt 56,
Saint Louis, MO 63105-2695 USA

McGwire, Mark D *Baseball Player*
16631 Carousel Ln, Huntington Beach,
CA 92649 USA

McHale, John *Baseball Player*
Detroit Tigers, 2014 NW Royal Fem Ct,
Palm City, FL 34990-8025 USA

McHale, Kevin E *Basketball Player*
20 Blue Jay Ln, N Oaks, MN 55127 USA

McHattie, Stephen *Actor*
Christopher Wright Management, 3340
Barham Blvd, Los Angeles, CA 90068

McHattle, Stephen *Actor*
Macklam Feldman Mgmt, 1505 W 2nd
Ave, #200, Vancouver, BC V6H 3Y4,
CANADA

McHenry, Donald F *Diplomat*
Georgetown University, Foreign Service
School, Washington, DC 20057 USA

McHenry, Vance *Baseball Player*
Seattle Mariners, 2396 Brown St, Durham,
CA 95938-9620 USA

McHugh, Heather *Writer*
University of Washington, English Dept,
PO Box 35330, Seattle, WA 98195 USA

Mcilvaine, Jim *Basketball Player*
811 Blaine Ave, Racine, WI 53405 USA

McInally, Pat *Football Player*
PO Box 17791, Covington, KY 41017
USA

McInnis, Marty *Hockey Player*
21 Peter Hobart Dr, Hingham, MA 02043
USA

McIntyre, Joe *Actor*
Rigberg-Rugolo Entertainment, 1180 S
Beverly Dr #601, Los Angeles, CA 90035
USA

McIntyre, Joey *Musician*
Management by Jaffe, 1560 Broadway,
#1103, New York, NY 10036 USA

McKagan, Duff Rose *Musician*
Big F D Entertainment, 301 Artzona Ave,
#200, Santa Monica, CA 90401 USA

McKagen, Duff
8647 Edwin Dr., Los Angeles, CA 90046

McKay, Cody *Baseball Player*
Oakland A's, 9702 E La Posada Cir,
Scottsdale, AZ 85255-3716 USA

McKay, Dave *Baseball Player*
Minnesota Twins, 9702 E La Posada Cir,
Scottsdale, AZ 85255-3716 USA

McKay, David S *Scientist*
NASA, Johnson Space Center, 2101 NASA
Road, Houston, TX 77058 USA

McKay, Gardner
252 Lumahai Pl., Honolulu, HI 96825-
2120

McKay, Heather *Athlete*
48 Nesbitt Dr, Toronto, ON M4W 2G3,
CANADA

McKay, Jim *Sportscaster*
Battlefield Farm, 2805 Sheppard Road,
Monkton, MD 21111 USA

McKay, Peggy *Actor*
8811 Wonderland Ave, Los Angeles, CA
90046 USA

McKean, Michael *Comedian, Actor*
3202 Club Dr, Los Angeles, CA 90064
USA

McKee, Frank S *Misc*
United Steelworkers Union, 5 gateway
Center, Pittsburgh, PA 15222 USA

McKee, Gina *Actor*
Rozane Vacca, 8 Silver Place, London,
W1R 3LJ, UNITED KINGDOM (UK)

McKee, Kinnaird R *Admiral*
7101 Bay Front Dr, #608, Annapolis, MD
21403 USA

McKee, Lucky *Director*
9300 Wilshire Blvd, Suite 555, Beverly Hills, CA 90212 USA

McKee, Maria *Musician*
Geffen Records, 10900 Wilshire Blvd, #1000, Los Angeles, CA 90024 USA

McKee, Rogers *Baseball Player*
Philadelphia Phillies, 409 Forest Hill Dr, Shelby, NC 28150-5520 USA

McKee, Theodore A *Judge*
US Appeals Court, US Couthouse, 601 Market St, Philadelphia, PA 19106 USA

McKee, Todd *Actor*
611 N Flores St, #2, West Hollywood, CA 90048 USA

McKeehan, Pat
PO Box 486, Louisville, TN 37777

McKeel, Walt *Baseball Player*
Boston Red Sox, 7637 Nc Highway 58 N, STantonsburg, NC 27883 USA

McKeever, Marlin *Football Player*
4000 E 2nd St, Long Beach, CA 90803 USA

McKellar, Danica *Actor*
10635 Santa Monica Blvd, #130, Los Angeles, CA 90025 USA

McKellen, Ian *Actor*
International Creative Management (ICM-LA), 8942 Wilshire Blvd, Beverly Hills, CA 90211 USA

McKenna, Andrew J *Business Person*
McDonald's Corp, 1 McDonald's Plaza, 1 Kroc Dr, Oak Brook, IL 60523 USA

McKenna, David (Dave) *Musician*
Thomas Cassidy, 11761 E Speedway Blvd, Tucson, AZ 85748 USA

McKenna, T P *Actor*
28 Claverley Grove, London, N3 2DH, UNITED KINGDOM (UK)

McKenna, Virginia *Actor*
8 Buckfast Court, Runcorn, Cheshire, WA7 1QJ, UNITED KINGDOM (UK)

McKenney, Donald H (Don) *Hockey Player*
16 Edgewater Dr, Norton, MA 02766 USA

McKennitt, Loreena *Musician*
Helter Skelter (UK), The Plaza, 535 Kings Rd, London, N13 5H, UNITED KINGDOM (UK)

McKennitt, Lorena *Musician, Songwriter*
Quinlan Road, PO Box 933, Stratford, ON N5A 7M3, CANADA

McKennon, Keith R *Business Person*
6079 N Paradise View Dr, Paradise Valley, AZ 85253 USA

McKenzie, Andrew *Misc*
Leather Goods Plastics Novelty Union, 265 W 14th St, New York, NY 10011 USA

McKenzie, Benjamin *Actor*
Gage Group, The (LA), 14724 Ventura Blvd #505, Los Angeles, CA 91403 USA

McKenzie, Constance
3360 Barham Blvd., Los Angeles, CA 90068

McKenzie, Dan P *Misc*
Bullard Labs, Madingley Rise, Madingley Road, Cambridge, CB3 0EZ, UNITED KINGDOM (UK)

McKenzie, Jacqueline *Actor*
Robyn Gardiner Mgmt, 397 Riley St, Surrey Hills, NSW, 2010, AUSTRALIA

McKenzie, Julia
Kingston Richmond Park, Surrey, ENGLAND

McKenzie, Kevin *Ballerina*
American Ballet Theatre, 890 Broadway, New York, NY 10003 USA

McKenzie, Reginald (Reggie) *Football Player*
3174 Outing Court, Green Bay, WI 54313 USA

McKenzie, Vashti *Religious Leader*
Payne Memorial Church, 1714 Madison Ave, #16, Baltimore, MD 21217 USA

McKeon, Doug *Actor*
818 6th St, #202, Santa Monica, CA 90403 USA

McKeon, Joel *Baseball Player*
Chicago White Sox, 1901 Pierce St Apt 7, Hollywood, FL 33020-4047 USA

McKeon, John A (Jack) *Baseball Player*
13453 Luna Dr, Redding, CA 96003 USA

McKeon, Matt *Soccer Player*
Kansas City Wizards, 2 Arrowhead Dr, Kansas City, MO 64129 USA

McKeon, Nancy *Actor*
PO Box 6778, Burbank, CA 91510 USA

McKeown, Bob *Commentator*
CBS-TV, News Dept, 51 W 52nd St, New York, NY 10019 USA

McKeown, Fintan *Actor*

McKeown, Fintan *Actor*
Saffron Management, 1701 N Beverly Dr, Beverly Hills, CA 90210 USA

McKeown, Les
27 Preston Grange Preston Pans, E. Lothian, SCOTLAND

McKeown, Leslie (Les) *Musician, Music Group*
Brian Gannon Mgmt, PO Box 106, Rochdale, OL, 16 4HW, UNITED KINGDOM (UK)

McKeown, M Margaret *Judge*
US Court of Appeals, US Courthouse, 1010 5th Ave, Seattle, WA 98104 USA

McKernan, John R Jr *Governor*
77 Sanderson Road, Cumberland Foreside, ME 04110 USA

McKey, Derrick *Basketball Player*
4243 Creekside Pass, Zionsville, IN 46077 USA

McKibbin, Nikki *Musician*
Fox Television Studios, 10201 W Pico Blvd, Bldg 41, Los Angeles, CA 90035

McKiernan, David *General*
Commanding General, 3rd Army, Fort PcPherson, GA 30330 USA

McKinley, John *Misc*
952 Bloomfield Village, Auburn Hills, MI 48326 USA

McKinley, Robin *Writer*
Writer's House, 21 W 26th St, New York, NY 10010 USA

McKinney, Greg
1800 Ave. of the Stars #400, Los Angeles, CA 90067

McKinney, Kurt
9200 Sunset Blvd. #1130, Los Angeles, CA 90069

McKinney, Mark *Actor*
William Morris Agency (WMA-LA), 1 William Morris Pl, Beverly Hills, CA 90212 USA

McKinney, Rich *Baseball Player*
Chicago White Sox, 2495 E Peterson Rd, Troy, OH 45373-7790 USA

McKinney, Tamara
4935 Parkers Mill Rd, Lexington, KY 40502

McKinnie, Bryant *Football Player*
Minnesota Vikings, 9520 Viking Dr, Eden Prairie, MN 55344 USA

McKinnney, Kurt *Actor*
5003 Tilden Ave, #206, Sherman Oaks, CA 91423 USA

McKinnney, Richard (Rick) *Athlete*
7659 Kavooras Dr, Sacramento, CA 95831 USA

McKinnney, Tamara *Skier*
4935 Parkers Mill Road, Lexington, KY 40513 USA

McKinnon, Bruce *Editor, Cartoonist*
Halifax Herald, Editorial Dept, PO Box 610, Halifax, NS B3J 2T2, CANADA

McKinnon, Dan *Hockey Player*
610 E River Dr, Warroad, MN 56763 USA

McKinnon, Ray *Actor*
Judy Schoen, 606 N Larchmont Blvd, #309, Los Angeles, CA 90004 USA

McKinny, Laura Hart
3224 Nottingham Rd, Winston Salem, NC 27104-1839

Mckinzie, Gordon *Engineer*
Boeing Co, 777 Program Po BOx 3707, Seattle, WA 98124 USA

McKissock, Gary S *General*
Deputy CofS for Installations/Logistics, HqUSMC, 2 Navy St, Washington, DC 20380 USA

McKnight, Brian *Musician, Songwriter*
William Morris Agency, 151 El Camino Dr, Beverly Hills, CA 90212 USA

McKnight, Clarence E Jr *General*
1624 Linway Park Dr, McLean, VA 22101 USA

McKnight, Jeff *Baseball Player*
New York Mets, 3296 Highway 92 W, Bee Branch, AR 72013-8937 USA

McKnight, Steven L *Biologist*
3717 Euclid Ave, Dallas, TX 75205 USA

McKnight, Tony *Baseball Player*
Houston Astros, 4214 Savannah Cir, Texarkana, AR 71854-1453 USA

McKuen, Rod *Writer, Musician, Songwriter*
PO Box 2783, Los Angeles, CA 90078 USA

McKusick, Victor A *Scientist*
221 Morthway, Baltimore, MD 21218
USA

McLachlan, Craig
Box 176, Potts Point, AUSTRALIA, NSW
2011

McLachlan, Sarah *Musician, Songwriter*
Nettwerk Mgmt, 1650 W 2nd Ave,
Vancouver, BC V6J 4R3, CANADA

McLafferty, Fred W *Scientist*
103 Needham Place, Ithaca, NY 14850
USA

McLagien, Andrew V *Director*
Stanmore Productions, PO Box 1056,
Friday Harbor, WA 98250 USA

McLaglen, Andrew
Box 1056, Friday Harbor, WA 98250

McLain, Dennis D (Denny) *Baseball
Player*
Detroit Tigers, 276 Redmaple Ln,
Brighton, MI 48116-2313 USA

McLain, Kevin *Football Player*
Calico Enterprises, 2551 State St, #222,
Carlsbad, CA 92008 USA

McLane, James P (Jimmy) Jr *Swimmer*
85 Pinckney St, Boston, MA 02114 USA

McLaren, Sally
28 Berkeley Sq., London, ENGLAND,
W1X 6HD

McLaughlin, Ann Dore *Secretary*
Urban Institute of Washington, 2100 M St
NW, Washington, DC 20037 USA

McLaughlin, Audrey *Government Official*
New Democratic Party, House of
Commons, Ottawa, ON K1A 0A6,
CANADA

McLaughlin, Carol *Musician*
Columbia Artists Mgmt Inc, 165 W 57th
St, New York, NY 10019 USA

McLaughlin, John *Government Official*
Central Intelligence Agency, Deputy
Director's Office, Washington, DC 20505
USA

McLaughlin, John J *Commentator*
Oliver Productions, 1211 Connecticut Ave
NW, Washington, DC 20036 USA

McLaughlin, Mike *Race Car Driver*
Joe Gibbs Racing, 13415 Reese Blvd W,
Huntersville, NC 28078 USA

McLean, A J *Musician, Actor*
The Firm, 9100 Wilshire Blvd, #100W,
Beverly Hills, CA 900210 USA

McLean, Barney *Skier*
11745 W 66th Place, #D, Arvada, CO
80004 USA

McLean, Don *Musician, Songwriter*
PO Box 102, Castline, ME 04421 USA

McLean, John L (Jackie) Jr *Musician,
Composer*
261 Ridgefield St, Hartford, CT 06112
USA

McLean, Rene *Musician*
Brad Simon Organization, 122 E 57th St,
#300, New York, NY 10022 USA

McLean, Sally *Actor, Producer*
Salmac Management, PO Box 526, Mt
Martha, VIC 3934, AUSTRALIA

Mclellan, Zoe *Actor*
Metropolitan Talent Agency (MTA), 4526
Wilshire Blvd, Los Angeles, CA 90010
USA

McLemore, LaMonte *Musician*
Sterling/Winters, 10877 Wilshire Blvd,
#15, Los Angeles, CA 90024 USA

McLemore, Mark *Baseball Player*
Po Box 92819, Southlake, TX 76092 USA

McLerie, Allyn Ann *Actor, Dancer*
3344 Campanil Dr, Santa Barbara, CA
93109 USA

McLish, Rachel *Actor, Athlete*
PO Box 1690, Rancho Mirage, CA 92270
USA

McIntosh, Joe *Baseball Player*
San Diego Padres, 1011 Western Ave Ste
803, Seattle, WA 98101-1083 USA

McIntosh, Tim *Baseball Player*
Milwaukee Brewers, 4325 E Norwich Ave,
Fresno, CA 93726-2643 USA

McIntyre, Donald C *Opera Singer*
Foxhill Farm, Jackass Lane Keston
Bromley, Kent, BR2 6AN, UNITED
KINGDOM (UK)

McMahon, Ed *Television Host, Entertainer*
12000 Crest Court, Beverly Hills, CA
90210 USA

McMahon, James R (Jim) *Football Player*
34 Bridlewood Road, Northbrook, IL
60062 USA

McMahon, Jenna
435 Palisades Ave, Santa Monica, 90402

McMahon, Julian *Actor*
Agency for Performing Arts, 9200 Sunset
Blvd, #900, Los Angeles, CA 90069 USA

McMahon, Shane *Wrestler*
World Wrestling Entertainment (WWE),
1241 E Main St, Stamford, CT 06905 USA

McMahon, Stephanie *Wrestler*
World Wrestling Entertainment (WWE),
1241 E Main St, Stamford, CT 06905 USA

McMahon, Vincent K *Misc*
47 Hurtingham Dr, Greenwich, CT 06831
USA

McMahon Jr, Vince
1241 E Main St, Stamford, CT 06905 USA

McManus, Don *Actor*
Principal Entertainment (LA), 1964
Westwood Blvd #400, Los Angeles, CA
90025 USA

McManus, Michelle *Musician*
Pop Idol (Fremantle Media), 2700
Colorado Ave #450, Santa Monica, CA
90404 USA

McMartin, John *Actor, Musician*
Artists Agency, 1180 S Beverly Dr, #301,
Los Angeles, CA 90035 USA

McMenamin, Mark *Misc*
Mount Holyoke College, Geology Dept,
South Hadley, MA 01075 USA

McMichael, Steve D *Football Player*
4250 N Marine Dr, #1027, Chicago, IL
60613 USA

McMichen, Robert S *Misc*
International Typographical Union, PO
Box 157, Colorado Springs, CO 80901
USA

McMillan, Nate *Basketball Player, Coach*
2520 39th Ave E, Seattle, WA 98112 USA

McMillan, Susan Carpenter
1744 Oak Lane, San Marino, CA 91108

McMillan, Terry *Writer*
PO Box 2408, Danville, CA 94526 USA

McMillan, William (Bill) *Misc*
1930 Sandstone Vista, Encinitas, CA
92024 USA

McMillen, C Thomas (Tom) *Basketball
Player*
1167 Jeffrey Dr, Crofton, MD 21114 USA

McMillian, Audray G *Football Player*
4015 Brightwood St, Missouri City, TX
77459 USA

McMillian, Michael *Actor*
Industry Entertainment, 955 S Carrillo Dr
#300, Los Angeles, CA 90048 USA

McMonagle, Donald R *Astronaut*
46 SW Riverway Blvd, Palm City, FL
34990 USA

McMullen, Curtis T *Mathematician*
Harvard University, Science Center,
Cambridge, MA 02138 USA

McMullin, Ernan V *Misc*
PO Box 1066, Notre Dame, IN 46556
USA

McMurray, Sam
11500 W. Olympic Blvd. #510, Los
Angeles, CA 90064-1524

McMurray, W Grant *Religious Leader*
Reorganized Church of Latter Day Saints,
PO Box 1059, Independence, MO 64051
USA

McMurtry, James *Musician, Songwriter*
High Road, 751 Bridgeway, #300,
Sausalito, CA 94965 USA

McMurtry, Larry *Writer*
PO Box 552, Archer City, TX 76351 USA

McMurtry, Tom
PO Box 273, Edwards AFB, CA 93523-
5000

McNabb, Donovan *Football Player*
100 Springsdale Road, A-3 #270, Cherry
Hill, NJ 08003 USA

McNair, Barbara *Musician*
Thomas Cassidy, 11761 E Speedway Blvd,
Tucson, AZ 85748 USA

McNair, Robert E *Governor*
RR 2 Box 310, Columbia, SC 29212 USA

McNair, Steve *Football Player*
Tenessee Titans, 460 Great Circle Road,
Nashville, TN 37228 USA

McNair, Sylvia *Opera Singer*
Kunstleragentur Raab & Bohm,
Plankengasse 7, Vienna, 1010, AUSTRIA

McNally, Kevin
162A Ladbrooke Grove, London,
ENGLAND, W10

McNally, Stephen (Ste) *Musician*
Day Time, Crown House, 225 Kensington
High St, London, W8 8SA, UNITED
KINGDOM (UK)

McNally, Terrence *Writer, Actor*
William Morris Agency, 1325 Ave of
Americas, New York, NY 10019 USA

McNamara, Brian *Actor*
11730 National Blvd., #19, Los Angeles, CA 90064 USA

McNamara, Eileen *Journalist*
Boston Globe, Editorial Dept, 135 W T Morrissey Blvd, Dorchester, MA 02125 USA

McNamara, John F *Baseball Player*
1206 Beech Hill Road, Brentwood, TN 37027 USA

McNamara, Julianne L *Gymnast, Actor*
Barry Axelrod, 2236 Encinitas Blvd, #A, Encinitas, CA 92024 USA

McNamara, Robert S *Secretary*
700 New Hampshire Ave NW, #101, Washington, DC 20037 USA

McNamara, William *Actor*
199 Maple Ave, Victor, NJ 14564 USA

McNaught, Judith *Writer*
Pocket Books, 1230 Ave of Americas, New York, NY 10020 USA

McNaughton, John D *Director*
1370 N Milwaukee Ave, Chicago, IL 60622 USA

McNaughton, Robert F Jr *Scientist*
2511 15th St, Troy, NY 12180 USA

McNeal, Donald (Don) *Football Player*
3311 Toledo Plaza, Coral Gables, FL 33134 USA

McNealy, Scott G *Business Person*
Sun Microsystems, 901 San Antonio Road, Palo Alto, CA 94303 USA

McNeeley, Big Jay *Misc*
Ray Lawrence, PO Box 1967, Studio City, CA 91614 USA

McNeeley, Brother Jay
PO Box 1987, Studio City, CA 91614

McNeely, Paulette
4518 Rodeo Lane #2, Los Angeles, CA 90016

McNeice, Ian *Actor*
Bauman Redanty & Shaul Agency, 5757 Wilshire Blvd #473, Los Angeles, CA 90036 USA

McNeil, Frederick A (Fred) *Football Player*
9667 W Olympic Blvd, #5, Beverly Hills, CA 90212 USA

McNeil, Freeman *Football Player*
A+ Technology Solutions, 4177 Merrick Road, Massapequa, NY 11758 USA

McNeil, Kate *Actor*
1743 N Dillon St, Los Angeles, CA 90026 USA

McNeil, Lori *Tennis Player*
Int'l Mgmt Group, 1 Erieview Plaza, 1360 E 9th St #1300, Cleveland, OH 44114 USA

McNeill, Robert Duncan *Actor*
Susan Smith, 121A N San Vicente Blvd, Beverly Hills, CA 90211 USA

McNeill, W Donald (Don) *Tennis Player*
2165 15th Ave, Vero Beach, FL 32960 USA

McNeish, Richard *Archaeologist*
Andover Archaeology Research Foundation, 1 Woodland Road, Andover, MA 01810 USA

McNerney, David H *War Hero*
20322 New Moon Trail, Crosby, TX 77532 USA

McPartlin, Ant *Television Host*
Pop Idol (Fremantle Media), 2700 Colorado Ave #450, Santa Monica, CA 90404 USA

McPartlnad, Marian M *Musician*
Abby Hoffer, 223 1/2 E 48th St, New York, NY 10017 USA

McPeak, Holly *Volleyball Player*
Women's Pro Volleyball Assn, 840 Apollo St, #204, El Segundo, CA 90245 USA

McPeak, Merrill A (Tony) *General*
17360 Grandview Court, Lake Oswego, OR 97034 USA

McPhee, John A *Writer*
475 Drake's Corner Road, Princeton, NJ 08540 USA

McPherson, Charles *Misc*
Joel Chriss, 300 Mercer St, #3J, New York, NY 10003 USA

McPherson, Don *Football Player*
360 Huntington Ave, Boston, MA 02115 USA

McPherson, Harry C Jr *Government Official*
10213 Montgomery Ave, Kensington, MD 20895 USA

McPherson, James M *Historian*
15 Randall Road, Princeton, NJ 08540 USA

McPherson, John *Cartoonist*
Universal Press Syndicate, 4520 Main St, Kansas City, MO 64111 USA

McPherson, Leon *Musician*
Pop Idol (Fremantle Media), 2700 Colorado Ave #450, Santa Monica, CA 90404 USA

McPherson, M Peter *Educator*
Michigan State University, President's Office, East Lansing, MI 48824 USA

McPherson, Rolf K *Religious Leader*
Church of Foursquare Gospel, 1100 Glendale Blvd, Los Angeles, CA 90026 USA

McQuagg, Sam *Race Car Driver*
8886 Hamilton Road, Midland, GA 31820 USA

McQueen, Alexander *Fashion Designer*
House of Givenchy, 3 Ave Saint George, Paris, 75008, FRANCE

McQueen, Chad *Actor*
8306 Wilshire Blvd, #438, Beverly Hills, CA 90211 USA

McQueen, Neile
2323 Bowmont Dr., Beverly Hills, CA 90210

McRae, Brian *Baseball Player*
2431 Landings Cir, Bradenton, FL 34209 USA

McRae, Harold O (Hal) *Baseball Player*
2431 Landing Circle, Bradenton, FL 34209 USA

McRaney, Gerald *Actor*
1012 Royal St, New Orleans, LA 70116 USA

McRee, Lisa
327 N. Orange Dr., Los Angeles, CA 90036-2613

McReynolds, Jim & Jesse
Box 304, Gallatin, TN 37066

McReynolds, Madison *Actor*
Kazarian/Spencer & Assoc, 11365 Ventura Blvd #100, Box 7403, Studio City, CA 91604 USA

McShane, Ian *Actor*
International Creative Mgmt, 76 Oxford St, London, W1N 0AX, UNITED KINGDOM (UK)

McShane, Jamie *Actor*
Select Artists Ltd (CA-Westside Office), 1138 12th Street, Suite 1, Santa Monica, CA 90403 USA

McShann, James C (Jay) *Musician*
Ozark Talent, 718 Schwarz Road, Lawrence, KS 66049 USA

McTeer, Janet *Actor*
Propaganda Films Mgmt, 1741 Ivar Ave, Los Angeles, CA 90028 USA

McTeer, Robert D Jr *Financier, Government Official*
Federal Reserve Bank, 2200 N Pearl St, Dallas, TX 75201 USA

McTiernan, John C *Director*
The Firm, 9100 Wilshire Blvd, #100W, Beverly Hills, CA 90210 USA

McVicar, Daniel *Actor*
1704 Oak St, Santa Monica, CA 90405 USA

McVie, Christine *Musician, Songwriter*
406 Poplar Dr, Wilmette, IL 60091 USA

McVie, John *Musician, Songwriter*
Boulevard Mgmt, 21650 Oxnard St, #1925, Woodland Hills, CA 91367 USA

McVie, Tom *Hockey Player*
Boston Bruins, 1 Fleet Center, Boston, MA 02114 USA

McWethy, John F *Commentator*
5028 30th St N, Arlington, VA 22207 USA

McWherter, Ned R *Governor*
321 Linden St, Dresdon, TN 38225 USA

McWhirter, Jillian *Actor*
PO Box 6308, Beverly Hills, CA 90212 USA

McWilliam, Edward *Artist*
8A Holland Villas Road, London, W14 8DP, UNITED KINGDOM (UK)

McWilliams, Brian *Misc*
Longshoremen/Warehousemen Union, 1188 Franklin St, San Francisco, CA 94109 USA

McWilliams, Caroline *Actor*
Premiere Artists, 1875 Century Park E, #2250, Los Angeles, CA 90067 USA

McWilliams, David *Football Player, Football Executive*
University of Texas, Athletic Dept, Austlin, TX 78712 USA

McWilliams, Fleming *Musician*
Michael Dixon Mgmt, 119 Pebble Creek Road, Franklin, TN 37064 USA

McWilliams, Robert H *Judge*
US COurt of Appeals, US Courthouse, 1929 Stout St, Denver, CO 80294 USA

MDO *Music Group*
Sony Music Miami, 605 Lincoln Rd,
Miami Beach, FL 33138 USA

Mead, Shepherd *Writer*
53 Rivermead Court, London, SW6 3RY,
UNITED KINGDOM (UK)

Meade, Carl J *Astronaut*
5711 Blenveneda Terrace, Palmdale, CA
93551 USA

Meade, Glenn *Writer*
Saint Martin's Press, 175 5th Ave, New
York, NY 10010 USA

Meade, Julia
101O Fifth Ave., New York, NY 10021

Meador, Eddle D (Ed) *Football Player*
1135 Padgett Hill Road, Natural Bridge,
VA 24578 USA

Meador, Vaughn
1096 Middle 2 Rock Rd., Petaluma, CA
94952

Meadows, Bernard W *Artist*
34 Belsize Grove, London, NW3, UNITED
KINGDOM (UK)

Meadows, Jayne *Actor*
16185 Woodvale Road, Encino, CA
91436 USA

Meadows, Stephen *Actor*
1760 Courtney Ave, Los Angeles, CA
90046 USA

Meadows, Tim *Actor, Comedian*
Brillstein/Grey, 9150 Wilshire Blvd, #350,
Beverly Hills, CA 90212 USA

Meagher, Mary T *Swimmer*
404 Vanderwall, Peachtree City, GA
30269 USA

Meaney, Colm *Actor*
11921 Laurel Hills Road, Studio City, CA
91604 USA

Meaney, Kevin *Actor, Comedian*
28 Beech Lane, Tarrytown, NY 10591
USA

Means, Natrone J *Football Player*
862 Kings Crossing Dr, Concord, NC
28027 USA

Means, Russell *Social Activist*
444 Crazy Horse Dr, Porcupine, SD
57772 USA

Meara, Anne *Actor, Comedian*
Innovative Artists (LA), 1505 Tenth St,
Santa Monica, CA 90401 USA

Mears, Casey *Race Car Driver*
Chip Ganassi Racing, 600 E Laburmum
Ave, Richmond, VA 23222 USA

Mears, Gary *Musician*
12170 Country Road 215, Tyler, TX
75707 USA

Mears, Rick *Race Car Driver*
1536 NW Buttonbush Circle, Palm City,
FL 34990 USA

Mears, Roger Sr *Race Car Driver*
PO Box 520, Terell, NC 28682 USA

Mears, Walter R *Journalist*
Associated Press, Editorial Dept, 2021 K St
NW, Washington, DC 20006 USA

Meat, Loaf *Musician, Actor*
Solo Agency, 252-260 Regent St, #100,
London, W1B 3BX, UNITED KINGDOM
(UK)

Mecchi, Irene *Actor*
Endeavor Agency LLC (LA), 9601 Wilshire
Blvd Fl 3, Beverly Hills, CA 90210 USA

Mecham, Evan *Governor*
Mecham Pontiac-AMC-Renault, 4510 W
Glendale Ave, Glendale, AZ 85301 USA

Mechem, Charles S Jr *Golfer, Business
Person*
United States Show, 1 Eastwood Dr,
Cincinnati, OH 45227 USA

Mechoso, Julio Oscar *Actor*
Gage Group, The (LA), 14724 Ventura
Blvd #505, Los Angeles, CA 91403 USA

Meciar, Vladimir *Prime Minister*
Urad Vlady SR, Nam Slobody 1,
Bratislava, 81370, SLOVAKIA

Mecir, Miloslav *Tennis Player*
Julova 1, Bratislava, 83101, CZECH
REPUBLIC

Medak, Peter *Director*
1355 N Laurel Ave, #9, West Hollywood,
CA 90046 USA

Medaris, J Bruce *General*
Po Box 415, Fem Park, FL 32751 USA

Medavoy, Mike *Producer*
Phoenix Pictures, 10202 W Washington
Blvd, Frankovich Bldg, Culver City, CA
90232 USA

Medcalf, Kim *Actor*
London Mgmt, 2-4 Noel St, London, W1V
3RB, UNITED KINGDOM (UK)

Meddick, Jim *Cartoonist*
United Feature Syndicate, 200 Madison
Ave, New York, NY 10016 USA

Medeiros, Glenn *Musician*
PO Box 8, Lawai, HI 96765 USA

Medgyessy, Peter *Prime Minister*
Prime Minister's Office, Kossuth Lajos Ter
1-3, Budapest, 1055, HUNGARY

Medina, Benny *Producer*

Medina, Patricia *Actor*
10787 Wilshire Blvd, #1503, Los Angeles,
CA 90024 USA

Medina Estevez, Jorge Arturo Cardinal
Religious Leader
Congregation for Divine Worship, Vatican
City, 00120, VATICAN CITY

Medley, Bill *Musician*
William Morris Agency (WMA-LA), 1
William Morris Pl, Beverly Hills, CA
90212 USA

Medley, Charles R O *Artist*
Charterhouse, Charterhouse Square,
London, EC1M 6AN, UNITED KINGDOM
(UK)

Medoff, Mark H *Writer*
PO Box 3072, Las Cruces, NM 88003
USA

Medrano, Frank *Actor*
Axiom Management, 10701 Wilshire Blvd
#1202, Los Angeles, CA 90024

Medress, Henry *Musician*
Brothers Mgmt, 141 Dunbar Ave, Fords,
NJ 08863 USA

Medved, Aleksandr V *Wrestler*
Central Soviet Sports Federation, Skatertny
p 4, Moscow, RUSSIA

Medvedev, Andrei *Tennis Player*
6352 Ellmau, Tirol, AUSTRIA

Medvedev, Zhores A *Biologist*
4 Osborn Gardens, London, NW7 1DY,
UNITED KINGDOM (UK)

Medwin, Michael *Actor*
International Creative Mgmt, 76 Oxford
St, London, W1N 0AX, UNITED
KINGDOM (UK)

Meehan, Thomas E *Writer, Musician*
Brook House, Obtuse Road, Newtown, CT
06470 USA

Meehl, Paul E *Misc*
1544 E River Terrace, Minneapolis, MN
55414 USA

Meek, Jeffrey
1801 Ave. of the Stars #902, Los Angeles,
CA 90067

Meeker, Howie *Hockey Player,
Sportscaster*
979 Dickenson Way, Parksville, BC V9P
1Z7, CANADA

Meeks, Aaron *Actor*
Showtime Networks (LA), 10880 Wilshire
Blvd #1600, Los Angeles, CA 90024 USA

Meely, Cliff *Basketball Player*
3240 Iris AVe, #204, Boulder, CO 80301
USA

Meena *Actor, Bollywood*
58 Second Street, Venkatesh Nagar,
Chennai, TN 600093, INDIA

Meese, Edwin III *Attorney General*
1075 Springhill Road, McLean, VA 22102
USA

Meester, Leighton *Actor*
Abrams Artists Agency (LA), 9200 Sunset
Blvd Fl 11, Los Angeles, CA 90069 USA

Meeuwsen, Terry *Religious Leader,
Television Host*
700 Club, 977 Centerville Tpke, Virginia
Beach, VT 23463 USA

Meggett, David L (Dave) *Football Player*
8 Brisbane Dr, Charleston, SC 29407 USA

Megnot, Roya *Actor*
House of Representatives, 400 S Beverly
Dr, #101, Beverly Hills, CA 90212 USA

Meher, Bill *Commentator, Comedian*
Agency for Performing Arts, 9200 Sunset
Blvd, #900, Los Angeles, CA 90069 USA

Mehl, Lance A *Football Player*
44920 Kacsmar Estates Dr, Saint
Clairsville, OH 43950 USA

Mehra, Prakash *Producer, Director,
Filmmaker, Bollywood*
30 Sumeet Bangalow 11th Road, JVPD
Scheme, Bombay, MS 400 049, INDIA

Mehrabian, Robert *Educator*
Carnegie Mellon University, President's
Office, Pittsburgh, PA 15213 USA

Mehregany, Mehran *Engineer*
Case Western Reserve University,
Electrical Engineer Dept, Cleveland, OH
44106 USA

Mehringer, David M *Astronomer*
University of Illinois, Astronomy Dept,
Champaign, IL 61820 USA

Mehta, Shailesh J *Business Person*
Providian Financial Corp, 201 Mission St, San Francisco, CA 94105 USA

Mehta, Sujata *Actor, Bollywood*
56 Dev Chhaya Tardeo Haji Ali Road, Tardeo, Bombay, MS 400 034, INDIA

Mehta, Ved *Writer*
139 E 79th St, New York, NY 10021 USA

Mehta, Zubin *Conductor*
Israel Philharmonic, 1 Huberman St, Tel Aviv, 61112, ISRAEL

Mehta (Metha) Saltzman, Deepa *Director, Producer, Editor, Writer*
Rigberg-Rugolo Entertainment, 1180 S Beverly Dr #601, Los Angeles, CA 90035 USA

Meier, Richard A *Architect*
Richard Meier Partners, 475 10th Ave, New York, NY 10018 USA

Meier, Waltraud *Opera Singer*
Festspielhugel 3, Bayreuth, 95445, GERMANY

Meinwald, Jerrold *Misc*
Cornell University, Chemistry Dept, Ithaca, NY 14853 USA

Meirelles, Fernando *Director, Producer*
Endeavor Agency LLC (LA), 9601 Wilshire Blvd Fl 3, Beverly Hills, CA 90210 USA

Meisel, Stephen *Photographer*
1271 Ave of Americas, New York, NY 10020 USA

Meiselas, Susan *Photographer*
256 Mott St, New York, NY 10012 USA

Meisner, Joachim Cardinal *Religious Leader*
Archbishop's Diocese, Marzellenstr 32, Cologne, 50668, GERMANY

Meisner, Randy *Musician*
3706 Eureka Dr, Studio City, CA 91604 USA

Meja *Musician*
Basic Music Mgmt, Norrtullsgatan 51, Stockholm, 113 45, SWEDEN

Mejdani, Rexhep *President*
President's Office, Keshilli i Ministrave, Tirana, ALBANIA

Mejia, Hipolito *President*
Palacio Nacional, Calle Moises Garcia, Santo Domingo, DOMINICAN REPUBLIC

Mejia, Jorge Maria Cardinal *Religious Leader*
Biblioteca Apostolica Vaticina, Vatican City, 00120, VATICAN CITY

Mejia, Paul R *Ballerina, Choreographer*
Fort Worth Ballet, 6848 Green Oaks Road, Fort Worth, TX 76116 USA

Mekka, Eddie *Actor*
Cosden Morgan, 129 W Wilson St, #202, Costa Mesa, CA 92627 USA

Melamed, Lisa
151 El Camino Dr., Beverly Hills, CA 90212

Melamld, Aleksandr *Artist*
Ronald Freeman Fine Arts, 31 Mercer St, New York, NY 10013 USA

Melanie *Musician, Songwriter*
53 Baymont St, #5, Clearwater Beach, FL 33767 USA

Melato, Mariangela *Actor*
Carol Levi Co, Via Giuseppe Pisanelli, Rome, 00196, ITALY

Melcher, John *Senator*
230 Maryland Ave NE, #B, Washington, DC 20002 USA

Melchionni, Bill *Basketball Player*
115 Whitehall Blvd, Garden City, NY 11530 USA

Melchior, Ib *Writer*
8228 Marmont Lane, Los Angeles, CA 90069 USA

Melendez, A J *Musician*
American Idol, 7800 Beverly Blvd #251, Los Angeles, CA 90036 USA

Melendez, Bill *Animator*
Bill Melendez Productions, 13400 Riverside Dr, #201, Sherman Oaks, CA 91423 USA

Melendez, Lisette *Musician*
Famous Artists Agency, 250 W 57th St, New York, NY 10107 USA

Melendez, Ron
12533 Woodgreen St, Los Angeles, CA 90066

Meler, Raymond *Photographer*
Raymond Meier Photography, 532 Broadway, New York, NY 10012 USA

Melinda *Artist*
M Entertainment, 120 E Flamingo Road, Las Vegas, NV 89109 USA

Mellanby, Scott *Hockey Player*
2559 Oak Springs Lane, Saint Louis, MO 63131 USA

Mellencamp, John *Musician, Songwriter*
PO Box 6777, Bloomington, IN 47407 USA

Mellers, Wilfrid H *Writer, Composer*
Oliver Sheldon House, 17 Aldwark, York, YO1 2BX, UNITED KINGDOM (UK)

Melles, Carl
Grunbergstr 4, Vienna, 1130, AUSTRIA

Mellinkoff, Sherman M *Educator, Physicist*
University of California, Med Center, 10833 LeConte Ave, Los Angeles, CA 90095 USA

Mello, Tamara *Actor*
Abrams Artists, 9200 Sunset Blvd, #1125, Los Angeles, CA 90069 USA

Mellons, Ken *Musician*
Buddy Lee Attractions Inc, 38 Music Square E #300, Nashville, TN 37203-4396 USA

Mellor, John W *Economist*
John Mellor Assoc, 801 Pennsylvania Ave NW, #PH18, Washington, DC 20004 USA

Mellor, Thomas (Tom) *Hockey Player*
63 Spoonhill Ave, Marlborough, MA 01752 USA

Melnick, Bruce E *Astronaut*
Boeing Aerospace, PO Box 21233, Kennedy Space Center, FL 32815 USA

Melnick, Daniel *Producer*
1123 Sunset Hills Dr, Los Angeles, CA 90069 USA

Melnikov, Vitaly V *Director*
Svetianovsky Proyezd 105, #20, Saint Petersburg, 195269, RUSSIA

Melody *Musician*
Sony Music Miami, 605 Lincoln Rd, Miami Beach, FL 33138 USA

Meloni, Christopher *Actor*
Gersh Agency, The (LA), 232 N Canon Dr, Beverly Hills, CA 90210 USA

Melrose, Barry J *Hockey Player, Coach*
ESPN-TV, Sports Dept, ESPN Plaza 935 Middle St, Bristol, CT 06010 USA

Melroy, Pamela A *Astronaut*
3910 Valley Green Court, Houston, TX 77059 USA

Melton, Sid *Actor*
PO Box 57933, Sherman Oaks, CA 91413 USA

Meltzer, Allan L *Economist*
Camegie Mellon University, Economics Dept, Pittsburgh, PA 15260 USA

Meluskey, Mitch *Baseball Player*
Houston Astros, 26 Meadowbrook Rd, Yakima, WA 98903-9505 USA

Melvill, Michael W *Astronaut*
24120 Jacaranda Dr, Tehachapi, CA 93561 USA

Melvin, Allan *Actor*
271 N Bowling Green Way, Los Angeles, CA 90049 USA

Melvin, Bob *Baseball Player*
Detroit Tigers, 5637 E Canyon Ridge North Dr, Cave Creek, AZ 85331-9319 USA

Melvin, Donnie
45 Overlook Terr., New York, NY 10033

Melvin, Murray
Joy Jameson, Plaza, 535 Kings Road, London, SW10 OSZ, UNITED KINGDOM (UK)

Melzack, Ronald *Misc*
51 Banstead Road, Montreal, QC, H4X 1P1, CANADA

Members, Swollen *Musician*
Agency Group, The (NY), 1775 Broadway #430, New York, NY 10019 USA

Men, Baha *Music Group*
Evolution Talent Agency LLC, 1776 Broadway Fl 15, New York, NY 10019 USA

Men At Work
1775 Broadway #433, New York, NY 10019

Menaker, Mitchell G
5062 Isleworth Country Club Dr, Windermere, FL 34786-8920 USA

Menand, Louis *Writer, Historian*
New Yorker Magazine, Editorial Dept, 4 Times Square, New York, NY 10036 USA

Menard, Renry W *Misc*
Scripps Institute of Oceanography, Geology Dept, La Jolla, CA 92093 USA

Mench, Kevin *Baseball Player*
Texas Rangers, 414 Saint Regis Dr, Newark, DE 19711-6107 USA

Menchu Tum, Rigoberta *Nobel Prize Laureate*
UN Working Group on Indigenous Populations, UN Plaza, New York, NY 10017 USA

Mendes, Eva *Actor*
Industry Entertainment, 955 Carillo Dr, #300, Los Angeles, CA 90048 USA

Mendes, Sam *Director*
Donmar Warehouse, 41 Earlham St, London, WC2H 9LD, UNITED KINGDOM (UK)

Mendes, Sergio *Musician*
PO Box 118, Los Angeles, CA 90053 USA

Mendez, Lucia *Actor*
TV Azteca, Periferico Sur 4121, Colonia Fuentes del Pedregal, DF, CP 14141, Mexico

Mendoza, June *Artist*
34 Inner Park Road, London, SW19 6DD, UNITED KINGDOM (UK)

Mendoza, Linda *Director*
Creative Artists Agency LCC (CAA-LA), 9830 Wilshire Blvd, Beverly Hills, CA 90212 USA

Mendoza, Mike *Baseball Player*
Houston Astros, 14207 S 20th St, Phoenix, AZ 85048-4519 USA

Mendoza, Minnie *Baseball Player*
Minnesota Twins, 2070 SW 57th Ct, Miami, FL 33155-2237 USA

Mendoza, Ramiro *Baseball Player, Athlete*
New York Yankees, 18706 Pepper Pike, Lutz, FL 33558-5303 USA

Mendte, Larry
330 Bob Hope Dr., Burbank, CA 91523

Menechino, Frank *Baseball Player*
Oakland A's, 522 Arlene St, Staten Island, NY 10314-3818 USA

Menendez, Erik
#1878449 CSP-Sac. Box 290066, Represa, CA 95671-0066

Menendez, Lyle
#1887106Calif. Correctional Inst. CCI-Box 1031, Tehachapi, CA 93581

Menendez, Tony *Baseball Player*
Cincinnati Reds, 18730 NW 48th Ct, Carol City, FL 33055-2536 USA

Meneses, Alex *Actor*
Abrams Artists Agency (LA), 9200 Sunset Blvd Fl 11, Los Angeles, CA 90069 USA

Meneses, Antonio *Musician*
Columbia Artists Mgmt Inc, 165 W 57th St, New York, NY 10019 USA

Menez, Bernard
119 Blvd. de Grenelle, Paris, FRANCE, 75015

Mengatti, John
8322 Beverly Blvd. #200, Los Angeles, CA 90048

Mengers, Sue
938 Bel Air Rd., Los Angeles, CA 90077

Menges, Chris *Cinematographer, Director*
Harmony Pictures, 420 S Beverly Dr, #1-100, Beverly Hills, CA 90212 USA

Menhart, Paul *Baseball Player*
Toronto Blue Jays, 4721 Thornwood Ct, Covington, GA 30016-8105 USA

Menichetti, Roberto *Fashion Designer*
3 Loc Monteleto, Gubbio, ITALY

Menke, Denis *Baseball Player*
Milwaukee Braves, 1246 Berkshire Ln, Tarpon Springs, FL 34688-7626 USA

Menken, Alan *Composer*
Shukat Co, 670 W End Ave, #8A, New York, NY 10025 USA

Mennea, Pietro *Track Athlete*
Via Cassia 1041, Rome, 00189, ITALY

Meno, Chorepiscopus John *Religious Leader*
263 Elm Ave, Teaneck, NJ 07666 USA

Menon, Mambillikalathil G K *Physicist*
C-63 Tarang Apts, Mother Dairy Road, Patparganj, Delhi, 110092, INDIA

Menotti, Gian Carlo
Gilford Haddington, E. Lothian, SCOTLAND, EH41 4jF

Menotti, Gian-Carlo *Composer*
Yester House, Gifford Haddington, East Lothian, EH41 4JF, SCOTTLAND

Menounos, Maria *Television Host*
Entertainment Tonight (ET), 5555 Melrose Ave, Mae West Bldg Fl 2, Hollywood, CA 90038 USA

Mensah, Peter *Actor*
Stone Manners Talent Agency, 6500 Wilshire Blvd, Ste 550, Los Angeles, CA 90048 USA

Menshov, Vladimir V *Actor, Director*
3D Tverskaya-Yamskaya 52, Moscow, 125047, RUSSIA

Mentez, Chris *Musician*
Arsisanian Assoc, 6671 Sunset Blvd, #1502, Los Angeles, CA 90028 USA

Menudo
2895 Biscayne Blvd. #455, Miami, FL 33137

Menzel, Idina *Actor, Musician*
Endeavor Talent Agency, 9701 Wilshire Blvd, #1000, Beverly Hills, CA 90212 USA

Menzel, Jiri *Director*
Studio 89, Kratky Film Jindrisska 34, Prague 1, 112 07, CZECH REPUBLIC

Menzies, Heather *Actor*
PO Box 1645, Park City, UT 84060 USA

Menzies, Peter G Jr *Cinematographer*
903 Tahoe Blvd, #802, Incline Village, NV 89451 USA

Meola, Eric *Photographer*
535 Greenwich St, New York, NY 10013 USA

Meola, Tony *Soccer Player*
488 Forest St, Keamy, NJ 07032 USA

Meoli, Christian *Actor*
Lichtman/Salners Company, 12216 Moorpark Street, Studio City, CA 91604 USA

Meoll, Rudy *Baseball Player*
California Angels, 8150 E Oak Ridge Cir, Anaheim, CA 92808-1941 USA

Merbold, Ulf *Astronaut*
Am Sonnenhang 4, Siegburg, 53721, GERMANY

Mercado, Orlando *Baseball Player*
Seattle Mariners, PO Box 1465, Arecibo, PR 00613-1465 USA

Mercante, Arthur *Referee*
135 Wickham Road, Garden City, NY 11530 USA

Merced, Orlando *Baseball Player*
Pittsburgh Pirates, 1246 W Stone Meadow Way, Springfield, MO 65810-1609 USA

Mercer, Kelvin *Artist, Musician*
Famous Artists Agency, 250 W 57th St, New York, NY 10107 USA

Mercer, Marian *Actor, Musician*
5250 Colodny Dr, #13, Argoura Hills, CA 91301 USA

Mercer, Mark *Baseball Player*
Texas Rangers, 10607 Penn Ave S, Minneapolis, MN 55431-3445 USA

Mercer, Ron *Basketball Player*
San Antonio Spurs, Alamodome, 1 SBC Center, San Antonio, TX 78219 USA

Mercer, Toby *Artist*
Mercer Studios, 316 E Reserve Dr, Kalispell, MT 59901 USA

Merchant, Andy *Baseball Player*
Boston Red Sox, Bates Lake Road, Malcolm, AL 36556 USA

Merchant, Ismail N *Producer*
Merchant-Ivory Productions, 46 Lexington St, London, W1P 3LH, UNITED KINGDOM (UK)

Merchant, Natalie *Musician, Songwriter*
Fort Apache, 51 the Square, Bellows Falls, VT 05101 USA

Mercker, Kent *Baseball Player*
Atlanta Braves, 5340 Mulrfield Ct, Dublin, OH 43017-7629 USA

Mercurio, Nicole *Actor*
Innovative Artists, 1505 10th St, Santa Monica, CA 90401 USA

Mercurio, Paul *Actor, Musician*
Beyond Films, 53-55 Brisbane St Surreyhills, Sydney, NSW, 2010, AUSTRALIA

Mercurio, Steven
Columbia Artists Mgmt Inc, 165 W 57th St, New York, NY 10019 USA

Mercurio, Tara *Actor*
9 Yards Entertainment, 8530 Wilshire Blvd Fl 5, Beverly Hills, CA 90211 USA

Meredith, Don
PO Box 597, Santa Fe, NM 87504-0597

Meredith, J Don *Football Player, Sportscaster*
PO Box 597, Santa Fe, NM 87504 USA

Meredith, James H *Misc*
929 Meadowbrook Road, Jackson, MS 39206 USA

Meredith, Richard *Hockey Player*
6520 Ridgeview Dr, Edina, MN 55439 USA

Meredith, William *Writer*
Connecticut College, PO Box 1498, New London, CT 06320 USA

Meri, Lennart *President*
President's Office, 39 Weizenberg St, Tallinn, 0100, ESTONIA

Merigan Jr, Thomas C *Scientist*
148 Goya Road, Portola Valley, CA 94028 USA

Meritano, Lorena *Actor*
Gabriel Blanco Iglesias (Mexico), Rio Balsas 35-32, Colonia Cuauhtemoc, DF, 06500, Mexico

Meriweather, Joe C *Basketball Player*
5816 NW 64th Terrace, Kansas City, MO 64151 USA

Meriweather, Lee *Actor, Beauty Pageant Winner*
12139 Jeanette Pl, Granada Hills, CA 91344 USA

Meriwether, Lee *Actor, Beauty Pageant Winner*
12139 Jeanette Place, Granada Hills, CA 91344 USA

Merkerson, S Epatha *Actor*
Alliance Talent, 9171 Wilshire Blvd, #441, Beverly Hills, CA 90210 USA

Merle, Carole *Skier*
Chalet La Calette, Super-Sauze, 04400, FRANCE

Merletti, Lewis C *Lawyer*
Cleveland Browns, 76 Lou Groza Blvd, Berea, OH 44017 USA

Merlin, Jan *Actor*
347 N California St, Burbank, CA 91505 USA

Merloni, Lou *Baseball Player*
Boston Red Sox, 56 E Bluff Rd, Ashland, MA 01721-2345 USA

Merlyn-Rees, Merlyn *Government Official*
House of Lords, Westminster, London, SW1A 0PW, UNITED KINGDOM (UK)

Mero, Rena (Sable) *Actor, Wrestler, Model*
PO Box 469, Geneva, FL 32732 USA

Meron, Neil *Producer*
William Morris Agency (WMA-LA), 1 William Morris Pl, Beverly Hills, CA 90212 USA

Merovich, Pete *Soccer Player*
945 Spruce St, Pittsburgh, PA 15234 USA

Merow, James F *Judge*
US Claims Court, 717 Madison Place NW, Washington, DC 20439 USA

Merrells, Jason *Actor*
QVoice, 8 Kings St, London, WC2E 8HN, UNITED KINGDOM (UK)

Merrick, Dawn
8281 Melrose Ave. #200, Los Angeles, CA 90046

Merrifield, R Bruce *Nobel Prize Laureate*
43 Mezzine Dr, Cresskill, NJ 07626 USA

Merrill, Catherine *Artist*
Old Church Pottery, 1456 Florida St, San Francisco, CA 94110 USA

Merrill, Dina *Actor*
Sue Siegel, 405 E 54th St #12A, New York, NY 10022 USA

Merrill, Edward W *Engineer*
90 Somerset St, Belmont, MA 02478 USA

Merrill, John O *Architect*
101 Gardner Place, Colorado Springs, CO 80906 USA

Merrill, Robert *Opera Singer*
Robert Merrill Assoc, 79 Oxford Road, New Rochelle, NY 10804 USA

Merrill, Stephen E (Steve) *Governor*
562 S Main, Farmington, NH 03855 USA

Merriman, Brent *Baseball Player*
Minnesota Twins, 241 S Equestrian Ct, Gilbert, AZ 85296-2156 USA

Merriman, Lloyd *Baseball Player*
Cincinnati Reds, 645 E Champlain #104, Fresno, CA 93720-1292 USA

Merriman, Randy
PO Box 70025, Houston, TX 77270

Merriman, Ryan *Actor*
William Morris Agency (WMA-LA), 1 William Morris Pl, Beverly Hills, CA 90212 USA

Merriman, Ryan *Actor*
Jamieson, PO Box 710025, Houston, TX 77270 USA

Merritt, Chris *Opera Singer*
George M Martynuk, 352 7th Ave, New York, NY 10001 USA

Merritt, Gilbert S *Judge*
US Court of Appeals, US Courthouse, 701 Broadway, Nashville, TN 37203 USA

Merritt, Jack N *General*
US Army Assn, 2425 Wilson Blvd, Arlington, VA 22201 USA

Merritt, James J (Jim) *Baseball Player*
Minnesota Twins, 833 Sandwagon Circle, Hemet, CA 92544-1891 USA

Merritt, Lloyd *Baseball Player*
St Louis Cardinals, 4703 Wlld Iris Dr Apt 301, Myrtle Beach, SC 29577-8718 USA

Merritt, Tift *Musician*
High Road Touring, 751 Bridgeway, 3rd Floor, Sausalito, CA 94965

Merrow, Susan *Misc*
Sierra Club, 85 2nd St, #200, San Francisco, CA 94105 USA

Merson, Michael *Government Official*
World Health Organization, Ave Appia, Geneva 27, 1211, SWITZERLAND

Merten, Lauri *Golfer*
105 Foulk Road, Wilmington, DE 19803 USA

Mertens, Alan *Misc*
PacWest Racing Group, 150 Gasoline Alley Road, Indianapolis, IN 46222 USA

Merton, Robert C *Nobel Prize Laureate*
Harvard University, Business School, Boston, MA 02163 USA

Mertz, Edwin T *Misc*
1504 Via Delta Scala, Henderson, NV 89052 USA

Mertz, Francis J *Educator*
Farleigh Dickinson University, President's Office, Teaneck, NJ 07666 USA

Merullo, Lennie *Baseball Player*
Chicago Cubs, 159 Summer Ave, Reading, MA 01867-2825 USA

Merullo, Matt *Baseball Player*
Chicago White Sox, 8 Fox Run Rd, Madison, CT 06443-2052 USA

Merwin, John D *Governor*
PO Box 2213, New London, NH 03257 USA

Merwin, William Stanley *Writer*
Farleigh Dickinson University Press, 285 Madison Ave, Madison, NJ 07940 USA

Merz, Suzanne (Sue) *Hockey Player*
5 Douglas Dr, Greenwich, CT 06831 USA

Mesa, Carlos *President*
President's Office, Palacio de Gobierno, Plaza Murilla, La Paz, BOLIVIA

Mesa, Jose *Baseball Player*
Baltimore Orioles, 13173 SW 51st St, Miramar, FL 33027-5522 USA

Meschery, Tom *Basketball Player*
PO Box 1297, Truckee, CA 96160 USA

Meselson, Matthew S *Misc*
Harvard University, Fairchild Biochemistry Laboratories, Cambridge, MA 02138 USA

Mesereau, Thomas *Lawyer*
1875 Century Park E, Los Angeles, CA 90067 USA

Mesguich, Daniel *Actor, Director*
Agence Monita Derrieux, 17-21 Rue Duret, Paris, 75116, FRANCE

Mesic, Stipe *President*
Presidential Palace, Pantovcak 241, Zagreb, 10000, CROATIA

Mesina Stanley, Dianne *Producer*
United Talent Agency (UTA), 9560 Wilshire Blvd, Beverly Hills, CA 90212 USA

Meskill, Thomas J *Governor, Judge*
218 Stony Mill Lane, East Berlin, CT 06023 USA

Mesnil Du Buisson, Robert *Archaeologist*
Chateau de Champobert, Par Exmes, Orne, 61310, FRANCE

Messager, Annette *Artist*
146 Blvd Camelinat, Colombier-Fontaine, 92240, FRANCE

Messenger, Melinda *Model*
Arcadia Mgmt, 2-3 Golden Square, London, W1R 3AD, UNITED KINGDOM (UK)

Messer, Thomas M *Misc*
1105 Park Ave, New York, NY 10128 USA

Messerschmid, Ernst *Astronaut*
Universitat Stuttgart, Pfaffenwaldring 31, Stuttgart, 70569, GERMANY

Messerschmidt, J Alexander (Andy) *Baseball Player*
200 Lagunita Dr, Soquel, CA 95073 USA

Messersmith, Andy *Baseball Player*
California Angels, 200 Lagunita Dr, Soquel, CA 95073-9594 USA

Messick, Dale *Cartoonist*
Tribune Media Services, 435 N Michigan Ave, #1500, Chicago, IL 60611 USA

Messier, Mark D *Hockey Player*
205 W 57th St, New York, NY 10019 USA

Messina, Jim *Musician, Songwriter*
Entertainment Artists, 2409 21st Ave S, #100, Nashville, TN 37212 USA

Messina, Jo Dee *Musician, Songwriter*
PO Box 8031, Hermitage, TN 37076 USA

Messing, Debra *Actor*
Gersh Agency, 232 N Canon Dr, Beverly Hills, CA 90210 USA

Messner, Heinrich (Heini) *Skier*
Huebenweg 11, Steinach, 6150, AUSTRIA

Messner, Johnny *Actor*
McKeon-Valeo Management, 9107 Wilshire Blvd #321, Beverly Hills, CA 90210 USA

Messner, Reinhold *Mountaineer*
Schloss Juval, Kastelbell, Tschars, 39040, ITALY

Messner (Baker), Tammy Faye *Religious Leader*
1527 Woody Creek Rd, Matthews, NC 28105-8834 USA

Meszaros, Maria *Director*
Malfilm Studio, Lumumba Utca 174, Budapest, 1149, HUNGARY

Metallica *Musician*
Q Prime Inc, 729 Seventh Ave Fl 16, New York, NY 10019 USA

Metcalf, Eric Q *Football Player*
7465 S 114th St, Seattle, WA 98178 USA

Metcalf, John *Writer*
128 Lewis St, Ottawa, ON K2P 0S7, CANADA

Metcalf, Joseph III *Admiral*
4658 Charleston Terrace NW, Washington, DC 20007 USA

Metcalf, Laurie *Actor*
109 E 950 S, Victor, ID 83455 USA

Metcalf, Mark *Actor*
Peter Strain & Associates Inc (LA), 5724 W 3rd St #302, Los Angeles, CA 90036 USA

Metcalf, Shelby *Coach*
Texas A & M University, Athletic Dept, College Station, TX 77843 USA

Metcalf, Terrance R (Terry) *Football Player*
5112 S Fountain St, Seattle, WA 98178 USA

Metcalf, Tom *Baseball Player*
New York Yankees, 1390 Wisconsin River Dr, Port Edwards, WI 54469-1042 USA

Metcalfe, Burt
11800 Brookdale Lane, Studio City, CA 91604

Metcalfe, Jesse *Actor*
TalentWorks (LA), 3500 W Olive Ave #1400, Burbank, CA 91505 USA

Metcalfe, Robert M *Scientist*
Polaris Venture Partners, 1000 Winter St, #3350, Waltham, MA 02451 USA

Metheny, Pat
Endeavor Agency LLC (LA), 9601 Wilshire Blvd Fl 3, Beverly Hills, CA 90210 USA

Metheny, Patrick B (Pat) *Musician, Composer*
Ted Kurland, 173 Brighton Ave, Boston, MA 02134 USA

Method Man *Musician*
International Creative Mgmt, 8942 Wilshire Blvd, #219, Beverly Hills, CA 90211 USA

Metrano, Art *Actor*
131 N Croft Ave, #402, Los Angeles, CA 90048 USA

Metro, Charlie *Baseball Player*
Detroit Tigers, 7890 Indiana St, Arvada, CO 80007-7123 USA

Mette-Marit, Princess *Royalty*
Det Kongelige, Slottet Drammensvein 1, Oslo, 0010, NORWAY

Metzenbaum, Howard M *Senator*
Consumer Federation of America, 1424 16th St NW, Washington, DC 20036 USA

Metzger, Butch *Baseball Player*
San Francisco Giants, 6573 Park Riviera Way, Sacramento, CA 95831-1085 USA

Metzger, Henry *Misc*
3410 Taylor St, Chevy Chase, MD 20815 USA

Metzger, Roger *Baseball Player*
Chicago Cubs, 3560 Bluebonnet Blvd, Brenham, TX 77833-7180 USA

Metzig, Bill *Baseball Player*
Chicago White Sox, 2129 57th St, Lubbock, TX 79412-2625 USA

Metzler, Jim
6300 Wilshire Blvd. #2110, Los Angeles, CA 90048

Meulens, Hensley *Baseball Player*
New York Yankees, Kaya Cupldo 7, Curacao-Netherlands, ANTILLES

Mewes, Jason *Actor*
Craig Entertainment Group, 9903 Santa Monica Blvd #531, Beverly Hills, CA 90212 USA

Mey, Reinhard
Sigismundkorso 63, Berlin, GERMANY, D-13465

Mey, Uwe-Jens *Speed Skater*
Vulkanstr 22, Berlin, 10367, GERMANY

Meyer, Alejandra *Actor*
Televisa, Blvd Adolfo Lopez Mateos 232, Colonia San Angel INN, DF, CP 01060, MEXICO

Meyer, Armin H *Diplomat*
4610 Reno Road NW, Washington, DC 20008 USA

Meyer, Bess
PO Box 5617, Beverly Hills, CA 90210

Meyer, Bob *Baseball Player*
New York Yankees, PO Box 3024, Mission Viejo, CA 92690-1024 USA

Meyer, Breckin *Actor*
Brillstein/Grey, 9150 Wilshire Blvd, #350, Beverly Hills, CA 90212 USA

Meyer, Brian *Baseball Player*
Houston Astros, 33 Bank St, Medford, NJ 08055-2635 USA

Meyer, Dan *Baseball Player*
Detroit Tigers, 2633 Fountainhead Dr, San Ramon, CA 94583-1735 USA

Meyer, Daniel J *Business Person*
Milacron Inc, 2090 Florence Ave, Cincinnati, OH 45206 USA

Meyer, Debbie
PO Box 2076, Carmichael, CA 95609-2076

Meyer, Dina *Actor*
2804 6th St, Santa Monica, CA 90405 USA

Meyer, Edward C *General*
1101 S Arlington Ridge Road, #1116, Arlington, VA 22202 USA

Meyer, Jerome J *Business Person*
Tektronix Inc, 26600 Southwest Parkway, Wilsonville, OR 97070 USA

Meyer, Joey *Baseball Player*
Milwaukee Brewers, 392 Kaimake Loop, Kallua, HI 96734-2019 USA

Meyer, Karl H *Misc*
642 Wyndham Road, Teaneck, NJ 07666 USA

Meyer, Lawrence H *Economist, Government Official*
Federal Reserve Board, 20th & Constitution NW, Washington, DC 20551 USA

Meyer, Nicholas *Director*
Creative Artists Agency, 9830 Wilshire Blvd, Beverly Hills, CA 90212 USA

Meyer, Raymond J (Ray) *Coach*
2518 Cedar Glen Dr, Arlington Heights, IL 60005 USA

Meyer, Robert K *Misc*
3 Rawlings Place, Fadden, ACT, 2904, AUSTRALIA

Meyer, Russ *Producer, Photographer*
3121 Arrowhead Dr, Los Angeles, CA 90068 USA

Meyer, Scott *Baseball Player*
Oakland A's, 15625 N 54th Pl, Scottsdale, AZ 85254-1722 USA

Meyer Reyes, Deborah E (Debbie) *Swimmer*
Po Box 2076, Carmichael, CA 95609 USA

Meyer's Drysdale, Ann E *Basketball Player, Sportscaster*
6621 Doral Dr, Huntington Beach, CA 92648 USA

Meyerowitz, Elliot M *Biologist*
California Institute of Technology, Biology Dept, Pasadena, CA 91125 USA

Meyerowitz, Joel *Photographer*
817 W End Ave, New York, NY 10025 USA

Meyerriecks, Jeffrey *Musical Director*
Lindy Martin Mgmt, 5 Lob Lolly court, Pinehurst, NC 28374 USA

Meyers, Anne Akiko *Musician*
ICM Artists, 40 W 57th St, New York, NY 10019 USA

Meyers, Ari *Actor*
17 E 96th St, #7B, New York, NY 10128 USA

Meyers, Augie *Musician*
Encore Talent, 2137 Zercher Road, San Antonio, TX 78209 USA

Meyers, Chad *Baseball Player*
Chicago Cubs, 17620 Marcy St, Omaha, NE 68118-3545 USA

Meyers, David *Director*
Evolution Entertainment, 901 N Highland Ave, Los Angeles, CA 90038 USA

Meyers, David (Dave) *Basketball Player*
40629 Carmelina Circle, Temecula, CA 92591 USA

Meyers, Josh *Comedian*
William Morris Agency (WMA-LA), 1 William Morris Pl, Beverly Hills, CA 90212 USA

Meyers, Nancy *Director*
Waverly Films/Nancy Meyers Productions, 10202 W Washington Blvd, Crawford Bldg, Culver City, CA 90232 USA

Meyers, Seth *Actor, Comedian*
William Morris Agency (WMA-LA), 1
William Morris Pl, Beverly Hills, CA
90212 USA

Meyerson, Martin *Educator*
2016 Spruce St, Philadelphia, PA 19103
USA

Meyfarth, Ulrike
Friedensweg 59, Wesseling, GERMANY,
D-50389

Meyfarth, Ulrike Nasse *Track Athlete*
Buschweg 53, Odenthal, 51519,
GERMANY

Meysel, Inge
Sudstrand 13, Bullenhausen, GERMANY,
D-21217

Mezentseva, Galina *Ballerina*
Kirov Ballet Theatre, 1 Ploshchad Iskusstr,
Saint Petersburg, RUSSIA

Mezlekia, Nega *Writer*
Picador USA Books, 175 5th Ave, New
York, NY 10010 USA

Mfume, Kweisi *Misc*
NAACP, President's Office, 4805 Mount
Hope Dr, Baltimore, MD 21215 USA

Miadich, Bart *Baseball Player*
Anaheim Angels, 17841 Hillside Dr, Lake
Oswego, OR 97034-7525 USA

Miami Sound Machine
6205 Bird Rd., Miami, FL 33155

Miceli, Danny *Baseball Player*
Pittsburgh Pirates, 8037 Hook Cir,
Orlando, FL 32836-5340 USA

Miceli, Joe
189 Vanderbilt Ave., Brentwood LI, NY
11717

Micell, Justine *Actor*
Don Buchwald, 6500 Wilshire Blvd,
#2200, Los Angeles, CA 90048 USA

Micelotta, Mickey *Baseball Player*
Philadelphia Phillies, 3266 Jog Park Dr
#11, Greenacres, FL 33467-2014 USA

Michael *King*
Villa Serena, 77 Chemin Louis-Degallier,
Versoix-Geneva, 1290, SWITZERLAND

Michael, Alum E *Government Official*
National Assembly for Wales, Cardiff Bay,
Cardiff, CF99 1NA, WALES

Michael, Archbishop *Religious Leader*
Antiochian Orthodox Christian Church,
358 Mountain Road, Englewood, NJ
07631 USA

Michael, Bob *Politician*
1029 N. Glenwood St., Peoria, IL 61606

Michael, Eugene R (Gene) *Misc*
49 Union Ave, Upper Saddle River, NJ
07458 USA

Michael, ex-King
77 Chemin Louis Degallier, Versoix,
SWITZERLAND, 1290

Michael, Gary G *Business Person*
Alberston's Inc, 250 E Parkcenter Blvd,
Boise, ID 83706 USA

Michael, Gene *Baseball Player*
Pittsburgh Pirates, 49 Union Ave, Upper
Saddle River, NJ 07458-2024 USA

Michael, George *Musician, Songwriter*
2 Elgin Mews, London, W9 1NN, UNITED
KINGDOM (UK)

Michael, Prince & Princess of Kent
Kensington Palace, London, ENGLAND,
W8 5AF

Michael, Ralph *Actor, Writer, Director*
Michael Slessinger & Assoc, 8730 Sunset
Blvd #270, Los Angeles, CA 90069 USA

Michaels, Al
47 W. 66th St, New York, NY 10023

Michaels, Alan R (Al) *Sportscaster*
ABC-TV, Sports Dept, 77 W 66th St, New
York, NY 10023 USA

Michaels, Beverly
11921 Weddington, No. Hollywood, CA
91601

Michaels, Bret *Musician*
3910 Brick Church Pike, Nashville, TN
37207-1504 USA

Michaels, Brett *Musician*
H K Mgmt, 9200 W Sunset Blvd, #530,
Los Angeles, CA 90069 USA

Michaels, Eugene H *Misc*
Alzheimer's Disease Research, 15825
Shady Grove Road, Rockville, MD 20850
USA

Michaels, Fern *Writer*
9 David Court, Edison, NJ 08820 USA

Michaels, James W *Editor*
Forbes Magazine, Editorial Dept, 60 5th
Ave, New York, NY 10011 USA

Michaels, Jason *Baseball Player*
Philadelphia Phillies, 8609 Leighton Dr,
Tampa, FL 33614-1723 USA

Michaels, Lorne *Producer, Writer*
Broadway Video, 1619 Broadway, #900,
New York, NY 10019 USA

Michaels, Louis A (Lou) *Football Player*
69 Grace St, Swoyersville, PA 18704 USA

Michaels, Marilyn
185 West End Ave., New York, NY 10023

Michaels, Michael
1640 S. Sepulveda Blvd. #218, Los
Angeles, CA 90025-7510

Michaels, Shawn *Wrestler*
World Wrestling Entertainment (WWE),
1241 E Main St, Stamford, CT 06905 USA

Michaels, Tammy Lynn *Actor*
Peter Strain & Associates Inc (LA), 5724 W
3rd St #302, Los Angeles, CA 90036 USA

Michaels, Walter (Walt) *Football Player,
Football Coach*
282 Michaels Road, Shickshinny, PA
18655 USA

Michaelsen, Kari *Actor*
Kazarian/Spencer, 11365 Ventura Blvd,
#100, Studio City, CA 91604 USA

Michalak, Chris *Baseball Player*
Arizona Diamondbacks, 14747 W
Hickory Ave, Lemont, IL 60439-7903 USA

Michaleczewski, Dariusz *Boxer*
Universum Box-Promotion, Am Stadtrand
27, Hamburg, 22047, GERMANY

Michals, Duane *Photographer*
109 E 19th St, New York, NY 10003 USA

Micheaux, Nicki *Actor*
MBST Entertainment, 345 N Maple D
#200, Suite 200, Beverly Hills, CA 90210
USA

Micheel, Shaun *Golfer*
Professional Golfer's Assn, PO Box
109601, Palm Beach Gardens, FL 33410
USA

Michel, Alex *Reality TV Star*
PO Box 46605, Los Angeles, CA 90046
USA

Michel, F Curtis *Astronaut*
2101 University Blvd, Houston, TX 77030
USA

Michel, Hartmut *Nobel Prize Laureate*
Max-Planck Institut, Heinrich-Hoffmann-
Str 7, Frankfort, 60528, GERMANY

Michel, Jean-Louis *Oceanographer,
Scientist*
IFREMER, Center de Toulon, La Seyne dur
Mer, Toulon, 83500, FRANCE

Michel, Paul R *Judge*
US Court of Appeals, 717 Madison Place
NW, Washington, DC 20439 USA

Michele, Michael *Actor*
PMK Public Relations, 8500 Wilshire
Blvd, #700, Beverly Hills, CA 90211 USA

Michele, Yvette
250 W. 57th St. #821, New York, NY
10107

Micheler, Elisabeth *Athlete*
Gruntenstr 45, Augsburg, 86163,
GERMANY

Michell, Keith *Actor*
Chatto & Linnit, Prince of Wales, Coventry
St, London, W1V 7FE, UNITED
KINGDOM (UK)

Michell, Roger *Director*
Duncan Heath, Paramount House, 162
Wardour, London, W1V 3AT, UNITED
KINGDOM (UK)

Michelle, Lisa *Stylist*
3Arts, 3176 Prairie Ave, Miami Beach, FL
33140 USA

Michelle, Sheley *Actor*
William Morris Agency (WMA-LA), 1
William Morris Pl, Beverly Hills, CA
90212 USA

Michelmore, Guy
72 Goldsmith Ave., London, ENGLAND,
W3 6HN

Michelmore, Lawrence *Government
Official*
4924 Sentinel Dr, Bethesda, MD 20816
USA

Michels, John J *Football Player*
10720 Nesbitt Ave S, Bloomington, MN
55437 USA

Michels, Rinus *Football Coach*
Hotel Breitenbacher Hof, H-Heine-Allee
36, Dusseldorf, 40213, GERMANY

Michener, Charles D *Misc*
1706 W 2nd St, Lawrence, KS 66044 USA

Michie, Donald *Scientist*
6 Inveralmond Grove, Cramond,
Edinburg, EH4 6RA, SCOTLAND

Michiko *Royalty*
Imperial Palace, 1-1 Chiyoda-ku, Tokyo, 100, JAPAN

Michnik, Adam *Editor*
Czerha 8/10, Warsaw, 00732, POLAND

Michos, Anastas N *Cinematographer*
Gersh Agency, 232 N Canon Dr, Beverly Hills, CA 90210 USA

Mickal, Abe *Football Player, Physicist*
774 Topaz St, New Orleans, LA 70124 USA

Mickelson, Ed *Baseball Player*
St Louis Cardinals, 1532 Charlemont Dr, Chesterfield, MO 63017-4604 USA

Mickelson, Phil *Golfer*
Gaylord Sports Mgmt, 14646 N Kierland Blvd, #230, Scottsdale, AZ 85254 USA

Mickens, Glenn *Baseball Player*
Brooklyn Dodgers, 5920 Kini Pl, Kapaa, HI 96746-8938 USA

Middendorf, J William II *Secretary, Diplomat*
565 W Main Road, Little Compton, RI 02837 USA

Middendorf, Tracy *Actor*
PO Box 480410, Los Angeles, CA 90048 USA

Middle of the Road
18 Irvine Dr. Linwood, Refrewshire, ENGLAND

Middlebrook, Jason *Baseball Player*
San Diego Padres, 3309 Glenview Ave, Austin, TX 78703-1446 USA

Middleton, Mike *Model*
Louisa Models, Ebersberger Str 9, Munich, 81679, GERMANY

Middleton, Rick *Hockey Player*
11 Wentworth Ave, Hampton, NH 03842 USA

Middleton, Terdell *Football Player*
1893 Prospect St, Memphis, TN 38206 USA

Midkiff, Dale *Actor*
11541 Morrison St, North Hollywood, CA 91601 USA

Midler, Bette *Musician, Actor*
Sussman Assoc, 1222 16th Ave S, #300, Nashville, TN 37212 USA

Midnight Fish
Samlandstr. 32, Munich, GERMANY, D-81825

Midnight Oil
Box 186 Glebe, Sydney, AUSTRALIA, NSW 2037

Midori *Musician*
Midori Foundation, 850 7th Ave, #705, New York, NY 10019 USA

Miechur, Thomas F *Misc*
Cement & Allied Workers Union, 2500 Brickdale, Elk Grove Village, IL 60007 USA

Mieczko, A J *Hockey Player*
295 Central Park W, #9G, New York, NY 10024 USA

Mielke, Gary *Baseball Player*
Texas Rangers, 1718 Orchid Dr S, Mankato, MN 56003-1435 USA

Mientkiewicz, Douglas (Doug) *Baseball Player*
Minnesota Twins, 21770 Southern Hills Dr Unit 202, Estero, FL 33928-7024 USA

Mierkowicz, Ed *Baseball Player*
Detroit Tigers, 7530 Macomb St Apt 1A, Grosse Ile, MI 48138-1522 USA

Mieske, Matt *Baseball Player*
Milwaukee Brewers, 3645 N Sonoran Hts, Mesa, AZ 85207-1826 USA

Mieto, Juha *Skier*
General Delivery, Mieto, FINLAND

Migenes, Julia *Opera Singer*
Artists Group, 10100 Santa Monica Blvd, #2490, Los Angeles, CA 90067 USA

Mighty Clouds of Joy
PO Box 570815, Tarzana, CA 91357

Mighty Morphin Power Rangers
26020-A Avenue Hall, Valencia, CA 91355

Mignola, Mike *Cartoonist*
Dark Horse Publishing, 10956 SE Main St, Portland, OR 97216 USA

Miguel, Luis *Musician*
William Morris Agency, 1325 Ave of the Americas, New York, NY 10019 USA

Mihaly, Andras *Composer*
Verhalom Ter 9B, Budapest II, 1025, HUNGARY

Mihm, Chris *Basketball Player*
Celeland Cavallers, Gund Arena, 1 Center Court, Cleveland, OH 44115 USA

Mihok, Dash *Actor*
Handprint Entertainment, 1100 Glendon Ave, #1000, Los Angeles, CA 90024 USA

Mikan, George L Jr *Basketball Player*
8776 E Shea Blvd, PO Box 3A317, Scottsdale, AZ 85260 USA

Mike-Mayer, Istvan (Steve) *Football Player*
681 Lincoln Ave, Glen Rock, NJ 07452 USA

Mike-Mayer, Nicholas (Nick) *Football Player*
681 Lincoln Ave, Glen Rock, NJ 07452 USA

Mikell, George
23 Shuttleworth Rd, London, ENGLAND, SW11

Mikhalchenko, Alla A *Ballerina*
Malaya Gruzinskaya St 12/18, Moscow, 123242, RUSSIA

Mikhalkov, Nikita *Director*
Maly Kozikhinksy Per 4, #16-17, Moscow, 103001, RUSSIA

Mikhalkov-Konchalovsky, Andrei S *Director*
Malaya Gruzinskaya 28 #130, Moscow, 123557, RUSSIA

Miki, Minouri *Composer*
1-11-6 Higashi Nogawa, Komae-shi, Tokyo, 201, JAPAN

Mikita, Stanley (Stan) *Hockey Player*
CSAS, PO Box 60036, RPO Glen Abbey, Oakville, ON L6M 3H2, CANADA

Mikkelsen, A Verner (Vern) *Basketball Player, Golfer*
17715 Breconville Road, Wayzata, MN 55391 USA

Miko, Isabella *Actor*
Evolution Talent, 1776 Broadway #1500, New York, NY 10019

Miko, Izabella *Actor*
Evolution Talent, 1776 Broadway #1500, New York, NY 10019 USA

Mikulski, Barbara *Senator*
1201 Pemberton Dr, Salisbury, MD 21801-2497 USA

Mikva, Abner J *Judge*
442 New Jersey Ave SE, Washington, DC 20003 USA

Milandro, Kristina
2518 Cardigan Ct., Los Angeles, CA 90077-1337

Milano, Alyssa *Actor*
25 Sea Colony Dr, Santa Monica, CA 90405 USA

Milano, Fred *Musician*
Paramount Entertainment, PO Box 12, Far Hills, NJ 07931 USA

Milbrett, Tiffeny *Soccer Player*
US Soccer Federation, 1801 S Prairle Ave, Chicago, IL 60616 USA

Milbury, Mike *Hockey Player, Coach*
98 Claydon Road, Garden City, NY 11530 USA

Milch, David *Writer, Producer*
Endeavor Talent Agency, 9701 Wilshire Blvd #1000, Beverly Hills, CA 90212 USA

Milchan, Arnon *Producer*
Regency Enterprises, 4000 Warner Blvd, #66, Burbank, CA 91522 USA

Mildren, L Jack Jr *Football Player, Football Executive*
1701 Guilford Lane, Nichols Hills, OK 73120 USA

Miledi, Ricardo *Biologist*
9 Gibbs Court, Irvine, CA 92612 USA

Miles, Darius *Basketball Player*
Cleveland Cavaliers, Gund Arena, 1 Center Court, Cleveland, OH 44115 USA

Miles, Joanna *Actor*
2062 N Vine St, Los Angeles, CA 90068 USA

Miles, John R (Jack) *Writer*
3568 Mountain View Ave, Pasadena, CA 91107 USA

Miles, John W *Geophysicist*
8448 Paseo del Ocaso, La Jolla, CA 92037 USA

Miles, Josephine *Writer*
2275 Virginia St, Berkeley, CA 94709 USA

Miles, Mark *Tennis Player, Misc*
Assn of Tennis Pros, 200 Tournament Players Road, Ponte Vedra Beach, FL 32082 USA

Miles, Sarah *Actor*
Chithurst Manor, Trotton near Petersfield, Hants, GU31 5EU, UNITED KINGDOM (UK)

Miles, Sylvia *Actor*
240 Central Park South, New York, NY 10019 USA

Miles, Vera *Actor*
PO Box 1599, Palm Desert, CA 92261 USA

Miles-Clark, Jearl *Track Athlete*
J J Clark, University of Florida, Athletic Dept, Gainsville, FL 32604 USA

Milgram, Stanley *Doctor*
City Universtiy of New York, Graduate Center, New York, NY 10036 USA

Milhoan, Michael *Actor*
Sanders/Armstrong Management, 2120 Colorado Blvd #120, Santa Monica, CA 90404 USA

Milian, Christina *Actor*
Innovative Artists (LA), 1505 Tenth St, Santa Monica, CA 90401 USA

Milian, Judge Marilyn
6922 Hollywood Blvd. #415, Hollywood, CA 90028

Milicevic, Ivana *Actor, Model*
United Talent Agency (UTA), 9560 Wilshire Blvd, Beverly Hills, CA 90212 USA

Milius, John F *Director, Writer*
888 Linda Flora Dr, Los Angeles, CA 90049 USA

Milken, Michael R *Financier*
4543 Tara Dr, Encino, CA 91436 USA

Milla, Roger *Soccer Player*
Federation Camerounaise de Football, BP 1116, Yaounde, CAMEROON

Millar, Jeffrey L (Jeff) *Cartoonist*
1301 Spring Oaks Circle, Houston, TX 77055 USA

Millar, Miles *Writer*
Millar/Gough Ink, 3800 Barham Blvd, Suite 503, Los Angeles, CA 90068 USA

Millcic, Darko *Basketball Player*
Detroit Pistons, Palace, 2 Championship Dr, Auburn Hills, MI 48326 USA

Millen, Matt G *Football Player, Football Executive*
PO Box 196, Durham, PA 18039 USA

Miller, Aaron *Hockey Player*
1501 10th St, Manhattan Beach, CA 90266 USA

Miller, Alan *Journalist*
Los Angeles Times, Editorial Dept, 202 W 1st St, Los Angeles, CA 90012 USA

Miller, Alice *Golfer*
Ladies Pro Golf Assn, 100 International Golf Dr, Daytona Beach, Fl, 32124 USA

Miller, Allan *Actor*
Douglas Gorman Rothacker Wilhelm, 1501 Broadway #703, New York, NY 10036 USA

Miller, Andre *Basketball Player*
Denver Nuggets, Pepsi Center, 1000 Chopper Circle, Denver, CO 80204 USA

Miller, Arthur *Writer*
RR 1 Box 320, Tophet Road, Roxbury, CT 06783 USA

Miller, Ben *Actor, Producer*
International Creative Management (ICM-UK), Oxford House, 76 Oxford St, London, W1N OAX, UNITED KINGDOM (UK)

Miller, Bode *Skier*
63 Eastern Valley Road, Franconia, NH 03580 USA

Miller, Brad *Basketball Player*
Sacramento Kings, Arco Arena, 1 Sports Parkway, Sacramento, CA 95834 USA

Miller, Buddy *Musician*
Mark Pucci Media, 5000 Oak Bluff Court, Atlanta, GA 30350 USA

Miller, C Arden *Doctor*
350 Caroline Meadows Villa, Capel Hill, NC 27517 USA

Miller, C Ray *Religious Leader*
United Brethren in Christ, 302 Lake St, Huntington, IN 46750 USA

Miller, Charles D *Business Person*
Avery Dennison Corp, 150 N Organge Grove Blvd, Pasadena, CA 91103 USA

Miller, Cheryl *Actor*
Fisherman Agency Inc, 6767 Forest Lawn Drive, #101, Los Angeles, CA 90068

Miller, Cheryl D *Basketball Player, Coach*
3206 Ellington Dr, Los Angeles, CA 90068 USA

Miller, Christa *Actor*
K&H, 1212 Ave of Americas, #3, New York, NY 10036 USA

Miller, Christine Cook *Judge*
US Claims Court, 717 Madison Place NW, Washington, DC 20439 USA

Miller, Coco *Basketball Player*
Washington Mystics, MCI Center, 601 F St NW, Washington, DC 20004 USA

Miller, Dan *Musician*
Trans Continental Records, 7380 Sand Lake Road, #350, Orlando, FL 32819 USA

Miller, David *Cartoonist*
167 Tremont St, Rehoboth, MA 02769 USA

Miller, Denise *Actor, Producer*
Bob Waters Agency, 9301 Wilshire Blvd, Suite 300, Beverly Hills, CA 90210 USA

Miller, Dennis *Actor, Comedian*
814 N Mansfield Ave, Los Angeles, CA 90038 USA

Miller, Denny *Actor*
9612 Gavin Stone Ave, Las Vegas, NV 89145 USA

Miller, Elizabeth C *Doctor, Educator*
1822 Masters Lane, Madison, WI 53719 USA

Miller, Eugene A *Financier*
Comerica Inc, 500 Woodward Ave, Detroit, MI 48226 USA

Miller, Frank *Actor, Writer*
Shapiro-Lichtman Talent Agency, 8827 Beverly Blvd, Los Angeles, CA 90048 USA

Miller, Frank *Cartoonist*
Dark House Publishing, 10956 SE Main St, Milwaukie, OR 97222 USA

Miller, G William *Secretary, Business Person*
G William Miller Co, 1215 19th St NW, Washington, DC 20036 USA

Miller, George *Producer, Director*
Kennedy/Miller Productions, 30 Orwell Street, Kings Cross, NSW, Sydney, 2011, Australia

Miller, George A *Doctor*
16 Willow St, Princeton, NJ 08542 USA

Miller, George D *General*
20 Phillips Pond South, Natick, MA 01760 USA

Miller, George T (Kennedy) *Director*
30 Orwell St, King's Cross, Sydney, NSW, 2011, AUSTRALIA

Miller, Glenn (Orchestra)
605 Crescent Exec. Ct. #300, Lake Mary, FL 32746

Miller, Glenn Birthplace Society
PO Box 61, Clarinda, IA 51632

Miller, Glenn Society
18 Crendon St., High Wycombe, Bucks., ENGLAND

Miller, Harvey R *Attorney General*
Weil Gotshal Manges, 797 5th Ave, New York, NY 10153 USA

Miller, J Ronald *Religious Leader*
Int'l Community Churches Council, 21116 Washington Parkway, Frankfort, IL 60423 USA

Miller, James C III *Government Official*
Citizens for Sound Economy, 1250 H St NW, Washington, DC 20005 USA

Miller, Jamir *Football Player*
331 Grenadine Way, Hercules, CA 94547 USA

Miller, Jeff
1301 Spring Oaks Circle, Houston, TX 77055

Miller, Jeremy *Actor*
5255 Vesper Ave, Sherman Oaks, CA 91411 USA

Miller, Jerry *Admiral*
Smithsonian Institution Press, 750 9th St NW #4300, Washington, DC 20560 USA

Miller, Jody *Musician*
PO Box 413, Blanchard, OK 73010 USA

Miller, Joel McKinnon *Actor*
Greene & Associates, 526 N Larchmont Blvd #201, Los Angeles, CA 90004 USA

Miller, John *Commentator*
ABC-TV, News Dept, 77 W 66th St, New York, NY 10023 USA

Miller, John L (Johnny) *Golfer*
1621 Ripley Run, Wellington, FL 33414 USA

Miller, Johnny
PO Box 2260, Napa, CA 94558

Miller, Johnny Lee
8730 Sunset Blvd. #490, Los Angeles, CA 90069

Miller, Jon *Sportscaster*
ESPN-TV, Sports Dept, ESPN Plaza 935 Middle St, Bristol, CT 06010 USA

Miller, Jonathan *Director*
63 Gloucester Crescent, London, NW1, UNITED KINGDOM (UK)

Miller, Jonny Lee *Actor*
I F A Talent Agency, 8730 Sunset Blvd,
#490, Los Angeles, CA 90069 USA

Miller, Joyce D *Misc*
Amalgamated Clothing & Textile Workers,
1710 Broadway, #3, New York, NY
10019 USA

Miller, Julie *Musician, Songwriter*
Mark Pucci Media, 5000 Oak Bluff Court,
Atlanta, GA 30350 USA

Miller, Keith H *Governor*
3605 Arctic Blvd, #1001, Anchorage, AK
99503 USA

Miller, Kelly *Basketball Player*
Indiana Fever, Conseco Fieldhouse, 125 S
Pennsylvania, Indianapolis, IN 46204 USA

Miller, Kenny
5312 Eagle Lake Dr., Palm Beach
Gardens, FL 33418

Miller, Kristen *Actor*
Lighthouse, 409 N Camden Dr, #202,
Beverly Hills, CA 90210 USA

Miller, Lajos *Opera Singer*
Balogh Adam Utca 28, Budapest, 1026,
HUNGARY

Miller, Larry *Actor, Comedian*
Spivak Entertainment, 11845 W Olympic
Blvd, #1125, Los Angeles, CA 90064 USA

Miller, Larry H *Misc*
Utah Jazz, Delta Center, 301 W South
Temple, Salt Lake City, UT 84101 USA

Miller, Lawrence (Larry) *Basketball Player*
1300 Paddock Dr, Releigh, NC 27609
USA

Miller, Lennox *Track Athlete*
1213 N Lake Ave, Pasadena, CA 91104
USA

Miller, Lenore *Misc*
Retail/Wholesale/Department Store Union,
30 E 29th St, New York, NY 10016 USA

Miller, Linda G
242 Conway Ave, Los Angeles, CA
90024-2602 USA

Miller, Linda Lael *Writer*
Pocket Star Books, 1230 Ave of Americas,
New York, NY 10020 USA

Miller, Mark *Musician*
Sawyer Brown Inc, 5200 Old Hardling
Road, Franklin, TN 37064 USA

Miller, Mark-Thomas
280 S. Beverly Dr. #400, Beverly Hills,
CA 90212

Miller, Marvin J *Misc*
211 E 70th St, New York, NY 10021 USA

Miller, Mike *Basketball Player*
Memphis Grizzlies, 175 Toyota Plaza,
#150, Memphis, TN 38103 USA

Miller, Mildred *Opera Singer*
PO Box 110108, Pittsburgh, PA 15232
USA

Miller, Mitch *Conductor, Musical Director*
345 W 58th St, New York, NY 10019
USA

Miller, Mulgrew *Musician*
3725 Farmersville Road, Easton, PA
18045 USA

Miller, Nancy (Ann) *Writer, Producer*
International Creative Management
(ICM-LA), 8942 Wilshire Blvd, Beverly
Hills, CA 90211 USA

Miller, Nate *Boxer*
1214 Allengrove St, Philadelphia, PA
19124 USA

Miller, Nicole J *Fashion Designer*
780 Madison Ave, New York, NY 10021
USA

Miller, Nolan *Fashion Designer*
Nolan Miller Collection, 241 S Robertson
Blvd, Beverly Hills, CA 90211 USA

Miller, Oliver *Basketball Player*
2912 S Meadow Dr, Fort WOrth, TX
76133 USA

Miller, Omar Benson *Actor*
MBST Entertainment, 345 N Maple D
#200, Suite 200, Beverly Hills, CA 90210
USA

Miller, Penelope Ann *Actor*
United Talent Agency, 9560 Wilshire
Blvd, #500, Beverly Hills, CA 90212 USA

Miller, Percy (Master P) *Musician, Actor*
Agency West Entertainment, 6255 West
Sunset Blvd, Suite 908, Hollywood, CA
90028 USA

Miller, Peter North *Business Person*
Dawson House, 5 Jewry St, London, EC3N
2EX, UNITED KINGDOM (UK)

Miller, Raymond R (Ray) *Baseball Player*
PO Box 41, New Athens, OH 43981 USA

Miller, Reginald W (Reggie) *Basketball
Player*
14301 East 113th St, Fortville, IN 46040
USA

Miller, Robert N (Red) *Football Coach*
3841 S Narcissis Way, Denver, CO 80237
USA

Miller, Shannon *Gymnast*
221 Magill Dr, Grafton, MA 01519 USA

Miller, Stanley L *Misc*
University of California, Chemistry Dept,
La Jolla, CA 92093 USA

Miller, Steve *Musician, Songwriter,
Musical Director*
PO Box 12680, Seattle, WA 98111 USA

Miller, Stuart L (Stu) *Baseball Player*
3701 Ocaso Court, Cameron Park, CA
95682 USA

Miller, Tangi *Actor*
Gersh Agency, 232 N Canon Dr, Beverly
Hills, CA 90210 USA

Miller, Ty *Actor*
David Shapira, 15821 Ventura Blvd #235,
Encino, CA 91436 USA

Miller, Valarie Rae
3500 W. Olive Ave. #1400, Burbank, CA
91505

Miller, Warren *Photographer*
505 Pler Ave, Hermosa Beach, CA 90254
USA

Miller, Wentworth *Actor*
Blue Max Management, 1802 North
Kenmore Avenue, Los Angeles, CA 90027
USA

Miller, Wiley *Cartoonist*
345 North Canon Dr, Santa Barbara, CA
93105 USA

Miller, Willie T *Football Player*
308 Martin Dr, Birmingham, AL 35215
USA

Miller-Lawrence, Christa *Actor*
Wolf/Kasteler PR, 335 N Maple Dr #351,
Beverly Hills, CA 90210 USA

Millett, Kate *Writer*
20 Old Overlook Rd, Poughkeepsie, NY
12603 USA

Millett, Lewis L *War Hero*
Korean War Memorial Patriotic Hall, 1816
Figueroa, #700, Los Angeles, CA 90015
USA

Millhauser, Steven *Writer*
235 Caroline St, Saratoga Springs, NY
12866 USA

Millionaire, Tony *Artist*
Fantagraphics Books, 7563 Lake City
Way, Seattle, WA 98115 USA

Millman, Irving *Inventor*
310 Windsor Circle, Cherry Hill, NY
08002 USA

Millo, Aprile E *Opera Singer*
Columbia Artists Mgmt Inc, 165 W 57th
St, New York, NY 10019 USA

Milloy, Lawyer *Football Player*
Buffalo Bills, 1 Bills Dr, Orchard Park, NY
14127 USA

Mills, Alley *Actor*
444 Carol Canal, Venice, CA 90291 USA

Mills, Billy *Track Athlete*
Billy Mills Speakers Bureau, The, 7760
Winding Way #723, Fair Oaks, CA 95628
USA

Mills, Curtis *Track Athlete*
328 Lake St, Lufkin, TX 75904 USA

Mills, Donna *Actor*
253 26th St, #259, Santa Monica, CA
90402 USA

Mills, Eddie
9200 Sunset Blvd. #1130, Los Angeles,
CA 90069

Mills, Erie *Opera Singer*
John J Miller, 801 W 18th St, #20, New
York, NY 10033 USA

Mills, Frank *Musician, Composer*
Rocklands Talent, PO Box 1282,
Peterborough, ON K9L 7H5, CANADA

Mills, Hayley *Actor, Musician*
Chatto & Linnit, Prince of Wales, Coventry
ST, London, W1V 7FE, UNITED
KINGDOM (UK)

Mills, Jordan
6500 Wilshire Blvd. #2200, Los Angeles,
CA 90048

Mills, Judson *Actor*
2401 West Olive Ave, Suite 290, Burbank,
CA 91506 USA

Mills, Juliet *Actor*
Waters & Nicolosi, 1501 Broadway, New
York, NY 10036 USA

Mills, Kyle *Writer*
William Morris Agency, 151 El Camino
Dr, Beverly Hills, CA 90212 USA

Mills, Mike *Musician*
REM/Athens Ltd, PO Box 8032, Athens, GA 30603 USA

Mills, Samuel D (Sam) Jr *Football Player*
Carolina Panthers, Ericsson Stadium, 800 S Mint St, Cahrlotte, NC 28202 USA

Mills, Sir John *Actor*
Hill House, Denham Village, Buckinghamshire, UNITED KINGDOM (UK)

Mills, Stephanie *Actor, Musician*
Associated Booking Corp, 1995 Broadway, #501, New York, NY 10023 USA

Mills, Terry *Basketball Player*
Indiana Pacers, Conseco Fieldhouse, 125 S Pennsylvania, Indianapolis, IN 46204 USA

Mills, William M (Billy) *Track Athlete*
7760 Winding Way, Fair Oaks, CA 95628 USA

Millsaps, Knox *Engineer*
323 NW 24th St, Gainesville, FL 32607 USA

Millwood, Kevin A *Baseball Player*
300 Leesville Ave, Bessemer City, NC 28016 USA

Milmoe, Caroline *Actor*
Nigel Martin-Smith, 41 S King St, Manchester, M2 6DE, UNITED KINGDOM (UK)

Milner, Anthony F D *Composer*
147 Heythorp St, Southfields, London, SW18 5BT, UNITED KINGDOM (UK)

Milner, Martin *Actor*
3106 Azahar Street, Carlsbad, CA 92009 USA

Milnes, Sherrill E *Opera Singer*
Herbert Barrett, 266 W 37th St, #2000, New York, NY 10018 USA

Milnor, John W *Mathematician*
3 Laurel Lane, Setauket, NY 11733 USA

Milo, Sandra
Viale Liegi 42, Rome, ITALY, I-00198

Milongo, Andre *Prime Minister*
Union for Democracy & Republic, Brazzaville, CONGO REPUBLIC

Milos, Sofia *Actor*
Untitled Entertainment (LA), 8436 W 3rd St #650, Los Angeles, CA 90048 USA

Milosz, Czeslaw *Nobel Prize Laureate*
University of California, Slavic Languages Dept, Berkeley, CA 94720 USA

Milow, Keith *Artist*
32 W 20th St, New York, NY 10011 USA

Milsap, Ronnie *Musician, Songwriter*
PO Box 40665, Nashville, TN 37204 USA

Milsome, Doug *Cinematographer*
Simth/Gosnell/Nicholson, PO Box 1156, Studio City, CA 91614 USA

Milstein, Elliott *Educator*
American University, President's Office, Washington, DC 20016 USA

Milton, DeLisha *Basketball Player*
Los Angeles Sparks, Staples Center, 1111 S Figueroa St, Los Angeles, CA 90015 USA

Milva
9 via Gabrio Serbelloni, Milan, ITALY, I-20122

Mimieux, Yvette *Actor*
Sterling/Winters, 10877 Wilshire Blvd, #15, L, CA 90024 USA

Mimoun, Alain *Track Athlete*
27 Ave Edouard-Jenner, Champigny-sur-Marne, 94500, FRANCE

Mims, Madeline Manning *Track Athlete*
7477 E 48th St, #83-4, Tulsa, OK 74145 USA

Min, Gao *Misc*
Olympic Committee, 9 Tuyuguan, Beijing, CHINA

Mincer, Jacob *Economist*
448 Riverside Dr, New York, NY 10027 USA

Mindel, Lee F *Architect*
Shelton Mindel Assoc, 216 W 18th St, New York, NY 10011 USA

Mindell, Earl *Writer*
Hay House, PO Box 5100, Carlsbad, CA 92018-5100

Minds, Simple *Music Group*
Solo Agency Ltd (UK), 55 Fulham High St, London, SW6 3JJ, United Kingdom

Minehan, Cathy E *Financier, Government Official*
Federal Reserve Bank, 600 Atlantic Ave, Boston, MA 02210 USA

Miner, Roger J *Judge*
US Court of Appeals, 445 Broadway, #414, Albany, NY 12207 USA

Miner, Steve *Director*
1137 2nd St, #103, Santa Monica, CA 90403 USA

Mineta, Norman Y *Secretary*
Transportation Department, 400 7th St SW, Washington, DC 20590 USA

Ming, Tsai *Chef*
Food Network, 1180 Ave of Americas, #1200, New York, NY 10036 USA

Ming-Na, Wen *Actor*
9903 Santa Monica, #575, Beverly Hills, CA 90212 USA

Minghella, Anthony *Director*
Judy Daish, 2 Saint Charles Place, London, W10 6EG, UNITED KINGDOM (UK)

Mingus, Charles
484 W. 43rd St. #43-S, New York, NY 10036

Minh, Tran *Dancer, Choreographer*
2014 NE 47th Ave, Portland, OR 97123 USA

Minisi, Anthony S (Skip) *Football Player*
300 Continental Lane, Paoli, PA 19301 USA

Mink, Rep *Politician*
PO Box 50144, Honolulu, HI 96850

Minkoff, Rob *Director*
Creative Artists Agency, 9830 Wilshire Blvd, Beverly Hills, CA 90212 USA

Minnelli, Liza *Musician, Actor*
Gersh Agency, The (LA), 232 N Canon Dr, Beverly Hills, CA 90210 USA

Minnifield, Frank *Football Player*
4809 Chaffey Lane, Lexington, KY 40515 USA

Minogue, Danil *Musician*
PO Box 46824, London, SW11 3WS, UNITED KINGDOM (UK)

Minogue, Dannii *Musician*
Shout! Promotions, Holden House #1 Holden Rd, Leigh, Greater Manchester, Wn7 1EX, UNITED KINGDOM (UK)

Minogue, Kylie *Musician, Actor*
Terry Blamey Mgmt, 329 Montague St, Albert Park, VIC, 3206, AUSTRALIA

Minor, Michael
280 S. Beverly Dr. #400, Beverly Hills, CA 90212

Minor, Rickey *Musical Director*
William Morris Agency (WMA-LA), 1 William Morris Pl, Beverly Hills, CA 90212 USA

Minor, Ronald R *Religious Leader*
Pentecostal Church of God, 4901 Pennsylvania, Joplin, MO 64804 USA

Minor, Shane *Musician*
ESP Mgmt, 838 N Doheny Dr, #302, West Hollywood, CA 90069 USA

Minoso, Minnie
805 Main Rd., Independence, MO 64056

Minoso, Saturino O A A (Minnie) *Basketball Player, Coach*
324 W 35th St, Chicago, IL 60616 USA

Minow, Newton N *Government Official*
179 E Lake Shore Dr, #15W, Chicago, IL 60611 USA

Minsky, Marvin L *Scientist*
Massachusetts Institute of Technology, Computer Sci Dept, Cambridge, MA 02139 USA

Minter, Kelly *Actor*
Marshak Wyckoff, 280 S Beverly Dr, #400, Beverly Hills, CA 90212 USA

Minter, Kristin *Actor*
Baumgarten, 1041 N Formosa Ave, #200, West Hollywood, CA 90046 USA

Mintoff, Dominic *Prime Minister*
Olives, Xintill St, Tarxien, MALTA

Minton, Yvonne F *Opera Singer*
Ingpen & Williams, 26 Wadham Road, London, SW15 2LR, UNITED KINGDOM (UK)

Mintz, Shiomo *Musician*
I C M Artists, 40 W 57th St, New York, NY 10019 USA

Miou-Miou *Actor*
VMA, 20 Ave Rapp, Paris, 75008, FRANCE

Mir, Isabelle *Skier*
Saint-Lary, 65170, FRANCE

Mira, George *Football Player*
19225 SW 128th Court, Miami, FL 33177 USA

Mirabella, Grace *Editor, Publisher*
Mirabella Magazine, 200 Madison Ave, New York, NY 10016 USA

Miracles, The
141 Dunbar Ave., Fords, NJ 08863

Miranda, Willie
5502 Whitwood Rd., Baltimore, MD 21208

Mirer, Rick
11220 NE 53rd St., Kirkland, WA 98033

Miriciolu, Nelly *Opera Singer*
53 Midhurst Ave, Muswell Hill, London, N10, UNITED KINGDOM (UK)

Mirikitani, Janice *Writer*
Glide Memorial United Methodist Church, 330 Ellis St, San Francisco, CA 94102 USA

Mirisch, Walter M *Producer*
647 Warner Ave, Los Angeles, CA 90024 USA

Mirkerevic, Dragen *Prime Minister*
Premier's Office, Vojvode Putnkia 3, Sarajevo, 71000, BOSNIA & HERZEGOVINA

Mirkin, David *Director, Actor*
Gersh Agency, The (LA), 232 N Canon Dr, Beverly Hills, CA 90210 USA

Mironov, Boris *Hockey Player*
New York Rangers, Madison Square Garden, 2 Penn Plaza, New York, NY 10121 USA

Mironov, Dmitri *Hockey Player*
Anahelm Mighty Ducks, 2000 E Gene Autry Way, Anaheim, CA 92806 USA

Mironov, Yevgeniy V *Actor*
Oleg Tabajiv Theater, Chaokygina Str 12A, Moscow, RUSSIA

Mirren, Helen *Actor*
Ken McReddie, 91 Regent St, London, W1R 7TB, UNITED KINGDOM (UK)

Mirrlees, James A *Nobel Prize Laureate*
Trinity College, Economics Dept, Cambridge, CB2 1TQ, UNITED KINGDOM (UK)

Mirzoev, Akbar *Prime Minister*
Prime Minister's Office, Dushaube, TAJIKISTAN

Mischka, Badgley *Fashion Designer*
525 Seventh Ave Fl 14, New York, NY 10018 USA

Mischka, James *Fashion Designer*
Badgley Mischka, 525 Fashion Ave, New York, NY 10018 USA

Mischke, Carl H *Religious Leader*
1034 Buena Vista Dr, Sun Prairie, WI 53590 USA

Misersky, Antje *Athlete*
Grenzgraben 3A, Stutzerbach, 98714, GERMANY

Misiano, Christopher *Director*
Creative Artists Agency LCC (CAA-LA), 9830 Wilshire Blvd, Beverly Hills, CA 90212 USA

Misiano, Vincent *Director*
Creative Artists Agency LCC (CAA-LA), 9830 Wilshire Blvd, Beverly Hills, CA 90212 USA

Misraki, Paul
35 av. Bugeaud, Paris, FRANCE, F-75116

Miss Teen USA
6420 Wilshire Blvd., Los Angeles, CA 90048

Missing Persons
11935 Laurel Hills Rd, Studio City, CA 91604

Mistral, Fernanda *Actor*
Telefe - Argentina, Pavon 2444 (C1248AAT), Buenos Aires, ARGENTINA

Mistry, Jimi *Actor*
Endeavor Agency LLC (LA), 9601 Wilshire Blvd Fl 3, Beverly Hills, CA 90210 USA

Miszak, Anna Cepinska *Beauty Pageant Winner*
Miss World Ltd, 21 Golden Sq, London, W1R 3PA, UNITED KINGDOM (UK)

Mitchell, Andrea *Commentator*
2710 Chain Bridge Rd NW, Washington, DC 20016 USA

Mitchell, Betsy *Swimmer*
Laurel High School, Athletic Dept, 1 Lyman Circle, Cleveland, OH 44122 USA

Mitchell, Beverley *Actor*
Creative Talent Group, PO Box 17062, Beverly Hills, CA 90209 USA

Mitchell, Beverly *Actor*
Forster Entertainment, 12533 Woodgreen St, Los Angeles, CA 90066 USA

Mitchell, Brian *Actor*
5307B Wilkinson Ave, #20, Valley Village, CA 91607 USA

Mitchell, Brian K *Football Player*
New York Giants, Giants Stadium, East Rutherford, NJ 07073 USA

Mitchell, Brian Stokes *Actor, Musician*
243 W 98th St, #5C, New York, NY 10025 USA

Mitchell, Darryl *Actor*
William Morris Agency, 151 El Camino Dr, Beverly Hills, CA 90212 USA

Mitchell, Daryl "Chill" *Actor*
William Morris Agency (WMA-LA), 1 William Morris Pl, Beverly Hills, CA 90212 USA

Mitchell, Don *Actor*
4139 Cloverdale Ave, Los Angeles, CA 90008 USA

Mitchell, Eddy
40 av. Sainte Foy, Neuilly, FRANCE, 92200

Mitchell, Edgar D *Astronaut*
PO Box 540037, Greenacres, FL 33454 USA

Mitchell, Elizabeth *Actor*
Paradigm Agency, 10100 Santa Monica Blvd, #2500, Los Angeles, CA 90067 USA

Mitchell, George J *Senator*
Walt Disney Company, The, 500 S Buena Vista St, Burbank, CA 91521 USA

Mitchell, Harris A *War Hero*
2701 Dees St, San Marcos, TX 78666 USA

Mitchell, Jack *Photographer*
1413 Live Oak St, New Smyma Beach, FL 32168 USA

Mitchell, James *Actor*
320 W 66th St, New York, NY 10023 USA

Mitchell, James Fitzallen *Royalty*
Premier's Office, Kingstown, Saint Vincent, SAINT VINCENT & GRENADINES

Mitchell, John Cameron *Actor, Director*
Innovative Artists (NY), 235 Park Ave S Fl 7, New York, NY 10003 USA

Mitchell, Joni *Musician, Writer*
624 Funchal Road, Los Angeles, CA 90077 USA

Mitchell, Keith C *Prime Minister*
Prime Minister's Office, Botonical Gardens, Saint George's, GRENADA

Mitchell, Kenneth *Actor*
Schachter Entertainment, 1157 S Beverly Dr Fl 3, Los Angeles, CA 90035 USA

Mitchell, Kim
41 Britain St. #305, Toronto, CANADA, Ont.M5A 1R

Mitchell, Leona *Opera Singer*
Columbia Artists Mgmt Inc, 165 W 57th St, New York, NY 10019 USA

Mitchell, Lydell D *Football Player*
702 Reservoir St, Baltimore, MD 21217 USA

Mitchell, Mike *Director*
Endeavor Agency LLC (LA), 9601 Wilshire Blvd Fl 3, Beverly Hills, CA 90210 USA

Mitchell, Mike *Basketball Player*
1510 Crescent Way, San Antonio, TX 78258 USA

Mitchell, Pat *Politician*
Public Broadcasting System, 1320 Braddock Place, Alexandria, VA 22314 USA

Mitchell, Radha *Actor*
William Morris Agency, 151 El Camino Dr, Beverly Hills, CA 90212 USA

Mitchell, Roger *Director*
Creative Artists Agency, 9830 Wilshire Blvd, Beverly Hills, CA 90212 USA

Mitchell, Roscoe E Jr *Musician, Composer*
SRO Artists, 6629 University Ave, #206, Middleton, WI 53562 USA

Mitchell, Russ *Television Host, Commentator*
CBS-TV, News Dept, 2020 M St NW, Washington, DC 20036 USA

Mitchell, Sam *Basketball Player, Coach*
Toronto Raptors, Air Canada Center, 40 Bay St, Toronto, ON M5J 2N8, CANADA

Mitchell, Sasha *Actor*
Flick East-West, 9057 A Nemo St, #A, West Hollywood, CA 90069 USA

Mitchell, Scott *Football Player*
5060 Franklin Road, Bloomfield Hills, MI 48302 USA

Mitchell, Shareen *Actor*
J Michael Bloom, 9255 Sunset Blvd, #710, Los Angeles, CA 90069 USA

Mitchell, Sharon
1122 White Rock, Dixon, IL 61021

Mitchell, Shirley
10635 Santa Monica Blvd. #130, Los Angeles, CA 90025

Mitchell, Steve *Actor*
Select Artists Ltd (CA-Westside Office), 1138 12th Street, Suite 1, Santa Monica, CA 90403 USA

Mitchell, Stump *Football Player*
Seattle Seahawks, 11220 NE 53rd St, Kirkland, WA 98033 USA

Mitchell, Susan *Writer*
Florida Atlantic University, English Dept,
Boca Raton, FL 33431 USA

Mitchell, Warren
28 Sheldon Ave., London, ENGLAND, N6

Mitchelson, Marvin *Attorney General*
2500 Apollo Dr, Los Angeles, CA 90046
USA

Mitchison, N Avrion *Biologist*
14 Belitha Villas, London, N1 1PD,
UNITED KINGDOM (UK)

Mitchum, Carrie *Actor*
Camden ITG Talent, 1501 Main St, #204,
Venice, CA 90291 USA

Mithun, Chakraborty *Actor, Bollywood*
Monarch Hotel, Ooty, TN INDIA

Mitra, Rhona *Actor*
Management 360, 9111 Wilshire Blvd,
Beverly Hills, CA 90210 USA

Mitsotakis, Constantine *Prime Minister*
1 Aravantinou St, Athens, 106 74,
GREECE

Mitta, Aleksander N *Director*
Malaya Gruzinskaya Str 28, #105,
Moscow, 123557, RUSSIA

Mittermaier, Rosi
Winklmoosalm, Reit im Winkl,
GERMANY, D-83242

Mittermaier-Neureuther, Rosi *Skier*
Winkelmoosalm, Reit Im Winkel, 83242,
GERMANY

Mittermayer, Tatjana *Skier*
Bucha 2A, Lenggries, GERMANY

Mitzelfeld, Jim *Journalist*
969 N Lebanon St, Arlington, VA 22205
USA

Mivelaz, Betty *Bowler*
6671 Shadygrove St, Tujunga, CA 91042
USA

Mix, Ronald J (Ron) *Football Player*
2317 Camino Recodo, San Diego, CA
92107 USA

Mix, Steve *Basketball Player*
25743 Willowbend Road, Newtown, PA
18940 USA

Mixon, J Wayne *Governor*
2219 Demeron Road, Tallahassee, FL
32308 USA

Miyamura, Hiroshi H *War Hero*
659 Kaimalino St, Kailua, HI 96734 USA

Miyazaki, Hayao *Animator*
Studio Ghibli, 1-4-25 Kajinocho,
Koganeishi, 184, JAPAN

Miyazawa, Kiichi *Prime Minister*
6-34-1 Jingu-Mae, Shibuyaku, Tokyo, 150,
JAPAN

Miyori, Kim *Actor*
Susan Smoth, 121A N San Vicente Blvd,
Beverly Hills, CA 90211 USA

Mize, John D *War Hero*
112 Sunset Dr, Belmond, IA 50421 USA

Mize, Larry *Golfer*
106 Graystone Court, Columbus, GA
31904 USA

Mize, Ola L *War Hero*
211 Hartwood Dr, Gadsden, AL 35901
USA

Mizerak, Steve *Billiards Player*
140 Alfred St, Edison, NJ 08820 USA

Mizerock, John J *Baseball Player*
PO Box 580, Punxsutawney, PA 15767
USA

Mizrahi, Isaac *Fashion Designer*
876 Centennial Ave, Piscataway, NJ
08854 USA

Mizzy, Vic
2170 Stradella Rd., Los Angeles, CA
90077

Mkapa, Benjamin William *President*
President's Office, State House, PO Box
9120, Dar es Salaam, TANZANIA

Mlkvy, Bill *Basketball Player*
586 Linton Hill Road, Newtown, PA
18940 USA

Mlodinow, Leonard *Writer*
Warner Books (Author Mail), 1271
Avenue of the Americas, New York, NY
10020

Mnookin, Robert H *Attorney General,
Educator*
10 Follen St, Cambridge, MA 02138 USA

Mnouchkine, Ariane *Director*
Theater du Soleil, Cartoucherie, Paris,
75012, FRANCE

Moats, David *Journalist*
Rutland Herald, Editorial Dept, PO Box
668, Rutland, VT 05702 USA

Mobley, Cuttino *Basketball Player*
Orlando Magic, Waterhouse Center, 8701
Maitland Summit Blvd, Orlando, FL
32810 USA

Mobley, Mary Ann *Actor, Beauty Pageant
Winner*
2751 Hutton Dr, Beverly Hills, CA 90210
USA

Mobley, William H *Educator*
9317 Grandview Dr, Denton, TX 76207
USA

Moby *Musician*
MVO Ltd, 307 Seventh Avenue, Suite 807,
New York, NY 10001 USA

Moceanu, Dominique *Gymnast*
Brown's Gymnastics Metro, 4676 McLeod
Road, Orlando, FL 32811 USA

Mochrie, Colin *Actor*
Jonas PR, 240 26th St #3, Santa Monica,
CA 90402 USA

Mochrie Pepper, Dorothy (Dottie) *Golfer*
15 Blazing Star Trail, Landrum, SC 29356
USA

Mocumbi, Pascoal *Prime Minister*
Prime Minister's Office, Avenida Julius
Nyerere 1780, Maputo, MOZAMBIQUE

Modano, Mike *Hockey Player*
200 Crescent Ct, #S600, Dallas, TX 75201
USA

Mode, Depeche *Music Group*
Creative Artists Agency LCC (CAA-LA),
9830 Wilshire Blvd, Beverly Hills, CA
90212 USA

Modell, Arthur B *Football Executive*
Baltimore Ravens, Ravens Stadium, 11001
Russell St, Baltimore, MD 21230 USA

Modell, Frank *Cartoonist*
115 Three Mile Course, Guilford, CT
06437 USA

Modern Talking
Modern Talking Fan Club, 56200 Hoehr-
Grenzhausen, GERMANY

Modernaires, The
11761 E. Speedway Blvd, Tucson, AZ
85748-2017

Modine, Matthew *Actor*
Untitled Entertainment (NY), 23 E 22nd St
Fl 3, New York, NY 10010 USA

Modrow, Hans *Prime Minister*
Frankfurter Tor 6, Berlin, 10243,
GERMANY

Modrzejewski, Robert J *War Hero*
4725 Oporto Court, San Diego, CA 92124
USA

Modzelewski, Richard B (Dick) *Football
Player*
1 Pier Pointe, New Bern, NC 28562 USA

Moe, Douglas E (Doug) *Basketball Player*
13 Arnold Palmer, San Antonio, TX 78257
USA

Moe, Thomas S (Tommy) *Skier*
1556 Hidden Lane, Anchorage, AK 99501
USA

Moe, Tommy
2138 Churchill Dr, Anchorage, AK 99517

Moe-Humphreys, Karen *Swimmer*
505 Augusta Dr, Moraga, CA 94556 USA

Moegle, Dickie
4047 Aberdeen Way, Houston, TX 77025

Moeller, Chuck *Actor*
Binder & Associates, 1465 Lindacrest Dr,
Beverly Hills, CA 90210 USA

Moeller, Dennis *Inventor*
25 Cobbie Ridge Dr, Chapel Hill, NC
27516 USA

Moellering, John H *General*
50130 Manly, Chapel Hill, NC 27517
USA

Moennig, Katherine *Actor*
Framework Entertainment (NY), 129 W
27th St Fl 12, New York, NY 10001 USA

Moffat, Donald *Actor*
151 El Camino Dr, Beverly Hills, CA
90212 USA

Moffat, Katherine (Kitty) *Actor*
Henderson/Hogan, 8285 W Sunset Blvd,
#1, West Hollywood, CA 21230 USA

Moffatt, Henry K *Mathematician, Physicist*
6 Banhams Close, Cambridge, CB4 1HX,
UNITED KINGDOM (UK)

Moffatt, John
59A Warrington St., London, ENGLAND,
W9

Moffatt, Katy *Musician, Songwriter*
PO Box 334, O Fallon, IL 62269 USA

Moffatts, The *Music Group*
Mascioli Entertainment Corp, 2202 Curry
Ford Rd #E, Orlando, FL 32806 USA

Moffett, D W *Actor*
Three Arts Entertainment, 9460 Wilshire
Blvd, #700, Beverly Hills, CA 90212 USA

Moffett, James R *Business Person*
Freeport-McMoRan Inc, 1615 Poydras St,
New Orleans, LA 70112 USA

Moffett, Randy
110 Lakeover Dr., Athens, GA 30606

Moffo, Anna *Opera Singer*
Columbia Artists Mgmt Inc, 165 W 57th
St, New York, NY 10019 USA

Mofford, Rose *Governor*
330 W Maryland Ave, #104, Phoenix, AZ
85013 USA

Mogae, Festus G *President*
President's Office, State House, Private
Bag 001, Gaborone, BOTSWANA

Mogenburg, Dietmar *Track Athlete*
Alter Garfen 34, Leverkusen, 51371,
GERMANY

Mogilevsky, Evgeny *Musician*
Columbia Artists Mgmt Inc, 165 W 57th
St, New York, NY 10019 USA

Mogilny, Alexander *Hockey Player*
Int'l Management Group, 801 6th St SW,
Calgary, AB T2P 3V8, CANADA

Mohacsi, Mary *Bowler*
15445 Sunset St, Livonia, MI 48154 USA

Mohammed VI *King*
Royal Palais, Rabat, MOROCCO

Mohan *Actor, Bollywood*
8 Mylai Ranganathan Street, T Nagar,
Chennai, TN 600017, INDIA

Mohmand, Abdul Ahad *Cosmonaut*
Potchta Kosmonavtov, Moskovkoi Oblasti,
Syvlsdny Goroduk, 141160, RUSSIA

Mohn, Reinhard *Business Person,
Publisher*
Bertelsmann AG, Carl-Bertelsmann-Str
256, Guetersloh, 33311, GERMANY

Mohoney, J Daniel *Judge*
US Court of Appeals, 40 FOley Square,
New York, NY 10007 USA

Mohoney, John *Actor*
International Creative Mgmt, 8942
Wilshire Blvd, #219, Beverly Hills, CA
90211 USA

Mohoney, Roger *Cartoonist*
King Features Syndicate, 888 7th Ave,
New York, NY 10106 USA

Mohony, Roger Cardinal *Religious Leader*
Archdiocese of Los Angeles, 3424
Wilshire Blvd, Los Angeles, CA 90010
USA

Mohr, Jay *Actor, Comedian*
New Wave Entertainment (LA), 2660 W
Olive Blvd, Burbank, CA 91505 USA

Mohr, Todd *Musician*
Morris Bliessner, 1658 York St, Denver,
CO 80206 USA

Mohri, Mamoru *Astronaut*
NASDA, 2-1-2 Sengen, Tukubashi,
Ibaraki, 305, JAPAN

Moine, Marc Forne *President*
President's Office, Casa de la Valle,
Andorra la Vella, ANDORRA

Moir, Richard *Actor*
Shanahan Mgmt, PO Box 1509,
Darlinghurst, NSW, 1300, AUSTRALIA

Moiseyev, Igor A *Director, Choreographer*
Moiseyev Dance Co, 20 Triumfalnaya Pl,
Moscow, RUSSIA

Mojslejenko, Ralf *Football Player*
11334 Baldwin Road, Bridgeman, MI
49106 USA

Mokri, Amir *Cinematographer*
Montana Artists, 625 Montana Ave, #200,
Santa Monica, CA 90403 USA

Mokrzynski, Jerzy *Architect*
Ul Marszalkowska 140 m 18, Warsaw, 00
061, POLAND

Mol, Gretchen *Actor*
1964 Westwood Blvd, #400, Los Angeles,
CA 90025 USA

Molden, Alex *Football Player*
3425 Brunswick Dr, Colorado Springs,
CO 80920 USA

Moldofsky, Philip J *Scientist*
Fox Chase Cancer Center, 7701 Burholme
Ave, Philadelphia, PA 19111 USA

Molina, Alfred *Actor*
Hyler Mgmt, 25 Sea Colony Dr, Santa
Monica, CA 90405 USA

Molina, Mario J *Nobel Prize Laureate*
8 Clematis Road, Lexington, MA 02421
USA

Molinaro, Al *Actor*
1530 Arboles Dr, Glendale, CA 91207
USA

Molinaro, Bobby
1 Harborside #2312, Del Rey Beach, FL
33483

Molitor, Paul L *Baseball Player, Coach*
34 Kirby Puckett Place, Minneapolis, MN
55415 USA

Moll, Georgia
229A v. Pineta Sacchetti, Rome, CA ITALY

Moll, John L *Engineer*
4111 Old Trace Road, Palo Alto, CA
94306 USA

Moll, Kurt *Opera Singer*
Voigtelstr 22, Cologne, 50933, GERMANY

Moll, Richard *Actor*
1119 Amalfi Dr, Pacific Palisades, CA
90272 USA

Molla, Jordi *Actor*
Kuranda Movies SL, Calle Segre 14,
Madrid, 28002, SPAIN

Moller, Andreas *Soccer Player*
Borussia Dortmund, Postfach 100509,
Dortmund, 44005, GERMANY

Moller, Frank *Athlete*
Sportclub Berlin, Weissenseer Weg 51-55,
Berlin, 13051, GERMANY

Moller, Gunnar
6 Cloverdale Rd., London, ENGLAND,
NW2

Moller, Hans *Artist*
2207 W Allen St, Allentown, PA 18104
USA

Moller, Paul *Inventor, Engineer*
Moller International, 1222 Research Park
Dr, Davis, CA 95616 USA

Moller-Gladisch, Silke *Track Athlete*
Lange Str 6, Rostock, 18055, GERMANY

Mollo-Christiansen, Erik L *Oceanographer*
10 Barberry Road, Lexington, MA USA

Molloy, Bryan B *Inventor*
7948 Beaumont Green Place,
Indianapolis, IN 46250 USA

Molloy, Irene
PO Box 5617, Beverly Hills, CA 90210

Molloy, Matt *Musician*
Macklam Feldman Mgmt, 1505 W 2nd
Ave, #200, Vancouver, BC V6H 3Y4,
CANADA

Moloney, Janel *Actor*
Untitled Entertainment (LA), 8436 W 3rd
St #650, Los Angeles, CA 90048 USA

Moloney, Paddy *Musician*
Macklam Feldman Mgmt, 1505 W 2nd
Ave, #200, Vancouver, BC V6H 3Y4,
CANADA

Molyneux, Juan Pablo *Architect*
J P Molyneux Studio, 29 E 69th St, New
York, NY 10021 USA

Mom Rajawong, Sirikit Kitiyarara *Royalty*
Royal Residence, Chirtalad a Villa,
Bangkok, Thailand

Momaday, N Scott *Writer*
University of Arizona, English Dept,
Tucson, AZ 85721 USA

Momoa, Jason *Actor*
DDO Artist Agency, 8322 Beverly Blvd
#301, Los Angeles, CA 90048 USA

Momper, ex-Mayor Walter
Fichtestr. 15, Berlin, GERMANY, D-10967

Momsen, Taylor *Musician*
Abrams Artists Agency (LA), 9200 Sunset
Blvd Fl 11, Los Angeles, CA 90069 USA

Monacelli, Amieto *Bowler*
Professional Bowlers Assn, 719 2nd Ave,
#701, Seattle, WA 98104 USA

Monaco, Kelly *Actor*
General Hospital, 4151 Prospect Ave, Los
Angeles, CA 90027 USA

Monaghan, Dominic *Actor*
Untitled Entertainment (LA), 8436 W 3rd
St #650, Los Angeles, CA 90048 USA

Monaghan, Marjorie
121 N. San Vicente Blvd., Beverly Hills,
CA 90211

Monaghan, Thomas L
3001 Earhart, Ann Arbor, MI 48106 USA

Monahan, Dan *Actor*
Cuzzins Management, 499 N Canon Dr,
Beverly Hills, CA 90210 USA

Monahan, David *Actor, Director*
Metropolitan Talent Agency (MTA), 4526
Wilshire Blvd, Los Angeles, CA 90010
USA

Monahan, Pat *Musician*
Jon Landau, 80 Mason St, Greenwich, CT
06830 USA

Monan, J Donald *Educator*
Boston College, President's Office,
Chestnut Hill, MA 02167 USA

Monbouquette, William C (Bill) *Baseball
Player*
46 Doonan St, Medford, MA 02155 USA

Moncrief, Sidney *Basketball Player*
4304 Carter Lane, Little Rock, AR 72223
USA

Moncrieff, Karen *Actor*
Brad Gross Agency, The, 6715 Hollywood
Blvd #236, Los Angeles, CA 90028 USA

Mond, Philip *Photographer*
PO Box 8906, Fort Lauderdale, FL 33310
USA

Mondale, Eleanor
282 Edge of Woods Rd, Southampton, NY
11968-2513

Mondale, Walter F *Vice President,
Senator*
50 S 6th, #1500, Minneapolis, MN 55402
USA

Mondavi, Robert G *Business Person*
Robert Mondavi Winery, 7801 St Helena
Highways, Oakville, CA 94562 USA

Monday, Rick
349 W. Pine St. #3D, Central Point, OR
97502

Monday, Robert J (Rick) *Baseball Player,
Sportscaster*
811 Gayleather Lane, Vero Beach, FL
32963 USA

Mondesi, Raul *Baseball Player, Athlete*
New York Yankees, Yankee Stadium,
161st Street & River Avenue, Bronx, NY
10451 USA

Monduzzi, Dino Cardinal *Religious
Leader*
Via Monfe della Farina 64, Rome, 00186,
ITALY

Moneo, J Fafael *Architect*
Calle Mino 5, Madrid, 28002, SPAIN

Monet, Daniella *Actor*
Abrams Artists Agency (LA), 9200 Sunset
Blvd Fl 11, Los Angeles, CA 90069 USA

Money, Don *Baseball Player*
282 Old Forest Rd, Vineland, NJ 08360

Money, Eddie *Musician*
International Creative Mgmt, 40 W 57th
St, #1800, New York, NY 10019 USA

Money, John W *Misc*
2104 E Madison St, Baltimore, MD 21205
USA

Money, Ken *Astronaut*
DCIEM, 1133 Sheppard Ave W, #2000,
Downsview, ON M3M 3B9, CANADA

Monhelt, Jane *Musician, Songwriter*
N-Coded Music/Warlock Records, 126 5th
Ave, #200, New York, NY 10011 USA

Monica *Musician*
Rowdy/Arista Records, 8750 Wilshire
Blvd, #300, Beverly Hills, CA 90211 USA

Monicelli, Mario *Director*
Via del Babuino 135, Rome, 00137,
ITALY

Monin, Clarence V *President*
Locomotive Engineers Brotherhood, 1370
Ontario St, Cleveland, OH 44113 USA

Moniz, Wendy *Actor*
Sanders/Armstrong Management, 2120
Colorado Blvd #120, Santa Monica, CA
90404 USA

Monk, Arthur (Art) *Football Player,
Sportscaster*
8251 Greensboro Dr, McLean, VA 22102
USA

Monk, Debra *Actor*
Gage Group, 315 W 57th St, #4H, New
York, NY 10019 USA

Monk, Meredith J *Choreographer,
Composer*
House Foundation for Arts, 131 Varick St,
New York, NY 10013 USA

Monk Jr, Thelonious
173 Brighton Ave, Boston, MA 02134
USA

Monkees, The *Music Group*
Primary Talent International (UK), 2-12
Pentonville Rd Fl 5, London, N1 9PL,
UNITED KINGDOM (UK)

Monkey See-Monkey Do
Feurigstr. 16, Berlin, GERMANY, D-10827

Monreal Luque, Alberto *Government
Official*
Eurotabac Monte Esquinza 28, Madrid,
28010, SPAIN

Monroe, A L (Mike) *Misc*
International Brotherhood pf Painters,
1750 New York NW, Washington, DC
20006 USA

Monroe, Betty *Actor*
TV Azteca, Periferico Sur 4121, Colonia
Fuentes del Pedregal, DF, CP 14141,
Mexico

Monroe, Earl (Pearl) *Basketball Player*
31 Meadowview Lane, Oneonta, NY
13620 USA

Monroe, Meredith *Musician*
Anonymous Content, 8522 National Blvd
#101, Culver City, CA 90232 USA

Monroe, Mircea *Actor*
Evolution Entertainment, 901 N Highland
Ave, Los Angeles, CA 90038 USA

Monroe, Richard *Publisher*
Atlanta Journal-Constitution, 72 Marietta
St, Atlanta, GA 30303 USA

Monson, Dan *Basketball Player, Coach*
University of Minnesota, Bierman Athletic
Building, Minneapolis, MN 55455 USA

Montagna, Joe
10415 Sarah St., Toluca Lake, CA 91602

Montagnier, Luc *Scientist*
Institut Pasteur, 25 Rue du Docteur, Paris
Cedux 15, 75015, FRANCE

Montague, Ashley
321 Cherry Hill Rd., Princeton, NJ 08540

Montague, Diana *Opera Singer*
91 Saint Martin's Lane, London, WC2,
UNITED KINGDOM (UK)

Montague, Lee *Actor*
Conway Van Gelder Robinson, 18-21
Jermyn St, London, SW1Y 6NB, UNITED
KINGDOM (UK)

Montague-Smith, Patrick W *Editor*
Brereton, 197 Park Road, Kingston-upon-
Thames, Surrey, UNITED KINGDOM (UK)

Montalban, Paolo *Actor*
Talent Entertainment Group, 9111
Wilshire Blvd, Beverly Hills, CA 90210
USA

Montalban, Ricardo *Actor*
1423 Oriole Dr, Los Angeles, CA 90069
USA

Montana, Claude *Fashion Designer*
131 Rue Saint-Denis, Paris, 75001,
FRANCE

Montana Jr, Joseph C (Joe) *Football Player*
3455 State Hwy 128, Calistoga, CA 94515
USA

Montazeri, Ayatollah Hussein Ali
Religious Leader
Madresseh Faizieh, Qom, IRAN

Monte, Chante
WMA, 1325 Ave. of the Americas, New
York, NY 1O0l9

Monteiro, Antonio M *President*
President's Office, Cia de la Republica,
Sao Tiago Praia, CAPE VERDE

Monteith, Kelly
PO Box 11669, Knoxville, TN 37939-
1669

Montermini, Andrea *Race Car Driver*
434 E Main St, Brownsburg, IN 46112
USA

Montero, Pablo *Actor*
Televisa, Blvd Adolfo Lopez Mateos 232,
Colonia San Angel INN, DF, CP 01060,
MEXICO

Monterola, Pablo *Musician*
BMG, 1540 Broadway, New York, NY
10036 USA

Montevecchi, Liliane *Musician*
Buzz Halliday, 8899 Beverly Blvd, #620,
Los Angeles, CA 90048 USA

Montez, Chris
6671 Sunset Blvd. #1502, Hollywood, CA
90028

Montgomerie, Colin S *Golfer*
Int'l Mgmt group, Pier House, Strand-on-
the-Green, London, W4 3NN, UNITED
KINGDOM (UK)

Montgomery, Anne *Sportscaster*
ESPN-TV, Sports Dept ESPN Plaza, 935
Middle St, Bristol, CT 06010 USA

Montgomery, Anthony *Actor*
Jerry Shandrew PR, 1050 South Stanley
Avenue, Los Angeles, CA 90019-6634
USA

Montgomery, Belinda *Actor*
Epstein-Wyckoff, 280 S Beverly Hills,
#400, Beverly Hills, CA 90212 USA

Montgomery, Chuck *Actor*
Don Buchwald & Associates Inc (LA),
6500 Wilshire Blvd #2200, Los Angeles,
CA 90048 USA

Montgomery, Clifford E (Cliff) *Football
Player*
362 I U Willets Road, Roslyn Heights, NY
11577 USA

Montgomery, David *Photographer*
11 Edith Grove #B, London, SW10,
UNITED KINGDOM (UK)

Montgomery, Eddie *Musician*
Hallmark Direction, 15 Music Square W,
Nashville, TN 37203 USA

Montgomery, James P (Jim) *Swimmer,
Coach*
3141 Westminster Ave, Dallas, TX 75205
USA

Montgomery, Jeff *Baseball Player*
2713 W 116th St, Leawood, KS 66211
USA

Montgomery, John Michael *Musician*
PO Box 128229, Nashville, TN 37212
USA

Montgomery, John W *Misc*
2 Rue de Rome, Starsbourg, 67000,
FRANCE

Montgomery, Melba *Musician*
Joe Taylor Artist Agency, 2802 Columbine
Place, Nashville, TN 37204 USA

Montgomery, Mike *Basketball Player,
Coach*
Golden State Warriors, 1001 Broadway,
Oakland, CA 94607 USA

Montgomery, Poppy *Actor*
Mindel/Donigan, 9057 C Nemo St, #C,
West Hollywood, CA 90069 USA

Montgomery, Wilbert N *Football Player*
950 Mid Point Dr, O Fallon, MO 63366
USA

Montgomery Jr, Dan *Actor*
Peter Strain & Associates Inc (LA), 5724 W
3rd St #302, Los Angeles, CA 90036 USA

Montiel, H Pierre
102 W 73rd St, New York, NY 10023
USA

Montminy, Marc R *Scientist*
Salk Institute, 10100 N Torrey Pines Road,
La Jolla, CA 92037 USA

Montoya, Al *Hockey Player*
New York Rangers, Madison Square
Garden, 2 Penn Plaza, New York, NY
10121 USA

Montoya, Juan *Race Car Driver*
Williams Grand Prix, Grove, Wontage,
Oxfordshire, OX12 0D0, UNITED
KINGDOM (UK)

Montross, Eric *Basketball Player*
4668 S NC Highway 150, Lexington, NC
27295 USA

Montsho, Este *Musician*
William Morris Agency, 1325 Ave of
Americas, New York, NY 10019 USA

Montvidas, Edgaras *Opera Singer*
Van Walsum Mgmt, 4 Addison Bridge
Place, London, W14 8XP USA

Montville, Leigh *Writer*
Boston Globe, Editorial Dept, 135 WT
Morrissey Blvd, Dorchester, MA 02125
USA

Monty, Harry
1600 N. Bronson Ave. #17, Hollywood,
CA 90028

Moody, James *Musician*
BPR, 230 12th St #118, Miami Beach, FL
33139 USA

Moody, Keith M *Football Player*
4632 Riverview Court, Tracy, CA 95377
USA

Moody, Lynne *Actor*
8708 Skyline Dr, Los Angeles, CA 90046
USA

Moody, Micky *Musician*
Int'l Talent Booking, 27A Floral St #300,
London, WC2E 9DQ, UNITED
KINGDOM (UK)

Moody, Orville *Golfer*
Int'l Mgmt group, 1 Erieview Plaza, 1360
E 9th St #1300, Cleveland, OH 44114
USA

Moody, Ron *Actor*
Eric Glass, 28 Berkeley Square, London,
W1X 6HD, UNITED KINGDOM (UK)

Moody Blues *Music Group*
Creative Artists Agency LCC (CAA-LA),
9830 Wilshire Blvd, Beverly Hills, CA
90212 USA

Moog, Andy *Hockey Player*
530 Rolling Hills Road, Coppell, TX
75019 USA

Moomaw, Donn D *Football Player*
3124 Corda Dr, Los Angeles, CA 90049
USA

Moon, H Warren *Football Player*
PO Box 22388, Houston, TX 77227 USA

Moon, Philip
449 N. Highland Ave., Los Angeles, CA
90036

Moon, Sun Myung *Religious Leader*
Unification Church, 4 W 43rd St, New
York, NY 10036 USA

Moon, Wallace W (Wally) *Baseball Player*
702 Ellen Lee Court, Bryan, TX 77802
USA

Moon, Wally
1415 Angeline Circle, College Station, TX
77840

Moon, Warren
1 Lakeside Estate Dr, Missouri City, TX
77459-4364

Mooney, Harold A *Biologist*
2625 Ramona St, Palo Alto, CA 94306
USA

Mooney, John *Musician*
Intrepid Artists, Midtown Plaza, 1300
Baxter St #405, Charlotte, NC 28204 USA

Mooney, Michael J *Educator*
Lewis & Clark College, President's Office,
Portland, OR 97219 USA

Mooney, Michael P (Mike) *Football Player*
4801 Diane Ave, Mount Airy, MD 21771
USA

Moonves, Leslie *Producer*
CBS-TV, 51 W 52nd St, New York, NY
10019 USA

Moordyukova, Nonna V *Actor*
Rublevskoye Shosse 34, Korp 2 #549,
Moscow, 121609, RUSSIA

Moore, Abra *Musician*
Haber Corp, 16830 Ventura Blvd, #501,
Encino, CA 91436 USA

Moore, Alan *Writer*
International Creative Management
(ICM-LA), 8942 Wilshire Blvd, Beverly
Hills, CA 90211 USA

Moore, Ann S *Publisher*
People Magazine, Publisher's Office, Time
& Life Building, New York, NY 10020
USA

Moore, Arch A Jr *Governor*
507 Jefferson Ave, Glen Dale, WV 26038
USA

Moore, Arthur *Misc*
Sheet Metal Workers Int'l Assn, 1750 New
York Ave NW, Washington, DC 20006
USA

Moore, Benjamin *Artist*
3123 39th Place S, Seattle, WA 98144
USA

Moore, Billie *Coach*
2247 Meadow Lane, Fullerton, CA 92831
USA

Moore, Bud *Race Car Driver*
4 Duck Lane, Isle of Palms, SC 29451
USA

Moore, Calvin C *Mathematician*
1408 Eagle Pointe Court, Lafayette, CA
94549 USA

Moore, Chante *Musician, Songwriter*
Artistic Control, 1350 Spring St NW,
#700, Atlanta, GA 30309 USA

Moore, Charles Jr *Track Athlete*
2018 Hillyer Place NW, Washington, DC
20009 USA

Moore, Chessie
PO Box 1516, Palatka, FL 32178-1516

Moore, Chris *Producer*
LivePlanet, 2644 30th St, Santa Monica,
CA 90405 USA

Moore, Christy *Musician*
It's a Gas Mgmt, 1184 Fischer Blvd #2B,
Toms River, NJ 08753 USA

Moore, Constance *Actor, Musician*
4729 Libbit Avenue, Encino, CA 91436
USA

Moore, Corey *Football Player*
Cincinnati Bengals, 1 Paul Brown
Stadium, Cincinnati, OH 45202 USA

Moore, Corwin *Writer*
3 Arts Entertainment Inc, 9460 Wilshire
Blvd Fl 7, Beverly Hills, CA 90212 USA

Moore, Demi *Actor*
Creative Artists Agency LCC (CAA-LA),
9830 Wilshire Blvd, Beverly Hills, CA
90212 USA

Moore, Derland P *Football Player*
925 Dove Park Road, Covington, LA
70433 USA

Moore, Dick *Cartoonist*
Dick Moore Assoc, 1560 Broadway, New
York, NY 10036 USA

Moore, Dickie
150 West End Ave. #26C, New York, NY
10023-5743

Moore, Dorothy *Musician*
Sirius Entertainment, 13531 Claimont Way
#8, Oregon City, OR 97045 USA

Moore, Earl
215 West End Blvd., Winston-Salem, NC
27101-1203

Moore, Eric P *Football Player*
2225 Lindsay Lane, Florissant, MO 63031
USA

Moore, George E *Doctor*
12048 S Blackhawk Dr, Conifer, CO
80433 USA

Moore, Herman J *Football Player*
265 Mount Hermon Circle, Danville, VA
24540 USA

Moore, J Jeremy *General*
Lloyds Bank, Cox's & King's Branch, 7 Pall Mall, London, SW1, UNITED KINGDOM (UK)

Moore, Jackie *Musician*
T-Best Talent Agency, 508 Honey Lake Court, Danville, CA 94506 USA

Moore, James E Jr *General*
18940 Joaquin Court, Salinas, CA 93908 USA

Moore, Jesse W *Engineer*
Ball Aerospace Corp, Boulder Industrial Park, Boulder, CO 80306 USA

Moore, Joe
2410 Memorial Dr. #3C, Bryan, TX 77802

Moore, John A *Biologist*
11522 Tulane Ave, Riverside, CA 92507 USA

Moore, John W *Educator*
Indiana State University, President's Office, Terre Haute, IN 47809 USA

Moore, Julianne *Actor*
Talent Entertainment Group, 9111 Wilshire Blvd, Beverly Hills, CA 90210 USA

Moore, Kenya *Actor*
Cunningham-Escott-Dipene & Associates Inc (CED-LA), 10635 Santa Monica Blvd #130, Los Angeles, CA 90025 USA

Moore, Leonard E (Lenny) *Football Player*
8815 Stonehaven Road, Randallstown, MD 21133 USA

Moore, LeRoi *Musician*
Red Light Mgmt, 3302 Lobban Place, Charlottesville, VA 22903 USA

Moore, Lorrie *Writer*
University of Wisconsin, English Dept, Madison, WI 53706 USA

Moore, Malcolm A S *Scientist*
Memorial Sloan-Dettering Cancer Center, 1275 York Ave, New York, NY 10021 USA

Moore, Mandy *Musician, Actor*
PO Box 6079, Bellingham, WA 98227 USA

Moore, Mary Tyler *Actor*
MTM, 1133 Ave of Americas, New York, NY 10022 USA

Moore, Melanie
3500 W. Olive Ave. #920, Burbank, CA 91505-4628

Moore, Melba *Actor, Musician*
Artist Services Inc, 1017 O St NW, #B, Washington, DC 20001 USA

Moore, Melissa Anne *Actor*
PO Box 55, Versailles, KY 40383 USA

Moore, Meredith
3500 W. Olive Ave. #920, Burbank, CA 91505-4628

Moore, Michael *Director*
Endeavor Agency LLC (LA), 9601 Wilshire Blvd Fl 3, Beverly Hills, CA 90210 USA

Moore, Michael (Mike) *Attorney General*
Attorney General's Office, PO Box 220, Jackson, MS 39205 USA

Moore, Michael K (Mike) *Prime Minister*
World Trade Organization, 154 Rue Lausanne, Geneva 21, 1211, SWITZERLAND

Moore, Nathanlel (Nat) *Football Player*
20041 E Oakmont Dr, Hialeah, FL 33015 USA

Moore, Patrick *Astronomer, Writer*
Farthings, 39 West St, Selsey, Sussex, PO20 9AAD, UNITED KINGDOM (UK)

Moore, Rachel *Actor, Model*
Exposure (Xposure) Public Relations, 9171 Wilshire Blvd #300, Beverly Hills, CA 90210 USA

Moore, Ralph *Musician*
Denon Records, 135 W 50th St, #1915, New York, NY 10020 USA

Moore, Richard *Actor*
London Mgmt, 2-4 Noel St, London, W1V 3RB, UNITED KINGDOM (UK)

Moore, Richard W (Dickie) *Hockey Player*
4955 Clemin Saint Francois, Saint Laurent, QC, 1P3, CANADA

Moore, Roger *Actor*
London Management, 2-4 Noel St, London, W1V 3RB, UNITED KINGDOM (UK)

Moore, Roger *Actor, Director, Producer*
GVA Talent Agency Inc, 9229 Sunset Blvd #320, Los Angeles, CA 90069 USA

Moore, Sam *Musician*
I'ma Da Wife Enterprises, 7119 E SHea Blvd, #109-436, Scottsdale, AZ 85254 USA

Moore, Scotty *Musician*
4104 Blueberry Hill Rd, Nashville, TN 37218 USA

Moore, Shawn *Football Player*
935 Blankenship Road #1, Martinsville, VA 24112 USA

Moore, Shemar *Actor*
A Management, 9107 Wilshire Blvd #650, Beverly Hills, CA 90210 USA

Moore, Tamara
Phoenix Mercury, American West Arena, 201 E Jefferson St, Phoenix, AZ 85004 USA

Moore, Terry *Producer*
Vin Di Bona Productions, 12233 West Olympic Blvd, Suite 170, Los Angeles, CA 90064 USA

Moore, Thomas *Writer*
Harper/Collins Publishers, 10 E 53rd St, New York, NY 10022 USA

Moore, Toby *Actor*
Sanders/Armstrong Management, 2120 Colorado Blvd #120, Santa Monica, CA 90404 USA

Moore, Tom *Director*
8283 Hollywood Blvd, Los Angeles, CA 90069 USA

Moore, W Edward C *Biologist*
1607 Boxwood Dr, Blacksburg, VA 24060 USA

Moore, Zeke *Football Player*
3422 Prudence Court, Houston, TX 77045 USA

Moore (Paxson), Melanie Deanne *Actor*
Metropolitan Talent Agency (MTA), 4526 Wilshire Blvd, Los Angeles, CA 90010 USA

Moore-Watkins, Pauline *Actor*
4077 SW Sunset Dr, #202, Lake Oswego, OR 97035 USA

Moorehouse, Adrian
St. Helier Bradford Rd. Bringley, W. York., ENGLAND, BD16 1PA

Moorer, Allison *Musician, Songwriter, Actor*
TKO Artist Mgmt, 1107 17th Ave S, Nashville, TN 37212 USA

Moorer, Michael *Boxer*
5000 Town Center, #2203, Southfield, MI 48075 USA

Moorse, Kiki *Musician*
K Records, 924 Jefferson St SE, #101, Olympia, WA 98501 USA

Mora, Gene *Cartoonist*
United Feature Syndicate, 200 Madison Ave, New York, NY 10016 USA

Mora, Jim
6928 Saint's Dr. Metairie, Los Angeles, CA 70003

Mora, Philippe *Director*
Altman Co, 9255 Sunset Blvd, #901, Los Angeles, CA 90069 USA

Mora Gramunt, Gabriel *Architect*
Passtage Sant Felip, 12 Bis, Barcelona, 08006, SPAIN

Mora Jr, James E (Jim) *Football Coach*
Atlanta Falcons, 4400 Falcon Parkway, Flowery Branch, GA 30542 USA

Morabito, Rocky *Photographer, Journalist*
3036 Gilmore St, Jacksonville, FL 32205 USA

Morahan, Christopher T *Director*
Highcombe, Devil's Punchbowl, Thursley, Godalming, Surrey, GU8 6NS, UNITED KINGDOM (UK)

Morales, Esai *Actor*
Don Buchwald & Associates Inc (LA), 6500 Wilshire Blvd #2200, Los Angeles, CA 90048 USA

Morales, Esal *Actor*
7527 Woodrow Wilson Dr, Los Angeles, CA 90046 USA

Morales, Jose M *Baseball Player*
17411 Fosgate Road, Montverde, FL 34756 USA

Morales, P Pablo *Swimmer*
University of Nebraska, Athletic Dept, Lincoln, NE 68588 USA

Moran, Erin *Actor*
PO Box 3261, Quartz Hill, CA 93586 USA

Moran, John *Religious Leader*
Missionary Church, PO Box 9127, Fort Wayne, IN 46899 USA

Moran, Julie *Sportscaster, Entertainer*
Creative Artists Agency, 9830 Wilshire Blvd, Beverly Hills, CA 90212 USA

Moran, Nick *Actor*
Brillstein-Grey Entertainment, 9150 Wilshire Blvd #350, Beverly Hills, CA 90212 USA

Moran, Pauline
275 Kensington Rd., London, ENGLAND, SW1 6BY

Moran, Richard J (Rich) *Football Player*
7252 Mimosa Dr, Carlsbad, CA 92009 USA

Moran, Tommy *Actor*
Creative Artists Agency LCC (CAA-LA), 9830 Wilshire Blvd, Beverly Hills, CA 90212 USA

Moranis, Rick *Actor*
101 Central Park West, #12B, New York, NY 10023 USA

Morante, Laura *Actor*
Carol Levi Co, Via Giuseppe Pisanelli, Rome, 00196, ITALY

Morasca, Jenna *Reality TV Star*
M Morasca, 6027 Belle Terre Ct, Bridgeville, PA 15017 USA

Morast, Daniel J *Misc*
International Wildlife Coalition, 634 N Falmouth Hwy, North Falmouth, MA 02556 USA

Morath, Max *Musician*
Producers Inc, 1186 N 56th St, Tampa, FL 33617 USA

Morauta, Mekere *Prime Minister*
Premier's Office, Marea Haus, Walgani, Port Moresby, PAPUA NEW GUINEA

Moravec, Ivan *Musician*
Cramer/Marder Artists, 3436 Springhill Road, Lafayette, CA 94549 USA

Morawetz, Cathleen S *Mathematician*
3298 Monteith Ave, Cincinnati, OH 45208 USA

Morceli, Noureddine *Track Athlete*
Youth & Sports Minitry, 3 Rue Mohamed Belouizdad, Algiers, ALGERIA

Morcheeba *Music Group*
Evolution Talent Agency LLC, 1776 Broadway Fl 15, New York, NY 10019 USA

Morcott, Southwood J *Business Person*
Dana Corp, PO Box 1000, Toledo, OH 43697 USA

Mordente, Tony
4541 Comber, Encino, CA 91316

Mordillo, Guillermo *Cartoonist*
Haye Top Present, Oberweg 8, Unterhacing, 82008, GERMANY

Mordkovitch, Lydia *Musician*
25B Belsize Ave, London, NW3 3BL, UNITED KINGDOM (UK)

More, Camilla *Actor*
Sharon Kemp, 477 S Robertson Blvd, #204, Beverly Hills, CA 90211 USA

Moreau, Jeanne *Actor*
Agence Intertalent, 5 Rue Clemont Marot, Paris, 75008, FRANCE

Moreau, Marguerite *Actor*
William Morris Agency, 151 El Camino Dr, Beverly Hills, CA 90212 USA

Moreau, Sylvie
11 av. Corentin Cariou, Paris, FRANCE, 75019

Moreira, Airto *Musician*
A Train Mgmt, PO Box 29242, Oakland, CA 94604 USA

Morelli, Oscar *Actor*
Televisa, Blvd Adolfo Lopez Mateos 232, Colonia San Angel INN, DF, CP 01060, MEXICO

Morello, Tom *Musician*
GAS Entertainment, 8935 Lindblade St, Culver City, CA 90232 USA

Morelos, Lisette *Actor*
Televisa, Blvd Adolfo Lopez Mateos 232, Colonia San Angel INN, DF, CP 01060, MEXICO

Moreno, Azucar *Music Group*
Sony Music Miami, 605 Lincoln Rd, Miami Beach, FL 33138 USA

Moreno, Isabel *Actor*
Gabriel Blanco Iglesias (Mexico), Rio Balsas 35-32, Colonia Cuauhtemoc, DF, 06500, Mexico

Moreno, Jaime *Musician*
New York/New Jersey Mtrostars, 1 Harmon Plaza, #300, Secaucus, NJ 07094 USA

Moreno, Jaime *Race Car Driver*
252 Montclaire Circle, Weston, FL 33326 USA

Moreno, Jorge *Musician*
Creative Artists Agency LCC (CAA-LA), 9830 Wilshire Blvd, Beverly Hills, CA 90212 USA

Moreno, Jose Elias *Actor*
Televisa, Blvd Adolfo Lopez Mateos 232, Colonia San Angel INN, DF, CP 01060, MEXICO

Moreno, Lea
4739 Lankershim Blvd., No. Hollywood, CA 91602-1803

Moreno, Rita *Actor*
Leonard Gordon, 160 Gravatt Dr, Berkeley, CA 94705 USA

Moretti, Fabrizio *Musician*
MVO Ltd, 370 7th Ave, #807, New York, NY 10001 USA

Morey, Bill *Actor*
Kazarian/Spencer, 11365 Ventura Blvd, #100, Studio City, CA 91604 USA

Morfogen, George *Actor*
Gersh Agency, The (LA), 232 N Canon Dr, Beverly Hills, CA 90210 USA

Morgan, Barbara R *Astronaut*
15602 River Maple Lane, Houston, TX 77062 USA

Morgan, Bob
175 Lakeshore, Asheville, NC 28804

Morgan, Chad *Actor*
Burstein Company, The, 15304 Sunset Blvd #208, Pacific Palisades, CA 90272 USA

Morgan, Cindy
280 S. Beverly Dr. #400, Beverly Hills, CA 90212

Morgan, Craig *Musician*
Neostar Management, 2 S University Dr #325, Plantation, FL 33324 USA

Morgan, Dan *Football Player*
Carolina Panthers, Ericsson Stadium, 800 S Mint St, Charlotte, NC 28202 USA

Morgan, Debbi *Actor*
Mitchell K Stubbs, 8675 Washington Blvd, #203, Culver City, CA 90232 USA

Morgan, Debelah *Musician*
DAS Communications, 83 Riverside Dr, New York, NY 10024 USA

Morgan, Donald M *Cinematographer*
15826 Mayall St, North Hills, CA 91343 USA

Morgan, Elaine
24 Aberford Rd. Mt. Ash, Glamorgan, ENGLAND

Morgan, Frank *Musician*
Integrity Talent, PO Box 961, Burlington, MA 01803 USA

Morgan, Gil *Golfer*
PO Box 806, Edmond, OK 73083 USA

Morgan, Glen *Director, Writer, Producer*
Original Film, 2045 S Barrington Ave, Los Angeles, CA 90025 USA

Morgan, Harry *Actor*
13172 Boca De Canon Lane, Los Angeles, CA 90049 USA

Morgan, James C *Business Person*
Applied Materials, 3050 Bowers Ave, Santa Clara, CA 95054 USA

Morgan, James N *Economist*
1217 Bydding Road, Ann Arbor, MI 48103 USA

Morgan, Jane *Musician*
27740 Pacific Coast Highway, Malibu, CA 90265 USA

Morgan, Jaye P *Musician, Actor*
1185 La Grange Ave, Newbury Park, CA 91320 USA

Morgan, Joseph *Actor*
International Creative Management (ICM-LA), 8942 Wilshire Blvd, Beverly Hills, CA 90211 USA

Morgan, Joseph M (Joe) *Baseball Player*
15 Oak Hill Dr, Walpole, MA 02081 USA

Morgan, Kim *Actor*
Artists Group, 10100 Santa Monica Blvd, #2490, Los Angeles, CA 90067 USA

Morgan, Lewis R *Judge*
US Court of Appeals, 25 Elmtree Dr, Sharpsburg, GA 30277 USA

Morgan, Lorrie *Musician*
Martin Assoc, 1207 17th Ave S, #101, Nashville, TN 37212 USA

Morgan, Marabel *Writer*
Total Woman Inc, 1300 NW 167th St, Miami, FL 33169 USA

Morgan, Michael *Scientist*
Wellcome Trust, 183 Euston Road, London, NW1 2BE, UNITED KINGDOM (UK)

Morgan, Michele *Actor, Musician*
5 Rue Jacques Dulud, Neuillysur-Seine, 92200, FRANCE

Morgan, Mike *Cartoonist*
Creators Syndicate, 5777 W Century Blvd, #1700, Los Angeles, CA 90045 USA

Morgan, Robert B *Senator*
PO Box 377, Lillington, NC 27546 USA

Morgan, Robin E *Editor, Writer*
Ms Magazine, Editorial Dept, 230 Park Ave, New York, NY 10169 USA

Morgan, Shelly Taylor *Actor*
Pakula/King, 9229 Sunset Blvd, #315, Los Angeles, CA 90069 USA

Morgan, Stanley D *Football Player*
PO Box 383048, Germantown, TN 38183 USA

Morgan, Tracy *Actor, Comedian*
William Morris Agency, 151 Camino Dr, Beverly Hills, CA 90212 USA

Morgan, Trevor *Actor*
Anonymous Content, 8522 National Blvd #101, Culver City, CA 90232 USA

Morgan, W Jason *Misc*
Princton University, Geophysic Dept, Princeton, NJ 08544 USA

Morgan, Walter T J *Misc*
57 Woodbury Dr, Sutton, Surrey, UNITED KINGDOM (UK)

Morgan, William N *Architect*
William Morgan Architects, 220 E Forsyth St, Jacksonville, FL 32202 USA

Morgan Chad
4526 Wilshire Blvd., Los Angeles, CA 90010

Morganna *Entertainer, Model*
PO Box 20281, Columbia, OH 43220 USA

Morgenson, Gretchen *Journalist*
New York Times, Editorial Dept, 229 W 43rd St, New York, NY 10036 USA

Morgenstern, Maia *Actor*
Catherine Davray Agency, 16 bis rue de l'Abbe de l'Epee, Paris, 75005, FRANCE

Morgenthau, Robert M *Attorney General*
1085 Park Ave, New York, NY 10028 USA

Morgenweck, Henry C *Referee*
33 Bogert St, Teaneck, NJ 07666 USA

Morgridge, John P *Business Person*
Cisco Systems, 170 W Tasan Dr, San Jose, CA 95134 USA

Mori, Hanae *Fashion Designer*
Hanae Mori Haute Couture, 17-19 Ave Montaigne, Paris, 75008, FRANCE

Mori, Yoshiro *Prime Minister*
Prime Minister's Office, 1-6-1 Nagatoicho, Chiyodaku, Tokyo, 100, JAPAN

Moriarty, Cathy *Actor*
Agency for the Performing Arts (APA-LA), 9200 Sunset Blvd #900, Los Angeles, CA 90069 USA

Moriarty, Evelyn
6251 Coldwater Canyon #102, No. Hollywood, CA 91606

Moriarty, Michael *Actor*
200 W 58th St, #3B, New York, NY 10019 USA

Moriarty, Phillip (Phil) *Coach*
12 Vista de Laguna, Fort Pierce, FL 34951 USA

Moriarty-Gentile, Cathy *Actor*
15300 Ventura Blvd, #315, Sherman Oaks, CA 91403 USA

Morimoto, Masaharu
105 Hudson St., New York, NY 10013-2331

Morin, Jim *Editor, Cartoonist*
Miami Herald, Editorial Dept, Herald Plaza, Miami, FL 33101 USA

Morin, Lee M E *Astronaut*
10 Marys Creek Lane, Friendswood, TX 77546 USA

Morin, Milt *Football Player*
45 N Maple St, #B, Hadley, MA 01035 USA

Morishima, Michio *Economist*
31 Greenway Hutton Mount, Brentwood, Essex, CM13 2NP, UNITED KINGDOM (UK)

Morison, Patricia *Actor, Musician*
Craig Mgmt, 125 S Sycamore Ave, Los Angeles, CA 90036 USA

Morissette, Alanis *Musician, Songwriter*
Atlas/Third Rail Entertainment, 9200 W Sunset Blvd, West Hollywood, CA 90069 USA

Morita, Noriyuki (Pat) *Actor*
Cunningham-Escott-Dipene & Associates Inc (CED-LA), 10635 Santa Monica Blvd #130, Los Angeles, CA 90025 USA

Moritz, Louisa
405 Cliffwood Ave., Los Angeles, CA 90049

Moriyama, Raymond *Architect*
32 Daveport Road, Toronto, ON 1H3, CANADA

Mork, Truis *Musician*
Harrison/Parrott, 12 Penzance Place, London, W11 4PA, UNITED KINGDOM (UK)

Morkis, Dorothy *Horse Racer*
17 Farm St, Dover, MA 02030 USA

Morley, Lawrence W *Geophysicist*
90 Hemlock St, Saint Thomas, ON N5R 1X9, CANADA

Morley, Malcolm *Artist*
Pace Gallery, 32 E 57th St, New York, NY 10022 USA

Morley, W I *Editor*
London Free Press, 369 York St, London, ON N6A 4G1, UNITED KINGDOM (UK)

Mornell, Sara
9300 Wilshire Blvd. #555, Beverly Hills, CA 90212

Moroder, Giorgio *Composer*
1880 Century Park East, #900, Los Angeles, CA 90067 USA

Morozov, Akexei *Hockey Player*
Pittsburgh Penguins, Mellon Arena, 66 Mario Lemieux Placa, Pittsburgh, PA 15219 USA

Morozov, Vladimir M *Opera Singer*
Kirov Opera, Mariinsky Theater, Reatralnaya 1, Saint Petersburg, RUSSIA

Morphet, David
101 Honor Oak Rd., London, ENGLAND, SE23 3LB

Morphine
48 Laight St., New York, NY 10013

Morrall, Earl *Football Player*
2751 68th St SW, Naples, FL 34105 USA

Morrell, David *Writer*
Warner Books, 1271 6th Ave, New York, NY 10020 USA

Morretti, Tobias *Actor*
ZBF Agentur, Ordensmeisterstr 15-16, Berling, 12099, GERMANY

Morrey, Charles B Jr *Mathematician*
210 Yale Ave, Kensington, CA 94708 USA

Morrice, Norman A *Ballerina, Choreographer*
Royal Ballet, Covent Garden, Bow St, London, WC2E 9DD, UNITED KINGDOM (UK)

Morricone, Ennio *Composer*
Viale delle Letteratura, #30, Rome, 00144, ITALY

Morris, Betty *Bowler*
225 Lemming Dr, Reno, NV 89523 USA

Morris, Byron (Bam) *Football Player*
251 NE 4th St, Cooper, TX 75432 USA

Morris, Colleen
8271 Melrose Ave. #110, Los Angeles, CA 90046

Morris, Desmond *Doctor*
78 Danbury Rd, Oxford, ENGLAND

Morris, Desmond J *Writer, Biologist*
Jonathan Cape Ltd, 20 Vauxhall Bridge Road, London, SW1V 2SA, UNITED KINGDOM (UK)

Morris, Dick
20 Beeholm Rd., West Redding, CT 06896

Morris, Edmund *Writer, Educator*
222 Central Park S, #14A, New York, NY 10019 USA

Morris, Errol *Director*
Endeavor Talent Agency, 9701 Wilshire Blvd, #1000, Beverly Hills, CA 90212 USA

Morris, Eugene (Mercury) *Football Player*
7000 SW 73rd Court, Miami, FL 33143 USA

Morris, Garret
8436 W. Third St. #740, Los Angeles, CA 90048-4100

Morris, Garrett *Actor, Musician*
Stone Manners, 6500 Wilshire Blvd, #550, Los Angeles, CA 90048 USA

Morris, Gary *Musician*
Gurley Co, 1204B Cedar Lane, Nashville, TN 37212 USA

Morris, George A *Football Player*
720 Fair Oaks Manor NW, Atlanta, GA 30327 USA

Morris, Howard *Comedian, Actor, Director*
742 N Sycamore Ave, Los Angeles, CA 90038 USA

Morris, James P *Opera Singer*
Colbert Artists, 111 W 57th St, New York, NY 10019 USA

Morris, Jan *Writer*
Trefan Morys, Llanystumdwy, Criccieth, Gwymedd, WALES

Morris, Jason *Athlete*
16 Gail St, Chelmsford, MA 01824 USA

Morris, Jenny *Musician*
Artist & Event Mgmt, PO Box 537, Randwick, NSW, 2031, AUSTRALIA

Morris, John S (Jack) *Baseball Player*
PO Box 2112, West Yellowstone, MT 59758 USA

Morris, Johnny *Football Player*
753 Shoreline Road, Lake Barrington, IL 60010 USA

Morris, Julianne *Actor*
Pakula/King & Associates, 9229 Sunset Blvd #315, Los Angeles, CA 90069 USA

Morris, Kathryn *Actor*
Mosaic Media Group, 9200 Sunset Blvd Fl 10, Los Angeles, CA 90069 USA

Morris, Keith *Musician*
International Creative Mgmt, 8942 Wilshire Blvd, #219, Beverly Hills, CA 90211 USA

Morris, Larry *Artist*
105 N Union St, #4, Alexandria, VA 22314 USA

Morris, Lawrence C (Larry) *Football Player*
4737 Upper Berkshire Road, Flowery Branch, GA 30542 USA

Morris, Mark W *Choreographer*
Mark Morris Dance Group, 3 Lafayette Ave, #504, Brooklyn, NY 11217 USA

Morris, Matthew C (Matt) *Baseball Player*
Saint Louis Cardinals, Busch Stadium, 250 Stadium Plaza, Saint Louis, MO 63102 USA

Morris, Mitch *Actor*
Bauer Company, The, 9300 Wilshire Blvd #PH, Beverly Hills, CA 90212 USA

Morris, Nathan *Musician*
Southpaw Entertainment, 10675 Santa Monica Blvd, Los Angeles, CA 90025 USA

Morris, Norval *Attorney General*
1207 E 50th St, Chicago, IL 60615 USA

Morris, Oswald (Ossie) *Cinematographer*
Holbrook Church St, Fontmell Magna, Shaftesbury, SP7 0NY, UNITED KINGDOM (UK)

Morris, Phil *Actor*
704 Strand, Manhattan Beach, CA 90266 USA

Morris, Reginald H *Cinematographer*
255 Bambaugh Circle #308, Scarborough, ON M1W 3T6, CANADA

Morris, Robert *Artist*
Hunter College, Art Dept, New York, NY 10021 USA

Morris, Ronald (Ron) *Track Athlete*
330 S Reese Place, Burbank, CA 91506 USA

Morris, Seth Irvin *Architect*
2 Waverly Court, Houston, TX 77005 USA

Morris, Shellee
RR #2 Box 138, Lake City, AR 72437

Morris, Wanya *Musician*
Creative Artists Agency LCC (CAA-LA), 9830 Wilshire Blvd, Beverly Hills, CA 90212 USA

Morris, Wayna *Musician*
Southpaw Entertainment, 10675 Santa Monica Blvd, Los Angeles, CA 90025 USA

Morris, Wingerter Pam *Swimmer*
PO Box 14381, New Bern, NC 28561 USA

Morrison, Christopher (Mink) *Director*
International Creative Management (ICM-LA), 8942 Wilshire Blvd, Beverly Hills, CA 90211 USA

Morrison, Ian (Scotty) *Misc*
Kennisis Lake, RR 1 PO Box 314, Haliburton, ON K0M 1S0, CANADA

Morrison, Jennifer *Actor*
Abrams Artists Agency (LA), 9200 Sunset Blvd Fl 11, Los Angeles, CA 90069 USA

Morrison, Mark *Musician*
Atlantic Records, 1290 Ave of Americas, New York, 10104 USA

Morrison, Philip *Astronomer, Physicist*
11 Bowden St, Cambridge, MA 02138 USA

Morrison, Robert S (Bob) *Business Person*
Quaker Oats Co, Quaker Tower, PO Box 049001, Chicago, IL 60604 USA

Morrison, Shelley *Actor*
Will & Grace, 4024 Radford Ave, Bungalow 3, Studio City, CA 91604 USA

Morrison, Toni *Nobel Prize Laureate*
185 Nassau St, Princeton, NJ 08542 USA

Morrison, Van *Musician, Songwriter*
#8 Glenthome, Hammersmith, London, W6 oLJ, UNITED KINGDOM (UK)

Morrissey *Music Group, Songwriter*
MVO Ltd, 307 7th Ave, #807, New York, NY 10001 USA

Morrissey, Bill *Musician, Songwriter*
Sage Productions, 1437 Firebird Way, Sunnyvale, CA 94087 USA

Morrissey, Neil *Actor*
International Creative Management (ICM-LA), 8942 Wilshire Blvd, Beverly Hills, CA 90211 USA

Morrone, Joe *Football Coach*
University of Connecticut, Athletic Dept, Storrs Mansfield, CT 06269 USA

Morrow, Bobby
Rt. 4 Box 57, San Benito, TX 78586

Morrow, Bobby Joe *Track Athlete*
PO Box 9, Beeville, TX 78104 USA

Morrow, Bruce (Cousin Brucie) *Entertainer*
CBS Radio Network, 51 W 52nd St, New York, NY 10019 USA

Morrow, Joshua *Actor*
Young and the Restless, The, 7800 Beverly Blvd, Ste 3305, Los Angeles, CA 90036 USA

Morrow, Kenneth (Ken) *Hockey Player*
39 Crystal Dr, Warwick, RI 02889 USA

Morrow, Mari *Actor*
Abrams-Rubaloff Lawrence, 8075 W 3rd St #303, Los Angeles, CA 90048 USA

Morrow, Rob *Actor*
Hofflund/Polone, 9465 Wilshire Blvd, #820, Beverly Hills, CA 90212 USA

Morse, Barry *Actor*
71 Charles St E, #506, Toronto, ON M4Y 2T3, CANADA

Morse, David *Actor*
Yvette Bikoff, 1040 1st Ave, #1126, New York, NY 10022 USA

Morse, David *Musician*
Agency for Performing Arts, 9200 Sunset Blvd, #900, Los Angeles, CA 90069 USA

Morse, David E *Publisher*
Christian Science Monitor, Publisher's Office, 1 Norway St, Boston, MA 02115 USA

Morse, Helen *Actor*
147 King St #A, Sydney, NSW, 2000, AUSTRALIA

Morse, John *Golfer*
9291 17 Mile Road, Marshall, MI 49068 USA

Morse, Natalie *Actor*
William Morris Agency, 52/53 Poland Place, London, W1F 7LX, UNITED KINGDOM (UK)

Morse, Philip M *Physicist*
126 Wildwood St, Winchester, MA 01890 USA

Morse, Ray
989 NW Spruce Ave. #207, Corvallis, OR 97330

Morse, Robert *Actor*
13830 Davana Terrace, Sherman Oaks, CA 91423 USA

Mortensen, Chris *Sportscaster*
ESPN-TV, Sports Dept ESPN Plaza, 935 Middle St, Bristol, CT 06010 USA

Mortensen, J D *Doctor*
Cardipulmonics Inc, 5060 W Amelia Earhart Dr, Salt Lake City, UT 84116 USA

Mortensen, Viggo *Actor*
Creative Artists Agency LCC (CAA-LA), 9830 Wilshire Blvd, Beverly Hills, CA 90212 USA

Mortier, Gerard *Opera Singer*
Saizburg Festpiele, Hofstallgasse 1, Saizburg, 5020, AUSTRIA

Mortimer, Barrett Angela *Tennis Player*
Oaks, Coombe Hill, Kingston-on-Thames, Surrey, UNITED KINGDOM (UK)

Mortimer, Emily *Actor*
Kelly Bush, 3859 Cardiff Ave, #200, Culver City, CA 90232 USA

Mortimer, John C *Writer*
Turville Heath Cottage, Henley-on-Thames, Oxon, UNITED KINGDOM (UK)

Mortimer, Kenneth P *Educator*
University of Hawaii Manoa, President's Office, Honolulu, HI 96822 USA

Mortita, Pat (Noriyuki) *Actor*
6399 Wilshire Blvd, #444, Los Angeles, CA 90048 USA

Morton, Bruce A *Commentator*
Cable News Network, News Dept, 820 1st St NE, Washington, DC 20002 USA

Morton, Joe *Actor*
Judy Schoen, 605 N Larchont Blvd, #309, Los Angeles, CA 90004 USA

Morton, John
119 Huse Dr., Annapolis, MD 21403

Morton, Johnnie *Football Player*
2911 Oakwood Lane, Torrance, CA 90505 USA

Morton, L Craig *Football Player*
500 S Eliseo Dr, #22, Greenbrae, CA 94904 USA

Morton, R Alastair *Business Person*
Senator House, 85 Queen St, London,
EC4V 4DP, UNITED KINGDOM (UK)

Morton, Samantha *Actor*
Conway Van Gelder Robinson, 18-21
Jermyn St, London, SW1Y 6NB, UNITED
KINGDOM (UK)

Morukov, Boris V *Cosmonaut*
Potcha Kosmonavtov, Moskovskoi Oblasti,
Syvisdny Goroduk, 141160, RUSSIA

Mosbacher, Robert A *Secretary*
Mosbacher Energy Co, 712 Main St,
#2200, Houston, TX 77002 USA

Moschen, Michael *Artist*
PO Box 178, Cornwall Bridge, CT 06754
USA

Moschitta Jr, John
11601 Dunston Way #206, Los Angeles,
CA 90049 USA

Moscow, David *Actor*
Robert Stein Management, 345 N Maple
Dr #317, Beverly Hills, CA 90210 USA

Mosdell, Kenneth *Hockey Player*
1695 Ave Surrey, Dorval, QC, H9P 1W7,
CANADA

Mosebar, Donald H (Don) *Football Player*
1713 Walnut Ave, Manhattan Beach, CA
90266 USA

Mosel, Tad *Writer*
149 East Side Dr, PO Box 249, Concord,
NH 03302 USA

Moseley, Jonny *Skier*
167 Trinidad Dr, Tiburon, CA 94920 USA

Moseley, Mark
16001 Berkeley Dr, Haymarket, VA
22079

Moseley, Roy
152 Ivor Ct Gloucester Pl., London,
ENGLAND, NW1

Moseley, T Michael (Buzz) *General*
Vice Cheif of Staff, HqUSAF Pentagon,
Washington, DC 20330 USA

Moser, Barry *Misc*
115 Pantry Rd, North Hatfield, MA 01066
USA

Moser, Donald B (Don) *Editor*
Smithsonian Magazine, Editorial Dept,
900 Jefferson SW, Washington, DC 20560
USA

Moser, Thomas *Opera Singer*
Lies Askonas, 6 Henrietta St, London,
WC2E 8LA, UNITED KINGDOM (UK)

Moser-Proll, Annemarie *Skier*
Moser Cafe-Bar, #92, Kleinari 115, 5602,
AUSTRIA

Moses, Albert
15 Overstone Rd, Harpenden Herts.,
ENGLAND, AL5 5PN

Moses, Billy E
409 N Camden Dr #202, Beverly Hills,
CA 90210 USA

Moses, Ed
One Olympic Plaza, Colorado Springs,
CO 80909-5770

Moses, Edwin
One Hoosier Dome, Indianapolis, IN
46225-1023

Moses, Edwin C *Track Athlete*
Robinson-Humphrey, 3333 Peachtree
Road NE, Atlanta, GA 30326 USA

Moses, Haven C *Football Player*
1140 Cherokee St, Denver, CO 80204
USA

Moses, Kim *Producer*
William Morris Agency (WMA-LA), 1
William Morris Pl, Beverly Hills, CA
90212 USA

Moses, Lincoln E *Mathematician*
Stanford University, Medical Center,
Statistics Dept, Stanford, CA 94305 USA

Moses, Rick *Actor, Musician*
Calder Agency, 19919 Redwing St,
Woodland Hills, CA 91364 USA

Moses, Robert (Bob) *Educator, Social Activist*
99 Bishop Allen Dr, Cambridge, MA
02139 USA

Moses, Yolanda T *Educator*
City College of New York, President's
Office, New York, NY 10031 USA

Moshammer, Rudolph
Maximilianstr. 14, Munich, GERMANY,
D-80539

Mosher, Gregory D *Director, Producer*
Lincoln Center Theater, 150 W 165th St,
New York, NY 10023 USA

Moshinsky, Elijah *Opera Singer*
28 Kidbrooke Groove, London, SE3 0LG,
UNITED KINGDOM (UK)

Mosimann, Anton *Chef*
Mosimann's, 11B W Halkin St, London,
SW1X 8JL, UNITED KINGDOM (UK)

Mosisilli, Pakalitha *Prime Minister*
Chairman's Office, Military Council, PO
Box 527, Maseru, 100, LESOTHO

Moskow, Michael *Financier, Government Official*
Federal Reserve Bank, 230 S LaSalle St,
Chicago, IL 60604 USA

Moskowitz, Robert *Artist*
81 Leonard St, New York, NY 10013 USA

Mosley, Brian *Actor*
After Dinner, Saga Court, S Heath G
Missenden, Bucks, HP16 9QQ, UNITED
KINGDOM (UK)

Mosley, J Brooke *Religious Leader*
1604 Foulkeways, Gwynedd, PA 19436
USA

Mosley, Max R *Race Car Driver*
Int'l Automobile Fed, 2 Chermin
Blandonnet, Geneva, 1215,
SWITZERLAND

Mosley, Roger E *Actor*
4470 Sunset Blvd, #107-342, Los Angeles,
CA 90027 USA

Mosley, Walter *Writer*
37 Carmine St, #275, New York, NY
10014 USA

Mosoke, Kintu *Prime Minister*
Prime Minister's Office, PO Box 341,
Kampala, UGANDA

Moss, Carrie-Anne *Actor*
William Morris Agency (WMA-LA), 1
William Morris Pl, Beverly Hills, CA
90212 USA

Moss, Cynthia *Misc*
African Wildlife Foundation, Mara Road,
PO Box 48177, Nairobi, KENYA

Moss, Elisabeth *Actor*
United Talent Agency, 9560 Wilshire
Blvd, #500, Los Angeles, CA 90212 USA

Moss, Elza *Religious Leader*
Primitive Advent Christian Church, 273
Frame Road, Elkview, WV 25071 USA

Moss, Eric Owen *Architect*
8557 Higuera St, Culver City, CA 90232
USA

Moss, Geoffrey *Cartoonist*
315 E 68th St, New York, NY 10021 USA

Moss, Jon
64 Knighton Park Rd, London, ENGLAND,
SE26 5RL

Moss, Kate *Model*
IMG Models, 304 Park Ave S Fl 12, New
York, NY 10010 USA

Moss, Randy *Football Player*
Minnesota Vikings, 9520 Viking Dr, Eden
Praire, MN 55344 USA

Moss, Ronn *Actor*
2401 Nottingham Ave, Los Angeles, CA
90027 USA

Moss, Santana *Football Player*
New York Jets, 1000 Fuiton Ave,
Hempstead, NY 11550 USA

Moss, Shirley *Artist*
Moss Studios, PO Box 18104, Anaheim,
CA 92817 USA

Moss, Sterling *Race Car Driver*
Stirling Moss Ltd, 46 Shephard St, Mayfair,
London, W1Y 8JN USA

Moss, Stirling
46 Shepherd St. Mayfair, London,
ENGLAND, W1Y 8JN

Mossbauer, Rudolf L *Nobel Prize Laureate*
Stumpflingstr 6A, Grunwald, 82031,
GERMANY

Mosser, Jonell *Musician*
Phil Mayo Co, PO Box 304, Bomoseen,
VT 05732 USA

Mossi, Donald L (Don) *Baseball Player*
23250 Canyon Lane, Caldwell, ID 83607
USA

Mossman, Doug
999 Kalapaki St., Honolulu, HI 96825

Most, Don *Actor*
6643 Buttonwood Ave, Agoura, CA 91301
USA

Most, Donny
280 S. Beverly Dr. #400, Beverly Hills,
CA 90212

Mosteller, Frederick *Mathematician*
Harvard University, Statistics Dept,
Cambridge, MA 02138 USA

Mostert, Dutch *Artist*
93696 Mallard Lane, North Bend, OR
97459 USA

Mostow, George D *Mathematician*
25 Beechwood Road, Woodbridge, CT
06525 USA

Mostow, Jonathan *Director*
Creative Artists Agency, 9830 Wilshire
Blvd, Beverly Hills, CA 90212 USA

Mota, Manny
4118 Ocean View Blvd., Montrose, CA
91020

Mota, Manuel R (Manny) *Baseball Player,*
Coach
1506 Canada Blvd, #3, Flendale, CA
91208 USA

Mota, Ross *Track Athlete*
R Teatro 194 4 Esq, Porto, 4100,
PORTUGAL

Mote, Bobby *Rodeo Rider*
20840 NW Kachina Ave, Redmond, OR
97756 USA

Mothersbaugh, Mark
2164 Sunset Plaza Dr., Los Angeles, CA
90069

Motion, Andrew *Writer*
University of East Anglia, English Dept,
Norwich, NR4 7TJ, UNITED KINGDOM
(UK)

Motley, Constance Baker *Judge*
US District Court, US Courthouse, Foley
Square, New York, NY 10007 USA

Motley, Isolde *Editor*
Life Magazine, Editorial Dept, Time-Life
Building, New York, NY 10020 USA

Motley Crue *Music Group*
Artist Group International (NY), 150 East
58th Street, Fl 19, New York, NY 10155
USA

Motorhead *Music Group*
98 Puddleton Cres Poole, Dorset,
ENGLAND, United Kingdom

Mott, Stewart R *Politician*
515 Madison Ave, New York, NY 10022
USA

Motta, Dick *Coach*
PO Box 4, Fish Haven, ID 83287 USA

Mottelson, Ben R *Nobel Prize Laureate*
Nordita, Blegdamsvei 17, Copenhagen,
2100, DENMARK

Mottola, Greg *Director, Writer*
United Talent Agency (UTA), 9560
Wilshire Blvd, Beverly Hills, CA 90212
USA

Mottola, Thomas (Tommy) *Business*
Person
Casablanca Records, 8255 Sunset Blvd.,
Los Angeles, CA 90046 USA

Motulsky, Amo G *Scientist*
4347 53rd St NE, Seattle, WA 98105 USA

Motyka, Christopher *Actor*
Bobby Ball Talent Agency, 4342
Lankershim Blvd, Universal City, CA
91602 USA

Motz, Diana Gribbon *Judge*
US Appeals Court, 101 W Lombard St,
Baltimore, MD 21201 USA

Motzfeldt, Jonathan *Prime Minister*
Greenland Home Rule Government, PO
Box 1015, Nuuk, 3900, GREENLAND

Mouawad, Jerry *Director*
Imago Theater, 17 SE 8th Ave, Portland,
OR 97214 USA

Mould, Bob *Musician, Songwriter*
High Road, 751 Bridgeway #300,
Sausalito, CA 94965 USA

Moulder-Brown, John
193 Wardour St., London, ENGLAND,
W1V 3FA

Moulds, Eric *Football Player*
5295 Briefcliff Dr, Hamburg, NY 14075
USA

Mouli *Actor, Bollywood*
12 Srinivasa Ave, Chennai, TN 600028,
INDIA

Moulton, Alexander E *Engineer*
Hall, Bradford-on-Avon, Wilts, BA15 1AJ,
UNITED KINGDOM (UK)

Moulton, Sara *Chef*
Food Network, 1180 Ave of Americas,
#1200, New York, NY 10036 USA

Moulton, Sarah *Television Host, Chef*
Sara's Secrets, 1180 6th Ave Fl 12, New
York, NY 10036 USA

Mounsey, Tara *Hockey Player*
24 E Sugar Ball Road, Concord, NH
03301 USA

Mounsey, Yvonne *Ballerina*
Westside School of Ballet, 1711 Stewart
St, Santa Monica, CA 90404 USA

Mount, Anson *Actor*
William Morris Agency, 1325 Ave of
Americas, New York, NY 10019 USA

Mount, Rick *Basketball Player*
904 Hopkins Road, Lebanon, IN 46052
USA

Mountcastle Jr, Vernon B *Misc*
15601 Carroll Road, Monkton, MD 21111
USA

Mourning, Alonzo *Basketball Player*
3525 Anchorage Way, Coconut Grove, FL
33133 USA

Mouse, Mickey Club
PO Box 10200, Lake Buena Vista, FL
32830-0200

Mouskouri, Nana
12 rue Gutenberg, Boulogne, FRANCE,
F-92100

Mouskouri, Nana J *Songwriter, Musician*
12 Rue Gitenberg, Boulogne, 92000,
FRANCE

Moussier, Sabine *Actor*
Televisa, Blvd Adolfo Lopez Mateos 232,
Colonia San Angel INN, DF, CP 01060,
MEXICO

Moustaki, Georges *Musician*
PolyGram Records, 20 Rue des Fosses-
Saint-Jacques, Paris, 75005, FRANCE

Mouton, Leslie *Journalist*
1333 Northland Drive, Mendota Heights,
MN 55120

Movessian, Victoria (Viki) *Hockey Player*
17 Webb St, Lexington, MA 02420 USA

Movita
2766 Motor Ave., Los Angeles, CA 90064

Mowat, Farley M *Writer*
18 King St, Port Hope, ON L1A 2R4,
CANADA

Mowerson, Robert *Swimmer*
2601 Kenzle Terrace, #324, Minneapolis,
MN 55418 USA

Mowlam, Marjorie *Government Official*
House of Commons, Westminster,
London, SW1 0AA, UNITED KINGDOM
(UK)

Mowrey, Caitlin *Actor*
William Morris Agency (WMA-LA), 1
William Morris Pl, Beverly Hills, CA
90212 USA

Mowrey, Dude *Musician*
Joe Taylor Artist Agency, 2802 Columbine
Place, Nashville, TN 37204 USA

Mowry, Tahj *Actor*
DDK Talent Representatives, 3800
Barham Blvd #303, Los Angeles, CA
90068 USA

Mowry, Tamara *Actor, Producer*
Metropolitan Talent Agency (MTA), 4526
Wilshire Blvd, Los Angeles, CA 90010
USA

Mowry, Tia *Actor*
DRM Management, PO Box 5009,
Woodland Hills, CA 91356 USA

Moxey, John Llewellyn *Director*
Shapiro-Lichtman, 8827 Beverly Blvd, Los
Angeles, CA 90048 USA

Moyer, Jamie *Baseball Player*
672 Mininger Road, Souderton, PA 18694
USA

Moyer, Paul *Commentator*
12742 Highwood St, Los Angeles, CA
90049 USA

Moyers, Bill D *Commentator*
151 Central Park W, New York, NY
10023 USA

Moyet, Alison *Musician*
Primary Talent, 2-12 Petonville Road,
London, N1 9PL, UNITED KINGDOM
(UK)

Moyle, Allan *Writer, Director*
Becsey Wisdom Kalajian, 9200 W Sunset
Blvd #820, Los Angeles, CA 90069 USA

Moynahan, Bridget *Actor, Model*
Endeavor Agency LLC (LA), 9601 Wilshire
Blvd Fl 3, Beverly Hills, CA 90210 USA

Moynihan, Christopher *Actor*
OmniPop Inc (LA), 10700 Ventura Blvd Fl
2, Studio City, CA 91604 USA

Moynihan, Colin B *Government Official*
Crown Reach, 16 Grosvenor Road,
London, SW1V 3JV, UNITED KINGDOM
(UK)

Moyroud, Louis M *Inventor*
202 Grove Way, Delray Beach, FL 33444
USA

Mphahele, Ezekiel *Writer*
5444 Zone 5, Pimville, Johannesburg,
SOUTH AFRICA

Mr, Cheeks *Musician*
Agency Group Ltd, 1775 Broadway, #430,
New York, NY 10019 USA

Mr Blackwell *Fashion Designer*
531 S Windsor, Los Angeles, CA 90020
USA

Mr T *Actor*
15208 La Maida St, Sherman Oaks, CA
91403-1921 USA

Mraz, Jason *Musician, Songwriter*
Elektra Records, 75 Rockefeller Plaza, New York, NY 10019 USA

Mroudjae, Ali *Prime Minister*
BP 58 Rond Point Gobadjou, Moroni, COMOROS

Msuya, Cleopa D *Prime Minister*
Prime Minister's Office, PO Box 980, Dodoma, TANZANIA

Mswati III *King*
Royal Palace, PO Box 1, Mbabane, SWAZILAND

Mu'all, Sheikh Rashid bin Ahmed al *Politician*
Ruler's Place, Umm Al Quwain, UNITED ARAB EMIRATES

Mubarak, Muhammad Hosni *President, General*
Presidential Palace, Abdeen, Cairo, EGYPT

Muccino, Gabriele *Director, Writer*
Creative Artists Agency LCC (CAA-LA), 9830 Wilshire Blvd, Beverly Hills, CA 90212 USA

Mucke, Manuela *Athlete*
Charlottenstr 13, Berlin, 10315, GERMANY

Muckler, John *Coach*
Ottawa Senators, 1000 Palladium Dr, Kanata, ON K2V 1A4, CANADA

Mudd, Howard E *Football Player, Coach*
Indianapolis Colts, 7001 W 56th St, Indianapolis, IN 46254 USA

Mudd, Jodie *Golfer*
7580 Manasota Key Road, Englewood, FL 34223 USA

Mudd, Roger
7167 Old Dominion Dr., McLean, VA 22101

Mudd, Roger H *Commentator*
7167 Old Dominion Dr, McLean, VA 22101 USA

Mudra, Darrell *Football Coach*
424 Tiger Hammock Road, Crawfordville, FL 32327 USA

Mudvayne *Music Group*
Anger Management, 6907 University Ave #199, Middleton, WI 53562-2763 USA

Muelier, Charles W *Business Person*
Ameren Corp, 1901 Chouteau Ave, Saint Louis, MO 63103 USA

Mueller, Don
11224 Mueller Lane, Maryland Heights, MO 63042

Mueller, George E *Engineer*
Kistler Aerospace Corp, 3760 Carillon Point, Kirkland, WA 98033 USA

Mueller-Stahl, Armin *Actor*
c/o ZBF, Ordensmeisterstr. 15-16, Berlin, GERMANY, D-12099

Muench, David *Photographer*
PO Box 30500, Santa Barbara, CA 93130 USA

Muetterties, Earl L *Misc*
University of California, Chemistry Dept, Berkeley, CA 94720 USA

Muetzelfeldt, Bruno *Religious Leader*
Lutheran World Federation, 150 Rt de Femey, Geneva 20, 1211, SWITZERLAND

Mugabe, Robert G *President*
President's Office, Munhumutapa Bldg, Samora Machel Ave, Harare, ZIMBABWE

Mugler, Thierry *Fashion Designer*
4-6 Rue Aux Ours, Paris, 75003, FRANCE

Muhammad, Elijah
7351 S. Stony Island, Chicago, IL 60617

Muhammad, Wallace D *Religious Leader*
American Muslim Mission, 7351 S Stony Island Blvd, Chicago, IL 60649 USA

Muir, Roger
10 Drewid Hill Ave., Methuen, MA 01844

Muir DeGraad, Karen *Swimmer*
Applebosch State Hospital, Ozwatini, Natal, SOUTH AFRICA

Muirhead, Brian *Astronomer, Scientist*
Jet Propulsion Laboratory, 4800 Oakgrove Dr, Pasadena, CA 91109 USA

Muirsheil of Kilmacolm, Viscount *Government Official*
Knapps, Kilmacolm, Renfrewshire, SCOTLAND

Mujica, Aylin *Actor*
TV Azteca, Periferico Sur 4121, Colonia Fuentes del Pedregal, DF, CP 14141, Mexico

Mukaddam, Ali *Actor*
Edward G Agency, 19 Isabella St, Toronto ON, M4Y 1M7, CANADA

Mukai, Chiaki Naito *Astronaut*
15836 Seahorse Dr, #253, Houston, TX 77062 USA

Mukhamedov, Irek J *Ballerina*
Royal Ballet, Covent Garden Bow St, London, WC2E 9DD, UNITED KINGDOM (UK)

Mukherjee, Bharati *Writer*
130 Rivoli St, San Francisco, CA 94117 USA

Mukherjee, Hrishikesh *Director, Producer, Filmmaker, Bollywood*
123A Anupama Carter Road, Bandra, Bombay, MS 400 050, INDIA

Mukherjee, Rani *Actor, Bollywood*
B/405 Shakti Apartments, Kaylan Complex Yari Road Versova, Mumbai, MS 400061, INDIA

Mulari, Tarja *Speed Skater*
Motion Oy, Vanhan Mankkaantie 33, Espoo, 02180, FINDLAND

Mularkey, Mike *Football Player*
2528 Lindenwood Dr, Wexford, PA 15090 USA

Mulcahy, Anne
Xerox Corp, 800 Long Ridge Road, Stamford, CT 06902 USA

Mulcahy, J Patrick *Business Person*
Raiston Purina Co, Checkerboard Square, Saint Louis, MO 63164 USA

Mulcahy, Russell *Director*
Agency For Performing Arts, 9200 W Sunset Blvd #900, Los Angeles, CA 90069 USA

Muldaur, Diana *Actor*
20 Cummings Way, Edgertown, MA 02539 USA

Muldaur, Maria *Musician, Songwriter*
Piedmont Talent, PO Box 680006, Charlotte, NC 28216 USA

Mulder, Mark *Baseball Player*
33196 N 74th Way, Scottsdale, AZ 85262 USA

Muldoon, Leslie L *Doctor*
Oregon Health Sciences University, Neurology Dept, Portland, OR 97201 USA

Muldoon, Patrick *Actor, Model*
11030 Ventura Blvd, #3, Studio City, CA 91604 USA

Muldoon, Paul B *Writer*
Princeton University, Creative Writing Program, Princeton, NJ 08544 USA

Muldowney, Dominic J *Composer*
Royal National Theater, Music Dept, South Bank, London, SE1 1PX, UNITED KINGDOM (UK)

Muldowney, Shirley *Race Car Driver*
79559 North Ave, Armada, MI 48005 USA

Mulgrew, Kate *Actor*
Marie Ambrosino Mgmt, 10351 Santa Monica Blvd, #220, Los Angeles, CA 90025 USA

Mulhern, Matt *Actor*
Gold Marshak Liedtke, 3500 W Olive Ave, #1400, Burbank, CA 91505 USA

Mulhern, Sinead *Opera Singer*
Van Walsum Mgmt, 4 Addison Bridge Place, London, W14 8XP, UNITED KINGDOM (UK)

Mulis, Kary B *Nobel Prize Laureate*
Vyrex, 2519 Avenida de la Palaya, La Jolla, CA 92037 USA

Mulkerin, Ted *Writer*
Endeavor Agency LLC (LA), 9601 Wilshire Blvd Fl 3, Beverly Hills, CA 90210 USA

Mulkey, Chris *Actor*
Paradigm Agency, 10100 Santa Monica Blvd, #2500, Los Angeles, CA 90067 USA

Mulkey-Robertson, Kim *Basketball Player, Coach*
Baylor University, Athletic Dept, Waco, TX 76798 USA

Mull, Martin *Actor*
338 S Chadbourne Ave, Los Angeles, CA 90049 USA

Mullally, Megan *Actor, Musician*
Baker/Winokur/Ryder, 9100 Wilshire Blvd, #600, Beverly Hills, CA 90212 USA

Mullan, Peter *Writer*
International Creative Management (ICM-LA), 8942 Wilshire Blvd, Beverly Hills, CA 90211 USA

Mullane, Richard M (Mike) *Astronaut*
1301 Las Lomas Road NE, Albuquerque, NM 87106 USA

Mullany, Mitch *Television Host*
New Wave Entertainment (LA), 2660 W Olive Blvd, Burbank, CA 91505 USA

Mullavey, Greg *Actor*
1818 Thayer Ave, #303, Los Angeles, CA 90025 USA

Mullavy, Greg
1818 Thayer Ave. #303, Los Angeles, CA 90025-4962

Mullen, Josep P (Joey) *Hockey Player*
126 Fieldgate Dr, Pittsburg, PA 15241 USA

Mullen, Larry Jr *Musician*
Principle Mgmt, 30-32 Sir John Rogerson Quay, Dublin, 2, IRELAND

Mullen, Michael G *Admiral*
Vice Chief of Naval Operations, HqUSN Pentagon, Washington, DC 20350 USA

Mullen, Nicole *Musician*
Creative Artists Agency LCC (CAA-LA), 9830 Wilshire Blvd, Beverly Hills, CA 90212 USA

Muller, Egon *Motorcycle Racer*
Dorfstr 17, Rodenbek, Kiel, 24247, GERMANY

Muller, Elisabeth
. Feld 14, Sempach/Lu, SWITZERLAND, 6204

Muller, Gerd *Soccer Player*
Neuestr 21, Munich, 81479, GERMANY

Muller, Jennifer *Dancer, Choreographer*
Muller/Works Foundation, 131 W 24th St, New York, NY 10011 USA

Muller, Jorg *Race Car Driver*
Insert Motorsport, Fassoldshof 1, Mainleus, 95336, GERMANY

Muller, K ALex *Nobel Prize Laureate*
IBM Research Laboratory, Saumerstr 4, Ruschlikon, 8803, SWITZERLAND

Muller, Leah Poulos *Speed Skater*
11455 N Mulberry Dr, Mequon, WI 53092 USA

Muller, Lillian *Model, Actor*
PO Box 20029-414, Encino, CA 91416 USA

Muller, Lisel *Writer*
LSU Press, PO Box 25053, Baton Rouge, LA 70894 USA

Muller, Marcia *Writer*
Mysterious Press, Warner Books, 1271 6th Ave, New York, NY 10020 USA

Muller, Michel *Actor, Writer*
ArtMedia, 20 Ave Rapp, Paris, 75007, FRANCE

Muller, Peter *Skier*
Haldenstr 18, Adliswil, 8134, SWITZERLAND

Muller, Peter *Architect*
PO Box 545, Clare, SA, 5453, AUSTRALIA

Muller, Richard S *Engineer*
University of California, Sensor/Acutator Center, Berkeley, CA 94720 USA

Muller, Robby *Cinematographer*
Smith/Gosnell/Nicholson, PO Box 1156, Studio City, CA 91614 USA

Muller, Robert *Misc*
Federal Bureau of Investigation, 9th & Pennsylvania NW, Washington, DC 20535 USA

Muller, Steven *Educator*
21st Century Foundation, 919 18th St NW #800, Washington, DC 20006 USA

Muller-Stahl, Armin *Actor*
Gartenweg 31, Sierksdorf, 23730, GERMANY

Muller-Westernhagen, Marius
Mittelweg 69, Hamburg, GERMANY, D-20149

Mulley of Manor Park, Frederick W
Government Official
House of Lords, Westminster, London, SW1A 0PW, UNITED KINGDOM (UK)

Mulligan, Gerry *Writer*
3 Arts Entertainment Inc, 9460 Wilshire Blvd Fl 7, Beverly Hills, CA 90212 USA

Mulligan, Richard C *Biologist*
11 Sumner Road, Cambridge, MA 02138 USA

Mulligan, Robert P *Director*
JV Broffman, 5150 Wilshire Blvd, #505, Los Angeles, CA 90036 USA

Mulliken, William (Bill) *Swimmer*
4216 N Keeler Ave, Chicago, IL 60641 USA

Mullin, Chris *Baseball Player*
116 Laurelwood Dr, Danville, CA 94506 USA

Mullin, Christopher P (Chris) *Basketball Player*
116 Laurelwood Dr, Danville, CA 94506 USA

Mullin, J Stanley *Skier*
Sheppard Mullin Richter Hampton, 333 S Hope St, Los Angeles, CA 90071 USA

Mullin, Leo F *Business Person*
Delta Air Lines, Hartsfield International Airport, Atlanta, GA 30320 USA

Mullins, Jeffrey (Jeff) *Basketball Player*
8866 N Sea Oaks Way, #202, Vero Beach, FL 32963 USA

Mullins, Larry *Model*
U2, 30-32 Sir John Rogerson's Quarry, Dublin, IRELAND

Mullins, Shawn *Musician, Songwriter*
High Road, 751 Bridgeway, #300, Sausalito, CA 94965 USA

Mullova, Viktoria Y *Musician*
Askonas Holt Ltd, 27 Chancery Lane, London, WC2A 1PF, UNITED KINGDOM (UK)

Mulloy, Gardner *Tennis Player*
800 NW 9th Ave, Miami, FL 33136 USA

Mulroney, Dermot *Actor*
5200 Linwood Dr, Los Angeles, CA 90027 USA

Mulroney, Kieran
6100 Wilshire Blvd. #1170, Los Angeles, CA 90048

Mulroney, M Brian *Prime Minister*
47 Forden Crescent, Westmount, QC, H3Y 2Y5, CANADA

Muluzi, Bakili *President*
President's Office, Private Bag 301, Capitol City, Lilongwe, 3, MALAWI

Mulva, James J *Business Person*
Conoco/Philips Inc, 600 N Daisy Ashford, Houston, TX 77029 USA

Mulvey, Grant *Hockey Player*
491 S Hampshire Ave, Elmhurst, IL 60126 USA

Mulvoy, Mark *Editor, Publisher*
Sports Illustrated Magazine, Rockefeller Center, New York, NY 10020 USA

Mumba, Samantha *Musician, Actor*
Polydor Records, 1 Sussex Place, London, W6 9XT, UNITED KINGDOM (UK)

Mumford, David B *Mathematician*
65 Milton St, Milton, MA 02186 USA

Mumy, Bill *Actor*
11333 Moorpark St, PO Box 433, Studio City, CA 91602 USA

Mumy, Billy *Actor*
11333 Moorpark St, PO Box 433, Studio City, CA 91602 USA

Muna, Solomon Tandeng *Prime Minister*
PO Box 15 Mbengwi, Mono Division, North West Province, CAMEROON

Munchak, Michael A (Mike) *Football Player*
9155 SAddlebow Dr, Brentwood, TN 37027 USA

Munchkins, The
PO Box 587, Farmingville, NY 11738

Muncie, Harry V (Chuck) *Football Player*
Chuck Muncie Youth Foundation, 3334 Woodview Court, Lafayette, CA 94549 USA

Mundae, Misty *Actor*
PO Box 447, Ringwood, NJ 07456

Mundell, Robert A *Nobel Prize Laureate*
35 Claremont Ave, New York, NY 10027 USA

Mundy, Carl E Jr *General*
9308 Ludgale Dr, Alexandria, VA 22309 USA

Munitz, Barry A *Educator*
California State University Syetem, 400 Golden Shore St, Long Beach, CA 90802 USA

Muniz, Frankie *Actor*
PO Box 55218, Sherman Oaks, CA 91413 USA

Munk, Peter *Business Person*
Barrick Gold Corp, 200 Bay St, Toronto, ON M5J 2J3, CANADA

Munk, Walter H *Geophysicist*
9530 La Jolta Shores, La Jolla, CA 92037 USA

Munn, Allison *Actor*
Sanders/Armstrong Management, 2120 Colorado Blvd #120, Santa Monica, CA 90404 USA

Munos, Maria *Television Host*
Entertainment Tonight (ET), 5555 Melrose Ave, Mae West Bldg Fl 2, Hollywood, CA 90038 USA

Munoz, M Anthony *Football Player, Sportscaster*
6529 Irwin Simpson Road, Mason, OH 45040 USA

Munro, Alice *Writer*
PO Box 1133, Clinton, ON N0M 1L0, CANADA

Munro, Caroline *Admiral*
PO Box 2589, London, W1A 3NQ,
UNITED KINGDOM (UK)

Munro, Dana G *Diplomat*
PO Box 317, Media, PA 19063 USA

Munro, Ian *Editor*
Annals of Internal Medicine, Editorial
Dept, 34 Beacon St, Boston, MA 02108
USA

Munro, J Richard *Publisher*
Time Warner Inc, Rockefeller Plaza, New
York, NY 10020 USA

Munro, Lochlyn *Actor*
International Creative Mgmt, 8942
Wilshire Blvd, #219, Beverly Hills, CA
90211 USA

Munsel, Patrice *Opera Singer*
PO Box 472, Schroon Lake, NY 12870
USA

Munson, John *Musician*
Monterey Peninsula Artists, 509 Hartnell
St, Monterey, CA 93940 USA

Muntyan, Mikhail *Opera Singer*
16 N Iorga Str, #13, Chisnau, 277012,
MOLDOVA

Muppets, The
PO Box 20750, New York, NY 10023-
1488

Murad, Ferid *Nobel Prize Laureate*
2121 W Holcombe Blvd, Houston, TX
77030 USA

Murad, Raza *Actor, Bollywood*
B 104 Mayfair Raviraj Oberoi Complex,
Near Lakxmi Industrial Estate New Link
Road Andheri, Bombay, MS 400 058,
INDIA

Muradov, Sakhat A *Government Official*
Turkmenistan Mejlis, 17 Gogol St,
Ashkhabad, 744017, TURKENISTAN

Murakami, Ryu *Writer*
Kodansha Books, 2-12-21 Otowa,
Bunkyoku, Tokyo, 112-8001, JAPAN

Murali *Actor, Bollywood*
3-77th Street, Chennai, TN 600083,
INDIA

Muraliyev, Amangeldy *Prime Minister*
Prime Minister's Office, Ul Perromayskaya
57, Bishkek, KYRGYZSTAN

Muratova, Kira G *Director*
Proletarsjy Blvd 14B, #15, Odessa,
270015, RUSSIA

Murayama, Makio *Scientist*
5010 Benton Ave, Bathesda, MD 20814
USA

Murayama, Tomiichi *Prime Minister*
3-2-2 Chiyomachi Oita, Oita, 870, JAPAN

Murcer, Bobby R *Baseball Player*
4323 NW 63rd St, #100, Oklahoma City,
OK 73116 USA

Murchison, Ira *Track Athlete*
10113 S Sangamon St, Chicago, IL 60643
USA

Murciano, Jr, Enrique *Actor*
IFA Talent Agency, 8730 Sunset Blvd
#490, Los Angeles, CA 90069 USA

Murdoch, K Rupert *Publisher*
News America Publishing, 1211 Ave of
Americas, New York, NY 10036 USA

Murdoch, Murray *Hockey Player*
190 Dessa Dr, Hamden, CT 06517 USA

Murdoch, Robert J (Bob) *Hockey Player,
Coach*
410 11th Ave S, Cranbrook, BC V1C 2P9,
CANADA

Murdoch, Rupert
1330 Angelo Dr., Beverly Hills, CA 90210

Murdoch, Stuart *Musician, Songwriter*
Legends of 21st Century, 7 Trinity Row,
Florence, MA 01062 USA

Murdock, David H *Business Person*
10900 Wilshire Blvd, #1600, Los Angeles,
CA 90024 USA

Murdock, George *Actor*
5733 Sunfield Ave, Lakewood, CA 90712
USA

Murdock, George P *Doctor*
Wynnewood Plaza, #107, Wynnewood,
PA 19096 USA

Murdock, Shirley *Musician*
Millennium Entertainment Group, 1319
Fifth Ave N, Nashville, TN 37208 USA

Muresan, Georghe *Basketball Player,
Actor*
New Jersey Nets, 390 Murray Hill
Parkway, East Rutherford, NJ 07073 USA

Muris, Timothy *Government Official*
Federal Trade Commission, Pennsylvania
Ave & 6th St NW, Washington, DC 20580
USA

Muris, Timothy J *Government Official,
Educator*
George Mason University, Law School,
Fairfax, VA 22030 USA

Murphey, Michael Martin *Musician,
Songwriter*
Wildfire Productions, PO Box 450,
Rancho de Taos, NM 87557 USA

Murphy, Ben *Actor*
2690 Rambla Pacifico St, Malibu, CA
90265 USA

Murphy, Bob *Sportscaster*
1401 Bonnie Lane, Bayside, NY 11360
USA

Murphy, Bob *Golfer*
Eddie Elias Enterprises, PO Box 5118,
Akron, OH 44334 USA

Murphy, Brian
265 Liverpool Rd, London, ENGLAND,
N1 1LX

Murphy, Brittany *Actor*
2545 Verbena Dr, Los Angeles, CA 90068
USA

Murphy, Calvin J *Basketball Player*
43 Sterling St, Sugar Land, TX 77479 USA

Murphy, Carolyn *Model*
I M G Models, 304 Park Ave S, #1200,
New York, NY 10010 USA

Murphy, Caryle M *Journalist*
Washington Post, Editorial Dept, 1150
15th St NW, Washington, DC 20071 USA

Murphy, Charles S *Government Official*
100 Bluff View Dr #503C, Belleair Bluffs,
FL 33770 USA

Murphy, Cillian *Actor*
United Talent Agency (UTA), 9560
Wilshire Blvd, Beverly Hills, CA 90212
USA

Murphy, Dale *Baseball Player*
Church Securities Corp, 605 Claremont
Ave, Decatur, GA 30030 USA

Murphy, David Lee *Musician*
D Mgmt, 1102 18th Ave S, Nashville, TN
37212 USA

Murphy, Diana E *Judge*
US Court of Appeals, 300 S 4th St,
Minneapolis, MN 55415 USA

Murphy, Donna *Actor, Musician*
Gerson Saines, 250 W 57th St, #2303,
New York, NY 10107 USA

Murphy, Ed *Basketball Player, Coach*
University of Mississippi, Smith Coliseum,
University, MS 38677 USA

Murphy, Eddie *Actor, Comedian*
William Morris Agency (WMA-LA), 1
William Morris Pl, Beverly Hills, CA
90212 USA

Murphy, Erin *Actor*
James/Levy/Jacobson, 3500 W Olive Ave,
#1470, Burbank, CA 91505 USA

Murphy, Lawrence T (Larry) *Hockey
Player*
927 S Bates St, Birmingham, MI 48009
USA

Murphy, Mark H *Musician*
Prince/SF Productions, 1450 Southgate
Ave #206, Daly City, CA 94015 USA

Murphy, Michael
9830 Wilshire Blvd, Beverly Hills, CA
90212

Murphy, Michael Martin
4077 State Hwy. 68, Rancho de Taos, NM
87557

Murphy, Michael R *Judge*
US Court of Appeals, Federal Building,
125 S State St, Salt Lake City, UT 84138
USA

Murphy, Mike *Hockey Player, Coach*
17072 Oak View Dr, Encino, CA 91436
USA

Murphy, Raymond D *War Hero*
4677 Sutton St NW, Albuquerque, NM
87114 USA

Murphy, Reg *Editor, Publisher*
National Geographic Society, 1145 17th
St NW, Washington, DC 20036 USA

Murphy, Richard W *Diplomat*
16 Sutton Place #9A, New York, NY
10022 USA

Murphy, Rosemary *Actor*
220 E 73rd St, New York, NY 10021 USA

Murphy, Sean *Golfer*
1004 June Place, Lovington, NM 88260
USA

Murphy, Terry *Entertainer*
Sherry Ingram, 3575 Cahuenga Blvd W,
#600, Los Angeles, CA 90068 USA

Murphy, Thomas (Tom) *Writer*
4 Garville Road, Dublin, 6, IRELAND

Murphy, Thomas S *Business Person*
Capitol Cities/ABC, 77 W 66th St, New
York, NY 10023 USA

Murphy, Troy *Basketball Player*
404 W Mountain Road, Sparta, NJ 07871
USA

Murphy-O'Connor, Cormac Cardinal
Religious Leader
Archbishop's House, Ambrosden Ave,
London, SW1P 1QJ, UNITED KINGDOM
(UK)

Murray, Albert L *Writer*
45 W 132nd St, New York, NY 10037
USA

Murray, Andy *Hockey Player*
Los Angeles Kings, Staples Center, 1111 S
Figueroa St, Los Angeles, CA 90015 USA

Murray, Anne *Musician*
Bruce Allen Talent, 406-68 Water St,
Vancouver, BC V6B 1A4, CANADA

Murray, Anne *Opera Singer*
Helge Rudolf Augstein, Sebastianplatz 3,
Munich, 80331, GERMANY

Murray, Bill *Actor, Comedian*
Creative Artists Agency, 9830 Wilshire
Blvd, Beverly Hills, CA 90212 USA

Murray, Brain Doyle *Actor*
Abrams Artists, 9200 Sunset Blvd, #1125,
Los Angeles, CA 90069 USA

Murray, Bruce C *Scientist*
Jet Propulsion Laboratory, 4800 Oak
Grove Dr, Pasadena, CA 91109 USA

Murray, Bryan C *Hockey Player*
2215 NE 32nd Ave, Fort Lauderdale, FL
33305 USA

Murray, Chad Michael *Actor*
Simmons & Scott Entertainment, 4110 W
Burbank Blvd, Burbank, CA 91505 USA

Murray, Charles A *Scientist*
American Enterprise Institute, 1150 17th
St NW, Washington, DC 20036 USA

Murray, Charles P Jr *War Hero*
5906 Northridge Road, Columbia, SC
29206 USA

Murray, Cherry A *Business Person,*
Physicist
Lucent technologies, 700 Mountain Ave,
New Providence, NJ 07974 USA

Murray, Chris *Misc*
IBM T J Watson Research Center, PO Box
218, Yorktown Heights, NY 10598 USA

Murray, Dave *Musician*
Sanctuary Music Mgmt, 82 Bishop's
Bridge Road, London, W2 6BB, UNITED
KINGDOM (UK)

Murray, David K *Musician*
Joel Chriss, 300 Mercer St, #3J, New York,
NY 10003 USA

Murray, Don *Actor*
1201 La Patera Canyon Road, Goleta, CA
93117 USA

Murray, Doug *Cartoonist*
Marvel Comic Group, 10 E 40th St, #900,
New York, NY 10016 USA

Murray, Eddie C *Baseball Player*
15319 Saddleback Road, Canyon Country,
CA 91387 USA

Murray, Edward P (Eddie) *Football Player*
1070 Forest Bay Dr, Waterford, MI 48328
USA

Murray, Elizabeth *Artist*
Paula Cooper Gallery, 534 W 21st, New
York, NY 10011 USA

Murray, Iain *Yachtsman*
Int'l Management Group, 75490 Fairway
Dr, Indian Wells, CA 92210 USA

Murray, James D *Biologist*
University of Washington, Applied Math
Dept, PO Box 352420, Seattle, WA 98195
USA

Murray, Jan *Actor, Comedian*
1157 Calle Vista Dr, Beverly Hills, CA
90210 USA

Murray, Joel
PO Box 5617, Beverly Hills, CA 90210

Murray, John E Jr *Educator*
Duquesne University, President's Office,
Pittsburg, PA 15282 USA

Murray, Jonathan *Producer*
Bunim/Murray Productions Inc, 6007
Sepulveda Blvd, Van Nuys, CA 91411
USA

Murray, Joseph E *Nobel Prize Laureate*
108 Abbott Road, Wellesley Hills, MA
02481 USA

Murray, Keith *Artist, Musician*
Famous Artists Agency, 250 W 57th St,
New York, NY 10107 USA

Murray, Maritza *Artist*
Sweeney Management, 8755 Lookout
Mountain Avenue, Los Angeles, CA 90046
USA

Murray, Michael *Musician*
1876 Northwest Blvd #B, Columbus, OH
43212 USA

Murray, Neil *Musician*
Int'l Talent Booking, 27A Floral St, #300,
London, WC2E 9DQ, UNITED
KINGDOM (UK)

Murray, Peg *Actor*
800 Light House Road, Southold, NY
11971 USA

Murray, Sean
8436 W. Third St. #740, Los Angeles, CA
90048-4100

Murray, Terence R (Terry) *Hockey Player*
Philadelphia Flyers, 1st Union Center,
3601 S Broad St, Philadephia, PA 19148
USA

Murray, Terrence (Terry) *Financier*
Fleet Boston Corp, 1 Federal Corp,
Boston, MA 02110 USA

Murray, Timothy V *Architect*
444 Springfield Road, Ottawa, ON K1M
0K4, CANADA

Murray, Tracy *Basketball Player*
4337 Marina City Dr, Marina del Rey, CA
90292 USA

Murray, Ty *Rodeo Rider*
1660 Private Road 1213, Stephenville, TX
76401 USA

Murray of Epping Forest, Lionel (Len)
Misc
29 Crescent, Loughton, Essex, 1G10 4PY,
UNITED KINGDOM (UK)

Murray-Leslie, Alex *Musician*
K Records, 924 Jefferson St SE, #101,
Olympia, WA 98501 USA

Murro, Noam *Director*
Management 360, 9111 Wilshire Blvd,
Beverly Hills, CA 90210 USA

Murtagh, Kate *Actor*
19557 Tribune St, Northridge, CA 91326
USA

Murukarni, Masanori *Baseball Player*
1-4-15-1506 Nisho Ohi Shinagawaku,
Tokyo, 140-0015, JAPAN

Musa, Said *Prime Minister*
Prime Minister's Office, East Bloc,
Belmopan, BELIZE

Musabayev, Talgat A *Cosmonaut*
Potcha Kosmonavtov, Moskovskoi Oblasti,
Syvisdny Goroduk, 141160, RUSSIA

Musante, Tony *Actor*
38 Bedford St, New York, NY 10014 USA

Musberger, Brent
47 W. 66th St., New York, NY 10023

Musburger, Brent W *Sportscaster*
286 Locha Dr, Jupiter, FL 33458 USA

Muscarello, Carl
720 NW 71st Ave., Ft. Lauderdale, FL
33317

Muse, William V *Educator*
Aubum University, President's Office,
Aubum University, AL 36849 USA

Museveni, Yoweri K *President*
President's Office, PO Box 7108,
Kampala, UGANDA

Musgrave, F Story *Astronaut*
8572 Sweetwater Trail, Kissimmee, FL
34747 USA

Musgrave, R Kenton *Judge*
US Court of International Trade, 1 Federal
Plaza, New York, NY 10278 USA

Musgrave, Ted *Race Car Driver*
175 Lakeside Dr E, Port Orange, FL 32128
USA

Musgrave, Thea *Composer*
Virginia Opera Assn, PO Box 2580,
Norfolk, VA 23501 USA

Musharraf, Parvez *President*
President's Office, Aiwan-e-Sadr, Mall &
Mayo Roads, Islamabad, PAKISTAN

Mushok, Mike *Musician*
William Morris Agency, 151 El Camino
Dr, Beverly Hills, CA 90212 USA

Musial, Stan
1655 Des Peres Rd. #125, St. Louis, MO
63131

Musial, Stanley F (Stan) *Baseball Player*
85 Trent Dr, Saint Louis, MO 63124 USA

Musiol, Bogdan *Athlete*
Fitness-Studio, Talstr 50, Zella-Mehlis,
98544, GERMANY

Musiq *Musician*
Def Soul Records, 825 8th Ave, #2700,
New York, NY 10019 USA

Musker, John *Director, Animator*
Walt Disney Productions, 500 S Buena
Vista St, Burbank, CA 91521 USA

Musonge, Pater Mafani *Prime Minister*
Prime Minister's Office, Yaounde, BP,
1057, CAMEROON

Mussa, Michael *Economist*
International Monetary Fund, 700 19th ST
NW, Washington, DC 20431 USA

Mussina, Michael C (Mike) *Baseball Player*
Ashton Group, 5 Shawan Road, #2, Hunt Valley, MD 21030 USA

Musso, Johnny *Football Player*
242 E 3rd St, Hinsdale, IL 60521 USA

Mussolini, Alessandra *Government Official*
Italian Social Movement (MSI), Chamber of Deputies, Rome, 00100, ITALY

Must *Music Group*
Wind-up Records, 72 Madison Ave, New York, NY 10016 USA

Mustaine, Dave *Musician*
ESP Mgmt, 838 N Doheny Dr #302, West Hollywood, CA 90069 USA

Mustalov, Abdulkhashim M *Prime Minister*
Government House, Tashkent, 700008, UZBEKISTAN

Mustan, Abbas *Actor, Bollywood*
119 Haveliwala Building 1st Floor, E R Road, Mumbai, MS 400003, INDIA

Muster, Thomas *Tennis Player*
370 Felter Ave, Hewlett, NY 11557 USA

Mustin, Henry C *Admiral*
2347 S Rolle St, Arlington, VA 22202 USA

Mustonen, Olli *Musician, Composer*
Shuman Assoc, 120 W 58th St, #8D, New York, NY 10019 USA

Mutchie, Marjorie Ann
1169 Mary Circle, La Verne, 91750

Mutchnick, Max *Producer*
Will & Grace, 4024 Radford Ave, Bungalow 3, Studio City, CA 91604 USA

Muteba II, Ronald Muwenda *King*
Royal Palace, Kampala, UGANDA

Muth, Ellen *Actor*
International Creative Management (ICM-LA), 8942 Wilshire Blvd, Beverly Hills, CA 90211 USA

Muth, Rene *Coach*
Pennsylvania State University, Athletic Dept, University Park, PA 16802 USA

Muthu, Kumari *Actor*
A-6 53 South West Boag Road, T Nagar, Chennai, TN 600 017, INDIA

Muti, Ornella *Actor*
33 Via Porta de Pinta, Bergamo, 24100, ITALY

Muti, Riccardo
Via Corti Alle Mura 25, Ravenna, 48100, ITALY

Muti, Richard
via Corti alle Mura 25, Ravenna, ITALY, 48100

Mutombo, Dikembe *Basketball Player*
1300 Valley Road, Villanova, PA 19085 USA

Mutschler, Carlfried *Architect*
E7, 7, Mannheim, 68159, GERMANY

Mutter, Anne-Sophie *Musician*
Effnerstr 48, Munich, 81925, GERMANY

Mutter, Carol A *General*
Women Marines Assn, PO Box 1907, Woodbridge, VA 22195 USA

Muxworthy, Jake *Actor*
United Talent Agency (UTA), 9560 Wilshire Blvd, Beverly Hills, CA 90212 USA

Muzorewa, Abel T *Religious Leader*
PO Box 353, Borrowdale, Harare, ZIMBABWE

Mwanawasa, Levy P *President*
President's Office, State House, PO Box 135, Lusaka, ZAMBIA

Mwinyi, Ali Hassam *President*
President's Office, State House, PO Box 9120, Dar es Salaam, TANZANIA

Mya *Musician, Actor*
PO Box 569, Glenn Dale, MD 20769 USA

Myers, A Maurice *Business Person*
Waste Management Inc, 1001 Fannin St, Houston, TX 77002 USA

Myers, Anne M *Religious Leader*
Church of the Brethren, 1451 Dundee Ave, Elgin, IL 60120 USA

Myers, Barton *Architect*
Barton Myers Assoc, 9348 Civic Center Dr, Beverly Hills, CA 90210 USA

Myers, Billie
PO Box 12198, Miami, FL 33101

Myers, Cynthia *Actor, Model*
PO Box 10, Liano, CA 93544 USA

Myers, Dale D *Engineer*
Dale Myers Assoc, PO Box 232518, Encinitas, CA 92023 USA

Myers, Danny *Race Car Driver*
Childress Racing, PO Box 1189, Industrial Dr, Welcome, NC 27374 USA

Myers, Dee Dee *Actor, Writer*
Endeavor Agency LLC (LA), 9601 Wilshire Blvd Fl 3, Beverly Hills, CA 90210 USA

Myers, Dwight (Heavy D)
Endeavor Agency LLC (LA), 9601 Wilshire Blvd Fl 3, Beverly Hills, CA 90210 USA

Myers, Jack D *Physicist*
University of Pittsburg, 1291 Scaife Hall, Pittsburg, PA 15261 USA

Myers, Lisa *Commentator*
NBC-TV, News Dept, 4001 Nebraska Ave NW, Washington, DC 20016 USA

Myers, Margaret J (Dee Dee) *Government Official*
Equal Time Show, CBS-TV, 1233 20th St NW #302, Washington, DC 20036 USA

Myers, Mike *Actor, Comedian*
Creative Artists Agency, 9830 Wilshire Blvd, Beverly Hills, CA 90212 USA

Myers, Norman *Scientist*
Upper Meadow Old Road, Headington, Oxford, OX3 8SZ, UNITED KINGDOM (UK)

Myers, Randall K (Randy) *Baseball Player*
15525 NE Caples Road, Brush Prairie, WA 98606 USA

Myers, Reginald R *War Hero*
PO Box 803, Annandale, VA 22003 USA

Myers, Richard *Scientist*
Stanford University, Human Genome Center, Stanford, CA 94305 USA

Myers, Richard B (Dick) *General*
Chairman Joint Chiefs of Staff, Pentagon, Washington, DC 20318 USA

Myers, Rochelle *Writer*
3827 California St, San Francisco, CA 94118 USA

Myers, Russell *Cartoonist*
Tribune Media Services, 435 N Michigan Ave, #1500, Chicago, IL 60611 USA

Myers, Terry-Jo *Golfer*
Ladies Pro Golf Assn, 100 International Golf Dr, Daytona Beach, FL 32124 USA

Myers, Tikalsky Linda *Skier*
RR 5 Box 2651, Santa Fe, NM 87506 USA

Myers, Walter Dean *Photographer*
Scholastic Press, 555 Broadway, New York, NY 10012 USA

Myers Jr, Harry J *Publisher*
46 W Ranch Trail, Morrison, CO 80465 USA

Myerson, Bess *Actor, Lawyer, Beauty Pageant Winner*
3 E 71st St, #9A, New York, NY 10021 USA

Myerson, Harvey *Attorney General*
Finley Kumble Wagner Assoc, 425 Park Ave, New York, NY 10022 USA

Myerson, Jacob M *Economist, Diplomat*
2 Rue Lucien-Gaulard, Paris, 75018, FRANCE

Myhre, Wencke
Im Vendla 22, Nesoya, NORWAY, N-1315

Myles, Alannah *Musician*
Miracle Prestige, 1 Water Lane, Camden Town, London, NW1 8N2, UNITED KINGDOM (UK)

Myles, Sophia *Actor*
Personal Management Company, 425 N Robertson Dr, Los Angeles, CA 90048 USA

Myre, Philippe (Phil) *Hockey Player*
101 Rue Dugas, Joliette, QC, J6E 4G7, CANADA

Myrick, Daniel *Director*
Artisan Entertainment, 2700 Colorado Ave, Santa Monica, CA 90404 USA

Myrin, Arden *Actor*
Sanders/Armstrong Management, 2120 Colorado Blvd #120, Santa Monica, CA 90404 USA

Mysen, Bjorn O *Misc*
Camegie Institution, 5221 Broad Branch Road, Washington, DC 20015 USA

Mystic *Musician*
WMA, 151 S El Camino Dr, Beverly Hills, CA 90212

Mystics
The88 Anador St., Staten Island, NY 10303

Mystikal *Musician*
International Creative Management (ICM-LA), 8942 Wilshire Blvd, Beverly Hills, CA 90211 USA

N

N Chandra *Director, Producer, Filmmaker, Bollywood*
Ankush 1 Belscot Units Lokhandwala Complex, Andheri Linking Road Andheri, Bombay, MS 400 058, INDIA

N'Dour, Youssou *Musician*
Konzertagentur Berthold Seliger, Nonnengasse 15, Fulda, 36037, GERMANY

Na-Ming
9903 Santa Monica Blvd. #575, Beverly Hills, CA 90212

Nabe, Ricky *Actor*
Envision Entertainment, 9255 Sunset Blvd #300, Los Angeles, CA 90069 USA

Naber, Jofin P *Swimmer*
PO Box 50107, Pasadena, CA 91115 USA

Naber, John
PO Box 50107, Pasadena, CA 91105-0107

Nabers, Drayton Jr *Business Person*
Protective Life Corp, 2801 Highway 280 S, Birmingham, AL 35223 USA

Nabokov, Evgeni *Hockey Player*
San Jose Sharks, San Jose Arena, 525 W Santa Clara St, San Jose, CA 95113 USA

Nabors, Jim *Actor, Musician*
PO Box 10364, Honolulu, HI 96816 USA

Nabors, Richard *Football Player*
1625 Brighton Court, Beaumont, TX 77706 USA

Naccarato, Vin *Musician*
Paramount Entertainment, PO Box 12, Far Hills, NJ 07931 USA

Nachamkin, Boris *Basketball Player*
350 E 62nd St, #5J, New York, NY 10021 USA

Nachbar, Bostjan *Basketball Player*
Houston Rockets, Toyota Center, 2 E Greenway Plaza, Houston, TX 77046 USA

Nachmansohn, David *Misc*
560 Riverside Dr, New York, NY 10027 USA

Nadeau, Jerry *Race Car Driver*
565 Pitts School Road, Concord, NC 28027 USA

Nader, Michael *Actor*
28 E 10th St, New York, NY 10003 USA

Nader, Ralph *Social Activist*
1600 20th St NW, Washington, DC 20009 USA

Nadiya *Actor, Bollywood*
A Block Door No 23, Anna Nagar, Chennai, TN 600102, INDIA

Naehring, Timothy J (Tim) *Baseball Player*
7300 Pinehurst Dr, Cincinnati, OH 45244 USA

Nafziger, Dana A *Football Player*
251 El Dorado Way, Pismo Beach, CA 93449 USA

Nagakura, Saburo *Misc*
2-7-13 Higashicho, Kichijoji, Musashino, Tokyo, 1800002, JAPAN

Nagano, Kent G
Van Walsum Mgmt, 4 Addison Bridge Place, London, W14 8XP, UNITED KINGDOM (UK)

Nagarjuna *Actor, Bollywood*
29 Kasturi Rangan Rd, Alwarpet, Madras, TN 600018, INDIA

Nagashima, Shigeo *Baseball Player*
3-29-19 Denenchofu, Ohtaku, Tokyo, 145, JAPAN

Nagel, Sidney R *Physicist*
4919 Blackstone Ave, Chicago, Il, 60615 USA

Nagel, Steven R *Astronaut*
16923 Cottonwood Way, Houston, TX 77059 USA

Nagel, Thomas *Misc*
New York University, Law School, 40 Washington Square S, New York, NY 10012 USA

Nagesh *Actor*
127 St Marys Road, Chennai, TN 600 018, INDIA

Naghma *Actor, Bollywood*
23 A Kalpak Aspen 1st Floor, Perry Cross Road Bandra, Bombay, MS 400 050, INDIA

Nagma *Actor, Bollywood*
43 Iind Street, Navarathna Gardens Ekkaduthangal, Chennai, TN 600017, INDIA

Nagra, Parminder *Actor*
ARG, 4 Great Portland St, London, W1W 8PA, UNITED KINGDOM (UK)

Nagy, Stanislaw Cardinal *Religious Leader*
Priests of Sacred Heart, Via Casale S Piov 20, Rome, 00126, ITALY

Nahan, Stu *Sportscaster*
11274 Canton Dr, Studio City, CA 91604 USA

Naharin, Ohad *Choreographer*
Dance Theater, Scheldeldoekshaven 60, Gravenhage, EN, 2511, NETHERLANDS

Nahyan, Sheikh Zayed bin Sultan al- *Royalty, President*
President's Office, Manhal Palace, Abu Dhabi, UNITED ARAB EMIRATES

Naifeh, Steven W *Writer*
335 Sumter St SE, Aiken, SC 29801 USA

Nail, Jimmy
76 Oxford St., London, ENGLAND, W1N 0AX

Naipaul, V S *Nobel Prize Laureate*
Aitken & Stone Ltd, 29 Fernshaw Road, London, SW10 0TG, UNITED KINGDOM (UK)

Nair, Mira *Director*
International Creative Mgmt, 8942 Wilshire Blvd, #219, Beverly Hills, CA 90211 USA

Naisbitt, John *Writer*
Spittelauer Platz 5A3A, Vienna, 1090, AUSTRIA

Naish, Bronwen *Musician*
Moelfre Xwm Pennant, Gamdolbenmaen, Gwunedd, North Wales, LL5 9AX, WALES

Najarian, John S *Doctor*
University of Minnesota, Health Center, Surgery Dept, Minneapolis, MN 55455 USA

Najee *Musician*
Associated booking Corp, 1995 Broadway, #501, New York, NY 10023 USA

Najera, Eduardo *Basketball Player*
Dallas Mavericks, 2909 Taylor St, Dallas, TX 75226 USA

Najimy, Kathy *Actor*
3366 Wrightwood Dr, Studio City, CA 91604 USA

Nakajiim, Tadashi *Astronomer*
California Institute of Technology, Astronomy Dept, Pasadena, CA 91125 USA

Nakama, Keo *Swimmer*
1344 9th Ave, Honolulu, HI 96816 USA

Nakano, Shinji *Race Car Driver*
Fernandez Racing, 6950 Guion Circle W, #E, Indianapolis, IN 46268 USA

Nakasone, Yasuhiro *Prime Minister*
3-22-7 Kamikitazawa, Setagayaku, Tokyo, JAPAN

Naked, Bif *Musician*
Crazed Mgmt, PO Box 779, New Hope, PA 18938 USA

Nalder, Eric C *Journalist*
Seattle Times, Editorial Dept, 1120 John St, Seattle, WA 98109 USA

Nalinikanth *Actor*
413 29th Street, 6th Sector, Chennai, TN 600 078, INDIA

Nall, N Anita *Swimmer*
PO Box 872505, Tempe, AZ 85287 USA

Nam, Leonardo *Actor*
Brookside Artists Management (LA), 450 N Roxbury Dr Fl 4, Beverly Hills, CA 90210 USA

Namaliu, Rabbie L *Prime Minister*
PO Box 6655, National Capital District, Boroko, PAPUA NEW GUINEA

Namath, Joseph W (Joe) *Football Player, Actor*
William Morris Agency, 151 El Camino Dr, Beverly Hills, CA 90212 USA

Nambiar, M N *Actor*
4 6th Street, Gopalapuram, Chennai, TN 600 086, INDIA

Nambu, Yoichiro *Physicist*
5535 University Ave, Chicago, IL 60637 USA

Namesnik, Eric *Swimmer*
114 Hickory St, Butler, PA 16001 USA

Nance, John J *Writer*
4512 8th Ave, West Tacorna, WA 98466 USA

Nance, Robin
5757 Wilshire Blvd. #510, Los Angeles, CA 90036

Nance, Todd *Musician*
Brown Cat Inc, 400 Foundary St, Athens, GA 30601 USA

Nancy, Ted L
Trident Media Group LLC, 41 Madison Ave Fl 33, New York, NY 10010 USA

Nanne, Louis V (Lou) *Hockey Player*
6982 Tupa Dr, Edina, MN 55439 USA

Nanni, Gianna
Carmenstr. 12, Zurich, SWITZERLAND, CH-8032

Nannini, Alessandro *Race Car Driver*
Via del Paradiso 4, Siena, 53100, ITALY

Nanoski, John (Jukey) *Soccer Player*
RR 1, Herkimer, NY 11350 USA

Nantucket
250 N. Kepler Rd. Deland, FL CA 33724

Nantz, Jim *Sportscaster*
CBS-TV, Sports Dept, 51 W 52nd St, New York, NY 10019 USA

Napier, Charles *Actor*
Star Route Box 60H, Caliente, CA 93518 USA

Napier, Hugo
2207 N. Beachwood Dr., Los Angeles, CA 90068

Napier, James *Actor*
Auckland Actors, PO Box 56460, Dominion Road, Auckland, NEW ZEALAND

Napier, John *Designer*
MLR Douglas House, 16-18 Douglas St, London, SW1P 4PB, UNITED KINGDOM (UK)

Napier, Wilfrid F Cardinal *Religious Leader*
Archbishop's House, 154 Gordon Road, Greyville, 4023, SOUTH AFRICA

Napoles, Jose *Boxer*
Cerrada De Tizapan 9-303 Ediciov, Codigo Postel, Mexico City, 06080, MEXICO

Narain, Nicole *Actor*
8033 Sunset Blvd #224, Hollywood, CA 90046

Naranjo, Monica *Musician*
Sony Music Miami, 605 Lincoln Rd, Miami Beach, FL 33138 USA

Narasimha, Rao P V *Politician*
Vangara Post, Karimnagar District, AP, INDIA

Narasimhan, V L *Actor*
9-6 L I C Staff Quarters, K K Nagar, Chennai, TN 600 078, INDIA

Narayanan, Kocheril Raman *President*
81 Lodhi Estate, New Delhi, 11003, INDIA

Narducci, Katherine
2843 Waterbury Ave., Bronx, NY 10461

Narducci, Tim *Musician*
Artists Group International, 9560 Wilshire Blvd, #400, Beverly Hills, CA 90212 USA

Narita, Hiro *Cinematographer*
2262 Magnolia Ave, Petatuma, CA 94952 USA

Narita, Richard
8831 Sunset Blvd. #304, Los Angeles, CA 90069

Narizzano, Silvio (Cas) *Director*
Al Parker, 55 Park Lane, London, W1Y 3DD, UNITED KINGDOM (UK)

Narleski, Raymond E (Ray) *Baseball Player*
1183 Chews Landing Road, Laurel Springs, NJ 08021 USA

Narron, Jerry A *Baseball Player*
206 Friendswood Dr, Goldsboro, NC 27530 USA

Naruhito *Royalty*
Imperial Palaca, 1-1 Chiyoda, Chiyoda-ku, Tokyo, JAPAN

Narvekar, Prabhakar R *Financier*
International Monetary Fund, 700 19th St NW, Washington, DC 20431 USA

Narz, Jack *Television Host*
1906 Beverly Place, Beverly Hills, CA 90210 USA

Nasclemento, Milton *Musician, Songwriter*
Tribo Producoes, Av A Lombardi 800, Rio de Janeiro, 22 640-000, BRAZIL

Naseeruddin, Shah *Actor, Bollywood*
204 Sand Pebbles, Perry X Road Bandra, Mumbai, MS 400050, INDIA

Nash, Charles F (Cotton) *Basketball Player, Baseball Player*
600 Summershade Circle, Lexington, KY 40502 USA

Nash, Chris *Actor*
Commercial Talent, 9255 Sunset Blvd, Suite 505, West Hollywood, CA 90069 USA

Nash, David *Artist*
Capel Rhiw Blanau, Flestiniog, Gwynedd Wales, LL41 3NT, WALES

Nash, Graham
14930 Ventura Blvd. #205, Sherman Oaks, CA 91403-3489

Nash, Graham W *Musician, Songwriter*
PO Box 838, Hanalei, HI 96714 USA

Nash, John F Jr *Nobel Prize Laureate*
Princeton University, Economics Department, Fine Hall, Princeton, NJ 08544 USA

Nash, Johnny *Musician, Songwriter*
Legacy Records, 550 Madison Ave, #1700, New York, NY 10022 USA

Nash, Keisha
344 E. 59th St., New York, NY 10022

Nash, Kevin *Wrestler*
World Wrestling Entertainment (WWE), 1241 E Main St, Stamford, CT 06905 USA

Nash, Niecy *Actor*
Agency for the Performing Arts (APA-LA), 9200 Sunset Blvd #900, Los Angeles, CA 90069 USA

Nash, Noreen *Actor*
4990 Puesta del Sol, Malibu, CA 90265 USA

Nash, Richard
19323 Oxnard St., Tarzana, CA 91356

Nash, Steve *Basketball Player*
BDA Sports Management (BDA-CA), 822 Ashley Ln #A, Walnut Creek, CA 94596 USA

Naslund, Markus *Hockey Player*
Mike Gillis Assoc, 154 Earl St, Kingston, ON K7L 2H2, CANADA

Naslund, Mats *Hockey Player*
6963 Progressona, SWITZERLAND

Naslund, Ron *Hockey Player*
2600 Cheyenne Circle, Minnetonka, MN 55305 USA

Nasr, Seyyed Hossein *Misc*
George Washington University, Gelman Library, Washington, DC 20052 USA

Nasser, Jacques A *Business Person*
One Equity Partners, 1st National Plaza, Chicago, IL 60607 USA

Nasser M *Actor*
245 Guhan Street, Kamakoti Nagar Valasarawakkam, Chennai, TN 600 087, INDIA

Nastase, Ilie *Tennis Player*
Calea Plevnei 14, Bucarest, HUNGARY

Nat, Marie-Jose
10 rue Royale, Paris, FRANCE, 75008

Natalicio, Diana S *Educator*
University of Texas at El Paso, President's Office, El Paso, TX 79968 USA

Nater, Swen *Basketball Player*
23006 SE 406th St, Enumclaw, WA 98022 USA

Nath, Alok *Actor, Bollywood*
901 Skydeck Oshiwara Complex, Off New Link Road Andheri, Mumbai, MS 400061, INDIA

Nathan, David G *Physicist*
Dana-Farber Cancer Institute, 44 Binney St, Boston, MA 02115 USA

Nathan, Joseph A *Business Person*
Compuware Corp, 1 Campus Martius, Detroit, MI 48226 USA

Nathan, S R *President*
President's Office, Orchard Road, Istana, Singapore, 0922, SINGAPORE

Nathan, Tony *Football Player, Coach*
15110 Dunbarton Pl, Miami Lake, FL 33016 USA

Nathan, Tony C *Football Player, Football Coach*
15110 Dunbarton Place, Miami Lakes, FL 33016 USA

Nathaniel (Popp), Bishop *Religious Leader*
Romanian Orthodox Episcopate, 2522 Grey Tower Road, Jackson, MI 49201 USA

Nathanson, Jeff *Writer*
United Talent Agency (UTA), 9560 Wilshire Blvd, Beverly Hills, CA 90212 USA

Nathanson, Roy *Musician*
Brad Simon Organization, 122 E 57th St, #300, New York, NY 10022 USA

Nathman, John B *Admiral*
Commander Naval Air Force Pacific, NAS North Island, San Diego, CA 92135 USA

Natividad, Charles
Star Rt Box 60H, Caliente, CA 93518

Natividad, Kitten
5917 Oak Ave. #148, Temple City, CA 91780

Natkin, Robert *Artist*
24 Mark Twain Lane, West Redding, CT 06896 USA

Natori, Josie C *Fashion Designer*
Natori Co, 40 E 34th St, New York, NY
10016 USA

Natsios, Andrew *Government Official*
US International Development Agency,
320 21st NW, Washington, DC 20523
USA

Natt, Calvin *Basketball Player*
4825 S Fraser St, Aurora, CO 80015 USA

Natter, Robert J *Admiral*
Commander, Atlantic Fleet, Norfolk, VA
23551 USA

Natural *Musician*
Official International Fan Club, PO Box
5097, Bellingham, WA 98227 USA

Naude, C F Beyers *Religious Leader*
26 Hoylake Road, Greenside, 2193,
SOUTH AFRICA

Naudet, Jules *Producer*
William Morris Agency (WMA-LA), 1
William Morris Pl, Beverly Hills, CA
90212 USA

Naughton, David *Actor*
5003 Tilden Ave, #202, Sherman Oaks,
CA 91423 USA

Naughton, James
8942 Wilshire Blvd, Beverly Hills, CA
90211

Naughton, Laurie *Actor*
OmniPop Inc (LA), 10700 Ventura Blvd Fl
2, Studio City, CA 91604 USA

Naughton, Naturi *Musician*
Pyramid Entertainment, 89 5th Ave, #700,
New York, NY 10003 USA

Naughty by Nature *Music Group*
Evolution Talent Agency LLC, 1776
Broadway Fl 15, New York, NY 10019
USA

Naulis, Willie *Basketball Player*
Chuck & Willie's Auto Agency, 13900
Hawthorne Blvd, Hawthorne, CA 90250
USA

Nauman, Bruce L *Artist*
4630 Rising Hill Road, Altadena, CA
91001 USA

Nava, Gregory *Director*
International Creative Mgmt, 8942
Wilshire Blvd, Beverly Hills, CA 90211
USA

Navaira, Emilio
15l El Camino Dr., Beverly Hills, CA
90212

Naval, Deepti *Actor, Bollywood*
603 Oceanic Seven Bungalows, Versova
Andheri, Mumbai, MS 400061, INDIA

Navarez, Alfred *Musician*
MPI Talent, 9255 Sunset Blvd, #407, Los
Angeles, CA 90069 USA

Navarro, Dave *Musician*
H K Mgmt, 9200 W Sunset Blvd, #530,
Los Angeles, CA 90069 USA

Navarro, Guillermo J *Cinematographer*
Lyons Sheldon Prosnit Agency, 800 S
Robertson Blvd, #6, Los Angeles, CA
90035 USA

Navas, Bibiana *Actor*
Gabriel Blanco Iglesias (Mexico), Rio
Balsas 35-32, Colonia Cuauhtemoc, DF,
06500, Mexico

Navasky, Victor S *Editor, Publisher*
33 W 67th St, New York, NY 10023 USA

Navon, Itzhak *President*
Education & Culture Ministry, Hakiria,
Jerusalem, ISRAEL

Navratilova, Martina *Tennis Player*
Int'l Mgmt group, 1 Erieview Plaza, 1360
E 9th St #1300, Cleveland, OH 44114
USA

Naylor, Gloria *Writer*
One Way Productions, 638 2nd St,
Brooklyn, NY 11215 USA

Naymenko, Gregg *Athlete*
2695 E Katella Ave, Anaheim, CA 92803-
6177

Nazam, Hisham *Government Official*
Ministry of Petroleum & Mineral
Resources, Riyadh, SAUDI ARABIA

Nazarbayev, Nursultan A *President*
President's Office, Pl Respublik, Astana,
480091, KAZAKHSTAN

Nazario, Ednita *Musician*
Sony Music Miami, 605 Lincoln Rd,
Miami Beach, FL 33138 USA

Nazario, Sonia *Journalist*
Los Angeles Times, Editorial Dept, 202 W
1st St, Los Angeles, CA 90012 USA

Ndayizeye, Domitien *President*
President's Office, Bujumbura, BURUNDI

Ndegeocello, Me'Shell *Musician*
Monetary Peninsula Artists, 509 Hartnell
St, Monetary, CA 93940 USA

Ndegeocello, Michelle *Musician*
Monterey Peninsula Artists (Monterey),
509 Hartnell St, Monterey, CA 93940 USA

Ndimira, Pascal Firmin *Prime Minister*
Prime Minister's Office, Bujumbura,
BURUNDI

Ne'eman, Yuval *Physicist*
Tel-Aviv University, Physics/Astronomy
Dept, Tel-Aviv, 69978, ISRAEL

Neagle, Dennis E (Denny) *Baseball Player*
945 Waugh Chapel Road, Gambrills, MD
21054 USA

Neagle, Denny *Baseball Player*
16254 Sandstone Dr, Morrison, CO
80465 USA

Neal, Dylan *Actor*
Pakula/King, 9229 Sunset Blvd, #315, Los
Angeles, CA 90069 USA

Neal, Edwin *Actor*
501 W Powell Lane, Austin, TX 78753
USA

Neal, Elise *Actor*
3626 Oakfield Dr, Sherman Oaks, CA
91423 USA

Neal, Fred (Curly) *Basketball Player*
PO Box 915415, Longwood, FL 32791
USA

Neal, James *Basketball Player*
803 Medora Dr, Greer, SC 29650 USA

Neal, James F *Attorney General*
Neal & Harwell, 3rd National Bank
Building, #800, Nashville, TN 37219 USA

Neal, Lloyd *Basketball Player*
8640 SE Causey Ave, Portland, OR 97266
USA

Neal, Patricia *Actor*
45 E End Ave, #4C, New York, NY 10028
USA

Neal, Philip M *Business Person*
Avery Dennison Corp, 150 N Orange
Grove Blvd, Pasadena, CA 91103 USA

Neal, Scott *Actor*
Ken McReddie Ltd, Paurelle House, 91
Regent St, London, W1R7TB, UNITED
KINGDOM (UK)

Neal, T Daniel (Dan) *Football Player*
5329 Briercliff Dr, Hamburg, NY 14075
USA

Neale, Gary L *Business Person*
Northern Indiana Service, 801 E 86th Ave,
Merrillville, IN 46410 USA

Nealon, Kevin *Comedian, Actor*
Agency for Performing Arts, 9200 Sunset
Blvd, #900, Los Angeles, CA 90069 USA

Nealy, Eddie *Basketball Player*
702 Lightstone Dr, San Antonio, TX 75258
USA

Neame, Christopher *Actor*
Borinstein Oreck Bogart, 3172 Dona
Susana Dr, Studio City, CA 91604 USA

Neame, Ronald *Director*
Kimridge Corp, 2317 Kimridge Ave,
Beverly Hills, CA 90210 USA

Near, Holly *Actor, Songwriter, Musician*
PO Box 236, Ukiah, CA 95482 USA

Neary, Martin G J *Musician*
2 Little Cloister, Westminster Abbey,
London, SW1P 3PL, UNITED KINGDOM
(UK)

Nebel, Dorothy Hoyt *Skier*
5340 Balfor Dr, Virginia Beach, VA 23464
USA

Neblett, Carol *Opera Singer*
Sardos Artists, 180 W End Ave, New York,
NY 10023 USA

Nebout, Claire *Actor*
Artmedia, 20 Ave Rapp, Paris, 75007,
FRANCE

Nechaev, Victor *Hockey Player*
6820 La Presa Dr, San Gabriel, CA 91775
USA

Ned, Derrick *Football Player*
430 Charles St, Eunice, LA 70535 USA

Nederlander, James M *Producer*
Netherlander Organization, 810 7th Ave,
New York, NY 10019 USA

Nedomansky, Vaclav *Hockey Player*
57 Crest Verde Lane, Rolling Hills Estates,
CA 90274 USA

Nedorost, Vaclav *Hockey Player*
Florida Panthers, 1 Panthers Parkway,
Sunrise, FL 33323 USA

Nedved, Petr *Hockey Player*
Edmonton Oilers, 11230 110th St,
Edmonton, AB T5G 3H7, CANADA

Needham, Connie *Actor*
19721 Castlebar Dr, Rowland Heights, CA
91748 USA

Needham, Hal *Director*
Laura Lizer Assoc, PO Box 46609, Los
Angeles, CA 90046 USA

Needham, James J *Business Person*
97 Coopers Farm Road, #1, Southampton,
NY 11968 USA

Needham, Tracey *Actor*
Badgley Connor Talent, 9229 Sunset Blvd,
#311, Los Angeles, CA 90069 USA

Needham, Tracy
9229 Sunset Blvd. #311, Los Angeles, CA
90069

Needleman, Jacob *Misc*
841 Wawona Ave, Oakland, CA 94610
USA

Neeleman, David *Business Person*
jetBlue Airways Corp, 80-02 Kew
Gardens, Floor 4, New York, NY 11415

Neelu *Actor*
G-5 Madhuram Flats Ururalagat Kuppam
5th Avenue, Besant Nagar, Chennai, TN
600 090, INDIA

Neely, Cam *Hockey Player*
76 Davison Dr, Lincoln, MA 01773 USA

Neely, Ralph E *Football Player*
6943 Sperry St, Dallas, TX 75214 USA

Neely Jr, Mark E *Historian*
Oxford University Press, 198 Madison
Ave, New York, NY 10016 USA

Neeson, Liam *Actor*
International Creative Mgmt, 40 W 57th
St, #1800, New York, NY 10019 USA

Nef, John U *Historian*
2726 N St NW, Washington, DC 20007
USA

Nef, Sonia *Skier*
Halten 345, Grub, 9035, SWITZERLAND

Neff, Francine I *Government Official*
1509 Sagebrush Trail SE, Albuquerque,
NM 87123 USA

Neff, William D *Psychic*
2080 Hideaway Court, Morris, IL 60450
USA

Negishi, Takashi *Economist*
2-10-5-301 Motoazabu, Minatoku, Tokyo,
106, JAPAN

Negoesco, Stephen *Coach*
University of San Francisco, Athletic Dept,
San Francisco, CA 94117 USA

Negri Sembilan, Yang Di-Pertuan Besar
President
Yang Di-Pertuan Agong's Residence,
Serembam, MALAYSIA

Negron, Chuck *Musician*
Mitch Schneider Organization, 14724
Ventura Blvd, #410, Sherman Oaks, CA
91403 USA

Negron, Taylor
8447 Wilshire Blvd. #206, Beverly Hills,
CA 90211-3246

Negroponte, John D *Diplomat*
US State Department, 2201 C St NW,
Washington, DC 20520 USA

Negroponte, Nicholas *Engineer*
69 Mount Vernon St, Boston, MA 02108
USA

Nehamas, Alexander *Misc*
Princeton University, Philosophy Dept,
Princeton, NJ 08544 USA

Nehemiah, Renaldo *Athlete*
1751 Pinnacle Dr, #1500, McLean, VA
22102 USA

Neher, Erwin *Nobel Prize Laureate*
Domane 11, Bovenden, 37120,
GERMANY

Nehmer, Meinhard *Athlete*
Vamkevitz, Altenkirchen, 18556,
GERMANY

Neid, Silvia *Soccer Player*
Betramstr 18, Frankfurt/Main, 60320,
GERMANY

Neidich, Charles *Musician*
Colbert Artists, 111 W 57th St, New York,
NY 10019 USA

Neighbors, William (Billy) *Football Player*
1904 Chippendale Dr SE, Huntsville, AL
35801 USA

Neil, Andrew F *Editor*
Glenbum Enterprises, PO Box 584,
London, SW7 3QY, UNITED KINGDOM
(UK)

Neil, Hildegarde *Actor*
Vernon Conway, 5 Spring St, London, W2
3RA, UNITED KINGDOM (UK)

Neil, Vince *Musician*
Ashley Talent, 2002 Hogback Road, #20,
Ann Arbor, MI 48105 USA

Neill, Mary Gardner *Director*
Seattle Art Museum, Volunteer Park,
Seattle, WA 98112 USA

Neill, Noel
331 Sage Lane, Santa Monica, CA 90402

Neill, Rolfe *Publisher*
Charlotte News-Observer, 600 S Tryon St,
Charlotte, NC 28202 USA

Neill, Sam *Actor*
Shanahan Mgmt, PO Box 1509,
Darlinghurst, NSW, 1300, AUSTRALIA

Neilson-Bell, Sandra *Swimmer*
3101 Mistyglen Circle, Austin, TX 78746
USA

Neiman, LeRoy *Artist*
1 W 67th St, New York, NY 10023 USA

Neinas, Charles M (Chuck) *Misc*
5344 Westridge Dr, Boulder, CO 80301
USA

Neis, Reagan Dale *Actor*
William Morris Agency (WMA-LA), 1
William Morris Pl, Beverly Hills, CA
90212 USA

Neizvestny, Ernst I *Artist*
81 Grand St, New York, NY 10013 USA

Nelkin, Stacey
2770 Hutton Dr., Beverly Hills, CA
90210-1216

Nelligan, Kate *Actor*
Innovative Artists, 1505 10th St, Santa
Monica, CA 90401 USA

Nellis, William J *Physicist*
Lawrence Livermore Laboratory, 7000 East
St, Livermore, CA 94550 USA

Nellssen, Roelof J *Financier, Government
Official*
PO Box 552, AN Laren, 1250,
NETHERLANDS

Nelly *Musician, Artist*
Team Lunatics, 1835 Beltway Dr, Saint
Louis, MO 63114 USA

Nelms, Michael (Mike) *Football Player*
Champion Chevrolet, 10411 James
Monroe Highway, Culpeper, VA 22701
USA

Nelson
15003 Greenleaf St, Sherman Oaks, CA
91403

Nelson, Barry *Actor*
120 W 58th St, #28, New York, NY
10019 USA

Nelson, Byron
Rt. 3 Box 5 Litsey Rd., Roanoke, TX
76262

Nelson, Cailin *Physicist*
Lawrence Livermore Laboratory, 7000 East
Ave, Livermore, CA 94550 USA

Nelson, Cordner *Misc*
USA Track & Field, 4341 Starlight Dr,
Indianapolis, IN 46239 USA

Nelson, Craig Richard *Actor*
Borinstein Oreck Bogart, 3172 Dona
Susana Dr, Studio City, CA 91604 USA

Nelson, Craig T *Actor*
Entertainment Tavel, 9171 Wllshire Blvd,
#406, Beverly Hills, CA 90210 USA

Nelson, Cynthia (Cindy) *Skier*
PO Box 1699, 0171 Larkspur Lane, Vail,
CO 81658 USA

Nelson, Daniel R *Financier*
West One Bancorp, 101 S Capitol Blvd,
Boise, ID 83702 USA

Nelson, Darrin *Football Player*
215 Marianne Court, Mountain View, CA
94040 USA

Nelson, David A *Judge*
US Court of Appeals, Courthouse
Building, 425 Walnut St, Cincinnati, OH
45202 USA

Nelson, David O *Actor, Director*
9 Yards Entertainment, 8530 Wilshire Blvd
Fl 5, Beverly Hills, CA 90211 USA

Nelson, Deborah *Journalist*
Seattle Times, Editorial Dept, 1120 John
St, Seattle, WA 98109 USA

Nelson, Donald A (Nellie) *Basketball
Player, Coach*
Dallas Mavericks, 2909 Taylor St, Dallas,
TX 75226 USA

Nelson, Dorothy W *Judge*
US Court of Appeals, 125 S Grand Ave,
Pasadena, CA 91105 USA

Nelson, Drew *Actor*
Select Artists Ltd (CA-Westside Office),
1138 12th Street, Suite 1, Santa Monica,
CA 90403 USA

Nelson, Ed *Actor*
1038 Marina Dr, Slidell, LA 70458 USA

Nelson, Edmund *Football Player*
1160 Billings Dr, Pittsburgh, PA 15241
USA

Nelson, Gaylord A *Governor, Senator*
3611 Calvend Lane, Kensington, MD
20895 USA

Nelson, George D *Astronaut*
AAAS Project, 1200 New York Ave NW,
#100, Washington, DC 20005 USA

Nelson, Glen D *Business Person*
Medtronic Inc, 7000 Central Ave NE,
Minneapolis, MN 55432 USA

Nelson, Gunnar
13030 Valleyheart Dr. #105, Studio City,
CA 91604

Nelson, Jameer *Basketball Player*
Orlando Magic, Waterhouse Center, 8701
Maitland Summit Blvd, Orlando, FL
32810 USA

Nelson, James E *Religious Leader*
Baha i Faith, 536 Sheridan Road,
Wilmette, IL 60091 USA

Nelson, Jerry E *Physicist, Astronomer*
University of California, Astronomy Dept,
Berkeley, CA 94720 USA

Nelson, Jim *Editor*
Gentlemen's Quarterly Magazine, 350
Madison Avenue, New York, NY 10017
USA

Nelson, Jimmy
10404 Greenhaven Parkway, Brecksville,
OH 44141-1625

Nelson, John Allen *Actor*
4960 Fulton Ave, Sherman Oaks, CA
91423 USA

Nelson, John R *Misc*
1111 Hermann Dr, #19A, Houston, TX
77004 USA

Nelson, John W
Astrid Schoerke, Monckebergallee 41,
Hanover, 30453, GERMANY

Nelson, Judd *Actor*
409 N Camden Dr, #202, Beverly Hills,
CA 90210 USA

Nelson, Judith *Opera Singer*
2600 Buena Vista Way, Berkeley, CA
94708 USA

Nelson, Kent C *Business Person*
United Parcel Service, 55 Glenlake
Parkway NE, Atlanta, GA 30328 USA

Nelson, Kirsten *Actor*
Himber Entertainment Inc, 211 S Beverly
Dr #208, Beverly Hills, CA 90212 USA

Nelson, Larry *Golfer*
421 Oakmont Circle, Marietta, GA 30067
USA

Nelson, Liza *Writer*
G P Putnam's Sons, 375 Hudson St, New
York, NY 10014 USA

Nelson, Lori *Actor*
13263 Ventura Blvd, #4, Studio City, CA
91604 USA

Nelson, Marilyn Carlson *Business Person*
Carlson Companies, Carlson Parkway, PO
Box 59159, Minneapolis, MN 55459 USA

Nelson, Matthew
12344 Moorpark St. #4, Studio City, CA
91604

Nelson, Ralph A *Misc*
Carle Foundation Hospital, 611 W Park St,
Urbana, IL 61801 USA

Nelson, Steven L (Steve) *Football Player,*
Coach
42 Noon Hill Ave, Box 132, Norfolk, MA
02056 USA

Nelson, Thomas G *Judge*
US Court of Appeals, 550 W Fort St,
Boise, ID 83724 USA

Nelson, Tim Blake *Actor*
I/D PR (NY), 155 Spring St Fl 6, New
York, NY 10013 USA

Nelson, Tracy *Actor*
13451 Galewood Dr, Sherman Oaks, CA
91423 USA

Nelson, William (Bill) *Senator, Astronaut*
Florida Insurance Dept, 200 E Gaines St,
Tallahassee, FL 32399 USA

Nelson, Willie *Musician, Songwriter*
Pedernails Studio, RR 1 Briarcliff TT,
Spicewood, TX 78669 USA

Nelson Jr, J Bryon *Golfer*
Fairway Ranch, RR 2 Box 5 Litsey Road,
Roanoke, TX 76262 USA

Nemchinov, Sergei *Hockey Player*
53 Walker Ave, Rye, NY 10580 USA

Nemcova, Petra *Model*
Next Management (NY), 23 Watts St, New
York, NY 10013 USA

Nemec, Corin *Actor*
859 N Hollywood Way, #104, Burbank,
CA 91505 USA

Nemecek, Bohumil *Boxer*
V Zahradkach 30, Usti Nad Labem, 400
00, CZECH REPUBLIC

Nemechek, Joe *Race Car Driver*
530 Mount Moriah Church Road, China
Grove, NC 28023 USA

Nemelka, Richard *Basketball Player*
1949 Sunridge Dr, Sandy, UT 84093 USA

Nemeth, Miklos *Prime Minister*
European Reconstruction Bank, 1
Exchange Square, London, EC2A 2EH,
UNITED KINGDOM (UK)

Nemov, AlekseiRGF
Lujnetskaya Nabereunaya 8, Moscow,
RUSSIA, 119.270

Nemov, Alexei *Gymnast*
Gymnastics Federation, Lujnetskaya
Nabereynaya 8, Moscow, 119270,
RUSSIA

Nennerman, Richard A *Editor*
PO Box 992, East Brunswick, NJ 08816
USA

Nenninger, Eric *Actor*
Roklin Management, 8265 Sunset Blvd
#101, Los Angeles, CA 90046 USA

Nepoleon *Actor*
12/5 Sandilya Apartments Jagathambal
Colony, II Street Royapettah, Chennai, TN
600 014, INDIA

NERD *Music Group*
Solo Agency Ltd (UK), 55 Fulham High St,
London, SW6 3JJ, United Kingdom

Nerem, Robert M *Engineer*
2950 Waverly Court, Atlanta, GA 30339
USA

Nerette, Joseph *President, Judge*
Supreme Court, Chief Justice's Office,
Port-au-Prince, HAITI

Neri, Francesca *Actor*
Blue Train Entertainment, 9100 Wilshire
Blvd #340W, Beverly Hills, CA 90212
USA

Nerl, Manuel *Artist*
greg Kucera Gallery, 212 3rd Ave S,
Seattle, WA 98104 USA

Nerl Vela, Rodolfo *Astronaut*
Playa Copacabana 131, Col Marte,
Mexico City, DF, 08830, MEXICO

Nerlove, Marc L *Economist*
University of Maryland, Agricultural/
Resource Economics, College Park, MD
20742 USA

Nerman, Maxens *Actor*
Continent II, 62, Rue des Grands Champs,
75020, PARIS

Nero, Franco *Actor*
Via di Monte del Gallo 26, Rome,
1-00165, ITALY

Nero, Peter *Musician*
202 Hidden Acres Lane, Media, PA 19063
USA

Nerud, John *Misc*
19 Pound Hollow Road, Glen Head, NY
11545 USA

Nesbitt, James *Actor*
Yakety Yak, 8 Bloomsbury Sq, London,
WC1A 2UA, UNITED KINGDOM (UK)

Neserovic, Radoslav *Basketball Player*
San Antonio Spurs, Alamodome, 1 SBC
Center, San Antonio, TX 78219 USA

Nesher, Avi *Director*
Gersh Agency, 232 N Canon Dr, Beverly
Hills, CA 90210 USA

Nesic, Alex *Actor*
Principato/Young Management, 9665
Wilshire Blvd #500, Beverly Hills, CA
90212 USA

Nesmith, Michael (Mike) *Musician*
Videoranch, 8 Harris Court, #C1,
Monterey, CA 93940 USA

Nespral, Jackie *Commentator*
NBC-TV, News Dept, 30 Rockefeller
Plaza, New York, NY 10112 USA

Ness, Norman F *Physicist*
9 Wilkinson Dr, Landenberg, PA 19350
USA

Ness, Rick *Musician*
Metropolitan Entertainment Group, 2 Penn
Plaza, #2600, New York, NY 10121 USA

Nessen, Ronald H (Ron) *Government*
Official, Commentator
6409 Walhonding Road, Bethesda, MD
20816 USA

Nesterenko, Eric *Hockey Player*
2395 Bald Mountain Road, Vail, CO
81657 USA

Nesterenko, Evgeny Y *Opera Singer*
Fruzenskaya Nab 24 Korp 1, #178,
Moscow, 119146, RUSSIA

Netanyahu, Benjamin *Prime Minister*
Likud Party, 38 Rehov King George, Tel-
Aviv, 61231, ISRAEL

Netherland, Joseph H *Business Person*
FMC Corp, 200 E Randolph Dr, Chicago, IL 60601 USA

Netravali, Arun N *Engineer*
10 Byron Court, Westfield, NJ 07090 USA

Nett, Robert B *War Hero*
5417 Kessington Dr, Columbus, GA 31907 USA

Nettles, Graig *Baseball Player*
4255 Parris Dr, Lenoir City, TN 37772 USA

Nettles, John *Actor*
Saraband Assoc, 265 Liverpool Road, London, N1 1LX, UNITED KINGDOM (UK)

Nettleton, Lois *Actor*
Susan Mann, 11762 Moorpark St, #G, Studio City, CA 91604 USA

Neubert, Keith
10000 Santa Monica Blvd. #305, Los Angeles, CA 90067

Neufeld, Elizabeth F *Misc*
University of California, Medical School, Biology Dept, Los Angeles, CA 90024 USA

Neufeld, Ray *Hockey Player*
RE/MAX Real Estate, 3919 Henderson Highway, Winnipeg, MB R2G 1P4, CANADA

Neugebauer, Marcia *Physicist*
7519 S Elliot Lane, Tucson, AZ 85747 USA

Neuharth, Allen H *Publisher*
Freedom Dorum, 1101 Wilson Blvd, Arlington, VA 22209 USA

Neuhaus, Max *Artist, Composer*
350 5th Ave, #3304, New York, NY 10118 USA

Neuhaus, Richard J *Religious Leader*
Center on Religion & Society, 152 Madison Ave, New York, NY 10016 USA

Neuhauser, Duncan V B *Misc*
2655 N Park Ave, Cleveland Heights, OH 44106 USA

Neuheisel, Richard (Rick) *Football Player, Football Coach*
University of Washington, Athletic Dept, Seattle, WA 98195 USA

Neumann, Liselotte *Golfer*
Int'l Mgmt Group, 1 Erieview Plaza, 1360 E 9th St #1300, Cleveland, OH 44114 USA

Neumann, Wolfgang *Opera Singer*
Opera et Concert, Maximilianstr 22, Munich, 80539, GERMANY

Neumark, Julie
900 E. First St. #314, Los Angeles, CA 90012

Neumeler, John *Choreographer*
Hamburg Ballet, 54 Caspar-Voght-Str, Hamburg, 20535, GERMANY

Neumeyer, Bobby *Producer*
Creative Artists Agency, 9830 Wilshire Blvd, Beverly Hills, CA 90212 USA

Neuner, Doris *Athlete*
6024 Innsbruck, AUSTRIA

Neuwelt, Edward A *Misc*
Oregon Health Sciences University, Neurology Dept, Portland, OR 97201 USA

Neuwirth, Bebe *Actor, Dancer, Musician*
144 Prospect Ave, Princeton, NJ 08540 USA

Nevil, Bobbie
20 Manchester Sq, London, W1M 5AE, ENGLAND

Neville, Aaron *Musician*
5771 Eastover Dr, New Orleans, LA 70128 USA

Neville, Arthel *Commentator, Television Host*
1840 Victory Blvd, Glendale, CA 91201 USA

Neville, Bill *Cartoonist*
506 Oakdale Road, Jamestown, NC 27282 USA

Neville, John *Actor, Director*
139 Winnett Ave, Toronto, ON M6C 3L7, CANADA

Neville, Katherine *Writer*
PO Box 788, Warrenton, VA 20188 USA

Neville, Robert C *Misc*
Boston University, Theology School, Boston, MA 02215 USA

Nevins, Claudette *Actor*
Gold Marshak Liedtke, 3500 W Olive Ave, #1400, Burbank, CA 91505 USA

Nevinson, Nancy
23 Mill Close Fishbourne, Chichester, ENGLAND

New Christy Minstrels, The
2112 Casitas Way, Palm Springs, CA 92264

New Edition
151 El Camino Dr., Beverly Hills, CA 90212

New Grass Revival
PO Box 128037, Nashville, TN 37212

New Order
72 Chancellor's Rd., London, ENGLAND, W6 9SG

New Radicals
645 Quail Ridge Rd., Aledo, TX 76008-2835

New Rascals, The
PO Box 1821, Ojai, CA 93023

New Riders of the Purple Sage
PO Box 3773, San Rafael, CA 94912-3773

New York Yankees
Yankee Stadium, 161st & River, Bronx, NY 10451 USA

Newbern, George *Actor*
Entertainment Tavel, 9171 Wilshire Blvd, #406, Beverly Hills, CA 90210 USA

Newberry, Thomas (Tom) *Football Player*
1140 Lugo Ave, Coral Gables, FL 33156 USA

Newbigging, William *Publisher*
Edmonton Journal, 10006 101st St, Edmonton, AB T5J 2S6, CANADA

Newborn, Ira *Composer*
Vangelos Mgmt, 15233 Ventura Blvd, #200, Sherman Oaks, CA 91403 USA

Newburn, George
PO Box 5617, Beverly Hills, CA 90210

Newcomb, Gerry *Artist*
7029 17th Ave NW, Seattle, WA 98117 USA

Newcomb, Jonathan *Publisher*
35 Pierrepont St, Brooklyn, NY 11201 USA

Newcombe, Don
4042 W. 226th St, Torrance, CA 90505

Newcombe, Donald (Don) *Baseball Player*
Paralysis Project, PO Box 627, Glendale, CA 91209 USA

Newcombe, John
PO Box 310469, New Braunfels, TX 78131-0469

Newcombe, John D *Tennis Player*
John Newcombe's Tennis Ranch, PO Box 310469, New Braunfels, TX 78131 USA

Newell, Horner E *Physicist*
2567 Nicky Lane, Alexandria, VA 22311 USA

Newell, James
20519 Rodax St., Canoga Park, CA 91306

Newell, Mike *Director, Actor, Producer*
Fifty Cannon Entertainment, 1950 Sawtelle Blvd #333, Los Angeles, CA 90025 USA

Newell, Norman D *Misc*
135 Knapp Terrace, Leonia, NJ 07605 USA

Newell, Peter F (Pete) *Coach*
16078 Via Viajera, Rancho Santa Fe, CA 92091 USA

Newfield, Heidi *Musician*
Creative Artists Agency, 9830 Wilshire Blvd, Beverly Hills, CA 90212 USA

Newgard, Christopher *Misc*
Southwestern Medical Center, Biochemistry Dept, Dallas, TX 75237 USA

Newhart, Bob *Actor, Comedian*
420 Amapola Lane, Los Angeles, CA 90077 USA

Newhouse, Bob
6847 Truxton, Dallas, TX 75231

Newhouse, Donald E *Publisher*
Advance Publications, 950 W Fingerboard Road, Staten Island, NY 10305 USA

Newhouse, Fred
816 Bantry Way, Benicia, CA 94510

Newhouse, Fredrick (Fred) *Track Athlete*
3003 Pine Lake Trail, Houston, TX 77068 USA

Newhouse, Robert F *Football Player*
6847 Truxton Dr, Dallas, TX 75231 USA

Newhouse Jr, Samuel I *Publisher*
Advance Publications, 950 W Fingerboard Road, Staten Island, NY 10305 USA

Newlin, Mike *Basketball Player*
1414 Horseshoe Dr, Sugar Land, TX 77478 USA

Newman, Alec *Actor*
Relativity Management, 8899 Beverly Blvd #510, Los Angeles, CA 90048 USA

Newman, Anthony *Musician, Conductor*
I C M Artists, 40 W 57th St, New York, NY 10019 USA

Newman, Arnold *Photographer*
33 W 67th St, New York, NY 10023 USA

Newman, Barry *Actor*
Greene & Associates, 526 N Larchmont Blvd #201, Los Angeles, CA 90004 USA

Newman, David *Composer*
Agency for Performing Arts, 9200 Sunset Blvd, #900, Los Angeles, CA 90069 USA

Newman, David(Fathead) *Musician*
Maxine Harvard, 7942 W Belt Road, Glendale, AZ 85308 USA

Newman, Edward (Ed) *Football Player*
10100 SW 140th St, Miami, FL 33176 USA

Newman, Edward K (Ed) *Football Player*
10100 SW 140th St, Miami, FL 33176 USA

Newman, Edwin
870 United Nations Plaza #16D, New York, NY 10017

Newman, Edwin H *Commentator*
870 United Nations Plaza, #18D, New York, NY 10017 USA

Newman, James H *Astronaut*
18583 Martinique Dr, Houston, TX 77058 USA

Newman, Jimmy C *Musician, Songwriter*
RR2, Christiana, TN 37037 USA

Newman, Johnny *Basketball Player*
Dallas Mavericks, 2909 Taylor St, Dallas, TX 75226 USA

Newman, Jon O *Judge*
US Court of Appeals, 450 Main St, Hartford, CT 06103 USA

Newman, Joseph M *Director*
10900 Winnetka Ave, Chatsworth, CA 91311 USA

Newman, Kevin *Commentator*
ABC-TV, News Dept, 77 W 66th St, New York, NY 10023 USA

Newman, Laraine *Actor, Comedian*
10480 Ashton Ave, Los Angeles, CA 90024 USA

Newman, Michael *Actor*
Morgan Agency

Newman, Nanette *Actor*
Seven Pines Wentworth, Surrey, GU25 4QP, UNITED KINGDOM (UK)

Newman, Oscar *Architect*
Community Design Analysis Institute, 66 Clover Dr, Great Neck, NY 11021 USA

Newman, Paul *Actor*
1120 5th Ave, #1C, New York, NY 10128 USA

Newman, Pauline *Judge*
US Court of Appeals, 717 Madison Place NW, Washington, DC 20439 USA

Newman, Phyllis *Actor, Musician*
Gage Group, 315 W 57th St, #4H, New York, NY 10019 USA

Newman, Randy *Musician, Songwriter*
1610 San Remo Dr, Pacific Palisades, CA 90272 USA

Newman, Ryan *Race Car Driver*
Tom Roberts PR, 123 Woodview Dr, Statesville, NC 28625 USA

Newman, Terence *Football Player*
Dallas Cowboys, 1 Cowboys Parkway, Irving, TX 75063 USA

Newman, Thomas *Composer*
Gorfaine/Schwartz, 13245 Riverside Dr, #450, Sherman Oaks, CA 91423 USA

Newman, Thomas *Actor*
Badgley Connor Talent, 9229 Sunset Blvd, #311, Los Angeles, CA 90069 USA

Newmar, Julie *Actor*
204 S Carmelina Ave, Los Angeles, CA 90049 USA

Newmyer (Newmeyer), Robert (Bobby) *Producer*
Outlaw Productions, 9155 Sunset Blvd, West Hollywood, CA 90069 USA

News, Huey Lewis & The *Musician*
Monterey Peninsula Artists (Monterey), 509 Hartnell St, Monterey, CA 93940 USA

Newsboys
PO Box 681668, Franklin, TN 37968-1668

Newsom, David *Actor*
Innovative Artists, 1505 10th St, Santa Monica, CA 90401 USA

Newsom, David D *Diplomat*
2409 Angus Road, Charlottesville, VA 22901 USA

Newsom, Tommy
19315 Wells Dr., Tarzana, CA 91356

Newsome, Gavin *Misc*
Mayor's Office, City Hall, 400 Van Ness Ave, San Francisco, CA 94102 USA

Newsome, Ozzie *Football Player*
6 Padonia Woods Court, Cockeysville, MD 21030 USA

Newsted, Jason *Musician*
205 Alamo View Place, Walnut Creek, CA 94595 USA

Newton, C M *Coach*
2 Olde Village Court, Nicholasville, KY 40356 USA

Newton, Christopher *Director*
22 Prideaux St, Niagara-on-the-Lake, ON L0S 1J0, CANADA

Newton, John Haymes *Actor*
Pakula/King & Associates, 9229 Sunset Blvd #315, Los Angeles, CA 90069 USA

Newton, Jon *Business Person*
American General Corp, 2929 Allen Parkway, Houston, TX 77019 USA

Newton, Juice *Musician, Songwriter*
OJ Mgmt, 4321 Reyes Dr, Tarzana, CA 91356 USA

Newton, Nate *Football Player*
1921 White Oak Clearing, Southlake, TX 76092 USA

Newton, Roger *Scientist*
Esperion Therapeutics, 695 KMS Place, 3621 S State St, Ann Arbor, MI 48108 USA

Newton, Thandie *Actor*
I/D PR (LA), 8409 Santa Monica Blvd, West Hollywood, CA 90069 USA

Newton, Thomas
9229 Sunset Blvd. #311, Los Angeles, CA 90069

Newton, Wayne *Musician, Actor*
Wayne Newton Mgmt, 6730 S Pecos Road, Las Vegas, NV 89120 USA

Newton-John, Olivia *Musician, Actor*
PO Box 2710, Malibu, CA 90265 USA

Ney, Edward N *Business Person, Diplomat*
Burson-Marsteller, 230 Park Ave S, New York, NY 10003 USA

Neyelova, Marina M *Actor*
Potapovsky Per 12, Moscow, 117333, RUSSIA

Neyra, Gianella *Actor*
Telefe - Argentina, Pavon 2444 (C1248AAT), Buenos Aires, ARGENTINA

Nezhat, Camran *Misc*
Fertility/Endocrinology Ctr, 5555 Peachtree Dunwoody Road NE, Atlanta, GA 30342 USA

Nguema, Tedoro Obiang *President*
President's Office, Malabo, EQUATORIAL GUINEA

Nguyen, Dustin *Actor*
1051 S Dunsmuir Ave, Los Angeles, CA 90019 USA

Nicastro, Michelle
1800 Ave. of the Stars #400, Los Angeles, CA 90067

Nicaud, Philippe
104 rue des Sablons, Mareil-Marly, FRANCE, 78750

Niccol, Andrew *Writer, Producer, Director*
Creative Artists Agency LCC (CAA-LA), 9830 Wilshire Blvd, Beverly Hills, CA 90212 USA

Nichol, Joseph McGinty (McG) *Writer, Producer, Musician*
Wonderland Sound and Vision, 8739 Sunset Blvd, W Hollywood, CA 90069 USA

Nicholas, Alison *Golfer*
Pat Darby, Badgar Farm House, Badgar near Wolverhampton, WV6 7LS, UNITED KINGDOM (UK)

Nicholas, Ben *Actor*

Nicholas, Denise *Actor*
932 Longwood Ave, Los Angeles, CA 90019 USA

Nicholas, Eric *Writer*
Gersh Agency, The (LA), 232 N Canon Dr, Beverly Hills, CA 90210 USA

Nicholas, Fayard *Actor, Dancer*
10153 1/2 Riverside Dr, #219, Toluca Lake, CA 91602 USA

Nicholas, Henry *Misc*
Hospital & Health Care Union, 330 W 42nd St, #1905, New York, NY 10036 USA

Nicholas, J D *Musician*
Management Assoc, 1920 Benson Ave, Saint Paul, MN 55116 USA

Nicholas, Peter M *Business Person*
Boston Scientific Corp, 1 Boston Scientific Place, Natick, MA 01760 USA

Nicholas, Thomas Ian *Actor*
Osbrink Talent, 4343 Lankershim Blvd, #100, North Hollywood, CA 91602 USA

Nicholas Jr, Nicholas J *Publisher*
Pluggers Inc, 1000 SW Broadway, #1850, Portland, OR 97205 USA

Nicholas(Smisko), Bishop *Religious Leader*
American Carpatho, 312 Garfield St, Johnstown, PA 15906 USA

Nicholls, Craig *Musician*
Winterman-Goldstein, 17 Holdsworth St, Newton, NSW, 2042, AUSTRALIA

Nichols, Austin *Actor*
Joan Green Management, 1836 Courtney Terr, Los Angeles, CA 90046 USA

Nichols, Bobby *Golfer*
8681 Glenlyon Court, Fort Myers, FL 33912 USA

Nichols, Dorothy L *Financier*
Farm Credit Administration, 1501 Farm Credit Dr, McLean, VA 22102 USA

Nichols, Hamilton J *Football Player*
11015 Kirkmead Dr, Houston, TX 77089 USA

Nichols, Joe *Musician*
Creative Artists Agency (CAA-Nashville), 3310 West End Ave Fl 5, Nashville, TN 37203 USA

Nichols, Kenwood C *Business Person*
Champion Int'l Corp, 1 Champion Plaza, Stamford, CT 06921 USA

Nichols, Kyra *Ballerina*
Peter Diggins Assoc, 133 W 71st St, New York, NY 10023 USA

Nichols, Larry *Designer*
Moleculon Research Corp, 139 Main St, Cambridge, MA 02142 USA

Nichols, Lorrie *Bowler*
1251 Lexington Dr, Algonquin, IL 60102 USA

Nichols, Marisol *Actor*
206 S Brand Blvd, Glendale, CA 91204 USA

Nichols, Mike *Director, Comedian*
Creative Artists Agency, 9830 Wilshire Blvd, Beverly Hills, CA 90212 USA

Nichols, Nichelle *Actor*
23281 Leonora Dr, Woodland Hills, CA 91367 USA

Nichols, Peter R *Writer*
Alan Brodie, 211 Piccadilly, London, W1V 9LD, UNITED KINGDOM (UK)

Nichols, Rachel *Actor*
Management 360, 9111 Wilshire Blvd, Beverly Hills, CA 90210 USA

Nichols, Stephen *Actor*
11664 National Blvd, #116, Los Angeles, CA 90064 USA

Nicholson, Bruce
PO Box 2573, Georgetown, SC 29442-2573

Nicholson, Jack *Actor*
Bresler Kelly & Associates, 11500 W Olympic Blvd #352, Los Angeles, CA 90064 USA

Nicholson, Jim *Diplomat*
US Embassy, Via delle Terme di Clare 26, Rome, 00162, ITALY

Nicholson, Julianne *Actor*
939 8th Ave, #609, New York, NY 10019 USA

Nicholson, Kathrin
9057-A Nemo St., W. Hollywood, CA 90069

Nickel Creek *Music Group*
William Morris Agency (WMA-TN), 2100 W End Ave #1000, Nashville, TN 37203 USA

Nickelback *Music Group*
Union Entertainment, 31225 La Baya Dr #213, Westlake Village, CA 91362-6333 USA

Nickerson, Hardy O *Football Player*
3319 Deer Hollow Dr, Danville, CA 94506 USA

Nickerson Jr, Donald A *Religious Leader*
Episcopal Church, 815 2nd Ave, New York, NY 10017 USA

Nicklaus, Gary
112 TPC Blvd., Ponte Vedra Beach, FL 32082

Nicklaus, Jack W *Golfer*
Golden Bear International, 11760 US Highway 1, North Palm Beach, FL 33408 USA

Nicks, John A W *Misc*
Ice Capades Chalet, 13211 Brooks Dr, #A, Baldwin Park, CA 91706 USA

Nicks, Regina *Musician*
Bobby Roberts, 909 Meadowlark Lane, Goodlettsville, TN 37072 USA

Nicks, Stevie *Musician, Songwriter*
H K Mgmt, 9200 W Sunset Blvd, #530, Los Angeles, CA 90069 USA

Nickson, Julia *Actor*
Elkins Entertainment, 8306 Wilshire Blvd, #438, Beverly Hills, CA 90211 USA

Nicol, Steve *Football Coach*
New England Revolution, CMGI Field, 1 Patriot Place, Foxboro, MA 02035 USA

Nicolaou, Kyriacos Costa *Misc*
Scripps Research Institute, 10550 N Torrey Pines Road, La Jolla, CA 92037 USA

Nicole
Im Pfarrwittum 1, Nohfelden, GERMANY, D-66625

Nicole Freeman, Jennifer *Actor*
Writers and Artists Group Intl (LA), 8383 Wilshire Blvd #550, Beverly Hills, CA 90211 USA

Nicolet, Aurele *Musician*
Hans Ulrich Schmid, Postfach 1617, Hanover, 30016, GERMANY

Nicoletti Susi
Goethegasse, Vienna, AUSTRIA, 1 A-1010

Nicollier, Claude *Astronaut*
18710 Martinique Dr, Houston, TX 77058 USA

Nicolson, Nigel *Writer*
Sissinghurst Castle, Kent, UNITED KINGDOM (UK)

Nicolucci, Guy *Writer*
Late Night with Conan O'Brien, 330 Bob Hope Dr, Burbank, CA 91523

Nicora, Attilio Cardinal *Religious Leader*
Patrimony of Apostolic See, Palazzo Apostolico, 00120, VATICAN CITY

Nidetch, Jean *Business Person*
Weight Watchers International, 3860 Crenshaw Blvd, Los Angeles, CA 90008 USA

Nieberg, Lars *Misc*
Gestit Waldershausen, Homberg, 35315, GERMANY

Nieder, William H (Bill) *Track Athlete*
PO Box 310, Mountain Ranch, CA 95246 USA

Niederhoffer, Victor *Misc*
Niederhoffer Cross Zeckhauser, 757 3rd Ave, New York, NY 10017 USA

Niedermayer, Scott *Hockey Player*
32 Prospect Ave, Montclair, NJ 07042 USA

Niedernhuber, Barbara *Athlete*
Schwarzeckstr 58, Ramsau, 83486, GERMANY

Niehaus, Dave *Sportscaster*
Seattle Mariners, Safeco Field, PO Box 4100, Seattle, WA 98194 USA

Niehaus, Lennie *Composer*
Robert Light Agency, 6404 Wilshire Blvd, #1225, Los Angeles, CA 90048 USA

Niekro, Joe
2707 Fairway Dr. So., Plant City, FL 33567

Niekro, Joseph F (Joe) *Baseball Player*
2707 Fairway Dr S, Plant City, FL 33566 USA

Niekro, Philip H (Phil) *Baseball Player*
6382 Nichols Rd, Flowery Branch, GA 30542 USA

Niel, Steve *Actor*
Central Artists, 269 W Alameda Ave #A, Burbank, CA 91502 USA

Nielsen, Brigitte *Actor, Model*
Bartels Co, PO Box 57593, Sherman Oaks, CA 91413 USA

Nielsen, Connie *Actor*
Lasher McManus Robinson, 1964 Westwood Blvd, #400, Los Angeles, CA 90025 USA

Nielsen, Gifford *Football Player*
10 Sarahs Cove, Sugar Land, TX 77479 USA

Nielsen, Leslie *Actor*
1622 Viewmont Dr, Los Angeles, CA 90069 USA

Nielsen, Rick *Musician*
Monterey Peninsula Artists, 509 Hartnell St, Monterey, CA 93940 USA

Niemann-Stirnemann, Gunda *Speed Skater*
Postfach 503, Erfurt, 99010, GERMANY

Niemeyer, Paul V *Judge*
US Court of Appeals, 101 W Lombard St, Baltimore, MD 21201 USA

Niemi, Lisa *Actor*
Flick East-West, 9057 Nemo St, #A, West Hollywood, CA 90069 USA

Nieminen, Toni *Skier*
Landen Kanava 99, vesijarvenkatu 74, Lahti, 15140, FINLAND

Nierman, Leonardo *Artist*
Amsterdam 43 PH, Mexico City 11, DF, MEXICO

Nies, Eric *Actor, Reality TV Star, Model*
Bunim/Murray Productions Inc, 6007 Sepulveda Blvd, Van Nuys, CA 91411 USA

Nieto, Adriana *Actor*
Televisa, Blvd Adolfo Lopez Mateos 232, Colonia San Angel INN, DF, CP 01060, MEXICO

Nieuwendyk, Joe *Hockey Player*
1493 Taughannock Blvd, Ithaca, NY 14850 USA

Nigam, Anjul *Actor*
Greene & Associates, 526 N Larchmont Blvd #201, Los Angeles, CA 90004 USA

Nigh, George P *Governor, Educator*
University of Central Oklahoma, 100 N University Dr, Edmond, OK 73034 USA

Nighy, Bill *Actor*
Markham & Froggatt, Julian House, 4 Windmill St, London, W1P 1HF, UNITED KINGDOM (UK)

Nigrelli, Ross F *Misc*
29 Barracuda Road, East Quogue, NY 11942 USA

Nihalani, Govind *Director, Producer, Filmmaker*
139 Aradhana Behind Bhavishya Nidhi, Bandra (E), Bombay, MS 400 051, INDIA

Niinimaa, Janne *Hockey Player*
2200-201 Portage Ave, Winnipeg, MB R3B 3L3, CANADA

Nikkanen, Kurt *Musician*
Columbia Artists Mgmt Inc, 165 W 57th St, New York, NY 10019 USA

Niklas, Jan
Konigsberger Str. 20, Munich, GERMANY, D-81927

Niklason, Laura A *Engineer*
Duke University Medical School, Durham, NC 27706 USA

Nikolishin, Andrei *Hockey Player*
105 Bloomfield Ave, Hartford, CT 06105 USA

Niland, John H *Football Player*
16058 Chalfont Court, Dallas, TX 75248 USA

Niles, John *Composer, Musician*
Magic Wing Music, PO Box 222, West Linn, OR 97068 USA

Niles, Nicholas H *Publisher*
Sporting News Publishing Co, 1212 N Lindbergh Blvd, Saint Louis, MO 63132 USA

Niles, Prescott *Musician*
Artists & Audience Entertainment, PO Box 35, Pawling, NY 12564 USA

Niles, Thomas M T *Diplomat*
National Defense Hdqs Library, 101 C By Dr, Ottawa, ON K1A 0K2, CANADA

Nilsson, Birgit M *Opera Singer*
Hammenhog, Hammenhog, 27050, SWEDEN

Nilsson, Inger
Box 12710, Stockholm, SWEDEN, 11294

Nilsson, Lennart *Photographer*
Pantheon Books, 201 E 50th St, New York, NY 10022 USA

Nimmo, Dirk *Actor*
Michael Whitehall, 125 Gloucester Road, London, SW7 4TE, UNITED KINGDOM (UK)

Nimoy, Leonard *Actor, Director*
Gersh Agency, The (LA), 232 N Canon Dr, Beverly Hills, CA 90210 USA

Nimri, Najwa *Actor, Musician*
Kuranda Management, 8626 Skyline, Los Angeles, CA 90046 USA

Nimziki, Joe *Director*
Paradigm Agency, 10100 Santa Monica Blvd, #2500, Los Angeles, CA 90067 USA

Nine Inch Nails (NIN) *Music Group*
Helter Skelter (UK), The Plaza, 535 Kings Rd, London, N13 5H, UNITED KINGDOM (UK)

Nininger, Harvey H *Misc*
PO Box 420, Sedona, AZ 86339 USA

Nipar, Yvette *Actor*
Irv Schechter, 9300 Wilshire Blvd, #410, Beverly Hills, CA 90212 USA

Nipon, Albert *Fashion Designer*
Leslie Faye Co, Albert Nipon Div, 1400 Broadway #1600, New York, NY 10018 USA

Nirenberg, Louis *Mathematician*
221 W 82nd St, New York, NY 10024 USA

Nirenberg, Marshall W *Nobel Prize Laureate*
7001 Omey Parkway, Bethesda, MD 20817 USA

Nirmala, Sister *Religious Leader*
Missionaries of Charity, 54A Lower Circular Road, Kolkata, WB, 700016, INDIA

Nirosha *Actor, Bollywood*
3 Paul Appasamy Street, T Nagar, Chennai, TN 600017, INDIA

Nirvana
151 El Camino Dr., Beverly Hills, CA 90212

Nisbet, Robert A *Historian, Social Activist*
6131 Purple Aster Lane NE, Albuquerque, NM 87111 USA

Nishizawa, Junichi *Engineer, Inventor*
Semiconductor Research Institute, Kawauchi, Aobaku, Sendai, 9800862, JAPAN

Nishizuka, Yasutomi *Physicist*
Kobe University, 7-5-1 Kusunokichochuoki, Kobe, 650-0017, JAPAN

Nishkian, Byron *Skier*
150 4th St, #PH, San Francisco, CA 94103 USA

Niskanen Jr, William A *Government Official, Economist*
Cato Institute, 1000 Massachusetts Ave NW, #6, Washington, DC 20001 USA

Nispel, Marcus *Director*
Endeavor Agency LLC (LA), 9601 Wilshire Blvd Fl 3, Beverly Hills, CA 90210 USA

Nissalke, Tom *Coach*
4569 S Thousand Oaks Dr, Salt Lake City, UT 84124 USA

Nissen, Steve *Doctor*
817 Hanover Road, Gates Mills, OH 44040 USA

Nithya *Actor, Bollywood*
37 Palayakaran Street, Chennai, TN 600024, INDIA

Nittmann, David *Artist*
PO Box 19065, Boulder, CO 80308 USA

Nitty Gritty Dirt Band *Music Group*
Monterey Peninsula Artists (Monterey), 509 Hartnell St, Monterey, CA 93940 USA

Nitze, Paul H *Secretary, Diplomat*
1619 Massachusetts Ave NW, #811, Washington, DC 20036 USA

Nitzkowski, Monte *Coach*
7041 Seat Circle, Huntington Beach, CA 92648 USA

Niven, Barbara
9300 Wilshire Blvd. #410, Beverly Hills, CA 90212

Niven, Kip *Actor*
9000 Sunset Blvd, #801, Los Angeles, CA 90069 USA

Niven, Laurence (Larry) *Writer*
11874 Macoda Lane, Chatsworth, CA 91311 USA

Niven Jr, David
1457 Blue Jay Way, Los Angeles, CA 90069 USA

Nivola, Alessandro *Actor*
More/Medavoy, 7920 W Sunset Blvd, #400, Los Angeles, CA 90046 USA

Niwa, Gail *Musician*
Siegel Artist Mgmt, 1416 Hinman Ave, Evanston, IL 60201 USA

Niwano, Nikkyo *Religious Leader*
Rissho Kosel-Kai, 2-11-1 Wada Suginamiku, Tokyo, 166, JAPAN

Nix, Matt *Writer*
Endeavor Agency LLC (LA), 9601 Wilshire Blvd Fl 3, Beverly Hills, CA 90210 USA

Nixon, Agnes *Writer, Producer*
774 Conestoga Rd, Bryn Mawr, PA 19010 USA

Nixon, Cynthia *Actor*
William Morris Agency, 1325 Ave of Americas, New York, NY 10019 USA

Nixon, Gary *Motorcycle Racer*
Gary Nixon Enterprises, 2408 Carroll Mill Road, Phoenix, MD 21131 USA

Nixon, Marni *Musician, Actor*
Agency for Performing Arts, 9200 Sunset Blvd, #900, Los Angeles, CA 90069 USA

Nixon, Norm
607 Marguerita Ave, Santa Monica, CA 90402

Nixon, Sam *Musician*
Pop Idol (Fremantle Media), 2700 Colorado Ave #450, Santa Monica, CA 90404 USA

Niyazov, Saparmurad *President*
President's Office, Karl Marx Str 24, Ashkabad, 744017, TURKMENISTAN

Nizhalgal, Raviee *Actor*
4 Sriram Nagar North Street, Chennai, TN 600 018, INDIA

Niznik, Stephanie *Actor*
Niad Literary & Talent Management, 3465
Coy Dr, Sherman Oaks, CA 91423 USA

NKOTB (New Kids on the Block)
27 Dudley St., Roxbury, MA 02132

No Doubt *Music Group*
Rebel Waltz Inc, 31652 Second Ave,
Laguna Beach, CA 92651 USA

Noah, John *Hockey Player*
3315 Prairiewood Dr W, Fargo, ND
58103 USA

Noah, Max W *General*
820 Arcturus-on-Potomac, Alexandria, VA
22308 USA

Noah, Yannick *Tennis Player, Coach*
20 Rue Billancourt, Boulogne, 92100,
FRANCE

Noakes, Michael *Artist*
146 Hamilton Terrace, Saint John's Wood,
London, NW8 9UX, UNITED KINGDOM
(UK)

Nobilo, Frank *Golfer*
Int'l Mgmt Group, 1 Erieview Plaza, 1360
E 9th St #1300, Cleveland, OH 44114
USA

Nobis, Thomas H (Tommy) Jr *Football
Player, Football Executive*
40 S Battery Placa NE, Atlanta, GA 30342
USA

Noble, Adrian K *Director*
Royal Shakespeare Co, Barbican Theater,
London, EC2Y 8BQ, UNITED KINGDOM
(UK)

Noble, Brian D *Football Player*
2912 Nikki Lee Court, Green Bay, WI
54313 USA

Noble, Chelsea *Actor*
PO Box 8665, Calabasas, CA 91372 USA

Noble, James *Actor*
113 Ledgebrook Dr, Norwalk, CT 06854
USA

Noble, John *Actor*
A A Williams Mgmt, PO Box 1397,
Darlinghurst, NSW, 1300, AUSTRALIA

Noblitt, Niles L *Business Person*
Biomet Inc, Airport Industrial Park, PO
Box 587, Warsaw, IN 46581 USA

Noboa, Gustavo *President, Educator*
Palacio de Gobierno, Garcia Moreno,
Quito, 1043, ECUADOR

Nodell, Mart *Cartoonist*
117 Lake Irene Dr, West Palm Beach, FL
33411 USA

Noe, Vergilius Cardinal *Religious Leader*
Piazza della Citta Leonina 1, Rome,
00193, ITALY

Noel, Chris
824 McIntosh St., West Palm Beach, FL
33405

Noel, Monique *Model, Actor*
PO Box 232058, Encinitas, CA 92023
USA

Noel, Philip W *Governor*
345 Channel View, #105, Warwick, RI
02889 USA

Nofziger, Lyn *Government Official*
2000 Pennsylvania Ave NW, #365,
Washington, DC 20037 USA

Noguchi, Soichi *Astronaut*
NASA, Johnson Space Center, 2101 NASA
Road, Houston, TX 77058 USA

Noguchi, Thomas *Doctor*
1110 Avoca Ave, Pasadena, CA 91105
USA

Nogulich, Natalia *Actor*
11841 Kiowa Ave #7, Los Angeles, CA
90049

Nogulich, Natalija *Actor*
11841 Kiowa Ave, #7, Los Angeles, CA
90049 USA

Noiret, Philippe *Actor*
104 Rue des Sablons, Mareil-Marly,
FRANCE, 78750, FRANCE

Nojima, Minoru *Musician*
John Gingrich Mgmt, PO Box 515, New
York, NY 10023 USA

Nokes, Matthew D (Matt) *Baseball Player*
13553 Poway Road, #181, Poway, CA
92064 USA

Nolan, Christopher *Writer*
158 Vernon Ave, Clontarf, Dublin, 3,
IRELAND

Nolan, Deanna *Basketball Player*
Detroit Shock, Palace, 2 Championship
Dr, Auburn Hills, MI 48326 USA

Nolan, Graham
162 Godfrey Terr., E. Aurora, NY 14052

Nolan, Kathleen
250 W. 57th St. #703, New York, NY
10107-0799

Nolan, Kathleen (Kathy) *Actor*
250 W 57th St, #703, New York, NY
10107 USA

Nolan, Michelle *Actor*
Hofflund/Polone, 9465 Wilshire Blvd
#820, Beverly Hills, CA 90212 USA

Nolan, Owen *Hockey Player*
5729 La Seyne Placa, San Jose, CA 95138
USA

Nolan, Richard C (Dick) *Football Player,
Coach*
4 Gentry Court, Trophy Club, TX 76262
USA

Nolan, Ted *Hockey Player, Coach*
269 Queen St E, Sault Sainte Marie, ON
P6A 1Y9, CANADA

Nolan, Thomas B *Scientist*
2219 California St NW, Washington, DC
20008 USA

Nolan, Tom
1335 N. Ontario St., Burbank, CA 91505

Noland, Kenneth C *Artist*
183 Park St, North Bennington, VT 05257
USA

Nolasco, Amaury *Actor*
Mitchell K Stubbs & Assoc (MKS), 8675 W
Washington Blvd #203, Culver City, CA
90232 USA

Nolin, Gena Lee *Actor*
6230 Wilshire Blvd, #171, Los Angeles,
CA 90048 USA

Noll, Charles H (Chuck) *Football Player,
Coach*
201 Grant St, Sewickley, PA 15143 USA

Noll, Chuck
2121 George Halas Dr. NW, Canton, OH
44708-2699

Nolte, Claudia *Government Official*
Mulgarten 28, Ilmenau, 98693,
GERMANY

Nolte, Nick *Actor*
Kingsgate Films, 6173 Bonsall Dr, Malibu,
CA 90265 USA

Nolting, Paul F *Religious Leader*
Church of Lutheran Confession, 620 E
50th St, Loveland, CO 80538 USA

Nomellini, Leo
520 St. Claire Dr., Palo Alto, CA 94306-
3050

Nomo, Hideo
126th & Roosevelt Avenues, Flushing, NY
11368

Nomura, Masayasu *Biologist*
74 Whitman Court, Irvine, CA 92612 USA

Nool, Erki *Track Athlete*
Regati 1, Tallinn, 11911, ESTONIA

Noonan, Chris *Actor*
Creative Artists Agency LCC (CAA-LA),
9830 Wilshire Blvd, Beverly Hills, CA
90212 USA

Noonan, Danny *Football Player*
Dallas Cowboys, 1 Cowboys Parkway,
Irving, TX 75063 USA

Noonan, John T Jr *Judge*
US Court of Appeals, Court Building, 95
7th St, San Francisco, CA 94103 USA

Noonan, Patrick F *Misc*
11901 Glen Mills Road, Potomac, MD
20854 USA

Noonan, Peggy *Writer*
Reagan Books, 10 E 53rd St, New York,
NY 10022 USA

Noonan, Robert W Jr *General*
Deputy Chief of Stafff for Intelligence,
HqUSA, Pentagon, Washington, DC
20310 USA

Noonan, Timothy J *Business Person*
Rite Aid Corp, 30 Hunter Lane, Camp
Hill, PA 17011 USA

Noone, Kathleen *Actor*
130 W 42nd St, #1804, New York, NY
10036 USA

Noone, Nora Jane *Actor*
International Creative Management
(ICM-UK), Oxford House, 76 Oxford St,
London, W1N OAX, UNITED KINGDOM
(UK)

Noone, Peter *Actor, Musician*
9265 Robin Lane, Los Angeles, CA 90069
USA

Noor, Queen
Baab al-Salem Palace, Amman, JORDAN

Noor Al-Hussein *Royalty*
Royal Palace, Amman, JORDAN

Norcross, Clayton
951 Galloway St., Pacific Palisades, CA
90272

Nordenberg, Mark A *Educator*
University of Pittsburgh, President's
Office, Pittsburgh, PA 15261 USA

Nordenstrom, Bjorn *Doctor*
Karolinska Institute, Radiology Dept,
Stockholm, SWEDEN

Nordheim, Arne *Composer*
Wergelandsveien 2, Oslo, 0167,
NORWAY

Nordlander, Mattias *Musician*
MOB Agency, 6404 Wilshire Blvd, #505,
Los Angeles, CA 90048 USA

Nordli, Odvar *Prime Minister*
Sanveien 4, Ottestad, 2312, NORWAY

Nordling, Jeffrey
100 Universal City Plaza Bidg. 507#3D,
Universal City, CA 91608

Nordsieck, Kenneth H *Astronaut*
University of Wisconsin, Space Astronomy
Laboratory, Madison, WI 53706 USA

Noren, Irving A (Irv) *Baseball Player,
Basketball Player*
3154 Camino Crest Dr, Oceanside, CA
92056 USA

Noren, Lars *Writer*
Ostermalmsgatan 33, Stockholm, 11426,
SWEDEN

Norgard, Erik C *Football Player*
60 Harbor View Dr, Sugar Land, TX
77479 USA

Noriander, John *Basketball Player*
801 9th St N, #102, Virginia, MN 55792
USA

Noriega, Carlos I *Astronaut*
13710 Shadow Falls Court, Houston, TX
77059 USA

Noriega, Eduardo *Actor*
Televisa, Blvd Adolfo Lopez Mateos 232,
Colonia San Angel INN, DF, CP 01060,
MEXICO

Noriega, Victor *Actor*
Televisa, Blvd Adolfo Lopez Mateos 232,
Colonia San Angel INN, DF, CP 01060,
MEXICO

Norman, Chris *Musician*
Denis Vaughan Mgmt, PO Box 28286,
London, N21 3WT, UNITED KINGDOM
(UK)

Norman, ChrisNL-
Venlo, THE NETHERLANDS, 5902 MA

Norman, Edie Jo *Bowler*
3544 Mariner Blvd, Spring Hill, FL 34609
USA

Norman, Greg *Golfer*
Great White Shark Enterprises, 501 N
Hwy A1A, Jupiter, FL 33477 USA

Norman, Gregory J (Greg) *Golfer*
Great White Shark Enterprises, 501 N
Highway A1A, Jupiter, FL 33477 USA

Norman, Jessye *Musician*
L'Orchidee, PO Box South, Crugers, NY
10521 USA

Norman, Ken *Basketball Player*
19020 Kelzie Ave, Homewood, IL 60430
USA

Norman, Marsha *Writer*
Abrams, 275 7th Ave, #2600, New York,
NY 10001 USA

Norman, Michael *Astronomer, Physicist*
University of California, Astronomy Dept,
La Jolla, CA 90293 USA

Norman, Monty *Composer*
PRS, 29/33 Berners St, London, W1P 4AA,
UNITED KINGDOM (UK)

Norman, Steve *Musician*
International Talent Group, 729 7th Ave,
#1600, New York, NY 10019 USA

**Norodom Sihanouk, Prince Samdech
Preah** *King*
Khemarindra Palace, Phnom Penh,
CAMBODIA

Norrington, Roger A C
Camerata Academica Salzburg, Bergstr 22,
Salzburg, 5020, AUSTRIA

Norris, Alan E *Judge*
US Court of Appeals, US Courthouse, 85
Marconi Blvd, Columbus, OH 43215 USA

Norris, Chuck *Actor*
Amadea Film Productions, 4024 Radford
Ave, #320, Studio City, CA 91604 USA

Norris, David Owen *Musician*
Aughton Rise, Collingbourne, Kingston
Wilts, SN8 3SA, UNITED KINGDOM (UK)

Norris, James R Jr *Misc*
University of Chicago, Chemistry Dept,
5735 S Ellis Ave, Chicago, IL 60637 USA

Norris, John *Journalist*
MTV News, 1515 Broadway Fl 29, New
York, NY 10036 USA

Norris, Michael K (Mike) *Baseball Player*
407 Perkins St, #105B, Oakland, CA
94610 USA

Norris, Michele *Commentator*
ABC-TV, News Dept, 5010 Creston St,
Hyattsville, MD 20781 USA

Norris, Paul J *Business Person*
WR Grace Co, 7500 Grace Dr, Columbia,
MD 21044 USA

Norris, Terry *Boxer*
Don King Productions, 968 Pinehurst Dr,
Las Vegas, NV 89109 USA

Norris, William A *Judge*
US COurt of Appeals, 312 N Springs St,
Los Angeles, CA 90012 USA

Norstrom, Mattais *Actor*
Los Angeles Kings

Norstrom, Mattias *Hockey Player*
2513 Laurel Ave, Manhattan Beach, CA
90266 USA

North, Andy *Golfer*
3289 High Point Road, Madison, WI
53719 USA

North, Chandra *Model*
Women Model Mgmt, 107 Greene St,
#200, New York, NY 10012 USA

North, Douglass C *Nobel Prize Laureate*
7569 Homestead Road, Benzonia, MI
49616 USA

North, J J
PO Box 614, Bloomfield, NJ 07003-0614
USA

North, Jay *Actor*
290 NE First Ave, Lake Butler, FL 32054
USA

North, Oliver L *General, Government
Official*
22570 Markley Circle, #240, Dulles, VA
20166 USA

North, Sheree *Actor*
Bessie Agency, 812 21st St, #C, Santa
Monica, CA 90403 USA

Northam, Jeremy *Actor*
International Creative Management
(ICM-LA), 8942 Wilshire Blvd, Beverly
Hills, CA 90211 USA

Northcutt, Dennis *Football Player*
Cleveland Browns, 76 Lou Groza Blvd,
Berea, OH 44017 USA

Northrop, Wayne *Actor*
37900 Road 800, Raymond, CA 93653
USA

Northrup, James T (Jim) *Baseball Player*
29508 Southfield Road, Southfield, MI
48076 USA

Northrup, Wayne
21919 W. Canon Dr., Topanga, CA 90290

Northrup, MD, Christiane *Writer*
Empowering Women's Wisdom, PO Box
199, Yarmouth, ME 04096

Northtrip, Richard A *Misc*
Cement & Allied Workers Union, 2500
Brickdale, Elk Grove Village, IL 60007
USA

Northway, Douglas (Doug) *Swimmer*
3239 E 3rd St, Tucson, AZ 85716 USA

Norton, Andre (Alice) *Writer*
HighHallack, 114 Eventide Dr,
Murfreesboro, TN 37130 USA

Norton, Edward *Actor*
Endeavor Agency LLC (LA), 9601 Wilshire
Blvd Fl 3, Beverly Hills, CA 90210 USA

Norton, Gale *Secretary*
Interior Department, 1849 C St NW,
Washington, DC 20240 USA

Norton, Gerard Ross (Toys) *War Hero*
PO Box 112, Banket, ZIMBABWE

Norton, Graham *Actor*
Talk Back Management, 20-21 Newman
St, London, W1T 1PG, UNITED
KINGDOM (UK)

Norton, James J *Misc*
Graphic Communications International,
1900 L St NW, Washington, DC 20036
USA

Norton, Jeff *Hockey Player*
1701 E Las Olas Blvd, #1, Fort
Lauderdale, FL 33301 USA

Norton, Ken
1 Hall of Fame Dr., Canastota, NY 13032

Norton, Kenneth H (Ken) *Boxer, Actor*
29 Gavina, Dana Point, CA 92629 USA

Norton, Peter *Designer*
225 Arizona Ave, #200W, Santa Monica,
CA 90401 USA

Norton, Virginia *Bowler*
11706 Mindanao St, Cypress, CA 90630
USA

Norville, Deborah *Commentator*
PO Box 426, Mill Neck, NY 11765 USA

Norvind, Nailea *Actor*
Televisa, Blvd Adolfo Lopez Mateos 232,
Colonia San Angel INN, DF, CP 01060,
MEXICO

Norwood, Brandy (Brandy) *Musician, Actor*
Norwood Kids Foundation, 1201 Baldwin St, Summit, MS 39666 USA

Norwood, Scott *Football Player*
14529 Picket Oaks Road, Centerville, VA 20121 USA

Nosbusch, Desiree
Mohrengasse 18, Hohenems, AUSTRIA, A-6845

Noseworthy, Jack
955 S. Carrillo Dr. #300, Los Angeles, CA 90048

Nossal, Gustav J V *Doctor*
46 Fellows St, Kew, VIC, 3101, AUSTRALIA

Nosseck, Noel *Director*
1435 San Ysidro Dr, Beverly Hills, CA 90210 USA

Notaro, Phyllis *Bowler*
20284 Brant Angota Road, Angola, NY 14006 USA

Notebaert, Richard *Business Person*
Quest Communications, 1801 California St, Denver, CO 80202 USA

Noth, Christopher *Actor*
United Talent Agency, 9560 Wilshire Blvd, #500, Beverly Hills, CA 90212 USA

Nothstein, Marty
One Olympic Plaza, Colorado Springs, CO 80909-5770

Notkins, Abner L *Scientist*
National Institute of Dental Research, 9000 Rockville Pike, Bethesda, MD 20892 USA

Noto, Lucio A *Business Person*
Mobil Corp, 3225 Gallows Road, Fairfax, VA 22037 USA

Nott, John W F *Government Official*
Hillsdown Holdings PLC, 32 Hampstead High St, London, NW3 1QD, UNITED KINGDOM (UK)

Nottebohm, Andreas *Artist*
Mentzstr 44, Mulheim An Der Ruhr, GERMANY

Nottingham, Robert
4348-B Coldwater Canyon, Studio City, CA 91604-5016

Nouhak, Phoumsavanh *President*
President's Office, Presidential House, Vientiane, LAOS

Nouri, Michael *Actor*
Burnstein, 15304 W Sunset Blvd, #208, Pacific Palisades, CA 90272 USA

Noury, Alain
Soyans s/Crest, FRANCE, 26400

Nouvel, Jean *Architect*
Architectures Jean Nouvel, 10 Cite d'Angouleme, Paris, 75011, FRANCE

Nova, Heather
Box 3704, London, ENGLAND, W4 4ZN

Nova, Nikki *Actor*
4331 E Baseline Road #B105, PO Box 431, Gilbert, AZ 85299 USA

Novacek, Jay *Athlete*
Jay Novacek Football Camp, PO Box 719, Burtonsville, MD 20866

Novack, K J *Business Person*
America Online, 22000 AOL Way, Dulles, VA 20166 USA

Novack, William
3 Ashton, Newton, MA 02159

Novak, David C *Business Person*
Tricon Global Restaurants, 1441 Gardiner Lane, Louisville, KY 40213 USA

Novak, John R *Inventor*
Engelhard Corp, Automotive Emissions Systems, 101 Wood Ave, Iselin, NJ 08830 USA

Novak, Kim *Actor*
5622 Valley View Lane, Klamath Falls, OR 97601 USA

Novak, Michael *Misc*
American Enterprise Institute, 1150 17th St NW, Washington, DC 20036 USA

Novak, Pablo *Actor*
Telefe - Argentina, Pavon 2444 (C1248AAT), Buenos Aires, ARGENTINA

Novak, Popper Ilona *Swimmer*
II Orso Utca 23, Budapest, HUNGARY

Novak, Robert *Commentator, Writer*
1750 Pennsylvania Ave NW, #1312, Washington, DC 20006 USA

Novarina, Maurice P J *Architect*
52 Rue Raynouard, Paris, 75116, FRANCE

Novelli, William *Misc*
American Association of Retired Persons, 601 E St NW, Washington, DC 20049 USA

Novello, Antonia C *Misc*
2700 Virginia Ave NW, #501, Washington, DC 20037 USA

Novello, Don
PO Box 245, Fairfax, CA 94930

Novello, Don (Fr Guido Sarducci) *Actor, Comedian*
Elizabeth Rush Agency, 100 Park St, #4, Montclair, NJ 07042 USA

Noveskey, Matt *Musician*
Ashley Talent, 2002 Hogback Road, #20, Ann Arbor, MI 48105 USA

Novoa, Rafael *Actor*
TV Caracol, Calle 76 #11 - 35, Piso 10AA, Bogota DC, 26484, COLOMBIA

Novosel, Michael J *War Hero*
202 Oakwood Dr, Enterprise, AL 36330 USA

Novotna, Jana *Tennis Player*
7834 Montvale Way, McLean, VA 22102 USA

Novotny, Dave *Musician*
Helter Skelter Plaza, 535 Kings Road, London, SW10 0S, UNITED KINGDOM (UK)

Nowak, Lisa M *Astronaut*
17123 Parsley Hawthome Court, Houston, TX 77059 USA

Nowak, Peter *Soccer Player, Coach*
DC United, 14120 Newbrook Dr, Chantilly, VA 20151 USA

Nowell, Peter C *Biologist*
345 Mount Alverno Road, Media, PA 19063 USA

Nowicki, Tom *Actor*
Davis Management, 4111 Lankershim Blvd, Studio City, CA 91602

Nowinksi, Christopher *Wrestler*
World Wrestling Entertainment (WWE), 1241 E Main St, Stamford, CT 06905 USA

Nowra, Louis *Writer*
Level 18 Plaza 11, 500 Oxford St, Bondi Junction, NSW, 2011, AUSTRALIA

Noxon, Marti *Writer*
Endeavor Agency LLC (LA), 9601 Wilshire Blvd Fl 3, Beverly Hills, CA 90210 USA

Noyce, Phillip *Director*
Cresswell, 163 Brougham St, Woolloomooloo, Sydney, 2011, AUSTRALIA

Noyd, R Allen *Religious Leader*
General Council, Christian Church, 1294 Rutledge Road, Transfer, PA 16154 USA

Noyes, Albert Jr *Misc*
5102 Fairview Dr, Austin, TX 78731 USA

Noyori, Ryoji *Nobel Prize Laureate*
135-417 Shinden, Umemoricho, Nisshin, Aichi, 470-0132, JAPAN

Nozieres, Philippe P G F *Physicist*
15 Route d Saint Nizier, Seyssins, 38180, FRANCE

Nri, Cyril *Actor*
Bosun House, 1 Deer Park Road, Merton, London, SW19 3TL, UK

Nsengiyremeye, Dismas *Prime Minister*
Prime Minister's Office, Kigali, RWANDA

Nsibanbi, Apolo *Prime Minister*
Premier's Office, International Conference Center, Kampala, UGANDA

NSYNC *Music Group*
Wright Entertainment Group (WEG), 7680 Universal Blvd #500, Orlando, FL 32819 USA

Ntombi *Royalty*
Royal Residence, PO Box 1, Lobamba, SWAZILAND

Ntoutoume, Jean-Francois *Prime Minister*
Prime Minister's Office, BP 546, Libreville, GABON

Nuami, Sheikh Humaid bin Rashid an- *King, Royalty*
Royal Palaca, PO Box 1, Ajman, UNITED ARAB EMIRATES

Nubla, Malou *Journalist*
KPIX TV, 855 Battery Street, San Francisco, CA 94111 USA

Nucci, Danny *Actor*
Gold Marshak Liedtke, 3500 W Olive Ave, #1400, Burbank, CA 91505 USA

Nucci, Leo *Opera Singer*
I C M Artists, 40 W 57th St, New York, NY 10019 USA

Nugent, Eddie
PO Box 1266, New York, NY 10150-1266

Nugent, Nelle *Producer*
Foxboro Entertainment, 133 E 58th St, #301, New York, NY 10022 USA

Nugent, Ted *Musician*
4008 W Michigan Ave, Jackson, MI 92516 USA

Nujoma, Sam S *President*
President's Office, State House, Mugabe Ave, Windhoek, 9000, NAMIBIA

Numan, Gary *Musician, Songwriter*
86 Staines Road, Wraysbury, N Staines, Middlesex, TW19 5A, UNITED KINGDOM (UK)

Numminen, Teppo *Hockey Player*
3422 E Palo Verde Dr, Paradise Valley, AZ 85253 USA

Nunez, Miguel Angel Jr *Actor*
Abrams Artists, 9200 Sunset Blvd, Los Angeles, CA 90069 USA

Nunez, Victor *Director*
Paul Kohner, 9300 Wilshire Blvd, #555, Beverly Hills, CA 90212 USA

Nuþez, Vladimir *Baseball Player*
Florida Marlins, 2269 Dan Marino Blvd, Miami, FL 33056 USA

Nunley, Frank *Football Player*
24632 Olive Tree Lane, Los Altos Hills, CA 94024 USA

Nunn, Michael *Boxer*
3517 W 47th St, #4, Davenport, IA 52806 USA

Nunn, Sam *Ex-Senator*
75 14th St NE #4810, Atlanta, GA 30309 USA

Nunn, Samuel A (Sam) *Senator*
75 14th St NE, #4810, Atlanta, GA 30309 USA

Nunn, Teri *Musician*
MOB Agency, 6404 Wilshire Blvd, #505, Los Angeles, CA 90048 USA

Nunn, Trevor R *Director*
Royal National Theater, South Bank, London, SE1 9PX, UNITED KINGDOM (UK)

Nurding, Louise *Actor*
42 Colwith Road, London, ENGLAND, W6 9EY

Nurmi, Maila (Vampira) *Actor*
4310 1/2 Gateway Ave, Los Angeles, CA 90029 USA

Nurse, Paul M *Nobel Prize Laureate*
Clare Hall Laboratories, Cell Cycle Control Lab, Herts, EN6 3LD, UNITED KINGDOM (UK)

Nussbaum, Danny *Actor*
Conway Van Gelder RObinson, 18-21 Jermyn St, London, SW1Y 6NB, UNITED KINGDOM (UK)

Nussbaum, Karen *Misc*
9-5 National Working Women Assn, 231 W Wisconsin, #900, Milwaukee, WI 53203 USA

Nussbaum, Martha C *Misc*
University of Chicago, Law School, 111 E 60th St, Chicago, IL 60637 USA

Nussiein-Volhard, Christiane *Nobel Prize Laureate*
Max Planck Biology Institute, Spenmannstr 35/III, Tubingen, 72076, GERMANY

Nutt, Jim *Artist*
1035 Greenwood Ave, Wilmette, IL 60091 USA

Nutter, Alice *Musician*
Doug Smith Assoc, PO Box 1151, London, W3 8ZJ, UNITED KINGDOM (UK)

Nutter, David *Director*
Shapiro-Lichtman, 8827 Beverly Blvd, Los Angeles, CA 90048 USA

Nutting, Wallace H *General*
PO Box 96, Biddeford Pool, ME 04006 USA

Nutzie, Futzie *Artist, Cartoonist*
PO Box 325, Aromas, CA 95004 USA

Nuwer, Hank *Writer, Journalist*
PO Box 31, Fairlane, IN 46126 USA

Nuxhall, Joe
5708 Lindenwood Lane, Fairfield, OH 45014

Nuxhall, Joseph H (Joe) *Baseball Player*
5706 Lingenwood Lane, Fairfield, OH 45014 USA

Nuyen, France *Actor*
PO Box 18437, Beverly Hills, CA 90209 USA

Nuzorewa, Abel Tendekayi *Prime Minister*
United African National Council, 40 Charter Road, Harare, ZIMBABWE

Nyad, Diana *Swimmer, Sportscaster*
Uptown Racquet Club, 151 E 86th St, New York, NY 10028 USA

Nyberg, Frederik *Skier*
Kaptensgatan 2C, Froson, 832 00, SWEDEN

Nyberg, Karen L *Astronaut*
2518 Lakeside Landing, Seabrook, TX 77586 USA

Nye, Bill
401 Mercer St., Seattle, WA 98109

Nye, Carrie *Actor*
Paradigm Agency, 200 W 57th St, #900, New York, NY 10019 USA

Nye, Erie *Business Person*
Texas Utilities Co, Energy Plaza, 1601 Bryan St, Dallas, TX 75201 USA

Nye, Louis *Actor, Comedian*
1241 Corsica Dr, Pacific Palisades, CA 90272 USA

Nye, Robert *Writer*
Thomfield, Kingsland, Ballinghassig, County Cork, IRELAND

Nyers, Rezso *Secretary*
Ozgida Utca 22/A, Budapest, 1025, HUNGARY

Nygaard, Richard L *Judge*
US Court of Appeals, 1st National Bank Building, 717 State St, Erie, PA 16501 USA

Nykvist, Sven V *Cinematographer*
Strandpromenaden 4, Saltjso-Duvnas, 131 50, SWEDEN

Nyland, William L *General*
Assistant Commander in Chief HqSMC, 2 Navy St, Washington, DC 20380 USA

Nyman, Michael L *Composer, Musician*
Michael Nyman Ltd, PO Box 430, High Wycombe, HP13 5QT, UNITED KINGDOM (UK)

Nystrom, Bob *Hockey Player*
475 Berry Hill Road, Oyster Bay, NY 11771 USA

Nystrom, Joakim *Tennis Player*
Torsgatan 194, Skellefteaa, 931 00, SWEDEN

O

O Town
7380 Sand Lake Rd.#350, Orlando, FL 32819

O'Bannon, Dan *Director*
Agency For Performing Arts, 9200 W Sunset Blvd #900, Los Angeles, CA 90069 USA

O'Bannon, Ed *Basketball Player*
11930 Agnes St, Cerritos, CA 90703 USA

O'Bard, Ronnie *Football Player*
27121 Puerta del Oro, Mission Viejo, CA 92691 USA

O'Boyle, Maureen *Entertainer*
30 Rockefeller Plaza, #820E, New York, NY 10112 USA

O'Brian, Hugh *Actor*
Hugh O'Brian Youth Foundation, 10880 Wilshire Blvd, #410, Los Angeles, CA 90024 USA

O'Brian, Richard *Actor*
Jonathan Alparas, 27 Floral St, London, C2E 9DP, UNITED KINGDOM (UK)

O'Brien, Austin *Actor*
Gersh Agency, 232 N Canon Dr, Beverly Hills, CA 90210 USA

O'Brien, Brian *Physicist*
PO Box 166, Woodstock, CT 06281 USA

O'Brien, Carl (Cubby) *Actor*
2530 Independence Ave, #2J, Bronx, NY 10463 USA

O'Brien, Cathy *Track Athlete*
19 Foss Farm Road, Durham, NH 03824 USA

O'Brien, Conan *Entertainer*
NBC-TV, 3000 W Alameda Ave, Burbank, CA 91523 USA

O'Brien, Conor Cruise *Writer, Diplomat*
Whitewater, Howth Summit, Dublin, IRELAND

O'Brien, Cubby
2839 N. Surrey Dr., Carrollton, TX 75004-4800

O'Brien, Dan *Track Athlete*
PO Box 9244, Moscow, ID 83843 USA

O'Brien, Dave *Football Player*
304 Newbury St, #349, Boston, MA 02115 USA

O'Brien, Ed *Musician*
Nasty Little Man, 72 Springs St, #1100, New York, NY 10012 USA

O'Brien, Edna *Writer*
Wylie Agency, 52 Knightsbridge, London, SW1X 7JP, UNITED KINGDOM (UK)

O'Brien, G Dennis *Educator*
PO Box 510, Middlebury, VT 05753 USA

O'Brien, George H Jr *War Hero*
2001 Douglas St, Midland, TX 79701 USA

O'Brien, Gregory M *Educator*
University of New Orleans, Chancellor's Office, New Orleans, LA 70148 USA

O'Brien, Jim *Basketball Player, Coach*
Philadelphia 76er's, 1 Union Center, 3601 S Broad St, Philadelphia, PA 19148 USA

O'Brien, John *Writer*
2 Columbine Placa, Delran, NJ 08075 USA

O'Brien, John T (Johnny) *Basketball Player, Baseball Player*
19504 92nd Ave NE, Bothell, WA 98011 USA

O'Brien, Keith M P Cardinal *Religious Leader*
Archdiocese, 113 Whitehouse Loan, Edinburgh, EH9 1BB, SCOTLAND

O'Brien, Kenneth J (Ken) Jr *Football Player*
201 Manhattan Ave, Manhattan Beach, CA 90266 USA

O'Brien, M Vincent *Horse Racer, Coach*
Ballydoyle House, Cashel, County Tipperary, IRELAND

O'Brien, Margaret *Actor*
440 Sepulveda Blvd, #305, Van Nuys, CA 91405 USA

O'Brien, Mark *Business Person*
Pulte Corp, 33 Bloomfield Hills Parkway, Bloomfield Hills, MI 48304 USA

O'Brien, Maureen *Actor*
Kate Feast, Primrose Hill Studios, Fitzroy Road, London, NW1 8TR, UNITED KINGDOM (UK)

O'Brien, Pat *Sportscaster, Entertainer*
CBS-TV, Sports Dept, 51 W 52nd St, New York, NY 10019 USA

O'Brien, Peter
397 Riley St., Surry Hills, AUSTRALIA, NSW 2010

O'Brien, Richard *Composer, Songwriter*
TimeWarp, 1 Elm Grove, Hildenborough, Tonbridge Kent, TN11 9HE, UNITED KINGDOM (UK)

O'Brien, Ron *Coach*
PO Box 784, Islamorada, FL 33036 USA

O'Brien, Soledad *Commentator*
Cable News Network, News Dept, 1050 Techwood Dr NW, Atlanta, GA 30318 USA

O'Brien, Thomas H *Financier*
PNC Bank Corp, 1 PNC Center, 249 5th Ave, Pittsburgh, PA 15222 USA

O'Brien, Thomas M *Financier*
North Side Savings Bank, 185 W 23st St, Bronx, NY 10463 USA

O'Brien, Tim *Track Athlete*
17 Partride Lane, Boxford, MA 01921 USA

O'Brien, Tina *Actor*
Creative Artists Agency LCC (CAA-LA), 9830 Wilshire Blvd, Beverly Hills, CA 90212 USA

O'Brien, Trever *Actor*
Emerald Talent Group, 6464 Sunset Blvd, Los Angeles, CA 90038 USA

O'Brien, Trevor *Actor*
Gersh Agency, 232 N Canon Dr, Beverly Hills, CA 90210 USA

O'Brien, W Parry *Track Athlete*
3415 Alginet Dr, Encino, CA 91436 USA

O'Bryan, Sean *Actor*
Alan Siegel Entertainment, 345 N Maple Dr #375, Beverly Hills, CA 90210 USA

O'Callaghan, Donald N (Mike) *Governor*
Las Vegas Sun, 2275 Corporate Circle, #300, Henderson, NV 89074 USA

O'Callahan, John (Jack) *Hockey Player*
101 Linden Ave, Glencoe, IL 60022 USA

O'Caroll, Sinead *Musician*
Clintons, 55 Drury Lane, Covent Garden, London, WC2B 5SQ, UNITED KINGDOM (UK)

O'Connell, Deirdre *Actor*
Himber Entertainment Inc, 211 S Beverly Dr #208, Beverly Hills, CA 90212 USA

O'Connell, Jerry *Actor*
Endeavor Talent Agency, 9701 Wilshire Blvd, #1000, Beverly Hills, CA 90212 USA

O'Connell, Maura *Musician*
Maura O'Connell Mgmt, 4222 Lindawood Ave, Nashville, TN 37215 USA

O'Conner, Tom
1 The Stiles Ormskirk, Lancashire, ENGLAND, L39 3QG

O'Connolly, James *Director*
61 Edith Grove, London, SW10, UNITED KINGDOM (UK)

O'Connolly, James *Astronaut*
1305 Lafayette Dr, Alexandria, VA 22308 USA

O'Connor, Bryan D
305 Lafayette Dr, Alexandria, VA 22308-1107 USA

O'Connor, Derrick *Actor*
Greene & Associates, 526 N Larchmont Blvd #201, Los Angeles, CA 90004 USA

O'Connor, Des
23 Eyot Gardens, London, ENGLAND, W6 9TR

O'Connor, Edmund F *General*
1169 Ironsides Ave, Melbourne, FL 32940 USA

O'Connor, Frances *Actor*
Creative Artists Agency LCC (CAA-LA), 9830 Wilshire Blvd, Beverly Hills, CA 90212 USA

O'Connor, Gavin *Director*
United Talent Agency, 9560 Wilshire Blvd, #500, Beverly Hills, CA 90212 USA

O'Connor, Glynnis *Actor*
Bill Treusch, 853 7th Ave, #9A, New York, NY 10019 USA

O'Connor, J Dennis *Educator*
Smithsonlan Institution, Provost's Office, Washington, DC 20560 USA

O'Connor, Mark *Musician*
CM Mgmt, 5749 Lanyan Dr, Woodland Hills, CA 91367 USA

O'Connor, Martin J *Religious Leader*
Palazzo San Carlo, Vatican City, 00120, VATICAN CITY

O'Connor, Maryanne *Basketball Player*
60 Romanock Place, Fairfield, CT 06825 USA

O'Connor, Patrick *Actor*
Select Artists Ltd (CA-Westside Office), 1138 12th Street, Suite 1, Santa Monica, CA 90403 USA

O'Connor, Patrick D (Pat) *Director*
International Creative Mgmt, 76 Oxford St, London, W1N 0AX, UNITED KINGDOM (UK)

O'Connor, Renee *Actor*
Progressive Artists Agency, 400 S Beverly Dr #216, Beverly Hills, CA 90212

O'Connor, Sandra Day *Judge*
US Supreme Court, 1 1st St NE, Washington, DC 20543 USA

O'Connor, Sinead *Musician, Songwriter*
Free Trade Agency, Chapel Place, Rivington St, London, EC21 3DQ, UNITED KINGDOM (UK)

O'Connor, Thom *Artist*
Moss Road, Voorheesville, NY 12186 USA

O'Connor, Tim *Actor*
PO Box 458, Nevada City, CA 95959 USA

O'Conor, John *Musician*
Columbia Artists Mgmt Inc, 165 W 57th St, New York, NY 10019 USA

O'Day, Alan *Musician, Songwriter*
Talent Consultants International, 1560 Broadway, #1308, New York, NY 10036 USA

O'Day, Anita *Musician*
Richard Barz, 21 Cobble Creek Dr, Tannersville, PA 18372 USA

O'Day, George *Yachtsman*
6 Turtle Lane, Dover, MA 02030 USA

O'Dell, Jennifer *Actor*
3500 West Olive Avenue, Suite 920, Burbank, CA 91505-4628 USA

O'Dell, Nancy *Television Host*
Access Hollywood, 3000 W Alameda Ave, Trailer E, Burbank, CA 91523 USA

O'Dell, Tawni *Writer*
Viking Press, 375 Hudson St, New York, NY 10014 USA

O'Dell, Tony
417 Griffith Park Dr., Burbank, CA 91506

O'Donnell, Annie *Actor*
Capital Artists, 6404 Wilshire Blvd, #950, Los Angeles, CA 90048 USA

O'Donnell, Charles (Chuck) *Bowler*
7354 Forest Haven E, Saint Louis, MO 63123 USA

O'Donnell, Chris *Actor*
Untitled Entertainment (LA), 8436 W 3rd St #650, Los Angeles, CA 90048 USA

O'Donnell, Daniel *Musician*
Public Broadcasting Service (PBS), 1320 Braddock Pl, Alexandria, VA 22314 USA

O'Donnell, John J *Misc*
Air Line Pilots Assn, 1625 Massachusetts Ave NW, Washington, DC 20036 USA

O'Donnell, Keir *Actor*
Visionary Entertainment, 8265 Sunset Blvd #104, Los Angeles, CA 90046 USA

O'Donnell, Mark *Writer*
202 Riverside Dr, #8E, New York, NY 10025 USA

O'Donnell, Neil K *Football Player*
PO Box 403, New Vernon, NJ 07976 USA

O'Donnell, Rosie *Actor*
International Creative Management (ICM-LA), 8942 Wilshire Blvd, Beverly Hills, CA 90211 USA

O'Donnell, William (Bill) *Horse Racer*
569 Penn Estate, East Stroudsburg, PA 18301 USA

O'Driscoll, Martha *Actor*
22 Indian Creek Island Road, Indian Creek Village, FL 33154 USA

O'Grady, Gail *Actor*
Agency for the Performing Arts (APA-LA), 9200 Sunset Blvd #900, Los Angeles, CA 90069 USA

O'Grady, Scott
3519 Wallingford Ave N #2, Seattle, WA 98103-9057 USA

O'Grady, Sean *Boxer*
Adoreable Promotions, PO Box 9, Bay City, MI 48707 USA

O'Hara, Catherine *Actor, Comedian*
Brillstein/Grey, 9150 Wilshire Blvd, #350, Beverly Hills, CA 90212 USA

O'Hara, Jamie
1025 16th Ave. So. #200, Nashville, TN 37212

O'Hara, Jenny *Actor*
8663 Wonderland Ave, Los Angeles, CA 90046 USA

O'Hara, Maureen *Actor*
PO Box 1400, Christeansted, Kingshill, VI 00851 USA

O'Hara, Terrence J *Director*
Armstrong/Hirsch, 1888 Century Park East, #1800, Los Angeles, CA 90067 USA

O'Hare, Denis *Actor*
Innovative Artists (LA), 1505 Tenth St, Santa Monica, CA 90401 USA

O'Hare, Michael *Actor*
E/W, 280 S Beverly Dr, #400, Beverly Hills, CA 90212 USA

O'Herlihy, Dan
24 W. 40th St. #1700, New York, NY 10018

O'Herlihy, Daniel *Actor*
Fifi Oscard, 110 W 40th St, #1500, New York, NY 10018 USA

O'Horgan, Thomas F (Tom) *Composer, Director*
Carl Goldstein, 9951 Seacrest Circle, #201, Boynton Beach, FL 33437 USA

O'Hurley, John *Actor*
11661 San Vicente Blvd, #307, Los Angeles, CA 90049 USA

O'Jays, The
1995 Broadway #501, New York, NY 10023

O'Keefe, Jeremiah J Sr *War Hero*
PO Box 430, Ocean Springs, MS 39566 USA

O'Keefe, Jodi Lyn *Actor*
Vincent Cirrincione Associates, 8721 Sunset Blvd #205, Los Angeles, CA 90069 USA

O'Keefe, Jodie Lyn *Actor*
J Michael Bloom, 9255 Sunset Blvd, #710, Los Angeles, CA 90069 USA

O'Keefe, Michael *Actor*
5850 W 3rd St, #144, Los Angeles, CA 90036 USA

O'Keefe, Miles *Actor*
Sharp/Karrys, 117 N Orlando Ave, Los Angeles, CA 90048 USA

O'Keefe, Paul
225 W. 83rd St. #9-5, New York, NY 10027

O'Keefe, Sean *Government Official*
national Aviation/Space Administration, 300 E St SW, Washington, DC 20024 USA

O'Koren, Mike *Basketball Player*
Washington Wizards, MCI Centre, 601 F St NW, Washington, DC 20004 USA

O'Leary, Brian T *Astronaut*
1993 S Kihei Road, #21200, Kihei, HI 96753 USA

O'Leary, George *Football Coach*
Central Florida University, Athletic Dept, Orlando, FL 32918 USA

O'Leary, Hazel R *Secretary*
Energy Department, 1000 Independence Ave SW, Washington, DC 20585 USA

O'Leary, John *Actor*
Gage Group, 14724 Venture Blvd, #505, Sherman Oaks, CA 91403 USA

O'Leary, Marrissa *Actor*
Select Artists Ltd (CA-Valley Office), PO Box 4359, Burbank, CA 91503 USA

O'Leary, Matthew *Actor*
Endeavor Agency LLC (LA), 9601 Wilshire Blvd Fl 3, Beverly Hills, CA 90210 USA

O'Leary, Michael *Actor*
38 Prospect Ave, Montclair, NJ 07042 USA

O'Leary, William *Actor*
House of Representatives, 400 S Beverly Dr, #101, Beverly Hills, CA 90212 USA

O'Loughlin, Gerald
PO Box 340832, Arleta, CA 91334-0832

O'Loughlin, Gerald S *Actor*
23388 Mulholland Dr, #204, Woodland Hills, CA 91364 USA

O'Malley, Mike *Actor*
Creative Artists Agency, 9830 Wilshire Blvd, Beverly Hills, CA 90212 USA

O'Malley, Peter *Baseball Player*
326 S Hudson Ave, Los Angeles, CA 90020 USA

O'Malley, Robert E *War Hero*
PO Box 775, Goldthwaite, TX 76844 USA

O'Malley, Sean Patrick *Religious Leader*
Archdiocese of Boston, 2121 Commonwealth Ave, Brighton, MA 02135 USA

O'Malley, Susan *Misc*
Washington Wizards, MCI Centre, 601 F St NW, Washington, DC 20004 USA

O'Malley, Thomas D *Business Person*
Tosco Corp, 1700 E Putnam Ave, #500, Old Greenwich, CT 06870 USA

O'Mara, Jason *Actor*
International Creative Management (ICM-LA), 8942 Wilshire Blvd, Beverly Hills, CA 90211 USA

O'Mara, Kate *Actor*
Michael Ladkin Mgmt, 1 Duchess St, #1, London, W1N 3DE, UNITED KINGDOM (UK)

O'Mara, Mark *Horse Racer, Coach*
6882 NW 65th Terrace, Parkland, FL 33067 USA

O'Meara, Mark *Golfer*
6312 Deacon Circle, Windermere, FL 34786 USA

O'Meara, Peter *Actor*
ROAR LLC, 2400 Broadway #350, Santa Monica, CA 90404 USA

O'Neal, Alexander *Musician, Songwriter*
Green Light Talent Agency, PO Box 3172, Beverly Hills, CA 90212 USA

O'Neal, E Stan *Financier*
Merrill Lynch Co, World Financial Center, 2 Vesey St, New York, NY 10007 USA

O'Neal, Griffin *Actor*
14209 Riverside Dr, Van Nuys, CA 91423 USA

O'Neal, Jamie *Musician, Songwriter*
Fitzgerald Hartley, 19078 Wedgewood Ave, Nashville, TN 37212 USA

O'Neal, Jermaine *Basketball Player*
Indiana Pacers, Conseco Fieldhouse, 125 S Pennsylvania, Indianapolis, IN 46204 USA

O'Neal, Leslie C *Football Player*
5617 Adobe Falls Road, #A, San Diego, CA 92120 USA

O'Neal, Ryan *Actor*
21368 Pacific Coast Highway, Malibu, CA 90265 USA

O'Neal, Shaquille R *Basketball Player*
Alliance Sports Marketing, 3960 Howard Hughes Pkwy #750, Las Vegas, NV 89109 USA

O'Neal, Tatum *Actor*
El Dorado Apartments, 300 Central Park West, #16G, New York, NY 10024 USA

O'Neal, Tatum *Actor*
Bill Treusch Assoc, 853 7th Ave #9A, New York, NY 10019 USA

O'Neil, John B (Buck) *Baseball Player, Coach*
3049 E 32nd St, Kansas City, MO 64128 USA

O'Neil, Lawrence *Director*
International Creative Mgmt, 8942 Wilshire Blvd, #219, Beverly Hills, CA 90211 USA

O'Neil, Ron
10100 Santa Monica Blvd. #2500, Los Angeles, CA 90067

O'Neil, Susie *Athlete, Swimmer*
177 Bridge Road, Richmond, Vic, 3121, Australia

O'Neil, Tatum *Actor*
Untitled Entertainment (LA), 8436 W 3rd
St #650, Los Angeles, CA 90048 USA

O'Neil, Tricia *Actor*
David Shapira, 15821 Ventura Blvd,
#235, Encino, CA 91436 USA

O'Neill, Brian *Hockey Player*
2600-1800 McGill College Ave, Montreal,
QC, H3A 3J6, CANADA

O'Neill, Ed *Actor*
2607 Grand Canal, Venice, CA 90291
USA

O'Neill, Eugene F *Engineer*
17 Dellwood Court, Middletown, NJ
07748 USA

O'Neill, Jennifer *Actor, Model*
7500 W Lake Mead Blvd, #492, Las
Vegas, NV 89128 USA

O'Neill, Kevin *Coach*
Toronto Raptors, Air Canada Center, 40
Bay St, Toronto, ON M5J 2N8, CANADA

O'Neill, Michael *Actor*
Mitchell K Stubbs & Assoc (MKS), 8675 W
Washington Blvd #203, Culver City, CA
90232 USA

O'Neill, Michael J *Editor*
23 Cayuga Road, Scarsdale, NY 10583
USA

O'Neill, Paul A *Baseball Player*
7785 Hartford Hill Lane, Cincinnati, OH
45242 USA

O'Neill, Paul H *Secretary*
3 Von Lent Place, Pittsburgh, PA 15232
USA

O'Neill, Susan (Susie) *Swimmer*
207 Kent St, #1800, Sydney, NSW, 2000,
AUSTRALIA

O'Neill, Terence P (Terry) *Photographer*
8 Warwick Ave, London, W2 1XB,
UNITED KINGDOM (UK)

O'Neill, William A *Governor*
Po Box 360, East Hampton, CT 06424
USA

O'Neill of Bengarve, O Sylvia *Misc*
NewHam College, Cambridge, CB3 9DF,
UNITED KINGDOM (UK)

O'Quinn, John M *Attorney General*
O'Quinn Kerensky McAnich, 2300 Lyric
Center, 440 Louisiana, Houston, TX
77002 USA

O'Quinn, Terry *Actor*
Innovative Artists, 1505 10th St, Santa
Monica, CA 90401 USA

O'Ree, William E (Willie) *Hockey Player*
7961 Anders Circle, La Mesa, CA 91942
USA

O'Reilly, Anthony *Business Person*
HJ Heinz Co, PO Box 57, Pittsburgh, PA
15230

O'Reilly, Anthony J F *Business Person,*
Publisher
HJ Heinz Co, Po Box 57, Pittsburgh, PA
15230 USA

O'Reilly, Bill *Commentator*
Fox-TV, News Dept, 205 E 67th St, New
York, NY 10021 USA

O'Reilly, Cyril *Actor*
Stone Manners, 6500 Wilshire Blvd, #550,
Los Angeles, CA 90048 USA

O'Reilly, Terry *Hockey Player, Coach*
PO Box 5544, Salisbury, MA 01952 USA

O'Riordan, Dolores *Musician*
Sendyk Leonard, 532 Colorado Ave, Santa
Monica, CA 90401 USA

O'Ross, Ed *Actor*
Whitaker Entertainment, 4924 Vineland
Avenue, N Hollywood, CA 91601 USA

O'Rourke, Charles C *Football Player*
220 Bedford St, #A7, Bridgewater, MA
02324 USA

O'Rourke, Tom *Actor*
Law & Order: SVU, 100 Universal City
Plz, Bldg 2252, Universal City, CA 91608
USA

O'Scannlain, Diarmuld F *Judge*
US Court of Appeals, Pionner Courthouse,
555 SW Yamhill St, Portland, OR 97204
USA

O'Shea, Kevin *Basketball Player, Coach*
87 Aquauista Way, San Francisco, CA
94131 USA

O'Shea, Milo *Actor*
Bancroft Hotel, 40 W 72nd St, #17A, New
York, NY 10023 USA

O'Sullevan, Peter J *Sportscaster, Writer*
37 Cranmer Court, London, SW3 3HW,
UNITED KINGDOM (UK)

O'Sullivan, Gilbert *Musician*
Park Promotions, PO Box 651, Park Road,
Oxford, OX2 9RB, UNITED KINGDOM
(UK)

O'Sullivan, Peter *Editor*
Houston Post, Editorial Dept, 4747
Southwest Freeway, Houston, TX 77027
USA

O'Sullivan, Richard *Actor*
Al Mitchell, 5 Anglers Lane, Kentish
Town, London, NW5 3DG, UNITED
KINGDOM (UK)

O'Sullivan, Shawn *Boxer*
231 Doniea Dr, Toronto, ON M4F 2N3,
CANADA

O'Sullivan, Sonia *Track Athlete*
Kim McDonald, 201 High St, Hampton
Hill, Middx, TW12 1NL, UNITED
KINGDOM (UK)

O'Toole, Annette *Actor*
11936 Gorham Ave, #106, Los Angeles,
CA 90049 USA

O'Toole, S Peter *Actor*
Stephen Kenis, Royalty House, 72-74
Dean St, London, W1D 3SG, UNITED
KINGDOM (UK)

O-Town *Music Group*
Official International Fan Club, PO Box
5488, Bellingham, WA 98227 USA

Oak Ridge Boys *Music Group*
William Morris Agency (WMA-TN), 2100
W End Ave #1000, Nashville, TN 37203
USA

Oakes, James L *Judge*
US Court of Appeals, PO Box 696,
Brattleboro, VT 05302 USA

Oakley, Charles *Basketball Player*
Washington Wizards, MCI Centre, 601 F
St NW, Washington, DC 20004 USA

Oasis
54 Linhope St., London, ENGLAND, NW1
6HL

Oates, Adam R *Hockey Player*
1480 S County Road, Osterville, MA
02655 USA

Oates, Bart S *Football Player, Sportscaster*
1 Silverbrook Dr, Morristown, NJ 07960
USA

Oates, John *Songwriter, Musician*
Creative Artists Agency, 9830 Wilshire
Blvd, Beverly Hills, CA 90212 USA

Oates, John L (Johnny) *Baseball Player*
20222 Eagle Cove Court, Petersburg, VA
23803 USA

Oates, Joyce Carol *Writer*
John Hawkins, 71 W 23rd St, #1600, New
York, NY 10010 USA

Oatway, Devin
10635 Santa Monica Blvd. #130, Los
Angeles, CA 90025

Obando, Bravo Miguel Cardinal *Religious*
Leader
Arzobispado, Apartado 3050, Managua,
NICARAGUA

Obasanjo, Olusegun *President, General*
President's Office, State House, Ribadu
Road Ikoyi, Lagos, NIGERIA

Obato, Gyo *Architect*
Helimuth Obato Kassabaum, 1
Metropolitan Square, #600, Saint Louis,
MO 63102 USA

Obee, Duncan *Football Player*
4488 283rd St, Toledo, OH 43611 USA

Obeid, Atef *Prime Minister*
Prime Minister's Office, PO Box 191, 1
Majlis El-Shaab St, Cairo, EGYPT

Obeidat, Ahmad Abdul-Majeed *Prime*
Minister
Law & Arbitration Center, PO Box
926544, Amman, JORDAN

Oberding, Mark *Basketball Player*
4131 Cliff Oaks St, San Antonio, TX
78229 USA

Oberg, Margo *Misc*
RR 1 Box 73, Koloa, Kaui, HI 96756 USA

Oberkfell, Ken
305 S. Donk St., Maryville, IL 62062

Oberlin, David W *Government Official*
800 Independence Ave SW, #814,
Washington, DC 20591 USA

Obermeyer, Klaus F *Fashion Designer*
Sport Obermeyer, 115 Atlantic Ave,
Aspen, CO 81611 USA

Oberoi, Vivek *Actor, Bollywood*
5 Kartar Kunj Golden Beach, Ruia Park
Juhu, Mumbai, MS 400 0049, INDIA

Obote, A Milton *President*
Uganda People's Congress, PO Box 1951,
Kampala, UGANDA

Obradors, Jacqueline *Actor*
Writers & Artists, 8383 Wilshire Blvd,
#550, Beverly Hills, CA 90211 USA

Obradovich, James R (Jim) *Football Player*
437 7th Place, Manhattan Beach, CA
90266 USA

Obraztsova, Elena V *Opera Singer*
Bolshoi Theater, Teatralnaya Pl 1,
Moscow, 103009, RUSSIA

Obregon, Alejandro *Artist*
Apartado Aereo 37, Barranquilla,
COLOMBIA

Obregon, Ana *Actor*
Paul Kohner, 9300 Wilshire Blvd, #555,
Beverly Hills, CA 90212 USA

Obst, Lynda *Producer*
Lynda Obst Productions, 5555 Melrose
Ave #210, Los Angeles, CA 90038

Ocampo Uria, Adriana C *Scientist*
National Aeronautics/Space
Administration, 300 E St SW, Washington,
DC 20456 USA

Ocasek, Ric *Songwriter, Musician*
Elektra Records, 75 Rockefeller Plaza,
New York, NY 10019 USA

Occhipinti, Andrea *Actor*
Carol Levi Co, Via Giuseppe Pisanelli,
Rome, 00196, ITALY

Ocean, Billy *Musician*
Laura Jay Enterprises, 32 Willesden Lane,
London, NW6 7ST, UNITED KINGDOM
(UK)

Ochirbat, Punsalmaagiyn *President*
Tengeriin Tsag Co, Olympic St 14, Ulan
Bator, MONGOLIA

Ochman, Wieslaw *Opera Singer*
Ul Miaczynska 46B, Warsaw, 02-637,
POLAND

Ochoa, Ellen *Astronaut*
11810 Mighty Redwood Dr, Houston, TX
77059 USA

Ockels, Wubbo *Astronaut*
ESTEC, Postbus 299, Noordwijk, AG,
2200, NETHERLANDS

ODB *Musician*
Famous Artists Agency, 250 W 57th St,
New York, NY 10107 USA

Oddsson, David *Prime Minister*
Prime Minister's Office, Stjo'maaroshusio,
Reykjavik, 150, ICELAND

Odelein, Selmar *Hockey Player*
Farm, Quill Lake, SK S0A 3E0, CANADA

Odell, Bob H *Football Player, Football
Coach*
340 Beth Ellen Dr, Lewisburg, PA 17837
USA

Odell, Deborah *Actor*
Characters Talent Agency, The (Toronto),
150 Carlton St Fl 2, Toronto ON, M5A
2K1, CANADA

Odell, Noel E *Mountaineer, Scientist*
5 Dean Court, Cambridge, UNITED
KINGDOM (UK)

Oden, Derrick *Football Player*
1805 S Barkley Dr, Mobile, AL 36606
USA

Odenkirk, Bob *Actor*
Endeavor Talent Agency, 9701 Wilshire
Blvd, #1000, Beverly Hills, CA 90212
USA

Odermatt, Robert A *Architect*
140 Camino Don Miguel, Orinda, CA
94563 USA

Odessa, Devon *Actor*
Writers & Artists, 8383 Wilshire Blvd
#550, Beverly Hills, CA 90211 USA

Odetta *Musician*
Douglas Yeager Productions, 300 W 55th
St, New York, NY 10019 USA

Odjig, Daphne *Artist*
102 Foresbrook Place, Penticton, BC V2A
7N4, CANADA

Odom, John Lee (Blue Moon) *Baseball
Player*
10343 Slater Ave, #204, Fountain Valley,
CA 92708 USA

Odom, Lamar *Basketball Player*
Los Angeles Lakers, Staples Center, 1111 S
Figueroa St, Los Angeles, CA 90015 USA

Odom, William E *General*
5112 38th St NW, Washington, DC 20016
USA

Odomes, Nathaniel B (Nate) *Football
Player*
900 Quail Creek Dr, Columbus, GA
31907 USA

Odoms, Riley M *Football Player*
834 1/2 Staffordshire Road, Stafford, TX
77477 USA

Odrowski, Gerry
Box 126, Trout Creek, CANADA, ON P0H
2L0

Oduber, Nelson O *Prime Minister*
Movimenti Electoral di Pueblo, Curnana
84, Oranjestad, ARUBA

Oe, Kenzaburo *Nobel Prize Laureate*
585 Seijo-Machi, Setagayaku, Tokyo,
JAPAN

Oedekerk, Steve *Director*
William Morris Agency, 151 El Camino
Drive, Beverly Hills, CA 90212 USA

Oefelein, William A *Astronaut*
1205 Hawkhill Dr, Friendswood, TX
77456 USA

Oenish, Dean *Doctor*
Preventive Medical Research Institute, 900
Bridgeway, #204, Sausalito, CA 94965
USA

Oerter, Al
5485 Avenieda Pescadera, Ft. Meyers, FL
33931-4209

Oerter, Alfred A (Al) *Track Athlete*
4745 Estero Blvd, #501, Fort Myres
Beach, FL 33931 USA

Oetiker, Phil *Cinematographer*
422 10th St, Brooklyn, NY 11215 USA

Oettinger, Anthony G *Mathematician*
65 Elizabeth Road, Belmont, NY 11215
USA

Offerdahl, John A *Football Player*
2749 NE 37th Dr, Fort Lauderdale, FL
33308 USA

Offerman, Jose A *Baseball Player*
Ed 81, Urb Anscaona Moscoso, San Pedro
de Marcos, DOMINICAN REPUBLIC

Offspring *Music Group*
Rebel Waltz Inc, 31652 Second Ave,
Laguna Beach, CA 92651 USA

Ogato, Sadako *Government Official*
United Nations Office for Refugees, CP
2500, Geneva 2, 1211, SWITZERLAND

Ogden, Jonathan (Jon) *Football Player*
Baltimore Ravens, Ravens Stadium, 11001
Russell St, Baltimore, MD 21230 USA

Ogi, Adolf *President*
Bundesiause-Nord, Kochergasse 10,
Berne, 3003, SWITZERLAND

Ogier, Bulle *Actor*
Artmedia, 20 Ave Rapp, Paris, 75007,
FRANCE

Ogilvie, Kelvin K *Educator*
Po Box 307, Canning, NS B0P 1X0,
CANADA

Ogilvie, Lana *Model*
Company Models, 17 Little West 12th St,
#333, New York, NY 10014 USA

Ogilvy, Ian *Actor*
Julian Belfarge, 46 Albermarle St, London,
W1X 4PP, UNITED KINGDOM (UK)

Ogle, Brett *Golfer*
Advantage International, 1751 Pinnacle
Dr, #1500, McLean, VA 22102 USA

Oglesby, Alfred L *Football Player*
111 Pendelton Place Circle, Sugar Land,
TX 77479 USA

Oglive, Benjamin A (Ben) *Baseball Player*
1012 E Sandpiper Dr, Tempe, AZ 85283
USA

Ogrin, David *Golfer*
37300 Golf Club Trail, Magnolia, TX
77355 USA

Ogrodnick, John *Hockey Player*
37034 Aldgate Court, Farmington Hills,
MI 48335 USA

Oh, Sadaharu *Baseball Player*
Fukuoka Dorne Daiei Hawks, 6F 2-2-2
Jigyohama, Chuo-Ku Fukouka, 810,
JAPAN

Oh, Sandra *Actor*
United Talent Agency (UTA), 9560
Wilshire Blvd, Beverly Hills, CA 90212
USA

Oh, Soon Teck
128 N. Kenwood St. #1, Burbank, CA
91505-4208

Oh, Soon-Teck *Actor*
128 N Kenwood St, #1, Burbank, CA
91505 USA

Ohl, Don *Basketball Player*
2 E Lockhaven Court, Edwardsville, IL
62025 USA

Ohlsson, Garrick *Musician*
International Creative Mgmt, 8942
Wilshire Blvd, #219, Beverly Hills, CA
90211 USA

Ohlund, Mattias *Hockey Player*
Vancouver Canucks, 800 Griffiths Way,
Vancouver, BC V6B 6G1, CANADA

Ohman, Jack *Editor, Cartoonist*
Portland Oregonian, Editorial Dept, 1320
SW Broadway, Portland, OR 97201 USA

Ohno, Apolo Anton *Speed Skater*
US Speedskating, PO Box 450639,
Westlake, OH 44145 USA

Ohrner, Tommy
Ortlinderstr. 6, Munich, GERMANY,
D-81927

Ohtani, Monshu Roshin *Religious Leader*
Horikawa-Dori, Hanayachosagaru
Shimogyoku, Kyoto, 600, JAPAN

Ohyama, Heilchiro *Conductor*
6305 Via Cabrera, La Jolla, CA 92037
USA

Oimeon, Casper *Skier*
540 S Mountain Ave, Ashland, OR 97520
USA

Oingo Boingo
3236 Prlmera Ave., Los Angeles, CA
90068

Oistrakh, Igor D *Musician*
Novolesnaya Str 3, Korp 2 #10, Moscow,
RUSSIA

Oiter, Bailey *President*
President's Office, Palikia, Pohnepei FM,
Kolonia, 96941, MICRONESIA

Ojeda, Miguel *Baseball Player*
San Diego Padres, 8880 Rio San Diego
Drive #400, San Diego, CA 92108 USA

Ojukwu, Chukwuerneka O *President,
General*
Vilaska Lodge, 29 Queen's Dr, Ikoyi,
Lagos State, NIGERIA

Oka, Takeshi *Misc*
1463 E Park Place, Chicago, IL 60637
USA

Okabe, Noroki *Engineer, Architect*
Kansai Airport, 1 Banchi Senshu-Kuko
Kita, Izumisanoshi, Osake, 549, JAPAN

Okafor, Emeka *Basketball Player*
Charlotte Bobcats, 129 W Trade St #700,
Charlotte, NC 28202 USA

Okamoto, Ayako *Golfer*
22627 Ladeene Ave, Torrance, CA 90505
USA

Okamura, Arthur *Artist*
210 Kale St, Bolinas, CA 94924 USA

Okhotnikoff, Nikolai P *Opera Singer*
Canal Griboedova 109, #13, Saint
Petersburg, 190068, RUSSIA

Okogie, Anthony Olubunmi Cardinal
Religious Leader
Archdiocese, PO Box 8, 19 Catholic
Mission St, Lagos, NIGERIA

Okolowicz, Jeff *Musician*
Living Eye Productions, PO Box 12956,
Rochester, NY 14612 USA

Okolowicz, Ted *Musician*
Living Eye Productions, PO Box 12956,
Rochester, NY 14612 USA

Okonedo, Sophie *Actor*
Markham and Froggatt Agency, 4
Windmill St, London, W1T 2H, England

Okoye, Christian E *Football Player*
10082 Big Pine Dr, Alta Loma, CA 91737
USA

Okubo, Susumu *Physicist*
1209 East Ave, Rochester, NY 14607 USA

Okuda, Hiroshi *Business Person*
Toyota Motor Corp, 1 Toyotacho, Toyota
City, Aichi Prefecture, 471, JAPAN

Okumura, Tomohiro *Musician*
Jecklin Assoc, 2717 Nichols Lane,
Davenport, IA 52803 USA

Okun, Daniel A *Engineer*
204 Carol Woods, 750 Weaver Dairy
Road, Chapel Hill, NC 27514 USA

Ol' Dirty Bastard
250 W. 57th St. #821, New York, NY
10021

Olafsson, Olafur J *Publisher*
Sony Electronics Publishing USA, 9 W
57th St, New York, NY 10019 USA

Olah, George A *Nobel Prize Laureate*
2252 Gloaming Way, Beverly Hills, CA
90210 USA

Olajuwon, Hakeem
10 Greenway Plaza E., Houston, TX
77046

Olander, Ed *War Hero*
61 Fox Farms Road, Florence, MA 01062
USA

Olander, Jimmy *Musician*
Dreamcatcher Artists Mgmt, 2908 Poston
Ave, Nashville, TN 37203 USA

Olandt, Ken *Actor*
Gold Marshak Liedtke, 3500 W Olive
Ave, #1400, Burbank, CA 91505 USA

Olay, Ruth
2700 Neilson Way #736, Santa Monica,
CA 90405

Olazabel, Jose Maria *Golfer*
Sergio Gomez, Apartado 26, San
Sebastian, 20080, SPAIN

Olberding, Mark *Basketball Player*
4131 Cliff Oaks St, San Antonio, TX
78229 USA

Olbermann, Keith *Sportscaster*
Cable News Network, Sports Dept, 1050
Techwood Dr NW, Atlanta, GA 30318
USA

Olczyk, Ed *Hockey Player, Coach*
Pittsburgh Penguins, Mellon Arena, 66
Mario Lemieux Place, Pittsburgh, PA
15219 USA

Old, Lloyd J *Biologist*
Ludwig Institute of Cancer Research, 1345
Ave of Americas, New York, NY 10105
USA

Oldenburg, Claes T *Artist*
556 Broome St, New York, NY 10013
USA

Oldenburg, Richard E *Director*
447 E 57th St, New York, NY 10022 USA

Oldendorf, William *Doctor*
University of California, Medical Center,
Neurology Dept, Los Angeles, CA 90024
USA

Older, Charles (Chuck) *War Hero*
930 Thayer Ave, Los Angeles, CA 90024
USA

Olderman, Murray *Writer*
832 Inverness Dr, Rancho Mirage, CA
92270 USA

Oldfield, Bruce *Fashion Designer*
27 Beauchamp Place, London, SW3,
UNITED KINGDOM(UK)

Oldfield, Mike *Actor, Director, Composer*
Air-Edel (UK), 18 Rodmarton Street,
London, W1H 3F, United Kingdom

Oldfield, Sally *Musician*
Global Artists Mgmt, Willy-Brandt-Str 39,
Erftstadt, 50374, GERMANY

Oldham, D Ray *Football Player*
1096 Harbor Landing Dr, Soddy Daisy,
TN 37379 USA

Oldham, John *Basketball Player, Coach*
2127 Sycamore Dr, Bowling Green, KY
42104 USA

Oldham, Tasha *Director*
Jerry Shandrew PR, 1050 South Stanley
Avenue, Los Angeles, CA 90019-6634
USA

Oldham, Todd *Fashion Designer*
120 Wooster St, New York, NY 10012
USA

Oldman, Gary *Actor, Director*
William Morris AGency, 151 El Camino
Dr, Beverly Hills, CA 90212 USA

Olds, Gabriel
PO Box 120551, Nashville, TN 37212-
0551

Olds, Robin *War Hero, Football Player*
PO Box 1478, Steamboat Springs, CO
80477 USA

Olds, Walter (Wally) *Hockey Player*
37296 Pincherry Road, Cohasset, MN
55721 USA

Oleksy, Jozef *Prime Minister*
Ul Wiktorii Wiedenskiej 5 M 4, Warsaw,
02-954, POLAND

Olerud, John G *Baseball Player*
1310 180th Ave NE, Bellevue, WA 98008
USA

Olesz, Rostislav *Hockey Player*
Florida Panthers, 1 Panthers Parkway,
Sunrise, FL 33323 USA

Olevsky, Julian *Musician*
68 Blue Hills Road, Amherst, MA 01002
USA

Oleynik, Larisa *Actor*
Savage Agency, 6212 Banner Ave, Los
Angeles, CA 90038 USA

Oliceira, Ana Cristina *Actor*
Ziffren Brittenham Branca Fischer Gilbert-
Lurie & Stiffman LLP, 1801 Century Park
W, Los Angeles, CA 90067 USA

Olin, Ken *Actor*
Endeavor Talent Agency, 9701 Wilshire
Blvd, #1000, Beverly Hills, CA 90212
USA

Olin, Lena *Actor*
Industry Entertainment, 955 Carillo Dr,
#300, Los Angeles, CA 90048 USA

Olin, Lina *Actor*
Industry Entertainment, 955 S Carrillo Dr
#300, Los Angeles, CA 90048 USA

Oliphant, Patrick B *Cartoonist*
Universal Press Syndicate, 4520 Main St,
Kansas City, MO 64111 USA

Oliphant, Randall *Business Person*
Barrick Gold Corp, 200 Bay St, Toronto,
ON M5J 2J3, CANADA

Olitski, Jules *Artist*
PO Box 440, Marlboro, VT 05344 USA

Oliu, Ingrid *Actor*
Cunningham-Escott-Dipene & Associates Inc (CED-LA), 10635 Santa Monica Blvd #130, Los Angeles, CA 90025 USA

Oliva, L Jay *Educator*
New York University, President's Office, New York, NY 10012 USA

Oliva, Sergio *Misc*
Oliva's Gym, 7383 Rogers Ave, Chicago, IL 60626 USA

Oliva, Tony
212 Spring Valley Dr., Bloomington, MN 55420

Olivares, Ruben *Boxer*
Geno Productions, PO Box 113, Montebello, CA 90640 USA

Olivas, John D *Astronaut*
2618 Sunset Blvd, Houston, TX 77005 USA

Oliveira, Elmar *Musician*
Cramer/Marder Artists, 3436 Springhill Road, Lafayette, CA 94549 USA

Oliveira, Nathan J *Artist*
785 Santa Maria Ave, Palo Alto, CA 94305 USA

Oliver, Albert (Al) *Baseball Player*
Po Box 1466, Portsmouth, OH 45662 USA

Oliver, Christian *Actor*
7211 Mulholland Dr, Los Angeles, CA 90068 USA

Oliver, Covey T *Attorney General, Diplomat*
Ingleton-on-Miles, RR 1 Box 194, Easton, MD 21601 USA

Oliver, Daniel *Government Official*
Heritage Foundation, 214 Massachusetts Ave NW, Washington, DC 20002 USA

Oliver, Dean *Race Car Driver*
21386 Notus Road, Greenleaf, ID 83626 USA

Oliver, Jamie *Chef*
15 Barmbles, Bishops Storford, Herts, CM23 4PX, UNITED KINGDOM (UK)

Oliver, Mary *Writer*
Molly Malone Cook Agency, PO Box U, Sweet Briar, VA 24595 USA

Oliver, Murray C *Hockey Player*
5505 McGuire Road, Minneapolis, MN 55439 USA

Oliver, Pam *Sportscaster*
Fox-TV, Sports Dept, 205 W 67th St, New York, NY 10021 USA

Oliveres, Rubin
PO Box 113, Montebello, CA 90640

Olivo, Joey *Boxer*
9628 Poinciana St, Pico Rivera, CA 90660 USA

Olivor, Jane *Music Group, Musician*
Ed Keane, 32 Saint Edwards Road, Boston, MA 02128 USA

Olkewicz, Walter *Actor*
Gold Marshak Liedtke, 3500 W Olive Ave #1400, Burbank, CA 91505 USA

Olmedo, Alex *Tennis Player*
5067 Woodley Ave, Encino, CA 91436 USA

Olmos, Edward James *Actor*
Olmos Productions, 18034 Ventura Blvd #228, Encino, CA 91316 USA

Olmstead, Matt *Producer*
International Creative Management (ICM-LA), 8942 Wilshire Blvd, Beverly Hills, CA 90211 USA

Olney, Claude W *Educator*
Olney 'A' Seminars, PO Box 686, Scottsdale, AZ 85252 USA

Olowaonkandi, Michael *Basketball Player*
Los Angeles Clippers, 1111 S Figueroa St, Los Angeles, CA 90015 USA

Olowokandi, Michael *Basketball Player*
Minnesota Timberwolves, Target Center, 600 1st Ave N, Minneapolis, MN 55403 USA

Olsen, Ashley *Actor*
DualStar Entertainment, 1801 Century Park E Fl 12, Los Angeles, CA 90067 USA

Olsen, David A *Financier*
Marsh & McLennan Co, 1166 Ave of Americas, New York, NY 10036 USA

Olsen, Eric Christian *Actor*
Ellen Meyer Entertainment, 8899 Beverly Blvd #616, Los Angeles, CA 90048 USA

Olsen, Gregory *Astronaut, Business Person*
Sensors Unlimited, 3490 US Route 1, Building 12, Princeton, NJ 08540 USA

Olsen, Kenneth H *Inventor*
111 Powder Mill Road, Maynard, MA 01754 USA

Olsen, Mary Kate *Actor*
DualStar Entertainment, 1801 Century Park E Fl 12, Los Angeles, CA 90067 USA

Olsen, Merlin J *Actor, Football Player, Sportscaster*
11755 Wilshire Blvd #2320, Los Angeles, CA 90025 USA

Olsen, Olaf *Archaeologist*
Strevelsiovedvej 2, Alro, Oder, 8300, DENMARK

Olsen, Paul E *Misc*
Columbia University, Lamont-Doherty Geological Laboratory, New York, NY 10027 USA

Olsen, Robert C Jr *Admiral, Educator*
Superintendent's Office, US Coast Guard Academy, New London, CT 06320 USA

Olsen, Stanford *Opera Singer*
Columbia Artists Mgmt Inc, 165 W 57th St, New York, NY 10019 USA

Olsen, Susan *Actor*
Manos Management, 8306 Wilshire Blvd, #3500, Beverly Hills, CA 90211 USA

Olshwanger, Ron *Photographer, Journalist*
1447 Meadowside Dr, Saint Louis, MO 63146 USA

Olson, Allen I *Governor*
9435 Libby Lane, Eden Prairie, MN 55347 USA

Olson, James *Actor*
250 W 57th St #803, New York, NY 10107 USA

Olson, Kaitlin *Actor*
Joan Green Management, 1836 Courtney Terr, Los Angeles, CA 90046 USA

Olson, Lisa *Writer*
New York Daily News, Editorial Dept, 220 E 42nd St, New York, NY 10017 USA

Olson, Mancur *Economist*
4316 Claggett Pine Way, University Park, MD 20782 USA

Olson, Mark *Songwriter, Musician*
Sussman Assoc, 1222 16th Ave S #300, Nashville, TN 37212 USA

Olson, Mark *Government Official, Economist*
Federal Reserve Board, 20th St & Constitution Ave, Washington, DC 20551 USA

Olson, Nancy *Actor*
945 N Alpine Dr, Beverly Hills, CA 90210 USA

Olson, R Lute *Basketball Player, Coach*
University of Arizona, McKate Memorial Center, Tucson, AZ 85721 USA

Olson, Richard E *Business Person*
Champion Int'l Corp, 1 Champion Plaza, Stamford, CT 06921 USA

Olson, Weldon *Hockey Player*
2623 Goldenrod Lane, Findlay, OH 45840 USA

Olstead, Renee
3013 Fountainview #240, Houston, TX 77057

Olszewski, Jan F *Prime Minister*
Biuro Poselskie, Al Ujazdowskie 13, Warsaw, 00-567, POLAND

Olyphant, Timothy *Actor*
William Morris Agency, 151 El Camino Dr, Beverly Hills, CA 90212 USA

Omakuchi, Narasimhann *Actor*
24 Vasudevapuram, Besant Road, Chennai, TN 600 005, INDIA

Oman, Qaboos Bin Said Sultan of
The Palace, Muscat, OMAN

Omar, Chamassi Said *Prime Minister*
Prime Minister's Office, BP 421, Moroni, COMOROS

Omar & The Howlers
PO Box 93, Austin, TX 78767

Omidyar, Pierre *Business Person*
eBay, 2145 Hamilton Ave, San Jose, CA 95125 USA

Onanian, Edward *Religious Leader*
Diocese of Armenian Church, 630 2nd Ave, New York, NY 10016 USA

Onarati, Peter *Actor*
Liberman Zerman, 252 N Larchmont Blvd, Los Angeles, CA 90004 USA

Onassis, Athina *Heir/Heiress*
88 av Foch, Paris, FRANCE, F-75116

Ondaatje, Michael *Writer*
Glendon College, English Dept, 2275 Bayview, Toronto, ON M4N 3M6, CANADA

Ondetti, Miguel A
79 Hemlock Circle, Princeton, NJ 08540 USA

Ondrasik, John *Musician, Songwriter*
Aware Records, 2336 W Belmont Ave, Chicago, IL 60618 USA

Ondricek, Miroslav *Cinematographer*
Nad Pomnikem 1, Prague 5, Smichow,
15200, CZECH REPUBLIC

Onetto, Victoria *Actor*
Telefe - Argentina, Pavon 2444
(C1248AAT), Buenos Aires, ARGENTINA

Onkotz, Dennis H *Football Player*
270 Walker Dr, State College, PA 16801
USA

Ono, Yoko *Artist, Filmmaker*
Studio One, 1 W 52nd St, New York, NY
10019 USA

Onodi, Henrietta *Gymnast*
Gymnastic Federation, Magyar Toma
Szovetseg, Budapest, 1143, HUNGARY

Onorati, Peter
252 N. Larchmont Blvd, Los Angeles, CA
90004

Ontiveros, Lupe *Actor*
Mitchell K Stubbs & Assoc (MKS), 8675 W
Washington Blvd #203, Culver City, CA
90232 USA

Ontkean, Michael *Actor*
PO Box 1241, Kilauea, HI 96754 USA

Onufriyenko, Yuri I *Astronaut, Misc*
Potchta Kosmonavtov, Moskovskoi
Oblasti, Syvisdny Goroduk, 141160,
RUSSIA

Oorvasi *Actor, Bollywood*
117 Solai Krishnan Street, Janaki Nagar,
Chennai, TN 600087, INDIA

Oosterhouse, Carter *Television Host*
Trading Spaces, The Learning Channel,
7700 Wisconsin Ave, Bethesda, MD
20814 USA

Oosterhuis, Peter *Golfer*
Riviera County Club, 1250 Capri Dr,
Pacific Palisades, CA 90272 USA

Opalinski-Harrer, Janice *Volleyball Player*
Women's Pro Volleyball Assn, 840 Apollo
St #204, El Segundo, CA 90245 USA

Opasik, Jim *Artist*
1914 Beverly Road, Baltimore, MD 21228
USA

Ophula, Marcel
10 rue Ernst-Deloison, Neuilly, FRANCE,
92200

Ophuls, Marcel *Director*
10 Rue Ernest Deloison, Neuilly-sur-Seine,
92200, FRANCE

Opie, John D *Business Person*
General Electric Co, 3135 Easton
Turnpike, Fairfield, CT 06828 USA

Opik, Ernst J *Astronomer*
University of Maryland, Physics &
Astronomy Dept, Colleger Park, MD
20742 USA

Oppel, Richard A *Editor*
Knight-Ridder, National Press Building,
529 14th St NW, Washington, DC 20045
USA

Oppenheim, Dennis A *Artist*
54 Franklin St, New York, NY 10013 USA

Oppenheim, Irwin *Physicist*
140 Upland Road, Cambridge, MA 02140
USA

Oppenheim-Barnes, Saily *Government Official*
Quietways Highlands, Painswick, Glos,
UNITED KINGDOM (UK)

Oppenheimer, Alan
1207 Beverly Green Dr., Beverly Hills, CA
90212

Oppenheimer, Allan *Actor*
1207 Beverly Green Dr, Beverly Hills, CA
90212 USA

Oppenheimer, Benjamin R *Astronomer*
California Institute of Technology,
Astronomy Dept, Pasadena, CA 91125
USA

Oppenheimer, Deborah *Producer*
United Talent Agency (UTA), 9560
Wilshire Blvd, Beverly Hills, CA 90212
USA

Opperman, Jan *Race Car Driver*
RR 1, Beaver Crossing, NE 68313 USA

Opry, Tonya
1525 E. Noble #160, Visalia, CA 93292

Orange, Walter (Clyde) *Music Group, Musician*
Management Assoc, 1920 Benson Ave,
Saint Paul, MN 55116 USA

Orbach, Jerry *Actor, Musician*
301 W 53rd St #20A, New York, NY
10019 USA

Orbach, Raymond L *Educator*
2950 Van Ness St NW #212, Washington,
DC 20008 USA

Orbelian, Konstantin A *Composer*
Demirchyan Str 27 #12, Yerevan,
3750002, ARMENIA

Orbit, William *Musician*
Creative Artists Agency LCC (CAA-LA),
9830 Wilshire Blvd, Beverly Hills, CA
90212 USA

Ord, Robert L (Bob) III *General*
3020 Ribera Road, Carmel, CA 93923
USA

Ordovos, Jose M *Scientist*
Tufts University, Nutrition Research
Center, Medford, MA 02155 USA

Ordway, Frederick I III *Writer*
2401 N Taylor St, Arlington, VA 22207
USA

Oremans, Miriam *Tennis Player*
Octagon, 1751 Pinnacle Dr #1500,
McLean, VA 22102 USA

Orend, Jack R
1808 Van Ness Ave, Hollywood, CA
90028-5674 USA

Orendi, Ron
6323 Salem Park Circle, Mechanicsburg,
PA 17055

Orenduff, J Michael *Educator*
New Mexico State University, President's
Office, Las Cruces, NM 88003 USA

Orenstein, Andrew *Producer*
United Talent Agency (UTA), 9560
Wilshire Blvd, Beverly Hills, CA 90212
USA

Oresko, Nicholas *War Hero*
31 Benjamin Road, Tenafly, NJ 07670
USA

Orgad, Ben-Zion *Composer*
14 Bloch St, Tel-Aviv, 64161, ISRAEL

Organ, H Bryan *Artist*
Stables, Marston Trussel near Market
Harborough, Leics, LE16 9TX, UNITED
KINGDOM (UK)

Orgy *Music Group*
Creative Artists Agency LCC (CAA-LA),
9830 Wilshire Blvd, Beverly Hills, CA
90212 USA

Orland, Frank J *Doctor*
519 Jackson Blvd, Forest Park, IL 60130
USA

Orlando, Geoarge J *Misc*
Distillery Wine & Allied Workers, 219
Paterson Ave, Little Falls, NJ 07424 USA

Orlando, Tony *Musician, Music Group*
Brokaw Co, 9255 Sunset Blvd #804, Los
Angeles, CA 90069 USA

Orleans, Joan *Musician*
PO Box 2596, New York, NY 10009 USA

Orlov, Yuri
Cornell Univ.Newman Lab., Ithaca, NY
14853-5001

Orman, Suze *Writer*
Riverhead Books, 375 Hudson Ave, New
York, NY 10014 USA

Orme, Stanley *Government Official*
8 Northwood Grove, Sale, Cheshire, M33
3DZ, UNITED KINGDOM (UK)

Ormond, Brian *Musician*
Pop Idol (Fremantle Media), 2700
Colorado Ave #450, Santa Monica, CA
90404 USA

Ormond, Julia *Actor*
Marmont Mgmt, Langham House, 302/8
Regent St, London, W1R 5AL, UNITED
KINGDOM (UK)

Ormond, Paul *Business Person*
Manor Care Inc, 333 N Summit St,
Toledo, OH 43604 USA

Ornish, Dean *Doctor, Writer*
Preventative Medicine Research Institue,
900 Bridgeway #2, Sausalito, CA 94965
USA

Ornstein, Donald S *Mathematician*
857 Tolman Dr, Stanford, CA 94305 USA

Orr, Bobby
300 Boylston St. #605, Boston, MA 02116

Orr, David A *Business Person*
Home Farm House Shackleford,
Godalming, Surrey, GU8 6AH, UNITED
KINGDOM (UK)

Orr, John (Johnny) *Coach*
5736 Gallery Court, West Des Moines, IA
50266 USA

Orr, Kay S *Governor*
1425 H St, Lincoln, NE 68508 USA

Orr, Louis *Coach*
14 Powell Dr, West Orange, NJ 07052
USA

Orr, Robert G (Bobby) *Hockey Player*
Woolf Assoc, 101 Huntington Ave,
#2575, Boston, MA 02199 USA

Orr, Terrence S *Dancer*
American Ballet Theatre, 890 Broadway,
New York, NY 10003 USA

Orr III, James E *Business Person*
UNUMProvident Corp, 2211 Congress St,
Portland, ME 04122 USA

Orr Jr, James E (Jim) *Football Player*
3104 Glynn Ave, Brunswick, GA 31520
USA

Orr-Cahall, Christina *Director*
Norton Gallery of Art, 1451 S Olive Ave,
West Palm Beach, FL 33401 USA

Orr-Ewing, Hamish *Business Person*
Fox Mill, Purton near Swindon, Wilts, SN5
9EF, UNITED KINGDOM (UK)

Orrall, Robert Ellis *Musician*
3 E 54th St, #1400, New York, NY 10022
USA

Orrico, Stacie *Musician*
Forefront Records, 230 Franklin Road,
Building 2A, Franklin, TN 37064 USA

Orser, Brian *Figure Skater*
1600 James Naismith Dr, Gloucester, ON
L1B 5N4, CANADA

Orser, Leland *Actor*
Brillstein-Grey Entertainment, 9150
Wilshire Blvd #350, Beverly Hills, CA
90212 USA

Orsin, Raymond *Cartoonist*
Cleveland Plain Dealer, 1801 Superior
Ave E, Cleveland, OH 44114 USA

Orsini, Myrna J *Artist*
Orsini Studios, 4411 N 7th St, Tacoma,
WA 98406 USA

Ortega, Gaspar
38 Branhaven Dr, East Haven, CT 06513

Ortega, Manuel *Actor*
Telefe - Argentina, Pavon 2444
(C1248AAT), Buenos Aires, ARGENTINA

Ortega Saavedra, Daniel *President*
Frente Sandinista de Liberacion National,
Managua, NICARAGUA

Ortega y Alamino, Jaime Cardinal
Religious Leader
Apartado 594, Calle Habana 152,
Havana, 10100, CUBA

Ortenberg, Arthur *Business Person*
Liz Claiborne Inc, 1441 Broadway, New
York, NY 10018 USA

Ortiz, Alejo *Actor*
Telefe - Argentina, Pavon 2444
(C1248AAT), Buenos Aires, ARGENTINA

Ortiz, Ana *Actor*
Gersh Agency, The (LA), 232 N Canon Dr,
Beverly Hills, CA 90210 USA

Ortiz, Carlos *Boxer*
2050 Seward Ave, #3C, Bronx, NY 10473
USA

Ortiz, Cristina *Musician*
Harrison/Parrott, 12 Penzance Place,
London, W11 4PA, UNITED KINGDOM
(UK)

Ortiz, Dave *Actor*
Anonymous Content, 8522 National Blvd
#101, Culver City, CA 90232 USA

Ortiz, David *Actor*
Anonymous Content, 8522 National Blvd
#101, Culver City, CA 90232 USA

Ortiz, Domingo *Misc*
Brown Cat Inc, 400 Foundry St, Athens,
GA 30601 USA

Ortiz, Manuel
1 Hall of Fame Dr., Canastota, NY 13032

Ortiz, Ramon *Baseball Player*
Anaheim Angels, Edison Field, 2000 Gene
Autry Way, Anaheim, CA 92806 USA

Ortiz Jr, Frank V *Diplomat*
663 Garcia St, Santa Fe, NM 87505 USA

Ortlieb, Patrick *Skier*
Hotel Montana, Obertech, Lech, 6764,
AUSTRIA

Ortner, Bev *Bowler*
Po Box 493, Odebolt, IA 51458 USA

Ortolani, Riz
Via Aurelia km 23 400, Torrimpietra,
ITALY, I-00050

Orton, Beth *Musician*
LBM, 155 Ave of Americas, #700, New
York, NY 10013 USA

Orton, Randy *Wrestler*
World Wrestling Entertainment (WWE),
1241 E Main St, Stamford, CT 06905 USA

Oruche, Phina *Actor*
Bauman Redanty & Shaul Agency, 5757
Wilshire Blvd #473, Los Angeles, CA
90036 USA

Oruviral, Krishna Rao *Actor*
4/1 Vellala Street, Kodambakkam,
Chennai, TN 600 024, INDIA

Orvick, George M *Religious Leader*
Evangelical Lutheran Synod, 6 Browns
Court, Mankato, MN 56001 USA

Ory, Meghan *Actor*
Pacific Artists Management, 1404-510 W
Hastings St, Vancouver, BC V6B 1L,
CANADA

Osborn, David V (Dave) *Football Player*
18067 Judicial Way N, Lakeville, MN
55044 USA

Osborn, Kassidy *Musician*
LGB Media, 1228 Pineview Lane,
Nashville, TN 37211 USA

Osborn, Kelsi *Musician*
LGB Media, 1228 Pineview Lane,
Nashville, TN 37211 USA

Osborn, Kristyn *Songwriter, Musician*
LGB Media, 1228 Pineview Lane,
Nashville, TN 37211 USA

Osborn, William A *Financier*
Northem Trust Corp, 50 S LaSalle St,
Chicago, IL 60675 USA

Osborne, Barrie M *Director, Producer*
Company Films, 2601 Second Street,
Santa Monica, CA 90405 USA

Osborne, Burl *Editor, Publisher*
Dallas Morning News, Editorial Dept,
Communications Center, Dallas, TX
75265 USA

Osborne, Burl *Religious Leader*
Salvation Army, 799 Bloomfield Ave,
Verona, NJ 07044 USA

Osborne, Jeffrey *Songwriter, Musician*
Entertainment Artists, 2409 21st Ave S,
#100, Nashville, TN 37212 USA

Osborne, Joan *Musician, Songwriter*
DAS Communications, 83 Riverside Dr,
New York, NY 10024 USA

Osborne, Mary Pope *Writer*
Random House, 1745 Broadway, #B1,
New York, NY 10019 USA

Osborne Brothers *Musician*
Billy Deaton Talent, 1300 Divisin Street,
Suite 102, Nashville, TN 37203

Osbourne, Jack *Reality TV Star*
Sharon Osbourne Management, 9292
Civic Center Dr, Beverly Hills, CA 90210
USA

Osbourne, Kelly *Musician*
Sharon Osbourne Management, 9292
Civic Center Dr, Beverly Hills, CA 90210
USA

Osbourne, Ozzy *Musician, Songwriter*
Sharon Osbourne Management, 9292
Civic Center Dr, Beverly Hills, CA 90210
USA

Osbourne, Sharon *Business Person*
Sharon Osbourne Management, 9292
Civic Center Dr, Beverly Hills, CA 90210
USA

Osby, Greg *Musician*
Bridge Agency, 35 Clark St, #A5, Brooklyn
Heights, NY 11201 USA

Oscar Scheld, Eusebio Cardinal *Religious Leader*
Archdiocese, Rua Benjamin Constant 23/
502, Rio de Janeiro, 20241, BRAZIL

Oseary, Guy *Producer*
Maverick Films, 9348 Wilshire Dr Fl 3,
Beverly Hills, CA 90210 USA

Osgood, Charles *Commentator*
CBS-TV, News Dept, 524 W 57th St, New
York, NY 10019 USA

Osgood, Charles E *Educator*
30 E Main St, Champaign, IL 61820 USA

Osgood, Chris *Hockey Player*
6382 Pembrook Dr, Westland, MI 48185
USA

Osheroff, Douglas D *Nobel Prize Laureate*
75 Ranch Road, Woodside, CA 94062
USA

Oshima, Nagisa *Director*
Oshima Productions, 2-15-7 Arasaka,
Minatoku, Tokyo, JAPAN

Osima, Nagisa
4-11-5 Kugenuma-Matsuaka, Fujisawa-
Shi, JAPAN, 251

Oslin, K T *Musician*
Moress-Nanas-Hart, 704 18th Ave S,
Nashville, TN 37203 USA

Osman, Mat *Musician*
Interceptor Enterprises, 98 White Lion St,
London, N1 9PF, UNITED KINGDOM
(UK)

Osman, Osman Ahmed *Engineer*
Osman Ahmed Osman Co, 34 Adly St,
Cairo, EGYPT

Osmar, Dean *Misc*
PO Box 32, Clam Gulch, AK 99568 USA

Osment, Emily *Actor*
Coast to Coast Talent Group, 3350
Barham Blvd, Los Angeles, CA 90068
USA

Osment, Haley Joel *Actor*
1420 Colina Dr, Glendale, CA 91208
USA

Osmond, Cliff *Actor, Director*
630 Benvenida Ave, Pacific Palisades, CA 90272 USA

Osmond, Donny *Musician*
PO Box 7122, Branson, MO 65615 USA

Osmond, Ken *Actor*
9863 Wornom Ave, Sunland, CA 91040 USA

Osmond, Marie *Actor, Musician*
Curb Records, 47 Music Square East, Nashville, TN 37203 USA

Osmond Boys
PO Box 7122, Branson, MO 65615

Osnes, Larry G *Educator*
Hamline University, President's Office, Saint Paul, MN 55104 USA

Osorio, Jorge Federico *Musician*
Columbia Artists Mgmt Inc, 165 W 57th St, New York, NY 10019 USA

Osrin, Raymond H *Cartoonist*
Cleveland Plain Dealer, Editorial Dept, 1801 Superior E, Cleveland, OH 44114 USA

Oss Jr, Arnold *Hockey Player*
8012 Pennsylvania Road, Bloomington, MN 55438 USA

Ossana, Diana
151 El Camino Dr., Beverly Hills, CA 90212

Ost, Friedheim *Government Official*
Heiersmauer 59, Paderborn, 33098, GERMANY

Ostaseski, Frank *Director*
Zen Hospice Project, 273 Page St, San Francisco, CA 94102 USA

Osteen, Claude W *Baseball Player*
624 Brent Dr, Arlington, TX 76012 USA

Osteen Jr, H M *Financier*
Bankers First Corp, 1 10th St, Augusta, GA 30901 USA

Osterbrock, Donald E *Astronomer*
120 Woodside Ave, Santa Cruz, CA 95060 USA

Osterhage, Jeff *Actor*
210-D N. Cordova, Burbank, CA 91505

Osteroth, Alexander
Steinsdorfstr. 20, Munich, GERMANY, 80538

Ostertag, Greg *Basketball Player*
1603 W 15th St, #202C, Lawrence, KS 66044 USA

Ostheim, Michael *Model*
Louisa Models, Ebersberger Str 9, Munich, 81679 USA

Ostin, Michael *Business Person*
DreamWorks SKG, 1000 Flower Street, Glendale, CA 91201

Ostin, Mo *Business Person*
Dreamworks SKG, Music Div, 100 Universal City Plaza, Universal City, CA 91608 USA

Ostler, Ryan *Fashion Designer*
Ostler Manta Enterprises, PO Box 92, Farmington, UT 84025 USA

Ostman, Arnold *Conductor*
Haydn Rawstron, 36 Station Road, London, SE20 7BQ, UNITED KINGDOM (UK)

Ostos, Javier *Swimmer*
FINA, Isabel La Catolica 13, Desp 401-2, Mexico City 1, DF, MEXICO

Ostriker, Jeremiah P *Physicist*
33 Philip Dr, Princeton, NJ 08540 USA

Ostrom, John H *Misc*
52 Hillhouse Road, Goshen, CT 06756 USA

Ostrosky, David *Actor*
Televisa, Blvd Adolfo Lopez Mateos 232, Colonia San Angel INN, DF, CP 01060, MEXICO

Ostrum, Peter *Actor*
6065 Duncan Road, Glenfield, NY 13343 USA

Ostwald, Martin *Educator*
408 Walnut Lane, Swarthmore, PA 19081 USA

Oswald, J Julian R *Admiral*
Naval Secretary, Victory Bldg, HM Naval Base, Portsmouth, PO1 3LS, UNITED KINGDOM (UK)

Oswald, Mark *Race Car Driver*
Championship Quest Motorsports, PO Box 99, Pfafftown, NC 27040 USA

Oswald, Mark *Opera Singer*
Herbert Barrett, 266 W 37th St, #2000, New York, NY 10018 USA

Oswald, Stephen S *Astronaut*
NASA, Johnson Space Center, 2101 NASA Road, Houston, TX 77058 USA

Oswalt, Patton *Actor*
William Morris Agency (WMA-LA), 1 William Morris Pl, Beverly Hills, CA 90212 USA

Oswalt, Roy *Baseball Player*
RR1 Box 156 A A, Weir, MS 39772 USA

Oszajca, John *Musician*
Interscope Records, 2220 Colorado Ave, Santa Monica, CA 90404 USA

Otaka, Tadaaki *Conductor*
Harold Holt, 31 Sinclair Road, London, W14 0NS, UNITED KINGDOM (UK)

Otellini, Paul *Business Person*
Intel Corp, 2200 Mission College Blvd, Santa Clara, CA 95054 USA

Oteri, Cheri *Comedian, Actor*
Endeavor Talent Agency, 9701 Wilshire Blvd, #1000, Beverly Hills, CA 90212 USA

Othenin-Girard, Dominque *Director*
327 Church Lane, Los Angeles, CA 90049 USA

Otis, Amos J *Baseball Player*
588 Preakness Stakes St, Henderson, NV 89015 USA

Otis, Carre *Actor, Model*
Goldman/Knell Agency, 1801 Century Park E, #2160, Los Angeles, CA 90067 USA

Otis, Glenn K *General*
3401 RR 9, Lake SHore Road, Peru, NY 12972 USA

Otis, James L (Jim) *Football Player*
14795 Greenleaf Valley Dr, Chesterfield, MO 63017 USA

Otis, Johnny *Songwriter, Musician*
7105 Baker Lane, Sebastopol, CA 95472 USA

Otman, Assed Mohamed *Prime Minister*
Villa Rissani, Route Oued Akrach, Souissi, Rabat, MOROCCO

Otstott, Charles P *General*
6152 Pohick Station Dr, Fairfax Station, VA 22039 USA

Otsuki, Tamayo *Actor*
Patterson Assoc, 20318 Hiawatha St, Chatsworth, CA 91311 USA

Ottey, Merlene
PO Box 120, Indianapolis, IN 46206-0120

Ottey-Page, Merlene *Track Athlete*
Jamaican Olympic Committee, Po Box 544, Kingston, 10, JAMAICA

Otto, August J (Gus) *Football Player*
8 Cool Meadows Dr, Ballwin, MO 63011 USA

Otto, Frei *Architect*
Berghalde 19, 7250 Leonberg, Warmbroun, 71229, GERMANY

Otto, James E (Jim) *Football Player*
00 Estates Dr, Auburn, CA 95602 USA

Otto, Joel *Hockey Player*
77 Sunset Way SE, Calgary, AB T2X 3C1, CANADA

Otto, Kristin *Swimmer*
ZDF Sportedaktion, Postfach 4040, Mainz, 55100, GERMANY

Otto, Michael *Business Person*
Spiegel Inc, 3500 Lacey Road, Downers Grove, IL 60515 USA

Otto, Miranda *Actor*
Shanahan Mgmt, PO Box 1509, Darlinghurst, NSW, 1300, AUSTRALIA

Otto, Sylke *Athlete*
BSD, An der Schiessstatte 4, Berchtesgaden, 83471, GERMANY

Otto Jr, A T *Misc*
Railroad Yardmasters Union, 1411 Peterson Ave, #201, Park Ridge, IL 60068 USA

Otwell, Ralph M *Editor*
2750 Hurd Ave, Evanston, IL 60201 USA

Ouaido, Nassour Guelengdoussia *Prime Minister*
Prime Minister's Office, N'Djamena, CHAD

Ouattara, Alassane D *Prime Minister, Financier*
International Monetary Fund, 700 19th St NW, #12-300H, Washington, DC 20431 USA

Ouchi, William G *Educator*
University of California, Graduate Management School, Los Angeles, CA 90024 USA

Ouedraogo, Gerard Kango *Prime Minister*
01 BP 347, Ouagadougou, BURKINA FASO

Ouedraogo, Idrissa *Director*
FEPACI, 01 BP 2524, Ouagadougou, BURKINA FASO

Ouedraogo, Kdre Desire *Prime Minister*
Prime Minister's Office, Parliament Building, Ouagadougou, BURKINA FASO

Ouellet, Joseph G N Cardinal *Religious Leader*
Archdiocese, 34 Rue de l'Eveche E, CP 730, Rimouski, QC, G5L 7C7, CANADA

Oureiro, Natalia *Musician*
BMG, 1540 Broadway, New York, NY 10036 USA

Ourisson, Guy *Misc*
10 Rue Geiler, Strasbourg, 67000, FRANCE

Ousland, Borge *Skier*
Axel Huitfeldts V5, Oslo, 1170, NORWAY

Outkast *Music Group*
William Morris Agency (WMA-LA), 1 William Morris Pl, Beverly Hills, CA 90212 USA

Outlar, Jesse *Writer*
116 Loblolly Circle, Peachtree City, GA 30269 USA

Outlaw, Charles (Bo) *Basketball Player*
14815 River Mill, San Antonio, TX 78216 USA

Outlaw, Travis *Basketball Player*
Portland Trail Blazers, Rose Garden, 1 Center Court St, Portland, OR 97227 USA

Outman, Tim *Artist*
57101 N Bank Road, McKenzie Bridge, OR 97413 USA

OV7 *Music Group*
Sony Music Miami, 605 Lincoln Rd, Miami Beach, FL 33138 USA

Ovchinikov, Vladmir P *Musician*
Manygate, 13 Cotswold Mews, 30 Battersea Square, London, SW11 3RA, UNITED KINGDOM (UK)

Ovechkin, Alexander *Hockey Player*
Washington Capitals, MCI Center, 601 F St NW, Washington, DC 20004 USA

Overall, Park *Actor*
33150 Drill Road, Santa Clarita, CA 91390 USA

Overath, Wolfgang
Auf dem Hummerich, Siegburg, GERMANY, D-53721

Overbeek, Jan T G *Misc*
Zweerslaan 35, Bilthoven, HN, 3723, NETHERLANDS

Overgard, Robert M *Religious Leader*
Church of Lutheran Brethren, PO Box 655, Fergus Falls, MN 56538 USA

Overgard, William *Cartoonist*
United Feature Syndicate, 200 Madison Ave, New York, NY 10016 USA

Overhauser, Albert W *Physicist*
236 Pawnee Dr, West Lafayette, IN 47906 USA

Overman, Ion
1801 Ave. of the Stars #902, Los Angeles, CA 90067

Overman, Larry E *Misc*
University of California, Chemistry Dept, Irvine, CA 92717 USA

Overmyer, Eric *Writer*
Yale University, English Dept, New Haven, CT 06520 USA

Overstreet, Paul *Songwriter, Musician*
White Horse Enterprises, 475 Annex Ave, Nashville, TN 37209 USA

Overstreet, Tommy *Songwriter, Musician*
PO Box 455, Brentwood, TN 37024 USA

Overton, Rick *Actor*
Don Buchwald & Associates Inc (LA), 6500 Wilshire Blvd #2200, Los Angeles, CA 90048 USA

Ovitz, Michael S *Business Person*
457 N Rockingham Ave, Los Angeles, CA 90049 USA

Ovshinsky, Stanford R *Engineer, Inventor*
Energy Conversion Devices, 2956 Waterview Dr, Rochester Hills, MI 48309 USA

Owen, Clive *Actor*
International Creative Mgmt, 8942 Wilshire Blvd, #219, Beverly Hills, CA 90211 USA

Owen, David A L *Government Official*
78 Narrow St, Limehouse, London, E14 8BP, UNITED KINGDOM (UK)

Owen, Edwyn (Bob) *Hockey Player*
3630 SW Stratford Road, Topeka, KS 66604 USA

Owen, Henry *Diplomat*
Brookings Institute, 1775 Massachusetts Ave NW, Washington, DC 20036 USA

Owen, Mark
Postfach 20 13 43, Hamburg, GERMANY, D-20243

Owen, Randy Y *Musician*
PO Box 529, Fort Payne, AL 35968 USA

Owen, Ray D *Biologist*
1583 Rose Villa St, Pasadena, CA 91106 USA

Owen, Terrell *Athlete*
San Francisco 49ers, 4949 Centennial Blvd, Santa Clara, CA 95054

Owens, Buck *Songwriter, Musician*
Buck Owens Productions, 3223 Sillect Ave, Bakersfield, CA 93308 USA

Owens, Burgess *Football Player*
1430 Telegraph Road, West Chester, PA 19380 USA

Owens, Charles W (Tinker) *Football Player*
4512 Hunters Hill Circle, Norman, OK 73072 USA

Owens, Chris *Actor*
Jerry Shandrew PR, 1050 South Stanley Avenue, Los Angeles, CA 90019-6634 USA

Owens, Cotton *Race Car Driver*
7605 White Ave, Spartanburg, SC 29303 USA

Owens, Gary *Entertainer*
17856 Via Vallarta, Encino, CA 91316 USA

Owens, James D (Jim) *Football Coach, Football Player*
PO Box 1749, Bigfork, MT 59911 USA

Owens, Rawleigh C (R C) *Football Player*
1533 Brook Dale Way, Manteca, CA 95336 USA

Owens, Rena *Actor, Model*
526 N Larchmont Blvd #201, Los Angeles, CA 90004 USA

Owens, Steve *Football Player*
812 Cedarbrook Dr, Norman, OK 73072 USA

Owens, Terrell *Football Player*
105 Emerson St, Alexander City, AL 35010 USA

Owens, William A *Admiral*
510 Lake St S, #B302, Kirkland, WA 98033 USA

Owensby, Earl
1 Motion Picture Blvd, Shelby, NC 28152

Owsley, Douglas *Misc*
Smithsonian Institute, 17th & M Sts NW, Washington, DC 20036 USA

Oxenberg, Catherine *Actor*
9461 Charleville Blvd, #380, Beverly Hills, CA 90212 USA

Oyakawa, Yoshinobu (Yoshi) *Swimmer*
4171 Hutchinson Road, Cincinnati, OH 45248 USA

Oz, Amos *Writer*
Ben Gurion University, PO Box 653, Beer-Sheva, 84195, ISRAEL

Oz, Frank R *Director*
Henson Co, PO Box 20726, New York, NY 10023 USA

Ozaki, Masashi *Golfer*
Bridgestone Sports, 14230 Lochridge Blvd, #G, Covington, GA 30014 USA

Ozaki, Satoshi *Physicist*
Brookhaven National Lab, Heavy Ion Collider, 2 Center St, Upton, NY 11973 USA

Ozark, Daniel L (Danny) *Misc*
PO Box 6666, Vero Beach, FL 32961 USA

Ozawa, Ichiro *Government Official*
Daiichi Giia Kaikan, Nagatacho Chiyodaku, Tokyo, 100, JAPAN

Ozawa, Seiji *Conductor*
Columbia Artists Mgmt Inc, 165 W 57th St, New York, NY 10019 USA

Ozbek, Rifat *Fashion Designer*
Ozbek Ltd, 18 Haunch of Venison Yard, London, W1Y 1AF, UNITED KINGDOM (UK)

Ozick, Cynthia *Writer*
Knopf Publishers, 201 E 50th St, New York, NY 10022 USA

Ozio, David *Bowler*
5915 Ventura Lane, Beaumont, TX 77706 USA

Ozolinsh, Sandis *Hockey Player*
Anaheim Mighty Ducks, 2000 E Gene Autry Way, Anaheim, CA 92806 USA

Ozomatli *Musician*
Creative Artists Agency LCC (CAA-LA), 9830 Wilshire Blvd, Beverly Hills, CA 90212 USA

Ozsan, Hal *Actor*
Brookside Artists Management (LA), 450 N Roxbury Dr Fl 4, Beverly Hills, CA 90210 USA

Ozzie, Raymond (Ray) *Designer*
33 Harbor St, Manchester-by-the-Sea, MA 01944 USA

P

Paabo, Svante *Director*
Evolutionary Anthropology Inst, Deutscher
Platz 6, Leipzig, 04103 USA

Paar, Jack *Entertainer*
9 Chateau Ridge Dr, Greenwich, CT
06831 USA

Paavola, Rodney *Hockey Player*
General Delivery, Hancock, MI 49930
USA

Pablo Cruise
PO Box 770850, Orlando, FL 32877

Pace, Darrell O *Athlete*
4394 Princeton Road, Hamilton, OH
45011 USA

Pace, Dominic *Actor*
Shapiro-Lichtman Talent Agency, 8827
Beverly Blvd, Los Angeles, CA 90048 USA

Pace, Judy *Actor*
4139 Cloverdale Ave, Los Angeles, CA
90008 USA

Pace, Justin *Actor*
McCabe/Justice, 247 S Beverly Dr #102,
Beverly Hills, CA 90212 USA

Pace, Lee *Actor*
Innovative Artists (LA), 1505 Tenth St,
Santa Monica, CA 90401 USA

Pace, Orlando *Football Player*
4203 Windham Place S, Sandusky, OH
44870 USA

Pace, Peter *General*
Vice Chairman, Joint Chiefs of Staff
Pentagon, Washington, DC 20318 USA

Pacheco, Abel *President*
Casa Presidencial, Apdo 520-2010, San
Jose, 1000, COSTA RICA

Pacheco, Ferdie *Sportscaster*
4151 Gate Lane, Miami, FL 33137 USA

Pacheco, Manuel T *Educator*
University of Arizona, President's Office,
Tucson, AZ 85721 USA

Pacino, Al *Actor*
Chal Productions, 301 W 57th St, #16C,
New York, NY 10019 USA

Packard, Kelly *Actor, Model*
2520 30th Dr, Astoria, NY 11102 USA

Packer, A William (Billy) *Sportscaster*
Bazel Group, 115 Penn Warren Dr #300-
329, Brentwood, TN 37027 USA

Packer, Kerry F B *Business Person*
Consolidated Press Holdings, 54 Park St,
Sydney, NSW, 2000, AUSTRALIA

Packwocd, Bob *Ex-Senator*
2201 Wisconsin Ave NW #C-120,
Washington, DC 20007-4128 USA

Packwood, Robert W (Bob) *Senator*
Sunrise Research, 2201 Wisconsin Ave
NW, Washington, DC 20007 USA

Pacula, Joanna *Actor*
Chuck Binder, 1465 Lindacrest Dr,
Beverly Hills, CA 90210 USA

Padalecki, Jared *Actor*
Evolution Entertainment, 901 N Highland
Ave, Los Angeles, CA 90038 USA

Padalka, Gennadi I *Cosmonaut*
Potchta Kosmonavtov, Moskovskoi
Oblasti, Syvisdny Goroduk, 141160,
RUSSIA

Paddock, John *Hockey Player, Coach*
1315 Penn Ave, Hershey, PA 17033 USA

Padilla, Douglas (Doug) *Track Athlete*
182 N 555 W, Orem, UT 84057 USA

Padilla, Vicente *Baseball Player*
Philadelphia Phillies, Veterans Stadium,
3501 South Broad Street, Philadelphia, PA
19148 USA

Padma-Nathan, Harin *Doctor*
1245 16th St, #312, Santa Monica, CA
90404 USA

Padmini *Actor, Bollywood*
9 Palot Madhavan Road,
Mahalingapuram, Chennai, TN 600034,
INDIA

Paez, Jorge (Maromero) *Boxer*
233 Paulin Ave, Calexico, CA 92231 USA

Paez, Richard A *Judge*
US Appellate Court, Court Building, 125 S
Grand Ave, Pasadena, CA 91105 USA

Pafko, Andrew (Andy) *Baseball Player*
1420 Blackhawk Dr, Mount Prospect, IL
60056 USA

Pafko, Andy *Athlete*
1420 Blackhawk Dr, Mt. Pleasant, IL
60056

Pagan, Jose *Athlete*
708 Spring Lake Blvd, Sebring, FL 33870

Paganelli, Robert P *Diplomat*
331 S Main St, Albion, NY 14411 USA

Pagano, Lindsay *Musician*
Azoff Music, 1100 Glendon Ave, #2000,
Los Angeles, CA 90024 USA

Page, Alan C *Football Player, Judge*
Po Box 581254, Minneapolis, MN 55458
USA

Page, Anita *Actor*
14840 Valerio St, Van Nuys, CA 91405
USA

Page, Ashley *Dancer, Choreographer*
Royal Ballet, Covent Garden, Bow St,
London, WC2E 9DD, UNITED KINGDOM
(UK)

Page, Bettie
2641 S. 53rd St., Kansas City, KS 66106

Page, Bettle *Model*
JL Swanson, PO Box 56176, Chicago, IL
60656 USA

Page, Corey *Actor*
Agency for Performing Arts, 9200 Sunset
Blvd, #900, Los Angeles, CA 90069 USA

Page, David *Artist*
3724 Greenmount Ave, Baltimore, MD
21218 USA

Page, David C *Misc*
Whitehead Institute, 9 Cambridge Center,
Cambridge, MA 02142 USA

Page, Erika *Actor*
Progressive Artists Agency, 400 S Beverly
Dr, #216, Beverly Hills, CA 90212 USA

Page, Genevieve *Actor*
52 Rue de Vaugirard, Paris, 75006,
FRANCE

Page, Greg *Boxer*
Don King Promotions, 968 Pinehurst Dr,
Las Vegas, NV 89109 USA

Page, Harrison *Actor*
S D B Partners, 1801 Ave of Stars, #902,
Los Angeles, CA 90067 USA

Page, Jimmy *Musician*
Trinifold Mgmt, 12 Oval Road, London,
NW1 7DH, UNITED KINGDOM (UK)

Page, Larry *Business Person, Scientist*
Google Inc, 2400 Bayshore Parkway,
Mountain View, CA 94043 USA

Page, Michael *Misc*
Po Box 229, North Salem, NY 10560 USA

Page, Murriel *Basketball Player*
Washington Mystics, MCI Center, 601 F St
NW, Washington, DC 20004 USA

Page, Oscar C *Educator*
Austin College, President's Office,
Sherman, TX 75090 USA

Page, Patti *Musician, Actor*
404 Loma Larga Dr, Solana Beach, CA
92075 USA

Page, Pierre *Coach, Hockey Player*
Anaheim Mighty Ducks, 2000 E Gene
Autry Way, Anaheim, CA 92806 USA

Page, Steven *Musician*
Nettwerk Mgmt, 8730 Wilshire Blvd,
#304, Beverly Hills, CA 90211 USA

Page, Tim *Journalist*
Washington Post, Editorial Dept, 1150
15th St NW, Washington, DC 20071 USA

Paget, Debra *Actor*
411 Kari Court, Houston, TX 77024 USA

Pagett, Nicola *Actor*
22 Victoria Road, Mortlake, London,
SW14, UNITED KINGDOM (UK)

Paglia, Camille *Writer, Educator*
University of the Arts, Humanities Dept,
320 S Broad St, Philadelphia, PA 19102
USA

Pagliarulo, Michael T (Mike) *Baseball
Player*
11 Fieldstone Dr, Winchester, MA 01890
USA

Pagnozzi, Thomas A (Tom) *Baseball
Player*
1710 W Park Ave, Chandler, AZ 85224
USA

Pagonis, William G *General*
25190 N Pawnee Road, Barrington, IL
60010 USA

Pahang *Misc*
Istana Abu Bakar, Pekan, Pahang,
MALAYSIA

Pahlavi, Ashraf
12 Ave. Montaigne, Paris, FRANCE,
75016

Paich, David *Musician*
Fitzgerald-Hartley, 34 N Palm St, Ventura,
CA 93001 USA

Paige, Betty
PO Box 56176, Chicago, IL 60656

Paige, Elaine *Actor, Musician*
DeWalden Court, 85 New Cavendish St,
London, W1M 7RA, UNITED KINGDOM
(UK)

Paige, Janis *Actor*
1700 Rising Glen Road, Los Angeles, CA 90069 USA

Paige, Jennifer *Musician, Songwriter*
Evolution Talent, 1776 Broadway, #1500, New York, NY 10019 USA

Paige, Mitchell *War Hero*
PO Box 2358, Palm Desert, CA 92261 USA

Paige, Peter *Actor*
3313 1/2 Barham Blvd, Los Angeles, CA 90068 USA

Paige, Rod *Secretary*
Education Department, 400 Maryland Ave SW, Washington, DC 20202 USA

Paik, Kun Woo *Musician*
Worldwide Artists, 12 Rosebery, Thomton Heath, Surrey, CR7 8PT, UNITED KINGDOM (UK)

Paik, Nam June *Artist*
Galerie Bonino, 48 Great Jones St, New York, NY 10012 USA

Pailes, William A *Astronaut*
105 LCR 409B, Mexia, TX 76667 USA

Paine, John *Musician*
Bob Flick Productions, 300 Vine, #14, Seattle, WA 98121 USA

Paintal *Actor, Bollywood, Comedian*
B 103 Sun Swept Lokhandwala Complex, Andheri, Bombay, MS 400 058, INDIA

Painter, John Mark *Musician*
Michael Dixon Mgmt, 119 Pebblecreek Road, Franklin, TN 37064 USA

Paisley, Brad *Musician*
PO Box 121113, Nashville, TN 37212 USA

Paisley, Ian *Religious Leader*
17 Cyprus Ave, Belfast, BT5 5NT, NORTHERN IRELAND

Paisley, Ian R K *Politician*
Parsonage, 17 Cyprus Ave, Belfast, BT5 5NT, NORTHERN IRELAND

Pak, Charles *Scientist*
University of Texas, Health Sciences Center, Dallas, TX 75235 USA

Pak, Se Ri *Golfer*
Steven Sung Yong Kil, 5817 Bent Pine Dr, #210, Orlando, FL 32822 USA

Pake, George E *Physicist*
13851 E Langtree Lane, Tucson, AZ 85747 USA

Pakeledinaz, Martin *Designer*
Gersh Agency, 232 N Canon Dr, Beverly Hills, CA 90210 USA

Paksas, Rolandus *Prime Minister*
President's Office, Gediminas 53, Vilnius, 232026, LITHUANIA

Palacios, Milt *Basketball Player*
Cleveland Cavaliers, Gund Arena, 1 Center Court, Cleveland, OH 44115 USA

Palade, George E *Nobel Prize Laureate*
University of California, Cellular & Molecular, La Jolla, CA 92093 USA

Paladecki, Jared *Actor*
Gilmore Girls, 4000 Warner Blvd, Building 2222, Burbank, CA 91522

Palance, Holly
2753 Roscomare Ave., Los Angeles, CA 90077

Palance, Jack *Actor*
Martin Hurwitz, 427 N Canon Dr, #215, Beverly Hills, CA 90210 USA

Palastra Jr, Joseph T *General*
RR 1 Box 267, Myrtle, MO 65778 USA

Palau, Doug *Producer*
Endeavor Agency LLC (LA), 9601 Wilshire Blvd Fl 3, Beverly Hills, CA 90210 USA

Palau, Luis *Misc*
1500 NW 167th Place, Beaverton, OR 97006 USA

Palazzari, Doug *Hockey Player*
4370 Dynasty Dr, Colorado Springs, CO 80918 USA

Palazzi, Lou *Football Player*
1521 W Gibson St, Scranton, PA 18504 USA

Palekar, Amol *Actor, Director, Bollywood*
Chire Bandee, 10th N S Road JVPD Scheme, Mumbai, MS 400049, INDIA

Palermo, Stephen M (Steve) *Misc*
7921 W 118th St, Overland Park, KS 66210 USA

Paleta, Ludwika *Actor*
Televisa, Blvd Adolfo Lopez Mateos 232, Colonia San Angel INN, DF, CP 01060, MEXICO

Paley, Albert R *Artist*
Paley Studio, 25 N Washington St, Rochester, NY 14614 USA

Paley, Grace *Writer*
PO Box 620, Thetford Hill, VT 05074 USA

Palias, Cecile *Actor*
P F D, Drury House, 34-43 Russell St, London, WC2B 5HA, UNITED KINGDOM (UK)

Palillo, Ron *Actor*
Spotlight, 322 Bowling Green, New York, NY 10274 USA

Palin, Michael *Actor, Writer*
Gurnby Corp, 68A Delancey St, Camden Town, London, NW1 7RY, UNITED KINGDOM (UK)

Pall, Gloria
12828 Victory Blvd #162, North Hollywood, CA 91606

Pall, Olga *Skier*
Fahrenweg 28, Absam, 6060, AUSTRIA

Palladino, Eric *Actor*
341 N Van Ness Ave, Los Angeles, CA 90004 USA

Palladino, Erik *Actor*
Evolution Entertainment, 901 N Highland Ave, Los Angeles, CA 90038 USA

Palladino, Vincent *Misc*
National Assn of Postal Supervisors, 1727 King St, Alexandria, VA 22314 USA

Pallavi *Actor, Bollywood*
14A Directors Colony, Kodambakkam, Chennai, TN 600024, INDIA

Palm, Siegfried
Gerhild Baron Mgmt, Dombacher Str 41/III/3, Vienna, 1170, AUSTRIA

Palmeiro, Rafael C *Baseball Player*
5216 Reims COurt, Colleyville, TX 76034 USA

Palmer, Arnold D *Golfer*
9000 Bay Hill Blvd, Orlando, FL 32819 USA

Palmer, Betsy *Actor*
8756 Wonderland Ave, Los Angeles, CA 90046 USA

Palmer, Byron
7044 Los Tilos Rd., Los Angeles, CA 90068

Palmer, C R *Business Person*
Rowan Companies, Transco Tower, 2800 Post Oak Blvd, Houston, TX 77056 USA

Palmer, Carl *Musician*
Asia, 9 Hillgate St, London, W8 7SP, UNITED KINGDOM (UK)

Palmer, Carson *Football Player*
Cincinnati Bengals, 1 Paul Brown Stadium, Cincinnati, OH 45202 USA

Palmer, Dave R *General, Educator*
4531 Blue RIdge Dr, Belton, TX 76513 USA

Palmer, Dean W *Baseball Player*
6420 Thomasville Road, Tallahassee, FL 32312 USA

Palmer, Geoffrey *Actor*
Marmont Mgmt, Langham House, 302/8 Regent St, London, W1R 5AL, UNITED KINGDOM (UK)

Palmer, Geoffrey W R *Prime Minister*
63 Roxburgh St, Mount Victoria, Wellington, NEW ZEALAND

Palmer, Gregg
5726 Graves Ave., Encino, CA 91316

Palmer, Gretchen
15301 Ventura Blvd. #345, Sherman Oaks, CA 91403

Palmer, James A (Jim) *Baseball Player, Sportscaster*
201 W Padonia Rd, #600, Timonium, MD 21093 USA

Palmer, Patsy *Actor*
International Artistes Limited, 235 Regent St - Fl Mezzanine, London, W1B 2AX, UNITED KINGDOM (UK)

Palmer, Peter *Actor*
216 Kingsway Dr, Temple Terrace, FL 33617 USA

Palmer, Reginald Oswald *Governor*
Government House, Saint George's, GRENADA

Palmer, Sandra *Golfer*
Ladies Pro Golf Assn, 100 International Golf Dr, Daytona Beach, FL 32124 USA

Palmer, William R *Publisher*
Detroit News, 615 W Lafayette Blvd, Detroit, MI 48226 USA

Palmieri, Eddie *Musician*
Berkeley Agency, 2608 9th St, #301, Berkeley, CA 94710 USA

Palmieri, Paul *Religious Leader*
Church of Jesus Christ, 6th & Lincoln Sts, Monongahela, PA 15063 USA

Palminteri, Chazz *Actor*
375 Greenwich St, New York, NY 10013 USA

Palmisano, Samuel J *Business Person*
IBM Corp, 1 N Castle Dr, Armonk, NY
10504 USA

Palms, John M *Educator*
University of South Carolina, President's
Office, Columbia, SC 29208 USA

Palomeque, Lincoln *Actor*
TV Caracol, Calle 76 #11 - 35, Piso
10AA, Bogota DC, 26484, COLOMBIA

Palomino, Carlos *Boxer*
14242 Burbank Blvd, #8, Sherman Oaks,
CA 91401 USA

Paltrow, Gwyneth *Actor*
Creative Artists Agency, 9830 Wilshire
Blvd, Beverly Hills, CA 90212 USA

Paltrow, Jake *Director*
Endeavor Agency LLC (LA), 9601 Wilshire
Blvd Fl 3, Beverly Hills, CA 90210 USA

Palumba, Joe *Football Player*
927 Old Garth Road, Charlottesville, VA
22901 USA

Pampanini, Sylvana
Via Flaminia 322, Rome, ITALY, I-00196

Pamuk, Orhan *Writer*
Farrar Straus Giroux, 19 Union Square W,
New York, NY 10003 USA

Pan, Hong *Actor*
Omei Film Studio, Tonghui Menwai,
Chengdu City, Sichuan Province, CHINA

Panafieu, Bernard L A Cardinal *Religious
Leader*
Archdiocese, 14 Place du Colonel-Edon,
Marseille Cedex 07, 13284, FRANCE

Pancholi, Aditya *Actor, Bollywood*
Hattes Bungalow, Gandhigram Road Juhu,
Mumbai, MS 400049, INDIA

Panday, Basdeo *Prime Minister*
Premier's Office, Eric Williams Plaza, Port
of Spain, TRINIDAD & TOBAGO

Pandey, Chunky *Actor, Bollywood*
1 A/B Monisha Apartments, St Andrews
Road Bandra, Mumbai, MS 400050,
INDIA

Pandian *Actor*
185/6 Bharatidasan Street, Baskar Colony,
Chennai, TN 600 093, INDIA

Pandian, Arun *Actor*
2A Bajaj Apartment, Nandanam, Chennai,
TN 600 035, INDIA

Panetierre, Hayden *Actor*
Brookside Artists Management (LA), 450 N
Roxbury Dr Fl 4, Beverly Hills, CA 90210
USA

Panetta, Leon E *Government Official*
15 Panetta Road, Carmel Valley, CA
93924 USA

Panettiere, Hayden *Actor*
Brookside Artists Management (LA), 450 N
Roxbury Dr Fl 4, Beverly Hills, CA 90210
USA

Pang, May
1619 Third Ave. #9D, New York, NY
10128

Panhofer, Walter *Musician*
Erdbergstr 35/9, Vienna, 1030, AUSTRIA

Panic, Milan *Prime Minister, Business
Person*
1050 Arden Road, Pasadena, CA 91106
USA

Panichas, George A *Writer*
PO Box AB, College Park, MD 20741
USA

Panish, Morton B *Misc*
9 Persimmon Way, Springfield, NJ 07081
USA

Pankey, Irv *Football Player*
348 Walker St, Aberdeen, MD 21001 USA

Pankin, Stuart *Actor*
1288 Bienevenda Ave, Pacific Palisades,
CA 90272 USA

Pankow, James *Musician*
3874 Puerco Canyon Road, Malibu, CA
90265 USA

Pankow, John *Actor*
Gersh Agency, 232 North Canon Dr,
Beverly Hills, CA 90210 USA

Panni, Marcello *Composer*
3 Piazza Borghese, Rome, 00186, ITALY

Panoff, Robert *Engineer*
1140 Connecticut Ave NW, Washington,
DC 20036 USA

Panofsky, Wolfgang K H *Physicist*
25671 Chapin Road, Los Altos Hills, CA
94022 USA

Panov, Valery M *Ballerina*
Carson Office, 119 W 57th St, #903, New
York, NY 10019 USA

Pantoliano, Joe (Joey Pants) *Actor*
United Talent Agency (UTA), 9560
Wilshire Blvd, Beverly Hills, CA 90212
USA

Pantotiano, Joe *Actor*
600 Willow Ave, #3, Hoboken, NJ 07030
USA

Panza dl Blumo, Giuseppe *Misc*
PO Box 3183, Lugano, 6901,
SWITZERLAND

Paola *Royalty*
Koninklijk Palais, Rue de Brederode,
Brussels, 1000, BELGIUM

Paolozzi, Eduardo L *President*
107 Dovehouse, London, SW3 6JZ,
UNITED KINGDOM (UK)

Papa, Tom *Comedian*
William Morris Agency (WMA-LA), 1
William Morris Pl, Beverly Hills, CA
90212 USA

Papa Doo Run Run
PO Box 255, Cuperino, CA 95015-0255

Papa Roach *Music Group*
Creative Artists Agency LCC (CAA-LA),
9830 Wilshire Blvd, Beverly Hills, CA
90212 USA

Papadopoulos, Tassos *President*
Presidential Palace, 5 Ioannis Ceridos St,
Nicosia, CYPRUS

Papamichael, Phedon M *Cinematographer*
Innovative Artists, 1505 10th St, Santa
Monica, CA 90401 USA

Papas, Irene *Actor*
38 Xenokratous St, Athens, 106 76,
GREECE

Papathanassiou, Aspassia *Actor*
38 Xenokratous St, Athens, 106 76,
GREECE

Papazian, Marty *Actor*
Chasin Agency, The, 8899 Beverly Blvd
#716, Los Angeles, CA 90048 USA

Papert, Seymour *Mathematician*
Massachusetts Institute of Technology, 20
Ames St, Cambridge, MA 02142 USA

Papis, Max *Race Car Driver*
30212 Tomas, Rancho Santa Margarita,
CA 92688 USA

Pappalardo, Salvatore Cardinal *Religious
Leader*
Arcibescovado, Via Matteo Bonello 2,
Palermo, 90134, ITALY

Pappano, Antonio
Royal Opera House, Covent Garden, Bow
St, London, WC2E 9DD, UNITED
KINGDOM (UK)

Pappas, George *Bowler*
21108 Blakely Shores Dr, Cornelius, NC
28031 USA

Pappas, Milt *Athlete*
RR 1 Box 154, Beecher, IL 60401

Pappas, Milton S (Milt) *Baseball Player*
502 Highlington Court, Beecher, IL 60401
USA

Pappenheimer, John R *Physicist*
66 Sherman St, #113, Cambridge, MA
02140 USA

Pappin, James J (Jim) *Hockey Player*
48947 Greasewood Lane, Palm Desert,
CA 92260 USA

Paquin, Anna *Actor*
The Firm, 9100 Wilshire Blvd, #100W,
Beverly Hills, CA 90210 USA

Paradis, Vanessa *Model, Musician, Actor*
14 Rue Lincoln, Paris, 75008, FRANCE

Paradise, Bob *Hockey Player*
1303 Beechwood Place, Saint Paul, MN
55116 USA

Parado, Alejandra *Actor*
Gabriel Blanco Iglesias (Mexico), Rio
Balsas 35-32, Colonia Cuauhtemoc, DF,
06500, Mexico

Parahia, Murray *Musician*
I M G Artists, 420 W 45th St, New York,
NY 10036 USA

Paraseghian, Ara
51767 Oakbrook Ct, Granger, IN 46539-
8731

Parazaider, Walter *Musician*
Front Line Mgmt, 8900 Wilshire Blvd,
#300, Beverly Hills, CA 90211 USA

Parazynski, Scott E *Astronaut*
2015 Wroxton Road, Houston, TX 77005
USA

Parcells, Duane C (Bill) *Football Coach*
Dallas Cowboys, 1 Cowboys Parkway,
Irving, TX 75063 USA

Pardee, Arthur B *Misc*
15 Buzzards Bay Ave, Woods Hole, MA
02543 USA

Pardee, Jack *Coach*
PO Box 272, Grause, TX 77857-0272

Pardee, John P (Jack) *Football Player, Football Coach*
Hawks Hill Ranch, PO Box 272, Gause, TX 77857 USA

Pardes, Herbert *Misc*
15 Claremont Ave, #93, New York, NY 10027 USA

Pardo, Don *Commentator*
NBC-TV, News Dept, 30 Rockefeller Plaza, New York, NY 10112 USA

Pardo, Jimmy *Comedian*
OmniPop Inc (LA), 10700 Ventura Blvd Fl 2, Studio City, CA 91604 USA

Pardue, Kip *Actor*
United Entertainment, 8436 W 3rd St, #650, Los Angeles, CA 90048 USA

Pare, Jessica *Actor*
3 Arts Entertainment (NY), 451 Greenwich St Fl 7, New York, NY 10013 USA

Pare, Michael *Actor*
Chasin Agency, The, 8899 Beverly Blvd #716, Los Angeles, CA 90048 USA

Paredes, Marisa *Actor*
Alsira Maroto Garcia, Gran Via 63, #3 Izda, Madrid, 28013, SPAIN

Parekh, Asha *Actor, Bollywood*
Azad Road, Juhu, Mumbai, MS 400049, INDIA

Parent, Bernard M (Bernie) *Hockey Player*
535 Route 38, Cherry Hill, NJ 08002 USA

Parent, Gail
2001 Mandeville Canyon, Los Angeles, CA 90024

Parent, Monique *Actor, Model*
PO Box 3458, Ventura, CA 93006 USA

Paret, Peter *Historian, Writer*
Institute for Advanced Studies, Historical Studies School, Princeton, NJ 08540 USA

Paretsky, Sara N *Writer*
1504 East 53rd Street, #302, Chicago, IL 60615 USA

Parfit, Derek A *Misc*
All Souls College, Philosophy Dept, Oxford, OX1 4AL, UNITED KINGDOM (UK)

Parfitt, Judy
8383 Wilshire Blvd. #550, Beverly Hills, CA 90211-2404

Parillaud, Anne *Actor*
Artmedia, 20 Ave Rapp, Paris, 75007, FRANCE

Parilli, Vito (Babe) *Football Player, Football Coach*
8060 E Girard Ave, #218, Denver, CO 80231 USA

Paris, Brandon *Actor*
Official International fan Club, PO Box 16045, 1199 Lynn Valley Road, North Vancouver, BC V7J 2P0, Canada

Paris, Johnny *Musician*
Atila Records, 195 Hannum Ave, Rossford, OH 43460 USA

Paris, Mica *Musician*
Richard Walters, 1800 Argyle Ave, #408, Los Angeles, CA 90028 USA

Paris, Twila *Musician, Songwriter*
Proper Mgmt, PO Box 150867, Nashville, TN 37215 USA

Parise, Louis *Misc*
National Maritime Union, 1125 15th St NW, Washington, DC 20005 USA

Parise, Robert L *Basketball Player*
20 Stonybrook Road, #1, Framingham, MA 01702 USA

Parise, Ronald A *Astronaut*
15419 Good Hope Road, Silver Spring, MD 20905 USA

Parise, Vanessa *Actor*
Lara Rosenstock Management, 8371 Blackburn Ave #1, Los Angeles, CA 90048 USA

Parisot, Dean *Director*
3 Arts Entertainment Inc, 9460 Wilshire Blvd Fl 7, Beverly Hills, CA 90212 USA

Parizeau, Jacques *Politician*
88 Grand Alle Est, Quebec, PQ G1A 1A2, CANADA

Park, Alyssa *Musician*
Columbia Artists Mgmt Inc, 165 W 57th St, New York, NY 10019 USA

Park, Chan Ho *Baseball Player*
2400 Hollister Terrace, Glendale, CA 91206 USA

Park, Charles R *Physicist*
5325 Stanford Dr, Nashville, TN 37215 USA

Park, D Bradford (Brad) *Hockey Player, Coach*
20 Stanley Road, Lynnfield, MA 01940 USA

Park, Grace *Golfer*
Gaylord Sports Mgmt, 14646 N Kierland Blvd, #230, Scottdale, AZ 85254 USA

Park, Linda *Actor*
SDB Partners Inc, 1801 Ave of the Stars #902, Los Angeles, CA 90067 USA

Park, Linkin *Musician*
Firm, The, 9465 Wilshire Blvd, Beverly Hills, CA 90212 USA

Park, Merle F *Ballerina*
Royal Ballet School, 144 Talgarth Road, London, W14 9DE, UNITED KINGDOM (UK)

Park, Nicholas W (Nick) *Animator, Director*
Aardvark Animation, Gas Ferry Road, Bristol, B51 6UN, UNITED KINGDOM (UK)

Park, Ray *Actor*
Gersh Agency, The (NY), 41 Madison Ave Fl 33, New York, NY 10010 USA

Park, Reg
Box 1002-Morningside 2057 Sandton, Gauteng, SOUTH AFRICA

Park, Steve *Race Car Driver*
1675 Coddle Creek Highway, Mooresville, NC 28115 USA

Parke, Dorothy *Actor*
AKA Talent Agency, 6310 San Vicente Blvd #200, Los Angeles, CA 90048 USA

Parke, Evan Dexter *Actor*
Essential Talent Management, 6399 Wilshire Blvd #400, Los Angeles, CA 90048 USA

Parkening, Christopher *Musician*
IMG Artists, 420 W 45th St, New York, NY 10036 USA

Parker, Alan W *Director*
Parker Film Co, Pinewood Studios, Iver Heath, Bucks, SL0 0NH, UNITED KINGDOM (UK)

Parker, Andrea *Actor*
Stan Rosenfield & Associates Ltd, 2029 Century Park East, Suite 1190, Los Angeles, CA 90067 USA

Parker, Anthony *Basketball Player*
Orlando Magic, Waterhouse Center, 8701 Maitland Summit Blvd, Orlando, FL 32810 USA

Parker, Bob *Skier*
408 Camino Don Miguel, Santa Fe, NM 87505 USA

Parker, Brant J *Cartoonist*
901 Glenwood Blvd, Waynesboro, VA 22980 USA

Parker, Bruce C *Biologist*
841 Hutchson Dr, Blacksburg, VA 24060 USA

Parker, Caryl Mack *Musician*
Scream Marketing, PO Box 120053, Nashville, TN 37212 USA

Parker, Chris *Actor*
Elstree Centre, Clarendon Road, Borehamwood, Herts, WD6 1JF, UK

Parker, Christopher *Actor*
Shepherd Mgmt, 13 Radnor Walk, London, SW3 4BP, UNITED KINGDOM (UK)

Parker, Clarence M (Ace) *Football Player*
210 Snead's Fairway, Portsmouth, VA 23701 USA

Parker, Clay
162 Willow Creek Dr., Soddy Daisy, TN 37379-4270

Parker, Corey *Actor*
Muse Mgmt, 429 Santa Monica Blvd #520, Santa Monica, CA 90401 USA

Parker, Craig *Actor*
International Creative Management (ICM-LA), 8942 Wilshire Blvd, Beverly Hills, CA 90211 USA

Parker, David G (Dave) *Baseball Player*
4036 Oak Tree Court, Loveland, OH 45140 USA

Parker, Denise *Athlete*
4801 Wallace Lane, Salt Lake City, UT 84117 USA

Parker, Eleanor *Actor*
2195 La Paz Way, Palm Springs, CA 92262 USA

Parker, Eugene N *Physicist*
1323 Evergreen Road, Homewood, IL 60430 USA

Parker, Fess *Actor, Musician*
Fess Parker Winery, PO Box 908, Los Olivos, CA 93441 USA

Parker, Franklin *Writer*
Western Carolina University, Education &
Psychology Dept, Cullowhee, NC 28723
USA

Parker, George M *Misc*
Glass Workers Union, 1440 S Byme Road,
Toledo, OH 43614 USA

Parker, Jack D (Jackie) *Football Player*
10623 65 Ave NW, Edmonton, AB T6H
1V5, CANADA

Parker, James T (Jim) *Football Player*
1902 Cedar Circle Dr, Catonsville, MD
21228 USA

Parker, Jameson *Actor*
Stone Manners, 6500 Wilshire Blvd, #550,
Los Angeles, CA 90048 USA

Parker, Jim
5448 Wingborne Ct, Columbia, MD
21045

Parker, Lara *Actor*
PO Box 1254, Topanga, CA 90290 USA

Parker, Lu
12222 Vance Jackson Rd. #734, San
Antonio, TX 78230-5941

Parker, Maceo *Musician*
Central Entertainment Services, 123
Harvard Ave, Staten Island, NY 10301
USA

Parker, Mary-Louise *Actor*
William Morris Agency, 1325 Ave of
Americas, New York, NY 10019 USA

Parker, Molly *Actor*
Macklam Feldman Mgmt, 1505 W 2nd
Ave, #200, Vancouver, BC V6H 3Y4,
CANADA

Parker, Nathanial
10100 Santa Monica Blvd. #2500, Los
Angeles, CA 90067

Parker, Nathaniel *Actor*
Markham & Froggatt, Julian House, 4
Windmill St, London, W1P 1HF, UNITED
KINGDOM (UK)

Parker, Nicole Ari *Actor*
Gersh Agency, The (NY), 41 Madison Ave
Fl 33, New York, NY 10010 USA

Parker, Noelle
9300 Wilshire Blvd. #555, Beverly Hills,
CA 90212

Parker, Oliver
76 Oxford St., London, ENGLAND, W1N
0AX

Parker, Olivia *Photographer*
Robert Klein, 38 Newbury St, #400,
Boston, MA 02116 USA

Parker, Paula Jai *Actor*
3 Arts Entertainment Inc, 9460 Wilshire
Blvd Fl 7, Beverly Hills, CA 90212 USA

Parker, Ray Jr *Musician*
Performers of the World, 8901 Melrose
Ave, #200, West Hollywood, CA 90069
USA

Parker, Robert A R *Astronaut*
Jet Propulsion Laboratory, 4800 Oak
Grove Blvd, Pasadena, CA 91109 USA

Parker, Robert B *Writer*
555 W 57th St, #1230, New York, NY
10019 USA

Parker, Sarah Jessica *Actor*
Creative Artists Agency, 9830 Wilshire
Blvd, Beverly Hills, CA 90212 USA

Parker, Scott *Motorcycle Racer*
6096 Grand Blanc Road, Swartz Creek,
MI 48473 USA

Parker, T Jefferson *Writer*
William Morris Agency, 151 El Camino
Dr, Beverly Hills, CA 90212 USA

Parker, Tony *Basketball Player*
San Antonio Spurs, Alamodome, 1 SBC
Center, San Antonio, TX 78219 USA

Parker, Trey *Writer, Animator*
6255 Sunset Blvd, #908, Los Angeles, CA
90028 USA

Parker-Bowles, Camilla *Misc*
Clarence House, Stable Yard Gate,
London, SW1, UNITED KINGDOM (UK)

Parkhill, Barry *Basketball Player*
3429 Cesford Grange, Keswick, VA 22947
USA

Parkhurst, Heather
8383 Wilshire Blvd. #954, Beverly Hills,
CA 90211

Parkhurst, Heather Elizabeth *Actor*
8491 Sunset Blvd, #440, West
Hollywood, CA 90069 USA

Parkins, Barbara
6399 Wilshire Blvd. #414, Los Angeles,
CA 90048

Parkinson, Bradford W *Business Person*
2780 Valley Circle, Meadow Vista, CA
95722 USA

Parkinson, Dian *Entertainer, Model*
Purrfect Productions, PO Box 777,
Pompano Beach, FL 33061 USA

Parkinson, Michael
58 Queen Anne St., London, ENGLAND,
W1M ODX

Parkinson, Robert
20 Kingston Lane Teddington, Middlesex,
ENGLAND

Parkinson, Robert L Jr *Business Person*
Abbott Laboratories, 100 Abbott Park
Road, Abbott Park, IL 60064 USA

Parkinson, Roger P *Publisher*
Minneapolis Star Tribune, 425 Portland
Ave, Minneapolis, MN 55488 USA

Parks, Andrew
1830 Grace Ave., Los Angeles, CA 90028

Parks, David W (Dave) *Football Player*
6629 Southpoint Dr, Dallas, TX 75248
USA

Parks, Maxie *Track Athlete*
4545 E Norwich Ave, Fresno, CA 93726
USA

Parks, Michael *Actor*
11684 Ventura Blvd, #476, Studio City,
CA 91604 USA

Parks, Michael *Editor*
Los Angeles Times, Editorial Dept, 202 W
1st, Los Angeles, CA 90012 USA

Parks, Rosa L *Social Activist*
814 Lomita Ave, Flint, MI 48505 USA

Parks, Suzan-Lori *Misc*
William Morris Agency, 151 El Camino
Dr, Beverly Hills, CA 90212 USA

Parks, Van Dyke *Composer*
267 S Arden Blvd, Los Angeles, CA 90004
USA

Parks, Wally *Misc*
National Hot Rod Assn, 2023 Financial
Way, Glendora, CA 91741 USA

Parmenter, Charles S *Misc*
Indiana University, Chemistry Dept,
Bloomington, IN 47405 USA

Parmet, Philip *Cinematographer*
1080 Hayworth Ave, Los Angeles, CA
90035 USA

Parnell, Chris *Actor*
Mosaic Media Group, 9200 Sunset Blvd Fl
10, Los Angeles, CA 90069 USA

Parnell, Lee Roy *Musician*
PO Box 23451, Nashville, TN 37202 USA

Parnell, LeRoy
PO Box 23451, Nashville, TN 37202

Parnell, Mel
700 Turquoise St., New Orleans, LA
70124

Parnell, Melvin L (Mel) *Baseball Player*
700 Turquoise St, New Orleans, LA 70124
USA

Parnell, Peter *Writer*
United Talent Agency (UTA), 9560
Wilshire Blvd, Beverly Hills, CA 90212
USA

Parnevik, Jesper *Golfer*
17553 SE Conch Bar Ave, Jupiter, FL
33469 USA

Parr, Carolyn Miller *Judge*
US Tax Court, 400 2nd St NW,
Washington, DC 20217 USA

Parr, Jerry S
4529 38th St NW, Washington, DC 20016
USA

Parr, Ralph S *War Hero*
14831 Heather Valley Way, Houston, TX
77062 USA

Parr, Robert G *Misc*
701 Kenmore Road, Chapel Hill, NC
27514 USA

Parra, Derek *Speed Skater*
US Speedskating, PO Box 450639,
Westlake, OH 44145 USA

Parrett, William *Business Person*
Deloitte Touche Tohmatsu, 433 Country
Club Road, New Canaan, CT 06840 USA

Parris, Fred *Musician*
Paramount Entertainment, PO Box 12, Far
Hills, NJ 07931 USA

Parrish, Bernard J (Bernie) *Football Player*
1633 NE 18th Place, Gainesville, FL
32609 USA

Parrish, Lance M *Baseball Player*
5141 Via Samuel, Yorba Linda, CA 92886
USA

Parrish, Larry A *Baseball Player*
234 Green Haven Lane W, Dundee, FL
33838 USA

Parros, Peter *Actor*
PO Box 241, Boonton, NJ 07005 USA

Parrot, Andrew
Jonathan Wentworth, 10 Fiske Place,
#530, Mount Vernon, NY 10550 USA

Parrott, Ian
Abermad nr. Aberystwyth, Dyfed Wales, ENGLAND, SY 23 4RS

Parry, Craig *Golfer*
Int'l Mgmt Group, 1 Erieview Plaza, 1360 E 9th St #1300, Cleveland, OH 44114 USA

Parry, Ken *Actor*
Billy Marsh Drama Ltd, 174-178 North Gower Street, London, NW1 2NB, United Kingdom

Parry, Robert T *Financier*
2 Ellis Court, Lafayette, CA 94549 USA

Parseghian, Ara *Sportscaster, Football Coach*
51767 Oakbridge Court, Granger, IN 46539 USA

Parseghian, Gregory *Business Person*
Federal Home Loan Mortgage, 8200 Jones Branch Dr, McLean, VA 22102 USA

Parshall, George W *Misc*
2504 Delaware Ave, Wilmington, DE 19806 USA

Parsky, Gerald L *Attorney General*
Aurora Capital Partners, 1800 Century Park East, Los Angeles, CA 90067 USA

Parsons, Alan *Musician*
Agency Group Ltd, 1775 Broadway, #430, New York, NY 10019 USA

Parsons, Benny *Race Car Driver*
2049 Country Club Dr, Port Orange, FL 32128 USA

Parsons, David *Choreographer*
Parsons Dance Foundation, 476 Broadway, New York, NY 10013 USA

Parsons, Estelle *Actor*
924 West End Ave, #T5, New York, NY 10025 USA

Parsons, John T *Inventor*
1456 Brigadoon Court, Traverse City, MI 49686 USA

Parsons, Karyn *Actor*
10351 Santa Monica Blvd, #211, Los Angeles, CA 90025 USA

Parsons, Nicholas *Actor*
Susan Shaper, 174/178 N Gower St, London, NW1 2NB, UNITED KINGDOM (UK)

Parsons, Phil *Race Car Driver*
18801 Windy Point Dr, Cornelius, NC 28031 USA

Parsons, Richard D *Business Person, Financier*
Time Warner Inc, 75 Rockefeller Plaza, New York, NY 10019 USA

Part, Arvo *Composer*
Universal Editions, Warwick House, 9 Warrick St, London, W1R 5RA, UNITED KINGDOM (UK)

Partee, Barbara H *Educator*
50 Hobart Lane, Amherst, MA 01002 USA

Parton, Dolly *Musician, Songwriter, Actor*
Dollywood, 1020 Dollywood Ln, Pigeon Ford, TN 37683 USA

Parton, Stella *Musician*
PO Box 120871, Nashville, TN 37212 USA

Partridge, Derek
96 Broadway Bexley Heath, Kent, ENGLAND, DA6 7DE

Partridge, John A *Architect*
20 Old Pye St, Westminster, London, SW1, UNITED KINGDOM (UK)

Parvanov, Georgi *President*
President's Office, 2 Dondukov Blvd, Sofia, 1123, BULGARIA

Pasanella, Giovanni *Architect*
Pasanella & Klein, 330 W 42nd St, New York, NY 10036 USA

Pasanella, Marco *Designer*
Pasanella Co, 45 W 18th St, New York, NY 10011 USA

Pasarell, Charles *Tennis Player*
78200 Miles Ave, Indian Wells, CA 92210 USA

Pascal, Adam *Actor*
Paradigm (LA), 10100 Santa Monica Blvd, Fl 25, Los Angeles, CA 90067 USA

Pascal, Francoise
89 Riverview Gardens, London, ENGLAND, SW12 9RA

Pascal, Olivia
Merzstr. 14, Munich, GERMANY, D-81679

Paschall, Jim *Race Car Driver*
RR 2 Box 450, Denton, NC 27239 USA

Paschke, Melanie *Track Athlete*
Asseweg 2, Braunschweig, 38124, GERMANY

Pasco, Richard *Actor*
Michael Whitehall, 125 Gloucester Road, London, SW7 4TE, UNITED KINGDOM (UK)

Pascoal, Hermeto *Musician*
Brasil Universo Prod, RVN Vitor Guisard 209, Rio de Janerio, 21832, BRAZIL

Pascual, Camilo *Baseball Player*
7741 SW 32nd St, Miami, FL 33155 USA

Pascual, Luis *Director*
Theatre de l'Europe, 1 Place Paul Claudel, Paris, 75006, FRANCE

Pascual, Mercedes *Biologist*
University of Michigan, Ecology & Biology Dept, Ann Arbor, MI 48109 USA

Pasdar, Adrian *Actor*
International Creative Mgmt, 8942 Wilshire Blvd, #219, Beverly Hills, CA 90211 USA

Pasik, Mario *Actor*
Telefe - Argentina, Pavon 2444 (C1248AAT), Buenos Aires, ARGENTINA

Pasillas, Jose *Musician*
ArtistDirect, 109000 Wilshire Blvd, #1400, Los Angeles, CA 90024 USA

Paskai, Laszio Cardinal *Religious Leader*
Uri Utca 62, Budapest, 1014, HUNGARY

Pasmore, E J Victor *Artist*
Dar Gamri, Gudja, MALTA

Pasqua, Dan *Baseball Player*
45 Silo Ridge Rd E, Orland Park, IL 60467 USA

Pasquale, Steven *Actor*
Brookside Artists Management (LA), 450 N Roxbury Dr Fl 4, Beverly Hills, CA 90210 USA

Pasqualoni, Paul *Football Coach*
Syracuse University, Athletic Dept, Syracuse, NY 13244 USA

Pasquin, John R *Filmmaker, Director, Producer*
Creative Artists Agency, 9830 Wilshire Blvd, Beverly Hills, CA 90212 USA

Passarelli, Pasquale *Wrestler*
Ander Froschlache 23, Munster, 4400, GERMANY

Passer, Ivan *Director*
Creative Road Corp, 8281 Melrose Ave, #300, Los Angeles, CA 90046 USA

Passions, The
141 Dunbar Ave., Fords, NJ 08863

Passmore, John A *Misc*
6 Jansz Crescent, Manuka, ACT, 2603, AUSTRALIA

Paster, Jessica *Stylist*
Luxe, 6442 Santa Monica Blvd #200-B, Los Angeles, CA 90038 USA

Pasternak, Michael *Actor*
Marc Bass Agency Inc, 415 N Crescent Dr #320, Beverly Hills, CA 90210 USA

Pasternak, Reagan *Actor*
Noble Caplan Agency, 1260 Yonge St Fl 2, Toronto ON, M4T 1W6, CANADA

Pastor, Amy Wynn *Actor*
Discover Networks, One Discovery Pl, Silver Spring, MD 20910-3354

Pastore, Vincent *Actor*
McGowan Management, 8733 W Sunset Blvd #103, W Hollywood, CA 90069 USA

Pastorell, Robert *Actor*
2751 Holly Ridge Dr, Los Angeles, CA 90068 USA

Pastorini, Darite A (Dan) Jr *Football Player*
10355 Old Stagecoach Road, Chappell Hill, TX 77426 USA

Pastrana, Arango Andres *President*
Palacio de Narino, Plaza de Bolivar, Carrera 8A, Bogota, DE COLUMBIA

Pataki, Governor George E *Politician*
State Capitol, Albany, NY 12224 USA

Patane, Giuseppe
Holbeinstr 6, Munich, 81679, GERMANY

Patasse, Ange-Felix *President*
Palais de Renaissance, Bangui, CENTRAL AFRICAN REPUBLIC

Patat, Frederic *Misc*
Faculte de Medecine, 2 Bis Blvd Tonnelle, Tours Cedex, 37032, FRANCE

Patchett, Ann *Writer*
Harcourt Brace, 525 B St, San Diego, CA 92101 USA

Pate, Jerry *Golfer*
5 Hyde Park Road, Pensacola, FL 32503 USA

Pate, Michael *Actor*
OAM, 130 Jenson Road, Wadalba, NSW, 2259, AUSTRALIA

Patekar, Nana *Actor, Bollywood*
304 Sheetal Apna Ghar Society, Samarth Nagar Andheri, Mumbai, MS 400053, INDIA

Patel, Anuradha *Actor, Bollywood*
1001D Abhishek Aptartments, Juhu Versova Road Andheri, Mumbai, MS 400058, INDIA

Patel, C Kumar N *Inventor*
1171 Roberto Lane, Los Angeles, CA 90077 USA

Patel, Piyush *Business Person*
Cabletron Systems, 35 Industrial Way, Rochester, NY 14614 USA

Patera, John A (Jack) *Football Player, Football Coach*
PO Box 812, Cle Elum, WA 98922 USA

Patera, Ken *Athlete*
6932 Stratford Road, Saint Paul, MN 55125 USA

Patera, Pavel *Hockey Player*
Minnesota Wild, Xcel Enegy Arena, 175 Kellogg Blvd W, Saint Paul, MN 55102 USA

Paterno, Joe
830 McKee St., State College, PA 16803

Paterno, Joseph V (Joe) *Football Coach*
830 McKee St, State College, PA 16803 USA

Paterson, Bill *Actor*
Kerry Gardner, 15 Kensington High St, London, W8 5NP, UNITED KINGDOM (UK)

Patillo, Maria
6300 Wilshire Blvd. #2110, Los Angeles, CA 90048

Patinkin, Mandy *Actor, Musician*
200 W 90th St, New York, NY 10024 USA

Patitz, Tatjana *Model*
Elite Model Management, 111 E 22nd St #200, New York, NY 10010

Patkau, John *Architect*
Patkau Architects, 560 Beaty St, #L110, Vancouver, BC V6B 2L3, CANADA

Patrese, Ricardo *Race Car Driver*
Via Umberto 1, Padova, 35100, ITALY

Patriarco, Earie *Opera Singer*
I C M Artists, 40 W 57th St, New York, NY 10019 USA

Patric, Jason *Actor*
501 21st Place, Santa Monica, CA 90402 USA

Patrick, Craig *Hockey Player, Coach*
Pittsburgh Penguins, Mellon Arena, 66 Mario Lemieux Place, Pittsburgh, PA 15219 USA

Patrick, Dan *Sportscaster*
ESPN-TV, Sports Dept ESPN Plaza, 935 Middle St, Bristol, CT 06010 USA

Patrick, Mary Anthony
56 Copsterhill Rd.Oldham, Manchester, ENGLAND

Patrick, Nicholas J M *Astronaut*
15923 Mesa Verde Dr, Houston, TX 77059 USA

Patrick, Pat *Misc*
Patrick Racing, 8431 Green Town Road, #400, Indianapolis, IN 46234 USA

Patrick, Richard *Musician*
Filter, Warner Bros Records, 3300 Warner Blvd, Burbank, CA 91510

Patrick, Robert *Actor*
2700 La Cuesta Dr, Los Angeles, CA 90046 USA

Patrick, Ruth *Educator*
Academy of Natural Sciences, 19th & Parkway, Philadelphia, PA 19103 USA

Patrick, Thomas M *Business Person*
Peoples Energy Corp, 130 E Randolph Dr, Chicago, IL 60601 USA

Patrick, Tom
Heimeranstr. 51, Munich, GERMANY, D-80339

Patrone, Shana
209 10th Ave. S. #229, Nashville, TN 37230

Patten, Christopher F *Governor*
Coutts Co, Campbells Office, 440 STrand, London, WC2R 0QS, UNITED KINGDOM (UK)

Patterson, Carly *Gymnast*
Worki Gymnastics Academy, 1937 W Parker Road, Plano, TX 75023 USA

Patterson, Donald Corey *Athlete, Basketball Player*
Chicago Cubs, Wrigley Field, 1060 West Addison Street, Chicago, IL 60613 USA

Patterson, Elvis V *Football Player*
3636 Alberta St, Houston, TX 77021 USA

Patterson, Floyd *Boxer*
Box 336, Springtown, New Paltz, NY 12561 USA

Patterson, Francine G (Penny) *Misc*
Gorilla Foudation, PO Box 620-640, Woodside, CA 94062 USA

Patterson, Gary *Cartoonist*
Patterson International, 25208 Malibu Road, Malibu, CA 90265 USA

Patterson, James *Writer, Business Person*
J Walter Thompson, 466 Lexington Ave, New York, NY 10017 USA

Patterson, Jarrod *Baseball Player*
Omaha Royals, PO Box 3665, Omaha, NE 68103

Patterson, John M *Governor*
Court of Judiciary, PO Box 30155, Montgomery, AL 36103 USA

Patterson, Katerine *Writer*
70 Wildersburgh Common, Barre, VT 05641 USA

Patterson, Lorna *Actor*
23852 Pacific Coast Highway #355, Malibu, CA 90265 USA

Patterson, Michael *Financier*
JP Morgan Chase, 270 Park Ave, New York, NY 10017 USA

Patterson, Neva
2498 Mandeville Canyon Rd., Los Angeles, CA 90049

Patterson, Percival J *Prime Minister*
Prime Minister's Office, 1 Devon Road, PO Box 272, Kingston 6, JAMAICA

Patterson, Richard North *Writer*
PO Box 183, West Tisbury, MA 02575 USA

Patterson, Robert M *War Hero*
907 Ironwood Dr, Henderson, KY 42420 USA

Patterson, Ross *Actor*
Paradigm (LA), 10100 Santa Monica Blvd, Fl 25, Los Angeles, CA 90067 USA

Patterson, Scott *Actor*
Gilmore Girls, 4000 Warner Blvd, Building 2222, Burbank, CA 91522

Patti, Sandi *Music Group, Musician*
Anderson Group, 2200 Madison Square, Anderson, IN 46011 USA

Pattillo, Linda *Commentator*
Cable News Network, News Dept, 820 1st St NE, Washington, DC 20002 USA

Patton, Antoine (Big Boi) *Artist, Musician, Music Group*
William Morris Agency, 1325 Ave of Americas, New York, NY 10019 USA

Patton, Donovan *Actor*
Glasser/Black Management, 283 Cedarhurst Ave, Cedarhurst, NY 11516 USA

Patton, Mel
2312 Via Del Aguagate, Fallbrook, CA 92028

Patton, Melvin (Mel) *Track Athlete*
2312 Via Del Aguagate, Fallbrook, CA 92028 USA

Patton, Will *Actor*
520 Washington Blvd #903, Marina del Rey, CA 90292 USA

Patty, Edward
14 Ave. de Jurigoz, Lausanne, SWITZERLAND, 1006

Patty, J Edward (Budge) *Tennis Player*
La Mame, 14 Ave de Jurigoz, Lausanne, 1006, SWITZERLAND

Patty, Sandi
PO Box 2940, Anderson, IN 46018

Patulski, Walter G (Walt) *Football Player*
4899 Abbottsbury Lane, Syracuse, NY 13215 USA

Patz, Arnall *Doctor*
Johns Hopkins Hospital, Wilmer Eye Institute, 600 N Wolfe, Baltimore, MD 21287 USA

Patzaichin, Ivan *Athlete*
SC Sportiv Unirea Tricolor, Soseaua Stefan Cel Mare 9, Bucharest, ROMANIA

Patzak, PeterJosef
Schottlgasse 23, Klosterneuburg, AUSTRIA, A-3400

Patzakis, Michele *Opera Singer*
Kunstleragentur Raab & Bohrn, Plandengasse 7, Vienna, 1010, AUSTRIA

Pauk, Gyorgy *Musician*
27 Armitage Road, London, NW11, UNITED KINGDOM (UK)

Paul, Aaron *Actor*
Santaur Entertainment, 581 N Crescent Heights Blvd, Los Angeles, CA 90046 USA

Paul, Adrian *Actor*
PO Box 4593, North Hollywood, CA 91617 USA

Paul, Alan *Musician, Music Group*
Columbia/CBS Records, 1801 Century Park West, Los Angeles, CA 90067 USA

Paul, Alexandra *Actor*
Innovative Artists, 1505 10th St, Santa Monica, CA 90401 USA

Paul, Billy *Musician*
8215 Winthrop St, Philadelphia, PA
19136 USA

Paul, Christi *Commentator*
Cable News Network, News Dept, 1050
Techwood Dr NW, Atlanta, GA 30318
USA

Paul, Don Michael *Actor, Director*
United Talent Agency (UTA), 9560
Wilshire Blvd, Beverly Hills, CA 90212
USA

Paul, Henry *Musician, Music Group*
Vector Mgmt, 1607 17th Ave S, Nashville,
TN 37212 USA

Paul, Jarrad *Actor*
McGowan Management, 8733 W Sunset
Blvd #103, W Hollywood, CA 90069 USA

Paul, John Michael *Actor*
United Talent Agency (UTA), 9560
Wilshire Blvd, Beverly Hills, CA 90212
USA

Paul, Les *Musician, Inventor*
78 Deerhaven Road, Mahwah, NJ 07430
USA

Paul, Oakenfold *Musician*
PO Box 19788, London, SW15 2FT,
UNITED KINGDOM (UK)

Paul, Robert *Figure Skater*
10675 Rochester Ave, Los Angeles, CA
90024 USA

Paul, Vinnie *Musician*
Concrete Mgmt, 361 W Broadway #200,
New York, NY 10013 USA

Paul, Wolfgang *Soccer Player*
Postfach 1324, Olsberg-Bigge, 59939,
GERMANY

Paul & Paula
7251 Lowell Dr. #200, Overland Park, KS
66204

Paula, Alejandro F (Jandi) *Prime Minister*
Primier's Office, Fort Amsterdam 17,
Willemstad, NETHERLANDS ANTILLES

Paulauskas, Arturas *President*
President's Office, Gediminas 53, Vilnius,
232026, LITHUANIA

Pauley, Jane *Commentator*
Jane Pauley Show, The, NBC, 30
Rockefeller Plz, New York, NY 10012
USA

Pauls, Raymond *Musician, Music Group,*
Composer
Veidenbaum Str 41/43 #26, Riga, 226001,
LATVIA

Paulsen, Robert (Rob) *Voice Over Artist*
Sutton Barth & Vennari Inc, 145 S Fairfax
#310, Los Angeles, CA 90036 USA

Paulson, Dennis *Golfer*
1721 Aryana Dr, Encinitas, CA 92024
USA

Paulson, Richard L *Business Person*
Potlatch Corp, 601 W Riverside Ave,
Spokane, WA 99201 USA

Paulson, Sarah *Actor*
10390 Santa Monica Blvd #300, Los
Angeles, CA 90025 USA

Paultz, Billy *Basketball Player*
7049 Spout Springs Road, Flowery
Branch, GA 30542 USA

Paup, Bryce E *Football Player*
1112 Moraine Way, Green Bay, WI
54303 USA

Paupua, Tomasi *Governor, General*
Governor General's Office, Government
House, Vaiaku, Funafuti, TUVALU

Pausini, Laura *Musician*
Creative Artists Agency LCC (CAA-LA),
9830 Wilshire Blvd, Beverly Hills, CA
90212 USA

Pavan, Marisa *Actor*
4 Allee des Brouillards, Paris, 75018,
FRANCE

Pavarotti, Luciano *Opera Singer*
Stradelho Nava u 8, Modena, 41199,
ITALY

Paven, Corey
2515 McKinney #930 Box 10, Dallas, TX
75201

Pavia, Ria
3500 W. Olive Ave. #1400, Burbank, CA
91505

Pavin, Corey *Golfer*
6505 Aladdin Dr, Orlando, FL 32818 USA

Pavletic, Viaiko *President*
Presidential Palace, Pantovcak 241,
Zagreb, 10000, CROATIA

Pavlovic, Aleksandar *Basketball Player*
Utah Jazz, Delta Center, 301 W South
Temple, Salt Lake City, UT 84101 USA

Pavlow, Muriel
2 Conduit St., London, ENGLAND, W1R
9TG

Pawelczyk, James A (Jim) *Astronaut*
NASA, Johnson Space Center, 2101 NASA
Road, Houston, TX 77058 USA

Paxman, Jeremy
56 Wood Lane, London, ENGLAND, W12
7RJ

Paxon, L William (Bill) *Misc*
Akin Gump Strauss Hauer Feld, 1333
New Hampshire NW, Washington, DC
20036 USA

Paxson, Jim *Basketball Player*
Cleveland Cavaliers, Gund Arena, 1
Center Court, Cleveland, OH 44115 USA

Paxson, John *Basketball Player, Misc*
125 Boardman Court, Lake Bluff, IL 60044
USA

Paxson, Melanie *Actor*
Brady Brannon & Rich/ VOX, 6300
Wilshire Blvd, Suite 900, Los Angeles, CA
90048 USA

Paxton, Bill *Actor*
742 La Gracia, Santa Maria, CA 93455
USA

Paxton, John *Editor*
Saint Martin's Press, 175 5th Ave, New
York, NY 10010 USA

Paxton, Sara *Actor*
Coast to Coast Talent Group, 3350
Barham Blvd, Los Angeles, CA 90068
USA

Paxton, Tom *Musician, Music Group,*
Songwriter
Fleming Tamulevich Assoc, 733 N Main
St, Ann Arbor, MI 48104 USA

Payette, Julie *Astronaut*
Space Agency, Rockliffe Base, Ottawa,
ON K1A 1A1, CANADA

Paymer, David *Actor*
327 19th St, Santa Monica, CA 90402
USA

Payne, Alexander *Writer*

Payne, Alexander *Writer*
Endeavor Agency LLC (LA), 9601 Wilshire
Blvd Fl 3, Beverly Hills, CA 90210 USA

Payne, Alexaner *Writer*
Endeavor Agency LLC (LA), 9601 Wilshire
Blvd Fl 3, Beverly Hills, CA 90210 USA

Payne, Allen *Actor*
Gersh Agency, The (LA), 232 N Canon Dr,
Beverly Hills, CA 90210 USA

Payne, Anthony E *Composer*
2 Wilton Square, London, N1 3DL,
UNITED KINGDOM (UK)

Payne, Bruce *Actor*
Gilbertson-Kincaid Management, 1330
Fourth St, Santa Monica, CA 90401 USA

Payne, David N *Engineer*
Southampton University, Highfield,
Southampton, SO17 1BJ, UNITED
KINGDOM (UK)

Payne, Dougie *Musician*
Wildlife Entertainment, 21 Heathmans
Road, London, SW6 4TJ, UNITED
KINGDOM (UK)

Payne, Freda *Music Group, Musician*
Ira Okun Entertainment, 708 Palisades Dr,
Pacific Palisades, CA 90272 USA

Payne, Harry C *Educator*
Williams College, President's Office,
Williamstown, MA 01267 USA

Payne, Henry *Editor, Cartoonist*
Detroit News, Editorial Dept, 615 W
Lafayette, Detroit, MI 48226 USA

Payne, Julie *Actor*
Pakula/King & Associates, 9229 Sunset
Blvd #315, Los Angeles, CA 90069 USA

Payne, Keith *War Hero*
2 Saint Bee's Ave, Bucasia, QLD, 4740,
AUSTRALIA

Payne, Ladell *Educator*
Randolph-Macon College, President's
Office, Ashland, VA 23005 USA

Payne, Roger S *Biologist, Misc*
191 Western Road, Lincoln, MA 01773
USA

Payne, Scherrie-
433 N. Camden Dr. #400, Beverly Hills,
CA 90210

Pays, Amanda *Actor*
Personal Management Company, 425 N
Robertson Dr, Los Angeles, CA 90048
USA

Payton, Benjamin F *Educator*
Tuskegee Institute, President's Office,
Tuskegee, AL 36088 USA

Payton, Christian *Actor*
William Morris Agency (WMA-LA), 1
William Morris Pl, Beverly Hills, CA
90212 USA

Payton, Gary *Basketball Player*
14003 SE 43rd St, Bellevue, WA 98006
USA

Payton, Gary E *Astronaut*
10140 Community Lane, Fairfax Station, VA 22039 USA

Payton, Melvin *Basketball Player*
17310 River Ave, Noblesville, IN 46060 USA

Payton, Nicholas *Musician*
Management Ark, 116 Village Blvd #200, Princeton, NJ 08540 USA

Pazienda, Vinnie
64 Waterman Ave., Cranston, RI 02910

Pazienza, Vinny *Boxer*
65 Waterman Ave, Cranston, RI 02910 USA

PC Quest
PO Box 720423, Norma[...]
4310

Peace, Our Lady *Musician*
Little Big Man Booking, Li[...]
Bldg, 155 6th Avenue, 6th [...]
York, NY 10013 USA

Peace, Terry *Actor*
PO Box 74, Allison Park, PA[...]

Peaches & Herb
1560 Broadway #1308, New Y[...]
10036

Peacock, Andrew S *Government [...]*
30 Monomeath Ave, Canterbury, Vi[...]
3126, AUSTRALIA

Peacocke, Arthur R *Misc*
Society of Ordained Scientists, St Mark Rectory, 11 Summer, Augusta, ME 0433[...] USA

Peake, Don *Musician*
Working Artists Agency, 13525 Ventura Blvd, Sherman Oaks, CA

Peake, James B *General*
Sergeon General US Army, 5109 Leesburg Pike, Falls Church, VA 22041 USA

Peaker, E J *Actor*
4935 Densmore Ave, Encino, CA 91436 USA

Peaks, Clarence *Football Player*
Creekside Apartments, 2500 Knights Road #3-2, Bensalem, PA 19020 USA

Pearce, Guy *Actor*
Shanahan Mgmt, PO Box 1509, Darlinghurst, NSW, 1300, AUSTRALIA

Pearce, Jacqueline *Actor*
Rhubarb Personal Mgmt, 6 Langley St #41, London, WC2H 9JA, UNITED KINGDOM (UK)

Pearce, Richard I *Director*
Bauer Co, 9465 Wilshire Blvd, Beverly Hills, CA 90212 USA

Pearl Jam *Musician*
Creative Artists Agency LCC (CAA-LA), 9830 Wilshire Blvd, Beverly Hills, CA 90212 USA

Pearlman, Rhea *Actor*
International Creative Management (ICM-LA), 8942 Wilshire Blvd, Beverly Hills, CA 90211 USA

Pearlstein, Philip *Artist*
361 W 36th St, New York, NY 10018 USA

Pearlstine, Norman *Editor*
Time Warner Inc, Magazines Division, Rockefeller Plaza, New York, NY 10020 USA

Pears, David F *Misc*
7 Sandford Road, Littlemore, Oxford, OX4 4PU, UNITED KINGDOM (UK)

Pearson, Albie
54-522 Shoal Creek, La Quinta, CA 92253

Pearson, Corey *Actor*
Original Film, 2045 S Barrington Ave, Los Angeles, CA 90025 USA

Pearson, David
PO B[...] [...]305

[...] [...]5052

[...] [...]2

[...] [...]ew

[...] [...]1406

[...] [...]n

[...] [...]vd

[...]es,

Peck, Josh *Actor*
Metropolitan Talent Agency (MTA), 4526 Wilshire Blvd, Los Angeles, CA 90010 USA

Peck, M Scott *Writer*
RR1, New Preston Marble Bliss Road, Washington Depot, CT 06793 USA

Peck, Tom
PO Box 249, McConnellsburg, PA 17233

Peeler, Anthony *Basketball Player*
Minnesota Timberwolves, Target Center, 600 1st Avenue North, Minneapolis, MN 55403 USA

Peeples, Nia *Actor*
Innovative Artists (LA), 1505 Tenth St, Santa Monica, CA 90401 USA

Peet, Amanda *Actor*
Management 360, 9111 Wilshire Blvd, Beverly Hills, CA 90210 USA

Peet, Lizzie *Actor*
952 Maltman Avenue, Suite 108, Los Angeles, CA 90026 USA

Peete, Rodney *Athlete, Football Player*
The HollyRod Foundation, 9171 Wilshire Blvd, Suite 440, Beverly Hills, CA 90210 USA

Peggy, Baby (Montgomery)
7220 Durango Circle, Carlsbad, CA 92008

Pei, I M
600 Madison Ave, New York, NY 10022 USA

Peirce, Kimberly Ane (Kim) *Director, Producer, Writer, Editor*
Creative Artists Agency LCC (CAA-LA), 9830 Wilshire Blvd, Beverly Hills, CA 90212 USA

Peirse, Sarah *Actor*
Peters Fraser & Dunlop (PFD - UK), Drury House, 34-43 Russell St, London, WC2 B5, UNITED KINGDOM (UK)

Pelaez, Juan *Actor*
Televisa, Blvd Adolfo Lopez Mateos 232, Colonia San Angel INN, DF, CP 01060, MEXICO

Peldon, Ashley
PO Box 57593, Sherman Oaks, CA 91403

Peldon, Courtney *Actor*
Binder & Associates, 1465 Lindacrest Dr, Beverly Hills, CA 90210 USA

Pele *Athlete, Soccer Player*
Rua Riachuelo 121-3, Andar-Fones 34-1633/35, Santos SP, Brazil

Pelikan, Lisa
PO Box 57593, Sherman Oaks, CA 91403

Pell, Claybourne *Ex-Senator*
3425 Prospect St NW, Washington, DC 20007-3219 USA

Pellegrini, Bob
567 Roslaire Dr., Hummelstown, PA 17036

Pellegrini, Margaret
5018 N. 61st Ave., Glendale, AZ 85301

Pellegrino, Mark *Actor*
Handprint Entertainment, 1100 Glendon Ave #1000, Los Angeles, CA 90024 USA

Pelley, Scott *Correspondent*
20/20, 147 Columbus Ave, New York, NY 10023, US

Pellicano, Anthony
9200 Sunset Blvd. #322, Los Angeles, CA 90069

Pellow, Marti *Musician*
Solo Agency Ltd (UK), 55 Fulham High St, London, SW6 3JJ, United Kingdom

Peltier, Leonard
PO Box 583, Lawrence, KS 66044

Peluce, Meeno
2713 N. Keystone, Burbank, CA 91504-1602

Pelzer, Dave
Box 1846, Rancho Mirage, CA 92270-1081

Pena, Alejandro
12635 Etris Rd., Roswell, GA 30075

Peḃa, Elizabeth *Actor*
Rigberg-Rugolo Entertainment, 1180 S Beverly Dr #601, Los Angeles, CA 90035 USA

Pena, Federico Secy
3517 Sterling Ave, Alexandria, VA 22304 USA

Pena, Jose
A. Flores #1116 NTE C Jiquilpan, Los Mochia Sinoloa, MEXICO

Pena, Michael *Actor*
Art Work Entertainment, 260 South Beverly Dr #205, Beverly Hills, CA 90210 USA

Pena, Orlando
1750 W. 46th St. #416, Hialeah, FL 33012

Pender, Mel
4910 Karl's Gate Dr., Marietta, GA 30062

Pendergrass, Teddy *Athlete*
1505 Flat Rock Rd, Narberth, PA 19072-1227 USA

Pendleton, Austin
155 E. 76th St., New York, NY 10021

Pendleton, Terry *Baseball Player*
300 Longvue Ct, Duluth, GA 30097 USA

Penghlis, Thaao *Actor*
Metropolitan Talent Agency (MTA), 4526 Wilshire Blvd, Los Angeles, CA 90010 USA

Penguins, The
24210 E. Fork Rd. #9, Azusa, CA 91702

Penhaligon, Susan
109 Jermyn St, London, ENGLAND, SW1

Peniche, Arturo *Actor*
Televisa, Blvd Adolfo Lopez Mateos 232, Colonia San Angel INN, DF, CP 01060, MEXICO

Penick, Trevor *Musician*
Trans Continental Records, 7380 Sand Lake Road, #350, Orlando, FL 32819 USA

Peniston, Ce Ce
250 W. 57th St. #821, New York, NY 10107

Peniston, CeCe *Musician*
250 W 57th St, #821, New York, NY 10107 USA

Penky, Joseph F *Engineer*
Purdue University, Chemical Engineering Dept, West Lafayette, IN 47907 USA

Penn *Comedian*
William Morris Agency, 151 El Camino Dr, Beverly Hills, CA 90212 USA

Penn, Arthur H *Director*
William Morris Agency, 151 El Camino Dr, Beverly Hills, CA 90212 USA

Penn, Chris
9560 Wilshire Blvd. #516, Beverly Hills, CA 90212

Penn, Christopher *Actor*
6728 Zumirez Dr, Malibu, CA 90265 USA

Penn, Irving *Photographer*
Irving Penn Studio, 89 5th Ave, New York, NY 10003 USA

Penn, Kal *Actor*
Evolution Entertainment, 901 N Highland Ave, Los Angeles, CA 90038 USA

Penn, Michael *Songwriter, Musician*
H K Mgmt, 9200 W Sunset Blvd, #530, Los Angeles, CA 90069 USA

Penn, Sean *Actor, Director*
Creative Artists Agency LCC (CAA-LA), 9830 Wilshire Blvd, Beverly Hills, CA 90212 USA

Penn & Teller *Comedian, Live Show*
4132 S Rainbow Blvd, Box 377, Las Vegas, NV 89103 USA

Pennacchio, Len A *Misc*
Stanford University, Human Genome Center, Stanford, CA 94305 USA

Pennario, Leonard *Musician*
Columbia Artists Mgmt Inc, 165 W 57th St, New York, NY 10019 USA

Pennebaker, Ed *Artist*
428 County Road 9351, Green Forest, AR 72638 USA

Pennell, Larry
15516 Sunset Blvd. #101, Pacific Palisades, CA 90272

Penner, Jonathan *Actor*
Writers & Artists, 8383 Wilshire Blvd #550, Beverly Hills, CA 90211 USA

Penner, Stanford S *Engineer*
5912 Avenida Chamnez, La Jolla, CA 92037 USA

Pennington, Ann
701 N. Oakhurst Dr., Beverly Hills, CA 90210

Pennington, Chad *Football Player*
New York Jets, 1000 Fulton Ave, Hempstead, NY 11550 USA

Pennington, Janice *Actor, Model*
PO Box 11402, Beverly Hills, CA 90213 USA

Pennington, Julia
PO Box 5617, Beverly Hills, CA 90210

Pennington, Michael *Actor*
Marmont Mgmt, Langham House, 302/8 Regent St, London, W1R 5AL, UNITED KINGDOM (UK)

Pennington, Ty *Television Host*
Cunningham-Escott-Dipene & Associates Inc (CED-LA), 10635 Santa Monica Blvd #130, Los Angeles, CA 90025 USA

Pennock, Chris *Actor*
25150 1/2 Malibu Road, Malibu, CA 90265 USA

Pennock of Norton, Raymond *Business Person*
Morgan Grenfell Group, 23 Great Winchester St, London, EC2P 2AX, UNITED KINGDOM (UK)

Penny, Joe *Actor*
10453 Sarah St, Toluca Lake, CA 91602 USA

Penny, Roger P *Business Person*
Bethlehem Steel, 1170 8th Ave, Bethlehem, PA 18016 USA

Penny, Sudney *Actor*
Baker/Winokur/Ryder, 9100 Wilshire Blvd, #600, Beverly Hills, CA 90212 USA

Penny, Sydney *Actor*
Stone Manners Talent Agency, 6500 Wilshire Blvd, Ste 550, Los Angeles, CA 90048 USA

Penny's
3220 Altura #106, La Crescenta, CA 91214

Penot, Jacques
9 rue de l'Isly, Paris, FRANCE, F-75008

Penrose, Craig R *Football Player*
1609 Camino Way, Woodland, CA 95695 USA

Penry Jones, Rupert *Actor*
Creative Artists Agency LCC (CAA-LA), 9830 Wilshire Blvd, Beverly Hills, CA 90212 USA

Penske, Roger S *Race Car Driver*
Penske Racing, 163 Rolling Hills Road, Mooresville, NC 28117 USA

Pentecost, Del *Actor*
Paradigm (LA), 10100 Santa Monica Blvd, Fl 25, Los Angeles, CA 90067 USA

Penthouse Pets
277 Park Ave., New York, NY 10172-0003

Pentland, Alex P *Scientist*
Massachusetts Institute of Technology, Media Laboratory, Cambridge, MA 02139 USA

Penzias, Arno A *Nobel Prize Laureate*
AT & T Bell Laboratories, 600 Mountain Ave, New Providence, NJ 07974 USA

People, Village *Musician*
William Morris Agency (WMA-LA), 1 William Morris Pl, Beverly Hills, CA 90212 USA

Peoples, John *Physicist*
Fermi Nat Acceleration Lab, CDF Collaboration, PO Box 500, Batavia, IL 60510 USA

Peoples, Woodrow (Woody) *Football Player*
1810 Eulaula Ave, Birmingham, AL 35208 USA

Pep, Willie *Boxer*
130 Hartford Ave, Wethersfield, CT 06109 USA

Pepitone, Joe
32 Lois Lane, Farmingdale, NY 11735-6003

Pepitone, Joseph A (Joe) *Baseball Player*
32 Lois Lane, Farmingdale, NY 11735 USA

Peplinski, Jim *Hockey Player*
Peplinski Auto Leasing, 212 Meridian Road NE, Calgary, AB T2A 2N6, CANADA

Pepper, Barry *Actor*
Paul Kohner, 9300 Wilshire Blvd, #555, Beverly Hills, CA 90212 USA

Pepper, Cynthia
3229 Canyon Lake Dr., Las Vegas, NV 89117-0119

Pepper, Dottie *Golfer*
Ladies Pro Golf Association (LPGA), 100 International Golf Drive, Daytona Beach, FL 32124 USA

Pepper, Gene *Football Player*
159 Cedar Mill Court, Saint Charles, MO 63304 USA

Peppers, Julius *Football Player*
Carolina Panthers, Ericsson Stadium, 800 S Mint St, Charlotte, NC 28202 USA

Peppers, Red Hot Chili *Music Group*
Creative Artists Agency LCC (CAA-LA), 9830 Wilshire Blvd, Beverly Hills, CA 90212 USA

Peppler, Mary Jo *Volleyball Player*
Coast Volleyball Club, 11526 Sorrento Valley Road, San Diego, CA 92121 USA

Perabo, Piper *Actor*
648 Broadway, #1002, New York, NY 10012 USA

Perak, Sultan of *King*
Sultan's Palace, Istana Bukit Serene, Kula
Lumpur, MALAYSIA

Perakis, Nicos
Isabellastr. 19, Munich, GERMANY,
D-80798

Peralta, Ricardo *Astronaut*
Ingeneria Instituto, Ciudad Universitaria,
Mexico City, DF, 04510, MEXICO

Percival, Lance *Actor*
PVA 2 High St, Westbury-on-Trim, Bristol,
BS9 3DU, UNITED KINGDOM (UK)

Percival, Troy E *Baseball Player*
28920 Greick Dr, Moreno Valley, CA
92555 USA

Percy, Charles H *Ex-Senator*
1691 34th St NW, Washington, DC 20007
USA

Perdue, Frank
PO Box 1656, Horsham, PA 19044-6656

Perdue, Franklin P (Frank) *Business
Person*
Perdue Farms, PO Box 1565, Horsham,
PA 19044 USA

Perdue, Will *Basketball Player*
3332 SE Salmon St, Portland, OR 97214
USA

Perec, Marie-Jose *Track Athlete*
Federacion d'Athletisme, 10 Rue du Fg
Poissonniere, Paris, 75480, FRANCE

Pereira, Aristides M *President*
PO Box 172, Praia, CAPE VERDE

Perek, Lubos *Astronomer*
Astronomical Institute, Budecska 6, Prague
2, CZECH REPUBLIC

Perelman, Ronald O *Business Person*
Revlon Group, 625 Madison Avenue,
New York, NY 10022 USA

Perelman, Vadim *Director*
Firm, The, 9465 Wilshire Blvd, Beverly
Hills, CA 90212 USA

Perenyi, Miklos *Musician*
Erdoalja Utca 1/B, Budapest, 1037,
HUNGARY

Peres, Shimon *Nobel Prize Laureate*
Aenot Law House, 8 Shaul Hamelech
Blvd, Tel Aviv, 64733, ISRAEL

Peretokin, Mark *Dancer*
Bolshoi Theater, Teatralnaya Pl 1,
Moscow, 103009, RUSSIA

Perez, Atanasio *Baseball Player*
1717 North Bayshore Drive, #2735,
Miami, FL 33132 USA

Perez, Atanasio R (Tony) *Baseball Player*
1717 N Bayshore Dr, #2735, Miami, FL
33132 USA

Perez, Chris *Musician*
Big FD Entertainment, 301 Arizona Ave,
#200, Santa Monica, CA 90401 USA

Perez, Eddie *Baseball Player*
Milwaukee Brewers, County Stadium, PO
Box 3099, Milwaukee, WI 53201 USA

Perez, Hugo *Soccer Player*
22018 Newbridge Dr, Lake Forest, CA
92630 USA

Perez, Luiz (Louie) *Musician*
Gold Mountain, 3575 Cahuenga Blvd W,
#450, Los Angeles, CA 90068 USA

Perez, Odalis A *Baseball Player*
Los Angeles Dodgers, Stadium, 1000
Elysian Park Ave, Los Angeles, CA 90012
USA

Perez, Oliver *Baseball Player*
San Diego Padres, 8880 Rio San Diego
Drive #400, San Diego, CA 92108 USA

Perez, Pascual *Baseball Player*
Salvador, Cucurulo #105, Santiago,
DOMINIC REPUBLIC

Perez, Rosie *Actor*
International Creative Management
(ICM-NY), 40 W 57th St, New York, NY
10019 USA

Perez, Scott *Cartoonist*
DC Comics, 1700 Broadway, New York,
NY 10019 USA

Perez, Timothy Paul *Actor*
Badgley Connor Talent, 9229 Sunset Blvd,
#311, Los Angeles, CA 90069 USA

Perez, Vincent *Actor*
Artmedia, 20 Ave Rapp, Paris, 75007,
FRANCE

Perez de Cuellar, Javier *General,
Secretary*
Avenida A Miro Quesada, Lima, 1071,
PERU

Perez Esquivel, Adolfo *Nobel Prize
Laureate*
Servicio Paz y Justicia, Piedras 730,
Buenos Aires, 1070, ARGENTINA

Perez Fernandez, Pedro *Government
Official*
PSOE, Ferraz 68 y 70, Madrid, 28008,
SPAIN

Perez Limon, Iyari *Actor*
Mitchell K Stubbs & Assoc (MKS), 8675 W
Washington Blvd #203, Culver City, CA
90232 USA

Perez-Brown, Maria *Producer*
William Morris Agency (WMA-LA), 1
William Morris Pl, Beverly Hills, CA
90212 USA

Perfect Circle, A *Music Group*
Spivak Sobol Entertainment, 11845 W
Olympic Blvd #1125, Los Angeles, CA
90064 USA

Perick, Christof *Conductor*
Kaylor Mgmt, 130 W 57th St, #8G, New
York, NY 10019 USA

Periyar, Dasan *Actor*
30 Muthaiappa Street, Shenoy Nagar,
Chennai, TN 600 030, INDIA

Perkins, David D *Biologist*
345 Vine St, Menlo Park, CA 94025 USA

Perkins, Edward J *Diplomat*
State Department, 2201 C St NW,
Washington, DC 20520 USA

Perkins, Elizabeth *Actor*
Brillstein-Grey Entertainment, 9150
Wilshire Blvd #350, Beverly Hills, CA
90212 USA

Perkins, John M *Social Activist*
1655 Saint Charles St, Jackson, MS 39209
USA

Perkins, Kathleen Rose *Actor*
Trademark Talent, 338 1/2 Ogden Dr, Los
Angeles, CA 90036 USA

Perkins, Kendrick *Basketball Player*
Boston Celtics, 151 Merrimac St, #1,
Boston, MA 02114 USA

Perkins, Lucian *Journalist*
3103 17th St NW, Washington, DC 20010
USA

Perkins, Millie *Actor*
2511 Canyon Dr, Los Angeles, CA 90068
USA

Perkins, Oz
7720 Sunset Blvd., Los Angeles, CA
90046

Perkins, Tex *Musician*
Stack/Polydor Records, 70 Universal City
Plaza, Universal City, CA 91608 USA

Perkins, W Ray *Football Player, Football
Coach*
57 Honors Lane, Hattiesburg, MS 39402
USA

Perkins Jr, Lawrence B *Architect*
Perkins Eastman Partners, 437 5th Ave,
New York, NY 10016 USA

Perkoff, Gerald T *Doctor*
1300 Torrey Pines Dr, Columbia, MO
65203 USA

Perl, Frank J *Cinematographer*
5020 Biloxi Ave, North Hollywood, CA
91601 USA

Perl, Martin L *Nobel Prize Laureate*
3737 El Centro Ave, Palo Alto, CA 94306
USA

Perle, George *Composer*
Queens College, Music Dept, Flushing,
NY 11367 USA

Perley, James *Misc*
American Assn of University Professors,
1012 14th St NW, Washington, DC 20005
USA

Perlich, Max *Actor*
Innovative Artists, 1505 10th St, Santa
Monica, CA 90401 USA

Perlman, Itzhak *Musician, Conductor*
I M G Artists, 420 W 45th St, New York,
NY 10036 USA

Perlman, Lawrence *Business Person*
Ceridian Corp, 3311 E Old Shakopee
Road, Minneapolis, MN 55425 USA

Perlman, Phil
439 S. Catalina Ave. #102, Pasadena, CA
91106

Perlman, Rhea *Actor*
PO Box 491246, Los Angeles, C, 90049
USA

Perlman, Ron *Actor*
Kritzer Entertainment, 12200 W Olympic
Blvd, #400, Los Angeles, CA 90064 USA

Perls, Tom *Misc*
2 Harrington Lane, Weston, MA 02493
USA

Perner, Wolfgang *Athlete*
Schildlehen 29, ramsau-D, 8972,
AUSTRIA

Pernice, Tom Jr *Golfer*
Gaylord Sports Mgmt, 14646 N Kierland
Blvd, #230, Scottsdale, AZ 85254 USA

Pero, Perry R *Financier*
Northern Trust Corp, 50 S La Salle St,
Chicago, IL 60675 USA

Peron, Isabelita Martinez de *President*
Moreto 3, Los Jeronimos, Madrid, 28014, SPAIN

Perot, Ross H *Business Person*
Perot Group, 2300 W Plano Pkwy, Plano, TX 75029 USA

Perot Jr, Henry Ross *Business Person*
Perot Group, 2300 W Plano Pkwy, Plano, TX 75029 USA

Perraneski, Ronald P (Ron) *Baseball Player*
3805 Indian River Dr, Vero Beach, FL 32963 USA

Perranoski, Ron
3805 Indian River Dr., Vero Beach, FL 32963

Perreau, Gigi *Actor*
5841 Cantaloupe Ave, Van Nuys, CA 91401 USA

Perreault, Gilbert (Gil) *Hockey Player*
4 Rue de la Serenite, Victoriaville, QC, G6P 6S2, CANADA

Perrella, James E *Business Person*
Ingersoll-Rand Co, 200 Chestnut Ridge Road, Woodcliff Lake, NJ 07677 USA

Perrier, Mireille *Actor*
Cineart, 36 Rue de Ponthieu, Paris, 75008, FRANCE

Perrin, Philippe *Astronaut*
11923 Mighty Redwood Dr, Houston, TX 77059 USA

Perrine, Valerie *Actor*
Bret Adams, 440 W 44th St, New York, NY 10036 USA

Perrineau Jr, Harold *Actor*
Handprint Entertainment, 1100 Glendon Ave #1000, Los Angeles, CA 90024 USA

Perrineau Jr, Harry *Actor*
Creative Artists Agency, 9830 Wilshire Blvd, Beverly Hills, CA 90212 USA

Perron, Jean *Coach*
5 Thomas Mellon Circle, San Francisco, CA 94134 USA

Perrotta, Tom *Writer*
Saint Martin's Press, 175 5th Ave, New York, NY 10010 USA

Perry, Anne *Writer*
Turn Vawr, Seafield Postmahomack, Rosshire, IV20 1RE, SCOTLAND

Perry, Barbara
6926 La Presa Dr., Los Angeles, CA 90068

Perry, Barry W *Business Person*
Engelhard Corp, 101 Wood Ave, Iselin, NJ 08830 USA

Perry, Charles O *Artist*
20 Shorehaven Road, Norwalk, CT 06855 USA

Perry, Chris *Golfer*
Clayton Hoskins, 1161 Gamblier Road, Mount Vernon, OH 43050 USA

Perry, Felton *Actor*
PO Box 931359, Los Angeles, CA 90093 USA

Perry, Fletcher (Joe) *Football Player*
1644 E Chicago St, Chandler, AZ 85225 USA

Perry, Gaylord J *Baseball Player*
PO Box 489, Spruce Pine, NC 28777 USA

Perry, Gerald *Football Player*
2940 Dell Dr, Columbia, SC 29209 USA

Perry, James E (Jim) *Baseball Player*
2608 S Ridgeview Way, Sjoux Falls, SD 57105 USA

Perry, Jeff *Actor*
2029 Century Park E #1060, Los Angeles, CA 90067 USA

Perry, Joe *Songwriter, Musician*
PO Box 2665, Duxbury, MA 02331 USA

Perry, John Bennett *Actor*
Judy Schoen, 606 N Larchmont Blvd, #309, Los Angeles, CA 90004 USA

Perry, John R *Misc*
Stanford University, Language & Information Study Center, Stanford, CA 94305 USA

Perry, Kenny *Golfer*
418 Quail Ridge Road, Franklin, KY 42134 USA

Perry, Linda *Musician, Songwriter*
Premier Talent, 3 E 54th St, #1100, New York, NY 10022 USA

Perry, Luke *Actor*
Himber Entertainment Inc, 211 S Beverly Dr #208, Beverly Hills, CA 90212 USA

Perry, Matthew *Actor*
Creative Artists Agency LCC (CAA-LA), 9830 Wilshire Blvd, Beverly Hills, CA 90212 USA

Perry, Michael Dean *Football Player*
19125 Peninsula Point Road, Cornelius, NC 28031 USA

Perry, Nickolas *Director, Writer*
William Morris Agency, 151 El Camino Dr, Beverly Hills, CA 90212 USA

Perry, Robert P *Biologist*
1808 Bustleton Pike, Churchville, PA 18966 USA

Perry, Ruth *Prime Minister*
Prime Minister's Office, Capitol Hill, Monrovia, LIBERIA

Perry, Steve *Writer*
1401 Pathfinder Ave, Thousand Oaks, CA 91362 USA

Perry, Steve *Musician*
William Morris Agency (WMA-LA), 1 William Morris Pl, Beverly Hills, CA 90212 USA

Perry, Steve *Musician*
3905 Peartree Place, Calabasas, CA 91302 USA

Perry, Troy D *Religious Leader*
Metropolitan Churches Fellowship, 5300 Santa Monica Blvd, Los Angeles, CA 90029 USA

Perry, William J *Secretary*
11210 Hooper Ln, Los Altos Hills, CA 94024 USA

Perry, Yvonne *Actor*
As World Turns Show, CBS-TV, 524 W 57th St, New York, NY 10019 USA

Perryman, Jill
4 Hillside Crescent, Gooseberry Hill, AUSTRALIA, 6076 W Aus

Perschy, Maria
Maxingstr. 30, Vienna, AUSTRIA, 1130

Persoff, Nahemiah *Actor*
5670 Moonstone Beach Dr, Cambria, CA 93428 USA

Persoff, Nehemiah
5847 Tampa Ave., Tarzana, CA 91356

Person, Chuck *Basketball Player*
Cleveland Cavaliers, Gund Arena, 1 Center Court, Cleveland, OH 44155 USA

Person, Wesley *Basketball Player*
8961 Golf Walk Circle S, Memphis, TN 38125 USA

Persson, Goeran *Prime Minister*
Statsradsberedningen, Rosenbad 4, Stockholm, 103 33, SWEDEN

Persson, Nina *Musician*
Motor SE, Gotabergs Gatan 2, Gothenburg, 400 14, SWEDEN

Persuaders, The
225 W. 57th St. #500, New York, NY 10019

Pertucceli, Valeria *Actor*
Telefe - Argentina, Pavon 2444 (C1248AAT), Buenos Aires, ARGENTINA

Pertwee, Bill
25 Whitehall, London, ENGLAND, SW1A 2BS

Perzigian, Jerry *Writer, Producer*
Creative Artists Agency LCC (CAA-LA), 9830 Wilshire Blvd, Beverly Hills, CA 90212 USA

Pescatelli, Tammy *Actor*
Gersh Agency, The (LA), 232 N Canon Dr, Beverly Hills, CA 90210 USA

Pesce, P J *Director, Writer*
Writers & Artists, 8383 Wilshire Blvd, #550, Beverly Hills, CA 90211 USA

Pesch, Doro & Warlock
Box 8721, Dusseldorf 1, GERMANY, D-(W) 4000

Pesci, Joe *Actor*
Falu Productions, PO Box 6, Lavallette, NJ 08735 USA

Pescia, Lisa *Actor*
Epstein-Wyckoff, 280 S Beverly Dr, #400, Beverly Hills, CA 90212 USA

Pescow, Donna *Actor*
8267 Paseo Canyon Dr, Malibu, CA 90265 USA

Pesek, Libor *Conductor*
I M G Artists, Media House, 3 Burlington Lane, London, W4 2TH, UNITED KINGDOM (UK)

Pesky, John M (Johnny) *Baseball Player*
2201 Edison Ave, Fort Myers, FL 33901 USA

Pestana, Simon *Actor*
Telefe - Argentina, Pavon 2444 (C1248AAT), Buenos Aires, ARGENTINA

Pestka, Sidney *Misc*
Robert Wood Johnson Medical School, 675 Hoes Lane, Piscataway, NJ 08854 USA

Peter, Paul & Mary
121 Mt. Herman Way, Ocean Grove, NJ 07756-1443

Peter, Valentine J *Religious Leader, Educator*
Father Flanagan's Boys Home, Boys Town, NE 68010 USA

Peter II, Edward C *General*
4521 Lake Dr, Lees Summit, MO 64064 USA

Peterdi, Gabor *Artist*
108 Highland Ave, Norwalk, CT 06853 USA

Peterman, Donald W *Cinematographer*
Gersh Agency, 232 N Canon Dr, Beverly Hills, CA 90210 USA

Peterman, Melissa *Actor*
Reba, 10201 W Pico Blvd, Bldg 38 Rm 125, Los Angeles, CA 90035 USA

Peters, Andy *Television Host*
BBC Artist Mail, PO Box 1116, Belfast, BT2 7AJ, United Kingdom

Peters, Anthony L (Tony) *Football Player*
2402 Boston St, Muskogee, OK 74401 USA

Peters, Barbara *Director*
1118 Magnolia Blvd, North Hollywood, CA 91601 USA

Peters, Bernadette *Musician, Actor*
MCA Records, 70 Universal City Plaza, Universal City, CA 91608 USA

Peters, Bob *Coach*
Bernidji State University, Athletic Dept, Bernidji, MN 56601 USA

Peters, Brock *Actor*
1420 Rising Glen Road, Los Angeles, CA 90069 USA

Peters, Charlie *Writer*

Peters, Clarke *Actor*
Writers and Artists Group Intl (NY), 19 W 44th St #1000, New York, NY 10036 USA

Peters, Dan *Musician*
Legends of 21st Century, 7 Trinity Row, Florence, MA 01062 USA

Peters, Elizabeth *Writer*
Avon Books, 1350 Ave of Americas, New York, NY 10019 USA

Peters, Emmitt *Dog Sled Racer*
General Delivery, Ruby, AK 99768 USA

Peters, Floyd *Football Player, Football Coach*
9222 Hyland Creek Road, Bloomington, MN 55437 USA

Peters, Gary C *Baseball Player*
7121 N Serenoa Dr, Sarasota, FL 34241 USA

Peters, Gordon
20 Elm Tree Ave., Ester Surrey, ENGLAND

Peters, Gretchen *Songwriter, Musician*
Purple Crayon Mgmt, PO Box 358, Hendersonville, TN 37077 USA

Peters, Jon *Producer*
9941 Tower Lane, Beverly Hills, CA 90210 USA

Peters, Maria Liberia *Prime Minister*
Prime Minister's Office, Fort Amsterdam, Willemstad, NETHERLANDS ANTILLES

Peters, Mary *Track Athlete*
Willowtree Cottage, River Road, Dunmurray, Belfast, NORTHERN IRELAND

Peters, Mike *Cartoonist*
PO Box 957, Bradenton, FL 34206 USA

Peters, Rick *Actor*
Metropolitan Talent Agency (MTA), 4526 Wilshire Blvd, Los Angeles, CA 90010 USA

Peters, Roberta *Actor, Opera Singer*
19356 Cedar Glen Dr, Boca Raton, FL 33434 USA

Peters, Tom *Business Person*
Tom Peters Group, 555 Hamilton Avenue, Palo Alto, CA 94301 USA

Peters Jr, Charles G *Editor*
Washington Monthly, 1611 Connecticut Ave NW, Washington, DC 20009 USA

Peters Jr, House
1202 Borden Rd Sp #91, Escondido, CA 92026 USA

Petersdorf, Robert G *Physicist*
8001 Sand Point Way NE, #C71, Seattle, WA 98115 USA

Petersen, Byron *Scientist*
University of Pittsburgh, Medical Center, Pittsburgh, PA 15260 USA

Petersen, Jan *Government Official*
Utenriksdepatementet, Postboks 8114 Dep, Oslo, 0032, NORWAY

Petersen, Niels Helveg *Government Official*
Drosselvej 72, Frederiksberg, 2000, DENMARK

Petersen, Pat
1634 Veteran Ave., Los Angeles, CA 90025

Petersen, Paul *Actor, Musician*
A Minor Consideration, 14530 Denker Ave, Gardena, CA 90247 USA

Petersen, Raymond J *Publisher*
Hearst Corp, 250 W 55th St, New York, NY 10019 USA

Petersen, Robert E *Publisher*
Petersen Publishing Co, 6420 Wilshire Blvd, #100, Los Angeles, CA 90048 USA

Petersen, Stewart
Box 64, Cokeville, WY 83114

Petersen, William L *Producer, Actor*
United Talent Agency, 9560 Wilshire Blvd, #500, Beverly Hills, CA 90212 USA

Petersen, Wolfgang *Director*
Radiant Productions, 914 Montana Ave Fl 2, Santa Monica, CA 90403 USA

Peterson, Bruce *Misc*
23792 Marguerite Parkway, #120, Mission Viejo, CA 92692 USA

Peterson, Buzz *Coach*
University of Tennessee, Athletic Dept, Knoxville, TN 37996 USA

Peterson, Cassandra (Elvira) *Actor, Writer*
Queen B Productions, PO Box 38246, Los Angeles, CA 90038 USA

Peterson, David C *Journalist*
4805 Pinehurst Court, Pleasant Hill, IA 50327 USA

Peterson, Debbi *Musician*
Bangles Mall, 1341 Fullerton Ave, Box 180, Chicago, IL 60614 USA

Peterson, Donald H
427 Pebblebrook, Seabrook, TX 77588 USA

Peterson, Donald R *Astronaut*
Aerospace Operations Consultants, 427 Pebblebrook Dr, Seabrook, TX 77586 USA

Peterson, Elly *Social Activist*
1515 M St NW, Washington, DC 20005 USA

Peterson, Forrest J *Misc*
17 Collins Meadow Dr, Georgetown, SC 29440 USA

Peterson, Fred I (Fritz) *Baseball Player*
PO Box 802, Dubuque, IA 52004 USA

Peterson, John *Wrestler*
457 19th Ave, Comstock, WI 54826 USA

Peterson, Lars *Doctor*
Sahlgrenska University Hospital, Surgery Dept, Goteborg, 413 45, SWEDEN

Peterson, Maggie
3310 W. Warm Springs Rd., Las Vegas, NV 89118

Peterson, Michael *Musician*
Falcon/Goodman Mgmt, 1103 17th Ave S, Nashville, TN 37212 USA

Peterson, Morris *Basketball Player*
Toronto Raptors, Air Canada Center, 40 Bay St, Toronto, ON M5J 2N8, CANADA

Peterson, Oscar E *Musician, Composer*
Regal Recordings, 2421 Hammond Road, Mississauga, ON L5K 1T3, CANADA

Peterson, Paul E *Scientist*
5 Midland Road, Wellesley, MA 05482 USA

Peterson, Peter G *Financier, Secretary*
Blackstone Group, 345 Park Ave, New York, NY 10154 USA

Peterson, Ray *Musician*
Lustig Talent, PO Box 770850, Orlando, FL 32877 USA

Peterson, Russell W *Governor*
11 E Mozart Dr, Wilmington, DE 19807 USA

Peterson, Seth *Actor*
3424 Blair Dr, Los Angeles, CA 90068 USA

Peterson, Steven *Architect*
Peterson/Littenberg Architecture, 131 E 66th St, New York, NY 10021 USA

Peterson, Todd *Football Player*
3249 Chatham Road NW, Atlanta, GA 30305 USA

Peterson, Vicki *Musician*
Bangles Mall, 1341 W Fullerton Ave, Box 180, Chicago, IL 60614 USA

Peterson, Walter R *Governor, Educator*
Po Box 3100, Peterborough, NH 03458 USA

Peterson, William L *Actor*
United Talent Agency, 9560 Wilshire Blvd, #500, Beverly Hills, CA 90212 USA

Petherbridge, Edward *Actor*
Jonathan Altaras, 13 Shorts Gardens, London, WC2H 9AT, UNITED KINGDOM (UK)

Petievich, Gerald *Producer, Writer*
Endeavor Agency LLC (LA), 9601 Wilshire Blvd Fl 3, Beverly Hills, CA 90210 USA

Petit, Philippe *Misc*
Cathedral of Saint John the Devine, 1047 Amsterdam Ave, New York, NY 10025 USA

Petit, Roland *Dancer*
20 Blvd Gabes, Marseilles, 13008, FRANCE

Petke, Mike *Soccer Player*
DC United, 14120 Newbrook Dr, Chantilly, VA 20151 USA

Peto, Richard *Misc*
Radcliffe Infirmary, Harkness Building, Oxford, ON OX2 6HE, UNITED KINGDOM (UK)

Petra, Yvon *Tennis Player*
Residence du Prieure, Saint Germain en Laye, 78100, FRANCE

Petrassi, Gottfredovia
Ferdinando di Savola 3, Rome, ITALY, 00196

Petrenko, Victor
1375 Hopmeadow St, Simsbury, CT 06070

Petrenko, Viktor *Figure Skater*
International Skating Center, PO Box 577, Sinsbury, CT 06070 USA

Petrey, Dan
1808 Cartlen Dr., Placentia, CA 92670

Petri, Michala *Musician*
Nordskraenten 3, Kokkedal, 2980, DENMARK

Petri, Nina *Actor*
Agentur Carola Studlar, Agnesstr 47, Munich, 80798, GERMANY

Petrie, Daniel M *Director*
Creative Artists Agency LCC (CAA-LA), 9830 Wilshire Blvd, Beverly Hills, CA 90212 USA

Petrie, Geoff *Basketball Player*
Sacramento Kings, Arco Arena, 1 Sports Parkway, Sacramento, CA 95834 USA

Petrie Jr, Daniel M *Director*
Richland/Wunsch/Hohman Agency, 9220 Sunset Blvd, #311, Los Angeles, CA 90069 USA

Petrie Sr, Daniel M *Director*
13201 Haney Place, Los Angeles, CA 90049 USA

Petrocelli, Americo P (Rico) *Baseball Player*
37 Green Heron Lane, Nashua, NH 03062 USA

Petrocelli, Daniel *Attorney General*
Mitchell Silverberg Krupp, 11377 W Olympic Blvd, Los Angeles, CA 90064 USA

Petrone, Rocco A *Engineer*
1329 Granvia Atlamira, Palos Verdes Estates, CA 90274 USA

Petrone, Shana *Musician*
Creative Artists Agency, 3310 W End Ave, #500, Nashville, TN 37203 USA

Petroni, Michael *Director*
United Talent Agency, 9560 Wilshire Blvd, #500, Beverly Hills, CA 90212 USA

Petronio, Stephen *Dancer, Choreographer*
95 Saint Marks Place, New York, NY 10019 USA

Petroske, John *Hockey Player*
Po Box 366, Side Lake, MN 55781 USA

Petrov, Andrei P *Composer*
Petrovskaya Str 42, #75, Saint Petersburg, 197046, RUSSIA

Petrov, Nikolai A *Musician*
Kutuzovsky Prosp 26, #23, Moscow, 121165, RUSSIA

Petrovics, Emil *Composer*
Attila Utca 29, Budapest, 1013, HUNDARY

Petrovics, Emil *Composer*
Attila Utca 29, Budapest, 1013, HUNGARY

Petrovsky, Daniel J *General*
Commanding General, UN Command Korea, APO, AE, 96343 USA

Petry, Daniel J (Dan) *Baseball Player*
1808 Cartlen Dr, Placentia, CA 92870 USA

Petsko, Gregory A *Misc*
8 Jason Road, Belmont, MA 02478 USA

Pett, Joel *Cartoonist*
Lexington Herald-Leader, 1010 New Circle Road NW, Lexington, KY 40511 USA

Pettengill, Gordon H *Physicist*
Massachusetts Institute of Technology, Space Research Ctr, Cambridge, MA 02139 USA

Petterson, Donald K *Diplomat*
American Embassy Khartoum, #63900, APO, AE, 09829 USA

Pettibon, Raymond *Artist*
Michael Kohn Gallery, 920 Colorado Ave, Santa Monica, CA 90401 USA

Pettibon, Richard A (Richie) *Football Player*
9628 Percussion Way, Vienna, VA 22182 USA

Pettiet, Christopher
9255 Sunset Blvd. #620, Los Angeles, CA 90069

Pettigrew, Antonio *Track Athlete*
Saint Augustine's College, Athletic Dept, Raleigh, NC 27610 USA

Pettigrew, L Eudora *Educator*
State University of New York, President's Office, Old Westbury, NY 11568 USA

Pettijohn, Francis J *Misc*
11630 Glen Arm Road, #V51, Glen Arm, MD 21057 USA

Pettinato, Rachelle *Actor*
Select Artists Ltd (CA-Westside Office), 1138 12th Street, Suite 1, Santa Monica, CA 90403 USA

Pettit, Bob *Basketball Player*
7 Garden Ln, New Orleans, LA 70124-1024

Pettit, Donald R *Astronaut*
2014 Country Ridge Dr, Houston, TX 77062 USA

Pettit Jr, Robert L (Bob) *Basketball Player*
7 Garden Lane, New Orleans, LA 70124 USA

Pettite, Andrew E (Andy) *Baseball Player*
2310 W Lawther Dr, Deer Park, TX 77536 USA

Pettitte, Andy
Yankee Stadium, Bronx, NY 10451

Petty, Kyle *Race Car Driver*
135 Longfield Dr, Mooresville, NC 28115 USA

Petty, Lori *Actor*
4001 W Alameda Ave, #301, Burbank, CA 91505 USA

Petty, Richard L *Race Car Driver*
Petty Enterprises, 311 Branson Mill Rd, Randleman, NC 27317 USA

Petty, Tom *Musician, Songwriter*
William Morris Agency (WMA-LA), 1 William Morris Pl, Beverly Hills, CA 90212 USA

Pevec, Katja *Actor*
Creative Management Group, 3815 Hughes Ave Fl 3, Culver City, CA 90232 USA

Peyroux, Madeline *Songwriter, Musician*
Bumstead Productions, PO Box 158, Station E, Toronto, ON M6H 4E2, CANADA

Peyser, Penny *Actor*
Epstein-Wyckoff, 280 S Beverly Dr, #400, Beverly Hills, CA 90212 USA

Peyton, Brad *Director*
Endeavor Agency LLC (LA), 9601 Wilshire Blvd Fl 3, Beverly Hills, CA 90210 USA

Peyton of Yeovil, John W W *Government Official*
Old Malt House, Hinton Saint George, Somerset, TA17 8SE, UNITED KINGDOM (UK)

Pezzano, Chuck *Writer*
27 Mountainside Terrace, Clifton, NJ 07013 USA

Pfaff, Judy *Artist*
Holly Solomon Gallery, 175 E 79th St, #2B, New York, NY 10021 USA

Pfann, George R *Football Player, Football Coach*
120 Warwick Place, Ithaca, NY 14850 USA

Pfeiffer, Dedee *Actor, Model*
Baker/Winokur/Ryder, 9100 Wilshire Blvd, #600, Beverly Hills, CA 90212 USA

Pfeiffer, Doug *Editor*
Po Box 1806, Big Bear Lake, CA 92315 USA

Pfeiffer, Michelle *Actor*
Creative Artists Agency LCC (CAA-LA), 9830 Wilshire Blvd, Beverly Hills, CA 90212 USA

Pfeiffer, Norman *Architect*
Hardy Holzman Pfeiffer, 811 W 7th St, Los Angeles, CA 90017 USA

Pflug, Jo Ann *Actor*
2865 Lenox Road NE, #509, Atlanta, GA 30324 USA

Pfund, Randy *Coach*
Miami Heat, American Airlines Arena, 601 Biscayne Blvd, Miami, FL 33132 USA

Phair, Liz *Musician, Actor, Songwriter*
Untitled Entertainment (LA), 8436 W 3rd
St #650, Los Angeles, CA 90048 USA

Pham, Tuan *Cosmonaut*
4C-1000-Soc Son, Hanoi, VIETNAM

Pham Dinh Tung, Paul J Cardinal
Religious Leader
Archdiocese, Toa Tong Giam Muc, Pho
Nha Chung, Hanoi, 40, VIETNAM

Pham Minh Man, Jean-Baptiste Cardinal
Religious Leader
Toa Tonggiam Muc, 180 Nguyen Dink
Chieu, Thanh-Pho Ho Chi Minh,
VIETNAM

Phan, Van Khai *Prime Minister*
Prime Minister's Office, Hoang Hoa Thum
St, Hanoi, VIETNAM

Phantog *Mountaineer*
Wuxi Sports & Physical Culture Comm,
Jiagnsu, CHINA

Phelan, Jim *Basketball Player, Coach*
16579 Old Emmitsburg Road,
Emmitsburg, MD 21727 USA

Phelps, Brian
1265 Coldwater Canyon Dr., Beverly
Hills, CA 90210

Phelps, Doug *Musician*
Mitchell Fox Mgmt, 212 3rd Ave N, #301,
Nashville, TN 37201 USA

Phelps, Edmund S *Economist*
45 E 89th St, New York, NY 10128 USA

Phelps, James *Actor*
JOP Project, PO Box 9765, Coldfield,
Sutton, B75 5XB, UNITED KINGDOM
(UK)

Phelps, Jaycie *Gymnast*
Cincinnati Gymnastics Academy, 3635
Woodridge Blvd, Fairfield, OH 45014
USA

Phelps, Kelly Joe *Musician*
Fleming/Tamulevich Assoc, 733 N Main
St, #35, Ann Arbor, MI 48104 USA

Phelps, Michael *Swimmer*
Octagon, 1751 Pinnacle Dr #1500,
McLean, VA 22102 USA

Phelps, Oliver *Actor*
JOP Project, PO Box 9765, Sutton
Coldfield, B75 5XB, United Kingdom

Phelps, Richard *Athlete*
ESPN, 935 Middle St, Bristol, CT 06010
USA

Phelps, Richard F (Digger) *Coach*
ESPN-TV, Sports Dept, ESPN Plaza 935
Middle St, Bristol, CT 06010 USA

Phelps Jr, Ashton *Publisher*
New Orleans Times-Picayune, 3800
Howard Ave, New Orleans, LA 70125
USA

Phifer, Mekhi *Actor*
William Morris Agency, 1325 Ave of
Americas, New York, NY 10019 USA

Phifer, Roman Z *Football Player*
1764 S Garth Ave, Los Angeles, CA 90035
USA

Philaret, Patriarch *Religious Leader*
10 Osvobozdeniya St, Minsk, 22004,
BELARUS

Philbin, Joy
101 W. 67th St. #51A, New York, NY
10023-5953

Philbin, Regis *Television Host*
Live With Regis & Kelly, 30 W 67th St Fl
9, New York, NY 10023 USA

Philip *Prince*
Buckingham Palace, London, SW1A 1AA,
UNITED KINGDOM (UK)

Philip, HRH Prince
Buckingham Palace, London, ENGLAND,
SW1

Philip, Primate *Religious Leader*
Antiochian Orthodox Christian Church,
358 Mountain Road, Englewood, NJ
07631 USA

Philipp, Stephanie *Model*
Agentur Margit de la Berg, Icking-Isartal,
82057, GERMANY

Philippe *Prince*
Koninklijk Palais, Rue de Brederode,
Brussels, 1000, BELGIUM

Philippe, Crown Prince *Royalty*
Koninklijk Palais, Rue de Brederode,
Brussels, 1000, Belgium

Philippoussis, Mark *Tennis Player*
Octagon, 1751 Pinnacle Dr, #1500,
McLean, VA 22102 USA

Philipps, Busy *Actor*
3 Arts Entertainment Inc, 9460 Wilshire
Blvd Fl 7, Beverly Hills, CA 90212 USA

Philips, Chuck *Journalist*
Los Angeles Times, Editorial Dept, 202 W
1st St, Los Angeles, CA 90212 USA

Philips, Emo *Actor*
OmniPop Inc (LA), 10700 Ventura Blvd Fl
2, Studio City, CA 91604 USA

Philips, Gina *Actor*
Immortal Entertainment, 12200 Olympic
Blvd, Suite 400, Los Angeles, CA 90064
USA

Phillippe, Ryan *Actor*
Paradigm Agency, 10100 Santa Monica
Blvd, #2500, Los Angeles, CA 90067 USA

Phillips, Anthony *Songwriter, Musician*
Solo Agency, 55 Fulham High St, London,
SW6 3JJ, UNITED KINGDOM (UK)

Phillips, Bijou *Actor, Model, Musician*
Evolution Talent, 1776 Broadway, #1500,
New York, NY 10019 USA

Phillips, Bill
Muscle Media, 444 Corporate Cir,
Golden, CO 80401-5600

Phillips, Bobbie *Actor*
UPN, 11800 Wilshire Blvd, West Los
Angeles, CA 90025 USA

Phillips, Brandon *Baseball Player*
2401 Ontario St, Cleveland, OH 44115-
4003

Phillips, Caryl *Writer*
Amherst College, English Dept, Amherst,
MA 01002 USA

Phillips, Chynna *Musician, Actor*
1007 Montana Avenue, #230, Santa
Monica, CA 90403 USA

Phillips, Emo *Comedian*
Harbour Agency, 63 William St, #300,
East Sydney, NSW, 1022, AUSTRALIA

Phillips, Ethan *Actor*
4212 McFarlane Ave, Burbank, CA 91505
USA

Phillips, Grace *Actor*
Framework Entertainment (LA), 9057
Nemo St #C, W Hollywood, CA 90069
USA

Phillips, Grant-Lee *Musician*
William Morris Agency, 151 El Camino
Dr, Beverly Hills, CA 90212 USA

Phillips, Harvey *Misc*
TubaRanch, 4769 S Harrell Road,
Bloomington, IN 47401 USA

Phillips, Howard *Misc*
Conservative Caucus, 47 West St, Boston,
MA 02111 USA

Phillips, James (Red) *Football Player*
1948 Wicker Point Road, Alexander City,
AL 35010 USA

Phillips, Jeffrey
8436 W. Third St. #740, Los Angeles, CA
90048-4100

Phillips, John *Coach*
University of Tulsa, Athletic Dept, Tulsa,
OK 74104 USA

Phillips, John L *Astronaut*
4422 Cedar Ridge Trail, Houston, TX
77059 USA

Phillips, Joseph C
8730 Sunset Blvd #480, Los Angeles, CA
90069 USA

Phillips, Julianne *Actor*
2227 Mandeville Canyon Road, Los
Angeles, CA 90049 USA

Phillips, Kate *Writer*
Houghton Mifflin, 222 Berkeley St, #700,
Boston, MA 02116 USA

Phillips, Kristie *Gymnast*
610 1st Ave, Asbury Park, NJ 07712 USA

Phillips, Lawrence *Football Player*
9527 Langdon Ave, North Hills, CA
91343 USA

Phillips, Leslie *Actor*
Storm Artists Mgmt, 47 Brewer St, London,
W1R 3FD, UNITED KINGDOM (UK)

Phillips, Lou Diamond *Actor*
Paradigm Agency, 10100 Santa Monica
Blvd, #2500, Los Angeles, CA 90067 USA

Phillips, Loyd *Football Player*
RR 3, Springdale, AR 72762 USA

Phillips, Mackenzie *Actor*
S D B Partners, 1801 Ave of Stars, #902,
Los Angeles, CA 90067 USA

Phillips, Michelie *Actor, Musician*
4350 Berryman Ave, #4, Los Angeles, CA
90066 USA

Phillips, Michelle
4350 Berryman Ave. #4, Los Angeles, CA
90035

Phillips, Norma *Social Activist*
Mothers Against Drunk Driving, PO Box
819100, Dallas, TX 75381 USA

Phillips, Owen M *Engineer*
23 Merrymount Road, Baltimore, MD
21210 USA

Phillips, Peter C B *Economist*
133 Concord Dr, Madison, CT 06443
USA

Phillips, Phil *Songwriter, Musician*
PO Box 105, Jennings, LA 70546 USA
Phillips, Princess Zara *Royalty*
Gatcombe Park, Minchinhampton, Stroud,
GL6 9AT, United Kingdom
Phillips, Sam *Songwriter, Musician*
Prager & Fenton, 12424 Wilshire Blvd,
#1000, Los Angeles, CA 90025 USA
Phillips, Scott *Musician*
Agency Group, 1776 Broadway, #430,
New York, NY 10019 USA
Phillips, Sean
153 Petherton Rd. Highbury, London,
ENGLAND, N5 2RS
Phillips, Sian *Actor*
8 Alexa Court, 78 Lexham Gardens,
London, ENGLAND, W8 6JL, UNITED
KINGDOM (UK)
Phillips, Stone *Commentator*
NBC-TV, News Dept, 30 Rockefeller
Plaza, New York, NY 10112 USA
Phillips, Susan M *Financier, Government
Official*
Federal Reserve Board, 20th St &
Constitution NW, Washington, DC 20551
USA
Phillips, Tari *Basketball Player*
New York Liberty, Madison Square
Garden, 2 Penn Plaza, New York, NY
10121 USA
Phillips, Teresa *Basketball Player, Coach*
Tennessee State University, Athletic Dept,
Nashville, TN 37209 USA
Phillips, Todd *Producer, Director, Actor,
Writer*
William Morris Agency (WMA-LA), 1
William Morris Pl, Beverly Hills, CA
90212 USA
Phillips, Wade *Football Coach*
San Diego Chargers, 4020 Murphy
Canyon Road, San Diego, CA 92123 USA
Phillips, Warren H *Publisher*
Bridge Works Publications, PO Box 1798,
Bridgehampton, NY 11932 USA
Phillips, Wendy *Actor*
1642 Westwood Blvd, #300, Los Angeles,
CA 90024 USA
Phillips, William D *Nobel Prize Laureate*
13409 Chestnut Oak Dr, Gaithersburg,
MD 20878 USA
Phillips Jr, J Dixon *Judge*
US Court of Appeals, 100 Europa Dr,
Chapel Hill, NC 27517 USA
Phillopusis, Mark *Tennis Player*
Octagon, 1751 Pinnacle Dr #1500,
McLean, VA 22102 USA
Phipps, Michael E (Mike) *Football Player*
2748 NE 26th St, Lighthouse Point, FL
33064 USA
Phipps, Sam
2346 Walgrove Ave, Los Angeles, CA
90066
Phish *Music Group*
Monterey Peninsula Artists (Monterey),
509 Hartnell St, Monterey, CA 93940 USA

Phoebus, Thomas H (Tom) *Baseball
Player*
2822 SW Lakemont Place, Palm City, FL
34990 USA
Phoenic, Robin *Musician*
Nine Inch Nails, 63 Main St, Cold Spring,
NY 10516
Phoenix, Joaquin *Actor*
Iris Burton Agency, 8916 Ashcroft Ave,
Los Angeles, CA 90048
Phoenix, Summer *Actor*
3 Arts Entertainment (NY), 451 Greenwich
St Fl 7, New York, NY 10013 USA
Pianalto, Sandra *Financier*
Federal Reserve Bank, 1455 E 6th St,
Cleveland, OH 44144 USA
Piano, Renzo *Architect, Nobel Prize
Laureate*
Renzo Piano Building Workshop, Via
Rubens 29, Genoa, 16158, ITALY
Piatkowski, Eric *Basketball Player*
Houston Rockets, Toyota Center, 2 E
Greenway Plaza, Houston, TX 77046 USA
Piazza, Michale J (Mike) *Baseball Player*
PO Box 864, Valley Forge, PA 19482 USA
Picard, Alexandre *Hockey Player*
Columbus Blue Jackets, Arena, 200 W
Nationwide Blvd, Columbus, OH 43215
USA
Picard, Robert
31831 Grand River Ave. #55, Farmington,
MI 48336
Picardo, Robert *Actor*
Don Buchwald, 6500 Wilshire Blvd,
#2200, Los Angeles, CA 90048 USA
Picasso, Paloma *Designer, Actor*
Quintana Ron Ltd, 291A Brompton Road,
London, SW3 2DY, UNITED KINGDOM
(UK)
Picatto, Alexandra *Actor*
Paradigm (LA), 10100 Santa Monica Blvd,
Fl 25, Los Angeles, CA 90067 USA
Piccard, Bertrand *Misc*
Media Impact, Rue de Lausanne 42,
Geneva, 1201, SWITZERLAND
Piccard, Jacques E J *Scientist*
Place d'Armes, Cully, 1096,
SWITZERLAND
Picco, Giandomenico
1 United Nations Plaza, New York, NY
10017
Piccoli, Camille *Actor*
Cineart, 36 Rue de Ponthieu, Paris,
75008, FRANCE
Piccoli, Michel *Actor*
11 Rue des Lions Saint Paul, Paris, 75004,
FRANCE
Piccone, Robin *Fashion Designer*
Piccone Apparel Corp, 1424 Washington
Blvd, Venice, CA 90291 USA
Picerni, Paul *Actor*
Po Box 572257, Tarzana, CA 91357 USA
Pichler, Joseph A *Business Person*
Kroger Co, 1014 Vine St, Cincinnati, OH
45202 USA
Pick, Amelie *Actor*
Artmedia, 20 Ave Rapp, Paris, 75007,
FRANCE

Pickard, Nancy *Writer*
2502 W 71st Terrace, Prairie Village, KS
66208 USA
Pickel, Bill *Football Player*
9 Autumn Ridge Road, South Salem, NY
10590 USA
Pickens, Carl M *Football Player*
623 Terrace Ave, Murphy, NC 28906 USA
Pickens, Jo Ann *Opera Singer*
Norman McCann Artists, 56 Lawrie Park
Gardens, London, SE26 6XJ, UNITED
KINGDOM (UK)
Pickens Jr, James
8436 W Third St #740, Los Angeles, CA
90048 USA
Pickens Jr, T Boone *Business Person*
1 Woodstone St, Amarillo, TX 79106 USA
Pickering, Byron *Artist*
6919 NE Highland Dr, Lincoln City, OR
97367 USA
Pickering, Donald
Back Court Manor House, Eastleach Glos,
ENGLAND
Pickering, Jeff *Cartoonist*
King Features Syndicate, 888 7th Ave,
New York, NY 10106 USA
Pickering, Thomas R *Diplomat, Business
Person*
Boeing Corp, PO Box 3707, Seattle, WA
98124 USA
Pickett, Bobby (Boris) *Musician*
4015 1/2 Alla Road, Los Angeles, CA
90066 USA
Pickett, Bobby Boris
707 Marr St. #205, Venice, CA 90291
Pickett, Cindy *Actor*
662 N Van Ness Ave, #305, Los Angeles,
CA 90004 USA
Pickett, Jay
24801 Eilat St., Woodland Hills, CA
91367-1036
Pickett, Rex
Trident Media Group LLC, 41 Madison
Ave Fl 33, New York, NY 10010 USA
Pickett, Ryan *Football Player*
Saint Louis Rams, 901 N Broadway, Saint
Louis, MO 63101 USA
Pickett, Wilson *Musician*
Talent Source, 1560 Broadway, #1308,
New York, NY 10036 USA
Pickford, Mary Foundation
9171 Wilshire Blvd. #512, Beverly Hills,
CA 90210
Pickitt, John L *General*
38 Sunrise Point Road, Lake Wylie, SC
29710 USA
Pickler, John M *General*
Director Army Staff, HqUSA Pentagon,
Washington, DC 20310 USA
Pickles, Christina *Actor*
137 S Westgate Ave, Los Angeles, CA
90049 USA
Pickles, Vivian
91 Regent St., London, ENGLAND, W1R
8RU
Pickup, Ronald
54 Crouch Hall Rd., London, ENGLAND,
N8 8HG

Pictor, Bruce *Musician*
Variety Artists, 1924 Spring St, Paso
Robles, CA 93446 USA

Pidgeon, Rebecca *Actor*
Julian Belfarge, 46 Albermarle St, London,
W1X 4PP, UNITED KINGDOM (UK)

Piech, Ferdinand *Business Person*
Volkswagenwerk AG, Braunschweiger Str
63, Schwulper, 38179, GERMANY

Pied Pipers, The
25 Cobble Creek Dr. RD #1 Box 91,
Tannersville, PA 18372

Piel, Gerard *Publisher, Editor*
Scientific American Magazine, 415
Madison Ave, New York, NY 10017 USA

Piel, Jonathan *Editor*
Scientific American Magazine, 415
Madison Ave, New York, NY 10017 USA

Pienaar, Jacobus F *Misc*
Rugby Football Union, PO Box 99,
Newlands, 7725, SOUTH AFRICA

Piene, Otto *Artist*
383 Old Ayer Road, Groton, MA 01450
USA

Pierce, Chester M *Psychic*
17 Prince St, Jamaica Plain, MA 02130
USA

Pierce, David Hyde *Actor*
4724 Cromwell, Los Angeles, CA 90027
USA

Pierce, Jill *Actor*
Extreme Team Productions, 15941 S
Harlem, #319, Tinley Park, IL 60477 USA

Pierce, Jonathan *Musician*
Muse Assoc, 330 Franklin Road, #135-8,
Brentwood, TN 37027 USA

Pierce, Lincoln *Cartoonist*
United Feature Syndicate, 200 Madison
Ave, New York, NY 10016 USA

Pierce, Mary *Tennis Player*
6023 26th St W, #113, Bradenton, FL
34207 USA

Pierce, Paul *Basketball Player*
Boston Celtics, 151 Merrimac St, #1,
Boston, MA 02114 USA

Pierce, Paul Anthony *Basketball Player*
Boston Celtics, 151 Merrimac Street, #1,
Boston, MA 02114 USA

Pierce, Stack *Actor*
Haeggstrom Office, 11288 Ventura Blvd,
#620, Studio City, CA 91604 USA

Pierce, W William (Billy) *Baseball Player*
1321 Baileys Crossing Dr, Lemont, IL
60439 USA

Pierce, Wendell *Actor*
Writers & Artists, 8383 Wilshire Blvd,
#550, Beverly Hills, CA 90211 USA

Pierce-Roberts, Tony *Cinematographer*
1 Princes Garden, London, W5 1SD,
UNITED KINGDOM (UK)

Piercy, Marge *Writer*
PO Box 1473, Wellfleet, MA 02667 USA

Pierpoint, Eric *Actor*
2199 Topanga Skyline Dr, Topanga, CA
90290 USA

Pierpoint, Robert *Commentator*
CBS-TV, News Dept, 2020 M St NW,
Washington, DC 20036 USA

Pierre, Andrew J *Scientist*
Carnegie Endowment for Peace, 1779
Massachusetts NW, Washington, DC
20036 USA

Pierre, Juan *Baseball Player*
2267 Dan Marino Blvd, Miami, FL 33056

Pierre of Normandy, Abbe *Religious
Leader, Social Activist*
La Halte d'Emmaus, Esteville, 76690,
FRANCE

Piersall, James A (Jimmy) *Baseball Player*
12462 N 72nd Place, Scottsdale, AZ
85260 USA

Piersall, Jimmy
1105 Oakview Dr, Wheaton, IL 60187

Pierson, Frank R *Director, Writer*
1223 Amalfi Dr, Pacific Palisades, CA
90272 USA

Pierson, Geoff *Actor*
Ambrosio/Mortimer, 165 W 46th St, New
York, NY 10036 USA

Pierson, Kate *Musician*
Direct Management Group, 947 N La
Cienega Blvd, #2, Los Angeles, CA 90069
USA

Pierson, Marcus *Artist*
Outwest, 7216 Washington St NE, #A,
Albuquerque, NM 87109 USA

Pierzynski, Anthony J (AJ) *Baseball Player*
5209 Pleasure Island Road, Orlando, FL
32809 USA

Pietrangeli, Nicola *Tennis Player*
Via Eustachio Manfredi, Rome, 15, ITALY

Pietrangelo, Frank *Hockey Player*
11 Buttonwood Lane, Avon, CT 06001
USA

Pietrus, Mickael *Basketball Player*
Golden State Warriors, 1001 Broadway,
Oakland, CA 94607 USA

Pietruski Jr, John M *Business Person*
27 Paddock Lane, Colts Neck, NJ 07722
USA

Pietrzykowski, Zbigniew *Boxer*
UI Gomicza 5, Bielsko-Blata, 43-409,
POLAND

Pietz, Amy *Actor*
Geddes Agency, 8430 Santa Monica Blvd,
#200, West Hollywood, CA 90069 USA

Piggott, Lester K *Jockey*
Beech Tree House, Tostock Bury Saint
Edmonds, Suffolk, 1P20 9NY, UNITED
KINGDOM (UK)

Pignatano, Joe
150 78th St., Brooklyn, NY 11209

Pigott, Mark C *Business Person*
PACCAR Inc, 777 106th Ave NE,
Bellevue, WA 98004 USA

Pigott-Smith, Tim *Actor*
P F D Drury House, 34-43 Russell St,
London, WC2B 5HA, UNITED KINGDOM
(UK)

Pihos, Peter L (Pete) *Football Player*
2755 Winslow Lane, Winston Salem, NC
27103 USA

Pikaizen, Viktor A *Musician*
Chekhova Str 31/22, #37, Moscow,
RUSSIA

Pike, Gary *Musician*
10031 Benares Place, Sun Valley, CA
91352 USA

Pike, Jim *Musician*
MPI Talent Agency, 9255 Sunset Blvd,
#407, Los Angeles, CA 90069 USA

Pike, Rosamund *Actor*
Peters Fraser & Dunlop (PFD - UK), Drury
House, 34-43 Russell St, London, WC2
B5, UNITED KINGDOM (UK)

Pikser, Jeremy *Actor*
Margaret Riley Management, 1041 N
Formosa Ave, Los Angeles, CA 90046

Pilarczyk, Daniel E *Religious Leader*
100 E 8th St, Cincinnati, OH 45202 USA

Pileggi, Mitch *Actor*
26893 Bouquet Canyon Road, #C237,
Santa Clarita, CA 91350 USA

Pileggi, Nicholas *Writer*
Creative Artists Agency, 9830 Wilshire
Blvd, Beverly Hills, CA 90212 USA

Pilic, Nicki *Tennis Player*
DTB, Otto-Fleck-Schneise 8, Frankfurt/
Maim, 60528, GERMANY

Piligian, Craig *Producer*

Pilkey, Dav *Writer*
Scholastic Press, 555 Broadway, New
York, NY 10012 USA

Pilkis, Simon J *Physicist*
State University of New York, Health
Sciences Center, Stony Brook, NY 11794
USA

Pill, Alison *Actor*
Burstein Company, The, 15304 Sunset
Blvd #208, Pacific Palisades, CA 90272
USA

Pilla, Anthony M *Religious Leader*
Catholic Bishops National Conference,
3211 4th St, Washington, DC 20017 USA

Pilliod Jr, Charles J *Diplomat, Business
Person*
494 Saint Andrews Dr, Akron, OH 44303
USA

Pillow, Ray *Musician*
Joe Taylor Artist Agency, 2802 Columbine
Place, Nashville, TN 37204 USA

Pillsbury, Edmund P *Director*
3601 Potomac Ave, Fort Worth, TX 76107
USA

Pilote, Pierre P *Hockey Player*
25 Mary Jane, Elmwood, ON L0L 2PO,
CANADA

Pilska, Paul *Opera Singer*
George M Martynuk, 352 7th Ave, New
York, NY 10001 USA

Pilson, Neal H *Producer*
CBS-TV, Sports Dept, 51 W 52nd St, New
York, NY 10019 USA

Pimenta, Simon Ignatius Cardinal
Religious Leader
Archbishop's House, 21 Nathalal Parekh
Marg, Mumbai, MS 400 039, INDIA

Pinal, Silvia
Av. de las Fuentes 629 Pedregal de San
Angel, Mexico DF, MEXICO

Pincay, Laffit
PO Box 250, Lexington, KY 40588-0250

Pincay Jr, Laffit *Jockey*
5200 Los Grandes Way, Los Angeles, CA
90027 USA

Pinchot, Bronson *Actor*
10061 Riverside Dr, Toluca Lake, CA
91602 USA

Pinckney, Ed *Basketball Player*
6 Coconut Lane, Miami, FL 33149 USA

Pinckney, Sandra *Chef*
Food Network, 1180 Ave of Americas,
#1200, New York, NY 10036 USA

Pinder, Michael (Mike) *Misc*
Moody Blues, 53-55 High St, Cobham,
Surrey, KT11 3DP, UNITED KINGDOM
(UK)

Pine, Courtney *Musician*
Elizabeth Rush Agency, 100 Park St, #4,
Montclair, NJ 07042 USA

Pine, Philip
7034 Costello Ave., Van Nuys, CA 91405

Pine, Robert *Actor*
4212 Ben Ave, Studio City, CA 91604
USA

Pineau-Valencienne, Didier *Business
Person*
Schneider, 64/70 J Baptiste Clement,
Boulogne-Billancourt, 92646, FRANCE

Pineda, Salvador *Actor*
TV Azteca, Periferico Sur 4121, Colonia
Fuentes del Pedregal, DF, CP 14141,
Mexico

Pinera, Mike *Musician*
18407 Chase St, Northridge, CA 91325
USA

Pines, Alexander *Misc*
University of California, Chemistry Dept,
Hildebrand Hall, Berkeley, CA 94720
USA

Pinette, John
International Creative Management
(ICM-LA), 8942 Wilshire Blvd, Beverly
Hills, CA 90211 USA

Ping Lu, Kun *Misc*
Beth Israel Deaconess Medical Center,
3300 Brookline Ave, Boston, MA 02215
USA

Pingel, John S *Football Player*
80 Celestial Way, #203, Juno Beach, FL
33408 USA

Pinger, Mark *Swimmer*
5201 Orduna Dr, #6, Coral Gables, FL
33146 USA

Piniella, Lou
1005 Taray De Avila, Tampa, FL 33613

Piniella, Louis V (Lou) *Baseball Player*
1005 Taray De Avila, Tampa, FL 33163
USA

Pink *Musician*
PO Box 390, 5701 E Circle Dr, Cicero,
NY 13039 USA

Pinkel, Donald P *Misc*
275 Martene Dr, San Luis Obispo, CA
93405 USA

Pinkel, Gary *Football Coach*
University of Missouri, Athletic Dept,
Columbia, MO 64211 USA

Pinkett, Allen *Football Player*
1849 Portsmouth St, Houston, TX 77098
USA

Pinkett Smith, Jada *Actor*
Brookside Artists Management (LA), 450 N
Roxbury Dr Fl 4, Beverly Hills, CA 90210
USA

Pinkham Jr, Daniel R *Composer*
150 Chilton St, Cambridge, MA 02138
USA

Pinkins, Tonya *Actor*
Innovative Artists, 1505 10th St, Santa
Monica, CA 90401 USA

Pinkney, Bill *Musician*
Superstars Unlimited, PO Box 371371,
Las Vegas, NV 89137 USA

Pinkston, Ryan *Actor*
MBST Entertainment, 345 N Maple D
#200, Suite 200, Beverly Hills, CA 90210
USA

Pinkston, Todd *Football Player*
1 Novacare Way, Philadelphia, PA 19145

Pinmonkey *Music Group*
William Morris Agency (WMA-TN), 2100
W End Ave #1000, Nashville, TN 37203
USA

Pinnock, Trevor *Musician, Conductor*
35 Gloucester Crescent, London, NW1
7DL, UNITED KINGDOM (UK)

Pino, Danny *Actor*
Firm, The, 9465 Wilshire Blvd, Beverly
Hills, CA 90212 USA

Pinos, Carmen *Architect*
Av Diagonal 490, #3/2, Barcelona, 08006,
SPAIN

Pinskey, Raleigh

Pinsky, Drew (Dr Drew) *Actor*
William Morris Agency (WMA-LA), 1
William Morris Pl, Beverly Hills, CA
90212 USA

Pinsky, Robert N *Writer*
Boston University, Creative Writing Dept,
236 Bay State Road, Boston, MA 02215
USA

Pinson, Julie *Actor*
13576 Cheltenham Dr, Sherman Oaks,
CA 91423 USA

Pinson, Vada
710 31st St., Oakland, CA 94609

Pintauro, Danny *Actor*
FHL, 10667 Adamsong Ave, Las Vegas,
NV 89135 USA

Pinter, Harold *Writer*
Judy Daish, 2 Saint Charles Place,
London, W10 6EG, UNITED KINGDOM
(UK)

Pintilie, Lucian *Director*
44 Mihail Kogalniceanu Blvd, Bucharest,
ROMANIA

Pintscher, Matthias *Composer*
Van Walsum Mgmt, 4 Addison Bridge
Place, London, W14 8XP, UNITED
KINGDOM (UK)

Piovanelli, Silvano Cardinal *Religious
Leader*
Piazzi S Glovanni 3, Florence, 50129,
ITALY

Piper, Jacki *Actor*
Lengford Assoc, 17 Westfields Ave,
Barnes, London, SW13 0AT, UNITED
KINGDOM (UK)

Piper, Rowdy Roddy *Wrestler, Actor*
18645 SW Farmington Rd, #312, Aloha,
OR 97007 USA

Pipes, Leah *Actor*
Identity Talent Agency (ID), 2050 Bundy
Dr #200, Los Angeles, CA 90025 USA

Pipes, R Byron *Educator*
Po Box 1147, Hudson, OH 44236 USA

Pippard, A Brian *Physicist*
30 Porson Road, Cambridge, CB2 2EU,
UNITED KINGDOM (UK)

Pippen, Scottie *Basketball Player*
Chicago Bulls, United Center, 1901 W
Madison St, Chicago, IL 60612 USA

Pippig, Uta *Track Athlete*
4279 Niblick Dr, Longmont, CO 80503
USA

Piquet, Nelson *Race Car Driver*
Autodromo, SEN/CDPM, Rua da Gasolina
#01, Brasilia, DF, 7007-400, BRAZIL

Pirae, Marcus Jean *Actor*
Visionary Entertainment, 8265 Sunset Blvd
#104, Los Angeles, CA 90046 USA

Piraro, Dan *Cartoonist*
United Feature Syndicate, 200 Madison
Ave, New York, NY 10016 USA

Pirates of the Mississippi
Box 17087, Nashville, TN 37217

Pirelli, Leopoldo *Business Person*
Via Gaetano Negri 10, Milan, 20123,
ITALY

Pires, Alexandre *Musician*
BMG, 1540 Broadway, New York, NY
10036 USA

Pires, Mary Joao *Musician*
Columbia Artists Mgmt Inc, 165 W 57th
St, New York, NY 10019 USA

Pires, Pedro V R *Prime Minister, General*
PAICV, CP 22, Praia, Santiago, CAPE
VERDE

Pires de Miranda, Pedro *Government
Official*
Avenida da India 10, Lisbon, 1300,
PORTUGAL

Pirner, Dave *Musician, Songwriter*
Monterey Peninsula Artists, 509 Hartnell
St, Monterey, CA 93940 USA

Piro, Stephanie *Cartoonist*
Po Box 605, Hampton, NH 03843 USA

Pirri, Jim
9300 Wilshire Blvd. #555, Beverly Hills,
CA 90212

Pischetsrider, Bernd *Business Person*
Bayerishe Motoren Werke, Petuelring 130,
Munich, 80788, GERMANY

Piscopo, Joe *Actor, Comedian*
PO Box 258, Bernardsville, NJ 07924 USA

Pisier, Marie-France *Actor*
Gaumont International, 30 Ave Charles de
Gaulle, Neuilly, 92200, FRANCE

Pister, Karl S *Educator*
University of California, Chancellor's
Office, Santa Cruz, CA 95064 USA

Pistone, Tom *Race Car Driver*
4405 Woodwind St, Charlotte, NC 28213
USA

Pitchford, Dean
1701 Queens Rd, Los Angeles, CA 90069

Pithart, Petr *Government Official*
Senate, Vakdstejnske Nam 4, Prague, 118
11, CZECH REPUBLIC

Pitillo, Maria *Actor*
William Morris AGency, 151 El Camino
Dr, Beverly Hills, CA 90212 USA

Pitino, Richard (Rick) *Coach*
University of Louisville, Crawford Gym,
Louisville, KY 40292 USA

Pitman, Jennifer S *Race Car Driver*
Weathercock House, Upper Lamboum
Hungerford, Berks, RG17 8QT, UNITED
KINGDOM (UK)

Pitney, Gene *Musician, Songwriter*
6201 39th Ave, Kenosha, WI 53142 USA

Pitoc, J P
1836 Courtney Terr, Los Angeles, CA
90046 USA

Pitoc, John Paul *Actor*
Don Buchwald & Associates Inc (LA),
6500 Wilshire Blvd #2200, Los Angeles,
CA 90048 USA

Pitou Zimmerman, Penny *Skier*
560 Sanborn Road, Sanbornton, NH
03269 USA

Pitt, Brad *Actor, Producer*
Brillstein/Grey, 9150 Wilshire Blvd, #350,
Beverly Hills, CA 90212 USA

Pitt, Eugene *Musician*
Paramount Entertainment, PO Box 12, Far
Hills, NJ 07931 USA

Pitt, Ingrid *Actor*
Langford, 17 Westfields Ave, London,
SW13 0AT, UNITED KINGDOM (UK)

Pitt, Michael *Actor*
United Talent Agency, 9560 Wilshire
Blvd, #500, Beverly Hills, CA 90212 USA

Pitt, William
9 rue Jean Mermoz, Paris, FRANCE,
F-75008

Pittenger, Mark F *Scientist*
Osrins Therapeutics, 2001 Aliceanna St,
Baltimore, MD 21231 USA

Pittman, Charles *Basketball Player*
16286 N 29th Dr, Phoenix, AZ 85053
USA

Pittman, R F *Publisher*
Tampa Tribune, 202 S Parker St, Tampa,
FL 33606 USA

Pittman, Richard A *War Hero*
5380 Dehesa Road, El Cajon, CA 92019
USA

Pittman Jr, James A *Misc*
5 Ridge Dr, Birmingham, AL 35213 USA

Pitts, Greg
8383 Wilshire Blvd. #550, Beverly Hills,
CA 90211

Pitts, Robert (R C) *Basketball Player*
12655 E Milburn Ave, Baton Rouge, LA
70815 USA

Pitts, Ron *Sportscaster*
Fox TV, Sports Dept, 205 W 67th St, New
York, NY 10021 USA

Pitts, Tyrone S *Religious Leader*
Progressive National Baptist Convention,
601 50th St NE, Washington, DC 20019
USA

Piven, Jeremy *Actor*
9 Yards Entertainment, 8530 Wilshire Blvd
Fl 5, Beverly Hills, CA 90211 USA

Piza, Arthur Luiz de *Artist*
16 Rue Dauphine, Paris, 75006, FRANCE

Pizarro, Artur *Musician*
Muscians Corporate Mgmt, PO Box 589,
Millbrook, NY 12545 USA

Piziou, Peter
16 Belsize Park, London, ENGLAND,
NW3 4ES

PJ & Duncan
PO Box 122Ashford, Kent, ENGLAND,
TN27 9BZ

Place, Mary Kay *Actor*
2739 Motor Ave, Los Angeles, CA 90064
USA

Placebo *Music Group*
Helter Skelter (UK), The Plaza, 535 Kings
Rd, London, N13 5H, UNITED
KINGDOM (UK)

Plachta, Leonard E *Educator*
Central Michigan University, President's
Office, Mount Pleasant, MI 48859 USA

Placido, Michele
. 5200 via San Cornelia, Formello-RM,
ITALY, 00060

Plager, Robert B (Bob) *Hockey Player,
Coach*
362 Branchport Dr, Chesterfied, MO
63017 USA

Plager, S Jay *Judge*
US Court of Appeals, 7171 Madison Place
NW, Washington, DC 20439 USA

Plain, Belva *Writer*
Houghton Mifflin, 215 Park Ave S, New
York, NY 10003 USA

Plainic, Zoran *Basketball Player*
New Jersey Nets, 390 Murray Hill
Parkway, East Rutherford, NJ 07073 USA

Plakson, Suzie *Actor*
302 N La Brea Ave, #363, Los Angeles,
CA 90036 USA

Plana, Tony *Actor*
Metropolian Talent Agency, 4526 Wilshire
Blvd, Los Angeles, CA 90010 USA

Planchon, Roger *Director, Writer*
Teatre National Populaire, 8 Pl Lazare
Goujon, Villeurbanne, 69627, FRANCE

Planinc, Milka *Prime Minister*
Fed Exec Council, Bul Lenjina 2, Novi
Belgrad, 11075, SERBIA-MONTENEGRO

Plank, Raymond *Business Person*
Apache Corp, 2000 Post Oak Blvd,
Houston, TX 77056 USA

Plank, Scott
151 El Camino Dr., Beverly Hills, CA
90212

Plano, Richard J *Physicist*
PO Box 5306, Sommerset, NJ 08875 USA

Plant, Robert *Musician, Songwriter*
Trinifold Mgmt, 12 Oval Road, London,
NW1 7DH, UNITED KINGDOM (UK)

Plante, Bruce *Cartoonist*
Chattanooga Times, Editorial Dept, 100 E
11th St #400, Chattanooga, TN 37402
USA

Plante, William M *Commentator*
CBS-TV, News Dept, 2020 M St NW,
Washington, DC 20036 USA

Plantu *Cartoonist*
Le Monde, Editorial Dept, 21 Bis Rue
Claude Bernard, Paris, 75005, FRANCE

Plaskett, Thomas G *Business Person*
5215 N O'Connor Blvd, #1070, Irving, TX
75039 USA

Plater-Zyberk, Elizabeth M *Architect*
Duany & Plater-Zyberk Architects, 1023
SW 25th Ave, Miami, FL 33135 USA

Platini, Michel
90 av. des Champs-Elysees, Paris,
FRANCE, F-75008

Platinli, Michel *Soccer Player*
World Cup Organization, 17-21 Ave Gen
Mangin, Paris Cedex, 75024, FRANCE

Platinum Blonde
Box 1223 Sta. F, Toronto, CANADA,
Ont.M4Y 2T

Platon, Nicolas *Archaeologist*
Leof Alexandras 126, Athens, 11471,
GREECE

Platov, Yevgeni *Dancer*
Connecticut Skating Center, 300 Alumni
Road, Newington, CT 06111 USA

Platt, Howard
9200 Sunset Blvd. #1130, Los Angeles,
CA 90069

Platt, Kenneth A *Doctor*
11435 Quivas Way, Westminster, CO
80234 USA

Platt, Lewis E (Lew) *Business Person*
Hewlett-Packard Co, 3000 Hanover St,
Palo Alto, CA 94304 USA

Platt, Nicholas *Diplomat*
131 E 69th St, New York, NY 10021 USA

Platt, Oliver *Actor*
Three Arts Entertainment, 9460 Wilshire
Blvd, #700, Beverly Hills, CA 90212 USA

Platters
2756 N. Green Valley Parkway #449, Las
Vegas, NV 89014-2100

Plavinsky, Dmitri P *Artist*
Arbat Str 51, Kotp 2 #97, Moscow,
121002, RUSSIA

Play *Music Group*
Music World Entertainment, 9898
Bissonnet, Suite 625, Houston, TX 77036
USA

Playboy Playmates
2112 Broadway, Santa Monica, CA
90404-2912

Player, Gary *Athlete*
3930 RCA Blvd #3001, Palm Beach
Gardens, FL 33410

Player, Gary J *Golfer*
3930 RCA Blvd #3001, Palm Beach
Gardens, FL 33410 USA

Playten, Alice *Actor*
33 5th Ave, New York, NY 10003 USA

Pleau, Lawrence W (Larry) *Hockey Player, Coach*
650 Spyglass Summit Dr, Chesterfield, MO 63017 USA

Plenty, Patty
1350 E. Flamingo Rd. #150, Las Vegas, NV 89118

Pleshette, John *Actor*
2643 Creston Dr, Los Angeles, CA 90068 USA

Pleshette, Suzanne *Actor*
10375 Wilshire Blvd, #5B, Los Angeles, CA 90024 USA

Pletcher, Eidon *Cartoonist*
210 Canberra Court, Slidell, LA 70458 USA

Pletnev, Mikhail V *Musician*
Starpkonyushenny Per 33, #16, Moscow, RUSSIA

Plimpton, Calvin H *Doctor*
Downstate Medical Center, 450 Clarkson Ave, Brooklyn, NY 11203 USA

Plimpton, Martha *Actor*
502 Park Ave, #15G, New York, NY 10022 USA

Plisetskaya, Maiya M *Ballerina*
Tverskaya 25/9, #31, Moscow, 103050, RUSSIA

Plotkin, Stanley A *Musician*
3940 Delancey St, Philadelphia, PA 19104 USA

Plott, Charles R *Economist*
881 El Campo Dr, Pasadena, CA 91107 USA

Plough, Thomas *Educator*
North Dakota State University, President's Office, Fargo, ND 58105 USA

Plowden, David *Writer, Photographer*
609 Cherry St, Winnetka, IL 60093 USA

Plowright, Joan A *Actor*
Malthouse, Horsham Road Ashurst Steying, West Sussex, BN44 3AR, UNITED KINGDOM (UK)

Plowright, Joan A *Opera Singer*
83 Saint Mark's Ave, Salisbury, Wilts, SP1 3DW, UNITED KINGDOM (UK)

Pluhar, Erika
Huschkagasse 5, Vienna, AUSTRIA, A-1190

Plum, Milton R (Milt) *Football Player*
1104 Oakside Court, Raleigh, NC 27609 USA

Plumb, Eve *Actor*
Edwards & Associates, 5455 Wilshire Blvd #1614, Los Angeles, CA 90036 USA

Plumer, Patricia (PattiSue) *Track Athlete*
USA Track & Field, 4341 Starlight Dr, Indianapolis, IN 46239 USA

Plummer, Amanda *Actor*
160 Prince St, #2, New York, NY 10012 USA

Plummer, Christopher *Actor, Musician*
49 Wampum Hill Road, Suite 480, Weston, CT 06883 USA

Plummer, Glenn *Actor*
Innovative Artists (LA), 1505 Tenth St, Santa Monica, CA 90401 USA

Plummer, Jake *Football Player*
3406 E Kachina Dr, Phoenix, AZ 85044 USA

Plummer, Scotty
909 Parkview Ave., Lodi, CA 95240

Plummer, Stephen B *General*
Deputy to Assistant Secretary, HqUSAF Pentagon, Washington, DC 20330 USA

Plunkett, Jim
51 Kilroy Way, Atherton, CA 94025

Plunkett, Maryann
10 E. 44th St., New York, NY 10017

Plunkett Jr, James W (Jim) *Football Player*
51 Kilroy Way, Atherton, CA 94027 USA

Plus One *Music Group*
Paradigm Management, 611 Lawrin Park, Franklin, TN 37069 USA

Plyushch, Ivan S *Misc*
Verkhovna Rada, M Hrushevskoho 5, Kiev, 252019, UKRAINE

PM Dawn
14 E. 4th St., New York, NY 10012

Pocklington, Peter H *Misc*
Edmonton Oilers, 11230 110th St, Edmonton, AB T5G 3H7, CANADA

Poderoso, Gozo *Musician*
William Morris Agency (WMA-LA), 1 William Morris Pl, Beverly Hills, CA 90212 USA

Podesta, John *Government Official*
White House, 1600 Pennsylvania Ave NW, Washington, DC 20500 USA

Podesta, Rosanna
Via Bartolomeo Ammannati 8, Rome, ITALY, I-00197

Podesta, Rossana *Actor*
Via Bartolomeo Ammanatti 8, Rome, 00187, ITALY

Podewell, Cathy *Actor*
17328 S Crest Dr, Los Angeles, CA 90035 USA

Podhoretz, Norman *Editor, Writer*
Commentary Magazine, Editorial Dept, 165 E 56th St, New York, NY 10022 USA

Podkopayeva, Lilia
Rue des Oeuches 10, Moutier, SWITZERLAND, CP 350 374

Podolak, Edward J (Ed) *Football Player*
2227 Emma Road, Basalt, CO 81621 USA

Podres, John J (Johnny) *Baseball Player*
1 Colonial Court, Glens Falls, NY 12804 USA

Podres, Johnny
1 Colonial Ct., Glen Falls, NY 12801

Poe *Songwriter, Musician*
Creative Artists Agency, 9830 Wilshire Blvd, Beverly Hills, CA 90212 USA

Poe, Gregory *Fashion Designer*
Dutch Courage, 1950 S Santa Fe Ave, Los Angeles, CA 90021 USA

Poe, Richard
10 Prospect Park SW #17, Brooklyn, NY 11215-5937

Poehler, Amy *Actor, Comedian*
Three Arts Entertainment, 9460 Wilshire Blvd, #700, Beverly Hills, CA 90212 USA

Pogorelich, Ivo *Musician*
Kantor Concert Mgmt, 67 Teignmouth Road, London, NW2 4EA, UNITED KINGDOM (UK)

Pogrebin, Letty Cottin *Editor, Writer, Social Activist*
33 W 67th St, New York, NY 10023 USA

Pogue, Donald W *Judge*
IS International Trade Court, 1 Federal Plaza, New York, NY 10278 USA

Pogue, William R *Astronaut*
4 Cromer Dr, Bella Vista, AR 72115 USA

Pohl, Dan
11609 S. Tusaya Ct., Phoenix, AZ 85044

Pohl, Don *Golfer*
3424 E Suncrest Court, Phoenix, AZ 85044 USA

Pohl, Frederick
855 S. Harvard Dr., Palatine, IL 60067-1026

Poindexter, Alan G *Astronaut*
2389 Calypso Lane, League City, TX 77573 USA

Poindexter, Buster *Musician*
Agency Group Ltd, 1775 Broadway, #430, New York, NY 10019 USA

Poindexter, Christian H *Business Person*
Constellation Energy Group, 39 W Lexington St, Baltimore, MD 21201 USA

Poindexter, John M *Admiral, Government Official*
10 Barrington Fare, Rockville, MD 20850 USA

Pointer, Anita *Musician*
12060 Crest Court, Beverly Hills, CA 90210 USA

Pointer, Bonnie *Musician*
T-Best Talent Agency, 508 Honey Lake Court, Danville, CA 94506 USA

Pointer, Noel *Musician*
Headline Talent, 1650 Broadway, #508, New York, NY 10019 USA

Pointer, Priscilla *Musician*
213 16th St, Santa Monica, CA 90402 USA

Pointer, Ruth *Musician*
William Morris AGency, 151 El Camino Dr, Beverly Hills, CA 90212 USA

Pointer Sisters *Music Group*
Morey Management Group, 9255 Sunset Blvd #600, Los Angeles, CA 90069 USA

Poirier, Anne
32 rue Lenine, Ivry, FRANCE, F-94200

Poirier, Patrick
32 rue Lenine, Ivry, FRANCE, F-94200

Poison *Music Group*
Agency for the Performing Arts (APA-LA), 9200 Sunset Blvd #900, Los Angeles, CA 90069 USA

Poitier, Sidney *Actor*
Creative Artists Agency, 9830 Wilshire Blvd, Beverly Hills, CA 90212 USA

Polaha, Kris *Actor*
3 Arts Entertainment (NY), 451 Greenwich St Fl 7, New York, NY 10013 USA

Polamalu, Troy *Football Player*
Pittsburgh Steelers, 3400 S Water St, Pittsburgh, PA 15203 USA

Polanski, Roman *Director*
Agents Associes Beaume, 201 Faubourg
Saint Honore, Paris, 75008, FRANCE

Polansky, Abraham
135 S. McCarty Dr.#4, Beverly Hills, CA
90212

Polansky, Mark *Astronaut*
2010 Hillside Oak Lane, Houston, TX
77062 USA

Polanyi, John C *Nobel Prize Laureate*
142 Collier St, Toronto, ON M4W 1M3,
CANADA

Polchinski, Joseph G *Physicist*
University of California, Physics Institute,
Santa Barbara, CA 93106 USA

Poledouris, Basil *Composer*
Kraft-Benjamin-Engel, 15233 Ventura
Blvd, #200, Sherman Oaks, CA 91403
USA

Poleshchuk, Alexander F *Cosmonaut*
Potchta Kosmonavtov Moskovskoi Oblasti,
Syvisdny Goroduk, 141160, RUSSIA

Poletiek, Noah *Actor*
Protege Management, 1025 N Kings Rd
#304, W Hollywood, CA 90069 USA

Poletto, Severino Cardinal *Religious
Leader*
Via Arcivescovado 12, Torino, 10121,
ITALY

Polgar, Laszlo *Opera Singer*
Abel Jeno Utca 12, Budapest, 1113,
HUNGARY

Polic, Henry II *Actor*
Sutton Barth Vennari, 145 S Fairfax Ave,
#310, Los Angeles, CA 90036 USA

Police, The
194 Kensington Park Rd., London,
ENGLAND, W11 2ES

Polish, Mark *Actor, Producer, Writer*
Endeavor Agency LLC (LA), 9601 Wilshire
Blvd Fl 3, Beverly Hills, CA 90210 USA

Polish, Michael *Director*
Endeavor Talent Agency, 9701 Wilshire
Blvd, #1000, Beverly Hills, CA 90212
USA

Polito, Jon *Actor*
Writers and Artists Group Intl (LA), 8383
Wilshire Blvd #550, Beverly Hills, CA
90211 USA

Politz, Henry A *Judge*
US Court of Appeals, 500 Fannin St,
Shreveport, LA 71101 USA

Polk, Steven R *General*
Vice Commander, Pacific Air Forces,
Hickam Air Force Base, HI 96853 USA

Polke, Sigmar *Artist*
Michael Werner, 4 E 77th St, #200, New
York, NY 10021 USA

Polkinghome, John C *Physicist*
Queen's College, Cambridge University,
Cambridge, CB3 9ET, UNITED
KINGDOM (UK)

Poll, Martin H *Producer*
Martin Poll Productions, 8961 Sunset
Blvd, #E, Los Angeles, CA 90069 USA

Polla, Dennis L *Engineer*
University of Minnesota, Electrical
Engineering Dept, Minneapolis, MN
55455 USA

Pollack, Andrea *Swimmer*
SSV, Postfach 420140, Kassel, 34070,
GERMANY

Pollack, Daniel *Musician*
University of Southern California, Music
Dept, Los Angeles, CA 90089 USA

Pollack, Jim *Actor*
Ericka Wain, 1418 N Highland Ave, #102,
Los Angeles, CA 90028 USA

Pollack, Joseph *Misc*
Insurance Workers Union, 1017 12th St
NW, Washington, DC 20005 USA

Pollack, Kevin *Actor*
International Creative Mgmt, 8942
Wilshire Blvd, #219, Beverly Hills, CA
90211 USA

Pollack, Sam *Misc*
6811 Monkland Ave, Montreal, QC, H4B
1J2, CANADA

Pollack, Sydney *Actor, Director*
The Firm, 9100 Wilshire Blvd, #100W,
Beverly Hills, CA 90210 USA

Pollak, Cheryl
275 S. Beverly Dr. #215, Beverly Hills,
CA 90212

Pollak, Cheryl A *Actor*
Kritzer, 12200 W Olympic Blvd, #400,
Los Angeles, CA 90064 USA

Pollak, Kevin *Actor, Comedian*
Calm Down Productions, 1360 N
Crescent Heights Blvd, Los Angeles, CA
90046 USA

Pollak, Lisa *Journalist*
Baltimore Sun, Editorial Dept, 501 N
Calvert St, Baltimore, MD 21202 USA

Pollan, Tracy *Actor*
Baker/Winokur/Ryder, 9100 Wilshire Blvd,
#600, Beverly Hills, CA 90212 USA

Pollard, Jonathan
Federal Reformatory, Marion, IL 62959

Pollard, Michael J *Actor*
520 S Burnside Ave, #12A, Los Angeles,
CA 90036 USA

Pollard, Scott *Basketball Player*
Indiana Pacers, Conseco Fieldhouse, 125
S Pennsylvania, Indianapolis, IN 46204
USA

Pollard, Su
24 Denmark St., London, ENGLAND,
WC2H 8NA

Polle, David R *Misc*
Nashville Predators, 501 Broadway,
Nashville, TN 37203 USA

Polle, Norman R (Bud) *Hockey Player,
Coach*
1509-2004 Fullerton Ave, North
Vancouver, BC V7P 3G8, CANADA

Pollen, Arabella R H *Fashion Designer*
Canham Mews, #8 Canham Road,
London, W3 7SR, UNITED KINGDOM
(UK)

Polley, Eugene J *Inventor*
202 W Berkshire Ave, Lombard, IL 60148
USA

Polley, Sarah *Actor*
10 Mary St, #308, Toronto, ON M4Y 1P9,
CANADA

Pollin, Abe *Baseball Player*
Centre Group, Capital Centre, 1 Truman
Dr, Landover, MD 20785 USA

Pollini, Maurizio *Musician*
RESIA, Via Manzoni 31, Milan, 20120,
ITALY

Pollock, Alex J *Business Person*
Federal Home Loan Bank, 111 E Wacker
Dr, Chicago, IL 60601 USA

Pollock, Channing
PO Box 36068, Los Angeles, CA 90036

Pollock, Michael P *Admiral*
Ivy House, Churchstoke Montgomery,
Powys, SY15 6DU, WALES

Polo, Ana Maria *Actor*
Telemundo, 2470 West 8th Avenue,
Hialeah, FL 33010 USA

Polo, Teri *Actor*
McGowan Management, 8733 W Sunset
Blvd #103, W Hollywood, CA 90069 USA

Polone, Gavin *Producer*
Endeavor Agency LLC (LA), 9601 Wilshire
Blvd Fl 3, Beverly Hills, CA 90210 USA

Poloujadoff, Michel E *Engineer*
8 Rue Roches, Buthiers, 77760, FRANCE

Polozkova, Lidia P *Speed Skater*
Solianka Str 14/2, Moscow, 109240,
RUSSIA

Polshak, James Stewart *Architect*
James Polshak Partners, 320 W 134th St,
#800, New York, NY 10030 USA

Polson, John *Actor*
RGM Associates (Australia), PO Box 128,
Surry Hills NSW, 2010, AUSTRALIA

Polyakov, Valeri V *Cosmonaut*
Health Ministry, Choroshevskoye
Chaussee 76A, Moscow, 123007, RUSSIA

Polyakov, Valery
141 160 Zvezdny Gorodok, Moscow Obl,
RUSSIA

Polynice, Olden *Basketball Player*
PO Box 220339, Newhall, CA 91322 USA

Pomers, Scarlett *Actor*
Platform Public Relations, 2133 Holly
Drive, Los Angeles, CA 90068 USA

Pommier, Jean-Bernard *Musician*
2 Chemin des Cotes de Montmoiret,
Lausanne, 1012, SWITZERLAND

Pomodora, Arnaldo *Artist*
Via Vigevano 5, Milan, 20144, ITALY

Pompedda, Mario Francesco Cardinal
Religious Leader
Palazzo della Cancelleria, Plazza della
Cancelleria 1, Rome, 00186, ITALY

Pompeo, Ellen *Actor*
P M K Public Relations, 8500 Wilshire
Blvd, #700, Beverly Hills, CA 90211 USA

Ponazecki, Joe *Actor*
Don Buchwald, 10 E 44th St, New York,
NY 10017 USA

Ponce, Carlos *Musician*
William Morris Agency (WMA-LA), 1
William Morris Pl, Beverly Hills, CA
90212 USA

Ponce, Enrile Juan *Government Official*
2305 Morado St, Dasmarinas Village
Makati, Metro Manila, PHILLIPPINES

Ponce, LuAnne *Actor*
Gold Marshak Liedtke, 3500 W Olive
Ave, #1400, Burbank, CA 91505 USA

Ponce, Ponce
13501 Delano St., Van Nuys, CA 91405

Ponce, Walter *Musician*
Columbia Artists Mgmt Inc, 165 W 57th
St, New York, NY 10019 USA

Poni-Tails, The
Box 262, Carteret, NJ 07008-0262

Pons, B Stanley *Misc*
University of Utah, Chemistry Dept,
Eyring Building, Salt Lake City, UT 84112
USA

Pons, Juan *Opera Singer*
Herbert Breslin, 119 W 57th St, #1505,
New York, NY 10019 USA

Pont, John *Football Coach*
482 White Oak Dr, Oxford, OH 45056
USA

Pontecorvo, Gillo *Director*
60 Thornhill Square, London, N1 1BE,
UNITED KINGDOM (UK)

Pontes, Marcos *Astronaut*
16807 Soaring Forest Dr, Houston, TX
77059 USA

Ponti, Cario *Producer*
Palazzo Colonna, 1 Piazza d'Ara Coell 1,
Rome, ITALY

Ponti, Carlo
6 rue Charles Bonnet, Geneva,
SWITZERLAND, CH-1206

Ponti, Michael *Musician*
Heubergstr 32, Eschenlohe, 83565,
GERMANY

Pontois, Noella-Chantal *Ballerina*
25 Rue de Maubeuge, Paris, 75009,
FRANCE

Ponty, Jean-Luc *Musician, Composer*
Monterey Peninsula Artists, 509 Hartnell
St, Monterey, CA 93940 USA

Pony, Trick *Music Group*
Creative Artists Agency (CAA-Nashville),
3310 West End Ave Fl 5, Nashville, TN
37203 USA

Ponzini, Anthony *Actor*
Gold Marshak Liedtke, 3500 W Olive
Ave, #1400, Burbank, CA 91505 USA

Ponzlov, Frederick *Writer*
Careyes Entertainment, 9000 Sunset blvd,
Suite 800, Los Angeles, CA 90069 USA

Pooja, Bhatt *Actor, Bollywood*
601 Kyle More Apartments, Behind
Mehboob Studios Bandra(W), Mumbai,
MS 400050, INDIA

Pook, Chris *Race Car Driver*
Championship Auto Racing, 5350
Lakeview Parkway S Dr, Indianapolis, IN
46268 USA

Pool, John L *Doctor*
560 Belden Hill Road, Wilton, CT 06897
USA

Poole, Brian *Musician*
67 Tower Drive, Neath Hill, Milton
Keynes, MK14 6JX, UNITED KINGDOM
(UK)

Poole, David J *Artist*
Trinity Flint Bam, Weston Lane, Petersfield
Hants, GU32 3NN, UNITED KINGDOM
(UK)

Poole, G Barney *Football Player*
213 E Railroad Ave, Gloster, MS 39638
USA

Poole, William *Government Official*
Federal Reserve Bank, 411 Locust St, Saint
Louis, MO 63102 USA

Pooley, Don *Golfer*
5251 N Camino Sumo, Tucson, AZ 85718
USA

Poons, Larry *Artist*
PO Box 115, Islamorada, FL 33036 USA

Poornam, Viswanatha *Actor*
7 Lodi Khan Street, T Nagar, Chennai, TN
600 017, INDIA

Poot, Marcel
Ave. Louis Lepoutre 72, Brussels,
BELGIUM, 1060

Pop, Iggy *Musician, Songwriter, Actor*
MVO Ltd, 307 7th Ave, #807, New York,
NY 10001 USA

Pope, Carly *Actor*
Handprint Entertainment, 1100 Glendon
Ave, #1000, Los Angeles, CA 90024 USA

Pope, Eddie *Soccer Player*
New York/New Jersey MetroStars, 1
Harmon Plaza, #300, Secaucus, NJ 07094
USA

Pope, Edwin *Writer*
Miami Herald Editorial Dept, 1 Herald
Plaza, Miami, FL 33132 USA

Pope, Everett P *War Hero*
16 Osprey Village Dr, Fernandina, FL
32034 USA

Pope, Marguez P *Football Player*
PO Box 470487, San Francisco, CA
94147 USA

Pope, Odeon *Musician*
Brad Simon Organization, 122 E 57th St,
#300, New York, NY 10022 USA

Pope Jr, Clarence C *Religious Leader*
Fort Worth Episcopal Church Diocese,
6300 Ridlea Place, Fort Worth, TX 76116
USA

Popiel, Poul P *Hockey Player*
2501 Peppermill Ridge Dr, Chesterfield,
MO 63005 USA

Popoff, A Jay *Musician*
Sepetys Entertainment, 1223 Wilshire
Blvd, #804, Santa Monica, CA 90403 USA

Popoff, Frank P *Business Person*
Dow Chemical, 2030 Dow Center,
Midland, MI 48674 USA

Popov, Aleksandr *Swimmer*
Swimming Assn, Sports House, Maitland
Road #7, Hackett, 2602, AUSTRALIA

Popov, Leonid I *Cosmonaut*
Potchta Kosmonavtov Moskovskoi Oblasti,
Syvisdny Goroduk, 141160, RUSSIA

Popovac, Gwynn *Artist*
17270 Robin Ridge, Sonora, CA 95370
USA

Popovich, Gregg *Coach*
San Antonio Spurs, Alamodome, 1 SBC
Center, San Antonio, TX 78219 USA

Popovich, Pavel R *Cosmonaut*
AIUS-Agroressurs, VNIZ, Bolshevitskij Per
11, Moscow, 101000, RUSSIA

Popowich, Paul *Actor*
Twice in A Lifetime, Marine Terminal 28
Studio 4, 175 Quee Quay East, Toronto,
Ontario Canada, M5A 1B6

Popp, Nathaniel *Religious Leader*
Romanian Orthodox Episcopate, PO Box
309, Grass Lake, MI 49240 USA

Poppe, Nils
Fredriksdale Theaterin Domsten,
Helsingborg, SWEDEN, 25590

Popper, John *Musician*
ArtistDirect, 10900 Wilshire Blvd, #1400,
Los Angeles, CA 90024 USA

Porcaro, Jeff
5247 Twin Oaks Rd., Hidden Hills, CA
91302

Porcaro, Steve *Composer*
13596 Contour Dr, Sherman Oaks, CA
91423 USA

Porcaro, Steve *Musician*
Fitzgerald-Hartley, 34 N Palm St, Ventura,
CA 93001 USA

Porcher, Robert *Football Player*
160 Grosvenor Dr, Rochester Hills, MI
48307 USA

Porfilio, John C *Judge*
US Court of Appeals, 1919 Stout St,
Denver, CO 80294 USA

Porizkova, Paulina *Actor, Model*
Paradigm (LA), 10100 Santa Monica Blvd,
Fl 25, Los Angeles, CA 90067 USA

Porras, German *Director*
Gabriel Blanco Iglesias (Colombia), Dg
127A #20-36, Conjunto Plenitud, Apto
132, Bogota, Colombia

Porretta, Matthew *Actor*
Damage Mgmt, 10 Southwick Mews,
London, W2, UNITED KINGDOM (UK)

Portale, Carl *Publisher*
Elle Magazine, Hachette Filipacchi, 1633
Broadway, New York, NY 10019 USA

Porteous, Peter
Glencot Parkside Cheam, Surrey,
ENGLAND, SM3 8BS

Porter, Alison
112 S. Almont Dr, Los Angeles, CA 90048

Porter, Billy *Musician*
William Morris AGency, 151 El Camino
Dr, Beverly Hills, CA 90212 USA

Porter, David H *Educator*
Skidmore College, President's Office,
Saratoga Springs, NY 12866 USA

Porter, Howard *Basketball Player*
1034 Iglehart Ave, Saint Paul, MN 55104
USA

Porter, Jean
3945 Westfall Dr., Encino, CA 91436

Porter, Jody *Musician*
MOB Agency, 6404 Wilshire Blvd, #505, Los Angeles, CA 90048 USA

Porter, Joey *Football Player*
1118 Virginia St, Bakersfield, CA 93305 USA

Porter, Marina Oswald
1850 WFM Rd. 550, Rockwall, TX 75087

Porter, Rick
943 Hartzell St., Pacific Palisades, CA 90272

Porter, Terry *Basketball Player, Coach*
Milwaukee Bucks, Bradley Center, 1001 N 4th St, Milwaukee, WI 53203 USA

Porterfield, Ellary Hume *Actor*
Marv Dauer Management, 11661 San Vicente Blvd #104, Los Angeles, CA 90049 USA

Portes, Richard D *Economist*
Economic Policy Centre, 90-98 Goswell Road, London, EC1V 7RR, UNITED KINGDOM (UK)

Portillo, Alfonso *President*
President's Office, Palacio Nacional, Guatemala City, GUATEMALA

Portis, Charles *Writer*
7417 Kingwood Road, Little Rock, AR 72207 USA

Portisch, Lajos *Misc*
Chess Federation, Nephadsereg Utca 10, Budapest, 1055, HUNGARY

Portishead *Music Group*
High Road Touring, 751 Bridgeway, 3rd Fl, Sausalito, CA 94965

Portland, Rene *Coach*
Pennsylvania State University, Greenberg Complex, University Park, PA 16802 USA

Portman, Natalie *Actor*
The Firm, 9100 Wilshire Blvd, #100W, Beverly Hills, CA 90210 USA

Portman, Rachel *Composer*
PRS, 29/33 Berners St, London, W1P 4AA, UNITED KINGDOM (UK)

Portman Jr, John C *Architect*
Charles Portman Assoc, 225 Peachtree St NE, #220, Atlanta, GA 30303 USA

Porto, James *Photographer*
601 W 26th St, #1321, New York, NY 10001 USA

Portwich, Ramona *Athlete*
KC Limmer, Stockhardweg 3, Hanover, 30453, GERMANY

Posada, Jorge R *Baseball Player*
Calle Ronda, Rio Piedras, PR 00926 USA

Poschl, Hanno
Singerstr. 13/15, Vienna, AUSTRIA, 1010

Posehn, Brian *Comedian*
William Morris Agency (WMA-LA), 1 William Morris Pl, Beverly Hills, CA 90212 USA

Poses, Frederic M *Business Person*
AlliedSignal Inc, PO Box 4000, Morristown, NJ 07962 USA

Posey, Parker *Actor*
1216 N 6th Ave, Laurel, MS 39440 USA

Posner, Richard A *Judge*
US Court of Appeals, 219 S Dearborn St, Chicago, IL 60604 USA

Posner, Vladimir
1125 16th St. NW, Washington, DC 20036

Posokhin, Mikhail M *Architect*
Mosproyekt-2, 2 Brestskaya Str 5, Moscow, 123056, RUSSIA

Post, Avery D *Religious Leader*
39 Boothman Lane, Randolph, NH 03593 USA

Post, Markie *Actor*
10153 1/2 Riverside Dr, #333, Toluca Lake, CA 91602 USA

Post, Mike *Composer*
Mike Post Productions, 1007 W Olive Ave, Burbank, CA 91506 USA

Post, Sandra *Golfer*
Ladies Pro Golf Assn, 100 International Golf Dr, Daytona Beach, FL 32124 USA

Post, Ted *Director*
Norman Blumenthal, 11030 Santa Monica Blvd, Los Angeles, CA 90025 USA

Post, William *Business Person*
Pinnacle West Capital, 400 E Van Buren St, PO Box 52132, Phoenix, AZ 85072 USA

Post III, Glen F *Business Person*
Centurytel Inc, 100 Century Park Dr, Monroe, LA 71203 USA

Poster, Steve *Cinematographer*
Smith/Gosnell/Nicholson, PO Box 1156, Studio City, CA 91614 USA

Postlethwaite, Pete *Actor*
Markham & Froggatt, Julian House, 4 Windmill St, London, W1P 1HF, UNITED KINGDOM (UK)

Postlewait, Kathy *Golfer*
A Thomason, 4355 Cobb Parkway, #R, Atlanta, GA 30339 USA

Postman, Marc *Astronomer*
3303 Lightfoot Dr, Pikesville, MD 21208 USA

Poston, Tom *Actor*
1 N Venice Blvd, #106, Venice, CA 90291 USA

Potente, Franka *Actor*
Presseburo Sohela Emani, Etterschlager Str 60, Steinebach, 82237, GERMANY

Pothan, Pratap *Actor*
8-C Peninsula Apartments, Tailers Road Kilpauk, Chennai, TN 600 010, INDIA

Poti, Tom *Hockey Player*
103 Alvarado Ave, Worcester, MA 01604 USA

Potrykus, Ingo *Scientist*
Eidgenossische Tech Hochshule, Plant Sci Dept, Zurich, 8093, SWITZERLAND

Potter, Carol
151 El Camino Dr, Beverly Hills, CA 90212

Potter, Chris *Actor*
565 Orwell St, Missigauga, ON L5A 2W4, CANADA

Potter, Chris *Musician*
Joel Chriss, 300 Mercer St, #3J, New York, NY 10003 USA

Potter, Cindy
1189 Ragley Hall Rd. NE, Atlanta, GA 30319

Potter, Cynthia (Cindy) *Swimmer, Sportscaster*
1188 Ragley Hall Road NE, Atlanta, GA 30319 USA

Potter, Dan M *Religious Leader*
21 Forest Dr, Albany, NY 12205 USA

Potter, Huntington *Scientist*
Harvard Medical School, 25 Shattuck St, Boston, MA 02115 USA

Potter, John *Government Official*
US Postal Service, 475 L'Enfant Plaza SW, Washington, DC 20260 USA

Potter, Monica *Actor*
United Talent Agency (UTA), 9560 Wilshire Blvd, Beverly Hills, CA 90212 USA

Potter, Nelson *Business Person*
Fleetwood Enterprises, 3125 Myers St, Riverside, CA 92503 USA

Potter, Philip A *Religious Leader*
3A York Castle Ave, Kingston, 6, JAMAICA

Pottinger, Stanley *Writer*
William Morris Agency, 151 El Camino Dr, Beverly Hills, CA 90212 USA

Pottios, Myron J (Mike) *Football Player*
71569 Sahara Road, Rancho Mirage, CA 92270 USA

Pottruck, David S *Financier*
Charles Schwab Co, 101 Montgomery St, San Francisco, CA 94104 USA

Potts, Annie *Actor*
PO Box 29400, Los Angeles, CA 90029 USA

Potts, Cliff *Actor*
PO Box 131, Topanga, CA 90290 USA

Potts, Erwin *Business Person*
McClatchy Newspapers, 2100, Sacramento, CA 95816 USA

Potts, MC
818 18th Ave. So., Nashville, TN 37203

Potts, Tony *Correspondent*
Access Hollywood, 3000 W Alameda Ave, Trailer E, Burbank, CA 91523 USA

Potvin, Denis *Hockey Player*
6820 NW 101st Terrace, Parkland, FL 33076 USA

Potvin, Felix *Hockey Player*
Boston Bruins, 1 Fleet Center, Boston, MA 02114 USA

Potvin, Jean R *Hockey Player*
24 Longwood Dr, Huntington Station, NY 11746 USA

Pouget, Ely *Actor*
Writers & Artists, 8383 Wilshire Blvd, #550, Beverly Hills, CA 90211 USA

Poul, Alan *Producer*
United Talent Agency (UTA), 9560 Wilshire Blvd, Beverly Hills, CA 90212 USA

Poulin, Dave *Hockey Player, Coach*
16771 Orchard Ridge Court, Granger, IN 46530 USA

Poulson, Josh *Actor*

Pound, Richard W D *Misc*
87 Arlington Ave, Westmount, QC, H3Y 2W5, CANADA

Pound, Robert V *Physicist*
87 Pinehurst Road, Belmont, MA 02478 USA

Pound, The Dog
8942 Wilshire Blvd., Beverly Hills, CA 90211

Pounder, C C H *Actor*
Susan Smith, 121A N San Vicente Blvd, Beverly Hills, CA 90211 USA

Poundstone, Paula *Actor, Comedian*
1223 Broadway, #162, Santa Monica, CA 90404 USA

Poupard, Paul Cardinal *Religious Leader*
Pontificium Consilium Pro Dialogo, 00120, VATICAN CITY

Pousette, Lena *Actor*
Atkins Assoc, 8040 Ventura Canyon Ave, Panorama City, CA 91402 USA

Poussaint, Alvin F *Educator*
Judge Baker Guidance Center, 295 Longwood Ave, Boston, MA 02115 USA

Povich, Manury R *Commentator, Entertainer*
Maury Povich Show, 1515 Broadway, #33-88, New York, NY 10036 USA

Povich, Maury *Talk Show Host*
Mo Po Productions, 1515 Broadway, #33-88, New York, NY 10036 USA

Powell, A J Philip *Architect*
16 Little Boltons, London, SW10, UNITED KINGDOM (UK)

Powell, Arthur (Art) *Football Player*
25221 Via Lido, Laguna Niguel, CA 92677 USA

Powell, Billy *Musician*
Vector Mgmt, 1607 17th Ave S, Nashville, TN 37212 USA

Powell, Brittany
145 S. Fairfax Ave. #310, Los Angeles, CA 90036

Powell, Brittney *Actor, Model*
Amset Eisenstadt Frazier, 5757 Wilshire Blvd, #510, Los Angeles, CA 90036 USA

Powell, Cecil *Misc*
939 Bobcat Blvd NE, Albuquerque, NM 87122 USA

Powell, Clifton *Actor*
Abrams Artists, 9200 Sunset Blvd, #1125, Los Angeles, CA 90069 USA

Powell, Colin L *General, Secretary*
1317 Ballantrae Farm Dr, McLean, VA 22101 USA

Powell, James R *Inventor*
Plus Ultra Technologies, 25 E Loop Road, Stony Brook, NY 11790 USA

Powell, Jane *Actor, Musician*
62 Cedar Road, Wilton, CT 06897 USA

Powell, Jesse *Musician*
Pyramid Entertainment, 89 5th Ave, #700, New York, NY 10003 USA

Powell, John *Composer*
Kraft-Benjamin-Engel, 15233 Ventura Blvd, #200, Sherman Oaks, CA 91403 USA

Powell, John G *Track Athlete*
John Powell Assoc, 10445 Mary Ave, Cupertino, CA 95014 USA

Powell, John W (Boog) *Baseball Player*
Boog's Barbeque, 333 W Camden St, Baltimore, MD 21201 USA

Powell, Joseph L (Jody) *Government Official, Journalist*
Powell Tate, 700 13th St NW, #1000, Washington, DC 20005 USA

Powell, Marvin *Football Player*
5441 8th Ave, Los Angeles, CA 90043 USA

Powell, Michael (Mike) *Track Athlete*
Team Powell, PO Box 8000-354, Alta Loma, CA 91701 USA

Powell, Michael K *Government Official*
Federal Communications Commission, 1919 M St NW, Washington, DC 20036 USA

Powell, Mike
1751 Pinnacle Dr. #1500, McLean, VA 22102-3833

Powell, Monroe *Musician*
Personality Presents, 880 E Sahara Ave, #101, Las Vegas, NV 89104 USA

Powell, Nicole *Basketball Player*
Charlotte Sting, 100 Hive Dr, Charlotte, NC 28217 USA

Powell, Randolph
2644 Highland Ave., Santa Monica, CA 90405

Powell, Robert *Actor*
10 Pond Place, London, W12 7RJ, UNITED KINGDOM (UK)

Powell, Sandy *Designer*
London Mgmt, 2-4 Noel St, London, W1V 3RB, UNITED KINGDOM (UK)

Powell, Susan *Actor*
6333 Bryn Mawr Dr, Los Angeles, CA 90068 USA

Powell III, Earl A (Rusty) *Misc*
National Gallery of Art, Constitution Ave & 4th St NW, Washington, DC 20565 USA

Powell Jr, D Duane *Cartoonist*
215 S McDowell St, Raleigh, NC 27601 USA

Power, J D (Dave) *Business Person*
J D Power Associates, 2625 Townsgate Road, Westlake Village, CA 91361 USA

Power, Romina(Brindise)
I-72020 Cellino, San Marco, ITALY

Power, Udana
1962 Beachwood Dr. #202, Los Angeles, CA 90068

Powers, Alexandra *Actor*
United Talent Agency, 9560 Wilshire Blvd, #500, Beverly Hills, CA 90212 USA

Powers, Dave
42995 Latisha Lane, Palm Desert, CA 92211-8209

Powers, James B *Religious Leader*
American Baptist Assn, 4605 N State Line, Texarkana, TX 75503 USA

Powers, Kim *Reality TV Star*
Survivor, 1661 Lincoln Blvd, Ste 200, Santa Monica, CA 90404

Powers, Mala *Actor*
10543 Valley Spring Lane, Toluca Lake, CA 91602 USA

Powers, Melvin *Business Person*

Powers, Ross *Skier*
PO Box 283, South Londonderry, VT 05155 USA

Powers, Stefanie *Actor*
Bartels Co, PO Box 57593, Sherman Oaks, CA 91413 USA

Powter, Susan *Writer*
Stop the Insanity, 6250 Ridgewood Road, Saint Cloud, MN 56395 USA

Poza, Jorge *Actor*
Televisa, Blvd Adolfo Lopez Mateos 232, Colonia San Angel INN, DF, CP 01060, MEXICO

Pozdnykova, Tatyana *Track Athlete*
4151 NW 43rd St, Gainesville, FL 32606 USA

Pozsgay, Imre *Government Official*
Parliament Buildings, Kossuth Lajos Ter 1, Budapest, 1055, HUNGARY

Prabhu *Actor*
16 Chevaliea Sivaji Ganesan Salai, T Nagar, Chennai, TN 600 017, INDIA

Prada, Aura Helena *Actor*
Gabriel Blanco Iglesias (Mexico), Rio Balsas 35-32, Colonia Cuauhtemoc, DF, 06500, Mexico

Praed, Michael
11500 W. Olympic Blvd. #510, Los Angeles, CA 90064

Pran *Actor, Bollywood*
25 Union Park, Khar, Bombay, MS 400 052, INDIA

Prance, Ghilean T *Misc*
Kew Royal Botanic Gardens, Richmond, Surrey, TW9 3AE, UNITED KINGDOM (UK)

Prange, Laurie
1519 Sargent Pl., Los Angeles, CA 90026

Pras *Musician*
DAS Communications, 83 Riverside Dr, New York, NY 10024 USA

Prasanna *Actor*
C4 Cauvery Apartments, 14 Brindavanam Street, Chennai, TN 600 004, INDIA

Prashanth *Actor*
No 40 North Usman Road, Thiagaraja Nagar, Chennai, TN 600 017, INDIA

Pratchett, Terry *Writer*
Colin Smythe, PO Box 67981, Gerrards Cross, Bucks, SL9 8XA, UNITED KINGDOM (UK)

Prather, Joan *Actor*
31647 Sea Level Dr, Malibu, CA 90265 USA

Pratiwi, Sudarmono *Astronaut*
Jalan Pegangsaan, Timur, Jakarta, 16, INDONESIA

Pratt, Awadagin *Musician*
Cramer/Marder Artists, 3436 Springhill Road, Lafayette, CA 94549 USA

Pratt, Chris *Actor*
Abrams Artists Agency (LA), 9200 Sunset Blvd Fl 11, Los Angeles, CA 90069 USA

Pratt, Judson
8745 Oak Park Ave., Northridge, CA 91325

Pratt, Kyla *Actor*
Acme Talent & Literary Agency (LA), 4727 Wilshire Blvd #333, Los Angeles, CA 90010 USA

Pratt, Kyle *Actor*
Acme Talent & Literary Agency (LA), 4727 Wilshire Blvd #333, Los Angeles, CA 90010 USA

Pratt, Roger *Cinematographer*
10 Nightingale Lane, Hornsey, London, N8 7QU, UNITED KINGDOM (UK)

Pratt, Vicky
1930 Yonge St. #1155 Toronto, CANADA, CA Ont. M4A 1

Pratt, Victoria *Actor*
Gilbertson-Kincaid Management, 1330 Fourth St, Santa Monica, CA 90401 USA

Preate Jr, Ernest D *Attorney General, Government Official*
Attorney General's Office, 4th & Walnut, Harrisburg, PA 17120 USA

Precourt, Charles J *Astronaut*
7015 Little Redwood Dr, Pasadena, TX 77505 USA

Predock, Antoine *Architect*
Antoine Predock Architect, 300 12th St, Northwest Albuquerque, NM 87102 USA

Preer Jr, John R *Biologist*
1414 E Maxwell Lane, Bloomington, IN 47401 USA

Pregerson, Harry *Judge*
US Court of Appeals, 21800 Oxnard St, Woodland Hills, CA 91367 USA

Pregulman, Merv *Football Player*
44 S Crest Road, Chattanooga, TN 37404 USA

Prejean, Patrick
B5 135 Poissonniere, Paris, FRANCE, F-75002

Prejean, Sister Helen *Social Activist, Writer*
Vintage Books, 201 E 50th St, New York, NY 10022 USA

Preki *Soccer Player*
Kansas City Wizards, 2 Arrowhead Dr, Kansas City, MO 64129 USA

Premice, Josephine
755 West End Ave., New York, NY 10023

Prendergast, Alan *Journalist*
William Morris Agency (WMA-LA), 1 William Morris Pl, Beverly Hills, CA 90212 USA

Prentice, Dean S *Hockey Player*
13-220 Salisbury Ave, Cambridge, ON N1S 1K5, CANADA

Prentiss, Lee
122 Middlesex St., London, ENGLAND, El 7HY

Prentiss, Paula *Actor, Comedian*
719 Foothill Road, Beverly Hills, CA 90210 USA

Prepon, Laura *Actor*
United Talent Agency (UTA), 9560 Wilshire Blvd, Beverly Hills, CA 90212 USA

Prescott, John L *Government Official*
365 Saltshouse Road, Sutton-on-Hull, North Humberside, UNITED KINGDOM (UK)

Presle, Micheline *Actor*
6 Rue Antoine Dubois, Paris, 75006, FRANCE

Presley, Brian *Actor*
International Creative Management (ICM-LA), 8942 Wilshire Blvd, Beverly Hills, CA 90211 USA

Presley, Lisa-Marie *Actor, Musician*
W Management, 266 Elizabeth St #1A, New York, NY 10012 USA

Presley, Priscilla *Actor*
1167 Summit Dr, Beverly Hills, CA 90210 USA

Presley, Reg *Musician*
Stan Green, PO Box 4, Dartmouth, Devon, TQ6 0YD, UNITED KINGDOM (UK)

Presley, Richard *Musician*
William Morris Agency, 151 El Camino Dr, Beverly Hills, CA 90212 USA

Presnell, Glenn E *Football Coach, Football Player*
510 Happy Hollow, Ironton, OH 45638 USA

Presnell, Harve *Actor, Musician*
Abrams Artists, 9200 Sunset Blvd, #1125, Los Angeles, CA 90069 USA

Press, Bill *Commentator*
Cable News Network, News Dept, 1050 Techwood Dr NW, Atlanta, GA 30318 USA

Press, Frank *Physicist*
2500 Virginia Ave, #616, Washington, DC 20037 USA

Pressey, Paul *Basketball Player, Coach*
8415 N Indian Creek Parkway, Milwaukee, WI 53217 USA

Pressler, H Paul *Attorney General, Judge*
3711 San Felipe St, #9J, Houston, TX 77027 USA

Pressler, Larry L *Senator*
2812 Davis Ave, Alexandria, VA 22302 USA

Pressler, Menahem M J *Musician*
Melvin Kaplan, 115 College St, Burlington, VT 05401 USA

Pressley, Robert *Race Car Driver*
6 Forestdale Dr, Ashville, NC 28803 USA

Pressly, Jaime *Actor, Model*
8265 Sunset Blvd, #101, West Hollywood, CA 90046 USA

Pressman, Edward R *Producer*
Edward Pressman Films, 130 El Camino Dr, Beverly Hills, CA 90212 USA

Pressman, Lawrence *Actor*
15033 Encanto Dr, Sherman Oaks, CA 91403 USA

Pressman, Michael *Director*
William Morris Agency, 151 El Camino Dr, Beverly Hills, CA 90212 USA

Preston, Billy *Songwriter, Musician*
Celebresearch, 7119 E Shea Blvd, #109-436, Scottsdale, AZ 85254 USA

Preston, Duncan
46 Hilltop House Hornsey Lane, London, ENGLAND, N6 5NW

Preston, J A *Actor*
Paradigm Agency, 10100 Santa Monica Blvd, #2500, Los Angeles, CA 90067 USA

Preston, Johhny
PO Box 1875, Gretna, LA 70054

Preston, Johnny *Musician*
Ken Keene Artists, PO Box 1875, Gretna, LA 70054 USA

Preston, Kelly *Actor*
15821 Ventura Blvd, #460, Encino, CA 91436 USA

Preston, Mike *Actor*
House of Representatives, 400 S Beverly Dr, #101, Beverly Hills, CA 90212 USA

Preston, Simon J *Musician*
Little Hardwick, Langton Green Tunbridge Wells, Kent, TN3 OEY, UNITED KINGDOM (UK)

Pretre, Georges *Conductor*
Chateau de Vaudricourt, A Naves, Par Casters, 81100, FRANCE

Preus, David W *Religious Leader*
2481 Como Ave, Saint Paul, MN 55108 USA

Previn, Andre G *Musician*
180 W 80th St, #206, New York, NY 10024 USA

Previn, Dory *Songwriter, Musician*
2533 Zorada Dr, Los Angeles, CA 90046 USA

Previn Andre
180 W. 80th St. #206, New York, NY 10024

Previte, Richard *Business Person*
Advanced Micro Devices, 1 AMD Place, PO Box 3453, Sunnyvale, CA 94088 USA

Prevost, Josette *Actor*
Tisherman Agency, 6767 Forest Lawn Dr, #101, Los Angeles, CA 90068 USA

Prew, William A *Swimmer, Business Person*
30600 Telegraph Road, #3110, Bingham Farms, MI 48025 USA

Pribilinec, Jozef *Track Athlete*
Moyzesova 75, Lutila, 966 22, SLOVAKIA

Price, Alan *Songwriter, Musician*
Lustig Talent, PO Box 770850, Orlando, FL 32877 USA

Price, Antony *Fashion Designer*
468 Kings Road, London, SW1, UNITED KINGDOM (UK)

Price, Frank *Misc*
Price Entertainment, 2425 Olympic Blvd, Santa Monica, CA 90404 USA

Price, Frederick K C *Religious Leader*
Crenshaw Christian Church, 7901 S Vermont Ave, Los Angeles, CA 90044 USA

Price, George C *Prime Minister*
House of Representatives, Belmopan, BELIZE

Price, Hillary *Cartoonist*
221 Pine St, #4G3, Florence, MA 01062 USA

Price, James G *Doctor*
12205 Mohawk Road, Leawood, KS
66209 USA

Price, James K
19 LaCresta Dr, Florence, KY 41042 USA

Price, Kelly *Musician*
JL Ent, 18653 Ventura Blvd, #340,
Tarzana, CA 91356 USA

Price, Larry C *Journalist*
1020 S Josephine St, Denver, CO 80209
USA

Price, Lindsay *Actor*
3033 Vista Crest, Los Angeles, CA 90068
USA

Price, Lloyd *Songwriter, Musician*
95 Horseshoe Hill Road, Pound Ridge, NY
10576 USA

Price, M V Leontyne *Opera Singer*
9 Van Dam St, New York, NY 10003 USA

Price, Marc *Actor*
8444 Magnolia Dr, Los Angeles, CA
90046 USA

Price, Margaret B *Opera Singer*
Ulf Tornqvist, Sankt Eriksgatan 100,
Stockholm, 113 31, SWEDEN

Price, Megyn *Actor*
United Talent Agency (UTA), 9560
Wilshire Blvd, Beverly Hills, CA 90212
USA

Price, Mike *Football Coach*
University of Texas, Athletic Dept, El
Paso, TX 79968 USA

Price, Molly *Actor*
Gersh Agency, The (NY), 41 Madison Ave
Fl 33, New York, NY 10010 USA

Price, Nick *Golfer*
300 S Beach Road, Hobe Souns, FL 33455
USA

Price, Noel *Hockey Player*
21 Windeyer Crescent, Kanata, ON K2K
2P6, CANADA

Price, Paul B *Physicist*
1056 Overlook Road, Berkeley, CA 94708
USA

Price, Peerless *Football Player*
Atlanta Falcons, 4400 Falcon Pkwy,
Flowery Branch, GA 30542 USA

Price, Ray *Musician*
Original Artists Agency, 1031 E Battlefield
Road, Springfield, MO 65807 USA

Price, Reynolds *Writer*
PO Box 99014, Durham, NC 27708 USA

Price, Richard *Writer*
Greater Talent Network, 437 5th Ave,
New York, NY 10016 USA

Price, Rod *Musician*
Lustig Talent, PO Box 770850, Orlando,
FL 32877 USA

Price, S H *Publisher*
Newsweek Inc, 251 W 57th St, New York,
NY 10019 USA

Price, W Mark *Basketball Player*
Georgia Institute of Technology, Athletic
Dept, Atlanta, GA 30332 USA

Price, Willard D *Misc*
814 Via Alhambra, #N, Laguna Hills, CA
92653 USA

Price II, Charles H *Diplomat, Business
Person*
1 W Armour Blvd, #300, Kansas City, MO
64111 USA

Prichard, Peter S *Editor*
USA Today, Editorial Dept, 1000 Wilson
Blvd, Arlington, VA 22209 USA

Priddy, Nancy *Actor*
11223 Sunshine Terrace, Studio City, CA
91604 USA

Pride, Charley
PO Box 670507, Dallas, TX 75367-0507

Pride, Charlie *Musician*
Cecca Productions, 3198 Royal Lane,
#200, Dallas, TX 75229 USA

Pride, Lynn *Basketball Player*
Minnesota Lynx, Target Center, 600 1st
Ave N, Minneapolis, MN 55403 USA

Priesand, Sally J *Religious Leader*
10 Wedgewood Circle, Eatontown, NJ
07724 USA

Priest, Judas *Musician*
International Talent Booking (ITB - UK),
27A Floral Street, Third Floor, Covent
Garden, London, WC2E 9, United
Kingdom

Priest, Maxi *Musician*
Virgin Records, 150 5th Ave, New York,
NY 10011 USA

Priest, Pat *Actor*
146 Huckleberry Lane, Buhl, ID 83316
USA

Priest, Steve *Musician*
DCM International, 296 Nether St,
Finchley, London, N3 1RJ, UNITED
KINGDOM (UK)

Priestley, Jason *Actor*
United Talent Agency, 9560 Wilshire
Blvd, #500, Beverly Hills, CA 90212 USA

Prieto, Rodrigo *Cinematographer*
2926 Nicada Dr, Los Angeles, CA 90077
USA

Primack, Joel R *Astronomer*
University of California, Astronomy Dept,
Santa Cruz, CA 95064 USA

Primatesta, Raul Francisco Cardinal
Religious Leader
Arzobispado, Ave H Irigoyen 98,
Cordoba, 5000, ARGENTINA

Primeau, Keith *Hockey Player*
2 Danforth Dr, Voorhees, NJ 08043 USA

Primis, Lance R *Publisher*
New York Times Co, 229 W 43rd St, New
York, NY 10036 USA

Primrose, Neil *Musician*
Wildlife Entertainment, 21 Heathmans
Road, London, SW6 4TJ, UNITED
KINGDOM (UK)

Primus, Barry
2735 Creston Dr., Los Angeles, CA 90068

Prince *Musician*
Lippin Group, The, 6100 Wilshire Blvd
#400, Los Angeles, CA 90048-5111 USA

Prince, Charles (Chuck) *Financier*
Citigroup Inc, 399 Park Ave, New York,
NY 10022 USA

Prince, Clayton
3500 W. Olive Ave. #1400, Burbank, CA
91505

Prince, Faith *Actor, Musician*
Innovative Artists, 1505 10th St, Santa
Monica, CA 90401 USA

Prince, Harold S (Hal) *Director, Producer*
Harold Prince Organization, 10
Rockefeller Plaza, #1009, New York, NY
10020 USA

Prince, Jonathan
526 N. Camden Dr., Beverly Hills, CA
90210

Prince, Karim
3313 1/2 Barham Blvd., Los Angeles, CA
90068

Prince, Larry L *Business Person*
Genuine Parts Co, 2999 Circle 75
Parkway, Atlanta, GA 30339 USA

Prince, Tayshaun *Basketball Player*
Detroit Pistons, Palace, 2 Championship
Dr, Auburn Hills, MI 48326 USA

Prince Jr, Gregory S *Educator*
Hampshire College, President's Office,
Amherst, MA 01002 USA

Prince-Bythewood, Gina *Writer, Director,
Producer*
Creative Artists Agency LCC (CAA-LA),
9830 Wilshire Blvd, Beverly Hills, CA
90212 USA

Princess Beatrice *Royalty*
Buckingham Palace, London, SW1A 1AA,
United Kingdom

Princess Eugenie *Royalty*
Buckingham Palace, London, SW1A 1AA,
United Kingdom

Principal, Victoria *Actor*
120 S Spalding Dr, #205, Beverly Hills,
CA 90212 USA

Principi, Anthony *Secretary*
Veteran Affairs Department, 810 Vermont
Ave NW, Washington, DC 20420 USA

Prine, Andrew *Actor*
3364 Longridge Ave, Sherman Oaks, CA
91423 USA

Prine, John *Songwriter, Musician*
Al Bunetta Mgmt, 33 Music Square W,
#102B, Nashville, TN 37203 USA

Pringle, Joan *Actor*
Gold Marshak Liedtke, 3500 W Olive
Ave, #1400, Burbank, CA 91505 USA

Prinosil, David *Athlete*
TC Wolfsberg, Am Schanzl 3, Amberg,
92224, GERMANY

Prinze Jr, Freddie *Actor*
4348 Ledge Ave, Toluca Lake, CA 91602
USA

Prinzi, Frank *Cinematographer*
571 W 113th St, #24, New York, NY
10025 USA

Prior, Anthony *Football Player*
12738 Longhorne Dr, Corona, CA 92880
USA

Prior, Maddy *Musician*
Park Promotions, PO Box 651, Park Road,
Oxford, OX2 9RB, UNITED KINGDOM
(UK)

Prior, Mark *Baseball Player*
3256 Casa Bonita Dr, Bonita, CA 91902
USA

Prior of Brampton, James M L
Government Official
36 Morpeth Mansions, London, SW1,
UNITED KINGDOM (UK)

Priory, Richard B *Business Person*
Duke Energy Co, 526 S Church St,
Charlotte, NC 28202 USA

Pritchard, Barry *Musician*
Lustig Talent, PO Box 770850, Orlando,
FL 32877 USA

Pritchard, David E *Physicist*
Massachusetts Institute of Technology,
Physics Dept, Cambridge, MA 02139 USA

Pritchard, Ron *Football Player*
690 E Park Ave, Gilbert, AZ 85234 USA

Pritchett, James *Actor*
53 W 74th St, New York, NY 10023 USA

Pritchett, Matt *Cartoonist*
London Daily Telegraph, 181 Marsh Wall,
London, E14 9SR, UNITED KINGDOM
(UK)

Pritchett, Sir Victor
12 Regent's Park Terrace, London,
ENGLAND, NW1

Pritha, Saratha *Actor, Bollywood*
2 1st Main Road, West Shenoy Nagar,
Chennai, TN 600030, INDIA

Prithiveeraj (Bablu) *Actor*
146 Anna Nagar (West), Chennai, TN 600
040, INDIA

Pritikin, Greg *Actor*
Catch 23 Management, 301 N Canon Dr
#207, Beverly Hills, CA 90210 USA

Pritkin, Roland I *Doctor*
4128 Grove Ave, Stickney, IL 60402 USA

Pritzker, Robert A *Business Person*
Marmon Group, 225 West Washington St,
Chicago, IL 60606 USA

Pritzker, Thomas *Business Person*
Hyatt Corp, 200 West Madison Street,
Chicago, IL 60606

Prix, Wolf *Architect*
Coop Himmelblau, 3526 Beethoven St,
Los Angeles, CA 90066 USA

Probert, Bob *Hockey Player*
2109 N Seminary Ave, Chicago, IL 60614
USA

Probst, Jeff *Talk Show Host*
Endeavor Agency LLC (LA), 9601 Wilshire
Blvd Fl 3, Beverly Hills, CA 90210 USA

Prochazka, Martin *Hockey Player*
Toronto Maple Leafs, 40 Bay St, Toronto,
ON M5J 2K2, CANADA

Prochnow, Jurgen *Actor*
Lamontstr 98, Munich, 81679, GERMANY

Prock, Markus *Athlete*
6142 Mieders, AUSTRIA

Proclaimers, The *Music Group*
Braw Music Management, 31 Hartington
Pl, Edinburgh, Lothian, EH10 4LF,
UNITED KINGDOM (UK)

Procol Harum
195 Sandycombe Rd., Kew, ENGLAND,
TW9 2EW

Procter, Emily *Actor*
Innovative Artists, 1505 10th St, Santa
Monica, CA 90401 USA

Proctor, Charles N *Skier*
100 Lockwood Lane, #238, Scotts Valley,
CA 95066 USA

Prodi, Romano *Prime Minister*
European Communities Commission, 200
Rue de la Loi, Brussels, BELGIUM

Prodigy *Musician*
Maverick Records, 9348 Civic Center Dr,
Beverly Hills, CA 90210-3606

Prodigy
205 Vickarage Hill Benfleet, Essex,
ENGLAND, SS7 1PF

Professor, Griff *Musician*
William Morris Agency, 151 El Camino
Dr, Beverly Hills, CA 90212 USA

Profumo, John D *Government Official*
28 Commercial St, London, E1 6LS,
UNITED KINGDOM (UK)

Pronger, Chris *Hockey Player*
10454 Ladue Road, Saint Louis, MO
63141 USA

Pronovost, R Marcel *Hockey Player*
4620 Dali Court, Windsor, ON N9G
2MB, CANADA

Proops, Greg *Actor*
Endeavor Agency LLC (LA), 9601 Wilshire
Blvd Fl 3, Beverly Hills, CA 90210 USA

Prophet, Billy *Musician*
Paramount Entertainment, PO Box 12, far
Hills, NJ 07931 USA

Prophet, Elizabeth Clare *Religious Leader*
Church Universal & Triumphant, Box A,
Livingston, MT 59047 USA

Prophet, Ronnie
1227 Saxon Dr., CA TN, 37215

Propp, Brian *Hockey Player*
5023 Church Road, Mount Laurel, NJ
08054 USA

Props, Rene *Actor*
Agency for Performing Arts, 9200 Sunset
Blvd, #900, Los Angeles, CA 90069 USA

Prosky, Robert *Actor*
309 9th St, Washington, DC 20003 USA

Prospal, Vaclav *Hockey Player*
Anaheim Mighty Ducks, 2000 E Gene
Autry Way, Anaheim, CA 92806 USA

Prospal, Vactav *Hockey Player*
Tampa Bay Lighting, Ice Palace, 401
Channelside Dr, Tampa, FL 33602 USA

Prosper, Sandra *Actor*
Mitchell K Stubbs & Assoc (MKS), 8675 W
Washington Blvd #203, Culver City, CA
90232 USA

Prosser, C Ladd *Misc*
101 W Windsor Road, #2106, Urbana, IL
61802 USA

Prosser, James *Musician*
Refugee Mgmt, 209 10th Ave S, #347
Cummins Station, Nashville, TN 37203
USA

Prosser, Robert *Religious Leader*
Cumberland Presbyterian Church, 1978
Union Ave, Memphis, TN 38104 USA

Prost, Alain M P *Race Car Driver*
Prost-Grand-Prix, 7 Ave Eugene Freyssinet,
Guyancourt, 78286, FRANCE

Prost, Sharon *Judge*
US Court of Appeals, 717 Madison Place
NW, Washington, DC 20439 USA

Protopopov, Oleg *Figure Skater*
Chalet Hubel, Grindelwald, 3818,
SWITZERLAND

Prouix, E Annie *Writer*
PO Box 230, Centennial, WY 82055 USA

Prout, Brian *Musician*
Oreamcatcher Artists Mgmt, 2908 Poston
Ave, Nashville, TN 37203 USA

Proval, David *Actor*
Incognito Management, 9440 Santa
Monica Blvd #302, Beverly Hills, CA
90210 USA

Provenza, Paul *Actor*
Patterson Assoc, 8271 Melrose Ave, #201,
Los Angeles, CA 90046 USA

Provine, Dorothy *Actor*
8832 Ferncliff NE, Bainbridge Island, WA
98110 USA

Provost, Jon
627 Montclair Dr., Santa Rosa, CA 95409

Prowse, David *Actor*
Spotlight, 7 Lelcester Place, London,
WC2H 7BP, United Kingdom

Proyas, Alex *Director*
International Creative Mgmt, 8942
Wilshire Blvd, #219, Beverly Hills, CA
90211 USA

Prudden, Bonnie *Misc*
PO Box 65240, Tucson, AZ 85728 USA

Prudhomme, Don *Race Car Driver*
1232 Distribution Way, Vista, CA 92081
USA

Prudhomme, Paul *Chef*
2424 Chartres, New Orleans, LA 70117
USA

Pruett, Harold
8904 Wonderland Ave., Los Angeles, CA
90046

Pruett, Jeanne *Songwriter, Musician*
Joe Taylor Artists Agency, 2802
Columbine Place, Nashville, TN 37204
USA

Pruett, Scott *Race Car Driver*
Arciero-Wells Racing, 30212 Tomas,
Rancho Santa Margarita, CA 92688 USA

Pruitt, Greg
99 Detering #100, Houston, TX 77007

Pruitt, Gregory D (Greg) *Football Player*
13851 Larchmere Blvd, Cleveland, OH
44120 USA

Pruitt, Michael(Mike) *Football Player*
472 S Mumaugh Road, Lima, OH 45804
USA

Pruitt Jr, Basil A *Doctor*
US Army Institute of Surgical Research,
Fort Sam Houston, TX 78234 USA

Prunariu, Dumitru D *Cosmonaut*
Str Sf Spiridon 12, #4, Bucharest, 70231,
ROMANIA

Prunskiene, Kazimiera *Politician*
Lithuanian-European Institute, Vilnius St
45-13, Vilnius, 2001, LITHUANIA

Prusiner, Stanley B *Nobel Prize Laureate*
University of California, Biochemistry
Dept, San Francisco, CA 94143 USA

Pryce, Jonathan *Actor, Musician*
Julian Belfarge, 46 Albermarle St, London,
ENGLAND, W1X 4PP, UNITED
KINGDOM (UK)

Pryce, Travor *Football Player*
Denver Broncos, 13655 E Broncos
Parkway, Englewood, CO 80112 USA

Pryor, David H *Senator*
2209 Julie Ann Lane, Paragould, AR
72450 USA

Pryor, Hubert *Editor, Publisher*
3560 S Ocean Blvd, #607, Palm Beach,
FL 33480 USA

Pryor, Nicholas *Actor*
S D B Partners, 1801 Ave of Stars, #902,
Los Angeles, CA 90067 USA

Pryor, Peter P *Editor*
Daily Variety, Editorial Dept, 5700
Wilshire Blvd #120, Los Angeles, CA
90036 USA

Pryor, Richard *Actor, Comedian*
16847 Bosque Dr, Encino, CA 91436 USA

Przybilla, Joel *Basketball Player*
Milwaukee Bucks, Bradley Center, 1001
N 4th St, Milwaukee, WI 53203 USA

Psycho, Les *Musician*
Agency Group Lts, 1775 Broadway, #430,
New York, NY 10019 USA

Ptacek, Louis *Misc*
University of Utah, Howard Hughes
Institute, Salt Lake City, UT 84112 USA

Ptak, Frank *Business Person*
Illinois Tool Works, 3600 W Lake Ave,
Glenview, IL 60025 USA

Ptashne, Mark S *Misc*
Harvard University, Biochemistry Dept,
Cambridge, MA 02138 USA

Puapua, Tomasi *Governor*
Governor General's Office, Vaiaku,
Funafuti, TUVALU

Public Enemy
298 Elizabeth St., New York, NY 10012

Pucci, Bert *Publisher*
Los Angeles Magazine, 1888 Century Park
East, Los Angeles, CA 90067 USA

Puck, Theodore T *Physicist*
10 S Albion St, Denver, CO 80246 USA

Puck, Wolfgang *Chef*
805 N Sierra Dr, Beverly Hills, CA 90210
USA

Puckett, Gary *Musician, Songwriter*
10710 Seminole Blvd, #3, Largo, FL
33778 USA

Puckett, Kirby *Baseball Player*
6625 West Trail, Minneapolis, MN 55439
USA

Puddle of Mud *Music Group*
Geffen Records, 2220 Colorado Ave,
Santa Monica, CA 90404 USA

Puemer, John P *Publisher*
Chicago Tribune, 435 N Michigan Ave,
Chicago, IL 60611 USA

Puenzo, Luis A *Director*
Cinematografia Nacional Instituto, Lima
319, Buenos Aires, 1073, ARGENTINA

Puerner, John P *Publisher*
Los Angeles Times, Editorial Dept, 202 W
1st St, Los Angeles, CA 90012 USA

Puett, Tommy *Actor*
16621 Cerulean Court, Chino Hills, CA
91709 USA

Pugacheva, Alia B *Musician*
State Variety Theater, Bersenevskaya Nab
20/2, Moscow, 109072, RUSSIA

Pugh, Jethro *Football Player*
1649 Glenlivet Dr, Dallas, TX 72518

Pugh, Larry *Football Player*
RR 4, New Castle, PA 16101 USA

Pugh Jr, Jethro *Football Player*
Gifts Inc, 1649 Glenlivet Dr, Dallas, TX
75218 USA

Pugsley, Don *Actor*
Lichtman/Salners, 12216 Moorpark St,
Studio City, CA 91604 USA

Pujats, Janis Cardinal *Religious Leader*
Metropolijas Jurija, Maza Pils Iela 2/A,
Riga, 1050, LATVIA

Pujol, Laetitia *Ballerina*
Paris Opera Ballet, Place de l'Opera,
Paris, 75009, FRANCE

Pujol I Soley, Jordi *Politician*
Generalitat Palau, Placa Sant Jaume S/N,
Barcelona, 2, SPAIN

Pujols, Alberto *Baseball Player*
Saint Louis Cardinals, Busch Stadium, 250
Stadium Plaza, Saint Louis, MO 63102
USA

Pujols, Luis B *Baseball Player*
3867 Jonathan Way, Lake Worth, FL
33462 USA

Pulcini, Robert *Director*
Creative Artists Agency LCC (CAA-LA),
9830 Wilshire Blvd, Beverly Hills, CA
90212 USA

Pulford, Robert J (Bob) *Hockey Player*
78 Coventry Road, Northfield, IL 60093
USA

Puljic, Vinko Cardinal *Religious Leader*
Nadbiskupski Ordinarijat, Kaptol 7,
Sarajevo, 71000, BOSNIA
HERZEGOVINA

Pullen, Melanie Clark *Actor*
Julian Belfrage & Associates, 42
Albermarle St, London, W1X 4P, UNITED
KINGDOM (UK)

Pulliam, Keisha Knight *Actor*
Endeavor Agency LLC (LA), 9601 Wilshire
Blvd Fl 3, Beverly Hills, CA 90210 USA

Pullman, Bill *Actor*
2599 Glen Green, Los Angeles, CA 90068
USA

Pullman, Philip *Writer*
24 Templar Road, Oxford, OX2 8LT,
UNITED KINGDOM (UK)

Pulver, Liselotte *Actor*
Villa Bip, Kanton Vaudois, Perroy, 1166,
SWITZERLAND

Punk, Daft *Composer, Writer*
Primary Talent International (UK), 2-12
Pentonville Rd Fl 5, London, N1 9PL,
UNITED KINGDOM (UK)

Punsley, Bernard *Actor*
1415 Granvia Altemeia, Palos Verdes
Estates, CA 90274 USA

Puppa, Daren *Hockey Player*
4526 Cheval Blvd, Lutz, FL 33558 USA

Puppies, The
15476 NW 77th Ct. #286, Miami Lakes,
FL 33016

Purcell, Dominic *Actor*
Untitled Entertainment (NY), 23 E 22nd St
Fl 3, New York, NY 10010 USA

Purcell, James N *Government Official*
6 Chateau-Banquet, Geneva, 1202,
SWITZERLAND

Purcell, Lee *Actor*
11101 Provence Lane, Tujunga, CA
91042 USA

Purcell, Patrick B *Publisher*
Boston Herald, 1 Herald St, Boston, MA
02118 USA

Purcell, Philip J *Financier*
Morgan Stanley Co, 1585 Broadway, New
York, NY 10036 USA

Purcell, Sarah *Actor*
6525 Esplanade St, Playa del Rey, CA
90293 USA

Purcell, William *Physicist*
Northwestern University, Astrophysics
Dept, Evanston, IL 60208 USA

Purdee, Nathan *Actor*
56 W 66th St, New York, NY 10023 USA

Purdom, Edmund *Actor*
Via Isonzo 42/C, Rome, 00198, ITALY

Purdy, Alfred *Writer*
Harbour Publishing, PO Box 219, Madeira
Park, BC V0N 2H0, CANADA

Purdy, James *Writer*
236 Henry St, Brooklyn, NY 11201 USA

Purefoy, James *Actor*
International Creative Mgmt, 76 Oxford
St, London, W1N 0AX, UNITED
KINGDOM (UK)

Puri, Amrish *Actor, Bollywood*
Vardhan Plot 45, 11th Road Juhu Scheme,
Mumbai, MS 400049, INDIA

Puri, Om *Actor*
703 Trishul II Seven Bangalows, Versova
Andheri, Bombay, MS 400 061, INDIA

Purim, Flora *Musician*
A Train Mgmt, PO Box 29242, Oakland,
CA 94604 USA

Purkey, Bob
5767 King School Rd., Bethel Park, PA
15102

Purkey, Robert T (Bob) *Baseball Player*
5767 Kings School Road, Bethel Park, PA
15102 USA

Purl, Linda *Actor*
Shelly & Pierce, 13775A Mono Way
#220, Sonora, CA 95370 USA

Purpura, Dominick P *Scientist*
Albert Einstein College of Medicine, 1300
Morris Park Ave, Bronx, NY 10461 USA

Purves, William *Financier*
87 Chester Square, London, SW1W 9HT,
UNITED KINGDOM (UK)

Purvis, Jeff *Race Car Driver*
4106 Roberta Road, Concord, NC 28027
USA

Puryear, Martin *Artist*
Nancy Drysdale Gallery, 700 New
Hampshire Ave NW, #917, Washington,
DC 20037 USA

Pusha, T *Musician*
Star Trax/Arista Records, 888 7th Ave,
#3800, New York, NY 10106 USA

Pushelberg, Glenn *Designer*
Yabu Pushelberg, 55 Booth Ave, Toronto,
ON M4M 2M3, CANADA

Putch, John *Actor*
3972 Sunswept Dr, Studio City, CA 91604
USA

Putilin, Nikolai G *Opera Singer*
Mariinsky Theater, Teatralnaya Square 1,
Saint Petersburg, 190000, RUSSIA

Putin, Vladimir V *President*
President's Office, Kremlin, Staraya Pl 4,
Moscow, 103132, RUSSIA

Putnam, Ashley *Opera Singer*
Maurice Mayer, 201 W 54th St, #1C, New
York, NY 10019 USA

Putnam, Duane *Football Player*
1545 Magnolia Ave, Ontario, CA 91762
USA

Putnam, Hilary W *Misc*
116 Winchester Road, Arlington, MA
02474 USA

Putterman, Seth J *Physicist*
University of California, Physics Dept, Los
Angeles

Putterman, Seth J *Physicist*
University of California, Physics Dept, Los
Angeles, CA 90024 USA

Puttnam, David T *Producer*
Engima Productions, 29A Tufton St,
London, SW1P 3QL, UNITED KINGDOM
(UK)

Puyana, Rafael *Musician*
88 Rue de Grenelle, Paris, 75007,
FRANCE

Pyavko, Vladislav I *Opera Singer*
Bryusov Per 2/14, #27, Moscow, 103009,
RUSSIA

Pye, William B *Artist*
43 Hambalt Road, Clapham, London,
SW4 9EQ, UNITED KINGDOM (UK)

Pyle, Andy *Musician*
Larry Page, 29 Ruston Mews, London,
W11 1RB, UNITED KINGDOM (UK)

Pyle, Michael J (Mike) *Football Player*
2436 Saranac Court, Glenview, IL 60025
USA

Pyle, Missi *Actor*
Paradigm (LA), 10100 Santa Monica Blvd,
Fl 25, Los Angeles, CA 90067 USA

Pyle, Missy *Actor*
Paradigm Agency, 10100 Santa Monica
Blvd, #2500, Los Angeles, CA 90067 USA

Pym of Sandy, Francis L *Government
Official*
Everton Park, Sandy, Beds, SG19 2DE,
UNITED KINGDOM (UK)

Pynchon, Thomas *Writer*
Henry Holt, 115 W 18th St, New York,
NY 10011 USA

Pyne, Natasha *Actor*
Kate Feast, Primrose Hill Studios, Fitzroy
Road, London, NW1 8TR, UNITED
KINGDOM (UK)

Pyne, Stephen J *Historian, Writer*
Arizona State University, History Dept,
Tempe, AZ 85287 USA

Pyott, David E I *Business Person*
Allergan Inc, 2525 Dupont St, Irvine, CA
92612 USA

Python, Monty
34 Thistlewaite Rd., London, ENGLAND,
E5 0QQ

Q

Q-Tip
9830 Wilshire Blvd., Beverly Hills, CA
90212

Qabas ibn Sa'id al Sa'id *King*
Royal Palace, PO Box 252, Muscat,
OMAN

Qarase, Laisenia *Prime Minister*
Prime Minister's Office, 6 Berkeley
Crescent, Suva, VITI LEVU, FIJI

Qasimi, Sheikh Saqr bin Muhammad al
President
Ruler's Palace, Ras Al Khaimah, UNITED
ARAB EMIRATES

Qasimi, Sheikh Sultan bin Muhammad al
President
Ruler's Palace, Sharjah, UNITED ARAB
EMIRATES

Qi, Shu *Actor*
Current Entertainment, 1411 Fifth St #405,
Santa Monica, CA 90401 USA

Quackenbush, Bill
54 Danielle Ct., Lawrenceville, NJ 08848-
1452

Quade, John *Actor*
Alex Brewis, 12429 Laurel Terrace Dr,
Studio City, CA 91604 USA

Quaid, Dennis *Actor*
11718 Barrington Court, #508, Los
Angeles, CA 90049 USA

Quaid, Randy *Actor*
Mirisch, 1801 Century Park East, #1801,
Los Angeles, CA 90067 USA

Quaintance, Rachel *Comedian*
OmniPop Inc (LA), 10700 Ventura Blvd Fl
2, Studio City, CA 91604 USA

Qualife, Pete *Musician*
Larry Page, 29 Ruston Mews, London,
W11 1RB, UNITED KINGDOM (UK)

Qualls, DJ *Actor*
Talent Group, 561 W Pike St, #100A,
Lawrenceville, GA 30045 USA

Quandt, Richard E *Economist*
162 Springdale Road, Princeton, NJ 08540
USA

Quann, Megan *Swimmer*
Thomas Quann, 8421 Woodland Ave E,
Puyallup, WA 98371 USA

Quant, Mary *Fashion Designer*
Mary Quant Ltd, 3 Ives St, London, SW3
2NE, UNITED KINGDOM (UK)

Quantrill, Paul *Baseball Player*
334 E Lake Rd, Palm Harbor, FL 34685
USA

Quarashi *Musician*
Creative Artists Agency LCC (CAA-LA),
9830 Wilshire Blvd, Beverly Hills, CA
90212 USA

Quaresma, Rhonda Lee *Misc*
PO Box 22033, Kingston, ON K7M 8S5,
CANADA

Quarrie, Donald (Don) *Track Athlete*
Jamaican Amateur Athletic Assn, PO Box
272, Kingston, 5, JAMAICA

Quarry, Mike *Boxer*
12728 Oxford Dr, La Mirada, CA 90638
USA

Quarry, Robert *Actor*
11032 Moorpark St, #A3, North
Hollywood, CA 91602 USA

Quarshie, Hugh *Actor*
PO Box 20092, London, NW2 6FJ,
UNITED KINGDOM (UK)

Quarterflash
5410 SW MacAdam Ave. #280, Portland,
OR 97201

Quarterman, Saundra *Actor*
Stone Manners Talent Agency, 6500
Wilshire Blvd, Ste 550, Los Angeles, CA
90048 USA

Quasha, Alan G *Business Person*
Hanover Direct Inc, 1509 Harbor Blvd,
Weehawken, NJ 07086 USA

Quastel, J Hirsch *Biologist, Scientist*
4585 Langara Ave, Vancouver, BC V6R
1C9, CANADA

Quasthoff, Thomas *Musician*
Cramer/Marser Artists, 3436 Springhill
Road, Lafayette, CA 94549 USA

Quate, Calvin F *Engineer*
340 Princeton Road, Menlo Park, CA
94025 USA

Quatro, Suzi *Songwriter, Musician*
Jive, 4 Pasteur Courtyard Whittle Road,
Corby, Norths, FL NN17 5DX, UNITED
KINGDOM (UK)

Quayle, Anna *Actor*
CDA, 47 Courtfield Road, London,
ENGLAND, SW7 4DB, UNITED
KINGDOM (UK)

Quayle, Danforth J (Dan) *Ex-Vice
President*
5395 Emerson Way, Indianapolis, IN
46226 USA

Quayle, Jenny *Actor*
Michelle Braidman Assoc, Lower John St
Fl 3 #10/11, London, W1F 9EB, UNITED
KINGDOM (UK)

Quayle, Marilyn Tucker
2929 E. Camelback Rd. #124, Phoenix,
AZ 85016-4425

Queen, Ida *Musician*
Traditional Arts Services, 16045 36th Ave
NE, Lake Forest Park, WA 98155 USA

Queen, Konga *Wrestler, Actor*
PO Box 5050, Carson, CA 90749 USA

Queens of the Stone Age *Music Group*
Creative Artists Agency LCC (CAA-LA), 9830 Wilshire Blvd, Beverly Hills, CA 90212 USA

Queensryche *Music Group*
Monterey Peninsula Artists (Chicago), 200 West Superior #202, Chicago, IL 60610 USA

Queffelec, Anne *Musician*
15 Ave Corneille, Maisons-Laffittle, 78600, FRANCE

Queler, Eve *Conductor*
Opera Orchestra of New York, 239 W 72nd St, #2R, New York, NY 10023 USA

Quellmatz, Udo *Athlete*
Friedhofstr 10, Omgolstandt, 85049, GERMANY

Queloz, Didier *Astronomer*
University of Geneva, Geneva Observatory, Geneva, SWITZERLAND

Quenneville, Joel *Hockey Player, Coach*
13039 Starbuck Road, Saint Louis, MO 63141 USA

Quenzrd, Nathalie *Actor*
Cineart, 36 Rue de Ponthieu, Paris, 75008, FRANCE

Quester, Hugues *Actor*
Cineart, 36 Rue de Ponthieu, Paris, 75008, FRANCE

Questlove *Musician*
Motown Records, 6255 Sunset Blvd, Los Angeles, CA 90028 USA

Questrom, Allen I *Business Person*
J C Penney Co, 6501 Legacy Dr, Plano, TX 75024 USA

Quezada, Milly *Musician*
Sony Music Miami, 605 Lincoln Rd, Miami Beach, FL 33138 USA

Quezada Toruno, Rodolfo Cardinal
Religious Leader
Archdiocese, 7A Avenida 6-21, Zona 1, Guatemala City, 01001, GUATEMALA

Quick, Clarence E *Musician, Songwriter*
376 Quincy St, Brroklyn, NY 11216 USA

Quick, Diana *Actor*
39 Seymour Walk, London, SW10, UNITED KINGDOM (UK)

Quick, James E (Jim) *Actor*
PO Box 12760, Scottsdale, AZ 85267 USA

Quick, Michael A (Mike) *Football Player*
13 Slab Branch Road, Marlton, NJ 08053 USA

Quick, Richard *Coach, Swimmer*
Stanford University, Athletic Dept, Stanford, CA 94305 USA

Quie, Albert H (Al) *Governor*
4209 Christy Lane, Hopkins, MN 55345 USA

Quiet Riot
2002 Hogback Rd. #20, Ann Arbor, MI 48105

Quigley, Austin E *Educator*
Columbia College, President's Office, New York, NY 10027 USA

Quigley, Dana *Golfer*
Crestwood Country Club, 90 Wheeler St, Rehoboth, MA 02769 USA

Quigley, Joan
1055 California St. #14, San Francisco, CA 94108

Quigley, Linnea *Actor*
2608-1 N. Ocean Blvd, #126, Pompano Beach, FL 33062 USA

Quigley, Philip J (Phil) *Business Person*
Pacific Telesis Group, 130 Keamy St, San Francisco, CA 94108 USA

Quik, D J *Musician*
International Creative Mgmt, 8942 Wilshire Blvd, #219, Beverly Hills, CA 90211 USA

Quill, Leonard W *Financier*
Wilmington Trust Corp, Rodney Square N, 1100 N Market St, Wilmington, DE 19801 USA

Quill, Timothy E *Social Activist*
University of Rochester, Medical & Dentistry School, Rochester, NY 14642 USA

Quillan, Frederick (Fred) *Football Player*
2924 Bailey Lane, Eugene, OR 97401 USA

Quindlen, Anna *Writer*
International Creative Management (ICM-LA), 8942 Wilshire Blvd, Beverly Hills, CA 90211 USA

Quindlen, Anna M *Misc*
Random House, 1745 Broadway, #B1, New York, NY 10019 USA

Quinlan, Kathleen *Actor*
PO Box 861, Rockaway, OR 97136 USA

Quinlan, Maeve *Actor*
Defining Artists, 4342 Lankershim Blvd, Universal City, CA 91602 USA

Quinlan, Maive
1123 N. Flores St., W. Hollywood, CA 90069

Quinlan, William D (Bill) *Football Player*
393 Mount Vernon St, Lawrence, MA 01843 USA

Quinn, Aidan *Actor*
Bumble Wald, 8383 Wilshire Blvd, #323, Beverly Hills, CA 90211 USA

Quinn, Aileen *Actor*
400 Madison Ave, #20, New York, NY 10017 USA

Quinn, Anthony *Actor, Producer, Director*
Untitled Entertainment (NY), 23 E 22nd St Fl 3, New York, NY 10010 USA

Quinn, Brian *Soccer Player, Coach*
San Jose Earthquakes, 3550 Stevens Creek Blvd, #200, San Jose, CA 95117 USA

Quinn, Carmel *Musician*
Jane Mathers Mgmt, 230 W Summit Ave, #1, Haddonfield, NJ 08033 USA

Quinn, Colin *Actor, Comedian*
Mosaic Media Group, 9200 Sunset Blvd Fl 10, Los Angeles, CA 90069 USA

Quinn, Colleen *Actor*
Bauman Assoc, 5750 Wilshire Blvd, #473, Los Angeles, CA 90036 USA

Quinn, Danny *Actor*
Don Buchwald, 6500 Wilshire Blvd, #2200, Los Angeles, CA 90048 USA

Quinn, David W *Business Person*
Centex Corp, 2728 N Harwood, Dallas, TX 75201 USA

Quinn, DeClan *Cinematographer*
22 Cherry Ave, Cornwall on Hudson, NY 12520 USA

Quinn, Ed *Actor*
Endeavor Talent Agency, 9701 Wilshire Blvd, #1000, Beverly Hills, CA 90212 USA

Quinn, Francesco *Actor*
3910 Woodcliff Road, Sherman Oaks, CA 91403 USA

Quinn, Freddy
Am Pfeilshof 35, Hamburg, GERMANY, D-22393

Quinn, Glenn *Actor*
Innovative Artists (LA), 1505 Tenth St, Santa Monica, CA 90401 USA

Quinn, J B Patrick (Pat) *Hockey Player, Coach*
Toronto Maple Leals, 40 Bay St, Toronto, ON M5J 2K2, CANADA

Quinn, Jane Bryant *Journalist*
Newsweek Magazine, Editorial Dept, 251 W 57th St, New York, NY 10019 USA

Quinn, Jim *Misc*
675 S Sierra Ave, #32, Solana Beach, CA 92075 USA

Quinn, John A *Engineer*
275 E Wynnewood Road, Merion Station, PA 19066 USA

Quinn, John C *Editor*
365 S Atlantic Ave, Cocoa Beach, FL 32931 USA

Quinn, Martha *Actor, Model*
Panacea Entertainment, 12020 Chandler Blvd, #300, North Hollywood, CA 91607 USA

Quinn, Sally *Journalist*
3014 N St NW, Washington, DC 20007 USA

Quinn, William F *Governor*
4340 Pahoa Ave, #13C, Honolulu, HI 96816 USA

Quinones, John *Correspondent*
20/20, 147 Columbus Ave, New York, NY 10023, US

Quintal, Stephane *Hockey Player*
1356A La Fontaine, Montreal, QC, H2L 1T5, CANADA

Quintana, Chela *Golfer*
Ladies Pro Golf Assn, 100 International Golf Dr, Daytona Beach, FL 32124 USA

Quiring, Frederic *Actor*
Cineart, 36 Rue de Ponthieu, Paris, 75008, FRANCE

Quirk, James P (Jamie) *Baseball Player*
12500 Aberdeen Road, Leawood, KS 66209 USA

Quirk, Michael J *War Hero*
1700 Kit Lane, Navarre, FL 32566 USA

Quiroga, Elena *Writer*
Agencia Balcells, Diagonal 580, Barcelona, 08021, SPAIN

Quiroga, Jorge (Tuto) *President*
President's Office, Palacio de Gobierno, Plaza Murllia, La Paz, BOLIVIA

Quist, Janet *Model*
13446 Poway Road, #239, Poway, CA 92064 USA

Quitones, John *Commentator*
ABC-TV, News Dept, 77 W 66th St, New York, NY 10023 USA

Quivar, Florence *Opera Singer*
Columbia Artists Mgmt Inc, 165 W 57th St, New York, NY 10019 USA

Quivers, Robin *Talk Show Host, Radio Personality, Actor, Entertainer*
350 E 79th St, #16H, New York, NY 10021 USA

Qureia, Ahmed *Prime Minister*
Prime Minister's Office, Gara City, Gaza Strip, Palestine, ISRAEL

R

R E M *Music Group*
170 College Ave, Athens, GA 30601, US

R M A, Bharathimohan *Actor*
31/8 Madley Lind Street, T Nagar, Chennai, TN 600 017, INDIA

R Pandiarajan *Actor*
18 Sivasailam Street, T Nagar, Chennai, TN 600 017, INDIA

R Partheepan *Actor*
Veerappa Nagar, Chennai, TN 600 093, INDIA

Raabe, Max *Opera Singer*
Klimperkasten, Thuyring 63, Berlin, 12101, GERMANY

Raabe, Meinhardt
PO Box 913, Penney Farms, FL 32079

Raaj Kumar, Puru *Actor, Bollywood*
57 Worli Sea Face, Bombay, MS 400 018, INDIA

Raakhee *Actor, Bollywood*
Muktangan Sarojini Naidu Road, Santacruz, Bombay, MS 400 054, INDIA

Raaurn, Gustav *Skier*
PO Box 700, Mercer Island, WA 98040 USA

Rabe, Pamela *Actor*
Shanahan Mgmt, PO Box 1509, Darlinghurst, NSW, 1300, AUSTRALIA

Rabin, Trevor *Composer*
Kraft-Benjamin-Engel, 15233 Ventura Blvd, #200, Sherman Oaks, CA 91403 USA

Rabinovitch, Benton S *Misc*
12530 42nd Ave NE, Seattle, WA 98125 USA

Rabinow, Jacob *Engineer, Inventor*
6920 Selkirk Dr, Bethesda, MD 20817 USA

Rabinowitz, Dorothy *Journalist*
Wall Street Journal, Editorial Dept, 200 Liberty St, New York, NY 10281 USA

Rabinowitz, Harry *Composer, Conductor*
11 Mead Road, Cranleigh, Surrey, GU6 7BG, UNITED KINGDOM (UK)

Rabinowitz, Jesse C *Misc*
University of California, Molecular & Cell Biology Dept, Berkeley, CA 94720 USA

Rabkin, Mitchell T *Doctor*
Beth Israel Deaconess Medical Center, 330 Brookline Ave, Boston, MA 02215 USA

Raby, Stuart *Physicist*
Ohio State University, Physics Dept, Columbus, OH 43210 USA

Racan, Ivica *Prime Minister*
Prime Minister's Office, Jordanovac 71, Zagreb, 41000, CROATIA

Racette, Patricia *Opera Singer*
Columbia Artists Mgmt Inc, 165 W 57th St, New York, NY 10019 USA

Rachin, Julian *Musician*
Columbia Artists Mgmt Inc, 165 W 57th St, New York, NY 10019 USA

Rachins, Alan *Actor*
1274 Capri Dr, Pacific Palisades, CA 90272 USA

Racicot, Marc F *Governor*
901 15th St S, #201, Arlington, VA 22202 USA

Racimo, Victoria *Actor*
Marion Rosenberg, PO Box 69826, West Hollywood, CA 90069 USA

Radatz, Richard R (Dick) *Baseball Player*
17 Hilltop Lane, #1, South Easton, MA 02375 USA

Radcliffe, Daniel *Actor*
PFD, Drury House, 34-43 Russell St, London, WC2B 5HA, UNITED KINGDOM (UK)

Raddatz, Carl
Stalluponer Allee 54, Berlin, GERMANY, 14055

Rademacher, Ingo *Actor*
S D B Partners, 1801 Ave of Stars, #902, Los Angeles, CA 90067 USA

Rademacher, Pete
5585 River Styx Rd., Medina, OH 44256

Rademacher, T Peter (Pete) *Boxer*
5585 River Styx Road, Medina, OH 44256 USA

Rader, Dotson C *Writer*
Parade Magazine, Editorial Dept, 750 3rd Ave, New York, NY 10017 USA

Rader, Douglas L (Doug) *Baseball Player*
1822 Sullins Way, Houston, TX 77058 USA

Rader, Randall R *Judge*
US Appeals Court, 717 Madison Place NW, Washington, DC 20439 USA

Rader, Stanley
360 Waverly Dr., Pasadena, CA 91105

Rader-Duval, Dean *Actor*
Don Gerler Agency, 3349 Cahuenga Blvd W #1, Los Angeles, CA 90068 USA

Radford, Mark *Basketball Player*
3423 NE, 22nd Ave, Portland, OR 97212 USA

Radford, Michael *Director*
38 Rickering Mews, London, W2 5AD, UNITED KINGDOM (UK)

Radha Ravi *Actor*
23 Poes Road, Teynampet, Chennai, TN 600 018, INDIA

Radhika *Actor, Bollywood*
3 Paul Appasamy Street, Abhirampuram, Chennai, TN 600018, INDIA

Radigan, Terry *Songwriter, Musician*
Frank Callan Corp, 6039 Robin Hill Road, Nashville, TN 37205 USA

Radiohead *Music Group*
Creative Artists Agency LCC (CAA-LA), 9830 Wilshire Blvd, Beverly Hills, CA 90212 USA

Radisic, Zivko *President*
President's Office, Marsala Titz 7, Sarajevo, 71000, BOSNIA & HERZEGOVINA

Radke, Brad W *Baseball Player*
Richard Radke, 3107 Emerson, Tampa, FL 33629 USA

Radko, Christopher *Artist*
PO Box 536, Elmsford, NY 10523 USA

Radmanovic, Vladimir *Basketball Player*
Seattle SuperSonics, 351 Elliott Ave W, #500, Seattle, WA 98119 USA

Radner, Roy *Economist*
30711 Overlook Run, Buena Vista, CO 81211 USA

Radnor, Josh *Actor*
Gersh Agency, The (NY), 41 Madison Ave Fl 33, New York, NY 10010 USA

Radojevic, Danilo *Dancer*
American Ballet Theatre, 890 Broadway, New York, NY 10003 USA

Raduege Jr, Harry D *General*
Director, Defense Information Systems Agency, Arlington, VA 22204 USA

Radwanski, George *Editor*
Toronto Star, Editorial Dept, 1 Yonge St, Toronto, ON M5E 1E6, CANADA

Rae, Cassidy *Actor*
24708 Riverchase Dr, #B-213, Valencia, CA 91355 USA

Rae, Charlotte *Actor*
10790 Wilshire Blvd, #903, Los Angeles, CA 90024 USA

Rae, Chris
122 Holland Park Ave., London, ENGLAND, W11 4UA

Rae, Robert K (Bob) *Politician*
Goodman Phillips Vineberg, 250 Yonge St, Toronto, ON M5B 2M6, CANADA

Rae Westley, Jennifer *Actor*
da Vinci Talent, 919 Marie Anne Est, Montreal QC, H2J 2B2, CANADA

Raekwon *Musician*
Famous Artists Agency, 250 W 57th St, New York, NY 10107 USA

Rafalski, Brian *Hockey Player*
New Jersey Devils, Continental Arena, 50 RR 120 N, East Rutherford, NJ 07073 USA

Rafelson, Bob *Director*
1543 Dog Team Road, 1022 Palm Ave. #3, New Haven, VT 05472 USA

Raffarin, Jean-Pierre *Prime Minister*
Premier's Office, Hotel Matignon, 57 Rue de Varenne, Paris, 75000, fr

Raffarin, Jean-Pierre *Prime Minister*
Premier's Office, Hotel Matignon, 57 Rue de Varenne, Paris, 75000, FRANCE

Rafferty, Thomas M (Tom) *Football Player*
1107 Travis Court, Southlake, TX 76092
USA

Raffi *Musician*
Agency for Performing Arts, 9200 Sunset
Blvd, #900, Los Angeles, CA 90069 USA

Raffin, Deborah *Actor*
301 N Canon Dr, #214, Beverly Hills, CA
90210 USA

Rafikov, Mars Z *Cosmonaut*
Ul M Gorkova 59, KV 44, Almaty, 480
002, KAZAKHSTAN

Rafko, Kaye Lani Rae
4932 Frary Lane, Monroe, MI 48161

Rafsanjani, Hashemi *Ex-President*
Ali Shariati Ave, Tehran, IRAN

Rafsanjani, Hojatoleslam H *President*
Expediency Council of Islamic Order,
Majilis, Teheran, IRAN

Rafshoon, Gerald
3028 Q St. NW, Washington, DC 20006

Rafter, Patrick *Tennis Player*
PO Box 1235, North Sydney, NSW, 2059,
AUSTRALIA

Raftery, S Frank *Misc*
Painters & Allied Trades Union, 1750
New York Ave NW, Washington, DC
20006 USA

Ragavendar *Actor*
2-C Palace View Apartments, 788
Santhome High Road, Chennai, TN 600
028, INDIA

Rage Against The Machine *Musician*
Creative Artists Agency LCC (CAA-LA),
9830 Wilshire Blvd, Beverly Hills, CA
90212 USA

Raggi, Florencia *Actor*
Telefe - Argentina, Pavon 2444
(C1248AAT), Buenos Aires, ARGENTINA

Raggio, Lisa
9300 Wilshire Blvd. #410, Beverly Hills,
CA 90212

Raghavan, V S *Actor*
6 School View Road, Mandavelli,
Chennai, TN 600 028, INDIA

Raghavi *Actor, Bollywood*
18 Crescent Park Road, T Nagar, Chennai,
TN 600017, INDIA

Raghuvaran *Actor*
D-1 Ist Floor Anandsree Apartments, 32
Hindi Prachar Saba Street, Chennai, TN
600 017, INDIA

Ragin, Derek Lee *Opera Singer*
Colbert Artists, 111 W 57th St, New York,
NY 10019 USA

Ragin, John S *Actor*
5706 Briarcliff Road, Los Angeles, CA
90068 USA

Rago, Pablo *Actor*
Telefe - Argentina, Pavon 2444
(C1248AAT), Buenos Aires, ARGENTINA

Ragsdale, William *Actor*
Innovative Artists, 1505 10th St, Santa
Monica, CA 90401 USA

Rahal, Bobby
PO Box 429, New Albany, OH 43054-
0429

Rahal, Robert W (Bobby) *Race Car Driver*
Team Rahal Racing, 4601 Lyman Dr,
Hilliard, OH 43026 USA

Rahlves, Daron *Skier*
PO Box 333, Truckee, CA 96160 USA

Rahm, Kevin *Actor*
3 Arts Entertainment, 9460 Wilshire Blvd,
#700, Beverly Hills, CA 90212 USA

Rahman Khan, Ataur *Prime Minister*
Bangladesh Jatiya League, 500 A
Dhanmondi R/A, Road 7, Dhaka,
BANGLADESH

Rahul, Roy *Actor, Bollywood*
502 Gildar Villa, 17 Master Vinayak X
Road Bandra, Mumbai, MS 400050,
INDIA

Rahzel *Musician*
Agency Group Ltd, 1775 Broadway, #430,
New York, NY 10019 USA

Rai, Aishwarya *Actor, Bollywood*
402 Ramalaxmi Niwas, 16th Road
Khar(W), Mumbai, MS 400054, INDIA

Rai, Rajeev *Director, Bollywood,
Filmmaker, Producer*
22 Sonmarg Nepean Sea Road, Bombay,
MS 400 006, INDIA

Rai, Rajiv *Bollywood, Producer, Director*
B-11 Commerce Center, Tardeo, Mumbai,
MS 400034, INDIA

Raichle, Marcus E *Doctor*
Washington University, Medical School,
Neurology Dept, Saint Louis, MO 63130
USA

Raider-Wexler, Victor *Actor*
Stone Manners Talent Agency, 6500
Wilshire Blvd, Ste 550, Los Angeles, CA
90048 USA

Raikkonen, Kimi *Race Car Driver*
Formula Management Ltd, PO Box 222,
Borehamwood, Herts, WD6 3FJ, United
Kingdom

Railsback, Steve *Actor*
11684 Ventura Blvd, #581, Studio City,
CA 91604 USA

Raimi, Sam *Director*
8381 Hollywood Blvd, #680, Los Angeles,
CA 90069 USA

Raimi, Ted
252 N. Larchmont Blvd. #200, Los
Angeles, CA 90004

Raimond, Jean-Bernard *Government
Official*
Servier SA, 22 Rue Garnier, Neuilly-sur-
Seine, 92200, FRANCE

Raimondi, Ruggero *Opera Singer*
M Gromof, 140 Bis Rue Lecourbe, Paris,
75015 USA

Rain, Misty
Box 67, Lakewood, CA 90714

Raine, Craig A *Writer*
New College, English Dept, Oxford, OX1
3BN, UNITED KINGDOM (UK)

Raine, Gillian
13 Billing Rd., London, ENGLAND, SW10

Rainer, Luise *Actor*
54 Eaton Square, London, SW1, UNITED
KINGDOM (UK)

Raines, Cristina
6399 Wilshire Blvd. #414, Los Angeles,
CA 90048

Raines, Franklin D *Government Official,
Financier*
Federal National Mortgage Assn, 3900
Wisconsin Ave NW, Washington, DC
20016 USA

Raines, Timothy (Tim) *Baseball Player*
310 Saddleworth Place, Lake Mary, FL
32746 USA

Rainey, Ford *Actor*
3821 Carbon Canyon Road, Malibu, CA
90265 USA

Rainey, Matt *Journalist*
Star-Ledger, Editorial Dept, 1 Star-Ledge
Plaza, Newark, NJ 07102 USA

Rainey, Wayne *Race Car Driver*
1660 Akron Peninsula Road, #201, Akron,
OH 44313 USA

Rainier, Crown Prince III *Prince*
Palais de Monaco, Boite Postale 518,
Monte Carlo Cedex, 98015, MONACO

Raintano, Natalie *Actor*
Artists Only Management, 1901 Avenue
of the Stars, Suite 605, Los Angeles, CA
90067 USA

Rainwater, G L *Business Person*
Ameren Corp, 1901 Chouteau Ave, Saint
Louis, MO 63103 USA

Rainwater, Gregg *Actor*
PO Box 291836, Los Angeles, CA 90029
USA

Rainwater, Keech *Musician*
Borman Entertainment, 1222 16th Ave S,
#23, Nashville, TN 37212 USA

Rainwater, Marvin *Musician*
36968 295th St, Aitkin, MN 56431 USA

Raitano, Natalie *Actor*
Much and House Public Relations, 8075
West Third Street, Suite 500, Los Angeles,
CA 90048

Raitt, Bonnie L *Songwriter, Musician*
3575 Cahuenga Blvd W, #590, Los
Angeles, CA 90068 USA

Raitt, John *Actor, Musician*
1164 Napoli Dr, Pacific Palisades, CA
90272 USA

Raj, Prakash *Actor*
183 Bharathidasan Street, Baskar Colony
Virugambakka, Chennai, TN 600 092,
INDIA

Raja *Actor*
6 Ranjith Road, Kotturpuram, Chennai,
TN 600 085, INDIA

Rajasulochana *Actor, Bollywood*
70 G N Chetty Road, T Nagar, Chennai,
TN 600017, INDIA

Rajat, Kapoor *Actor, Bollywood*
Unit No 140 Andheri Indl Est, Off Veera
Desai Road Andheri (W), Mumbai, MS
400053, INDIA

Rajeev *Actor*
12/V Ambedkar Street Gandhi Nagar,
Saligramam, Chennai, TN 600 093, INDIA

Rajeevi *Actor, Bollywood*
32 Raman Street, T Nagar, Chennai, TN
600017, INDIA

Rajendran, S S *Actor*
3/3 Eldams Road, Chennai, TN 600 018, INDIA

Rajesh *Actor*
7 Kannappa Salai, Ashok Nagar, Chennai, TN 600 083, INDIA

Rajinikanth *Actor*
18 Raghava Veera Avenue, Poes Garden, Chennai, TN 600 086, INDIA

Rajkiran *Actor, Bollywood*
145/5 North Boag Road, T Nagar, Chennai, TN 600017, INDIA

Rajkumar, Puru *Actor, Bollywood*
57 Worli Sea Face, Worli, Mumbai, MS 400018, INDIA

Rajna, Thomas *Composer, Musician*
10 Wyndover Road, Claremont, Cape, 7700, SOUTH AFRICA

Rajnikant *Actor, Bollywood*
18 Ragava Veera Avenue, Poes Garden, Madras, TN 600 086, INDIA

Rajskub, Mary Lynn *Actor*
Endeavor Agency LLC (LA), 9601 Wilshire Blvd Fl 3, Beverly Hills, CA 90210 USA

Rakhmonov, Emomali *President*
President's Office, Supreme Soviet, Dushanbe, TAJIKISTAN

Raki, Laya *Actor*
Atkins Assoc, 8040 Ventura Canyon Ave, Panorama City, CA 91402 USA

Rakim *Musician*
Padell Nadell Fine Wineberger, 156 W 56th St, #400, New York, NY 10019 USA

Rakotomavo, Pascal *Prime Minister*
Prime Minister's Office, Mahazoarivo, Antananarivo, MADAGASCAR

Rakowski, Mieczyslaw F *Prime Minister*
Miesiecznik Dzis, Ul Poznanska 3, Warsaw, 00-680, POLAND

Rales, Steven M *Business Person*
Danaher Corp, 1250 24th St NW, Washington, DC 20037 USA

Rall, Gunther *War Hero*
Schmalschlagerstr 17, Bad Reichenhall, 83435, GERMANY

Rall, J Edward *Doctor*
3947 Baltimore St, Kensington, MD 20895 USA

Rall, Ted *Cartoonist*
Chronicle Features, 901 Mission St, San Francisco, CA 94103 USA

Rallis, George J *Prime Minister*
4 Kanari St, Athens, 10671, GREECE

Ralph, Christopher *Actor*
Evolution Entertainment, 901 N Highland Ave, Los Angeles, CA 90038 USA

Ralph, Richard P *Governor*
Governor's Office, Government House, Stanley, FALKLAND ISLANDS

Ralph, Sheryl Lee *Actor, Musician*
938 S Longwood Ave, Los Angeles, CA 90019 USA

Ralston, Bob
17027 Tennyson Pl., Granada Hills, CA 91344-1225

Ralston, Dennis *Tennis Player*
2005 San Vicente Dr, Concord, CA 94519 USA

Ralston, John R *Football Player, Football Coach*
5958 Dry Oak Dr, San Jose, CA 95120 USA

Ralston, Steve *Soccer Player*
New England Revolution, CMGI Field, 1 Patriot Place, Foxboro, MA 02035 USA

Ram, C Venkata *Doctor*
Texas Southwestern Medical Center, 5323 Harry Hines Blvd, Dallas, TX 75390 USA

Rama IX *King*
Chitralada Villa, Bangkok, THAILAND

Rama Rau, Santha *Writer*
496 Leedsville Road, Amenia, NY 12501 USA

Ramage, Rob *Hockey Player*
16127 Wilson Manor Dr, Chesterfield, MO 63005 USA

Ramahata, Victor *Prime Minister*
PO Box 6004, Antanarivo, 101, MADAGASCAR

Raman, Priya *Actor, Bollywood*
Plot No 69, Part II VGP Sea View Palavakkam, Chennai, TN 600041, INDIA

Raman, Ragha *Actor, Bollywood*
Flat 202 II Floor, 167 Eldams Road Teynampet, Chennai, TN 600018, INDIA

Ramani, Karthik *Engineer*
3421 Crawford St, West Lafayette, IN 47906 USA

Ramaphosa, M Cyril *Government Official*
New Africa Investments, PO Box 782922, Sandton, 2416, SOUTH AFRICA

Ramarajan *Actor*
1 Ramakrishna Street, T Nagar, Chennai, TN 600 017, INDIA

Ramasami, V. K. *Bollywood, Actor*
26 Tilak Street, T Nagar, Chennai, TN 600017, INDIA

Ramazzotti, Eros *Musician*
Via Vittoria Colonna, Milan, ITALY, I-20149

Ramba *Actor, Bollywood*
184 Bharathidasan Salai, Baskaran Colony Saligramam, Chennai, TN 600092, INDIA

Ramba *Actor*
44/1 Navaneethammal Street, Saligramam, Chennai, TN 600 093, INDIA

Rambahadur, Limbu *War Hero*
Box 420, Bandar Seri Begawan, Negara Brunei Darussalam, BRUNEI

Rambert, Charles J J *Architect*
179 Rue de Courcelles, Paris, 75017, FRANCE

Rambis, Kurt *Basketball Player, Coach*
20 Chatham, Manhattan Beach, CA 90266 USA

Rambo, David L *Religious Leader*
Christian & Missionary Alliance, PO Box 35000, Colorado Springs, CO 80935 USA

Rambo, John *Track Athlete*
1847 Myrtle Ave, Long Beach, CA 90806 USA

Rambola, Tony *Musician*
William Morris Agency, 151 El Camino Dr, Beverly Hills, CA 90212 USA

Ramey, Louis *Actor, Comedian*
William Morris Agency (WMA-LA), 1 William Morris Pl, Beverly Hills, CA 90212 USA

Ramey, Samuel E *Opera Singer*
320 Central Park West, New York, NY 10025 USA

Ramgoolam, Navinchandra *Prime Minister*
85 Sir Seewilsagur Ramgoolam St, Port Louis, MAURITIUS

Ramgoolam, Seewosagur *Prime Minister*
85 Desforges St, Port Louis, MAURITIUS

Ramirez, Carolina *Actor*
Gabriel Blanco Iglesias (Mexico), Rio Balsas 35-32, Colonia Cuauhtemoc, DF, 06500, Mexico

Ramirez, Manny *Baseball Player*
Boston Red Sox, Fenway Park, 4 Yawkey Way, Boston, MA 02215 USA

Ramirez, Manuel A (Manny) *Baseball Player*
29315 Regency Circle, Westlake, OK 44145 USA

Ramirez, Michael P (Mike) *Cartoonist*
Los Angeles Times, Editorial Dept, 202 W 1st St, Los Angeles, CA 90012 USA

Ramirez, Pedro J *Editor*
El Mundo, Calle Pradillo 42, Madrid, 28002, SPAIN

Ramirez, Raul *Tennis Player*
Avenida Ruiz, 65 Sur Ensenada, Baja California, MEXICO

Ramirez, RaulAvenida Ruiz
65 Sur Ensenada, Baja, California MEXICO

Ramirez, Twiggy *Musician*
Mitch Schnelder Organization, 14724 Ventura Blvd, #410, Sherman Oaks, CA 91403 USA

Ramirez Vazquez, Pedro *Architect*
Ave de la Fuentes 170, Mexico City, DF, 01900, MEXICO

Ramis, Harold *Director, Actor*
160 Euclid Ave, Glencoe, IL 60022 USA

Rammstein *Music Group*
Feinstein Management, 420 Lexington Ave #2150, New York, NY 10170

Ramo, Simon *Business Person*
9200 Sunset Blvd, #401, West Hollywood, CA 90069 USA

Ramon, Haim *Government Official*
Knesset, Jerusalem, 91010, ISRAEL

Ramone, Phil
3301 Barham Blvd. #201, Los Angeles, CA 90068

Ramones, The *Music Group*
Kurfirst/Blackwell Management, 601 W 26th St, Fl 11, New York, NY 10001

Ramos, Del *Musician*
Variety Artists, 1924 Spring St, Paso Robles, CA 93446 USA

Ramos, Diego *Actor*
Gabriel Blanco Iglesias (Mexico), Rio Balsas 35-32, Colonia Cuauhtemoc, DF, 06500, Mexico

Ramos, Fidel *President*
Malacanang Palace, Manila, PHILIPPINES

Ramos, Jorge *Actor*
Univision, 314 Main St, Chico, CA 95928
USA

Ramos, Mando *Boxer*
1252 W Park Western Dr, #91, San Pedro,
CA 90732 USA

Ramos, Mel *Artist*
5941 Ocean View Dr, Oakland, CA
94618 USA

Ramos, Monica *Musician*
MNW Records Group, PO Box 535, Taby,
183 25, SWEDEN

Ramos, Rudy
280 S. Beverly Dr. #400, Beverly Hills,
CA 90212

Ramos, Tab *Soccer Player*
William Morris Agency, 151 El Camino
Dr, Beverly Hills, CA 90212 USA

Ramos Jr, Hilario (Larry) *Musician*
Variety Artists, 1924 Spring St, Paso
Robles, CA 93446 USA

Ramos-Horta, Jose *Nobel Prize Laureate*
Rua Sao Lazoro 16, #1, Lisbon, 1150,
PORTUGAL

Rampling, Charlotte *Actor*
1 Ave Emile Augier, Croissy-sur-Seine,
78290, FRANCE

Ramsay, Anne
PO Box 5617, Beverly Hills, CA 90210

Ramsay, Bruce
9150 Wilshire Blvd. #350, Beverly Hills,
CA 90212-3427

Ramsay, Craig *Hockey Player, Coach*
9701 NW 58th Court, Parkland, FL 33076
USA

Ramsay, John T (Jack) *Coach*
444 Ridgeway Road, Lake Oswego, OR
97034 USA

Ramsay, Keshu *Filmmaker, Director,
Producer*
Maharaja Surajmal 'C', New Versova Link
Road Andheri, Bombay, MS 400 058,
INDIA

Ramsay, Wayne *Hockey Player*
General Delivery, Oak River, MB R0K
1T0, CANADA

Ramsey, David *Actor*
Agency for the Performing Arts (APA-LA),
9200 Sunset Blvd #900, Los Angeles, CA
90069 USA

Ramsey, Garrard S (Buster) *Football
Player*
4102 Highway 411S, Maryville, TN
37801 USA

Ramsey, John & Patsy
100 Peachtree St. #2140, Atlanta, GA
30303-1912

Ramsey, Logan
12923 Killion St., Van Nuys, CA 91401

Ramsey, Mary *Musician*
Agency for Performing Arts, 9200 Sunset
Blvd, #900, Los Angeles, CA 90069 USA

Ramsey, Michael (Mike) *Hockey Player*
445 W 79th St, Chanhassen, MN 55317
USA

Ramsey, Ray *Football Player*
1612 Sequoria Dr, Chatham, IL 62629
USA

Ramsey, Ray *Songwriter, Musician*
Elbchaussee 118, Hamburg, 22763,
GERMANY

Ramsey, Wes *Actor*
Creative Management Group (CMG),
9465 Wilshire Blvd #335, Beverly Hills,
CA 90212 USA

Ramsey, William E *Admiral*
825 Bayshore Dr, Pensacola, FL 32507
USA

Ramsey Jr, Frank V *Basketball Player,
Coach*
363 Buckner Ridge Lane, Madisonville,
KY 42431 USA

Ramsey Jr, Norman F *Nobel Prize
Laureate*
24 Monmouth Court, Brookline, MA
02446 USA

Ran, Shulamit *Composer*
University of Chicago, Music Dept, 5845
S Ellis Ave, Chicago, IL 60637 USA

Rana, Ashutosh *Actor, Bollywood*
23 Bharat Petroleum Colony, Aziz Baug
Chembur, Mumbai, MS 400074, INDIA

Rancic, Bill *Reality TV Star*
Esterman Events, 220 Park Rd, Riva, MD
21140 USA

Rand, Marvin *Photographer*
Marvin Rand Assoc, 1310 Abbot Kinney
Blvd, Venice, CA 90291 USA

Rand, Reese Mary *Track Athlete*
6650 Los Gatos, Atascadero, CA 93422
USA

Rand, Robert W *Educator*
Good Samaritan Hospital, Neurosciences
Institute, Los Angeles, CA 90017 USA

Randa, Joe *Baseball Player*
W236N1150 Archery Dr, Waukesha, WI
53188 USA

Randall, Alice *Writer*
Creative Artists Agency LCC (CAA-LA),
9830 Wilshire Blvd, Beverly Hills, CA
90212 USA

Randall, Carolyn D *Judge*
US Court of Appeals, 515 Rusk St,
Houston, TX 77002 USA

Randall, Claire *Religious Leader*
10015 W Royal Oak Road, #120, Sun
City, AZ 85351 USA

Randall, Frankie *Boxer*
355 Fish Hatchery Road, #02,
Morristown, TN 37813 USA

Randall, Jon *Musician*
Joe's Garage, 4405 Belmont Park Terrace,
Nashville, TN 37215 USA

Randall, Josh *Actor*
I F A Talent Agency, 8730 Sunset Blvd,
#490, Los Angeles, CA 90069 USA

Randall, Rebel *Actor*
Women United Int'l, 32969 Shifting Sands
Trail, Cathedral City, CA 92234 USA

Randell, Ron
133 S. Oakhurst Dr. #102, Beverly Hills,
CA 90212-3500

Randi, James *Misc*
12000 NW 8th St, Plantation, FL 33325
USA

Randie, John *Football Player*
PO Box 489, Harrisonburg, VA 22803
USA

Randle, Betsy
9300 Wilshire Blvd. #555, Beverly Hills,
CA 90212

Randle, Theresa *Actor*
Personal Management Company, 425 N
Robertson Dr, Los Angeles, CA 90048
USA

Randle, Theresa *Actor*
350 S Catalina St, #307, Los Angeles, CA
90020 USA

Randle, Ulmo (Sonny) *Football Player*
2361 Meadow Court, Harrisonburg, VA
22801 USA

Randolph, A Raymond *Judge*
US Court of Appeals, 333 Constitution
NW, Washington, DC 20001 USA

Randolph, Boots *Musician*
541 Richmar Dr, Nashville, TN 37211
USA

Randolph, Carl *Musician*
David Levin Mgmt, 200 W 57th St, #308,
New York, NY 10019 USA

Randolph, Jackson H *Business Person*
Cinergy Corp, 139 E 4th St, Cincinnati,
OH 45202 USA

Randolph, Joyce
295 Central Park W. #18-A, New York,
NY 10024

Randolph, Judson G *Doctor*
111 Michigan Ave NW, Washington, DC
20010 USA

Randolph, Willie L *Baseball Player*
648 Juniper Place, Franklin Lakes, NJ
07417 USA

Randolph, Zach *Basketball Player*
Portland Trail Blazers, Rose Garden, 1
Center Court St, Portland, OR 97227 USA

Randrup, Michael *Misc*
10 Fairlawn Road, Lythamst Annes,
Lancashire, FY8 5PT, UNITED KINGDOM
(UK)

Rands, Bernard *Composer*
Harvard University, Music Dept,
Cambridge, MA 02138 USA

Ranford, William (Bill) *Hockey Player*
Coquitlam Express, 633 Poirier St,
Coquitlam, BC V3J 6B1, CANADA

Ranganathan, Suman *Actor, Bollywood*
Gilder Building, Turner Road Bandra,
Mumbai, MS 400050, INDIA

Rangel, Charles B *Politician*
74 W. 132nd St., New York, NY 10037

Ranger, Doug *Songwriter*
New Frontier Mgmt, 1921 Broadway,
Nashville, TN 37203 USA

Rani *Actor, Bollywood*
Anubhav Apts, Arunachalam Road,
Chennai, TN 600083, INDIA

Rania *Royalty*
Royal Palace, Amman, JORDAN

Raniers, Massimo
via Giovanni Battista Tiepolo 34, Rome,
ITALY, 00196

Ranis, Gustav *Economist*
7 Mulberry Road, Woodbridge, CT 06525
USA

Ranjani *Actor, Bollywood*
78/a Moubrews Road, Alwarpet, Chennai,
TN 600018, INDIA

Ranjeet *Actor, Bollywood*
14 Silver Beach A B Nair Road, Juhu,
Bombay, MS 400 049, INDIA

Ranki, Dezso *Musician*
OrdogoromLejto 11/B, Budapest, 1112,
HUNGARY

Rankin, Chris *Actor*
Ken McReddie Ltd, Paurelle House, 91
Regent St, London, W1R7TB, UNITED
KINGDOM (UK)

Rankin, Judy *Golfer*
2715 Racquet Club Dr, Midland, TX
79705 USA

Rankin, Kenny *Songwriter, Musician*
Absolute Artists, 530 Howard St, #200,
San Francisco, CA 94105 USA

Rankin Jr, Alfred M *Business Person*
NACCO Industries, 5875 Landerbrook Dr,
Mayfield Heights, OH 44124 USA

Rankine, Terry *Architect*
Cambridge Seven Assoc, 1050
Massachusetts Ave, Cambridge, MA
02138 USA

Ranks, Shabba *Musician*
Epic Records, 550 Madison Ave, #2500,
New York, NY 10022 USA

Ranney, Helen M *Doctor*
6229 La Jolla Mesa Dr, La Jolla, CA
92037 USA

Ransdell, Gary *Educator*
Western Kentucky University, President's
Office, Bowling Green, KY 42101 USA

Ransey, Kelvin *Basketball Player*
3195 Monterey Dr, Tupelo, MS 38801
USA

Ransome, Prunella
59 Frith St., London, ENGLAND, W1

Rao, Ashok *Actor*
28 17th Cross Malleswaram, Bangalore,
KA, INDIA

Rao, C N Ramchandra *Misc*
JNC President's House, Indian Science
Institute, Bangalore, KA, 560012, INDIA

Rao, Calyampudi R *Mathematician*
826 W Aaron Dr, State College, PA 16803
USA

Rao, T Rama *Actor, Director, Filmmaker,
Producer, Bollywood*
No 14 1st Balaji Street Balaji Avenue, T
Nagar, Madras, TN 600 017, INDIA

Rapaport, Michael *Actor*
Innovative Artists, 1505 10th St, Santa
Monica, CA 90401 USA

Raper, Kenneth B *Misc*
602 N Segoe Road, Madison, WI 53705
USA

Raphael *Actor*
Kaduri Agency, 16125 NE 18th Ave,
North Miami Beach, FL 33162 USA

Raphael, Fredric M *Writer*
Largadeile, Saint Lauraent la Vallee,
Belves, 24170, FRANCE

Raphael, Sally Jessy *Entertainer*
249 Quaker Hill Road, Pawling, NY
12564 USA

Raposo, Greg *Musician*
PO Box 434, Glen Head, NY 11545

Rapp, Antony *Actor*
Paradigm (NY), 500 5th Ave Fl 37, New
York, NY 10110 USA

Rappeneau, Jean-Paul *Director*
24 Rue Henri Barbusse, Paris, 75005,
FRANCE

Rapping 4-Tay *Musician*
Richard Walters, 1800 Argyle Ave, #408,
Los Angeles, CA 90028 USA

Rappuoli, Rino *Scientist*
Sclavo Research Center, Via Fiorentina 1,
Siena, 53100, ITALY

Rapson, Ralph *Architect*
1 Seymour Ave, Minneapolis, MN 55414
USA

Rare, Vanessa *Actor*
Auckland Actors, PO Box 56460,
Dominion Road, Auckland, NEW
ZEALAND

Rarick, Cindy *Golfer*
Ladies Pro Golf Assn, 100 International
Golf Dr, Daytona Beach, FL 32124 USA

Rasa Don *Musician*
William Morris Agency, 1325 Ave of
Americas, New York, NY 10019 USA

Rascal Flatts *Music Group*
William Morris Agency (WMA-TN), 2100
W End Ave #1000, Nashville, TN 37203
USA

Rasche, David *Actor*
687 Grove Lane, Santa Barbara, CA
93105 USA

Rascon, Alfred V *War Hero*
10397 Derby Dr, Laurel, MD 20723 USA

Rash, Steve *Director*
Broder Kurland Webb Uffner, 9242
Beverly Blvd, #200, Beverly Hills, CA
90210 USA

Rashad, Ahmad *Football Player,
Sportscaster*
NBA Ent, 450 Harmon Meadow Blvd,
Secaucus, NJ 07094 USA

Rashad, Phylicia *Actor*
25 Magnolia Ave, Mount Vernon, NY
10553 USA

Rasheeda *Musician*
International Creative Mgmt, 8942
Wilshire Blvd, #219, Beverly Hills, CA
90211 USA

Rashid, Karim *Designer*
357 W 17th St, New York, NY 10011
USA

Rasi *Actor, Bollywood*
28B Main Road, Zakkaria Colony
Saligramam, Chennai, TN 600094, INDIA

Raskin, Alex *Journalist*
Los Angeles Times, Editorial Dept, 202 W
1st St, Los Angeles, CA 90012 USA

Raskin, David *Composer*
Robert Light, 6404 Wilshire Blvd, Los
Angeles, CA 90012 USA

Rasmussen, Anders Fogh *Prime Minister*
prins Jorgens Gard 11, Copenhagen K,
2000, DENMARK

Rasmussen, Poul Nyrup *Prime Minister*
Aliegade 6A, Frederiksberg, 2000,
DENMARK

Raspberry, Larry *Musician*
Craig Nowag Attractions, 6037
Haddington Place, Memphis, TN 38119
USA

Raspberry, William J *Journalist*
Washington Post, Editorial Dept, 1150
15th St NW, Washington, DC 20071 USA

Rasuk, Victor *Actor*
Washington Square Arts (LA), 1041 N
Formosa Ave, Writers Bldg #305, West
Hollywood, CA 90046 USA

Ratchford, Jeremy *Actor*
Paradigm Agency, 10100 Santa Monica
Blvd, #2500, Los Angeles, CA 90067 USA

Ratcliffe, John A *Astronomer*
193 Huntingdon Road, Cambridge, CB3
0DL, UNITED KINGDOM (UK)

Ratelle, J G Y Jean *Hockey Player*
1200 Salem St, #111, Lynnfield, MA
01940 USA

Rather, Dan *Correspondent, Television
Host, Commentator*
CBS-TV, News Dept, 51 W 52nd St, New
York, NY 10019 USA

Rathke, Henrich K M H *Religious Leader*
Schleifmuhlenweg 11, Schwering, 19061,
GERMANY

Rathmann, George B *Business Person*
ICOS Corp, 22021 20th Ave SE, Bothell,
WA 98021 USA

Rathmann, Jim *Race Car Driver*
14 Marina Isles Blvd, #14G, Indian
Harbor Beach, FL 32937 USA

Rathnam, Mani *Director, Bollywood*
3 First Cross Road, Venus Colony,
Alwarpet, Madras, 600018, INDIA

Ratleff, Ed *Basketball Player*
4202 Paseo de Oro, Cypress, CA 90630
USA

Ratliff, Theo *Basketball Player*
Portland Trail Blazers, Rose Garden, 1
Center Court St, Portland, OR 97227 USA

Ratner, Brett *Director*
William Morris Agency, 151 El Camino
Dr, Beverly Hills, CA 90212 USA

Ratner, Ellen
6127 Glen Tower, Los Angeles, CA 90068

Ratner, Helmer *Director*
Creative Artists Agency, 9830 Wilshire
Blvd, Beverly Hills, CA 90212 USA

Ratner, Mark A *Misc*
615 Greenleaf Ave, Glencoe, IL 60022
USA

Ratnoff, Oscar D *Doctor*
1801 Chestnut Hills Dr, Cleveland, OH
44106 USA

Rato, Rodrigo *Government Official*
International Monetary Fund, 700 19th St
NW, Washington, DC 20431 USA

Ratser, Dmitri *Musician*
Naxim Gershunoff, 1401 NE 9th St, #38,
Fort Lauderdale, FL 33304 USA

Ratsiraka, Didier *President, Admiral*
President's Office, Iavoloha, Antananarivo, MADAGASCAR

RATT
1818 Illion St., San Diego, CA 92110

Ratterman, George *Football Player*
6745 S Cook St, Centennial, CO 80122 USA

Rattle, Simon D *Conductor*
Frank Salomon, 201 W 54th St, #1C, New York, NY 10019 USA

Ratushinskaya, Irina B *Writer*
Vargius Publishing House, Kuzakova Str 18, Moscow, 107005, RUSSIA

Ratzenberger, John *Actor*
Shelter Entertainment, 9255 Sunset Blvd, #1010, Los Angeles, CA 90069 USA

Ratzinger, Joseph A Cardinal *Religious Leader*
Palazzo del S Uffizio II, Rome, 00193, ITALY

Rau, Doug
Rt. 1 Box 154-A, Columbus, TX 78934

Rau, Johannes *Politician, President*
Haroldstr 2, Dusseldorf, 47057, GERMANY

Rauch, John (Johnny) *Football Coach, Football Player*
30 Tads Trail, Oldsmar, FL 34677 USA

Rauch, Siegfried
Weilheimerstr. 6, Untersochering, GERMANY, D-82395

Raup, David M *Musician*
RR1 Box 168Y, Washington Island, WI 54246 USA

Rauschenberg, Robert *Artist*
381 Lafayette Street, New York, NY 10003 USA

Rautio, Nina *Opera Singer*
Herbert Breslin, 119 W 57th St, #1505, New York, NY 10019 USA

Ravalec, Blanche *Actor*
Babette Pouget, 6 Square Villaret de Joyeuse, Paris, 75017, FRANCE

Ravali *Actor, Bollywood*
159 Thirupathi Nagar, Valasaravakkam, Chennai, TN 600087, INDIA

Ravalomanana, Marc *President*
President's Office, Iavoloha, Antananarivo, MADAGASCAR

Raveena, Tondon *Actor, Bollywood*
Nippon Society, Juhu Church, Mumbai, MS 400049, INDIA

Raven *Wrestler*
3665 Wintershill Dr, Atlanta, GA 30380 USA

Raven, Eddy *Songwriter, Musician*
Great American Talent, PO Box 2476, Hendersonville, TN 37077 USA

Raven, Peter H *Misc*
Missouri Botanical Garden, PO Box 299, Saint Louis, MO 63166 USA

Raven, Robert D *Lawyer*
Morrison & Forester, 345 California St, #3500, San Francisco, CA 94104 USA

Raven-Symone *Actor*
International Creative Mgmt, 8942 Wilshire Blvd, #219, Beverly Hills, CA 90211 USA

Ravenscroft, Thurl
2527 Brea Blvd. #116, Fullerton, CA 92625

Raver, Kim *Actor*
Innovative Artists (NY), 235 Park Ave S Fl 7, New York, NY 10003 USA

Ravitch, Diane S *Historian*
New York University, Press Building, Washington Place, New York, NY 10003 USA

Ravony, Francisque *Prime Minister*
Union des Forces Vivas Democratiques, Antananarivo, MADAGASCAR

Rawail, Rahul *Director, Filmmaker, Producer, Bollywood*
B103 Kailash Juhu Church Road, Juhu, Bombay, MS 400 049, INDIA

Rawal, Paresh *Actor, Comedian, Bollywood*
11 Sea Breeze Apartments 12th Road, JVPD Scheme, Bombay, MS 400 049, INDIA

Rawat, Navi *Actor*
Joan Green Management, 1836 Courtney Terr, Los Angeles, CA 90046 USA

Rawlings, Adrian *Actor*
Ken McReddie Ltd, 91 Regent St, London, W1R 7TB, ENGLAND

Rawlins, V Lane *Educator*
Washington State University, President's Office, Pullman, WA 99164 USA

Rawlinson of Ewell, Peter A G
Government Official
Wardour Castle, Tisbury, Wilts, SP3 6RH, UNITED KINGDOM (UK)

Rawls, Betsy
4613 Sylvanus Dr., Wilmington, DE 19803-4813

Rawls, Elizabeth E (Betsy) *Golfer*
501 Country Club Dr, Wilmington, DE 19803 USA

Rawls, Lou *Actor, Musician*
8428 E Preserve Way, Scottsdale, AZ 85262 USA

Rawls, Sam *Cartoonist*
King Features Syndicate, 888 7th Ave, New York, NY 10106 USA

Ray, Alexa *Actor*
The Agency, 1800 Ave of Stars, #400, Los Angeles, CA 90067 USA

Ray, Amy *Musician, Songwriter*
Russell Carter Artist Mgmt, 315 Ponce de Leon Ave, #756, Decatur, GA 30030 USA

Ray, Edward J *Educator*
Oregon State University, President's Office, Corvallis, OR 97331 USA

Ray, Fred Olen *Director*
PO Box 3563, Van Nuys, CA 91407 USA

Ray, Jeanne *Writer*
Harmony Books, 201 E 50th St, New York, NY 10022 USA

Ray, Jimmy *Musician*
Nineteen Music/Mgmt, 35-37 Parkgate Road, London, SW11 4NP, UNITED KINGDOM (UK)

Ray, Lisa *Actor*
Victory Productions, 9663 Santa Monica Blvd #7700, Beverly Hills, CA 90210

Ray, Marguerite *Actor*
1329 N Vista, #106, Los Angeles, CA 90046 USA

Ray, Rachael *Chef*
Food Network, 1180 6th Ave Fl 12, New York, NY 10036 USA

Ray, Rachel *Chef*
Food Network, 1180 Ave of Americas, #1200, New York, NY 10036 USA

Ray, Robert D *Governor*
Blue Cross/Blue Shield of Iowa, 636 Grand Ave, Des Moines, IA 50309 USA

Ray, Ronald E *War Hero*
4324 Belle Vista Dr, Saint Petersburg Beach, FL 33706 USA

Ray, Sugar
Pinnacle Entertainment, 30 Glenn St, White Plains, NY 10603 USA

Raybon, Marty *Musician*
Hallmark Direction, 15 Music Square W, Nashville, TN 37203 USA

Raycroft, Andrew *Hockey Player*
Boston Bruins, 1 Fleet Center, Boston, MA 02114 USA

Raye, Collin *Musician*
Scott Dean Mgmt, 612 Humboldt St, Reno, NV 89509 USA

Raye, Lisa *Actor*
JMG Management, 18000 Coastline Drive, Suite 8, Malibu, CA 90265 USA

Rayhal, Bobby
934a Crescent Blvd., Glenellyn, IL 60137

Rayl, Jim *Basketball Player*
201 West Boulevard, Kokcmo, IN 46902 USA

Raymo, Maureen *Misc*
Boston University, Geology Dept, Boston, MA 02215 USA

Raymond, Guy *Actor*
550 Erskine Dr, Pacific Palisades, CA 90272 USA

Raymond, Kenneth N *Misc*
University of California, Chemistry Dept, Berkeley, CA 94720 USA

Raymond, Lee R *Business Person*
Exxon Corp, 5959 Las Colinas Blvd, Irving, TX 75039 USA

Raymond, Lisa *Tennis Player*
Octagon, 1751 Pinnacle Dr, #1500, McLean, VA 22102 USA

Raymond, Paula *Actor*
PO Box 86, Beverly Hills, CA 90213 USA

Raymond, Ralph *Coach*
USA Softball, 1 Olympia Plaza, Colorado Springs, CO 80909 USA

Raymond, Usher *Musician*
3 Arts Entertainment Inc, 9460 Wilshire Blvd Fl 7, Beverly Hills, CA 90212 USA

Rayner, Chuck
116-5710 201st St., Langley, CANADA, BC V3A 8A6

Raynor, Bruce *Politician*
Unite, 275 7th Ave, New York, NY 10001
USA

Raz, Kavi *Actor*
Dale Garrick, 8831 Sunset Blvd, #402,
Los Angeles, CA 90069 USA

Raza, S Atiq *Business Person*
Advanced Micro Devices, 1 AMD Place,
Sunnyvale, CA 94085 USA

**Razafindratandra, Armand Gaetan
Cardinal** *Religious Leader*
Archeveche, Andohalo, Antananarivo,
101, MADAGASCAR

Razanamasy, Guy *Prime Minister*
Prime Minister's Office, Mahazoarivo,
Antananarivo, MADAGASCAR

Razborov, A A *Mathematician*
Princeton University, Mathematics Dept,
Princeton, NJ 08540 USA

Re, Giovanni Battsti Cardinal *Religious
Leader*
Palazzo delle Congregazioni, Piazza Pio
XII #10, Rome, 00193, ITALY

Rea, Chris *Musician*
Real Life, 122 Holland Park Ave, London,
W11 4UA, UNITED KINGDOM (UK)

Rea, Peggy *Actor*
10331 Riverside Dr, #204, Toluca Lake,
CA 91602 USA

Rea, Stephen *Actor*
861 Sutherland Ave, London, W9,
UNITED KINGDOM (UK)

Read, James *Actor*
3713 Hitchcock Ranch Road, Santa
Barbara, CA 93105 USA

Read, Nicolas *Actor*
Capocom Entertainment, 8970 Norma Pl,
Los Angeles, CA 90069 USA

Read, Richard *Journalist*
Portland Oregonian, Editorial Dept, 1320
SW Broadway, Portland, OR 97201 USA

Read, Sister Joel *Educator*
Alvermo College, President's Office, PO
Box 343922, Milwaukee, WI 53234 USA

Read-Martin, Dolly
30765 Pacific Coast Hwy. #103, Malibu,
CA 90265-3643

Readdy, William F (Bill) *Astronaut*
NASA, Johnson Space Center, 2101 NASA
Road, Houston, TX 77058 USA

Reagan, Bernice Johnson *Musician*
American University, History Dept,
Washington, DC 20016 USA

Reagan, Michael
4740 Allott Ave., Sherman Oaks, CA
91403

Reagan, Nancy D *Actor, First Lady*
10880 Wilshire Blvd, #870, Los Angeles,
CA 90024 USA

Reagan Jr, Ron
2612 28th Ave W, Seattle, WA 98199-
3320 USA

Real, Roxanne *Musician*
Headline Talent, 1650 Broadway, #508,
New York, NY 10019 USA

Reality, Maxim *Musician*
Midi Mgmt, Jenkins Lane, Great
Hallinsbury, Essex, CM22 7QL, UNITED
KINGDOM (UK)

Rearden, Kenny
568 Grosvenor Ave., Westmount,
CANADA, PQ H3Y 4Z3

Reardon, Jeffrey J (Jeff) *Baseball Player*
5 Marlwood Lane, Palm Beach Gardens,
FL 33418 USA

Reardon, Kenneth J (Ken) *Baseball Player*
568 Ave Grosvenor, Westmount, QC,
H3Y 2S7, CANADA

Reaser, Elizabeth *Actor*
Gersh Agency, The (LA), 232 N Canon Dr,
Beverly Hills, CA 90210 USA

Reason, Rex *Actor*
Roadside Productions, 20105 Rhapsody
Road, Walnut Creek, CA 91789 USA

Reason, Rhodes
PO Box 503, Gladstone, OR 97027

Reasons, Gary P *Football Player*
16303 Perry Pass Court, Spring, TX 77379
USA

Reaux, Angelina *Opera Singer*
Herbert Breslin, 119 W 57th St, #1505,
New York, NY 10019 USA

Reaves, Shawn *Actor*
Glasser/Black Management, 283
Cedarhurst Ave, Cedarhurst, NY 11516
USA

Reaves, Stephanie *Race Car Driver*
PO Box 55, Bar Mills, ME 04004 USA

Reaves, T Johnson (John) *Football Player,
Football Coach*
4830 NW 43rd St, #3A, Gainesville, FL
32606 USA

Rebagliati, Ross
One Erieview Plaza #1300, Cleveland,
OH 44114

Rebardo, Joe *Musician*
Billy Paul Mgmt, 8215 Winthrop St,
Philadelphia, PA 19136 USA

Rebekah *Musician*
Int'l Talent Booking, 27A Floral St, #300,
London, WC2E 9DQ, UNITED
KINGDOM (UK)

Rebhorn, James *Actor*
145 West 45th St, #1204, New York, NY
10036 USA

Rebroff, Ivan
Agil Anagire, Skopelos/Magnisias, GREECE

Recchi, Mark *Hockey Player*
Pittsburgh Penguins, Mellon Arena, 66
Mario Lemieux Place, Pittsburgh, PA
15219 USA

Rechichar, Albert (Bert) *Football Player*
141 W McClain Road, Belle Vernon, PA
15012 USA

Rechin, Bill *Cartoonist*
North American Syndicate, 235 E 45th St,
New York, NY 10017 USA

Rechter, Yacov *Architect*
150 Arlozorov St, Tel Aviv, 62098, ISRAEL

Reckell, Peter *Actor*
PO Box 2704-462, Huntington Beach, CA
92647 USA

Rector, Jeff *Actor*
10748 Aqua Vista St, North Hollywood,
CA 91602 USA

Rector, Milton G *Misc*
National Council on Crime &
Delinquency, 288 Monroe, River Edge, NJ
07661 USA

Redbone, Leon *Musician*
Red Shark Inc, 2169 Aquetong Road, New
Hope, PA 18938 USA

Redd, Michael *Basketball Player*
Milwaukee Bucks, Bradley Center, 1001
N 4th St, Milwaukee, WI 53203 USA

Reddicliffe, Steven *Editor*
TV Guide Magazine, Editorial Dept, 100
Matsonford Road, Radnor, PA 19080 USA

Redding, Juli
PO Box 1806, Beverly Hills, 90212

Reddy, D Raj *Scientist*
Robotics Institute, Carnegie-Mellon
University, Pittsburgh, PA 15213 USA

Reddy, Helen *Musician*
Helen Reddy Inc, 2029 Century Park E,
#600, Los Angeles, CA 90067 USA

Redeker, Quinn *Actor*
8075 Third St, #303, Los Angeles, CA
90048 USA

Redfield, James *Writer*
Warner Books, 1271 6th Ave, New York,
NY 10020 USA

Redford, Paul *Writer, Producer*
Broder Webb Chervin Silbermann Agency,
The (BWCS), 9242 Beverly Blvd #200,
Beverly Hills, CA 90210 USA

Redford, Robert *Actor, Director*
RR 3 Box 837, Provo, UT 84604 USA

Redgrave, Corin *Actor*
Kate Feast, Primrose Hill Studios, Fitzroy
Road, London, NW1 8TR, UNITED
KINGDOM (UK)

Redgrave, Jemma *Actor*
Conway Van Gelder Robinson, 18-21
Jermyn St, London, SW1Y 6NB, UNITED
KINGDOM (UK)

Redgrave, Lynn *Actor*
P F D Drury House, 34-43 Russell St,
London, WC2B 5HA, UNITED KINGDOM
(UK)

Redgrave, Vanessa *Actor*
Gavin Barker Assoc, 2D Wimpole St,
London, W1G 0EB, UNITED KINGDOM
(UK)

Reding, Juli *Actor*
PO Box 1806, Beverly Hills, CA 90213
USA

Redman *Musician*
International Creative Mgmt, 8942
Wilshire Blvd, #219, Beverly Hills, CA
90211 USA

Redman, Dewey *Musician, Composer*
Joel Chriss, 300 Mercer St, #3J, New York,
NY 10003 USA

Redman, Joshua *Musician, Composer*
Wilkins Mgmt, 323 Broadway,
Cambridge, MA 02139 USA

Redman, Joyce *Actor*
P F D Drury House, 34-43 Russell St, London, WC2B 5HA, UNITED KINGDOM (UK)

Redman, Michele *Golfer*
Ladies Pro Golf Assn, 100 International Golf Dr, Daytona Beach, FL 32124 USA

Redman, Richard C (Rick) *Football Player*
153 Prospect St, Seattle, WA 98109 USA

Redmann, Teal *Actor*
Metropolitan Talent Agency (MTA), 4526 Wilshire Blvd, Los Angeles, CA 90010 USA

Redmond, Marge *Actor*
Abrams Artists, 9200 Sunset Blvd, #1125, Los Angeles, CA 90069 USA

Redmond, Markus *Actor*
Writers & Artists, 8383 Wilshire Blvd, #550, Beverly Hills, CA 90211 USA

Redmond, Michael E (Mickey) *Hockey Player*
30699 Harlincin Court, Franklin, MI 48025 USA

Redmond, Mike *Athlete*
2269 NW 199th St, Miami, FL 33056

Redpath, Jean *Musician*
Sunny Knowe, Promenade, Leven, Fife, SCOTLAND

Redstone, Summer M *Business Person*
Viacom Inc, 1515 Broadway, New York, NY 10036 USA

Redstone, Sumner
200 Elm St., Dedham, MA 02026

Redwine, Jarvis J *Football Player*
2707 W 79th St, Inglewood, CA 90305 USA

Redwine, Tim
3518 Cahuenga Blvd. W. #200, Los Angeles, CA 90068

Reece, Beasley *Football Player, Sportscaster*
717 S Columbus Blvd, #821, Philadelphia, PA 19147 USA

Reece, Daniel (Danny) *Football Player*
24610 S Avalon Blvd, Wilmington, CA 90744 USA

Reece, Gabrielle
5111 Ocean Front Walk #4, Marina del Rey, CA 90291

Reece, Gabrielle (Gabby) *Volleyball Player, Model*
PO Box 2246, Malibu, CA 90265 USA

Reece, Thomas L *Business Person*
Dover Corp, 280 Park Ave, New York, NY 10017 USA

Reed, Andre D *Football Player*
PO Box 9383, Rancho Santa Fe, CA 92067 USA

Reed, Ben
151 El Camino Dr., Beverly Hills, CA 90212

Reed, Brandy *Basketball Player*
Phoenix Mercury, American West Arena, 201 E Jefferson St, Phoenix, AZ 85004 USA

Reed, Brian *Songwriter, Musician*
Turner Management Group, 374 Poli St, #205, Ventura, CA 93001 USA

Reed, Eric *Musician*
Joel Chriss, 300 Mercer St, #3J, New York, NY 10003 USA

Reed, Herb *Musician*
Platters Mgmt, 990 Massachusetts Ave, Arlington, MA 02476 USA

Reed, Jerry *Songwriter, Actor, Musician*
Jerry Lee Enterprises, PO Box 3586, Brentwood, TN 37024 USA

Reed, John H *Governor*
410 O St NW, Washington, DC 20024 USA

Reed, John S *Financier*
Citigroup Inc, 399 Park Ave, New York, NY 10022 USA

Reed, Johnny *Musician*
Jackson Artists, 7251 Lowell Dr, #200, Overland Park, KS 66204 USA

Reed, Kira
PO Box 251255, Los Angeles, CA 90025

Reed, Lou *Songwriter, Musician*
Three Artist Mgmt, 2550 Laurel Pass, Los Angeles, CA 90046 USA

Reed, Margaret
524 W. 57th St. #5330, New York, NY 10019

Reed, Mark A *Doctor*
Yale University, Electrical Engineering Dept, PO Box 2157, New Haven, CT 06520 USA

Reed, Nikki *Actor*
Booh Schut Company, 11350 Ventura Blvd #200, Studio City, CA 91604 USA

Reed, Pamela *Actor*
Innovative Artists, 1505 10th St, Santa Monica, CA 90401 USA

Reed, Ralph *Religious Leader*
1801 Sarah Drive, #L, Chesapeake, VA 23320 USA

Reed, Rex *Critic*
Dakota Hotel, 1 W 72nd St, #86, New York, NY 10023 USA

Reed, Richard A (Rick) *Baseball Player*
2205 Jefferson Ave, Huntington, WV 25704 USA

Reed, Richard J *Misc*
University of Washington, Atmospheric Sciences Dept, Seattle, WA 98195 USA

Reed, Ronald L (Ron) *Baseball Player, Basketball Player*
2613 Cliffview Dr, Lilbum, GA 30047 USA

Reed, Shanna *Actor*
1327 Brinkley Ave, Los Angeles, CA 90049 USA

Reed, Thomas C *Government Official*
Quaker Hill Development Corp, PO Box 2240, Healdsburg, CA 95448 USA

Reed, Walter
3400 Paul Sweet Rd. #B-209, Santa Cruz, CA 95065

Reed Jr, Alan
3455 Laurelvale Dr, Studio City, CA 91604 USA

Reed Jr, Willis *Baseball Player, Coach*
New Orleans Hornets, New Orleans Arena, 1501 Girod St, New Orleans, LA 70113 USA

Reeds, Mark *Hockey Player*
7823 Cardinal Ridge Court, Saint Louis, MO 63119 USA

Reedus, Norman *Actor, Model*
527 Hudson St, New York, NY 10014 USA

Reel & Reel
Box 480 High Wycombe, Bucks., ENGLAND, PH12 4LH

Rees, Andrew *Opera Singer*
Van Walsum Mgmt, 4 Addison Bridge Place, London, W14 8XP, UNITED KINGDOM (UK)

Rees, Angharad *Actor*
James Sharkey, 21 Golden Square, London, W1R 3PA, UNITED KINGDOM (UK)

Rees, Dai *Fashion Designer*
Dai Rees, 6 Blackstock Mews, Blackstock Road, London, England, N42BT, United Kingdom

Rees, Eberhard *Physicist*
69 Revere Way, Huntsville, AL 35801 USA

Rees, Jed *Actor*
Elizabeth Hodgson Mgmt Group, 525 Seymour St #550, Vancouver BC, V6B 3H7, CANADA

Rees, John *Musician*
TPA, PO Box 124, Round Corner, NSW, 2158 USA

Rees, Martin J *Astronomer*
King's College, Astronomy Institute, Cambridge, CB2 1ST, UNITED KINGDOM (UK)

Rees, Mina *Mathematician*
301 E 66th St, New York, NY 10021 USA

Rees, Norma S *Educator*
California State University, President's Office, Hayward, CA 94542 USA

Rees, Roger *Actor*
Innovative Artists, 1505 10th St, Santa Monica, CA 90401 USA

Rees Jr, Clifford H (Ted) *General*
1620 Mayflower Court, #B414, Winter Park, FL 32792 USA

Rees-Jones, Trevor
Oswestry, Shropshire, ENGLAND

Rees-Mogg of Hinton Bleweet, William *Publisher*
3 Smith Square, London, SW1, UNITED KINGDOM (UK)

Reese, Della *Actor, Musician*
55 W 900 S, Salt Lake City, UT 84101 USA

Reese, Eddie *Swimmer, Coach*
University of Texas, Athletic Dept, Austin, TX 78712 USA

Reese, Miranda *Ballerina*
New York City Ballet, Lincoln Center Plaza, New York, NY 10023 USA

Reeser, Autumn *Actor*
Identity Talent Agency (ID), 2050 Bundy Dr #200, Los Angeles, CA 90025 USA

Reeve, Christopher *Actor*
500 Morris Ave, Springfield, NJ 07081 USA

Reeve, Dana
RR #2, Bedford, NY 10506

Reeves, Bryant *Basketball Player*
memphis Grizzlies, 175 Toyota Plaza, #150, Memphis, TN 38103 USA

Reeves, Del *Songwriter, Musician*
Billy Deaton Talent, 5811 Still Hollow Road, Nashville, TN 37215 USA

Reeves, Diane
PO Box 66, Englishtown, NJ 07726

Reeves, Dianne *Musician*
Po Box 66, Englishtown, NJ 07726 USA

Reeves, Julie
PO Box 300, Russell, KY 41169

Reeves, Keanu *Actor*
Three Arts Entertainment, 9460 Wilshire Blvd, #700, Beverly Hills, CA 90212 USA

Reeves, Martha *Musician*
Mars Talent, 27 L'Ambiance Court, Bardonia, NY 10954 USA

Reeves, Melissa
6520 Platt Ave. #634, West Hills, CA 91307-3218

Reeves, Perrey *Actor*
Prophet, 1640 S Sepulveda Blvd, #218, Los Angeles, CA 90025 USA

Reeves, Phil *Actor*
Bauman Redanty & Shaul Agency, 5757 Wilshire Blvd #473, Los Angeles, CA 90036 USA

Reeves, Richard *Misc*
Universal Press Syndicate, 4520 Main St, Kansas City, MO 64111 USA

Reeves, Ronna
5114 Albert Dr., Brentwood, TN 37021

Reeves, Saskia *Actor*
Markham & Froggatt, Julian House, 4 Windmill St, London, W1P 1HF, UNITED KINGDOM (UK)

Reeves, Scott *Actor*
6520 Platt Ave, #634, West Hills, CA 91307 USA

Regaibuto, Joe *Actor*
724 24th St, Santa Monica, CA 90402 USA

Regalbuto, Joe
724 24th St., Santa Monica, CA 90402

Regan, Brian *Actor, Comedian*
Conversation Co, 697 Middle Neck Road, Great Neck, NY 11023 USA

Regan, Chris *Writer*
Principato/Young Management, 9665 Wilshire Blvd #500, Beverly Hills, CA 90212 USA

Regan, Donald T
240 McLaws Cir #142, Williamsburg, VA 23185 USA

Regan, Gerald A *Government Official*
PO Box 828, Station B, Ottawa, ON K1P 5P9, CANADA

Regan, Judith *Writer, Talk Show Host*
New Enterprises, 1211 Ave of Americas, New York, NY 10036 USA

Regan, Larry *Hockey Player*
4A-260 Metcalfe St, Ottawa, ON K2P 1R6, CANADA

Regan, Laura *Actor*
TMT Entertainment Group, 648 Broadway #1002, New York, NY 10022 USA

Regan, Philip R (Phil) *Baseball Player*
1375 108th St, Byron Center, MI 49315 USA

Regazzoni, Clay *Race Car Driver*
Via Monzoni 13, Lugano, 6900, SWITZERLAND

Regehr, Duncan *Actor*
2501 Main St, Santa Monica, CA 90405 USA

Regen, Elizabeth *Actor*
Abrams Artists Agency (LA), 9200 Sunset Blvd Fl 11, Los Angeles, CA 90069 USA

Reger, Nate *Writer*
Principato/Young Management, 9665 Wilshire Blvd #500, Beverly Hills, CA 90212 USA

Reggiani, Serge *Actor, Musician*
Charley Marouani, 4 Ave Hoche, Paris, 75008, FRANCE

Reggio, Godfrey *Director*
Regional Education Institute, PO Box 2404, Santa Fe, NM 87504 USA

Regina, Paul
2911 Canna St., Thousand Oaks, CA 91360-1718

Regine *Business Person*
502 Park Ave, New York, NY 10022 USA

Regis, John *Track Athlete*
67 Fairby Road, London, SE12, UNITED KINGDOM (UK)

Regnier, Charles *Actor, Director*
Neherstr 7, Munich, 81675, GERMANY

Rehm, Jack D *Publisher*
19 Neponset Ave, #9A, Old Saybrook, CT 06475 USA

Rehm Jr, Daniel R *War Hero*
1043 Del Norte St, Houston, TX 77018 USA

Rehn, Trista *Reality TV Star*
ABC Entertainment Television Group, 500 S Buena Vista St, Burbank, CA 91521

Rehnquist, William H *Judge*
2329 N Glebe Road, Arlington, VA 22207 USA

Rehr, Frank *Cartoonist*
United Feature Syndicate, 200 Madison Ave, New York, NY 10016 USA

Reich, Charles A *Lawyer, Educator*
Crown Publishers, 225 Park Ave S, New York, NY 10003 USA

Reich, Frank M *Football Player*
8820 Covey Rise Court, Charlotte, NC 28226 USA

Reich, Jason *Writer*
Kaplan-Stahler-Gumer Agency, 8383 Wilshire Blvd #923, Beverly Hills, CA 90211 USA

Reich, John *Director*
724 Bohemia Parkway, Sayville, NY 11782 USA

Reich, Robert B *Secretary*
4 Mercer Circle, Cambridge, MA 02138 USA

Reich, Steve M *Composer*
Nonesuch Records, 75 Rockefeller Plaza, New York, NY 10019 USA

Reichel, Robert *Hockey Player*
Toronto Maple Leafs, 40 Bay St, Toronto, ON M5J 2K2, CANADA

Reichert, Jack F *Business Person*
580 Douglas Dr, Lake Forest, IL 60045 USA

Reichert, Tanja *Actor*
Pacific Artists, 1404-510 W Hastings St, Vancouver, BC V6B 1L8, CANADA

Reichl, Ruth M *Editor*
Gourmet Magazine, Editorial Dept, 4 Times Square, New York, NY 10036 USA

Reichman, Fred *Artist*
1235 Stanyan St, San Francisco, CA 94117 USA

Reichman, MD, Judith *Doctor, Journalist, Writer*
NBC Television (LA), 3000 W Alameda Ave #5366, Burbank, CA 91523

Reichs, Kathy *Writer*
Charles Scribner's Sons, 866 3rd Ave, New York, NY 10022 USA

Reid, Andy *Football Coach*
Philadelphia Eagles, 1 Novacare Way, Philadelphia, PA 19145 USA

Reid, Antonio (L A) *Writer*
Kear Music, Carter Turner Co, 9229 W Sunset Blvd, West Hollywood, CA 90069 USA

Reid, Daphne Maxwell *Actor*
10520 Wilshire Blvd, #1507, Los Angeles, CA 90024 USA

Reid, Don S *Songwriter, Musician*
American Major Talent, 8747 Highway 304, Hernando, MS 38632 USA

Reid, Elliott
1850 N. Whitley Ave, Los Angeles, CA 90028

Reid, Frances *Actor*
235 Oceano Dr, Los Angeles, CA 90049 USA

Reid, Harold W *Songwriter, Musician*
American Major Talent, 8747 Highway 304, Hernando, MS 38632 USA

Reid, J R *Basketball Player*
121 Cemetary St, Chester, SC 29706 USA

Reid, LA *Producer*
La Face Records, 3350 Peachtree Road NE, Suite 1500, Atlanta, GA 30326

Reid, Michael B (Mike) *Football Player, Composer*
825 Overton Lane, Nashville, TN 37220 USA

Reid, Norman R *Misc*
50 Brabourne Rise, Park Langley Beckenham, Kent, UNITED KINGDOM (UK)

Reid, Odgen R *Journalist, Diplomat*
Ophir Hill, Purchase, NY 10577 USA

Reid, Ogden
Ophir Hill, Purchase, NY 10577

Reid, Robert *Basketball Player, Coach*
Washington Wizards, MCI Centre, 601 F St NW, Washington, DC 20004 USA

Reid, Robert *Skier*
Dixfield Health Care Center, Dixfield, ME 04224 USA

Reid, Stephen E (Steve) *Football Player, Doctor*
800 S River Road, #1017, Des Plaines, IL 60016 USA

Reid, Tara *Actor*
124 W 60th St, #39D, New York, NY 10023 USA

Reid, Terry *Musician*
Blumenauer, PO Box 343, Burbank, CA 91503 USA

Reid, Tim *Actor, Director*
1 New Millennium Dr, Petersburg, VA 23805 USA

Reidy, Carolyn K *Publisher*
Simon & Schuster, 1230 Ave of Americas, New York, NY 10020 USA

Reifsnyder, Robert H (Bob) *Football Player*
681 Ocean Parkway, Berlin, MD 21811 USA

Reightler Jr, Kenneth S *Astronaut*
1602 Honeysuckle Ridge Court, Annapolis, MD 21401 USA

Reilly, Charles Nelson *Actor, Director*
2341 Gloaming Way, Beverly Hills, CA 90210 USA

Reilly, Gabrielle *Model*
PO Box 3145, Shawnee, KS 66203-0145 USA

Reilly, Jennifer
345 N. Maple Dr. #397, Beverly Hills, CA 90210

Reilly, John *Actor*
335 N Maple Dr, #3360, Beverly Hills, CA 90210 USA

Reilly, John C *Actor*
United Talent Agency, 9560 Wilshire Blvd, #500, Beverly Hills, CA 90212 USA

Reilly, William K *Government Official*
Stanford University, International Studies Institute, Stanford, CA 94305 USA

Reilly II, James F *Astronaut*
15903 Lake Lodge Dr, Houston, TX 77062 USA

Reimer, Dennis J (Denny) *General*
MIPT, PO Box 889, Oklahoma City, OK 73101, us3

Reimer, Dennis J (Denny) *General*
MIPT, PO Box 889, Oklahoma City, OK 73101 USA

Reimer, Roland *Religious Leader*
mennonite Brethren Churches Conference, 8000 W 21st St N, Wichita, KS 67205 USA

Reincke, Heinz
Hof 38, Mondsee, AUSTRIA, A-5310

Reineck, Thomas *Athlete*
Graf-Bernadotte-Str 4, Essen, 45133, GERMANY

Reinemund, Steven S *Business Person*
Pepsi Co Inc, 700 Anderson Hill Road, Purchase, NY 10577 USA

Reiner, Carl *Actor, Director*
714 N Rodeo Dr, Beverly Hills, CA 90210 USA

Reiner, ex-DA Ira
1290 Sunset Plaza Dr., Los Angeles, CA 90069

Reiner, John *Cartoonist*
Parade Magazine, Editorial Dept, 750 3rd Ave, New York, NY 10017 USA

Reiner, Rob *Actor, Director*
Castle Rock Entertainment, 335 North Maple Dr #135, Beverly Hills, CA 90210-3867

Reinhard, Robert R (Bob) *Football Player*
37230 NW Soap Creek Road, Corvallis, OR 97330 USA

Reinhardt, John E *Diplomat*
4200 Massachusetts Ave NW, #702, Washington, DC 20016 USA

Reinhardt, Stephen R *Judge*
US Court of Appeals, 312 N Spring St, Los Angeles, CA 90012 USA

Reinharz, Jehuda *Educator*
Brandeis University, President's Office, Waltham, MA 02254 USA

Reinhold, Judge *Actor, Director*
Paradigm Agency, 10100 Santa Monica Blvd, #2500, Los Angeles, CA 90067 USA

Reinking, Ann *Actor, Dancer, Director*
International Creative Mgmt, 40 W 57th St, #1800, New York, NY 10019 USA

Reiser, Jerry *Architect*
28 S Washington Ave, Dobbs Ferry, NY 10522 USA

Reiser, Paul *Actor*
Creative Artists Agency, 9830 Wilshire Blvd, Beverly Hills, CA 90212 USA

Reiser, Rock
9014 Melrose Ave., W. Hollywood, CA 90069-5610

Reisman, Garrett E *Astronaut*
1715 Hedgecroft Dr, Seabrook, TX 77586 USA

Reiss, Howard *Misc*
16656 Oldham St, Encino, CA 91436 USA

Reisz, Michael *Actor*
William Morris Agency (WMA-LA), 1 William Morris Pl, Beverly Hills, CA 90212 USA

Reiter, Mario *Skier*
Hauselweg 5, Rankweil, 6830, AUSTRIA

Reiter, Thomas *Astronaut*
Europe Astronaut Center, Linder Hohe, Box 906096, Cologne, 51127, GERMANY

Reitman, Ivan *Director, Producer*
900 Cold Springs Road, Montecito, CA 93108 USA

Reitz, Bruce *Doctor*
Johns Hopkins Hospital, 600 N Wolfe St, Baltimore, MD 21287 USA

Rekha *Actor, Bollywood*
Sea Springs Bungalow 2, Band Stand Bandra, Mumbai, MS 400050, INDIA

Reklow, Jesse *Cartoonist*
2415 College Ave, #20, Berkeley, CA 94704 USA

Relient K *Music Group*
Alabaster Arts Inc, PO Box 210098, Nashville, TN 37221 USA

Relman, Arnold S *Editor, Doctor*
New England Journal of Medicine, 860 Winter St, #2, Waltham, MA 02451 USA

Relph, Michael *Producer*
71 Maltings Westgate, Chichester, West Sussex, PO19 2DN, UNITED KINGDOM (UK)

Remar, James *Actor*
409 N Camden Dr, #202, Beverly Hills, CA 90210 USA

Remedios, Alberto T *Opera Singer*
21 Lanhill Road, London, W9 2BS, UNITED KINGDOM (UK)

Remedy
225 Crossroads #107, Carmel, CA 93923

Remek, Vladimir *Cosmonaut*
Veletrzni 17, Prague 7, 17000, CZECH REPUBLIC

Remigino, Lindy *Track Athlete*
22 Paris Lane, Newington, CT 06111 USA

Remington, Deborah W *Artist*
309 W Broadway, New York, NY 10013 USA

Remini, Leah *Actor*
Gold Marchak Liedtke, 3500 W Olive Ave, #1400, Burbank, CA 91505 USA

Remnick, David *Writer*
Creative Artists Agency LCC (CAA-LA), 9830 Wilshire Blvd, Beverly Hills, CA 90212 USA

Remnick, David J *Writer, Editor*
257 W 86th St, #11A, New York, NY 10024 USA

Remo, Ken
121 S. Orange Dr., Los Angeles, CA 90036

Rempt, Rodney *Admiral, Educator*
Superintendent, US Naval Academy, Annapolis, MD 21402 USA

Remy, Gerald P (Jerry) *Baseball Player*
33 Viles St, Weston, MA 02493 USA

Renaud, Line *Musician*
5 Rue du Bois-de-Boulogne, Paris, 75116, FRANCE

Renault, Dennis *Cartoonist*
Sacramento Bee, Editorial Dept, 21st & Q Sts, Sacramento, CA 95852 USA

Renay, Liz
3708 San Angelo Ave., Las Vegas, NV 89102

Renbourn, John *Musician*
Folklore Inc, 1671 Appian Way, Santa Monica, CA 90401 USA

Rendall, Mark *Actor*
Artist Management Inc, 550 Queen St E #315, Toronto ON, M5A 1V2, CANADA

Rendell, Majorie O *Judge*
US Court of Appeals, US Courthouse, 601 Market St, Philadelphia, PA 19106 USA

Rendell, Ruth
Nusstead's Polstead Suffolk, Colchester, ENGLAND, CO6 5DN

Rendell of Barbergh, Ruth B *Writer*
Nussteads Polstead, Suffolk, Colchester, CO6 5DN, UNITED KINGDOM (UK)

Rene, France-Albert *President*
President's Office, State House, Victoria, Mahe, SEYCHELLES

Reneau, Daniel D *Educator*
Louisiana Tech University, President's
Office, Ruston, LA 71272 USA

Renee Clunie, Michelle *Actor*
Abrams Artists, 9200 Sunset Blvd #1125,
Los Angeles, CA 90069 USA

Renfrew of Kaimsthorn, Andrew C
Archaeologist
McDonald Archaeological Institute,
Downing St, Cambridge, CB2 3ER,
UNITED KINGDOM (UK)

Renfro, Brad *Actor*
Power Entertainment, 12200 W Olympic
Blvd #499, Los Angeles, CA 90064 USA

Renfro, Mel
220 W. Irving Blvd., Irving, TX 75060-
2958

Renfro, Melvin L (Mel) *Football Player*
6060 N Central Expressway, #560, Dallas,
TX 75206 USA

Renfroe, Jay *Producer*
Renegade 83 Entertainment, 5700
Wilshire Blvd, 6th Floor, Los Angeles, CA
90036 USA

Renger, Annemarie *Government Official*
Bundestag, Bundestag, Platz der Republik
1, Berlin, 11011, GERMANY

Renick, Jesse (Cab) *Basketball Player,
Coach*
2656 SE, Washington Blvd, Bartlesville,
OK 74006 USA

Renier, Jeremie *Actor*
Artmedia, 20 Ave Rapp, Paris, 75007,
FRANCE

Renk, Silke *Track Athlete*
Erhard-Hubner-Str 13, Halle/S, 06132,
GERMANY

Renko, Steven (Steve) *Baseball Player*
PO Box 3566, West Palm Beach, FL
33402 USA

Renna, Eugene A *Business Person*
Mobil Corp, 3225 Gallows Road, Fairfax,
VA 22037 USA

Renne, Paul *Misc*
Berkeley Geochronology Center, 2445
Ridge Road, Berkeley, CA 94709 USA

Rennebohm, J Fred *Religious Leader*
Congregational Christian Churches Assn,
PO Box 1620, Oak Creek, MI 53154 USA

Rennebohm, J Fred *Misc*
Holbeinstr 58, Berlin, 12203, GERMANY

Renner, Jeremy *Actor*
Untitled Entertainment (LA), 8436 W 3rd
St #650, Los Angeles, CA 90048 USA

Rennert, Gunther *Director, Opera Singer*
Holbeinstr 58, Berlin, 12203, GERMANY

Renney, Tom *Coach*
New York Rangers, Madison Square
Garden, 2 Penn Plaza, New York, NY
10121 USA

Renni, Gino *Actor*
Telefe - Argentina, Pavon 2444
(C1248AAT), Buenos Aires, ARGENTINA

Reno, Jack
PO Box 1001, Florence, KY 41042

Reno, Janet *Attorney General*
11200 N Kendall Dr, Miami, FL 33176
USA

Reno, Jean *Actor*
CBC M C1 Besson, 11 Rue de la Croix
Boissee, Mennecy, 79154, FRANCE

Reno, William H *General*
2706 S Ives St, Arlington, VA 22202 USA

Renoth, Heldi *Skier*
Lercheckerweg 23, Berchtesgaden, 83471,
GERMANY

Rense, Paige *Editor*
Architectural Digest, Editorial Dept, 5900
Wilshire Blvd, Los Angeles, CA 90036
USA

Renteria, Edgar *Baseball Player*
1408 N West Shore Blvd, #512, Tampa,
FL 33607 USA

Rentmeester, Co *Photographer*
PO Box 1562, West Hampton Beach, NY
11978 USA

Renton of Mount Harry, R Timothy
Government Official
House of Lords, Westminster, London,
SW1A 0PW, UNITED KINGDOM (UK)

Rentzel, T Lance *Football Player*
Trust Data Corp, 159 Almanden Blvd,
#500, San Jose, CA 95113 USA

Rentzepis, Peter M *Misc*
University of California, Chemistry Dept,
Irvine, CA 92717 USA

Renucci, Robin
64 rue Condorcet, Paris, FRANCE, 75009

Renvall, Johan *Dancer*
American Ballet Theatre, 890 Broadway,
New York, NY 10003 USA

Renyi, Thomas A *Financier*
Bank of New York, 1 Wall St, New York,
NY 10286 USA

Repeta, Nina *Actor*
Gage Group, 14724 Ventura Blvd, Suite
505, Los Angeles, CA 91403 USA

Repin, Vadim V *Musician*
Eckholdtweg 2A, Lubeck, 23566,
GERMANY

Rerych, Stephen (Steve) *Swimmer*
445 Baltimore Ave, Ashville, NC 28801
USA

Resch, Alexander *Athlete*
BSD, An der Schiessstatte 4,
Berchtesgaden, 83471, GERMANY

Rescher, Nicholas *Misc*
5818 Aylesboro Ave, Pittsburgh, PA
15217 USA

Rescigno, Nicola *Conductor*
Robert Lombardo, 61 W 62nd St, #6F,
New York, NY 10023 USA

Resin, Dan *Actor*
Don Buchwald, 6500 Wilshire Blvd,
#2200, Los Angeles, CA 90048 USA

Resnais, Alain *Director*
70 Rue des Plantes, Paris, 75014, FRANCE

Resnik, Regina *Opera Singer*
American Guild of Musical Arts, 1430
Broadway, New York, NY 10018 USA

Ressler, Glenn E *Football Player*
1524 Woodcreek Dr, Mechanicsburg, PA
17055 USA

Ressler, Robert
PO Box 187, Spotsylvania, VA 22553

Restani, Jane A *Judge*
US Court of International Trade, 1 Federal
Plaza, New York, NY 10278 USA

Restani, Kevin *Basketball Player*
16 Lyndhurst Dr, San Francisco, CA
94132 USA

Reswick, James B *Engineer*
1834 Calf Mountain Road, Crozet, VA
22932 USA

Retore, Guy *Director*
Theatre de l'Est Parislen, 159 Ave
Gambetta, Paris, 75020, FRANCE

Retton, Mary Lou *Gymnast*
114 White Ave, Fairmont, WV 26554
USA

Retzer, Otto W *Director*
Justinus-Kerner-Str 10, Munich, 80686,
GERMANY

Retzlaff, Palmer (Pete) *Football Player*
669 New Road, Gilbertsville, PA 19525
USA

Reuben, David R *Writer*
Scott Meredith, 1675 Broadway, New
York, NY 10019 USA

Reuben, Gloria *Actor*
William Morris Agency, 151 El Camino
Dr, Beverly Hills, CA 90212 USA

Reubens, Paul *Actor, Comedian*
PO Box 29373, Los Angeles, CA 90029
USA

Reuschel, Ricky E (Rick) *Baseball Player*
PO Box 143, Renfrew, PA 16053 USA

Reuss, Jerry *Baseball Player*
350 SW 1st St, Des Moines, IA 50309
USA

Reusser, Ken L *War Hero*
17345 SW Reusser Court, Aloha, OR
97007 USA

Reutemann, Carlos
San Martin 3233, Santa Fe, ARGENTINA

Reuter, Edzard *Business Person*
Daimler-benz AG, Postfach 800230,
Stuttgart, 70546, GERMANY

Reutersward, Carl Fredrik *Artist*
6 Rue Montilieu, Bussigny/Lausanne,
1030, SWITZERLAND

Revathi *Actor, Bollywood*
7 1st Crescent Road, GandhiNagar Adyar,
Chennai, TN 600020, INDIA

Revel, Jean-Francois *Writer*
55 Quai de Bourbon, Paris, 75004,
FRANCE

Revell, Graeme *Composer*
APRA, PO Box 567, Crow's Nest, NSW,
2065, AUSTRALIA

Revere, Paul *Musician*
Paradise Artists, 108 E Matilija St, Ojai,
CA 93023 USA

Reverho, Christine *Actor*
Artmedia, 20 Ave Rapp, Paris, 75007,
FRANCE

Revill, Clive *Actor*
15029 Encanto Dr, Sherman Oaks, CA
91403 USA

Rex *Musician*
Concrete Mgmt, 361 W Broadway, #200,
New York, NY 10013 USA

Rex, Simon (Sebastian) *Actor, Television Host*
9 Yards Entertainment, 8530 Wilshire Blvd Fl 5, Beverly Hills, CA 90211 USA

Rey, Paola *Actor*
Gabriel Blanco Iglesias (Mexico), Rio Balsas 35-32, Colonia Cuauhtemoc, DF, 06500, Mexico

Rey, Reynaldo *Actor, Comedian, Writer*
Starwil Talent, 433 N Camden Dr, #400, Beverly Hills, CA 90210 USA

Reyes, Judy *Actor*
Paradigm (LA), 10100 Santa Monica Blvd, Fl 25, Los Angeles, CA 90067 USA

Reyes, Sandra *Actor*
TV Caracol, Calle 76 #11 - 35, Piso 10AA, Bogota DC, 26484, COLOMBIA

Reyes Jr, Ernie
12561 Willard St, N Hollywood, CA 91605 USA

Reymundo, Alex *Comedian*
Edmonds Management, 1635 N Cahuenga Blvd Fl 5, Los Angeles, CA 90028 USA

Reynold, Catherine B *Business Person*
Catherine B Reynolds Foundation, PO Box 11346, McLean, VA 22102 USA

Reynolds, Alastair *Writer*
P F D Drury House, 34-43 Russell St, London, WC2B 5HA, UNITED KINGDOM (UK)

Reynolds, Albert *Prime Minister*
Mount Carmel House, Dublin Road, Longford, IRELAND

Reynolds, Anna *Opera Singer*
Peesten 9, Kasendorf, 95359, GERMANY

Reynolds, Burt *Actor, Director*
PO Box 3288, Tequesta, FL 33469 USA

Reynolds, David S *Writer, Historian*
16 Linden Lane, Old Westbury, NY 11568 USA

Reynolds, Dean *Commentator*
ABC-TV, News Dept, 5010 Creston St, Hyattsville, MD 20781 USA

Reynolds, Debbie *Actor, Musician*
1700 Coldwater Canyon Dr, Beverly Hills, CA 90210 USA

Reynolds, Ed *Football Player*
12136 East Run Dr, Lawrenceville, NJ 08648

Reynolds, Gene *Actor, Producer*
2034 Castilian Dr, Los Angeles, CA 90068 USA

Reynolds, Glenn F *Inventor*
242 Edgewood Ave, Westfield, NJ 07090 USA

Reynolds, Harry (Butch) *Track Athlete*
Advantage International, 1025 Thomas Jefferson NW, #450, Washington, DC 20007 USA

Reynolds, J Guy *Admiral*
1605 Fox Hunt Court, Alexandria, VA 22307 USA

Reynolds, Jamai *Football Player*
Green Bay Packers, PO Box 10628, Green Bay, WI 54307 USA

Reynolds, Jamal *Football Player*
Cleveland Browns, 76 Lou Groza Blvd, Berea, OH 44017 USA

Reynolds, James *Actor*
1925 Hanscom Dr, South Pasadena, CA 91030 USA

Reynolds, Jerry O *Coach*
Sacramento Kings, Arco Arena, 1 Sports Parkway, Sacramento, CA 95834 USA

Reynolds, John R *Physicist, Educator*
University of California, Physics Dept, Berkeley, CA 94720 USA

Reynolds, Kevin
151 El Camino Dr., Beverly Hills, CA 90212

Reynolds, Patti
PO Box 530, Fontana, WI 53125

Reynolds, R Shane *Baseball Player*
23 Beacon Hill, Sugarland, TX 77479 USA

Reynolds, Rachel *Actor, Model*
Price Is Right, The, 2700 Colorado Ave Fl 4, Santa Monica, CA 90404 USA

Reynolds, Randolph N *Business Person*
Reynolds Metal Co, 6601 Broad St, PO Box 27003, Richmond, VA 23261 USA

Reynolds, Richard V *General*
Commander Aeronautical Systems, Wright-Patterson Air Force Base, OH 45433 USA

Reynolds, Robert *Musician*
AristoMedia, 1620 16th Ave S, Nashville, TN 37212 USA

Reynolds, Ryan *Actor*
Endeavor Talent Agency, 9701 Wilshire Blvd, #1000, Beverly Hills, CA 90212 USA

Reynolds, Sheldon *Musician*
Great Scott Productions, 137 N Wetherly Dr, #403, Los Angeles, CA 90048 USA

Reynolds, W Ann *Educator*
City University of New York, Chancellor's Office, New York, NY 10021 USA

Reynolds Booth, Nancy *Skier*
3197 Padaro Lane, Carpinteria, CA 93013 USA

Reynolds Jr, Thomas A *Lawyer*
Winston & Strawn, 1 First National Plaza, 45 W Wacker Dr, Chicago, IL 60601 USA

Reza, Yasmina *Writer, Actor*
Marta Andras, 14 Rue des Sablons, Paris, 75116, FRANCE

Reznor, Trent *Musician*
Artists & Audience Entertainment, PO Box 35, Pawling, NY 12564 USA

Rhames, Ving *Actor*
1158 26th St, #549, Santa Monica, CA 90403 USA

Rhea, Caroline *Comedian, Actor*
3 Arts Entertainment Inc, 9460 Wilshire Blvd Fl 7, Beverly Hills, CA 90212 USA

Rheaume, Manon *Hockey Player*
University of Minnesota, Athletic Dept, Duluth, MN 55812 USA

Rhett, Alicia *Actor*
PO Box 700, Charleston, SC 29402-0700 USA

Rhind-Tutt, Julian *Actor*
Peters Fraser & Dunlop (PFD - UK), Drury House, 34-43 Russell St, London, WC2 B5, UNITED KINGDOM (UK)

Rhines, Peter B *Oceanographer*
5753 61st Ave NE, Seattle, WA 98105 USA

Rhoades, Barbara *Actor*
90 Old Redding Road, Weston, CT 06883 USA

Rhoads, George *Artist*
1478 Mecklenburg Road, Ithaca, NY 14850 USA

Rhoads, James B *Misc*
1300 Fox Run Trail, Platte City, MO 64079 USA

Rhoden, Richard A (Rick) *Baseball Player*
8009 Whisper Lake Lane E, Ponte Vedra, FL 32082 USA

Rhodes, Cynthia *Actor, Dancer*
15260 Ventura Blvd, #2100, Sherman Oaks, CA 91403 USA

Rhodes, Donnelly *Actor*
Gold Marshak Liedtke, 3500 W Olive Ave, #1400, Burbank, CA 91505 USA

Rhodes, Dusty
240 Datura St., Henderson, NV 89104-8894

Rhodes, Frank H T *Educator*
Cornell University, Geology Dept, Snee Hall, Ithaca, NY 14853 USA

Rhodes, Mark *Musician*
Pop Idol (Fremantle Media), 2700 Colorado Ave #450, Santa Monica, CA 90404 USA

Rhodes, Nick *Musician*
DD Productions, 93A Westbourne Park Villas, London, W2 5ED, UNITED KINGDOM (UK)

Rhodes, Philip *Musician*
William Morris Agency, 2100 W End Ave, #1000, Nashville, TN 37203 USA

Rhodes, Ray *Football Coach, Football Player*
25812 NE 4th Place, Sammamish, WA 98074 USA

Rhodes, Richard L *Writer*
Janklow & Nesbit, 445 Park Ave, #1300, New York, NY 10022 USA

Rhodes, Tom *Actor, Comedian*
William Morris Agency, 151 El Camino Dr, Beverly Hills, CA 90212 USA

Rhodes, Zandra *Fashion Designer*
79-85 Bermondsey St, London, SE1 3XF, UNITED KINGDOM (UK)

Rhome, Gerald B (Jerry) *Football Player, Football Coach*
3883 Morning Meadow Lane, Buford, GA 30519 USA

Rhone, Earriest C (Ernie) *Football Player*
6102 Sleepy Hollow Ave, Texarkana, TX 75503 USA

Rhone, Sylvia *Business Person*
Elektra Entertainment Group, 75 Rockefeller Plaza, 15th Floor, New York, NY 10019

Rhymes, Busta *Musician*
Violator Mgmt, 205 Lexington Ave, #400, New York, NY 10016 USA

Rhys, Paul *Actor*
Gersh Agency, 232 N Canon Dr, Beverly Hills, CA 90210 USA

Rhys, Phillip *Actor*
3 Arts Entertainment Inc, 9460 Wilshire Blvd Fl 7, Beverly Hills, CA 90212 USA

Rhys-Davies, John *Actor*
3428 Oak Glen Dr, Los Angeles, CA 90068 USA

Rhys-Jones, HRH Sophie (Duchess of Wessex)
Bagshot Park, Surrey, ENGLAND, GUl9 5PN

Rhys-Meyer, Jonathan
Velvets Town House Butteront, County Cork, IRELAND

Rhys-Meyers, Jonathan *Actor*
United Talent Agency (UTA), 9560 Wilshire Blvd, Beverly Hills, CA 90212 USA

Rhythm Syndicate
6255 Sunset Blvd. #2100, Los Angeles, CA 90028

Ri Jong Ok *Vice President*
Vice President's Office, Pyongyang, NORTH KOREA

Ri'chard, Robert *Actor*
Tollin/Robbins Management, 10960 Ventura Blvd Fl 2, Studio City, CA 91604 USA

Ribas Reig, Oscar *Government Official*
Governmental Offices, Andorra la Vella, ANDORRA

Ribbons, Rosie *Musician*
Pop Idol (Fremantle Media), 2700 Colorado Ave #450, Santa Monica, CA 90404 USA

Ribbs, Willy T *Race Car Driver*
2343 Ribbs Lane, San Jose, CA 95116 USA

Ribeau, Sidney A *Educator*
Bowling Green State University, President's Office, Bowling Green, OH 43403 USA

Ribeiro, Alfonso *Actor*
19122 Halstead St, Northridge, CA 91324 USA

Ribeiro, Andre *Race Car Driver*
Tasman Motor Spoerts Group, 4192 Weaver Court, Hillard, OH 43026 USA

Ribeiro, Ignacio *Fashion Designer*
Clements Ribejro Ltd, 48 S Molton St, London, W1X 1HE, UNITED KINGDOM (UK)

Ribisi, Giovanni *Actor*
William Morris Agency (WMA-LA), 1 William Morris Pl, Beverly Hills, CA 90212 USA

Ribisi, Giovanni *Actor*
William Morris Agency, 151 El Camino Dr, Beverly Hills, CA 90212 USA

Ribisi, Marissa *Actor*
4121 Wilshire Blvd, #415, Los Angeles, CA 90010 USA

Ricardo Y Alberto *Music Group*
Sony Music Miami, 605 Lincoln Rd, Miami Beach, FL 33138 USA

Ricci, Christina *Actor*
International Creative Mgmt, 8942 Wilshire Blvd, #219, Beverly Hills, CA 90211 USA

Ricci, Ruggiero *Musician*
2930 E Delhi Road, Ann Arbor, MI 48103 USA

Ricciarelli, Katia *Opera Singer*
Via Magellana 2, Corsica, 20097, ITALY

Rice, Alex *Actor*
Imparato Fay Management, 1122 S Roxbury Dr, Los Angeles, CA 90035 USA

Rice, Anne *Writer*
1239 1st St, New Orleans, LA 70130 USA

Rice, Bobby G
505 Canton Pass, Madison, TN 37115 USA

Rice, Buddy *Race Car Driver*
Team Rahal, 4601 Lyman Dr, Hilliard, OH 43026 USA

Rice, Christopher *Writer*
C/O Hyperion Editorial Department, 77 West 66th Street, 11th Floor, New York, NY 10023

Rice, Condoleezza *Government Official*
National Security Council, 1600 Pennsylvania Ave NW, Washington, DC 20500 USA

Rice, Elizabeth *Actor*
Hansen Jacobson Teller & Hoberman, 450 N Roxbury Dr Fl 8, Beverly Hills, CA 90210 USA

Rice, Gene D *Religious Leader*
Church of God, PO Box 2430, Cleveland, TN 37320 USA

Rice, Gigi *Actor*
14951 Alva Dr, Pacific Palisades, CA 90272 USA

Rice, Glen
9492 Doral Blvd, Miami, FL 33178

Rice, James E (Jim) *Baseball Player*
35 Bobby Jones Dr, Andover, MA 01810 USA

Rice, James R *Geophysicist*
Harvard University, Applied Science Division, Cambridge, MA 02138 USA

Rice, Jerry L *Football Player*
222 S Central Ave, #1008, Clayton, MO 63105 USA

Rice, Norman B *Politician*
Mayor's Office, Municipal Building, 600 4th Ave, Seattle, WA 98104 USA

Rice, Simeon *Football Player*
2777 E Camelback Road, #300, Phoenix, AZ 85016 USA

Rice, Stuart A *Misc*
5517 S Kimbark Ave, Chicago, IL 60637 USA

Rice, Susan *Writer*
International Creative Management (ICM-LA), 8942 Wilshire Blvd, Beverly Hills, CA 90211 USA

Rice, Thomas M *Physicist*
Theoretische Physik, ETH-Hoggerberg, Zurich, 8093, SWITZERLAND

Rice, Timothy M B *Musician*
Lewis & Golden, 40 Queen Anne Street, London, England, W1M 0EL

Rice, Timothy M B (Tim) *Musician*
Chiltens, France-Hill Dr Camberley, Surrey, GU153-30A, UNITED KINGDOM (UK)

Rice-Hughes, Donna
PO Box 888, Fairfax, VA 22030

Rich, Adam *Actor*
4814 Lemona Ave, Sherman Oaks, CA 91403 USA

Rich, Adrienne *Writer*
Stanford University, English Dept, Stanford, CA 94305 USA

Rich, Alexander *Misc*
2 Walnut Ave, Cambridge, MA 02140 USA

Rich, Allan *Actor*
225 E 57th St, New York, NY 10022 USA

Rich, Christopher *Actor*
Bresler Kelly Assoc, 11500 W Olympic Blvd, #510, Los Angeles, CA 90064 USA

Rich, Claude
18 Chemin de la Butte, Orgeval, FRANCE, F-78630

Rich, Clayton *Doctor*
University of Oklahoma, Health Services Center, Oklahoma City, OK 73190 USA

Rich, Denise *Musician*
IGD Music & Media, 785 5th Avenue, New York, NY 10022-1012

Rich, Elaine
500 S. Sepulveda Blvd, Los Angeles, CA 90049-3540

Rich, Frank H *Critic*
New York Times, Editorial Dept, 229 W 43rd St, New York, NY 10036 USA

Rich, John
2501 Colorado Ave. #350, Santa Monica, CA 90404

Rich, Katie
1O100 Santa Monica Blvd. #2490, Los Angeles, CA 90067

Rich, Lee *Business Person*
Lee Rich Productions, Warner, 75 Rockefeller Plaza, New York, NY 10019 USA

Rich, Matty
9560 Wilshire Blvd. #500, Beverly Hills, CA 90212

Rich, The Tony Project
14724 Ventura Blvd. #410, Sherman Oaks, CA 91403

Rich, Tony *Musician*
Prestige, 220 E 23rd St, #303, New York, NY 10010 USA

Richard, Cliff *Musician*
Harley House, Portsmouth Road Box 46C, Esher, Surrey, KT10 9AA, UNITED KINGDOM (UK)

Richard, Henri *Hockey Player*
905-4300 Place de Cageux, Ile Paton Laval, QC, H7W 4Z3, CANADA

Richard, Ivor S *Government Official*
11 South Square, Gray's Inn, London, WC1R 5EU, UNITED KINGDOM (UK)

Richard, James Rodney (J R) *Baseball Player*
5134 Bungalow Lane, Houston, TX 77048 USA

Richard, Jean
Ermenonville, FRANCE, 60950

Richard, Little *Musician*
William Morris Agency (WMA-LA), 1
William Morris Pl, Beverly Hills, CA
90212 USA

Richard, Pierre
6 rue de Vieux-Moulin, Droue-sur-
Drouette, FRANCE, 28230

Richard, Wendy
5 Denmark St., London, ENGLAND, WCl
8LP

Richard III, Oliver G *Business Person*
Columbia Energy Group, 200 Civic Center
Dr, Columbus, OH 43215 USA

Richards, Ann W *Politician*
98 San Jacinto Blvd #1440, Austin, TX
78701

Richards, Ariana *Actor*
Don Buchwald, 6500 Wilshire Blvd,
#3300, Los Angeles, CA 90048 USA

Richards, Bob *Doctor*
1616 Estates Dr, Waco, TX 76712 USA

Richards, Brad *Hockey Player*
809 Seddon Cove Way, Tampa, FL 33602
USA

Richards, Brooke *Model*
9242 Beverly Blvd, Beverly Hills, CA
90210

Richards, D Ann W *Governor*
98 San Jacinto Blvd, #1440, Austin, TX
78701 USA

Richards, Denise *Actor*
Gersh Agency, 232 N Canon Dr, Beverly
Hills, CA 90210 USA

Richards, Emelie
PO Box 7052, Arlington, VA 22207

Richards, Evan
1800 Ave. of the Stars #400, Los Angeles,
CA 90067

Richards, Frederic M *Misc*
69 Andrews Road, Guilford, CT 06437
USA

Richards, I Vivian A (Viv) *Cricketer*
West Indian Cricket Board, PO Box 616,
Saint John's, ANTIGUA & BARBUDA

Richards, J August *Actor*
PO Box 99, China Spring, TX 76633 USA

Richards, J R *Musician*
William Morris Agency, 1325 Ave of
Americas, New York, NY 10019 USA

Richards, Keith *Musician*
William Morris Agency (WMA-LA), 1
William Morris Pl, Beverly Hills, CA
90212 USA

Richards, Kim *Actor*
10326 Orion Ave, Los Angeles, CA 90064
USA

Richards, Lloyd G *Director*
18 W 95th St, New York, NY 10025 USA

Richards, Lou
2467 Brighton Dr. #2-B, Valencia, CA
91355

Richards, Mark *Misc*
755 Hunter St, Newcastle, NSW, 2302,
AUSTRALIA

Richards, Michael *Comedian, Actor*
International Creative Management
(ICM-LA), 8942 Wilshire Blvd, Beverly
Hills, CA 90211 USA

Richards, Paul G *Misc*
Lamont-Doherty Geological Observatory,
Palisades, NY 10964 USA

Richards, Paul W *Astronaut*
NASA, Johnson Space Center, 2101 NASA
Road, Houston, TX 77058 USA

Richards, Renee *Tennis Player*
1604 Union St, San Francisco, CA 94123
USA

Richards, Rex E *Misc*
13 Woodstock Close, Oxford, OX2 8DB,
UNITED KINGDOM (UK)

Richards, Richard N *Astronaut*
NASA, Johnson Space Center, 2101 NASA
Road, Houston, TX 77058 USA

Richards, Robert E (Bob) *Track Athlete*
1616 Estates Dr, Waco, TX 76712 USA

Richards, Stephanie *Actor*
H David Moss, 733 Seward St, #PH, Los
Angeles, CA 90038 USA

Richards, Viv *Cricketer*
West Indies Cricket Club, PO Box 616, St
John's, ANTIGUA

Richards, Warren J
PO Box 2496, Salt Lake City, UT 84110
USA

Richardson, Ashley *Model*
Ford Model Agency, 142 Greene St, #400,
New York, NY 10012 USA

Richardson, Bill
799 United Nations Plaza, New York, NY
10017 USA

Richardson, Bill *Secretary*
1000 Independence SW, Washington, DC
20585 USA

Richardson, Cameron *Actor*
United Talent Agency (UTA), 9560
Wilshire Blvd, Beverly Hills, CA 90212
USA

Richardson, Cheryl *Actor*
8900 Amestoy Ave, Northridge, CA 91325
USA

Richardson, Dan *Musician*
Agency Group Ltd, 1775 Broadway, #430,
New York, NY 10019 USA

Richardson, Donna *Misc*
Anchor Bay Entertainment, 500 Kirts Blvd,
Troy, MI 48084 USA

Richardson, Dorothy (Dot) *Misc*
USC Medical Center, 1200 N State St,
#GH3900, Los Angeles, CA 90089, us

Richardson, Dorothy (Dot) *Misc*
USC Medical Center, 1200 N State St,
#GH3900, Los Angeles, CA 90089 USA

Richardson, Earl *Educator*
Morgan State University, President's
Office, Baltimore, MD 21239 USA

Richardson, Eliot
1100 Crest Lane, McLean, VA 22101

Richardson, Gordon W H *Financier*
Morgan Stanley, 25 Cabot Square, Canary
Wharf, London, E14 4QA, UNITED
KINGDOM (UK)

Richardson, Greg *Boxer*
382 Camden Ave, Youngstown, OH
44505 USA

Richardson, Hamilton *Tennis Player*
870 United Nations Plaza, New York, NY
10017 USA

Richardson, Howard *Writer*
207 Columbus Ave, New York, NY 10023
USA

Richardson, Ian W *Actor*
131 Lavender Sweep, London, SW11,
UNITED KINGDOM (UK)

Richardson, Jack *Artist*
12171 Sunset Ave, Grass Valley, CA
95945 USA

Richardson, Jake *Actor*
Coast to Coast Talent Group, 3350
Barham Blvd, Los Angeles, CA 90068
USA

Richardson, Jason *Basketball Player*
Golden State Warriors, 1001 Broadway,
Oakland, CA 94607 USA

Richardson, Joely *Actor*
P F D Drury House, 34-43 Russell St,
London, WC2B 5HA, UNITED KINGDOM
(UK)

Richardson, John T *Educator*
2233 N Kenmore Ave, Chicago, IL 60614
USA

Richardson, Kevin *Musician*
The Firm, 9100 Wilshire Blvd, #100W,
Beverly Hills, CA 90210 USA

Richardson, Kevin Michael *Actor*
Haeggstrom Office, The, 11288 Ventura
Blvd #620, Studio City, CA 91604

Richardson, LaTanya *Actor, Producer*
Paradigm (LA), 10100 Santa Monica Blvd,
Fl 25, Los Angeles, CA 90067 USA

Richardson, Linda *Opera Singer*
Van Walsum Mgmt, 4 Addison Bridge
Place, London, W14 8XP, UNITED
KINGDOM (UK)

Richardson, Midge T *Editor*
Seventeen Magazine, Editorial Dept, 850
3rd Ave, New York, NY 10022 USA

Richardson, Miranda *Actor*
Kerry Gardner Mgmt, 7 Saint George's
Square, London, SW1V 2HX, UNITED
KINGDOM (UK)

Richardson, Natasha *Actor*
International Creative Management
(ICM-LA), 8942 Wilshire Blvd, Beverly
Hills, CA 90211 USA

Richardson, Natasha J *Actor, Musician*
30 Brackenburg Ave, London, W6,
UNITED KINGDOM (UK)

Richardson, Nolan *Coach*
2539 E Joyce St, Fayetteville, AR 72703
USA

Richardson, Patricia *Actor*
11718 Barrington Ct #510, Los Angeles,
CA 90049 USA

Richardson, Quentin *Basketball Player*
Los Angeles Clippers, Staples Center,
1111 S Figueroa St, Los Angeles, CA
90015 USA

Richardson, Robert *Cinematographer*
Skouras Agency, 725 Arizona Ave, #406,
Santa Monica, CA 90401 USA

Richardson, Robert C *Nobel Prize Laureate*
4 Hunter Lane, Ithaca, NY 14850 USA

Richardson, Robert C (Bobby) *Baseball Player*
47 Adams Ave, Sumter, SC 29150 USA

Richardson, Sam *Artist*
4121 Sequoyah Road, Oakland, CA 94605 USA

Richardson, W Franklyn *Religious Leader*
National Baptist Convention, 52 S 6th Ave, Mount Vernon, NY 10550 USA

Richardson, Willam C *Educator*
W K Kellogg Foundation, 1 Michigan Ave E, Battle Creek, MI 49017 USA

Richardson of Lee, John S *Doctor*
Windcutter, Lee, North Devon, EX34 8LW, UNITED KINGDOM (UK)

Richardson-Whitfield, Salli *Actor*
Blueprint Management, 5670 Wilshire Blvd #2525, Los Angeles, CA 90036 USA

Richer, Stephane *Hockey Player*
New Jersey Devils, Continental Arena, 50 RR 120 N, East Rutherford, NJ 07073 USA

Richert, Nate *Actor*
Iris Burton Agency, 8916 Ashcroft Ave, Los Angeles, CA 90048 USA

Richey, Cliff *Tennis Player*
2936 Cumberland Dr, San Angelo, TX 76904 USA

Richey, Jennifer *Actor*
Bobby Ball Talent, 4342 Lankershim Blvd, North Hollywood, CA 91602 USA

Richey, Kim
209 10th Ave. #322, Nashville, TN 37203

Richey, Nancy *Tennis Player*
2936 Cumberland Dr, San Angelo, TX 76904 USA

Richie, Lionel *Musician, Songwriter*
Creative Artists Agency LCC (CAA-LA), 9830 Wilshire Blvd, Beverly Hills, CA 90212 USA

Richie, Nicole *Reality TV Star, Heir/Heiress*
Creative Artists Agency LCC (CAA-LA), 9830 Wilshire Blvd, Beverly Hills, CA 90212 USA

Richie, Shane *Actor*
Qdos Entertainment, 8 King St, Covent Garden, London, WC2 8HN, UNITED KINGDOM

Richman, Caryn *Actor*
16 1/2 Mast St, Marina del Rey, CA 90292 USA

Richman, Jonathan *Musician, Actor*
High Road, 751 Bridgeway, #300, Sausalito, CA 94965 USA

Richman, Peter Mark *Actor*
5114 Del Moreno Dr, Woodland Hills, CA 91364 USA

Richmond, Branscombe *Actor*
5706 Calvin Ave, Tarzana, CA 91356 USA

Richmond, Julius B *Doctor*
PO Box 996, West Tisbury, MA 02575 USA

Richmond, Mitch *Basketball Player*
25548 Kingston Court, Calabasas, CA 91302 USA

Richmond, Tequan *Actor*
Nancy Chaidez & Associates, 6399 Wilshire Blvd #424, Los Angeles, CA 90048

Richt, Mark *Football Coach*
University of Georgia, Athletic Dept, PO Box 1472, Athens, GA 30603 USA

Richter, Andy *Actor, Comedian*
315 S Beverly Dr, #216, Beverly Hills, CA 90212 USA

Richter, Burton *Nobel Prize Laureate*
Stanford University, Linear Accelerator Center, PO Box 4349, Stanford, CA 94309 USA

Richter, Gerhard *Artist*
Bismarckstr 50, Cologne, 50672, GERMANY

Richter, Hans
In der Wasserschopp 43, Heppenheim, GERMANY, D-64646

Richter, James A (Jim) *Football Player*
8620 Bournemouth Dr, Raleigh, NC 27615 USA

Richter, Jason James *Actor*
United Talent Agency, 9560 Wilshire Blvd, #500, Beverly Hills, CA 90212 USA

Richter, Leslie A (Les) *Football Player*
1405 Via Valiarta, Riverside, CA 92506 USA

Richter, Michael T (Mike) *Hockey Player*
314 Mount Holly Road, Katonah, NY 10536 USA

Richter, Pat V *Football Player, Football Executive*
45 Cambridge Road, Madison, WI 53704 USA

Richwine, Maria *Actor*
Abrams-Rubaloff Lawrence, 8075 W 3rd St, #303, Los Angeles, CA 90048 USA

Ricker, Robert S *Religious Leader*
Baptists Conference, 2002 Arlington Heights Road, Arlington Heights, IL 60005 USA

Rickles, Don *Comedian, Actor*
10249 Century Woods Dr, Los Angeles, CA 90067 USA

Rickman, Alan *Actor*
Creative Artists Agency, 9830 Wilshire Blvd, Beverly Hills, CA 90212 USA

Rickter, Alicia *Actor*
Innovative Artists (LA), 1505 Tenth St, Santa Monica, CA 90401 USA

Ricoeur, Paul *Misc*
18 Rue Henri Marrou, Chatenay Malabry, 92290, FRANCE

Ridder, Eric *Publisher*
Piping Rock Road, Locust Valley, NY 11560 USA

Ridder, P Anthony *Business Person, Publisher*
Knight-Ridder Inc, 50 W San Fernando St, San Jose, CA 95113 USA

Riddick, Frank A Jr *Physicist*
1923 Octavia St, New Orleans, LA 70115 USA

Riddick, Steven (Steve) *Track Athlete*
7601 Crittenden, #F2, Philadelphia, PA 19118 USA

Riddiford, Lynn M *Biologist*
16324 51st Ave SE, Bothell, WA 98012 USA

Riddles, Libby *Dog Sled Racer*
PO Box 15253, Fritz Creek, AK 99603 USA

Ride, Sally
9500 Gillman Dr MS 0221, La Jolla, CA 92093-0221 USA

Ride, Sally K *Astronaut*
California Space Institute, PO Box 0221, 9500 Gilman Dr, La Jolla, CA 92093 USA

Rider, Isaiah (J R) *Basketball Player*
PO Box 121R, Montchanin, DE 19710 USA

Rider, Thomas J (Tom) *Secretary, Governor*
Homeland Security Department, Washington, DC 20528 USA

Riders In The Sky
38 Music Sq. E. #300, Nashville, TN 37203

Riders of the Purple Sage
PO Box 1987, Studio City, CA 91604

Ridgeley, Andrew *Musician*
8800 Sunset Blvd, #401, Los Angeles, CA 90069 USA

Ridgeway, Frank *Cartoonist*
King Features Syndicate, 888 7th Ave, New York, NY 10106 USA

Ridgley, Bob *Actor*
20th Century Artists, 4605 Lankersham Blvd, #305, North Hollywood, CA 91602 USA

Ridgway, Brunilde S *Archaeologist*
Bryn Mawr College, Archaeology Dept, Bryn Mawr, PA 19010 USA

Ridker, Paul *Doctor*
Brigham & Women's Hospital, 75 Francis St, Boston, MA 02115 USA

Ridley, John *Writer*
Endeavor Talent Agency, 9701 Wilshire Blvd, #1000, Beverly Hills, CA 90212 USA

Ridnour, Luke *Basketball Player*
Seattle SuperSonics, 351 Elliot Ave W, #500, Seattle, WA 98119 USA

Riedel, Deborah *Opera Singer*
Columbia Artists Mgmt Inc, 165 W 57th St, New York, NY 10019 USA

Riedel, Lars *Track Athlete*
LAC Chemnitz, Reichenhainer Str 154, Chemnitz, 09125, GERMANY

Riedlbauch, Vaclav *Composer*
Revoluci 6, Prague 1, 110 00, CZECH REPUBLIC

Rieger, Max *Skier*
Innsbrucker Str 12, Mittenwald, 82481, GERMANY

Riegert, Peter *Actor*
Innovative Artists, 1505 10th St, Santa Monica, CA 90401 USA

Riegle, Donald W Jr *Senator*
352 S Saginaw St, Flint, MI 48502 USA

Riegle, Gene *Horse Racer, Coach*
1162 Fort Jefferson Ave, Greenville, OH
45331 USA

Riehle, Richard *Actor*
Abrams Artists, 9200 Sunset Blvd, #1125,
Los Angeles, CA 90069 USA

Rienstra, John *Football Player*
1374 Top of the Rock Way, Monument,
CO 80132 USA

Riepe, James S *Business Person*
T Rowe Price Assoc, 100 E Pratt St,
Baltimore, MD 21202 USA

Ries, Christopher D *Artist*
Keelersburg Road, Tunkhannock, PA
18657 USA

Riese, Randall
PO Box 691239, Los Angeles, CA 90069

Riess, Adam *Physicist, Astronomer*
Space Telescope Science Institute, 3700
San Martin Dr, Baltimore, MD 21218 USA

Riessen, Marty *Tennis Player*
PO Box 5444, Santa Barbara, CA 93150
USA

Rieu, Andre *Musician*
Polygram Holland, Mozartlaan 25,
Hilversum, CM, 1217, NETHERLANDS

Rife, Rikki
520 Washington Blvd. #924, Marina del
Rey, CA 90292-5442

Riff
PO Box 7257, Paterson, NJ 07509

Rifkin, Jeremy *Writer, Social Activist*
1660 L St NW, #216, Washington, DC
20036 USA

Rifkin, Ron *Actor, Musician*
500 S Sepulveda Blvd, Los Angeles, CA
90049 USA

Rifkind, Joshua *Musician, Conductor*
100 Montgomery St, Cambridge, MA
02140 USA

Rigali, Justin F Cardinal *Religious Leader*
Archdiocese, 222 N 17th St, Philadelphia,
PA 19103 USA

Rigby, Amy *Musician, Songwriter*
Press Network, 1229 17th Ave S,
Nashville, TN 37212 USA

Rigby, Cathy
110 E. Wilshire #200, Fullerton, CA
92632

Rigby, Jean P *Opera Singer*
Harold Holt, 31 Sinclair Road, London,
W14 0NS, UNITED KINGDOM (UK)

Rigby, McCoy Cathy *Gymnast, Actor*
McCoy/Rigby Entertainment, 110 E
Wilshire Ave, #200, Fullerton, CA 92832
USA

Rigby, Paul *Cartoonist*
119 Monterey Pointe Dr, West Palm
Beach, FL 33418 USA

Rigby, Randall Jr *General*
Deputy CG, US Army Training/Doctrine
Command, Fort Monroe, VA 23651 USA

Rigg, Diana *Actor*
London Mgmt, 2-4 Noel St, London, W1V
3RB, UNITED KINGDOM (UK)

Rigg, Rebecca *Actor*
June Cann Mgmt, 110 Queen St,
Woollahra, NSW, 2025, AUSTRALIA

Riggins, John *Football Player*
2332 Hill Place, Falls Church, VA 22043
USA

Riggio, Leonard *Business Person*
Barnes & Noble Inc, 122 5th Ave, New
York, NY 10011 USA

Riggleman, James D (Jim) *Baseball Player*
14950 Gulf Blvd, #1003, Madeira Beach,
FL 33708 USA

Riggs, Gerald *Football Player*
2574 Bright Court, Decatur, GA 30034
USA

Riggs, Lorrin A *Misc*
80 Lyme Road, #104, Hanover, NH
03755 USA

Righetti, Amanda *Actor*
MBST Entertainment, 345 N Maple D
#200, Suite 200, Beverly Hills, CA 90210
USA

Righetti, David A (Dave) *Baseball Player*
552 Magdalena Ave, Los Altos Hills, CA
94024 USA

Right Said Fred
PO Box 891135, Edam, NETHERLANDS,
ZJ

Righteous Bros *Music Group*
William Morris Agency (WMA-LA), 1
William Morris Pl, Beverly Hills, CA
90212 USA

Rights, Graham H *Religious Leader*
Moravian Church Southern Province, 459
S Church St, Winston Salem, NC 27101
USA

Rijker, Lucia *Actor*
Sports Placement Service, 5458 Wilshire
Blvd, Los Angeles, CA 90036 USA

Rikaart, Greg *Actor*
TalentWorks (LA), 3500 W Olive Ave
#1400, Burbank, CA 91505 USA

Riker, Albert J *Misc*
2760 E 8th St, Tucson, AZ 85716 USA

Riker, Robin *Actor*
Don Buchwald & Associates Inc (LA),
6500 Wilshire Blvd #2200, Los Angeles,
CA 90048 USA

Riklis, Meshulam *Business Person*
Riklis Family Corp, 2901 Las Vegas Blvd
S, Las Vegas, NV 89109 USA

Riley, Bill *Hockey Player*
286 Buckingham Ave, Riverview, NB E1B
2P2, CANADA

Riley, Bridget L *Artist*
Mayor Rowan Gallery, 31A Bruton Place,
London, W1X 7A8, UNITED KINGDOM
(UK)

Riley, Gerald (Jerry) *Dog Sled Racer*
General Delivery, Nenana, AK 99760
USA

Riley, H John Jr *Business Person*
Cooper Industries, 600 Travis, Houston,
TX 77002 USA

Riley, Jack *Actor*
House of Representatives, 400 S Beverly
Dr, #101, Beverly Hills, CA 90212 USA

Riley, James C *General*
Commanding General, V Corps, APO, AE,
09079 USA

Riley, Jeannie C *Musician*
906 Granville Road, Franklin, TN 37064
USA

Riley, John P (Jack) *Hockey Player, Coach*
185 Mistic Dr, Marstone Mills, MA 02648
USA

Riley, Michael
9200 Sunset Blvd. #900, Los Angeles, CA
90069

Riley, Mike *Football Coach*
Oregon State University, Athletic Dept,
Corvallis, OR 97331 USA

Riley, Pat
180 Arvida Parkway, Miami, FL 33156

Riley, Patrick J (Pat) *Basketball Player,
Coach*
180 Arvida Parkway, Coral Gables, FL
33156 USA

Riley, Richard D *Misc*
16 Boathouse Road, Laconia, NH 03246
USA

Riley, Ruth *Athlete*
3777 Lapeer Rd, Auburn Hills, MI 48326-
1733

Riley, Teddy *Musician, Songwriter*
Future Enterprise Records, 70 Universal
City Plaza, Universal City, CA 91608 USA

Riley, Terry M *Composer, Musician*
Shri Moonshine Ranch, 13699 Moonshine
Road, Camptonville, CA 95922 USA

Rilling, Helmuth
Int'l Bach Academy, Johann-Sebastian-
Bach-Platz, Stuttgart, 70178, GERMANY

Rimando, Nick *Soccer Player*
DC United, 14120 Newbrook Dr,
Chantilly, VA 20151 USA

Rimer, Jeff *Sportscaster*
3629 Spanish Oak Point, Davie, FL 33328
USA

Rimes, LeAnn *Musician*
193 Carronbridge Way, Franklin, TN
37067 USA

Rimington, Stella *Government Official*
PO Box 1604, London, SW1P 1XB,
UNITED KINGDOM (UK)

Rimmel, James E *Religious Leader*
Evangetical Presbyterian Church, 26049
Five Mile Road, Detroit, MI 48239 USA

Rinaldi, Kathy *Tennis Player*
Advantage International, 1025 Thomas
Jefferson NW, #450, Washington, DC
20007 USA

Rinaldo, Benjamin *Skier*
Ski World, 2680 Buena Park Dr, North
Hollywood, CA 91604 USA

Rincon, Ricardo *Baseball Player*
Oakland Athletics, 7000 Coliseum Way,
Oakland, CA 94621 USA

Rinearson, Peter M *Journalist*
Seattle Times, Editorial Dept, 1120 John
St, Seattle, WA 98109 USA

Rinehart, Kenneth *Misc*
University of Illinois, Chemistry Dept,
Urbana, IL 61801 USA

Rines, Robert H *Inventor*
17 Ripley Road, Belmont, MA 02478 USA

Ringadoo, Veerasamy *President*
Corner of Farquhar & Sir Celicourt
Antelme Sts, Quatre-Bornes, MAURITIUS

Ringer, Jennifer *Ballerina*
New York City Ballet, Lincoln Center
Plaza, New York, NY 10023 USA

Ringer, Robert J *Writer, Publisher*
Stratford Press, 1880 Century Park East,
Los Angeles, CA 90067 USA

Ringling Brothers Barnum & Bailey Circus
8607 Westwood Cir, Vienna, VA 22182,
US

Ringo, James S (Jim) *Football Player*
408 Montross Court, Chesapeake, VA
23323 USA

Ringwald, Molly *Actor*
Writers & Artists, 19 W 44th St, #1000,
New York, NY 10036 USA

Rinna, Lisa *Actor*
B & B Entertainment, 1640 S Sepulveda
Blvd, #530, Los Angeles, CA 90025 USA

Rinser, Luise
via di Marino 49, Rocca di Papa, ITALY,
I-00040

Rintoul, David
91 Regent St., London, ENGLAND, W1R
7TB

Rintzler, Marius A *Opera Singer*
Friedingstr 18, Dusseldorf, 40625,
GERMANY

Riordan, ex-Mayor Richard
141 N. Bristol Ave, Los Angeles, CA
90049

Riordan, Marjorie
1833 Pelham Ave., Los Angeles, CA
90025

Riordan, Mike *Basketball Player*
Riordan's Saloon, 26 Market Place,
Annapolis, MD 21401 USA

Riordan, Richard J *Politician*
141 N Bristol Ave, Los Angeles, CA 90049
USA

Rios, Alberto *Writer*
Arizona State University, English Dept,
Tempe, AZ 85287 USA

Rios, Alexis *Baseball Player*
Yale Field, 252 Derby Ave, West Haven,
CT 06516 USA

Rios, Marcelo *Tennis Player*
Int'l Mgmt Group, Via Augusta 200, #400,
Barcelona, 08021, SPAIN

Rios, Montt Efrain *President, General*
6A Avenida A 3-18 Zona 1, Guatamela
City, GUATEMALA

Rios, Osvaldo *Actor*
TV Caracol, Calle 76 #11 - 35, Piso
10AA, Bogota DC, 26484, COLOMBIA

Riotta, Vincent *Actor*
Scott Marshall, 54 Poland St #9, London,
UNITED KINGDOM (UK)

Ripa, Kelly *Actor*
646 Juniper Place, Franklin Lakes, NJ
07417 USA

Ripert, Eric *Chef*
Le Bernardin, 787 7th Ave, New York, NY
10019 USA

Ripken, Calvin E (Cal) Jr *Baseball Player*
10801 Tony Dr, #A, Lutherville, MD
21093 USA

Ripley, Alice *Actor, Musician*
Douglas Gorman ROthacker Wilhelm,
1501 Broadway, #703, New York, NY
10036 USA

Rippey, Rodney Allan *Actor*
3941 Veselich Ave, #4-251, Los Angeles,
CA 90039 USA

Rippey, Rodney Allen
3939 Veselich Ave. #351, Los Angeles,
CA 90039-1435

Ripple, Kenneth F *Judge*
US Court of Appeals, 204 S Main St,
South Bend, IN 46601 USA

Ris, Hans *Biologist*
5542 Riverview Dr, Waunakee, WI 53597
USA

Risebrough, Doug *Hockey Player, Coach*
5809 Schaefer Road, Edina, MN 55436
USA

Risen, Arnie *Basketball Player*
3217 Bremerton Rd, Pepper Pike, OH
44125

Risen, Arnold (Arnie) *Basketball Player*
3217 Bremerton Road, Pepper Pike, OH
44124 USA

Risien, Cody L *Football Player*
209 Spanish Oak Trail, Dripping Springs,
TX 78620 USA

Risk, Thomas N *Financier*
10 Belford Place, Edinburgh, EH4 3DH,
SCOTLAND

Rispoli, Michael *Actor*
Gersh Agency, The (LA), 232 N Canon Dr,
Beverly Hills, CA 90210 USA

Rist, Robbie
PO Box 867, Woodland Hills, CA 91365

Ristorucci, Lisa *Actor*
Progressive Artists Agency, 400 S Beverly
Dr, #216, Beverly Hills, CA 90212 USA

Ritcher, James A (Jim) *Football Player*
8620 Boumemouth Dr, Raleigh, NC
27615 USA

Ritchie, Daniel L *Educator, Television
Host*
University of Denver, Chancellor's Office,
Denver, CO 80208 USA

Ritchie, Guy *Director*
SKA Films, 1 Horse & Dolphin Yard,
London, W1V 7LG, UNITED KINGDOM
(UK)

Ritchie, Ian *Architect*
110 Three Colt St, London, E14 8A2,
UNITED KINGDOM (UK)

Ritchie, Jill *Actor*
Rigberg-Rugolo Entertainment, 1180 S
Beverly Dr #601, Los Angeles, CA 90035
USA

Ritchie, Jim *Artist*
Adelson Galleries, Mark Hotel, 25 E 77th
St, New York, NY 10021 USA

Ritchie, John H *Architect*
Mount Heswall, Wirrai, L60 4RD,
UNITED KINGDOM (UK)

Ritchie Family, The
4100 W. Flagler St. #B-2, Miami, FL
33134

Ritenour, Lee *Musician, Composer*
11808 Dorothy St, #108, Los Angeles, CA
90049 USA

Ritger, Dick *Bowler*
804 Valley View Dr, River Falls, WI
54022 USA

Ritter, C Dowd *Financier*
AmSouth Bancorp, AmSouth Sonat Tower,
1900 5th Ave N, Birmingham, AL 35203
USA

Ritter, Huntley *Actor*
Agency for the Performing Arts (APA-LA),
9200 Sunset Blvd #900, Los Angeles, CA
90069 USA

Ritter, Jason *Actor*
Burstein Company, The, 15304 Sunset
Blvd #208, Pacific Palisades, CA 90272
USA

Ritts, Jim *Golfer, Television Host*
Ladies Pro Golf Assn, 100 International
Golf Dr, Daytona Beach, FL 32124 USA

Ritz, David
Trident Media Group LLC, 41 Madison
Ave Fl 33, New York, NY 10010 USA

Ritzenhaler, Henry Leon
1617 Pearson Rd., Paradise, CA 95969

Riutta, Ernest R *Admiral*
Commander, US Coast Guard Pacific,
Coast Guard Island, Alameda, CA 94501
USA

Riva, Emmanuelle
37 rue de la Harpe, Paris, FRANCE,
F-75005

Rivaldo *Soccer Player*
AC Milan, Via Turati 3, Milan, 20221,
ITALY

Rivas, Gonzalo *Actor*
Televisa, Blvd Adolfo Lopez Mateos 232,
Colonia San Angel INN, DF, CP 01060,
MEXICO

Rivas Montaþo, Hanna *Actor*
Televisa, Blvd Adolfo Lopez Mateos 232,
Colonia San Angel INN, DF, CP 01060,
MEXICO

Rivera, Ana Liz *Actor*
Televisa, Blvd Adolfo Lopez Mateos 232,
Colonia San Angel INN, DF, CP 01060,
MEXICO

Rivera, Angelica *Actor*
Televisa, Blvd Adolfo Lopez Mateos 232,
Colonia San Angel INN, DF, CP 01060,
MEXICO

Rivera, Chita *Actor, Musician, Dancer*
99 Greenbush Road, Blauvell, NY 10913
USA

Rivera, Geraldo *Entertainer*
2200 Fletcher Ave, Fort Lee, NJ 07024
USA

Rivera, Gina
PO Box 5617, Beverly Hills, CA 90210

Rivera, Jerry *Musician*
BMG, 1540 Broadway, New York, NY
10036 USA

Rivera, Lupillo *Music Group*
Sony Music Miami, 605 Lincoln Rd, Miami Beach, FL 33138 USA

Rivera, Mariano *Baseball Player*
Casa 3666, Calle El Puerto, Puerto Caimito, PANAMA

Rivera, Ron *Football Player*
17 Saddlehorn Dr, Cherry Hill, NJ 08003 USA

Rivera Carrera, Norberto Cardinal
Religious Leader
Curia Arzobispal, Aptdo Postal 24-4-33, Mexico City, DF, 06700, MEXICO

Rivero, Jorge *Actor*
H David Moss, 733 Seward St, #PH, Los Angeles, CA 90038 USA

Rivers, Glenn (Doc) *Basketball Player, Coach*
861 Bonita Dr, Winter Park, FL 32789 USA

Rivers, Joan *Comedian, Entertainer*
William Morris Agency (WMA-LA), 1 William Morris Pl, Beverly Hills, CA 90212 USA

Rivers, Johnny *Musician, Songwriter*
3141 Coldwater Canyon Lane, Beverly Hills, CA 90210 USA

Rivers, Melissa *Talk Show Host*
William Morris Agency (WMA-LA), 1 William Morris Pl, Beverly Hills, CA 90212 USA

Rivers, Mickey
350 NW 48th St., Miami, FL 33127

Rivers, Philip *Football Player*
San Diego Chargers, 4020 Murphy Canyon Road, San Diego, CA 92123 USA

Riverside, Vincent
5757 Wilshire Blvd. #2200, Los Angeles, CA 90036

Rivette, Jacques *Director*
20 Blvd de la Bastille, Paris, 75012, FRANCE

Riviere, Marie
5 rue Edmond Gondinet, Paris, FRANCE, 75013

Rivlin, Alice M *Government Official*
2842 Chesterfield Place, Washington, DC 20008 USA

Rizzo, Patti *Golfer*
2455 Provence Circle, Weston, FL 33327 USA

Rizzotti, Jennifer *Basketball Player, Coach*
University of Hartford, Athletic Dept, West Hartford, CT 06117 USA

Rizzuto, Phil
912 Westminster Ave., Hillside, NJ 07205

Rizzuto, Philip F (Phil) *Baseball Player, Sportscaster*
912 Westminster Ave, Hillside, NJ 07205 USA

Roa Bastos, Augusto *Writer*
Berutti 2828, Martinez, Buenos Aires, ARGENTINA

Roach, Jay *Director*
International Creative Mgmt, 8942 Wilshire Blvd, #219, Beverly Hills, CA 90211 USA

Roach, Maxwell L (Max) *Musician*
Fat City Artists, 1906 Chet Atkins Place, #502, Nashville, TN 37212 USA

Roach, Steve *Musician*
Hearts of Space, PO Box 5916, Sausalito, CA 94966 USA

Roache, Linus *Actor*
Endeavor Agency LLC (LA), 9601 Wilshire Blvd Fl 3, Beverly Hills, CA 90210 USA

Roaf, William L (Willie) *Football Player*
1900 E 38th Ave, Pine Bluff, AR 71601 USA

Roark, Terry P *Educator*
1752 Edward Dr, Laramie, WY 82072 USA

Roath, Stephen D *Business Person*
Longs Drug Stores, 141 N Civic Dr, Walnut Creek, CA 94596 USA

Robards, Jake
350 Willow St., Southport, CT 06840

Robards, Karen *Writer*
Pocket Books, 1230 Ave of Americas, New York, NY 10020 USA

Robards, Sam *Actor*
Rigberg Roberts Rugolo, 1180 S Beverly Dr, #601, Los Angeles, CA 90035 USA

Robb, Annasophia *Actor*
Cunningham-Escott-Dipene & Associates Inc (CED-LA), 10635 Santa Monica Blvd #130, Los Angeles, CA 90025 USA

Robb, David *Actor*
William Morris Agency, 151 El Camino Dr, Beverly Hills, CA 90212 USA

Robb, Doug *Musician*
Island Def Jam Records, 8920 Sunset Blvd, #200, Los Angeles, CA 90069 USA

Robb, Lynda Johnson
612 Chain Bridge Rd., McLean, VA 22101

Robb, Walter L *Business Person, Inventor*
1358 Ruffner Road, Niskayuna, NY 12309 USA

Robbe-Grillet, Alain *Writer, Director*
18 Blvd Maillot, Neuilly-sur-Seine, 92200, FRANCE

Robbie, Seymour
9980 Liebe Dr., Beverly Hills, CA 90210

Robbie, Timothy J (Tim) *Football Executive*
Miami Dolphins, 7500 SW 30th St, Davie, FL 33314 USA

Robbins, Amy *Actor*
Artists Rights Group (ARG London), 4 Great Portland St, London, W1W 8PA, UNITED KINGDOM (UK)

Robbins, Barret *Football Player*
5980 laurel Creek Dr, Pleasanton, CA 94588 USA

Robbins, Brian *Director*
7743 Woodrow Wilson Dr, Los Angeles, CA 90046 USA

Robbins, Deanna *Actor*
630 N Keystone St, Burbank, CA 91506 USA

Robbins, Jane *Actor*
Scott Marshall Mgmt, 44 Perry Road, London, W3 7NA, UNITED KINGDOM (UK)

Robbins, Kelly *Golfer*
1025 Lincoln Dr, Weidman, MI 48893 USA

Robbins, Mary
PO Box 641032, Miami, FL 33164-9998

Robbins, Randy *Athlete*
1131 E Valle Vista Dr, Nogales, AZ 85621-1229

Robbins, Tim *Actor, Director*
International Creative Mgmt, 40 W 57th St, #1800, New York, NY 10019 USA

Robbins, Tom *Writer*
PO Box 338, La Conner, WA 98257 USA

Robbins, Tony *Writer*
Jennifer Martinez, 9888 Carrole Center, San Diego, CA 92126 USA

Robby Krieger Band *Music Group*
dv8 Entertainment & Productions, 208 Main Street, Suite 202, Asbury Park, NJ 07712 USA

Robelot, Jane *Commentator*
CBS-TV, News Dept, 51 W 52nd St, New York, NY 10019 USA

Robens of Woldingham, Alfred
Government Official, Educator
2 Laleham Abbey, Staines, Middx, TW18 1SZ, UNITED KINGDOM (UK)

Roberson, Irvin (Bo) *Track Athlete*
820 N Raymond Ave, #47, Pasadena, CA 91103 USA

Roberson, James W *Cinematographer*
PO Box 121013, Big Bear Lake, CA 92315 USA

Robert, Jacques F *Attorney General*
14 Villa Saint-Georges, Antony, 92160, FRANCE

Robert, Rene *Hockey Player*
4020 Rue Savard, Troie Rivieres, QC, G8Y 4B8, CANADA

Roberts, Bernard *Musician*
Uwchlaw'r Coed, Llanbedr, Gwynedd, LL45 2NA, WALES

Roberts, Bert C Jr *Business Person*
MCI WorldCom Inc, 500 Clinton Dr, Clinton, MS 39056 USA

Roberts, Beverly
30912 Ariana Lane, Laguna Niguel, CA 92677

Roberts, Beverly *Actor*
30912 Ariana Lane, Laguna Niguel, CA 92677 USA

Roberts, Brad *Musician*
Macklam Feldman Mgmt, 1505 W 2nd Ave, #200, Vancouver, BC V6H 3Y4, CANADA

Roberts, Brian L *Business Person*
Storer Communications, 1500 Market St, Philadelphia, PA 19102 USA

Roberts, Bruce *Musician, Songwriter*
Gorfaine/Schwartz, 13245 Riverside Dr, #450, Sherman Oaks, CA 91423 USA

Roberts, Cecil *Misc*
United Mine Workers, 8315 Lee Highway, #500, Fairfax, VA 22031 USA

Roberts, Chalmers M *Journalist*
6699 MacArthur Blvd, Bethesda, MD 20816 USA

Roberts, Corrine (Cokie) *Commentator*
5315 Bradley Blvd, Bethesda, MD 20814
USA

Roberts, Danny *Reality TV Star*
Bunim/Murray Productions Inc, 6007
Sepulveda Blvd, Van Nuys, CA 91411
USA

Roberts, David (Dave) *Track Athlete*
14310 SW 73rd Ave, Archer, FL 32618
USA

Roberts, Dee *Artist*
2012 N 19th St, Boise, ID 83702 USA

Roberts, Doris *Actor*
Innovative Artists (LA), 1505 Tenth St,
Santa Monica, CA 90401 USA

Roberts, Emma *Actor*
Sweeney Management, 8755 Lookout
Mountain Avenue, Los Angeles, CA 90046
USA

Roberts, Eric *Actor*
United Talent Agency, 9560 Wilshire
Blvd, #500, Beverly Hills, CA 90212 USA

Roberts, Eugene L Jr *Educator*
New York Times, Editorial Dept, 229 W
43rd St, New York, NY 10036 USA

Roberts, Gary *Hockey Player*
Wooden Sticks, PO Box 848 Station Main,
Uxbridge, PM, L9P 1N2, CANADA

Roberts, Gordon R *War Hero*
445 Ward-Koebel Road, Oregonia, OH
45054 USA

Roberts, H Edward (Ed) *Designer*
Bleckley Memorial Hospital, 408 Peacock
St, Cochran, GA 31014 USA

Roberts, Jake
Box 3859, Stamford, CT 06905

Roberts, James A (Jim) *Hockey Player,
Coach*
137 Ridgecrest Dr, Chesterfield, MO
63017 USA

Roberts, Joan
114 W. 44th St., New York NY, 10036

Roberts, John *Commentator*
CBS-TV, News Dept, 51 W 52nd St, New
York, NY 10019 USA

Roberts, John *Director*
International Creative Mgmt, 76 Oxford
St, London, W1N 0AX, UNITED
KINGDOM (UK)

Roberts, John D *Misc*
California Institute of Technology,
Chemistry Dept, Pasadena, CA 91125
USA

Roberts, John D (J D) *Football Player,
Football Coach*
6708 Trevi Court, Oklahoma City, OK
73116 USA

Roberts, Julia *Actor*
386 Park Ave S, #1000, New York, NY
10016 USA

Roberts, Kenny *Motorcycle Racer*
KR Marketing, 419 Medina Road, Medina,
OH 44256 USA

Roberts, Kevin *Business Person*
Saatchi & saatchi Worldwide, 375
Hudson St, New York, NY 10014 USA

Roberts, Lawrence G *Scientist*
Caspian Networks, 170 Baytech Dr, San
Jose, CA 95134 USA

Roberts, Leonard *Actor*
Kohner Agency, The, 9300 Wilshire Blvd
#555, Beverly Hills, CA 90212 USA

Roberts, Leonard *Business Person*
Tandy Corp, 100 Throckmorton St, Fort
Worth, TX 76102 USA

Roberts, Loren *Golfer*
3311 Tournament Dr S, Memphis, TN
38125 USA

Roberts, Louie
2401 12th Ave. So., Nashville, TN 37203

Roberts, Lynn
PO Box 4125, Calabash, NC 28467

Roberts, M Brigitte *Writer*
Atkins & Stone, 29 Fernshaw Road,
London, SW10 0TG, UNITED KINGDOM
(UK)

Roberts, Marcus *Musician*
Columbia Artists Mgmt Inc, 165 W 57th
St, New York, NY 10019 USA

Roberts, Michael
76 Oxford St., London, ENGLAND, W1N
0AX

Roberts, Michele *Writer*
Henry Holt, 115 W 18th St, New York,
NY 10011 USA

Roberts, Nora *Writer*
19239 Burnside Bridge Road, Keedysville,
MD 21756 USA

Roberts, Oral *Misc*
Oral Roberts University, 7777 S Lewis
Ave, Tulsa, OK 74171 USA

Roberts, Paul H *Mathematician*
PO Box 951567, Los Angeles, CA 90095
USA

Roberts, Pernell *Actor*
20395 Seaboard Rd, Malibu, CA 90265
USA

Roberts, R Michael *Scientist*
2213 Hominy Branch Court, Columbia,
MO 65201 USA

Roberts, Rachel *Model, Actor*
IMG Models, 304 Park Ave S Fl 12, New
York, NY 10010 USA

Roberts, Ralph J *Business Person*
Comcast Corp, 1500 Market St,
Philadelphia, PA 19102 USA

Roberts, Richard J *Nobel Prize Laureate*
New England Biolabs, 32 Tozer Road,
Beverly, MA 01915 USA

Roberts, Richard L *Educator*
Oral Roberts University, President's
Office, 7777 S Lewis Ave, Tulsa, OK
74171 USA

Roberts, Rick
9150 Wilshire Blvd. #350, Beverly Hills,
CA 90212-3427

Roberts, Robin *Sportscaster*
ESPN-TV, Sports Dept ESPN Plaza, 935
Middle St, Bristol, CT 06010 USA

Roberts, Robin E *Baseball Player*
504 Terrace Hill Road, Temple Terrace,
FL 33617 USA

Roberts, Stanley *Basketball Player*
1192 Congaree Road, Hopkins, SC 29061
USA

Roberts, Steven
5315 Bradley Blvd., Bethesda, MD 20814

Roberts, Tanya *Actor*
8410 Allenwood Road, Los Angeles, CA
90046 USA

Roberts, Tawny *Adult Film Star*
11208 Vista Sorrento Pkwy #207, San
Diego, CA 92130-7621 USA

Roberts, Tony *Actor*
970 Park Ave, #8N, New York, NY 10028
USA

Roberts, Trish *Basketball Player*
218 Carver Dr, Monroe, GA 30655 USA

Roberts, Xavier *Business Person, Designer*
PO Box 1438, Cleveland, GA 30528 USA

Robertson, Alvin C *Basketball Player*
3 Bimam Oaks, San Antonio, TX 78248
USA

Robertson, Belinda *Fashion Designer*
BR Cashmere, 22 Palmerston Place,
Edinburgh, EH12 5AL, SCOTLAND

Robertson, Cliff *Actor*
325 Dunemere Dr, La Jolla, CA 92037
USA

Robertson, Dale *Actor*
PO Box 850707, Yukon, OK 73085 USA

Robertson, Davis *Dancer*
Joffrey Ballet, 70 E Lake St, #1300,
Chicago, IL 60601 USA

Robertson, DeWayne *Football Player*
New York Jets, 1000 Fulton Ave,
Hempstead, NY 11550 USA

Robertson, Ed *Musician, Songwriter*
Nettwerk Mgmt, 8730 Wilshire Blvd,
#304, Beverly Hills, CA 90211 USA

Robertson, Georgina *Model*
Compagny, 270 Lafayette, #1400, New
York, NY 10012 USA

Robertson, Gordon *Religious Leader,
Television Host*
700 Club, 977 Centerville Tpke, Virginia
Beach, VT 23463 USA

Robertson, Isiah *Football Player*
1115 N Florida St, Covington, LA 70433
USA

Robertson, Jamie Robbie *Actor, Producer,
Musician*
Creative Artists Agency LCC (CAA-LA),
9830 Wilshire Blvd, Beverly Hills, CA
90212 USA

Robertson, Jenny *Actor*
Shelter Entertainment, 9255 Sunset Blvd,
#1010, Los Angeles, CA 90069 USA

Robertson, Kathleen *Actor*
Three Arts Entertainment, 9460 Wilshire
Blvd, #700, Beverly Hills, CA 90212 USA

Robertson, Kimmy *Actor*
Commercials Unlimited, 8383 Wilshire
Blvd, #850, Beverly Hills, CA 90211 USA

Robertson, Leslie E *Engineer*
Robertson Fowler Assoc, 211 E 46th St,
New York, NY 10017 USA

Robertson, Lisa
1365 Enterprise Dr., West Chester, PA
18380

Robertson, M G (Pat) *Misc*
Christian Broadcast Network, 100 Centerville Tumpike, Virginia Beach, VA 23463 USA

Robertson, Marcus A *Football Player*
3218 Cypress Point, Missouri City, TX 77459 USA

Robertson, Oscar
621 Tusculum Ave., Cincinnati, OH 45226-1771

Robertson, Oscar P *Basketball Player*
621 Tusculum Ave, Cincinnati, OH 45226 USA

Robertson, Pat *Religious Leader, Television Host*
700 Club, 977 Centerville Tpke, Virginia Beach, VT 23463 USA

Robertson, Robbie *Musician, Songwriter*
323 14th St, Santa Monica, CA 90402 USA

Robes, Ernest C (Bill) *Skier*
3 Mile Road, Etna, NH 03750 USA

Robie, Carl *Swimmer*
2525 Sunnybrook Dr, Sarasota, FL 34239 USA

Robinowitz, Joseph R *Editor, Publisher*
TV Guide Magazine, Editorial Dept, 100 Matsonford Road, Radnor, PA 19080 USA

Robins, Lee N *Scientist*
Washington University, Medical School, Psychiatry Dept, Saint Louis, MO 63110 USA

Robinson, Alexia
3500 W. Olive #920, Burbank, CA 91505

Robinson, Andrew *Actor*
2671 Byron Place, Los Angeles, CA 90046 USA

Robinson, Ann *Actor*
1357 Elysian Park Dr, Los Angeles, CA 90026 USA

Robinson, Anne *Entertainer*
19 Victoria Grove, London, W8 5RW, UNITED KINGDOM (UK)

Robinson, Arthur H *Misc*
7707 N Brookline Dr, #302, Madison, WI 53719 USA

Robinson, Brooks *Athlete*
PO Box 1168, Baltimore, MD 21203

Robinson, Brooks C *Baseball Player*
9210 Baltimore National Pike, Ellicot, MD 21042 USA

Robinson, Bumper *Actor*
1551 Majesty St, Upland, CA 91784 USA

Robinson, Charles
10000 Santa Monica Blvd. #305, Los Angeles, CA 90067

Robinson, Charles Knox
10637 Burbank Blvd., No. Hollywood, CA 91601

Robinson, Chip *Race Car Driver*
3034 Lake Forest Dr, Augusta, GA 30909 USA

Robinson, Chris *Actor*
3800 Barham Blvd, #303, Los Angeles, CA 90068 USA

Robinson, Chris *Actor*
Milch Schneider Organization, 14724 Ventura Blvd, #410, Sherman Oaks, CA 91403 USA

Robinson, Clarence (Arnie) *Track Athlete*
2904 Ocean View Blvd, San Diego, CA 92113 USA

Robinson, Cliff *Basketball Player*
57 Fire Flicker Place, The Woodlands, TX 77381 USA

Robinson, Clifford *Basketball Player*
PO Box 3357, San Ramon, CA 94583 USA

Robinson, David W *Basketball Player*
1 Admirals Way, San Antonio, TX 78257 USA

Robinson, Dawn *Musician*
William Morris Agency, 151 El Camino Dr, Beverly Hills, CA 90212 USA

Robinson, Dwight P *Financier*
Government National Mortgage Assn, 451 7th St SW, Washington, DC 20410 USA

Robinson, Elizabeth
12706 E. Pacific Circle #202, Aurora, CO 80014

Robinson, Emily Erwin *Football Player*
Atlanta Falcons, 4400 Falcon Parkway, Flowery Branch, GA 30542 USA

Robinson, Fatima
Fatima, 8306 Wilshire Blvd, PMB 833, Beverly Hills, CA 90211 USA

Robinson, Flynn *Basketball Player*
11875 Manor Dr, #1, Hawthome, CA 90250 USA

Robinson, Frank *Baseball Player*
15557 Aqua Verde Dr, Los Angeles, CA 90077 USA

Robinson, Glenn *Basketball Player, Coach*
Franklin & Marshall College, Athletic Dept, Lancaster, PA 17604 USA

Robinson, Jackie (Rachel) *Athlete*
3 W 35th St, New York, NY 10001 USA

Robinson, Janice *Musician*
Flavor Unit Entertainment, 155 Morgan St, Jersey City, NJ 07302 USA

Robinson, Jay *Actor*
13757 Milbank Ave, Sherman Oaks, CA 91403 USA

Robinson, John A *Football Coach*
45 Anthem Creek Circle, Henderson, NV 89052 USA

Robinson, Johnny N *Football Player*
3209 S Grand St, Monroe, LA 71202 USA

Robinson, Keith *Actor*
Stone Manners Talent Agency, 6500 Wilshire Blvd, Ste 550, Los Angeles, CA 90048 USA

Robinson, Keith *Musician*
New York Entertainment, 1776 Broadway #2001, New York, NY 10019 USA

Robinson, Kenneth *Government Official*
12 Grove Terrace, London, NW5, UNITED KINGDOM (UK)

Robinson, Koren *Football Player*
12 Henry Ave, Belmont, NC 28012 USA

Robinson, Larry *Hockey Player, Coach*
3211 Stevenson St, Plant City, FL 33566 USA

Robinson, Laura *Actor*
Henderson/Hogan, 8285 W Sunset Blvd, #1, West Hollywood, CA 90046 USA

Robinson, Leon (Leon) *Actor, Producer*
Rigberg-Rugolo Entertainment, 1180 S Beverly Dr #601, Los Angeles, CA 90035 USA

Robinson, Madeleine
63 av. de Chillon, Territet-Veytaux, SWITZERLAN, D1820

Robinson, Mary *President*
Aras an Uachtarain, Phoenix Park, Dublin, 8, IRELAND

Robinson, Nichole *Actor*
Evolution Entertainment, 901 N Highland Ave, Los Angeles, CA 90038 USA

Robinson, Patrick *Fashion Designer*
Ann Klein Co, 11 W 42nd St, #2300, New York, NY 10036 USA

Robinson, Paul Michael
11300 W. Olympic Blvd. #610, Los Angeles, CA 90064-1643

Robinson, Randall
1744 R St .NW, Washington, DC 20009

Robinson, Rich *Musician*
Milch Schneider Organization, 14724 Ventura Blvd, #410, Sherman Oaks, CA 91403 USA

Robinson, Richard D (Dave) *Football Player*
406 S Rose Blvd, Akron, OH 44320 USA

Robinson, Rumeal *Basketball Player*
Detroit Pistons, Palace, 2 Championship Dr, Auburn Hills, MI 48326 USA

Robinson, Shaun *Correspondent*
Access Hollywood, 3000 W Alameda Ave, Trailer E, Burbank, CA 91523 USA

Robinson, Shawna *Race Car Driver*
Performance One, 545C Pitts School Road NW, Concord, NC 28027 USA

Robinson, Smokey *Musician, Songwriter*
Milch Schneider Organization, 14724 Ventura Blvd, #410, Sherman Oaks, CA 91403 USA

Robinson, Stephen K *Astronaut*
2405 Airline Dr, Friendswood, TX 77546 USA

Robinson, T Wayne
PO Box 249, McConnellsburg, PA 17233 USA

Robinson, V Gene *Religious Leader*
Saint Paul's Church, 21 Centre St, Concord, NH 03301 USA

Robinson, Wendy Raquel *Actor*
HWA Talent, 3500 West Olive Avenue, Suite 1400, Burbank, CA 91505

Robinson of Woolwich, John *Religious Leader*
Trinity College, Cambridge, CB2 1TQ, UNITED KINGDOM (UK)

Robinson-Peete, Holly *Actor*
11964 Crest Place, Beverly Hills, CA 90210 USA

Robisch, Dave *Basketball Player*
1401 Guemes Court, Springfield, IL 62702 USA

Robison, Bruce *Songwriter, Musician*
Artists Envoy Agency, 1016 16th Ave S, #101, Nashville, TN 37212 USA

Robison, Charlie *Musician, Songwriter*
Steve Hoiberg Organization, 2021 21st Ave S, #120, Nashville, TN 37212 USA

Robison, Paula *Musician*
Matthew Sprizzo, 477 Durant Ave, Staten Island, NY 10308 USA

Robitaille, Luc *Hockey Player*
13801 Ventura Blvd, Sherman Oaks, CA 91423 USA

Robles, Jorge *Actor*
Televisa, Blvd Adolfo Lopez Mateos 232, Colonia San Angel INN, DF, CP 01060, MEXICO

Robles, Marisa *Musician*
38 Luttrll Ave, London, SW15 6PE, UNITED KINGDOM (UK)

Robles, Mike *Producer*
ICM, 8942 Wilshire Blvd, Beverly Hills, CA 90212

Roboz, Zsuzsi *Artist*
6 Bryanston Court, George St, London, W1H 7HA, UNITED KINGDOM (UK)

Robson, Bryan *Soccer Player*
Middlesbrough FC, Riverside Stadium, Midds, Cleveland, TS3 6RS, UNITED KINGDOM (UK)

Robson, Wade *Dancer*
Creative Artists Agency LCC (CAA-LA), 9830 Wilshire Blvd, Beverly Hills, CA 90212 USA

Robuchon, Joel *Chef*
Societe de Gestion Culinaire, 67 Blvd du Gen M Valin, Paris, 75015, FRANCE

Robustelli, Andrew R (Andy) *Football Player*
30 Spring St, Stamford, CT 06901 USA

Robustelli, Andy
30 Spring St., Stamford, CT 06901

Robyn *Musician*
Lifeline, 73C Saint Charles Square, London, W10 6EJ, UNITED KINGDOM (UK)

Rocard, Michel L L *Prime Minister*
Hotel de Ville, 63 Rue M Berteaux, Conflans-Sainte-Honorine, 78700, FRANCE

Rocca, Constantino *Golfer*
Golf Products International, 5719 Lake Lindero Dr, Agoura Hills, CA 91301 USA

Rocca, Mo *Commentator*
Creative Artists Agency LCC (CAA-LA), 9830 Wilshire Blvd, Beverly Hills, CA 90212 USA

Rocca, Peter *Swimmer*
534 Hazel Ave, San Bruno, CA 94066 USA

Rocco, Alex *Actor*
PO Box 302, Carpinteria, CA 93014 USA

Rocco, Rinaldo *Actor*
Carol Levi Co, Via Giuseppe Pisanelli, Rome, 00196, ITALY

Rocha, Enrique *Actor*
Televisa, Blvd Adolfo Lopez Mateos 232, Colonia San Angel INN, DF, CP 01060, MEXICO

Rocha, Ephraim (Red) *Basketball Player, Coach*
3045 NW Roosevelt Dr, Corvallis, OR 97330 USA

Rochberg, George *Composer*
3500 West Chester Pike, #CH118, Newtown Square, PA 19073 USA

Roche, Anthony D (Tony) *Tennis Player*
5 Kapiti St, Saint Ives, NSW, 2075, AUSTRALIA

Roche, E Kevin *Architect*
Roche Dinkeloo Assoc, 20 Davis St, Hamden, CT 06517 USA

Roche, George A *Financier*
T Rowe Price Assoc, 100 E Pratt St, Baltimore, MD 21202 USA

Roche, James G *Secretary*
Air Force Department, Secretary's Office, Pentagon, Washington, DC 20310 USA

Roche, John *Basketball Player*
6401 E 6th Ave, Denver, CO 80220 USA

Rochefort, Jean *Actor*
Le Chene Rogneaux, Grosvre, 078125, FRANCE

Rochon, Debbie *Actor*
PO Box 1299, New York, NY 10009

Rochon, Lela *Actor*
Gersh Agency, 232 N Canon Dr, Beverly Hills, CA 90210 USA

Rock *Wrestler, Actor*
World Wrestling Entertainment, Titan Towers, 1241 E Main St, Stamford, CT 06902 USA

Rock, Angela *Volleyball Player*
4134 Lymer Dr, San Diego, CA 92116 USA

Rock, Chris *Comedian, Actor*
ML Management Assoc, 1740 Broadway, #1500, New York, NY 10019 USA

Rock, Tony *Comedian*
William Morris Agency (WMA-LA), 1 William Morris Pl, Beverly Hills, CA 90212 USA

Rock, The *Actor*
Baker Winokur Ryder (BWR-LA), 9100 Wilshire Blvd Fl 6, W Tower, Beverly Hills, CA 90212 USA

Rockburne, Dorothea G *Artist*
140 Grand St, New York, NY 10013 USA

Rockefeller, David *Financier*
1 Chase Manhattan Plaza, New York, NY 10005 USA

Rockefeller, Laurance S *Misc*
Rockefeller Bros Fund, 30 Rockefeller Plaza, #5600, New York, NY 10112 USA

Rockefeller, Sharon Percy
1940 Shepherd St NW, Washington, DC 20011

Rocker, John *Baseball Player*
1425 Old Forsyth Road, Macon, GA 31210 USA

Rockers, The
PO Box 3859, Stamford, CT 06905

Rockett, Charles
10100 Santa Monica Blvd. #2500, Los Angeles, CA 90067

Rockett, Rikki *Musician*
H K Mgmt, 9200 W Sunset Blvd, #530, Los Angeles, CA 90069 USA

Rockwell, Martha *Skier, Coach*
Dartmouth College, PO Box 9, Hanover, NH 03755 USA

Rockwell, Robert
18428 Coastline Dr., Malibu, CA 90265

Rockwell, Sam *Actor*
9 Desbrosses St, #200, New York, NY 10013 USA

Rockwood, Marcia *Editor*
Reader's Digest, Editorial Dept, PO Box 100, Pleasantville, NY 10572 USA

Rodan, Jay *Actor*
William Morris Agency (WMA-LA), 1 William Morris Pl, Beverly Hills, CA 90212 USA

Rodd, Marcia *Actor*
11738 Moorpark St, #C, Studio City, CA 91604 USA

Roddam, Franc *Director*
William Morris Agency, 52/53 Poland Place, London, W1F 7LX, UNITED KINGDOM (UK)

Roddick, Andy *Tennis Player*
1499 Las Casas Road, Boca raton, FL 33486 USA

Roderick, Brande *Actor, Model*
Untitled Entertainment (LA), 8436 W 3rd St #650, Los Angeles, CA 90048 USA

Rodgers, Anton
The White House Lower Basildon, Berkshire, ENGLAND

Rodgers, Bill
535 N. Marketplace, Boston, MA 02109

Rodgers, Jimmie
PO Box 685, Forsyth, MO 65653-0685

Rodgers, Michael *Actor*
Anthem Entertainment, 6100 Wilshire Blvd #1170, Los Angeles, CA 90069 USA

Rodgers, Paul *Musician*
Work Hard PR, 19D Pinhold Road, London, SW16 5GD, United Kingdom

Rodin, Judith S *Educator*
35 Hillhouse Ave, New Haven, CT 06511 USA

Rodman, Dennis *Athlete*
Prince Marketing Group, 454 Prospect Avenue, Suite 74, West Orange, NJ 07052

Rodriguez, Adam *Actor*
Magus Entertainment, 9107 Wilshire Blvd #650, Beverly Hills, CA 90210 USA

Rodriguez, Alexander E (Alex) *Baseball Player*
New York Yankees, Yankee Stadium, 161st St & River Ave, Bronx, NY 10451 USA

Rodriguez, Chi Chi *Athlete*
3916 Clock Pointe Trail, #101, Stow, OH 44224

Rodriguez, Freddie *Actor*
Innovative Artists (LA), 1505 Tenth St, Santa Monica, CA 90401 USA

Rodriguez, Freddy *Actor*
Kass & Stokes Management, 9229 Sunset Blvd #504, Los Angeles, CA 90069 USA

Rodriguez, Genesis *Actor*
Select Artists Ltd (CA-Valley Office), PO Box 4359, Burbank, CA 91503 USA

Rodriguez, Ivan (Pudge) *Baseball Player*
Florida Marlins, 2269 Dan Marino Blvd, Miami, FL 33056 USA

Rodriguez, Jai *Television Host*
Queer Eye for the Straight Guy, 119 Braintree St, Boston, MA 02134

Rodriguez, Javier *Actor*
Select Artists Ltd (CA-Valley Office), PO Box 4359, Burbank, CA 91503 USA

Rodriguez, Johnny
PO Box 23162, Nashville, TN 37202

Rodriguez, Jose Luis (El Puma) *Musician*
BMG, 1540 Broadway, New York, NY 10036 USA

Rodriguez, Juan (Chi Chi) *Athlete*
Eddie Elias Enterprises, 3916 Clock Pointe Trail #101, Stow, OH 44224

Rodriguez, Michelle *Actor*
Baker Winokur Ryder (BWR-LA), 9100 Wilshire Blvd Fl 6, W Tower, Beverly Hills, CA 90212 USA

Rodriguez, Paul *Actor*
International Creative Management (ICM-LA), 8942 Wilshire Blvd, Beverly Hills, CA 90211 USA

Rodriguez, Robert *Director, Producer*
International Creative Management (ICM-LA), 8942 Wilshire Blvd, Beverly Hills, CA 90211 USA

Roe, Elwin
204 Wildwood Terr., West Plains, MO 65775

Roe, Tommy
PO Box 26037, Minneapolis, MN 55426

Roebuck, Daniel
1314 Scott Rd., Burbank, CA 91501

Roeg, Nicolas
14 Courtnell St, London, ENGLAND, W2 5BX

Roenicke, Ron *Athlete*
2212 Avenida Las Ramblas, Chino Hills, CA 91709-1362

Roeske, Emily *Actor*
PO Box 10911, Burbank, CA 91510

Roethlisberger, Ben *Football Player*
Pittsburgh Steelers, 3400 S Water St, Pittsburgh, PA 15203 USA

Rogan, Joe *Comedian*
United Talent Agency (UTA), 9560 Wilshire Blvd, Beverly Hills, CA 90212 USA

Rogen, Seth
522 So. Genesee Ave, Los Angeles, CA 90036

Roger, John *Religious Leader*
John Roger Foundation, 2101 Wilshire Blvd, Santa Monica, CA 90403 USA

Rogers, Amerie M M *Musician*
International Creative Management (ICM-NY), 40 W 57th St, New York, NY 10019 USA

Rogers, Bill
353 The Marketplace Faneuil Hall, Boston, MA 02109

Rogers, Jane
1485 S. Beverly Dr. #8, Los Angeles, CA 90035

Rogers, Joy
4141 W. Kling St. #3, Burbank, CA 91505-3309

Rogers, Kenny *Musician*
Kenny Rogers Inc, 2910 Poston Ave, Nashville, TN 37203

Rogers, Melody
2051 Nichols Canyon Rd., Los Angeles, CA 90046

Rogers, Mimi *Actor*
United Talent Agency (UTA), 9560 Wilshire Blvd, Beverly Hills, CA 90212 USA

Rogers, Paul *Actor*
9 Hillside Gardens, London, ENGLAND, N6 5SU, United Kingdom

Rogers, Peter *Producer*
Peter Rogers Productions, 52 Queen Anne St, London, W1M 0LA, UNITED KINGDOM (UK)

Rogers, Reg *Actor*
Brookside Artists Management (LA), 450 N Roxbury Dr Fl 4, Beverly Hills, CA 90210 USA

Rogers, Shorty
PO Box 1711, Bellingham, WA 98227

Rogers, Stephen D (Steve) *Baseball Player*
3746 S Madison Ave, Tulsa, OK 74105 USA

Rogers, Suzanne *Actor*
11266 Canton Dr, Studio City, CA 91604 USA

Rogers, Tristan *Actor*
Don Buchwald, 6500 Wilshire Blvd, #2200, Los Angeles, CA 90048 USA

Rogers, Wayne *Actor*
11828 La Grange Ave, Los Angeles, CA 90025 USA

Rogerson, Kate *Golfer*
Debra Oberg, 42 Nelson St, Harrington Park, NJ 07640 USA

Rogge, Jacques *Misc*
Int'l Olympic Committee, Chateau de Vidy, Lausanne, 1007, SWITZERLAND

Roggin, Fred
3000 W. Alameda Ave., Burbank, CA 91523

Rogin, Gilbert L *Editor*
21 W 10th St, #5A, New York, NY 10011 USA

Rogoff, Ilan *Musician*
Apdo 1098, Palma de Mallorca, 07080, SPAIN

Rogow, Stan *Producer*
International Creative Management (ICM-LA), 8942 Wilshire Blvd, Beverly Hills, CA 90211 USA

Rohde, Bruce *Business Person*
ConAgra Inc, 1 ConAgra Dr, Omaha, NE 68102 USA

Rohde, David *Journalist*
Chrsitian Science Monitor, Editorial Dept, 1 Norway St, Boston, MA 02115 USA

Rohde, Kristen *Actor*
Gersh Agency, The (LA), 232 N Canon Dr, Beverly Hills, CA 90210 USA

Rohini *Actor, Bollywood*
D-1 Ist Floor Anandsree Apartments, 32 Hindi Prachara Saba Street, Chennai, TN 600017, INDIA

Rohlander, Uta *Track Athlete*
Liebigstr 9, Leuna, 06237, GERMANY

Rohm, Elisabeth *Actor*
Brillstein/Grey, 9150 Wilshire Blvd, #350, Beverly Hills, CA 90212 USA

Rohmer, Eric *Director*
Films du Losange, 22 Ave Pierre-de-Serbie, Paris, 75116, FRANCE

Rohner, Clayton
6924 Treasure Trail, Los Angeles, CA 90068

Rohner, Georges *Artist*
Galerie Framond, 3 Rue des Saints Peres, Paris, 75006, FRANCE

Rohr, James E *Financier*
PNC Bank Corp, 1 PNC Plaza, 249 5th Ave, Pittsburgh, PA 15222 USA

Rohrer, Heinrich *Nobel Prize Laureate*
IBM Research Laboratory, Saumerstr 4, Ruschilkon, 8803, SWITZERLAND

Roizman, Bernard *Biologist*
5555 S Everett Ave, Chicago, IL 60637 USA

Roizman, Owen *Cinematographer*
17533 Magnolia Blvd, Encino, CA 91316 USA

Roja *Actor, Bollywood*
8 Saravana Mudali Street, T.Nagar, Chennai, TN 600017, INDIA

Roja *Actor*
12 43rd Street, 6th Avenue Ashok Nagar, Chennai, TN 600 083, INDIA

Rojas, Nydia *Musician*
Silverlight Entertainment, 9171 Wilshire Blvd, #426, Beverly Hills, CA 90210 USA

Rojas, Octavio R (Cookie) *Baseball Player*
19195 Mystic Pointe Dr, #Loop 2, Aventura, FL 33180 USA

Rojcewicz, Susan (Sue) *Basketball Player*
48 Elena Circle, San Rafael, CA 94903 USA

Rojo, Ana Patricia *Actor*
Televisa, Blvd Adolfo Lopez Mateos 232, Colonia San Angel INN, DF, CP 01060, MEXICO

Rojo, Gustavo *Actor*
Televisa, Blvd Adolfo Lopez Mateos 232, Colonia San Angel INN, DF, CP 01060, MEXICO

Roker, Al *Entertainer*
CNBC-TV, 2200 Fletcher Ave, Fort Lee, NJ 07024 USA

Rokk, Marika
Mozartstr. 15, Baden, AUSTRIA, A-2500

Rokke, Ervin J *General*
79 W Church St, Bethlehem, PA 18018 USA

Roland, Ed *Musician, Songwriter*
Spivak Entertainment, 11845 W Olympic Blvd, #1125, Los Angeles, CA 90064 USA

Roland, Johnny E *Football Player, Coach*
8701 S Hardy Dr, Tempe, AZ 85284 USA

Rolandi, Gianna *Opera Singer*
Columbia Artists Mgmt Inc, 165 W 57th
St, New York, NY 10019 USA

Rolen, Scott B *Baseball Player*
638 Dundee Lane, Holmes Beach, FL
34217 USA

Roles-Williams, Barbara *Figure Skater*
3790 Leisure Lane, Las Vegas, NV 89103
USA

Rolfe, Dale
365 Hughson St., Gravenhurst, CANADA,
ON P1P 1G8

Rolfe, Johnson Anthony *Opera Singer*
I C M Artists, 40 W 57th St, New York,
NY 10019 USA

Rollin, Betty *Writer, Commentator*
NS Bienstack Inc, 1740 Broadway, New
York, NY 10019 USA

Rollins, Ed
William Morris Agency (WMA-LA), 1
William Morris Pl, Beverly Hills, CA
90212 USA

Rollins, Henry *Actor*
7615 Hollywood Blvd, Los Angeles, CA
90046 USA

Rollins, Henry *Musician, Songwriter*
Three Artists Mgmt, 14260 Ventura Blvd,
#201, Sherman Oaks, CA 91423 USA

Rollins, James (Jimmy) *Baseball Player*
Philadelphia Phillies, Veterans Stadium,
3501 S Broad, Philadelphia, PA 19148
USA

Rollins, Kenneth (Kenny) *Basketball Player*
Gardens, 220 Hibiscus Way, Parrish, FL
34219 USA

Rollins, Kenny
2370 Bryant Rd, .Lexington, KY 40509

Rollins, Sonny
193 Brighton Ave., Boston, MA 02134

Rollins, Theodore W (Sonny) *Musician,
Composer*
RR 9G, Germantown, NY 12526 USA

Rollins, Wayne (Tree) *Basketball Player,
Coach*
2107 Westover Reserve Blvd,
Windermere, FL 34786 USA

Roloff, Matt
23985 Grossen Rd., Hillsboro, OR 97124

Roloson, Dwayne *Hockey Player*
Minnesota Wild, Xcel Energy Arena, 175
Kellogg Blvd W, Saint Paul, MN 55102
USA

Rolston, Holmes III *Misc*
Colorado State University, Philosophy
Dept, Fort Collins, CO 80523 USA

Rolston, Matthew *Photographer*
Venus Entertainment, 3630 Eastham Dr,
Culver City, CA 90232 USA

Roman, Joseph *Misc*
Glass & Ceramic Workers Union, 556 E
Town St, Columbus, OH 43215 USA

Roman, Lauren
170 Flanders Drakestown Rd., Flanders,
NJ 07036-9736

Roman, Petre *Prime Minister*
Str Gogol 2, Sector 1, Bucharest,
ROMANIA

Roman, Phil
10635 Riverside Dr., Toluca Lake, CA
91602

Roman, Ric
2967 E. 3rd St, Los Angeles, CA 90033

Roman Holiday
Box 475, London, ENGLAND

Romanek, Mark *Director*
Creative Artists Agency LCC (CAA-LA),
9830 Wilshire Blvd, Beverly Hills, CA
90212 USA

Romanenko, Roman Y *Cosmonaut*
Polchta Kosmonavtov, Moskovskoi
Oblasti, Syvisdny Goroduk, 141160,
RUSSIA

Romanenko, Yuri V *Cosmonaut*
Polchta Kosmonavtov, Moskovskoi
Oblasti, Syvisdny Goroduk, 141160,
RUSSIA

Romano, Christy Carlson *Actor*
International Creative Management
(ICM-LA), 8942 Wilshire Blvd, Beverly
Hills, CA 90211 USA

Romano, John *Misc*
212 Valley Road, Merion Station, PA
19066 USA

Romano, Larry *Actor*
Gold Marshak Liedtke, 3500 W Olive
Ave, #1400, Burbank, CA 91505 USA

Romano, Pete *Cinematographer*
HydroFlex Inc, 5335 McConnell Ave, Los
Angeles, CA 90066 USA

Romano, Ray *Actor, Comedian*
Conversation Co, 1044 Northern Blvd,
#304, Roslyn, NY 11576 USA

Romano, Umberto *Artist*
162 E 83rd St, New York, NY 10028 USA

Romanos, John J (Jack) Jr *Publisher*
Pocket Books, 1230 Ave of Americas,
New York, NY 10020 USA

Romanov, Pyotr V *Government Official*
Communist Party, Bolshoy Komsomlsky
Per 8/7, Moscow, 10100, RUSSIA

Romanov, Stephanie *Actor*
Diverse Talent Group, 1875 Century Park
E #2250, Los Angeles, CA 90067 USA

Romanowski, William T (Bill) *Football
Player*
9239 E Star Hill Trail, Lone Tree, CO
80124 USA

Romansky, Monroe J *Doctor*
5600 Wisconsin Ave, Chevy Chase, MD
20815 USA

Romantics, The
1924 Spring St., Paso Robles, CA 93446

Romanus, Richard *Actor*
Chasin Agency, 8899 Beverly Blvd, #716,
Los Angeles, CA 90048 USA

Romario *Soccer Player*
Fluminense FC, Rua Alvaro Chaves 41,
Rio de Janiero, 22231-200, BRAZIL

Romashin, Anatoliy V *Actor*
Vspolny Per 16 Korp 1, #60, Moscow,
103101, RUSSIA

Romelfanger, Charles *Misc*
Pattern Makers League, 4106 34th Ave,
Moline, IL 61265 USA

Romeo, Lil' *Musician*
Lil' Romeo, 8351 Ontario St, Vancouver
BC, V5X 3E8, Canada

Romer, Roy R *Governor*
Los Angeles School District, 333 S
Beaudry Ave, Los Angeles, CA 90017 USA

Romer, Suzanne F C *Prime Minister*
Prime Minister's Office, Willemstad,
Curacao, NETHERLANDS ANTILLES

Romero, Angel *Musician*
Thea Dispeker Artists, 59 E 54th St, New
York, NY 10022 USA

Romero, Celino *Musician*
Columbia Artists Mgmt Inc, 165 W 57th
St, New York, NY 10019 USA

Romero, Danny Jr *Boxer*
800 Salida Sandia SW, Albuquerque, NM
87105 USA

Romero, George
PO Box 5617, Beverly Hills, CA 90210

Romero, Ned *Actor*
19438 Lassen Ave, Northridge, CA 91324
USA

Romero, Pepe *Musician*
Frank Salomon, 201 W 54th St, #1C, New
York, NY 10019 USA

Romero, Richard *Actor*
Select Artists Ltd (CA-Valley Office), PO
Box 4359, Burbank, CA 91503 USA

Romijn-Stamos, Rebecca *Model, Actor*
Three Arts Entertainment, 9460 Wilshire
Blvd, #700, Beverly Hills, CA 90212 USA

Rominger, Kent V *Astronaut*
16211 Elmwood Park Court, Houston, TX
77059 USA

Rommel, Ex-Mayor Manfred
Eduard-Steinle-Str 60, Stuttgart,
GERMANY, D-70619

Romo, Daniela *Actor*
Televisa, Blvd Adolfo Lopez Mateos 232,
Colonia San Angel INN, DF, CP 01060,
MEXICO

Rompre, Robert *Hockey Player*
316 W Maple Ave, Beaver Dam, WI
53916 USA

Ron, Moo-hyun *President*
President's Office, Chong Wa Dae, 1
Sejong-no, Seoul, SOUTH KOREA

Ronaldo *Soccer Player*
Real Madrid FC, Avda Concha Espina 1,
Madrid, 28036, SPAIN

Ronan, William J *Engineer*
525 S Flagler Dr, West Palm Beach, FL
33401 USA

Ronettes, The
855 E. Twain #123411, Las Vegas, NV
89109

Roney, Paul H *Judge*
US Court of Appeals, 100 1st Ave S, Saint
Petersburg, FL 33701 USA

Ronney, Paul D *Astronaut*
613 Ranchito Road, Monrovia, CA 91016
USA

Ronning, Cliff *Hockey Player*
316 Newton Dr, RR 3, Penticton, BC V2A
8Z5, CANADA

Ronningen, Jon *Wrestler*
Mellomasveien 132, Trollasen, 1414,
NORWAY

Rono, Peter *Track Athlete*
Mount Saint Mary's College, Athletic
Dept, Emmitsburg, MD 21727 USA

Ronson, Len
2006 SW Eastwood Ave, Gresham, OR
97060

Ronstadt, Linda *Musician*
Trident Media Group LLC, 41 Madison
Ave Fl 33, New York, NY 10010 USA

Roocroft, Amanda *Opera Singer*
Ingpen & Williams, 26 Wadham Road,
London, SW15 2LR, UNITED KINGDOM
(UK)

Roof, Michael *Actor*
3 Arts Entertainment Inc, 9460 Wilshire
Blvd Fl 7, Beverly Hills, CA 90212 USA

Rook, Susan *Commentator*
Cable News Network, News Dept, 1050
Techwood Dr NW, Atlanta, GA 30318
USA

Rooker, Michael *Actor*
275 S Beverly Hills, #215, Beverly Hills,
CA 90212 USA

Rooney, Andrew A (Andy) *Commentator*
PO Box 48, Rensselaervie, NY 12147 USA

Rooney, Andy *Correspondent*
60 Minutes, 524 W 57th St, New York,
NY 10019 USA

Rooney, Daniel M *Football Executive*
940 N Lincoln Ave, Pittsburgh, PA 15233
USA

Rooney, Jim *Soccer Player*
New England Revolution, CMGI Field, 1
Patriot Place, Foxboro, MA 02035 USA

Rooney, Joe Don *Musician*
LGB Media, 1228 Pineview Lane,
Nashville, TN 37211 USA

Rooney, Kevin *Actor*
Metropolitan Talent Agency (MTA), 4526
Wilshire Blvd, Los Angeles, CA 90010
USA

Rooney, Mickey *Actor*
Ruth Webb, 10580 Des Moines Ave,
Northridge, CA 91326 USA

Rooney, Patrick W *Business Person*
Cooper Tire & Rubber Co, Lima &
Western Ave, Findlay, OH 45840 USA

Roos, Don *Actor, Producer*
Endeavor Agency LLC (LA), 9601 Wilshire
Blvd Fl 3, Beverly Hills, CA 90210 USA

Rooster, The Red
PO Box 3859, Stamford, CT 06905

Root, Bonnie
8383 Wilshire Blvd. #550, Beverly Hills,
CA 90211-2404

Root, Stephen (Steven) *Actor*
Paradigm (LA), 10100 Santa Monica Blvd,
Fl 25, Los Angeles, CA 90067 USA

Roots, Melvin H *Misc*
Plasters & Cement Workers Union, 1125
17th St NW, Washington, DC 20036 USA

Roots, The *Music Group*
William Morris Agency (WMA-LA), 1
William Morris Pl, Beverly Hills, CA
90212 USA

Roper, Dee Dee (Spinderella) *Musician*
Nest Plateau Records, 1650 Broadway,
#1130, New York, NY 10019 USA

Rorem, Ned *Composer, Writer*
PO Box 764, Nantucket, MA 02554 USA

Rorty, Richard M *Misc*
402 Peacock Dr, Charlottesville, VA
22903 USA

Rosa, John *General, Educator*
Superintendent, US Air Force Academy,
Colorado Springs, CO 80840 USA

Rosa, Robi Draco *Musician, Producer,
Composer*
Tanner Mainstain Assoc, 10866 Wilshire
Blvd, #10000, Los Angeles, CA 90024
USA

Rosa, Rosa
6640 Sunset Blvd. #110, Los Angeles, CA
90028

Rosado, Eduardo *Opera Singer*
Calle 3, Ave Cupules 112A Col G
Giberes, Menda, Yucatan, 97070,
MEXICO

Rosamund, John
4 Dean's Yard, London, ENGLAND,
SW1P

Rosand, David *Historian*
560 Riverside Dr, New York, NY 10027
USA

Rosas, Cesar *Musician, Songwriter*
Monterey International, 200 W Superior,
#202, Chicago, IL 60610 USA

Rosato, Genesia *Ballerina*
Royal Ballet, Covent Garden, Bow St,
London, WC2E 9DD, UNITED KINGDOM
(UK)

Rosberg, Keke *Race Car Driver*
7 Rue Gabian, Monte Carlo, 9800,
MONACO

Rosburg, Bob *Golfer*
49425 Avenida Club La Quinta, La
Quinta, CA 92253 USA

Roschkov, Victor *Editor, Cartoonist*
Toronto Star, Editorial Dept, 1 Yonge St,
Toronto, ON M5E 1E5, CANADA

Rose, Axl *Musician, Songwriter*
5055 Latigo Canyon Road, Malibu, CA
90265 USA

Rose, Charles (Charlie) *Commentator*
Rose Communications, 499 Park Ave,
#1500, New York, NY 10022 USA

Rose, Charlie *Television Host*
Rose Communications Inc, 499 Park Ave
Fl 15, New York, NY 10022 USA

Rose, Chris *Television Host*
Best Damned Sports Show Period, The,
10201 W Pico Blvd, Trailer 103, Los
Angeles, CA 90035 USA

Rose, Clarence *Golfer*
405 Walnut Creek Dr, Goldsboro, NC
27534 USA

Rose, Cristine *Actor*
Paradigm Agency, 10100 Santa Monica
Blvd, #2500, Los Angeles, CA 90067 USA

Rose, H Michael *General*
Coldstream Guards, Wellington Barracks,
London, SW1E 6HQ, UNITED KINGDOM
(UK)

Rose, Jalen *Basketball Player*
Toronto Raptors, Air Canada Center, 40
Bay St, Toronto, ON M5J 2N8, CANADA

Rose, Jamie *Actor*
Marshak/Zachary Company, The, 8840
Wilshire Blvd Fl 1, Beverly Hills, CA
90211 USA

Rose, Lee *Director, Producer*
Broder Webb Chervin Silbermann Agency,
The (BWCS), 9242 Beverly Blvd #200,
Beverly Hills, CA 90210 USA

Rose, Marie *Actor*
6916 Chisholm Ave, Van Nuys, CA 91406
USA

Rose, Matthew *Business Person*
Burlington North/Santa Fe, 2650 Lou
Menk Dr, Fort Worth, TX 76131 USA

Rose, Murray *Swimmer*
77 Berry Level 3, North Sydney, NSW,
2060, AUSTRALIA

Rose, Peter E (Pete) *Baseball Player*
8144 W Glades Road, Boca Raton, FL
33434 USA

Rose, Peter H *Business Person*
Krytek Corp, 2 Centennial Dr, Peabody,
MA 01960 USA

Rose, Richard *Scientist*
Bennochy, 1 E Abercromby St,
Helensburgh, Dunbartonshire, G84 7SP,
SCOTLAND

Rose, Sherrie *Actor, Model*
1758 Laurel Canyon Blvd, Los Angeles,
CA 90046 USA

Rose Marie
6916 Chisholm Ave., Van Nuys, CA
91406

Roseau, Maurice E D *Engineer*
144 Bis Ave du General Leclerc, Sceaux,
92330, FRANCE

Roseboro, John
957 Ariole Way, Los Angeles, CA 90077-
2601

Rosegarten, Rory *Producer*
William Morris Agency (WMA-LA), 1
William Morris Pl, Beverly Hills, CA
90212 USA

Roselle, David P *Educator*
47 Kent Way, Newark, DE 19711 USA

Roselli, Jimmy
64 Division Ave., Levittown, NY 11756

Rosellini, Albert D *Governor*
5936 6th Ave S, Seattle, WA 98108 USA

Roseman, Saul *Scientist*
8206 Cranwood Court, Baltimore, MD
21208 USA

Rosemont, Romy *Actor*
Don Buchwald & Associates Inc (LA),
6500 Wilshire Blvd #2200, Los Angeles,
CA 90048 USA

Rosen, Albert (Al) *Conductor*
Corbett Arts Mgmt, 2101 California St, #2,
San Francisco, CA 94115 USA

Rosen, Albert L (Al) *Baseball Player*
15 Mayfair Dr, Rancho Mirage, CA 92270
USA

Rosen, Benjamin M *Business Person*
Compaq Computer, 20555 State Highway
249, Houston, TX 77070 USA

Rosen, Charles W *Musician*
101 W 78th St, New York, NY 10024
USA

Rosen, Harold A *Engineer, Inventor*
Rosen Electrical Equipment, 8226 E
Whittier Blvd, Pico Rivera, CA 90660 USA

Rosen, Milton W *Engineer, Physicist*
5610 Alta Vista Road, Bethesda, MD
20817 USA

Rosen, Nathaniel *Musician*
4555 Henry Hudson Parkway, #1110,
Bronx, NY 10471 USA

Rosenbaum, Edward E *Physicist*
333 NW 23rd St, Potland, OR 97210 USA

Rosenbaum, Michael *Actor*
Tollins/Robbins, 10960 Ventura Blvd,
#200, Studio City, CA 91604 USA

Rosenberg, Alan
PO Box 5617, Beverly Hills, CA 90210

Rosenberg, Howard *Misc*
5859 Larboard Lane, Agoura Hills, CA
91301 USA

Rosenberg, Michael *Producer*
Imagine Entertainment, 9465 Wilshire
Blvd Fl 7, Beverly Hills, CA 90212 USA

Rosenberg, Pierre M *Director*
Musee du Louvre, 34-36 Quai du Louvre,
Paris, 75068, FRANCE

Rosenberg, Scott *Writer*
Creative Artists Agency LCC (CAA-LA),
9830 Wilshire Blvd, Beverly Hills, CA
90212 USA

Rosenberg, Steven A *Doctor*
10104 Iron Gate Road, Potomac, MD
20854 USA

Rosenberg, Stuart *Director*
1984 Coldwater Canyon Dr, Beverly Hills,
CA 90210 USA

Rosenberg, Tina *Writer*
New School for Social Research, World
Policy Institute, New York, NY 10011
USA

Rosenblath, Marshall N *Physicist*
2311 Via Siena, La Jolla, CA 92037 USA

Rosenblatt, Dana *Boxer*
1850 Beacon St, #603, Brookline, MA
02445 USA

Rosenblum, Robert *Educator*
New York University, Fine Arts Dept, New
York, NY 10003 USA

Rosenbluth, Leonard (Lennie) *Basketball
Player*
14654 SW 140th Court, Miami, FL 33186
USA

Rosenburg, Saul A *Doctor*
Stanford University, Oncology Division,
Stanford, CA 94305 USA

Rosendahl, Heidemarie (Heide) *Track
Athlete*
Burscheider Str 426, Leverkusen, 51381,
GERMANY

Rosenfeld, Arnold S *Editor*
Cox Newspapers, PO Box 105720,
Atlanta, GA 30348 USA

Rosenfeld, Isadore *Physicist*
Warner Books, 1271 Ave of Americas,
New York, NY 10020 USA

Rosenfield, John Max *Educator*
75 Coolidge Road, Arlington, MA 02476
USA

Rosenman, Leonard *Composer*
Elizabeth Dworkin, PO Box 248, Bedford
Hills, NY 10507 USA

Rosenmeyer, Grant *Actor*
DreamWorks SKG, 1000 Flower St,
Glendale, CA 91201

Rosenn, Max *Judge*
US Court of Appeals, US Courthouse, 197
S Main St, Wilkes Barre, PA 18701 USA

Rosenquist, James A *Artist*
PO Box 4, 420 Broadway, Aripeka, FL
34679 USA

Rosenstein, Samuel M *Judge*
US Court of International Trade, 2200 S
Ocean Lane, Fort Lauderdale, FL 33316
USA

Rosenthal, Abraham (A M) *Editor, Writer*
New York Times, Editorial Dept, 229 W
43rd St, New York, NY 10036 USA

Rosenthal, Albert J *Attorney General,
Educator*
15 Oak Way, Scarsdale, NY 10583 USA

Rosenthal, David S *Director, Writer*
1801 Century Park E #2160, Los Angeles,
CA 90067

Rosenthal, Jacob (Jack) *Journalist*
New York Times, Editorial Dept, 229 W
43rd St, New York, NY 10036 USA

Rosenthal, Joe *Photographer, Journalist*
15 Curtis Ave, San Rafael, CA 94901 USA

Rosenthal, Mark D *Writer*
Endeavor Agency LLC (LA), 9601 Wilshire
Blvd Fl 3, Beverly Hills, CA 90210 USA

Rosenthal, Philip *Producer*
Creative Artists Agency LCC (CAA-LA),
9830 Wilshire Blvd, Beverly Hills, CA
90212 USA

Rosenthal, Richard L (Rick) *Director,
Producer*
Whitewater Films, 2232 South Cotner
Avenue, Los Angeles, CA 90064 USA

Rosenthal, Robert J *Editor*
Philadelphia Inquirer, Editorial Dept, 400
N Broad St, Philadelphia, PA 19130 USA

Rosenthal, Tony *Artist*
173 E 73rd St, New York, NY 10021 USA

Rosenzweig, Barney *Producer*
2311 Fisher Island Dr, Miami Beach, FL
33109 USA

Rosenzweig, Mark R *Misc*
University of California, Psychology Dept,
Tolman Hall, Berkeley, CA 94720 USA

Rosenzweig, Robert M *Educator*
1462 Dana Ave, Palo Alto, CA 94301
USA

Roses, Allen D *Doctor*
Duke University, Medical Center, Bryan
Research Center, Durham, NC 27706
USA

Rosewall, Ken *Tennis Player*
Turramurra, 111 Pentacost Ave, Sydney,
NSW, 2074, AUSTRALIA

Rosewoman, Michele *Musician*
Abby Hoffer, 223 1/2 E 48th St, New
York, NY 10017 USA

Roshan, Hrithik *Actor, Bollywood*
Filmkraft Mayur, Tilak Road Santa cruz
(W), Mumbai, MS 400054, INDIA

Roshan, Hritik *Actor, Bollywood*
Filmkraft Mayur Tilak Road, Santacruz
(W), Bombay, MS 400 054, INDIA

Roshan, Rakesh *Actor, Bollywood,
Producer, Director*
Kavita 10th Road, JVPD Scheme, Mumbai,
MS 400049, INDIA

Rosi, Francesco
Via Gregoriana 36, Rome, ITALY,
1-00187

Rosin, Walter L *Religious Leader*
Lutheran Church Missouri Synod, 1333 S
Kirkwood Road, Saint Louis, MO 63122
USA

Rosinski, Edward J *Inventor*
2305 Arnold Ave, Yorkville, NY 13495
USA

Roskill of Newtown, Eustace W *Judge*
New Court, Temple, London, EC4,
UNITED KINGDOM (UK)

Rosman, Mackenzie *Actor*
7th Heaven, 5700 Wilshire Blvd #575,
Los Angeles, CA 90036 USA

Rosner, Robert *Astronomer*
4950 S Greenwood Ave, Chicago, IL
60615 USA

Rosnes, Renee *Musician*
Integrity Talent, PO Box 961, Burlington,
MA 01803 USA

Ross, Al *Cartoonist*
2185 Bolton St, Bronx, NY 10462 USA

Ross, Annie *Actor*
Artists Group (LA), 10100 Santa Monica
Blvd #2490, Los Angeles, CA 90067 USA

Ross, Ben *Director*
United Talent Agency, 9560 Wilshire
Blvd, #500, Beverly Hills, CA 90212 USA

Ross, Betsy *Sportscaster*
ESPN-TV, Sports Dept, ESPN Plaza 935
Middle St, Bristol, CT 06010 USA

Ross, Brian *Correspondent*
20/20, 147 Columbus Ave, New York, NY
10023, US

Ross, Charlotte *Actor*
Abrams Artists, 9200 Sunset Blvd, #1125,
Los Angeles, CA 90069 USA

Ross, Daniel R (Dan) *Football Player*
10 Manasquan Circle, Londonderry, NH
03053 USA

Ross, David A *Director*
Whitney Museum of American Art, 945
Madison Ave, New York, NY 10021 USA

Ross, Diana *Musician, Actor*
PO Box 11059, Glenville Station,
Greenwich, CT 06831 USA

Ross, Don *Athlete*
PO Box 981, Venice, CA 90294 USA

Ross, Donald R *Judge*
US Court of Appeals, Federal Building, PO Box 307, Omaha, NE 68101 USA

Ross, Douglas T *Scientist*
Softech Inc, 2 Highwood Dr, #200, Tewksbury, MA 01876 USA

Ross, Fairbanks Anne *Swimmer*
10 Grandview Ave, Troy, NY 12180 USA

Ross, Gary *Director*
Creative Artists Agency, 9830 Wilshire Blvd, Beverly Hills, CA 90212 USA

Ross, Herbert
8383 Wilshire Blvd. #550, Beverly Hills, CA 90211

Ross, Ian M *Engineer*
5 Blackpoint Road, Horsehoe, Rumson, NJ 07760 USA

Ross, Jeffrey (Jeff) *Actor*
Creative Artists Agency LCC (CAA-LA), 9830 Wilshire Blvd, Beverly Hills, CA 90212 USA

Ross, Jerry L *Astronaut*
NASA, Johnson Space Center, 2101 NASA Road, Houston, TX 77058 USA

Ross, Jim *Wrestler*
19 Juhasz Rd, Norwalk, CT 06854

Ross, Jimmy D *General*
4981 Maple Glen Road, Lake Forest, FL 32771 USA

Ross, John *Misc*
738 Mayfield Ave, Palo ALto, CA 94305 USA

Ross, Jonathan
34/42 Cleveland St., London, ENGLAND, W1P 5SB

Ross, Karie *Sportscaster*
ESPN-TV, Sports Dept, ESPN Plaza 935 Middle St, Bristol, CT 06010 USA

Ross, Katharine
33050 Pacific Coast Hwy, Malibu, CA 90265

Ross, Katherine *Actor*
33050 Pacific Coast Highway, Malibu, CA 90265 USA

Ross, Marion *Actor*
21755 Ventura Blvd, PO Box 144, Woodland Hills, CA 91365 USA

Ross, Robert J (Bobby) *Football Coach*
US Millitary Academy, Athletic Dept, West Point, NY 10996 USA

Ross, Stan
1410 N. Gardner, Los Angeles, CA 90046

Ross, Tracee Ellis *Actor*
Rogers & Cowan PR, 1888 Century Park E #500, Los Angeles, CA 90067 USA

Ross, Yolanda *Actor*
RK Talent Management Group, 235 Park Avenue South, 10th Floor, New York, NY 10003 USA

Rossdale, Gavin
10900 Wilshire Blvd. #1230, Los Angeles, CA 90024

Rosselli, Jimmy
344 Paterson Plank Rd, Jersey City, NJ 07307

Rossellini, Isabella *Actor*
Untitled Entertainment (NY), 23 E 22nd St Fl 3, New York, NY 10010 USA

Rossen, Carol
1119 23rd St. #8, Santa Monica, CA 90403

Rossi, Tony (Ray) *Actor*
Wallis Agency, 4444 Riverside Dr #105, Burbank, CA 91505 USA

Rossio, Terry *Writer*
Creative Artists Agency LCC (CAA-LA), 9830 Wilshire Blvd, Beverly Hills, CA 90212 USA

Rossovich, Rick
PO Box 5617, Beverly Hills, CA 90210

Rossum, Emmy *Actor*
Essential Talent Management, 6399 Wilshire Blvd #400, Los Angeles, CA 90048 USA

Rostenkowski, Dan *Politician*
1372 W. Evergreen St., Chicago, IL 60622

Rostow, Walt
1 Wildwind Point, Austin, TX 78746

Rote, Kyle
24700 Deepwater Pt. Dr. #14, St. Michaels, MD 21663

Rote, Tobin
7590 Lighthouse Rd, Port Hope, MI 48468-9760

Rote Jr, Kyle
6075 Poplar Ave #920, Memphis, TN 38119-4717 USA

Roth, Andrea
4526 Wilshire Blvd., Los Angeles, CA 90010

Roth, David Lee *Musician*
International Creative Management (ICM-LA), 8942 Wilshire Blvd, Beverly Hills, CA 90211 USA

Roth, Eli *Writer, Producer*
3 Arts Entertainment Inc, 9460 Wilshire Blvd Fl 7, Beverly Hills, CA 90212 USA

Roth, Matt
PO Box 5617, Beverly Hills, CA 90210

Roth, Tim *Actor*
Polaris PR, 8135 West 4th Street, 2 Floor, Los Angeles, CA 90048 USA

Rothenberger, Anneliese *Opera Singer*
Quellenhof, Salenstein, TG, 8268, SWITZERLAND

Rothery, Teryl *Actor*
Twenty First Century Artists, 501 - 825 Granville St, Vancouver BC, V6Z 1K9, CANADA

Rothman, John
9229 Sunset Blvd. #710, Los Angeles, CA 90069

Rothrock, Cynthia
20670 Callon Drive, Topanga, CA 90290-3712

Rotunno, Giuseppe
Via Crescenzio 58, Rome, ITALY, 00193

Rouillard, Richard
11750 Sunset Blvd. #117, Los Angeles, CA 90049

Roundtree, Richard *Actor*
Kohner Agency, The, 9300 Wilshire Blvd #555, Beverly Hills, CA 90212 USA

Rourke, Jack
PO Box 1706, Burbank, CA 91507

Rourke, Mickey (Marielito) *Actor*
International Creative Management (ICM-LA), 8942 Wilshire Blvd, Beverly Hills, CA 90211 USA

Rouse, Irving *Misc*
12 RIdgewood Terrace, North Haven, CT 06473 USA

Rouse, Jeff
302 Gerber Dr., Fredericksburg, VA 22408

Rouse, Jeffrey (Jeff) *Swimmer*
302 Gerber Dr, Fredericksburg, VA 22408 USA

Rouse, Mitch *Actor*
Three Arts Entertainment, 9460 Wilshire Blvd, #700, Beverly Hills, CA 90212 USA

Rousellot, John
2111 Wilson Blvd. #850, Arlington, VA 22201

Roush, Jack *Misc*
Roush Racing, 122 Knob Hill Road, Mooresville, NC 28115 USA

Roussell, Thierry
Villa Crystal, St. Moritz, SWITZERLAND, CH-7500

Rousselot, Philippe *Cinematographer*
Gersh Agency, 232 N Canon Dr, Beverly Hills, CA 90210 USA

Rousset, Christophe *Musician*
Trawick Artists, 1926 Broadway, New York, NY 10023 USA

Roustabouts, The
PO Box 25371, Charlotte, NC 28212

Routledge, Alison *Actor*
Marmont Mgmt, Langham House, 302/8 Regent St, London, W1R 5AL, UNITED KINGDOM (UK)

Routledge, Patricia *Actor*
Marmont Mgmt, Langham House, 302/8 Regent St, London, W1R 5AL, UNITED KINGDOM (UK)

Roux, Albert H *Chef*
Le Gavroche, 43 Upper Brook St, London, W1Y 1PF, UNITED KINGDOM (UK)

Roux, Jean-Louis *Director, Actor*
4145 Blueridge Crescent, #2, Montreal, QC, H3H 1S7, CANADA

Roux, Michel A *Chef*
Waterside Inn, Ferry Road, Bray, Berks, SL6 2AT, UNITED KINGDOM (UK)

Rove, Karl *Government Official*
White House, 1600 Pennsylvania Ave NW, Washington, DC USA

Rovick, Sheriff John
3531 Clifton Pl., Glendale, CA 91206

Rowan, Carl T
3116 Fessenden St NW, Washington, DC 20008 USA

Rowan, Kelly
Levine Management, 9028 W Sunset Blvd #PH1, Los Angeles, CA 90069 USA

Rowden, William H *Admiral*
55 Pinewood Court, Lancaster, VA 22503 USA

Rowe, Alan
8 Sherwood Close, London, ENGLAND, SW13

Rowe, Brad *Actor*
1327 Brinkley Ave, Los Angeles, CA 90049 USA

Rowe, Jack *Writer*
Pocket Books, 1230 Ave of Americas, New York, NY 10020 USA

Rowe, John W *Business Person*
Unicom Corp, 10 S Dearborn St, Chicago, IL 60603 USA

Rowe, John W *Business Person*
Aetna Inc, 151 Farmington Ave, Hartford, CT 06156 USA

Rowe, Maggie *Comedian*
International Creative Management (ICM-LA), 8942 Wilshire Blvd, Beverly Hills, CA 90211 USA

Rowe, Misty *Actor*
2193 River Road, Egg Harbor Cay, NJ 08215 USA

Rowe, Nicolas
52 Shaftesbury Ave, London, ENGLAND, WIV 7DE

Rowe, Red
79 Margarita, Camarillo Springs, CA 93010

Rowe, Sandra M *Editor*
Portland Oregonian, Editorial Dept, 1320 SW Broadway, Portland, OR 97201 USA

Rowe-Jackson, Debbie
435 N. Roxbury Dr., Beverly Hills, CA 90210

Rowell, Victoria *Actor*
Third Hill Entertainment, 195 S Beverly Dr #400, Beverly Hills, CA 90212

Rowland, Betty *Dancer*
125 N Barrington Ave, #103, Los Angeles, CA 90049 USA

Rowland, Dave
PO Box 121089, Nashville, TN 37212

Rowland, F Sherwood *Nobel Prize Laureate*
4807 Dorchester Road, Corona del Mar, CA 92625 USA

Rowland, J David *Business Person*
National Westminster Bank, 41 Lothbury, London, EC2P 2BP, UNITED KINGDOM (UK)

Rowland, James A *General*
17 Pindari Ave, Mosman, NSW, 2088, AUSTRALIA

Rowland, John W *Misc*
Amalgamated Transit Union, 5025 Wisconsin Ave NW, Washington, DC 20016 USA

Rowland, Kelly *Musician*
Creative Artists Agency, 9830 Wilshire Blvd, Beverly Hills, CA 90212 USA

Rowland, Landon H *Business Person*
Kansas City Southern, PO Box 219335, Kansas City, MO 64121 USA

Rowland, Rodney *Actor, Model*
Booh Schut, 11350 Ventura Blvd, #206, Studio City, CA 91604 USA

Rowlands, Gena *Actor*
7917 Woodrow Wilson Dr, Los Angeles, CA 90046 USA

Rowlands, Patsy
265 Liverpool Rd., London, ENGLAND, N1 1LX

Rowlands, Sherry
5055 Seminary Rd, Alexandria, VA 22311

Rowley, Cynthia *Fashion Designer*
498 Fashion Ave, New York, NY 10018 USA

Rowley, Janet D *Physicist*
5310 S University Ave, Chicago, IL 60615 USA

Rowling, J K *Writer*
Scholastic Entertainment, 557 Broadway, New York, NY 10012 USA

Rowling, J K (Jo) *Writer*
Levine/Scolastic Press, 55 Broadway, New York, NY 10012 USA

Rowlinson, John S *Misc*
12 Pullens Field, Headington, OX3 0BU, UNITED KINGDOM (UK)

Rowny, Edward L *General*
2700 Calvert St NW, #813, Washington, DC 20008 USA

Roxburgh, Richard *Actor, Music Group*
Shanahan Mgmt, PO Box 1509, Darlinghurst, NSW, 1300, AUSTRALIA

Roxton, Steve
6 Thornton Rd. Leytonstone, London, ENGLAND, E11

Roy *Misc*
Beyond Belief, 1639 N Valley Dr, Las Vegas, NV 89108 USA

Roy, Arundhati *Writer*
Random House, 1745 Broadway, #B1, New York, NY 10019 USA

Roy, James D *Financier*
Federal Hone Loan Bank, 601 Grant St, Pittsburgh, PA 15219 USA

Roy, John *Comedian*
Metropolitan Talent Agency (MTA), 4526 Wilshire Blvd, Los Angeles, CA 90010 USA

Roy, Patrick *Hockey Player*
5340 S Race Court, Greenwood Village, CO 80121 USA

Roy, Reena *Actor, Bollywood*
Pam Villa D'Monte Park Road, Bandra, Bombay, MS 400 050, INDIA

Royal, Billy Joe *Musician, Songwriter*
304 Somerset Way, Newport, NC 28570 USA

Royal, Darrell K *Football Player, Football Coach*
3752 Crestone Dr, Loveland, CO 80537 USA

Royce, Kenneth
3 Abbott's Close Andover, Hants., ENGLAND, SP11 7NP

Royce, Mike *Comedian*
United Talent Agency (UTA), 9560 Wilshire Blvd, Beverly Hills, CA 90212 USA

Roylance, Pamela
221 S. Gale Dr. #403, Beverly Hills, CA 90211

Royo, Sanchez Aristides *President*
Morgan & Morgan, PO Box 1824, Panama City, 1, PANAMA

Royster, Jeron K (Jerry) *Baseball Player*
1 Brewers Way, Milwaukee, WI 53214 USA

Rozanov, Evgeny G *Architect*
Int'l Architecture Academy, Bolshara Dmitrovka 24, Moscow, 103284, RUSSIA

Rozelle, Pete
PO Box 9686, Rancho Santa Fe, 92067

Rozhdestvensky, Gennady N
Victor Hochhauser Ltd, 4 Oak Hill Way, London, NW3, UNITED KINGDOM (UK)

Rozhdestvensky, Valery I *Cosmonaut*
Potchta Kosmonavtov, Moskovskoi Oblasti, Syvisdny Goroduk, 141160, RUSSIA

Rozier, Clifford *Basketball Player*
Toronto Raptors, Air Canada Center, 40 Bay St, Toronto, ON M5J 2N8, CANADA

Rozier, Mike *Football Player*
9 Hidden Hollow Lane, Sicklerville, NJ 08081 USA

Rubalcaba, Gonzalo *Musician*
Eardrums Music, 5930 NW 201st St, Miami, FL 33105 USA

Rubbia, Carlo *Nobel Prize Laureate*
CERN, Particle Physics Laboratory, Geneva 23, 1211, SWITZERLAND

Ruben, Joseph P (Joe) *Director*
250 W 57th St, #1905, New York, NY 10107 USA

Rubens, Bernice
16A Belsize Park Gardens, London, ENGLAND, NW3 4LD

Rubenstein, Ann *Commentator*
NBC-TV, News Dept, 30 Rockefeller Plaza, New York, NY 10112 USA

Rubenstein, David *Business Person*
Carlyle Group, 1001 Pennsylvania Ave NW, Washington, DC 20004 USA

Rubenstein, Edward *Physicist*
Stanford University Medical School, Surgery Dept, Stanford, CA 94305 USA

Rubiano, Saenz Pedro Cardinal *Religious Leader*
Arzubispado, Carrera 7A N 10-20, Santafe de Bogota, DC 1, COLOMBIA

Rubik, Erno *Inventor*
Rublik Erno, Varosmajor Utca 74, Budapest, 1122, HUNGARY

Rubin, Amy *Actor*
Hervey/Grimes, PO Box 64249, Los Angeles, CA 90064 USA

Rubin, Benjamin A *Inventor*
1329 173rd St, Hazel Crest, IL 60429 USA

Rubin, Chanda
708 So. St. Antoine St., Lafayette, LA 70501

Rubin, Chandra *Tennis Player*
708 S Saint Antoine St, Lafayette, LA 70501 USA

Rubin, Ellis *Lawyer*
4141 NE 2nd Ave, #203A, Miami, FL 33137 USA

Rubin, Gloria *Actor*
International Creative Management (ICM-LA), 8942 Wilshire Blvd, Beverly Hills, CA 90211 USA

Rubin, Harry *Biologist*
University of California, Molecular
Biology Dept, Berkeley, CA 94720 USA

Rubin, Jennifer
3200 Bonnie Hill Dr., Los Angeles, CA
90068

Rubin, Leigh *Cartoonist*
Creators Syndicate, 5777 W Century Blvd,
#700, Los Angeles, CA 90045 USA

Rubin, Louis D Jr *Writer*
702 Ginghoul Road, Chapel Hill, NC
27514 USA

Rubin, Robert *Misc*
Massachusetts General Hospital, 32 Fruit
St, Boston, MA 02114 USA

Rubin, Robert E *Secretary, Financier*
Citigroup Inc, 399 Park Ave, New York,
NY 10022 USA

Rubin, Stephen E *Publisher*
Doubleday Co, 1540 Broadway, New
York, NY 10036 USA

Rubin, Theodore I *Misc*
219 E 62nd St, New York, NY 10021 USA

Rubin, Vanessa *Musician*
Joel Chriss, 300 Mercer St, #3J, New York,
NY 10003 USA

Rubin, Vera C *Astronomer*
Carnegie Institution, 5241 Broad Branch
Road NW, Washington, DC 20015 USA

Rubin, William *Misc*
Museum of Modern Art, 11 W 53rd St,
New York, NY 10019 USA

Rubin-Vega, Daphne *Actor*
300 Park Ave S, #300, New York, NY
10010 USA

Rubinek, Saul *Actor*
Gersh Agency, 232 North Canon Dr,
Beverly Hills, CA 90210 USA

Rubini, Cesare *Coach*
Federazione Italian Pallacanestro, Via
Fogliano 15, Rome, 00199, ITALY

Rubino, Frank A *Lawyer*
2601 S Bayshore Dr, Miami, FL 33133
USA

Rubinoff, Ira *Biologist*
Smithsonian Tropical Research Institute,
Unit 0848, APO, AA, 34002 USA

Rubinoff, Marla *Actor*
Commercial Talent, 9255 Sunset Blvd,
Suite 505, West Hollywood, CA 90069
USA

Rubinstein, John *Actor*
4417 Leydon Ave, Woodland Hills, CA
91364 USA

Rubinstein, Zeida *Actor*
The Agency, 1800 Ave of Stars, #400, Los
Angeles, CA 90067 USA

Rubinstein, Zelda
8730 Sunset Blvd. #270, Los Angeles, CA
90069

Rubio, Maria
2238Blvd. Adolfo Lopez Mateo 5
Placopac San Angel, Mexico DF,
MEXICO, 01040

Rubio, Paulina *Musician*
Universal Records, 825 8th Avenue, New
York, NY 10019 USA

Ruby & The Romantics
1650 Broadway #508, New York, NY
10119-6833

Ruccolo, Richard *Actor*
ER Talent, 301 W 53rd St, #4K, New
York, NY 10019 USA

Ruch, Charles *Educator*
Boise State University, President's Office,
Boise, ID 83725 USA

Rucinsky, Martin *Hockey Player*
Vancouver Canucks, 800 Griffiths Way,
Vancouver, BC V6B 6G1, CANADA

Ruck, Alan *Actor*
Innovative Artists, 1505 10th St, Santa
Monica, CA 90401 USA

Ruckelshaus, William D *Business Person,*
Government Official
PO Box 76, Median, WA 98039 USA

Ruckenstein, Eli *Engineer*
94 North Dr, Buffalo, NY 14226 USA

Rucker, Anja *Track Athlete*
TUS Jena, Wollnitzer Str 42, Jena, 07749,
GERMANY

Rucker, Darius *Musician*
FishCo Mgmt, PO Box 5656, Columbia,
SC 29250 USA

Rucker, Reginald J (Reggie) *Football*
Player
3128 Richmond Road, Beachwood, OH
44122 USA

Rudbottom, Roy R Jr *Diplomat*
7831 Park Lane, #213A, Dallas, TX 75225
USA

Rudd, Paul *Actor*
9465 Wilshire Blvd, #517, Beverly Hills,
CA 90212 USA

Rudd, Ricky *Race Car Driver*
124 Summerville Dr, Mooresville, NC
28115 USA

Ruddle, Francis H *Biologist*
Yale University, Biology Dept, New
Heaven, CT 06511 USA

Ruddock, Donovan (Razor) *Boxer*
7379 NW 34th St, Lauderhill, FL 33319
USA

Ruddy, Al
1601 Clearview Dr., Beverly Hills, CA
90210

Rudel, Julius
101 Central Park West, #11A, New York,
NY 10023 USA

Rudenstine, Neil L *Educator*
41 Armour Road, Princeton, NJ 08540
USA

Ruder, David S *Government Official,*
Educator
Baker & McKenzie, 1 Prudential Plaza,
130 E Randolph Dr, Chicago, IL 60601
USA

Rudi, Joseph O (Joe) *Baseball Player*
17667 Deer Park Loop, Baker City, OR
97814 USA

Rudie, Evelyn *Actor*
Santa Monica Playhouse, 7514
Hollywood Blvd, Los Angeles, CA 90046
USA

Rudin, Scott *Producer, Filmmaker*
Scott Rudin Productions, 120 W 45th St,
New York, NY 10036 USA

Rudman, Warren *Ex-Senator*
1615 L St NW #1300, Washington, DC
20036-5626 USA

Rudman, Warren B *Senator*
327 10th St SE, Washington, DC 20003
USA

Rudner, Rita *Actor, Comedian*
2877 Paradise Road, #1605, Los Angeles,
CA 89109 USA

Rudnick, Paul *Writer*
Creative Artists Agency, 9830 Wilshire
Blvd, Beverly Hills, CA 90212 USA

Rudoff, Sheldon *Religious Leader*
Union of Orthodox Jewish Congregations,
333 7th Ave, New York, NY 10001 USA

Rudolph, Alan
15760 Ventura Blvd. #16, Encino, CA
91436

Rudolph, Alan S *Director*
International Creative Mgmt, 8942
Wilshire Blvd, #219, Beverly Hills, CA
90211 USA

Rudolph, Donald E *War Hero*
33799 Shamrock Dr, Bovey, MN 55709
USA

Rudolph, Frederick *Historian*
234 Ide Road, Williamstown, MA 01267
USA

Rudolph, Larry *Producer*
ReignDeer Entertainment, 432 Park Ave S
Fl 2, New York, NY 10016 USA

Rudolph, Maya *Actor*
United Talent Agency (UTA), 9560
Wilshire Blvd, Beverly Hills, CA 90212
USA

Rudometkin, John *Basketball Player*
6181 Wise Road, Newcastle, CA 95658
USA

Rudzinski, Witold *Composer*
Ul Narbutta 50 m 6, Warsaw, 02-541,
POLAND

Rue, Sara *Actor*
Innovative Artists, 1505 10th St, Santa
Monica, CA 90401 USA

Ruehe, Volker *Government Official*
Bundesministerium Der Verteidigunj,
Hardthoehe, Honn, 53125, GERMANY

Ruehl, Mercedes *Actor*
United Talent Agency, 9560 Wilshire
Blvd, #500, Beverly Hills, CA 90212 USA

Ruelas, Gabriel (Gabe) *Boxer*
1242 S Tremaine Ave, Los Angeles, CA
90019 USA

Ruelle, David P *Mathematician*
1 Ave Charles-Cormar, Bures-sur-Yvette,
91440, FRANCE

Ruether, Rosemary R *Misc*
530 Mayflower Road, Claremont, CA
91711 USA

Ruettgers, Ken *Football Player*
69550 Deer Ridge Road, Sisters, OR
97759 USA

Ruettgers, Michael C *Business Person*
ECM Corp, 35 Parkway Dr, Hopkinton,
MA 01748 USA

Ruff, Howard J *Economist, Writer*
PO Box 441, Orem, UT 84059 USA

Ruff, Lindy *Hockey Player, Coach*
4980 Shadow Rock Lane, Clarence, NY
14031 USA

Ruffalo, Mark *Actor*
William Morris Agency, 151 El Camino
Dr, Beverly Hills, CA 90212 USA

Ruffin, Jimmy
. 102 Ryder's Lane, East Brunswick, NJ
08816

Ruffini, Attilio *Government Official*
Camera dei Deputati, Via della Missione
10, Rome, 00187, ITALY

Ruffo, Victoria *Actor*
Televisa, Blvd Adolfo Lopez Mateos 232,
Colonia San Angel INN, DF, CP 01060,
MEXICO

Rufus
7250 Beverly Blvd. #200, Los Angeles, CA
90036

Ruge, John A *Cartoonist*
240 Nronxville Road, #B4, Bronxville, NY
10708 USA

Rugolo, Pete
3955 Pacheco Dr, Sherman Oaks, CA
91403

Ruivivar, Anthony Michael *Actor*
Gersh Agency, The (LA), 232 N Canon Dr,
Beverly Hills, CA 90210 USA

Ruiz, Jose Carlos *Actor*
Televisa, Blvd Adolfo Lopez Mateos 232,
Colonia San Angel INN, DF, CP 01060,
MEXICO

Ruiz, Mark
201 S. Capitol Ave. #430, Indianapolis, IN
46225

Ruiz, Rodrigo *Actor*
Televisa, Blvd Adolfo Lopez Mateos 232,
Colonia San Angel INN, DF, CP 01060,
MEXICO

Rulli, Sebastian *Actor*
Gabriel Blanco Iglesias (Mexico), Rio
Balsas 35-32, Colonia Cuauhtemoc, DF,
06500, Mexico

Rumsfeld, Donald *Business Person*
Defense Department, Pentagon,
Washington, DC 20301 USA

Run D M C *Music Group*
250 W 57th St #821, New York, NY
10107, US

Rundgren, Todd *Musician*
Paradise Artists, PO Box 1821, Ojai, CA
93024 USA

Runrig
55 Wellington St., Aberdeen, SCOTLAND,
AB2 1BX

Runyan, Marla
PO Box 120, Indianapolis, IN 46206-0120

Runyon, Jennifer *Actor*
5922 SW Amberwood Ave, Corvalis, OR
97333 USA

RuPaul
1501 Broadway #1301, New York, NY
10036

Rupp, Debra Jo *Actor*
Stephen Hanks Management, 252 North
Larchmont Blvd, Suite 200, Los Angeles,
CA 90004 USA

Ruprecht, Tom *Writer*
3 Arts Entertainment Inc, 9460 Wilshire
Blvd Fl 7, Beverly Hills, CA 90212 USA

Rush *Music Group*
Artist Group International (NY), 150 East
58th Street, Fl 19, New York, NY 10155
USA

Rush, Barbara *Actor*
1709 Tropical Avenue, Beverly Hills, CA
90210 USA

Rush, Deborah
PO Box 5617, Beverly Hills, CA 90210

Rush, Geoffrey *Actor*
Creative Artists Agency LCC (CAA-LA),
9830 Wilshire Blvd, Beverly Hills, CA
90212 USA

Rush, Jennifer
145 Central Park W, New York, NY
10023

Rush, Rudy *Comedian*
International Creative Management
(ICM-LA), 8942 Wilshire Blvd, Beverly
Hills, CA 90211 USA

Rush, Sarah *Actor*
Acme Talent & Literary Agency (LA), 4727
Wilshire Blvd #333, Los Angeles, CA
90010 USA

Rush, Tom *Musician*
Maple Hill Productions Inc, PO Box 1570,
Wilson, WY 83014-1570 USA

Rushdie, A Salman *Writer*
Wylie Agency, 42 Knightsbridge, London,
SW1S 7JR, UNITED KINGDOM (UK)

Rushen, Patrice
PO Box 6278, Altadena, CA 91003

Rusler, Robert
112 S. Almont Dr., Los Angeles, CA
90048

Russ, Tim
8436 W. Third St. #740, Los Angeles, CA
90048-4100

Russ, William
2973 Passmore Dr., Los Angeles, CA
90068

Russek, David *Actor*
Koenigsberg Management/ AsIS
Productions, 200 North Larchmont Blvd,
Suite 2, Hollywood, CA 90004 USA

Russell, Betsy
13926 Magnolia Blvd, Sherman Oaks, CA
91423-1230

Russell, Bill *Basketball Player*
1641 Santa Rosa Ave, Glendale, CA
91208 USA

Russell, Bing
229 E. Gainsborough Rd., Thousand
Oaks, CA 91360

Russell, Brenda
9000 Sunset Blvd. #1200, Los Angeles,
CA 90069

Russell, David O *Writer, Director, Actor,
Producer*
Endeavor Agency LLC (LA), 9601 Wilshire
Blvd Fl 3, Beverly Hills, CA 90210 USA

Russell, Eric *Actor*

Russell, Jane *Actor*
2340 Ridgemark Dr, Santa Maria, CA
93455-1518 USA

Russell, Johnny
Box Drawer 37, Hendersonville, TN
37077

Russell, Ken
7 Bellmount Wood Lane Warford, Herts.,
ENGLAND

Russell, Keri *Actor*
Burstein Company, The, 15304 Sunset
Blvd #208, Pacific Palisades, CA 90272
USA

Russell, Kimberly
11617 Laurelwood Dr, Studio City, CA
91604-3818

Russell, Kurt *Actor, Producer*
Cosmic Entertainment, 9255 Sunset Blvd
#1010, Los Angeles, CA 90069

Russell, Leon
PO Box 24455, New Orleans, LA 70184

Russell, Mark
3201 33rd Pl .NW, Washington, DC
20008

Russell, Nipsey
1650 Broadway #1410, New York, NY
10019

Russell, Ragina *Actor*
Don Gerler Agency, 3349 Cahuenga Blvd
W #1, Los Angeles, CA 90068 USA

Russell, T E
8271 Melrose Ave #110, Los Angeles, CA
90046 USA

Russell, Theresa *Actor*
Untitled Entertainment (LA), 8436 W 3rd
St #650, Los Angeles, CA 90048 USA

Russert, Tim *Television Host*
CNBC (DC), 1025 Connecticut Ave NW
#800, Washington, DC 20036 USA

Russi, Bernhard
6490 Andermatt, SWITZERLAND

Russo, Anthony *Writer, Director, Producer*
United Talent Agency (UTA), 9560
Wilshire Blvd, Beverly Hills, CA 90212
USA

Russo, James
8306 Wilshire Blvd. #438, Beverly Hills,
CA 90211-2304

Russo, Joe *Writer, Director, Producer*
United Talent Agency (UTA), 9560
Wilshire Blvd, Beverly Hills, CA 90212
USA

Russo, John
218 Euclid Ave., Glassport, PA 15045-
1331

Russo, Patricia *Business Person*
Lucent Technologies Inc, 600 Mountain
Ave, New Providence, NJ 07974 USA

Russo, Rene *Actor, Model*
253A 26th St, #199, Santa Monica, CA
90401 USA

Russo, Richard *Writer*
Vintage Press, 1111 Rancho Conejo Blvd,
Newbury Park, CA 91320 USA

Rutan, Elbert L (Burt) *Designer*
14329 Rutan Road, Mojave, CA 93501
USA

Rutan, Richard G (Dick) *Designer*
2833 Delmar Ave, Mojave, CA 93501
USA

Ruth, Lauren *Cartoonist*
PO Box 200206, New Heaven, CT 06520
USA

Ruth, Mike *Football Player*
85 Jenkins Road, Andover, MA 01810
USA

Rutherford, Ann *Actor*
PO Box 5028, Westlake Village, CA
91359 USA

Rutherford, John S (Johnny) III *Race Car
Driver*
4819 Black Oak Lane, River Oaks, TX
76114 USA

Rutherford, Johnny *Race Car Driver*
4919 Black Oak Ln, Ft. Worth, TX 76114

Rutherford, Kelly *Actor*
PO Box 1380, Beverly Hills, CA 90213
USA

Rutherford, Mike *Musician*
Solo Agency, 55 Fulham High St, London,
SW6 3JJ, UNITED KINGDOM (UK)

Rutigliano, Sam *Football Coach*
Liberty University, Athletic Dept,
Lynchburg, VA 24506 USA

Rutledge, Jeffrey R (Jeff) *Football Player,
Football Coach*
Vanderbilt University, Athletic Dept,
Nashville, TN 37240 USA

Rutschman, Adolph (Ad) *Football Coach*
2142 NW Pinehurst Dr, McMinnville, OR
97128 USA

Ruttan, Susan *Actor*
PO Box 7345, Burbank, CA 91510 USA

Rutter, John M *Composer*
Old Lacey's, Saint John's Church,
Duxford, Cambridge, UNITED KINGDOM
(UK)

Ruttgers, Jurgen *Government Official*
BM fur Bildung/Technologie,
Heinemannstr 2, Bonn, 53175,
GERMANY

Rutting, Barbara
Sommerholz 30, Neumarkt, AUSTRIA,
5202

Ruttman, Joe
3 Knob Hill Rd., Mooresville, NC 28115

Ruud, Birger *Skier*
Munstersvei 20, Kongsberg, 3600,
NORWAY

Ruud, Sigmund *Skier*
Kirkeveien 57, Oslo, 3, NORWAY

Ruuska, Percy Sylvia *Swimmer*
4216 College View Way, Carmichael, CA
95608 USA

Ruusuvuori, Aarno E *Architect*
Annankalu 15 B 10, Helsinki 12, 00120,
UNITED KINGDOM (UK)

Ruutel, Arnold *President*
Koidula Str 3-5, Tallinn, 0010, ESTONIA

Ruwe, Robert P *Judge*
US Tax Court, 400 2nd St NW,
Washington, DC 20217 USA

Ruzicka, Vladimir *Hockey Player*
17 Highland Court, Needham, MA 02492
USA

Ruznak, Josef *Director*
Writers & Artists, 8383 Wilshire Blvd,
#550, Beverly Hills, CA 90211 USA

Ryan, Arthur F *Business Person*
Prudential Insurance, Prudential Plaza,
751 Broad St, Newark, NJ 07102 USA

Ryan, Blanchard *Actor*
Anonymous Content, 8522 National Blvd
#101, Culver City, CA 90232 USA

Ryan, Buddy
8701 S. Hardy Dr., Tempe, AZ 85284

Ryan, Dave *Musician*
Agency Group Ltd, 1775 Broadway, #430,
New York, NY 10019 USA

Ryan, Debbie *Comedian*
University of Virginia, Athletic Dept, PO
Box 3785, Charlottesville, VA 22903 USA

Ryan, Fran
4204 Woodland, Burbank, CA 91505

Ryan, Jeri *Actor*
Original Film, 2045 S Barrington Ave, Los
Angeles, CA 90025 USA

Ryan, Lee *Musician*
Concorde Intl Artists Ltd, 101 Shepherds
Bush Rd, London, W6 7LP, UNITED
KINGDOM (UK)

Ryan, Lisa *Religious Leader, Television
Host*
700 Club, 977 Centerville Tpke, Virginia
Beach, VT 23463 USA

Ryan, Lisa Dean *Actor*
Pakula/King & Associates, 9229 Sunset
Blvd #315, Los Angeles, CA 90069 USA

Ryan, Marisa *Actor*
McGowan Management, 8733 W Sunset
Blvd #103, W Hollywood, CA 90069 USA

Ryan, Mark *Actor*
Henderson Hogan, 247 S Beverly Dr
#102, Beverly Hills, CA 90212

Ryan, Max *Actor*
Mosaic Media Group, 9200 Sunset Blvd Fl
10, Los Angeles, CA 90069 USA

Ryan, Meg *Actor*
William Morris Agency (WMA-LA), 1
William Morris Pl, Beverly Hills, CA
90212 USA

Ryan, Mitchell *Actor*
30355 Mulholland Dr, Cornell, CA 91301
USA

Ryan, Nolan *Baseball Player*
2925 S Loop 35, Alvin, TX 77511 USA

Ryan, Norbert R Jr *Admiral*
Cheif of Naval Porsonnel, 2 Navy St,
Washington, DC 20370 USA

Ryan, Patrick G *Business Person*
Aon Corp, 200 East Randolf St, Chicago,
IL 60601 USA

Ryan, Peggy *Actor*
1821 E Oakley Blvd, Las Vegas, NV
89104 USA

Ryan, Shawn *Producer*
International Creative Management
(ICM-LA), 8942 Wilshire Blvd, Beverly
Hills, CA 90211 USA

Ryan, Terry *Writer*
Simon & Schuster, 1230 Ave of Americas,
New York, NY 10020 USA

Ryan, Thomas M *Business Person*
CVS Corp, 1 CVS Dr, Woonsocket, RI
02895 USA

Ryan, Timothy T (Tim) *Football Player*
4901 Sugar Creek Dr, Evansville, IN
47715 USA

Ryan, Tom K *Cartoonist*
North American Syndicate, 235 E 45th St,
New York, NY 10017 USA

Ryazanov, Eldar A *Director*
Bolshoi Tishinski Per 12 #70, Moscow,
123557, RUSSIA

Rybczynski, Witold *Writer*
Charles Scribner's Sons, 866 3rd Ave,
New York, NY 10022 USA

Rybkin, Ivan *Government Official*
National Security Council, 4 Staraya
Poischad, Moscow, 103073, RUSSIA

Rybska, Agnieszka *Musician, Music
Group*
RPM Music Productions, 130 W 57th St
#9D, New York, NY 10019 USA

Rydal, Emma *Actor*
Peters Fraser & Dunlop (PFD - UK), Drury
House, 34-43 Russell St, London, WC2
B5, UNITED KINGDOM (UK)

Rydell, Bobby *Actor, Musician, Music
Group*
917 Bryn Mawr Ave, Narberth, PA 19072
USA

Rydell, Christopher *Actor*
911 N Sweetzer #C, Los Angeles, CA
90069 USA

Rydell, Mark *Director*
Concourse Productions, 3110 Main St
#220, Santa Monica, CA 90405 USA

Ryder, Mitch *Musician, Music Group*
Entertainment Services Int'l, 6400 Pleasant
Park Dr, Chanhassen, MN 55317 USA

Ryder, Thomas O *Publisher*
Reader's Digest Assn, PO Box 100,
Pleasantville, NY 10572 USA

Ryder, Winona *Actor*
STarr Co, 350 Park Ave, #900, New York,
NY 10022 USA

Ryder, Winoria *Actor*
721 N Fairview St, Burbank, CA 91505
USA

Ryders, Ruff *Music Group*
International Creative Management
(ICM-LA), 8942 Wilshire Blvd, Beverly
Hills, CA 90211 USA

Rydze, Richard *Misc*
125 7th St, Pittsburgh, PA 15222 USA

Ryerson, Ann
935 Gayley Ave., Los Angeles, CA 90024

Ryff, Frankie
2055 McGraw, Bronx, NY 10462

Rykiel, Sonia F *Fashion Designer*
175 Blvd Saint Germain, Paris, 75006,
FRANCE

Ryknow *Musician*
Agency Group Ltd, 1775 Broadway #430,
New York, NY 10019 USA

Rylance, Mark *Actor, Director*
Shakespeare's Globe, Southwark, London,
SE1, UNITED KINGDOM (UK)

Ryman, Robert T *Artist*
17 W 16th St, New York, NY 10011 USA

Rymer, Pamela Ann *Judge*
US Court of Appeals, 125 S Grand Ave,
Pasadena, CA 91105 USA

Rynkiewicz, Mariusz *Artist, Misc*
12401 Alexander Road, Everett, WA
98204 USA

Rypdal, Terje *Musician*
PJP as, Utragata 16, Voss, 5700,
NORWAY

Rypien, Mark R *Football Player*
5855 W Riverside Dr, Post Falls, ID
83854 USA

Rysanek, Leony
Altenbeuren, GERMANY, D-88682

Ryumin, Valery V *Astronaut, Misc*
Potchta Kosmonavtov, Moskovskoi
Oblasti, Syvsdny Goroduk, 141160,
RUSSIA

Ryun, James R (Jim) *Track Athlete*
PO Box 62B, Lawrence, KS 66044 USA

Ryun, Jim
Rt. 3Box 62-B, Lawrence, KS 66044

Ryzhkov, Nikolai I *Misc*
State Duma, Okhotny Ryad 1, Moscow,
103009, RUSSIA

RZA *Artist, Musician, Music Group*
Famous Artists Agency, 250 W 57th St,
New York, NY 10107 USA

Rzeznik, Johnny *Musician*
Mosaic Media Group, 9200 Sunset Blvd Fl
10, Los Angeles, CA 90069 USA

S

S Club 7 *Music Group*
Creative Artists Agency LCC (CAA-LA),
9830 Wilshire Blvd, Beverly Hills, CA
90212 USA

S Jayaram *Actor*
7-Majestic Terrace 48 Arcot Road,
Saligramam, Chennai, TN 600 098, INDIA

Saadiq, Raphael *Musician*
Family Tree Entertainment, 135 E 57th St
#2600, New York, NY 10022 USA

Saakashvili, Mikhail *President*
President's Office, Rustaveli Prosp 29,
Tbilsi, 380008, GEORGIA

Saar, Bettye *Artist*
8074 Willow Glen Road, Los Angeles, CA
90046 USA

Saari, Roy A *Swimmer*
PO Box 7086, Mommoth Lakes, CA
93546 USA

Saatchi, Charles *Business Person*
36 Golden Square, London, W1R 4EE,
UNITED KINGDOM (UK)

Saatchi, Maurice *Business Person*
36 Golden Square, London, W1R 4EE,
UNITED KINGDOM (UK)

Sabah, Joe

Sabah, Sheikh Jaber al-Ahmed al-Jabar al
Misc
Sief Palace, Amiry Diwan, Kuwait City,
KUWAIT

Sabah, Sheikh Saad al-Abdullah al-Salem
Prince, Prime Minister
Prime Minister's Office, PO Box 4, Safat,
Kuwait City, 13001, KUWAIT

Saban, Haim *Producer*
Saban Entertainment, 10960 Wilshire
Blvd, 22nd Floor, Los Angeles, CA 90024
USA

Saban, Lou *Football Coach*
Lousiana State University, Baton Rouge,
LA 70803 USA

Saban, Louis H (Lou) *Football Player,
Coach*
177 Lake Laurel Dr, Dohlonega, GA
30533 USA

Saban, Nick *Athlete*
Chowan College, Chowan College,
Athletic Dept, Murfreesboro, NC 27855

Sabara, Daryl *Actor*
Endeavor Talent Agency, 9701 Wilshire
Blvd, #1000, Beverly Hills, CA 90212
USA

Sabates, Felix *Race Car Driver, Misc*
Sabco Racing, PO Box 560579, Charlotte,
NC 28258 USA

Sabathia, C C *Baseball Player*
Cleveland Indians, Jacobs Field, 2401
Ontario St, Cleveland, OH 44115 USA

Sabatini, Gabriela *Tennis Player*
35/35 Grosvenor St, London, W1K 4QX,
UNITED KINGDOM (UK)

Sabatino, Michael *Actor*
13538 Valleyheart Dr, Sherman Oaks, CA
91423 USA

Sabato, Antonio Jr *Actor, Model*
Alan Siegel Entertainment, 345 N Maple
Dr #375, Beverly Hills, CA 90210 USA

Sabato, Ernesto *Writer*
Severino Langeri 3135, Santos Lugares,
ARGENTINA

Sabbah, Michel *Religious Leader*
Latin Patriarch Office, PO Box 14152,
Jerusalem, ISRAEL

Sabelle *Musician, Music Group,
Songwriter*
Sarmast Entertainment, 241 W 36th St
#2R, New York, NY 10018 USA

Saberhagen, Bret W *Baseball Player*
5535 Amber Circle, Calabasas, CA 91302
USA

Saberhagen, Brett *Baseball Player*
5535 Amber Circle, Calabasas, CA 91302
USA

Sabihy, Kyle *Actor*
Stein Entertainment Group, 11271 Ventura
Blvd #477, Studio City, CA 91604 USA

Sabiston, David C Jr *Doctor*
1528 Pinecrest Road, Durham, NC 27705
USA

Sabo, Christopher A (Chris) *Baseball
Player*
7455 Stonemeadow Lane, Cincinnati, OH
45242 USA

Saca, Elias Antonio *President*
Casa Presidencial Avda Cuba, Barrosan
Jacinto, San Salvador, El SALVADOR

Sacchi, Robert
203 N. Gramercy Pl, Los Angeles, CA
90004

Sacco, Joe *Artist*
Fantagraphics Books, 7563 Lake City
Way, Seattle, WA 98115 USA

Sacco, Michael *Misc*
Seafarers International Union, 5201 Auth
Way, Suitland, MO 20746 USA

Saccone, Viviana *Actor*
Telefe - Argentina, Pavon 2444
(C1248AAT), Buenos Aires, ARGENTINA

Sachar, Louis *Writer*
Foster Books/Farrar Straus Giroux, 19
Union Square W, New York, NY 10003
USA

Sachdev, Asha *Actor, Bollywood*
18B Sunset Heights, 59 Pali Hill Bandra,
Mumbai, MS 40050, INDIA

Sachenbacher, Evi *Skier*
WSV Reit im Winkl, Rthausplatz 1, Reit
im Winkl, 83242, GERMANY

Sachin *Actor, Bollywood, Director,
Filmmaker*
B609 Pearl Apartments 33 Swami Samarth
Nagar, Cross Road No 3 Andheri,
Bombay, MS 400 058, INDIA

Sachs, Andrew *Actor*
Richard Stone, 2 Henrietta St, London,
WC2E 8PS, UNITED KINGDOM (UK)

Sachs, Gloria *Fashion Designer*
117 E 57th St, New York, NY 10022 USA

Sachs, Gunter
101 E. 63rd St., New York, NY 10021

Sachs, Jeffrey D *Economist*
Harvard University, International
Development Institute, Cambridge, MA
02138 USA

Sachs, Richard *Doctor*
6 Saint Ronan Terrace, New Haven, CT
06511 USA

Sachs, William *Director*
3739 Montuso Place, Encino, CA 91436
USA

Sachu *Actor, Bollywood*
78 Sairam Colony, Alwarpet, Chennai, TN
600018, INDIA

Sack, Kevin *Journalist*
Los Angeles Times, Editorial Dept, 202 W
1st St, Los Angeles, CA 90012 USA

Sack, Steve *Cartoonist*
Minneapolis Star-Tribune, 425 Portland
Ave, Minneapolis, MN 55488 USA

Sackheim, Daniel *Director, Producer,
Editor*
Creative Artists Agency LCC (CAA-LA),
9830 Wilshire Blvd, Beverly Hills, CA
90212 USA

Sackhoff, Kate *Actor*
Envision Entertainment, 9255 Sunset Blvd
#300, Los Angeles, CA 90069 USA

Sacks, Greg *Race Car Driver*
6092 Sabal Creek Blvd, Port Orange, FL
32128 USA

Sacks, Jonathan H *Religious Leader*
735 High Road, London, N12 0US,
UNITED KINGDOM (UK)

Sacks, Oliver W *Doctor, Writer*
2 Horatio St #3G, New York, NY 10014
USA

Sadanah, Kamal *Actor, Bollywood*
Jal Kamal Plot 202, 23rd Road Bandra,
Mumbai, MS 400050, INDIA

Sadat, Jehan El- *Social Activist*
University of Maryland, Int'l Development
Center, College Park, MD 20742 USA

Sadat, Madame Jehan
NW2310 Decatur Pl., Washington, DC
20008

Saddler, Donald E *Choreographer, Dancer*
Coleman-Rosenberg Agency, 210 E 58th
St, New York, NY 10022 USA

Sade *Musician, Songwriter*
1 Red Place, London, W1Y 3RE, UNITED
KINGDOM (UK)

Sadeckl, Raymond M (Ray) *Baseball
Player*
4237 E Clovis Ave, Mesa, AZ 85206 USA

Sadik, Nafis *Government Official*
United Nations Population Fund, 220 E
42nd St, New York, NY 10017 USA

Sadler, Elliott *Race Car Driver*
PO Box 871, Emporia, VA 23847 USA

Sadler, William
10474 Santa Monica Blvd, Suite 380, Los
Angeles, CA 90025 USA

Sadoulet, Bernard *Astronomer*
2824 Forest Ave, Berkeley, CA 94705
USA

Safdie, Moshe *Architect*
100 Rev Nazareno Properzi Way,
Somerville, MA 02143 USA

Safer, Morley *Commentator*
CBS-TV, News Dept, 51 W 52nd St, New
York, NY 10019 USA

Saffiotti, Umberto *Doctor*
5114 Wissioming Road, Bathesda, MD
20816 USA

Saffman, Philip G *Mathematician*
California Institute of Technology,
Firestone Hall, Pasadena, CA 91125 USA

Safin, Marat *Tennis Player*
TC Weiden am Postkeller, Schirmitzer
Weg, Weiden, 92637, GERMANY

Safina, Alessandro *Opera Singer*
Interscope Records, 2220 Colorado Ave,
Santa Monica, CA 90404 USA

Safina, Carl *Biologist*
Living Oceans Program, Audubon Society,
100 W Main St, East Islip, NY 11730 USA

Safire, William *Journalist, Writer*
6200 Elmwood Road, Chevy Chase, MD
20815 USA

Safuto, Dominick (Randy) *Musician,
Music Group*
PO Box 656507, Fresh Meadows, NY
11365 USA

Safuto, Frank *Musician, Music Group*
PO Box 656507, Fresh Meadows, NY
11365 USA

Sagal, Jean *Actor*
Progressive Artists Agency, 400 S Beverly
Dr #216, Beverly Hills, CA 90212 USA

Sagal, Katey *Actor*
7095 Hollywood Blvd #792, Los Angeles,
CA 90028 USA

Sagal, Liz
4526 Wilshire Blvd., Los Angeles, CA
90010

Sagan, Francoise
Equemauville, Honfleur, 14600, FRANCE

Sagansky, Jeff
145 Ocean Ave., Santa Monica, CA
90402

Sagar, Ramanand *Actor, Director,
Filmmaker, Producer*
Natraj Studios 194 M V Road, Andheri (E),
Bombay, MS 400 069, INDIA

Sagdeev, Roald Z *Physicist*
Space Research Institute, Profsoyuznaya
84/32, Moscow B485, 11780, RUSSIA

Sage, William *Actor*
Gersh Agency, 232 N Canon Dr, Beverly
Hills, CA 90210 USA

Sagebrecht, Marianne *Actor*
Kaulbachstr 61, Ruckgeb, Munich, 80539,
GERMANY

Sagemiller, Melissa *Actor*
Abrams Artists, 9200 Sunset Blvd #1125,
Los Angeles, CA 90069 USA

Sager, Carole Bayer *Songwriter, Musician,
Music Group*
10761 Bellagio Road, Los Angeles, CA
90077 USA

Sager, Craig *Sportscaster*
3064 Spring Hill Road, Smyrna, GA
30080 USA

Saget, Bob *Actor*
William Morris Agency (WMA-LA), 1
William Morris Pl, Beverly Hills, CA
90212 USA

Saglio, Laura *Actor*
Cineart, 36 Rue de Ponthieu, Paris,
75008, FRANCE

Sagnier, Ludivine *Actor*
Don Buchwald & Associates Inc (LA),
6500 Wilshire Blvd #2200, Los Angeles,
CA 90048 USA

Sagona, Katie *Actor*
Wilhelmina Creative Mgmt, 300 Park Ave
S #200, New York, NY 10010 USA

Sahagun, Elena *Actor*
Artists Agency, 1180 S Beverly Dr #301,
Los Angeles, CA 90035 USA

Sahgal, Ajay *Actor, Producer, Writer*
International Creative Management
(ICM-LA), 8942 Wilshire Blvd, Beverly
Hills, CA 90211 USA

Sahgal, Nayantara *Writer*
181B Rajpur Road, Dehra Dun, Uttar
Pradesh, 248009, INDIA

Sahi, Deepa *Actor, Bollywood*
466 Laxmi Bhuvan Sardar Patel Road,
Mumbai, MS 400004, INDIA

Sahl, Mort *Actor, Comedian*
1441 3rd Ave #12-C, New York, NY
10028 USA

Sahm, Hans-Werner *Artist*
Zur Wasserburg 7, Bidingen, Schwab,
GERMANY

Sailer, Anton (Toni) *Skier*
Gundhabing 19, Kitzbuhl, 6370, AUSTRIA

Sailer, Toni
Gundhabing 19, Kitzbuhel, AUSTRIA,
A-6370

Sailors, Kenny (Ken) *Basketball Player*
1614 Shoestring Road, Gooding, ID
83330 USA

Saimes, George *Football Player, Football
Executive*
2307 Beechmoor Dr NW, North Canton,
OH 44720 USA

Sain, John F (Johnny) *Baseball Player*
2S707 Ave Latour, Oak Brook, IL 60523
USA

Sain, Johnny
2 So. 707 Ave. Latour, Oakbrook, IL
60521

Sainsbury of Preston Candover, John D
Business Person
J Sainsbury PLC, Stamford House,
Stamford St, London, SE1 9LL, UNITED
KINGDOM (UK)

Sainsbury of Turville, David J *Business
Person*
4 Charterhouse Mews, Charterhouse
Square, London, EC1M 6BB, UNITED
KINGDOM (UK)

Saint, Crosbie E *General*
1116 N Pitt St, Alexandria, VA 22314
USA

Saint, Eva Marie *Actor*
10590 Wilshire Blvd #408, Los Angeles,
CA 90024 USA

Saint, Laurent Yves *Fashion Designer*
7 Rue Leonce Reynaud, Paris, 75116,
FRANCE

Saint, Silva *Adult Film Star*
Atlas Multimedia Inc, 22940 Burbank
Blvd, Woodland Hills, CA 91367 USA

Saint, Sylvia
Suze.net, 26500 W Agoura Rd #389,
Calabasas, CA 91302

Saint James, Sara
289 So. Robertson Blvd. #259, Beverly
Hills, CA 90212

Saint James, Susan *Actor*
174 West St #54, Litchfield, CT 06759
USA

Saint-Subber, Arnold *Producer*
116 E 64th St, New York, NY 10021 USA

Sainte-Marie, Buffy *Musician, Music
Group, Songwriter*
1191 Kuhio Highway, Kapaa, HI 96746
USA

Sainz, Salvador *Actor, Director*
Ave Prat de la Riba 43, Reus (Tarragona),
43201, SPAIN

Sajak, Pat *Entertainer*
Whell of Fortune Show, 3400 Riverside Dr
#201, Burbank, CA 91505 USA

Sajawal, Aziz *Actor, Bollywood, Director,
Filmmaker*
S303 Sameer Society JP Road, Seven
Bungalows Andheri, Mumbai, MS
400058, INDIA

Sajko, Kristina *Model*
Karin Models, 6 W 14th St #300, New York, NY 10011 USA

Sakamoto, Ryoichi *Composer*
Columbia Artists Mgmt Inc, 165 W 57th St, New York, NY 10019 USA

Sakamoto, Soichi *Swimmer, Coach*
768 McCully St, Honolulu, HI 96826 USA

Sakamura, Ken *Inventor*
University of Tokyo, Information Science Dept, Tokyo, JAPAN

Sakato, George T *War Hero*
6369 Katherine Way, Denver, CO 80221 USA

Sakharov, Alik *Cinematographer*
6050 Boulevard E #4D, West New York, NJ 07093 USA

Sakic, Joe *Hockey Player*
4785 S Franklin St, Englewood, CO 80113 USA

Sakmann, Bert *Nobel Prize Laureate*
Max Planck Institute, Jehnstr 39, Heidelberg, 69120, GERMANY

Saks, Gene *Actor, Director*
International Creative Mgmt, 40 W 57th St #1800, New York, NY 10019 USA

Sakshaug, Eugene C *Engineer*
18 Grove Ave, Pittsfield, MA 01201 USA

Sala, Edoardo *Actor*
Carol Levi Co, Via Giuseppe Pisanelli, Rome, 00196, ITALY

Sala, Oskar
Leistikowstr. 5, Berlin, GERMANY, 14050

Sala, Richard *Cartoonist*
3131 College Ave, Berkeley, CA 94705 USA

Salaam, Rashaan *Football Player*
8132 Brookhaven Road, San Diego, CA 92114, u

Salac, Joe
2205 Avenue Colisee Quebec, PQ CANADA, GIL 4W7

Salad Hassan, Abdikassim *President*
President's Office, People's Palace, Mogadishu, SOMALIA

Salamanca & Garcia *Writer*
Gabriel Blanco Iglesias (Mexico), Rio Balsas 35-32, Colonia Cuauhtemoc, DF, 06500, Mexico

Salans, Lester B *Doctor*
Sandoz Research Institute, RR 10, Hanover, NJ 07936 USA

Salazar, Alberto *Track Athlete*
Int'l Mgmt Group, 1 Erieview Plaza, 1360 E 9th St #1300, Cleveland, OH 44114 USA

Salazar, Arion *Musician*
Eric Godtland Mgmt, 5715 Claremont Ave #C, Oakland, CA 94618 USA

Salazar, Eliseo *Race Car Driver*
2310 Rippling Way S, Indianapolis, IN 46260 USA

Saldana, Theresa *Actor*
Tamara Villa, 12190 1/2 Ventura Blvd #361, Studio City, CA 91604 USA

Saldana, Zoe *Actor*
Gersh Agency, The (NY), 41 Madison Ave Fl 33, New York, NY 10010 USA

Saldarini, Giovanni Cardinal *Religious Leader*
Archdiocese of Turin, Via dell'Archivescovado 12, Turin, 10121, ITALY

Sale, Jamie *Dancer*
12116 NW 128th St, Edmonton, AB T5L 1C3, CANADA

Saleh, Ali Abdullah *President, General*
President's Office, Zubairy St, Sana'a, YEMEN ARAB REPUBLIC

Saleh, Jaime H *Governor*
Fort Amsterdam 1, Willemstad, Curacao, NETHERLANDS ANTILLES

Salem, Dahlia *Actor*
Innovative Artists, 1505 10th St, Santa Monica, CA 90401 USA

Salem, Marc *Actor, Comedian*
William Morris Agency, 151 El Camino Dr, Beverly Hills, CA 90212 USA

Salenger, Meredith *Actor*
Shelter Entertainment, 9255 Sunset Blvd #1010, Los Angeles, CA 90069 USA

Salerno-Sonnenberg, Nadja *Musician*
Columbia Artists Mgmt Inc, 165 W 57th St, New York, NY 10019 USA

Sales, Eugenio de Araujo Cardinal *Religious Leader*
Palacio Sao Joaquim, Rua Gloria 446, Rio de Janeiro RJ, 20241-150, BRAZIL

Sales, Nykesha *Basketball Player*
Connecticut Sun, Mohegan Sun Arena, Uncasville, CT 06382 USA

Sales, Soupy *Actor, Comedian*
245 E 35th St, New York, NY 10016 USA

Salgado, Michael *Musician*
Sony Music Miami, 605 Lincoln Rd, Miami Beach, FL 33138 USA

Salgado, Sabastiano R *Photographer*
Instituto Terra, Fazenda Bulcao, Minas Gerais, BRAZIL

Saliba, Metropolitan Primate Philip *Religious Leader*
Antiochian Orthodox Christian Diocese, 358 Mountain Road, Englewood, NJ 07631 USA

Saliers, Emily *Musician, Songwriter*
Russell Carter Artist Mgmt, 315 Ponce de Leon Ave #755, Decatur, GA 30030 USA

Salim, Salim Ahmed *Prime Minister*
Organization of African Unity, PO Box 3243, Addis Ababa, ETHIOPIA

Salinas, Carmen *Actor*
Televisa, Blvd Adolfo Lopez Mateos 232, Colonia San Angel INN, DF, CP 01060, MEXICO

Salinas, Jorge *Actor*
Televisa, Blvd Adolfo Lopez Mateos 232, Colonia San Angel INN, DF, CP 01060, MEXICO

Salinas, Maria Elena *Actor*
Univision, 314 Main St, Chico, CA 95928 USA

Salinas, Nora *Actor*
Televisa, Blvd Adolfo Lopez Mateos 232, Colonia San Angel INN, DF, CP 01060, MEXICO

Salinger, Diane *Actor*
The Agency, 1800 Ave of Stars #400, Los Angeles, CA 90067 USA

Salinger, Emmanuel *Actor*
Cineart, 36 Rue de Ponthieu, Paris, 75008, FRANCE

Salinger, Jerome David (J D) *Writer*
RR 3 Box 176, Comish Flat, NH 03745 USA

Salinger, Matt *Actor*
Bresler Kelly Assoc, 11500 W Olympic Blvd #510, Los Angeles, CA 90064 USA

Salinger, Pierre E G *Senator, Journalist*
La Bastiderose, 99 Cherin Des Croupieres, Le Thor, 84250, FRANCE

Salkind, Ilya *Producer*
Pinewood Studios, Iverheath, Iver, Bucks, SL0 0NH, UNITED KINGDOM (UK)

Salle, David *Artist*
Larry Gagosian Gallery, 980 Madison Ave #PH, New York, NY 10021 USA

Salles, Walter *Producer, Director*
Endeavor Agency LLC (LA), 9601 Wilshire Blvd Fl 3, Beverly Hills, CA 90210 USA

Salley, John *Basketball Player, Television Host*
Salley Foundation Inc, The, 5230 Winding Glen Dr, Lithonia, GA 30038 USA

Sallinen, Aulis H *Composer*
Runneberginkatu 37A, Helsinki 10, 00100, FINLAND

Sallis, Peter *Actor*
Jonathan Altaras, 13 Shorts Gardens, London, WC2H 9AT, UNITED KINGDOM (UK)

Salminen, Matti *Opera Singer*
Mariedi Anders Artists, 535 El Camino del Mar, San Francisco, CA 94121 USA

Salming, Borje *Hockey Player*
Borje Salming Assoc, Box 45438, Stockholm, 104 31, SWEDEN

Salmon, Colin *Actor*
Markham & Froggatt, Julian House, 4 Windmill St, London, W1P 1HF, UNITED KINGDOM (UK)

Salmon, Tim
6061 E. Sunnyside Dr., Scottsdale, AZ 85254-4977

Salmon, Timothy J (Tim) *Baseball Player*
24767 Masters Cup Way, Valencia, CA 91355 USA

Salmons, John *Basketball Player*
Philadelphia 76ers, 1st Union Center, 3601 S Broad St, Philadelphia, PA 19148 USA

Salmons, Steve *Volleyball Player*
1717 N El Dorado Ave, Ontario, CA 91764 USA

Salo, Mika *Race Car Driver*
TWI Formula One, Leafield, Whitney, Oxon, OX8 5PF, UNITED KINGDOM (UK)

Salomon, Mikael *Cinematographer*
PO Box 2230, Los Angeles, CA 90078 USA

Salomon, Sandy *Actor*
Cineart, 36 Rue de Ponthieu, Paris, 75008, FRANCE

Salonen, Esa-Pekka *Composer*
Los Angeles Philharmonic, Music Center, 135 N Grand Ave, Los Angeles, CA 90012 USA

Salonga, Lea *Actor, Music Group, Musician*
Writers & Artists, 8383 Wilshire Blvd #550, Beverly Hills, CA 90211 USA

Salopek, Paul *Journalist*
Chicago Tribune, Editorial Dept, 435 N Michigan Ave, Chicago, IL 60611 USA

Salpeter, Edwin E *Physicist*
116 Westbourne Lane, Ithaca, NY 14850 USA

Salt, Jennifer *Actor*
9045 Elevado St, West Hollywood, CA 90069 USA

Salt-N-Peppa
250 W. 57th St. #821, New York, NY 10107

Salter, Hans
3658 Woodhill Canyon, Studio City, CA 91604

Saltpeter, Edwin E *Misc*
Comell University, Physical Sciences Dept, Ithaca, NJ 14853 USA

Saltykov, Aleksey A *Director*
Institute Mosfilmosvsky, Per 4A #104, Moscow, 119285, RUSSIA

Saltykov, Boris G *Economist, Government Official*
Bryusov Per 11, Moscow, 103009, RUSSIA

Salva, Victor *Director*
Gersh Agency, The (LA), 232 N Canon Dr, Beverly Hills, CA 90210 USA

Salvador, Henri
6 place Vendome, Paris, FRANCE, 75001

Salvay, Bennett *Composer*
Gorfaine/Schwartz, 13245 Riverside Dr #450, Sherman Oaks, CA 91423 USA

Salvino, Carmen *Bowler*
65 Stevens Dr, Schaumburg, IL 60173 USA

Salzman, Marc *Writer*
Knopf Publishers, 201 E 50th St, New York, NY 10022 USA

Sam the Sham *Musician*
6123 Old Brunswick Road, Arlington, TN 38002 USA

Samaranch, Juan Antonio
Avenida Pau Casals 24, Barcelona, SPAIN, E-08021

Samaranch Torello, Juan Antonio *Misc*
Avenida Pau Casals 24, Barcelona 6, 08021, SPAIN

Samaras, Lucas *Artist, Photographer*
Pace Gallery, 32 E 57th St, New York, NY 10022 USA

Sambora, Richie *Musician, Music Group, Songwriter*
4970 Summit View Dr, Westlake Village, CA 91362 USA

Samios, Nicholas P *Physicist, Misc*
Brookhaven National Laboratory, Directors's Office, 2 Center St, Upton, NY 11973 USA

Samis, Phil
1509 Rue Sherbrooke O, Montreal, CANADA, QC H3G 1M1

Sammie *Actor*
Green Light Talent Agency, PO Box 3172, Beverly Hills, CA 90212 USA

Samms, Emma *Actor*
2934 1/2 N Beverly Glen Circle #417, Los Angeles, CA 90077 USA

Samoilova, Tatiana Y *Actor*
Spiridonyevsky Per 8/11, Moscow, 103104, RUSSIA

Samotsvetov, Anatoly *Hockey Player*
Nashville Predators, 501 Broadway, Nashville, TN 37203 USA

Sampaio, Jorge *President*
President's Office, Palacio de Belem, Lisbon, 1300, PORTUGAL

Sample, Joe *Musician*
Patrick Ralns Assoc, 220 W 93rd St #7B, New York, NY 10025 USA

Sample, Steven B *Educator*
University of Southern California, President's Office, Los Angeles, CA 90089 USA

Samples, Keith *Producer, Director, Writer*
Creative Artists Agency LCC (CAA-LA), 9830 Wilshire Blvd, Beverly Hills, CA 90212 USA

Sampras, Pete *Tennis Player*
William Morris Agency (WMA-LA), 1 William Morris Pl, Beverly Hills, CA 90212 USA

Sampson, Kelvin *Basketball Player, Coach*
University of Oklahoma, Lloyd Noble Complex, Norman, OK 73019 USA

Sampson, Ralph L Jr *Basketball Player, Coach*
10831 W Broad St, Glen Allen, VA 23060 USA

Sampson, Robert *Actor*
20th Century Artists, 4605 Lankershim Blvd #305, North Hollywood, CA 91602 USA

Sams, Dean *Musician*
Borman Entertainment, 1222 16th Ave #23, Nashville, TN 37212 USA

Sams, Jeffrey D *Actor*
Abrams Artists, 9200 Sunset Blvd, #1125, Los Angeles, CA 90069 USA

Sams, Russell *Actor*
William Morris Agency (WMA-LA), 1 William Morris Pl, Beverly Hills, CA 90212 USA

Samuels, Chris *Football Player*
Washington Redskins, 21300 Redskin Park Dr, Ashburn, VA 20147 USA

Samuels, Ron
PO Box 1690, Rancho Mirage, CA 92270-1058

Samuelson, Pamela *Attorney General*
University of California, Center for Law/Technology, Berkeley, CA 94720 USA

Samuelson, Paul A *Nobel Prize Laureate*
94 Somerset St, Belmont, MA 02478 USA

Samuelsson, Bengt I *Nobel Prize Laureate*
Karolinska Institute, Chemistry Dept, Stockholm, 171 77, SWEDEN

Samuelsson, Kjell *Hockey Player*
5 Simsbury Dr, Voorhees, NJ 08043 USA

Samuelsson, Ulf *Hockey Player*
11 Deerfield Terrace, Moorestown, NJ 08057 USA

San Basilio, Paloma *Music Group*
Sony Music Miami, 605 Lincoln Rd, Miami Beach, FL 33138 USA

San Giacomo, Laura *Actor*
Baker Winokur Ryder (BWR-NY), 909 3rd Ave Fl 9, New York, NY 10022 USA

Sanabria, Marilyn *Actor*
Central Artists, 269 W Alameda Ave #A, Burbank, CA 91502 USA

Sanborn, David *Musician*
Patrick Rains Assoc, 220 W 93rd St #7B, New York, NY 10025 USA

Sanches, Stacy *Model*
Playboy Entertainment Group Inc, 2706 Media Center Dr, Los Angeles, CA 90065

Sanchez, Eduardo *Director*
Artisan Entertainment, 2700 Colorado Ave, Santa Monica, CA 90404 USA

Sanchez, Emilio *Tennis Player*
Sabiono de Avena 28, Barcelona 46, SPAIN

Sanchez, Jose T Cardinal *Religious Leader*
Via Rusticucci 13, Rome, 00193, ITALY

Sanchez, Juan (Pepe) *Basketball Player*
Detroit Pistons, Palace, 2 Championship Drive, Auburn Hills, MI 48326 USA

Sanchez, Kiele *Actor*
Evolution Entertainment, 901 N Highland Ave, Los Angeles, CA 90038 USA

Sanchez, Marco *Actor*
Stone Manners, 6500 Wilshire Blvd #550, Los Angeles, CA 90048 USA

Sanchez, Monika *Actor*
Gabriel Blanco Iglesias (Mexico), Rio Balsas 35-32, Colonia Cuauhtemoc, DF, 06500, Mexico

Sanchez, Pancho *Musician*
PO Box 59236, Norwalk, CA 90652 USA

Sanchez, Pedro *Scientist*
Columbia University, Earth Institute, New York, NY 10027 USA

Sanchez, Pepe *Director*
Gabriel Blanco Iglesias (Colombia), Dg 127A #20-36, Conjunto Plenitud, Apto 132, Bogota, Colombia

Sanchez, Roselyn *Actor*
400 N Gardner St, Los Angeles, CA 90036 USA

Sanchez Azuara, Rocio *Actor*
TV Azteca, Periferico Sur 4121, Colonia Fuentes del Pedregal, DF, CP 14141, Mexico

Sanchez Gijon, Aitana *Actor*
Alsira Garcia Maroto, Gran Via 63 #3, Izda, Madrid, 28013, SPAIN

Sanchez-Vicario, Arantxa *Tennis Player*
Sabino de Arana 28 #6-1A, Barcelona, 08028, SPAIN

Sanchez-Vilella, Roberto *Governor*
414 Ave Munoz Rivera #7A, Stop 31-1/2, San Juan, PR 00918 USA

Sand, Paul *Actor*
Paradigm Agency, 10100 Santa Monica Blvd #2500, Los Angeles, CA 90067 USA

Sand, Shauna
345 N. Maple Dr. #185, Beverly Hills, CA 90210

Sand, Todd *Figure Skater*
2973 Harbor Blvd #468, Costa Mesa, CA 92626 USA

Sanda, Dominique
201 rue du Faubourg St. Honore, Paris, FRANCE, F-75008

Sandage, Allan R *Astronomer*
8319 E Josard Road, San Gabriel, CA 91775 USA

Sandberg, Ryne D *Baseball Player*
3630 E Coconino Court, Phoenix, AZ 85044 USA

Sander, Casey
145 S. Fairfax Ave. #310, Los Angeles, CA 90036

Sander, Ian *Producer*
William Morris Agency (WMA-LA), 1 William Morris Pl, Beverly Hills, CA 90212 USA

Sander, Jil *Fashion Designer*
Osterfeldstr 32-34, Hamburg, 22529, GERMANY

Sanderling, Kurt *Conductor*
Am Iderfenngraben 47, Berlin, 13156, GERMANY

Sanders, Beverly *Actor*
12218 Morrison St, Valley Village, CA 91607 USA

Sanders, Bill *Cartoonist*
PO Box 661, Milwaukee, WI 53201 USA

Sanders, Charles A (Charlie) *Football Player, Football Coach, Coach*
3418 Palm Aire Court, Rochester Hills, MI 48309 USA

Sanders, Chris *Director*
William Morris Agency (WMA-LA), 1 William Morris Pl, Beverly Hills, CA 90212 USA

Sanders, Deion L *Football Player, Baseball Player*
10200 Deer Run Farms Rd, Fort Myers, FL 33912 USA

Sanders, Doug *Golfer*
Doug Sanders Enterprises, 8828 Sandringham Dr, Houston, TX 77024 USA

Sanders, Frank *Hockey Player*
670 Lade View Dr, Saint Paul, MN 55129 USA

Sanders, Jay O *Actor*
165 W 46th St, #409, New York, NY 10036 USA

Sanders, Jonathan (Jon) *Yachtsman*
28 Portland St, Redlands, WA 6009, AUSTRALIA

Sanders, Mariene *Commentator*
WNET-TV, News Dept, 356 W 58th St, New York, NY 10019 USA

Sanders, Marlene
175 Riverside Dr., New York, NY 10024

Sanders, Pharoah *Musician*
Joel Chriss, 300 Mercer St #3J, New York, NY 10003 USA

Sanders, Reggie
1764 Williamsburg Circle, Florence, SC 29501

Sanders, Richard *Actor*
Halpem Assoc, PO Box 5597, Santa Monica, CA 90409 USA

Sanders, Scott G *Baseball Player*
10403 Sandlewood Lane, Northridge, CA 91326 USA

Sanders, Summer *Swimmer*
160 W 86th St #11A, New York, NY 10024 USA

Sanders, Thomas (Satch) *Basketball Player, Misc*
114 Fenway, Boston, MA 02115 USA

Sanders, W J (Jerry) III *Business Person*
Advanced Micro Devices, 1 AMD Place, PO Box 3453, Sunnyvale, CA 94088 USA

Sanderson, Cael *Wrestler*
Steve Sanderson, 1380 Valley Hills Blvd, Heber City, UT 84032 USA

Sanderson, Derek M *Hockey Player*
267 Manning St, Needham, MA 02492 USA

Sanderson, Geoff *Hockey Player*
1988 Berkshire Road, Upper Arlington, OH 43221 USA

Sanderson, Peter *Artist*
1105 Shell Gate Plaza, Alameda, CA 94501 USA

Sanderson, Theresa (Tessa) *Track Athlete*
Tee-Dee Promotion, Atles Center, Oxgate Lane, London, NW2 7HU, UNITED KINGDOM (UK)

Sanderson, William *Actor*
4251 W Sarah St, Burbank, CA 91505 USA

Sandeson, William S *Editor, Cartoonist*
119 W Sherwood Terrace, Fort Wayne, IN 46807 USA

Sandford, John *Writer*
G P Putnam's Sons, 375 Hudson St, New York, NY 10014 USA

Sandiford, L Erskine *Prime Minister*
Hillvista, Porters, Saint James, BARBADOS

Sandin, Bill *Inventor*
University of Illinois, Electronic Visualization Lab, Chicago, IL 60607 USA

Sandit, Tom *Athlete*
540 S Ashland Ave, La Grange, IL 60525-2811

Sandler, Adam *Actor, Comedian*
Brillstein/Grey, 9150 Wilshire Blvd #350, Beverly Hills, CA 90212 USA

Sandler, Herbert M *Financier*
Golden West Financial, 1901 Harrison St, Oakland, CA 94612 USA

Sandler, Marion O *Financier*
Golden West Financial, 1901 Harrison St, Oakland, CA 94612 USA

Sandlund, Debra *Actor*
Innovative Artists, 1505 10th St, Santa Monica, CA 90401 USA

Sandor, Gyorgy *Musician*
Jack Brennan, 500 E 85th St #31, New York, NY 10028 USA

Sandoval, Arturo *Musician*
PO Box 660335, Miami Springs, FL 33266 USA

Sandoval, Hope *Musician, Music Group*
Rough Trade Mgmt, 66 Golbarne Road, London, W10 5PS, UNITED KINGDOM (UK)

Sandoval, Miguel *Actor*
Paradigm Agency, 10100 Santa Monica Blvd #2500, Los Ageles, CA 90067 USA

Sandoval, Sonny *Musician*
East West America Records, 75 Rockefeller Plaza, New York, NY 10019 USA

Sandoval Iniguez, Juan Cardinal *Religious Leader*
Morelos 244, San Pedro Tlaquepaque, 45500, MEXICO

Sandow, Nick *Actor*
Sweet Mud Group, 648 Broadway #1002, New York, NY 10012 USA

Sandre, Didier *Actor*
Agents Associes Beaume, 201 Faubourg Saint Honore, Paris, 75008, FRANCE

Sandrelli, Stefania *Actor*
TNA, Viale Parioli 41, Rome, 00197, ITALY

Sandrich, Jay *Director*
610 N Maple Dr, Beverly Hills, CA 90210 USA

Sands, Julian *Actor*
1287 Ozeta Terrace, Los Ageles, CA 90069 USA

Sands, Tommy *Actor, Musician*
225 N Evergreen St #301, Burbank, CA 91505 USA

Sandstrom, Sven *Financier*
World Bank Group, 1818 H St NW, Washington, DC 20433 USA

Sandstrom, Tomas *Hockey Player*
156 Iron Run Road, Bethel Park, PA 15102 USA

Sandusky, Alexander B (Alex) *Football Player*
636 Oakland Hills Dr #2A, Arnold, MD 21012 USA

Sandy, Baby (Sandra Magee)
6846 Haywood, Tujunga, CA 91042

Sandy, Gary *Actor*
PO Box 818, Cynthiana, KY 41031 USA

Sandy B *Musician*
Atlantic Entertainment Group, 2922 Atlantic Ave #200, Atlantic City, NJ 08401 USA

Sandy Jr, Alomar *Baseball Player*
4635 Prestwick Xing, Westlake, OH 44145 USA

Sanford, Ed *Hockey Player*
18 Clearwater Rd, Winchester, MA 01890-4011

Sanford, Jack
2300 Presidential Way, West Palm Beach, FL 33401

Sanford, Lucius M *Football Player*
1350 Allegheny St SW, Atlanta, GA 30310 USA

Sanford, Meredith *Athlete*
2800 Highway 389, Starkville, MS 39759-8379

Sanford, Richard M (Rick) *Football Player*
335 Lemonts Road, Chapin, SC 29036 USA

Sangavi *Actor, Bollywood*
20 4th Street, Dr. Subraya Nagar Kodambakkam, Chennai, TN 600024, INDIA

Sangeetha *Actor, Bollywood*
26A Brindavan Apartments, Karumari Amman Koil Street Vadapalani, Chennai, TN 600026, INDIA

Sanger, David J *Musician*
Old Wesleyan Chapel, Embleton Near Cockermouth, Cumbria, CA13 9YA, UNITED KINGDOM (UK)

Sanger, Frederick *Nobel Prize Laureate*
Far Leys Fen Lane, Swaffham Bulbeck, Cambridge, CB5 0NJ, UNITED KINGDOM (UK)

Sanger, Stephan W *Business Person*
General Mills Inc, 1 General Mills Blvd, PO Box 1113, Minneapolis, MN 55440 USA

SanGiacomo, Laura *Actor*
Rigberg Roberts Rugolo, 1180 S Beverly Dr #601, Los Ageles, CA 90035 USA

Sangster, Jimmy *Writer*
1590 Lindercrest Dr, Beverly Hills, CA 90210 USA

Sangster, Thomas *Actor*
Marcus & McCrimmon Management, 4 Fitzwarren Gardens, Highgate, London, UNITED KINGDOM (UK)

Sangueli, Andrei *Prime Minister*
Parliament House, Prosp 105, Kishineau, 277073, MOLDOVA

Sanguinetti Cairolo, Julio Maria *President*
Partido Colorado, Andres Martinez Trueba 1271, Montevideo, URUGUAY

Sanha, Malam Bacai *President*
President's Office, Bissau, GUINEA-BISSAU

SanJuan, Olga *Actor*
O'Brien, 12100 Sunset Blvd #2, Los Ageles, CA 90049 USA

Sanjukta, Singh *Actor, Bollywood*
4th Floor Mona Apts, Breach Candy, Mumbai, MS 400036, INDIA

Sano, Roya A *Religious Leader*
United Methodist Church, PO Box 320, Nashville, TN 37202 USA

Sanobar, Kabir *Actor, Bollywood*
402 Karan Building Yari Road, Versova Andheri (W), Mumbai, MS 400061, INDIA

Sansom, Bruce *Ballerina*
Royal Ballet, Convent Garden, Bow St, London, WC2E 9DD, UNITED KINGDOM (UK)

Sansom, Chip *Cartoonist*
204 Long Beach Road, Centerville, MA 02632 USA

Sant, Alfred *Prime Minister*
National Labor Center, Mills End Road, Hannum, MALTA

Santa Rosa, Gilberto *Musician*
Universal Attractions, 225 W 57th St #500, New York, NY 10019 USA

Santamaria, Eduardo *Actor*
Gabriel Blanco Iglesias (Mexico), Rio Balsas 35-32, Colonia Cuauhtemoc, DF, 06500, Mexico

Santana, Carlos *Musician, Songwriter*
Santana Mgmt, 121 Jordan St, San Rafael, CA 94901 USA

Santana, Manuel *Tennis Player*
International Tennis Hall of Fame, 194 Bellevue Ave, Newport, RI 02840 USA

Santer, Jacques *Misc*
69 Rue J P Huberty, 1742, LUXEMBOURG

Santiago, Benito R *Baseball Player*
12503 NW 23rd St, Pembroke Pines, FL 33028 USA

Santiago, Daniel *Basketball Player*
Phoenix Suns, 201 East Jefferson Street, Phoenix, AZ 85004 USA

Santiago, Eddie *Musician*
Sony Music Miami, 605 Lincoln Rd, Miami Beach, FL 33138 USA

Santiago, Tessie *Actor*
Untitled Entertainment (LA), 8436 W 3rd St #650, Los Angeles, CA 90048 USA

Santiago-Hudson, Ruben *Actor*
Gersh Agency, 232 N Canon Dr, Beverly Hills, CA 90210 USA

Santo, Ron *Athlete, Baseball Player*
1721 Meadow Lane, Bannockburn, IL 60015 USA

Santo, Ronald E (Ron) *Baseball Player*
1721 Meadow lane, Bannockbum, IL 60015 USA

Santo & Johnny
217 Edgewood Ave., Clearwater, FL 34615

Santoni, Reni *Actor*
Henderson/Hogan, 8285 W Sunset Blve #1, West Hollywood, CA 90046 USA

Santorelli, Frank *Actor*
Stone Meyer & Genow, 9665 Wilshire Blvd #510, Beverly Hills, CA 90212 USA

Santorini, Paul E *Physicist, Engineer*
PO Box 49, Athens, GREECE

Santoro, Rodrigo *Actor*
William Morris Agency (WMA-LA), 1 William Morris Pl, Beverly Hills, CA 90212 USA

Santorum, Rick *Senator*
1101 Landerset Dr, Herndon, VA 20170-2083 USA

Santos, Al *Actor*
Don Buchwald & Associates Inc (LA), 6500 Wilshire Blvd #2200, Los Angeles, CA 90048 USA

Santos, Joe *Actor*
1444 Queens Dr, Los Angeles, CA 90069 USA

Santos, Pablo *Actor*
Don Buchwald & Associates Inc (LA), 6500 Wilshire Blvd #2200, Los Angeles, CA 90048 USA

Santos, Rey-Phillip *Actor*
Dramatic Artists Agency, 50-16th Avenue, WA 98033

Santos de Oliveira, Alessandra *Basketball Player*
Washington Mystics, MCI Center, 601 F St NW, Washington, DC 20004 USA

Sanz, Alejandro *Musician, Songwriter*
RLM Intl, 800 Ocean Dr #19, Miami Beach, FL 33139 USA

Sanz, Horatio *Actor*
3 Arts Entertainment Inc, 9460 Wilshire Blvd Fl 7, Beverly Hills, CA 90212 USA

Saper, Clifford *Doctor*
Beth Israel Hospital, Neurology Dept, 330 Brookline Ave, Boston, MA 02215 USA

Saperstein, David *Writer, Director, Producer*
Fran Saperstein Organization, Marina del Rey, CA 90292 USA

Sapienza, Al
10474 Santa Monica Blvd. #380, W. Los Angeles, CA 90025

Saplenza, Al *Actor*
PO Box 691240, West Hollywood, CA 90069 USA

Sapp, Bob *Actor, Wrestler*
Writers and Artists Group Intl (LA), 8383 Wilshire Blvd #550, Beverly Hills, CA 90211 USA

Sapp, Carolyn
1840 41st Ave. #102-227, Capitola, CA 95010-2513

Sapp, Warren *Football Player*
16609 Villalenda de Avila, Tampa, FL 33613 USA

Sara, Mia *Actor*
2311 Alto Oak Dr, Los Ageles, CA 90068 USA

Sarachan, Dave *Soccer Player, Coach*
Chicago Fire, 980 N Michigan Ave #1998, Chicago, IL 60611 USA

Sarafanov, Gennadi V *Misc*
Potchta Kosmonavtov, Moskovskol Oblasti, Syvisdny Goroduk, 141160, RUSSIA

Sarafian, Richard C *Director, Actor, Writer*
Leavitt Talent Group, 6404 Wilshire Blvd, Suite 950, Los Angeles, CA 90048 USA

Sarah, Duchess of York
Birch Hall, Windlesham Surrey, ENGLAND, GU2O 6BN

Saraiva Martins, Jose Cardinal *Religious Leader*
Via Pancrazio Pfeiffer 10, Rome, 00193, ITALY

Saralegui, Cristina *Commentator*
William Morris Agency, 151 El Camino Dr, Beverly Hills, CA 90212 USA

Saramago, Jose *Writer*
Los Topes 3, 35572 Tias/Lansarote, Canaries, SPAIN

Sarandon, Chris *Actor*
9540 Hidden Valley Road, Beverly Hills, CA 90210 USA

Sarandon, Susan *Actor*
International Creative Mgmt, 40 W 57th St
#1800, New York, NY 10019 USA

Saranya *Actor, Bollywood*
17A Rajaram Directors Colony,
Kodambakkam, Chennai, TN 600024,
INDIA

Saraste, Jukka-Pekka
Van Walsum Mgmt, 4 Addison Bridge
Place, London, W14 8XP, UNITED
KINGDOM (UK)

Sarbanes, Paul *Senator*
320 Suffolk Rd, Baltimore, MD 21218-
2521 USA

Sarcev, Ursula
PO Box 25738, Los Angeles, CA 90025

Sardi, Vincent Jr *Business Person*
Sardi's Restaurant, 234 W 44th St, New
York, NY 10036 USA

Sare, Chris
21100 Erwin St., Woodland Hills, CA
91367

Sarfatl, Alain *Architect*
28 Rue Barbet du Jouy, Paris, 75007,
FRANCE

Sargent, Ben *Editor, Cartoonist*
Austin American-Statesman, 166 E
Riverside Dr, Austin, TX 78704 USA

Sargent, John T *Producer*
Hasley Lane, Watermill, NY 11976 USA

Sargent, Joseph *Director, Producer*
27432 Latigo Bay View Dr, Malibu, CA
90265 USA

Sargent, Ronald L *Business Person*
Staples Inc, PO Box 9265, Framingham,
MA 01701 USA

Sargent, Wallace *Astronomer*
400 S Berkeley Ave, Pasadena, CA 91107
USA

Sargeson, Alan M *Misc*
National University, Chemistry Dept,
Canberra, ACT, 0200, AUSTRALIA

Sari, Gabriela *Actor*
Telefe - Argentina, Pavon 2444
(C1248AAT), Buenos Aires, ARGENTINA

Saritha *Actor, Bollywood*
Karthik Apartments III Floor, No.46,
Vijayaraghava Road, T. Nagar, Chennai,
TN 600017, INDIA

Sarkisian, Alex *Football Player*
1604 E 142nd St, East Chicago, IN 46312
USA

Sarna, Craig *Hockey Player*
1375 Brown Road S, Wayzata, MN 55391
USA

Sarne, Tanya *Fashion Designer*
Ghost, Chapel 263 Kensal Road, London,
W10 5DB, UNITED KINGDOM (UK)

Sarner, Craig *Hockey Player*
1375 Brown Road S, Wayzata, MN 55391
USA

Sarni, Vincent A *Baseball Player, Misc*
Pittsburgh Pirates, PNC Park, 115 Federal
St, Pittsburgh, PA 15212 USA

Sarnoff, Liz *Actor*
Creative Artists Agency LCC (CAA-LA),
9830 Wilshire Blvd, Beverly Hills, CA
90212 USA

Sarnoff, William *Publisher*
Warner Publishing Inc, 1325 Ave of
Americas, New York, NY 10019 USA

Sarojadevi *Actor, Bollywood*
351 4th Main Road, Sadasivanagar,
Bangalore, KA, 560080, INDIA

Sarosi, Imre *Swimmer, Coach*
1033 Bp Harrer Dal Utca 4, HUNGARY

Sarrazin, Michael *Actor*
9696 Culver Blvd #203, Culver City, CA
90232 USA

Sarsgaard, Peter *Actor*
Creative Artists Agency, 9830 Wilshire
Blvd, Beverly Hills, CA 90212 USA

Sartzetakis, Christos *President*
Presidential Palace, 7 Vas Georgiou B,
Odos Zalokosta 10, Athens, GREECE

Sarven, Allan (Al Snow) *Wrestler*
World Wrestling Entertainment (WWE),
1241 E Main St, Stamford, CT 06905 USA

Sarzo, Rudy
1155 N. La Cienega Blvd. #506, Los
Angeles, CA 90069

Sasaki, Kazuhiro *Baseball Player*
Seattle Mariners, Safeco Field, PO Box
4100, Seattle, WA 98194 USA

Sasdy, Peter *Director*
Cleves, 21 Matham Rd E, Molesey, Surrey,
KT8 0SX, ENGLAND

Sasikala *Actor, Bollywood*
D-10 Parsan Apartments, 204 T.T.K. Road
Alwarpet, Chennai, TN 600018, INDIA

Sassano, C E *Business Person*
Bausch & Lomb, 1 Bausch & Lomb Place,
Rochester, NY 14604 USA

Sassard, Jacqueline
54 av. Montaigne, Paris, FRANCE,
F-75008

Sasselov, Dimitar *Astronomer*
Harvard-Smithsonian Astrophysics Center,
60 Garden St, Cambridge, MA 02138 USA

Sasser, Clarence E *War Hero*
13414 FM 521, Rosharon, TX 77583 USA

Sasso, Will *Comedian, Actor*
InnerAct Entertainment, 141 S Barrington
Ave #E, Los Ageles, CA 90049 USA

Sasson, Debra *Opera Singer*
Erlenhaupstr 10, Bensheim, 64625,
GERMANY

Sassoon, Beverly *Model*
1511 SE 2nd St, Fort Lauderdale, FL
33301 USA

Sassoon, David *Fashion Designer*
Bellville Sassoon, 18 Culford Gardens,
London, SW3 2ST, UNITED KINGDOM
(UK)

Sassoon, Vidal *Stylist*
1163 Calle Vista Dr, Beverly Hills, CA
90210 USA

Sassou-Nguesso, Denis *President*
President's Office, Brazzaville, CONGO
REPUBLIC

Sastre, Ines *Actor*
International Creative Management
(ICM-LA), 8942 Wilshire Blvd, Beverly
Hills, CA 90211 USA

Satanowski, Robert *Conductor*
Ul Madalinskiego 50/52 m 1, Warsaw,
02-581, POLAND

Satcher, David *Misc*
Kaiser Family Foundation, 2400 Sand Hill
Road, Menlo Park, CA 94025 USA

Satcher, Leslie *Musician, Music Group,
Songwriter*
Warner Bros Records, 3300 Warner Blvd,
Burbank, CA 91505 USA

Satchwell, Brooke *Actor*
Darren Gray Management, 2 Marston
Lane, Portsmouth, Hampshire, England,
PO3 5TW

Sather, Glen C *Hockey Player, Coach*
505 Buffalo St, Banff, AB T0L 0C0,
CANADA

Sathiyaraj *Actor*
13-A Pirakathambal Street, Chennai, TN
600 034, INDIA

Sato, Kazuo *Economist*
300 E 71st St #15H, New York, NY 10021
USA

Satra, Sonia *Actor*
Innovative Artists, 1505 10th St, Santa
Monica, CA 90401 USA

Satre, Philip G *Business Person*
Harrah's Entertainment, 1023 Cherry
Road, Memphis, TN 38117 USA

Satriani, Joe *Musician, Music Group*
Bill Graham Mgmt, 360 17th St, Oakland,
CA 94612 USA

Satterfield, Paul *Actor*
PO Box 6945, Beverly Hills, CA 90212
USA

Satturno, William *Archaeologist*
University of New Hampshire, Archaelogy
Dept, Durham, NH 03824 USA

Saubert, Jean M *Skier*
147 Harbor Heights Blvd, Bigfork, MT
59911 USA

Saud, Prince Sultan Bin Abdulaziz al
Government Official
Defense Ministry, PO Box 26731, Airport
Road, Riyadh, 11165, SAUDI ARABIA

Saudek, Jan *Photographer*
Blodkova 6, Prague 3, 130 00, CZECH
REPUBLIC

Sauer, George H Jr *Football Player*
2608 E 8th St #201, Sioux Falls, SD
57103 USA

Sauer, Hank
207 Vallejo Ct., Millbrae, CA 94030

Sauer, Louis *Architect*
3472 Marlowe St, Montreal, QC, H4A
2L7, CANADA

Sauer, Richard J *Educator*
National 4-H Council, 7100 Connecticut
Ave, Bethesda, MD 20815 USA

Sauerlander, Willibald P W *Historian*
Zentralinstitut fyr Kunstgeschichte,
Meiserstr 10, Munich, 80333, GERMANY

Sauers, Gene
19 Herons Nest, Savannah, GA 31410-
3331

Saul, April *Journalist*
Philadelphia Inquirer, Editorial Dept, 400
N Broad St, Philadelphia, PA 19130 USA

Saul, John
Robin Straus, 229 E 79th St, New York, NY 10021

Saul, John W III *Writer*
The Firm, 9100 Wilshire Blvd #100W, Beverly Hills, CA 90210 USA

Saul, Ralph S *Business Person*
805 Oxford Crest, Villanova, PA 19085 USA

Saul, Richard R (Rich) *Football Player*
127 G St, Newport Beach, CA 92661 USA

Saul, Stephanie *Journalist*
Newsday, Editorial Dept, 235 Pinelawn Road, Melville, NY 11747 USA

Sauli, Daniel *Actor*
Firm, The, 9465 Wilshire Blvd, Beverly Hills, CA 90212 USA

Sauls, Don *Religious Leader*
Pentecostal Free Will Baptist Church, PO Box 1568, Dunn, NC 28335 USA

Saum, Sherri *Actor*
Jerry Shandrew PR, 1050 South Stanley Avenue, Los Angeles, CA 90019-6634 USA

Saunders, Cicely *Misc*
Saint Christopher's Hospice, 51 Lawreie Park Road, Sydenham, 6DZ, UNITED KINGDOM (UK)

Saunders, Doug
43 Saint Kitts, Dana Point, CA 92629

Saunders, George *Writer*
Random House, 1745 Broadway #B1, New York, NY 10019 USA

Saunders, George L Jr *Attorney General*
179 E Lake Shore Dr, Chicago, IL 60611 USA

Saunders, Jennifer *Actor*
P F D, Drury House, 34-43 Russell St, London, WC2B 5HA, UNITED KINGDOM (UK)

Saunders, John *Cartoonist*
King Features Syndicate, 888 7th Ave, New York, NY 10106 USA

Saunders, John *Sportscaster*
ESPN-TV, Sports Dept, ESPN Plaza 935 Middle St, Bristol, CT 06010 USA

Saunders, John R *Race Car Driver*
Watkins Glen Speedway, PO Box 500F, Watkins Glen, NY 14891 USA

Saunders, Lori *Actor*
Lori's Friends, 99 La Vuelta Road, Santa Barbara, CA 93108 USA

Saunders, Phil (Flip) *Basketball Player, Coach*
Minnesota Timberwolves, Target Center, 600 1st Ave N, Minneapolis, MN 55403 USA

Saunders, Rachel
PO Box 993, Bonifay, FL 32425

Saunders, Townsend *Wrestler*
733 Chantilly Dr, Sierra Vista, AZ 85635 USA

Saura, Carlos *Director*
Antonio Duran, Calle Arturo Soria 52, #Edif 2 1-5A, Madrid, 28027, SPAIN

Sauve, Robert (Bob) *Hockey Player*
Jandec Inc, 803-3080 Boul le Carrefour, Laval, QC, H7T 2R5, CANADA

Savage, Ann *Actor*
1541 N Hayworth Ave #203, Los Angeles, CA 90046 USA

Savage, Ben *Actor*
International Creative Mgmt, 8942 Wilshire Blvd #219, Beverly Hills, CA 90211 USA

Savage, Chantay *Musician, Music Group*
Famous Artists Agency, 250 W 57th St, New York, NY 10107 USA

Savage, Fred *Actor*
Original Film, 2045 S Barrington Ave, Los Angeles, CA 90025 USA

Savage, John *Actor*
5584 Bonneville Road, Hidden Hills, CA 91302 USA

Savage, Michael *Radio Personality*
6 Knoll Ln #E, Mill Valley, CA 94941 USA

Savage, Randy (Macho Man) *Wrestler*
7650 Bayshore Dr #10038, Treasure Island, FL 33706 USA

Savage, Randy Macho Man
7650 Bayshore Dr. #10038, St. Petersburg, FL 33706

Savage, Rick *Musician*
Q Prime Mgmt, 729 7th Ave #1400, New York, NY 10019 USA

Savage, Tracie
6212 Banner Ave., Los Angeles, CA 90038

Savage Garden
9255 Sunset Blvd. #411, W. Hollywood, CA 90069

Saval, Dany
131 rue de l'Universite, Paris, FRANCE, 75007

Savant, Doug *Actor*
1015 E Angeleno Ave, Burbank, CA 91501 USA

Savard, Denis *Hockey Player*
Chicago Blackhawks, United Center, 1901 W Madison St, Chicago, IL 60612 USA

Savard, Serge A *Hockey Player*
1790 Ch du Golf, RR 1, Saint Bruno, QC, J3V 4P6, CANADA

Savary, Jerome *Director*
Theatre National de Chaillot, 1 Place du Trocadero, Paris, 75116, FRANCE

Savchenko, Arkadly M *Opera Singer*
8-358 Storozhovskaya Str, Minsk, 220002, BELARUS

Saveleva, Lyudmila M *Actor*
Tverskaya Str 19, #76, Moscow, 103050, RUSSIA

Saves the Day *Music Group*
Jeff Hanson Management & Promotions, 2813 South Hiwassee Road, #307, Orlando, FL 32835 USA

Savident, John *Actor*
Coronation Street, Granada Television, Quay Street, Manchester, M60 9EA, UNITED KINGDOM (UK)

Savidge, Jennifer *Actor*
2705 Glenower Ave, Los Angeles, CA 90027 USA

Savile, David
28 Colomb St., London, ENGLAND, SW10 9EW

Saville, Curtis *Misc*
RFD Box 44, West Charleston, VT 05872 USA

Saville, Fleur *Actor*
Auckland Actors, PO Box 56460, Dominion Road, Auckland, NEW ZEALAND

Saville, Kathleen *Misc*
RFD Box 44, West Charleston, VT 05872 USA

Savini, Tom
311 Taylor St., Pittsburgh, PA 15224

Savinykh, Viktor P *Misc*
Moscow State University, Gorochovskii 4, Moscow, 103064, RUSSIA

Savitskaya, Svetalana Y *Misc*
Russian Association, Khovanskaya Str 3, Moscow, 129515, RUSSIA

Savitsky, George M *Football Player*
350 E Seabright Road, Ocean City, NJ 08226 USA

Savitt, Dick
19 E. 80th St., New York, NY 10021-0109

Savitt, Richard (Dick) *Tennis Player*
19 E 80th St, New York, NY 10021 USA

Savoy, Gene
643 Ralston St., Reno, NV 89503

Savoy, Guy *Chef*
101 Blvd Pereire, Paris, 75017, FRANCE

Savvina, Iya S *Actor*
Bolshaya, Grunzinskaya St 12 #43, Moscow, 123242, RUSSIA

Saw, Maung *Prime Minister, General*
Prime Minister's Office, Yangon, MYANMAR

Sawa, Devon *Actor*
7201 Melrose Ave #202, Los Angeles, CA 90046 USA

Sawalha, Julia *Actor*
P F D, Drury House, 34-43 Russell St, London, WC2B 5HA, UNITED KINGDOM (UK)

Sawalha, Nadia *Talk Show Host*
BBC, Broadcasting House, Portland Place, London, W1A 1AA

Sawallisch, Wolfgang *Musician, Conductor*
Hinterm Bichi 2, Grassau, 83224, GERMANY

Sawyer, Amos *President*
President's Office, Executive Mansion, PO Box 9001, Monrovia, LIBERIA

Sawyer, Charles H *Misc*
466 Tuallitan Road, Los Angeles, CA 90049 USA

Sawyer, Daine *Commentator*
147 Columbus Ave #300, New York, NY 10023 USA

Sawyer, Diane *Television Host*
Good Morning America, 147 Columbus Ave Fl 6, New York, NY 10023 USA

Sawyer, Elton *Race Car Driver*
Akins Motorsports, 185 McKenzie Road, Mooresville, NC 28115 USA

Sawyer, Forrest *Commentator*
NBC-TV, News Dept, 30 Rockefeller Plaza, New York, NY 10112 USA

Sawyer, James L *Misc*
Leather Workers Union, 11 Peabody Square, Peabody, MA 01960 USA

Sawyer, Paul *Race Car Driver*
Richmond International Raceway, PO Box 9257, Richmond, VA 23227 USA

Sawyer, Robert E *Religious Leader*
Moravian Church Southern Province, 459 S Church St, Winston Salem, NC 27101 USA

Sawyer Brown *Music Group*
Monterey Peninsula Artists (Nashville), 124 12th Ave S #410, Nashville, TN 37203 USA

Sax, Stephen L (Steve) *Baseball Player*
201 Wesley Court, Roseville, CA 95661 USA

Sax, Steve
201 Wesley Ct., Roseville, CA 95661

Saxbe, William H *Attorney General, Senator*
4600 N Ocean Blvd #200, Boynton Beach, FL 33435 USA

Saxe, Adrian *Artist*
4835 N Figueroa St, Los Angeles, CA 90042 USA

Saxon, David S *Physicist*
1008 Hilts Ave, Los Angeles, CA 90024 USA

Saxon, Edward *Producer*
Creative Artists Agency LCC (CAA-LA), 9830 Wilshire Blvd, Beverly Hills, CA 90212 USA

Saxon, James E *Football Player*
RR 3 Box 34X, Beaufort, SC 29906 USA

Saxon, James E (Jimmy) *Football Player*
1 Mulberry Lane, Austin, TX 78746 USA

Saxon, John *Actor*
2432 Banyan Dr, Los Angeles, CA 90049 USA

Saxton, Johnny *Boxer*
Crystal Palms, 1710 4th Ave N, Lake Worth, FL 33460 USA

Saxton, Shirley Childress *Music Group, Musician*
Sweet Honey Agency, PO Box 600099, Newtonville, MA 02460 USA

Say, Peggy
438 Lake Shore Dr., Cadiz, KY 42211

Sayed, Mostafa Amr El *Misc*
579 Westover Dr NW, Atlanta, GA 30305 USA

Sayer, Leo *Musician, Music Group, Songwriter*
Mission Control, Business Center, Lower Road, London, SE16 2XB, UNITED KINGDOM (UK)

Sayers, E Roger *Educator*
University of Alabama, President's Office, Tuscaloosa, AL 35487 USA

Sayers, Gale *Football Player*
1313 N Ritchie Court #407, Chicago, IL 60610 USA

Saykally, Richard J *Misc*
University of California, Chemistry Dept, Latimer Hall, Berkeley, CA 94720 USA

Sayles, John T *Director*
130 W 25th St #12A, New York, NY 10001 USA

Sayre, Anne
1268 E. 14th St., Brooklyn, NY 11230

Sbarge, Raphael
4526 Wilshire Blvd., Los Angeles, CA 90010

Scaasi, Arnold *Fashion Designer*
16 E 52nd St, New York, NY 10022 USA

Scacchi, Greta *Actor*
P F D, Drury House, 34-43 Russell St, London, WC2B 5HA USA

Scaduto, Al *Cartoonist*
250 Chapel St, Milford, CT 06460 USA

Scaggs, Boz *Musician*
9460 Wilshire Blvd. #310, Beverly Hills, CA 90212

Scaggs, William R (Boz) *Musician, Music Group, Songwriter*
H K Mgmt, 9200 W Sunset Blvd #530, Los Angeles, CA 90069 USA

Scales, Dwight *Football Player*
6112 Rosevelt Circle NW, Huntsville, AL 35810 USA

Scales, Prunella *Actor*
Conway Van Gelder Robinson, 18-21 Jermyn St, London, SW1Y 6NB, UNITED KINGDOM (UK)

Scalia, Jack *Actor*
16260 Ventura Blvd, Encino, CA 91436 USA

Scalia, Justice Antonin *Judge*
US Supreme Court, 1 1st St NE, Washington, DC 20543 USA

Scalians, Bret *Musician*
Media Five Entertainment, 3005 Brodhead Read #170, Bethlehem, PA 18020 USA

Scalzo, Tony *Music Group, Musician*
Russell Carter Artists, 315 Ponce de Leon Blvd #755, Decatur, GA 30030 USA

Scaminace, Joseph M *Business Person*
Sherwin-Williams Co, 101 W Prospect Ave, Cleveland, OH 44115 USA

Scancarelli, Jim *Cartoonist*
Mark J Cohen, PO Box 1892, Santa Rosa, CA 95402 USA

Scandiuzzi, Roberto *Opera Singer*
Opera et Concert, Maximilianstr 22, Munich, 80539, GERMANY

Scanga, Italo *Artist*
7127 Olivetas, La Jolla, CA 92037 USA

Scanlan, Hugh P S *Misc*
23 Seven Stones Dr, Broadstairs, Kent, UNITED KINGDOM (UK)

Scarabelli, Michele *Actor*
9157 Sunset Blvd #215, Los Angeles, CA 90069 USA

Scarbath, John C (Jack) *Football Player*
736 Calvert Road, Rising Sun, MD 21911 USA

Scarbrough, W Carl *Misc*
Furniture Workers Union, 1910 Airlane Dr, Nashville, TN 37210 USA

Scardelletti, Robert A *Misc*
Transportation Communications Union, 3 Research Place, Rockville, MD 20850 USA

Scardino, Albert J *Journalist*
19 Empire House, Thurloe Place, London, SW7 2RU, UNITED KINGDOM (UK)

Scarf, Herbert E *Economist*
88 Blake Road, Hamden, CT 06517 USA

Scarface *Musician*
American Talent Agency, 173 Main St, Ossining, NY 10562 USA

Scarfe, Gerald A *Cartoonist*
10 Cheyne Walk, London, SW3, UNITED KINGDOM (UK)

Scarfe, Jonathan
4739 Lankershim Blvd., No. Hollywood, CA 91602-1803

Scargill, Arthur *Misc*
National Union of Mineworkers, 2 Huddersfield Road, Bamsley, UNITED KINGDOM (UK)

Scarpelli, Glenn
3480 Barham Blvd. #320, Los Angeles, CA 90068

Scarwid, Diana *Actor*
PO Box 3614, Savannah, GA 31414 USA

Scates, Al *Volleyball Player, Coach*
8433 Apple Hill Court, Las Vegas, NV 89128 USA

Scattini, Monica *Actor*
Carol Levi Co, Via Giuseppe Pisanelli, Rome, 00196, ITALY

Scelba-Shorte, Mercedes *Reality TV Star*
Ty Ty Baby Productions, 8346 W Third St #650, Los Angeles, CA 90048 USA

Schaaf-Behle, Petra
Am Rodeland 22, Willingen, GERMANY, D-34508

Schaal, Richard *Actor*
612 Gulf Blvd #9, Indian Rocks Beach, FL 33785 USA

Schaal, Wendy *Actor*
Gage Group, 14724 Ventura Blvd #505, Shreman Oaks, CA 91403 USA

Schaap, Dick
77 W. 66th St., New York, NY 10023

Schacher, Mel *Musician*
Lustig Talent, PO Box 770850, Orlando, FL 32877 USA

Schachman, Howard K *Biologist*
University of California, Molecular Biology Dept, Berkeley, CA 94720 USA

Schacht, Henry B *Business Person*
Lucent Technologies Inc, 600 Mountain Ave, New Providence, NJ 07974 USA

Schachter, Norm *Referee*
7716 Westlawn Ave, Los Angeles, CA 90045 USA

Schachter, Steven *Director, Writer*
Writers and Artists Group Intl (LA), 8383 Wilshire Blvd #550, Beverly Hills, CA 90211 USA

Schachter Sisters
182-06 Midland Park Blvd., Jamaica Estates, NY 11432

Schachter-Shalomi, Zalman *Religious Leader*
Spiritual Eldering Institute, 970 Aurora Ave, Boulder, CO 80302 USA

Schadler, Jay *Commentator*
ABC-TV, News Dept, 77 W 66th St, New York, NY 10023 USA

Schadt, James P *Publisher*
Reader's Digest Assn, Reader's Digest Road, Pleasantville, NY 10570 USA

Schaech, Johnathon *Actor*
Lee Daniels Entertainment, 625 Broadway #6M, New York, NY 10012 USA

Schaech, Jonathan *Actor*
9055 Hollywood Hills Road, Los Angeles, CA 90046 USA

Schaefer, Ernst J *Scientist*
Tufts University, Nutrition Research Center, Medford, MA 02155 USA

Schaefer, George A Jr *Financier*
Fifth Third Bancorp, 38 Fountain Square Plaza, Cincinnati, OH 45263 USA

Schaefer, Henry F III *Misc*
University of Georgia, Computational Quantum Chemistry Center, Athens, GA 30602 USA

Schaefer, Molly *Publisher*
Town & Country Magazine, 1700 Broadway, New York, NY 10019 USA

Schaefer, Roberto *Cinematographer*
Innovative Artists, 1505 10th St, Santa Monica, CA 90401 USA

Schaefer, William D *Governor*
7184 Springhouse Lane, Baltimore, MD 21226 USA

Schaeffer, Eric *Actor, Director*
Writers & Artists, 8383 Wilshire Blvd #550, Beverly Hills, CA 90211 USA

Schaeffer, George
1040 Woodland Dr., Beverly Hills, CA 90210

Schaeffer, Leonard *Business Person*
WellPoint Health Networks, 1 Wellpoint Way, Westlake Village, CA 91362 USA

Schaefzel, John R *Writer*
2 Bay Tree Lane, Bethesda, MD 20816 USA

Schaffel, Lewis *Basketball Player, Misc*
Miami Heat, American Airlines Arena, 601 Biscayne Blvd, Miami, FL 33132 USA

Schaffer, Eric *Musician, Music Group*
Kennedy Center for Performing Arts, Washington, DC 20011 USA

Schafrath, Dick *Football Player*
3040 Shad Dr E, Mansfield, OH 44903 USA

Schakper, Allison *Writer*
Endeavor Agency LLC (LA), 9601 Wilshire Blvd Fl 3, Beverly Hills, CA 90210 USA

Schall, Alvin A *Judge*
US Appeals Court, 717 Madison Place NW, Washington, DC 20439 USA

Schaller, George B *Biologist*
90 Sentry Hill Road, Roxbury, CT 06783 USA

Schaller, Willie *Soccer Player*
3283 S Indiana St, Lakewood, CO 80228 USA

Schallert, William *Actor*
14920 Ramos Pl, Pacific Palisades, CA 90272 USA

Schally, Andrew V *Nobel Prize Laureate*
5025 Kawanee Ave, Metairie, LA 70006 USA

Schama, Simon M *Historian, Writer*
Minda de Gunzburg European Studies Center, Adolphus Hall, Cambridge, MA 02138 USA

Schamehorn, Kevin *Hockey Player*
25379 W Fan River Rd, Sturgis, MI 49091-9747

Schanberg, Sydney H *Journalist*
164 W 79th St #12D, New York, NY 10024 USA

Schank, Roger C *Scientist, Doctor*
Northwestern University, Learning Sciences Institute, Evanston, IL 60201 USA

Schanz, Heidi *Actor*
Gersh Agency, 232 N Canon Dr, Beverly Hills, CA 90210 USA

Schapp, Dick *Sportscaster*
ESPN-TV, Sports Dept, ESPN Plaza 935 Middle St, Bristol, CT 06010 USA

Scharansky, Natan *Social Activist, Scientist*
Trade & Industry Ministry, 30 Rehov Agron, Jerusalem, 91002, ISRAEL

Scharar, Erich *Athlete*
Grutstrasse 63, Herrliberg, 8074, SWITZERLAND

Scharping, Rudolf *Government Official*
Wilhelmstr 5, Lahnstein, 56112, GERMANY

Schatz, Albert *Biologist*
Rutgers University, Research/Endowment Foundation, New Brunswick, NJ 08903 USA

Schatz, Gottfried *Biologist, Misc*
Basle University, Klingelbergstr 70, Basle, 4056, SWITZERLAND

Schatz, Howard *Photographer*
435 W Broadway #2, New York, NY 10012 USA

Schatzberg, Jerry N *Director*
International Creative Mgmt, 8942 Wilshire Blvd #219, Beverly Hills, CA 90211 USA

Schatzman, Evry *Physicist*
11 Rue de l'Eglise, Domplerre, Maignelay-Montigny, 60420, FRANCE

Schaudt, Martin *Horse Racer, Athlete*
Gerhardstr 10/2, Albstadt, 72461, GERMANY

Schaufuss, Peter *Ballerina, Director*
Papoutsis Representation, 18 Sundial Ave, London, SE25 4BX, UNITED KINGDOM (UK)

Schayes, Adolph (Dolph) *Basketball Player*
PO Box 156, DeWitt, NY 13214 USA

Schayes, Danny *Basketball Player*
PO Box 665, Windermere, FL 34786 USA

Scheck, Barry *Attorney General, Educator*
Yeshiva University, Law School, 55 5th Ave, New York, NY 10003 USA

Scheckter, Jody D *Race Car Driver*
39 Ave Princess Grace, Monte Carlo, MONACO

Schedeen, Anne *Actor*
Metropolitan Talent Agency, 4526 Wilshire Blvd, Los Angeles, CA 90010 USA

Scheffczyk, Leo Cardinal *Religious Leader*
PD Comboni 2, Rome, ITALY

Scheffer, Victor B *Biologist*
14806 SE 54th St, Bellevue, WA 98006 USA

Scheffler, Israel *Misc*
Harvard University, Larsen Hall, Cambridge, MA 02138 USA

Scheibel, Arnold B *Doctor*
16231 Morrison St, Encino, CA 91436 USA

Scheider, Roy *Actor*
PO Box 364, Sagaponack, NY 11962 USA

Schein, Philip S *Doctor*
6212 Robinwood Road, Bethesda, MD 20817 USA

Schekman, Randy W *Scientist*
Howard Hughes Institute, 4000 Jones Bridge Road, Chevy Chase, MD 20815 USA

Schell, Catherine *Actor*
Postfach 800504, Cologne, 51005, GERMANY

Schell, Jonathan *Journalist*
Newsday, Editorial Dept, 235 Pinelawn Road, Melville, NY 11747 USA

Schell, Jozef S *Biologist, Scientist*
College de France, 11 Pl Marcelin-Berthelot, Paris Cedex 05, 75231, FRANCE

Schell, Maria *Actor*
Preitenegg, 9451, AUSTRIA

Schell, Maximilian *Actor*
2869 Royston Place, Beverly Hills, CA 90210 USA

Schell, Ronnie
1888 Century Park E. #622, Los Angeles, CA 90067

Schellenbach, Kate *Musician*
Metropolitan Entertainment, 2 Penn Plaza #2600, New York, NY 10121 USA

Schellenberg, August *Actor*
Gold Marshak Liedtke, 3500 W Olive Ave #1400, Burbank, CA 91505 USA

Schellhase, Dave *Basketball Player*
31139 Wrencrest Dr, Zephyrhills, FL 33543 USA

Schelling, Gunther F K *Engineer*
Graz University, Rechbauerstr 12, Graz, 8010, AUSTRIA

Schelling, Thomas C *Economist*
University of Maryland, Economics Dept, College Park, MD 20742 USA

Schellman, John A *Misc*
65 W 30th Ave #508, Eugene, OR 97405 USA

Schelmerding, Kirk *Race Car Driver, Misc*
Childress Racing, PO Box 1189, Industrial Dr, Welcome, NC 27374 USA

Schemansky, Norbert *Misc*
24826 New York St, Dearborn, MI 48124 USA

Schembechler, Bo
1904 Boulder Dr., Ann Arbor, MI 48104

Schembechler, Glenn E (Bo) Jr *Football Player, Coach*
1904 Boulder Dr, Ann Arbor, MI 48104 USA

Schemling, Bill
PO Box 11308, Portland, OR 97211-0308

Schenk, Franziska *Speed Skater*
DSEG, Mensinger Str 68, Munich, 80992, GERMANY

Schenkel, Chris *Sportscaster*
7101 N Kalorama Road, Leesburg, IN 46538 USA

Schenkenberg, Markus *Model, Actor*
Wilhelmina Models, 300 Park Ave S #200, New York, NY 10010 USA

Schenkkan, Robert F *Writer*
Dramatist Guild, 1501 Broadway #701, New York, NY 10036 USA

Schenkman, Eric *Musician*
DAS Communications, 84 Riverside Dr, New York, NY 10024 USA

Schepisi, Fred *Director*
William Morris Agency (WMA-LA), 1 William Morris Pl, Beverly Hills, CA 90212 USA

Schepisl, Frederic A *Director*
Film House, 159 Eastern Road, South Melbourne, VIC, 3205, AUSTRALIA

Scherbo, Vitali *Gymnast*
8308 Aqua Spray Ave, Las Vegas, NV 89128 USA

Scherbo, Vitaly
8308 Aqua Spray Ave, Las Vegas, NV 89128-7432

Scherega, Harold A *Misc*
212 Homestead Terrace, Ithaca, NY 14850 USA

Scherrer, Jean-Louis *Fashion Designer*
51 Ave du Montaigne, Paris, 75008, FRANCE

Scherrer, Tom *Golfer*
Gaylord Sports Mgmt, 14646 N Kierland Blvd #230, Scottsdale, AZ 85254 USA

Scherza, Chuck *Hockey Player*
51 Manistee St, Pawtucket, RI 02861-4011

Scheuer, Paul J *Misc*
3271 Melemele Place, Honolulu, HI 96822 USA

Schevill, James *Writer*
1309 Oxford St, Berkeley, CA 94709 USA

Schiavelli, Vincent *Actor*
450 N Rossmore Ave #206, Los Angeles, CA 90004 USA

Schiavo, Mary *Government Official, Social Activist*
Ohio State University, Public Policy Dept, Columbus, OH 43210 USA

Schiavone, Carmine
271 Central Park W., New York, NY 10024

Schickel, Richard *Writer, Critic*
9051 Dicks St, Los Angeles, CA 90069 USA

Schickele, Peter *Comedian, Composer*
International Creative Mgmt, 40 W 57th St #1800, New York, NY 10019 USA

Schiebold, Hans *Artist*
13705 SW 118th Court, Tigard, OR 97223 USA

Schieffer, Bob *Commentator*
CBS-TV, 51 W 52nd St, New York, NY 10019 USA

Schiff, Andras *Musician*
Shirley Kirshbaum, 711 W End Ave #5KN, New York, NY 10025 USA

Schiff, Heinrich *Musician*
Astrid Schoerke, Monckegergallee 41, Hannover, 30453, GERMANY

Schiff, John J Jr *Financier*
Cincinnati Financial Corp, 6200 S Gilmore Road, Fairfield, OH 45014 USA

Schiff, Mark *Actor, Comedian*
Gail Stocker Presents, 1025 N Kings Road #113, Los Angeles, CA 90069 USA

Schiff, Richard *Actor*
537 N June St, Los Angeles, CA 90004 USA

Schiff, Robin *Writer*
Broder Webb Chervin Silbermann Agency, The (BWCS), 9242 Beverly Blvd #200, Beverly Hills, CA 90210 USA

Schiffer, Claudia *Model*
Singer Weisberg & Assoc, 60 E 42nd St #1841, New York, NY 10165-1841 USA

Schiffer, Eric *Writer*
6965 El Camino Real #105, PMB 517, Carlsbad, CA 92009

Schiffer, Menahem M *Mathematician*
6404 Ruffin Road, Chevy Chase, MD 20815 USA

Schiffer, Michael *Actor*
Harvest Mgmt, 132 W 80th St #3F, New York, NY 10024 USA

Schiffner, Travis *Actor*
Bohemia Entertainment Group, 8170 Beverly Blvd #102, Los Angeles, CA 90048 USA

Schiffrin, Andre *Publisher*
New Press, 201 E 50th St, New York, NY 10022 USA

Schifrin, Lalo *Composer*
710 N Hillcrest Road, Beverly Hills, CA 90210 USA

Schillebeeckx, Edward *Religious Leader, Misc*
Crossroad Publishing Co, 575 Lexington Ave, New York, NY 10022 USA

Schiller, Harvey W *Misc*
Turner Sports, 1050 Techwood Dr NW, Atlanta, GA 30318 USA

Schiller, Lawrence J *Director, Writer*
5430 Oakdale Ave, Woodland Hills, CA 91364 USA

Schilling, Curtis M (Curt) *Baseball Player*
105 Blackshire Road, Kennet Square, PA 19348 USA

Schilling, Peter
Geiselgasteigstr. 76, Munich, GERMANY, 81545

Schilling, William
626 N. Valley St., Burbank, CA 91505

Schimberg, Henry R *Business Person*
Coca-Cola Enterprises, 2500 Windy Ridge Parkway, Atlanta, GA 30339 USA

Schimberni, Mario *Business Person*
Armando Curcio Editore SpA, Via IV Novembre, Rome, 00187, ITALY

Schimmel, Paul R *Biologist, Misc*
Scripps Research Institute, 10550 N Torrey Pines Road, La Jolla, CA 92037 USA

Schindelholz, Lorenz *Athlete*
Hardstr 184, Herbetswil, 4715, SWITZERLAND

Schinkel, Kenneth (Ken) *Hockey Player*
19927 Beaulieu Court, Fort Myers, FL 33908 USA

Schino, Dominic *Producer*
Magic Touch Records, 12-15 36th Avenue, #4-E, Long Island City, NY 11106 USA

Schipper, Ron *Football Coach*
2406 Orchard Ave, Holland, NI, 49424 USA

Schirinowskij, Wladmir
Sokolnitscheskij wal 38-114, Moscow, RUSSIA, 107113

Schirra Jr, Walter M *Astronaut*
PO Box 73, 16834 Via de Santa Fe, Rancho Santa Fe, CA 92067 USA

Schirripa, Steven R *Actor*
Stone Manners Talent Agency, 6500 Wilshire Blvd, Ste 550, Los Angeles, CA 90048 USA

Schisgal, Murray J *Writer*
International Creative Mgmt, 40 W 57th St #1800, New York, NY 10019 USA

Schissler, Les *Bowler*
3060 E Bridge St #20, Brighton, CO 80601 USA

Schlafly, Phyllis *Social Activist*
68 Fairmont Ave, Alton, IL 62002 USA

Schlag, Edward W *Misc*
Osterwaldstr 91, Munich, 80805, GERMANY

Schlamme, Thomas *Actor*

Schlamme, Thomas *Actor*
Industry Entertainment, 955 S Carrillo Dr #300, Los Angeles, CA 90048 USA

Schlatmann, Gert Jan
Oostzeedijk Gen 39a, Rotterdam, HOLLAND, NL 3062 WK

Schlatter, Charlie *Actor*
638 Lindero Canyon Road #322, Oak Park, CA 91377 USA

Schlatter, George
400 Robert Lane, Beverly Hills, CA 90210

Schleech, Russ *Misc*
21634 Paseo Maravia, Mission Viejo, CA 92962 USA

Schlegel, Hans W *Astronaut*
DLR Astronaulenburo Linder Hohe, Postfach 906058, Cologne, 51140, GERMANY

Schlegel, John P *Educator*
University of San Francisco, President's Office, San Francisco, CA 94117 USA

Schlein, Dov C *Financier*
Republic New York Corp, 452 5th Ave, New York, NY 10018 USA

Schlesinger, Adam *Musician, Music Group, Songwriter*
MOB Agency, 6404 Wilshire Blvd #505, Los Angeles, CA 90048 USA

Schlesinger, Arthur M Jr *Historian*
455 E 51st St, New York, NY 10022 USA

Schlesinger, James R *Secretary*
Georgetown University, 1800 K St NW #400, Washington, DC 20006 USA

Schlesinger, Laura *Radio Personality*
Premier Radio Network, 15260 Ventura Blvd, Suite 500, Sherman Oaks, CA 91403

Schlesinger Jr, Arthur
33 W 42nd St, New York, NY 10036 USA

Schlessinger, Laura *Doctor*
25065 Ashley Ridge Road, Hidden Hills, CA 91302 USA

Schleyer, Paul Von R *Misc*
Frederich-Alexander-Universtat, Henkestr 41, Erlangen, 91469, GERMANY

Schlichtmann, Jan *Attorney General*
359 Hale St, Beverly Farms, MA 01915 USA

Schlondorff, Volker *Director*
Studio Babelsberg, Postfach 900361, Potsdam, 14439, GERMANY

Schloredt, Robert S (Bob) *Football Player*
Nestle-Beich, 1827 N 167th St, Shoreline, WA 98133 USA

Schlossberg, Edwin
641 Ave. of the Americas, New York, NY 10011

Schlossberg, Katie *Actor*
Talent Group, 6300 Wilshire Blvd #2100, Los Angeles, CA 90048 USA

Schlossberg, Katle *Actor*
Talent Group, 5670 Wilshire Blvd, #820, Los Angeles, CA 90036 USA

Schlueter, Dale *Basketball Player*
15555 SW Harcourt Terrace, Portland, OR 97224 USA

Schluter, Poul H *Prime Minister*
Frederiksberg Allee 66, Frederiksberg C, 1820, DENMARK

Schmautz, Bobby
15544 SE Webster Rd., Portland, OR 97267

Schmeichel, Peter *Soccer Player*
Aston Villa, Villa Park, Trinity Road, Birmingham, B6 6HE, UNITED KINGDOM (UK)

Schmeling, Max *Boxer*
Sonnenweg 1, Hollenstedt, D-21279, GERMANY

Schmeling, Maximilian (Max) *Boxer*
Sonnenweg 1, Hollenstedt, 21279, GERMANY

Schmemann, Serge *Journalist*
New York Times, Editorial Dept, 229 W 43rd St, New York, NY 10036 USA

Schmid, Dave
17173 Rayen St., Northridge, CA 91325-2908

Schmid, Kyle *Actor*
Martin Chase Productions, 500 S Buena Vista St, Animation 2E-6, Burbank, CA 91521 USA

Schmid, Rudi *Misc*
211 Woodland Road, Kentfield, CA 94904 USA

Schmid, Sigi *Soccer Player, Coach*
Los Angeles Galaxy, 1010 Rose Bowl Dr, Pasadena, CA 91103 USA

Schmidgall, Jennifer *Hockey Player*
3850 Xenium Court N, Minneapolis, MN 55441 USA

Schmidly, David J *Educator*
Texas Tech University, President's Office, Lubbock, TX 79409 USA

Schmidt, Andreas *Opera Singer*
Fossredder 51, Hamburg, 22359, GERMANY

Schmidt, Benno C Jr *Educator*
Edison Project, 375 Park Ave, New York, NY 10152 USA

Schmidt, Dave *Baseball Player*
7172 N Serenoa Dr, Sarasota, FL 34241 USA

Schmidt, Eric E *Business Person, Engineer*
Google Inc, 2400 Bayshore Parkway, Mountain View, CA 94043 USA

Schmidt, Harald *Track Athlete*
Schulstr 11, Hasselroth, 63594, GERMANY

Schmidt, Helmut *Misc*
Neuberger Weg 80, Hamburg, 22419, GERMANY

Schmidt, Jason D *Baseball Player*
35 View Ridge Circle, Longview, WA 98632 USA

Schmidt, Joe *Football Player*
29600 Northwestern Hwy, PO Box 2210, Southfield, MI 48034-1016 USA

Schmidt, John *Football Player*
2 Mayflower Rd, Brookville, NY 11545 USA

Schmidt, Joseph P (Joe) *Football Player*
226 Norcliff Dr, Bloomfield Hills, MI 48302 USA

Schmidt, Kathryn (Kate) *Track Athlete*
1008 Dexter St, Los Angeles, CA 90042 USA

Schmidt, Maarten *Astronomer*
California Institue of Technology, Astronomy Dept, Pasadena, CA 91125 USA

Schmidt, Michael J (Mike) *Baseball Player*
373 Eagle Dr, Jupiter, FL 33477 USA

Schmidt, Mike *Athlete, Baseball Player*
373 Eagle Drive, Jupiter, FL 33477 USA

Schmidt, Milt *Hockey Player*
10 Logwood Dr #376, Westwood, MA 02090-1144

Schmidt, Milton C (Milt) *Hockey Player*
10 Longwood Dr #376, Westwood, MA 02090 USA

Schmidt, Ole *Composer, Conductor*
Puggaardsgade 17, Copenhagen, 1573, DENMARK

Schmidt, Richard *Doctor*
University of Pennsylvania, 3400 Spruce St, Philadelphia, PA 19104 USA

Schmidt, Steve *Race Car Driver*
8405 E 30th St, IndianapolisI, IN 46219 USA

Schmidt, Terry *Football Player*
36809 N Magnolia, Gurnee, IL 60031 USA

Schmidt, William (Bill) *Track Athlete*
1809 Devonwood Court, Knoxville, TN 37922 USA

Schmidt, Wolfgang *Track Athlete*
Birkheckenstr 116B, Stuttgart, 70599, GERMANY

Schmidt, Wolfgang *Opera Singer*
Kunstleragentur Raab & Bohm, Plankengasse 7, Vienna, 1010, AUSTRIA

Schmidt-Nielsen, Knut *Doctor*
Kuke University, Zoology Dept, Durham, NC 27706 USA

Schmidtmer, Christiane *Model, Actor*
Postfach 120617, Heidelberg, 69067, GERMANY

Schmidtt, Harrison *Ex-Senator*
PO Box 90730, Albuquerque, NM 87199-0730 USA

Schmiege, Marilyn *Opera Singer*
Opera et Concert, Maximilianstr 22, Munich, 80539, GERMANY

Schmiegel, Klaus K *Inventor*
4507 Stoughton Dr, Indianapolis, IN 46226 USA

Schmit, Timothy B *Musician*
William Morris Agency, 1325 Ave of Americas, New York, NY 10019 USA

Schmitt, Harrison H (Jack) *Senator*
PO Box 90730, Albuquerque, NM 87199 USA

Schmitt, Martin *Skier*
Muhleschweg 4, VA-Tannehim, 78052, GERMANY

Schmitz, John A (Johnny) *Baseball Player*
526 W Union Ave, Wausau, WI 54401 USA

Schmitz, Johnny *Baseball Player*
526 E Union Ave, Wausau, WI 54403 USA

Schmoeller, David *Director*
3910 Woodhill Ave, Las Vegas, NV 89121 USA

Schnabel, Julian *Artist, Director*
Pace Gallery, 32 E 57th St, New York, NY 10022 USA

Schnabel, Marco *Director*
Firm, The, 9465 Wilshire Blvd, Beverly Hills, CA 90212 USA

Schnackenberg, Roy L *Artist*
1919 N Orchard St, Chicago, IL 60614 USA

Schnarre, Monika *Actor, Model*
Alex Stevens, 137 N Larchmont #259, Los Angeles, CA 90004 USA

Schnebli, Dolf *Architect*
Sudstr 45, Zurich, 8008, SWITZERLAND

Schneer, Charles *Producer*
8 Ilchester Place, London, W14 8AA, UNITED KINGDOM (UK)

Schneider, Andrew *Journalist*
Pittsburgh Press, Editorial Dept, 34 Blvd of Allies, Pittsburgh, PA 15230 USA

Schneider, Bernd *Race Car Driver*
Team AMG Mercedes, Daimlerstr 1, Affalterbach, 71563, GERMANY

Schneider, Fred *Musician, Music Group, Songwriter*
Direct Management Group, 947 N La Cienega Blvd #2, Los Angeles, CA 90069 USA

Schneider, Helen
12 L.W. Church Rd., Washingon Depot, CT 06794

Schneider, Helge
Prinz-Regent-Str. 50-60, Bochum, GERMANY, 44795

Schneider, Howie *Cartoonist*
United Feature Syndicate, 200 Madison Ave, New York, NY 10016 USA

Schneider, John *Actor, Musician*
30169 Alexander Dr, Cathedral City, CA 92234 USA

Schneider, Lew *Producer, Comedian*
Everybody Loves Raymond, 4000 Warner Blvd, Bldg 131, Burbank, CA 91522

Schneider, Maria
81 bd. Richard Lenoir, Paris, FRANCE, F-75011

Schneider, Mathieu *Hockey Player*
1311 6th St, Manhattan Beach, CA 90266 USA

Schneider, Rob *Actor, Comedian*
Borinstein Oreck Bogart, 3172 Dona Susana Dr, Studio City, CA 91604 USA

Schneider, Vreni *Skier*
Dorf, Elm, 8767, SWITZERLAND

Schneider, William (Buzz) *Hockey Player*
5656 Turtle Lake Road, Shoreview, MN 55126 USA

Schneider, William G *Misc*
National Research Council, 65 Whitemart Dr #2, Ottawa, ON K1L 8J9, CANADA

Schneiderman, David A *Publisher, Editor*
Village Voice, President's Office, 36 Cooper Square, New York, NY 10003 USA

Schneiderman, Leon
1578 N. Topanga Skyline Dr., Topanga, CA 90290

Schneidman, Herm *Football Player*
1811 S 24th St #5, Quincy, IL 62301-6950

Schnelker, Bob *Coach*
85 Silver Oaks Cir #6102, Naples, FL 34119 USA

Schnellbacher, Otto O *Football Player, Basketball Player*
2010 SW Bowman Court, Topeka, KS 66604 USA

Schnelldorfer, Manfred *Figure Skater*
Seydlitzstr 55, Munich, 80993, GERMANY

Schnellenberger, Howard *Football Coach*
5109 N Ocean Blvd #G, Ocean Ridge, FL 33435 USA

Schnetzer, Stephen
448 W. 44th St., New York, NY 10036

Schnittker, Richard (Dick) *Basketball Player*
2303 E Las Granadas, Green Valley, AZ 85614 USA

Schobel, Frank
Sterntalerstr. 16, Berlin, GERMANY, D-12555

Schochet, Bob *Cartoonist*
6 Sunset Road, Highland Mills, NY 10930 USA

Schock, Gina *Musician*
PO Box 4398, North Hollywood, CA 91617 USA

Schock, Ron *Hockey Player*
1360 Whalen Rd, Penfield, NY 14526 USA

Schockemohle, Alwin *Horse Racer*
Munsterlandstr 51, Muhlen, 49439, GERMANY

Schoelen, Jill *Actor*
Gold Marshak Liedtke, 3500 W Olive Ave #1400, Burbank, CA 91505 USA

Schoellkopf, Carolyn Hunt
100 Crescent #1700, Dallas, TX 75201

Schoen, Gerry *Baseball Player*
1717 Nero St, Metairie, LA 70005 USA

Schoen, Max H *Doctor*
5818 S Sherbourne Dr, Los Angeles, CA 90056 USA

Schoenbaechler, Andreas *Skier*
Muhlrustistr 2, Affoltern a A, 8910, SWITZERLAND

Schoenborn, Christoph Cardinal *Religious Leader*
Wollzeile 2, Vienna, 1010, AUSTRIA

Schoenfeld, Gerald *Producer*
Shubert Organization Inc, 225 W 44th St, New York, NY 10036 USA

Schoenfeld, Jim *Hockey Player, Coach*
11745 E Cortez Dr, Scottsdale, AZ 85259 USA

Schoenfield, Al *Swimmer, Misc*
2731 Pecho Road, Los Osos, CA 93402 USA

Schoenfield, Dana *Swimmer*
7734 Lakeview Trail, Orange, CA 92869 USA

Schoffer, Nicolas *Artist*
Villa Des Arts, 15 Rue Hegesippe-Moreau, Paris, 75018, FRANCE

Schofield, Annabel *Actor*
Special Artists Agency, 345 N Maple Dr #302, Beverly Hills, CA 90210 USA

Schofield, Dwight *Hockey Player*
5900 N Illinois St, Fairview Heights, IL 62206-2700

Schofield, Phillip
56 Wood Lane, London, ENGLAND, W12 7RJ

Scholder, Fritz *Artist*
118 Cattletrack Road, Scottsdale, AZ 85251 USA

Scholes, Clarke *Swimmer*
1360 Somerset Ave, Grosse Pointe Woods, MI 48230 USA

Scholes, Myron S *Nobel Prize Laureate*
Stanford University, Graduate Business School, Stanford, CA 94305 USA

Schollander, Don
3576 Lakeview Blvd, Lake Oswego, OR 97035

Schollander, Donald A (Don) *Swimmer*
3576 Lakeview Blvd, Lake Oswego, OR 97035 USA

Scholten, Jim *Musician, Music Group*
Sawyer Brown Inc, 5200 Old Harding Road, Franklin, TN 37064 USA

Scholz, Rupert *Government Official*
Postfach 1328, Bonn 1, 5300, GERMANY

Scholz, Tom *Musician*
Agency for Performing Arts, 9200 Sunset Blvd #900, Los Angeles, CA 90069 USA

Schomberg, A Thomas *Artist*
4923 S Snowberry Lane, Evergreen, CO 80439 USA

Schon, Jan Hendrik *Inventor*
Lucent Technology Bell Laboratory, 600 Mountain Ave, New Providence, NJ 07974 USA

Schon, Kyra *Actor*
930 N Sheridan Ave, Pittsburgh, PA 15206 USA

Schon, Neal *Musician*
Artists & Audience Entertainment, PO Box 35, Pawling, NY 12564 USA

Schon, Neil *Musician*
William Morris Agency (WMA-LA), 1 William Morris Pl, Beverly Hills, CA 90212 USA

Schonberg, Claude-Michel *Composer*
Stephen Tenenbaum, 605 3rd Ave, New York, NY 10158 USA

Schone, Lydia
2020 Broadway, Santa Monica, CA 90404

Schonhuber, Franz *Commentator*
Europaburo, Fraunhoferstr 23, Munich, 80469, GERMANY

Schoofs, Mark *Journalist*
Village Voice, Editorial Dept, 32 Cooper Square, New York, NY 10003 USA

Schoolnik, Gary *Biologist*
Stanford University, Medical School, Microbiology Dept, Stanford, CA 94305 USA

Schools, Dave *Musician*
Brown Cat Inc, 400 Foundry St, Athens, GA 30601 USA

Schoomaker, Peter J (Pete) *General*
Chief of Staff HqUSA, Pentagon, Washington, DC 20310 USA

Schopf, J William *Biologist*
University of California, Study of Evolution Center, Los Angeles, CA 90024 USA

Schorer, Jane *Journalist*
Des Moines Register, Editorial Dept, PO Box 957, Des Moines, IA 50304 USA

Schorr, Bill *Cartoonist*
United Feature Syndicate, 200 Madison Ave, New York, NY 10016 USA

Schorr, Daniel *Journalist, Writer*
3113 Woodley Road, Washington, DC 20008 USA

Schorske, Carl E *Historian, Writer*
106 Winant Road, Princeton, NJ 08540 USA

Schotte, Jan P Cardinal *Religious Leader*
Sinodo Dei Vescovi, 00120, VATICAN CITY

Schottenheimer, Martin E (Marty)
Football Coach, Sportscaster
San Diego Chargers, 4020 Murphy
Canyon Road, San Diego, CA 92123 USA

Schou, Mogens *Doctor*
Aarhus University, Institute of Psychiatry,
Aarhus, DENMARK

Schowalter, Edward R Jr *War Hero*
913 Bibb Ave #312, Auburn, AL 36830
USA

Schrader, Ken *Race Car Driver*
PO Box 325, East Flat Rock, NC 28726
USA

Schrader, Maria *Actor*
Davien Littlefield Management, 939
Eighth Ave #609, New York, NY 10019
USA

Schrader, Paul *Actor, Director, Writer*
Parseghian/Planco LLC, 23 E 22nd St Fl 3,
New York, NY 10010 USA

Schrader, Paul J *Director, Writer*
9696 Culver Blvd #203, Culver City, CA
90232 USA

Schram, Bitty *Actor*
Metropolitan Talent Agency (MTA), 4526
Wilshire Blvd, Los Angeles, CA 90010
USA

Schramm, David *Actor*
3521 Berry Dr, Studio City, CA 91604
USA

Schramm, Tex
9355 Sunnybrook, Dallas, TX 75220

Schranz, Karl *Skier*
Hotel Garni, Saint Anton, 6580, AUSTRIA

Schreiber, Avery
6399 Wilshire Blvd. #414, Los Angeles,
CA 90048

Schreiber, Liev *Actor*
William Morris Agency, 151 El Camino
Dr, Beverly Hills, CA 90212 USA

Schreiber, Martin J *Governor*
2700 S Shore Dr #B, Milwaukee, WI
53207 USA

Schreler, Peter *Opera Singer, Conductor*
Calberlastr 13, Dresdon, 01326,
GERMANY

Schrempf, Detlef *Basketball Player*
4025 94th Ave NE, Bellevue, WA 98004
USA

Schrempp, Jurgen E *Business Person*
Daimler-Chrysler AG, Plieningerstra,
Stuttgart, 70546, GERMANY

Schreyer, Edward R *Governor, General*
250 Wellington Crescent #401, Winnipeg,
MB R3M 0B3, CANADA

Schrieffer, John R *Nobel Prize Laureate*
Florida State University, 1800 E Paul
Dirac Dr, Tallahassee, FL 32310 USA

Schrier, Eric W *Editor*
Reader's Digest, Editorial Dept, PO Box
100, Pleasantville, NY 10572 USA

Schriesheim, Alan *Misc*
1440 N Lake Shore Dr #31AC, Chicago,
IL 60610 USA

Schriever, Bernard A *General*
2300 M St NW #900, Washington, DC
20037 USA

Schrimshaw, Nevin S *Doctor*
Sandwich Notch Farm, Thompton, NH
03223 USA

Schriner, David
3216 Upland Pl. NW Calgary, Alb.,
CANADA

Schrock, Richard R *Misc*
Massachusetts Institute of Technology,
Chemistry Dept, Cambridge, MA 02139
USA

Schroder, Ernst A *Actor*
Podere Montalto, Castellina In Chianti,
Siena, 53011, ITALY

Schroder, Gerhard
Bundeskanzleramt, Berlin, GERMANY,
11012

Schroder, Jochen
Postfach 10 23 46, Bochum, GERMANY,
D-44723

Schroder, Rick *Actor*
William Morris Agency (WMA-LA), 1
William Morris Pl, Beverly Hills, CA
90212 USA

Schroeder, Barbet *Director, Producer*
8033 W Sunset Blvd #51, West
Hollywood, CA 90046 USA

Schroeder, Carly *Actor*
KWAC, 1875 Century Park E #700,
Century City, CA 90067 USA

Schroeder, Frederick R (Ted) Jr *Tennis
Player*
1010 W Muirlands Dr, La Jolla, CA 92037
USA

Schroeder, Gerhard *Misc*
Bundeskanzlerant, Willy-Brandt-Str 1,
Berlin, 10557, GERMANY

Schroeder, Jay
322 Center St., El Segundo, CA 90245

Schroeder, Jim *Bowler*
3 Greenhaven Terrace, Tonawanda, NY
14150 USA

Schroeder, John H *Educator*
University of Wisconsin, Chancellor's
Office, Milwaukee, WI 53211 USA

Schroeder, Kenneth L *Business Person*
KLA-Tencor Corp, 160 Rio Robles, San
Jose, CA 95134 USA

Schroeder, Manfred R *Physicist*
Rieswartenweg 8, Gottingen, 37073,
GERMANY

Schroeder, Mary M *Judge*
US Court of Appeals, 230 N 1st Ave,
Phoenix, AZ 85025 USA

Schroeder, Patricia S *Misc*
William Morris Agency, 151 El Camino
Dr, Beverly Hills, CA 90212 USA

Schroeder, Paul W *Writer*
University of Illinois, History Dept, 810 S
Wright St, Urbana, IL 61801 USA

Schroeder, Steven A *Doctor, Misc*
10 Paseo Mirasol, Bel Tiburon, CA 94920
USA

Schroeder, Ted
1010 W. Muirlands Dr., La Jolla, CA
92037

Schroeder, Terry *Athlete, Coach*
4901 Lewis Road, Agoura Hills, CA 91301
USA

Schrom, Kenneth M (Ken) *Baseball Player*
4733 Rosinante Road, El Paso, TX 79922
USA

Schruefer, John J *Doctor*
Georgetown University Hospital, Ob-Gyn
Dept, Washington, DC 20007 USA

Schuba, Beatrice (Trixi) *Figure Skater*
Giorgengasse 2/1/8, Vienna, 1190,
AUSTRIA

Schubb, Mark
9744 Wilshire Blvd. #308, Beverly Hills,
CA 90212

Schubert, Mark *Swimmer, Coach*
PO Box 479, Surfside, CA 90743 USA

Schubert, Richard F *Misc*
6615 Madison McLean Dr, McLean, VA
22101 USA

Schuck, Anett *Athlete*
Defoestry 6A, Leipzig, 04159, GERMANY

Schuck, John *Actor*
1501 Broadway #703, New York, NY
10036 USA

Schueler, Jon R *Artist*
40 W 22nd St, New York, NY 10010 USA

Schuenke, Donald J *Business Person*
Nortel Networks Corp, 8200 Dixie Road,
Brampton, ON L6T 5P6, CANADA

Schuessel, Wolfgang *Misc*
Chancellor's Office, Ballhausplatz 2,
Vienna, 1014, AUSTRIA

Schuessler, Jack *Business Person*
Wendy's International, 4288 W Dublin-
Granville Road, Dublin, OH 43017 USA

Schuh, Harry F *Football Player*
2309 Massey Road, Memphis, TN 38119
USA

Schul, Robert (Bob) *Track Athlete*
320 Wisteria Dr, Dayton, OH 45419 USA

Schulberg, Budd
Brookside, PO Box 707, Westhampton
Beach, NY 11978 USA

Schuler, Carolyn *Swimmer*
26552 Via del Sol, Mission Viejo, CA
92691 USA

Schulhofer, Scotty *Misc*
PO Box 1581, Waynesville, NC 28786
USA

Schull, Rebecca *Actor*
Writers & Artists, 8383 Wilshire Blve
#550, Beverly Hills, CA 90211 USA

Schuller, Grete *Artist*
8 Barstow Road #7G, Great Neck, NY
11021 USA

Schuller, Gunther *Composer, Conductor*
Margun Music, 167 Dudley Road,
Newton Center, MA 02459 USA

Schuller, Robert *Religious Leader*
Crystal Cathedral Ministries, 12141 Lewis
St, Garden Grove, CA 92840 USA

Schult, Jurgen *Track Athlete*
Drosselweg 6, Leuna, 19069, GERMANY

Schultz, Axel *Boxer*
Axel Schultz Mgmt, Kloetzrstr 15, Riesa,
01587, GERMANY

Schultz, Dave *Hockey Player*
329 Oxford Place, Macungie, PA 18062
USA

Schultz, Dave *Race Car Driver*
2365 Lazy River Lane, Fort Myers, FL
33905 USA

Schultz, Dean *Financier*
Federal Home Laon Bank, 1079
Hutchinson Road, Walnut Creek, CA
94598 USA

Schultz, Dwight *Actor*
Borinstein Oreck Bogart, 3172 Dona
Susana Dr, Studio City, CA 91604 USA

Schultz, Flip *Comedian*
International Creative Management
(ICM-LA), 8942 Wilshire Blvd, Beverly
Hills, CA 90211 USA

Schultz, Frederick H *Government Official*
PO Box 1200, Jacksonville, FL 32201 USA

Schultz, Howard *Business Person*
Starbucks Corp, 2401 Utah Ave S, Seattle,
WA 98134 USA

Schultz, Howard H (Howie) *Basketball
Player, Baseball Player*
1333 McKusick Road Lane W, Stillwater,
MN 55082 USA

Schultz, Michael A *Director*
Chrystalite Productions, PO Box 1940,
Santa Monica, CA 90406 USA

Schultz, Peter C *Inventor*
Heraeus Amersil Inc, 3473 Satellite Blvd
#300, Duluth, GA 30096 USA

Schultz, Peter G *Misc*
Salk Research Institute, 10550 N Torrey
Pine Road, La Jolla, CA 92037 USA

Schultz, Richard D *Misc*
US Olympic Committee, 1 Olympia
Plaza, Colorado Springs, CO 80909 USA

Schultze, Charles L *Government Official*
Brookings Institute, 1775 Massachusetts
Ave NW, Washington, DC 20036 USA

Schulz, Axel
Zehmeplatz 10, Frankfurt/Oder,
GERMANY, D-15230

Schulz, William *Editor*
Reader's Digest, Editorial Dept, PO Box
100, Pleasantville, NY 10572 USA

Schulze, Matt *Actor*
Gersh Agency, 232 N Canon Dr, Beverly
Hills, CA 90210 USA

Schulze, Paul *Actor*
Kyle Fritz Management, 1979 Grace Ave
#5A, Hollywood, CA 90068 USA

Schulze, Richard M *Business Person*
Best Buy Co, 7601 Penn Ave S,
Minneapolis, MN 55423 USA

Schumacher, Joel *Director*
Greenfield & Selvaggi, 11766 Wilshire
Blvd #1610, Los Angeles, CA 90025 USA

Schumacher, Kelly *Basketball Player*
Indiana Fever, Conseco Fieldhouse, 125 S
Pennsylvania, Indianapolis, IN 46204 USA

Schumacher, Michael *Race Car Driver*
Via Ascari 55-57, Maranello, 40153,
ITALY

Schumacher, Ralf *Race Car Driver*
Weber Mgmt, Trankestr 11, Stuttgart,
70597, GERMANY

Schuman, Allan L *Business Person*
Ecolab Inc, Ecolab Center, 370 Wabasha
St N, Saint Paul, MN 55102 USA

Schuman, Melissa *Actor*
Elements Entertainment, 2401 W Olive
Ave #290, Burbank, CA 91506 USA

Schuman, Tom *Musician*
Crosseyed Bear Productions, 926
Haverstraw Road, Suffem, NY 10901 USA

Schumann, Jochen *Yachtsman*
Birkenstr 88, Penzberg, 48336,
GERMANY

Schumann, Ralf *Misc*
Steomach 22, Stockheim, 97640,
GERMANY

Schur, Michael *Writer*
3 Arts Entertainment Inc, 9460 Wilshire
Blvd Fl 7, Beverly Hills, CA 90212 USA

Schurmann, Petra *Swimmer*
Max-Emanuel-Str 7, Starnberg, 82319,
GERMANY

Schurr, Harry W *War Hero*
1178 Davis Dr, Fairborn, OH 45324 USA

Schussler Florenza, Elisabeth *Writer, Misc*
Notre Dame University, Theology Dept,
Notre Dame, IN 46556 USA

Schuster, Rudolf *President*
President's Office, Nam Slobody 1,
Bratislava, 91370, SLOVAKIA

Schute, Anja
Parkstr. 37, Erfstadt, GERMANY, D-50374

Schutz, Klaus *Government Official*
9 Konstanzerstr, Berlin, 10707,
GERMANY

Schutz, Stephen *Artist*
Blue Mountain Arts Inc, PO Box 4549,
Boulder, CO 80306 USA

Schutz, Susan Polis *Writer*
Blue Mountain Arts Inc, PO Box 4549,
Boulder, CO 80306 USA

Schutze, Jim *Writer, Journalist*
Avon Books, 1350 Ave of Americas, New
York, NY 10019 USA

Schuur, Diane *Music Group, Musician*
Paul Canter Enterprises, 33042 Ocean
Ridge, Dana Point, CA 92629 USA

Schwab, John J *Doctor*
6217 Innes Trace Road, Louisville, KY
40222 USA

Schwabb, Charles R *Financier*
Charles Scwab Co, 101 Montgomery
Street, San Francisco, CA 94104 USA

Schwarthoff, Florian *Track Athlete*
Fischweiher 51, Heppenheim, 64646,
GERMANY

Schwartsman, John *Cinematographer*
Mirisch Agency, 1801 Century Park E
#1801, Los Angeles, CA 90067 USA

Schwartz, Gene

Schwartz, Jacob T *Scientist*
New York University, Courant Math
Sciences Institute, New York, NY 10012
USA

Schwartz, Josh *Writer, Producer*
OC, The, 1600 Rosecrans Ave, Bldg 6A Fl
2, Manhattan Beach, CA 90266 USA

Schwartz, Lloyd *Journalist*
27 Pennsylvania Ave, Somerville, MA
02145 USA

Schwartz, Maxime *Misc*
Institut Pasteur, 25-28 Rue du Docteur-
Roux, Paris Cedex 15, 75724, FRANCE

Schwartz, Melvin *Nobel Prize Laureate*
PO Box 5068, Ketchum, ID 83340 USA

Schwartz, Neil
3044 Pearl Harbor Dr, Las Vegas, NV
89117 USA

Schwartz, Neil J *Actor*
3044 Pearl Harbor Dr, Las Vegas, NV
89117 USA

Schwartz, Norton A *General*
Commander, 11th Air Force, Elmendorf
Air Force Base, AK 99506 USA

Schwartz, Sherwood
1865 Carla Ridge Dr, Beverly Hills, CA
90210

Schwartz, Stephen L *Composer,
Songwriter, Music Group, Musician*
Chaplin Entertainment, 545 8th Ave, #14,
New York, NY 10018 USA

Schwartz, Thomas A *General*
Commander, United Nations
Command/US Forces Korea, APO, AP,
96205 USA

Schwartz, Tony *Misc*
455 W 56th St, New York, NY 10019
USA

Schwartzman, Jason *Actor*
Baker Winokur Ryder (BWR-LA), 9100
Wilshire Blvd Fl 6, W Tower, Beverly
Hills, CA 90212 USA

Schwartzman, John *Cinematographer*
Mirisch Agency, 1801 Century Park E,
#1801, Los Angeles, CA 90067 USA

Schwartzman, Robert *Actor*
William Morris Agency (WMA-LA), 1
William Morris Pl, Beverly Hills, CA
90212 USA

Schwarz, Gerard R *Conductor*
New York Chamber Symphony, 1395
Lexington Ave, New York, NY 10128 USA

Schwarz, Hanna *Opera Singer*
Opera et Concert, Maximilianstr 22,
Munich, 80539, GERMANY

Schwarz, John H *Physicist*
California Institute of Technology, Physics
Dept, Pasadena, CA 91125 USA

Schwarz-Shilling, Christian *Government
Official*
Post-Telecomm Ministry, Heinrich-von-
Stephanstr 1, Bonn, 53175, GERMANY

Schwarzbein, Diana *Doctor, Writer*
Health Communications, 3201 SW 15th
St, Deerfield Beach, FL 33442 USA

Schwarzenegger, Arnold *Actor, Governor,
Misc*
Creative Artists Agency LCC (CAA-LA),
9830 Wilshire Blvd, Beverly Hills, CA
90212 USA

Schwarzkopf, Elisabeth
Rebhusstr. 29, Zumikon, SWITZERLAND,
CH-8126

Schwarzkopf, H Norman *General*
Black Summit, 400 N Ashley Dr #3050,
Tampa, FL 33602 USA

Schwebel, Stephen M *Judge*
PO Box 356, Woodstock, VT 05091 USA

Schweickart, Russell L *Astronaut*
PO Box 381, Sea Ranch, CA 95497 USA

Schweig, Eric *Actor*
Prime Talent, PO Box 5163, Vancouver, BC V7B 1M4, CANADA

Schweiger, Til *Actor*
Agentur Players, Sophienstr 21, Berlin, 10178, GERMANY

Schweiker, Richard S *Secretary*
8890 Windy Ridge Way, McLean, VA 22102 USA

Schweikert, J E *Religious Leader*
Old Roman Catholic Church, 4200 N Kedvale Ave, Chicago, IL 60641 USA

Schweikher, Paul *Architect*
3222 E Missouri Ave, Phoenix, AZ 85018 USA

Schwertsik, Kurt *Composer*
Doblinger Music, Dorotheerhgasse 10, Vienna, 1011, AUSTRIA

Schwery, Henry Cardinal *Religious Leader*
Bishoporic of Sion, CP 2068, Sion 2, 1950, SWITZERLAND

Schwimmer, David *Actor*
Talent Entertainment Group, 9111 Wilshire Blvd, Beverly Hills, CA 90210 USA

Schwinden, Ted *Governor*
401 N Fee St, Helena, MT 59601 USA

Schwitters, Roy F *Physicist*
1718 Cromwell Hill, Austin, TX 78703 USA

Schygulla, Hanna *Actor*
ZBF Agentur, Leopoldstr 19, Munich, 80802, GERMANY

Scialfa, Patti
17 E. 76th St., New York, NY 10021

Scialfa, Patty *Music Group, Musician*
1224 Benedict Canyon, Beverly Hills, CA 90210 USA

Sciarra, John M *Football Player*
4220 Woodleigh Lane, La Canada Flintridge, CA 91011 USA

Sciascia, Leonardo
Viale Scaduto 10/B, Palermo, ITALY, 1-90144

Sciorra, Anabella *Actor*
Writers & Artists, 8383 Wilshire Blvd #550, Beverly Hills, CA 90211 USA

Sciorra, Annabella *Actor*
United Talent Agency (UTA), 9560 Wilshire Blvd, Beverly Hills, CA 90212 USA

Scioscia, Michael L (Mike) *Baseball Player*
1915 Falling Star Ave, Westlake Village, CA 91362 USA

Scioscia, Mike
444 Fargo St., Thousand Oaks, CA 91360-1515

Scirica, Anthony J *Judge*
US Court of Appeals, US Courthouse, 601 Market St, Philadelphia, PA 19106 USA

Sciutto, Nellie *Actor*
Schachter Entertainment, 1157 S Beverly Dr Fl 3, Los Angeles, CA 90035 USA

Scofield, Dean
12304 Santa Monica Blvd. #104, Los Angeles, CA 90025

Scofield, Dino *Actor*
3330 Barham Blvd #103, Los Angeles, CA 90068 USA

Scofield, John *Musician*
Ted Kurland, 173 Brighton Ave, Boston, MA 02134 USA

Scofield, Paul *Actor*
Gables, Balcombe, Sussex, RH17 6ND, UNITED KINGDOM (UK)

Scofield, Richard M (Dick) *General*
3661 Grandview Circle, Shingle Springs, CA 95682 USA

Scoggins, Matt *Swimmer*
4900 Calhoun Canyon Loop, Austin, TX 78735 USA

Scoggins, Tracy *Actor*
Jorgensen & Rogers, 10100 Santa Monica Blvd #410, Los Angeles, CA 90067 USA

Scogin, Mack *Architect*
Scogin Elam Bray, 1819 Peachtree Road NE, #700, Atlanta, GA 30309 USA

Scola, Angelo Cardinal *Religious Leader*
Archdiocese, S Marco 320/Ã, Venezia, 30124, ITALY

Scola, Ettore *Director*
Via Bertoloni 1/E, Rome, 00197, ITALY

Scolari, Peter *Actor*
Artists Agency, 1180 S Beverly Dr #301, Los Angeles, CA 90035 USA

Scolnick, Edward M *Scientist, Doctor*
811 Wickfield Road, Wynnewood, PA 19096 USA

Scooters, The
15190 Encanto Dr., Sherman Oaks, CA 91403

Score, Herbert J (Herb) *Baseball Player, Sportscaster*
12700 Lake Ave, Lakewood, OH 44107 USA

Scorpions *Music Group*
Famous Artists Agency, 250 W 57th St, New York, NY 10107 USA

Scorsese, Martin *Director*
445 Park Ave #700, New York, NY 10022 USA

Scorsese, Nicolette *Actor*
Orange Grove Group Inc, 12178 Ventura Blvd #205, Studio City, CA 91604 USA

Scorupco, Izabella *Actor, Model, Music Group, Musician*
Vourimiehenkatu 20, Helsinki, 00150, FINLAND

Scott, Adam *Actor*
Metopolitan Talent Agency, 4526 Wilshire Blvd, Los Angeles, CA 90010 USA

Scott, Andy *Musician*
DCM International, 296 Nether St, Finchley, London, N3 1RJ, UNITED KINGDOM (UK)

Scott, Ashley *Actor*
Original Film, 2045 S Barrington Ave, Los Angeles, CA 90025 USA

Scott, Byron *Basketball Player, Coach*
405 Murray Hill Parkway, East Rutherford, NJ 07073 USA

Scott, Camilla
23773 Via Canon #201, Newhall, CA 91321

Scott, Campbell *Actor*
3211 Retreat Court, Malibu, CA 90265 USA

Scott, Charles (Charlie) *Basketball Player*
300 Chastain Manor Dr, Norcross, GA 30071 USA

Scott, Clarence *Football Player*
216 Sisson Ave NE, Atlanta, GA 30317 USA

Scott, Clyde L (Smackover) *Football Player, Track Athlete*
12840 Rivercrest Dr, Little Rock, AR 72212 USA

Scott, Coltin
195 S. Beverly Dr. #400, Beverly Hills, CA 90212-3044

Scott, David
1300-B Manhattan Ave., Manhattan Beach, CA 90266

Scott, David R *Astronaut*
Merces, VC Johnson, 30 Hackamore Lane #1, Bell Canyon, CA 91307 USA

Scott, Deborah L *Fashion Designer*
Gersh Agency, 232 N Canon Dr, Beverly Hills, CA 90210 USA

Scott, Debralee *Actor*
1180 S Beverly Dr #608, Beverly Hills, CA 90212 USA

Scott, Dennis *Basketball Player*
5425 Palm Lake Circle, Orlando, FL 32819 USA

Scott, Donovan *Actor*
Talent Group, 6300 Wilshire Blvd #2100, Los Angeles, CA 90048 USA

Scott, Dougray *Actor*
P F D, Drury House, 34-43 Russell St, London, WC2B 5HA, UNITED KINGDOM (UK)

Scott, Eric
11934 River Grove Ct, . Moorpark, CA 93021

Scott, Freddie *Musician*
Headline Talent, 1650 Broadway #508, New York, NY 10019 USA

Scott, Freddie L *Football Player*
29209 Northwestern Highway #694, Southfield, MI 48034 USA

Scott, Gavin *Writer*
Original Artists (LA), 9465 Wilshire Blvd, Suite 840, Beverly Hills, CA 90212 USA

Scott, Gene *Doctor*
1615 Glendale Ave, Glendale, CA 91205 USA

Scott, Geoffrey
1126 Hollywood Way #203-A, Burbank, CA 91505

Scott, George *Baseball Player*
1216 Fair Park Blvd, Harlingen, TX 78550 USA

Scott, Gloria Dean Randle *Educator*
Bennett College, President's Office, Greensboro, NC 27401 USA

Scott, Gordon *Actor*
116 Santa Monica Blvd, Santa Monica, CA 90401 USA

Scott, H Lee Jr *Business Person*
Wal-Mart Stores, 702 SW 8th St, Bentonville, AR 72712 USA

Scott, Irene F *Judge*
US Tax Court, 400 2nd St NW,
Washington, DC 20217 USA

Scott, Jack *Music Group, Musician,
Songwriter*
34039 Coachwood Dr, Sterling Heights,
MI 48312 USA

Scott, Jacob E (Jake) Jr *Football Player*
PO Box 857, Hanalei, HI 96714 USA

Scott, Jacqueline *Actor*
Lichtman/Salners, 12216 Moorpark St,
Studio City, CA 91604 USA

Scott, Jane *Critic*
Cleveland Plain Deater, 1801 Superior
Ave, Cleveland, OH 44114 USA

Scott, Jean Bruce *Actor*
144 N Westerly Dr, Los Angeles, CA
90048 USA

Scott, Jerry *Cartoonist*
Creators Syndicate, 5777 W Century Blvd
#700, Los Angeles, CA 90045 USA

Scott, Jill *Musician*
Rhythm Jazz Entertainment, 4465 Don
Milagro Dr, Los Angeles, CA 90008 USA

Scott, Jimmy *Musician, Music Group*
J's Way Jazz, 175 Prospect St #20D, East
Orange, NJ 07017, ITALY

Scott, Josey *Musician, Music Group*
Helter Skelter, Plaza, 535 Kings Road,
London, SW10 0S, UNITED KINGDOM
(UK)

Scott, Judson
10000 Santa Monica Blvd. #305, Los
Angeles, CA 90067

Scott, Kathryn Leigh *Actor*
3236 Bennett Dr, Los Angeles, CA 90068
USA

Scott, Klea *Actor*
Talent Entertainment Group, 9111
Wilshire Blvd, Beverly Hills, CA 90210
USA

Scott, Larry *Misc*
148 N Main St, Kaysville, UT 84037 USA

Scott, Lary R *Business Person*
Carolina Freight Corp, PO Box 1000,
Cherryville, NC 28021 USA

Scott, Lizabeth *Actor*
8277 Hollywood Blvd, Los Angeles, CA
90069 USA

Scott, Melody Thomas *Actor*
12068 Crest Court, Beverly Hills, CA
90210 USA

Scott, Michael W (Mike) *Baseball Player*
28355 Chat Dr, Laguna Niguel, CA 92677
USA

Scott, Paul *Writer*
33 Drumsheugh Gardens, Edinburgh,
SCOTLAND

Scott, Pippa *Actor*
10850 Wilshire Blvd #250, Los Angeles,
CA 90024 USA

Scott, Ray *Basketball Player, Coach*
Colonial Life Insurance, 33200 Schoolcraft
Road, Livonia, MI 48150 USA

Scott, Richard U (Dick) *Football Player*
3369 Upland Court, Adamstown, MD
21710 USA

Scott, Ridley *Director*
Scott Free, 42/44 Beak St, London, W1R
3DA, UNITED KINGDOM (UK)

Scott, Robert L Jr *War Hero, Writer*
96 Ridgecrest Place, Warner Robins, GA
31088 USA

Scott, Robert W *Governor, Educator*
North Carolina Community College
System, 200 W Jones St, Raleigh, NC
27603 USA

Scott, Seann William *Actor*
Creative Artists Agency LCC (CAA-LA),
9830 Wilshire Blvd, Beverly Hills, CA
90212 USA

Scott, Shelby *Misc*
American Federation of TV/Radio Artists,
260 Madison Ave, New York, NY 10016
USA

Scott, Stephen *Musician*
Bridge Agency, 35 Clark St #A5, Brooklyn
Heights, NY 11201 USA

Scott, Steven M (Steve) *Track Athlete*
4106 La Portalada Dr, Carlsbad, CA
92008 USA

Scott, Thomas C (Tom) *Football Player*
3259 Kirkwood Court, Keswick, VA
22947 USA

Scott, Tom *Musician*
Performers of the World, 8901 Melrose
Ave #200, West Hollywood, CA 90069
USA

Scott, Tom Everett *Actor*
United Talent Agency, 9560 Wilshire Blvd
#500, Beverly Hills, CA 90212 USA

Scott, Tony *Director*
Totem Productions, 8009 Santa Monica
Blvd, West Hollywood, CA 90046 USA

Scott, W Richard *Misc*
940 Lathrop Place, Stanford, CA 94305
USA

Scott, Willard *Television Host*
NBC Television (NY), 30 Rockefeller
Plaza, New York, NY 10112 USA

Scott, Willard W Jr *General, Educator*
9115 McNair Dr, Alexandria, VA 22309
USA

Scott, William Lee
Sager Management, 260 South Bevely
Drive, Suite 205, Beverly Hills, CA 90210
USA

Scott, Winston E *Astronaut*
PO Box 1192, Cape Canaveral, FL 32920
USA

Scott Brown, Denise *Architect*
Venturi Scott Brown Assoc, 4236 Main St,
Philadelphia, PA 19127 USA

Scott Thomas, Kristin *Actor*
P M K Public Relations, 8500 Wilshire
Blvd #700, Beverly Hills, CA 90211 USA

Scott-Brown, Denise *Architect*
Venturi Scott Brown Assoc, 4236 Main St,
Philadelphia, PA 19127 USA

Scott-Heron, Gil *Musician, Music Group,
Songwriter*
PO Box 31, Malverne, NY 11565 USA

Scotti, Nick *Actor, Musician*
Untitled Entertainment (NY), 23 E 22nd St
Fl 3, New York, NY 10010 USA

Scotto, Renata *Opera Singer*
Robert Lombardo, Harkness Plaza, 61 W
62nd St #6F, New York, NY 10023 USA

Scotto, Renato
61 W. 62nd St. #6F, New York, NY
10023

Scottoline, Lisa *Writer*
Harper Collins Publishers, 10 E 53rd St,
New York, NY 10022 USA

Scouler, Angela *Actor*
Daly Gagan, 60 Old Brompton Road,
London, SW7 3LQ, UNITED KINGDOM
(UK)

Scovell, Nell *Producer*
William Morris Agency (WMA-LA), 1
William Morris Pl, Beverly Hills, CA
90212 USA

Scowcroft, Brent *Government Official,
General*
350 Park Ave #2600, New York, NY
10022 USA

Scranton, Nancy *Golfer*
Int'l Mgmt Group, 1 Erieview Plaza, 1360
E 9th St #1300, Cleveland, OH 44114
USA

Scranton, William W *Governor*
PO Box 116, Dalton, PA 18414 USA

Scratch *Artist, Musician*
William Morris Agency, 1325 Ave of
Americas, New York, NY 10019 USA

Scream3 *Music Group*
Wind-up Records, 72 Madison Ave, New
York, NY 10016 USA

Scribner, Bucky *Football Player*
512 Georgina Ave, Santa Monica, CA
90402-1912

Scribner, Rick *Race Car Driver*
8904 Amerigo Ave, Orangevale, CA
95662 USA

Scrimm, Angus *Actor*
PO Box 5193, North Hollywood, CA
91616 USA

Scrimshaw, Nevin S *Doctor*
Sandwich Mountain Farm, PO Box 330,
Campton, NH 03223 USA

Scripps, Charles E *Publisher*
10 Grandin Lane, Cincinnati, OH 45208
USA

Scruggs, Earl *Musician, Songwriter*
774 Elysian Road, Nashville, TN 37204
USA

Scruggs, Randy *Musician*
Creative Artists Agency (CAA-Nashville),
3310 West End Ave Fl 5, Nashville, TN
37203 USA

Scudamore, Peter *Jockey*
Mucky Cottage Grangehill, Naunton
Cheltenham, Glos, GL54 3AY, UNITED
KINGDOM (UK)

Scully, Sean P *Artist*
Timothy Taylor Gallery, 1 Bruton Place,
London, W1X 7AB, UNITED KINGDOM
(UK)

Scully, Vincent E (Vin) *Sportscaster*
Los Angeles Dodgers, Stadium, 1000
Elysian Park Ave, Los Angeles, CA 90012
USA

Scully-Power, Paul D *Astronaut*
Civil Aviation Safety Authority, Box 2005, Canberra, ACT, 2600, AUSTRALIA

Sculthorpe, Peter J *Composer*
91 Holdsworth St, Woollahra, NSW, 2025, AUSTRALIA

Scutt, Der *Architect*
Der Scutt Architect, 44 W 28th St, New York, NY 10001 USA

Seabra, Verissimo Correia *President, General*
President's Office, Bissau, GUINEA-BISSAU

Seacrest, Ryan *Radio Personality, Television Host*
William Morris Agency (WMA-LA), 1 William Morris Pl, Beverly Hills, CA 90212 USA

Seaforth-Hayes, Susan *Actor*
4528 Beck Ave, North Hollywood, CA 91602 USA

Seaga, Edward P G *Prime Minister*
24-26 Grenada Crescent, New Kingston, Kingston 5, JAMAICA

Seagal, Steven *Actor*
3288 Foxridge Dr, Jasper, IN 47546 USA

Seagrave, Jocelyn *Actor*
Perspective Film, 15030 Ventura Blvd, Sherman Oaks, CA 91403 USA

Seagraves, Ralph *Race Car Driver*
RR 10 Box 413, Winston Salem, NC 27127 USA

Seagren, Bob
One Hoosier Dome, Indianapolis, IN 46225-1023

Seagren, Robert L (Bob) *Track Athlete*
21902 Velicata St, Wooland Hills, CA 91364 USA

Seagrove, Jenny *Actor*
Marmont Mgmt, Langham House, 302/8 Regent St, London, W1R 5AL, UNITED KINGDOM (UK)

Seal
56 Beethoven St., London, ENGLAND, W10 4LG

Seal *Musician*
Atlas/Third Rall Entertainment, 9200 W Sunset Blvd, West Hollywood, CA 90069 USA

Seale, Bobby *Politician*
Cafe Society, 302 W Chelton Ave, Philadelphia, PA 19144 USA

Seale, John C *Cinematographer*
Mirisch Agency, 1801 Century Park E, Los Angeles, CA 90067 USA

Seals, Brady
2100 West End Ave. #1000, Nashville, TN 37203

Seals, Dan *Musician, Music Group, Songwriter*
Morningstar Productions, 153 Sanders Ferry Road, Hendersonville, TN 37075 USA

Seals, Son *Music Group, Musician*
Bad Axe Entertainment, 14514 San Francisco, Posen, IL 60469 USA

Seals & Croft *Music Group*
4STAR Entertainment LLC, 520 East 88th Street, Suite 2A, New York, NY 10128, United Kingdom

Seaman, Christopher *Conductor*
25 Westfield Dr, Glasgow, G52 2SG, SCOTLAND

Seaman, David *Soccer Player*
Arsenal London, Avenell Road, Highbury, London, N5 1BU, UNITED KINGDOM (UK)

Seamans, Robert C Jr *Engineer*
Sea Meadow, 675 Hale St, Beverly Farms, MA 01915 USA

Sean Paul *Musician*
William Morris Agency (WMA-LA), 1 William Morris Pl, Beverly Hills, CA 90212 USA

Searchers, The
2514 Build America Dr., Hampton, VA 22666

Searcy, Leon *Football Player*
3841 Biggin Church Road, Jacksonville, FL 32224 USA

Searcy, Nick *Actor*
Abrams Artists Agency (LA), 9200 Sunset Blvd Fl 11, Los Angeles, CA 90069 USA

Searfoss, Richard A *Astronaut*
24480 Silver Creek Way, Tehachapi, CA 93561 USA

Searle, Jackie
7214 Chestwood Dr., Tujunga, CA 91042

Searle, John R *Misc*
109 Yosemite Road, Berkeley, CA 94707 USA

Searle, Ronald *Cartoonist, Animator*
Elaine McMahon Agency, PO Box 1062, Bayonne, NJ 07002 USA

Searles, John *Writer*
Avon/William Morrow, 1350 Ave of Americas, New York, NY 10019 USA

Sears, Paul B *Misc*
17 Las Milpas, Taos, NM 87571 USA

Sears, Victor W (Vic) *Football Player*
2501 Webb Chapel Extension 9105, Dallas, TX 75220 USA

Sears, Dr, William
34761 Doheny Place, Capistrano Beach, CA 92624

Seau, Tiana (Junior) Jr *Football Player*
1904 Via Casa Alta, La Jolla, CA 92037 USA

Seaver, G Thomas (Tom) *Baseball Player*
1761 Diamond Mountain Road, Calistoga, CA 94515 USA

Seaver, Tom
1761 Diamond Mountain Rd., Calistoga, CA 94515-9636

Seavey, David *Editor, Cartoonist*
USA Today, Editorial Dept, 1000 Wilson Blvd, Arlington, VA 22209 USA

Seaward, Tracey *Producer*
International Creative Management (ICM-LA), 8942 Wilshire Blvd, Beverly Hills, CA 90211 USA

Seaward, Tracy *Producer*
International Creative Management (ICM-UK), Oxford House, 76 Oxford St, London, W1N OAX, UNITED KINGDOM (UK)

Seawell, William T *Business Person*
21 Westridge Dr, Pine Bluff, AR 71603 USA

Sebaldt, Maria
Geranienstr. 3, Grunwald, GERMANY, D-82031

Sebastian, Cuthbert *Governor, General*
Governor General's House, Basseterre, SAINT kITTS & NEVIS

Sebastian, John *Musician*
Lustig Talent, PO Box 770850, Orlando, FL 32877 USA

Sebastiani, Sergio Cardinal *Religious Leader*
Palazzo delle Congregazioni, Lardo del Colonnato 3, Rome, 00193, ITALY

Sebestyen, Marta *Musician, Music Group*
Konzertgentur Berthold Seliger, Nonnengasse 15, Fulda, 36037, GERMANY

Sebold, Alice *Writer*
Little Brown, 3 Center Plaza, Boston, MA 02108 USA

Secada, Jon *Musician*
PO Box 145247, Coral Gables, FL 33114 USA

Seck, Idrissa *Prime Minister*
Prime Minister's Office, Ave Leopold Sedar Senghor, Dakar, SENEGAL

Secor, Kyle *Actor*
Brillstein/Grey, 9150 Wilshire Blvd #350, Beverly Hills, CA 90212 USA

Secord, Al *Hockey Player*
950 Ginger St, Southlake, TX 76092-6063

Secord, John *Musician, Music Group*
Making Texas Music, Old Putnam Bank Building, PO Box 1013, Putnam, TX 76469 USA

Secord, Richard V *General*
Computerized Thermal Imaging, 1719 W 2800 S, Ogden, UT 84401 USA

Secret GardenContinental AS, Marcus
Thranesgate 2b, Oslo, NORWAY, 0473

Secrets, No *Music Group*
Official International Fan Club, PO Box 5247, Bellingham, WA 98227 USA

Secunda, Andrew *Writer*
Late Night with Conan O'Brien, 330 Bob Hope Dr, Burbank, CA 91523

Seda, Jon *Actor*
Anthem Entertainment, 6100 Wilshire Blvd #1170, Los Angeles, CA 90069 USA

Sedaka, Neil *Musician*
Sedaka Music, 201 E 66th St #3N, New York, NY 10021 USA

Sedaris, Amy *Actor*
Paradigm (LA), 10100 Santa Monica Blvd, Fl 25, Los Angeles, CA 90067 USA

Sedaris, David *Writer*
Doubleday Press, 1540 Broadway, New York, NY 10036 USA

Seddon, M Rhea
1709 Shagbark Trail, Murfreesboro, TN
37130 USA

Seddon, Margaret Rhea *Astronaut*
1709 Shagbark Trail, Murfreesboro, TN
37130 USA

Sedelmaier, J Josef (Joe) *Director,
Animator*
Sedelmaier Film Productions, 858 W
Armitage Ave #267, Chicago, IL 60614
USA

Sedgman, Frank *Tennis Player*
28 Bolton Ave, Hampton, VIC, 3188,
AUSTRALIA

Sedgwick, Kyra *Actor*
PO Box 668, Sharon, CT 06069 USA

Sedgworth, Bill
1811 Volusia Ave., Daytona Beach, FL
32015

Sedney, Jules *Prime Minister*
Maystreet 24, Paramaribo, SARINAME

Sedykh, Yuri G *Track Athlete*
Russian Light Athletics Federation,
Luzhnetskaya Nab 8, Moscow, RUSSIA

See, Carolyn *Writer*
17339 Tramonto Dr #303, Pacific
Palisades, CA 90272 USA

Seear, Beatrice N S *Government Official*
189B Kennington Road, London, SE11
6ST, UNITED KINGDOM (UK)

Seegal, Denise *Business Person*
Liz Claiborne Inc, 1441 Broadway, New
York, NY 10018 USA

Seeger, Michael
PO Box 1592, Lexington, VA 24450

Seeger, Pete *Music Group, Musician,
Songwriter*
PO Box 431, Dutchess Junction, Beacon,
NY 12508 USA

Seehorn, Rhea *Actor*
Epstein Wyckoff Corsa Ross & Assoc (LA),
280 S Beverly Dr #400, Beverly Hills, CA
90212 USA

Seelenfreund, Alan *Business Person*
McKesson HBOC Inc, 1 Post St, San
Francisco, CA 94104 USA

Seeler, Uwe *Soccer Player*
HSV, Rothenbaumchaussee 125,
Hamburg, 20149, GERMANY

Seeling, Angelle *Motorcycle Racer*
Star Performance Suzuki Racing Team, PO
Box 1240, Americus, GA 31709 USA

Seely, Jeannie *Musician, Music Group,
Songwriter*
Tessier-Marsh Talent, 2825 Blue Book Dr,
Nashville, TN 37214 USA

Seelye, Talcott W *Diplomat*
5510 Pembroke Road, Bethesda, MD
20817 USA

Seema *Actor, Bollywood*
25 Madhavan Nair Road,
Mahalingapuram, Chennai, TN 600034,
INDIA

Seether *Music Group*
Wind-up Records, 72 Madison Ave, New
York, NY 10016 USA

Seffrin, John R *Misc*
American Cancer Society, 1599 Clifton
Road NE, Atlanta, GA 30329 USA

Sega, Ronald M *Astronaut, Engineer*
711 Staters Lane #B, Alexandria, VA
22314 USA

Segal, Erich *Writer*
Wolfson College, English School, Oxford,
OX2 6UD, UNITED KINGDOM (UK)

Segal, Fred *Fashion Designer*
Fred Segal Jeans, 8100 Melrose Ave, Los
Angeles, CA 90046 USA

Segal, George *Actor*
515 N Robertson Blvd, West Hollywood,
CA 90048 USA

Segal, Jason *Actor*
United Talent Agency (UTA), 9560
Wilshire Blvd, Beverly Hills, CA 90212
USA

Segal, Jonathan
PO Box 3059, Tel Aviv, ISRAEL, 61030

Segal, Michael
27 Cyprus Ave Finchley, London,
ENGLAND, N3 1SS

Segal, Peter *Director*
William Morris Agency, 151 El Camino
Dr, Beverly Hills, CA 90212 USA

Segal, Uri
MA Artists Mgmt, 28 Sheffield Terrace,
London, W8 7NA, UNITED KINGDOM
(UK)

Segall, Pamela
1450 S. Robertson Blvd., Los Angeles, CA
90035

Seganti, Paolo *Actor*
PFD, Drury House, 34-43 Russell St,
London, W8 7NA, UNITED KINGDOM
(UK)

Seger, Bob *Musician, Music Group,
Songwriter*
Capitol Records, 1750 N Vine St, Los
Angeles, CA 90028 USA

Seger, Shea *Musician, Music Group*
Helter Skelter, Plaza, 535 Kings Road,
London, SW10 0S, UNITED KINGDOM
(UK)

Segerstam, Leif S *Composer*
Garvey & Ivor, 59 Lansdowne Place,
Hove, BN3 1FL, UNITED KINGDOM (UK)

Segui, David V *Baseball Player*
13421 Leavenworth Road, Kansas City, KS
66109 USA

Segui, Diego P *Baseball Player*
7520 King St #J, Shawnee Mission, KS
66214 USA

Segura, Francisco (Pancho) *Tennis Player*
Rancho La Costa Hotel & Spa, 7690
Camino Real, Carlsbad, CA 92009 USA

Segura, Pancho
. La Costa Hotel, Costa Del Mar Rd,
Carlsbad, 92009

Seguso, Robert *Tennis Player*
Advantage International, 1025 Thomas
Jefferson NW #450, Washington, DC
20007 USA

Seibou, Ali *President, General*
Chairman's Office, National Orientation
Higher Council, Niamey, NIGER

Seidel, Kelly
8441 Balboa Blvd. #36, Northridge, CA
91325

Seidel, Martie *Musician, Music Group*
Senior Mgmt, 56 Lindsey Ave, Nashville,
TN 37210 USA

Seidelman, Susan *Director*
Michael Shedler, 225 W 34th St #1012,
New York, NY 10122 USA

Seidenberg, Ivan G *Business Person*
Bell Atlantic Corp, 1095 Ave of Americas,
New York, NY 10036 USA

Seidler, Harry *Architect*
2 Glen St, Milsons Point, NSW, 2061,
AUSTRALIA

Seidman, L William *Government Official,
Business Person*
1025 Connecticut Ave NW #800,
Washington, DC 20036 USA

Seifert, George G *Football Coach,
Sportscaster*
1908 Bay Flat Road, Bodega Bay, CA
94923 USA

Seigenthaler, John L *Publisher*
Tennessean, 1100 Broadway, Nashville,
TN 37203 USA

Seigner, Emmanuelle *Actor*
Artmedia, 20 Ave Rapp, Paris, 75007,
FRANCE

Seigner, Mathilde *Actor*
Artmedia, 20 Ave Rapp, Paris, 75007,
FRANCE

Seignoret, Clarence H A *President*
24 Cork St, Roseau, DOMINICA

Seikaly, Rony *Basketball Player*
27 E Dilido Dr, Miami Beach, FL 33139
USA

Seiko
9200 Sunset Blvd. #PH-15, W.
Hollywood, CA 90069-3502

Seilacher, Adolf *Geophysicist*
Yale University, Geology/Geophysics
Laboratory, New Haven, CT 06520 USA

Seinfeld, Jerry *Actor, Comedian*
211 Central Park W, New York, NY
10024 USA

Seinfeld, John H *Engineer*
363 Patrician Way, Pasadena, CA 91105
USA

Seiple, Larry *Football Player*
1361 W Golfview Dr, Pembroke Pines, FL
33026 USA

Seitz, Frederick *Politician, Educator*
Rockefeller University, Physics Dept, 1230
York Ave, New York, NY 10021 USA

Seitz, Raymond G H *Diplomat*
Lehman Brothers International, 1
Broadgate, London, EC2M 7HA, UNITED
KINGDOM (UK)

Seiwald, Robert J *Inventor*
59 Burnside Ave, San Francisco, CA
94131 USA

Seixas, E Victor (Vic) Jr *Tennis Player*
8 Harbor Point Dr #207, Mill Valley, CA
94941 USA

Seixas, Vic
8 Harbor Point Dr. #207, Mill Valley, CA
94941

Seizinger, Katja *Skier*
Rudolf-Epp-Str 48, Eberbach, 69412, GERMANY

Seka
1122 White Rock, Dixon, IL 60121

Sekka, Johnny
35315 Glenwall St, Agua Dulce, CA 91350

Sela, Michael *Doctor, Misc*
Weizmann Science Institute, Immunology Dept, Rehovot, 76100, ISRAEL

Selanne, Teemu *Hockey Player*
31731 Madre Selva Lane, Trabuco Canyon, CA 92679 USA

Selby, David *Actor*
International Creative Mgmt, 8942 Wilshire Blvd #219, Beverly Hills, CA 90211 USA

Selby, Philip *Composer*
Hill Cottage, Via 1 Maggio 93, Rignano Flaminio, Rome, 00068, ITALY

Seldes, Marian
210 Central Park S., New York, NY 10019

Seldin, Donald W *Doctor*
Texas Southwestern Medical Center, 5323 Harry Hines Blvd, Dallas, TX 75390 USA

Seldon, Bruce *Boxer*
Don King Productions, 968 Pinehurst Dr, Las Vegas, NV 89109 USA

Sele, Aaron H *Baseball Player*
5760 NE Gunderson Road, Poulsbo, WA 98370 USA

Seles, Monica *Tennis Player*
2895 Dick Wilson Dr, Sarasota, FL 34240 USA

Seley, Jason *Artist*
Cornell University, Art Dept, Ithaca, NY 14853 USA

Self, Bill *Basketball Player, Coach*
University of Kansas, Athletic Dept, Allen Fieldhouse, Lawrence, KS 66045 USA

Selig, Allan H (Bud) *Baseball Player, Misc*
Baseball Commissioner's Office, 245 Park Ave #3100, New York, NY 10167 USA

Seliger, Mark *Photographer*
Little Brown, 3 Center Plaza, Boston, MA 02108 USA

Seligman, Martin E P *Doctor*
University of Pennsylvania, Psychology Dept, Philadelphia, PA 19104 USA

Selkirk, George N *Government Official*
Rose Lawn Coppice, Wimborne, Dorset, UNITED KINGDOM (UK)

Selkoe, Dennis J *Doctor*
Brigham & Women's Hospital, 221 Longwood Ave, Boston, MA 02115 USA

Sellars, Peter *Director*
Creative Artists Agency, 9830 Wilshire Blvd, Beverly Hills, CA 90212 USA

Selldorf, Annabelle *Architect*
Selldorf Architects, 62 White St, New York, NY 10013 USA

Selleca, Connie *Actor*
15050 Ventura Blvd #916, Sherman Oaks, CA 91403 USA

Selleck, Tom *Actor*
Agency for Artists, 9939 Robbins Dr, Beverly Hills, CA 90212 USA

Seller, Peg *Swimmer, Coach*
72 Monkswood Crescent, Newmarket, ON L3Y 2K1, CANADA

Sellers, Franklin *Religious Leader*
Reformed Episcopal Church, 2001 Frederick Road, Baltimore, MD 21228 USA

Sellers, Larry *Actor*
Vaughn Hart & Associates, 8899 Beverly Blvd, Los Angeles, CA 90048 USA

Sellers, Michael *Producer, Writer, Actor*
Quantum Entertainment, 3599 Cahuenga Blvd #319, Los Angeles, CA 90068 USA

Sellers, Piers J *Astronaut*
16011 Craighurst Dr, Houston, TX 77059 USA

Sellers, Ron F *Football Player*
4109 Hickory Dr, Palm Beach Gardens, FL 33418 USA

Sellers, Victoria
1927 Vista Del Mar Ave., Hollywood, CA 90068

Sellick, Phyllis *Musician*
Beverly House, 29A Ranelagh Ave, Barnes, SW13 0BN, UNITED KINGDOM (UK)

Selmon, Dewey W *Football Player*
2725 S Berry Road, Norman, OK 73072 USA

Selmon, Lee Roy *Football Player*
15350 Amberty Dr #624, Tampa, FL 33647 USA

Selmon, Lucious *Football Player, Coach*
Jacksonville Jaguars, 1 AllTell Stadium Place, Jacksonville, FL 32202 USA

Selten, Reinhard *Nobel Prize Laureate*
Hardtweg 23, Konigswinter, 53639, GERMANY

Seltz, Rolland *Basketball Player*
3328 Oswego Heights Road, Shoreview, MN 55126 USA

Seltzer, David *Director, Writer*
Shady Acres, Universal Studios, Universal City Plaza, Universal City, CA 91608 USA

Selvy, Franklin D (Frank) *Basketball Player*
305 Honey Horn Dr, Simpsonville, SC 29681 USA

Selya, Bruce M *Judge*
US Court of Appeals, US Courthouse, Providence, RI 02903 USA

Selzer, Milton *Actor*
1751 Emerald Isle Way, Oxnard, CA 93035 USA

Selzer, Richard *Writer, Doctor*
6 Saint Ronan Terrace, New Haven, CT 06511 USA

Selznick, Albie
2800 Nielsen Way, Santa Monica, CA 90405-4025

Semak, Michael W *Photographer*
1796 Spruce Hill Road, Pickering, ON L1V 1S4, CANADA

Sembello, Michael *Musician, Songwriter*
Talent Consultants International, 1560 Broadway, #1308, New York, NY 10036 USA

Sembene, Ousmane *Director*
PO Box 8087, Yoff, SENEGAL

Sembier, Melvin F *Diplomat*
Sembler Co, 5858 Central Ave, Saint Petersburgh, FL 33707 USA

Semenov, Anatoli *Hockey Player*
8825 E Crestview Lane, Anaheim, CA 92808 USA

Semenova, Juliana *Basketball Player*
Zalalela 4-35, Riga, 1010, LATVIA

Semenyaka, Lyudmila *Ballerina*
Bolshoi Theater, Teatralnaya Pl 1, Moscow, 103009, RUSSIA

Semiz, Teata *Bowler*
3131 Kennedy Blvd, North Bergen, NJ 07047 USA

Semizorova, Nina L *Ballerina*
2 Zhukovskaya St, #8, Moscow, RUSSIA

Semkow, Jerzy G
Ul Dynasy 6 m 1, Warsaw, 00-354, POLAND

Semler, Dean *Cinematographer, Director*
4260 Arcola Ave, Toluca Lake, CA 91602 USA

Semmelrogge, Martin
Terhallestr. II, Munich, GERMANY, D-81545

Sempe, Jean-Jacques *Cartoonist*
Editions Denoel, 9 Rue du Cherche-Midi, Paris, 75006, FRANCE

Semple, Robert B Jr *Journalist*
New York Times, Editorial Dept, 229 W 43rd St, New York, NY 10036 USA

Semyonov, Vladilen G *Ballerina*
15/17-504 Roubinshteina St, Saint Petersburg, 191002, RUSSIA

Sen, Amartya K *Nobel Prize Laureate*
Trinity College, Economics Dept, Cambridge, CB2 1TP, UNITED KINGDOM (UK)

Sen, Dog *Musician*
William Morris Agency, 151 El Camino Dr, Beverly Hills, CA 90212 USA

Sen, Moon Moon *Actor*
Ruia Park Flat No 62 'B', Juhu, Bombay, MS 400 049, INDIA

Sen, Mrinal *Director*
4E Motilal Nehru Road, Culcutta, 700029, INDIA

Sen, Riya *Actor, Bollywood*
62-B Ruia Park, Juhu, Mumbai, MS 400049, INDIA

Sen, Sushmita *Actor, Bollywood*
6th Floor Beach Queen, Yari Road Versova Andheri (W), Mumbai, MS 400061, INDIA

Sena, Dominic *Director*
International Creative Management (ICM-LA), 8942 Wilshire Blvd, Beverly Hills, CA 90211 USA

Sena, Suzanne
6310 San Vicente Blvd. #200, Los Angeles, CA 90048

Sendak, Maurice
200 Chestnut Hill Rd., Ridgefield, CT 06877-1200

Sendak, Maurice B *Writer, Misc*
200 Chestnut Hill Road, Ridgefield, CT
06877 USA

Sendel, Peter *Athlete*
Zallaer Str 9, Oberhof, 98599, GERMANY

Sendel, Sergio *Actor*
Televisa, Blvd Adolfo Lopez Mateos 232,
Colonia San Angel INN, DF, CP 01060,
MEXICO

Senderens, Alain *Chef*
Restaurant Lucas Carton, 9 Place de la
Madeleine, Paris, 75008, FRANCE

Senff, Dina (Nida) *Swimmer*
DW Coutuner-Senff, Praam 122,
Amstelveen, 1186 TL, NETERLANDS

Sennewald, Robert W *General*
426 S Pitt St, Alexandria, VA 22314 USA

Sentelle, David B *Judge*
US Court of Appeals, 333 Constitution
Ave NW, Washington, DC 20001 USA

Seow, Yit Kin *Musician*
8 North Terrace, London, SW3 2BA,
UNITED KINGDOM (UK)

Sepe, Crescenzio Cardinal *Religious Leader*
Piazza della Citta Leonina 9, Rome,
00193, ITALY

Septimus, Jake *Producer*
Creative Artists Agency LCC (CAA-LA),
9830 Wilshire Blvd, Beverly Hills, CA
90212 USA

Sepulveda, Charlie *Musician*
Ralph Mercado Mgmt, 568 Broadway
#608, New York, NY 10012 USA

Sequeira, Luis *Scientist, Biologist*
10 Appomattox Court, Madison, WI
53705 USA

Serafini, Tito A *Biologist*
University of California, Neurobiology
Dept, San Francisco, CA 94143 USA

Seraphin, Oliver *Prime Minister*
44 Green's Lane, Goodwill, DOMINICA

Serbedzija, Rade *Actor*
P F D, Drury House 34-43 Russell St,
London, WC2B 5HA, UNITED KINGDOM
(UK)

Serebrier, Jose *Composer*
20 Queensgate Gardens, London, SW7
5LZ, UNITED KINGDOM (UK)

Serebrov, Alexander A *Misc*
Potchta Kosmonavtov, Moskovskoi
Oblasti, Syvisdny Goroduk, 141160,
RUSSIA

Serembus, John *Misc*
Upholsterers Union, 25 N 4th St,
Philadelphia, PA 19106 USA

Serendipity Singers, The
PO Box 142, Wauconda, IL 60084

Sereno, Paul *Scientist*
University of Chicago, Paleontology Dept,
Chicago, IL 60537 USA

Seresin, Michael *Cinematographer*
59 North Wharf Road, London, W2 1LA,
UNITED KINGDOM (UK)

Sereys, Jacques
84 bd. Malesherbes, Paris, FRANCE,
F-75008

Sergei, Ivan *Actor*
Burstein Company, The, 15304 Sunset
Blvd #208, Pacific Palisades, CA 90272
USA

Serig, Jennifer *Fashion Designer*
Perception Public Relations LLC, 13333
Ventura Blvd #203, Sherman Oaks, CA
91423 USA

Serious, Yahoo *Actor*
12/33 E Crescent St, McMahons Point,
NSW, 2060, AUSTRALIA

Serkin, Peter A *Musician*
Manne Music College, 150 W 85th St,
New York, NY 10024 USA

Serkis, Andy *Actor*
Gersh Agency, The (LA), 232 N Canon Dr,
Beverly Hills, CA 90210 USA

Serlemitsos, Peter J *Astronomer*
BBXRT Project, Goddard Space Flight
Center, Greenbelt, MD 20771 USA

Sermon, Eric *Musician*
Richard Walters, 1800 Argyle Ave, #408,
Los Angeles, CA 90028 USA

Serna, Assumpta *Actor*
8306 Wilshire Blvd #438, Beverly Hills,
CA 90211 USA

Serna, Diego *Soccer Player*
Los Angeles Galaxy, 1010 Rose Bowl Dr,
Pasadena, CA 91103 USA

Serna, Pepe *Actor*
127 Ruby Ave, Newport Beach, CA 92662
USA

Serota, Nicholas A *Director*
Tate Gallery, Millbank, London, SW1P
4RG, UNITED KINGDOM (UK)

Serra, Eduardo *Cinematographer*
4324 Promenade Way #109, Marina del
Rey, CA 90292 USA

Serra, Pablo *Writer*
Gabriel Blanco Iglesias (Mexico), Rio
Balsas 35-32, Colonia Cuauhtemoc, DF,
06500, Mexico

Serra, Richard *Artist*
173 Duane St, New York, NY 10013 USA

Serrano, Diego *Actor*
McKeon-Valeo Management, 9107
Wilshire Blvd #321, Beverly Hills, CA
90210 USA

Serrano, Juan *Musician*
Prince/SF Productions, 1450 Southgate
Ave #206, Daly City, CA 94015 USA

Serrano, Nestor *Actor*
InnerAct Entertainment, 141 Barrington
Ave #E, Los Angeles, CA 90049 USA

Serrault, Michel L *Actor, Musician*
MS Productions, 12 Rue Greuze, Paris,
75116, FRANCE

Serrauot, Michel
201 rue Du Fauboug-St.-Honore, Paris,
FRANCE, F-75008

Serre, Jean-Pierre *Mathematician*
6 Ave de Montespan, Paris, 75116,
FRANCE

Serreau, Coline *Director*
Artmedia, 20 Ave Rapp, Paris, 75007,
FRANCE

Serrin, James B *Mathematician*
4422 Dupont Ave S, Minneapolis, MN
55409 USA

Servan-Schreiber, Jean-Claude *Journalist*
147 Bis Rue d'Alesia, Paris, 75014,
FRANCE

SerVass, Cory J *Editor*
Saturday Evening Post Magazine, 1100
Waterway Blvd, Indianapolis, IN 46202
USA

Server, Josh *Actor*
Amsel Eisenstadt & Frazier Inc, 5757
Wilshire Blvd #510, Los Angeles, CA
90036 USA

Sesame Street
1 Lincoln Plaza, New York, NY 10022

Sessions, John
4 Windmill St., London, ENGLAND, W1P
1HF

Sessions, William S *Judge*
112 E Pecan #2900, San Antonio, TX
78205 USA

Sessler, Gerhard M *Inventor*
Fichtenstra 30B, Darmstadt, 64285,
GERMANY

Setari, Robert *Actor*
Vessel Entertainment, 10989 Bluffside Dr
#3210, Studio City, CA 91604

Seter, Mordecai *Composer*
1 Kamy St, Ramat Aviv, Tel-Aviv, ISRAEL

Seth, Joshua *Actor*
Sutton Barth & Vennari Inc, 145 S Fairfax
#310, Los Angeles, CA 90036 USA

Seth, Oliver *Judge*
US Court of Appeals, PO Box 1, Santa Fe,
NM 87504 USA

Seth, Vikram *Writer*
Phoenix House, Orion House, 5 Upper St,
London, WC2H 9EA, UNITED KINGDOM
(UK)

Sethi, Parmeet *Actor, Bollywood*
702/B-1 Sundervan, Off Lokhandwala
Road Andheri (W), Mumbai, MS 400053,
INDIA

Sethna, Homi N *Engineer*
Old Yacht Club, Chatrapati Shivaji
Maharaj, Bombay, 400 038, INDIA

Setlow, Richard B *Biologist*
4 Beachland Ave, East Quogue, NY 11942
USA

Settle, Matthew *Actor*
Untitled Entertainment (LA), 8436 W 3rd
St #650, Los Angeles, CA 90048 USA

Setzer, Brian *Music Group, Musician*
Haber Corp, 16830 Ventura Blvd #501,
Encino, CA 91436 USA

Setziol, LeRoy I (Roy) *Artist*
30450 Moriah Lane, Sheridan, OR 97378
USA

Sevastyanov, Vitayi I *Misc*
Potchta Kosmonavtov, Moskovskoi
Oblasti, Syvisdny Goroduk, 141160,
RUSSIA

Seven, Johnny *Actor*
11213 McLennan Ave, Granada Hills, CA
91344 USA

Severance, Joan *Actor*
Agency for the Performing Arts (APA-LA), 9200 Sunset Blvd #900, Los Angeles, CA 90069 USA

Severeid, Suzanne *Model, Actor*
PO Box 4171, Malibu, CA 90264 USA

Severin, G Timothy (Tim) *Misc*
Inchy Bridge, Timoleague, County Cork, IRELAND

Severino, John C *Misc*
Prime Ticket Network, 401 S Prairie St, Inglewood, CA 90301 USA

Severinsen, Carl H (Doc) *Musician, Conductor*
4275 White Pine Lane, Santa Ynez, CA 93460 USA

Sevier, Corey *Actor*
Innovative Artists (LA), 1505 Tenth St, Santa Monica, CA 90401 USA

Sevigny, Chloe *Actor*
Brillstein/Grey, 9150 Wilshire Blvd #350, Beverly Hills, CA 90212 USA

Sevilla, Carmen
Plaza de Pablo Ruiz Picasso s/n Torre Picasso Planto 36, Madrid, SPAIN, 2800

Sevsec, Pedro *Actor*
Telemundo, 2470 West 8th Avenue, Hialeah, FL 33010 USA

Seward, George C *Attorney General*
Seward & Kissel, 1 Battery Park Plaza, New York, NY 10004 USA

Sewell, George *Actor*
Peter Charlesworth, 68 Old Brompton Road, London, SW7 3LQ, UNITED KINGDOM (UK)

Sewell, Harley *Football Player*
104 W Lily Lane, Arlington, TX 76010 USA

Sewell, Rufus *Actor*
Julian Belfarge, 46 Albemarle St, London, W1X 4PP, UNITED KINGDOM (UK)

Seweryn, Andrzej *Actor*
Comedie Francaise, Place Colette, Paris, 75001, FRANCE

Sex Pistols
100 Wilshire Blvd. #1830, Santa Monica, CA 90401

Sexsmith, Ron *Musician, Songwriter*
Michael Dixon Mgmt, 119 Pebblecreek Road, Franklin, TN 37064 USA

Sexson, Richie *Athlete*
17913 NE 28th St, Vancouver, WA 98682 USA

Sexto, Camilo *Musician*
BMG, 1540 Broadway, New York, NY 10036 USA

Sexton, Charlie *Musician*
Courage Artists, 310 Water St, #201, Vancouver, BC V6B 1B6, CANADA

Sexton III, Brendan *Actor*
Gersh Agency, The (LA), 232 N Canon Dr, Beverly Hills, CA 90210 USA

Seydoux, Geraldine *Biologist*
Johns Hopkins University, Molecular Biology Dept, Baltimore, MD 21218 USA

Seyferth, Dietmar *Misc*
Massachusetts Institute of Technology, Chemistry Dept, Cambridge, MA 02139 USA

Seyler, Athene *Actor*
Coach House, 26 Upper Mall Hammersmith, London, W8, UNITED KINGDOM (UK)

Seymour, Cara *Actor*
Davien Littlefield Management, 939 Eighth Ave #609, New York, NY 10019 USA

Seymour, Caroline *Actor*
Langford Assoc, 17 Westfields Ave, London, SW13 0AT, UNITED KINGDOM (UK)

Seymour, Carolyn *Actor*
Chasin Agency, 8899 Beverly Blvd #716, Los Angeles, CA 90048 USA

Seymour, Jane *Actor*
Metropolitan Talent Agency (MTA), 4526 Wilshire Blvd, Los Angeles, CA 90010 USA

Seymour, John *Senator*
46393 Blackhawk Dr, Indian Wells, CA 92210 USA

Seymour, Lesley Jane *Editor*
Redbook Magazine, Editorial Dept, 224 W 57th St, New York, NY 10019 USA

Seymour, Lynn *Ballerina*
Artistes in Action, 16 Balderton St, London, W1Y 1TF, UNITED KINGDOM (UK)

Seymour, Paul C *Football Player*
4188 Shoals Dr, Okemos, MI 48864 USA

Seymour, Richard *Football Player*
1156 Cate Road, Eastover, SC 29044 USA

Seymour, Stephanie *Model*
5415 Oberlin Dr, San Diego, CA 92121 USA

Seymour, Stephanie K *Judge*
US Court of Appeals, US Courthouse, 333 W 4th St, Tulsa, OK 74103 USA

Seynhaeve, Ingrid
111 E. 22nd St. #200, New York, NY 10010

Sezer, Ahmet Necdet *President*
President's Office, Cumhurbaskanlgl Kosku, Cankaya, Ankara, TURKEY

Sfar, Rachid *Prime Minister*
278 Ave de Tervuren, Brussels, 1150, BELGIUM

Sfeir, Nasrallah Pierre Cardinal *Religious Leader*
Patriarcat Maronite, Bkerke, LEBANON

Sgouros, Dimitris *Musician*
Tompazi 28 Str, Piraeus, 18537, GREECE

Shack, Edward S P (Eddie) *Hockey Player*
508 Fairlawn Ave, North York, ON M5M 1V2, CANADA

Shack, William A *Misc*
2597 Hilgard Ave, Berkeley, CA 94709 USA

Shackelford, Ted *Actor*
12305 Valley Heart Dr, Studio City, CA 91604 USA

Shackouls, Bobby S *Business Person*
Burlington Resources, 5051 Westheimer, Houston, TX 77056 USA

Shad-Kydd, Frances
Althorpe House Gr. Brington, Northamptonshire, ENGLAND, NN7 4HQ

Shadyac, Tom *Director*
United Talent Agency, 9560 Wilshire Blvd #500, Beverly Hills, CA 90212 USA

Shafer, Martin *Business Person*
Castle Rock Entertainment, 335 North Maple Dr #135, Beverly Hills, CA 90210-3867

Shafer, R Donald *Religious Leader*
Brethren in Christ Church, PO Box 290, Grantham, PA 17027 USA

Shaffer, David H *Publisher*
MacMillan, 1177 Ave of Americas, #1965, New York, NY 10036 USA

Shaffer, Paul *Musician, Music Group*
Panacea Entertainment, 12020 Chandler Blvd, #300, North Hollywood, CA 91607 USA

Shaffer, Peter *Writer*
Lantz, 888 7th Ave #2500, New York, NY 10106 USA

Shagan, Steve *Writer*
285 W Via Lola, Palm Springs, CA 92262 USA

Shagari, Alhaji Shehu Usman Aliu *President*
22 Shehu Crescent, PO Box 162 Adarawa, Sokoto State, NIGERIA

Shaggy *Musician*
Artist Group International, 9560 Wilshire Blvd #400, Beverly Hills, CA 90212 USA

Shah, Idries *Writer*
AP Watt Ltd, 26/28 Bedford Row, London, WC1R 4HL, UNITED KINGDOM (UK)

Shah, Satish *Actor, Bollywood, Comedian*
30A Anand Nagar, Forjeet Street, Bombay, MS 400 036, INDIA

Shahan, Gil *Musician*
ICM Artists, 40 W 57th St, New York, NY 10019 USA

Shahi, Sara *Actor*
Paradigm (LA), 10100 Santa Monica Blvd, Fl 25, Los Angeles, CA 90067 USA

Shahmatova, Larissa *Musician*
Julliard Music School, Lincoln Center Plaza, New York, NY 10023 USA

Shaiman, Marc *Composer*
8476 Brier Dr, West Hollywood, CA 90046 USA

Shakespeare, Frank J Jr *Television Host, Diplomat*
303 Coast Blvd, La Jolla, CA 92037 USA

Shakira *Musician*
Sony Music, CI 94 A 11 A-50, Bogota DF, COLOMBIA

Shakur, Kula
39-A Gramercy Park N. #1-C, New York, NY 10010

Shakurov, Sergei K *Actor*
Bibliotechnava Str 27, #94, Moscow, 109544, RUSSIA

Shal-Houd, Tony
9560 Wilshire Blvd. #516, Beverly Hills, CA 90212

Shalala, Donna *Secretary*
University of Miami, President's Office, Coral Gables, FL 33124 USA

Shalamar
707 18th Ave. So., Nashville, TN 37203

Shales, Thomas W *Journalist*
Washington Post, Editorial Dept, 1150 15th St NW, Washington, DC 20071 USA

Shales, Tom
1650 Kirby Rd., McLean, VA 22101

Shalhoub, Tony *Actor*
United Talent Agency, 9560 Wilshire Blvd #500, Beverly Hills, CA 90212 USA

Shalikashvili, John M (Shali) *General*
55 Chapman Loop, Steilacoom, WA 98388 USA

Shalim *Musician*
Sony Music Miami, 605 Lincoln Rd, Miami Beach, FL 33138 USA

Shalit, Gene *Critic*
NBC-TV, News Dept, 30 Rockefeller Plaza, New York, NY 10112 USA

Shamask, Ronaldus *Fashion Designer*
Moss Shamask, 39 W 37th St, New York, NY 10018 USA

Shamir, Yitzhak *Prime Minister*
Beit Amot Mishpat, 8 Shaul Hamelech Blvd, Tel Aviv, 64733, ISRAEL

Shan Kuo-Hsi, Paul Cardinal *Religious Leader*
Bishop's House, 125 Szu-Wie 3rd Road, Kaohsiung, 80203, TAIWAN

Shanahan, Brendan *Hockey Player*
473 Puritan Ave, Birmingham, MI 48009 USA

Shanahan, Mike *Football Coach*
Denver Broncos, 13655 E Broncos Parkway, Englewood, CO 80112 USA

Shand, Remy *Musician, Music Group, Songwriter*
Universal Records, 2550 Victoria Park, Toronto, ON M2J 4A2, CANADA

Shandling, Garry *Comedian, Actor*
Endeavor Talent Agency, 9701 Wilshire Blvd #1000, Beverly Hills, CA 90212 USA

Shandrowsky, Alex *Misc*
Marine Engineer Beneficial Assn, 444 N Capitol St NW, Washington, DC 20001 USA

Shane, Bob *Music Group, Musician*
9410 S 46th St, Phoenix, AZ 85044 USA

Shange, Ntozake *Writer*
Saint Martin's Press, 175 5th Ave, New York, NY 10010 USA

Shangri-La's, The
27 L'Ambiance Ct, Bardonia, NY 10954

Shanice *Musician*
Richard Walters, 1800 Argyle Ave #408, Los Angeles, CA 90028 USA

Shank, Bud
PO Box 948, Townsend, WA 98368

Shank, Clarence E (Bud) *Musician*
PO Box 70128, Tucson, AZ 85737 USA

Shank, Roger C *Scientist*
Northwestern University, Learning Sciences Institute, Evanston, IL 60201 USA

Shankar, Anoushka *Musician*
International Creative Management (ICM-LA), 8942 Wilshire Blvd, Beverly Hills, CA 90211 USA

Shankar, Naren *Producer*
CSI, 25135 Anza Dr, Stage 6, Santa Clarita, CA 91355 USA

Shankar, Ravi
17 Warden Ct Gowalia Tank Rd., Bombay, INDIA, 36

Shanker, Ravi *Musician, Composer*
17 Warden Court, Gowalia Tank Road, Bonbay, 36, INDIA

Shankley, Amelia
2-4 Noel St., London, ENGLAND, W1V 3RB

Shankman, Adam *Comedian, Director*
Brillstein-Grey Entertainment, 9150 Wilshire Blvd #350, Beverly Hills, CA 90212 USA

Shanks, Michael *Actor*
Characters Talent Agency, The (Toronto), 150 Carlton St Fl 2, Toronto ON, M5A 2K1, CANADA

Shanley, John Patrick *Director, Writer*
Creative Artists Agency LCC (CAA-LA), 9830 Wilshire Blvd, Beverly Hills, CA 90212 USA

Shannon *Music Group, Musician*
Big Mgmt, 226 5th Ave, New York, NY 10001 USA

Shannon, Elaine *Writer*
Penguin USA, 375 Hudson St, New York, NY 10014 USA

Shannon, Mem *Music Group, Musician, Songwriter*
Miasma Mgmt, PO Box 27037, Los Angeles, CA 90027 USA

Shannon, Michael *Actor*
Endeavor Agency LLC (LA), 9601 Wilshire Blvd Fl 3, Beverly Hills, CA 90210 USA

Shannon, Michael E *Business Person*
Ecolab Inc, Ecolab Center, 370 Wabasha St N, Saint Paul, MN 55102 USA

Shannon, Molly *Actor, Comedian*
Innovative Artists, 1505 10th St, Santa Monica, CA 90401 USA

Shannon, Vicellous Reon *Actor*
Talent Entertainment Group, 9111 Wilshire Blvd, Beverly Hills, CA 90210 USA

Shantz, Robert C (Bobby) *Baseball Player*
152 E Mount Pleasant Ave, Ambler, PA 19002 USA

Shanze, Michael
Fichtenweg 8, Feldafing, GERMANY, D-82340

Shapar, Howard K *Government Official*
4610 Langdrum Lane, Chevy Chase, MD 20815 USA

Shapiro, Ascher H *Engineer*
111 Perkins St, Jamaica Plain, MA 02130 USA

Shapiro, Dani *Writer*
Random House, 1745 Broadway, #B1, New York, NY 10019 USA

Shapiro, Debbie *Actor*
Agency for Performing Arts, 9200 Sunset Blvd, #900, Los Angeles, CA 90069 USA

Shapiro, Harold T *Educator*
10 Campbelton Circle, Princeton, NJ 08540 USA

Shapiro, Irwin I *Physicist*
17 Lantern Lane, Lexington, MA 02421 USA

Shapiro, James *Doctor*
University of Alberta, 114th St & 89th Ave, Edmonton, T6G 2M7, CANADA

Shapiro, Joel E *Artist*
Pace Gallery, 32 E 57th St, New York, NY 10022 USA

Shapiro, Mary L *Government Official*
Securities & Exchange Commission, 450 5th St NW, Washington, DC 20001 USA

Shapiro, Maurice M *Physicist*
5809 Nicholson Lane, #801, Rockville, MD 20852 USA

Shapiro, Mel *Writer*
University of California, Theater Film/TV Dept, Los Angeles, CA 90024 USA

Shapiro, Neal *Horse Racer*
22 Floyd Place, East Norwich, NY 11732 USA

Shapiro, Richard & Esther
617 N. Alta Dr., Beverly Hills, CA 90210

Shapiro, Robert B *Business Person*
Monsanto Co, 800 N Lindergh Blvd, Saint Louis, MO 63167 USA

Shapiro, Robert L *Lawyer*
1421 Ambassador St, #206, Los Angeles, CA 90035 USA

Shapley, Lloyd S *Mathematician, Economist*
University of California, Economics Dept, Los Angeles, CA 90024 USA

Sharapova, Maria *Tennis Player*
Int'l Mgmt Group, 1 Erieview Plaza, 1360 E 9th St #1300, Cleveland, OH 44114 USA

Share, Charlie (Chuck) *Basketball Player*
12922 Twin Meadows Court, Saint Louis, MO 63146 USA

Sharif, Omar *Actor*
BP 41, Bougival, Yvelines, 78380, FRANCE

Sharipov, Sallzhan S *Cosmonaut*
Potchta Kosmonavtov, Moskovskoi Oblasti, Syvisdny Goroduk, 141160, RUSSIA

Sharma, Barbara *Actor*
PO Box 29125, Los Angeles, CA 90029 USA

Sharma, Kawal *Actor, Bollywood*
A 502 Janak Deep Seven Bangalows, Versova Andheri, Bombay, MS 400 049, INDIA

Sharma, Rakesh *Cosmonaut*
Hindustan Aeronautics, Bangalore, KA, 560037, INDIA

Sharman, Bill
7510 W. 81st St., Playa del Rey, CA 90293

Sharman, Helen *Cosmonaut*
12 Stratton Court, Adelade Road Surbiton, Surrey, UNITED KINGDOM (UK)

Sharman, Jim *Director*
M&L, 49 Daringhurst St, Kings Cross, NSW, 2100, AUSTRALIA

Sharman, William W (Bill) *Basketball Player, Coach*
7510 W 81st St, Playa del Rey, CA 90293 USA

Sharmila *Actor, Bollywood*
5 Narsimhan 1st CrossStreet, B.N. Reddy Road T.Nagar, Chennai, TN 600017, INDIA

Sharmili *Actor, Bollywood*
5/A, Karnan Street, SVT Maligai Rangarajapuram, Chennai, TN 600024, INDIA

Sharon, Ariel *President*
President's Office, 3 Hanassi, Jeruslam, 92188, ISRAEL

Sharp, Dee Dee *Musician*
Cape Entertainment, 1161 NW 76th Ave, Plantation, FL 33322 USA

Sharp, Don
80 Castelnau, London, ENGLAND, SW13 9EX

Sharp, Kevin *Musician*
Rising Star, 1415 River Landing Way, Woodstock, GA 30188 USA

Sharp, Lesley
76 Oxford St., London, ENGLAND, WlN OAX

Sharp, Leslie *Actor*
International Creative Mgmt, 8942 Wilshire Blvd, #219, Beverly Hills, CA 90211 USA

Sharp, Linda K *Coach*
Phoenix Mercury, American West Arena, 201 E Jefferson St, Phoenix, AZ 85004 USA

Sharp, Marsha *Coach*
Texas Tech University, Athletic Dept, Lubbock, TX 79409 USA

Sharp, Mitchell W *Government Official*
33 Monkland Ave, Ottawa, ON K1S 1Y8, CANADA

Sharp, Phillip A *Nobel Prize Laureate*
36 Fairmont Ave, Newton, MA 02458 USA

Sharp, Richard L *Business Person*
Circuit City Group, 9950 Maryland Dr, Richmond, VA 23233 USA

Sharpe, Rochelle P *Journalist*
94 Dudley St, #2, Brookline, MA 02445 USA

Sharpe, Shannon *Football Player*
204 Jay St, Glennville, GA 30427 USA

Sharpe, Thomas R (Tom) *Writer*
38 Tunwells Lane, Great Shelford, Cambridge, CB2 5LJ, UNITED KINGDOM (UK)

Sharpe, William F *Nobel Prize Laureate*
532 Orange Ave, Los Altos, CA 94022 USA

Sharpe Jr, Luis E *Football Player*
12641 S 34th Place, Phoenix, AZ 85044 USA

Sharper, Darren *Football Player*
10707 Bluebell Dr, Glen Allen, VA 23060 USA

Sharper, Jamie *Football Player*
10707 Bluebill Dr, Glen Allen, VA 23060 USA

Sharpless, K Barry *Nobel Prize Laureate*
Scripps Research Institute, 10650 Torrey Pines Road, La Jolla, CA 92037 USA

Sharpton, Al *Religious Leader, Social Activist*
1941 Madison Ave, #2, New York, NY 10035 USA

Sharqi, Sheikh Hamad bin Muhammad al *President*
Royal Palace, Emiri Court, PO Box 1, Fujairah, UNITED ARAB EMIRATES

Shatalov, Vladimir A *Cosmonaut*
Potchta Kosmonavtov, Moskovskoi Oblasti, Syvisdny Goroduk, 141160, RUSSIA

Shatkin, Aaron J *Biologist*
Center for Advanced Biotechnology, 679 Hoes Lane, Piscataway, NJ 08854 USA

Shatner, Melanie *Actor*
Henderson/Hogan, 8285 W Sunset Blvd, #1, West Hollywood, CA 90046 USA

Shatner, William *Actor*
William Shatner Connection, 7059 Atoll Ave, North Hollywood, CA 91605 USA

Shatraw, David
Stone Manners Talent Agency, 6500 Wilshire Blvd, Ste 550, Los Angeles, CA 90048 USA

Shattuck, Kim *Musician*
International Creative Mgmt, 40 W 57th St, #1800, New York, NY 10019 USA

Shaud, Grant *Actor*
8738 Appian Way, Los Angeles, CA 90046 USA

Shaud, John A *General*
Air Force Aid Society, 1745 Jefferson Davis Highway, #202, Arlington, VA 22202 USA

Shaughnessy, Charles *Actor*
534 15th St, Santa Monica, CA 90402 USA

Shavelson, Mel
11947 Sunshine Terrace, No. Hollywood, CA 91602

Shavelson, Melville *Writer, Producer*
William Morris Agency, 151 El Camino Dr, Beverly Hills, CA 90212 USA

Shaver, Billy Joe *Songwriter, Musician*
435 N Martell Ave, Los Angeles, CA 90036 USA

Shaver, Helen *Actor*
Innovative Artists, 1505 10th St, Santa Monica, CA 90401 USA

Shavers, Ernie *Boxer*
30 Doreen Ave Moretown Wirral, Merseyside, CH46 6DN, UNITED KINGDOM (UK)

Shaw, Artie *Musician*
2127 W Palos Court, Newbury Park, CA 91320 USA

Shaw, Bernard *Commentator*
7526 Heatherton Lane, Potomac, MD 20854 USA

Shaw, Brian *Basketball Player*
540 Brickell Key Dr, #1513, Miami, FL 33131 USA

Shaw, Bryant *Athlete*
1115 Elizabeth Ln, Richardson, TX 75080-5928

Shaw, Carolyn Hagner *Publisher*
Social Register, 2620 P St NW, Washington, DC 20007 USA

Shaw, David L *Journalist*
Los Angeles Times, Editorial Dept, 202 W 1st St, Los Angeles, CA 90012 USA

Shaw, Fiona *Actor*
International Creative Mgmt, 76 Oxford St, London, W1N 0AX, UNITED KINGDOM (UK)

Shaw, Jason *Actor, Model*
Burstein Company, The, 15304 Sunset Blvd #208, Pacific Palisades, CA 90272 USA

Shaw, Jeffrey L (Jeff) *Baseball Player*
465 Carolyn Road, Washington Court House, OH 43160 USA

Shaw, John H *Geophysicist*
Harvard University, Geophysics Dept, Cambridge, MA 02138 USA

Shaw, Kenneth A *Educator*
Syracuse University, President

Shaw, Kenneth A *Educator*
Syracuse University, President's Office, Syracuse, NY 13244 USA

Shaw, Mariena *Musician*
Berkeley Agency, 2608 9th St, Berkeley, CA 94710 USA

Shaw, Martin *Actor*
204 Belswins Lane, Hemel, Hempstead, Herts, UNITED KINGDOM (UK)

Shaw, Robert J (Bob) *Baseball Player*
2225 US Highway 1, #208, Tequesta, FL 33469 USA

Shaw, Run Run *Producer*
Shaw House, Lot 220 Clear Water Bar Road, Kowloon, Hong Kong, CHINA

Shaw, Scott *Journalist*
20771 Lake Road, Cleveland, OH 44116 USA

Shaw, Stan *Actor*
Innovative Artists, 1505 10th St, Santa Monica, CA 90401 USA

Shaw, Tim
5315 River Ave., Newport Beach, CA 92663

Shaw, Timothy A (Tim) *Swimmer*
5315 River Ave, Newport Beach, CA 92663 USA

Shaw, Tommy *Musician, Songwriter*
Alliance Artists, 1225 Northmeadow Parkway, #100, Roswell, GA 30076 USA

Shaw, Vernon *President*
President's Office, Morne Bruce, Victoria St, Roseau, DOMINICA

Shaw, Victoria *Songwriter, Musician*
PO Box 120512, Nashville, TN 37212
USA

Shaw, Vinessa *Actor*
Industry Entertainment, 955 Carillo Dr,
#300, Los Angeles, CA 90048 USA

Shaw, William L (Billy) *Football Player*
3427 Old Rothell Road, Toccoa, GA
30577 USA

Shaw Jr, Brewster H *Astronaut*
4123 University Blvd, Houston, TX 77005
USA

Shawkat, Alia *Actor*
Don Buchwald, 6500 Wilshire Blvd,
#2200, Los Angeles, CA 90048 USA

Shawn, Wallace *Actor, Writer*
Gersh Agency, 232 N Canon Dr, Beverly
Hills, CA 90210 USA

Shawyer, David
16 Rylett Rd., London, ENGLAND, W12

Shaye, Lin *Actor*
Paul Kohner, 9300 Wilshire Blvd, #555,
Beverly Hills, CA 90212 USA

Shaye, Robert *Business Person*
New Line Cinema, 578 8th Ave, New
York, NY 10018 USA

Shaye, Skyler *Actor*
Artists Only Management, 1901 Avenue
of the Stars, Suite 605, Los Angeles, CA
90067 USA

Shchedrin, Rodion K *Composer*
Tverskaya St, #31, Moscow, 103050,
RUSSIA

Shea, Eric *Actor*
27710 Jubilee Run Road, Pearblossom,
CA 93553 USA

Shea, George Beverly
1300 Harmon Pl., Minneapolis, MN
55403

Shea, Jere *Actor*
SMS Talent, 8730 Sunset Blvd, #440, Los
Angeles, CA 90069 USA

Shea, John *Actor*
Mutant X, 40 Carl Hall Road, Toronto,
ON M3K 2B8, CANADA

Shea, Joseph F *Scientist*
15 Dogwood Road, Weston, MA 02493
USA

Shea, Judith *Artist*
Barbara Krakow Gallery, 10 Newbury St,
Boston, MA 02116 USA

Shea, Katt *Actor*
International Creative Mgmt, 8942
Wilshire Blvd, #219, Beverly Hills, CA
90211 USA

Shea, Robert M *General*
Director Cmd Control Communications,
HqUSMC 2 Navy St, Washington, DC
20380 USA

Shea, Terry *Football Coach*
San Jose State University, Athletic Dept,
San Jose, CA 95192 USA

Shear, Jules *Songwriter, Musician*
Concerted Efforts, 59 Parsons St, West
Newton, MA 02465 USA

Shear, Rhonda *Actor, Comedian, Model*
9297 Burton Way, #6, Beverly Hills, CA
90210 USA

Sheard, Michael *Actor*
Summerdale Pubs, 46 West St, Chichester,
West Sussex, P019 1RP, UK

Shearer, Al *Actor, Reality TV Star*
Dolores Robinson Entertainment, 112 S
Almont Dr, Los Angeles, CA 90048 USA

Shearer, Alan *Soccer Player*
Newcastle United FC, Saint James Park,
Newcastle-Tyne, NE1 4ST, UNITED
KINGDOM (UK)

Shearer, Harry *Actor, Comedian*
1900 W Pico Blvd, Santa Monica, CA
90405 USA

Shearer, Moira *Ballerina, Actor*
Rogers Coleridge White, 2 Powis Mews,
London, W11 1JN, UNITED KINGDOM
(UK)

Shearer, Peter M *Geophysicist*
Scripps Oceanography Institute,
Geophysics Dept, La Jolla, CA 92093 USA

Shearer, S Bradford (Brad) *Football Player*
1909 Lakeshore Dr, #B, Austin, TX 78746
USA

Shearing, George A *Musician, Composer*
350 5th Ave, #6215, New York, NY
10118 USA

Shearmur, Edward (Ed) *Composer,
Musician*
Gorfaine/Schwartz Agency, The, 13245
Riverside Dr #450, Sherman Oaks, CA
91423 USA

Shearsmith, Reece *Actor*
Hamilton Hodell Ltd, 24 Hanway St Fl 24,
London, W1T 1UH, UNITED KINGDOM
(UK)

SheDaisy
PO Box 150638, Nashville, TN 37215

Sheed, Wilfrid J J *Writer*
General Delivery, Sag Harbor, NY 11963
USA

Sheedy, Ally *Actor*
Don Buchwald, 6500 Wilshire Blvd,
#2200, Los Angeles, CA 90048 USA

Sheehan, Doug *Actor*
Innovative Artists, 1505 10th St, Santa
Monica, CA 90401 USA

Sheehan, Jeremiah J *Business Person*
Reynolds Metals Co, 6601 Broad St, PO
Box 27003, Richmond, VA 23261 USA

Sheehan, Neil *Journalist*
4505 Klingle St NW, Washington, DC
20016 USA

Sheehan, Patricia A (Patty) *Golfer*
2300 Skyline Blvd, Reno, NV 89509 USA

Sheehan, Patty *Golfer*
Ladies Pro Golf Association (LPGA), 100
International Golf Drive, Daytona Beach,
FL 32124 USA

Sheehan, Susan *Writer*
4505 Klingle St NW, Washington, DC
20016 USA

Sheehy, Gail H *Writer*
300 E 57th St, #18D, New York, NY
10022 USA

Sheehy, Timothy (Tim) *Hockey Player*
4 Boswell Lane, Southborough, MA 01772
USA

Sheen, Charles *Actor*
Jeffrey Ballard, 4814 Lemara Ave,
Sherman Oaks, CA 91403 USA

Sheen, Charlie *Actor*
Evolution Entertainment, 901 N Highland
Ave, Los Angeles, CA 90038 USA

Sheen, Martin *Actor*
29351 Bluewater Road, Malibu, CA
90265 USA

Sheen, Michael *Actor*
Personal Management Company, 425 N
Robertson Dr, Los Angeles, CA 90048
USA

Sheen, Ramon
6916 Dume Dr., Malibu, CA 90265

Sheer, Ireen
Yachthof B-22, Waldeck, GERMANY,
D-34513

Sheerer, Gary *Athlete*
1557 Country Club Dr, Los Altos Hills, CA
94024 USA

Sheets, Ben *Baseball Player*
11234 George Lambert Road, Saint
Amant, LA 70774 USA

Sheffer, Craig *Actor*
5699 Kanan Dr, #275, Agoura, CA 91301
USA

Sheffield, Gary A *Baseball Player*
2247 Queensborough Lane, Los Angeles,
CA 90077 USA

Sheffield, John M (Johnny) *Actor*
834 1st Ave, Chula Vista, CA 91911 USA

Sheffield, Johnny
834 1st Ave., Chula Vista, CA 91911

Sheffield, William J (Bill) *Governor*
PO Box 91476, Anchorage, AK 99509
USA

Sheibler, Jim
PO Box 60, Venice, CA 90294

Sheik, Duncan *Songwriter, Musician*
Nonesuch Records, 75 Rockefeller Plaza,
New York, NY 10019 USA

Sheikh, Farooque *Actor, Bollywood*
Rafi Mansion 28th Road, Bandra,
Mumbai, MS 400050, INDIA

Sheila E *Musician*
Ofoove Ent, 1005 N Alfred St, #2, West
Hollywood, CA 90069 USA

Sheindlin, Judge Judy *Judge, Actor*
PO Box 949, Los Angeles, CA 90078 USA

Sheindlin, Judy (Judge) *Entertainer, Judge*
PO Box 949, Los Angeles, CA 90078 USA

Sheiner, David S *Actor*
1827 Veteran Ave, #19, Los Angeles, CA
90025 USA

Sheinfeld, David *Composer*
112 Ash Way, San Rafael, CA 94903 USA

Shelby, Carol *Race Car Driver*
19020 Anelo Ave, Gardena, CA 90248

Shelby, Carroll *Race Car Driver*
19020 Anelo Ave, Gardena, CA 90248
USA

Shelby, Mark *Composer, Musician*
Thomas Cassidy, 11761 E Speedway Blvd,
Tucson, AZ 85748 USA

Sheldon, Jack *Musician*
7095 Hollywood Blvd, #617, Los Angeles, CA 90028 USA

Sheldon, Sidney *Actor, Director, Producer, Writer*
10250 W Sunset Blvd, Los Angeles, CA 90077 USA

Shell, Art *Athlete*
2318 Walker Drive, Lawrenceville, GA 30043-6018 USA

Shell, Arthur (Art) *Football Coach, Football Player*
7090 Island Queen Court, Sparks, NV 89436 USA

Shell, Donnie *Football Player*
2945 Shandon Road, Rock Hill, SC 29730 USA

Shellen, Stephen
615 Yonge St. #401, Toronto, CANADA, Ont. M4Y l

Shelley, Barbara *Actor*
Ken McReddie, 91 Regent St, London, W1R 7TB, UNITED KINGDOM (UK)

Shelley, Carole *Actor*
333 W 56th St, New York, NY 10019 USA

Shelley, Howard G *Musician, Conductor*
38 Cholmeley Park, London, N6 5ER, UNITED KINGDOM (UK)

Shelley, Rachel *Actor*
Personal Management Company, 425 N Robertson Dr, Los Angeles, CA 90048 USA

Shelton, Abigail *Actor*
Dale Garrick, 8831 Sunset Blvd, #402, Los Angeles, CA 90069 USA

Shelton, Blake *Musician*
Hallmark, 1 Music Square West, Nashville, TN 37203

Shelton, Deborah *Actor*
2265 Westwood Blvd, #251, Los Angeles, CA 90064 USA

Shelton, Lonnie *Basketball Player*
860 S 8th Ave, Kingsburg, CA 93631 USA

Shelton, Marley *Actor*
United Talent Agency (UTA), 9560 Wilshire Blvd, Beverly Hills, CA 90212 USA

Shelton, Peter *Architect*
Shelton Mindel Assoc, 216 W 18th St, New York, NY 10011 USA

Shelton, Ricky Van *Musician, Songwriter*
PO Box 683, Lebanon, TN 37087 USA

Shelton, Ron
2364 Hermits Glen, Los Angeles, CA 90046

Shelton, Ronald W *Director*
15200 Friends St, Pacific Palisades, CA 90272 USA

Shelton, Samantha *Actor*
Innovative Artists (LA), 1505 Tenth St, Santa Monica, CA 90401 USA

Shelton, William E *Educator*
Eastern Michigan University, President's Office, Ypsilanti, MI 48197 USA

Shen, Parry *Actor*
Lichtman/Salners Company, 12216 Moorpark Street, Studio City, CA 91604 USA

Shenandoah
PO Box 1547, Goodlettsville, TN 37070-1547

Shenandoh, Joanne *Songwriter, Musician*
Oneida Nation Territory, PO Box 450, Oneida, NY 13421 USA

Shenkman, Ben *Actor*
James Suskin Management, 253 West 72nd Street, Suite 1014, New York, NY 10023 USA

Shepard, Dax *Reality TV Star, Actor*
Endeavor Agency LLC (LA), 9601 Wilshire Blvd Fl 3, Beverly Hills, CA 90210 USA

Shepard, Devon *Writer*
Agency for the Performing Arts (APA-LA), 9200 Sunset Blvd #900, Los Angeles, CA 90069 USA

Shepard, Jean *Musician*
Billy Deaton Talent, 5811 Still Hollow Road, Nashville, TN 37215 USA

Shepard, Kenny Wayne *Musician*
Ken Shephard Co, 4361 Youree Dr, #200, Shreveport, LA 71105 USA

Shepard, Kiki *Actor*
Cunningham-Escott-Dipene & Associates Inc (CED-LA), 10635 Santa Monica Blvd #130, Los Angeles, CA 90025 USA

Shepard, Roger N *Psychic*
5775 Montclair Ave, Marysville, CA 95901 USA

Shepard, Sam
8942 Wilshire Blvd., Beverly Hills, CA 90211

Shepard, Samuel K (Sam) *Writer, Actor*
1801 Martha St, Encino, CA 91316 USA

Shepard, Vonda *Actor, Songwriter, Musician*
William Morris Agency, 151 El Camino Dr, Beverly Hills, CA 90212 USA

Sheperd, Ben *Musician*
Susan Silver Mgmt, 6523 California Ave SW, #348, Seattle, WA 98136 USA

Sheperd, Cybill *Actor, Model*
PO Box 261503, Encino, CA 91426 USA

Sheperd, Elizabeth *Actor*
London Mgmt, 2-4 Noel St, London, W1V 3RB, UNITED KINGDOM (UK)

Sheperd, Morgan *Race Car Driver*
57 Rhody Creek Loop, Stuart, VA 24171 USA

Shephard, Gillian P *Government Official*
House of Commons, Westminster, London, SW1A 0AA, UNITED KINGDOM (UK)

Shepherd, Chris *Writer, Director*
Slinky Pictures, Old Truman Brewery, 91 Brick Ln, London, E16 QN, UNITED KINGDOM (UK)

Shepherd, Cybill
Hofflund/Polone, 9465 Wilshire Blvd #820, Beverly Hills, CA 90212 USA

Shepherd, Kenny Wayne
4361 Youree Dr., Shreveport, LA 71105-3339

Shepherd, Sherrie *Cartoonist*
United Feature Syndicate, 200 Madison Ave, New York, NY 10016 USA

Shepherd, William M *Astronaut*
18623 Prince William Lane, Houston, TX 77058 USA

Shepherd (Sheperd), Sherri *Actor*
Untitled Entertainment (LA), 8436 W 3rd St #650, Los Angeles, CA 90048 USA

Shepis, Tiffany
PO Box 1077, Venice, CA 90294-1077

Sheppard, Alfred J *Business Person*
Court Mead, 6 Guildown Ave Guilford, Surrey, GU2 5HB, UNITED KINGDOM (UK)

Sheppard, Anna *Fashion Designer*
International Creative Mgmt, 8942 Wilshire Blvd, #219, Beverly Hills, CA 90211 USA

Sheppard, Jonathan *Misc*
287 Lamborn Town Road, West Grove, PA 19390 USA

Sheppard, Julian *Comedian*
Gersh Agency, The (LA), 232 N Canon Dr, Beverly Hills, CA 90210 USA

Sheppard, Mark *Actor*
Stone Manners Talent Agency, 6500 Wilshire Blvd, Ste 550, Los Angeles, CA 90048 USA

Sheppard, Mike *Football Coach*
University of New Mexico, Athletic Dept, Albuquerque, NM 87131 USA

Sheppard, T G *Musician*
RJ Kaltenbach Mgmt, 35W741 Valley View Road, Dundee, IL 60118 USA

Sheps, Cecil G *Biologist*
388 Carolina Meadows Villa, Chapel Hill, NC 27517 USA

Sher, Antony *Actor*
Conway Van Gelder Robinson, 18-21 Jermyn St, London, SW1Y 6NB, UNITED KINGDOM (UK)

Shera, Mark *Actor*
PO Box 15717, Beverly Hills, CA 90209 USA

Sheraton, Mimi *Writer*
Random House, Inc, 1540 Broadway, New York, NY 10036

Sherba, John *Musician*
Kronos Quartet, 1235 9th Ave, San Francisco, CA 94122 USA

Sherbedgia, Rade *Actor*
Innovative Artists, 1505 10th St, Santa Monica, CA 90401 USA

Sherffius, John *Cartoonist*
Saint Louis Post Dispatch, Editorial Dept, 900 N Tucker, Saint Louis, MO 63101 USA

Sheridan, Bonnie
18011 Martha St., Encino, CA 91316

Sheridan, Bonnie Bramlett *Actor, Musician*
18011 Martha St, Encino, CA 91316 USA

Sheridan, Dave C *Actor, Writer*
Management 360, 9111 Wilshire Blvd, Beverly Hills, CA 90210 USA

Sheridan, Dinah *Actor*
International Creative Mgmt, 76 Oxford St, London, W1N 0AX, UNITED KINGDOM (UK)

Sheridan, Jamey *Actor*
Sames/Rollnick Assoc, 250 W 57th St, New York, NY 10107 USA

Sheridan, Jim *Director, Producer*
Creative Artists Agency, 9830 WIlshire Blvd, Beverly Hills, CA 90212 USA

Sheridan, Lisa *Actor*
Burstein Company, The, 15304 Sunset Blvd #208, Pacific Palisades, CA 90272 USA

Sheridan, Liz *Actor*
11333 Moorpark #427, West Hollywood, CA 91602

Sheridan, Nicole *Adult Film Star*
Atlas Multimedia Inc, 22940 Burbank Blvd, Woodland Hills, CA 91367 USA

Sheridan, Nicolette *Actor*
Gersh Agency, 232 N Canon Dr, Beverly Hills, CA 90210 USA

Sheridan, Rondell *Actor*
Gail Stocker Presents, 1025 N Kings Road, #113, Los Angeles, CA 90069 USA

Sheridan, Tony *Musician*
Gems, PO Box 1031, Montrose, CA 91021 USA

Sheriff, Haja *Actor*
20/1 Desikar Street, Chennai, TN 600 026, INDIA

Sherk, Jerry M *Football Player*
1819 Bel Air Terrace, Encinitas, CA 92024 USA

Sherlock, Nancy J *Astronaut*
NASA, Johnson Space Center, 2101 NASA Road, Houston, TX 77058 USA

Sherlock-Currie, Nancy
2101 NASA Rd, Houston, TX 77058 USA

Sherman, Alex (Allie) *Football Player, Football Coach*
New York Off Track Betting Corp, 1501 Broadway, #1000, New York, NY 10036 USA

Sherman, Bobby *Musician, Actor*
1870 Sunset Plaza Dr, Los Angeles, CA 90069 USA

Sherman, Cindy *Photographer*
Metro Pictures, 519 W 24th St, New York, NY 10011 USA

Sherman, Edgar A *Football Coach*
681 Nancy Lane, Newark, OH 43055 USA

Sherman, Mike *Football Coach*
Green Bay Packers, PO Box 10628, Green Bay, WI 54307 USA

Sherman, Richard M *Composer, Musician*
PO Box 17740, Beverly Hills, CA 90209 USA

Sherman, Vincent *Director*
6355 Sycamore Meadows Dr, Malibu, CA 90265 USA

Sherman-Palladino, Amy *Writer, Producer, Director*
Endeavor Agency LLC (LA), 9601 Wilshire Blvd Fl 3, Beverly Hills, CA 90210 USA

Shernoff, William M *Attorney General*
600 S Indian Hill Road, Claremont, CA 91711 USA

Sherrard, Michael W (Mike) *Football Player*
30130 Cuthbert Road, Malibu, CA 90265 USA

Sherrill, Jackie W *Football Coach*
Mississippi State University, Athletic Dept, Mississippi State, MS 39762 USA

Sherrin, Edward G (Ned) *Director*
4 Cornwall Mansions, Ashburnham Road, London, SW10 0PE, UNITED KINGDOM (UK)

Sherrington, Georgina *Actor*
JGM, 15 Lexham Mews, London, W8 6JW, UNITED KINGDOM (UK)

Sherry, Lawrence (Larry) *Baseball Player*
27181 Arena Lane, Mission Viejo, CA 92691 USA

Sherry, Paul H *Religious Leader*
United Church of Christ, 700 Prospect Ave, Cleveland, OH 44115 USA

Sherwood, Brad *Actor*
Super Artists, 12021 Wilshire Blvd, Los Angeles, CA 90025

Sheshadri, Meenakshi *Actor, Bollywood*
601 Sheshadri Moonbeam, Union Park Khar (W), Mumbai, MS 400052, INDIA

Shesol, Jeff *Cartoonist*
Creators Syndicate, 5777 W Century Blvd, #700, Los Angeles, CA 90045 USA

Shestakova, Tatyana B *Actor*
Maly Drama Theatre, Rubinstein St 18, Saint Petersburgh, RUSSIA

Shetty, Shilpa *Actor, Bollywood*
12 Dev Darshan, 262 St Anthony Road Chembur, Mumbai, MS 400071, INDIA

Shetty, Sunil *Actor, Bollywood*
18/B Prithvi Apartments, Altamont Road, Mumbai, MS 400026, INDIA

Shevchenko, Arkady N *Politician*
Alfred Knopf/Ballantine/Fawcett Publishers, 201 East 50th Street, New York, NY 10022

Shi, David E *Educator*
Furman University, President's Office, Greenville, SC 29613 USA

Shicoff, Neil *Opera Singer*
Opera et Concert, Maximilianstr 22, Munich, 80539, GERMANY

Shields, Ben *Actor*
10965 Fruitland Drive, Suite 102, Studio City, CA 91604 USA

Shields, Brooke *Actor, Model*
Christa Inc, 10061 Riverside Dr, #1013, Toluca Lake, CA 91602 USA

Shields, Perry *Judge*
US Tax Court, 400 2nd St NW, Washington, DC 20217 USA

Shields, Robert *Misc*
Robert Shields Designs, PO Box 10024, Sedona, AZ 86339 USA

Shields, Will H *Football Player*
Kansas City Chiefs, 1 Arrowhead Dr, Kansas City, KS 64129 USA

Shiely, John S *Business Person*
Briggs & Stratton, PO Box 702, Milwaukee, WI 53201 USA

Shifty, Shellshock *Musician*
Q Prime, 729 7th Ave, #1600, New York, NY 10019 USA

Shigeta, James *Actor*
10635 Santa Monica Blvd, #130, Los Angeles, CA 90025 USA

Shih, Wen Yann *Actor*
Vincent Cirrincione Associates, 8721 Sunset Blvd #205, Los Angeles, CA 90069 USA

Shikler, Aaron *Artist*
44 W 77th St, New York, NY 10024 USA

Shiley, Newhouse Jean *Track Athlete*
1100 Sunnybrae Ave, Chatsworth, CA 91311 USA

Shilton, Justin *Actor*
Writers and Artists Group Intl (LA), 8383 Wilshire Blvd #550, Beverly Hills, CA 90211 USA

Shilton, Peter *Soccer Player*
Hubbards Cottage, Bentley Lane, Maxstoke near Coleshill, B46 2QR, UNITED KINGDOM (UK)

Shima, Masatoshi *Engineer*
Shima Co, 260 Tsurumaki, Omika Haramachishi, Fukushima, 975-0049, JAPAN

Shimada, Yoko
7245 Hillside Ave. #415, Los Angeles, CA 90046

Shimell, William *Opera Singer*
I M G Artists, 3 Burlington Lane, Chiswick, London, W4 2TH, UNITED KINGDOM (UK)

Shimerman, Armin *Actor*
Innovative Artists, 1505 10th St, Santa Monica, CA 90401 USA

Shimkis, Joanna
9255 Doheny Rd., Los Angeles, CA 90069-3201

Shimkus, Joanna *Actor*
Creative Artists Agency LCC (CAA-LA), 9830 Wilshire Blvd, Beverly Hills, CA 90212 USA

Shimmerman, Armin *Actor*
Innovative Artists (LA), 1505 Tenth St, Santa Monica, CA 90401 USA

Shimono, Sab *Actor*
12711 Ventura Blvd, #440, Studio City, CA 91604 USA

Shin, Yong Moon *Biologist*
National University, Sillimdong, Gwanakgu, Seoul, 151-742, SOUTH KOREA

Shindle, Kate
2 Ocean Way #1000, Atlantic City, NJ 08401-4163

Shine, Michael (Mike) *Track Athlete*
508 Royal Road, State College, PA 16801 USA

Shinefield, Henry R *Misc*
2240 Hyde St, #2, San Francisco, CA 94109 USA

Shinn, Christopher *Comedian*
Gersh Agency, The (LA), 232 N Canon Dr, Beverly Hills, CA 90210 USA

Shinnick, Donald (Don) *Football Player*
3721 Northampton Lane, Modesto, CA 95356 USA

Shinoda, Mike *Musician*
Artist Group International, 9560 Wilshire Blvd, #400, Beverly Hills, CA 90212 USA

Shipler, David K *Journalist*
4005 Thornapple St, Bethesda, MD 20815 USA

Shipley, Walter V *Financier*
Chase Manhattan Corp, 270 Park Ave, New York, NY 10017 USA

Shipman, Clarie *Commentator*
ABC-TV, News Dept, 77 W 66th St, New York, NY 10017 USA

Shipp, E R *Misc*
New York Daily News, Editorial Dept, 220 E 42nd St, New York, NY 10017 USA

Shipp, Jerry *Basketball Player*
PO Box 370, Kingston, OK 73439 USA

Shipp, John Wesley *Actor*
1219 Sunset Plaza Dr, West Hollywood, CA 90069 USA

Shirakawa, Hideki *Nobel Prize Laureate*
University of Tsukuba, Chemistry Dept, Sakura-Mura, Ibaraki, 305, JAPAN

Shirayanagi, Peter Seiichi Cardinal *Religious Leader*
Archbishop's House, 3-16-15 Sekiguchi, Bunkyoku, Tokyo, 112, JAPAN

Shire, David L *Composer*
19 Ludlow Ave, Palisades, NY 10964 USA

Shire, Talia *Actor, Director*
10730 Beliagio Road, Los Angeles, CA 90077 USA

Shirelles, The
PO Box 100, Clifton, NJ 07011

Shirley, George I *Opera Singer*
University of Michigan, Music School, Ann Arbor, MI 48109 USA

Shirley, J Dallas *Referee*
5324 Pommel Dr, Mount Airy, MD 21771 USA

Shirley Temple, Black *Actor, Diplomat*
Motion Picture Arts-Sciences Acad, 8949 Wilshire Blvd, Beverly Hills, CA 90211 USA

Shirley-Quirk, John S *Opera Singer*
6062 Red Clover Lane, Clarksville, MD 21029 USA

Shirodkar, Namrata *Actor, Bollywood*
Venkatesh Vihar, 7th Road Khar, Mumbai, MS 400052, INDIA

Shirodkar, Shilpa *Actor, Bollywood*
Venkatesh Vihar, 4th Floor 7th Road Khar, Mumbai, MS 400050, INDIA

Shivpuri, Himani *Actor*
16A/24 PGM Colony Poonam Nagar, Mahakali Caves Road Andheri (E), Bombay, MS 400 093, INDIA

Shivpuri, Ritu *Actor, Bollywood*
12 Poonam 29/30 Pali Hill Union Bank, Khar, Bombay, MS 400 052, INDIA

Shlaudeman, Harry W *Diplomat*
7006 Pebble Beach Way, San Luis Obispo, CA 93401 USA

Shlyapina, Galina A *Ballerina*
Bolshoi Theater, Teatralnaya Pl 1, Moscow, 103009, RUSSIA

Shnayerson, Robert B *Editor*
118 Riverside Dr, New York, NY 10024 USA

Shobana *Actor, Bollywood*
77/5 Gulmohar Avenue, Velachery High Road, Chennai, TN 600032, INDIA

Shobana, Maganadhi *Actor, Bollywood*
A P 198, 16th Street 2nd Sector, Chennai, TN 600078, INDIA

Shobert, Bubba *Race Car Driver*
8905 153rd St, Wolfforth, TX 79382 USA

Shocked, Michelle *Musician*
Siddons Assoc, 584 N Larchmont Blvd, Los Angeles, CA 90004 USA

Shockley, Jeremy *Football Player*
New York Giants, Giants Stadium, East Rutherford, NJ 07073 USA

Shockley, William *Actor*
6345 Balboa Blvd, #375, Encino, CA 91316 USA

Shoecraft, John A *Misc*
Shoecraft Contracting Co, 7430 E Stetson Dr, Scottsdale, AZ 85251 USA

Shoeffling, Michael
PO Box 2563, Canyon Country, CA 91351

Shoemaker, Bill
250 W. Main St. #1820, Lexington, KY 40502-1733

Shoemaker, Carolyn S *Astronomer*
Lowell Observatory, 1400 W Mars Hill Road, Flagstaff, AZ 86001 USA

Shoemaker, Craig *Actor*
Rick Dorfman Management, 450 W 15th St #500, New York, NY 10011 USA

Shoemaker, Robert M *General*
PO Box 768, Belton, TX 76513 USA

Shoemaker, Sydney S *Misc*
104 Northway Road, Ithaca, NY 14850 USA

Shoemate, C Richard *Business Person*
Bestfoods, International Plaza, 700 Sylvan Ave, Englewood Cliffs, NJ 07632 USA

Shofner, Delbert M (Del) *Football Player*
1665 Del Mar Ave, San Marino, CA 91108 USA

Shofner, James (Jim) *Football Player*
9620 Champions Dr, Granbury, TX 76049 USA

Shoji, Dave *Coach*
University of Hawaii, Athletic Dept, Hilo, HI 96720 USA

Shonekan, Ernest A O *President*
12 Alexander Ave, Ikoyi, Lagos, NIGERIA

Shonin, Georgi S *Cosmonaut, General*
Potchta Kosmonavtov, Moskovskoi Oblasti, Syvisdny Goroduk, 141160, RUSSIA

Shoop, Ron
PO Box 92, Rural Valley, PA 16249

Shope, Allan *Architect*
Shope Reno Wharton, 18 W Putnam Ave, Greenwich, CT 06830 USA

Shore, Howard *Actor, Musician, Composer*
Gortaine/Schwartz, 13245 Riverside Dr, #450, Sherman Oaks, CA 91423 USA

Shore, Pauly *Actor, Comedian*
8491 W Sunset Blvd, #700, West Hollywood, CA 90069 USA

Shore, Roberta
PO Box 71639, Salt Lake City, UT 84171-0639

Shorr, Lonnie
707 18th Ave. So., Nashville, TN 37203

Short, Bobby *Actor, Musician*
444 E 57th St, #9E, New York, NY 10022 USA

Short, Martin *Actor, Comedian, Musician*
J/P/M, 760 N La Cienega Blvd, #200, Los Angeles, CA 90069 USA

Short, Nigel *Misc*
Daily Telegraph, Peterborough Court, Marsh Wall, London, E14, UNITED KINGDOM (UK)

Short, Purvis *Basketball Player*
8111 Fondren Lake Dr, Houston, TX 77071 USA

Short, Thomas C *Misc*
Theatrical Stage Employees Alliance, 1515 Broadway, New York, NY 10036 USA

Shorter, Frank *Track Athlete*
558 Utica Court, Boulder, CO 80304 USA

Shorter, Wayne *Musician, Composer*
International Music Network, 278 S Main St, #400, Gloucester, MA 01930 USA

Shorthill, Richard W *Engineer*
University of Utah, Mechanical Engineering Dept, Salt Lake City, UT 84112 USA

Shortridge, Steve *Actor*
1707 Clearview Dr, Beverly Hills, CA 90210 USA

Shostakovich, Maxim D *Musician*
PO Box 273, Jordanville, NY 13361 USA

Shou, Robin *Actor*
Paradigm Agency, 10100 Santa Monica Blvd, #2500, Los Angeles, CA 90067 USA

Show, Grant *Actor*
937 S Tremaine Ave, Los Angeles, CA 90019 USA

Showalter, Buck
7501 Jefferson Ave., Century, FL 32535

Showalter, William N (Buck) III *Misc*
3839 W Madura Road, Gulf Breeze, FL 32563 USA

Shower, Kathy *Actor, Model*
Provenca 23 1-1, Barcelona, SPAIN

Shreve, Anita *Writer*
Creative Artists Agency LCC (CAA-LA), 9830 Wilshire Blvd, Beverly Hills, CA 90212 USA

Shreve, Susan R *Writer*
3319 Newark St NW, Washington, DC 20008 USA

Shribman, David M *Journalist*
Boston Globe, Editorial Dept, 1130
Connecticut Ave NW, Washington, DC
20036 USA

Shrimpton, Jean *Actor, Model*
Abbey Hotel Penzance, Cornwall,
UNITED KINGDOM (UK)

Shriner, Kin *Actor*
Don Buchwald, 6500 Wilshire Blvd,
#2200, Los Angeles, CA 90048 USA

Shriner, Wil *Entertainer*
5313 Quakertown Ave, Woodland Hills,
CA 91364 USA

Shriver, Anthony
100 SE 2nd St. #1990, Miami, FL 33131

Shriver, Bobby
501 Colorado Ave. #200, Santa Monica,
CA 90401

Shriver, Duward F *Scientist*
1100 Colfax St, Evanston, IL 60201 USA

Shriver, Eunice Kennedy *Business Person*
9109 Harnington Dr, Potomac, MD
20854 USA

Shriver, Loren J *Astronaut*
108 Charleston St, Friendswood, TX
77456 USA

Shriver, Maria *Commentator, Television
Host*
Dateline NBC, 30 Rockefeller Plz, New
York, NY 10112 USA

Shriver, Mark Kennedy
10015 Carter Rd, Bethesda, MD 20817

Shriver, Pam
Pam Shriver Tennis Challenge, 8742
Mylander Ln #R, Towson, MD 21286-
2102

Shriver, Pamela H (Pam) *Tennis Player*
509 S Gretna Green Way, Los Angeles,
CA 90049 USA

Shriver, R
1325 G St NW, Washington, DC 20005
USA

Shriver Jr, R Sargent *Government Official*
Special Olympics Int'l, 1325 G St NW,
#500, Washington, DC 20005 USA

Shroff, Jackie *Actor, Bollywood*
1302 Le Pepeyon, Mount Mary Road
Bandra, Mumbai, MS 400050, INDIA

Shrontz, Frank A *Business Person*
2949 81st Place, #P, Mercer Island, WA
98040 USA

Shrowder, Lisa *Race Car Driver*
1650 E Golf Road, Schaumburg, IL 60196
USA

Shroyer, Sonny *Actor*
12725 Ventura Blvd, #F, Studio City, CA
91604 USA

Shtalenkov, Mikhail *Hockey Player*
501 Broadway, Nashville, TN 37203 USA

Shtokolov, Boris T *Opera Singer*
Mariinsky Theater, Teatralnaya Pl 1, Saint
Petersburg, RUSSIA

Shuart, James M *Educator*
Hofstra University, President's Office,
Hempstead, NY 11550 USA

Shubin, Neil H *Biologist*
Harvard University, Biology Dept,
Cambridge, MA 02138 USA

Shue, Andrew *Actor*
Do Something, 423 W 55th St, #800,
New York, NY 10019 USA

Shue, Elisabeth *Actor*
Creative Artists Agency, 9830 Wilshire
Blvd, Beverly Hills, CA 90212 USA

Shue, Gene *Coach*
4338 Redwood Ave, #B303, Marina del
Rey, CA 90292 USA

Shugart, Alan F *Inventor*
Seagate Technologies, 920 Disc Dr, Scotts
Valley, CA 95066 USA

Shukovsky, Joel *Writer*
Shukovsky-English Ent, 4024 Radford Ave,
Studio City, CA 91604 USA

Shula, David D (Dave) *Coach*
10805 Indian Trail, Cooper City, FL 33328
USA

Shula, Don
16 Indian Creek Island, Miami, FL 33154-
2904

Shula, Donald F (Don) *Football Coach,
Football Player*
16 Indian Creek Island Road, Indian Creek
Village, FL 33154 USA

Shula, Mike *Football Player, Football
Coach*
7518 Spinnaker Ave NE, Tuscaloosa, AL
35406 USA

Shuler, Mickey C *Football Player*
332 Belle Vista Dr, Marysville, PA 17053
USA

Shuler Jr, Ellie G (Buck) *General*
32 Willow Way W, Alexander City, AL
35010 USA

Shulgin, Alexander *Scientist*
1483 Shulgin Road, Lafayette, CA 94549
USA

Shulman, Lawrence E *Scientist*
3726 Tudor Arms Ave, Baltimore, MD
21211 USA

Shulman, Robert G *Biologist*
333 Cedar St, New Haven, CT 06510
USA

Shultz, George P *Politician, Secretary*
776 Dolores St, Stanford, CA 94305 USA

Shumaker, John W *Educator*
University of Louisville, President's Office,
Louisville, KY 40292 USA

Shumate, John *Basketball Player, Coach*
306 E Calle de Arco S, Tempe, AZ 85284
USA

Shumate, Rachel *Actor*
Imparato Fay Management, 1122 S
Roxbury Dr, Los Angeles, CA 90035 USA

Shumway, Norman E *Doctor*
Stanford University, Medical Center, 300
Pasteur Dr, Palo Alto, CA 94304 USA

Shutt, Steve *Hockey Player, Coach*
Cimco Refrigeration, 65 Villiers, Toronto,
ON M5A 3S1, CANADA

Shuttleworth, Mark *Astronaut*
HBD Ventura Capital, PO Box 1159,
Durbanville, 7551, SOUTH AFRICA

Shuttz, George P
776 Dolores St, Stanford, CA 94305 USA

Shyamalan, M Night *Director*
Blinding Edge Pictures, 100 Four Falls
Corporate Center #102, Conshohocken,
PA 19428 USA

Shydner, Ritch *Comedian*
Agency for the Performing Arts (APA-LA),
9200 Sunset Blvd #900, Los Angeles, CA
90069 USA

Shyer, Charles R *Writer, Director*
227 N Glenroy Ave, Los Angeles, CA
90049 USA

Sia, Beau *Actor*
Creative Artists Agency LCC (CAA-LA),
9830 Wilshire Blvd, Beverly Hills, CA
90212 USA

Siana *Model*
PO Box 4957, Virginia Beach, VA 23454

Siani, Michael J (Mike) *Football Player*
748 Conifer Court, Myrtle Beach, SC
29572 USA

Sias, John B *Publisher*
Chronicle Publishing Co, 901 Mission St,
San Francisco, CA 94103 USA

Sibbett, Jane *Actor*
2144 Nichols Canyon Road, Los Angeles,
CA 90046 USA

Siberry, Jane *Songwriter, Musician*
Sheeba, 238 Davenport Road, #291,
Toronto, ON M5R 1J6, CANADA

Sibley, Antoinette *Ballerina*
Royal Dancing Academy, 36 Battersea
Square, London, SW11 3LT, UNITED
KINGDOM (UK)

Sibley, David *Actor*
Select Artists Ltd (CA-Westside Office),
1138 12th Street, Suite 1, Santa Monica,
CA 90403 USA

Sicard, Pedro *Actor*
Gabriel Blanco Iglesias (Mexico), Rio
Balsas 35-32, Colonia Cuauhtemoc, DF,
06500, Mexico

Sichting, Jerry *Basketball Player*
3190 Country Club Road, Martinsville, IN
46151 USA

Siddiqui, Farouge *Director, Filmmaker*
16/24 Old Collector Compound, Malvani
Colony Gate No 5 Malad, Bombay, MS
400 095, INDIA

Siddons, Ann Rivers *Writer*
60 Church St, Charleston, SC 29401

Siddons, Anne R *Writer*
767 Vermont Road, Atlanta, GA 30319
USA

Sidenbladh, Goran *Architect*
Narvagen 23, Stockholm, 114 60,
SWEDEN

Sider, Harvey R *Religious Leader*
Brethren in Christ Church, PO Box 290,
Grantham, PA 17027 USA

Sidey, Hugh
1050 Connecticut Ave, Washington, DC
20036

Sidgmore, John *Business Person*
WorldCom, 500 Clinton Center Dr,
Clinton, MS 39056 USA

Sidime, Lamine *Prime Minister*
Prime Minister's Office, Conakry, GUINEA

Sidlin, Murry *Conductor*
Catholic University, Music School,
Washington, DC 20064 USA

Sidney, Laurin
PO Box 105366, Atlanta, GA 30348-5366

Sidransky, David *Scientist, Doctor*
Baylor Medical Center, 1200 Moursand
Ave, Houston, TX 77030 USA

Sieber, Christopher *Actor*
Abrams Artists Agency (NY), 275 Seventh
Ave Fl 26, New York, NY 10001

Siebert, Sonny
2583 Brush Creek, St. Louis, MO 63129

Siebert, Wilfred C (Sonny) *Baseball Player*
2555 Brush Creek, Saint Louis, MO 63129
USA

Siega, Marcos *Director*
Endeavor Agency LLC (LA), 9601 Wilshire
Blvd Fl 3, Beverly Hills, CA 90210 USA

Siegal, Bernard *Writer*
61 0x Bow Ln, Woodbridge, CT 06525-
1525

Siegal, Jay *Music Group, Musician*
Brothers Mgmt, 141 Dunbar Ave, Fords,
NJ 08863 USA

Siegbahn, Kai M B *Nobel Prize Laureate*
University of Uppasala, Physics Institute,
Box 530, Uppasala, 75 121, SWEDEN

Siegel, Barry *Journalist*
Los Angeles Times, Editorial Dept, 202 W
1st St, Los Angeles, CA 90012 USA

Siegel, Bernie S *Doctor, Writer*
61 Oxbow Lane, Woodbridge, CT 06525
USA

Siegel, Eric *Actor*
Pure Arts Entertainment, 1925 Century
Park East, Suite 2320, Los Angeles, CA
90067 USA

Siegel, Herbert J *Business Person*
Chris-Craft Industries, 767 5th Ave, New
York, NY 10153 USA

Siegel, Ira T *Publisher*
16589 Senterra Dr, Delray Beach, FL
33484 USA

Siegel, Janis *Musician*
International Creative Mgmt, 40 W 57th St
#1800, New York, NY 10019 USA

Siegel, Joel *Commentator*
Good Morning America, 147 Columbus
Ave Fl 6, New York, NY 10023 USA

Siegel, L Pendleton *Business Person*
Potlatch Corp, 601 W Riverside Ave,
Spokane, WA 99201 USA

Siegel, Robert C *Commentator*
National Public Radio, News Dept, 2025
M St NW, Washington, DC 20036 USA

Siegfried *Magician*
Beyond Belief, 1639 N Valley Dr, Las
Vegas, NV 89108 USA

Siegfried, Larry *Basketball Player*
4178 Covert Road, Perrysville, OH 44864
USA

Siekevitz, Philip *Biologist*
290 W End Ave, New York, NY 10023
USA

Siemaszko, Casey *Actor*
Gersh Agency, 232 N Canon Dr, Beverly
Hills, CA 90210 USA

Siemon, Jeffrey G (Jeff) *Football Player*
5401 Londonderry Road, Edina, MN
55436 USA

Siepi, Cesare *Opera Singer*
12095 Brookfield Club Dr, Russwell, GA
30075 USA

Siering, Lauri *Swimmer*
3829 Rotterdam Ave, Modesto, CA 95356
USA

Sierra, Gregory *Actor*
8050 Selma Ave, Los Angeles, CA 90046
USA

Sierra, Ruben A *Baseball Player*
1500 Copeland Road, Arlington, TX
76011 USA

Sierra, Rubin
Ed 25 #2501 Jardines Selles, Rio Piedras,
PR 00924

Siers, Kevin *Editor, Cartoonist*
Charlotte Observer, Editorial Dept, 600 S
Tryon St, Charlotte, NC 28202 USA

Sievers, Roy E *Baseball Player*
11505 Belle Fontaine Road, Saint Louis,
MO 63138 USA

Sieverts, Thomas C W *Architect*
Buschstr 20, Bonn, 53113, GERMANY

Sifford, Charlie *Golfer*
PO Box 43128, Highland Heights, OH
44143 USA

Sific, Mokdad *Prime Minister*
Prime Minister's Office, Government
Palais, Al-Moradia, Algiers, ALGERIA

Sigel, Beanie *Musician*
International Creative Mgmt, 8942
Wilshire Blvd, #219, Beverly Hills, CA
90211 USA

Sigel, Jay *Golfer*
1284 Farm Road, Berwyn, PA 19312 USA

Sigel, Tom *Cinematographer*
International Creative Mgmt, 8942
Wilshire Blvd #219, Beverly Hills, CA
90211 USA

Sigholtz, Bob
5425 Shirley Ave., Tarzana, CA 91356

Sigler (Discala), Jamie-Lynn *Actor*
Brax Management, 130 W 42nd St #904,
New York, NY 10036 USA

Sigman, Stan *Business Person*
Cingular Creative Mgmt, 5565 Glenridge
Connector, Atlanta, GA 30342 USA

Sigoloff, Sanford
320 Cliffwood Ave., Los Angeles, CA
90004

Sigwart, Ulrich *Doctor*
Centre Hospitalier Universitaire Vaudois,
Lausanne, SWITZERLAND

Siilasvuo, Ensio *General*
Castrenikatu 6A17, Helsinki 53, 00530,
FINLAND

Sikahema, Vai *Football Player*
28 Abington Road, Mount Laurel, NJ
08054 USA

Sikes, Alfred C *Government Official*
3214 Kirwans Neck Road, Church Creek,
MD 21622 USA

Sikes, Cynthia *Actor*
250 N Delfern, Los Angeles, CA 90077
USA

Sikharulidze, Anton *Figure Skater*
Ice House Skating Rink, 111 Midtown
Bridge Approach, Hackensack, NJ 07601
USA

Sikking, James B *Actor*
258 S Carmelina Ave, Los Angeles, CA
90049 USA

Sikma, Jack *Basketball Player*
8005 SE 28th St, Mercer Island, WA
98040 USA

Silas, James *Basketball Player*
823 Congress Ave, #610, Austin, TX
78701 USA

Silas, Paul *Basketball Player, Coach*
14 Colony Lane, Cleveland, OH 44108
USA

Silatolu, Ratu Timoci *Prime Minister*
Prime Minister's Office, 6 Berkeley
Crescent, Suva, Viti Levu, FIJI

Silber, John R *Educator*
132 Carlton St, Brookline, MA 02446 USA

Silberling, Bradley (Brad) *Director,
Producer*
Creative Artists Agency, 9830 Wilshire
Blvd, Beverly Hills, CA 90212 USA

Silberman, Charles E *Writer*
535 E 86th St, New York, NY 10028 USA

Silberman, Laurence H *Judge, Diplomat*
US Court of Appeals, 3rd & Constitution
NW, Washington, DC 20001 USA

Silberstein, Diane Wichard *Publisher*
New Yorker Magazine, Publisher's Office,
4 Times Square, New York, NY 10036
USA

Silbey, Robert J *Misc*
Massachusetts Institute of Technology,
Chemistry Dept, Cambridge, MA 02139
USA

Silia, Felix *Actor*
8927 Snowden Ave, Arleta, CA 91331
USA

Silja, Anja *Opera Singer*
Colbert Artists, 111 W 57th St, New York,
NY 10019 USA

Silk *Artist, Musician*
Creative Artists Agency, 9830 Wilshire
Blvd, Beverly Hills, CA 90212 USA

Silk, David (Dave) *Hockey Player*
4 Glen Ridge Terrace, Norwell, MA
02061 USA

Silk, George *Photographer*
27 Owenoke Park, Westport, CT 06880
USA

Silla, Felix
8927 Snowden Ave., Arleta, CA 91331

Sillas, Karen *Actor*
PO Box 725, Wading River, NY 11792
USA

Silliman, Michael B (Mike) *Basketball
Player*
6602 Deep Creek Dr, Prospect, KY 40059
USA

Sillitoe, Alan *Writer*
14 Ladbroke Terrace, London, W11 3PG,
UNITED KINGDOM (UK)

Sills, Beverly *Opera Singer, Director*
Rural Farm Delivery, Lambert's Cove
Road, Vinegard Haven, MA 02568 USA

Sills, Douglas *Actor, Musician*
Gold Marshak Liedike, 3500 W Olive Ave, #1400, Burbank, CA 91505 USA

Sills, Stephen *Architect, Designer*
Sills Huniford Assoc, 30 E 67th St, New York, NY 10021 USA

Silva, Gilberto *Football Player*
Arsenal Stadium, Highbury, London, N5 1BU, ENGLAND

Silva, Henry *Actor*
8747 Clifton Way #305, Beverly Hills, CA 90211 USA

Silva, Jackie *Volleyball Player*
Marcia Esposito, PO Box 931416, Los Angeles, CA 90093 USA

Silva, Tom *Entertainer*
This Old House Show, PO Box 2284, South Burlington, VT 05407 USA

Silver, Casey *Business Person*
Universal Pictures, Universal City Plaza, Universal City, CA 91608 USA

Silver, Claudia *Producer*
Writers and Artists Group Intl (LA), 8383 Wilshire Blvd #550, Beverly Hills, CA 90211 USA

Silver, Edward J *Religious Leader*
Bible Way Church, 5118 Clarendon Road, Brooklyn, NY 11203 USA

Silver, Harvey *Actor*
Michael Slessinger & Assoc, 8730 Sunset Blvd #270, Los Angeles, CA 90069 USA

Silver, Horace *Musician, Composer*
Bridge Agency, 35 Clark St #A5, Brooklyn, NY 11201 USA

Silver, Jeffrey *Producer*
Outlaw Productions, 9155 Sunset Blvd, West Hollywood, CA 90069 USA

Silver, Joan Macklin *Director*
Silverfilm Productions, 510 Park Ave #9B, New York, NY 10022 USA

Silver, Joel *Producer*
Creative Artists Agency, 9830 Wilshire Blvd, Beverly Hills, CA 90212 USA

Silver, Michael B
9229 Sunset Blvd #315, Los Angeles, CA 90069 USA

Silver, Robert S *Engineer*
Oakbank, Breadalbane St, Tobermory, Isle of Mull, SCOTLAND

Silver, Ron *Actor*
6116 Tyndall Ave, Bronx, NY 10471 USA

Silverchair
Box 15, Merewether, AUSTRALIA, NSW 2291

Silverman, Al *Publisher*
411 E 53rd St, 16H, New York, NY 10022 USA

Silverman, Barry G *Judge*
US Court of Appeals, 230 N 1st St, Phoenix, AZ 85025 USA

Silverman, Fred
1642 Mandeville Canyon, Los Angeles, CA 90049

Silverman, Henry R *Business Person*
Cendant Corp, 9 W 57th St, New York, NY 10019 USA

Silverman, Jonathan *Actor*
Untitled Entertainment (LA), 8436 W 3rd St #650, Los Angeles, CA 90048 USA

Silverman, Kenneth E *Writer, Educator*
New York University, English Dept, 19 University Place, New York, NY 10003 USA

Silverman, Sarah *Comedian*
Mosaic Media Group, 9200 Sunset Blvd Fl 10, Los Angeles, CA 90069 USA

Silvers, Robert *Artist*
Henry Holt, 115 W 18th St, New York, NY 10011 USA

Silverstein, Elliott *Director*
Gersh Agency, 232 N Canon Dr, Beverly Hills, CA 90210 USA

Silverstein, Joseph H *Musician, Conductor*
Utah Symphony Orchestra, 123 W South Temple, Salt Lake City, UT 84101 USA

Silverstone, Alicia *Actor*
2947 Woodwardia Dr, Los Angeles, CA 90077 USA

Silverstone, Ben *Actor*
London Management, 2-4 Noel St, London, W1V 3RB, UNITED KINGDOM (UK)

Silvestre, Armando
Cerro Macultepec 273Col. Campestre Churubusco, Mexico DF, MEXICO

Silvestri, Alan A *Composer*
Gorfaine/Schwartz, 13245 Riverside Dr #450, Sherman Oaks, CA 91423 USA

Silvestrini, Achille Cardinal *Religious Leader*
Oriental Churches Congregation, Via Conciliazione 34, Rome, 00193, ITALY

Silvia *Royalty*
Kungliga Slottet, Stottsbacken, Stockholm, 111 30, SWEDEN

Silvstedt, Victoria *Model, Actor*
Andy Gould Mgmt, 8484 Wilshire Blvd #425, Beverly Hills, CA 90211 USA

Sim, Gerald *Actor*
Associated Internationl Mgmt, 7 Great Russell St, London, W1D 1BS, UNITED KINGDOM (UK)

Sim, Sheila
Old Friars Richmond Greene, Surrey, ENGLAND

Simanek, Robert E *War Hero*
25194 Westmoreland Dr, Farmington Hills, MI 48336 USA

Simcoe, Anthony *Actor*
Farscape, PO Box 20726, New York, NY 10023-1488 USA

Sime, David W (Dave) *Track Athlete, Doctor*
240 Harbor Dr, Key Biscayne, FL 33149 USA

Simeon II *King, Prime Minister*
Prime Minister's Office, 1 Dondukov Blvd, Sofia, 1000, BULGARIA

Simeoni, Sara *Track Athlete*
Via Castello Rivoli Veronese, Verona, 37010, ITALY

Simic, Charles *Writer*
PO Box 192, Strafford, NH 03884 USA

Simitis, Costas *Prime Minister*
35 Akadanuas St, Athens, 106 72, GREECE

Simmel, Johannes Mario
Bohlgutsch 3, Zug, SWITZERLAND, CH-6300

Simmer, Charlie *Hockey Player*
17635 N 52nd Place, Scottsdale, AZ 85254 USA

Simmonds, Kennedy A *Prime Minister*
PO Box 167, Earle Mome Development, Basseterre, SAINT KITTS & NEVIS

Simmons, Chelan *Actor*
Pacific Artists Management, 1404-510 W Hastings St, Vancouver, BC V6B 1L, CANADA

Simmons, Curtis T (Curt) *Baseball Player*
200 Park Road, Ambler, PA 19002 USA

Simmons, Dick
3215 Silver Cliff Dr., Prescott, AZ 86303

Simmons, Earl (DMX) *Musician*
William Morris Agency (WMA-LA), 1 William Morris Pl, Beverly Hills, CA 90212 USA

Simmons, Floyd (Chunk) *Track Athlete*
2330 Pembroke Ave #8, Charlotte, NC 28207 USA

Simmons, Gene *Musician*
McGhee Entertainment, 8730 Sunset Blvd #195, Los Angeles, CA 90069 USA

Simmons, Henry *Actor*
PO Box 5617, Beverly Hills, CA 90210 USA

Simmons, J K *Actor*
Gersh Agency, The (LA), 232 N Canon Dr, Beverly Hills, CA 90210 USA

Simmons, Jaason *Actor*
Gilbertson & Kincaid Mgmt, 1330 4th ST, Santa Monica, CA 90401 USA

Simmons, Jean *Actor*
636 Adelaide Place, Santa Monica, CA 90402 USA

Simmons, John E *Basketball Player, Baseball Player*
9 Lee Dr, Farmingdale, NY 11735 USA

Simmons, Joseph *Musician, Artist*
Entertainment Artists, 2409 21st Ave S, #100, Nashville, TN 37212 USA

Simmons, Kimora Lee *Fashion Designer*
Phat Fashions LLC, 512 Seventh Ave, New York, NY 10018 USA

Simmons, Lionel J *Basketball Player*
108 Wellesley Court, Mount Laurel, NJ 08054 USA

Simmons, Richard *Misc*
9306 Civic Center Dr, Beverly Hills, CA 90210 USA

Simmons, Richard D *Publisher*
Int'l Herald Tribune, 181 Ave Charles de Gaulie, Neuilly, 92521, FRANCE

Simmons, Richard P *Business Person*
Allegheny Teledyne, 1000 6 PPG Place, Pittsburgh, PA 15222 USA

Simmons, Russell *Producer*
International Creative Management (ICM-NY), 40 W 57th St, New York, NY 10019 USA

Simmons, Ruth *Educator*
Brown University, President's Office, Providence, RI 02912 USA

Simmons, Shadia *Actor*
265 GA Hwy 30 West, Americus, GA 31709 USA

Simmons, Ted L *Baseball Player*
PO Box 26, Chesterfield, MO 63006 USA

Simms, Joan *Actor*
MGA, Southbank House, Black Prince Road, London, SE1 7SJ, UNITED KINGDOM (UK)

Simms, Kimberley *Actor*
House of Representatives, 400 S Beverly Dr, #101, Beverly Hills, CA 90212 USA

Simms, Larry *Actor*
1043 Keeho Marina, Honolulu, HI 96819 USA

Simms, Phil
252 W. 71st St., New York, NY 10023

Simms, Philip (Phil) *Football Player, Sportscaster*
David Fishof Productions, 252 W 71st St, New York, NY 10023 USA

Simms, Primate George Otto *Religious Leader*
62 Cypress Grove Road, Dublin, 6, IRELAND

Simollardes, Drew *Musician*
David Levin Mgmt, 200 W 57th St, #308, New York, NY 10019 USA

Simon, Bob *Commentator*
CBS-TV, News Dept, 2020 M St NW, Washington, DC 20036 USA

Simon, Carly *Musician, Songwriter*
C Winston Simone Mgmt, 1790 Broadway, 1000, New York, NY 10019 USA

Simon, Claude *Nobel Prize Laureate*
Place Vieille, Satses, Rivesaltes, 66600, FRANCE

Simon, David *Producer, Actor, Writer*
Creative Artists Agency LCC (CAA-LA), 9830 Wilshire Blvd, Beverly Hills, CA 90212 USA

Simon, Dick *Race Car Driver*
Dick Simon Racing, 701 S Girls School Road, Indianapolis, IN 46231 USA

Simon, George W *Astronaut*
PO Box 62, Sunspot, NM 88349 USA

Simon, John I *Critic*
New York Magazine, Editorial Dept, 444 Madison Ave, New York, NY 10022 USA

Simon, Josette *Actor*
Conway Van Gelder Robinson, 18-21 Jermyn St, London, SW1Y 6NB, UNITED KINGDOM (UK)

Simon, Neil *Writer*
William Morris Agency (WMA-LA), 1 William Morris Pl, Beverly Hills, CA 90212 USA

Simon, Paul *Musician, Songwriter*
Michael Tannen, 36 E 61st St, New York, NY 10021 USA

Simon, Roger M *Writer*
Baltimore Sun, Editorial Dept, 1627 K St NW, Washington, DC 20006 USA

Simon, Scott *Commentator*
NBC-TV, News Dept, 30 Rockefeller Plaza, New York, NY 10112 USA

Simon, Simone *Actor*
5 Rue de Tilsitt, Paris, 75008, FRANCE

Simone, Albert J *Educator*
Rochester Institute of Technology, President's Office, Rochester, NY 14623 USA

Simoneau, Yves
151 El Camino Dr., Beverly Hills, CA 90212

Simonini, Edward (Ed) *Football Player*
6617 E 113th St S, Bixby, OK 74008 USA

Simonis, Adrianus J Cardinal *Religious Leader*
Aartbisdom, BP 14019 Maliebaan, Utrecht, SB, 3508, NETHERLANDS

Simonon, Paul *Musician*
Premier Talent, 3 E 54th St, #1100, New York, NY 10022 USA

Simonov, Yuriy I *Conductor*
Moscow Conservatory, Gertsema St 13, Moscow, RUSSIA

Simons, Elwyn L *Misc*
Duke University, Primate Center, 3705 Erwin Road, Durham, NC 27705 USA

Simons, Lawrence B *Government Official*
Powell Goldstein Frazier, 1001 Pennsylvania Ave NW, Washington, DC 20004 USA

Simons, Paullina *Writer*
Avon/William Morrow, 1350 Ave of Americas, New York, NY 10019 USA

Simonsen, Renee *Actor, Model*
Ford Model Agency, 142 Greene St, #400, New York, NY 10012 USA

Simple Plan *Music Group*
Creative Artists Agency LCC (CAA-LA), 9830 Wilshire Blvd, Beverly Hills, CA 90212 USA

Simpson, Alan *Educator*
Yellow Gate Farm, Little Compton, RI 02837 USA

Simpson, Alan K *Senator*
1201 Sunshine Ave, PO Box 270, Cody, WY 82414 USA

Simpson, Arnelle
11661 San Vicente Blvd. #632, Los Angeles, CA 90049

Simpson, Ashlee *Actor, Musician*
Creative Artists Agency LCC (CAA-LA), 9830 Wilshire Blvd, Beverly Hills, CA 90212 USA

Simpson, Carole *Commentator*
ABC-TV, News Dept, 77 W 66th St, New York, NY 10023 USA

Simpson, Charles R *Judge*
US Tax Court, 400 2nd St NW, Washington, DC 20217 USA

Simpson, Geoffrey *Cinematographer*
PO Box 3194, Bellevue Hills, NSW, 2023, AUSTRALIA

Simpson, Jason
11661 San Vicente Blvd. #632, Los Angeles, CA 90049

Simpson, Jessica *Musician*
Top Entertainment, 156 W 56th St, #500, New York, NY 10019 USA

Simpson, Jimmi *Actor*
Agency for the Performing Arts, 485 Madison Ave, New York, NY 10022 USA

Simpson, Joanne G *Scientist*
NASA/GSFC, Mail Code 912, Earth Sciences Center, Greenbelt, MD 20771 USA

Simpson, Juliene Brazinski *Basketball Player*
PO Box 1267, Stroudsburg, PA 18360 USA

Simpson, Louis A M *Writer*
PO Box 119, Setauket, NY 11733 USA

Simpson, Orenthal James (OJ) *Football Player, Actor, Sportscaster*
9450 SW 112th St, Miami, FL 33176 USA

Simpson, Ralph *Basketball Player*
5189 Fraser St, Denver, CO 80239 USA

Simpson, Scott *Golfer*
15778 Paseo Hermosa, Poway, CA 92064 USA

Simpson, Stern Carol *Misc*
American Assn of University Professors, 1012 14th St NW, Washington, DC 20005 USA

Simpson, Suzi *Actor, Model*
24338 El Toro Road, #E315, Laguna Woods, CA 92653 USA

Simpson, Terry *Coach*
Anaheim Mighty Ducks, 2000 E Gene Autry Way, Anaheim, CA 92806 USA

Simpson, Tim *Golfer*
6750 Polo Dr, Cumming, GA 30040 USA

Simpson, Valerie *Songwriter, Musician*
Associated Booking Corp, 1995 Broadway, #501, New York, NY 10023 USA

Simpson, Wayne K *Baseball Player*
330 E Collamer Dr, Carson, CA 90746 USA

Simpson Sr, John F *Race Car Driver*
Mount Morris Star Route, Waynesburg, PA 15370 USA

Simpy Red *Music Group*
Lee & Thompson, 15 St Christopher's Pl, London, W1M 5HE, UNITED KINGDOM (UK)

Simran *Actor*
C/o Hotel Residency, Thyagaraya Nagar, Chennai, TN 600 017, INDIA

Sims, Billy R *Football Player*
PO Box 3147, Coppell, TX 75019 USA

Sims, Joan
17 Esmond Ct.Thackery St., London, ENGLAND, WE 5HB

Sims, Kenneth W *Football Player*
PO Box 236, Kosse, TX 76653 USA

Sims, Molly *Actor*
Endeavor NY, 23 Watts St Fl 6, New York, NY 10013 USA

Sin, Jaime L Cardinal *Religious Leader*
121 Arzobispo St Entramuros, PO Box 132, Manila, 10099, PHILIPPINES

Sinatra, Nancy *Actor, Musician*
7215 Williams Road, Lansing, MI 48911
USA

Sinatra, Ray
1234 S. 8th Pl., Las Vegas, NV 89104

Sinatra Jr, Frank *Musician, Actor*
Jack Grenier Productions, 32630 Concord
Dr, Madison Heights, MI 48071 USA

Sinbad *Comedian, Actor*
Creative Artists Agency, 9830 Wilshire
Blvd, Beverly Hills, CA 90212 USA

Sinceros
25 Buliver St.Shephard's Bush, London,
ENGLAND, W12 8AR

Sinclair, Clive M *Inventor*
Sinclair Research, 7 York Central, 70 York
Way, London, N1 9AG, UNITED
KINGDOM (UK)

Sinclair, Harry *Director, Writer*
International Creative Management
(ICM-LA), 8942 Wilshire Blvd, Beverly
Hills, CA 90211 USA

Sindelar, Jerry
213 Prospect Hill Rd, Horseheads, NY
14845

Sindelar, Joey *Golfer*
PGA Tour, 112 PGA Tour Blvd, Ponte
Vedra Beach, FL 32082 USA

Sinden, Donald A *Actor*
Rats Castle, Isle of Oxney, Kent, TN30
7HX, UNITED KINGDOM (UK)

Sinden, Harry *Hockey Player*
9 Olde Village Dr, Winchester, MA 01890
USA

Sinfelt, John H *Misc*
Exxon Research & Engineering, Clinton
Township, RR 22E, Annadale, NJ 08801
USA

Singer, Bryan *Director*
William Morris Agency (WMA-LA), 1
William Morris Pl, Beverly Hills, CA
90212 USA

Singer, Isadore M *Mathematician*
Massachusetts Institute of Technology,
Mathematics Dept, Cambridge, MA 02139
USA

Singer, Lori *Actor*
Chuck Binder, 1465 Linda Crest Dr,
Beverly Hills, CA 90210 USA

Singer, Marc *Actor*
11218 Canton Dr, Studio City, CA 91604
USA

Singer, Maxine F *Educator*
5410 39th St NW, Washington, DC 20015
USA

Singer, Peter A D *Misc*
Princeton University, Human Values
Center, Princeton, NJ 08544 USA

Singer, S Fred *Physicist*
4084 University Dr, #101, Fairfax, VA
22030 USA

Singer, William R (Bill) *Baseball Player*
1119 Mallard Marsh Dr, Osprey, FL
34229 USA

Singh, Amrita *Bollywood, Actor*
Bungalow 5, Lokhandwala Complex
Andheri Link Road, Mumbai, MS 400058,
INDIA

Singh, Archana Puran *Actor, Bollywood*
G426 Anjali Apartments, Seven
Bungalows Anheri, Mumbai, MS 400061,
INDIA

Singh, Bipin *Dancer, Choreographer*
Manipuri Nartanalaya, 15A Bipin Pal
Road, Kolkata, WB, 700026, INDIA

Singh, Chandrachur *Actor, Bollywood*
6th Floor Oakland Park, Off Lokhandwala
Complex Versova, Mumbai, MS 400049,
INDIA

Singh, Dara *Actor, Bollywood*
Dara Villa Mamta Apartments, Ground
Floor A. B. Nair Road Juhu, Mumbai, MS
400049, INDIA

Singh, Manmohan *Prime Minister*
Premier's Office, South Block, Safdarjung
Road, New Delhi, Delhi, 110011, INDIA

Singh, Sukhmander *Engineer*
Santa Clara University, Civil Engineering
Dept, Santa Clara, CA 95053 USA

Singh, Tjinder *Musician*
Legends of 21st Century, 7 Trinity Row,
Florence, MA 01062 USA

Singh, Vijay *Golfer*
Int'l Mgmt Group, 1 Erieview Plaza, 1360
E 9th St #1300, Cleveland, OH 44114
USA

Singh, Vishwanath Pratap *Prime Minister*
1 Teen Murti Marg, New Delhi, ND
110001, INDIA

Singletary, Daryl
1000 18th Ave. So., Nashville, TN 37212

Singletary, Michael (Mike) *Football Player*
8 Dipping Pond Court, Lutheerville
Timon, MD 21093 USA

Singletary, Mike
PO Box 3224, Barrington, IL 60010

Singleton, Chris *Football Player*
1461 W Hawk Way, Chandler, AZ 85248
USA

Singleton, Doris
344 Dalehurst Ave., Los Angeles, CA
90024

Singleton, Isaac *Actor*
Richard Schwartz Management, 2934-1/2
Beverly Glen Cir #107, Los Angeles, CA
90077

Singleton, John D *Director, Writer,
Producer*
PO Box 92547, Pasadena, CA 91109 USA

Singleton, Kenneth W (Kenny) *Baseball
Player*
10 Sparks Farm Road, Sparks, MD 21152
USA

Singleton, Margie *Musician*
PO Box 567, Hendersonville, TN 37077
USA

Sinha, Mala *Actor*
8 Turner Road, Bandra, Bombay, MS 400
050, INDIA

Sinha, Shatrughan *Actor, Bollywood,
Politician*
104 Green Star Apts Rizvi Complex,
Sherly Rajan Road Bandra, Bombay, MS
400 050, INDIA

Sinise, Gary *Actor*
PO Box 6704, Malibu, CA 90264 USA

Sinner, George A *Governor*
101 3rd St N, Moorhead, MN 56560 USA

Sinowatz, Fred *Government Official,
Governor*
Loewelstr 18, Vienna, 1010, AUSTRIA

Sinton, Nell *Artist*
484 Lake Park Ave, #189, Oakland, CA
94610 USA

Sinyavskaya, Tamara I *Opera Singer*
Kunstleragentur Raab & Bohm,
Plankengasse 7, Vienna, 1010, AUSTRIA

Siouxsie & The Banshees
1325 Ave. of the Americas, New York, NY
10019

Siouzsie, Sioux *Musician*
Helter Skelter, Plaza, 535 Kings Road,
London, SW10 0S, UNITED KINGDOM
(UK)

Sipchen, Bob *Journalist*
Los Angeles Times, Editorial Dept, 202 W
1st St, Los Angeles, CA 90012 USA

Sipe, Brian W *Football Player*
1630 Luneta Dr, Del Mar, CA 92014 USA

Siphandon, Khamtay *President, General*
President's Office, Vientiane, LAOS

Sipinen, Arto K *Architect*
Arkkitehtitoimistro Arto Sipinen Ky,
Ahertajantie 3, Espoo, 02100, FINLAND

Sippy, G P *Actor*
3/G Naaz Building, Lamington Road,
Bombay, MS 400 004, INDIA

Sippy, Raj *Director, Filmmaker, Producer,
Bollywood*
101 Jal Tarang Kishore Kumar Ganguly
Marg, Juhu Tara Road, Bombay, MS 400
049, INDIA

Sippy, Ramesh *Director, Filmmaker,
Producer, Bollywood*
379 Sathe House 14th Road, Khar,
Bombay, MS 400 052, INDIA

Sir Douglas Quintet
59 Parsons St., Newtonville, MA 02160

Sir Mix-A-Lot *Artist, Musician*
Richard Walters, 1800 Argyle Ave, #408,
Los Angeles, CA 90028 USA

Siren, Heikki *Architect*
Tiirasaarentie 35, Heisinki, 00200,
FINLAND

Siren, Katri A H *Architect*
Tiirasaarentie 35, Heisinki, 00200,
FINLAND

Sirgo, Otto *Actor*
Televisa, Blvd Adolfo Lopez Mateos 232,
Colonia San Angel INN, DF, CP 01060,
MEXICO

Sirhan, Sirhan
#B21014Corcoran State Prison Box 8800,
Corcoran, CA 93212

Siri Singh Sahib *Religious Leader*
Sikh, PO Box 351149, Los Angeles, CA
90035 USA

Sirico, Tony *Actor*
McGowan Management, 8733 W Sunset
Blvd #103, W Hollywood, CA 90069 USA

Sirikit *Royalty*
Chritrada Villa, Bangkok, THAILAND

Sirtis, Marina *Actor*
Metropolitan Talent Agency, 4526 Wilshire Blvd, Los Angeles, CA 90010 USA

Sisco, Joseph J *Engineer, Government Official*
5630 Wisconsin Ave, Chevy Chase, MD 20815 USA

Sisemore, Jerald G (Jerry) *Football Player*
1730 Whipporwill Trail, Leander, TX 78641 USA

Sislen, Myrna *Musician*
Lindy Martin Mgmt, 5 Lob Lolly Court, Pinehurst, NC 28374 USA

Sisqo *Musician*
Evolution Talent, 1776 Broadway, #1500, New York, NY 10019 USA

Sissel *Musician*
Stageway Impressario, Skuteviksboder 11, Bergen, 5035, NORWAY

Sissel, George A *Business Person*
Ball Corp, 10 Longs Peak Dr, Broomfield, CO 80021 USA

Sissi *Actor*
Univision, 314 Main St, Chico, CA 95928 USA

Sissons, Kimber *Actor*
412 Amaz Dr, #204, Los Angeles, CA 90048 USA

Sister, Max *Fashion Designer*
Mount Everest Centre for Buddhist Studies, Kathmandu, NEPAL

Sister Sledge *Music Group*
Tony Denton Promotions Limited (UK), 19 South Molton Way, London, W1K 5LE, United Kingdom

Sisters of Mercy
28 Kensington Church St., London, ENGLAND, W8 4EP

Sisti, Sebastian D (Sibby) *Baseball Player*
38 Clifford Heights, Amherst, NY 14226 USA

Sisto, Jeremy *Actor*
Innovative Artists, 1505 10th St, Santa Monica, CA 90401 USA

Sistrunk, Otis *Football Player*
PO Box 372, Dupont, WA 98327 USA

Sites, Brian *Actor*
Innovative Artists (LA), 1505 Tenth St, Santa Monica, CA 90401 USA

Sites, James W *Producer*
American Legion Magazine, 700 N Pennsylvania St, Indianapolis, IN 46204 USA

Sithara *Actor, Bollywood*
556 I Floor, 2nd Block 2nd Cross R T Nagar, Bangalore, KA, 560032, INDIA

Sitkovetsky, Dmitry *Musician*
Columbia Artists Mgmt Inc, 165 W 57th St, New York, NY 10019 USA

Sitter, Charles R *Business Person*
Exxon Corp, 5959 Las Collinas Blvd, Irving, TX 75039 USA

Sittler, Darrell *Athlete, Hockey Player*
84 Buttonwood Court, East Amherst, NY 14051 USA

Sittler, Darryl G *Hockey Player*
84 Buttonwood Court, East Amherst, NY 14051 USA

Sittler, Walter *Actor*
Agentur Heppeler, Seinstr 54, Munich, 81667, GERMANY

Sivad, Darryl
400 So. Beverly Dr. #101, Beverly Hills, CA 90212

Sivam, Peeli *Actor*
43 Parthasarathy Pettai, II Street, Chennai, TN 600 086, INDIA

Sivaranjani (Ooha) *Actor, Bollywood*
7 Vivekananda Nagar, Nesapakkam, Chennai, TN 600092, INDIA

Six Shooter
PO Box 53, Portland, TN 37148

Sixx
9255 Sunset Blvd. #200, Los Angeles, CA 90069-3309

Sixx, Nikki *Musician*
936 Vista Ridge Lane, Westlake Village, CA 91362 USA

Siza, Alvaro *Architect*
Oporto University, Architecture School, Oporto, PORTUGAL

Sizemore, Tom *Actor*
United Talent Agency, 9560 Wilshire Blvd, #500, Beverly Hills, CA 90212 USA

Sizemore, Tom *Educator*
Brown University, Essential Schools Coalition, Providence, RI 02912 USA

Sizova, Alla I *Ballerina*
Universal Ballet School, 4301 Harewood Road NE, Washington, DC 20017 USA

Sjoberg, Patrik *Track Athlete*
Hokegatan 17, Goteberg, 416 66, SWEDEN

Sjoman, Vilgot *Director*
Banergatan 53, Stockholm, 115 22, SWEDEN

Skaggs, Ricky *Musician*
380 Forest Retreat, Hendersonville, TN 37075 USA

Skah, Khalid *Track Athlete*
Boite Postale 2577, Fez, MOROCCO

Skala, Brian T *Actor*
Osbrink Talent Agency, 4343 Lankershim Blvd #100, Universal City, CA 91602 USA

Skarsgard, J Stellan *Actor*
Hogersgatan 40, Stockholm, 118 26, SWEDEN

Skarsgard, Stellan
Hogbergsgatan 40 II, Stockholm, SWEDEN, S-118 26

Skarsten, Rachel *Actor*
Lovett Management, 1327 Brinkley Ave, Los Angeles, CA 90049 USA

Skayskal, Wayne
PO Box 191, Tampa, FL 33601

Skeggs, Leonard T Jr *Misc*
10212 Blair Lane, Kirtland, OH 44094 USA

Skeie, Andris *Prime Minister*
Prime Minister's Office, Brivibus Bulv 36, Riga, PDP, 226170, LATVIA

Skelton, Byron G *Judge*
US Court of Appeals, 717 Madison Ave NW, Washington, DC 20439 USA

Skelton, Richard K (Rich) Jr *Rodeo Rider*
1139 County Road 312, Liano, TX 78643 USA

Skerritt, Tom *Actor*
United Talent Agency, 9560 Wilshire Blvd, #500, Beverly Hills, CA 90212 USA

Skibbie, Lawrence F *General*
2309 S Queen St, Arlington, VA 22202 USA

Skibniewska, Halina *Architect*
Wydzlat Architektury Politechniki, Ul Koszykowa 55, Warsaw, 00-659, POLAND

Skid Row *Music Group*
McGhee Entertainment, 8730 Sunset Blvd #175, Los Angeles, CA 90069

Skilling, Hugh H *Engineer*
11720 E Shore Dr, Whitmore Lake, MI 48189 USA

Skinner, Jimmy *Hockey Player, Coach*
2860 Askin Ave, Windsor, ON N9E 3H9, CANADA

Skinner, Joel P *Baseball Player*
24310 Lake Road, Cleverland, OH 44140 USA

Skinner, Jonty *Swimmer, Coach*
University of Alabama, Athletic Dept, Tuscaloosa, AL 35487 USA

Skinner, Mike *Race Car Driver*
Lisa Shealy, 218 Sease Hill Road, Lexington, SC 29073 USA

Skinner, Robert R (Bob) *Baseball Player*
1576 Diamond St, San Diego, CA 92109 USA

Skinner, Samuel K *Secretary, Business Person*
Commonwealth Edison, 1 First National Plaza, PO Box 767, Chicago, IL 60690 USA

Skinner, Val *Golfer*
Debbie Massey, PO Box 116, Cheboygan, MI 49721 USA

Skjelbreid, Ann-Elen *Athlete*
5640 Eikelandsosen, NORWAY

Skladany, Thomas E (Tom) *Football Player*
6666 Highland Lakes Place, Westerville, OH 43082 USA

Sklvorecky, Josef *Writer*
Erindale College, English Dept, Toronto, ON M5S 1A5, CANADA

Skol, Michael *Diplomat*
PO Box 596, Dennis, MA 02638 USA

Skolimowski, Jerzy *Director*
Film Polski, Ul Mazowiecka 6/8, Warsaw, 00-048, POLAND

Skolnick, Mark H *Scientist*
University of Utah, Medical Center, Genetics Dept, Salt Lake City, UT 84112 USA

Skoog, Meyer (Whitey) *Basketball Player, Coach*
35689 398th Lane, Saint Peter, MN 56082 USA

Skopil Jr, Otto R *Judge*
US Court of Appeals, Pionner Courthouse, 555 SW Yamhill St, Portland, OR 97204 USA

Skorich, Nicholas L *Football Coach, Football Player*
8 Briarwood Court, Columbus, NJ 08022 USA

Skorupan, John P *Football Player*
142 Crossing RIdge Trail, Cranberry Township, PA 16066 USA

Skotheim, Robert A *Misc*
2120 Place Road, Port Angeles, WA 98363 USA

Skou, Jens C *Nobel Prize Laureate*
Rislundvej 9, Risskov, 8240, DENMARK

Skouras, Thanos *Economist*
8 Chlois St, Athens, 145 62, GREECE

Skovhus, Bo *Opera Singer*
Balmer & Dixon Mgmt, Granitweg 2, Zurich, 8006, SWITZERLAND

Skowron, Bill *Baseball Player*
1118 Beachcomber Dr, Schaumburg, IL 60193

Skowron, Moose
1118 Beachcomber Dr., Schaumburg, IL 60193

Skowron, William J (Moose) *Baseball Player*
1118 Beachcomber Dr, Schaunmurg, IL 60193 USA

Skrebneski, Victor *Photographer*
1350 N LaSalle Dr, Chicago, IL 60610 USA

Skrepenak, Greg *Football Player*
301 Madison St, Wilkes Barre, PA 18705 USA

Skrovan, Steve *Comedian*
William Morris Agency (WMA-LA), 1 William Morris Pl, Beverly Hills, CA 90212 USA

Skrowaczewski, Stanislaw *Composer*
Minnesota Symphony, 1111 Nicollet Mail, Minneapolis, MN 55403 USA

Skrypnk, Metropolitan Mstyslav S *Religious Leader*
Ukranian Orthodox Church, PO Box 445, South Bound Brook, NJ 08880 USA

Skvorecky, Josef V *Writer*
487 Sackville St, Montreal, ON M4X 1T6, CANADA

Sky, Alison *Architect*
Site, 65 Bleecker St, New York, NY 10012 USA

Sky, Jennifer *Actor*
12533 Woodgreen, Los Angeles, CA 90066 USA

Skye, Azura *Actor*
Baker Winokur Ryder (BWR-LA), 9100 Wilshire Blvd Fl 6, W Tower, Beverly Hills, CA 90212 USA

Skye, Ione *Actor*
8794 Lookout Mountain Ave, Los Angeles, CA 90046 USA

Skyrms, Brian *Misc*
University of California, Philosophy Dept, Irvine, CA 92717 USA

Slade, Bernard N *Writer*
345 N Saltair Ave, Los Angeles, CA 90049 USA

Slade, Chris *Musician*
11 Leominster Road, Morden, Surrey, SA4 6HN, UNITED KINGDOM (UK)

Slade, Mark *Actor*
38 Joppa Road, Worcester, MA 01602 USA

Slade, Roy *Artist*
Cranbrook Academy Art Museum, PO Box 801, Bloomfield Hills, MI 48303 USA

Slagle, James R
13630 Barryknoll Lane, Houston, TX 77079 USA

Slaney, Mary Decker *Track Athlete*
2923 Flintlock St, Eugene, OR 97408 USA

Slash *Musician*
801 N Roxbury Dr, Beverly Hills, CA 90210 USA

Slater, Christian *Actor*
Brillstein-Grey Entertainment, 9150 Wilshire Blvd #350, Beverly Hills, CA 90212 USA

Slater, Helen *Actor*
1327 Brinkley Ave, Los Angeles, CA 90049 USA

Slater, Jock C K (John) *Admiral*
Naval Secretary, Victory Bldg, HM Naval Base, Portsmouth, PO1 3LS, UNITED KINGDOM (UK)

Slater, Kelly *Athlete, Actor*
SLAM Management, 31652 2nd Ave, Laguna Beach, CA 92651 USA

Slater, Ryan
3500 W. Olive Ave. #1400, Burbank, CA 91505

Slater, Suzanne
10000 Riverside Dr. #10, Toluca Lake, CA 91602

Slatkin, Leonard E *Conductor*
Washington National Symphony, Kennedy Center, Washington, DC 20011 USA

Slaton, Tony *Football Player*
122 E Childs Ave, Merced, CA 95340 USA

Slattery, John *Actor*
Gersh Agency, The (LA), 232 N Canon Dr, Beverly Hills, CA 90210 USA

Slattery, John M Jr *Actor*
Gersh Agency, 232 N Canon Dr, Beverly Hills, CA 90210 USA

Slattvik, Simon *Athlete*
Bankgata 22, Lillehammer, 2600, NORWAY

Slatzer, Robert F
3033 Hollycrest Dr #2, Los Angeles, CA 90068 USA

Slaughter *Music Group*
Artist Representation & Management, 1257 Arcade St, St Paul, MN 55106

Slaughter, Frank *Doctor*
Box 14 Ortega Station, Jacksonville, FL 32210 USA

Slaughter, J Mack *Actor*
3 Arts Entertainment Inc, 9460 Wilshire Blvd Fl 7, Beverly Hills, CA 90212 USA

Slaughter, John B *Educator*
Occidental College, President's Office, Los Angeles, CA 90041 USA

Slaughter, Karin *Writer*
Harper Collins Publishers, 10 E 53rd St, New York, NY 10022 USA

Slavin, Randall *Actor*
Gold Marshak Liedtke, 3500 W Olive Ave, #1400, Burbank, CA 91505 USA

Slavitt, David R *Writer*
35 West St, #5, Cambridge, MA 02139 USA

Slay, Brandon *Wrestler*
6155 Lehman Ave, Colorado Springs, CO 80918 USA

Slayton, Bobby *Comedian*
Artist's Agency, The (LA), 1180 S Beverly Dr #301, Los Angeles, CA 90035 USA

Sledge, Percy *Musician*
PO Box 220082, Great Neck, NY 11022 USA

Sleep, Wayne *Dancer, Actor, Choreographer*
22 Queensberry Mews West, London, SW7 2DY, UNITED KINGDOM (UK)

Slegr, Jiri *Hockey Player*
Vancouver Canucks, 800 Griffiths Way, Vancouver, BC V6B 6G1, CANADA

Slegr, Jirl *Hockey Player*
Boston Bruins, 1 Fleet Center, Boston, MA 02114 USA

Slezak, Erika *Actor*
International Creative Mgmt, 40 W 57th St, #1800, New York, NY 10019 USA

Slichter, Charles P *Physicist*
61 Chestnut Court, Champaign, IL 61822 USA

Slichter, Jacob *Musician*
Monterey Peninsula Artists, 509 Hartnell St, Monterey, CA 93940 USA

Slick, Grace *Musician, Songwriter*
Bill Thompson Mgmt, 2051 3rd St, San Francisco, CA 94107 USA

Slick, Rick *Musician*
Famous Artists Agency, 250 W 57th St, New York, NY 10107 USA

Sliger, Bernard F *Educator*
3341 E Lakeshore Dr, Tallahassee, FL 32312 USA

Slipknot *Musician*
Agency Group, The (NY), 1775 Broadway #430, New York, NY 10019 USA

Sliwa, Curtis
628 W 28th St., New York, NY 10001-1151

Sloan, Gerald E (Jerry) *Basketball Player, Coach*
300 S Washington St, McLeansboro, IL 62859 USA

Sloan, Holly Goldberg *Director*
Sanford-Beckett-Skouras, 1015 Gayley Ave, #300, Los Angeles, CA 90024 USA

Sloan, P F *Musician, Songwriter*
All the Best, PO Box 164, Cedarhurst, NY 11516 USA

Sloan, Stephen C (Steve) *Football Player, Football Coach*
University of Central Florida, Athletic Dept, Orlando, FL 32816 USA

Sloan Jr, Robert B *Educator*
Bayor University, President's Office, Waco, TX 76798 USA

Sloane, Carol *Musician*
Magi Productions, 705 Centre St, #300, Boston, MA 02130 USA

Sloane, Lindsay *Actor*
Abrams Artists, 9200 Sunset Blvd, #1125, Los Angeles, CA 90069 USA

Sloatman, Lala
11917 Vose St., No. Hollywood, CA 91605

Slobodyanik, Alexander *Musician*
Columbia Artists Mgmt Inc, 165 W 57th St, New York, NY 10019 USA

Slocombe, Douglas *Cinematographer*
London Mgmt, 2-4 Noel St, London, W1V 3RB, UNITED KINGDOM (UK)

Slocumb, Reathcliff (Heath) *Baseball Player*
1045 Arthur St, Uniondale, NY 11553 USA

Slon, Steve *Editor*
AARP Magazine, 601 E St NW, Washington, DC 20049 USA

Slonimsky, Sergey M *Composer*
9 Kanal Griboedova, #97, Saint Petersburg, RUSSIA

Slotnick, Bernard *Publisher*
DC Comics Group, 355 Lexington Ave, New York, NY 10017 USA

Slotnick, Joey *Actor*
Gersh Agency, 232 N Canon Dr, Beverly Hills, CA 90210 USA

Slotnick, Mortimer H *Artist*
43 Amherst Dr, New Rochelle, NY 10804 USA

Slotnick, R Nathan *Doctor*
825 Fairfax Ave, Norfolk, VA 23507 USA

Slovan, Eric *Comedian*
William Morris Agency (WMA-LA), 1 William Morris Pl, Beverly Hills, CA 90212 USA

Slover, Karl
904 S. Lakeview Dr, Tampa, FL 33609-5310

Slovin, Eric *Writer*
Principato/Young Management, 9665 Wilshire Blvd #500, Beverly Hills, CA 90212 USA

Sloviter, Dolores K *Judge*
US Court of Appeals, US Courthouse, 601 Market St, Philadelphia, PA 19106 USA

Sloyan, James *Actor*
920 Kagawa St, Pacific Palisades, CA 90272 USA

Sluman, Jeff *Golfer*
808 McKinley Lane, Hinsdale, IL 60521 USA

Slutsky, Lorie A *Misc*
New York Community Trust, 2 Park Ave, New York, NY 10016 USA

Sly, Darryl *Hockey Player*
Blue Mountain Chrysler, Highway 26, Collingwood, ON L9Y 1W6, CANADA

Smagorinsky, Joseph *Misc*
72 Gabriel Court, Hillsborough, NJ 08844 USA

Smale, Stephen *Mathematician*
68 Highgate Road, Kensington, CA 94707 USA

Small, Brendan *Comedian*
Brillstein-Grey Entertainment, 9150 Wilshire Blvd #350, Beverly Hills, CA 90212 USA

Small, Lawrence W *Financier*
Smithsonian Institution, 1000 Jefferson Dr SW, Washington, DC 20560 USA

Small, Mary
165 W. 66th St., New York, NY 10023

Small, Marya *Actor*
CL Inc, 843 N Sycamore Ave, Los Angeles, CA 90038 USA

Small, William N *Admiral*
1605 Bluecher Court, Verginia Beach, VA 23454 USA

Smalley, Richard E *Nobel Prize Laureate*
1816 Bolsolver St, Houston, TX 77005 USA

Smalley, Roy F Jr *Baseball Player*
6319 Timber Trail, Edina, MN 55439 USA

Smallwood, Dwana *Dancer*
Alvin Ailey American Dance Foundation, 211 W 61st St #300, New York, NY 10023 USA

Smallwood, Richard *Musician, Music Group*
Sierra Mgmt, 1035 Bates Court, Hendersonville, TN 37075 USA

Smart, Amy *Actor*
Endeavor Talent Agency, 9701 Wilshire Blvd #1000, Beverly Hills, CA 90212 USA

Smart, Jean *Actor*
17351 Rancho St, Encino, CA 91316 USA

Smart, Keith *Basketball Player, Coach*
5306 Asterwood Dr, Dublin, CA 94568 USA

Smart, Pamela
#93G0356 Bedford Hills Corr. Fac., Bedford Hills, NY 10507-2496

Smash Mouth *Musician*
Creative Artists Agency LCC (CAA-LA), 9830 Wilshire Blvd, Beverly Hills, CA 90212 USA

Smashing Pumpkins
9830 Wilshire Blvd., Beverly Hills, CA 90212

Smathers, George A *Senator*
Alred I du Pont Building, 169 E Flager St, Miami, FL 33131 USA

Smeal, Eleanor
900 N. Stafford St. #1217, Arlington, VA 22003

Smeal, Eleanor C *Social Activist, Misc*
900 N Stafford St #1217, Arlington, VA 22203 USA

Smeaton, Bruce
585 Nepean Hwy. Carrum, Victoria, AUSTRALIA, 3197

Smedley, Geoffrey *Artist*
RR 3, Gambier Island, Gibsons, BC V0N 1V0, CANADA

Smedvig, Rolf *Musician*
Columbia Artists Mgmt Inc, 165 W 57th St, New York, NY 10019 USA

Smehlik, Richard *Hockey Player*
8824 Hearthstone Dr, East Amherst, NY 14051 USA

Smerlas, Frederick C (Fred) *Football Player*
400 Main St, Waltham, MA 02452 USA

Smid, Ladislav *Hockey Player*
Anaheim Mighty Ducks, 2000 E Gene Autry Way, Anaheim, CA 92806 USA

Smigel, Irwin *Doctor*
Smigel Research, 635 Madison Ave, New York, NY 10022 USA

Smiley, Jane G *Writer*
316 Mid Valley Center #273, Carmel, CA 93923 USA

Smiley, John P *Baseball Player*
208 W 3rd Ave, Collegeville, PA 19426 USA

Smiley, Rickey *Comedian*
International Creative Management (ICM-LA), 8942 Wilshire Blvd, Beverly Hills, CA 90211 USA

Smiley, Tavis *Radio Personality*
International Creative Management (ICM-LA), 8942 Wilshire Blvd, Beverly Hills, CA 90211 USA

Smirnoff, Yakov *Actor, Comedian*
Comrade Entertainment, 3750 W 76 Country Blvd, Branson, MO 65616 USA

Smirnov, Nikolai I *Admiral*
Ministry of Defense, 4 Staraya Pl, Moscow, 103073, RUSSIA

Smith, Adrian *Musician*
Chipster Entertainment, 1976 E High St #101, Pottstown, PA 19464 USA

Smith, Adrian *Basketball Player*
2829 Saddleback Dr, Cincinnati, OH 45244 USA

Smith, Akili *Football Player*
7771 Gribble St, San Diego, CA 92114 USA

Smith, Alexander J C *Financier*
Marsh & McLennan Co, 1166 Ave of Americas, New York, NY 10036 USA

Smith, Alexis *Artist*
1907 Lincoln Blvd, Venice, CA 90291 USA

Smith, Allison *Actor*
Innovative Artists, 1505 10th St, Santa Monica, CA 90401 USA

Smith, Amber *Actor, Model*
Shelter Entertainment, 9255 Sunset Blvd #1010, Los Angeles, CA 90069 USA

Smith, Andrea *Artist*
Lahaina Gallery, 728 Front St, Lahaina, HI 96761 USA

Smith, Ann *Tennis Player*
2 Rivers Edge Road, Hull, MA 02045 USA

Smith, Anna Deavere *Actor*
Creative Artists Agency, 9830 Wilshire Blvd, Beverly Hills, CA 90212 USA

Smith, Anna Nicole *Model, Actor*
200 Ashdale Ave, Los Angeles, CA 90049 USA

Smith, Anne Mollegen *Editor*
451 W 24th St, New York, NY 10011 USA

Smith, Anthony W *Educator*
4316 Marina City Dr, #727C, Marina del Rey, CA 90292 USA

Smith, April *Writer*
427 7th St, Santa Monica, CA 90402 USA

Smith, Arthur K Jr *Educator*
5346 Mcculloch Circle, Houston, TX 77056 USA

Smith, B *Television Host*
B Smith With Style, 168 Park Ave, Harrison, NY 10528 USA

Smith, Beau *Cartoonist*
Flying Fist Ranch, PO Box 706, Ceredo, WV 25507 USA

Smith, Ben *Hockey Player, Coach*
47 Norwood Heights, Gloucester, MA 01930 USA

Smith, Ben *Cartoonist*
King Features Syndicate, 888 7th Ave, New York, NY 10106 USA

Smith, Ben *Football Player*
1127 Riverbend Club Dr SE, Atlanta, GA 30339 USA

Smith, Bennett W *Religious Leader*
Progressive National Baptist Convention, 601 50th St NE, Washington, DC 20019 USA

Smith, Billy *Hockey Player*
8356 Quail Meadow Way, West Palm Beach, FL 33412 USA

Smith, Billy Ray Jr *Football Player*
14755 Caminito Porta Delgada, Del Mar, CA 92014 USA

Smith, Bob *Golfer*
Signature Sports Group, 4150 Olson Memorial Highway, Minneapolis, MN 55422 USA

Smith, Bobby *Hockey Player*
10800 E Cactus Road, #46, Scottdale, AZ 85259 USA

Smith, Brad *Musician*
Shapiro Co, 9229 Sunset Blvd, #607, Los Angeles, CA 90069 USA

Smith, Brooke *Actor*
1860 N Fuller Ave #104, Los Angeles, CA 90046 USA

Smith, Bruce *Football Player*
20473 Tappahannock Place, Sterling, VA 20165 USA

Smith, Bruce W *Director*
Jambalaya Studio, 111 N Maryland Ave #300, Glendale, CA 92206 USA

Smith, Bubba
5178 Sunlight Pl., Los Angeles, CA 90016 USA

Smith, C Reginald (Reggie) *Baseball Player*
22239 1/2 Erwin St, Woodland Hills, CA 91367 USA

Smith, Calvin *Track Athlete*
16703 Sheffield Park Dr, Lutz, FL 33549 USA

Smith, Carl *Musician*
2510 Franklin Road, Nashville, TN 37204 USA

Smith, Carl R *General*
2345 S Queen St, Arlington, VA 22202 USA

Smith, Carolyn Renee
PO Box. 813, No. Hollywood, CA 91603

Smith, Chad *Musician*
Q Prime, 729 7th Ave #1600, New York, NY 10019 USA

Smith, Charles A (Bubba) *Football Player, Actor*
6085 Adobe Summit Ave, Las Vegas, NV 89110 USA

Smith, Charles Martin *Actor, Director*
980 Cedarcliff Court, Westlake Village, CA 91362 USA

Smith, Chelsi
335 E. San Augustine St., Deer Park, TX 77536-4127

Smith, Clifford (Method Man) *Musician, Television Host*
Native Pictures, 6605 Hollywood Blvd, Suite 100B, Los Angeles, CA 90028 USA

Smith, Clinton J (Clint) *Hockey Player*
501-1919 Bellview Ave, West Vancouver, BC V7V 1B7, CANADA

Smith, Connie *Musician, Music Group*
Gurley Co, 1204B Cedar Lane, Nashville, TN 37212 USA

Smith, Cotter *Actor*
15332 Antioch St #800, Pacific Palisades, CA 90272 USA

Smith, D Brooks *Judge*
US Court of Appeals, Penn Traffic Bldg, 319 Washington St, Johnstown, PA 15901 USA

Smith, Danny *Actor*
Endeavor Agency LLC (LA), 9601 Wilshire Blvd Fl 3, Beverly Hills, CA 90210 USA

Smith, Dante (Mos Def) *Musician, Actor*
Brookside Artists Management (NY), 250 W 57th St #2303, New York, NY 10107 USA

Smith, Darden *Musician, Music Group, Songwriter*
AGF Entertainment, 30 W 21st St #700, New York, NY 10010 USA

Smith, David
1104 Lakeside Dr. #E-3, Union, SC 29379-9676

Smith, Dean E *Basketball Player, Coach*
University of North Carolina, PO Box 2126, Chapel Hill, NC 27515 USA

Smith, Dennis *Football Player*
2450 Achilles Dr, Los Angeles, CA 90046 USA

Smith, Derek *Hockey Player*
201 Bramblewood Lane, East Amherst, NY 14051 USA

Smith, Dick *Swimmer, Coach*
5810 N 59th Ave, Glendale, AZ 85301 USA

Smith, Doug *Basketball Player*
21930 Winchester St, Southfield, MI 48076 USA

Smith, Doug *Football Player, Football Coach*
University of Southern California, Heritage Hall, Los Angeles, CA 90089 USA

Smith, Dylan *Actor*
TalentWorks (LA), 3500 W Olive Ave #1400, Burbank, CA 91505 USA

Smith, Elmore *Basketball Player*
33065 Cedar Road, Mayfield Heights, OH 44124 USA

Smith, Emil L *Physicist, Biologist*
University of California, Medical School, Los Angeles, CA 90024 USA

Smith, Emmett
1 Cowboys Parkway, Irving, TX 75063

Smith, F Dean *Track Athlete*
PO Box 71, Breckenridge, TX 76424 USA

Smith, Floyd *Hockey Player*
138 Stonehenge Dr, Orchard Park, NY 14127 USA

Smith, Forry
3500 W. Olive #1400, Burbank, CA 91505

Smith, Frederick W *Business Person*
FDX Corp, 942 S Shady Grove Road, Memphis, TN 38120 USA

Smith, G E
24 Thorndike St, Cambridge, MA 02141-1882 USA

Smith, G Elaine *Religious Leader*
American Baptist Churches USA, PO Box 851, Valley Forge, PA 19482 USA

Smith, Gary *Hockey Player*
Villa Cortina, 4451 Albert St #102, Burnaby, BC V5C 2G4, CANADA

Smith, George *Cartoonist*
Universal Press Syndicate, 4520 Main St, Kansas City, MO 64111 USA

Smith, Gerald *Misc*
World Tennis Assn, 133 1st St NE, Saint Petersburg, FL 33701 USA

Smith, Gerald C *Government Official*
2425 Tracy Place NW, Washington, DC 20008 USA

Smith, Gregory *Actor*
4570 Van Nuys Blvd #171, Sherman Oaks, CA 91403 USA

Smith, Gregory Edward *Actor*
Anonymous Content, 8522 National Blvd #101, Culver City, CA 90232 USA

Smith, Gregory White *Writer*
129 1st Ave SW, Aiken, SC 29801 USA

Smith, Hamilton O *Nobel Prize Laureate*
13607 Hanover Road, Reisterstown, MD 21136 USA

Smith, Harry *Commentator*
CBS-TV, News Dept, 51 W 52nd St, New York, NY 10019 USA

Smith, Harry *Bowler*
580 E Cuyahoga Falls Ave, Akron, OH 44310 USA

Smith, Harry E (Black Jack) *Football Player, Football Coach, Coach*
805 Leawood Terrace, Columbia, MO 65203 USA

Smith, Hedrick L *Journalist*
4204 Rasemary St, Chevy Chase, MD 20815 USA

Smith, Hillary B
8730 Sunset Blvd #480, Los Angeles, CA 90069 USA

Smith, Hulett C *Governor*
2105 Harper Road, Beckley, WV 25801 USA

Smith, Ian
Gwenoro Farm, Shurugwi, ZIMBABWE

Smith, Ian D *Prime Minister*
Gwenoro Farm, Selukwe, ZIMBABWE

Smith, Ilan Mitchell
104-60 Queens Blvd. #10C, Fox Hills, NY 11375

Smith, Ivor *Architect*
Station Officer's House, Prawle Pointe Kingsbridge, Devon, TQ7 2BX, UNITED KINGDOM (UK)

Smith, Jackie L *Football Player*
1566 Walpole Dr, Chesterfield, MO 63017 USA

Smith, Jaclyn *Actor*
10398 Sunset Blvd #1200, Los Angeles, CA 90077 USA

Smith, Jacob *Actor*
Agency for the Performing Arts (APA-LA), 9200 Sunset Blvd #900, Los Angeles, CA 90069 USA

Smith, James (Bonecrusher) *Boxer*
355 Keith Hills Road, Lillington, NC 27546 USA

Smith, Jamie Renee *Actor*
Hervey/Grimes Talent Agency, 10561 Missouri Avenue, #2, Los Angeles, CA 90025 USA

Smith, Jean Kennedy
500 Fifth Ave., New York, NY 10110

Smith, Jennifer M *Prime Minister, Misc*
Premier's Office, Cabinet Building, 105 Front St, Hamilton, HM, 12, BERMUDA

Smith, Jerry *Judge*
US Court of Appeals, 515 Rusk Ave, Houston, TX 77002 USA

Smith, Jim Ray *Football Player*
7049 Cliffbrook Dr, Dallas, TX 75254 USA

Smith, Jimmy O *Musician*
2761 Lacy Lane, Sacramento, CA 95821 USA

Smith, Joe *Basketball Player*
7639 Leafwood Dr, Norfolk, VA 23518 USA

Smith, John *Actor*
IFA Talent Agency, 8730 Sunset Blvd #490, Los Angeles, CA 90069 USA

Smith, John L *Football Coach*
Michigan State University, Daugherty Field House, East Lansing, MI 48824 USA

Smith, John W *Wrestler*
5315 S Sangre Road, Stillwater, OK 74074 USA

Smith, Josh *Misc*
University of Pennsylvania, 240 S 33rd St, Philadelphia, PA 19104 USA

Smith, Justin *Football Player*
Cincinnati Bengals, 1 Paul Brown Stadium, Cincinnati, OH 45202 USA

Smith, Karin
2300 Palisades St, Los Osos, CA 93402

Smith, Kathy *Misc*
PO Box 491433, Los Angeles, CA 90049 USA

Smith, Katie *Basketball Player*
Minnesola Lynx, Target Center, 600 1st Ave N, Minneapolis, MN 55403 USA

Smith, Keely
2705 Cricket Hollow Ct, Henderson, NV 89014-1924

Smith, Keely Shaye *Actor*
24955 Pacific Coast Hwy, Suite C-205, Malibu, CA 90265-4759 USA

Smith, Kellita *Actor*
Vincent Cirrincione Associates, 8721 Sunset Blvd #205, Los Angeles, CA 90069 USA

Smith, Ken *Architect*
80 Warren St, #28, New York, NY 10007 USA

Smith, Kenneth L *Basketball Player*
4042 Panama St, Pasadena, TX 77504 USA

Smith, Kerr *Actor*
Sharp Assoc, 8721 Sunset Blvd, Los Angeles, CA 90069 USA

Smith, Kevin *Actor, Producer, Director, Writer*
View Askew Productions, 69 Broad St, #B, Red Bank, NJ 07701 USA

Smith, Kurtwood *Actor*
1146 N Central Ave, #521, Glendale, CA 91202 USA

Smith, Lane *Actor*
Paradigm Agency, 10100 Santa Monica Blvd, #2500, Los Angeles, CA 90067 USA

Smith, Larry *Basketball Player*
4118 Waterview Court, Missouri City, TX 77459 USA

Smith, Lawrence Leighton
Louisville Symphony, 611 W Main St, Louisville, KY 40202 USA

Smith, Lee A *Baseball Player*
2124 Highway 507, Castor, LA 71016 USA

Smith, Lewis
8271 Melrose Ave. #110, Los Angeles, CA 90046

Smith, Liz *Writer*
William Morris Agency (WMA-LA), 1 William Morris Pl, Beverly Hills, CA 90212 USA

Smith, Lois *Actor*
Abrams Artists, 420 Madison Ave, #1400, New York, NY 10017 USA

Smith, Loren A *Judge*
US Claims Court, 717 Madison Place NW, Washington, DC 20439 USA

Smith, Louise *Race Car Driver*
12 Cartton Ave, Greenville, SC 29611 USA

Smith, Lovie *Football Player, Football Coach*
Chicago Bears, 1000 Football Dr, Lake Forest, IL 60045 USA

Smith, M Elizabeth (Liz) *Writer*
160 E 38th St, New York, NY 10016 USA

Smith, Madeline *Actor*
Joan Gray, Sunbury Island, Sunbury on Thames, Middx, UNITED KINGDOM (UK)

Smith, Maggie *Actor*
International Creative Mgmt, 76 Oxford St, London, W1N 0AX, UNITED KINGDOM (UK)

Smith, Margo *Musician, Songwriter*
PO Box 1169, Franklin, TN 37065 USA

Smith, Marilynn *Golfer*
2503 Bluebonnet Dr, Richardson, TX 75082 USA

Smith, Martha *Actor, Model*
9690 Heather Road, Beverly Hills, CA 90210 USA

Smith, Marvin (Smitty) *Musician*
Joel Chriss, 300 Mercer St, #3J, New York, NY 10003 USA

Smith, Melanie *Actor*
Innovative Artists, 1505 10th St, Santa Monica, CA 90401 USA

Smith, Michael Bailey *Actor*
Sharp/Karrys, 117 N Orlando Ave, Los Angeles, CA 90048 USA

Smith, Michael W *Musician, Songwriter*
GET Mgmt, 25 Music Square W, Nashville, TN 37203 USA

Smith, Mike *Cartoonist*
Las Vegas Sun, Editorial Dept, 2275 Corporate Circle Dr, Henderson, NV 89074 USA

Smith, Mike *Misc*
Names Project Foundation, 310 Townsend St, San Francisco, CA 94107 USA

Smith, Mindy *Musician, Songwriter*
Vanguard Records, 2700 Pennsylvania Ave, Santa Monica, CA 90404 USA

Smith, Moishe *Artist*
Utah State University, Art Dept, Logan, UT 84322 USA

Smith, Nicholas *Actor*
Michelle Braidman, 10/11 Lower John St, London, ENGLAND, W1R 3PE, UNITED KINGDOM (UK)

Smith, O C
1650 Broadway #508, New York, NY 10019 USA

Smith, O Guinn *Track Athlete*
2164 Hyde St, #306, San Francisco, CA 94109 USA

Smith, Orin R *Business Person*
Engelhard Corp, 101 Wood Ave S, Iselin, NJ 08830 USA

Smith, Orlando (Tubby) *Coach*
University of Kentucky, Athletic Dept, Lexington, KY 40536 USA

Smith, Osborne E (Ozzie) *Baseball Player, Sportscaster*
PO Box 164, Saint Albans, MO 63073 USA

Smith, Patti *Songwriter*
High Road, 751 Bridgeway, #300, Sausalito, CA 94965 USA

Smith, Paul *Fashion Designer*
Paul Smith Ltd, 43 Heard St, London, ENGLAND, WC2E 9DH

Smith, Paul B *Fashion Designer*
Paul Smith Ltd, 41/44 Floral St, Covent Garden, London, WC2E 9DG, UNITED KINGDOM (UK)

Smith, Putter
318 Fairview Ave., South Pasadena, CA 91030

Smith, Quinn *Actor*
1738 N Whitley Ave, Hollywood, CA 90028

Smith, R Jackson *Swimmer*
122 Palmers Hill Road, #3101, Stamford, CT 06902 USA

Smith, Ralph *Cartoonist*
King Features Syndicate, 888 7th Ave, New York, NY 10106 USA

Smith, Randy *Basketball Player*
1542 Amherst Ave, Buffalo, NY 14214 USA

Smith, Ray E *Religious Leader*
Open Bible Standard Churches, 2020 Bell Ave, Des Moines, IA 50315 USA

Smith, Raymond W *Financier, Business Person*
Rothschild North America, 1251 Ave of Americas, New York, NY 10020 USA

Smith, Rex *Actor*
16986 Encino Hills Dr, Encino, CA 91436 USA

Smith, Richard A *Publisher*
Harcourt general, 275 Washington St, Newton, MA 02458 USA

Smith, Richard M *Editor*
Newsweek Magazine, Editorial Dept, 251 W 57th St, New York, NY 10019 USA

Smith, Ricky *Musician, Reality TV Star*
American Idol, 7800 Beverly Blvd #251, Los Angeles, CA 90036 USA

Smith, Riley *Actor*
Innovative Artists (LA), 1505 Tenth St, Santa Monica, CA 90401 USA

Smith, Robert C (Bob) *Senator*
5768 Ferrara Dr, Sarasota, FL 34238 USA

Smith, Robert C *Editor*
TV Guide Magazine, Editorial Dept, 100 Matsonford Road, Radnor, PA 19080 USA

Smith, Robert Gray (Graysmith)
Cartoonist
San Francisco Chronicle, 901 Mission St, San Francisco, CA 94103 USA

Smith, Robert Lee *Musician*
Speer Entertainment Services, PO Box 49612, Atlanta, GA 30359 USA

Smith, Robert S *Football Player*
5668 Harrison Ave, Maple Heights, OH 44137 USA

Smith, Robyn *Jockey*
1155 San Ysidro Dr, Beverly Hills, CA 90210 USA

Smith, Rod *Football Player*
821 W 4th St, Charlotte, NC 28202 USA

Smith, Roger *Actor*
2707 Benedict Canyon Dr, Beverly Hills, CA 90210 USA

Smith, Roger Guenveur *Actor*
Wiliiam Morris Agency, 151 El Camino Dr, Beverly Hills, CA 90212 USA

Smith, Rolland *Commentator*
CBS-TV, News Dept, 524 W 57th St, New York, NY 10019 USA

Smith, Ron
7060 Hollywood Blvd. #1215, Los Angeles, CA 90028

Smith, Ronnie Ray *Track Athlete*
752 W Athens Blvd, Los Angeles, CA 90044 USA

Smith, Royce *Football Player*
404 S College St, Claxton, GA 30417 USA

Smith, Russell *Musician*
LC Media, PO Box 965, Antioch, TN 37011 USA

Smith, Sammi *Musician*
RR 4 Box 362, Bristow, OK 74010 USA

Smith, Shawnee *Actor*
Diverse Talent, 1875 Century Park E, #2250, Los Angeles, CA 90067 USA

Smith, Shawntel
PO Box 1620, Muldrow, OK 74918

Smith, Shelley *Actor*
4184 Colfax Ave, Studio City, CA 90212 USA

Smith, Siniin *Volleyball Player*
Assn of Volleyball Pros, 330 Washington Blvd, #400, Marina del Rey, CA 90292 USA

Smith, Stan
194 Bellevue Ave., Newport, RI 02840-3515

Smith, Stanley R (Stan) *Tennis Player*
ProServe, 1101 Woodrow Wilson Blvd, #1800, Arlington, VA 22209 USA

Smith, Steve *Producer*
S&S Productions, 212 King St W #205, Toronto ON, M5H 1K5, CANADA

Smith, Steven *Misc*
National Rural Letter Carriers Assn, 1630Duke St, Alexandria, VA 22314 USA

Smith, Steven D (Steve) *Basketball Player*
24 Champions Trail, San Antonio, TX 78258 USA

Smith, Steven L *Astronaut*
15728 Lake Lodge Dr, Houston, TX 77062 USA

Smith, Susan
Leath Correctional Institution, Leath Correctional Institution, 2809 Airport Rd, Greenwood, SC 29649

Smith, Taran *Actor*
Full Circle Mgmt, 12665 Kling St, North Hollywood, CA 91604 USA

Smith, Tasha *Actor*
Writers & Artists, 8383 Wilshire Blvd, #550, Beverly Hills, CA 90211 USA

Smith, Tommie *Track Athlete, Football Player*
13338 Lilac St, Chino, CA 91710 USA

Smith, Tony *Artist*
Pace Gallery, 32 E 57th St, New York, NY 10022 USA

Smith, Vernon L *Nobel Prize Laureate*
3830 9th St N, #PH 1E, Arlington, VA 22203 USA

Smith, Vince *Musician*
Process Talent Management, 439 Wiley Ave, Franklin, PA 16323 USA

Smith, Wallace B *Religious Leader*
Reorganized Church of Latter Day Saints, PO Box 1059, Independence, MO 64051 USA

Smith, Walter *Designer, Engineer*
Microsoft Corp, 1 Microsoft Way, Redmond, WA 98052 USA

Smith, Walter H F *Oceanographer*
Nat'l Oceanic/Atmospheric Administration, Commerce Dept, Washington, DC 20230 USA

Smith, Wilbur *Writer*
Charles Pick Constituency, 3 Bryanston Place, #3, London, W1H 7FN, UNITED KINGDOM (UK)

Smith, Will *Actor, Musician*
Overbrook Entertainment, 450 N Roxbury Dr Fl 4, Beverly Hills, CA 90210 USA

Smith, William *Actor*
3202 Anacapa St, Santa Barbara, CA 93105 USA

Smith, William D *Admiral*
7025 Fairway Oaks, Fayetteville, PA 17222 USA

Smith, William Jay *Writer*
62 Luther Shaw Road, RR 1 Box 151, Cummington, MA 01026 USA

Smith, William Y *General*
6541 Brooks Place, Falls Church, VA 22044 USA

Smith, Willie *Football Player*
Baltimore Ravens, Ravens Stadium, 11001 Russell St, Baltimore, MD 21230 USA

Smith, Yeardley *Actor*
Bresler Kelly Assoc, 11500 W Olympic Blvd, #510, Los Angeles, CA 90064 USA

Smith, Zadie *Writer*
Random House, 1745 Broadway, #B1, New York, NY 10019 USA

Smith Court, Margaret *Tennis Player*
21 Lewanna Way, City Beach, Perth, WA 6010, AUSTRALIA

Smith III, Emmitt J *Football Player*
15001 Winnwood Road, Dallas, TX 75254 USA

Smith Jr, John F (Jack) *Business Person*
General Motors Corp, 100 Renaissance Center, Detroit, MI 48243 USA

Smith Jr, Lonnie Liston *Musician*
Associated Booking Corp, 1995 Broadway, #501, New York, NY 10023 USA

Smith Jr, William (Bill) *Swimmer*
46-049 Alii Aneta Place, #1726, Kaneohe, HI 96744 USA

Smith Jr, William R *Lawyer*
1 Harbour Place, PO Box 3239, Tampa, FL 33601 USA

Smith Osborne, Madolyn *Actor*
United Talent Agency, 9560 Wilshire Blvd #500, Beverly Hills, CA 90212 USA

Smither, Beri *Model*
Flutie Entertainment, 270 Lafayette St, #1400, New York, NY 10012 USA

Smithers, William
2202 Anacapa St., Santa Barbara, CA 93105

Smithies, Oliver *Misc*
318 Urnstead Dr, Chapel Hill, NC 27516
USA

Smitrovich, Bill *Actor*
5075 Amestoy Ave, Encino, CA 91316
USA

Smitrovich, William *Actor*
Lighthouse Entertainment, 409 North
Camden Drive #202, Beverly Hills, CA
90210 USA

Smits, Jimmy *Actor*
El Sendero, PO Box 49922, Barrington
Station, Los Angeles, CA 90049 USA

Smogolski, Henry R *Financier*
Northwestern Savings & Loan, 2300 N
Western Ave, Chicago, IL 60647 USA

Smokie
Box 2711, Venlo, NETHERLANDS, NL-
5902 MA

Smolan, Rick *Photographer*
Workman Publishers, 708 Broadway, New
York, NY 10003 USA

Smolinski, Mark *Football Player*
3300 Country Club Road, Petoskey, MI
49770 USA

Smolka, James W *Misc*
PO Box 2123, Lancaster, CA 93539 USA

Smoltz, John A *Baseball Player*
5950 State Bridge Road, #H303, Duluth,
GA 30097 USA

Smoot, George F III *Physicist*
Lawrence Berkeley Laboratory, 1
Cyclotron Blvd, Berkeley, CA 94720 USA

Smothers, Dick *Actor, Comedian*
6442 Coldwater Canyon Ave, #107B,
North Hollywood, CA 91606 USA

Smothers, Tom *Actor, Comedian*
6442 Coldwater Canyon Ave, #107B,
North Hollywood, CA 91606 USA

Smothers Brothers, The *Comedian*
William Morris Agency (WMA-LA), 1
William Morris Pl, Beverly Hills, CA
90212 USA

Smuin, Michael *Ballerina, Choreographer*
Smuin Ballets, 1314 34th Ave, San
Francisco, CA 94122 USA

Smurfit, Victoria
76 Oxford St., London, ENGLAND, W1N
0AX

Smyl, Stan *Hockey Player*
202-130 W 5th St, North Vancouver, BC
V7M 1J8, CANADA

Smyth, Charles P *Misc*
245 Prospect Ave, Princeton, NJ 08540
USA

Smyth, Craig H *Historian*
Po Box 39, Cresskill, NJ 07626 USA

Smyth, Joe *Music Group, Musician*
Sawyer Brown Inc, 5200 Old Harding
Road, Franklin, TN 37064 USA

Smyth, Patty *Musician*
23712 Malibu Colony Road, Malibu, CA
90265 USA

Smyth, Randy *Yachtsman*
17136 Bluewater Lane, Huntington Beach,
CA 92649 USA

Smyth, Ryan *Hockey Player*
Newport Sports, 601-201 City Centre Dr,
Mississauga, ON L5B 2T4, CANADA

Smythe, Marcus
10635 Santa Monica Blvd. #130, Los
Angeles, CA 90025

Snapcase
PO Box 711966, Salt Lake City, UT 84171

Snead, J C
1751 Pinnacle Dr #1500, McLean, VA
22102 USA

Snead, Jesse Caryle (J C) *Golfer*
PO Box 782170, Wichita, KS 67278 USA

Snead, Norman B (Norm) *Football Player*
3951 Gulf Shore Blvd #303, Naples, FL
34103 USA

Snead, W T Sr *Religious Leader*
Baptist Convention Missionary, 1404 E
Firestone Blvd, Los Angeles, CA 90001
USA

Snedden, Stephen
1925 Century Park E. #750, Los Angeles,
CA 90067

Sneed, Floyd *Musician*
McKenzie Accountancy, 5171 Caliente St
#134, Las Vegas, NV 89119 USA

Sneed, Joseph T *Judge*
US Court of Appeals, Court Building, 95
7th St, San Francisco, CA 94103 USA

Snelder, Richard L *Diplomat*
211 Central Park West, New York, NY
10024 USA

Snell, Esmond E *Misc*
970 Aurora Ave #A202, Boulder, CO
80302 USA

Snell, Matthews (Matt) *Football Player*
Snell Construction, 175 Clendenny Ave,
Jersey City, NJ 07304 USA

Snell, Peter *Track Athlete*
6452 Dunston Lane, Dallas, TX 75214
USA

Sneva, Tom *Race Car Driver*
3301 E Valley Vista Lane, Paradise Valley,
AZ 85253 USA

Snicket, Lemony *Writer*
Harper Collins Publishers, 10 E 53rd St,
new York, NY 10022 USA

Snider, Dee *Musician*
Pooch, 9511 Weldon Circle #316, Fort
Lauderdale, FL 33321 USA

Snider, Edward M (Ed) *Hockey Player*
200 W Montgomery Ave, Ardmore, PA
19003 USA

Snider, Edwin D (Duke) *Baseball Player*
3037 Lakemont Dr, Fallbrook, CA 92028
USA

Snider, Mike
PO Box 140710, Nashville, TN 37214

Snider, R Michael *Scientist*
Pfizer Pharmaceuticals, Eastern Point
Road, Groton, CT 06340 USA

Snider, Todd *Musician, Music Group,
Songwriter*
Al Bunneta Mgmt, 33 Music Square W
#102B, Nashville, TN 37203 USA

Snipes, Wesley *Actor*
Nadashingha, PO Box 490, New York, NY
10014 USA

Snitzier, Larry *Musician*
Lindy Martin Mgmt, 5 Lob Lolly Court,
Pinehurst, NC 28374 USA

Snodgrass, William D *Writer*
3061 Hughes Road, Erieville, NY 13061
USA

Snoop Doggy Dog *Musician, Artist*
Firstars Mgmt, 14724 Ventura Blvd #PH,
Sherman Oaks, CA 91403 USA

Snow *Artist, Songwriter, Musician*
Hype Music, 2076 Sherobee Road #510,
Mississauga, ON L5A 4C4, CANADA

Snow, Brittany *Actor*
Innovative Artists (LA), 1505 Tenth St,
Santa Monica, CA 90401 USA

Snow, Eric *Basketball Player*
Philadelphia 76ers, 1st Union Center,
3601 S Broad St, Philadelphia, PA 19148
USA

Snow, Jack T *Football Player*
205 Los Lomas, Palm Desert, CA 92260
USA

Snow, Jack T (J T) *Baseball Player*
351 Fairfax Ave, San Mateo, CA 94402
USA

Snow, John W *Secretary*
Treasury Department, 1500 Pennsylvania
Ave NW, Washington, DC 20220 USA

Snow, Mark *Composer*
Gorfaine/Schwartz, 13245 Riverside Dr
#450, Sherman Oaks, CA 91423 USA

Snow, Michelle *Basketball Player*
Houston Comets, 2 Greenway Plaza
#400, Houston, TX 77046 USA

Snow, Percy L *Football Player*
2010 48th St NE, Canton, OH 44705 USA

Snow, Phoebe *Musician*
Day After Day, 2458 Zorada Dr, Los
Angeles, CA 90046 USA

Snow, Richard F *Editor*
American Heritage Magazine, Editorial
Dept, 60 5th Ave, New York, NY 10011
USA

Snowden, Alison *Writer*
Endeavor Agency LLC (LA), 9601 Wilshire
Blvd Fl 3, Beverly Hills, CA 90210 USA

**Snowden, Earl of (A C R Armstrong-
Jones)** *Photographer*
22 Launceston Place, London, W8 5RL,
UNITED KINGDOM (UK)

Snowden, Lisa *Model*
Susan Smith, 121A N San Vincente Blvd,
Beverly Hills, CA 90211 USA

Snowdon, Lord
22 Lauceston Pl, London, ENGLAND, W1

Snyder, Allan W *Scientist*
National University, Optical Science
Center, Canberra, ACT, 2601, AUSTRALIA

Snyder, Ben *Comedian*
Gersh Agency, The (LA), 232 N Canon Dr,
Beverly Hills, CA 90210 USA

Snyder, Bill *Football Coach*
Kansas State University, Athletic Dept,
Manhattan, KS 66506 USA

Snyder, Clayton *Actor*
Strong/Morrone Entertainment, 9100
Wilshire Blvd #503E, Beverly Hills, CA
90212 USA

Snyder, Daniel *Football Executive*
Washington Redskins, 21300 Redskin Park Drive, Ashburn, VA 20147 USA

Snyder, Dick *Basketball Player*
4621 E Mockingbird Lane, Paradise Valley, AZ 85253 USA

Snyder, Evan *Doctor*
Harvard Medical School, 25 Shattuck St, Boston, MA 02115 USA

Snyder, Fonda *Actor*
William Morris Agency (WMA-LA), 1 William Morris Pl, Beverly Hills, CA 90212 USA

Snyder, Gary S *Writer*
18442 MacNab Cypress Road, Nevada City, CA 95959 USA

Snyder, J Cory *Baseball Player*
696 S 1200 E, Mapleton, UT 84664 USA

Snyder, Joan *Artist*
Hirschi & Adler Modern, 21 E 70th St, New York, NY 10021 USA

Snyder, Joshua *Actor*
Amsel Eisenstadt & Frazier Inc, 5757 Wilshire Blvd #510, Los Angeles, CA 90036 USA

Snyder, Liza
121 N. San Vicente Blvd., Beverly Hills, CA 90211

Snyder, Solomon H *Doctor*
3801 Canterbury Road #1001, Baltimore, MD 21218 USA

Snyder, Suzanne *Actor*
Premiere Artists Agency, 1875 Century Park E #2250, Los Angeles, CA 90067 USA

Snyder, Tom *Commentator*
9536 Wilshire Blvd #500, Beverly Hills, CA 90212 USA

Snyder, William *Journalist*
508 Young St, Dallas, TX 75202 USA

Snyder, William D *Photographer, Journalist*
Dallas Morning News, Communivations Center, Editorial Dept, Dallas, TX 75265 USA

Snyder, Zack *Director, Writer*
Michael Black Management, 5750 Wilshire Blvd #640, Los Angeles, CA 90036 USA

Snyderman, Nancy *Doctor, Entertainer*
ABC-TV, News Dept, 77 W 66th St, New York, NY 10023 USA

So, Linda *Model*
6130 W Tropicana Blvd #280, Las Vegas, NV 89103

So Solid Crew *Music Group*
Mission Control Artists Agency, 50 City Business Centre, Lower Road, London, SE16 2XB, UNITED KINGDOM (UK)

Soares, Mario A N L *President*
Rue Dr Joao Soares #2-3, Lisbon, 1600, PORTUGAL

Sobel, Barry
9000 Sunset Blvd. #1200, Los Angeles, CA 90069

Sobers, Garfield S (Gary) *Cricketer*
Cricket Board, 9 Appleblossom, Petit Valley, Diego Martin, TRINIDAD

Sobieski, Leelee *Actor*
Kane Assoc, 125 2nd Ave #12, New York, NY 10003 USA

Soble, Ron *Actor*
Tyler Kjar, 4637 Willowcrest Ave, North Hollywood, CA 91602 USA

Sobule, Jill *Songwriter, Musician*
Evolution Talent, 1776 Broadway, #1500, New York, NY 10019 USA

Sochor, James (Jim) *Football Coach*
1018 Kent Dr, Davis, CA 95616 USA

Socolofsky, Shelley *Artist*
3285 Sumac Dr S, Salem, OR 97302 USA

Sodano, Angelo Cardinal *Religious Leader*
Office of Secretary of State, Palazzo Apostolico, 00120, VATICAN CITY

Soderbaum, Kristina
St.-Jakobs-platz 10 D-, Munich, GERMANY, 80331

Soderberg, E Loren *Photographer*
PO Box 313, Sausalito, CA 94966 USA

Soderbergh, Steven *Director*
4335 Emory Ave, Baton Rouge, LA 70808 USA

Soderstrom, Elisabeth *Opera Singer*
19 Hersbyvagen, Lidingo, 181 42, SWEDEN

Soderstrom, Elizabeth
19 Jersbyvagen, Lidingo, SWEDEN, 181-42

Sofaer, Abraham D *Lawyer*
120 Bryant St, Palo Alto, CA 94301 USA

Sofer, Rena *Actor*
Metropolitan Talent Agency, 4526 Wilshire Blvd, Los Angeles, CA 90010 USA

Sofie von Otter, Anne *Musician*
International Creative Management (ICM-LA), 8942 Wilshire Blvd, Beverly Hills, CA 90211 USA

Softley, Iain *Director*
32A Camaby St, London, W1V 1PA, UNITED KINGDOM

Sohmer, Steve
2625 Larmar Rd., Los Angeles, CA 90068

Sohn Kee-Chung *Track Athlete*
Korean Olympic Committee, International PO Box 1106, Seoul, SOUTH KOREA

Soklosky, Bing *Cinematographer*
4654 Cartwright Ave, Toluca Lake, CA 91602 USA

Sokol, Marilyn *Actor*
24 W 40th St #1700, New York, NY 10018 USA

Sokoloff, Louis *Misc*
National Mental Health Institute, 9000 Rockville Pike, Bethesda, MD 20892 USA

Sokoloff, Marla *Actor*
The Firm, 9100 Wilshire Blvd #100W, Beverly Hills, CA 90210 USA

Sokolov, Grigory L *Musician*
Trawick Artists, 1926 Broadway, New York, NY 10023 USA

Sokolove, James G *Lawyer*
1 Boston Place, Boston, MA 02108 USA

Sokomanu, A George *President*
Mele Village, PO Box 1319, Port Villa, VANUATU

Sokurov, Alexander N *Director*
Smolenskaya Nab 4 #222, Saint Petersburg, 199048, RUSSIA

Sol Hudson, Slash *Musician*
5664 Cahuenga Blvd #246, N Hollywood, CA 91601 USA

Solana Madariaga, Javier *Government Official*
European Union Foreign Office, Rue de la Loi, Brussels, 1048, BELGIUM

Solano, Jose *Actor*
House of Representatives, 400 S Beverly Dr #101, Beverly Hills, CA 90212 USA

Solars, Stephen
241 Dover St., Brooklyn, NY 11235

Solberg, Magnar *Athlete*
Stabellvn 60, Trondheim, 7000, NORWAY

Soleil, Stella *Music Group, Musician*
Kurfirst/Blackwell, 350 W End Ave #1A, New York, NY 10024 USA

Soler, Juan *Actor*
Televisa, Blvd Adolfo Lopez Mateos 232, Colonia San Angel INN, DF, CP 01060, MEXICO

Soleri, Paolo *Architect*
Cosanti Foundation, 6433 Doubletree Road, Scottsdale, AZ 85253 USA

Solh, Rashid *Prime Minister*
Chambre of Deputes, Place de I'Etoile, Beirut, LABANON

Solich, Frank *Football Coach*
University of Nebraska, Athletic Dept, Lincoln, NE 68588 USA

Solis, Christina
9300 Wilshire Blvd. #555, Beverly Hills, CA 90212

Sollscher, Goran *Musician*
Kunstleragentur Raab & Bohm, Plankengasse 7, Vienna, 1010, AUSTRIA

Soloman, Anthony M *Financier*
535 Park Ave, New York, NY 10021 USA

Soloman, Freddie *Football Player*
803 Turtle River Court, Plant City, FL 33567 USA

Solomon, Arthur K *Physicist*
27 Cragie St, Cambridge, MA 02138 USA

Solomon, Bruce
3518 Cahuenga Blvd. W. #316, Los Angeles, CA 90068

Solomon, David H *Scientist*
2103 Ridge Dr, Los Angeles, CA 90049 USA

Solomon, Edward I *Misc*
Stanford University, Chemistry Dept, Stanford, CA 94305 USA

Solomon, Harold *Tennis Player*
Int'l Mgmt Group, 1 Erieview Plaza, 1360 E 9th St #1300, Cleveland, OH 44114 USA

Solomon, Richard H *Scientist, Diplomat*
US Institute for Peace, 1200 17th St NW, #200, Washington, DC 20036 USA

Solomon, Susan *Misc*
National Oceanic & Atmospheric Admin, 325 Broadway, Boulder, CO 80305 USA

Solomon, Yonty *Musician*
56 Canonbury Park N, London, N1 2JT, UNITED KINGDOM (UK)

Solondz, Todd *Director, Writer*
Industry Entertainment, 955 Carillo Dr, #300, Los Angeles, CA 90048 USA

Soloviyev, Vladimir A *Cosmonaut*
Khovanskaya Ui D 3, Kv 28, Moscow, 129515, RUSSIA

Solovyev, Anatoli Y *Cosmonaut*
Potchta Kosmonavtov, Moskovskoi Oblasti, Syvisdny Goroduk, 141160, RUSSIA

Solovyev, Sergei A *Director, Writer*
Akademika Pilyugina Str 8, Korp 1 #330, Moscow, 11393, RUSSIA

Solow, Robert M *Nobel Prize Laureate*
528 Lewis Wharf, Boston, MA 02110 USA

Soloway, Jill *Producer*
International Creative Management (ICM-LA), 8942 Wilshire Blvd, Beverly Hills, CA 90211 USA

Soltan, Jerzy *Architect*
6 Shady Hill Square, Cambridge, MA 02138 USA

Soltau, Gordon (Gordy) *Football Player*
1290 Sharon Park Dr, Mento Park, CA 94025 USA

Soltau, Gordy
1111 Hamilton Ave, Palo Alto, CA 94301

Soluna *Music Group*
Creative Artists Agency LCC (CAA-LA), 9830 Wilshire Blvd, Beverly Hills, CA 90212 USA

Solvay, Jacques *Business Person*
Solvay Cie SA, Rue de Prince Albert 33, Brussels, 1050, BELGIUM

Solymosi, Zoltan *Dancer*
Royal Ballet, Covent GArden, Bow St, London, WC2E 9DD, UNITED KINGDOM (UK)

Solyom, Janos P *Musician*
Norr Malarstrand 54, VII, Stockholm, 11220, SWEDEN

Solzhenitsyn, Aleksandr I *Nobel Prize Laureate*
Farrar Straus Giroux, 19 Union Square W, New York, NY 10003 USA

Solzhenitsyn, Ignat *Musician*
Columbia Artists Mgmt Inc, 165 W 57th St, New York, NY 10019 USA

Somare, Michael T *Prime Minister*
Assembly House, Karan, Murik Lakes, East Sepik, PAPUA NEW GUINEA

Sombrotto, Vincent R *Misc*
National Letter Carriers Assn, 100 Indiana Ave NW, Washington, DC 20001 USA

Somerhalder, Ian *Actor*
1505 10th St, Santa monica, CA 90401 USA

Somers, Brett *Actor*
4 Willow Wall, Westport, CT 06880 USA

Somers, Gwen *Actor, Model*
Alice Fries Agency, 1927 Vista Del Mar Ave, Los Angeles, CA 90068 USA

Somers, Suzanne *Actor*
Port Carling Productions, 23679 Calabasas Rd, Suite 663, Calabasas, CA 91302 USA

Somerset, Willie *Basketball Player*
PO Box 314, Monmouth Junction, NJ 08852 USA

Somerville, Bonnie *Actor*
McKeon-Valeo Management, 9107 Wilshire Blvd #321, Beverly Hills, CA 90210 USA

Something Corporate *Music Group*
Agency for the Performing Arts (APA-LA), 9200 Sunset Blvd #900, Los Angeles, CA 90069 USA

Sommars, Julie *Actor*
S D B Partners, 1801 Ave of Stars, #902, Los Angeles, CA 90067 USA

Sommaruga, Cornelio *Misc*
International Red Cross, 19 Ave de la Paix, Genoa, 1202, SWITZERLAND

Sommer, Elke *Actor*
Atzelaberger Str 46, Marloffstein, D-91080, GERMANY

Sommers, Gordon L *Religious Leader*
Moravian Church Northem Province, 1021 Center St, bethlehem, PA 18018 USA

Sommers, Joanie *Musician*
Xentel, 900 SE 3rd Ave, #201, Fort Lauderdale, FL 33316 USA

Sommers, Stephen *Director*
William Morris Agency (WMA-LA), 1 William Morris Pl, Beverly Hills, CA 90212 USA

Sommore *Comedian*
International Creative Management (ICM-LA), 8942 Wilshire Blvd, Beverly Hills, CA 90211 USA

Somogyi, Jeannie R *Ballerina*
New York City Ballet, Lincoln Center plaza, New York, NY 10023 USA

Somogyi, Jozsef *Artist*
Marton Utca 3/5, Budapest, 1038, HUNGARY

Somorjai, Gabor A *Misc*
665 San Luis Road, Berkeley, CA 94707 USA

Sondeckis, Saulls *Conductor*
Ciurlionio 28, Vilnius, LITHUANIA

Sondheim, Stephen *Musician, Composer*
300 Park Ave #1700, New York, NY 10022 USA

Sondheim, Stephen J *Composer, Musician*
300 Park Ave, #1700, New York, NY 10022 USA

Song, Brenda *Actor*
Curtis Talent Management, 9607 Arby Dr, Beverly Hills, CA 90210 USA

Song, Xiaodong *Misc*
Columbia University, Lamont-Doherty Earth Observatory, New York, NY 10027 USA

Songaila, Antoinette *Astronomer*
University of Hawaii, Astronomy Dept, Honolulu, HI 96822 USA

Sonja *Royalty*
Det Kongelige Slott, Drammensveien 1, Oslo, 0010, NORWAY

Sonnenfeld, Barry *Director*
Endeavor Talent Agency, 9701 Wilshire Blvd, #1000, Beverly Hills, CA 90212 USA

Sonnenschein, Hugo F *Educator*
University of Chicago, President's Office, Chicago, IL 60637 USA

Sonnenschein, Klaus
Breisgauer Str. 15a, Berlin, GERMANY, D-14129

Sonnier, Jo-El *Musician*
Entertainment Artists, 2409 21st Ave S, #100, Nashville, TN 37212 USA

Sons of the Desert *Music Group*
William Morris Agency (WMA-TN), 2100 W End Ave #1000, Nashville, TN 37203 USA

Sons of the Pioneers
117 Berms Circle 45 #4, Branson, MO 65616-3744

Sonsini, Larry W *Lawyer*
Wilson Sonsini Goodrich Rosati, 650 Page Mill Road, Palo Alto, CA 94304 USA

Sontag, Susan *Writer*
470 W 24th St, New York, NY 10011 USA

Sophia *Royalty*
Palacio de la Zarzuela, Madrid, 28071, SPAIN

Sopko, Michael D *Business Person*
Inco Ltd, 145 King St W, Toronto, ON M5H 4B7, CANADA

Soraya *Musician*
Firstars Mgmt, 14724 Ventura Blvd, #PH, Sherman Oaks, CA 91403 USA

Sorbo, Kevin *Actor*
Mosaic Media Group, 9200 Sunset Blvd Fl 10, Los Angeles, CA 90069 USA

Sorel, Edward *Artist*
156 Franklin St, New York, NY 10013 USA

Sorel, Jean *Actor*
Cineart, 36 Rue de Ponthieu, Paris, 75008, FRANCE

Sorel, Louise *Actor*
10808 Lindbrook Dr, Los Angeles, CA 90024 USA

Sorensen, Jacki F *Misc*
Jacki's Inc, 129 1/2 N Woodland Blvd, #5, Deland, FL 32720 USA

Sorensen, Theodore C *Attorney General, Government Official*
Paul Weiss Rifkind Assoc, 1285 Ave of Americas, New York, NY 10019 USA

Sorenson, Dave *Basketball Player*
19000 Lake Road #723, Rock River, OH 44116 USA

Sorenson, Heidi *Actor, Model*
Shelly & Pierce, 13775A Mono Way #220, Sonora, CA 95370 USA

Sorenson, Paul *Actor*
11802 Lindbrook Dr, Los Angeles, CA 90024 USA

Sorenson, Richard K *War Hero*
3393 Skyline Blvd, Reno, NV 89509 USA

Sorenson, Theodore
1285 Ave. of the Americas, New York, NY 10019

Sorenstam, Annika *Golfer*
Int'l Mgmt Group, 1 Erieview Plaza, 1360
E 9th St #1300, Cleveland, OH 44114
USA

Sorgers, Jana *Athlete*
Potsdamer RG, An Der Pirschheide,
Potsdam, 14471, GERMANY

Soriano, Alfonso *Baseball Player*
New York Yankees, Yankee Stadium,
161st Street & River Avenue, Bronx, NY
10451 USA

Soriano, Alfonso G *Baseball Player*
Texas Rangers, 1000 Ballpark Way,
Arlington, TX 76011 USA

Soriano, Edward *General*
Vice Commander, I Corps/Fort Lewis, Fort
Lewis, WA 98433 USA

Sorkin, Aaron *Writer, Producer*
Endeavor Talent Agency, 9701 Wilshire
Blvd #1000, Beverly Hills, CA 90212 USA

Sorkin, Arleen *Actor*
623 S Beverly Glen Blvd, Los Angeles, CA
90024 USA

Sorlie, Donald M *Misc*
14612 44th Ave NW, Gig Harbor, WA
98332 USA

Sorokin, Peter P *Physicist*
5 Ashwood Road, South Salem, NY 10590
USA

Soros, George *Financier*
Soros Fund Mgmt, 888 7th Ave, #3300,
New York, NY 10106 USA

Soroya, Princess
Ave. Montaigne, Paris, FRANCE, 75008

Sorrento, Paul A *Baseball Player*
5918 Mont Blance Place NW, Issaquah,
WA 98027 USA

Sorsa, T Kalevi *Prime Minister*
Hakaniemenranta 16D, Helsinki, 00530,
FINLAND

Sorte, Maria *Actor*
Televisa, Blvd Adolfo Lopez Mateos 232,
Colonia San Angel INN, DF, CP 01060,
MEXICO

Sorvino, Mira *Actor*
200 Park Ave S, #800, New York, NY
10003 USA

Sorvino, Paul *Actor*
110 E 87th St, New York, NY 10128 USA

Sosa, Mercedes *Songwriter, Musician*
Blue Moon Art Mgmt, 270 Ave of
Americas, New York, NY 10014 USA

Sosa, Samuel (Sammy) *Baseball Player*
505 N Lake Shore Dr, #5500, Chicago, IL
60611 USA

Sossaman, Shannyn *Actor*
Dash Group, The, 550 North Larchmont
Blvd, Suite 201, Los Angeles, CA 90004
USA

Sossamon, Shannyn *Actor*
550 N Larchmont Blvd, #201, Los
Angeles, CA 90004 USA

Soter, Paul *Comedian*
United Talent Agency (UTA), 9560
Wilshire Blvd, Beverly Hills, CA 90212
USA

Sotin, Hans *Opera Singer*
Schulheide 10, Bendestorf, 21227,
GERMANY

Sotirhos, Michael A *Diplomat*
American Embassy, A Leoforos Vassilisis
Sofias 91, Athens, 106 60, GREECE

Sotkilava, Zurab L *Opera Singer*
Bolshoi Theater, Teatralnaya Pi 1,
Moscow, 103009, RUSSIA

Soto, Freddy *Comedian*
Brillstein-Grey Entertainment, 9150
Wilshire Blvd #350, Beverly Hills, CA
90212 USA

Soto, Gabriel *Actor*
Televisa, Blvd Adolfo Lopez Mateos 232,
Colonia San Angel INN, DF, CP 01060,
MEXICO

Soto, Jock *Dancer*
New York City Ballet, Lincoln Center
Plaza, New York, NY 10023 USA

Soto, Mario M *Baseball Player*
Joachs-Lachaustegui #42, Sur-Bani,
DOMINICAN REPUBLIC

Soto, Talisa *Actor, Model*
Flick East-West, 9057 Nerno St, #A, West
Hollywood, CA 90069 USA

Sotomayor, Antonio *Artist*
3 LeRoy Place, San Francisco, CA 94109
USA

Sotomayor Sanabria, Javier *Track Athlete*
Int'l Mgmt Group, 1 Erieview Plaza, 1360
E 9th St #1300, Cleveland, OH 44114
USA

Sottsass Jr, Ettore *Designer*
Via Manzoni 14, Milan, 20121, ITALY

Souchak, Mike *Golfer*
79 Pelican Place, Belleair, FL 33756 USA

Soul, David *Actor, Musician*
Innovative Artists, 1505 10th St, Santa
Monica, CA 90401 USA

Soul Asylum
955 S. Carrillo Dr. #300, Los Angeles, CA
90048

Soul II Soul *Music Group*
Profile Artists Agency, Unit 10, J Block,
Tower Bridge Business Complex, 110
Clements Road, London, SE16 4DG,
United Kingdom

Soulages, Pierre *Artist*
18 Rue des Trois-Portes, Paris, 75005,
FRANCE

SoulDecision *Music Group*
SL Feldman & Associates, 1505 W 2nd
Ave #200, Vancouver BC, V6H 3Y,
CANADA

Soundarya *Actor, Bollywood*
Bangalore, KA, INDIA

Sousa, Mauricio de *Cartoonist*
Mauricio de Sousa Producoes, Rua do
Curtume 745, Sao Paulo SP, BRAZIL

Soutar, Dave *Bowler*
6910 Chickasaw Falls Ave, Bradenton, FL
34203 USA

Soutar, Judy *Bowler*
3914 102nd Place N, Clearwater, FL
33762 USA

Soutendijk, Renee *Actor*
Marion Rosenberg, PO Box 69826, West
Hollywood, CA 90069 USA

Souter, David H *Judge*
US Supreme Court, 1 1st St NE,
Washington, DC 20543 USA

South, Joe *Songwriter, Musician*
3051 Claremont Road NE, Atlanta, GA
30329 USA

South, Leonard J *Cinematographer*
6208 Orion Ave, Van Nuys, CA 91411
USA

South, Mike
PO Box 1288, Tucker, GA 30084

Souther, J D *Songwriter, Musician*
8263 Hollywood Dr, Los Angeles, CA
90069 USA

Southern, Silas (Eddie) *Track Athlete*
1045 Rosewood Dr, Desoto, TX 75115
USA

Southern Belles
11150 W. Olympic Blvd. #1100, Los
Angeles, CA 90064

Souza, Francis N *Artist*
148 W 67th St, New York, NY 10023
USA

Souzay, Gerard M *Opera Singer*
26 Rue Freycinet, Paris, 75116, FRANCE

Sova, Peter M *Cinematographer*
1492 Roses Brook Road, South Kortright,
NY 13842 USA

Sovern, Michael I *Educator*
Columbia University, Law School, 435 W
116th St, New York, NY 10027 USA

Sovey, William P *Business Person*
Newell Co, 20 E Milwaukee St #212,
Janesville, WI 53545 USA

Sowell, Arnold (Arnie) *Track Athlete*
1647 Waterstone Lane, #1, Charlotte, NC
28262 USA

Sowell, Thomas *Economist*
Stanford University, Hoover Institution,
Stanford, CA 94305 USA

Soyer, David *Musician*
PO Box 307, Brattleboro, VT 05302 USA

Soyinka, Wole *Nobel Prize Laureate*
University of Nevada, Creative Writing
Dept, Las Vegas, NV 89154 USA

Soyster, Harry E *General*
4706 Duncan Dr, Annandale, VA 22003
USA

Spaak, Catherine
Viale Parioli 59, Rome, ITALY, 00197

Spacek, Jaroslav *Hockey Player*
Columbus Blue Jackets, Arena, 200 W
Nationwide Blvd, Columbus, OH 43215
USA

Spacek, Sissy *Actor*
Beau Val Farm, Box 22 #640, Cobham,
VA 22929 USA

Spacey, Kevin *Actor*
Trigger Street Productions, 755A N La
Cienega Blvd, Los Angeles, CA 90069
USA

Spaddky, Boris V *Misc*
State Committee for Sports, Skatertny
Pereulok 4, Moscow, RUSSIA

Spade, David *Actor, Comedian*
International Creative Mgmt, 8942 Wilshire Blvd, #219, Beverly Hills, CA 90211 USA

Spade, Kate *Fashion Designer*
Kate Spade LLC, 48 W 25th St Fl 4, New York, NY 10010 USA

Spader, James *Actor*
International Creative Management (ICM-LA), 8942 Wilshire Blvd, Beverly Hills, CA 90211 USA

Spafford, Eugene *Educator*
Purdue University, Education Research Center, West Lafayette, IN 47907 USA

Spagnola, John S *Football Player*
414 Hillbrook Road, Bryn Mawr, PA 19010 USA

Spahn, Ryan *Actor*
Stein Entertainment Group, 11271 Ventura Blvd #477, Studio City, CA 91604 USA

Spahr, Charles E *Business Person*
800 Beach Road, Vero Beach, FL 32963 USA

Spain, Douglas *Actor*
Innovative Artists, 1505 10th St, Santa Monica, CA 90401 USA

Spali, Timothy *Actor*
Markham & Froggatt, Julian House, 4 Windmill St, London, W1P 1HF, UNITED KINGDOM (UK)

Spall, Timothy *Actor*
Markham and Froggatt Agency, 4 Windmill St, London, W1T 2H, England

Spanarkel, Jim *Basketball Player*
436 Edgewood Place, Rutherford, NJ 07070 USA

Spander, Art *Writer*
San Francisco Examiner, Editorial Dept, 110 5th Ave, San Francisco, CA 94118 USA

Spanger, Amy *Actor*
New Wave Entertainment (LA), 2660 W Olive Blvd, Burbank, CA 91505 USA

Spanic, Gabriela *Actor*
Televisa, Blvd Adolfo Lopez Mateos 232, Colonia San Angel INN, DF, CP 01060, MEXICO

Spanjers, Martin *Actor*
8 Simple Rules for Dating My Teenage Daughter, 500 S Buena Vista, Stage 6 Fl 5, Burbank, CA 91521

Spano, Joe *Actor*
EC Assoc, 10315 Woodley Ave, #110, Granada Hills, CA 91344 USA

Spano, Robert *Musician*
International Creative Management (ICM-LA), 8942 Wilshire Blvd, Beverly Hills, CA 90211 USA

Spano, Vincent *Actor*
More/Medavoy, 7920 W Sunset Blvd, #400, Los Angeles, CA 90046 USA

Spark, Muriel S *Writer*
David Higham, 5-8 Lower John St, Golden Square, London, W1R 4H4, UNITED KINGDOM (UK)

Sparks
106 N. Buffalo St. #200, Warsaw, IN 46580

Sparks, Dana *Actor*
VOX, 5670 Wilshire Blvd, #820, Los Angeles, CA 90036 USA

Sparks, Hal *Actor, Comedian, Musician*
Writers & Artists, 8383 Wilshire Blvd, #550, Beverly Hills, CA 90211 USA

Sparks, Hayley
5757 Wilshire Blvd. #512, Los Angeles, CA 90036

Sparks, Kylie *Actor*
Myrna Lieberman Management, 3001 Hollyridge Drive, Hollywood, CA 90068 USA

Sparks, Mike *Referee*
World Wrestling Entertainment (WWE), 1241 E Main St, Stamford, CT 06905 USA

Sparks, Nicholas *Writer*
Warner Books, 1271 Ave of Americas, New York, NY 10020 USA

Sparlis, Alexander (Al) *Football Player*
13206 Mindanao Way, Marina del Rey, CA 90292 USA

Sparv, Camilla *Actor*
957 Cole Ave, Los Angeles, CA 90038 USA

Spassky, Boris
Skatertny Pereulok 5, Moscow, CA RUSSIA

Speakman-Pitt, William *War Hero*
Victoria Cross Assn, Old Admiralty Building, London, SW1A 2BL, UNITED KINGDOM (UK)

Speaks, Ruben L *Religious Leader*
African Methodist Episcopal Zion Church, PO Box 32843, Charlotte, NC 28232 USA

Spear, Laurinda H *Architect*
Arquitectonica International, 550 Brickell Ave, #200, Miami, FL 33131 USA

Spears, Aries *Actor*
International Creative Management (ICM-LA), 8942 Wilshire Blvd, Beverly Hills, CA 90211 USA

Spears, Billie Jo *Musician*
PO Box 23470, Nashville, TN 37202 USA

Spears, Billy Jo *Musician*
2802 Columbine Place, Nashville, TN 37204

Spears, Britney *Musician, Actor*
Rudolph & Beer, 432 Park Ave S, New York, NY 10016 USA

Spears, William D *Football Player*
63 Waterbridge Place, Ponte Vedra Beach, FL 32082 USA

Specter, Arlen *Senator*
310 Spruce St, Scranton, PA 18503-1413 USA

Spector, Elisabeth (Lisa) *Government Official*
Resolution Trust Corp, 801 17th St NW, Washington, DC 20232 USA

Spector, Phil *Business Person, Songwriter*
686 S Arroyo Parkway, #175, Pasadena, CA 91105 USA

Spector, Ronnie *Musician*
Absolute Artists, 8490 W Sunset Blvd, #403, West Hollywood, CA 90069 USA

Speech *Musician, Artist*
William Morris Agency, 1325 Ave of Americas, New York, NY 10019 USA

Speed, Lake *Race Car Driver*
4027 Old Salisbury Road, Kannapolis, NC 28083 USA

Speed, Lizz *Producer*
Jackoway Tyerman Wertheimer Austen Mandelbaum & Morris, 1888 Century Park E Fl 18, Los Angeles, CA 90067 USA

Speedman, Scott *Actor*
Endeavor Agency LLC (LA), 9601 Wilshire Blvd Fl 3, Beverly Hills, CA 90210 USA

Speedwagon, REO *Musician*
Creative Artists Agency LCC (CAA-LA), 9830 Wilshire Blvd, Beverly Hills, CA 90212 USA

Speers, Ted *Hockey Player*
61515 Brookway Dr, South Lyon, MI 48178-7056

Speier, Chris E *Baseball Player*
6240 30th Place, Phoeniz, AZ 85016 USA

Speight, Lester (Rasta) *Actor*
Endeavor Agency LLC (LA), 9601 Wilshire Blvd Fl 3, Beverly Hills, CA 90210 USA

Speir, Chris
6114 E. Montecito, Scottsdale, AZ 85251

Speiser, Jerry *Musician*
TPA, PO Box 124, Round Corner, NSW, AUSTRALIA

Speler, Justin *Baseball Player*
Colorado Rockies, Coors Field, 2001 Blake Street, Denver, CO 80205 USA

Spelke, Elizabeth S *Doctor*
Harvard University, Psychology Dept, Cambridge, MA 02138 USA

Spelling, Aaron *Producer*
Aaron Spelling Productions, 5700 Wilshire Blvd, #575, Los Angeles, CA 90036 USA

Spelling, Randy *Actor*
Aaron Spelling Productions, 5700 Wilshire Blvd, #575, Los Angeles, CA 90036 USA

Spelling, Tori *Actor*
594 N Mapleton Dr, Los Angeles, CA 90024 USA

Spellman, Alonzo R *Football Player*
1300 Marigold Way, Pflugerville, TX 78660 USA

Spellman, John D *Governor*
7048 51st Ave NE, Seattle, WA 98115 USA

Spelvin, Georgina
3121 Ledgewood Dr, Hollywood, CA 90060

Spence, A Michael *Nobel Prize Laureate*
768 Mayfield Ave, Stanford, CA 94305 USA

Spence, Dave *Misc*
Horseshores Union, RR 2 Box 71C, Englishtown, NJ 07726 USA

Spence, Gerry *Lawyer*
Spence Moriarity Schuster, 15 South Jackson Street, Jackson, WY 83001 USA

Spence, Jonathan D *Historian, Writer*
691 Forest Road, West Haven, CT 06516 USA

Spence, Roger F *Religious Leader*
Reformed Episcopal Church, 2001 Jackson St, Jackson, WY 83001 USA

Spence, Sebastian *Actor*
1005 Cambie St, Vancouver, BC V6B 5L7, CANADA

Spencer, Bud *Actor*
Mistral Film Group, Via Archmede 24, Rome, 00187, ITALY

Spencer, Chris
10100 Santa Monica Blvd. #2490, Los Angeles, CA 90067

Spencer, Danielle *Actor*
Robert Barnham Mgmt, 432 Tygarah Road, Myocum, NSW, 2481, AUSTRALIA

Spencer, Daryl
2740 Larkin Dr., Wichita, KS 67216

Spencer, Earl Charles
Althorpe House Gr. Brington, Northamptonshire, ENGLAND, NN7 4HQ

Spencer, Elizabeth *Writer*
402 Longleaf Dr, Chapel Hill, NC 27517 USA

Spencer, Elmore *Basketball Player*
1770 Foxlair Trail, Atlanta, GA 30349 USA

Spencer, F Gilman *Editor*
Denver Post, Editorial Dept, 1560 Broadway, Denver, CO 80202 USA

Spencer, Felton *Basketball Player*
New York Knicks, Madison Square Garden, 2 Penn Plaza, New York, NY 10121 USA

Spencer, Frank Cole *Doctor, Educator*
560 1st Ave, New York, NY 10016 USA

Spencer, Jesse *Actor*
RGM Associates (Australia), PO Box 128, Surry Hills NSW, 2010, AUSTRALIA

Spencer, Jimmy *Race Car Driver*
18326 Mainsail Pointe Dr, Huntersville, NC 28078 USA

Spencer, John *Misc, Athlete*
17 Knowles St, Radcliffe, Lancs, M26 0DN, UNITED KINGDOM (UK)

Spencer, Melvin J *Religious Leader, Attorney General*
5910 N Shawnee Ave, Oklahoma City, OK 73112 USA

Spencer, Octavia *Actor*
Greene & Associates, 526 N Larchmont Blvd #201, Los Angeles, CA 90004 USA

Spencer, Roderick
602 Bay St., Santa Monica, CA 90405

Spencer, Susan *Commentator*
CBS-TV, News Dept, 2020 M St NW, Washington, DC 20036 USA

Spencer, Timothy (Tim) *Football Player*
1435 Sherborne Lane, Powell, OH 43065 USA

Spencer, Tracie *Musician*
Rogers & Cowan, 6340 Breckenridge Run, Rex, GA 30273 USA

Spencer-Churchill, Victor
6 Cumberland Geo. St., London, ENGLAND, W1

Spencer-Devlin, Muffin *Golfer*
Linda Stoick, 425 California St, #1900, San Francisco, CA 94104 USA

Spender, Percy C *Judge*
Headingley House, 11 Wellington St Woolhara, Sydney, NSW, 2025, AUSTRAILIA

Sperber, Wendie Jo *Actor*
Bresler Kelly Assoc, 11500 W Olympic Blvd, #510, Los Angeles, CA 90064 USA

Sperber Carter, Paula *Bowler*
9895 SW 96th St, Miami, FL 33176 USA

Spergel, David *Misc*
Princeton University, Astrophysicist Dept, Princeton, NJ 08544 USA

Sperling, Gene *Politician, Government Official*
National Economic Council, 1600 Pennsylvania Ave NW, Washington, DC 20506 USA

Spero, Nancy
530 La Guardia Place, New York, NY 10012 USA

Spheeris, Penelope *Director*
PO Box 1128, Studio City, CA 91614 USA

Spice
338 N. Foothill Rd., Beverly Hills, CA 90210

Spice 1 *Artist, Musician*
JL Entertainment, 18653 Ventura Blvd #340, Tarzana, CA 91356 USA

Spice Girls
35 Parkgate Rd. #32 Ransome Dock, London, ENGLAND, SW11 4NP

Spicer III, William E *Physicist*
785 Mayfield Road, Palo Alto, CA 94305 USA

Spidia, Vladimir *Prime Minister*
Kancelar Presidenta Republiky, Hradecek, Prague 1, 119 08, CZECH REPUBLIC

Spidlik, Tomas Cardinal *Religious Leader*
Society of Jesus, Borgo S Spirito 4, CP 6139, Rome-Prati, 00195, ITALY

Spiegel, Henry W *Economist*
6848 Nashville Road, Lanham Seabrook, MD 20706 USA

Spiegelman, Art *Writer*
Raw Books & Graphics, 27 Greene St, New York, NY 10013 USA

Spielberg, David *Actor*
10537 Cushdon Ave, Los Angeles, CA 90064 USA

Spielberg, Steven *Director, Producer*
DreamWorks SKG, 100 Universal City Plaza, Universal City, CA 91608 USA

Spielman, C Christopher (Chris) *Football Player, Sportscaster*
2094 Edgemont Road, Columbus, OH 43212 USA

Spier, Peter E *Artist*
PO Box 566, Shoreham, NY 11786 USA

Spier, Wolfgang
Kaiserdamm 98, Berlin, GERMANY, 14057

Spiers, Judi
1-3 Charlotte St., London, ENGLAND, W1P 1HD

Spiers, Ronald I *Diplomat*
1176 Middletown Road, South Londonderry, VT 05155 USA

Spikes, Jack E *Football Player*
9537 Highland View Dr, Dallas, TX 75238 USA

Spikes, Takeo *Football Player*
3475 Oak Valley Road NE, #130, Atlanta, GA 30326 USA

Spilker, Angela
425 N. Oakhurst Dr., Beverly Hills, CA 90210

Spillane, Mickey *Writer, Actor*
PO Box 265, Murrells Inlet, SC 29576 USA

Spiller, Michael A *Cinematographer*
2418 Roscornare Road, Los Angeles, CA 90077 USA

Spin Doctors, The
83 Riverside Dr., New York, NY 10024

Spinal Tap *Music Group*
Harriet Sternberg Management, 4530 Gloria Avenue, Encino, CA 91436 USA

Spindt, Capp *Inventor*
SRI International, 333 Ravenswood Ave, Menlo Park, CA 94025 USA

Spinella, Stephen *Actor*
William Morris Agency, 1325 Ave of Americas, New York, NY 10019 USA

Spiner, Brent *Actor*
Essential Talent Management, 6399 Wilshire Blvd #400, Los Angeles, CA 90048 USA

Spinetta, Jean-Cyril *Business Person*
Group Air France, 45 Rue de Paris, Roissy CDG Cedex, 95747, FRANCE

Spinetti, Victor *Actor*
15 Devonshire Place, Brighton, Sussex, UNITED KINGDOM (UK)

Spinks, Leon *Boxer*
209 Jones St, Holister, MO 65672 USA

Spinks, Michael *Boxer*
1240 Chateau Ave, Saint Louis, MO 63103 USA

Spinners, The
65 W. 55th St. #6C, New York, NY 10019

Spinotti, Dante *Cinematographer*
Smith/Gosnell/Nicholson, PO Box 1156, Studio City, CA 91614 USA

Spiro, Lev L *Director*
Endeavor Agency LLC (LA), 9601 Wilshire Blvd Fl 3, Beverly Hills, CA 90210 USA

Spirtas, Kevin *Actor*
Stone Manners Talent Agency, 6500 Wilshire Blvd, Ste 550, Los Angeles, CA 90048 USA

Spittka, Marko *Athlete*
Judo Club 90, Zielona-Gora-Str 9, Frankfurt/Ober, 15230, GERMANY

Spitz, Mark A *Swimmer*
383 Dalehurst Ave, Los Angeles, CA 90024 USA

Spitzer, Robert *Psychic, Doctor*
Columbia University, Psychiatry School, New York, NY 10027 USA

Spivakov, Vladmir T *Musician*
Vspolny Per 17, #14, Moscow, RUSSIA

Spizzirri, Angelo *Actor*
Metropolitan Talent Agency, 4526 Wilshire Blvd, Los Angeles, CA 90010 USA

Splatt, Rachel *Race Car Driver*
12629 N Tatum Blvd, #184, Phoenix, AZ
85032 USA

Split Ends
136 New Kings Rd., London, ENGLAND,
SW6

Splittorff Jr, Paul W *Baseball Player*
4204 Hickory Lane, Blue Springs, MO
64015 USA

Spohr, Arnold T *Director*
Royal Winnipeg Ballet, 380 Graham Ave,
Winnipeg, MB R3C 4K2, CANADA

Spoiler, The
3615 W. Waters Box 110, Tampa, FL
33614

Sponenburgh, Mark *Artist*
5562 NW Pacific Coast Highway, Seal
Rock, OR 97376 USA

Spong, John S *Religious Leader*
24 Puddingdtone Road, Morris Plains, NJ
07950 USA

Spooner, John *Writer, Financier*
Houghton Miffin, 222 Berkeley St, #700,
Boston, MA 02116 USA

Spoonhour, Charles (Charlie) *Coach*
University of Nevada, Athletic Dept, Las
Vegas, NV 89154 USA

Sporkin, Stanley *Government Official,
Judge*
US District Court, Courthouse, 3rd &
Constitution NW, Washington, DC 20001
USA

Sporleder, Gregory *Actor*
Don Buchwald & Associates Inc (LA),
6500 Wilshire Blvd #2200, Los Angeles,
CA 90048 USA

Spottiswoode, Roger *Director*
132 Spaulding Dr, #217, Beverly Hills, CA
90212 USA

Spound, Michael *Actor*
James/Levy/Jacobson, 3500 W Olive Ave,
#1470, Burbank, CA 91505 USA

Spradlin, Danny *Football Player*
1011 Laurie St, Maryville, TN 37803 USA

Spradlin, G D *Actor*
La Familia Ranch, PO Box 1294, San Luis
Obispo, CA 93406 USA

Spratlan, Lewis *Composer*
Amherst College, Music Dept, Amherst,
MA 01002 USA

Sprayberry, James M *War Hero*
426 Holiday Dr, Titus, AL 36080 USA

Sprewell, Latrell *Basketball Player*
4340 Purchase St, Purchase, NY 10577
USA

Spring, Sherwood C *Astronaut*
5427 Point Longstreet Way, Burke, VA
22015 USA

Springer, Jerry *Entertainer, Misc*
454 N Columbus Dr #200, Chicago, IL
60611 USA

Springer, Michael *Golfer*
1482 E Forest Oaks Dr, Fresno, CA 93720
USA

Springer, Robert C *Astronaut*
202 Village Dr, Sheffield, AL 35660 USA

Springfield, Rick *Musician, Actor*
Ron Weisner, 515 Ocean Ave, Santa
Monica, CA 90402 USA

Springs, Alice *Photographer*
7 Ave Saint-Ramon #T1008, Monte Carlo,
MONACO

Springs, Shawn *Football Player*
Washington Redskins, 21300 Redskin Park
Dr, Ashbum, VA 20147 USA

Springsteen, Bruce *Musician, Songwriter*
1224 Benedict Canyon Dr, Beverly Hills,
CA 90210 USA

Sprinkel, Beryl W *Government Official*
20140 Saint Andrews Dr, Olympia Fields,
IL 60461 USA

Sprinkle, Edward A (Ed) *Football Player*
3 Saint Moritz Dr, Palos Park, IL 60464
USA

Sprouse, Cole *Actor*
Evolution Entertainment, 901 N Highland
Ave, Los Angeles, CA 90038 USA

Sprouse, Dylan *Actor*
Evolution Entertainment, 901 N Highland
Ave, Los Angeles, CA 90038 USA

Sprouse, James M *Judge*
US Court of Appeals, PO Box 401, 122 N
Court St, Lewisburg, WV 24901 USA

Spurrier, Paul
Beccles Rd. 47, Lowestoft/Norfolk,
ENGLAND

Spurrier, Stephen O (Steve) *Football
Player, Football Coach*
17050 Silver Charm Pl, Leesburg, VA
20176 USA

Spurrior, Stephen O (Steve) *Football
Player, Coach*
17050 Silver Charm Place, Leesburg, VA
20176 USA

Spuzich, Sandra *Golfer*
Ladies Pro Golf Assn, 100 International
Gold Dr, Daytona Beach, FL 32124 USA

Spyro Gyro
200 W. Superior #202, Chicago, IL 60610

Squier, Billy *Musician, Songwriter*
PO Box 231251, New York, NY 10023
USA

Squierek, Jack *Football Player*
4051 Vezbar Dr, Seven Hills, OH 44131
USA

Squirrel Nut Zippers
2756 N. Green Valley Parkway #449, Las
Vegas, CA 89014-2100

Squyres, Steven W *Scientist*
Comell University, Planetary Science
Dept, Ithaca, NY 14853 USA

SR-71 *Music Group*
Jeff Hanson Management & Promotions,
2813 South Hiwassee Road, #307,
Orlando, FL 32835 USA

Sranowski, Wally
Mill Rd., Toronto, CANADA, Ont M9C 1Y

Srb, Adrian M *Misc*
411 Cayuga Heights Road, Ithaca, NY
14850 USA

Sri Chinmoy *Religious Leader*
85-45 Sri Chinmoy St, Jamaica, NY 11432
USA

Sridevi *Actor, Bollywood*
Green Acres, 7 Bungalows Lokhandwala
Complex Andheri(W), Mumbai, 400058,
MS INDIA

Sridevi *Actor, Bollywood*
1 Bishop Wallers South Avenue, C I T
Colony, Chennai, TN 600004, INDIA

Sripriya *Actor, Bollywood*
10 Muthu Pandian Avenue, Santhome,
Chennai, TN 600004, INDIA

Srividhya *Actor, Bollywood*
22 North Street, Sriram Nagar, Chennai,
TN 600018, INDIA

St, Clair Carl
Pacific Symphony Orchestra, 1231 E Dyer
Road, Santa Ana, CA 92705 USA

St Clair, Bob *Football Player*
PO Box 750369, Petaluma, CA 94975-
0369

St Clair, Robert B (Bob) *Football Player*
Clover Stornetta Farms, PO Box 750369,
Petaluma, CA 94975 USA

St Florian, Friedrich G *Architect*
Rhode Island School of Design,
Architecture Dept, Providence, RI 02903
USA

St George, William R *Admiral*
862 San Antonio Place, San Diego, CA
92106 USA

St James, Lyn *Race Car Driver*
LSJ Racing, 57 Gasoline Alley, #D,
Indianapolis, IN 46222 USA

St James, Rebecca *Musician, Actor*
Richard De La Font Agency, 4845 S
Sheridan Rd, Tulsa, OK 74145 USA

St Jean, Garry *Basketball Player, Coach*
Golden State Warriors, 1001 Broadway,
Oakland, CA 94607 USA

St John, Jill *Actor*
Borinstein Oreck Bogart, 3172 Dona
Susana Dr, Studio City, CA 91604 USA

St John, Kristoff *Actor*
3443 Violet Trail, Calabasas, CA 91302
USA

St John, Lara *Musician*
Columbia Artists Mgmt Inc, 165 W 57th
St, New York, NY 10019 USA

St John, Mia *Boxer*
Amsel Eisenstadt & Frazier Inc, 5757
Wilshire Blvd #510, Los Angeles, CA
90036 USA

St John of Fawsley, Norman A F
Government Official
Old Rectory Preston Capes, Daventry,
Northants, NN11 6TE, UNITED
KINGDOM (UK)

St Laurent, Yves
5 Ave du Marceau, Paris, FRANCE,
75016, FRANCE

St Louis, Martin *Hockey Player*
Tampa Bay Lighting, Ice Palace, 401
Channelside Dr, Tampa, FL 33602 USA

St Patrick, Mathew *Actor*
Writers and Artists Group Intl (LA), 8383
Wilshire Blvd #550, Beverly Hills, CA
90211 USA

St Patrick, Matthew *Actor*
Untitled Entertainment (LA), 8436 W 3rd
St #650, Los Angeles, CA 90048 USA

Staab, Rebecca *Actor*
Don Buchwald, 6500 Wilshire Blvd,
#2200, Los Angeles, CA 90048 USA

Staats, Elmer B *Government Official*
Truman Scholarship Foundation, 712
Jackson Place NW, Washington, DC
20006 USA

Stabile, Nick
Jerry Shandrew PR, 1050 South Stanley
Avenue, Los Angeles, CA 90019-6634
USA

Stabler, Ken
260 N. Joachim St., Mobile, AL 36603

Stabler, Ken M (Kenny) *Football Player*
Stabler Co, PO Box 460, Orange Beach,
AL 36561 USA

Stacey Q *Actor, Music Group, Musician*
641 S Palm St #D, La Habra, CA 90631
USA

Stack, Brian *Writer*
3 Arts Entertainment Inc, 9460 Wilshire
Blvd Fl 7, Beverly Hills, CA 90212 USA

Stack, Timothy
10635 Santa Monica Blvd. #130, Los
Angeles, CA 90025

Stackhouse, Jerry *Basketball Player*
2124 Oakridge Dr, Kinston, NC 28504
USA

Stackpole, H C (Hank) *General*
Asia-Pacific Security Studies Center, 2058
Maluhia Road, Honolulu, HI 96815 USA

Stacomb, Kevin *Basketball Player*
14 Florida Ave, Jamestown, RI 02835 USA

Stacy, Hollis *Golfer*
9400 W 10th Ave, Lakewood, CO 80215
USA

Stacy, James *Actor*
478 Severn Ave, Tampa, FL 33606 USA

Stadler, Craig *Golfer*
1 Cantitoe Lane, Englewood, CO 80113
USA

Stadler, Sergei V *Musician*
Kaiserstr 43, Munich, 80801, GERMANY

Stadtman, Earl R *Misc*
16907 Redland Road, Derwood, MD
20855 USA

Stadtman, Thressa C *Misc*
16907 Redland Road, Derwood, MD
20855 USA

Staff, Kathy
17 Maple Mews, London, ENGLAND,
NW6

Stafford, Harrison *Football Player*
RR 1 Box 216, Edna, TX 77957 USA

Stafford, James Francis Cardinal *Religious
Leader*
Pontifical Council for the Laity, Piazza S
Calisto 16, Rome, 00153, ITALY

Stafford, Jim *Musician, Music Group,
Songwriter*
PO Box 6366, Branson, MO 65616 USA

Stafford, Jimmy *Musician*
Jon Landau, 80 Mason St, Greenwich, CT
06830 USA

Stafford, Jo *Musician*
2339 Century Hill, Los Angeles, CA
90067 USA

Stafford, John R *Business Person*
American Home Products, 5 Giralda
Farms, Madison, NJ 07940 USA

Stafford, Michelle *Actor*
606 N Larchmont Blvd #210, Los Angeles,
CA 90004 USA

Stafford, Nancy *Actor*
PO Box 11807, Marina del Rey, CA
90295 USA

Stafford, Robert T *Governor, Senator*
1 Sugarwood Hill Road, RR 1 Box 3954,
Rutland, VT 05701 USA

Stafford, Thomas
1006 Cameron St, Alexandria, VA 22314-
2427

Stafford, Thomas P *Astronaut, General*
AVD, PO Box 604, Glenn Dale, MD
20769 USA

Stagliano, John
14141 Covello St., Van Nuys, CA 91405

Stagus, Gus *Swimmer, Coach*
University of Michigan, Athletic Dept,
Ann Arbor, MI 48104 USA

Stahl, Jerry *Actor, Writer*
United Talent Agency (UTA), 9560
Wilshire Blvd, Beverly Hills, CA 90212
USA

Stahl, Lesley *Commentator*
CBS-TV, News Dept, 51 W 52nd St, New
York, NY 10019 USA

Stahl, Lisa *Actor*
Don Buchwald, 6500 Wilshire Blvd
#2200, Los Angeles, CA 90048 USA

Stahl, Nick *Actor*
1122 S Roxbury Dr, Los Angeles, CA
90035 USA

Stahl, Norman H *Judge*
US Appeals Court, McCormack Federal
Building, Boston, MA 02109 USA

Stahl, Richard *Actor*
Richard Sindell, 1910 Holmby Ave, #1,
Los Angeles, CA 90025 USA

Stahler, Jeff *Editor, Cartoonist*
Cincinnati Post, Editorial Dept, 125 E
Court St, Cincinnati, OH 45202 USA

Staind *Music Group*
William Morris Agency (WMA-LA), 1
William Morris Pl, Beverly Hills, CA
90212 USA

Staite, Jewel *Actor*
Elements Entertainment, 2401 W Olive
Ave #290, Burbank, CA 91506 USA

Stajola, Enzo
Piazza Augusto Albini 5, Rome, ITALY,
I-00154

Staley, Dawn M *Basketball Player, Coach*
1228 Callowhill St #603, Philadelphia, PA
19123 USA

Staley, Gerald A (Gerry) *Baseball Player*
2517 NE 100th, Vancouver, WA 98686
USA

Staley, Jerry *Athlete*
2517 NE 100th St, Vancouver, WA 98686

Staley, Joan *Actor*
24516 Windsor Dr, #B, Valencia, CA
91355 USA

Staley, Matthew R *Actor, Musician*
PO Box 590, New York, NY 10108-0590
USA

Staley, Walter *Hockey Player*
214 Teal Lake Road, Mexico, MO 65265
USA

Staller, Ilona
Via Cassia 1818, Rome, ITALY, I-00123

Stallings, George *Religious Leader*
African American Catholic Congregation,
1015 St NE, Washington, DC 20002 USA

Stallings, Larry *Football Player*
207 S Mason Road, Saint Louis, MO
63141 USA

Stallone, Frank
10668 Eastborne Ave. #206, Los Angeles,
CA 90025

Stallone, Jackie
323 San Vicente Blvd. #8, Santa Monica,
CA 90402

Stallone, Sasha
9 Beverly Park, Beverly Hills, CA 90210

Stallone, Sylvester *Actor*
Firm, The, 9465 Wilshire Blvd, Beverly
Hills, CA 90212 USA

Stallworth, Johnny L (John) *Football
Player*
188 Boulton Court, Madison, AL 35756
USA

Stalmaster, Lynn
12400 Wilshire Blvd. #920, Los Angeles,
CA 90025

Stamatopoulos, Dino *Writer*
International Creative Management
(ICM-LA), 8942 Wilshire Blvd, Beverly
Hills, CA 90211 USA

Stamler, Jonathan *Misc*
Duke University, Medical Center,
Hematology Dept, Durham, NC 27708
USA

Stamm, Michael (Mike) *Swimmer*
23 Wildwood Road, Orinda, CA 94563
USA

Stamos, John *Actor*
Brillstein-Grey Entertainment, 9150
Wilshire Blvd #350, Beverly Hills, CA
90212 USA

Stamos, Theodoros *Artist*
37 W 83rd St, New York, NY 10024 USA

Stamp, Terence *Actor*
Markham & Froggatt, Julian House, 4
Windmill St, London, W1P 1HF, UNITED
KINGDOM (UK)

Stanat, Dug *Artist*
46828 Bradley St, Fremont, CA 94534
USA

Standhardt, Kenneth *Artist*
620 Elmwood Dr, Eugene, OR 97401 USA

Standiford, Les *Writer*
Harper/Collins, 10 E 53rd St, New York,
NY 10022 USA

Standing, John *Actor*
International Creative Mgmt, 76 Oxford
St, London, W1N 0AX, UNITED
KINGDOM (UK)

Stanfel, Richard (Dick) *Football Player, Coach*
1104 Juniper Parkway, Libertyville, IL 60048 USA

Stanfill, Dennis
908 Oak Grove Ave., San Marino, CA 91108

Stanfill, William T (Bill) *Football Player*
111 Amelia Lane, Leesburg, GA 31763 USA

Stanford, Aaron *Actor*
Cyrena Esposito Management, 437 West 48th Street, Suite D, New York, NY 10036 USA

Stang, Arnold *Actor*
PO Box 920386, Needham, MA 02492 USA

Stang, Peter J *Misc*
University of Utah, Chemistry Dept, Salt Lake City, UT 84112 USA

Stangassinger, Thomas *Skier*
Hofgasse 19, Durenberg-Hallein, 5422, AUSTRIA

Stange, A Lee *Baseball Player*
436 Dolphin St, Melbourne Beach, FL 32951 USA

Stange, Maya *Actor*
Peters Fraser & Dunlop (PFD - UK), Drury House, 34-43 Russell St, London, WC2 B5, UNITED KINGDOM (UK)

Stangel, Eric *Writer, Producer*
3 Arts Entertainment Inc, 9460 Wilshire Blvd Fl 7, Beverly Hills, CA 90212 USA

Stangel, Justin *Writer, Producer*
3 Arts Entertainment Inc, 9460 Wilshire Blvd Fl 7, Beverly Hills, CA 90212 USA

Stanhope, Doug *Comedian*
Agency for the Performing Arts (APA-LA), 9200 Sunset Blvd #900, Los Angeles, CA 90069 USA

Stanis, Bernadette *Actor*
Nancy Chaidez & Associates, 6399 Wilshire Blvd #424, Los Angeles, CA 90048

Stankalla, Stefan *Skier*
Furstenstr 14, Gramisch-Partenkirchen, 82467, GERMANY

Stankovic, Borislav (Boris) *Basketball Player, Misc*
PO Box 7005, Munich, 81479, GERMANY

Stankowski, Paul *Golfer*
Cornerstone Sports, 14646 N Kierland Blvd #230, Scottsdale, AZ 85254 USA

Stanlch, George *Track Athlete, Basketball Player*
15816 Marigold Ave, Gardena, CA 90249 USA

Stanler, John W *Misc*
Coutts & Co, 440 Strand, London, SC2R 0QS, UNITED KINGDOM (UK)

Stanley, Allan H *Hockey Player*
RR 3, Fennelon Falls, ON K0M 1N0, CANADA

Stanley, Frank *Cinematographer*
Po Box 2230, Los Angeles, CA 90078 USA

Stanley, James *Producer*
United Talent Agency (UTA), 9560 Wilshire Blvd, Beverly Hills, CA 90212 USA

Stanley, Marianne Crawford *Coach*
New York Liberty, Madison Square Garden, 2 Penn Plaza, New York, NY 10121 USA

Stanley, Marlanne Crawford *Basketball Player, Coach*
Washington Mystics, MCI Center, 601 F St NW, Washington, DC 20004 USA

Stanley, Mitchell J (Mickey) *Baseball Player*
5319 Timberbend Dr, Brighton, MI 48116 USA

Stanley, Paul *Musician*
McGhee Entertainment, 8730 Sunset Blvd #195, Los Angeles, CA 90069 USA

Stanley, Ralph *Musician, Music Group*
Press Office, 2607 Westwood Dr, Nashville, TN 37204 USA

Stanley, Steven M *Misc*
1305 Malvern Ave, Baltimore, MD 21204 USA

Stanley Jr, Julian C *Psychic*
Johns Hopkins University, Blumberg Center, Baltimore, MD 21218 USA

Stansfield, Claire
9300 Wilshire Blvd. #555, Beverly Hills, CA 90212

Stansfield, Lisa *Songwriter, Musician, Music Group*
PO Box 59, Ashwell, Herts, SG7 5NG, UNITED KINGDOM (UK)

Stansfield Smith, Colin *Architect*
Three Ministers House, 76 High St Winchester, Hants, SO23 8UL, UNITED KINGDOM (UK)

Stansky, Peter D L *Historian*
375 Pinehill Road, Hillsborough, CA 94010 USA

Stantis, Scott *Editor, Cartoonist*
Birmingham News, Editorial Dept, 2200 4th Ave N, Birmingham, AL 35203 USA

Stanton, Andrew *Director, Writer, Animator*
Pixar, 1200 Park Ave, Emeryville, CA 94608 USA

Stanton, Frank N *Misc*
25 W 52nd St, New York, NY 10019 USA

Stanton, Harry Dean *Actor*
14527 Mulholland Dr, Los Angeles, CA 90077 USA

Stanton, Jeff *Race Car Driver*
1137 Athens Road, Sherwood, MI 49089 USA

Stanton, Molly *Actor*
Stone Manners Talent Agency, 6500 Wilshire Blvd, Ste 550, Los Angeles, CA 90048 USA

Stanton, Paul *Hockey Player*
39 Phillips St, Marblehood, MA 01945 USA

Stanton, Phil *Entertainer*
Blue Man Group, Luxor Hotel, 3900 Las Vegas Blvd S, Las Vegas, NV 89119 USA

Stapinski, Helene *Writer*
Saint Martin's Press, 175 5th Ave, New York, NY 10010 USA

Staple Singers, The
PO Box 170429, San Francisco, CA 94117

Staples, Mavis *Musician, Music Group*
PO Box 498360, Chicago, IL 60649 USA

Stapleton, Jean *Actor*
Bauman-Hiller, 5757 Wilshire Blvd #512, Los Angeles, CA 90036 USA

Stapleton, Kevin *Actor*
Gersh Agency, 232 N Canon Dr, Beverly Hills, CA 90210 USA

Stapleton, Maureen *Actor*
1 Morgan Manor #14, Lenox, MA 01240 USA

Stapleton, Oliver *Cinematographer*
MacCorkindale & Holton, 1640 5th St #205, Santa Monica, CA 90401 USA

Stapleton, Walter K *Judge*
US Court of Appeals, Federal Building, 844 N King St, Wilmington, DE 19801 USA

Stapp, Scott *Musician*
Agency Group, 1776 Broadway #430, New York, NY 10019 USA

Star, Darren *Writer*
William Morris Agency (WMA-LA), 1 William Morris Pl, Beverly Hills, CA 90212 USA

Star Sailor *Musician*
Solo Agency Ltd (UK), 55 Fulham High St, London, SW6 3JJ, United Kingdom

Starbird, Kate *Basketball Player*
Indiana Fever, Conseco Fieldhouse, 125 S Pennsylvania, Indianapolis, IN 46204 USA

Starbuck, Jo Jo *Figure Skater*
33 Pomeroy Road, Madison, NJ 07940 USA

Starck, Philippe *Architect, Designer*
3 Rue Faisans, Shiltigheim, 67300, FRANCE

Starfield, Barbara H *Doctor*
Johns Hopkins University, Hygiene School, 624 N Broadway, Baltimore, MD 21205 USA

Stargell, Tony
PO Box 53500, Indianapolis, IN 46253

Stark, Collin *Actor*
Impact Artists Group LLC, 10508 La Maida St, Toluca Woods, CA 91601 USA

Stark, Don *Actor*
Halpern & Associates, 12304 Santa Monica Blvd #104, Los Angeles, CA 90025 USA

Stark, Freya M *Writer, Misc*
Via Canova, Asolo, Treviso, ITALY

Stark, Graham *Actor*
International Creative Mgmt, 76 Oxford St, London, W1N 0AX, UNITED KINGDOM (UK)

Stark, Koo *Actor*
Rebecca Blond, 52 Shaftesbury Ave, London, W1V 7DE, UNITED KINGDOM (UK)

Stark, Melissa *Sportscaster, Commentator*
NBC-TV, News Dept, 30 Rockefeller
Plaza, New York, NY 10112 USA

Stark, Nathan J *Lawyer*
4000 Cathedral Ave NW #132,
Washington, DC 20016 USA

Stark, Rohn T *Football Player*
PO Box 10067, Lahaina, HI 96761 USA

Starke, Anthony *Actor*
Don Buchwald & Associates Inc (LA),
6500 Wilshire Blvd #2200, Los Angeles,
CA 90048 USA

Starker, James
1241 Winfield Rd., Bloomington, IN
47401

Starker, Janos *Musician*
1241 Winfield Road, Bloomington, IN
47401 USA

Starkweather, Gary K *Engineer*
10274 Parkwood Dr #7, Cupertino, CA
95014 USA

Starling, James D *General*
5336 Dawn Oak Lane, Fair Oaks, CA
95628 USA

Starn, Douglas *Photographer*
Stux Gallery, 163 Mercer St #1, New
York, NY 10012 USA

Starn, Mike *Photographer*
Stux Gallery, 163 Mercer St #1, New
York, NY 10012 USA

Starner, Shelby *Musician, Music Group*
Morebam Music, 30 Hillcrest Ave,
Morristown, NJ 07960 USA

Starr, Albert *Doctor*
5050 SW Patton Road, Portland, OR
97221 USA

Starr, B Bartlett (Bart) *Football Player*
2065 Royal Fern Lane, Birmingham, AL
35244 USA

Starr, Bart
2647 Rocky Ridge Lane, Birmingham, AL
35216

Starr, Brenda K *Musician, Music Group*
Brothers Mgmt, 141 Dunbar Ave, Fords,
NJ 08863 USA

Starr, Chauncey *Engineer*
95 Stern Lane, Atherton, CA 94027 USA

Starr, Fredro *Actor, Artist, Musician*
Writers & Artists, 8383 Wilshire Blvd
#550, Beverly Hills, CA 90211 USA

Starr, Kay *Musician, Music Group*
Ira Okun Entertainment, 708 Palisades Dr,
Pacific Palisades, CA 90272 USA

Starr, Kenneth *Judge, Government Official*
Pepperdine Law School, 24255 Pacific
Coast Highway, Malibu, CA 90263 USA

Starr, Leonard *Cartoonist*
Tribune Media Services, 435 N Michigan
Ave #1500, Chicago, IL 60611 USA

Starr, Martin *Actor*
Paradigm Agency, 10100 Santa Monica
Blvd #2500, Los Angeles, CA 90067 USA

Starr, Mike *Artist*
1505 10th St., Santa Monica, CA 90401

Starr, Paul E *Misc*
Princeton University, Sociology Dept,
Green Hall, Princeton, NJ 08544 USA

Starr, Randy *Musician, Music Group,
Songwriter*
DDS, 230 Park Ave, New York, NY 10169
USA

Starr, Ringo *Musician, Actor, Music
Group*
David Fishof Presents, 252 W 71st St,
New York, NY 10023 USA

Starr, Ryan *Musician*
Kazarian/Spencer & Assoc, 11365 Ventura
Blvd #100, Box 7403, Studio City, CA
91604 USA

Starr, Steve *Photographer, Journalist*
720 Arcadia Place, Colorado Springs, CO
80903 USA

Starship
9850 Sandalfoot Blvd. #458, Boca Raton,
FL 33428

Starzewski, Tomasz *Fashion Designer*
House of Tomasz Trarzewski, 15-17 Pont
St, London, SW1X 9EH, UNITED
KINGDOM (UK)

Starzl, Thomas E *Doctor*
University of Pittsburgh, Medical School,
Surgery Dept, Pittsburgh, PA 15261 USA

Stastny, Anton *Hockey Player*
Montoileu 11, Bussigney-Lausanne, 1030,
SWITZERLAND

Stastny, Peter *Hockey Player*
465 S Mason Road, Saint Louis, MO
63141 USA

Stata, Raymond S *Business Person*
Analog Devices Inc, 1 Technology Way,
Norwood, MA 02062 USA

Statham, Jason *Actor*
Current Entertainment, 1411 Fifth St #405,
Santa Monica, CA 90401 USA

Static, Wayne *Musician*
Andy Gould Mgmt, 9100 Wilshire Blvd
#400W, Beverly Hills, CA 90212 USA

Statler Brothers
Box 492, Hernando, MS 38632 USA

Staton, Candi *Musician, Music Group*
Capital Entertainment, 1201 N St NW
#A5, Washington, DC 20005 USA

Staton, Dakota *Musician, Music Group*
Hot Jazz, 328 W 43rd St #4FW, New
York, NY 10036 USA

Status Quo
Pinewood Rd. Ivor, Buckinghamshire,
ENGLAND

Staub, Daniel J (Rusty) *Baseball Player*
WWOR-Radio, 9 Broadcast Plaza,
Secaucus, NJ 07094 USA

Staubach, Roger T *Football Player*
6912 Edelweiss Circle, Dallas, TX 75240
USA

Stauber, Liz *Actor*
Creative Artists Agency, 9830 Wilshire
Blvd, Beverly Hills, CA 90212 USA

Stauffer, William A (Bill) *Basketball Player*
3920 Grand Ave #301, Des Moines, IA
50312 USA

Staunton, Imelda *Actor*
P F D, Drury House, 34-43 Russell St,
London, WC2B 5HA, UNITED KINGDOM
(UK)

Stautner, Ernest A (Ernie) *Football Player,
Coach*
801 Greenvalley Lane, Highland Village,
TX 75077 USA

Staveley, William D M *Admiral*
Thames Health Authority, 40 Eastbourne
Terrace, London, W2 3QR, UNITED
KINGDOM (UK)

Stavropoulos, William S *Business Person*
Dow Chemical, 2030 Dow Center,
Midland, MI 48674 USA

Stayskal, Wayne *Editor, Cartoonist*
Tampa Tribune, Editorial Dept, 200 S
Parker St, Tampa, FL 33606 USA

Staysniak, Joseph A (Joe) *Football Player*
10640 LaGrange Road, Elyria, OH 44035
USA

Stead, Eugene A Jr *Doctor*
5113 Townsville Road, Bullock, NC
27507 USA

Steadman, Alison *Actor*
P F D, Drury House, 34-43 Russell St,
London, WC2B 5HA, UNITED KINGDOM
(UK)

Steadman, J Richard *Doctor*
Steadman Hawkins Clinic, 181 W
Meadows Dr #400, Vail, CO 81657 USA

Steadman, Mark *Writer*
450 Pin-du-Lac Dr, Central, SC 29630
USA

Steadman, Ralph I *Cartoonist*
Old Loose Court, Loose Valley Maidstone,
Kent, ME15 9SE, UNITED KINGDOM
(UK)

Steadman, Robert L *Cinematographer*
15925 Temecula St, Pacific Palisades, CA
90272 USA

Stearns, Cheryl *Misc*
613 Saddlebred Lane, Raeford, NC 28376
USA

Stearns, Jeff
9200 Sunset Blvd. #1130, Los Angeles,
CA 90069

Stecher, Renate Meissner- *Track Athlete*
Haydnstr 11, #526/38, Jena, 07749,
GERMANY

Stecher, Theodore P *Astronomer*
UIT Project, Goddard Space Flight Center,
Greenbelt, MD 20771 USA

Steckler, Ray Dennis *Director*
2375 E Tropicana Ave, Las Vegas, NV
89119 USA

Steding, Katy *Basketball Player*
Warner Pacific College, Athletic Dept,
2219 SE 68th Ave, Portland, OR 97215
USA

Steeb, Carl-Uwe
18 chemin des Jardillets, Hauterive,
SWITZERLAND, CH-2068

Steel, Amy *Actor*
Innovative Artists, 1505 10th St, Santa
Monica, CA 90401 USA

Steel, Danielle
PO Box 1637 Murray Hill Sta., New York,
NY 10156

Steel, Danielle F *Writer*
330 Bob Hope Dr, Burbank, CA 91523
USA

Steel, David M S *Government Official*
Aikwood Tower, Ettrick Bridge, Selkirkshire, SCOTLAND

Steel, John *Musician*
Lustig Talent, PO Box 770850, Orlando, FL 32877 USA

Steele, Allan
1640 S. Sepulveda Blvd. #218, Los Angeles, CA 90025-7510

Steele, Barbara *Actor*
2460 Benedict Canyon, Beverly Hills, CA 90210 USA

Steele, Cassie *Actor*
Noble Caplan Agency, 1260 Yonge St Fl 2, Toronto ON, M4T 1W6, CANADA

Steele, Danielle *Writer*
United Talent Agency (UTA), 9560 Wilshire Blvd, Beverly Hills, CA 90212 USA

Steele, Larry *Basketball Player*
139 Del Prado St, Lake Oswego, OR 97035 USA

Steele, Michael *Musician*
Bangles Mall, 1341 W Fullerton Ave, Box 180, Chicago, IL 60614 USA

Steele, Richard *Referee, Boxer*
2438 Antler Point Dr, Henderson, NV 89074 USA

Steele, Shelby *Writer*
San Jose State University, English Dept, San Jose, CA 95192 USA

Steele, Tommy *Actor, Musician*
IMG, Media House, 3 Burlington Lane, London, W4 2TH, UNITED KINGDOM (UK)

Steele, William M (Mike) *General*
Commanding General, Combined Arms Center, Fort Leavenworth, KS 66207 USA

Steele-Perkins, Christopher H
Photographer
5 Saint John's Buildings, Canterbury St, London, SW9 7QB, UNITED KINGDOM (UK)

Steely Dan *Music Group*
Howard Rose Agency Ltd, The, 9460 Wilshire Blvd #310, Beverly Hills, CA 90212 USA

Steen, Jessica *Actor*
Innovative Artists, 1505 10th St, Santa Monica, CA 90401 USA

Steenburgen, Mary *Actor*
165 Copper Cliff Lane, Sedona, AZ 86336 USA

Stefan, Greg *Hockey Player*
37648 Baywood Dr #33, Farmington Hills, MI 48335 USA

Stefani, Gwen *Musician, Songwriter*
PO Box 8899, Anaheim, CA 92812 USA

Stefanich, Jim *Bowler*
1025 N Prairie Ave, Joliet, IL 60435 USA

Stefanson, Leslie *Actor*
9271 1/2 W Norton Ave, West Hollywood, CA 90046 USA

Stefanyshyn-Piper, Heidemarie M
Astronaut
3722 W Pine Brook Way, Houston, TX 77059 USA

Steffes, Kent *Volleyball Player*
11106 Ave de Cortez, Pacific Palisades, CA 90272 USA

Steffy, Joseph B (Joe) Jr *Football Player*
25 Water Way, Newburgh, NY 12550 USA

Steger, Joseph A *Educator*
University of Cincinnati, President's Office, Cincinnati, OH 45221 USA

Steger, Will *Misc*
International Arctic Project, 990 3rd St E, Saint Paul, MN 55106 USA

Stegman, Millie *Actor*
Telefe - Argentina, Pavon 2444 (C1248AAT), Buenos Aires, ARGENTINA

Steiger, Ueli *Cinematographer*
2222 Kenilworth Ave, Los Angeles, CA 90039 USA

Stein, Ben *Actor, Comedian*
4549 Via Vienta, Malibu, CA 90265 USA

Stein, Bob *Basketball Player, Misc*
Minnesota Timberwolves, Target Center, 600 1st Ave N, Minneapolis, MN 55403 USA

Stein, Chris *Musician*
Shore Fire Media, 32 Court St #1600, Brooklyn, NY 11201 USA

Stein, Ed *Editor, Cartoonist*
Rocky Mountain News, Editorial Dept, 400 W Colfax Ave, Denver, CO 80204 USA

Stein, Elias M *Mathematician*
132 Dodds Lane, Princeton, NJ 08540 USA

Stein, Gilbert (Gil) *Hockey Player, Misc*
National Hockey League, 650 5th Ave #3300, New York, NY 10019 USA

Stein, Horst *Conductor*
Mariedi Anders Artists, 535 El Camino del Mar, San Francisco, CA 94121 USA

Stein, Howard *Financier*
Dreyfus Corp, 200 Park Ave, New York, NY 10166 USA

Stein, James *Business Person*
Fluor Corp, 3353 Michelson Dr, Irvine, CA 92612 USA

Stein, Joseph *Writer*
1130 Park Ave, New York, NY 10128 USA

Stein, Mark *Music Group, Musician*
Future Vision, 280 Riverside Dr #12L, New York, NY 10025 USA

Stein, Pamela Jean
2112 Broadway, Santa Monica, CA 90404-2912

Stein, Robert *Editor*
McCall's Magazine, Editorial Dept, 375 Lexington Ave, New York, NY 10017 USA

Steinbach, Alice *Journalist*
Baltimore Sun, Editorial Dept, 501 N Calvert St, Baltimore, MD 21202 USA

Steinbach, Terry L *Baseball Player*
750 Boone Ave N #109, Golden Valley, MN 55427 USA

Steinberg, David *Actor, Comedian, Director*
15332 Longbow Dr, Sherman Oaks, CA 91403 USA

Steinberg, Leigh *Attorney General*
Steinberg Moorad Dunn, 500 Newport Center Dr #800, Newport Beach, CA 92660 USA

Steinberg, Leo *Historian*
165 W 66th St, New York, NY 10023 USA

Steinberg, Paul *Cartoonist*
New Yorker Magazine, Editorial Dept, 4 Times Square, New York, NY 10036 USA

Steinberg, Saul P *Business Person*
Reliance Group Holdings, 5 Hanover Square #1700, New York, NY 10004 USA

Steinberger, Jack *Nobel Prize Laureate*
25 Chemin des Merles, 1213 Onex, Geneva, SWITZERLAND

Steinbrenner, George
PO Box 25077, Tampa, FL 33622-5077

Steinbrenner III, George M *Baseball Player, Misc*
PO Box 25077, Tampa, FL 33622 USA

Steinem, Gloria *Social Activist, Editor*
118 E 73rd St, New York, NY 10021 USA

Steiner, Andre *Athlete*
Bismarckstr 4, Berlin, 14109, GERMANY

Steiner, George *Writer*
32 Barrow Road, Cambridge, UNITED KINGDOM (UK)

Steiner, Paul *Cartoonist*
Washington Times, 3600 New York Ave NE, Washington, DC 20002 USA

Steiner, Peter *Cartoonist*
New Yorker Magazine, Editorial Dept, 4 Times Square, New York, NY 10036 USA

Steiner, Reed *Producer*
William Morris Agency (WMA-LA), 1 William Morris Pl, Beverly Hills, CA 90212 USA

Steiner, Tommy
Ettenbergstr. 20, Aalen, GERMANY, D-73432

Steiner, Tommy Shane *Music Group, Musician*
Collinsworth, 50 Music Square W #702, Nashville, TN 37203 USA

Steines, Mark *Television Host*
Entertainment Tonight (ET), 5555 Melrose Ave, Mae West Bldg Fl 2, Hollywood, CA 90038 USA

Steinfeld, Jake
622 Toyopa Dr., Pacific Palisades, CA 90272-4471

Steinfield, Jake *Actor, Wrestler, Misc*
622 Toyopa Dr, Pacific Palisades, CA 90272 USA

Steinhardt, Arnold *Musician*
Herbert Barrett, 266 W 37th St #2000, New York, NY 10018 USA

Steinhardt, Paul J *Physicist*
1000 Cedargrove Road, Wynnewood, PA 19096 USA

Steinhardt, Richard *Biologist*
University of California, Biology Dept, Berkeley, CA 94720 USA

Steinhauer, Sherri *Golfer*
Rick Lepley, 4675 SW 74th St, Coral Gables, FL 33143 USA

Steinkraus, William (Bill) *Horse Racer*
PO Box 3038, Darien, CT 06820 USA

Steinkuhler, Dean E *Football Player*
1135 Oak St, Syracuse, NE 68446 USA

Steinman, Jim *Songwriter*
DAS Communications, 83 Riverside Dr,
New York, NY 10024 USA

Steinmetz, Richard *Actor*
Personal Management Company, 425 N
Robertson Dr, Los Angeles, CA 90048
USA

Steinsaltz, Adin *Religious Leader*
Israel Talmudic Publications Institute, PO
Box 1458, Jerusalem, ISRAEL

Steinseifer Bates, Carrie *Swimmer*
9309 Benzon Dr, Pleasanton, CA 94588
USA

Steitz, Joan A *Misc*
45 Prospect Hill Road, Branford, CT
06405 USA

Stella, Frank P *Artist, Misc*
17 Jones St, New York, NY 10014 USA

Stelle, Kellogg S *Physicist*
Imperial College, Prince Consort Road,
London, SW7 2BZ, UNITED KINGDOM
(UK)

Stempel, Robert C *Business Person*
Energy Conversion Devices, 1647 W
Maple Road, Troy, MI 48084 USA

Stenberg, Brigitta
11484th St. #116, Santa Monica, CA
90403

Stenerud, Jan *Football Player*
3180 Shieks Place, Colorado Springs, CO
80904 USA

Stenmark, Ingemar *Skier*
Residence l'Annonciade, 17 Av de
l'Anncenciade, Monte Carlo, 98000,
MONACO

Stent, Gunther S *Biologist*
145 Purdue Ave, Kensington, CA 94708
USA

Stepanova, Maria *Basketball Player*
Phoenix Mercury, American West Arena,
201 E Jefferson St, Phoenix, AZ 85004
USA

Stepashin, Sergei V *Prime Minister,
General*
Government of Russia, Kasnopresneskaya
Embankment 2, Moscow, 103274,
RUSSIA

Stephanie *Royalty*
Maison Clos St Martin, Saint Remy de
Provence, FRANCE

Stephanopolous, Constantine (Costis)
President
Presidential Palace, 7 Vas Georgiou B,
Odos Zalokosta 10, Athens, GREECE

Stephanopolous, George R *Journalist,
Government Official*
151 E 83rd St #6E, New York, NY 10028
USA

Stephanopoulos, George *Journalist,
Government Official*
This Week with George Stephanopoulos,
1717 DeSales St NW, Washington, DC
20036-4401 USA

Stephens, James
8271 Melrose Ave. #110, Los Angeles, CA
90046

Stephens, Janaya *Actor*
Noble Caplan Agency, 1260 Yonge St Fl
2, Toronto ON, M4T 1W6, CANADA

Stephens, Laraine
10800 Chalon Rd., Los Angeles, CA
90077

Stephens, Olin James II *Architect,
Yachtsman, Designer*
80 Lyme Road #160, Hanover, NH 03755
USA

Stephens, Robert *Business Person*
Adaptec Inc, 691 S Milpitas Blvd,
Milpitas, CA 95035 USA

Stephens, Stanley G (Stan) *Governor*
4 Capitol Court, Helena, MT 59601 USA

Stephens, Toby *Actor*
International Creative Mgmt, 76 Oxford
St, London, W1N 0AX, UNITED
KINGDOM (UK)

Stephenson, Debra
2 Henrietta St., London, ENGLAND,
WC2E 8PS

Stephenson, Dwight E *Football Player*
1180 S Powerline Road #208, Pampano
Beach, FL 33069 USA

Stephenson, Garrett *Baseball Player*
503 Gem Dr, Kimberly, ID 83341 USA

Stephenson, Gordon *Architect*
55/14 Albert St, Claremont, WA 6010,
AUSTRALIA

Stephenson, Jan *Golfer*
PO Box 705, Windermere, FL 34786 USA

Stephenson, Neal T *Writer*
Avon Books, 1350 Ave of Americas, New
York, NY 10019 USA

Stephenson, Van *Musician, Music Group,
Songwriter*
Vector Mgmt, 1607 17th Ave S, Nashville,
TN 37212 USA

Stepnoski, Mark M *Football Player*
3001 Shelton Way, Plano, TX 75093 USA

Stepp, Craig
6310 San Vicente Blvd. #520, Los
Angeles, CA 90048

Steppenwolf (John Kay)
108 E. Matilija, Ojai, CA 93023

Steppling, John *Writer*
William Morris Agency, 151 El Camino
Dr, Beverly Hills, CA 90212 USA

Steranko, Jim *Cartoonist*
PO Box 974, Reading, PA 19603 USA

Sterban, Richard A *Musician, Music
Group*
329 Rockland Road, Hendersonville, TN
37075 USA

Stereo Fuse *Music Group*
Wind-up Records, 72 Madison Ave, New
York, NY 10016 USA

Stereophonics *Music Group*
Nettwerk Management (Canada), 1850 W
Second Ave, Vancouver BC, V6J 4R3,
CANADA

Sterkel, Jill *Swimmer*
3025 Snoddy Road, Bloomington, IN
47401 USA

Sterling, Annette *Musician, Music Group*
Soundedge Personal Mgmt, 332
Southdown Road, Lloyd Harbor, NY
11743 USA

Sterling, Mindy *Actor*
7307 Melrose Ave, Los Angeles, CA
90046 USA

Sterling, Nici *Adult Film Star*
Atlas Multimedia Inc, 22940 Burbank
Blvd, Woodland Hills, CA 91367 USA

Sterling, Robert *Actor*
121 S Bentley Ave, Los Angeles, CA
90049 USA

Sterling, Tisha *Actor*
PO Box 788, Ketchum, ID 83340 USA

Stern, Andrew L *Misc*
Service Employees International Union,
1313 L St NW, Washington, DC 20005
USA

Stern, Bert *Photographer*
330 E 39th St, New York, NY 10016 USA

Stern, Daniel *Actor*
PO Box 6788, Malibu, CA 90264 USA

Stern, David J *Basketball Player, Misc*
National Basketball Assn, Olympic Tower,
122 E 55th St, New York, NY 10022 USA

Stern, Dawn
400 S. Beverly Dr. #101, Beverly Hills,
CA 90212

Stern, Fritz R *Historian*
15 Claremont Ave, New York, NY 10027
USA

Stern, Gary H *Financier, Government
Official*
Federal Reserve Bank, PO Box 291,
Minneapolis, MN 55480 USA

Stern, Gerald *Writer*
W W Norton, 500 5th Ave, New York,
NY 10110 USA

Stern, Howard *Entertainer*
Don Buchwald, 10 E 44th St, New York,
NY 10017 USA

Stern, Joseph *Producer, Actor*
Creative Artists Agency LCC (CAA-LA),
9830 Wilshire Blvd, Beverly Hills, CA
90212 USA

Stern, Leonard B *Producer*
1709 Angelo Dr, Beverly Hills, CA 90210
USA

Stern, Michael (Mike) *Musician*
Tropix International, 163 3rd Ave #206,
New York, NY 10003 USA

Stern, Richard G *Writer*
University of Chicago, English Dept,
Chicago, IL 60637 USA

Stern, Robert A M *Architect*
Robert A M Stern Architects, 460 W 34th
St, New York, NY 10001 USA

Stern, Shoshannah *Actor*
Perception Public Relations LLC, 13333
Ventura Blvd #203, Sherman Oaks, CA
91423 USA

Sternbach, Leo H *Misc*
10 Woodmont Road, Montclair, NJ 07043
USA

Sternberg, Thomas *Business Person*
Staples Inc, PO Box 9265, Framingham,
MA 01701 USA

Sternecky, Neal *Cartoonist*
52 Bluebird Lane, Naperville, IL 60565
USA

Sternfeld, Reuben *Financier*
Inter-American Development Bank, 1300
New York Ave NW, Washington, DC
20577 USA

Sternhagen, Frances *Actor*
152 Sutton Manor Road, New Rochelle,
NY 10801 USA

Sternin, Joshua *Actor*
International Creative Management
(ICM-LA), 8942 Wilshire Blvd, Beverly
Hills, CA 90211 USA

Sterrett, Samuel B *Judge*
US Tax Court, 400 2nd St NW,
Washington, DC 20217 USA

Sterzinsky, Georg Maximilian Cardinal
Religious Leader
Archdiocese of Berlin, Wundstr 48/50,
Berlin, 14057, GERMANY

Stetson, Mark *Special Effects Designer*
International Creative Management
(ICM-LA), 8942 Wilshire Blvd, Beverly
Hills, CA 90211 USA

Stetter, Karl *Biologist*
Universtat Regensburg, Universitatsstr 31,
Regensburg, 93053, GERMANY

Steussie, Todd E *Football Player*
34793 Emigrant Trail, Shingletown, CA
96088 USA

Stevens, Andrew *Actor*
Irv Schechter, 9300 Wilshire Blvd #410,
Beverly Hills, CA 90212 USA

Stevens, April *Musician, Music Group*
19530 Superior St, Northridge, CA 91324
USA

Stevens, Bob *Producer*
United Talent Agency (UTA), 9560
Wilshire Blvd, Beverly Hills, CA 90212
USA

Stevens, Brinke *Actor*
PO Box 8900, Universal City, CA 91618
USA

Stevens, Cat
Steinhauser Str. 3, Munich, GERMANY,
81677

Stevens, Cat (Yusef Islam) *Musician,
Music Group, Songwriter*
Ariola Steinhauser Str 3, Munich, 81667
USA

Stevens, Chuck *Photographer*
PO Box 422782, San Francisco, CA
94142 USA

Stevens, Connie *Actor, Music Group,
Musician*
Forever Spring, 426 S Robertson Blvd, Los
Angeles, CA 90048 USA

Stevens, Dorit *Actor, Model*
206 S Brand Blvd, Glendale, CA 91204
USA

Stevens, Eileen *Social Activist*
126 Marion St, Sayville, NY 11782 USA

Stevens, Fisher *Actor*
329 N Orange Grove, Los Angeles, CA
90036 USA

Stevens, George Jr *Producer*
New Liberty Productions, John F Kennedy
Center, Washington, DC 20566 USA

Stevens, John Paul *Judge*
US Supreme Court, 1 1st St NE,
Washington, DC 20543 USA

Stevens, Kaye *Actor, Musician, Music
Group*
Ruth Webb, 10580 Des Moines Ave,
Northridge, CA 91326 USA

Stevens, Kenneth N *Engineer*
7 Larchwood Lane, Natick, MA 01760
USA

Stevens, Kevin M *Hockey Player*
38 Bay Pond Road, Duxbury, MA 02332
USA

Stevens, Laraine
10800 Chalon Rd., Los Angeles, CA
90077

Stevens, Mick
PO Box 344, West Tisbury, MA 02575-
0344

Stevens, Ray *Music Group, Musician,
Songwriter*
William Morris Agency, 2100 W End Ave
#1000, Nashville, TN 37203 USA

Stevens, Rise *Opera Singer*
930 5th Ave, New York, NY 10021 USA

Stevens, Robert B *Educator*
Covington/Burling, Leconfield House,
Curzon St, London, W1Y 8AS, UNITED
KINGDOM (UK)

Stevens, Robert J *Business Person*
Lockheed Martin Corp, 6801 Rockledge
Dr, Bethesda, MD 20817 USA

Stevens, Robert M *Cinematographer*
1920 S Beverly Glen Blvd #106, Los
Angeles, CA 90025 USA

Stevens, Rogers *Musician*
Shapiro Co, 9229 Sunset Blvd #607, Los
Angeles, CA 90069 USA

Stevens, Ronnie *Actor*
Caroline Dawson, 125 Gloucester Road,
London, SW7 4IE, UNITED KINGDOM
(UK)

Stevens, Scott *Hockey Player*
102 Oval Road, Essex Falls, NJ 07021
USA

Stevens, Shadoe *Radio Personality*
2934 N. Beverly Glen Circle #399, Los
Angeles, CA 90077 USA

Stevens, Shakin' *Musician, Music Group,
Songwriter*
Mgmt Gerd Kehren, Postfach 1455,
Erkelenz, 41804, GERMANY

Stevens, Stella *Actor, Model*
Stella Visions, 1608 N Cahuenga Blvd
#649, Los Angeles, CA 90028 USA

Stevens, Steve *Musician*
J H Cohn LLP, 720 Palisade Ave,
Englewood Cliffs, NJ 07632 USA

Stevens, Steven *Actor*
Stevens Group, 3518 Cahuenga Blvd W,
Los Angeles, CA 90068 USA

Stevens, Tabitha *Adult Film Star*
Atlas Multimedia Inc, 22940 Burbank
Blvd, Woodland Hills, CA 91367 USA

Stevens, Tony *Musician*
Lustig Talent, PO Box 770850, Orlando,
FL 32877 USA

Stevens, Warren *Actor*
14155 Magnolia Blvd #27, Sherman
Oaks, CA 91423 USA

Stevenson, Adlai E III *Senator*
20 N Clark St #750, Chicago, IL 60602
USA

Stevenson, Cynthia *Actor*
William Morris Agency (WMA-LA), 1
William Morris Pl, Beverly Hills, CA
90212 USA

Stevenson, DeShawn *Basketball Player*
Utah Jazz, Delta Center, 301 W South
Temple, Salt Lake City, UT 84101 USA

Stevenson, Juliet *Actor*
68 Pall Mall, London, SW1Y 5ES, UNITED
KINGDOM (UK)

Stevenson, Parker *Actor*
10100 Santa Monica Blvd #400, Los
Angeles, CA 90067 USA

Stevenson, Teofilo
Hotel Havana Libre, Havana, CUBA

Stevenson Lorenzo, Teofilo *Boxer*
Comite Olimppicu, Hotel Havana, Libre,
Havana, CUBA

Stever, H Guyford *Engineer, Educator*
59 Randolph Hill Road, Randolph, NH
03593 USA

Steward, Emanuel *Boxer, Misc*
19244 Bretton Dr, Detroit, MI 48223 USA

Steward, Robert L
2864 S Circle Dr #800, Colorado Springs,
CO 80906 USA

Stewart, Al *Musician, Music Group,
Songwriter*
Chapman & Co, 14011 Ventura Blvd
#405, Sherman Oaks, CA 91423 USA

Stewart, Alana *Actor*
13480 Firth Dr, Beverly Hills, CA 90210
USA

Stewart, Alec *Cricketer*
Surrey County Cricket Club, Kennington
Oval, London, SE11 5SS, UNITED
KINGDOM (UK)

Stewart, Alexandra
37 Ave. de la Dame Blanche, Fontenay-
Bois, FRANCE, 94120

Stewart, Amy *Actor*
Burstein Company, The, 15304 Sunset
Blvd #208, Pacific Palisades, CA 90272
USA

Stewart, Bill *Musician*
Blue Note Records, 6920 Sunset Blvd, Los
Angeles, CA 90028 USA

Stewart, Catherine Mary *Actor*
350 DuPont St, Toronto, ON M5R 1Z9,
CANADA

Stewart, David A (Dave) *Musician*
Arista Records, 8750 Wilshire Blvd #300,
Beverly Hills, CA 90211 USA

Stewart, David K (Dave) *Baseball Player*
17762 Vineyeard Lane, Poway, CA 92064
USA

Stewart, Freddie
4862 Excelente Dr., Woodland Hills, CA
91364

Stewart, French *Actor*
United Talent Agency, 9560 Wilshire Blvd #500, Beverly Hills, CA 90212 USA

Stewart, Ian *Government Official*
House of Commons, Westminster, London, SW1A 0AA, UNITED KINGDOM (UK)

Stewart, Jackie
24 Rte. de Divonne, Nyon, SWITZERLAND, 1260

Stewart, James B *Journalist*
Wall Street Journal, Editorial Dept, 200 Liberty St, New York, NY 10281 USA

Stewart, James C *War Hero*
8793 Grape Wagon Circle, San Jose, CA 95135 USA

Stewart, Jermaine *Musician, Music Group*
Richard Walters, 1800 Argyle Ave #408, Los Angeles, CA 90028 USA

Stewart, John *Musician*
Fuji Productions, 2480 Williston Dr, Charlottesville, VA 22901 USA

Stewart, John Y (Jackie) *Race Car Driver*
Stewart GP, 16 Tanners Dr, Blakelands, Milton Keynes, MK14 5BW, UNITED KINGDOM (UK)

Stewart, Jon *Comedian, Actor*
Daily Show with Jon Stewart, The, 2049 Century Park E #4170, Los Angeles, CA 90067 USA

Stewart, Josh *Actor*
Roklin Management, 8265 Sunset Blvd #101, Los Angeles, CA 90046 USA

Stewart, Kristen *Actor*
Gersh Agency, The (LA), 232 N Canon Dr, Beverly Hills, CA 90210 USA

Stewart, Lisa *Musician*
Friedman & LaRosa, 1344 Lexington Ave, New York, NY 10128 USA

Stewart, Martha K *Publisher, Entertainer*
19 Newtown Turnpike #6, Westport, CT 06880 USA

Stewart, Mary *Writer*
House of Letterawe, Lock Awe, Argyll, PA33 1AH, SCOTLAND

Stewart, Maxine
545 Lucero Ave., Pacific Palisades, CA 90272

Stewart, Melvin Jr *Swimmer*
1311 Lake Lauden Blvd, Knoxville, TN 37916 USA

Stewart, Natalie *Musician, Songwriter*
DreamWorks Records, 9268 W 3rd St, Beverly Hills, CA 90210 USA

Stewart, Nick
1285 S. La Brea Ave . #203, Los Angeles, CA 90019

Stewart, Patrick *Actor*
William Morris Agency, 151 El Camino Dr, Beverly Hills, CA 90212 USA

Stewart, Paul Anthony
10635 Santa Monica Blvd. #130, Los Angeles, CA 90025

Stewart, Peggy *Actor*
11139 Hortense St, Toluca Lake, CA 91602 USA

Stewart, Potter *Judge*
US Court of Appeals, US Courthouse, 100 E 5th St, Cincinnati, OH 45202 USA

Stewart, Ray *Golfer*
Scott McWilliams, 2947 34th Ave W, Vancouver, BC V6N 2J9, CANADA

Stewart, Robert L *Astronaut, General*
815 Sun Valley Dr, Woodland Park, CO 80863 USA

Stewart, Roderick D (Rod) *Musician*
23 Beverly Park Terrace, Beverly Hills, CA 90210 USA

Stewart, Ronald G (Ron) *Hockey Player*
4010 N 11th St, #3, Phoenix, AZ 85014 USA

Stewart, Shannon H *Baseball Player*
18460 SW 78th Place, Miami, FL 33157 USA

Stewart, Thomas J Jr *Opera Singer*
Columbia Artists Mgmt Inc, 165 W 57th St, New York, NY 10019 USA

Stewart, Tonea *Actor*
Alabama State University, Theater Arts Dept, Montgomery, AL 36101 USA

Stewart, Tony *Race Car Driver*
13415 Reese Blvd W, Huntersville, NC 28078 USA

Stewart, Tyler *Musician*
Nettwerk Mgmt, 8730 Wilshire Blvd #304, Beverly Hills, CA 90211 USA

Stewart, Will Foster *Actor*
8730 Santa Monica Blvd #1, Los Angeles, CA 90069 USA

Stewart-Hardway, Donna *Actor*
PO Box 777, Pinch, WV 25156 USA

Stezer, Philip *Musician*
I M G Artists, 3 Burlington Lane, Chiswick, London, W4 2TH, UNITED KINGDOM (UK)

Stich, Michael *Tennis Player*
Ernst-Barlach-Str 44, Elmshom, 25336, GERMANY

Sticht, J Paul *Business Person*
11732 Lake House Court, North Palm Beach, FL 33408 USA

Stickel, Fred A *Publisher*
Portland Oregonian, 1320 SW Broadway, Portland, OR 97201 USA

Stickler, Alfons M Cardinal *Religious Leader*
Piazza del S Uffizio 11, Rome, 00193, ITALY

Stickles, Montford (Monty) *Football Player*
1363 3rd Ave, San Francisco, CA 94122 USA

Stickles, Ted *Swimmer*
1142 Sharynwood Dr, Baton Rouge, LA 70808 USA

Sticky, Fingaz *Artist, Musician*
International Creative Mgmt, 8942 Wilshire Blvd #219, Beverly Hills, CA 90211 USA

Stieb, David (Dave) A *Baseball Player*
10860 Shay Lane, Reno, NV 89511 USA

Stieber, Tamar *Journalist*
Albuquerque Journal, Editorial Dept, 7777 Jefferson NE, Albuquerque, NM 87109 USA

Stiefel, Ethan *Ballerina*
American Ballet Theatre, 890 Broadway, New York, NY 10003 USA

Stiegler, Josef (Pepi) *Skier*
PO Box 290, Teton Village, WY 83025 USA

Stielike, Uli
Case Postale 78, Neuchatel, SWITZERLAND, CH-2000

Stiers, David Ogden *Actor*
Stubbs, 8675 W Washington Blvd #203, Culver City, CA 90232 USA

Stigers, Curtis *Musician*
C Winston Simone Mgmt, 1790 Broadway #1000, New York, NY 10019 USA

Stiglitz, Joseph E *Nobel Prize Laureate*
Columbia University, International Affairs Building, New York, NY 10027 USA

Stigwood, Robert
122 E. 42nd St., New York, NY 10017

Stigwood, Robert C *Producer*
Barton Manor, Whippingham, East Cowes, Isle of Wight, PO32 6LB, UNITED KINGDOM (UK)

Stiles, Jackie *Basketball Player*
Patrick J Stiles, 115 E Hamilton, Claffin, KS 67525 USA

Stiles, Julia *Actor*
Bryan Zuriss, 409 N Camden Dr #202, Beverly Hills, CA 90210 USA

Stiles, Ryan *Actor, Comedian*
AKA Talent Agency, 6310 San Vicente Blvd #200, Los Angeles, CA 90048 USA

Stilgoe, Richard *Songwriter*
Noel Gray Artists, 24 Denmark St, London, WC2H 8NJ, UNITED KINGDOM (UK)

Still, Arthur B (Art) *Football Player*
20002 Missouri City Road, Liberty, MO 64068 USA

Still, Ken *Golfer*
1210 Princeton St, Fircrest, WA 98466 USA

Still, Ray *Musician, Conductor*
858 Scenic Hills Way, Annapolis, MD 21401 USA

Still, Susan L *Astronaut*
NASA, Johnson Space Center, 2101 NASA Road, Houston, TX 77058 USA

Still, William C Jr *Misc*
Columbia University, Chemistry Dept, New York, NY 10027 USA

Stiller, Ben *Actor, Director, Comedian*
United Talent Agency, 9560 Wilshire Blvd #500, Beverly Hills, CA 90212 USA

Stiller, Jerry *Actor, Comedian*
118 Riverside Dr #5A, New York, NY 10024 USA

Stiller, Stephen *Music Group, Musician*
17525 Ventura Blvd #210, Encino, CA 91316 USA

Stillman, Whit *Director*
International Creative Mgmt, 8942
Wilshire Blvd, #219, Beverly Hills, CA
90211 USA

Stills, Chris *Musician*
Atlantic Records, 9229 Sunset Blvd, #900,
Los Angeles, CA 90069 USA

Stills, Stephen
191 N. Phelps Ave., Winter Park, FL
32789

Stillwagon, Jim R *Football Player*
3999 Parkway Lane, Hilliard, OH 43026
USA

Stillwell, Richard D *Opera Singer*
1969 Rockingham St, McLean, VA 22101
USA

Stillwell, Roger *Football Player*
25 Woodland Court, Novato, CA 94947
USA

Stilson, Jeff *Producer*
Creative Artists Agency LCC (CAA-LA),
9830 Wilshire Blvd, Beverly Hills, CA
90212 USA

Stine, Richard *Editor, Cartoonist*
PO Box 4699, Rollingbay, WA 98061
USA

Stine, Robert L (R L) *Writer*
Scholastic Book Services, 555 Broadway,
New York, NY 10012 USA

Sting *Musician, Actor, Music Group,
Songwriter*
Outlandos, 2 Grove, Highgate Village,
London, N16, UNITED KINGDOM (UK)

Stingley, Darryl *Football Player*
400 E Randolph St #K125, Chicago, IL
60601 USA

Stipe, Michael *Musician, Songwriter*
REM/Athens Ltd, 170 College Ave, Athens,
GA 30601 USA

Stiritz, William P *Business Person*
Ralston Purina Co, Checkerboard Square,
Saint Louis, MO 63164 USA

Stirling, Rachel *Actor*
Management Inc, 2032 Pinehurst Rd, Los
Angeles, CA 90068

Stirling, Steve *Hockey Player, Coach*
New York Islanders, Nassau Coliseum,
Hempstead Trunpike, Uniondate, NY
11553 USA

Stitch, Stephen P *Misc*
Rutgers University, Philosophy Dept, New
Brunswick, NJ 08901 USA

Stith, Bryant *Basketball Player*
20697 Governor Harrison Parkway,
Freeman, VA 23856 USA

Stobart, John *Artist*
613/4 Bat Club Dr, Fort Lauderdale, FL
33308 USA

Stobbs, Charles K (Chuck) *Baseball Player*
1731 Rivera Circle, Sarasota, FL 34232
USA

Stock, Barbara *Actor*
19045 Sprague St, Tarzana, CA 91356
USA

Stock-Poynton, Amy *Actor*
Artists Group, 10100 Santa Monica Blvd,
#2490, Los Angeles, CA 90067 USA

Stockdale, Gretchen
520 Washington Blvd. #248, Marina del
Rey, CA 90292

Stockdale, James
Hoover Inst, Stanford, CA 94305-6010
USA

Stockdale, James B *Admiral, War Hero*
547 A Ave, Coronado, CA 92118 USA

Stockhausen, Karl-Heinz
Stockhausen-Verlag, Kuerten, GERMANY,
D-51515

Stockhausen, Karlheinz *Composer*
Stockhausen-Vertag, Kurten, 51515,
GERMANY

Stockman, David A *Government Official,
Financier*
Blackstone Group, 345 Park Ave, New
York, NY 10154 USA

Stockman, Shawn *Music Group, Musician*
Southpaw Entertainment, 10675 Santa
Monica Blvd, Los Angeles, CA 90025 USA

Stockmayer, Walter H *Doctor, Misc*
Willey Hill, Norwich, VT 05055 USA

Stockton, Dave K *Golfer*
222 Escondido Dr, Redlands, CA 92373
USA

Stockton, Dick *Sportscaster*
2519 NW 59th St, Boca Raton, FL 33496
USA

Stockton, John H *Basketball Player*
Utah Jazz, Delta Center, 301 West South
Temple, Salt Lake City, UT 84101 USA

Stockton, Richard L (Dick) *Tennis Player*
715 Stadium Dr, San Antonio, TX 78212
USA

Stockwell, Dean *Actor*
95723 Highway 99 W, Junction City, OR
97448 USA

Stockwell, Jeff *Writer*
United Talent Agency (UTA), 9560
Wilshire Blvd, Beverly Hills, CA 90212
USA

Stockwell, John *Actor*
United Talent Agency, 9560 Wilshire Blvd
#500, Beverly Hills, CA 90212 USA

Stoddard, Brandon
241 N. Glenroy Ave., Los Angeles, CA
90049

Stoicheff, Boris P *Physicist*
66 Collier St #6B, Toronto, ON M4W
1L9, CANADA

Stoitchkov, Hristo *Soccer Player*
DC United, 14120 Newbrook Dr,
Chantilly, VA 20151 USA

Stojko, Elvis *Figure Skater*
Mentor Marketing, 2 Saint Clair Ave E,
Toronto, ON M4T 2T, CANADA

Stokes, Chris *Business Person, Musician,
Director*
Tobin & Associates PR, 6565 Sunset Blvd,
Suite 301, Hollywood, CA 90028 USA

Stokes of Leyland, Donald G *Business
Person*
2 Branksome Cliff, Westminster Road
Poole, Dorset, BH13 6JW, UNITED
KINGDOM (UK)

Stokkan, Bill *Race Car Driver*
Championship Auto Racing, 5350
Lakeview Parkway S Dr, Indianapolis, IN
46268 USA

Stoklos, Randy *Volleyball Player*
Assn of Volleyball Pros, 330 Washington
Blvd #400, Marina del Rey, CA 90292
USA

Stole, Mink *Actor*
3155 Ettrick St, Los Angeles, CA 90027
USA

Stolhanske, Erik *Comedian*
United Talent Agency (UTA), 9560
Wilshire Blvd, Beverly Hills, CA 90212
USA

Stolle, Frederick S *Tennis Player*
Turnberry Isle Yacht & Racquet Club,
19735 Turnberry Way, Miami, FL 33180
USA

Stoller, Mike *Composer*
Leiber/Stoller Entertainment, 9000 W
Sunset Blvd, West Hollywood, CA 90069
USA

Stollery, David *Actor*
3203 Bern Court, Laguna Beach, CA
92651 USA

Stolley, Paul D *Doctor*
6424 Brass Knob, Columbia, MD 21044
USA

Stolley, Richard B *Editor*
Time Inc, Time-Life Building, Rockefeller
Center, New York, NY 10020 USA

Stolojan, Theodor *Prime Minister*
World Bank, 1818 H St NW, Washington,
DC 20433 USA

Stolper, Pinchas *Religious Leader*
Orthodox Jewish Congregations Union, 11
Broadway, New York, NY 10004 USA

Stoltz, Eric *Actor*
7575 Mulholland Dr, Los Angeles, CA
90046 USA

Stoltzman, Richard L *Musician*
Frank Salomon, 201 W 54th St #1C, New
York, NY 10019 USA

Stolze, Lena *Actor*
Agentur Carola Studlar, Neuroeder Str 1C,
Planegg, 82152, GERMANY

Stomare, Peter
1129 N. Poinsettia Dr., W. Hollywood,
CA 90046

Stone, Albert L *Race Car Driver*
700 Central Ave, PO Box 8427, Louisville,
KY 40208 USA

Stone, Andrew L *Director*
2132 Century Park Lane #212, Los
Angeles, CA 90067 USA

Stone, Angie *Musician*
Creative Artist Agency, 9830 Wilshire
Blvd, Beverly Hills, CA 90212 USA

Stone, Dee Wallace *Actor*
23035 Cumorah Crest Dr, Woodland
Hills, CA 91364 USA

Stone, Doug *Musician, Music Group,
Songwriter*
PO Box 943, Springfield, TN 37172 USA

Stone, Edward C Jr *Physicist*
Jet Propulsion Laboratory, 4800 Oak
Grove Dr #180-904, Pasadena, CA 91109
USA

Stone, George H *Baseball Player*
1206 Eastland Ave, Ruston, LA 71270
USA

Stone, Jack *Religious Leader*
Church of Nazarene, 6401 Paseo, Kansas
City, MO 64131 USA

Stone, James L *War Hero*
1279 Cedarland Plaza Dr, Arlington, TX
76011 USA

Stone, Joss *Musician, Songwriter*
S-Curve Records, 150 5th Ave, #900, New
York, NY 10011 USA

Stone, Kelly
1531 Sunset Plaza Dr. #315, Los Angeles,
CA 90069

Stone, Leonard *Actor*
Capital Artists, 6404 Wilshire Blvd #950,
Los Angeles, CA 90048 USA

Stone, Matt *Writer, Animator*
Barnes Morris Klein Young, 1424 2nd St
#3, Santa Monica, CA 90401 USA

Stone, Nikki *Skier*
Podium Enterprises, PO Box 680-332,
Park City, UT 84068 USA

Stone, Oliver *Director, Producer*
Ixtlan, 1207 Fourth St, Penthouse 1, Santa
Monica, CA 90401

Stone, Oliver W *Director, Writer*
Steven Pines, 520 Broadway #600, Santa
Monica, CA 90401 USA

Stone, Rob
8033 Sunset Blvd. #450, Los Angeles, CA
90046

Stone, Robert A *Writer*
Donadio & Ashworth, 121 W 27th St
#704, New York, NY 10001 USA

Stone, Roger D *Politician*
34 W 88th St, New York, NY 10024 USA

Stone, Sammy
PO Box 2825, Port Arthur, TX 77642

Stone, Sharon *Actor*
P M K Public Relations, 8500 Wilshire
Blvd #700, Beverly Hills, CA 90211 USA

Stone, Sly *Musician, Music Group,*
Songwriter
Richard Walters, 1800 Argyle Ave #408,
Los Angeles, CA 90028 USA

Stone, Steven M (Steve) *Baseball Player,*
Sportscaster
8340 E Cheryl Dr, Scottsdale, AZ 85258
USA

Stone Temple Pilots *Music Group*
William Morris Agency (WMA-LA), 1
William Morris Pl, Beverly Hills, CA
90212 USA

Stonecipher, David A *Financier*
Jefferson-Pilot Corp, 100 N Greene St,
Greensboro, NC 27401 USA

Stonecipher, Harry C *Business Person*
Boeing Co, PO Box 3707, Seattle, WA
98124 USA

Stoneman, Ronl *Musician*
111 Redberry Road, Smyma, TN 37167
USA

Stoner, Alyson *Musician*
Osbrink Talent Agency, 4343 Lankershim
Blvd #100, Universal City, CA 91602 USA

Stones
4790 Irvine Blvd. #105, Irvine, CA 92720-
1998

Stones, Dwight E *Track Athlete*
4790 Irvine Blvd #105, Irvine, CA 92620
USA

Stones, Rolling *Musician*
Rogers & Cowan PR NYC, 640 Fifth Ave
Fl 5, New York, NY 10019 USA

Stones People Europe
1217 JT, Hilversum, THE NETHERLANDS
(HOL

Stonesipher, Don *Football Player*
1502 Canberry Court, Wheeling, IL 60090
USA

Stonestreet, Eric *Actor*
TalentWorks (LA), 3500 W Olive Ave
#1400, Burbank, CA 91505 USA

Stookey, Paul *Musician, Music Group,*
Songwriter
Newworld, RR 175, South Blue Hill Falls,
ME 04615 USA

Stoops, Bob *Football Coach*
University of Oklahoma, Athletic Dept,
108 Brooks St, Norman, OK 73069 USA

Stoops, Mike *Football Coach*
Arizona State University, Athletic Dept,
Tempe, AZ 85287 USA

Stoppard, Tom S *Writer*
P F D, Drury House, 34-43 Russell St,
London, WC2B 5HA, UNITED KINGDOM
(UK)

Storaro, Vittorio *Cinematographer*
Via Divino Amore 2, Frattocchie Merino,
00040, ITALY

Storch, Larry *Actor*
330 W End Ave #17F, New York, NY
10023 USA

Storey, David M *Writer*
2 Lyndhurst Gardens, London, NW3,
UNITED KINGDOM (UK)

Storey, June
338 Morgan Pl., Vista, CA 92083-8018

Stork, Gilbert *Misc*
188 Chestnut St, Englewood Cliffs, NJ
07632 USA

Stork, Jeff *Volleyball Player*
Pepperdine University, Athletic Dept,
24255 Pacific Coast Hwy, Malibu, CA
90263 USA

Storke, Adam *Actor*
Personal Management Company, 425 N
Robertson Dr, Los Angeles, CA 90048
USA

Storm, Crystal
2139 University Dr. #297, Coral Springs,
FL 33071

Storm, Gale *Actor, Musician*
23831 Bluehill Bay, Dana Point, CA
92629 USA

Storm, Hannah *Commentator, Sportscaster*
CBS-TV, News Dept, 51 W 52nd St, New
York, NY 10019 USA

Storm, Jim
13576 Cheltenham Dr., Sherman Oaks,
CA 91423

Storm, Tempest *Dancer*
PO Box 2095, Helendale, CA 92342 USA

Stormare, Peter *Actor*
1129 Poinsettia Dr, West Hollywood, CA
90046 USA

Stormer, Horst L *Nobel Prize Laureate*
20 E 9th St #14P, New York, NY 10003
USA

Storms, Kirsten *Actor*
Elements Entertainment, 2401 W Olive
Ave #290, Burbank, CA 91506 USA

Storraro, Vittorio *Cinematographer*
International Creative Management
(ICM-LA), 8942 Wilshire Blvd, Beverly
Hills, CA 90211 USA

Story, Liz *Musician, Songwriter*
SRO Artists, PO Box 9532, Madison, WI
53715 USA

Story, Ralph *Commentator*
3425 Wonderview Dr, Los Angeles, CA
90068 USA

Story, Tim *Director*
William Morris Agency (WMA-LA), 1
William Morris Pl, Beverly Hills, CA
90212 USA

Stossel, John *Commentator*
Beresford Apartments, 211 Central Park
West #15K, New York, NY 10024 USA

Stott, Kathryn L *Musician*
Mire House, West Martor near Skipton,
Yorks, BD23 3UQ, UNITED KINGDOM
(UK)

Stott, Nicole P *Astronaut*
NASA, Johnson Space Center, 2101 NASA
Road, Houston, TX 77058 USA

Stottlemyre, Mel
26004 SE 27th St., Issaquah, WA 98029

Stottlemyre, Melvin L (Mel) *Baseball*
Player
1007 Tower Dr, Edgewater, NJ 07020
USA

Stotts, Terry *Coach*
Golden State Warriors, 1001 Broadway,
Oakland, CA 94607 USA

Stoudamire, Damon *Basketball Player*
4114 N Vancouver Ave, Portland, OR
97217 USA

Stoudemire, Amare *Basketball Player*
Phoenix Suns, 201 E Jefferson St, Phoenix,
AZ 85004 USA

Stouder, Sharon M *Swimmer*
144 Loucks Ave, Los Altos, CA 94022
USA

Stoudt, Bud *Bowler*
431 Lehman St, Lebanon, PA 17046 USA

Stoudt, Cliff *Football Player*
326 Doe Run Circle, Henderson, NV
89012 USA

Stovall, Jerry L *Football Player*
417 Highland Trace Dr #D, Baton Rouge,
LA 70810 USA

Stove, Betty *Tennis Player*
Advantage International, 1025 Thomas
Jeffferson NW #450, Washington, DC
20007 USA

Stover, George *Actor*
PO Box 10005, Baltimore, MD 21285
USA

Stover, Irwin Russ Juno *Swimmer, Misc*
512 Lanai Circle, Union City, CA 94587
USA

Stowe, David H Jr *Business Person*
Deere Co, John Deere Road, Moline, IL
61265 USA

Stowe, Madeleine *Actor*
United Talent Agency (UTA), 9560
Wilshire Blvd, Beverly Hills, CA 90212
USA

Stowe, Medeleine *Actor*
United Talent Agency, 9560 Wilshire Blvd
#500, Beverly Hills, CA 90212 USA

Stoyanov, Krasimir M *Misc*
Potchta Kosmonavtov, Moskovskoi
Oblasti, Syvisdny Goroduk, 141160,
RUSSIA

Stoyanov, Michael
3172 Dona Susana Dr, Studio City, CA
91604-4536

Stoyanovich, Peter (Pete) *Football Player*
1429 SE 2nd Court, Fort Lauderdale, FL
33301 USA

Stracey, John *Boxer*
Van Laeken 4, Norsey Road Billericay,
Essex, CM11 2AD, UNITED KINGDOM
(UK)

Strachan, Rod *Swimmer*
11632 Ranch Hill, Santa Ana, CA 92705
USA

Strader, Cam *Race Car Driver*
9913 Liberty Bell Court, Charlotte, NC
28269 USA

Stradford, Troy *Football Player*
20636 NE 7th Court, Miami, FL 33179
USA

Stradlin, Izzy *Musician*
Big FD Entertainment, 301 Arizona Ave
#200, Santa Monica, CA 90401 USA

Stradling, Harry A Jr *Cinematographer*
3664 Avenida Callada, Calabasas, CA
91302 USA

Strahan, Michael A *Football Player*
New York Giants, Giants Stadium, East
Rutherford, NJ 07073 USA

Straight, Bering *Music Group*
Creative Artists Agency (CAA-Nashville),
3310 West End Ave Fl 5, Nashville, TN
37203 USA

Strain, Julie *Actor, Model*
Candy Entertainment Management, 8981
West Sunset Blvd, Ste 310, Hollywood,
CA 90069 USA

Strain, Sammy *Musician, Music Group*
Associated Booking Corp, 1995 Broadway
#501, New York, NY 10023 USA

Strait, Donald *War Hero*
6 Burning Tree Place, Jackson Springs, NC
27281 USA

Strait, George *Musician*
Erv Woolsey Agency, The, 1000 18th Ave
S, Nashville, TN 37212 USA

Straka, Martin *Hockey Player*
Pittsburgh Penguins, Mellon Arena, 66
Mario Lemieux Place, Pittsburgh, PA
15219 USA

Stram, Hank
194 Belle Terre Blvd, Covington, LA
70483

Stram, Henry L (Hank) *Football Coach,
Sportscaster*
194 Belle Terre Blvd, Covington, LA
70433 USA

Strampe, Bob *Bowler*
5875 W Michigan Ave, Saginaw, MI
48603 USA

Strand, Mark *Writer*
Knopf Publishers, 201 E 50th St, New
York, NY 10022 USA

Strand, Robin *Actor*
4118 Elmer Ave, North Hollywood, CA
91602 USA

Strane, John *War Hero*
18230 Mirasol Dr, San Diego, CA 92128
USA

Strang, Deborah *Actor*
Henderson/Hogan, 8285 W Sunset Blvd
#1, West Hollywood, CA 90046 USA

Strang, William G *Mathematician*
7 Southgate Road, Wellesley, MA 02181
USA

Strange, Curtis N *Golfer, Sportscaster*
137 Thomas Dale, Williamsburg, VA
23185 USA

Strange, Sarah *Actor*
Agency for the Performing Arts (APA-LA),
9200 Sunset Blvd #900, Los Angeles, CA
90069 USA

Strange-Hansen, Martin *Actor*
Gersh Agency, The (LA), 232 N Canon Dr,
Beverly Hills, CA 90210 USA

Strasser, Robin *Actor*
PO Box 1892, Ojai, CA 93024 USA

Strasser, Teresa *Comedian, Television
Host*
OmniPop Inc (LA), 10700 Ventura Blvd Fl
2, Studio City, CA 91604 USA

Strassman, Marcia *Actor*
5115 Douglas Fir Road #E, Calabasas, CA
91302 USA

Stratas, Teresa *Opera Singer*
Vincent Farrell Assoc, 481 8th Ave #340,
New York, NY 10001 USA

Strathairn, David *Actor*
United Talent Agency (UTA), 9560
Wilshire Blvd, Beverly Hills, CA 90212
USA

Stratham, Jason *Actor*
International Creative Mgmt, 8942
Wilshire Blvd #219, Beverly Hills, CA
90211 USA

Strathiam, David *Actor*
United Talent Agency, 9560 Wilshire Blvd
#500, Beverly Hills, CA 90212 USA

Stratton, Frederick P Jr *Business Person*
Briggs & Stratton, PO Box 702,
Milwaukee, WI 53201 USA

Stratton, Gil
4227 Colfax Ave. #B, Studio City, CA
91604-2953

Stratus, Trish *Wrestler*
World Wrestling Entertainment (WWE),
1241 E Main St, Stamford, CT 06905 USA

Straub, Peter
53 W. 85th St., New York, NY 10026

Straub, Peter F *Writer*
53 W 85th St, New York, NY 10024 USA

Straus, Robert *Scientist*
656 Raintree Road, Lexington, KY 40502
USA

Straus Jr, William L *Philanthropist*
7111 Park Heights Ave, #506, baltimore,
MD 21215 USA

Strauss, Peter *Actor*
Wolf/Kasteller, 335 n Maple Dr, #351,
Beverly Hills, CA 90210 USA

Strauss, Robert S *Politician, Diplomat*
Akin Gump Strauss Hauer Feld, 1700
Pacific Ave, #4100, Dallas, TX 75201
USA

Straw, John W (Jack) *Government Official*
House of Commons, Westminster,
London, SW1A 0AA, UNITED KINGDOM
(UK)

Straw, Syd *Musician*
Agency Group Ltd, 1775 Broadway, #430,
New York, NY 10019 USA

Strawberry, Darryl E *Baseball Player*
5118 Rue Vendorne, Lutz, FL 33558 USA

Strawberry Blondes
Box 33 Pontypool, Gwent, ENGLAND,
NP4 6YU

Strawser, Neil *Commentator*
130 E St SE, Washington, DC 20003 USA

Streep, Meryl *Actor*
Creative Artists Agency, 9830 Wilshire
Blvd, Beverly Hills, CA 90212 USA

Street, John *Politician*
Mayor's Office, City Hall, 23 N Juniper St,
Philadelphia, PA 19107 USA

Street, Picabo *Skier*
PO Box 321, Hailey, ID 83333 USA

Street, Rebecca *Actor*
225 S Gramercy Place, Los Angeles, CA
90004 USA

Streetman, Ben G *Engineer*
3915 Glengarry Dr, Austin, TX 78731
USA

Streisand, Barbra *Musician, Producer,
Director, Actor*
160 W 96th St, New York, NY 10025
USA

Streit, Clarence K *Journalist*
2853 Ontario Road NW, Washington, DC
20009 USA

Streitwieser Jr, Andrew *Misc*
University of California, Chemistry Dept,
berkeley, CA 94720 USA

Strekalov, Gennadi M *Cosmonaut*
Federation Peace Committee, 36 Mira
Prospekt, Moscow, 129090, RUSSIA

Stretton, Ross *Dancer*
American Ballet Theatre, 890 Broadway,
New York, NY 10003 USA

Stricker, Steve *Golfer*
1629 N Golf Glen, Madison, WI 53704
USA

Strickland, Amzie *Actor*
1329 N Ogden Dr, Los Angeles, CA
90046 USA

Strickland, Gail *Actor*
14732 Oracle Place, Pacific Palisades, CA
90272 USA

Strickland, KaDee *Actor*
United Talent Agency (UTA), 9560
Wilshire Blvd, Beverly Hills, CA 90212
USA

Strickland, Rod *Basketball Player*
114 W Glenview Dr #300, San Antonio,
TX 78228 USA

Stringer, C Vivian *Coach*
Rutgers University, Athletic Dept, New
Brunswick, NJ 08903 USA

Stringer, Howard *Television Host*
186 Riverside Dr, New York, NY 10024
USA

Stringfield, Sherry *Actor*
United Talent Agency (UTA), 9560
Wilshire Blvd, Beverly Hills, CA 90212
USA

Stritch, Elaine *Musician, Actor*
Michael Whitehall, 125 Gloucester Road,
London, SW7 4TE, UNITED KINGDOM
(UK)

Strobel, Eric *Hockey Player*
6617 129th St W, Apple Valley, MN
55124 USA

Strock, Donald J (Don) *Football Player,
Football Coach*
1512 Passion Vine Circle, Weston, FL
33326 USA

Strock, Herbert L *Director*
1630 Hilts Ave, #205, Los Angeles, CA
90024 USA

Stroessner, Alfredo *President, General*
Lago Sul, Brasilia, BRAZIL

Strohmayer, Tod *Astronomer*
Goddard Space Flight Center, NASA/
GSFC, Greenbelt, MD 20771 USA

Strolz, Hubert *Skier*
6767 Warth 19, AUSTRIA

Strom, Brock T *Football Player*
4301 W 110th St, Leawood, KS 66211
USA

Strominger, Jack L *Misc*
Dana Faber Cancer Institute, Biochemistry
Dept, 44 Binney St, Boston, MA 02115
USA

Strong, Brenda *Actor*
S D B Partners, 1801 Ave of Stars, #902,
Los Angeles, CA 90035 USA

Strong, Danny *Actor*
Koopman Management, 851 Oreo Pl,
Pacific Palisades, CA 90272 USA

Strong, Johnny *Actor*
Anonymous Content, 8522 National Blvd
#101, Culver City, CA 90232 USA

Strong, Maurice F *Government Official*
255 Consummers Road, #401, Toronto,
ON M2J 5B6, CANADA

Strong, Rider *Actor*
Yorke & Harper, 800 S Robertson Blvd,
#2, Los Angeles, CA 90035 USA

Strong, Tara *Actor*
International Creative Management
(ICM-LA), 8942 Wilshire Blvd, Beverly
Hills, CA 90211 USA

Stroock, Daniel W *Mathematician*
55 Frost St, Cambridge, MA 02140 USA

Strossen, Nadine *Lawyer*
57 Worth St, New York, NY 10013 USA

Stroud, Carlos *Misc*
Rockefeller University, Physics Dept, 1230
York Ave, Cambridge, MA 02138 USA

Stroud, Don *Actor*
1347 Gates Ave, Manhattan Beach, CA
90266 USA

Stroup Jr, Theodore G (Ted) *General*
2085 Hopewood Dr, Falls Church, VA
22043 USA

Strouse, Charles *Composer*
171 W 57th St, New York, NY 10019
USA

Strube, Juergen F *Business Person*
BASF Corp, Carl-Bosch Str 38,
Ludwigshafen, 67063, GERMANY

Struber, Larry *Producer*
William Morris Agency (WMA-LA), 1
William Morris Pl, Beverly Hills, CA
90212 USA

Struchkova, Raisa S *Ballerina*
Sovetskiy Ballet, Tverskaya 22B, Moscow,
103050, RUSSIA

Struever, Stuart M *Misc*
200 Sheridan Road, Evanston, IL 60208
USA

Strug, Kerri *Gymnast, Athlete*
2801 N Camino Principal, Tucson, AZ
85715 USA

Strugnell, John *Misc*
Harvard University, Divinity School, 45
Francis Ave, Cambridge, MA 02138 USA

Strus, Lusia *Actor*
Himber Entertainment Inc, 211 S Beverly
Dr #208, Beverly Hills, CA 90212 USA

Struthers, Sally *Actor*
8721 W Sunset Blvd, #210, Los Angeles,
CA 90069 USA

Struycken, Carel *Actor*
1665 E Mountain St, Pasadena, CA 91104
USA

Stryker, Bradley *Actor*
House of Representatives, 400 S Beverly
Dr #101, Beverly Hills, CA 90212 USA

Strykert, Ron *Musician*
TPA, PO Box 124, Round Corner, NSW,
2158, AUSTRALIA

Stuart, Barbara *Actor*
11156 Valley Spring Lane, North
Hollywood, CA 91602 USA

Stuart, Gloria *Actor*
884 S Bundy Dr, Los Angeles, CA 90049
USA

Stuart, Jason *Comedian, Actor*
Bonny Dore Management, 8530 Wilshire
Blvd #400, Beverly Hills, CA 90211

Stuart, Lyle *Publisher*
1530 Palisade Ave, #6L, Fort Lee, NJ
07024 USA

Stuart, Marty *Musician, Songwriter*
Gurley Co, 1204B Cedar Lane, Nashville,
TN 37212 USA

Stuart, Maxine *Actor*
S D B Partners, 1801 Ave of Stars, #902,
Los Angeles, CA 90067 USA

Stuart, Roy *Actor*
4948 Radford Ave, North Hollywood, CA
91607 USA

Stubbins Jr, Hugh Asher *Architect*
6110 N Ocean Blvd, Boynton Beach, FL
33435 USA

Stubblefield, Dana W *Football Player*
420 E State St, Columbus, OH 43215 USA

Stubbs, Imogen M *Actor*
International Creative Mgmt, 76 Oxford
St, London, W1N 0AX, UNITED
KINGDOM (UK)

Stubbs, Levi *Musician*
William Morris Agency, 151 El Camino
Dr, Beverly Hills, CA 90212 USA

Stuck, Hans-Joachim *Race Car Driver*
Harmstatt 3, Ellmau/Tirol, 6352, AUSTRIA

Stuckey, James (Jim) *Football Player*
2044 Egret Lane, Charleston, SC 29414
USA

Studdard, Ruben *Musician*
J Records (Division of BMG
Entertainment), 745 Fifth Avenue, New
York, NY 10151 USA

Studds, Gerry *Politician*
146 Main St., Hyannis, MA 02601

Studenroth, Carl W *Misc*
Molders & Allied Workers Union, 1225 E
McMillan St, Cincinnati, OH 45206 USA

Studer, Cheryl *Opera Singer*
Columbia Artists Mgmt Inc, 165 W 57th
St, New York, NY 10019 USA

Studi, Wes *Actor*
Michael Mann Talent Mgmt, 617 S Olive
St #510, Los Angeles, CA 90014 USA

Studstill, Patrick L (Pat) *Football Player*
2235 Linda Flora Dr, Los Angeles, CA
90077 USA

Studt, Amy *Musician*
19 Management Ltd, 33 Ransomes Dock,
35-37 Parkgate Rd, London, SW11 4NP,
UNITED KINGDOM (UK)

Stuhr, Jerzy *Actor, Director*
Graffutu Ltd, Ul SW Gertrudy 5, Cracow,
31-107, POLAND

Stults, Geoff *Actor*
3 Arts Entertainment Inc, 9460 Wilshire
Blvd Fl 7, Beverly Hills, CA 90212 USA

Stults, George *Actor*
Warren Cowan & Associates PR, 8899
Beverly Blvd #919, Los Angeles, CA
90048 USA

Stump, David *Cinematographer*
HFWD Creative Representation, 394 E
Glaucus St, Encinitas, CA 92024 USA

Stumpf, Kenneth E *War Hero*
16528 State Highway 131, Tomah, WI
54660 USA

Stumpf, Paul K *Misc*
764 Elmwood Dr, Davis, CA 95616 USA

Stumps, Kathy *Actor*
Gersh Agency, The (LA), 232 N Canon Dr, Beverly Hills, CA 90210 USA

Sturckow, Frederick W (Rick) *Astronaut*
RR 2 Box 14, Dickinson, TX 77539 USA

Sturdivant, John N *Misc*
American Government Employees Federation, 80 F St NW, Washington, DC 20001 USA

Sturdivant, Thomas V (Tom) *Baseball Player*
1324 SW 71st St, Oklahoma City, OK 73159 USA

Sturdivant, Tom
1324 SW 71st St., Oklahoma City, OK 73159

Sturgeon, Bob
3903 Lewis Ave., Long Beach, CA 90807

Sturgess, Shannon *Actor*
1223 Wilshire Blvd, #577, Santa Monica, CA 90403 USA

Sturm, John F *Misc*
Newspaper Assn of America, 1921 Gallows Road, #4, Vienna, VA 22182 USA

Sturm, Yfke *Model*
Elite Model Mgmt, 111 E 22nd St, #200, New York, NY 10010 USA

Sturman, Eugene *Artist*
1108 W Washington Blvd, Venice, CA 90291 USA

Sturr, Jimmy *Musician*
United Polka Artists, PO Box 1, Florida, NY 10921 USA

Sturridge, Charles *Director*
PFD, Drury House, 34-43 Russell St, London, WC2B 5HA, UNITED KINGDOM (UK)

Sturtevant, Julian M *Misc*
14025 3rd Ave, NW, Seattle, WA 98177 USA

Sturza, Ion *Prime Minister*
Premier's Office, Piaca Maril Atuner Nacional, Chishinev, 277033, MOLDOVA

Stuttering John *Radio Personality*
Howard Stern Show WXRK (K-Rock), 40 West 57th Street, 14th Floor, New York, NY 10019 USA

Stutzmann, Nathalie *Opera Singer*
Herbert Breslin, 119 W 57th St, #1505, New York, NY 10019 USA

Styler, Kara
PO Box 8002, Honolulu, HI 96820

Styler, Trudie *Actor, Producer, Director*
Xingu Films, 12 Cleveland Row, St James, London, SW1A 1DH, UNITED KINGDOM (UK)

Styron, Alexandra *Writer*
Little Brown, 3 Center Plaza, Boston, MA 02108 USA

Styron, William
12 Rucum Rd., Roxbury, CT 06783

Styron Jr, William C *Writer*
12 Rucum Road, Roxbury, CT 06783 USA

Styx *Musician*
Creative Artists Agency LCC (CAA-LA), 9830 Wilshire Blvd, Beverly Hills, CA 90212 USA

Suarez, Carlos *Actor*
Televisa, Blvd Adolfo Lopez Mateos 232, Colonia San Angel INN, DF, CP 01060, MEXICO

Suarez Gomez, Hector *Actor*
Gabriel Blanco Iglesias (Mexico), Rio Balsas 35-32, Colonia Cuauhtemoc, DF, 06500, Mexico

Suarez Gonzalez, Adolfo *Prime Minister*
Sagasta, 33, Madrid, 4, SPAIN

Suarez Rivera, Adolfo A Cardinal
Religious Leader
Apartado Postal 7, Loma Larga 2429 Sierra Madre, Monterrey, 64000, MEXICO

Suau, Anthony *Journalist*
Denver Post, PO Box 1709, Denver, CO 80201 USA

Subhash, B *Actor, Bollywood*
1 Coelho House, Juhu Tara Road Juhu, Mumbai, MS 400049, INDIA

Subotnick, Morton L *Composer*
25 Minetta Lane, #4B, New York, NY 10012 USA

Such, Alec John *Musician*
Bon Jovi Mgmt, 248 W 17th St, #501, New York, NY 10011 USA

Suchet, David *Actor*
Ken McReddie, 91 Regent St, London, W1R 7TB, UNITED KINGDOM (UK)

Suchocka, Hanna *Prime Minister*
Urzad Rady Ministrow, Al Ujazdowskie 1/3, Warsaw, 00-567, POLAND

Sudakis, Bill
16641 Algonquin, Huntington Beach, CA 92649

Sudan, Madhu *Scientist*
81 Benton Road, Somerville, MA 02143 USA

Sudduth, Jill *Swimmer*
15910 Sunnyside Ave, Morgan Hill, CA 95037 USA

Sudduth, Skip *Actor*
Writers and Artists Group Intl (LA), 8383 Wilshire Blvd #550, Beverly Hills, CA 90211 USA

Sudduth, Skipp *Actor*
Writers & Artists, 8383 Wilshire Blvd, #550, Beverly Hills, CA 90211 USA

Sudersham, Ennackel *Physicist*
University of Texas, Physics Dept, Austin, TX 78713 USA

Sudharmono *General, Government Official*
Senopati St 44B, Jakarta Selatan, INDONESIA

Suede
PO Box 3431, London, ENGLAND, N1 7LW

Sues, Alan *Actor*
9014 Dorrington Ave, West Hollywood, CA 90048 USA

Suess, Hans E *Misc*
University of California, Chemistry Dept, La Jolla, CA 92093 USA

Suganya *Actor, Bollywood*
4/5 Oorur Alcot, 5thAvenue Besant Nagar, Chennai, TN 600090, INDIA

Sugar, Bert Randolph *Writer*
6 Southview Road, Chappaqua, NY 10514 USA

Sugar, Leo T *Football Player*
7161 Golden Eagle Court, #1012, Fort Myers, FL 33912 USA

Sugarcult *Actor*
Kio Novina Management & Booking, 545 N Rossmore Ave, #3, Los Angeles, CA 90004

Sugarman, Burt *Producer*
Giant Group, 9440 Santa Monica Blvd, #407, Beverly Hills, CA 90210 USA

Sugarman, Joe

Sugarman, Josh *Social Activist*
1650 Harvard St NW, Washington, DC 20009 USA

Sugden, Mollie
Hazel Cottage Wheeler End Commons Lane End, Bucks, ENGLAND, HP14 3NL

Sugg, Diana K *Journalist*
Baltimore Sun, Editorial Dept, 501 N Calvert St, Baltimore, MD 21202 USA

Suggs, Louise
2000 S. Ocean Blvd., Del Ray Beach, FL 33483

Suggs, M Louise *Golfer*
424 Royal Crescent Court, Saint Augustine, FL 32092 USA

Suggs, Terrell *Football Player*
Baltimore Ravens, Ravens Stadium, 11001 Russell St, Baltimore, MD 21230 USA

Suharto, Mohamed *General, President*
8 Jalan Cendana, Jakarta, INDONESIA

Suhey, Matthew J (Matt) *Football Player*
550 Carriage Way, Deerfield, IL 60015 USA

Suhl, Harry *Physicist*
University of California, Physics Dept, 9500 Gilman Dr, La Jolla, CA 92093 USA

Suhonen, Alpo *Coach*
Chicago Blackhawks, United Center, 1901 W Madison St, Chicago, IL 60612 USA

Suhor, Yvonne *Actor*
J Michael Bloom, 233 Park Ave S, #1000, New York, NY 10003 USA

Suhr, August R (Gus) *Baseball Player*
4516 E Marion Way, Phoenix, AZ 85018 USA

Suhrheinrich, Richard F *Judge*
US Court of Appeals, 315 W Allegan, Lansing, MI 48933 USA

Suhrstedt, Timothy *Cinematographer*
Gersh Agency, 232 N Canon Dr, Beverly Hills, CA 90210 USA

Sui, Anna *Fashion Designer*
Anna Sui Corp, 275 W 39th St, New York, NY 10018 USA

Suitner, Otmar
Platanestr 13, Berlin-Niederschonhausen, 13156, GERMANY

Suits, Julla *Cartoonist*
Creators Syndicate, 5777 W Century Blvd, #700, Los Angeles, CA 90045 USA

Suk, Josef *Musician*
Karlovo Namesti 5, Prague 2, 12000, CZECH REPUBLIC

Sukawaty, Andrew *Business Person*
Sprint PCS Group, PO Box 11315, Kensas City, KS 66111 USA

Sukova, Helena *Tennis Player*
1 Ave Grande Bretagne, Monte Carlo, MONACO

Sukowa, Barbara *Actor*
Artmedia, 20 Ave Rapp, Paris, 75007, FRANCE

Sukselainen, Vieno J *Prime Minister*
Palvattarenpolku 2, Tapiola, 02100, FINALND

Sulaiman, Jose *Misc*
World Boxing Council, Genova 33, Colonia Juarez, Cuahtetemoc, 0660, MEXICO

Suleymanoglu, Naim *Wrestler*
Olympic Committee, Sisli, Buyukdere Cad 18 Tankaya, Istanbul, TURKEY

Suliotis, Elena *Opera Singer*
Villa il Poderino, Via Incontri, Florence, 38, ITALY

Sullivan, Daniel *Writer, Producer*
Jackoway Tyerman Wertheimer Austen Mandelbaum & Morris, 1888 Century Park E Fl 18, Los Angeles, CA 90067 USA

Sullivan, Danny *Race Car Driver*
434 E Cooper St, #201, Aspen, CO 81611 USA

Sullivan, Dennis P *Mathematician*
Queens College, Mathematics Dept, 33 W 42nd St #308, New York, NY 10036 USA

Sullivan, Erik Per *Actor*
Jodi Peikoff Law Office, 76 Greene Street, Suite 3B, New York, NY 10012 USA

Sullivan, Frank *Athlete*
PO Box 1873, Lihue, HI 96766

Sullivan, Franklin L (Frank) *Baseball Player*
PO Box 1873, Lihue, HI 96766 USA

Sullivan, Greg *Musician*
David Levin Mgmt, 200 W 57th St, #308, New York, NY 10019 USA

Sullivan, Kathleen *Commentator*
1025 N Kings Road, #202, West Hollywood, CA 90069 USA

Sullivan, Kathryn D *Astronaut*
795 Old Oak Trace, Columbus, OH 43235 USA

Sullivan, Kevin *Journalist*
Washington Post, Editorial Dept, 1150 15th St NW, Washington, DC 20071 USA

Sullivan, Louis W *Secretary*
Morehouse College, Medical School, 720 Westview Dr SW, Atlanta, GA 30310 USA

Sullivan, Michael J (Mike) *Governor*
1140 S Center St, Casper, WY 82601 USA

Sullivan, Mike *Hockey Player, Coach*
9 Gardner Road, Duxbury, MA 02332 USA

Sullivan, Nicole *Actor*
ODE, 5842 Sunset Blvd, Building 11, Beverly Hills, CA 90212 USA

Sullivan, Pattrick J (Pat) *Football Player, Football Coach*
1717 Indian Creek Dr, Birmingham, AL 35243 USA

Sullivan, Susan *Actor*
8642 Allenwood Road, Los Angeles, CA 90046 USA

Sullivan, Tim *Director*
Agency for Performing Arts, 9200 Sunset Blvd, #900, Los Angeles, CA 90069 USA

Sullivan, Timothy J *Educator*
College of William & Mary, President's Office, Williamsburg, VA 23187 USA

Sullivan, William J *Educator*
Seattle University, President's Office, Seattle, WA 98122 USA

Sullivan Jr, Brendan V *Lawyer*
Williams & Connolly, 725 12th St NW, Washington, DC 20005 USA

Sullivan Jr, Brendon V
725 12th St NW, Washington, DC 20005 USA

Sulston, John E *Nobel Prize Laureate*
39 Mingle Lane, Stapleford, Cambridge, CB2 5BG, UNITED KINGDOM (UK)

Sultan, Altoon *Artist*
PO Box 2, Groton, VT 05046 USA

Sultan, Donald K *Artist*
19 E 70th St, New York, NY 10021 USA

Sultan of Brunei
Bandar Seri, Begawan, BRUNEI

Sultan Salman, Abdulaziz Al-Saud *Astronaut*
PO Box 18368, Riyadh, 11415, SAUDI ARABIA

Sultanov, Alexel *Musician*
Columbia Artists Mgmt Inc, 165 W 57th St, New York, NY 10019 USA

Sultonov, Outkir T *Prime Minister*
Prime Minister's Office, Mustarilik 5, Tashkent, 70008, UZBEKISTAN

Sulzberger, Arthur Ochs
229 W. 43rd St., New York, NY 10036

Sulzberger Jr, Arthur O *Publisher, Business Person*
New York Times Co, 229 W 43rd St, New York, NY 10036 USA

Sum 41 *Music Group*
Nettwerk Management (LA), 8730 Wilshire Blvd #304, Beverly Hills, CA 90211 USA

Sumac, Yma *Musician*
Absolute Artists, 8490 W Sunset Blvd, #403, West Hollywood, CA 90069 USA

Suman, Shekhar *Actor, Bollywood, Comedian, Talk Show Host, Television*
1 Krishna Apartments 168 Sher-E-Punjab Colony, Mahakali Caves Road Andheri (E), Bombay, MS 400 093, INDIA

Sumaye, Frederick T *Prime Minister*
Prime Minister's Office, PO Box 980, Dodoma, TANZANIA

Sumerfelt, Josh
6550 Yucca #310, Los Angeles, CA 90028

Sumino, Naoko *Astronaut*
NASDA, Tsukuba Space Center, 2-1-1 Sengen Tukubashi, Ibaraka, 305, JAPAN

Summar, Trent *Musician*
Grassroots Media, 800 18th Ave S, #B, Nashville, TN 37203 USA

Summer, Cree *Actor*
Monterey Peninsula Artists, 509 Hartnell St, Monterey, CA 93940 USA

Summer, Donna *Musician*
18171 Eccles St, Northridge, CA 91325 USA

Summer-Francks, Cree
PO Box 5617, Beverly Hills, CA 90210

Summerleigh, George A (Pat) *Football Player*
710 S White Chapel Blvd, Southlake, TX 76092 USA

Summers, Andy *Musician*
21A Noel St, London, W1V 3PD, UNITED KINGDOM (UK)

Summers, Carol *Artist*
2817 Smith Grade, Santa Cruz, CA 95060 USA

Summers, Dana *Cartoonist*
Orlando Sentinel, Editorial Dept, 633 N Orange Ave, Orlando, FL 32801 USA

Summers, Jerry *Musician*
American Promotions, 2011 Ferry Ave, #U19, Camden, NJ 08104 USA

Summers, Lawrence H (Larry) *Secretary, Educator*
Harvard University, President's Office, Cambridge, MA 02138 USA

Summers, Marc *Chef*
Food Network, 1180 Ave of Americas, #1200, New York, NY 10036 USA

Summers, Yale *Actor*
Screen Actors Guild (SAG-LA), 5757 Wilshire Blvd, Los Angeles, CA 90036 USA

Summitt, Pat Head *Coach*
3720 River Trace Lane, Knoxville, TN 37920 USA

Sumners, Rosalynn *Figure Skater*
International Management Group, 22 E 71st St, New York, NY 10021 USA

Sumpter, Jeremy *Actor*
Mark Robert Management, 14014 Moorpark St #316, Sherman Oaks, CA 91423 USA

Sun Dao Lin *Actor, Director*
Shanghai Film Studio, 595 Tsao Hsi North Road, Shanghai, 200030, CHINA

Sun Yun-Hsuan *Prime Minister*
10 Lane 6, Chung South Rd Section 2, Taipei, 100, TAIWAN

Sundance, Robert *Social Activist*
California Indian Alcoholism Commission, 225 W 8th St, Los Angeles, CA 90014 USA

Sundin, Mats *Hockey Player*
Int'l Management Group, 801 6th St SW, #235, Calgary, AB T2P 3V8, CANADA

Sundlun, Bruce G *Governor*
Seawood Cliff Ave, Newport, RI 02840 USA

Sundvold, Jon *Basketball Player*
2700 Westbrook Way, Columbia, MO 65203 USA

Sung, Elizabeth *Actor*
GVA Talent, 9229 Sunset Blvd, #320, Los Angeles, CA 90069 USA

Sunjata, Daniel *Actor*
Principal Entertainment (LA), 1964
Westwood Blvd #400, Los Angeles, CA
90025 USA

Sununu, John H *Ex-Governor,*
Government Official
24 Samoset Dr, Salem, NH 03079 USA

Supernaw, Doug *Songwriter, Musician*
Red & Rio, PO Box 411, Bellville, TX
77418 USA

Supertramp
16530 Ventura Blvd. #201, Encino, CA
91436

Suplee, Ethan *Actor*
Don Buchwald, 6500 Wilshire Blvd,
#2200, Los Angeles, CA 90048 USA

Suppes, Patrick *Psychic*
678 Mirada Ave, Stanford, CA 94305 USA

Supremes, The *Music Group*
PO Box 1821, Ojai, CA 93024

Suquia Goicoechea, Angel Cardinal
Religious Leader
El Cardenal Arxobispo, San Justo 2,
Madrid, 28074, SPAIN

Sura, Bob *Basketball Player*
Atlanta Hawks, 190 Marietta St SW,
Atlanta, GA 30303 USA

Sure, Al B *Musician*
International Creative Management
(ICM-LA), 8942 Wilshire Blvd, Beverly
Hills, CA 90211 USA

Surhoff, William J (BJ) *Baseball Player*
221 Oakland Beach Ave, Rye, NY 10580
USA

Surin, Bruny *Track Athlete*
PO Box 2, Succ Saint Michel, Montreal,
QC, H2A 3L8, CANADA

Surnow, Joel *Producer*
Principal Entertainment (LA), 1964
Westwood Blvd #400, Los Angeles, CA
90025 USA

Surovy, Nicolas *Actor*
Susan Smith, 121A N San Vicente Blvd,
Beverly Hills, CA 90211 USA

Sursok, Tammin *Actor*
Channel Seven, Mobbs Lane, Epping,
2121, AUSTRALIA

Surtain, Patrick *Football Player*
380 Sweet Bay Ave, Plantation, FL 33324
USA

Surtees, Bruce *Cinematographer*
36 Linda Vista Place, Monterey, CA
93940 USA

Surtees, John *Race Car Driver*
Team Surtees, Fircroft Way, Edenbridge,
Kent, TN8 6EJ, UNITED KINGDOM (UK)

Survivor
PO Box 1821, Ojai, CA 93024

Susa, Conrad *Composer*
433 Eureka St, San Francisco, CA 94114
USA

Susana, Marta *Actor*
Univision, 314 Main St, Chico, CA 95928
USA

Suschitzky, J Peter *Cinematographer*
13 priory Road, London, NW6 4NN,
UNITED KINGDOM (UK)

Suschitzky, Wolfgang *Cinematographer*
Douglas House, 6 Maida Ave #11,
London, W2 1TG, UNITED KINGDOM
(UK)

Susclick, Kenneth S *Misc*
University of Illinois, Chemistry Dept,
Champaign, IL 61820 USA

Susco, Stephen *Writer, Producer*
Evolution Entertainment, 901 N Highland
Ave, Los Angeles, CA 90038 USA

Susi, Carol Ann *Actor*
846 N Sweetzer Ave, Los Angeles, CA
90069 USA

Susman, Todd *Actor*
Pakula/King, 9229 Sunset Blvd, #315, Los
Angeles, CA 90069 USA

Sussman, Susan
927 Noyes St., Evanston, IL 60201

Sutcliffe, David *Actor*
Innovative Artists (LA), 1505 Tenth St,
Santa Monica, CA 90401 USA

Sutcliffe, Richard L (Rick) *Baseball Player*
25911 99th St, Lees Summit, MO 64086
USA

Sutcliffe, Rick
25911 99th St., Lee's Summit, MO 64053

Suter, Bob *Hockey Player*
4332 McConnell St, Fitchburg, WI 53711
USA

Suter, Gary *Hockey Player*
2128 County Road D, Lac du Flambu, WI
54538 USA

Sutera, Paul
11365 Ventura Blvd. #100, Studio City,
CA 91604-7403

Sutherland, Bill *Actor*
Select Artists Ltd (CA-Westside Office),
1138 12th Street, Suite 1, Santa Monica,
CA 90403 USA

Sutherland, Catherine *Actor*
Lichtman/Salners Company, 12216
Moorpark Street, Studio City, CA 91604
USA

Sutherland, Dame Joan *Opera Singer*
Chalet Monet Rt De Son, Les Avants,
ICH-18, SWITZERLAND

Sutherland, Donald *Actor, Musician,*
Producer, Writer
Creative Artists Agency, 9830 Wilshire
Blvd, Beverly Hills, CA 90212 USA

Sutherland, Kiefer *Actor*
Wolf/Kasteller, 335 N Maple Dr, #351,
Beverly Hills, CA 90210 USA

Sutherland, Kristine *Actor*
Silver Massetti & Szatmary (SMS-LA),
8730 Sunset Blvd #440, Los Angeles, CA
90069 USA

Sutherland, Peter D *Government Official*
68 Eglinton Road, Dublin, 4, IRELAND

Sutherland, Thomas
229 Columbine Ct., Ft. Collins, CO 80521

Sutorius, James
14014 Milbank St. #1, Sherman Oaks, CA
91423

Sutter, Brent *Hockey Player*
2551 Thaddeus Circle, #S, Glen Ellyn, IL
60137 USA

Sutter, Brian *Hockey Player, Coach*
Chicago Blackhawks, United Center, 1901
W Madison St, Chicago, IL 60612 USA

Sutter, Darryl *Hockey Player, Coach*
Calgary Flames, PO Box 1540, Station M,
Calgary, AB T2P 3B9, CANADA

Sutter, Duane *Hockey Player*
3703 High Plne Dr, Coral Springs, FL
33065 USA

Sutter, H Bruce *Baseball Player*
1368 Hamilton Road, Kennesaw, GA
30152 USA

Sutterluty, Elizabeth *Actor*
Cineart, 36 Rue de Ponthleu, Paris,
75008, FRANCE

Sutton, Don
1145 Mountain Ivy Dr, Roswell, GA
30075

Sutton, Donald H (Don) *Baseball Player,*
Sportscaster
14412 Club Circle, Alpharetta, GA 30004
USA

Sutton, Eddie *Coach*
Oklahoma State University, Athletic Dept,
Stillwater, OK 74078 USA

Sutton, Hal *Golfer*
212 Texas St, #117, Shreveport, LA 71101
USA

Sutton, Michael *Actor*
Somers Teitelbaum David, 8840 Wilshire
Blvd, #200, Beverly Hills, CA 90211 USA

Sutton, Percy E *Politician*
10 W 135th St, New York, NY 10037
USA

Suvalatsumi *Actor*
58 2nd Street Venkatesh Nagar,
Virugambakkam, Chennai, TN 600 092,
INDIA

Suvaluxmi *Actor, Bollywood*
Matri Aasis 22/1/1/1 Monohar Pukur
Road, PO Rash Behari Avenue, Kolkata,
WB, 700029, INDIA

Suvari, Mena *Actor*
United Talent Agency, 9560 Wilshire
Blvd, #500, Beverly Hills, CA 90212 USA

Suwa, Gen *Misc*
University of California, Human
Evolutionary Science Lab, Berkeley, CA
94720 USA

Suwyn, Mark A *Business Person*
Louisiana-Pacific Corp, 111 SW 5th Ave,
Portland, OR 97204 USA

Suzman, Janet *Actor*
Faircroft, 11 Keats Grove, Hampstead,
London, NW3, UNITED KINGDOM (UK)

Suzuki, David *Scientist, Commentator,*
Writer
211-3905 Springtree Dr, Vancouver, BC
V6L 2E2, CANADA

Suzuki, Ichiro *Baseball Player*
Seattle Mariners, Safeco Field, PO Box
4100, Seattle, WA 98194 USA

Suzuki, Pat
343 E. 30th St, New York, NY 10016

Suzuki, Robert *Educator*
California State University, President's
Office, Bakersfield, CA 93311 USA

Suzy *Writer*
18 E 68th St, #1B, New York, NY 10021
USA

Svankmajer, Jan *Director*
Ceminska 5, Prague 1, 118 00, CZECH
REPUBLIC

Svare, Harland *Football Player, Football
Coach*
6127 Paseo Jaguita, Carlsbad, CA 92009
USA

Svenden, Birgitta *Musician*
Ulf Tomqvist, Sankt Eriksgatan 100,
Stockholm, 113 31, SWEDEN

Svendsen, George *Football Player*
163 Wayzata Blvd W, #315, Wayzata,
MN 55391 USA

Svendsen, Louise A *Misc*
16 Park Ave, New York, NY 10016 USA

Sveningsson, Magnus *Musician*
Motor SE, Gotabergs Gatan 2,
Gothenburg, 400 14, SWEDEN

Svenson, Bo *Actor*
247 S Beverly Dr, #102, Beverly Hills, CA
90212 USA

Svensson, Peter *Musician, Songwriter*
Motor SE, Gotabergs Gatan 2,
Gothenburg, 400 14, SWEDEN

Sverak, Jan *Director*
PO Box 33, Prague 515, 155 00, CZECH
REPUBLIC

Svoboda, Petr *Hockey Player*
1119 S Jefferson St, Allentown, PA 18103
USA

Swados, Elizabeth A *Writer, Composer*
360 Central Park West, #16G, New York,
NY 10025 USA

Swagerty, Jane *Swimmer*
9128 N 70th St, Paradise Valley, AZ
85253 USA

Swaggart, Jimmy L *Misc*
8919 World Ministry Ave, Baton Rouge,
LA 70810 USA

Swaggert, Jimmy
8912 World Ministry Ave, Baton Rouge,
LA 70810

Swail, Julie *Athlete, Coach*
University of California, Athletic Dept,
Irvine, CA 92697 USA

Swaim, Caskey
1605 N. Cahuenga Blvd. #202, Los
Angeles, CA 90028

Swain, Brennan *Athlete*
Jerry Shandrew PR, 1050 South Stanley
Avenue, Los Angeles, CA 90019-6634
USA

Swain, Dominique *Actor*
International Creative Mgmt, 8942
Wilshire Blvd, #219, Beverly Hills, CA
90211 USA

Swaminathan, Monkombu S *Scientist*
MS Swaminathan Foundation, 3 Cross St,
Taramani, Chennai, TN 600113, INDIA

Swan, Billy *Musician, Songwriter*
Muirhead Mgmt, 202 Fulham Road,
Chelsea, London, SW10 9PJ, UNITED
KINGDOM (UK)

Swan, John W D *President*
Swan Building, 26 Victoria St, Hamilton,
HM12, BERMUDA

Swan, Michael *Actor*
13576 Cheltenham Dr, Sherman Oaks,
CA 91423 USA

Swan, Richard G *Mathematician*
700 Melrose Ave, #M3, Winter Park, FL
32789 USA

Swank, Hilary *Actor*
Baker Winokur Ryder (BWR-LA), 9100
Wilshire Blvd Fl 6, W Tower, Beverly
Hills, CA 90212 USA

Swank, Hillary *Actor*
Baker/Winokur/Ryder, 9100 Wilshire Blvd,
#600, Beverly Hills, CA 90212 USA

Swann, Eric J *Football Player*
PO Box 790, Cornelius, NC 28031 USA

Swann, Lynn C *Football Player,
Sportscaster*
Swann Inc, 600 Grant St, #4870,
Pittsburgh, PA 15219 USA

Swanson, August G *Physicist*
3146 Portage Bay Place E, #H, Seattle,
WA 98102 USA

Swanson, Jackie *Actor*
15155 Albright St, Pacific Palisades, CA
90272 USA

Swanson, Judith *Actor*
Persona Mgmt, 40 E 9th St, New York, NY
10003 USA

Swanson, Kristy *Actor, Model*
2934 1/2 N Beverly Glen Circle, #416,
Los Angeles, CA 90077 USA

Swanson, Steven R *Astronomer*
16403 Bougainville Lane, Friendswood,
TX 77546 USA

Sward, Melinda *Actor*
Osbrink Talent Agency, 4343 Lankershim
Blvd #100, Universal City, CA 91602 USA

Swardson, Nick *Actor*
Brillstein-Grey Entertainment, 9150
Wilshire Blvd #350, Beverly Hills, CA
90212 USA

Swaroop, Shikha *Actor, Bollywood*
13/14 Atmanand Saraswat Colony,
Santacruz, Mumbai, MS 400054, INDIA

Swartz, Jacob T *Scientist*
New York University, 251 Mercer St, New
York, NY 10012 USA

Swatek, Barret *Actor*
Personal Management Company, 425 N
Robertson Dr, Los Angeles, CA 90048
USA

Swathi *Actor, Bollywood*
Flat No 4-42, 47th Street 9thAvenue
Ashok Nagar, Chennai, TN 600083,
INDIA

Sway *Television Host*
MTV Networks (NY), 1515 Broadway,
New York, NY 10036 USA

Swayze, Don
247 S. Beverly Dr. #102, Beverly Hills,
CA 90212

Swayze, Patrick *Actor*
William Morris Agency (WMA-LA), 1
William Morris Pl, Beverly Hills, CA
90212 USA

Swe, U Ba *Prime Minister*
84 Innes Road, Yangon, MYANMAR

Swearingen, John E Jr *Business Person*
1420 Lake Shore Dr, Chicago, IL 60610
USA

Sweat, Keith *Musician, Songwriter*
PO Box 1002, Bronx, NY 10466 USA

Swedberg, Heidi *Actor*
Writers & Artists, 8383 Wilshire Blvd,
#550, Beverly Hills, CA 90211 USA

Swedlin, Rosalie *Producer*
Jackoway Tyerman Wertheimer Austen
Mandelbaum & Morris, 1888 Century
Park E Fl 18, Los Angeles, CA 90067 USA

Sweeney, Alison *Actor*
Days of Our Lives, 3000 W Alameda Ave,
Burbank, CA 91523 USA

Sweeney, D B *Actor*
International Creative Mgmt, 8942
Wilshire Blvd, #219, Beverly Hills, CA
90211 USA

Sweeney, James (Jim) *Football Coach*
119 Justabout Road, Venetia, PA 15367
USA

Sweeney, John J *Politician*
AFL-CIO, 1750 New York Ave NW,
Washington, DC 20006 USA

Sweeney, Julia *Comedian*
187 North Larchmont Blvd #214, Los
Angeles, CA 90004 USA

Sweeney, Michael J (Mike) *Baseball
Player*
2802 E Tam O'Shanter Court, Ontario, CA
91761 USA

Sweeney, Pepper
1930 Century Park W. #403, Los Angeles,
CA 90067

Sweeney, Walter F (Watt) *Football Player*
1040 Martin Ave, #A, South Lake Tahoe,
CA 96150 USA

Sweet, Matthew *Musician, Songwriter*
Russell Carter Artists Mgmt, 315 W Ponce
De Leon Ave, #755, Decatur, GA 30030
USA

Sweet, Rachel *Producer*
Endeavor Agency LLC (LA), 9601 Wilshire
Blvd Fl 3, Beverly Hills, CA 90210 USA

Sweet, Sharon *Opera Singer*
Columbia Artists Mgmt Inc, 165 W 57th
St, New York, NY 10019 USA

Sweet, Shay *Adult Film Star*
Atlas Multimedia Inc, 22940 Burbank
Blvd, Woodland Hills, CA 91367 USA

Sweeten, Madylin *Actor*
Innovative Artists (LA), 1505 Tenth St,
Santa Monica, CA 90401 USA

Sweethearts of the Rodeo
5101 Overton Rd., Nashville, TN 37220

Sweetin, Jodie *Actor*
Savage Agency, 6212 Banner Ave, Los
Angeles, CA 90038 USA

Sweetlin, Jodie
6212 Banner Ave., Los Angeles, CA
90038

Sweetney, Mike *Basketball Player*
New York Knicks, Madison Square
Garden, 2 Penn Plaza, New York, NY
10121 USA

Swensen, Joseph A *Composer, Conductor*
Van Walsum Mgmt, 4 Addison Bridge
Place, London, W14 8XP, UNITED
KINGDOM (UK)

Swenson, August
1702 Azores Dr., Pflurgerville, TX 78880

Swenson, Inga *Actor, Musician*
3351 Halderman St, Los Angeles, CA
90066 USA

Swenson, Rick *Dog Sled Racer*
PO Box 16205, Two Rivers, AK 99716
USA

Swenson, Robert C (Bob) *Football Player*
910 Cypress Lane, Louisville, CO 80027
USA

Swenson, Ruth Ann *Opera Singer*
Columbia Artists Mgmt Inc, 165 W 57th
St, New York, NY 10019 USA

Swensson, Earl S *Architect*
Earl Swensson Assoc, 2100 W End Ave,
#1200, Nashville, TN 37203 USA

Swerling Jr, Jo
25745 Vista Verde Dr, Calabasas, CA
91302-2165 USA

Swett, James E *War Hero*
PO Box 327, Trinity Center, CA 96091
USA

Swiatek, Kazimierz Cardinal *Religious Leader*
Pl Swobody 9, Minsk, 220030, BELARUS

Swiczinsky, Helmut *Architect*
Coop Himmelblau, Seilerstatte 16/11A,
Vienna, 81010, AUSTRIA

Swienton, Gregory T *Business Person*
Ryder System Inc, 3600 NW 82nd Ave,
Miami, FL 33166 USA

Swift, Clive *Actor*
Roxane Vacca Mgmt, 8 Silver Place,
London, W1R 3LJ, UNITED KINGDOM
(UK)

Swift, Graham C *Writer*
AP Watt, 20 John St, London, WC1N
2DR, UNITED KINGDOM (UK)

Swift, Hewson H *Biologist*
University of Chicago, Cell Biology Dept,
Chicago, IL 60637 USA

Swift, Staphanie
PO Box 9864, Canoga Park, CA 91309

Swift, Stephen J *Judge*
US Tax Court, 400 2nd St NW,
Washington, DC 20217 USA

Swift, Stromile *Basketball Player*
Memphis Grizziles, 175 Toyota Plaza,
#150, Memphis, TN 38103 USA

Swift, William C (Bill) *Baseball Player*
5880 E Sapphire Lane, Paradise Valley,
AZ 85253 USA

Swilling, Pat *Football Player*
Patrick's Place, E 6711 Tara Ln 11B, New
Orleans, LA 70127

Swilling, Patrick T (Pat) *Football Player*
Patrick's Place East, 6780 Bundy Road,
New Orleans, LA 90127 USA

Swindell, F Gregory (Greg) *Baseball Player*
9625 N 55th St, Paradise Valley, AZ
85253 USA

Swindells, William Jr *Business Person*
Williamette Industries, 1300 SW 5th Ave,
Portland, OR 97201 USA

Swindle, Orson
500 University Ave. #309, Honolulu, HI
96826

Swindolls, Charles R *Writer*
Insight for Living, 211 Imperial Highway,
Fullerton, CA 92835 USA

Swing Out Sister
132 Liverpool Rd Islington, London,
ENGLAND, N1 1LA

Swingley, Doug *Dog Sled Racer*
General Delivery, Lincoln, MT 59634
USA

Swink, James E (Jim) *Football Player*
1201 8th Ave, Fort Worth, TX 76104 USA

Swinny, Wayne *Musician*
Helter Skelter Plaza, 535 Kings Road,
London, SW10 0S, UNITED KINGDOM
(UK)

Swinton, Tilda *Actor*
Lorraine Hamilton, 76 Oxford St, London,
W1N 0AT, UNITED KINGDOM (UK)

Swisher, Carl C *Misc*
Institute of Human Origins, 1288 9th St,
Berkeley, CA 94710 USA

Swisten, Amanda *Actor*
Exposure (Xposure) Public Relations, 9171
Wilshire Blvd #300, Beverly Hills, CA
90210 USA

Swit, Loretta *Actor*
23852 Pacific Coast Highway, Malibu, CA
90265 USA

Switchfoot *Music Group*
William Morris Agency (WMA-LA), 1
William Morris Pl, Beverly Hills, CA
90212 USA

Switzer, Barry *Football Player, Coach*
700 W Timberdell Road, Norman, OK
73072 USA

Switzer, Barry *Basketball Player*
PO Box 43021, Lubbock, TX 79409 USA

Swoboda, Ron
4847 Chestnut St., New Orleans, LA
70115

Swoopes, Sheryl *Basketball Player*
PO Box 43021, Lubbock, TX 79409

Swope, Tracy Brooks
8730 Sunset Blvd. #480, Los Angeles, CA
90069

SWV
6464 Sunset Blvd. #610, Hollywood, CA
90028-8013

Swygert, H Patrick *Educator*
Howard University, President's Office,
Washington, DC 20059 USA

Syberberg, Hans-Jurgen *Director*
Genter Str 15A, Munich, 80805,
GERMANY

Sybil *Musician*
Mission Control, Business Center, Lower
Road, London, SE16 2XB, UNITED
KINGDOM (UK)

Sykes, Eric *Actor*
Norma Farnes, 9 Orme Court, London,
W2 4RL, UNITED KINGDOM (UK)

Sykes, Lynn R *Geophysicist*
RR 1 Box 248, 100 Washington Spring
Road, Palisades, NY 10964 USA

Sykes, Peter *Director*
International Creative Mgmt, 76 Oxford
St, London, W1N 0AX, UNITED
KINGDOM (UK)

Sykes, Phil *Hockey Player*
2312 Hill Lane, Redondo Beach, CA
90278 USA

Sykes, Wanda *Comedian*
13949 Ventura Blvd, #309, Oaks, CA
91423 USA

Sylbert, Anthea *Designer*
13949 Ventura Blvd, #309, Oaks, CA
91423 USA

Sylvester, George H *General*
4571 Conicville Road, Mount Jackson, VA
22842 USA

Sylvester, Harold *Actor*
International Creative Mgmt, 8942
Wilshire Blvd, #219, Beverly Hills, CA
90211 USA

Sylvester, Michael *Opera Singer*
Columbia Artists Mgmt Inc, 165 W 57th
St, New York, NY 10019 USA

Sylvia *Musician*
So Much More Media, PO Box 120426,
Nashville, TN 37212 USA

Symington, J Fife III *Governor*
1700 W Washington St, Phoenix, AZ
85007 USA

Symms, Steven D *Senator*
127 S Fairfax St, #137, Alexandria, VA
22314 USA

Symonds, Anthony *Fashion Designer*
Anthony Symonds, 17B Clerkenwell Road,
London, England, EC1M 5RD, United
Kingdom

Symone, Raven *Actor*
That's So Raven, 1040 N Las Palmas, Bldg
33, Los Angeles, CA 90038

Symphony X *Music Group*

Syms, Sylvia *Actor*
Barry Brown, 47 West Square, London,
SE11 4SP, UNITED KINGDOM (UK)

Syreeta
6255 Sunset Blvd. #1800, Los Angeles,
CA 90028

Syron, Richard F *Financier, Government Official*
American Stock Exchange, 86 Trinity
Place, New York, NY 10006 USA

Sytsma, John F *Politician*
Locomotive Engineers Brotherhood, 1370
Ontario Ave, Cleveland, OH 44113 USA

Szabo, Istvan *Director*
Objektiy Fil Studio-MAFILM, Rona Utca
174, Budapest, 1149, HUNGARY

Szasz, Thomas S *Doctor*
4739 Limberlost Lane, Manlius, NY 13104
USA

Szczerbiak, Wally *Basketball Player*
521 River St, Minneapolis, MN 55401
USA

Szekely, Eva *Swimmer*
Szepvolgyi Utca 4/B, Budapest, 1025,
HUNGARY

Szekessy, Karen *Photographer*
Haynstr 2, Hamburg, 20249, GERMANY

Szep, Paul M *Editor, Cartoonist*
12760 Indian Rocks Road, #1071, Largo, FL 33774 USA

Szewczenki, Tanya *Figure Skater*
Niederbeerbacher Str 10, Muhital, 64367, GERMANY

Szigmond, Vilmos *Cinematographer*
PO Box 2230, Los Angeles, CA 90078 USA

Szmanda, Eric *Actor*
Untitled Entertainment (LA), 8436 W 3rd St #650, Los Angeles, CA 90048 USA

Szoka, Edmund C Cardinal *Religious Leader*
Prefecture for Economic Affairs, Vatican City, 00120, VATICAN CITY

Szymanski, Richard (Dick) *Football Player*
5270 Forest Edge Court, Lake Forest, FL 32771 USA

Szymborska, Wislawa *Nobel Prize Laureate*
Stowarzyszenie Pissarzy Polskich, Ul Kanonicza 7, Cracow, 31-002, POLAND

T

T, Mr *Actor*
15203 La Maida St, Sherman Oaks, CA 91403 USA

T Hooft, Gerardus *Nobel Prize Laureate*
Leuvenlaan 4, Postbus 80.195, Utrecht, 3508, NETHERLANDS

T Rajendar *Actor*
33 Hindi Prachar Sabha Road, T Nagar, Chennai, TN 600 017, INDIA

Tabachnik, Michel *Composer, Conductor*
Garvey & Ivor, 59 Lansdowne Place, Hove, BN3 1FL, UNITED KINGDOM (UK)

Tabackin, Lewis B (Lew) *Musician*
38 W 94th St, New York, NY 10025 USA

Tabai, Ieremia T *President*
South Pacific Forum Secretariat, Ratu Su Kuna Rd, GPO Box 856, Suva, FIJI

Tabakov, Oleg P *Actor, Director*
Chemysherskogo 39, #3, Moscow, 103062, RUSSIA

Tabaksblat, Morris *Business Person*
Unilever NV, Weena 455, Rotterdam, DK, 3000, NETHERLANDS

Tabassum *Actor, Talk Show Host, Television Host, Bollywood, Com*
11A Pooja Apartments Master Vinayak Road, Bandra, Bombay, MS 400 050, INDIA

Taber, Carol A *Publisher*
Working Woman Magazine, 230 Park Ave, New York, NY 10169 USA

Tabitha, Masentle *Royalty*
Royal Palace, PO Box 524, Maseru, LESOTHO

Tabone, Anton *President*
33 Carmel St, Slierna, MALTA

Tabor, David *Physicist*
8 Rutherford Road, Cambridge, CB2 2HH, UNITED KINGDOM (UK)

Tabor, Herbert *Scientist*
National Institute of Health, 8 Center Dr, Bethesda, MD 20892 USA

Tabori, Kristoffer *Actor*
International Artists, 235 Regent St, London, W1R 8AX USA

Tabori, Laszlo *Track Athlete*
2221 W Olive Ave, Burbank, CA 91506 USA

Tabu *Actor, Bollywood*
Anukool 2nd Floor, 7 Bungalows Versova Andheri (W), Mumbai, MS 400058, INDIA

Tacha, Deanell R *Judge*
US Court of Appeals, 4830 W 15th St, Lawrence, KS 66049 USA

Taco *Musician*
8124 W 3rd St, #204, Los Angeles, CA 90048 USA

Taddei, Giuseppe *Opera Singer*
Metropolitan Opera Assn, Lincoln Center Plaza, New York, NY 10023 USA

Tademy, Lalita *Writer*
Warner Books, 1271 Ave of the Americas, New York, NY 10020 USA

Tadic, Boris *President*
President's Office, Nemanjina 11, Belgrade, 11000, SERBIA

Taeger, Ralph
5619 Mother Lode, Placerville, CA 95667

Taff, Russ
PO Box 570815, Tarzana, CA 91357-0815

Tafoya, Michele *Sportscaster*
CBS-TV, Sports Dept, 51 W 52nd St, New York, NY 10019 USA

Taft, Robert
4300 Drake Rd., Cincinnati, OH 45243-4210

Taft, William H IV *Government Official*
1001 Pennsylvania Ave NW, Washington, DC 20004 USA

Tagawa, Cary-Hiroyuki *Actor*
Jerry Shandrew PR, 1050 South Stanley Avenue, Los Angeles, CA 90019-6634 USA

Taghmaoui, Said *Actor*
Lee Daniels Entertainment, 625 Broadway #6M, New York, NY 10012 USA

Tagliabue, Paul *Football Executive*
National Football League, 280 Park Ave #12W, New York, NY 10017

Tagliabue, Paul J *Football Executive*
National Football League, 280 Park Ave, #12W, New York, NY 10017 USA

Taglianetti, Peter *Hockey Player*
67 Merion Court, Bridgeville, PA 15017 USA

Tahil, Dalip *Actor, Bollywood*
19 Deepali St Cyril Road, Bandra, Mumbai, MS 400050, INDIA

Tai, Kobe *Adult Film Star*
Atlas Multimedia Inc, 22940 Burbank Blvd, Woodland Hills, CA 91367 USA

Taillibert, Roger R *Architect*
163 Rue de la Ponpe, Paris, 75116, FRANCE

Taimak *Actor*
Chasin Agency, The, 8899 Beverly Blvd #716, Los Angeles, CA 90048 USA

Tait, John E *Business Person*
Penn Mutual Life, Independence Square, Philadelphia, PA 19172 USA

Tait, Tristan *Actor*
Paradigm Agency, 10100 Santa Monica Blvd, #2500, Los Angeles, CA 90067 USA

Taittinger, Jean *Business Person*
58 Blvd Gouvion, Saint-Cyr, Paris, 75017, FRANCE

Tak, Saawan Kumar *Director, Filmmaker, Producer, Bollywood*
A/11 Dakshina Park 10th Road, Juhu, Bombay, MS 400 049, INDIA

Taka, Miiko
14560 Round Valley Dr., Sherman Oaks, CA 91403

Takac, Robby *Musician*
Atlas/Third Rail Entertainment, 9200 W Sunset Blvd, West Hollywood, CA 90069 USA

Takacs, Tibor *Director*
IP, 104 Richview Ave, Toronto, ON M5P 3E9, CANADA

Takacs-Nagy, Gabor *Musician*
Case Postale 196, Collonge-Bellerive, 1245, SWITZERLAND

Takahashi, Joseph S *Scientist*
Northwestern University, Neurobiology Dept, 2153 N Campus Dr, Evanston, IL 60208 USA

Takahashi, Michiaki *Scientist*
Osaka University, Microbe Diseases Research Institute, Osaka, JAPAN

Takamatsu, Shin *Architect*
Shin Takamatsu Assoc, 195 Jobodaiincho Takeda, Kyoto, JAPAN

Take Six
89 Fifth Ave. #700, New York, NY 10003

Take That
69-79 Fulham High St., London, ENGLAND, SW6 3JW

Takei, George *Actor*
Hosato Enterprises, 419 N Larchmont Blvd, #41, Los Angeles, CA 90004 USA

Takenouchi, Naoko *Artist*
Kathleen Gaffney, Art Glass Int'l, PO Box 58922, Renton, WA 98058 USA

Takezawa, Kyoko *Musician*
I C M Artists, 40 W 57th St, New York, NY 10019 USA

Tal, Josef *Composer, Musician*
3 Dvira Haneviyah St, Jerusalem, ISRAEL

Talalay, Paul *Scientist*
5512 Boxhill Lane, Baltimore, MD 21210 USA

Talalay, Rachel *Director*
1047 Grant St, Santa Monica, CA 90405 USA

Talancon, Ana Claudia *Actor*
Creative Artists Agency LCC (CAA-LA), 9830 Wilshire Blvd, Beverly Hills, CA 90212 USA

Talavera, Tracee *Gymnast*
106 Mandala Court, Walnut Creek, CA 94598 USA

Talbert, Billy *Athlete*
194 Bellevue Avenue, Newport, RI 02840 USA

Talbot, Diron V *Football Player*
3803 B F Terry Blvd, Rosenberg, TX
77471 USA

Talbot, Don *Swimmer, Coach*
Sports Federation, 333 River Road, Vanier,
Ottawa, ON K1L 8B9, CANADA

Talbot, Nita *Actor*
3420 Merrimac Road, Los Angeles, CA
90049 USA

Talbot, Susan *Actor*
Media Artists Group, 6300 Wilshire Blvd,
#1470, Los Angeles, CA 90048 USA

Talbott, Gloria *Actor*
2066 Montecito Dr, Glendale, CA 91208
USA

Talbott, John H *Doctor*
Commodore Club, 177 Ocean Lane Dr,
Key Biscayne, FL 33149 USA

Talbott, Michael *Actor*
10340 Santa Monica Blvd, Los Angeles,
CA 90025 USA

Talbott, Strobe *Journalist*
State Department, 2201 C St NW,
Washington, DC 20520 USA

Talese, Gay *Writer*
154 E Atlantic Blvd, Ocean City, NJ
08226 USA

Taliaferro, George *Football Player*
Innovative Health Systems, 3013 S
Stratfield Dr, Bloonington, IN 47401 USA

Talking Back Sunday *Music Group*
Kenmore Agency, The, PO Box 15643,
Boston, MA 02215

Tallchief, Maria *Dancer*
48 Prospect, Highland Park, IL 60035
USA

Talley, Darryl V *Football Player*
8713 Lake Tibet Court, Orlando, FL
32836 USA

Talley, Gary *Musician*
Horizon Mgmt, PO Box 8770, Endwell, NJ
13762 USA

Talley, Joel E *War Hero*
20 Lakeshore Dr, Shalimar, FL 32579 USA

Tallman, Patricia *Actor*
PMB 2161, 1801 E Tropicana, #9, Las
Vegas, NV 89119 USA

Tallman, Richard C *Judge*
US Court of Appeals, US Courthouse,
1010 5th Ave, Seattle, WA 98104 USA

Talor, Vanessa
11271 Ventura Blvd. #396, Studio City,
CA 91604

Talsania, Tiku *Actor, Bollywood*
22-A Shruti Yashudham Enclave, Filmcity
Rd Goregaon (E), Mumbai, MS 400053,
INDIA

Tam, Vivienne *Fashion Designer*
550 Fashion Ave, New York, NY 10018
USA

Tamahori, Lee W *Director*
International Creative Mgmt, 8942
Wilshire Blvd, #219, Beverly Hills, CA
90211 USA

Tamaro, Janet *Journalist*
Endeavor Agency LLC (LA), 9601 Wilshire
Blvd Fl 3, Beverly Hills, CA 90210 USA

Tamayo, Mendez Amaldo *Cosmonaut*
Calle 16, #504 C/5A y 7MA, Miramar,
Ciudad Havana, 11300, CUBA

Tamberino, Paul *Referee*
349 Homeland Southway, Baltimore, MD
21212 USA

Tambiah, Stanley J *Misc*
Harvard University, Anthropology Dept,
Cambridge, MA 02138 USA

Tamblyn, Amber *Actor*
Endeavor Agency LLC (LA), 9601 Wilshire
Blvd Fl 3, Beverly Hills, CA 90210 USA

Tamblyn, Russ *Actor, Dancer*
1221 N King's Road, #PH 405, West
Hollywood, CA 90069 USA

Tambor, Jeffrey *Actor*
Bragman/Nyman/Cafarelli, 9171 Wilshire
Blvd #300, Beverly Hills, CA 90210 USA

Tambor, Jeffrey *Actor*
Brillstein/Grey, 9150 Wilshire Blvd, #350,
Beverly Hills, CA 90212 USA

Tamia *Musician*
International Creative Mgmt, 8942
Wilshire Blvd, #219, Beverly Hills, CA
90211 USA

Tamke, George W *Business Person*
Emerson Electric Co, PO Box 4100, Saint
Louis, MO 63136 USA

Tamm, Peter *Publisher*
Elbchaussee 277, Hamburg, 22605,
GERMANY

Tan, Amy *Writer*
Steven Barclay Agency, 12 Western Ave,
Petaluma, CA 94952 USA

Tan, Dun *Composer*
Columbia University, Arts School, Dodge
Hall, New York, NY 10027 USA

Tan, Melvyn *Musician*
Valerie Barber Mgmt, 4 Winsley St, #305,
London, W1N 7AR, UNITED KINGDOM
(UK)

Tanaev, Nikoly *Prime Minister*
Prime Minister's Office, Ul Perromayskaya
57, Bishkek, KYRGYZSTAN

Tanaka, Koichi *Nobel Prize Laureate*
Shimadzu Corp, 1 Nishinokyo-
Kuwabaracho, Nakagoku, Kyoto, 604-
8511, JAPAN

Tanaka, Shoji *Physicist*
Superconductivity Laboratory, 1-10-13
Shinonome, Kotoku, Tokyo, 135, JAPAN

Tanana, Frank D *Baseball Player*
28492 S Harwich Dr, Farmington Hills,
MI 48334 USA

Tandon, Raveena *Actor, Bollywood*
Tandon House Nippon Society, Juhu
Church, Mumbai, MS 400049, INDIA

Tandon, Ravi *Director, Filmmaker,
Producer, Bollywood*
B/58 Ravi Kiran, New Linking Road,
Bombay, MS 400 058, INDIA

Tanford, Charles *Doctor*
Tarlswood, Back Lane, Easingwold, York,
YO6 3BG, UNITED KINGDOM (UK)

Tange, Kenzo *Architect*
Kenzo Tange Assoc, 7-2-21 Akasaka,
Minato-ku, Tokyo, JAPAN

Tangerine Dream
PO Box 29242, Oakland, CA 94604

Tani, Daniel M *Astronaut*
3703 Montvale Dr, Houston, TX 77059
USA

Taniguchi, Tadatsugu *Biologist*
University of Osaka, Molecular & Cellular
Biology Dept, Osaka, JAPAN

Tankian, Serj *Musician*
Velvet Hammer, 9911 W Pico Blvd, #350,
Los Angeles, CA 90035 USA

Tanksley, Steven D *Scientist*
Cornell University, Plant Genetics Dept,
Emerson Hall, Ithaca, NY 14853 USA

Tannenwald, Theodore Jr *Judge*
US Tax Court, 400 2nd St NW,
Washington, DC 20217 USA

Tanner, Alain *Director*
Chemin Point-du-Jour 12, Geneva, 1202,
SWITZERLAND

Tanner, Charles W (Chuck) *Baseball
Player*
34 E Maitland Lane, New Castle, PA
16105 USA

Tanner, Joseph R *Astronaut*
1519 Seaget Lane, Houston, TX 77062
USA

Tanner, Roscoe
1109 Gnome Trail, Lookout Mountain, TN
37350

Tannous, Afif I *Government Official*
6912 Oak Court, Annandale, VA 22003
USA

Tanuja *Actor, Bollywood*
14 Usha Kiran 15, M L Dhahanukar Marg,
Mumbai, MS 400026, INDIA

Tanumafili, Malietoa II *President*
Government House, Valima, Apia,
SAMOA

Tanzi, Vito *Economist*
5912 Walhondine Road, Bethesda, MD
20816 USA

Taofinu'u, Pio Cardinal *Religious Leader*
Cardinal's Office, PO Box 532, Apia,
WESTERN SAMOA

Tape, Gerald F *Physicist*
9707 Old Georgetown Road, #2518,
Bethesda, MD 20814 USA

Tapert, Robert *Producer, Writer, Director*
Renaissance Pictures, 11684 Ventura Blvd
#226, Studio City, CA 91604 USA

Tapia, Johnny *Boxer*
2009 Foothill Dr SW, Albuquerque, NM
87105 USA

Tappan V, Alfredo *Director*
Gabriel Blanco Iglesias (Mexico), Rio
Balsas 35-32, Colonia Cuauhtemoc, DF,
06500, Mexico

Tappert, Horst
Geigerstr. 21, Grafelfing, GERMANY,
D-82166

Tapscott, Mark
5663 Ruthwood Dr., Calabasas, CA
91302

Tarand, Andres *Prime Minister*
Riigikogu, Lossi Plats 1A, Tallinn, 10130,
ESTONIA

Tarantina, Brian *Actor*
HWA Talent, 3500 West Olive Avenue, Suite 1400, Burbank, CA 91505

Tarantino, Quentin *Actor, Director, Producer, Writer*
A Band Apart, 7966 Beverly Blvd Fl 3, Los Angeles, CA 90048 USA

Taranu, Cornel *Composer, Conductor*
Str Nicolae Iorga, Ckuj-Napoca, 3400, ROMANIA

Tarasova, Tatiana *Figure Skater, Coach*
Connecticut Skating Center, 300 Alumni Road, Newington, CT 06111 USA

Tarbuck, Jimmy
118 Beaufort St., London, ENGLAND, SW3 6BU

Tardiff, Marc *Hockey Player*
6070 Boul du Jardin, Charlesbourg Toyota, Charlesbourg, PQ G1G 3Z8, CANADA

Tarjan, Robert E *Mathematician*
18 Lake Lane, Princeton, NJ 08540 USA

Tarkan *Musician*
Mydonose Productions, No 22 K 14, Park Plaza Eski Buyukdere Cad, Maslak, Istanbul, Turkey

Tarkenton, Fran
3340 Peachtree Rd. NE #2570, Atlanta, GA 30326

Tarkenton, Francis A (Fran) *Football Player, Business Person*
Tarkenton Co, 3340 Peachtree Road NE, #2570, Atlanta, GA 30326 USA

Tarpey, Erin
77 W. 66th St., New York, NY 10023

Tarpley, Roy *Basketball Player*
2250 Justin Road, #108-303, Highland Village, TX 75077 USA

Tarr, Curtis W *Government Official, Business Person*
Intermet Corp, 5445 Corporate Dr, #200, Troy, MI 48098 USA

Tarr, Robert J Jr *Publisher*
3 Commonwealth Ave, #2, Boston, MA 02116 USA

Tarrant, Chris *Game Show Host*
Who Wants to Be a Millionaire, 30 W 67th St, New York, NY 10023

Tarses, Matt *Producer*
Endeavor Agency LLC (LA), 9601 Wilshire Blvd Fl 3, Beverly Hills, CA 90210 USA

Tartabull, Danilio (Dan) *Baseball Player*
16840 NW 79th Place, Hialeah, FL 33016 USA

Tartabull, Danny *Baseball Player*
PO Box 811449, Boca Raton, FL 33481 USA

Tartakovsky, Genndy *Writer, Director, Producer*
William Morris Agency (WMA-LA), 1 William Morris Pl, Beverly Hills, CA 90212 USA

Tarter, Jill *Astronomer, Physicist*
Seti Institute Research Center, 2035 Mountain View, Mountain View, CA 94043 USA

Tartt, Donna *Writer*
Knopf Publishers, 201 E 50th St, New York, NY 10022 USA

Tarver, Antonio *Boxer*
5102 Belmere Parkway, #608, Tampa, FL 33624 USA

Tarzier, Carol *Artist*
1217 32nd St, Oakland, CA 94608 USA

Tashima, A Wallace *Judge*
US Court of Appeals, 125 S Grand Ave, Pasadena, CA 91105 USA

Tasker, Steven J (Steve) *Football Player, Sportscaster*
44 Gypsy Lane, East Aurora, NY 14052 USA

Tatar, Jerome F *Business Person*
Mead Corp, Courthouse Plaza N, Dayton, OH 45463 USA

Tate, Albert Jr *Judge*
US Court of Appeals, 600 Camp St, New Orleans, LA 70130 USA

Tate, Bruce *Musician*
David Harris Enterprises, 24210 E Fork Road, #9, Azusa, CA 91702 USA

Tate, Frank *Boxer*
12731 Water Oak Dr, Missouri City, TX 77489 USA

Tate, James V *Writer*
16 Jones Road, Pelham, MA 01002 USA

Tate, Jeffrey P
English Chamber Orchestra, 2 Coningsby Road, London, W5 4HR, UNITED KINGDOM (UK)

Tate, Kevin
6834 Hollywood Blvd. #303, Hollywood, CA 90028-6175

Tate, Lahmard *Actor*
Identity Talent Agency (ID), 2050 Bundy Dr #200, Los Angeles, CA 90025 USA

Tate, Larena
4116 W. Magnolia Blvd. #101, Burbank, CA 91505-2700

Tate, Larenz *Actor*
Sanders/Armstrong Management, 2120 Colorado Blvd #120, Santa Monica, CA 90404 USA

Tate, Randy *Politician*
Chrsitian Coalition, 100 Centerville Tumpike, Virginia Beach, VA 23463 USA

Tatel, David S *Judge*
US Court of Appeals, 333 Constitution Ave NW, Washington, DC 20001 USA

Tatiana *Model*
Ford Model Agency, 142 Greene St, #400, New York, NY 10012 USA

Tatrai, Vilmos *Musician*
R Wallenberg Utca 4, Budapest XIII, 1136, HUNGARY

Tattersall, David *Cinematographer*
Lucasfilm, PO Box 2459, San Rafael, CA 94912 USA

TATU *Music Group*
Sound Management, 1525 S Winchester Blvd, San Jose, CA 95128 USA

Tatum, Bradford
1505 10th St., Santa Monica, CA 90401

Tatum, Earl
6915 W. Fond du Lac, Milwaukee, WI 53218

Tatum, John D (Jack) *Football Player*
10620 Mark St, Oakland, CA 94605 USA

Tatupu, Mosi *Football Player*
71 Walnut St, Plainville, MA 02762 USA

Taube, Henry *Nobel Prize Laureate*
441 Gerona Road, Stanford, CA 94305 USA

Taube, Sven-Bertil
113 Cheyne Walk, London, ENGLAND, SWl0 OES

Taubman, A Alfred *Business Person*
Taubman Co, 200 E Long Lake Road, Bloomfield Hills, MI 48304 USA

Taufa'ahau, Tupou IV *King*
Royal Palace, PO Box 6, Nuku'alofa, TONGA

Taupin, Bernie *Musician, Songwriter*
2905 Roundup Road, Santa Ynez, CA 93460 USA

Tauran, Jean-Louis Cardinal *Religious Leader*
Palazzo Apostolico, Vatican City, 00120, VATICAN CITY

Taurasi, Diana *Basketball Player*
Tri Star Sports/Entertainment Group, 104 E Park Dr, #104, Brentwood, TN 37027 USA

Taurel, Sidney *Business Person*
Eli Lilly Co, Lilly Corporate Center, Indianapolis, IN 46285 USA

Tauscher, Hansjorg *Skier*
Schwand 7, Oberstdorf, 87561, GERMANY

Tautou, Audrey *Actor*
ArtMedia, 20 Ave Rapp, Paris, 75007, FRANCE

Tauziat, Nathalie *Tennis Player*
Federation de Tennis, 1 Ave Gordon Bennett, Paris, 75016, FRANCE

Tavard, Georges H *Misc*
330 Market St, Brighton, MA 02135 USA

Tavare, Jay *Actor*
International Arts Entertainment, 8899 Beverly Blvd #800, Los Angeles, CA 90048

Tavener, John H *Football Player*
241 N Oregon St, Johnstown, OH 43031 USA

Tavener, John K *Composer*
Chester Music, 8-9 Firth St, London, W1V 5TZ, UNITED KINGDOM (UK)

Taverner, Sonia *Ballerina*
PO Box 129, Stony Plain, AB CANADA

Tavernier, Bertrand R M *Director*
Little Bear Productions, 7-9 Rue Arthur Groussler, Paris, 75010, FRANCE

Taviani, Paolo *Director*
Instituto Luce SPA, Via Tuscolana 1055, Rome, 00173, ITALY

Taviani, Vittorio *Director*
Instituto Luce SPA, Via Tuscolana 1055, Rome, 00173, ITALY

Taxier, Arthur *Actor*
Pakula/King, 9229 Sunset Blvd, #315, Los Angeles, CA 90069 USA

Taya, Maawiya Ould Sid'Ahmed *President*
President's Office, Boite Postale 184, Nouakchott, MAURITANIA

Taylor, Andy *Musician*
DD Productions, 93A Westbourne Park Villas, London, W2 5ED, UNITED KINGDOM (UK)

Taylor, Arthur R *Educator, Business Person*
Muhlenburg College, President's Office, Allentown, PA 18104 USA

Taylor, Benedict
4 Great Queen St., London, ENGLAND, WC28 5DG

Taylor, Bob "Hawk" *Athlete*
136 Skyway Dr, Murray, KY 42071

Taylor, Brian *Basketball Player*
3622 Green Vista Dr, Encino, CA 91436 USA

Taylor, Bruce L *Football Player*
6 Cascade Court W, Burr Ridge, IL 60527 USA

Taylor, Buck *Actor*
1305 Clyde Dr, Marrero, LA 70072 USA

Taylor, Carl E *Physicist*
Bittersweet Acres, 1201 Hollins Lane, Baltimore, MD 21209 USA

Taylor, Cecil P *Musician, Composer*
Joel Chriss, 300 Mercer St, #3J, New York, NY 10003 USA

Taylor, Chad *Musician*
Freedman & Smith, 1790 Broadway, #131, New York, NY 10019 USA

Taylor, Charles R (Charley) *Football Player, Football Executive*
12032 Canter Lane, Reston, VA 20191 USA

Taylor, Christian *Actor*

Taylor, Christine *Actor*
United Talent Agency, 9560 Wilshire Blvd, #500, Beverly Hills, CA 90212 USA

Taylor, Christy *Actor*
10990 Massachusetts Ave, #3, Los Angeles, CA 90024 USA

Taylor, Chuck
242 Oak Grove Ave., Atherton, CA 94025

Taylor, Clarice *Actor*
380 Elkwood Terrace, Englewood, NJ 07631 USA

Taylor, Dana *Actor*
100 S Sunrise Way, #468, Palm Springs, CA 92262 USA

Taylor, Dave *Hockey Player*
18920 Pasadero Dr, Tarzana, CA 91356 USA

Taylor, Delores *Actor*
PO Box 840, Moorpark, CA 93020 USA

Taylor, Elizabeth *Actor*
PO Box 55995, Sherman Oaks, CA 91413 USA

Taylor, Eric *Artist*
13 Tredgold Ave, Branhope near Leeds, West Yorkshire, LS16 9BS, UNITED KINGDOM (UK)

Taylor, Femi *Actor*
Paul Telford Mgmt, 23 Noel St, London, W1V 3RD, UNITED KINGDOM (UK)

Taylor, Fred *Football Player*
13750 Bronley Point Dr, Jacksonville, FL 32225 USA

Taylor, Gilbert *Cinematographer*
Cinematography Society, 11 Croft, Gerrards Cross, Bucks, SL9 9E, UNITED KINGDOM (UK)

Taylor, Glen *Basketball Player*
Minnesota Timberwolves, Target Center, 600 1st Ave N, Minneapolis, MN 55403 USA

Taylor, Henry S *Writer*
6930 Selkirk Dr, Bethesda, MD 30817 USA

Taylor, Holland *Actor*
2676 Hollyridge Dr, Los Angeles, CA 90068 USA

Taylor, J Herbert *Biologist*
110 Wood Road, #H210, Los Gatos, CA 95030 USA

Taylor, J T *Musician*
Famous Artists Agency, 250 W 57th St, New York, NY 10107 USA

Taylor, Jackie Lynn *Actor*
PO Box 3182, Citrus Heights, CA 95611 USA

Taylor, James *Musician, Songwriter*
Borman Entertainment, 1250 6th St, #401, Santa Monica, CA 90401 USA

Taylor, James A *War Hero*
PO Box 284, Trinity Center, CA 96091 USA

Taylor, James C (Jim) *Football Player*
7840 Walden Road, Baton Rouge, LA 70808 USA

Taylor, Jason *Football Player*
2342 SW 132nd St, Davie, FL 33325 USA

Taylor, Jay *Business Person*
Placer Dorne Inc, 1600-1055 Dunsmuir St, Vancouver, BC V7X 1P1, CANADA

Taylor, Jim *Writer*
William Morris Agency (WMA-LA), 1 William Morris Pl, Beverly Hills, CA 90212 USA

Taylor, John *Actor*
Left Bank Mgmt, 9255 Sunset Blvd #200, West Hollywood, CA 90069 USA

Taylor, John *Football Player*
5682 E Shepherd Ave, Clovis, CA 93611 USA

Taylor, Jonathan *Producer*
United Talent Agency (UTA), 9560 Wilshire Blvd, Beverly Hills, CA 90212 USA

Taylor, Joseph H Jr *Nobel Prize Laureate*
272 Hartley St, Princeton, NJ 08540 USA

Taylor, Josh
422 S. California Ave., Burbank, CA 91505

Taylor, Josh *Actor*
422 S California Ave, Burbank, CA 91505 USA

Taylor, Judson H *Educator*
State University of New York College, President's Office, Cortland, NY 13045 USA

Taylor, Karen *Comedian*
Avalon Management, 4A Exmoor St, London, W10 6BD, UNITED KINGDOM (UK)

Taylor, Kenneth N *Publisher*
1515 E Forest Ave, Wheaton, IL 60187 USA

Taylor, Kitrick L *Football Player*
18215 Foothill Blvd, #94, Fontana, CA 92335 USA

Taylor, Koko *Musician*
PO Box 60234, Chicago, IL 60660 USA

Taylor, Lance J *Economist*
PO Box 378, Old County Road, Washington, DC 04574 USA

Taylor, Lauriston S *Physicist*
10450 Lottsford Road, #1-5, Bowie, MD 20721 USA

Taylor, Lawrence *Football Player*
122 Canterburg Place, Williamsburg, VA 23188 USA

Taylor, Lili *Actor*
William Morris Agency, 1325 Ave of Americas, New York, NY 10019 USA

Taylor, Lionel *Football Player, Football Coach*
6593 Sahchu Lane, Cochiti Lake, NM 87083 USA

Taylor, Livingston *Musician*
Fat City Artists, 1906 Chet Atkins Place, #502, Nashville, TN 37212 USA

Taylor, Marianne *Actor*
Jack Scagnatti, 5118 Vineland Ave, #102, North Hollywood, CA 91601 USA

Taylor, Mark L *Actor*
7919 Norton Ave, West Hollywood, CA 90046 USA

Taylor, Maurice *Basketball Player*
Houston Rockets, Toyota Center, 2 E Greenway Plaza, Houston, TX 77046 USA

Taylor, Meldrick *Boxer*
1158 N York Road, Warminster, PA 18974 USA

Taylor, Meshach *Actor*
6300 Wilshire Blvd, #900, Los Angeles, CA 90048 USA

Taylor, Mick *Musician*
Jacobson & Colin, 19 W 21st St, #603A, New York, NY 10010 USA

Taylor, Natascha *Actor*
International Creative Management (ICM-LA), 8942 Wilshire Blvd, Beverly Hills, CA 90211 USA

Taylor, Nicole R (Niki) *Model*
8362 Pines Blvd, #334, Pembroke Pines, FL 33024 USA

Taylor, Noah *Actor*
June Cann Mgmt, 110 Quenn St, Woolahra, NSW, 2025, AUSTRALIA

Taylor, Paul B *Dancer, Choreographer*
Paul Taylor Dance Co, 552 Broadway, New York, NY 10012 USA

Taylor, Penny *Basketball Player*
Cleveland Rockers, Gund Arena, 1 Center Court, Cleveland, OH 44115 USA

Taylor, Regina *Actor*
PO Box 2015, North Highlands, CA 95660 USA

Taylor, Renee *Actor*
Judy Schoen, 606 N Larchmont Blvd,
#309, Los Angeles, CA 90004 USA

Taylor, Richard E *Nobel Prize Laureate*
757 Mayfield Ave, Stanford, CA 94305
USA

Taylor, Rip *Actor, Comedian*
1133 N Clark St, Los Angeles, CA 90069
USA

Taylor, Robert *Track Athlete*
1010 S Glenwood Blvd, Tyler, TX 75701
USA

Taylor, Rod *Actor*
2375 Bowmont Dr, Beverly Hills, CA
90210 USA

Taylor, Roger *Musician*
DD Productions, 93A Westbourne Park
Villas, London, W2 5ED, UNITED
KINGDOM (UK)

Taylor, Roger *Tennis Player*
39 Newstead Way, Wimbledon, SW19,
UNITED KINGDOM (UK)

Taylor, Roger M *Musician*
Neil Levin, 15260 Ventura Blvd, #1700,
Sherman Oaks, CA 91403 USA

Taylor, Roosevelt *Football Player*
1821 Arts St, New Orleans, LA 70117
USA

Taylor, Sandra *Actor, Model*
IPA Network, 231 E Alessandro Blvd,
#A355, Riverside, CA 92508 USA

Taylor, Stephen Monroe *Actor*
MC Talent Management, 4821 Lankershim
Blvd #F329, N Hollywood, CA 91601
USA

Taylor, Tamara *Actor*
PMK/HBH Public Relations (PMK-LA),
8500 Wilshire Blvd #700, Beverly Hills,
CA 90211 USA

Taylor, William O *Publisher*
Affiliated Publications, 135 William
Morrissey Blvd, Dorchester, MA 02125
USA

Taylor, Wilson H *Business Person*
CIGNA Corp, 1 Liberty Place, 1650
Market St, Philadelphia, PA 19192 USA

Taylor Jr, William (Billy) *Musician,
Composer*
555 Kappock St, Bronx, NY 10463 USA

Taylor-Grauman, Joan
9920 Robin Dr., Los Angeles, CA 90069

Taylor-Taylor, Courtney *Musician*
Monqui Records, PO Box 5908, Portland,
OR 97228 USA

Taylor-Young, Leigh *Actor*
11300 W Olympic Blvd, #610, Los
Angeles, CA 90064 USA

Taymor, Julie *Director*
International Creative Mgmt, 40 W 57th
St, #1800, New York, NY 10019 USA

Tchaikovsky, Aleksandr V *Musician,
Composer*
Leningradsky Prosp 14, #4, Moscow,
125040, RUSSIA

Tcherkassky, Marianna *Ballerina*
American Ballet Theatre, 890 Broadway,
New York, NY 10003 USA

Te Kanawa, Kiri *Opera Singer*
Jules Haelliger Impressario, Postfach 4113,
Lucerne, 6002, SWITZERLAND

Teaff, Grant *Football Coach*
8265 Forest Ridge Dr, Waco, TX 76712
USA

Teagle, Terry *Basketball Player*
2111 Heatherwood Dr, Missouri City, TX
77489 USA

Teague, Lewis
2190 N. Beverly Glen Blvd., Los Angeles,
CA 90077

Teague, Marshall *Actor*
Pinnacle Commercial Talent, 5757
Wilshire Blvd #510, Los Angeles, CA
90036

Teannaki, Teatao *President*
President's Office, PO Box 68, Bairiki,
Tarawa Atoll, KIRBATI

Tear, Robert *Opera Singer*
11 Ravenscourt Court, London, W6,
UNITED KINGDOM (UK)

Tears For Fears *Music Group*
Creative Artists Agency LCC (CAA-LA),
9830 Wilshire Blvd, Beverly Hills, CA
90212 USA

Teasdale, Joseph P *Governor*
Commerce Tower, 911 Main St #1210,
Kansas City, MO 64105 USA

Teasley, Nikki *Basketball Player*
Los Angeles Sparks, Staples Center, 1111
S Figueroa St, Los Angeles, CA 90015
USA

Tebaldi, Renata *Opera Singer*
Piazzetta della Guastalla 1, Milan, 20122,
ITALY

Tebbets, Birdie
229 Oak Ave., Anna Maria, FL 33501

Tebbit of Chingford, Norman B
Government Official
House of Lords, Westminsiter, London,
SW1A 0PW, UNITED KINGDOM (UK)

Tebbutt, Arthur R *Mathematician*
1511 Pelican Point Dr, Sarasota, FL 34231
USA

Techine, Andre J F *Director*
Artmedia, 20 Ave Rapp, Paris, 75007,
FRANCE

Technotronic
89 Fifth St.7th Flr., New York, NY 10003

Tedeschi, Susan *Musician*
Blue Sky Artists, 761 Washington Ave N,
Minneapolis, MN 55401 USA

Tedford, Travis *Actor*
Acme Talent & Literary Agency (LA), 4727
Wilshire Blvd #333, Los Angeles, CA
90010 USA

Teevens, Buddy *Football Coach*
Stanford University, Athletic Dept,
Stanford, CA 94395 USA

Tefkin, Blair *Actor*
Lucie Gamelon, 8022 Sunset Blvd #4049,
Los Angeles, CA 90046 USA

Tegan and Sara *Music Group*

Tegan and Sara *Music Group*
Paquin Entertainment Agency, 110 Bond
St, Toronto ON, M5B 1X8, CANADA

Tegart Dalton, Judy *Tennis Player*
72 Grange Road, Toorak, VIC, 3412,
AUSTRALIA

Teich, Malvin C *Engineer*
Boston University, Electrical/Computer
Engineering Dept, Boston, MA 02215 USA

Teicher, Louis (Lou) *Musician*
Avant-Grade Records, 12224 Avila Dr,
Kansas City, MO 64145 USA

Teichner, Helmut *Skier*
4250 Marine Dr, #2101, Chicago, IL
60613 USA

Teitel, Robert *Producer*
Creative Artists Agency LCC (CAA-LA),
9830 Wilshire Blvd, Beverly Hills, CA
90212 USA

Teitelbaum, Philip *Doctor*
University of Florida, Psychology Dept,
Gainesville, FL 32611 USA

Teitell, Conrad L *Lawyer*
16 Marlow Court, Riverside, CT 06878
USA

Teitler, William *Producer*
International Creative Management
(ICM-LA), 8942 Wilshire Blvd, Beverly
Hills, CA 90211 USA

Tejada, Miguel O M *Baseball Player*
Oakland Athletics, NA Coliseum, 7000
Coliseum Way, Oakland, CA 94621 USA

Tejera, Michael *Baseball Player*
Florida Marlins, 2269 Dan Marino Blvd,
Miami, FL 33056 USA

Tekulve, Kenton C (Kent) *Baseball Player*
1531 Sequoia Dr, Pittsburgh, PA 15241
USA

Telgdi, Valentine L *Physicist*
Eidgenossosche Technische Hochschule,
Houggerberg, Zurich, SWITZERLAND

Tellep, Daniel M *Business Person*
Lockheed Corp, PO Box 5118, Thousand
Oaks, CA 91359 USA

Teller *Musician*
William Morris Agency, 151 El Camino
Dr, Beverly Hills, CA 90212 USA

Teller, Edward *Doctor*
Box 808, Livermore, CA 94550 USA

Telles, Rick
2934 1/2 S. Beverly Glen Circle #107, Los
Angeles, CA 90077

Telnaes, Ann *Cartoonist*
Tribune Media Services, 435 N Michigan
Ave, #1500, Chicago, IL 60611 USA

Teltscher, Eliot *Tennis Player, Coach*
Pepperdine University, Athletic Dept,
Malibu, CA 90265 USA

Temchen, Sybil *Actor*
9 Yards Entertainment, 8530 Wilshire Blvd
Fl 5, Beverly Hills, CA 90211 USA

Temesvari, Andrea *Tennis Player*
ProServe, 1101 Woodrow Wilson Blvd,
#1800, Arlington, VA 22209 USA

Temirkanov, Yuri K
State Philharmonia, Mikhailovskaya 2,
Saint Petersburg, RUSSIA

Temko, Allan B *Journalist*
San Francisco Chronicle, Editorial Dept,
901 Mission, San Francisco, CA 94103
USA

Templeman of White Lackington, Sydney W *Judge*
Manor Heath, Know Hill Woking, Surrey, GU22 7HL, UNITED KINGDOM (UK)

Templesman, Maurice
529 Fifth Ave., New York, NY 10017

Templeton, Ben *Cartoonist*
Tribune Media Services, 435 N Michigan Ave, #1500, Chicago, IL 60611 USA

Templeton, Christopher
11333 Moorpark St., No. Hollywood, CA 91602

Templeton, Garry L *Baseball Player*
13552 Del Poniente Road, Poway, CA 92064 USA

Templeton, John M *Financier*
Lyford Cay Club, Box N7776, Nassau, BAHAMAS

Temptations, The *Music Group*
International Creative Management (ICM-LA), 8942 Wilshire Blvd, Beverly Hills, CA 90211 USA

Ten Thousand Maniacs
509 Hartnell St., Monterey, CA 93940

Tenace, F Gene *Baseball Player*
2650 Cliff Hawk Court, Redmond, OR 97756 USA

Tendulkar, Priya *Actor, Bollywood*
1 Anookul Apartments Harminder Singh Marg, Seven Bangalows Versova Andheri, Bombay, MS 400 061, INDIA

Teng-Hui, Lee *President*
Chaehshou Hall Chung King South Rd., Taipei, 10728, TAIWAN

Tengbom, Anders *Architect*
Kornhaminstorg 6, Stockholm, 11127, SWEDEN

Tenison, Renee *Actor, Model*
Tension Group, 171 Pier Ave, #403, Santa Monica, CA 90405 USA

Tennant, Stella *Model*
Select Model Mgmt, Archer House, 43 King St, London, WC2E 8RJ, UNITED KINGDOM (UK)

Tennant, Veronica *Ballerina*
National Ballet of Canada, 157 King St E, Toronto, ON M5C 1G9, CANADA

Tennant, Victoria *Actor*
PO Box 929, Beverly Hills, CA 90213 USA

Tenner, Judge Jack
218 N. Glenroy Pl., Los Angeles, CA 90049

Tenney, Jon *Actor*
United Talent Agency, 9560 Wilshire Blvd, #500, Beverly Hills, CA 90212 USA

Tennille, Toni *Musician*
7123 Franktown Road, Carson City, NV 89704 USA

Tennison, Chalee *Musician*
Tanasi Entertainment, 1204 17th Ave S, Nashville, TN 37212 USA

Tenorio, Pedro P *Governor*
Governor's Office, Capitol Hill, Chalan Kanoa, Saipan, CM, 96950 USA

Tenuta, Judy *Actor, Comedian*
Super Artists, 12021 Wilshire Blvd, #612, Los Angeles, CA 90025 USA

Tepper, Lou *Football Coach*
University of Illinois, Assembly Hall, Champaign, IL 61820 USA

Tequila Sunrise
4630 Deepdale Dr., Corpus Christi, TX 78413

Ter Horst, Jerald F *Government Official, Journalist*
7815 Evening Lane, Alexandria, VA 22306 USA

Ter-Petrosyan, Levon A *President*
Marshal Baghramjan Prospect 19, Yerevan, 375016, ARMENIA

Teran, Arlet *Actor*
Gabriel Blanco Iglesias (Mexico), Rio Balsas 35-32, Colonia Cuauhtemoc, DF, 06500, Mexico

Teraoka, Masami *Artist*
41-048 Kaulu St, Waimanalo, HI 96795 USA

TerBlanche, Esta *Actor*
Paradigm (LA), 10100 Santa Monica Blvd, Fl 25, Los Angeles, CA 90067 USA

Terekhova, Margarita B *Actor*
Bolshaya Gruzinskaya Str 57, #92, Moscow, 123056, RUSSIA

Terentyeva, Nina N *Opera Singer*
Bolshoi Theater, Teatralnaya Pl 1, Moscow, 103009, RUSSIA

Tereschenko, Sergei A *Prime Minister*
Prime Minister's Office, Dom Pravieelstra, Alma-Ata, 148008, KAZAKHSTAN

Tereshkova, Valentina V *Cosmonaut*
Int'l Co-operation Assn, Vozdvizhenka Str 14-18, Moscow, 103885, RUSSIA

Tergesen, Lee *Actor*
Gersh Agency, 232 N Canon Dr, Beverly Hills, CA 90210 USA

Terkel, Studs L *Writer*
850 W Castlewood Terrace, Chicago, IL 60640 USA

Terlesky, John *Actor*
14229 Dickens, #5, Sherman Oaks, CA 91423 USA

Termeer, Henricus A *Business Person*
Genzyme Corp, 1 Kendall Square, Cambridge, MA 02139 USA

Terminator X *Musician*
William Morris Agency, 151 El Camino Dr, Beverly Hills, CA 90212 USA

Termo, Leonard *Actor*
Baumgarten/Prophet, 1041 N Formosa Ave, #200, West Hollywood, CA 90046 USA

Terra, Scott *Actor*
DMG, 505 N Robertson Blvd, Los Angeles, CA 90048 USA

Terrace, Herbert S *Misc*
17 Campfire Road, Chappaqua, NY 10514 USA

Terrani, Lucia Valenti
Via Venti Settembre 72, Padova, ITALY, I-35122

Terranova, Joe *Musician*
Joe Taylor Mgmt, PO Box 1017, Turnersville, NJ 08012 USA

Terranova, Phil *Boxer*
30 Bogardus Place, New York, NY 10040 USA

Terrasson, Jacky *Musician*
Joel Chriss, 300 Mercer St, #3J, New York, NY 10003 USA

Terrazas Sandoval, Julio Cardinal *Religious Leader*
Arzobispado Casilla 25, Calle Ingavi 49, Santa Cruz, BOLIVIA

Terrell, David *Football Player*
196 N Main St, Roanoke, IN 46783 USA

Terrell, Ernie
11136 So. Parnell, Chicago, IL 60628

Terreri, Chris *Hockey Player*
170 Dezenso Lane, West Orange, NJ 07052 USA

Terrero, Jessy *Director, Producer*
William Morris Agency (WMA-LA), 1 William Morris Pl, Beverly Hills, CA 90212 USA

Terrile, Richard *Astronomer*
2121 E Woodlyn Road, Pasadena, CA 91104 USA

Terrio, Deney *Dancer, Entertainer*
Paramount Entertainment, PO Box 12, Far Hills, NJ 07931 USA

Terrio, Denny
1560 Broadway #1308, New York, NY 10036

Terris, Malcolm
14 England's Lane, London, ENGLAND, NW3

Terry, Clark *Musician*
420 Ivy Ave, Haworth, NJ 07641 USA

Terry, Hilda *Cartoonist*
8 Henderson Place, New York, NY 10028 USA

Terry, Jason *Basketball Player*
Atlanta Hawks, 190 Marietta St SW, Atlanta, GA 30303 USA

Terry, John *Actor*
25 W 5200 N, Park City, UT 84098 USA

Terry, John Q *Architect*
Old Exchange Dedham, Colchester, Essex, CO7 6HA, UNITED KINGDOM (UK)

Terry, Megan D *Writer*
2309 Hansom Blvd, Omaha, NE 68105 USA

Terry, Nigel *Actor*
BBC Artist Mail, PO Box 1116, Belfast, BT2 7AJ, United Kingdom

Terry, Ralph W *Baseball Player*
801 Park St, Larned, KS 67550 USA

Terry, Randall A *Social Activist*
Operation Rescue National, PO Box 360221, Melbourne, FL 32936 USA

Terry, Richard E *Business Person*
Peoples Energy Corp, 130 E Randolph Dr, Chicago, IL 60601 USA

Terry, Ruth *Actor, Musician*
622 Hospitality Dr, Rancho Mirage, CA 92270 USA

Terry, Tony *Musician*
Richard Walters, 1800 Argyle Ave, #408, Los Angeles, CA 90028 USA

Terzian, Jacques *Artist*
PO Box 883753, San Francisco, CA
94188 USA

Terzieff, Laurent D A *Actor, Director*
8 Rue du Dragon, Paris, 75006, FRANCE

Tesh, John *Musician, Composer,
Entertainer*
PO Box 6010, Sherman Oaks, CA 91413
USA

Teske, Rachel *Golfer*
Gaylord Sports Mgmt, 14646 N Kierland
Blvd, #230, Scottsdale, AZ 85254 USA

Tess, John *Business Person*
Heritage, 123 NW Second Avenue, Suite
200, Portland, OR 97209

Tessler-Lavigne, Marc *Doctor*
361 Ridgeway Road, Woodside, CA
94062 USA

Testa, M David *Financier*
T Rowe Price Assoc, 100 E Pratt St,
Baltimore, MD 21202 USA

Testaverde, Vincent F (Vinny) *Football
Player*
15 Tall Oak Court, Syosset, NY 11791
USA

Tester, Hans
6310 San Vicente Blvd. #401, Los
Angeles, CA 90048

Testi, Fabio
Via Francesco Siacci 38, Rome, ITALY,
I-00197

Testl, Fabio *Actor*
Via Siacci 38, Rome, 00197, ITALY

Tetley, Glen *Director, Choreographer*
15 W 9th St, New York, NY 10011 USA

Tetrault, Roger E *Business Person*
McDermott International, 1450 Polydras
St, New Orleans, LA 70112 USA

Tettamanzi, Dlonigi Cardinal *Religious
Leader*
Arclvescovado, Plazza Matteotti 4, Genoa,
16123, ITALY

Tettleton, Mickey L *Baseball Player*
52 W Royal Oak Road, Pauls Valley, OK
73075 USA

Tetzlaff, Christian *Musician*
Shuman Assoc, 120 W 58th St, #80, New
York, NY 10019 USA

Tewell, Doug *Golfer*
6301 Oak Tree Dr, Edmond, OK 73003
USA

Tewes, Lauren *Actor*
157 W 57th St, #604, New York, NY
10019 USA

Tewkesbury, Joan F *Director, Writer*
201 Ocean Ave, #B1702, Santa Monica,
CA 90402 USA

Tewksbury, Mark
2380 Pierre Depuy Ave, Montreal,
CANADA, PQ H3C 3R4

Tews, Andreas *Boxer*
Hamburger Allee 1, Schwerin, 19063,
GERMANY

Texada, Tia *Actor*
Evolution Entertainment, 901 N Highland
Ave, Los Angeles, CA 90038 USA

Thabu *Actor, Bollywood*
Ankul II Floor, 7 Bungalows Andheri
West, Mumbai, MS 400054, INDIA

Thacker, Brian M *War Hero*
11413 Monterey Dr, Wheaton, MD 20902
USA

Thackery, Jimmy *Musician*
Mongrel Music, 743 Center Blvd, Fairfax,
CA 94930 USA

Thaddeus, Patrick *Physicist*
58 Garfield St, Cambridge, MA 02138
USA

Thagard, Norman E *Astronaut, Physicist*
502 N Ride, Tallahassee, FL 32303 USA

Thain, John *Financier*
New York Stock Exchange, 11 Wall St,
New York, NY 10005 USA

Thaksin, Shinawatra *Prime Minister*
Premier's Office, Govt House, Luke Road,
Bangkok, 10300/2, THAILAND

Thalia *Musician, Actor*
William Morris Agency, 151 El Camino
Dr, Beverly Hills, CA 90212 USA

Than, Shwe *General, Prime Minister*
Prime Minister's Office, Theinbyu Road,
Botahtaung, Yangon, MYANMAR

Thani, Sheikh Abdul Aziz Ibn Khalifa al
Prime Minister
Prime Minister's Office, Dohar, QATAR

Thani, Sheikh Hamad bin Khalifa al
Royalty
Royal Palace, PO Box 923, Dohar,
QATAR

Thapa, Surya Bahadur *Prime Minister*
Tangal, Kathmandu, NEPAL

Tharp, Twyla *Dancer, Choreographer*
Twyla Tharp Productions, 336 Central
Park W, #17B, New York, NY 10025 USA

Thatcher, Baroness Margaret
Chester Sq Belgravia, London, ENGLAND

Thatcher of Lincolnshire, Margaret H
Prime Minister
11 Dutwich Gate, Dulwich, London,
SE12, UNITED KINGDOM (UK)

Thaves, Bob *Cartoonist*
PO Box 67, Manhattan Beach, CA 90267
USA

Thaxter, Phyllis *Actor*
Artist's Agency, The (LA), 1180 S Beverly
Dr #301, Los Angeles, CA 90035 USA

Thayer, Bill *Misc*
PO Box 233, Snohomish, WA 98291 USA

Thayer, Brynn *Actor*
House of Representatives, 400 S Beverly
Dr, #101, Beverly Hills, CA 90212 USA

Thayer, Bryrn
400 S. Beverly Dr. #101, Beverly Hills,
CA 90212

Thayer, Helen *Skier*
PO Box 233, Snohomish, WA 98291 USA

Thayer, W Paul *Government Official,
Business Person*
10200 Hollow Way, Dallas, TX 75229
USA

Theberge, James D *Diplomat*
4462 Cathedral Ave NW, Washington,
DC 20016 USA

Thedford, Marcello *Actor*
Overview, 15453 Lemay Street, Van
Nuys, CA 91406 USA

Theile, David *Swimmer*
84 Woodville St, Hendea, Brisbane, QLD,
4011, AUSTRALIA

Theismann, Joe *Football Player,
Sportscaster*
JRT Associates, 5661 Columbia Pike, Suite
200, Falls Church, VA 22041 USA

Theismann, Joseph R (Joe) *Football
Player, Sportscaster*
5661 Columbia Pike, #200, Falls Church,
VA 22041 USA

Thelan, Jodi
8428-C Melrose Pl., Los Angeles, CA
90069

Theodorakis, Mikis *Composer*
Epifanous 1, Akropolis, Athens, GREECE

Theodore, Donna
10000 Santa Monica Blvd. #305, Los
Angeles, CA 90067

Theodore, Jose *Hockey Player*
Montreal Canadiens, 1260 de la
Gauchetiere W, Montreal, QC, H3B 5EB,
CANADA

Theodorescu, Monica *Athlete*
Gestit Lindenhof, Sassenberg, 48336,
GERMANY

Theodosakis, Jason *Writer, Doctor*
Saint Martin's Press, 175 5th Ave, New
York, NY 10010 USA

Theodosius, Primate Metropolitian
Religious Leader
Orthodox Church in America, PO Box
675 RR 25A, Syosset, NY 11791 USA

Theron, Charlize *Actor, Model*
United Talent Agency (UTA), 9560
Wilshire Blvd, Beverly Hills, CA 90212
USA

Theroux, Justin *Actor*
3 Arts Entertainment Inc, 9460 Wilshire
Blvd Fl 7, Beverly Hills, CA 90212 USA

Theroux, Louis *Television Host*
BBC Artist Mail, PO Box 1116, Belfast,
BT2 7AJ, United Kingdom

Theroux, Paul E *Writer*
35 Elsynge Road, London, SW18 2NR,
UNITED KINGDOM (UK)

Theus, Reggie *Basketball Player*
Sanders Agency, 241 Ave of Americas,
#11H, New York, NY 10014 USA

Thewlis, David *Actor*
William Morris Agency (WMA-LA), 1
William Morris Pl, Beverly Hills, CA
90212 USA

Thiandoum, Hyacinthe Cardinal *Religious
Leader*
Archeveche, Ave Jean XXIII, Dakar, 1908,
SENEGAL

Thibaudet, Jean-Yves *Musician*
3601 Griffith Park Blvd, Los Angeles, CA
90027 USA

Thibault, Charles *Doctor*
4 Place Jussieu, Paris, 75005, FRANCE

Thibiant, Aida *Fashion Designer*
Institut de Beaute, 449 N Canon Dr,
Beverly Hills, CA 90210 USA

Thibodeaux, Keith *Actor*
5372 Jamaica Dr, Jackson, MS 39211-4057 USA

Thicke, Alan *Actor*
10505 Sarah St, Toluca Lake, CA 91602 USA

Thiedemann, Fritz *Misc*
Ostreherweg 28, Heide, 25746, GERMANY

Thiele, Gerhard P J *Astronaut*
ESA/EAC, Linder Hohe, Cologne, 51147, GERMANY

Thielemann, Ray C (R C) *Football Player*
210 Rose Meadow Lane, Alpharetta, GA 30005 USA

Thielemans, Jean B (Toots) *Musician*
Peter Levinson Communications, 2575 Palisade Ave, #11H, Bronx, NY 10463 USA

Thielen, Gunter *Business Person*
Bertelsmann AG, Carl-Bertelsmann-Str 270, Guetersloh, 33311, GERMANY

Thiemann, Charles Lee *Financier*
Federal Home Loan Bank, PO Box 598, Cincinnati, OH 45201 USA

Thieme, Paul *Misc*
Tubingen University, Wilhelmstr 7, Tubingen, 72074, GERMANY

Thier, Samuel O *Educator, Physicist*
99-20 Florence St, #4B, Chestnut Hill, MA 02467 USA

Thierry, John F *Football Player*
1431 Federal Road, Opelousas, LA 70570 USA

Thiess, Ursula *Actor*
1940 Bel Air Road, Los Angeles, CA 90077 USA

Thiessen, Tiffani *Actor*
3523 Wrightwood Court, Studio City, CA 91604 USA

Thigpen, Yancey D *Football Player*
3305 Greystone Dr, Rocky Mountain, NC 27804 USA

Thimmesch, Nicholas *Journalist*
6301 Broad Branch Road, Chevy Chase, MD 20815 USA

Thinnes, Roy *Actor*
Mail Center, 1910 Madison Ave, Memphis, TN 38104 USA

Third Day *Music Group*
Creative Artists Agency LCC (CAA-LA), 9830 Wilshire Blvd, Beverly Hills, CA 90212 USA

Third Eye Blind *Music Group*
Eric Godtland Management, 1040 Mariposa St #200, San Francisco, CA 94107 USA

Third World
151 El Camino Dr., Beverly Hills, CA 90212

Thirsk, Robert B *Astronaut*
Space Agency, 6767 Route de Aeroport, Saint-Hubert, QC, J3Y 8Y9, CANADA

Thode, Henry G *Scientist*
McMaster University, Nuclear Research Dept, Hamilton, ON L8S 4M1, CANADA

Thoma, Dieter *Skier*
Am Rossleberg 35, Hinterzarten, 79856, GERMANY

Thoma, Georg *Skier*
Bisten 6, Hinterzarten, 79856, GERMANY

Thomalla, Georg *Actor*
Hans Nefer, Bad Gastein, 5640, AUSTRIA

Thomas, Andrew S W (Andy) *Astronaut*
NASA, Johnson Space Center, 2101 NASA Road, Houston, TX 77058 USA

Thomas, Aurelius *Football Player*
PO Box 91157, Columbus, OH 43209 USA

Thomas, B J *Musician, Songwriter*
Gloria Thomas, 1324 Crownhill Dr, Arlington, TX 76012 USA

Thomas, Barbara S *Government Official*
News International, 1 Virginia St, London, E1 9XY, UNITED KINGDOM (UK)

Thomas, Betty *Director, Actor*
Creative Artists Agency, 9830 Wilshire Blvd, Beverly Hills, CA 90212 USA

Thomas, Billy M *General*
2387 Spanish Oak Terrace, Colorado Springs, CO 80920 USA

Thomas, BJ *Musician*
Gloria Thomas Inc, 1424 Crownhill Drive, Arlington, TX 76012 USA

Thomas, Blair *Football Player*
723 Belvoir Road, Plymouth Meeting, PA 19462 USA

Thomas, Broderick *Football Player*
16123 Padons Trace Court, Missouri City, TX 77489 USA

Thomas, Bruce *Actor*
Jerry Shandrew PR, 1050 South Stanley Avenue, Los Angeles, CA 90019-6634 USA

Thomas, Cal *Television Host*
After Hours with Cal Thomas, 1211 Ave of the Americas, Level C-1, New York, NY 10036-8701 USA

Thomas, Carl *Musician*
William Morris Agency (WMA-LA), 1 William Morris Pl, Beverly Hills, CA 90212 USA

Thomas, Carla *Musician*
Talent Consultants International, 1560 Broadway, #1308, New York, NY 10036 USA

Thomas, Carotine Bedell *Physicist*
2401 Calvert St NW, #504, Washington, DC 20008 USA

Thomas, Chris *Musician*
Associated Booking Corp, 1995 Broadway, #501, New York, NY 10023 USA

Thomas, Craig *Actor*
Granada Television, Quay Street, Manchester, M60 9EA, UK

Thomas, Damien
31 Kensington Church St., London, ENGLAND, W8 4LL

Thomas, Dave *Comedian*
MBST Entertainment, 345 N Maple D #200, Suite 200, Beverly Hills, CA 90210 USA

Thomas, David *Musician*
74 Hyde Vale, Greenwich, London, SE10 8HP, UNITED KINGDOM (UK)

Thomas, Debi
22 E. 71st St., New York, NY 10021

Thomas, Debra J (Deb) *Figure Skater*
Mentor Mgmt, 202 S Michigan St, #810, South Bend, IN 46601 USA

Thomas, Dennis (D T) *Musician*
Pyramid Entertainment, 89 5th Ave, #700, New York, NY 10003 USA

Thomas, Dominic R *Religious Leader*
Church of Jesus Christ, 6th & Lincoln Sts, Monongahela, PA 15063 USA

Thomas, Donald A *Astronaut*
311 Shadow Creek Dr, Seabrook, TX 77586 USA

Thomas, Donald Michael (D M) *Writer*
Coach House, Rashleigh Vale Tregolls Rd, Truro, Cornwall, TR1 1TJ, UNITED KINGDOM (UK)

Thomas, E Donnall *Nobel Prize Laureate*
Hutchinson Cancer Research Center, PO Box 19024, Seattle, WA 98109 USA

Thomas, Eddie Kaye *Actor*
3 Arts Entertainment Inc, 9460 Wilshire Blvd Fl 7, Beverly Hills, CA 90212 USA

Thomas, Elizabeth Marshall *Writer*
80 E Mountain Road, Petersborough, NH 03458 USA

Thomas, Ernest *Actor*
Coast to Coast Talent, 3350 Barham Blvd, Los Angeles, CA 90068 USA

Thomas, Etan *Basketball Player*
Washington Wizards, MCI Center, 601 F St NW, Washington, DC 20004 USA

Thomas, Frank E *Baseball Player*
2521 N Bosworth Ave, Chicago, IL 60614 USA

Thomas, Frank J *Baseball Player*
118 Doray Dr, Pittsburgh, PA 15237 USA

Thomas, Franklin R (Frank) *Animator*
Animation Celection, 1002 Prospect St, La Jolla, CA 92037 USA

Thomas, Fred *Lawyer, Government Official*
Metropolitan Police Dept, 300 Indiana Ave NW, Washington, DC 20001 USA

Thomas, Gareth *Actor*
Julian Belfrage & Associates, 42 Albermarle St, London, W1X 4P, UNITED KINGDOM (UK)

Thomas, Gareth *Engineer*
University of California, Materials Science Dept, Berkeley, CA 94720 USA

Thomas, Heather *Actor*
Lymberopoulos, 13601 Ventura Blvd, #354, Sherman Oaks, CA 91423 USA

Thomas, Heidi *Actor*
Lichtman/Salners, 12216 Moorpark St, Studio City, CA 91604 USA

Thomas, Helen A *Journalist*
2501 Calvert St NW, Washington, DC 20008 USA

Thomas, Henry *Actor*
International Creative Mgmt, 8942 Wilshire Blvd, #219, Beverly Hills, CA 90211 USA

Thomas, Henry L Jr *Football Player*
16811 Southern Oaks Dr, Houston, TX
77068 USA

Thomas, Henry W *Writer*
3214 Warder St NW, Washington, DC
20010 USA

Thomas, Irma *Musician*
Emile Jackson, PO Box 26126, New
Orleans, LA 70186 USA

Thomas, J Gorman *Baseball Player*
759 Tallwood Road, Charleston, SC
29412 USA

Thomas, Jack Ward *Government Official,*
Biologist
University of Montana, Biology Dept,
Missoula, MT 59812 USA

Thomas, Jake *Actor*
Stan Rogow Productions, 846 N
Cahuenga Blvd, Bldg D, Los Angeles, CA
90038 USA

Thomas, Jay *Actor*
Gersh Agency, 232 N Canon Dr, Beverly
Hills, CA 90210 USA

Thomas, Jean *Artist*
1427 Summit Road, Berkeley, CA 94708
USA

Thomas, Jeremy *Producer, Filmmaker*
Recorded Picture Co, 8-12 Broadwick St,
London, W1V 1FH, UNITED KINGDOM
(UK)

Thomas, John *Basketball Player*
Toronto Raptors, Air Canada Center, 40
Bay St, Toronto, ON M5J 2N8, CANADA

Thomas, John C *Track Athlete*
51 Mulberry St, Brockton, MA 02302 USA

Thomas, John M *Scientist*
Royal Institution, 21 Albemarle St,
London, W1X 4BS, UNITED KINGDOM
(UK)

Thomas, Jonathan Taylor *Actor*
Management 360, 9111 Wilshire Blvd,
Beverly Hills, CA 90210 USA

Thomas, Justice Clarence *Judge*
US Supreme Court, 1 1st St NE,
Washington, DC 20543 USA

Thomas, Khleo *Actor*
Beverly Hecht Agency, 12001 Ventura
Place, Suite 320, Studio City, CA 91604
USA

Thomas, Kleo *Musician*
American Idol, 7800 Beverly Blvd #251,
Los Angeles, CA 90036 USA

Thomas, Kurt *Gymnast*
1184 N Hillcrest Road, Beverly Hills, CA
90210 USA

Thomas, Kurt *Basketball Player*
1826 Brook Terrace Trail, Dallas, TX
75232 USA

Thomas, Larry
4924 Vineland Ave., No. Hollywood, CA
91601

Thomas, LaToya *Basketball Player*
San Antonio Silver Stars, 1 SBC Center,
San Antonio, TX 78219 USA

Thomas, Mark A *Football Player*
556 Hillsboro St, Monticello, GA 31064
USA

Thomas, Marlo *Actor*
420 E 54th St, #28G, New York, NY
10022 USA

Thomas, Mary *Musician*
Superstars Unlimited, PO Box 371371,
Las Vegas, NV 89137 USA

Thomas, Michael Tilson *Conductor,*
Musician
San Francisco Symphony, Davies
Symphony Hall, San Francisco, CA 94102
USA

Thomas, Michelle Rene *Actor*
Agency for Performing Arts, 9200 Sunset
Blvd #900, Los Angeles, CA 90069

Thomas, Pamela *Business Person*
CNBC, 900 Sylvan Ave, Englewood Cliffs,
NJ 07632 USA

Thomas, Pat *Football Player*
612 Middle Cove Dr, Plano, TX 75023
USA

Thomas, Philip Michael *Actor*
PO Box 3714, Brooklyn, NY 11202 USA

Thomas, Randy *Voice Over Artist*
Innovative Artists (LA), 1505 Tenth St,
Santa Monica, CA 90401 USA

Thomas, Ray *Nobel Prize Laureate*
Insight Mgmt, 1222 16th Ave S, #300,
Nashville, TN 37212 USA

Thomas, Reginald
18 Belgrave Mews West, London,
ENGLAND, SW1X 8HT

Thomas, Richard *Actor*
3219 Fairpoint St, Pasadena, CA 91107
USA

Thomas, Rob *Musician, Songwriter*
Creative Artists Agency, 9830 Wilshire
Blvd, Beverly Hills, CA 90212 USA

Thomas, Robert D *Publisher*
223 Mariomi Road, New Canaan, CT
06840 USA

Thomas, Robin *Actor*
Marshak/Zachary Company, The, 8840
Wilshire Blvd Fl 1, Beverly Hills, CA
90211 USA

Thomas, Rozonda (Chili) *Music Group*
Diggit Entertainment, 6 W 18th St, #800,
New York, NY 10011 USA

Thomas, Sean Patrick *Actor*
Endeavor Agency LLC (LA), 9601 Wilshire
Blvd Fl 3, Beverly Hills, CA 90210 USA

Thomas, Serena Scott *Actor*
S M S Talent, 8730 Sunset Blvd, #440, Los
Angeles, CA 90069 USA

Thomas, Steve *Entertainer*
This Old House Show, PO Box 2284,
South Burlington, VT 05407 USA

Thomas, Ted

Thomas, Thurman L *Football Player*
7018 Robertson Road, Missouri City, TX
77489 USA

Thomas, Tra *Football Player*
Philadelphia Eagles, 1 Novacare Way,
Philadelphia, PA 19145 USA

Thomas, Wayne *Hockey Player*
Cleveland Barons, 200 Hudson Road E,
Cleveland, OH 44115 USA

Thomas, William H Jr *Football Player*
2401 Echo Dr, Amarillo, TX 79107 USA

Thomas, Zach *Football Player*
1051 NW 122nd Ave, Planation, FL
33323 USA

Thomas III, Isiah L *Athlete, Basketball*
Player, Business Person, Coach
PO Box 43136, Detroit, MI 48243 USA

Thomas of Swynnerton, Hugh S *Historian*
Well House, Sudbourne, Suffolk, UNITED
KINGDOM (UK)

Thomason, Harry *Producer*
Mozark Productions, 4024 Radford Ave,
Bldg 5 #104, Studio City, CA 91604

Thomason, Harry Z *Producer*
10732 Riverside Dr, North Hollywood,
CA 91602 USA

Thomason, Marsha *Actor*
Personal Management Company, 425 N
Robertson Dr, Los Angeles, CA 90048
USA

Thomassin, Florence *Actor*
Artmedia, 20 Ave Rapp, Paris, 75007,
FRANCE

Thome, James H (Jim) *Baseball Player*
6137 Greenhill Road, New Hope, PA
18938 USA

Thomerson, Tim *Actor*
2635 28th St, #14, Santa Monica, CA
90405 USA

Thomopoulos, Anthony *Business Person*
10727 Wilshire Blvd, #1602, Los Angeles,
CA 90024 USA

Thomopoulos, Tony
1280 Stone Canyon Rd., Los Angeles, CA
90077-2920

Thompson, Andrea
PO Box 105366, Atlanta, GA 30348

Thompson, Anthony *Football Player,*
Football Coach
Indiana University, Athletic Dept,
Bloomington, IN 47405 USA

Thompson, Bennie *Football Player*
Baltimore Ravens, Ravens Stadium, 11001
Russell St, Baltimore, MD 21230 USA

Thompson, Bobby
122 Sunlit Dr., Watchung, NJ 07060

Thompson, Brian
1010 Olive Lane, La Canada, CA 91011

Thompson, Brooks *Basketball Player*
Orlando Magic, Waterhouse Center, 8701
Maitland Summit Blvd, Orlando, FL
32810 USA

Thompson, Caroline W *Writer, Director*
William Morris Agency, 151 El Camino
Dr, Beverly Hills, CA 90212 USA

Thompson, Christopher *Astronomer*
University of North Carolina, Astrophysics
Dept, Chapel Hill, NC 27599 USA

Thompson, Clifford *Hockey Player, Coach*
3 Summit Dr, #16, Reading, MA 01867
USA

Thompson, Daley *Athlete*
1 Church Row Wandsworth Plain,
London, ENGLAND, SW18 1ES

Thompson, David O *Basketball Player*
5045 Strawberry Hill Dr, #C, Charlotte,
NC 28211 USA

Thompson, David R *Judge*
US Court of Appeals, 940 Front St, San Diego, CA 92101 USA

Thompson, David W *Scientist*
Orbital Science Corp, 21839 Atlantic Blvd, Sterling, VA 20166 USA

Thompson, Edward K *Editor*
Rock Ledge Farm, RR 8 Box 350 Union Valley Road, Mahopac, NY 10541 USA

Thompson, Edward T *Editor*
11 Cotswold Dr, North Salem, NY 10560 USA

Thompson, Emma *Actor*
Hamilton Asper Mgmt, 24 Hanway St, London, W1P 9DD, UNITED KINGDOM (UK)

Thompson, Ernest
Rt. #1 Box 3248, Ashland, NH 03217

Thompson, F M (Daley) *Track Athlete*
Olympic Assn, 1 Wadsworth Plain, London, SW18 1EH, UNITED KINGDOM (UK)

Thompson, Fred Dalton *Actor*
Abrams Artists Agency (LA), 9200 Sunset Blvd Fl 11, Los Angeles, CA 90069 USA

Thompson, G Kennedy *Financier*
First Union Corp, 1 First Union Center, Charlotte, NC 28288 USA

Thompson, G Ralph *Religious Leader*
Seventh-Day Adventists, 12501 Old Columbia Pike, Silver Spring, MD 20904 USA

Thompson, Gary *Basketball Player*
2531 Park Vista Circle, Arnes, IA 50014 USA

Thompson, Gary Scott *Writer, Producer*
William Morris Agency (WMA-LA), 1 William Morris Pl, Beverly Hills, CA 90212 USA

Thompson, Gina *Musician*
Richard Walters, 1800 Argyle Ave, #408, Los Angeles, CA 90028 USA

Thompson, Hank *Musician, Songwriter*
2000 Vista Road, Roanoke, TX 76262 USA

Thompson, Hilarie
13202 Weddington St., Van Nuys, CA 91401

Thompson, Hugh L *Educator*
Washburn University, President's Office, Topeka, KS 66621 USA

Thompson, Hunter S *Journalist, Writer*
PO Box 220, Woody Creek, CO 81656 USA

Thompson, Ian
44 Perryn Rd, London, ENGLAND, W3 7NA

Thompson, J Lee
9595 Lime Orchard Rd, Beverly Hills, CA 90210 USA

Thompson, Jack *Football Player*
2507 29th Ave W, Seattle, WA 98199 USA

Thompson, Jack *Actor*
June Cann Mgmt, 110 Queen St, Woollahra, NSW, 2025, AUSTRALIA

Thompson, Jack E *Business Person*
Homestake Mining Co, 650 California St, San Francisco, CA 94108 USA

Thompson, James B Jr *Misc*
1010 Waltham St, #F1, Lexington, MA 02421 USA

Thompson, James R (Jim) Jr *Governor*
Winston & Strawn, 25 W Wacker Dr, Chicago, IL 60601 USA

Thompson, James R Jr *Misc*
416 Randolph Ave SE, Huntsville, AL 35801 USA

Thompson, Jason D *Baseball Player*
1358 Forest Bay Dr, Waterford, MI 48328 USA

Thompson, Jennifer (Jenny) *Swimmer*
USA Swimming, 1 Olympia Plaza, Colorado Springs, CO 80909 USA

Thompson, Jenny
One Olympic Plaza, Colorado Springs, CO 80909-5770

Thompson, Jill *Cartoonist*
DC Comics, 1700 Broadway, New York, NY 10019 USA

Thompson, John B *Basketball Player, Coach, Sportscaster*
3636 16th St NW, #B1161, Washington, DC 20010 USA

Thompson, John G *Mathematician*
University of Florida, Mathematics Dept, Gainesville, FL 32611 USA

Thompson, John M *Business Person*
IBM Corp, 1 N Castle Dr, Armonk, NY 10504 USA

Thompson, Kenan *Actor*
Endeavor Agency LLC (LA), 9601 Wilshire Blvd Fl 3, Beverly Hills, CA 90210 USA

Thompson, Kenneth L *Scientist*
AT & T Bell Lucent Laboratory, 600 Mountain Ave, New Providence, NJ 07974 USA

Thompson, Lea *Actor*
6061 Longridge Ave, Van Nuys, CA 91401 USA

Thompson, Leonard *Golfer*
9010 Marsh View Court, Ponte Vedra, FL 32082 USA

Thompson, Linda *Actor*
25254 Eldorado Meadows Road, Hidden Hills, CA 91302 USA

Thompson, Linda *Musician*
High Road, 751 Bridgeway, #300, Sausalito, CA 94965 USA

Thompson, Lonnie *Scientist*
Ohio State University, Geology Dept, Columbus, OH 43210 USA

Thompson, Mike *Editor, Cartoonist*
Detroit Free Press, Editorial Dept, 600 W Fort St, Detroit, MI 48226 USA

Thompson, Obadele *Track Athlete*
Amateur Athletics Assn, PO Box 46, Bridgetown, BARBADOS

Thompson, Paul H *Educator*
Weber State University, President's Office, Ogden, UT 84408 USA

Thompson, Richard *Musician, Songwriter*
Elizabeth Rush Agency, 100 Park St, #4, Montclair, NJ 07042 USA

Thompson, Richard K *Religious Leader*
African Methodist Episcopal Zion Church, PO Box 32843, Charlotte, NC 28232 USA

Thompson, Robert G K *General*
Pitcott House, Winsford Minehead, Somerset, UNITED KINGDOM (UK)

Thompson, Robert R (Robby) *Baseball Player*
4438 Gun Club Road, West Palm Beach, FL 33406 USA

Thompson, Sada *Actor*
PO Box 490, Southebury, CT 06488 USA

Thompson, Scott
9150 Wilshire Blvd. #350, Beverly Hills, CA 90212

Thompson, Shawn
5319 Biloxi Ave., No. Hollywood, CA 91601

Thompson, Sophie *Actor*
Jonathan Altaras, 13 Shorts Gardens, London, WC2H 9AT, UNITED KINGDOM (UK)

Thompson, Starley L *Scientist*
National Atmospheric Research Center, PO Box 3000, Boulder, CO 80307 USA

Thompson, Sue *Musician*
Curb Entertainment, 3907 W Alameda Ave, #200, Burbank, CA 91505 USA

Thompson, Susanna
PO Box 15717, Beverly Hills, CA 90209-1717

Thompson, Tina *Basketball Player*
Houston Comets, 2 Greenway Plaza, #400, Houston, TX 77046 USA

Thompson, Tommy *Football Player*
PO Box 687, Calico Rock, AR 72519 USA

Thompson, Tommy G *Secretary*
Health/Human Service Department, 200 Independence SW, Washington, DC 20201 USA

Thompson, Wilbur (Moose) *Track Athlete*
11372 Martha Ann, Los Alamitos, CA 90720 USA

Thompson, William P *Religious Leader*
World Council of Churches, 475 Riverside Dr, New York, NY 10115 USA

Thompson Twins
9 Eccleston St., London, ENGLAND, SW1W 9LX

Thomsen, Ulrich *Actor*
Paradigm Agency, 10100 Santa Monica Blvd, #2500, Los Angeles, CA 90067 USA

Thomson, Anna *Actor*
Innovative Artists, 1505 10th St, Santa Monica, CA 90401 USA

Thomson, Bobby
122 Sunlit Dr., Watchung, NJ 07060

Thomson, Brian E *Designer*
5 Little Dowling St, Paddington, NSW, 2021, AUSTRALIA

Thomson, Cyndi *Musician*
The Firm, 9100 Wilshire Blvd, #100W, Beverly Hills, CA 90210 USA

Thomson, Dorrie
3349 Cahuenga Blvd. W. #2, Los Angeles, CA 90068

Thomson, Gordon *Actor*
3914 Fredonia Dr, Los Angeles, CA 90068 USA

Thomson, H C (Hank) *Misc*
PO Box 38, Mullet Lake, MI 49761 USA

Thomson, James A *Biologist*
University of Wisconsin, Medical School, Biology Dept, Madison, WI 53706 USA

Thomson, June *Commentator*
KNBC-TV, News Dept, 3000 W Alameda Ave, Burbank, CA 91523 USA

Thomson, Peter W *Golfer*
Carmel House, 44 Mathoura Road, Toorak, VIC, 3142, AUSTRALIA

Thomson, Robert B (Bobby) *Baseball Player*
122 Sunlit Dr, Watchung, NJ 07069 USA

Thomson of Fleet, Kenneth R *Publisher*
Thompson Newspapers, 65 Queen St NW, Toronto, ON M5H 2M8, CANADA

Thon, Olaf *Social Activist*
FC Schalke 04, Postfach 200861, Gelsenkirchen, 45843, GERMANY

Thone, Charles *Governor*
Erickson & Sederstrom, 301 S 13th St, #400, Lincoln, NE 68508 USA

Thoni, Gustav *Skier, Coach*
39026 Prato Allo, Stelvio-Prao, BZ, ITALY

Thora *Actor*
CunninghamEscottDipene, 10635 Santa Monica Blvd, #130, Los Angeles, CA 90025 USA

Thorburn, Clifford C D (Cliff) *Billiards Player*
31 West Side Dr, Markham, ON L3P 7J5, CANADA

Thorell, Clarke *Actor*
Bauman Redanty & Shaul Agency, 5757 Wilshire Blvd #473, Los Angeles, CA 90036 USA

Thorin, Christopher *Musician*
Shapiro Co, 9229 Sunset Blvd, #607, Los Angeles, CA 90069 USA

Thorin, Donald E Sr *Cinematographer*
15260 Ventura Blvd, #1040, Sherman Oaks, CA 91403 USA

Thorn, Gaston *Prime Minister*
1 Rue de la Forge, Luxembourg, LUXEMBOURG

Thorn, Rod *Basketball Player*
20 Loewen Court, Rye, NY 10580 USA

Thorn, Tracey *Musician*
JFD Mgmt, Acklam Worshops, 10 Acklam Road, London, W10 5QZ, UNITED KINGDOM (UK)

Thornburgh, Richard *Ex-Governor*
2540 Massachusetts Ave NW #405, Washington, DC 20005-2832 USA

Thornburgh, Richard L (Dick) *Attorney General, Governor*
Kirkpatrick & Lockhart, 1800 Massachusetts Ave NW, #900, Washington, DC 20036 USA

Thorne, Dyanne *Actor*
8721 Sunset Blvd, #101, Los Angeles, CA 90069 USA

Thorne, Frank *Cartoonist*
1967 Grenville Road, Scotch Plains, NJ 07076 USA

Thorne, Gary *Commentator*
ABC-TV, Sports Dept, 77 W 66th St, New York, NY 10023 USA

Thorne, Kip S *Physicist*
California Institute of Technology, Physics Dept, Pasadena, CA 91125 USA

Thorne-Smith, Courtney *Actor, Model*
Paradigm Agency, 10100 Santa Monica Blvd, #2500, Los Angeles, CA 90067 USA

Thornell, Jack R *Photographer, Journalist*
6815 Madewood Dr, Metairie, LA 70003 USA

Thornhill, Arthur H Jr *Publisher*
50 S School St, Portsmouth, NH 03801 USA

Thornhill, Leeroy *Dancer*
Midi Mgmt, Jenkins Lane, Great Hallinsburry, Essex, CM22 9QL, UNITED KINGDOM (UK)

Thornhill, Lisa *Actor*
208-11 Anin St, Bedford Nova, Scotia, B4A 4E3, CANADA

Thornton, Billy Bob *Actor, Director*
Creative Artists Agency LCC (CAA-LA), 9830 Wilshire Blvd, Beverly Hills, CA 90212 USA

Thornton, Frank *Actor*
David Daly, 586A King Road, London, SW6 2DX, UNITED KINGDOM (UK)

Thornton, Kathryn C *Astronaut*
100 Bedford Place, Charlottesville, VA 22903 USA

Thornton, Sigrid *Actor*
International Casting Services, 147 King St, Sydney, NSW, 2000, AUSTRALIA

Thornton, William E *Astronaut*
7640 Pimilco Lane, Boerne, TX 78015 USA

Thornton, Zach *Soccer Player*
Chicago Fire, 980 N Michigan Ave, #1998, Chicago, IL 60611 USA

Thorogood, George *Musician*
Michael Donahue Mgmt, PO Box 807, Lewisburg, VA 24901 USA

Thorpe, Ian *Swimmer*
PO Box 427, Milsons Point, NSW, 2061, AUSTRALIA

Thorpe, James *Director*
20 Loeffler Road, #T320, Bloomfield, CT 06002 USA

Thorpe, Jeremy J *Government Official*
2 Orme Square, Bayswater, London, W2, UNITED KINGDOM (UK)

Thorpe, Jim *Golfer*
1612 Kersley Circle, Heathrow, FL 32746 USA

Thorpe, Otis H *Basketball Player*
PO Box 400, Canfield, OH 44406 USA

Thorsell, William *Editor*
Toronto Globe & Mail, 444 Front St W, Toronto, ON M5V 2S9, CANADA

Thorsness, Leo K *War Hero*
64915 E Brassie Dr, Tucson, AZ 85739 USA

Thorson, Linda *Actor*
S M S Talent, 8730 Sunset Blvd, #440, Los Angeles, CA 90069 USA

Thout, Pierre
6606 Patrick Ct., Centreville, VA 21020

Thranhardt, Carlo
Brauweilerstr. 14, Koln, GERMANY, D-50859

Threadgill, Henry L *Musician, Composer*
Joel Chriss, 300 Mercer St, #3J, New York, NY 10003 USA

Threatt, Sedale *Basketball Player*
5359 Newcastle Lane, Calabasas, CA 91302 USA

Three Degrees
19 The Willows Maidenhead Rd., Windsor Berkshire, ENGLAND

Three Dog Night
5171 Caliente St. #134, Las Vegas, NV 89119

Threlfall, David *Actor*
James Sharkey Assoc, 15 Golden Sq Fl 3, London, W1R 3PA, UNITED KINGDOM (UK)

Threlkeld, Richard D *Commentator*
CBS-TV, News Dept, 51 W 52nd St, New York, NY 10019 USA

Threshie, R David Jr *Publisher*
Orange County Register, 625 N Grand Ave, Santa Ana, CA 92701 USA

Thrice *Music Group*
Nick Ben-Meir CPA, 652 N Doheny Dr, West Hollywood, CA 90069 USA

Throne, Malachi *Actor*
11805 Mayfield Ave, #306, Los Angeles, CA 90049 USA

Thumann, Chad *Writer*
Jericho Entertainment, 2121 Ave of the Stars #2900, Los Angeles, CA 90067

Thunman, Nils R *Admiral*
1516 S Willemore Ave, Springfield, IL 62704 USA

Thuot, Pierre
21700 Atlantic Blvd., Dulles, VA 21066

Thuot, Pierre J *Astronaut*
6606 Patrick Court, Centreville, VA 20120 USA

Thurm, Maren *Actor*
ZBF Agentur, Ordensmeisterstr 15-16, Berlin, 12099, GERMANY

Thurman, Dennis L *Football Player*
3447 W 59th Place, Los Angeles, CA 90043 USA

Thurman, Uma *Actor*
Creative Artists Agency LCC (CAA-LA), 9830 Wilshire Blvd, Beverly Hills, CA 90212 USA

Thurman, William E *General*
10 Firestone Dr, Pinehurst, NC 28374 USA

Thurmond, Nate *Basketball Player*
5094 Diamond Heights Blvd, #B, San Francisco, CA 94131 USA

Thurow, Lester C *Economist*
Massachusetts Institute of Technology, Economics Dept, Cambridge, MA 02139 USA

Thurston, Frederick C (Fuzzy) *Football Player*
2 Watercolor Way, Naples, FL 34113 USA

Thurston, Joe *Athlete*
PO Box 2887, Vero Beach, FL 32961

Thyssen, Greta *Actor*
444 E 82nd St, New York, NY 10028 USA

Tian, Jiyun *Government Official*
Vice President's Office, State Council, Beijing, CHINA

Tiant, Luis C *Baseball Player*
67 Pine Hill Road, Southborough, MA 01772 USA

Tibbets, Paul W
5574 Knollwood Dr, Columbus, OH 43227 USA

Tibbets, Paul W Jr *War Hero*
5574 Knollwood Dr, Columbus, OH 43232 USA

Tice, George A *Photographer*
581 Kings Highway E, Atlantic Hills, NJ 07716 USA

Tice, Michael P (Mike) *Football Player*
6708 Galway Dr, Minneapolis, MN 55439 USA

Tichnor, Alan *Religious Leader*
United Synagogues of Conservative Judaism, 155 5th Ave, New York, NY 10010 USA

Tickner, Charles (Charlie) *Figure Skater*
5410 Sunset Dr, Littleton, CO 80123 USA

Ticotin, Rachel *Actor*
William Morris Agency (WMA-LA), 1 William Morris Pl, Beverly Hills, CA 90212 USA

Tiddy, Kim *Actor*
Bosun House, 1 Deer Park Rd, Merton, London, SW19 9TL, ENGLAND

Tidwell, Moody R III *Judge*
US Claims Court, 717 Madison Place NW, Washington, DC 20439 USA

Tiefenbach, Dov *Actor*
Firm, The, 9465 Wilshire Blvd, Beverly Hills, CA 90212 USA

Tiegs, Cheryl *Model*
457 Cuesta Way, Los Angeles, CA 90077 USA

Tiemann, Norbert T *Governor*
7511 Pebbiestone Dr, Dallas, TX 75230 USA

Tierney, Maura *Actor*
Creative Artists Agency, 9830 Wilshire Blvd, Beverly Hills, CA 90212 USA

Tiffany *Musician, Model*
Universal Attractions, 225 W 57th St, #500, New York, NY 10019 USA

Tiffin, Pamela *Actor*
15 W 67th St, New York, NY 10023 USA

Tigar, Kenneth *Actor*
642 Etta St, Los Angeles, CA 90065 USA

Tiger, Lionel *Scientist*
248 W 23rd St, #400, New York, NY 10011 USA

Tigerman, Stanley *Architect*
Tigerman McCurry Architect, 444 N Walls St, Chicago, IL 60610 USA

Tighe, Kevin *Actor*
PO Box 453, Sedro Woolley, WA 98284 USA

Tikkanen, Esa *Hockey Player*
New York Rangers, Madison Square Garden, 2 Penn Plaza, New York, NY 10121 USA

Tilghman, Shirley M C *Educator, Biologist*
Princeton University, President's Office, Princeton, NJ 08544 USA

Tilker, Ewald *Athlete*
2767 40th Ave, San Francisco, CA 94116 USA

Tiller, Joe *Football Coach*
Purdue University, Athletic Dept, W Lafayette, IN 47907 USA

Tiller, Nadja *Actor*
Via Tamporiva 26, Castagnola, 6976, SWITZERLAND

Tilley, Patrick L (Pat) *Football Player, Football Coach*
3 Lake Point Place, Shreveport, LA 71119 USA

Tillis, Mel *Musician, Songwriter*
Mel Tillis Enterprises, 2527 State Highway 248, Branson, MO 65616 USA

Tillis, Pam *Musician, Songwriter*
Fitzgerald Hartley Co, 1908 Wedgewood Ave, Nashville, TN 37212 USA

Tillman, Robert L *Business Person*
Lowe's Companies, 1605 Curtis Bridge Road, Wilkesboro, NC 28697 USA

Tillman Jr, George *Producer, Director*
Creative Artists Agency, 9830 Wilshire Blvd, Beverly Hills, CA 90212 USA

Tillotson, Johnny *Musician*
American Mgmt, 19948 Mayall St, Chatsworth, CA 91311 USA

Tilly, Jennifer *Actor*
1050 Stone Canyon Road, Los Angeles, CA 90077 USA

Tilly, Meg *Actor*
321 S Beverly Dr, #M, Beverly Hills, CA 90212 USA

Tilson, Joseph (Joe) *Artist*
2 Brook Street Mansions, 41 Davies St, London, W1Y 1FJ, UNITED KINGDOM (UK)

Tilton, Charlene *Actor*
Wilkinson/Lipsman, 8075 W 3rd St, #500, Los Angeles, CA 90048 USA

Tilton, Glenn F *Business Person*
UAL Corp, 1200 E Algonquin Road, Arlington Heights, IL 60005 USA

Tilton, Martha *Musician, Actor*
2257 Mandeville Canyon Road, Los Angeles, CA 90049 USA

Tilton, Robert *Misc*
Robert Tilton Ministries, PO Box 819000, Dallas, TX 75381 USA

Timbaland & Magoo *Music Group*
Virgin Records (NY), 304 Park Avenue South, New York, NY 10010 USA

Timberlake, Justin *Musician*
Just-in-Time, PO Box 1070, Windermere, FL 34786 USA

Timberlake, Robert W (Bob) *Football Player*
2219 E Jarvis St, Milwaukee, WI 53211 USA

Timchal, Cindy *Coach*
University of Maryland, Athletic Dept, College Park, MD 20742 USA

Timken, William R Jr *Business Person*
Timken Co, 1835 Dueber Ave SW, Canton, OH 44706 USA

Timlin, Mike *Baseball Player*
4874 Cross Pointe Dr, Oldsmar, FL 34677 USA

Timme, Robert *Architect*
Taft Architects, 2370 Rice Blvd, #112, Houston, TX 77005 USA

Timmermann, Ulf *Track Athlete*
Conrad Blenkle Str 34, Berlin, 1055, GERMANY

Timmins, Call *Actor*
The Agency, 1800 Ave of Stars, #400, Los Angeles, CA 90067 USA

Timmons, Harold
PO Box 140571, Nashville, TN 37214

Timmons, Jeff *Musician*
DAS Communications, 83 Riverside Dr, New York, NY 10024 USA

Timmons, Margo *Musician*
Macklam Feldman Mgmt, 1505 W 2nd Ave, #200, Vancouver, BC V6H 3Y4, CANADA

Timmons, Michael *Musician, Songwriter*
Macklam Feldman Mgmt, 1505 W 2nd Ave, #200, Vancouver, BC V6H 3Y4, CANADA

Timmons, Peter *Musician*
Macklam Feldman Mgmt, 1505 W 2nd Ave, #200, Vancouver, BC V6H 3Y4, CANADA

Timofeev, Valeri *Artist*
464 Blue Mountain Lake, East Stroudsburg, PA 18301 USA

Timofeyeva, Nina V *Ballerina*
Bolshoi Theater, Teatralnaya Pl 1, Moscow, 103009, RUSSIA

Timonen, Kimmo *Hockey Player*
920 Cherry Plum Court, Nashville, TN 37215 USA

Timpson, Michael D *Football Player*
4722 Saint Simon Dr, Coconut Creek, FL 33073 USA

Tin Tin, Rin
PO Box 27, Crockett, TX 75835

Tindermans, Leo *Prime Minister*
Jan Verbertiel 24, Edegem, 2520, BELGIUM

Tindle, David *Astronaut*
Redfern Gallery, 20 Cork St, London, W1, UNITED KINGDOM (UK)

Ting, Samuel C C *Nobel Prize Laureate*
2 Eliot Place, Jamaica Plain, MA 02130 USA

Ting, Walasse *Artist*
100 W 25th St, New York, NY 10001 USA

Tinglehoff, H Michael (Mick) *Football Player*
19288 Judicial Road, Prior Lake, MN 55372 USA

Tinker, Grant *Business Person*
10727 Wilshire Blvd, #1604, Los Angeles, CA 90024 USA

Tinkham, Michael *Physicist*
98 Rutledge Road, Belmont, MA 02478 USA

Tinoco, Joe
118 N. Keeler, Olathe, KS 66061

Tinsley, Bruce *Editor, Cartoonist*
King Features Syndicate, 888 7th Ave, New York, NY 10106 USA

Tinsley, Jackson B (Jack) *Editor*
Fort Worth Star-Telegram, Editorial Dept, 400 W 7th St, Fort Worth, TX 76102 USA

Tinsley, Jamaal *Basketball Player*
Indiana Pacers, Conseco Fieldhouse, 125 S Pennsylvania, Indianapolis, IN 46204 USA

Tippet, Andre B *Football Player*
17 Knob Hill St, Sharon, MA 02067 USA

Tippett, Dave *Hockey Player, Coach*
260 Breakers Lane, Stratford, CT 06615 USA

Tippett, Sir Michael
48 Great Marborough St., London, ENGLAND, W1V 2BN

Tippin, Aaron *Musician, Songwriter*
Tip Top Mgmt, Po Box 41689, Nashville, TN 37204 USA

Tipton, Daniel *Religious Leader*
Churches of Christ in Christian Union, PO Box 30, Circleville, OH 43113 USA

Tiriac, Ion *Tennis Player, Coach*
Blvd. D'Italie 44, Monte Carlo, MONACO

Tirico, Mike *Sportscaster*
ABC-TV, Sports Dept, 77 W 66th St, New York, NY 10023 USA

Tirimo, Martino *Musician*
1 Romeyn Road, London, SW16 2NU, UNITED KINGDOM (UK)

Tirole, Jean M *Economist*
Institut D'Economie Industrielle, Toulouse, FRANCE

Tisch, James S *Business Person*
Loews Corp, 667 Madison Ave, New York, NY 10021 USA

Tisch, Preston R *Business Person, Government Official*
Loews Corp, 667 Madison Ave, New York, NY 10021 USA

Tisch, Steve *Writer*
1162 Tower Road, Beverly Hills, CA 90210 USA

Tisdale, Wayman *Basketball Player*
4710 S Wheeling Ave, Tulsa, OK 74105 USA

Tishby, Noa *Actor*
McGowan Management, 8733 W Sunset Blvd #103, W Hollywood, CA 90069 USA

Tishchenko, Boris I *Composer*
79 Rimsky-Korsakoff Ave, #10, Saint Petersburg, 190121, RUSSIA

Titanic Historical Society
PO Box 51053, Indian Orchard, MA 01151

Titchmarsh, Alan *Talk Show Host*
Alan Titchmarsh Products, New Mills, Slad Rd, Stroud, Gloucestershire Engl, GL5 1RN, UNITED KINGDOM (UK)

Tito, Dennis *Astronaut*
1800 Alta Mura Road, Pacific Palisades, CA 90272 USA

Tito, Teburoro *President*
President's Office, Tarawa, KIRIBATI

Titov, German *Hockey Player*
Anaheim Mighty Ducks, 2000 E Gene Autry Way, Anaheim, CA 92806 USA

Titov, Vladimir
3 Hovanskaya Str. 8, Moscow, RUSSIA, 129515

Titov, Vladimir G *Cosmonaut*
Potcha Kosmonavtov, Moskovskoi Oblasti, Syvisdny Goroduk, 141160, RUSSIA

Titov, Yuri E *Gymnast*
Kolokolnikov Per 6, #19, Moscow, 103045, RUSSUA

Tits, Jacques L *Mathematician*
12 Rue du Moulin des Pres, Paris, 75013, FRANCE

Tittle, Y A
PO Box 571, Lebanon, IN 46052 USA

Tittle, Yelberton A (Y A) *Football Player*
2500 E Camino Real, Palo Alto, CA 94306 USA

Titus, Christopher *Writer*
OmniPop Inc (LA), 10700 Ventura Blvd Fl 2, Studio City, CA 91604 USA

Titus-Carmel, Gerard *Artist*
La Grand Maison, Oulchy Le Chateau, 02210, FRANCE

Tixby, Dexter *Musician*
David Harris Enterprises, 24210 E Fork Road, #9, Azusa, CA 91702 USA

Tizard, Catherine A *Governor*
12A Wallace St, Herne Bay, Auckland, 1, NEW ZEALAND

Tizon, Albert *Journalist*
Seattle Times, Editorial Dept, 1120 John St, Seattle, WA 98109 USA

Tizzio, Thomas R Sr *Business Person*
American Int'l Group, 70 Pine St, New York, NY 10270 USA

Tjeknavorian, Loris-Zare *Composer, Conductor*
State Philharmonia, Mashtotsi Prospekt 46, Yerevan, ARMENIA

Tjoflat, Gerald B *Judge*
US Court of Appeals, 311 W Monroe St, Jacksonville, FL 32202 USA

Tkachuk, Keith *Hockey Player*
11243 Hunters Pond Road, Creve Coeur, MO 63141 USA

Tkaczuk, Ivan *Religious Leader*
Ukrainian Orthodox Church, 3 Davenport Ave, #2A, New-Rochelle, NY 10805 USA

Tkaczuk, Walter R (Walt) *Hockey Player*
River Valley Golf & Country Club, RR 3, Saint Mary's, On, N0M 2G0, CANADA

TLC *Music Group*
Creative Artists Agency LCC (CAA-LA), 9830 Wilshire Blvd, Beverly Hills, CA 90212 USA

To, Tony *Director*
CAA, 9830 Wilshire Blvd, Beverly Hills, CA 90212

Toback, James *Director*
International Creative Mgmt, 8942 Wilshire Blvd, #219, Beverly Hills, CA 90211 USA

Tober, Barbara D *Editor*
Bride Magazine, Editorial Dept, 4 W 42nd St, New York, NY 10036 USA

Tobey, David (Dave) *Basketball Player, Referee, Coach*
Naismith Basketball Hall of Fame, 1150 W Columbus Ave, Springfield, MA 01105 USA

Tobey, James *Actor*
Paradigm Agency, 10100 Santa Monica Blvd, #2500, Los Angeles, CA 90067 USA

Tobian, Gary
9174 Belted Kingfisher Rd., Blaine, WA 98230

Tobian, GAry M *Misc*
9171 Belted Kingfisher Road, Blaine, WA 98230 USA

Tobias, Andrew *Writer*
Micro Education Corp of America, 285 Riverside Ave, Westport, CT 06880 USA

Tobias, Oliver *Actor*
Gavin Barker Assoc, 2D Wimpole St, London, W1G 0EB, UNITED KINGDOM (UK)

Tobias, Phillip V *Scientist*
Witwatersrand University, 7 York Road, Johannesburg, 2193, SOUTH AFRICA

Tobias, Randall L *Business Person*
Eli Lilly Co, Lilly Corporate Center, Indianapolis, IN 46285 USA

Tobias, Robert M *Misc*
National Treasury Employees Union, 901 E St NW, Washington, DC 20004 USA

Tobias, Stephen C *Business Person*
Norfolk Southern Corp, 3 Commercial Place, Norfolk, VA 23510 USA

Tobin, Don *Cartoonist*
12312 Ranchwood Road, Santa Ana, CA 92705 USA

Tobin, Vince *Football Coach*
16359 N 109th Way, Scottdale, AZ 85255 USA

Tobolowsky, Stephen *Actor*
William Morris Agency, 151 El Camino Dr, Beverly Hills, CA 90212 USA

Tobymac *Musician*
Creative Artists Agency (CAA-Nashville), 3310 West End Ave Fl 5, Nashville, TN 37203 USA

Tocchet, Rick *Hockey Player*
692 Highpointe Dr, Pittsburgh, PA 15220 USA

Tochi, Brian *Actor*
247 S Beverly Dr, #102, Beverly Hills, CA 90212 USA

Toczyska, Stefania *Opera Singer*
Columbia Artists Mgmt Inc, 165 W 57th
St, New York, NY 10019 USA

Todd, Rachel *Actor*
6310 San Vicente Blvd, #520, Los
Angeles, CA 90048 USA

Todd, Hallie *Actor*
Ann Morgan Guilbert, 550 Erskine Dr,
Pacific Palisades, CA 90272 USA

Todd, James R (Jim) *Baseball Player*
21639 Hill Gail Way, Parker, CO 80138
USA

Todd, Josh *Musician*
The Firm, 9100 Wilshire Blvd, #100W,
Beverly Hills, CA 90210 USA

Todd, Mark *Horse Racer*
PO Box 507, Cambridge, NEW ZEALAND

Todd, Richard *Actor*
Chinham Farm, Faringdon, Oxon, SN7
8EZ, UNITED KINGDOM (UK)

Todd, Richard *Football Player*
PO Box 471, Shelfield, AL 35660 USA

Todd, Tony *Actor*
Innovative Artists, 1505 10th St, Santa
Monica, CA 90401 USA

Todd, Virgil H *Religious Leader*
Memphis Theological, 168 E Parkway S,
Memphis, TN 38104 USA

Todorov, Stanko *Prime Minister*
Narodno Sobranie, Sofia, BULGARIA

Todorovsky, Piotr Y *Director*
Vernadskogo Prospect 70A, #23, Moscow,
117454, RUSSIA

Toennies, Jan Peter *Physicist*
Ewaldstr 7, Gottingen, 37075, GERMANY

Toerzs, Gregor *Actor*
Richard Schwartz Management, 2934-1/2
Beverly Glen Cir #107, Los Angeles, CA
90077

Toews, Jeffrey M (Jeff) *Football Player*
11924 SW 44th St, Davie, FL 33330 USA

Tofani, Loretta A *Journalist*
Philadelphia Inquirer, Editorial Dept, 400
N Broad St, Philadelphia, PA 19130 USA

Toffel, Alvin
2323 Bowmont Dr., Beverly Hills, CA
90210

Toffler, Alvin *Writer*
Randon House, 1745 Broadway, #B1,
New York, NY 10019 USA

Toft, Rod *Bowler*
11350 12th St N, Lake Elmo, MN 55042
USA

Tognini, Gina *Actor*
Innovative Artists (LA), 1505 Tenth St,
Santa Monica, CA 90401 USA

Tognini, Michel *Cosmonaut*
5413 Newcastle St, Bellaire, TX 77401
USA

Togo, Jonathan *Actor*
Gersh Agency, The (LA), 232 N Canon Dr,
Beverly Hills, CA 90210 USA

Togunde, Victor *Actor*
Christopher Nassif Agency, 1925 Century
Park West, #750, Los Angeles, CA 90067
USA

Tokarev, Valeri I *Cosmonaut*
Potcha Kosmonavtov, Moskovskoi Oblasti,
Syvisdny Goroduk, 141160, RUSSIA

Tokes, Laszlo *Religious Leader, Politician*
Calvin Str 1, Oradea, 3700, ROMANIA

Tokody, Ilona *Opera Singer*
Hungarian State Opera, Andrassy Utca 22,
Budapest, 1062, HUNGARY

Tokyo Rose (Iva Toguri)
1443 Winnemac St. W., Chicago, IL
60640

Tolan, Robert (Bobby) *Baseball Player*
804 Woodstock St, Bellaire, TX 77401
USA

Toland, John
1 Long Ridge Rd., Danbury, CT 06810

Tolar, Kevin *Baseball Player*
PO Box 2365, Pawtucket, RI 02861

Tolbert, Tony L *Football Player*
475 S White Chapel Blvd, Southlake, TX
76092 USA

Toledo, Alejandro *President*
Palacio de Gobierno S/N, Plaza de Armas
S/N, Lima, 1, PERU

Toles, Thomas G (Tom) *Editor, Cartoonist*
4625 46th St NW, Washington, DC 20016
USA

Tolkan, James *Actor*
Paradigm Agency, 10100 Santa Monica
Blvd, #2500, Los Angeles, CA 90067 USA

Tolsky, Susan *Actor*
10815 Acama St, North Hollywood, CA
91602 USA

Tolson, Billy
2710 N. Stemmons Frwy. #700, Dallas,
TX 75207

Tom, Braatz *Football Player*
3131 NE 55th Court, Fort Lauderdale, FL
33308 USA

Tom, David
3033 Vista Crest, Los Angeles, CA 90068

Tom, Heather *Actor*
740 N Evergreen, Burbank, CA 91505
USA

Tom, Kiana *Model*
PO Box 1111, Sunset Beach, CA 90742
USA

Tom, Lauren *Actor*
Gersh Agency, 232 N Canon Dr, Beverly
Hills, CA 90210 USA

Tom, Nicholle *Actor*
3033 Vista Crest Drive, Los Angeles, CA
90068 USA

Tom, Nicolle
3033 Vista Crest, Los Angeles, CA 90068

Toma, David
PO Box 854, Clark, NJ 07066

Tomanovich, Dara
8016 Willow Glen Rd., Los Angeles, CA
90046

Tomasic, Andrew J (Andy) *Football
Player, Baseball Player*
688 Maryland Ave, Whitehall, PA 18052
USA

Tomasson, Helgi *Ballerina, Director*
San Francisco Ballet, 455 Franklin St, San
Francisco, CA 94102 USA

Tomba, Alberto *Skier*
Castel dei Britti, Bologna, 40100, ITALY

Tomczak, Michael J (Mike) *Football
Player*
108 Bell Acres Estate, Sewickley, PA
15143 USA

Tomei, Concetta *Actor*
765 Linda Flora Dr, Los Angeles, CA
90049 USA

Tomei, Marisa *Actor*
United Talent Agency (UTA), 9560
Wilshire Blvd, Beverly Hills, CA 90212
USA

Tomel, Marisa *Actor*
Three Arts Entertainment, 9460 Wilshire
Blvd, #700, Beverly Hills, CA 90212 USA

Tomey, Dick *Football Coach*
San Francisco 49ers, 4949 Centennial
Blvd, Santa Clara, CA 95054 USA

Tomfohrde, Heinn F *Business Person*
GAF Corp, 1361 Alps Road, Wayne, NJ
07470 USA

Tomita, Stan *Photographer*
2439 Saint Louis Dr, Honolulu, HI 96816
USA

Tomita, Tamlyn *Actor*
Artists Group (LA), 10100 Santa Monica
Blvd #2490, Los Angeles, CA 90067 USA

Tomjanovich, Rudolph (Rudy) *Basketball
Player, Coach*
3142 Canterbury Lane, Montgomery, TX
77356 USA

Tomkins, Darlene
15413 Hall Rd. #230, Macomb, MI 48044

Tomko, Jozef Cardinal *Religious Leader*
Villa Betania, Via Urbano VIII-16, Rome,
00165, ITALY

Tomlin, Lily *Actor, Comedian*
1800 Argyle Ave, #300, Los Angeles, CA
90028 USA

Tomlinson, Charles *Writer*
Bristol University, English Dept, Bristol,
BS8 1TH, UNITED KINGDOM (UK)

Tomlinson, John *Opera Singer*
Music International, 13 Ardilaun Road,
Highbury, London, N5 2QR, UNITED
KINGDOM (UK)

Tomlinson, LaDainian *Football Player*
San Diego Chargers, 4020 Murphy
Canyon Road, San Diego, CA 92123 USA

Tomlinson, Mel A *Ballerina*
790 Riverside Dr, #6B, New York, NY
10032 USA

Tomowa-Sintow, Anna *Opera Singer*
Columbia Artists Mgmt Inc, 165 W 57th
St, New York, NY 10019 USA

Tompkins, Angel *Actor*
Hurkos, 11935 Kling St, #10, Valley
Village, CA 91607 USA

Tompkins, Dariene *Actor*
15413 Hall Road, #230, Macomb, MI
48044 USA

Tompkins, Darlene
15413 Hall Rd. #230, Macomb, MI 48044

Tompkins, Susie *Fashion Designer*
2500 Steiner St, #PH, San Francisco, CA
94115 USA

Toms, David *Golfer*
820 S MacArthur Blvd, #105-383, Coppell, TX 75019 USA

Tomsco, George *Musician*
Fireballs Entertainment, 1224 Cottonwood, Raton, NM 87740 USA

Tomsic, Dubravka *Musician*
Trawick Artists, 1926 Broadway, New York, NY 10023 USA

Tomsic, Ronald (Ron) *Basketball Player*
448 Isabella Terrace, Corona del Mar, CA 92625 USA

Toneff, Robert (Bob) *Football Player*
18 Dutch Valley Lane, San Anselmo, CA 94960 USA

Tonegawa, Susumu *Nobel Prize Laureate*
Massachusetts Institute of Technology, Biology Dept, Cambridge, MA 02139 USA

Toner, Mike *Journalist*
Atlanta Journal-Constitution, Editorial Dept, 72 Marietta, Atlanta, GA 30303 USA

Toney, Andrew *Basketball Player*
Philadelphia 76ers, 1st Union Center, 3601 S Broad St, Philadelphia, PA 19148 USA

Toney, James
6305 Wellesley, West Bloomfield, MI 48322

Toney, Sedric *Basketball Player*
3831 Sweetwater Dr, Cleveland, OH 44141 USA

Tong, Stanley *Director*
William Morris Agency (WMA-LA), 1 William Morris Pl, Beverly Hills, CA 90212 USA

Tonini, Ersilio Cardinal *Religious Leader*
Via Santa Teresa 8, Ravenna, 48100, ITALY

Tony! Toni! Tone!
1995 Broadway #501, New York, NY 10023

Too, Short *Artist*
Pyramid Entertainment, 89 5th Ave, #700, New York, NY 10003 USA

Too, Slim *Musician*
New Frontier Mgmt, 1921 Broadway, Nashville, TN 37203 USA

Tooker, George *Artist*
PO Box 385, Hartland, VT 05048 USA

Toomey, Bill
2227 Del Mar Scenic, Parkway Del Mar, CA 92014

Toomey, William A (Bill) *Track Athlete*
1755 Hi Mountain Road, Arroyo Grande, CA 93420 USA

Toomin Straus, Amy *Writer*
United Talent Agency (UTA), 9560 Wilshire Blvd, Beverly Hills, CA 90212 USA

Toon, Al *Football Player*
4827 Enchanted Valley Road, Middleton, WI 53562 USA

Toon, Malcolm *Diplomat*
375 PeeDee Road, Southern Pines, NC 28387 USA

Toots & The Maytals
151 El Camino Dr., Beverly Hills, CA 90212

Top, Carrot *Actor, Comedian*
Carrot Top Inc, 420 Sylvan Dr, Winter Park, FL 32789 USA

Topfer, Morton L *Business Person*
Dell Computer Corp, 1 Dell Way, Round Rock, TX 78682 USA

Toploader *Music Group*
Helter Skelter (UK), The Plaza, 535 Kings Rd, London, N13 5H, UNITED KINGDOM (UK)

Topol, Chaim *Actor*
22 Vale Court Maidville, London, W9 1RT, UNITED KINGDOM (UK)

Topper, John *Musician*
Monterey Peninsula Artists, 509 Hartnell St, Monterey, CA 93940 USA

Topping, Seymour *Editor*
5 Heathcote Road, Scarsdale, NY 10583 USA

Toppo, Telesphore P Cardinal *Religious Leader*
Archdiocese, PO Box 5, Purulia Road, Ranchi, Jharkhand, 834001, INDIA

Toradze, Alexander *Musician*
Columbia Artists Mgmt Inc, 165 W 57th St, New York, NY 10019 USA

Torborg, Jeffrey A (Jeff) *Baseball Player*
5208 Siesta Cove Dr, Sarasota, FL 34242 USA

Torgensen, Paul E *Educator*
Virginia Polytechnic Institute, President's Office, Blacksburg, VA 24061 USA

Torgeson, LaVern *Football Player*
17672 Gainsford Lane, Huntington Beach, CA 92649 USA

Tork, Peter *Musician*
524 Anselmo Ave, #102, San Anselmo, CA 94960 USA

Torkildsen, Justin
7800 Beverly Blvd. #3371, Los Angeles, CA 90036

Torn, Rip *Actor*
118 S Beverly Dr, #504, Beverly Hills, CA 90212 USA

Torp, Niels A *Architect*
Industrigaten 59, PO Box 5387, Oslo, 0304, NORWAY

Torrance, Sam *Golfer*
Carnegie Sports, Glassmill, Battersea Bridge Rd, London, SW11 3BZ, UNITED KINGDOM (UK)

Torrance, Thomas F *Religious Leader, Educator*
37 Braid Farm Road, Edinburgh, EH10 6LE, SCOTLAND

Torre, Arath de la *Actor*
Televisa, Blvd Adolfo Lopez Mateos 232, Colonia San Angel INN, DF, CP 01060, MEXICO

Torre, Joe *Athlete*
20 Lawrence Lane, Harrison, NY 10528 USA

Torre, Jose Maria *Actor*
Televisa, Blvd Adolfo Lopez Mateos 232, Colonia San Angel INN, DF, CP 01060, MEXICO

Torre, Joseph P (Joe) *Baseball Player*
20 Lawrence Lane, Harrison, NY 10528 USA

Torrence, Dean *Musician, Songwriter*
221 Main St, #P, Huntington Beach, CA 92648 USA

Torrence, Gwendolyn (Gwen) *Track Athlete*
Gold Medal Mgmt, 1750 14th St, Boulder, CO 80302 USA

Torrens, David *Actor*
Gabriel Blanco Iglesias (Mexico), Rio Balsas 35-32, Colonia Cuauhtemoc, DF, 06500, Mexico

Torres, Dara *Swimmer, Model*
Wilhelmina Models, 300 Park Ave, #200, New York, NY 10010 USA

Torres, Diego *Musician*
Fenix Prod, Av Figueroa Alcorta 3221, Buenos Aires, 1215, ARGENTINA

Torres, Gina *Actor*
Badgley Connor Talent, 9229 Sunset Blvd, #311, Los Angeles, CA 90069 USA

Torres, Harold *Musician*
Brothers Mgmt, 141 Dunbar Ave, Fords, NJ 08863 USA

Torres, Jose *Boxer*
364B Greenwich St, #B, New York, NY 10013 USA

Torres, Liz *Musician, Actor*
Siegel, 1680 N Vine St, #617, Hollywood, CA 90028 USA

Torres, Oscar *Basketball Player*
Houston Rockets, 2 East Greenway Plz #400, Houston, TX 77046 USA

Torres, Raffi *Hockey Player*
Edmonton Oilers, 11230 110th St, Edmonton, AB T5G 3H7, CANADA

Torres, Tico *Musician*
Bon Jovi Mgmt, 248 W 17th St, #501, New York, NY 10011 USA

Torres, Tommy *Musician*
Sony Music Miami, 605 Lincoln Rd, Miami Beach, FL 33138 USA

Torretta, Gino L *Football Player*
All American Speakers, 365 W King Road, #200, Ithaca, NY 14850 USA

Torrey, Bill *Misc*
2740 Clubhouse Pointe, West Palm Beach, FL 33409 USA

Torrey, Rich *Cartoonist*
King Features Syndicate, 888 7th Ave, New York, NY 10106 USA

Torrijos, Martin *President*
Palaclo Presidencial, Valija 50, Panama City, 1, PANAMA

Torrissen, Birger *Skier*
PO Box 216, Lakeville, CT 06039 USA

Torruella, Juan R *Judge*
US Court of Appeals, 150 Ave Cartos Chardon, #119, San Juan, PR 00918 USA

Torry, Guy *Actor, Comedian*
William Morris Agency (WMA-LA), 1 William Morris Pl, Beverly Hills, CA 90212 USA

Torry, Joe *Comedian*
William Morris Agency (WMA-LA), 1 William Morris Pl, Beverly Hills, CA 90212 USA

Torteller, Yan Pascal *Musician*
MA de Valmalete, Building Gaceau, 11 Ave Delcasse, Paris, 75635, FRANCE

Torti, Robert *Actor*
5722 Ranchito Ave, Van Nuys, CA 91401 USA

Tortorella, John *Coach*
2801 Northwood Hills Dr, Valrico, FL 33594 USA

Torvaids, Linus *Designer*
Transmeta Corp, 3990 Freedom Circle, Santa Clara, CA 95054 USA

Torvalds, Linus *Designer, Engineer*
Open Source Development Labs, 12725 SW Millikan Way, Beaverton, OR 97005 USA

Torvill, Jayne *Dancer*
Sue Young, PO Box 32, Heathfield, East Sussex, TN21 0BW, UNITED KINGDOM (UK)

Tory, Guy *Actor*
William Morris Agency, 151 El Camino Dr, Beverly Hills, CA 90212 USA

Tosca, Carlos *Misc*
2831 Timber Knoll Dr, Valrico, FL 33594 USA

Tosh, Daniel *Comedian*
William Morris Agency (WMA-LA), 1 William Morris Pl, Beverly Hills, CA 90212 USA

Toski, Bob *Golfer*
160 Essex St, Newark, OH 43055 USA

Totenberg, Nina *Commentator*
National Public Radio, News Dept, 615 Main Ave NW, Washington, DC 20024 USA

Toto
5O W. Main St., Ventura, CA 93001

Totten, Robert *Director*
PO Box 7180, Big Bear Lake, CA 92315 USA

Totter, Audrey *Actor*
Motion Picture Country Home, 23388 Mulholland Dr, Woodland Hills, CA 91364 USA

Totushek, John B *Admiral*
Commander, Naval Reserve Force HqUSN, Pentagon, Washington, DC 20350 USA

Toulouse, Gerard *Physicist*
Laboratoire de Physique de I'ENS, 24 Rue Lhomond, Paris, 75231, FRANCE

Tountas, Pete *Bowler*
10100 N Calle del Camero, Tucson, AZ 85737 USA

Touraine, Jean-Louis *Biologist*
Edouard-Herriot Hopital, Place d'Arsonval, Lyons Cedex 03, 69437, FRANCE

Toure, Younoussi *Prime Minister*
Union Economique/Monetaire, 01 BP 543, Quagadougou 01, Burkina Faso, MALI

Tournier, Michel *Writer*
Le Presbytree Choisel, Chevreuse, 78460, FRANCE

Toussaint, Allen *Musician, Composer*
3264 Frey Place, New Orleans, LA 70119 USA

Toussaint, Beth
11333 Moorpark St. PMB 156, Studio City, CA 91602-2618

Toussaint, Coleman Beth *Actor*
Don Buchwald, 6500 Wilshire Blvd, #2200, Los Angeles, CA 90048 USA

Toussaint, Lorraine *Actor*
William Morris Agency, 151 S El Camino Dr, Beverly Hills, CA 90212 USA

Tovar, Lupita
1527 N. Tigertail Rd, Los Angeles, CA 90049

Tovar, Steven E (Steve) *Football Player*
17203 Sandalwood Dr, Wildwood, FL 34785 USA

Tovoli, Luciano *Cinematographer*
United Talent Agency, 9560 Wilshire Blvd, #500, Beverly Hills, CA 90212 USA

Towe, Monte *Basketball Player, Coach*
7434 Canal Blvd, New Orleans, LA 70124 USA

Tower, Joan P *Composer*
Bard College, Music Dept, Annandale-on-Hudson, NY 12504 USA

Tower of Power
654 N. Sepulveda Blvd. #14, Los Angeles, CA 90049

Towers, Constance *Actor*
2100 Century Park W, #10263, Los Angeles, CA 90067 USA

Towers, Kenneth *Editor*
Chicago Sun-Times, Editorial Dept, 401 N Wabash, Chicago, IL 60611 USA

Towle, Stephen R (Steve) *Football Player*
609 NE Lake Pointe Dr, Lees Summit, MO 64064 USA

Towles, Tom *Actor*
Blueprint Management, 5670 Wilshire Blvd #2525, Los Angeles, CA 90036 USA

Town, Crazy *Musician*
Creative Artists Agency LCC (CAA-LA), 9830 Wilshire Blvd, Beverly Hills, CA 90212 USA

Towne, Katharine *Actor*
United Talent Agency, 9560 Wilshire Blvd, #500, Beverly Hills, CA 90212 USA

Towne, Robert *Writer, Director*
1417 San Remo Dr, Pacific Palisades, CA 90272 USA

Towner, Ralph N *Musician*
Ted Kurtland, 173 Brighton Ave, Boston, MA 02134 USA

Townes, Charles H *Nobel Prize Laureate*
1988 San Antonio Ave, Berkeley, CA 94707 USA

Townsend, Colleen *Actor*
National Presbyterian Church, 4101 Nebraska Ave NW, Washington, DC 20016 USA

Townsend, John W Jr *Scientist*
6532 79th St, Cabin John, MD 20818 USA

Townsend, Robert *Actor*
2934 1/2 N Beverly Glen Circle, #407, Los Angeles, CA 90077 USA

Townsend, Roscoe *Religious Leader*
Evangelical Friends, 2018 Maple St, Wichita, KS 67213 USA

Townsend, Stuart *Actor*
Endeavor Agency LLC (LA), 9601 Wilshire Blvd Fl 3, Beverly Hills, CA 90210 USA

Townshend, Pete
The Boathouse Ranelagh Dr., Twickenham, ENGLAND, TW1 1Q2

Townshend, Peter D B *Musician, Songwriter*
Boathouse, Ranelagh Dr, Twickenham, Middx, TW1 1QZ, UNITED KINGDOM (UK)

Toya *Musician*
CEG, 485 Madison Avenue, 21st Floor, Ormond Beach, NJ 10022

Toye, Wendy *Choreographer, Ballerina*
London Mgmt, 2-4 Noel St, London, W1V 3RB, UNITED KINGDOM (UK)

Toyoda, Shoichiro *Business Person*
Keidanren, 1-9-4 Ohtemachi, Chuyodaku, Tokyo, 100, JAPAN

Tozzi, Giorgio *Opera Singer*
BMG Ricordi SpA, Via Berchet 2, Milan, 20100, ITALY

Tozzi, Umberto
Heussweg 25, Hamburg, GERMANY, D-20255

Traa *Musician*
East West America Records, 75 Rockefeller Plaza, New York, NY 10019 USA

Trabert, M Anthony (Tony) *Tennis Player*
115 Knotty Pine Trail, Ponte Vedra Beach, FL 32082 USA

Trabert, Tony
115 Knotty Pine Trail, Ponte Vedra, FL 32082

Tracey, Margaret *Ballerina*
New York City Ballet, Lincoln Center Plaza, New York, NY 10023 USA

Trachsel, Stephen P (Steve) *Baseball Player*
4141 Ricardo Dr, Yorba Linda, CA 92886 USA

Trachta, Jeff *Actor*
1327 Cordova Ave, Glendale, CA 91207 USA

Trachte, Don *Cartoonist*
King Features Syndicate, 888 7th Ave, New York, NY 10106 USA

Trachtenberg, Lyle
18619 Collins St. #F-7, Tarzana, CA 91356

Trachtenberg, Michelle *Actor*
Framework Entertainment (LA), 9057 Nemo St #C, W Hollywood, CA 90069 USA

Trachtenberg, Stephen J *Educator*
George Washington University, President's Office, Washington, DC 20052 USA

Tracy, James E (Jim) *Baseball Player*
3535 Arlington Ave, Hamilton, OH 45015 USA

Tracy, Keegan Connor *Actor*
SMS Talent, 8730 Sunset Blvd, #440, Los Angeles, CA 90069 USA

Tracy, Michael C *Director, Dancer*
Pilobolus Dance Theater, PO Box 388, Washington Depot, CT 06794 USA

Tracy, Paul *Race Car Driver*
9700 Highridge Dr, Las Vegas, NV 89134 USA

Trafficant, James *Politician*
125 Market St., Youngstown, OH 45503-1780

Trager, Milton *Doctor*
Trager Institute, 3800 Park East Dr, #100, Beachwood, OH 44122 USA

Trager, William *Biologist*
Rockefeller University, Parasitology Lab, 1230 York Ave, New York, NY 10021 USA

Train *Musician*
Creative Artists Agency LCC (CAA-LA), 9830 Wilshire Blvd, Beverly Hills, CA 90212 USA

Train, Harry D II *Admiral*
401 College Place, #10, Norfolk, VA 23510 USA

Train, Russell E *Government Official*
World Wildlife Fund, 1250 24th St NW, Washington, DC 20037 USA

Trainor, Bernard E *General*
80 Potter Pond, Lexington, MA 02421 USA

Trammell, Alan S *Baseball Player*
191 22nd St, Del Mar, CA 92014 USA

Trammell, Terry *Doctor*
Orthopedics-Indianapolis, 1801 N Senate Blvd, #200, Indianapolis, IN 46202 USA

Tramps, The
102 Ryders Lane, East Brunswick, NJ 08816

Tran, Duc Luong *President*
President's Office, Hoang Hoa Tham St, St Hanoi, VIETNAM

Trang, Thuy
209 N. Kenilworth Ave, Glendale, CA 91203

Trani, Eugene P *Educator*
Virginia Commonwealth University, President's Office, Richmond, VA 23284 USA

Trask, Thomas E *Religious Leader*
Assemblies of God, 1445 Boonville Ave, Springfield, MO 65802 USA

Traub, Charles *Photographer*
39 E 10th St, New York, NY 10003 USA

Trauth, AJ *Actor*
Innovative Artists (LA), 1505 Tenth St, Santa Monica, CA 90401 USA

Trautmann, Richard *Athlete*
Horemansstr 29, Munich, 80636, GERMANY

Trautwig, Al *Sportscaster*
ABC-TV, Sports Dept, 77 W 66th St, New York, NY 10023 USA

Travalena, Fred *Actor, Comedian*
4515 White Oak Place, Encino, CA 91316 USA

Travanti, Daniel J *Actor*
1077 Melody Road, Lake Forest, IL 60045 USA

Travers, Mary *Musician*
Fritz/Byers Mgmt, 1455 N Doheny Dr, Los Angeles, CA 90069 USA

Travers, Pat *Musician*
ARM, 1257 Arcade St, Saint Paul, MN 55106 USA

Travis *Music Group*
Helter Skelter (UK), The Plaza, 535 Kings Rd, London, N13 5H, UNITED KINGDOM (UK)

Travis, Cecil H *Baseball Player*
2260 Highway 138, Riverdale, GA 30296 USA

Travis, Kylie *Model, Actor*
1196 Summit Dr, Beverly Hills, CA 90210 USA

Travis, Nancy *Actor*
231 S Cliffwood Ave, Los Angeles, CA 90049 USA

Travis, Randy *Musical Director, Songwriter*
William Morris Agency (WMA-LA), 1 William Morris Pl, Beverly Hills, CA 90212 USA

Travis, Stacey *Actor*
Pakula/King & Associates, 9229 Sunset Blvd #315, Los Angeles, CA 90069 USA

Travolta, Ellen *Actor*
5923 Wilbur Ave, Tarzana, CA 91356 USA

Travolta, Joey
4975 Chimineas Ave., Tarzana, CA 91356-4301

Travolta, John *Actor*
1504 Live Oak Lane, Santa Barbara, CA 93105 USA

Traylor, B Keith *Football Player*
Chicago Bears, 1000 Football Dr, Lake Forest, IL 60045 USA

Traylor, Robert *Basketball Player*
New Orleans Hornets, New Orleans Arena, 1501 Girod St, New Orleans, LA 70113 USA

Traylor, Susan *Actor*
Propaganda Films Mgmt, 1741 Ivar Ave, Los Angeles, CA 90028 USA

Traynor, Jay *Musician*
Jet Music, 17 Pauline Court, Rensselaer, NY 12144 USA

Traywick, Joel
10100 Santa Monica Blvd. #2490, Los Angeles, CA 90067

Treach *Musician*
International Creative Mgmt, 8942 Wilshire Blvd, #219, Beverly Hills, CA 90211 USA

Treacy, Philip *Fashion Designer*
Philip Treacy Ltd, 69 Elizabeth St, London, SW1W 9PJ, UNITED KINGDOM (UK)

Treadway, Edward A *Politician*
Elevator Constructors Union, 5565 Sterret Place, Columbia, MD 21044 USA

Treadway, James C Jr *Government Official*
Laurel Ledge Farm, Croton Lake Road, RR 4, Mount Kisco, NY 10549 USA

Treadway, Kenneth *Misc*
Phillips Petroleum Co, Adams Building, Bartlesville, OK 74003 USA

Treadway, Nick *Baseball Player*
16 Scarlet Oak Court, Troy, MO 63379 USA

Treadway, Ty *Actor*
The Agency, 11350 Ventura Blvd, Suite 100, Studio City, CA 91604 USA

Trebek, Alex *Entertainer*
3405 Fryman Road, Studio City, CA 91604 USA

Trebelhorn, Thomas L (Tom) *Baseball Player*
4344 SE 26th Ave, Portland, OR 97202 USA

Tree, Michael *Musician*
45 E 89th St, New York, NY 10128 USA

Treen, David C *Governor*
Deutsch Kerrigan Stile, 755 Magazine St, New Orleans, LA 70130 USA

Trefilov, Andrei
Calgary Flames, PO Box 1540, Station M, Calgary, AB T2P 3B9, CANADA

Trejo, Danny *Actor*
Amsel Eisenstadt & Frazier, 5757 Wilshire Blvd, #510, Los Angeles, CA 90036 USA

Trejos, Fernandez Jose J *President*
Apartado 10 096, San Jose, 1000, COSTA RICA

Trelford, Donald G *Editor*
15 Fowler Road, London, N1 2EA, UNITED KINGDOM (UK)

Tremblay, Mario *Hockey Player, Coach*
714 Mistassini, Lachenaie, QC, J6W 5H2, CANADA

Tremblay, Michel *Writer*
294 Carre Saint Louis, #5E, Montreal, QC, H2X 1A4, CANADA

Tremko, Anne
10100 Santa Monica Blvd. #2500, Los Angeles, CA 90067

Tremlett, David R *Artist*
Broadlawns, Chipperfield Road, Bovingdon, Herts, UNITED KINGDOM (UK)

Tremont, Ray C *Religious Leader*
Volunteers of America, 3939 N Causeway Blvd, #400, Metairie, LA 70002 USA

Tremonti, Mark *Musician, Songwriter*
Agency Group, 1776 Broadway, #430, New York, NY 10019 USA

Trendy, Bobby *Designer*
Marshak/Zachary Company, The, 8840 Wilshire Blvd Fl 1, Beverly Hills, CA 90211 USA

Trenhaile, John
4 Wailands Crescent Lewes, E. Sussex, ENGLAND, BNT 2QT

Treniers, The
520 N. Camden Dr., Beverly Hills, CA 90210

Trent, Gary *Basketball Player*
2905 Bookout St, Dallas, TX 75201 USA

Treschev, Sergei Y *Cosmonaut*
Potchta Kosmonavtov, Moskovskoi Oblasti, Syvisdny Goroduk, 141160, RUSSIA

Trese, Adam
8912 Burton Way, Beverly Hills, CA 90211

Tresh, Tom
4208 E. Wing Rd. RR #8, Mt. Pleasant, MI 48216

Tressel, Jim *Football Coach*
Ohio State University, Athletic Dept, Columbus, OH 43210 USA

Tretlak, Vladislav *Hockey Player, Coach*
Transglobal Sports, 94 Festival Dr, Toronto, ON M2R 3V1, CANADA

Tretyak, Ivan *General*
Ministry of Defense, 34 Manerezhnaya M Thoreza, Moscow, RUSSIA

Trevanian *Writer*
Jove Books, Berkeley Publishing Group, 375 Hudson St, New York, NY 10014 USA

Trever, John *Editor, Cartoonist*
Albuquerque Journal, Editorial Dept, 717 Silver Ave SW, Albuquerque, NM 87102 USA

Treves, Frederick
5 St. Catherine's Mews Milner St., London, ENGLAND, SW3 2PX

Trevi, Gloria *Musician*
Leisil Entertainment, Avenida Parque 67 Napoles, Mexico City, DF, 03810, MEXICO

Trevino, Lee
1901 W. 47th Pl. #200, Westwood, KS 66205-1834

Trevino, Lee B *Golfer*
1901 W 47th Place, #200, Westwood, KS 66205 USA

Trevino, Rick *Musician*
William Morris Agency, 2100 W End Ave, #1000, Nashville, TN 37203 USA

Trevor, William *Writer*
P F D, Drury House, 34-43 Russell St, London, WC2B 5HA, UNITED KINGDOM (UK)

Triandos, C Gus *Baseball Player*
165 Blossom Hill Road, #488, San Jose, CA 95123 USA

Tribbitt, Sherman W *Governor*
39 Hazel Road, Dover, DE 19901 USA

Tribe, Laurence H *Attorney General, Educator*
Harvard University, Law School, Griswold Hall, Cambridge, MA 02138 USA

Trible, Paul S Jr *Senator, Educator*
Christopher Newport University, 50 University Place, Newport News, VA 23606 USA

Trichter, Judd
10264 Rochester Ave, Los Angeles, CA 90024-5331

Trick, Cheap *Musician*
Monterey Peninsula Artists (Monterey), 509 Hartnell St, Monterey, CA 93940 USA

Trick Daddy *Music Group*
Atlantic Recording Corporation, 1290 Avenue of the Americas, New York, NY 10104 USA

Trickey, Paula
PO Box 261098, Encino, CA 91426

Trickle, Dick *Race Car Driver*
PO Box 645, Skyland, NC 28776 USA

Trickside *Music Group*
Wind-up Records, 72 Madison Ave, New York, NY 10016 USA

Tricky *Musician, Songwriter*
Little Big Man, 155 Ave of Americas, #700, New York, NY 10013 USA

Triffle, Carol *Director*
Imago Theater, 17 SE 8th Ave, Portland, OR 97214 USA

Trigger, Sarah *Actor*
Paradigm Agency, 10100 Santa Monica Blvd, #2500, Los Angeles, CA 90067 USA

Triggs, Trini
3178 Allen Marthaville Rd., Robeline, LA 71469

Trillin, Calvin M *Writer*
New Yorker Magazine, Editorial Dept, 4 times Square, New York, NY 10036 USA

Trimble, David *Nobel Prize Laureate*
2 Queen St, Lurgen, County Arnagh, BT66 8BQ, NORTHERN IRELAND

Trimble, Vance H *Editor*
25 Oakhurst St, Wewoka, OK 74884 USA

Trimble, Vivian *Musician*
Metropolitan Entertainment, 2 Penn Plaza, #2600, New York, NY 10121 USA

Trina *Musician*
Pyramid Entertainment Group, 89 Fifth Ave Fl 7, New York, NY 10003 USA

Trinh, Eugene *Astronaut*
NASA Headquarters, 300 E St SW, Washington, DC 20546 USA

Trinidad, Felix (Tito) *Boxer*
RR 6 Box 11479, Rio Piedras, PR 00926 USA

Trinkaus, Erik *Biologist*
Washington University, Paleontology Dept, Saint Louis, MO 63130 USA

Trinneer, Connor *Actor*
Abrams Artists Agency (LA), 9200 Sunset Blvd Fl 11, Los Angeles, CA 90069 USA

Trintignant, Jean-Louis *Actor*
Artmedia, 20 Ave Rapp, Paris, 75007, FRANCE

Triola, Michelle
23215 Mariposa De Oro, Malibu, CA 90265

Triple H *Wrestler*
Braverman/Bloom Company, 6399 Wilshire Blvd #901, Los Angeles, CA 90048 USA

Triplet, Kirk *Golfer*
8141 E Overlook Dr, Scottsdale, AZ 85255 USA

Tripp, Linda
27285 Boyce Mill Rd., Greensboro, MD 21639

Trippi, Charles L (Charlie) *Football Player*
125 Riverhill Court, Athens, GA 30606 USA

Trippi, Charley
125 Riverhill Ct., Athens, GA 30606

Tripplehorn, Jean *Actor*
ID Public Relations, 8409 Santa Monica Blvd, West Hollywood, CA 90069 USA

Tripucka, Frank *Football Player*
21 Walnut Dr, Spring Lake, NJ 07762 USA

Tripucka, Kelly *Basketball Player*
14 Devon Road, Boonton, NJ 07005 USA

Tritt, Travis *Musician, Songwriter*
PO Box 2044, Hiram, GA 30141 USA

Trixter
210 Westfield Ave, Clark, NJ 07066

Troccoli, Kathy *Musician, Songwriter*
William Morris Agency, 2100 W End Ave, #1000, Nashville, TN 37203 USA

Troche, Rose *Actor, Writer, Director, Producer*
Gersh Agency, The (NY), 41 Madison Ave Fl 33, New York, NY 10010 USA

Troger, Christian-Alexander *Swimmer*
I Muncher SC, Josefstr 26, Deisenhofen, 82941, GERMANY

Troisgros, Pierre E R *Business Person*
Place Jean Troisgros, Roanne, 42300, FRANCE

Troitskaya, Natalia L *Opera Singer*
Klostergasse 37, Vienna, 1170, AUSTRIA

Troliope, Joanna *Writer*
P F D, Drury House, 34-43 Russell St, London, WC2B 5HA, UNITED KINGDOM (UK)

Trondheim, Lewis *Artist*
Fantagraphics Books, 7563 Lake City Way, Seattle, WA 98115 USA

Trone, Roland (Don) *Musician*
Mars Talent, 27 L'Ambiance Court, Bardonia, NY 10954 USA

Trosper, Jennifer Harris *Scientist*
Jet Propulsion Laboratory, 4800 Oak Grove Dr, Pasadena, CA 91109 USA

Trost, Barry M *Scientist*
24510 Amigos Court, Los Altos Hills, CA 94024 USA

Trost, Carlisle A H *Admiral*
11 Compromise St, Annapolis, MD 21401 USA

Trott, Stephen S *Judge*
US Court of Appeals, US Courthouse, 550 W Fort St, Boise, ID 83724 USA

Trottier, Bryan
3868 Forest Dr., Doylestown, PA 18901-5425

Trottier, Bryan J *Hockey Player, Coach*
356 Birdsong Way, Doylestown, PA 18901 USA

Trouble, Valli *Musician*
Q Prime, 729 7th Ave, #1600, New York, NY 10019 USA

Troup, Tom
8829 Ashcroft Ave., Los Angeles, CA 90048

Troupe, Tom *Actor*
8829 Ashcroft Ave, West Hollywood, CA 90048 USA

Troutt, William E *Educator*
Belmont University, President's Office, Nashville, TN 37212 USA

Trova, Ernest T *Artist*
6 Laylon Terrace, Saint Louis, MO 63124 USA

Trowbridge, Alexander B Jr *Secretary*
1823 23rd St NW, Washington, DC 20008 USA

Trower, Robin *Musician*
Stardust Enterprises, 4600 Franklin Ave, Los Angeles, CA 90027 USA

Troxel, Gary
11471 Earle Dr, Nount Vernon, WA 98273 USA

Troyat, Henri *Writer*
Academie Francaise, 23 Quai de Conti, Paris, 75006, FRANCE

Troyer, Verne *Actor*
Simanton/Fondacaro Mgmt, 18032 Lenon Dr, #C, Yorba Linda, CA 92886 USA

Truax, Billy *Football Player*
PO Box 96, Gulfport, MS 39502 USA

Trucco, Michael *Actor*
Rising Stars, PO Box 99, China Springs, TX 76633 USA

Trucks, Virgil *Athlete*
1016 Waterford Tr, Calera, AL 35040

Trucks, Virgil O (Fire) *Baseball Player*
1016 Waterford Trail, Calera, AL 35040 USA

Trudeau, Garry *Cartoonist*
459 Columbus Ave, #200, New York, NY 10024 USA

Trudeau, Jack F *Football Player*
9150 Timberwolf Lane, Zionsville, IN 46077 USA

True, Rachel
PO Box 5617, Beverly Hills, CA 90210 USA

True Vibe *Music Group*
Creative Artists Agency LCC (CAA-LA), 9830 Wilshire Blvd, Beverly Hills, CA 90212 USA

Trueba, Fernando *Director*
CAA

Truesdale, Yanic *Actor*
Nancy Iannios PR, 8271 Melrose Avenue, Suite 102, Los Angeles, CA 90046 USA

Trufant, Marcus *Football Player*
Seattle Seahawks, 11220 NE 53rd St, Kirkland, WA 98033 USA

Truhitte, Dan
4630 Sapp Rd., Concord, NC 28027

Truitt, Anne D *Artist*
3506 35th St NW, Washington, DC 20016 USA

Trujillo, Chadwick *Astronomer*
California Institute of Technology, Astronomy Dept, Pasadena, CA 91125 USA

Trujillo, Solomon D *Business Person*
US West Inc, 1801 California St, Denver, CO 80202 USA

Truly, Richard N *Astronaut, Admiral*
25078 Foothills Dr N, Lakewood, CO 80401 USA

Truman, Dan *Musician*
Dreamcatcher Artists Mgmt, 2908 Poston Ave, Nashville, TN 37203 USA

Truman, James *Editor*
Conde Nast Publications, Editorial Dept, 4 Times Square, New York, NY 10036 USA

Trumbo, Karen *Actor*
Creative Artists Management (OR), 909 SW Saint Clair Avenue, Portland, OR 97205-1330 USA

Trumka, Richard L *Politician*
AFL-CIO, 1750 New York Ave NW, Washington, DC 20006 USA

Trump, Blaine
166 Avenue of the Americas, New York, NY 10013

Trump, Donald J *Business Person*
Trump Organization, 725 5th Ave, New York, NY 10022 USA

Trump, Ivana *Business Person, Model*
PO Box 8104, West Palm Beach, FL 33407 USA

Trump, Ivanka *Model*
PO Box 8095, West Palm Beach, FL 33407 USA

Trumpy, Robert T (Bob) Jr *Football Player, Sportscaster*
75 Oak St, Cincinnati, OH 45246 USA

Trundy, Natalie *Actor*
2109 S Wilbur Ave, Walla Walla, WA 99362 USA

Truran, James W Jr *Physicist*
210 Wysteria Dr, Olympia Fields, IL 60461 USA

Truscott, Lucian K IV *Writer*
Avon/William Morrow, 1350 Ave of Americas, New York, NY 10019 USA

Truth, Hurts *Songwriter, Actor*
Aftermath/Interscope Records, 2220 Colorado Ave, Santa Monica, CA 90404 USA

Trynin, Jennifer *Musician, Songwriter*
Vector Mgmt, 1607 17th Ave S, Nashville, TN 37212 USA

Tsakalidis, Iakovos (Jake) *Basketball Player*
Memphis Grizzlies, 175 Toyota Plaza, #150, Memphis, TN 38103 USA

Tsang, Bion *Musician*
Columbia Artists Mgmt Inc, 165 W 57th St, New York, NY 10019 USA

Tsantiris, Len *Football Player*
University of Connecticut, Athletic Dept, Storrs Mansfield, CT USA

Tsao, I Fu *Engineer*
University of Michigan, Chemical Engineering Dept, Ann Arbor, MI 48109 USA

Tschechowa, Vera
Gosslerstr 2, Berlin, GERMANY, D-12161

Tschetter, Kris *Golfer*
Legends Inc, 7458 Sommerset Shores COurt, Orlando, FL 32819 USA

Tschumi, Bernard *Architect*
7 Rue Pecquay, Paris, 75004, FRANCE

Tsibliyev, Vasili V *Cosmonaut*
Potchta Kosmonavtov, Moskovskoi Oblasti, Syvisdny Goroduk, 141160, RUSSIA

Tskitishvili, Nikoloz *Basketball Player*
Denver Nuggets, Pepsi Center, 1000 Chopper Circle, Denver, CO 80204 USA

Tsoucalas, Nicholas *Judge*
US Court of International Trade, 1 Federal Plaza, New York, NY 10278 USA

Tsu, Irene
3349 Cahuenga Blvd. W. #1, Los Angeles, CA 90068

Tsui, Daniel C *Nobel Prize Laureate*
2 Newlin Road, Princeton, Nj, 08540 USA

Tsui, Hark *Director, Producer, Writer*
International Creative Management (ICM-LA), 8942 Wilshire Blvd, Beverly Hills, CA 90211 USA

Tsui, Lap-Chee *Biologist*
Sick Children Hospital, 555 University Ave, Toronto, ON M5G 1X8, CANADA

Tu, Francesa
Beethovenstr. 48, Sarstedt, GERMANY, D-31157

Tuanku, Salehuddin Abdul Aziz Shah *King, Royalty*
Sultan's Palace, Istana Bukit Serene, Kuala Lumpur, 50502, MALAYSIA

Tubbs, Billy *Coach*
Lamar University, Athletic Dept, Beaumont, TX 77710 USA

Tubbs, Gerald J (Jerry) *Football Player*
3813 Centenary Ave, Dallas, TX 75225 USA

Tubert, Marcelo *Actor*
Richard Schwartz Management, 2934-1/2 Beverly Glen Cir #107, Los Angeles, CA 90077

Tuberville, Tommy *Football Coach*
Auburn University, Athletic Dept, Auburn University, AL 36849 USA

Tubes, The
903 10th Ave. So., Nashville, TN 37212

Tucci, Michael *Actor*
1425 Irving Ave, Glendale, CA 91201 USA

Tucci, Roberto Cardinal *Religious Leader*
Palazzo Pio, Piazza Pia 3, Rome, 00193, ITALY

Tucci, Stanley *Actor, Director*
Creative Artists Agency, 9830 Wilshire Blvd, Beverly Hills, CA 90212 USA

Tuchman, Maurice *Misc*
150 E 57th St, #PH 1A, New York, NY 10022 USA

Tuck, Jessica *Actor*
Brett Adams, 448 W 44th St, New York, NY 10036 USA

Tucker, Bill *Boxer*
26126 Meadowcrest Blvd, Huntington Woods, MI 48070 USA

Tucker, Chris *Comedian, Actor*
19133 Briarfield Way, Tarzana, CA 91356 USA

Tucker, Corin *Musician*
Legends of 21st Century, 7 Trinity ROw, Florence, MA 01062 USA

Tucker, Ira Sr *Musician*
Thrill Entertainment Group, Po Box 57090, Hayward, CA 94545 USA

Tucker, Marcia *Misc*
New Museum of Contemporary Art, 583 Broadway, New York, NY 10012 USA

Tucker, Marshall Band
315 S. Beverly Dr. #206, Beverly Hills, CA 90212

Tucker, Michael *Actor*
197 Oakdale Ave, Mill Valley, CA 94941 USA

Tucker, Michael *Biologist*
Reproductive Biology Assoc, 5505 Peachtree Dunwoody, Atlanta, GA 30342 USA

Tucker, Robert L (Bob) Jr *Football Player*
8 Hunter Road, Hazleton, PA 18201 USA

Tucker, Tanya *Musician*
Curtis Co, 109 Westpark Dr, #400, Brentwood, TN 37027 USA

Tucker, Tony *Boxer*
Club Prana, 1619 7th Ave, Ybor City, Tampa, FL 33605 USA

Tucker, William E *Educator*
Texas Christian University, Chancellor's Office, Fort Worth, TX 76129 USA

Tucker, Y Arnold *Football Player*
10835 SW 86th Ave, Ocala, FL 34481 USA

Tuckwell, Barry E
13140 Fountain Head Road, Hagerstown, MD 21742 USA

Tudor, John T *Baseball Player*
31 Upton Hills Lane, Middleton, MA 01949 USA

Tudyk, Alan *Actor*
Endeavor Agency LLC (LA), 9601 Wilshire Blvd Fl 3, Beverly Hills, CA 90210 USA

Tueting, Sarah *Hockey Player*
488 Ash St, Winnetka, IL 60093 USA

Tufeld, Dick
11020 Wrightwood Pl., Studio City, CA 91604

Tuiasosopo, Marques *Football Player*
5569 Gold Creek Dr, Castro Valley, CA 94552 USA

Tuibahadur, Pun *War Hero*
Victoria Cross Assn, Old Admiralty Building, London, SW1A 2BL, UNITED KINGDOM (UK)

Tuilaepa, Sailele Maljelegaio *Prime Minister*
Prime Minister's Office, PO Box 193, Apia, SAMOA

Tully, Darrow *Publisher*
9862 Bridgeton Dr, Tampa, FL 33626 USA

Tully, Susan
265 Liverpool Rd., London, ENGLAND, N1 1LX

Tulving, Endel *Misc*
45 Baby Point Crescent, York, ON M6S 2B7, CANADA

Tumi, Christian W Cardinal *Religious Leader*
Archveche, BP 179, Douala, CAMEROON

Tune, Thomas J (Tommy) *Dancer, Actor*
1501 Broadway, #1508, New York, NY 10036 USA

Tune, Tommy
50 E. 89th St., New York, NY 10128

Tung, Chee-Hwa *Misc*
Asia Pacific Finance Tower, 3 Garden Road, Hong Kong, CHINA

Tunie, Tamara *Actor*
Paradigm (LA), 10100 Santa Monica Blvd, Fl 25, Los Angeles, CA 90067 USA

Tunney, John V *Senator*
304 Chautauqua Blvd, Pacific Palisades, CA 90272 USA

Tunney, Robin *Actor*
Borinstein Oreck Bogart, 3172 dona Susana Dr, Studio City, CA 91604 USA

Tunnick, George *Misc*
National Assn of Female Executives, 127 W 24th St, New York, NY 10011 USA

Tupa, Thomas J (Tom) *Football Player*
6542 Lloyd Dr, Brecksville, OH 44141 USA

Tupou, King IV
Palace Officiale, Nuku'alofa, TONGA

Tupouto'a *Prince*
Royal Palace, PO Box 6, Nuku'alofa, TONGA

Turco, Marty *Hockey Player*
841 Shorewood Dr, Coppell, TX 75019 USA

Turco, Paige *Actor*
Gersh Agency, 232 N Canon Dr, Beverly Hills, CA 90210 USA

Turco, Richard P *Scientist*
R&D Assoc, 4340 Admiralty Way, Marina del Rey, CA 90292 USA

Turcotte, Donald L (Don) *Geophysicist*
27104 Middle Golf Dr, El Macero, CA 95618 USA

Turcotte, Jean-Claude Cardinal *Religious Leader*
1071 Rue de la Cathedrale, Montreal, QC, H2B 2V4, CANADA

Turcotte, Ron *Jockey*
82 Seattle Slew Dr, Howell, NJ 07731 USA

Turgeon, Pierre *Hockey Player*
4073 Bryn Mawr Dr, Dallas, TX 75225 USA

Turk, Stephen *Cartoonist*
927 Westbourne Dr, Los Angeles, CA 90069 USA

Turkel, Ann *Actor*
9877 Beverly Grove Dr, Beverly Hills, CA 90210 USA

Turkoglu, Hidayet *Basketball Player*
San Antonio Spurs, Alamodome, 1 SBC Center, San Antonio, TX 78219 USA

Turkson, Peter K A Cardinal *Religious Leader*
Archdiocese, PO Box 112, Cape Coast, GHANA

Turley, Bob
15470 Thorntree Run, Alpharetta, GA 30201-2647

Turley, Robert L (Bob) *Baseball Player*
11053 Big Canoe, Big Canoe, GA 30143 USA

Turlington, Christy *Model*
United Talent Agency, 9560 Wilshire Blvd, #500, Beverly Hills, CA 90212 USA

Turman, Glynn *Actor, Director, Musician*
Elkins Management, 8306 Wilshire Blvd #438, Beverly Hills, CA 90211 USA

Turnage, Mark-Anthony *Composer*
Schott Co, Great Marlborough St, London, W1V 2BN, UNITED KINGDOM (UK)

Turnbull, David *Physicist*
29 Concord Ave, #715, Cambridge, MA 02138 USA

Turnbull, Renaldo A *Football Player*
88 Oriole St, New Orleans, LA 70124 USA

Turnbull, Wendy *Tennis Player*
822 Boylston Dt, #203, Chestnut Hill, MA 02467 USA

Turnbull, William *Artist*
Waddington Galleries, 11 Cork St, London, W1, UNITED KINGDOM (UK)

Turner, Bree *Actor*
Osbrink, 4343 Lankershim, #100, North Hollywood, CA 91602 USA

Turner, Cathy *Speed Skater*
251 East Ave, Hilton, NY 14468 USA

Turner, Cecil *Football Player*
4820 Scott St, Houston, TX 77004 USA

Turner, Debbye *Doctor*
PO Box 12450, St. Louis, MO 63132-0150 USA

Turner, Edwin L *Physicist*
Princeton University, Astrophysical Sciences Dept, Princeton, NJ 08544 USA

Turner, Fred L *Business Person*
McDonald Corp, McDonald's Plaza, 1 Kroc Dr, Oak Brook, IL 60523 USA

Turner, Grant
PO Box 414, Brentwood, TN 37027

Turner, Guinevere *Actor*
Gersh Agency, 41 Madison Ave, #3300, New York, NY 10010 USA

Turner, Hamp *Football Player*
430172 Milledge Terrace, Athens, GA 30605 USA

Turner, Ike *Musician, Songwriter*
905 Viewpoint Dr, San Marcos, CA 92069 USA

Turner, James A (Jim) *Football Player*
14155 W 59th Place, Arvada, CO 80004 USA

Turner, James Jr *Business Person*
General Dynamics, 3190 Fairview Park Dr, Falls Church, VA 22042 USA

Turner, James T *Judge*
US Claims Court, 717 Madison Place NW, Washington, DC 20439 USA

Turner, Janine *Actor, Model*
Patricola Lust, 8271 Melrose Ave, #101, Los Angeles, CA 90046 USA

Turner, Jesse
1502 N. 5th St., Boise, ID 83702-3703

Turner, Jim *Actor*
David Shapira & Associates, 15821 Ventura Blvd #235, Encino, CA 91436 USA

Turner, John N *Prime Minister*
27 Dunice Road, Toronto, ON M4V 2W4, CANADA

Turner, Josh *Musician*
Monterey Peninsula Artists (Nashville), 124 12th Ave S #410, Nashville, TN 37203 USA

Turner, Karri *Actor*
Premiere Artists Agency, 1875 Century Park E, #2250, Los Angeles, CA 90067 USA

Turner, Kathleen *Actor*
International Creative Management (ICM-LA), 8942 Wilshire Blvd, Beverly Hills, CA 90211 USA

Turner, Keena *Football Player, Football Coach*
8200 W Erb Way, Tracy, CA 95304 USA

Turner, Kriss *Producer*
William Morris Agency (WMA-LA), 1 William Morris Pl, Beverly Hills, CA 90212 USA

Turner, Lowri *Actor*
Noel Gay Artists, 19 Denmark St, London, WC2H 8NA, United Kingdom

Turner, Michael *Artist*
Top Cow Productions Inc, 10390 Santa Monica Blvd, #110, Los Angeles, CA 90025

Turner, Morrie *Cartoonist*
PO Box 3004, Berkeley, CA 94703 USA

Turner, Norv *Football Coach*
Oakland Raiders, 1220 Harbor Bay Parkway, Alameda, CA 94502 USA

Turner, Stansfield
600 New Hampshire Ave NW #800, Washington, DC 20037 USA

Turner, Ted *Business Person*
Ted Turner Pictures, 133 Luckie St NW, Floor 7, Atlanta, GA 30303 USA

Turner, Tina *Musician*
Keith Sherman & Associates, 1776 Broadway #1200, New York, NY 10019 USA

Turner, Tyrin *Actor*
Agency for the Performing Arts (APA-LA), 9200 Sunset Blvd #900, Los Angeles, CA 90069 USA

Turney, Maura
PO Box 5617, Beverly Hills, CA 90210

Turow, Scott
Sears Tower #8000, Chicago, IL 60606

Turtles, The
PO Box 1821, Ojai, CA 93024

Turturro, Aida
9057C Nemo St., W. Hollywood, CA 90069

Turturro, John *Actor*
International Creative Management (ICM-NY), 40 W 57th St, New York, NY 10019 USA

Turturro, Nicholas *Actor*
Agency for the Performing Arts (APA-LA), 9200 Sunset Blvd #900, Los Angeles, CA 90069 USA

Turturro, Nick *Actor*
Writers and Artists Group Intl (LA), 8383 Wilshire Blvd #550, Beverly Hills, CA 90211 USA

Tush, Bill
1 City CNN Center Box 105366, Atlanta, GA 30348-5366

Tushingham, Rita
4 Kingly St, London, ENGLAND, W1R 5LF

Tuten, Rick
1315 SE 22nd Ave., Ocala, FL 34471-2659

Tutin, Dame Dorothy
13 St. Martin's Rd., London, ENGLAND, SW9 0SP

Tutu, Desmond *Religious Leader*
7981 Orlando West Box 1131, Johannesburg, SOUTH AFRICA

Twain, Shania *Musician*
Q Prime Inc, 729 Seventh Ave Fl 16, New York, NY 10019 USA

Tweed, Shannon *Actor*
Allman/Rea Management, 141 Barrington #E, Los Angeles, CA 90049 USA

Tweeden, Leeann *Model*
William Morris Agency (WMA-LA), 1 William Morris Pl, Beverly Hills, CA 90212 USA

Twilley, Howard J Jr *Football Player*
3109 S Columbia Circle, Tulsa, OK 74105 USA

Twilly, Dwight
PO Box 1821, Ojai, CA 93024

Twohy, David *Actor*
International Creative Management (ICM-LA), 8942 Wilshire Blvd, Beverly Hills, CA 90211 USA

Twohy, Mike *Cartoonist*
605 Beloit Ave, Kensington, CA 94708 USA

Twohy, Robert *Cartoonist*
New Yorker Magazine, Editorial Dept, 4 Times Square, New York, NY 10036 USA

Twombly, Cy *Artist*
Gagosian Gallery, 980 Madison Ave, New York, NY 10021 USA

Twyman, John K (Jack) *Business Person, Basketball Player*
8955 Indian Ridge Lane, Cincinnati, OH 45243 USA

Tydings, Alexandra *Actor*
Writers & Artists, 8383 Wilshire Blvd, #550, Beverly Hills, CA 90211 USA

Tydings, Joseph D *Senator*
2705 Pocock Road, Monkton, MD 21111 USA

Tyers, Kathy *Writer*
Martha Millard Agency, 204 Park Ave, Madison, NJ 07940 USA

Tykwer, Tom *Director, Writer, Actor*
Creative Artists Agency, 9830 Wilshire Blvd, Beverly Hills, CA 90212 USA

Tyler, Aisha *Actor, Comedian*
Endeavor Talent Agency, 9701 Wilshire Blvd, #1000, Beverly Hills, CA 90212 USA

Tyler, Anne *Writer*
222 Tunbridge Road, Baltimore, MD 21212 USA

Tyler, Bonnie *Musician, Songwriter*
David Aspden Mgmt, Coach House, S Holmwood, Dorking, RH5 4LJ, UNITED KINGDOM (UK)

Tyler, Cory
9955 Balboa Blvd., Northridge, CA 91325

Tyler, Harold R Jr *Attorney General*
Patterson Belknap Webb Tyler, 30 Rockefeller Plaza, New York, NY 10112 USA

Tyler, James Michael *Actor*
Friends

Tyler, Liv *Actor*
William Morris Agency (WMA-LA), 1 William Morris Pl, Beverly Hills, CA 90212 USA

Tyler, Nikki
4F So. Main St. PMB 307, West Bridgewater, MA 02379

Tyler, Richard *Fashion Designer*
Richard Tyler, 2001 Saturn St, Los Angeles, CA 91755 USA

Tyler, Robert *Actor*
Innovative Artists, 1505 10th St, Santa Monica, CA 90401 USA

Tyler, Steven *Musician, Songwriter*
Monterey Peninsula Artists, 509 Hartnell St, Monterey, CA 93940 USA

Tyler, Wendell A *Football Player*
2541 Still Meadow Lane, Lancaster, CA 93536 USA

Tyler, Willie
1650 Broadway #705, New York, NY 10019

Tylo, Hunter *Actor*
11684 Ventura Blvd. #910, Studio City, CA 91604-2613

Tylo, Michael *Actor*
11684 Ventura Blvd, #910, Studio City, CA 91604 USA

Tynan, Ronan
Trident Media Group LLC, 41 Madison Ave Fl 33, New York, NY 10010 USA

Tyne, George
1449 Benedict Canyon, Beverly Hills, CA 90210

Tyner, Charles *Actor*
Dade/Schultz, 6442 Coldwater Canyon Ave, #206, Valley Green, CA 91606 USA

Type O Negative *Music Group*
Helter Skelter (UK), The Plaza, 535 Kings Rd, London, N13 5H, UNITED KINGDOM (UK)

Tyra, Charles (Charlie) *Basketball Player*
901 Stoneykirk Dr, Louisville, KY 40223 USA

Tyree, Omar *Writer*
Omar Tyree Books, P.O. Box 41918, Philadelphia, PA 19101

Tyrell, Steve *Musician*
William Morris Agency (WMA-LA), 1 William Morris Pl, Beverly Hills, CA 90212 USA

Tyrell, Susan
1489 Scott Ave., Los Angeles, CA 90026

Tyrrell, Susan *Actor*
Abrams Artists, 9200 Sunset Blvd, #1125, Los Angeles, CA 90069 USA

Tysoe, Ronald W *Business Person*
Federated Department Stores, 151 W 34th Ave, New York, NY 10001 USA

Tyson, Cathy *Actor*
P F D Drury House, 34-43 Russell St, London, WC2B 5HA, UNITED KINGDOM (UK)

Tyson, Cicely *Actor*
315 W 70th St, New York, NY 10023 USA

Tyson, Ian *Musician*
Richard Flohil Assoc, 60 McGill St, Toronto, ON M5B 1H2, CANADA

Tyson, Neil de Grasse *Physicist*
Hayden Planetarium, W 81st St & Central Park, New York, NY 10024 USA

Tyson, Richard *Actor*
Kritzer, 12200 W Olympic Blvd, #400, Los Angeles, CA 90064 USA

Tyurin, Mikhail *Cosmonaut*
Potcha Kosmonavtov, Moskovskoi Oblasti, Syvisdny Goroduk, 141160, RUSSIA

Tyus, Wyomia *Track Athlete*
1102 Keniston Ave, Los Angeles, CA 90019 USA

Tyzack, Margaret *Actor*
Joyce Edwards, 275 Kennington Road, London, SE1 6BY, UNITED KINGDOM (UK)

Tzadua, Paulos Cardinal *Religious Leader*
PO Box 2141, Addis Abeba, ETHIOPIA

Tzekova, Polina *Basketball Player*
Houston Comets, 2 Greenway Plaza, #400, Houston, TX 77046 USA

U

U-God *Artist*
Famous Artists Agency, 250 W 57th St, New York, NY 10107 USA

U2 *Musician*
30-32 Sir John Rogerson's Quarry, Dublin, IRELAND

UB 40
Kensal House 553-579 Harrow Rd., London, ENGLAND, W10 4RH

UB40 *Music Group*
International Talent Booking (ITB - UK), 27A Floral Street, Third Floor, Covent Garden, London, WC2E 9, United Kingdom

Ubach, Alanna *Actor*
8730 Sunset Blvd, #490, Los Angeles, CA 90069 USA

Ubriaco, Gene *Coach*
Chicago Wolves, 2301 Ravine Way, Glenview, IL 60025 USA

Uchida, Irene A *Scientist*
20 North Shore Blvd W, Burlington, ON L7T 1A1, CANADA

Uchida, Mitsuko *Musician*
Arts Management Group, 1133 Broadway, #1025, New York, NY 10010 USA

Udenio, Fabiana *Actor*
Michael Slessinger, 8730 Sunset Blvd, #220W, Los Angeles, CA 90069 USA

Uderzo, Albert
26 av. Victor Hugo, Paris, FRANCE, F-75116

Udvari, Frank *Referee*
2-379 Gage Ave, Kitchener, ON N2M 5E1, CANADA

Udy, Helene *Actor*
Sterling/Winters, 10877 Wilshire Blvd, #15, Los Angeles, CA 90024 USA

Ueberroth, John A *Business Person*
Carlson Cos Inc, 12755 State Highway 55, Minneapolis, MN 55441 USA

Ueberroth, Peter
184 Emerald Bay, Laguna Beach, CA 92651

Ueberroth, Peter V *Misc*
Doubletree Hotels Corp, 755 Crossover Lane, Memphis, TN 38117 USA

Uecker, Bob
201 S. 46th St., Milwaukee, WI 53214

Uecker, Gunther *Artist*
Dusseldorfer Str 29A, Dusseldorf, 40545, GERMANY

Uecker, Robert G (Bob) *Baseball Player, Actor, Sportscaster*
31N7867 N Country Lane, Menomonee Falls, WI 53051 USA

Uelses, John *Track Athlete*
30660 Rolling Hills Dr, Valley Center, CA 92082 USA

Uelsmann, Jerry N *Photographer*
5701 SW 17th Dr, Gainesville, FL 32608 USA

Ueltschi, Albert L *Business Person*
Flight Safety Int'l, Marine Air Terminal, LaGuardia Airport, Flushing, NY 11371 USA

Ufland, Len *Actor, Director*
4400 Hillcreat Dr, #901, Hollywood, FL 33021 USA

UFO
10 Sutherland, London, ENGLAND, W9 24Q

Uggams, Leslie *Musician, Actor*
Entertainment Unlimited, 72 N Village Ave, Rockville Centre, NY 11570 USA

Ughi, Uto *Musician*
Cannareggio 4990/E, Venice, 30121, ITALY

Uhl, George *Biologist*
Johns Hopkins University, Medical Center, Genetics Dept, Baltimore, MD 21218 USA

Uhl, Petr *Social Activist*
Anglicka 8, Prague 2, 120 00, CZECH REPUBLIC

Uhlenbeck, Karen K *Mathematician*
University of Texas, Mathematics Dept, Austin, TX 78712 USA

Uhlenhake, Jeffrey A (Jeff) *Football Player*
4125 NW 24th Terrace, Boca raton, FL 33431 USA

Uhlig, Anneliese
1519 Escalona Dr., Santa Cruz, CA 95060

Uhry, Alfred F *Writer*
Marshall Purdy, 226 W 47th St, #900, New York, NY 10036 USA

Ujiie, Junichi *Financier*
Normura Securities, 2 World Financial Center, 200 Liberty, New York, NY 10281 USA

Ukropina, James R *Business Person, Attorney General*
O'Melveny & Myers, 400 S Hope St, Los Angeles, CA 90071 USA

Ulene, Art *Doctor*
10810 Via Verona, Los Angeles, CA 90024 USA

Ulevich, Neal *Photographer, Journalist*
2841 Perry St, Iowa City, IA 52245 USA

Ulf, Gunnar Ekberg
Ace of Base, 9975 Santa Monica Blvd, Beverly Hills, CA 90212

Ulinski, Ed *Football Player*
2860 Lander Road, Cleveland, OH 44124 USA

Ulion, Gretchen *Hockey Player*
22181 Toro Hills Dr, Salinas, CA 93908 USA

Ullman, Norman V A (Norm) *Hockey Player*
819-25 Austin Dr, Unionville, ON L3R 8H4, CANADA

Ullman, Ricky *Actor*
Nani/Saperstein Management, 481 8th Ave #1575, New York, NY 10001 USA

Ullman, Tracey *Actor, Comedian*
815 E Colorado St, #210, Glendale, CA 91205 USA

Ullmann, Liv J *Actor*
101 W 79th St, #8F, New York, NY 10024 USA

Ullsten, Ola *Prime Minister*
Folkpartiet, PO Box 6508, Stockholm, 11383, SWEDEN

Ulmar, Bin Hassan *Musician*
Agency Group, 1775 Broadway, #433, New York, NY 10019 USA

Ulmer, Kristen *Athlete*
3671 Willow Canyon Dr, Salt Lake City, UT 84121 USA

Ulrich, Henry *Admiral*
Commander, Naval Striking Force Central Europe & 6th Fleet, FPO, AE, 09609 USA

Ulrich, Kim Johnston *Actor*
S D B Partners, 1801 Ave of Stars, #902, Los Angeles, CA 90067 USA

Ulrich, Lars *Musician*
Q Prime Inc, 729 7th Ave, #1600, New York, NY 10019 USA

Ulrich, Laurel T *Historian*
University of New Hampshire, History Dept, Durham, NH 03824 USA

Ulrich, Robert *Business Person*
Target Corporation, 1000 Nicollet Mall, Minneapolis, MN 55403-2467

Ulrich, Robert J *Business Person*
Daytone Hudson, 1000 Nicollet Mall, Minneapolis, MN 55403 USA

Ulrich, Skeet *Actor*
International Creative Mgmt, 8942
Wilshire Blvd, #219, Beverly Hills, CA
90211 USA

Ulrich, Thomas *Boxer*
Brunsbutteler Damm 29, Berlin, 13581,
GERMANY

Ultang, Don *Photographer, Journalist*
3500 Lower West Branch Road, #121,
Iowa City, IA 52245 USA

Ultra, Nate *Musician*
Peach Bisquit, 451 Washington Ave, #5A,
Brooklyn, NY 11238 USA

Ulufa'alu, Bartholomew *Prime Minister*
Premier's Office, Legakiki Ridge, Honiara,
Guadacanal, SOLOMON ISLANDS

Ulusu, Bulent *Prime Minister, Admiral*
Ciftehavuzlar Yesilbahar 50K 8/27,
Kadikoy/Istanbul, TURKEY

Ulvaeus, Bjorn *Musician, Composer*
Gorel Hanser, Sodra Brobanken 41A,
Skeppsholmen, Stockholm, 11149,
SWEDEN

Ulvang, Vegard *Skier*
Fiellveien 53, Kirkenes, 9900, NORWAY

Ulyanov, Mikhail A *Actor, Director*
Theater Vakhtango, 26 Arbat, Moscow,
121002, RUSSIA

Umana, Christina *Actor*
TV Caracol, Calle 76 #11 - 35, Piso
10AA, Bogota DC, 26484, COLOMBIA

Umermoto, Nanako *Architect*
118 E 59th St, New York, NY 10022 USA

Umrao, Singh *War Hero*
Victoria Cross Assn, Old Admirally
Building, London, SW1A 2BL, UNITED
KINGDOM (UK)

Unanue, Emil R *Misc*
Washington University, Medical School,
Pathology Dept, Saint Louis, MO 63110
USA

Uncle Kracker *Music Group*
Helter Skelter (UK), The Plaza, 535 Kings
Rd, London, N13 5H, UNITED
KINGDOM (UK)

Underwood, Blair *Actor*
PO Box 55665, Sherman Oaks, CA 91413
USA

Underwood, Jacob *Musician*
Trans Continental Records, 7380 Sand
Lake Road, #350, Orlando, FL 32819 USA

Underwood, Jay *Actor*
6100 Wilshire Blvd, #1170, Los Angeles,
CA 90048 USA

Underwood, Ron *Director*
United Talent Agency, 9560 Wilshire
Blvd, #500, Beverly Hills, CA 90212 USA

Underwood, Scott *Musician*
Jon Landua, 80 Mason St, Greenwich, CT
06830 USA

Ungaro, Emanuel M *Fashion Designer*
2 Ave du Montaigne, Paris, 75008,
FRANCE

Ungaro, Susan Kelliher *Editor*
Family Circle Magazine, Editorial Dept,
375 Lexington Ave, New York, NY 10017
USA

Unger, Brian
5750 Wilshire Blvd., Los Angeles, CA
90036

Unger, Brian *Television Host*
Extra (LA), 1840 Victory Blvd, Glendale,
CA 91201 USA

Unger, Deborah *Actor*
International Creative Management
(ICM-LA), 8942 Wilshire Blvd, Beverly
Hills, CA 90211 USA

Unger, Deborah Kara *Actor*
International Creative Mgmt, 8942
Wilshire Blvd, #219, Beverly Hills, CA
90211 USA

Unger, Garry D *Hockey Player*
5315 E 93rd St, Tulsa, OK 74137 USA

Unger, Jim *Cartoonist*
Universal Press Syndicate, 4520 Main St,
Kansas City, MO 64111 USA

Unger, Kay *Fashion Designer*
Saint Gillian Sportswear, 498 Fasion Ave,
New York, NY 10018 USA

Unger, Leonard *Diplomat*
31 Amherst Road, Belmont, MA 02478
USA

Ungers, Oswald M *Architect*
Belvederestr 60, Cologne, 50933,
GERMANY

Union, Gabrielle *Actor*
Strong/Morrone Entertainment, 9100
Wilshire Blvd #503E, Beverly Hills, CA
90212 USA

Union, Sarah *Actor*
William Morris Agency (WMA-LA), 1
William Morris Pl, Beverly Hills, CA
90212 USA

Unkefer, Ronald A *Business Person*
Good Guys Inc, 1600 Harbor Bay
Parkway, Alameda, CA 94502 USA

Uno, Osamu *Business Person*
1-46 Showacho, Hamadera Sakai, Osaka,
592, JAPAN

Unruh, James A *Business Person*
5426 E Morrison Lane, Paradise Valley,
AZ 85253 USA

Unseld, Westley S (Wes) *Basketball
Player, Coach*
2210 Cedar Dr, Baltimore, MD 21228
USA

Unser, Al *Race Car Driver*
7625 Central NW, Albuquerque, NM
87121

Unser, Alfred (Al) *Race Car Driver*
7625 Central Ave NW, Albuquerque, NM
87121 USA

Unser, Alfred (Al) Jr *Race Car Driver*
PO Box 56696, Albuquerque, NM 87187
USA

Unser, Robert W (Bobby) *Race Car Driver*
7700 Central Ave SW, Albuquerque, NM
87121 USA

Unser Jr, Al
6847 Rio Grande Blvd, Albuquerque, NM
87107 USA

Unser Jr, Bobby
PO Box 25047, Albuquerque, NM 87125
USA

Upatnieks, Juris *Engineer*
Applied Optics, 2662 valley Dr, Ann
Arbor, MI 48103 USA

Upchurch, Rickie (Rick) *Football Player*
988 S Avenida del Oro W, Pueblo, CO
81007 USA

Updike, John H *Writer*
675 Hale St, Beverly Farms, MA 01915
USA

Uphoff-Becker, Nicole *Horse Racer*
Freiherr-von-Lanen-Str 15, Warendorf,
48231, GERMANY

Upshaw, Dawn *Opera Singer*
Columbia Artists Mgmt Inc, 165 W 57th
St, New York, NY 10019 USA

Upshaw, Eugene (Gene) *Football Player*
1102 Pepper Tree Dr, Great Falls, VA
22066 USA

Upshaw, Gene
1102 Pepper Tree Dr, Great Falls, VA
22066

Upshaw, Regan *Football Player*
Washington Redskins, 21300 Redskin Park
Dr, Ashbum, VA 20147 USA

Upton, Arthur C *Physicist*
7743 S Galileo Lane, Tucson, AZ 85747
USA

Urb, Johann *Actor*
3 Arts Entertainment Inc, 9460 Wilshire
Blvd Fl 7, Beverly Hills, CA 90212 USA

Urban, Amanda
ICM, 40 W 57th St, New York, NY 10019

Urban, Karl *Actor*
Auckland Actors, PO Box 56460,
Dominion Road, Auckland, 1030, NEW
ZEALAND

Urban, Keith *Musician*
PO Box 40185, Nashville, TN 37204 USA

Urban, Thomas N *Business Person*
Pioneer Hi-Bred Int'l, Capital Square, 400
Locust St, Des Moines, IA 50309 USA

Urbanchek, Jon *Coach*
University of Michigan, Athletic Dept,
Ann Arbor, MI 48109 USA

Urbanek, Karel *President*
Kvetna 54, Brno, CZECHOSLOVAKIA

Urbano, Mike *Musician*
Creative Artists Agency, 9830 Wilshire
Blvd, Beverly Hills, CA 90212 USA

Urbanova, Eva *Opera Singer*
National Theater, Narodni Divadlo,
Prague 1, CZECH REPUBLIC

Urbanski, Douglas *Writer*
Creative Artists Agency, 9830 Wilshire
Blvd, Beverly Hills, CA 90212 USA

Urbina, Ugueth U *Baseball Player*
Rojas Conj Res Las Aca Lias 2, Ocumare
Del Troy, VENEZUELA

Ure, Midge *Musician*
#8 Glenthome 115A Glenhome,
Hammersm, London, W6 0LJ, UNITED
KINGDOM (UK)

Uremovich, Emil P *Football Player*
2935 S County Road 210, Knox, In,
46534 USA

Urguhart, Lawrence M *Business Person*
English China Clays, Business Park, Theale, Reading, RG7 4SA, UNITED KINGDOM (UK)

Uribe, Diane *Actor*
23874 Via Jacara, Valencia, CA 91355 USA

Urich, Justin *Actor*
Talent Group, 5670 Wilshire Blvd, #820, Los Angeles, CA 90036 USA

Urkal, Oklay *Boxer*
Bautzener Str 4, Berlin, 10829, GERMANY

Urlacher, Brian *Football Player*
310 Belle Forest, Lake Bluff, IL 60044 USA

Urmanov, Aleksei *Figure Skater*
Union of Skaters, Luzhnetskaya Nab 8, Moscow, 119871, RUSSIA

Urmanov, Alexei
Luzhnetskaya nab. 8, Moscow, RUSSIA, 119871

Urmson, Claire *Model*
Ford Model Agency, 142 Greene St, #400, New York, NY 10012 USA

Urquhart, Brian E *Diplomat*
Howard Farms, Jerusalem Road, Tyringham, MA 01264 USA

Urry, Lew *Inventor*
Energizer Corp, 800 Chouteau Ave, Saint Louis, MO 63164 USA

Urseth, Bonnie *Actor*
Gage Group, 14724 Ventura Blvd, #505, Sherman Oaks, CA 91403 USA

Urshan, Nathaniel A *Religious Leader*
United Pentecostal Church International, 8855 Dunn Road, Hazelwood, MO 63042 USA

Ursi, Corrado Cardinal *Religious Leader*
Via Capodimonte 13, Naples, 80136, ITALY

Usachyov, Yuri V *Cosmonaut*
Potcha Kosmonavtov, Moskovskoi Oblasti, Syvisdny Goroduk, 141160, RUSSIA

Usaher *Actor, Artist*
J Pat Mgmt, 3996 Pleasantville Road, #104A, Dovaville, GA 30340 USA

Used, The *Music Group*
Freeze Artist Management, 27783 Hidden Trail Rd, Laguna Hills, CA 92653

Usery, William J Jr *Secretary*
1101 S Arlington Ridge Road, Arlington, VA 22202 USA

Usgaonkar, Varsha *Actor, Bollywood*
2

Usgaonkar, Varsha *Actor, Bollywood*
2C-24 Wild Wood Park Yari Road, Versova Andheri (W), Bombay, MS 400 061, INDIA

Usher *Musician, Actor*
International Creative Mgmt, 8942 Wilshire Blvd, #219, Beverly Hills, CA 90211 USA

Usher, Thomas J *Business Person*
USX Corp, 600 Grant St, Pittsburgh, PA 15219 USA

Usova, Maya *Figure Skater*
Connecticut Skating Center, 300 Alumni Road, Newington, CT 06111 USA

Ustvolskaya, Galina I *Composer*
Prospect Gagarina 27, #72, Saint Petersburg, 196135, RUSSIA

Ut, Nick *Photographer*
Associated Press, Photo Dept, 221 S Figueroa St #300, Los Angeles, CA 90012 USA

Utay, William *Actor*
Days of Our Lives, 3000 W Alameda Ave, Burbank, CA 91523 USA

Uteem, Cassam *President*
President's Office, Le Redult, Port Louis, MAURITIUS

Utley, Adrian *Musician*
Fruit, Saga Centre, 326 Kensal Road, London, W10 5BZ, UNITED KINGDOM (UK)

Utley, Garrick *Commentator*
ABC-TV, News Dept, 8 Carburton St, London, W1P 7DT, UNITED KINGDOM (UK)

Utley, Mike *Football Player*
PO Box 458, Orondo, WA 98843 USA

Utley, Stan *Golfer*
4504 Laramie Court, Columbia, MO 65203 USA

Utzon, Jorn *Architect*
General Delivery, Hellebaek, 3150, DENMARK

Uyeda, Seiya *Geophysicist*
2-39-6 Daizawa, Setagayaku, Tokyo, 113, JAPAN

Uzawa, Hirofumi *Economist*
Higashi 1-3-6 Hoya, Tokyo, JAPAN

V

V Gopalakrishnan *Actor*
11D4 Habibullah Road, T Nagar, Chennai, TN 600 017, INDIA

V M T Chaarllee *Actor*
Plot No 11 Kamarajar Nagar, II Street Sathya Gardens Saligramam, Chennai, TN 600 093, INDIA

Vaca, Joselito *Soccer Player*
Dallas Burn, 14800 Quorum Dr, #300, Dallas, TX 75254 USA

Vacano, Jost *Cinematographer*
Leoprechtingstr 18, Munich, 81739, GERMANY

Vacanti, Charles A *Doctor*
Massachusetts University Med Center, Anesthesiology Dept, Worcester, MA 02139 USA

Vacariou, Nicolae *Prime Minister*
Romanian Senate, Piata Revolutiei, Bucharest, 71243, ROMANIA

Vaccaro, Brenda *Actor*
Gold Marshak Liedtke, 3500 W Olive Ave, #1400, Burbank, CA 91505 USA

Vachon, Christine *Producer*
Killer Films, 380 Layfayette St #302, New York, NY 10003 USA

Vachon, Louis-Albert Cardinal *Religious Leader*
Seminaire de Quebec, 1 Rue des Remparts, Quebec, QC, G1R 5LY, CANADA

Vachon, Paul *Wrestler*
RR 4, Mansonville, QC, J0E 1X0, CANADA

Vachon, Rogatien R (Rogie) *Hockey Player, Coach*
47385 Via Florence, La Quinta, CA 92253 USA

Vachss, Andrew H *Writer*
299 Broadway, #1800, New York, NY 10007 USA

Vadivukkarasi *Actor, Bollywood*
49/1A Sadulla Street, Chennai, TN 600017, INDIA

Vaduva, Leontina *Opera Singer*
Luisa Petrov, Glaburgstr 95, Frankfurt, 60318, GERMANY

Vaea of Houma, Baron *Prime Minister*
Prime Minister's Office, Nuku'alofa, TONGA

Vagelos, P Roy *Business Person, Biologist*
1 Crossroads Dr, 500 Building A, Bedminster, NJ 07921 USA

Vago, Constantin *Misc*
University of Sciences, Place Eugene Bataillon, Montpellier, 34095, FRANCE

Vahi, Tiit *Prime Minister*
Coalition Party Eesti Koonderakond, Kuhlbarsi 1, Tallinn, 0104, ESTONIA

Vai, Steve *Musician*
Septys Entertainment, 1223 Wilshire Blvd, #804, Santa Monica, CA 90403 USA

Vaidyanathan, Aparna *Actor, Bollywood*
520 19th Cross 14th Main, Benasankari 2nd Stage, Bangalore, KA, 560070, INDIA

Vail, Justina *Actor*
UPN, 5555 melrose Ave, Los Angeles, CA 90038 USA

Vail, Thomas *Editor*
Cleveland Plain Dealer, Editorial Dept, 1801 Superior, Cleveland, OH 44114 USA

Vaishnavi *Actor, Bollywood*
2 Sambandam Street, G N Chetty Road, Chennai, TN 600017, INDIA

Vajiralongkorn *Prince*
Royal Residence, Chirtalad a Villa, Bangkok, THAILAND

Vajna, Andrew *Producer, Filmmaker*
Cinergi Productions, 2308 Broadway, Santa Monica, CA 90404 USA

Vajna, Andy *Producer*
Bumble Ward & Associates, 8383 Wilshire Blvd #340, Beverly Hills, CA 90211 USA

Vajpayee, Atal Bihari *Prime Minister*
6 Raisina Road, New Delhi, Delhi, 110011, INDIA

Valabik, Boris *Hockey Player*
Atlanta Thrashers, Philips Arena, 13 South Ave SE, Atlanta, GA 30315 USA

Valance, Holly *Musician*
Warner Music UK Limited (WMI-UK), The Warner Building, 28 Kensington Church Street, London, W8 4EP, United Kingdom

Valandrey, Charlotte *Actor*
Artmedia, 20 Ave Rapp, Paris, 75007, FRANCE

Valar, Paul *Skier*
34 Hubertus Ring, Franconia, NH 03580 USA

Valasquez, Nadine *Actor*
Don Buchwald & Associates Inc (LA), 6500 Wilshire Blvd #2200, Los Angeles, CA 90048 USA

Valderrama, Carlos *Soccer Player*
Colorado Rapids, 555 17th St, #3350, Denver, CO 80202 USA

Valderrama, Wilmer *Actor*
Rigberg Roberts Rugolo, 1180 S Beverly Dr, #601, Los Angeles, CA 90035 USA

Valdes, Ismael *Baseball Player*
Texas Rangers, 1000 Ballpark Way, Arlington, TX 76011 USA

Valdes, Jesus (Chucho) *Musician*
IMN, 278 Main St, Gloucester, MA 01930 USA

Valdes, Maximiano *Conductor*
Cramer/Marder Artists, 3436 Springhill Road, Lafayette, CA 94549 USA

Valdez, Luis *Writer*
El Teatro Capesino, 705 4th St, San Juan Bautista, CA 95045 USA

Vale, Angelica *Actor*
Televisa, Blvd Adolfo Lopez Mateos 232, Colonia San Angel INN, DF, CP 01060, MEXICO

Vale, Jerry *Musician*
40960 Glenmore Dr, Palm Desert, CA 92260 USA

Vale, Tina *Musician*
DreamWorks Records, 9268 W 3rd St, Beverly Hills, CA 90210 USA

Vale, Virginia
4039 Edenhurst Ave, Los Angeles, CA 90039-1469

Valek, Vladimir *Conductor*
Na Vapennem 6, Prague 4, 140 00, CZECH REPUBLIC

Valen, Nancy *Actor*
Metropolitan Talent Agency, 4526 Wilshire Blvd, Los Angeles, CA 90010 USA

Valensi, Nick *Musician*
MVO Ltd, 370 7th Ave, #807, New York, NY 10001 USA

Valente, Benita *Opera Singer*
Maurice Mayer, 201 W 54th St, #1C, New York, NY 10019 USA

Valente, Catarina *Musician*
Villa Corallo Via ai Ronci, Bissone, 6816, SWITZERLAND

Valente, Caterina
Casella Postale 77, Bissone, SWITZERLAND, CH-6816

Valenti, Carl M *Publisher*
Information Services, Dow Jones Telerate, 200 Liberty St, New York, NY 10281 USA

Valenti, Jack *Misc*
Motion Picture Assn, 4635 Ashby St NW, Washington, DC 20007 USA

Valentin, Barbara *Actor*
Hans-Sachs-Str 22, Munich, 80469, GERMANY

Valentin, Dave *Musician*
Turi's Music Enterprises, 103 Westwood Dr, Miami Springs, FL 33166 USA

Valentine, Dan *Business Person*
C-Cube Microsystems, 1551 McCarthy Blvd, Milpitas, CA 95035 USA

Valentine, Darnell *Basketball Player*
7546 SW Ashford St, Tigard, OR 97224 USA

Valentine, Donald T *Business Person*
Network Appliance Inc, 495 E Java Dr, Sunnyvale, CA 94089 USA

Valentine, Gary *Comedian, Actor*
William Morris Agency, 151 El Camino Dr, Beverly Hills, CA 90212 USA

Valentine, Gary *Musician*
Shore Fire Media, 32 Court St, #1600, Brooklyn, NY 11201 USA

Valentine, James W *Biologist*
1351 Glendale Ave, Berkeley, CA 94708 USA

Valentine, Karen *Actor*
PO Box 1410, Washington Depot, CT 06793 USA

Valentine, Raymond C *Misc*
University of California, Plant Growth Laboratory, Davis, CA 95616 USA

Valentine, Robert J (Bobby) *Baseball Player*
71 Wynnewood Lane, Stamford, CT 06903 USA

Valentine, Scott *Actor*
17465 Flanders St, Granada Hills, CA 91344 USA

Valentine, Stacy *Adult Film Star*
200 W Houston St, New York, NY 10014 USA

Valentine, Steve *Actor*
Opus Entertainment, 5225 Wilshire Blvd #905, Los Angeles, CA 90036 USA

Valentine, Victoria
PO Box 12324, La Crescenta, CA 91224

Valentine, William N *Doctor*
2128 Quail Point Circle, Medford, OR 97504 USA

Valentino *Fashion Designer*
Palazzo Mignanelli, Piazza Mignanelli 22, Rome, 00187, ITALY

Valenza, Tasia *Actor*
Artists Group, 10100 Santa Monica Blvd, #2490, Los Angeles, CA 90067 USA

Valenzuela, Fernando *Baseball Player*
2123 N Beachwood Dr, Los Angeles, CA 90068 USA

Valeriani, Richard G *Commentator*
23 Island View Dr, Sherman, CT 06784 USA

Valetta, Amber *Model*
Wilhelmina Models, 300 Park Ave S, #200, New York, NY 10010 USA

Valiant, Leslie G *Scientist*
50 Tyler Road, Belmont, MA 02478 USA

Valiee, Bert L *Doctor*
300 Boyksti St, #712, Boston, MA 02116 USA

Valle, Aurora *Actor*
TV Azteca, Periferico Sur 4121, Colonia Fuentes del Pedregal, DF, CP 14141, Mexico

Vallely, James (Jim) *Writer*
Creative Artists Agency LCC (CAA-LA), 9830 Wilshire Blvd, Beverly Hills, CA 90212 USA

Valletta, Amber *Actor, Model*
Boss Models, 1 Gansevoort St, New York, NY 10014 USA

Valley, Mark *Actor*
International Creative Management (ICM-LA), 8942 Wilshire Blvd, Beverly Hills, CA 90211 USA

Valli, Alida *Actor*
G Perrone Elisabetta Morea, Viale Liegi 42, Rome, ITALY, 00198, ITALY

Valli, Frankie *Musician*
Agency for Performing Arts, 9200 Sunset Blvd, #900, Los Angeles, CA 90069 USA

Vallone, Raf
Viale R. Bacone 14, Rome, ITALY

Valot, Daniel L *Business Person*
Total Petroleum, 900 19th St, Denver, CO 80202 USA

Valtman, Edmund S *Editor, Cartoonist*
80 Loeffler Road, #G301, Bloomfield, CT 06002 USA

Valverde, Rawley
15207 Magnolia #106, Sherman Oaks, CA 91403

Van, Allen *Hockey Player*
4890 Ashley Lane, #206, Inver Grove Heights, MN 55077 USA

Van, Joey
48607 Presidential Dr. #2., Macomb Twp, MI 48044

Van Allan, Richard
18 Octavia St., London, ENGLAND, SW11 3DN

Van Ark, Joan *Actor*
William Morris Agency (WMA-LA), 1 William Morris Pl, Beverly Hills, CA 90212 USA

Van Buren, Abigail *Writer*
Phillips-Van Buren Inc, 1900 Ave of the Stars #2710, Los Angeles, CA 90067 USA

Van Dam, Rob *Actor*
Coast to Coast Talent Group, 3350 Barham Blvd, Los Angeles, CA 90068 USA

van den Hoogenband, Pieter *Swimmer*
PO Box 302, Arnhem, NETHERLANDS, 6800 AH

Van Der Beek, James *Actor*
Original Film, 2045 S Barrington Ave, Los Angeles, CA 90025 USA

Van Der Meer, Johnny
4005 Leona Ave., Tampa, FL 33606

Van Derbur-Alter, Marilyn
1401 17th St. #600, Denver, CO 80202

Van Devere, Trish
3211 Retreat Ct., Malibu, CA 90265

Van Dien, Casper *Actor*
Agency for the Performing Arts (APA-LA),
9200 Sunset Blvd #900, Los Angeles, CA
90069 USA

Van Doren, Mamie *Actor*
3419 Via Lido #184, Newport Beach, CA
92663 USA

Van Dusen, Granville
10974 Alta View Dr., Studio City, CA
91604

Van Dyke, Barry *Actor*
27800 Blythdale Rd, Agoura, CA 91301
USA

Van Dyke, Dick *Actor*
William Morris Agency (WMA-LA), 1
William Morris Pl, Beverly Hills, CA
90212 USA

Van Dyke, Jerry
PO Box 2130, Benton, AR 72018-2130

Van Dyke, Leroy
Rt. 1 Box 271, Smithton, MO 65350

Van Eeghen, Mark *Football Player*
90 Woodstock Ln, Cranston, RI 02920

Van Eman, Charles
12304 Santa Monica Blvd. #104, Los
Angeles, CA 90025

Van Gorkum, Harry *Actor*
2552 Dearborn Drive, Los Angeles, CA
90068 USA

Van Halen, Alex
12024 Summit Circle, Beverly Hills, CA
90210

Van Halen, Eddie *Musician*
United Talent Agency (UTA), 9560
Wilshire Blvd, Beverly Hills, CA 90212
USA

Van Holt, Brian *Actor*
Thruline Entertainment, 9250 Wilshire
Blvd, Ground Floor, Beverly Hills, CA
90210 USA

Van Horn, Kelly *Producer, Writer*
Mirisch Agency, 1801 Century Park E
#1801, Los Angeles, CA 90067 USA

Van Horn, Patrick
9200 Sunset Blvd. #1130, Los Angeles,
CA 90069

Van Horne, Keith *Basketball Player*
Philadelphia 76ers, 1st Union Center,
3601 South Broad Street, Philadelphia, PA
19148

Van Houten, Leslie
#W13378 Bed #1B314U CA Inst. for
Women16756 Chino Corona, Frontera,
CA 91720

van Johnson, Rodney *Actor*
Passions, 4024 Radford Ave, Studio City,
CA 91604 USA

Van Kemp, Merete
10000 Santa Monica Blvd. #305, Los
Angeles, CA 90067

Van Lowe, Ehrich *Producer, Writer*
Sweet Lorraine Productions, 8060 Melrose
Ave Fl 4, Los Angeles, CA 90046 USA

Van Patten, Dick
13920 Magnolia Blvd, Sherman Oaks, CA
91423

Van Patten, James
14411 Riverside Dr. #15, Sherman Oaks,
CA 91423

Van Patten, Joyce
2005 Sierra Pl., Glendale, CA 91208-2428

Van Patten, Nels
14411 Riverside Dr. #18, Sherman Oaks,
CA 91423

Van Patten, Tim *Director*
CAA, 9830 Wilshire Blvd, Beverly Hills,
CA 90212

Van Patten, Timothy
13920 Magnolia Blvd, Sherman Oaks, CA
91423

Van Patten, Vincent
13926 Magnolia Blvd, Sherman Oaks, CA
91423-1230

Van Peebles, Mario *Actor*
United Talent Agency (UTA), 9560
Wilshire Blvd, Beverly Hills, CA 90212
USA

Van Praagh, James *Actor, Writer,
Producer*
William Morris Agency (WMA-NY), 1325
Ave of the Americas, New York, NY
10019 USA

Van Sant, Doug G *Director*
William Morris Agency (WMA-LA), 1
William Morris Pl, Beverly Hills, CA
90212 USA

Van Sant, Gus *Director, Writer, Producer,
Actor*
Sawtooth, 1300 NW Northrup Ave Fl 3,
Portland, OR 97209 USA

Van Susteren, Greta *Television Host*
On the Record with Greta Van Susteren,
1211 Ave of the Americas, New York, NY
10036 USA

Van Valkenburgh, Deborah
2025 Stanley Hills Dr, Los Angeles, CA
90046

Van Vooren, Monique
165 E. 66th St., New York, NY 10021

Van Zandt, Steve *Actor*
Writers and Artists Group Intl (LA), 8383
Wilshire Blvd #550, Beverly Hills, CA
90211 USA

Van Zandt, Steven *Actor*
Writers and Artists Group Intl (LA), 8383
Wilshire Blvd #550, Beverly Hills, CA
90211 USA

VanAllen, James A *Physicist*
5 Woodland Mounds Road, RFD 6, Iowa
City, IA 52245 USA

VanAllen, Richard *Opera Singer*
18 Octavia St, London, SW11 3DN,
UNITED KINGDOM (UK)

VanAlmsick, Franziska (Franzi) *Swimmer*
Eichhom, Bizetstr 1, Berlin, 13088,
GERMANY

VanAmerongen, Jerry *Cartoonist*
10926 Owensmouth Ave, Chatsworth, CA
91311 USA

VanArk, Joan *Actor*
10950 Alta View Dr, Studio City, CA
91604 USA

VanArsdale, Dick *Basketball Player*
5816 N Dragoon Lane, Paradise Valley,
AZ 85253 USA

VanArsdale, Tom *Basketball Player*
3930 E Camelback Road, Phoenix, AZ
85018 USA

VanAuken, John A *Misc*
Canadian Tennis Technology, PO Box
1538, Sydney, NS B1P 6R7, CANADA

VanBasten, Marco *Soccer Player*
AC Milan, Via Turati 3, Milan, 20121,
ITALY

VanBerg, John C (Jack) *Coach*
420 Fair Hill Dr, #1, Elkton, MD 21921
USA

Vanbiesbrouck, John *Hockey Player*
PO Box 1514, Sault Sainte Marie, MI
49783 USA

VanBreda, Kolff Jan *Basketball Player,
Coach*
New Orleans Hornets, New Orleans
Arena, 1501 Girod St, New Orleans, LA
70113 USA

VanBreda, Kolff Willem (Butch)
Basketball Player, Coach
1005 Warwick Court, Sun City Center, FL
33573 USA

VanBuren, Abigail *Writer*
Philips-Van Buren Inc, 1900 Ave of Stars,
#2710, Los Angeles, CA 90067 USA

VanCamp, Emily *Actor*
International Creative Management
(ICM-LA), 8942 Wilshire Blvd, Beverly
Hills, CA 90211 USA

Vance, Courtney B *Actor*
Creative Artists Agency, 9830 Wilshire
Blvd, Beverly Hills, CA 90212 USA

Vance, Cyrus
425 Lexington Ave., New York, NY 10017

Vance, Kenny *Musician*
PO Box 116, Fort Tilden, NY 11695 USA

Vance, Robert S *Judge*
US Court of Appeals, 1800 5th Ave N,
Birmingham, AL 35203 USA

VanCitters, Robert L *Psychic*
University of Washington, Medical
School, Physiology Dept, Seattle, WA
98815 USA

VanClief, D G *Race Car Driver*
Breeders Cup Ltd, 2525 Harrodsburg
Road, Lexington, KY 40504 USA

VanCulin, Samuel *Religious Leader*
All Hallows Church, 43 Trinity Square,
London, EC3N 4DJ, UNITED KINGDOM
(UK)

VanDam, Jose *Opera Singer*
Zurich Artists, Rutistr 52, Zurich,
Gockhausen, 8044, SWITZERLAND

VanDamme, Jean-Claude *Actor*
International Creative Mgmt, 8942
Wilshire Blvd, #219, Beverly Hills, CA
90211 USA

VanDantzig, Rudi *Choreographer*
Emma-Straat 27, Amsterdam,
NETHERLANDS

Vandeman, George
1600 Waverly Rd., San Marino, CA 91108

VandenBerg, Lodewijk *Astronaut*
Constellation Technology Corp, 7887 Bryan Dairy Road, #100, Largo, FL 33777 USA

VandenBergh, M A *Business Person*
Royal Dutch Petroleum, 30 Van Bylandtlaan, Hague, HR, 2596, NETHERLANDS

Vandenburgh, Jane *Writer*
North Point Press, 1563 Solano Ave, #353, Berkeley, CA 94707 USA

VanDenHoogenband, Pieter *Swimmer*
PO Box 302, Amhem, AH, 6800, NETHERLANDS

Vander, Jagt Guy *Misc*
Baker & Hostetler, 1050 Connecticut Ave NW, Washington, DC 20036 USA

Vander, Musetta *Actor*
Agency for Performing Arts, 9200 Sunset Blvd, #900, Los Angeles, CA 90069 USA

VanDerBeek, James *Actor*
2945 S Barrington Ave, Los Angeles, CA 90025 USA

Vanderberg Shaw, Helen *Coach*
Heaven's Fitness, 301 14th St NW, Calgary, AB T2N 2A1, CANADA

Vanderhoef, Larry N *Educator*
University of California, President's Office, Davis, CA 95616 USA

Vanderloo, Mark *Model*
Wilhelmina Models, 300 Park Ave S, #200, New York, NY 10010 USA

VanDerMeer, Simon *Nobel Prize Laureate*
4 Chemin des Corbillettes, Saconnex, GD, 1218, SWITZERLAND

Vandermeersch, Bernard *Misc*
University of Bordeaux, Anthropology Dept, Bordeaux, FRANCE

Vanderveen, Loet *Artist*
Lime Creek 5, Big Sur, CA 93920 USA

VanDerveer, Tara *Coach*
1036 Cascade Dr, Menlo Park, CA 94025 USA

VandeSande, Theo A *Cinematographer*
2337 High Oak Dr, Los Angeles, CA 90068 USA

Vandeweghe, Kiki
4 Pennsylvania Plaza, New York, NY 10019

VandeWetering, John E *Educator*
17 Cricket Hill Dr, Pittsford, NY 14534 USA

Vandis, Titos
1930 Century Park W. #303, Los Angeles, CA 90067

Vandross, Luther *Musician*
Artist Group International (NY), 150 East 58th Street, Fl 19, New York, NY 10155 USA

VanDusen, Granville *Actor*
10974 Alta View Dr, Studio City, CA 91604 USA

Vangelis
195 Queensgate, London, ENGLAND, W1

VanHalen, Eddie *Musician*
20411 Chapter Dr, Woodland Hills, CA 91364 USA

VanHorn, Buddy *Director*
4409 Ponca Ave, Toluca Lake, CA 91602 USA

VanHorn, Keith *Basketball Player*
Milwaukee Bucks, Bradley Center, 1001 N 4th St, Milwaukee, WI 53203 USA

Vanilla Fudge
141 Dunbar Ave., Fords, NJ 08863

Vannelli, Gino
28205 Agoura Rd., Agoura Hills, CA 91301

Vanner, Sue
26 Wellesley Rd. Cheswick, London, ENGLAND, W4 4BN

Vanous, Lucky *Actor, Model*
28345 La Calenta Mission, Vlejo, CA 92692 USA

VanPatten, Joyce *Actor*
2005 Sierra Place, Glendale, CA 91208 USA

VanValkenburgh, Deborah *Actor*
Gaye West, PO Box 1515, Studio City, CA 91614 USA

Vapors, The
44 Valmoral Dr. Woking, Surrey, ENGLAND

Varda, Agnes *Director*
Cine-Tamaris, 86 Rue Daguerre, Paris, 75014, FRANCE

Vardalos, Nia *Actor*
United Talent Agency, 9560 Wilshire Blvd, #500, Beverly Hills, CA 90212 USA

Varela, Leonor *Actor*
Endeavor Agency LLC (LA), 9601 Wilshire Blvd Fl 3, Beverly Hills, CA 90210 USA

Varga, Imre *Artist*
Bartha Utca 1, Budapest XII, HUNGARY

Vargas, Elizabeth *Commentator*
ABC-TV, News Dept, 77 W 66th St, New York, NY 10023 USA

Vargas, Jacob *Actor*
9 Yards Entertainment, 8530 Wilshire Blvd Fl 5, Beverly Hills, CA 90211 USA

Vargas, Jay R *War Hero*
12466 Thombrush Court, San Diego, CA 92131 USA

Vargas, Ramon *Opera Singer*
Columbia Artists Mgmt Inc, 165 W 57th St, New York, NY 10019 USA

Vargas, Valentina *Actor*
5 Rue Norvins, Paris, 75018, FRANCE

Vargo, Tim *Business Person*
AutoZone Inc, 123 S Front St, Memphis, TN 38103 USA

Varian, Hal R *Economist*
1198 Estate Dr, Lafayette, CA 94549 USA

Varley of Chesterfield, Eric G
Government Official
Coalite Group, Buttermilk Lane, Bolsover, Derbyshire, S44 6AB, UNITED KINGDOM (UK)

Varmus, Harold E *Nobel Prize Laureate*
Memorial Sloan-Kettering Cancer Center, 1275 York Ave, New York, NY 10021 USA

Varo, Marton *Artist*
Phillips Gallery, PO Box 5807, Carmel, CA 93921 USA

Varoni, Miguel *Director*
TV Caracol, Calle 76 #11 - 35, Piso 10AA, Bogota DC, 26484, COLOMBIA

Varrella, Leonor *Actor*
Endeavor Talent Agency, 9701 Wilshire Blvd, #1000, Beverly Hills, CA 90212 USA

Varrichione, Frank
55 Dinsmore Ave. #103, Framingham, MA 01701

Varrichone, Frank *Football Player*
55 Dinsmore Ave, #103, Framingham, MA 01702 USA

Varshavsky, Alexander *Biologist*
California Institute of Technology, Cell Biology Dept, Pasadena, CA 91125 USA

Vartan, Michael *Actor*
252 N Larchmont Blvd, #201, Los Angeles, CA 90004 USA

Vartan, Sylvie *Musician*
Scotti, 706 N Beverly Dr, Beverly Hills, CA 90210 USA

Varty, Keith *Fashion Designer*
Bosco di San Francesco #6, Sirolo, ITALY

Varvatos, John *Fashion Designer*
Soho New York, 149 Mercer St, New York, NY 10012 USA

Vasarely, Victor
83 rue aux Religues, Annet-sur-Marne, FRANCE, F-77410

Vasary, Tamas *Musician*
9 Village Road, London, N3, UNITED KINGDOM (UK)

Vasile, Radu *Prime Minister*
Premier's Office, Piata Vicotriel 1, Bucharest, 71201, ROMANIA

Vasilyev, Vladimir V *Ballerina, Dancer*
Bolshoi Theater, Teatralnaya Pl 1, Moscow, 103009, RUSSIA

Vasquez, Juan F *Judge*
US Tax Court, 400 2nd St NW, Washington, DC 20217 USA

Vasquez, Rana Mario *Publisher*
El Sol de Mexico, Guillermo Prieto 7, Mexico City, DF, MEXICO

Vasquez, Randy
10600 Holman Ave. #1, Los Angeles, CA 90024

Vass, Joan *Fashion Designer*
Joan Vass Inc, 36 E 31st St, New York, NY 10016 USA

Vasser, Jimmy *Race Car Driver*
2398 Broadway St, San Francisco, CA 94115 USA

Vassey, Liz *Actor*
Endeavor Agency LLC (LA), 9601 Wilshire Blvd Fl 3, Beverly Hills, CA 90210 USA

Vassilieva, Sofia *Actor*
William Morris Agency (WMA-LA), 1 William Morris Pl, Beverly Hills, CA 90212 USA

Vassillou, George V *President*
PO Box 874, 21 Academiou Ave, Aglandjia, Nicosia, CYPRUS

Vasu, P *Actor, Bollywood*
25 D Tilak Street, T Nagar, Chennai, TN 600017, INDIA

Vaswani, Vivek *Actor, Bollywood*
141 142 Dalamal Park, Cuffe Parade, Bombay, MS 400 005, INDIA

Vasyuchenko, Yuri *Ballerina, Dancer*
Bolshoi Theater, Teatralnaya Pl 1, Moscow, 103009, RUSSIA

Vasyutin, Vladimir V *Cricketer*
Potcha Kosmonavtov, Moskovskoi Oblasti, Syvisdny Goroduk, 141160, RUSSIA

Vaughan, Denis E *Musician*
Schofer/Gold, 50 Riverside Dr, New York, NY 10024 USA

Vaughan, Greg
William Morris Agency (WMA-LA), 1 William Morris Pl, Beverly Hills, CA 90212 USA

Vaughan, Jimmie *Musician*
2300 S 3rd St, Austin, TX 78704 USA

Vaughan, Martha *Biologist*
11608 W Hill Dr, Rockville, MD 20852 USA

Vaughan, Norman *Mountaineer*
Schulin Lake Trail, Talkeetna, AK 99676 USA

Vaughan, Peter *Actor*
International Creative Mgmt, 76 Oxford St, London, W1N 0AX, UNITED KINGDOM (UK)

Vaughn, David *Basketball Player*
New Jersey Nets, 390 Murray Hill Parkway, East Rutherford, NJ 07073 USA

Vaughn, Gregory L (Greg) *Baseball Player*
6309 Thresher Court, Elk Grove, CA 95758 USA

Vaughn, Jacque *Basketball Player*
Atlanta Hawks, 190 Marietta St SW, Atlanta, GA 30303 USA

Vaughn, Jimmie *Musician*
Mark I Mgmt, PO Box 29480, Austin, TX 78755 USA

Vaughn, John H (Johnny) *Football Player, Coach*
Highway 6 W, Oxford, MS 38655 USA

Vaughn, Jonathan S (Jon) *Football Player*
2263 Franham Lane, Florissant, MO 63033 USA

Vaughn, Linda *Race Car Driver*
2865 S Eagle Road, Newtown, PA 18940 USA

Vaughn, Maurice S (Mo) *Baseball Player*
8008 Sacramento St, Fair Oaks, CA 95628 USA

Vaughn, Moe
8008 Sacramento St, Fair Oaks, CA 95628-7547

Vaughn, Ned *Actor*
James/Levy/Jacobson, 3500 W Olive Ave, #920, Burbank, CA 91505 USA

Vaughn, Robert *Actor*
PO Box 2071, Los Angeles, CA 90028 USA

Vaughn, Terri J *Actor*
Siegal Company, The, 445 S Beverly Dr #100, Beverly Hills, CA 90212 USA

Vaughn, Vince *Actor*
United Talent Agency, 9560 Wilshire Blvd, #500, Beverly Hills, CA 90212 USA

Vaugier, Emmanuelle *Actor*
Innovative Artists (LA), 1505 Tenth St, Santa Monica, CA 90401 USA

Vavra, Otakar *Director, Writer*
Music & Arts Academy, Smetanova Nabrezo 2, Prague 1, 11000, CZECH REPUBLIC

Vazquez, Javier *Baseball Player*
Montreal Expos, PO Box 500, Station M, Montreal, H1V 3P, Canada

Veale, Robert A (Bob) *Baseball Player*
2833 Bush Blvd, Birmingham, AL 35208 USA

Veasey, Josephine *Opera Singer*
5 Meadow Biew, Whitechurch, Hunts, RG28 7BL, UNITED KINGDOM (UK)

Vecchione, Mike *Scientist*
Nat'l Oceanic/Atmosphere Admin, 14th & Constitution, Washington, DC 20230 USA

Vecsei, Eva H *Architect*
Vecsei Architects, 1425 Rue du Fort, Montreal, QC, H3H 2C2, CANADA

Vecsey, George S *Writer, Sportscaster*
New York Times, Editorial Dept, 229 W 43rd St, New York, NY 10036 USA

Vedder, Eddie *Musician*
Creative Artists Agency LCC (CAA-LA), 9830 Wilshire Blvd, Beverly Hills, CA 90212 USA

Vee, Bobby *Musician, Songwriter*
Rockhouse Studio, PO Box 41, Sauk Rapids, MN 56379 USA

Veerapha, P S *Actor, Bollywood*
Porur, Chennai, TN 600116, INDIA

Vega, Alexa *Actor, Musician*
S D B Partners, 1801 Ave of Stars, #902, Los Angeles, CA 90067 USA

Vega, Suzanne *Musician*
William Morris Agency (WMA-NY), 1325 Ave of the Americas, New York, NY 10019 USA

Vegas, Dirty *Music Group*
Creative Artists Agency LCC (CAA-LA), 9830 Wilshire Blvd, Beverly Hills, CA 90212 USA

Veil, Simone *Government Official*
11 Place Vauban, Paris, 75007, FRANCE

Vejar, Chico *Boxer*
56 Glenbrook Road, #3214, Stamford, CT 06902 USA

Vejtasa, Stanley W (Swede) *War Hero*
1649 Summit Lane, Escondido, CA 92025 USA

Vel Johnson, Reginald *Actor*
DGRW, 1501 Broadway, Suite 703, New York, NY 10036

Velarde, Randy *Baseball Player*
4902 Thames Ct, Midland, TX 79705 USA

Velasquez, Jaci *Musician*
Jaci Inc, PO Box 3568, Brentwood, TN 37024 USA

Velasquez, Jorge
770 Allerton Ave., Bronx, NY 10467

Velasquez, Jorge L Jr *Jockey*
770 Allerton Ave, Bronx, NY 10467 USA

Velasquez, Nadine *Actor*
Don Buchwald & Associates Inc (LA), 6500 Wilshire Blvd #2200, Los Angeles, CA 90048 USA

Velasquez, Patricia *Actor, Model*
Lasher McManus Robinson, 1964 Westwood Blvd, #400, Los Angeles, CA 90025 USA

Velazquez, Patricia *Actor*
Mosaic Media Group, 9200 Sunset Blvd Fl 10, Los Angeles, CA 90069 USA

Velez, Eddie *Actor*
Stone Manners Talent Agency, 6500 Wilshire Blvd, Ste 550, Los Angeles, CA 90048 USA

Velez, Lauren *Actor*
Gersh Agency, 232 N Canon Dr, Beverly Hills, CA 90210 USA

Velga, Carlos A Wahnon de C *Prime Minister*
Prime Minister's Office, Varzea CP 16, Praia, Santiago, CAPE VERDE

Velgos, Alicia *Actor*
William Morris Agency, 151 El Camino Dr, Beverly Hills, CA 90212 USA

Velikhov, Yevgeni P *Physicist*
Kurchatovskiy Institute, Kurchatova Pl 1, Moscow, 12182, RUSSIA

Veljohnson, Reginald *Actor*
9637 Allenwood Dr, Los Angeles, CA 90046 USA

Vella, John *Football Player*
5350 Willow Glen Place, Castro Valley, CA 94546 USA

Veloso, Caetano *Musician, Songwriter*
Natasha Records/Shows, Rua Marquis Sao Vincente, Rio de Janiero, BRAZIL

Veltman, Martinus J G *Nobel Prize Laureate*
Sachubertiaan 15, Bilthoven, 3723, NETHERLANDS

Velvet, Jimmy
PO Box 808, Lititz, PA 17543

Venables, Terry F *Football Coach*
Terry Venables Holdings, 213 Putney Bridge Road, London, SW15 2NY, UNITED KINGDOM (UK)

Vendetta Red *Music Group*
Spivak Sobol Entertainment, 11845 W Olympic Blvd #1125, Los Angeles, CA 90064 USA

Venditti, Antonello
Via Zara 12, Rome, ITALY

Veneman, Ann *Secretary*
Agriculture Department, 14th St & Independence Ave SW, Washington, DC 20250 USA

Venet, Bernar *Artist*
533 Canal St, New York, NY 10013 USA

Vengerov, Maxim *Musician*
Lies Askonas, 6 Henrietta St, London, WC2E 8LA, UNITED KINGDOM (UK)

Venitucci, Michele *Actor*
Carol Levi Co, VIa Giuseppe Pisanelli, Rome, 00196, ITALY

Venkataraman, Ramaswamy *Ex-President*
Pothigal, Greenways Road, Chennai, TN 600028, INDIA

Venniraadai, Murthy *Actor, Bollywood*
44 4th Main Road, Kottur Garden,
Chennai, TN 600085, INDIA

Venora, Diane *Actor*
Innovative Artists, 1505 10th St, Santa
Monica, CA 90401 USA

Ventimiglia, John
9150 Wilshire Blvd. #350, Beverly Hills,
CA 90212

Ventimiglia, Jon *Actor*
Gersh Agency, The (NY), 41 Madison Ave
Fl 33, New York, NY 10010 USA

Ventimiglia, Milo *Actor*
Much and House Public Relations, 8075
West Third Street, Suite 500, Los Angeles,
CA 90048

Ventimilia, Jeffrey *Actor*
International Creative Management
(ICM-LA), 8942 Wilshire Blvd, Beverly
Hills, CA 90211 USA

Ventresca, Vincent *Actor*
Mindel/Donigan, 9057 Nemo St, #C, West
Hollywood, CA 90069 USA

Ventura, Jesse *Politician*
Jesse Ventura's America, 1 MSNBC Plaza,
Secaucus, NJ 07094 USA

Ventura, Robin *Baseball Player*
2755 Coast View Dr, Arroyo Grande, CA
93420 USA

Ventura, Robin M *Baseball Player*
106 Dingletown Road, Greenwich, CT
06830 USA

Ventures, The *Music Group*
11761 E Speedway Blvd, Tucson, AZ
85748-2017 USA

Venturi, Ken *Golfer*
161 Waterford Circle, Rancho Mirage, CA
92270 USA

Vera, Audry *Actor*
Televisa, Blvd Adolfo Lopez Mateos 232,
Colonia San Angel INN, DF, CP 01060,
MEXICO

Verastegui, Eduardo *Actor*
The Firm

Verbinski, Gore *Director, Producer*
Endeavor Agency LLC (LA), 9601 Wilshire
Blvd Fl 3, Beverly Hills, CA 90210 USA

Verdugo, Elena
PO Box 2048, Chula Vista, CA 92012

Vereen, Ben *Actor, Dancer, Musician*
424 W End Ave #18C, New York, NY
10024 USA

Vergara, Sofia *Actor, Musician*
Latin World Entertainment Agency, 2800
Biscayne Blvd, Miami, FL 33137 USA

Verhoeven, Lis
Merzstrasse 14, Munich, GERMANY,
D-81679

Verhoeven, Paul *Director, Writer*
Provident Management, 10345 W
Olympis Blvd, Los Angeles, CA 90064
USA

Verica, Tom *Actor*
20 Ironsides St, #18, Marina del Rey, CA
90292 USA

Verma, Deven *Actor, Bollywood*
7B Todiwala Road, Pune, MS 400041,
INDIA

Vermeil, Dick *Coach*
Kansas City Chiefs, 1 Arrowhead Dr,
Kansas City, MO 64129 USA

Vernon, John
5751 Stansbury Ave., Van Nuys, CA
91401-4238

Vernon, Kate
1505 10th St., Santa Monica, CA 90401

Verraros, Jim *Musician*
Fox Television Studios, 10201 W Pico
Blvd, Bldg 41, Los Angeles, CA 90035

Versace, Donatella *Fashion Designer*
Gianni Versace SPA, Via Della Spige 25,
Milan, 20221, ITALY

Versini, Marie
23 res. Elysses 78170 La Celle-St, Cloud,
FRANCE

Verve Pipe, The *Music Group*
Monterey Peninsula Artists (Monterey),
509 Hartnell St, Monterey, CA 93940 USA

Verveen, Arie *Actor*
Stone Meyer & Genow, 9665 Wilshire
Blvd #510, Beverly Hills, CA 90212 USA

Vessey, Tricia *Actor*
Brillstein-Grey Entertainment, 9150
Wilshire Blvd #350, Beverly Hills, CA
90212 USA

Vest, R Lamar *Religious Leader*
Church of God, PO Box 2430, Cleveland,
TN 37320 USA

Vetri, Victoria *Actor*
7045 Hawthorn Ave, #206, Los Angeles,
CA 90028 USA

Vetrov, Aleksandr *Ballerina, Dancer*
Bolshoi Theater, Teatralnaya Pl 1,
Moscow, 103009, RUSSIA

Vettori, Ernst *Skier*
Fohrenweg 1, Absam, Eichat, 6060,
AUSTRIA

Vettrus, Richard J *Religious Leader*
Church of Lutheran Brethren, 707
Crestview Dr, West Union, IA 52175 USA

Vez, El
3322 Hamilton Way, Los Angeles, CA
90026-2112

Vicario, Arantxa Sanchez
22 E. 71st St., New York, NY 10021

Vichitra *Actor, Bollywood*
821 Jeevanandam Salai, Chennai, TN
600078, INDIA

Vick, Michael *Football Player*
5108 West Creek Court, Suffolk, VA
23435 USA

Vickaryous, Scott *Actor*
Foundation Management, 2121 Avenue of
the Stars, 29th Floor, Los Angeles, CA
90067 USA

Vickers, Brian *Race Car Driver*
27 High Tech Blvd, Thomasville, NC
27360 USA

Vickers, Jonathan S (Jon) *Opera Singer*
Collingtree, 18 Riddlells Bay Road,
Warwick, WK 04, BERMUDA

Vickers, Steve *Hockey Player*
209 Washington Ave, Batavia, NY 14020
USA

Vickers, Yvette
PO Box 292479, Phelan, CA 92329-2479

Victor, James
1944 N. Whitley Ave. #306, Los Angeles,
CA 90036

Victoria *Royalty*
Royal Palace, Kung Slottet, Stottsbacken,
Stockholm, 11130, SWEDEN

Victorin (Ursache), Archbishop *Religious
Leader*
Romanian Orthodox Church, 19959
Riopelle St, Detroit, MI 48203 USA

Vidal, Christina *Actor*
McGowan Management, 8733 W Sunset
Blvd #103, W Hollywood, CA 90069 USA

Vidal, Deborah *Golfer*
Tony Criscuolo, 8425 NW 222nd Ave,
Alachua, FL 32615 USA

Vidal, Gore *Writer*
Via Fusco 20, Ravello, SA, 84010, ITALY

Vidal, Jean-Pierre *Skier*
Ski Federation, 50 Rue de Marquisats, BP
51, Annecy Cedex, 74011, FRANCE

Vidal, Lisa *Actor*
William Morris Agency, 151 El Camino
Dr, Beverly Hills, CA 90212 USA

Vidal, Ricardo J Cardinal *Religious Leader*
Chancery, PO Box 52, Cebu City, 6401,
PHILIPINES

Vidal, Rodrigo *Actor*
Televisa, Blvd Adolfo Lopez Mateos 232,
Colonia San Angel INN, DF, CP 01060,
MEXICO

Vidali, Lynn *Swimmer*
14750 Mosegard, Morgan Hills, CA
95037 USA

Vidmar, Peter *Gymnast*
23832 Via Roble, Coto De Caza, CA
92679 USA

Vidro, Jose A C *Baseball Player*
Montreal Expos, Olympic Stadium,
Montreal, QC, H1V 3N7, CANADA

Vie, Richard C *Business Person*
PO Box 191, Lake Forest, IL 60045 USA

Viehboeck, Franz *Cosmonaut*
Brunnerbergstr 3021, Perchtoldsdorf,
2380, AUSTRIA

Vieillard, Roger *Artist*
7 Rue de l'Estrapade, Paris, 75005,
FRANCE

Vieira, Meredith *Commentator*
ABC- TV, News Dept, 77 W 66th St, New
York, NY 10023 USA

Vieluf, Vince *Actor*
Endeavor Agency LLC (LA), 9601 Wilshire
Blvd Fl 3, Beverly Hills, CA 90210 USA

Viener, John *Actor*
Don Buchwald & Associates Inc (LA),
6500 Wilshire Blvd #2200, Los Angeles,
CA 90048 USA

Viera, Joey
4253 Navajo Ave., No. Hollywood, CA
91602

Viereck, Peter *Writer*
12 Silver St, South Hadley, MA 01075
USA

Viertel, Peter Wyhergut
7250 Klosters, Grisons, SWITZERLAND

Vieth, Michelle *Actor*
Televisa, Blvd Adolfo Lopez Mateos 232, Colonia San Angel INN, DF, CP 01060, MEXICO

Vieyra, Veronica *Actor*
Telefe - Argentina, Pavon 2444 (C1248AAT), Buenos Aires, ARGENTINA

Vig, Butch *Musician*
Borman Entertainment, 1250 6th St, #401, Santa Monica, CA 90401 USA

Vigman, Gillian *Actor*
Hansen Jacobson Teller & Hoberman, 450 N Roxbury Dr Fl 8, Beverly Hills, CA 90210 USA

Vigneault, Alain *Hockey Player, Coach*
Saint Louis Blues, Sawis Center, 1401 Clark Ave, Saint Louis, MO 63103 USA

Vigneron, Thierry *Track Athlete*
Adidas USA, 5675 N Blackstock Road, Spartanburg, SC 29303 USA

Vignesh *Actor, Bollywood*
AP 210 9th Street, 2nd Sector, Chennai, TN 600078, INDIA

Vigoda, Abe *Actor*
Scott Sandler, 13701 Riverside Dr, #201, Sherman Oaks, CA 91423 USA

Viguerie, Richard
7777 Leesburg Pike, Falls Church, VA 22043

Vijay, S A *Actor, Bollywood*
64 Kaveri Street, Saligramam, Chennai, TN 600093, INDIA

Vijaya K R *Actor, Bollywood*
9 Raman Street, Chennai, TN 600018, INDIA

Vijayakanth *Actor, Bollywood*
54 Kannambal Street, Kannapiran Colony Saligramam, Chennai, TN 600093, INDIA

Vijayakumar, Manjula *Actor, Bollywood*
236 & 237 8th Street, Asthalakshmi Nagar, Chennai, TN 600116, INDIA

Vila, Bob *Actor, Producer, Television Host*
115 Kingston Street, #300, Boston, MA 02111

Vilanch, Bruce *Writer*
Bragman/Nyman/Cafarelli, 9171 Wilshire Blvd #300, Beverly Hills, CA 90210 USA

Vilanich, Bruce *Comedian*
William Morris Agency (WMA-LA), 1 William Morris Pl, Beverly Hills, CA 90212 USA

Vilar, Tracy
9200 Sunset Blvd. #1130, Los Angeles, CA 90069

Vilas, Guillermo
86 av. Foch F-75116, Paris, FRANCE

Vilasuso, Jordi *Actor*
Innovative Artists (LA), 1505 Tenth St, Santa Monica, CA 90401 USA

Vilella, Edward
905 Lincoln Blvd., Miami, FL 33139

Viljoen, Marais *President*
PO Box 5555, Pretoria, 0001, SOUTH AFRICA

Villapiano, Phillip J (Phil) *Football Player*
21 Riverside Dr, Rumson, NJ 07760 USA

Villari, Guy *Musician*
293 Airport Road, Liberty, NY 12754 USA

Villarroel, Vernoica *Opera Singer*
Columbia Artists Mgmt Inc, 165 W 57th St, New York, NY 10019 USA

Villella, Edward J *Ballerina, Choreographer*
Miami City Ballet, 2200 Liberty Ave, Miami Beach, FL 33139 USA

Villeneuve, Jacques *Race Car Driver*
BAR Team, PO Box 5014, Brackley, Northants, NN13 7YY, UNITED KINGDOM (UK)

Villiers, Christopher *Actor*
Hillman Trelfall, 33 Brookfield, Highgate W Hill, London, N6 6AT, UNITED KINGDOM (UK)

Villiers, James *Actor*
International Creative Mgmt, 76 Oxford St, London, W1N 0AX, UNITED KINGDOM (UK)

Vimond, Paul M *Architect*
91 Ave Niel, Paris, 75017 USA

Vinatieri, Adam *Football Player*
PO Box 2779, Attleboro Falls, MA 02763 USA

Vince, Pruitt Taylor *Actor*
520 Salemo Dr, Pacific Palisades, CA 90272 USA

Vince, Taylor *Misc*
20160 NW 9th Dr, Pembroke Pines, FL 33029 USA

Vincent, Amy *Cinematographer*
5932 Graciosa Dr, Los Angeles, CA 90068 USA

Vincent, Jan-Michael *Actor*
Artists Group, 10100 Santa Monica Blvd #2490, Los Angeles, CA 90067 USA

Vincent, Jay *Basketball Player*
PO Box 27459, Lansing, MI 48909 USA

Vincent, June
1541 Via Entrada del Lago, Lake San Marcos, CA 92069

Vincent, Marjorie
1325 Boardwalk, Atlantic City, NJ 08401

Vincent, Rhonda *Musician*
Keith Case Assoc, 1025 17th Ave S #200, Nashville, TN 37212 USA

Vincent, Richard F *Misc*
House of Lords, Westminster, London, SW1A 0PW, UNITED KINGDOM (UK)

Vincent, Rick *Songwriter, Musician*
Carter Career Mgmt, 1028 18th Ave S, #B, Nashville, TN 37212 USA

Vincent, Sam *Basketball Player*
PO Box 27459, Lansing, MI 48909 USA

Vincent, Troy *Football Player*
460 Roeloffs Road, Yardley, PA 19067 USA

Vincent, Virginia *Actor*
1001 Hammond St, Los Angeles, CA 90069 USA

Vincz, Melanie *Actor*
2212 Earle Court, Redondo Beach, CA 90278 USA

Vineetha *Actor, Bollywood*
Flat No 3B Chandrika Apartments, 5 & 6 Ashok Avenue Directors Colony Kodambakkam, Chennai, TN 600024, INDIA

Vines, C Jerry *Religious Leader*
First Baptist Church, 124 W Ashley St, Jacksonville, FL 32202 USA

Vines, Ellsworth
4680 Irvine Blvd. #203, Irvine, CA 92620

Vines, The *Music Group*
Creative Artists Agency LCC (CAA-LA), 9830 Wilshire Blvd, Beverly Hills, CA 90212 USA

Vining, David *Doctor, Scientist*
1725 Briar Lake Road, Winston Salem, NC 27103 USA

Vinith, R *Actor, Bollywood*
Flat G 1, 68 Halls Road Kilpauk, Chennai, TN 600010, INDIA

Vinnie *Artist, Music Group*
International Creative Mgmt, 8942 Wilshire Blvd #219, Beverly Hills, CA 90211 USA

Vinogradov, Oleg M *Ballerina*
Mariinsky Theater, Teatralnaya Square 1, Saint Petersburg, 190000, RUSSIA

Vinogradov, Pavel V *Misc*
Potchta Kosmonavtov, Moskovskol Oblasti, Syvisdny Goroduk, 141160, RUSSIA

Vinoly, Rafael *Architect*
1016 5th Ave, New York, NY 10028 USA

Vinothini *Actor, Bollywood*
3 Alagar Perumal Koil Street, Chennai, TN 600026, INDIA

Vinson, James S *Educator*
University of Evansville, President's Office, Evansville, IN 47722 USA

Vint, Jesse
10637 Burbank Blvd, No. Hollywood, CA 91601

Vint, Jesse Lee III *Actor*
Film Artists, 13563 1/2 Ventura Blvd #200, Sherman Oaks, CA 91423 USA

Vintas, Gustavo *Actor*
Artists Group (LA), 10100 Santa Monica Blvd #2490, Los Angeles, CA 90067 USA

Vinton, Bobby *Musician*
MPI Talent Agency, 9255 Sunset Blvd #804, Los Angeles, CA 90069 USA

Vinton, Will *Animator*
William Morris Agency, 151 El Camino Dr, Beverly Hills, CA 90212 USA

Viola, Bill *Artist*
282 Granada Ave, Long Beach, CA 90803 USA

Viola, Frank
844 Sweetwater Island Circle, Longwood, FL 32779-2345

Viola, Frank J Jr *Baseball Player*
9868 Kilgore Road, Orlando, FL 32836 USA

Viola, Lisa *Dancer*
Paul Taylor Dance Co, 552 Broadway, New York, NY 10012 USA

Virata, Cesar E *Prime Minister*
63 E Maya Dr, Quezon City, PHILIPPINES

Virdon, William C (Bill) *Baseball Player*
1311 E River Road, Springfield, MO 65804 USA

Viren, Lasse *Track Athlete*
Suomen Urhellulirto Ry, Box 25202, Helsinki 25, 00250, FINLAND

Virts, Terry W Jr *Astronaut*
1904 Edgewater Court, Friendswood, TX 77546 USA

Virtue, Doreen *Writer*
Angel Therapy, PO Box 5100, Carlsbad, CA 92018

Virtue, Frank *Musician*
8309 Rising Sun Ave, Philadelphia, PA 19111 USA

Virtue, Thomas (Tom) *Actor*
Gage Group, The (LA), 14724 Ventura Blvd #505, Los Angeles, CA 91403 USA

Virzaladze, Elizo K *Musician, Music Group*
Moscow Conservatory, Bolshaya Nikitskaya Str 13, Moscow, RUSSIA

Vis, Anthony *Religious Leader*
Reformed Church in America, 475 Riverside Dr, New York, NY 10115 USA

Viscardi, Johnston Catherine *Publisher*
Mirabella Magazine, 200 Madison Ave, New York, NY 10016 USA

Visculo, Sal
6491 Ivarene Ave., Los Angeles, CA 90068

Viscuso, Sal *Actor*
6491 Ivarene Ave, Los Angeles, CA 90068 USA

Vise, David A *Journalist*
Washington Post, Editorial Dept, 1150 15th St NW, Washingfon, DC 20071 USA

Vishnevskaya, Galina P *Opera Singer*
Gazetny Per 13 #79, Moscow, 103009, RUSSIA

Vishnyova, Diana V *Ballerina*
Maninsky Theater, Teatralnaya Square 1, Saint Petersburg, 190000, RUSSIA

Visitor, Nana *Actor*
Gersh Agency, 232 N Canon Dr, Beverly Hills, CA 90210 USA

Visnjic, Goran *Actor*
United Talent Agency, 9560 Wilshire Blvd #500, Beverly Hills, CA 90212 USA

Viso, Michel *Misc*
7 Domaine Chateau-Gaillard, Maison-d' Alfort, 94700, FRANCE

Visscher, Maurice B *Doctor*
120 Melbourne Ave SE, Minneapolis, MN 55414 USA

Visser, Angela
819 N. Sycamore Ave, Los Angeles, CA 90038-3816

Visser, Lesley *Sportscaster*
CBS-TV, Sports Dept, 51 W 52nd St, New York, NY 10019 USA

Visu *Actor, Bollywood*
11 Agastheya Nagar, Kilpaul Garden, Chennai, TN 600012, INDIA

Vitale, Carol *Actor, Model*
1516 S Bundy Dr #309, Los Angeles, CA 90025 USA

Vitale, Dick *Sportscaster, Basketball Player, Coach*
ESPN-TV, Sports Department ESPN Plaza, 935 Middle St, Bristol, CT 06010 USA

Vitale, Joe

Vitamin-C *Musician, Actor*
International Creative Mgmt, 8942 Wilshire Blvd #219, Beverly Hills, CA 90211 USA

Viterbi, Andrew J *Engineer, Scientist*
QUALCOMM Inc, 5775 Morehouse Dr, San Diego, CA 92121 USA

Vitez, Michael *Journalist*
Philadelphia Inquirer, Editorial Dept, 400 N Broad St, Philadelphia, PA 19130 USA

Vithayathil, Varkey Cardinal *Religious Leader*
Syro-Malabar Archiepiscopal Curia, Bharath Matha College, Kerala, INDIA

Vitolo, Dennis *Race Car Driver*
2130 Intracoastal Dr, Fort Lauderdale, FL 33305 USA

Vitousek, Peter M *Misc*
Stanford University, Biological Science Dept, Stanford, CT 94305 USA

Vittadini, Adrienne *Fashion Designer*
Adrienne Vittadini Inc, 575 Fashion Ave, New York, NY 10018 USA

Vitti, Monica *Actor*
IPC, Via F Siacci 38, Rome, 00197, ITALY

Vittori, Roberto *Astronaut*
Europe Astronaut Center, Linder Hole, Box 906096, Cologne, 51127, GERMANY

Vitukhnovskaya, Alina A *Writer*
Leningradskoye Shosse 80 #89, Moscow, 125565, RUSSIA

Vivas, Juan Carlos *Actor*
Gabriel Blanco Iglesias (Mexico), Rio Balsas 35-32, Colonia Cuauhtemoc, DF, 06500, Mexico

Vivek *Actor, Bollywood*
9 Subhiksha Apts, 5 Tank Street U.I. Colony, Chennai, TN 600024, INDIA

Viviano, Joseph P *Business Person*
Hershey Foods Corp, 100 Crystal A Dr, Hershey, PA 17033 USA

Vizquel, Omar E *Baseball Player*
Blvd Del Cafetel, Res Adroana 6 Pisa, Caracas, VENEZUELA

Vlacil, Frantisek *Director*
Cinska 5, Prague 6, 160 00, CZECH REPUBLIC

Vladeck, Judith P *Attorney General*
Vladeck Waidman Elias Engelhard, 1501 Broadway, New York, NY 10036 USA

Vlady, Marina *Actor*
10 Ave de Marivaux, Mission Lafitte, 78800, FRANCE

Vlardo, Vladimir V *Musician*
457 Piedmont Road, Cresskill, NJ 07626 USA

Vlassic, Robert
1910 Rothmor Rd., Bloomfield, MI 48304

Vlk, Miloslav Cardinal *Religious Leader*
Arcibiskupstvi, Hradcanske Nam 16/56, Prague 1, 119 02, CZECH REPUBLIC

Vo Nguyen Giap *General*
Dang Cong San Vietnam, 1C Blvd Hoang Van Thu, Hanoi, VIETNAM

Vo Van Kiet *Prime Minister*
Prime Minister's Office, Hoang Hoa Thum, Hanoi, VIETNAM

Voevodsky, Vladimir *Mathematician*
22 Earle Lane, Princeton, NJ 08540 USA

Vogel, Dariene *Actor*
Michael Slessinger, 8730 Sunset Blvd #220W, Los Angeles, CA 90069 USA

Vogel, Darlene *Actor*
Michael Slessinger & Assoc, 8730 Sunset Blvd #270, Los Angeles, CA 90069 USA

Vogel, Hans-Jochen *Government Official*
Stresemanstr 6, Bonn-Bad Godesberg, 53123, GERMANY

Vogel, Mark *Composer*
Gorfaine/Schwartz, 13245 Riverside Dr #450, Sherman Oaks, CA 91423 USA

Vogel, Mike *Actor, Skateboarder*
Management 360, 9111 Wilshire Blvd, Beverly Hills, CA 90210 USA

Vogel, Mitch *Actor*
3335 Honeysuckle Ave, Palmdale, CA 93550 USA

Vogelstein, Bert *Doctor, Scientist*
Johns Hopkins University, Medical School, Oncology Center, Baltimore, MD 21218 USA

Vogler, Karl Michael
Auweg 8, Seehausen, GERMANY, D-82418

Vogt, Lars *Musician*
I C M Artists, 40 W 57th St, New York, NY 10019 USA

Vogt, Paul *Actor*
Coppage Company, The, 5411 Camellia Ave, N Hollywood, CA 91601 USA

Vogt, Peter K *Scientist, Misc*
LA County/USC Medical School, 2011 Zonal Ave, Los Angeles, CA 90089 USA

Vogt, Rochus E *Physicist, Astronomer*
California Institute of Technology, Bridge Laboratory, Pasadena, CA 91125 USA

Vogts, Hans-Hubert (Berti) *Soccer Player*
Mozartweg 2, Korschenbroich, 41352, GERMANY

Voight, Jon *Actor*
9660 Oak Pass Road, Beverly Hills, CA 90210 USA

Voigt, Cynthia *Writer*
Atheneum Publishers, 866 3rd Ave, New York, NY 10022 USA

Voigt, Deborah *Opera Singer*
Columbia Artists Mgmt Inc, 165 W 57th St, New York, NY 10019 USA

Voinovich, George V *Governor, Senator*
601 Lakeside Ave E, Cleveland, OH 44114 USA

Voiselle, William S (Bill) *Baseball Player*
105 Lowell St, Ninety Six, SC 29666 USA

Voisine, Rich
1505 W. 2nd Ave. #200, Vancouver, CANADA, BC V6H 3Y4

Volberding, Paul *Scientist*
General Hospital AIDS Activities Dept, 995 Potrero Ave, San Francisco, CA 94110 USA

Volcker, Paul *Government Official*
151 E 79th St, New York, NY 10021 USA

Voldstad, John *Actor*
24812 Van Owen St, West Hills, CA 91300 USA

Volibracht, Michaele *Fashion Designer, Artist*
General Delivery, Safety Harbor, FL 34695 USA

Volk, Igor P *Misc*
Potchta Kosmonavtov, Moskovskoi Oblasti, Syvisdny Goroduk, 141160, RUSSIA

Volk, Patricia *Writer*
Gloria Loomis, 133 E 35th St, New York, NY 10016 USA

Volk, Phil *Musician*
Paradise Artists, 108 E Matilija St, Ojai, CA 93023 USA

Volk, Richard R (Rick) *Football Player*
13605 Bardon Road, Phoenix, MD 21131 USA

Volker, Sandra *Swimmer*
DESG, Mensingen Str 68, Munich, 80992, GERMANY

Volkert, Stephan *Athlete*
Semmelweisstr 42, Cologne, 51061, GERMANY

Volkmann, Elisabeth *Opera Singer*
Sonnenstr 20, Munich, 80331, GERMANY

Volkov, Aleksandr A *Misc*
Potchta Kosmonavtov, Moskovskoi Oblasti, Syvisdny Goroduk, 141160, RUSSIA

Voll, Rich *Actor*
Career Management Corp, 1850 Sawtelle Blvd #450, Los Angeles, CA 90025

Vollebak, Knut *Government Official*
Royal Norwegian Embassy, 2720 34th St NW, Washington, DC 20008 USA

Vollenweider, Andreas *Musician*
Sempacher Str 16, Zurich, 8032, SWITZERLAND

Volodos, Arcadl *Musician*
Columbia Artists Mgmt Inc, 165 W 57th St, New York, NY 10019 USA

Voloshin, Valeri *Cosmonaut*
Potchta Kosmonavtov, Moskovskoi Oblasti, Syvisdny Goroduk, 141160, RUSSIA

Volpe, Joseph (Joe) *Opera Singer, Misc*
Metropolitan Opera Assn, Lincoln Center Plaza, New York, NY 10023 USA

Volstad, John
15924 Leadwell St., Van Nuys, CA 91406

Volynov, Boris V *Misc*
Potchta Kosmonavtov, Moskovskoi Oblasti, Syvisdny Goroduk, 141160, RUSSIA

Volz, Nedra
5606 E. Fairfield St., Mesa, AZ 86205-5522

Volz, Wolfgang
Konstanzer Str. 8, Berlin, GERMANY, D-10707

Von Bulow, Claus
960 Fifth Ave., New York, NY 10021

von Damm-Gurtler, Helene
Hotel Sacher bei der Oper, Vienna, AUSTRIA, 1010

von Daniken, Eric
CH-Baselstr. 1, Feldbrunnen, Switzerland, 4532

von Detten, Erik *Actor*
Reel Talent Management, 980 N Bundy, Los Angeles, CA 90049 USA

von Dohlen, Lenny
N 121 San Vicente Blvd, . Beverly Hills, CA 90211

Von Erick's, The
145 Columbia St. W #9, Waterloo, CANADA, Ont. N2L 3

Von Furstenberg, Betsy
230 Central Park W., New York, NY 10028

Von Furstenberg, Diane *Fashion Designer*
745 Fifth Ave #2400, New York, NY 10151 USA

Von Furstenberg, Diane *Designer*
389 West 12th Street, New York, NY 10014 USA

von Habsburg, Otto
Hindenburgstr. 15, Pocking, GERMANY, D-82343

von Kusserow, Ingeborg
16-D Avercorn Pl., London, ENGLAND, NW8

von Oy, Jenna *Actor*
19 Saddle Ridge Rd., Newtown, CT 06470-2417

Von Scherler Mayer, Daisy *Director*
Endeavor Agency LLC (LA), 9601 Wilshire Blvd Fl 3, Beverly Hills, CA 90210 USA

Von Sydow, Max *Actor*
United Talent Agency (UTA), 9560 Wilshire Blvd, Beverly Hills, CA 90212 USA

von Trier, Lars *Writer, Director*
Anonymous Content, 8522 National Blvd #101, Culver City, CA 90232 USA

Von Trotta, Margarethe *Director*
Turkenstr 91, Munich, 80799, GERMANY

von Weizsacker, Carl
Alpenstr. 15, Socking, GERMANY, D-82319

von Weizsacker, Richard *Ex-President*
Meisenstr 6, Berlin, D-14195, GERMANY

von Wietersheim, Sharon
Leopoldstr. 19, Munich, GERMANY, D-80802

VonAroldingen, Karin *Ballerina*
New York City Ballet, Lincoln Center Plaza, New York, NY 10023 USA

VonBulow, Vicco (Loriot) *Actor*
Hohenweg 19, Munsing-Ammerland, 82451, GERMANY

VonDerHeyden, Karl I M *Business Person*
PepsiCo Inc, 700 Anderson Hill Road, Purchase, NY 10577 USA

VonDetten, Erik *Actor*
William Morris Agency, 151 El Camino Dr, Beverly Hills, CA 90212 USA

VonDohnanyi, Christoph *Conductor*
Cleveland Orchestra, Severance Hall, Cleveland, OH 44106 USA

VonErich, Waldo *Wrestler*
Columbia Sports Med Center, 9-145 Columbia W, Waterloo, ON N2L 3L2, CANADA

VonEschenbach, Andrew *Doctor*
National Cancer Institute, 9000 Rockville Pike, Bethesda, MD 20892 USA

VonFurstenberg, Betsy *Actor*
230 Central Park West, New York, NY 10024 USA

VonFurstenberg, Diane *Fashion Designer*
389 W 12th St, New York, NY 10014 USA

VonFurstenberg, Egon *Fashion Designer*
50 E 72nd St, New York, NY 10021 USA

VonGarnier, Katja *Director*
Creative Artists Agency, 9830 Wilshire Blvd, Beverly Hills, CA 90212 USA

VonGerkan, Manon *Model*
Shamballa Jewels, 92 Thompson St, New York, NY 10012 USA

VonGerkan, Meinhard *Architect*
Elbchaussee 139, Hamburg, 22763, GERMANY

VonGrunigen, Michael *Skier*
Chalet Sunneblick, Schonried, 3778, SWITZERLAND

VonHabsburg-Lothringem, Otto *Government Official*
Hindenburgstr 14, Pocking, 82343 USA

VonHippel, Peter H *Misc*
1900 Crest Dr, Eugene, OR 97405 USA

Vonk, Hans *Conductor*
Intermusic Artists, 16 Duncan Terrace, London, N1 8BZ, UNITED KINGDOM (UK)

VonKlitzing, Klaus *Nobel Prize Laureate*
Max Planck Institute, Heisenbergstr 1, Stuttgart, 70569, GERMANY

VonMehren, Arthur T *Attorney General, Educator*
68 Sparks St, Cambridge, MA 02138 USA

VonMehren, Arthur T *Attorney General*
925 Park Ave, New York, NY 10028 USA

Vonnegut, Kurt Jr *Writer*
Washington Square/Simon & Schuster, 1230 Ave of Americas, New York, NY 10020 USA

Vonoimoana, Eric
715 S. Circle Dr., Colorado Springs, CO 80910

VonOtter, Anne Sofie *Opera Singer*
I C M Aritsts, 40 W 57th St, New York, NY 10019 USA

VonOy, Jenna *Actor*
19 Saddle Ridge Road, Newtown, CT 06470 USA

VonPierer, Heinrich *Business Person*
Seimens AG, Wittelsbacherplatz 2, Munich, 80333, GERMANY

VonQuast, Veronika *Actor*
ZBF Agentur, Leopoldstr 19, Munich, 80802, GERMANY

VonRunkle, Theodora *Fashion Designer*
8805 Lookout Mountain Road, Los Angeles, CA 90046 USA

VonSaltza Olmstead, S Christine (Chris) *Swimmer*
7060 Fairway Place, Carmel, CA 93923 USA

VonStade, Frederica *Opera Singer*
1200 San Antonio Ave, Alameda, CA
94501 USA

VonStrateen, Frans *Artist*
Samuel Muller Plein 17C, Rotterdam,
3023, DENMARK

VonWeizsacker, Carl Friedrich *Misc*
Aplenstr 15, Socking, 82319, GERMANY

VonWeizsacker, Richard *President*
Meisenstr 6, Berlin, 14195, GERMANY

Voog, Ana *Music Group, Musician,
Songwriter*
MCA Records, 1755 Broadway, New
York, NY 10019 USA

Voorhees, John J *Doctor*
3965 Waldenwood Dr, Ann Arbor, MI
48105 USA

Voorhies, Lark *Actor*
10635 Santa Monica Blvd #130, Los
Angeles, CA 90025 USA

Vorgan, Gigi *Actor*
3637 Stone Canyon, Sherman Oaks, CA
91403 USA

Vorhies, Lark *Actor*
Brillstein-Grey Entertainment, 9150
Wilshire Blvd #350, Beverly Hills, CA
90212 USA

Voris, Roy M (Butch) *Misc*
14 Greenwood Way, Monterey, CA
93940 USA

Voronin, Vladimir *President*
President's Office, 23 Nicolae Iorge Str,
Chishinev, 277033, MOLDOVA

Vosloo, Arnold *Actor*
804 E 16th St, Los Angeles, CA 90021
USA

Voss, Brian *Bowler*
340 Banyon Brook Point, Roswell, GA
30076 USA

Voss, James S *Astronaut*
4207 Indian Sunrise Court, Houston, TX
77059 USA

Voss, Janice E *Astronaut*
14803 Flowerwood Dr, Houston, TX
77062 USA

VosSavant, Marilyn *Writer*
Parade Publications, 711 3rd Ave, New
York, NY 10017 USA

Votaw, Ty *Golfer*
Ladies Pro Golf Assn, 100 International
Golf Dr, Daytona Beach, FL 32124 USA

Voznesensky, Andrei A *Writer*
Kotelnicheskaya Nab 1/15, BI W #62,
Moscow, 109240, RUSSIA

Vraa, Sanna *Model, Actor*
Irv Schechter, 9300 Wilshire Blvd #410,
Beverly Hills, CA 90212 USA

Vraciu, Alexander (Alex) *War Hero*
309 Merrille Place, Danville, CA 94526
USA

Vranes, Danny *Basketball Player*
7105 Highland Dr, Salt Lake City, UT
84121 USA

Vranitzky, Franz
Ballhausplatz 2, Vienna, AUSTRIA, 1015

Vuarnet, Jean *Skier*
Chalet Squaw Peak, Auoriaz, 74110,
FRANCE

Vuckovich, Peter D (Pete) *Baseball Player*
309 Keiper Lane, Johnstown, PA 15909
USA

Vuitton, Henri-Louis *Fashion Designer*
78 Bis Ave Marceau, Paris, 75000,
FRANCE

Vujtek, Vladimir *Hockey Player*
Pittsburgh Penguins, Mellon Arena, 66
Mario Lemieux Place, Pittsburgh, PA
15219 USA

Vukovich, George
615 Summer Grass Lane, Roswell, GA
30075-7103

Vuono, Carl E *General*
5796 Westchester St, Alexandria, VA
22310 USA

Vyent, Louise *Model*
Pauline's Talent Corp, 379 W Broadway
#502, New York, NY 10012 USA

W

Waadataar, Paar *Musician*
Banada Mgmt, 11 Elvaston Place #300,
London, SW 7 5QC, UNITED KINGDOM
(UK)

Waalkes, Otto
Papenhuder Str. 61, Hamburg,
GERMANY, D-22087

Wach, Caitlin *Actor*
Writers and Artists Group Intl (LA), 8383
Wilshire Blvd #550, Beverly Hills, CA
90211 USA

Wachowski, Andy *Producer, Director,
Writer*
William Morris Agency (WMA-LA), 1
William Morris Pl, Beverly Hills, CA
90212 USA

Wachowski, Larry *Director, Producer,
Writer*
Circle of Confusion LLC (NY), 107-23 71st
Road, Suite 300, Forest Hills, NY 11375
USA

Wachs, Caitlin *Actor*
Cunningham-Escott-Dipene & Associates
Inc (CED-LA), 10635 Santa Monica Blvd
#130, Los Angeles, CA 90025 USA

Wachtel, Christine *Track Athlete*
Rostock Sports Club, Rostock,
Mecklenburg-Vorpommoem, GERMANY

Wachter, Anita *Skier*
Gantschierstr 579, Schruns, 6780,
AUSTRIA

Waddell, Ernest *Actor*
Writers and Artists Group Intl (LA), 8383
Wilshire Blvd #550, Beverly Hills, CA
90211 USA

Waddell, John Henry *Artist*
Star Route 2273, Oak Creek Village Road,
Cornville, AZ 86325 USA

Waddell, Justine *Actor*
International Creative Mgmt, 8942
Wilshire Blvd #219, Beverly Hills, CA
90211 USA

Waddington, Steven *Actor*
Kerry Gardner, 15 Kensington High St,
London, W8 5NP, UNITED KINGDOM
(UK)

Waddington of Read, David *Governor,
General*
Stable House Sabden, Clitheroe, Lanc,
BB7 9HP, UNITED KINGDOM (UK)

Wade, Abdoulaye *President*
President's Office, Ave Roume, Dakar, BPI
168, SENEGAL

Wade, Adam *Musician*
118 E 25th St #600, New York, NY 10010
USA

Wade, Ben
1165 Medford Rd, Pasadena, CA 91107

Wade, Dwayne *Basketball Player*
Miami Heat, American Airlines Arena,
601 Biscayne Blvd, Miami, FL 33132 USA

Wade, Edgar L *Religious Leader*
4466 Elvis Presley Blvd, #222, Memphis,
TN 38116 USA

Wade, Jason *Musician*
DreamWorks Records, 9268 W 3rd St,
Beverly Hills, CA 90210 USA

Wade, Kevin *Writer*
Endeavor Agency LLC (LA), 9601 Wilshire
Blvd Fl 3, Beverly Hills, CA 90210 USA

Wade, Russell
47-287 W. Eldorado Dr., Indian Wells, CA
92260

Wade, Todd *Football Player*
217 Hendricks Isle, #302, Fort
Lauderdale, FL 33301 USA

Wade, Virginia *Tennis Player*
Sharstead Court, Sittingbourne, Kent,
UNITED KINGDOM (UK)

Wade, William J (Bill) Jr *Football Player*
PO Box 210124, Nashville, TN 37221
USA

Wadhams, Wayne *Musician*
73 Hemenway, Boston, MA 02115 USA

Wadhawan, Avinash *Actor, Bollywood*
305 Skyway Shastri Nagar, Off J P Road
Andheri, Mumbai, MS 400058, INDIA

Wadkins, Bobby *Golfer*
5815 Harbour Hill Place, Midlothian, VA
23112 USA

Wadkins, Lanny *Golfer*
6002 Kettering Court, Dallas, TX 75248
USA

Wadsworth, Charles W *Musician*
PO Box 157, Charleston, SC 29402 USA

Waelsch, Salome G *Doctor, Scientist*
90 Morningside Dr, New York, NY 10027
USA

Wages, Robert E *Misc*
Oil Chemical Atomic Workers
International Union, PO Box 2812,
Denver, CO 80201 USA

Wages, William *Cinematographer*
Innovative Artists, 1505 10th St, Santa
Monica, CA 90401 USA

Waggoner, Lyle *Actor*
1124 Oak Mirage Place, Westlake Village,
CA 91362 USA

Waggoner, Paul E *Misc*
314 Vineyard Point Road, Guilford, CT
06437 USA

Wagner, Amanda
PO Box 1294, Los Alamos, NM 87544-
1294

Wagner, Bruce *Writer*
United Talent Agency, 9560 Wilshire Blvd #500, Beverly Hills, CA 90212 USA

Wagner, Chuck *Actor, Musician*
1200 Maldonado Dr, Pensacola Beach, FL 32561 USA

Wagner, Dajuan *Basketball Player*
Cleveland Cavaliers, Gund Arena, 1 Center Court, Cleveland, OH 44115 USA

Wagner, Fred *Cartoonist*
King Features Syndicate, 888 7th Ave, New York, NY 10106 USA

Wagner, Harold A *Business Person*
Air Products & Chemicals, 7201 Hamilton Blvd, Allentown, PA 18195 USA

Wagner, Helen
1268 E. 141st St., Brooklyn, NY 11230

Wagner, Jack *Actor, Musician*
314 Waverly Place Court, Chesterfield, MO 63017 USA

Wagner, Jane
PO Box 27700, Los Angeles, CA 90027

Wagner, John *Cartoonist*
Hallmark Cards, Shoebox Division, 101 McDonald Dr, Lawrence, KS 66044 USA

Wagner, Katey *Actor*
1500 Old Oak Road, Los Angeles, CA 90049 USA

Wagner, Lindsay *Actor*
Bartels Co, PO Box 57593, Sherman Oaks, CA 91413 USA

Wagner, Lou *Actor*
21224 Celtic St, Chatsworth, CA 91311 USA

Wagner, Louis C Jr *General*
6309 Chaucer Lane, Alexandria, VA 22304 USA

Wagner, Matt *Cartoonist*
DC Comics, 1700 Broadway, New York, NY 10019 USA

Wagner, Melinda *Composer*
Theodore Presser, 588 N Gulph Road, King of Prussia, PA 19406 USA

Wagner, Michael R (Mike) *Football Player*
McCandless, 800 Wyngold Dr, Pittsburgh, PA 15237 USA

Wagner, Paula *Producer*
Cruise/Wagner Productions (C/W), 5555 Melrose Ave, Bldg 200, Los Angeles, CA 90038 USA

Wagner, Philip M *Writer*
32 Montgomery St, Boston, MA 02116 USA

Wagner, Robert J *Actor*
Binder & Associates, 1465 Lindacrest Dr, Beverly Hills, CA 90210 USA

Wagner, Robert T *Educator*
24497 N Playhouse Rd, Keystone, SD 57751 USA

Wagner, Robin S A *Designer*
Robin Wagner Studio, 890 Broadway, New York, NY 10003 USA

Wagner, William E (Billy) *Baseball Player*
2607 Iris Court, Pearland, TX 77584 USA

Wagner, Wolfgang M M *Opera Singer, Director*
Bayreuth Festival, Postfach 100262, Bayreuth, 95402, GERMANY

Wagoner, Dan *Dancer, Choreographer*
Contemporary Dance Theater, 17 Duke's Road, London, WC1H 9AB, UNITED KINGDOM (UK)

Wagoner, David R *Writer*
5416 154th Place SW, Edmonds, WA 98026 USA

Wagoner, G Richard *Business Person*
General Motors Corp, 100 Renaissance Center, Detroit, MI 48243 USA

Wagoner, Harold E *Architect*
331 Lindsey Dr, Berwyn, PA 19312 USA

Wagoner, Porter *Musician, Songwriter*
Porter Wagoner Enterprises, PO Box 290785, Nashville, TN 37229 USA

Wahl, Ken *Actor*
William Morris Agency, 151 El Camino Dr, Beverly Hills, CA 90212 USA

Wahlberg, Donnie *Actor, Musician*
6441 Langdon Ave, Van Nuys, CA 91406 USA

Wahlberg, Mark *Actor, Musician, Model*
Leverage Mgmt, 3030 Pennsylvania Ave, Santa Monica, CA 90404 USA

Wahlen, George E *War Hero*
3437 W 5700 South, Roy, UT 84067 USA

Wahlgren, Olof G C *Editor*
Nicoloviusgatan 5B, Malmo, 217 57, SWEDEN

Wahlquist, Heather *Actor*
Endeavor Agency LLC (LA), 9601 Wilshire Blvd Fl 3, Beverly Hills, CA 90210 USA

Wahlstrom, Jarl H *Religious Leader*
Borgstrominkuja 1A10, Helsinki 84, 00840, FINLAND

Waigel, Theodor *Government Official*
Oberrohr, Ursberg, 86513, GERMANY

Waihee, John D III *Governor*
745 Fort Street Mall #600, Honolulu, HI 96813 USA

Wain, Bea *Musician*
9955 Durant Dr #305, Beverly Hills, CA 90212 USA

Wainwright, James *Actor*
Lew Sherrell, 937 N Sinova, Mesa, AZ 85205 USA

Wainwright, Loudon *Actor*
Harriet Sternberg Management, 4530 Gloria Avenue, Encino, CA 91436 USA

Wainwright, Loudon III *Musician, Songwriter*
Teddy Wainwright, 521 SW Halpatiokee St, Stuart, FL 34994 USA

Wainwright, Rufus *Musician*
United Talent Agency (UTA), 9560 Wilshire Blvd, Beverly Hills, CA 90212 USA

Waite, John *Musician, Songwriter*
Rascoff/Zysblat, 110 W 57th St #300, New York, NY 10019 USA

Waite, Liam
Gersh Agency, The (LA), 232 N Canon Dr, Beverly Hills, CA 90210 USA

Waite, Ralph *Actor*
73317 Ironwood St, Palm Desert, CA 92260 USA

Waite, Terence H (Terry) *Religious Leader*
Wheelrights Green Harvest, Bury Saint Demunds, Suffolk, IP29 4DH, UNITED KINGDOM (UK)

Waite, Terry
The Green Harvest Bury St. Edmunds, Suffolk, ENGLAND, 1P29 4DH

Waits, Tom *Musician, Music Group, Songwriter*
Mitch Schneider Organization, 14724 Ventura Blvd #410, Sherman Oaks, CA 91403 USA

Waitt, Theodore W (Ted) *Business Person*
Gateway Inc, 4545 Towne Centre Court, PO Box 2000, San Diego, CA 92121 USA

Waitz, Grete *Track Athlete*
Birgitte Hammers Vei 15G, Oslo, 1169, NORWAY

Waitz, Richard H *Cinematographer*
405 Zenith Ave, Lafayette, CO 80026 USA

Wajda, Andrezei
u1 Jezefa Hauke Boska 14, Warsaw, POLAND, 01-540

Wajda, Andrzej *Director*
Ul Konopnickiej 26, Cracow, 30-302, POLAND

Wakasugi, Hiroshi
Astrid Schoerke, Monckebergallee 41, Hanover, 30453, GERMANY

Wakata, Koichi *Astronaut*
NASA, Johnson Space Center, 2101 NASA Road, Houston, TX 77058 USA

Wakeham of Maldon, John *Government Official*
House of Lords, Westminster, London, SW1A 0PW, UNITED KINGDOM (UK)

Wakeley, Amanda *Fashion Designer*
79-91 New Kings Road, London, SW6 4SQ, UNITED KINGDOM (UK)

Wakeman, Frederic E Jr *Historian*
702 Gonzalez Dr, San Francisco, CA 94132 USA

Wakeman, Rick *Musician, Songwriter*
Bajonor House, 2 Bridge St Peel, Isle of Man, UNITED KINGDOM (UK)

Wako, Gabriel Zubeir Cardinal *Religious Leader*
Archdiocese, PO Box 49, Khartoum, SUDAN

Wakoski, Diane *Writer*
607 Division St, East Lansing, MI 48823 USA

Waks, Aisha *Actor*
Writers & Artists, 8383 Wilshire Blvd #550, Beverly Hills, CA 90211 USA

Walcott, Derek A *Nobel Prize Laureate*
71 Saint Mary's Court, Brookline, MA 02446 USA

Walcott, Gregory *Actor*
22246 Saticoy St, Canoga Park, CA 91303 USA

Walcutt, John *Actor*
MC Talent Management, 4821 Lankershim Blvd #F329, N Hollywood, CA 91601 USA

Wald, Charles F *General*
Deputy CofS for Air/Space Operations, HqUSAF Pentaton, Washington, DC 20330 USA

Wald, Jeff *Producer*
Jeff Wald Entertainment, 3000 W Olympic Blvd, Bldg 2 #1400, Santa Monica, CA 90404 USA

Wald, Patricia M *Judge*
US Court of Appeals, 3rd & Constitution NW, Washington, DC 20001 USA

Waldegrave, William *Government Official*
66 Palace Gardens Terrace, London, W8 4RR, UNITED KINGDOM (UK)

Walden, Lynette *Actor*
Metropolitan Talent Agency, 4526 Wilshire Blvd, Los Angeles, CA 90010 USA

Walden, Robert *Actor*
1450 Arroyo View Dr, Pasadena, CA 91103 USA

Walden, Robert E (Bobby) *Football Player*
1403 E Douglas Dr, Bainbridge, GA 39819 USA

Waldheim, Kurt *President*
1 Lobkowitz Platz, Vienna, 1010, AUSTRIA

Waldhorn, Gary *Actor*
London Mgmt, 2-4 Noel St, London, W1V 3RB, UNITED KINGDOM (UK)

Waldie, Marc *Volleyball Player*
13290 Ocean Vista Road, San Diego, CA 92130 USA

Waldman, Myron *Cartoonist*
3660 Lufberry Ave, Wantagh, NY 11793 USA

Waldner, Jan-Ove *Tennis Player, Athlete*
Banda, Skiulstagatan 1O, Eskilstuna, 632 29, SWEDEN

Waldo, Janet
15735 Royal Oak Rd, Encino, CA 91316

Waldorf, Duffy *Golfer*
International Golf Partners, 3300 PGA Blvd #820, West Palm Beach, FL 33410 USA

Waldron, Jeremy J *Educator*
1061 Keith Ave, Berkeley, CA 94708 USA

Wales, Ross *Swimmer*
2730 Walsh Road, Cincinnati, OH 45208 USA

Walesa, Lech *Nobel Prize Laureate, President*
Ul Polanki 54, Gdansk-Oliwa, 80-308, POLAND

Walheim, Rex J *Astronaut*
142 Hidden Lake Dr, League City, TX 77573 USA

Walia, Sonu *Actor, Bollywood*
20 The Anchorage Juhu-Versova Link Road, Andheri(W), Bombay, MS 400 058, INDIA

Walkabouts, The
PO Box 360524, Berlin, GERMANY, 10975

Walken, Christopher *Actor*
International Creative Mgmt, 40 W 57th St #1800, New York, NY 10019 USA

Walker, Alan *Misc*
Johns Hopkins, Medical School, Cell Biology/Anatomy Dept, Baltimore, MD 21205 USA

Walker, Alice *Social Activist, Writer*
670 San Luis Road, Berkeley, CA 94707 USA

Walker, Alice M *Social Activist, Writer*
670 San Luis Road, Berkeley, CA 94707 USA

Walker, Ally *Actor*
More/Medavoy, 7920 W Sunset Blvd #400, Los Angeles, CA 90046 USA

Walker, Anetia
19551 Turtle Ridge Lane, Northridge, CA 91326-3808

Walker, Antoine *Basketball Player*
Dallas Mavericks, 2909 Taylor St, Dallas, TX 75226 USA

Walker, Arnetia *Actor*
19551 Turtle Ridge Lane, Northridge, CA 91326 USA

Walker, B J *Financier*
First Union Corp, 1 First Union Center, Charlotte, NC 28288 USA

Walker, Billy *Musician*
PO Box 618, Hendersonville, TN 37077 USA

Walker, Bree
3347 Tareco Dr., Los Angeles, CA 90068

Walker, Brian *Cartoonist*
King Features Syndicate, 888 7th Ave, New York, NY 10106 USA

Walker, Butch *Musician*
Progressive Global Agency, 103 W Tyne Dr, Nashville, TN 37205 USA

Walker, Catherine *Fashion Designer*
65 Sydney St, Chelsea, London, SW3 6PX, UNITED KINGDOM (UK)

Walker, Charles D *Astronaut*
Boeing Co, 1200 Wilson Blvd, MC RS00, Arlington, VA 22209 USA

Walker, Charlie *Musician*
Tessier-Marsh Talent, 2825 Blue Book Dr, Nashville, TN 37214 USA

Walker, Charls E *Economist*
10120 Chapel Road, Potomac, MD 20854 USA

Walker, Chet *Basketball Player*
124 Fleet St, Marina del Rey, CA 90292 USA

Walker, Chris *Actor*
Roll Kruger, 121 Gloucester Place, London, W1H 3PJ, UNITED KINGDOM (UK)

Walker, Clay *Musician*
TBA Ent, 300 10th Ave S, Nashville, TN 37203 USA

Walker, Colleen *Golfer*
Players Group, 5 Cathy Place, Menlo Park, CA 94025 USA

Walker, Darrell *Basketball Player, Coach*
16122 Patriot Dr, Little Rock, AR 72212 USA

Walker, David *Government Official*
General Accounting Office, 441 G St NW, Washington, DC 20548 USA

Walker, Derek *Architect*
2 General Sage Dr, Santa Fe, NM 87505 USA

Walker, Derrick *Race Car Driver, Misc*
Walker Racing, 147 Midland Rd Royston, Bamsley, S York, S71 4B1, UNITED KINGDOM (UK)

Walker, Eamonn *Actor*
William Morris Agency, 151 El Camino Dr, Beverly Hills, CA 90212 USA

Walker, Fiona
13 Despard Rd., London, ENGLAND, 5NP

Walker, George T Jr *Composer*
323 Grove St, Montclair, NJ 07042 USA

Walker, Greg *Cartoonist*
King Features Syndicate, 888 7th Ave, New York, NY 10106 USA

Walker, Harry
RR #2Box 145, Leeds, AL 35094

Walker, Herschel J *Football Player*
1360 E 9th St, Cleveland, OH 44114 USA

Walker, Hershell
19 West St., New York, NY 10004

Walker, Hezekiah *Musician*
Covenant Agency, 1011 4th St #315, Santa Monica, CA 90403 USA

Walker, James E *Educator*
Middle Tennessee State University, President's Office, Murfreesboro, TN 37132 USA

Walker, James L (Jimmy) *Misc*
Fireman & Oilers Brotherhood, 1100 Circle 75 Parkway, Atlanta, GA 30339 USA

Walker, Jerry Jeff *Musician, Songwriter*
Tried & True Music, PO Box 39, Austin, TX 78767 USA

Walker, Jimmie *Actor, Comedian*
88 Roxiticus Rd, Far Hills, NJ 07931-2222

Walker, Jimmie (J J) *Actor, Comedian*
Nationwide Entertainment, 2756 N Green Valley Parkway, Henderson, NV 89014 USA

Walker, Joe Louis *Musician*
Rick Bates Mgmt, 714 Brookside Lane, Sierra Madre, CA 91024 USA

Walker, John *Track Athlete*
Jeffs Road, RD Papatoetoe, NEW ZEALAND

Walker, John E *Nobel Prize Laureate*
MRC Molecular Biology Laboratory, Hills Road, Cambridge, CB2 2QH, UNITED KINGDOM (UK)

Walker, Junior
141 Dunbar Ave., Fords, NJ 08863

Walker, Kenny *Basketball Player*
2252 Terrace Woods Park, Lexington, KY 40513 USA

Walker, Kenyatta *Football Player*
Tampa Bay Buccaneers, 1 W Buccaneer Place, Tampa, FL 33607 USA

Walker, Larry *Baseball Player*
21642 River Road, Maple Ridge, BC V2X 2B7, CANADA

Walker, LeRoy T *Coach, Educator*
1208 Red Oak Ave, Durham, NC 27707 USA

Walker, Marcy *Actor*
David Shapira & Associates, 15821 Ventura Blvd #235, Encino, CA 91436 USA

Walker, Mort *Cartoonist*
61 Studio Court, Stamford, CT 06903 USA

Walker, Nicholas
1900 Ave. of the Stars #1640, Los Angeles, CA 90067

Walker, Paul *Actor*
International Creative Mgmt, 8942 Wilshire Blvd #219, Beverly Hills, CA 90211 USA

Walker, Paul L *Religious Leader*
Church of God, PO Box 2430, Cleveland, TN 37320 USA

Walker, Peter *Director*
23 Bentick St, London, W1, UNITED KINGDOM (UK)

Walker, Polly *Actor*
Markham & Froggatt, Julian House, 4 Windmill St, London, W1P 1HF, UNITED KINGDOM (UK)

Walker, Robert M *Physicist*
1 Brookings Dr #CB1105, Saint Louis, MO 63130 USA

Walker, Roger N *Architect*
8 Brougham St, Mount Victoria, Wellington, NEW ZEALAND

Walker, Ronald C *Publisher*
Smithsonian Magazine, 900 Jefferson Dr SW, Washington, DC 20560 USA

Walker, Sandra *Opera Singer*
Columbia Artists Mgmt Inc, 165 W 57th St, New York, NY 10019 USA

Walker, Sarah E B *Opera Singer*
152 Inchmery Road, London, SE6 1DF, UNITED KINGDOM (UK)

Walker, Wally *Basketball Player*
154 Lombard St #58, San Francisco, CA 94111 USA

Walker, Wesley D *Football Player*
PO Box 20438, Huntington Station, NY 11746 USA

Walker, William D *Business Person*
Tektronix Inc, 26600 Sourtwest Parkway, Wilsonville, OR 97070 USA

Walker Jr, Robert *Actor*
TOPS, 23410 Civic Center Way #C-1, Malibu, CA 90265 USA

Walker of Worchester, Peter E
Government Official
Abbots Morton Manor, Grooms Hill Abbots Morton, Worc, WR7 4LT, UNITED KINGDOM (UK)

Wall, Brian A *Artist*
306 Lombard St, San Francisco, CA 94133 USA

Wall, Carolyn *Publisher*
Newsweek Magazine, 251 W 57th St, New York, NY 10019 USA

Wall, David *Ballerina*
Royal Ballet, Covent Garden, Bow St, London, WC2E 9DD, UNITED KINGDOM (UK)

Wall, Frederick T *Misc*
8515 Costa Verde Blvd #606, San Diego, CA 92122 USA

Wall, John F *General*
507 Hanover St, Fredericksburg, VA 22401 USA

Wallace, Anthony F C *Misc*
University of Pennsylvania, Anthropology Dept, Philadelphia, PA 19014 USA

Wallace, Aria *Actor*
Discover Inc Management, 11425 Moorpark St, Studio City, CA 91602 USA

Wallace, B Steven (Steve) *Football Player*
4455 Harris Trail NW, Atlanta, GA 30327 USA

Wallace, Ben *Basketball Player*
Detroit Pistons, Palace, 2 Championship Dr, Auburn Hills, MI 48326 USA

Wallace, Bruce *Doctor, Scientist*
940 McBryde Dr, Blacksburg, VA 24060 USA

Wallace, Carol *Editor*
People Magazine, Editorial Dept, Time-Life Building, New York, NY 10020 USA

Wallace, Chris *Correspondent*
20/20, 147 Columbus Ave, New York, NY 10023, US

Wallace, Christopher (Chris)
Commentator
Fox-TV, News Dept, 205 E 67th St, New York, NY 10021 USA

Wallace, Craig K *Doctor*
National Institutes of Health, 9000 Rockville Pike, Bethesda, MD 20892 USA

Wallace, David Foster *Writer*
Illinois State University, English Dept, Normal, IL 61761 USA

Wallace, George *Comedian*
Magus Entertainment, 9107 Wilshire Blvd #650, Beverly Hills, CA 90210 USA

Wallace, Gerald *Basketball Player*
Sacramento Kings, Arco Arena, 1 Sports Parkway, Sacramento, CA 95834 USA

Wallace, Ian *Actor, Opera Singer*
P F D, Drury House, 34-43 Russell St, London, WC2B 5HA, UNITED KINGDOM (UK)

Wallace, Jane *Entertainer*
Cosgrove-Meurer Productions, 4303 W Verdugo Ave, Burbank, CA 91505 USA

Wallace, Jerry
. 1161 NW 76th Ave., Ft Lauderdale, FL 33322

Wallace, Jessie *Actor*

Wallace, Julie T *Actor*
Annette Stone, 9 Newburgh St, London, W1V 1LH, UNITED KINGDOM (UK)

Wallace, Kenny *Race Car Driver*
8929 Harris Rd, Concord, NC 28027 USA

Wallace, Laurie
PO Box 3023, Guttenberg, NJ 07093

Wallace, Marcia *Actor*
Artists Group, 10100 Santa Monica Blvd #2490, Los Angeles, CA 90067 USA

Wallace, Mike *Commentator*
CBS-TV, News Dept, 51 W 52nd St, New York, NY 10019 USA

Wallace, Randall *Writer, Producer, Director, Actor*
Wheelhouse, The, 15464 Ventura Blvd, Sherman Oaks, CA 91403-3002

Wallace, Rasheed *Basketball Player*
01905 SW Greenwood Road, Portland, OR 97219 USA

Wallace, Rheagan *Actor*
Abrams Artists Agency (LA), 9200 Sunset Blvd Fl 11, Los Angeles, CA 90069 USA

Wallace, Rusty *Race Car Driver*
Penske Racing, 136 Knob Hill Road, Mooresville, NC 28117 USA

Wallace, Tommy Lee *Director*
Innovative Artists, 1505 10th St, Santa Monica, CA 90401 USA

Wallace, Will *Actor*
Origin Talent, 3393 Barham Blvd, Los Angeles, CA 90068 USA

Wallace, William *General*
Commanding General, V Corps, APO, AE, 09079 USA

Wallach, Eli *Actor*
Paradigm Agency, 200 W 57th St #900, New York, NY 10019 USA

Wallach, Evan J *Judge*
US International Trade Court, 1 Federal Plaza, New York, NY 10278 USA

Wallach, Timothy C (Tim) *Baseball Player*
10762 Holly Dr, Garden Grove, CA 92840 USA

Wallechinsky, David *Writer*
Avon/William Morrow, 1350 Ave of Americas, New York, NY 10019 USA

Wallenberg, Raoul Committee
823 UN Plaza 8th Flr., New York, NY 10017

Wallendas, The Great
138 Frog Hollow Rd, Churchville, PA 18966

Waller, Charlie *Musician*
Lendel Agency, 9188 James Madison Highway, Warrenton, VA 20186 USA

Waller, Gordon *Musician*
7 Passage St, Powey, Cornwall, PL23 1DE, UNITED KINGDOM (UK)

Waller, Michael *Editor*
Hartford Courant Co, 285 Broad St, Hartford, CT 06115 USA

Waller, Peter
7 Passage St. owley, Cornwall, ENGLAND, PL23 IDE

Waller, Rik *Musician*
Pop Idol (Fremantle Media), 2700 Colorado Ave #450, Santa Monica, CA 90404 USA

Waller, Robert James *Writer*
Aaron Priest Literary Agency, 708 3rd Ave #2300, New York, NY 10017 USA

Waller, Ron *Football Player*
900 Concord Road, Seaford, DE 19973 USA

Waller, William L *Governor*
220 S President St, Jackson, MS 39201 USA

Wallerstein, Ralph G *Misc*
3447 Clay St, San Francisco, CA 94118 USA

Wallflowers, The *Music Group*
Creative Artists Agency LCC (CAA-LA), 9830 Wilshire Blvd, Beverly Hills, CA 90212 USA

Walling, Camryn *Actor*
Stein Entertainment Group, 11271 Ventura Blvd #477, Studio City, CA 91604 USA

Walling, Cheves T *Misc*
PO Box 537, Jaffrey, NH 03452 USA

Wallis, Shani *Actor*
15460 Vista Haven, Sherman Oaks, CA 91403 USA

Walliser, Maria *Skier*
Selfwingert, Malans, 7208, SWITZERLAND

Wallop, Malcolm *Senator*
58 Canyon Ranch Road, Big Horn, WY 82833 USA

Walls, Denise (Nee-C) *Musician, Songwriter*
2113 South Ave, Youngstown, OH 44502 USA

Walls, Everson C *Football Player*
5927 Tree Shadow Court, Dallas, TX 75252 USA

Walmsley, Jon *Actor*
13810 Magnolia Blvd, Sherman Oaks, CA 91423 USA

Walpot, Heike *Astronaut*
DLR, Abt Raumflugbetrieb, Cologne, 51170, GERMANY

Walser, Don *Musician, Songwriter*
Nancy Fly Agency, 6618 Wolfcreek Pass, Austin, TX 78749 USA

Walser, Martin
Zum Hecht 36, Uberlingen, GERMANY, D-88662

Walsh, Addie *Writer*
William Morris Agency (WMA-LA), 1 William Morris Pl, Beverly Hills, CA 90212 USA

Walsh, Arthur
12360 Riverside Dr., No. Hollywood, CA 91607

Walsh, David M *Cinematographer*
15436 Valley Vista Blvd, Sherman Oaks, CA 91403 USA

Walsh, Diana Chapman *Educator*
Wellesley College, President's Office, Wellesley, MA 02181 USA

Walsh, Don *Misc, Swimmer*
International Maritime Inc, 14758 Sitkum Lane, Myrtle Point, OR 97458 USA

Walsh, Donnie *Basketball Player, Coach*
Indiana Pacers, Conseco Fieldhouse, 125 Pennsylvania, Indianapolis, IN 46204 USA

Walsh, Dylan *Actor*
McGowan Agency, 370 Lexington Ave #802, New York, NY 10017 USA

Walsh, Fran *Producer*
WingNut Films, PO Box 15208, Miramar, Wellington, 6003, NEW ZEALAND

Walsh, Gwynyth *Actor*
12304 Santa Monica Blvd #104, Los Angeles, CA 90025 USA

Walsh, Joe *Musician, Songwriter*
PO Box 1188, Eaton, PA 18044 USA

Walsh, John *Television Host*
3111 S Dixie Highway #244, West Palm Beach, FL 33405 USA

Walsh, John Jr *Misc*
J Paul Getty Museum, Getty Center, 1200 Getty Center Dr, Los Angeles, CA 90049 USA

Walsh, Kate *Actor*
PO Box 261067, Encino, CA 91426 USA

Walsh, Lawrence E *Government Official, Attorney General*
1902 Bedford St, Nichols Hills, OK 73116 USA

Walsh, M Emmet *Actor*
4173 Motor Ave, Culver City, CA 90232 USA

Walsh, Martin *Misc*
National Organization on Disability, 910 16th St NW, Washington, DC 20006 USA

Walsh, Matt *Comedian*
United Talent Agency (UTA), 9560 Wilshire Blvd, Beverly Hills, CA 90212 USA

Walsh, Patrick C *Doctor*
Johns Hopkins University, Brady Urological Institute, Baltimore, MD 21205 USA

Walsh, Stephen J (Steve) *Football Player*
1921 Flagler Estates Dr, West Palm Beach, FL 33411 USA

Walsh, Steve
Box 6 Wickford, Essex, ENGLAND, SS12 9D0

Walsh, Sydney *Actor*
Innovative Artists, 1505 10th St, Santa Monica, CA 90401 USA

Walsh, Tom *Artist*
PO Box 133, Philomath, OR 97370 USA

Walsh, William E (Bill) *Football Coach*
12 Vineyard Hill Road, Woodside, CA 94062 USA

Walske, Steven *Business Person*
Parametric Technology, 140 Kendrick St, Needham Heights, MA 02494 USA

Walsman, Leanna *Actor*
International Creative Management (ICM-LA), 8942 Wilshire Blvd, Beverly Hills, CA 90211 USA

Walter, Jessica *Actor*
27 W 87th St #2, New York, NY 10024 USA

Walter, Lisa Ann *Comedian, Actor*
United Talent Agency, 9560 Wilshire Blvd #500, Beverly Hills, CA 90212 USA

Walter, Paul H L *Misc*
3 Benedictine Retreat, Savannah, GA 31411 USA

Walter, Robert D *Business Person*
Cardinal Health, 7000 Cardinal Place, Dublin, OH 43017 USA

Walter, Tracey *Actor*
257 N Rexford Dr, Beverly Hills, CA 90210 USA

Walter, Ulrich *Astronaut*
IBM Germany, Schonaicherstr 220, Boblingen, 71032, GERMANY

Walters, Barbara *Commentator*
ABC-TV News Dept, 77 W 66th St, New York, NY 10023 USA

Walters, Charles *Director*
23922 De Ville Way #A, Malibu, CA 90265 USA

Walters, David L *Governor*
RR 2, Watts, OK 74964 USA

Walters, Dottie

Walters, Harry N *Government Official*
DHC Holdings Corp, 125 Thomas Dale, Williamsburg, VA 23185 USA

Walters, Hugh
15 Christchurch Ave, London, ENGLAND, NW6 7QP

Walters, Jamie *Actor, Musician*
4702 Ethel Ave, Sherman Oaks, CA 91423 USA

Walters, Julie *Actor*
International Creative Mgmt, 76 Oxford St, London, W1N 0AX, UNITED KINGDOM (UK)

Walters, Melora *Actor*
United Talent Agency, 9560 Wilshire Blvd #500, Beverly Hills, CA 90212 USA

Walters, Minette *Writer*
G P Putnam's Sons, 375 Hudson St, New York, NY 10014 USA

Walters, Peter I *Business Person*
22 Hill St, London, W1X 7FU, UNITED KINGDOM (UK)

Walters, Roger T *Architect*
46 Princess Road, London, NW1 8JL, UNITED KINGDOM (UK)

Walters, Susan *Actor*
1505 10th St, Santa Monica, CA 90401 USA

Walters, Tome H Jr *General*
Defense Security Cooperation Agency, 1111 Davis Highway, Arlington, VA 22202 USA

Walthall, Romy *Actor*
Defining Artists, 4342 Lankershim Blvd, Universal City, CA 91602 USA

Walther, Herbert *Physicist*
Egenhoferstr 7A, Munich, 81243, GERMANY

Walton, Anthony J (Tony) *Designer*
International Creative Mgmt, 40 W 57th St #1800, New York, NY 10019 USA

Walton, Bill
1010 Myrtle Way, San Diego, CA 92103-5123

Walton, Cedar A Jr *Musician*
Bridge Agency, 35 Clark St #A5, Brooklyn Heights, NY 11201 USA

Walton, Helen R *Business Person*
Wal-Mart Stores, 702 SW 8th St, Bentonville, AR 72716 USA

Walton, Jess *Actor*
4716 Woodman Ave, Sherman Oaks, CA 91423 USA

Walton, Joseph (Joe) *Football Player, Football Coach, Coach*
8 Windy Crest Dr, Beaver Falls, PA 15010 USA

Walton, S Robson (Rob) *Business Person*
Wal-Mart Stores, 702 SW 8th St, Bentonville, AR 72716 USA

Walton, William T (Bill) III *Basketball Player, Sportscaster*
1010 Myrtle Way, San Diego, CA 92103 USA

Waltrip, Darrell L *Race Car Driver*
PO Box 381, Harrisburg, NC 28075 USA

Waltrip, Michael (Mike) *Race Car Driver*
PO Box 5065, Concord, NH 28027 USA

Waltrip, Robert L *Business Person*
Service Corp International, 1929 Allen Parkway, Houston, TX 77019 USA

Waltz, Lisa *Actor*
Writers & Artists, 8383 Wilshire Blvd #550, Beverly Hills, CA 90211 USA

Walworth, Arthur *Writer*
North Hill, 865 Central Ave E #206, Needham, MA 02492 USA

Walz, Carl E *Astronaut*
129 Lake Point Dr, League City, TX 77573 USA

Wamala, Emmanuel Cardinal *Religious Leader*
PO Box 14125, Mengo, Kampala, UGANDA

Wambaugh, Joseph *Writer*
3520 Kellogg Way, San Diego, CA 92106 USA

Wambold, Richard L *Business Person*
Pactiv Corp, 1900 W Field Court, Lake Forest, IL 60045 USA

Wan, Li *Government Official*
State Council, People's Congress, Tian An Men Square, Beijing, CHINA

Wanamaker, Zoe *Actor*
Conway Van Gelder Robinson, 18-21 Jermyn St, London, SW1Y 6NB, UNITED KINGDOM (UK)

Wang, Garrett *Actor*
7049 Macapa Dr, Los Angeles, CA 90068 USA

Wang, Henry Y *Engineer*
University of Michigan, Chemical Engineering Dept, Ann Arbor, MI 48109 USA

Wang, Jida *Artist*
7612 35th Ave #3E, Jackson Heights, NY 11372 USA

Wang, Junxia *Track Athlete*
Athletic Assn, 9 Tiyuguan Road, Chongwen District, Beijing, 10061, CHINA

Wang, Taylor G *Astronaut, Physicist*
1224 Amo Dr, Sierra Madre, CA 91024 USA

Wang, Tian-Ren *Artist*
Shaanxi Sculpture Institute, Longshoucun, Xi'am, Shaanxi, 710016, CHINA

Wang, Vera *Fashion Designer*
Vera Wang Bridal House, 225 W 39th St #1000, New York, NY 10018 USA

Wang, Wayne *Director*
1888 Century Park E, #1888, Los Angeles, CA 90067 USA

Wang, Zhen-Yi *Doctor, Scientist*
Hopital de Shanghai, Rul Jin Road 11, Shanghai, 200025, CHINA

Wang Zhl Zhi *Basketball Player*
Miami Heat, American Airlines Arena, 601 Biscayne Blvd, Miami, FL 33132 USA

Wangchuck, Dasho Jigme Khesar Namgyal *Prince*
Royal Palace, Tashichhodzong, Thimpu, BHUTAN

Wangchuck, Jigme Singye *King*
Royal Palace, Tashichhodzong, Thimpu, BHUTAN

Wanner, H Eric *Misc*
Russell Sage Foundation, 112 E 64th St, New York, NY 10021 USA

Wannsdedt, David R (Dave) *Football Coach*
12600 N Stonebrook Circle, Davie, FL 33330 USA

Wansel, Dexter *Musician*
Walt Reeder Productions, PO Box 27641, Philadelphia, PA 19118 USA

Wanzer, Robert F (Bobby) *Basketball Player*
28 Greenwood Park, Pittsford, NY 14534 USA

Waples, Keith *Horse Racer*
PO Box 632, Durham, ON N0G 1R0, CANADA

Waples, Ron *Horse Racer, Coach*
7 Mill Run W, Highstown, NJ 08520 USA

Wapner, Joseph A *Judge, Actor*
2388 Century Hill, Los Angeles, CA 90067 USA

War
250 W. 57th St. #407, New York, NY 10019-3202

Warburton, Patrick *Actor*
William Morris Agency, 151 El Camino Dr, Beverly Hills, CA 90212 USA

Ward, Anita *Musician*
Richard Walters, 1800 Argyle Ave, #408, Los Angeles, CA 90028 USA

Ward, Burt *Actor*
Boy Wonder Visual Effects, 8611 Hayden Pl, Culver City, CA 90232 USA

Ward, Burton *Race Car Driver*
Bill Davis Racing, 301 Old Thomasville Road, Winston Salem, NC 27107 USA

Ward, Charlie *Basketball Player, Football Player*
109 Heisman Way, Thomasville, GA 31792 USA

Ward, Christopher L (Chris) *Football Player*
PO Box 1365, Inglewood, CA 90308 USA

Ward, Dale *Musician*
A Crosse the World, PO Box 23066, London, W11 3FR, UNITED KINGDOM (UK)

Ward, David *Opera Singer*
1 Kennedy Crescent, Lake Wanaka, NEW ZEALAND

Ward, Fred *Actor*
1215 Cabrillo Ave, Venice, CA 90291 USA

Ward, Hines *Football Player*
150 Acadian Dr, Stockbridge, GA 30281 USA

Ward, John F *Business Person*
Russell Corp, 755 Lee St, Alexander City, AL 35010 USA

Ward, John Milton *Educator*
20 Follen St, Cambridge, MA 02138 USA

Ward, Jon P *Business Person*
RR Donnelley & Sons, 77 W Wacker Dr, Chicago, IL 60601 USA

Ward, Jonathan *Actor*
Auckland Actors, Po Box 56460, Dominion Road, Auckland, 1030, NEW ZELAND

Ward, Lala *Actor*
London Mgmt, 2-4 Noel St, London, W1V 3RB, UNITED KINGDOM (UK)

Ward, Maitland *Actor*
Shelter Entertainment, 9255 Sunset Blvd, #1010, Los Angeles, CA 90069 USA

Ward, Mary *Actor*
Melbourne Artists, 643 Saint Kilda Road, Melbourne, VIC, 3004, AUSTRALIA

Ward, Mary B *Actor*
Innovative Artists, 1505 10th St, Santa Monica, CA 90401 USA

Ward, Megan *Actor*
PO Box 481219, Los Angeles, CA 90036 USA

Ward, Michael P *Mountaineer, Doctor*
Saint Andrews's Hospital, Bow St, London, E3 3NT, UNITED KINGDOM (UK)

Ward, R Duane *Baseball Player*
4505 Pacific St, Farmington, NM 87402 USA

Ward, Rachel *Actor*
Himber Entertainment, 211 S Beverly Dr #208, Beverly Hills, CA 90212 USA

Ward, Robert *Composer*
2701 Pickett Road #4022, Durham, NC 27705 USA

Ward, Robert R (Bob) *Football Player*
PO Box 535, Riva, MD 21140 USA

Ward, Ronald L (Ron) *Hockey Player*
3178 W 140th St, Cleveland, OH 44111 USA

Ward, Sela *Actor*
289 S Robertson Blvd #469, Beverly Hills, CA 90211 USA

Ward, Simon *Actor*
Shepherd & Ford, 13 Radner Walk, London, SW3 4BP, UNITED KINGDOM (UK)

Ward, Sterling *Religious Leader*
Brethren Church, 524 College Ave, Ashland, OH 44805 USA

Ward, Susan *Actor*
Howie Simon, 8219 Norton Ave #6, West Hollywood, CA 90046 USA

Ward, Turner M *Baseball Player*
232 Autumn Dr, Saraland, AL 36571 USA

Ward, Vincent *Director*
PO Box 423, Kings Cross, Sydney, NSW, 2011, AUSTRALIA

Ward, Wendy *Golfer*
12845 Sassin Station Road N, Edwall, WA 99008 USA

Ward, Zach *Actor*
Diverse Talent Group, 1875 Century Park
E, #2250, Los Angeles, CA 90067 USA

Warden, Jack *Actor*
23604 Malibu Colony Road, Malibu, CA
90265 USA

Warden, John *Attorney General*
Sullivan & Cromwell, 125 Broad St, New
York, NY 10004 USA

Wardlaw, Kim McLane *Judge*
US Court of Appeals, 125 S Grand Ave,
Pasadena, CA 91105 USA

Ware, Andre *Football Player*
3910 Wood Park, Sugar Land, TX 77479
USA

Ware, Chris *Artist*
Fantagraphics Books, 7563 Lake City
Way, Seattle, WA 98115 USA

Ware, Clyde
1252 N. Laurel Ave., Los Angeles, CA
90046

Ware, Herta *Actor*
PO Box 151, Topanga Canyon, CA 90290
USA

Warfield, Paul D *Football Player*
Jamesco Inc, 15476 NW 77th Court #347,
Hialeah, FL 33016 USA

Wargo, Tom *Golfer*
2801 Putter Lane, Centralia, IL 62801
USA

Warhols, James *Writer*
PO Box 748, Rhinebeck, NY 12572 USA

Wariner, Steve *Musician, Songwriter*
Steve Wariner Productions, PO Box 1647,
Franklin, TN 37065 USA

Waring, Amanda
8 Chester Close Queens Ride, Barnes,
ENGLAND

Waring, Richard
1 Chester Close Queens Ride, London,
ENGLAND, SW13 OJE

Waring, Todd *Actor*
Artists Agency, 1180 S Beverly Dr #301,
Los Angeles, CA 90035 USA

Wark, Robert R *Misc*
Huntington Library & Art Gallery, 1151
Oxford Road, San Marino, CA 91108 USA

Warlock, Billy *Actor*
Pakula/King, 9229 Sunset Blvd #315, Los
Angeles, CA 90069 USA

Warmenhoven, Daniel *Business Person*
Network Appliance Inc, 495 E Java Dr,
Sunnyvale, CA 94089 USA

Warmerdam, Cornelius
3976 N. 1st St., Fresno, CA 93726

Warnecke, John Carl *Architect*
300 Broadway St, San Francisco, CA
94133 USA

Warnecke, Mark *Swimmer*
Am Schichtmeister 100, Witten, 58453,
GERMANY

Warner, Chris *Cartoonist*
Dark House Publishing, 10956 SE Main
St, Portland, OR 97216 USA

Warner, Curt *Football Player*
Curt Warner Chevrolet, 10811 SE Mill
Plain Blvd, Vancouver, WA 98664 USA

Warner, Dan *Actor*

Warner, Dan *Actor*
Players Talent Agency, 13033 Ventura
Blvd # N, Studio City, CA 91604 USA

Warner, David *Actor*
Julian Belfarge, 46 Albermarle St, London,
W1X 4PP, UNITED KINGDOM (UK)

Warner, Douglas A III *Financier*
JP Morgan Chase, 270 Park Ave, New
York, NY 10017 USA

Warner, Jane
166 Ditching Rd., Brighton, CA BN1 6JA
EN

Warner, John *Senator*
Atoka Farms PO Box 1320, Middleburg,
VA 20118-1320 USA

Warner, Julie *Actor*
5850 W 3rd St #128, Los Angeles, CA
90036 USA

Warner, Kurt *Football Player*
PO Box 249, Chesterfield, MO 63006
USA

Warner, Malcolm-Jamal *Actor*
PO Box 69646, Los Angeles, CA 90069
USA

Warner, Margaret *Commentator*
News Hour Show, 2700 S Quincy St,
Arlington, VA 22206 USA

Warner, T C *Actor*
S D B Partners, 1801 Ave of Stars #902,
Los Angeles, CA 90067 USA

Warner, Todd *Artist*
8799 Boyne City Road, Charlevoix, MI
49720 USA

Warner, Tom *Producer*
Carsey-Warner Productions, 4024 Radford
Ave, Building 3, Studio City, CA 91604
USA

Warner, Ty *Designer*
Ty Inc, PO Box 5377, Oak Brook, IL
60522 USA

Warner, William W *Writer*
2243 47th St NW, Washington, DC 20007
USA

Warnes, Jennifer *Musician, Songwriter*
Donald Miller, 12746 Kling St, Studio
City, CA 91604 USA

Warnke, Paul
5037 Garfield St. NW, Washington, DC
20016

Warnock, John *Business Person*
Adobe Systems, 345 Park Ave, San Jose,
CA 95110 USA

Warrant
15216 Burbank Blvd. #103, Van Nuys, CA
91411

Warren, Daine *Songwriter*
1896 Rising Glen Road, Los Angeles, CA
90069 USA

Warren, Diane *Musician*
Realsongs, 6363 Sunset Blvd #810, Los
Angeles, CA 90028

Warren, Estalia *Model, Actor*
AGS, 200 Park Ave #800, New York, NY
10036 USA

Warren, Estella *Actor, Model*
AGS, 200 Park Ave #800, New York, NY
10036 USA

Warren, Fran *Musician*
Richard Barz, 21 Cobble Creek Dr,
Tannersville, PA 18372 USA

Warren, Frederick M *Architect*
65 Cambridge Terrace, Christchurch 1,
NEW ZEALAND

Warren, Gerard *Football Player*
Cleveland Browns, 76 Lou Groza Blvd,
Berea, OH 44017 USA

Warren, Gloria *Actor, Musician*
16872 Bosque Dr, Encino, CA 91436 USA

Warren, Jennifer *Actor*
1675 Old Oak Road, Los Angeles, CA
90049 USA

Warren, Kenneth S *Doctor, Scientist*
Picower Medical Research Institute, 350
Community Dr, Manhasset, NY 11030
USA

Warren, Kiersten *Actor*
Stubbs, 8675 W Washington Blvd #203,
Culver City, CA 90232 USA

Warren, L D *Editor, Cartoonist*
1815 William Howard Taft Road #203,
Cincinnati, OH 45206 USA

Warren, Lesley Ann *Actor*
Relativity Management, 8899 Beverly Blvd
#510, Los Angeles, CA 90048 USA

Warren, Michael
11500 W. Olympic Blvd #510, Los
Angeles, CA 90064

Warren, Michael (Mike) *Actor, Basketball
Player*
21216 Escondido St, Woodland Hills, CA
91364 USA

Warren, Rosanna *Writer*
11 Robinwood Ave, Needham, MA 02492
USA

Warren, Thomas L *Misc*
National Wildlife Federation, 11100
Wildlife Center Dr, Reston, VA 20190
USA

Warren, Tom *Athlete*
2393 La Marque St, San Diego, CA 92109
USA

Warren, Ty *Football Player*
New England Patriots, Gillette Stadium,
RR1 60 Washington, Foxboro, MA 02035
USA

Warren Brothers
PO Box 120479, Nashville, TN 37212
USA

Warren Brothers, The *Music Group*
Creative Artists Agency (CAA-Nashville),
3310 West End Ave Fl 5, Nashville, TN
37203 USA

Warren G *Artist, Music Group, Musician*
Richard Walters, 1800 Argyle Ave #408,
Los Angeles, CA 90028 USA

Warren Jr, Christopher C (Chris) *Football
Player*
1020 W Casino Road, Everett, WA 98204
USA

Warren-Green, Christopher *Musician,
Conductor*
Columbia Artists Mgmt Inc, 165 W 57th
St, New York, NY 10019 USA

Warrenskjold, Dorothy
165 W. 57th St., New York, NY 10019

Warrick, Peter *Football Player*
2166 Western Ave, Cincinnati, OH 45214
USA

Warrick, Ruth *Actor*
903 Park Ave, New York, NY 10021 USA

Warsi, Arshad *Actor, Bollywood*
Kohinoor Apartments 503 Yari Road,
Versova Andheri, Mumbai, MS 400061,
INDIA

Warwick, Dionne *Musician*
World Entertainment Assoc, 297101
Kinderkamack Road #128, Oradell, NJ
07649 USA

Was, Don *Composer, Musician*
10984 Bellagio Road, Los Angeles, CA
90077 USA

Washburn, Barbara *Misc*
1010 Waltham St #F22, Lexington, MA
02421 USA

Washburn, Beverly *Actor*
215 Chiquis Court, Henderson, NV 89074
USA

Washburn, Jarod *Baseball Player*
4334 Deerpath Rd, Danbury, WI 54830
USA

Washburn, Jarrod M *Baseball Player*
4334 E Deerpath Road, Danbury, WI
54830 USA

Washburn, Ray C *Baseball Player*
19001 131st Dr SE, Snohomish, WA
98296 USA

Washburn Jr, H Bradford *Misc*
1010 Waltham St #F22, Lexington, MA
02421 USA

Washington, Alonzo *Cartoonist*
Omega 7, PO Box 171046, Kansas City,
KS 66117 USA

Washington, Baby *Musician*
Headline Talent, 1650 Broadway #508,
New York, NY 10019 USA

Washington, Claudell *Baseball Player*
4067 Hardwick St, Lakewood, CA 90712
USA

Washington, Denzel *Actor*
International Creative Management
(ICM-LA), 8942 Wilshire Blvd, Beverly
Hills, CA 90211 USA

Washington, Dwayne (Pearl) *Basketball Player*
206 Grenadier Dr #206C, Liverpool, NY
13090 USA

Washington, Eugene (Gene) *Football Player*
2625 N Jewell Lane, Plymouth, MN
55447 USA

Washington, Gene A *Football Player*
4087 Cripps Ave, Palo Alto, CA 94306
USA

Washington, Hayma *Producer*
Innovative Artists (LA), 1505 Tenth St,
Santa Monica, CA 90401 USA

Washington, Isaiah *Actor*
International Creative Mgmt, 8942
Wilshire Blvd #219, Beverly Hills, CA
90211 USA

Washington, Joe D *Football Player*
First Union Securities, 2350 W Joppa
Road, Lutherville, MD 21093 USA

Washington, Kermit *Basketball Player*
2242 NW 45th Ave, Carnas, WA 98607
USA

Washington, Kerry *Actor*
Abrams Artists Agency (LA), 9200 Sunset
Blvd Fl 11, Los Angeles, CA 90069 USA

Washington, Lionel *Football Player*
Green Bay Packer's, PO Box 10628,
Green Bay, WI 54307 USA

Washington, MaliVai *Tennis Player*
5 S Roscoe Blvd, Ponte Vedra Beach, FL
32082 USA

Washington, Mike L *Football Player*
3235 Hernon Road, Montgomery, AL
36106 USA

Washington, Theodore (Ted) *Football Player*
3522 E 26th Ave, Tampa, FL 33605 USA

Wasilewski, Paul *Actor*
Brillstein-Grey Entertainment, 9150
Wilshire Blvd #350, Beverly Hills, CA
90212 USA

Wasim, Akram *Cricketer*
Lancashire Cricket Club, Old Trafford,
Manchester, M16 0PX, UNITED
KINGDOM (UK)

Waskow, Thomas C *General*
Commander, US Forces Japan & 5th Air
Force Unit 5068, APO, AP, 96328 USA

Wasmeier, Markus *Skier*
Breitensteinstr 14B, Schliersee-Neuhaus,
83727, GERMANY

Wass, Ted *Actor*
3354 Longridge Terrace, Sherman Oaks,
CA 91423 USA

Wasserburg, Gerald J *Geophysicist*
1207 Arden Road, Pasadena, CA 91106
USA

Wasserman, Dale *Writer*
Casa Blanca Estates, #37, Paradise Valley,
AZ 95253 USA

Wasserman, Dan *Editor, Cartoonist*
Boston Globe, Editorial Dept, 135 William
Morrissey Blvd, Dorchester, MA 02125
USA

Wasserman, Lew
911 N. Foothill Rd., Beverly Hills, CA
90210

Wasserman, Rob *Musician*
Leslie Wiener Financial Services, PO Box
245, Sausalito, CA 94966 USA

Wasserman, Robert H *Doctor*
Cornell University, Veterinary Medicine
College, Ithaca, NY 14853 USA

Wasserstein, Wendy *Writer*
Royce Carlton Inc, 866 United Nations
Plaza, #4030, New York, NY 10017 USA

Wasson, Craig *Actor*
E/W, 280 S Beverly Dr, #400, Beverly
Hills, CA 90212 USA

Wasson, Erin *Model*
I M G Models, 304 Park Ave S #1200,
New York, NY 10010 USA

Watanabe, Gedde
1632 Westerly Terr, Los Angeles, CA
90026-1234

Watanabe, Ken *Actor*
ROAR LLC, 2400 Broadway #350, Santa
Monica, CA 90404 USA

Watanabe, Milio *Scientist*
Nippon Electric Co, Computer Labs,
5-33-1 Shiba, Tokyo, JAPAN

Watanabe, Sadao *Musician*
International Music Network, 278 S Main
St #400, Gloucester, MA 01930 USA

Watanabe, Youji *Architect*
1-6-13 Hirakawacho, Chiyodaku, Tokyo,
JAPAN

Waterboys
3 Monmouth Rd., London, ENGLAND,
W2

Waterman, Denis
D&J Arlon, Pinewood Studios, Iverheath,
Iver, SL0 0NH, UNITED KINGDOM (UK)

Waterman, Felicity *Actor*
280 Mott St #4R, New York, NY 10012
USA

Waterman, Hannah *Actor*
EastEnders, BBC Elstree Centre, Clarendon
Road, Borehamwood, Herts, UNITED
KINGDOM

Waterman, Pete *Actor*
Pop Idol (Fremantle Media), 2700
Colorado Ave #450, Santa Monica, CA
90404 USA

Waters, Alice *Chef*
Chez Panisse, 1517 Shattuck Ave,
Berkeley, CA 94709 USA

Waters, Charles T (Charlie) *Football Player, Football Coach, Coach*
2838 Woodside St, Dallas, TX 75204 USA

Waters, Crystal *Musician*
270 Lafayette St #602, New York, NY
10012 USA

Waters, Frank (Muddy) *Football Coach*
5337 E Hidden Lake Dr, East Lansing, MI
48823 USA

Waters, John *Director*
10 W Highfield Road, Baltimore, MD
21218 USA

Waters, John B *Government Official*
405 Burridge Waters Edge, Sevierville, TN
37862 USA

Waters, Lou *Commentator*
Cable News Network, News Dept, 1050
Techwood Dr NW, Atlanta, GA 30318
USA

Waters, Mark *Director*
Miramax Films, 11 Beach St, New York,
NY 10013 USA

Waters, Richard *Publisher*
20 Somerset Downs, Saint Louis, MO
63124 USA

Waters, Roger *Musician*
Agency Group, 370 City Road, London,
EC1V 2QA, UNITED KINGDOM (UK)

Waterston, James *Actor*
Essential Entertainment Management,
6121 Santa Monica Blvd #201,
Hollywood, CA 90038 USA

Waterston, Robert *Biologist*
Washington University Medical School,
Biology Dept, Saint Louis, MO 63130
USA

Waterston, Sam *Actor*
RR Box 197, Easton St, West Cornwall, CT 06796 USA

Wathan, John D *Baseball Player*
1401 Deer Run Trail, Blue Springs, MO 64015 USA

Watkin, David *Cinematographer*
6 Sussex Mews, Brighton, BN2 1GZ, UNITED KINGDOM (UK)

Watkins, Carlene *Actor*
104 Fremont Place W, Los Angeles, CA 90005 USA

Watkins, Dean A *Inventor, Business Person*
Watkins-Johnson Co, 401 River Oaks Parkway, San Jose, CA 95134 USA

Watkins, James D *Admiral, Secretary*
2021 Indian Circle, Saint Leonard, MD 20685 USA

Watkins, Lloyd I *Economist*
PO Box 111, Bloomington, IL 61702 USA

Watkins, Marilyn
217 No. San Marino Ave, San Gabriel, CA 91775

Watkins, Michelle *Actor*
Capital Artists, 6404 Wilshire Blvd, #950, Los Angeles, CA 90048 USA

Watkins, Tasker *War Hero, Judge*
5 Pump Court, Middle Temple, London, EC4, UNITED KINGDOM (UK)

Watkins, Tionne (T-Boz) *Artist, Musician*
Diggit Entertainment, 6W 18th St, #800, New York, NY 10011 USA

Watkins, Tuc
9229 Sunset Blvd. #311, Los Angeles, CA 90069

Watkins, William D *Business Person*
Seagate Technology, 920 Disc Dr, Scotts Valley, CA 95066 USA

Watkinson of Working, Harold A *Government Official*
Tyma House, Bosham near Chichester, Sussex, UNITED KINGDOM (UK)

Watley, Jody *Musician*
Baker Winokur Rider, 9100 Wilshire Blvd #600, Beverly Hills, CA 90212 USA

Watling, Deborah
183 Trevelyan Rd, London, ENGLAND, SW17 9LW

Watros, Cynthia *Actor*
Principal Entertainment (LA), 1964 Westwood Blvd #400, Los Angeles, CA 90025 USA

Watrous Jr, William R (Bill) *Musician*
GNP/Crescendo Records, 8480 Sunset Blvd #A, Los Angeles, CA 90069 USA

Watson, A J *Race Car Driver, Engineer*
5420 Crawfordsville Road, Indianapolis, IN 46224 USA

Watson, Albert M *Photographer*
777 Washington St, New York, NY 10014 USA

Watson, Alberta *Actor*
Cathy Atkinson, 2629 Main Street, PMB 129, Santa Monica, CA 90405 USA

Watson, Alexander F *Diplomat*
Nature Conservancy International, 4245 Fairfax Dr #100, Arlington, VA 22203 USA

Watson, Angela *Actor*
Chasin Agency, The, 8899 Beverly Blvd #716, Los Angeles, CA 90048 USA

Watson, Barry *Actor*
Creative Artists Agency LCC (CAA-LA), 9830 Wilshire Blvd, Beverly Hills, CA 90212 USA

Watson, Cecil J *Doctor*
Abbott Northwestern Hospital, 2727 Chicago Ave, Minneapolis, MN 55407 USA

Watson, Dale *Musician*
Crowley Artist Mgmt, 602 Wayside Dr, Wimberley, TX 78676 USA

Watson, Dennis
420 San Marco Dr., Ft. Lauderdale, FL 33301

Watson, Doc *Musician*
CM Mgmt, 5479 Larryon Dr, Woodland Hills, CA 91367 USA

Watson, Elizabeth M *Judge*
Houston Police Department, Chief's Office, 1200 Travis St, Houston, TX 77002 USA

Watson, Emily *Actor*
William Morris Agency, 151 El Camino Dr, Beverly Hills, CA 90212 USA

Watson, Emma *Actor*
PO Box 3000, Laevesden Harts, London, WD25 ZLF, UNITED KINGDOM (UK)

Watson, Gene *Musician*
Bobby Roberts, 909 Meadowlark Lane, Goodlettsville, TN 37072 USA

Watson, James D *Nobel Prize Laureate*
Bungtown Road, Cold Spring Harbor, NY 11724 USA

Watson, Kenneth M *Physicist, Oceanographer*
8515 Costa Verde Blvd #2008, San Diego, CA 92122 USA

Watson, Martha *Track Athlete*
5509 Royal Vista Lane, Las Vegas, NV 89149 USA

Watson, Max P Jr *Business Person*
BMC Software, 2101 CityWest Blvd, Houston, TX 77042 USA

Watson, Mills *Actor*
2824 Dell Ave, Venice, CA 90291 USA

Watson, Paul *Misc*
Sea Shepherd Conservation Society, Po Box 2616, Friday Harbor, WA 98250 USA

Watson, Paul *Photographer, Journalist*
Toronto Star, Editorial Dept, 1 Yonge St, Toronto, ON M5E 1E6, CANADA

Watson, Polly Jo *Misc*
Washington University, Anthropology Dept, Saint Louis, MO 63130 USA

Watson, Robert A *Religious Leader*
Salvation Army, 615 Slaters Lane, Alexandria, VA 22314 USA

Watson, Robert M (Bobby) Jr *Musician*
Split Second Timing, 11 Ridge Road, Chappaqua, NY 10514 USA

Watson, Russell *Musician*
Box 806, Manchester, M60 2XS, UNITED KINGDOM (UK)

Watson, Stephen E *Business Person*
Dayton Hudson, 1000 Nicollet Mall, Minneapolis, MN 55403 USA

Watson, Thomas S (Tom) *Golfer*
1901 W 47th Place #200, Mission, KS 66205 USA

Watson, Wayne *Musician*
TBA Artist Mgmt, 300 10th Ave S, Nashville, TN 37203 USA

Watson Jr, Jack H *Government Official*
Long Aldridge Norman, 1900 K St NW, Washington, DC 20006 USA

Watson Richardson, Lillian (Pockey) *Swimmer*
4960 Maunalani Circle, Honolulu, HI 96816 USA

Watson-Johnson, Vernee *Actor*
Gage Group, 14724 Ventura Blvd #505, Sherman Oaks, CA 91403 USA

Watt, Ben *Musician, Songwriter*
JFD Mgmt, Acklam Workshops, 10 Acklam Road, London, W10 5QZ, UNITED KINGDOM (UK)

Watt, James G *Secretary, Designer*
PO Box 3705, Jackson Hole, WY 83001 USA

Watt, Mike *Musician*
Agency Group, The (NY), 1775 Broadway #430, New York, NY 10019 USA

Watt, Tom *Hockey Player, Coach*
Calgary Flames, PO Box 1540, Station M, Calgary, AB T2P 3B9, CANADA

Wattenberg, Ben J *Misc*
American Enterprise Institute, 1150 17th St NW, Washington, DC 20036 USA

Watters, Richard J (Rickie) *Football Player*
11100 NE 8th St #600, Bellevue, WA 98004 USA

Watters, Richard J (Ricky) *Football Player*
11100 NE 8th St #600, Bellevue, WA 98004 USA

Watters, Tim *Hockey Player*
804 Oak Grove Parkway, Houghton, MI 49931 USA

Watterson, Bill *Artist*
General Delivery, Hudson, OH 44236 USA

Watterson, John B (Brett) *Astronaut*
2508 Via Anacapa, Palos Verdes Estates, CA 90274 USA

Wattleton, A Faye *Entertainer*
Fischer-Ross Agency, 250 W 57th St, New York, NY 10107 USA

Watts, Andre *Musician*
205 W 57th St, New York, NY 10019 USA

Watts, Charles R (Charlie) *Musician*
Rupert Lowenstein, 2 King St, London, SW1Y 6QL, UNITED KINGDOM (UK)

Watts, Charlie
Half Moon Chambers Chapel Walks, Manchester, ENGLAND, M2 1HN

Watts, D Henry *Business Person*
Norfolk Southern Corp, 3 Commercial Place, Norfolk, VA 23510 USA

Watts, Ernest J (Ernie) *Musician*
DeLeon Artists, 4031 Panama Court, Piedmont, CA 94611 USA

Watts, Ernie *Designer, Director*
International Creative Mgmt, 40 W 57th St #1800, New York, NY 10019 USA

Watts, Heather *Ballerina*
New York City Ballet, Lincoln Center Plaza, New York, NY 10023 USA

Watts, Helen J *Opera Singer*
Rock House Wallis, Ambleston Haverford-West, Dyfed, SA62 5RA, WALES

Watts, Kristi *Religious Leader, Television Host*
700 Club, 977 Centerville Tpke, Virginia Beach, VT 23463 USA

Watts, Naomi *Actor*
June Cann Mgmt, 110 Queen St, Woollahra, NSW, 2025, AUSTRALIA

Watts, Quincy *Track Athlete*
First Team Marketing, PO Box 67581, Los Angeles, CA 90067 USA

Watts III, Claudius E *Educator, General*
Citadel, President's Office, Charleston, SC 29409 USA

Waugh, Jim *Baseball Player*
8151 Spruce Valley Dr, Ft Worth, TX 76137-1296

Waugh, John S *Misc*
Massachusetts Institute of Technology, Chemistry Dept, Cambridge, MA 02139 USA

Waugh, Stephen (Steve) *Cricketer*
Octagon, 1751 Pinnacle Dr #1500, McLean, VA 22102 USA

Wax, Ruby *Actor, Comedian*
Old Christchurch Road, Bournemouth, BH1 1LG, UNITED KINGDOM (UK)

Waxenberg, Alan M *Publisher*
Good Housekeeping Magazine, 959 8th Ave, New York, NY 10019 USA

Waxman, Henry *Politician*
6913 Ayr Lane, Bethesda, MD 20817

Wayans, Damien Dante *Actor*
William Morris Agency (WMA-LA), 1 William Morris Pl, Beverly Hills, CA 90212 USA

Wayans, Damon *Actor*
Creative Artists Agency, 9830 Wilshire Blvd, Beverly Hills, CA 90212 USA

Wayans, Keenan Ivory *Actor, Writer, Producer, Director*
Wayans Brothers Entertainment, 500 S Buena Vista St, Stage 7 Floor 5, Burbank, CA 91521 USA

Wayans, Keenen Ivory *Actor, Director*
16405 Mulholland Dr, Los Angeles, CA 90049 USA

Wayans, Kim *Actor*
1742 Granville Ave #2, Los Angeles, CA 90025 USA

Wayans, Marlon *Actor, Comedian*
Gold-Miller Mgmt, 9220 Sunset Blvd #320, Los Angeles, CA 90069 USA

Wayans, Shawn *Actor*
Gold-Miller Mgmt, 9220 Sunset Blvd #320, Los Angeles, CA 90069 USA

Wayda, Stephen *Photographer*
Playboy Magazine, Reader Service, 680 N Lake Shore Dr, Chicago, IL 60611 USA

Wayne, Fredd
117 Strand St., Santa Monica, CA 90405

Wayne, Jimmy *Musician*
William Morris Agency (WMA-TN), 2100 W End Ave #1000, Nashville, TN 37203 USA

Wayne, June *Artist*
1108 N Tamarind Ave, Los Angeles, CA 90038 USA

Wayne, Lil *Musician*
JL Entertainment Inc, 18653 Ventura Blvd, #340, Tarzana, CA 91356

Wayne, Patrick *Actor*
10502 Whipple St, Toluca Lake, CA 91602 USA

Wayne, Reggie *Football Player*
Indianapolis Colts, 7001 W 56th St, Indianapolis, IN 46254 USA

Wazed, Sheik Hasina *Prime Minister*
Sere-e Bangla Nagar, Gono Bhaban, Sher-e-Banglanagar, Dakar, BANGLADESH

Weah, George *Soccer Player*
AC Milan, Via Turati 3, Milan, 20221, ITALY

Weatherill, B Bruce *Government Official*
Emmets House, Ide Hill, Kent, TN14 6BA, UNITED KINGDOM (UK)

Weatherly, John Michael
3300 Buckeye Rd. #405, Atlanta, GA 30431

Weatherly, Michael *Actor*
United Talent Agency, 9560 Wilshire Blvd, #500, Beverly Hills, CA 90212 USA

Weatherly, Shawn
9229 Sunset Blvd. #311, Los Angeles, CA 90069

Weatherly, Shwan *Actor, Beauty Pageant Winner*
135 N Westgate Ave, Los Angeles, CA 90049 USA

Weathers, Carl *Actor*
4241 Redwood Ave #2205, Los Angeles, CA 90066 USA

Weatherspoon, Clarence *Basketball Player*
PO Box 117, Crawford, MS 39743 USA

Weatherspoon, Teresa G *Basketball Player*
Los Angeles Sparks, Staples Center, 1111 S Figueroa St, Los Angeles, CA 90015 USA

Weatherwax, Bob
16133 Soledad Canyon Rd., Canyon Country, CA 91351

Weatherwax, Jim *Football Player*
636 Cucharas Mountain Dr, Livermore, CO 80536 USA

Weaver, Dennis *Actor, Musician*
13869 County Road 1, Ridgeway, CO 81432 USA

Weaver, Earl S *Baseball Player*
3000 SW 62nd Ave, Miami, FL 33155 USA

Weaver, Fritz *Actor*
161 W 75th St, New York, NY 10023 USA

Weaver, Jason *Actor*
Don Buchwald & Associates Inc (LA), 6500 Wilshire Blvd #2200, Los Angeles, CA 90048 USA

Weaver, Reg *Misc*
National Education Assn, 1201 16th St NW, Washington, DC 20036 USA

Weaver, Robby *Actor*
Artists Group, 10100 Santa Monica Blvd #2490, Los Angeles, CA 90067 USA

Weaver, Rufus *Inventor*
77 Adelaide St, New London, CT 06320 USA

Weaver, Sigourney *Actor*
Goat Cay Productions, Po Box 38, New York, NY 10150 USA

Weaver, Warren E *Misc*
7607 Horsepen Road, Richmond, VA 23229 USA

Weaver, Wayne *Football Executive*
Jacksonville Jaguars, 1 AllTel Stadim Place, Jacksonville, FL 32202 USA

Weaving, Hugo *Actor*
Shanahan Mgmt, PO Box 1509, Darlinghurst, NSW, 1300, AUSTRALIA

Webb, Chloe *Actor*
1015 Main St, Venice, CA 90291 USA

Webb, Christiaan *Musician, Songwriter*
SuperVision Mgmt, 109B Regents Park Road, London, NW1 8UR, UNITED KINGDOM (UK)

Webb, James R (Jimmy) *Football Player*
1319 S Prairie Flower Road, Turlock, CA 95380 USA

Webb, Jimmy *Musician, Songwriter*
1560 N Laurel Ave #109, Los Angeles, CA 90046 USA

Webb, Justin *Musician, Songwriter*
SuperVision Mgmt, 109B Regents Park Road, London, NW1 8UR, UNITED KINGDOM (UK)

Webb, Karrie *Golfer*
725 Presidential Dr, Boynton Beach, FL 33435 USA

Webb, Lee *Religious Leader, Television Host*
700 Club, 977 Centerville Tpke, Virginia Beach, VT 23463 USA

Webb, Lucy *Actor, Comedian*
1360 N Crescent Heights #38, West Hollywood, CA 90046 USA

Webb, Richmond J *Football Player*
4120 Humphrey Dr, Dallas, TX 75216 USA

Webb, Russell (Russ) *Misc, Athlete*
2362 Walnut Ave, Upland, CA 91784 USA

Webb, Tamilee *Physicist*
PO Box 676107, Rancho Santa Fe, CA 92067 USA

Webb, Veronica *Actor, Model*
Ford Model Agency, 142 Greene St #400, New York, NY 10012 USA

Webb, Wayne *Bowler*
4413 McGuire St, North Las Vegas, NV 89031 USA

Webb, Wellington E *Misc*
Mayor's Office, City-County Building, 1437 Bannock St, Denver, CO 80202 USA

Webb, William H *Business Person*
Altria Group, 120 Park Ave, New York, NY 10017 USA

Webber, Chris *Basketball Player*
Sacramento Kings, Arco Arena, 1 Sports Parkway, Sacramento, CA 95834 USA

Webber, Julian Lloyd *Musician*
Columbia Artists Mgmt Inc, 165 W 57th St, New York, NY 10019 USA

Webber, Lord Andrew Lloyd *Producer, Director, Writer*
725 Fifth Avenue, New York, NY 10022 USA

Webber, Mark *Actor*
Handprint Entertainment, 1100 Glendon Ave #1000, Los Angeles, CA 90024 USA

Webber, Tristan *Fashion Designer*
Brower Lewis, 74 Gloucester Place, London, W1H 3HN, UNITED KINGDOM (UK)

Weber, Amy *Actor*
Select Artists Ltd (CA-Westside Office), 1138 12th Street, Suite 1, Santa Monica, CA 90403 USA

Weber, Arnold R *Educator*
Northwestern University, Chancellor's Office, Evanston, IL 60208 USA

Weber, Bruce *Photographer*
Robert Miller Gallery, 526 W 26th St #10A, New York, NY 10001 USA

Weber, Eberhard *Musician, Composer*
Ted Kurland, 173 Brighton Ave, Boston, MA 02134 USA

Weber, Eugen J *Historian*
11579 Sunset Blvd, Los Angeles, CA 90049 USA

Weber, George B *Misc*
Chemin Moise-Duboule 19, Geneva, 1209, SWITZERLAND

Weber, Jack *Actor*
Gersh Agency, 232 N Canon Dr, Beverly Hills, CA 90210 USA

Weber, Jake *Actor*
Gersh Agency, 232 N Canon Dr, Beverly Hills, CA 90210 USA

Weber, Mark *Actor*
Handprint Entertainment, 1100 Glendon Ave #1000, Los Angeles, CA 90024 USA

Weber, Mary E *Astronaut*
14 Hawkview St, Portola Valley, CA 94028 USA

Weber, Peter D (Pete) *Bowler*
10500 Saint Xavier Lane, Saint Ann, MO 63074 USA

Weber, Richard A (Dick) *Bowler*
1305 Arlington Dr, Florissant, MO 63033 USA

Weber, Robert M (Bob) *Cartoonist*
New Yorker Magazine, Editorial Dept, 4 Times Square, New York, NY 10036 USA

Weber, Stephen L *Educator*
State University of New York, President's Office, Oswego, NY 13126 USA

Weber, Steven *Actor*
1615 N Wilcox Ave #469, Los Angeles, CA 90028 USA

Weber, Vin *Misc*
Empower America, 1776 I St NW, Washington, DC 20006 USA

Weber Jr, Bob *Cartoonist*
King Features Syndicate, 888 7th Ave, New York, NY 10106 USA

Webre, Septime *Choreographer*
Washington Ballet, 3515 Wisconsin Ave NW, Washington, DC 20016 USA

Webster, Alexander (Alex) *Football Player, Football Coach, Coach*
8461 SE Palm Hammock Lane, Hobe Sound, FL 33455 USA

Webster, George D *Football Player*
5623 Tallow Lane, Houston, TX 77021 USA

Webster, Marvin *Basketball Player*
8819 Stonehaven Road, Randallstown, MD 21133 USA

Webster, R Howard *Publisher, Baseball Player*
Toronto Globe & Mail, 444 Front St W, Toronto, ON M5V 2S9, CANADA

Webster, Robert D (Bob) *Swimmer, Misc*
800 Energy Center Blvd #3414, Northport, AL 35473 USA

Webster, Tom *Hockey Player, Coach*
1750 Longfellow Dr, Canton, MI 48187 USA

Webster, Victor *Actor*
Benderspink, 6735 Yucca Street, Hollywood, CA 90028 USA

Webster, William H *Government Official*
4777 Dexter St NW, Washington, DC 20007 USA

Wechsler, Nick *Actor*
BBA, 4342 Lankershim Blvd, N Hollywood, CA 91602 USA

Wecht, Cyril H
5420 Darlington Rd, Pittsburgh, PA 15217 USA

Weck, Peter
Bambauer Keplerstr. 2, Munich, GERMANY, D-81679

Wecker, Andreas *Gymnast*
Am Dorfplatz 1, Klein-Ziethen, 16766, GERMANY

Weddington, Sarah R *Attorney General*
709 W 14th St, Austin, TX 78701 USA

Wedeen, Kelsey *Actor*
Select Artists Ltd (CA-Westside Office), 1138 12th Street, Suite 1, Santa Monica, CA 90403 USA

Wedel, Dieter *Director*
Tonndorfer Strand 2, Hamburg, 22045, GERMANY

Weder, Gustav *Athlete*
Haltenstr 2, Stachen/TG, SWITZERLAND

Wedge, Eric M *Baseball Player*
31 Abington Road, Danvers, MA 01923 USA

Wedgeworth, Ann *Actor*
70 Riverside Dr, New York, NY 10024 USA

Wedman, Scott *Basketball Player*
7912 NW Scenic Dr, Kansas City, MO 64152 USA

Wee Kim Wee *President*
25 Siglap Plain, Singapore, 456014, SINGAPORE

Weed, Kent *Director, Producer, Writer*
Arthur Smith & Co, 1811 Centinela Ave, Santa Monica, CA 90404 USA

Weed, Maurice James *Composer*
308 Overlook Road #55, Asheville, NC 28803 USA

Weege, Reinhold *Producer*
2035 Via Don Berito, La Jolla, CA 92037 USA

Weeks, Claire
11048 Chimineas Ave, Northridge, CA 91326

Weeks, John D *Misc*
15301 Watergate Road, Silver Spring, MD 20905 USA

Weeks, John R *Architect*
39 Jackson's Lane, Highgate, London, N6 5SR, UNITED KINGDOM (UK)

Weeks, Rollo *Actor*
Artists Independent Network (NY), 270 La Fayette St #402, New York, NY 10012 USA

Weese, Miranda *Ballerina*
New York City Ballet, Lincoln Center Plaza, New York, NY 10023 USA

Weezer *Music Group*
Creative Artists Agency LCC (CAA-LA), 9830 Wilshire Blvd, Beverly Hills, CA 90212 USA

Wefald, Jon *Educator*
Kansas State University, President's Office, Manhattan, KS 66506 USA

Wegman, William G *Artist, Photographer*
239 W 18th St, New York, NY 10011 USA

Wegner, Hans J *Designer*
Tinglevej 17, Gentofte, 2820, DENMARK

Wehling, Ulrich *Athlete*
Skiverband, Hubertusstr 1, Munich, 81477, GERMANY

Wehrli, Roger R *Football Player*
46 Fox Meadows Court, Saint Charles, MO 63303 USA

Wei, Dan-Wen *Musician*
Columbia Artists Mgmt Inc, 165 W 57th St, New York, NY 10019 USA

Wei, James *Engineer*
571 Lake St, Princeton, NJ 08540 USA

Weibel, Robert *Doctor*
University of Pennsylvania, Med School, Pediatrics Dept, Philadelphia, PA 19104 USA

Weibring, D A *Golfer*
1315 Garden Grove Court, Plano, TX 75075 USA

Weich, Gillian *Musician*
DS Mgmt, 1017 16th Ave S, Nashville, TN 37212 USA

Weicker, Lowell P Jr *Governor, Senator*
200 Duke St, Alexandria, VA 22314 USA

Weida, Johnny *General, Educator*
Superintendent, US Air Force Academy, Colorado Springs, CO 80840 USA

Weide, Bob *Director*
CAA, 9830 Wilshire Blvd, Beverly Hills, CA 90212

Weide, Robert B *Producer, Director*
MBST Entertainment, 345 N Maple D #200, Suite 200, Beverly Hills, CA 90210 USA

Weidemann, Jakob *Artist*
Ringsveen, Lillehammer, 2600, NORWAY

Weidenbaum, Murray L *Government Official, Economist*
6231 Rosebury Ave, Saint Louis, MO 63105 USA

Weidenfeld of Chelsea, Arthur G *Publisher*
9 Chelsea Embankment, London, SW3 4LE, UNITED KINGDOM (UK)

Weider, Joe *Publisher*
Weider Health & Fitness, 21100 Erwin St, Woodland Hills, CA 91367 USA

Weidinger, Christine *Opera Singer*
John J Miller, 801 W 181st St #20, New York, NY 10033 USA

Weidlinger, Paul *Engineer*
Weidlinger Assoc, 375 Hudson Ave, New York, NY 10014 USA

Weigel, Teri *Actor, Model*
6433 Topanga Canyon Blvd #103, Woodland Hills, CA 91303 USA

Weight, Doug *Hockey Player*
Saint Louis Blues, Sawis Center, 1401 Clark Ave, Saint Louis, MO 63103 USA

Weihenmayer, Erik *Mountaineer*
682 Partridge Circle, Golden, CO 80403 USA

Weikel, M Keith *Business Person*
Manor Care Inc, 333 N Summit St, Toledo, OH 43604 USA

Weikl, Bernd *Opera Singer*
Ulf Torgvist, Sankt Eriksgatan 100, Stockholm, 113 31, SWEDEN

Weil, Andrew *Doctor*
University of Arizona, Medical Center, 1501 N Campbell Ave, Tucson, AZ 85724 USA

Weil, Bruno *Composer, Conductor*
Kaylor Mgmt, 130 W 57th St #8G, New York, NY 10019 USA

Weil, Cynthia *Songwriter*
Gorfaine/Schwartz, 13245 Riverside Dr #450, Sherman Oaks, CA 91423 USA

Weil, Frank A *Misc*
Smithsonian Institution, 900 Jefferson Dr SW, Washington, DC 20560 USA

Weil, Liza *Actor*
Creative Artists Agency, 9830 Wilshire Blvd, Beverly Hills, CA 90212 USA

Weiland, Scott *Musician, Songwriter*
Q Prime, 729 7th Ave #1600, New York, NY 10019 USA

Weill, Claudia B *Director*
2800 Seattle Dr, Los Angeles, CA 90046 USA

Weill, David (Dave) *Track Athlete*
120 Mountain Spring Ave, San Francisco, CA 94114 USA

Weill, Sanford I (Sandy) *Business Person*
Citigroup Inc, 399 Park Ave, New York, NY 10022 USA

Wein, George *Producer*
Festival Productions, 311 W 74th St, New York, NY 10023 USA

Weinbach, Arthur F *Business Person*
Automatic Data Processing, 1 ADP Blvd, Roseland, NJ 07068 USA

Weinbach, Lawrence A *Business Person*
Unisys Corp, Unisys Way, Blue Bell, PA 19424 USA

Weinberg, Alvin M *Physicist*
111 Moylan Lane, Oak Ridge, TN 37830 USA

Weinberg, John L *Financier*
Goldman Sachs Co, 85 Broad St, New York, NY 10004 USA

Weinberg, Max *Musician*
Panacea Entertainment, 12020 Chandler Blvd #300, North Hollywood, CA 91607 USA

Weinberg, Mike *Actor*
Reel Talent Management, 980 N Bundy, Los Angeles, CA 90049 USA

Weinberg, Robert A *Scientist, Doctor*
Whitehead Institute, 9 Cambridge Center, Cambridge, MA 02142 USA

Weinberg, Steven *Nobel Prize Laureate*
University of Texas, Physics Dept, 2613 Wichita St, Austin, TX 78712 USA

Weinberger, Caspar *Secretary, Publisher*
Rogers & Wells, 2001 K St NW, Washington, DC 20006 USA

Weinbrecht, Donna *Skier*
General Delivery, West Milford, NJ 07480 USA

Weiner, Art E *Football Player*
404 Kimberly Dr, Greensboro, NC 27408 USA

Weiner, Eric *Writer, Producer*
Writers and Artists Group Intl (LA), 8383 Wilshire Blvd #550, Beverly Hills, CA 90211 USA

Weiner, Gerry *Government Official*
40 Fredmir St, Dollard-des-Ormeaux, PQ H9A 2R3, CANADA

Weiner, Timothy E (Tim) *Journalist*
New York Times, Editorial Dept, 1627 I St NW, Washington, DC 20006 USA

Weingarten, David M *Architect*
Ace Architects, 330 2nd St, Oakland, CA 94607 USA

Weingarten, Reid *Attorney General*
Steptoe & Johnson, 4603 Harrison St, Chevy Chase, MD 20815 USA

Weinger, Scott *Actor*
9255 Sunset Blvd #1010, West Hollywood, CA 90069 USA

Weinke, Chris *Football Player*
Carolina Panthers, Ericsson Stadium, 800 S Mint St, Charlotte, NC 28202 USA

Weinman, Roz *Producer*
Wolf Films Inc, 100 Universal City Plz, Bldg 2252, Universal City, CA 91608 USA

Weinstein, Arnold A *Writer, Songwriter*
Columbia University, English Dept, New York, NY 10027 USA

Weinstein, Bob *Producer*
Miramax Films (LA), 8439 Sunset Blvd, West Hollywood, CA 90069

Weinstein, Diane Gilbert *Judge*
US Court of Claims, 717 Madison Place NW, Washington, DC 20439 USA

Weinstein, Harvey *Producer*
Miramax Films (LA), 8439 Sunset Blvd, West Hollywood, CA 90069

Weinstein, Robert (Bob) *Producer*
Miramax Films, 7920 Sunset Blvd, Los Angeles, CA 90046 USA

Weinstein, Sidney T *General*
11936 Holly Branch Court, Great Falls, VA 22066 USA

Weintraub, Carl
10390 Santa Monica Blvd. #300, Los Angeles, CA 90025

Weintraub, Jerry *Producer*
27740 Pacific Coast Highway, Malibu, CA 90265 USA

Weir, Arabella *Actor*
Lip Service Casting Ltd, 4 Kingly St, Soho, W1B 5PE, UNITED KINGDOM (UK)

Weir, Bill *Commentator*
ABC-TV, News Dept, 77 W 66th St, New York, NY 10023 USA

Weir, Bob *Musician*
Grateful Dead, PO Box 1073, San Rafael, CA 94915 USA

Weir, Gillian C *Musician*
78 Robin Way, Tilehurst, Berks, RG3 5SW, UNITED KINGDOM (UK)

Weir, Judith *Composer*
Chester Music, 8/9 Frith St, London, W1V 5TZ, UNITED KINGDOM (UK)

Weir, Mike *Golfer*
Taboo Muskoka Sands, Muskoka Beach Road, Gravenhurst, ON P1P 1R1, CANADA

Weir, Peter *Director*
Salt Pan Films, PO Box 29, Palm Beach, NSW, 2108, AUSTRALIA

Weis, Heidelinde
Schleissheimer Str. 207, Munich, GERMANY, D-80809

Weis, Joseph F Jr *Judge*
US Court of Appeals, US Courthouse, 700 Grant St, Pittsburgh, PA 15219 USA

Weisberg, Ruth *Artist*
11452 W Washington Blvd, Los Angeles, CA 90066 USA

Weisberg, Tim *Musician*
Pyramid Entertainment, 89 5th Ave #700, New York, NY 10003 USA

Weisel, Heidi *Fashion Designer*
202 W 40th St, New York, NY 10018 USA

Weiser-Most, Franz *Conductor*
Van Walsum Mgmt, 4 Addison Bridge Place, London, W14 8XP, UNITED KINGDOM (UK)

Weishoff, Paula *Volleyball Player*
20021 Colgate Circle, Huntington Beach, CA 92646 USA

Weiskopf, Tom *Golfer*
7580 E Gray Road, Scottsdale, AZ 85260 USA

Weiskrantz, Lawrence *Doctor*
Oxford University, Experimental Psychology Dept, Oxford, OX1 3UD, UNITED KINGDOM (UK)

Weisman, Annie *Comedian*
Gersh Agency, The (LA), 232 N Canon Dr, Beverly Hills, CA 90210 USA

Weisman, Ben *Composer*
4527 Alla Road #3, Marina del Rey, CA 90292 USA

Weisman, Kevin *Actor*
Metropolitan Talent Agency (MTA), 4526 Wilshire Blvd, Los Angeles, CA 90010 USA

Weisman, Sam *Actor, Director*
United Talent Agency, 9560 Wilshire Blvd, #500, Beverly Hills, CA 90212 USA

Weisner, Maurice F *Admiral*
351 Woodbine Dr, Pensacola, FL 32503 USA

Weiss, Barry *Business Person*
Zomba Recording Corporation, 137-139 West 25th Street, New York, NY 10001

Weiss, Eric *Actor*
Brant Rose Agency, The, 10537 Santa Monica Blvd #305, Los Angeles, CA 90025

Weiss, Glenn *Director*
William Morris Agency (WMA-LA), 1 William Morris Pl, Beverly Hills, CA 90212 USA

Weiss, Heinz
Rosskopfstr. 10, Grunwald, GERMANY, D-82031

Weiss, Janet *Musician*
Legends of 21st Century, 7 Trinity Row, Florence, MA 01062 USA

Weiss, Julie *Designer*
International Creative Mgmt, 8942 Wilshire Blvd, #219, Beverly Hills, CA 90211 USA

Weiss, Melvyn I *Attorney General*
Milberg Weiss Bershad, 1 Pennsylvania Plaza, New York, NY 10119 USA

Weiss, Michael *Figure Skater*
PO Box 12311, Burke, VA 22009 USA

Weiss, Michael T *Actor*
Endeavor Talent Agency, 9701 Wilshire Blvd #1000, Beverly Hills, CA 90212 USA

Weiss, Morry *Business Person*
American Greetings Corp, 1 American Road, Cleveland, OH 44144 USA

Weiss, Robert W (Bob) *Basketball Player, Coach*
1600 Windermere Dr E, Seattle, WA 98112 USA

Weiss, Roberta *Actor*
Sarnoff Co, 3500 W Olive Ave #300, Burbank, CA 91505 USA

Weiss, Walter W *Baseball Player*
1275 Castlepoint Circle, Castle Rock, CO 80108 USA

Weissenberg, Alexis *Musician*
Michael Schmidt, 59 E 54th St #83, New York, NY 10022 USA

Weisser, Morgan
1030 Superba Ave., Venice, CA 90291

Weissflog, Jens *Skier*
Markt 2, Kurort Oberweisenthal, 09484, GERMANY

Weissman, Irving L *Biologist, Doctor*
Stanford University, Pathology Dept, Beckman Center, Stanford, CA 94305 USA

Weissman, Robert *Business Person*
IMS Health Inc, 1499 Post Road, Fairfield, CT 06824 USA

Weissman, Steven *Artist*
Fantagraphics Books, 7563 Lake City Way, Seattle, WA 98115 USA

Weisz, Paul B *Engineer, Physicist*
University of Pennsylvania, Bio-Engineering Dept, Philadelphia, PA 19104 USA

Weisz, Rachel *Actor*
Creative Artists Agency LCC (CAA-LA), 9830 Wilshire Blvd, Beverly Hills, CA 90212 USA

Weithaas, Antje *Musician*
Harrison/Parrott, 12 Penzance Place, London, W11 4PA, UNITED KINGDOM (UK)

Weitz, Bruce *Actor*
18826 Erwin St, Tarzana, CA 91335 USA

Weitz, Chris *Writer*
William Morris Agency (WMA-LA), 1 William Morris Pl, Beverly Hills, CA 90212 USA

Weitz, Paul *Writer*
William Morris Agency (WMA-LA), 1 William Morris Pl, Beverly Hills, CA 90212 USA

Weitz, Paul J *Astronaut*
3086 N Tam Oshanter Dr, Flagstaff, AZ 86004 USA

Weitzman, Howard *Attorney General*
Katten Muchin Zavis Weitzman, 1999 Ave of Stars #1400, Los Angeles, CA 90067 USA

Weizman, Ezer *President, General*
Beit Amot Mishpat, 8 Shaul Hamelech Blvd, Tel-Aviv, 64733, ISRAEL

Wejbe, Jolean *Actor*
McGowan Management, 8733 W Sunset Blvd #103, W Hollywood, CA 90069 USA

Wel, Hul *Writer*
Pocket Books, 1230 Ave of Americas, New York, NY 10020 USA

Welch, Gillian *Musician*
DS Mgmt, 1017 16th Ave S, Nashville, TN 37212 USA

Welch, Jack *Astronomer*
University of California, Electrical Engineering Dept, Berkeley, CA 94720 USA

Welch, Justin *Musician*
CMO Mgmt, Ransomes Dock, 35037 Parkgate Road, London, SW11 4NP, UNITED KINGDOM (UK)

Welch, Kevin *Musician, Songwriter*
Press Network, 1035 16th Ave S #200, Nashville, TN 37212 USA

Welch, Lenny *Musician*
Brothers Mgmt, 141 Dunbar Ave, Fords, NJ 08863 USA

Welch, Michael *Actor*
Curtis Talent Management, 9607 Arby Dr, Beverly Hills, CA 90210 USA

Welch, Raquel *Actor*
9903 Santa Monica Blvd #514, Beverly Hills, CA 90212 USA

Welch, Robert L (Bob) *Baseball Player*
11055 E Gold Dust Ave, Scottsdale, AZ 85259 USA

Welch, Tahnee *Actor, Model*
PO Box 823, Beverly Hills, CA 90213 USA

Welch Jr, John F *Business Person*
General Electric Co, 3135 Easton Turnpike, Fairfield, CT 06828 USA

Weld, Tuesday *Actor*
Agency for the Performing Arts (APA-LA), 9200 Sunset Blvd #900, Los Angeles, CA 90069 USA

Weld, William F *Governor*
Hale & Dorr, 60 State St, Boston, MA 02109 USA

Weldon, Fay *Writer*
24 Ryland Road, London, NW5 3EA, UNITED KINGDOM (UK)

Weldon, Joan *Actor*
67 E 78th St, New York, NY 10021 USA

Weldon, W Casey *Football Player*
Washington Redskins, 21300 Redskin Park Dr, Ashburn, VA 20147 USA

Welk, Lawrence (All Stars)
901 Winding River Rd., Vero Beach, FL 32963

Welker, Frank
10635 Santa Monica Blvd. #130, Los Angeles, CA 90025

Welland, Colin *Actor, Writer*
Peter Charlesworth, 68 Old Brompton Road, London, SW7 3LQ, UNITED KINGDOM (UK)

Wellborn, Joe *Football Player*
809 Paulus St, Schulenburg, TX 78956-1424

Weller, Freddie *Musician, Songwriter*
Ace Productions, PO Box 428, Portland, TN 37148 USA

Weller, Mary Louise *Actor*
1416 N Hayvenhurst Dr #11, West Hollywood, CA 90046 USA

Weller, Michael *Writer*
Rosenstone/Wender, 38 E 29th St, New York, NY 10016 USA

Weller, Paul *Musician*
Variety Artists International Inc, 1924 Spring St, Paso Robles, CA 93446-1620 USA

Weller, Peter *Actor*
8401 Cresthill Road, Los Angeles, CA 90069 USA

Weller, Rene
Kelterstr. 18 Grafenhausen, Birkenfeld, GERMANY, D-75217

Weller, Robb
4249 Beck Ave., Studio City, CA 91604

Weller, Thomas H *Nobel Prize Laureate*
56 Winding River Road, Needham, MA
02492 USA

Weller, Watter *Musician*
Doblinger Hauptstr 40, Vienna, 1190,
AUSTRIA

Welles, Terri *Actor, Model*
PO Box 2549, Del Mar, CA 92014 USA

Wellford, Harry W *Judge*
US Court of Appeals, Federal Building,
167 N Main St, Memphis, TN 38103 USA

Welling, Tom *Actor*
Creative Artists Agency, 9830 Wilshire
Blvd, Beverly Hills, CA 90212 USA

Wellings, Bob
40 Kent Gardens Ealing, London,
ENGLAND, W13 8BW

Wellington, Harry H *Educator*
New York Law School, 57 Worth St, New
York, NY 10013 USA

Welliver, Titus *Actor*
Fenton-Kritzer Entertainment, 12200 W
Olympic Blvd #400, Los Angeles, CA
90064 USA

Wellman Jr, William *Actor*
410 N Barrington Ave, Los Angeles, CA
90049 USA

Wells, Annie *Photographer, Journalist*
Press Democrat, Editorial Dept, 427
Mendocino Ave, Santa Rosa, CA 95401
USA

Wells, Audrey *Writer, Director*
Endeavor Talent Agency, 9701 Wilshire
Blvd #1000, Beverly Hills, CA 90212 USA

Wells, Carole *Actor*
Burton Moss, 8827 Beverly Blvd #L, Los
Angeles, CA 90048 USA

Wells, Cory
3853 Carbon Canyon Road, Malibu, CA
90265 USA

Wells, David (Dave) *Baseball Player*
2519 N McMullen Booth Road #510-198,
Clearwater, FL 33761 USA

Wells, Dawn *Actor*
4616 Ledge Ave, Toluca Lake, CA 91602
USA

Wells, John *Producer*
John Wells Productions, 4000 Warner
Blvd, Bldg 1, Burbank, CA 91522-

Wells, Kitty *Musician*
Midnight Special Productions, PO Box
916, Hendersonville, TN 37077 USA

Wells, LLewellyn *Producer*
United Talent Agency (UTA), 9560
Wilshire Blvd, Beverly Hills, CA 90212
USA

Wells, Mark *Hockey Player*
27619 Harrison Woods Lane, Harrison
Township, MI 48045 USA

Wells, Patricia *Journalist*
Harper Collins Publishers, 10 E 53rd St,
New York, NY 10022 USA

Wells, Thomas B *Judge*
US Tax Court, 400 2nd St NW,
Washington, DC 20217 USA

Wells-Hawkes, Sharlene
24-C Maria Ave., Southbridge, MA 01550

Wellstone, Paul *Senator*
417 Litchfield Ave SW, Wilmar, MN
56201-3241 USA

Welsch, Jiri *Basketball Player*
Boston Celtics, 151 Merrimac St #1,
Boston, MA 02114 USA

Welser-Most, Franz *Conductor*
Cleveland Symphony, Severance Hall,
11001 Euclid Ave, Cleveland, OH 44106
USA

Welsh, Moray M *Musician*
28 Somerfield Ave, Queens Park, London,
NW6 6JY, UNITED KINGDOM (UK)

Welsh, Stephanie *Photographer, Journalist*
PO Box 277, Wayne, ME 04284 USA

Welsom, Elleen *Journalist*
Albuquerque Tribune, Editorial Dept,
7777 Jefferson NE, Albuquerque, NM
87109 USA

Welti, Lisa *Actor*
Select Artists Ltd (CA-Westside Office),
1138 12th Street, Suite 1, Santa Monica,
CA 90403 USA

Welty, John D *Educator*
4411 N Van Ness Blvd, Fresno, CA 93704
USA

Wen, Jinbao *Prime Minister, Misc*
Premier's Office, Zhonganahai, Beijing,
CHINA

Wendelstedt Jr, Harry H *Baseball Player,
Referee*
88 S Saint Andrews Dr, Ormond Beach,
FL 32174 USA

Wenden, Michael *Swimmer*
Palm Beach Currmbin Center, Thrower
Dr, Palm Beach Queens, AUSTRALIA

Wenders, Wim *Director*
Road Movies Filmproduton,
Clausewitzstra 4, Berlin, 10629,
GERMANY

Wendkos, Gina *Writer*
Industry Entertainment, 955 S Carrillo Dr
#300, Los Angeles, CA 90048 USA

Wendt, George *Actor*
3856 Vantage Ave, Studio City, CA 91604
USA

Wenge, Ralph *Commentator*
Cable News Network, News Dept, 1050
Techwood Dr NW, Atlanta, GA 30318
USA

Wengren, Mike *Musician*
Mitch Scneider Organization, 14724
Ventura Blvd #410, Sherman Oaks, CA
91403 USA

Wenham, David *Actor*
William Morris Agency (WMA-LA), 1
William Morris Pl, Beverly Hills, CA
90212 USA

Wenner, Jann S *Publisher*
Wenner Media, 1290 Ave of the
Americas, New York, NY 10104 USA

Went, Joseph J *General*
9204 Kristin Lane, Fairfax, VA 22032 USA

Wente, Jean R *Business Person*
California State Automobile Assn, PO Box
422940, San Francisco, CA 94142 USA

Wentworth, Alexandra *Actor, Comedian*
Gersh Agency, 232 N Canon Dr, Beverly
Hills, CA 90210 USA

Wenzel, Andreas *Skier*
Oberhul 151, Liechtenstein-Gamprin,
LIECHENSTEIN

Wenzel, Hanni Weirather- *Skier*
Fanalwegle 4, Schaan, 9494,
LIECHENSTEIN

Wepner, Chuck *Boxer*
153 Ave E, Bayonne, NJ 07002 USA

Wepper, Fritz
Lamonstr. 9, Munich, GERMANY,
D-81679

Werbach, Adam *Misc*
Sierra Club, 85 2nd St #200, San
Francisco, CA 94105 USA

Werber, William M (Bill) *Baseball Player*
5800 Old Providence Road #5732A,
Charlotte, NC 28226 USA

Werner, Anna *Commentator*
KHOU, News Department, 1945 Allan
Parkway, Houston, TX 77019 USA

Werner, Marianne *Track Athlete*
Gauseland 2A, Dortmund, 44227,
GERMANY

Werner, Michael *Misc*
Michael Werner Ltd, 21 E 67th St, New
York, NY 10021 USA

Werner, Roger L Jr *Television Host, Misc*
Prime Sports Ventures, 10000 Santa
Monica Blvd, Los Angeles, CA 90067 USA

Werner, Tom *Producer*
Carsey-Werner-Mandabach, 4024 Radford
Ave, Bldg 3, Studio City, CA 91604

Wersching, Raimund (Ray) *Football Player*
18 Buttercup Lane, San Carlos, CA 94070
USA

Werth, Isabell *Horse Racer*
Winterswicker Feld 4, Rheinberg, 47495
USA

Wertheim, Jorge *Misc*
UNESCO, Director's Office, UN Plaza,
New York, NY 10017 USA

Wertheimer, Fredric M *Misc*
3502 Macomb St NW, Washington, DC
20016 USA

Wertheimer, Linda *Commentator*
National Public Radio, News Dept, 2025
M St NW, Washington, DC 20036 USA

Wertimer, Ned *Actor*
Acme Talent, 4727 Wilshire Blvd #333,
Los Angeles, CA 90010 USA

Wertmuller, Lina *Director*
Piazza Clotilde, Rome, 00196, ITALY

Wesker, Arnold *Writer*
37 Ashley Road, London, N19 3AG,
UNITED KINGDOM (UK)

Wesley, Norman *Business Person*
Fortune Brands Inc, 300 Tower Parkway,
Lincolnshire, IL 60069 USA

Wesselmann, Tom *Artist*
RR 1 Box 36, Long Eddy, NY 12760 USA

West, Adam *Actor*
Chasin Agency, The, 8899 Beverly Blvd
#716, Los Angeles, CA 90048 USA

West, Chandra
955 S. Carrillo Dr.#300, Los Angeles, CA 90048

West, Cornel *Social Activist, Misc*
Harvard University, Afro American Studies Dept, Cambridge, MA 02138 USA

West, David *Basketball Player*
New Orleans Hornets, New Orleans Arena, 1501 Girod St, New Orleans, LA 70113 USA

West, Dominic *Actor*
Creative Artists Agency LCC (CAA-LA), 9830 Wilshire Blvd, Beverly Hills, CA 90212 USA

West, Doug *Basketball Player*
15 Holly Road, Wheeling, WV 26003 USA

West, Ernest E *War Hero*
912 Adams Ave, Wurtland, KY 41144 USA

West, Jake *Misc*
International Assn of Iron Workers, 1750 New York Ave NW, Washington, DC 20006 USA

West, James E *Inventor*
724 Berkeley Ave, Plainfield, NJ 07062 USA

West, Jerome A (Jerry) *Basketball Player*
Memphis Grizzlies, 175 Toyota Plaza #150, Memphis, TN 38103 USA

West, Jerry
1150 W. Columbus Ave, Springfield, MA 01105

West, Joel *Model*
William Morris Agency, 1325 Ave of Americas, New York, NY 10019 USA

West, Jon Fredric *Opera Singer*
Opera et Concert, Maximillianstr 22, Munich, 80539, GERMANY

West, Leslie *Musician*
James Faith Entertainment, 318 Wynne Lane, Port Jefferson, NY 11777 USA

West, Lizzie *Musician*
Warner Bors Records, 3300 Warner Blvd, Burbank, CA 91505 USA

West, Mark *Basketball Player*
715 E Forest Hills Dr, Phoenix, AZ 85022 USA

West, Nathan *Actor*
Strong/Morrone Entertainment, 9100 Wilshire Blvd #503E, Beverly Hills, CA 90212 USA

West, Paul *Writer*
Elaine Markson, 44 Greenwich Ave, New York, NY 10011 USA

West, Peter
4708 Largo Way, Las Vegas, NV 89121

West, Red *Actor*
6676 Memphis-Arlington, Bartlett, TN 38135

West, Richard L *War Hero*
1603 Morningside Dr, Chillicothe, MO 64601 USA

West, Sam
34-43 Russell, London, ENGLAND, WC2B 5HA

West, Samuel *Actor*
P F D, Drury House, 34-43 Russell St, London, WC2B 5HA, UNITED KINGDOM (UK)

West, Shane *Actor*
Strong/Morrone, 9100 Wilshire Blvd, # 503E, Beverly Hills, CA 90212 USA

West, Shelly *Musician*
West Hood Entertainment, PO Box 158718, Nashville, TN 37215 USA

West, Simon *Director*
Rogers & Cowan PR, 1888 Century Park E #500, Los Angeles, CA 90067 USA

West, Timothy L *Actor*
Gavin Barker Assoc, 2D Wimpote St, London, W1G 0EB, UNITED KINGDOM (UK)

West Jr, Togo D *Secretary*
922 N Cameron Ave, Winston Salem, NC 27101 USA

Westbrook, Bryant *Football Player*
7710 Hunters Point Dr, Sugar Land, TX 77479 USA

Westbrook, Michael *Football Player*
Cincinnati Bengals, 1 Paul Brown Stadium, Cincinnati, OH 45202 USA

Westerberg, Paul *Musician, Songwriter*
Mitch Scneider Organization, 14724 Ventura Blvd #410, Sherman Oaks, CA 91403 USA

Westerfield, Putney *Publisher*
10 Green View Lane, Hillsborough, CA 94010 USA

Westfall, Ed
PO Box 39, Locust Valley, NY 11560

Westfall, V Edward (Ed) *Hockey Player*
699 Hillside Ave, New Hyde Park, NY 11040 USA

Westfeldt, Jennifer *Actor*
PMK/HBH

Westhead, Paul *Basketball Player, Coach*
2217 Via Alamitos, Palos Verdes Estates, CA 90274 USA

Westheimer, David K *Writer*
11722 Darlington Ave #2, Los Angeles, CA 90049 USA

Westheimer, Frank H *Misc*
3 Berkeley St, Cambridge, MA 02138 USA

Westheimer, Gerald *Doctor, Misc*
582 Santa Barbara Road, Berkeley, CA 94707 USA

Westheimer, Mary

Westheimer, Ruth S *Doctor*
900 West 190th St, New York, NY 10040 USA

Westlake, Donald E *Writer*
Knox Burger Assoc, 425 Madison Ave, New York, NY 10017 USA

Westlife *Music Group*
BMG, 1540 Broadway, New York, NY 10036 USA

Westling, Jon *Educator*
285 Goddard Ave, Brookline, MA 02445 USA

Westmore, McKenzie *Actor*
3904 Laurel Canyon Blvd, #766, Studio City, CA 91604 USA

Westmoreland, James *Actor*
8019 1/2 W Norton Ave, West Hollywood, CA 90046 USA

Westmoreland, William C *General*
1 Gadsden Way #CTG, Charleston, SC 29412 USA

Weston, Celia *Actor*
Innovative Artists, 1505 10th St, Santa Monica, CA 90401 USA

Weston, David
123-A Grosvenor Rd., London, ENGLAND, SW1

Weston, J Fred *Educator*
258 Tavistock Ave, Los Angeles, CA 90049 USA

Weston, Kim *Musician*
Powerplay, 5434 W Sample Road, PMB 533, Pompano Beach, FL 33073 USA

Weston, P John *Government Official*
13 Denbigh Gardens, Richmond, Surrey, TW10 6EN, UNITED KINGDOM (UK)

Weston, Randolph (Randy) *Musician*
PO Box 749, Maplewood, NJ 07040 USA

Westphal, James A *Scientist*
California Institute of Technology, Platary Sciences Dept, Pasadena, CA 91125 USA

Westphal, Paul D *Basketball Player, Coach*
16640 Cumbre Verde Court, Pacific Palisades, CA 90272 USA

Westwood, Vivienne *Fashion Designer*
Westwood Studios, 9-15 Elcho St, London, SW11 4AU, UNITED KINGDOM (UK)

Wetherbee, James D *Astronaut*
710 Huntercrest St, Seabrook, TX 77586 USA

Wetherell, T R *Educator*
Florida State University, Athletic Dept, Tallahassee, FL 32306 USA

Wetherill, George W *Geophysicist*
Camergie Institution, Terrestrial Magnetism Dept, Washington, DC 20015 USA

Wethington, Charles T Jr *Educator*
2926 Four Pines Dr, Lexington, KY 40502 USA

Wetnight, Ryan S *Football Player*
2752 E Fremont Ave, Fresno, CA 93710 USA

Wetter, Friedrich Cardinal *Religious Leader*
Kardinal-Faulhaber-Str 7, Munich, 80333, GERMANY

Wettig, Patricia *Actor*
522 Arbamar Place, Pacific Palisades, CA 90272 USA

Wetton, John *Musician*
Entourage Talent, 133 W 25th St #500, New York, NY 10001 USA

Wetzel, Gary G *War Hero*
PO Box 84, Oak Creek, WI 53154 USA

Wetzel, John *Basketball Player, Coach*
13011 N Sunrise Canyon Lane, Marana, AZ 85653 USA

Wetzel, Robert L *General*
1425 Dartmouth Road, Columbus, GA 31904 USA

Wetzel, Rosemarie
111 E. 22nd St. #200, New York, NY 10010

Wexler, Anne *Government Official*
1317 F St NW #600, Washington, DC 20004 USA

Wexler, Haskell *Cinematographer*
1247 Lincoln Blvd #585, Santa Monica, CA 90401 USA

Wexler, Jacqueline G *Educator*
222 Park Ave S, New York, NY 10003 USA

Wexner, Leslie H *Business Person*
Limited Inc, 3 Limited Parkway, PO Box 16000, Columbus, OH 43216 USA

Weyand, Frederick C *General*
5002 Maunalani Circle, Honolulu, HI 96816 USA

Weyerhaeuser, George *Business Person*
Weyerhaeuser Co, 33663 32nd Ave S, Federal Ave, WA 98023 USA

Weymouth, Tina *Musician*
Premier Talent, 3 E 54th St #1100, New York, NY 10022 USA

Whalen, Laurence J *Judge*
US Tax Court, 400 2nd St NW, Washington, DC 20217 USA

Whalen, Lindsay *Basketball Player*
Connecticut Sun, Mohegan Sun Arena, Uncasville, CT 06382 USA

Whaley, Frank *Actor*
Shelter Entertainment, 9255 Sunset Blvd #1010, Los Angeles, CA 90069 USA

Whaley, Joanne
9830 Wilshire Blvd, Beverly Hills, CA 90212

Whaley, Suzi *Golfer*
1 Essex Court, Farmington, CT 06032 USA

Whalin, Justin
3604 Holboro Dr., Los Angeles, CA 90027

Whalley, Joanne *Actor*
1435 Lindacrest Dr, Beverly Hills, CA 90210 USA

Whalum, Kirk *Musician*
Cole Classic Mgmt, PO Box 231, Canoga Park, CA 91305 USA

Whang, Suzanne *Actor*
Kragen & Company, 1112 N Sherbourne Dr, Los Angeles, CA 90069

Wharton, Bernard *Architect*
Shope Reno Wharton, 18 W Putnam Ave, Greenwich, CT 06830 USA

Whatmore, Sarah *Musician*
Pop Idol (Fremantle Media), 2700 Colorado Ave #450, Santa Monica, CA 90404 USA

Wheatley, E H *Publisher*
Vancouver Sun, 2250 Granville St, Vancouver, BC V6H 3G2, CANADA

Wheatley, Tyrone *Football Player*
4794 Woodrose Circle, Dublin, CA 94568 USA

Wheaton, David *Tennis Player*
20045 Cottagewood Ave, Excelsior, MN 55331 USA

Wheaton, Wil *Actor*
2603 Seapine Lane, La Crescenta, CA 91214 USA

Whedon, Joss *Writer, Producer, Director*
Mutant Enemy, PO Box 900, Beverly Hills, CA 90212 USA

Wheeler, Blake *Hockey Player*
Philadelphia Flyers, 1st Union Center, 3601 S Broad St, Philadelphia, PA 19148 USA

Wheeler, Charles F *Cinematographer*
79125 Jack Rabbit Trail, La Quinta, CA 92253 USA

Wheeler, Cheryl *Musician, Songwriter*
Morningstar Mgmt, PO Box 1770, Hendersonville, TN 37077 USA

Wheeler, Daniel S *Editor*
American Legion Magazine, 700 N Pennsylvania St, Indianapolis, IN 46204 USA

Wheeler, Ellen
13576 Cheltenham Dr, Sherman Oaks, CA 91423

Wheeler, H Anthony *Architect*
Hawthombank House, Dean Village, Edinburgh, EH4 3BH, SCOTLAND

Wheeler, John *Actor*
Levin Agency, 8484 Wilshire Blvd #745, Beverly Hills, CA 90211 USA

Wheeler, John A *Physicist*
1904 Meadow Lane, Highstown, NJ 08542 USA

Wheeler, Margaret
4950 Cahuenga Blvd., No. Hollywood, CA 91607

Whelan, Bill *Composer*
Sony Records, 2100 Colorado Ave, Santa Monica, CA 90404 USA

Whelan, Jill *Actor*
Scott Stander & Associates, 13701 Riverside Dr #201, Sherman Oaks, CA 91423 USA

Whelan, Julia *Actor*
International Creative Mgmt, 8942 Wilshire Blvd, #219, Beverly Hills, CA 90211 USA

Whelan, Wendy *Ballerina*
New York City Ballet, Lincoln Center Plaza, New York, NY 10023 USA

Whelchel, Lisa *Actor*
8221 Navisota Dr, Lantana, TX 76226 USA

Wheless, Jamy *Animator*
405 Fair St, Pefaluma, CA 94952 USA

Whibley, Deryck *Musician*
Nettwerk Management (LA), 8730 Wilshire Blvd #304, Beverly Hills, CA 90211 USA

Whicker, Alan D *Commentator*
Le Gallais Chambers, Saint Helier, Jersey, UNITED KINGDOM (UK)

Whigham, Shea *Actor*
Original Film, 2045 S Barrington Ave, Los Angeles, CA 90025 USA

Whinnery, Barbara *Actor*
Baier/Kleinman, 3575 Cahuenga Blvd #500, Los Angeles, CA 90068 USA

Whinnery, John R *Engineer*
1804 Wales Dr, Walnut Creek, CA 94595 USA

Whipple, Fred L *Astronomer*
35 Elizabeth Road, Belmont, MA 02478 USA

Whirry, Shannon *Actor*
Shapiro-Lichtman, 8827 Beverly Blvd, Los Angeles, CA 90048 USA

Whishaw, Anthony *Artist*
7A Albert Place, Victoria Road, London, W8 5PD, UNITED KINGDOM (UK)

Whisler, J Steven *Business Person*
Phelps Dodge Corp, 1 N Central Ave, Phoenix, AZ 85004 USA

Whiston, Don *Hockey Player*
2 Jeffreys Neck, Ipswich, MA 01938 USA

Whitacre, Edward E Jr *Business Person*
SBC Communications, 175 E Houston, San Antonio, TX 78205 USA

Whitaker, Forest *Actor, Director*
Three Arts Entertainment, 9460 Wilshire Blvd #700, Suite 700, Beverly Hills, CA 90212 USA

Whitaker, Jack *Sportscaster*
500 Berwyn Baptist Road #L-Fleur, Devon, PA 19333 USA

Whitaker, Jack *Golfer*
Int'l Golf Partners, 3300 PGA Blvd #820, West Palm Beach, FL 33410 USA

Whitaker, Johnny
4924 Vineland Ave., No. Hollywood, CA 9l60l

Whitaker, Lou
4781 Highland Pl., Lakeland, FL 33813

Whitaker, Louis R (Lou) Jr *Baseball Player*
4781 Highland Place, Lakeland, FL 33802 USA

Whitaker, Mark *Editor*
Newsweek Magazine, Editorial Dept, 251 W 57th St, New York, NY 10019 USA

Whitaker, Meade *Judge*
US Tax Court, 400 2nd St NW, Washington, DC 20217 USA

Whitaker, Pernell *Boxer*
3808 Cranberry Court, Virginia Beach, VA 23456 USA

Whitaker, Roger
1730 Tree Blvd. #2, St. Augustine, FL 32086

Whitbread, Fatima *Track Athlete*
Chafford Information Ctr, Elozabeth Road, Grays, Essex, RM16 6QZ, UNITED KINGDOM (UK)

Whitcomb, Bob *Race Car Driver*
Whitcomb Racing, 9201 Garrison Road, Charlotte, NC 28278 USA

Whitcomb, Edgar D *Governor*
15415 Rome Road, Rome, IN 47574 USA

Whitcomb, Ian *Songwriter, Musician*
PO Box 451, Altadena, CA 91003 USA

Whitcomb, Richard T *Inventor*
119 Tide Mill Lane, Hampton, VA 23666 USA

White, Alan *Musician*
Ignition Mgmt, 54 Linhope St, London, NW1 6HL, UNITED KINGDOM (UK)

White, Alvin S (Al) *Misc*
14254 N Fawnbrooke Dr, Tucson, AZ
85737 USA

White, Anna
9950 Durant Dr. #402, Beverly Hills, CA
90212

White, Betty *Actor, Comedian*
PO Box 491965, Los Angeles, CA 90049
USA

White, Bradley
8730 Sunset Blvd. #480, Los Angeles, CA
90069

White, Bryan *Musician, Songwriter*
Holly Co, 3415 W End Ave #101G,
Nashville, TN 37203 USA

White, Charles R *Football Player*
University of Southern California, Heritage
Hall, Los Angeles, CA 90089 USA

White, Cheryl *Musician*
PO Box 270067, Houston, TX 77277 USA

White, Chris *Musician*
Lustig Talent, PO Box 770850, Orlando,
FL 32877 USA

White, Devon M *Baseball Player*
6440 E Sierra Vista Dr, Paradise Valley,
AZ 85253 USA

White, DeVoreaux
4505 Santa Rosalia Dr, Los Angeles, CA
90008

White, Dwight *Football Player, Financier*
406 Landon Gate, Pittsburgh, PA 15238
USA

White, Ed
1225 Grand View Dr., Berkeley, CA
94705-1629

White, Edmund V *Writer*
Maxine Groffsky, 25th Ave, New York,
NY 10011 USA

White, Edward A (Ed) *Football Player*
PO Box 1437, Julian, CA 92036 USA

White, Frank *Baseball Player*
5335 W 96th St, Shawnee Mission, KS
66207 USA

White, Gilbert F *Misc*
624 Pearl St #302, Boulder, CO 80302
USA

White, Jahidi *Athlete, Basketball Player*
Washington Wizards, MCI Center, 601 F
Street NW, Washington DC, 20004 USA

White, Jai *Actor*
Baumgarten Merims Entertainment, 1640
South Sepulveda, Suite 218, Los Angeles,
CA 90025 USA

White, Jaleel *Actor*
8916 Ashcroft Ave, West Hollywood, CA
90048

White, James
7529 Franklin Ave, Los Angeles, CA
90046-2241

White, James B *Attorney General,
Educator*
1606 Morton Ave, Ann Arbor, MI 48104
USA

White, Jamie *Radio Personality*
Star 98.7 FM, 3500 West Olive Avenue,
Suite 250, Burbank, CA 91505 USA

White, John H *Photographer, Journalist*
Chicago Sun-Times, Editorial Dept, 401 N
Wabash Ave, Chicago, IL 60611 USA

White, John Patrick *Actor*
Metropolitan Talent Agency, 4526
Wilshire Blvd, Los Angeles, CA 90010
USA

White, Jordie *Musician*
Marilyn Manson, 83 Riverside Dr, New
York, NY 10024

White, Joseph (Jo Jo) *Basketball Player*
2 Mansfield Road, Middleton, MA 01949
USA

White, Joy Lynn *Musician*
Buddy Lee, 38 Music Square E #300,
Nashville, TN 37203 USA

White, Judith M *Biologist*
University of San Francisco, Biology Dept,
San Francisco, CA 94117 USA

White, Julie *Actor*
4129 Laurelgrove Ave, Studio City, CA
91604 USA

White, Karyn *Musician*
Warner Bors Records, 3300 Warner Blvd,
Burbank, CA 91505 USA

White, Kate *Editor*
Cosmopolitan Magazine, Editorial Dept,
224 W 57th St, New York, NY 10019
USA

White, L Robert (Bob) *Football Player*
1044 Grouse Way, Venice, FL 34285 USA

White, Lari *Actor*
William Morris Agency (WMA-LA), 1
William Morris Pl, Beverly Hills, CA
90212 USA

White, Larri *Musician, Songwriter*
Carter Career Mgmt, 1028 18th Ave S #B,
Nashville, TN 37212 USA

White, Marco P *Chef*
The Restaurant, 66 Knightsbridge, London,
SW1X 7LA, UNITED KINGDOM (UK)

White, Marilyn *Track Athlete*
9605 6th Ave, Inglewood, CA 90305 USA

White, Mark *Musician*
DAS Communications, 84 Riverside Dr,
New York, NY 10024 USA

White, Martha G *Publisher*
London Free Press, 369 York St, London,
ON N6A 4G1, CANADA

White, Meg *Music Group, Musician*
Jack White Productions, Muenchner Str
45, Unterfoehring, 85774, GERMANY

White, Michael Jai *Actor*
Baumgarten, 1640 S Sepulveda Blvd,
#218, Los Angeles, CA 90025 USA

White, Michael R *Misc*
11794 Blue Ridge Road,
Newcornerstown, OH 43832 USA

White, Michael S *Producer*
48 Dean St, London, W1V 5HL, UNITED
KINGDOM (UK)

White, Mike *Football Coach*
Kansas City Chiefs, 1 Arrowhead Dr,
Kansas City, KS 64129 USA

White, Miles D *Business Person*
Abbott Laboratories, 100 Abbott Park
Road, Abbott Park, IL 60064 USA

White, Nera D *Basketball Player*
RR 3 Box 165, Lafayette, TN 37083 USA

White, Persia *Actor*
Acme Talent & Literary Agency (LA), 4727
Wilshire Blvd #333, Los Angeles, CA
90010 USA

White, Peter *Actor*
S M S Talant, 8730 Sunset Blvd #440, Los
Angeles, CA 90069 USA

White, Randy L *Football Player*
5000 E FM 1461, Prosper, TX 75078 USA

White, Raymond P Jr *Doctor*
1506 Velma Road, Chapel Hill, NC 27514
USA

White, Reggie
501 Nelson Pl., Nashville, TN 37214

White, Reginald H (Reggie) *Football
Player*
PO Box 11475, Green Bay, WI 54307
USA

White, Reglnald E (Reggie) *Football Player*
501 Nelson Place, Nashville, TN 37214
USA

White, Robert M *General*
PO Box 2488, APO, AE, NY 09063 USA

White, Robert M *Misc*
Somerset House II, 5610 Wisconsin Ave
#1506, Bethesda, MD 20815 USA

White, Robert M II *Journalist*
4871 Glenbrook Road NW, Washingon,
DC 20016 USA

White, Rodney *Basketball Player*
Denver Nuggets, Pepsi Center, 1000
Chopper Circle, Denver, CO 80204 USA

White, Ron *Comedian*
International Creative Management
(ICM-LA), 8942 Wilshire Blvd, Beverly
Hills, CA 90211 USA

White, RoseDenville Hall
62 Ducks Hill Rd. Northwood, Middlesex,
ENGLAND, HA6 2SB

White, Roy H *Baseball Player*
1001 2nd St, Sacramento, CA 95814 USA

White, Sharon
380 Forest Retreat, Hendersonville, TN
37075

White, Shernan E (Sherm) *Football Player*
PO Box 1856, Pebble Beach, CA 93953
USA

White, Steven A *Admiral, Business Person*
Stone & Webster Engineering Corp, 245
Summer St, Boston, MA 02210 USA

White, Thelma *Actor*
Motion Picture Country Home, 23388
Mulholland, Woodland Hills, CA 91364
USA

White, Timothy D *Misc*
University of California, Hiuman
Evolutionary Studies Lab, Berkeley, CA
94720 USA

White, Tony L *Business Person*
PE Corp, 710 Bridgeport Ave, Shelton, CT
06484 USA

White, Vanna *Model, Entertainer*
"Wheel of Fortune" Show, 10202 W
Washington Blvd #5300, Culver City, CA
90232 USA

White, Verdine *Musician*
Atlas/Third Rail Entertainment, 9200 W Sunset Blvd, West Hollywood, CA 90069 USA

White, W Daniel (Danny) *Football Player*
902 E San Angelo Ave, Gilbert, AZ 85234 USA

White, Willard W *Opera Singer*
10 Montague Ave, London, SE4 1YP, UNITED KINGDOM (UK)

White, William B (Bill) *Baseball Player*
8517 Bam Owl, San Antonio, TX 78255 USA

White, Willye B *Track Athlete*
7221 S Calumet Ave, Chicago, IL 60619 USA

White Jr, Josh *Musician*
23625 Ripple Creek, Novi, MI 48375 USA

White of Rhymney, Eirene L *Government Official*
64 Vandon Court, Petty France, London, SW1H 9HF, UNITED KINGDOM (UK)

White Stripes, The *Music Group*
Agency Group, The (NY), 1775 Broadway #430, New York, NY 10019 USA

White's
PO Box 2158, Hendersonville, TN 37075

Whitehead, Alfred K *Misc*
International Assn of Fire Fighters, 1750 New York Ave NW, Washington, DC 20006 USA

Whitehead, Geoffrey
81 Shaftesbury Ave., London, ENGLAND, W1

Whitehead, George W *Mathematician*
53 Hill Road #706, Belmont, MA 02478 USA

Whitehead, Jerome *Basketball Player*
1543 Merritt Dr, El Cajon, CA 92020 USA

Whitehead, John C *Government Official, Financier*
131 Old Chester Road, Essex Fells, NJ 07021 USA

Whitehead, John C *Scientist*
Brookings Institute, 1775 Massachusetts Ave NW, Washington, DC 20036 USA

Whitehead, Paxton *Actor*
Abrams Artists, 9200 Sunset Blvd #1125, Los Angeles, CA 90069 USA

Whitehead, Richard F *Admiral*
American Cage & Machine Co, 135 S LaSalle St, Chicago, IL 60674 USA

Whitehurst, C David *Football Player*
11010 Linbrook Lane, Duluth, GA 300097 USA

Whitelaw, Billie *Actor*
Rose Cottage Plum St, Glensford, Suffolk, C010 7PX, UNITED KINGDOM (UK)

Whitemore, Hugh *Writer*
Creative Artists Agency LCC (CAA-LA), 9830 Wilshire Blvd, Beverly Hills, CA 90212 USA

Whitemore, Willet F Jr *Doctor, Scientist*
2 Hawthorne Lane, Plandome, NY 11030 USA

Whiten, Richard *Actor*
247 S Beverly Dr, #102, Beverly Hills, CA 90212 USA

Whiteread, Rachel *Artist*
Anthony d'Offay, 22 Dering St, London, W1R 9AA, UNITED KINGDOM (UK)

Whitesell, Emily *Writer, Producer*
Endeavor Agency LLC (LA), 9601 Wilshire Blvd Fl 3, Beverly Hills, CA 90210 USA

Whitesell, Sean *Actor*
United Talent Agency (UTA), 9560 Wilshire Blvd, Beverly Hills, CA 90212 USA

Whitesides, George M *Misc*
124 Grasmere St, Newton, MA 02458 USA

Whitesnake *Music Group*
International Talent Booking (ITB - UK), 27A Floral Street, Third Floor, Covent Garden, London, WC2E 9, United Kingdom

Whitfield, Dondre T *Actor*
Writers & Artists, 8383 Wilshire Blvd #550, Beverly Hills, CA 90211 USA

Whitfield, Fred *Misc*
PO Box 489, Hockley, TX 77447 USA

Whitfield, Lynn *Actor*
William Morris Agency, 151 El Camino Dr, Beverly Hills, CA 90212 USA

Whitfield, Mal
1 Hoosier Dome, Indianapolis, IN 46225-1023

Whitfield, Malvin G (Mal) *Track Athlete*
1225 Harvard St NW, Washington, DC 20009 USA

Whitford, Brad *Musician*
PO Box 869, Norwell, MA 02061 USA

Whitford, Bradley *Actor*
5761 Valley Oak Dr, Los Angeles, CA 90068 USA

Whiting, Barbara
1085 Waddington St., Birmingham, MI 48009

Whiting, Leonard
7 Leicester Pl., London, ENGLAND, WC2H 7BP

Whiting, Margaret *Musician*
41 W 58th St #5A, New York, NY 10019 USA

Whitlam, Gough *Prime Minister*
Westfiel Towers, 100 William St, Sydney, NSW, 2001, AUSTRALIA

Whitley, Chris *Musician, Songwriter*
Feinstein Mgmt, 420 Lexington Ave #2150, New York, NY 10170 USA

Whitley, Keith Society
Box 222, Sandy Hook, KY 41171

Whitman, Kari *Actor, Model*
1155 N La Cienega Blvd #104, West Hollywood, CA 90069 USA

Whitman, Mae *Actor*
CunninghamEscottDipene, 10635 Santa Monica Blvd #130, Los Angeles, CA 90025 USA

Whitman, Marina Von Neumann *Economist*
University of Michigan, Public Policy School, Ann Arbor, MI 48109 USA

Whitman, Meg *Business Person*
eBay, 2145 Hamilton Ave, San Jose, CA 95125 USA

Whitman, Slim *Musician*
3830 Old Jennings Road, Middleburg, FL 32068 USA

Whitman, Stuart *Actor*
749 San Ysidro Road, Santa Barbara, CA 93108 USA

Whitmore, James *Actor*
4990 Puesta del Sol, Malibu, CA 90265 USA

Whitmore, Kay *Hockey Player*
16 Springwood Road, Farmington, CT 06032 USA

Whitmore Jr, James *Actor*
1284 La Brea St, Thousand Oaks, CA 91362 USA

Whitney, Ashley *Swimmer*
125 Villa View Court, Brentwood, TN 37027 USA

Whitney, CeCe *Actor*
1145 Barham Dr #217, San Marcos, CA 92078 USA

Whitney, Jane *Entertainer*
5 TV Place, Needham, MA 02494 USA

Whitney-Lee, Grace *Actor*
PO Box 79, Coarsegold, CA 93614 USA

Whitson, Peggy A *Astronaut*
306 Lakeview Circle, Seabrook, TX 77586 USA

Whittaker, James (Jim) *Mountaineer*
2023 E Sims Way #277, Port Townsend, WA 98368 USA

Whittaker, Roger *Musician, Songwriter*
BML Mgmt, 426 Marsh Point Circle, Saint Augustine, FL 32080 USA

Whittingham, Charles A *Publisher*
11 Woodmill Road, Chappaqua, NY 10514 USA

Whittinghill, Dick
11310 Valley Spring Lane, Toluca Lake, CA 91602

Whitton, Margaret *Actor*
William Morris Agency, 151 El Camino Dr, Beverly Hills, CA 90212 USA

Whitwam, David R *Business Person*
Whirlpool Corp, 2000 N State St, RR 63, Benton Harbor, MI 49022 USA

Whitworth, Kathrynne A (Kathy) *Golfer*
1735 Misletoe Dr, Flower Mound, TX 75022 USA

Whitworth, Kathy
5990 Lindenshire Lane #101, Dallas, TX 75230-2726

Who, The *Musician*
William Morris Agency (WMA-LA), 1 William Morris Pl, Beverly Hills, CA 90212 USA

Wholey, Dennis *Television Host*
Dennis Wholey Enterprises, 1333 H St NW, Washington, DC 20005-4704 USA

Whoppers, Wendy *Actor*
Wow Entertainment Inc, 8362 Pines Blvd #296, Pembroke Pines, FL 33024 USA

Whyte, Sandra *Hockey Player*
81 Golden Hills Road, Saugus, MA 01906 USA

Wiberg, Kenneth B *Misc*
160 Carmalt Road, Hamden, CT 06517 USA

Wiberg, Pernilla *Skier*
Katterunsvagen 32, Norrkopping, 60 210, SWEDEN

Wick, Charles Z *Government Official*
US Information Agency, 400 C St SW, Washington, DC 20024 USA

Wicker, Thomas G (Tom) *Writer, Journalist*
PO Box 361, Rochester, VT 05767 USA

Wicker, Tom
229 W. 43rd St., New York, NY 10036

Wickham, John A Jr *General*
13590 N Fawnbrooke Dr, Tucson, AZ 85737 USA

Wicki-Fink, Agnes *Actor*
Weisgerberstr 2, Munich, 80805, GERMANY

Wickman, Robert J (Bob) *Baseball Player*
PO Box 105, Abrams, MI 54101 USA

Wicks, Ben *Editor, Cartoonist*
38 Yorkville Ave, Toronto, ON M4W 1L5, CANADA

Wicks, Sidney *Basketball Player*
1030 S La Jolla Ave, Los Angeles, CA 90035 USA

Wicks, Sue *Basketball Player*
New York Liberty, Madison Square Garden, 2 Penn Plaza, New York, NY 10121 USA

Widby, G Ronald (Ron) *Football Player, Basketball Player*
542 Mahler Road, Wichita Falls, TX 76310 USA

Widdoes, Kathleen *Actor*
"As the World Turns" Show, CBS-TV, 524 W 57th St 5330, New York, NY 10019 USA

Widdoes, Kathleen *Actor*
24 E 11th St, New York, NY 10003 USA

Widdrington, Peter N T *Business Person*
Laidlaw Inc, 3221 N Service Road, Burlington, ON L7R 3Y8, CANADA

Wideman, John Edgar *Writer*
University of Massachusetts, Englesh Dept, Amherst, MA 01003 USA

Widener, H Emroy Jr *Judge*
US Court of Appeals, PO Box 868, Abrington, VA 24212 USA

Widman, Herbert (Herb) *Swimmer, Athlete*
844 Monarch Circle, San Jose, CA 95138 USA

Widmark, Richard *Actor*
PO Box 232, Woodland Hills, CA 91365 USA

Widom, Benjamin *Misc*
204 The Parkway, Ithaca, NY 14850 USA

Wiebe, Susanne *Fashion Designer*
Amalienstr 39, Munich, 80799, GERMANY

Wiedemann, Josef *Architect*
Im Eichgeholz 11, Munich, 80997, GERMANY

Wiedlin, Jane *Musician*
Nick Ben-Meir, 652 N Doheny Dr, Los Angeles, CA 90069 USA

Wiedorfer, Paul J *War Hero*
2506 Moore Ave, Baltimore, MD 21234 USA

Wiegart, Zach *Football Player*
3747 Saltmeadow Court S, Jacksonville, FL 32224 USA

Wiehl, Christopher *Actor*
Gersh Agency, The (LA), 232 N Canon Dr, Beverly Hills, CA 90210 USA

Wielicki, Krzysztof *Mountaineer*
Ul A Frycza Modrzewskiego 21, Tychy, 43-100, POLAND

Wieman, Carl E *Nobel Prize Laureate*
University of Colorado, 440 Physics Campus Box, Boulder, CO 80309 USA

Wiener, Jacques L Jr *Judge*
US Court of Appeals, Federal Buliding, 500 Fannin St, Shreveport, LA 71101 USA

Wier, Murray *Basketball Player, Coach*
118 Goodwater St, Georgetown, TX 78628 USA

Wieschaus, Eric F *Nobel Prize Laureate*
11 Pelham St, Boston, MA 02118 USA

Wiese, John P *Judge*
US Claims Court, 717 Madison Place NW, Washington, DC 20439 USA

Wiesel, Elie *Writer, Nobel Prize Laureate*
200 E 64th St, New York, NY 10021 USA

Wiesen, Bernard *Director*
Weisgerberstr 2, Munich, 80805, GERMANY

Wiesenthal, Simon *Social Activist*
Jewish Documentation Center, Salztorgasse 6, Vienna, 1010, AUSTRIA

Wiesner, Kenneth (Ken) *Track Athlete*
3601 Meta Lake Road, Eagle River, WI 54521 USA

Wiest, Dianne *Actor*
59 E 54th St, #22, New York, NY 10022 USA

Wiggin, Paul *Football Player, Football Coach, Coach*
5013 Ridge Road, Edina, MN 55436 USA

Wiggins, Audrey *Musician*
William Morris Agency, 2100 W End Ave #1000, Nashville, TN 37203 USA

Wiggins, John *Musician*
William Morris Agency, 2100 W End Ave #1000, Nashville, TN 37203 USA

Wigglesworth, Marian McKean *Skier*
General Delivery, Wilson, WY 83014 USA

Wiggs, Susan *Writer*
PO Box 4469, Rolling Bay, WA 98061 USA

Wightman, Arthur S *Mathematician, Physicist*
16 Balsam Lane, Princeton, NJ 08540 USA

Wightman, Donald E *Misc*
Utility Workers Union, 815 16th Ave NW, Washington, DC 20006 USA

Wigle, Ernest D *Doctor*
101 College St, Toronto, ON M56 1L7, CANADA

Wiig, Kristen *Actor*
Odenkirk Talent Management, Raleigh Studios, 650 N Bronson Ave Bldg B145, Los Angeles, CA 90004 USA

Wiik, Sven *Skier*
PO Box 774484, Steamboat Springs, CO 80477 USA

Wijdenbosch, Jules A *President*
Presidential Palace, Onafhankelikheidsplein 1, Paramaribo, SURINAME

Wilander, Mats *Tennis Player*
Einar Wilander, Vickervagen 2, Vaxjo, 352 53, SWEDEN

Wilber, Doreen V H *Athlete*
1401 W Lincoln Way, Jefferson, IA 50129 USA

Wilbraham, John H G *Musician*
9 D Cuthbert St, Wells, Somerset, BA5 2AW, UNITED KINGDOM (UK)

Wilbur, Richard C *Judge*
US Tax Court, 400 2nd St NW, Washington, DC 20217 USA

Wilbur, Richard P *Writer*
88 Dodswell Road, Cummington, MA 01026 USA

Wilbur, Richard S *Doctor*
985 Hawthome Place, Lake Forest, IL 60045 USA

Wilburn Brothers
Box 50, Goodlettsville, TN 37072-0050 USA

Wilby, James *Actor*
William Morris Agency, 52/53 Poland Place, London, W1F 7KX, UNITED KINGDOM (UK)

Wilcox, Chris *Basketball Player*
Los Angeles Clippers, Staples Center, 1111 S Figueroa St, Los Angeles, CA 90015 USA

Wilcox, Christopher *Editor*
Reader's Digest Magazine, Reader's Digest Road, Pleasantville, NY 10570 USA

Wilcox, Collin
121 N. San Vicente Blvd., Beverly Hills, CA 90211

Wilcox, David *Music Group, Musician, Songwriter*
Elizabeth Rush Agency, 100 Park St #4, Montclair, NJ 07042 USA

Wilcox, Davie (Dave) *Football Player*
94471 Willamette Dr, Junction City, OR 97448 USA

Wilcox, Larry *Actor*
10 Appaloosa Lane, Bell Canyon, CA 91307 USA

Wilcox, Lisa *Actor*
Stone Manners, 6500 Wilshire Blvd #550, Los Angeles, CA 90048 USA

Wilcox, Shannon *Actor*
1753 Centinela Ave #A, Santa Monica, CA 90404 USA

Wilcutt, Terence W (Terry) *Astronaut*
1216 Red Wing Dr, Freindswood, TX 77546 USA

Wild, Earl *Musician, Composer*
2233 Femleaf Lane, Columbus, OH 43235 USA

Wild, Jack *Actor*
A Jay Hawthorns, L Littleworth, Amberley, Stroud Glouc, GL5 5AW, UNITED KINGDOM (UK)

Wild Orchid
PO Box 90370, City of Industry, CA 91715-0370

Wilde, Kim *Songwriter, Musician*
Dance Crazy Mgmt, 294-296 Nether St, Finchley, Lake Forest, N31 RJ, UNITED KINGDOM (UK)

Wilde, Olivia *Actor*
Lloyd and Kass Entertainment, 10202 West Washington Blvd, Astaire Bldg Room 2210, Culver City, CA 90232 USA

Wilde, Patricia *Artist, Director, Ballerina*
Pittsburgh Ballet Theater, 2900 Liberty Ave, Pittsburgh, PA 15201 USA

Wilder, Alan *Musician*
Reach Media, 295 Greenwich St #109, New York, NY 10007 USA

Wilder, Don *Cartoonist*
North American Syndicate, 235 E 45th St, New York, NY 10017 USA

Wilder, Gene *Actor, Director*
Lovett Management, 1327 Brinkley Ave, Los Angeles, CA 90049 USA

Wilder, James *Football Player*
14406 Burgundy Square, Tampa, FL 33613 USA

Wilder, James *Actor*
Stone Manners, 6500 Wilshire Blvd, #550, Los Angeles, CA 90048 USA

Wilder, L Douglas *Governor, Educator*
3650 Monon St #313, Los Angeles, CA 90027 USA

Wilder, Yvonne
11836 Hesby St., No. Hollywood, CA 91607

Wilding Jr, Michael
34 Ellis Ranch Rd, Santa Fe, NM 87505-1415 USA

Wildman, George *Cartoonist*
1640 Shepard Ave, Hamden, CT 06518 USA

Wildman, Valerie *Actor*
110 Hurricane St #305, Marina del Rey, CA 90292 USA

Wildmon, Donald *Social Activist*
National Federation of Decency, PO Box 1398, Tupelo, MS 38802 USA

Wildung, Richard K (Dick) *Football Player*
10368 Rich Road, Bloomington, MN 55437 USA

Wiles, Andrew J *Mathematician*
Princeton University, Mathematics Dept, Princeton, NJ 08544 USA

Wiles, Jason *Actor*
Rigberg-Rugolo Entertainment, 1180 S Beverly Dr #601, Los Angeles, CA 90035 USA

Wiley, Lee *Musician*
Country Crossroads, 7787 Monterey St, Gilroy, CA 95020 USA

Wiley, Marcellus *Football Player*
San Diego Chargers, 4020 Murphy Canyon Road, San Diego, CA 92123 USA

Wiley, Michael E *Business Person*
Atlantic Richfield Co, 333 S Hope St, Los Angeles, CA 90071 USA

Wiley, William T *Artist*
PO Box 661, Forest Knolls, CA 94933 USA

Wilford, John Noble Jr *Journalist*
232 W 10th St, New York, NY 10014 USA

Wilhelm, John W *Misc*
Hotel & Restaurant Employees Union, 1219 28th St NW, Washington, DC 20007 USA

Wilhelm, Kati *Athlete*
SC Motor Zella-Mehlis, Bierbachstr 68, Zella-Mehlis, 98544 USA

Wilhoite, Kathleen
PO Box 5617, Beverly Hills, CA 90210

Wilk, Brad *Musician*
GAS Entertainment, 8935 Lindblade St, Culver City, CA 90232 USA

Wilkening, Laurel L *Educator*
University of California, Chancellor's Office, Irvine, CA 92717 USA

Wilkens, Lanny
2660 Peachtree Rd. W #39F, Atlanta, GA 30305-3683

Wilkens, Leonard R (Lenny) Jr *Basketball Player, Coach*
3429 Evergreen Point Road, Medina, WA 98039 USA

Wilkerson, Bobby *Basketball Player*
4012 Zinfadel Way, Indianapolis, IN 46254 USA

Wilkerson, Brad *Baseball Player*
Montreal Expos, Olympic Stadium, Montreal, QC, H1V 3N7, CANADA

Wilkerson, Isabel *Journalist*
New York Times, Editorial Dept, 229 W 43rd St, New York, NY 10036 USA

Wilkes, Donna
16228 Maplegrove St, La Puente, CA 91744

Wilkes, Glenn *Basketball Player, Coach*
Stetson University, Athletic Dept, Campus Box 8359, DeLand, FL 32720 USA

Wilkes, Jamaal *Basketball Player*
7846 W 81st St, Playa del Rey, CA 90293 USA

Wilkes, Maurice V *Engineer*
Olivetti Research Ltd, 24A Trumpington St, Cambridge, CB2 1QA, UNITED KINGDOM (UK)

Wilkie, Chris *Musician*
Primary Talent Int'l, 2-12 Petonville Road, London, N1 9PL, UNITED KINGDOM (UK)

Wilkie, David *Swimmer*
Oaklands Queens Hill, Ascot, Berkshire, UNITED KINGDOM (UK)

Wilkin, Richard E *Religious Leader*
Winebrenner Theological Seminary, 950 N Main St, Findlay, OH 45840 USA

Wilkins, J Dominique *Basketball Player*
Atlanta Hawks, 1 CNN Center #405, Atlanta, GA 30303

Wilkins, Laisha *Actor*
Televisa, Blvd Adolfo Lopez Mateos 232, Colonia San Angel INN, DF, CP 01060, MEXICO

Wilkins, Maurice (Mac) *Track Athlete*
PO Box 1058, 328 Coldbrook Lane, Soquel, CA 95073 USA

Wilkins, Maurice H F *Nobel Prize Laureate*
30 Saint John's Park, London, SE3, UNITED KINGDOM (UK)

Wilkins, Roger *Journalist*
George Mason University, 207 East Building, Fairfax, VA 22030 USA

Wilkins, William W Jr *Judge*
US Court of Appeals, PO Box 10857, Greenville, SC 29603 USA

Wilkinson, Adrienne *Actor*
9157 Sunset Blvd, #215, W. Hollywood, CA 90069 USA

Wilkinson, Amanda *Music Group, Musician*
Fitzgerald-Hartley, 1908 Wedgewood Ave, Nashville, TN 37212 USA

Wilkinson, Dan *Football Player*
Detroit Lions, 222 Republic Dr, Allen Park, MI 48101 USA

Wilkinson, Geoffrey *Nobel Prize Laureate*
Imperial College, Chemistry Dept, London, SW7 2AY, UNITED KINGDOM (UK)

Wilkinson, J Harvie III *Judge*
US Court of Appeals, 255 W Main St, Charlottesville, VA 22902 USA

Wilkinson, Joseph B Jr *Admiral*
340 Chesapeake Dr, Great Falls, VA 22066 USA

Wilkinson, June *Actor, Model*
1025 N Howard St, Glendale, CA 91207 USA

Wilkinson, Laura *Swimmer, Misc*
201 S Capitol Ave, #300, Indianapolis, IN 46225 USA

Wilkinson, Leon *Musician*
Alliance Artists, 6025 Corners Parkway #202, Norcross, GA 30092 USA

Wilkinson, Signe *Editor, Cartoonist*
Philadelphia Daily News, Editorial Dept, 400 N Broad, Philadelphia, PA 19130 USA

Wilkinson, Steve *Musician*
Fitzgerald Hartley, 1908 Wedgewood Ave, Nashville, TN 37212 USA

Wilkinson, Tom *Actor*
Lou Coulson, 37 Berwick St, London, W1V 3RF, UNITED KINGDOM (UK)

Wilkinson, Tyler *Musician*
Fritzgerald Hartley, 1908 Wedgewood Ave, Nashville, TN 37212 USA

Will, George *Writer*
9 Grafton St, Chevy Chase, MD 20815 USA

Will-Halpin, Maggie *Golfer*
178 Tall Trees Court, Sarasota, FL 34232 USA

Willard, Fred *Actor, Comedian*
William Morris Agency, 151 El Camino Dr, Beverly Hills, CA 90212 USA

Willard, Kenneth H (Ken) *Football Player*
Ken Willard Assoc, 3071 Viewpoint Road, Midlothian, VA 23113 USA

Willcocks, David V *Musician*
13 Grange Road, Cambridge, CB3 9AS, UNITED KINGDOM (UK)

Willcox, Toyah *Actor*
Roseman Organisation, The, 51 Queen Anne St, London, W1G 9HS, UNITED KINGDOM (UK)

Willebrands, Johannes Cardinal *Religious Leader*
Council for Promoting Christian Unity, Via dell'Erba I, Rome, 00120, ITALY

Willem-Alexander *Prince*
Huis ten Bosch, Hague, NETHERLANDS

Willerth, Jeffrey
6615 W. Tamarack Ave., Sun Valley, CA 91352

Willet, E Crosby *Artist*
Willet Stained Glass Studios, 10 E Moreland Ave, Philadelphia, PA 19118 USA

Willets, Kathy
3251 Spanish River Dr, Pompano Beach, FL 33062

Willett, Chad
PO Box 5617, Beverly Hills, CA 90210

Willett, Malcolm *Cartoonist*
Universal Press Syndicate, 4520 Main St, Kansas City, MO 64111 USA

Willett, Walter *Doctor, Scientist*
Harvard Medical School, 25 Shattuck St, Boston, MA 02115 USA

Willette, Jo Ann
9300 Wilshire Blvd. #400, Beverly Hills, CA 90212

Willey, Kathleen
2642 New Timer Way, Powhattan, VA 23139-5320

Willhite, Gerald *Football Player*
10464 Iliff Court, Rancho Cordova, CA 95670 USA

William *Prince*
Clarence House, Stable Yard Gate, London, SW1, UNITED KINGDOM (UK)

William, David *Actor, Director*
194 Langarth St E, London, ON N6C 1Z5, CANADA

William, Edward *Religious Leader*
Bible Way Church, 5118 Clarendon Road, Brooklyn, NY 11203 USA

Williams, W Clyde *Religious Leader*
Christian Methodist Episcopal Church, 4466 E Presley Blvd, Memphis, TN 38116 USA

Williams, Adrian *Basketball Player*
Phoenix Mercury, American West Arena, 201 E Jefferson St, Phoenix, AZ 85004 USA

Williams, Aeneas D *Football Player*
11978 Charter House Lane, Saint Louis, MO 63146 USA

Williams, Alfred H *Football Player*
7602 Las Flores Dr, Houston, TX 77083 USA

Williams, Alvin *Basketball Player*
Toronto Raptors, Air Canada Center, 40 Bay St, Toronto, ON M5J 2N8, CANADA

Williams, Andy *Musician*
161 Berms Circle, #3, Branson, MO 65616 USA

Williams, Anson *Actor*
24615 Skyline View Dr, Malibu, CA 90265 USA

Williams, Anthony A *Politician*
Mayor's Office, District Building, 14th & E Sts NW, Washington, DC 20004 USA

Williams, Barbara *Actor*
Innovative Artists, 1505 10th St, Santa Monica, CA 90401 USA

Williams, Barry *Actor, Musician*
2337 Roscomare Rd #2-242, Los Angeles, CA 90077 USA

Williams, Bernabe (Bernie) *Baseball Player*
5 Hallock Place, Armonk, NY 10504 USA

Williams, Bert *Actor*
Susan Nathe, 8281 Melrose Ave, #200, Los Angeles, CA 90046 USA

Williams, Betty *Nobel Prize Laureate*
Orchardville Gardens, Finaghy, Belfast, 10, NORTHERN IRELAND

Williams, Billy *Cinematographer*
Coah House, Hawkshill Place Esher, Surrey, KT10 9HY, UNITED KINGDOM (UK)

Williams, Billy Dee *Actor*
18411 Hatteras St, #204, Tarzana, CA 91356 USA

Williams, Billy Dee *Actor*
Artist's Agency, The (NY), 230 W 55th St #29D, New York, NY 10019

Williams, Billy L *Baseball Player*
586 Prince Edward Road, Glen Ellyn, IL 60137 USA

Williams, Bob A *Football Player*
602 Stone Bam Road, Towson, MD 21286 USA

Williams, Branden *Actor*
Creative Management Group (CMG), 9465 Wilshire Blvd #335, Beverly Hills, CA 90212 USA

Williams, Brian *Television Host, Commentator*
NBC-TV, News Dept, 30 Rockefeller Plaza, New York, NY 10112 USA

Williams, Bruce *Entertainer*
PO Box 547, Elfers, FL 34680 USA

Williams, C K *Writer*
Princeton University, English Dept, Princeton, NJ 08544 USA

Williams, Cara *Actor*
Dann, 9903 Santa Monica Blvd, #606, Beverly Hills, CA 90212 USA

Williams, Chris *Actor*
Artist Management, 1118 15th St #1, Santa Monica, CA 90403

Williams, Christy *Artist*
PO Box 849, Lopez Island, WA 98261 USA

Williams, Cindy *Actor*
Sterling/Winters, 10877 Wilshire Blvd, #15, Los Angeles, CA 90024 USA

Williams, Clarence *Journalist*
Los Angeles Times, Editorial Dept, 202 W 1st St, Los Angeles, CA 90012 USA

Williams, Cliff *Musician*
11 Leominster Road, Morden, Surrey, SA4 6HN, UNITED KINGDOM (UK)

Williams, Clyde *Religious Leader*
Christian Methodist Episcopal Church, 4466 E Presley Blvd, Memphis, TN 38116 USA

Williams, Colleen *Commentator*
KNBC-TV, News Dept, 3000 W Alameda Ave, Burbank, CA 91523 USA

Williams, Cress *Actor*
William Morris Agency (WMA-LA), 1 William Morris Pl, Beverly Hills, CA 90212 USA

Williams, Curtis *Musician*
Neal Hollander Agency, 9966 Majorca Place, Boca Raton, FL 33434 USA

Williams, Cynda *Actor*
Innovative Artists, 1505 10th St., Santa Monica, CA 90401 USA

Williams, Dafydd R (David) *Astronaut*
NASA, Johnson Space Center, 2101 NASA Road, Houston, TX 77058 USA

Williams, Dana *Musician*
Dreamcatcher Artists Mgmt, 2908 Poston Ave, Nashville, TN 37203 USA

Williams, Daniel *General*
Governor General's Office, Botanical Gardens, Saint George's, GRENADA

Williams, Darnell *Actor*
Stone Manners, 6500 Wilshire Blvd, #550, Los Angeles, CA 90048 USA

Williams, David *Athlete, Football Player*
109 East Oxford Street, Valley Stream, NY 11580 USA

Williams, David G T *Educator*
Emmanuel College, Cambridge, CB2 3AP, UNITED KINGDOM (UK)

Williams, David W *Football Player*
108 E Oxford St, Valley Stream, NY 11580 USA

Williams, Deniece *Musician*
Green Light Talent Agency, PO Box 3172, Beverly Hills, CA 90212 USA

Williams, Dick
3680 Madrid St., Las Vegas, NV 89121

Williams, Dick Anthony *Actor*
Abrams Artists, 9200 W Sunset Blvd, #1125, Los Angeles, CA 90069 USA

Williams, Don *Musician, Songwriter*
Kathy Gangwisch, 5100 Harris Ave, Kansas City, MO 64133 USA

Williams, Donald E *Astronaut*
Science Applications Int'l, 2200 Space Park Dr, #200, Houston, TX 77058 USA

Williams, Doug *Comedian*
JKA Talent & Literary Agency, 8033 Sunset Blvd #115, Los Angeles, CA 90046 USA

Williams, Douglas L (Doug) *Football Player, Football Coach*
Tampa Bay Buccaneers, 1 W Buccaneer Place, Tampa, FL 33607 USA

Williams, Dudley *Dancer*
Alvin Alley American Dance Foundation, 211 W 61st St, #300, New York, NY 10023 USA

Williams, E Virginia *Director, Choreographer*
Boston Ballet, 19 Clarendon St, Boston, MA 02116 USA

Williams, Easy *Actor*
Judy Schoen, 606 N Larchmont Blvd, #309, Los Angeles, CA 90004 USA

Williams, Edy *Actor, Model*
PO Box 6325, Woodland Hills, CA 91365 USA

Williams, Elmo *Director, Producer*
1249 Iris St, Brookings, OR 97415 USA

Williams, Eric *Basketball Player*
Boston Celtics, 151 Merrimac St, #1, Boston, MA 02114 USA

Williams, Esther *Actor, Swimmer*
9377 Readcrest Dr, Beverly Hills, CA 90210 USA

Williams, Frank *Basketball Player*
New York Knicks, Madison Square Garden, 2 Penn Plaza, New York, NY 10121 USA

Williams, Freeman *Basketball Player*
450 W 4 1st Place, Los Angeles, CA 90037 USA

Williams, Gary *Basketball Player, Coach*
University of Maryland, Athletic Dept, College Park, MD 20742 USA

Williams, Gary Anthony *Actor*
Innovative Artists (LA), 1505 Tenth St, Santa Monica, CA 90401 USA

Williams, Gluyas *Cartoonist*
New Yorker Magazine, Editorial Dept, 4 Times Square, New York, NY 10036 USA

Williams, Greg *Actor*
1680 Vine St, #604, Los Angeles, CA 90028 USA

Williams, Greg Alan *Actor*
Sandy Schnarr Assoc, 8281 Melrose Ave, #200, Los Angeles, CA 90046 USA

Williams, Gregg *Football Coach*
Buffalo Bills, 1 Bills Dr, Orchard Park, NY 14127 USA

Williams, Hal *Actor*
Marter, PO Box 14227, Palm Desert, CA 92255 USA

Williams, Harland *Actor*
Brillstein/Grey, 9150 Wilshire Blvd, #350, Beverly Hills, CA 90212 USA

Williams, Harold M *Misc*
J Paul Getty Museum, Getty Center, 1200 Getty Center Dr, Los Angeles, CA 90049 USA

Williams, Harvey L *Football Player*
RR 2 Box 234A, Hempstead, TX 77445 USA

Williams, Herb *Basketball Player*
4500 Bentley Dr, Plano, TX 75093 USA

Williams, Hershel W *War Hero*
3450 Wire Branch Road, Ona, WV 25545 USA

Williams, Howard E (Howie) *Basketball Player*
1940 Hamilton Lane, Carmel, CA 46032 USA

Williams, Howard L (Howie) *Football Player*
4731 Proctor Ave, Oakland, CA 94618 USA

Williams, Hype *Director, Producer*
Creative Artists Agency, 9830 Wilshire Blvd, Beverly Hills, CA 90212 USA

Williams, Ivy *Writer*
Mediachase, 834 N Harper Ave, Los Angeles, CA 90046 USA

Williams, Jack K *Misc*
Texas Medical Center, 1133 M D Anderson Blvd, Houston, TX 77030 USA

Williams, Jaimie *Actor*
1019 Kane Concourse, #202, Bay Harbour Islands, FL 33154 USA

Williams, Jamal *Football Player*
San Diego Chargers, 4020 Murphy Canyon Road, San Diego, CA 92123 USA

Williams, James A *General*
8928 Maurice Lane, Annandale, VA 22003 USA

Williams, James A (Froggy) *Football Player*
296 Sugarberry Circle, Houston, TX 77024 USA

Williams, James D *Admiral*
1111A N Stuart St, Arlington, VA 22201 USA

Williams, James F (Jimmy) *Baseball Player*
1401 Olde Post Road, Palm Harbor, FL 34683 USA

Williams, James O *Football Player*
330 S Western Ave, Lake Forest, IL 60045 USA

Williams, Jay *Basketball Player*
Chicago Bulls, United Center, 1901 W Madison St, Chicago, IL 60612 USA

Williams, Jayson *Basketball Player, Sportscaster*
NBC-TV, Sports Dept, 30 Rockefeller Plaza, New York, NY 10112 USA

Williams, Jeffrey N *Astronaut*
2721 Moss Court, Seabrook, TX 77586 USA

Williams, Jerome *Basketball Player*
Toronto Raptors, Air Canada Center, 40 Bay St, Toronto, ON M5J 2N8, CANADA

Williams, Jerry *Football Player*
1501 E Riviera Dr, Chandler, AZ 85249 USA

Williams, Jessica *Musician*
T-Best, Talent Agency, 508 Honey Lake Court, Danville, CA 94506 USA

Williams, Jimy *Baseball Player*
1401 Olde Post Rd, Palm Harbor, FL 34683-1470

Williams, JoBeth *Actor*
Innovative Artists, 1505 10th St, Santa Monica, CA 90401 USA

Williams, Jody *Nobel Prize Laureate*
663 Lancaster St, Fredericksburg, VA 22405 USA

Williams, John *Musician, Composer*
Askonas Holt Ltd, 27 Chancery Lane, London, WC2A 1PF, UNITED KINGDOM (UK)

Williams, John A *Writer*
693 Forest Ave, Teaneck, NJ 07666 USA

Williams, John C *Athlete*
718 David Road, Santa Maria, CA 93455 USA

Williams, John L *Football Player*
1709 Husson Ave, Palatka, FL 32177 USA

Williams, John M *Football Player*
2222 Victory Memorial Dr, Minneapolis, MN 55412 USA

Williams, John T *Musician, Composer, Conductor*
333 Loring Ave, Los Angeles, CA 90024 USA

Williams, Joseph R *Publisher*
Memphis Commercial Appeal, 495 Union Ave, Memphis, TN 38103 USA

Williams, Kameelah *Musician*
Creative Artists Agency, 9830 Wilshire Blvd, Beverly Hills, CA 90212 USA

Williams, Katt *Actor, Comedian*
William Morris Agency (WMA-LA), 1 William Morris Pl, Beverly Hills, CA 90212 USA

Williams, Kelli *Actor, Musician*
Innovative Artists, 1505 10th St, Santa Monica, CA 90401 USA

Williams, Kevin *Football Player*
Minnesota Vikings, 9520 Viking Dr, Eden Prairie, MN 55344 USA

Williams, Kiely *Musician*
Pyramid Entertainment, 89 5th Ave, #700, New York, NY 10003 USA

Williams, Kiely Alexis *Actor, Musician*
Writers and Artists Group Intl (LA), 8383 Wilshire Blvd #550, Beverly Hills, CA 90211 USA

Williams, Kimberly *Actor, Producer*
Beyond Talent Agency, 330 Bob Hope Dr, #C109, Burbank, CA 91523 USA

Williams, Lee E *Football Player*
11651 NW 4th St, Plantation, FL 33325 USA

Williams, Lewis T *Scientist*
Howard Hughes Medical Institute, 5323 Harry Hines Blvd, Dallas, TX 75390 USA

Williams, Lorenzo *Basketball Player*
2731 Via Capri, #924, Clearwater, FL 33764 USA

Williams, Lucinda *Musician, Songwriter*
Azoff Music, 1100 Glendon Ave, #2000, Los Angeles, CA 90024 USA

Williams, Lynn R *Misc*
Harvard University, Politics Institute, 79 Kennedy St, Cambridge, MA 02138 USA

Williams, Maiya *Producer*
Principal Entertainment (LA), 1964 Westwood Blvd #400, Los Angeles, CA 90025 USA

Williams, Malinda *Actor*
Agency West Entertainment, 6255 West Sunset Blvd, Suite 908, Hollywood, CA 90028 USA

Williams, Mark *Bowler*
Professional Bowlers Assn, 719 2nd Ave, #701, Seattle, WA 98104 USA

Williams, Mary Alice *Commentator*
NYNEX Corp, Public Relations Dept, 1113 Westchester Ave, White Plains, NY 10604 USA

Williams, Mason *Composer, Musician*
PO Box 25, Oakridge, OR 97463 USA

Williams, Matt *Writer*
Zeiderman, 211 E 48th St, New York, NY 10017 USA

Williams, Maurice J *Misc*
Overseas Development Council, 1875 Connecticut Ave NW, Washington, DC 20009 USA

Williams, Merriwether *Artist*
Endeavor Agency LLC (LA), 9601 Wilshire Blvd Fl 3, Beverly Hills, CA 90210 USA

Williams, Michael *Actor*
Michael Whitehall, 125 Gloucester Road, London, SW7 4TE, UNITED KINGDOM (UK)

Williams, Michael D (Mike) *Baseball Player*
240 Horseshoe Farm Road, Pembroke, VA 24136 USA

Williams, Michael J *General*
Assistant Commander in Chief, HqUSMC 2 Navy St, Washington, DC 20380 USA

Williams, Michael L *Actor*
Julian Belfarge, 46 Albermarle St, London, W1X 4PP, UNITED KINGDOM (UK)

Williams, Micheal *Basketball Player*
1415 Reynoldston Lane, Dallas, TX 75232 USA

Williams, Michelle *Actor*
United Entertainment, 8436 W 3rd St, #650, Los Angeles, CA 90048 USA

Williams, Michelle *Musician*
Creative Artists Agency, 9830 Wilshire Blvd, Beverly Hills, CA 90212 USA

Williams, Mike *Football Player*
Buffalo Bills, 1 Bills Dr, Orchard Park, NY 14127 USA

Williams, Milan *Musician*
Management Assoc, 1920 Benson Ave, Saint Paul, MN 55116 USA

Williams, Montel B *Actor, Talk Show Host, Producer, Director*
Letnom Productions, 1104 Hayworth Avenue South, Los Angeles, CA 90035 USA

Williams, Natalie *Basketball Player*
Indiana Fever, Conseco Fieldhouse, 125 S Pennsylvania, Indianapolis, IN 46204 USA

Williams, Natashia *Actor*
Beverly Hecht Agency, 12001 Ventura Place, Suite 320, Studio City, CA 91604 USA

Williams, O L *Religious Leader*
United Free Will Baptist Church, 1101 University St, Kinston, NC 28501 USA

Williams, Olivia *Actor*
International Creative Mgmt, 76 Oxford St, London, W1N 0AX, UNITED KINGDOM (UK)

Williams, Otis *Musician*
Barry Pollock Associates, 9255 Sunset Blvd, #404, Los Angeles, CA 90069 USA

Williams, Patrick *Musician*
3156 Mandeville Canyon Road, Los Angeles, CA 90049 USA

Williams, Paul
8545 Franklin Ave, Los Angeles, CA 90069-1401

Williams, Paul H *Actor, Songwriter*
8545 Franklin Ave, Los Angeles, CA 90069 USA

Williams, Pharell *Actor, Composer*
Creative Artists Agency LCC (CAA-LA), 9830 Wilshire Blvd, Beverly Hills, CA 90212 USA

Williams, Pharrell *Musician*
Creative Artists Agency LCC (CAA-LA), 9830 Wilshire Blvd, Beverly Hills, CA 90212 USA

Williams, Phillip L *Publisher*
Los Angeles Times, Editorial Dept, 202 W 1st St, Los Angeles, CA 90012 USA

Williams, Prince Charles *Boxer*
Boxing Ministry, 3675 Polley Dr, Austintown, OH 44515 USA

Williams, R J
1505 10th St, Santa Monica, CA 90401 USA

Williams, Randy *Track Athlete*
5655 N Marty Ave, #204, Fresno, CA 93711 USA

Williams, Reggie *Basketball Player*
2016 Calloway St, Temple Hills, MD 20748 USA

Williams, Reginald (Reggie) *Football Player*
503 Jennifer Lane, Windermere, FL 34786 USA

Williams, Richard H (Dick) *Baseball Player*
394 Steprock Court, Henderson, NV 89014 USA

Williams, Ricky *Football Player*
4901 Palin St, San Diego, CA 92113 USA

Williams, Robbie *Musician*
EE Management, 111 Frithville Gardens, London, W12 7JG, UNITED KINGDOM (UK)

Williams, Robert *Artist*
Fantagraphics Books, 7563 Lake City Way, Seattle, WA 98115 USA

Williams, Robert Cary
Robert Cary Williams, 5 Claremont Villas, Southampton Way, Camberwell, London, England, 8E4 96W, United Kingdom

Williams, Robert J (Ben) *Football Player*
5961 Huntview Dr, Jackson, MS 39206 USA

Williams, Robin *Comedian, Actor*
Blue Wolf Productions, 3145 Geary Blvd #524, San Francisco, CA 94118 USA

Williams, Roderick *Opera Singer*
Van Walsum Mgmt, 4 Addison Bridge Place, London, W14 8XP, UNITED KINGDOM (UK)

Williams, Roger *Musician*
16150 Clear Valley Place, Encino, CA 91436 USA

Williams, Ron *Basketball Player*
610 Arcadia Terrace, #302, Sunnyvale, CA 94085 USA

Williams, Rowan *Religious Leader*
Lambert Palace, London, SE1 9JU, UNITED KINGDOM (UK)

Williams, Roy *Coach*
University of North Carlonia, PO Box 2126, Chapel Hill, NC 27515 USA

Williams, Roy *Football Player*
Dallas Cowboys, 1 Cowboys Parkway, Irving, TX 75063 USA

Williams, Sam B *Inventor*
Williams International, 2280 W Maple Road, Walled Lake, MI 48390 USA

Williams, Scott *Basketball Player*
Phoenix Suns, 201 E Jefferson St, Phoenix, AZ 85004 USA

Williams, Serena *Tennis Player*
313 Grand Key Terrace, West Palm Beach, FL 33418 USA

Williams, Simon *Actor*
Rebecca Blond Assoc, 69A Kings Road, London, SW3 4NX, UNITED KINGDOM (UK)

Williams, Stanley W (Stan) *Baseball Player*
4702 Hayter Ave, Lakewood, CA 90712 USA

Williams, Stephanie E *Actor*
S M S Talent, 8730 Sunset Blvd, #440, Los Angeles, CA 90069 USA

Williams, Stephen *Misc*
1017 Foothills Trail, Santa Fe, NM 87505 USA

Williams, Stephen F *Judge*
US Court of Appeals, 333 Constitution NW, Washington, DC 20001 USA

Williams, Steven *Actor*
Geddes Agency, 8430 Santa Monica Blvd, #200, West Hollywood, CA 90069 USA

Williams, Sunita L *Astronomer*
16810 Clear Oak Way, Houston, TX 77058 USA

Williams, T Franklin *Doctor*
Monroe Community Hospital, Director's Office, Rochester, NY 14620 USA

Williams, Tamika *Basketball Player*
Minnesota Lunx, Target Center, 600 1st Ave N, Minneapolis, MN 55403 USA

Williams, Terrie *Biologist*
University of California, Biology Dept, Santa Cruz, CA 95064 USA

Williams, Terry *Musician*
Damage Mgmt, 16 Lambton Place, London, W11 2SH, UNITED KINGDOM (UK)

Williams, Terry Tempest
Brandt & Brandt Literary Agency, 1501 Broadway, New York, NY 10036

Williams, Thomas S Cardinal *Religious Leader*
Viard, 21 Eccleston Hill Po Box 198, Wellington, 1, NEW ZELAND

Williams, Todd *Baseball Player*
6244 Fly Road, East Syracuse, NY 13057 USA

Williams, Tonya Lee *Actor*
Artists Agency, 1180 S Beverly Dr, #301, Los Angeles, CA 90035 USA

Williams, Treat *Actor*
One Entertainment (LA), 9220 W Sunset Blvd #306, Los Angeles, CA 90069 USA

Williams, Ulis *Track Athlete*
2511 29th St, Santa Monica, CA 90405 USA

Williams, Van *Actor*
Pierce & Shelly, 612 Lighthouse Ave, #220, Pacific Grove, CA 93950 USA

Williams, Vanessa *Actor*
17621 Gilmore St, Van Nuys, CA 91406 USA

Williams, Vanessa L *Musician, Actor*
MCC, 15030 Ventura Blvd, #710, Sherman Oaks, CA 91403 USA

Williams, Venus *Athlete, Tennis Player*
313 Grand Key Terrace, West Palm Beach, FL 33418 USA

Williams, Victoria *Songwriter, Musician*
PO Box 342, Joshua Tree, CA 92252 USA

Williams, Walt *Basketball Player*
3240 Beaumont St, Temple Hills, MD 20748 USA

Williams, Walter *Musician*
Associated Booking Corp, 1995 Broadway, #501, New York, NY 10023 USA

Williams, Wendy Lian *Swimmer*
Advantage International, 1025 Thomas Jefferson NW, #450, Washington, DC 20007 USA

Williams, William A *Astronaut*
Environmental Protection Agency, 200 SW 35th St, Corvallis, OR 97333 USA

Williams & Ree
PO Box 163, Hendersonville, TN 37077

Williams III, Clarence *Actor*
Flick East-West, 9057 Nemo St, #A, West Hollywood, CA 90069 USA

Williams III, Hank *Songwriter, Musician*
Gold Mountain, 3575 Cahuenga Blvd W, #450, Los Angeles, CA 90068 USA

Williams Jr, B John *Judge*
Morgan Lewis Bockius, 1800 M St NW, Washington, DC 20036 USA

Williams Jr, Hank *Musician, Songwriter*
Merle Kilgore Mgmt, 2 Music Circle S, Nashville, TN 37203 USA

Williams Jr, Redford B *Misc*
Duke University, Medical School, Box 3708, Durham, NC 27706 USA

Williams Jr, Robin M *Scientist*
414 Oak Ave, Ithaca, NY 14850 USA

Williams Jr, Walter Ray *Bowler*
6503 NW 223rd St, Micanopy, FL 32667 USA

Williams of Crosby, Shirley V T B *Government Official*
House of Lords, Westminster, London, SW1A 0PW, UNITED KINGDOM (UK)

Williams of Elvel, Charles C P *Government Official*
48 Thurloe Square, London, SW7 2SX, UNITED KINGDOM (UK)

Williams-Dourdan, Roshumba *Model*
Bethann Model Mgmt, 36 N Moore St, #36N, New York, NY 10013 USA

Williamson, Corliss *Basketball Player*
Detroit Pistons, Palace, 2 Championship Dr, Auburn Hills, MI 48326 USA

Williamson, Fred *Actor, Football Player*
H David Moss, 733 Seward St, #PH, Los Angeles, CA 90038 USA

Williamson, Keith A *Misc*
National Westminster Bank, Fakenham, Norfolk, UNITED KINGDOM (UK)

Williamson, Kevin *Director, Producer, Writer*
International Creative Mgmt, 8942 Wilshire Blvd, #219, Beverly Hills, CA 90211 USA

Williamson, Marianne *Doctor*
Los Angeles Center for Living, 8265 W Sunset Blvd, Los Angeles, CA 90046

Williamson, Marianne *Writer*
Los Angeles Center for Living, 8265 W Sunset Blvd, West Hollywood, CA 90046 USA

Williamson, Martha *Producer*
Broder Webb Chervin Silbermann Agency, The (BWCS), 9242 Beverly Blvd #200, Beverly Hills, CA 90210 USA

Williamson, Matthew *Fashion Designer*
Beverly Cable, 11 Saint Christopher's Place, London, W1M 5HB, UNITED KINGDOM (UK)

Williamson, Michael *Writer*
10400 Hutting Place, Silver Spring, MO 20902 USA

Williamson, Michael *Journalist*
Washington Post, Editorial Dept, 1150 15th St NW, Washington, DC 20071 USA

Williamson, Mykelti *Actor*
Paradigm (LA), 10100 Santa Monica Blvd, Fl 25, Los Angeles, CA 90067 USA

Williamson, Nicol *Actor*
Jonathan Altaras, 13 Shorts Gardens, London, WC2H 9AT, UNITED KINGDOM (UK)

Williamson, Oliver E *Economist*
University of California, Economics Dept, Berkeley, CA 94720 USA

Williamson, Shaun *Actor*
McIntosh Rae Management, Thornton House, Thornton Road, London, SW19 4NG, ENGLAND

Williamson Jr, Samuel R *Educator*
University of the South, President's Office, Sewanee, TN 37375 USA

Willingham, Tyrone *Football Coach*
Notre Dame University, Athletic Dept, PO Box 518, Notre Dame, IN 46556 USA

Willis, Alicia Leigh
11364 Ventura Blvd. #100, Studio City, CA 91604

Willis, Bruce W *Actor*
Cheyenne Enterprises, 406 Wilshire Blvd, Santa Monica, CA 90401 USA

Willis, Gordon *Cinematographer*
11849 W Olympic Blvd, #100, Los Angeles, CA 90064 USA

Willis, Jim *Artist*
5323 SW 53rd Court, Portland, OR 97221 USA

Willis, Kelly *Songwriter*
4007 Lullwood Road, Austin, TX 78722 USA

Willis, Kevin A *Basketball Player*
4970 Carriage Lake Dr, Roswell, GA 30075 USA

Willis, Mark *Musician*
William Morris Agency (WMA-TN), 2100 W End Ave #1000, Nashville, TN 37203 USA

Willis, Pete *Musician*
Q Prime Mgmt, 729 7th Ave, #1400, New York, NY 10019 USA

Willis, William K (Bill) *Football Player*
1158 S Waverly St, Columbus, OH 43227 USA

Willison, Mike *Musician*
Metropolitan Entertainment Group, 2 Penn Plaza, #2600, New York, NY 10121 USA

Willman, David *Journalist*
Los Angeles Times, Editorial Dept, 202 W 1st St, Los Angeles, CA 90012 USA

Willms, Andre *Athlete*
Rennebogen 94, Magdeburg, 39130, GERMANY

Willoch, Kare I *Prime Minister*
Fr Nansens V 17, Lysaker, 1324, NORWAY

Willoughby, Bill *Basketball Player*
350 W Englewood Ave, Englewood, NJ 07631 USA

Wills, Garry *Writer, Historian*
Northwestern University, History Dept, Evanston, IL 60201 USA

Wills, Mark *Musician*
Rasky-Baerlein Group, 1808 W End Ave #516, Nashville, TN 37203 USA

Wills, Maurice M (Maury) *Athlete, Baseball Player*
3200 La Rotonda Dr, #303, Rancho Palos Verdes, CA 90275 USA

Wills, Rick *Musician*
Hard to Handle Mgmt, 16501 Ventura Blvd, #602, Encino, CA 91436 USA

Willson, John *Business Person*
Placer Dome Inc, 1600-1055 Dunsmuir St, Vancouver, BC V7X 1P1, CANADA

Willson-Piper, Marty *Musician*
Globeshine, 101 Chamberlayne Road, London, NW10 3ND, UNITED KINGDOM (UK)

Willumstad, Robert *Financier*
Citigroup Inc, 399 Park Ave, New York, NY 10022 USA

Wilmarth, Dick *Misc*
1111 F St, Anchorage, AK 99501 USA

Wilmer, Douglas *Actor*
Julian Belfarge, 46 Albermarle St, London, W1X 4PP, UNITED KINGDOM (UK)

Wilmer, Harry A *Psychic*
Texas Health Science Center, Psychiatric Dept, San Antonio, TX 78284 USA

Wilmore, Barry E *Astronaut*
1502 Regency Court, Friendswood, TX 77546 USA

Wilmut, Ian *Misc*
Roslin Institute, Roslin Bio Centre, Midlothian, EH25 9PS, SCOTLAND

Wilson, A N *Writer*
21 Arlington Road, London, NW1 7ER, UNITED KINGDOM (UK)

Wilson, Al *Musician*
Talent Consultants International, 1560 Broadway, #1308, New York, NY 10036 USA

Wilson, Alexander G (Sandy) *Composer, Writer*
2 Southwell Gardens, #4, London, SW7 4SB, UNITED KINGDOM (UK)

Wilson, Alexandra *Actor*
GVA Talent Agency Inc, 9229 Sunset Blvd #320, Los Angeles, CA 90069 USA

Wilson, Allan B *Biologist*
University of California, Molecular Biology Dept, Berkeley, CA 94724 USA

Wilson, Ann *Musician*
H K Mgmt, 9200 W Sunset Blvd, #530, Los Angeles, CA 90069 USA

Wilson, August *Writer*
600 1st Ave, #301, Seattle, WA 98104 USA

Wilson, Billy *Football Player*
Whitehawk Ranch, PO Box 84, Clio, CA 96106 USA

Wilson, Blaine
201 S. Capitol Ave. #300, Indianapolis, IN 46225

Wilson, Blenda J *Educator*
California State University, President's Office, Northridge, CA 91330 USA

Wilson, Bob *Baseball Player*
806 Cabot Ln, Madison, WI 53711

Wilson, Brian D *Musician, Songwriter*
Rogers & Cowan, 1888 Century Park E, #500, Los Angeles, CA 90067 USA

Wilson, C A S John *Architect*
John Wilson Assoc, 27 Horsell Road, London, N5 1XL, UNITED KINGDOM (UK)

Wilson, Carnie *Musician*
Levine/Scheider, 433 N Camden Dr, Beverly Hills, CA 90210 USA

Wilson, Cassandra *Musician*
Dream Street Mgmt, 4346 Redwood Ave, #307, Marina del Rey, CA 90292 USA

Wilson, Cindy *Musician*
Direct Management Group, 947 N La Cienega Blvd, #2, Los Angeles, CA 90069 USA

Wilson, Colin H *Writer*
Tetherdown Trewallock Lane, Gorran Haven, Cornwall, UNITED KINGDOM (UK)

Wilson, Craig *Misc*
1423 Lake Blvd, David, CA 95616 USA

Wilson, Dan *Songwriter, Musician*
Monterey Peninsula Artists, 509 Hartnell St, Monterey, CA 93940 USA

Wilson, Daniel A (Dan) *Baseball Player*
1933 E Blaine St, Seattle, WA 98112 USA

Wilson, David *Actor*
Susan Smith, 121A N San Vicente Blvd, Beverly Hills, CA 90211 USA

Wilson, De'Angelo *Actor*
Brookside Artists Management (LA), 450 N Roxbury Dr Fl 4, Beverly Hills, CA 90210 USA

Wilson, Demond *Actor*
LAX & Company, CA USA

Wilson, Dick
2705 Cricket Hollow Ct., Henderson NV, 89014-1924

Wilson, Don The Dragon
178 S. Victory Blvd. #205, Burbank, CA 91502-2881

Wilson, Dorien *Actor*
Innovative Artists (LA), 1505 Tenth St, Santa Monica, CA 90401 USA

Wilson, Doug *Hockey Player*
18580 Petunia Court, Saratoga, CA 95070 USA

Wilson, Earle L *Religious Leader*
Wesleyan Church, PO Box 50434, Indianapolis, IN 46250 USA

Wilson, Edward O *Writer*
1010 Waltham St, #A208, Lexington, MA 02421 USA

Wilson, Elizabeth
200 W. 57th St. #900, New York, NY 10019

Wilson, Eric C T *War Hero*
Woodside Cottage, Stowell Sherbome, Dorset, UNITED KINGDOM (UK)

Wilson, Eugene *Skier*
25775 Ranchview Lane N, #1, Plymouth, MN 55447 USA

Wilson, F Paul *Writer*
PO Box 33, Allenwood, NJ 08720 USA

Wilson, F Perry *Engineer*
225 N 56th St, #217, Lincoln, NE 68504 USA

Wilson, Frank *Race Car Driver*
North Carlonia Motor Speedway, PO Box 500, Rockingham, NC 28380 USA

Wilson, Gahan *Writer*
New Yorker Magazine, Editorial Dept, 4 Times Square, New York, NY 10036 USA

Wilson, George *Basketball Player*
3900 Rose Hill Ave, Cincinnati, OH 45229 USA

Wilson, Georges *Director*
Moulin de Vilgris, Rambouillet, 78120, FRANCE

Wilson, Gerald S *Composer, Musician*
4625 Brynhurst Ave, Los Angeles, CA 90043 USA

Wilson, Harry C *Religious Leader*
Wesleyan Church Int'l Center, 6060 Castleway West Dr, Indianapolis, IN 46250 USA

Wilson, Hugh *Director*
William Morris Agency, 151 El Camino Dr, Beverly Hills, CA 90212 USA

Wilson, J Tylee *Business Person*
PO Box 2057, Ponte Vedra Beach, FL 32004 USA

Wilson, James B *Admiral*
40 Windermere Way, Kennett Square, PA 19348 USA

Wilson, James M *Misc*
University of Pennsylvania, Med Center, Genetics Dept, Philadelphia, PA 19104 USA

Wilson, James Q *Educator*
University of California, Graduate Management School, Los Angeles, CA 90024 USA

Wilson, Jean D *Doctor*
Texas Southwestern Medical Center, 5323 Harry Hines Blvd, Dallas, TX 75390 USA

Wilson, Jeannie *Actor*
General Delivery, Ketchum, ID 83340 USA

Wilson, Jennifer
1947 Lakeshore Dr., Branson, MO 65616

Wilson, Julie *Actor, Musician*
Stan Scotland Entertainment, 157 E 57th St, #188, New York, NY 10022 USA

Wilson, Justin *Musician*
David Levin Mgmt, 200 W 57th St, #308, New York, NY 10019 USA

Wilson, Kenneth G *Nobel Prize Laureate*
Ohio State University, Physics Dept, 174 W 18th Ave, Columbus, OH 43210 USA

Wilson, Kim *Musician*
Ricci Assoc, 28205 Agoura Road, Agoura Hills, CA 91301 USA

Wilson, Kristen *Actor*
Writers and Artists Group Intl (LA), 8383 Wilshire Blvd #550, Beverly Hills, CA 90211 USA

Wilson, Lambert *Actor*
Principal Entertainment (LA), 1964 Westwood Blvd #400, Los Angeles, CA 90025 USA

Wilson, Lanford *Writer*
PO Box 891, Sag Harbor, NY 11963 USA

Wilson, Lawrence F (Larry) *Football Player*
11834 N Blackheath Road, Scottsdale, AZ 85254 USA

Wilson, Luke *Actor*
Creative Artists Agency, 9830 Wilshire Blvd, Beverly Hills, CA 90212 USA

Wilson, Mara *Actor*
TalentWorks (LA), 3500 W Olive Ave #1400, Burbank, CA 91505 USA

Wilson, Marc D *Football Player*
113113 Mount Wallace Court, Alta Loma, CA 91737 USA

Wilson, Marie
6 Oakdale, Irvine, CA 92604

Wilson, Mary *Musician*
Borman Entertainment, 1250 6th St #401, Santa Monica, CA 90401 USA

Wilson, Melanie *Actor*
Irv Schechter, 9300 Wilshire Blvd, #410, Beverly Hills, CA 90212 USA

Wilson, Michael H *Government Official*
Industry & Science Dept, 235 Queen's St, Ottawa, ON K1A OH5, CANADA

Wilson, Nancy *Musician*
H K Management, 9200 W Sunset Blvd, #530, Los Angeles, CA 90069 USA

Wilson, Nancy *Musician*
MPI Talent Agency, 9255 Sunset Blvd, #407, Los Angeles, CA 90069 USA

Wilson, Neal C *Religious Leader*
Seventh-Day Adventists, 12501 Old Columbus Pike, Silver Spring, MD 20904 USA

Wilson, Olin C *Astronomer*
1508 Circa del Lago, B110, San Marcos, CA 92069 USA

Wilson, Owen C *Actor*
ID Public Relations, 8409 Santa Monica Blvd, West Hollywood, CA 90069 USA

Wilson, Patrick *Actor*
Creative Artists Agency LCC (CAA-LA), 9830 Wilshire Blvd, Beverly Hills, CA 90212 USA

Wilson, Paul
5255 Ventura Canyon, Van Nuys, CA 91401

Wilson, Peta *Actor*
June Cann Mgmt, 73 Jersey Road, Woollahra, NSW, 2025, AUSTRALIA

Wilson, Preston J R *Baseball Player*
Colorado Rockies, Coors Field, 2001 Blake St, Denver, CO 80205 USA

Wilson, Rainn *Actor*
3 Arts Entertainment Inc, 9460 Wilshire Blvd Fl 7, Beverly Hills, CA 90212 USA

Wilson, Ralph C Jr *Misc*
Buffalo Bills, 1 Bills Dr, Orchard Park, NY 14127 USA

Wilson, Rick *Race Car Driver*
Henderson Motorsports, 566 E Main St, Abingdon, VA 24210 USA

Wilson, Rick *Hockey Player, Coach*
166 E Bethel Road, Coppell, TX 75019 USA

Wilson, Rita *Actor*
PO Box 1650, Pacific Palisades, CA 90272 USA

Wilson, Robert E (Bobby) *Football Player*
1034 Liberty Park Dr, #408R, Austin, TX 78746 USA

Wilson, Robert M *Actor*
RW Work, 131 Varick St, #908, New York, NY 10013 USA

Wilson, Robert N *Business Person*
Johnson & Johnson, 1 Johnson & Johnson Plaza, New Brunswick, NJ 08933 USA

Wilson, Robert W *Nobel Prize Laureate*
94 Lucille Ave, Dumont, NJ 07628 USA

Wilson, Robin *Musician*
William Morris Agency, 2100 W End Ave, #1000, Nashville, TN 37203 USA

Wilson, Roger *Actor*
Joel Stevens Entertainment, 11524 Amanda Dr, Studio City, CA 91604 USA

Wilson, Ron *Hockey Player, Coach*
San Jose Sharks, San Jose Arena, 525 W Santa Clara St, San Jose, CA 95113 USA

Wilson, Ryan *Actor*
Osbrink Talent Agency, 4343 Lankershim Blvd #100, Universal City, CA 91602 USA

Wilson, Samuel W *Educator, General*
Hampden-Sydney College, President's Office, Hampden-Sydney, VA 23943 USA

Wilson, Sarah *Religious Leader*
Friends United Meeting, 101 Quaker Hill Dr, Richmond, IN 47374 USA

Wilson, Scott
PO Box 5617, Beverly Hills, CA 90210

Wilson, Sheree J *Actor*
7218 S Jan Mar Court, Dallas, TX 75230 USA

Wilson, Stephanie D *Astronaut*
14910 Hollydale Dr, Houston, TX 77062 USA

Wilson, Stuart *Actor*
International Creative Management (ICM-UK), Oxford House, 76 Oxford St, London, W1N OAX, UNITED KINGDOM (UK)

Wilson, Tom *Cartoonist*
Universal Press Syndicate, PO Box 419149, Kansas City, MO 64141 USA

Wilson, Torrie *Wrestler, Model*
5214 E Longboat Blvd, Tampa, FL 33615 USA

Wilson, William J *Social Activist*
Harvard University, Kennedy Government School, Cambridge, MA 02138 USA

Wilson, Woody *Cartoonist*
King Features Syndicate, 888 7th Ave, New York, NY 10106 USA

Wilson David, Mackenzie *Director*
Lifeboat House, Castletown, Isle of Man, IM9 1LD, UNITED KINGDOM (UK)

Wilson Jr, George B (Mike) *Football Player, General*
1062 E Lancaster Ave, Bryn Mawr, PA 19010 USA

Wilson Jr, Louis H *War Hero, General*
100 University Park Dr, Birmingham, AL 35209 USA

Wilson of Tillyorn, David C *Government Official*
House of Lords, Westminster, London, SW1A 0PW, UNITED KINGDOM (UK)

Wilson Phillips
1290 Ave. of the Americas #4200, New York, NY 10104

Wilson-Johnson, David R *Opera Singer*
28 Englefield Road, London, N1 4ET, UNITED KINGDOM (UK)

Wilson-Sampras, Bridgette *Actor*
Brillstein/Grey, 9150 Wilshire Blvd, #350, Beverly Hills, CA 90212 USA

Wimmer, Brian *Actor*
RR 3 Box H1, Provo, UT 84604 USA

Wimmer, Kurt *Actor, Writer, Producer, Director*
Endeavor Agency LLC (LA), 9601 Wilshire Blvd Fl 3, Beverly Hills, CA 90210 USA

Winans
1420 Coleman Rd., Franklin, TN 37064

Winans, BeBe *Musician*
Covenant Agency, 1011 4th St, #315, Santa Monica, CA 90403 USA

Winans, CeCe *Musician*
Wellspring Mgmt, 2300 Franklin Road, #2B, Franklin, TN 37064 USA

Winans, Vicki *Musician*
Convenant Agency, 1011 4th St, #315, Santa Monica, CA 90403 USA

Winbush, Angela *Songwriter, Musician*
Joyce Agency, 370 Harrison Ave, Harrison, NY 10528 USA

Winbush, Troy *Actor*
Paradigm (LA), 10100 Santa Monica Blvd, Fl 25, Los Angeles, CA 90067 USA

Wincer, Simon *Director, Producer*
Creative Artists Agency LCC (CAA-LA), 9830 Wilshire Blvd, Beverly Hills, CA 90212 USA

Wincer, Simon G *Director*
PO Box 241, Toorak, VIC, 3142, AUSTRALIA

Winchell, Paul *Actor*
4607 Rio Bravo Court, Moorpark, CA 93021 USA

Winchester, Jesse *Songwriter, Musician*
Keith Case Assoc, 1025 17th Ave S, #200, Nashville, TN 37212 USA

Winchester, Simon *Writer*
Harper Collins Publishers, 10 E 53rd St, New York, NY 10022 USA

Wincott, Jeff P *Actor*
Judy Shane & Associates, 606 N Larchmont Blvd, Los Angeles, CA 90004

Wincott, Michael *Actor*
Brillstein-Grey Entertainment, 9150 Wilshire Blvd #350, Beverly Hills, CA 90212 USA

Winders, Rich *Bowler*
720 Augusta St, Racine, WI 53402 USA

Winders, Wim *Director*
Paul Kohner, 9300 Wilshire Blvd, #555, Beverly Hills, CA 90212 USA

Windle, William F *Misc*
229 Cherry St, Granville, OH 43023 USA

Windom, William *Actor*
House of Representatives, 400 S Beverly Dr, #101, Beverly Hills, CA 90212 USA

Windon, Stephen *Cinematographer*
PO Box 659, Northbridge, Sydney, NSW, 2063, AUSTRALIA

Windsor, Barbara *Actor, Comedian*
104 Crouch Hill, London, NB 9EA, UNITED KINGDOM (UK)

Windsor-Smith, Barry *Artist*
Fantagraphics Books, 7563 Lake City Way, Seattle, WA 98115 USA

Wine, David M *Religious Leader*
Church of Brethren, 1451 Dundee Ave, Elgin, IL 60120 USA

Winfield, Dave *Athlete, Baseball Player*
2235 Stratford Circle, Los Angeles, CA 90077 USA

Winfield, David M (Dave) *Baseball Player*
2235 Stratford Circle, Los Angeles, CA 90077 USA

Winfield, Peter *Actor*
Screen Actors Guild (SAG-LA), 5757 Wilshire Blvd, Los Angeles, CA 90036 USA

Winfrey, Oprah *Talk Show Host, Producer, Actor*
Harpo Productions, Harpo Studios, 110 N Carpenter St, Chicago, IL 60607 USA

Winfrey, W C (Bill) *Misc*
7802 Sierra Trail, Spring Lake, NC 28390 USA

Wing-Merrill, Toby
Box 889, Matthews, VA 23109

Winger, Debra *Actor*
Parseghian/Planco LLC, 23 E 22nd St Fl 3, New York, NY 10010 USA

Winger, Kip *Musician*
Joseph Minkes Assoc, 2740 W Magnolia Blvd, #204, Burbank, CA 91505 USA

Wingreen, Jason
4224 Teesdale Ave., No. Hollywood, CA 91604

Wink, Chris *Entertainer*
Blue Man Group, Luxor Hotel, 3900 Las Vegas Blvd S, Las Vegas, NV 89119 USA

Winkleman, Sophie *Actor*
Creative Artists Agency LCC (CAA-LA), 9830 Wilshire Blvd, Beverly Hills, CA 90212 USA

Winkler, Angela
Schanzenstr. 24 rautsand, Drochtersen, GERMANY, D-21706

Winkler, David *Director*
Rigberg Roberts Rugoto, 1180 S Beverly Dr, #604, Los Angeles, CA 90035 USA

Winkler, Gerard *Actor*
Alsertra 26-3A, Vienna, 1090, AUSTRIA

Winkler, Hans-Gunter *Misc*
Dr Rau Allee 48, Warendorf, 48231, GERMANY

Winkler, Henry *Actor, Producer*
PO Box 49914, Los Angeles, CA 90049 USA

Winkler, Irwin *Director, Producer*
Irwin Winkler Productions, 211 S Beverly Dr, #220, Beverly Hills, CA 90212 USA

Winkler, Mel *Actor*

Winkles, Bobby B *Misc*
78452 Calle Huerta, La Quinta, CA 92253 USA

Winn, D Randolph (Randy) *Baseball Player*
59 Leeds Court E, Danville, CA 94526 USA

Winner, Michael R *Director, Producer*
31 Melbury Road, London, W14 8AB, UNITED KINGDOM (UK)

Winningham, Mare *Actor*
United Talent Agency, 9560 Wilshire Blvd, #500, Beverly Hills, CA 90212 USA

Winograd, Shmuel *Scientist, Mathematician*
235 Glendale Road, Scarsdale, NY 10583 USA

Winokur, Marissa Jaret *Actor*
McKeon-Valeo Management, 9107 Wilshire Blvd #321, Beverly Hills, CA 90210 USA

Winslet, Kate *Actor*
P F D, Drury House, 34-43 Russell St, London, CA WC2B 5HA, UNITED KINGDOM (UK)

Winslow, Dan *Musician*
3807 114th Lane NE, Minneapolis, MN 55449 USA

Winslow, Kellen B *Football Player*
5173 Waring Road, #312, San Diego, CA 92120 USA

Winslow, Michael *Actor, Comedian*
1327 Ocean Ave, #J, Santa Monica, CA 90401 USA

Winsor, Jackie *Artist*
Paula Cooper Gallery, 534 W 21st St, New York, NY 10011 USA

Winstead, Mary Elizabeth *Actor*
Anonymous Content, 8522 National Blvd #101, Culver City, CA 90232 USA

Winston, George *Composer, Musician*
Dancing Cat Productions, PO Box 639, Santa Cruz, CA 95061 USA

Winston, Hattie *Actor*
13025 Jarvis Ave, Los Angeles, CA 90061 USA

Winston, Patrick H *Scientist, Engineer*
Massachusetts Institute of Technology, Technology Square, Cambridge, MA 02139 USA

Winston, Roland *Physicist*
3384 Locksley Court, Merced, CA 95340 USA

Winston, Roy C *Football Player*
1541 S Elaine Dr, Baton Rouge, LA 70815 USA

Winston, Stan *Producer, Director, Writer, Artist*
7032 Valiean Ave, Van Nuys, CA 91406 USA

Winstone, Ray *Actor*
IFA Talent Agency, 8730 Sunset Blvd #490, Los Angeles, CA 90069 USA

Winter, Alex *Actor*
Tavel Entertainment, 9171 Wilshire Blvd #406, Beverly Hills, CA 90210 USA

Winter, Edgar
26033 Mulholland Hwy, Calabasas, CA 91302

Winter, Edgar *Musician*
Hooker Enterprises, 26033 Mulholland Highway, Calabasas, CA 91302 USA

Winter, Edward D *Actor*
4230 Whitsett Ave, #1, Studio City, CA 91604 USA

Winter, Eric *Actor*
Days of Our Lives, 3000 W Alameda Ave, Burbank, CA 91523 USA

Winter, Fred (Tex) *Coach*
Los Angeles Lakers, Staples Center, 1111 S Figueroa St, Los Angeles, CA 90015 USA

Winter, Harrison L *Judge*
US Court of Appeals, 101 W Lombard St, Baltimore, MD 21201 USA

Winter, Johnny *Musician*
Slatus Mgmt, 35 Hayward Ave, Colchester, CT 06415 USA

Winter, Judy
Merzstr. 14, Munich, GERMANY, D-81679

Winter, Olaf *Athlete*
An der Pirschheide 28, Potsdam, 14471, GERMANY

Winter, Paul T *Musician*
Living Music Records, PO Box 72, Litchfield, CT 06759 USA

Winter, Ralph *Producer*
Ralph Winter Productions, 10201 W Pico Blvd, Bldg 6 #101, Los Angeles, CA 90035 USA

Winter, Terence *Producer*
Creative Artists Agency LCC (CAA-LA), 9830 Wilshire Blvd, Beverly Hills, CA 90212 USA

Winter, Terrence *Writer, Producer*
Sopranos, The, 42-22 22nd St Fl 3, Long Island City, NY 11101 USA

Winter, William F *Governor*
633 N State St, Jackson, MS 39202 USA

Winter Jr, Ralph K *Judge*
US Court of Appeals, 55 Whitney Ave, New Haven, CT 06510 USA

Winterbottom, Michael *Director, Writer, Producer*
Revolution Films, 10 Little Turnstile, London, WC1V 70X, UNITED KINGDOM (UK)

Winters, Brian *Basketball Player, Coach*
2303 Tree Creek Place, Danville, CA 94526 USA

Winters, Dean *Actor*
Gersh Agency, The (LA), 232 N Canon Dr, Beverly Hills, CA 90210 USA

Winters, Jonathan *Comedian, Actor*
945 Lilac Dr, Santa Barbara, CA 93108 USA

Winters, Scott William *Actor*
Abrams Artists Agency (LA), 9200 Sunset Blvd Fl 11, Los Angeles, CA 90069 USA

Winters, Shelley *Actor*
Gladys Hart Assoc, 1244 11th St, #A, Santa Monica, CA 90401 USA

Wintour, Anna *Editor*
Vogue Magazine, Editorial Dept, 350 Madison Ave, New York, NY 10017 USA

Winwood, Steve *Musician*
Trinley Cottage, Tirley, Gloucs, GL19 4EU, UNITED KINGDOM (UK)

Winzenried, Jesse D *Financier*
Securities Investor Protection, 805 15th St NW, Washington, DC 20005 USA

Wire II, William S *Business Person*
6119 Stonehaven Dr, Nashville, TN 37215 USA

Wirth, Billy *Actor, Director*
Michael Slessinger, 8730 Sunset Blvd, #220W, Los Angeles, CA 90069 USA

Wirth, Timothy E *Senator*
United Nations Foundation, 1301 Connecticut Ave NW, Washington, DC 20036 USA

Wirtz, W Willard *Secretary*
1211 Connecticut Ave NW, Washington, DC 20036 USA

Wirtz, William W (Bill) *Misc*
181 De Windt Road, Winnetka, IL 60093 USA

Wisdom, Norman *Actor, Comedian*
Ballalaugh, Lhen Andreas Ramsey, Isle of Man, IM7 3EH, UNITED KINGDOM (UK)

Wisdom, Robert *Actor*
Evolution Entertainment, 901 N Highland Ave, Los Angeles, CA 90038 USA

Wisdom, Sir Norman
The Lhen, Andreas Ramsay ISLE OF MAN, UK, 1M7 3EH

Wise, Ray *Actor*
Gold Marshak Liedtke, 3500 W Olive Ave, #1400, Burbank, CA 91505 USA

Wise, Richard C (Rick) *Baseball Player*
662 SW 201st Ave, #66, Beaverton, OR 97006 USA

Wise, Robert *Director, Producer*
Robert E Wise Productions, 2222 Ave of the Stars, #2303, Los Angeles, CA 90067 USA

Wise, William A *Business Person*
El Paso Energy Corp, 1001 Louisiana St, Houston, TX 77002 USA

Wise, Willie *Basketball Player*
5232 215th St SE, Woodinville, WA 98072 USA

Wisecarver, Ellsworth (Sonny)
305 Mill Creek Rd, Mentone, CA 92359

Wiseman, Frederick *Producer*
Zipporah Films, 1 Richdale Ave, #4, Cambridge, MA 02140 USA

Wiseman, Joseph *Actor*
382 Central Park West, New York, NY 10025 USA

Wiseman, Len *Director, Writer*
International Creative Management (ICM-LA), 8942 Wilshire Blvd, Beverly Hills, CA 90211 USA

Wiseman, Mac *Musician*
PO Box 17028, Nashville, TN 37217 USA

Wish Bone *Musician*
Creative Artists Agency, 9830 Wilshire Blvd, Beverly Hills, CA 90212 USA

Wishart III, Leonard P *General*
19360 Magnolia Grove Square, #315, Leesburg, VA 20176 USA

Wisner, Frank G *Diplomat*
American International Group, 70 Pine St, #1800, New York, NY 10270 USA

Wisniewski, Andreas *Actor*
Gage Group, 14724 Ventura Blvd, #505, Sherman Oaks, CA 91403 USA

Wisniewski, Stephen A (Steve) *Football Player*
36 El Alamo Court, Danville, CA 94526 USA

Wisoff, Peter J K (Jeff) *Astronaut*
4268 Brindisi Place, Pleasanton, CA 94566 USA

Wistert, Albert A (Ox) *Football Player*
256 Gunnell Road, Grants Pass, OR 97526 USA

Wistert, Alvin L (Moose) *Football Player*
10250 W Seven Mile Road, Northville, MI 48167 USA

Wistrom, Grant *Football Player*
683 Spyglass Summit Dr, Chesterfield, MO 63017 USA

with Spencer Davis, Strawberry Alarm Clock *Music Group*
Geoffrey Blumenauer Artists, PO Box 343, Burbank, CA 91503-0343 USA

Withers, Bill *Musician, Songwriter*
PO Box 16698, Beverly Hills, CA 90209 USA

Withers, Googie *Actor*
Larry Dalzall, 17 Broad Court, London, WC2B 5QN, UNITED KINGDOM (UK)

Withers, Jane *Actor*
Scott Stander, 13701 Riverside Drive, #201, Sherman Oaks, CA 91423 USA

Withers, Pick *Musician*
Damage Mgmt, 16 Lambton Place, London, W11 2SH, UNITED KINGDOM (UK)

Witherspoon, Jimmy
223 1/2 E. 48th St., New York, NY 10017

Witherspoon, John *Actor*
T-Boyds Boy Inc, 12400 Ventura Blvd, Box 354, Studio City, CA 91604 USA

Witherspoon, Reese *Actor, Producer*
Nancy Ryder, 9111 Wilshire Blvd, #600W, Beverly Hills, CA 90210 USA

Witherspoon, Tim *Boxer*
Dennis Rappaport Productions, 22501 Linden Blvd, Cambridge Heights, NY 11411 USA

Witkin, Isaac *Artist*
Bennington College, Art Dept, Bennington, VT 05201 USA

Witkin, Joel-Peter *Photographer*
1707 Five Points Road SW, Albuquerque, NM 87105 USA

Witkop, Bernhard *Misc*
3807 Montrose Driveway, Chevy Chase, MD 20815 USA

Witt, Alicia *Actor*
Booth Schut, 11350 Ventura Blvd, #206, Studio City, CA 91604 USA

Witt, Katarina *Figure Skater*
Reichenheimer Str, Chemnitz, 09023, GERMANY

Witt, Michael A (Mike) *Baseball Player*
37 Poppy Hills Road, Laguna Nigel, CA 92677 USA

Witt, Paul J *Writer*
16032 Valley Vista Blvd, Encino, CA 91436 USA

Witt, Robert E *Educator*
University of Alabama, President's Office, Tuscaloosa, AL 35487 USA

Witten, Edward *Physicist*
Institute for Advanced Study, Einstein Lane, Princeton, NJ 08540 USA

Witter, Karen *Actor, Model*
H/H/M, 247 S Beverly Dr, #102, Beverly Hills, CA 90212 USA

Witting, Steve *Actor*
Artist's Agency, The (LA), 1180 S Beverly Dr #301, Los Angeles, CA 90035 USA

Wittman, Randy *Basketball Player, Coach*
8646 French Curve, Eden Prairie, MN 55347 USA

Wixted, Kevin
101001 Santa Monica Blvd. #700, Los Angeles, CA 90067

Wobst, Frank *Financier*
Huntington Bancshares, Huntington Center, 41 S High St, Columbus, OH 43287 USA

Wocket-Eckert, Barbel *Athlete*
Im Bangert 61, Lutzelbach, 64750, GERMANY

Woese, Carl R *Biologist*
806 W Delaware Ave, Urbana, IL 61801 USA

Woessner, Mark M *Business Person, Publisher*
Erich-Kastner-Str 25, Gutersloh, 33332, GERMANY

Woetzel, Damian *Dancer, Choreographer*
New York City Ballet, Lincoln Center Plaza, New York, NY 10023 USA

Wofford, Harris L *Senator*
260 Burch Dr, Coraopolos, PA 15108 USA

Wogan, Gerald N *Misc*
Massachusetts Institute of Technology, Toxicology Div, Cambridge, MA 02139 USA

Woggon, Bill *Cartoonist*
2724 Cabot Court, Thousand Oaks, CA 91360 USA

Wohl, Dave *Basketball Player, Coach*
23 Tompkins Road, East Brunswick, NJ 08816 USA

Wohlers, Mark E *Baseball Player*
135 Old Cedar Lane, Alpharetta, GA 30004 USA

Wohlhuter, Richard C (Rick) *Track Athlete*
175 Dickinson Dr, Wheaton, IL 60187 USA

Woit, Dick *Misc*
Lehmann Sports Center, 2700 N Lehmann Court, Chicago, IL 60614 USA

Woiwode, Larry *Writer*
State University of New York, English Dept, Binghamton, NY 13901 USA

Wojciehowicz, Alex
105 Silway Dr., Forked River, NJ 08731

Wojtowicz, R P *Misc*
Railway Carmen Union, 3 Research Place, Rockville, MD 20850 USA

Wolaner, Robin P *Publisher*
Sunset Publishing Corp, 80 Willow Road, Mento Park, CA 94025 USA

Wolcott, Charles
Box 155, Haifa, ISRAEL

Wolf, David A *Astronaut*
1714 Neptune Lane, Houston, TX 77062 USA

Wolf, Dick *Producer, Writer, Actor*
United Talent Agency, 9560 Wilshire Blvd, #500, Beverly Hills, CA 90212 USA

Wolf, Frank *Publisher*
Seventeen Magazine, 850 3rd Ave, New York, NY 10022 USA

Wolf, Naomi *Writer*
Random House, 1745 Broadway, #B1, New York, NY 10019 USA

Wolf, Peter *Musician*
Nick Ben-Meir, 652 N Doheny Dr, Los Angeles, CA 90069 USA

Wolf, Randall C (Randy) *Baseball Player*
7266 Angela Ave, West Hills, CA 91307 USA

Wolf, Scott *Actor*
Brillstein-Grey Entertainment, 9150 Wilshire Blvd #350, Beverly Hills, CA 90212 USA

Wolf, Sigrid *Skier*
Elbigenalp 45 A, 6652, AUSTRIA

Wolf, Stephen M *Business Person*
US Airways Group, 2345 Crystal Dr, Arlington, VA 22202 USA

Wolfe, George C *Director*
Shakespeare Festival, 425 Lafayette St, New York, NY 10003 USA

Wolfe, Kenneth L *Business Person*
Hershey Foods Corp, 100 Crystal A Dr, Hershey, PA 17033 USA

Wolfe, Michael
41 Lansdowne Rd., London, ENGLAND, W11 26Q

Wolfe, Naomi *Writer*
Royce Carlton Inc, 866 United Nations Plaza, New York, NY 10017 USA

Wolfe, Ralph S *Biologist*
University of Illinois, Microbiology Dept, Burnill Hall, Urbana, IL 61801 USA

Wolfe, Sterling *Actor*
2609 Wyoming Ave, #A, Burbank, CA 91505 USA

Wolfe, Thad A *General*
5207 Dunleigh Dr, Burke, VA 22015 USA

Wolfe, Tom
21 E. 79th St, New York, NY 10021

Wolfe Jr, Thomas K (Tom) *Writer*
21 E 79th St, New York, NY 10021 USA

Wolfenden of Westcott, John F *Educator*
White House, Guildford Road Westcott near Dorking, Surrey, UNITED KINGDOM (UK)

Wolfensohn, James D *Financier*
World Bank Group, 1818 H St NW, Washington, DC 20433 USA

Wolfenstein, Lincoln *Physicist*
Camegie-Mellon University, Physics Dept, Pittsburgh, PA 15213 USA

Wolfermann, Klaus *Track Athlete*
Fasenenweg 13A, Herzogenaurach, 91074, GERMANY

Wolff, Christian
Zinnkopfstr. 6, Aschau/Chiemsee, GERMANY, D-83229

Wolff, Christoph J *Educator*
182 Washington St, Belmont, MA 02478 USA

Wolff, Hugh *Conductor*
Van Walsun Mgmt, 4 Addison Bridge Place, London, W14 8XP, UNITED KINGDOM (UK)

Wolff, Jon A *Misc*
1122 University Bay Dr, Madison, WI 53705 USA

Wolff, Sanford I *Misc*
8141 Broadway, New York, NY 10023 USA

Wolff, Toblas J A *Writer*
Stanford University, English Dept, Stanford, CA 94305 USA

Wolff, Torben *Biologist*
Hesseltoften, Hellerup, 2900, DENMARK

Wolfowitz, Paul D *Government Official*
Defense Department, Pentagon, Washington, DC 20301 USA

Wolfson, Louis E *Business Person*
10205 Collins Ave, Bal Harbour, FL 33154 USA

Wolken, Jonathan *Dancer, Artist, Director*
Pilobolus Dance Theater, PO Box 388, Washington Depot, CT 06794 USA

Wolkowyski, Ruben *Basketball Player*
Seattle Supersonics, 351 Elliott Avenue W #500, Seattle, WA 98119 USA

Woll, Tom

Wollman, Harvey L *Governor*
RR 1 Box 43, Hitchcock, SD 57348 USA

Wollman, Roger L *Judge*
US Court of Appeals, Federal Building, 400 S Phillips, Sioux Falls, SD 57104 USA

Wolman, M Gordon *Geophysicist*
2104 W Rogers Ave, Baltimore, MD 21209 USA

Wolper, David L *Producer*
617 N Rodeo Dr, Beverly Hills, CA 90210 USA

Wolpert, Julian *Geophysicist*
188 E 64th St, #2304, New York, NY 10021 USA

Wolszczan, Aleksander *Astronomer*
Pennsylvania State University, Astronomy Dept, University Park, PA 16802 USA

Wolter, Sherilyn *Actor*
128 Old Topanga Canyon Rd, Topanga, CA 90290

Wolters, Kara *Basketball Player*
137 Westfield Dr, Holliston, MA 01746 USA

Womack, Bobby *Songwriter, Musician*
Richard Walters, 1800 Argyle Ave, #408, Los Angeles, CA 90028 USA

Womack, James E *Scientist*
2105 Farley, College Station, TX 77845 USA

Womack, Lee Ann *Musician*
Erv Woolsey, 1000 18th Ave S, Nashville, TN 37212 USA

Woman, Nancy
PO Box 3601, Torrance, CA 90510

Wonder, Stevie *Musician, Songwriter*
Steveland Morris Music, 4616 W Magnolia Blvd, Burbank, CA 91505 USA

Wong, Albert *Engineer*
26796 Vista Terrace, Lake Forest, CA 92630 USA

Wong, B D *Actor*
Innovative Artists (LA), 1505 Tenth St, Santa Monica, CA 90401 USA

Wong, James *Director, Writer, Producer*
Original Film, 2045 S Barrington Ave, Los Angeles, CA 90025 USA

Wong, Russell *Actor*
International Creative Mgmt, 8942 Wilshire Blvd, #219, Beverly Hills, CA 90211 USA

Wong-Staal, Flossie *Biologist*
University of California, Molecular Biology Dept, La Jolla, CA 92093 USA

Woo, John *Director, Producer*
Endeavor Talent Agency, 9701 Wilshire Blvd, #1000, Beverly Hills, CA 90212 USA

Wood, Brenton *Musician*
PO Box 4127, Inglewood, CA 90309 USA

Wood, C Norman *General*
5440 Mount Corcoran Place, Burke, VA 22015 USA

Wood, Carolyn *Swimmer*
4380 SW 86th Ave, Portland, OR 97225 USA

Wood, Charles G *Writer*
London Mgmt, 2-4 Noel St, London, W1V 3RB, UNITED KINGDOM (UK)

Wood, Danny
496 Adams St., Dorchester, MA 02122

Wood, Elijah *Actor*
PO Box 10459, Burbank, CA 91510 USA

Wood, Evan Rachel *Actor*
International Creative Mgmt, 8942 Wilshire Blvd, #219, Beverly Hills, CA 90211 USA

Wood, Gene
PO Box 805, Culver City, CA 90232-0805

Wood, Glen *Race Car Driver*
57 Rhody Creek Loop, Stuart, VA 24171 USA

Wood, Gordon S *Historian*
77 Keense St, Providence, RI 02906 USA

Wood, James *Business Person*
Great A & P Tea Co, 2 Paragon Dr, Montvale, NJ 07645 USA

Wood, James N *Director*
Art Institute of Chicago, 111 S Michigan Ave, Chicago, IL 60603 USA

Wood, Janet *Actor*
Acme Talent, 4727 Wilshire Blvd, #333, Los Angeles, CA 90010 USA

Wood, John *Actor*
Royal Shakespeare Co, Barbican Center, Silk St, London, EC2Y 8DS, UNITED KINGDOM (UK)

Wood, John A *Physicist, Geophysicist*
1716 Cambridge St, #16, Cambridge, MA 02138 USA

Wood, Jon *Race Car Driver*
Hendrick Motorsports, 4400 Papa Joe Hendrick Blvd, Charlotte, NC 28262 USA

Wood, Kerry L *Baseball Player*
15832 E Richwood Ave, Fountain Hills, AZ 85268 USA

Wood, Kimba M *Judge*
US District Court House, 40 Foley Square, New York, NY 10007 USA

Wood, Lana *Actor*
868 Masterson Dr, Thousand Oaks, CA 91360 USA

Wood, Leon *Basketball Player*
4217 Faculty Ave, Long Beach, CA 90808 USA

Wood, Maurice *Doctor*
RR 2 Box 543B, Hot Springs, VA 24445 USA

Wood, Oliver *Cinematographer*
2018 N Vine St, Los Angeles, CA 90068 USA

Wood, Rachel Hurd *Actor*
Paradigm (LA), 10100 Santa Monica Blvd, Fl 25, Los Angeles, CA 90067 USA

Wood, Robert C *Secretary*
66 Pinewood Ave, Sudbury, MA 01776
USA

Wood, Robert E *Publisher*
Peninsula Times Tribune, 435 N Michigan
Ave, #1609, Chicago, IL 60611 USA

Wood, Robert J *Astronaut*
McDonnell Douglas Corp, PO Box 516,
Saint Louis, MO 63166 USA

Wood, Ron
Sandy Mount House, County Kildare S.,
IRELAND

Wood, Ronald (Ron) *Musician*
Monroe Sounds, 5 Church Row,
Wandsworth Plain, London, SW18 1ES,
UNITED KINGDOM (UK)

Wood, Sharon *Misc*
PO Box 1482, Canmore, AB T0L 0M0,
CANADA

Wood, Sidney B B *Tennis Player*
300 Murray Place, Southampton, NY
11968 USA

Wood, Stuart (Woody) *Musician*
27 Preston Grange Road, Preston Pans E,
Lothlan, SCOTLAND

Wood, Thomas H *Publisher*
Atlanta Constitution, 72 Marietta St NW,
Atlanta, GA 30303 USA

Wood, Tom
6310 San Vicente Blvd. #520, Los
Angeles, CA 90048

Wood, Wilbur F *Baseball Player*
3 Elmsbrook Road, Bedford, MA 01730
USA

Wood, William V (Willie) *Football Player*
Willie Wood Mechanical Systems, 7941
16th St NW, Washington, DC 20012 USA

Wood III, William B *Biologist*
University of Colorado, Molecular Biology
Dept, Boulder, CO 80309 USA

Wood Jr, Harlington *Judge*
US Court of Appeals, 600 E Monroe St,
Springfield, IL 62701 USA

Woodall, Jerry M *Engineer, Inventor*
Yale University, Microelectronic Materials
Ctr, 105 Wall, New Haven, CT 06511
USA

Woodard, Alfre *Actor*
602 Bay St, Santa Monica, CA 90405 USA

Woodard, Bob *Writer*
2907 Q Street NW, Washington, DC
20007 USA

Woodard, Charlayne *Actor, Writer*
Agency for Performing Arts, 9200 Sunset
Blvd, #900, Los Angeles, CA 90069 USA

Woodard, Lynette *Basketball Player*
University of Kensas, Allen Fieldhouse,
Lawrence, KS 66045 USA

Woodard, Rickey *Musician*
JVC Music, 3800 Barham Blvd, #409, Los
Angeles, CA 90068 USA

Woodard, Steven L (Steve) *Baseball
Player*
800 Frost Court SW, Hartselle, AL 35640
USA

Woodbine, Bokeem *Actor*
19351 Ventura Blvd, Tarzana, CA 91356
USA

Woodbridge, Todd *Tennis Player*
Advantage International, PO Box 3297,
North Burnley, VIC, 3121, AUSTRALIA

Woodburn, Danny *Actor*
TalentWorks (LA), 3500 W Olive Ave
#1400, Burbank, CA 91505 USA

Woodcock, Leonard
2404 Vinewood, Ann Arbor, MI 48104

Wooden, John *Basketball Player, Coach*
17711 Margate St, #102, Encino, CA
91316 USA

Woodforde, Mark *Tennis Player*
Octagon, 1751 Pinnacle Dr, #1500,
McLean, VA 22102 USA

Woodhead, Cynthia *Swimmer*
PO Box 1193, Riverside, CA 92502 USA

Woodiwiss, Kathleen E *Writer*
Avon Books, 959 8th Ave, New York, NY
10019 USA

Woodland, Lauren
Jerry Shandrew PR, 1050 South Stanley
Avenue, Los Angeles, CA 90019-6634
USA

Woodlawn, Holly
PO Box 27766, Los Angeles, CA 90027

Woodmansee Jr, John W *General*
6609 Shady Creek Circle, Plano, TX
75024 USA

Woodring, Jim *Artist*
Fantagraphics Books, 7563 Lake City
Way, Seattle, WA 98115 USA

Woodring, Wendell P *Misc*
6647 El Colegio Road, Goleta, CA 93117
USA

Woodruff, Billie *Actor*
Gersh Agency, The (NY), 41 Madison Ave
Fl 33, New York, NY 10010 USA

Woodruff, Blake *Actor*
Hines and Hunt Entertainment, 1213 W
Magnolia Blvd, Burbank, CA 91506 USA

Woodruff, Bob *Songwriter, Musician*
Jim Della Croce Mgmt, 1229 17th Ave S,
Nashville, TN 37212 USA

Woodruff, Frank
170 N. Crescent Dr., Beverly Hills, CA
90210

Woodruff, John Y *Track Athlete*
9 Dennison Dr, #J, East Windsor, NJ
08520 USA

Woodruff, Judy C *Television Host,
Commentator*
Cable News Network, News Dept, 820 1st
St NE, Washington, DC 20002 USA

Woods, Aubrey *Actor*
James Sharkey, 21 Golden Square,
London, W1R 3PA, UNITED KINGDOM
(UK)

Woods, Barbara Alyn *Actor*
Honey Prod, 2930 Falaise Ave SW, #H1,
Calgary, AL T3E 7J2, CANADA

Woods, Elbert (Ickey) *Football Player*
7031 Fairpark Ave, Cincinnati, OH 45216
USA

Woods, Eldrick T (Tiger) *Golfer*
Tiger Woods Foundation, 4281 Katella
Ave, #111, Los Alamitos, CA 90720 USA

Woods, George *Track Athlete*
7631 Green Hedge Road, Edwardsville, IL
62025 USA

Woods, James *Actor*
Guttman Assoc, 118 S Beverly Dr, #201,
Beverly Hills, CA 90212 USA

Woods, Jerome *Football Player*
Kansas City Chiefs, 1 Arrowhead Dr,
Kansas City, KS 64129 USA

Woods, Michael *Actor*
1608 Courtney Ave, Los Angeles, CA
90046 USA

Woods, Paul *Hockey Player*
4276 S Shore St, Waterford, MI 48323-
1157

Woods, Philip (Phil) *Composer, Musician*
PO Box 278, Delaware Water Gap, PA
18327 USA

Woods, Qyntel *Basketball Player*
Portland Trail Blazers, Rose Garden, 1
Center Court St, Portland, OR 97227 USA

Woods, Robert S *Actor*
ITA, 227 Central Park W, #5A, New York,
NY 10024 USA

Woods, Rosemary *Secretary*
3700 S Union Ave, Alliance, OH 44601
USA

Woods, Stuart *Writer*
Harper Collins Publishers, 10 E 53rd St,
New York, NY 10022 USA

Woods, Tiger *Golfer*
IMG (Sports), 1360 E 9th St #100,
Cleveland, OH 44114 USA

Woodside, DB *Actor*
Paradigm Agency, 10100 Santa Monica
Blvd, #2500, Los Angeles, CA 90067 USA

Woodson, Abraham B (Abe) *Football
Player*
3680 Waynesvill St, Las Vegas, NV 89122
USA

Woodson, Alli *Musician*
Superstars Unlimited, PO Box 371371,
Las Vegas, NV 89137 USA

Woodson, Charles *Football Player*
Oakland Raiders, 1220 Harbor Bay
Parkway, Alameda, CA 94502 USA

Woodson, Darren R *Football Player*
5315 Ambergate Lane, Dallas, TX 75287
USA

Woodson, Herbert H *Engineer*
1034 Libert Park Dr, Austin, TX 78746
USA

Woodson, Marv *Football Player*
2218 Bienville St, New Orleans, LA
70119 USA

Woodson, Michael (Mike) *Basketball
Player*
19918 Parsons Green Court, Katy, TX
77450 USA

Woodson, Robert L *Social Activist*
National Neighborhood Enterprise Center,
1424 16th St NW, Washington, DC 20036
USA

Woodson, Roderick K (Rod) *Football
Player*
434 Heights Dr, Gibsonia, PA 15044 USA

Woodson, Warren V *Football Coach*
12680 Hillcrest Road, #1106, Dallas, TX 75230 USA

Woodville, Kate *Actor*
27320 Winding Way, Malibu, CA 90265 USA

Woodward, Bob
2907 Q St. NW, Washington, DC 20007

Woodward, Edward *Actor, Musician*
Ravens Court Calstock, Cornwall, PL18 9ST, UNITED KINGDOM (UK)

Woodward, Joanne *Actor*
International Creative Management (ICM-LA), 8942 Wilshire Blvd, Beverly Hills, CA 90211 USA

Woodward, Joanne G *Actor*
1120 5th Ave, #1C, New York, NY 10128 USA

Woodward, Kenneth L *Writer*
Simon & Schuster/Pocket/Summit, 1230 Ave of Americas, New York, NY 10020 USA

Woodward, Kirsten *Fashion Designer*
Kirsten Woodward Hats, 26 Portobello Green Arcade, London, W10, UNITED KINGDOM (UK)

Woodward, Louise
Elton, ENGLAND

Woodward, Morgan *Actor*
2111 Rockledge Road, Los Angeles, CA 90068 USA

Woodward, Peter
84 Park Rd Kingston Gate, Surrey, ENGLAND, KT2 5JZ

Woodward, Robert D (Bob) *Journalist*
2907 Q St NW, Washington, DC 20007 USA

Woodward, Roger R *Composer, Musician, Conductor*
LH Productions, 2/37 Hendy Ave, Coogee, NSW, 2034, AUSTRALIA

Woodward III, Neil W *Astronaut*
18603 Carriage Court, Houston, TX 77058 USA

Woodwell, George M *Scientist*
Woods Hole Research Center, 13 Church St, Woods Hole, MA 02543 USA

Woody, Paul *Misc*
New Frontier Mgmt, 1921 Broadway, Nashville, TN 37203 USA

Woogon, Bill *Cartoonist*
2724 Cabot Court, Thousand Oaks, CA 91360 USA

Wool, Christopher *Artist*
Luhring Augustine Gallery, 531 W 24th St, New York, NY 10011 USA

Wooldridge, Dean E *Business Person*
4545 Via Esperanza, Santa Barbara, CA 93110 USA

Woolery, Chuck *Actor, Entertainer*
2555 Silver Cloud Dr, Park City, UT 84060 USA

Woolfolk, Andre *Football Player*
Tennessee Titans, 460 Great Circle Road, Nashville, TN 37228 USA

Woolfolk, Harold (Butch) *Football Player*
3138 N Richards St, Milwaukee, WI 53212 USA

Woolford, Donnell *Football Player*
792 Old Shirley Road, Central, SC 29630 USA

Woolley, Catherine *Writer*
PO Box 71, Higgins Hollow Road, Truro, MA 02666 USA

Woolley, Kenneth F *Architect*
790 George St, LV 5, Sydney, NSW, 2000, AUSTRALIA

Woolley, Sheb
123 Walton Ferry Rd. #200, Hendersonville, TN 37075

Woolridge, Orlando *Basketball Player, Coach*
16656 Cumbre Verde Court, Pacific Palisades, CA 90272 USA

Woolridge, Susan
4 Windmill St., London, ENGLAND, W1P 1HF

Woolsey, Elizabeth D *Skier*
Trail Creek Ranch, Wilson, WY 83014 USA

Woolsey, R James *Lawyer*
Shea & Gardner, 1800 Massachusetts Ave NW, Washington, DC 20036 USA

Woolsey, Ralph A *Cinematographer*
23388 Mulholland Dr, #109, Woodland Hills, CA 91364 USA

Woolstenhulme, Rick *Musician*
Untitled Entertainment (LA), 8436 W 3rd St #650, Los Angeles, CA 90048 USA

Woomble, Roddy *Musician*
Agency Group Ltd, 370 City Road, London, EC1V 2QA, UNITED KINGDOM (UK)

Woosnam, Ian H *Golfer*
Dyffryn, Morda Rd, Oswestry, Shropshire, SY11 2AY, WALES

Woosnam, Phil *Misc*
1255 Fairfield E, Atlanta, GA 30338 USA

Wooten, Jim *Commentator*
ABC-TV, News Dept, 5010 Creston St, Hyattsville, MD 20781 USA

Wooten, Morgan *Coach*
De Matha High School, Athletic Dept, Hyattsville, MD 20781 USA

Wooten, Nicholas *Producer*
Endeavor Agency LLC (LA), 9601 Wilshire Blvd Fl 3, Beverly Hills, CA 90210 USA

Wooten, Victor *Musician*
Skyline Music, PO Box 31, Lancaster, NH 03584 USA

Wootton, Charles G *Diplomat*
Chevron Corp, 555 Market St, San Francisco, CA 94105 USA

Wopat, Tom *Actor, Musician*
Po Box 128031, Nashville, TN 37212 USA

Word, Weldon R *Engineer*
633 Private Road 7908, Hawkins, TX 75765 USA

Worden, Alfred M *Astronaut*
PO Box 8065, Vero Beach, FL 32963 USA

Worden, Marc *Actor*
Burstein Company, The, 15304 Sunset Blvd #208, Pacific Palisades, CA 90272 USA

Worgull, David *Religious Leader*
Wisconsin Evangelical Lutheran Synod, 1270N Dobson Road, Chandler, AZ 85224 USA

World Wrestling Entertainment (WWE)
1241 E Main St, Stamford, CT 06902

Worlds Apart
PO Box 21, London, ENGLAND, W10 6BR

Worley, Darryl *Musician*
William Morris Agency, 2100 W End Ave, #1000, Nashville, TN 37203 USA

Worley, Jo Anne *Actor*
PO Box 2054, Toluca Lake, CA 91610 USA

Worndl, Frank *Skier*
Burgsiedlung 19C, Sonthofen, 87527, GERMANY

Woronov, Mary *Actor*
4350 1/4 Beverly Blvd, Los Angeles, CA 90004 USA

Worsley, Lorne J (Gump) *Hockey Player*
421 Bonaire Ave, Beloeil, QC, H3G L1L, CANADA

Worth, Maurice *Business Person*
Della Air Lines, Hartsfield International Airport, Atlanta, GA 30320 USA

Worthen, John E *Educator*
Ball State University, President's Office, Muncie, IN 47306 USA

Worthington, Cal
3815 Florin Rd., Sacramento, CA 95823

Worthington, Melvin L *Religious Leader*
Free Will Baptists, PO Box 5002, Antioch, TN 37011 USA

Worthington, Sam
9830 Wilshire Blvd., Beverly Hills, CA 90212

Worthy, James *Basketball Player, Sportscaster*
11821 Henley Lane, Los Angeles, CA 90077 USA

Worthy, Rick (Richard) *Actor*
Silver Massetti & Szatmary (SMS-LA), 8730 Sunset Blvd #440, Los Angeles, CA 90069 USA

Wottie, David J (Dave) *Track Athlete*
9245 Forest Hill Lane, Germantown, TN 38139 USA

Wottle, Dave
9245 Forest Hill Lane, Germantown, TN 38139-7906

Wouk, Herman *Writer*
303 Crestview Dr, Palm Springs, CA 92264 USA

Woytowicz-Rudnicka, Stefania *Musician*
Al Przyiaciol 2 m, Warsaw, 00-565, POLAND

Wozniak, Steve *Designer, Inventor*
300 Santa Rosa Dr, Los Gatos, CA 95032 USA

Wragg, John *Artist*
6 Castle Lane, Devizes, Wilts, SN10 1HJ, UNITED KINGDOM (UK)

Wrangler, Jack
41 W. 58th St. #5A, New York, NY 10019

Wray, Gordon R *Designer, Engineer*
Stonestack Rempstone, Loughborough, Leics, LE12 6RH, UNITED KINGDOM (UK)

Wray, Link *Musician*
Absolute Artists, 8490 W Sunset Blvd, #403, West Hollywood, CA 90069 USA

Wregget, Ken *Hockey Player*
120 Devon Road, Bllomfield Hills, MI 48302 USA

Wren, Claire
5757 Wilshire Blvd. #473, Los Angeles, CA 90036

Wright, Ben *Sportscaster*
CBS-TV, Sports Dept, 51 W 52nd St, New York, NY 10019 USA

Wright, Betty *Musician*
Rodgers Redding, 1048 Tatnall St, Macon, GA 31201 USA

Wright, Bonnie *Actor*
P F D Drury House, 34-43 Russell St, London, WC2B 5HA, UNITED KINGDOM (UK)

Wright, Bruce A *General*
Vice Commander, Air Combat Command, Langley Air Force Base, VA 23665 USA

Wright, Chely *Musician*
TBA Artist Mgmt, 300 10th Ave S, Nashville, TN 37203 USA

Wright, Clyde *Baseball Player*
528 S Jeanine St, Anaheim, CA 92806 USA

Wright, Craig M *Architect*
C M Wright Inc, 700 N La Cienega Blvd, Los Angeles, CA 90069 USA

Wright, Dick *Cartoonist*
Columbus Dispatch, Editorial Dept, 34 S 3rd St, Columbus, OH 43215 USA

Wright, Donald C (Don) *Cartoonist*
PO Box 1176, Palm Beach, FL 33480 USA

Wright, Ernie H *Football Player*
1414 Lauren Court, Encinitas, CA 92024 USA

Wright, Felix *Football Player*
2698 Wakefield Lane, Westlake, OH 44145 USA

Wright, Felix E *Business Person*
Leggett & Platt Inc, 1 Leggett Road, Carthage, MO 64836 USA

Wright, Gary *Songwriter, Musician*
Artists & Audience Entertainment, PO Box 35, Pawling, NY 12564 USA

Wright, Geoffrey *Actor*
Innovative Artists, 1505 10th St, Santa Monica, CA 90401 USA

Wright, Gerald *Director*
Guthrie Theatre, 725 Vineland Place, Minneapolis, MN 55403 USA

Wright, Heather
1 Sunnyside Wimbledon, London, ENGLAND, SW19

Wright, Hugh *Musician*
William Morris Agency, 2100 W End Ave, #1000, Nashville, TN 37203 USA

Wright, Ian *Television Host*
Public Broadcasting Service (PBS), 1320 Braddock Pl, Alexandria, VA 22314 USA

Wright, Irving S *Doctor*
25 E End Ave, New York, NY 10028 USA

Wright, J Oliver *Diplomat*
Burstow Hall, Hortey, Surrey, H6 9SR USA

Wright, Jay *Writer*
General Delivery, Piermont, NH 03779 USA

Wright, Jeffrey *Actor*
Creative Artists Agency, 9830 Wilshire Blvd, Beverly Hills, CA 90212 USA

Wright, Jenny *Actor*
Paul Kohner, 9300 Wilshire Blvd, #555, Beverly Hills, CA 90212 USA

Wright, Judith A *Writer*
17 Devonport St, #1, Lyons, ACT, 2060, AUSTRALIA

Wright, Laura
51 W. 52nd St., New York, NY 10019

Wright, Lawrence A *Judge*
US Tax Court, 400 2nd St NW, Washington, DC 20217 USA

Wright, Louis B *Historian*
3702 Leland St, Chevy Chase, MD 20815 USA

Wright, Louis D *Football Player*
Digi-Tec, Seismic Corp, 3140 S Peoria St #K274, Aurora, CO 80014 USA

Wright, Mary K (Mickey) *Golfer*
2972 SE Treasure Island Road, Port Saint Lucie, FL 34952 USA

Wright, Max *Actor*
Bresler Kelly Assoc, 11500 W Olympic Blvd, #510, Los Angeles, CA 90064 USA

Wright, Michael
10000 Santa Monica Blvd. #305, Los Angeles, CA 90067

Wright, Michael W *Business Person*
Super Valu Inc, 11840 Valley View Road, Eden Prairie, MN 55344 USA

Wright, Michelle *Musician*
Savannah Music, 205 Powell Place, #214, Brentwood, TN 37027 USA

Wright, Mickey
2972 SE Treasure Island Rd, Port St. Lucie, FL 34952-5773

Wright, N'Bushe
1505 10th St., Santa Monica, CA 90401

Wright, Nathaniel (Nate) *Football Player*
11247 Zorita Court, San Diego, CA 92124 USA

Wright, Pat *Musician*
Superstars Unlimited, PO Box 371371, Las Vegas, NV 89137 USA

Wright, Peter R *Dancer, Choreographer*
10 Chiswick Wharf, London, W4 2SR, UNITED KINGDOM (UK)

Wright, Petra *Actor*
One Entertainment (LA), 9220 W Sunset Blvd #306, Los Angeles, CA 90069 USA

Wright, Rayfield *Football Player*
PO Box 30513, Phoenix, AZ 85046 USA

Wright, Raymond R *War Hero*
10 Holt Circle, Fletcher, NC 28732 USA

Wright, Rick *Musician*
Agency Group, 370 City Road, London, EC1V 2QA, UNITED KINGDOM (UK)

Wright, Samuel E *Actor*
Gilla Roos Ltd, 16 West 22nd Street, New York, NY 10010 USA

Wright, Steven *Actor*
United Talent Agency (UTA), 9560 Wilshire Blvd, Beverly Hills, CA 90212 USA

Wright, Teresa *Actor*
571 Tolland Tumpike, Manchester, CT 06040 USA

Wright, Trevor *Actor*
James/Levy/Jacobson Management, 3500 W Olive Ave #1470, Burbank, CA 91505 USA

Wright, Van Earl *Actor*
William Morris Agency (WMA-LA), 1 William Morris Pl, Beverly Hills, CA 90212 USA

Wright Jr, Charles P *Writer*
940 Locust Ave, Charlottesville, VA 22901 USA

Wright Jr, Cobina *Actor*
1326 Dove Meadow Road, Solvange, CA 93463 USA

Wright Jr, James C (Jim) *Misc*
Texas Christian University, Fort Worth, TX 76129 USA

Wright Jr, John M *General*
21227 George Brown Ave, Riverside, CA 92518 USA

Wright Penn, Robin *Actor*
Creative Artists Agency, 9830 Wilshire Blvd, Beverly Hills, CA 90212 USA

Wrightman, Robert
125 S. Kings Rd., Los Angeles, CA 90048

Wrightman, Tim *Football Player*
3505 S Dension Ave, San Pedro, CA 90731 USA

Wrightson, Bernard (Bernie) *Swimmer*
924 Birch Ave, Escondido, CA 92027 USA

Wrigley Jr, William *Business Person*
William Wrigley Jr Co, 410 N Michigan Ave, Chicago, IL 60611 USA

Wriston, Walter B *Financier*
Citicorp Center, 425 Park Ave, #300, New York, NY 10022 USA

Wszola, Jacek *Track Athlete*
Ul Chrzanowskiego 7 m 70, Warsaw, 04-381, POLAND

Wu, Alice *Writer*
Creative Artists Agency LCC (CAA-LA), 9830 Wilshire Blvd, Beverly Hills, CA 90212 USA

Wu, Gordon Y S *Business Person*
Hopewell Holdings, Hopewell Center, 183 Queen Road East, Hong Kong, CHINA

Wu, Madame Sylvia
1515 N. Capri Dr., Pacific Palisades, CA 90272

Wu, Sau Lan *Physicist*
35 Robinson St, Cambridge, MA 02138 USA

Wu, Tai Tsun *Physicist*
35 Robinson St, Cambridge, MA 02138 USA

Wu Yigong *Director*
52 Yong Fu Road, Shanghai, CHINA

Wu-Tang
BMG/RCA, 1540 Broadway #3500, New York, NY 10036

WuDunn, Sheryl *Journalist*
New York Times, Editorial Dept, 229 W 43rd St, New York, NY 10036 USA

Wuethrich, Kurt *Nobel Prize Laureate*
Federal Institute of Technology, ETH Zentrum, Zurich, 8092, SWITZERLAND

Wuhl, Robert *Actor*
Paradigm Agency, 10100 Santa Monica Blvd, #2500, Los Angeles, CA 90067 USA

Wuhrer, Kari *Actor*
PO Box 69188, Los Angeles, CA 90069 USA

Wunderlich, Paul *Artist*
Haynstr 2, Hamburg, 20949, GERMANY

Wunsch, Carl I *Oceanographer*
78 Washington Ave, Cambridge, MA 02140 USA

Wuorinen, Charles P *Composer*
Howard Stokar Mgmt, 870 W End Ave, New York, NY 10025 USA

Wurtzel, Elizabeth *Actor, Writer*
Artist's Agency, The (NY), 230 W 55th St #29D, New York, NY 10019

Wurz, Alexander *Race Car Driver*
McLaren Int'l Working Park, Albert Dr, Woking, Surrey, GU21 5JY, UNITED KINGDOM (UK)

Wuycik, Dennis *Basketball Player*
31 Rogerson Dr, Chapel Hill, NC 27517 USA

Wyatt, Jane *Actor*
651 Siena Way, Los Angeles, CA 90077 USA

Wyatt, Jennifer *Golfer*
Carolina Group, 2321 Devine St, #A, Columbia, SC 29205 USA

Wyatt, Keke *Musician*
Universal Attractions, 145 W 57th St, #1500, New York, NY 10019 USA

Wyatt, Leslie *Educator*
Arkansas State University, President's Office, State University, AR 72467 USA

Wyatt, Shannon *Actor*
8949 Falling Creek Court, Annandale, VA 22003 USA

Wyatt, Sharon *Actor*
16830 Ventura Blvd, #300, Encino, CA 91436 USA

Wyatt Jr, Oscar S *Business Person*
Coastal Corp, 6955 Union Park Ave, #540, Midvale, UT 84047 USA

Wyche, Samuel D (Sam) *Football Coach, Sportscaster*
PO Box 1570, Pickens, SC 29671 USA

Wycheck, Frank *Football Player*
4674 Sunrise Ave, Bensalem, PA 19020 USA

Wycoff, Brooks *Athlete*
1 Mohegan Sun Blvd, Uncasville, CT 06382

Wyeth, Andrew N *Artist*
10000 Brintons Bridge Road, Chadds Ford, PA 19317 USA

Wyeth, James Browning *Artist*
Lookout Farm, 701 Smiths Bridge Road, Wilmington, DE 19807 USA

Wylde, Chris
3313 1/2 Barham Blvd., Los Angeles, CA 90068

Wylde, Zakk *Musician*
Agency Group, The (LA), 8490 Sunset Blvd #403, W Hollywood, CA 90069 USA

Wyle, Noah *Actor, Producer*
PO Box 27380, Los Angeles, CA 90027 USA

Wyler, Gretchen *Actor*
11754 Barranca Road, Camarillo, CA 93012 USA

Wylie, Adam
14011 Ventura Blvd. #202, Sherman Oaks, CA 91423

Wylie, Paul *Figure Skater*
170 Estey Ave, Hyannis, MA 02601 USA

Wyludda, Ilke *Track Athlete*
LAC Chemnitz, Relchengainer Str 154, Chemnitz, 09125, GERMANY

Wyman, Bill *Musician*
Ripple Productions, 344 Kings Road, London, SW3 5UR USA

Wyman, Jane *Actor*
14 Kavenish Dr, Rancho Mirage, CA 92270 USA

Wyman, Joel *Producer, Writer*

Wymore, Patrice *Actor*
Port Antonio, JAMAICA, BWI, WEST INDIES

Wyn-Davies, Geraint *Actor*
Oscars Abrams Zimel, 438 Queen St E, Toronto, ON M5A 1T4, CANADA

Wynalda, Eric *Soccer Player*
2313 Stomcroft Court, Westlake Village, CA 91361 USA

Wynant, H M
300 S Raymond Ave #11, Pasadena, CA 91105 USA

Wyner, George *Actor*
3450 Laurie Place, Studio City, CA 91604 USA

Wyngaarden, James B *Doctor*
NAS, 2101 Columbus Ave NW, Washington, DC 20418 USA

Wyngarde, Peter *Actor*
41, 4 Acre Lane, Clock Face Saint Helen's, Lancash, WA9 4DZ, UNITED KINGDOM (UK)

Wynn, Bob *Golfer*
78455 Calle Orense, La Quinta, CA 92253 USA

Wynn, Renaldo *Football Player*
19805 Rothschild Court, Ashburn, VA 20147 USA

Wynn, Stephen A *Business Person*
Desert Inn Hotel, 3245 Las Vegas Blvd S, Las Vegas, NV 89109 USA

Wynn, Steve *Chef, Business Person*
Desert Inn Hotel, 3245 Las Vegas Blvd S, Las Vegas, NV 89109

Wynn, Tracy Keenan
700 W. Third St., Los Angeles, CA 90048

Wynter, Dana *Actor*
Contemporary Artists, 610 Santa Monica Blvd, #202, Santa Monica, CA 90401 USA

Wynter, Sarah *Actor*
Mosaic Media Group, 9200 Sunset Blvd Fl 10, Los Angeles, CA 90069 USA

Wyss, Amanda *Actor*
Badgley Connor Talent, 9229 Sunset Blvd, #311, Los Angeles, CA 90069 USA

X

Xiaoshuang, Li
Rue Tiyukuan 9, Beijing, Peoples Republic of China

Xie Bingxin *Writer*
Central Nationalities Institute, Residential Qtrs, Beijing, 100081, CHINA

Xie Jin *Director*
Shanghai Film Studio, 595 Caoxi Beilu, Shanghai, CHINA

Xu Bing *Artist*
540 Metropolitan Ave, Brooklyn, NY 11211 USA

Xu Shuyang *Artist*
Zheijang Academy of Fine Arts, PO Box 169, Hangzhou, CHINA

Xue Wei *Musician*
134 Sheaveshill Ave, London, NW9, UNITED KINGDOM (UK)

Xuereb, Emanuel *Actor*
Artists Group (LA), 10100 Santa Monica Blvd #2490, Los Angeles, CA 90067 USA

Xuereb, Salvator *Actor*
Metropolitan Talent Agency, 4526 Wilshire Blvd, Los Angeles, CA 90010 USA

Xzibit *Musician*
William Morris Agency (WMA-LA), 1 William Morris Pl, Beverly Hills, CA 90212 USA

Y

Yabians, Frank *Producer*
88 Bull Path, East Hampton, NY 11937 USA

Yablans, Frank
100 Bull Path, East Hampton, NY 11937-4601

Yablokov, Alexey V *Biologist*
Koltsove Biology Institute, Vaviloca Str 26, Moscow, 117808, RUSSIA

Yaeger, Andrea *Tennis Player*
1490 S Ute Ave, Aspen, CO 81611 USA

Yaffe, Martin *Physicist*
University of Toronto, Biophysics Dept, Toronto, ON M4W 1J3, CANADA

Yager, Faye *Social Activist*
Children of the Underground, 902 Curlew Court NW, Atlanta, GA 30327 USA

Yager, Rick *Cartoonist*
North American Syndicate, 235 E 45th St, New York, NY 10017 USA

Yagher, Jeff
15057 Sherview Pl., Sherman Oaks, CA 91403

Yago, Gideon *Television Host*
MTV Networks (NY), 1515 Broadway,
New York, NY 10036 USA

Yaguda, Stan *Musician*
Joyce Agency, 370 Harrison Ave,
Harrison, NY 10528 USA

Yagudin, Alexei *Figure Skater*
Connecticut Skating Center, 300 Alumini
Road, Newington, CT 06111 USA

Yake, Terry *Hockey Player*
3 Stratford Park, Bloomfield, CT 06002
USA

Yakovlev, Aleksandr N *Government
Official*
Prisoner Rehabilitation Commission, Ul
Iljinka 8/4, Moscow, 103132, RUSSIA

Yallop, Frank *Coach*
San Jose Earthquakes, 3550 Stevens Creek
Blvd, #200, San Jose, CA 95117 USA

Yalow, Rosalyn S *Nobel Prize Laureate*
3242 Tibbett Ave, Bronx, NY 10463 USA

Yalow, Roslyn
3242 Tibbett Ave., Bronx, NY 10463-
3801

Yamagata, Hiro *Artist*
1080 Ave D, Redondo Beach, CA 90277
USA

Yamaguchi, Kristi T *Figure Skater*
2500 E Las Olas Blvd, #502, Fort
Lauderdale, FL 33301 USA

Yamaguchi, Roy *Business Person*
Roy's Restaurant, Kai Corporate Plaza,
6600 Kalaniaole Hwy, Honolulu, HI
96825 USA

Yamame, Marlene Mitsuko *Actor*
Herb Tannen, 10801 National Blvd, #101,
Los Angeles, CA 90064 USA

Yamamoto, Keith R *Biologist*
332 Douglass St, San Francisco, CA
94114 USA

Yamamoto, Kenichi *Business Person*
Mazda Motor Corp, 4-6-19 Funairi-
Minami, Minamiku, Hiroshima, JAPAN

Yamamoto, Takuma *Business Person*
Fujitsu Ltd, 1-6-1 Marunouchi, Chiyodaku,
Tokyo, 100, JAPAN

Yamamoto, Yohji *Fashion Designer*
14-15 Conduit St, London, W1R 9TG,
UNITED KINGDOM (UK)

Yamanaka, Tsuyoshi *Swimmer*
6-10-33-212 Akasaka, Minatoku, Tokyo,
JAPAN

Yamani, Sheikh Ahmed Zaki *Government
Official*
Chermignon near Crans-Montana, Valais,
SWITZERLAND

Yamaoka, Seigen H *Religious Leader*
Buddhist Churches of America, 1710
Octavia St, San Francisco, CA 94109 USA

Yamasaki, Taro M *Journalist*
People Magazine Editorial Dept, Time-Life
Building, New York, NY 10020 USA

Yamashita, Yasuhiro *Athlete, Coach*
1117 Kitakaname, Hitatsuka Kanagawa,
259-1207, JAPAN

Yan, Romina *Actor*
Telefe - Argentina, Pavon 2444
(C1248AAT), Buenos Aires, ARGENTINA

Yancey, Emily
247 S. Beverly Dr. #102, Beverly Hills,
CA 90212

Yancy, Emily *Actor*
Henderson/Hogan, 8285 W Sunset Blvd,
#1, West Hollywood, CA 90046 USA

Yanez, Edwardo *Actor*
Dolores Robinson Entertainment, 112 S
Almont Dr, Los Angeles, CA 90048 USA

Yang, C K
PO Box 7855-39 Tsoying, Kaoshking,
TAIWAN R.O.C., TAIWAN R O C

Yang, Chen Ning *Nobel Prize Laureate*
3 Victoria Court, Saint James, NY 11780
USA

Yang, Chuan-Kwang (C K) *Track Athlete*
PO Box 7855-39, Tsoying, Kaohsking,
TAIWAN

Yang, Jerry *Business Person, Engineer*
Yahoo!, 701 First Ave, Sunnyvale, CA
94089 USA

Yang, Liwei *Misc*
Satellite Launch Center, Jiuquan, Gansu
Province, CHINA

Yang, Shang-Fa *Misc*
118 Villanova Dr, Davis, CA 95616 USA

Yankelovich, Daniel *Scientist*
Public Agenda Foundation, 6 E 39th St,
#900, New York, NY 10016 USA

Yankovic, Al (Weird Al) *Actor, Comedian,
Songwriter, Musician*
1631 Magnetic Terrace, Los Angeles, CA
90069 USA

Yankovic, Weird Al
5725 Green Oak Dr., Los Angeles, CA
90068-2505

Yankovsky, Oleg I *Actor*
Komsomolsky Prospekt 41, #10, Moscow,
119270, RUSSIA

Yannas, I V *Engineer, Scientist*
Massachusetts Institute of Technology,
Engineering School, Cambridge, MA
02139 USA

Yanni *Musician, Songwriter*
PO Box 46996, Eden Prairie, MN 55344
USA

Yanofsky, Charles *Biologist*
725 Mayfield Ave, Stanford, CA 94305
USA

Yanukovich, Victor *Prime Minister*
Prime Minister's Office, Hrushevskoga
12/2, Kiev, 252008, UKRAINE

Yao, Ming *Basketball Player*
Houston Rockets, Toyota Center, 2E
Greenway Plaza, Houston, TX 77046 USA

Yarborough, Cale
2723 W. Palmetto St. Florence, SC CA
29501-5929

Yarborough, Glenn
PO Box 158, Malibu, CA 90265-0158

Yarborough, W Caleb (Cale) *Race Car
Driver*
Yarborough Racing, 2723 W Palmetto St,
Florence, SC 29501 USA

Yarborough, William P *General*
160 Hillside Road, Southern Pines, NC
28387 USA

Yarbrough, Curtis *Religious Leader*
General Baptists Assn, 100 Stinson Dr,
Poplar Bluff, MO 63901 USA

Yarbrough, Glenn *Songwriter, Musician*
150 Avenida Presidio, San Clemente, CA
92672 USA

Yard, Mollie
1000 16th St. W, Washington, DC

Yardbirds, The
PO Box 1821, Ojai, CA 93024

Yardley, George *Basketball Player*
George Yardley Co, 17260 Newhope St,
Fountain Valley, CA 92708 USA

Yared, Gabriel *Composer*
Gortaine/Schwartz, 13245 Riverside Dr,
#450, Sherman Oaks, CA 91423 USA

Yarlett, Claire *Actor*
1540 Skylark Lane, Los Angeles, CA
90069 USA

Yarnall, Celeste *Actor*
2899 Agoura Road, #315, Westlake, CA
91361 USA

Yarnell, Lorene *Misc*
Arthur Shafman International, PO Box
352, Pawling, NY 12564 USA

Yarrow, Peter *Musician, Songwriter*
27 W 67th St, #5E, New York, NY 10023
USA

Yary, A Ronald (Ron) *Football Player*
15650 El Prado Road, Chino, CA 91710
USA

Yasbeck, Amy *Actor*
11601 Wilshire Blvd, #2200, Los Angeles,
CA 90025 USA

Yashin, Alexei *Hockey Player*
New York Islanders, Nassau Coliseum,
Hempstead Turnpike, Uniondale, NY
11553 USA

Yastrzemski, Carl M *Baseball Player*
8 Whittier Place, #7C, Boston, MA 02114
USA

Yasutake, Patti
145 S. Fairfax Ave. #310, Los Angeles, CA
90036

Yates, Albert C *Educator*
Colorado State University System,
President's Office, Denver, CO 80202
USA

Yates, Bill *Cartoonist*
King Features Syndicate, 888 7th Ave,
New York, NY 10106 USA

Yates, Cassie *Actor*
260 S Beverly Dr, #210, Beverly Hills, CA
90212 USA

Yates, Jim *Race Car Driver*
Commonwealth Service & Supply, 4740
Eisenhower Ave, Alexandria, VA 22304
USA

Yates, Peter
3340 Caroline Ave, Culver City, CA
90230

Yates, Peter J *Director*
334 Caroline Ave, Culver City, CA 90232
USA

Yates, Ronald W (Ron) *General*
525 Silhouette Way, Monument, CO
80132 USA

Yau, Shing-Tung *Mathematician*
Harvard University, Mathematics Dept, 1
Oxford St, Cambridge, MA 02138 USA

Yauch, Adam (MCA) *Artist*
GAS Entertainment, 8935 Lindblade St,
Culver City, CA 90232 USA

Yavneh, Cyrus *Producer*
International Creative Management
(ICM-LA), 8942 Wilshire Blvd, Beverly
Hills, CA 90211 USA

Ybarra y Churruca, Emilio de *Financier*
Banco Bilbao-Vizcaya, Plaza de San
Nicolas 4, Bilboa, 48005, SPAIN

Yeager, Andrea
3137 Devlin Dr., Grand Junction, CO
81504

Yeager, Bunny *Model, Photographer*
9301 NE 6th Ave, #B201, Miami Shores,
FL 33138 USA

Yeager, Charles E (Chuck) *General*
PO Box 579, Penn Valley, CA 95946 USA

Yeager, Cheryl L *Ballerina*
American Ballet Theatre, 890 Broadway,
New York, NY 10003 USA

Yeager, Jeana *Misc*
3695 Highway 50, Campbell, TX 75422
USA

Yeager, Stephen W (Steve) *Baseball
Player*
PO Box 34184, Granada Hills, CA 91394
USA

Yeager, Steve
PO Box 34184, Granada Hills, CA 91394
USA

Yeagley, Jerry *Coach*
1418 S Sare Road, Bloomington, IN
47401 USA

Yeagley, Susan *Actor*
OmniPop Inc (LA), 10700 Ventura Blvd Fl
2, Studio City, CA 91604 USA

Yeakel, G Scott *Astronaut*
12184 E Poinsettia Dr, Scottsdale, AZ
85259 USA

Yearley, Douglas C *Business Person*
Phelps Dodge Corp, 1 N Central Ave,
Phoenix, AZ 85004 USA

Yearwood, Trisha *Musician*
William Morris Agency (WMA-TN), 2100
W End Ave #1000, Nashville, TN 37203
USA

Yeghiayan, Lori *Actor*
Kyle Fritz Management, 1979 Grace Ave
#5A, Hollywood, CA 90068 USA

Yelchin, Anton *Actor*
International Creative Management
(ICM-LA), 8942 Wilshire Blvd, Beverly
Hills, CA 90211 USA

Yeliseyev, Aleksei S *Cosmonaut*
Baurman Higher Technical School,
Baumanskaya Ul 5, Moscow, 107005,
RUSSIA

Yellen, Janet L *Financier, Government
Official*
683 San Luis Road, Berkeley, CA 94707
USA

Yellen, Linda B *Producer, Director*
3 Sheridan Square, New York, NY 10014
USA

Yellowjackets
9220 Sunset Blvd. #320, Los Angeles, CA
90069

Yeltsin, Boris N *Ex-President*
Belji Don, Krascnopresneskaj Nab 2,
Moscow, 103274, RUSSIA

Yen, Donnie *Actor*
Paradigm (LA), 10100 Santa Monica Blvd,
Fl 25, Los Angeles, CA 90067 USA

Yeoh, Michelle *Actor*
William Morris Agency, 151 El Camino
Dr, Beverly Hills, CA 90212 USA

Yeohlee *Fashion Designer*
Yeohlee Designs, 530 Fashion Ave, New
York, NY 10018 USA

Yeoman, William F (Bill) *Football Player,
Football Coach*
3030 Country Club Blvd, Sugar Land, TX
77478 USA

Yeosock, John J *General*
223 Newport Dr, Peachtree City, GA
30269 USA

Yepremian, Garabed S (Garo) *Football
Player*
1 E Mount Vernon St, Oxford, PA 19363
USA

Yerby, Frank
Avenida del America 37, Madrid, SPAIN,
E-28002

Yerman, Jack *Track Athlete*
753 Camellia, Paradise, CA 95969 USA

Yes *Music Group*
10th Street Entertainment, 700 San
Vicente Blvd #G410, W Hollywood, CA
90069 USA

Yeston, Maury *Composer*
Yale University, Music Dept, New Haven,
CT 06520 USA

Yetnikoff, Walter
Trident Media Group LLC, 41 Madison
Ave Fl 33, New York, NY 10010 USA

Yeutter, Clayton K *Secretary*
10955 Martingale Court, Potomac, MD
20854 USA

Yevtushenko, Yevgeny A *Writer*
Kutuzovski Prospekt 2/1, #101, Moscow,
121248, RUSSIA

Yewcic, Thomas (Tom) *Football Player,
Baseball Player*
31 Cherokee Road, Arlington, MA 02474
USA

Yilmaz, A Mesut *Prime Minister*
Basbakanlik, Bakanliklar, Ankara, TURKEY

Yip, David
15 Golden Square #315, London,
ENGLAND, W1R 3AG

Yip, Vern *Designer*
Trading Spaces, The Learning Channel,
7700 Wisconsin Ave, Bethesda, MD
20814 USA

Ylonen, Juha *Hockey Player*
Ottawa Senators, 1000 Palladium Dr,
Kanata, ON K2V 1A4, CANADA

Yo Yo Ma *Actor, Musician*
International Creative Management
(ICM-LA), 8942 Wilshire Blvd, Beverly
Hills, CA 90211 USA

Yo-Yo *Musician*
William Morris Agency, 1325 Ave of
Americas, New York, NY 10019 USA

Yoakam, Dwight *Songwriter, Musician*
Fitzgerald Hartley, 1908 Wedgewood
Ave, Nashville, TN 37212 USA

Yoakum, Dwight *Musician*
Borman Entertainment, 1250 6th St #401,
Santa Monica, CA 90401

Yoba, Malik *Actor*
Gersh Agency, The (NY), 41 Madison Ave
Fl 33, New York, NY 10010 USA

Yoba, Malk *Actor*

Yoccoz, Jean-Christophe *Mathematician*
University of Paris-Sud (Orsey), Orsay-
Cedex-Bait, 91405, FRANCE

Yock, Robert J *Judge*
US Claims Court, 717 Madison Place NW,
Washington, DC 20439 USA

Yodoyman, Joseph *Prime Minister*
Prime Minister's Office, N'Djamena,
CHAD

Yogaraj *Actor, Bollywood*
18 34th Street, Ashok Nagar, Chennai, TN
600083, INDIA

Yoken, Mel B *Writer*
261 Carroll St, New Bedford, MA 02740
USA

Yonaker, John *Football Player*
20450 Lake Shore Blvd, Cleveland, OH
44123 USA

Yoo, Paula *Writer*
International Creative Management
(ICM-LA), 8942 Wilshire Blvd, Beverly
Hills, CA 90211 USA

York, Francine *Actor*
6430 Sunset Blvd, #1205, Los Angeles,
CA 90028 USA

York, Glen P *War Hero*
1620 E Driftwood Dr, Tempe, AZ 85283
USA

York, Herbert F *Physicist*
6110 Camino de la Costa, La Jolla, CA
92037 USA

York, John J *Actor*
4804 Laurel Canyon Blvd, #212, Valley
Village, CA 91607 USA

York, Kathleen *Actor*
Bresler Kelly Assoc, 11500 W Olympic
Blvd, #510, Los Angeles, CA 90064 USA

York, Michael *Actor*
9100 Cordell Dr, Los Angeles, CA 90069
USA

York, Michael (Mike) *Hockey Player*
Edmonton Oilers, 11230 110th St,
Edmonton, AB T5G 3H7, CANADA

York, Michael M *Journalist*
Lexington Herald-Leader, Editorial Dept,
Main & Midland, Lexington, KY 40507
USA

York, Morgan *Actor*
Coast to Coast Talent Group, 3350
Barham Blvd, Los Angeles, CA 90068
USA

York, Ray *Jockey*
27918 Taft Highway, Taft, CA 93268 USA

York, Susannah *Actor*
P F D Drury House, 34-43 Russell St, London, WC2B 5HA, UNITED KINGDOM (UK)

Yorke, Thom *Musician*
Nasty Little Man, 72 Springs St, #1100, New York, NY 10012 USA

Yorkin, Alan (Bud) *Producer, Director*
Bud Yorkin Productions, 250 Delfem Dr, Los Angeles, CA 90077 USA

Yorkin, Bud
250 N. Delfern Dr., Los Angeles, CA 90077

Yorkin, Peg *Politician*
Fund for Feminist Majority, 1600 Wilson Blvd, #704, Arlington, VA 22209 USA

Yorn, Pete *Musician*
William Morris Agency (WMA-LA), 1 William Morris Pl, Beverly Hills, CA 90212 USA

Yorn, Peter *Songwriter, Musician*
The Firm, 9100 Wilshire Blvd, #100W, Beverly Hills, CA 90210 USA

Yorzyk, William A (Bill) *Swimmer*
162 W Sturbridge Road, #7, East Brookfield, MA 01515 USA

Yoseliani, Otar D *Director*
Mitskewitch 1 Korp, 1 #38, Tbilisi, 380060, GEORGIA

Yost, Dennis
PO Box 8770, Endwell, NY 13762

Yost, E Frederick (Ned) *Baseball Player*
N46W28654, Willow Brook Court, Hartland, WI 53029 USA

Yost, Eddie
48 Oakridge Rd, Wellesley, MA 02181

Yost, Edward F J (Eddie) *Baseball Player*
48 Oakridge Road, Wellesley, MA 02481 USA

Yost, Paul A Jr *Admiral*
James Medison Memorial Foundation, 200 K St NW, Washington, DC 20001 USA

Yothers, Tina *Actor, Musician*
12368 Apple Dr, Chino, CA 91710 USA

Young, Aden *Actor*
June Cann Mgmt, 110 Queen St, Woollahra, NSW, 2025, AUSTRALIA

Young, Adrian *Musician*
Rebel Waltz Inc, 31652 2nd Ave, Laguna Beach, CA 92651 USA

Young, Alan *Actor*
24072 La Hermosa, Laguna Niguel, CA 92677 USA

Young, Andrew *Diplomat, Religious Leader*
National Council of Churches, 924 N Magnolia Ave, #304, Orlando, FL 32803 USA

Young, Angus *Musician, Songwriter*
East-West Records, 46 Kensington Court St, London, W8 5DP, UNITED KINGDOM (UK)

Young, Barbara
23-B Deodar Rd., London, ENGLAND, SWl5- 2NP

Young, Bellamy *Actor*
Untitled Entertainment (LA), 8436 W 3rd St #650, Los Angeles, CA 90048 USA

Young, Bob *Cartoonist*
King Features Syndicate, 888 7th Ave, New York, NY 10106 USA

Young, Boyd *Misc*
United Paperworkers Union, 3340 Perimeter Hill Dr, Nashville, TN 37211 USA

Young, Brian *Musician*
MOB Agency, 6404 Wilshire Blvd, #505, Los Angeles, CA 90048 USA

Young, Bryant C *Football Player*
601 Primrose Lane, Matteson, IL 60443 USA

Young, Burt *Actor*
Agency for Performing Arts, 9200 Sunset Blvd, #900, Los Angeles, CA 90069 USA

Young, Charle E *Football Player*
16035 Mink Road NE, Woodinville, WA 98077 USA

Young, Chris T
5959 Triumph St, Commerce, CA 90040-1688 USA

Young, Christoper *Composer*
Kraft-Benjamin-Engel, 15233 Ventura Blvd, #200, Sherman Oaks, CA 91403 USA

Young, Colville N *General, Governor*
Governor General's Office, Belize House, Belnopan, BELIZE

Young, Corey
11553 Sunshine Terrace, Studio City, CA 91604

Young, Curt *Baseball Player*
400 Ballpark Dr, West Sacramento, CA 95691

Young, Dean *Cartoonist*
King Features Syndicate, 888 7th Ave, New York, NY 10106 USA

Young, Earl *Track Athlete*
4344 Livingston Ave, Dallas, TX 75205 USA

Young, Eric O *Baseball Player*
28 Regina Dr, Hattiesburg, MS 39402 USA

Young, Frank E *Scientist, Government Official*
Food & Drug Administration, 5600 Fishers Lane, Rockville, MD 20852 USA

Young, Fred *Musician*
Mitchell Fox Mgmt, 212 3rd Ave, #301, Nashville, TN 37201 USA

Young, Fredd *Football Player*
4200 Real del Sur, Las Cruces, NM 88011 USA

Young, George L *Track Athlete*
8926 N Cox Road, Casa Grande, AZ 85222 USA

Young, H Edwin *Religious Leader*
Southern Baptist Convention, 901 Commerce St, Nashville, TN 37203 USA

Young, Howard (Howie) *Hockey Player*
5527 N 22nd Dr, Phoenix, AZ 85015 USA

Young, J Steven (Steve) *Football Player*
261 E Broadway, Salt Lake City, UT 84111 USA

Young, J Warren *Publisher*
Boys Life Magazine, 1325 Walnut Hill Road, Irving, TX 75038 USA

Young, Jacob *Actor*
International Creative Management (ICM-LA), 8942 Wilshire Blvd, Beverly Hills, CA 90211 USA

Young, James *Musician*
Alliance Artists, 1225 Northmeadow Parkway, #100, Roswell, GA 30076 USA

Young, Jerry *Religious Leader*
Grace Brethren Church Fellowship, 855 Tumbull St, Deltona, FL 32725 USA

Young, Jesse Colin *Songwriter, Musician*
Skyline Music, PO Box 31, Lancaster, NH 03584 USA

Young, Jewell L *Basketball Player*
4480 Fairways Blvd, Building 8 #203, Bradenton, FL 34209 USA

Young, Jim *Football Coach*
US Military Academy, Athletic Dept, West Point, NY 10966 USA

Young, John A *Business Person*
Norvell Inc, 122 E 1700 S, provo, UT 84606 USA

Young, John W *Astronaut*
NASA, Johnson Space Center, 2101 NASA Road, Houston, TX 77058 USA

Young, John Zachary *Misc*
1 Crossroads, Brill, Bucks, HP18 9TL, UNITED KINGDOM (UK)

Young, Kathy *Musician*
Cape Entertainment, 1161 NW 76th Ave, Plantation, FL 33322 USA

Young, Keone *Actor*
Gage Group, 14724 Ventura Blvd, #505, Sherman Oaks, CA 91324 USA

Young, Kevin *Track Athlete*
8860 Corban Ave, Northridge, CA 91324 USA

Young, Laurence Retman *Astronaut*
217 Thorndike St, #108, Cambridge, MA 02141 USA

Young, Lee Thompson *Actor*
Firm, The, 9465 Wilshire Blvd, Beverly Hills, CA 90212 USA

Young, M Adrian *Football Player*
10300 4th St, #100, Rancho Cucamonga, CA 91730 USA

Young, Malcolm *Songwriter, Musician*
11 Leominister Road, Morden, Surrey, SA4 6HN, UNITED KINGDOM (UK)

Young, Martin D *Misc*
1110 Marshall Road, #2007, Greenwood, SC 29646 USA

Young, MC *Musician*
Evolution Talent, 1776 Broadway, #1500, New York, NY 10019 USA

Young, Melissa *Actor*
Badgley Connor Talent, 9229 Sunset Blvd, #311, Los Angeles, CA 90069 USA

Young, Mighty Joe *Musician*
Jay Reil, 3430 Bayberry Dr, Northbrook, IL 60062 USA

Young, Neil *Musician*
PO Box 410, Holualoa, HI 96725 USA

Young, Nina *Actor*
BBC Television Centre, Incoming Mail, Wood Lane, London, W12 7RJ, UNITED KINGDOM (UK)

Young, Paul *Musician*
What Mgmt, PO Box 1463, Culver City, CA 90232 USA

Young, Ray *Misc*
3360 Barham Blvd, Los Angeles, CA 90068 USA

Young, Raymond
7 Church St., Littlehampton, ENGLAND, BN1Y 5EL

Young, Richard
1275 Westwood Blvd., Los Angeles, CA 90024

Young, Richard E *Scientist*
Jet Propulsion Laboratory, 4800 Oak Grove Dr, Pasadena, CA 91109 USA

Young, Richard S *Educator*
137 Saint Croix Ave, Cocoa Beach, FL 32931 USA

Young, Richard S *Photographer*
110 Highlever Road, London, W10 6PL, UNITED KINGDOM (UK)

Young, Robert (Bob) *Track Athlete*
8705 Fairfield Dr, Bakersfield, CA 93311 USA

Young, Scott *Hockey Player*
17 Sandy Ridge Road, Sterling, MA 01564 USA

Young, Sean *Actor*
Cathy Atkinson, 2629 Main Street, PMB 129, Santa Monica, CA 90405 USA

Young, Steve *Misc*
American Federation of Musicians, 1501 Broadway, #800, New York, NY 10036 USA

Young, Tom *Coach*
Washington Wizards, MCI Centre, 601 F St NW, Washington, DC 20004 USA

Young, Vincent *Actor*
Don Buchwald, 6500 Wilshire Blvd, #2200, Los Angeles, CA 90048 USA

Young, Will *Musician*
Pop Idol (Fremantle Media), 2700 Colorado Ave #450, Santa Monica, CA 90404 USA

Young, William Allen *Actor*
5519 S Holt Ave, Los Angeles, CA 90056 USA

Young, Wise *Scientist*
Rutgers University, Collaborative Neuroscience Center, New Brunswick, NJ 08901 USA

Young Jr, Walter R *Business Person*
Champion Enterprises, 2710 University Dr, Auburn Hills, MI 48326 USA

Young Ochowicz, Sheila G *Speed Skater*
2805 N University Dr, Waukesha, WI 53188 USA

Youngblood, H Jackson (Jack) *Football Player, Sportscaster*
4377 Steed Terrace, Winter Park, FL 32792 USA

Youngblood, Jack
4377 Steed Terrace, Winter Park, FL 32792-7630

Youngblood, Jimmy L (Jim) *Football Player*
534 N Manhattan Place, Los Angeles, CA 90004 USA

Youngblood, Rob
1604 N. Vista Ave., Los Angeles, CA 90046

Youngblood, Sydney
Postfach 20 13 43, Hamburg, GERMANY, D-29243

Younger, Ben *Director, Writer*
Creative Artists Agency LCC (CAA-LA), 9830 Wilshire Blvd, Beverly Hills, CA 90212 USA

Youngerman, Jack *Artist*
PO Box 508, Bridgehampton, NY 11932 USA

Younis, Waqar *Cricketer*
Surrey County Cricket Club, Kennington Oval, London, SE11 5SS, UNITED KINGDOM (UK)

Yount, Robin R *Baseball Player*
5001 E Arabian Way, Paradise Valley, AZ 85253 USA

Youssoufi, Abdderrahmane El *Prime Minister*
Prime Minister's Office, Rabat, MOROCCO

Yu, Ronnie *Director, Writer, Producer*
Gersh Agency, The (LA), 232 N Canon Dr, Beverly Hills, CA 90210 USA

Yu Chuan Yong *Architect*
Urban/Rural Construction Committee, 149 Guangming Road, Weihai PR, CHINA

Yuan Enfeng *Musician*
Provincial Broadcasting/TV Station, Xian, Shaanxi, CHINA

Yuan Zhongyi *Archaeologist, Misc*
Qin Shi Huang's Terracotta Army Museum, Lintong, Xi'an, CHINA

Yuasa, Joji *Composer*
1517 Shields Ave, Encinitas, CA 92024 USA

Yuba, Malika
230 Park Ave. #550, New York, NY 10069

Yudkin, Marcia

Yudof, Mark G *Educator*
University of Minnesota, President's Office, Minneapolis, MN 55455 USA

Yue Jingyu *Swimmer*
Physical Culture/Sports Bureau, 9 Tiyuguan Road, Beijing, CHINA

Yuen, Corey *Actor, Director*
Current Entertainment, 1411 Fifth St #405, Santa Monica, CA 90401 USA

Yulin, Harris *Actor*
40 W 86th St, #5C, New York, NY 10024 USA

Yun-Fat, Chow *Actor*
PO Box 71288, Kowloon Central, Hong Kong, CHINA

Yune, Johnny
1921 Scenic Sunrise Dr., Las Vegas, NV 89117

Yune, Rick *Actor*
Innovative Artists, 1505 10th St, Santa Monica, CA 90401 USA

Yunis, Jorge J *Misc*
Thomas Jefferson University, Jefferson Medical College, Philadelphia, PA 19107 USA

Yurchikhin, Fyodor N *Cosmonaut*
NASA, Johnson Space Center, 2101 NASA Road, Houston, TX 77058 USA

Yushkevich, Dmitri *Hockey Player*
International Sports Advisors, 878 Ridge View Way, Franklin Lakes, NJ 07417 USA

Yuvarani *Actor, Bollywood*
Plot No 28 Annamalai Colony, Virugambakkam, Chennai, TN 600092, INDIA

Yzaguirre, Raul *Social Activist*
National Council of La Raza, 1111 19th St NW, #1000, Washington, DC 20036 USA

Yzerman, Steve *Hockey Player*
PO Box 488, Bloomfield Hills, MI 48303 USA

Z

Z, Jenna *Model*
PO Box 39624, N Ridgeville, OH 44039 USA

Zaa, Charlie *Musician*
Sony Music Miami, 605 Lincoln Rd, Miami Beach, FL 33138 USA

Zabaleta, Nicanor *Musician*
Villa Izar, Aldapeta, San Sebasatian, 20009, SPAIN

Zabarain, Ines *Actor*
TV Caracol, Calle 76 #11 - 35, Piso 10AA, Bogota DC, 26484, COLOMBIA

Zabel, Mark *Athlete*
Grosse Fischerei 18A, Calbe/Saale, 39240, GERMANY

Zabel, Steven G (Steve) *Football Player*
6000 Oak Tree Road, Edmond, OK 73003 USA

Zaborowski, Robert R J M *Religious Leader*
Mariavite Old Catholic Church, 2803 10th St, Wyandotte, MI 48192 USA

Zabriskie, Grace *Actor*
1800 S Robertson Blvd, #426, Los Angeles, CA 90035 USA

Zachara, Jan *Boxer*
Sladkovicova 13, Nova Dubnica, 01851, CZECH REPUBLIC

Zacharius, Walter *Publisher*
475 Park Ave S, New York, NY 10016 USA

Zacherle, John *Actor*
125 W 96th St, #4B, New York, NY 10025 USA

Zadan, Craig *Producer*
William Morris Agency (WMA-LA), 1 William Morris Pl, Beverly Hills, CA 90212 USA

Zadeh, Lofti A *Scientist*
904 Mendocino Ave, Berkeley, CA 94707 USA

Zadel, C William *Business Person*
Millipore Corp, 80 Ashby Road, Bedford, MA 01730 USA

Zadora, Pia *Actor, Musician, Model*
1143 Summit Dr, Beverly Hills, CA 90210
USA

Zaentz, Saul *Producer*
Saul Zaentz Co, 2600 10th St, Berkeley,
CA 94710 USA

Zaffaroni, Alejandro C *Misc*
Alza Corp, 1950 Charleston Road,
Mountain View, CA 94043 USA

Zafferani, Rosa *Misc*
Co-Regent's Office, Government Palace,
47031, SAN MARINO

Zagaria, Anita *Actor*
Carol Levi Co, Via Giuseppe Pisanelli,
Rome, 00196, ITALY

Zaglmann-Willinger, Cornelia *Director*
Siegfriedstr 9, Munich, 80802, GERMANY

Zagorin, Perez *Historian*
2990 Beaumont Farm Road,
Chartottesville, VA 22901 USA

Zahn, Geoffrey C (geof) *Baseball Player*
6536 Walsh Road, Dexter, MI 48130 USA

Zahn, Paula *Talk Show Host,
Commentator*
Cable News Network, News Dept, 1050
Techwood Dr NW, Atlanta, GA 30318
USA

Zahn, Steve *Actor*
Principal Entertainment (LA), 1964
Westwood Blvd #400, Los Angeles, CA
90025 USA

Zahn, Wayne *Bowler*
2143 E Center Lane, Tempe, AZ 85281
USA

Zaklinsky, Konstantin *Dancer*
Mariinsky Theater, Teatralnaya Square 1,
Saint Petersburg, 190000, RUSSIA

Zaks, Jerry *Director*
Helen Merrill, 337 W 22nd St, New York,
NY 10011 USA

Zal, Roxana *Actor*
P M K Public Relations, 8500 Wilshire
Blvd, #700, Beverly Hills, CA 90211 USA

Zalapski, Zarley *Hockey Player*
308 Kingsberry Circle, Pittsburgh, PA
15234 USA

Zale, Richard N *Misc*
724 Santa Ynez St, Stanford, CA 94305
USA

Zalyotin, Sergei V *Cosmonaut*
Potchta Kosmonavtov, Moskovskoi
Oblasti, Syvisdny Goroduk, 141160,
RUSSIA

Zamba, Frieda *Misc*
2706 S Central Ave, Flagler Beach, FL
32136 USA

Zamecnik, Paul *Misc*
101 Chestnut St, Boston, MA 02108 USA

Zamecnik, Paul C *Doctor*
Worcester Experimental Biology
Foundation, 222 Maple St, Shrewbury,
MA 01545 USA

Zamka, George D *Astronaut*
144 Lake Point Dr, League City, TX 77573
USA

Zampini, Carina *Actor*
Telefe - Argentina, Pavon 2444
(C1248AAT), Buenos Aires, ARGENTINA

Zanardi, Alex *Race Car Driver*
Target Canaddi Racing, 7777 Woodland
Dr, Indianapolis, IN 46278 USA

Zander, Robin *Musician*
Monterey Peninsula Artists, 509 Hartnell
St, Monterey, CA 93940 USA

Zander, Thomas *Wrestler*
Grundfeldstr 23, Aalen, 73432,
GERMANY

Zane, Billy *Actor*
450 N Rossmore Ave, #1001, Los
Angeles, CA 90004 USA

Zane, Lil *Musician*
JL Entertainment Inc, 18653 Ventura Blvd,
#340, Tarzana, CA 91356

Zane, Lisa *Actor*
209 S Orange Dr, Los Angeles, CA 90036
USA

Zanes, Dan *Songwriter, Musician*
Harriet Stemberg Mgmt, 4530 Gloria Ave,
Encino, CA 91436 USA

Zanetti, Eugenio *Actor, Director*
Sandra Marsh Management, 9150
Wilshire Blvd #220, Beverly Hills, CA
90212 USA

Zano, Nick *Actor*
3 Arts Entertainment Inc, 9460 Wilshire
Blvd Fl 7, Beverly Hills, CA 90212 USA

Zanuck, Lili Fini *Director, Producer*
Zanuck Co, 9465 Wilshire Blvd, #308,
Beverly Hills, CA 90212 USA

Zanuck, Richard D *Producer*
Zanuck Co, 9465 Wilshire Blvd, #308,
Beverly Hills, CA 90212 USA

Zanussi, Krzysztof *Director*
Ul Kaniowska 114, Warsaw, 01-529,
POLAND

Zapata, Carmen *Actor*
6107 Ethel Ave, Van Nuys, CA 91401
USA

Zapata, Laura *Actor*
Televisa, Blvd Adolfo Lopez Mateos 232,
Colonia San Angel INN, DF, CP 01060,
MEXICO

Zappa, Dweezil *Actor, Musician*
7885 Woodrow Wilson Dr, Los Angeles,
CA 90046 USA

Zappa, Moon
PO Box 5265, No. Hollywood, CA 91616

Zappa, Moon Unit *Actor, Musician*
10377 Oletha Lane, Los Angeles, CA
90077 USA

Zarate, Carlos *Boxer*
Gene Aguilera, PO Box 113, Montebello,
CA 90640 USA

Zarnas, August C (Gust) *Football Player*
850 Jennings St, Bethlehem, PA 18017
USA

Zaslow, Jeffrey L (Jeff) *Writer, Journalist*
Chicago Sun-Times, Editorial Dept, 401 N
Wabash, Chicago, IL 60611 USA

Zatopkova, Dana *Track Athlete*
Nad Kazankov 3, Prague 7, 171 00,
CZECH REPUBLIC

Zaveri, Anjala *Actor, Bollywood*
604 Jupiter Apts Yari Road, Andheri (W),
Mumbai, MS 400058, INDIA

Zaveri, Anjali *Actor, Bollywood*
604 Jupiter Apartments, Yari Road,
Andheri, Mumbai, 400058, India

Zawinul, Josef (Joe) *Composer, Musician*
International Music Network, 278 S Main
St, #400, Gloucester, MA 01930 USA

Zawoluk, Robert (Zeke) *Basketball Player*
325 W 17th St, New York, NY 10011
USA

Zayak, Elaine *Figure Skater*
298 McHenry Dr, Paramus, NJ 07652
USA

Zea, Natalie *Actor*
Platform Public Relations, 2133 Holly
Drive, Los Angeles, CA 90068 USA

Zeal, Meredith *Actor*
Marv Dauer Management, 11661 San
Vicente Blvd #104, Los Angeles, CA
90049 USA

Zeamer Jr, Jay *War Hero*
PO Box 602, Boothbay Harbor, ME 04538
USA

Zech, Rosel
Agensstr. 47, Munich, GERMANY, 80798

Zeckendorf Jr, William *Business Person*
502 Park Ave, New York, NY 10022 USA

Zeckhauser, Richard J *Economist*
138 Irving St, Cambridge, MA 02138 USA

Zedillo Ponce de Leon, Ernesto *Politician,
President*
Institutional Revolutionary, Insurges N 61,
Mexico City, DF, 06350, MEXICO

Zefferelli, Franco
91 Regent St., London, ENGLAND, W1R
7TB

Zeffirelli, G Franco *Director*
Via Appia Pignatelli 448, Rome, 00178,
ITALY

Zegers, Kevin *Actor*
Agency for Performing Arts, 9200 Sunset
Blvd, #900, Los Angeles, CA 90069 USA

Zeglis, John D *Business Person*
AT & T Corp, 32 Ave of Americas, New
York, NY 10013 USA

Zeh, Geoffrey N *Misc*
Maintenance of Way Employees
Brotherhood, 12050 Woodward, Detroit,
MI 48203 USA

Zehetner, Nora *Actor*
Mosaic Media Group, 9200 Sunset Blvd Fl
10, Los Angeles, CA 90069 USA

Zeidel, Larry *Hockey Player*
101 Millcreek Rd, Ardmore, PA 19003-
1537

Zeidler, Eberard H *Architect*
Zeidler Roberts Architects, 315 Queen St
W, Toronto, ON M5V 2X2, CANADA

Zeigler, Heidi *Actor*
Mary Gardy Agency, 221 E Walnut St,
#130, Pasadena, CA 91101 USA

Zeigler, Larry
10620 Woodchase Circle, Orlando, FL
32836-5885

Zeile, Todd E *Baseball Player*
New York Yankees, Yankee Stadium,
161st St & River Ave, Bronx, NY 10451
USA

Zeilic, Mauricio *Actor*
Telemundo, 2470 West 8th Avenue, Hialeah, FL 33010 USA

Zeitlin, Zvi *Musician*
204 Warren Ave, Rochester, NY 14618 USA

Zelensky, Igor *Dancer*
New York City Ballet, Lincoln Center Plaza, New York, NY 10023 USA

Zelepukin, Valeri *Hockey Player*
Chicago Blackhawks, United Center, 1901 W Madison St, Chicago, IL 60612 USA

Zelezny, Jan *Track Athlete*
Rue Armady 683, Boleslav, CZECH REPUBLIC

Zell, Samuel *Business Person*
Itel Corp, 2 N Riverside Plaza, Chicago, IL 60606 USA

Zeller, Hank
2120 Greentree Rd. #100E, Pittsburgh, PA 15220

Zellweger, Renee *Actor*
Creative Artists Agency, 9830 Wilshire Blvd, Beverly Hills, CA 90212 USA

Zelman, Aaron *Writer*
International Creative Management (ICM-LA), 8942 Wilshire Blvd, Beverly Hills, CA 90211 USA

Zelmani, Sophie *Musician*
United Stage Artists, PO Box 11029, Stockholm, 100 61, SWEDEN

Zeman, Jacklyn *Actor*
STone Manners, 6500 Wilshire Blvd, #550, Los Angeles, CA 90048 USA

Zeman, Milos *Prime Minister*
Premier's Office, Nabrezi E Benese 4, Prague 1, 118 01, CZECH REPUBLIC

Zemanova, Veronica *Model*
Veronica Zemanova Management, G Noodtstr 12 SW, Nijmegen, 6511, NETHERLANDS

Zembriski, Walter *Golfer*
7231 Moss Leaf Lane, Orlando, FL 32819 USA

Zemeckis, Robert L *Writer, Director, Producer*
100 Universal City Plaza, #Building 484, Universal City, CA 91608 USA

Zenawi, Hailu *Prime Minister*
Prime Minister's Office, PO Box 1013, Addis Ababa, ETHIOPIA

Zenawi, Meles *President*
President's Office, PO Box 5707, Addis Ababa, ETHIOPIA

Zender, Hans *Composer*
Am Rosenheck, Bad Soden, 65812, GERMANY

Zender, Stuart *Musician*
Searles, Chapel, 26A Munster St, London, SW6 4EN, UNITED KINGDOM (UK)

Zentmyer Jr, George A *Misc*
955 S El Camino Real, #216, San Mateo, CA 94402 USA

Zentner, Sy
4825 Fairfax Ave., Las Vegas, NV 89120

Zepeda, David *Actor*
Osbrink Talent Agency, 4343 Lankershim Blvd #100, Universal City, CA 91602 USA

Zeppelin, Dread *Musician*
The M.O.B Agency, 6404 Wilshire Blvd, suite 700, Los Angeles, CA 90048

Zeppelin, Led *Musician*
46 Kensington Ct St, London, ENGLAND, W8 5DP

Zerbe, Anthony *Actor*
411 W 115th St, #51, New York, NY 10025 USA

Zerhouni, Elias A *Government Official, Doctor*
National Institutes of Health, 9000 Rockville Pike, Bethesda, MD 20892 USA

Zernial, Gus E *Baseball Player*
687 Coventry Ave, Clovis, CA 93611 USA

Zero, Mark *Musician*
PO Box 656507, Fresh Meadows, NY 11365 USA

Zervas, Nicholas T *Doctor*
100 Canton Ave, Milton, MA 02186 USA

Zeta Jones, Catherine *Actor*
Milkwood Films, 3000 W Olympic Blvd, Bldg 5, Santa Monica, CA 90404 USA

Zettler, Michael E *General*
Deputy Chief of Staff for Logistics, HqUSA Pentagon, Washington, DC 20310 USA

Zettler, Rob *Hockey Player*
31 Tadcaster Place, Saulte Sainte Marie, ON P6B 5E3, CANADA

Zewail, Ahmed H *Nobel Prize Laureate*
871 Winston Ave, San Marino, CA 91108 USA

Zhamnov, Alexei *Hockey Player*
1950 N Orchard St, Chicago, IL 60614 USA

Zhang, Aiping *Government Official, General*
Ministry of Defense, State Council, Beijing, CHINA

Zhang, Xianliang *Writer*
Ningxia Writers Assn, Yinchuan City, CHINA

Zhang, Yimou *Director*
Xi'an Film Studio, Xi'an City, Shanxi Province, CHINA

Zhang, Ziyl *Actor*
William Morris Agency, 151 El Camino Dr, Beverly Hills, CA 90212 USA

Zhe-Xi Lo *Misc*
Camegie Natural History Museum, 4400 Forbes Ave, Pittsburgh, PA 15213 USA

Zhenan, Bao *Inventor*
AT & T Bell Lucent Laboratory, 600 Mountain Ave, New Providence, NJ 07974 USA

Zheng, Wei *Astronomer*
Johns Hopkins Universities, Astronomy Dept, Baltimore, MD 21218 USA

Zhirinovsky, Vladimir V *Government Official*
Liberal Democratic Party, 1st Basmanny Per 3, Moscow, 103045, RUSSIA

Zhislin, Grigory Y *Musician*
25 Whiteball Gardens, London, W3 9RD, UNITED KINGDOM (UK)

Zhitnik, Alexel *Hockey Player*
Buffalo Sabres, HSBC Arena, 1 Seymour St, Buffalo, NY 14210 USA

Zholobov, Vitall M *Cosmonaut*
Ul Yanvarskovo Vostaniya D 12, Klev, 252010, UKRAINE

Zhou Long *Composer*
University of Missouri, Music Dept, Kansas City, MO 64110 USA

Zhudov, Vyacheslav D *Cosmonaut*
Potchta Kosmonavtov, Moskovskoi Oblasti, Syvisdny Goroduk, 141160, RUSSIA

Zhumaliyev, Kubanychbek M *Cosmonaut*
Parliament Buildings, Bishkek, 7200003, KYRGYZSTAN

Zhvanetsky, Mikhail M *Actor, Writer*
Lesnaya Str 4, #63, Moscow, 125047, RUSSIA

Zia, B Khaleda *Prime Minister*
Sere-e Bangla Nagar, Gono, Bhaban Sher-e-Banglanagar, Dakah, BANGLADESH

Ziblijew, Wassili *Cosmonaut*
Potchta Kosmonavtov, Moskovskoi Oblasti, Syvisdny Goroduk, 141160, RUSSIA

Zidane, Zinedine *Soccer Player*
Real Madrid FC, Avda Concha Espina 1, Madrid, 28036, SPAIN

Ziegler, Dolorea *Opera Singer*
Lynda Kay, 2702 Crestworth Lane, Buford, GA 30519 USA

Ziegler, Jack *Cartoonist*
New Yorker Magazine, Editorial Dept, 4 Times Square, New York, NY 10036 USA

Ziegler, Larry *Golfer*
10315 Luton Court, Orlando, FL 32836 USA

Ziegler, Ron
413 N. Lee St. #1417-D49, Alexandria, VA 22314-2301

Ziegler Jr, John A *Misc*
Dickinson Wright, 38525 Woodward Ave, Bloomfield, MI 48304 USA

Ziemann, Sonia *Actor*
Via del Alp Dorf, Saint Moritz, 7500, SWITZERLAND

Ziemann, Sonja
Neherstr. 7, Munich, GERMANY, D-81675

Zien, Chip *Actor*
Gersh Agency, The (LA), 232 N Canon Dr, Beverly Hills, CA 90210 USA

Ziering, Ian *Actor*
2700 Jalmia Dr, West Hollywood, CA 90046 USA

Ziering, Nikki Schieler *Actor*
Shapiro-Lichtman Talent Agency, 8827 Beverly Blvd, Los Angeles, CA 90048 USA

Ziff Jr, William B *Publisher*
Ziff-Davis Publishing Co, 1 Park Ave, New York, NY 10016 USA

Ziffren, Kenneth *Lawyer*
Ziffren Brittenham Branca, 1801 Century Park West, Los Angeles, CA 90067 USA

Ziglar, Zig *Business Person*
Success'94 Seminars, General Delivery, Hawkins, TX 75765 USA

Zigler, Edward F *Educator*
Yale University, Bush Child Development Center, New Haven, CT 06520 USA

Zikarsky, Bengt *Swimmer*
SV Wurzburg 05, Oberer Bogenweg 1, Wurzburg, 97074, GERMANY

Zikarsky, Bjorn *Swimmer*
555 California St, #2600, San Francisco, CA 94104 USA

Zikes, Les *Bowler*
424 S Stuart Lane, Palatine, IL 60067 USA

Zilinskas, Annette *Musician*
Creative Artists Agency, 9830 Wilshire Blvd, Beverly Hills, CA 90212 USA

Zils, John *Engineer*
N1513 Shore Haven Dr, Fontana, WI 53125 USA

Zim Zum *Musician*
Mitch Schneider Organization, 14724 Ventura Blvd, #410, Sherman Oaks, CA 91403 USA

Zima, Madeline *Actor*
Innovative Artists (LA), 1505 Tenth St, Santa Monica, CA 90401 USA

Zimbalist, Stephanie *Actor*
Blake Agency, 1333 Ocean Ave, Santa Monica, CA 90401 USA

Zimbalist III, Efrem *Business Person*
Times Mirror Co, Times Mirror Square, Los Angeles, CA 90053 USA

Zimbalist Jr, Efrem *Actor*
1448 Holsted Dr, Solvang, CA 93463 USA

Zimerman, Krystian *Musician*
Columbia Artists Mgmt Inc, 165 W 57th St, New York, NY 10019 USA

Zimm, Bruno H *Misc*
2522 Horizon Way, La Jolla, CA 92037 USA

Zimmer, Constance *Actor*
Sweeney Management, 8755 Lookout Mountain Avenue, Los Angeles, CA 90046 USA

Zimmer, Don
10124 Yacht Club Dr., St. Petersburg, FL 33706

Zimmer, Donald W (Don) *Baseball Player*
10124 Yacht Club Dr, Treasure Island, FL 33706 USA

Zimmer, Hans *Composer*
1547 14th St, Santa Monica, CA 90404 USA

Zimmer, Kim *Actor*
15561 Almendra Dr, Santa Clarita, CA 91355 USA

Zimmer, Norma
661 Woodlake Dr., Brea, CA 92621

Zimmerer, Wolfgang *Athlete*
Schwaigangerstr 22, Mumau, 82418, GERMANY

Zimmerman, Gary W *Football Player*
17450 Skyliners Road, Bend, OR 97701 USA

Zimmerman, H Leroy *Football Player*
808 Willis Ace, Madera, CA 93637 USA

Zimmerman, Howard E *Misc*
7813 Westchester Dr, Middleton, WI 53562 USA

Zimmerman, James M *Business Person*
Federated Department Stores, 151 W 34th St, New York, NY 10001 USA

Zimmerman, John T *Scientist*
University of Colorado, Medical School, Neurology Dept, Denver, CO 80202 USA

Zimmerman, Kent *Publisher*
Friendly Exchange Magazine, 1999 Shepard Road, Saint Paul, MN 55116 USA

Zimmerman, Mary Beth *Golfer*
Ladies Pro Golf Assn, 100 International Golf Dr, Daytona Beach, FL 32124 USA

Zimmerman, Matt
562 Eastern Ave. Ilford, Essex, ENGLAND, 1G2 6PH

Zimmerman, Philip (Phil) *Designer*
Network Assoc, 4677 Old Ironside Dr, Santa Clara, CA 95054 USA

Zimmermann, Egon *Skier*
Hotel Krisberg, Am Arlberg, 67644, AUSTRIA

Zimmermann, Frank P *Musician*
Riaskoff Mgmt, Concertgebouwplein 15, Amsterdam, 1071 LL, NETHERLANDS

Zimmermann, Markus *Athlete*
Waldhauserstr 51-33, Schonau am Konigsee, 83471, GERMANY

Zimmermann, Udo *Composer*
Operhaus Leipzig, Augustusptatz, Leipzig, 04109, GERMANY

Zinder, Norton D *Misc*
450 E 63rd St, New York, NY 10021 USA

Zindler, Marvin *Commentator*
KTRK-TV News Dept, 3310 Bissonnet, Houston, TX 77005 USA

Zinke, Olaf *Speed Skater*
Johannes Bobrowski Str 22, Berlin, 12627, GERMANY

Zinkernagel, Rolf M *Nobel Prize Laureate*
Rebhusstr 47, Zumikon, 8126, SWITZERLAND

Zinman, David J *Conductor*
Baltimore Symphony, 1212 Cathedral St, Baltimore, MD 21201 USA

Zinta, Preity *Actor, Bollywood*
C-10/A Ranwar Wadora Road, Off Hill Road Bandra (W), Mumbai, MS 400050, INDIA

Zippel, David *Musician*
Kraft-Benjamin-Engel, 15233 Ventura Blvd, #200, Sherman Oaks, CA 91403 USA

Zisk, Richard W (Richie) *Baseball Player*
4231 NE 26th Terrace, Lighthouse Point, FL 33064 USA

Ziskin, Laura
William Morris Agency (WMA-LA), 1 William Morris Pl, Beverly Hills, CA 90212 USA

Zito, Barry *Baseball Player*
10175 Spring Mountain Road, Las Vegas, NV 89117 USA

Zivi, Zhang
151 El Camino Dr., Beverly Hills, CA 90212

Zivkovic, Zoran *Prime Minister*
Prime Minister's Office, Nemanjina 11, Belgrade, 11000, SERBIA

Ziyi, Zhang *Actor*
I/D PR (LA), 8409 Santa Monica Blvd, West Hollywood, CA 90069 USA

Zlatoper, Ronald J (Zap) *Admiral*
1001 Kamokila Blvd, Kapolei, HI 96707 USA

Zlotoff, Lee *Director*
Niad Literary & Talent Management, 3465 Coy Dr, Sherman Oaks, CA 91423 USA

Zmed, Adrian *Actor*
12186 Laurel Terr, Studio City, CA 91604 USA

Zmeskal, Kim *Gymnast*
Cincinnati Gymnastics Academy, 3635 Woodridge, Fairfield, OH 45014 USA

Zmievskaya Petrenko, Galina (Nina) *Coach*
International Skating Center, PO Box 577, Simsbury, CT 06070 USA

Zoeller, Frank (Fuzzy) *Golfer*
4146 Lakeside Dr, Sellersburg, IN 47172 USA

Zoeller, Fuzzy
418 Deer Run Terr., Floyd's Knobs, IN 47119-8505

Zoellick, Robert *Government Official*
US Trade Representatives Office, 600 17th St NW, Washington, DC 20506 USA

Zoffinger, George R *Financier*
CoreStates (NJ) Bank, 370 Scotch Rd, Pennington, NJ 08534 USA

Zohn, Ethan *Reality TV Star*
Survivor, 1661 Lincoln Blvd, Ste 200, Santa Monica, CA 90404

Zombie, Rob

Zombo, Rick *Hockey Player*
557 Vista Hills Ct, Eureka, MO 63025

Zook, John E *Football Player*
9425 Riviera Rd, Roswell, GA 30075 USA

Zook, Ron *Football Coach*
9425 Rivera Rd, Roswell, GA 30075 USA

Zophres, Mary *Designer*
United Talent Agency (UTA), 9560 Wilshire Blvd, Beverly Hills, CA 90212 USA

Zoran *Fashion Designer*
157 Chambers St #1200, New York, NY 10007 USA

Zorich, Christopher R (Chris) *Football Player*
1429 S Clark St, Chicago, IL 60605 USA

Zorich, Louis *Actor*
Susan Smith Company, The, 121 A North San Vicente Blvd, Beverly Hills, CA 90211 USA

Zorn, James A (Jim) *Football Coach*
2006 W Mercer Way, Mercer Island, WA 98040 USA

Zorrilla, Alberto *Swimmer*
580 Park Ave, New York, NY 10021 USA

Zorrilla, China *Actor*
Telefe - Argentina, Pavon 2444 (C1248AAT), Buenos Aires, ARGENTINA

Zsigmond, Vilmos *Cinematographer*
Spyros Skouras, 631 Wilshire Blvd #2C, Santa Monica, CA 90401 USA

Zubak, Kresimir *President*
Presidency, Marsala Titz 7A, Sarajevo, 71000, BOSNIA-HERZEGOVINA

Zuber, Maria *Geophysicist*
Massachusetts Institute of Technology, Geophysics Dept, Cambridge, MA 02139 USA

Zucker, David *Producer, Director*
Zucker/Netter Productions, 1411 Fifth St #402, Santa Monica, CA 90401 USA

Zucker, Irwin *Business Person*

Zucker, Jerry *Producer, Director*
Zucker Productions, 1250 Sixth St #201, Santa Monica, CA 90401

Zuckerman, Josh *Actor*
Saffron Management, 1701 N Beverly Dr, Beverly Hills, CA 90210 USA

Zuckerman, Mortimer *Publisher*
Boston Properties, 599 Lexington Ave, New York, NY 10022 USA

Zuckerman, Pinchas *Musician, Conductor*
Shirley Kirshbaum Assoc, 711 W End Ave #5KN, New York, NY 10025-8843 USA

Zugsmith, Albert *Director*
23388 Mulholland Dr, Woodland Hills, CA 91364 USA

Zuiker, Anthony E *Producer*
Creative Artists Agency LCC (CAA-LA), 9830 Wilshire Blvd, Beverly Hills, CA 90212 USA

Zukav, Gary *Writer*
Fireside/Simon & Schuster, 1230 Ave of the Americas, New York, NY 10020 USA

Zukerman, Eugenia *Musician*
Brooklyn College of Music, Bedford & H Aves, Brooklyn, NY 11210 USA

Zukerman, Pinchas *Musician, Conductor*
Shirley Kirshbaum & Associates, 711 W End Ave #5KN, New York, NY 10025 USA

Zullo, Alan *Cartoonist*
Tribune Media Services, 435 N Michigan Ave #1500, Chicago, IL 60611 USA

Zuniga, Daphne *Actor*
Untitled Entertainment (LA), 8436 W 3rd St #650, Los Angeles, CA 90048 USA

Zuniga, Jose *Actor*
Sanders/Armstrong Management, 2120 Colorado Blvd #120, Santa Monica, CA 90404 USA

Zuniga, Miles *Musician*
Russell Carter Artist Management, 315 West Ponce De Leon Avenue, Suite 755, Decatur, GA 30030 USA

Zurbriggen, Pirmin *Skier*
Hotel Larchenhof, 3905 Saas-Almagell, SWITZERLAND

Zvereva, Natalya *Tennis Player*
Women's Tennis Association, 133 First St NE, St Petersburg, FL 33701 USA

Zwanzig, Robert *Scientist*
5314 Sangamore Rd, Bethesda, MD 20816 USA

Zweig, George *Physicist*
Los Alamos National Laboratory, MS B276, PO Box 1663, Los Alamos, NM 87544 USA

Zwerling, Darrell *Actor*
CLInc Talent, 843 N Sycamore Ave, Los Angeles, CA 90038 USA

Zwick, Charles J *Financier*
4210 Santa Maria St, Coral Gables, FL 33146 USA

Zwick, Edward M *Producer, Director, Actor, Writer*
Bedford Falls Company, The, 409 Santa Monica Blvd #PH, Santa Monica, CA 90401 USA

Zwick, Joel *Director*
Irv Schechter Company, 9460 Wilshire Blvd, Suite 300, Beverly Hills, CA 90212 USA

Zwilich, Ellen Taaffe *Composer*
Music Association of America, 224 King St, Englewood, NJ 07631 USA

Zycinski, Jozef *Religious Leader*
Ul Prumasa St Wyszynskiego 2, Skr Poczt 198, Lublin, 20-950, POLAND

Zydeco, Buckwheat *Musician*
Concerted Efforts, 59 Parsons St, W Newton, MA 02465 USA

Zykina, Lyudmila G *Musician*
Kotelnicheskaya Nab Y15 Korp B #64, Moscow, RUSSIA

Zylberstein, Elsa *Actor*
Agence Intertalent, 5 Rue Clement Marot, Paris, 75008, FRANCE

Zylis-Gara, Teresa *Opera Singer*
16A Blvd de Belgique, Monaco-Ville, MONACO

ZZ Top *Musician*
Creative Artists Agency LCC (CAA-LA), 9830 Wilshire Blvd, Beverly Hills, CA 90212 USA

Quick & Easy Order Form

Additional copies of *The Celebrity Black Book* may be ordered directly from the publisher. Simply mail or fax us the completed form below. Your order will be filled immediately with the most recent published edition. You may also order online at www.contactanycelebrity.com!

....

BILLING ADDRESS:

First Name: _____ Last Name: _____

Company: _____

Address: _____

City: _____ State: _____ Zip: _____

Country: _____ Phone: _____

SHIPPING ADDRESS: [ ] Check this box if the same address as above.

First Name: _____ Last Name: _____

Company: _____

Address: _____

City: _____ State: _____ Zip: _____

Country: _____ Phone: _____

Please send me _____ copies of *The Celebrity Black Book* at $49.95 each.
Shipping to U.S.: $5.00 for the first copy, $3.00 each additional.
Shipping to Canada: $7.00 for the first copy, $5.00 each additional.
Shipping to Everywhere Else: $10.00 for the first copy, $7.00 each additional.

TOTAL ENCLOSED: $ _____
Payment must be made in U.S. funds and drawn on a U.S. Bank.

PAYMENT METHOD: [ ] Check/Money Order (Make payable to Contact Any Celebrity.)
                    [ ] Visa [ ] MasterCard [ ] American Express [ ] Discover

Card #: _____ Exp.: _____

Signature: _____ CVV2 #: _____ (see below)

(The CVV2 # is the last 3 digits on the back of your card, at the end of the signature strip. For American Express it is the four digits printed alone on the front of the card on the right side.)

Mail to: Contact Any Celebrity, 8721 Santa Monica Blvd. #431, West Hollywood, CA 90069-4507
Or order online, by phone or by fax 24 hours a day, 7 days a week!
Online: www.contactanycelebrity.com **Phone:** (888) 267-0204 or (310) 691-5466
Fax: (310) 362-8771 (24 hours)

Give a great gift--place your order now!

www.contactanycelebrity.com